CENTRAL PROCESS	PRIME ADAPTIVE EGO QUALITY	CORE PATHOLOGY	APPLIED TOPIC
			Abortion
Mutuality with the caregiver	Hope	Withdrawal	The role of the parents
Imitation	Will	Compulsion	Child care
Identification	Purpose	Inhibition	School readiness
Education	Competence	Inertia	Violence in the lives of children
Peer pressure	Fidelity to others	Dissociation	Adolescent alcohol and drug use
Role experimentation	Fidelity to values	Repudiation	Dropping out of college
Mutuality among peers	Love	Exclusivity	Divorce
Person-environment interaction and creativity	Care	Rejectivity	Discrimination in the workplace
Introspection	Wisdom	Disdain	Retirement
Social support	Confidence	Diffidence	Meeting the needs of the frail elderly

THIRTEENTH EDITION

DEVELOPMENT THROUGH LIFE

A Psychosocial Approach

Barbara M. Newman
University of Rhode Island

Philip R. Newman
University of Rhode Island

CENGAGE
Learning®

Australia • Brazil • Mexico • Singapore • United Kingdom • United States

Development Through Life: A Psychosocial Approach, **Thirteenth Edition**
Barbara Newman and Philip Newman

Product Director: Marta Lee-Perriard

Product Manager: Star Burruto

Content Developer: Nedah Rose

Product Assistant: Katie Chen

Media Developer: Jaclyn Hermesmeyer

Marketing Manager: James Finlay

Content Project Manager: Ruth Sakata Corley

Art Director: Vernon Boes

Manufacturing Planner: Karen Hunt

Production and Composition: MPS Limited

Photo and Text Researcher: Lumina Datamatics

Text and Cover Designer: Cheryl Carrington

Cover Image: Claude and Paloma Drawing;
    Claude et Paloma Dessinant, 1954 (oil on
    canvas),

Picasso, Pablo (1881–1973) / Private Collection /
    Bridgeman Images

For product information and technology assistance, contact us at
Cengage Learning Customer & Sales Support, 1-800-354-9706.

For permission to use material from this text or product,
submit all requests online at **www.cengage.com/permissions.**
Further permissions questions can be e-mailed to
permissionrequest@cengage.com

Library of Congress Control Number: 2017933381

Student Edition:

ISBN: 978-1-337-09814-4

Loose-leaf Edition:

ISBN: 978-1-337-11872-9

Cengage Learning
20 Channel Center Street
Boston, MA 02210
USA

Cengage Learning is a leading provider of customized learning solutions with employees residing in nearly 40 different countries and sales in more than 125 countries around the world. Find your local representative at **www.cengage.com**

Cengage Learning products are represented in Canada by Nelson Education, Ltd.

To learn more about Cengage Learning Solutions, visit **www.cengage.com**

Purchase any of our products at your local college store or at our preferred online store **www.cengagebrain.com**

Printed in the United States of America
Print Number: 01   Print Year: 2017

Brief Contents

Contents

3   Psychosocial Theory   55

4   The Period of Pregnancy and Prenatal Development   81

5   Infancy (First 24 Months)   129

6 Toddlerhood (Ages 2 to 4 Years)   183

7 Early School Age (4 to 6 Years) 229

8 Middle Childhood (6 to 12 Years) 271

9 Early Adolescence (12 to 18 Years) 317

10 Later Adolescence (18 to 24 Years) 373

11 Early Adulthood (24 to 34 Years) 417

12   Middle Adulthood (34 to 60 Years) 469

13 Later Adulthood (60 to 75 Years) 513

14 Elderhood (75 Until Death) 551

15 Understanding Death, Dying, and Bereavement 587

The first edition of *Development Through Life* was published in 1975. Since that time, an expanding scientific study of human development and increases in longevity have converged to create a remarkable revision of our understanding of the life course. Insights about human development have emerged in a vibrant research environment with new interdisciplinary approaches to research, greater inclusion of diverse samples in the United States and internationally, new statistical techniques to manage multiple observations and multiple variables, and a growing acceptance of qualitative studies.

Today, the years of infancy and childhood comprise a smaller percentage of the life span than was the case in 1975. Researchers look in much greater detail at the prenatal stage as a dynamic period when learning begins, the environment impacts the developmental trajectory, and conditions of pregnancy influence fetal growth. Genetic studies now recognize the role of the environment in silencing or enhancing gene expression in ways that can be transmitted from one generation to the next. Research on infant development, particularly in the first days and weeks of life, has flourished, resulting in greater appreciation for the cognitive and sensory capacities of the newborn. The expanding field of evolutionary psychology has shed new light on the adaptive capacities of infants and the features of the parent-infant relationships that contribute to survival and long-term growth. There is a growing consensus about what constitutes effective or "good" parenting and the cascading negative impact of harsh or neglectful parenting.

The application of developmental systems theory has provided many new insights into the way change occurs. We view development as a product of the interaction of many levels at once, each potentially altering the others. For example, neuroimaging studies illustrate how various areas of the brain interact and influence each other. As a person engages in cognitive tasks, such as problem solving or risk assessment, areas of the brain involved in emotion regulation, attention, motor activity, and sensory processing are all recruited.

In the current edition of *Development Through Life*, we have included discussions about conditions of life in other industrialized countries. We are troubled to note many ways in which life in the United States, as exciting and promising as it is, does not compare favorably. As you read, you will find that infant mortality, student performance in math and science, teen pregnancies, school dropouts, children and adolescents who are victims of violent crime, children in poverty, children who experience multiple parental transitions, debt-burden in later adolescence and early adulthood, homelessness, and the health and longevity of the elderly are all less favorable in the United States than in many other countries. These comparisons lead us to urge scholars in

human development to be more active advocates for policies that promote optimal development through the life span.

One of the troubling realities of the current historical period is extreme income inequality in the United States and associated disparities in health, educational attainment, and occupational opportunities. Despite the knowledge about effective interventions and best practices, greed among the very top segment of the population is preventing the level of investment in programs that would improve many of the conditions mentioned above. From a psychosocial perspective, we see evidence of stagnation among the very wealthy that has serious implications for future societal well-being.

The Stage Approach

The text provides a thorough chronological introduction to the study of human development from conception through elderhood. We examine physical, intellectual, social, and emotional growth in each of 11 stages, emphasizing that development results from the interdependence of these areas at every stage. This strategy gives attention to important developmental themes that recur in different stages of life. For each life stage, the process of development is linked to internal conflicts, changing self-awareness, and a dynamic social environment. As a result, students gain a sense of a multidimensional person, striving toward new levels of competence and mastery, embedded in multiple contexts.

In our stage approach, we cover two stages of adolescence, early adolescence with the psychosocial crisis of group identity versus alienation, and later adolescence, with the psychosocial crisis of individual identity versus identity confusion. We are witnessing an ever more gradual transition out of adolescence into adulthood so that the period we call later adolescence is lasting well into the decade of the 20s. Research on educational and occupational attainment, relationships with family, and the formation of intimate bonds all point to the idea that the life commitments that used to be formed in the decade of the 20s are being forestalled for many young people into their late 20s and 30s. Studies of brain development lend support to this view of a more gradual transition from adolescence to adulthood as capacities for executive function become increasingly coordinated with other brain regions governing emotional reactions and responses to stress.

Life expectancy in the United States has changed over the past 40 years so that today those who are already age 65 can expect to live an average of another 19 years. As a result, we cover two stages of later life: later adulthood and elderhood. Those in the period of elderhood (ages 75 and beyond) are the fastest-growing segment of the U.S. population. As the baby boomers age, they will contribute to an even greater proportion of the population in elderhood. These elders will experience a period of life that is more active, more informed about healthy lifestyle practices, and less constrained by traditional gender and family role scripts than ever before. At the same time, a burst in commercialism is targeting older adults and making them potentially vulnerable to exploitation and poor quality care.

Advantages of the Psychosocial Framework

Psychosocial theory provides an organizing conceptual framework, highlighting the continuous interaction and integration of individual competencies with the demands and resources of culture. Development is viewed as a product of genetic, maturational, societal, and self-directed factors. The psychosocial framework helps students think about how people make meaning of their experiences and how efforts at meaning making change over the life span. Applying the psychosocial framework to an analysis of human development has the following advantages:

- Helps to identify and emphasize themes and directions of growth across the life span.
- Helps readers assess the influence of experiences during earlier life stages on later development.
- Clarifies how one's past, present, and expectations of the future are systematically connected to the lives of people who are older and younger, highlighting intergenerational transmission and the reciprocal influences of the generations.
- Offers a hopeful outlook on the total life course, including positive psychological capacities such as hope, purpose, love, and caring.
- Offers insight into human vulnerabilities at each life stage, embracing these negative poles as potentially adaptive while recognizing the possibility that they can result in an outlook of extreme cautiousness, self-doubt, or social withdrawal.
- Clarifies how a personal worldview develops within the context of cultural influences and historical events.
- Locates development within a framework of significant relationships, emphasizing the simultaneous and complementary processes of autonomy and connection.

The Life-Span Perspective

When we wrote the first edition of *Development Through Life*, we had just completed graduate study, had two young children, and were in the midst of early adulthood. Now, at the publication of the 13th edition, we have just celebrated the birth of our fifth grandchild; our three adult children are all married, living in cities across the country and thriving in their careers; and we are experiencing the challenges of later adulthood.

The psychosocial life-span perspective has been a valuable orienting framework for our scholarly work as well as our personal lives. It has provided insights into the birth and parenting of our children and grandchildren; the deaths of our parents; the successes, disappointments, and transitions of our work lives; and the conflicts and delights of our relationship as husband and wife. The themes of this book have allowed us to anticipate and cope with the challenges of adult life and to remain resilient in the face of

crises. We hope that the ideas presented in this text will provide these same benefits to you.

In addition to enhancing self-understanding, the life-span perspective provides a broader worldview. The ego strengths and developmental competences of those in early, middle and later adulthood provide the resources that are needed to care for and nurture the young. The way that elders find meaning in their longevity and approach the end of life inspire those in younger stages to live their life with hopefulness. And now, in the context of rapidly changing electronic media, younger children and adolescents are increasingly able to guide their elders in embracing new technologies. The life-span perspective helps steer interactions with others so they can be optimally sensitive, supportive, and facilitative for growth at each life stage.

Effects of Cultural and Historical Contexts

The developing person exists in a changing cultural and historical context. Studying development over the course of life requires awareness of the ways societies change over time. The population of the U.S. has increased from 216 million in 1975 to 324 million in 2016. The diversity of this population has changed as well. For example, in 1970 4% of the population was Hispanic; today 16% are Hispanic. Life expectancy in the U.S. in 1970 was 69 for men, 77 for women; in 2010 this had increased to 76 for men and 81 for women. People are waiting longer to marry, family size has decreased, and more adults are voluntarily childless, resulting in an aging population. In this context, people like to say "60 is the new 40." For the field of human development this means that we have to revise our ideas about chronological age and expectations for behavior.

In 1975 there were no cell phones, no desk top computers in the home, and, of course, no email, texting, Facebook, or Twitter. Cell phones are now tiny hand-held computers that dramatically alter the way we connect with one another, entertain ourselves, and gather information. With every kind of streaming resource, people can create their own electronic environment and take it with them, making the notion of "environment" highly personalized.

And amid this swirling technological change, where robots are taking on many of the tasks that used to be done by human hands, the world of work is in flux, and social values are also changing. Dual earner couples are the norm, the boundary between home and work is extremely permeable, there is a great diversity of family structures, more acceptance of lifestyle choices, and fewer constraints about gender roles and sexuality. The task of tracing patterns and pathways of development over the lifespan is becoming increasingly challenging.

Effects of Poverty, Discrimination, and Other Forms of Societal Oppression

The National Center for Children in Poverty at Columbia University estimates that a family of four actually needs twice the income of the poverty level, which was $24,250 a year in 2015, to cover basic expenses. Using this statistic, the Center estimates that 45% of children live in low-income families. The impact of poverty cascades through life from increased risks during the prenatal period through disruptions in physical, cognitive, and emotional development in infancy, childhood, adolescence, and into adult life.

As income inequality increases and scientific evidence about the impact of poverty on health, educational attainment, employment, housing, and longevity accumulates, a number of nongovernmental groups are taking independent actions to form coalitions, raise awareness, and create local programs to deliver services and support the well-being of low-resource families.

Numerous examples of the ways that poverty, discrimination, and various forms of societal oppression affect individual development are interwoven throughout the text. At the same time, research on resilience illustrates the remarkable capacities for growth and adaptation at every period of life.

Organization

Guided by psychosocial theory, we return again and again to the ideas that human development is a social enterprise, that meaning making emerges in social and cultural contexts, and that individuals play a role in shaping the direction of their development. We use case material, boxes on diversity, international data, and cultural examples to emphasize these themes. The following summarizes the basic organization of the text.

Introducing the Field: Chapters 1 to 3

Chapter 1 describes the orientation and assumptions of the text, introduces the psychosocial life-span perspective, and introduces data about longevity and life expectancy, setting the stage for the idea that the lifespan unfolds in a changing historical context. Chapter 2 introduces the role of theory in human development and the questions that a theory of human development is expected to address. The chapter outlines significant ideas about change and growth from seven theoretical perspectives. The presentation of each theory emphasizes its basic features, implications for the study of human development, and links to the psychosocial framework. Chapter 3 introduces basic concepts of psychosocial theory, including an analysis of its strengths and weaknesses.

The Latest on Pregnancy and Prenatal Development: Chapter 4

In Chapter 4, fetal development is presented, highlighting the bidirectional influences of the fetus and the pregnant woman within her social and cultural environments. Continuing discoveries in the field of behavioral genetics have been included in this revision. The chapter traces changes in physical and sensory development across the three trimesters. The chapter covers issues of infertility, alternative reproductive techniques, and ethical considerations surrounding their implementation. We have emphasized research on the health and well-being of pregnant women and their partners, as well as risks to fetal development associated with a pregnant woman's exposure to a wide range of substances, especially nicotine, alcohol, caffeine, other drugs, and environmental toxins. Poverty is discussed as a context that increases risks for suboptimal development. This chapter includes a detailed description of cultural differences in the way pregnancy and childbirth are conceptualized, providing a model for considering the psychosocial process as it will unfold in subsequent chapters. The applied topic of this chapter is abortion; an issue that clearly illustrates the relevance of the field of human development for salient personal, social and cultural perspectives.

Growth and Development from Infancy to Elderhood: Chapters 5 to 14

Chapters 5 through 14 trace basic patterns of normal growth and development in infancy, toddlerhood, early school age, middle childhood, early adolescence, later adolescence, early adulthood, middle adulthood, later adulthood, and elderhood. In these chapters we consider how individuals organize and interpret their experience, noting changes in their behavior, attitudes, worldview, and the coping strategies they use in the face of changing environmental demands.

Each chapter begins with an examination of four or five of the critical developmental tasks of the stage. These tasks reflect global aspects of development, including physical maturation, sensory and motor competence, cognitive maturation, emotional development, social relationships, and self-understanding. We consider the psychosocial crisis of each stage in some detail. We also show how successfully resolving a crisis helps individuals develop a prime adaptive ego quality and how unsuccessful resolution leads to a core pathology. Although most people grow developmentally—albeit with pain and struggle—others do not. People who acquire prime adaptive ego qualities are more likely to lead active, flexible, agentic lives, and be resilient in the face of stressors. People who acquire core pathologies are more likely to lead withdrawn, guarded lives; they are more vulnerable to stressors resulting in greater risk of mental and physical health problems.

Applied Topics at the End of Each Chapter

We conclude each chapter by applying research and theory to a topic of societal importance. These applied topics provide an opportunity for students to link the research and theory about normative developmental processes to the analysis of pressing social concerns. Table 3.1 contains an overview of the basic tasks, crises, and applied topics for each stage of life.

Understanding Death, Dying, and Bereavement: Chapter 15

Chapter 15 addresses end-of-life issues within a psychosocial framework. As with the developmental stage chapters, the topic illustrates the interaction of the biological, psychological, and societal systems as they contribute to the experiences of dying, grieving, and bereavement. The chapter includes definitions of death, the process of dying, death-related rituals, grief, and bereavement, including a focus on the role of culture in shaping ideas about death and expressions of grief. The chapter ends with a discussion of the opportunities for psychosocial growth that are a result of bereavement and the considerations of one's own mortality.

Research Appendix

The Research Appendix highlights basic principles of the scientific process, including the positivist and qualitative approaches to inquiry. The Appendix reviews basic topics in research design including sampling, research methods, and designs for studying development. A section on evaluating research highlights the need to approach the results of research as a critical and informed consumer, recognizing some of the limitations and biases that may be imbedded in the research process. Finally, we review ethical guidelines for conducting research with human participants.

New to This Edition

The 13th edition has retained the basic structure and positive developmental emphasis of previous editions. We continue to strive to make the text clear, readable, and thought provoking, while capturing the complexities and novel concepts that make the study of human development so fascinating. In this edition, each chapter begins with case material that helps bring important themes from the chapter into focus. References to these introductory cases are spread throughout the chapter, providing opportunities to apply concepts to real-world examples. In addition, new first-person quotations have been incorporated to highlight the process of meaning-making that takes place as individuals face the developmental challenges of their stage of life.

The chapters have been rewritten with an effort to streamline and reorganize the material to ensure a clearer and more focused discussion. The text has been completely updated. New research findings, recent census data, updated results of ongoing studies that collect data on new cohorts, and results of ongoing longitudinal studies have been integrated into the narrative. The results of studies using large data sets are summarized as well as some discussion about the difficulties associated with these studies.

The 13th edition is published in a vibrant, new 4-color format. The Picasso paintings, which have been so intimately woven into earlier editions, are now in full color. We hope these wondrous works help students see the connection between the creative enterprise in art, with its experimentation, whimsy, innovation, and insight, and the imaginative, playful and innovative forces at work in creating a life. The 4-color format also improves readability, bringing increased attention to features such as section headings, tables, figures, photographs, and boxes.

On the advice of reviewers, three contemporary research themes have been expanded in this edition: 1. developmental neuroscience; 2. health, fitness, and disability; and 3. the impact of the electronic media environment. Research findings, boxes, tables, and case material have been introduced to extend coverage of these themes across the lifespan. Some examples of these additions are listed below:

Updates on risks associated with prescription drugs during pregnancy.

New information on food safety and nutrition during pregnancy.

New approaches and data on outcomes of assisted reproductive technologies.

Mental health stressors and possible psychological reactions to childbirth for new immigrants highlighting the interaction of culture with mental and physical health.

A box on the neuroscience of attachment.

The dynamic interaction of neurological structures and systems in the coordination of decision-making, risk assessment, and responses to stress.

Robbie Case's theory of Central Conceptual Structures, which integrates cognitive neuroscience and information processing with a constructivist approach to cognitive development.

The impact of poverty on health, including the long-term consequences of early childhood poverty on adult health.

The impact of harsh and neglectful parenting on brain development.

The nature of autism spectrum disorder and its treatment in toddlerhood.

The nature and prevalence of electronic media use in infancy, toddlerhood, early childhood and adolescence.

New insights about sexuality and gender in childhood, adolescence, and adulthood.

Research on transgender issues in childhood, adolescence, and adulthood.

Update on the impact of media on moral development in early school age.

Data on the percent of young children who engage in various types of daily media activities.

The nature and impact of cyber bullying.

Disability and gender atypicality as factors that make children targets of bullying.

The use of computer-assisted match-making and dating sites in adolescence and early adulthood.

Issues faced by new immigrants, especially concerns with family stability, academic success, and physical and mental health.

Added cross-cultural research that highlights social relationships, parenting practices, academic achievement, the role of the elderly, and approaches to death, dying, and bereavement.

The impact of disability on career choice and employment.

The importance of exercise and its contribution to mental and physical health, life satisfaction, and cognitive capacities across the lifespan.

An evaluation of computer games on cognitive functioning in later adulthood.

The relationship of health, fitness, and disability to life acceptance and well-being in later adulthood.

Neuroplasticity, cognitive functioning, and aging.

The importance of nutrition, exercise, and fitness as aspects of lifestyle.

The role of neighborhood resources and design on exercise and fitness in later life.

Features That Support Learning

Several features are included in the 13th edition that we expect will contribute to the learning process.

1. **Organizational Chart:** There is a chart, Table 3.1, which provides a two-page overview of the organization of the text.

2. **Chapter Outlines:** A detailed outline of the chapters is provided at the beginning of the book. An outline is also presented at the start of each chapter.

3. **Chapter Learning Objectives:** Each chapter begins with Learning Objectives. These objectives have been stated using the six thinking processes: remember, understand, apply, analyze, evaluate, and create.

   These objectives are restated at the opening of each related section to help highlight the primary goal for that section of the text and are stated again in the chapter summary to help students review and integrate concepts from the chapter.

4. **Opening Case:** Each chapter starts with a case that brings to life one or more issues addressed in the chapter. These cases are followed by a set of questions labeled "Case Analysis: Using What You Know." The purpose of these cases is threefold: to help students become more personally attached to the concepts of the chapter; to provide a shared life experience that can serve as a basis for class discussion; and to encourage the application of concepts from the text and the course.

5. **Further Reflection:** At the end of each section within the chapter, one or more suggestions are labeled "Further Reflection." These are intended to prompt students to stop and think a bit about what they have just read. These suggestions and questions encourage students to engage in critical thinking, evaluate the information, and link the information to related concepts and/or to personal life experiences.

6. **Boxes:** Two types of boxes are included in the chapters: **Applying Theory and Research to Life** and **Human Development and Diversity**. At the end of each box, a series of critical thinking questions encourage students to evaluate and apply information. The boxes are intended to provide added detail to the text. In the boxes labeled **Applying Theory and Research to Life**, students are encouraged to see the relevance of human development theory and research to issues in contemporary life. In the boxes labeled **Human Development and Diversity**, topics that are covered in the text are expanded to illustrate how differences in culture, ethnicity, family structure, economic resources, and disability can influence developmental pathways.

7. **Case material:** Throughout the chapters longer cases and short vignettes complement the descriptions of developmental issues. These cases highlight the real-life experiences of individuals, sometimes illustrating how individuals cope with challenges at various points in life; and sometimes illustrating the diversity of experiences that are possible at a certain period of life.

8. **End of Chapter Summary:** The chapter summaries are organized around the learning objectives. These summary paragraphs are intended to remind the reader of the big ideas but do not replace a careful reading of the text.

9. **Key Terms:** Key terms are boldfaced in the text, typically defined within the text, and also defined in the glossary.

10. **Glossary:** A comprehensive glossary with brief definitions can be found at the end of the text.

11. **References:** A detailed list of references is provided including references to books, chapters, articles, and websites.

12. **Index:** There is both an author index and a subject index.

Acknowledgments

The works of Erik Erikson and Robert Havighurst have guided and inspired our own intellectual development. Their writings shaped the basic direction of psychosocial theory and have guided an enormous amount of research in human development. They directed us to look at the process of growth and change across the life span. They recognized the intimate interweaving of the individual's life story with a sociohistorical context, emphasizing societal pressures that call for new levels of functioning at each life stage. In their writing, they communicated an underlying optimism about each person's resilience, adaptability, and capacity for growth, an outlook that finds new expression in the work of positive psychology. At the same time, they wrote with a moral passion about our responsibility as teachers, therapists, parents, scholars, and citizens to create a caring society. We celebrate these ideas and continue their expression in the 13th edition of *Development Through Life*.

We want to acknowledge the hundreds of scholars upon whose work this revision is based. The science of human development is a growing, multidisciplinary field. Over the many editions of *Development Through Life*, we have been gratified to see the increasing use of basic concepts from the psychosocial perspective to inform the research agenda. Key constructs including developmental tasks, psychosocial crisis, the radius of significant relationships (social support), trust, autonomy, shame and guilt, industry, competence, group identity, personal identity, intimacy, isolation, generativity, integrity and wisdom have become cornerstones of the life-span perspective on development.

We want to express our thanks to our many students, colleagues, and friends who share their experiences and expertise. We are so appreciative of the faculty who continue to use this book; they are supportive of the psychosocial stage approach and let us know about the ways the book contributes to their students' learning. Through the years, our mentors, Bill McKeachie and Jim Kelly, were voices of wisdom, reminding us of the values of good scholarship and a generous heart. In the early part of our careers, a few friends stand out as people who encouraged us and trusted in our ability to forge this collaboration: Catherine Chilman, Margaret and Harold Feldman, Gisela Konopka, Anne McCreary Juhasz, and Freda Rebelsky. Our former students Brenda Lohman and Laura Landry Meyer were excellent collaborators on our life-span development case book. With each new edition, we turn to our children and their families to offer new observations, try out ideas, and talk over controversies. At each stage, they bring new talents and perspectives that enrich our efforts.

The 13th edition was produced under the guidance of our product manager Star Burruto and content developers Jasmin Tokatlian and Nedah Rose. Their advice, encouragement, support, and vision have been instrumental in bringing this edition to fruition. We are very lucky to have had the benefit of their creative energy. In addition, we would like to express our appreciation to the other professionals at Cengage who have helped make this book possible: Ruth Sataka-Corley, Content Production Manager; Vernon Boes, Art Director; and James Findlay, Marketing Manager.

Finally, we acknowledge the thoughtful, constructive comments and suggestions of the following reviewers: for this 13th edition, Diane Davis Ashe, Valencia College; Judy A. Daniels, University of Hawaii at Manoa; and Tracy A. Phillips. In earlier editions, we received feedback from Verneda Hamm Baugh, Kean University; Dianna G. Cooper, University of Indianapolis; Lisa C. Davies, Nashville State Community College; Tobi DeLong Hamilton, Lewis-Clark State College; Kalinda Jones, Saint Xavier University; Monica Miller-Smith, University of Connecticut-Stamford; Angel Brock Murphy, Eastern Gateway Community College; Alex Schwartz, Santa Monica College.

Supplements: Video and Electronic

Development Through Life: A Psychosocial Approach, 13th edition, is accompanied by supplementary resources prepared for both the instructor and student.

For the Instructor

Online PowerPoint® Slides

These vibrant Microsoft® PowerPoint® lecture slides for each chapter assist you with your lecture by providing concept coverage using images, figures, and tables directly from the textbook.

Online Instructor's Manual

This detailed manual provides sample syllabi, course guidelines, in-class exercises, and chapter objectives to assist instructors in teaching the course.

Cengage Learning Testing, powered by Cognero® Instant Access

Cengage Learning Testing Powered by Cognero® is a flexible, online system that allows you to: import, edit, and manipulate content from the text's test bank or elsewhere, including your own favorite test questions; create multiple test versions in an instant; and deliver tests from your LMS, your classroom, or wherever you want.

MindTap® Psychology, 1 term (6 months) Instant Access for Newman/Newman's Development Through Life: A Psychosocial

MindTap® Psychology for Newman/Newman's Development Through Life: A Psychosocial Approach, 13th Edition is the digital learning solution that powers students from memorization to mastery. It gives you complete control of your course—to provide engaging content, to challenge every individual, and to build their confidence. Empower students to accelerate their progress with MindTap. MindTap: Powered by You. MindTap propels students from memorization to mastery, beginning with Mastery Training as the first activity in each chapter. Investigate Development cases provide engaging real-life stories, with activities that ask students to summarize, analyze evidence, and apply what they have learned to reach conclusions. MindTap gives you complete ownership of your content and learning experience. Customize the interactive syllabi, emphasize the most important topics, and add your own material or notes in the eBook. The outcome-driven application helps you challenge every student, build their confidence, and empower them to be unstoppable.

LMS Integrated MindTap® Psychology

This access code will provide your with seamless access to their MindTap® Psychology resources from within your campus Learning Management System. Students will be prompted to enter this access code the first time that they click on a link in your course that includes Cengage content.

For the Student

Life-Span Development: A Case Book
ISBN-13: 9780534597672

Written by Barbara M. Newman (University of Rhode Island), Philip R. Newman (University of Rhode Island), Laura Landry-Meyer (Bowling Green State University), and Brenda J. Lohman (Iowa State University), *LIFE-SPAN DEVELOPMENT: A CASE BOOK* uses lively, contemporary case studies to illustrate development transitions and challenges in every stage of life. The authors have chosen these cases for their ability to fascinate, engage, and stimulate. Together with thought-provoking questions for analysis, the case studies create a learning experience that helps readers use multiple perspectives to analyze and interpret life events.

MindTap for Psychology

MindTap for *Development Through Life: A Psychosocial Approach* puts everything you need for class in one, easy-to-navigate place. MindTap includes an integrated eBook, assignments, practice quizzes, videos, and more, all designed to help you be a more successful student. MindTap for *Development Through Life: A Psychosocial Approach* can be purchased at www.cengagebrain.com.

About the Authors

Philip R. Newman (Ph.D., University of Michigan) is a social psychologist whose research has focused on the transition to high school as well as on group identity and alienation. His current project is a book about how high schools can better meet the psychosocial needs of adolescents. He has taught courses in introductory psychology, adolescence, social psychology, developmental psychology, counseling, and family, school, and community contexts for development. He served as the director for research and evaluation of the Young Scholars Program at the Ohio State University and as the director of the Human Behavior Curriculum Project for the American Psychological Association. He is a fellow of the American Psychological Association, the Society for the Psychological Study of Social Issues (SPSSI), and the American Orthopsychiatric Association. For fun, Phil enjoys photography, reading mysteries, attending concerts and Broadway plays, and watching baseball. He homeschooled his three children through elementary and middle school.

Barbara M. Newman (Ph.D., University of Michigan) is a professor emeritus in the department of Human Development and Family Studies at the University of Rhode Island. She has also been on the faculty at Russell Sage College and the Ohio State University, where she served as department chair in Human Development and Family Science and as associate provost for faculty recruitment and development. She has taught courses in life-span development, adolescence, human development and family theories, and the research process. Dr. Newman's current research focuses on the sense of belonging among college students, with particular attention to students in minoritized groups. She is a member of an inter-university research team investigating the developing sense of purpose among students with disabilities. For fun, Barbara enjoys reading mysteries, practicing the piano, making up projects with her grandchildren, taking walks along Narragansett Bay and Block Island Sound, and spending time with her family.

Courtesy of Philip and Barbara Newman

Together, the Newmans have worked on programs to bring low-income minority youth to college and have studied the processes involved in their academic success. They are co-authors of 13 books, including a recent book on theories of human development, and numerous articles in the field of human development. They met by the Mason Hall elevator at the University of Michigan, fell in love at first sight, and have been married for 50 years.

Human development is a social enterprise. Ideally, lives unfold in a network of caring relationships as people engage in productive action within stimulating, safe environments. The young ones observe and imitate their elders; the older ones care for and encourage the young. We strive to understand the ways that individuals make meaning and shape the direction of their lives from the creative, playful work of childhood to the inspiring wisdoms of elderhood.

1. Explain the basic assumptions that guide the orientation of the text.

2. Describe the psychosocial approach to the study of development, including the interrelationship among the biological, psychological, and societal systems.

3. Compare historical changes in life expectancy. Analyze individual and group factors that contribute to longevity.

THE DEVELOPMENT THROUGH LIFE PERSPECTIVE

1

— CASE STUDY Ruth Hamilton —

Ruth Hamilton was born in 1898 and died in 2008. Over her long life, she was a teacher, wife, mother, businesswoman, radio talk-show host, legislator, and world traveler. Ruth's advice: "No matter what your age, keep learning. Put this motto on your mirror so that you'll see it: Every day without learning something is a day lost" (Enkelis, 2000, p. 95).

Ruth grew up in the farming town of Alta, Iowa, where she graduated from high school and went on to Iowa State Teacher's College. "At that time, they needed teachers so badly in the country schools that they had crash courses," Ruth recalls. "We could get the two years of training that was needed for a teaching certificate in twelve weeks, but we had to go to school night and day to do it" (Enkelis, 2000, pp. 91–92). She began teaching in a one-room country schoolhouse with children in first, second, fourth, and eighth grades. "All the kids could hear all of the recitations. It was fascinating. I think all the kids benefited," Ruth noted (Enkelis, p. 92).

In July 1920, Ruth met Carter Hamilton while she was watching a sandlot baseball game during a 4th of July celebration. She and Carter fell in love. Carter had been drafted by the Cleveland Indians, and when he came to say goodbye, he said he'd like her to come with him, but he knew her parents wouldn't agree unless they were married, so he thought getting married would be a good idea. Ruth took a half day off from teaching, and they went to Des Moines and were married 8 months after they met. Since married women couldn't teach (a widespread practice in the United States at the turn of the 20th century), she tried to keep it a secret. But her students found out and told other teachers. She had to go before the school board, and they agreed to change the rules.

Carter played baseball in the summers and went to college and later to medical school in the off-season. Once Carter completed his internship they settled in Iowa for a while. Carter wanted Ruth to give up teaching and stay at home, but Ruth could never accept this role. She was an energetic, curious, and active person. Even after they adopted their son Peter, she continued to pursue her own interests.

While in Iowa, Ruth continued teaching. Then Carter's specialization as a radiologist took them to Philadelphia. When they moved to Philadelphia, Ruth expanded her professional life by teaching over the radio. In the 1930s, Ruth was one of America's first female radio talk-show hosts. On a whim, Ruth got a loan and bought a building where she set up a women's dress shop. She operated the shop successfully for two years and then sold the building for $2,000 profit. With that money, she bought a log cabin and 10 acres of land in New Hampshire, where she and her husband vacationed.

In 1937, Ruth began what was to become a life-long interest in travel. She took a 2 month trip to Europe to explore her family history, including travel to Denmark and Sweden. At this time, she went to Berlin where she remembers seeing Adolph Hitler and having a glimpse of his magnetism and the way women swooned when they saw him. She became well aware of how dangerous he was and tried to talk to people back home about this.

Following Carter's death in 1948, Ruth moved into the cabin in New Hampshire. From the ages of 50 to 90, Ruth developed a life of international travel and political leadership. She traveled extensively beginning in the 1950s through 1990, giving lectures and writing articles about the countries she visited. She became involved in politics, including the political campaigns of Eugene McCarthy, George McGovern, and Jimmy Carter. She was the first woman elected to the New Hampshire legislature, where she was elected twice from 1964 to 1973. She took an active role in legislative issues, including reducing the legal voting age, issues related to wiretapping and eavesdropping, and legislation to have inspections and licensing for residential homes that care for senior citizens. In 1986, she was honored as an "Unsung Heroine" by the Claremont New Hampshire Commission on the Status of Women.

In her 90s Ruth moved to an assisted living community in Florida where she became a member of "Growing Bolder," a social networking site for older adults. At age 109, she was recognized on that site as the world's oldest video blogger. You can watch her blog about the power of curiosity at https://www.growingbolder.com/ruth1898-on-the-power-of-curiosity-1499/.

Ruth was an amazingly active, enthusiastic, outgoing person. She once said, "I just wish I could live to be one thousand years old because there are so many things that I want to see improved" (Enkelis, p. 95).

Imagine for a moment living for more than 100 years into an unknowable future. Think of Ruth Hamilton, starting out as a teacher in a one-room country school and eventually sharing her thoughts over the Internet as a video blogger. Finding love in a most unexpected way, adopting a son, hosting a radio talk show, traveling the world, building a new political career after the early death of her husband, advocating for the young and the old—these are all segments of a life built on intelligence, resilience, and optimism. Ruth's sense of agency—her ability to set goals and make things happen to achieve these goals—her curiosity, and her love of learning propelled her through challenges, losses, and accomplishments from one chapter of her life to the next.

If you are intrigued by the life of Ruth Hamilton, if you wonder how and why people make the choices that they make, how they cope with adversity, and how they maintain a sense of purpose, you have come to the right place—the study of human development. You are about to explore theory and research that have accumulated over the years about how individuals make sense of their experiences, make decisions and take actions to adapt to their environments, cope with challenges, and continue to develop from one period of life to the next. This process is as individual as each person's life story. It is influenced by the quality of one's social relationships, as well as such factors as gender, ethnicity, cultural identity, health, socioeconomic status, education, sexual orientation, physical abilities and disabilities, and historical and social contexts. Even though each person's life is unique, common patterns of experience and meaning allow us to

Growth occurs at every stage of life. Within a large family, we have opportunities to observe family resemblances and individual differences, patterns of continuity from year to year, as well as evidence of maturation and change.

know and care for one another and contribute to one another's well-being. As you study the life-span approach to human development, you will learn to identify and evaluate patterns of transition and transformation from one period of life to another. In this process, you will come to recognize that there are both intergroup differences and individual variations within groups.

Several features of the chapters are intended to foster your critical thinking and to broaden your ability to link the theories and research presented in the text to important social issues. Boxes labeled "Applying Theory and Research to Life" and "Human Development and Diversity" end with a set of critical thinking questions. Case studies are followed by prompts entitled "Using What You Know." And interspersed in the text are encouragements for "Further Reflection." All these features are designed to engage you as an active reader and to help you link what you are reading about to your own personal life experiences.

This chapter provides a brief introduction to three topics that are central to the study of the **life span**. First, we outline six **assumptions** about human development that guide the orientation of the text. Second, we introduce the concept of a **psychosocial approach** to development. Third, we review data about **life expectancy** to start you thinking in a concrete way about the course of your life and the decisions you make that may directly influence your life story. ●

Assumptions of the Text

OBJECTIVE 1   Explain the basic assumptions that guide the orientation of the text.

Our perspective on development through life makes the following six assumptions that are critical to the orientation of this book:

1. *Growth occurs at every period of life, from conception through elderhood.* At each period, new capacities emerge, new roles are undertaken, new challenges must be faced, and, as a result, a new orientation toward

self and society unfolds. The concept of life-span development implies **plasticity**, a capacity for adaptive reorganization at the neurological, psychological, and behavioral levels.

2. *Individual lives show both continuity and developmental change over time.* An awareness of the processes that contribute to both continuity and change is central to an understanding of human development. **Continuity** refers to stability in characteristics from one period of life to another. It also refers to a sense of sameness over time built on a history of memories, identity, and reflected self. **Developmental change** refers to patterns of growth and reorganization. Change may be attributed to biological maturation, systematic socialization, self-directed striving, and the interaction of these forces.

3. *We need to understand the whole person, because we function in an integrated manner.* To achieve such an understanding, we need to study the major developments in physical, social, emotional, and cognitive capacities and their interrelationships. For example, what people think about moving to a new town is influenced by their social roles, their expectations and goals, their feelings in the situation, and their physical health or limitations. Each system serves as a stimulus for the others, requiring an integration of all these capacities in order to produce an adaptive response.

4. *Behavior must be interpreted in the context of relevant settings and personal relationships.* Human beings are highly skilled in adapting to their environments. The meaning of a given behavior pattern or behavior change must be interpreted in light of the significant physical and social environments in which it occurs. While individuals are changing, so are their environments. As children grow older, they may have new siblings; their parents will age; and they may encounter new technologies, health care interventions, or educational approaches that alter the nature of daily life. As a result, we need to be able to consider how changes in the nature of the person are impacted by changes in the environments in which they function.

5. *People contribute actively to their development.* These contributions take many forms, including the expression of tastes and preferences, choices and goals, and one's willingness to embrace or resist cultural and societal expectations. One of the most critical ways in which a person contributes to his or her development is through the creation of significant social relationships, which then form a context for social support and socialization. Some societies offer more opportunities for choice and promote a person's ability to mold the direction of development, whereas others have fewer resources, are more restrictive, or place less value on individuality (Veenhoven, 2000).

6. *Diversity is a product of the interaction of the biological, the psychological, and the societal systems.* Diversity refers to the differences that exist among people. Diversity is built into the architecture of the human genome.

It increases as individuals encounter new settings and make unique meaning of their experiences. Social identities, economic resources, and educational opportunities are all aspects of the societal system that contribute to diversity. The differences that exist among people are part of what protects the human species and allows it to adapt across a wide and changing range of environments. Throughout the chapters, we highlight the nature of individual, group, and cultural differences and feature some specific examples in the **Human Development and Diversity** boxes.

FURTHER REFLECTION: Describe three examples of assumption 5, illustrating how people's decisions and goals influence the course of their development.

A Psychosocial Approach: The Interaction of the Biological, Psychological, and Societal Systems

OBJECTIVE 2 Describe the psychosocial approach to the study of development, including the interrelationship among the biological, psychological, and societal systems.

Erik Erikson (1963, p. 37) wrote that human life as the individual experiences it is produced by the interaction and modification of three major systems: the biological system, the psychological system, and the societal system. Each system can be examined for patterns of continuity and change over the life course. Each system can be modified by self-guided choices. The integration of the biological, psychological, and societal systems leads to a complex, **biopsychosocial** dynamic portrait of human thought and behavior.

In many developmental analyses of behavior, you may come across the terms "nature" and "nurture." These terms are often used as shorthand for thinking about the roles of genetics and environments in guiding development. Typically, nature refers to genetic predispositions or potentials and inborn or innate qualities that guide the unfolding of capacities and traits. Nurture refers to the patterns of socialization and care that the person receives. The science of development has often been presented as the study of the ways nature and nurture interact to produce a certain outcome, for example intelligence, assertiveness, or hopefulness.

In *Development Through Life* we take a somewhat different approach by expanding the analysis to three interrelated systems: the biological, the societal, and the psychological systems. Rather than thinking of the developing person as passively shaped by forces of nature and nurture, we think of the person as actively engaged in the developmental process through the application of the psychological system. The psychological system is the **meaning-making** system that seeks out information, integrates information from many sources, and evaluates experiences as positive or negative, encouraging or threatening. Depending on their experiences and predispositions, some people are more likely to take the initiative in shaping the course of their development while others are more passive. The psychosocial approach is an attempt to sketch the ways that a person's worldview and sense of self in society change as a product of the interaction of these three dynamic systems over the course of life.

The Biological System

The **biological system** includes all those processes necessary for the physical functioning of the organism and for mental activity (see FIGURE 1.1 ▶). The brain and spinal cord (the central nervous system) and the peripheral nervous system are components of the biological system through which all sensory information is received, processed, and transmitted to guide behavior. Biological processes develop and change as a consequence of genetically guided maturation; environmental stimulation and resources, including social interactions, cognitive challenges, and nutrition; exposure to environmental toxins; encounters with accidents and diseases; and lifestyle patterns of behavior.

We can imagine that when Ruth Hamilton fell in love with Carter, this resulted in many changes to her biological system including changes in hormones, sexual behavior, eating and sleeping patterns, and physical activity. Falling in love is a major change factor that brings out a cascade of modifications to the biological system. As a result of some feature of the biological system which is not disclosed in the case, Ruth and Carter were not able to have children. This biological problem posed new challenges to Ruth's self-concept and led to the eventual decision to adopt a son, thereby altering her social role.

Some components of the biological system influence the maturation of other components of the biological system. For example, when the infant's limbs achieve a certain length and

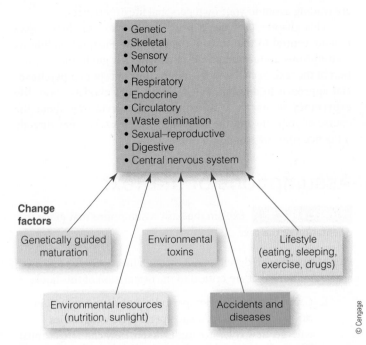

FIGURE 1.1 ▶ THE BIOLOGICAL SYSTEM

muscle strength, the baby is able to reach out from a sitting position to begin crawling—a new form of locomotion. This results in new opportunities for exploration of the environment which in turn results in new neural networks and changes in the organization of the brain. The biological system is itself a multilevel, dynamic system in which maturation at one level can have profound, and sometimes unexpected, consequences for maturation at another level.

Cultures differ in their support of physical growth and health, depending on the availability of adequate nutritional resources, approaches to the treatment of illness, exposure to environmental toxins and hazardous conditions, and the availability of information about healthy lifestyle choices.

In the case of Ruth Hamilton, two examples of the influences of the biological system on her life experiences are her **longevity** and her good **health**. Looking at Figure 1.1, try to formulate a list of other aspects of the biological system that may have been important in shaping Ruth Hamilton's life story. The theme of health is synergistically integrated throughout the text. At each stage of life, health care practices, access to health care resources and knowledge, and individual differences in health-related risks and resilience have an impact on a person's developmental trajectory.

The Psychological System

The **psychological system** includes those mental processes central to a person's ability to make meaning of experiences and take action (see FIGURE 1.2 ▶). Emotion, memory, perception, motivation, thinking and reasoning, language, symbolic abilities, and one's orientation to the future are examples of psychological processes. When these processes are integrated, they provide the resources for processing information, solving problems, and navigating reality. In the case of Ruth Hamilton, we can appreciate the influence of the psychological system in her motivation,

persistence, independence, ingenuity, personal goals, and feelings of self-determination.

Like the biological processes, psychological processes develop and change over one's life span. Psychological change is guided in part by genetic information. The capacity for intellectual functioning and the direction of cognitive maturation are genetically guided. Some genetic diseases result in intellectual impairment and a reduced capacity for learning. Psychological change also results from the accumulation of experiences and from encounters with various educational settings that impact brain development and result in new cognitive structures and new approaches to problem solving. Psychological processes can be enhanced by numerous life experiences including the quality of parenting one receives; interactions with friends; opportunities for play of all types; travel; reading; exposure to music, art, poetry, and the dramatic arts; and schooling.

Finally, psychological change can be self-directed. A person can decide to pursue a new interest, learn another language, or adopt a new set of ideas. Ruth Hamilton took time for self-discovery through travel, which expanded her worldview. By retreating to New Hampshire after the death of her husband, she gave herself time for reflection and recovery in a place that she and Carter enjoyed together. People can strive to achieve new levels of **self-insight**, to be more aware of their thoughts and feelings, and to be less defensive. Meditation and mindfulness practice are examples of techniques people are using to achieve these goals. There is evidence to suggest that self-insight is a vital component of positive mental health (Wilson, 2009). What strategies do you use to alter your worldview or achieve new levels of self-insight?

Meaning Making

The meaning we make of our experiences changes over the course of life. Think about the concept of love as an example. In infancy, love is almost entirely physical. It is the pervasive sense of comfort and security that we feel in the presence of our caregivers. By adolescence, the idea of love includes loyalty, emotional closeness, and sexuality. In adulthood, the concept of love may expand to include a new emphasis on companionship and open communication. The need to be loved and to give love remains important throughout life, but the self we bring to a loving relationship, the context within which the relationship is established, and the signs we look for as evidence of love change with age.

Meaning is created out of efforts to interpret and integrate the experiences of the biological, psychological, and societal systems. A primary focus of this meaning making is the search for **identity**. Humans struggle to define themselves—to achieve a sense of identity—through a sense of connectedness with certain other people and groups and through feelings of distinctiveness from others. We establish categories that define to whom we are connected, about whom we care, and which of our own qualities we admire. We also establish categories that define those to whom we are not connected, those about whom we do not care, and those qualities of our own that we reject or deny. These categories provide us with an orientation toward certain kinds of people and away from others, toward certain life choices and away from others. The psychosocial perspective brings to light the dynamic

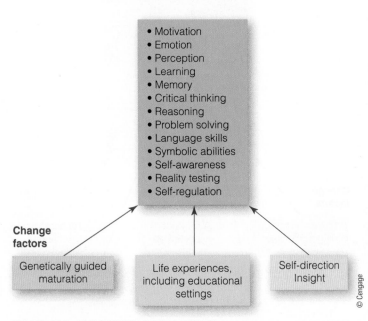

Change factors

- Motivation
- Emotion
- Perception
- Learning
- Memory
- Critical thinking
- Reasoning
- Problem solving
- Language skills
- Symbolic abilities
- Self-awareness
- Reality testing
- Self-regulation

Genetically guided maturation

Life experiences, including educational settings

Self-direction Insight

© Cengage

FIGURE 1.2 ▶ THE PSYCHOLOGICAL SYSTEM

The desire to experience a loving relationship remains strong throughout life. However, the self one brings to a loving relationship changes at each stage. How might experiences of love change from adolescence to early adulthood to later adulthood?

interplay of the roles of the self and the others, the I and the We, as they contribute to the emergence of identity over the life course.

The Societal System

The **societal system** includes social roles; social support; **culture**, including rituals, myths, and social expectations; media; leadership styles; communication patterns; family organization; ethnic and subcultural influences; political ideologies and forms of government; religions; patterns of economic prosperity or **poverty**; conditions of war or peace; and exposure to racism, sexism, and other forms of discrimination, intolerance, or intergroup hostility. The societal system encompasses those processes that foster or disrupt a person's sense of social integration and social identity (see FIGURE 1.3 ▶). Through laws and public policies, political and economic structures, and educational opportunities, societies influence the psychosocial development of individuals and alter the life course for future generations (de St. Aubin, McAdams, & Kim, 2004). Societal processes may change over one's life span. The process of modernization may bring exposure to new levels of education, new technologies, encounters with more diverse groups of people, and new forms of work. These changes are likely to result in more individualistic values, new priorities about which skills are valued, and changing patterns of family life (Greenfield, 2009).

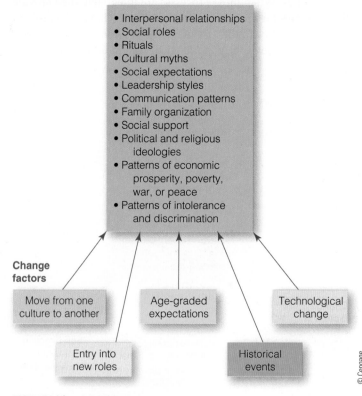

- Interpersonal relationships
- Social roles
- Rituals
- Cultural myths
- Social expectations
- Leadership styles
- Communication patterns
- Family organization
- Social support
- Political and religious ideologies
- Patterns of economic prosperity, poverty, war, or peace
- Patterns of intolerance and discrimination

Change factors

Move from one culture to another

Entry into new roles

Age-graded expectations

Historical events

Technological change

FIGURE 1.3 ▶ THE SOCIETAL SYSTEM

Technological innovations can modify the societal system. For example, television, cell phones, personal computers, and the Internet are technological innovations that have modified people's access to information and relationships. These technologies have altered children's roles, providing them with resources that can allow them to function at new levels of autonomy and competence. In many families, children teach their parents and grandparents how to make use of new technologies, thus expanding their role. Cell phones reduce barriers to communication, a change that has multiple impacts on patterns of communication—some positive and some negative.

Historical events can also influence the societal system, altering social roles, access to resources, economic conditions, and one's sense of personal safety or security. Events such as the destruction of the World Trade Towers in 2001, the economic collapse of 2008, the devastation of Hurricane Katrina and Hurricane Sandy, the bombing at the Boston Marathon, and the shooting at the Sandy Hook Elementary School have an enduring influence on people's sense of safety, economic security, and confidence in key social institutions. Positive events, such as the Supreme Court rulings regarding marriage equality and the passage of the Affordable Health Care Act have provided social validation and access to resources that contribute to a more secure, predictable life.

In this text, the role of culture is emphasized as it contributes to the pattern, pace, and direction of development. Societies differ in their **worldviews**, including the emphasis placed on collectivism or individualism, ideas about the major sources of stress and ways to alleviate stress, and beliefs about which groups are viewed as more powerful or more important than others. Societies differ in their emphasis on and belief in science, spirituality, and fatalism. They differ in their **age-graded expectations**, such as when a person is considered to be a child, an adult, or an elder, and how people in these age roles should be treated. They differ in their definitions of morality, beauty, bravery, wealth, and other ideals that may define individual and group aspirations. As you read the text, you will encounter **Human Development and Diversity** boxes. These boxes provide examples of how norms of development might be viewed differently in different cultures or ethnic groups. We hope these examples will help sensitize you to the role of culture in defining what may be viewed as appropriate, optimal, or normal behavior.

The societal system is illustrated in several ways in the case of Ruth Hamilton. Women did not have the right to vote in the United States until 1920. By then, Ruth was 22. Early in her life, there was a teacher shortage. The societal system responded by providing training opportunities, and Ruth took advantage of this program. When she married Carter, the policies of the school prohibited married women from teaching. In the early part of the 20th century it was considered improper for married women to work. Although many women were trained as teachers, they were forced to leave their profession once they were married (Enkelis, 2000). Ruth, however, pushed back against these restrictions, hoping to continue in her work. Due to her good performance and the need for teachers in her town, the societal system changed in order to keep her in the school. This specific example illustrates that the societal system can impose constraints, but that there are many ways that individuals and groups can alter the societal system.

The Psychosocial Impact of Poverty

In thinking about the impact of societal factors on development, we want to highlight the context of poverty as a major obstacle to optimal development. (See the **Applying Theory and Research to Life** box Poverty.) Racism, sexism, ageism, homophobia, and discrimination against individuals with physical, intellectual, and emotional disabilities are other examples. However, under conditions of poverty, individuals have fewer options and less opportunity to escape or avoid these other societal deterrents. Poverty has powerful and potentially pervasive effects on the biological and psychological systems across the life span.

The government, as an arm of the societal system, defines poverty in order to determine who is eligible for certain resources and services. The **poverty threshold** is defined as the minimum cash income needed to support a person or a family in meeting basic needs of daily living. The poverty threshold varies by family size, number of children, and the age of the householder (Bishaw, 2012). Certain terms are used in the literature to refer to the level or intensity of poverty: Extreme poverty—income less than 50 percent of the poverty threshold; Poverty—income less than 100 percent of the poverty threshold; and Low income—income less than 200 percent of the poverty threshold.

The original definition of the poverty threshold was created in the 1960s. It was formulated based on the idea that under subsistence conditions, a family would need to spend about one third of its income on basic food needs; so the poverty threshold was set at three times the cost of a basic food budget. Each year, the dollar value of this minimum level is recalculated based on the cost of living index. Critics argue that this approach to defining poverty is inadequate in today's economy. The cost of food has remained relatively low in comparison to the cost of housing, transportation, health care, energy, and child care (for families with young children). They suggest that the poverty threshold should be more like five times the cost of a basic food budget. Furthermore, the cost of living and employment opportunities vary by states and regions of the country, but the basic poverty threshold is set at a national level and is applied without consideration for these regional variations (Grusky, Mattingly, & Varner, 2015). Based on the definition used by the U.S. Census Bureau, in 2014 there were 46.7 million people in poverty (U.S. Census Bureau, 2015).

In and of itself, poverty does not place inevitable limits on development. There are many instances of children who grew up in poverty and achieved eminence (Harrington & Boardman, 2000). Many children flourish under conditions of meager family resources. However, it is well documented that poverty increases the risks that individuals face, including risks associated with malnutrition, poor quality health care, living in poor quality and overcrowded housing, living in a hazardous or dangerous neighborhood, and attending ineffective schools. Poverty is linked with reduced access to basic resources associated with health and survival (Crosnoe & Huston, 2007; Yoo, Slack, & Holl, 2009). Exposure to these risk factors early and continuously throughout childhood is associated with higher incidences of health problems, greater challenges in achieving the developmental tasks of each life stage, disruptions in family and work trajectories, and reduced life expectancy (Hayward, Crimmins, Miles, & Yang, 2000; Knitzer, 2007).

Poverty

Conditions Leading to Poverty

A number of societal factors contribute to the percentage of families living in poverty: (1) the decline in well-paying manufacturing and management jobs due to downsizing and outsourcing; (2) large numbers of single-mother households; (3) the erosion of the economic safety net for poor families, including the decline in cash transfers and benefits to families in the Transitional Assistance to Needy Families (TANF) program; (4) natural disasters such as hurricanes and floods; and (5) the decline in the purchasing power of the minimum wage. The actual buying power of the minimum wage has declined by over 30 percent since the 1960s (Siegmund, 2015).

Poverty is transitory for some families—such as when a wage earner becomes unemployed and then finds new work—but persistent over the life course for others. For unmarried women who become mothers in adolescence, poverty is often a result of interrupted education, the inability to work full time (usually because of time needed to care for their children), and the low-paying jobs that are available to those with limited educational attainment. Furthermore, many of these young mothers are growing up in families that are already living in poverty. Eighty-six percent of children whose parents do not have a high-school diploma live in low-income families (Jiang, Ekono, & Skinner, 2015).

Divorce places many women and their children into poverty. In many instances, the family was already encountering financial strain, one of the primary factors associated with divorce. However, following divorce, it is not uncommon for women to experience a substantial drop in family income (Gadalla, 2009). The poverty rate of custodial mothers in 2011 (32 percent) was significantly higher than the poverty rate for custodial fathers (16 percent). The level of poverty experienced by newly divorced women is aggravated by the failure of many fathers to pay child support (Putze, 2014). Poverty after divorce may be transitory if women

remarry and their family income returns to pre-divorce levels (Reilly, 2009). With increases in women's education and career prospects, and laws enforcing the payment of child support, women may be more likely to emerge from poverty after divorce in the future than was the case in the past.

Negative Consequences of Poverty

Persistent poverty and exposure to poverty during infancy and early childhood are associated with greater vulnerability and more negative consequences to physical health, cognitive development and school achievement, and mental health. Specific family characteristics increase the likelihood that children in poor and low-income families will experience negative academic and health outcomes. These include:

Households without English speakers
Large families
Low parental education
Residential mobility
Single-parent families
Teen mothers
Unemployed parents

Children with three or more of these risk factors are the most vulnerable to early and continuing negative outcomes (Robbins, Stagman, & Smith, 2012).

Physical Health. Exposure to poverty during the prenatal period is associated with increased risks for having premature babies and babies that are small for gestational age (Nepomnyaschy, 2009). Children in low-income families are more likely to be in fair or poor health and lack access to quality health care. Children in low-income families often lack treatment for existing physical health problems, such as asthma, or go untreated for infections that then become more serious and can result in long-term chronic conditions. For a family in poverty, a visit to a doctor that costs $75 is a significant and possibly prohibitive expense.

A person's health is not only related to their current level of income, but also to their exposure to economic

hardship from childhood through adulthood. Conditions of poverty create a heightened level of wear and tear on the body, brought about by the need to continuously respond to stress. Over time, the cumulative impact of these conditions results in accelerated physical deterioration leading to increased rates of diseases and an earlier age of death (Fuller-Rowell, Evans, & Ong, 2012; Williams, 2012).

Academic Achievement. Higher family income is consistently associated with higher academic achievement. Children in low-income families begin kindergarten with a substantial disadvantage with regard to specific academic skills such as counting, recognizing letters of the alphabet, and reading. By the time they are in the third grade, children in low-income families have an average vocabulary of 4,000 words compared to a vocabulary of 12,000 words for children from middle-income families (Klein & Knitzer, 2007).

Research on seasonal fluctuations in learning shows that children from low-income families and low-resource communities have substantially fewer opportunities over the summer than their middle-income peers. Year after year, they begin school behind their middle-income peers. In addition, inequities in school resources and educational opportunities across communities are well documented. As a result, by the time children from low-income families reach the ninth grade, they have significantly lower test scores, are less likely to be placed in college-preparatory tracks, and are more likely to drop out of high school than their higher socioeconomic (SES) peers (Alexander, Entwisle, & Olson, 2007).

In schools with students from a diversity of economic backgrounds, the students from low-income families tend to be viewed as less competent by the teachers and their wealthier classmates. This may create an added burden on their academic self-concept and result in lower academic performance (Crosnoe, 2009). Fewer adolescents who live in low-income families apply to and attend college than their middle and higher income peers. A national longitudinal study followed students from 2002 when they were in tenth grade, through 2012, when they were age 24. Students could be linked to their families' socioeconomic (SES) group based on their parents' income, education, and occupation. Fourteen percent of the low SES group had a bachelor's degree or higher compared to 29 percent of the middle SES group, and 60 percent of the high SES group (U.S. Department of Education, 2015).

Mental Health. Early experiences shape the establishment of neural networks, including the way the brain processes information and manages emotions. A key ingredient of early brain development is the quality of caregiving relationships, especially the ability of caregivers to be appropriately nurturing, responsive, and stimulating. Children from low-income families are more likely to be exposed prenatally to factors such as maternal malnutrition, cigarette smoke, alcohol, and environmental toxins that disrupt neural development. Infants and young children in impoverished families are more likely to be exposed to parental depression, other diagnosable mental disorders, and parental adversities including domestic violence, substance abuse, and residential instability or homelessness that disrupt or destabilize caregiving. In addition, threats to safety are of special concern to children living in low-income neighborhoods where exposure to uncontrollable violence

Poverty is a powerful characteristic of the societal system. Children growing up in poverty are exposed to stressors and hazards that can severely restrict development.

on the streets and near the school is associated with symptoms of post-traumatic stress (Caughy, Nettles, O'Campo, & Lohrfink, 2006).

A combination of parental mental health problems, neighborhood instability, and chaotic school environments all contribute to the emergence of short- and long-term mental health consequences including depression, acting-out behaviors, difficulty concentrating, and school problems. Living in poverty is associated with higher rates of learning problems and diagnosable disorders in older children (Knitzer & Cooper, 2006).

These often lead to juvenile justice involvement and higher school dropout rates.

Critical Thinking Questions

1. Explain what is meant by the phrase "the cycle of poverty."

2. Create a table that shows how the experiences of growing up in poverty might influence a person's physical health, academic achievement, and mental health as an adolescent and as an adult.

3. Propose some immediate steps that a society could take to reduce the negative consequences of poverty.

With 45 percent of children growing up in low-income families, the United States faces a serious long-term challenge (DeNavas, Walt, & Proctor, 2015; Jiang, Ekono, & Skinner, 2015). Evidence suggests that children growing up in poverty are likely to experience multiple physical and mental health problems, which often grow worse as they encounter the stressors of poverty in adolescence and adulthood. Problems in cognitive and behavioral functioning have implications for academic achievement, job acquisition and performance, and the formation of long-term, stable relationships. The challenge for the field of human development is to inform policies and programs that will buffer children and families from the negative consequences of poverty (Yoshikawa, Aber, & Beardslee, 2012).

Because of the complex and pervasive impact of poverty on development, we introduce it as a fundamental societal theme. Issues related to the impact of poverty on patterns of individual

development and family life will be addressed in more detail in subsequent chapters.

Overview of the Psychosocial Approach

The psychosocial approach seeks to understand development as a product of interactions among biological, psychological, and societal processes. Changes in one of the three systems (biological, psychological, or societal) generally bring about changes in the others. As an example, the psychological capacities for thinking about oneself and others develop over time as the social information-processing areas of the brain are stimulated (Adolphs, 2009; Grossman, 2013). The biological system recognizes and processes social stimulation. The societal system creates the contexts for social interactions and introduces complex patterns of values and priorities for social behavior. Further, the psychological system internalizes these values and assigns unique meaning to social events. So, for example, researchers find that in a task that requires recognition of one's own face and the face of a familiar other, Westerners, who tend to emphasize self-related events, recognize their own face more quickly, and East Asians, who tend to emphasize social connections among people, recognize the familiar other more quickly (Sui, Liu, & Han, 2009).

Throughout life, personal relationships occupy our attention. Some of these relationships are more important than others, but their quality and diversity provide a basis for the study of one's psychosocial development. As we progress through the stages of life, most of us develop an increasing capacity to initiate new relationships and to innovate in our thoughts and actions so as to direct the course of our lives.

At each period of life, people strive to master a unique group of psychological tasks that provides essential learning for social adaptation within their society. Each life stage brings a normative crisis, which is viewed as a tension between one's competencies and the new demands of society. People try to reduce this tension by using a variety of familiar coping strategies and by learning new ones. A positive resolution of each crisis yields new social abilities and a new understanding of the self and others that enhance a person's capacity to adapt successfully in succeeding stages. A negative resolution of each crisis typically results in defensiveness, rigidity, or withdrawal, which decreases a person's ability for successful social adaptation in succeeding stages.

— CASE STUDY Rose —

The case of Rose provides an opportunity to apply the concepts that were presented about the biological, the psychological, and the societal systems and their interactions to a real-life example.

Rose is a 60-year-old woman who has been having serious attacks of dizziness and shortness of breath as Thanksgiving approaches. Rose is usually active and energetic. In the past, she looked forward to entertaining her family, which used to include three married daughters, one married son, their spouses, and their children. However, her son has recently been divorced. Feelings between him and his ex-wife are bitter. Any attempts on Rose's part to communicate with her former daughter-in-law or granddaughter are met with outbursts of hostility from her son. Although Rose is very fond of her daughter-in-law and granddaughter, she knows that she cannot invite them to the family gathering without stirring up intense conflict with her son. Rose's daughters suggest having the dinner at one of their homes in order to prevent further conflict. They hope this solution will take some of the pressure off their mother and ease the attacks. Rose agrees, but her attacks continue.

Case Discussion

How are the biological, psychological, and societal systems involved in Rose's situation? We might hypothesize that her physical symptoms—dizziness and shortness of breath—are due to an inability to resolve a difficult family conflict. Psychological and societal demands may elicit responses from the biological system, as they commonly do in people under stress. The biological system often alerts a person to the severity of a threat or crisis through the development of physical symptoms. Rose might visit her family doctor in order to evaluate whether her symptoms are a result of high blood pressure or early signs of heart disease. There may be medication that can help reduce these symptoms, allowing Rose to feel less anxious and more confident about her role in the family.

Rose's psychological system is involved in interpreting her son's behavior, which she views as forcing her to choose between him and her daughter-in-law and granddaughter. She might also use psychological processes to try to arrive at a solution to the conflict. So far, Rose has not identified any satisfactory solution. Although she can avoid the conflict most of the time, the impending Thanksgiving dinner is forcing her to confront it directly.

The psychological system includes Rose's self-concept as well as her emotional state. Through memory, Rose retains a sense of her family at earlier periods, when they enjoyed greater closeness. Having to face a Thanksgiving dinner at which she will feel angry at her son or guilty about excluding her daughter-in-law and granddaughter places her in a fundamental conflict. The Thanksgiving meal is also a symbolic event, representing Rose's idea of family unity, which she cannot achieve. Rose will lose the sense of family unity that she has tried to preserve.

The societal system influences the situation at several levels. First, there are the societal expectations regarding the mother role: Mother is nurturing, loving, and protecting. But Rose cannot be nurturing without sending messages of rejection either to her son or to her daughter-in-law and granddaughter. Second, social norms for relating to various family members after a divorce are unclear. How should Rose behave toward her son's former spouse? How should she relate to her grandchild if her son is no longer the child's custodial parent? Rose is confused about what to do. Third, the Thanksgiving celebration has social, religious, and cultural significance. This family ritual was performed in Rose's home when she was a child, and she has carried it through in her own home as an adult. Now, however, she is being forced to pass the responsibility for this gathering to her daughter before she is ready to do so and, as a result, Rose is likely to feel a special sense of loss.

CASE ANALYSIS Using What You Know

1. How does this case illustrate the interconnections among the biological, psychological, and societal systems?
2. Given what you know about the assumptions of psychosocial theory, how might Rose's stage of development influence her perceptions of this situation and her approach to coping with this conflict?
3. How might you pose a research question based on the information raised in this case study? (For example, how likely is it that parents experience health problems following their child's divorce?)

4. How might Rose's social support system, especially her daughters, be involved in helping her cope with this conflict?

5. How might the current conflict impact future psychosocial development for Rose? Consider the assumptions of the text as you try to answer this question.

FURTHER REFLECTION From your own experiences, what are two examples of how the biological, the psychological, and the societal systems interact?

How does your culture view the stages of life? For example, what messages from your family, community, or ethnic group influence your understanding of the distinctions between childhood, adolescence, adulthood, and elderhood?

How do these cultural beliefs influence the way you make meaning of your current stage of life?

The Life Span

OBJECTIVE 3 Compare historical changes in life expectancy. Analyze individual and group factors that contribute to longevity.

Many of our most important life decisions are made with either an implicit or explicit assumption about how long we expect to live. These assumptions have an impact on our behavior, self-concept, attitudes, and outlook on the future. For example, Colleen expects to live to be about 80 years old. She reasons that there is no rush about getting married because, even if she waits until she is 40, she will still have 40 years of married life, and that is a long time to get along with one partner. In contrast, Tyler expects to live to be about 25. Several of his older brothers' friends died of gunshot wounds, others died from drug overdoses, and some died in prison. He believes that he may as well take all the risks and have all the fun he can in life, because his time is short. He hopes to have lots of babies by many women so that some part of him will live on. Marie is celebrating her 90th birthday. She had expected to live to about age 75. Most of her friends and all her older siblings are dead. She is puzzled by the idea of having lived so long and sometimes wonders about the purpose of her long life.

People's expectations about how long they will live influence their life planning and what they think they need to accomplish in order to provide some security in adulthood and old age. There are national trends, but there are also regional, racial/ethnic, gender, and economic differences in longevity that can influence people's expectations about length of life, life planning, and the timing of transitions into adulthood.

Life Expectancy

Life expectancy is a statistical projection of the number of years one can expect to live. The task of mapping one's future depends on how long one expects to live. Naturally, for specific individuals, we can make only rough predictions. We know that some lives may be cut short by a disaster, an accident, or an illness. On the other hand, some people, like Ruth Hamilton, are exceptionally long lived.

As the life expectancy has changed, a complex network of policies and practices are coming into question. These include the idea of retirement, the age of retirement, the nature of adult retirement communities, dating and remarriage in later life, second or third careers, and educational opportunities for elders.

In the 1930s, the U.S. government set 65 as the age of retirement in the Social Security system. The selection of this age was a combination of a pragmatic decision based on the typical age for retirement in a few private and state-based systems as well as actuarial data. In the late 1930s and 1940s, slightly over 50 percent of men survived from age 21 to age 65, and those who survived to age 65 had about another 13 years to live. In 2010, those who reached age 65 could expect an average of another 19 years of life. People have to think about how to support themselves for 20 or 30 years, leading to new ideas about retirement and financial independence in later life.

As people come to expect that life will last into the 80s and 90s, their ideas about the ideal age for assuming adult roles change. A longer life expectancy seems to be related to a more gradual transition into adulthood, including a later age at marriage, older age for having children, and more occupational transitions. A healthier later life changes ideas about the nature of retirement or even the whole concept of retirement. Many older adults in their 70s do not feel "too old" to work. There is some evidence to suggest that working actually helps sustain cognitive well-being in later life.

Life expectancy is also a useful "bellwether" of societal modernization and progress. Improvements in education, nutrition, water quality, infant and maternal health, and access to medical care are all associated with gains in longevity. We use average length of life as one indication that a country is doing well or doing poorly in meeting basic human needs.

Table 1.1 presents data on the average life expectancy of people in the United States during eight time periods from 1900 to 2010. Look at the top row of the table, labeled "At birth." The average life expectancy of people born at the beginning of the 20th century was about 49 years. Over the course of the 20th century, we observed increasingly longer life expectancies. In the year 2010, people had a life expectancy at birth of 79 years, 30 years longer than they had in 1900, a 61 percent increase in average life expectancy in a little over one century!

How can we know about the life expectancy of people who were born in the year 2010? Not many years have passed to record deaths and life expectancy estimates for this group. The National Center for Health Statistics calculates life expectancy tables based on the number of deaths at each age for a particular year, information from the U.S. Census Bureau about the number of people who are alive at each age, and information from the Medicare program about the likelihood of dying among those aged 85 years and older (Arias, 2007). So whereas the life expectancy for people born in 1900 is based on the actual rates of death experienced by that group over time, the life expectancy projections for people born in 2008 are based on a summary of the death rates in the year 2008 for people at each age.

The next few lines in Table 1.1 give the average remaining years of life for people who have reached an advanced age of 65, 75, or 80 years. For example, a person born in 1900 could expect

Table 1.1	Average Remaining Lifetime at Various Ages, 1900–2010							
Age	2010	1989	1978	1968	1954	1939–1941	1929–1931	1900–1902
At birth	78.7	75.3	73.3	70.2	69.6	63.6	59.3	49.2
65 years	19.1	17.2	16.3	14.6	14.4	12.8	12.3	11.9
75 years	12.1	10.9	10.4	9.1	9.0	7.6	7.3	7.1
80 years	9.1	8.3	8.1	6.8	6.9	5.7	5.4	5.3

Source: Arias, 2014; U.S. Census Bureau, 1984, 1992, 1997, 2000, 2003.

to live until age 49, but a person who was already 65 in 1900 could expect to live an additional 12 years to age 77. Hazards encountered during the early and middle years of life shorten the average life expectancy at birth. Infant mortality was a major factor in limiting life expectancy at the turn of the 20th century. Furthermore, many women died in childbirth. Respiratory diseases and heart disease were serious threats to life during the middle adult years. If one survived these common killers, chance for a long later life increased.

Over the past 100 years, the U.S. population has changed from one shaped like a pyramid to one shaped more like a rectangle (see FIGURE 1.4 ▶). In 1900 the population had a large number of children and adolescents and relatively fewer adults at each advanced age. In 2010 the population had a relatively smaller percentage of children and adolescents and a relatively larger percentage of adults including a growing percentage of those in advanced old age. These changes have implications for a wide range of social policies regarding education, employment, retirement, health care, and Social Security benefits.

Group Differences in Life Expectancy

Although life expectancy has increased for the population as a whole, significant group differences persist (see Table 1.2). Overall, women outlive men and Hispanics outlive Anglos and African Americans (Arias, 2014). For Anglos without a high

school diploma, life expectancy actually declined between 1990 and 2008. Within this subgroup of people without a high school degree, African American women had a longer life expectancy than Anglo women. Although the size of this group of less well-educated whites is decreasing, they appear to be a particularly vulnerable population characterized by high rates of smoking, prescription drug overdoses, obesity, lack of physical exercise, and lack of access to health insurance and health care services (Olshansky et al., 2012).

Gender Differences. Men die at younger ages than women in countries around the world. Since 1979, the gap in life expectancy between males and females has decreased from 7.8 years to 5 years. There are biological, societal, and behavioral explanations for women's longevity advantage, but this discrepancy is not fully understood and is still being investigated. Although more male than female infants are born, more males die at each age than females. Some researchers suggest that estrogen has a protective effect that helps reduce women's risk of heart disease during the childbearing years. Others suggest that because men are physically larger on average than women, their cells must reproduce more often and are at greater risk of exhausting their regenerative potential. Although women suffered higher mortality rates during childbirth at the beginning of the 20th century, the risks associated with childbirth have been substantially reduced. In contrast, men continue to be exposed to more risks associated

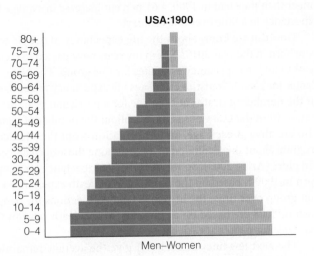

USA:1900

Men—Women

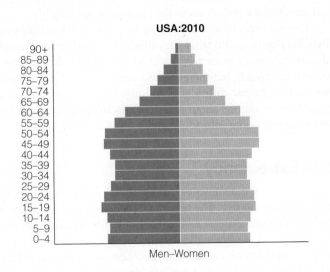

USA:2010

Men—Women

FIGURE 1.4 ▶ U.S. POPULATION PYRAMID: 1900 AND 2010

Source: U.S. Census Bureau, 1910, 2010.

Table 1.2	Estimated Life Expectancy at Birth by Race/Ethnicity and Sex, 2010	
Race	Male	Female
Anglo	76.5	81.3
African American	71.8	78.0
Hispanic	78.7	83.8

Source: Arias, 2014, Table 19.

Note: Hispanic is an ethnicity; Hispanics can be of any race.

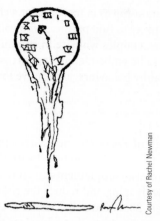

Age is relative, as is time. As the life span increases, the way we calculate our sense of maturity and aging changes. How old do you feel you are? In what way does your sense of being old depend on the situation?

with physical labor, military service, accidents, and injuries than women. One of the most commonly cited explanations for men's greater risk of heart disease and lung cancer is their more widespread exposure to cigarette smoking. Some researchers suggest that the change in cigarette smoking, both the increase in the number of women who smoke and the reduction in the number of men who smoke, contributes to the narrowing of the longevity advantage of women (Shrestha, 2006).

Racial/Ethnic Differences.
In the United States, Hispanic females have the longest life expectancy at birth (83.8 years), and African American males have the shortest (71.8 years) (Arias, 2014). The discrepancy in longevity between the African Americans and other racial/ethnic groups in the United States can be seen in higher rates of death among the African American population from a wide range of causes including cardiovascular diseases, infections, lung disease, diabetes, and traumatic injuries associated with motor vehicle accidents, other accidents, and homicide. These health disparities can be attributed to the confounding of factors, many of which are associated with lifelong exposure to poverty and inadequate access to health care resources. Starting in infancy, more African American babies are born with low birth weight, making them more vulnerable to infant mortality. Poverty is associated with prenatal and infant malnutrition. African American men are more likely to work in hazardous conditions where they may be exposed to toxins and injury, and, at the same time, where employers do not provide health insurance benefits. Across all economic groups, exposure to racial discrimination is itself a lifelong source of stress that can have deleterious psychological and physiological consequences (Arias, 2014; Lewis, Cogburn, & Williams, 2015).

Factors That Contribute to Longevity

We can think of longevity as a product of the interaction of the biological, the psychological, and the societal systems. As an example, improvements in longevity over the past 50 years have been attributed to major reductions in the death rates from diseases of the heart and cerebrovascular diseases (commonly referred to as stroke). These improvements have been brought about by medical advances in diagnosis, emergency treatment, new medicines, and new patterns of care; changes in individual behavior patterns, especially smoking cessation and management of high blood pressure; and changes in social policies that provide greater access to medical resources, especially the introduction of Medicare and Medicaid.

Projections of longevity reflect overall changes in the U.S. population. Over the past 50 years, the population has become substantially larger, older, and culturally more diverse (Shrestha & Heisler, 2011). When you try to estimate your own life expectancy, you must consider projections for people in your country, region, and state, and in your age, educational, racial, and sex groups. Furthermore, research with identical twins finds that some components of longevity are genetically guided. People with long-lived ancestors are likely to be long lived themselves. Moreover, individual lifestyle factors have a great impact on longevity. Among these, four of the most powerful influences are education, social integration, diet, and exercise.

Education

Of the many factors that have been studied, education has consistently been linked to health and longevity. Across many societies with many different models of educational opportunity, increases in years of schooling predict added years of life. The benefit of more years of education for longevity has been observed among African Americans and Anglos, men and women. These benefits are explained in part by the relationship of education and wealth. People with more schooling have higher paying jobs. In addition, people with better paying jobs may have greater control over their time and less exposure to dangerous work conditions. Finally, more schooling is associated with better decision-making skills that may influence health care, risk taking, and better self-monitoring of one's health status (Lieras-Muney, 2005; National Center for Health Statistics, 2012).

Social Integration

Social integration has been identified as a factor that influences health and longevity across the life span, from childhood through elderhood (Berkman, Glass, Brissette, & Seeman, 2000; Kolata, 2007; Uchino, Cacciopo, & Kiekolt-Glaser, 1996). Social integration refers to being comfortably involved and connected to meaningful interpersonal associations and friendships and experiencing a sense of belonging. One aspect of social integration that has been linked to improved health and longevity is being in a committed relationship as in marriage, or a civil union. Healthy adults are more likely to find partners who will commit to them. At the same time, couples who are in committed relationships are more likely to be embedded in supportive social networks, to engage in healthy behaviors, and to live longer (Winkelby & Cubbin, 2004).

Diet

A growing body of research emphasizes the potential benefits of a well-balanced diet combined with the strategic use of vitamin and mineral supplements to slow the cellular damage associated with aging and reduce the risks of inflammatory disease (Aronson, 2009; Cannella, Savina & Donini, 2009). The government hosts a website that addresses the relationship of nutrition to specific health concerns, such as diabetes, allergies, cancer, and heart health (see http://www.nutrition.gov /nutrition-and-health-issues).

Exercise

Other research highlights the value of daily activity—even 20 to 30 minutes of exercise and movement—for promoting health and longevity. A modest amount of leisure-time physical activity can add 3 or 4 years to one's life expectancy. Even for people who are obese, those who are physically active have a longer life than those who are inactive (Moore et al., 2012).

As we look to the future, advances in medical technology and treatment coupled with improved support services for older adults can lead to higher standards of living and new levels of functioning in later life. On the other hand, inequities in the distribution of health care services and other societal supports may result in a growing disparity in the quality of later life for various segments of the population.

FURTHER REFLECTION *How long do you think you will live? What are you doing now to increase your chances of living a long, healthy life?*

Explain why education is associated with longevity. What benefits might education provide that could support better health practices and/or access to care?

What are some implications of the increase in life expectancy for social policies? For example, how might the Social Security system, retirement benefits, or community health care services need to change to reflect the needs of an aging population?

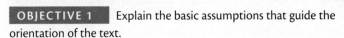

CHAPTER SUMMARY

OBJECTIVE 1 Explain the basic assumptions that guide the orientation of the text.

This book presents the story of human development across the life span. The analysis is based on six assumptions: (1) Growth occurs at every period of life, from conception through very old age. (2) Individual lives show continuity and change as they progress through time. (3) We need to understand the whole person because we function in an integrated manner. (4) Every person's behavior must be analyzed in the context of relevant settings and personal relationships. (5) People contribute actively to their development. (6) Diversity is a product of the interaction of the biological, the psychological, and the societal systems.

OBJECTIVE 2 Describe the psychosocial approach to the study of development, including the interrelationship among the biological, psychological, and societal systems.

Psychosocial theory, which provides the organizing framework for the book, emphasizes interaction among the biological, psychological, and societal systems. As a result of maturation and change in each of these systems, individuals' beliefs about themselves and their relationships are modified. Although each life story is unique, we can identify important common patterns, allowing us to anticipate the future and to understand one another.

OBJECTIVE 3 Compare historical changes in life expectancy. Analyze individual and group factors that contribute to longevity.

Demographic information about the life span stimulates thought about one's own life expectancy. In the United States, the average life expectancy increased by more than 50 percent during the 20th century. This dramatic change affects how each of us views our own future. We need to study human development in a constantly changing context. We can never be satisfied that the information from earlier periods will hold true for future generations.

Picasso experiments with strategies to convey the inner and outer worlds of his subjects. Here he shares a glimpse into his private home life using vivid colors and bold outlines. While Jacqueline seems contemplative, their dog seems to be giving us a bit of a smirk. Like abstract art, theories provide ways of understanding behavior by introducing processes and constructs that are not directly observable.

1. Explain the concept of theory and discuss how theories contribute to the study of development.

2. Explain the basic concepts of seven major theories and examine the implications of each theory for the study of human development:

   2a. Evolutionary theory

   2b. Psychoanalytic theory

   2c. Cognitive developmental theories

   2d. Theories of learning

   2e. Cultural theory

   2f. Social role theory

   2g. Systems theory

MAJOR THEORIES FOR UNDERSTANDING HUMAN DEVELOPMENT

2

Jack Manasky has been widowed for 6 years. He still writes letters to his beloved wife Anna, keeping her up to date on the events of his life. In the following letter, Jack writes of a small episode, but a lot is revealed about Jack's life, his sense of self, and his relationship with his adult daughter.

Dear Anna,

I am writing this from a coffee shop. My seat is by the window. Why, you are thinking, am I sitting in a coffee shop when I have a perfectly good house to sit in? Okay, I will tell you.

Marilyn, our dear daughter, may she have a long and wonderful life, this dear child of ours who is no longer a child, decided last month to cure me. Cure me of what, I do not know. I did not ask. One day she came in. A day no different from any other. I was sitting in the living room watching the television news.

Marilyn went into the kitchen to empty her grocery bags. "Dad," she said. "I bought you new coffee. It's decaffeinated." "What does this mean, decaffeinated?" I asked. This I said from my chair; why should I walk into the kitchen? "Unleaded, Dad. You shouldn't be drinking regular coffee. It's a diuretic."

By this time she was standing in the doorway of the kitchen, folding her paper bag. "It means it takes too much water out of you. You're too old for that."

Nu? Decaffeinated? Diuretic? Too much water? Let her do what she wants. What did I care?

I forgot about it. The next day, I got up, I fed the birds, read the newspaper, and drank my coffee. No big deal. But that afternoon, a headache. And what a headache, loud, pounding, I could not think. This was not so new to me. Headaches. They come, they go. But this one, it was different. The next day, it was still with me. And the next day also. Like a black cloud, it filled my head with thunder, everywhere I went.

When Marilyn came on the third day, I remembered. "Marilyn," I said, "this decaffeinated coffee, however you call it, it is killing me."

"Ha, ha," she laughed. "It's not killing you, Dad. It's good for you."

"It's murdering me. Go, buy me some coffee. Or tomorrow you will be pouring this decaffeinated coffee on my grave."

"Dad," she said. "You have a headache? You'll get over it. It's not the decaf that's giving it to you. It's from no caffeine. It'll stop soon." She laughed again, and then she was gone. This is what she does. Comes into my house, checks things off her list, and then disappears.

I sat down. "Okay." I said to the floor. "I will buy my own coffee."

Source: From Starboys by Elissa Goldberg in *Families in Later Life: Connections and Transitions*, by Alexis J. Walker et al., pp. 250–251. Copyright 2001 Pine Forge Press.

Y̶ou may know people just like Jack Manasky and Marilyn— people with good intentions who have different outlooks on a situation; people who have different goals that guide their actions.

And you may have your own personal ideas about why conflicts among parents and their children arise. The purpose of this chapter is to introduce a diverse "basket" of concepts that help to account for the nature of development over the life span. The theories were selected for their significant impact in guiding research and intervention in the field of human development. Many theories presented here continue to be evaluated and challenged as new and competing ideas about human behavior emerge.

First, we consider the role of theory in the study of human development, including a definition of theory and an analysis of what a theory of development is likely to explain. Then we present basic concepts of seven major theories of human development. The *theory of evolution* provides a broad picture of species change over long time periods. Evolutionary theory places the study of individual development in the context of the history of the species. It links humans with other animal species and suggests ways of thinking about key periods in the life span that are critical for species survival. *Psychoanalytic theory* explains the relationship of mental activity to changing needs, wishes, and drives, with a particular focus on the role of sexual and aggressive needs. *Cognitive developmental theory* describes the maturation of capacities for logical thought. *Learning theories*, *cultural theory*, *social role theory*, and *developmental systems theory* each introduce mechanisms that explain how environments guide the content and direction of growth.

In each section, a brief explanation of the theory and a few major constructs are presented, along with an analysis of the theory's contributions to the study of development and links to the psychosocial approach. In subsequent chapters, additional ideas from many of the theories will be presented as they relate to specific topics.

At the end of the explanation of each theory, there is a section called Case Analysis: Using What You Know. These sections present questions that are intended to help you gain insights into the case of Jack Manasky and Marilyn, and to think about it through the lens of each theoretical perspective. By trying to answer these questions, you will begin the process of using what you know to build a conceptual bridge between theory and application. ●

What Is a Theory?

OBJECTIVE 1 Explain the concept of theory and discuss how theories contribute to the study of development.

A **theory** is a logical system of concepts that helps explain observations and contributes to the development of a body of knowledge. We all have our informal, intuitive theories about social life. For example, the adage "The acorn doesn't fall far from the tree" is an informal theory that predicts that children are going to grow up to behave a lot like their parents. However, the idea of a scientific theory is quite different from an informal set of beliefs. In order for a set of ideas to reach the level of a formal scientific theory, it has to be supported by extensive evidence, including systematic experimentation and observation (Zimmerman, 2009). A formal scientific theory is a set of interconnected statements, including assumptions, definitions, and hypotheses that explain and interpret observations. The function of this set of interconnected statements is to describe unobservable structures, mechanisms, or processes and to relate them to one another and to observable events.

In the field of human development, theory is differentiated from research and from facts. The research process, which is described in some detail in the appendix, may be guided by theory. However, the research process is a separate approach to building a knowledge base. For example, Piaget's cognitive developmental theory introduced the idea that through direct interaction with the physical world, infants gradually construct a scheme for the permanent object, an understanding that objects do not cease to exist even when they are out of sight. A growing body of research stimulated by this theory has led to a more differentiated view of what infants know about objects depending on the nature of the task, the kind of response the baby is required to make, and the setting where the baby is being studied. Thus, research often uncovers a more detailed analysis than is presented in the original theoretical formulation.

Facts are distinct from the theories that might try to explain or account for them. For example, in chapter 1, we pointed out that life expectancy at birth in the United States has increased considerably from 1900 to the present. This fact is indisputable. There may be several theories about factors that account for changes in longevity. Each theory might influence the direction of research about longevity. However, these theories do not change the facts.

Major theories reorganize the way we think about and understand the world. Einstein's theory of relativity showed us that matter and energy are two forms of the same thing rather than totally distinct. Freud's theory of psychosexual development showed us that emotional conflicts can be expressed unconsciously through physical symptoms. Once a scientific theory is introduced, it leads the way for testing and elaboration through additional research.

Requirements of a Theory

A formal theory should meet certain requirements. It should be *logical* and *internally consistent*, with no contradictory statements. The hypothetical constructs should be translatable into *testable* hypotheses that can be explored through systematic research. As you read each theory, look for ways that the abstract concepts of the theory can be observed and measured. For example, a theory of learning might suggest that a behavior is more likely to occur when it is followed by a reinforcement. You can test this theory by monitoring a specific behavior, creating a specific reinforcement, and observing whether or not a person performs the behavior more often once the reinforcement has been presented.

The theory should be *parsimonious*, which means that the theory should be simple, relying on as few assumptions, constructs, and propositions as possible while still accurately accounting for the observations. Parsimony is relative. For example, Freud hypothesized that there were five stages of development; Erikson hypothesized that there were eight stages of development. Using the principle of parsimony, one might conclude that Freud's theory is a better one. However, Erikson's

theory provides a more differentiated view of adulthood and aging, and, as a result, his theory offers more insight into the process of development over the life span. On the other hand, a theory that suggests 30 or 40 stages of life might be viewed as overly complex and less parsimonious than one that provides a smaller number of integrated periods. Finally, a theory should integrate previous research, and it should deal with a relatively large area of science (P. H. Miller, 2016).

In order to understand a theory, we must answer three questions:

1. **Which phenomena is the theory trying to explain?**
   Understanding the focus of the theory helps to identify its **range of applicability**. There are many different types of theories, each with its own range of applicability. For example, there are theories of personality, learning, decision making, conflict resolution, group dynamics, leadership, counseling, social work practice, and family formation. Just within the field of human development, there are many theories including those that account for language development, theories that focus on emotional bonds between parents and their children, and theories that address processes of change from one generation to the next. Although principles from one theory may have relevance to another area of knowledge, a theory is evaluated in terms of the behavior it was originally intended to explain.

2. **What assumptions does the theory make?**
   Assumptions are the guiding premises underlying the logic of a theory. In order to evaluate a theory, you must first understand what its assumptions are. Charles Darwin assumed that lower life forms "progress" to higher forms in the process of evolution. Freud assumed that all behavior is motivated and that the unconscious is a "storehouse" of motives and wishes. The assumptions of any theory may be challenged or modified over time. For example, we do not necessarily think of a progression from lower to higher life forms as Darwin discussed them. Life forms have unique adaptive capacities—owls have exceptional night vision; bats have unusual hearing; humans have unique cognitive capacities. In Darwin's time, humans were thought to be a higher life form; now we recognize the diverse adaptive advantages of varied species. Assumptions may be influenced by the following:

   The cultural context that dominates the theorist's period of history

   The sample of observations from which the theorist has drawn inferences

   The current knowledge of the field

   The intellectual capacities, values, religion, and education of the theorist

3. **What does the theory predict?**
   Theories add new levels of understanding by suggesting causal relationships, unifying diverse observations, and identifying the importance of events that may have gone unnoticed. Theories of human development offer

explanations regarding the origins and functions of human behavior, predictions about changes that can be expected in behavior from one period of life to the next, and hypotheses about the mechanisms or processes that account for change.

Requirements for Theories of Development

A theory of development usually helps explain how people change and grow over time, as well as how to account for continuity. We expect a theory of human development to provide explanations for six questions:

1. **What is the *direction* of change over the life span?**
   We assume that there is a direction to development, that it is not random. Development is not the same as changing one's hairstyle or deciding one day to play tennis and the next day to play soccer. Theories of development offer some big ideas about maturity and shed light on important ways in which thought, self-understanding, the capacity for social relationships, and the capacity for adaptation become increasingly complex and integrated through the course of life. Some theories suggest that change takes place in a sequence of stages or qualitatively distinct periods of life. Other theories suggest processes that account for gradual change or highlight significant events that result in transitions at various points in life.

2. **What are the *mechanisms* that account for growth from conception through old age? Do these mechanisms vary across the life span?**
   Theories of development identify the processes or experiences that bring about systematic change. In this chapter and throughout the text, we will present and explain a variety of mechanisms theorists offer for how growth and development occur. Some theories emphasize a biologically based, genetically guided plan for development. Others emphasize the role of the environment in shaping behavior and providing roles or settings that support new levels of functioning. Still other theories emphasize the ongoing interaction of biological and environmental factors, characterizing development as a process of adaptive self-organization.

3. **How relevant are *early experiences* for later development?**
   Theories of development offer different ideas about the significance of early experiences for the psychological and behavioral organization of later periods of life. Some theories suggest that incidents from infancy and childhood play a powerful role in guiding the direction of development well into adulthood. Other theories emphasize the influence of contemporary events in guiding development by viewing the person as continuously adapting to new demands and new opportunities.

   One important question that emerges in the study of development is the degree to which individuals can

be characterized as **resilient** in the face of early stresses or deprivation. Current work in cognitive neuroscience suggests that there is a high degree of plasticity in the human brain. In cases of injury, one area of the brain can reorganize to take over functions of another area. Plasticity is observed across the life span, well into later life. The human brain has evolved to have a great degree of flexibility, being able to adapt to a wide range of family, cultural, language, and environmental conditions. At the same time, there is a growing literature about the risks of early exposure to harsh parenting and the long-term consequences of these early negative experiences. This research suggests that events that unfold early in life may set a person on a trajectory that intensifies certain ways of thinking and feeling and narrows the options for recovery.

4. **How do *physical, cognitive, emotional, and social* functions interact?**
   Most theories of human development focus on a specific domain such as cognition, learning, social relationships, or the expression and management of emotions. However, they also consider the interplay of other domains. For example, according to social learning theory, feelings of tension or anxiety in the learning situation can influence a person's confidence about whether a new skill can be mastered. According to cognitive theory, emotions can contribute to the person's attention and motivation to persist in seeking the solution to a problem.

5. **How do the *environmental* and *social contexts* affect individual development?**
   Individuals develop in social and physical **contexts**. Theories of human development differ in the ways they conceptualize settings and relationships, and in which aspects of these contexts are especially important in shaping the directions of growth. Should we focus on interactions with mother as context? Father? Both parents? Siblings? Friends? Spouse? School? Work? The physical environment of home or neighborhood? How do social constructions, including social class, race, ethnicity, and religion, become integrated into a person's life story? How and in what ways do they matter?

   Research on the interaction of environment and genetic predisposition illustrates the complexity of these questions. For example, some genes are highly responsive to environmental influences. A serotonin transporter gene, *5 HTTLPR*, has a short and long allele. Earlier studies had linked the gene to vulnerability to depression. Recent studies have shown that individuals who have two short alleles are more vulnerable to depression as young adults if they grew up in a cold, emotionally distant, or harsh family environment. Individuals with this same genetic makeup are less likely than others to experience depression if they grew up in a warm, nurturing, and supportive environment (Taylor et al., 2006). This kind of research illustrates the need for theories of development to consider the interactions of biological factors and environmental conditions that may be relevant at particular periods of life.

6. **What factors are likely to place the person *at risk* at specific periods of the life span?**

Although humans have an enormous capacity for adaptation, some combination of conditions is likely to impede optimal growth. Each theory of human development provides constructs that help us understand the nature of risks as well as predictions about conditions that increase risks. Some theories also offer differentiated views of risk across the life span or at different critical life transitions.

Each of the seven theories reviewed in this chapter provides concepts that can be applied to these questions. No single theory is currently accepted as the unifying explanation for the process of development; however, taken as a whole they offer concepts that guide research, intervention, and programming. As you read each theory, keep in mind the assumption that development is a product of the interaction of the biological, the psychological, and the societal systems. Try to identify the ways each theory incorporates these systems in its approach to explaining processes of continuity and change. Consider how you might apply these concepts. For example, imagine that you had to explain development to a new parent. What mechanisms or processes do the seven theories offer to explain how children grow up and change from infancy to adulthood? What ideas from each of the theories might be most useful in supporting the parenting process?

The Theory of Evolution

OBJECTIVE 2a Explain the basic concepts of the theory of evolution and examine its implications for the study of human development.

The theory of evolution focuses on how diverse and increasingly complex life forms come to exist. The law of **natural selection** explains how those individuals who are best suited to the immediate features of their environment are most likely to survive and reproduce. Over generations, species gradually change to respond to changing environmental conditions. Darwin referred to this process as **adaptation** (Darwin, 1859/1979).

The phrase "survival of the fittest" is sometimes associated with Darwin's theory of evolution. A common interpretation of this expression is that those who are the strongest or most powerful will survive. In fact, the term "fitness" has a more nuanced meaning—it refers to the idea of reproductive success.

Reproductive success, called **fitness**, varies among members of a species (Archer, 1991). Every species produces more offspring than can survive to reproduce because of limitations of the food supply and natural dangers. Darwin observed that there was quite a bit of variability among members of the same species in any given location. Some individuals are better suited to their immediate environment than others and, thus, are more likely to survive, mate, and produce offspring. These offspring are more likely to have characteristics appropriate for that location. Over

time, those members of a species that have a selective advantage are more likely to survive and reproduce, thus passing their genetic characteristics on to future generations.

If the environment changes (e.g., in climate), only certain variations of organisms will survive. Failure to adapt will lead to species **extinction**. In the context of changing environmental conditions, the fact that there is variability within a species ensures the species will continue or develop into new forms. Evolutionary change takes place slowly and incrementally as individual organisms adapt and populations with similar adaptive characteristics come to dominate an environment or **ecological niche**.

Darwin described two aspects of evolution (Mayr, 1991). One is the gradual change within a species over time from earlier to later forms. For example, even though they are the same species, chimpanzees alive today are not identical to the chimpanzees that lived thousands of years ago. The second form of evolution involves the breaking away from an earlier evolutionary lineage and the establishment of a new species. This is the process of **speciation** that contributes to biological diversity. For example, some combination of events led to the separation of the hominids from Homo erectus to Homo sapiens thousands of years ago (Stringer, 2012).

The concept of **inclusive fitness** suggests that a characteristic can be selected if the genes are passed along to the next generation by promoting the survival and reproductive success of others who carry those genes (Hamilton, 1964). In human groups, behaviors that support one's family members or that make it possible for one's kin to be more attractive in the mating process would be considered examples of inclusive fitness. This concept highlights the adaptive advantage of supportive kin networks that selectively direct their resources toward members of their family, kinship network, tribe, or ethnic group.

Advances in the field of genetics coupled with advances in neuroscience have begun to shed new light on the evolutionary process. By analyzing the human genome, one can better compare humans to primates and other mammals, leading to a clearer understanding of the likely points at which the brains of various species diverged. For example, in an analysis of the Y chromosome in a variety of populations, researchers have estimated that all humans alive today are descendants of a small group of about 4,000 men and women who left Africa less than 100,000 years ago and settled throughout the rest of the world. These humans carried the *FOXP2* gene that supports advanced language capacity and other symbolic and representational arts (Drake, 2015; Enard et al., 2002; Underhill et al., 2000).

Ethology

Two subspecialties that have emerged from evolutionary theory are *ethology* and *evolutionary psychology*. **Ethology** is the comparative study of behavior in its social contexts in order to understand the immediate causes of these behaviors and their adaptive significance. Ethologists focus on describing the unique adaptive behaviors of specific species, such as mating, caregiving, play, or strategies for obtaining resources. They are especially interested in behaviors that appear to be spontaneous and that provide some type of adaptive advantage. An example is the infant's smile. Smiles occur early in the postnatal period. They function as a powerful signal that evokes a caregiving response. Over time, the infant's smile takes on a more complex meaning within the social context. Yet smiling begins as an unlearned behavior that has important survival value in producing caregiving (Fogel et al., 2006).

Through comparisons among species, the study of the conditions that evoke and maintain adaptive behaviors helps to clarify the role of behavior in the long-term survival of the species. Many areas of human behavior that are functionally relevant to the fitness of individuals and groups are potential targets of study in the field of human ethology (Charlesworth, 1992; Eibl-Eibesfeldt, 2007). They include:

Reproductive strategies, such as having few or many sex partners
Infant immaturity requiring prolonged care
Infant–caregiver attachment
Parent–child conflicts
Sibling rivalry
Peer group formation and functions, especially cooperation, competition, dominance, and submission
Peer bonding and mate selection
Helping behaviors and altruism
Learning as adaptive behavior
Individual creation and modification of the environment
Elaboration of rites, rituals, and religions

Evolutionary Psychology

Evolutionary psychology is the study of the evolutionary origins of mental structures, emotions, and social behavior. Whereas ethology focuses on analyzing adaptive behavior patterns across species, evolutionary psychology draws on principles of evolution to understand the human mind. Cosmides and Tooby (1997) stated: "The mind is a set of information processing machines that were designed by natural selection to solve adaptive problems faced by our hunter-gatherer ancestors." This focus takes us to a time when humans lived in small, nomadic groups, traveling from place to place to find sources of food and trying to protect themselves from the dangers of predatory animals, weather, illness, and other humans. This way of life existed for more than 2 million years, during which time various human species (along with their human minds) emerged. From this perspective, the mind is highly adapted to solve the problems faced by these human ancestors, but it may not be well adapted to solve the new problems that have emerged in our recent industrial and postindustrial way of life.

From an evolutionary perspective, any behavior can be assessed by asking a few basic questions: What behavior is necessary to achieve a goal? How much energy is needed to achieve the goal? When should the organism stop the activity? What should the organism do next? These questions suggest that the organism has to recognize the nature of a problem, apply the best "tool" needed to solve the problem, and be mindful of the extent to which efforts to achieve a goal are using up resources (Neese, 2001). There are start-up costs to beginning any new

behavior. Once a behavior has been started, the organism has to assess how hard and how long to persist at the task. There is risk in putting too much energy into one problem and ignoring other important tasks.

The work of David Buss on mating strategies provides an example of the approach that evolutionary psychology takes to understanding human behavior. According to evolutionary theory, one of the key components of fitness is the mating process.

Successful mating requires solutions of a number of difficult adaptive problems. These include selecting a fertile mate, out-competing same-sex rivals in attracting a mate, fending off mate poachers (those who try to lure one's mate away), preventing the mate from leaving, and engaging in all of the necessarily sexual and social behaviors required for successful conception to take place. (Buss, 2006, p. 239)

The work of John and Stephanie Cacioppo focuses on the adaptive value of social connections (Cacioppo, J., & Cacioppo, S., 2012; Cacioppo, S., & Cacioppo, J., 2012). Human beings are social animals whose evolutionary survival depended on being well integrated into a social group. The human brain is organized to monitor social connections and to detect inadequate social bonds as potential sources of threat. When people perceive that their social connections are inadequate, they experience loneliness. And loneliness has significant, measureable consequences including sleep disturbances, longer time for wound healing, difficulty

From an evolutionary perspective, the attachment behavioral system is central to the offspring's survival. Adults have strategies for monitoring and protecting their young, and infants have capacities for alerting their caregivers when they are frightened or upset. What behaviors in human infant–mother pairs help them stay connected in times of distress?

with communication, and depression. Perceptions of being lonely may be especially strong when relationships that are expected to be supportive, such as relationships between marital partners, parents and children, or close friends, become strained or distant.

Implications for Human Development

Darwin's theory of evolution by means of natural selection provided the foundational theoretical framework for much of American psychology through its influences on William James, G. Stanley Hall, John Dewey, and their students. An underlying premise of natural selection is that new or emerging capacities are retained as a result of their adaptive value. This perspective was elaborated by William James in defense of consciousness itself. James argued that consciousness evolved and has been preserved among humans because it contributes positively to the chances of survival. By being able to set a goal, plan a course of action, assess progress toward that goal, and modify actions as needed, consciousness and its corollary, free will, increase the ability of human beings to adapt effectively to whatever environments or environmental changes they encounter (Dewey, 1896; Green, 2009; James, 1890).

With its focus on reproductive success, evolutionary theory highlights three phases of the life span: (1) healthy growth and development leading up to the reproductive period; (2) success in mating and the conception of offspring; and (3) the ability to parent offspring so they can survive, reach reproductive age, and bear offspring of their own (Charlesworth, 1992).

Humans are most vulnerable during infancy and childhood. Children require nurture and care in order to survive to reproductive age. Biological capacities and the environments in which they can be expressed operate together to produce behavior. A genetic plan, shaped through hundreds of generations, guides infants' predispositions, capacities, and sensitivities. Evolutionary theory points out that infants come into the world with a range of innate capacities and potentials. They are able to establish social contact, organize information, and recognize and communicate their needs.

The genetic potential of human infants is much greater than the behaviors actually exhibited in any particular cultural context. Infants have to be able to respond to the specific language environment, diet, parenting behaviors, and other physical and social contexts in which they are born. Particular environments are likely to take advantage of certain genetic predispositions and not others. Infants must adapt to a variety of environmental conditions including differences in the quality of parenting, adequacy of resources, and competition for resources with other siblings. Childhood experiences shape the future of the human species by providing the context for the establishment of attachments, meaningful social competence, and problem-solving capacities. These in turn have a bearing on an individual's behavior in adulthood—particularly the ability to form intimate relationships and to parent one's offspring.

In adolescence and adulthood, the evolutionary focus shifts to emerging reproductive capacities—the ability to find a mate, to reproduce, and to rear one's young so they can reach their own reproductive age. With advanced age, the forces of selection weaken. Because early humans died at a relatively young age due to predators, diseases, and environmental hazards, the selective advantage of characteristics that might be noticeable in later life was not preserved. As a result, the genome does not guide the direction of development to preserve high levels of functioning in later life as it so clearly does in infancy, childhood, and the transition through puberty to reproductive adulthood (Baltes, 1997). More rests on culture, lifestyle, and social resources to support successful aging.

The evolutionary perspective draws attention to the interconnection between an individual's life history and the long-range history of the species. Principles of natural selection operate slowly over generations. However, the reproductive success of individuals over the course of their own life span determines whether their genetic material continues to be represented in the larger population. The evolutionary perspective also directs attention to the importance of variability for a species' survival. These differences help explain how the human species adapts successfully across a wide variety of environmental conditions.

Links to the Psychosocial Approach

The psychosocial approach translates the idea of species adaptation to the individual level. Individuals encounter a necessary developmental struggle between their own traits and capacities and the requirements and demands of the environment. Each generation within a society faces similar challenges to cycle critical resources to the young, form enduring social bonds that will result in a reproductive environment, nurture competence and a capacity for caring in the new generation of adults, and inspire younger generations with hope and anticipation about the prospects of growing old. Within cultural groups, rites and rituals serve to protect and preserve resources, direct the rearing of children, and assist individuals through key transitions. Groups that adapt successfully are those that effectively sustain their resources so they can be available for future generations, integrate new members, and pass along information that will help individuals cope with future challenges. For a list of the key concepts of evolutionary theory, see Table 2.1.

Table 2.1	Basic Concepts of Evolutionary Theory
Law of Natural Selection	
Fitness	
Inclusive fitness	
Adaptation	
Contexts	
Extinction	
Ecological niche	
Speciation	
Ethology	
Evolutionary psychology	

© Cengage

1. The case of Jack Manasky and Marilyn focuses on the life and behaviors of someone in the stage of elderhood. What is the adaptive benefit of longevity? What does survival into elderhood contribute to species survival?

2. What aspects of fitness are illustrated in the case of Jack Manasky and Marilyn? How can evolutionary theory account for Marilyn's motivation to care for her aging father?

3. What adaptive problems is Jack dealing with? What are his coping strategies? Does Marilyn understand Jack's problem-solving efforts? Why or why not?

Psychoanalytic Theory

OBJECTIVE 2b Explain the basic concepts of psychoanalytic theory and examine its implications for the study of human development.

Evolutionary theory emphasizes the importance of reproductive functions as they contribute to fitness and long-term species adaptation. In contrast, psychoanalytic theory focuses on the impact of sexual and aggressive drives on the individual's psychological functioning. It distinguishes between the impact of drives on mental activity and their effect on reproductive functions. The theory assumes that very young children have strong sexual and aggressive drives that find unique modes of expression through successive stages of psychosexual development. Throughout childhood, adolescence, and adult life, sexual and aggressive drives operate to direct aspects of one's fantasies, self-concept, problem-solving strategies, and social interactions.

A unique feature of psychoanalytic theory is the importance placed on childhood experiences for shaping adult thoughts and behavior. The theory focuses on both normative and pathological patterns of growth and development that result from the socialization pressures that act on biologically based drives. The theory highlights the relevance of certain primary social ties, especially the mother–child and father–child relationships, for their roles in determining the expression and gratification of needs and the internalization of moral standards. Many contributions of psychoanalytic theory continue to influence the study of development and approaches to therapeutic interventions.

Five Components of Psychoanalytic Theory

Five components of psychoanalytic theory are reviewed in the chapter: (1) motivation and behavior, (2) domains of consciousness, (3) the structure of personality, (4) stages of development, and (5) defense mechanisms. Two extensions of the theory, object relations theory and ego psychology, are briefly explained.

Motivation and Behavior

Freud assumed that all behavior (except that resulting from fatigue) is motivated. He thought that all behavior has meaning; it does not occur randomly or without purpose. A related assumption of psychoanalytic theory is that there is an area of the mind called the **unconscious** that is a storehouse of powerful, primitive motives of which the person is unaware. Unconscious as well as conscious motives may motivate behavior simultaneously. Thus, behaviors that may appear to be somewhat unusual or extremely intense are described as **multiply determined**—that is, a single behavior expresses many motives, some of which the person can recognize and control and others that are guided by unconscious thought.

Freud's analysis of development and mental illness are derived from his understanding of the ways that sexual and aggressive drives press for expression and are inhibited or given various outlets in thoughts, dreams, behaviors, and symptoms. The term *drive* is sometimes referred to as psychic energy, tension, instincts, or *libido*. **Drives** can be thought of as sexual and aggressive forces that have a biological or somatic origin—they are a result of some metabolic functions but are also intimately linked to psychological processes. The energy behind the drives builds up as it seeks satisfaction. The psychic energy that is embodied in these drives can be expressed in a variety of ways, but the energy itself will not be destroyed.

Drives have a power or force along a continuum from mild to strong. Drives have an aim—a desire to be satisfied. When possible, drives are satisfied immediately to reduce tension and achieve a state of equilibrium. Drives have an object—a person or thing that allows the drive to achieve its aim. The object of the drive is closely linked to the specific environment in which the child functions.

Imagine that Kevin, who is three, comes home from preschool. The first thing his mother says is, "Kevin, do you need to go potty?" Kevin says "No," and starts to play with his train set. A half hour later, Kevin's mother says, "Kevin, you need to go potty and wash up before dinner." Kevin yells, "No, I'm busy with trains; I can go later. I know how to go when I need to." According to the theory, Kevin takes pleasure in holding on or letting go by controlling his anal functions. His drive to control these body experiences is strong. Now that he has his toilet habits pretty well developed, Kevin gets pleasure from knowing that he can enjoy letting go when he wants to. Having his mother repeatedly remind him about toileting competes with his own drive for physical pleasure associated with elimination. When he yells at her, and tells her "NO!" he gains some expression of his aggressive drives. In order to understand how drives are satisfied, one must have a concrete understanding of the social and physical resources that are available to a child at a specific developmental period. With maturity, a person becomes able to delay satisfaction of the drives and finds increasingly flexible and socially appropriate ways to achieve satisfaction.

Domains of Consciousness

Freud thought the human mind was like an iceberg (see FIGURE 2.1 ▶). **Conscious processes** are the tip that protrudes out of the water; they make up only a small part of the mind. Our conscious thoughts are fleeting. We can have only a few of them at any one time. As soon as energy is diverted from a thought or image, it disappears from consciousness.

The **preconscious** is analogous to the part of the iceberg near the waterline. Material in the preconscious can be made conscious

FIGURE 2.1 ▶ TOPOGRAPHY OF MENTAL ACTIVITY: DOMAINS OF CONSCIOUSNESS

if attention is directed to it. Preconscious thoughts are readily accessible to consciousness through focused attention. You may not be thinking about your hometown or favorite desserts right now, but if someone were to ask you about either of them you could readily recall and discuss them.

The unconscious, like the rest of the iceberg, is hidden from view. It is a vast network of content and processes that are actively barred from consciousness. Freud hypothesized that the content of the unconscious, including wishes, fears, impulses, and repressed memories, plays a major role in guiding behavior even though we cannot explain the connections consciously. Through certain techniques used in psychotherapy, the link between unconscious wishes and fears and overt behaviors can often be established.

Three Structures of Personality

Freud (1933/1964) described three components of personality: the id, the ego, and the superego. Freud suggested a developmental progression in which id exists alone at birth, ego emerges during infancy, and the superego takes shape in early childhood.

Id. The **id,** including instincts and impulses, is the primary source of psychic energy, and exists from birth. Freud believed that newborn infants' mental processes were comprised completely of id impulses and that the ego and superego emerged later, drawing their energy from the id.

The id expresses its demands according to the **pleasure principle**: People are motivated to seek pleasure and avoid pain. Its rule is to achieve the immediate satisfaction of impulses and to discharge energy without regard to the feelings of others. When you lie to a friend to protect your image, or when you cut ahead of people in line so you won't have to wait, you are operating according to the pleasure principle.

The logic of the id is called **primary process thought**. It is characterized by a lack of concern for the constraints of reality.

In primary process thought, there are no negatives. Everything is yes. There is no time. Nothing happens in the past or in the future. Everything is now. Symbolism becomes flexible. One object may symbolize many things, and many different objects may mean the same thing. Many male faces can all represent the father. The image of a house may be a symbol for one's mother, a lover, or the female genitalia as well as for a house.

Ego. **Ego** is a term that has two related meanings. One is the idea of ego as a person's self, including one's physical self, self-concept, self-esteem, and mental representations of the self in relation to others. This sense of ego emerges as psychic energy and is directed toward the self—a process that is sometimes called **primary narcissism**. The idea is that the sense of self is born out of self-love, an enthusiasm and excitement for one's body, one's experiences, and one's emerging sense of agency. The second idea of ego refers to all mental functions that have to do with the person's relation to the environment. It includes a multitude of cognitive processes such as perception, learning, memory, judgment, self-awareness, and language skills that allow a person to take in information, process it, assess its implications, and select a course of action. Freud thought the ego begins to develop in the first 6 or 8 months of life and is well established by the age of 2 or 3.

The ego operates according to the **reality principle**. Under this principle, the ego protects the person by waiting to gratify id impulses until a socially acceptable form of expression or gratification can be found. In the ego, primary process thought becomes subordinated to a more reality-oriented thinking, called **secondary process thought**, the kind of logical, sequential thinking that we usually mean when we discuss thinking. It allows people to plan and act in order to engage the world and to achieve gratification in personally and socially acceptable ways. It enables people to delay gratification. It helps people assess plans by examining whether they will really work.

Superego. The **superego** includes both a punishing and a rewarding function. The **conscience** includes ideas about which behaviors and thoughts are improper, unacceptable, and wrong. It carries out the punishing function. The **ego ideal**, which includes ideas about what behaviors and thoughts are admirable, acceptable, and worthy of praise, carries out the rewarding function. Because it is formed during early childhood, the superego tends to be harsh and unrealistic in its demands. It is often just as illogical and unrelenting in its search for proper behavior as the id is in its search for pleasure. When a child thinks about behaving in a morally unacceptable way, the superego sends a warning by producing feelings of anxiety and guilt.

Freud thought that the superego does not begin to develop until the age of 5 or 6 and is probably not firmly established until several years later. Other theorists have suggested that the roots of the superego emerge in infancy as the child becomes differentiated from the caregiver and aware of the possibility of disrupting the close bond with this loving object (Klein, 1948).

What Is the Relationship of Id, Ego, and Superego? Ego processes work toward satisfying id impulses through thoughts and actions without generating strong feelings of guilt in the superego. In one sense, ego processes serve both the id and the superego, striving to provide gratification, but in morally and socially acceptable ways. In another sense, ego is the executive of personality. The strength of the ego determines the person's effectiveness in meeting needs, handling the demands of the superego, and dealing with the demands of reality. If the ego is strong and can establish a good balance among id, superego, and environmental demands, the person is satisfied and free from immobilizing guilt and feelings of worthlessness.

When id and superego are stronger than the ego, the person may be tossed and turned psychologically by strong desires for pleasure and strong constraints against attaining those desires. When environmental demands are strong and the ego is weak, a person may also be overwhelmed. According to psychoanalytic theory, it is the breakdown of the ego that leads to mental disorder.

Stages of Development

According to psychoanalytic theory, the most significant developments in personality take place during five life stages from infancy through adolescence with the primary emphasis given to the first 5 or 6 years of life. During those years, the essential pattern for expressing and controlling impulses is established. Later life serves primarily to uncover new modes of gratification and new sources of frustration.

The five psychosexual stages are the oral, anal, phallic, latent, and genital stages. These stages reflect the emphasis on **sexuality** as a driving force. During the **oral stage**, in the first year of life, the mouth is the site of sexual and aggressive gratification. Babies use their mouths to explore the environment, to express tension, and to experience pleasure. As infants learn to delay gratification, they become aware of the distinction between the self and others. With this awareness comes the realization that all wishes cannot be satisfied.

In the **anal stage**, during the second year of life, the anus is the most sexualized body part. With the development of the sphincter muscles, a child learns to expel or withhold feces at will. The conflict at this stage focuses on the subordination of the child's will to the demands of the culture (via parents) for appropriate toilet habits.

The **phallic stage** begins during the third year of life and may last until the child is 6. It is a period of heightened genital sensitivity in the absence of the hormonal changes that accompany puberty. At this stage, children direct sexualized activity toward both sexes and engage in self-stimulation. This is the stage during which the Oedipal or Electra complex is observed.

The **Oedipal complex** in boys and the **Electra complex** in girls result from ambivalence surrounding heightened sexuality. The child has a strong, sexualized attraction to the parent of the opposite sex, and the same-sex parent becomes a fantasized rival. The child may desire to have the exclusive attention of one parent and may fantasize that the other parent will leave, or perhaps die. At the same time, the child fears that amorous overtures toward the desired parent may result in hostility or retribution from the parent of the same sex. The child also worries that this beloved, same-sex parent will withdraw love. Parental threats intended to prevent the child from masturbating and fantasies of the possibility of castration or bodily mutilation may add to the child's fears that sexualized fantasies are going to result in **punishment** or withdrawal of love.

In a successful resolution of the Oedipal or Electra conflict, the superego emerges as a strong structure that aids the ego in controlling unacceptable impulses. Through a process of **identification** with one's parents' moral and ethical values, the child achieves a new level of autonomy and at the same time receives the admiration and approval of both parents who see the child as moving in the direction of maturity and self-control. Most of the intense and painful conflicts of this period are repressed, and the ego emerges with a new degree of self-esteem and confidence about the child's place in the family structure.

Once the Oedipal or Electra conflict is resolved, the child enters a period of **latency**. During this stage, which lasts from about 7 years until puberty, no new significant conflicts or impulses arise. The primary personality development during this period is the maturation of the ego.

A final stage of development begins with the onset of puberty: the **genital stage**. During this period, the person finds ways of satisfying sexual impulses in mature, dyadic relationships. Adolescence brings about a reawakening of Oedipal or Electra conflicts and a reworking of earlier childhood identifications. Freud explained the tension of adolescence as the result of the sexual threat that the mature adolescent poses to the family unit. In an effort to avoid this threat, adolescents may withdraw from their families or temporarily devalue their parents. With the formation of a romantic attachment to someone outside the family, the threat of intimacy between young people and their parents diminishes. At the end of adolescence, a more autonomous relationship with one's parents becomes possible.

Freud believed that the psychological conflicts that arise during adolescence and adulthood result from a failure to satisfy or express specific childhood wishes. At any of the childhood stages, sexualized impulses may have been so frustrated or overindulged that the person continues to seek their gratification at later stages of life. The term **fixation** refers to continued use of pleasure-seeking or anxiety- reducing behaviors appropriate to an earlier stage of development. Because no person can possibly satisfy all wishes at every life stage, normal development depends on the ability to channel the energy from those impulses into activities that either symbolize the impulses or express them in a socially acceptable form. This process is called **sublimation**. During adolescence and early adulthood, patterns of impulse expression, fixation, and sublimation crystallize into a life orientation. From this point on, the content of the id, the regulating functions of the superego, and the executive functions of the ego rework the struggles of childhood through repeated episodes of engagement, conflict, and impulse gratification or frustration.

Defense Mechanisms

Much of the ego's work involves mediating the conflicts between the id's demands for gratification and the superego's demands for good behavior. This work is conducted outside the person's awareness. When unconscious conflicts threaten to break through into consciousness, the person experiences anxiety. If the ego functions effectively, it pushes these conflicts into the unconscious, thereby protecting the person from unpleasant emotions.

When the ego is unable to resolve these conflicts, a person may experience intense anxiety, and symptoms may emerge. A person who feels a desire that is thought to be very "bad," such as an unconscious wish to harm a parent or to be sexually intimate with a sibling, may experience anxiety without recognizing its source. The unexpressed drive continues to seek gratification. The unpleasant emotional state may preoccupy the person and make it difficult to handle the normal demands of day-to-day life.

Defense mechanisms protect the person from anxiety so that effective functioning can be preserved. They distort, substitute, or completely block out the source of the conflict. They are usually initiated unconsciously. The defense mechanism used depends on a person's age and the intensity of the perceived threat. Younger children tend to use denial and repression (pushing thoughts from awareness). A more diverse set of defenses, requiring greater cognitive complexity, becomes available in the course of development. In situations of greatest threat, denial is often the initial defense used, regardless of age.

According to Freud, the basic defense mechanism is **repression**, a process whereby unacceptable impulses are pushed into the unconscious. With unacceptable thoughts and impulses far from awareness, the person is protected from uncomfortable feelings of anxiety and may devote the remaining psychic energy to interchange with the interpersonal and physical environments. This defensive strategy has two major costs. First, it takes energy to continue to protect the conscious mind from these thoughts, thereby reducing the amount of mental energy available to cope with other daily demands. Second, if too many thoughts and feelings are relegated to repression, the person loses the use of the emotional system as a means of monitoring and evaluating reality.

Defense mechanisms not only reduce anxiety but also may lead to positive social outcomes. Physicians who use isolation may be able to function effectively because they are able to apply their knowledge without being hindered by their feelings. Children who rationalize defeat may be able to protect their self-esteem by viewing themselves favorably. The child who projects angry feelings onto someone else may find that this technique stimulates a competitive orientation that enhances performance.

Regression is an interesting example of a defense mechanism when considered from a developmental perspective. Regression means that a person (child or adult) reverts to an earlier form of drive satisfaction, immature forms of relationships with others, lower moral standards, or more simplistic ways of thinking and solving problems. Regression can serve ego development if it is not met with extreme disapproval (Blos, 1967; A. Freud, 1965). Sometimes it is necessary to return to an earlier mode of functioning in order to resolve conflicts that were inadequately resolved at that time, or to engage in a kind of playful childishness in order to achieve a new level of mastery. Most obviously, in the creative process, a certain amount of regressive fantasy can unlock possible associations that make sense according to primary process thinking but are censored in secondary process thinking.

Object Relations Theory

Object relations theory is an adaptation of psychoanalytic theory that places less emphasis on aggression and sexuality and more emphasis on human relationships as the primary motivational

force in life (Kernberg, 2005). The term *object* means a person or thing that allows the drive to achieve its aim. Object relations theory stresses that humans have basic needs for connection, contact, and meaningful interpersonal relationships throughout life (Borden, 2000; Safran, 2012). In this view, infants have a very limited sense of self. The self is formed in relationships with primary objects, especially the mother, father, or other close and continuous caregivers.

Margaret Mahler (Mahler & Furer, 1968; Mahler, Pine, & Bergman, 1975) described the self as taking shape in three stages over the first 2 years of life. At first, the infant simply enjoys the isolated events of the caregiving relationship. In this context, drives are satisfied and a sense of frustration is followed by a sense of satisfaction when needs are met. In the second phase, infants enjoy engaging in more rhythmic interactions with the primary caregiver, initiating interactions that are social and not necessarily focused solely around meeting basic needs. In the final stage, a process of separation and individuation occurs that continues throughout infancy and into adolescence and adult life. In this phase, a tension arises between wanting to explore the environment beyond the primary caregiver, yet wanting to be reassured of the primary caregiver's continuous presence. During this time, infants have a hard time making meaning of the positive and negative interactions they have with their caregivers. This may lead to the creation of a mental scheme for a good and loving caregiver, and a mental scheme for a bad and neglectful caregiver.

By about 24 months, the child is able to integrate the frustrating, angry, and loving memories of interactions with mother

The infant builds a sense of self and other through the accumulation of many, many interactions with the caregiver. When these interactions are mostly positive, a child will internalize the representation of a loving caregiver that can be used in times of stress for self-control.

or other primary caregiver into a stable representation of self and other. The internalization of the loving other contributes positively to the child's sense of self-esteem, enabling the child to think, "I am someone who is safe, loved, and valued."

The path toward maturity requires that the person achieve a sense of vitality, stability, and inner cohesiveness that is formulated through interpersonal transactions. Psychopathology or dysfunction arises when a person internalizes rigid, rejecting, or neglectful relational experiences and then uses these internalizations to anticipate or respond to real-life social encounters. Since the internalized relational pattern is familiar and well-learned, the person is reluctant to give it up even if it leads to feelings of isolation, anxiety, or self-loathing. The result is recurring maladaptive interpersonal relations, which are evidenced in contemporary friendship, family, work, and intimate contexts and are typically observed in the therapeutic relationship as well (Levenson, 2010; Messer & Warren, 1995).

Ego Psychology

In Freud's psychoanalytic theory, the ego has a variety of functions including managing the expression of impulses, negotiating between the id and the superego, striving to attain goals embedded in the ego ideal, and assessing reality. Anna Freud took these ideas further in *The Ego and the Mechanisms of Defense* (1936/1946), outlining new ego capacities that emerge from infancy through adolescence. She highlighted the various threats that the id poses to the ego at each stage of development and provided a classification of the defense mechanisms the ego uses to protect itself from unruly and unacceptable impulses. **Ego psychology** has become a study of the development and differentiation of the ego as integrative, adaptive, and goal directed (Blanck & Blanck, 1986; Loevinger, 1976).

Anna Freud gave special attention to the period of adolescence as a time of increased sexual and aggressive energy that is linked to the biological changes of puberty. At this time, children are likely to be overwhelmed by their impulses and the ego is more or less fighting for its life. Anger and aggression become more intense, sometimes to the point of getting out of hand. Previously successful defense mechanisms threaten to fall to pieces as intense sexual impulses emerged. During this period, the ego may employ very rigid defenses in order to deny the instinctual drives. Adolescents may waiver in their behavior from loving to mean, compliant to rebellious, and self-centered to altruistic as the ego tries to assert itself in the midst of conflicting and newly energized impulses.

Peter Blos identified the coping mechanisms that emerge in adolescence as young people find ways of adapting psychologically to the physical transitions of puberty. By the end of adolescence, those ego conflicts present at the beginning of puberty are transformed into more manageable aspects of identity construction and expression.

Not all aspects of the ego's functioning arise out of conflict between id and superego. Heinz Hartmann (1939/1964) thought that the concepts of ego, id, and superego were more accurately viewed as three interrelated components of mental functioning that could expand or contract under the influence of one another. He offered a developmental picture of the ego, describing a shift from early self-love to investment in others, and the eventual achievement of adaptive, reality-based thinking.

Building on Hartmann's work, Edith Jacobson (1964) explained how the self is shaped through identification with others. Adolescents achieve new levels of autonomy through the incorporation of moral codes and ethical values. According to Jacobson, the superego is not always a threat to the ego. It can become a stimulus for new levels of ego development when anxiety or guilt signals a need for a new standard of moral behavior.

Implications for Human Development

Psychoanalytic theory emphasizes the tension between interpersonal demands and internal psychological demands in shaping personality. The ego develops skills for dealing with the realities of the interpersonal world. It also develops skills for satisfying personal needs and for imposing personal standards and aspirations about the way these needs are satisfied. The expectations of others—particularly parents—are internalized and given personal meaning in the formation of the superego, thereby accounting for how a child translates the demands of the interpersonal world into a personal way of functioning.

Psychoanalytic theory was unique in its focus on early experiences of childhood, stages of development, family interactions, and unresolved family conflicts as explanations for ongoing adult behavior. Freud's emphasis on the importance of parenting practices and their implications for development has provided one of the few theoretical frameworks for examining parent–child relationships. Many of the early empirical studies in developmental psychology focused on issues that derived from psychoanalytic theory, such as childrearing and discipline practices, moral development, and childhood aggression. These topics will all be taken up in more detail in subsequent chapters.

The psychoanalytic approach recognizes the importance of motives, emotions, and fantasies that guide behavior. Within this framework, human behavior springs at least as much from emotional needs as from reason. The theory suggests that unconscious motives and wishes explain behaviors that appear irrational, self-destructive, or contradictory. Many domains of mental activity—including fantasies, dreams, primary process thoughts and symbols, and defense mechanisms—influence how individuals make meaning from their experiences. The idea that development involves efforts to find acceptable outlets for strong, often socially unacceptable impulses still guides therapeutic interventions with children, adolescents, and adults.

Another significant contribution is recognition of the role of sexual impulses during childhood. Freud believed that a sexual relationship with a loving partner is important for healthy adult functioning. Sexual impulses have a direct outlet in behavior during adult life. However, Freud argued that children also have needs for sexual stimulation and satisfaction. Today, we are more aware of a child's need for hugging, snuggling, and physical warmth with loving caregivers, but most adults still find it difficult to acknowledge that young children have sexual impulses. Childhood wishes and needs, bottled up in the unconscious, guide behavior indirectly through symbolic expression, dreams, or, in some cases, the symptoms of mental disorders.

Throughout adulthood, childhood fantasies and impulses continue to press for expression. Sometimes this childlike behavior can serve a positive function, promoting playfulness, creativity, and joy. Of course, sometimes these impulses can get you into trouble.

We need only look at a daily newspaper to recognize that the acceptance and expression of sexual impulses continue to be points of conflict in modern society. Controversies over sex education and providing contraception to teens, as well as the prevalence of disordered sexual behaviors and the use of sex for the expression of aggression in rape and sexual abuse illustrate the difficulties that people have in dealing with the expression of their sexual impulses.

Links to the Psychosocial Approach

Both psychoanalytic theory and psychosocial theory are stage theories that address basic, qualitative changes in self-understanding and social orientation. Psychoanalytic theory deals with conflicts that the child experiences in satisfying basic needs and impulses, especially sexual and aggressive impulses, within socially acceptable boundaries. The psychosocial approach expands this view by considering the broad range of social demands and expectations that confront people at each point in development as well as the wide variety of competencies and social resources that individuals have for meeting those demands.

Both the psychosocial approach and psychoanalytic theory describe characteristics and functions of the ego system. However, the psychosocial approach goes beyond childhood and adolescence, suggesting the direction for ego development in early, middle, and later adulthood. The psychosocial approach gives a greater role to the individual in guiding and shaping the direction of development through the use of coping strategies that redefine conflicts and identify new resources.

Psychoanalytic theory suggests that basic issues of personal development are in place by adolescence. The results of this development are then played out for the remainder of adult life in a person's defensive style, fixations, typical sexual behavior and sexual fantasies, and the strategies for sublimating sexual and aggressive impulses. In contrast, the psychosocial approach assumes that development goes on throughout life. The skills resulting from accomplishing new developmental tasks are learned, and new social abilities are achieved. The radius of significant relationships expands, bringing new expectations and new sources of social support. As new conflicts arise, they stimulate new growth, and new ego qualities emerge as a result of successfully coping with each new challenge. For a list of the key concepts of psychoanalytic theory, see Table 2.2.

CASE ANALYSIS Using What You Know

1. Analyze the role of the id, the ego, and the superego in Jack Manasky's behavior; in Marilyn's behavior.
2. What evidence is there in the case that unconscious drives are motivating the behavior of Jack and Marilyn?
3. What drives does Jack Manasky satisfy by writing letters to his deceased wife?
4. How might the relationship between Jack and Marilyn be explained through the lens of object relations theory?

Table 2.2	Basic Concepts of Psychoanalytic Theory
Drives	
Preconscious	
Unconscious	
Id	
Ego	
Ego psychology	
Superego	
Conscience	
Ego ideal	
Primary narcissism	
Primary process thought	
Pleasure principle	
Reality principle	
Reality testing	
Regression	
Secondary process thought	
Stages of development: oral, anal, phallic, latency, genital	
Identification	
Oedipal conflict	
Electra conflict	
Defense mechanisms	
Object relations theory	

© Cengage

Cognitive Developmental Theories

OBJECTIVE 2c Explain the basic concepts of cognitive developmental theories and examine their implications for the study of human development.

Cognition is the process of organizing and making meaning of experience. In psychoanalytic theory, this function was assigned to the ego. Interpreting a statement, solving a problem, synthesizing information, critically analyzing a complex task—all of these are cognitive activities. Cognitive developmental theory focuses specifically on how knowing emerges and is transformed into logical, systematic capacities for reasoning and problem solving. Perhaps the most widely known and influential of the modern cognitive theorists is Jean Piaget (Beins, 2012). His concepts provide the initial focus of this section. Recent interest in the social framework within which cognition develops has been stimulated by the work of L. S. Vygotsky. Several of his important contributions, introduced toward the end of this section, complement and expand the developmental perspective on how cognition emerges and changes over the life course (Lourenço, 2012).

Basic Concepts in Piaget's Theory

According to Piaget, every organism strives to achieve equilibrium. **Equilibrium** is a balance of organized structures, whether motor, sensory, or cognitive. When structures are in equilibrium, they provide effective ways of interacting with the environment. Whenever changes in the organism or in the environment require a revision of the basic structures, they are thrown into **disequilibrium** (Piaget, 1978/1985). Piaget focused on how equilibrium is achieved with the environment through the formation of **schemes** (the structure or organization of action in thought) and **operations** (the mental manipulation of schemes and concepts) that form systematic, logical structures for comprehending and analyzing experience, and on how equilibrium is achieved within the schemes and operations themselves.

Equilibrium is achieved through adaptation—a process of gradually modifying existing schemes and operations in order to take into account changes or discrepancies between what is known and what is being experienced. Adaptation is a two-part process in which the continuity of existing schemes and the possibility of altering schemes interact. One part of adaptation is **assimilation**—the tendency to interpret new experiences in terms of an existing scheme. Assimilation contributes to the continuity of knowing. The second part of adaptation is **accommodation**—the tendency to modify familiar schemes in order to account for new dimensions of the object or event that are revealed through experience. Assimilation operates to preserve existing structures by incorporating new information and confirming that what is already known is useful in making sense of new experiences. Accommodation operates to alter existing structures in light of new information, thereby creating the basis for future assimilation (van Geert, 1998).

Stages of Development

Piaget hypothesized that cognitive development occurs in four stages, each of which is characterized by a unique capacity for organizing and interpreting information. At each new stage, competencies of the earlier stages are not lost but are

Adaptation = Assimilation + Accommodation

This infant is exploring and experimenting with the properties of the fruit basket. Visual, tactile and motor senses are all in use as the basket becomes a new hat. What are some examples of sensorimotor exploration that you continue to use?

integrated into a qualitatively new approach to thinking and knowing. The essential features of these stages are introduced here. They will be discussed in greater detail in subsequent chapters. Piaget's theory describes the path in the development of cognition from direct action on objects in infancy to mental actions (operations) and the relationships among mental operations in adolescence.

The first stage, **sensorimotor intelligence**, begins at birth and lasts until approximately 18 months of age. This stage is characterized by the formation of increasingly complex sensory and motor schemes that allow infants to organize and exercise some control over their environment.

The second stage, **preoperational thought**, begins when the child learns a language and ends at about age 5 or 6. During this stage, children develop the tools for representing schemes symbolically through language, imitation, imagery, symbolic play, and symbolic drawing. Their knowledge is still very much tied to their own perceptions.

The third stage, **concrete operational thought**, begins at about age 6 or 7 and ends in early adolescence, around age 11 or 12. During this stage, children begin to appreciate the logical necessity of certain causal relationships. They can manipulate categories, classification systems, and hierarchies in groups. They are more successful at solving problems that are clearly tied to physical reality than at generating hypotheses about purely philosophical or abstract concepts.

The final stage of cognitive development, **formal operational thought**, begins in adolescence and persists through adulthood. This level of thinking permits a person to conceptualize about many simultaneously interacting variables. It allows for the creation of a system of laws or rules that can be used for problem solving. Formal operational thought reflects the quality of intelligence on which science and philosophy are built.

Implications of Piaget's Theory for Human Development

Piaget's theory has had an enormous influence on our understanding of cognition and the way we think about the reasoning capacities of infants and young children. Six implications of the theory for the study of child development are discussed here. First, the theory suggests that cognition has its base in the biological capacities of the human infant—that knowledge is derived from action. For example, infants learn about the features of objects by grasping and sucking on them. Knowledge is constructed rather than passively absorbed. Children as well as adults select, explore, and experiment with objects and later with ideas. They create their knowledge through this active engagement.

As the knower changes, so does what is known. For example, an infant may know a ball through its touch, how it feels in the hand or mouth, through its appearance, and through its response to the infant's actions. A toddler may become aware of the functions of a ball by kicking, throwing, rolling, and bouncing it. At later ages, children understand more about the physical properties of a ball and can link it to other shapes and categories of objects. With each more advanced level of motor, symbolic, and interpersonal capacity, the knower creates a new meaning of

Cognitive Developmental Theories   **33**

objects, people, and the interactions among them. Because of natural interest and through exposure to a wide range of materials, stimuli, and experiences, infants and young children "teach themselves" a great deal of what they know. This perspective has been integrated into instructional strategies in which children are encouraged to construct meaning through direct experience. Through free exploration, which typically requires the coordination of perspectives and the manipulation of interconnected elements, an understanding of the integration of coordinated factors is naturally acquired (Kamii et al., 2001; Kamii, Rummelsburg, & Kari, 2005).

Second, discrepancies between existing schemes and contemporary experiences promote cognitive development. Encounters with all types of novelty—especially experiences that are moderately distinct rather than widely different from what is already known—are important for advancing new ideas and new ways of organizing thought. Extending this idea, encounters with differences in opinion through discussion and reading are just as important in adolescence and adulthood as encounters with different types of sensory materials in infancy and toddlerhood.

Third, infants have the capacity for thinking and problem solving. Although infants do not make use of symbolic strategies, they are able to establish certain logical connections between means and ends that guide their problem-solving efforts.

Fourth, infants, toddlers, and school-age children think in different ways, and the ways they think are different from the ways adults think. This does not mean that their thinking is unorganized or illogical, but the same principles of logic that typically govern adult thought do not govern the thinking of young children.

Fifth, beginning with the period of concrete operations, children can approach problems using many of the principles that are fundamental to scientific reasoning. They can also begin to reason about their reasoning—introducing the importance of **metacognition**, the many strategies used to guide the way we organize and prepare ourselves to think more clearly and effectively.

Sixth, thinking about the social world is regulated by many of the same principles as thinking about objects in the physical world. As we learn about the principles that govern objects and physical relationships, we are also learning about ourselves and others.

Vygotsky's Concepts of Cognitive Development

Although Piaget acknowledged the significance of social factors, especially parents and peers, in the cognitive process, his theory focused on what he believed to be universal processes and stages in the maturation of cognition from infancy through adolescence. In contrast, Vygotsky, often referred to as an interactionist, argued that development can be understood only within a social-historical framework. At the heart of his work is a focus on thinking, especially in childhood, which he links to the development of language and speech.

The development of the child's thinking depends on his mastery of the social means of thinking, that is, on mastery of speech. . . . This thesis stems from our *comparison* of the development of inner speech and verbal thinking in man with the development of speech and intellect as it occurs in the animal world and the earliest stages of childhood. This comparison demonstrates that the former does not represent a simple continuation of the latter. The very type of development changes. It changes from a biological form of development to a socio-historical form of development. (Vygotsky, 1987, p. 120)

Lower and Higher Mental Processes

Vygotsky was trying to account for the development of higher mental processes from their simpler forms. He saw development as following a continuous path from other animals to humans, and also a discontinuous path. This was captured in his view of *natural* or **lower mental processes**, which could be observed in animal behavior and in the problem-solving behaviors of infants and very young children, and higher mental processes, which arise as children encounter and master the cultural tools of their society. He viewed human beings across cultures as similar to the extent that they shared basic physical characteristics and natural psychological processes, and different depending upon the cultural symbol systems to which they are exposed.

Higher mental processes, particularly language and meaning, emerge from the child's ongoing interactions within social, historical, and cultural contexts, as well as from the child's biological maturation. The child and the culture are intricately interwoven through the process of social interaction. New levels of understanding begin at an interpersonal level as two individuals, initially an infant and an adult, coordinate their interactions. Eventually interpersonal collaboration becomes internalized to shape a child's thinking. Through continuous interactions with others, especially adults and older children, children revise and advance their levels of understanding. Over time, the mastery of **cultural tools,** including symbol systems, permits individuals to alter their environments and guide, regulate, and redefine themselves.

Four key concepts in Vygotsky's theory are introduced here: (1) culture as a mediator of cognitive structuring, (2) movement from the intermental to the intramental, (3) inner speech, and (4) the zone of proximal development.

Culture as a Mediator of Cognitive Structuring

Vygotsky argued that cognitive development can be understood only in the context of culture. Of the many elements of culture that shape cognition, one that was of special interest to Vygotsky was the idea of tools as human inventions that shape thought. *Technical tools*, such as plows, cars, weapons, and computers, and *psychological tools*, such as symbolic systems, counting systems, and strategies for remembering, modify a person's relationship to the environment. Through the use of tools, humans change the way they organize and think about the world. For example, having a cell phone frees people from thinking that they have to be in a specific location, like their home or office, in order to talk with someone. Cell phones change the way people think about the manner and location of interpersonal communications. Vygotsky viewed tools as a means through which the human mind is shaped and modified over the course of history.

Movement from Intermental to Intramental

Perhaps contrary to common sense, Vygotsky argued that high-level mental functions begin in external activity that is gradually reconstructed and internalized. He gave the example of *pointing*. Vygotsky claimed that initially an infant will reach toward an object that is out of reach, stretching the hand in the direction of the object and making grasping motions with the fingers. This is a movement directed to the object. As soon as the caregiver recognizes that the child wants the object and is able to satisfy the child's request, the child begins to modify the reaching and grasping motion into a socially meaningful gesture—pointing. The caregiver's understanding of the gesture and the **intermental** coordination between caregiver and infant result in an **intramental** process for the infant—an understanding of the special relationship between the desired goal, the caregiver as mediator, and pointing as a meaningful sign.

Inner Speech

Vygotsky (1978) argued that speech plays a central role in self-regulation, self-directed goal attainment, and practical problem solving. He described the problem-solving behaviors of toddlers as involving both speech and action. Toddlers use what was described by Piaget (1952) as **egocentric speech** to accompany their behavior. They talk out loud but do not seem to be concerned about whether anyone can hear them or understand them. He described the talk as egocentric because it did not seem to have any social intention. Piaget suggested that the development of communication began with inner thinking of a very private nonsocialized nature. In toddlerhood, he viewed egocentric speech as evidence of the relative absence of social life and the great extent of nonsocialized thoughts that the child is unable to express.

Vygotsky (1987) proposed a completely different developmental pathway to account for egocentric speech and its function. He viewed speech as beginning in the social interactions between children and adults or other children. The first and foremost function of speech is social. Egocentric speech is a transformation of this social speech inward. The child uses speech that was initially acquired through interactions with others to guide personal behaviors. It does not have a social intention; rather, it is a tool that helps to guide problem solving. Vygotsky viewed egocentric speech and actions as part of the same problem-solving function. The more difficult the problem, the more speech is necessary for the child to find a solution. He observed, "Children solve practical tasks with the help of their speech, as well as their eyes and hands" (Vygotsky, 1978a, p. 26). Eventually, the egocentric speech

Ronnie Kaufman/Blend Images/Larry Hirshowitz/Getty Images

Vygotsky's theory emphasizes the social context of cognitive development. Why might an older sibling be effective for promoting learning in the zone of proximal development?

of an audible nature dwindles (but does not disappear entirely) and becomes **inner speech**.

The Zone of Proximal Development

Taking the idea of internalization further, Vygotsky offered the concept of the zone of proximal development to explain how learning and development converge. The **zone of proximal development** is "the distance between the actual developmental level as determined by independent problem solving and the level of potential development as determined through problem solving under adult guidance or in collaboration with more capable peers" (Vygotsky, 1978b, p. 86).

We have all experienced situations in which we were able to solve a task only with the assistance and advice of someone else. The typical efforts of parents to help a child put together a jigsaw puzzle by suggesting strategies, such as selecting all the straight-edged pieces first to make the border, or sorting the many pieces into those with a similar color, are examples of how learning takes place within the zone. Vygotsky suggested that the level of competence a person can reach when taking advantage of the guidance of others reflects the functions that are in the process of maturation, as contrasted to those that have already matured. Learning within the zone of proximal development sets into motion the reorganization and internalization of existing developmental competencies, which then become synthesized at a new, higher intramental level.

Implications of Vygotsky's Theory for Human Development

Vygotsky's theory suggests that the boundaries between the individual and the environment are much less clear than one might infer from most other theories of human development.

Cognitive Developmental Theories **35**

Vygotsky directs attention to the guiding role of social interaction and culture in shaping and orienting cognition, thus bringing the study of cognitive development into much greater harmony with the concepts of psychosocial theory than are seen in Piaget's theory.

Several specific implications of Vygotsky's work can be inferred (Davydov, 1995; R. Miller, 2011). First, in contrast to Piaget, who viewed the emergence of logical thought as largely a universal process, Vygotsky considered the nature of reasoning and problem solving as culturally created. Because of the way in which intermental experiences and networks structure intramental events, one's family and others who influence and control the child's early learning and problem-solving experiences will have a strong influence on the structure of one's thinking.

Second, Vygotsky highlighted the role of language as a cultural tool that links each new generation of children with the history and cultural meaning of their ancestors. Language, especially the spoken word, is a bridge between the interpersonal environment and the child's private thoughts.

Third, the concept of a zone of proximal development links development and learning. It assumes a critical role for adults in the child's environment who can identify where a child is with regard to any particular skill area and can then introduce questions, suggestions, tasks, and strategies to help move them to a new level of competence. Vygotsky believed in the interconnection of the learning and teaching processes, arguing that children could never discover everything in a culture's knowledge base just through exploration and experimentation. They need the guidance of more skillful peers and adults.

Finally, individuals can promote their own cognitive development by seeking interactions with others who can help draw them to higher levels of functioning within their zone of proximal development.

Links to the Psychosocial Approach

Piaget's cognitive developmental theory and the psychosocial approach focus on development as a product of discrepancies, referred to as *disequilibrium* in cognitive developmental theory and as *psychosocial crises* in psychosocial theory. Piaget's theory, like the psychosocial approach, proposes a set of stages of development, with each stage growing from and integrating the achievements of earlier stages. Piaget's theory did not offer any hypotheses about the qualitative changes that might follow the period of formal operational reasoning, whereas the psychosocial approach makes clear predictions about the direction of ego development in early, middle, and later adulthood.

Piaget focused on the cognitive domain—especially on the process of knowledge acquisition and logical reasoning. The meaning a person makes of a situation depends largely on the stage of mental development attained. Feelings, social relationships, and self-understanding are viewed as cognitive schemes that are constructed with the same logic that the person applies to the understanding of objects. In the psychosocial approach, cognitive development is referred to as ego development—an understanding of how the self emerges and shapes a personal identity with goals, values, beliefs, and strategies for achieving goals within the constraints of the society. Ego development involves planning, making decisions, coping with challenges, and facing the future with a sense of purpose.

Vygotsky's theory provides an important link from Piaget's emphasis on the maturation of logical reasoning to the emphasis of the psychosocial approach on the maturation of self in society by emphasizing the interpersonal nature of cognition. The idea of a zone of proximal development relates closely to the idea of an expanding network of social relationships, capturing the unique interpersonal and cultural context of all aspects of knowing, whether it is knowing about the logic of the physical world or about the logic of relationships. Vygotsky's theory shares with the psychosocial approach a strong emphasis on the role of culture in guiding social and cognitive development. The two theories view development as an ongoing interaction of the person and the cultural context. One might think of Vygotsky's notion of movement from the intermental to the intramental as a forerunner of the psychosocial concept of identity—a gradual internalization and integration of the roles and social expectations of others into a meaningful sense of one's role in society. For a list of the key concepts of cognitive developmental theory, see Table 2.3.

Table 2.3	Basic Concepts of Cognitive Developmental Theory
Piaget's Theory	
Equilibrium	
Adaptation	
Assimilation	
Accommodation	
Disequilibrium	
Operations	
Schemes	
Sensorimotor intelligence	
Preoperational thought	
Concrete operational thought	
Formal operational thought	
Metacognition	
Vygotsky's Theory	
Culture	
Cultural tools	
Language	
Intermental processes	
Intramental processes	
Speech	
Inner speech	
Egocentric speech	
Zone of proximal development	

© Cengage

1. How is Jack Manasky using his formal operational reasoning to explain his new symptoms of headaches?
2. How might Marilyn use the concepts of assimilation and accommodation to influence Jack's thinking about trying a new kind of coffee?
3. Think about Jack's letters to his wife. How are the concepts of cultural tools and inner speech related to these letters?
4. Given their interactions, would you say that Jack and Marilyn are products of the same culture? How might changes in culture over time alter cognitive reasoning?

Theories of Learning

OBJECTIVE 2d Explain the basic concepts of learning theories and examine their implications for the study of human development.

Human abilities are diverse, flexible, and can be coordinated or integrated to achieve many different goals. An understanding of the processes of learning and teaching requires concepts that are not linked to specific goals but can be applied broadly across many problem areas (Premack, 2010). For example, observational learning is a common mode through which humans can learn a vast array of behaviors, such as eating with a fork, swinging a bat, speaking in a polite tone of voice, or sharing toys with friends. Learning theorists have proposed mechanisms to account for the relatively permanent changes in behavior that occur as a result of experience. Underlying human beings' extensive capacity to adapt to changes in their environments is their flexible ability to learn. Two theories of learning that have made significant contributions to the study of human development are social learning and cognitive behaviorism.

Social Learning Theory

The concept of **social learning** evolved from the awareness that much learning takes place as a result of **observation** and **imitation** of other people's behavior (Bandura & Walters, 1963). Changes in behavior can occur without being linked to a specific pattern of positive or negative reinforcement. They can also occur without numerous opportunities for trial-and-error practice. A person can watch someone perform a task or say a new expression and imitate that behavior accurately on the first try. The person being observed is called the **model**; the process is called **modeling**.

Early research in social learning theory was devoted to identifying conditions that determine whether a child will imitate a model (Bandura, 1971/2006, 1977, 1986). Children have been found to imitate aggressive, altruistic, helping, and stingy models. They are most likely to imitate models who appear to be powerful and prestigious, in other words, models who control resources or who are themselves rewarded. Bandura and Walters (1963) suggested that children not only observe the behaviors carried out by a model, but they also watch what happens to the model. When the model's behavior is rewarded, the behavior is more likely to

JGI/Jamie Grill/Blend Images/Getty Images

Social learning theory emphasizes the role of observation and imitation as means of learning new behaviors. Can you think of a new response that you recently learned through imitation?

be imitated; when the model's behavior is punished, the behavior is more likely to be avoided. This process is called **vicarious reinforcement**. When naughty behaviors go unpunished, they too are likely to be imitated. Through observational learning, a child can learn a behavior and also acquire the motivation to perform that behavior or to resist performing that behavior depending on what is learned about the consequences linked to that behavior. Thus, observational learning can hold the key to self-regulation and to the internalization of standards for resisting certain behaviors as well as for enacting behaviors (Grusec, 1992).

Bandura (1977) pointed out the distinction between learning and performance. A learner might understand features of a task or demands in a situation that are not evident in the learner's behavior. Social learning theory assumes that a great deal of learning goes on through observation, but that much of it is not observed in behavior unless the reinforcement conditions are conducive.

Social learning theory has taken an increasingly cognitive orientation, sometimes referred to as social cognitive theory (Bandura, 1989, 1991, 2001, 2012). Through observational learning, the child becomes acquainted with the general nature of the situation as well as with the specific behaviors. Direct reinforcement or non-reinforcement provides information about how to behave in a certain situation. Moreover, people watch others, learn about the consequences of their actions, and remember what others have told or shown them and what they have read or learned about the situation. Over time, one forms a symbolic representation for the situation, the required behaviors, and the expected outcomes. A worker may learn that with one type of supervisor, it is appropriate to ask lots of questions and offer suggestions for ways of solving problems, whereas with another supervisor, it is better to remain quiet and try not to be noticed. The rules for behavior in each setting are abstracted from what has been observed in watching others, what happened following one's own behavior in the past, and what one understands about the demands in the immediate situation. Through social learning, individuals develop an understanding of the social consequences of behavior, leading to new patterns of behavioral expression and self-regulation. The culmination of this learning process is what Bandura (2001, 2008) referred to as **efficacy**, including planning intentional actions, guiding and directing one's own behaviors toward a goal, and reflecting on one's actions to assess their quality, impact, and purpose.

Implications of Social Learning Theory for Human Development

The principles of social learning theory are assumed to operate in the same way throughout life. The concept of social learning highlights the relevance of models' behavior in guiding the behavior of others. These models may be parents, older siblings, peers, entertainment stars, or sports heroes. Because new models may be encountered at any life stage, new learning through the process of observational learning is always possible. Exposure to a certain array of models and a certain pattern of rewards or punishments results in the encouragement to imitate some behaviors and to inhibit the performance of others. The similarity in behavior among people of the same age reflects their exposure to a common history of models, rewards, and punishments. Recognition of the potential impact one has as a model for others—especially in the role of parent, teacher, clinician, counselor, or supervisor—ought to impart a certain level of self-conscious monitoring about the behaviors one exhibits and the strategies one employs in the presence of those who are likely to perceive one as a model for new learning.

Cognitive Behaviorism

Cognitive behaviorism is the study of the many thoughts, ideas, and memories that influence behavior. In addition, it is a study of the ways people represent behavior in thought. For example, athletes think about their performance and visualize the actions needed to perform well. This is a cognitive representation of actions. Edward Tolman (1932/1967, 1948) introduced the notion of a **cognitive map**—a mental representation of the learning environment. According to Tolman, individuals who perform a specific task in a certain environment attend primarily to that task, but they also

form a representation of the setting. The cognitive map includes expectations about the reward system, existing spatial relationships, and the behaviors that are most highly valued in that setting.

An individual's performance in a situation represents only part of what has been learned in the setting. Imagine that you are going to your local grocery store to buy some milk and eggs. You know exactly where they are located in the store. If another shopper asks you where the coffee is, you can tell them the location since you have been in that store many times. You have a cognitive map of the store that is more extensive than the path you will take to get the milk and eggs.

According to Walter Mischel (1973, 1979; Mischel & Shoda, 1995), six types of cognitive and emotional factors influence a person's behavior in a situation and account for continuity in how people respond across situations: encodings, expectancies and beliefs, affects (feelings and emotional responses), goals and values, competencies, and self-regulatory plans (see FIGURE 2.2 ▶). **Encodings** refer to constructs or schemes the person has about the self, the situation, and others in the situation. **Expectancies** refer to cognitive assessments about one's ability to perform, ideas about the consequences of one's behavior, and the meaning of events in one's environment.

Affects are the feelings and emotional reactions or physiological responses that are associated with a situation. Feelings of anger, fear, arousal, excitement, or jealousy might interact with expectancies and encodings to guide behavior. **Goals** and **values** are related to the relative importance one places on the outcomes of situations. One person may value high levels of task performance, whereas another may value success in social situations. One's behavior in a situation is influenced by how one values its possible outcomes. **Cognitive competencies** consist of knowledge, skills, and abilities.

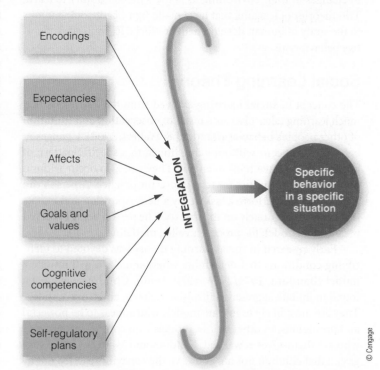

© Cengage

FIGURE 2.2 ▶ SIX COGNITIVE AND AFFECTIVE DIMENSIONS THAT INFLUENCE BEHAVIOR

Cognitive Behavioral Therapy

Building on the traditions of cognitive developmental theory, cognitive behaviorism, and attribution theory, cognitive behavioral therapy (CBT) is a general term that applies to a variety of therapies that share certain similarities. A premise of cognitive behavioral therapy is that our thoughts cause our feelings or reactions to events, not the events themselves. This is important because we can alter the way we think about events much more readily than we can alter the events themselves (Clark, Holifield, Leahy, & Beck, 2009). Since people differ in the way they categorize and evaluate a stimulus, the same situation might create feelings of discouragement and depression in some people and feelings of determination in others. For example, one person might react to a bad grade on a test as evidence that she is not smart enough to do well; another person might react to the same grade as evidence that she needs to study harder.

Aaron Beck (1976/1979), the founder of cognitive therapy, began his work in the treatment of depression. He found that patients suffering from depression spoke consistently of themes of loss, incompetence, and failure. They viewed themselves as failures; they perceived their efforts to alter their situation as useless, and their expectancies of the future as bleak. Beck began to focus his therapeutic effort on guiding patients to examine their emotional reactions and learn new ways of reacting.

CBT is based on the scientifically supported assumption that most emotional and behavioral reactions are learned. Therefore, the goal of CBT is to teach clients ways of unlearning their problematic reactions and to learn a new way of reacting by examining their thoughts in light of new information or alternative interpretations (National Association of Cognitive Behavioral Therapists, 2014). The therapy takes an inductive approach, encouraging clients to consider their thoughts as hypotheses that can be questioned or tested and then changed in order to be more appropriately adapted to reality. The therapist focuses on teaching the client rational, self-counseling skills that can be practiced through weekly homework and applied to daily situations outside of the therapy session. The therapy also teaches clients to examine their problems with a degree of calm detachment. If a person is upset about a problem, then the person actually has two problems, the troubling situation and the distress associated with their reaction to it. Finding ways to reduce the distress allows the person to examine the problem using higher order cognitive skills rather than affect-driven stress reduction responses.

Cognitive behavioral therapy has been shown to be effective in the treatment of depression, panic disorder, bulimia (an eating disorder), and post-traumatic stress disorder (Baker, McFall, & Shoham, 2009; Hofmann, Asnaani, Vonk, Sawyer, & Fang, 2012). A number of clinical studies have shown that cognitive behavioral therapy is more long lasting as a treatment for these disorders than treatment using medication. In other words, once the treatment has ended, patients who have had cognitive behavioral therapy are substantially less likely to relapse than those who were treated with medication. The implication is that for these conditions, a therapeutic process can result in a relatively permanent change in thought, affect, and specific behaviors designed to help the client achieve goals.

Critical Thinking Questions

1. What are the links between the six elements of cognitive behaviorism (Figure 2.2) and cognitive behavioral therapy?

2. Based on what you know about psychoanalytic theory and cognitive behaviorism, what might be some similarities and differences in the therapeutic approaches of these two theories?

3. What are some ways in which cognitive behavioral therapy builds on Piaget's cognitive developmental theory? How might the therapy be viewed in terms of Vygotsky's idea of the zone of proximal development?

4. What are some limitations to cognitive behavioral therapy? What are some features of the client or the problem that would not lend themselves well to cognitive behavioral therapy?

Self-regulatory plans are strategies for achieving one's goals, including techniques for managing internal emotional states, creating a plan, and putting the plan into action (Kross, Mischel, & Shoda, 2010; Mischel, 2012). Self-regulation is especially important in situations where temptations, frustrations, or self-doubt threaten to pull one away from important goals (Mischel & Ayduk, 2002). As people become increasingly aware of the effects of stimuli on their behavior, they can learn to overcome, channel, or eliminate those influences that tempt them to abandon their goals. The box, **Applying Theory and Research to Life box** Cognitive Behavioral Therapy, illustrates how the principles of cognitive behaviorism have been incorporated into a therapeutic approach to help clients alter unwanted or distressing thoughts, affect, and behavior.

Implications of Cognitive Behaviorism for Human Development

Cognitive behaviorism suggests that the learner acquires an outlook on the learning situation that influences subsequent learning and performance. This outlook influences the learner's feeling of familiarity with the task, motivation to undertake the task, optimism about performing the task successfully, and strategies for approaching the task. In addition to everything a parent, teacher, or supervisor might do to structure a learning environment, one must always take into account the outlook that the learner brings to the task. Differences in expectancies, self-control strategies, values, emotional reactions, and goals all influence the way individuals approach a learning situation and the behaviors they are likely to exhibit in the situation.

In order to understand why people behave as they do in a specific situation, one needs to understand the meaning they give to the situation. Although information or skills can be learned, they will not be expressed in action unless expectations about the self and the environment justify their enactment.

Links to the Psychosocial Approach

The psychosocial approach assumes that growth and change continue throughout the life span; however, it does not account for the exact processes by which new behaviors, new coping strategies, or new ego strengths are acquired. The learning theories provide explanations for the ways in which the patterns of daily events shape the direction of adaptation and growth. They offer insight into the processes through which society's rules, norms, and customs become internalized and translated into habits, preferences, and expectations, which become generalized across common situations. The learning theories emphasize the significance of the immediate environment in directing the course of growth. They help to explain why habits or patterns of behavior may be difficult to change, even when they appear to be dysfunctional. The key terms introduced by social learning theory and cognitive behaviorism are listed in Table 2.4.

CASE ANALYSIS Using What You Know

1. Using the concepts in Figure 2.2, develop an approach that Marilyn might use to modify her father's coffee-drinking behavior.
2. Speculate about how the two different settings—Jack's living room and the coffee shop—might influence Jack's behavior. What might be some differences and some consistencies in his behavior in these two settings?

Table 2.4	Basic Concepts of Social Learning Theory and Cognitive Behaviorism	
---	---	
Social Learning	**Cognitive Behaviorism**	
Observation	Cognitive map
Imitation	Encodings
Model	Expectancies
Modeling	Affects
Vicarious reinforcement	Goals
Social learning	Values
Efficacy	Cognitive competencies
	Self-regulatory plans

© Cengage

3. Explain how concepts from social learning theory, including modeling, imitation, and vicarious reinforcement, might apply to the development of behavioral habits, like drinking coffee or smoking cigarettes.

Cultural Theory

OBJECTIVE 2e Explain the basic concepts of cultural theory and examine its implications for the study of human development.

The concept of **culture**, although defined in a variety of ways by anthropologists, political scientists, sociologists, and psychologists, refers here to the learned systems of meanings and patterns of behaviors that are shared by a group of people and transmitted from one generation to the next. **Physical culture** encompasses the objects, technologies, structures, tools, and other artifacts of a culture. **Social culture** consists of norms, roles, beliefs, values, rites, and customs (Betancourt & Lopez, 1993; Herkovits, 1948; Rohner, 1984; Triandis, 1994; Triandis et al., 1980).

Culture has been described as a **worldview**—a way of making meaning of the relationships, situations, and objects encountered in daily life. Basic ideas, such as whether people are considered to be in control of nature or a part of nature, who is included in the definition of family, what characteristics are considered signs of mental health or mental illness, which acts are construed as hostile or nurturing, which aspects of the environment are considered dangerous or safe—all these and many other mental constructions are shaped by culture (Kagitcibasi, 1990). Culture guides development, not only through encounters with certain objects, roles, and settings, but also through the meanings linked to actions.

Weisner and Lowe (2004) clarify this process using the term **cultural pathways**. According to this view, adults in each culture have values and goals for themselves and for their children that shape and organize the socialization process and activities of daily life. They state, "Activities are made up of values and goals; resources needed to make the activity happen; people in relationships; the tasks the activity is there to accomplish; emotions and feelings of those engaged in the activity; and a script defining the appropriate, normative way we expect to do that activity" (Weisner & Lowe, 2004, p. 6).

The idea that engaging in the specific routines and activities of daily life shaped developmental pathways was captured early in the field of cultural anthropology through the work of Ruth Benedict. She introduced the principle of **cultural determinism** (Benedict, 1934/1950), which suggests that the individual's psychological experiences are shaped by the expectations, resources, and challenges posed by one's specific cultural group. Cultural determinism suggests that an individual's development is shaped through **enculturation**. **Culture carriers**, such as parents, teachers, religious leaders, and elders, use strategies to transmit critical practices and values. For example, in Japanese culture, infants and their mothers are expected to establish a sense of closeness and interdependence. This is achieved by keeping the infant physically close to the mother. Mothers and infants practice co-sleeping, co-bathing, and very few experiences of physical separation.

In European American culture in the United States, by contrast, mothers are expected to foster autonomy in their infants. This is achieved by encouraging exploration, choice, and early experiences of physical separation from the mother for sleeping and play. The two cultures have different worldviews and different values about interpersonal and family relationships. These values are transmitted through their childrearing practices (Bornstein, Cote, Haynes, Suwalsky, & Bakeman, 2012). Two theoretical dimensions that allow one to compare cultures are presented here: cultural continuity and discontinuity, and individualism and collectivism.

Cultural Continuity and Discontinuity

The extent to which development is viewed as distinct stages of life depends on the degree to which socialization within a culture is characterized by continuity or discontinuity. Cultural **continuity** is found when a child is given information and responsibilities that apply directly to that child's future adult behavior. For example, Margaret Mead (1928/1950) observed that in Samoan society, girls of 6 or 7 years of age commonly took care of their younger

Dressed in her ball gown and wearing the traditional tiara, Lucinda dances with her father at her Quinceañera. This cultural celebration is a rite of passage at the 15th birthday, marking a girl's transition into womanhood.

siblings. As they grew older, their involvement in the caregiving role increased; however, the behaviors that were expected of them were not substantially changed. When there is continuity, development is a gradual, fluid transformation, in which adult competencies are built directly on childhood accomplishments.

Cultural **discontinuity** is found when a child is either barred from activities that are open only to adults or is forced to "unlearn" information or behaviors that are accepted in children but considered inappropriate for adults. The change from expectations of virginity before marriage to expectations of sexual responsiveness after marriage is an example of discontinuity. Cultures that have discrete, age-graded expectations for people at different periods of life produce a pattern of development in which age groups have distinct characteristics and appear to function at different skill levels. These societies are likely to be marked by public ceremonies, graduations, and other **rites of passage** from one stage to the next.

Individualism and Collectivism

The dimensions of individualism and collectivism provide another lens for comparing cultures (Triandis, 1990, 1995, 1998). **Individualism** refers to a worldview in which social behavior is guided largely by personal goals, ambitions, and pleasures, which may or may not coincide with the interests of the group. Independence and personal achievement are valued. When conflicts arise between group and personal goals, it is considered acceptable and perhaps expected that personal goals will come first.

Collectivism refers to a worldview in which social behavior is guided largely by goals that are shared by a collective, such as a family, tribe, work group, or political or religious association. Interdependence and group solidarity are valued. The ingroup creates norms, goals, and beliefs that are enculturated and endorsed by its members. When conflicts arise between group goals and personal goals, a person is expected to act in the best interest of the group.

People from different cultures process social information somewhat differently, influenced in part by the collectivist or individualistic orientation of the culture. For example, both native Chinese and Western adults process information about characteristics of the self in the same area of the prefrontal cortex. However, Chinese adults also process information about characteristics of their mothers in this same area of the brain, an area that in Western adults is involved only in thinking about the self. The implication is that for Chinese adults, a strong cultural tie between self and others is supported by a neural pathway for thinking about self and significant others (Ambady & Bharucha, 2009; Zhu, Zhang, Fan, & Han, 2007).

Across cultures, people have to achieve some of the same basic developmental tasks, but the degree to which the culture is collectivistic or individualistic will influence what the people in a culture think is the ideal state and what is necessary to achieve that state. All cultures have some expectations for the formation of social relationships and social bonds, but the pathways that are emphasized as high quality or most desirable are different. In an individualistic developmental pathway, social obligations are constructed through agreements among the individual participants in the relationship. Opportunities to decide with whom you want

Implications of Individualism and Collectivism for Parenting Practices

The constructs of individualism and collectivism refer to two different value systems that characterize a culture. Individualism encourages and celebrates individual accomplishments and self-expression; collectivism encourages and celebrates interdependence and the strength of the community. Every society requires some blend or balance between these two perspectives. In order to survive, a group must be able to support both the *I* and the *We*, the individual person and the group. However, as one interacts with people from different cultural backgrounds, it is helpful to be aware of the dominant orientation toward either individualism or collectivism in order to achieve greater insight into the person's likely motivations, goals, and sense of moral obligation (Greenfield, Trumbull, & Rothstein-Fisch, 2003). Table 2.5 summarizes the features of these two orientations.

These contrasting values have implications for the behaviors that parents value and the ways athey interact with their children. Individualist cultures encourage more independent play. They foster a child's autonomy

and self-expression by allowing greater physical distance between the child and the caregiver, asking for the child's opinions, and allowing children to have a voice in decision making. Children are praised for doing things on their own and moving toward self-reliance. In both subtle and specific ways, children in individualist cultures are encouraged to compete with each other and to feel pride in their individual achievements.

Children in collectivist cultures are kept closer to their parents or caregivers during infancy. They are more likely to be nurtured through longer periods of breastfeeding, carried or held closely during infancy, and socialized through gentle encouragement and indulgences well into childhood. Families in collectivist cultures usually include extended kinship groups that all play an active role in a child's comfort, socialization, and care. Children are taught to be respectful of their elders and to show deference for adults' opinions and decisions. A strong value for sharing and cooperation leads to encouragement for children to share their belongings and to learn from one another. Children are praised for

behaviors that evidence responsibility for others, a sense of duty, and commitment to the family (Bornstein & Lansford, 2010; Greenfield, Suzuki, & Rothstein-Fisch, 2006).

Critical Thinking Questions

1. Joan and Dave get married and have a child. Joan comes from a cultural background that has a collectivist orientation. Dave comes from a cultural background that has an individualist orientation. They are discussing how to discipline their young child.
   a. What kinds of strategies might Joan elect to use?
   b. What kinds of strategies might Dave elect to use?
   c. Under what circumstances might they find themselves in conflict over their approach to childrearing?
   d. What kinds of childrearing approaches might they devise that would be acceptable to both of them?
2. Some researchers take issue with the idea that cultures can be characterized as collectivist or individualist. What are the limitations of these concepts? Are they overly simplistic? Do they reflect real differences in people's attitudes and beliefs? Do they help explain differences in the behaviors of people from various cultural backgrounds? What kinds of evidence would you want to have in order to be confident about using these constructs?
3. Aside from the ideas of individualism and collectivism, what other ideas do you find useful in characterizing cultural orientations that are transmitted from one generation to the next?

Table 2.5	A Comparison of Individualism and Collectivism
Individualism	**Collectivism**
Fosters independence	Fosters interdependence
Values individual achievement	Values group success
Promotes self-expression	Promotes adherence to norms
Values individual thinking	Values group consensus
Associated with egalitarian relationships	Associated with hierarchical roles and respect for elders
Associated with private property and individual ownership	Associated with shared property and group ownership

© Cengage

to have relationships and how to behave within those relationships are maximized. As a result, there is considerable variability in the nature and quality of interpersonal relationships. In the collectivistic or interdependent developmental pathway, social obligations and responsibilities are more important, and more clearly defined. There is greater consistency in the scripts for specific

relationships and greater agreement about the importance of preserving those relationships, even when those obligations require personal sacrifice (Greenfield, Keller, Fuligni, & Maynard, 2003). For example, arranged marriages are more common in collectivistic cultures, whereas marriages based on romantic love and personal choice are more common in individualistic cultures.

Typically, societies marked by greater complexity, affluence, social mobility, and cultural diversity tend to be more individualistic in their worldview (Greenfield, 2009). Factors including greater exposure to education, increased access to technology, and increased globalization tend to move cultures away from the collectivistic and toward the individualistic pathways.

People within cultures can also be described as adhering to more individualist or collectivist values. Thus, not everyone in a collectivist culture equally endorses the collectivist worldview. Subgroups within a society may differ in how much their values reflect the dominant individualist or collectivist orientation of the larger society. The **Human Development and Diversity** box Implications of Individualism and Collectivism for Parenting Practices provides a discussion of the implications of individualism and collectivism for parenting.

Implications for Human Development

Culture and biological development interact to determine how each period of life is experienced. This concept is illustrated by the ways in which different cultures mark an adolescent girl's first menstruation (Mead, 1949/1955). In some societies, people fear menstruation and treat the girl as if she were dangerous to others. In other societies, she is viewed as having powerful magic that will affect her own future and that of the tribe so she is treated with new reverence. In still others, the perceived shamefulness of sex requires that the menstruation be kept as secret as possible. The culture thus determines how a biological change is marked by others and how it is experienced by the person.

Societies vary in the extent to which people are expected to make significant decisions during each life period and in the range of choices that are available. The United States is a highly individualistic culture. American adolescents are expected to make decisions regarding sex, work, politics, religion, marriage, and education. In each of these areas, the alternatives are complex and varied. As a result, adolescence is prolonged, and the risk of leaving this period without having answers is great.

People who migrate to the United States from more collectivistic cultures or who are members of more collectivistic **subcultures** may experience even more stress during this period as their values for family and group allegiances and their scripts for behavior come into conflict with the individualistic orientation of the larger cultural context. In cultures that offer fewer choices and provide a clearer path from childhood to adulthood, adolescence may be brief and relatively free of psychological stress.

Cultures not only differ from one another, but also some societies are more culturally diverse than others. The process of **globalization** includes "the rapid spread of materials and products, ideas, images, capital flows, and people across spaces and borders (national or otherwise) that formerly were far more difficult if not impossible to connect" (Weisner & Lowe, 2004, p. 6). With increased global travel, migration, global communication systems, and opportunities to study or work in other cultures, most contemporary societies are becoming more culturally diverse than in the past. This means that there may be tensions between dominant and minority cultures as well as conflicts among ethnic groups. There are also new opportunities for the emergence of mixed cultural identities. The intermingling of cultural practices and related values could lead to new forms of adaptation and new worldviews (Kagitcibasi, 2007/2009).

Links to the Psychosocial Approach

The psychosocial approach is based on the assumption that culture contributes fundamentally to individual development. Basic cultural values regarding generosity, self-control, independence, or cooperation can be interpreted from infant caregiving practices. Psychosocial theory assumes that individual development is a product of continuous interaction between the developing person and the demands and resources of the cultural environment.

Using the metaphor of cultural pathways, we assume that individuals in all cultures have to address certain developmental tasks, such as the establishment of interpersonal relationships, but the way their pathways are structured, the activities that are included along the path, and the ideals or goals that adults strive to achieve differ across cultures. According to the psychosocial approach, all cultures must be able to adapt to changes in economic, environmental, and intercultural conditions in order to survive. Individual development is interwoven with the ability of the society to adapt and continue. For a list of the key concepts of cultural theory, see Table 2.6.

CASE ANALYSIS Using What You Know

1. From the case of Jack Manasky and Marilyn, deduce the cultural norms for the relationship of an adult daughter and an aging father.

2. Describe a hypothetical cultural context in which Jack and Marilyn might have a very different type of relationship and a different style of interaction.

3. Explain how the cultural value of individualism and independence are expressed in this case.

Table 2.6	Basic Concepts from Cultural Theory
Culture	Continuity
Physical culture	Discontinuity
Social culture	Rites of passage
Worldview	Collectivism
Cultural pathways	Individualism
Cultural determinism	Globalization
Culture carriers	Subcultures
Enculturation	

© Cengage

Social Role Theory

OBJECTIVE 2f Explain the basic concepts of social role theory and examine its implications for the study of human development.

Social role theory traces the process of socialization and personality development through the person's participation in increasingly diverse and complex social roles (Brim, 1966; Parsons & Bales, 1955). A social role is any set of behaviors that has a socially agreed-upon function and an accepted code of norms (Biddle, 1979; Biddle & Thomas, 1966; Brown, 1965).The term *role* was taken from the context of the theater. In a play, actors' behaviors are distinct and predictable because each actor has a part to play and follows a script. You will recall this metaphor from Shakespeare's analysis in *As You Like It*: "All the world's a stage, / and all the men and women merely players. / They have their exits and their entrances, / and one man in his time plays many parts" (Act 2, scene 7).

Role theory applies this same framework to social life (Biddle, 1986). The three elements of concern to role theory are the patterned characteristics of social behavior (**role enactment**); the parts or identities a person assumes (**social roles**); and the scripts or shared expectations for behavior that are linked to each part (**role expectations**). Social roles serve as a bridge between the individual and the society. Every society has a range of roles, and individuals learn about the expectations associated with them. As people enter new roles, they modify their behavior to conform to these role expectations. Each role is usually linked to one or more related or **reciprocal roles**. The student and the teacher, the parent and the child, and the salesperson and the customer are reciprocal roles. Each role is partly defined by the other roles that support it. The function of the role is determined by its relation to the surrounding role groups to which it is allied.

Four dimensions are used to analyze the impact of social roles on development: the *number* of roles a person occupies; the *intensity* of role involvement, or how deeply the person identifies with the role; the amount of *time* the role demands; and the extent to which the expectations associated with each role are either highly *structured* or *flexible* and open to improvisation. These features help account for experiences of role strain and role overload at various periods of life when the demands and intensity of multiple roles converge (see the **Applying Theory and Research to Life** box Role Strain and Parenthood).

Implications for Human Development

All cultures offer new roles that await individuals as they move from one stage of life to another. Some of these roles may be directly associated with age, such as the role of a high school

The social role of healer can be found in most cultures. Although the costumes and techniques may differ, healers typically have access to knowledge not shared by most of the people in the society. The role of healer exists in coordination with the reciprocal role of patient or a person seeking a cure. What are some of the role expectations associated with healers in our society?

Role Strain and Parenthood

A recurring theme in the literature on parenthood is the experience of role strain. **Role strain** is defined as a sense of difficulty in meeting perceived role expectations or balancing competing role demands (Biddle, 1986). Each of the following dimensions of social roles may contribute to parental role strain: role intensity, time required, the structure or flexibility of the role, and the number and characteristics of other roles. Because the parent role has great intensity, the sense of involvement in all the behaviors associated with the role intensifies, and so does anxiety about failure to meet the expectations of the role. First-time parents especially may have little confidence in their ability to fulfill their roles, and the level of worry associated with the role rises accordingly.

The parent role takes a lot of time. Most first-time parents underestimate how much time infants and toddlers require. When new parents reflect on the time they spend in a variety of social roles, they point to the parent role as more time consuming than any other role, now or in the past.

Role strain linked with parenting is related to the structure of the role. Some adults have very clear ideas about how they should enact their parent role, but many are unsure. Partners are likely to differ in their views on childrearing techniques. These differences require time to resolve. Because of the hardships or distress they recall from their own childhoods, many adults do not want to raise their children the way they were raised themselves. They have to learn a new script for this role.

When parenting is added to other adult roles, especially those of worker and spouse, the demands of the new parental role may seem overwhelming. Most parents are also enacting a worker role. Workplace conditions that allow demands of the work role to spill over into family life can be a cause of work–family conflict and role strain. With corporate downsizing, many workers find that they have much more to do, more functions to fill, and increased pressure to do work after hours or at home. The need to make a long commute to work, expectations to bring work home, and expectations to be available for telephone or online interactions from home are all examples of work demands that can increase parental role strain (Voydanoff, 2005). Societies differ in the extent to which family responsibilities come into conflict with one's worker role. In more collectivist cultures, it is likely that family commitments place substantial strains on individuals who are also engaged in demanding work settings (Allen, French, Dumani, & Shockley, 2015).

There are at least five ways to minimize role strain associated with the parent role (Allen, 2001; Bornstein, 2012; Cowan & Cowan, 2012; Newman, 2000):

1. Focus on a small number of expectations for the parenting role and focus on finding pleasure in meeting those expectations rather than worrying about the many expectations that are not being met.
2. Delegate role responsibilities can reduce role strain. Parents who can hire others to help with some of the parenting responsibilities or who can turn to family members or friends for help will experience less role strain than those who are solely responsible for the parenting role. Couples who can flexibly alter and share household responsibilities in response to the demands of parenting will experience more satisfaction and less strain.
3. Integrate several aspects of the role in one activity to reduce role strain. Some parents become quite inventive about ways to maintain contact with their infant while carrying out household chores and other work and also preserving time with each other.
4. Role strain is reduced when partners reach consensus about their parent roles. New parents who have resolved their differences regarding childrearing philosophy, child care activities, and the division of household responsibilities experience less role strain and a higher level of marital satisfaction than those who continue to have opposing views on these issues.
5. Either find a work environment that has supportive attitudes and policies regarding work–family coordination, or take steps to change the existing work culture to be more flexible and positive toward workers who are trying to balance concurrent family and work roles and responsibilities.

Critical Thinking Questions

1. Identify the behaviors you would be likely to observe if parents are experiencing role strain. What types of emotional states might you observe?
2. Hypothesize how parental role strain might influence one's relationships with other family members. How might it influence one's performance as a worker?
3. Discuss the factors that might make it difficult for partners to reach consensus about childrearing in order to reduce role strain.
4. Predict how characteristics of the child or children in the family might contribute to parental role strain. What are some of these characteristics?
5. Analyze some demands of the work role that might produce work–family conflict and parental role strain. What are some characteristics of the workplace that might reduce parental role strain?

student. Other roles may be accessible only to those of a certain age who demonstrate other relevant skills, traits, or personal preferences. In many elementary schools, for example, the fifth-grade students become eligible to serve in the role of crossing guard to help the younger children get across the streets near the school. Families, organizations, and the larger community have implicit theories of development that determine what role positions open up for individuals in each age group. Some of the most important life roles persist across several stages, including child, parent, and sibling. The expectations for role performance remain the same in some respects, but change in others. We can begin to see how social roles provide consistency to life experiences and how they prompt new learning.

Involvement in personal relationships and social groups contributes to the formation of one's **social identity**—that aspect of the self-concept that is based on membership in a group or groups and on the importance and emotional salience of that membership (Tajfel, 1981). Some of these role relationships are personal—based on family, friendship, or intimate relationships. Others are political, religious, or ethnic. Some aspects of one's social identity may be associated with a stigmatized group, such as being homeless, unemployed, or poor (Lott, 2012). In modern societies, people are members of many groups and form complex social identities; many roles and their varying meanings and values are balanced and synthesized. Understanding a person's social identity helps account for which groups a person may view as in-groups and out-groups, why a person might discriminate against certain out-groups, or how a person's views of fairness and justice may be shaped (Simon & Klandermans, 2001).

The idea that one's social identity is crafted from experiences in a variety of roles is illustrated in the following discussion about people who undergo the process of naturalization to become U.S. citizens.

> Several people I talked to implicitly compared citizenship status to other social divisions, particularly race. In thinking about changes brought about by naturalization, these respondents emphasized that while they were being formally incorporated into membership, they would remain outsiders because citizenship status is not a visible characteristic. A thirty-year-old Taiwanese immigrant explained his experience of racialization: "Well, sometimes, being American is not something you say about yourself. You have to depend on people's point of view and perspective. How people see me, because I don't look like American. So I would say I am American after I finish the process (*of naturalization*) but still it's so hard to reach people that I am American especially when I am walking along a road and one of the cops stops me and I don't think he looks at me like I am American".... Despite demographic realities, whiteness continues to be associated with being a real American. (Aptekar, 2015, p. 80)

This narrative illustrates the complexity of social identity, in this case for people who decide to pursue a path to citizenship in a new country. Their experience of naturalization, and its

Table 2.7	Basic Concepts from Social Role Theory
Social role	
Role enactment	
Role expectations	
Reciprocal roles	
Social identity	
Role strain	

© Cengage

accompanying status as an American citizen, has to be integrated with other social categories including ethnicity, race, social class, and gender.

Links to the Psychosocial Approach

Role relationships provide a central mechanism through which the socialization process takes place. In the psychosocial approach, one might think of the radius of significant relationships as an interconnected web of reciprocal roles and role relationships through which the expectations and demands of society make themselves known. The idea of reciprocity in roles is closely linked to the concept of interdependence of people at different psychosocial stages. The capacity of adults to cope with the challenges of their life stages and to achieve new ego strengths is intricately linked to the ability of children and youth to flourish and grow. Social role theory helps clarify why this is so important, because children and adults occupy many reciprocal roles.

In the following chapters, we describe a number of life roles especially related to family, school, and work. As the number of roles increases, individuals must learn some of the skills of role-playing, role differentiation, and role integration. The developmental crisis of individual identity versus identity confusion emphasizes the challenge of being able to integrate several diverse roles in order to preserve a sense of personal continuity. With each new role, one's self-definition changes and one's potential for influencing the world increases. For a list of the key concepts of social role theory, see Table 2.7.

CASE ANALYSIS Using What You Know

1. In the case of Jack Manasky and Marilyn, describe how Marilyn may be defining her role as the adult child of a widowed father.

2. Hypothesize factors that may contribute to role strain for adult children who are trying to care for their aging parents. What evidence do you see for this in the case of Jack Manasky and Marilyn?

3. Explain the idea of reciprocal roles. What evidence of reciprocal roles do you see in the case of Jack Manasky and Marilyn? How might the concept of reciprocal roles help explain some of the stresses associated with widowhood?

Systems Theory

OBJECTIVE 2g Explain the basic concepts of systems theory and examine its implications for the study of human development.

A **system**—whether it is a cell, an organ, an individual, a family, or a corporation—is composed of interdependent elements that share some common goals, interrelated functions, boundaries, and an identity. Systems theories attempt to describe and account for the characteristics of systems and the relationships among the component parts found within the system. Systems theories take the position that the whole is more than the sum of its parts. The system cannot be fully understood by identifying each of its component parts. A language system, for example, is more than the capacity to make vocal utterances, use grammar, and acquire vocabulary. It is the coordination of these elements in a useful way in a context of shared meaning.

Characteristics of Open Systems

Individuals, families, communities, schools, and societies are all examples of open systems. Open systems are in ongoing interaction with their environments. These systems have boundaries that help establish their identity: A cell has a cell wall; a team has a roster of members; a family has a sense of itself as an emotionally connected group. Resources, including information, food, friends, or sources of energy, can impact the system, yet the system has ways of managing and monitoring its boundaries so that it is not overwhelmed by external forces. As energy or resources are used, the open system has ways of acquiring new resources from adjoining systems. An isolated system has a very tight, impermeable boundary that does not allow outside forces to enter. When the energy or resources of an isolated system are used up, it is difficult for the system to acquire new resources.

Adaptation is a fundamental process in system maintenance and change. A system uses **feedback** mechanisms to monitor and communicate among the elements within the

The neighborhood is a microsystem. Children adapt their play to the physical characteristics and resources of their neighborhood.

David Grossman/The Image Works

system, and between the system and its environment. The more information about the environment the system is capable of detecting, the more complex these feedback mechanisms must be. For example, when the oxygen level of the environment is reduced, you tend to grow sleepy. While you sleep, your breathing slows, and you use less oxygen. This is a feedback mechanism that protects the system. Some adjustments are managed unconsciously by the organization of biological systems. Others are managed more deliberately by efforts to minimize the effects of environmental changes. Most systems have a capacity for storing or saving resources so that temporary shortages do not disrupt their operations. This is called **adaptive self-regulation**.

When open systems are confronted by new or changing environmental conditions, they have the capacity for **adaptive self-organization**. For example, when corporations have unexpected profits, they may create a new philanthropic arm to support some charitable goals, or create a new research and development wing to create new products. When an organization faces uncertainties related to new technologies or new markets, it may need to create new teams or redefine its goals. Similarly, when a family experiences illness of a family member, a person may withdraw from some aspect of work to spend more time with the person who is ill. When a child starts having new difficulties in school, parents may start to spend more time giving the child help with homework, or hire a tutor. The ability to withdraw from certain goals or to engage in new goals shows both aspects of adaptive self-organization (Wrosch, Amir, & Miller, 2011). In the face of change, the system retains its essential identity by creating new subsystems, revising the relationships among the components, or creating new, higher levels of organization that coordinate existing subsystems.

From the systems perspective, the components and the whole are always in tension. What one understands and observes depends on where one stands in this complex set of interrelationships. All living entities are both parts and wholes. A person is a part of a family, a classroom or work group, a friendship group, and a society. A person is also a whole—a coordinated, complex system composed of physical, cognitive, emotional, social, and self subsystems. Part of the story of human development is told in an analysis of the adaptive regulation and organization of those subsystems. Simultaneously, the story is told in the way larger systems fluctuate and impinge on individuals, forcing adaptive regulation and reorganization.

Ecological Systems Theory

In an effort to elaborate and clarify the set of interlocking systems in which human behaviors take place, Urie Bronfenbrenner (1979, 1995, 1999) developed ecological systems theory. According to this theory, individual development takes place in a complex set of interconnected systems, some of which the person is participating in directly, like the family, school, or workplace; and some of which impact the person indirectly because of the policies, resources, or expectations that influence the person's life. Four levels of systems are highlighted (see FIGURE 2.3 ▶):

1. A **microsystem** is a setting with particular physical characteristics and resources. Microsystems are characterized by patterns of activities, roles, and interpersonal relations experienced by the developing person. A child may function in multiple microsystems, such as a family, child care setting, and playground. One might expect that as people mature, they become involved in a larger number of microsystems with varying patterns of resources and expectations for behavior.

2. A **mesosystem** comprises the interrelations among two or more settings in which the developing person actively participates. For a child, this might be the relations among home, school, and neighborhood peer group. For an adult, this might be the relationships among family, work, community, and friendships. The demands of one setting, such as work, may require so much time and effort that the person is not able to meet expectations in another setting. Or the rewards of one setting are so highly valued that the person begins to neglect responsibilities in another setting.

3. An **exosystem** refers to one or more settings that do not involve the developing person as an active participant, but in which events occur that affect—or are affected by—what happens in the setting containing the developing person. A woman gets a promotion at work, which means more travel and time at corporate conferences. As a result, her partner has to spend more time at home caring for the children, and the children have fewer opportunities to interact with their mother. The partner and the children have no contact with the woman's work setting, but decisions made there have an impact on their lives.

4. The **macrosystem** refers to the culture or society that frames the structures and relationships among the systems. The macrosystem has laws and law enforcement practices, government agencies, social policies, health care resources, economic systems, educational resources, media, and many symbolic forms of influence that create the social, political, and financial contexts for development (Bronfenbrenner, 1979, pp. 22, 25, 26). For example, in 2007–2008, the United States experienced a major financial crisis. Many people lost their retirement savings, companies laid off tens of thousands of employees, and thousands of people experienced foreclosure on their homes. These events, brought about by mismanagement and greed at the macrosystem level, led to dramatic disruption at the family and community levels. The extreme and sudden nature of the financial losses required adaptive reorganization on the part of individuals and families as they disengaged from certain goals and re-engaged in alternatives.

Both the individual and the systems in which that person is embedded change over time. What is more, the relationships among the systems change over **time**. Some of these changes are patterned, developmental transformations, such as the change in a child's capacity for coordinated movement and voluntary, goal-directed action. Other changes are societal, such as a community decision to restructure a school system from an elementary (Grades K–6), junior high (Grades 7–9), and high school (Grades 10–12) system to an elementary (Grades K–5), middle school (Grades 6–8), and high school (Grades 9–12) system. Finally, some changes reflect the decline or improvement of resources in a

FIGURE 2.3 ▶ A TOPOGRAPHY OF THE RELATIONSHIP AMONG SYSTEMS   This is a hypothetical model of a person's ecological contexts. Over time, the specific microsystems change, and a person becomes involved in new microsystems. The impact of previous systems may continue to influence a person as a result of learning, memories, and internalized values. The two-way arrows suggest that individuals influence their contexts and contexts influence the individuals who participate in them.

Source: Adapted from Bronfenbrenner, 1979.

setting over time, as when a neighborhood becomes transformed through urban development. As resources of an environment change, the setting may become more or less supportive of continuing development.

In his later writings, Bronfenbrenner modified his theory, focusing on the ways individuals influence their environments (Bronfenbrenner, 2004; Bronfenbrenner & Morris, 2006). Both personal characteristics such as intelligence, temperament, or physical appearance, and activities in which the person engages, such as social interactions, physical activities, or maintenance tasks, can modify the environment and alter its impact. Some people are more intentional than others about trying to alter their environments. Repeated efforts to alter one's environment may improve a person's ability to effect change.

In these writings, Bronfenbrenner emphasized the central role of processes as the basic engines that account for development. He described a **process** as any of a wide range of interactions between a person and the environment. These processes, which are activity based, connect the active, growing person with the people, objects and symbolic representations in the environment. In order for the processes to have an impact on development, they must take place frequently or regularly over relatively long periods of time. Over time, the maturing person may become engaged in the process in new ways, and the process itself may be modified to become more complex. Think about the process of reading books. In infancy, even before a baby can talk, a parent might read a book or two before bedtime. This process of reading begins as a time for physical closeness, shared attention, auditory and visual stimulation. With advancing development, infants can select books, turn pages, point to pictures, and imitate words and sounds from books. Reading becomes a cognitive process as the child recalls stories, selects favorite books, and pretends to read. The process of reading is gradually transformed from something initiated by an adult to something sought after and performed by the child.

Implications for Human Development

Systems theory has been applied to the study of the life span through **developmental systems theory** (Molenaar, Lerner, & Newell 2014). This perspective emphasizes the ongoing interaction and integration across many levels of the human organism from the genetic to the behavioral level. **Plasticity,** the capacity for change, is at the heart of this approach. The **person in the setting** is the focus of analysis. The challenge to developmental systems theory is to understand the **bidirectional** regulation of the person and the environment over time. How is the person shaped and defined by the contexts in which the person functions? How does the person influence these contexts to foster more optimal environments for growth?

The boundary between the person and the environment is fuzzy. As an open system, a person is continuously influenced by information and resources from the environment and, at the same time, creates or modifies the environment to preserve system functioning. In this view, the self is a flexible construct, constantly being modified by the nature of social roles, relationships and interactions.

> We carry on a whole series of different relationships to different people. We are one thing to one [*person*] and one thing to another... We divide ourselves up in all sorts of different selves with reference to our acquaintances. We discuss politics with one and religion with another. There are all sorts of different selves answering to all sorts of different social reactions. (Mead, 1934, p. 142)

A Systems View of Families

Systems theory has also been applied to the analysis of family functioning. Family systems theories focus on how families establish and maintain stable patterns of functioning. Families are viewed as emotional units identifiable by certain boundaries and rules (Broderick, 1993). The **boundaries** of the family determine who is considered to be a family member and who is an outsider. Some families have very strict **rules** that maintain a narrow boundary around the family. Few sources of information or contact are admitted. Other families extend the sense of belonging to a wide range of people who bring ideas and resources to the family system.

Family systems are maintained by patterns of communication (Vogl-Bauer, 2003). Positive and negative **feedback loops** operate to stabilize, diminish, or increase certain types of interactions. For example, a feedback loop is positive when a child offers a suggestion and a parent recognizes and compliments the child on that suggestion. As a result, the child is encouraged to continue to offer suggestions, and the parent comes to view the child as someone who has valuable suggestions to offer. A feedback loop is negative if a parent ignores the child's suggestions or scolds the child for making them. The child is less likely to make further suggestions, and the parents' view of the child as someone who has no valuable ideas to offer is confirmed. Many positive and negative feedback loops operate in families to sustain the qualities of the system, such as the power hierarchy, level of conflict, and balance between autonomy and dependence among the members.

One of the most commonly noted characteristics of family systems is the **interdependence** of the family members. Changes in one family member are accompanied by changes in the others. Imagine for a moment that family members are standing in a circle and holding a rope. Each person is trying to exert enough tension on the rope to keep it tight and preserve the circular shape. The amount of tension each person must exert depends on what every other person is doing. Now imagine that one member of the family lets go of the rope and steps away. In order to retain the shape and tension of the rope, everyone else has to adjust his or her grip. Letting go of the rope is an analogy for many kinds of changes that can occur in a family—a parent becomes ill, a child goes off to college, or a parent takes on a demanding job outside of the home. The system adjusts by redefining relationships, modifying patterns of communication, and adjusting its boundaries. The family systems perspective offers a distinct approach to clinical problems. A person who has been identified as dysfunctional is treated not as a lone individual, but as part of a family system. The assumption is that the person's problems are a product of the interactions among family members. The only way to bring about changes in that person's functioning is to alter the functioning of the *other* members of the system as well. If the person is underfunctioning—that is, acting irresponsibly, not communicating, not performing at a level of capability, withdrawing, or acting impulsively—one assumes that others in the family are overfunctioning—that is, assuming many of the person's roles and responsibilities in order to take up the slack. The dysfunctional behavior is maintained because it is a component of an emotional unit. Dysfunction belongs neither to the person nor to the other family members, but to the particular interdependence among the family members that operates to preserve the viability of the family system as a whole (Bowen, 1978; Gilbert, 2006).

Links to the Psychosocial Approach

The psychosocial approach is quite compatible with the basic assumption of systems theory—an understanding of development requires an analysis of the person embedded in a number of interrelated systems. Systems theory predicts that systems change through adaptive self-regulation and adaptive self-organization. The direction of this change is not necessarily patterned, except that it is expected to move in the direction of creating new, higher levels of organization to coordinate newly developed substructures. The nature of change is a product of efforts to retain a sense of system identity and boundaries in the face of multiple demands and shifts in environments.

According to psychosocial theory, however, change is patterned. At each new stage of life, a person is propelled into increasingly complex social systems and encounters new stimulation for growth through participation in a greater variety of social relationships. As they mature, individuals develop new coping skills and devise strategies for new levels of participation in the social system. Eventually, they create innovative approaches for modifying the social system itself.

Building on the assumption that development is a product of ongoing interactions between the person and society, the psychosocial approach suggests that both the diversity of microsystems in which one is embedded and the quality of one's connections to those microsystems will influence the direction of development. Feelings of belonging, attachment, and connection to particular microsystems are associated with lower levels of anxiety, depression, and antisocial behavior. For example, in a study of middle-school-age adolescents, those who had a positive connection to home, school, and neighborhood had

Table 2.8	Basic Concepts of Systems Theory
System
Open system
Adaptation
Adaptive self-regulation
Adaptive self-organization
Developmental systems theory
Feedback
Microsystem
Mesosystem
Exosystem
Macrosystem
Process
Time
Boundaries
Rules
Interdependence

© Cengage

better grades in school than those who had low connection to these contexts. A positive connection to at least one of these microsystems serves as a protective factor, providing a basis for self-esteem and a buffer against depression (Witherspoon, Schotland, Way, & Hughes, 2009). The specific configuration of microsystems and one's role or place in those systems contribute to the positive or negative direction of development over the life span.

For a summary of the key concepts of systems theory, see Table 2.8.

CASE ANALYSIS Using What You Know

1. Explain the usefulness of the concept of a family system in trying to understand the relationship of Jack Manasky, his daughter Marilyn, and his deceased wife Anna.

2. Evaluate the feedback mechanisms between Jack Manasky and Marilyn. How does communication between these two family members encourage or discourage certain behaviors?

3. Hypothesize the ways that the macrosystem may influence Jack and Marilyn's approach to food, nutrition, and health.

Table 2.9 provides an overview of the primary emphasis and aspects of development highlighted in each of the theories.

OBJECTIVE 1 Explain the concept of theory and discuss how theories contribute to the study of human development.

A theory is a logical system of concepts that helps explain observations and points to underlying processes or relationships that are not readily observable. In order to understand a theory, one must consider which phenomena the theory is trying to explain, the assumptions that underlie the theory, and the theory's predictions about causal relationships or systematic associations. A theory of human development typically addresses several of the following questions: What is the direction of change over the life span? What are the mechanisms that account for continuity and change? What is the relevance of early experiences for later development? How do physical, cognitive, emotional, and social functions interact? How do the physical and social environments impact development? What factors typically place the person at risk for problems in development at various periods of life?

The seven theoretical perspectives reviewed in this chapter each take a distinct approach to explaining continuity and change across the life span.

OBJECTIVE 2a Explain the basic concepts of the theory of evolution and examine its implications for the study of human development.

Evolutionary theory provides a framework for understanding individual development within the broad perspective of the biological evolution of the human species. Although a life span of 85 or 90 years may seem long, it is just a flicker in the millions of years of biological adaptation. Evolutionary theory highlights the genetically governed aspects of growth and development. The environment provides the specific conditions that require adaptation. However, adaptive change can occur only if it is supported by the genetically based characteristics of the organism. The basic mechanism that accounts for species change over many generations is natural selection.

Table 2.9	Overview of Seven Theories of Development	
Theory	**Emphasis**	**Specific Aspects of Human Development**
Evolutionary theory	The emergence and modification of species as a result of natural selection	Fitness and inclusive fitness; the adaptive value of species' characteristics
Psychoanalytic theory	The origins and development of mental life	Personality development, emotions, motivation, impulse control, morality
Cognitive developmental theories	The origins and development of cognition	The development of reasoning and logical thought from infancy through adolescence; the role of culture and the teaching/learning process
Learning theories	The formation of relatively permanent changes in behavior as a result of experience	Learned behaviors, observational learning, the distinction between learning and performance, affects, expectancies, values, goals, and plans
Cultural theory	Learned systems of meanings and patterns of behavior shared by groups and transmitted from one generation to the next	The nature and direction of culturally guided developmental pathways; diversity in worldview
Social role theory	Socially constructed roles and role relationships that bridge the individual and society	The development of the self in social life; role gain, role loss, and the enactment of multiple roles
Systems theory	Processes that account for continuity and change in complex systems	The interdependence of elements within and between systems; emergence of new properties and behaviors as a result of self-regulation and self-organization; bidirectional nature of influence across system boundaries

© Cengage

Ethology, the study of evolutionarily significant behaviors, provides a systematic approach to analyzing reproductive practices, caregiving behaviors, strategies for obtaining resources, and other behaviors that contribute to individual and species survival. Evolutionary psychology focuses on understanding the human mind in terms of the problems of survival it has been shaped to solve.

OBJECTIVE 2b Explain the basic concepts of psychoanalytic theory and examine its implications for the study of human development.

According to psychoanalytic theory, development follows a biologically determined path in which patterns of social relationships change as a result of emerging sexual and aggressive impulses and the sexualization of body zones. Culture plays a major role in establishing the taboos and acceptable patterns of sexual gratification that lead to conflicts, fixations, and strategies for sublimation. The content of the unconscious—including sexual impulses, wishes, and fears—guides behavior and gives it meaning. Psychoanalytic theory emphasizes the years of infancy and childhood as those in which basic personality patterns are established. It also identifies the family, especially the parent–child relationship, as the primary context within which conflicts related to the socialization of sexual impulses are resolved. In contemporary psychoanalytic theory, interpersonal needs and the relational context of ego development are highlighted in contrast to the drive-based perspective of traditional psychoanalytic theory.

OBJECTIVE 2c Explain the basic concepts of cognitive developmental theories and examine their implications for the study of human development.

Cognitive developmental theories focus on the etiology of rational thought and the capacity for scientific reasoning. Piaget's cognitive theory, like psychoanalytic theory, views development as the product of a biologically guided plan for growth and change. The elements that make cognitive growth possible are all present in the genetic information that governs the growth of the brain and nervous system. However, the process of intellectual growth requires interaction with a diverse and responsive environment. Cognitive development is fostered by the recognition of discrepancies between existing schemes and new experiences. Through the reciprocal processes of assimilation and accommodation, schemes are modified and integrated to form the basis for organizing and explaining experience. The child is viewed as actively constructing knowledge through sensory, motor, and representational exploration.

Vygotsky's contribution to cognitive theory places the development of higher mental processes in a dynamic social context. Although thinking and reasoning are dependent on biologically based capacities, the way in which mental activity is organized reflects unique characteristics of the social context, especially as culture is transmitted through language, tools, and social relationships.

OBJECTIVE 2d Explain the basic concepts of learning theories and examine their implications for the study of human development.

Learning theories focus on the mechanisms that permit individuals to respond to their diverse environments and the changes in thought and behavior that accompany changes in the environment. Behavior can be shaped and modified by systematic changes in environmental conditions. According to learning theorists, human beings have an especially flexible behavioral system. No assumptions are made about universal stages of growth. As conditions in the environment change, response patterns also change. Similarity among individuals at a particular period of life is explained by the fact that they are exposed to similar environmental conditions, patterns of reinforcement, and models. Consistent contingencies between behaviors and their consequences result in the formation of cognitive expectations as well as behaviors.

OBJECTIVE 2e Explain the basic concepts of cultural theory and examine its implications for the study of human development.

Cultural theory, like the learning theories, emphasizes the role of the environment in directing the course of development. However, within the cultural theory framework, the focus is on the patterns of meaning that are given to biological maturation as well as the activities and routines that shape developmental pathways. Cultural theory recognizes certain constants in developmental tasks, but the ideal direction and socialization processes for guiding development differ widely across cultural groups. What one defines as the normal or natural pattern and tempo of change in competence, roles, and status depends largely on the way a society recognizes and treats individuals of different ages, sexes, and degrees of kinship.

OBJECTIVE 2f Explain the basic concepts of social role theory and examine its implications for the study of human development.

Social role theory suggests that learning is organized around key social functions called roles. As people enact roles, they integrate their behavior into meaningful units. Meaning is provided by the definition of the role and by the expectations of those in reciprocal roles. Development is a product of entry into an increasing number of complex roles over the life span. As children acquire and lose roles, they change their self-definitions and their relationships with social groups. Most societies define roles that are linked with gender, age, marital status, and kinship. These roles provide patterning to the life course. However, the patterns are understood to be products of the structures and functions of the society rather than of genetic information.

OBJECTIVE 2g Explain the basic concepts of systems theory and examine its implications for the study of human development.

Systems theory emphasizes the multidimensional sources of influence on individuals and the simultaneous influence of individuals on the systems of which they are a part. Each person is at once a component of one or more larger systems, and a system unto the self. One must approach the study of development from many angles, identifying the critical resources, the flow of resources, and the transformation of resources that underlie an adaptive process of reorganization and growth. This perspective has been applied to an analysis of families and family change as well as to individual development over the life span. Ecological systems theory highlights the layered nature of environments and the salient processes or activities that link individuals with their settings over time.

CASEBOOK

For additional case material related to this chapter, see the case of "A School Debate," on page 13 of *Life Span Development: A Case Book*, by Barbara and Philip Newman, Laura Landry-Meyer, and Brenda J. Lohman. This case focuses on the opinions of teachers and the school principal at a middle school about how to increase school attendance and reduce student tardiness. The varying suggestions reflect the application of different theories of human development to the solution of an important real-world problem. The case provides practice in linking theoretical ideas about causes of behavior to potential strategies for intervention.

This painting, The Family of Philip IV, no. 42, was inspired by the famous masterpiece Las Meninas, painted by Velázquez in 1656. Picasso first saw this painting when he was 14 years old. In 1957 he spent four months exploring many facets of the work, ultimately producing numerous interpretations. We are witnessing psychosocial evolution through art—the transmission of inspiration across centuries. Picasso's work conveys the intimacy of family life, adding a feeling of movement and chaos between adults and children as they try to get the little girl dressed for the day while the dog scampers underfoot. As implied in psychosocial theory, development is a product of ongoing interactions among people and their physical and social environments.

1. Explain the rationale for using psychosocial theory as an organizing framework for the study of human development.

2. Define the six basic concepts of psychosocial theory: stages of development, developmental tasks, psychosocial crisis, central process for resolving the crisis, radius of significant relationships, and coping.

3. Evaluate psychosocial theory, pointing out its strengths and weaknesses.

PSYCHOSOCIAL THEORY

3

In this chapter we introduce the basic concepts of psychosocial theory that provide the integrating framework for our approach to the study of human development. Psychosocial theory accounts for patterns of individual development that emerge from a biopsychosocial process. The theory covers the entire life span from infancy through elderhood, offering a guide for thinking about essential life issues such as the importance of parent–infant interactions, the role of school in promoting a sense of competence, the emergence of a personal identity, the formation of loving relationships in adulthood, and the relationship of meaningful work to personal well-being. It provides concepts that help explain the complex interplay between individuals and their societies, including insights into understanding why some people soar and thrive while others struggle and withdraw.

The Rationale for Emphasizing Psychosocial Theory

Explain the rationale for using psychosocial theory as an organizing framework for the study of human development.

We have selected **psychosocial theory** as an organizing framework for the text because of its range and scope. Having read chapter 2, you understand that psychosocial theory is not the only or most widely accepted theory for studying human development. However, it combines three features that make it especially useful as we strive to link the broad field of human development to applications in health, human services, education, and social welfare (Green, 2008):

1. Psychosocial theory addresses growth across the life span, identifying and differentiating central issues from infancy through elderhood.
2. Psychosocial theory assumes that individuals have the capacity to contribute to their own psychological development at each stage of life. People have the ability to integrate, organize, and conceptualize their experiences in order to protect themselves, cope with challenges, and direct the course of their lives. Therefore, the direction of development is shaped by self-regulation as well as by the ongoing interaction of biological and societal influences.
3. Psychosocial theory takes into consideration the active contribution of **culture** to individual growth. At each life stage, cultural goals, aspirations, and social expectations and requirements make demands that evoke individual reactions. These reactions influence which of a person's capabilities will be developed further. This vital link between the individual and the culture is a key mechanism of development. Each society has its own view of the qualities that reflect maturity. These qualities are infused into the lives of individuals and help determine the direction of growth within the society.

The person who identified and developed psychosocial theory was Erik H. Erikson. He was initially trained as a

Although Erik Erikson's name is typically associated with psychosocial theory, the work is a product of an active collaboration between Erik and his wife Joan.

Ted Streshinsky Photographic Archive/Getty Images

psychoanalyst. His theory was influenced by the work of many others, including Sigmund and Anna Freud, Peter Blos, Robert White, Jean Piaget, and Robert Havighurst, whose ideas you will encounter throughout this book. His wife Joan was an important intellectual collaborator as well. Erik and Joan worked together to formulate the first presentation of psychosocial theory and its eight stages of development in 1950 (J. M. Erikson, 1988).

The case study, which was written by Erikson, gives us a brief look into his early life and leads us to speculate about how his life experiences may have guided the direction of his theoretical work. Just like other great thinkers of his time, being an outsider seems to have had some advantages for Erikson, allowing him to approach the study of human development from a unique, multidisciplinary and creative point of view (Dunbar, 2000).

The psychosocial approach that guides the organization of this book expands on Erikson's theory, integrating the literature in human development, especially the idea of developmental tasks, to help explain the multidimensional competences needed to address each of the psychosocial crises. The book also expands on the number of stages, including a focus on prenatal development, two stages of adolescence, and two stages of later life. These additions are a product of the growing body of evidence about the genetic and environmental factors that shape prenatal life, the increasingly complex nature of society that requires an extended period of adolescence, and the expanding length of life and the vitality of many who live well beyond their original life expectancy.

FURTHER REFLECTION *What is the focus or range of applicability of psychosocial theory? What is this theory about?*

— **CASE STUDY** Erik H. Erikson —

Erik Erikson (1902–1994) illustrates the psychosocial perspective by describing the personal, family, and societal factors that contributed to his own identity crisis.

There is first of all the question of origin, which often looms large in individuals who are driven to be original. I grew up in Karlsruhe in southern Germany as the son of a pediatrician, Dr. Theodor Homburger, and his wife Karla, née Abrahamsen, a native of Copenhagen, Denmark. All through my earlier childhood, they kept secret from me the fact that my mother had been married previously; and that I was the son of a Dane who had abandoned her before my birth. They apparently thought that such secretiveness was not only workable (because children then were not held to know what they had not been told) but also advisable, so that I would feel thoroughly at home in their home. As children will do, I played in with this and more or less forgot the period before the age of three, when mother and I had lived alone. Then her friends had been artists working in the folk style of Hans Thoma of the Black Forest. They, I believe, provided my first male imprinting before I had to come to terms with that intruder, the bearded doctor, with his healing love and mysterious instruments. Later, I enjoyed going back and forth between the painters' studios and our house, the first floor of which, in the afternoons, was filled with tense and trusting mothers and children. My sense of being "different" took refuge (as it is apt to do even in children without such acute life problems) in fantasies of how I, the son of much better parents, had been altogether a foundling. In the meantime, however, my adoptive father was anything but the proverbial stepfather. He had given me his last name (which I have retained as a middle name) and expected me to become a doctor like himself.

Identity problems sharpen with that turn in puberty when images of future roles become inescapable. My stepfather was the only professional man (and a highly respected one) in an intensely Jewish small bourgeois family, while I (coming from a racially mixed Scandinavian background) was blond and blue-eyed, and grew flagrantly tall. Before long, then, I was referred to as "goy" in my stepfather's temple; while to my schoolmates I was a "Jew." Although during World War I, I tried desperately to be a good German chauvinist, I became a "Dane" when Denmark remained neutral.

At the time, like other youths with artistic or literary aspirations, I became intensely alienated from everything my bourgeois family stood for. At that point, I set out to be different. After graduation from the type of high school called a humanistic Gymnasium . . . I went to art school, but always again took to wandering. . . . And in those days

every self-respecting stranger in his own (northern) culture drifted sooner or later to Italy, where endless time was spent soaking up the southern sun and the ubiquitous sights with their grand blend of artifact and nature. I was a "Bohemian" then.

Source: Erikson, 1975.

CASE ANALYSIS Using What You Know

As you think about this autobiographical case, consider the following questions:

1. Describe why Erikson feels like a "stranger in his own culture."
2. Analyze the biological, psychological, and societal factors that contributed to Erikson's identity crisis.
3. Speculate about factors from childhood which appear to be influencing his experiences as an adolescent.
4. Evaluate the role of the significant figures in Erikson's life, the radius of significant others, and the parts they played in defining how he should behave and who he should strive to become.
5. Hypothesize about the factors that might have contributed to Erikson's ability to cope with the challenges of this period of his life, so that he could eventually discover a sense of direction and meaning.

Basic Concepts of Psychosocial Theory

OBJECTIVE 2 Define the six basic concepts of psychosocial theory: stages of development, developmental tasks, psychosocial crisis, central process for resolving the crisis, radius of significant relationships, and coping.

Psychosocial theory offers an organizational framework for considering individual development within the larger perspective of psychosocial evolution. **Psychosocial evolution**, a construct proposed by Julian Huxley (1941, 1942), refers to the human abilities that allow us to gather knowledge from our ancestors and transmit it to our descendants. Childrearing practices, education, and modes of communication are examples of mechanisms that transmit information from earlier generations to the present time. Meanwhile, new information, new ways of thinking, and new ways of teaching are developed. The transmission of values and knowledge across generations requires the maturation of individuals who are capable of creating knowledge, symbolizing it, adapting it, and transferring it to others.

Psychosocial theory accounts for systematic change over the life span using six basic concepts: (1) stages of development, (2) developmental tasks, (3) psychosocial crises, (4) central processes for resolving the crisis at each stage, (5) networks of significant relationships, and (6) coping—the process through which people generate new behaviors to meet new challenges. These concepts will be defined in the following sections. However, each concept includes stage-specific content that will be discussed in greater detail in subsequent chapters. Table 3.1 provides an

Table 3.1   The Organization of the Text

Life Stage	Developmental Tasks	Psychosocial Crisis
PRENATAL (CONCEPTION TO BIRTH) CHAPTER 4		
INFANCY (FIRST 24 MONTHS) CHAPTER 5	Maturation of sensory/perceptual, and motor functions Sensorimotor intelligence: Processing, organizing and using information Communication Attachment Emotional development	Trust versus mistrust
TODDLERHOOD (2 TO 4) CHAPTER 6	Elaboration of locomotion Language development Fantasy play Self-control	Autonomy versus shame and doubt
EARLY SCHOOL AGE (4 TO 6) CHAPTER 7	Gender identification Early moral development Self-theory Peer play	Initiative versus guilt
MIDDLE CHILDHOOD (6 TO 12) CHAPTER 8	Friendship Concrete operations Skill learning Self-evaluation Team play	Industry versus inferiority
EARLY ADOLESCENCE (12 TO 18) CHAPTER 9	Physical maturation Formal operations Emotional development Membership in the peer group Romantic and sexual relationships	Group identity versus alienation
LATER ADOLESCENCE (18 TO 24) CHAPTER 10	Autonomy from parents Gender identity Internalized morality Career choice	Individual identity versus identity confusion
EARLY ADULTHOOD (24 TO 34) CHAPTER 11	Exploring intimate relationships Childbearing Work Lifestyle	Intimacy versus isolation
MIDDLE ADULTHOOD (34 TO 60) CHAPTER 12	Managing a career Nurturing an intimate relationship Expanding caring relationships Managing the household	Generativity versus stagnation
LATER ADULTHOOD (60 TO 75) CHAPTER 13	Accepting one's life Promoting intellectual vigor Redirecting energy toward new roles Developing a point of view about death	Integrity versus despair
ELDERHOOD (75 UNTIL DEATH) CHAPTER 14	Coping with the physical changes of aging Developing a psychohistorical perspective Traveling uncharted territory: Life structures of the very old	Immortality versus extinction

Central Process	Prime Adaptive Ego Quality	Core Pathology	Applied Topic
			Abortion
Mutuality with the caregiver	Hope	Withdrawal	The role of the parents
Imitation	Will	Compulsion	Child care
Identification	Purpose	Inhibition	School readiness
Education	Competence	Inertia	Violence in the lives of children
Peer pressure	Fidelity to others	Dissociation	Adolescent alcohol and drug use
Role experimentation	Fidelity to values	Repudiation	Dropping out of college
Mutuality among peers	Love	Exclusivity	Divorce
Person–environment interaction and creativity	Care	Rejectivity	Discrimination in the workplace
Introspection	Wisdom	Disdain	Retirement
Social support	Confidence	Diffidence	Meeting the needs of the frail elderly

overview of the life stages, summarizing the content of the basic concepts for each stage of life. In addition, for each stage there is a discussion of an applied topic of current interest that illustrates how a psychosocial perspective can help us to analyze the topic and shape directions for action.

Take a moment to study the table. You can use it as a guide and study aid to help identify the major themes of the text. It may help you to see the connections among the topics in a chapter and to trace threads of continuity over several periods of life. You may also use this table in constructing a life map for yourself that will reveal areas of emerging competence, potential tension, and the major psychosocial factors that are currently affecting your self-concept and your relationships with others.

Stages of Development

A **developmental stage** is a period of life that is characterized by a specific underlying organization. At every stage, some characteristics differentiate that stage from the preceding and succeeding stages. Stage theories propose a specific direction for development. At each stage, the accomplishments from the previous stages provide resources for mastering the challenges of the new stage. Each stage is unique and leads to the acquisition of new skills related to new capabilities. In the process of development, it is not uncommon to observe plateaus, where the

level of competence remains steady while the person integrates new abilities, followed by a spurt of rapid reorganization as the person attains a new, more complex level of functioning (Dawson-Tunick, Commons, Wilson, & Fischer, 2005).

Within the framework of psychosocial theory, the concept of stages of development refers to a pattern of changes in the self-concept based on new cognitive capacities, new learning, and the acquisition of new relationship skills. At each stage, the biological, psychological, and societal systems converge around a set of defining challenges that require a new view of the self in society and a new way of relating to others (Whitbourne, Sneed, & Sayer, 2009). You can verify the stage concept through reflection on your own past. You can probably recall earlier periods when you were very preoccupied by efforts first to gain your parents' approval, then to win acceptance by your peers, and later to experience self-acceptance. Each of these concerns may have appeared all-encompassing at the time, but eventually each gave way to a new preoccupation. At each stage, you were confronted with a unique set of problems that required the integration of your personal needs and skills with the social demands of your culture.

Erikson (1963) proposed eight stages of psychosocial development. His formulation can be traced in part to the stages of psychosexual development proposed by Freud and in part to his own observations and rich mode of thinking. FIGURE 3.1 ▶ shows the chart that Erikson (1963) produced in *Childhood and*

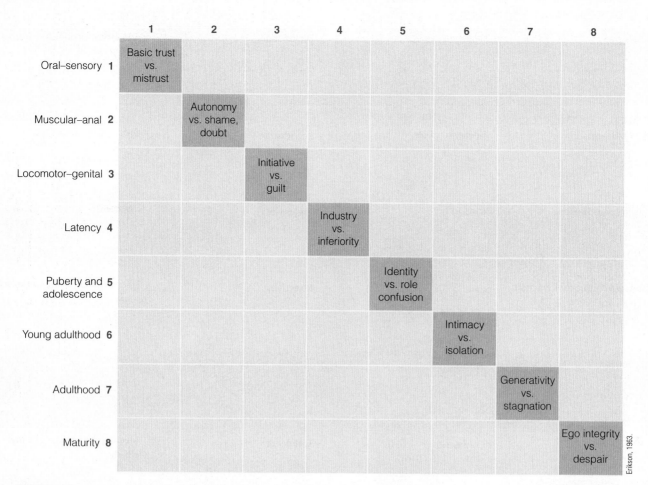

FIGURE 3.1 ▶ ERIKSON'S MODEL OF THE PSYCHOSOCIAL STAGES OF DEVELOPMENT

Society to describe the stages of psychosocial development. The shaded boxes identify the main psychosocial conflicts of each stage. If the conflict of a stage is handled well, a new sense of mastery and competence emerges. In Erikson's original model, the periods of life are given names, such as oral–sensory or puberty and adolescence, but no ages. This approach reflects Erikson's emphasis on an individual timetable for development, guided by both biological maturation and cultural expectations rather than by a strict chronological time frame for development.

Erikson (1963) proposed that the stages of development follow the **epigenetic principle**—a biological plan for growth that allows each function to emerge systematically until the fully functioning organism has developed. An assumption of this and other stage theories is that the stages form a sequence. Although one can anticipate challenges that will occur at a later stage, one passes through the stages in an orderly pattern of growth. In the logic of psychosocial theory, the entire life span is required for all the functions of psychosocial development to appear and become integrated. There is no going back to an earlier stage because experience makes retreat impossible. In contrast to other stage theories, however, Erikson suggested that one can review and reinterpret previous stages in the light of new insight or new experiences.

Furthermore, the themes of earlier stages may reemerge at any point. Through reflection and insight, a person can find new meaning and new resolutions to earlier conflicts. Joan Erikson reflects on the fluidity and hopefulness in this perspective:

> This sequential growth . . . is now known to be more influenced by the social milieu than was in previous years considered possible. . . . Where a strength is not adequately developed according to the given sequence for

its scheduled period of critical resolution, the supports of the environment may bring it into appropriate balance at a later period. Hope remains constant throughout life that more sturdy resolutions of the basic confrontation may be realized. (J. M. Erikson, 1988, pp. 74–75)

The concept of life stages permits us to consider the various aspects of development, such as physical growth, social relationships, and cognitive capacities, at a given period of life and to speculate about their interrelation. It also encourages a focus on the experiences that are unique to each life period—experiences that deserve to be understood both in their own right and for their contribution to subsequent development. When programs and services are designed to address critical needs in such areas as education, health care, housing, and social welfare, the developmental stage approach allows the designers to focus on the needs and resources of the particular population to be served.

Despite the usefulness of a stage approach, one must avoid thinking of stages as pigeonholes. Being in a given stage does not mean that a person cannot function at other levels. It is not unusual for people to anticipate later challenges before they become dominant. Many children of toddler and preschool age, for example, play house, envisioning having a husband or a wife and children. You might say that, in this play, they are anticipating the issues of intimacy and generativity that lie ahead. The experience of having a child—whether this occurs at age 18, 25, or 35—is likely to raise issues of generativity, even if the theory suggests that this theme is not in its peak ascendancy until middle adulthood. Whereas some elements of each psychosocial theme can be observed at all ages, the intensity with which they are expressed at certain times marks their importance in the definition of a developmental stage. Erikson, Erikson, and Kivnick (1986) put it this way:

> The epigenetic chart also rightly suggests that the individual is never struggling only with the tension that is focal at the time. Rather, at every successive developmental stage, the individual is also increasingly engaged in the anticipation of tensions that have yet to become focal and in re-experiencing those tensions that were inadequately integrated when they were focal; similarly engaged are those whose age-appropriate integration was then, but is no longer, adequate. (p. 39)

As one leaves a stage, the achievements of that period are neither lost nor irrelevant to later stages. Important ego strengths emerge from the successful resolution of conflicts at every stage. Some of these strengths may be challenged or reorganized as events take place later in life that call into question the essential beliefs established in an earlier period. For example, the psychosocial conflict during early school age is initiative versus guilt. Its positive outcome, a sense of initiative, is a joy in innovation and experimentation and a willingness to take risks in order to learn more about the world. Once achieved, the sense of initiative provides a positive platform for the formation of social relationships and for further creative intellectual inquiry and discovery. However, experiences in a highly authoritarian school environment or in a very judgmental, shaming personal

Lawrence Migdale/Science Source

The epigenetic principle assumes that it takes the entire life span, from the prenatal period through elderhood, for all facets of human capacity to emerge. In later adulthood and elderhood grandparents transmit the wisdom of their generation to their grandchildren by teaching them stories, songs, customs, and beliefs.

relationship may inhibit one's sense of initiative or mask it with a facade of indifference.

The concept of the psychosocial stages of development is very good as far as it goes, but Erikson's road map seems incomplete. Three criticisms of this layout of the life span have been raised. First, although the boxes in the figure look very even and comparable, each stage is actually of very different length. Second, the figure suggests discrete shifts from one stage to the next, when in fact the themes of these stages overlap (McAdams & de St. Aubin,1992). Transitions from stage to stage are not instantaneous. Movement from one stage to the next is the result of changes in several major systems that take place gradually. Third, if the idea of psychosocial evolution has validity—and we believe it does—new stages can be expected as a culture evolves.

In this text, we have identified 11 stages of psychosocial development, each with the following approximate age range: (1) *prenatal*, from conception to birth; (2) *infancy*, from birth to 2 years; (3) *toddlerhood*, 2 to 4 years; (4) *early school age*, 4 to 6 years; (5) *middle childhood*, 6 to 12 years; (6) *early adolescence*, 12 to 18 years; (7) *later adolescence*, 18 to 24 years; (8) *early adulthood*, 24 to 34 years; (9) *middle adulthood*, 34 to 60 years; (10) *later adulthood*, 60 to 75 years; and (11) *elderhood,* 75 until death.

By discussing a prenatal stage, two stages of adolescent development rather than one, and elderhood, we are adding three stages to those proposed by Erikson. This revision is a product of our analysis of the research literature, observations through research and practice, discussions with colleagues, and suggestions from other stage theorists. The addition of these three new stages provides a good demonstration of the process of theory construction.

FIGURE 3.2 ▶ shows the 11 stages of psychosocial development as presented in this textbook. The age range given for each stage is only an approximation. Each person has a uniquely personal timetable for growth. Differences associated with poverty, health, cultural group (e.g., differing rates of longevity), and exposure to environmental risks also lead to different timetables. The lengths of the stages vary, from the 9 months of the prenatal period to the roughly 26 years of middle adulthood.

FURTHER REFLECTION Explain how psychosocial theory treats biological maturation and experience as forces guiding development.

Evaluate the concept of stages of development. How might this concept prove useful in the contexts of education, counseling, or human services?

Developmental Tasks

Robert J. Havighurst first introduced the concept of **developmental tasks**. He believed that human development is a process in which people attempt to learn the tasks required of them by the society to which they are adapting. These tasks change with age because each society has **age-graded expectations** for behavior. As Havighurst observed, "Living in a modern society is a long series of tasks to learn" (1972, p. 2). In Havighurst's view, the person who learns well receives satisfaction and reward; the person who does not suffers unhappiness and social disapproval.

Although Havighurst's view of development emphasized the guiding role of society in determining which skills need to be acquired at a certain age, he did not totally ignore the role of physical maturation. Havighurst believed that there are **sensitive periods** for learning developmental tasks—that is, times when the person is most ready to acquire a new ability. Havighurst called these periods **teachable moments**. Most people learn developmental tasks at the time and in the sequence appropriate in their society. If a particular task is not learned during the sensitive period, it may be much more difficult to learn later on.

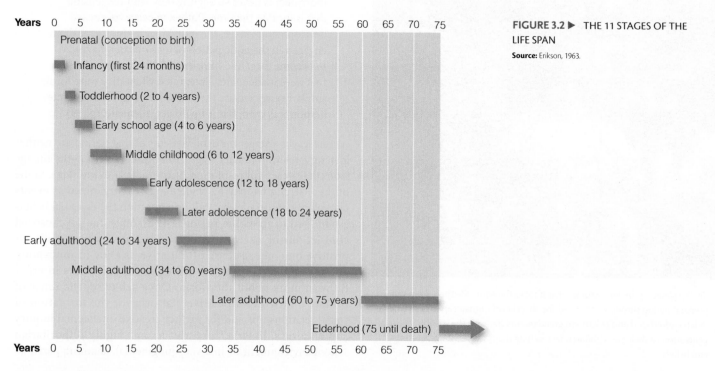

FIGURE 3.2 ▶ THE 11 STAGES OF THE LIFE SPAN

Source: Erikson, 1963.

At each stage of life, one faces new developmental tasks that contribute to increased mastery over one's environment. These tasks reflect areas of accomplishment in physical, cognitive, social, and emotional development, as well as development of the self-concept. The specific tasks we identify differ from those outlined in Havighurst's writings. Our choice of tasks is based on broad areas of accomplishment that have been identified by researchers as critical to psychological and social growth at each stage of life in a modern, technological culture.

We often think of mastery of developmental tasks, especially in childhood, as being fostered as parents and teachers encourage, educate, and model new levels of functioning for their children and students. However, as they move into early adolescence, young people are increasingly likely to invent novel strategies to advance their competence. The Internet provides a rich and diverse environment in which adolescents explore interests, form and strengthen social relationships, and find outlets for the expression of their opinions (Borca, Bina, Keller, Gilbert, & Begotti, 2015).

Societal expectations for mastery of a developmental task may change over time. These changes may be gradual, occurring over generations. For example, we identify emotional development as a task that begins in infancy and is a focus of attention again in early adolescence. The content of this task changes markedly across developmental stages, and society has changed in its expectations about the nature of this task. Lauren, an American Indian mother describes how her approach to emotional expression with her children differs from the way she was raised:

> We are more open with our children; we allow them to express themselves, a lot more than we were allowed as children ourselves. Basically, if we had something to say, we felt like we wanted to say something about our emotions, we were like told, "I don't want to hear anything about that" You know, we were not given a voice. Whereas children today are not only given a voice, but are given plenty of opportunity to express that voice. (Parker et al., 2012, p. 77)

Changing societal expectations that impact developmental tasks may also occur rapidly, as happened during the radical political transformation of the 1990s in many countries of central and eastern Europe and the former Soviet Union. Young people experienced new freedoms that encouraged more autonomy of expression, travel, and political engagement. They also faced new challenges related to employment and economic uncertainties. These societal changes did not alter the importance of basic developmental tasks of adolescence and early adulthood, but led to a postponement of the timing of traditional transitions into family and career roles (Tomasik & Silbereisen, 2012).

The basic premise associated with the concept of developmental tasks, regardless of their specific content, is that a relatively small number of major psychosocial challenges dominate a person's problem-solving efforts and learning during a given stage of life. As these tasks are mastered, new competencies enhance the person's ability to engage in more complex social relationships and advanced problem solving. Effective mastery of the developmental tasks of a specific stage of life provides building

Toddlerhood is a sensitive period for language development, when parent–child conversations are especially critical.

blocks for mastery of the tasks of future stages (Masten, Obrdovic, & Burt, 2006; McCormick, Kuo, & Masten, 2011).

Successful cultures will stimulate behavior that helps its members learn what they need to know for both their own survival and that of the group. In the case presented earlier in the chapter, Erikson provides an example of how the culture supports a person's work on the developmental tasks of a particular life stage. As he was entering later adolescence following graduation from Gymnasium, Erikson took advantage of a culturally accepted period of exploration by traveling to Italy. During this period, he was able to work on several of the developmental tasks of later adolescence, especially gaining greater autonomy from his family, experimenting with possible career paths, and clarifying his values and beliefs by becoming a "Bohemian."

Keep in mind that a person is maturing in a few important domains at once during each period of life. Tasks involving physical, emotional, intellectual, and social growth, as well as growth in one's self-concept, all contribute to one's resources for dealing with the challenges of life. Table 3.2 shows the developmental tasks we have identified as areas of learning for most people in modern society and the stages during which each set of tasks is of primary learning value. There are 42 developmental tasks on the list. Whereas the infant is learning orientations and skills related to the first 5, a person at the

Table 3.2	Developmental Tasks Associated with the Life Stages	
Life Stages*	**Developmental Tasks**
Infancy (first 24 months)	Maturation of sensory/perceptual and motor functions
	Sensorimotor intelligence: Processing, organizing, and using information
	Communication
	Attachment
	Emotional development
Toddlerhood (2 to 4)	Elaboration of locomotion
	Language development
	Fantasy play
	Self-control
Early school age (4 to 6)	Gender identification
	Early moral development
	Self-theory
	Peer play
Middle childhood (6 to12)	Friendship
	Concrete operations
	Skill learning
	Self-evaluation
	Team play
Early adolescence (12 to18)	Physical maturation
	Formal operations
	Emotional development
	Membership in the peer group
	Romantic and sexual relationships
Later adolescence (18 to 24)	Autonomy from parents
	Gender identity
	Internalized morality
	Career choice
Early adulthood (24 to 34)	Exploring intimate relationships
	Childbearing
	Work
	Lifestyle
Middle adulthood (34 to 60)	Managing a career
	Nurturing an intimate relationship
	Expanding caring relationships
	Managing the household
Later adulthood (60 to 75)	Accepting one's life
	Redirecting energy toward new roles and activities
	Promoting intellectual vigor
	Developing a point of view about death
Elderhood (75 until death)	Coping with physical changes of aging
	Developing a psychohistorical perspective
	Traveling through uncharted terrain

*We do not consider the concept of developmental tasks appropriate to the prenatal stage.

© Cengage

early adulthood stage has already acquired skills related to 27 tasks from the previous stages. New learning may continue in these areas as well as in the 4 new developmental tasks faced by the young adult. This helps one appreciate that by the time people reach early adulthood, they have a considerable repertoire of competencies that can be used to cope with the challenges of life. By the stage of elderhood a person has all the areas of previous learning to draw from while working on three new tasks.

FURFER REFLECTION   Describe a developmental task that may have changed in content or focus from the time of your grandparents to your parents or from your parents to you. What are some of these changes? What may have led to these changes?

Psychosocial Crisis

A **psychosocial crisis** refers to a state of tension that results from the discrepancies between the person's competences at the beginning of a stage and the society's expectations for behavior at that period of life (Erikson, 1963). For example, in toddlerhood, the second stage of development from roughly ages 2 to 4, the psychosocial crisis is autonomy versus shame and doubt. At the beginning of this stage, the toddler may have established a strong, positive, and trusting relationship with the caregiver. Now the child is expected to function more independently, to take care of some basic needs, and exercise new levels of self-control. These expectations for new levels of autonomy may be accompanied by new experiences of shame. A child may overreach by asserting too much autonomy.

> In an attempt to do something on her own, Mindy tries to pour her own glass of milk from the carton and spills milk all over the counter. Her mother says, "What a mess! You should have waited for me to help you."
>
> On the other hand, a child may be shamed for being overly dependent.
>
> Brad is trying to get Lewis ready for preschool. They have to leave by 8:00 a.m. in order to get there on time. Lewis is just sitting on the floor, playing with his Legos. "Lewis, I need you to get your shoes on so we can get going. You are old enough to do this on your own. You shouldn't need me to remind you every morning about how to get ready to go."

At each developmental stage, the sense of crisis arises because one must make psychological efforts to adjust to the demands of the social environment. The word *crisis* in this context refers to a normal set of stresses and strains rather than to an extraordinary set of events.

Societal demands vary from stage to stage. People experience these demands as mild, but persistent expectations for behavior. They may be demands for greater self-control, further development of skills, or a stronger commitment to goals. Before the end of each stage of development, the individual tries to achieve a resolution, adjust to society's demands, and at the same time translate those demands into personal terms. This process produces a state of tension that the individual must reduce in order to proceed to the next stage.

Mastery of the developmental tasks and resolution of the psychosocial crises interact to produce individual life stories. The skills learned during a particular stage as a result of work on its developmental tasks provide the tools for the resolution of the psychosocial crisis of that stage. This resolution orients the person toward new experiences, a new aptitude for relationships, and new feelings of personal worth as the challenges of the next stage's developmental tasks begin.

Psychosocial Crises of the Life Stages

Table 3.3 lists the psychosocial crisis of each stage of development from infancy through elderhood. This scheme, derived from Erikson's model shown in Figure 3.2, depicts the crises as polarities—for example, trust versus mistrust, and autonomy versus shame and doubt. These contrasting conditions suggest the underlying dimensions along which each psychosocial crisis is resolved. According to psychosocial theory, most people experience both positive and negative elements of the continuum. For example, even within a loving, caring family environment that promotes trust, an infant will experience some moments of frustration or disappointment that result in mistrust.

The outcome of the crisis at each stage is an integration of the two opposing forces. For each person, the relative frequency and significance of positive and negative experiences will contribute to a resolution of the crisis. The likelihood of a completely positive or a completely negative resolution is small. Most individuals resolve the crises in a generally positive direction, supported by a combination of positive experiences and natural maturational tendencies. At each successive stage, however, the likelihood of a negative resolution mounts as the developmental tasks become more complex and the chances of encountering societal barriers to development increase.

To understand the process of growth at each life stage, we have to consider the negative as well as the positive pole of each crisis. The dynamic tension between the positive and negative forces reflects the struggles a person encounters to restrain powerful impulses, overcome fears and doubts, and look past one's own needs to consider the needs of others.

In every psychosocial crisis, experiences at both the positive and negative poles contribute to the total range of a person's adaptive capacities. Although a steady diet of mistrust is undesirable, for example, it is important that a trusting person be able to evaluate situations and people for their trustworthiness. This ability is based in part on experiences of mistrust, which help a person recognize cues about safety or danger in any encounter.

Why conceptualize life in terms of crises? Does this idea adequately portray the experience of the individual, or does it overemphasize conflict and abnormality? The term *crisis* implies that tension and conflict are necessary to the developmental process; crisis and its resolution are viewed as normative, biologically based components of life experience at every stage.

The term *psychosocial* draws attention to the fact that the crises are, in part, the result of cultural pressures and expectations. Individuals will experience tension because of the culture's need to socialize and integrate its members. The concept acknowledges the dynamic conflicts between individuality and group membership at each period of life.

Looking back to the opening case, Erikson attributes the psychosocial crisis around his personal identity to a convergence of biological, psychological, and societal factors. He is physically different from his Jewish family members; he is identified as a religious outsider by his friends; and he is an object of traditional, middle-class family values and expectations that he rejects. As he emerges into later adolescence, he finds his transitional identity as an artist, an identity that he explores for several years before discovering his potential as a teacher, therapist, and theorist.

The exact nature of the psychosocial crisis is not the same at each stage. However, as reflected in the epigenetic principle, the succession of crises occurs in a predictable sequence over the life course. Although Erikson did not specify the exact ages for each crisis, the theory hypothesizes an age-related progression, in which each crisis has its time of special significance. The research described in the **Applying Theory and Research to Life** box Using Autobiographical Memories to Explore Psychosocial Stages of Life illustrates one approach for exploring the empirical basis of this concept.

Unforeseen Crises

In addition to the predictable psychosocial crises, any number of unforeseen stressors may arise. These stressors may impact individuals and families, such as parental divorce, death of a sibling, or unexpected job loss. Unforeseen crises may extend more broadly to communities or nations, as in national disasters, acts of terrorism, famine, or war. Although these events may foster growth and new competencies, they may also result in anxiety, defensiveness, regression, or dread. The need to cope with them may overwhelm a person and may require coordinated intervention. For example, experts from eight European countries have formed a consortium to provide guidelines on mental health and psychosocial support for people in crisis. Their work is especially targeted for people in communities that have been exposed to natural or man-made disasters. Interventions are designed to consider the special needs of children, adolescents, disabled

Table 3.3	The Psychosocial Crises
Life Stage*	**Psychosocial Crisis**
Infancy (first 24 months)	Trust versus mistrust
Toddlerhood (2 to 4)	Autonomy versus shame and doubt
Early school age (4 to 6)	Initiative versus guilt
Middle childhood (6 to 12)	Industry versus inferiority
Early adolescence (12 to 18)	Group identity versus alienation
Later adolescence (18 to 24)	Individual identity versus identity confusion
Early adulthood (24 to 34)	Intimacy versus isolation
Middle adulthood (34 to 60)	Generativity versus stagnation
Later adulthood (60 to 75)	Integrity versus despair
Elderhood (75 until death)	Immortality versus extinction

© Cengage

*We do not consider the concept of psychosocial crisis appropriate to the prenatal stage.

Using Autobiographical Memories to Explore Psychosocial Stages of Life

Psychosocial theory predicts that the self-concept and worldview are reorganized at each stage of life to highlight new goals and a new relationship of self and society. To explore this idea further, Martin Conway and Alison Holmes (2004) asked adults between the ages of 62 and 89 to recall memories for each decade of their lives from the first 10 years through the decade of the 60s. The participants were asked about the decades in a random order and were given 5 minutes per decade to write down up to three memories from that time of life. Each memory was dated to the

nearest year and month within the decade. The memories were then coded for the degree to which they reflected themes inherent in the psychosocial crises.

Fifty participants produced 552 memories. The two decades from ages 10 to 19 and 20 to 29 produced the largest number of memories (FIGURE 3.3 ▶). As predicted, memories tied to early psychosocial crises (wanting to be or being nurtured, helped, and taught; having fun and playing; encounters with parents, family members, and teachers) were most frequently recalled in

association with the first decade of life. Memories associated with identity and identity confusion were most frequent in the second decade of life. Memories related to intimacy were of greatest frequency in the third decade. In contrast to childhood memories that decline noticeably from the first decade of life, memories associated with generativity increased gradually from the 20s to the 40s and continued to be prominent in the decades of the 50s and the 60s. Relatively few memories were coded as reflecting the themes of integrity and despair, but those memories were tied primarily to the decade of the 60s. These findings use biographical memory recall to support the view that the self is reorganized around different goals and preoccupations at various stages of life that reflect the demands and satisfactions associated with the psychosocial crises of those stages.

Critical Thinking Questions

1. Evaluate the strengths and limitations of using autobiographical memory to study psychosocial development over the stages of life.
2. Given the detailed conceptualization of psychosocial theory presented in this chapter, propose a list of additional variables you might want to measure in order to determine the salience of specific psychosocial crises at various periods of life.
3. Describe other approaches to measurement you might use aside from memory recall to study the question of patterns of psychosocial development.

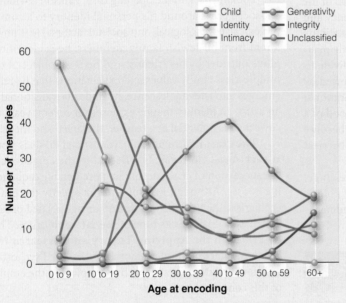

FIGURE 3.3 ▶ LIFE-SPAN MEMORY DISTRIBUTION CURVES FOR MEMORIES CLASSIFIED BY PSYCHOSOCIAL STAGE OVER SEVEN DECADES OF LIFE

Source: From "Psychosocial stages and the accessibility of autobiographical memories across the life cycle," by M.A Conway and A.Holmes, 2004, Journal of Personality, 72,pp. 461480.

individuals, and the elderly. This work is also sensitive to the mental health and psychosocial needs of volunteers and first responders (OPSIC, 2015).

The impact of an unpredictable crisis will depend in part on whether the person is in a state of psychosocial crisis at the time. For example, the unexpected death of a sibling might be exceptionally disruptive for someone who is also in a period of questioning their personal identity, where matters of family loyalties and commitments to values and beliefs are unresolved.

A person who has resolved the psychosocial crisis in a positive direction is likely to have greater resilience and ego strength to cope with this difficult loss (Svetina, 2014).

The combination of predictable crises, unpredictable crises, and unique historical pressures may lead to the resurfacing of prior crises that require reorganization. For example, during early adulthood, when issues of intimacy versus isolation are most important, it is common to find a reworking of industry versus inferiority as well. While striving to form

The devastating earthquake in Nepal left ruins in Kathmandu city, resulting in death, injury, and homelessness. 800,000 homes were damaged or destroyed. Children, adults, and the aged cope differently with these unexpected crises; communities differ in their ability to reassure and rebuild.

not be directly observable, that takes place in small increments over time and leads to a natural transformation. This concept is similar to Bronfenbrenner's use of the term to refer to basic mechanisms that connect an active, growing person with the people, objects, and symbolic representations in the environment as discussed in chapter 2. In the physical world, we are familiar with processes such as evaporation, condensation, and breathing. In psychosocial theory, each central process suggests a means by which the person recognizes new social pressures and expectations, gives these expectations personal meaning, and gradually changes.

The process, unfolding over time, results in a new relationship between self and society. For example, in toddlerhood, the psychosocial crisis raises the question of how children increase their sense of autonomy without risking too many experiences that provoke a sense of shame and doubt. We suggest that **imitation** is the central process for psychosocial growth during toddlerhood (ages 2 to 4). Children expand their range of skills by imitating adults, siblings, television models, playmates, and even animals. Movement toward a sense of autonomy in toddlerhood is facilitated by the child's readiness to imitate the variety of

meaningful, close relationships, young adults also encounter the challenges of establishing themselves in the labor market and achieving self-sufficiency. The outcome of this reworking of an earlier crisis depends in part on historical factors, such as the economic and materialistic orientation of the society as a specific age group enters early adulthood. It also depends on additional individual factors—especially on whether the adult is able to forge a meaningful occupational role that is consistent with personal and community values (Thomasik & Silbereisen, 2012; Whitbourne, Sneed, & Sayer, 2009). Thus, the psychosocial crises are not resolved and put to rest once and for all. Each crisis is played and replayed both during ongoing developmental changes and when life events challenge a balance that was achieved earlier.

FURTHER REFLECTION *What is the psychosocial crisis associated with your current stage of life? What thoughts and feelings can you identify that relate to these themes? How do these thoughts and feelings impact your self-concept and your relationships with others?*

The Central Process for Resolving the Psychosocial Crisis

Every psychosocial crisis reflects some discrepancy between the person's developmental competencies at the beginning of the stage and new societal pressures for more effective functioning. How is the discrepancy resolved? What experiences or processes permit the person to interpret the expectations and demands of society and to internalize them in order to support change? We have identified a **central process** through which each psychosocial crisis is resolved. The central process suggests a way that the person takes in or makes sense of cultural expectations and, as a result, changes the self-concept. The term **process** refers to an ongoing operation or activity, which may

Pablo Picasso's son is shown in deep concentration as he sketches at his desk. Through imitation, a child takes ownership of actions and skills that are observed when among adults. It is little wonder that Paulo, surrounded by his father's ongoing artistic activity, would be drawn to imitate it.

Basic Concepts of Psychosocial Theory **67**

Table 3.4	The Central Process for Resolving Each Psychosocial Crisis
Life Stage*	Central Process
Infancy (first 24 months)	Mutuality with caregiver
Toddlerhood (2 to 4)	Imitation
Early school age (4 to 6)	Identification
Middle childhood (6 to 12)	Education
Early adolescence (12 to 18)	Peer pressure
Later adolescence (18 to 24)	Role experimentation
Early adulthood (24 to 34)	Mutuality among peers
Middle adulthood (34 to 60)	Person–environment fit and creativity
Later adulthood (60 to 75)	Introspection
Elderhood (75 until death)	Social support

*We do not consider the concept of central process appropriate to the prenatal stage.

© Cengage

models available for observation, and the variety of behaviors the child has the opportunity to observe. Through persistent imitative activity, children expand their self-initiated behavior and control over their actions. Repetitive experiences of this kind allow children to believe that they can do more things on their own; this advances their sense of personal autonomy.

The central process for coping with the challenges of each life stage provides both personal and societal mechanisms for taking in new information and reorganizing existing information. It also suggests the means that are most likely to lead to a revision of the psychological system so that the crisis of that particular stage can be resolved. Each central process results in an intensive reworking of the psychological system, including a reorganization of boundaries, values, and images of oneself and others. Table 3.4 shows the central process that leads to the resolution of the psychosocial crisis at each life stage.

Radius of Significant Relationships

Age-related demands on individuals are communicated through **significant relationships** (Erikson, 1982, p. 31) (see FIGURE 3.4 ▶). Initially, a person focuses on a small number of relationships. During childhood, adolescence, and early adulthood, the number of relationships expands, and the quality of these relationships takes on greater variety in depth and intensity. In later adulthood, the person often returns to a small number of extremely important

relationships that provide opportunities for great depth and intimacy. Figure 3.4 suggests that each layer in the radius of significant relationships is a neat circle of individuals. But in fact, the circles are comprised of complex **networks** of individuals who interact with each other as well as with the target person. You might think of these circles as intermingling vines, much like holiday wreaths, where people from various families, neighborhoods, and groups communicate. This network of relationships plays a major role at every stage of life, impacting cognitive and emotional development, self-understanding, family and career roles, and physical health.

Mildred, a woman in her late 70s, is an active, retired professor of mathematics. She lives alone but with family and friends nearby. In the spring, she had a stroke. Luckily, her son was able to get her to the hospital quickly. After some days of hospitalization, she returned home. She was surrounded by family and friends who came to visit, brought books and movies, food, and good conversation to speed along her convalescence. She had a strong and positive relationship with her family doctor. By September, she was almost fully recovered and back to her active life.

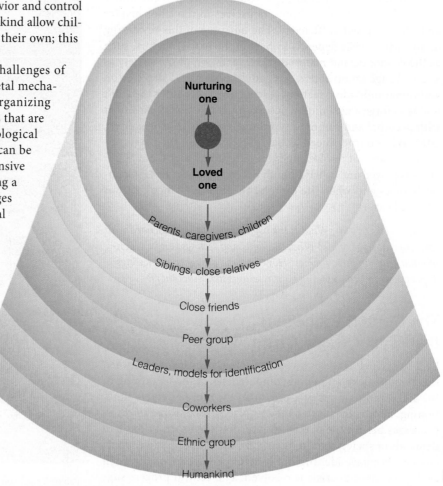

FIGURE 3.4 ▶ THE RADIUS OF SIGNIFICANT RELATIONSHIPS

Source: © Cengage

In Erikson's case study, he recalls a network of artists who may have influenced him at a very early age while he was living with his mother. Then, the radius of significant relationships shifted to include his father, Dr. Homburger, who was a trusted and respected professional. As he moved into later adolescence, he found a network of like-minded young people with artistic and literary ambitions who supported his feelings of alienation from his traditional family and offered a milieu of acceptance and care. Subsequently he became immersed in a network of professional analysts who educated and trained him and offered him a new professional identity.

At each stage of life, the network of significant relationships determines the demands that will be made, how the person will be taken care of, conflicts the person is exposed to, and the meaning that could be derived from these relationships. The quality of these relationships is determined in part by the psychosocial maturity of the people who populate these networks. Often, the people in these relationships serve as role models and resources for the developing person. However, in some cases, the person experiences significant relationships that are intrusive, negative, or undermining to optimal development. For example, some children experience harsh, intimidating interactions with parents, grandparents, older siblings, or peers. As a result, the developing person may learn to be aggressive with others. Some children experience interactions with adults who are very self-absorbed and narcissistic. As a result, they may learn not to expect much from others. The point is that the quality of the interactions in this radius of significant relationships transmits information about how the person is valued and what to expect in social exchanges. The relationship network varies individually, but each person has a network of significant relationships and an increasing readiness to enter into a more complex social life (Christakis & Fowler, 2009). The quality of these relationships and the norms for interaction are influenced by the nature of the specific social context. Family, culture, and ethnic group are three of the major network contexts through which the radius of significant relationships transmits its influences. In addition to these historically acknowledged contexts, there is growing interest in how social media, including Facebook, Twitter, Instagram, and other cyber technologies, have become contexts for social influence.

Contexts of Development

One way of thinking about the impact of the societal system is to consider individuals as embedded in a kaleidoscope of changing, interconnected systems. Children are members of families. Parents and other relatives are members of other important work and community groups that can influence families. As they get older, children may become members of other institutions, such as child care programs, schools, religious groups, community clubs, or athletic teams. Communities are nested in cities, counties, states, and nations. An understanding of development requires insight into each level of social organization as well as the culture as a whole. These organizations influence what is expected of its members, the resources available to meet these expectations, the roles individuals play, the activities they engage in, and the risks they may encounter.

The **contexts of development** include social, economic, and historical factors. Events such as war, political revolution, famine, or economic collapse may temporarily alter the prevailing childrearing values, opportunities for education or employment, and the availability of resources. Furthermore, these events may increase exposure to violence and separation of family members or provide exposure to other unpredictable stressors that may disrupt the course of development.

Families. All over the world, children are raised by small groups or families. Family is the universal primary social context of childhood. The family continues to be a meaningful context throughout life, especially as we think of the relationship of adults with their aging parents, the formation of new families in adulthood, and the lifelong connections among siblings. Historically, the term **family** has referred to a group of people, usually related by blood, marriage, or adoption. In contemporary U.S. society, however, people who view themselves as members of a family may have no legal relationship or shared ancestral bond. The composition and nature of the relationships among members of modern families is diverse. The psychosocial meaning of family, however, continues to be defined as individuals who share a common destiny and who experience a sense of emotional intimacy. Ideally, people in a family care about one another and take care of one another (Price, Price, & McKenry, 2010). As we see throughout the book, there are vast differences in the ways family members define their roles and treat one another.

Culture. Culture refers to the socially standardized ways of thinking, feeling, and acting that are shared by members of a

As a newborn, Max is the center of a radius of significant relationships, including his mother, father, older brother, grandparents, aunts, and uncles.

society. Culture includes the concepts, habits, skills, arts, technology, religion, and government of a people. It encompasses the tools and symbol systems that give structure and meaning to experience. Cultures have implicit theories about the stages of life, the expectations for behavior as one matures, and the nature of one's obligations to the older and younger members of the cultural group. A culture exerts influence directly through families as well as through networks of interacting individuals who may belong to common social organizations such as churches, clubs, or schools. As is true for other nations, the United States' culture has a strong, unifying impact on its citizens. Within the United States, there are also noticeable regional cultural patterns marked by unique vocabulary and dialect, mannerisms, and styles of social interaction. Throughout this book, we will note the great differences in what life—including family life—is like in different cultures and note how the integration of person and culture produces distinctive personal experiences for individuals in various cultures.

Ethnic Groups.

In addition to the common threads of culture that affect everyone who grows up or lives for a long time in the United States, there are also persistent subcultural forces that shape the daily lives of children and adults. The United States is a complex society made up of people from a vast array of cultures throughout the world. We call these groups ethnic subcultures or **ethnic groups**. People who belong to ethnic groups share ways of thinking, feeling, and acting with other members of their group. Holidays such as St. Patrick's Day, Oktoberfest, or Kwanzaa are examples of public occasions that celebrate the ethnic heritage of particular groups.

Research has focused on the development of ethnic identity, particularly the ways in which one's ethnic heritage and cultural values are integrated into one's personal identity. Ethnic values may include views about family cohesiveness, the importance of certain religious practices, the role and meaning of education, attitudes toward elders, or efforts to preserve a language and customs. The influence of one's ethnic heritage is likely to change from one generation to another. Studies examine the role of ethnic values and beliefs for first-generation immigrants as compared to second- and third-generation offspring (Coll & Marks, 2009; Portes & Rumbaut, 2014). Increasing attention is being given to the lifestyles, identity development, parenting practices, and family values of ethnic groups, particularly the challenges facing immigrants to the United States as they strive to integrate their cultural and ethnic beliefs and practices into contemporary U.S. life (Coll & Marks, 2012).

Many people in the United States acknowledge mixed ethnic ancestry, resulting in experiences of ambiguous and/or multi-ethnic identities (Ho, 2015). According to the U.S. Census Bureau, the population reporting mixed racial heritage (9.0 million) grew by 32.0 percent from 2000 to 2010 (Jones & Bullock, 2012). Thus, a person's radius of significant relationships may include people who convey diverse cultural, religious, and/or ethnic values, some of which are more salient or comfortably integrated than others. In subsequent chapters we will address the contributions of ethnicity and mixed ethnicity to developmental pathways.

Social Media.

Evidence about the impact or influence of social media on development is contradictory. Some studies find that people who use social media frequently feel more connected, whereas other studies find that the frequent use of social media is associated with stress, reduced feelings of happiness, and stronger feelings of loneliness and depression (Barth, 2015; Brooks, 2015). These differences may relate to the motivation for engaging in the use of social media. Many people make use of social media to stay connected to their family and friends, especially when they are separated by distance. They are preserving and strengthening their existing radius of significant relationships. Others use social media primarily as a way to connect to like-minded others whom they do not know in a face-to-face relationship (Murthy, Gross, & Pensavalle, 2015). Social media can also be used l to promote one's business or to foster one's professional reputation. Still others use social media for dating, to spread gossip, or to try to establish their popularity within their peer culture.

Social media are contexts through which individuals create and are influenced by their radius of significant relationships. People get more excited, pleased and rewarded by being recognized among their social media contacts; and more discouraged, depressed, and hurt by being rejected, ignored, or maligned by their contacts (Barth, 2015).

Social networking sites can provide information in order to make social comparisons (Vogel, Rose, Okdie, Eckles, & Franz, 2015). By checking in with "friends" on Facebook or following people on Twitter, a person can assess whether his or her daily life, accomplishments, and/or adventures are as successful or thrilling as those of others. Some students describe their preoccupation with social media as linked to a fear of missing out on the fun, gossip, or plans that are being formulated among their peers. Some people are more prone to seek social comparison than others, needing more reassurance and feedback in order to feel confident about their worth. As a result they are more likely to make frequent use of their social media contexts, trying to reduce their anxiety and self-doubt (Nesi & Prinstein, 2015). Many adolescents and adults "follow" television and movie stars, athletes, or popular music artists on social media. This kind of connection may strengthen their identification with these role models, providing a stronger bond of influence. Some of these media personalities offer advice through blogs on parenting, financial decisions, career advice, or political views, which can influence the beliefs and values of their "followers."

Coping

Coping refers to people's conscious, adaptive efforts to manage stressful events or situations and their efforts to manage the emotions associated with these stressors (Aldwin, 2011). Coping is a process that begins with an **appraisal** of the situation. This includes answers to the following questions: What is the nature of this stressor? How much of a threat is it? How much time do I have to deal with this challenge? How much control do I have over the situation?

Following the appraisal, one must enlist cognitive, affective, and behavioral **coping strategies** to manage the stress. Lazarus and Folkman (1984) distinguished between coping strategies that intend to change something about the source of stress (*problem-focused coping*) and strategies that intend to manage or control one's emotions in the face of the stressor (*emotion-focused coping*). Often, these strategies are used together.

For example, Claire, who has taken a week of vacation, has returned to work to find a basket full of mail, 40 voice messages, and 180 email messages. She still has her usual daily workload. She decides to take a short lunch and stay an hour late in order to catch up. At the same time, she tries to remain calm and think about the wonderfully relaxing time she had on her vacation so that she does not become anxious as she faces this backlog of work. She uses both problem-focused and emotion-focused strategies to manage the demands of this situation.

In order to understand how a person copes with a stressful situation, one must consider (1) the nature of the stressor, (2) how it is perceived by the person, and (3) the range of resources that are available to address the situation (Hobfoll, 2011; Lazarus, 2000; McCubbin & Patterson, 1982). The coping process depends on the specific stressful situation. One does not cope the same way if the house is on fire or if the baby has a high fever. In the situation of bereavement, for example, there are no actions the grieving person can take to bring the lost loved one back to life. Survivors must find ways to reconcile themselves to the situation and carry on with their own lives. Depending on the circumstances of the loss, survivors need to develop effective coping strategies in order to preserve their health, and continue to form meaningful ties with others (Stroebe, 2011; Wortman & Boerner, 2007).

One's approach to coping also depends on the values, beliefs, and goals of the person or family involved and how these values, beliefs, and goals lead to a particular interpretation of the stressor event. For example, in one family, the announcement that an oldest child decides to enlist in the military may be greeted with great joy and pride; in another family, that same announcement may be greeted with dismay and disappointment. Both families will worry about the child's safety and will experience the stress of the child's absence. However, the family's beliefs and goals will determine the meaning given to a child's decision to join the military.

Finally, individuals and families differ in the resources that are available to cope with a difficult situation. Resources include such things as social support, educational background, information, professional advice, financial resources, and a sense of humor. In the research literature, the term **socioeconomic status (SES)** is used to refer to a combination of resources including income, education, and occupation. Fewer resources, or the lack of appropriate resources,

may impede the coping process. In a study exploring how people cope with financial stress, problem-focused coping was found to be more effective in reducing distress than emotion-focused coping (Caplan & Schooler, 2007). Among those participating in this study, those with fewer social and economic resources (referred to as low SES) were found to use more emotion-focused coping strategies and, as a result, had higher levels of distress. The path from low SES to distress over financial strain is brought about largely through perceived lack of control, which interferes with the mobilization of problem-focused coping.

Coping behavior is an important concept in psychosocial theory because it explains how unique and inventive behaviors occur. An important aspect of coping is the ability to redefine or *reappraise* the situation in a positive way. This suggests creating or reemphasizing the meaning, values, and opportunities embedded in the stressful situation (Folkman & Moskowitz, 2000).

For example, as Robert cared for his partner who had AIDS, he took special pleasure in routine, daily events such as planning an enjoyable meal that they shared together. In the face of feelings of helplessness about the uncontrollable changes in his partner's condition, Robert also took steps to set attainable goals, such as creating a video library of favorite movies that he and his partner could enjoy together. Thus, even while Robert was experiencing many negative emotions, he also found positive experiences in the context of the stress.

Some people are better able to cope with the challenges they are faced with than others. The term **resilience** is often used to characterize individuals who exhibit positive outcomes in the face of serious threats to development. They may have experienced prolonged, severe poverty; they may have a parent with a serious mental illness; or they may have been exposed

Despite significant physical challenges, these young men are coping by developing new skills and engaging in competitive sports. Their sense of competence contributes to feelings of well-being and joy in life.

to ongoing abuse or violence. Faced with these or other difficulties, resilient individuals show low levels of psychological symptoms and function effectively in the basic developmental tasks expected for their stage of life (Masten, Obradović, & Burt, 2006). Over time, they create lives that integrate their own personal strengths with the resources and opportunities of their community, meeting the community's expectations for maturity. Although the story of resilience is highly individual, reflecting unique patterns of life challenges and coping strategies, the notion of resilience underscores a widely shared capacity to recover from adversity. There appears to be a small number of factors that support resilience including "connections to competent and caring adults in the family and community; cognitive and self-regulation skills; positive views of self; and motivation to be effective in the environment" (Masten, 2001, p. 13).

Over time, effective coping contributes to development. As a result of experiencing mastery and competence through coping, one builds a more positive expectation about being able to face new challenges, an outlook that contributes to the positive resolution of subsequent psychosocial crises. The positive consequences of coping help to sustain individuals during prolonged stressors. In the face of threat, coping behavior allows an individual to act effectively, rather than merely to maintain equilibrium or become disorganized.

New coping strategies can be learned. You will recall that approaches to coping with difficult emotions is a focus of cognitive behavioral therapy (See chapter 2). The goal of this therapy is to teach clients to examine unwanted ways of reacting to stressful situations and to develop new ways of reacting. This includes examining troubling situations with a degree of calm detachment, examining the facts of the situation, and using new information to formulate a new interpretation of the situation. Each of these strategies can be learned with practice and repetition. Over life, a person encounters new stressors that require new coping strategies. There is no single coping strategy that is appropriate for every situation. But a first step is learning to be calm so that you can apply your best rational strategies to the assessment of the situation. Learning to recognize whether a difficult situation can be changed, or one's interpretation and reaction to the situation must change, is a lifelong challenge.

According to psychosocial theory, at each stage of life, consistent efforts to face and cope with the psychosocial crisis of the period result in the formation of basic adaptive capacities, referred to as the **prime adaptive ego qualities**. When coping is unsuccessful and the challenges of the period are not adequately mastered, individuals are likely to form maladaptive orientations, referred to as **core pathologies**.

Prime Adaptive Ego Qualities

Erikson (1978) postulated prime adaptive ego qualities that develop from the positive resolution of the psychosocial crisis of a given stage and provide resources for coping with the next. He described these qualities as *mental states* that shape the interpretation of life experiences. The idea of adaptive ego qualities suggests that a person's core beliefs about the self are positive, well grounded in meaningful social relationships, and useful for interpreting real life events. Ego strengths support resilience in the face of stressors and position the person to make effective choices as they face new societal demands.

The prime adaptive ego qualities and their definitions are listed in Table 3.5. These ego qualities contribute to the person's dominant **worldview**, which is continuously reformulated to accommodate new ego qualities. With maturity, as one makes positive resolutions of each psychosocial stage, the ego strengths accumulate and become integrated. The person becomes increasingly hopeful, purposeful, competent, and committed to relationships and ideals. These strengths contribute to the way the person makes meaning and adapts to life conditions.

The importance of many of the prime adaptive ego qualities, including hope, purpose, competence, love, and wisdom, has been verified by research (Lopez & Snyder, 2003). For example, a measure, *The Psychosocial Inventory of Ego Strengths*, was developed to assess the relationship of the prime adaptive ego strengths to psychosocial well-being. As anticipated, higher scores on the psychosocial inventory were correlated with identity achievement, self-esteem, locus of control, empathic concern, and perspective taking (Markstrom, Sabino, Turner, & Berman, 1997; Markstrom & Marshall, 2007).

Focusing specifically on the ego quality of *hope,* Erikson and his colleagues found that people in later life who were hopeful about their own future and that of their children were more intellectually vigorous and psychologically resilient than those who were less hopeful (Erikson et al., 1986). People with a hopeful attitude have a better chance of maintaining their spirits and strength in the face of crisis than people who are pessimistic. For both young and older adults, the ego strength of hope has been found to be a significant predictor of life satisfaction (Isaacowitz, Vaillant, & Seligman, 2003).

Core Pathologies

Although most people develop the prime adaptive ego qualities, a potential core pathology may also emerge as a result of ineffective, negatively balanced resolution of the psychosocial crisis at each stage (Erikson, 1982; see Table 3.5). Like the prime adaptive ego qualities, core pathologies also serve as guiding orientations for behavior. These pathologies move people away from others, tend to prevent further exploration of interpersonal relations, and obstruct the resolution of subsequent psychosocial crises. As the core pathologies accumulate, the person becomes more withdrawn, compulsive, and inhibited. Fearfulness and self-doubt may lead to an increasingly rigid approach to life challenges. The energy that would normally be directed toward mastering the developmental tasks of a stage is directed instead toward resisting or avoiding change.

The core pathologies are not simply passive limitations or barriers to growth. They are energized worldviews leading to strategies that protect people from further unwanted association with the social system and its persistent, tension-producing demands. These strategies may find expression in attitudes that are rejecting and disdainful of others in efforts to disguise undermining negative feelings such as social rejection, disconnectedness, or lack of worth.

Table 3.5 Prime Adaptive Ego Qualities and Core Pathologies

Life Stage	Ego Quality and Core Pathology	Definition
Infancy (first 24 months)	Hope	An enduring belief that one can attain one's deep and essential wishes
	Withdrawal	Social and emotional detachment
Toddlerhood (2 to 4)	Will	A determination to exercise free choice and self-control
	Compulsion	Repetitive behaviors motivated by impulse or by restrictions against the expression of impulse
Early school age (4 to 6)	Purpose	The courage to imagine and pursue valued goals
	Inhibition	A psychological restraint that prevents freedom of thought, expression, and activity
Middle childhood (6 to 12)	Competence	The free exercise of skill and intelligence in the completion of tasks
	Inertia	A paralysis of action and thought that prevents productive work
Early adolescence (12 to 18)	Fidelity to others	The ability to freely pledge and sustain loyalty to others
	Dissociation	An inability to connect with others
Later adolescence (18 to 24)	Fidelity to values	The ability to freely pledge and sustain loyalty to values and ideology
	Repudiation	Rejection of roles and values that are viewed as alien to oneself
Early adulthood (24 to 34)	Love	A capacity for mutuality that transcends childhood dependency
	Exclusivity	An elitist shutting out of others
Middle adulthood (34 to 60)	Care	A commitment to concern about what has been generated
	Rejectivity	Unwillingness to include certain others or groups of others in one's generative concern
Later adulthood (60 to 75)	Wisdom	A detached yet active concern with life itself in the face of death
	Disdain	A feeling of scorn for the weakness and frailty of oneself and others
Elderhood (75 until death)	Confidence	A conscious trust in oneself and assurance about the meaningfulness of life
	Diffidence	An inability to act because of overwhelming self-doubt

© Cengage

FURTHER REFLECTION   Explain the concept of coping in your own words. Examine an example of problem-focused coping that you have observed in yourself or others. Describe how the actions influenced the outcome of the situation.

Hypothesize how people at different stages of psychosocial development might cope with the same life stressor such as unemployment or the death of a parent.

Imagine that a teacher or social worker has identified a child who exhibits evidence of one or more core pathologies, such as withdrawal, compulsion, or inhibition. What steps can the concerned adult take to help alleviate or modify these characteristics?

Evaluation of Psychosocial Theory

OBJECTIVE 3   Evaluate psychosocial theory, pointing out its strengths and weaknesses.

Although we believe that psychosocial theory provides a useful theoretical framework for organizing the vast array of observations in the field of human development, we recognize that it has weaknesses as well as strengths. As a student of development, you must begin to form your own independent judgment of its usefulness. The strengths and weaknesses of psychosocial theory that are discussed in the following sections are listed in Table 3.6.

Strengths

Psychosocial theory highlights the social nature of human development. Human beings depend for their survival on their capacity to form social bonds and to recognize and respond to social messages. Although the field of psychology has traditionally focused on the thoughts and behaviors of individuals, a growing body of research emphasizes the social nature of mental functioning. Thus, the basic view of development offered by psychosocial theory as a product of interactions between the individual and the social environment is gaining increasing support.

Psychosocial theory provides a broad, integrative context within which to study life-span development (Hopkins, 1995; Kiston, 1994). The theory links the process of child development to stages of adult life, individual development to the nature of culture and society, and the personal and historical past to the personal and societal future. Although many scholars agree that such a broad perspective is necessary, few other theories attempt to address the interplay between individual development and society (Miller, 2011).

Table 3.6	Strengths and Weaknesses of Psychosocial Theory	
Strengths	**Weaknesses**
The theory provides a broad, integrative framework within which to study the life span.	Explanations for the mechanisms of crisis resolution and process of moving from one stage to the next need to be developed more fully.
The theory provides insight into the directions of healthy development across the life span.	The idea of a specific number of stages of life and their link to a genetic plan for development is disputed.
Many of the basic ideas of the theory have been operationalized using traditional and novel approaches to assessment.	The theory and much of its supporting research have been dominated by a male, Eurocentric perspective that gives too much emphasis to individuality and not enough attention to connection and social relatedness.
The concept of psychosocial crises, including the positive and negative poles of the crisis, offers a model for considering individual differences within a framework of normal development.	The specific ways that culture encourages or inhibits development at each stage of life are not clearly elaborated.
The concept of the psychosocial crisis identifies predictable tensions between socialization and maturation.	
Longitudinal studies support the general direction of development hypothesized by the theory.	

Source: Based on Erikson, 1982.

© Cengage

Psychosocial theory provides a framework for tracing the process through which self-concept, self-esteem, and self-other boundaries become integrated into a positive, adaptive, socially engaged person (Hamachek, 1985, 1994). Emphasizing the normal, hopeful, and creative aspects of coping and adaptation, the theory has taken the study of development beyond the deterministic position of psychoanalytic theory or the mechanistic view of behaviorism, providing an essential conceptual framework for the emergence of positive psychology.

Some have argued that a weakness of psychosocial theory is that its basic concepts were presented in language that is abstract and difficult to examine empirically (Crain, 2011; Miller, 2016). However, over the past 20 years, such terms as *hope, inhibition, autonomy, personal identity, intimacy, generativity,* and *integrity*—to name a few—have been operationalized (Bohlin, Bengtsgard, & Andersson, 2000; Christiansen & Palkovitz, 1998; de St. Aubin, McAdams, & Kim, 2003; Kroger, 2007; Lopez & Snyder, 2003; Marcia, 2002, 2007; McAdams & de St. Aubin, 1998; Snyder, 2002). Concepts central to the theory—such as trust, autonomy, identity achievement, coping, well-being, social support, and intergenerational interdependence—have become integrated into contemporary human development scholarship. Researchers have created instruments to trace the emergence of psychosocial crises and their resolution in samples varying in age from adolescence to later adulthood (Constantinople, 1969; Darling-Fisher & Leidy, 1988; Domino & Affonso, 1990; Hawley, 1988; Markstrom & Marshall, 2007; Waterman & Whitbourne, 1981; Whitbourne et al., 1992; Whitbourne et al., 2009).

Unlike some other theories, psychosocial theory identifies tensions that may disrupt development at each life stage, providing a framework for considering individual differences in development. The positive and negative poles of each psychosocial crisis offer a way of thinking about differences in self-concept development at each stage of life as well as a model for considering cumulative differences across the life span. This matrix of crises and stages provides a useful tool for approaching psychotherapy, counseling, and social work. Recent applications are directed toward leadership development and executive training.

In a business context, for example, the concept of generativity highlights the importance of contributing to the development and mentoring of younger workers by their more senior supervisors in order to ensure the continuity of leadership for the organization.

The concept of normative psychosocial crises is a creative contribution that identifies predictable tensions between socialization and maturation throughout life. Societies, with their structures, laws, roles, rituals, and sanctions, are organized to guide individual growth toward a particular ideal of mature adulthood. However, every society faces problems striving to balance the needs of the individual with the needs of the group. All individuals face some strains as they attempt to experience their individuality while maintaining the support of their groups and attempting to fit into their society. Psychosocial theory offers concepts for exploring these natural tensions.

Longitudinal research using psychosocial theory as a framework for studying patterns of personality change and self-concept development has found support for many of its basic concepts. Changes in psychological outlook that reflect the major themes of the theory—such as industry, identity, intimacy, and generativity—appear to emerge and become consolidated over time (Whitbourne et al., 2009). There is also evidence of a preview of themes prior to their period of maximum ascendancy (Peterson & Steward, 1993) and evidence for the notion of revisitation through which adults are stimulated to rework and reorganize the resolutions of earlier issues (Shibley, 2000).

Weaknesses

One weakness of psychosocial theory is that the explanations of the mechanisms for resolving crises and moving from one stage to the next are not well developed (Miller, 2016). Think of Lillian who is 19 years old, has a close, loving relationship with a partner, is expecting her first child but has not yet settled on a career and lives with her parents. We can think of Lillian as straddling the boundary between later adolescence and early adulthood. Having made commitments regarding her partner and parenthood, does she already perceive herself as well grounded in the period of adulthood or is she still struggling with ambiguity regarding her personal identity?

The theory does not offer a universal mechanism for crisis resolution or a detailed picture of the kinds of experiences that are necessary at each stage if one is to cope successfully with the crisis of that stage. We have addressed this weakness by including the concepts of developmental tasks and a central process for each stage. The developmental tasks suggest some of the major achievements that permit a person to meet the social expectations of each stage. The central process identifies the primary mechanism through which the person encounters societal expectations and integrates them into a revised sense of self. Using these two constructs, one can begin to clarify the process of movement from one stage to the next.

The specific number of stages and their link to a biologically based plan for development has been criticized. The stages of life unfold in a cultural context. For example, in some societies, the transition from childhood to adulthood is swift, leaving little time or expectation for identity exploration. In many traditional societies, parents choose one's marital partner, there are few occupational choices, and one is guided toward one's vocation from an early age. Thus, although there is always a biological period of pubescence that marks the transition from childhood to adulthood, there may be little justification for two stages of adolescence when the identity formation process is societally constrained (Thomas & Schwarzbaum, 2011). In contrast, in our highly technological society, adolescence appears to be extended for some, especially as the age at first marriage is delayed and the complexity of preparing for and entering the labor market increases. As a reflection of this extension of modern adolescence, we have treated the period from puberty through about age 24 as two stages rather than one, each with its own psychosocial crisis and developmental tasks.

Along this same line of criticism, some scholars have taken a more differentiated view of the stages of adulthood and later life. In later life, health status, life circumstances, and culture interact to produce increasing variation in life stories. Distinctions are made between people of the same chronological age who are referred to as the "young-old" and the "old-old" depending upon their health status and their capacity to manage tasks of daily life (Aldwin, Spiro, & Park, 2006; Poon & Harrington, 2006).

In other research, distinctions are made on the basis of chronological age. For example, Leonard Poon has written extensively about the differences between centenarians (people who are 100 or more), octogenarians (people in their 80s), and sexagenarians (people in their 60s). Each cohort of older adults has been exposed to different historical crises, educational, health, and occupational opportunities, and shifting societal values. Therefore, it is likely that the normative patterns used to describe development in adulthood and later life will become outdated and need reexamination as each younger cohort enters later adulthood and elderhood (Randall, Martin, Bishop, Johnson, & Poon, 2012; Siegler, Poon, Madden, & Welsh, 1996).

We have addressed this concern in part by extending the traditional psychosocial stage approach to adulthood from three stages to four, adding a period called elderhood. In the chapters on adulthood, we address differences in lifestyle and life course that are attributable to historical events, medical advances, and cultural trends. Nevertheless, the increasing life expectancy, accompanied by a longer period of healthy later life and the elaboration of lifestyles, makes it difficult to chart a normative life course from early adulthood into elderhood (Aldwin & Gilmer, 2013).

In this book, you will also read about the important developmental issues of the prenatal period—a stage that Erikson's theory does not consider, but one that clearly plays a central role in setting the stage for a lifetime of vulnerabilities and competencies. These expansions of the stages of development demonstrate the natural evolution of a theoretical framework.

Finally, psychosocial theory and related research have been criticized as being dominated by a male, Eurocentric, individualistic perspective that emphasizes the ability to originate plans and take action, called **agency**, over the commitment to and consideration for the well-being of others, called **communion** (Abele & Wojciszke, 2007). Critics have argued that the themes of autonomy, initiative, industry, and personal identity, which reflect individuality, have been equated with psychological maturity. They suggest that relatively little attention has been given to the development of interpersonal connection and social relatedness. These latter themes have been identified as central for an

Courtesy of Philip and Barbara Newman

The positive relationships established between parents and their children are passed along from one generation to the next, fostering strong feelings of affection and care.

understanding of the psychosocial maturity of girls and young women. These themes also emerge in the study of collectively oriented ethnic groups, as discussed in chapter 2, cultures in which maturity is equated with one's ability to support and sustain the success of the family or the extended family group rather than with one's own achievement of status, wealth, or recognition (Boykin, 1994; Josselson, Lieblich, & McAdams, 2007).

Within the framework of psychosocial theory, the theme of connection is addressed directly through the first psychosocial crisis of trust versus mistrust in infancy. Then the thread is lost until early adolescence and early and middle adulthood, when group identity, intimacy, and generativity direct the focus back to the critical links that individuals build with others. The concept of the radius of significant relationships serves to maintain the perspective of the person interwoven in a tapestry of relationships, focusing especially on family and friends in childhood; the family, peer group, love relationships, and close friends in early and later adolescence; and on intimate partners, family, friends, and coworkers in adult life. A basic premise of psychosocial theory is that the self-concept is taking shape in constant interaction with the community (Schlein, 1987, 2007).

To extend the theme of connection, this book elaborates on developing capabilities for social interaction and differences in socialization practices and outcomes for men and women in our society. A variety of social abilities, including empathy, prosocial behavior, interaction skills, and components of social cognition, are traced as they emerge in the context of family relationships, friendships, peer groups, and work. This book considers ethnic groups as well as broader social influences on development and the importance of a collective orientation toward responsibility in caring for children and creating a sense of community.

FURTHER REFLECTION *Analyze how well psychosocial theory meets the criteria for a scientific theory that were presented in chapter 2.*

A Recap of Psychosocial Theory

FIGURE 3.5 ▶ shows development as a building process that incorporates the six constructs of psychosocial theory. The structure grows larger as the radius of significant relationships expands and as the achievements of earlier stages are integrated into the behavior of the next stage of development.

How can you tell when a stage change has occurred? The resolution of the psychosocial crisis of a previous stage provides the ego strengths and skill acquisition needed to face the challenges and expectations of the next stage. Once a person is fully engaged in all the tasks of a new period of life, a new stage of life has begun. The person's energy, motivation, and concerns about self and others are directed toward new goals, and the expectations others have for the person's level of functioning shift. Just as we no longer applaud the 4-year-old for the ability to crawl, we no longer applaud the 30-year-old for the ability to hold a steady job. Evidence of a stage change can be marked by new preoccupations and plans, new worries, and a new approach to building and maintaining relationships. A wonderful aspect of human development is the continuing redirection of energy to new ambitions, building upon the satisfactions of prior achievements.

At the beginning of chapter 2, we introduced three questions one must ask in order to understand a theory. Let us now answer these questions with respect to psychosocial theory.

> *Which phenomena is the theory trying to explain?* Psychosocial theory attempts to explain human development across the life span—especially patterned changes in self-concept development that are reflected in self-understanding, identity formation, social relationships, and worldview.
>
> *What assumptions does the theory make?* Human development is a product of three interacting factors: biological maturation, the interaction between individuals and

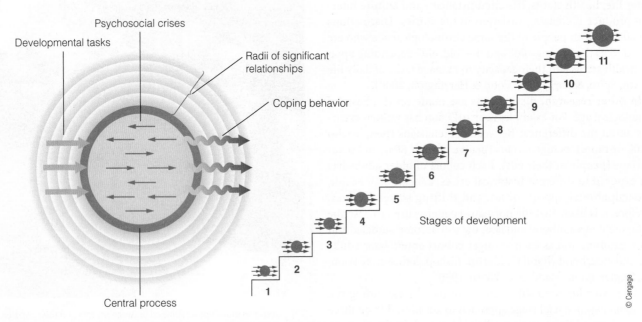

FIGURE 3.5 ▶ THE SIX BASIC CONCEPTS OF PSYCHOSOCIAL THEORY

Source: © Cengage

social groups, and the contributions that individuals make to their own psychological growth.

The theory makes the following six assumptions:

1. Growth occurs at every period of life, from conception through elderhood.
2. Individual lives show continuity and change as they progress through time.
3. In order to understand behavior, one must consider the integration of cognitive, physical, social, and emotional competencies, since these domains influence one another.
4. Every person's behavior must be analyzed in the context of relevant settings and personal relationships.
5. People contribute actively to their own development.
6. Diversity is a product of the interaction of the biological, the psychological, and the societal systems.

What does the theory predict?

1. There are 11 stages of development, which emerge in an ordered sequence. Issues of later stages can be previewed at an earlier time, but each issue has its period of ascendance. It takes the entire life span, from the prenatal period through elderhood, for all aspects of the person's potential to be realized.
2. Developmental tasks are dictated by the interaction of the biological, psychological, and societal systems during each stage.
3. A normal crisis arises at each stage of development, and a central process operates to resolve this crisis. The resolution of the crisis at each stage determines one's coping resources, with a positive resolution contributing to ego strengths and a negative resolution contributing to core pathologies.
4. Each person is part of an expanding network of significant relationships that convey society's expectations and demands. These relationships also provide encouragement in the face of challenges.

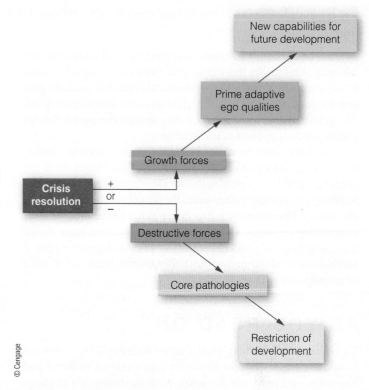

FIGURE 3.6 ▶ THE MECHANISM FOR POSITIVE AND NEGATIVE PSYCHOSOCIAL DEVELOPMENT

5. Development will be optimal if a person can create new behaviors and relationships as a result of skill acquisition and successful crisis resolution during each stage of growth. Lack of development and core pathologies result from tendencies that restrict behavior (especially social behavior) in general and new behavior in particular. The mechanisms for positive and negative development are diagrammed in FIGURE 3.6 ▶.

CHAPTER SUMMARY

OBJECTIVE 1 Explain the rationale for using psychosocial theory as an organizing framework for the study of human development.

Psychosocial theory offers a life-span view in which development is a product of the interactions between individuals and their social environments. The needs and goals of both the individual and society must be considered in conceptualizing human development. Predictability is found in the sequence of psychosocial stages, the central process involved in the resolution of the psychosocial crisis at each stage, and the radius of significant relationships. Individuality is expressed in the achievement of the developmental tasks, the balance of the positive and negative poles of each psychosocial crisis and the resulting worldview, and

the style and resources for coping that a person brings to each new life challenge.

Connectivity is achieved in the way the person learns to relate in a radius of significant others who make demands, convey social expectations, and offer social rewards. Over time, the person becomes engaged in increasingly complex social groups and institutions. A person's worldview at a particular age is a product of past identifications and the resolution of previous psychosocial crises, contemporary pressures and opportunities, and hopes for the future. In our society, there is great diversity in the outcomes of this psychosocial process and in the transmission of social expectations from one generation of adults to the next generation of children.

Psychosocial theory accounts for systematic change over the life span through six basic concepts: (1) stages of development, (2) developmental tasks, (3) psychosocial crises, (4) a central process for resolving the crisis at each stage, (5) a radiating network of significant relationships, and (6) coping—the new behavior people generate to meet new challenges.

The basic concepts of psychosocial theory provide the framework for analyzing development across 11 life stages from the prenatal period through elderhood. Development is viewed as a building process that incorporates the six constructs of psychosocial theory. The structure grows larger as the radius of significant relationships expands, and coping strategies become more varied and complex as the developmental tasks of each stage are mastered and become available to face the challenges and psychosocial crisis of the next stage of life.

Psychosocial theory provides a broad, integrative context within which to study life-span development. The strengths and weaknesses of the theory are summarized in Table 3.6. The theory provides insights into the direction of development over the life span, highlighting human strengths and vulnerabilities and predictable shifts in worldview and self-understanding at each stage. The theory offers a framework for considering the ongoing interaction of individuals and their societies, pointing to the interconnections of people at various stages of life. The theory has been criticized for its lack of clarity about the mechanisms that explain change from one stage to the next. The psychosocial crises have been criticized as overemphasizing values of individuality as compared to values of connection and interdependence.

AS YOU READ ON . . .

Each chapter of this text, from chapter 4 through 14, is devoted to one life stage. Chapter 15 covers topics related to death and bereavement across the life span. With the exception of chapter 4, on pregnancy and prenatal development, each life-stage chapter starts with a discussion of the developmental tasks of that life stage. By tracing developments in physical growth, emotional growth, intellectual skills, social relationships, and self-understanding, you can recognize the interrelationships among all of these dimensions during each period of life.

In the second section of each chapter, the psychosocial crisis of that life stage is described, accounting for the tension by examining the individual's needs and personal resources in light of the dominant societal expectations. In addition to defining the crisis, we conceptualize the central process by which it is resolved. The resolution of the crisis at each stage is tied to new ego strengths and new core pathologies.

At the end of each chapter, we draw on the material we have discussed to analyze a topic that is of persistent concern to our society. These topics are controversial, and they may generate sentiment as they deepen understanding. We intend these sections to stimulate the application of developmental principles to real-world concerns.

CASEBOOK

For additional case material related to this chapter, see the case of "Ayesha and the Dinosaurs," in *Life Span Development: A Case Book*, by Barbara and Philip Newman, Laura Landry Meyer, and Brenda J. Lohman, page 100. This case of an engaging 10-year-old illustrates ways in which the psychosocial strengths of trust, autonomy, initiative, and industry come together to support effective problem solving. The case provides an opportunity to discuss the usefulness of the central concepts of psychosocial theory for guiding understanding about positive development.

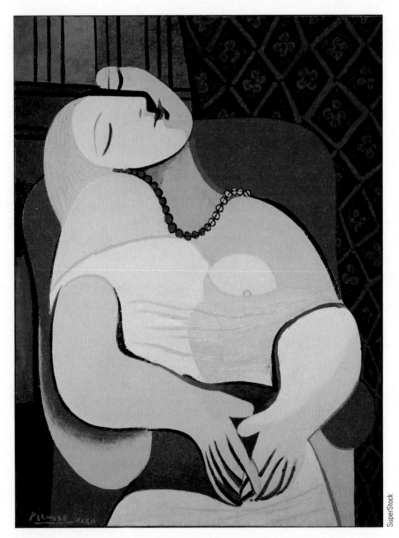

SuperStock

The period of pregnancy and prenatal development involves ongoing interactions between the fetus and the pregnant woman. Fetal development is guided by genetic factors in the context of the mother's health, social support, emotional well-being, and culture.

1. Summarize the process through which genetic information is transmitted from one generation to the next.

2. Differentiate the contributions of genetic factors to individuality through their role in controlling the rate of development, their influences on individual traits, and the genetic sources of abnormalities.

3. Trace the process of prenatal development from fertilization through three trimesters of pregnancy, including an understanding of infertility, alternative means of reproduction, and related ethical considerations.

4. Describe the birth process and analyze factors that contribute to infant mortality.

5. Analyze ways that the pregnant woman and the developing fetus influence each other, focusing on how pregnancy affects a childbearing woman and expectant father, and the impact of environmental influences on fetal growth, such as a woman's age, drug use, nutrition, environmental toxins, and stress.

6. Examine the impact of culture on pregnancy and childbirth.

7. Apply the psychosocial perspective to the topic of abortion, including the legal context, its social and emotional impact on women, and men's views.

THE PERIOD OF PREGNANCY AND PRENATAL DEVELOPMENT

4

The experiences of pregnancy and childbirth provide a wonderful example of the interconnections of the biological, the psychological, and the societal systems. The following interview takes place when Katherine is in her eighth month of pregnancy. Katherine is married and has two children.

Interviewer: How have you been doing?

Katherine: Fine! Last month, I was nauseous and tired, but now I feel good.

Interviewer: Did you plan to have the baby?

Katherine: No.

Interviewer: How did it happen?

Katherine: We jokingly say it was an immaculate conception. I was using a diaphragm, but since I'm regular, I didn't use it the first few days after my period and the doctors said that can happen.

Interviewer: How did you feel when it happened?

Katherine: I was basically happy, and then scared—mainly shocked, I felt, "Me! How could it happen?" The other two were so carefully planned. Of course, unconsciously maybe I wanted it.

Interviewer: What has it felt like being pregnant?

Katherine: I haven't had the euphoria that I had with the first one, when everyone treats you special, and you feel so good. Because now, I'm mainly with mothers and they do it all and it's not so special to be pregnant. I feel heavy and fat.

Interviewer: How will you feel when you're no longer pregnant?

Katherine: I'll probably still feel heavy and fat! (laughs)

Interviewer: Will you miss being pregnant at all?

Katherine: With my other two, I didn't miss being pregnant, but I did miss it when I stopped nursing. I felt very sad then. There are times when I just lie there and love the feel of the baby inside me, but I don't relish being pregnant.

Source: From *Pregnancy, Birth, and Parenthood*, by F. K. Grossman, L. S. Eichler, S. A. Winickoff,. with M. K. Anzalone, M. H., Gofseyeff, and S. P. Sargent, 1980, pp. 25, 26, 40, San Francisco: Jossey-Bass.

CASE ANALYSIS Using What You Know

1. Describe the interactions among the biological, the psychological, and the societal systems as they relate to Katherine's experience of pregnancy.

2. Speculate about the impact of this unplanned pregnancy on other members of the family, including Katherine's husband and her two children.

3. Think about being pregnant. List some of the positive and negative aspects of this life experience.

4. How might Katherine have been better educated about the risks associated with not using her diaphragm in the first few days of her menstrual cycle? Evaluate the current quality of family planning information for most U.S. couples. Where do they receive this information? How well is it understood?

When does an individual's life story begin? At birth? At conception? At the births of one's parents or one's grandparents? We are each linked back in time, through a lifeline comprising our ancestry, culture, and genetic makeup. This chapter begins the story of development at the molecular level of genes and chromosomes, moves to the physical maturation of the fetus during the prenatal period, and then expands the view of early development by considering the psychosocial, interpersonal, and cultural contexts of the period of pregnancy.

Genetic factors guide the tempo of growth and the emergence of individual characteristics. As the human fetus grows, sensory and motor competencies emerge. The psychosocial environment provides both resources for and challenges to healthy development. Cultural attitudes toward pregnancy and childbirth, poverty and the associated stressors, support from the child's father and other significant family members, maternal nutrition, and exposure to toxins or drugs are among the factors that affect fetal growth.

The chapter ends with the Applied Topic Abortion. As you read about the contributions of genetic factors to development, the process of fertilization, normal fetal development, and the psychosocial and cultural contexts of pregnancy and childbirth, you will gain a more complex, nuanced understanding of this topic and the controversies that surround it. ●

Genetics and Development

OBJECTIVE 1 Summarize the process through which genetic information is transmitted from one generation to the next.

Variability, which is so essential for human survival, is guaranteed, in part, by the complexity of the human *genome* (all the genetic material in the chromosomes of a human being) and the mechanisms for genetic inheritance. In this section, we briefly review the biology of genetics and the laws that govern the transmission of genetic information from one generation to the next. As parents, teachers, and human service professionals, we are encouraged to value and respond to human diversity. The growing knowledge about human genetics provides a foundation for appreciating the biological basis of this diversity. An excellent source of information and links about the history, results, ethics, and future applications of the Human Genome Project can be found on the Human Genome Project website sponsored by the U.S. Department of Energy at genomics.energy.gov.

Chromosomes and Genes as Sources of Genetic Information

Genetic information links each new person to the human species in general and also to a specific genetic ancestry. The term "inherited characteristics" refers to two different kinds of heredity. The first includes all the genetic information that comes to us

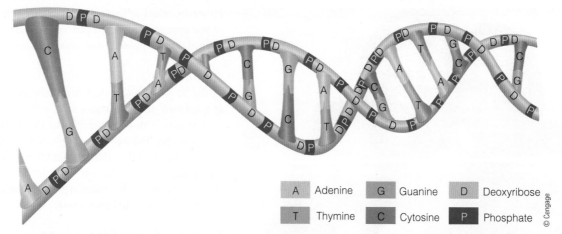

A	Adenine	G	Guanine	D	Deoxyribose
T	Thymine	C	Cytosine	P	Phosphate

FIGURE 4.1 ▶ DIAGRAM OF A SMALL PART OF A DNA MOLECULE   The biochemical basis of genetic information is the DNA (deoxyribonucleic acid) molecule, which has the shape of a double helix (i.e., it looks somewhat like a twisted rope ladder). The sides of this ladder comprise alternating units of sugar (deoxyribose) and phosphate, and its rungs are made up of pairs of nitrogen bases (so named because they contain the element nitrogen as well as hydrogen and carbon). The four nitrogen bases involved are adenine (A), guanine (G), cytosine (C), and thymine (T). They are often referred to by their initial letters A, G, C, and T and are called the genetic alphabet.

as members of the human species. Most inherited genetic information is shared by *all* human beings, such as patterns of motor behavior (e.g., walking upright), brain size, and body structure, including the proportional size of the head, torso, and limbs. Two of the most relevant of these species-related characteristics are the readiness to learn and the ability to participate in social interactions. The second kind of heredity consists of characteristics that have been transmitted through a specific *ancestry*. Hair color, skin color, blood group, and height result from the genetic information passed on from one generation to the next.

Chromosomes, the long, thin strands of genetic material located in the cell nucleus, are formed from chains of DNA molecules (see FIGURE 4.1 ▶). Most single **genes** are composed of a piece of DNA that codes for the production of one protein and occupies a specific place on a chromosome. An estimate based on **genome** mapping places the number of these genes at about 20,500, which is less than 10 percent of the entire genome (Powledge, 2014; Rands, Meader, Ponting, & Lunter, 2014). In addition to the functional regions that specify the code for making proteins, some sequences of DNA have a regulatory function. They control or modify the activity of the nearby genes and contribute to basic processes that allow copies of DNA to be replicated during cell division. Recent technologies and studies of the genome have revealed that there are many variations in the structure of the genomes among healthy individuals. These variations include insertions, deletions, rearrangements, and differences in the location of gene sequences. The consequence of these variations for normal development and disease are not entirely known (Zhang et al., 2013).

The important work of the genes is to produce proteins, which then guide cellular formation and functioning. Proteins, which are large, complex molecules comprised of amino acids, perform most life functions and make up the majority of cellular structures. The group of all proteins in a cell is called its **proteome**. "Unlike the relatively unchanging genome, the dynamic proteome changes from minute to minute in response to tens of thousands of intra- and extracellular environmental signals. A protein's chemistry and behavior are specified by the gene sequence and by the number and identities of other proteins made in the same cell at the same time and with which it associates and reacts" (U.S. Department of Energy, 2003). Therefore, at the cellular level, genetic and environmental sources of information are continuously interacting to influence the functions of the cells.

In each chromosome pair, one chromosome comes from the father and one from the mother. The chromosome pairs differ in size. In 22 pairs of chromosomes, both members are similar in shape and size. They also contain the same kinds of genes. The 23rd pair of chromosomes is a different story: Female humans have two X chromosomes, and male humans have one X and one Y chromosome. The X and Y notation is used because these chromosomes differ in shape and size (the X chromosome is longer than the Y chromosome). There are very few similarities in the genes present on the X and Y chromosomes.

One common misconception is that there is one gene for each specific trait such as sociability, intelligence, or criminality. Single genes do not determine most human behaviors. Only certain rare disorders such as Huntington's disease have a simple mode of transmission in which a specific mutation confers the certainty of developing the disorder. Most types of behavior have no such clear-cut pattern and depend on interplay between environmental factors and multiple genes (McGuffin, Riley, & Plomin, 2001).

The Principles of Heredity

Certain basic ideas about the process by which information is transmitted from parent to offspring were discovered by Gregor Mendel (1866), a monk who studied the inherited characteristics of plants, particularly garden peas. Mendel chose the garden pea plant as his focus of study because he was able to follow two generations of plants in a single growing season. Today most studies of genetics use the fruit fly, which reproduces every two weeks,

Family resemblance is influenced by the transmission of genes that guide the production of melanin, which can be detected in similarity of hair color, eye color, and skin tones.

Monkey Business Images/Shutterstock.com

However, many of these basic ideas are still fundamental to our appreciation of the process through which genetic information is passed from one generation to the next.

Alleles

In the 22 pairs of identical chromosomes, each gene has at least two possible states or conditions, one on each chromosome in the pair. These alternative states are called **alleles**. Whatever the allelic state of the gene from one parent, the other parent's allele for that gene may be either the same or different. If both alleles are the same, the gene is said to be **homozygous**. If the alleles are different, the gene is **heterozygous**.

Genotype and Phenotype

The genetic information about a trait is called the **genotype** (e.g., the genetic information that encodes skin color). The observed characteristic (e.g., one's actual skin color) is called the **phenotype.** The phenotype is a result of the genotype and development in the environment. Genotype can influence phenotype in three different ways. First, the differences in the allelic states of several genes sometimes result in a **cumulative relation**, in which more than one pair of alleles influences the trait. An example of this kind of relation is the genetic contribution to height. The genotype for height is based on a number of genes. A person whose alleles of different genes are mostly for tallness will be tall; a person who receives many alleles of different genes for shortness will be short. Most people receive a mix of alleles for both tallness and shortness and are of average height.

Second, the differences between alleles may result in **codominance**, in which both genes are expressed in the new cell. An example of codominance is the AB blood type that results from the joining of an A blood type allele from one parent and a B blood type allele from the other parent. This blood type is not a mixture of A and B, nor is A subordinate to B or B to A; instead, a distinct blood type, AB, is formed.

Third, differences in the allele states of a gene may result in a **dominance** relation. Dominance means that if one allele is present, its characteristic is predominantly observed whether the other allele of the pair is the same or not. The allele that dominates is called the *dominant* allele. The other allele that is present, but whose characteristic is masked by the dominant allele, is called the *recessive* allele. Eye color is the result of a dominance relation. The allele for brown eyes (B) is dominant over the allele for blue eyes (b). The probability that the recessive trait of blue eyes will emerge in the offspring of two heterozygous parents is illustrated in FIGURE 4.2 ▶. The possible combinations of the gene related to brown or blue eye color are BB, Bb, bB, and bb. Only one combination, bb, which will occur on the average in only 25 percent of the offspring, results in a child with blue eyes. The other three genotypes result in one phenotype—brown eyes.

Epigenetics

Adding to the complexity of the laws of heredity are the processes of **epigenetics**. Epigenetics is the study of mechanisms that turn genes on and off. These are changes in gene expression that can be

or certain bacteria that reproduce every 3 to 5 hours. Imagine the patience and care that were needed for Mendel to follow the path of certain characteristics over multiple generations of plants. In his work, he observed plants that had readily distinguishable traits, like the color of the flowers they produced or the color of their seeds. From his experiments, in which he combined plants with certain features in systematic ways, he was able to deduce the basic principles of how information is passed along from one generation to the next. These principles, which were gathered from the research on garden peas, also apply to humans.

1. The inheritance of specific traits occurs as units of information (now called genes) are passed from the parent generation to the child.
2. A person has two units of information about each trait. The person inherits one unit related to each trait from each parent (these are referred to as alleles).
3. A trait that was present in the parent may not show up in the child, but it is still present and can be passed along to the next generation.
4. In the process of reproduction, only one of the parent's alleles for each trait is passed along to the offspring. (We now know that this happens in the formation of the sex cells, which carry only one of each chromosome pair.)
5. Alleles for different traits are passed along independently. The information regarding eye color is not passed along with the information about blood type. (We now know that genes related to different characteristics are found on different chromosomes.)

As the study of genetics and the principles of heredity has progressed, our understanding of the dynamic nature of genes and the factors that can influence their expression has advanced.

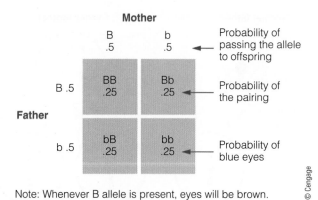

Mother

	B .5	b .5	← Probability of passing the allele to offspring
B .5	BB .25	Bb .25	← Probability of the pairing
b .5	bB .25	bb .25	← Probability of blue eyes

Father

© Cengage

Note: Whenever B allele is present, eyes will be brown.

FIGURE 4.2 ▶ PROBABILITY OF HETEROZYGOUS BROWN-EYED PARENTS PRODUCING BLUE-EYED OFFSPRING

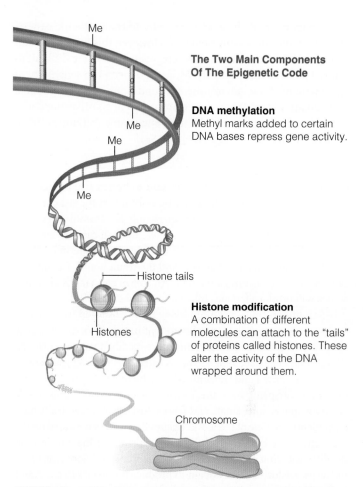

The Two Main Components Of The Epigenetic Code

DNA methylation
Methyl marks added to certain DNA bases repress gene activity.

Histone modification
A combination of different molecules can attach to the "tails" of proteins called histones. These alter the activity of the DNA wrapped around them.

FIGURE 4.3 ▶ EPIGENETIC MECHANISMS   Environmental conditions such as a rich diet following a period of starvation can alter gene expression. These changes can turn genes on or off and may affect what gets passed down to succeeding generations.

Source: "From Epigenetics: UnfinishedSymphony," by J. Qiu, 2006, Nature, 441, no. 7090, pp. 143–145.

transmitted from one generation to the next but do not alter the genome itself. In other words, these processes influence the phenotype (gene expression) but not the genotype. You will recall that in psychosocial theory, the epigenetic principle refers to a biological plan for growth that allows each function to emerge systematically until the fully functioning organism has developed. In the early 1940s, this term was used to consider the role of genetics in guiding development. Here, the same term is used to consider the ways that the environment can modify gene expression.

Two epigenetic processes are imprinting and epigenetic marks. **Imprinting** is a condition in which genes from either the mother or the father are silenced. For most genes, we inherit two working copies, one from mother and one from father. However, for imprinted genes, only one working copy is inherited; the other is silenced by the presence of a chemical tag that sits along the gene (Genetics Science Learning Center, 2014; Kelsey & Bartolomei, 2012). Under conditions of imprinting, the genes from both parents are present on the DNA strands and are copied by the RNA, but only the genes from one parent are used in making proteins. As a result, even though there are two alleles in the genotype, only the mother's or the father's allele is expressed in the phenotype. There is an assumed adaptive advantage to having some genetic information silenced selectively depending on its origin from the paternal or maternal genetic source, but the mechanisms that might explain or account for this advantage are not yet clear. Many developmental disorders and diseases are linked to imprinted genes. For example, in a certain gene related to growth, the father's allele is expressed and the mother's allele is silenced. If for some reason the imprinting is disrupted and both alleles are expressed, the cell is likely to become cancerous. Future study of imprinted genes is expected to contribute significantly to our understanding of the genetic and epigenetic basis of disease (Jirtle & Weidman, 2007).

Epigenetic marks are chemicals that sit on top of the genes and instruct them to switch on or off (FIGURE 4.3 ▶). These marks can be influenced by environmental factors such as overabundant eating, smoking cigarettes at an early age, taking particular vitamins during the prenatal period, or exposure to extremely stressful conditions. When the epigenetic marks are altered, the impact is seen in subsequent generations. For example, researchers studied the long-term impact of famine and feast

in a small Swedish community. They found that the children and grandchildren of those children who had experienced periods of near starvation followed by a year of overeating had substantially shorter lives than the offspring of those who experienced only the famine, but no overeating. In contrast to the slow process of genetic modification through natural selection, epigenetic studies show how exposure to critical environmental factors at key periods of life can predispose one's children and grandchildren to genetically based vulnerabilities. These environmental influences are distinct from the prenatal exposure of the fetus to malnutrition or toxins, discussed later in this chapter, which may result in developmental delay or disruption. Epigenetic studies link developmentally time-sensitive exposure to environmental conditions to the gene expression in one or more generations of offspring (Pembrey, 2008; Pembrey, Bygren et al., 2006).

The study of intergenerational inheritance due to epigenetic marks is still in its infancy. Research with animal models suggests that some of a grandparent's experiences with nurturing and/or harsh and neglectful parenting can be passed on to their children and grandchildren (Weaver, Cervoni et al., 2004). In the field of behavioral epigenetics, particular focus has been given to

Genetics and Development   **85**

the impact of child abuse and exposure to traumatic life experiences that alter the brain chemistry. However, this research is still considered controversial because epigenetic marks are difficult to trace. They can form quickly. Moreover, given the sensitivity of epigenetic marks to environmental conditions, it is also possible that sensitivities that are passed from parent to offspring could be modified by exposure to different environments (Hurley, 2013; Genetic Science Learning Center, 2015a).

Sex-Linked Characteristics

Certain genetic characteristics are said to be **sex linked** because the gene for the specific characteristic is found on the sex chromosomes (X and Y). The female ova carry only X chromosomes. Half of the male sperm carry Y chromosomes, and half carry X chromosomes. Male children can be produced only when a sperm carrying a Y chromosome fertilizes an egg, and the result is an XY combination in the 23rd chromosome pair. All sperm carrying X chromosomes will produce female children.

Sex-linked traits are more likely to be observed in male offspring, even though they may be present in the genotype of female offspring. You will understand this more readily if you visualize the XY chromosome pair. When a trait is carried on the Y chromosome, it will be inherited and transmitted only by male offspring, because only male offspring have the Y chromosome. Interestingly, the Y chromosome is quite small, and few exclusively Y-linked traits have been identified. One of the few key genes that has been located on the Y chromosome is SRY, which is responsible for setting into motion the differentiation of the testes during embryonic development. Once the testes are formed, they begin to produce hormones that account for further differentiation of the male reproductive system.

Sex-linked traits that are carried on the X chromosome are more likely to be observed in male offspring than in female offspring, because male children do not have a second X chromosome to offset the effects of an X-linked trait. Hemophilia A, the most common type of hemophilia, is an example of such a sex-linked trait. Individuals with hemophilia lack a specific blood protein that causes blood to clot after receiving a wound (Medline Plus, 2014). The allele for hemophilia is a recessive trait carried on the X chromosome; however, it is most likely to affect men (see FIGURE 4.4 ▶). Half (50 percent) of the male offspring of female carriers have the disease, and 50 percent of their female offspring are carriers. All female children of a man with hemophilia are carriers of the trait. This disease affects approximately 1 in 5,000 men.

Other genes are expressed exclusively in one sex but are not found on the sex chromosomes per se. For example, the genes for male beard development and female breast development are not located on the sex chromosomes. However, these characteristics will emerge only in the presence of the appropriate hormonal environment, which is directed by the sex chromosomes.

Genetic Sources of Individual Differences

OBJECTIVE 2 Differentiate the contributions of genetic factors to individuality through their role in controlling the rate of development, their influences on individual traits, and the genetic sources of abnormalities.

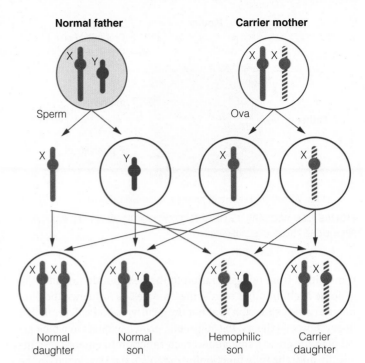

FIGURE 4.4 ▶ SEX-LINKED INHERITANCE OF HEMOPHILIA   The allele for hemophilia is carried on the X chromosome. If the allele is either heterozygous or homozygous for the dominant trait (normal blood clotting), a female child will have normal blood-clotting capabilities. Only if she is homozygous for the recessive trait (a very rare occurrence) will she be hemophilic. A male child, on the other hand, has only one allele for the clotting gene, which he inherits from his mother. If that allele is dominant, his blood will clot normally, but if it is recessive, he will be hemophilic.

Source: From "The Molecular Genetics of Hemophilia," by R. M. Lawn and G. A. Vehar, 1986, *Scientific American*, 254, p. 50. Copyright © 1986.

The study of genetics reveals that individual variability is due to the combination of the many variations in environments and experiences that confront a growing person and the variability built into the biological mechanisms of heredity. Each adult couple has the potential for producing a great variety of genetically distinct children. Four areas in which genetic factors contribute to individual variability are *mutations, rate and sequence of development, individual traits,* and *abnormal development.*

Mutations

Every time a cell divides its DNA is copied. A **mutation** refers to a natural process that changes some aspect of the DNA sequence; it is like a *typo* in the reproduction or copying process. These errors may be a result of a normal process of cell division. However, they may also result from exposure to radiation, chemicals, or infection by viruses. Cells have the ability to repair these errors. Unrepaired mutations that occur in body cells are not passed on to offspring. However, if a change goes unrepaired in an egg or sperm cell, it may be passed along to the next generation. This means that some aspects of the DNA of the offspring are a bit different from the DNA from either parent. In this way, mutations contribute to genetic variation, especially when they occur within genes, rather than in the large amount of DNA that falls between the genes.

Genetic mutations are a source of variation at the level of the allele. If the variation contributes to fitness and increases the probability of the offspring's survival, we could say it was a positive mutation. If the variation disrupts important protein development, causes disease or vulnerability, or prevents reproductive success, we could say it was a negative mutation. However, many mutations, like those that contribute to variations in skin color, blood type, or the shape of one's ears, are neither good nor bad. They are just sources of differences between individuals (Genetics Home Reference, 2015a; Genetics Science Learning Center, 2015b).

Genetic Determinants of the Rate and Sequence of Development

Genes regulate the rate and sequence of maturation. The concept of an epigenetic plan for growth and development is based on the assumption that a genetically guided system promotes or restricts the growth of cells over the life span. Genetic factors have been found to play a role in behavioral development, including the onset of various levels of reasoning, language, and social orientation (Moore, 2015; Plomin, DeFries, Knopik, & Neiderhiser, 2012).

Evidence for the role of genetics in guiding the rate and sequence of development comes largely from studies of identical twins (who have the same genotype). The rates at which identical twins develop are highly correlated. A number of characteristics—including the timing of the acquisition of motor skills, personality development, changes in intellectual capacity among aged twins, and the timing of physical maturation—show a strong genetic influence (Bouchard & Pederson, 1999; Segal, 2010; Segal & Johnson, 2009).

Genes can be viewed as internal regulators that set the pace for maturation. They signal the onset of significant developmental changes throughout life, such as growth spurts, the eruption of teeth, puberty, and menopause. They also appear to set the limits of the life span. A small number of genes influence how many times the cells of a specific organism can divide and replicate.

Differences in the rate of development contribute to our understanding of psychosocial growth. For example, you may encounter charts and websites that offer milestones about the age at which infants and young children are expected to perform various motor skills or language abilities. However, these and other capacities evidence considerable variability in the timing and rate of development. Differences in age at crawling or walking, for example, bring children into contact with new aspects of their environments and provide them with changing capacities for exploration at different chronological ages.

Genetic Determinants of Individual Traits

Genes contain specific information about a wide range of human characteristics, from eye color and height to the ability to taste a particular substance called phenylthiocarbamide (PTC) (which to tasters is bitter, but to nontasters has no taste at all). Have you ever wondered why some people are very picky eaters, and others will eat anything? One hypothesis has to do with difference in the PTC gene. Tasters seem to have more food aversions. This might come in handy if the food sources are spoiled or tainted, but it might be a disadvantage if there are limited food supplies.

Some characteristics are controlled by a single gene. However, most significant characteristics, such as height, weight, blood group, skin color, and intelligence, are guided by the combined action of several genes. When multiple genes are involved in the regulation of a trait, the possibilities for individual differences in that trait increase. Because many characteristics are regulated by multiple genes, the variety of human phenotypes is enormous.

Genetic factors also play a substantial role in individual differences in personality traits (Barondes, 2011; Borkenau, Riemann, Angleitner, & Spinath, 2001; Plomin & Spinath, 2004). Traits such as *sociability* (a tendency to be outgoing), *inhibition* (a tendency to be cautious and socially shy or withdrawn), and *neuroticism* (a tendency to be anxious and emotionally sensitive) are pervasive dimensions of personality that appear to have strong genetic components. Even in rather specific areas of personality, such as political attitudes, aesthetic preferences, and sense of humor, identical twins show greater similarity than fraternal twins. Research on the biological basis of sexual orientation suggests that genes influence the development of the part of the brain that guides sexual behavior. Identical twins are more likely to have the same sexual orientation than are fraternal twins or adoptive siblings (Bailey & Pillard, 1991, 1994; LeVay, 1991, 2011; Ngun & Vilain, 2014).

The notion that genetic factors influence personality and behavior has led to extensive research to identify specific genes responsible for particular traits such as cooperativeness, impulse regulation, or vulnerability to stress. In this search, an important perspective has emerged for understanding how genes and the environment interact. As discussed above, differing environmental conditions at a molecular, biological, or behavioral level can alter the expression of one or more genes through epigenetic marks, resulting in vulnerabilities or resilience. You have probably met people who seem to just "roll with the punches" whereas others seem to get ruffled by even minor disturbances. Genetic factors can influence whether individuals are more or less distressed by their environments (Belsky, 2011; Caspi, Hariri, Holmes, Uher, & Moffitt, 2010). What is more, people with the same genotype can demonstrate different phenotypes depending on their exposure to harsh or nurturing parenting (see Figure 4.5 ▶).

As people mature and become increasingly assertive in selecting certain experiences and rejecting others, their own temperaments, talents, intelligence, and level of sociability will guide the kinds of environments they select, strengthening certain genetic predispositions while dampening others. The more control a person has over decisions affecting lifestyle, work and leisure activities, and relationships, the greater impact certain innate or genetically guided preferences are likely to have on these decisions.

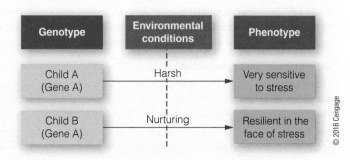

FIGURE 4.5 ▶ EXPRESSION OF SAME GENE IN DIFFERENT ENVIRONMENTS

© 2018 Cengage

Genetic Determinants of Abnormal Development

In addition to characteristics such as physical appearance, temperament, talent, and intellectual capacity, a wide variety of abnormalities, or *anomalies*, have a genetic cause. The most dramatic anomalies result in a spontaneous abortion of the fetus early in the pregnancy. Pregnancy loss that occurs on its own before 20 weeks of gestation is referred to as a **miscarriage**. Approximately 10 percent to 25 percent of diagnosed pregnancies end in miscarriage (American Pregnancy Association, 2015). The risk of miscarriage is lower for women under age 30, increases to 20 percent to 35 percent among women ages 35–45, and is as high as 50 percent among women age 45 and over (American Pregnancy Association, 2015). The majority of these early-term miscarriages are due to chromosomal abnormalities in the fertilized zygotes (the developing organism formed from the father's sperm and the mother's egg) that prevent normal fetal development.

Of those infants who survive the neonatal period, an estimated 3 percent to 5 percent have one or more major recognizable anomalies or birth defects (Cunningham et al., 2014). The incidence of anomalies increases to 6 percent to 7 percent as some disorders are diagnosed later in childhood. Some birth defects are linked to a specific chromosome or to a single gene. Other birth defects are linked solely to environmental factors, such as drugs, medications, and fetal and maternal infections. Most malformations, however, result from the interaction of genetic vulnerabilities and environmental hazards or are of unknown origin (Moore, Persaud, & Torchia, 2015). Some birth defects, such as respiratory distress associated with underdeveloped lungs, can be corrected through medical interventions. Others, such as injury of the small or large intestines, which disrupts digestion and creates a site for repeated infections, may remain a source of life-long illness and/or disability (Institute of Medicine, 2007).

Examples of genetic and **chromosomal disorders** are listed in Table 4.1. The disorders are presented in two broad

Table 4.1 Examples of Genetic and Chromosomal Disorders
Genetic Disorders
Autosomal dominant gene
Huntington's chorea: Rapid, jerky, involuntary movements; deterioration of muscle coordination and mental functioning. Symptoms usually do not appear until age 35–50. Caused by genetic defect on chromosome 4.
Marfan's syndrome: Elongated fingers; deformed chest and spine; abnormal heart. Tendons, ligaments, and joint capsules are weak.
Autosomal recessive gene
Albinism: Hair, skin, and eyes lack the pigment melanin. Often accompanied by visual problems and a susceptibility to skin cancer.
Cystic fibrosis: Certain glands do not function properly. The glands in the lining of the bronchial tubes produce excessive amounts of thick mucus, which leads to chronic lung infections. Failure of the pancreas to produce enzymes necessary for the breakdown of fats and their absorption from the intestines leads to malnutrition. Sweat glands are also affected. Often fatal by age 30. Caused by missing base pairs on chromosome 7.
Sickle-cell anemia: Malformation of red blood cells reduces the amount of oxygen they can carry. Results in fatigue, headaches, shortness breath on exertion, pallor, jaundice, pain, and damage to kidneys, lungs, intestine, and brain.
Tay-Sachs disease: Absence of a certain enzyme results in the buildup of harmful chemicals in the brain. Results in death before age 3.
X-linked recessive gene
Color blindness: Defect of light-sensitive pigment in one or more classes of cone cells in the retina of the eye or an abnormality in or reduced number of cone cells themselves. The two common types are reduced discrimination of light wavelengths within the middle (green) and long (red) parts of the visible spectrum.
Hemophilia: Absence of a blood protein (factor VIII) reduces effectiveness of blood clotting. Severity of disorder varies. Bleeding episodes likely to begin in toddlerhood.
Chromosomal Disorders
Autosomal abnormality
Down syndrome: Additional 21st chromosome; also called trisomy 21. The extra chromosome results in physical and intellectual abnormalities, including IQ in the range of 30–80; distinctive facial features, heart defects, intestinal problems, hearing defects; susceptibility to repeated ear infections. Tendency to develop narrowing of the arteries in adulthood, with attendant increase in risk of heart disease.
Sex-chromosome abnormalities
Turner syndrome: Usually caused by a lack of one X chromosome in a girl; sometimes one of two X chromosomes is defective; occasionally some base pairs are missing on an X chromosome. These abnormalities result in defective sexual development and infertility, short stature, absence or retarded development of secondary sex characteristics, absence of menstruation, narrowing of the aorta, and a degree of mental retardation.
Klinefelter syndrome: One or more extra X chromosomes in a boy. This abnormality results in defective sexual development, including enlarged breasts and small testes, infertility, and often mental retardation.

This table is derived from information available at the National Institute of Health website, Genetics Home Reference(2015b) http://www.genome.gov/10001204

categories: those associated with specific genes and those associated with chromosomal abnormalities. Within those categories, some disorders are found on 1 of the 22 pairs of autosomal chromosomes (chromosomes other than the sex chromosomes), and others are on one of the sex chromosomes. There are more than 1,100 genes for which at least one disease- related mutation or alternate allele has been identified using the map-based approach to gene discovery. However, many diseases are thought to involve multiple genes in some form of interaction. Moreover, many diseases that have an identified genetic basis— such as hypertension, schizophrenia, or coronary artery disease—are expressed in certain environments, including the prenatal environment, and not in others (Fox, Hane, & Pine, 2007; Peltonen & McKusick, 2001).

Certain genetic diseases are linked directly to our ancestry; therefore, their incidence is higher in certain populations than in others (National Institutes of Health, 2015a). For example, the incidence of Tay-Sachs disease is especially frequent in Jews who settled in Eastern Europe. One in every 27 Jews in the United States carries the gene. Thalassemia, a disease involving faulty production of hemoglobin (which carries oxygen in the blood), is found most often in people of Mediterranean, Middle Eastern, and Southeast Asian origins. The variety of genetic abnormalities serves to broaden the range of individual variability. Many of these irregularities pose a challenge both to the adaptive capacities of the affected person and to the caregiving capacities of the adults involved.

Larry has a family history of cystic fibrosis. He and Leila have come to talk with a genetic counselor to help them evaluate the likelihood that their children would have this condition, and how to deal with this situation.

Genetic Technology and Psychosocial Evolution

Psychosocial evolution has typically been differentiated from biological evolution in that change is accomplished by social mechanisms, such as parenting, education, and the media, rather than incorporated in the genetic structure. As a result of scientific knowledge, however, we are entering an era when it is possible to intervene to influence the genotype. One such intervention is **genetic counseling** (Medline Plus, 2015). Individuals and couples with a family history of a genetic disease—or who for some other reason worry about the possibility of transmitting a genetic disease to their children—can have blood tests to identify genes that may result in the inherited disorder. The locations of the genes that account for such abnormalities as Tay-Sachs disease, sickle-cell anemia, Duchenne muscular dystrophy, and cystic fibrosis have been identified. Couples who have reason to believe that they may carry genes for one of these diseases can be advised about the probability of having children who may be afflicted. If significant numbers of the carriers of genetic diseases decided not to reproduce, the incidence of these diseases in the population would decline over time. Thus, a psychosocial intervention would modify the gene pool.

Ethical Considerations

Gene transfer; the patenting of new life forms created through genetic engineering; genetic fingerprinting, which is used to help identify criminal suspects; and cloning from an adult mammal are some of the topics that are raising new ethical concerns. There is consensus that the use of gene therapy to try to treat serious diseases such as severe combined immunodeficiency (SCID) or cancer is ethical. This type of gene therapy targets body cells such as bone marrow or blood cells. However, there is less agreement about germline gene therapy in which genes are inserted into gametes to try to prevent or modify the characteristics of offspring. Germline gene therapy is intended to modify disease-causing-genes in order to prevent their expression in the offspring or reduce the risk of passing certain mutations from one generation to the next. You can read more about the ethical controversies surrounding germline gene therapy at yourgenome.org (YourGenome.org, 2015).

Even the advances in identifying genetic markers for specific diseases can lead to ethical dilemmas. Three sources of federal legislation address prevention of discrimination based on genetic information. The Genetic Information Nondiscrimination Act of 2008 and the 2000 Executive Order prohibit discrimination in federal employment based on genetic discrimination. The 2010 Affordable Care Act contains further anti-discrimination measures including prevention of health insurers from refusing individuals coverage because of pre-existing conditions, including genetic diseases, and prevention of adjustment of premiums because of medical conditions (U.S. Department of Energy, 2013). State laws addressing discrimination on the basis of genetic diseases or the requirement for genetic testing as a condition of employment are less consistent.

The possibility of reproducing genetically identical clones from human tissue has stirred the conscience of the religious, political, and medical communities. Is it ethical to clone human genes so that great scholars, scientists, and artists can walk the Earth again? Should cloning become an approved technology for coping with infertility?

The debate about cloning has extended to include human stem cell research. Stem cells are unspecialized cells that have the potential to develop into any type of organ in the body. In the 3- to 5-day-old human embryo, these stem cells become the basis for all the organs that emerge during gestation. In some adult tissues, including bone marrow, muscle, and lungs, stem cells can generate replacement for cells that have been lost through wear and tear, injury, or disease (NIH, 2015b). In the early work, stem cells were derived from human embryos that were not going to be used for reproductive purposes. Now, however, adult somatic cells can be genetically manipulated to return them to an "unprogrammed" state, allowing them to take on the same properties as embryonic stem cells. This approach avoids much of the ethical controversy about the use of embryonic stem cells, allowing the research in this field to expand (Brind' Amour, 2010; NIH, 2015b).

Gene X Environment Interactions and Behavior

Forget the idea of nature versus nurture. Genes cannot be expressed without an appropriate environment, including the biological environment at the cellular level and the physical and social environments at the larger systems levels. For a genotype to be fully expressed in the phenotype, many environmental supports must be in place. For example, a human being needs to breathe oxygen. If an infant is deprived of oxygen for a long time in the prenatal period or during the birth process, the genetic potential for intelligence will be compromised. As illustrated in the discussion of epigenetic marks, individuals and their environments are in a state of dynamic interaction and change, each modifying the other. As the study of the human genome continues, we are appreciating that there is significant individual variability in sensitivity to the environment and the possibility of changing sensitivities to the environment at various points in the life span.

Genetics and Intelligence

One area that has received considerable attention is the relative contributions of genetic and environmental factors to **intelligence**. To what extent is a person's intelligence set by hereditary factors? To what extent is it a product of experience? Intelligent behavior requires the successful integration of both. It relies on the structure of the central nervous system and the sense receptors, which are products of genetically guided information. However, the healthy functioning of these systems requires adequate nutrition, rest, and freedom from disease—conditions that vary with the environment. Intelligent behavior builds on experiences with diverse stimuli, social interactions, and schooling—all elements of the physical and social environment.

The influence of genetic factors on intelligence may be observed in three ways. First, specific genetic anomalies, such as Down syndrome, are known to disrupt the development of the

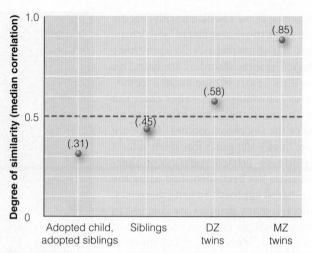

FIGURE 4.6 ▶ SIMILARITY IN INTELLIGENCE AMONG SIBLINGS AT FOUR LEVELS OF RELATIONSHIP

Source: From "Familial Studies of Intelligence: A Review," by T. J. Bouchard and M. McGue, 1981, Science, 212, pp.1055–1059.

central nervous system and interfere with cognitive functioning. Second, the contributions of genetics to intelligence are observed through the study of family relationships. Family members may be related closely or distantly. The closer the biological relationship, the more similar the genetic makeup. If intelligence is influenced by genetics, close relatives should be more similar in intelligence than distant relatives. FIGURE 4.6 ▶ shows the degree of similarity found in more than 100 studies of intelligence in siblings at four different degrees of relationship (Bouchard & McGue, 1981). Similarity in intelligence increases with the degree of genetic relatedness. The correlation between pairs of monozygotic (identical) twins is 0.85, providing striking evidence of the contribution of genetics to intelligence. Fraternal, dizygotic (DZ) twins who share the same prenatal environment, home, and childrearing environments show much less similarity than do MZ twins and not much more than non-twin siblings. Third, recent research using Genome-wide Complex Trait Analysis (GCTA) in large samples allows for the quantitative analysis of genotypes and their relationship to measured intelligence (Plomin & Deary, 2015).

An overview of studies that have attempted to evaluate the contribution of genetic factors to cognitive ability suggests that genetics accounts for 50 percent of the variance, shared environmental factors for 33 percent of the variance, unshared environmental factors for 17 percent of the variance, and measurement error for 10 percent of the variance in intelligence (Gottesman, 1997). One might expect that genetic factors would play a smaller role in measured intelligence with age. However, the data suggest the opposite. The role of genetic factors associated with the inheritance of intelligence increases with age (Plomin & Deary, 2015; Plomin & Spinath, 2004). In other words, identical twins are more alike in intelligence in their adulthood and elderhood than they were as infants and young children.

The fact that intelligence is strongly influenced by genetic factors does not imply that environments have no impact or that intelligence is fixed or unchangeable. Through the field of cognitive neuroscience, we are learning more about the role of genes in the structure and functions of the brain and the ways that various genes are related to cognitive capacities. As we will discuss later in the chapter, both the prenatal and postnatal environments have potential impact on the developing nervous system. Access to adequate nutrition, exposure to toxins, and birth trauma can all alter the phenotype with regard to intelligence. Moreover, tested IQ is only one way of conceptualizing intelligence, a concept that is widely debated in the social sciences. The question of how to think about and study the relationship of genetics and intelligence is moving into new and exciting areas of investigation (Plomin, 2004).

The Norm of Reaction

One way to think about the influence of genetics on behavior is to view the phenotype or observed behavior as a **norm of reaction**— that is, a pattern of possible phenotypes that are likely to be observed under different environmental conditions. This way of thinking about development highlights the importance of the concept of plasticity. **Plasticity** can be conceptualized as the degree of flexibility or variation that can be expressed at the level of an organ, a capacity, or a broad, developmental trajectory. Consider the example of handedness. If you are left- handed, and you break your left hand, you can learn to feed yourself with your right hand. It's not as smooth, but it's possible. So handedness, which is genetically influenced, is also plastic. And some people are more readily able to switch from one hand to the other than others; we call them ambidextrous.

Some characteristics of personality, intelligence, and emotional response are more plastic than others; that is, they are more sensitive to environmental stimulation or the conditions of childrearing than others. For example, whereas some children are very highly attuned to the social messages and childrearing practices of their parents, others are more resistant to parenting strategies and seem to grow up in tune with their own inner plan (Belsky & Pluess, 2009). Plasticity suggests that specific characteristics can be modified under various environmental conditions, and that some individuals are more responsive to the impact of the environment (for better or worse) than others.

FIGURE 4.7 ▶ shows the possible ranges of intelligence for three children under different nutritional conditions. Child A has greater genetic potential for intelligence than Child B, who has greater potential than Child C. Imagine a continuum of prenatal nutrition from very inadequate food resources to a very adequate diet. Some women living in very poor countries where there is widespread famine may have little to eat while they are pregnant. For other women, food supplies are plentiful. Now, imagine that after the child's birth, there is also a continuum of access to food. Some babies who were malnourished in the prenatal period continue to be malnourished in the early months of infancy. Other babies who were malnourished in the prenatal period begin to have access to an adequate diet after birth. And still other babies never experience food deprivation. Figure 4.7 provides a way of thinking about how levels of malnutrition may interact with the genotype for intelligence to produce different phenotypes.

When all three children are in food-deprived environments both prenatally and after birth, their IQs develop at the lower end of their potential range and the differences among the three phenotypes are reduced. When all three children are in environments where nutritional resources are plentiful both before and after birth, their IQs develop toward the upper end of their potential range and the differences among the three phenotypes are accentuated. Each child's intellectual ability can be expressed as a range of probable levels that are likely given the child's genetic potential and the quality of the nutritional environment. The more plastic a characteristic, such as intelligence, the more the phenotype will reflect environmental variation. The more channeled or constrained the characteristic, such as the shape of one's eyes or the length of one's fingers, the less environmental factors will influence the expression of the genotype in the phenotype.

Some genotypes flourish under certain conditions but not others. For example, consider the genotype for behavioral inhibition (Fox, Hane, & Pine, 2007). Behaviorally inhibited children are likely to stop their activity and seek proximity to their caregiver when faced with novel stimuli. Whereas some children have a genotype for intense inhibition, others have a genotype for low levels of inhibition. They are more active, outgoing, and exploratory and less disrupted or distressed by novelty. Now consider cultural differences that might interact with these predispositions for high or low inhibition. In cultures where children are expected to learn through observation and imitation, and where close physical contact between caregivers and mothers is the norm, one might expect the behaviorally inhibited children to be viewed as more normal and to thrive. The outgoing, exploratory, uninhibited children may be perceived as difficult, disruptive, and may experience more efforts on the part of caregivers to control or constrain their behavior. Children with a genotype that predisposes them to be outgoing and active might experience high levels of distress and self-doubt in this type of environment. In other cultures, where the norm is toward early independence and encouragement for exploratory behavior, the inhibited infants will require especially sensitive and supportive caregiving in order to thrive. Some parents may add to their inhibited infant's distress by rejecting these infants or conveying impatience with their infant's sensitivity, perceived clinginess, and avoidant behavior.

The concept of the norm of reaction can be seen clearly in the outlook for children with Down syndrome. This condition, which occurs in about 1 of every 700 live births, is the most common chromosomal cause of mental retardation in the United States (Parker, Mai, Canfield et al., 2010). In the early part of the 20th century, children born with Down syndrome had a life expectancy of 9 years. Today, the average life expectancy of a person with Down syndrome is 50 and beyond (National Institutes of Health, 2014). Medical care, early and constant educational intervention, physical therapy, and a nurturing home environment have significant positive results for children with Down syndrome (Hazlett, Hammer, Hooper, & Kamphaus, 2011). Participation in a mainstreamed classroom environment has been shown to have significant benefits for these children's vocabulary, grammar, and certain memory skills. Under optimal conditions, individuals with Down syndrome are able to achieve a moderate degree of independence and to participate actively in the life of their schools, communities, and families. Although Down syndrome constrains the probable phenotype, there is a norm of reaction that results from a child's exposure to various degrees of environmental support (National Down Syndrome Society, 2013). Thus, the norm of reaction depends on the specific dynamic interaction of a given genotype in a particular environment.

FURTHER REFLECTION *What do you know about your genetic makeup? How would you find out more if you were interested?*

Based on your reading, how do you evaluate the contribution of genetics and environment to human behaviors? How do genetics and environment contribute to areas of human functioning such as intelligence, creativity, leadership, or sense of humor?

John Henley/Corbis/Getty Images

Even though children with Down syndrome have mild to moderate disabilities, they also have many talents and abilities. They benefit enormously from early intervention services, including physical, speech, and developmental therapies. Children with Down syndrome enjoy and benefit from social interactions with their typically developing peers.

Normal Fetal Development

OBJECTIVE 3 Trace the process of prenatal development from fertilization through three trimesters of pregnancy, including an understanding of infertility, alternative means of reproduction, and related ethical considerations.

In the three trimesters of pregnancy, development unfolds from the cellular level of two merging gametes to the formation of complex physical, sensory, and neurological capacities.

Fertilization

One normal ejaculation contains several hundred million sperm. This large number is necessary to ensure **fertilization** because most sperm die on the way through the vagina and the uterus. Each microscopic sperm is composed of a pointed head and a tail. The head contains the genetic material necessary for reproduction. The tail moves like a whip as the sperm swims through the cervix and uterus and into the fallopian tubes. Swimming at the rate of 1 inch every 8 minutes, sperm may reach the egg in as little as 30 minutes, but the journey usually takes about 6 hours; sperm can stay alive in the uterus for up to 5 days.

In contrast to a man, who produces billions of sperm in a lifetime, a woman ordinarily releases just one ovum, or egg, each month, midway through the menstrual cycle. In a lifetime of approximately 40 fertile years, the average woman releases roughly 450 eggs. Each woman is born with her complete supply of eggs.

Like the sperm, the ovum is a single cell that contains genetic material. In comparison with body cells, the ovum is quite large

(0.12 millimeters), about the size of the period at the end of this sentence. When the ovum is mature, it is encased in a sac of fluid and floats to the surface of the ovary. The sac ruptures and releases the ovum into one of the two fallopian tubes. Millions of feathery, hair-like structures in the fallopian tube sweep around the ovum and gently move it toward the uterus.

Only one sperm can enter the egg. As the first sperm passes through the egg's cell membrane, a rapid change in the membrane's chemistry effectively locks out other sperm. If the ovum is not fertilized within the first 24 hours of its maturity, it begins to disintegrate and is shed along with the lining of the uterus in the next menstrual period.

Once inside the egg cell, the sperm loses its tail, and the head becomes a normal cell nucleus. The egg cell also goes through a final change in preparation for fertilization. The **gametes** (egg and sperm cells) contain 23 chromosomes, rather than the full set of 23 pairs. When the cell nuclei of the sperm and the ovum meet in the egg cytoplasm, their separate chromosomal material is integrated into a single set of 23 pairs of chromosomes. At this moment, all the information necessary to activate growth is contained in a single cell.

Identical twins have the same genotype; fraternal twins are no more alike genetically than other siblings. However, both kinds of twins share the same prenatal environment. These twins smile for a group photo at the 32nd annual Twins Days Festival in Twinsburg, Ohio.

Twins

The cell produced when the sperm has fertilized the egg is referred to as a **zygote**. The zygote travels down the fallopian tube and divides as it travels toward the uterus without growing larger. After about a week, this mass of cells implants in the uterus. Occasionally, this growing mass of cells divides in two and separates, forming two individuals with the same chromosomal composition. These individuals are referred to as **monozygotic** (MZ) twins, because they come from a single zygote. They are always of the same sex and are strikingly similar in physical appearance, a characteristic leading to the term **identical twins**.

Fraternal twins occur as a result of multiple ovulations in the same cycle. Each egg develops separately in the ovary, is shed and fertilized individually, and develops separately in the uterus. The result is **dizygotic** (DZ) twins—that is, two-egg twins. Actually, these twins are littermates and may be of different sexes. Genetically, they bear no more resemblance to one another than other children of the same parents. However, they share the same prenatal environment and a more common parenting environment than do most siblings who are born one or more years apart. This may account for the greater similarity in intelligence between DZ twins as compared to siblings shown in Figure 4.6. Approximately 34 in 1,000 live births are twins; 113.5 births in 100,000 are triplets or more. This rate for triplets is the lowest in 20 years. The ratio of multiple births is notably higher among mothers over age 30, possibly because older mothers are more likely to be using some type of fertility therapy (Hamilton et al., 2015).

Infertility and Alternative Means of Reproduction

Infertility, or the inability to conceive, can result from problems in the reproductive system of the man, the woman, or both. An estimated 12 percent of women in the United States between the ages of 15 and 44 face problems of infertility. The risk of infertility increases with age and is associated with exposure to toxins, including cigarette smoke, pesticides, chemical solvents, and fumes from anesthesia (NICHD, 2012a). Research on the emotional impact of infertility suggests that it is a major source of stress. The discovery of infertility may force a couple to reassess the meaning and purpose of their marriage. It may raise doubts in the couple about their self-worth; it often disrupts their satisfaction with their sexual relationship; and it often isolates them because of the difficulty of discussing this personal family problem with others (Haynes & Miller, 2003).

I have been trying to conceive for 2 years. Each month, at ovulation, I am so sure this will be "the month." And then, like clockwork, my period comes and I spend at least a day feeling depressed. Sex has even become a chore for both me and my partner. This whole infertility roller coaster is definitely hurting our relationship and sex life. Well-meaning friends tell me it will happen when the time is right, but I don't know how to help our relationship in the meantime. (Peterson, 2001)

When couples perceive similar levels of distress about their infertility and are able to communicate with each other about it, they report higher levels of marital satisfaction (Peterson, Newton, & Rosen, 2003). However, it is not uncommon for husbands and wives to have different reactions to infertility and different levels of distress about it, which results in more strained marital relationships. The stressors associated with infertility may go on over a long period. Some couples undergo fertility treatments for years before conceiving or giving up on their hopes for a biologically related child. Over time, the impact of infertility can become increasingly stressful, leading to high levels of depression as various alternatives are tried and fail (Covington, 2015; M. P. McCarthy, 2008).

Although much of the literature focuses on the experiences of women, men have strong feelings of their own as the infertility persists (E. McCarthy, 2013). Edward describes one aspect of his distress, the lack of male friends or family with whom he can share his feelings.

> As infertility dragged on, my heart yearned to share my feelings with an understanding peer, another man who had either been where I was or one who was on the infertility roller coaster himself. I had experienced this type of mutual support during my training days as a chaplain, but now, I couldn't find the same type of safe haven to express my sense of utter loss, my anger, my grief, and my frustration that swirled around like a hurricane in my soul. In general, men experiencing grief have a lack of kinship with peers. (Dake, 2002, p. 49)

In addition to the emotional costs of treatment, there are substantial financial costs amounting to tens of thousands of dollars, most of which is not covered by insurance. Moreover, many procedures are unsuccessful. During 1 year of unprotected sexual relations, 90 percent of healthy couples achieve pregnancy. Data from 467 U.S. clinics reporting to the National Center for Chronic Disease Prevention and Health Promotion in 2013 provide a picture of the likelihood that a reproductive cycle using an **assisted reproductive technology** (ART) results in a live birth. The cycle begins with the fertilization of one or more ova using one of the techniques described in the **Applying Theory and Research to Life** box Reproductive Technologies. The 190,733 ART cycles performed at these reporting clinics resulted in 54,323 live births (deliveries of one or more living infants) and 67,996 infants. Over 1.5 percent of all infants born in the United States are now conceived using some form of ART (Centers for Disease Control and Prevention, 2015a). For more information about infertility and reproductive technologies, you may want to visit the website of the International Council on Infertility Information Dissemination at www.inciid.org.

On an encouraging note, longitudinal studies have compared children conceived through **artificial insemination**, **surrogacy**, and **in vitro fertilization** and those who are a product of natural conception. Results of these studies find that there are no differences in child adjustment in infancy, toddlerhood, or early school age among these groups (Golombok, Murray, Jadva, MacCallum, & Lycett, 2004; Golombok et al., 2011).

Families with children conceived through alternative reproductive technologies have been compared with families with naturally conceived and adopted children. In general, parents of children conceived through both types of assisted reproduction showed more warmth and involvement with their children, higher levels of interaction, and lower levels of stress than the parents of children who were conceived naturally. Parents of adopted children typically scored in between the levels of the other two groups. In a comparison of parenting experiences for couples who conceived through a successful ART procedure and couples who conceived spontaneously, mothering experiences during the child's first year of life were more positive for the ART mothers. Difficulties with the birth, challenges associated with low-birth-weight babies, and difficulties soothing the babies were perceived as less stressful for the ART mothers than for mothers who conceived through spontaneous fertility (Repokari et al., 2006). In general, the research to date suggests a positive developmental trajectory for mother–infant relationships for infants conceived through in vitro fertilization.

Ethical Considerations of ART

ARTs have raised many legal and ethical questions.

1. One of these focuses on equitable access to these new technologies (Beckman & Harvey, 2005). A variety of social, medical, financial, and legal practices have resulted in limited access to ART for certain groups of marginalized women including unmarried women, women with alternative sexual orientations, poor women, and women whose ability to rear children is questioned, especially women with certain disabilities and older women (Brezina & Zhao, 2012; Kissel & Davey, 2012; Peterson, 2005). There is wide variability in funding for ART, including government and insurance sources, and insurers differ in the extent of coverage they will provide for these interventions.

2. As a result of fertility intervention, women in their 60s are having babies (*Sydney Morning Herald*, 2011). Ethical considerations have been raised about the use of medical technology to keep the birth window open at this advanced age. Concerns focus on the medical complications associated with pregnancy in older women and on whether older men and women can sustain effective parenting as their children move into adolescence while they enter later adulthood.

3. Another ethical concern involves attitudes about the acceptable use of reproductive technologies. For example, there is a debate about whether couples should be allowed to use reproductive technologies to select the sex of their child or to select for or against certain genetic conditions that are not life threatening such as deafness or Down syndrome (Hollingsworth, 2005; Johnston, 2005).

4. A fourth ethical concern involves the lack of information for consumers in order to make a reasoned decision about whether to elect to use reproductive technologies. Information about risks, costs, legal considerations,

Reproductive Technologies

Much of the data about reproductive technology focuses on strategies for artificially fertilizing ova and transferring them to the uterus for the prenatal period. Many websites are available for advice, exchange of information, and encouragement to individuals who are using or thinking about using these new technologies. The following sections describe reproductive technologies in use today.

Artificial Insemination

This is an old form of reproductive technology that is commonly used in animal husbandry and more recently has been applied to human fertilization. Sperm that have been donated and frozen are injected into a woman at the time of her ovulation. The most successful approach is to inject the sperm directly into the uterus (IUI, *intrauterine insemination*), thus bypassing the potentially destructive cervical environment.

Typically, the male partner is the source of the sperm; however, this is not necessary. Some sperm banks keep the donors' characteristics on file, which enables the woman to select the sperm of a donor whose features she desires in her offspring. Other banks blend sperm, so that the recipient cannot trace the donor's identity. In one recent case, a woman froze her husband's sperm and was able to conceive his child using artificial insemination after his death. Success rate: 5 percent to 30 percent per cycle using IUI (IVF-infertility.com, 2013).

Fertility Drugs

Ovulation induction is the artificial stimulation of the ovaries to produce eggs using **fertility drugs**. There is about a 90 percent chance that the ovaries can be made to work with the right drug(s) as long as the woman is not suffering ovarian failure (IVF-infertility.com, 2013). The administration of fertility drugs usually results in the release of multiple eggs at a cycle, increasing the chances that one egg will be fertilized. In about 20 percent of cases, multiple births

result. Most other assisted reproductive technologies begin with this step (i.e., using some form of medication to stimulate the ovaries to produce eggs). If this is successful, decisions must be made about how many eggs to fertilize and how many embryos to transfer to the uterus. For male infertility, when the cause of the infertility is diagnosed as due to a specific infection, or chemical or hormonal imbalance, medical treatments can be successful (UCSF Medical Center, 2015).

In Vitro Fertilization (Fertilization in an Artificial Environment)

In vitro fertilization occurs when eggs are removed from the ovary and placed in a petri dish inside an incubator. A few drops of sperm are then added to the dish. If the eggs are fertilized and the cells begin to divide, they are returned to the woman's uterus or implanted in the uterus of another woman for subsequent development. Typically, two or three embryos are transferred at once in hopes that at least one will implant and mature. Success rates for this type of ART can vary depending on whether the eggs are donated or from a nondonor woman, the age of the woman who is donating the eggs, and whether the embryo is implanted immediately or after having been frozen. The overall success rate for live births resulting from ART cycles started in 2013 was 33 percent. This figure reflects only cycles intended to be used for immediate implantation, not cycles intended to be frozen and stored for later use (Centers for Disease Control and Prevention, 2015).

Intracytoplasmic Sperm Injection

A modification of in vitro fertilization is intracytoplasmic sperm injection, in which a sperm is injected directly into the egg. This procedure is used when there is a very low sperm count or nonmotile sperm. Embryos produced by in vitro fertilization can be frozen for future use if the initial pregnancy does not reach full term.

Gamete Intrafallopian Transfer (GIFT)

Gamete intrafallopian transfer (GIFT), involves using a fiber optic instrument called a laparoscope to guide the transfer of unfertilized eggs and sperm (gametes) into the woman's fallopian tubes through small incisions in her abdomen. Fertilization takes place as it normally would, within the woman's reproductive system. These eggs and sperm may come from the couple or from other donors. Thus, the fetus may be genetically related to the man or the woman in the couple or to neither.

In Vivo Fertilization (Fertilization in a Living Body)

In vivo fertilization (fertilization in a living body) is when partners involve another woman in the conception. The second woman, who has demonstrated her fertility, is artificially inseminated with the man's sperm. Once an embryo has formed, it is transferred to the first woman's uterus, which becomes the gestational environment. The child is therefore genetically related to the man, but not to the woman.

Surrogate Mother

There are two types of surrogacy, traditional and gestational. In the traditional surrogacy, sperm from an infertile woman's husband are injected into the surrogate mother during the time of her monthly ovulation. This is repeated each month until the surrogate becomes pregnant. The surrogate mother bears the child and returns it to the couple at birth. In gestational surrogacy, the couple produces the embryo through IVF and the resulting embryo is implanted in the surrogate. Surrogacy is an expensive and legally complicated procedure. Not all states allow surrogacy, and each state has its own regulations regarding its execution. Although the use of surrogacy appears to be increasing, there are no official statistical data available to the public about the number of births in the United States

(Continued on next page)

attributed to surrogacy. One report found that the number of births in the United States through gestational surrogacy increased from 738 in 2004 to 1,593 in 2011 (Cohen, 2013).

Critical Thinking Questions

1. Summarize the costs associated with these various ARTs. You will have to go to other sources beyond this book to find out about this.

2. Evaluate the risks associated with each method. Again, you will have to draw on additional resources and use your critical thinking skills to address this question.

3. Explain the different reasons that people may have for wanting to explore ARTs. What medical or personal circumstances might lead to an individual or a couple to choose one method over another?

4. Imagine that you are advising someone who is thinking about using ART. Describe the factors you would want the person to be aware of. What would you point out related to health risks, costs, and success rates?

5. Based on your reading and your experiences, hypothesize why someone might prefer to use one of these technologies instead of adopting a child.

---

and effectiveness is often not available or not accurate (Wingert, Harvey, Duncan, & Berry, 2005).

5. Questions are raised about the limits that should be placed on the production and use of embryos in vitro. Should scientists be permitted to produce embryos from frozen sperm and egg cells for purposes other than implantation? Thousands of frozen embryos are held in various medical and laboratory facilities in the United States. Research on embryos is important for further understanding of the expression of genetic diseases, for understanding the factors associated with miscarriages, and for improving reproductive technologies. Various countries as well as states within the United States differ in their laws governing the use, preservation, and ownership of embryos produced through ART. Ethical and legal questions are being raised about the rights of parents to determine the fate of these embryos, the embryos' rights to protection and inheritance, and the responsibility of institutes and laboratories to ensure the proper use of the embryos (Krones et al., 2006).

6. Issues regarding claims to parenthood are called into question. The husband of a woman who is planning to be artificially inseminated must consent to the procedure and agree to assume legal guardianship of the offspring. But are there parental rights associated with being sperm and egg donors? Surrogacy is a growing international practice that has complex ethical implications, including the legal, financial, and kinship aspects of giving birth to another couple's child.

Countries differ in the extent to which they have developed comprehensive guidelines and legislation to address these varied ethical considerations. The state of Victoria, Australia, was a leader in introducing comprehensive legislation to regulate the use of ART in 1988. Contemporary ART legislation in Victoria is guided by the following ethical principles:

(1) the welfare and interests of persons born or to be born as a result of treatment procedures are paramount; (2) at no time should the use of treatment procedures be for the purpose of exploiting, in trade or otherwise (a) the reproductive capabilities of men or women, or (b) children born as a result of treatment procedures; (3) children born as a result of the use of donated gametes have a right to information about their genetic parents; (4) the health and wellbeing of persons undergoing treatment procedures must be protected at all times; and (5) persons seeking to undergo treatment procedures must not be discriminated against on the basis of their sexual orientation, marital status, race or religion. (Johnson, 2014)

Adoption

Adoption is an alternative to biological reproduction for those who want to be parents. In 2014, 107,918 children in foster care in the United States were waiting to be adopted. In that year, 50,644 or slightly less than 50 percent were adopted. For these children, the median length of time from the end of their parents' rights to the time they were adopted was 8.7 months (U.S. Department of Health and Human Services, 2015).

Adoption options include international adoption, adoption from a child in foster care, and adoption from a private agency. A national survey of parents of over 1.8 million adopted children conducted by the National Center for Family and Marriage Research found that across all three of these alternatives, the most common reasons parents gave for adopting a child were: (1) the desire to give a permanent family and home to a child in need; (2) a desire to expand their family; and (3) an inability to have a biologically related child (Ela, 2011).

Most agencies that provide adoption services suggest that couples who have undergone treatment for infertility need to cope with the grief and disappointment of unsuccessful outcomes before engaging in the adoption process. Once the alternative of adoption is being considered, new decisions must be faced including international versus domestic adoption, age of child, racial preferences, and adoption from a private service or a public agency. The adoption process typically includes a 3- to 6-month home study in which a social worker gathers information about the adoptive parents. This process allows the adoptive parents to consider the decision to adopt from many angles and also allows the agency to reach an informed assessment of whether the prospective parents will be able to provide a caring, supportive family for the adoptive child (Arcus & Chambers, 2008; Pertman, 2011).

FURTHER REFLECTION *Imagine that you were faced with the challenge of infertility. How might you cope? What alternatives would you be willing to consider: childlessness, adoption, fertility drugs, artificial reproductive technologies, surrogacy? How important is it to you to have a genetically related child?*

Development in the First Trimester

The period of pregnancy—typically 40 weeks after the last menstrual period, or 38 weeks from ovulation—is often conceptualized in three 3-month periods called **trimesters**. Perhaps because development is so rapid and dramatic during the first trimester, it is divided further into the **germinal period**, the **embroynic period**, and the **fetal period**. Each trimester brings changes in the status of the developing fetus and its supporting systems (Moore, Persaud, Torchia, 2015). These changes are summarized briefly in Table 4.2. The pregnant woman also experiences changes during the trimesters. In the first trimester, many women are not certain that they are pregnant. By the last trimester, though, the woman is usually certain, and so is everyone else! There are many apps available to follow the process of pregnancy and prenatal development. Four that are widely recommended are WebMdPregnancy, The pregnancy companion, The Ovia, and I am totally pregnant. These apps help women and their partners understand the biological changes associated with pregnancy, likely physical symptoms, images and characteristics of the developing fetus, questions to ask one's physician, suggestions for maintaining good health and fitness during pregnancy, and access to additional resources.

The Germinal Period

After fertilization, the egg begins to divide. At this time, the cell material is referred to as a zygote until implantation. The first series of cell divisions does not increase the mass of the cells, nor do the cells take on specialized functions; rather, the cell material is redistributed among several parts. These are the cells referred to earlier in the chapter as *stem cells*. When implantation is successful, by the 6th day after fertilization, the egg makes contact with the lining of the uterus and begins to attach itself there. At this point, the cells are referred to as an **embryo**. Sometimes, the egg does not reach the uterus but attaches itself to the fallopian tube or even to some area of the intestine. This can be a life-threatening condition. The embryo may grow in these locations until the organ ruptures.

The Embryonic Period

The 3 weeks following implantation are devoted primarily to elaboration of the supportive elements that will house the embryo. An **amniotic sac** surrounds the embryo and fills with a clear, watery fluid. This fluid acts as a cushion that buffers the embryo and permits it to move about and change position. Once the embryo is firmly implanted in the uterus, special cells in the placenta produce a hormone that maintains the uterine lining. This hormone is excreted through the kidneys, so a urine sample can be evaluated to determine its presence. Home pregnancy tests are based on the detection of this hormone in a small drop of urine and are accurate 1 or 2 days after implantation. A large number of pregnancies are spontaneously aborted in these early weeks, usually as a result of some major abnormalities of the embryo.

The **placenta** is an organ that is newly formed with each pregnancy and is expelled at birth. Nutrients necessary for the embryo's growth pass through the placenta, as does the embryo's waste, which then passes into the mother's blood. Thus, the placenta is an exchange station at which adult material is synthesized for the embryo's use and foreign materials harmful to the embryo's development can be screened out. However, this screening is imperfect. Even though the mother's blood and the embryo's blood are separated by independent systems, the placenta permits the two systems to come close enough that oxygen and nutrients from the mother's blood can enter the fetal system and waste products from the fetal system can be removed. In the process, certain substances in the mother's system may affect the fetal system.

Agents that can produce malformations in the fetus while the tissues and organs are forming are referred to as **teratogens**. Teratogens have a wide variety of forms, such as viruses; medicines, alcohol, and other drugs that a pregnant woman takes; and **environmental toxins**. During the first trimester—especially weeks 3 through 9—the embryo is particularly sensitive to the disruptive influences of teratogens (see FIGURE 4.8 ▶).

Table 4.2	Major Developments in Fetal Growth During the Three Trimesters	
First Trimester	**Second Trimester**	**Third Trimester**
Fertilization	Sucking and swallowing	Nervous system matures
Growth of the amniotic sac	Preference for sweet taste	Coordination of sucking and swallowing
Growth of the placenta	Skin ridges on fingers and toes	Mechanisms for regulating body temperature
Emergence of body parts	Hair on scalp, eyebrows, back, arms, legs	More efficient digestion and excretion
Differentiation of sex organs	Sensitivity to touch, taste, light	Degeneration of the placenta toward the end of the ninth month
Initial formation of central nervous system	Sucks thumb	
Movement	6-month average size: 10 inches, 2 pounds	9-month average size: 20 inches, 7 to 7½ pounds
Grasp reflex		
Babinski reflex		
Heartbeat		
3-month average size: 3 inches, about 2/5 ounce		

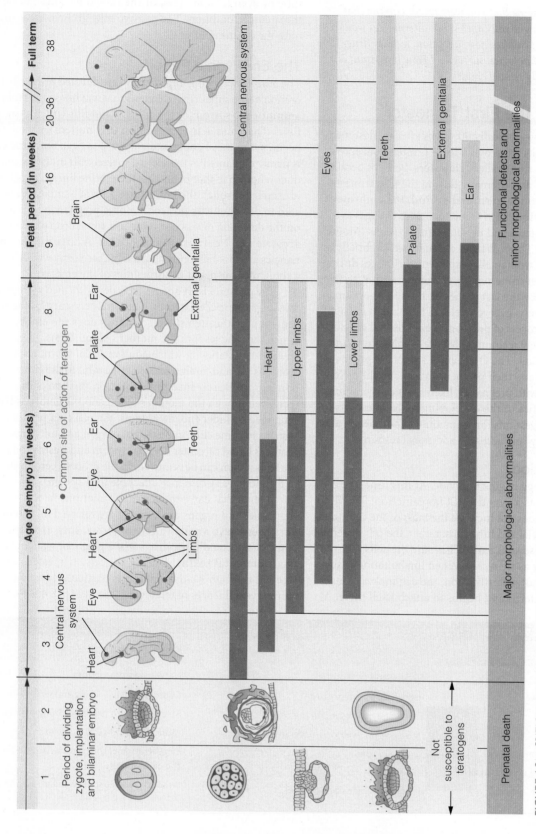

FIGURE 4.8 ▶ CRITICAL PERIODS IN PRENATAL DEVELOPMENT During the first 2 weeks of development, the embryo is usually not susceptible to teratogens. During these predifferentiation stages, a substance either damages all or most of the cells of the embryo, resulting in its death, or damages only a few cells, allowing the embryo to recover without developing defects. Dark bars denote highly sensitive periods for particular organs or organ systems; light bars indicate stages that are less sensitive to teratogens. Severe mental retardation may result from the exposure of the embryo or fetus to teratogenic agents, such as high levels of radiation, from the 8th to the 16th week.

Source: Rathus, Childhood and Adolescence, 6e, 9781305504592, page 96 figure 3.05

In the third and fourth weeks, the embryo's cells differentiate rapidly, taking on the specialized structures that will permit them to carry out their unique functions in the body. Similar cells are grouped into tissues that gradually emerge as body organs. The first essential changes include the establishment of the body form as an elongated cylinder and the formation of structures that will eventually become the brain and the heart. The neural tube, which is the structural basis of the central nervous system (CNS), begins to take shape at the end of the third week after conception. Cells in the neural tube are produced at the miraculous rate of 250,000 a minute over the first 5 weeks, as the tube is differentiated into five bulges that are the forerunners of the major subdivisions of the brain.

The central nervous system begins to develop early in the prenatal period and continues to develop throughout childhood and adolescence. Most of the neurons that will make up the cerebral cortex are produced by the end of the second trimester. By birth, the infant's brain contains roughly 100 billion neurons, ready to be linked and organized into networks as the infant responds to environmental stimulation and patterned experience (Aoki & Siekevitz, 1988; Lagercrantz, Hanson, Ment, & Peebles, 2010).

By the end of the fourth week, the head, the upper trunk, and the lower trunk are visible, as are the limb buds and the forerunners of the forebrain, midbrain, hindbrain, eyes, and ears. The embryo has increased 50 times in length and 40,000 times in weight since the moment of fertilization.

By the end of the second month, the embryo looks quite human. It weighs about 2.25 grams and is about 28 millimeters (1 inch) long. Almost all the internal organs are formed, as are the external features of the face, limbs, fingers, and toes. At 8 weeks, the embryo will respond to mild stimulation. The embryonic period ends about 10 weeks after the last menstrual period—most of the essential structures are formed by this time. The term **fetus** is used from this point until birth.

The Fetal Period

In the third month, the fetus grows to 3 inches, and its weight increases to 14 grams. The head is about one third of the total body length. During this month, the fetus assumes the *fetal position*, arms curled up toward the face and knees bent in to the stomach. The eyelids are fused.

A dramatic change takes place in the sex organs during this period. All embryos go through a bisexual stage, during which no sex-linked characteristics can be discerned. Both female and male embryos have a surface mass that becomes the testes in male fetuses and eventually deteriorates in female fetuses, when new sex cells grow to form the ovaries. Both male and female embryos have two sets of sex ducts. In male fetuses, the sperm ducts develop and the female ducts dissolve. In female fetuses, the fallopian tubes, the uterus, and the vagina develop, and the other ducts degenerate. Finally, both male and female embryos have a conical area that is the outlet for the bladder duct. In males this area forms into the penis and scrotum. In females, it remains to form the clitoris, which is surrounded by the genital swellings of the labia majora.

Differentiation of the male and female genitalia is guided by genetic information. In the presence of the maleness gene, SRY, the undifferentiated embryonic tissue is transformed into the testes. The testes then produce gonadal steroid hormones that facilitate the further elaboration of male genitalia and internal reproductive structures. Genes carried on the X chromosome are thought to guide the formation of the ovaries (Crooks & Baur, 2016).

The genetic factors that produce the differentiation of the fetus as male or female appear to influence more than the formation of the reproductive organs and the production of hormones. Research on the organization and structure of the brain suggests that during fetal and early postnatal development, sex hormones direct male and female brains along slightly different paths.

The brain is in reality not a unitary organ like the liver or the kidney. It is a compilation of multiple independent yet interacting groups of cells that are subject to both external and internal factors. .... As a result, it is quite literally impossible for the brain to take on a uniform "maleness" or "femaleness." Instead, the brain is a mix of relative degrees of masculinization in some areas and feminization in others. On average, there are likely to be some areas that are more strongly feminized in a female and others that are more strongly masculinized in a male, but averages are never predictive of an individual's profile. Moreover, a mosaic is not a blend—there is not a continuum of maleness to femaleness—and there are many parameters that are neutral in regard to sex, with no consistent differences between males and females.

Evolutionarily, the creation of a **maleness–femaleness** mosaic within one brain makes sense, providing organisms with greater variability and therefore adaptability to changing environments. (McCarthy, 2015)

Although males and females are very similar in most psychological variables, and in particular have similar distributions in measured intelligence, studies by numerous researchers have shown that sex differences in hormonal levels influence differences in specific problem-solving areas and intellectual strengths. Some of the areas in which males and females have been shown to differ include verbal ability, visual-spatial ability, and mathematical ability. We are still not sure what the route is from the developing fetal brain structure to cognitive functioning in childhood and beyond, but it is increasingly clear that anatomical variations in regions of the brain and their interconnections are tied to sex-linked variations in certain specialized problem-solving capacities (Kimura, 2002, 2004).

The 3-month-old fetus moves spontaneously and has both a grasp reflex and a Babinski reflex, in which the toes extend and fan out in response to a mild stroke on the sole of the foot. When an amplified stethoscope, called a Doppler, is placed on the mother's abdomen, the fetal heartbeat can be heard through the uterine wall by the expectant parents as well as the physician and nurse. For expectant parents, listening to the fetal heartbeat is one of the first experiences that transforms the fetus from something abstract and remote to a concrete, vital reality.

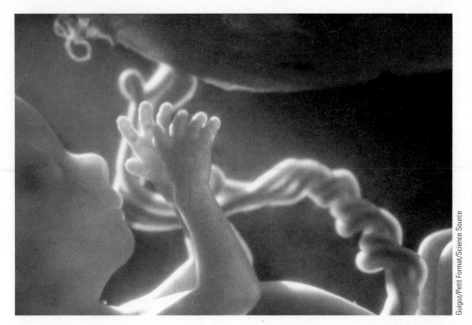

At 16 weeks, the fetus is about 6.4 inches (16 cm) long and is clearly recognizable as a human child. The fetus has assumed what is known as the "fetal position"—arms curled up near the head and legs bent in toward the stomach—a position that remains part of the human behavioral repertoire throughout life.

fills with amniotic fluid; thus, the sense of smell is probably not functional until birth.

The external ear canal is filled with fluid. The fetus does not respond to sound until the third trimester; however, the semicircular canals of the inner ear are sensitive to stimulation. The nerve fibers that connect the retina to the brain are developed by 6 months, and infants born prematurely at this time respond to light.

At 25 weeks, the fetus functions well within its uterine environment. It swallows, digests, excretes, moves about, sucks its thumb, rests, and grows. However, the nervous system, which begins to develop at 3 weeks, is still not mature enough to coordinate the many systems that must function simultaneously to ensure survival. The outlook for survival of the 22- to 24-week-old fetus is improving, especially if the infant is treated in a special care center

Development in the Second Trimester

During the second trimester, the average fetus grows to 10 inches and increases in weight to almost 2 pounds. The fetus continues to grow at the rate of about an inch every 10 days from the fifth month until the end of the pregnancy. During this trimester, the uterus itself begins to stretch and grow. It rises into the mother's abdominal cavity and expands until, by the end of the ninth month, it is pushing against the ribs and diaphragm. The reality of a growing life becomes more evident to the pregnant woman during this trimester as she observes the changes in her body and experiences the early fetal movements, called **quickening**. These movements first feel like light bubbles or twitches; later, they can be identified as the foot, elbow, or fist of the restless resident.

During the fourth month, the fetus begins to suck and swallow. Whenever the fetus opens its mouth, amniotic fluid enters and cycles through the system. This fluid provides some nutrients in addition to those absorbed through the placenta. The 4-month-old fetus shows some preference for a sweet taste: If sugar is introduced into the amniotic fluid, it will swallow the fluid at a faster rate.

In the fifth month, the skin begins to thicken, and a cheesy coating of dead cells and oil, the *vernix caseosa*, covers the skin. The individuality of the fetus is marked by the pattern of skin ridges on the fingers and toes. Hair covers the scalp, eyebrows, back, arms, and legs.

The sensory receptors of the fetus are well established by the end of the sixth month. The fetus is sensitive to touch and may react to it with a muscle movement. It will also stick out its tongue in response to a bitter taste. Throughout the sixth month, the nostrils are plugged by skin cells. When these cells dissolve, the nose

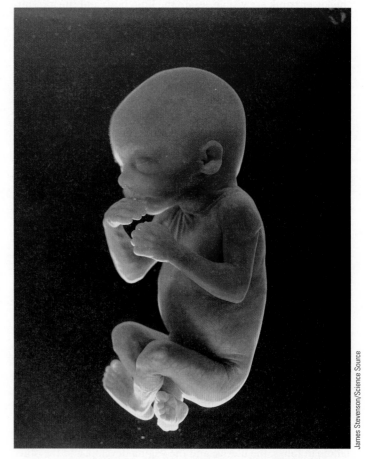

At 23 weeks, the fetus is about 12 inches (30 cm) long, still small enough to have room to swim about in the expanding uterus. As any pregnant woman will tell you, the fetus is active at this stage, kicking, grasping, waving its arms, and turning over.

where more aggressive interventions are applied. In one study, 39 percent of infants born at 22 to 24 weeks of gestational age survived, with survival rates varying notably depending on the kind of center where the infants were treated. For infants born at 25 to 27 weeks, the survival rate was 81 percent (Smith et al., 2012). Researchers in the United Kingdom have found that the 22- to 24-week-old babies who are born at medical centers that specialize in the care of very small babies have a better chance of survival than those who are transferred from smaller hospitals to these centers after birth (Salter, 2014). These advances in the treatment of extremely pre-term infants are raising new questions about policies related to fetal viability and its relationship to abortion practices.

Development in the Third Trimester

In the last trimester, the average fetus grows from 10 to 20 inches and increases in weight from 2 to 7 or 7½ pounds. These increases in body size and weight are paralleled by a maturation of the central nervous system. From 20 to 28 weeks of gestational age, fetal heart rate declines and variability and accelerations in heart rate increase. In the third trimester, there are longer periods of quiet between fetal movements. By combining recordings from ultrasound and monitoring of fetal heart rate, patterns of fetal behavioral states have been documented. They include periods of quiet, similar to non-REM sleep in newborns; periods of frequent movement with sleep-like heartbeat, similar to REM sleep; periods of quiet wakefulness; and periods of active wakefulness (Nijhuis, 2003). Moreover, fetal heart rate and fetal movement become increasingly coordinated. These patterns suggest a critical integration of the somatic and cardiac processes within the central nervous system. At some point between 28 and 32 weeks, these patterns of increase stop and are replaced by a leveling off or slight decrease. This pattern is interpreted to mean that a certain critical level of neurological maturation is in place by 32 weeks. Evidence to support this idea is found in the cognitive competence of pre-term infants who are born at about 32 weeks (DiPietro et al., 2004; DiPietro et al., 2010).

Additional evidence of cognitive maturation is provided by studies of fetal memory. By the age of 30 weeks gestational age, the fetus appears to recognize and remember the sensation of a vibroacoustic stimulus that is applied to the mother's abdomen. Fetal movement in the second following the stimulus is taken as evidence of a response. The absence of fetal movement on four trials following several consecutive positive responses is taken as evidence of habituation or familiarity with the stimulus. By 38 weeks of gestational age, the fetus recognizes these vibro-acoustic stimuli even 4 weeks after the last testing session (Dirix, Nijhuis, Jongsma, & Hornstra, 2009).

Research on fetal sensitivity to sound has a long history. A number of studies have demonstrated that the fetus is sensitive to auditory stimulation in the form of music as well as speech. A fetus experiences its mother's speech sounds during the third trimester, becoming familiar with the sound of her voice and the features of her spoken language (DeCasper et al., 1994). Neural networks sensitive to properties of the mother's voice and

native-language speech are being formed during the prenatal period (Kisilevsky et al., 2009).

In one study, pregnant women played a recording of *Twinkle Twinkle Little Star* five times a week at loud volume beginning in the eighth month of gestational age. At birth, and again at 4 months after birth, evidence from EEG recordings demonstrated that the babies recognized the melody, and reacted differently when notes were identical or changed from the tune they heard prenatally (Partanen, Kujala, Tervaniemi, & Huotilainen, 2013). Studies of 36- to 39-week-old fetuses have found that they are sensitive to changes in low-pitched musical notes, to pulsing as compared to continuous sounds, and to changes in speech sounds (Byers-Heinlein, Burns, & Werker, 2010: Groome et al., 2000; Lecanuet, Graniere- Deferre, Jacquet, & DeCasper, 2000).

Advantages of a Full-Term Fetus

The advantages that a full-term fetus has over a premature, 28-week-old fetus include (1) the ability to begin and maintain regular breathing; (2) a stronger sucking response; (3) well-coordinated swallowing movements; (4) stronger peristalsis and, therefore, more efficient digestion and waste excretion; and (5) a more fully balanced control of body temperature.

The full-term fetus has been able to take advantage of minerals in the mother's diet for the formation of tooth enamel. As the placenta begins to degenerate in the last month of pregnancy, antibodies against various diseases that have been formed in the mother's blood pass into the fetal bloodstream. They provide the fetus with immunity to many diseases during the first few months of life.

The uterus cannot serve indefinitely as the home of the fetus. Several factors lead to the eventual termination of the fetal-uterine relationship. First, as the placenta degenerates, antibodies that form in both the mother's and the fetus's blood would destroy the blood of the other. Second, because the placenta does not grow much larger than 2 pounds, the fetus, as it reaches its maximum size, cannot obtain enough nutrients to sustain life. Third, the fetal head cannot grow much larger than the pelvic opening without endangering the brain in the birth process. Even though soft connecting membranes permit the skull plates to overlap, head size is a factor that limits fetal growth. The photo in this section shows the footprints of an infant born prematurely and an infant who has reached full gestational age.

Late in pregnancy, the fetal brain begins to produce hormones that increase the production of estrogen in the placenta. This, in turn, leads to a shift from mild to strong uterine contractions, which result in dilation of the cervix, rupture of the amniotic sac, and delivery (Cunningham et al., 2014; Nathanielsz, 1996). The approximate time from conception to birth is 38 weeks. However, there is variability in the duration of pregnancies and in the size of full-term infants, even infants born to the same mother.

FURTHER REFLECTION Suppose your work exposed you to environmental toxins that might have a negative impact on your unborn child. What would you do?

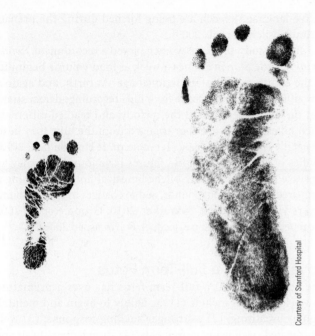

These are the birth footprints of a baby born prematurely at 23 weeks, and one born at a full 40-week gestational age.

The Birth Process

OBJECTIVE 4 Describe the birth process and analyze factors that contribute to infant mortality.

Birth is initiated by involuntary contractions of the uterine muscles, commonly referred to as **labor**. The length of time from the beginning of labor to the birth of the infant is highly variable. The average time is 14 hours for women undergoing their first labor and 8 hours for women undergoing later labors.

The uterine contractions serve two central functions: *effacement* and *dilation*. **Effacement**, or thinning, is the shortening of the cervical canal. **Dilation** is the gradual enlargement of the cervix from an opening only millimeters wide to one of about 10 centimeters—large enough for the baby to pass through. Effacement and dilation occur without deliberate effort by the mother. Once the cervix is fully enlarged, the mother can assist in the birth by exerting pressure on the abdominal walls of the uterus. The baby, too, helps in the birth process by squirming, turning its head, and pushing against the birth canal.

Stages of Labor

The medical profession describes three stages of labor. The first stage begins with the onset of uterine contractions and ends with the full dilation of the cervix; this is the longest stage. The second stage involves the expulsion of the fetus. It begins at full dilation and ends with the delivery of the baby. The third stage begins with delivery and ends with the expulsion of the placenta. This stage usually lasts 5 to 10 minutes.

These three stages of labor do not precisely parallel the personal experience of childbirth. For example, although the expulsion of the placenta is considered a unique stage of labor in the medical model, it is rarely mentioned in women's accounts of their birth experiences. On the other hand, many of the signs of impending labor that occur in the last weeks of pregnancy are often included in women's accounts of labor.

In terms of the psychological adaptation to the birth process, labor can be viewed as having five phases: (1) early signs that labor is approaching; (2) strong, regular uterine contractions, signaling that labor has begun and generally accompanied by a move from the home to the hospital or birthing center; (3) the transition phase, during which contractions are strong, rest times between contractions are short, and women experience the greatest difficulty or discomfort; (4) the birth process, which allows the mother's active participation in the delivery and is generally accompanied by a move from the labor area to the more sterile delivery room; and (5) the postpartum period, which involves the initial interactions with the newborn, physiological changes that mark a return to the prepregnant state, and the return home.

Cesarean Delivery

Sometimes a normal, spontaneous vaginal delivery would be dangerous to the mother or the newborn (Cunningham et al., 2014). One alternative is to remove the baby surgically through an incision in the uterine wall, a procedure called **cesarean section**. The incidence of cesarean deliveries in the United States increased from 5.5 percent of births in 1970 to 33 percent in 2013 (Martin et al., 2015). Cesarean deliveries may be planned or unplanned. The procedure may be used if labor is severely prolonged and the fetus appears to be at risk due to lack of oxygen. It may also be used when the infant is in the breech position (feet or buttocks first rather than head first) or if the mother's pelvis is too small for the infant's head to pass through. Physicians often recommend a repeat cesarean if the woman has delivered by cesarean section before. The rate of cesarean deliveries is higher for mothers age 30 and older than for younger mothers.

The cesarean delivery makes childbirth a surgical procedure, requiring anesthetics, intravenous feeding of the mother, and a prolonged recovery period. Although the procedure undoubtedly saves many infants and mothers who would not survive vaginal childbirth, there is some concern that it is being misused for the convenience of health professionals or busy mothers who want to be able to schedule deliveries and thus avoid waiting for the unpredictable onset of labor. In a national goal statement, *Healthy People 2020*, the U.S. Public Health Service called for a reduction of the national cesarean rate for both first-time deliveries and for births following a cesarean to an overall rate of 15 percent (U.S. Department of Health and Human Services, 2010)—a goal implying that a substantial number of the current cesarean procedures are not necessary.

Infant Mortality

The **infant mortality rate** is the number of infants who die during the first year of life per 1,000 live births during that year. In 2013, the U.S. rate was estimated at 5.96 deaths per 1,000 live births (Mathews, MacDorman, & Thoma, 2015). The rate for non-Hispanic Black babies in the United States in 2013—11.11 deaths per 1,000 live births—was higher than the infant mortality rates in countries such as Chile, Botswana, Cuba, Serbia, and Poland that are considered economically emergent nations (Central Intelligence Agency, 2015).

Roughly two thirds of infant deaths occur during the first month after birth. Most of these deaths result from severe birth defects, premature birth, or **sudden infant death syndrome** (SIDS), in which apparently healthy babies are put to bed and are later found dead with no clear explanation, even after autopsy.

Infant mortality rates are influenced by many factors, including the (1) frequency of birth complications; (2) robustness of the infants who are being born, which is influenced by their prenatal nutrition and degree of exposure to viruses or bacteria, damaging X rays, drugs, and other teratogens; (3) mother's age; and (4) facilities that are available for prenatal and newborn care. Infant mortality rates are 25 times higher for infants born at birth weights below 2500 grams than for infants born at 2500 grams or more. If the conditions leading to prematurity and associated low birth weight could be altered, the U.S. infant mortality rate would be significantly improved (Mathews, MacDorman, & Thoma, 2015).

Infant mortality rates vary from one country and region of the world to another. In 2015, the infant mortality rate in Japan was 2.08, but in that same year, the infant mortality rate in 13 other countries of the world was more than 70 (The Central Intelligence Agency, 2015). The United States, with all its resources and advanced technology, ranks behind other industrialized countries, including Australia, Canada, France, Germany, Israel, Italy, Japan, the Netherlands, South Korea, Spain, Switzerland, and the United Kingdom. Within the United States, regional infant mortality rates range from a low of 4.18 per 1,000 in the state of Massachusetts, to a high of 9.60 in Mississippi (Mathews, MacDorman, & Thoma, 2015).

The density of low-income populations, availability of educational materials on the impact of diet and drugs on the developing fetus, and adequacy of medical facilities for high-risk newborns all contribute to the regional variations in infant death rates among populations of different incomes. Children conceived in poverty are at the greatest risk of infant mortality. Their mothers receive poorer quality prenatal care and are exposed to more dangerous environmental and health factors during the prenatal period than are mothers of children conceived in more advantaged families. The chances that any one infant will survive the stresses of birth depend on the convergence of biological, environmental, cultural, and economic influences on the child's intrauterine growth, delivery, and postnatal care.

FURTHER REFLECTION How do you account for the fact that the United States is behind so many other industrialized countries in the rate of infant mortality? Design an intervention that would contribute to lowering infant mortality rates in the United States.

The Mother, the Fetus, and the Psychosocial Environment

OBJECTIVE 5 Analyze ways that the pregnant woman and the developing fetus influence each other, focusing on how pregnancy affects a childbearing woman and expectant father, and the impact of environmental influences on fetal growth, such as a woman's age, drug use, nutrition, environmental toxins, and stress.

The course of prenatal development is guided by genetic information that unfolds in the context of the pregnant woman's biopsychosocial environment. A woman's health, her attitudes toward pregnancy and childbirth, her lifestyle, the resources available to her during her pregnancy, and the behavior demanded of her by her culture all influence her sense of well-being. Many of these same factors may directly affect the health and growth of the fetus. In the next section, we discuss the impact of the fetus on the pregnant woman, including how the pregnancy might affect the infant's father and his relationship to the mother. The subsequent section focuses on the impact of the pregnant woman on the fetus and the many factors that contribute to the quality of the intrauterine environment.

The Impact of the Fetus on the Pregnant Woman

Consider some of the ways in which a fetus influences a pregnant woman. In the following sections we consider physical changes, changes in roles and status, and changes in the woman's emotional state. Pregnancy initiates sweeping hormonal changes that prepare the uterus to host the developing fetus. Over the months of pregnancy, the uterus changes in size and shape, altering the woman's physical appearance and placing new pressures on internal organs. Beginning in the second trimester, women experience fetal movement. Research that focused on the synchrony between fetal movement and maternal heart rate showed that after about 20 weeks **gestational age** (the age of the fetus from the time of conception until birth), a regular pattern could be observed in which fetal movement is followed after 2 or 3 seconds by an increase in maternal heart rate. Fetal movement occurs about once every minute. Even when the pregnant woman is not aware of the movement, changes in heart rate following movement were observed. One can think of the fetus as making repeated and continuous signals that engage the mother's autonomic nervous system and thereby begin a process through which the mother's level of arousal is linked to the infant's state (DiPietro et al., 2006).

Pregnancy alters a woman's body image and her sense of well-being. Some women feel especially vigorous and energetic during much of their pregnancy; others experience distressing symptoms such as nausea, backache, swelling, headache, and irritability. Some women say they have difficulty remembering things during their last trimester. In some cases, pregnancy is accompanied by serious illnesses that threaten the mother's health. To learn more about physical changes that accompany pregnancy and recommendations for maintaining one's health during pregnancy, you may want to visit the website on pregnancy from Medline Plus, the resource of the U.S. National Library of Medicine, https://www.nlm.nih.gov/medlineplus/pregnancy.html.

Changes in Roles and Social Status

Women who become pregnant may be treated in new ways by people close to them and by their broader communities. Usually, fathers become more concerned for and supportive of their pregnant partners, and pregnant women may also be viewed in a new light by their peers. In some communities, adolescent girls who become pregnant feel ashamed or guilty and may be scorned. In others, becoming pregnant during adolescence is

Ariel Skelley/Blend Images/Getty Images

Laurie's experience of pregnancy is closely tied to the reactions of her loving partner and the enthusiastic curiosity of her daughter, who will soon become an older sib.

viewed by the peer group as an accomplishment, a sign of maturity. Work settings differ in the ways they respond to the needs of pregnant women. Some settings may accommodate pregnant women by giving them lighter duties or fewer responsibilities. In other settings, pregnant women may be forced to take unpaid leave if they cannot perform physical tasks or to avoid exposure to harmful chemicals. Pregnancy may be viewed as an annoyance, something that is likely to interfere with productivity, or it may be viewed as one of many physical conditions that must be accommodated.

Within her family, a pregnant woman is likely to be treated with new levels of concern and care. By giving birth to a first child, a woman transforms her mother and father into grandparents and her brothers and sisters into uncles and aunts. Moreover, pregnancy may strengthen the gender identity of the baby's mother or father. Just as infertility threatens one's gender identity, becoming pregnant may be viewed as confirmation of a woman's femininity and a man's virility in impregnating her.

In some societies, pregnancy and childbirth confer special status on a woman. In Japan, for example, traditional values place motherhood above all other women's roles. When they become mothers, Japanese women begin to have an impact on government, community, and public life as the people who are especially responsible for molding and shaping the next generation. For Mexican American women, childbearing is likely to be viewed within a broad religious context. Despite their difficult economic and social conditions, women who are Mexican immigrants in the United States have relatively fewer low-birthweight babies than mothers from other low-income groups. One explanation is that the strong value for *familialism* in Latino/a families brings forth substantial family support that buffers the pregnant woman from the adverse effects of poverty (Campos, et al., 2008; Sagrestano et al., 1999; Sherraden & Barrera, 1996). See the **Applying Theory and Research to Life** box that discusses the positive effects for the mother of having a doula or supportive companion during the labor and delivery.

Being Pregnant Changes a Woman's Emotional State

For most people, being pregnant is a very powerful experience. Thus it is no surprise that mothers and fathers have strong emotional reactions to pregnancy. A woman's attitude toward her unborn child may be pride, excitement, acceptance, or rejection. In most normal pregnancies, women may experience negative feelings such as anxiety and depression as well as positive feelings such as excitement and hopefulness. The normal physical changes of pregnancy may become a source of stress for a pregnant woman. These changes include feelings of nausea, being tired, having indigestion, or backaches. Changing hormone levels may result in sleeplessness, mood swings, and irritability.

In addition to these troubling physical symptoms, the expectant woman has recurring worries and fears about the childbirth experience, whether the baby will be healthy, and her own well-being. These fears may be accentuated if the woman has heard about problems with childbirth from friends, relatives, or health care professionals (March of Dimes, 2013). In one study, women who had attended childbirth classes were interviewed 4 weeks after they gave birth. Thirty-four percent of the women reported that their childbirth experience was traumatic, including many who had symptoms of post-traumatic stress disorder (Soet, Brack, & Dilorio, 2003). Among women who have had previous pregnancies, worries may focus on recollections about the difficulties of delivery and the health and care of the new baby (Melender, 2002). Some women receive troubling information during an ultrasound screening about possible fetal abnormalities. This information adds to anxiety during pregnancy (Brisch et al., 2003).

Certain psychosocial factors are associated with increased anxiety and depression during pregnancy, including exposure to stressors, lack of resources, the absence of a supportive partner, and experiencing an unwanted pregnancy. It is not uncommon for depression to be higher in the early months of pregnancy and then to decline in the months after the baby is born. Women who show the greatest drop in depression over the pregnancy have relatively more financial resources, more social support, and fewer other life stressors (Ritter, Hobfoll, Lavin, Cameron, & Hulsizer, 2000).

The Doula or Birth Companion

The idea of having a supportive companion available to women during childbirth has been formalized in the role of **doula**. The term *doula* comes from a Greek word for handmaiden, referring to the primary servant for the woman of the household. Before the introduction of hospital deliveries, most cultures had a role for a close female companion who accompanied a woman during childbirth. The contemporary doula is trained to offer information as well as physical and emotional support during labor, delivery, and the early weeks following childbirth. Her role is to remain at the side of the laboring mother to help her have a safe, reassuring childbirth experience. She does not take the place of the midwife, obstetrician, nurses, or the mother's partner (Doulas of North America, 2013). According to the Doula of North America website, when a doula is present during and after childbirth, "women report greater satisfaction with their birth experience, make more positive assessments of their babies, have fewer caesareans and

requests fewer medical interventions, and (experience) less postpartum depression."

A review of 15 studies involving more than 12,000 women examined additional empirical support for the contribution of the doula in childbirth (Hodnett, 2003). The studies were conducted in Australia, Belgium, Botswana, Canada, Finland, France, Greece, Guatemala, Mexico, South Africa, and the United States, under very different hospital conditions. All of the studies contrasted the childbirth experiences of women who did and did not have a supportive companion available during labor and delivery. Mothers who were accompanied by a supportive companion had shorter labors and fewer obstetrical difficulties. The presence of the doula has been shown to reduce the incidence of low-birth weight infants. The presumption is that a woman who is attended by a doula has lower levels of anxiety, thus reducing the release of hormones that might contribute to obstetrical difficulties and neonatal distress

(Corter & Fleming, 2002; Kozhimannil, Almanza, Vogelsang, & Hardeman, 2015).

The presence of a doula is especially valuable in cases where women would ordinarily labor alone with just the presence of the medical staff. In a study of low-income women who were at risk for adverse birth outcomes, one group that received support from a doula was compared to a group that chose not to receive this support. All the mothers had been enrolled in a *Healthy Moms, Healthy Babies* childbirth class for at least three sessions. Doula-assisted mothers were four times less likely to have a low birth weight (LBW) baby, two times less likely to experience a birth complication involving themselves or their baby, and significantly more likely to initiate breastfeeding (Gruber, Cupito, & Dobson, 2013). The benefit of the doula appears to endure beyond childbirth, contributing to increased maternal responsiveness and competence in the months following the birth ((McComish & Visger, 2009, Nommsen-Rivers, Mastergeorge, Hansen, Cullum, & Dewey, 2009). To find out more about doulas and their role as birth companions, visit DONA International at www.DONA.org.

Critical Thinking Questions

1. Explain why and how the presence of a supportive companion might shorten labor and ease delivery.
2. List some characteristics that would make a person an effective doula.
3. Design a study to evaluate the benefits of a doula in childbirth.
4. Analyze the characteristics of the U.S. birth culture that might prevent or support the inclusion of a doula as a component of prenatal care and childbirth.

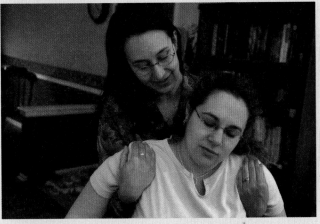

This certified labor doula is helping Leanne prepare for the upcoming childbirth experience.

Karl Gehring/Getty Images

Fathers' Involvement During Pregnancy

Just like women, men have diverse reactions to the idea of having children. Their reproductive behaviors reflect their own psychosocial maturity, their perceptions about the quality and stability of the relationships they are in, the stability of their employment, and their readiness to embrace the responsibilities of fatherhood. Some men worry about the economic ramifications of the impending birth. If they are unemployed or underemployed, they may worry about money, have low confidence, feel they are not worth much, or be fearful that the mother's income will decrease. And some men do not seem to take any responsibility for the pregnancy they are responsible for. In a study of an ethnically diverse sample of low-income men, 171 were aware of their responsibility for 424 pregnancies (Augustine, Nelson, & Edin, 2009). Among this sample, 47 percent described the pregnancies a result of "just not thinking." These men did not have a plan to have a child and did nothing to prevent it. In contrast, some men reported that having a child brought them a new level of self-respect. Dante, a 38-year-old African American father who had been living a high-risk lifestyle before the birth of his child, told researchers, "I know for a fact that if it wasn't for my son and I was just a single guy [without kids] my life would be chaos!" (Augustine et al., 2009, p. 109).

The many different types of relationships that are possible between a woman and her partner have implications for both the emotional state of the mother during pregnancy and the psychosocial development of the child. Research supports the idea of continuity between the quality of the relationship between the partners during the prenatal period and the quality of their parenting in the early years of childhood. This continuity in turn has implications for the child's growth and development. Partners who show high levels of negative interaction or detachment during the prenatal period have trouble providing an emotionally secure environment for their newborn child. Anger, mistrust, or avoidance between partners are all likely to be a source of stress for a pregnant woman.

In contrast, couples characterized by positive mutuality, partner autonomy, and the ability to confront problems and regulate negative affect create a positive emotional climate for the pregnancy. Feelings of safety, security, and being loved and valued within a relationship can contribute to a woman's ability to manage the other worries that are associated with her pregnancy and delivery.

In the first trimester, involved fathers are able to hear the fetal heartbeat amplified through the Doppler. Through the use of ultrasound, fathers are able to visualize the developing fetus. During the second trimester, a father is able to make contact with his unborn child as he places his hand on his partner's abdomen and feels the life and movement within. For many men, this is a time of great joy, as the prospect of fatherhood becomes more than abstract empathy with his partner's experiences. Investment in the new life begins to increase as the reality of the fetus becomes more concrete. These times can provide the basis for a new kind of intimacy for the expectant couple as they begin to talk about their plans and hopes for the child, share their feelings about the pregnancy and upcoming birth, and explore their feelings related to assuming responsibility for the care and protection of their child.

However, some men turn away from the mother during her pregnancy. They may find features of pregnancy repugnant. They may fear losing their place in the mother's affection. They may become depressed, feeling that they cannot live up to the expectations for caring for and supporting their partner and the child (Deater-Deckard, Pickering, Dunn, & Golding, 1998). A father's depression may, in turn, have a negative effect on the mother, leaving her depressed and aware that she is without the support she was expecting.

Fathers are becoming increasingly involved in supporting their partner's pregnancy and delivery. This support is both an important aspect of identification with the father role and a great emotional comfort to the mother.

In some circumstances, men think that the fetus and then the baby threaten their own position with the mother, and they feel resentful and competitive toward the woman and the unborn infant. This resentment may lead to violence. The incidence of intimate partner violence (IPV) is difficult to summarize, due to differences in sample size, measurement approaches, and the timing of the assessment in reported studies. However, the problem of IPV during pregnancy appears to be widespread. One study of a rural sample of U.S. women reported that 81 percent of prenatal patients at a family practice clinic reported some type of IPV during pregnancy; 28 percent reported physical IPV, and 20 percent reported sexual violence (Bailey, 2007). Many studies find higher rates of prematurity and low birth weight in infants born to women who were victims of IPV (Bailey, 2010).

A growing awareness of the challenges facing expectant fathers has led to the publication of an assortment of advice books and websites. Unfortunately many of these resources tend to focus on the instrumental roles of fathers: Keep your job, know how to assemble the crib, be ready to be the family photographer and IT expert, get the nursery painted, install the car seat, etc. Not enough attention is given to the psychosocial issues facing men as they approach the new role of fatherhood. These resources could do more to provide expectant fathers with reassurance and encouragement about their ability to form a close, loving relationship with their baby, and the best ways to support their partner during the months leading up to the birth, as well as during the post-partum period. Men may need guidance and support from others as they reflect on their own experiences of being parented. These early experiences may provide good models for their approach to fatherhood; but they may also need revision. Men may need to alter their approach to balancing work and family life in order to enact a fulfilling father role. And they may need guidance about how to express the tender, caring, and loving aspects of their role within the framework of their masculine identity.

Fathers' Involvement in Labor and Delivery

Trends in the United States have shifted dramatically toward greater involvement of fathers during labor and delivery (Reed, 2005). Expectant fathers often attend childbirth classes to learn to assist their partners during the delivery. The father's presence during labor and delivery is typically a great comfort to the pregnant woman. When the father is present, women tend to have shorter labors, report experiencing less pain, use less medication, and feel more positive about themselves and their childbirth experience. Many fathers also describe their participation in the birth as a peak experience. They feel they are most helpful to their wives during labor, and they find the birth experience to be extremely powerful (Nichols, 1993).

Birthing experiences are commonly set in the context of a medical environment in which fathers may be viewed as assistants, but they may also be viewed as getting in the way. Negative experiences for men during childbirth occur when they are unsure what their role is during the delivery or when hospital personnel treat them rudely, as a disruption, stereotype them as unable to manage the events of childbirth, or fail to provide them with the information they want during the labor and delivery process (Johnson, 2002). When there are complications during the birth process, or if the birth is performed with cesarean delivery, it is likely that the father will be asked to leave the birth setting, often left alone until the birthing process is complete. This can lead to emotional turmoil for the father, resulting in post-traumatic stress disorder or depression and doubts about the ability to comfort and care for his partner and his baby. Little attention is given to men's needs as they make a psychological transition to fatherhood. We do not know how negative experiences in childbirth may impact subsequent interactions between a man and his partner or his children.

— **CASE STUDY** A Father's Recollections About His Daughter's Birth —

The sentiments of frustration and joy are captured in this description of a father's experiences during labor and delivery. The text was taken from a bulletin board discussion about fathers' views of whether they should be present at their child's birth on Blacknet. com, a place for dialogue and communication within the Black community of the United Kingdom.

Gonna remenise about when my first child was born, I remember being dragged out of work on a Wednesday am because my then wife had gone into labour. Someone however forgot to inform me that women needed to dialate. geeez.

So after rushing to Guys hospital I'm told Baby not ready. Anyway I'm waiting for said wife to get big enough so to speak. All flippin day, All day man watching the paint dry.

I was like Donkey in Shrek 2 'Are we there yet?' every five minutes, then night falls I think ok, maybe it will be a night birth. Oh nooo, nooo such luck.

So here am i holding my wifes hand, or was that her squeezing the blood out of my hand. hmmm yes that was it. I'm giving the 'i'm in control mans' talk you know 'come on darling its ok, breath breath' My girl is in full contractions now about 20 mins apart. So the top half of me is trying to be firm and calm, the bottom half is trying hard not to piss mi pants.

Then the nurse mentioned Epidural, oh my days I know i nearly passed out at the sight of the needle going into the spinal column, all the while that wretch is screaming blue murder in the next room. 'get it out'.

Anyway after waiting ALL day (do I still sound vex?) and ALL night with a hardback chair for a bed, you know I'm happy right?... next thing I know doctor come in approx 8:40 am ish. 'ok lets do it'. Next thing I know they pull out these stirrups out of nowhere and got my wife with both legs in the air like she's riding an invisable horse whilst lying on her back.

Then a whole heap of student doctors and nurses come into the room, and I mean a whole heap. So here's the wife with legs up in the air, fanny out of door, and all these strangers peering right up it. Now you know man is about to cuss right.

Anyway before I could get into it, baby starts to be delivered and out she pops, 9 am in the morning. she pops out. can't describe how i felt but it was as close to perfection as i will ever get. bonded with her and we've been close not matter what 21 years later.

Source: Kunjufu, (2004).

CASE ANALYSIS Using What You Know

1. Given all the stress of the situation, what might account for the very positive feelings reported by Kunjufu at the moment of birth?

2. Summarize the different roles that men can play during the childbirth process. What roles is Kunjufu playing?

3. How does the case illustrate reasons why some men might not want to be present during labor and delivery?

4. Assess how hospital personnel may influence the experiences of fathers during childbirth.

5. Explain how childbirth preparation classes might influence the experiences of fathers during childbirth.

The Impact of the Pregnant Woman on the Fetus

Among the factors that influence the fetus's development are the mother's age, use of drugs during pregnancy and delivery, exposure to environmental toxins, maternal depression, infections encountered during pregnancy, diet, and stress. The quality of a pregnant woman's physical and emotional health before and during pregnancy are linked to her own knowledge about, and preparation for, pregnancy as well as to her culture's attitudes and practices associated with childbearing. One of the most harmful influences of the psychosocial environment on fetal development is poverty. Embedded in the conditions of poverty are many of the individual factors mentioned above that are associated with suboptimal prenatal development.

The Impact of Poverty

Perhaps the most powerful psychosocial factor that influences the life chances of the developing fetus is poverty (Lipina & Colombo, 2009). Women living in poverty are likely to experience the cumulative effects of many of the factors associated with infant mortality and developmental vulnerabilities. Poverty is directly linked to poor prenatal care. Women who live in poverty are likely to begin having babies at an earlier age and to have repeated pregnancies into their later adult years—practices that are associated with low birth weight. Women who have had little education are less likely to be aware of the risks of smoking, alcohol, and drug use for their babies and are more likely to use or abuse these substances. Women living in poverty are less likely to have been vaccinated against some of the infectious diseases (e.g., rubella) that can harm the developing fetus. Poverty is linked with food insecurity; lack of safe, affordable housing; lack of health insurance; higher instances of infection; and higher rates of diabetes and cardiovascular disease, which are all linked to the infant's low birth weight and physical vulnerability (Burgard & King, 2015; MacDonald & Seshia, 2016).

Many of the risks that face infants born to women who live in poverty are preventable. One of the Millennium Development Goals established under the auspices of the United Nations was to reduce global maternal mortality rates 75 percent by the year 2015. A key element in achieving this goal was to dramatically increase the percentage of births attended by skilled medical personnel. Impoverished and rural women are currently far less likely than their wealthier urban counterparts to receive skilled care during childbirth. Inequality in access to skilled care between urban and rural women is especially notable in Sub-Saharan Africa where wealthier women are three times more likely to deliver with the assistance of skilled birth professionals than the poorest women. While the Millennium Goal was not achieved, significant progress was made. By 2015, the maternal mortality rate was reduced by 45 percent (United Nations, 2012, 2015).

A well-organized, accessible system of regional medical care facilities combined with an effective educational program on pregnancy and nutritional support can significantly improve the health and vigor of babies born to women in poverty. One of the central elements in delivering effective prenatal and continuing services to women in poverty is the establishment of a caring relationship between the woman and the health care provider. This caring relationship provides emotional support to the woman, encouraging her to feel valued as a client, as a mother, and as an adult in the community (Barnard & Morisset, 1995; Massey, Rising, & Ickovics, 2005).

Comprehensive prenatal care programs can improve birth outcomes even in a high-risk population. Delivery of coordinated care involves more than providing prenatal checkups and information about health care during pregnancy. It recognizes the complex challenges that face women in poverty, including violence, hazardous living conditions, poor quality services, and unstable or disruptive social relationships. Effective interventions must include nonmedical support services, such as making sure the woman has access to food stamps; is part of the Women, Infants, and Children (WIC) food program; has the transportation needed for prenatal and postnatal health care appointments; and receives housing assistance or job training as necessary (California Department of Public Health, 2016; McAllister & Boyle, 1998).

Living in a high-poverty neighborhood has been associated with poor pregnancy outcomes. However, disrupting a pregnant woman's housing arrangements, for example, by closing or dismantling a public housing project and forcing women to relocate, has also been found to increase the risk for having preterm, low-birth-weight babies (Kramer, Waller, Dunlop, & Hogue, 2012). The life chances and quality of survival of infants born in poverty are a reflection of the value that a society places on social justice.

Mother's Age

The capacity for childbearing begins about 1 to 1½ years after menarche (the beginning of regular menstrual periods) and normally ends at the climacteric, or menopause (the ending of regular menstrual periods, usually between the ages of 48 and 55). Thus, a woman is potentially fertile for 35–40 years of her life. Pregnancy and childbirth can occur at various times during this period. The effects of childbirth on the physical and psychological well-being of a mother vary with her age and emotional commitment to the mother role. Similarly, these factors also contribute significantly to the survival and well-being of her infant. In later chapters, we will discuss the psychosocial consequences of childbearing for adolescents and adults. Here we point out the birth outcomes and risks to mothers and infants that are associated with the age of the mother during pregnancy.

Women between the ages of 16 and 35 tend to provide a better uterine environment for the developing fetus and to give birth with fewer complications than do women under 16 or over 35. Particularly when it is their first pregnancy, women over 35 are likely to have a longer labor than younger women, and the labor is more likely to result in the death of either the infant or the mother. As expected, the two groups with the highest probability of giving birth to premature babies are women over 35 and those under 16 (Behrman & Butler, 2007). In an analysis of over 180,000 deliveries, the risk of having a preterm delivery increased with age for women living in poor neighborhoods, African American women, and women who smoked (Holzman et al., 2009).

Mothers under 16 tend to receive less adequate prenatal care and to be less biologically mature. Young mothers are likely to engage in other high-risk behaviors, including alcohol and drug use, that have negative consequences for fetal development. In addition, adolescent mothers are more likely than older mothers to be exposed to violence in their communities, homes, and in the context of intimate relationships, thus increasing their level of stress and an associated increased use of tobacco, alcohol, drugs, and antidepressants, all of which can have negative consequences for the developing fetus (Kennedy, 2006). As a result of these interacting factors, premature children of teenage mothers are more likely than those of older mothers to have neurological defects that will influence their coping capacities. Evidence suggests that good medical care, nutrition, and social support improve the childbirth experiences of adolescent mothers who are over 16. However, the physical immaturity of those under 16 puts the mother and infant at greater risk even with adequate medical and social supports (Behrman & Butler, 2007).

A primary risk for infants of mothers who are over 40 is Down syndrome. It is hypothesized that the relatively high incidence of Down syndrome in babies born to older women is the result, in part, of deteriorating ova. However, older women are also likely to have male partners who are their age or older. Even though new sperm are produced daily, some evidence suggests that among older men, the rate of genetically defective sperm increases. Thus, aging in one or both partners may contribute to the increased incidence of Down syndrome in babies born to older women. These explanations are not entirely satisfactory, however, because older women who have had multiple births are not as likely to have a baby with Down syndrome as are women who have their first child at an older age. Moreover, many babies with Down syndrome are born to women who are under 35. It is likely that in some cases, Down syndrome is a result of errors that occur during cell division and that in others, it is a result of a genetically transmitted condition (National Down Syndrome Society, 2013).

FIGURE 4.9 ▶ shows the rate of live births to women in the age range from 10 to 49 between 1960 and 2013. Overall, women are somewhat older today at the time of their first

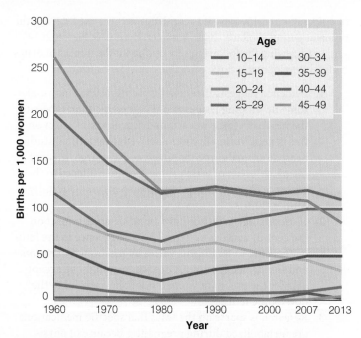

FIGURE 4.9 ▶ LIVE BIRTHRATES BY AGE OF MOTHER, 1960–2013
Source: U.S. Census Bureau, 1986, 1989, 1992, 2003, 2007e, 2010e; Martin et al., 2015

birth (Mean=26.0 years) than was the case in the past. With the exception of the very youngest and the very oldest women, the birth rate dropped substantially from 1960 to 1980. Current trends show a shift from the 1960s, when the highest birth rate was among women ages 20–24, to the present when the highest rate was among women 25–29. In comparison to the 1980s, the current trend shows an increase in childbearing for women in their 30s. Although there is a lot of concern about risks associated with teen pregnancy, the birth rate for the very youngest group (ages 10–14) is comparatively low, and the birth rate for those ages 15–19 has dropped notably since the 1990s (Martin et al., 2015) .

Maternal Drug Use

The range of drugs used by pregnant women is enormous. Iron, diuretics, antibiotics, hormones, tranquilizers, appetite suppressants, and other drugs are prescribed for or are purchased over-the-counter by pregnant women. Furthermore, women influence the fetal environment through their voluntary use of such drugs as alcohol, nicotine, caffeine, marijuana, cocaine, and other narcotics. Studies of the effects of specific drugs on fetal growth suggest that many drugs ingested by pregnant women are in fact metabolized in the placenta and transmitted to the fetus. Furthermore, although the impact of a specific dosage of a drug on the pregnant woman may be minimal, the impact on the fetus may be quite dramatic.

Male-mediated effects of drugs on fetal development are also documented but less well publicized. Drug abuse among men may produce abnormalities of the sperm that can account for birth defects in their offspring. Current studies are examining the possibility that addictive drug use by men and women prior to conception can have deleterious effects on the physical and behavioral development of offspring through the formation of epigenetic marks, even if these drugs are not used during the prenatal period (Pollard, 2000; Vassoler, Byrnes, & Pierce, 2014).

In reviewing the following sections about the impact of drugs on fetal development, three principles must be considered:

1. Evidence suggests that genetic predisposition may make some developing fetuses more vulnerable than others to the negative effects of certain drugs or toxins. Data on this genetic variability were derived from animal studies because animals are more likely to have large litters of offspring, some of which show greater resilience to the presence of prenatal teratogens than others (O'Rahilly & Muller, 2001).

2. Most teratogens do not have an all-or-none impact on the central nervous system. The consequence to the fetus of exposure to teratogens varies by the *dosage*, *duration*, and *timing* of exposure. A dosage that might be acceptable for the pregnant woman might be harmful to the developing fetus.

3. Research is sparse on the ways that specific medications are metabolized during pregnancy. Because of physiological changes during pregnancy, some medications may be metabolized so quickly that they do not treat the condition for which they were prescribed. In an effort to avoid harming the pregnant woman or the fetus, some serious conditions such as asthma or depression may be left untreated, thereby placing the pregnant woman and the fetus at risk for additional complications (Lyerly, Little, & Faden, 2009).

Nicotine. Smoking cigarettes is one of the most common, preventable causes of reduced fertility, conception delay, and negative birth outcomes (Centers for Disease Control and Prevention, 2012b). Women who smoke are at greater risk for miscarriages, stillbirths, preterm deliveries, low-birth-weight babies, and infant mortality. Children born to mothers who smoke are at increased risk for cleft lip and cleft palate, ear infections, and respiratory diseases, including asthma. Neurological examinations of babies exposed to nicotine during the prenatal period showed decreased levels of arousal and responsiveness at 9 and 30 days after birth. Infants of smokers have a three to four times greater risk of SIDS before 2 months of age. Although there is clearly a benefit to stopping smoking before pregnancy, research suggests that stopping smoking during pregnancy can also be associated with reduced health risks to the newborn.

Alcohol. The evidence is conclusive that alcohol is a teratogen. Prenatal exposure to alcohol can disrupt brain development, interfere with cell development and organization, and modify the production of neurotransmitters, which are critical to the maturation of the central nervous system (Sokol, Delaney-Black, & Nordsstrom, 2003). The complex impact of alcohol on fetal development has been given the name **fetal alcohol spectrum disorders** (Centers for Disease Control and Prevention, 2015d). Fetal alcohol spectrum disorders (FASDs) is an umbrella term for the range of effects that can occur in an individual whose mother drank alcohol during pregnancy. These effects include physical, mental, behavioral, and learning disabilities with possible lifelong implications. FASDs include **fetal alcohol syndrome (FAS)**, as well as other conditions in which individuals have some, but not all, of the clinical signs, which include abnormal facial features, growth deficiencies, and central nervous system (CNS) problems.

Damage to brain structures by alcohol can be detected through changes in fetal habituation at 35 weeks of gestational age (Hepper, Doman, & Lynch, 2012). The impact of FASD may become more notable as children reach the elementary and middle school grades as they face more challenging academic tasks. The compromised CNS may result in problems with learning, memory, attention span, communication, vision, hearing, or a combination of these. These problems often lead to difficulties in school and problems getting along with others. Individuals who were diagnosed with FAS in infancy continue to be at greater risk for health and mental health problems well into adulthood (Popova, Lange, Burd, & Rehm, 2012).

FAS is a permanent condition. At a rate of 0.2 to 1.5 infants affected per 1,000 live births, fetal alcohol syndrome is the greatest source of environmentally caused developmental disruption in the prenatal CNS. For every child born with FAS, an estimated three more children are born who suffer some of the neurological complications associated with fetal exposure to alcohol (Centers for Disease Control and Prevention, 2015d). Estimates of the costs associated with the educational, health care, and behavioral supports for people with FASDs are in the billions of dollars. The Centers for Disease Control and Prevention has a valuable website about FASDs that provides detailed information about diagnosis, treatment, statistics, research articles, and educational tools: http://www.cdc.gov/ncbddd/fasd/index.html.

Both of these children show the facial characteristics of fetal alcohol syndrome: eyes widespread, with an epicanthic fold; short nose; small midface; and thin upper lip.

We emphasize the risks associated with prenatal exposure to alcohol because it is so widely used in American society and because even what many adults perceive to be a safe or socially acceptable amount of alcohol during pregnancy can have a negative effect on the fetus. In a national survey of pregnant women, 1 in 10 reported any alcohol use and 1 in 33 reported binge drinking in the past 30 days (Centers for Disease Control and Prevention, 2015d). According to the National Institute on Alcohol Abuse and Alcoholism, "there is no known safe amount of alcohol to drink while pregnant. Studies show that even drinking small amounts of alcohol during pregnancy may affect fetal brain development" (NIAA, 2011). In 2005, the U.S. Surgeon General advised all women who are pregnant or trying to get pregnant to abstain from alcohol consumption in order to prevent fetal exposure to alcohol. Because of discoveries that even minimal alcohol consumption could result in some disruption in fetal development, the old advice of limiting one's alcohol consumption during pregnancy has been revised. In order to prevent any possible damaging effects of alcohol, the advice is to abstain from alcohol consumption entirely (Centers for Disease Control and Prevention, 2015d).

Narcotics. The use of narcotics, especially heroin and cocaine, as well as methadone (a drug used in the treatment of heroin addiction), has been linked to increased risks of birth defects, low birth weight, and higher rates of infant mortality. Cocaine has both an indirect and direct impact on fetal development. Complications of pregnancy and fetal development occur when a pregnant woman uses cocaine. Cocaine increases a woman's blood pressure and constricts blood vessels at the site where the uterus and the placenta are connected, resulting in a decrease in the oxygen supply to the fetus, which can lead to fetal anomalies. What is more, cocaine crosses the placenta, resulting in direct effects on fetal blood circulation, with potential consequences for cell death in the brain or intestines, cardiac disorders, and other disruptions in organ development and function (Tantibancha-chai & Zhang, 2015).

Shortly after birth, infants who have been exposed prenatally to opiates, cocaine, and methadone show evidence neonatal abstinence syndrome, otherwise referred to as withdrawal. This syndrome can include symptoms such as neurological disorganization, fever, sleep disturbances, feeding problems, muscle spasms, and tremors (Bard et al., 2000; Farid, Dunlop, Tait, & Hulse, 2008).

Prenatal cocaine exposure has been linked to cortisol reactivity. Cortisol is a hormone that contributes to a person's ability to manage and regulate the responses to the stressors of daily life. Babies who were exposed to cocaine prenatally were observed at 7 months of age. They had elevated cortisol levels, which leads to greater reactivity to stress, and disruptions in the ability to self-regulate. The disruptive consequences of cocaine exposure were more serious when the caregiving situation was unstable, suggesting that the infants who were physiologically predisposed to having difficulties in managing arousal and stress suffered even further when they were not able to rely on a consistent context of care (Eiden, Veira, & Granger, 2009). Longer range studies found that some children who were exposed to addictive drugs in the prenatal period continued to show problems with fine motor coordination, had difficulty focusing and sustaining their attention, and, perhaps as a result, had more school adjustment problems (Ben-Dat Fisher et al., 2007). In a study that followed children from birth to mid-adolescence, prenatal exposure to cocaine was related to poorer perceptual organization IQ, visual–spatial information processing, attention, language, executive function, and behavior regulation through early adolescence (Singer et al., 2015).

Of course, it is difficult to separate the direct prenatal effects of these drugs on the nervous system from the effects of other negative teratogens on fetal development, such as alcohol and nicotine use, maternal malnutrition, or sexually transmitted diseases. Long-term consequences of prenatal exposure to teratogens are also confounded with post-natal conditions associated with being parented by a drug-abusing mother, or exposure to a violent or neglectful home environment (National Institute on Drug Abuse, 2010). One study focused on the caregiving environment of 2-year-old children who had been prenatally exposed to cocaine. Those who were in nonparental caregiving environments were doing much better at age 2 with respect to physical development, cognitive and language skills, and social and emotional functioning than those who continued in the care of their cocaine-using birth mothers (Brown et al., 2004a).

In a similar study, children who were exposed prenatally to methamphetamine were evaluated again at age 5. The children who had been prenatally exposed to methamphetamine were more than twice as likely as a comparison group to have significant externalizing behavior problems (i.e., problems managing their impulses, including expressions of anger, harming others, and breaking things). Those children who continued living with their biological mothers had more behavioral problems than those similarly exposed who were separated from their biological mothers and placed in the hands of a calmer, responsive caregiver. The results of this research suggest that in addition to the direct harm of prenatal drug exposure, these babies are also more sensitive to the potentially disruptive impact of harsh, neglectful, or inconsistent care after birth (Twomey et al., 2013).

Should women who use illegal substances also be charged with child abuse or child endangerment? Currently, one state, Tennessee, has criminalized maternal substance abuse during pregnancy. Supreme courts in Alabama and South Carolina have found that drug use while pregnant is considered the criminal endangerment/abuse of a child. However, 18 states have altered their child welfare statues and guidelines so that prenatal drug use can be grounds for ending parental rights based on child abuse or endangerment. Moreover, 18 states require health care professionals to report any suspected prenatal drug use to the state child welfare agency. Four states require health professionals to do testing for drug use as well as reporting. Recognizing the neurobehavioral consequences of prenatal exposure to cocaine and other opiates, 19 states are funding drug treatment programs specifically for pregnant women (Guttmacher Institute, 2016).

Prescription Drugs. Some drugs are administered to women during pregnancy as part of the treatment of a medical or psychological condition. Some drugs are administered to help sustain the pregnancy. Studies examining the dose and timing of these drugs suggest that they can have temporary or long-term consequences for fetal development by altering the blood supply to the fetus, interfering with neurological development, and altering the functioning of the placenta, thereby restricting nutrition and growth. The effects of some kinds of drugs may persist long after birth, either by directly altering the CNS or by influencing the pattern of caregiver–infant interactions. In some cases, women who have had certain drugs prescribed for pain, anxiety, sleep disturbances, or hyperactivity become dependent upon these medications and take them in greater doses, or beyond the time for which they were prescribed. Abuse of prescription drugs is among the causes of low birth weight and fetal abnormalities. The American Pregnancy Association provides information about potentially harmful prescription drugs and guidelines to determine if one is abusing these drugs (American Pregnancy Association, 2015b).

A recent controversy focuses on decisions about the treatment of depression among pregnant women. Estimates of the prevalence of depression among pregnant women suggest that about 6 percent experience major depression; and 16.6 percent experience minor depression. Whereas the risk of major depression is about the same for pregnant and nonpregnant women, the risk of minor depression is substantially greater for pregnant women (Ashley et al., 2015). What is more, 30 percent to 40 percent of women who have a history of major depression prior to pregnancy experience a relapse during the perinatal period (Dimidjian et al., 2016).

Antidepressant medications are prescribed to help relieve symptoms of depression. The hormonal changes of pregnancy can make it more difficult to cope with depressive thoughts and emotions. The decision to stop taking these medications during pregnancy could lead to health risk behaviors including an increase in smoking or alcohol use, poor eating or sleeping patterns, or a general indifference to one's health. On the other hand, there are some risks associated with certain antidepressant medications. For example, Paxil has been associated with an increased risk of fetal heart defects; certain other antidepressants have been linked to limiting fetal growth. Moreover, infants born to women who have been taking antidepressants during pregnancy have been found to show some withdrawal symptoms following birth. While the risks of many antidepressants are low, women and their health care providers have to consider how best to manage this situation (Mayo Clinic, 2015).

Caffeine. Caffeine freely crosses the placenta. It is commonly consumed in coffee and coffee-flavored ice creams, certain sodas, energy drinks, teas, and chocolates. An estimated 200 foods and food products contain caffeine. Caffeine raises the heart rate and acts as a diuretic, resulting in loss of fluids and the possibility of dehydration. Heavy caffeine consumption—defined in one study as more than 300 milligrams, or roughly three cups of coffee per day—is associated with an increased risk of low birth weight, and there is a modest relationship to prematurity. Babies exposed to high doses of caffeine have been found to have a higher heart rate, more startles and tremors, and are more difficult to soothe (Howell, 2005).

The impact of caffeine on fetal development is not fully understood. Most medical and health sources suggest that pregnant women should be cautious in their intake of caffeine, limiting the amount to 200 mg per day. (An 8 oz. cup of coffee has about 95 mgs of caffeine.) In striving to limit caffeine, women need to check the content in drinks, foods, and over-the-counter and prescription medications, such as cough and cold products. This can be challenging. For example, the U.S. Food and Drug Administration does not require manufacturers of energy drinks to put the amount of caffeine in their products on the label. Some energy drinks have large amounts of caffeine as well as other ingredients that may be harmful to the developing fetus (March of Dimes, 2016; Mayo, 2014).

Environmental Toxins

Because of the large number of women in the workplace, including many who assume nontraditional work roles, concern about the hazards of work settings for fetal development continues to grow. It is difficult to assess the causal links between exposure to specific chemicals and their impact on reproductive health in humans. The levels of exposure to environmental toxins that may be considered safe or acceptable for adults may still have a negative impact on fetal development. What is more, it is difficult to control for the possible accumulation of toxins that might be present in a person's system due to workplace exposure, water, air, and diet. Current reports from the National Safety Council and the National Institute for Occupational Safety and Health identify a long list of agents that pose potential harm to reproductive health for women and men. Furthermore, childbearing women whose partners are exposed to these substances may suffer from secondary exposure that can have a harmful impact on the developing fetus (National Safety Council, 2013; *Science Daily*, 2005).

The workplace is not the only setting in which pregnant women may be exposed to environmental toxins. For example, mercury, used in the manufacture of a variety of products, finds its way into the air and then into oceans and waterways where it is ingested by fish. Large fish, like tuna and swordfish, eat the smaller fish, thereby accumulating greater concentrations of mercury. When these fish are eaten by humans, the mercury acts as a neurotoxin, harming the brain and nervous system. Exposure to mercury is especially harmful for fetal development due to its impact on brain development. Pregnant women who eat a lot of fish have to be particularly careful about the source of those fish and the amount they eat (National Resources Defense Council, 2013). All communities must be sensitive to the quality of their water, air, and soil. Each new generation depends on its predecessors for protection from environmental hazards.

Mother's Diet

The notion that no matter what a pregnant woman eats, the fetus will get what it needs for growth is simply not true. Providing adequate nutrition for fetal development requires both a balanced diet for the mother and the capacity to transform nutrients into a form that the fetus can ingest through the placenta (Tanner & Finn-Stevenson, 2002).

Because of ethical problems involved in experimentally modifying the diets of pregnant women, much of the research on the effects of maternal malnutrition on fetal development has been conducted with animal models, primarily rats. The impact of prenatal malnutrition on rats shows that when the mother is malnourished, fewer nutrients cross the placenta. The fetal brain receives comparatively more of the limited nutritional resources than the other organs; however, the central nervous system (CNS) is disrupted. The consequences, for those fetuses that survive, include delayed skeletal development, impaired reflexes, and cognitive deficits (Galler & Tonkiss, 1998; Lukas & Campbell, 2000).

The impact of prenatal malnutrition on human development depends on its timing, severity, and the particular nutrients that are absent from the mother's diet. Prenatal malnutrition has an immediate negative impact on fetal growth including the growth of organs, organ functions, and the CNS. Babies who experience prenatal malnutrition are likely to be small for their gestational age and are more likely to suffer birth complications.

Prenatal malnutrition is also associated with longer term health and behavioral problems including learning disabilities, mental illness, and motor impairments. Studies of children born during a severe food shortage in the Dutch Hunger Winter of 1944–45 found that these individuals had impaired glucose tolerance and a greater incidence of coronary heart disease and elevated blood pressure in adulthood (Langley-Evans, 2006; Neugebauer, Hoek, & Susser, 1999).

One of the nutrients of grave concern because of its role in the maturation of the CNS is iron. The brain uses iron to help support the speed of neural firing. Iron deficiency is a widespread nutrient disorder, with an estimated 20 percent to 25 percent of babies worldwide suffering from **iron deficiency anemia**. During pregnancy, iron deficiency is common since a woman's blood has to serve her own increased blood volume as well as be a source of hemoglobin for the maturing fetus. Babies who have severe iron deficiencies test lower in motor and cognitive development and show evidence of fearfulness, fatigue, and wariness. Even with postnatal iron-enriched treatment, these behavioral consequences have been found to persist (Georgieff, 2008; National Research Council and Institute of Medicine, 2000).

Programs targeted at pregnant women who are at risk for malnutrition often supplement the diet with foods that are rich in protein and high in calories. These supplements have been found to be effective in reducing infant mortality, birth defects, and the number of babies born small for gestational age. In order for these interventions to be truly effective, they must be coupled with efforts to reduce the continued effects of poverty after birth. Children who are at risk for malnutrition are likely to experience more illness, lethargy, and withdrawal; delayed physical growth; and, in consequence, delayed intellectual growth. Some of these negative effects of malnutrition can be offset if infants are adequately nourished after birth (Tanner & Finn-Stevenson, 2002).

Pregnant women have to be especially careful about the preparation and safety of the foods they eat. During pregnancy, a woman's immune system may be weaker, and the immune system of the fetus is not fully developed. As a result, both the woman and the fetus may be especially vulnerable to bacteria, viruses, and parasites that can cause food-borne illnesses. Pregnant women are advised to avoid eating raw eggs and unpasteurized milk, juice, and cheese products, to thoroughly cook meats, and to thoroughly wash fruits and vegetables to prevent eating foods that may have come into contact with contaminants. The U.S. government has produced an informational website and guidelines about some of the potential risks of various foods to pregnant women and their unborn children (Foodsafety.gov, 2016) (see FIGURE 4.10 ▶).

Stress and Fetal Development

Strong emotional reactions in mothers—such as prolonged anxiety or depression—may influence the fetal environment directly through the maternal hormones that cross the placental barrier. A review of existing literature suggests that among humans, prenatal stress is associated with higher rates of spontaneous abortion, preterm labor and delivery, and growth delay among babies (Mulder et al., 2002). Stress-related changes in endocrine levels during pregnancy are associated with motor development, cognitive development, and immune functioning in babies. Research is focusing on ways in which stress-induced physiological changes in the mother might influence fetal growth and nervous system development (DiPietro, 2004, 2012; Field et al., 2003).

What are the sources of stress for pregnant women that can have an impact on the developing fetus? Studies have explored the role of women's exposure to psychosocial stress and racism on birth outcomes. Prenatal anxiety is higher among those women who have a less positive outlook about their pregnancy and who are undergoing a large number of challenging life events during pregnancy. In a comparison of European American, African American, and Latina women, the sources of prenatal anxiety were different for women of the different racial/ethnic groups. Income inadequacy was the primary source of prenatal anxiety for European American women. For African American women, both childhood and current exposure to racism was significantly related to pregnancy stress. For Latinas, a sense of mastery and support from the baby's father were factors that reduced levels of pregnancy stress (Dominguez et al., 2008; Gurung et al., 2005).

Another source of stress is related to a woman's working conditions. Although it is generally positive for women to be employed and to have work-related income, work-related strain can have a negative impact on fetal development. The following work conditions were identified as especially stressful: working 32 hours a week or more early in their pregnancy; a demanding work pace, including time pressures and expectations to do multiple tasks as once; and physically demanding, strenuous work. These work conditions were associated with greater risk for having low-birth-weight babies or babies who were small for their gestational age (Vrijkotte, van der Wal, van Eijsden, & Bonsel, 2009).

A mother's emotional state during pregnancy has an impact beyond the events of childbirth. Women who experience severe anxiety or depression during pregnancy are more likely to continue feeling depressed after giving birth and are more likely to have additional depressive symptoms in the 5 years following childbirth. Clinicians who focus on the causes and treatment of

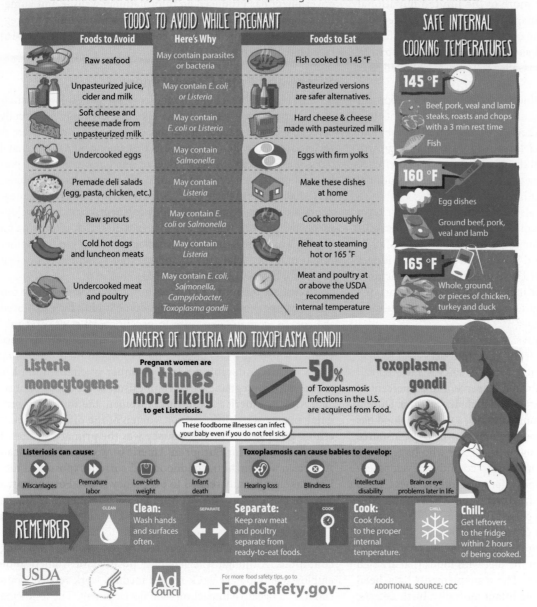

FIGURE 4.10 ▶ FOOD SAFETY FOR BABY AND ME

Source: Foodsafety.gov. Retrieved from http://www.foodsafety.gov/risk/pregnant/

depression in women emphasize that the period of pregnancy and childbirth should be a time for preventive intervention (Le, Munoz, Ippen, & Stoddard, 2003).

Summary

The many risk factors we have reviewed, including maternal age, exposure to drugs and environmental toxins, exposure to medications, inadequate nutritional resources, and stress, can occur singly or in combination. The greater the number of risk factors the fetus encounters, the greater the chance for disruption in neurological and behavioral development. As suggested by the model for the differential effect of the childrearing environment presented earlier in the chapter (Figure 4.6), psychosocial processes can contribute to growth and new resources for coping or to disruption and limitations on coping. Within the prenatal environment, a child's genetic potential may encounter a supportive, healthy, optimizing environment or an environment in which one or more conditions place fetal development at risk. For infants who carry the genetic markers for anomalies, the expression of these conditions may be less severe when fetal development has taken place in a healthy, fully resourced uterine environment. In contrast, even infants who would otherwise be healthy may suffer long-term negative consequences when they are exposed to a combination of teratogens and disruptive uterine conditions.

FURTHER REFLECTION Based on what you have read, what is your view about whether pregnant women should work? Describe what you consider to be the best work environments for a pregnant woman and her partner, and the least desirable environments.

The central nervous system is a work in progress that matures throughout pregnancy. As you review the sections above, make a list of the many ways that the baby's CNS may be influenced by the fetal environment.

The Cultural Context of Pregnancy and Childbirth

OBJECTIVE 6 Examine the impact of culture on pregnancy and childbirth.

Julan is a Hmong, now living in Australia. She has just had a baby, and she and her family are preparing for the soul-calling ceremony on the third day after the baby's birth. Once completed, she will feel that she has done what is needed to protect the baby and link it to its living as well as its supernatural world. The Hmong believe that each of us has three souls—one that enters the body when the infant is conceived, one that enters as the baby takes its first breath during childbirth, and one that enters on the third day after birth. The soul-calling ceremony secures these souls in the infant's body and thus ensures the baby's well-being. (Rice, 2000)

Cultures differ in the ways they "script" pregnancy and birth. The beliefs, values, and guidelines for behavior regarding pregnancy and childbirth have been referred to as the **birth culture** (Gross & Pattison, 2007). The decision to have a child, the social and physical experiences of pregnancy, the particular style of help that is available for the delivery of the child, and the care and attitudes toward mother, father, and baby after delivery are all components of the birth culture. Not everyone in a cultural group adheres to the full script of the birth culture, but at the very least, these guidelines are part of the mythology or lore that surfaces as a woman and her partner experience the events of pregnancy. Within larger countries, it is common to find a diversity of cultural groups, each of which has its own birth culture. This requires new levels of cultural competence and sensitivity among health care providers in order to provide optimal prenatal and childbirth services for a culturally diverse population.

Reactions to Pregnancy

Many cultures share the assumption that the behavior of expectant parents will influence the developing fetus and the ease or difficulty of childbirth. Of the 64 cultures studied by Ford (1945), 42 prescribed certain behaviors for expectant parents and prohibited others. Many such restrictions were dietary.

In many Asian, Mediterranean, and Central and South American cultures, pregnancy is believed to be affected by the balance of hot and cold foods in a woman's diet. For example, during pregnancy, Vietnamese women are likely to follow dietary practices that permit "hot" foods such as ginger and black pepper in the first trimester and avoid "cold" foods such as lemon, melon, or pineapple. Pregnant Vietnamese women often use traditional plant and herbal medicines to support their health and the health of their babies (Queensland Government, 2012).

A culture's view of pregnancy determines the kinds and severity of the symptoms associated with it, the types of treatment or medical assistance sought during pregnancy, and the degree to which pregnancy is responded to as a life stressor. Attitudes toward pregnant women can be characterized along two dimensions: (1) **solicitude versus shame** and (2) **adequacy versus vulnerability** (Mead & Newton, 1967). A syndrome of fathers' reactions to a wife's pregnancy, called couvade, is discussed in the following **Human Development and Diversity** box Couvade.

Solicitude Versus Shame

Solicitude toward the pregnant woman is shown in the care, interest, and help of others. For example, when Chinese women are pregnant, they are likely to take on a "sick role" in which they rely heavily on others for help. This role is expected; other members of the family offer comfort and encourage her to rely on older relatives at this time (Queensland Government, 2012). Earlier in the chapter we noted the low incidence of birth complications and low birth weight among Mexican immigrant women, despite their limited economic resources. Their positive childbirth experiences are attributed in large part to the value placed on family relations and the support shown to pregnant women by their kinship network. The Korean beliefs called **Taegyo** assume that the fetus is able to feel what the mother feels. As a result, a very detailed set of guidelines were established that encourage the creation of a peaceful, comfortable surrounding for pregnant women as well as recommendations for the woman's diet, activities, and exposure to positive, beautiful stories, songs, and paintings (Kim, 2002).

At the other end of this spectrum are the cultures that convey shame through their practices. They keep pregnancy a secret as long as possible. This custom may stem from a fear that damage will come to the fetus through supernatural demons or from shyness about the sexual implications of pregnancy.

Societies that demonstrate solicitude increase the care given to the pregnant woman and fetus. These attitudes emphasize the importance of birth as a mechanism for replenishing the group, and additional resources are likely to be provided to the pregnant woman. By keeping the pregnancy a secret, cultures that instill a sense of shame in the woman do not promote the health of the mother or the fetus and may not encourage couples to have children.

Couvade

Couvade, or sympathetic pregnancy, is a syndrome in which otherwise healthy men whose partners are pregnant experience pregnancy-related symptoms (Nippldt, 2016). Couvade has been observed in two forms. The first is a deliberate enactment of rituals expected for men whose partners are pregnant. In the formal cultural practice of couvade, the expectant father takes to his bed and observes very specific taboos during the period shortly before birth. Among the Arapesh of New Guinea, childbearing is believed to place as heavy a burden and drain of energy on the father as on the mother. Some cultures believe that by following the ritual of couvade, fathers distract the attention of evil spirits, so that the mother and baby can go through the childbirth transition more safely (Helman, 2007).

The second form of couvade is a more unconscious emergence of pregnancy-related symptoms (Bauer, 2014; Brennan, Ayers, Marshall-Lucette, & Ahmed, 2007; Klein, 1991).

"My husband is experiencing constipation, gas, bloating, irritability, and nausea right along with me," says one BabyCenter mom-to-be. And dad Mathew Erickson admits, "During my wife's pregnancy, I gained 15 pounds and had severe swelling in my hands." (Lack, 2016)

One source reported that 31 percent of expectant Australian fathers experienced eight or more physical and psychological couvade symptoms, such as general fatigue, weight gain, food cravings, stomach cramps, nausea, dizziness, or backache. Symptoms often begin toward the end of the first trimester, are noticeable again toward the end of pregnancy, and end with childbirth (Brennan, 2010).

One study participant indicated that a number of his symptoms occurred concurrently with his partner's pregnancy most particularly, stomach pain/cramps, increased appetite and weight gain.

"Stomach pains were not so much pains as weird movements in my stomach that I had never felt before. I felt much hungrier and have just started to work on losing the weight I put on whilst my wife was pregnant. … have not put on this much weight before. I have put an average of 5 kilos more on than usual." (Brennan, 2010)

Trethowan (1972), one of the first to document the nature and extent of couvade symptoms in the normal population, suggested that these physical symptoms are the product of a man's emotional ambivalence toward his wife during her pregnancy. The expectant father may experience empathy and identify with his wife's pregnant state. At the same time, he may experience some jealousy of his wife, resentment of the loss or potential loss of intimacy in their relationship, repulsion by his wife's physical appearance, or some envy of his wife's ability to bear a child. These psychological conflicts, many of which are probably unconscious or unexpressed, are amplified by an expectant father's conscious worries about the health and well-being of his wife and their baby. Contemporary ob-gyn physicians recognize the couvade syndrome and suspect that a combination of empathy and stress, each of which can be accompanied by unique hormonal changes, may account for some of the couvade symptoms (Lack, 2016).

Critical Thinking Questions

1. Investigate societies in which couvade is routinely practiced. What are some characteristics of these societies?
2. Evaluate the functions that might be served by couvade rituals.
3. Interpret why a woman's pregnancy may create conflict for her male partner.
4. In addition to the explanations for couvade symptoms presented in this box, what other explanations can you think of?
5. Explore the literature to see if there is any evidence of couvade symptoms for lesbian, gay, bisexual, or transsexual (LGBT) couples who are expecting a child.

Adequacy Versus Vulnerability

In many societies, pregnancy is a sign of sexual prowess and a means of access to social status. Some cultures do not arrange a wedding until after the woman has become pregnant. In a polygynous family—one in which a man has more than one wife—the pregnant wife receives the bulk of her husband's attention and may prevent her husband from taking an additional wife (Grandquist, 1950). Among Melanesian Fijians, the status of a married woman rises when she becomes pregnant. The community comes together to support Fijian women during pregnancy and in the months after childbirth, providing both emotional and material resources (Queensland Government, 2012).

The other end of this continuum is the view that *child-making* is exhausting, pregnant women are vulnerable, and women grow more frail with each pregnancy. Among Samoans, many women believe that pregnancy is an illness. A lone pregnant woman is vulnerable to evil spirits and should avoid going out alone or being in the house alone. Samoan women may believe that a variety of practices, such as wearing earrings or floral arrangements around the neck, may result in disfiguring or harming the fetus (Queensland Government, 2012). Many cultures teach that during pregnancy, the woman and the fetus are more readily exposed to evil spirits. In several cultures, the forces of life and death are thought to be engaged in

In an effort to reduce infant and maternal mortality in Nepal, community volunteers visit women in the countryside to teach expectant mothers about safe practices. This is an example of an increasing effort toward solicitude and care in a developing nation.

PRAKASH MATHEMA/AFP/Getty Images

mother and the infant until the ninth day after birth (MacCormack, 1994).

In most traditional cultures, childbirth takes place in a familiar setting, either at home or in a nearby birthing hut. If the birth takes place at home, a woman may be separated from others by a curtain for privacy, but she knows that her family members are close at hand. Women typically give birth standing, squatting, or sitting and reclining against something or someone. The Western birth custom of lying on one's back with one's feet propped up in the air has no counterpart in traditional birth cultures, nor are women expected to be moved from one setting or room to another during the phases of labor. That appears to be a ritual reserved for women in modern, industrialized societies. Views about the birth itself range from an extreme negative pole, where birth is seen as dirty and defiling, to an extreme positive pole, where it is seen

a particularly intense competition for the mother and the fetus around the time of delivery.

Solicitude versus shame and adequacy versus vulnerability are two dimensions that create a matrix within which the birth culture of any society or subculture can be located. Within this framework, pregnancy may be viewed as a time of great rejoicing or a time for caution and privacy; a time for feeling sexually powerful or extremely vulnerable. One might describe the U.S. medical birth culture as being characterized by solicitude and vulnerability. Pregnant women are usually treated with increased concern and care and are often placed in a medical system that increases their sense of dependency. Attitudes in the workplace also contribute to the sense of vulnerability when pregnancy is viewed as incompatible with serious dedication to the job. In the workplace, women are likely to be devalued when they are pregnant, especially if they are engaged in jobs that are typically held by men (Hebl, King, Glick, Singletaary, & Kazama, 2007).

as a personal achievement. The view of childbirth as a normal physical event is the midpoint on this continuum (Stone & Selin, 2009).

When birth is viewed as dirty, as it is by the Arapesh of New Guinea and the Kadu Gollas of India, the woman must go to an area away from the village to deliver her child. Many cultures, such as that of the ancient Hebrews, require extensive purification rituals after childbirth. Vietnamese villagers believe that mothers should not bathe or shampoo their hair for a month after giving birth so that the baby will not "fall apart," and that the new mother must not have sexual intercourse for 100 days (Stringfellow, 1978).

A slightly more positive orientation toward childbirth is to identify it as a sickness. This view causes a pregnant Cuna Indian woman to visit her medicine man for daily medication. The midpoint of this spectrum—what we might most appropriately describe as natural childbirth—is a setting in which the mother delivers her baby in the presence of many members of the community, without much expression of pain and with little magic or obstetrical mechanics. Clark and Howland (1978) described childbirth for Samoan women as follows:

Reactions to Childbirth

Childbirth is an important event in most societies, marked by the presence of specially designated attendants, a specified location, and certain ceremonies and rituals intended to support the miraculous emergence of the newborn into the society (Dundes, 2003). In traditional societies, the delivery is usually attended by two or more assistants with specific assigned roles. They are usually women who have had children themselves and are respected members of their community. In Jamaica, the *nana*, or midwife, is one of the key figures in the village. She is called on to assist in many family crises. During pregnancy and childbirth, the nana provides assistance in the many rituals and taboos that mark the rebirth of the woman as a mother, and she usually cares for the

The process of labor is viewed by Samoan women as a necessary part of their role and a part of the life experience. Since the baby she is producing is highly valued by her culture, the mother's delivery is also commendable and therefore ego-satisfying. Pain relief for labor may well present the patient with a conflict. She obviously experiences pain as demonstrated by skeletal muscle response, tossing and turning, and fixed body positions, but her culture tells her that she does not need medication. It is the "spoiled" palagi [Caucasian] woman who needs pain-relieving drugs. Moreover, the culture clearly dictates that control is expected of a Samoan woman, and no overt expressions of pain are permissible. (p. 166)

At the most positive end of the scale, birth is seen as a proud achievement. Among the Ila of Northern Zimbabwe, women attending childbirth were observed to shout praises of the woman who had a baby. They all thanked her, saying, "I give thanks to you today that you have given birth to a child" (Mead & Newton, 1967, p. 174).

A similar sentiment is expressed in Marjorie Karmel's (1983) description of the Lamaze method of childbirth:

> From the moment I began to push, the atmosphere of the delivery room underwent a radical transformation. Where previously everyone had spoken in soft and moderate tones in deference to my state of concentration, now there was a wild encouraging cheering section, dedicated to spurring me on. I felt like a football star, headed for a touchdown. (pp. 93–94)

The American view of childbirth is evolving toward an emphasis on safety for mother and child and convenience for mothers and medical professionals. In comparison with the medical practices of the 1940s and 1950s, there is greater involvement of fathers or other birth coaches during labor and delivery and more immediate contact between newborns and their parents. There are more opportunities for the newborn baby to spend much of the day with the mother and for siblings to visit. Hospital stays are short—one or two days. Many hospitals have birth centers that provide a home-like environment where fewer technical interventions are used and the birth is attended by a midwife or obstetrical nursing team.

Couples are advised about the best way to promote the healthy development and safe delivery of their child as follows: (1) make early and regular visits to their obstetrician during the prenatal period; (2) attend childbirth classes; (3) observe recommendations for diet and use of drugs; and (4) avoid exposure to certain environmental hazards that may harm the fetus. In the United States, 99 percent of births take place in hospitals or hospital-affiliated centers, and 91 percent are attended by physicians (BabyCenter.com, 2007). Despite the fact that the overwhelming majority of women giving birth are healthy and could expect an uncomplicated birth, over half of women surveyed in 2006 experienced an induced labor or cesarean delivery, thereby exposing themselves and their babies to a variety of drugs and surgical interventions that bypass spontaneous labor (Declercq, Sakala, Corry, & Applebaum, 2006).

> I had a lot of pressure from the nursing staff to take Pitocin and to have an epidural. I felt like the birth experience was severely impacted by this pressure, as if the most important thing to the nurses was for me to have the baby quickly. My doctor is a big fan of induction which is not my cup of tea. (Childbirthconnection.org, 2007)

It is reasonable to speculate that events at the time of the birth influence a mother's feelings about herself and her parenting

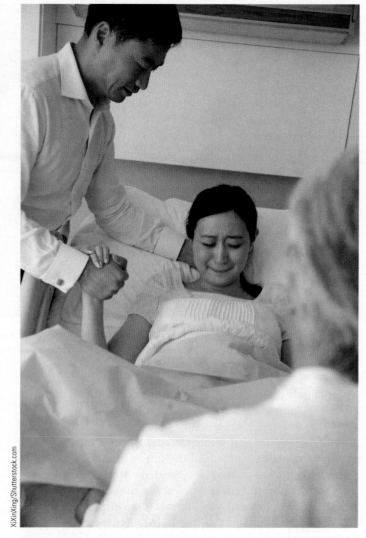

XiXinXing/Shutterstock.com

Modern birth cultures favor less use of obstetrical medications so that the mother is awake, the father is involved, and medical staff are part of the support team.

ability. Efforts by her community—especially family members, close friends, and health care professionals—to foster a woman's competence in, and control of, parenting and to express care and support for her seem to promote a woman's positive orientation toward herself and her mothering role. On the other hand, messages of social rejection, doubts about a woman's competence, and attempts to take away control or to isolate the mother from her infant or social support system may undermine the woman's self-esteem and interfere with her effectiveness as she approaches the demanding and exhausting task at hand (Dunkel-Schetter, 2009; Dunkel-Schetter, Sagrestano, Feldman, & Killingsworth, 1996).

Each country has a distinct approach to medical care during childbirth and the management of a birthing environment. These differences influence what a woman and her partner are likely to expect, and their comfort with the procedures during labor and delivery. For example, research on the birth settings in hospitals in the United States, Germany, France, and Italy found that each country had a somewhat different focus on the woman's ability to have control over the birth process, the types of emotional and technical support provided, the availability of childbirth preparation classes, and the focus given to mother–child and father–child bonding in each setting (Scopesi, Zanobini, & Carossino, 1997). In a comparison of childbirth experiences in seven countries, Canada, the United States, the United Kingdom, Azerbaijan, Lithuania, the Russian Federation, and Moldova, significant differences in medical practice were observed. Practices in the United States and Canada were the most "medicalized." Practices in the former Soviet countries were the least, with the United Kingdom in between. These differences included the frequency of induced labor, the use of fetal heart monitors during labor, the rates of cesarean deliveries, and the presence of a partner during labor and delivery. Over all, only about half the women were very satisfied with their birth experiences (Chalmers 2012).

Studies of immigrants giving birth in a new country examine problems of communication between women, their families, and the childbirth professionals that undercut the woman's sense of confidence and control. Table 4.3 summarizes some

Table 4.3	Mental Health Stressors and Possible Psychological Reactions
Pre-immigration experiences	• Psychological issues related to past experiences of war, displacement, rape, torture, survival in refugee camps, death of close relatives • Post-traumatic stress disorder (fear, nightmares, lack of control over a situation, depression, hopelessness) • Powerlessness over decision to migrate
Adjustment	• Stress related to the loss of job, housing, financial problems, lack of English language skills, lack of knowledge and skills for everyday activities, stress related to lack of knowledge of services
Wellbeing of overseas family	• Feelings of guilt for not contributing enough to family overseas • Family members may be missing or living in difficult or dangerous circumstances
Lack of knowledge of antenatal care system and birthing practices	• Fear of difference in health care and birthing practices in host country • Inability to navigate the health system due to cultural or language barriers
Traditional beliefs	• Fear of illnesses due to not practicing traditional practices • Fear of being cursed by overseas relatives • Fear to displease relatives and/or ancestral spirits • Adjustment stress due to practicing traditional practices
Female genital mutilation	• Stigma, feeling different from others, fear of potential procedures, lack of voice • Confusion. Some women feel proud of being circumcised. When entering western culture, the woman may feel different or incomplete and this may impact on mental health.
Antenatal testing, genetic counselling	• Fear of tests, lack of choice about continuing or terminating a pregnancy due to religious beliefs
Sex preference	• Negative emotions linked to having a female fetus, lack of choice about continuing or terminating a pregnancy due to family pressure
Arranged/early marriage, unwanted/unplanned pregnancy	• Hopelessness, lack of personal voice, lack of choice about continuing or terminating a pregnancy, lack of choice about remaining married, or separation or divorce due to family pressure and religious beliefs
Inflicted violence	• Post-traumatic stress disorder (fear, emotional distress, lack of control, frequent use of psychotropic medication)
Lack of support	• Loneliness, isolation, nostalgic feelings, burden of care for the newborn infant, lack of extended family support in Australia
Lack of knowledge and skills to care for newborn child	• Fear that the infant might die due to inadequate care, anxiety and fear that something is not right with the infant, self-blame for inadequate care, fear of reactions to immunization
Breast feeding problems	• Stress related to insufficient lactation, fear that the infant is hungry, stress related to introducing formula and solid foods

of the stressors that face immigrant women and their partners in Australia as they go through pregnancy and childbirth in a new, unfamiliar birthing environment. Some of these stressors relate to difficulties such as poor health care or exposure to violence that precede the transition to a new country; others relate to the lack of trust in or understanding of contemporary health care practices. Immigrant women are especially distressed by behaviors that they perceive to be unkind, rushed, or unsupportive during their labor and delivery (Queensland Government, 2012). Efforts should be made to provide information about the key elements of the birth culture for women who are not familiar with it in order to foster trust and improve birth outcomes.

FURTHER REFLECTION *What do you know about cultural rituals, practices, and beliefs about pregnancy in your family, ethnic group, or community? How would you describe these cultural practices along the dimensions of solicitude vs. shame or adequacy vs. vulnerability?*

Applied Topic: Abortion

OBJECTIVE 7 Apply the psychosocial perspective to the topic of abortion, including the legal context, its social and emotional impact on women, and men's views.

What Is Abortion?

Abortion is the termination of a pregnancy before the fetus is able to live outside the uterus. We want to encourage you to analyze the applied topic of abortion from a biopsychosocial perspective. Abortion is a biological process that impacts living beings, including fetus and mother. Information from the chapter about genetic inheritance, fetal development, and the physiological experiences of pregnancy are all related to the biological system. Abortion is a psychological process, involving decision making, fears, hopes and other emotional responses, life plans, and goals. Abortion is also a social, cultural, and societal process, embedded in a complex context of relationships, beliefs, laws, regulations, resources, and community norms.

Each year, thousands of pregnancies are terminated through spontaneous abortion, usually referred to as miscarriage. However, the focus of this section is on the *voluntary* termination of pregnancy. In obstetrical practice, abortions are induced differently depending on the time from the woman's last menstrual period. In the first trimester, medical and surgical abortions can be performed. In the second trimester, several different types of surgical procedures are considered. In the third trimester, abortions are only performed under specific medical circumstances. Guidelines for these abortions differ across the states and depend on the evaluation of fetal viability, maternal health-related risks, and state law (American Pregnancy Association, 2015c; Cunningham et al., 2014).

A nonsurgical approach to abortion, sometimes referred to as medical abortion, was developed in France in 1988 with the drug RU-486, now called mifepristone. The drug was approved by the Food and Drug Administration (FDA) in the United States in 2000 to be prescribed by a physician who can make a referral to a hospital or surgeon should a surgical abortion be required ("Congress and RU-486," 2001). The drug, called Mifeprex, combines two drugs: mifepristone, which blocks the hormone that sustains the uterine lining, and misoprostol, which causes uterine contractions. The combination of these drugs ends the pregnancy. Administration of Mifeprex typically requires several clinic visits. Based on data from 1.5 million women, the drug was found to be 92 percent to 95 percent effective in ending pregnancy within the first 49 to 63 days (Boonstra, 2013).

The Legal and Political Context of Abortion in the United States

At the heart of the abortion controversy in the United States is the conflict between society's responsibility to protect the health and reproductive rights of a woman and its responsibility to protect the rights of an unborn child. On one side are those who argue that a woman's human rights include self-determination and reproductive autonomy, including the right to privacy in consultations with her health care providers, and the right to choose or reject motherhood. In countries where legal abortions are restricted or prohibited, thousands of women resort to illegal procedures, resulting in death or impaired sexual and reproductive health. Since women bear the physical consequences of unintended pregnancies, access to the benefits of medical science to end those pregnancies is a central component of the case for legalized abortions.

On the other side are those who seek to treat fertilized eggs, embryos, and fetuses as separate legal persons deserving of the state's protection since they are incapable of protecting their own interests. This argument includes recognition of the prenatal embryo/fetus as a person who is legally entitled to the same parental support and protection as a child after birth. Those who oppose abortion from a religious perspective view it as a sin, violating a holy commandment against taking a human life. Since the well-being of a woman and her unborn fetus are intimately entwined, some argue that we cannot truly separate the well-being of one from the other (Fried, 2013).

A key developmental concept requiring clarification in the abortion controversy is the age at which the embryo is considered an individual and thus entitled to protection by the state. In 1973, in the case of *Roe* v. *Wade*, the U.S. Supreme Court proposed a developmental model to address that issue. The court supported the division of pregnancy into three trimesters and considered abortion a woman's right in the first trimester, guarded by the U.S. Constitution's protection of privacy. The court said that in the second trimester, some restrictions could be placed on access to abortion because of its risk to the mother; however, the fetus's rights were still not an issue during this period. In the final trimester, when the fetus was regarded as having a good chance of surviving outside the uterus, states could choose not to permit

The abortion controversy continues to highlight the social, political, religious, and cultural significance of the prenatal period. What do you see as the eventual resolution of this controversy in the United States?

abortion. This ruling endorsed a woman's right to full control over the abortion decision until the fetus reached a point of **developmental viability**. At that point, the court ruled, society's responsibility to the unborn child outweighs the woman's right to freedom and privacy.

As we discussed earlier in the chapter, medical practices and new technologies are having an impact on fetal viability. Whereas in the past, 24 weeks of gestational age was considered a lower threshold for viability, interventions at some specialized centers are successful in saving some babies at 22 to 24 weeks, leaving open the question of viability and related policy implications.

In the years since the *Roe v. Wade* decision, the Supreme Court has ruled unconstitutional the state laws that tried to regulate abortions. However, the states have a wide range of regulations, some permitting and others prohibiting restrictions of various types. The main areas where restrictions have been imposed are as follows: restrictions on abortion after a specified point related to **fetal viability**, abortion reporting requirements, clinic access, parental involvement, mandatory delay and state-directed counseling, restrictions on insurance coverage of abortion, state funding of abortion for Medicaid recipients, partial-birth abortion bans, and restrictions on later abortions. For details about the restrictions that apply in each state, visit the website of the Guttmacher Institute, www.guttmacher.org.

In general, the U.S. Supreme Court has ruled that states ought not to impose an undue burden on a woman by placing major obstacles in her way if she seeks an abortion before the fetus has reached viability. However, from 2010 t0 2015, states have enacted a total of 282 provisions restricting some aspect of access to abortion. According to a report issued by the American College of Obstetricians and Gynecologists (ACOG, 2014), many of these restrictions are neither evidence-based nor ethical:

> Abortion, although still legal, is increasingly out of reach because of numerous government-imposed restrictions targeting women and their health care providers. Recent years have seen a dramatic increase in the number and scope of legislative measures restricting abortion, with 22 states enacting 70 measures restricting abortion care in 2013. The greatest number of state-level restrictions ever enacted in 1 year was in 2011, with 92 restrictions. Health care providers face laws inappropriately unique to the provision of abortion that mandate procedures and counseling that are not evidence-based or ethical. The College, along with other medical organizations, opposes such interference with the patient–provider relationship, confirming the importance of this relationship in the provision of high-quality medical care. (ACOG, 2014)

Many states require counseling and informed consent, often with a mandatory waiting period, before the abortion can be performed. Restrictions also focus on the requirement for minors to get parental consent before having an abortion. Most states require reporting from physicians who perform abortions; some states require physicians to have specific hospital admitting privileges in order to perform abortions. At present, women are not required to have the consent of their husbands or the child's father before having an abortion (Nash, Gold, Rathbun, & Vierboom, 2015).

The impact of the anti-abortion movement has been to limit women's access to abortion resources across the country. By attacking and even killing physicians who perform abortions, by intimidating women as they approach clinics, by supporting measures that result in the loss of funding for clinics, and by pressing for legislation that impacts abortion practices, the availability of safe, legal abortion services has declined. One report found only 51 percent of obstetrics and gynecology residency programs routinely offer abortion training. What is more, although family medicine physicians are the most likely to serve women who are in the early stages of pregnancy and may be considering abortions, only 5 percent of family medicine residency programs include abortion training (ACOG, 2014). From 1982 to 2005, the number of abortion providers declined almost 50 percent. Most abortion clinics are located in urban areas. In 2014, 89 percent of U.S. counties lacked a single licensed abortion provider. This has had a differential impact on rural and low-income women (American College of Obstetricians and Gynecologists, 2014; Yanow, 2013).

Statistics About Legal Abortions and the Women Who Have Them

The number of reported legal abortions in the United States increased dramatically after the *Roe v. Wade* decision, from 745,000 in 1973 to 1,554,000 in 1980 (U.S. Census Bureau, 1999). Since then, the trend has been a decline in the number of abortions and in the ratio of abortions to live births. Based on data from 2012, the number of abortions in that year was 699,202, with an abortion ratio of 13.2 abortions per 1,000 women ages 14 to 44 (Pazol, Creanga, & Jamieson, 2015). This decline is attributed to a number of factors, including changes in attitudes toward abortion, decline in access to abortion clinics, more effective contraceptive use, and a resulting decline in the number of unwanted pregnancies especially among adolescents.

Some of the characteristics of U.S. women who had legal abortions in 2012 are summarized in Table 4.4. The data suggest that women who have abortions come from a variety of socioeconomic, developmental, and family contexts. Based on this diversity, one can infer that women have different reasons for having an abortion. The age group from 20 to 24 years old had the highest rate of abortions (32.8 percent of all abortions), followed by those from 25 to 29 (25.4 percent of all abortions) and 30 to 34 (16.4 percent of all abortions). White non-Hispanic women had 37.6 percent of all legal abortions. Most of the abortions were performed at less than 13 weeks gestation. Roughly one in three women had experienced two or more prior abortions.

The Psychosocial Impact of Abortion

What do we know about the impact of abortions on women? Are abortions medically risky? The mortality rate for women who experience a legal, induced abortion (0.6 per 100,000 women who have an abortion) is substantially lower than the

Table 4.4	Legal Abortions in the United States: Selected Characteristics, 2012
Total legal abortions in 2012:	699,202
Abortion ratio (no. of abortions per 1,000 women ages 14–44):	13.2
Age of women having abortions (%)	
Under 15	0.4
15–19	12.2
20–24	32.8
25–29	25.4
30–34	16.4
35–39	9.1
40 and over	3.7
Marital status of women having abortions (%)	
Married	14.7
Unmarried	85.3
Ethnicity of women having abortions (%)	
Non-Hispanic White	37.6
Non-Hispanic Black	36.7
Non-Hispanic Other	7
Hispanic	17.4
Number of prior live births for women having abortions (%)	
None	40.3
1	26.2
2	19.6
3	8.7
4 or more	5.3
Number of prior induced abortions (%)	
None	55.7
1	24.6
2	11
3 or more	8.6
Weeks of gestation at time of abortion (%)	
Less than 13 weeks	91.5

Source: Pazol, Creanga, & Jamieson, 2015.

mortality rate for women who carry a pregnancy to term and deliver a live baby (8.8 per 100,000 live births) (Raymond & Grimes, 2012).

How do women cope emotionally with the experience of abortion? Although the physical risks of abortion are less than those associated with childbirth, this still leaves unanswered questions about the emotional or psychological risks. Despite a substantial body of research, these questions are difficult to answer. Research on the emotional and mental health consequences of abortion continues to face methodological criticisms and inconsistent findings (Cougle, Reardon, & Coleman, 2005; Schmiege & Russo, 2005). Methodological questions include the following:

1. What are some differences between women who have had abortions and are willing to participate in research and those who are not?
2. What are the appropriate comparison groups in studies of abortion? For example, how do reactions to abortion compare with the mental health consequences associated with elective plastic surgery, breast reconstruction, or other surgeries?
3. What are the appropriate outcome measures?
4. When, how often, and for how long should the consequences of abortion be assessed?
5. How should differences in age, family status, and economic status be considered in this research?
6. How should differences in the reasons for having an abortion be considered in this research?

— CASE STUDY   Karen and Don —

This case explores the decision about giving birth to an infant with severe genetic anomalies.

A young couple, whom we will call Karen and Don, wanted to start a family but were troubled by a puzzling coincidence. A few years before, Don's sister had given birth to a daughter with abnormalities that matched a pattern in Don's younger brother: a heart defect, a double thumb, a club foot, and severe mental retardation.

Karen and Don went to a human genetics clinic and began a process of discovery. With the help of a counselor, they constructed a family tree … identified potential carriers of the disorder in Don's family, and [the counselor] persuaded them to get a blood test. Don's test confirmed the young couple's worst fear: He was a carrier and potential children were at risk. …

The impact of these discoveries on Don's family was profound. When blood testing revealed that his mother was not a carrier, she was relieved of a burden of guilt she had secretly carried for years… The same information implicated Don's father; his reaction to it can be gauged by his refusal to have a blood test … Don himself fell into guilty silence. Not only was he the carrier of a genetic defect, he was disappointing his wife, who desperately wanted to have a baby.

He thought of artificial insemination, rejected the idea, and came close to abandoning altogether the idea of having children. Then, suddenly and surprisingly, after beginning to look into adoption, Karen discovered she was pregnant. …

A process of intervention began for Karen and Don when amniocentesis revealed that theirs was to be a child with severe abnormalities. "Maybe I should go ahead and have the child," she remembered thinking, "because it could be the only one I'll ever have." But they had already decided under what conditions they would terminate their pregnancy.

Karen's abortion was no easy matter for her. "It's not like I just lost the baby, I had a miscarriage. I willfully went in and terminated a pregnancy, and it was hard for people to deal with it. Some people think it was the kind of thing … you go in and you're knocked out and you wake up and you're not pregnant anymore. And that's not the way it was at all. They induced labor, and I was in labor for ten hours, and I delivered a child. I was awake. My mother called to find out how I was doing afterward, but then dropped the subject. When I went back to work, everyone acted like things should be normal, like nothing had ever happened, and I was definitely mourning.

Source: From "Intergenerational Buffers: The Damage Stops Here," by J. Kotre and K. B. Kotre, 1998, pp. 367–389, in D. P. McAdams and E. de St. Aubin (Eds.), *Generativity and Adult Development: Psychosocial Perspectives on Caring for and Contributing to the Next Generation,* Washington, DC: The American Psychological Association.

CASE ANALYSIS Using What You Know

1. Try to put yourself in the roles of the main characters in this case: Karen, Don, Karen's mother, Don's mother, Don's father. How might you react?
2. Analyze how the biological, psychological, and societal systems are involved in understanding the issues faced by Karen and Don.
3. Compare how these experiences might influence the marital relationship for Karen and for Don.
4. Evaluate the ethical considerations in this case.
5. Examine the case through a cultural lens. In what ways do cultural issues related to pregnancy, childbirth, and abortion come into play in this case?

Findings of a task force convened by the American Psychological Association on Mental Health and Abortion reviewed numerous studies. After evaluating their methodological strengths and weaknesses, the task force reached the following conclusions:

1. The majority of women who terminate their pregnancy through a legal, first-trimester abortion do not have any mental health problems.
2. There is no systematic evidence that having an abortion causes mental health problems.
3. The risks of mental health problems associated with the first trimester termination of an unwanted pregnancy are about the same as risks for mental health problems among women who deliver an unwanted child (Major et al., 2009).

In addition, the task force found that "other risk factors, including poverty, prior exposure to violence, a history of emotional problems, a history of drug or alcohol use, and prior unwanted births place women at risk of experiencing both unwanted pregnancies and mental health problems after a pregnancy, irrespective of how the pregnancy is resolved. Failures to control for these co-occurring risk factors may lead to reports of associations between abortion history and mental health problems that are misleading" (TFMHA, 2008).

The typical emotional reactions of women who have had abortions are both positive and negative: relief at having taken control over one's situation by ending an unwanted pregnancy, and regret over the loss (Fergusson, Horwood, & Boden, 2009). In a study of more than 400 women 2 years after they had an abortion, 70 percent felt they had made the right decision. Especially when the pregnancy was unwanted and the abortion was performed within the first 12 weeks, women generally resolve any negative feelings and thoughts they may have had soon after the abortion (Adler et al., 1990). However, roughly 30 percent of women experience some emotional distress as they look back on their decision (Bradshaw & Slade, 2003).

Women differ in the reasons they give for having an abortion. In one study, 80 Norwegian women were interviewed at 10 days, 6 months, and 2 years after their abortion. Some of the reasons they gave as most important for the decision to have an abortion were education, job, finances, being tired and worn out, having enough children, the partner does not want children, and pressure from the male partner to have an abortion. At 6 months and 2 years, the strongest predictor of women's emotional distress associated with the abortion was feeling pressure from their partners to have the abortion. Women who said they had enough children had somewhat better psychological outcomes at 2 years than others (Broen, Moum, Bodtker, & Ekeberg, 2005).

Another factor related to post-abortion adjustment is a woman's views about the acceptability of abortion within the cultural context of her family's and community's beliefs (Wang & Buffalo, 2004). Some women perceive that having an abortion is unacceptable among their family and friends. They may even go so far as to try to keep the abortion a secret because they believe others will despise them for their decision. Not surprisingly, women who believe that abortion is an acceptable solution to an unwanted pregnancy and that abortion is also acceptable to their friends, family, and partner are less likely to experience strong feelings of regret or emotional upset following an abortion. Religious beliefs, childbearing motives, and the woman's awareness of community opinions influence her own attitudes toward abortion.

A review by the Academy of Medical Royal Colleges in London (AMRC, 2011) examined the results of all studies published between 1990 and 2011 on the emotional reactions to abortion. Following consideration of the limitations in these studies, the AMRC offered the following conclusions about the literature:

- Unwanted pregnancy increases a woman's risk of problems with her mental health.
- A woman with an unwanted pregnancy is as likely to have mental health problems from abortion as she is from giving birth.

- A woman with a history of mental health problems before abortion is more likely to have mental health problems after abortion.
- Circumstances, conditions, behaviors, and other factors associated with mental health problems are similar for women following abortion and women following childbirth.
- Pressure from a partner to terminate a pregnancy, negative attitudes about abortion, and negative attitudes about a woman's experience of abortion may increase a woman's risk of mental health problems after abortion.

Based on their assessment of the literature, the AMRC suggested that whereas legal abortion is a relatively mild procedure that does not threaten a woman's health, more attention should be given to the psychological and societal circumstances that are associated with unwanted pregnancies.

Men's Reactions to Abortion

Although abortion is often construed as a women's issue, women and their unborn babies are not the only people affected by the abortion decision. In 1976, the Supreme Court ruled that a woman did not need the consent of her husband or the child's father to have an abortion. Since that decision, the Supreme Court has supported a woman's independence from her husband or a child's father with regard to reproductive decision making. Men do not have a right to be notified about a woman's decision to have an abortion nor do they have a right to prevent an abortion. Even when men object to a woman's decision to carry a baby to term, they may still be required to contribute financially to the support of the child. Informal agreements between partners can allow men to have a greater role in the abortion decision. For example, if a woman wants an abortion, but the child's father is opposed, the couple can create a binding agreement that the man will cover the medical expenses of childbirth and assume legal parenthood (FindLaw, 2016). However, questions about the legal rights of fathers to determine the fate of their unborn children are still being raised, and the laws will probably continue to be challenged as fathers become increasingly committed to participation in parenting or resistant to the financial obligations associated with supporting an unwanted child.

Men clearly play a role in many women's decisions about whether or not to have an abortion. They also have their own reactions to the situation. For both of these reasons, there is a need to pursue systematic research about men's reactions to abortion, including their emotional responses and the consequences of the abortion for their future reproductive behavior.

Research suggests that men have ambivalent reactions to their partner's abortion including relief, grief, and sadness, and a desire to support their partners. Men also express a need for counseling programs for the male partners of women undergoing abortion (Coyle, 2007).

In a qualitative study of men's experiences with unintended pregnancy and abortion, a range of reactions were identified. Men differ in the degree to which they take responsibility for the pregnancy. In some cases, they viewed the unintended pregnancy as entirely the responsibility of their female partner. In other cases, they accepted shared responsibility. Similarly, men differed in the perception of the role they played regarding the pregnancy outcome. Some believed that their female partner made the decision, excluding them entirely; others felt that the decision was reached together; and still others claimed that they convinced their partner to end the pregnancy through abortion (Reich & Brindis, 2006).

Some research has focused especially on adolescent fathers who may experience feelings of anxiety, anger, and moral conflicts about abortion. Young men feel that they need to be strong for their girlfriends, even if they are feeling their own sense of confusion or loss. Just as for women, the response of men is embedded in their value system and in their relationship with the baby's mother. For young fathers, issues of secrecy and consideration for the girlfriend may prevent them from seeking support for their own feelings.

Research on men's influences on women's reproductive health suggests that women are concerned about their partners' attitudes, especially if they think that having a child or not having a child might result in abandonment (Dudgeon & Inhorn, 2004). Abuse by a partner may be one reason women choose to have an abortion. Women who believe that their partner will love them and their unborn child are more likely to give birth. However, most of the research on the role of men in the abortion decision is based on what women say about how they have taken their partner into account in reaching their decision. More research is needed to learn what shapes men's reactions to unintended pregnancy, their attitudes about abortion, how men contribute to the abortion decision, and how abortion experiences may influence a man's future approach to sexual relationships and paternity. This research needs to be approached from a cultural perspective, recognizing the dynamic interplay of gender roles, family structure, and religious and ethnic values.

The debate surrounding the legalization and availability of abortion services is an excellent example of a psychosocial controversy. Embedded in this controversy are key human development issues: When does human life begin? When is a fetus viable—that is, capable of life outside the uterus? What is society's responsibility to unborn children? To women of childbearing age? What is the impact of an abortion on a woman's physical health, psychological well-being, and future childbearing? What is the impact of bearing and rearing an unwanted child on a woman's physical health and psychological well-being? What is the impact of being an unwanted child? What are the rights of fathers with respect to a woman's decision to have an abortion? What are the rights and responsibilities of parents in regard to an adolescent's abortion? The politicization of the abortion controversy often overshadows the personal dilemmas that face women and men as they confront this difficult decision.

FURTHER REFLECTION Summarize your understanding of the politics of abortion. Why is this a political topic? Why would a person's views on abortion be relevant to how he or she would serve as a member of the state or federal legislature? How does your understanding of the content of this chapter on pregnancy and the prenatal period influence your own thinking about a woman's reproductive decisions?

CHAPTER SUMMARY

OBJECTIVE 1   Summarize the process through which genetic information is transmitted from one generation to the next.

Genetic inheritance links each new infant to a specific ancestry and to the evolutionary history of the species. The important work of the genes is to produce proteins, which then guide cellular formation and functioning. The laws of heredity explain how genetic information is passed from parents to their offspring. The genotype is the biochemical information encoded in the DNA; the phenotype is the expression of that information, which can be influenced by patterns of interacting genes, or the interaction of genes and the surrounding cellular, social, and physical environment. Epigenetic marks and mutations can alter the expression of genes in the person and in his or her offspring.

OBJECTIVE 2   Differentiate the contributions of genetic factors to individuality through their role in controlling the rate of development, their influences on individual traits, and the genetic sources of abnormalities.

Individual differences are due to a combination of the many variations in environment and experience that confront a growing person and the variability built into the biological mechanisms of heredity. Genetic factors contribute to differences in the rate and timing of development, to patterns of individual characteristics such as temperament or intelligence, and to anomalies that may result in abnormal development. The norm of reaction is a way of conceptualizing the probabilistic outcome of various phenotypes given a particular genotype. Through advances in scientific technologies, we are entering an era when it is possible to intervene to influence the genotype, thereby modifying its contribution to individual differences. These advances are accompanied by significant ethical considerations. The more we study human genetics, the more we learn about the dynamic and ongoing interplay of genetic information and environmental factors.

OBJECTIVE 3   Trace the process of prenatal development from fertilization through three trimesters of pregnancy, including an understanding of infertility, alternative means of reproduction, and related ethical considerations.

The 38 weeks of prenatal development, including the germinal period, the embryonic period, and the fetal period, involve a rapid differentiation of body organs and a gradual integration of survival functions, especially the ability to suck and swallow, the regulation of breathing and body temperature, and the maturation of the digestive system. Sense receptors are prepared to respond to stimulation long before they are put to use. The CNS, which begins to take shape in the third and fourth weeks after conception, continues to develop and change throughout the prenatal period and into childhood and adolescence. The newborn's neurobehavioral capacities are influenced by the quality of the prenatal environment, including potential disruptions to the CNS. During weeks 3 through 9 of the prenatal period, fetal development is especially vulnerable to the disruptive impact of teratogens, a wide range of viruses, medications, and environmental toxins that can harm organ differentiation and the maturation of the CNS. Medical advances are providing a range of increasingly effective alternative approaches for reproduction for couples who are unable to conceive and do not want to adopt a child. Each of these alternatives is accompanied by complex ethical considerations about the nature of parental rights and the fate of artificially produced embryos.

OBJECTIVE 4 Describe the birth process and analyze factors that contribute to infant mortality.

Childbirth is described in five stages: early signs that labor is approaching, the onset of labor, transition from labor to delivery, birthing, and the postpartum period. The length of labor is quite variable, with first births usually taking longer than subsequent births. Infant mortality rates are influenced by the quality of prenatal care, the availability of quality medical facilities for newborns, and risks associated with low birth weight often coupled with preterm births. The United States ranks behind many industrialized countries in the number of infants who die before the age of 1.

OBJECTIVE 5 Analyze ways that the pregnant woman and the developing fetus influence each other, focusing on how pregnancy affects a childbearing woman and expectant father, and the impact of environmental influences on fetal growth, such as a woman's age, drug use, nutrition, environmental toxins, and stress.

During pregnancy, the mother and the fetus are interdependent. The fetus alters the mother's physical state, fetal movements provide an ongoing source of stimulation, and pregnancy can introduce new risks to maternal health. Pregnancy affects a woman's social roles and social status. Pregnancy influences how people, including the baby's father, treat a woman and what resources become available to her. A woman's physical well-being and emotional state along with her attitude toward her pregnancy and her developing attachment to her unborn child set the stage for the quality of her parenting after the child is born.

Characteristics of the mother, her lifestyle, and her physical and cultural environments all influence fetal development. Of special concern are the mother's age, any drugs she takes during her pregnancy, her exposure to certain diseases and environmental toxins, exposure to stress, adequacy a woman's diet, and safety of the food she eats. Whereas each of these factors is known to have an impact on fetal development, increasing attention is being given to their cumulative impact. Infants conceived by women living in poverty are exposed to many of the environmental hazards that are known to result in low birth weight and physical abnormalities. Expectant fathers have different reactions, which influence their own well-being as well as the emotional and physical well-being of their pregnant partners. Men's outlook on their impending fatherhood reflects their own psychosocial maturity, their perceptions about the quality and stability of the relationships they are in, the stability of their employment, and their readiness to embrace the responsibilities of fatherhood.

OBJECTIVE 6 Examine the impact of culture on pregnancy and childbirth.

The experiences of pregnancy and childbirth occur in a cultural context. The birth culture provides a set of guidelines for behavior, attitudes toward and beliefs about restrictions on the woman's activities, the availability of resources, and the treatment of a pregnant woman by others. Cultures vary in their attitudes toward pregnancy along dimensions of solicitude versus shame and adequacy versus vulnerability. Even within cultures, there may be variability in attitudes depending on the age and social status of a woman and the timing of her pregnancy. Health providers are urged to be sensitive to cultural expectations about pregnancy and childbirth when providing care to recent immigrants or to women who are going through childbirth in an unfamiliar cultural context.

OBJECTIVE 7 Apply the psychosocial perspective to the topic of abortion, including the legal context, its social and emotional impact on women, and men's views.

The applied topic of abortion illustrates the integration of the biological, psychological, and societal systems as they impact an important issue in the field of human development. The decision to abort reflects the mother's attitude toward childbirth; her criteria for a healthy, normal child; her age and economic resources; and her access to a safe means of ending the pregnancy. Decisions about abortion are often tied to a woman's perceptions about her partner and his attitudes toward the unborn child. Decisions about abortion also reflect the culture's attitudes about the moral implications of ending a life after conception and the legal principles about when the fetus itself has a right to society's protection. Finally, the decision to abort is related to the safety, accessibility, and expense of the procedure. The research on abortion-related decision making and the mental health consequences of abortion are replete with difficulties. Men do not have a legal right to impose their views about a partner's abortion-related decision; however, they may work with their partner to create informal agreements about this decision.

The stage is now set to consider the remaining life stages in a psychosocial context. In this chapter, we have discussed the emergence of a child into an existing family, community, and cultural network. Although much attention has been given to the early period of childhood (birth through age 3) for subsequent cognitive, social, and emotional development, the analysis of the prenatal period suggests that the dynamic epigenetic process is already under way before birth. The care provided for expectant parents is intimately connected to the potential for optimal development in their offspring.

CASEBOOK

For additional cases related to this chapter, see the case of "Lonita and Tano," in *Life Span Development: A Case Book*, by Barbara and Philip Newman, Laura Landry-Meyer, and Brenda J. Lohman, pp. 32–37. This case introduces the challenges of supporting a healthy pregnancy for a new immigrant couple with few financial resources.

In 1921, Picasso's first son Paulo was born. In that year, he painted at least 13 works focusing on mother and child. In this image, a large, monumental style canvas, Picasso brings the classical tradition of Greek and Roman sculpture together with the intimacy of a loving relationship. The mother provides safety, security, and a calming affection. The baby gazes peacefully in her arms. We see the process of mutual adaptation as mother and infant establish patterns of meaningful interaction and build a foundation for trust.

1. Describe characteristics of newborns and explain the challenges facing low-birth-weight babies.

2. Identify important milestones in the maturation of the sensory/perceptual and motor systems. Describe the interactions among these systems during the first 2 years of life. Explain how brain development in infancy is tied to the maturation of the sensory and motor systems.

3. Discuss the development of sensorimotor intelligence, including an analysis of how infants process information, organize experiences, conceptualize causality, and understand the properties and functions of objects.

4. Summarize the beginnings of language competence from birth through the first 2 years of life.

5. Analyze social attachment, the process through which infants develop strong emotional bonds with others, and describe the dynamics of attachment formation during infancy.

6. Examine the nature of emotional development, including emotional differentiation, the interpretation of emotions, and emotional regulation. Analyze the concept of temperament as an organized aspect of emotional reactivity.

7. Explain the psychosocial crisis of trust versus mistrust; the central process through which the crisis is resolved, mutuality with the caregiver; the prime adaptive ego quality of hope; and the core pathology of withdrawal.

8. Evaluate the critical role of parents and caregivers during infancy, with special attention to issues of safety and nutrition; optimizing cognitive, social, and emotional development; and the role of parents and caregivers as advocates for their infants.

INFANCY (FIRST 24 MONTHS)

5

CASE STUDY   A Close Look at a Mother–Infant Interaction —

Systems theory invites us to look at infants as dynamic systems, striving to make meaning in the context of numerous daily caregiver–infant interactions. Infants gather information through their sensory and motor actions, monitor the reactions of others, and use that information to form increasingly coherent and complex ideas about themselves and others. In the following interchange between a mother and her 6-month -old infant, we get a glimpse into the kinds of situations that lead to an infant's formation of expectations about the world and his or her place in it.

The mother bends down to nuzzle the infant with her hair. The baby tightly grabs her hair and won't let go when she tries to disengage herself. The mother vocalizes in genuine pain ("Ow") and pulls back with an angry, bared-tooth facial expression. Although the mother's vocal and facial display of anger lasts less than half a second, the infant immediately responds in a defensive fashion. He brings his hands up in front of his face and turns away…The mother's angry display is not just an interesting or novel display or one with no significance; rather it has meaning for the infant. The infant appears to be apprehending danger. The mother immediately perceives the meaning of her infant's change in behavior and quickly changes what she is doing. She uses soothing, cajoling actions and vocalizations to try to repair the interactive rupture. At first, the infant stays behind his hands; then he tentatively peeks out at her. Gradually, over the next 30 to 40 seconds, he begins to smile, and then he smiles and looks at her, until they return to a state of mutual positive engagement.

Source: From "Infants' Meaning-Making and the Development of Mental Health Problems," by E. Tronick, and M. Beeghly, 2011, *American Psychologist, 66*, pp. 109–110.

CASE ANALYSIS Using What You Know

1. Explain the idea of the infant as an open system. What are the resources that the infant needs from the environment? What strategies does an infant have to obtain these resources?

2. Explain the role of facial expressions in this case. What roles do facial expressions play as infants and caregivers strive to understand each other?

3. Describe the sequence of meaning-making that takes place in this case. How might the meaning of this interaction alter future interactions?

4. Can you attribute motivation to the infant's action of pulling his mother's hair? What might it be? How might the mother's understanding of her infant's behavior alter the way she reacts to it?

Infancy is a period of strikingly rapid development. During the first year of life, the infant's birth weight almost triples. (Imagine if your weight tripled within 1 year at any other time in your life!) The baby seems to grow before your very eyes. Parents will remark that they go to work in the morning and their baby seems to have changed by the time they return in the evening. Along with this extraordinary rate of physical growth comes a remarkable increase in control and purposefulness. By the age of 2, the fundamentals of movement, language, and concept formation can be observed.

Infants are marvelously flexible. They do not know the culture or family into which they will be born. They have to be ready to adapt to the practices and customs of their early family or caregiving environment. Thus, we begin to appreciate the central role of culture as it shapes neural pathways and behavioral patterns from the very first days of life.

At the turn of the 20th century, many infants died before their first birthday. As a result, many parents did not invest emotionally in their infants. For example, they often did not name an infant until they were sure that the infant would live. Today, with vast improvements in infant survival each child is taken much more seriously. Safety concerns have prompted laws about car seats for infants, guidelines for putting babies to sleep on their back or side, and the widespread use of monitors in the baby's room to catch signals of infant distress. The medical community is devising complex technologies for saving the lives of babies who are born weighing 1,000 grams (32 oz.) or less. The psychological community is giving attention to infant temperament and the origins of personality, the emergence of language and problem solving abilities, and the potential impact of early stress on development. Research focuses on individual differences among infants even in the very first weeks of life. The Internet is filled with websites and blogs for expectant and new parents. A growing baby industry offers special equipment, foods, toys, books, and other paraphernalia. Sometimes in their exuberance to make a profit from a receptive target market, companies produce infant equipment, toys, and medications that are flawed and dangerous and have to be recalled.

Understanding development during infancy requires that one keep in mind that a genetically guided pattern of growth and development is in continuous interaction with complex and changing social and physical environments. The infant's capacities change, bringing the baby into interaction with new facets of the environment. The burgeoning field of cognitive neuroscience provides insights into the intimate interactions of sensory, motor, and social experiences and neural development. The repetition of daily experiences shape the infant's neural pathways, sculpting patterns of thought and behavior.

Five major developmental tasks are especially critical during infancy:

- Establishment and coordination of the sensory, perceptual, and motor systems
- Elaboration of information-processing capacities and sensorimotor intelligence
- Emergence of early communication skills
- Formation of attachments
- Differentiation of the emotional system

This chapter begins with a description of the physical status of the newborn and then discusses each of the five developmental tasks. The psychosocial crisis of infancy—trust versus mistrust—is explored as a way of thinking about the foundational orientation toward self and society. The applied topic at the end of the chapter analyzes how parents and caregivers can play key roles in promoting optimal development in infancy while laying the foundation for future growth. ●

Newborns

OBJECTIVE 1 Describe characteristics of newborns and explain the challenges facing low-birth-weight babies.

In the United States, the average full-term baby weighs 3,300 grams (7 to 7.5 pounds) and is 51 centimeters (20 inches) long. Boys are slightly heavier and longer than girls. At birth, girls' nervous systems and bones are about 2 weeks more mature than boys'.

In the first minute after birth, and then again at 5 minutes, the newborn's life signs are evaluated using the **Apgar scoring method**, named for its originator Virginia Apgar (see Table 5.1). Five life signs are scored on a scale from 0 to 2: heart rate, respiratory effort, muscle tone, reflex irritability, and body color. A score of 7 to 10 means the infant is in good condition. Scores of 4 to 6 mean the infant is in fair condition and may require the administration of supplemental oxygen. Scores of 0 to 3 suggest an extremely poor condition and the need for resuscitation. Even among the infants who score 7 to 10, those with scores of 7 or 8 show less efficient attention and poorer cognitive processing than the higher scoring infants. The most important use of the Apgar scoring method is for evaluating the need for immediate intervention; not as a means of assessing subsequent development. The Apgar score does not explain the source of the difficulty; it provides an indication about whether some level of intervention is needed (U.S. National Library of Medicine, 2014).

Babies differ in their physical maturity and appearance at birth. Differences in physical maturity have important consequences for the capacity to regulate survival functions such as breathing, digesting, waking, and sleeping. Infants who weigh less than 2,500 grams (about 5 pounds, 8 ounces) are called **low-birth-weight babies**. Low birth weight may result from prematurity (i.e., being born before the full period of gestation). It may also result from the mother's inadequate diet, smoking, or use of drugs, as discussed in chapter 4. These factors tend to lower the fetus's weight for a given gestational age. Babies who are **small for their gestational age** (SGA) are at greater risk for health problems than those who are born prematurely but are of average weight for their gestational age.

Preterm births—that is, births before 38 weeks of gestational age—now comprise about 10 percent of all live births.

Although many interventions have been devised to increase the survival of preterm infants, preterm birth is the most common cause of infant mortality. It is associated with a range of medical complications that result in the risk of serious disabilities including cerebral palsy, vision and hearing impairments, and neurological impairments. The earlier the baby is born, the greater the risks of these complications (Center for Disease Control and Prevention, 2015).

The care for preterm infants typically takes place in a neonatal intensive care unit (NICU) of a hospital. Monitoring and management of their breathing, temperature regulation, and heart rate and creation of appropriate stimulation and nurturing in the hospital all contribute to improved chances for survival. Skin-to-skin contact between mothers or fathers and their infants, sometimes referred to as *Kangaroo Care*, has been shown to have benefits for the newborn as well as for parents. It provides a variety of sensory stimulation to the infant and increases the caregivers' confidence and comfort in caring for their baby. Preterm babies who receive *Kangaroo Care* as well as other forms of gentle touching and massage gain weight faster, have improved temperature regulation, and improved alertness as compared to babies who do not receive the systematic comfort of human touch (Feldman, 2011; Feldman & Eidelman, 2004; C. S. Mott Children's Hospital-University of Michigan Health System, 2015).

During the third prenatal trimester, especially between 30 and 34 weeks of gestation, certain self-regulatory functions related to self-calming in the face of unpleasant stimuli and organization of wake-sleep cycles become integrated and synchronized. Babies born before 30 weeks do not have the benefit of positive features of the uterine environment that support these aspects of **self-regulation**. **The Applying Theory and Research to Life** box about very small babies discusses some of the risks for developmental disabilities among babies weighing less than 1,500 grams. Renewed efforts are needed to determine the causes of low birth weight and to prevent as many preterm births as possible.

FURTHER REFLECTION: Summarize the developmental advantages for full-term babies and the risks for babies who are small for their gestational age. Thinking back to chapter 4, what steps might be taken to reduce the incidence of preterm and SGA babies in the United States?

Table 5.1	The Apgar Scoring Method		
	Score		
Sign	**0**	**1**	**2**
Heart rate	Absent	Slow (less than 100 beats/minute)	More than 100 beats/minute
Respiratory effort	Absent	Slow or irregular breathing	Good crying, strong breathing
Muscle tone	Flaccid or limp	Weak; some flexion of extremities	Active motion, strong flexion of extremities
Reflex irritability	No response	Weak cry, grimace, cough, or sneeze	Vigorous cry, grimace, cough, or sneeze
Color	Blue, pale	Body pink, extremities blue	Completely pink

Source: Apgar, 1953.

Very Small Babies

Many babies are born before they reach full gestational maturity. Modern technology has pushed back the boundary of fetal viability to about 24 weeks of gestational age, or a weight of about 500 grams (slightly more than 1 pound). These tiny babies, not much bigger than the palm of your hand, receive weeks of round-the-clock care in their struggle to survive. Hours of intensive care combined with new medical technologies increase the life chances for very tiny babies, yet many of them are at high risk for developmental disabilities associated with their extremely low birth weight and related physical immaturity. In one study of over 4,000 babies born between 22 and 25 weeks of gestational age, 49 percent died and 30 percent lived with disabilities; only 21 percent lived without disabilities (Lee et al., 2010).

Infants who are born at very low birth weights (less than 1500 grams) combined with a low gestational age (under 32 weeks) are much more likely to face chronic health risks including cerebral palsy, asthma, impaired vision, developmental delays, and cognitive impairment compared to babies born at normal weight and full term. Thus extreme prematurity is associated with increased risk of a range of neurological difficulties and disabilities requiring increased levels of medical, educational, and parental care (Hack et al., 2005). However, with improved medical interventions, many of these associated difficulties can be prevented. In a Finnish study, 155 very-low-birth-weight (VLBW) babies were compared to 129 full-term babies. Roughly two thirds of the VLBW babies did *not* have medical complications associated with prematurity (Huhtala et al., 2016).

Very-low-birth-weight babies are clearly different from full-term babies. They are less physically attractive; have higher pitched, unpleasant cries; are more easily overstimulated and more difficult to soothe; and are less able to establish rhythmic patterns of social interaction. In a longitudinal study, Ruth Feldman (2007) compared three groups: high-risk, very small babies born at less than 1,000 grams; low-risk preterm infants (1,700– 1,850 grams); and full-term infants. She was interested in how the coordination of two important biological rhythms, the sleep-wake cycle and vagal tone, differed for the very small babies, and how these biological rhythms might relate to the infant's ability to orient to and react to stimuli.

Vagal tone is a process through which changes in heart rate vary during changes in environmental conditions. Typically, when you breathe in, heart rate increases; when you breathe out, heart rate decreases. Under conditions when a task requires attention and concentration, heart rate increases, which allows for the adaptive mobilization of resources. When the situation becomes more intense or threatening, heart rate slows, leading to conservation of resources and the ability to achieve a more calm state. The vagal system contributes to regulation of arousal and reactivity and is considered to be a basic neural component of self-regulation, information processing, and emotion (Bornstein & Suess, 2000). Feldman hoped to learn whether these biological rhythms would predict infants' ability to modify their reactions to stimuli and to engage in coordinated interactions with their mothers at 3 months.

The first comparison of the three groups was based on data collected at 37 weeks gestational age for the preterm babies and at the second day after birth for the full-term babies. The full-term babies had the most mature sleep-wake cycle and the most mature vagal tone. The low-risk preterm babies scored next, and the high-risk preterm babies had the poorest scores. Both the sleep-wake cycle and vagal tone were related to neurobehavioral orientation.

At 3 months, the infants who showed the poorest vagal tone were more likely to show distress and crying in response to a sequence of stimuli and were less likely to engage in synchronous interactions with their mothers. The study supports the important role of full gestation in allowing for the organization of critical neurobiological rhythms and their subsequent role in fostering emotional

regulation, attention, and social interactions. It also helps to account for some of the difficulties parents experience in social interactions with their very small babies.

Several factors help account for the risks that VLBW infants face in subsequent cognitive development. Infants who are born weighing less than 1,500 grams are likely to suffer brain hemorrhages. Moreover, their undeveloped lungs cannot deliver an adequate supply of oxygen to the brain. Chronic lung disease, frequently associated with prematurity, results in breathing problems, feeding difficulties, lung infections, and disrupted flow of oxygen. These insults to the nervous system have an impact on a variety of information-processing skills that can be measured in newborns, including regulation of arousal and attention, visual recognition of familiar stimuli, and reactivity to novel stimuli (Huhtala et al., 2016; Grunewaldt et al., 2014).

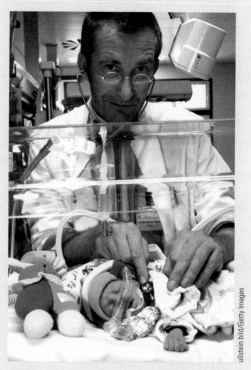

Improvements in neonatal intensive care units (NICUs) include providing a more stimulating, infant-adapted environment while still monitoring basic functions and intervening to enhance chances of survival.

In the Finnish study noted previously, if the VLBW premature babies had none of the medical conditions typically associated with prematurity, their health and quality of life at age 7 was comparable to that of children born full term. However, if the babies had one or more health complications associated with being VLBW, they had notably lower scores on nine dimensions of health and quality of life at age 7 including vision, hearing, breathing, eating, speech, excretion, learning and memory, appearance, and concentration.

Other studies of VLBW babies have begun to focus on the specific aspects of brain architecture that may be compromised as a result of prematurity. Rapid maturation in the CNS takes place during the last prenatal weeks and the first 2 years after birth. When babies born extremely prematurely were compared to full term infants at age 10, many showed evidence of deficits in brain volume and cortical surface area that negatively impacted working memory, motor skills, attention, and self-regulation (Gruenwaldt et al., 2014).

Given the significant challenges faced by very-low-birth-weight babies and their families, research has also focused on evaluating evidence-based programs that provide support and early intervention. First and foremost, chances for survival are improved when very premature babies are delivered in a Level III neonatal intensive care hospital unit. All states have early intervention programs, authorized through the Individuals with Disabilities Education Act, that provide coordinated care for families with infants who are at risk for developmental delays or physical disabilities (National Dissemination Center for Children with Disabilities, 2013).

Critical Thinking Questions

1. List the reasons that very small babies are at risk for impairments of cognitive and sensorimotor functioning.
2. Drawing on information provided in chapter 4, describe neurological development in the last trimester that may be disrupted by preterm birth.
3. Hypothesize why the consequences of neurological damage due to prematurity might become more evident as children get older.
4. What advice would you give to parents of premature infants about how to evaluate their child's developmental level and how to foster a developmentally appropriate set of childrearing expectations?

Developmental Tasks

The Development of Sensory/Perceptual and Motor Functions

OBJECTIVE 2 Identify important milestones in the maturation of the sensory/perceptual and motor systems. Describe the interactions among these systems during the first 2 years of life. Explain how brain development in infancy is tied to the maturation of the sensory and motor systems.

In chapter 4, you learned about the emerging sensory, perceptual, and motor capacities that have been observed during the prenatal period. Depending on his/her gestational age, a newborn has already experienced some vital sensory/perceptual and motor stimulation in utero. However, once the infant encounters the diversity of stimuli in the external environment, the sensory/perceptual system—vision, hearing, taste, smell, touch, motion sensitivity, and responsiveness to internal cues (*proprioception*)—develops rapidly; much more quickly than the motor system. Because most muscle movements are not under the infant's voluntary control in the early months of life, researchers have had to apply considerable ingenuity to study infants' sensory/perceptual competencies. How can you know if an infant detects the difference between the color red and the color orange, or between the mother's voice and the voice of a stranger? We cannot simply ask an infant to point to a circle or press a button to respond to a certain change in color or image. Behaviors such as gazing time, changes in heart rate, strength or frequency of sucking, facial action, head turning, observations of neural firing, and habituation are used as indicators of infants' interest or change in response to stimuli.

Habituation means that the infant's response decreases after each presentation of an identical stimulus. Habituation is one of the most primitive forms of learning and is observed in many mammalian species. Habituation allows the infant to shift attention to new aspects of the environment as certain elements become familiar. When a new stimulus is presented, such as a new level of loudness, or the same tone presented to a different ear, the infant shows an increase in alert responsiveness.

Habituation is one way to determine whether an infant can discriminate between two different stimuli. The researcher first habituates the infant to one stimulus; then a second stimulus is presented. Signs of renewed interest or alertness, measured by changes in heart rate, gazing time, or eye movements, are taken as evidence that the infant has detected a difference between the two stimuli. If the infant shows no new signs of interest or responsiveness, this is taken as evidence that the differences between the two stimuli were too slight to be perceived. Research supports the notion that young infants are capable of forming and retaining a memory for sensory experiences against which they can compare new events.

Brain Development in Infancy

Most infants are born with intact sensory organs and a well-formed brain. The infant's brain contains about 100 billion **neurons**, or nerve cells, which are already connected in pathways that are designed to execute functions related to sensation, perception, and motor behavior as well as to regulate internal systems such as respiration, circulation, digestion, and temperature control (FIGURE 5.1 ▶). The basic architecture of the brain, including regions of the brain and their interconnections, serves as the foundation for all subsequent learning, behavior, and health. The fundamental organization of the brain does not

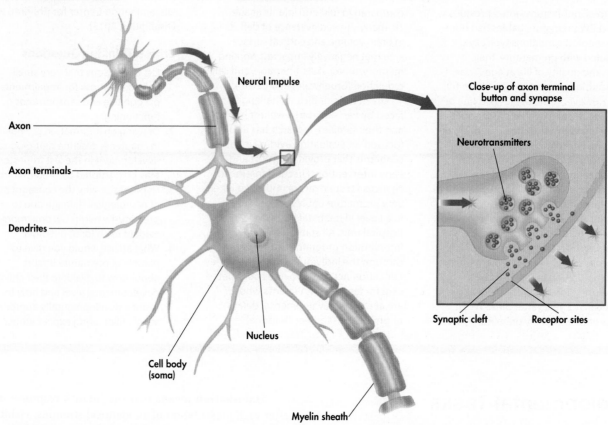

FIGURE 5.1 ▶ MODEL OF NEURON

Source: From Rathus. Psychology, 8E. © 2007 South-Western, a part of Cengage Learning, Inc. Reproduced by permission. www.cengage.com/permissions

change after birth, but details of its structure demonstrate **plasticity** (Center of the Developing Child at Harvard University, 2016).

What is **neural plasticity**? It can be thought of in two different but related ways. First, there are all the changes in the interconnections among neurons that occur as a result of learning and experience:

- The formation of neurons.
- The continuing growth of axons and dendrites.
- The formation of synapses, the connections between the axons of one cell and the dendrites of another.
- The sculpting or **pruning** of synapses.
- The production of neurotransmitters, the chemicals that stimulate or inhibit the firing of specific neurons.
- Myelination, the white fatty substance that insulates the neurons and increases the speed of firing from one neuron to the next.
- The production of glial cells that provide stability for the neural network.

The human brain is genetically designed to take in information and use it to guide further thought and action through the establishment of neural pathways. This allows humans to form neural connections that take into account the unique features of their environments and cultures. In the prenatal period, brain cells are formed and the initial organization of the brain structures takes place. Neurons are produced at an astounding rate, and axons and dendrites are formed as the nerve cells begin to link up with each other.

Transient exuberance is the term given to this rapid increase in the number of neurons, dendrites, and synapses that form during the first 2 years of life. As the term suggests, the growth is exceptional, producing far more neurons than will actually be used, and the rate of growth is temporary, preparing the brain to be shaped and organized through experience. Throughout infancy the interconnections among neurons and the speed of firing increase. Changes in the central nervous system improve the infant's ability to organize and use information and to regulate behavior. The early years are the most active period for establishing neural connections, but new connections can form throughout life and unused connections continue to be pruned. Connections that form early provide either a strong or weak foundation for the connections that form later. However, the connections among neurons are not fixed; they can be modified and strengthened through repeated experiences and deliberate practice. These connections are a biological underpinning of all new learning.

Second, neural plasticity can refer to the variety of ways that the brain compensates for injury by making use of alternative resources. For example, severe damage to the left cerebral cortex, where many language-related functions have been located, does not result in lasting language deficits if it occurs prenatally or in the very early postnatal period. As long as the damage does not impact both hemispheres, the infant's language capacities can mature without significant or noticeable disruption or delay (Bates & Roe, 2001).

During the first 3 years, the brain triples in weight and creates about 1,000 trillion connections among the neurons. Different areas of the brain experience an overproduction of synapses at different times, with the visual cortex taking the lead, followed by areas related to hearing and language and the prefrontal cortex where higher level thought and problem solving take place. Then, the pathways are gradually paired down. As a result of early experiences, sights, smells, sounds, tastes, touches, and postures activate and strengthen specific neural pathways, whereas other pathways are not used and decay. The frequency and speed with which nerves fire across a synapse strengthen the stability of the synapse. In the visual and auditory regions, this pruning seems to be completed during the preschool and early childhood periods. In the prefrontal cortex, however, sculpting continues to about age 24, suggesting a much longer window for the organization of higher order reasoning capacities (Giedd et al., 2012).

The process of pruning or sculpting leads to a reduction in plasticity. Although we do not know the exact timing for each area of sensory or motor competence, it is believed that there is much greater plasticity during the period of overproduction of synapses and reduced plasticity once the number of synapses reaches its adult level. For example, in the development of language, all infants are capable of recognizing and uttering sounds from a wide universe of languages. However, after repeated interactions with family members and caregivers, the infant develops strong neural connections for the sounds of the language(s) spoken in the home environment. The neural connections associated with sounds from other languages decay with disuse (Friederici, 2008). Significant injuries or deficiencies in experiences required for optimal functioning become harder to correct as the system becomes more finely organized.

In addition to the production and loss of synaptic connections among neurons, brain development advances through the production of **neurotransmitters**, the chemicals that influence how the nerves grow, how they respond to stimulation, and whether they result in the firing or the inhibition of firing of the neurons. These chemicals influence the growth in dendrites and synapses in various parts of the brain, they alter synaptic strength, and they change in strength following trauma to aid in repair. Experiences such as skin-to-skin contact, which was described as an intervention for preterm infants, contribute to the release of certain chemicals, including oxytocin, that help relieve pain, reduce stress, and provide a sense of security (Carter, 2014). There is a growing interest in how specific aspects of early nurturing might influence the neurochemical environment and thereby alter brain development. The box on **Applying Theory and Research to Life** addresses the role of early stress on brain development.

APPLYING THEORY AND RESEARCH TO LIFE

The Impact of Early Life Stress on Subsequent Brain Development

An infant's brain is especially vulnerable to exposure to stress. Responding to stressors is an important aspect of normal adaptation and development. You can image many possible sources of stress in an infant's daily life such as being hungry, being wet or cold, feeling overstimulated, or wanting physical or social contact. In the face of stress, the body prepares us to respond by increasing the heart rate, blood pressure, and stress hormones, such as cortisol. When an infant's stress response systems are activated within an environment of supportive relationships, these physiological effects are buffered and brought back down to baseline. The result is the development of healthy stress response systems (Center on the Developing Child, 2007). You may recall from chapter 2 that one contribution of object relations theory is the idea that the caregiver creates an interpersonal environment that helps an infant interpret and respond to stress. Thus, in a caring, responsive environment, exposure to stressors can create neural networks that link the stress responses to systems that help to soothe and calm the aroused emotional and physical states.

However, when the stressors are intense and prolonged, without the support of a caring, responsive social environment, the stress response may be prolonged. The accompanying respiratory, circulatory, and hormonal reactions do not return readily to a calm state. Prolonged activation of the stress response system can disrupt the development of brain architecture, increasing the risk for stress-related disease and cognitive impairment.

A violent, neglectful, or erratic caregiving environment may be one of the most central sources of this type of toxic stress. For example, researchers studied the brain functioning of 6- to 12-month-old infants who had been exposed to various levels of inter-parental conflict. Higher levels of inter-parental conflict were associated with changes in the infant's brain architecture associated with more negative emotionality (Graham et al., 2015). Another study explored the relationship of infant attachment status and brain development in early adulthood. Secure attachment is known to emerge in the context of responsive and synchronous caregiving. Those adults who had been characterized as having an insecure attachment in infancy were found to have an enlarged amygdala in early adulthood (Moutsiana et al., 2015). These and other studies provide further evidence of a link between exposure to a stressful parenting environment and brain architecture.

Critical Thinking Questions

1. What are some specific ways that supportive parenting helps infants manage stress?
2. Why might exposure to inter-parental conflict be a source of stress for infants?
3. What might be some links between excessive hormonal activation in infancy, brain architecture, and later cognitive functioning?
4. What is an example of a policy or program that might improve the positive interpersonal environment of infants and young children? How does it work?

As we continue to understand the relationship of brain development to changes in motor behavior, cognition, emotional expression and inhibition, language and communication, interpersonal or social behavior, and self-awareness, keep these two important principles in mind: First, through interactions with the immediate stimulus environment each infant shapes the organization of neural connections, creating very early patterns of familiarity and meaning. Thus, infants contribute to their own brain development by repeating certain actions, attending to certain stimuli more than others, and producing responses in caregivers (Center on the Developing Child, 2016).

Second, throughout childhood, adolescence, and adulthood, more complex cognitive functions, including organized and abstract thought; self-control; appreciation for subtle forms of communication such as sarcasm; capacities for poetry, music, and symbolic art; spatial reasoning; and cognitive flexibility, will emerge. Even though a lot of attention has been given to the importance of brain development in the first 3 years of life, advanced reasoning and expert knowledge require continued maturation of specific areas of the cortex as well as the synchronization of systems in the periods of adolescence and adulthood (Lebel & Beaulieu, 2011; Rubia et al., 2006).

Sensory/Perceptual Development

FIGURE 5.2 ▶ provides a map of the sensory and motor areas of the brain that are related to the infant's emerging capacities. The map suggests that specific functions are guided by activity in certain areas of the brain. However, that is an oversimplification. Early experiences create neural networks that link areas of the brain. For example, movement, body sensations, perception, hearing, and vision are all stimulated as an infant nurses or sucks from a bottle. The more frequently an experience occurs, the stronger and more rapidly the neural connections are made, linking these regions of the brain. Over time, as networks become strengthened through memory and associated emotions, they form foundational neural systems upon which other associations and links can be built. More complex processes such as decision making, learning and memory,

emotional expression and recognition, planning, and participation in meaningful social interactions require the interaction and feedback among several areas, including increasing engagement of the prefrontal cortex, a process that unfolds over time with experience and practice (Buschman & Miller, 2007).

It would be difficult to review the full range and detail of sensory capacities that emerge and develop during infancy. Maturation in these domains is breathtaking. Our discussion focuses on those abilities that permit infants to participate in and adapt to their social environment. From birth, sensory/perceptual capacities are vital resources that help infants establish interpersonal ties with their caregivers, gather information about their environment, and cope with sources of stress. Although we provide information on each of the sensory modalities, keep in mind that they typically function together as a multimodal system. Infants not only hear their caregivers, but they also see, smell, and touch them. Voices are normally associated with faces; tastes are linked to smells and textures. Sensory meaning-making takes place with the benefit of information from multiple sources.

Hearing. You may be surprised to learn that hearing rather than vision is the sense that provides the very earliest link between newborns and their mothers. Research has confirmed that the fetus is sensitive to auditory stimulation in utero (Porcaro, 2006). Before birth, the fetus hears the mother's heartbeat. This sound continues to be soothing to the infant in the days and weeks after birth. Newborns show a preference for the sound of their mother's voice over an unfamiliar voice. The speed with which they recognize their mother's voice suggests both increased attention and clear memory for this type of auditory stimulus (Kisilevsky et al., 2009; Purhonen et al., 2005). Infants show a preference for the sound of melodies that their mother sang during the pregnancy and even for the sound of prose passages she read during the prenatal period. An infant's indication of preference for these auditory stimuli is most likely based on familiarity with the sounds from exposure in utero (DeCasper & Fifer, 1980; DeCasper, Granier-Deferre, Fifer, & Moon, 2011; DeCasper & Spence, 1986).

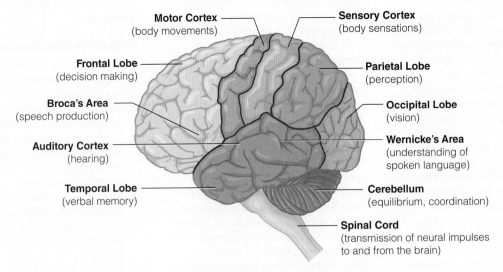

FIGURE 5.2 ▶ SENSORY AND MOTOR AREAS OF THE HUMAN CORTEX

Source: From D. A. Shaffer and K. Kipp, *Developmental Psychology, Childhood & Adolescence*, 7th ed., Fig. 6.6, p. 202, © 2007, Wadsworth/Thomson.

Even in the first weeks of life, a newborn is taking in sensory information about her mother's face, the sound of her voice, her scent, and the way it feels to be cuddled in her arms.

Young infants can distinguish changes in the loudness, pitch, duration, and location of sounds. They can use auditory information to differentiate objects from one another and to track the location of objects (Bahrick, Lickliter, & Flom, 2006; Wilcox, Woods, Tuggy, & Napoli, 2006). Many of these capacities are present among newborns but become increasingly sensitive by 6 months. In one study, infants ages 4 to 6 months were exposed to a looming sound that appeared to come closer or recede from them at a slow or rapid pace. When the sound loomed toward them quickly, the babies leaned back in a defensive strategy to escape the anticipated threat. This suggests that infants have the ability to use auditory information to detect relative speed and distance (Freiberg, Tually, & Crassini, 2001).

The human voice is one of the earliest stimuli to evoke an infant's smile. Infants appear to be particularly sensitive to language sounds (Benasich & Leevers, 2003). In a comparison of newborns and babies 3 months old, the newborns were equally interested in human and monkey vocalizations, and preferred these sounds to synthetic sounds. By 3 months, however, babies showed a clear preference for human over monkey vocalizations, suggesting that human auditory preferences take shape rapidly in the first months of life (Vouloumanos, Hauser, Werker, & Martin, 2010).

Very young babies are able to differentiate basic sound distinctions used in human speech throughout the world. Infants from all language environments are able to perceive and distinguish among the speech sounds that could be used in one or more of the world's languages. By 6 months of age, however, infants prefer to listen to sequences of words spoken in the mother's language rather than in a foreign language, especially if the two

languages differ in their overall tone, pauses, and rhythm (Fava, Hull, & Bortfeld, 2014).

During the second 6 months of life, speech perception becomes more tied to the native language. After exposure to a native language, the infant's ability to perceive and produce some sound distinctions declines. Infants begin to produce babbling sounds and attach meaning to certain sound combinations they hear around them, indicating a reorganization of sensory capabilities as the child learns to listen to people speaking a particular language (Altvater-Mackensen, Mani, & Grossman, 2016; Bornstein, 2012; Werker, Yeung, & Yoshida, 2012). This is an example of the plasticity referred to earlier—a fine-tuning of the neural network as a result of experience.

Vision. For sighted, normally developing infants, gazing provides an early and continuing source of information that guides social interactions and learning about the physical environment (Hoehl et al., 2009). Newborns and their caregivers gaze into each other's eyes. Mutual gazing has been shown to have a calming effect on distressed babies. Babies also actively avert their gaze when they need to reduce or withdraw from stimulation. By 4 months of age, babies can follow the gaze of another person toward an object and by 9 months, they use the gaze and head-turning cues of others to direct their attention. By gazing at others and following the gaze of others, babies use vision to form social connections, focus attention, and gain information from others about important objects and activities in their environment (Akhtar & Gernsbacher, 2008; Moore, 2008).

The vast majority of research on sensory development in infancy has concentrated on assessing the acuity or sensitivity of vision. Infants respond to a variety of visual dimensions, including movement, color, brightness, complexity, light-dark contrast, contours, depth, and distance. **Visual acuity** improves rapidly during the first 4 months. Infants are born with a variety of skills for detecting visual stimuli, which matures rapidly into the coordination of visual perception. Pattern and movement perception mature as well. By 2 months, infants form an expectation of a visual sequence. As they watch a pattern of events, they show evidence of anticipating the next event in the sequence (MacMurray & Aslin, 2004). Four-month-old babies perceive objects as adults would. They recognize shapes and colors, and detect complex patterns of motion such as human walking. However, the process of visual cognition—that is, understanding the nature of objects and their physical properties—requires further experience and experimentation.

Visual behaviors also offer a way to assess the infant's cognitive capacities. For instance, the time an infant takes to scan an object and the length of time spent fixating on a novel object are indications of infant intelligence. Shorter fixation time indicates greater speed and efficiency in neural processing (Iliescu & Dannemiller, 2008).

Faceness. Faces are especially salient visual stimuli. Research shows that there is a region of the brain that is active in processing faces; specific nerves fire exclusively in response to faces and not to other visual stimuli. Moreover, among those neurons, some are triggered by particular features of faces such as the round shape, the arrangement and distance between the eyes, or the size of the iris (Nakato et al., 2011; Tsao, 2006). It is as if the brain is organized to build an increasingly complex perception of faces by integrating the recognition of a variety of specific features.

Infants show preference for face-like stimuli (Nelson, 2001). In the early weeks following birth, infants have optimal focus on objects that are about 20 cm away— approximately the distance between the mother's face and her baby cradled in her arms. Newborns can shift focus to scan and keep track of a moving target, but not as easily and smoothly as older babies. Young infants focus their attention on the contours or external borders of objects rather than on the internal details. Thus, if you were holding a young baby, the child might appear to be staring at your hairline or your chin rather than at your mouth.

Faces have many of the properties that infants prefer. The hairline is a type of contour, the eyes provide a light-dark contrast, and the facial expressions provide a changing, moving stimulus. Some 2-day-old infants discriminate between their mother's face and the face of a stranger. By 3 months, almost all infants can distinguish a parent's face from that of a stranger (Nakato et al., 2011). These visual perceptual skills illustrate the highly developed capacities for orienting toward social stimuli that permit infants to participate readily in the social context on which their survival depends.

An experiment with newborns who were 25 to 73 hours old demonstrated that one aspect of a face that is important to babies is the top-heavy configuration of the features (Cassia, Turati, & Simion, 2004). FIGURE 5.3 ▶ shows the comparisons that support this conclusion. Babies preferred the upright to the upside-down face and the top-heavy scrambled face to the bottom-heavy scrambled face. By 6 or 7 months of age, infants treat **faceness** as a special visual category, showing surprise when facial features are disorganized or upside down (Cashon, 2011).

In addition to the form, shape, and movement of the human face, certain facial expressions appear to have meaning to very young babies. One- and 2-day-old babies are able to discriminate and imitate the happy, sad, and surprised expressions of a live model. This very early capacity for imitation wanes and is replaced between the ages of 1 and 2 months with a voluntary capacity for imitation of facial expressions when the model is not present. Sometime between 4 and 7 months, infants are able to recognize and classify some expressions such as happiness, fear, and anger (DeHaan & Carver, 2013; McClure, 2000).

Lack of motion in an adult face has a disturbing effect on infants. When adults pose with a still face, babies stop looking at the adult and, in some cases, begin grimacing or showing other signs of discomfort. This reaction suggests that infants anticipate a certain normal sequence of facial movements in a human interaction. The absence of facial movements is not simply noted as novel, but distressing (Adams, Franklin, Nelson, & Stevenson, 2010; Muir & Lee, 2003).

Of course, sights and sounds typically go together. When people speak, their mouths change shape and their faces move. By 3 months of age, infants recognize familiar voice-face associations. They show surprise when a familiar face is paired with an unfamiliar voice (Brookes et al., 2001). So while babies are making sense of their visual environment, they are also using vision as a source of information about language and communication. The visual sense plays a key role in helping babies connect and communicate with others. Through vision, babies are able to recognize their familiar caregivers, observe changes in their caregivers' emotions, and maintain contact through tracking and gazing long before they are able to crawl or walk.

Taste and Smell. Taste and smell are closely linked sensory capacities that contribute to our experience of flavor in food. Although we have only a limited number of taste receptors, possibly five or six, we are able to recognize and differentiate hundreds of different smells. Newborns can tell the difference among sweet,

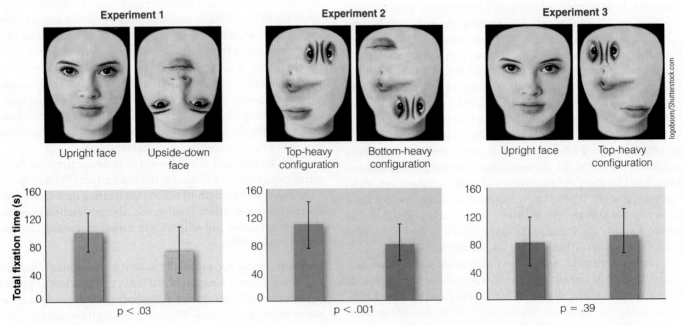

FIGURE 5.3 ▶ STIMULUS PAIRS FROM THREE EXPERIMENTS ON INFANTS' PREFERENCE FOR TOP-HEAVY CONFIGURATIONS For each experiment, the total fixation time toward each stimulus is shown along with the p value for comparison between the two stimuli.

Source: From "Can a Nonspecific Bias Toward Top-Heavy Patterns Explain Newborns' Face Preference?" by V. M. Cassia, C. Turati, and F. Simion, 2004, *Psychological Science, 15*, pp. 379–383.

salty, bitter, and sour tastes. Evidence of preference for sweet and salt over bitter and sour can be seen in their facial expressions as well as in the eagerness with which they consume various foods. Certain preferences, especially for sweet and salt, appear to be innate; however, these preferences can be modified as a result of prenatal and early postnatal exposure (Beauchamp & Mennella, 2009).

The food choices a pregnant woman makes influence the flavor of the amniotic fluid. Experiences with these flavors impact a baby's taste preferences. In one study, women were randomly assigned to groups that either drank carrot juice in the last trimester of pregnancy or refrained from eating anything involving carrots. The infants whose mother drank carrot juice showed a clear preference for carrot-flavored cereal in comparison to babies whose mothers did not eat carrots (Beauchamp & Mennella, 2011). Similar studies have demonstrated the impact of taste preferences for anise, mint, vanilla, and blue cheese (Bakalar, 2012).

Taste preferences continue to be influenced by the flavors that are transferred from the lactating mother's diet to her breast milk. Human milk has both nutrients and flavor. Exposure to a variety of smells and tastes through breast milk introduces novelty and diversity of flavor experiences, which result in a greater willingness to eat various foods when babies make the transition from milk to solid foods. The early flavor experiences of breast-fed babies may account for why breast-fed babies have been observed to be less "picky" and more willing to try new foods than formula-fed babies (Beauchamp & Mennella, 2011). These observations suggest a link between very early experiences of taste and smell with later food preferences and the establishment of eating habits (Mennella & Trabulsi, 2012).

In addition to the role of taste in shaping flavor and food preferences, sweet flavors have a pain-reducing impact. In a review of many studies, babies who were given a sweet solution just prior to a painful procedure were compared to babies who had a placebo or no solution. In 93 percent of the studies, babies who received the sweet solution had a much milder response to the pain than did babies in the comparison groups (Harrison, Bueno, Yamada, Adams-Webber, & Stevens, 2010).

The sense of smell plays a role in linking a newborn to his or her mother. Babies recognize the odor of their mother's milk. This familiarity strengthens feelings of comfort and increases the willingness to suck, both of which contribute to the infant's survival (Raimbault, Saliba, & Porter, 2007).

Touch. The skin is the largest sensory organ and the earliest to develop. Touch has a communication function, providing an early form of caregiver–infant interaction. Playful touch, like tickling or tapping, might be used to evoke an infant's smile, whereas holding the baby upright or adjusting their position might have the goal of helping the baby to interact with the environment (Jean, Stack, &

Fogel, 2009). Gentle handling, such as rocking, stroking, and cuddling, has soothing effects on a baby. Swaddling—the practice of wrapping a baby snugly in a soft blanket—is a common technique for soothing a newborn across many cultures. One of the effective techniques for caring for low-birth-weight babies is to introduce regular gentle stroking, rocking, and other forms of soothing touch. As mentioned earlier in the chapter, Kangaroo Care exploits the premature infant's sense of touch to stimulate sensory systems and reduce stress.

Touch is an active as well as a passive sense; babies use it to explore objects, people, and their own bodies. Sucking and mouthing are early forms of exploratory touch. Babies can recognize the qualities of objects from the way they feel in their mouths—nubbly or smooth, chewy and flexible, or rigid. For older infants, most tactile information comes through touching with the hands and bringing objects to the face in order to take a closer look or to explore them with the mouth. By 5 or 6 months of age, infants can use their hands for the controlled examination of objects. They finger surfaces to explore small details and transfer objects from one hand to the other to detect corners, shapes, and the flexibility of surfaces as well as the object's size, temperature, and weight (Streri, 2005).

The Interconnected Nature of Sensory/Perceptual Capacities

The sensory/perceptual capacities function as an interconnected system to provide a variety of information about the environment (Calvert, Spence, & Stein, 2004; Murray & Wallace, 2012; Stein, 2012). Listening to a person's voice provides clues to their identity and stimulates an area of the brain that is also associated with face recognition. Research on multisensory perception suggests that the brain integrates information from the various sensory regions

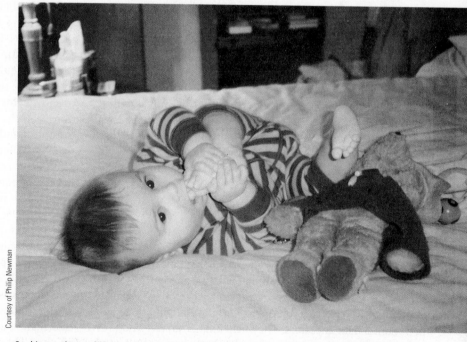

Courtesy of Philip Newman

Sucking and mouthing are important ways of exploring objects. Fists and toes are the first easy targets.

to improve recognition and to compensate when one region is impaired or restricted (Rosenblum, 2013).

Consider the situation when an infant is being nursed. At first, the mother guides the baby toward her breast, but the baby makes use of vision, touch, smell, and movement to find and grab hold of the nipple. If very hungry, the baby may close the eyes in order to concentrate exclusively on bursts of sucking behavior, coordinating sucking and swallowing as efficiently as possible. But as the initial swallows of milk satisfy strong hunger pangs, the baby pauses to take in other aspects of the situation. The baby may then gaze at the contours of the mother's face, playfully lick the milk dripping from the mother's breast, smell the milk's fragrance, taste its special sweet taste, and listen to the sound of the mother's voice offering comfort or inviting conversation. The baby may reach up to explore the mother's skin or relax in the comfort of the mother's gentle embrace. All the sensory information becomes integrated to create familiarity with this experience, including a growing recognition of the mother and a rich mixture of sensory impressions associated with this special situation in which hunger is satisfied.

The sensory/perceptual regions of the brain show evidence of integration in infancy, providing essential adaptive benefits for attention, recognition, and appropriate behavioral responses. This sensory integration improves with age, with optimal functioning achieved at around age 15 (Burr & Gori, 2012). Given the multi-modal nature of most complex cognitive tasks, it is not surprising that multisensory integration deficits have been associated with various neurodevelopmental disorders, especially dyslexia and attention deficit disorder (Dionne-Dostie, Paquette, Lassonde, & Gallagher, 2015).

FURTHER REFLECTION: Describe some examples of how hearing, vision, touch, and smell work together to help infants form schemes about their world. Imagine that one of these senses was impaired, vision or hearing, for example. How might the other senses fill the gap as an infant strives to gather information about his or her world?

Motor Development

Motor development refers to all the changes in a child's ability to control and direct movement, including movement of the eyes and head, as well as movement of fingers, arms, legs, and torso. Movement is involved in just about every aspect of observable behavior, from a smile or grimace to arm waving and leg kicking. Motor development begins during the prenatal period as the fetus twitches, hiccups, waves its arms, kicks its legs, sticks out its tongue and orients its body within the amniotic fluid. These prenatal movements lay the groundwork for neural pathways that will eventually sustain more coordinated movement after birth.

Many of the observable early motor behaviors are **reflexes**, meaning that a specific stimulus evokes a particular motor response without any voluntary control or direction. Reflexes are thought to have an evolutionary origin, linking humans to their mammalian ancestors. They help infants survive and provide a platform upon which they develop more complicated

sequences of voluntary behaviors. The sucking reflex is a good example. At birth, inserting something in an infant's mouth produces a sucking reflex. This helps infants gain nourishment relatively easily before sucking behavior is under their voluntary control. Before long, infants become skillful at controlling the strength and sensitivity of sucking behavior. They also use sucking and mouthing as strategies for exploration. Infants use their mouths to explore objects that they can then identify visually, thus transferring information from the sense of touch to the visual sense.

Table 5.2 describes a number of common infant reflexes, the evoking stimulus, and the response. Infant reflexes include sucking, grasping, rooting (turning the head in the direction of the cheek that is stroked), coughing, and stepping. With time, many of these behaviors make a transition from an involuntary to a voluntary behavior. Eventually infants blend several of these new movements into increasingly coordinated and complex patterns. Reaching and grasping is a good example.

Reaching and Grasping. In the first weeks of life, we see a strong, involuntary grasp reflex. If you put something, like a finger or a rattle handle in a baby's hand, the hand closes tightly. Over time, this involuntary reflex is transformed into purposeful, goal-directed reaching and grasping. Advances in reaching and grasping result from an ongoing interaction among sensory and perceptual abilities, motor skills, cognitive capacities, social interactions, and cultural contexts (Diamond, 2007). Infants practice controlled, coordinated muscle movements, guided by visual and auditory cues—particularly cues about size, distance, and direction.

In the first few months of life, babies cannot achieve much in the way of voluntary reaching because they cannot yet keep their head up or their torso from collapsing. When babies are propped up in an infant chair, you may observe them wave their arms and shake their hands in the direction of an object. At first, this arm flapping and waving is not connected to the goal of reaching for a toy. But over time, as the shoulder and elbow become more developed, and as the arm waving results in reaching a toy, the frequency and stability of hand–toy contact improves. By the time they are able to sit independently, they also begin to show evidence of coordinated reaching, grasping, and handling objects. They make a large movement in the direction of the object and then modify their hands in order to grab hold of the object. Between 5 and 7 months, babies become increasingly accurate at reaching and grasping a moving object, anticipating the direction of its movement, and alternating their hands to intercept it (Adolph & Robinson, 2015; Robin, Berthier, & Clifton, 1996; Rochat, 1989).

By 12 months, babies have mastered the pincer grasp, using their index finger and thumb to pick up tiny things, such as string and thread, pieces of dry cereal, and spaghetti noodles. With this advance, they can also manipulate things by lifting latches, turning knobs, and placing small things inside bigger things and trying to get them out again. These motor skills provide new information about how objects work and how they relate to one another. The development of fine motor skills contributes to the

Table 5.2	Some Infant Reflexes	
Reflex	**Evoking Stimulus**	**Response**
Reflexes that facilitate adaptation and survival		
Sucking reflex	Pressure on lips and tongue	Suction produced by movement of lips and tongue
Pupillary reflex	Weak or bright light	Dilation or constriction of pupil
Rooting reflex	Light touch to cheek	Head movement in direction of touch
Startle reflex	Loud noise	Similar to Moro reflex (below), with elbows flexed and fingers closed
Swimming reflex	Neonate placed prone in water	Arm and leg movement
Reflexes linked to competences of related species		
Creeping reflex	Feet pushed against a surface	Arms and legs drawn under, head lifted
Flexion reflex	Pressure on sole of foot	Involuntary bending of leg
Grasp reflex	Pressure on fingers or palm	Closing and tightening of fingers
Moro reflex	Infant lying on back with head raised—rapidly release head	Extension of arms, head thrown back, spreading of fingers, crossing arms across body
Springing reflex	Infant held upright and slightly forward	Arms extended forward and legs drawn up
Stepping reflex	Infant supported under the arms above a flat surface	Rhythmical stepping movement
Abdominal reflex	Tactile stimulation	Involuntary contraction of abdominal muscles
Reflexes of unknown function		
Achilles tendon reflex	Blow to Achilles tendon	Contraction of calf muscles and downward bending of foot
Babinski reflex	Mild stroke on sole of foot	Fanning and extension of toes
Tonic neck reflex	Infant on back with head turned to one side	Arm and leg on side toward which head is facing are extended, other arm and leg flexed

© Cengage

infant's sense of mastery and can be a source for positive emotions. At the same time, they may cause new conflicts between the baby and the caregiver, who knows that tiny things shouldn't go into the mouth, and that certain objects ought not to be touched, moved, and manipulated.

Motor Milestones

Motor skills develop as a result of physical growth and maturation in combination with perceptual information and opportunities for exploration of the environment. The infant's drive to explore and master the environment as well as encouragement from caregivers contribute to the rate and sequence of motor development (Adolph & Robinson, 2015). Table 5.3 lists the milestones of motor development and a typical sequence of accomplishments during the first year of life. Usually, during the first 12 months, babies begin to hold their heads up and roll over by themselves; they learn to reach for things and grasp them; they sit, crawl, stand, and walk.

However, research has documented substantial variability in the sequence and rate at which infants acquire these skills. Individual children grow in spurts, interspersed with times of slow growth and some periods of regression (Adolph, Berger, & Leo, 2011). Not all children crawl before they walk. Some

scoot along on their bottoms; others slide or slither on their tummies. Children in some cultures sit, stand unassisted, and walk at a much younger age than in other cultures. Parental expectations and the ways parents treat their babies, including the ways they massage, stretch, or exercise them, seem to influence the timing of the onset for some of these milestones (Adolph & Berger, 2011).

During the second year, walking becomes increasingly steady. Crawling may be used for play but is no longer the preferred method for locomotion. One might wonder why babies give up the stable, well-developed strategy of crawling for the more shaky, precarious approach of walking. Several explanations seem relevant. First, a social explanation suggests that babies recognize that all the older adults around them are walking. And they receive social encouragement for walking. In addition, as they gain the skills of walking, they can cover ground more quickly, engage in exploration with objects further away, and encounter different kinds of social interactions (Adolph & Tamis-LaMonda, 2014). During the second year, babies explore stairs, climbing up and down using a variety of strategies. They start to slide or jump down from modest heights. Each of these accomplishments requires practice, refinement, struggle, and, finally, mastery (Adolph et al., 2012).

Table 5.3	Motor Development Milestones—First 24 months			
1 Month	**3 Months**	**4–7 Months**	**8–12 Months**	**12–24 Months**
• Strong reflex movements • Makes jerky, quivering arm thrusts • Brings hands within range of eyes and mouth • Moves head from side to side while lying on stomach • Head flops backward if unsupported • Keeps hands in tight fists	• Raises head and chest when on stomach • Stretches and kicks on back • Opens and shuts hands • Brings hand to mouth • Grasps and shakes toys	• Rolls both ways • Sits with and without support of hands • Supports whole weight on legs • Reaches with one hand • Transfers object from hand to hand • Uses raking grasp	• Gets to sitting position without help • Crawls forward on belly • Assumes hands-and-knees position • Gets from sitting to crawling position • Pulls self up to stand • Walks holding onto furniture	• Walks alone • Pulls toys behind her while walking • Carries large toy or several toys while walking • Begins to run • Stands on tiptoe • Kicks a ball • Climbs onto and down from furniture unassisted • Walks up and down stairs holding onto support

Table constructed from information derived from American Academy of Pediatrics, Ages and stages. Retrieved February. 8, 2013, from http://www.healthychildren.org/English/ages-stages/Pages/default.aspx

The Contributions of Nature and Nurture in Motor Development

Motor development provides an excellent illustration of the interaction between the genetically guided plan for growth and experience. The unfolding of motor capacities is guided by genetics, beginning as it does with the presence of a wide range of reflexes that are hardwired, so to speak, into the infant's neurological system. At the same time, within this plan, one observes both individual and group differences. Not only are babies different from one another at birth, but they also show different rates of motor advancement. For example, one study examined how babies adapted their locomotor strategy for going down a slope. Thirty-one infants, all 14 months old, were recruited for the study. Even though they were all the same chronological age, their prior experience with walking ranged from 10 days to 137 days (Adolph & Eppler, 2002).

In addition to individual differences in the timing and tempo of motor development, cultures differ in the opportunities provided for motor exploration. In a longitudinal study of almost 16,000 infants living in the United Kingdom (England, Wales, Scotland, and Northern Ireland), cultural differences in the attainment of motor milestones were noted. Black Caribbean infants, Black African infants, and Indian infants were on average more advanced in motor development than White infants. Advantages of the babies of Caribbean, African, and Indian ethnicity could not be accounted for by financial factors. A combination of parental expectations and parenting practices associated with cultural tradition, such as holding the babies upright, stretching and massaging their legs, helped support advanced motor development in these groups (Kelly, Sacker, Schoon, & Nazroo, 2006).

Researchers now regard the regularities in motor behavior as a result of a dynamic process in which infants coordinate their physical actions with the demands and opportunities of the situation and the expectations of the culture. The combination of a maturing central nervous system, growth in strength and

coordination, opportunities for various types of movements, and the emergence of cognitions to understand and anticipate actions underlies an ongoing process of self-correcting, adaptive movement (Adolph, 2008). Perception and action work hand in hand, giving the infant information about the physical properties of the situation and feedback about the consequences of a specific motor strategy. Over time and with practice in similar situations, infants discover the combination of action, intensity, direction, and speed that will create the desired outcome. With additional practice, this pattern becomes most likely and increasingly efficient (Thelen, 1995). (See the **Applying Theory and Research to Life** box on the stepping reflex.)

Most babies reach a point when they rock in a stationary position on all fours before they can crawl. In repeated observations of 15 infants, they first showed a clear hand preference before they made the transition to crawling. When infants fell from a seated position onto their hands, they tended to fall onto their non-preferred hand, so that the preferred hand was available to reach out and begin crawling. Confidence in being able to maintain one's body weight on one arm and two legs while reaching out with the preferred hand is part of the motor sequence necessary for forward crawling (Adolph, Vereijken, & Denny, 1998; Goldfield, 1989). What is more, in a systematic observation of crawling, it appears that infants intersperse crawling with sitting. After short bouts of crawling, they typically turn to a sitting position, possibly to rest or to reorient themselves in space before moving on (Soska, Robinson, & Adolph, 2015). This observation illustrates how new behaviors may emerge from or build upon earlier milestones. Crawling, which tends to be regarded as natural and easily performed in infancy, is in fact achieved by long and patient effort in the coordination of head and shoulder movement, reaching, and kicking. As the baby changes from crawling to walking, new strategies for navigating the environment have to be invented.

Infants gain greater motor control with each motor milestone from sitting and crawling to standing and walking. At the

The Dynamic Development of Stepping

At some point within the first 2 or 3 weeks of life, when you hold an infant upright under the arms, the infant makes stepping motions that look very much like walking (Barbu-Roth et al., 2009). This stepping response is evoked by a number of stimuli, including the posture in which the baby is held, tactile stimulation to the feet, and visual information about the relationship of the body to the surface below. By the age of 2 or 3 months, this stepping behavior seems to disappear. Initial explanations for this loss of the stepping response were that the reflex is inhibited by higher level cortical functions. The assumption was that the stepping reflex was a vestigial behavior from some earlier evolutionary primate period, and that true stepping and walking were products of voluntary movement genetically programmed to emerge with more advanced cortical development.

The idea that a behavior that is so closely related to walking would disappear and then reappear was puzzling. Esther Thelen and Donna Fisher (1982) designed research to examine the relationship of the biomechanics of infant stepping and its relation to the infant's posture and physical growth. They used video recordings and electromyography (EMG) of four muscle groups to capture data on patterns of muscle activation associated with various movements. Their first goal was to explore the similarities between infant stepping while held upright and infant kicking while the infants were lying on their backs. The former seems to disappear and the latter becomes stronger and more coordinated over time. Their second goal was to consider the biomechanical conditions that might constrain the stepping response and increase the kicking response.

The infants who participated in the study were all under 2 weeks old. Of 13 infants, 8 showed both stepping and kicking during the recording session. Both the stepping and kicking showed alternating right- and left-leg action. The EMG data (an electronic technique for recording muscles at rest and when they are contracting) for the two types of movement were quite similar. The timing of the flexion and extension phases of the kick and the step were also similar. Thelen and Fisher argued that neonatal stepping and kicking while lying on the back are essentially the same movement patterns.

The key to the disappearance of stepping and the increase in kicking is in the role of gravity as infants' legs gain mass. As the legs gain in fat, the muscle strength needed to lift the legs against the force of gravity is not sufficient to permit the stepping action. However, in the prone position, the kicking action is actually supported

According to research on motor development, the stepping reflex remains intact and plays a role in upright walking when babies are strong enough to lift their legs against the force of gravity.

by the force of gravity. During the first months of life, the growth of body fat outpaces the growth of muscle mass, so the babies cannot lift their legs in the upright position. However, the action itself is not lost and in fact is practiced actively when babies are lying down. When slightly older babies were submerged waist-high in water, overcoming the constraints of body mass and gravity, the stepping pattern was observed (Thelen, Fisher, & Ridley-Johnson, 1984). Thus, the shift from stepping to no stepping was actually a dynamic adaptation to the combination of changing physical characteristics in a particular physical context (Thelen & Smith, 1994). The results of this research led to a transformation in the way we think about motor development. Studies of infant care in other cultures, especially in Africa and Central America, find a more common practice of holding infants upright rather than laying them down in a cradle or crib. Infants in these cultures have been observed to walk at an earlier age than Western infants. Thelen and Fisher suggested that infants who are given more experience in an upright position strengthen their leg muscles, leading to an earlier use of legs for support in standing and walking.

Critical Thinking Questions

1. Explain how this research on stepping significantly altered our understanding of motor development.
2. Describe the interactions of neurological, physical, and experiential aspects of motor behavior that are illustrated in this research on stepping.
3. Apply the principles of development illustrated in this research to other examples of behaviors that might be better understood from a dynamic systems perspective.

same time, each new motor capacity permits the exploration of a more varied environment. As a result, infants have to be able to make immediate assessments of the relationship between their physical abilities and the environmental conditions in order to decide whether to avoid action, take familiar actions, or try to invent some new, adapted action. The evidence for this flexibility can be seen as babies experiment with descending slopes and slides. Some try going headfirst and then slide backwards; others try to go down with a crablike crawl and then switch over to their bottoms; and still others won't go down at all (Adolph & Eppler, 2002). Infant motor behavior requires flexibility because of the rapid changes in physical size and strength and the variety of contexts for movement.

FURTHER REFLECTION: Summarize the contributions of each of the motor milestones to the infant's ability to explore the environment and enter into the social life of the family.

Sensorimotor Intelligence: Processing, Organizing, and Using Information

OBJECTIVE 3 Describe the development of sensorimotor intelligence, including an analysis of how infants process information, organize experiences, conceptualize causality, and understand the properties and functions of objects.

What is sensorimotor intelligence? Think for a moment of a familiar experience, such as tying your shoelaces. The pattern of tying shoelaces unfolds with little, if any, language involved. In fact, the task of explaining to a young child how to tie shoelaces is particularly difficult because very few words or concepts are part of the process. This kind of motor routine is an example of **sensorimotor intelligence**.

According to Piaget's (1970) theory of cognitive development that was introduced in chapter 2, the growth of intelligence during infancy is based on **sensorimotor adaptation**. From the very earliest days of life, infants use their reflexes to make contact with the environment. At the same time, they gradually alter their reflexive responses to take into account the unique properties of objects around them. When infants adapt their sucking reflex to make it more effective, or when they use different techniques of sucking on the breast and the bottle, they are demonstrating sensorimotor intelligence. The familiar scheme for sucking is modified so that it takes into account the special properties of the breast and the bottle, depending on the situation.

Infants do not use the conventional symbolic system of language to organize experience. Rather, they form concepts through perception and direct investigation of the environment. Sensorimotor intelligence encompasses the elaboration of patterns of movement and sensory experiences that the infant recognizes in association with specific environmental events. In the sections that follow, we will describe the infant's information-processing abilities, their emerging ability to understand causality, and their approach to exploring and categorizing objects.

Information-Processing Abilities

Whereas Piaget emphasized the process of sensorimotor exploration and adaptation, other theorists incorporate evidence from neuroscience to explain how development of the central nervous system constrains or facilitates cognitive functioning. As children get older, they can keep more information in the mind at once, thereby allowing them to organize, coordinate, and compare data in order to solve problems (Case, 1998; Morra, Gobbo, Marini, & Sheese, 2008; Young, 2011).

Four basic information-processing abilities provide the cognitive resources that support the maturation of sensorimotor intelligence. They include attention, processing speed, memory, and representational abilities (Rose, Feldman, & Jankowski, 2009).

Attention refers to the infant's ability to focus on an object or task as well as to shift or redirect focus from one object or task to another. Attention is a foundational cognitive ability that allows infants to follow the gaze of another person, track the path of a moving object, and participate in alternating interactions. Attention is typically measured by noting how long an infant looks at an object and how often the infant shifts gaze from one object to another when comparing objects. Problems in attention can be early signs of developmental delay. For example if the 1-month-old baby does not track an object as it moves from side to side and this inability to track moving objects continues into the second or third month, caregivers are advised to contact their pediatrician (American Academy of Pediatrics, 2014).

Processing speed is the time it takes to identify a stimulus and figure out its meaning. The faster the processing speed, the more quickly one can incorporate a stream of information. Processing speed is often assessed with reaction time tasks. The time elapsed from presentation of the stimulus to response is taken as evidence of processing speed.

Memory is a complex capacity that includes recognizing something as similar to something one has seen or experienced in the past, holding information in mind for a brief period before using it and recalling information as needed (Flom & Bahrick, 2010). One way of studying memory in infancy is through the use of habituation tasks. Memory is inferred from an infant's ability to compare a stimulus with something that was experienced in the past.

Representational skills are those cognitive abilities that allow a child to let one thing stand for something else. Representational skills are involved when a child uses a word or a gesture to indicate an object or when a child pretends, such as when using a block to feed a doll or giving it a sip of pretend water from a pretend cup. The idea is that the child has a mental image or representation of an object or action, and the child is able to work with this image, expressing it in words, actions, or pretense.

Taken together, these information-processing skills— attention, processing speed, memory, and representational skills—support an infant's ability to form increasingly complex schemes about objects, people, actions, and the relationships among them. Changes in the demand properties of one aspect of a task, such as processing speed or memory, may influence attention or representational competence. For example, immature memory capacities may make it difficult for infants to accurately represent and categorize new objects (Oakes, 2009).

According to an emerging view, sometimes referred to as the *theory theory*, infants form theories about how their world operates and modify these theories as new information is gathered (Wellman, 2014). The infant starts out with some basic sensory, motor, and cognitive organizational structures. With new information, a process of adaptation results in the revision of basic schemes to better predict and interpret experience (Xu & Kushnir, 2013). For example, Ruby, who is 12 months old, may be surprised and upset when her grandmother scolds her as she reaches for a shiny glass bowl on the table. Grandmother knows that the bowl will break if Ruby pushes it off the table. By 16 months, Ruby warily watches her grandmother's face as she reaches for the bowl and may withdraw her hand if she sees Grandma frown or hears the sharp "No!" that has come to be associated with "Don't touch." Ruby has developed a theory that she should not touch the bowl, which she cautiously tests by reaching for it and watching for the response.

Causal Schemes

One of the most important components of sensorimotor intelligence occurs when infants make things happen. Causal schemes refer to the capacity to anticipate that certain actions will have specific consequences. Infants develop an understanding of **causality** based largely on sensory and motor experiences. By 9 months of age, infants show evidence that they anticipate the direction of an action, like pouring a liquid into a glass or using a spoon to bring soup to the mouth, and are surprised when the action is not completed or takes an unexpected twist. This understanding leads to goal-directed behavior; infants become increasingly intentional and purposeful in their behaviors (Reid et al., 2009). Babies discover that if they cry, Mama will come to them; if they kick a chair, it will move; and if they let go of a spoon, it will fall to the floor. These predictable sequences are learned through repetition and experimentation. The predictability of the events depends on the consistency with which objects or people in their world respond as well as on the child's initiation of the action. Babies learn to associate specific actions with regularly occurring outcomes. They also experiment with their own actions to determine the variety of events that a single behavior may cause. Eventually, they are able to work backward: They can select a desirable outcome and then perform the behavior that will produce it.

The achievement of complex, purposeful, causal behaviors develops gradually during the first 2 years of life. The dynamic process of establishing a complex causal scheme is illustrated in a study of the emergence of the use of a spoon as a tool for eating (Connolly & Dalgleish, 1989). Infants were observed once a month for 6 months in their home during a mealtime. At first, actions involving the spoon appeared to focus on exploration of the spoon itself. The infants banged the spoon, sucked it, or rubbed it in their hair. Then the babies showed an understanding of the purpose of the spoon as a tool by repeating the action sequence of dipping the spoon in the dish and bringing it to the mouth. However, no food was on the spoon. In the third phase, babies began to integrate the function and the action by loading the spoon with food and then bringing it to the mouth. During this phase, they made so many errors that very little food actually got to the mouth via the spoon. Finally, babies were able to coordinate the action and the function by using the other hand to steady the bowl, altering the angle of the spoon, picking up food they had dropped, and devising other strategies to enhance the function, depending on the type of food involved. Here we see a demonstration of how one complex motor behavior becomes part of a problem-solving action sequence during the sensorimotor period of development.

Piaget and Inhelder (1966/1969) described six phases in the development of **causal schemes** (see Table 5.4). In Phase 1, *reflexes*, cause and effect are linked through the involuntary reflexive responses. The built-in stimulus-response systems of key reflexes are viewed as the genetic origin of intelligence. Babies suck, grasp, and root in response to specific types of stimulation. Piaget viewed these reflexes as adaptive learning systems. In detailed observations of his youngest child, Laurent, he noted daily changes in sucking behavior during the first month of life. Laurent became increasingly directed in groping for the breast, forming early associations between those situations in which he would be fed and those in which he would not (Piaget, 1936/1952).

Table 5.4	Six Phases in the Development of Sensorimotor Causality		
Phase	**Approximate Age**	**Characteristic**	**Example**
1. Reflexes	From birth	Reflexive responses to specific stimuli	Grasp reflex
2. First habits	From 2nd week	Use of reflexive responses to explore new stimuli	Grasp rattle
3. Circular reactions	From 4th month	Use of familiar actions to achieve new goals	Grasp rattle and make banging noise on table
4. Coordination of means and ends	From 8th month	Deliberate use of actions to achieve new goals	Grasp rattle and shake to play with dog
5. Experimentation with new means	From 11th month	Modifications of actions to reach goals	Use rattle to bang a drum
6. Insight	From 18th month	Mental recombination of means and ends	Use rattle and string to make a new toy

© Cengage

In the second phase, *first habits*, the reflexive responses are used to explore a wider range of stimuli. Babies explore toys, fingers, parents' noses, and blankets by sucking on them. Gradually, they discover the unique properties of objects and modify their responses according to the demands of the specific objects. The fact that a baby can satisfy the need to suck by bringing an object to the mouth is a very early form of purposive causal behavior.

The third and fourth phases involve coordination of means and ends, first with familiar situations and then with new ones. In the third phase, *circular reactions*, babies connect an action with an expected outcome. They shake a rattle and expect to hear a noise; they drop a spoon and expect to hear a noise when it hits the floor; they pull Daddy's beard and expect to hear "ouch." They do not understand why a specific action leads to the expected outcome, but they show surprise when the expected outcome does not follow.

In the fourth phase, *coordination of means and ends*, infants use familiar actions or means to achieve new outcomes. They may shake a rattle to startle Mommy or pull Daddy's beard to force him to look away from the television set. The means and the outcomes have become quite distinct. There can be no question about the purposiveness of behavior at this point. At this stage, coordination of means and ends are closely tied to a specific context. For example, a baby may know how to make certain kicking motions to move a mobile or to get a toy to jiggle in the crib. But in another room with the same toy, the baby may not make the same connection. This may explain why babies perform less competently in the laboratory environment than they do at home. Many causal strategies that become part of a baby's daily repertoire are supported by the context of a familiar environment (Baillargeon, 2004, 2008).

The fifth phase, *experimentation with new means*, begins as children experiment with familiar means to achieve new goals. When familiar strategies do not work, children will modify them in light of the situation. One can think of this stage as sensorimotor problem solving. Children will try to reach a drawer by standing on a box, fix a broken toy with a string, or make a gift by wrapping a toy in a piece of tissue.

The last phase in the development of sensorimotor causality, *insight*, involves mental manipulation of means–end relationships. Instead of actually going through a variety of physical manipulations, children carry out trial-and-error problem-solving activities and planning in their minds, anticipating outcomes. They can sort out possible solutions and reject some without actually having to try them. The result is insight: Mental experimentation brings the child to the best solution, which is the only one necessary to enact.

The capacity to perceive oneself as a causal agent and to predict the outcome of one's actions are essential to the development of a sense of competence, which involves investigation of the environment, directed problem solving, and persistence toward a goal. At later stages, the abilities to formulate a plan, execute it, and evaluate its outcome depend on these skills.

Understanding the Nature of Objects and Creating Categories

Babies are active explorers of their environment (Bruner, 2001). From birth, they track objects visually, altering their gaze to maintain contact with them. As they get older, they use combinations of mouthing, looking at, and manipulating objects as a type of exploratory behavior that provides infants with a scheme for gathering information about novel objects (Diamond, 2007). As products of this active engagement with the object world, two related but independent aspects of infant intelligence develop: an understanding of the nature of objects, and the ability to categorize similar ones.

The Nature of Objects. Through looking, manipulating, and examining, infants establish that objects have basic properties. In the discussion of vision, we pointed out that very young babies recognize the contours of objects and that by 4 months they seem to perceive objects just as adults would. That is, babies see objects as separate from each other, defined by boundaries, taking up space, having depth, and having certain attributes of weight, color, malleability, texture, and the capacity to contain something else or not. All these properties influence the types of actions that infants use to explore the objects and the ways they are eventually woven into other actions (Xu, 2003).

Object Permanence. Piaget (1954) argued that understanding the properties of objects was one of the foundations of logical thought. One of the most carefully documented of these properties is **object permanence**—the concept that objects in the environment are permanent and do not cease to exist when they are out of reach or out of view. A permanent object retains its physical properties even when it cannot be seen.

Piaget suggested that initially, the infant is aware of only those objects that are in the immediate perceptual field. If a 6-month-old girl is playing with a rattle, it exists for her. If the rattle drops

Through mouthing and grasping, Olivia is exploring the fuzzy blanket.

out of her hand or is taken away, she may show some immediate distress but will not pursue the rattle. The attainment of the concept of the permanent object frees children from reliance on only what they can see. The ability to hold the image of an object in the mind is a critical step in the emergence of complex representational thinking.

Piaget suggested that the capacity to understand that objects continue to exist requires a level of representational or symbolic thinking that would permit an infant to hold the idea of the object in mind while it was hidden. It also requires a combination of sensorimotor capacities that permit the infant to become actively engaged in reaching, tracking, and uncovering hidden objects and learning about the spatial properties of objects in the environment. Thus, according to Piaget, the first real evidence that infants have the ability to pursue a hidden object could not really be observed much before 8 or 9 months of age when babies begin to crawl, and the full confidence in an object's permanence could probably not emerge much before 16 to 18 months when infants have access to representational thinking. By this age, infants can imagine various movements and displacements of objects without actually viewing them.

A growing body of research has focused on what infants know and expect about objects well before they can crawl or pursue objects through space. In a series of experiments, Renée Baillargeon (2008) has tried to determine how infants evaluate objects that are hidden from view. One of the features of her experiments is that she has deleted the motor search component that is required in Piaget's studies of object permanence. Most of her experiments use habituation in pretest conditions and a change in looking time as evidence for infants' reactions to an unexpected outcome. At very early ages, before infants can search for and retrieve objects, they appear to have a memory for the locations of objects. Infants can follow an object through at least three different ways of hiding it: by placing the object in a container, by moving the object behind a screen, or by covering the object (Baillargeon, 2004).

Young infants have a well-developed sense of objects as distinct, permanent structures that will be set into motion when they are pushed, knocked, or launched in some other way by another object. They also expect that, once in motion, an object will follow a prescribed trajectory (Belanger & Desrochers, 2001). The infant's ability to anticipate an object's trajectory behind a screen is an early step in a sequence of abilities that will produce the complex search process that Piaget described.

The Categorization of Objects. Physical objects have basic properties:

1. Objects have a location and a path and speed of motion.
2. Objects have mechanical properties that include how they move and their relation to other objects.
3. Objects have features, such as their size, shape, and color.
4. Objects have functions; this is what objects do or how they are used (Wilcox, Schweinle, & Chapa, 2003).

As infants explore and experiment with objects, they begin to devise schemes for grouping objects together. They modify these schemes to add new items to the category and to differentiate one category from another. Categories can be based on the physical properties of objects, such as smooth and rough, or on the functions of objects, as in something to sit on and something to dig with. The classification of objects and events into categories is one method infants have for coping with the array of new experiences they encounter.

Categorization is an aid to information processing. By treating certain individual objects as similar because they belong to the same basic grouping, like two individual red blocks or two wiggly goldfish, the potential amount of information to process is reduced. Categories can be specific, such as cups, chairs, and cars, or abstract, such as tools, food, or animals. If an item is classified as a member of a category, then all the information that has been accumulated regarding that category can automatically be applied to the specific object. This process aids in the storage and recall processes of memory, in reasoning and problem solving, and in the acquisition of new information. Classification of objects into categories is a cognitive capacity that becomes increasingly sophisticated over the childhood years.

One category that has special meaning for infants is *faceness*. By 6 months of age, infants attribute clear expectations to faces. They expect faces to be organized in certain patterns and to move and respond in special ways. Six-month-old infants can categorize faces as attractive or unattractive (Zebrowitz, Bronstad & Montepare, 2010).

A second related category is the distinction between people and inanimate objects (Atkinson, Heberlein, & Adolphs, 2010; Rakison & Poulin- Dubois, 2001). Infants have been observed to smile, vocalize, and become more active when interacting with people as compared to things. By 3 months of age, infants show their ability to categorize stimuli as people or things by smiling almost exclusively at people. Infants may look with equal interest at inanimate objects, especially novel ones, but their smiles are reserved for people. This distinction between the social and the nonsocial realm can be considered a **foundational category**. It provides evidence for the unique role of social relationships in the process of adaptation and growth. From this basic distinction between a person and a thing, many further categories, such as father and mother, familiar and stranger, or adult and child, emerge that begin to differentiate the infant's social world.

Research on infant categorization skills typically involves sorting objects or images into groups. Using a habituation-type methodology, the earliest form of categorization can be observed. When 4.5-month-old babies see an object alone and then placed next to a different object, they respond in a way that indicates their recognition that the two objects are different (Needham, 2001). Using visual silhouettes, 3- and 4-month-old babies were able to distinguish between images of cats and dogs, primarily through a comparison of the information in the shape and features of the silhouette heads (Quinn, Doran, Reiss, & Hoffman, 2009; Quinn, Eimas, & Tarr, 2001). Thus, at very early ages, infants are able to differentiate and group people and objects in their environment.

The categorization process advances over the first 24 months as features of objects are differentiated and linked to concepts and functions. Information about the shape and size of objects seems to guide an infant's identification and categorization of objects by 4.5 months. At 7.5 months, infants make use of information based on differences in pattern, and by 11.5 months they incorporate color and shininess as features that help guide categorization (Woods & Wilcox, 2010).

By 15 months, babies will touch all the objects that belong to one category and then touch all the objects in another category. By 18 months of age, children can perform multidimensional categorization tasks (e.g., sorting eight objects, such as four brightly colored yellow rectangles and four human-shaped plastic figures, into two distinct groups) (Gopnik & Meltzoff, 1987, 1992, 1997). This kind of sorting does not require the ability to give names to the objects. However, by 20 months, infants will use both visual cues and names to categorize objects. The larger the infant's vocabulary, the more likely the baby is to use names to help group objects together (Nazzi & Gopnick, 2001). Thus, categorizing and naming appear to be closely linked. By the close of the second year of life, babies know that objects have certain stable features, that some objects belong with others, and that objects have names. With these achievements, infants impose a new degree of order and predictability on their daily experiences.

The Prefrontal Cortex and Infant Intelligence

The cognitive skills that we have described in the preceding sections—causal schemes, object permanence, and the categorization of objects—are all evidence of a capacity to generalize principles and devise abstract rules from experience. One hallmark of human intelligence is the ability to derive abstract concepts, rules, and generalizations from sensory and motor experiences and to apply them in new situations. The area of the brain that appears to be responsible for supporting these capacities is the **prefrontal cortex**.

The prefrontal cortex is more developed in humans than in other species, and, within humans, continues to develop into the mid-20s. It has been viewed as the brain's executive, an area of the brain that is highly interconnected with all the sensory and motor systems and with areas of the brain associated with emotion, memory, and reward (Kolb et al., 2012; Miller, Freedman, & Wallis, 2002). The neurons in the prefrontal cortex can be activated from all the sensory domains in anticipation of events, during actions, and during memory of past events.

One of the key features of neurons in the prefrontal cortex is their ability to sustain mental activity for several seconds without additional stimulation. As a result, the neurons of the prefrontal cortex are able to guide actions for the period of time it takes to transmit signals to other related brain areas in order to accomplish a task. This longer "hold" time also plays a role in the ability to delay responses and resist distractions. From 6 to 12 months, infants perform increasingly better on tasks that require them to resist distractions (Holmboe et al., 2010).

Neuroimaging studies of infants find that the prefrontal cortex is involved in language processing, identification of novel stimuli, working memory, goal-oriented reasoning, and categorization of objects. Studies of the neurodevelopment of categorization suggest that the lower brain regions, especially the basal ganglia, are involved in the recognition of individual stimuli and related responses. The prefrontal cortex links the details of these individual experiences together to form general representations. After repeated exposure, the prefrontal cortex plays a leading role,

recognizing individual stimuli as examples of more general categories and associating them with appropriate responses (Antzoulatos & Miller, 2014; Seger & Miller, 2010).

There are both benefits and costs to the long maturational time and plasticity of the prefrontal cortex. The neural connections and pathways within the prefrontal cortex as well as from the prefrontal cortex to other areas of the brain can be shaped by many environmental factors, both prenatally and over the course of childhood and adolescence. The early years of synaptic production in the prefrontal cortex establish a structure upon which subsequent cognitive, affective, and social adaptation are based. Rich sensory and motor stimulation, comforting touch, responsive parenting, and opportunities for peer play are all examples of early experiences that are known to have beneficial consequences for the formation of neural development in the prefrontal cortex. However, the sensitivity of the prefrontal cortex to environmental conditions also contributes to vulnerability when the infant or young child is exposed to disruptive factors including sensory deprivation, stress, harsh handling, and parental deprivation or neglect (Kolb et al., 2012).

FURTHER REFLECTION: Imagine that you are advising parents of infants about how to promote their child's cognitive development. What caregiving practices are most likely to foster an infant's ability to develop a sense of causality? What caregiving practices are most likely to help infants understand and categorize objects?

Communication

OBJECTIVE 4 Summarize the beginnings of language competence from birth through the first 2 years of life.

After birth, infants see and hear people talking, making gestures, and combining language with actions. So even though infants may not be active partners in the spoken language of their home and culture from birth, they do participate in rhythmic communication exchanges through gazing, smiling, cooing, and coordinated play. Research on language development has focused on the many forerunners of language competence that emerge from birth through the first 2 years of life (Parish-Morris, Golinkoff & Hirsh-Pasek, 2013).

Thought and language travel independent courses that typically intersect during the second year of life. Before that time, babies exhibit meaningful communication that does not require speech, such as pointing and gesturing and vocalizations that are not meaningful, such as babbling and cooing. A rare genetic disease, Williams syndrome, illustrates that the capacities for language and cognition are distinct. Children with Williams syndrome are typically very talkative and sociable; they develop a large vocabulary and speak in grammatically correct sentences. Although their speech indicates some developmental abnormalities, it is much further advanced than their other cognitive functions. For example, children with Williams syndrome may have difficulty with tasks that are easy for most middle-school-age children, like tying their shoes, subtracting 2 from 4, or writing their street address (Schultz, Grelotti, & Pober, 2001). This genetic condition forces one to think about language competence separate from other cognitive abilities. Of course, one does not have to go to the extreme of people with Williams syndrome to find examples of people whose speech seems disconnected from their ability to think and reason.

Language Perception

Infants are able to recognize sounds and differentiate between sound combinations long before they are able to produce language or understand word meaning. This capacity to recognize language sounds, including the combinations of sounds made by letters and words and the rise and fall of pitch as words and sentences are spoken, is called **language perception** (Tsao, Liu, & Kuhl, 2004). Young infants are able to hear and distinguish among the major language sounds used in natural language. By 5 months of age, infants are able to recognize the difference between words that emphasize the first syllable, like *father*, and words that emphasize the second syllable, like *begin*. By this age, they also recognize the sound of their own name (Mandel, Jusczyk, & Pisoni, 1995; Weber, Hahne, Friedrich, & Friederici, 2004). Over the first year of life, there is a universal process of narrowing, in which infants become less sensitive to the sound distinctions that are not present in the spoken language of their family. This mechanism contributes to language acquisition by attuning the infant's ear to the important and possibly subtle distinctions of their native language (Plamer, Fais, Golinkoff, & Werker, 2012).

Babbling

Babbling, initially characterized by sounds used in many languages, begins to reflect the sounds and intonation infants are most likely to hear. By about 6 months of age, sounds they do not hear dropout of their babbling and, at about this same time, they become less able to tell the differences among sounds not found in their native language (Hoff, 2013). This environmental shaping of language competence provides another example of the plasticity of brain functions. Some networks grow and become strengthened by experience, whereas others wither.

At around 6 to 10 months, babbling begins to take on a special character, connecting consonants and vowels and repeating these combinations. Although parents may eagerly receive this type of babbling as evidence of first words (i.e., *baba*, *mama*, *dada*), there is debate about whether these repetitions of babbling sounds have a symbolic value.

One sound that is especially important in the parenting process is "Mama." The infant word for mother has many similarities across hundreds of language groups. In a study of "Mama" sounds, a pediatrician asked 75 parents of newborns in his practice to listen for *mama* sounds (Goldman, 2001). If they heard one, he asked them to note the infant's age; the circumstances of the sound (time of day, etc.); if they could determine whether the infant wanted something, and if so, what; and if the sound was directed at anyone, to whom it was directed. Of the 75 parents, 52 spoke only English. Other languages included Spanish, Hindi, Italian, Russian, Hebrew, Ibo, Chinese, and some combinations of Spanish and Greek or Italian. Fifty-five of the parents heard a *mama* sound, often as part of a cry. Thirty-two infants made the *mama* sound for the first time in the first 2 months of life. It became more distinct and more of a whine or call as it was repeated over the first 6 months. For those babies who made *mama* sounds, the sound was interpreted as an indication of wanting—especially wanting to be picked up, wanting attention, or wanting to be taken out of the crib or infant seat and entertained. An implication of this research is that by 2 months, many infants have the ability to use a non-crying vocalization to serve as a call that brings caregiver attention.

Studies using brain scans of infants as they listened to nonsense syllables found that very young infants, only 2 and 3 days old, were more responsive to words with repeated syllables (e.g. penana) than to word sounds that did not have repeated syllables (e.g. penaku). Brain activity increased when the words with repeated sounds were played. The implication is that infants across cultures are ready to attend to these kinds of word sounds and find them interesting, giving words like "mama" and "dada" a favored position in the ocean of language sounds in which they are immersed (Live Science Staff, 2011).

Communication with Gestures

By 8 months, infants use sounds like grunting and whining in combination with **gestures** to achieve a goal. Sounds combined with gestures and looks in a certain direction become part of purposeful **communication**—trying to get the caregiver to reach a cookie or get a certain toy off the shelf. A common first gesture is to raise the arms up toward the caregiver in a desire to be picked up. Gestures may also be used to express emotion or to get someone's attention. When Jakob was about 14 months, he used the gesture of shaking his hands to signal that he was all done with his food. This was much preferred to having him throw the food on the floor!

Three other communicative strategies emerge at about 9 to 11 months. Infants begin to seek adult interest and attention by *showing* them objects and thereby initiating an interaction. Soon after showing, the infant begins *giving* objects. Adults who are willing to engage in this type of exchange will find the baby bringing them a whole variety of toys, utensils, and pieces of dirt or dust for inspection. Following giving, a common next key gesture is *pointing*. There is some debate about whether pointing is a form of reaching or a way of getting an adult's attention to notice an object. In either case, it is an example of an infant's ability to set up a shared focus with another person on the same object, thereby creating a common point of reference. This is called **intersubjectivity**—a condition in which two conscious minds have the same thought or feeling. The role of gestures in establishing intersubjectivity is an excellent example of the interdependence of motor, social, and psychological systems as they combine to support language development (Gallagher, 2013).

Gestures are a way for a nonverbal child to ask for additional information. Pointing or reaching may be precursors of asking a question like "What is this?" or "Where is this?" This preverbal question-asking behavior is fundamental to the knowledge acquisition process and illustrates the child's early active role in seeking information (Chouinard, 2007). Gestures can also be a child's way to get additional reassurance, or to communicate needs and interests. The way that adults respond to these gestures, by ignoring them, responding to them, or providing additional information once the initial request or question has been addressed, illustrates

Kissing, nose rubbing, and hugging are early gestures that communicate affection between mother and baby.

[SMACKING LIPS], "flower" [SNIFFING], "bird" [FLAPPING ARMS], "airplane" [SWOOPING HAND MOVEMENT], "frog" [FIST OPEN AND CLOSE], "Where is it?" [PALMS UP AND OUT], "more" [FINGER TO OPPOSITE PALM], and "all gone" [PALM DOWN, BACK AND FORTH]. Families were encouraged to invent their own additional gestures and were also given toys to take home that corresponded to the target words in order to encourage the use of gestures. Follow-up telephone interviews were conducted every 2 weeks to learn about how often and in what contexts the gesturing was taking place. Infants were tested at 11 months to establish their initial level of use for gestures or words. They were tested again at 15, 19, 24, 30, and 36 months to evaluate both expressive and receptive language. This group was compared to two other groups of infants who did not receive training in early gestures (Goodwyn, Acredolo, & Brown, 2000).

In the follow-up phone conversations it was determined that the infants had acquired an average of 20 gestures that were initiated by the infant and were used regularly. Babies showed advanced performance in expressive and receptive language as well as advances in their ability to use two-word combinations at 15, 19, and 24 months. There were no significant differences between the symbolic gesture group and the control group at 36 months.

The value of early signing for hearing infants may not be its advantage for eventual long-term language competence, but for its contribution to a caregiver's increased understanding of an infant's needs. Parents who recognize an infant's sign for "all done," "more" or "water" can respond more readily and appropriately to the infant's needs (Acredolo, Goodwyn, & Abrams, 2009). Needless to say, the use of signs and gestures plays an intricate role in communication with deaf infants as part of a rich, multidimensional approach to pre-symbolic language acquisition (Günther & Hennies, 2012).

the parents' active role in establishing a child's confidence that communications will be recognized and reciprocated.

Baby Signs. Building on the emerging capacity of infants to invent gestures for shared communication, Linda Acredolo and Susan Goodwyn began to study the role of symbolic gestures in preverbal infants. During the second year of life, it is not uncommon for infants and their caregivers to use symbolic gestures, like waving bye-bye, putting the thumb to the mouth to request or refer to a bottle, or using a throwing motion to suggest playing ball. Infants are avid observers of such action-meaning combinations, and once established, parents seem enthusiastic about using them to enhance communication. Following these naturalistic observations of symbolic gestures, Acredolo and Goodwyn conducted experimental research to increase parents' use of symbolic gestures with their infants and to evaluate the impact of this intervention on subsequent language development. One question their research addressed was whether exposure to an expanded capacity for symbolic gestures might replace a child's need for spoken language and thereby delay language production.

In one study, healthy, 11-month-old babies were taught gestures for five objects and three nonobject concepts: "fish"

Early Grammar Recognition

Grammar refers to rules that guide the combination of words and phrases in order to preserve meaning. In English, for example, sentences are usually formed from nouns (people, places, or things) or noun phrases, followed by verbs (actions) or verb phrases (e.g., "The girl reads the book"). Certain cues about the way words are used in a sentence or their order in a sentence convey their meaning. For example, the word "the" is a signal that a noun will follow.

By 7 to 8 months of age, infants show the ability to recognize the specific regularities in spoken speech and to detect rules about the combination of language sounds. For example, babies were habituated to 2 minutes of a grammar in which sentences followed an ABA form, such as *ga ti ga*, or a grammar that followed the ABB form, such as *ga ti ti*. In the test situation, babies recognized the difference between the grammar to which they were habituated and an inconsistent grammar made up of entirely different sounds (Marcus, 2000). The implication of these findings is that long before babies can produce words, word phrases, or grammatically correct sentences, they are gathering information about the rules that hold sounds and phrases together in order to make meaning (Rabagliati, Senghas, Johnson, & Marcus, 2012).

First Words

Between 12 and 18 months of age **words** emerge as more salient than gestures as a way to refer to objects (Namy & Waxman, 2002). Around the age of 8 months, infants understand the meanings of some individual words and phrases. This ability to understand words, called **receptive language**, precedes **language production**, the ability to produce spoken words and phrases. You can direct a baby's glance by saying, "Look at the flowers," or "Do you want candy?" At this age, babies can go through their paces in the ever delightful game of "point to your nose, eyes, ears," and so on. The number of words infants understand increases rapidly after 12 months. According to one analysis, 16-month-olds have a receptive vocabulary of between 92 and 321 words (Fenson et al., 1994).

One of the first significant events in the development of language production is the *naming* of objects. With repetition, a sound or word becomes associated with a specific object or a set of related objects. For example, a child may say *ba* whenever she sees her bottle. If she is thirsty and wants her bottle, she may try saying *ba* in order to influence her caregiver to produce the bottle. Gestures, actions, and facial expressions often accompany the baby's word, which help establish its meaning in the caregiver's mind. If the baby's word has meaning to the caregiver and serves to satisfy the baby's needs, it will probably be retained as a sign. The word *ba* may come to mean "bottle" and other liquids such as juice, water, or milk.

The important characteristic of **first words** is their shared meaning. Even though *ba* is not a real word, it functions in the same way that any noun does—it names a person, place, or thing. These single-word utterances accompanied by gestures, actions, vocal intonation, and emotion are called **holophrases**. They convey the meaning of an entire sentence. For example, saying "ba, ba" in a pleading tone while pointing to the refrigerator and bouncing up and down conveys the meaning "I need a bottle," or "Get me the bottle." Gradually, the child discovers that every object, action, and relationship has a name. Rapid progress occurs between 12 and 16 months in the naming of objects. By 16 months a typical infant has a productive vocabulary of 26 words. Table 5.5 provides a summary of milestones in language over the first 18 months of life.

Young children first talk about what they know and what they are interested in. Common first words include important people (*Mama, Dada*, names of siblings), foods, pets, toys, body parts (*eye, nose*), clothes (*shoe, sock*), vehicles (*car*), favorite objects (*bottle, blanket, phone*), other objects in the environment (*keys, trees*), actions (*up, bye-bye, yes, no, please, down, more*), pronouns (*you, me*), and states (*hot, hungry*). One hypothesis is that first words are those that are rich with imagery. Whether words are nouns or verbs is not as important as whether an infant has been able to form a mental representation of what the word refers to (McDonough, Song, Hirsha-Pasek, Golinkoff, & Lannon, 2011). Lois Bloom (2004) has suggested that a "principle of relevance" guides the early acquisition of new words. Babies pay special attention to words and expressions that are most closely linked with what they are doing and thinking about at the time. For that reason, the actual vocabulary that is acquired during infancy is quite idiosyncratic, reflecting the themes and experiences of each child's everyday life (Polka, Rvatchew, & Mattock, 2009).

FURTHER REFLECTION Analyze the role of gestures in early communication. What is the importance of gestures? How do they contribute to the establishment of intersubjectivity? How much and in what contexts do you continue to rely on gestures to convey meaning?

Attachment

OBJECTIVE 5 Analyze social attachment, the process through which infants develop strong emotional bonds with others, and describe the dynamics of attachment formation during infancy.

Have you ever wondered how feelings of love and connectedness form between babies and their caregivers? At birth, an infant has some familiarity with the sound and rhythm of the mother's voice, but a newborn does not show evidence of a specific emotional preference for the biological mother over other responsive adults. By the end of the first year of life, however, babies not only know their caregivers but also have very strong emotional preferences for these adults over all others. **Attachment** is the process through which people develop specific, positive emotional bonds with others. John Bowlby proposed the notion

Table 5.5	Early Communication Milestones		
By the End of 3 Months	**By the End of 6 Months**	**By the End of 12 Months**	**By the End of 18 Months**
Smile when you appear.	Make gurgling sounds when playing with you or left alone.	Try to imitate words.	Point to an object or picture when it is named.
Startle upon hearing loud sounds.	Babble repetitive syllables such as ba, ba or ma, ma.	Say a few words, such as dada, mama, and oh, oh.	Recognize names of familiar people, objects, and body parts.
Make cooing sounds.	Use voice to express pleasure and displeasure.	Understands about 50 words and simple instructions, such as "please drink your milk."	Follow simple directions accompanied by gestures.
Quiet or smile when spoken to.	Move eyes in the direction of sounds.	Understands "no."	Say as few as 8 to 10 and as many as 180 words (great degree of normal variability in spoken vocabulary at this age).
Seem to recognize your voice.	Respond to changes in the tone of your voice.	Turn and look in the direction of sounds.	
Cry differently for different needs.	Notice that some toys make sounds.		
	Pay attention to music.		

This table is adapted from information on the Mayo Clinic website, Language Development: Speech Milestones for Babies, www.mayoclinic.com/health/infant-development/AN01026

Close physical contact during nursing provides infants with a combination of sensory stimuli—sight, sound, smell, and touch—that contribute to the formation of an early scheme for their mother.

this attachment/caregiving system is a foundation of survival. Through repeated sensory, motor, and communication experiences, it creates the embodiment of a social-emotional relational context that is forged and reinforced in the establishment of neural pathways, interconnections, and biochemical processes. These biological and neural responses are associated with threat reduction, comfort or discomfort, and sensitive or insensitive care. Infants' experiences, especially under conditions of threat or distress, set the stage for their own ability to regulate their emotions and to establish significant relationships over the next stages of life (Schore, 2013).

The Development of Attachment

Attachment theorists have described a sequence of stages in the formation of the attachment relationship (Ainsworth, 1973, 1985; Bowlby, 1969/1982, 1988; Marvin & Britner, 2009) (see Table 5.6). Many of the sensory and motor competencies described earlier in this chapter contribute to an infant's ability to establish a vivid mental representation of the primary caregiver and to stimulate caregiving behaviors. During the first 3 months of life, infants engage in a variety of behaviors, including sucking, rooting, grasping, smiling, gazing, cuddling, crying, and visual tracking or following, which serve to maintain closeness with a caregiver or bring the caregiver to the infant. Through these contacts, babies learn about the unique features of their caregivers. Caregivers, for their part, use a variety of strategies including eye contact, touching and holding, and vocalizing as means of establishing and maintaining social engagement with their infants (Akhtar & Gernsbacher, 2008). Caregivers and infants experience repeated interactions that result in the formation of predictable patterns. Rhythmic patterns of interaction lay the foundation for expectations about communication.

From about 3 to 6 months, an infant's attachment is expressed through preferential responsiveness to a few familiar figures. Infants smile more at the familiar person than at a stranger. They show more excitement at that person's arrival and appear to be upset when that person leaves. During this phase, babies initiate more interactions toward the familiar caregiver. They are able to control the interaction by linking a chain of behaviors into a more complex sequence. In Stage 1, for example, the baby may look intently at the primary caregiver. In Stage 2, the baby looks intently, reaches toward the caregiver's face, and pulls the caregiver's hair.

of the **attachment behavior system** as an organized pattern of infant signals and adult responses that lead to a protective, trusting relationship during the very earliest stage of development. The nurturing responses of the caregiver form a corresponding behavioral system referred to as **parenting** or **caregiving** (Ainsworth, 1985; Bowlby, 1988).

From ethological and neurobiological perspectives, the coordinated attachment and caregiving systems form a pattern of mutual regulation through which the infant alerts the caregiver to distress, and the caregiver provides protection, comfort, and care. Given the prolonged dependent status of human infants,

Table 5.6	Five Stages in the Development of Attachment	
Stage	Age	Characteristics
1	Birth to 3 months	Infant uses sucking, rooting, grasping, smiling, gazing, cuddling, crying, and visual tracking to maintain closeness with caregivers.
2	3 to 6 months	Infant is more responsive to familiar figures than to strangers.
3	6 to 9 months	Infant seeks physical proximity and contact with objects of attachment.
4	9 to 12 months	Infant forms internal mental representation of object of attachment, including expectations about the caregiver's typical responses to signals of distress.
5	12 months and older	Child uses a variety of behaviors to influence the behavior of the objects of attachment in ways that will satisfy needs for safety and closeness.

© Cengage

With Dad nearby, Jakob can begin to explore this new environment and return to his secure base as needed.

From about 6 to 9 months, babies want to be physically close to the object(s) of attachment. The ability to crawl and to coordinate reaching and grasping contribute to greater control over the outcomes of their actions. In this phase, babies experiment with finding an optimal distance from the caregiver. They may crawl away, look back, and then, depending on the caregiver's perceived availability, crawl back to the caregiver or smile and continue exploring. If the caregiver is preoccupied or out of sight, the baby may cry to bring the caregiver closer or to reestablish contact.

From about 9 to 12 months, babies form mental representations of their caregivers. This mental picture provides the first robust **working model of an attachment** relationship. Specific characteristics of a caregiver and expectations about how the caregiver will respond to the infant's actions are organized into a complex attachment scheme that includes expectations about how the caregiver will respond when the child is frightened, hurt, or distressed.

In toddlerhood and later, young children use a variety of behaviors to influence the behavior of their parents and other objects of attachment in order to satisfy their own needs for closeness. Bowlby described this new and important capacity as the creation of a **goal-corrected partnership**. Children may ask to be read to, cuddled at bedtime, and taken along on errands. These and other strategies produce caregiver behaviors that will satisfy a child's continuing needs for physical contact, reassurance, closeness, and love.

As children get older, they begin to think about new risks and threats to their security. They may initiate new strategies for maintaining closeness to the objects of their attachment. Especially when they are experiencing unusual stress, as in times of illness, divorce, or rejection, children of any age may try to activate the attachment system by sending signals that are intended to evoke the caregiver's comfort and closeness.

Stranger Anxiety

During the second half of the first year, two signs of a child's growing attachment to a specific person are observed: stranger anxiety and separation anxiety. **Stranger anxiety** refers to the baby's discomfort or tension in the presence of unfamiliar adults. By 6 months of age, most babies can distinguish a picture of their mother from a picture of a stranger (Swingler, Sweet, & Carver, 2010). Babies vary in how they express their protest to strangers and in how intensely they react (Rieser-Danner, 2003). They may cling to their parents, refuse to be held, stiffen at the stranger's touch, or merely avert their eyes from the stranger's face.

The baby's response to a stranger depends on specific features of the situation, including how close the caregiver is, how the stranger approaches the baby, and how the caregiver responds to the stranger. For example, if a mother speaks in a positive tone of voice to her baby about a stranger, the baby's response to the stranger is likely to be positive. In contrast, if the mother interacts with the stranger in a socially anxious manner, the baby will be more fearful of the stranger. This effect is especially notable in infants who are temperamentally more fearful and inhibited (deRosnay, Cooper, Tsigaras, & Murray, 2006).

The baby's response to a stranger will also be influenced by the amount of prior experience with unfamiliar adults. Strangers are more unfamiliar to infants in some cultures and contexts than in others (Rothbaum, Morelli & Rusk, 2011). In some parts of the world, babies rarely come into contact with anyone outside of their small village. In contrast, some children are in child care arrangements where adults frequently come and go. Normally, wariness of strangers is considered a positive developmental sign—that is, babies are able to detect the differences between their parents and adults they do not know. Wariness of strangers continues to be expressed throughout life. In fact, one often sees stronger expressions of suspiciousness or fear among adults encountering strangers than among babies.

Separation Anxiety

At about 9 months, infants give another indication of the intensity of their attachment to their parents. They express rage and despair when their parents leave them. This reaction is called **separation anxiety**. Just as with stranger anxiety, a baby's response to separation depends on the conditions. Infants are less distressed when their primary caregiver leaves them alone in a room at home than when they do so in a laboratory. They are less likely to protest if the caregiver leaves the door to the room open than if she closes the door as she leaves. Separation from the mother for periods of 30 minutes has been identified as a distinct source of stress for babies 9 months of age and older. Neurological and biochemical evidence of stress, including increases in adrenocortical activity and concentrations of cortisol in the saliva, were associated with 30 minutes of separation from the mother in a laboratory situation. The impact of stressful separations can be seen in the disruption of basic physical patterns, especially sleep disturbances, and in regression to more immature forms of play behavior, aimless wandering, and altered interactions with peers and teachers in the child care setting (Coan, 2016).

A baby's responses to separation and reunion have been used as key behavioral indicators of attachment quality. Babies who are described as having an insecure attachment are more distressed when they are separated from their mothers, and the mothers appear to be less responsive in calming their babies following separation (Harel & Scher, 2003).

Over time, most babies become more flexible in response to parents' temporary departures. Young children learn to tolerate brief separations. By the age of 3, children may even look forward to a night with a babysitter or an afternoon at grandfather's house. Once the attachment is fully established, many children can comfort themselves by creating mental images of their parents and by remembering their parents' love for them. During infancy, however, the parents' physical presence remains a focal point of attention and concern.

Formation of Attachments with Mother, Father, and Others

Most infants have more than one caring person with whom they form an attachment. Most commonly, the first object of attachment is the mother, but fathers, older siblings, grandparents, and child care professionals also become objects of attachment. Several factors have been identified as important for predicting which people will form the infant's hierarchy or radius of significant attachment figures (Cassidy, 2016; Howes & Spieker, 2016):

1. The amount of time the infant spends in the care of the person.
2. The quality and responsiveness of the care provided by the person.
3. The person's emotional investment in the infant.
4. The presence of the person in the infant's life across time.

Patterns of Attachment

It is important to distinguish between the presence of an attachment and the quality of that attachment. According to attachment theory, if an adult is present to interact with the infant, an attachment will be formed. However, individual differences emerge in the quality of that attachment depending on the accumulation of information the infant gathers over many instances when the infant is seeking reassurance, comfort, or protection from threat (Weinfield, Sroufe, Egeland, & Carlson, 2008). The adults' acceptance of the infant and their ability to respond to the child's varying communications are important to forming a positive, secure attachment. The caregivers' patterns of expressing affection and rejection will influence how well babies can meet their strong needs for reassurance and comfort.

The Strange Situation. Early research on individual differences in the quality of attachment was carried out through systematic observations of babies and their caregivers in a standard laboratory procedure called the strange situation (Ainsworth, Blehar, Waters, & Wall, 1978; Bretherton, 1990). Much of this research involved babies with their mothers. As a consequence, results are typically reported in regard to the attachment styles of infants and their mothers. During an approximately 20-minute period, the child is exposed to a sequence of events that are likely to stimulate the attachment behavior system (see Table 5.7). The situation introduces several potentially threatening experiences, including the presence of a stranger, the departure of the mother,

Table 5.7	The Strange Situation Laboratory Procedure		
Episode	**Duration**	**Participants***	**Events**
1	30 seconds	M, B, O	O shows M and B into the room, instructs M on where to put B down and where to sit; O leaves.
2	3 minutes	M, B	M puts B down close to her chair, at a distance from the toys. She responds to B's social bids but does not initiate interaction. B is free to explore. If B does not move after 2 minutes, M may take B to the toy area.
3	3 minutes	M, B, S	This episode has three parts. S enters, greets M and B, and sits down opposite M without talking for 1 minute. During the second minute, S engages M in conversation. S then joins B on the floor, attempting to engage B in play for 1 minute. At the end of this episode, M leaves "unobtrusively" (B usually notices).
4	3 minutes	B, S	S sits on her chair. She responds to B's social bids but does not initiate social interaction. If B becomes distressed, S attempts to comfort B. If this is not effective, M returns before 3 minutes are up.
5	3 minutes	M, B	M calls B's name outside the door and enters (S leaves unobtrusively). If B is distressed, M comforts B and tries to reengage B in play. If B is not distressed, M goes to sit on her chair, taking a responsive, noninitiating role. At the end of the episode, M leaves, saying, "Bye-bye; I'll be back."
6	3 minutes	B	B remains alone. If B becomes distressed, the episode is curtailed and S enters.
7	3 minutes	B, S	S enters, comforting B if required. If she cannot comfort B, the episode is curtailed. If B calms down or is not distressed, S sits on her chair, taking a responsive role as before.
8	3 minutes	M, B	M returns (S leaves unobtrusively). M behaves as in episode 5.

*O = observer; M = mother; B = baby; S = stranger.

Source: Data from "Open Communication and Internal Working Models: Their Roles in the Development of Attachment Relationships," by I. Bretherton, in R. Dienstbier and R. A. Thompson (eds.), *Nebraska Symposium on Motivation, 1988: Socioemotional Development, 36,* pp. 60–61.

being left alone with a stranger, and being left completely alone—all in the context of an unfamiliar laboratory setting. During this sequence, researchers have the opportunity to make systematic observations of the child's behaviors, the caregiver's behaviors, and the characteristics of their interactions. Four infant behaviors were of special importance: contact maintenance, proximity seeking, avoidance, and resistance. These behaviors were coded and compared across varying segments of the procedure.

Four Patterns of Attachment. Using the strange situation method, four patterns of attachment behavior have been identified: (1) secure attachment, (2) avoidant attachment, (3) resistant attachment, and (4) disorganized attachment.

Infants who have a **secure attachment** actively explore the laboratory setting and interact with strangers while their mothers are present. After separation, the babies actively greet their mothers or seek interaction. If the babies were distressed during separation, once the mothers return the infants go to the mothers for comfort, and the mothers effectively reduce their distress. Then the babies resume exploring the environment.

When observed at home, babies who have a secure attachment cry less than other babies (Ainsworth, 1985; Tracy & Ainsworth, 1981). They greet their mothers more positively on reunion after everyday separations and respond more cooperatively to their mothers' requests. One can sense that securely attached babies have a working model of attachment in which they expect their caregiver to be accessible and responsive. Mothers of infants who have secure attachments are able to talk openly and coherently about their own childhood attachment figures and attachment behaviors (van Ijzendoorn, 1995).

Infants who show an **avoidant attachment** avoid contact with their mothers during the reunion segment following separation or ignore their efforts to interact. They appear to expect that their mothers will not be there when needed. They show less distress at being alone than other babies. Mothers of babies who were characterized as avoidant seem to reject their babies. It is almost as if they were angry at their babies. They spend less time holding and cuddling their babies than other mothers, and more of their interactions are unpleasant or even hurtful. At home, these babies cry a lot, they are not readily soothed by contact with the caregiver, and yet they are quite distressed by separations. Mothers of infants who show an avoidant attachment are often dismissive or devaluing of their own childhood attachment experiences (Main & Solomon, 1990).

Infants who show a **resistant attachment** are very cautious in the presence of the stranger. Their exploratory behavior is noticeably disrupted by the caregiver's departure. When the caregiver returns, the infants appear to want to be close to the caregiver, but they are also angry so they are very hard to soothe or comfort. Infants who are characterized as resistant have mothers who are inconsistent in their responsiveness. Sometimes, these mothers ignore clear signals of distress. At other times, they interfere with their infants in order to make contact. These infants do not know if their needs will be attended to. Although these mothers enjoy close physical contact with their babies, they do not necessarily do so in ways appropriate to the baby's needs. The result is the formation of an internal working model of attachment that is highly unpredictable. These babies try to maintain proximity and avoid unfamiliar situations that increase uncertainty about accessibility to their caregiver. Caregivers of infants who have formed a resistant attachment are overly preoccupied with conflicts around their own childhood attachment issues.

In the **disorganized attachment**, babies' responses are particularly notable in the reunion sequence. These babies have no consistent strategy for managing their distress. They behave in contradictory, unpredictable ways that seem to convey feelings of extreme fear or utter confusion (Belsky, Campbell, Cohn, & Moore, 1996). Observations of mothers and infants who are described as having a disorganized attachment highlight two different patterns. Some mothers are negative, intrusive, and frighten their babies in bursts of intense hostility. Other mothers are passive and helpless, rarely showing positive or comforting behaviors. These mothers appear to be afraid of their babies, perhaps not trusting their own impulses to respond appropriately (Lyons-Ruth, Lyubchik, Wolfe, & Bronfman, 2002). The mothers often have experiences of loss or abuse in their childhood that have disrupted their own attachment experiences. Only a small percentage of infants show the disorganized pattern. Research has suggested links between the disorganized attachment and serious mental health problems in later childhood and beyond, including depression, borderline personality, and dissociative reactions (Fonagy, 2003; Lyons-Ruth et al., 2002; Lyons-Ruth & Jacobvitz, 2016).

Although categories of attachment style are still widely used in the developmental literature, the idea of attachment types or categories has come under some criticism (Waters & Beauchaine, 2003). The strange situation and its related script and coding system may constrain features of the attachment system, resulting in the emergence of a typology. In real-life situations, the expression of attachment behaviors is likely to be more fluid, adapted to the changing nature of the caregiver's responses and the conditions that provoke infant distress. Some authors prefer to think of attachment as characterized by underlying dimensions. For example, Fraley and Spieker (2003) suggested that individual differences in infant attachment can be captured along two dimensions: (1) proximity seeking versus avoidance and (2) anger and resistance. Children who are high on proximity seeking and low on anger might be thought of as secure. Children who are high on proximity seeking and high on anger might be thought of as resistant. But the exact nature of a child's working model of attachment may be more accurately characterized as some combination of these dimensions.

Parental Sensitivity and the Quality of Attachment

How can we account for differences in the quality of attachment? A cornerstone in the formation of a secure attachment is caregiver sensitivity. **Sensitivity** is defined as attentiveness to the infant's state, accurate interpretation of the infant's signals, and well-timed responses that promote mutually rewarding interactions (Mesman, Oster, & Camras, 2012). A sensitive caregiver is able to recognize the infant's emotional state, empathize with it, and make an appropriate response. An insensitive parent might recognize that the infant is distressed but be too busy or preoccupied to respond and provide effective comfort.

Caregivers who are psychologically available, responsive, consistent, and warm in their interactions with their babies—especially during the first 6 months of the baby's life—are found to be most successful in establishing a secure attachment relationship that can be measured by the time the baby is 12 months old (Braungart-Rieker, Garwood, Powers, & Wang, 2001). The way caregivers respond when infants are distressed is uniquely related to the formation of a secure attachment independent of how they respond to other infant cues (Leerkes, Blankson, & O'Brien, 2009). This makes sense since the attachment system is theorized to be especially adapted to protecting infants from threat. The **Applying Theory and Research to Life** box discusses the possibility that there may be a sensitive period for the development of attachment.

APPLYING THEORY AND RESEARCH TO LIFE

Is There a Sensitive Period for Attachment?

A **sensitive period** is a time of utmost readiness for the development of certain skills or behavior patterns. The particular skill or behavior pattern is not likely to emerge before the onset of the period, and it is extremely difficult if not impossible to establish once the sensitive time period has passed. The successful emergence of any behavior that has a sensitive period for development depends on the coordination of the biological readiness of the organism and environmental supports (Scott, 1987).

Konrad Lorenz (1935, 1937/1961) described a process of social attachment among birds that he called imprinting. In this process, the young bird establishes a comparatively permanent bond with its mother. In her absence, however, the young bird will imprint on other available targets, including a model of its mother or a human being. For birds, the onset of this sensitive period coincides with the time at which they are able to walk and ends when they begin to fear strangers. After this point, no new model or species can be substituted as a target for imprinting.

Is there a time when infants are most likely to form such an attachment to their primary caregiver? Is there a point after which such attachments cannot be formed? The answer to these questions is especially relevant for policies related to foster care and adoption. We need to know about the plasticity of social attachment in order to support optimal social and emotional development.

Evidence to address these questions has been drawn from real-life situations in which mother–infant relationships have been disrupted. Leon Yarrow (1963, 1964, 1970) observed 100 infants who were shifted from foster mothers to adoptive mothers. The infants who were separated from their foster mothers at 6 months or earlier showed minimal distress. They did not express prolonged anger or depression over the separation if their physical and emotional needs continued to be met. In contrast, all the infants who were transferred from foster mothers to adoptive mothers at 8 months or older showed strong negative reactions, including angry protest and withdrawal. These infants found the disruption of their earlier relationships very stressful.

Later research by John Bowlby (1980) focused on adolescents who had moved repeatedly from one foster home or institution to another. These children never had an opportunity to form an enduring, loving relationship with a caring adult. As adolescents, they were described as affectionless and unable to form close relationships with others. Subsequent studies of adopted children have confirmed that children who spend their infancy in institutions where the turnover in caregivers is high show disruptions in social functioning, including indiscriminate friendship formation, difficulty in forming close relationships, and difficulty in finding emotional support from peers (Rutter, 2012).

In the 1990s, a large number of orphans from Romania were adopted by families in the United States, Canada, and several European countries. While they were in the Romanian orphanages, these children had been exposed to a variety of neglectful conditions including poor nutrition, little attention or adult interaction, and long periods of time in their cribs with little opportunity for stimulation or play. Those who were

Konrad Lorenz inadvertently became the target of imprinting for these geese. They followed him as if he were their mother.

Nina Leen/Time & Life Pictures/Getty Images

adopted by 4 months of age seemed to develop quite normally. However those who were adopted at 8 months of age or older had a wide range of cognitive and affective problems that lasted into childhood. In particular, those who had longer exposure to the Romanian orphanages had disrupted social competence characterized by an overly friendly style of interaction, regardless of whether the person was a familiar caregiver or a complete stranger, and a lack of close connection to their adoptive parents (Carlson & Earls, 1997; Gunnar, 2000; Rutter et al., 2010).

In a study of children who spent their first years of life in an institution where the quality of care was good but staff turnover was high, children who were adopted at age 2 were able to form secure attachments to their adoptive parents. However, at later observations at ages 8 and 16, the children showed evidence of difficulty in peer relations similar to the children who remained in the institution (Hodges & Tizard, 1989).

From these real-world examples of inconsistent or disrupted caregiving relationships, we can say that a sensitive period for attachment must begin at about 6 months of age. Whereas lack of continuity in caregiving during infancy is likely to produce long-lasting disruptions in relationship formation, it is not clear if there is a time after which a secure attachment can no longer be established.

Critical Thinking Questions

1. Design a research study to evaluate whether there is a sensitive period for the formation of a secure attachment. What kinds of evidence would be needed to determine whether there is a sensitive period for attachment?
2. In your research plan, explain how you could determine whether the problems arising from disruptions in early caregiving were a result of a lack of attachment or some other explanation such as poor nutrition or lack of stimulation.
3. Identify other aspects of infant development that might be characterized as having a sensitive period.
4. Apply what you have read about attachment to policies that guide practices related to foster care and adoption.

Four factors come into play in producing the kind of sensitivity that underlies secure attachments: (1) cultural and subcultural pathways, (2) the caregiver's personal life story, (3) contemporary factors, and (4) characteristics of the infant (see FIGURE 5.4 ▶).

Cultural and Subcultural Pathways. Cultural and subcultural pathways are integrated into one's mental representation of a parent or caregiver. The culture's beliefs about infants, including how fragile or vulnerable they are, how best to help infants cope with distress, and what skills or temperamental qualities are most valued, are likely to shape a caregiver's practices (Coll, 2004). For example, Japanese mothers keep close, continuous proximity to their infants. Separations are infrequent, and infants are expected to monitor their mothers' reactions in order to assess people and objects in the environment. Japanese mothers subtly direct their infants' play behavior through gestures and facial expressions. Independent play is not especially valued, and the

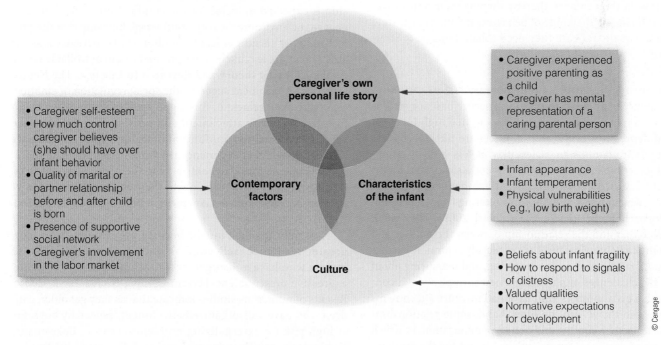

- Caregiver self-esteem
- How much control caregiver believes (s)he should have over infant behavior
- Quality of marital or partner relationship before and after child is born
- Presence of supportive social network
- Caregiver's involvement in the labor market

Caregiver's own personal life story

Contemporary factors

Characteristics of the infant

Culture

- Caregiver experienced positive parenting as a child
- Caregiver has mental representation of a caring parental person

- Infant appearance
- Infant temperament
- Physical vulnerabilities (e.g., low birth weight)

- Beliefs about infant fragility
- How to respond to signals of distress
- Valued qualities
- Normative expectations for development

© Cengage

FIGURE 5.4 ▶ FACTORS CONTRIBUTING TO CAREGIVER SENSITIVITY

idea that children would handle separation and reunion with the mother with little distress is not expected by Japanese caregivers (Okimoto, 2001).

In-depth observations of behaviors central to the survival of a group, such as caregiving strategies, establish that many cultures practice shared child care. When many adults and older siblings share responsibility for infant care, a child's needs can readily be met. When mothers expect to be able to share the tasks of infant care with others, they may also have a different ideal about the quality of infant attachment, a model that is less exclusive and possibly less emotionally intense. As a result, infants emerge with a more confident mental representation about the willingness of others to protect and care for them (Seymour, 2004).

The Caregiver's Personal Life Story. Aspects of the caregiver's personal life story contribute to being able to serve as a secure base for a child. Adults who recall their own parents as accepting, responsive, and available are more likely to be able to transmit those qualities as they enact the caregiver role. Adults who have experienced early loss or disruption of an attachment relationship have more difficulty providing a secure base for their offspring (Ainsworth & Eichberg, 1991). Some studies find that parents who have experienced significant loss in the recent past may behave in frightening or frightened ways that undermine the infant's ability to form a stable attachment representation (Stovall-Mcclough & Dozier, 2016).

Studies suggest that the internal working model of an attachment relationship may be transmitted across generations. Mothers and fathers draw on the model of an attachment they formed as infants and young children, which then guides their perceptions of infant cues and their own responses (Bornstein, 2012; George & Solomon, 2008). Parents' early life experiences establish patterns of reaction to the positive and negative cues they observe in their infants, thereby shaping their responsiveness and influencing the kinds of behaviors infants engage in to draw out the quality of care they need (Shah, Fonagy, & Strathearn 2010).

Contemporary Factors. Contemporary factors can influence the ability of an adult to provide a secure base for attachment. For example, some mothers experience high levels of postnatal depression. Depressed mothers are likely to be less attuned to their infants' signals, less playful, less verbally stimulating, more irritable, and generally less enthusiastic and happy as they interact with their infants. Attachment insecurity is more likely when infants' mothers are suffering from depression (Toth, Rogosch, Sturge-Apple, & Cicchetti, 2009). The role of the child's father and the relationship between the mother and father or the caregiving partners are especially central. A partner who is supportive, involved in caregiving, and reassuring about meeting the challenges of parenting a newborn provides a context in which even mothers who have had insecure attachments themselves can thrive. On the other hand, some relationships are characterized by conflict and poor communication, in which the partner may even compete with the infant for the mother's

care or impede the mother's efforts to care for her infant. Other contemporary factors that influence the caregiver's sensitivity to the infant include the caregiver's self-esteem, the degree of control the caregiver believes is necessary to have over the infant's behavior, the presence of a supportive social network that validates the person's caregiving efforts, the person's involvement in the labor market, and financial worries (Belsky, 2006; George & Solomon, 2008).

Infant Characteristics. The quality of attachment can also be influenced by the characteristics of the infant. Infants born with physical abnormalities are more likely to evoke responses of rejection or neglect from caregivers (Azar, 2012). Physical conditions such as colic can test the parents' commitment to caregiving and create a cycle of anxiety and fearfulness. Babies with colic may not find comfort in their caregivers' efforts to soothe them, and caregivers may not experience a sense of efficacy in their ability to calm their child.

Certain aspects of the infant—especially fearfulness, sociability, and the intensity of negative emotions—may influence the way the attachment relationship is established (Vaugh, Bost, & van Ijzendoorn, 2008). Infants who are irritable are often difficult for parents to respond to. Over time, some parents may respond to difficult infants harshly or by withdrawing. These behaviors may produce an insecure attachment for the infant (Putnam, Sanson, & Rothbart, 2012).

The Relevance of Attachment to Subsequent Development

The nature of one's attachment and the related internal working models of attachment influence expectations about the self, others, and the nature of relationships (Shaver, Collins, & Clark, 1996). Moreover, the formation of a secure attachment relationship is expected to influence the child's ability to explore and engage the environment with confidence, knowing that the protective "other" is near at hand. Children who experience a secure attachment are less likely to be exposed to uncontrollable stress. As the **Applying theory and Research to Life** box, The Neuroscience of Attachment suggests, the social regulation of emotion, especially management of threat and associated stress, is a major feature of a secure attachment and provides the link between supportive social relationships and health. Children who have a secure attachment experience rhythmic, meaningful, and predictable interactions that contribute to their social competences. As a result, they are *hopeful* about their ability to form positive relationships with others (Weinfield, Sroufe, Egeland, & Carlson, 2008).

Securely attached infants become preschoolers who show greater resilience, self-control, and curiosity. In contrast, infants who have a disorganized attachment are very hostile, aggressive preschoolers (Hazan, Campa, & Gur-Yaish, 2006). Results of numerous studies indicate that as they get older, children who have a disorganized attachment, especially boys, are at high risk for externalizing problems (Fearon, Bakermans-Kranenburg, van IJzendoorn, Lapsley, & Roisman, 2010).

The Neuroscience of Attachment

A growing body of research is addressing two intriguing questions: How does the brain support the attachment system? How is the brain altered in the context of social contacts related to attachment?

There is no single neural system that aligns in a one-to-one relationship with the construct of attachment. As Coan (2016) suggests, you can think of the whole brain as an attachment system that uses its hearing, vision, touch, smell, and movement sensory areas as well as memory, affect regulation, and stress/threat responses to form an integrated internal working model of the object of attachment. Many of the ideas we have introduced in the chapter thus far help to account for the way that filial affection unfolds rapidly and unconditionally in the infant.

1. The capacity to recognize the familiar emerges very early. Our discussion of habituation as an early form of learning confirms this idea. A preference for the familiar is supported by the production of dopamine. Positive stimuli act as reinforcers through the release of dopamine. We can understand that with repeated interactions with a familiar caregiver, a chain of dopamine activation takes place, reinforcing the pleasure of experiencing this familiarity and motivating the desire to experience this contact again and again.
2. The amygdala is a complex set of structures that is intimately associated with emotion, especially signs of threat. Given the importance of threat assessment for survival, it is not surprising that the amygdala can be quickly activated through sensory information. But it also sends information to the prefrontal cortex, which can result in appraisal and reinterpretation of the threat. The amygdala is especially sensitive to facial expressions, promoting the capacity for social referencing. The infant can use a caregiver's facial expressions to assess emotionally charged situations, especially fear.
3. The amygdala may tag a social interaction as emotionally salient, but the hippocampus will consolidate the memory of that interaction and preserve it in long-term memory.
4. The hypothalamus regulates many metabolic processes, linking the central nervous system and the endocrine system. The hypothalamus receives signals from the amygdala, the hippocampus, and the prefrontal cortex. When these signals suggest a threat, a sequence of neural systems, known as the hypothalamic-pituitary adrenal (HPA) axis is activated to produce cortisol. Cortisol is circulated throughout the body, influencing the following systems:

   - Blood sugar (glucose) levels
   - Fat, protein, and carbohydrate metabolism to maintain blood glucose
   - Immune responses
   - Anti-inflammatory actions
   - Blood pressure
   - Heart and blood vessel tone and contraction
   - Central nervous system activation

   In the context of caregiving behaviors, especially social soothing, the hypothalamus can regulate the production of cortisol, returning it to baseline levels. Looking at this list, you can appreciate the role of effective nurturing and secure attachment for long-term health.
5. The prefrontal cortex is connected to all systems mentioned above. It plays a role in interpreting or appraising emotional information, regulating emotional responses, directing attention, and integrating current information with long-term memory.
6. In the first 2 years, during a period of rapid production of axons, dendrites, and synapses, the neural organization that takes place is particularly sensitive to the caregiving context. Basic, largely automatic emotional assessments and related responses are gradually modulated and interpreted by voluntary cognitive control processes. But in first months of life, efforts that the caregiver makes to comfort, soothe, and respond to infant distress shape the neural pathways associated with memory of care, instigate cues for the release of hormones, and build an embodied set of expectations about the nature of this social contact (Schore, 2013; Vatička & Vuilleumier, 2012).

Two forms of attachment disorder have been identified by the DSM-5 (Attachment and Trauma Network, 2014):

1. **Reactive Attachment Disorder** – A consistent pattern of inhibited, emotionally withdrawn behavior toward adult caregivers, manifested by both of the following:
   - The child rarely or minimally seeks comfort when distressed.
   - The child rarely or minimally responds to comfort when distressed.

A persistent social or emotional disturbance characterized by at least two of the following:

- Minimal social and emotional responsiveness to others
- Limited positive affect
- Episodes of unexplained irritability, sadness, or fearfulness that are evident even during nonthreatening interactions with adult caregivers

2. **Disinhibited Social Engagement Disorder** – A pattern of behavior in which a child actively approaches and

interacts with unfamiliar adults and exhibits at least two of the following:

- Reduced or absent reticence in approaching and interacting with unfamiliar adults
- Overly familiar verbal or physical behavior (that is not consistent with culturally sanctioned and with age-appropriate social boundaries)
- Diminished or absent checking back with adult caregiver after venturing away, even in unfamiliar settings
- Willingness to go off with an unfamiliar adult with little or no hesitation

In addition to these clinical diagnoses, a third form of attachment disorder has been identified as developmental trauma disorder, to be distinguished from post-traumatic stress disorder (van der Kolk, 2005). According to experts who work in the field of stress and trauma, the symptoms associated with developmental trauma disorder occur when a child or adolescent has experienced or witnessed multiple or prolonged adverse events over a period of at least 1 year beginning in childhood or early adolescence, including:

- Direct experience or witnessing of repeated and severe episodes of interpersonal violence, and
- Significant disruptions of protective caregiving as the result of repeated changes in primary caregiver, repeated separation from the primary caregiver, or exposure to severe and persistent emotional abuse.

As a result of these experiences, children who experience developmental trauma disorder have significant difficulties regulating arousal and self-soothing, difficulties managing attention, preoccupation with threat, and difficulties managing social relationships including those with caregivers and peers.

From a life-span perspective, the quality of the attachment formed in infancy influences the formation of later relationships. Children who have formed secure attachments in infancy are likely to find more enjoyment in close peer friendships during their preschool years. In an analysis of the results of more than 60 studies of the relationship of parent–child attachment and peer relations, the quality of attachment with the mother was consistently predictive of the quality of close peer friendships well into middle school and early adolescence (Schneider, Atkinson, & Tardif, 2001). Children who have secure attachments are more likely to attribute positive intentions to peers, whereas children with anxious attachments are more likely to view peers with wariness.

The attachment construct has been used to help explain the nature of adolescent and adult love relationships as well as characteristics of adult parenting behaviors. These topics will be covered in chapter 11, Early Adulthood.

Critique of the Attachment Paradigm

The attachment paradigm and its measurement using the strange situation have significant limitations especially when viewed from a cross-cultural or comparative cultural lens. Three criticisms are discussed here; you may think of others.

The attachment construct continues to be evident in adult, loving relationships. This mother and daughter enjoy physical closeness, comfort each other, and look to each other for reassurance in times of stress.

1. The strange situation analyzes the child–caregiver attachment based on how the infant copes with the stressors associated with separation from the caregiver. Although one might assume that infant–caregiver separation is a universal problem, it is much more common in some cultures than others. For example, in many parts of Asia, Africa, and South America, infants sleep with their mothers and are carried on the mother's back or side throughout the day. Close physical contact is a culture's way of conveying warmth and safety. The prolonged physical separation that would occur if a baby sleeps in a bassinet or in a separate room would be considered harsh or cruel parenting. Thus, the premise that attachment can be assessed by how well a baby copes with separation may be a poor yardstick in cultures where infant–mother separation is rare and not highly valued (Greenfield, Keller, Fuligni, & Maynard, 2003).

2. The attachment framework and the strange situation emphasize the nature of the mother–infant dyad as the prototype of an attachment relationship. Although some research has been carried out to compare attachment to mothers and fathers, or mothers and caregivers, the focus is on a dyadic attachment. However, in many cultures, the infant is cared for by a cluster or collective of older siblings, cousins, aunts, fathers, and uncles, as well as the mother and other specially designated caregivers. In these cultures, the ability of the child to feel safe and secure depends on the coordinated care of many members of the family or village rather than exclusive care by the mother. The strange situation in particular and the attachment paradigm more generally do not capture the fluid nature of this collective caregiving context and the degree to which it is effective in supporting a child's feelings of safety and security (Lewis, 2005).

3. Infant–caregiver interactions can be understood as an introduction to the nature of valued social relationships which, over time, will contribute to the child's survival and successful integration into the social community. One of the assumptions of the attachment framework is that a secure attachment provides a safe harbor from which the child feels free to explore the environment. From this view, attachment is a foundation for subsequent independence. However, autonomy, exploration, and self-reliance are not primary goals of socialization in all cultures. Societies marked by greater value for interdependence view the formation of infant attachment as a precursor to obedience, intragroup harmony, and acceptance of cultural norms and values.

Thus, while the need to ensure the survival of the young through sensitive and responsive care may be a cultural universal, the socialization goals that follow from the formation of a secure attachment may differ from one culture to the next depending upon the culture's goals, values, and traditions (Mesman, van IJzendoorn, & Sagi-Schwartz, 2016; Weisner, 2005).

FURTHER REFLECTION: Explain the evolutionary basis for the attachment behavior system. In this light, hypothesize why very small babies might be vulnerable to the formation of insecure attachments.

Describe the concept of sensitive caregiving. How might contemporary life events disrupt an adult's ability to provide sensitive care?

Emotional Development

OBJECTIVE 6   Examine the nature of emotional development, including emotional differentiation, the interpretation of emotions, and emotional regulation. Analyze the concept of temperament as an organized aspect of emotional reactivity.

Emotional development during infancy can be understood along four dimensions. First, new emotions emerge. Infants express these emotions at different levels of intensity—for example, from a whimper or fussy noise to a full-blown angry rage, or from a happy cooing gurgle to outright laughter. Second, with cognitive maturation, a child interprets events differently. New emotions may become attached to familiar situations. An experience that may once have caused wariness, such as a new toy or a loud noise, may become a source of excitement or joy as the child gains a new understanding of the situation. Third, children develop strategies for regulating their emotions so that they are not overwhelmed by emotional intensity. Fourth, emotions serve as a channel for adult–infant communication.

Emotional Differentiation

New emotions gradually emerge during the first 2 years of life. Peter Wolff (1966) described seven states of arousal in newborn infants: regular sleep, irregular sleep, periodic sleep, drowsiness,

At 3 months of age, infants can communicate their emotional state using different facial expressions. Sensitive caregivers can detect happiness, excitement, wariness, sadness, and frustration.

alert inactivity, waking activity, and crying. Each is characterized by a different pattern of breathing, muscle tone, motor activity, and alertness. In these states, one observes the earliest distinct emotions of distress (*crying*), interest (*alert inactivity*), and excitement (*waking activity*). A newborn's state of arousal influences the capacity to respond to the environment. Changes in arousal also prompt responses from caregivers. Crying usually brings an effort to comfort or soothe. Visual alertness is likely to prompt social interactions with caregivers who use a variety of strategies to sustain contact such as smiling, making cooing sounds, or shaking a toy or rattle.

Crying is an especially important emotional expression that contributes to the infant's survival. Until about 6 or 7 months of age, the infant's mobility is quite limited. The cry is one of the primary signals available that will bring the caregiver to the infant. Infant cries vary in pitch as well as in tempo and duration. Adults have measurable emotional reactions to infant crying, including changes in heart rate, breathing, and perspiration, which indicate that the cry serves as a stressor. Studies from laboratory and natural field settings and across cultures suggest that high-pitched cries are considered more upsetting to the caregiver and are treated as a signal of a more urgent need than are low-pitched cries. Moreover, information is contained in the pauses between cries. Cries that involve shorter pauses between crying sounds are perceived by adults as more arousing and unpleasant (Groh & Roisman, 2009; Zeskind, Klein, & Marshall, 1992).

Emotional responses during the first month are closely tied to the infant's internal state. Physical discomfort, arousal, pain, and changing tension in the central nervous system are the major sources of emotions. During the period from 1 to 6 months, emotions begin to reflect the infant's awareness of features of the environment. Babies smile at familiar faces; they show interest in and curiosity about novel stimuli. They express rage when nursing is disrupted or when they are prevented from viewing an activity they have been intently watching.

From 1 to 6 months, the intensity of emotional expression becomes more varied. For example, four different kinds of infant smiles have been observed: the simple smile in which a baby's mouth curves upward at the corner; the Duchenne smile, which involves crinkling eyes, raised cheeks, and an open, smiling mouth; the play smiles in which the jaw drops and the mouth stays open; and the duplay smiles in which the jaw drops and the cheeks are raised (Fogel et al., 2006). The simple smile is considered a signal of happy social engagement, whereas the Duchenne, play, and duplay smiles reflect different levels of intensity in play that accompany such activities as tickling, peek-a-boo, and playful interactions with familiar caregivers.

The period from 6 to 12 months reflects a greater awareness of the context of events. Emotions of joy, anger, and fear are tied to a baby's ability to recall previous experiences and to compare them with an ongoing event. These emotions also reflect the ability to exercise some control over the environment and frustration when goals are blocked. Fearfulness, assessed several times from 4 to 12 months, increases steadily over the first year. Babies who are less fearful at 4 months show a steeper increase in fear than babies who are already quite fearful at a very young age (Gartstein et al., 2010).

The dimension of wariness–fear becomes more differentiated during the second year. Wariness is viewed as an early feature of the attachment process, especially as it relates to stranger anxiety at about 6 months and separation anxiety at about 9 months. Fear responses are relatively rare among young infants. It may be that fear needs to be learned as babies gain experiences that result in the appraisal of threat. Fear of a more nonspecific form begins to be observed during the second year. Babies begin to anticipate negative experiences and express fear of objects or events that have been associated with negative experiences in the past. In the image on the left below, the fear response is evoked when a nurse returns for the second of two inoculations. In some instances, as in the image on the right, one sees the expression of fear blended with surprise, as when a novel toy emits a loud noise or a dog makes a sudden move toward the infant (Sullivan & Lewis, 2003).

By the end of the first year, the extent of an infant's negative emotions, such as irritability and fear, are influenced by the caregiver's depression and anxiety. The impact of maternal depression on infants' psychosocial development has received a great deal of attention in the literature, demonstrating that there are

A fear expression in response to approach of a nurse following inoculation (a) and a fear blend in response to the sudden appearance of a stimulus (b).

distinct differences in the emotional expressiveness and social engagement of infants of depressed mothers. Higher levels of maternal depression and anxiety in infancy are linked to greater increases in fearfulness at the end of infancy, and more symptoms of anxiety at age 2 (Gartstein et al., 2010). Positive emotions are not as clearly tied to the caregiver's characteristics (Pauli-Pott, Mertesacker, & Beckman, 2004).

Emotions that are observed during the second year of life, 12 to 24 months—especially anxiety, pride, defiance, and shame—suggest an emerging sense of self. Infants recognize that they can operate as causal agents. They also begin to respond to the emotions of others. They can give love to others through hugs, kisses, and tender pats. They can share toys, comfort another distressed infant, and imitate another person's excitement. In becoming a more distinct being, an infant achieves a new level of awareness of the capacity to give and receive pleasure as well as the vulnerability of self and others.

Emotions as a Key to Understanding Meaning

An infant's emotional reactions provide a channel for determining the meaning the child is giving to a specific situation. Often, these reactions are studied by the systematic coding of facial expressions. One example of how emotions provide a window on meaning comes from a study of infants in an operant conditioning experiment. Infants at ages 2, 4, and 6 months were observed while they learned an operant arm-pulling task. A string was attached to the infant's wrist. When the string was pulled, it activated a switch that turned on a color slide of an infant smiling accompanied by the sound of children singing the *Sesame Street* theme song. During the learning phase, pulling the string produced the visual and auditory stimulus. During the extinction phase, nothing happened when the string was pulled. Even as young as 2 months old, the babies' expressions changed from interest and enjoyment during the learning phase to anger and sadness during the extinction phase. The study illustrates that infants' anger is associated with violation of their expectations and that expressions of interest and enjoyment are associated with learning and increased control (Sullivan, Lewis, & Alessandri, 1992).

An infant's smile can have a wide variety of meanings and can be produced in response to many stimuli. *Social smiles* begin to be observed at about 5 weeks of age. These smiles are first produced in response to a wide range of stimuli: familiar faces and voices (especially the mother's), strangers, and nonhuman objects. Games such as tickle and peek-a-boo bring on open-mouth smiles and laughter (Fogel et al., 2006). The social smile conveys both recognition of familiarity and an invitation to further communication or interaction.

The *cognitive smile* develops alongside the social smile. Infants smile in response to their own behaviors, as if they were expressing satisfaction with their accomplishments or self-recognition. In a study of infants over the period from 7 to 20 weeks, babies were observed to show the *coy smile*—smiling while averting their gaze—when they were successful in getting attention or renewing attention from an adult (Reddy, 2000). As evidenced in the string-pulling task described previously, infants make a *mastery smile* when they are able to make something happen.

In the second year of life, smiling is associated with a primitive form of *humor*. Babies smile when they recognize an incongruity, such as seeing their mother drinking from a baby bottle or crawling on her hands and knees. They also smile and laugh when they violate a caregiver's expectations. These smiles suggest that the baby appreciates something about the discrepancy between what is being presented and what is normally observed (Loizou, 2005).

The Ability to Regulate Emotions

Emotional regulation refers to a variety of processes that allow infants to control the intensity of their emotional state and reduce feelings of distress. These abilities, which mature over the first 2 years, have important implications for a child's successful social participation in preschool and later childhood (Calkins & Leerkes, 2011). Infants develop a range of techniques for coping with intense emotions, both positive and negative. Even newborns have some strategies for reducing the intensity of distress, such as turning the head away, sucking on their hands or lips, or closing their eyes. As infants gain new motor coordination and control, they can move away, distract themselves with other objects, or soothe themselves by rocking, stroking, or thumb sucking (Kopp, 1989). One study compared 3-, 5-, and 7-month old infants as they reacted to their mother and their father who were showing them the "still face." Infants who looked away or who engaged in some kind of self-soothing activity showed at decrease in distress; infants who engaged in intense motor activity showed an increase in distress (Ekas, Lickenbrock, & Braungart-Rieker, 2013). There are many instances when infants are not able to regulate the intensity of their emotions. Researchers who work with infants often note the number of babies who had to be eliminated from their study because they simply could not be calmed enough in the experimental procedure to attend to the task. The way an infant reacts to environmental stimuli and the intensity of that reaction is often conceptualized as a reflection of the concept of temperament.

Temperament. **Temperament** is a theoretical construct that refers to relatively stable characteristics of response to the environment and patterns of self-regulation (Putnam, Sanson, & Rothbart, 2012; Thomas & Chess, 1980).

> Temperament traits are early emerging basic dispositions in the domains of activity, affectivity, attention, and self-regulation, and these dispositions are the product of complex interactions among genetic, biological, and environmental factors across time. (Shiner et al., 2012, p. 2)

Temperament is a significant source of individual differences. When we describe babies as active, cheerful, quiet, or fussy, we are making reference to what scholars study as temperament. One of the underlying questions is the extent to which infant temperament is predictive of adult personality. Although aspects of temperament that might be observed in infancy are quite different from the features of adult personality, it is possible that features of temperament, such as inhibition or wariness, and features of adult personality, such as shyness or social anxiety, may be reflections of a common underlying dimension. Theorists have offered different views about the specific features of temperament and what accounts for the stability of these features over time

Table 5.8	Three Types of Infant Temperaments	
Type	**Description**	**% of Total Sample**
Easy	Positive mood, regular body functions, low or moderate intensity of reaction, adaptability, positive approach rather than withdrawal from new situations	40
Slow to warm up	Low activity level, tendency to withdraw on first exposure to new stimuli, slow to adapt, somewhat negative in mood, low intensity of reaction to situations	15
Difficult	Irregular body functions, unusually intense reactions, tendency to withdraw from new situations, slow to adapt to change, generally negative mood	10

Note: Some researchers prefer terms such as flexible and active, cautious, and feisty rather than easy, slow to warm up, and difficult, which have judgmental connotations.

Source: From "The Origin of Personality," by A. Thomas, S. Chess, and H. Birch, 1970, *Scientific American*, 223, pp. 102–109.

(Vaughn & Bost, 2016). The following section reviews four views of temperament.

Dimensions of Temperament. Thomas, Chess, and Birch (1970; Thomas & Chess, 1977) used observations of nine dimensions to classify infants into three temperamental groupings: *easy, slow to warm up,* and *difficult*. Table 5.8 summarizes the characteristics of each of these temperaments and the percentages of the sample that could be clearly identified as one of the three types. Roughly 35 percent of the sample could not be classified. Some researchers use different labels to describe these types, reflecting an understanding that some aspects of infant behavior are difficult for some parents but easy for others. In newer work, the types are labeled "resilient," "undercontrolled," and "overcontrolled," terms that capture features of self-regulation, and seem less judgmental (Caspi & Shiner, 2006).

Buss and Plomin (1984/2015; 1986) identified three aspects of temperament—activity level, sociability, and emotionality— that they thought were influenced largely by genetic factors. Further work has included impulsivity, a trait comprising difficulties with emotional and behavioral control, persistence, and planfulness as showing a strong genetic basis (Gagne & Saudino, 2010; Saudino & Zapfe, 2008). Patterns of electrical activity in the frontal cortex in infancy have been associated with individual differences in these features of temperament, particularly distinguishing between babies who are more able to regulate their emotions, who are easily soothed, and who seem to be relatively positive as contrasted to the babies who are easily distressed, difficult to soothe, and have difficulty focusing their attention (Schmidt, Fox, Perez-Edgar, & Hamer, 2009). These dimensions—especially emotionality and activity level—show modest stability over adjacent periods of infancy and toddlerhood (Henderson, Fox, & Rubin, 2001). Genetic factors appear to account for stability in temperament across different settings (e.g. laboratory and home). However, genetics and

environment also interact, especially when considering possible prenatal influences on development, and the differential sensitivity of infants to nurturing versus harsh parenting (Braungart, Plomin, DeFries, & Fulker, 1992; Goldsmith & Campos, 1986; Goldsmith et al., 1987; Shiner et al., 2012; Wilson & Matheny, 1986).

Another view of temperament focuses on the construct of **behavioral inhibition**, a combination of fearfulness, a low threshold for arousal in the presence of novel or unusual stimuli, and general cautiousness. A method of assessing behavioral inhibition involves presenting infants with a set of unusual stimuli and observing their reactions. Some infants seem to think this is great fun. They smile, coo, and respond with positive excitement. Other infants get very distressed. They cry, struggle, arch their backs, and try to escape the situation. These early reactions in the laboratory setting at 4 months of age are predictors of toddler behavior. The infants who react positively to the novel stimuli are likely to become active, busy, exploratory toddlers. The infants who react with distress to the novel stimuli are likely to become fearful, shy, and socially wary toddlers (Kagan & Snidman, 2004).

Rothbart (1981; Rothbart & Bates, 2006) characterized temperament as "constitutionally based individual differences in reactivity and self-regulation in the domains of affect, activity, and attention" (Rothbart & Bates, 2006, p. 100). Rothbart's research led to the identification of three overarching dimensions of temperament: surgency/extroversion, negative affectivity, and effortful control. These dimensions, viewed as present in infancy, undergo maturation associated with the emerging neural basis for attention and self-regulation. Studies of mothers' and fathers' observational ratings of their infants support the stability of these dimensions from infancy to toddlerhood, with the exception that orienting/regulating is observed in very young infants as the precursor to effortful control in toddlers (Casalin, Luyten, Vliegen, & Meurs, 2012).

A child's temperament influences the tone of interactions, the frequency with which interactions take place, the way others react to the child, and the way the child reacts to the reactions of others. Highly active, sociable children are likely to initiate interactions and to respond positively to the attention of others. More passive, inhibited, or fearful children will be less likely to initiate interactions and may withdraw when other children or adults direct attention to them. There is growing concern that infants and toddlers who are temperamentally shy, fearful, and readily distressed by novel or unfamiliar situations may be vulnerable to subsequent difficulties regulating anxiety and depression (Moffitt et al., 2007).

The kind of caregiving a child receives will depend in part on the parental context. For example, Thomas and Chess (1977, 1986) found that when parents were calm and allowed their difficult children to adapt to novelty at a leisurely pace, the children grew more comfortable and had an easier time adapting to new routines. However, if parents were impatient and demanding, then their difficult children remained difficult and had a hard time adjusting to new situations as they grew older. A mother's age, her economic resources, the nature of the neighborhood where she lives, and characteristics such as depression, stress, or a sense of parenting efficacy might each influence how patient and supportive a mother may be with a child who has an emotionally negative or irritable temperament (Paulussen-Hoogeboom, Stams, Hemranns, & Peetsma, 2007).

Is this baby showing evidence of a difficult temperament or is the protest a result of the father's lack of attention? What observations would you need to make in order to answer this question?

Child outcomes are understood as a product of child temperament and parenting strategies (Rothbart & Bates, 2006). Many studies emphasize the relevance of the fit or match between the parent's temperament and that of the child (Rettew et al., 2006). Depending on the caregiving they receive and the environments they encounter, shy children can become sociable, fearful children can become secure explorers of their surroundings, and highly exuberant children can develop considerable self-control (National Research Council and Institute of Medicine, 2000,p. 389). In all likelihood, temperamental characteristics are modified as they come into contact with socialization pressures at home and at school, as well as with new internal capacities to regulate behavior.

A few examples of this kind of interaction follow:

- Gentle, low-power discipline techniques are more effective in socializing infants who are relatively fearful and inhibited; these techniques do not work well with temperamentally fearless infants who respond better to socialization strategies that emphasize positive feelings between the mother and child (Kochanska, Aksan, & Joy, 2007).
- Children who are fearful are more likely to be inhibited with their peers when their mothers are overprotective, but more confident with their peers when their mothers

are reassuring and supportive of the child's autonomy (Rubin, Hastings, Stewart, Henderson, & Chen, 1997).
- Parental use of harsh punishment is not predictive of aggressive behavior for children who are flexible and low in reactivity but is strongly linked to aggressiveness among children who are inflexible and highly reactive (Patterson & Sanson, 1999).

These and other findings create a complex picture of differential sensitivity and reactivity to the features of the caregiving environment. Children differ in the extent to which they detect and react to environmental demands or threats (Moore & Depue, 2016). A modest level of parental dominance or assertiveness may be frightening and intimidating for a child with high behavioral inhibition, and completely insignificant for a child with low behavioral inhibition (Gilissen et al., 2007). Consider the role of temperament in the case study on the Cotton family.

— **CASE STUDY** The Cotton Family —

Nancy and Paul Cotton are a professional couple who gave birth to their first child, Anna, after they had been married for 7.5 years.

Nancy said, "We wanted a baby but couldn't decide when to have one. Finally we realized that we could not control everything, or time things perfectly. No one can predict the future. So we finally decided to go ahead and have a child as soon as possible. ... By the time we had Anna, I was thirty-three, and our marriage and careers were established. We felt secure.

"Being an optimistic person, I guess I expected nirvana. Anna was difficult to deliver, and breastfeeding was a nightmare. Every time she nursed, it hurt. But I didn't want to miss the opportunity. I was so determined. I used a stopwatch to make sure Anna got enough milk, and I gave her a pacifier for recreation. When she was five weeks old, I went off to our summer house on Martha's Vineyard. I wondered if it was the right decision because there was less in the way of family and friends for support. But we worked things out together that summer. She was energetic from the first, and I was constantly sleep-deprived, but we were oh! so close. I found ways to make it easier for us. I used the 'Swyngomatic' so that I could eat a warm supper every once in a while, and I learned to give Anna pacifiers or bottles to soothe herself."

Paul interjected: "She was like a miracle to me. She was fabulous! Miraculous! She even looked like me. I did as much for her as Nancy did, not out of guilt, but because I couldn't keep my hands off her. I took her with me everywhere when I was off work. At the Stop-and-Shop, all the ladies crowded around me, 'How do you do it? You're so good with her!' I learned all about babies from her. I can bathe a kid faster than anyone in the world."

"Anna fit," said Nancy. "From the time she was born, we'd pick her up and just go. As you can see, going is pretty important in our family, and Anna thrived on it. We were not the only ones who enjoyed her; my own mother thought she was fabulous. She took care of her part-time after I went back to work. I had a chance to see my mother be loving and kind, a good mother to Anna. It was like reliving my own childhood—another kind of miracle. You see, I'd had a sister, Ginny, who had died. Anna gave my mother an opportunity to heal the pain of Ginny's death. This was true for me, too."

CASE ANALYSIS Using What You Know

1. Describe Anna's temperament. What problems might the Cotton family have faced if Anna had been a more passive, reserved, and inhibited child?

2. Evaluate the ways that Anna was expected to adapt to the Cotton family lifestyle.

3. List some of the challenges Nancy and Paul faced as new parents. How did they cope with these challenges?

4. Describe and assess Paul's enactment of the father role. Describe and assess Nancy's enactment of the mother role. How well do they match the features of sensitive parenting?

5. Anna seems to be influencing the well-being of her mother, father, and her grandmother. What impact does Anna have on each of these family members?

How Caregivers Help Infants Manage Their Emotions. One of the most important elements in the development of emotional regulation is the way caregivers assist infants to manage their strong feelings. Caregivers can provide direct support when they observe that a child is distressed. They may cuddle, hug, rock, or swaddle a baby. They may offer food or a pacifier to the baby or nurse her as a means of comfort. Through words and actions, the caregiver may help a child interpret the source of the stress or suggest ways to reduce the stress.

In a longitudinal study of maternal comforting strategies, mothers were observed as they tried to comfort their children following an inoculation at 2 and 6 months of age. The intensity and duration of infant crying decreased over this 4-month period. At the younger age, mothers used affection and soothing as comforting strategies when their babies cried after the shot; at 6 months, they used vocalization and distracting strategies more often, taking advantage of the infant's more developed capacities for attention and playfulness. For all levels of infant distress, the most effective method of soothing was a combination of holding/rocking and vocalizing, combining the sense of touch and the rhythmic movement of rocking with the calming features of the mother's voice (Jahromi, Putnam, & Stifter, 2004).

Concern has focused on babies who show intense negative emotionality early in infancy. Babies who show high levels of motor activity and who cry a lot at 4 months of age have been found to show high levels of wariness, fearfulness, and shyness at later ages. Babies who show high levels of fearfulness appear to be at risk for later problems with social anxiety (Buss, 2011). Studies have analyzed individual differences in negative emotionality and the family characteristics that might be associated with changes in negativity over the first year of life (Calkins & Howse, 2004; Pauli-Pott et al., 2004). In a longitudinal analysis of the relationship of parenting environments and infant temperament among a sample of over 2,000 Canadian families, exposure to more positive parenting reduced

behavior problems in children with difficult/undercontrolled temperaments. Contextual factors including neighborhood problems, neighborhood cohesion, social support, and maternal depression influenced the ability of parents to provide positive, sensitive parenting for those infants with more undercontrolled temperaments (Gallitto, 2015).

Caregivers' approaches to infant emotional regulation vary with the culture (Kitayama, Karasawa, & Mesquita, 2004; Mesquita, De Leersnyder, & Albert, 2014). In some cultures, caregivers regulate emotions by preventing a child from being exposed to certain arousing situations. Japanese mothers, for example, try hard to prevent their children from being exposed to anger and avoid frustrating them. Furthermore, parents rarely express anger to their young children, especially in public. Thus, Japanese parents try to regulate anger by minimizing the child's experiences with it. Cultural values influence how mothers respond to infants' distress and what they teach their babies about how to regulate feelings of wariness, fear, and anxiety.

Infants achieve emotional regulation by observing emotional reactions of others. Children observe anger, pride, shame, or sadness in others, often in response to their own emotional expressions. For example, Connie stumbles and falls in trying to take a step on her own. She looks up at her mother. If her mother looks upset and frightened, Connie may begin to cry. On the other hand, if her mother laughs or speaks to her in a comforting tone, Connie may get up and try again. Children can be distracted from their sadness by seeing laughter and joy in someone else. Through empathy, they can reduce their angry feelings toward someone else by seeing how sad or frightened the other person is.

As children understand the consequences or implications of a situation, they have new motives for regulating or failing to regulate their emotions. Children may extend or expand their signals of distress if they think it will help them achieve their goals, such as special attention or nurturing. Children may try to disguise their distress if they think it will provoke additional pain. Emotional regulation, like emotional signaling, takes place in an interpersonal context.

Emotions as a Channel for Adult-Infant Communication

Emotions provide a two-way channel through which infants and their caregivers can establish **intersubjectivity**. An infant has the capacity to produce a range of emotional expressions, including fear, distress, disgust, surprise, excitement, interest, joy, anger, and sadness. Parents and other caregivers rely on facial, vocal, and behavioral cues related to these emotions as ways of determining an infant's inner states and goals, and responding to them. Using techniques for recording neural electrical activity, studies find that infant smiles and cries stimulate different areas of the caregiver's brain. Both biological and adoptive mothers react with special sensitivity to their infant's crying (Doi & Shinohara, 2012).

The mirror neuron system provides infants and adults with the capacity to link seeing and doing. This system is activated both when we perform an action and when we see someone else perform that action. Thus it creates an early neural bridge for social understanding of behavior. Mirror neurons support an infant's capacity to imitate adult expressions, and for adults to recognize and interpret infants' expressions. Mirror neuron processes are needed for social connection but are not adequate for the co-construction of meaning. This is gradually supplemented by joint attention, shared emotional referencing, and the attached association of positive or negative reactions that provide approach and/or avoidance cues and create a framework for shared values (Rochat & Passos-Ferreira, 2009).

Babies can detect and differentiate the affective expressions of others including fear, anger, happiness, sadness, and surprise. They can recognize facial expressions at 4 months of age, but they require further time to understand the meanings of these expressions (Grossman, 2013; Kaneshige & Haryu, 2015). In cycles of interaction, responsive caregivers monitor changes in a baby's affect as a way of determining whether their interventions are effective (Meins, 2011).

Think of a 6-month-old baby who wants a toy that is out of reach. The baby waves her arms in the direction of the toy, makes fussy noises, and looks distressed. As her father tries to figure out what the baby wants, he watches her expressions in order to discover whether he is on the right track. Parents who are attuned to this form of communication are more likely to help babies to achieve their goals, and babies are more likely to persist in attempts to communicate because they have experienced success in such interactions. Through a shared repertoire of emotions, babies and their caregivers are able to understand one another and create common meanings. Thus, emotional expression becomes a building block of trust (Trevarthen & Aitken, 2001).

Social Referencing. One of the most notable ways that infants and adults have of co-constructing their reality is the mechanism of **social referencing** in which infants gather information about a situation or an object by assessing their parent's or caregiver's reactions. Social referencing involves three coordinated processes: (1) The infant coordinates attention between the adult and an ambiguous object or situation; (2) the infant understands that the adult's emotional reaction refers to the specific object or

situation; (3) the infant uses the information from the adult's emotional reaction to guide behavior toward the object (Feinman et al., 1992; Hornik & Gunnar, 1988; Murray et al., 2008). By 12 months of age, infants can draw upon all of these abilities to use the emotional responses of another person to guide their own behavior (Carver & Vaccaro, 2007). They often use their mothers as a *social reference*, but other adults can serve this function as well. As infants approach an unfamiliar adult, an ambiguous situation, or a novel object, they look to their mother and use her facial expression or verbal expressions as a source of information about the situation. If the mother expresses wariness or a negative emotion, the infant is more likely to withdraw or to explore with caution. On the other hand, if the mother expresses a positive emotion, the infant is more likely to approach the situation or the unfamiliar person with confidence. By 12 months of age, infants consistently use this mechanism to try to appraise an ambiguous situation (de Rosnay, Cooper, Tsigaras, & Murray, 2006; Rosen, Adamson, & Bakeman, 1992).

In an extension of the social referencing concept, researchers wondered whether infants could gather information by observing how adults interacted with each other in relation to an object (Repacholi & Meltzoff, 2007). In an experimental situation, infants observed while one adult (the experimenter) performed specific activities with an object and a second adult (the emoter) expressed either an angry or a neutral reaction to the first adult. For example, the angry adult might say to the experimenter who was demonstrating an activity with an object, "That's aggravating! That's so annoying," while speaking in an angry tone of voice and using angry facial expressions. Then the infants were given an opportunity to touch the object while the experimenter and the emoter sat quietly in the room. Infants who observed the angry emoter were less likely to imitate the activity, slower to touch the object, and more likely to look at the angry adult who remained in the room, even though the adult was now calm and neutral in behavior. In the angry emoter condition, the infants had fewer positive facial expressions during the time when they were

allowed to explore the object. The results of this research suggest that infants can gather and retain information about how to interact with objects in their environment based on what they observe of the emotional reactions of others to these objects, even when the responses are not directed toward them.

Social referencing illustrates how members of a cultural group build a shared view of reality during infancy (Halberstadt & Lozada, 2011). Infants actively request information by looking to their mothers or other adults. They also eavesdrop on adults, watching and listening to the emotional tone of their interactions. The adult's expression, either positive or negative, cues the infant about whether to approach or withdraw. In an experimental study, it was demonstrated that infants could detect the stress level of their mothers, which in turn created heightened stress in the infants. This research illustrates the role of emotional reciprocity and potential

Emotions provide a channel of communication before speech and language. The exchange of playful laughing and smiling is an early form of conversation.

contagion, especially negative of emotions, in the caregiver–infant dyad (Waters, West, & Mendes, 2014).

Infants reduce their uncertainty and begin to appraise their world in the context of the emotional responses of their caregivers. You can probably imagine the wide range of objects and situations that can be evaluated through this mechanism. Foods, toys, people, animals, sounds, plants, and objects of all sorts can be discerned as positive and approachable or negative and a cause for wariness. Depending on the cultural outlook, infants in different societies will begin to categorize their experiences differently based in part on these early appraisals derived from social referencing.

FURTHER REFLECTION: Explain how infants and caregivers use emotional communication to create meaning. Give some examples that reflect positive and negative emotion states.

The Psychosocial Crisis: Trust Versus Mistrust

OBJECTIVE 7 Explain the psychosocial crisis of trust versus mistrust; the central process through which the crisis is resolved, mutuality with the caregiver; the prime adaptive ego quality of hope; and the core pathology of withdrawal.

At each stage of life, the psychosocial crisis is expressed as a struggle between the positive and negative poles of a critical dimension. In infancy, the specific nature of the crisis—trust versus mistrust—focuses on the fundamental nature of an infant's sense of connection to the social world.

Trust

In adult relationships, **trust** refers to an appraisal of the availability, dependability, and sensitivity of another person. Trust emerges in the course of a relationship as one person discovers those traits in another person. As the level of trust grows, the partners may take some risks by disclosing information or feelings that may lead to rejection. Relationships that endure through periods of risk grow in feelings of trust. However, trust is more than a summary of the past: It is a faith that the relationship will survive in an unpredictable future. This faith begins in infancy. A trusting relationship links confidence about the past with faith about the future.

For infants, trust is an emotion—a positive state of confidence that their needs will be met and that they are valued. Trust is inferred from the infant's increasing capacity to delay gratification and from the warmth and delight that are evident in interactions with family members. This sense expands from trust of the immediate figures in the social environment to trust in the supportiveness and responsiveness of the broader social and physical world. Infants also learn to trust their sensory systems as they process stimulation from the environment. Thus, the sense of trust extends to learning to trust oneself.

The sense of basic trust is related but not identical to Bowlby's concept of attachment. Attachment refers to the behavioral system that ensures safety and security for the infant. Over time, the internal representation of the attachment relationship generalizes

to other relationships, especially where issues of intimacy and protection are relevant. Trust is a broader, more abstract construct. It not only refers to the infant–caregiver relationship but also includes the orientation of the infant to the wider social network of trustable and caring others. As such, it establishes the infant's first model or way of thinking about social integration. Trust becomes a basic orientation toward the self and others; it conveys a belief that "I am safe and loved; I can extend my self toward others and count on them to be dependable and caring."

Infants establish an assessment of the central social figures in their world as trustable or untrustable; they also achieve a sense of their own value and trustworthiness. Over time, a basic sense of trust expands to a general sense of optimism about how one expects to be treated by others and about one's ability to cope with life's challenges. Trust is an integrating force that helps synthesize emotions, cognitions, and actions under conditions of uncertainty, allowing the person to pursue goals with a belief that things will work out well.

Given the key role of trust in forming and sustaining human social bonds, it makes sense to think that there is a biological basis for trusting in interpersonal interactions. Recent research has identified the role of **oxytocin** in the neuroscience of trust. Oxytocin, a hormone that plays a key role in social attachment, produces a general sense of calm relaxation, reducing wariness and increasing approach behavior (Baumgartner et al., 2008).

It is likely that positive social interactions stimulate the production of oxytocin. When a person perceives a combination of certain interpersonal cues such as facial expressions, especially smiling and laughter, rhythmic gestures, and tone of voice in a specific context, oxytocin is released. The release of oxytocin then triggers a set of neural networks that reduces wariness and fear of others and increases willingness to trust the other person (Damasio, 2005; Kirsch et al., 2005; Mayo Clinic, 2014).

Mistrust

During infancy, experiences of **mistrust** can arise from at least three sources: infant wariness, lack of confidence in the caregiver, and doubt in one's own lovableness. First, wariness, one of the earliest infant emotions, is linked initially to at least two infant reflexes, the startle response in reaction to loud noises and the Moro reflex in response to sudden loss of support (see Table 5.2). All infants are prewired neurologically to be alert to certain environmental dangers. Infants are able to use sensory information, especially the ability to interpret facial expressions and the ability to differentiate auditory cues, to assess interpersonal anger or threat. By 6 months of age, most infants show evidence of stranger anxiety, another indication of normal capacities for wariness. Two of the caregiver's functions are to minimize the infant's exposure to stimuli that evoke these responses and to comfort and reassure the infant after exposure to threatening stimuli.

Second, babies can lack confidence in the good intentions of others. Most parents contribute to experiences of mistrust because they inevitably make some mistakes in responding to their infant's signs of distress, particularly when the baby is young. They may first try the bottle, and, if the crying continues, they may change the diaper, give water, move the baby to another room, or put the baby to bed—trying a variety of things until something works.

Molly can't get her mother's attention. Her mother is worn out and unable to make any appropriate response to Molly's distress. Over time, this inability to evoke a parent's caring response can generate mistrust.

Over time, however, sensitive caregivers learn to interpret their child's signals correctly and respond appropriately, thereby fostering the infant's sense of trust in the environment.

Some caregivers are unable to identify their infant's needs or frequently respond inappropriately to them. Others are indifferent or unusually harsh. Under conditions of maltreatment, seeds of doubt may grow about the trustworthiness of the environment. Abused infants become especially sensitive to cues that suggest hostility or anger in their environment, and are more likely to fixate on those cues, even when the threat has passed (Pollak, 2008).

Infants are not only aware of threats expressed toward them but are also sensitive to expressions of anger or hostility among other members of the household. Infants are attuned to angry, negative interactions that, at some level, threaten their security. Under conditions of interpersonal conflict, infants may try to intervene by crying or by sidling up to one of the adults; or they may try to escape by crawling away. Chronic exposure to interpersonal conflict creates a level of insecurity in the child who may feel that needs cannot be met when the adults in the family, especially attachment figures, are engaged in angry interactions with each other (Davies & Woitach, 2008).

Third, babies experience the power of their own rage. In some children, self-regulatory abilities are poorly developed, which leads to frequent outbursts of negativity and frustration. They may learn to doubt their own lovableness as they encounter the intensity of their own capacity for anger.

Feelings of doubt or anxiety about the bond of trust are more common than may have been expected. About one third of American infant–mother pairs who have been systematically observed show evidence of an insecure attachment. Cross-cultural research provides further evidence that a significant proportion of infants have difficulty deriving emotional comfort or security from their caregivers (Mesman, van IJzendoorm, & Sagi-Schwartz, 2016; Posada et al., 1995; van IJzendoorn & Kroonenberg, 1988).

In addition to the mistrust that emerges in the context of inconsistent, unresponsive, or harsh caregiving, there are cases in which the mother–infant relationship is disrupted. This can happen in conditions of war, parental imprisonment, parental death due to disease or accident, or lengthy hospitalization. In all these situations, an infant is at risk for experiencing a strong sense of mistrust.

Mistrust may manifest itself in the infant by withdrawal from interaction and by symptoms of depression and grief, which include sobbing, lack of emotion, lethargy, and loss of appetite. It may also be revealed later on in development in the expressions of interpersonal distress observed in the angry, anxious, and resistant behaviors of children with insecure attachments or in the inability to form close, satisfying relationships with others as adolescents and adults. Mistrust may provide a foundation for the emergence of a negative scheme about the self—a scheme that is elaborated over time by defining the self with a cluster of closely related, negative attributes such as cautiousness, nervousness, or introversion (Malle & Horowitz, 1995).

All infants experience some aspects of mistrust, either as a result of mismatches between their needs and the caregiving strategies they receive or as a product of their own difficulties in modulating strong feelings of wariness or anger. Just as there is a neurobiological basis for trust in the production of oxytocin, another brain-stimulating chemical, vasopressin may cause suspicion and trigger social anxiety or aggression (Neumann & Landgraf, 2012). The resolution of the crisis in the direction of trust reflects a biopsychological achievement in which infants are able to minimize their wariness of the environment and regulate their own anxiety.

Over the life span, the sense of trust is transformed and provides an operating principle that guides a person's daily life and relationships with others. The sense of trust is essential for the maintenance of complex organizations and communities. Parents trust schools to educate their children; consumers trust manufacturers to produce safe products; banks trust customers to pay back their loans. The nature of social life is built on hopefulness about positive transactions that will take place in an uncertain future (Cook, Levi, & Hardin, 2009). Among older adults who have a strong sense of trust, many of life's disappointments and complexities are minimized by a growing religious faith. Their basic sense of trust evolves into a powerful belief in a great source of goodness and love in the universe, a force that can transcend the pain of daily tragedies and give integrity and meaning to their dying as well as to their living (Erikson et al., 1986).

The Central Process for Resolving the Crisis: Mutuality with the Caregiver

To resolve the crisis of trust versus mistrust, an infant must establish **mutuality with a caregiver**. Mutuality is a characteristic of a relationship. Initially it is built on the consistency with which the caregiver responds appropriately to the infant's needs. The caregiver comes to appreciate the variety of an infant's needs, and the infant learns to expect that personal needs will be met. Within families, the establishment of mutuality differs with each child, depending on infant characteristics and parental responses (Deater-Deckard & O'Connor, 2000).

An infant and a caregiver learn to regulate the amount of time that passes between the expression of a need and its satisfaction. Bell and Ainsworth (1972) observed mothers' responses to infant crying during the first year of life. Over the course of the year, the infants' crying decreased, and the mothers tended to respond more quickly to their cries. This finding suggests a process of mutual adaptation by mothers and infants. Some mothers came quickly and ignored few cries. Other mothers waited a long time and ignored much of the crying. The longer mothers delayed in responding to their infants' cries, the more crying the infants did in later months. Babies whose mothers responded promptly in the first 6 months of life cried less often in the second 6 months. The results of this early research have been supported in many studies of parent–infant interactions. Infants learn to cope with the demands and variations of adult/family interactions, and adults provide the socialization environment that helps to support an infant's emotional appraisals and self-control (Thompson, 2014).

Coordination, Mismatch, and Repair of Interactions

The study of mutuality with the caregiver has focused in some detail on patterns and rhythms of social interaction, especially coordination between the infant and caregivers (Tronick, 2003). Infants are striving to make meaning of their social situation. They do not have language, so they use all the sensory, motor and cognitive resources available to gather information about how to behave, how to sustain and end interactions, and how to get what they need. For example, infants use social referencing to decide if they should approach or avoid an object or another person (Stenberg, 2013).

Infants form expectations for social interactions based in part on their observations of contingencies. They come to recognize that the behavior of one participant in an interaction is predictable based on the behavior of the other. Eventually these observations of contingent interactions become integrated into coordinated patterns of mutuality. For example, in a study of mother–infant vocal interactions, from 4 to 10 months of age, vocalizations became increasingly coordinated. At 4 months, infants were most likely to vocalize at the same time as their mothers vocalized, not when the mothers paused in their vocalizations. In contrast, mothers were more likely to vocalize when the infants were silent, demonstrating the more typical pattern of turn-taking in conversation. However, over time, there were fewer instances of co-vocalization by the infants, and more instances of turn-taking. This research indicates a period of continued development from 4 months and beyond when coordination in vocal interactions will likely show additional evidence of mutual co-regulation (Harder Lange, Hansen, Væver, & Køppe, 2015).

Adult caregivers are also learning to read their infant's signals and to provide appropriate care. Some caregivers are better at this than others. Depressed mothers, for example, have been shown to be less expressive and less responsive to their babies than nondepressed mothers (Field, Diego, & Hernandez-Reif, 2009). In the context of thousands of small daily interactions, it is common that the intentions and meanings of the partners are at odds—the infant shifts his or her attention, the caregiver misinterprets the infant's signals, the interaction lasts too long or is over too quickly. These early interactions are often recognized as being mismatched, and there is some attempt at repair. The work of creating mutuality of communication is characterized as a process of coordination, mismatch, and repair (Tronick & Beeghly, 2011).

Coordination refers to two related characteristics of interaction: matching and synchrony. **Matching** means that the infant and the caregiver are involved in similar behaviors or states at the same time. They may be playing together with an object, cooing and smiling at each other, or fussing and angry at each other. **Synchrony** means that the infant and caregiver move fluidly from one state to the next. When infants are paying attention to their caregivers, the caregivers attempt to stimulate them. As babies withdraw attention, the caregivers learn to reduce stimulation and wait until the infants are ready to engage again. Normally, caregiver–infant interactions are typically mismatched (Tronick, 2009). In fact, matched interactions appear to become mismatched rather quickly. Babies are developing rapidly. Their efforts to understand their situation and their changing sensory, emotional, cognitive, and motor abilities all work to bring new intentions and new meaning to social interactions. Caregivers' past experiences in trying to meet their infants' needs do not always adequately inform how to meet the new, changing nature of their infant's behaviors. However, periods of **mismatch** are usually followed by **communication repairs**, As a result, it is not surprising that infants and caregivers continue to experience this "dance" of coordination, mismatch, and repair.

Why is caregiver–infant communication so frequently disrupted? The explanation may lie partly in the infant's inability to sustain coordinated attention with the caregiver, partly in a rapid shift of need states, and partly in the inability of adults to sustain long periods of nonverbal communication. The moments of coordination become a prototype for the positive feelings of connection that people enjoy in social relationships. Long before infants can use language to convey their feelings or needs, they experience the satisfaction of social connection through these cycles of communication. As a caregiver and baby move into renewed moments of coordination, their sense of pleasure increases, leaving a memory of such moments to guide future conversations (Goleman, 2006). Moments of **repair** that follow mismatch are also evidence that interactions that were not well coordinated can be rectified. This leads to hopefulness about the potential in future interactions and persistence even in the face of interactions that seem to veer off course.

At a biological level, what appears to occur through experiences of coordination, mismatch, and repair is the establishment of a neurochemical pattern: Networks of synapses are established; oxytocin is released; pleasurable feelings ensue; and the amygdala is impacted, resulting in reduced arousal and a greater sense of calm. Over time, as a product of experiences of receiving sustained, sensitive caregiving, the infant's complex neurological social capacity for trust is strengthened. Even though the brain is prewired to recognize and respond to certain types of social stimulation, actual caregiving experiences establish more or less likely patterns of social engagement. Infants who experience disrupted, harsh, withdrawn, or neglectful care do not develop the same underlying neurochemical structures for patterns of social behavior as do babies whose caregivers are psychologically available and warm. As they grow older, these children may experience a wide range of problems in social behavior, emotional development, and cognitive development, especially in areas of language and communication competence.

Establishing a Functional Rhythm in the Family

The match or mismatch between an infant's rhythms and the family's rhythms is an important factor in the overall adjustment of a family to a new baby. Some babies are quite predictable; the timing of their sleeping, eating, playtime, and even fussy periods follows a clear pattern. Other babies are much less regular. All babies are changing rapidly during the first 24 months of life, so daily patterns are bound to change, and families must make frequent adjustments in order to continue to meet the infant's needs.

In American culture, by the end of the first year of life, babies are typically expected to modify their schedule of needs so that they sleep when the rest of the family sleeps, play when the rest of the family is awake, and eat three or at most four times a day, generally when the other family members eat. During the second year of life, the demands of parenting change. Babies become more mobile and have new capacities to initiate activities. Their attention span increases, they have new requirements for stimulation, and they have new areas of wariness and resistance—things they don't want to do (like take a nap) or people they don't want to be with (like a certain babysitter). These and other changes require adaptation on the part of parents in order to sustain the mutuality that has been achieved or to rectify problems in attachment and trust that may now be evident. The stable features in mutual relationships are the caregiver's effort to be responsive to the child's changing capacities and needs, and the child's ongoing monitoring of and responsiveness to the caregiver's cues.

Parents with Psychological Problems

The importance of reciprocal interactions in building trust and hope during infancy is highlighted by studies of parents with psychological problems. Sensitivity to an infant's emotional states, the ability to respond appropriately to an infant's needs, and the quality of common, daily interactions can all be impaired by family risk factors. As an example, research has compared interactions between depressed and nondepressed mothers and their infants. Interactions between the depressed mothers and their infants appear to be stressful and mutually unsatisfying (Field, Hernandez-Reif, & Diego, 2006). Depressed mothers have been observed to be unresponsive, emotionally unavailable, and unable to sustain smooth communication with their babies. Compared with nondepressed mothers and their infants, depressed mothers have fewer positive matched states with their babies, and it takes them longer to repair those mismatched states (Reck et al., 2011). Depressed mothers are less likely to show animated, positive facial expressions. Typical efforts at fostering an infant's emotional regulation, commonly observed in nondepressed mothers—such as introducing stimulating toys and games, touching and talking, and the efforts at reducing arousal through appropriate soothing and comforting—are not as common in depressed mothers. For their part, the infants of depressed mothers have few expressions of interest, show more sad and angry expressions, show less ability to match a happy face with a happy vocal expression, and are less able to regulate their emotions (Bornstein, Arteberry, Mash, & Manian, 2011).

The Prime Adaptive Ego Quality and the Core Pathology

Hope

Erikson (1982) theorized that the positive resolution of the psychosocial crisis of trust versus mistrust leads to the adaptive ego quality of **hope**. As you will recall from chapter 3, the prime adaptive ego qualities shape a person's outlook on life in the direction of greater openness to experience and information, greater capacity to identify a variety of pathways to achieve one's goals, more willingness to assert the self and to express one's wishes and views, and a positive approach to the formation of close relationships. Even in the face of difficulties and stressful life events, these qualities contribute to higher levels of functioning and well-being.

As the first of the prime adaptive ego qualities, hope pervades the entire life story. It is a global cognitive orientation that one's goals and dreams can be attained and that events will turn out for the best. As Erikson described it, "Hope bestows on the anticipated future a sense of leeway inviting expectant leaps, either in preparatory imagination or in small initiating actions. And such daring must count on basic trust in the sense of a trustfulness that must be, literally and figuratively, nourished by maternal care and—when endangered by all-too-desperate discomfort—must be restored by competent consolation" (1982, p. 60).

Hopefulness combines the ability to think of one or more paths to achieve a goal with a belief in one's ability to move along that pathway toward the goal (Snyder, Cheavens, & Sympson, 1997). The roots of hopefulness lie in the infant's understanding of the self as a causal agent. Each time a baby takes an action to achieve an outcome, the sense of hope grows. When babies encounter obstacles or barriers to their goals, sensitive caregivers find ways to remove the obstacles or lead them along a new path toward the goal. The infant's sense of the self as a causal agent combined with the caregiver's sensitivity create the context for the emergence of hope.

Research with adults shows that people who have a hopeful, optimistic outlook about the future have different achievement beliefs and emotional reactions in response to actual achievement than do people who have a pessimistic outlook (Seligman, 2011). People who have higher levels of hopefulness undertake a larger number of goals across life areas and select tasks that are more difficult thus leading to higher overall levels of performance (Snyder, 2002). Hopefulness is essential for behavior change in that it combines a desire to achieve new goals and a belief that one will be able to find successful paths toward those goals. Feelings of hope help people deal with difficult challenges, including coping with their own serious injury or illness, parenting children with developmental disabilities, or facing the end of life (Einav, Levi, & Margalit, 2012; Sullivan, 2003).

Within the psychosocial framework, hope provides the platform from which very young children take certain leaps of faith. When an infant overcomes doubts and hesitancy in taking a first independent step, you see the dividend of hope. When a toddler clambers over the bars of her crib and drops several inches to the floor, you see the dividend of hope. As a parent, when you give your adolescent the keys to the car, you see the dividend of hope. Without hope, neither the individual nor the society could bear the weight of uncertainty in our changing world. With hope, individuals can envision a better society and come together in actions to reach the collective good (Braithwaite, 2004).

Withdrawal

As a core pathology, **withdrawal** refers to a general orientation of wariness toward people and objects. This is especially disturbing because, during infancy, healthy development is a pattern of outward motion, extension, and increasing engagement with the social and physical worlds. Infants typically reach and grasp, crawl, stand, and walk. They explore through gazing, mouthing, and manipulating objects. Their behavior is typically characterized by interest in novelty, joy in learning, and frustration at encountering barriers to goal achievement. Over the first year, babies become increasingly connected to significant figures in their social world, following them about, devising strategies to engage them in interaction, and looking to them for consolation when they are distressed.

Infants who are characterized by withdrawal may show evidence of passivity, lethargy, and neutral or negative affect. They are not readily engaged in social interaction and do not show the signs of self-directed exploration that are typical of most healthy infants. Withdrawal may have some of its roots in genetically determined temperamental characteristics. Some babies have a very low threshold for pain. They are highly sensitive to sensory stimulation and recoil from the kinds of handling that other babies find comforting or pleasurable. Some babies are more passive than others, requiring little in the way of stimulation and showing less evidence of exploratory behavior than active babies.

One of the earliest descriptions of withdrawal in infancy was provided by Rene Spitz's (1945, 1946) analysis of children who had been institutionalized before 1 year of age. The babies who suffered the most had been placed in a foundling home in which eight babies were cared for by one nurse. These babies went through a phase of initial rage, followed by a period of physical and emotional withdrawal. They lay passively in their cribs, showing limited motor exploration and little emotionality. Furthermore, they rarely smiled or showed excitement. The babies' babbling and language were extremely delayed. They deteriorated physically. Their measured developmental level dropped substantially over a year's time. These babies suffered from a combination of a loss of their attachment figure, a lack of meaningful social interaction, and an absence of appropriate sensory stimulation—all of which produced what Spitz called *anaclitic depression*.

Not all instances of withdrawal are as severe as the anaclitic depression syndrome. However, a growing literature focuses on the links between disrupted mother–infant interaction, violent parental interactions, and infant social withdrawal (Crockenberg, Leerkes, & Kekka, 2007; Gerhold et al., 2002). Temperamental factors including behavioral inhibition and a low threshold for sensory stimulation, an anxious-avoidant attachment, and a lack of contingent, responsive caregiving can combine to produce mistrust and the formation of the core pathology of withdrawal. Social withdrawal can become such a severe social deficit that it interferes with adaptive functioning and requires clinical treatment (Calkins & Fox, 2002).

FURTHER REFLECTION: Explain the connection between trust and hope; between mistrust and withdrawal. How are these concepts related?

How might the sense of trust and the ego strength of hope play a role in the enactment of later life roles such as friend, teacher, supervisor, parent, or political leader?

Applied Topic: The Role of Parents

OBJECTIVE 8 Evaluate the critical role of parents and caregivers during infancy, with special attention to issues of safety and nutrition; optimizing cognitive, social, and emotional development; and the role of parents and caregivers as advocates for their infants.

In this chapter, we have portrayed infants as active, adaptive, and eager to master the environment. At the same time, the immaturity of human infants at birth necessitates a long period of dependence on adults. The few instinctive behaviors of human infants in comparison with the infants of other species are compensated for by their enormous capacity to learn. For this potential to be realized, infants must rely on their parents to maintain their health, provide stimulation, and protect them from danger. During the period of dependence, infants become entwined in complex social systems and develop strong emotional bonds with their caregivers. The quality of these early relationships provides infants with mental representations that guide their later development of friendships, intimacy, and relationships with their own children.

Infancy, just like pregnancy and childbirth, is culturally constructed. The content of experience and the way the period of infancy is viewed depend on cultural traditions, beliefs, and technologies. Some of the ways that culture defines infancy include the infant's sleeping arrangements, the choice of clothing, the choice of the infant's name and the naming process, the selection of foods, and access to nursing from mothers and other lactating women. Parents transmit the culture through their care, and by enacting certain rituals and practices, they introduce and integrate their infant into the cultural community.

Infancy is culturally constructed. Cora rises early each morning, ties her infant to her back, and walks to the market to sell flowers. She expects her baby to be calm and quiet while she earns her living.

The **Human Development and Diversity** box Sensitive Care in Two Cultures provides a contrast between features of sensitive care for U.S. mothers and Colombian mothers.

Five aspects of the parental role promote optimal development in infancy: ensuring safety and providing adequate nutrition; fostering socioemotional and cognitive development; coordinating the roles of father and mother; acting as **advocates** with other societal systems; and connecting with other sources of social support.

Safety and Nutrition

Safety

One of the central responsibilities parents face is to protect infants from environmental dangers. The nature of home and neighborhood influences the kinds of dangers to which infants are exposed and the kinds of practices that families and cultures invent to protect their children. In addition to physical risks, some dangers are linked to superstitions, religious beliefs, and matters of the spirit world. In many parts of the world, parents take special precautions to prevent their infants from coming under the influence of an evil eye. The eye gaze may be viewed as a vehicle through which a person may deliberately or inadvertently transmit harmful feelings of jealousy, revenge, or unbridled pride (Galt, 1991). The presence of dangers or risks in the environment usually elicits some effort to restrict a child's movement. Swaddling, carrying the baby in a sling, or placing the baby in a playpen are examples. Because of concern about dangers, caregivers may invoke certain prohibitions, such as telling the child, "No, don't touch that," or pulling the child away from something dangerous. As infants become more mobile in the second half of their first year, the need to monitor and limit exploratory activities increases. Depending on the cultural values concerning independent exploration, caregivers may heighten their restrictions and prohibitions or they may try to modify the environment to permit safe, unrestricted exploration.

Certain childrearing practices arise from a desire to protect young children from known dangers. For example, Robert LeVine (1977) described the practice of many African cultures of carrying infants 18 months and older on the back, even though they were able to walk around. This practice was used to prevent toddlers from getting burned on the open cooking fires at an age when they were mobile enough to walk or stumble into the fire and yet not old enough to know how to inhibit their movements. Other hazards, such as falling off steep cliffs or into lakes, rivers, or wells, prompted this same carrying behavior.

In industrialized countries, infants may face different types of hazards, such as electrical outlets, steep stairs, and open containers of insecticides, cleaning agents, and other poisons. Lead is a known neurotoxin. Lead poisoning has an especially negative impact on infants and young children, resulting in life-long cognitive and behavioral impairments. Lead can leach into drinking water from lead-based plumbing and contaminated water sources, a condition that is particularly dangerous for infants whose formula is made with water from the tap (Hanna-Attisha, LaCance, Sadler, & Schnepp, 2016).

Some families protect babies from danger by putting gates at a doorway or the top of a stairway, or by placing an infant in a crib or playpen to restrict exploration. In other homes, the strategy is to *baby proof* the home by

Sensitive Care in Two Cultures

Socialization toward culturally valued goals is a primary focus of parenting. This socialization process begins in infancy and is expressed through the beliefs parents have about what children should be able to do and what they should know or understand in the period of infancy. These beliefs are translated into caregiving strategies (Lamm & Keller, 2007). A primary assumption of attachment theory is that the quality of early care, and especially sensitive caregiving, promotes attachment security, an assumption that has been supported in a large number of studies (De Wolff & van IJzendoorn, 1997). However, the behavioral components of sensitive caregiving and how it might be expressed in various cultures has not been explored in great detail. A study by German Posada and colleagues (2002), which contrasted maternal care in two middle-class samples, one in Denver, Colorado, and the other in Bogota, Colombia, was designed to clarify this topic.

Although men's and women's roles are changing in Latin America, especially among the urban middle class, the Colombian culture is considered more collectivistic and interdependent than the U.S. culture,

which is viewed as more individualistic and independent. Two questions guided the research: (1) Are the features outlined in the attachment literature that define sensitive care descriptive of care in both cultures? (2) Are there features of care that might be unique to the specific cultures that are related to attachment security?

The researchers used an ethnographic methodology to formulate categories of maternal behaviors. Two researchers observed mother–infant pairs at home for two 2-hour visits. Following the visits, the observers used a Q-sort technique to describe the mothers' behaviors. This technique involved sorting 90 cards that describe maternal behavior into three piles: characteristic, neither characteristic nor uncharacteristic, and uncharacteristic. Each of the three piles is then further sorted into categories rated from 1 (most uncharacteristic) to 9 (most characteristic).

From this rating process, eight categories of care were identified. Four of these categories were very similar to features of sensitive care outlined in the basic attachment research: (1) sensitive responding to infant signals

and communication; (2) accessibility, which reflects a mother's ability to consider the baby's needs despite other competing demands; (3) acceptance of the infant, which is reflected in the mother's positive emotional tone when interacting with the baby; and (4) interference, a mother's intrusive or non-coordinated interactions with the baby. Two categories were observed that had not been captured in the literature as related to sensitive care: active, energetic interactions with the baby and creating an interesting environment for the baby. One category was observed in each cultural group that was unique to that culture: For the U.S. mothers it was close-intimate interactions involving cuddling and close affectionate touching; for the Colombian mothers it was concern with the baby's physical appearance, including concern that the baby was getting messy during feeding and that the baby was messy or soiled during play.

Mothers from the United States and Colombia were very similar in their scores on sensitive responding, accessibility, and acceptance, and all these dimensions were predictive of infants' secure attachments. Mothers from Colombia were less interfering and more active and energetic in their interactions than the U.S. mothers. Mothers from the United States scored higher on creating an interesting environment for the baby. Of these three dimensions, interfering was negatively related to secure attachments for the U.S. sample, but not for the Colombian sample, and being active and energetic was positively related to secure attachment for the Colombian sample but not for the U.S. sample.

The results of this study highlight several points about the role of parents during infancy. First, certain features of parenting appear to have beneficial consequences for infants in both cultures. When combined with results from many other studies, these features are becoming accepted as universally supportive of the attachment process—attuned response to the

It is typical for mothers in the United States to create a stimulating environment for their babies by providing lots of toys and other interesting objects for exploration and play.

Vasiliy Koval/Shutterstock.com

infant's signals, accessibility in the face of competing demands, and acceptance or the positive emotional tone of mother–infant interactions. Second, some features of parenting are observed across cultures but not always related to attachment security in every culture. Third, some features of parenting may be culturally or contextually specific and, while important for early socialization, may not be specifically relevant for the formation of a secure attachment.

Critical Thinking Questions

1. Based on this study, list the basic features that are essential for sensitive caregiving across both cultures.
2. Evaluate whether the differences in caregiving between the U.S. and Colombian samples fit with characterizations of these cultures as more individualistic or collectivistic.
3. The research has captured a few features of caregiving that are distinct between the U.S. and Colombian cultures. Discuss the implications of these differences for infant socialization and subsequent socialization.
4. Evaluate the strengths and weaknesses of the Q-sort methodology for assessing features of the caregiving environment. Design another approach that might be used to capture cultural differences in caregiving.

removing as many known dangers as possible so that the baby has maximum freedom for exploration. These two different strategies reflect different values concerning childrearing—both with the same goal of providing maximum safety and protection from danger. In the former, parents try to preserve their adult environment. Children must modify their behavior in order to fit into the home. In the latter, parents modify the environment to accommodate the baby's developmental needs. For more information about child safety, you may want to visit the website of the U.S. Consumer Product Safety Commission section on safety for kids and babies. This agency publishes reports on recalls, statistics on injuries and deaths, as well as guidelines for child safety and toy safety.

Nutrition

In addition to protecting children from dangers and preventing injuries, parents are responsible for providing an age-appropriate diet that supports the infant's changing nutritional needs. An estimated 30 percent of children under the age of 5 in developing countries suffer from malnutrition, which is known to result in stunted growth as well as disruptions in brain structures associated with cognitive and behavioral development (Venables & Raine, 2016). Infant nutrition and health are significantly associated with childhood and adult intelligence (Kanazawa, 2015).

The American Academic of Pediatrics recommends exclusive breastfeeding for the first 6 months of life (American Academy of Pediatrics, 2012; 2016). Human milk is sufficient to provide the baby's nutritional needs. In addition, breastfeeding is associated with many health benefits including reduced risk of ear infections, fewer respiratory infections, fewer infections that inflame the intestines, lower risk of chronic diseases such as asthma and diabetes, reduced risk of childhood obesity, and lower risk of sudden infant death syndrome. Newborns may nurse every 2 to 4 hours; by 4 months of age, babies may nurse 4 to 6 times in 24 hours. If the baby is breastfeeding, mothers have to be careful about how their own diet and medications might affect their breast milk. If they are using formula, they have to be careful about the water quality that is used. In some areas of the world, poor water quality makes the use of powdered formula a serious health risk for infants.

The transition to solid foods, sometime around 4 to 6 months, leads to both safety and dietary concerns. Babies need to be strong enough to hold their heads up and to sit with some support so they do not choke on solid foods. Typically, parents are instructed to introduce some type of iron-fortified rice cereal mixed with breast milk or formula as the first solid food. New foods are introduced one at a time, giving the baby a few days to become accustomed to the new taste, watching for signs that the baby is able to digest the new food, and also ensuring that the baby is not allergic to the food. Most resources on pediatric nutrition advise against giving infants honey, which can cause botulism.

Safety concerns related to food include: avoid foods that are likely to cause choking like nuts, raisins, or large pieces of meat; avoid giving bottles with milk, juice, or sweetened beverages, which can cause tooth decay, at bedtime; avoid feeding the baby from the jar in order to prevent bacteria from the baby's saliva from contaminating unused portions of the food; and avoid keeping opened jars of baby food (Foodsafety.gov, 2016).

Many first-time parents are unsure about how to provide adequate, safe nutrition for their babies. This is a source of some anxiety because it is an area in which the infant so obviously depends on caring adults for health, safety, and survival. Many excellent resources are available to inform parents about infant nutrition, including online resources such as the Mayo Clinic and the MedLine Plus of the National Institutes of Health. The WIC (Women, Infants, and Children) program provides federal grants to states to make supplemental foods, health care referrals, and nutrition education available for low-income pregnant, breastfeeding, and non-breastfeeding postpartum women, and to infants and children up to age 5 who are found to be at nutritional risk (USDA, 2016).

Fostering Socioemotional and Cognitive Development

Another component of the parents' role during infancy is the promotion of socioemotional and cognitive development. Much of the behavior that appears to be important in the development of strong emotional bonds between infants and parents is also central to fostering intellectual growth. Three features of parenting quality have been found to support optimal development, including children's language, literacy, cognition, autonomy, self-efficacy, and school readiness. They are (1) parenting sensitivity, (2) cognitive stimulation, and (3) warmth (Lugo-Gil & Tamis-LeMonda, 2008). As was discussed earlier, parenting sensitivity refers to the way parents respond to their infant's distress, emotional expressions, interests, and abilities, effectively balancing the infant's needs for comfort and reassurance with the infant's needs for autonomy and self-control. Cognitive stimulation refers to parents' efforts to teach their child, to enrich the child's language and cognitive development, and to provide an interesting, age-appropriate environment. Warmth refers to the parents' expressions of affection, admiration, and respect for their child.

Parents foster both emotional and intellectual growth by structuring the stimulus environment to suit the infant's developmental level (Bornstein, 2012). Part of the parents' function is to initiate interactions and not just respond to their infants' demands for attention. Parents need to create what they perceive to be a suitable environment—one that allows a variety of experiences, a reasonable amount of challenge, and adequate opportunities to experience success. Furthermore, parents should be attuned to their infant's developing skills and alter the environment appropriately. As their children mature, parents must provide more complex stimuli, more opportunities for autonomy, and more encouragement for tolerating frustration. By providing experiences that are attuned to the infant's level of cognitive functioning, parents are also supporting emotional satisfaction, confidence, and joy.

Parents use a variety of methods to help their infants regulate their emotions. Through physical and verbal play, they increase the baby's arousal and orient the baby toward objects in the environment. Through soothing and comforting, they help their infants regain a calm state after distress. As babies mature, parents increase their use of language to guide behavior and provide new problem-solving strategies. Infants are constantly watching their parents, observing their emotional reactions as well as their novel behaviors. As a negative example, we have discussed how infants of depressed mothers become passive and inhibited in their reactions to the environment as they observe their mothers' passive or angry depressive symptoms. Another example is the influence of harsh parenting or maltreatment on infants' emotional negativity,

especially fearfulness and anxiety, and problems in emotional regulation.

U.S. parents of infants have made enormous expenditures for special toys, music, videos, and infant stimulation programs intended to foster intellectual development. A desire to provide resources to promote infant stimulation in the period from birth to 3 years of age in order to ensure optimal cognitive growth is probably important. However, in their desire to support optimal development, parents need to be wary of fads and hypes that make it seem as if some specific form of stimulation is essential for their baby's growth. In an international study of caregiving practices, Bornstein and colleagues identified six basic caregiving practices that are associated with optimal psychosocial development in the first 12 months of infancy: read books to the baby; tell the baby stories; name objects, count, and/or draw with the baby; play with the baby; sing songs with the baby; and take the baby outside (Bornstein, Putnick, Lansford, Deater-Deckard, & Bradley, 2015). These practices, which are observed in a range of 38 low- and middle-income countries, highlight the value of face-to-face processes that promote infant attention, emphasize a positive emotional tone, and engage the infant in the objects and resources of their near environment.

Parents and other sensitive caregivers are the most valuable sensory and emotional assets a baby can have. Rhythmic interactions, positive tone, comfort and soothing care under conditions of distress, and playful, relaxed interactions that allow babies to initiate as well as to follow are among the most valuable forms of stimulation for promoting social, emotional, and cognitive growth in infancy.

Fathers' and Mothers' Parental Behaviors

Do fathers and mothers differ in how they enact the parent role with infants? Babies form strong attachments to their fathers as well as to their mothers. Fathers may be just as involved in and sensitive to their babies' needs as mothers. However, the daily interactions between mothers and their babies and those between fathers and their babies are distinct. In a national time use survey, mothers and fathers who had children under the age of 6 were compared, based on their employment status (Table 5.9). Regardless of their employment status, mothers spend more time each day on the care of their young children than fathers. The

Table 5.9	Average Hours per Day Spent with Children under Age 6 by Mothers and Fathers by Employment Status				
	Married Mothers			Married Fathers	
Activity	Employed Full Time	Employed Part Time	Not Employed	Employed Full Time	Not Employed
Overall caring for and helping children	1.29	1.73	2.47	.87	1.46
Physical care	.55	.67	.95	.27	.41
Education-related activities	.11	.17	.29	.07	.15
Reading	.04	.06	.07	.03	.04
Playing/doing hobbies	.25	.33	.60	.29	.41

Source: Bureau of Labor Statistics (2016). American Time Use Survey, 2009-2013, Table A6.

difference is especially notable in the time spent on physical care, where mothers spend almost twice as much time as fathers (U.S. Bureau of Labor Statistics, 2016). Fathers, who spend less time overall with their babies, tend to focus more on play—especially physical play. They use their strength and physical activity as resources as they interact with their babies. When mothers play with their babies, the play tends to be with words or with toys, as opposed to rough-and-tumble activity (Laflamme et al., 2002).

Cameron, a stay-at-home father of two daughters (an infant and a two-year-old), speaks about how he thinks fathers are different from mothers: "I find I am very playful with the girls. I become the play structure you know. I will have them sitting on me. We'll sing 'the people on the bus' and *I'm the bus!* I'm the slide.' I don't think I've ever really seen my wife do that. I will do it for hours at a time throughout the day. They are climbing all over me all day long" (Doucet, 2009, pp. 86–87).

The experience of parenting results in changes in the brain, particularly neural regions that are associated with parental motivation. Fathers form mental representations of their infants that stabilize from the prenatal period through the first months of an infant's life. When presented with images of their young infants, a network of brain regions are activated, accompanied by the release of hormones that are associated with parental sensitivity and reciprocity (Kim et al., 2014; Kuo, Carp, Light, & Grewen, 2012; Vreeswijk et al., 2014).

Both fathers and mothers have strategies for soothing their infants. However, the quality of interaction between fathers and infants depends on the context. When mothers are present, for example, fathers interact less with their babies. When fathers are alone with their babies, they are more engaged and sensitive play companions. Men who are not overly stressed at work, have strong positive identification with their own fathers, and are in satisfying, harmonious marriages, achieve greater levels of inter-subjectivity with their babies. Fathers who are in relationships that they describe as very satisfying are also observed to engage in more responsive, sensitive interactions with their infants (Barnett, Deng, Mills-Koonce, Willoughby, & Cox, 2008). What is more, when fathers are actively engaged in parenting, their involvement contributes to a mother's confidence. Women whose husbands share in the care and comfort of their infants are better able to cope with their infants' distress (Dayton, Walsh, Oh, & Volling, 2015).

Even fathers who are not married to their baby's mother seem to be involved in the baby's life in the early months after birth. Many of these fathers, especially those who are cohabiting or are romantically involved with the mother but live apart from her, provide direct and indirect support, want their name on the child's birth certificate, and say they want to help in the child's care. Unfortunately, this level of involvement often does not persist into the child's toddlerhood or early childhood. As the relationship between the parents dissolves, the father's involvement with his child also diminishes. By the time the child is 5 years old, only half of the non-resident fathers had seen their child in the past month (Fragile Families and Child Welfare Study, 2016).

Despite the gender stereotypes it is clear that fathers can be gentle and soothing with their infants, and mothers can enjoy moments of silly tickling and play.

The quality of the relationship between the parents is vital for an infant's well-being. When adults are in constant conflict or when there is physical violence, loud yelling, or emotional abuse between the partners, infants suffer. In these families, infants may be at risk for direct abuse and/or neglect, but they may also be at risk simply through exposure to inter-parental aggression. As a result, infants may experience anxiety, disruption of executive functions, and problems with emotional regulation, which are associated with a range of mental health problems. The link between parental dysfunction and child outcomes will be explored further in subsequent chapters.

Parents as Advocates

In addition to providing care themselves, more and more parents are responsible for arranging supplemental care for their infants. As a result, parents become advocates for their child. Parents must review the child care services available to them and select a setting that will meet their infant's needs and accommodate their work requirements and economic resources. Family day care, in-home babysitting, and center-based care are three common alternatives.

To function as advocates for their children, parents may have to engage in an unfamiliar kind of thinking. They may even feel unqualified to make the kinds of judgments required. For example, parents must evaluate the competence and motivation of the adults who will care for their child. They must estimate how successful these caregivers will be in meeting their child's needs for security and stimulation. And they must consider the degree to which alternative caregivers reflect their own parental values, beliefs, and strategies.

Even when pressures to continue a caregiving arrangement are very strong, parents must be able to assess its impact on their children. They must judge whether their children are in the kind of responsive, stimulating environment that will enhance their development. In the best situations, alternative care settings actually complement a parent–infant relationship. In the worst settings, infants may be neglected and abused. It is essential for parents to maintain communication with the alternative caregivers, assess the quality of the care, and intervene promptly when necessary to ensure their infant's well-being.

Another situation in which parents serve as advocates for their infants occurs when the children have some form of chronic illness, developmental delay, or disability. These children may require coordinated health care, therapeutic interventions, mental health services, and educational supports. The Individuals with Disabilities Education Act (IDEA) requires every state to provide early intervention programs to support parents and help them understand the nature, prognosis, and treatment of the infant's condition from birth through age 2. Although each state has some discretion in the way they implement early intervention services, the program typically assigns case managers to families to help connect parents and infants with physicians and other health professionals. Case managers may also provide home services, identify the least restrictive environments for infants who need care, and assist in the identification of appropriate community resources (U.S. Department of Education, 2016). However, parents are ultimately responsible for making sure that the services match the child's changing needs.

The Importance of Social Support

The infant's physical, cognitive, social, and emotional development are fostered through the loving care of mothers, fathers, other family members, and community caregivers who are able to create supportive relationships with one another and with the infant. Infant mental health and optimal development are intimately entwined with the mental health of caregivers (Fay-Tammbach, Hawes, & Meredith, 2014; Karevold, Røysamb, Ystrom, & Kristin, 2009; Weatherston, 2001). A variety of factors play a part in parents' ability to promote their child's optimal development. Adults who had difficult experiences with their own caregivers may come to the parental role with special challenges. They may not have experienced the comfort, responsiveness, or appropriate stimulation that are essential for effective parenting. Some factors, however, help to make up for these deficits. The quality of one's intimate relationship with a loving partner is important in sustaining positive parent–child relationships. Couples who experience mutuality and trust in their own relationship are better able to create a predictable, supportive, and caring family environment for their children (Crockenberg, Leerkes, & Lekka, 2007).

Sources of **social support** beyond the intimate partner may also enhance one's effectiveness as a parent. This support may come from the child's grandparents and other family members, friends, and health care and mental health professionals (Bornstein & Tamis-LeMonda, 2010). Both men and women can benefit from talking with their friends about how to care for their infants. This seems to be easier for women to do than for men, but when men are able to talk freely with other men about their father role, it provides tremendous reassurance and can enhance their sense of parental efficacy (Bagnini, 2014).

The effective use of a social support network ensures that adults will not be isolated as parents, and that others will be available to help the parents identify and interpret childrearing problems. Often, the help is very direct—for example, child care or sharing of clothes, playthings, and furniture. Support may also take the form of companionship and validation of the importance of the parental role. However, social support cannot fully compensate for the lack of partner support or for the stresses on parenting caused by economic pressures that prevent parents from meeting basic life needs.

In reviewing this chapter, you can begin to appreciate the demanding nature of the parental role in promoting optimal development during infancy. The elements of effective parenting that we have identified or implied are listed in Table 5.10. As a parent, one must rely heavily on one's own psychological well-being and on the encouragement of one's spouse, caring friends, and family to sustain the ego strengths and emotional resources necessary to the task.

The way parents conceive of their role has a major influence on the direction and rate of their infants' development. Parenting also allows adults opportunities for creative problem solving,

Table 5.10	Optimizing an Infant's Development
Spend time with the child; be available when the child needs you.	
Provide warmth and affection; express positive feelings toward the baby in many ways—verbally, through touching and hugging, and through playful interactions.	
Play with the baby; sing songs; make up little games.	
Communicate often, directly with the child; engage the child in verbal interaction.	
Read to the baby; tell the baby stories.	
Provide stimulation.	
Encourage the child's active engagement in and exploration of the indoor and outdoor environments.	
Help the child understand that he or she causes things to happen.	
Help the child engage in directed problem solving. Encourage the child to persist in efforts to reach a goal.	
Keep things predictable, especially when the infant is very young.	
Guide language development by using words to name, sort, and categorize objects and events.	
Accept the child's efforts to achieve closeness.	
Be sensitive to the child's state; learn to interpret the child's signals accurately; time your responses appropriately.	
Find effective ways to soothe and comfort the child in times of distress.	
Help the child interpret sources of distress and find ways to regulate distress. Minimize the child's exposure to intensely negative, hostile, and frightening events.	
Be aware of the visual and auditory cues you send when you interact with the child.	
Pay attention to how the child is changing over time.	
Monitor the child's emotional expressions to evaluate the success of specific actions and interventions.	

© Cengage

empathy, physical closeness, and self-insight. Enacting the parent role makes considerable physical, cognitive, and emotional demands, but attachment to a child also promotes the parent's own psychosocial development. These contributions to adult development are described further in chapters 11 (Early Adulthood) and 12 (Middle Adulthood).

FURTHER REFLECTION: Hypothesize how life conditions such as poverty, the dual-earner family, single parenting, or having a very-low-birth-weight baby might influence a person's ability to function as an advocate for his or her infant.

Summarize how infants may influence and even enhance the lives of their family members.

CHAPTER SUMMARY

The genetic plan plays a major role in guiding physical and sensory/perceptual maturation during infancy. There is also considerable evidence for plasticity in neurological development as an infant interacts with the social and physical environments. During infancy, a child rapidly develops sensory and motor skills, social relationships, and emotional and conceptual skills. Babies are born with the capacity to perceive their environment and to evoke responses from their caregivers. They are ready to respond to a wide array of caregiving conditions. Caregivers convey cultural beliefs and values through their childrearing practices, thereby shaping the infant's experiences along particular cultural pathways. The result is a blend of many universal features of infancy, such as reflexes, motor development, attachment processes, and sensorimotor reasoning, with the specific experiences

infants have in their culture of care. Some of these experiences are a result of socialization goals, such as sleeping arrangements or types of food that are given to the infant. Some of the experiences are a result of the language, communication patterns, and social interactions that accompany care. Other experiences are a result of individual differences in the caregivers' sensitivity and ability to meet infants' needs.

OBJECTIVE 1 Describe characteristics of newborns and explain the challenges facing low-birth-weight babies.

Babies differ in their physical maturity and appearance at birth. Differences in physical maturity have distinct consequences for the capacity to regulate survival functions such as breathing, digesting, waking, and sleeping. The Apgar scoring method is used to evaluate the newborn's need for immediate intervention. Infants who weigh less than 2,500 grams (about 5 pounds, 8 ounces) are called low-birth-weight babies. Babies who are small for their gestational age (SGA) are at greater risk for health problems than those who are born prematurely but are of average weight for their gestational age. Babies born before 30 weeks do not have the benefit of positive features of the uterine environment that support the maturation of various aspects of self-regulatory functions.

OBJECTIVE 2 Identify important milestones in the maturation of the sensory/perceptual and motor systems. Describe the interactions among these systems during the first 2 years of life. Explain how brain development in infancy is tied to maturation of the sensory and motor systems.

It makes sense to think of infants as newly developing systems that require continuous support for ongoing growth and refinement. The synapses in their brains become more elaborated in the context of engagement in a stimulating and responsive environment. As regions of the brain become more organized, they influence each other, leading to new cognitive capacities and abilities for goal-oriented behavior and self-regulation. The infant brain, including capacities for social connection, sensory processing, motor behavior, and emotional regulation and expression, is emerging in an ongoing, fluid process of exchange of information with its social and physical environments. What begins as an explosion of possible meanings and connections gradually becomes sculpted into certain patterns and preferred responses, but with a continuous potential for new interconnections into childhood and beyond.

During the first months of life, the sensory/perceptual system—vision, hearing, taste, smell, touch, motion sensitivity, and responsiveness to internal cues (*proprioception*)—is developing rapidly and functions at a more advanced level than the motor system. Young infants can distinguish changes in the loudness, pitch, duration, and location of sounds. They can use auditory information to differentiate objects from one another and to track the location of objects. Infants respond to a variety of visual dimensions, including movement, color, brightness, complexity, light-dark contrast, contours, depth, and distance. By 6 or 7 months of age, infants treat faceness as a special visual category. Newborns can differentiate sweet, sour, bitter, and salty tastes. Touch is an active as well as a passive sense; babies use it to explore objects, people, and their own bodies. Over the first year, infants' voluntary motor functions mature rapidly. Many motor functions are present in a reflexive form and emerge more fully as a result of continuing muscle development, motor coordination, and practice. Stepping is one example of this dynamic emergence.

OBJECTIVE 3 Discuss the development of sensorimotor intelligence, including an analysis of how infants process information, organize experiences, conceptualize causality, and understand the properties and functions of objects.

Sensorimotor intelligence begins with the use of motor and sensory/perceptual capacities to explore and understand the environment. Four basic information-processing abilities provide the cognitive resources that support the maturation of sensorimotor intelligence: attention, processing speed, memory, and representational abilities. Of the many schemes that are established during this period, the emergence of an increasingly complex sense of causal relationships, the establishment of the concept of object permanence, and the formation of categories of objects are achievements that impose order and predictability on experience.

OBJECTIVE 4 Summarize the beginnings of language competence from birth through the first 2 years of life.

Evidence of both language perception and language production can be traced to infancy. Auditory and visual cues contribute to an awareness of the structure and rhythm of spoken language. Infants are able to recognize sounds and differentiate between sound combinations. They communicate through babbling and gestures before using spoken words. Around the age of 8 months, infants understand the meanings of some individual words and phrases. By 16 months, an infant has a receptive vocabulary of between 90 and 300 words and a productive vocabulary of about 26 words.

OBJECTIVE 5 Analyze social attachment, the process through which infants develop strong emotional bonds with others, and describe the dynamics of attachment formation during infancy.

A social attachment forms between the infant and the primary caregiver, creating the basic mental representation for subsequent intimate relationships. The attachment has physical as well as social and emotional characteristics. Sensory/perceptual and motor experiences with the caregiver's voice, touch, aroma, facial expressions, soothing, and playfulness are all part of what become integrated into the mental representation of the object of attachment. Depending upon the sensitivity of the caregiver, attachments can be secure, resistant, avoidant, or disorganized.

OBJECTIVE 6 Examine the nature of emotional development, including emotional differentiation, the interpretation of emotions, and emotional regulation. Analyze the concept of temperament as an organized aspect of emotional reactivity.

Emotions are an early and continuous means of achieving intersubjectivity between infants and their caregivers. Emotions become increasingly differentiated in intensity and meaning. Emotional regulation provides a critical underpinning for subsequent cognitive functioning and social competence. Temperament refers to relatively stable ways that infants have of responding to stimulation, regulating their reactions, and engaging objects and people in the environment. Several models or approaches to characterizing temperament are described. A child's temperament influences the tone of interactions, the frequency with which interactions take place, the way others react to the child, and the way the child reacts to the reactions of others.

OBJECTIVE 7 Explain the psychosocial crisis of trust versus mistrust; the central process through which the crisis is resolved, mutuality with the caregiver; the prime adaptive ego quality of hope; and the core pathology of withdrawal.

The establishment of trust between the infant and the caregiver is significant in both intellectual and social development. Through repeated interactions with caregivers, the infant develops a concept of the adult as both separate and permanent. Parental sensitivity is an underlying factor in determining the quality of attachment. Factors that appear to influence sensitivity are the adult's past experiences, including how the parent was cared for as a young child; contemporary factors that influence the caregiver's well-being, self-esteem, and emotional availability, such as the quality of the parental dyad and experiences at work; and characteristics of the infant. Once established, the trusting relationship

between the infant and the caregiver becomes a source of security for the infant's further explorations of the environment and a framework for future close relationships. Trust serves as a basis for an orientation toward hopefulness.

OBJECTIVE 8 Evaluate the critical role of parents and caregivers during infancy, with special attention to issues of safety and nutrition; optimizing cognitive, social, and emotional development; and the role of parents and caregivers as advocates for their infants.

Infants are skilled at adapting to their environment, but they cannot bring about major changes in it. Parents and other caregivers are ultimately responsible for structuring the environment so that it is maximally suited to the infant. Infants count on their caregivers to create a safe environment, to provide safe and adequate nutrition, to protect them from distress, to promote their health and physical growth, and to rally appropriate social support and community resources as needed. Parents must act as advocates for their infants and for themselves in the parental role.

CASEBOOK

For additional case material related to this chapter, see the case of "Marcie and Mom," in *Life Span Development: A Case Book*, by Barbara and Philip Newman, Laura Landry-Meyer, and Brenda J. Lohman, pp. 54–55. The case offers a starting point for discussing a common parenting routine—bedtime—and how infant temperament, mother's parenting style, and context interact to create a parenting environment.

A hallmark of toddlerhood is the emerging capacity for pretense. It begins with the imitation of activities the child has observed at home and evolves into complex fantasy play. Maya can take care of her baby, feed her, soothe her, and put her to sleep. Imagination, language, and physical skills all contribute to the expression of symbolic play.

1. Describe the expansion of motor skills during toddler-hood, and explain their importance for the child's capacity to explore the environment and to experience opportunities for mastery.

2. Summarize the accomplishments in language development and outline the features of the language environment that support communicative competence.

3. Explain the development of fantasy play and its importance for cognitive and social development.

4. Examine the factors that contribute to the development of self-control, including impulse management and goal attainment.

5. Define the psychosocial crisis of autonomy versus shame and doubt, the central process of imitation, the prime adaptive ego strength of will, and the core pathology of compulsion.

6. Evaluate the impact of poverty on development in toddlerhood.

7. Apply a psychosocial analysis to the topic of child care, emphasizing the impact of the kind of care and the quality of care on development during toddlerhood.

TODDLERHOOD (AGES 2 TO 4 YEARS)

6

Harrison was 27 months old when he joined the toddler room. After a few days, Harrison began to have conflicts just after arriving in the morning. He would not wash his hands or come to the breakfast table. When teacher Rena tried to invite him, he worked himself into a rage, yelling the F word (with his own particular pronunciation) and throwing things. Because his behavior distressed the other toddlers, Rena had to physically move him to a far corner of the room, and hold him until he calmed down.

When Harrison repeated this behavior over the following days, Rena talked with Betty, his young mom, whom she had met only a few days earlier. Rena said she enjoyed having Harrison in her group. But, she told Betty, he was having a problem, especially after he arrived, and she wanted to help him.

Betty shared that their house was small, and the activities of some family members often kept Harrison from settling down and getting to sleep. From their conversation, Rena concluded that the toddler's aggressive behavior was due to lack of sleep related to conditions at home.

Over that first month, Rena developed a relationship with Betty, who disclosed a bit more about the family's home situation. Rena learned that two male members of the family were particularly affected by poverty and clinical depression.

Harrison was clearly bringing a high stress level to the toddler room. Rena guessed that the stress was largely due to Harrison's having to transition from one chaotic situation at home to what he perceived as another chaotic situation in the classroom.

Rena worked out a strategy with Betty and the other staff. When Harrison arrived in the morning, she approached him in a low-key way and gave him the choice of getting ready for breakfast or snuggling. Harrison usually chose snuggling and occasionally fell asleep. During the day, Rena gave him choices between two activities. Harrison began making choices and participating more. Rena and the two assistant teachers also sought out opportunities for one-on-one snuggling and contact talks—a few minutes of shared quality time— with him throughout each day.

Gradually, Harrison accepted the toddler routine. Rena remained open to his need for a morning snuggle, but Harrison needed closeness on arrival only some days. The staff realized that while they could not change Harrison's home environment, they could help him feel safe and welcome in the toddler room and maintain a positive relationship with his mother.

Source: Gartrell, D. (2011), Aggression, the prequel preventing the need. *Young Children,* 66, p. 62.

CASE ANALYSIS Using What You Know

1. Analyze the features of toddlerhood that are captured in this case. How does the case relate to the developmental tasks of locomotion, language, and self-control?

2. Evaluate Rena's interpretation of Harrison's behavior. What evidence supports the link between lack of sleep, stressful home environment, and a child's aggressive behavior? What alternative interpretations can you think of to explain Harrison's behavior?

3. Explain the relationship of attachment security to a child's ability to cope with stress.

4. How are Rena and the staff using guidance strategies to support Harrison's successful adjustment to toddler care? What might be some long-term benefits of these approaches for Harrison?

Toddlers seem to bubble with unpredictable, startling thoughts and actions that keep adults in a state of puzzled amazement. Toddlers are extremely busy—talking, moving, fantasizing, and planning all the time. Their outpouring of physical activity is remarkable for its vigor, constancy, and complexity. Equally impressive is the flood of cognitive accomplishments, especially language production and unique forms of playful fantasy.

Building on a foundation of trust and optimism formed during infancy, toddlerhood brings a flowering of the sense of personal **autonomy**, an enjoyment and confidence in doing things for oneself and expressing one's will. The successful blending of these two basic capacities for trust and autonomy provides a strong, protective shield for the young child's ego system. From this foundation, children are able to venture into satisfying and meaningful social relationships, engage in playful problem solving, and face their future with an outlook of hopefulness and assertiveness.

The chances for such a positive conclusion to the period of toddlerhood rest largely on the quality of the home environment. Toddlers, with their high energy level, improbable ideas, impish willfulness, and needs for mastery, run headlong into the full range of limits in their physical and social environment. Parenting during toddlerhood is like paddling a canoe through the rapids. It requires vigilance, good communication between the bow and the stern, flexibility, and a certain *joie de vivre* that keeps the whole trip fun. A child's cognitive and social development during this period of life can be facilitated by the parents' own ego development, their style of parenting, and the quality of their relationship. The degree to which discord and conflict introduce stress into the lives of parents brings special risks for some toddlers. ●

Developmental Tasks

The use of the word *toddler* to describe development for 2- and 3-year-olds is in itself a clue to the important part that locomotion plays. In fact, it is only during the first year of this stage that the child actually toddles. By age 3, the child's walk has changed from the precarious, determined, half-humorous toddle to a more graceful, continuous, effective stride. Removal of diapers plays an important role in the progress of a child's walk. When toddlers no longer have a large wad of padding between their legs, they quickly make the transition from ugly duckling to swan.

The developmental tasks of toddlerhood—expanded locomotion, language and communication skills, fantasy play, and self-control—all contribute to the child's emerging independence within the boundaries of the social group. Some theorists refer to this as the first individuation process (Blos, 1979; Mahler, Pine, & Bergman, 1975). Obviously, 3-year-olds are not ready to set out for life alone in the big city, but they are ready to express independent thoughts, exercise some control in making choices, and do some things independently. The psychosocial crisis during this period of life—autonomy versus shame and doubt—refers to the child's struggle to establish a sense of separateness without disrupting the bonds of affection and protection that are crucial to a young child's physical survival and emotional connection to the family. In many cultures, expectations for new levels of self-sufficiency are brought about by the birth of the next child. Typically, this takes place with the support of older siblings, neighboring children, and extended family members who model and encourage more mature behavior.

Elaboration of Locomotion

OBJECTIVE 1 Describe the expansion of motor skills during toddlerhood, and explain their importance for the child's capacity to explore the environment and to experience opportunities for mastery.

Locomotion plays a central role in the toddler's psychosocial development by helping children translate their ideas into actions and by fostering new types of interactions with the social and physical environments. Imagine Harrison, kicking, throwing things, whirling around, pushing and hitting, asserting himself through the use of his motor skills to express his frustration. As locomotor skills develop, the child has new ways of remaining close to the objects of attachment, new avenues for investigating the environment, new opportunities for play, and new strategies for coping with stressful situations. For many toddlers, when frustrations build up, their anger is expressed in **tantrums**, often including an outpouring of unrestrained physical actions including hitting, kicking, flailing arms and legs, head banging, or throwing oneself on the floor. As a child's language and self-control improve, tantrums typically become less frequent, especially if adults do not inadvertently reward or reinforce them (Mayo Clinic, 2015).

Locomotion and Cognition

Growth in locomotion and cognition go hand in hand. An understanding of space, distance, and the relationship of one place to the next expand as children maneuver through their environments (Gibson & Pick, 2000). Motor activity involves continuous decision making. Functional motor activities, like getting dressed, climbing up the ladder on a slide, or pumping to make the swing go higher requires gathering information, using feedback to modify actions, and refining movement patterns to achieve desired goals. One study found that when people think about the future, their leg muscles react as if they are moving ahead, and when they think about the past, their leg muscles react as if they are moving backward (Miles, Nind, & Macrae, 2010). In toddlerhood, sensorimotor exploration may serve as the physical basis for subsequent thinking about the future (moving ahead through

space) and thinking about the past (moving backward through space). Actions become increasingly goal directed and adapted to the demands of the situation. Early movements may seem jerky, unbalanced, and ineffective, but over time they become more fluid, smooth, and rhythmic. From among the variety of movement strategies that toddlers use, a few are selected and gradually coordinated. However, locomotion is always adapted to a specific environment, so when a toddler is faced with a new setting, like getting onto a swing, or crawling through a tunnel, the diversity of actions that have been cast aside may come back into use (Adolph & Robinson, 2015).

Dynamic Systems Theory and Locomotion

Dynamic systems theory has guided the contemporary view of motor development. Five factors interact to support the emergence of motor skills: (1) physical characteristics of the limbs, joints, and muscles involved in the movement; (2) changes in body weight and muscle mass; (3) new capacities in the central nervous system that improve coordination of feedback from the limbs and guide the amount of effort needed to achieve a motor goal; (4) the nature of behavioral goals; and possibly the most important of all (5) opportunities for repetition and practice (Adolph & Berger, 2006; Thelen & Smith, 1994). These factors are integrated through repeated action; as one factor changes, the others must change. In addition, these motor skills are adapted to various physical environments. Walking on sidewalks requires a different set of actions than walking in sand or on unpaved, dirt paths. As a result, although most toddlers eventually achieve the same kinds of gross motor skills, the exact path toward proficiency differs for different children and across cultural groups.

Landmarks of Motor Development

Some landmarks of motor development that are reached from ages 2 to 6—walking and running, jumping, hopping, throwing and catching, pedaling and steering—are described in Table 6.1. The development and perfection of these skills depend on opportunity and encouragement as well as on the maturation of the neurological, cognitive, and motor systems (Adolph & Robinson, 2015).

As walking becomes a more comfortable form of locomotion, new skills are added to the child's repertoire. Running and jumping are the first to emerge. By the age of 4, children are likely to leap from stairways, porches, or ladders. They have begun to imagine what it might be like to fly. Jumping is their closest approximation to flying. The actions involved in jumping form a pattern that remains stable throughout childhood and into adulthood (Clark, Phillips, & Petersen, 1989).

Children's locomotor abilities become more elaborated all through toddlerhood. For example, in films used to study the emergence of running, it appears that for toddlers, running and walking are very much alike, with little increase in velocity and little or no flight (the time when both feet are off the ground) in running. At first, toddlers appear to be running because they are moving a bit faster, but their action is not similar to adult running. Over time, however, the movements smooth out as flight time and velocity increase (Whitall & Getchell, 1995). These examples of jumping and running suggest how important early

Table 6.1   Changes in Gross Motor Skills During Toddlerhood and Early School Age

Age	Walking and Running	Jumping	Hopping	Throwing and Catching	Pedaling and Steering
2–3 years	Walks rhythmically; opposite arm–leg swing appears. Hurried walk changes to true run.	Jumps down from step. Jumps several inches off floor with both feet, no arm action.	Hops 1 to 3 times on same foot with stiff upper body and nonhopping leg held still.	Throws ball with forearm extension only; feet remain stationary. Awaits thrown ball with rigid arms outstretched.	Pushes riding toy with feet; does little steering.
3–4 years	Walks up stairs, alternating feet. Walks downstairs, leading with one foot. Walks in a straight line.	Jumps off floor with coordinated arm action. Broad jumps about 1 foot.	Hops 4 to 6 times on same foot, flexing upper body and swinging nonhopping leg.	Throws ball with slight body rotation but little or no transfer of weight with feet. Flexes elbows in preparation for catching; traps ball against chest.	Pedals and steers tricycle.
4–5 years	Walks downstairs, alternating feet. Runs more smoothly. Gallops and skips with one foot.	Improved upward and forward jumps. Travels greater distance.	Hops 7 to 9 times on same foot. Improved speed of hopping.	Throws ball with increased body rotation and some transfer of weight forward. Catches ball with hands; if unsuccessful, may still trap ball against chest.	Rides tricycle rapidly, steers smoothly.
5–6 years	Increased speed of run. Gallops more smoothly. True skipping appears.	Jumps off floor about 1 foot. Broad jumps 3 feet.	Hops 50 feet on same foot in 10 seconds. Hops with rhythmical alternation (2 hops on one foot and 2 on the other).	Has mature throwing and catching pattern. Moves arm more and steps forward during throw. Awaits thrown ball with relaxed posture, adjusting body to path and size of ball.	Rides bicycle with training wheels.

Source: From *Infants, Children, and Adolescents,* 3rd ed., by Laura E. Berk, Boston: Allyn and Bacon. Copyright © 1999 by Pearson Education.

locomotor activity is in establishing motor skills that become elements of more complex athletic abilities in later childhood, adolescence, and adult life.

Locomotion and Play

Locomotor skills figure prominently in the increasing complexity of play. At first, youngsters may run for the sake of running. They practice over and over again. Later in toddlerhood, running changes from a kind of game in itself to a valuable component of many other games. The absolute speed of toddlers is limited by their somewhat precarious balance and short legs. This does not discourage them, however, from devoting a great deal of time and energy to running. The goals of mastery and getting to new places for exploration are too strong to dampen their enthusiasm. Locomotor play provides practice for coordinated movement in a risk-free context. Through locomotor play, toddlers can develop new skills and perfect actions that become useful for later activities, such as running to catch the bus or hopping over a big mud puddle. Locomotor play eventually becomes incorporated into the games and sports of early and middle childhood (Pellegrini, 2011).

Toddlers are often exposed to a wide variety of forms of locomotion, such as swimming, skiing, skating, sledding, and dancing. Children seem eager to use their bodies in a variety of ways, and they learn quickly (Goodway, Ozmun, & Gallahue, 2012). As their physical coordination improves, children engage in new large-muscle activities: climbing, sliding, swinging, pounding,

Toddlerhood brings tremendous advances in movement, coordination, and balance. You can see the sense of accomplishment in Micah's face, having climbed up the big log blocks and getting ready to leap off.

digging, and rough-and-tumble play. Locomotor play provides immediate benefits to children in terms of physical fitness, including increased bone density, cardiovascular fitness, and flexibility (Pellegrini, 2009). Certain forms of physical activity provide an important source of information about the physical self. Toddlers enjoy their bodies and are generally joyful when in the midst of physical play. Thus, physical activity contributes in an essential way to the toddler's self-concept.

To the extent that coping involves the ability to maintain freedom of movement under conditions of threat, locomotor skills acquired during toddlerhood provide resources for lifelong strategies for fight or flight. Advanced locomotor skills may also increase conflicts with caregivers, introducing new struggles of willfulness and new parental constraints.

> When Ellen was about 2½ years old, she enjoyed watching her older brother climbing up a tree in the neighbor's yard. She would beg her brother to lift her up so she could get into the tree with him. One afternoon, Ellen's brother lifted her into the tree and then ran off to play with a friend. Ellen tried to get down from the tree, but she got her foot stuck in a crack between the branches. She cried and yelled until her mom came to get her. Ellen's mom scolded her for being in the tree and warned her never to go up there again. But the next afternoon, Ellen was back trying to figure out how to climb into the tree on her own.

From this example, one can see that when locomotor skills occur early in a developmental period, before the maturation of verbal and cognitive competence, toddlers may find themselves at odds with caregivers who must limit locomotion to protect the child's safety. Caregivers may also have to limit a toddler's locomotion to secure the safety of other people and objects in the environment.

Motor Impairments

Children who lack muscle strength or coordination may experience strong feelings of frustration as they struggle to keep their balance, throw or catch a ball, or use their hands and feet to perform new tasks. A number of conditions, including motor skills impairment (sometimes referred to as motor dyspraxia) and neurological diseases such as muscular dystrophy or cerebral palsy, impede the maturation of locomotion and other motor skills. Although children may be diagnosed with the same motor impairment condition, the exact impact on their functional capacity for locomotion can differ. For example, some children with motor skill impairment are described as clumsy; they may drop items or run into walls and furniture. Some may have difficulty using a cup, spoon, or fork to eat or have difficulty holding a pencil and learning to print. Others have frequent accidents due to motor planning difficulties (eMedicinehealth, 2015).

Young children with these conditions can benefit from guided activity-focused interventions that improve their ability to participate in functional activities, allowing them to enjoy interacting with family members and peers. With the help of physical and occupational therapists and parents, specific interventions can be designed to enhance functional motor activity,

and improve coordination and control. Three steps are suggested to help design interventions that will foster motor advances (Valvano & Rapport, 2006, p. 294):

1. Develop activity-related goals and objectives in cooperation with the family's priorities and values that will increase a child's ability to participate in daily routines.
2. Plan activity-focused interventions that include frequent opportunities for practice throughout each day. These interventions should be designed to address impairments due directly to the diagnosed disorder, but incorporate the child's strengths and interests, as well as principles observed in typically developing children.
3. Integrate impairment-focused interventions that include remediating possible secondary impairments such as weakness from disuse, muscle strain, or postural problems that have emerged over time in efforts to cope with the primary limitations.

Since functional movement is intricately connected to the environmental conditions, interventions need to incorporate environmental modifications that make it possible for a child to experience success. These might include creating physical supports for upright sitting, positioning objects at a level that allows the child to reach them without losing balance, or creating a nonskid surface to enhance walking. Over time, as the child's abilities improve, these environmental parameters may be altered or eliminated. In the end, movements need to be flexibly adapted to achieve goals in varied environments. Thus, interventions have to incorporate opportunities for children to use their problem solving abilities to modify their approaches, even when impairments constrain certain actions.

FURTHER REFLECTION *What do you remember from your childhood about locomotor activities? Do you recall riding a tricycle, swinging, running, going down the slide, or swimming? In what ways do motor skills continue to contribute to your sense of autonomy and mastery as an adult?*

What observations would lead you to think that a toddler had a motor impairment? Who would you contact to help identify this kind of problem? What interventions might be possible?

Language Development

OBJECTIVE 2 Summarize the accomplishments in language development and outline the features of the language environment that support communicative competence.

Jean Piaget (1970) described the years from about 2 to 5 or 6 as the stage of **preoperational thought**. During this stage, the sensorimotor schemes that were developed during infancy are represented internally. The most significant achievement of this new stage of cognitive development is the capacity for semiotic or *representational* thinking—understanding that one thing can stand for another.

In **semiotic thinking**, children learn to recognize and use symbols and signs. **Symbols** are usually related in some way to the objects for which they stand. The cross, for example, is a

How the Brain Processes Language

With the use of positron emission tomography (PET) and functional magnetic resonance imaging (fMRI), one can observe different areas of activity in the brain related to varying language activities, including speaking, seeing words, and hearing words. The areas of the brain that become more visible following a task are assumed to have been activated by the task (Campbell, MacSweeney & Waters, 2007).

In infancy, both hemispheres are involved in language perception. By the end of the third year, for the vast majority of right-handed children, the essential aspects of speaking and understanding spoken language typically become focused in the left hemisphere of the brain. For left-handed children and those who are ambidextrous, these aspects of language are focused in the right hemisphere (Oates, Karmiloff-Smith, & Johnson, 2012).

The nondominant hemisphere becomes important for understanding features of language such as interpreting the emotional tone of the speaker, humor, and metaphor. However, neuroimaging studies have demonstrated that many regions of the brain are involved in language production and comprehension (Gernsbacher & Kaschak, 2003; see FIGURE 6.1 ▶).

You can appreciate how complex language comprehension is and why it must engage many brain areas. In what seems like an instant, the sounds someone else makes are heard and interpreted. This requires attention, recognition of word sounds and meanings, and the flexibility to recognize language from a variety of speakers who use different expressions, tones of voice, and dialects in their speech (Cutler, 2012). Studies that monitor brain activity find that nouns and verbs, the kinds of words that are especially important for conveying meaning, are associated with different patterns of activity than prepositions and conjunctions, the kinds of words that are more important for grammatical information.

Damage to localized areas of the brain leads to a loss of the ability to speak referred to as **aphasia**. Damage to Broca's area results in an inability to produce speech, but language comprehension remains functional. Damage to Wernicke's area does not affect the ability to produce language, but understanding is lost. People with Wernicke's aphasia can produce words clearly, but the words do not make sense. People who have damage to the arcuate fasciculus can understand language, but their speech does not make sense, and they cannot repeat words. In a condition called *aprosodia*, people have difficulty talking about their emotions when there is damage to the area of the right hemisphere that mirrors the area of the left hemisphere that is used for language.

Speech is different from other cognitive functions related to communication, such as word meaning or symbolizing an idea by drawing a picture (Sanders, Weber-Fox, & Neville, 2008). In addition to the areas of the brain identified in Figure 6.1 as especially key for language production and comprehension, speaking involves the motor cortex, reading involves the visual cortex, and understanding spoken language involves the auditory cortex. The task of reading aloud involves the visual cortex, motor cortex, and Broca's area.

What about sign languages? Are they processed in the brain the same way as spoken language? Studies of this question are leading to the following conclusion: Both spoken language and sign language engage the same left hemisphere areas for language production and comprehension, including Broca's area and Wernicke's area. The right hemisphere supports other aspects of language, especially appreciation for how sentences or phrases are linked together, and the rhythm or melody of the communication. It is also activated in social communication, including the pragmatics of language, facial expressions, gestures, and tone of voice. This is true whether the person is a native speaker or a native signer. However, there is some evidence that sign language engages more of the right hemisphere, especially the simultaneous processing of visual/spatial information and the large grain information contained in gestures (Campbell, MacSweeney, & Waters, 2007).

Language production capacities of the brain demonstrate both sensitive periods and remarkable plasticity. Sensitivity is evidenced by the impact of delayed exposure to language on disruptions in grammar. Sensitivity is also

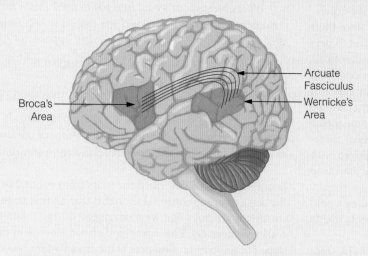

Broca's Area — Arcuate Fasciculus — Wernicke's Area

FIGURE 6.1 ▶ Three Areas of the Brain That Are Intimately Related to Speech: Broca's Area, Wernicke's Area, and the Arcuate Fasciculus, a bundle of nerve fibers that connects the two.

symbol of Christianity. In pretend play, a scarf or a blanket may be a symbol for a pillow or a dress. **Signs** stand for things in a more abstract, arbitrary way. **Words** are signs; there is no direct relation between the word *dog* and the animal to which the word refers, yet the word stands for the object. For adults, it seems natural to use matchsticks or little squares of cardboard to represent people or buildings, but for children, the idea that a stick may be a car or a horse is a dramatic change in thinking that emerges gradually during the preoperational period.

Five representational skills allow children to manipulate objects mentally rather than by actual behavior: (1) imitation in the absence of the model, (2) mental images, (3) symbolic drawing, (4) symbolic play, and (5) language. **Representational skills** allow children to share their experiences with others and to create imagined experiences. These skills also free children from communicating only through gestures and opens up opportunities to communicate about the past or the future as well as the present. Children can express relationships they may have known in the past by imitating them, drawing them, talking about them, or acting them out in fantasy. They can also portray events and relationships that they wish would occur or that they wish to alter (Nelson, 2010). In this and the following sections, we focus on two of these representational skills, language and fantasy play, which are among the most notable achievements of toddlerhood and are foundational for psychosocial development across the life span.

Communicative Competence

In the process of language development, children acquire **communicative competence**. They become adept at using all the aspects of language that permit effective participation in the **language environment** of their culture (Hill & Kuczaj, 2011; MacWhinney, 2015). This includes producing the sounds of the language; understanding the system of meanings, the rules for word formation, and the rules for sentence formation; developing a rich vocabulary; making adjustments to the social setting that are necessary to produce and interpret communication (*pragmatics*); and acquiring the ability to express thoughts in written as well as oral form. Through the achievement of communicative competence, children become increasingly integrated into their culture. They learn the expressions, tones of voice, and gestures that link them intimately to the language environment of their home and community. They learn when to speak and when to remain silent. They learn how to communicate with peers, parents, and authority figures. They learn the terms applied to kin, close friends, acquaintances, and strangers; the words that are used to disparage or devalue; and the words that are used to recognize and praise. Although much of communication is intended to create shared meaning between the sender and the receiver of messages, sometimes communicative competence is used to deceive, mislead, or intimidate (Fiedler, 2008). If nurturing is the primary vehicle for cultural socialization in infancy, communication is the primary vehicle in toddlerhood. A discussion of how the toddler's brain processes language is presented in the **Applying Theory and Research to Life** box.

Communicative competence begins during infancy and develops across the entire life span. Vocabulary, grammar, and pragmatics continue to be refined as one engages in formal schooling and diverse social settings where specific words, expressions, and styles of interaction are in use. But toddlerhood is the time of a dramatic expansion in verbal competence when remarkable achievements are made in an exceptionally brief period. The following discussion of language and communication is divided into two major sections: (1) language milestones and (2) the language environment. The first section outlines the pattern of communication accomplishments of toddlerhood, including the expanded use of words with meaning, the formation of two-word sentences, and more complex sentence formation. The second section identifies factors in the psychosocial environment that help facilitate and optimize communicative competence.

Language Milestones in Toddlerhood

The text provides an overview of patterns of accomplishment in language and communication from infancy through about age 4. As you may remember, many of the precursors of spoken language, including language perception, babbling, and gesturing, were discussed in chapter 5. Certain sequences or developmental milestones appear to be quite common among children from many language environments. Communicative gestures precede the production of spoken words, and the production of a substantial vocabulary of spoken words precedes the linking of words into two-word sentences. However, it is important to recognize the wide variability in the development of communicative skills.

The timing of the onset of various abilities and their rate of growth vary from child to child. At 20 months, Sadie would talk about her experiences in a rapid profusion of sounds and expressions that were completely unintelligible. She was telling her story in her own private vocalizations. By 30 months, Sadie could tell you in "real" words and phrases what she does or does not want to eat or wear, what happened in school, or when she wants to go outside, read a book, or play a certain game. In contrast, many toddlers at this same age are poorly understood even by family members and have a very limited vocabulary. In a large national study of infant/toddler language, word production for 12-month-old infants ranged from the 90th percentile, who used 26 words or more, to the 10th percentile, who produced no words (see FIGURE 6.2 ▶). By 16 months of age, those in the 90th percentile were using 180 words, and those in the 10th percentile produced 10 words or less (Fenson et al., 1994). All these children were healthy, normal children, with no known history of developmental delay, prematurity, or genetic disease. As you read about typical patterns, try to remember that these patterns disguise important variations.

Language development in toddlerhood brings rapid acquisition of a wide-ranging vocabulary and the initial use of a primitive grammar that is quickly transformed into the grammar of the spoken language. The typical developmental progression in language competence is characterized by three common patterns: (1) an acceleration in the production of single words, followed by two-word combinations; (2) a predominance of nouns in the vocabulary followed by the addition of verbs, adjectives, and prepositions; and (3) two-word utterances followed by longer strings of words organized by use of grammatical rules that include indicators of meaning, such as possession, plural, and past, present, and future (Owens, 2015).

A universal capacity for language matures rapidly in the first 4 years of life. Each of the approximately 6,000 languages spoken in the world today is capable of doing roughly the same thing, conveying ideas. However, each language has its own vocabulary

and grammar, which have to be learned specifically. Whereas there may be a universal capacity to recognize certain facial expressions as happy or sad, or even certain gestures that mean "give me" or "pick me up," there is no universal human code that links objects, ideas, or actions to spoken words and sentences. Each human child has to learn a particular spoken language. This uniqueness of language contributes to its flexibility, leading to the creative use of language and its capacity to express novel thoughts and ideas (Wargo, 2008).

Vocabulary. During the period from 12 to 16 months, infants make significant progress in learning the names of objects and applying them to pictures or real examples. There is a rapid expansion of vocabulary during these 4 months from few or no spoken words to about 26. Vocabulary continues to expand at a rapid rate throughout the toddler and early school years (Booth, 2009). The average toddler of 30 months has a spoken vocabulary of about 570 words. In order to accomplish this feat, children seem to *fast-map* new meanings as they experience words in conversation. To **fast-map** is to quickly form an initial, partial understanding of a word's meaning. It is an information-processing technique in which children relate the new word to the known vocabulary by linking it to known words and concepts that are already well understood. The child has to hear the new word only a few times in a context that makes its meaning clear. In day-to-day life, children hear thousands of words, many over and over again, without necessarily knowing their meaning. However, once children recognize the link between a word's sound and its meaning, they can quickly associate other familiar word sounds with their meanings (Swingley, 2007). Thus, without direct word-by-word tutoring, children accumulate numerous samples of their culture's language from the speech they hear and attach a minimally satisfactory definition to each word or phrase. This vocabulary burst is associated with speed of processing in word recognition. Young children who recognize words with greater speed also seem to have a greater vocabulary. The combination of speed of word recognition and vocabulary size in early toddlerhood are strong predictors of subsequent language and cognitive skills in middle childhood (Marchman & Fernald, 2008).

The early phase of vocabulary development seems to focus on broad semantic categories—animals, vehicles, fruits, clothes, and so on. New words, particularly nouns, are treated like the name of a category of things rather than of only one specific object or a part of it. For example, when a child learns the word *cup*, it is used to refer to all objects that have the general shape and function of a cup. A much slower process of vocabulary development occurs as children and adults learn the distinctions among words within categories (McDonough, 2002). Toddlers may have a clear idea about the difference between dogs and cats and use these words correctly, but they do not yet know about the distinctions among the various types or breed of cats or dogs. This requires careful observation and new learning. Many books written for young children take up this kind of vocabulary building by presenting pictures of the many different types of a larger category—the different animals at the zoo; the different flowers in the garden.

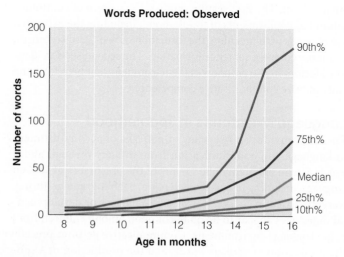

Words Produced: Observed

FIGURE 6.2 ▶ Word Production from 8 to 16 Months

Source: From "Variability in Early Communicative Development," by L. Fenson et al., 1994, *Monographs of the Society for Research in Child Development,* 1994, 59 (5), 38. Copyright © 1994 The Society for Research in Child Development, Inc.

Two-Word Sentences. At 16 months of age, few children make two-word sentences, but by 30 months almost all children make them (Fenson et al., 1994). These two-word sentences are referred to as **telegraphic speech**. Children merge two words into phrases that are essential to communicate what they intend to say. Just as in a telegram, however, other words—verbs, articles, prepositions, pronouns, conjunctions—are left out. A child will say, "my ball," "more juice," and "Daddy gone." Before this point, children tend to utter single words accompanied by gestures and actions. By stringing two words together, they convey more meaning through verbal communication and rely less heavily on gestures and actions. The acquisition of telegraphic speech allows a child to make greater use of the symbolism inherent in language to communicate meaning (Powers, 2002).

Children are quite innovative in using two-word sentences. They continue to understand more than they are able to say, but they appear to use their limited vocabulary and the newfound ability to combine them to get their point across. Children may convey different meanings with the same sentence. "Daddy go," for example, may be used to tell someone that Daddy has left, or it may be used to tell Daddy to leave. Children often indicate their meanings by tone of voice or by the words they stress. The use of two-word sentences is characteristic of toddler-age language learners in many cultures (MacWhinney, 2015).

Martin Braine (1976) analyzed the first word combinations spoken by children in English, Samoan, Finnish, Hebrew, and Swedish. His goal was to identify the kinds of rules or patterns that governed these early combinations. Ten patterns of word combination were embedded in those early language samples:

1. Making reference to something: See + X (*see mother*)
2. Describing something: Hot + X (*hot stove*)
3. Possession: X has a Y (*Billy has a bottle*)
4. Plurality: Two + X (*two dogs*)
5. Repetition or other examples: More + X (*more up*)
6. Disappearance: All gone + X (*all gone milk*)
7. Negation: No + X (*no sleep*)
8. Actor-action relations: Person + X (*Daddy sleep*)
9. Location: X + here (*Grandma here*)
10. Requests: Have + X (*have it, ball*)

Braine found that he could identify some common patterns of word combinations. However, these combinations were not guided by the grammatical categories of the spoken language. Rather, they were guided by the meanings the child wished to express and by the variety of objects, people, and interactions in the immediate environment. The patterns of word combinations used by some children did not overlap at all with those used by other children in the same culture.

Early language is closely tied to the representation of sensorimotor schemes—the activities that dominate the child's life, such as eating, sleeping, playing games with mommy or daddy or siblings, going places, coming back home, and so on. It expresses the properties and relationships of the objects and people that are important in a child's life. Language use emerges within a larger communication system and reflects a child's cognitive capacities. At the same time, it reflects the perceptual and functional characteristics of the environment. Vocabulary and grammar grow hand in hand. As toddlers learn more words, they use them in combination to express more complex ideas (Bates & Goodman, 2001). Underlying this remarkable blossoming of language expression is the child's motivation to become part of his or her social community. Language brings children closer to those they love by allowing them to share thoughts and feelings in ways that can be understood (Nelson, 2007).

Grammatical Transformations. By combining words according to the rules of **grammar** for a given language, a person can produce a limitless number of messages that can be understood by another person. Remarkably, by the age of 4, children appear to be able to structure their sentences using most of these rules without any direct instruction. Consider the difference in meaning between "The boy hit the ball" and "The ball hit the boy." The simple matter of word order in a sentence is critical for preserving meaning. The basic format of an English sentence—noun phrase followed by verb phrase—is a central part of its grammar. In order to ask a question or produce a negative sentence, the speaker transforms this word order according to a specific set of rules (e.g., "You are going" versus "Are you going?"). The addition of certain inflections and modifiers conveys information about time, possession, number, and relation. As children learn the grammatical transformations of their language, they become much more effective in conveying exactly what they have in mind.

A surprising observation is that children use correct transformations for the past tense of irregular verbs (*went, gave, run*) before they use correct inflections of regular verbs (*talked, walked, jumped*). It appears that children first learn the past tense of irregular verbs through rote memory. Once they learn the rule for expressing the past tense by adding *ed*, they occasionally **overregularize** this rule and begin making errors in the past tense. Thus, a 2-year-old is likely to say "I ran fast," but a 3-year-old may say "I runned fast." According to a model proposed by Gary Marcus, children recognize and have a symbolic category for words that are verbs. They establish a default rule: "To form the past tense, add *ed* to any word that can be categorized as a verb." They also memorize the past forms of the irregular verbs as they encounter them. When an irregular verb is required, its irregular past tense form is always used if the child can recall it. However, if the child cannot recall the past tense, or if the word is novel, the default rule is called into play. In a study of preschoolers, the rate of overregularization was 4.5 percent. This fell to 2.5 percent for first graders and 1 percent for fourth graders, suggesting that as a child's vocabulary grows, the need to apply the default rule to unfamiliar verbs declines (Marcus, 1996).

The grammatical errors that young children make alert us to the fact that they are working to figure out a system of rules with which to communicate meaning. It is unlikely that these errors result from imitation of adult speech. Children say such things as "My do it" or "Dose mines." They have certainly not copied those expressions from adults; rather, these errors suggest the beginning of a grammar that becomes more specialized and accurate as children acquire the opportunity to match their speech to that of others. One can catch toddlers in the act of building their grammar by listening to them revise their own speech. From the age of 2 to 4, as their grammar matures, toddlers will pause in midsentence and revise their speech to make a more complex or complete expression. Aware of linguistic alternatives, they stop to select one that best expresses their thoughts in a specific language environment (Rispoli, 2003).

The milestones in language development from 24 months to age 4 are summarized in Table 6.2. In the second year of life, babies understand words and phrases. They develop a vocabulary and begin to form two-word phrases. During the third year, language is definitely used to communicate ideas, observations, and needs. Comprehension of spoken language seems almost complete. Some speech may not be easily understood by people outside the family, partly because these children are unable to produce clear phonetic sounds and also because their knowledge of adult grammar is limited. During the fourth year, most children acquire an extensive vocabulary. They can create sentences that reflect most of the basic rules of grammar. Their language is a vehicle for communicating complex thoughts that are usually understood by children and adults outside the family. They can use their communicative skills to participate in social exchanges with other children, talk about their experiences, make plans, and resolve conflicts.

The pattern of language milestones is common across languages and similar for toddlers who are learning a second language. In an investigation of international adoptees, researchers compared English language acquisition for children who had been adopted from China and U.S.-born monolingual (one language) infants (Snedeker, Geren, & Shafto, 2007). The Chinese children were between the ages of 2½ and 5½ when they were adopted. They were compared to U.S. infants between the ages of 1½ and 2¾. Language competence was assessed every 3 months until the Chinese children had been in the United States 18 months. These adopted children were learning English in much the same way that babies of English-speaking parents learn the language—from exposure to English in the family environment. They had the advantage of more advanced cognitive maturation and experience learning a first language and the disadvantage of delayed exposure to English during infancy.

Three features of language learning were observed among the Chinese adoptees: (1) They showed the same pattern of language production as monolingual infants, using one-word utterances at first, which were mostly nouns with other kinds of words added over time. (2) During their first 3 months in the United States, the adopted children acquired English vocabulary at a rate four times faster than comparable monolingual infants. This suggests that prior experience coupled with advanced understanding of the object-word link contributed to an accelerated process of vocabulary learning. (3) Both adopted children and monolingual infants showed the same positive correlation between vocabulary size and sentence complexity. Neither infants nor adoptees whose vocabulary was less than 300 words produced multiword expressions. Thus, despite their advanced cognitive maturation and prior exposure to another language, adoptees seemed to go through the same sequence of problem-solving steps to build grammatically complex sentences that are characteristic of monolingual infant language learners.

Table 6.2	Milestones in Language Development from 24 Months to 4 Years
At the Completion of	**Language Skills**
24 months	Enjoys listening to and hearing stories; speaks about 50 words; links two or more words together; makes up language using their own creations (e.g. "No paper daddy."); uses some adjectives like *big* or *silly*; speaks clearly enough for parents to understand.
30 months	Vocabulary of more than 300 items (some children seem to be able to name everything in the environment); many new additions every day; no babbling; uses two- and three-word phrases to talk about and ask for things; definite increase in communicative behavior and interest in language; use of linguistic suffixes for possession, plural, and past tense; frequent use of irregular plural noun (foot/feet) and irregular verbs; comprehension is not very good yet by those unfamiliar with the child's speech.
36 months	Vocabulary of 500–1,000 words; speaks in three- and four-word sentences; uses pronouns like *I, you,* and *we*; asks for and directs attention to objects and activities by naming them; can follow multiple requests (e.g., "bring me the book and sit on the couch"); speech is understood more readily by familiar language partners.
48 months	Answers simple questions; speaks in complete sentences; uses parts of speech like other native speakers; talks about activities that took place at child care, with friends, or in other settings; people outside the family can usually understand the child's speech.

Adapted from Mayo Clinic Infant and Toddler Health, 2013. American Speech-Language Hearing Association, 2013.

Pragmatics. Children use language to participate in social interactions. A child may have a rich vocabulary and may be able to form grammatically correct sentences that are understood by others, and still use language inappropriately. **Pragmatics** includes three basic skills: using language for different purposes such as asking a question, giving information, or asking for help; changing language depending on the listener, for example, speaking to a younger child or an adult, or speaking to a class of other children as compared to one friend; and following cultural rules for language, for example, taking turns in a conversation or using appropriate facial expressions and gestures to supplement one's verbal communications (American Speech-Language-Hearing Association, 2016).

Language is a tool for explaining your thoughts and getting what you need from others. It is a source of entertainment through storytelling, reading books, singing, poetry, jokes, and games. As children become increasingly embedded in their culture and community, the pragmatics of their language matures. They learn politeness rules, rules for inferring information from someone's communications, and rules for taking part in dyadic and small group conversations (Hwa-Froelich, 2015). As you review the language milestones in Table 6.2, notice certain features of pragmatics, including a child's ability to answer questions about a story, respond to a request, ask for things, retell an experience, and tell stories to others.

Language Development Beyond Toddlerhood. Although the fundamentals of language are well established by age 4, vocabulary and accompanying word meaning are still far from complete. For example, Mary may raise a fuss about wanting the biggest piece of cake. If you allow her to make a choice, she selects a piece with lots of frosting. Clearly, the word *biggest* is not being used correctly. Even though Mary is able to memorize and repeat the words *big, bigger,* and *biggest,* she does not yet fully understand the concept to which they refer.

As the process of fast-mapping implies, young children may add a word to their vocabulary without understanding the several meanings that this word has in different contexts. During the periods of early and middle childhood, considerable time and attention are devoted to exploring vocabulary, correcting some meanings that were incorrectly learned, and expanding the full range of meanings and underlying concepts that are linked to the many words that were acquired so rapidly during toddlerhood. One estimate is that the reading vocabulary or comprehension of dictionary entries of a 10-year-old child is close to 40,000 words, with another 40,000 proper names, places, and expressions unique to the child's own family, neighborhood, and cultural group (Anglin, 1993).

After toddlerhood, children become increasingly able to use language to guide and control their behavior. Two- and three-year-olds have difficulty using verbal instructions to control or guide their behavior. They may be able to tell themselves to "stop" or "go slow," but these commands are not effective in slowing them down. As their vocabulary and cognitive abilities increase, children become better at using language to reinforce, modify, or disrupt their behavior. The development of language is an integral feature of the maturation of self-control, a developmental task that is discussed further on in this chapter (Beaver, DeLisi, Vaughn, Wright, & Boutwell, 2008; Hebert-Myers, Guttentag, Swank, Smith, & Landry, 2006; Vallotton & Ayoub, 2011).

Important language functions develop more fully during early and middle childhood. As their understanding of the self and the social environment expands, older children use language to plan a problem-solving strategy, guide a complex series of motor activities, or identify the relationships among objects. Vocabulary expands, and words are used more frequently in the ways they are used in adult speech. Depending on the nature of their conversational partners at home and school, children's sentences become more complex, including conditional and descriptive clauses. The irregular verbs and nouns are learned and used correctly. As children attend school, they learn to conceptualize the grammatical structure of their language. Pragmatics also

Toddlers can use their language to enhance play and foster cooperation.

matures. Children learn patterns of polite speech as well as slang. They learn to distinguish between expressions that communicate *probability* (e.g. "I'll try to be there to pick you up at 4:30," or "The ball may have rolled under the couch") versus *certainty* (e.g. "I'll be there promptly at 4:30," or "The ball rolled under the couch") (Ozturk & Papafragou, 2015). Language skills contribute to a child's ability to interact with peers, planning, coordinating, and explaining their ideas in the context of play.

Beyond the formal elements of vocabulary, grammar, pragmatics, reading, and writing, language becomes a vehicle for creative expression. Children write poems, essays, and stories. They begin to use sarcasm, puns, and metaphors to elaborate their speech. They create secret codes with their special friends. Children make up riddles and jokes, put on plays and puppet shows, work on school newspapers, and leave enigmatic or corny messages in their friends' yearbooks. As children move into early and later adolescence, they begin to supplement their communication with the use of social media. They may use new codes or symbols to share private information with peers. Through the use of text messaging and Twitter, forms of expression have been invented that abbreviate or condense meaning. If you participate in these modes of communication, you quickly learn the meanings of these symbols and signs.

Language plays a critical role in the resolution of subsequent psychosocial crises, especially the establishment of group identity, intimacy, and generativity. It is primarily through the quality of one's spoken language that one achieves the level of disclosure that sustains friendships and subsequent intimate relationships. Language also serves as a mechanism for resolving conflicts and for building a sense of cohesiveness within groups, whether of friends, coworkers, or family members.

The Language Environment

In this section, we focus primarily on the nature of the interaction between toddlers and their caregivers, with some attention to the issue of bilingualism and the relationship of the language environment at home and school. Language is a cultural tool, a means for socializing and educating young children. It is one of many inventions for creating a sense of group identity and for passing the mythology, wisdom, and values of the culture from one generation to the next. Competence in the use of language solidifies the young child's membership in the immediate family and in the larger cultural group.

Although there is strong evidence for genetically based origins of the capacity for language learning, the specific content and tone of a child's communication are strongly influenced by the language environment. In many industrialized cultures, children are separated from the world of adult work. Special educational settings are created to prepare children for the tasks of adulthood, and adults interact with children in specific ways that differ from their interactions with other adults. In other cultures, children are present in the midst of ongoing adult activities. Children are encouraged to become active listeners and observers, gradually participating in conversations and work as their abilities permit. Thus, the nature of the interactive language environment, the expectations for children to participate, and the kinds of communications that children are likely to engage in can vary based on the broad cultural orientation about the place and role of children in the larger society (Rogoff & Angelillo, 2002; Rogoff, Morelli, & Chavajay, 2010; Rogoff, Paradise, Arauz, Correa-Chavez, & Angelillo, 2003).

Interaction and Language Development.
Of all the many ways that caregivers contribute to a child's cognitive growth, possibly the most important is the opportunity for language interactions. Brain development in infancy and toddlerhood is stimulated by exposure to adult language through conversation, baby talk, and reading aloud. Language development emerges in a social context. Caregivers and children engage in a dynamic pattern of talk: Infants make vocalizations to which caregivers respond; caregivers engage in a flow of infant-directed talk to which infants respond. Contingent interactions are a powerful tool for promoting language learning (Ko, Seidl, Cristia, Reimchen, & Soderstrom, 2015). An interactive human being can respond to a child's questions, provide information, react in unexpected ways and surprise the child, explain plans or strategies, and offer praise or criticism. The frequency and quality of parent–child interactions are closely associated with children's social and cognitive competence (Hart, Newell, & Olsen, 2003). The **Human Development and Diversity** box discusses **bilingualism**, the complex learning process that takes place in children who are brought up in families that speak two languages.

The link between the frequency of parent–child interactions and the child's verbal competence is well established. Three different explanations have been suggested to account for this link:

1. Parents and their offspring share a genetic predisposition for verbal competence that is evident in the frequency of parent–child interactions and in the early acquisition of verbal skills.
2. Parents who interact frequently with their children provide a rich array of verbal stimuli and thereby promote high levels of verbal comprehension and production.
3. Children who are more verbally competent stimulate more interaction from their caregivers; this establishes a more active and diverse verbal environment.

Certain characteristics of a language partner facilitate a child's language acquisition and communication skills (Singh,

Morgan, & Best, 2002; Snow, 1984). When using infant-directed speech, adults tend to speak in a high pitch, use shorter sentences, speak slowly, use a limited vocabulary, use attention-getting strategies, and speak in a friendly, positive tone. Even older children will modify their speech when interacting with toddlers to hold their attention and guide their behavior. Caregivers have been observed to modify their speech in the following ways so that they are more likely to be understood (Golinkoff, Can, Soderstrom, & Hirsh-Pasek, 2015; Mitchell, 2001; Soderstrom, 2007):

1. They simplify utterances to correspond with the toddler's interests and comprehension level.
2. They emphasize the here and now.
3. They use a more restricted vocabulary.
4. They do a lot of paraphrasing.
5. They use simple, well-formed sentences.
6. They use frequent repetitions.
7. They use a slow rate of speech with pauses between utterances and after the major content words.

These characteristics of caregiver speech are not universal; rather they reflect cultural norms for addressing infants and toddlers. They are most typically observed in middle-class, European American families. In one cross-cultural analysis, for example, African American adults in the rural South were observed in interaction with their children (Heath, 1989). Adults did not simplify or censor their speech for young children. They frequently did not address children directly but expected the children to hear what they said and to interrupt if they had something to add. Adults and children directed one another's behavior with specific commands. It was just as acceptable for a toddler to command an adult as the other way around. Adults teased children, especially in the presence of others, in order to give the children a chance to show off their quick wit and to practice assertiveness. Within this language environment, children had the opportunity to hear a variety of opinions, gather information to extend their direct experience, and observe shifts in language tone and style that accompany changes in the topic or purpose of the conversation. This example illustrates the variation in communication styles that characterize the language-learning environments of American families.

Other research describes variations in the nature and amount of parent–child interaction that take place during a typical day (Huttenlocher, Vasilyeva, Waterall, Vevea, & Hedges, 2007). In one longitudinal study, 40 families were observed once per month over 2½ years (Hart & Risley, 1992). The observations covered the period shortly before, during, and after the child was learning to talk. The results of the study illustrate the differences in language environments in families. The number of words spoken to a child in an hour varied from 232 to 3,606; the percentage of time that parents were in the same room as the child ranged from 38 percent to 99 percent; and the average number of times that parents and children took turns in an interaction ranged from 1.8 to 17.4.

In addition to documenting differences in the amount of parent speech directed toward children, the study found that the quality of a parent's speech toward the child was positively related to the child's IQ at 37 months of age. A systematic relationship was

Bilingualism

Children all over the world speak more than one language without any problems. The rise in the number of Asian and Latino immigrants to the United States has led researchers to investigate the process through which young children manage the challenges of learning and speaking two or more languages. Children who grow up in multi-lingual families and who continue to have access to multiple languages in early childhood appear to benefit, as evidenced by fewer internalizing and externalizing problems as they enter middle childhood (Han & Huang, 2010).

Young bilingual children are adept at switching from one language to another as the conversational situation demands. This is referred to as **code switching**. In one study of bilingual Latino children in Miami, Florida, the children had access to two vocabularies, one in Spanish and one in English. Rather than knowing two words for the same thing, these vocabularies did not overlap much. Knowing the two languages actually expanded the concepts children could use to express their thoughts in comparison to children who spoke English or Spanish

only (Umbel, Pearson, Fernandez, & Oller, 1992).

Code switching begins at a very early age. Infants growing up in multilingual families begin to acquire first words in both languages and are soon able to use these words appropriately, for example, speaking Spanish to their Spanish-speaking caregiver and English to their English-speaking grandmother (Holowaka, Brosseau-Lapré, & Pettito, 2002). In a study of a bilingual English-Portuguese infant at play with his mother and father, the child switched languages to fill in the gaps in his vocabulary. If he did not know the word for something in one language, he used the other. Similarly, his parents switched languages in order to provide words that were the best match with the child's level of understanding.

Bilingual families can use their language environment to the child's advantage, providing alternative communication strategies to improve communication and understanding (Nicoladis, 1998; Nicoladis & Secco, 2000). The richer the language environment in the two languages, the more readily children will develop bilingual competence. The more opportunities children have to hear

and practice using multiple languages in everyday situations with multiple language partners, the more proficient they become (Silven & Rubinov, 2010).

How do bilingual individuals prevent one language from interfering with another? Research using functional magnetic resonance imaging (fMRI) explored the process by which bilingual individuals inhibit one language while drawing on another (Rodriguez-Fornells, Rotte, Heinze, Nosselt, & Munte, 2002). Individuals who were bilingual from infancy were compared to those who were monolingual. The task involved focusing on words in one language even when words from other languages were presented. Bilinguals could identify the stimuli as words, but they did not process the words for meaning if the word was not in the language they had been instructed to pay attention to. None of the brain areas that are associated with word meaning were activated when the words in the nontarget language were displayed. The implication is that early bilingualism stimulates additional plasticity in brain organization and function to accomplish tasks that require language separation.

Regardless of which language is being spoken, the same regions of the cortex are used to produce and understand spoken language. However, when words from different languages are spoken or presented visually, an additional brain area is activated which is sensitive to monitoring and controlling the language that is in use (Crinion et al., 2006). You can think of this process as a recognition switch that toggles back and forth, alerting the person to which language they are using and suppressing interfering meaning making from other languages.

There appear to be some costs as well as benefits associated with bilingualism. Bilingual children have a smaller vocabulary overall, and in controlled experiments they are a bit slower in tasks that require thinking of words that name a picture. Benefits of bilingualism are evident in many tasks that are associated with executive control, including focusing attention, resisting distractions,

These young children are learning English as a second language. An early exercise is matching letters, their names, and sounds.

Jeffry Myers/Getty Images

monitoring changes in stimuli, and changing strategies between tasks. Bilingualism requires paying attention to a variety of communication cues. As a result, bilingual children are especially adept at integrating multiple sources of information to understand and interpret a speaker's intentions. Bilingualism is viewed as a context that stimulates early and ongoing advantages in cognitive flexibility, selectivity, and control

(Bialystok & Craik, 2010; Kovács & Mehler, 2009; Yow & Markman, 2015).

Critical Thinking Questions

1. Evaluate the following statement: "The human brain has the capacity for a great deal more language competence than is typically observed."

2. Based on the information presented here, propose a plan for parents who want to promote bilingualism in their children. How should they organize the language environment for their children?

3. Examine the potential advantages and disadvantages of bilingualism for young children.

4. Describe how the study of bilingualism contributes to the broader understanding of language development.

---

observed between the quality of a parent's speech toward the child and the family's socioeconomic status. Children in lower socio-economic status families experienced less time with their parents, fewer moments of joint play, and exposure to fewer words. In these families, children were less likely to have their speech repeated or paraphrased by their parents, less likely to be asked questions, and more likely to experience prohibitions placed on their behavior.

Poverty and language development. The relationship of poverty and social class to language development is a topic of some complexity. Exposure to poverty at any point in a child's early years may have a negative impact on language development and cognitive competence. This relationship is primarily a result of disruptions in the quality of parent–child interactions (Allhusen et al., 2006). The stressors associated with poverty often create a home environment that is harsh, where parent–child interactions are infrequent, and the child has difficulty establishing a sense of meaningful connections with adults (Bradley, McKelvey, & Whiteside-Mansell, 2011). Other studies have emphasized that it is not socioeconomic status per se, but the features of parent–child interactions that are typical in lower and higher SES families that influence language development. Four features of parent–child interaction differentiate high SES and lower SES family interactions: the amount of talking, the use of a varied vocabulary, the early use of gestures to convey meaning, and the use of more complex sentences. The way parents talk to their infants and toddlers is closely related to the child's vocabulary by age 4 (Rowe & Goldin-Meadow, 2009). Within socioeconomic groups, the more children experience responsive, stimulating, and symbol-infused interactions with caregivers in the home, the further advanced their language abilities (Hirsh-Pasek et al., 2015).

The language environment can also be undermined by competing auditory events. For example, when parents have the television playing, even when it is just playing in the background, the amount of parent–child interaction is decreased. Studies have shown that when the television is playing in the background at home, toddlers' social behavior declines and their parents engage in fewer conversations with them and are less responsive (Kirkorian, Pempek, Murphy, Schmidt, & Anderson, 2009). As result of a habitual reliance on having the television playing, some parents inadvertently create environments that are disruptive to their toddler's optimal language development.

Question-asking. One component of parent–child interaction that has been studied in detail is **question-asking** by the child. Children as young as 18 months ask questions in order to gather information and accomplish other goals, such as asking permission or clarifying a situation. In one intensive study of four children, they asked an average of 107 questions an hour while engaged in conversations with adults (Chouirnard, 2007). The ability to ask questions of parents begins early in infancy and may be a universal strategy that infants use for information gathering. However, the extent to which question-asking is encouraged depends on the nature of parental responses and the way parents themselves use question-asking in daily conversation. Mothers and fathers use question-asking and requests for clarification to elicit children' speech. Frequent question-asking on the part of adults is related to toddlers' vocabulary and their own question-asking (Leech, Salo, Rowe & Cabrera, 2013; Rowland, Pine, Lieven, & Theakston, 2003).

In middle-class families, children are more likely to persist in sustained questioning where one question is followed by an answer, is followed by another question, and so on. When a child asks a lot of questions and the parent answers and gives additional information, this guides how the child builds a knowledge base and understands the world. A relationship exists between child and parent that allows the child to keep asking questions and to expect informative answers even if a question has to be asked several times in order for the parent to understand it (Harris, 2007). The ability to ask questions allows the child to gain information, trusting that it is all right to do this rather than to be rejected or rebuked with an angry response. By creating this interactive relationship around inquiry and information sharing, the child and parent create a secure base regarding access to information that offers the emotional security from which new and more exploratory forms of curiosity can grow.

Competence of partners. In learning vocabulary, children appear to be sensitive to the competence of their language partners. For example, in one study, 3- and 4-year-olds participated in an experiment where the experimenter appeared to be either knowledgeable and confident or uncertain about the name for a given toy. In the confident situation, the experimenter said things like, "I know right where my friend left her *blinket*." In the uncertain situation, the experimenter said, "I'd like to help my friend, but I don't know what a *blinket* is." Even though the children in both situations learned how the toy worked, they used the name of the toy only if the experimenter appeared confident (Sabbagh & Baldwin, 2001). The implication of this work is that by age 3, children are able to assess the expertise and confidence of the language partner before incorporating words into their vocabulary.

Scaffolding and Other Strategies for Enhancing Language Development.

The process of language learning involves upward **scaffolding** and a process of mutual regulation. Scaffolding is a metaphor for providing assistance in helping someone reach a new, higher level of functioning. Verbal scaffolding refers to the variety of ways that adults help children reach a more advanced level of language competence, for example, by repeating words, offering new words, restating a child's expressions in different words, correcting a child's mistakes, or encouraging a child to say more about his or her ideas (Rodgers & Rodgers, 2004). With assistance, children can be more effective in learning vocabulary and expressing their ideas.

Sometimes a child may be misunderstood because the child's pronunciation is so discrepant from the real word (*ambiance* for *ambulance*; *tommick cake* for *stomach ache*). Adults can scaffold the child's expression by modeling the correct pronunciation. Sometimes an adult will use a word that is a little more advanced than the word the child is using, which helps the child link known vocabulary to the new word or idea. For example, "We call that kind of car that has a top that goes down a *convertible*." Scaffolding is closely related to Vygotsky's idea of the **zone of proximal development**. By interacting with a more verbally competent adult or peer, children are able to reach new levels of linguistic ability (Gregory, Kim, & Whiren, 2003; Landry, Miller-Loncar, Smith, & Swank, 2002; Rowe, 2012).

Adults do not always interact with children by encouraging the child to express ideas in a more mature form. Sometimes, adults restate or simplify their expressions to make sure they are being understood. Through frequent interactions, adults encourage language development by establishing a good balance between modifying their speech somewhat and modeling more complex, accurate speech for their children. Children respond to the scaffolding by expressing themselves in more complete sentences and by using a larger vocabulary. This reflects the idea of mutual regulation.

Adults make use of several strategies to clarify a child's meaning when the speech is unclear. One is **expansion**, or the elaboration of the child's expressions:

CHILD: Doggie wag.
PARENT: Yes, the dog is wagging her tail.

Another strategy is **prompting**, often in the form of a question. Here the parent urges the child to say more:

CHILD: More crackel.
PARENT: You want more what?

In both of these interactions, the adult is helping the child to communicate more effectively by expanding on or asking the child to elaborate on something of interest to the child. The kinds of sentences that parents use help children see how they can produce new sentences that are more grammatically correct and therefore more meaningful to others. These interactions help children express their thoughts and share their experiences with others. This has the benefit of binding the child more closely to his or her social community, while at the same time allowing others to know and understand the child more accurately (Nelson, 2010).

Pre-Literacy and the Language Environment.

Socially interactive rituals, such as telling stories, playing word games, verbal joking and teasing, and reading books together, enhance language development, especially by building vocabulary and preparing children to use language comfortably in social situations. Reading aloud has been identified as an especially important language activity that helps expand a child's language skills and provides preparation for literacy (Hammer, 2001; Wood, 2002). During toddlerhood, an adult may start out by reading picture books and asking the child questions about the pictures. The adult may try to relate the picture to some event in the child's life or ask the child to tell something about the pictures. Thus, just as in scaffolding with respect to language, reading along with an experienced reader can scaffold the child's literacy skills (Leech & Rowe, 2014; Verhoeven, 2001). Over time, the child becomes more and more the storyteller, while the adult listens, encourages, and expands the tale. Some books are read aloud so often that the toddler begins to "read" them from memory or retell the story in the child's own words from the pictures. Books can become a starting point for talk about people, places, and things that can be symbolized through words, even though they are not physically present—e.g. places they have visited, people they care about, or toys and games they enjoy (Rowe, 2013).

By reading aloud and pointing to pictures, parents and their toddlers create an environment for the development of literacy.

As children enter early school age, this type of ritualized reading activity provides a framework for the child's concept of what it means to be a reader. A common list of **pre-literacy** skills includes the following:

Vocabulary—Words and their meanings
Print motivation—Enjoying and being interested in books
Print awareness—Understanding how a book is read, top to bottom, left to right (in English)
Narrative skills—Understanding and telling stories
Letter knowledge—Naming the letters and the sounds they make
Phonological awareness—The small sounds that make up words

Certain language skills, including attention, phonological awareness, and early language comprehension, have been shown to be important predictors of reading ability in the school-age years (Overby, Trainin, Smit, Bernthal, & Nelson, 2012; Walcott, Scheemaker, & Bielski, 2010).

Reading aloud introduces the notion that printed letters make up words; stories usually have a beginning, middle, and end; and printed words and spoken words are similar in some ways. Experiences with handling books, becoming aware of the link between letters and their sounds, beginning to recognize printed words, and practicing the actions associated with reading all contribute to early reading proficiency (Hammill, 2004). Depending on the context in which children read, they may also realize that you can learn things from printed words that you cannot always know from the pictures. They discover that reading is a way to learn about the world beyond what you can know through direct experiences.

Children and parents often engage in language games that expand the child's use of words and phrases. These games are usually part of ongoing family life. They are introduced not as a separate activity, but as an extension of a related activity. The quality of toys, social games, and conversation between mothers and their infants predicts the level of the child's language development at ages 2 and 3 (Lacroix, Pomerleau, Malcuit, Seguin, & Lamarre, 2001). As an example, one mother described one of her 3½-year-old son David's spontaneous games that began to build the bridge from speech to literacy. As the game developed, the object was for David to point to road signs as he rode with his mother to nursery school and for her to read as many of the signs as possible while they were driving along. David had created this game, and his mother played along willingly (Hoffman, 1985).

On the way to nursery school, David said, "Let's talk about signs! What does that sign say?" I answered, "Right turn signal."

David proceeded with, "And what does that yellow and red shell say?"

I answered him, "It says 'Shell'—that's a gasoline station."

He asked, "Does it have seashells in it?"

I answered, "No."

We proceeded to read signs. I read the majority as he requested. However, David read "Speed Limit 35," "Bike Route," and "No Parking Any Time." When we came to "No Parking This Side of Street," he thought it was "No Parking Any Time."

These were the signs that I was able to read as he requested while I was driving. They were not the only ones on the route.

Speed Limit 40	Watch Children
Bike Route (2 times)	No Parking Any Time (20 times)
Speed Limit 35 (12 times)	Signal Ahead (3 times)
No Turn on Red (3 times)	School Speed Limit (2 times)
No Littering	No Parking on This Side
Driveway	of Street (7 times)

By telling stories, reading aloud, and playing word games, children and their caregivers begin to explore a vast array of topics. Books and stories can be a starting point to talk about needs such as hunger or wanting to be comforted, or fears and frustrations. Parents and toddlers can travel along the paths of emotions such as anger, sadness, delight, pride, and shame. They talk playfully with one another, examining new objects, discussing kinship relations, and creating fantasies. Furthermore, adults and young children begin to talk about philosophical and moral questions like lying, helping, "what ifs," and the question "how would you feel if it happened to you?" As children speak from their own inner world, revealing their own point of view, parents begin to know and appreciate their children's concerns and needs in a new way. Similarly, children begin to hear and understand their family's talk in a new way. They can question what they do not understand and expand what they know through family talk.

Talk About Feelings. One area that has received special attention is the role of family conversation about feelings and its relation to a child's ability to express feelings and to identify feelings in others. Talking about feelings is closely related to experiences of validation and feelings of being understood. Consider a child who is afraid to go to sleep in the dark. Think about the difference in a child's experience between hearing a parent say "There's nothing to be afraid of," and hearing a parent say, "Tell me how you feel; let's find a way to help you feel safe." Children's use of words to refer to feelings and to describe emotions increases notably at 3 and 4 years of age. At the same time, children become more skilled at recognizing feelings in others and in understanding how a person might feel in a certain situation (Brown & Dunn, 1992). Acknowledging and talking about feelings are central to the expanding capacity for empathy and self-control. In fact, a common parenting strategy in toddlerhood is to encourage children to "use their words" instead of kicking, hitting, or biting when they feel angry. In contrast, rejecting or suppressing a child's talk about feelings are links to the emergence of a sense of shame and doubt. Toddlers who have frequent experiences of talking with their mothers when they are in distress or conflict appear to be more effective at the age of 6 in understanding the

Doug hopes that by talking with his son about his feelings, they will build a strong basis for communication in the years ahead.

point of view of others and in anticipating others' needs (Dunn, Brown, & Beardsall, 1991).

Some families have a practice of reviewing the events of the day, asking children to tell what was important to them that day and how those events made them feel. These kinds of conversations let children know that adults in the family care about their experiences and want to know more about how they are processing the events of their daily life. Children who grow up in families that are open to identifying and talking about emotions are more likely to carry on this kind of talk at later ages and to show sensitivity to others in relationships outside the family (Jenkins, Turrell, Kogushi, Lollis, & Ross, 2003).

FURTHER REFLECTION *Reflect on the words* language, thought, *and* speech. *What are the differences among these three? How are they interconnected?*

Describe the process through which language acquisition binds a child to his or her culture and social group.

Fantasy Play

OBJECTIVE 3 Explain the development of fantasy play and its importance for cognitive and social development.

Fantasy play and language are contrasting forms of representation. For language to be effective, children must use the same words and grammar as the older members of the family, discovering how to translate their thoughts into existing words and sentences. Fantasy serves almost the opposite function. In fantasy, children create characters and situations that may have a very private meaning. They play with the dolls in their doll house, arranging the baby in the crib or putting grandma doll in the rocking chair. They put little cars on the brick walkway and pretend to race them to the sidewalk. There are probably many times when children have strong feelings but lack the words to express them. They may be frustrated by their helplessness or angry at being overlooked. They can express and soothe these feelings in the

world of imagination, even though the feelings may never become part of a shared conversation (Erikson, 1972). The worlds of make-believe, poetry, fairy tales, and folklore—domains we often associate with childhood—open up to toddlers as their ability for symbolization expands. Pretend play is not possible without semiotic thinking, which underlies the capacity for imagination, for allowing objects and people to take on new identities and new meaning.

The Nature of Pretend Play

During infancy, play often consists of the repetition of a motor activity. Infants delight in sucking their toes or dropping a spoon from the high chair. These are typical **sensorimotor play** activities. Toward the end of infancy, sensorimotor play includes the deliberate imitation of parental acts. Children who see their caregiver washing the dishes may enjoy climbing up on a chair and getting their hands wet, too. At first, these imitations occur only when they are stimulated by the sight of the parent's activity. As children enter toddlerhood, they begin to imitate parental activities when they are alone. A vivid mental image of an action permits them to copy what they recall instead of what they see. This is the beginning of symbolic play. Before the period of pre-operational thought, children do not really pretend because they cannot let one thing stand for something else. Once the capacity for symbolic thought emerges, children become increasingly flexible in allowing an object to take on a wide variety of pretend identities.

Most 2-year-olds are able to understand the context of a pretend situation. Using pretend props, they can pretend to feed a hungry animal or give a drink to a thirsty animal. They can assign a pretend function to a substitute prop, treating a wooden block as if it were a banana or a piece of cake. And they can follow through with the consequences of a pretend situation, like pretending to wipe up pretend spilled tea with a towel. Toddlers can construct a make-believe world in which objects are assigned a pretend meaning (toy blocks can be bananas) and words are used in pretend ways ("feed the monkey a banana" is acted out by putting a toy block up to the mouth of a toy monkey) (Harris & Kavanaugh, 1993).

The Capacity for Pretense

Sometimes, adults wonder whether children can distinguish between reality and **pretense**. The line between make-believe and reality may become blurred for all of us, for example when watching television. Which televised images are pretend and which are real? Are the images and messages used to advertise products real or pretend? Is a television news story real or pretend? Are dramatic reenactments of historical events real or pretend? Are reality shows real or pretend?

In simplified situations, children as young as 2 can tell when someone is pretending and can follow the transformations in a pretend sequence (Rakoczy, Tomasello, & Striano, 2004; Walker-Andrews & Harris, 1993). For example, an investigator might tell a child that she is going to fill two bowls with cereal and then pretend to fill the bowls. The investigator then pretends to eat all of the cereal in her bowl, saying something at the end to indicate that all the cereal is gone. She then asks the child to feed a doll its cereal. Many 2-year-olds and most 3-year-olds can follow this type of scenario, selecting the bowl that is still full of pretend cereal and feeding it to the doll.

Studies about pretense lead to further speculations about what toddlers understand about someone else's mental state. For example, what do toddlers think is going on in someone else's mind as they are pretending? In judging whether someone else is pretending or not, toddlers tend to focus on the way the person is acting and the context of the situation rather than on what the person's intentions might be. Toddlers are quite accurate about judging when someone is engaging in make-believe or in a realistic activity, but they may not be able to tell you what the person is thinking about (Ganea, Lillard, & Turkheimer, 2004; Rosen, Schwebel, & Singer, 1997; Sobel, 2004).

Toddlers know the difference between what an object really is and what someone is pretending that it is (Flavell, Flavell, & Green, 1987). For example, 3-year-olds understand that a sponge is really a sponge, but they can pretend it is a boat floating in the water or a car driving along the road. Three-year-olds also understand the difference between knowing something and pretending something. If they see a rabbit, they know it is real, but they also know that they do not have to have seen a rabbit in order to imagine one. However, compared with older children, 3-year-olds are more convinced that imagination reflects reality. If they imagine something, like a fire-breathing dragon or a horse with wings, they think it may actually exist. In contrast, 4-year-olds understand that something that is imagined may not have a counterpart in reality (Woolley & Wellman, 1993). However, even though most 3- and 4-year-olds know the difference between what a real person or object can or cannot do, they continue to believe in certain imaginary characters like Santa Clause or the Tooth Fairy, who clearly defy many of these "rules" about reality.

How Fantasy Play Changes During Toddlerhood

Toddlers can direct their play in response to mental images that they have generated by themselves. At first, their symbolic play is characterized by the simple repetition of familiar activities. Pretending to sweep the floor, to be asleep, to be a dog or a cat, and to drive a car are some of the early play activities of toddlers. Fantasy play changes in four ways during toddlerhood (Lucariello, 1987; Tamis-LeMonda, Uzgiris, & Bornstein, 2012):

1. The action component becomes more complex as children integrate a sequence of actions.
2. Children's focus shifts from the self to fantasies that involve others and the creation of multiple roles.
3. The play involves the use of substitute objects, including objects children only pretend to have, and eventually the invention of complex characters and situations.
4. The play becomes more socially interactive, more organized and planned, and play leaders emerge.

Early pretense is typically action based. Gradually, children combine a number of actions into a play sequence. From pretending to sweep the floor or take a nap, they devise strings of activities that are part of a complex play sequence. An early sequence might include changing the baby's diapers, giving the baby a bottle, singing the baby a song, and putting the baby down for a nap. In a more advanced sequence, while playing firefighter, children may pretend to be the fire truck, the hose, the ladder, the engine, the siren, the people being rescued, and the firefighters. All the elements of the situation are brought under the children's control through this fantasy enactment.

Second, children become increasingly able to include others in their play and to shift the focus of the play from the self to the others (Howes, 1987; Howes, Unger, & Seidner, 1989). One can see a distinction here between solitary pretense, social play, and **social pretend play**. Children engaged in solitary pretense are involved in their own fantasy activities, such as pretending that they are driving a car or giving a baby a bath. Children engaged in social play join with other children in some activity.

In social pretend play, children have to coordinate their pretense. Play companions' interactions are interdependent. What one child does influences the others. They establish a fantasy structure, take roles, agree on the make-believe meaning of props, and solve pretend problems. As you may guess, participation in social pretend play and creativity are closely related in toddlerhood. The fact that 3- and 4-year-olds can participate in this type of coordinated fantasy play is remarkable, especially given their very limited use of language to establish and sustain coordination (Mottweiler & Taylor, 2014; Rubin, Bukowski, & Parker, 2006).

Third, fantasy play changes as children become more flexible in their use of substitute objects in their play. Fantasy play begins in the areas closest to children's daily experience. They use real objects or play versions of those objects as props in their pretense. For example, they pick up a toy telephone and pretend to call Grandma, or they pretend to have a picnic with toy cups and plates and plastic foods. But as they develop their fantasy skills, these props are no longer essential. Children can create novel uses for common objects like using a bowl for a hat or a scarf for a baby blanket. Sometimes they pretend to have an object when they have nothing, gesturing as if they have a gun or a sword. Despite these remarkably inventive capacities to impose meaning on neutral objects, children's toys have become increasingly more realistic, reflecting the nature of modern technology. Whereas experts in early childhood education continue to recommend the use of flexible, open-ended play materials for young children like blocks or clay, toy makers appear to be enthusiastic about producing realistic play materials like plastic cell phones, kitchens, computers, and carpenter's tools.

Play moves away from common daily experiences to invented worlds, which are often based on stories, television programs, movies, or purely imagined characters and situations. Cultural, religious, and entertainment heroes, heroines, and stories filtered through the cognitive interpretations of young children become the content for pretense. Three-year-olds may generate negative as well as positive imaginary images, including fears about supernatural creatures, witches, ghosts, zombies, and monsters. Children may take the roles of characters with extraordinary powers. They may pretend to fly, become invisible, or transform themselves into other shapes with the aid of a few secret words or gestures. Their identification with a particular fantasy hero or heroine may last for days or even weeks as they involve the characters of the story in a variety of fantasy situations.

The cell phone has become a common resource for pretense as well as for real communication.

Fourth, fantasy play becomes more socially interactive. It becomes more planned and organized as children try to coordinate their pretend play with others. There are new discoveries about what makes pretend play most fun, and a desire to make sure that those components are included in the play. In a preschool or child care group, certain children are likely to take the lead in organizing the direction of fantasy play. They may set the play in motion or give it direction by suggesting the use of certain props, assigning roles, or working out the context of the play. Social skill development and social pretense influence each other. The more socially skilled children are likely to take a leadership role in the coordination of group pretense; as other children participate in these coordinated play scenarios, their social competence is also likely to improve (Li, Hestenes, & Wang, 2016). In the example below, a child demonstrates this kind of leadership:

> STUART (climbing up on a tractor tire): This will be our shark ship, OK? Get on quick, Jeremy! The sharks will eat you!
>
> JEREMY: No! This is my police helicopter!
>
> STUART: Well, OK. We're police. But we need to chase the sharks, OK? I see the sharks way down there! Come on!
>
> JEREMY: OK. Let's get 'em! (They both make helicopter noises and swat at make-believe sharks with plastic garden tools.) (Trawick-Smith, 1988, p. 53)

Some theorists distinguish symbolic role-playing from games with rules, implying that the latter are guided by a formal set of mental operations that constrain play, whereas the former is open and flexible. However, it is clear that pretend play operates within a rule-bound structure (Harris & Kavanaugh, 1993; Vygotsky, 1978c). In order to coordinate **symbolic play** with a partner, children have to come to some mutual understanding about the situation, props, characters, and plot. The players have to limit their behavior in ways that conform to the unspoken or latent rules of the pretense. For example, if the children decide that certain leaves are the pretend food, then no one can use the leaves as bricks to build a house or as hats. If one player is supposed to be

the mommy, that player has to act like the mommy and not like the baby. In games with rules, the rules are more readily spelled out, but in both types of play, part of what makes it fun is to function within the boundaries of certain kinds of constraints.

Dramatic role-playing, in which a child takes on the role of another person or creates a fantasy situation, increases steadily from the ages of 3 through 5. By the age of 6, however, children become involved in games with rules. They may use their fantasy skills during play by making up new games or new rules rather than by engaging in pretend play. If one is looking for the experts in diversified, elaborated fantasy, observe 4- and 5-year-olds.

Theoretical Views about the Contributions of Fantasy Play to Development

Fantasy play is not simply a diversion. Children use fantasy to experiment with and understand their social and physical environments and to expand their thinking (Pellegrini & Bjorklund, 2004). Theoretical views of the importance and value of fantasy play vary widely. Here we consider how Piaget, Vygotsky, and Erikson understood the role of fantasy play.

Piaget (1962) emphasized the assimilative value of play. He believed that through fantasy and symbolic play, children are able to make meaning of experiences and events that are beyond their full comprehension. Fantasy play is a private world to which the rules of social convention and the logic of the physical world do not necessarily apply. From this perspective, fantasy play frees the child from the immediacy of reality, permitting mental manipulations and modifications of objects and events. One cognitive benefit of fantasy play is the opportunity to engage in role reversal, taking turns playing the various characters, which helps to advance perspective taking among play companions.

Vygotsky (1978c) saw fantasy play quite differently.

> Play creates a zone of proximal development of the child. In play a child always behaves beyond his average age, above his daily behavior; in play it is as though he were a head taller than himself. As in the focus of a magnifying glass, play contains all developmental tendencies in a condensed form and is itself a major source of development. (p. 102)

Vygotsky used the term zone of proximal development to refer to the distance between the actual level of a child's performance and the potential level that a child is capable of reaching with help from a more skilled peer or adult. Normally adults—especially parents and teachers—and more advanced peers promote development by engaging children in activities and problem-solving tasks that draw children into their zone of proximal development—the new directions along which their capacities are moving. However, in play, Vygotsky saw a cognitive process that captures a foreshadowing of the child's next higher level of functioning.

In pretense, children address areas where they do not yet feel competent in their lives and try to act as if they were competent. They set rules for their performance, and commit themselves to function according to them. So if a child is pretending to be a good mother, she brings forward all the ideas she has about how to be a good mother and applies them to the pretend situation.

Similarly, if a child is pretending to be a superhero, she imposes all the rules of power, goodness, and helpfulness that she knows of and tries to limit her actions to those rules. Vygotsky regarded fantasy play as a window into the areas of competence that the child is striving to master but are still out of reach.

Erikson (1972) considered fantasy play vital in promoting personality and social development. He valued play as a mechanism for dramatizing the psychological conflicts that children are struggling with, such as angry feelings toward their siblings or parents, or jealousy over a friend's new toys. According to Erikson, the play often not only represents the problem but also offers a solution so that children experience some new sense of resolution and a reduction in the tension associated with the conflict. For example, Leslie is frustrated because her older brother, Harold, got to go with his dad to the movies, and she had to stay home with a babysitter. In play, Leslie goes to the movies, and her doll has to stay home. Symbolic play provides a certain flexibility or leeway in structuring the situation and, at the same time, imposes some limits so that children may experience a new mastery of issues that are perplexing or overwhelming in real life. One way that children use pretend play to explore relationship issues and mastery of puzzling questions involves creating an imaginary companion to serve as a play partner (see the **Applying Research and Theory to Life** box Imaginary Companions).

Pretend play is a form of representational thought—a way that children experiment with the relationships of objects and social roles. For children who have some forms of language delay, observations of their pretense provide insight into their cognitive capacities. Research suggests that high-quality pretend play actually fosters cognitive, emotional, and social development (Bergen, 2002). Children who have well-developed pretending skills tend to be well liked by their peers and viewed as leaders. This may be linked to their advanced communication skills, their greater ability to take the point of view of others, and their ability to reason about social situations. Children who have been encouraged in a playful, imaginative approach to the manipulation and exploration of materials and objects through fantasy show more complex language use and more flexible approaches to problem solving. Children who have frequent opportunities for pretend play—especially with a more experienced play partner—are better able to express their feelings, show higher levels of empathy, and are more aware of their emotional states (Galyer & Evans, 2001; Lindsey & Colwell, 2003).

Pretend play emerges through the coordination of cognitive, motor, and emotional development. At the same time, pretense appears to contribute to the further maturation of these domains. In the context of the preschool, pretense is not the sole contributor to advances in learning, but it contributes to a joyful environment in which new learning can occur. It supports social interactions with peers and adults, and offers a comfortable context in which children can express new ideas, integrate information from life events, and arrive at new insights about important questions they face in daily life (Hopkins, Dore, & Lillard, 2015; Lillard et al., 2013; Snow, 2016).

Fantasy play is essential for the full social, intellectual, and emotional development of young children. Some parents and teachers want to define a young child's cognitive growth in terms of the acquisition of words and concepts that seem relevant to the real world. They emphasize the importance of learning numbers and letters, memorizing facts, and learning to read. However, research on cognitive development suggests that gains in the capacity for symbolic play provide essential foundations for subsequent intellectual abilities, such as abstract reasoning, creativity, and inventive problem solving. What is more, by integrating pretense as a teaching/learning strategy, opportunities for play enhance children's motivation to learn, improve their ability to sustain their attention, and provide practice in using new concepts in innovative contexts (Singer, Golinkoff, & Hirsh-Pasek, 2006).

The Role of Play Companions

Cognitive developmental theory emphasizes representational thought and symbolic play as the natural outcomes of cognitive maturation during toddlerhood. However, the quality of that play as well as its content depend in part on the behavior of a child's **play companions**. Consider the following incident:

> In a university preschool where college students were having their first supervised experience as teachers of young children, a child of 3 made a bid for some pretend play with a student teacher. The child picked up the toy telephone and made ringing noises. The student teacher picked up another phone and said, "Hello." The child asked, "Is Milly there?" The student teacher said, "No" and hung up the phone. Rather than extending the pretense into a more elaborate social pretend situation by saying something like "Who is calling?" or pretending to put Milly on the phone, the student teacher brought the scenario to a close.

As play companions, parents, siblings, peers, and child care professionals can significantly enrich a child's fantasy play. Play companions can elaborate a child's capacity for fantasy, legitimize fantasy play, and help the child explore new domains of fantasy. When mothers are available as play companions, the symbolic play of their 2-year-old children is more complex and lasts longer (Slade, 1987; Tamis-LeMonda, Uzgiris, & Bornstein, 2012). Parents may engage in pretend actions with their toddlers, like pretend eating, caring for the doll baby, or creating the pretend town where the bus or the train travels along, gathering up passengers. As a toddler's capacity for pretense improves, parents' active engagement in the pretense may change, possibly helping to set up the resources for play or talking about the play rather than joining in the play (Ban & Uchiyama, 2015).

When adults are trained to engage in and encourage pretend play, the toddlers show a higher level of ability to coordinate their responses with those of the adults. Toddlers become increasingly skillful in directing an adult's behavior and negotiating changes in kinds of play. Early and frequent opportunities to pretend with older siblings, peers, and parents contribute to a young child's ability to understand other people's feelings and beliefs. As toddlers experiment with pretend roles, construct fantasy situations, and manipulate objects with a play companion, they establish new channels of shared meaning, thus fostering a new degree of awareness about self and others. Frequent opportunities for social pretend play with peers is associated with advances in early learning (Bulotsky-Shearer et al., 2012).

Imaginary Companions

Probably the most sophisticated form of symbolic play is the creation of an **imaginary companion**. An imaginary friend, which may be an animal, a child, or some other creature, springs complete in concept from the mind of the child. It occupies space. It has its own personality, which is consistent from day to day. It has its own likes and dislikes, which are not necessarily the same as those of its creator. Although not all children who have imaginary companions will disclose this information to adults, some studies have shown that as many as 65 percent of young children have imaginary companions, and some children have more than one (Singer & Singer, 1990).

In one study in the United Kingdom, 1,800 children were asked about past or present experience with imaginary companions. Roughly 46 percent said they had one (Pearson et al., 2001). When parents were surveyed about their children, those with imaginary companions were more likely to be firstborn or only children, were judged by parents to be very imaginative in other aspects of their play, and to enjoy magical or fantasy play as compared to other forms of play. Children who have imaginary companions also report a more vivid imagery when daydreaming or engaging in pretend play and more mythical creatures in their dreams (Bouldin, 2006).

Children who have imaginary companions tend to have more extensive language competence that is observable in conversations with their invisible friend (Bouldin & Pratt, 1999; Gleason, Sebanc, & Hartup, 2003). They are also more likely to engage in covert private speech (Davis, Meins, & Fernyhough, 2013). One by-product of having ongoing conversations with an imaginary companion and telling others about one's adventures with an imaginary companion is that children gain practice in storytelling. As a result, children who have imaginary companions also have advanced abilities to produce verbal narratives as evidenced in the way they retell stories, explain past situations to others, and expand on their experiences in social conversations (Trifoni & Reese, 2009). Another by-product is a greater self-knowledge. Compared to children who do not have an imaginary companion, those who do are more likely to understand that they have unobservable thoughts, feelings, and dreams of which adults are unaware (Davis, Meins, & Fernyhough, 2011).

Several functions may be served by an imaginary friend: It takes the place of other children when there are none around; it serves as a play companion for pretend play; it serves as a confidant for children's private expression; it helps to overcome boredom and loneliness; it provides support when children face difficult situations; and it is often involved in their efforts to differentiate between right and wrong (Majors, 2013;

Taylor & Mannering, 2006). Children can distinguish the social relationship they have with their imaginary companion from the relationships they have with parents, siblings, and best friends. Imaginary companions and real friends are viewed as similar in many ways, but children are more likely to comfort and nurture their imaginary friend than their real friend (Gleason, 2002).

Critical Thinking Questions

1. Explain how imaginary friends might get created. What experiences, ideas, or mental states might be necessary in order for an imaginary companion to be invented?

2. Imagine that you are 3 or 4 years old. What type of imaginary companion would you create for yourself? Why? Could you have an imaginary companion now? Is there an equivalent of an imaginary companion in the lives of adults? What functions do they fill?

3. Design a study to explore the similarities and differences between imaginary friends and real friends. What approach might you take to investigate this question? What would be some challenges you would need to overcome in order to pursue this problem?

4. Do you think that having an imaginary friend in childhood has any relationship to creativity and imagination in adulthood? How could you find out about this?

For many children, the child care setting is where they interact with play companions. When children are with the same group of teachers and classmates over time, their play becomes more complex. Because toddlers rely so heavily on imitation and nonverbal signals to initiate and develop their social pretend play, the more time they have together, the more complex their fantasy play will be. Children who have had many changes in their child care arrangements, or who are in settings where there is frequent staff or student turnover are less likely to engage in complex social pretense (Eckerman & Didow, 1996; Hirsh-Pasek, Golinkoff, Berk, & Singer, 2009).

The importance of pretense and the way pretend play is nurtured depends in part on the meaning it is given in one's culture. For example, among the Ijaw of Nigeria, children under 5 are thought to have a special link with the female creator spirit. Adults may watch a young child playing alone, interacting with imaginary companions by giving out pretend food, or speaking to them in a happy tone. Rather than dismissing this activity as child's play, the adults believe that the child is interacting with the spirit world and will take care not to disrupt the activity. An Ijaw woman who wants to become pregnant might try to appeal to a small child, hoping that if she is kind to the child, the child will use this special link to the spirit world to help bring about the pregnancy (Valsiner, 2000). In most U.S. families, the idea that children have imaginary companions may be considered quaint or amusing. But in some cultures, the ability of children to interact with an invented world is viewed with great respect. Among scholars of child development, this ability to create and sustain an imaginary companion is considered evidence of advanced symbolic representation, an emerging sense of self, and a strategy for achieving new levels of self-control.

FURTHER REFLECTION Describe how the capacity for pretense contributes to development in childhood. Evaluate the value contemporary U.S. society places on fantasy play in childhood; in adulthood. What would you expect to observe in a culture that places great importance on individuals' imaginative play?

Self-Control

OBJECTIVE 4 Examine the factors that contribute to the development of self-control, including impulse management and goal attainment.

Do you ever find that you hit the snooze button and roll over for 10 more minutes of sleep even when you know you should get out of bed? Does your mind wander when you need to be paying attention? Do you go for that extra helping of cake when you are trying to lose 5 pounds? These are just a few examples of lapses in self-control. Self-control is frequently noted as a marker of maturity. The ability to control impulses, direct action toward a goal, express and inhibit the expression of emotions, and resist temptation are all evidence of this capacity (Myrseth & Fishbach, 2009). Over time, self-control becomes a foundation for moral behavior.

In toddlerhood, rapid changes in language, motor skills, and purposeful behavior come together as children strive to become meaningfully integrated into their families and communities. At the same time, toddlers encounter new demands to limit their actions, suppress their strong emotions, and modify their requests in coordination with the needs of others. For toddlers, **self-control** is observed in the ability to comply with a request, modify behavior according to the situation, initiate or postpone action, and behave in a socially acceptable way without having to be guided or directed by someone else (Brownell & Kopp, 2007a). In the following sections we consider two components of self-control: (1) control of impulses—a form of self-control directed inward toward managing one's emotional states and drives (see the **Applying Theory and Research to Life** box for a discussion of the expression and control of angry feelings) and (2) self-directed goal attainment—a form of self-control directed outward in action toward mastery of the environment (Carver & Scheer, 2016).

Control of Impulses

Early in infancy, self-control is usually understood as the infant's ability to prevent the disorganization of behavior brought on by overstimulation and to recover from emotional distress. Babies have a variety of internal regulating strategies (Brownell & Kopp, 2007b). For example, by sucking or rocking, babies can soothe themselves. They can also resist overstimulation by turning away from the source of stimulation, crying, or going to sleep.

During toddlerhood, children improve their ability to modify and control their impulses. The case of Colin illustrates how

toddlers may fail to control their impulses. Sometimes, they simply cannot interrupt an ongoing action, even one they know is inappropriate. Colin, age 2 years 9 months, is just starting preschool:

In his relations with children, Colin progressed quickly from a quiet, friendly, watching relationship on the first few days to actively hugging the other children. The hugging seemed to be in an excess of friendliness and was only mildly aggressive. Having started hugging, he didn't know how to stop, and usually just held on until he pulled the child down to the floor. This was followed very closely by hair pulling. He didn't pull viciously, but still held on long enough to get a good resistance from the child. He grabbed toys from others. When stopped by an adult from any of these acts, he was very responsive to reason, would say, smiling, "I won't do it any more," would tear around the room in disorganized activity, and then return to hugging or pulling hair. (Murphy, 1956, pp. 11–12)

From ages 2 to 4, most children are increasingly able to modify and control their impulses and withstand delays in gratification. They also become more willing to modify their behavior because they do not want to cause distress to others. The ability to regulate or restrain behavior is a product of changing cognitive, social, and emotional competencies. As executive functions in the prefrontal cortex mature, toddlers are better able to focus their attention and slow their behavioral reactions. Children become increasingly sensitive to the negative consequences of impulsive acts. At the same time, they develop new strategies to help manage feelings of frustration, such as distracting themselves and redirecting their attention to some alternative activity or toy, creating a pretend scenario in which they soothe themselves through conversation with a fantasy character, using some physical soothing or comforting strategy like thumb sucking or cuddling with a blanket, and seeking comfort or distraction from a parent or play companion (Berger, 2011).

It takes a lot of self- control to cope with her baby sister's screaming. Annie holds her ears and stays calm, hoping someone will come soon to soothe her sister or at least get her out of the bed.

iStockphoto.com/Lisa5201

The Expression and Control of Angry Feelings

The expression of anger, which is important to the child's development of a sense of autonomy, typically generates tension between parents and children. Toddlers get angry for many reasons, including inability to perform a task, parental restrictions on behavior, and peer or sibling rivalry. As toddlers become increasingly involved in directing the outcomes of their activities, they get angry when someone interrupts them or offers unrequested assistance. Toddlers are likely to get angry when they are tired, or when forced to make a transition from something they are enjoying to something someone else wants them to do.

Studies involving observational and mothers' reports provide evidence that during the second year of life, children begin to use physical aggression toward other children. This is especially likely when children want something that another child has or in retaliation if a child hits them (Baillargeon et al., 2007). The most common forms of physical aggression at this age are kicking, biting, pushing, and hitting. Between ages 2 and 5, the frequency of physical aggression declines as children develop effective strategies for self-control.

In addition to physical aggression, some children use relational aggression to harm others. In toddlerhood, **relational aggression** involves behaviors that result in social exclusion by refusing to let a child join in a play activity, making fun of another child, telling another child that you don't want to be his or her friend, or failing to invite one child to a party when many other children in the class or group are invited (Murray-Close & Ostrov, 2009).

Some children are temperamentally more aggressive than others. Although occasional acts of aggression are not uncommon among toddlers, only a small percentage of toddlers are frequently aggressive and irritable (Paulussen-Hoogeboom, Stams, Hermanns, & Peetsma, 2007; Tremblay et al., 2004). These children are characterized by negative emotionality and difficulties in emotion regulation. They are more frequently in a negative mood, get angry

easily, have a highly intense negative reaction to any type of limit-setting, and when upset, have a hard time recovering or returning to a calm state (Calkins & Dedmon, 2000).

Children rely on their parents as models for learning how to express and control anger. The times when parents are angry are very important. Children learn as much or more about the expression of anger from watching their parents when they are angry as they do from verbal explanations or punishment (Bandura, 1977). Children are sensitive to angry expressions directed toward them through both verbal and nonverbal behavior. In some parent–child dyads, anger is a dominant theme in the parenting interactions. Parents who are angry and abusive toward their children provide a model for the imitation of angry behavior. Children are also sensitive to anger between their parents, even when it is not directed at them. Parents' hostility to each other, expressed through quarrels, sarcasm, or physical abuse, increases children's sensitivity to anger and is closely related to disturbances in development (Kochanska, Aksan, & Joy, 2007).

Exposure to parental aggression not only provides a model for the expression of aggression but also creates a stressful environment that is accompanied by physiological reactions, especially activation of the hypothalamic-pituitary-adrenocortical (HPA) axis and the autonomic nervous system (ANS). It is probable that repeated engagement of these stress-response systems results in conflict sensitization, a heightened reaction to conflict that can be experienced as "arousal, anger, anxiety, or the desire to avoid confrontation" (Margolin, Ramos, Timmons, Miller, & Han, 2016, p. 16). For many children, the punitive or hostile family environment creates a lower threshold to the perception of threat and a heightened physiological reaction, which they are less able to regulate. A combination of a lack of parental supports that help children recover from stressors and the dysregulation of internal physiological

responses create a pattern of reactions to conflict that are carried forward into later aggressive behaviors, especially in relationships with peers, love relationships, and parenting (Berlin, Appleyard, & Dodge, 2011; Margolin, Ramos, Timmons, Miller, & Han, 2016).

Not all parenting efforts are directed at inhibiting the expression of anger. In an ethnographic study of the socialization of anger and aggression, three 2-year-old girls and their mothers from a working-class neighborhood of Baltimore were studied in detail. The mothers considered assertiveness and self-defense essential to survival in their neighborhood. Along with socialization strategies that focused on controlling inappropriate aggression, the mothers found many ways to model aggressiveness toward others and to reward certain displays of toughness and assertiveness in the girls' behavior (Miller & Sperry, 1987).

Children who can express anger without losing control make tremendous gains in the development of autonomy. Anger or conflict with parents gives toddlers evidence that they are indeed separate from their parents and that this separateness is legitimate. Children who are severely punished or ridiculed for their anger are left in a state of doubt. They see models for the expression of anger in the way their parents respond to them, and yet they are told that anger is not appropriate for them. The goal in the socialization of angry feelings is to help children find legitimate expressions of anger without hurting themselves or others.

Recall from the opening case how Rena used her tone of voice, physical comfort, and giving Harrison a few choices to help him manage his anger in the classroom. In some preschools there is a "peace table." Typically the peace table has an object that represents peacefulness. The child who is speaking holds the object, and then gives it over to the other child to have a turn to speak. The peace table slows things down so children can step away from the conflict, take time to say what is bothering them, and listen to each other. When children are having angry conflicts, they might be reminded to try using the peace table where they can talk about the problem and try to resolve the conflict.

Different strategies can help young children regulate or reduce the intensity of their anger. These strategies have to be coordinated with the child's temperament and the ecological context in which the anger takes place (Brinkmeyer & Eyberg, 2003; Kochanska, Aksan, & Joy, 2007; Thompson, 1990).

- Increase a child's experiences of positive, responsive interactions with caregivers through playfulness, conversations, positive tone of voice, or comforting touch. This has been found to increase a child's sense of security and willingness to cooperate with parental requests.
- Provide a brief time-out in a nearby quiet area to help children return to a calm state.
- Arouse feelings that are incompatible with anger, especially empathy for a

possible target for one's aggressive impulses.
- Minimize exposure to stimuli that arouse aggressive or fearful impulses.
- Explain the consequences of a child's aggressive actions for others.
- Suggest ideas about acceptable ways to express or release angry feelings such as drawing, going for a run or a bicycle ride, or digging in the yard.
- Model strategies for nonaggressive responses to frustration and conflict. Use peaceful language and talk about peaceful ways of resolving conflict.

Critical Thinking Questions

1. How does the expression of anger help a toddler achieve autonomy? What functions might the expression of anger serve in later stages of development?
2. Why is anger both difficult to express and difficult to control once it is expressed?

3. How does the expression of angry feelings fit in with your ideas about optimal childrearing strategies and socialization goals?
4. There are temperamental differences in the tendency to get angry, and these differences might be accentuated by certain parenting practices. Imagine that you are advising parents about how to respond to their child's anger. What different advice would you give if you thought that the child was especially anger-prone as compared to a child who was especially fearful and inhibited?
5. What might be some gender differences in the experiences of anger and in societal preferences for the expression and control of anger? Do you think there is a biological basis for gender differences in aggressive behavior? What evidence would you need to support your conclusion?

Increasing Sensitivity to the Distress of Others

Toddlers can observe and empathize with distress expressed in others, both children and adults. Moreover, they begin to understand when they have been the cause of someone else's distress (Hay & Cook, 2007; Hoffman, 2007; Zahn-Waxler et al., 1992; Zahn-Waxler, Robinson, & Emde, 1992). Often, the socialization environment helps to focus toddlers' attention on these instances when parents or teachers point out their actions and the consequences. The following observation from a study of family interaction shows how a conversation about negative consequences and a child's concern over his mother's distress contributed to the self-regulation of impulses:

Danny is 33 months old. He and his mother are at the sink washing dishes. Danny blows a handful of suds at his mother and some gets in her eyes. Danny is laughing at this new game.

Mother: No! Nuh uh, Danny. Danny, you got it in my eye. (mild negative affect)

Danny stops laughing.

Mother: Don't do that in my eye, OK? It hurts to get soap in your eye.

Danny: (very serious) I won't. (Brown & Dunn, 1992, pp. 347–348)

Parents and teachers play an important role in socializing toddlers toward concern about the impact of their behavior on

others. Through their talk about feelings and their explanations about what causes happy, sad, or angry feelings, they alert toddlers to the possibility that their actions can have positive and negative consequences for others. Language skills, feelings of guilt and the desire to make reparation, and cognitive capacities including the ability to focus attention and inhibit or modify their actions contribute to toddlers' ability to regulate their behavior in order to consider the other person (Brownell & Kopp, 2007b; Colasante, Zuffiano, Bae, & Malti, 2014; Rhee et al., 2013).

Discipline Strategies and Impulse Control. In toddlerhood, the immediate aim of discipline is to achieve compliance (Edwards & Liu, 2012; Kochanska, Aksan, & Koenig, 1995). A parent typically wants children to stop doing something ("Don't touch those figurines; they might break") or to do something ("Help me put the toys away now; it's time to go to bed"). If the child complies, a parent might respond positively by smiling, patting the child or giving a hug, or complimenting the child for being good, helpful, or obedient. If the child does not comply, a parent may try some form of distraction or offer some choice ("You can help clean up the toys or help me fold the laundry"). Sometimes, when the child is doing something else, a parent may give a "five minute warning" ("In five minutes it will be time to wash up and get ready for bed"). But if compliance is not forthcoming, some type of discipline is likely to ensue. Many parents use a combination of techniques including verbal instruction, verbal warnings, time-out, and praise to encourage compliance (Kremer, Smith, & Lawrence, 2010).

Discipline practices have been described in three general categories (Hoffman, 1977; 2000):

1. **Power assertion:** Physical punishment, shouting, attempts to physically move a child or inhibit behavior, taking away privileges or resources, or threatening any of these things. Any action that takes advantage of a parent's greater power in the parent–child relationship, whether it is due to physical size, control of resources, or threats of violence, can be interpreted as power assertion.

2. **Love withdrawal:** Expressing anger, disappointment, or disapproval; refusing to communicate; walking out or turning away. Love withdrawal implies that a parent's love is conditional upon a child's good behavior. It can be given or taken away.

3. **Inductions:** Explaining why the behavior was wrong; pointing out the consequences of the behavior to others; redirecting the behavior by appealing to the child's sense of mastery, fair play, or love of another person. Inductions build on the child's cognitive understanding of the situation and their empathy for others.

In addition to these three general categories of discipline techniques, parental warmth, modeling desired behaviors, and praise of acceptable or desired behaviors contribute to the development of internal control (Callahan, Stevens, & Eyberg, 2010; Maccoby, 1992). In order to correct their behavior, children must know what acts are considered appropriate as well as how to inhibit their inappropriate acts. Modeling and reinforcement aid children in directing their behavior; discipline serves to inhibit or redirect it.

The manner in which discipline is carried out over time is associated with child outcomes, especially increases in self-regulation, compliance, prosocial behavior, and the eventual internalization of moral standards; or increases in noncompliance, aggressiveness, and low levels of moral reasoning. On the one hand, when parents make greater use of inductions, their children have fewer problems managing their angry feelings or harming others. On the other hand, when children behave in a very angry, aggressive way, their parents are increasingly likely to use power-assertive tactics to limit or control the child's behavior (Choe, Olson, & Sameroff, 2013).

Three features of the approach to discipline appear to be important (O'Leary, 1995):

1. The discipline should be immediate or as close in time to the situation as possible. Laxness in discipline, such as laughing at an undesirable behavior, waiting too long to respond, reprimanding the child sometimes but not at other times for the same misconduct, or inadvertently rewarding a child for misconduct are all practices that are likely to increase rather than decrease the undesired behavior.

2. The discipline for a toddler should be brief. It is important to make sure that the toddler understands what the misbehavior was and why it was wrong, but

the explanation should be concise and presented at the toddler's level of understanding. Punishment involving love withdrawal is especially likely to be carried on too long. The parent should make sure the toddler knows when the punishment is over and not let the child spend hours thinking the parent is still angry.

3. The discipline should be appropriately firm, but not overreactive. The response to noncompliance should be coordinated with the child's behavior, focusing on expressing concern for the harm that was done, engaging the child in talking about how to repair the situation, and setting the stage for what the child might do next (Edwards & Liu, 2012). Practices that are intensely harsh, abusive, or cruel, whether they involve physical, verbal, or emotional intensity, are associated with increases in problem behaviors. Infrequent use of power-assertive punishment in an overall context of a warm, nurturing relationship may be effective in fostering compliance. However, intense and frequent harsh punishment is associated with a variety of maladaptive consequences for children including problems in emotional regulation and poor inhibitory control (Hallquist, Hipwell, & Steppe, 2015; Lucassen et al., 2015; Repetti, Taylor, & Seeman, 2002; Weiss, Dodge, Bates, & Petit, 1992).

Where Does Time-Out Fit as a Discipline Strategy?

Time-out is a widely used strategy to reduce disruptive or noncompliant behavior among young children. Its proper and sensible use is recommended in many programs established to support parenting, especially parenting young children and children who have conduct problems. **Time-out** is generally defined as a specific period of time when a child is removed from opportunities for desired reinforcements such as social interaction, play, or parental attention. There are many variations in the implementation of time-out. The Clark family was very enthusiastic about hockey. They referred to time out as time in the "penalty box." This renaming allowed the family to help their child interpret time out as part of a system of rules about behavior: When the rules are broken, there is a penalty—it has a limited duration and then you can rejoin the group.

As a discipline strategy, we see time out as a combination of power assertion and love withdrawal. The parent/caregiver calmly but insistently directs the child to a nonreinforcing environment—possibly a nearby chair, a specific location in the room, or another room. During the specific period of time-out the child is separated from the reinforcing attention and affection of the parent/caregiver. The more interesting and loving the "time-in" environment is, the more salient the time-out experience will be, and the less often it will need to be invoked. However, the proper use of time-out is in coordination with other discipline strategies, especially explanations about why the behavior was unacceptable, and why the child is being sent to "time-out." The technique has been found effective when the parent is able to remain calm, the time-out period is brief, the reunion re-establishes warmth and communication, and the technique is used in combination with other positive guidance strategies (Morawska & Sanders, 2011).

Harsh Discipline. Harsh discipline, including physical punishment like spanking or use of the strap, yelling, angry and prolonged time-outs, and threatening violence are all associated with negative outcomes. In a national survey of U.S. parents, 22 percent say they often raise their voice or yell at their kids; 17 percent say they use spanking as a form of discipline at least some of the time (Pew Research Center, 2015). Children who are exposed to **harsh discipline** are more likely to show difficulties in aggressive behaviors, noncompliance, difficulties in emotion regulation, and anxiety associated with perceptions of the world as a fearful, threatening place. Thinking back to the attachment system, it is especially disruptive for young children to experience fear of their primary caregiver, since the primary caregiver is supposed to be the source of comfort and security under conditions of threat, not the source of threat itself. The relationship of harsh discipline to emotional and behavior problems has been observed across social and economic groups, and in cross-national comparisons (Olson et al., 2011; Runyan et al., 2010).

Economic hardship produces emotional distress among parents, which is likely to result in harsh, neglectful, or erratic parent–child interactions (McLoyd, 1990). Mothers living in poverty are more likely than more affluent mothers to use power assertion and physical punishment as a form of discipline. Studies of the relationship of poverty to parenting practices and children's mental health have found that the amount of spanking parents use is directly related to the family's current level of poverty. Under conditions of extreme poverty, family conflict and parental stress are most likely to undermine a parent's coping strategies and result in the use of harsh discipline (Pereira, Negräo, Soares, & Mesman, 2015). The conditions of poverty that contribute to harsh parenting are moderated by parental characteristics, such as poor executive functioning, depression, and exposure to harsh parenting as a child; child characteristics such as oppositional behavior, disability, or poor emotional regulation; and neighborhood stressors such as high crime rates; unsafe, chaotic streets; or hazardous housing (Barajas-Gonzalez & Brooks-Gunn, 2014; Deater-Deckard, Wang, Chen, & Bell, 2012; Norlin, Axberg, & Broberg, 2014).

Regardless of their socioeconomic level, the more parents use spanking and harsh discipline—especially when it is used without accompanying emotional support or warmth—the more likely their children are to show signs of emotional distress (depression, fearfulness, and crying) and externally directed behaviors such as arguing, disobedience, destructiveness, and impulsiveness (Conger et al., 2002; McLeod & Shanahan, 1993; McLoyd & Smith, 2002). Infants and toddlers whose home environments are characterized by high levels of conflict, anger, and aggression and who are targets of harsh, cold, unsupportive, and neglectful parenting are at great risk for disruptions in self-regulation. Early experiences of abuse produce repeated physiological responses of fear, anxiety, and stress. Over time, these stress responses result in greater fearfulness, dysregulation of the natural systems that are helpful in calming and controlling emotions, and difficulty regulating anxiety and depression. Toddlers have fewer chances to observe or model effective strategies for handling conflict and are more likely to behave in aggressive ways with peers. The lack of social competence that is caused by harsh parenting is likely to result in peer rejection, weak social relationship skills, and low levels of social integration (Repetti, Taylor, & Seeman, 2002; Repetti, Robles, & Reynolds, 2011).

Individual Differences in the Ability to Control Impulses. The ability to control one's impulses matures over the period from 2 to 4. Nonetheless, some children are better able to inhibit their impulses than others. Two concepts have been used to evaluate how well children can manage their impulses: effortful control and delay of gratification. Both of these aspects of impulse control show individual differences as well as maturation over the toddler years.

Three factors account for differences in toddlers' impulse control (see FIGURE 6.3 ▶). First, toddlers differ in their capacity to empathize with the distress of others. Some children appear to be callous, showing little regard for others and little willingness to make reparations when they are the cause of others' distress. Other children are quick to recognize signs of distress in others, offering care and comfort. Individual differences in sensitivity to the distress of others leads to differences in how upset children might be when their behavior causes someone else's suffering, how eager they are to make reparations, and in how willing the child may be to curb that behavior in the future (Colasante, Zuffianò, Bae, & Malti, 2014).

Empathy has both genetic and environmental foundations. In a study of identical and fraternal twins who were 2 years old, the identical twins showed greater similarity in their emotional concern about and response to others' distress than did the fraternal twins. Moreover, harsh or nurturing parenting is related to a child's concern for others. Mothers who showed a stronger concern for others in their childrearing strategies had children whose empathy was more fully developed. Furthermore, girls were observed to be more empathic than boys (Rhee et al., 2013; Waller et al., 2012; Zahn-Waxler, Robinson, & Emde, 1992).

Second, differences in temperament affect self-control. Children who are more aggressive, active, or socially outgoing may experience more situations in which their actions are viewed as disruptive or in need of control. In contrast, children who are more socially inhibited, withdrawn, or passive may encounter fewer expectations to curb or restrict their behavior.

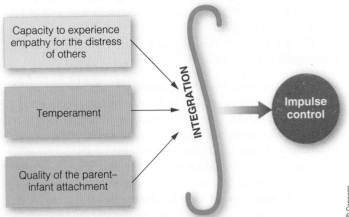

FIGURE 6.3 ▶ Factors Associated with the Ability to Control Impulses

The temperamental characteristic described as **effortful control** refers to a child's ability to regulate his or her response to situations, particularly to inhibit or suppress an automatic response like throwing one's food on the floor and instead to perform a non-automatic response, like saying or gesturing "all done." For example, even when Riley wants to shout out loud, he can talk in a whisper because he sees that Grandpa is napping and he does not want to wake Grandpa. Those infants who are less emotionally intense in their expressions of anger or joy, and who are more cautious in a novel situation, have been found to have greater effortful control in toddlerhood (Kochanska & Knaack, 2003).

Effortful control includes the ability to slow down one's actions on request and suppress movement in response to instructions (e.g., sit still; stop fidgeting; walk, don't run). One measure of effortful control requires a child to move a toy turtle and a toy rabbit along a curved path toward a barn. Effortful control is demonstrated in the child's ability to move the rabbit quickly and the turtle slowly along the same path.

Children show substantial improvement in their effortful control over the period from ages 2 to 4, supported in large part by the continued maturation of executive functions including attention focusing abilities and the capacity for regulating emotional and motor reactions (Li-Grining, 2007; Rothbart & Bates, 2006). However, there are also consistent individual differences that have genetic as well as environmental origins. In a study of identical and fraternal twins, genetic influences accounted for over 60 percent of the variance in the way parents rated their 2-year-olds' ability to inhibit their impulses, with identical twins showing much greater similarity than fraternal twins. However, by age 3, the fraternal twins were becoming much more alike, suggesting that environmental factors were playing a new role. Parents may be expecting their children to function more independently and to show greater patience, and many children are participating in early child care programs where the inhibition of impulses is required in a more structured environment (Gagne & Saudino, 2016).

Third, the capacity for self-regulation may depend on the quality of the parent–infant attachment. Caregiver responsiveness, emotional expressiveness, and a sense of connection are associated with a child's ability to delay gratification. Sensitive caregiving, in which the parent and toddler are able to coordinate their interactions to sustain longer periods of mutually responsive interaction, is associated with an enhanced capacity for self-regulation. Toddlers who experience this rhythmic co-regulation are better able to distract themselves and deliberately guide their attention away from tempting objects that they are not allowed to touch (Kochanska et al., 2010; Li-Grining, 2007).

Since the early 1960s, Walter Mischel and his colleagues have investigated the process by which children delay gratification. To delay gratification, a child must exert willpower in order to resist a strong immediate pull or temptation. This requires shifting attention or distancing oneself from the immediate situation and redirecting attention or action in order to achieve a different goal (Mischel & Ayduk, 2002). For example, when they were at the zoo, Kelly asked for ice cream. Her mother said she could either have ice cream now or go to McDonalds for dinner when they left the zoo. Kelly agreed to wait and go to McDonalds. At age

4, children who delay gratification longer tend to be more intelligent, more likely to resist temptation, demonstrate greater social responsibility, and have higher achievement strivings.

According to Mischel's research, a 4-year-old's ability to use self-regulatory strategies to delay gratification has enduring effects. You have probably watched some version of the famous Mischel marshmallow experiment. Children are asked to wait in a room by themselves where a single marshmallow is sitting in front of them. They are told that when the experimenter returns, they can eat the marshmallow and have another. Children who waited longer in this experimental situation that required a self-imposed **delay of gratification** at age 4 were described more than 10 years later as socially and academically more competent than their peers. Their parents rated these children as more verbally fluent and able to express ideas, using and responding to reason, and more competent and skillful. These children were more attentive and able to concentrate, plan, and think ahead, and they were also seen as better able to cope with frustration and resist temptation (Mischel & Ayduk, 2011; Mischel, Shoda, & Rodriguez, 1989; Morf & Mischel, 2002).

Other longitudinal studies have supported the link between self-control in toddlerhood and subsequent social competence. Children who are able to regulate their emotional reactions and resist temptations in toddlerhood are less likely to violate parental rules, are more likely to plan as they approach new tasks, and as a result, are more likely to be successful in school settings where cooperation and compliance are highly valued (Rothbart, Ahadi, & Evans, 2000; Tangney, Baumeister, & Boone, 2004). Children's self-regulatory competence is associated with many positive outcomes, including better scholastic performance, more successful social functioning, and fewer behavior problems. By adolescence, self-control is a better predictor of academic performance than IQ (Duckworth & Seligman, 2005; Eisenberg, Fabes, Guthrie, & Reiser, 2002). Children who are able to resist temptations are demonstrating that they can outwit their desires, using a variety of strategies to achieve longer-term goals that may be in conflict with immediate pleasure.

As a result of a combination of biological and environmental factors, some children have more difficulty regulating their impulses than others. Children's temperament, the ease with which they become frustrated as well as their inability to focus their attention, interacts with their parents' harsh parenting to compromise the emergence of self-control (Lengua, 2009). Some children show evidence of overcontrol, intense worries and fears, and suppression of emotions. These children who experience unusually intense anxiety are described as having **internalizing problems**. Other children show a lack of ability to suppress their impulses. They experience intense anger in conditions of frustration, an inability to delay gratification, and lack of empathy. Children who experience frequent outbursts of anger are described as having **externalizing problems**. Longitudinal studies link the toddler's inability to manage impulses and later internalizing and externalizing problems (Lengua, Honorado, & Bush, 2007).

The Role of Language and Fantasy in Impulse Control.
Language and fantasy are children's most useful tools for managing impulses. Talking about feelings and needs enables adults

to help children understand more about their emotions and to devise strategies for self-regulation. Although we tend to think of self-control as internally initiated and managed, there are many social prompts that foster self-control and help children manage their impulses (Fitzsimons & Finkel, 2010). Thompson (1990) identified four ways that caregivers use talking about emotions to help young children gain impulse control. First, parents articulate the family or cultural rules about emotional expression: "Don't get so excited; calm down!" or "Stop that fussing; big boys don't whine and cry!" These messages give young children an idea about the acceptable levels of impulses or emotional intensity and about the types of emotions that need to be regulated.

Second, adults help modify the intensity of emotions through reassuring or distracting talk. They may try to distract a child who is worried about getting an injection, try to convince the child that the shot won't hurt, or that it will be just a little sting. They may try to comfort a sobbing child by talking about some happy event that will distract the child.

Third, adults give children ideas for ways to manage their impulses. "Why don't you count to 50, and then I'll be ready to go outside with you." They might suggest that the child think of pleasant times from the past or sing a cheerful song. Adults teach children superstitions, rituals, songs, and stories about how people handle their strong feelings. "Whenever I feel afraid, I hold my head erect, and whistle a happy tune, so no one will suspect, I'm afraid" (from *The King and I*).

Fourth, children listen to and imitate adults who talk about their own strong emotions and impulses. Parents have an outlook about whether or not emotions can be expressed, and this outlook permeates the home environment. One father described it this way:

At least in our household, there is stability. I think with us, there is this stability and this comfort level, so I think some of those emotions that are not necessarily allowed to be showed elsewhere because you don't have security, they can feel comfortable having those emotions because it is a safe place. (Parker et al., 2012, p. 55)

Toddlers who can talk to themselves may be able to control their fears, modify their anger, and soften their disappointments. They may repeat their parents' comforting words, or develop their own verbal strategies for reducing pain and suffering.

The development of symbolic fantasy allows children to create imaginary situations in which disturbing problems can be expressed and resolved. Through fantasy play, toddlers can control situations that are far beyond their real-world capacities (Singer & Singer, 1990; Singer & Singer, 2008). They can punish and forgive, harm and heal, fear and conquer fear—all within the boundaries of their own imagination. Children can use the context of pretense to manage strong feelings and to preserve their emotional control (Galyer & Evans, 2001). When Robbie feels bad about something, he whispers to himself, "Superheroes don't cry." He is making use of fantasy and language to control his emotional state. When children are asked to resist temptation, they use a variety of verbal strategies, including talking quietly to themselves and singing songs to distract themselves (Mischel, Shoda, & Rodriguez, 1989).

Self-Directed Goal Attainment

The second sense in which self-control develops involves toddlers' feelings that they can direct their own behavior and the behavior of others to achieve intended outcomes. During infancy, children become increasingly aware of themselves as causal agents. They make things happen. In toddlerhood, children become much more assertive about their desire to initiate actions, persist in activities, and determine when these activities should stop.

Benjamin at 27 months, 17 days:

When I put him to bed tonight he bellowed at the top of his lungs for a good five minutes from sheer rage that I wouldn't let him get down on the floor and go on playing with his car. What he wants and doesn't want he can be very noisy about—but he can also obviously be rather confused as to what he does want.... This is especially true in the afternoon after his nap. He may wake up demanding a ride or a walk. By the time he gets downstairs, it has switched to "Want to pway bwocks." (Church, 1966, p. 157)

Toddlers' sense of agency—their view of themselves as the originators of action—expands to include a broad array of behaviors. Children want to participate in decisions about bedtime, the clothes they wear, the kinds of foods they eat, and family activities. They want to do things they see their parents and older siblings doing. They also want to direct the behavior of others—taking you by the hand to show you something, giving you some of their cheesy crackers to taste, or bringing a book and climbing up on the couch for some reading. Their confidence in their own ability to handle difficult tasks is not modified by a realistic assessment of their own skills. According to toddlers, "Anything you can do, I can do better." When they have opportunities to do some of these new and complex things and they succeed, they gain confidence in themselves and their abilities. Toddlers feel themselves to be valuable members of the family as they contribute to routine household tasks, like cooking, washing dishes, or sweeping up crumbs. Their feelings of confidence and value are matched by the acquisition of a wide variety of complex, coordinated skills.

You can see how serious Micah is as she helps her dad prepare a healthy smoothie.

The Role of Language in Self-Directed Goal Attainment.
Toddlers use what was described by Piaget (1952) as **egocentric speech** to accompany their behavior. They talk aloud but do not seem to be concerned about whether anyone can hear them or understand them. He described the talk as egocentric because it did not seem to have any social intention. Piaget suggested that the development of communication began with inner thinking of a very private nature.

Vygotsky (1987) proposed a completely different developmental pathway to account for egocentric speech and its function. He represented the scheme as follows:

Social speech → egocentric speech → inner speech

Vygotsky viewed speech as beginning in the social interactions between children and adults or other children. In his view, the first and foremost function of speech is social. Egocentric speech is a transformation of this social speech inward. The child uses speech, initially acquired through interactions with others, to guide behaviors. This speech does not have a social intention; rather, it is a tool for problem solving. Vygotsky viewed egocentric speech and actions as part of the same problem-solving function. The more difficult the problem, the more speech is necessary for the child to find a solution. He noted, "Children solve practical tasks with the help of their speech, as well as their eyes and hands" (Vygotsky, 1978a, p. 26). Eventually, the egocentric speech of an audible nature dwindles (but does not disappear entirely) and becomes inner speech.

The language that guides problem solving emerges from the social interactions with adults and eventually becomes **inner speech**. Often, when young children try to figure out how to work something or how to get something that is out of reach, they turn to adults for help. The talk that adults use as they guide young children is then used by the children themselves to support and guide their own behaviors. Vygotsky referred to this process as the internalization of social speech. In a sense, a child's capacity for self-directed goal attainment depends on what the child has taken in of the spoken, practical advice and guidance given by adults and older peers who have tried to help the child solve problems in the past. In adulthood, these speech-like cognitions are not typically audible; they are experienced as inner talk, or self-talk, that help organize complex tasks (e.g., *first make an outline*), encourage persistence (e.g., *concentrate, stay focused*), or review and revise (e.g., *doesn't fit, try the bigger one*).

Inner speech gives children a new degree of freedom, flexibility, and control in approaching tasks and working toward a goal. They can use words to call to mind tools that are not visible. When striving to solve a difficult problem, young children use private speech both to focus attention on the cognitive aspects of the task, and to manage or regulate their emotions (Damianov, Lucas, & Sullivan, 2012). They can plan steps toward a goal and repeat them to guide their actions. They can use words like *slowly, be careful*, or *hold tight* to control their behavior as they work on a task. Even when engaging in social communication, inner speech may help children regulate their emotions (e.g. *don't yell; stay calm*) or clarify their communication (e.g. *find another word; talk louder*) (San Martin Martinez, Boada i Calbet, & Feigenbaum, 2011). Language skills and self-control operate together to help

children inhibit negative emotions and disruptive behavior during times of frustration (Lynam & Henry, 2001).

In summary, we have reviewed two rather different phenomena under the developmental task of self-control. Children's ability to control their impulses is closely linked to the psychoanalytic concept of delay of gratification, as Freud (1905/1953) used it to describe development during the oral and anal stages. Self-directed goal attainment, sometimes referred to as agency, accounts for children's efforts to increase their competence through persistent investigation and skillful problem solving (Harter, 1982; White, 1960). Self-determination theory assumes that very young children have a natural desire to explore their environment, extend their skills, and achieve new levels of mastery. However, their desire for autonomy and self-directed goal attainment need to be supported and scaffolded by sensitive parenting (Deci & Ryan, 2000). Autonomy-supportive parents foster their toddler's goals, interests, and choices, rather than controlling their behaviors. They may give hints or suggestions as their child tries to accomplish a task, and give encouragement, rather than taking over the task or just telling the child to "work it out on your own" (Whipple, Bernier, & Magneau, 2011).

To function effectively as family members, toddlers must feel confident in their ability to control the inner world of their feelings and impulses and the outer world of decisions and tasks. As toddlers discover that they can tolerate stress, express or withhold their anger as appropriate, and approach difficult tasks and succeed at them, they also lay claim to a growing sense of selfhood.

The more toddlers can do by themselves, the more confidence they have in their ability to control the outcomes of their actions and achieve their goals. Over time, the sense of self-control that is formed during toddlerhood is integrated into adult capacities to overcome obstacles to achieve important goals and to engage in acts of generosity and kindness even when these acts conflict with their own immediate needs.

FURTHER REFLECTION Why is self-control emphasized as a primary developmental task in toddlerhood? How does it relate to the theme of autonomy versus shame and doubt?

Do you know people who have limited self-control? Others who appear to be "over-controlled"? Speculate about how individual differences in self-control play out in later stages of childhood, adolescence, and adulthood.

The Psychosocial Crisis: Autonomy Versus Shame and Doubt

OBJECTIVE 5 Define the psychosocial crisis of autonomy versus shame and doubt, the central process of imitation, the prime adaptive ego strength of will, and the core pathology of compulsion.

During toddlerhood, children become aware of their separateness. Through a variety of experiences, they discover that their parents do not always know what they want and do not always understand their feelings. In early toddlerhood, children use rather primitive devices to explore their independence. They may say "no" to everything offered to them, whether they want it or not. This is the period that people often refer to as the terrible twos. Toddlers seem very demanding and insist on having things done their own way.

Autonomy

The positive pole of the psychosocial crisis of toddlerhood is autonomy. During this period of life, autonomy refers to the ability to behave independently—to perform actions on one's own. Children do not just prefer to do most things on their own, they *insist* on it. Once children begin to work on a task, such as putting on pajamas or tying shoelaces, they will struggle along, time after time, until they have mastered it. They may adamantly reject help and insist they can manage on their own. They will allow someone else to help them only when they are sure that they can progress no further by themselves.

In most cultures, expectations for autonomy are expressed as encouragement for children to perform daily tasks, such as dressing and feeding themselves, playing alone or with peers, and sleeping apart from parents. The exact list of expectations and the age at which these behaviors are to be accomplished varies from one society to the next. Within U.S. society, pressures for autonomy are often expressed in early expectations for skill acquisition and verbal expressiveness. Families in the United States are especially enthusiastic about fostering autonomy, starting with early weaning and separate sleeping arrangements for infants and continuing with efforts to support early locomotion with walkers, scooters, and other toys that foster toddlers' independent movement.

In many non-Western cultures, *interdependence* rather than independence is the valued goal of socialization. Children are likely to experience pressures toward autonomy with the birth of a sibling. Rather than pressing for separateness and distance from the caregiver, toddlers may hover near their mother, distressed at her new lack of availability. Through guidance from older siblings and peers, young children learn to participate in the ongoing activities of the household, watching intently, imitating others, and contributing as they can to daily tasks. Within this cultural context, expectations for autonomy may emphasize the ability to demand less of the mother, to become sensitive to the needs of others, and to function cooperatively with peers (Edwards & Liu, 2012; Harkness & Super, 2012).

The establishment of a sense of autonomy requires not only tremendous effort by the child, but also extreme patience and support from parents. Toddlers' demands for autonomy are often exasperating. They challenge their parents' good sense, goodwill, and good intentions. Parents must learn to teach, cajole, absorb insults, wait, and praise. Sometimes, they must allow their children to try things that the children may not be able to do. By encouraging their children to engage in new tasks, parents hope to promote their sense of competence.

Autonomy-supportive parenting has been defined as incorporating the following characteristics (Joussemet, Landry & Koestner, 2008):

1. Providing rationale and explanation for behavioral requests
2. Recognizing the feelings and perspective of the child
3. Offering choices and encouraging initiative
4. Minimizing the use of controlling techniques

Autonomy-supportive parenting is distinguished from controlling parenting, in which parents use more commands and insist on immediate compliance (Harvey et al., 2016), and from permissive parenting in that it includes active engagement with the child and clear expectations for behavior (Joussemet, Landry, & Koestner, 2008). An underlying motivation is to foster the child's emerging self-regulation and internal motivation, not simply to insist on compliance. Autonomy-supportive parenting has been found to be predictive of higher levels of self-regulation and social competence in toddlerhood as well as subsequent school achievement and socioemotional development in later childhood and early adolescence (Bindman, Pomerantz, & Roisman 2015; Matte-Gagné, Harvey, Stack, & Serbin, 2015).

In the development of autonomy, toddlers may go through a period of somewhat rigid, ritualized, unreasonable nay-saying, but eventually they establish a more enthusiastic, energetic desire for independent action (Erikson, 1963). The behavior of older toddlers is characterized by the phrase "I can do it myself." Toddlers demonstrate an increasing variety of skills. Each new accomplishment gives them great pride. When doing things independently leads to positive results, the sense of autonomy grows. Toddlers begin to create an image of themselves as people who can manage situations competently and who can satisfy many of their own needs. Children who have been allowed to experience autonomy should, by the end of toddlerhood, have a strong foundation of self-confidence and feelings of delight in behaving independently.

Courtesy of Philip Newman

At 2 ½, Sadie is already getting ready to engage in some autonomous scooting, not too fast, but on her own.

Shame and Doubt

Some children fail to emerge from toddlerhood with a sense of autonomy. Because of their failure at most attempted tasks, because of continual discouragement and criticism from caregivers, or most likely because of both, some children develop an overwhelming sense of shame and self-doubt. This is the negative resolution of the psychosocial crisis of toddlerhood (Erikson, 1963). **Shame** is an intense negative emotion that focuses on a negative evaluation of the self. Often it is accompanied by a sense of having been exposed or ridiculed and made to feel inferior to others. When young children were observed in a shame-inducing situation, they exhibited physical tension, avoided eye contact, and were reluctant to talk (Bafunno & Camodeca, 2013). Feelings of shame do not have to occur in the presence of an audience; however, they usually involve at least an imagined notion of how one's behavior might look to others (Tangney, 2001). The literature often discusses shame and guilt as two negative "moral" emotions. But they are really distinct emotions with different precursors and quite distinct relationships to moral development. We will consider the nature of guilt as a feature of the psychosocial crisis of early school age in chapter 7.

One source of shame is social ridicule or criticism. You can probably recall feelings of shame for having had some kind of accident—you spilled your milk or wet the bed or got dirt on your new outfit. Early experiences of shaming are often linked to toilet training (see the **Human Development and Diversity** box Toilet Training). Shame generally originates in an interpersonal interaction in which a child is made to feel embarrassed or ridiculed for behaving in a stupid, thoughtless, or clumsy way (Tangney, Wagner, Fletcher, & Gramzow, 1992). The child may have acted without considering the consequences or was unable to control his or her actions. When you are shamed, you feel small, humiliated, and helpless. Some cultures rely heavily on shame coupled with opportunities for restitution as a means of social control. Children in these cultures grow up with a strong concern about how their behaviors might reflect on their family or result in disrupting the social bond with their community. One of their greatest fears is to be publicly accused of immoral or dishonorable actions that would bring disgrace to their family (Scamier, Schmader, & Lickel, 2009; Scheff, 2003).

The quality of early attachment relationships can also contribute to experiences of shame. Attachment theory suggests that in the process of ongoing interactions between infants and their caregivers, children form an internal working model of self and other. If the child's working model of the parent is rejecting, indifferent, or unpredictable, this is likely to be linked to a sense of the self as unworthy or unlovable. In toddlerhood, the child's representations of self and other become more readily observable in the way they talk about themselves and in their fantasy play. Children whose earlier attachments were insecure are more likely to form a negative representation of the self, including expressing anger, blame, or shame about their actions or feelings (Toth, Rogosch, Sturge-Apple, & Cicchetti, 2009).

As children construct an idea of what it means to be a good, decent, capable person, they build a mental image of an ideal person. Children feel shame when their behavior does not meet the standards of their ideal, even though they have not broken a rule or done anything naughty. In general, shame is associated with feelings that the whole self is bad or worthless. It makes one want to disappear from the eyes of others. Children who have frequently been shamed by their parents in toddlerhood are also likely to exhibit early signs of depression. These two emotions, depression reflecting feelings of worthlessness and helplessness and shame reflecting experiences of parental disappointment or humiliation, are likely to go hand in hand (Luby et al., 2009).

Shame is extremely unpleasant. In order to avoid it, children may refrain from all kinds of new activities. Children who feel shame lack confidence in their abilities and expect to fail at what they do. The acquisition of new skills becomes slow and painful when feelings of self-confidence and worth are replaced by constant doubt. Children who have a pervasive sense of **doubt** feel comfortable only in highly structured and familiar situations in which the risk of failure is minimal. Intense feelings of shame and doubt do not generally result in restitution or prosocial behavior. Rather, shame and doubt often motivate denial, defensiveness, anger, and aggression (Tangney & Dearing, 2002; Tangney & Mashek, 2004). Children's proneness to shame and guilt has been found to predict risky and illegal behaviors in young adulthood (Stuewig et al., 2015).

All children experience some failures amid their many successes. In the process of achieving a new level of separateness, children may discover that they have harmed a loved one, broken a treasured toy, or wandered too far away and become separated from the caregiver at a crowded store or an unfamiliar park. Toddlers often exhibit periods of ambivalent dependency alternating with unrealistic self-assurance as they try to establish a comfortable level of independence from the loved one. The successful outcome to this process requires flexibility and warmth on the part of caregivers who accept and welcome the emerging selfhood of their child while building support for appropriate levels of self-control.

The Central Process: Imitation

Imitation is one of the most widely used and efficient mechanisms for learning. Along with teaching and practice, imitation is a basic mechanisms that supports cultural transmission over generations. Children observe their more skillful parents, siblings, and peers. Each successive generation benefits from observing the skilled behaviors of the previous generation (Caldwell & Millen, 2009). Imitation plays a role in skill learning as well as in social cognition, allowing one person to observe and reproduce the actions, expressions, and gestures of others. Although imitation requires the presence of active models, its outcome is a shift of the action from the model to the imitator. Once toddlers succeed in imitating a certain skill, that skill belongs to them, and they can use it for any purpose they like.

Toddlers seem driven to imitate almost everything they observe. Toddlers' vocabularies expand markedly through their imitation of the words they hear in adult conversations, on television, and in stories. Their interest in dancing, music, and other activities stems from imitation of parents and peers. When one

Toilet Training

Every human culture has practices to remove waste products from close proximity to the social group. The effort to teach children how to dispose of human waste in a culturally appropriate fashion is the focus of what we in the United States refer to as *toilet training* or *potty training*. Any approach to this task reflects a combination of technology, beliefs, and practices. One of the basic issues is whether one believes that the regulation of this training should be left to the child, drawing on a sense of developmental readiness, or given over to others, which usually suggests a training program (Valsiner, 2000).

In psychoanalytic theory, toilet training symbolizes the classic psychological conflict between individual autonomy and social demands for conformity. Children must subordinate their autonomy to expectations for a specific routine regarding elimination. In the United States, the contemporary approach to this dichotomy between autonomy and conformity is advocated by the American Academy of Pediatrics (American Academy of Pediatrics, 2016; Stadtler, Gorski, & Brazelton, 1999). The American Academy of Pediatrics website has an extensive list of articles addressing various aspects of toilet training, including readiness, choosing a potty, and dealing with accidents (https://www.healthychildren.org/English/ages-stages/toddler/toilet-training/pages/default.aspx).

Their advice about toilet training combines waiting until the child is ready and introducing toileting in a guided, systematic fashion. They suggest three areas of readiness: physical maturation, including the ability to sit, walk, dress, and undress; cognitive maturation, including the ability to understand and comply with directions; and social maturation, including the desire to imitate and identify with adults as well as a desire for self-determination and mastery. The process is expected to begin at around 18 months when infants show some interest in the potty and be complete by around age 4 when toddlers will

Spencer is able to relax on a potty just his size, taking advantage of a few quiet moments for reading as he develops his toilet habits.

be able to accomplish both day time and night time toileting. Even when they are managing well during the day, many children continue to have difficulty staying dry through the night well into their middle childhood years.

Experts suggest starting with bowel training and then moving on to urinating in the potty by allowing the child to play near the potty, dropping the contents of the dirty diaper in the potty so the child sees the connection, reminding the child to use the potty when needed, but not to show disappointment when he or she misses or forgets. Patience, reassurance, and praise are suggested while the caregiver encourages increasing compliance with toileting practices (Mayo Clinic, 2014).

This approach, which you may find extremely sensible and right, can be contrasted with the practices of the Digo, a group living in coastal Kenya and Tanzania. The Digo live in huts with mud floors. The smell of urine mixed with the mud is extremely unpleasant and difficult to remove. So the Digo are eager to have their infants urinate

out of the hut as early as possible. Training begins at 2 to 3 weeks of age. The caregiver sits on the ground outside the hut with feet outstretched and places the baby in the appropriate position for urinating. The baby is placed on the caregiver's feet, facing away from the caregiver but supported by the caregiver. While in this position, the caregiver makes a low sound ("shuus"), which serves as a conditioned stimulus for urination. This is repeated frequently, day and night, until the baby urinates in this position following the sound. When this happens, the baby is rewarded with breastfeeding. By the age of 4 to 5 months, Digo babies are trained to urinate only in the culturally approved position and setting (De Vries & De Vries, 1977). In contrast to the recommendations of the American Academy of Pediatrics, this approach places a strong emphasis on training and shows a perception of readiness that is much earlier than the perception of readiness held in the United States and other Western cultures.

Critical Thinking Questions

1. Apply what you have read about toddlerhood, including physical, cognitive, language, and emotional development, to the process of toilet training. What are some developmentally appropriate practices that could support this important goal?

2. Explain how toilet training is related to the themes of autonomy versus shame and doubt.

3. Discuss the role of self-control, including self-regulation and self-directed goal attainment, in toilet training.

4. Compare and contrast the cultural beliefs and goals implied by the U.S. and the Digo approaches to toilet training.

5. Discuss possible caregiver reactions to toileting. Include ways they may foster autonomy or create feelings of shame and doubt.

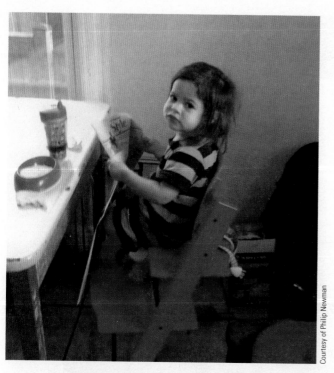

Every morning Micah sees her dad read the paper. Now she likes to do this herself even though she can't read yet.

child in a play group makes a funny noise or performs a daring act, other children seem compelled to recreate this novel behavior.

The imitative behavior of toddlers is different from the socially induced conformity observed in older children. Toddlers are not aware of a great many social norms and therefore feel little pressure to conform to them. Their imitative behavior is really a vehicle for learning. Every act becomes their own, even if it has been inspired by others. There are two complementary motives for imitation during toddlerhood: One is the drive for mastery and skill learning; the other is the drive to feel connected to the social group (Over & Carpenter, 2013).

> Jess liked to imitate adult tasks. When his mother cleaned the house, he followed her with a cloth, trying to dust the tables. When Mark (*Jess's older brother*) fed the dog, Jess helped him by getting the dog's dish. When his father shaved in the morning, Jess took a toothbrush to imitate his father with lathering and shaving motions. He was learning to brush his teeth, even though his span of attention was short at this job and the cleansing ineffective. (Brazelton, 1974, pp. 139–140)

Imitation is a means of participating in and sustaining social interactions, and advancing social cognition (Meltzoff, 2010). In a peer setting, imitation emerges as a strategy for children to coordinate their behaviors with those of other toddlers. Before verbal communication becomes a truly useful tool for establishing or maintaining social contact, toddlers use imitation to feel connected to one another and begin to invent coordinated games. Imitation advances empathy. By watching and repeating the actions of others, toddlers begin to gain insight into the other person's experiences and emotional state (Rogers & Williams, 2006). Imitation can

also be a way to reestablish a sense of belonging after experiences of exclusion or rejection. By mimicking others, especially those the child wants to be connected to, the child increases the target's feelings of liking, closeness, and trust (Lakin, Chartrand, & Arkin, 2008; Watson-Jones, Whitehouse, & Legare, 2016).

The emphasis on imitation highlights the central role of culture at this period of life. In many cultures, adults orient young children toward important tasks and expect them to watch and learn in a process of imitation and shared problem solving (Rogoff, Mistry, Goncu, & Mosier, 1993). Daily events provide models for imitation and reflect the culture of families and communities. Toddlers rapidly accumulate the vocabulary of speech and action that belongs to their cultural group. How visitors are greeted when they arrive at the home; how adults groom themselves, dress, and speak to one another; how household tasks and chores are performed; how older children amuse themselves; how young people and older people treat each other—the thousands of words, gestures, and rituals of daily life make up the culture absorbed by watchful toddlers as they arm themselves with the resources to press toward autonomy.

Given its pervasive role in the early development of children, it is not surprising to learn that imitation is supported by specific neural mechanisms. Research has identified a **mirror neuron system** that underlies a person's ability to observe and then recreate the actions of others as well as to understand the emotions and intentions of others (Iacoboni & Dapretto, 2006; Iacoboni, 2009). The mirror neuron system in humans is a coordinated network of three areas: One area gathers visual information; one recognizes and processes the motor components of the visual information; and one processes the goal of the action. Information from the goal-oriented area is sent back through the system to match up with the original visual information to guide motor behavior. The system supports sensory and motor integration while the person is observing others, imitating others, and being imitated by others. These neurons show activity during observation, and even greater activity while one performs an action that was observed when watching others—in other words, when one is imitating something one is watching. The mirror neurons are sensitive to the intention of the action as well as to the actions themselves. For example, a different pattern of neural firing in the mirror neuron system is observed when a grasping action is linked to drinking from a cup and when grasping is linked to taking the cup away from the table to clean up. The mirror neuron system is considered to be a key to clarifying empathy and our ability to understand others through imitation of facial expressions, body posture, and gestures. Disruptions of the mirror neuron system may be implicated in the social deficits associated with autism (Gallese, 2006).

The Prime Adaptive Ego Quality and the Core Pathology

As a result of the resolution of the psychosocial crisis of autonomy versus shame and doubt, toddlers emerge with the prime adaptive ego quality of will or the core pathology of compulsion.

The ego quality of will provides a sense of being in control of one's thoughts and actions. It is vital to emerging capacities for self-expression, self-direction, and eventually self-fulfillment. In contrast, the core pathology of compulsion reflects pervasive anxiety. Thoughts impose themselves; actions must be carried out over and over. The will is taken hostage by unbidden impulses that must be satisfied.

Will

Erikson et al. (1986) identified the prime adaptive ego quality that emerges through the successful resolution of the psychosocial crisis of toddlerhood as **will**—the capacity of the mind to direct and control action. It is closely linked to the idea of self-directed goal attainment. Will is the inner voice, focusing attention, encouraging, and urging one on, especially in the face of obstacles. It provides the psychological energy that allows people to press harder in competition, work to surpass previous achievements, and reach for new goals. In the face of disability, it is the force that urges the person to make peace with the loss and focus on alternate goals. In the face of crisis, people often refer to their will to survive as the fundamental strength that kept them looking for new solutions or that prevented them from giving up hope. In older people who experience potentially spirit-crushing, painful losses or disabilities, will is the force that provides buoyancy as they learn to accept their decline, and look for areas of continued mastery.

Sometimes, we think of will in a negative way, as associated with stubbornness or overbearing dominance, that is, bending to someone's will. But the meaning of will in the psychosocial context refers to the sense of inner determination and purpose that permits a person to set goals freely and make persistent efforts to achieve them. It reflects the positive connotation of the term *willpower,* the ability to sustain effort and delay gratification in order to achieve a long-term goal (Mischel & Ayduk, 2011). Will leads to a positive belief in oneself as someone who can make things happen. When you see a child struggling to carry a heavy box or drag a wagon filled with toys up a steep hill, you see will in action. When you watch an older child chew and twist a pencil trying to figure out a tough math problem, you see will in action. And when you go to the high school swimming pool at 6:00 in the morning and see students working out or swimming laps to get ready for an upcoming meet, you see will in action.

Compulsion

Will provides a voluntary energy and focus to action. In contrast, **compulsions** are repetitive behaviors that are motivated by impulse or by restrictions on the expression of it. They are nonspontaneous and unchanging. Compulsions are a close relative to the *ritualization* that is developed in toddlerhood. Children at this stage typically devise some well-ordered rituals, especially around important transitions such as going to bed, getting dressed, and leaving the house. They insist that these rituals be followed precisely and become distressed if the rituals are violated. Rituals are efforts to bring control and order to the environment. They are

Will reflects an inner determination to persist toward a goal. Micah shows her will as she pedals fast to reach the neighbor's house, leaving Papa and Grandma far behind.

often associated with fears, such as fear of strangers or separation from loved ones for younger children, or fears of environmental threats such as burglars or illness in somewhat older children (Evans, Gray, & Leckman, 1999). Rituals help provide feelings of sameness and continuity during changes in setting or state that may threaten toddler's feelings of selfhood.

Benjamin at 27 months, 17 days:

His bedtime rituals are changing but still evident. He must be read to—as many books as the reader will stand for—and his music-box must be wound up. And I don't think he knows it's even possible to sleep any way except on the stomach. But he doesn't ask for his three old favorite stories to be told to him any more (thank heaven) and he doesn't always ask to be sung to—sometimes he wants one of three or four particular songs, but by no means always. (Church, 1966, p. 159)

Toddlers' rituals usually do not repeat adult ways of doing things; they are not mere imitations of adult rituals. Their rituals, however, like those of adults, serve the important psychological function of bringing order and a sense of mastery to the unknown or the unpredictable. In comparison to adaptive rituals that actually provide a sense of comfort and relief from uncertainty, compulsions must be carried out again and again, never adequately resolving the anxiety that motivates them.

Obsessive-compulsive disorder (OCD) is a clinical diagnosis of an anxiety disorder that has been increasingly observed among children and adolescents. **Obsessions** are persistent, repetitive *thoughts* that serve as mechanisms to focus anxiety. An obsession is a disturbing idea that cannot be set aside, even if the person realizes that the idea is unreasonable or unlikely. Compulsions are repetitive, ritualized *actions*. A person may try to get rid of a worrisome obsession by carrying out a ritualized set of behaviors. However, the thoughts that trigger anxiety are not permanently resolved through the actions, so the cycle of thoughts and actions have to be repeated again and again. For instance, a person with an obsessive-compulsive disorder may become committed to repeated handwashing to rid the self of preoccupying thoughts about uncleanness. The compulsive handwasher "scrubs his hands in tortured solitude, until they become raw, and yet he never feels clean" (Erikson, 1977, p. 78). Over time, a neurosis may become disruptive to daily life because it takes a lot of time, makes it hard to concentrate on tasks, and the person feels a loss of control.

Cases of OCD have been documented as young as 4 years of age. The pattern of symptoms observed in children and adolescents tends to differ from the pattern observed in adults, and among children the number and severity of symptoms can be quite diverse. Common groups of OCD symptoms among children include (1) mental rituals, touching, and ordering, (2) contamination and cleaning, (3) superstitions, (4) obsessions/checking and confessing, and (5) somatic concerns (Ivarsson & Valderhaug, 2006). One case study described a child who had obsessive fears of choking on a big object at age 4 and needed repeated reassurances that this would not happen. By age 9, the child was diagnosed with OCD (Geffken, Sajid, & MacNaughton, 2005). An overview about the nature of OCD can be found in the brochure published by the National Institute of Mental Health: *Obsessive-Compulsive Disorder: When Unwanted Thoughts Take Over* (NIMH, 2010).

In a sense, people who suffer from obsessions and compulsions have a damaged will. Their ability to willfully direct their thoughts and actions toward a goal is impaired. Rather, they feel that their thoughts and actions are being controlled by some powerful force outside their voluntary control. It is not the same as a hallucination. People with compulsions or obsessions do not think that someone from outer space or some voice from the spirit world is telling them what to do. They recognize the directive as coming from their mind, but not from their will.

Compulsions represent the ego's attempts to provide some structure to reality, but they do not work to promote further development because they are not meaningful (Erikson, 1982). The experience of the doubt-filled, shame-ridden person tends to be continuously unpleasant, uncertain, and sometimes tortuous. Life is enacted around carefully orchestrated patterns of meaningless, compulsive behaviors. The **Human Development and Diversity** box explores autism spectrum disorders, a complex array of developmental disabilities that typically include symptoms involving intense, repetitive behaviors and difficulties with social communication.

FURTHER REFLECTION *How does culture influence the expression of the psychosocial crisis of autonomy versus shame and doubt?*

What are the societal forces that foster the sense of autonomy in toddlerhood? What are the forces that create a sense of shame and doubt?

What are some adaptive functions of rituals? How can you determine if a toddler's rituals are a symptom of a more serious mental disorder?

The Impact of Poverty on Psychosocial Development in Toddlerhood

OBJECTIVE 6 Evaluate the impact of poverty on development in toddlerhood.

In 2014, approximately 47 percent of U.S. children under the age of 6 lived in low-income families (family income is up to 200 percent above the poverty threshold) and 24 percent (5.5 million children) lived in poor families (the family income is at the poverty threshold or below). In 2014, the federal poverty level for a family of three with one child was $19,055 or less. In fact, this is much less than it costs to meet basic needs for housing, food, transportation, health care, and child care expenses. The National Center for Children in Poverty estimates that a family of three would need roughly twice this amount to meet basic needs, an amount that varies by regions of the country as well as urban, suburban, and rural communities (Jiang, Ekono, & Skinner, 2016). In a comparison of 20 rich countries around the world, the United States has the dubious distinction of having the highest percentage of children (21.1 percent) living in poverty (Gornick & Jäntti, 2016).

Poverty and Brain Development

Poverty is associated with conditions that are disruptive to optimal development, including food insecurity, poor nutrition, inadequate health care, poor mental health, limited parental education, child abuse and neglect, lack of stimulating parent–child interactions, and harsh punishment (Yoshikawa, Aber, & Beardslee, 2012). In the first years of life, rapid growth and interdependence among cognitive, social, and physical domains mean that significant modifications in any one system can have a substantial impact on the others. Early malnutrition, iron deficiency, exposure to environmental toxins such as lead, lack of adequate stimulation, and exposure to harsh or neglectful parenting can all impact brain development, including reactivity to stress, ability to regulate anxiety, executive control, memory, and attention (Rodier, 2004; Semeniuk, 2013). It is not surprising that living in poverty, especially conditions that create heightened stress for parents, is associated with high rates of cognitive challenges for children, particularly difficulties with inhibitory control and attention regulation (Lempinen, 2012).

Poverty and Health

Many children from low-income families have no regular source of health care and have not been immunized for measles and

Autism Spectrum Disorder

What Is Autism Spectrum Disorder (ASD)?

ASD is a general term that refers to a range of complex neurodevelopmental disorders characterized by (1) social impairment, (2) communication difficulties, and (3) restricted, repetitive, stereotyped patterns of behavior. According to the CDC, 1 child out of every 68 has some form of ASD.

What Are the Symptoms or Signs of ASD?

The symptoms associated with ASD are typically observed by the age of 2. They may range from mild to severe. In some cases, children may develop normally in infancy, and then show symptoms in toddlerhood. They stop using language, playing, or enjoying interacting with others.

Symptoms observed in infancy, often by 18 months:

Unresponsive to others
Focuses on one item intently to the exclusion of all else
Does not respond when called by name
Avoids eye contact

Symptoms observed in toddlerhood:

Delayed use of language
Lack of empathy
Difficulty interpreting or responding to what others are feeling
Difficulty understanding social cues
Special attachment to one particular object
Likes to line things up; have objects in a specific order
Repetitive movements; self-harming behaviors
Refers to self by name, instead of me or I

Autism intensifies the nature of tantrums

Tantrums do not subside readily
The child may appear not to be able to control behaviors
The child does not respond to parental soothing, talk, or threats
Intense responses: Screaming, crying, resisting contact, pushing others away

Sensory sensitivities

Unusual sensitivity to light, touch, smell, sounds, or taste
Over- or under-reaction to pain or loud noises
Distinctive food preferences

What Causes ASD?

As the term implies, ASD is a complex condition with a variety of symptoms of varying intensity. The condition is considered to be primarily caused by genetic factors, but the root causes are not fully known.

- Twin studies show that if one twin has ASD, there is a 90 percent chance that the other identical twin will also be affected. This supports a genetic basis for ASD.
- Irregularities in brain development, including abnormal levels of serotonin and other neurotransmitters, suggest genetically-based problems in how brain cells communicate with each other.
- These genetic predispositions may be activated by certain environmental conditions in the prenatal period, especially the presence of a virus, or paternal age.

Even if the condition has a genetic basis, it is unlikely that most cases of autism can be traced to one gene. Researchers are identifying a large number of genes that are associated with ASD. What is more, autism has been linked to new mutations in the sperm or egg cells that form the offspring, suggesting some problem in DNA replication, not a condition that is inherited from the parents (Makin, 2015).

What Treatments Are Effective for ASD?

There is no cure and no single best treatment. This is a lifelong condition. However, early screening and early intervention have the best chance for reducing the severity of symptoms and supporting normal development. Common treatment methods include:

- Behavioral management to reinforce desired behaviors and to minimize undesired behaviors.
- Speech and language therapy, occupational therapy, physical therapy.
- Special services within schools: one-to-one or small group instruction,

design of an IEP and ongoing evaluation of progress.
- Medications to reduce anxiety and control hyperactivity

Controversies Around ASD

Although ASD is considered a developmental disability, people with ASD are also known to have many strengths including (NIMH, 2016):

- Having above-average intelligence: the CDC reports 46 percent of ASD children have above average intelligence
- Being able to learn things in detail and remember information for long periods of time
- Being strong visual and auditory learners
- Exceling in math, science, music, or art

Thus, some prefer to use the term "neurodiversity" rather than disorder or disability, suggesting that ASD is one expression of a wide range of neurobiological differences in human cognitive functioning that can be adaptive in some contexts and disruptive in others.

There is a burgeoning literature on ASD. You can find more information at the Center for Disease Control and Prevention website, http://www.cdc.gov/ncbddd/autism, and the Eunice Kennedy Shriver National Institute of Child Health and Human Development (NICHD) website, http://www.nichd.nih.gov/health/topics/autism/Pages/default.aspx.

Critical Thinking Questions

1. What are the signs and symptoms of autism spectrum disorder that you might look for in infants and toddlers?
2. What community resources are available if you suspect that a child has an autism- related condition?
3. What are the pros and cons of thinking of ASD as neurobiological diversity as contrasted with a developmental disability?
4. There is a great deal of ongoing research into the causes and possible treatments of ASD. Using your Internet search skills, what can you find out about new discoveries in this field?

These Cambodian boys help their mother scavenge for resources in the garbage dump near their village. You can imagine all the health risks associated with this activity and their impact on the boys' development.

Sean Sprague/Alamy Stock Photo

Poverty and Academic Outcomes

Early exposure to poverty can have lasting consequences for adult outcomes, especially outcomes related to academic achievement and cognitive abilities. A combination of factors tied to family poverty, including exposure to harsh parenting, disruptions in emotional regulation, and the absence of positive interactions with adults, results in a lack of school readiness and a trajectory of lower academic motivation and subsequent disengagement from school. The benefits of attending high quality preschool for children in low-income families are well known. Preschool enrollment contributes to school readiness, positive attitudes toward schooling, and a reduced risk of dropping out of school. Yet, for a variety of reasons, many parents do not enroll their young children in Head Start or other high quality programs: difficulty in finding *high-quality, affordable* programs in low-income neighborhoods; the number of young children in the family; parental education; and constraints associated with a mother's work schedule (Crosnoe, Purtell, Davis-Kean, Ansari, & Benner, 2016; Pew Research Center, 2015b).

The link between childhood poverty and life-long educational and career attainment is well-documented. A clear connection was found between exposure to poverty in the first 5 years of life and reduced income and hours of work after age 25 (Duncan, Ziol-Guest, & Kalil, 2010). One model for explaining this process focuses on the likelihood that extreme poverty brings with it exposure to **toxic stress**, intense and frequent traumatic events that persistently activate the stress response. Toxic stress in childhood is associated with disruptions in the neurobiological systems that contribute to learning, memory, and cognitive and emotional control. These problems are linked to difficulties in academic performance, heightened risks of mental health disorders associated with anxiety and depression, and maladaptive coping strategies that impact health such as substance abuse and overeating in the absence of energy needs (Hill et al. 2016). You can appreciate how childhood exposure to toxic stress might result in reduced educational attainment, mental health and physical health problems, and impaired cognitive functioning, limiting occupational opportunities and forcing the young person to remain in the impoverished community where continued exposure to toxic stress is likely (Shern, Blanch, & Steverman, 2016).

Poverty Worldwide

In a worldwide analysis Sally Grantham-McGregor and her colleagues estimated that over 200 million children under the age of 5 are exposed to such extreme conditions of poverty, malnutrition, and neglectful care that they are at critical risk for disrupted developmental outcomes (Grantham-McGregor et al., 2007). Poverty for these children is associated with inadequate food supplies, poor sanitation, increased infections and illness, and growth retardation. The mothers of these children have had limited education, and the home environment is barren and unstimulating.

In many countries around the world, poor families live in high-risk neighborhoods where children are likely to be exposed to toxic stress and chaotic conditions, including disruptions in basic services such as water or electricity, violence, and family instability (Ceballo & McLoyd, 2002; Evans et al., 2005). Even in

other infectious diseases. Repeated bouts of illness combined with poor nutrition detract from a child's energy. The combination of malnutrition and illness has multiple consequences, including the possibility of structural brain damage, lethargy, delayed physical growth, and, as a result, minimal exploration of the environment. All these factors taken together produce what has been observed as delayed psychomotor and cognitive development in toddlerhood (Brown & Pollitt, 1996; Pollitt, 1994). Poor health in childhood has a lasting impact on adult health (Halfon, Inkelas, & Hochstein, 2000).

Poverty Impacts the Parenting Environment

Families in poverty are a diverse group, characterized by a range of conditions that could present challenges to optimal development. Think about Harrison who came from a chaotic home environment, but whose mother placed him in a caring preschool. With the support of thoughtful early childhood teachers, Harrison was able to manage his outbursts, become more relaxed, and enjoy being part of the preschool group. Love, caring, warmth, and responsiveness can produce children who emerge from impoverished conditions with great strengths.

The specific consequences of poverty depend on the ways in which poverty impacts the childrearing environment. For example, young mothers whose education is disrupted by early childbearing and mothers who are suffering from depression are also likely to have reduced financial resources. However, educational level and depression are associated with different consequences for children. Mothers' educational attainment is strongly associated with their children's vocabulary and school achievement. Among low-income families, children whose mothers have had fewer years of school have lower levels of school readiness and do worse on standard measures of academic achievement. Maternal depression is a different risk factor, associated with the child's social skills. Children whose mothers are depressed are less cooperative, less compliant, and show more evidence of oppositional or defiant behaviors in preschool (Perry & Fantuzzo, 2010).

the United States, parents whose incomes are $30,000 or below are more likely to describe their neighborhoods as dangerous places. They are more likely to worry that their children will get beat up, attacked, or shot, or that they might get in trouble with the law (Pew Research Center, 2015a). In many poor communities, schools are inadequate, adults have completed fewer years of schooling, and there is relatively little encouragement for education. As a result, the children who live in extreme poverty will attend fewer years of school and have less earning potential as adults. As they enter adulthood, they will have more children than adults who had more years of education and be less able to provide the educational or economic resources for their children that will support optimal growth in the next generation. Investment in the nurturance, safety, education, health, and nutrition of young children worldwide is critical in order to alter the trajectory of an intergenerational pattern of lost developmental potential.

FURTHER REFLECTION *What are some implications of Grantham-McGregor's assessment that 200 million children worldwide are exposed to conditions of extreme poverty? Given what you know about development in infancy and toddlerhood, how might early and ongoing exposure to poverty impact a country's economic, social, and political future?*

What do you think might be the most effective two or three policies that could buffer children from the negative long-term impact of poverty on development?

Applied Topic: Child Care

OBJECTIVE 7 Apply a psychosocial analysis to the topic of child care, emphasizing the impact of the kind of care and the quality of care on development during toddlerhood.

Every person who expects to combine parenting and employment or schooling must give some thought to how to provide **child care**. In the United States, child care arrangements are highly diverse. Child care in the United States is covered by minimal federal and state regulations. Thus, children are in the care of a wide range of caregivers with varying types of education and training, from no specific background and training at all to bachelor's and master's degrees.

Because of the growing national need for child care and the wide choice of child care arrangements, parents, educators, and policymakers are asking such critical questions as: What is the optimal child care arrangement for specific children, especially for infants versus toddlers and for children with particular disabilities or temperaments? How does child care influence the development of young children? What is our obligation to ensure quality child care for the children of working parents? What is our obligation as a society to meet the health, nutrition, and safety needs of the children of poor parents?

In 2011, 61 percent of children under the age of 5 were in some type of child care arrangement. This means that a parent or guardian identified one or more types of arrangements that were used at least once a week. The remaining 39 percent of children

had no regular arrangement, meaning that they might be in school, in self-care, or in arrangements that varied from week to week (Laughlin, 2013).

In the national survey of child care arrangements, child care providers were classified as relatives or nonrelatives of children. *Relatives* included mothers, fathers, siblings, and grandparents; *other relatives* were aunts, uncles, and cousins. *Nonrelatives* included in-home babysitters, neighbors, friends, and other nonrelatives providing care in either the child's or the provider's home. Another subcategory of nonrelative care was *family day care providers* who care for two or more children outside of the child's home. *Organized child care facilities* included day care or child care centers, nursery schools, preschools, and Head Start programs. Kindergarten/grade school was also included in the organized care total for children 0 to 4 years of age. The largest group, 42 percent, was in care with a relative; 23.5 percent in some type of organized center-based care; and 11 percent in some form of nonrelative care. Eighteen percent were in multiple arrangements on a regular weekly basis (Laughlin, 2013). Fathers and grandparents were especially important sources of care for young children, particularly for those whose mothers are employed full time.

Organized child care facilities reflect a variety of philosophies about the care of young children, wide differences in curriculum, and a wide range of physical settings. As opposed to the public schools where there are state standards and regulations about the curriculum, time and amount of instruction, and certification of teachers, the U.S. approach to the care of infants and toddlers is highly variable. Whatever arrangements a child's parents can patch together seem to be acceptable. However, most early childhood experts agree that there are markers of quality care that have an impact on children's daily experiences as well as on their long-term cognitive, emotional, and social development. These markers include:

- Advanced training in the field of child development and early childhood education for the caregivers
- A small caregiver-to-child ratio and smaller group size
- A safe, clean environment
- Sensitive, developmentally appropriate interactions between caregivers and children
- Strong, respectful, positive relationships with children's families (Honig, 2012; Watson, Koehn, & Desrochers, 2012)

Table 6.3 lists the 10 standards for accreditation by the National Association for the Education of Young Children. This list provides an idea of what families might look for in trying to evaluate whether a center is likely to support positive developmental outcomes for their child. The question of how to evaluate the quality of child care and its relationship to child outcomes is not as obvious as one might think. At least four dimensions need to be considered: (1) What is the definition of quality and how is it measured? (2) What is the child's exposure to this care? For example, how many months and for how many hours per day are the children in care? (3) Who are the children in question? For example, how old are the children? Are they from low-resource families? Are they in multiple care arrangements? (4) What specific outcomes are being measured?

Table 6.3	NAEYC Standards for Accreditation of Quality Child Care Centers and Preschool Programs
Standard	**Definition**
1. Relationships	The program promotes positive relationships among all children and adults, and encourages each child's sense of individual worth as well as belonging to and contribution to the community.
2. Curriculum	The program implements a curriculum that promotes learning and development in social, emotional, physical, language, and cognitive domains.
3. Teaching	The program uses developmentally, culturally, and linguistically appropriate teaching approaches that recognize differences in learning styles, needs, interests, and backgrounds to help all children learn.
4. Assessment of Child Progress	The program is informed by ongoing systematic, formal, and informal assessment within the context of reciprocal communications with families and sensitivity of cultural contexts. The assessments are helpful to guide curriculum planning, to tailor instruction to children's strengths and needs, and to identify children with developmental disabilities in order to ensure that they receive appropriate services.
5. Health	The program promotes nutrition, safety, and health.
6. Teachers	The program employs and supports a teaching staff with the educational qualifications, knowledge, and professional commitment needed to promote children's learning and development and to support families' diverse needs and interests.
7. Families	The program establishes and maintains collaborative relationships with each child's family, being sensitive to family composition, language, and culture and striving to create bonds of mutual trust and respect.
8. Community Relationships	The program establishes relationships and uses resources in the children's communities to support program goals.
9. Physical Environment	The program has a safe and healthy environment including both indoor and outdoor facilities, equipment, and materials to support learning and development.
10. Leadership and Management	The program effectively implements policies, procedures and systems that support staff, fiscal management, program delivery, and compliance with licensing regulations.

Source: Adapted from NAEYC, 2016, The 10 NAEYC Program Standards.

Assessments of child care's effects on young children generally focus on intellectual abilities, socioemotional development, and peer relations. Research has tended to emphasize the impact of child care on the children of families living in poverty because they are at a higher risk for school failure, illiteracy, and subsequent minimal employment or unemployment, even though they are less likely to be enrolled in center-based care than families with more resources. Many studies focus on Head Start—a federally funded early childhood program that has a complex mission, including education, health, mental health, and family support. However, not all child care programs have the same educational emphasis or developmental curriculum as Head Start. Many studies that investigate the impact of child care do not systematically control for the differences in program focus, services, and hours of service that exist among public and private child care and preschool programs.

Efforts to assess the impact of early child care arrangements on subsequent development are often discussed as causal relationships (e.g., participation in quality early child care results in cognitive benefits). However, these causal statements should be treated cautiously. About 18 percent of young children experience a combination of care arrangements including parental and family member care as well as center-based and nonrelative care, and these arrangements may change from year to year. Experiences with multiple care arrangements and frequent changes in arrangements have been found to be associated with behavioral difficulties even when the settings are of good quality (Morrissey, 2009). The quality of care a child experiences can be assessed, but the many factors that might account for why some children are in high-quality care and others are in poor-quality care, or why some children are in care for many hours a day and others are in care for few hours a day cannot be fully measured or controlled. As a result, it is best to think of studies that evaluate the impact of early child care arrangements as associational rather than causal.

The Impact of Child Care on Intelligence, Cognition, and Academic Achievement

Results of a growing body of research suggest that the effect of quality child care on toddlers' cognitive development is positive but modest (Auger et al., 2014; Ludwig & Phillips, 2007). Data from model programs show that quality child care contributes to intellectual achievement, as reflected in higher IQ scores, both during the preschool years and during the first grade (Burchinal et al., 2000).

Because of the questionable validity of IQ scores for very young children and for children from various racial and ethnic subgroups, the focus on IQ as an indication of program impact may be inadequate. Thus, studies have focused on more specific competencies such as language ability, pre-reading and pre-writing skills, vocabulary, cognitive problem solving, and motivation for school and school achievement as evidence of the long-term impact of child care on intellectual development (Love, Chazan-Cohen, Raikes, & Brooks-Gunn, 2013). Studies of participation in Head Start or Early Head Start (a program for infants to age 3) find initial cognitive benefits in vocabulary, reading, math, and general school readiness. However, by early elementary school, children who were in control or comparison groups were performing at about the same level as those in the Head Start interventions. Certain subgroups of children may benefit more from participation in high quality Head Start programs, especially those whose mothers are recent immigrants, where English is not their primary language spoken at home, and whose mothers have not had much education prior to immigration (Cooper & Lanza, 2014; Love, Chazan-Cohen, Raikes, & Brooks-Gunn, 2013).

Even studies that did not find lasting cognitive advantages in elementary school found evidence for later benefits in school engagement, school completion, attitudes toward learning, and health. For example, children who attended center-based care in pre-kindergarten were less likely to be chronically absent in kindergarten (Gottfried, 2015; Puma et al., 2012).

The National Institute of Child Health and Human Development (NICHD) began a longitudinal study of the effects of early child care in 1991 (National Institutes of Health, 2000). The primary aim of the study was to learn what impact child care has on developmental outcomes above and beyond the influence of family and home environment. In this study, 1,300 children under 1 month of age and their families were identified as participants from 10 sites across the United States. The study followed children into early adolescence, ages 14 and 15. Families varied by race, income, family structure, mother's education and employment status, and the number of hours children spent in nonparental care. The quality of care was measured with a focus on caregiver interactions that are expected to promote positive emotions, social competence, and cognitive and language skills. For more detailed information about this national longitudinal study, look for the SECCYD study on the NICHD website.

Findings from this research suggest that family variables were *more important* predictors of a child's development than the quality of child care in infancy, toddlerhood, and even in middle school. "Higher levels of parenting quality predicted greater levels of tested reading, math, and vocabulary achievement in fifth grade, and lower levels of teacher-rated externalizing problems and conflict and high levels of social skills, social-emotional functioning, and work habits in the sixth grade" (Belsky et al., 2007, p. 693).

However, there were some benefits of participation in quality child care. After all the family factors were taken into account, the quality of language stimulation directed to the child in the child care setting made a significant additional contribution to children's language and cognitive competence. Children in higher quality care had higher scores on measures of cognitive development, language, and school readiness (National Institutes of Health, 2000; NICHD, 2006).

Follow-up studies have found evidence of long-term consequences of exposure to early child care. By the sixth grade, a positive relationship was observed between experiences in quality care and measured vocabulary (Belsky et al., 2007). By age 15, there was continued evidence of a benefit to high-quality care as measured in adolescents' academic performance (Vandell et al., 2010).

For children from low-income families, experiences in high-quality child care can partially offset the negative associations between poverty and subsequent math and reading skills. High-quality child care proved to be a benefit with regard to school readiness at age 3, which was then strongly associated with higher scores in measures of math, reading, applied problem solving, and language skills in grades 5 and 6 (Dearing, McCartney, & Taylor, 2009). In an Australian sample, a positive relationship between center-based care providers and young children was found to improve their vocabulary and reduce behavior difficulties, especially for children from low-income families (Gialamas et al., 2015).

In addition to test score benefits, children who have participated in model programs and Head Start are less likely to be placed in special education classrooms or to be held back a grade. These advantages are of significance in thinking about the tradeoff in costs and benefits of providing early educational experiences to children at risk of school failure (Ludwig & Phillips, 2007).

The Perry Preschool Project, a model program that has carried out extensive longitudinal research on its participants, has documented a number of indications of academic success. In the mid-1960s, 123 African American children from very-low-income families were selected to participate in this program. They were randomly assigned to a quality preschool intervention or to no preschool. At age 19, children who had attended a quality preschool program had higher grades, fewer failing grades, a more positive attitude toward school, and a higher literacy rate than a comparable group of young adults living in poverty who had not participated in a quality child care program (Schweinhart et al., 2005; Schweinhart & Weikart, 1988). Most (95 percent) of those who had participated in the study were re-interviewed at age 27. The group that had the preschool experience continued to show evidence of the benefits of their early childhood education. Those who had attended the quality preschool were 30 percent more likely to have graduated from high school or received their GED. They were four times more likely to be earning $2,000 or more per month, and three times more likely to own their own homes (High/Scope, 2003).

The Impact of Child Care on Social Competence

Quality care is also associated with higher levels of social competence, self-esteem, and empathy. Children who interact positively with adults in their child care settings are more likely to continue to interact positively and comfortably with their teachers and classmates in the elementary grades. Children who experience frequent, high quality interactions with their care providers at ages 2 and 3 are better able to focus their attention and regulate their emotions when they are in early elementary school. Especially for low-income children, frequent positive interactions with care providers over longer periods of time are associated with fewer behavioral problems in the elementary grades (Burchinal, Magnuson, Powel, & Hong, 2015; Gialamas et al., 2014).

Some studies have found that children with more hours of child care experience are less compliant with their parents' wishes than children who have not been in day care. The study conducted by NICHD helps explain these findings. The more time children spent in nonmaternal care, the less responsive mothers were to their children at 15 and 36 months, and the less affectionate the child was to the mother at 24 and 36 months (NICHD Early Child Care Research Network, 2002). These findings were strongest for children who were in low-quality care for the longest time periods. Even when children were adolescents, the consequences of experiences in poor quality care and long hours of care continued to be observed. By age 15, the more hours a child spent in nonfamily care as a toddler, the more they were observed to have difficulties controlling their impulses as an adolescent (Vandell et al., 2010). However, this relationship is moderated by parental sensitivity. Over the years from preschool to adolescence, children who have spent long hours in poor quality care are more likely to be observed as impulsive and as having problems with behavioral control when they also have parents who demonstrate insensitive care (Burchinal, Lowe Vandell, & Belsky, 2014).

Some children are more affected by the quality of their early child care experiences than others (Pluess & Belsky, 2010). Children who were characterized as having a difficult temperament in infancy, especially high levels of negativity and irritability at 6 months, were compared to children who were characterized as low in negativity at 6 months. In sixth grade, these two groups of children were rated by teachers on behavior problems and teacher–child conflicts. For the children who had low levels of negativity, there was no relationship between their experiences in high- or low-quality child care and the way teachers rated their behavior in sixth grade. For the children who had high levels of negativity as infants, the experiences in high- or low-quality child care made a big difference. If the children who had a more difficult temperament also experienced low-quality child care in toddlerhood, they had many more behavior problems and teacher–child conflicts. If the children who had a more difficult temperament were in high-quality child care, they had fewer behavior problems and teacher conflicts than the low-negative children, even those who had been in high-quality care. When evaluating the long-term consequences of early child care experiences, it is important to take into account variations in children's susceptibility to environmental conditions.

Quality child care also has an impact on peer relations. Children benefit from opportunities to interact with a variety of peers in settings where adults are readily available to help them make choices and resolve differences. The quality and complexity of social play are especially enhanced when children remain in the same child care setting rather than moving from one arrangement to another. In stable conditions, toddlers, whose verbal skills are limited, expand their strategies for coordinating their play with others and for exploring shared fantasies. Children who are growing up in difficult and impoverished life circumstances are especially likely to benefit from stable, consistent caregiving practices where they can form a secure attachment to the caregivers and experience calm, friendly interactions with peers (Ritchie & Howes, 2003). Long-term benefits for peer relations were observed for the participants of the Perry Preschool Project when, at age 19, they were more likely to report that they provided help to their friends and family than were comparison participants, but less likely to volunteer without pay for community service (Schweinhart & Weikart, 1988; Schweinhart et al., 2005).

Few of the evaluations of model programs or Head Start have addressed long-term social consequences. However, results from the Perry Preschool Project showed that by age 19, fewer of the children studied had committed delinquent acts or had been processed by the courts, fewer had been on welfare, and more had

In quality child care, the learning environment combines positive social interactions with many opportunities to foster children's natural curiosity. Armed with their magnifying glasses, these boys bring a new sense of wonder to their observation of a snail.

been employed (Barnett, 1996). In the follow-up at age 27, those who had been enrolled in the quality preschool program were less likely to have been arrested for drug dealing, men had been married longer, and women were more likely to be married and less likely to have had a child out of wedlock (High/Scope, 2003).

Child Care and Physical Activity

Concerns are being raised about the need for young children to have more physical activity in their daily routine. According to the U.S. Office of Disease Prevention and Health Promotion, children should have at least 60 minutes of moderate to vigorous physical activity a day (ODPHP, 2016). Vigorous physical activity contributes to aerobic capacity as well as muscle and bone strength. For toddlers and preschoolers, health experts suggest at least 30 minutes of adult-guided activity and 60 minutes of free-play activity daily. Toddlers should not be sedentary for more than 60 minutes at a time except when they are asleep (KidsHealth, 2014).

Given these recommendations, researchers have been examining the amount and quality of physical activity among toddlers and preschoolers in various types of early child care. Children who are in some type of child care setting are typically more physically active while they are at their center or preschool than when they are at home (Hesketh, Griffin, Simon, & van Sluijs, 2015). In a study of physical activity in 35 U.S. centers, children were observed to spend an average of 9 minutes per waking hour in moderate to vigorous physical activity (Henderson, Grode, O'Connell, & Schwartz, 2015). The strongest predictors of frequent physical activity in centers include encouragement for free play, time spent in outdoor play, suitability of the indoor play spaces for large muscle activity, and encouragement from teachers for active play. We think of toddlers as naturally active. However, observational research suggests that children in care will not get the amount of vigorous physical activity they need unless there is focused attention on motor development as a part of the curriculum and the design of the environment.

Benefits Associated with Head Start

Head Start is more comprehensive than most preschool or child care programs. As a result, it has the potential for a broader range of benefits to children and families than other programs. The Head Start program standards include requirements for the staff to provide children and families with comprehensive services related to health and nutrition. Staff must assist parents in using available resources for immunization; regular checkups; screening for health, vision, and behavioral problems; and regular preventive dental care (U.S. Code of Federal Regulations, 2002, 2015). In 30 studies that reported on the health impact of Head Start, the data showed that participating children are more likely to get a wide variety of examinations and assessments covering medical and dental health, speech and hearing, vision, and nutrition. Because Head Start provides meals, young children in the program have a much higher daily nutritional intake than similar children who are not in the program (Zigler & Styfco, 2004). All of these opportunities allow a direct response to young children's physical needs when their parents may not be aware of emerging problems or are unsure how to address them. The following health benefits have been documented through systematic research (NHSA, 2016):

- Mortality rates for 5- to 9-year-old children who had attended Head Start are 33 to 50 percent lower than the rates for comparable children who were not enrolled in Head Start (Ludwig & Miller, 2007).
- Head Start children are more likely to receive dental checkups and have healthy eating patterns than nonparticipants (Lee et al., 2013).
- Head Start children have lower Body Mass Index (BMI) scores and are less likely to be overweight compared to children in nonparental care (Lee et al., 2013).
- Preschool age children who were obese, overweight, or underweight and who participated in Head Start had a significantly healthier BMI by kindergarten entry than control children (Lumeng et al., 2015).
- Head Start improves adult health status for graduates; they are 7 percent less likely to be in poor health as adults than their siblings who did not attend (Deming, 2009; Johnson, 2010).
- As adults, Head Start graduates are 19 percent less likely to smoke than their siblings who did not attend,- and savings from reduced health costs are equal to 36 percent to-141 percent of the program costs (Anderson et al., 2010).
- The Head Start Trauma Smart program integrates training for program staff and parents, support groups, classroom consultation, and individual child treatment to support children who have experienced trauma; the program has decreased children's need for special education services (Holmes et al., 2015).

As an additional benefit, Head Start has a positive impact on families and communities. A key area of Head Start programming is parent education and parent involvement. Parents whose children are in Head Start are less likely to spank their children and spend more time reading to their children than parents whose children are in other kinds of child care programs (Puma et al., 2005). Head Start has provided education, training, and career development for millions of parents and community members. It has mobilized over a million community volunteers to assist in Head Start classrooms, and most of these volunteers were once Head Start or Early Head Start parents. Head Start has created hundreds of thousands of jobs, the majority of which are held by people who live in the low-resource communities where the programs are located. Thus, Head Start contributes to the advancement and engagement of community adults, drawing on their talents to contribute to the quality of education in their communities (NHSA.org, 2016).

Directions for the Future of Child Care in the United States

In his 2013 State of the Union address, President Obama proposed creating a universal pre-kindergarten program. The program would include several components:

> "financial assistance to help parents pay for infant and toddler care; additional investment in the Early Head Start programs; and a proposal to partner with states, matching their investments dollar-for-dollar, with a goal of subsidizing preschool based on income" (Cohn, 2013). Prekindergarten would not be required for all children, but it would be accessible and affordable for all.

Given the current political climate, the probability of any immediate action on this proposal is low. States vary widely in their support of pre-kindergarten access. There are 50 programs in 40 states plus DC that offer state-funded pre-kindergarten programs. Four-year olds are the primary target, making up 86 percent of the children enrolled. At present, these programs are far from universal. If we consider children enrolled in state-funded pre-kindergarten, Head Start, and special education preschool programs, 41.5 percent of 4 year olds and 14.5 percent of 3 year olds are enrolled (Barnett et al., 2015).

Concerns about the need for affordable, quality child care are expressed by parents who are in the labor market as well as by those who would like to be in the labor market. Worries about child care arrangements are a significant source of stress for working parents. Concerns about child care continue throughout toddlerhood and well into the elementary school years when children need adult companionship and supervision before and after school hours. Services for certain groups, including children with disabilities, those whose parents have evening work schedules, children who are ill, and those who need year-round programs, are in short supply. Many families living in low-income communities do not have access to quality care.

National welfare policies add pressure on the need for affordable, quality child care services. In the past, for example, Head Start programs, which have been an important resource to children in low-income families, have not offered full day care. However, because mothers of young children who were previously receiving welfare benefits are required to enter the labor market, they need to find full day care for their children. Consider the dilemma of a woman who was trying to locate quality care for her child:

> I called child care agencies. . . . And I interviewed all the people they [the state] gave me with licenses. I sat in some of the places for quite a while. I saw drugs being sold in and out of those places. I found one place I thought my daughter would be secure. She was sexually abused. I think that was the thing that really gave it to me then: I quit my job and went fully back on the welfare system. (Scarbrough, 2001, p. 267)

Quality, affordable child care is one of the primary resources that single parents rely on in order to stay off welfare. Without some form of child care subsidy, women cannot support themselves and their families on what they are typically able to earn in jobs that pay a minimum wage. Even with such a subsidy, the likelihood of finding a high-quality setting is low, and the risks to toddlers of spending time in a poor-quality setting are great.

FURTHER REFLECTION Imagine that you have to decide about child care arrangements for your child. Given what you have read about the developmental tasks and the psychosocial crisis of toddlerhood, what features of the child care arrangement are most important for optimizing development for your child?

Given what you know about the diversity of U.S. families and the current economic and political environment, what do you think are the most likely trends for child care arrangements in the coming 10 years?

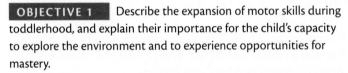

CHAPTER SUMMARY

OBJECTIVE 1 Describe the expansion of motor skills during toddlerhood, and explain their importance for the child's capacity to explore the environment and to experience opportunities for mastery.

The developmental tasks of toddlerhood support children's ability to express themselves through action, language, fantasy, and self-directed goal attainment. The tasks of toddlerhood all contribute to a child's ability to participate in and feel a sense of connection to the social group. Locomotive skills heighten toddlers' sense of mastery and expand their boundaries of experience. Advanced motor skills highlight the dynamic interaction of brain development, physical growth, opportunity, and practice.

OBJECTIVE 2 Summarize the accomplishments in language development and outline the features of the language environment that support communicative competence.

Language is both a tool for the expression of feelings and concepts and a primary mechanism of socialization. Communicative competence relies on both genetically-based capacities for symbolic representation and exposure to a language system. Certain language skills are more vulnerable to the timing of exposure than others, illustrating an important feature of plasticity. Toddlers' use of language gives us clues as to their cognitive and social development. Through language, children gain access to worlds of information, learn new strategies for the control and expression of their impulses, and form meaningful connections with others.

OBJECTIVE 3 Explain the development of fantasy play and its importance for cognitive and social development.

The emergence of fantasy provides toddlers with an internal, personal form of symbolic representation. Fantasy allows a pseudomastery in which barriers are overcome and the limitations of reality are less important. In fantasy, toddlers experiment symbolically with objects, roles, and events that occur in their daily lives. Conflicts can be acted out, and pretend solutions can be found. Fantasy may be enhanced by language, but it thrives even in the absence of words.

OBJECTIVE 4 Examine the factors that contribute to the development of self-control, including impulse management and goal attainment.

Efforts at self-control—both impulse regulation and self-directed goal attainment—begin in toddlerhood and continue through life. Temperamental differences in negative emotionality, anger proneness, fearfulness, and activity level can all influence the child's ability to achieve self-control. At the same time, these differences are shaped by parenting practices that help or disrupt children's capacities for regulation. Self-control is a foundational capacity that predicts subsequent adaptive functioning in school, peer relationships, and moral behavior.

OBJECTIVE 5 Define the psychosocial crisis of autonomy versus shame and doubt, the central process of imitation, the prime adaptive ego strength of will, and the core pathology of compulsion.

The psychosocial crisis of autonomy versus shame and doubt reflects the child's needs for self-expression and mastery in the context of their social group. Young children develop individuality by exercising the skills that develop during toddlerhood. Self-doubts result from repeated ridicule, shame, and failure. The adaptive ego quality of will, directly linked to self-directed goal attainment, emerges in a positive resolution of this crisis. In the context of shame and doubt, the child is likely to rely more and more on compulsive, ritualized behaviors.

Autonomy and individuation are given different values across cultures. Within the context of parent–child relationships, children learn in what ways they are expected to become self-sufficient and self-expressive and to what extent they are expected to fit in or blend in with others. Toddlers are avid observers, imitating and incorporating parental behaviors and values into their own routines. Parental interaction, acceptance, and discipline all contribute to a child's emerging sense of individuality and connection.

OBJECTIVE 6 Evaluate the impact of poverty on development in toddlerhood.

Living in poverty poses challenges to optimal development during the prenatal period and infancy, and these risks continue throughout toddlerhood. Poor nutrition, lack of health care, harsh or neglectful parenting, and exposure to chaotic neighborhoods can all influence the direction of cognitive development, emotional regulation, social competence, and sense of control. Growing up in a very poor community increases the likelihood that parents will be psychologically unavailable or will use harsh, restrictive disciplinary strategies that produce shame or unexpressed rage in their young children.

OBJECTIVE 7 Apply a psychosocial analysis to the topic of child care, emphasizing the impact of the kind of care and the quality of care on development during toddlerhood.

Increasing numbers of young children are being cared for in group settings. The impact of child care depends largely on the quality of the personnel, the nature of the program, and an appropriate physical environment. The most important predictor of children's social and cognitive maturation is the quality of parenting they receive. Nonetheless, many studies find a consistent relationship between quality child care and cognitive development, especially in the area of language acquisition. Whereas the contributions of quality child care are modest but positive, the consequences of poor quality care can be seriously disruptive. A major policy concern is how to expand affordable, high-quality care for those families that need it.

CASEBOOK

For additional case material related to this chapter, see the case of "Little Raymond," in *Life Span Development: A Case Book*, by Barbara and Philip Newman, Laura Landry-Meyer, and Brenda J. Lohman, pp. 77–80. The case illustrates ways in which a toddler uses language and fantasy to cope with frustration when his mom's boyfriend interferes with his play.

Starting school brings an expansion of the child's social world: encounters with new adults and peers, new social norms, higher expectations, and new information. Each of these changes has an effect on the child's self-concept.

1. Describe the process of gender identification during early school age and explain its importance for the way a child interprets experiences.

2. Summarize the process of early moral development, drawing from theories and research to explain how knowledge, emotion, and action combine to produce internalized morality.

3. Analyze changes in the self-theory, with special focus on the theory of mind and self-esteem during the early-school-age years.

4. Describe the features of peer play, including group games, media play, and friendship in the early-school-age years.

5. Explain the psychosocial crisis of initiative versus guilt, the central process of identification, the prime adaptive ego quality of purpose, and the core pathology of inhibition.

6. Define the concept of school readiness, and analyze its relation to the developmental tasks of early school age. Summarize obstacles that may prevent children from being able to adapt and learn in the school environment.

EARLY SCHOOL AGE (4 TO 6 YEARS)

7

— CASE STUDY Gloria Remembers Being 5 Years Old —

Gloria Johnson-Powell recalls growing up, a middle child among five siblings, in an African American family living in a predominantly white neighborhood in Boston. As an adult, she studied medicine, became a psychiatrist, and joined the faculty at UCLA and then Harvard medical schools. Going back to live in Boston after many years away, the conflicting memories of her early years stimulate a reconstruction of her view of self in society as a small child.

Going to nursery school was a major event for me, but I'm not certain if all of my siblings had the exciting experience of going to St. Mark's Congregational Church on Townsend Street for nursery school. It was only a block away from our house on Elbert Street and, on some occasions, I was allowed to walk that block while my mother stood at the corner and watched. I can remember feeling so grown-up, almost as big as the big kids—Barbara and Alice (*her older sisters*).

I can remember that as early as 5 years old I decided that I did not want to grow up. The glimpses into the adult world that I perceived were too complex and troubling for me. As a child I had minimal responsibilities. I could think what I pleased without any contention, and was free to play, to dream, and to learn at will. I even had my own closet where I would go to play or to daydream, but most often to read without disturbance. I loved the cocoon in which I lived and had no desire for any transitions except my promotions in school. Indeed, my scholarly pursuits became the security cloak to protect me from having to enter the real world where I felt I could not compete with my dark skin and my long, very thin body. Besides, black was not beautiful in a predominantly white world. (Johnson-Powell, 1996, p. 56).

CASE ANALYSIS Using What You Know

1. Gloria recalls with some pride being able to walk by herself from home to school. Do you have any similar memories of your own sense of initiative and purposeful behavior in the ages 4–6? Any recollections of other activities that made you feel "grown up"?

2. Gloria had a special private place where she felt safe to imagine and to read. Do you recall any similar spot where you felt protected from the demands of the adult world? Explain why a child might need this kind of place.

3. Gloria reflects on certain aspects of her self-concept, especially her appearance, her race, and being the "little sister." Try to recall the features of your own self-concept that were taking shape at this age. Were some a source of shame? Were some a source of pride?

4. Analyze this case from the perspective of the biological, the psychological, and the societal systems. How does each of these systems contribute to the sense of self that is emerging for Gloria in her early childhood?

The period of early school age brings children face to face with new and complex socialization forces. By the age of 6, virtually all children in the United States are enrolled in school. Before they start kindergarten, most children have school-like experiences in child care, nursery school, early childhood programs, or prekindergarten to prepare them for the environment and demands of school. School brings new information and experiences, new opportunities for success and failure, and new settings for peer group formation. School is a source of influence on the child beyond the family. Beliefs and practices followed at home may be challenged by teachers or classmates. Parents' personal hopes and aspirations for their children may be tempered by the reality of their children's school performance. Although the law requires children to attend school, many are found to be lacking the cognitive, emotional, and/or behavioral maturity to do well. This leads to the question of what it takes to be ready to go to school.

Most early-school-age children exhibit wide-ranging curiosity about all facets of life. "How does this work?" "Why is that the rule?" "Why can't I do that?" The child's self-concept is transformed in coordination with exposure to new socialization voices. In addition to family and school, the peer group, neighborhood, and television all influence children's self-concept during early school age. Once children become aware of alternatives to their own families' rules and patterns, they may begin to question familiar notions. The press toward *independence of action* seen in the toddler is now accompanied by a new *independence of thought* in the early-school-age child. ●

Developmental Tasks

During the early-school-age period, between the ages of 4 and 6, children are constructing an overview of how their interpersonal world is structured and where they fit in. They are devising a scheme for self in society. Because children's life experiences are limited and they are still highly impressionable, the nature of this initial worldview is likely to be very compelling, permeating their outlook in the years ahead. The lessons from early childhood about what it means to be a good person, to be a good boy or girl, man or woman, to be cherished or despised are established at a deep emotional and cognitive level. These ideas are intertwined with feelings of being safe, loved, and admired or neglected, rejected, or abused. As a result, the basic beliefs about oneself and others that are formed at this time are often difficult to change.

In this chapter, four developmental tasks are discussed that contribute to a child's capacity to construct a worldview: gender identification, moral development, self-theory, and peer play. The topic of gender identification includes a discussion of the neurobiological, physical, cognitive, emotional, and social domains as they become integrated into an early scheme for thinking of oneself as male or female. Issues of right and wrong surface constantly as a result of the child's newly acquired abilities for independent thought and exposure to a wide range of social influences. These experiences provide the basis for early moral development. The self-concept expands markedly during early school age. This developmental task centers on the acquisition of a personal self-theory that becomes increasingly

In early school age, children's worlds expand as they spend more time playing with friends, going to school, and exploring their neighborhoods.

complex because it is being stimulated by many new social influences. Accompanying the development of the self-theory is the development of a set of complex feelings about self-worth called self-esteem. A fourth area involves new levels of participation in friendship and peer play. Through the process of learning the rules and playing cooperatively with others, children begin to form meaningful friendships and mental representations of ways of participating in groups.

Gender Identification

OBJECTIVE 1 Describe the process of gender identification during early school age and explain its importance for the way a child interprets experiences.

Every human society has patterns of organization based partially on gender. Male and female individuals are often assigned different roles, engage in different tasks, have access to different resources, and are viewed as having different powers and attributes. The specific content of these gender roles varies from one culture to another. As children form their concept of gender identity, they must integrate their own physical experiences, knowledge, and observations with the socialization messages coming to them from parents, siblings, peers, and other salient voices of the culture.

In this and other discussions of **gender identification**, you will want to differentiate among three concepts: sex, gender, and sexual orientation. **Sex** refers to a person's biological maleness or femaleness, which is determined by chromosomal information. An infant's external genitalia are typically used as the evidence to determine sex. In most cases, the chromosomes and the hormones that are produced in the prenatal period converge to produce an unambiguous sex. However, there are exceptions. The term **intersex** is used to refer to conditions in which a person's external genital anatomy does not match their genetic chromosomal status. Researchers are discovering that biological sex is more of a spectrum than the generally accepted dichotomy between male and female would suggest. Recent studies have identified 25 genes that contribute to sexual diversity. The expression of these genes may be observed in genital abnormalities at birth, but in some cases they are not recognized until puberty, or when problems with infertility arise in adulthood. An estimated 1 in 100 people have some type of intersex condition, resulting in a growing advocacy for a more differentiated view of sex than the current social and legal systems support (Ainsworth, 2015).

Gender refers to the integrated cognitive, social, emotional, and behavioral patterns associated with being a boy or girl, man or woman in one's culture. In childhood, gender identification includes learning to identify oneself as a boy or girl in one's family, friendship group, and community; learning and internalizing the community's expectations for how boys and girls ought to behave; and sensing how well one meets the social expectations for a boy or girl. Some children, described as transgender or gender nonconforming, demonstrate mannerisms, choice of clothes, activity preferences, or use of self-referents that conflict with social expectations associated with the sex they are were assigned at birth (Lev & Alie, 2012; Olson, Key, & Easton, 2015).

Sexual orientation refers to one's preference for and attraction to sexually intimate partners. Sexual orientation can be thought of as ranging along a continuum from exclusive attraction to the same sex to exclusive attraction to the other sex. Four sexual orientations discussed in the literature are *heterosexual*, *homosexual*, *bisexual*, and *asexual* (American Psychological Association, 2008). In the acronym LGBTQ, L stands for Lesbian (females whose primary sexual attraction is other females); G stands for Gay (males whose primary sexual attraction is other males); and B stands for Bisexual (females or males who are attracted to both females and males). T stands for Transgender and refers to one's gender, not one's sexual orientation. Q may stand for Queer or Questioning. It is an umbrella term to reflect that the person identifies as outside the societal norm, but does not want to be constrained by a specific label. The term Queer provides a link to a community of people who accept gender and sexual diversity.

> Why does it matter how I'm different, when I'm different, or why I'm different? Just let there be a place in this society for difference—of any sort—and accept me any way that I am or am not. Accept me as queer. (PFLAG, 2016)

Sexual orientation is not a primary topic of discussion in this chapter. However, it is important to appreciate the distinction between sexual orientation and gender identity, particularly in this chapter because of questions raised in research on the relationship of the sexual orientation of parents to the gender identity of their children.

— **CASE STUDY** Gender Identification in Early Childhood —

Lee, a mother of six children, recalls with warmth and humor her early childhood years growing up in New Mexico in the 1920s and 1930s.

I was born in the southern part of New Mexico in Ruidoso. The town was up in the pines in the mountains and was mostly just a main street that followed the river. There was a meadow on one side of the river with a lot of Indian arrowheads and shards and the biggest grasshoppers in the world. I used to go catch grasshoppers and find arrowheads, and my cousin Bob and I would wander around by ourselves.

My father was a carpenter and my mother had planned to be a nurse until she stopped and got married. I think my father must have really wanted a son because I was quite a tomboy and grew up as his only son. I helped him dig and move rocks instead of learning how to cook and sew. We had a large family, uncles and aunts and a grandmother and great aunt, with houses right next to each other and big, traditional holiday dinners with everybody there.

My cousin Bob was two years younger than I was and we were inseparable.…He was a rough, tough little kid. We ran around without coats in the winter and hardly ever got sick. . . . It was almost like two boys because we used to go to the river and fish with our hands and churn the fish over a little fire and try to eat it. We just grew up like little wild things. My parents expected me to be on the premises by nightfall, but that was about it. We played cowboys and Indians with the other kids in the neighborhood, and we never played with girls at all; they were really something to be scorned. But he was allowed to cuss and have good tantrums that I wasn't allowed to have.

My mother always provided books and she would tell stories about Huckleberry Finn. The river in our town was much too small for a raft; it was rocky and was just a stream, but we'd pretend rafts and imagine running away. One time I got tied up on an Indian raid and left there, and I was too stubborn to call for help, so I was there past supper time and my mother found me and brought me in. I was always tearing up my clothes, and my mother was always tearing me up about that. I think she would have liked to have a daughter. It wasn't until my sister Barbara was born that she had a daughter. Barbara had long curls and was pretty feminine. That way mother had the daughter to play with and daddy had the son and everything was all right.

Source: Excerpt from *Dignity: Lower Income Women Tell of Their Lives and Struggles*, by F. L. Buss, pp. 173–174. Copyright 1985 University of Michigan Press.

CASE ANALYSIS Using What You Know

1. Summarize the aspects of the formation of gender identification that are captured in this narrative.

2. Describe the mental representations of her mother and father with which Lee may have identified.

3. Analyze the role that the context of the physical environment may have played in Lee's experiences of gender identification.

4. Hypothesize about factors that contributed to Lee's preference for rough-and-tumble play. What role do you attribute to her desire to be "the son" for her father? What role do you attribute to her temperament and other aspects of her personality?

5. From what you have read, and drawing on your own experiences, imagine how Lee's gender identification at this period

of her life might influence her later relationships with male and female peers and her capacity to form intimate relationships in later adolescence or early adulthood.

A Framework for Thinking About Gender Identification

Our goal in the discussion that follows is to explore how young children begin to understand gender. Gender is a dimension of the self-concept, an organizing principle of social life, and a guide to behavior. We do not expect a lifetime's work on gender identity to have been completed by 6 years of age. During this stage, however, significant cognitive, emotional, and social changes make gender more meaningful and highlight the relevance of gender for a child's overall self-concept. Gender is among the very early social categories upon which children base inferences about others. Establishment of gender identification links a child to others of their gender reference group and influences their interests, preferences, and social interactions (Ruble et al., 2004).

Gender identification is a product of the interaction of the biological, the psychological, and the societal systems. Biological factors including brain organization and physical capacities combine with socialization pressures and a child's own understanding of the demands of the situation to create experiences of positive, enjoyable action. In one culture, a 4-year-old girl may feel happy and competent when she is playing with a toy loom, learning to weave as her older sisters and her mother do, while in another culture a 4-year-old girl may feel happy and competent when she is playing pretend school with a friend. These gendered states are emotionally and behaviorally satisfying. They draw on cognitive and motor skills that are well developed for girls and are socially encouraged by adults and peers in the community. As a result, there is a desire to repeat them. Over time, these experiences become increasingly more likely and draw the child into a pattern of gendered interpersonal interactions, play, and learning activities. However, they are not inflexible. A girl who most enjoys playing pretend school with friends can engage in rough-and-tumble play if her male cousins come over for a visit or when her dad comes home from work. As in the case of Lee, a girl can experience rough-and-tumble play as her most pleasurable activity, and still know that she is a girl.

Our analysis of gender identification focuses on four components: (1) understanding the concept of gender, (2) learning gender-role standards and stereotypes, (3) identifying with parents, and (4) forming a gender preference.

Children are actively constructing their gender identity in light of their physical body, unique talents and preferences, socialization messages, temperament, and the gendered behaviors of others (Martin & Ruble, 2010). Children of this age ask a lot of questions about reproductive and sexual topics, take great interest in the nature of household and family roles, and try to figure out how their status as a male or female fits into their self-theory. The outcome of this work will differ from child to child. Most of the literature on gender differences acknowledges that differences within groups of males or females are greater than the average differences between males and females (Hyde, 2005). We believe that these intragroup variations have their origin in the unique ways

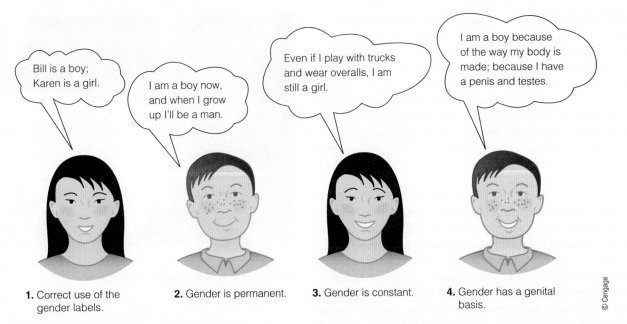

FIGURE 7.1 ▶ Four Components for Understanding Gender

1. Correct use of the gender labels.
2. Gender is permanent.
3. Gender is constant.
4. Gender has a genital basis.

that boys and girls create personal mental representations of gender during the early-school-age period. (See FIGURE 7.1 ▶.)

Understanding Gender

Understanding one's gender involves four components that emerge in a developmental sequence from toddlerhood through early school age (Kohlberg, 1966; Martin, Ruble, & Szkrybalo, 2002): (1) applying the correct gender label to oneself and others, (2) understanding that gender is permanent, (3) understanding gender constancy, and (4) understanding the genital basis of gender (see Figure 7.1). According to this analysis, children create the personal meaning of gender in much the same way that they form other cognitive schemes.

The correct use of **gender labels** is the earliest component of gender identification to be achieved. The recognition of people as male and female is a natural category, much like the recognition of the difference between familiar people and strangers or between people and inanimate objects, as discussed in chapter 5. Even before the abstract categories *male* and *female* are understood, children learn to refer to themselves as boys or girls by imitating their parents. From infancy, parents make continual reference to a child's gender in such statements as "That's a good boy" or "That's a good girl."

As early as 21 months, a majority of infants produce at least one gender label, such as boy or girl. By the age of 2½, children can accurately label other children as boys or girls, and by the age of 3, they can accurately sort photographs of boys and girls. They can also apply gender labels such as *Mommy* and *Daddy*, *brother* and *sister*, and *boy* and *girl* accurately. These verbal labels become useful for guiding a child's attention to important distinctions between males and females (Dunham, Baron, & Banaji, 2008; Dunham, Baron, & Carey, 2011; Gelman, Taylor, & Nguyen, 2004). Once they know these labels, children seek out cues to help them make these distinctions correctly, like hair style, clothes, or

body shape. Their attention is directed to the differences between male and female individuals. When children have words or labels for gender categories, they can further understand these categories and their appropriate applications (Nelson, 2012; Waxman & Lidz, 2006). What is more, when children begin to use gender labels, they also increase their gender-typed play, suggesting that the representation of oneself as a boy or a girl motivates and guides their gender-typed behaviors (Zosuls et al., 2009). As children recognize themselves as boys or girls, they begin to feel some affinity for their group. This means a greater liking for girls if you are a girl, or for boys if you are a boy. This is the very beginning of what emerges later as in-group bias.

Understanding **gender permanence** and **gender constancy** emerge somewhat later, usually between ages 4 and 7 (Levy, 1998; Serbin, Powlishta, & Gulko, 1993). Permanence refers to an appreciation that a boy grows up to be a man and a girl grows up to be a woman. One's sex is permanent over time, even though many other things about one might change. Constancy refers to an appreciation that one's sex is unchanged by clothing, hairstyle, play activities, and other day-to-day alterations. Even if a boy puts on a wig and dresses up in a fancy dress, pretending to be a princess, he is still a boy. Even if a girl puts on a helmet and shoulder pads and pretends to be a football player, she is still a girl.

Understanding the **genital basis of gender labels** provides a fundamental context for understanding that gender is permanent and constant. In research involving 3-, 4-, and 5-year-olds, the majority of children who understood the genital differences between the sexes could also tell that a child's sex did not change simply because the child was dressed up to look like a member of the opposite sex. These young children understood that gender is a constant feature of a person, no matter how the person is dressed or whether the hair is long or short. In contrast, the majority of the children who had no knowledge of genital differences were unable to respond correctly to questions about constancy (Bem, 1989).

Gender-Role Standards and Sex Stereotypes

Gender-role standards are cultural expectations about appropriate behavior for boys and girls and for men and women. One might consider these *sex stereotypes*. If you had no information about a person other than whether the person was male or female, what qualities would you attribute to that person? How would you expect the person to behave? Gender-role standards tell us what the culture considers typical and admirable for girls and boys, men and women (Eagly, 2009). For young children, this usually means the kinds of toys, clothes, and activities that would be preferred by boys or girls.

In research on gender-role standards, children are typically asked to identify whether certain activities, occupations, or traits are more frequently associated with male individuals, female individuals, or both. For example, in the *Sex-Role Learning Index*, children are shown drawings of 20 objects traditionally associated with gender roles—10 for the male gender role (such as a hammer, a shovel, and a fire helmet) and 10 for the female gender role (such as an iron, a stove, and dishes). By age 7, most children make a perfect score on this type of test, illustrating that they know how their society links a person's sex to activities or occupations (Beere, 1990; Levy, 1998; Serbin et al., 1993). Knowledge of gender-typed personality traits, such as gentle and affectionate or adventurous and self-confident, emerges somewhat later. In one study of more than 550 children, sixth graders answered about 90 percent of these types of questions correctly (Serbin et al., 1993).

An early-school-age child's knowledge about gender-role standards shapes the child's preferences and behaviors. For example, once children identify certain toys as more appropriate for girls and others as more appropriate for boys, their own toy preferences are guided by these standards. Conversely, when they like a toy that is not obviously sex-stereotyped, they are inclined to think that other children of their sex would like that toy as well (Martin, Eisenbud, & Rose, 1995). One consequence of this gender-typed thinking is that it may limit a child's willingness to play with certain toys and games and therefore reduces the child's opportunities to learn from a variety of play experiences.

One expression of gender stereotyping is a child's rigid insistence on wearing gender-stereotyped clothing. Little girls might insist on wearing skirts or dresses; little boys reject any clothes that have bows, frills, or "girly" designs. One study found that across diverse ethnic groups, the more children positively identified with their natal sex and understood the idea of gender stability, the more likely they were to want to wear gender-stereotyped clothing (Halim et al., 2014).

The nature of parental influences on children's gender role stereotyping is very complex. Some parents believe that boys should be assertive and fight for their rights. Others believe that boys should think carefully about what is right and wrong and guide their actions by reason rather than by impulsive aggression. Each of these sets of parents has a conception of male attributes that is communicated to their sons over a long period. The toys that parents give their children, the experiences to which they expose them, and the activities in which they encourage their children's participation all reflect dimensions of the parents'

Although early-school-age children are familiar with gender stereotypes, they are also likely to be flexible in their gender-role play.

gender-role standards. By the time children reach school age, they have been encouraged to adopt those standards and may have been shamed or chided for what their parents have viewed as gender-inappropriate behavior. Young girls may be shamed for their assertiveness by being told that they are acting bossy, and young boys may be warned to stop acting like a sissy.

As the cognitive underpinnings related to the concept of gender mature, children form **gender schemes**, or personal theories about cultural expectations and stereotypes related to gender. Children look for clues about gender, seeking information from their social environment about what activities they should or should not engage in ("Boys don't dance," "Girls don't play with trucks," "Pink scooters are for girls; blue scooters are for boys"); whom they should play with; and what information is especially relevant for them as boys or girls. They use this information to organize their perceptions, focus their attention, and interpret information in such a way as to be consistent with their gender scheme. For example, 4-year-old children use information about gender to decide which other children they would like to be friends with (Shutts, Roben, & Spelke, 2013). When young children are placed in a situation where they are uncertain about how to use a certain piece of equipment or when they are trying to understand a new bit of information, they are more likely to turn to an adult of their own gender to get new information (Ma & Wooley, 2013; Martin & Ruble, 2004).

Not all children are equally rigid in applying gender-role standards to themselves or to others. Flexibility in the application of gender-role standards to oneself and others appears to be influenced by both cognitive factors and socialization. Preschool-age children are more flexible than older children. For example, they are likely to see gender-role transgressions (e.g., boys playing with dolls or girls pretending to be firefighters) as more permissible than do older children, ages 6 and 7 (Lobel & Menashri, 1993; Smetana, 1986). Young children who have more advanced abilities to differentiate between moral norms (e.g., telling the truth) and social norms (e.g., saying "please" and "thank you") are also less sex-stereotyped in their play activities and toy choices (Lobel & Menashri, 1993).

Variations in family environments and socialization influence children's thinking about gender-role norms. In most countries around the world, women/mothers are more involved in caregiving activities than men/fathers for both boys and girls. Thus, if children are looking for evidence about gender role stereotypes, it is not surprising to think that they might associate being a female with the caregiving role. Children whose mothers perform nontraditional tasks develop a more flexible attitude, seeing more activities and occupations as appropriate for both men and women (Serbin et al., 1993). However, when looking at how mothers interact with their male and female children, few differences have been observed. One notable exception is that in countries characterized by an overall low level of socioeconomic development, parents were more likely to take their boys outside to play, read to them, and engage them in naming things, counting, and drawing. In these countries, young girls were more likely to be involved in child labor than young boys (Bornstein, Putnick, Deater-Dekcard, Lansford, & Bradley, 2016).

Identification with Parents

The third component of gender identification involves **parental identification**. Identification is the process through which one person incorporates the values and beliefs of another. To identify with someone is to increase one's sense of allegiance and closeness with that person. Through the process of identification, ideals, values, and standards of the family and community are internalized so that they become a part of the individual's own belief system.

During early school age, most children admire and want to be like their parents. Young children are enthusiastic observers of their parents as models, they are emotionally invested in their parents' reactions to them, and they are eager to internalize parental values. Young children integrate parental values and behaviors as part of their gender scheme. When parents have more traditional views about gender, their young children's ideas about gender are more stereotyped, both about themselves and about others (Tennenbaum & Leaper, 2002). Children identify with their parents' gender-related beliefs through conversations that they have about books, movies, and television programs. When parents challenge the gender stereotypes that are portrayed in these media, the children are likely to have a less stereotyped view of gender (Friedman, Leaper, & Bigler, 2007).

Parents can make deliberate efforts to encourage more flexibility in gender-role conceptualization and preferences by deliberately modeling counter-stereotyped activities—fathers making dinner or mothers mowing the lawn—and including more counter-stereotypical comments in conversations with their children (Friedman, Leaper, & Bigler, 2007). Parents can also balance their child's toys and play activities, introducing gender-neutral games and toys, as well as introducing toys and games that may be associated with boys (e.g., playing with toy trucks and cars on a track) and others that are associated with girls (e.g., playing pretend school) (Leaper, 2000).

Parents devise their beliefs and parenting practices out of their own internalized cultural script about gender. So even if they endorse gender flexibility, they may not be able to carry through entirely with their beliefs. For example, many studies focus on how parents talk to their children. The results of this work suggest that mothers are generally both more supportive and more negative with their children—that is, more expressive—whereas fathers are more directive, or task oriented. Furthermore, daughters receive more verbal interaction than do sons, especially from mothers. Finally, fathers are more assertive than mothers, and children are more assertive with their mothers than with their fathers (Leaper, Anderson, & Sanders, 1998). Thus, the family environment is *gendered* through patterns of communication that give children different role models for the behavior of mothers and fathers and provide boys and girls with opportunities to develop different approaches to social interaction.

In addition to the enactment of scripts for how to interact, most adults have deeply held standards about how men and women, boys and girls ought to behave. Consider the following:

> [A family] with three children (5-year-old Dan, 7-year-old Lyle, and 3.5-year-old Amy) in which the mother had always believed that her children should be exposed to all types of experiences, with no distinction indicated between "boy's kind" and "girl's kind." She encouraged her older son's play with dolls. . . . The boys were not allowed to play "aggressive" sports (American football) and were redirected by parents toward ballet and soccer. Yet the mother herself reported being "taken to the limits":

> . . . watching her [the mother] play with Amy, the mother was painting Amy's fingernails, Dan asked his mother to paint his fingernails too. "I could only bring myself to paint two [nails]. I knew it was ridiculous, but it just bothered me." (MacKain, 1987, p. 120)

This example illustrates how strongly internalized the standards about gender distinctions can be. Even for parents who want to minimize gender distinctions, some prohibitions or constraints are difficult to disregard (Valsiner, 2000).

The **Applying Theory and Research to Life** box discusses children raised by gay or lesbian parents. The research finds no differences in gender-role behavior, gender identity, or emotional well-being between children raised by heterosexual or homosexual parents.

Gender Preference

The fourth component of gender identification is the development of a personal preference for the kinds of activities and attitudes associated with masculine or feminine roles. Preferences for gender-typed play activities and same-sex play companions have been observed among preschoolers as well as older children (Hoffmann & Powlishta, 2001). Egan and Perry (2001) conceived of gender preference as a combination of gender typicality and gender contentedness. **Gender typicality** refers to whether a child fits in with others of the same sex, likes to do the same kinds of things as others of the same sex, is good at the same kinds of things as others of the same sex, and in general displays the typical traits of being a girl or a boy. **Gender contentedness** means that a child likes being the sex proscribed at birth, does not think it would be more fun to be the opposite sex, and does not spend time wishing to do things that members of the

Children Raised by LGBT Parents

A growing number of LGBT couples are raising children. In many cases, the children were conceived in heterosexual marriages. Then one parent established a new relationship and continued to raise the child. Some couples have children conceived through artificial insemination, surrogacy, or other assisted reproductive technologies; other couples have assumed the parent role through adoption (Brodzinsky & Pertman, 2012; Richards, Pennings, & Appleby, 2012).

The emergence of this unique family structure provides an opportunity to better understand the process of gender-role socialization and the development of sexual orientation. Over 30 years of research has addressed the adjustment and development of children raised by LGBT parents. Many questions about child-rearing environments and child outcomes can be posed.

Do LGBT parents differ from heterosexual parents in their parenting strategies or parental-roles? When compared to heterosexual couples, lesbian couples exhibit more sensitive parenting and more egalitarian role relationships. Open disclosure of the lesbian relationship, the ability to maintain ties with the rest of the child's family, and a perception that the partners share equally in the tasks associated with household and child care all contribute to the child's emotional well-being (Patterson, 1995; Tasker, 2005).

How relevant is a parent's sexual orientation in shaping a child's gender-role identification and psychological well-being? In general, studies of the well-being, cognitive levels, and emotional adjustment of children growing up with LGBT parents find no differences between these children and those growing up in heterosexual families (Fitzgerald, 1999; Golombok, 2013; Lamb, 2012; Patterson, 2006). The children have gender-role preferences that are very similar to those of children growing up in heterosexual families (Patterson, 2009). Some studies of girls who are raised by lesbian mothers have observed that these young girls are more flexible in their play preferences (e.g. enjoying play with pretend firetrucks

and carpenter's tools as well as with dolls and tea sets), and more likely to aspire to male-dominated occupations than girls raised by heterosexual mothers (Fulcher, Sutfin, & Patterson, 2008). No differences in gender identity or psychological well-being were observed.

One report reviewed findings from 23 studies of children of lesbian and gay parents (Anderssen, Amlie, & Ytteroy, 2002). Of these studies, most were conducted in North America, but four focused on European samples. Twenty studies reported on children of lesbian mothers; three on children of gay fathers. The results of these studies were discussed in terms of seven outcomes: emotional functioning, sexual preference, stigmatization, gender-role behavior, behavioral adjustment, gender identity, and cognitive functioning. Not all studies measured all of these variables, and even when studies focused on common outcomes, they used a variety of methods to measure the same variables. The studies of children of gay fathers focused only on sexual preferences and stigmatization.

Despite the variations in approaches to sampling, measurement, and design, the studies reported quite similar results. Children of lesbian mothers did not differ from other children with respect to emotional or behavioral problems, gender identity, gender-role behavior, or cognitive functioning. Children's sexual preference was not related to their parents' sexual orientation. There was some greater sensitivity to stigmatization among children of lesbian and gay parents, with children in some studies reporting being teased about being gay or lesbian. Also, children gave more thought to whom they would tell about their parents' sexual orientation. However, these experiences were not associated with higher rates of emotional or behavioral difficulties. The authors concluded that the research, with its many flaws, provides a picture of basic similarity between children reared in gay or lesbian families and those reared by heterosexual families.

Research on transgendered parents and their children is relatively new. A

few studies report that the child's well-being is supported when the transition happens at a young age, when the parents preserve a positive relationship, when the transition takes place in a well-planned and open process, and when the child can preserve a close, positive relationship with both parents (Coolhart, 2014; White & Ettner, 2007). In legal cases where the transgendered parent's custody or visitation rights are questioned, parents are encouraged to focus on evidence supporting the position that there is nothing about being transgender that limits a person's ability to be a warm, responsive parent and to raise a healthy, well-adjusted child (Cooper, 2013; Hippensteele, 2011).

Three aspects of family life have been found to promote a child's well-being: (1) the quality of the child's relationship with parents and parental figures, with particular emphasis on sensitivity and warmth; (2) the quality of the relationship between the parents, especially the importance of harmonious as contrasted with hostile relationships; and (3) the availability of adequate economic, social, and physical resources (Lamb, 2012). These factors are predictive of well-being and positive adjustment across all types of family structures and family kinship relations. The sexual orientation of parents is not a significant predictor of a child's gender identification, future sexual orientation, or well-being (Herek, 2006). Given this conclusion, it makes sense to stop comparing LGBT families to heterosexual families and to begin exploring the unique characteristics of diverse families that contribute to their enactment of effective parenting, positive adult relationships, and their access to essential financial, social, and community resources.

With regard to LGBT families, children whose parents have formed a positive gender identity including acknowledgment and disclosure of their sexual orientation will be more comfortable talking about these topics with their children. Young children who perceive that their parents are guarded or threatened because of their sexual orientation may internalize this

Courtesy of Philip Newman

Parental warmth, sensitivity, and responsiveness; close, loving relationships between the partners; and adequate financial and social resources support a child's adjustment and well-being across all types of family structures.

bonds in LGBT families is broadening and enriching our understanding of basic constructs such as family, parenting, mother and father, kinship, and gender (Golombok, 2015; Hicks, 2013).

Critical Thinking Questions

1. Based on what you have read about gender identification, describe the role you would expect a parent's sexual orientation to play in the way gender identification is formed.
2. Same-sex couples must take a highly planned, and sometimes very expensive, approach to having children. Hypothesize about how this might influence their approach to parenting.
3. If you were asked to design research to study the child-rearing practices and gender socialization of LGBT parents, what factors would you want to take into account? What would you measure? Who would be your comparison group? Why?
4. Describe the features of the community that might make it more comfortable or more difficult for gay and lesbian parents to disclose their sexual orientation and for their children to talk comfortably about the unique features of their families.

sense of fear, even though they do not have a full understanding of its origin or how to cope with it (Telingator & Patterson, 2008). As the legal and societal environments have shifted to affirm marriage equality, more LGBT adults can live openly in their community, disclosing their identities without fear of threat or social isolation. The growing literature on parent–child relationships and kinship

opposite sex can do. In their research, Egan and Perry found a strong and consistent relationship between gender typicality and measures of self-esteem, social competence, and acceptance from both male and female peers. The greater social pressure children felt to conform to gender-role norms, the more important gender contentedness was in sustaining self-esteem and perceived social competence. Those children who were not content about being a boy or a girl and also perceived a lot of pressure to conform to gender stereotypes experienced lower self-esteem.

Generally, there is more latitude or flexibility around the behaviors that are viewed as acceptable for young girls than for young boys. Little boys are more frequently stigmatized for acting in what is considered girlish ways and are more likely to experience peer rejection if their behaviors are deemed gender atypical. As a result, a nonconforming gender preference is more likely to be a source of distress for boys (Hegarty, 2009; Wallien, vanGoozen, & Cohen-Kettenis, 2007).

Both boys and girls can have experiences, like those described by Lee in the case study Gender Identification in Early Childhood, when their personal preferences for play behaviors, friends, and interests do not seem to fit with the cultural standards or stereotypes for their sex. In most cases, children and adults recognize these preferences as expressions of a child's unique temperament

or personality. The term "tomboy" reflects this idea, as it refers to girls who prefer activities and clothes that are typically associated with boys. Girls who identify themselves as tomboys have been found to describe themselves as less like a typical girl, and less content about gender expectations for being a girl. At the same time, they had fewer biases about same-sex and other-sex behaviors and were more accepting of other children who engaged in behavior that violated gender-related norms (Ahlqvivst, Halim, Greulich, Lurye, & Ruble, 2013).

Gender preference can be influenced by environmental cues as to the value of one sex or the other. The cues may emanate from the family, ethnic and religious groups, the media, social institutions (such as the schools), and other culture carriers. Many cultures have traditionally valued men more than women and have given men higher status. For example, among Japanese immigrants who came to the United States between the 1890s and early 1900s, a strong value was the commitment to a hierarchical and male-head-of-household view of the family (Ishii-Kuntz, 1997):

The Issei (*first-generation immigrant families*) customarily designated their eldest son the successor to the family business. . . . Accordingly, the eldest Nisei (*second-generation*) son usually received special treatment and privileges from his parents. In many Issei families, he was the second to be served at meals, after his father, and he was generally indulged by his mother. . . . Younger siblings were instructed to obey his directions, and even older sisters were expected to defer to him. (Ishii-Kuntz, 1997, p. 138)

To the extent that a cultural preference for males is communicated to children, boys are likely to establish a firmer preference for their sex group, and girls are likely to experience some ambivalence toward, if not rejection of, their sex group. Parental preference for one sex over the other can influence the quality of parent–child interactions and the resources, interactions, and opportunities available to boys and girls as they are growing up. The attainment of gender preference is a more complex and dynamic accomplishment than might be imagined. In fact, one's gender preference may fluctuate at different stages of life, particularly as one perceives gender-based changes in access to roles, resources, and social status (Maccoby, 2002).

In contrast to gender-nonconforming children who resist the constraints imposed on their gender, some children say they want to be the opposite sex. They may have a strong aversion to some or all of the physical characteristics and/or social and cultural expectations associated with the sex they were assigned at birth. The term **transgender** reflects this feeling of disconnect between one's gender preference and one's assigned sex. This conscious confusion about one's basic gender identity is undoubtedly a source of some distress. However, it appears that many transgender children are able to express their gender role preferences clearly (Olson, Key, & Eaton, 2015). When parents understand and affirm their child's reality, talk openly about it, and find ways to advocate for their child in the family and school contexts, they can reduce the child's feelings of isolation and minimize exposure to harassment and discrimination (Pyne, 2016). However, when children are subjected to parental and/or peer rejection, discrimination, and stigmatization around their nonconforming gender identity, they are more likely to experience symptoms associated with **gender dysphoria**, including intense distress, anxiety, and depression often accompanied by negative self-image and social withdrawal (APA Task Force on Gender Identity and Gender Variance, 2009; American Psychiatric Association, 2016).

We have reviewed four components of gender identification: (1) developing an understanding of gender, including learning and using gender labels, understanding gender stability and constancy, and understanding the genital basis of gender; (2) learning gender-role standards and stereotypes, and applying them to play activities, preferences for toys and clothes, and attributing them to others; (3) identifying with parents; and (4) establishing a gender preference, which may or may not coincide with one's assigned sex. What was once viewed as a predominantly biological process of sex role differentiation unfolding into a socially scripted gender role is now viewed as a product of each person's active integration of biological, cognitive, behavioral, and social factors.

A child's gender identity becomes a basic cognitive scheme that influences the interpretation of experiences (Leaper & Bigler, 2011). Children learn that people are grouped into two sexes—male and female. In our society, this dichotomy imposes itself on a wide array of social situations, including work, play, school, and politics—arenas where one's genital sex is not especially relevant. Once children learn this powerful category, they go about the business of figuring out how to apply it to themselves and others. They form expectations based on this categorization—that certain toys, interests, and behaviors are appropriate for boys and others are appropriate for girls; that certain activities, dispositions, and occupations are appropriate for men and others for women. These expectations are generally reinforced by the beliefs of the older children and adults with whom children interact. Some children do not conform to the gender norms and expectations associated with their assigned sex. They may resist these expectations or express a preference to reject their assigned sex altogether. The gender schemes that are conceived during childhood guide a child's daily activities and shape a preliminary vision of oneself in the future. Gender-based beliefs may become integrated into moral development, so that children begin to believe that it is morally right to adhere to certain gender-role standards and morally wrong to violate these standards.

FURTHER REFLECTION: Consider the biological, psychological, and societal factors that contribute to whether a young child is viewed as "gender typical" or "gender atypical." What might be some consequences for subsequent development of being gender typical or gender atypical in early school age?

Early Moral Development

OBJECTIVE 2   Summarize the process of early moral development, drawing from theories and research to explain how knowledge, emotion, and action combine to produce internalized morality.

The moral dilemmas facing young children are not about plagiarism or cloning or abortion. Rather, they are about understanding that lying, cheating, stealing, hurting others, or making fun of other children's differences are morally wrong and that telling the truth, playing fairly, sharing, being helpful, and respecting people's differences are morally right. The following analysis of moral development focuses on how children learn moral standards and apply them to their own behavior as well as the behavior of others. For early-school-age children, achievements in moral development include changes in three interrelated domains:

1. *Emotions.* (a) Experiencing the array of emotions that foster caring about others and that produce anxiety, guilt, and remorse when a moral standard has been violated; and (b) recognizing these emotions in others.
2. *Knowledge.* Learning the moral code of one's family and community and making judgments about whether something is good or bad, right or wrong.
3. *Action.* Taking appropriate actions to inhibit negative impulses, to act in accordance with rules and requests, to obey parents and other authorities, and to act in a caring, helpful manner, depending on the situation.

Internalization

Early moral development involves a process called **internalization**, which means behaving according to parental standards, rules, and values without external monitoring and constant reminders. This process, sometimes referred to as the formation of a conscience, requires that the child experience moral emotions, understand the family and community's moral code, and be able to take appropriate actions to either inhibit bad behavior or enact good behavior (Aksan & Kochanska, 2005).

Toddlers typically feel that demands for proper behavior do not come from within themselves, but from parents and other adults or older siblings. During early school age, standards and limits gradually become part of a child's self-concept. Specific values may be acquired primarily from parents, but they become integrated elements of the child's worldview.

Internalized morality includes both inhibiting harmful or socially unacceptable impulses and striving to do what is right. This is often characterized as the *want versus should conflict*. A child *wants* to indulge impulses for immediate expression or pleasure but knows that there *should* be a consideration for the consequences of those behaviors (Milkman, Rogers, & Bazerman, 2008). For example, a 5-year-old boy may take great delight in teasing his dog by threatening it with a stick. During one of these attacks, his mother scolds him. She insists that he stop and explains that it is cruel to hurt or frighten the dog. She may have to remind the boy on several other occasions that hitting the dog is not permitted. He may see the dog lying calmly in the sun and, with a gleam in his eye, begin to pick up a stick. He wants to hit the dog. At that moment, his behavior is interrupted by a feeling of tension, which is accompanied by the thought that he shouldn't hit the dog. If the standard has been successfully internalized, the emotional tension and the thought will be sufficient to inhibit the boy from hitting the dog. Internalization of the moral code is accompanied by increased control over one's behavior.

The following sections address various ways of understanding how the process of internalization unfolds in childhood. First, we review five theoretical perspectives that address aspects of moral development: learning theories, cognitive developmental theory, psychoanalytic and object relations theories, and evolutionary theory. Second, we review the related concepts of empathy, care, and perspective taking as they contribute to the internalization of morality. Third, we consider how a parent's discipline strategies may influence a child's morality. Finally, we consider media, including television and video games, as influences on moral development.

Five Theoretical Perspectives on Moral Development

The five theoretical approaches presented here—learning theories, cognitive developmental theory, psychoanalytic and object relations theories, and evolutionary theory—each offer distinct views about the way morality becomes internalized. You may find it helpful to refer back to chapter 2 (Major Theories for Understanding Human Development) to review the basic concepts of these theories.

These theories focus on the *process* of moral development, not the content. Each culture or subcultural group has its own set of moral standards. For example, in many Asian cultures, children are taught that teachers should be highly revered. Children learn to show respect to a teacher and to view their teachers as important role models. Children who are disrespectful of a teacher would be shamed. In the United States, the role of teacher does not have high status in comparison to many other occupations. Parents may express criticism of teachers openly in front of their children. They may write excuses for children's absences or failure to complete their homework, even though both the children and parents know these excuses are fabrications. Children may learn that some teachers are fair and helpful, but others are not. They may not consider it immoral to ignore a teacher's request or to make fun of a teacher with the other children. The theories that follow suggest how children internalize moral standards; they do not explain what the standards are or suggest what they should be.

Learning Theories. The focus of learning theories is on the conditions that support moral behaviors or actions. Moral behavior and the process of internalization are viewed as responses to environmental reinforcements and punishments. Moral behaviors can be shaped by the *consequences* that follow them. A positive, prosocial behavior, like helping to put the toys away or comforting another child who is distressed, is likely to be repeated if it is reinforced. In contrast, if a behavior is ignored or punished, it is less likely to occur again. If a child performs a misdeed or defies an authority and suffers negative consequences, these consequences ought to reduce the likelihood that such behavior will recur. If a child is in an unpleasant or painful environment and performs a behavior that reduces or eliminates the unpleasantness, the child is more likely to perform this same behavior again in similar situations. For example, if a child says, "I'm sorry. I'll try to do better next time," and this apology reduces the parent's anger or irritability, this behavior is likely to be repeated at other times when the parent is angry at the child. According to learning theory, internalization results as the behaviors that lead to a more comfortable, less threatening environment become more common and the behaviors that produce parental anger or conflict disappear.

The special case of **avoidance conditioning** is a paradigm for understanding how internalization is sustained. Having been disciplined in the past for wrong-doings, a child contemplating a misdeed should feel tension. Avoiding or inhibiting the impulse to misbehave reduces the tension and is therefore reinforcing. This process may occur even when the person who was involved in administering the discipline is absent. In other words, the scenario of thinking about a wrong or naughty action, feeling the anxiety that is associated with past discipline, and reducing that anxiety by exercising restraint may take place mentally, without any observable behavior. Over time, the reinforcement of tension reduction that is linked to controlling a wrongful impulse strengthens the tendency to inhibit it, and the child's behavior becomes less impulsive.

Social learning theory adds another mechanism for moral learning: the **observation of models**. By observing and imitating helpful models, children can learn prosocial behavior. When a child observes someone else perform a kind, generous, or selfless

According to learning theory, Martin's willingness to do his chores and help around the house is strengthened because he receives a reward for his efforts. According to this theory, what would happen if Martin's father stopped giving him the reward?

act, it produces an uplifting emotional response. If the opportunity for positive or altruistic actions occurs, the child who has observed someone else's generosity is likely to be more caring or helpful as a result of having observed this positive action by others (Schnall, Roper, & Fessler, 2010).

By observing the negative consequences that follow the misdeeds of models, they can also learn to inhibit their own misbehavior. Their moral behavior is not limited to the actions they have performed—it may be based on expectations formulated from observations of how the conduct of relevant models has been rewarded or punished (Bandura, 1991). For example, early-school-age children are more likely to judge an act of televised violence as *right* if the act goes unpunished. If a police officer in a television episode hits a suspect and threatens them in order to get a confession, the police officer is typically not punished in the program. Having viewed such unpunished acts, children formulate abstract rules, concepts, and sets of propositions about when aggressive behavior is justified (Kremar & Cooke, 2001). According to this theoretical perspective, the specific situation will influence the extent to which moral behavior is displayed. Moral behavior is built on the accumulation of many experiences across different situations day after day where children learn which behaviors are acceptable and which are not.

Cognitive Developmental Theory. In comparison to the learning theories, cognitive developmental theorists focus more on **moral reasoning** than on moral behavior. They emphasize a child's active construction of moral meaning, focusing on developmental changes in the ways children make judgments and reason about morally relevant situations. Piaget (1932/1948) described the major transition in moral judgment as a shift from heteronomous to autonomous morality. In **heteronomous morality**, rules are understood as fixed, unchangeable aspects of social reality. Children's moral judgments reflect a sense of subordination to authority figures. An act is judged as right or wrong depending on the letter of the law, the amount of damage that was done, and whether or not the act was punished.

In **autonomous morality**, children see rules as products of cooperative agreements. Moral judgments reflect a child's participation in a variety of social roles and in egalitarian relationships with friends. Give-and-take with peers highlights mutual respect and mutual benefit as rewards for holding to the terms of agreement or abiding by the law. Piaget posed situations like the following to young children in order to help clarify the difference between heteronomous and autonomous morality.

> Mark rushes into the kitchen, pushing open the door. Although he did not realize it, his mother had left a set of 10 cups and saucers on a stool behind the door. When he pushed the door open, the cups and saucers fell off the stool and broke.
>
> Matt was climbing up on the kitchen counter to reach some cookies that his mother told him he was not supposed to eat. While climbing on the counter, he broke 1 cup and saucer.
>
> Who committed the more serious moral transgression? Which boy should be more severely punished?

Children operating with a heteronomous morality believe that the child who breaks 10 cups by accident has committed a much more serious transgression than the child who broke only 1. Children who have achieved an autonomous morality believe that the child who disobeyed and violated his mother's trust committed the more serious transgression. In general, younger children are likely to judge the moral seriousness of an action based on the magnitude and nature of the consequences. If an action, no matter what the intent, produced harm, it should be punished. Older children are able to consider both the intention and the consequences in making a moral judgment. If an action was intended to harm and produced harm, it should definitely be punished (Helwig, Zelazo, & Wilson, 2001).

Expanding on the distinction between heteronomous and autonomous morality, cognitive developmental theorists have described a sequence of stages of moral thought (Kohlberg, 1976; Smetana, Jambone, & Ball, 2013). As children become increasingly skillful in evaluating the abstract, logical components of a moral dilemma, their moral judgments change. At the core of this change is the mechanism called **equilibration**—efforts to reconcile new perspectives and ideas about basic moral concepts, such as justice, intentionality, and social responsibility, with existing views about what is right and wrong. Children's reasoning may be thrown into disequilibrium by external sources, such as their parents' use of explanations and inductions regarding a moral dilemma or encounters with friends who reason differently about a moral conflict. Children's own cognitive maturation, especially the ability to think abstractly and hypothetically about interrelated variables, determines how their reasoning about moral dilemmas will be structured (Piaget, 1978/1985; Walker, Gustafson, & Hennig, 2001).

As summarized in Table 7.1, Kohlberg (1969, 1976) described three levels of moral thought, each characterized by two stages of moral judgment. Each level reflects a more cognitively abstract approach to matters of justice, fairness, and social responsibility. At Level I, **preconventional morality**, Stage 1 judgments of justice are based on whether a behavior is rewarded or punished. Stage 2 judgments are based on an instrumental view of whether the consequences will be good for "me and my family." The first and, to some degree, the second stage of Level I characterize children of early school age. Level II, **conventional morality**, is concerned with maintaining the approval of authorities at Stage 3 and with upholding the social order at Stage 4. Level III, **postconventional morality,** brings an acceptance of moral principles that are viewed as part of a person's own ideology rather than simply being imposed by the social order. At Stage 5, justice and morality are determined by a democratically derived social contract. At

Table 7.1	Stages in the Development of Moral Judgment

LEVEL I: PRECONVENTIONAL

Stage 1 Judgments are based on whether behavior is rewarded or punished.

Stage 2 Judgments are based on whether the consequences result in benefits for self or loved ones.

LEVEL II: CONVENTIONAL

Stage 3 Judgments are based on whether authorities approve or disapprove.

Stage 4 Judgments are based on whether the behavior upholds or violates the laws of society.

LEVEL III: POSTCONVENTIONAL

Stage 5 Judgments are based on preserving social contracts based on cooperative collaboration.

Stage 6 Judgments are based on ethical principles that apply across time and cultures.

© Cengage

Source: Based on Kohlberg, 1969, 1976.

Stage 6, a person develops a sense of universal ethical principles that apply across history and cultural contexts.

According to this theory, the stages form a logical hierarchy. At each new stage, individuals reorganize their view of morality, realizing the inadequacy of the preceding stage. For example, once a person sees morality in terms of a system that upholds and protects the social order (Stage 4), then the reasoning that argues for an act as moral because it was rewarded or immoral because it was punished is seen as inadequate. The stages form an invariant sequence, moving from a very idiosyncratic, personal view of morality to a view in which rules and laws are obeyed because they have been established by an authority or a society, and finally to an understanding of rules and laws as created to uphold basic principles of fairness, justice, and humanity (Boom, Brugman, & van der Heijden, 2001).

Consistent with this theory of moral development, early-school-age children can be expected to reason about moral situations at Level I, preconventional morality, which is dominated by concerns about the consequences of their behavior. This is quite consistent with the learning theory view that morality is shaped by the consequences that follow behavior in specific situations. However, children understand that not all misbehavior involves a moral transgression. Some behaviors violate social norms or expectations, sometimes called social transgressions, that are situation specific: "Don't talk with your mouth full," "Take your empty plate to the kitchen," or "Say 'Thank You' to the waitress when she brings you your food." Young children understand the difference between moral transgressions like lying, hitting, or taking something that doesn't belong to you, and social transgressions, which are violations of social convention (Smetana, Schlagman, & Adams, 1993; Turiel, 2002).

Moreover, a child's moral reasoning can be altered by exposure to an environment that encourages children to participate actively in creating the moral climate. For example, in the preschool and early primary grades, children can function at a more flexible, autonomous level when the moral atmosphere

Hannah got in trouble in school today for talking back to her teacher. Now her mother is trying to explain that it is wrong to be disrespectful to teachers. At the preconventional level of morality, Hannah just thinks it's wrong if you get punished. Lots of other kids are disrespectful to the teacher and nothing ever happens to them.

consistently emphasizes mutual respect. Classrooms where children are involved in rule making and conflict resolution give children an opportunity to appreciate each other's perspectives and to construct a social order that is largely regulated by the children themselves (DeVries, Hildebrandt, & Zan, 2000).

The notion that people move through a hierarchical sequence of stages of moral reasoning prompted by a process of cognitive disequilibrium has been challenged on a number of fronts. The direction of development over the stages has been viewed as too linear, valuing justice over social cooperation. It has been criticized as embodying a Western cultural orientation and a male-oriented value system that places the individual good and individual freedoms above the good of the group or community (Arnold, 2000). For example, in the African Ubuntu/Botho community, "actions are right roughly insofar as they are a matter of living harmoniously with others or honoring communal relations" (Metz & Gaie, 2010). However, cross-cultural comparisons have found support for the idea that as people mature, they find increasingly sophisticated ways of approaching moral situations. A study of more than 500 high school and university students in Taiwan found that the students showed evidence of high levels of postconventional reasoning, even though they adopted a culturally collectivist Chinese moral ethic (Gielen & Miao, 2000). Longitudinal studies in a variety of countries have observed an evolution of moral thought much like that proposed by Kohlberg, in which the reasoning shifts from an idiosyncratic to a more principled approach to evaluating moral conflicts (Gielen & Markoulis, 2001).

Psychoanalytic and Object Relations Theories. The psychoanalytic theorists focus on the ability of children to control their impulses and resist temptation, rather than on their cognitive reasoning about what constitutes a moral transgression. This theoretical perspective addresses moral emotions, especially guilt about having harmful or naughty impulses and pride in behaving in accord with one's ideals, as they contribute to moral behavior. According to psychoanalytic theory, a moral sense develops as a result of strong parental identification. Classical psychoanalytic theory views a child's conscience, or **superego,** as an internalization of parental values and moral standards. It holds that the superego is formed during the phallic stage, between the ages of about 4 and 7, as a result of the conflict between a child's sexual and aggressive impulses and the ways in which the parents deal with the behavioral manifestations of those impulses.

Freud (1925/1961) suggested that the more severely a parent forced a child to inhibit impulses, the stronger the child's superego would be. Research on the development of conscience has failed to support Freud's hypothesis. The children of parents who use harsh physical punishment do not have higher levels of internalization. These children are likely to inhibit impulsive behaviors in the presence of their parents, but when they are observed with their peers away from home, they tend to be physically aggressive and do not control their behavior well. Parental warmth, limited use of power assertion, involving children in decision making, and modeling resistance to temptation contribute to high levels of prosocial behavior and social responsibility.

In contrast to Freud's views on the formation of conscience, **object relations theory** views the critical time for moral

According to the psychoanalytic view, young children act on their impulses. As the superego develops, they are more successful at resisting temptation.

development as infancy rather than the early-school-age years (Klein, 1932/1975; Kohut, 1971; Mahler, 1963; Winnicut, 1958). Infants develop an awareness of three domains: the body and its physical experiences and needs, the existence of others, and the relations between the self and others (Sharp, Fonagy, & Goodyer, 2008). All subsequent psychological growth must be assimilated into these three domains. According to this view, the origins of moral reasoning and behavior have links to early feelings about the self and its needs, especially feelings of pleasure and pain, and the way these feelings are mirrored or accepted by the loving caregiver.

Morality has a basis in a young child's awareness of valued others and in behaviors that strengthen or threaten the bonds between the self and these others. All humans are seen as confronted by a dynamic tension between positive and negative emotions—love and hate, kindness and cruelty. One basis of early morality lies in the child's own sense of self-love, a wish to enhance and not harm or violate the self. Another basis is the extension of this self-love to the other and the wish to preserve feelings of connection, trust, and security that have been established in the early parent–infant relationship.

Through experiences with sensitive caregiving, infants become increasingly aware of the loved object as an integrated whole with feelings, motives, and goals as well as a physical reality. At the same time, this realization about the other fosters the child's own awareness of his or her inner mental life. When a child is distressed, for example, a calm, reassuring caregiver will use a certain tone of voice, facial expressions, and comforting strategies to help the child cope with the difficulty. This gives the child a chance to feel safe about experiencing the inner world of painful emotions. The loving caregiver allows the child an intimate context in which to encounter these impulses, emotions, and fears. As a result, the child does not have to split off from his or her angry, vengeful self or project it onto others. By seeing the loved other as both good and bad, and the self as both good and bad, the child's capacity for caring and empathy expands (Fonagy, Gergely, & Target, 2010; Fonagy, Luyten, Allison, & Campbell, 2016).

Longitudinal studies have provided support for the link between experiences of mutually responsive care in infancy and later moral emotion and behaviors (Kochanska, Forman, Aksan, & Dunbar, 2005). Children whose relationship with their mothers was characterized as mutually responsive in infancy showed stronger moral emotions, including greater distress over another person's pain and distress, and greater remorse after having damaged a valued toy. These children also showed greater restraint in resisting temptation and higher levels of compliance with requests from a parent or an experimenter when they were left alone. The early experiences of mutuality with a caregiver are transformed over time into enjoyment during child–caregiver interactions, greater willingness for compliance, and less need for the use of power assertion or monitoring to ensure compliance.

Evolutionary Theory. The evolutionary perspective emphasizes an emotional as well as a cognitive aspect to morality. Haidt (2007, 2008) characterized these components as **moral intuition** and moral reasoning. The emotional or intuitive component is a more primitive, immediate, almost automatic system that evaluates experiences as positive or negative, good or bad, without going through steps of searching for more information or weighing evidence. The moral reasoning component is thought to have evolved later, along with language, and is used to reach a moral judgment or decision. According to the evolutionary view, the moral reasoning component is slower than moral intuition and is often used to justify the initial moral intuition.

Certain areas of the brain, especially the amygdala and insula, produce emotional alarms, signaling fear or danger, as well as positive responses to stimuli. Social emotions, including lust and disgust, pride, humiliation, and guilt, which are processed in the insula, contribute to moral intuition. These affective areas operate to produce an orienting emotion that colors subsequent judgments. When people are told a moral story or dilemma, they typically have an immediate emotional reaction. They then begin to use reason to justify this reaction. Sometimes, they can override the initial intuitive reaction, most commonly when they interact with others who might stimulate a different, alternative emotional reaction to the situation.

According to an evolutionary view, morality, especially altruism and care for others, and fairness and reciprocity in social interactions, helps to sustain families and bind members of groups together. If you think about human evolution, you can appreciate that human infants have a relatively long period of dependence; and human infants can be born relatively close together. So it is likely that in early human families, parents had to care for several infants and young children at the same time. In order for a family to survive, slightly older children, even as young as 3, would need to contribute to the functional requirements of the family, such as carrying water, collecting firewood, or watching an infant sibling. As a result, helping behavior can be viewed as contributing to an adaptive advantage that has carried forward to contemporary human children. The motivation to help and the skills associated with helping behaviors can be observed very early in childhood across many cultures (Warneken, 2015).

Early human groups that were able to create a moral code that rewarded and increased behaviors beneficial to the group and that punished or reduced selfishness would have been more successful in attracting new members and fighting off competing groups. Thus, morality is thought to have co-evolved with the formation of larger human communities in which individuals are tied together beyond the basis of immediate kinship. As part of this process, rites, rituals, and institutions have emerged that link emotions, motor behaviors, and states of consciousness of large groups of people such that they are more attuned to one another than to members of out-groups and more willing to share resources, behave in a caring way, and exhibit loyalty to others in their group (Hauser, 2006).

Whereas the cognitive developmental and psychoanalytic perspectives focus on individuals and how they manage to control their antisocial impulses, the evolutionary emphasis is on the benefit of moral emotions for the protection and preservation of the group. Five components have been found to be incorporated in the moral codes of many cultures: (1) a belief that one should protect one's kin and members of one's group from harm and provide care for them; (2) a belief that one should behave fairly and exercise reciprocity (an equal give and take) with members of one's group; (3) a belief that one should be loyal to members of one's group; (4) a belief in respect and obedience to authority; and (5) a belief that one should follow practices that preserve bodily and spiritual purity, living in sacred or sanctioned, not a disgraceful or disgusting, way (Graham et al., 2011; Haidt, 2007, p. 1001). These content areas are elaborated to varying degrees by each cultural group, given more or less prominence in various religious teachings, and passed along from generation to generation through parental socialization, stories, and rituals. All five of these moral domains operate to build and strengthen communal bonds, creating a framework for how people should treat others, how they expect others to treat them, and how they should function in a larger social group.

— **CASE STUDY** Early Learning About
Obedience —

Jung Chang describes the moral environment to which she was exposed in her early childhood years through interactions with her grandmother.

For my grandmother, all flowers and trees, the clouds and the rain were living beings with a heart and tears and a moral sense. We would be safe if we followed the old Chinese rule for children, *ting-hua* ("heeding the words," being obedient). Otherwise all sorts of things would happen to us. When we ate oranges my grandmother would warn us against swallowing the seeds. "If you don't listen to me, one day you won't be able to get into the house. Every little seed is a baby orange tree, and he wants to grow up, just like you. He'll grow quietly inside your tummy, up and up, and then one day, Ai-ya! There he is, out from the top of your head! He'll grow leaves, and bear more oranges, and he'll become taller than our door. . . ."

The thought of carrying an orange tree on my head fascinated me so much that one day I deliberately swallowed a seed—one, no more. I did not want an orchard on my head; that would be too heavy. For the whole day, I anxiously felt my skull every other minute to see whether it was still in one piece. Several times I almost asked my grandmother whether I would be allowed to eat the oranges on my head, but I checked myself so that she would not know I had been disobedient. I decided to pretend it was an accident when she saw the tree. I slept very badly that night. I felt something was pushing up against my skull. (Chang, 1991, pp. 208–209)

CASE ANALYSIS Using What You Know

1. Describe the moral lesson of this case.
2. Explain how the case illustrates the themes of moral emotion, knowledge, and action.
3. Discuss how this case illustrates the particular orientation of early-school-age children to moral dilemmas.
4. Analyze this case as it relates to the psychosocial crisis of initiative versus guilt.

The study of moral development has been expanded through research in several directions. The research on empathy and perspective taking focuses on how children come to know and understand others. These abilities are essential for moral action. The research on parental discipline highlights the socialization process that supports self-regulation and internalization of moral values, including the passing on of a moral code from one generation to the next. The research on media, including television and video games, illustrates the co-evolution of morality and culture.

Empathy, Caring, and Perspective Taking

Empathy, caring, and perspective taking are factors that contribute to a child's ability to care about another person's distress, to consider the other person's needs and intentions when judging a moral act, and to respond in a helpful way.

Empathy. **Empathy** has been defined as the ability to understand and feel the perceived emotions of another person, for example feeling sad when someone else is sad. This definition emphasizes one's emotional reaction to the observation of another person's emotional condition. By merely observing the facial expressions, body attitudes, and vocalizations of another person, a child can identify that person's emotion and feel it personally. The range of emotions with which one can empathize depends on the clarity of the cues the other person sends and on one's own prior experiences. Research on the mirror neuron system discussed in chapter 6 suggests that humans are neurologically and psychologically prepared to synchronize their feelings and movements with others, thus enhancing the capacity for empathy. The capacity for empathy is deeply embedded in our evolutionary history, suggesting adaptive advantages for groups where the capacity for empathy is genetically passed along from one generation to the next (Dalai Lama & Ekman, 2008).

The capacity for empathy begins in infancy. Infant imitation, observed in the first months of life, provides an initial link between the observation of emotional expressions in another person and the expression of that emotion (Meltzoff, 2010). Infants appear to be able to recognize and interpret auditory and facial cues that suggest emotional expressions in others. In the newborn nursery, when one infant starts to wail, the other infants begin to cry. Following from object relations theory, the intimate infant–caregiver relationship forms an early framework for empathy. The coordination of rhythmic interactions, the creation of joint attention, and the achievement of intersubjectivity through early gestures and words provide infants with an understanding of their caregiver's state. In a study of 125 firstborn girls, empathic concern for their mothers' distress was observed to increase from 16 months to 22 months of age. In contrast, empathic concern for a stranger was observed to decrease. In infancy, empathy for others appears to be situational, requiring an ability to overcome wariness or fearfulness in order to offer comfort to another person (van der Mark, van IJzendoorn, & Bakermans-Kranenburg, 2002).

Early-school-age children can usually identify the circumstances that may have produced another child's emotional response, especially anger and distress, and they can understand and empathize with another child's feelings. Children are most likely to think that external events produce emotional reactions: "The teacher made her put her toys away," or "He tripped over the blocks." But they can also think about internal states that may produce strong emotions: "He's mad because he didn't get a turn," or "She's sad because her stomach hurts." The ability to understand the emotions and mental state of another person allows children to justify someone's moral behavior and perhaps to forgive a transgression: "The dad just spilled juice on his paper, so he yelled at his daughter. He was upset; he didn't really mean it." The ability to identify pleasurable and unpleasurable emotions in others and to empathize with them makes the child receptive to moral teachings.

Caring. It is one thing to feel empathy for someone else, and yet another to take action to help that person. The **principle of care** refers to a sense of duty or obligation to help someone who is in need. Caring may build upon the emotions aroused by empathy. However, the principle of care also requires a cognitive evaluation of the other person's situation and an action component—the desire or intention to do something to help. From a developmental perspective, the principle of care reflects a greater degree of cognitive awareness than empathic distress and an internalized moral standard that one should do what one can to reduce another

Young children can be very caring and supportive in comforting others, especially if they understand the reason behind another child's distress.

person's distress (Eisenberg, Fabes, & Spinard, 2006; Wilhelm & Bekkers, 2010). Even at very young ages, as young as 18 months or 2 years, many infants are able to help others and seem to want to do this. They can pick up an object that someone else has dropped, or reach under a chair or table to retrieve something that is out of reach. The capacity and motivation for helping both adults and peers matures rapidly between the ages of 2 and 5 (Hepach, Vaish, & Tomasello, 2012).

Although most children who experience empathy are also inclined toward caring actions, some children are characterized by callousness and disregard for others. Not surprisingly, these characteristics in early childhood have been found to predict antisocial behavior in middle childhood and adolescence. The origins for this deficit in caring are not fully understood. Twin studies suggest possible genetic origins, and studies of harsh parenting implicate environmental influences (Rhee et al., 2013; Waller et al., 2012).

Perspective Taking. The terms *empathy* and *perspective taking* are sometimes confused. Empathy typically refers to the ability to identify and experience the *emotional* state of another person. **Perspective taking** refers to the *cognitive* capacity to consider a situation from the point of view of another person. This requires a recognition that someone else's point of view may differ from one's own. It also requires the ability to analyze the factors that may account for these differences (Flavell, 1974; Piaget, 1932/1948). Perspective taking is closely linked to a child's theory of mind. It requires a child to consider what another person might know or feel, especially when that person's experiences differ from the child's own point of view.

Imagine a child who wants to play with another child's toy. If the first child thinks, "If I had that toy, I would be happy, and if I am happy, everyone is happy," then that child may take the toy without anticipating that the other child will be upset. This is evidence of a lack of perspective taking. Whereas empathy provides an emotional bridge that enables children to discover the similarities between self and others, it does not teach them about differences. Recognizing these differences requires perspective taking. The capacity to take another person's perspective is achieved gradually through parental inductions, peer interaction, social pretend play, conflict, and role-playing.

Children at ages 4 and 5 frequently exhibit prosocial behaviors that evidence an understanding of others' needs. The most common of these behaviors are sharing, cooperating, and helping. Two examples illustrate the nature of this kind of social perspective taking:

> The path of a child with an armload of play dough was blocked by two chairs. Another child stopped her ongoing activity and moved the chair before the approaching child reached it.
>
> A boy saw another child spill a puzzle on the floor and assisted him in picking it up. (Iannotti, 1985, p. 53)

Many moral dilemmas require that children subordinate their personal needs for someone else's sake. To resolve such situations, children must be able to separate their personal wants from the other person's. One longitudinal study followed children from the ages of 4 and 5 into early adulthood. Those children who showed spontaneous sharing, helping, and other prosocial behaviors in the early childhood years continued to exhibit prosocial behavior, sympathy, and perspective taking over the course of adolescence and early adulthood (Eisenberg et al., 1999). A combination of a genetically based social orientation, an ability to regulate or inhibit one's impulses, and a consistent socialization environment contribute to a young child's sympathetic response toward others' distress. Over time, this outlook combines with a more mature capacity for moral reasoning and deepening social ties that help sustain a prosocial orientation.

Although the capacity for perspective taking appears to be universal, some cultures rely on it more than others. For example, East Asian cultures, which tend to have a more collectivist orientation, emphasize the value of interdependence. As a result, from early childhood, East Asian children are encouraged to observe others carefully to determine signs of intentions and distress. In an experimental study, Chinese and American participants were paired up in a communication game. Chinese players were much more tuned in to their partners' nonverbal communications and intentions than were the American players, suggesting a cultural socialization that fosters perspective taking (Wu & Keysar, 2007).

Parental Discipline

Parents are a child's first teachers about the content of the moral code the child will be expected to internalize. Through their approach to discipline, parents make a stand for certain values, beliefs, and behaviors that embody their ideas about a moral way of life. When disciplining a child, parents emphasize that certain behaviors are wrong and should be inhibited; other behaviors are right and should be repeated. This distinction between good and bad behaviors and the accompanying parental approval or disapproval forms the content of a child's moral code. Ideally, the socialization process as well as the specific moral teaching should support a child's belief in a caring, just, and fair community. Discipline strategies that are unduly harsh or erratic are likely to undermine these values and produce a set of moral beliefs focusing on power, domination, and self-interest (Arsenio & Gold, 2006). What is more, as discussed in chapter 6, harsh discipline undermines a child's capacity for self-regulation, making it more difficult to exercise inhibitory control.

Parents use specific discipline techniques to bring about compliance with the moral code. Four elements are important in determining the impact of these techniques on a child's future behavior. The discipline should

1. Help the child interrupt or inhibit the forbidden action.
2. Point out a more acceptable form of behavior so that the child will know what is right in a future instance.
3. Provide some reasons, understandable to the child, why one action is inappropriate and the other more desirable.
4. Stimulate the child's ability to empathize with the victim of the misdeed. In other words, children are asked to put themselves in their victim's place in order to see how much they dislike the feelings they caused in the other person.

In considering discipline as a mechanism for teaching morality, one becomes aware of the many interacting and interrelated components of a moral act. The discipline techniques that are most effective in teaching morality to children are those that help children control their own behavior, understand the meaning of their behavior for others, and expand their feelings of empathy. Discipline techniques that do not include these characteristics, such as power assertion, may succeed in inhibiting undesired behavior but may fail to achieve the long-term goal of incorporating moral values into future behavior.

The child's temperament is often overlooked in determining the likely effectiveness of certain disciplinary techniques. For example, children who are especially fussy and irritable as infants are more likely to be spanked by their parents (Berlin et al., 2009). Children who are temperamentally fearful and inhibited in response to novel stimuli and who choose to stay close to their mothers during toddlerhood are especially sensitive to messages of disapproval. For these children, a small dose of parental criticism is adequate to promote moral internalization, and too much power assertion appears to be counterproductive. In contrast, children who are highly active and who are insensitive to messages of disapproval require more focused and directive discipline, especially a consistent program of recognizing and rewarding good behaviors and minimizing the situations and stimuli that may provoke impulsive or aggressive actions (Kim & Kochanska, 2012). In the face of anger-arousing events or distressing situations, some children are better able to regulate their emotions and return to a calm state than others. Children who are able to exercise emotional control and manage the physical conditions associated with mild distress are also more likely to be able to show prosocial behavior by expressing concern and trying to comfort others who are distressed (Scrimgeour, Davis, & Buss, 2016).

In addition to their use of discipline, parents guide moral development by modeling positive, prosocial behaviors and by talking with their children about moral issues. In chapter 6, we discussed the use of scaffolding to promote more effective communicative competence. In the same way, parents can scaffold their child's moral reasoning by talking with their children, raising questions about moral decisions their children are facing, and introducing new arguments or alternative views as their children think about moral conflicts. Security in the child–caregiver attachment, the expression of warmth and affection in the relationship, and a parent's willingness to talk about feelings and moral concerns all contribute to a child's early moral development (Dunn, 2006; Laible & Thompson, 2000).

For example, Beth's mother asks her to help pick up the toys and put them away. Beth says that her brother made the mess, and he should pick up the toys. Beth's mother might acknowledge Beth's frustration about picking up after her little brother, but then she could point out that Beth would be helping her by picking up the toys, and that at some time in the future, she will want her brother to help clean up a mess that Beth made. Meanwhile, it is important to pick up the toys so they do not get broken and so no one trips or falls over them. The idea that helping in a family is not just about what each person does, but about what is good for the family as a whole, challenges Beth's moral reasoning and encourages her to move to a new level of moral reasoning.

Parents encounter many examples when their children behave well and show signs of kindness, caring, and truthfulness. They also encounter times when their children misbehave, exhibiting selfishness, anger, or cruelty. Especially at times when children are experiencing emotional distress, parents teach and model positive moral behavior through their tone of voice, their willingness to hear a child's explanations, their willingness to provide explanations for their rules, and their ability to maintain open communication, even during conflict. Depending on the situation, parents may try to sooth the child with physical comfort, encourage the child to talk about his or her feelings, try to distract a distressed child, or try to reframe the situation to change the way the child is thinking or feeling about the problem. All these strategies can help children manage their distress and regain emotional control (Scrimgeour, Davis, & Buss, 2016). They convey a sense that we are all imperfect, that we continue to strive toward a moral ideal, and that we can forgive and try again.

The Impact of Media, Including Television and Video Games, on Moral Development

Moral influences extend beyond the family to include schools, religious institutions, and the community. Among the societal influences that have been a focus of research and policy is the impact of the media, especially television, video games, and Internet play, on children's attitudes and behaviors. Some people suggest that we need to think about the television as a part of the family system. In about 80 percent of homes, the television is on even when no one is watching. Family interactions are different in the presence of the television, involving less talking and

Steven is completely engrossed in his video game. Even though he is an active child, he can sit like this for long stretches. His mother has to set the timer to limit his play.

more touching. Images, information, and dramatic situations portrayed on television influence family members, resulting in new kinds of behaviors, shared experiences, points of discussion, and exposure to distressing images that may require comforting or interpretation (Gentile & Walsh, 2002). In families with siblings, it is not uncommon for younger children to "watch up" to the television interests of the older sibling. As a result, younger children may be exposed to programs when they are less able to understand them.

Violent Programming. What is the impact of exposure to *media violence* on the beliefs and behaviors of young children (Huesmann & Skoric, 2003)? Concern about media violence is particularly meaningful in the context of the child's growing moral consciousness. More than 30 years of laboratory experiments, field experiments, and analyses of naturally occurring behaviors have led to the conclusion that televised and video game violence has definite negative consequences for young children's behaviors and beliefs. Nonetheless, in 2011 the U.S. Supreme Court ruled that video games are protected as free speech and that the sale of these games to minors cannot be regulated or curtailed (Ferguson, 2013). As a result, the responsibility for establishing viewing practices rests entirely with families.

Those who monitor contemporary television viewing estimate that in the United States, children ages 2 to 5 watch an average of 32 hours of video and other recorded screen media each week (Nielsen, 2009). In comparison to older children, young children also tend to watch their favorite programs over and over again using alternative recording devices. An analysis of music television videos found that almost one fourth of the videos included images of violence and carrying weapons. Video games are especially permeated with violent themes. Many video games require children to become increasingly adept at killing off characters with the use of special weapons or superpowers. Studies suggest that long-term exposure to violent video game play is associated with lower empathy for others, increased aggressive behavior, and desensitization to real-life violence (Carnagey & Anderson, 2004; Funk, Baldacci, Pasold, & Baumgardner, 2004; Swing & Anderson, 2007).

The American Academy of Pediatrics issued a policy statement on television viewing in which they make the following recommendations (American Academy of Pediatrics, 2013):

1. Discourage television viewing for all children under age 2.
2. Remove televisions and Internet connected devices from children's bedrooms.
3. Limit children's total entertainment media time (television, video games, Internet play) to no more than 1 to 2 hours per day.
4. Monitor the media and programs that children are viewing, including websites and social media; focus on programs and games that are informational, educational, and nonviolent.
5. View TV, movies, and other media programs along with children and discuss the content.
6. Since children's viewing is often influenced by parents' viewing habits, establish family guidelines and limits for media use at home, such as a time away from media during mealtime or a nighttime close-off time for cell phones and devices.

These recommendations are based on research suggesting that about two thirds of current television programming contains a great amount of violence, and portrayals of violence are often glamorized and go unpunished. As a result, watching television and playing video games that have violent content have a strong impact on a child's willingness to engage in real-life violence, or they may be frightened by these violent images (Federman, 1998; Wilson et al., 2002). What is more, children's viewing patterns are associated with the amount of time parents watch television or other media and their choice of media content (Bleakley, Jordan, & Hennessy, 2013). This supports the notion that media violence can become an integrated aspect of the family system, influencing a young child's beliefs and values about aggressive behaviors.

At least three processes are at work that may increase the level of aggressiveness in children who are exposed to media violence (Bushman, Huesmann, & Whitaker, 2009) (see Table 7.2). First, children observe role models who perform aggressive actions. Especially when the hero is provoked and retaliates with aggression that goes unpunished, the child is likely to imitate the aggressive actions. Thus, viewing media violence adds new violent behaviors to the child's repertoire. Moreover, when the hero

Table 7.2	Three Processes That May Increase the Level of Aggression in Children Who Watch Media Violence
Process	**Possible Consequence**
Observing role models who engage in aggressive actions.	Imitation of violent action is likely when hero is provoked and retaliates with aggression.
	Hero is rewarded for violent actions.
	New violent behaviors added to repertoire.
Viewing aggressive actions leads to heightened level of arousal.	Brings network of aggressive thoughts, feelings, memories, and action tendencies into consciousness.
	Repeated stimulation strengthens this network.
	Stimulation interacts with aggressive temperament to increase the likelihood of aggressive action.
Viewing aggression affects beliefs and values.	Aggressive behavior is seen as an acceptable way to resolve conflicts.
	Viewers are hardened to the use of aggression in peer interactions.
	Aggression is used as a response to frustration.
	Viewers expect others to be aggressive toward them.
	Viewers worry about being victims of aggression.
	Viewers see the world as a dangerous place.

© Cengage

is rewarded or viewed as successful because of violent actions, children's tendencies to express aggression are increased.

Second, exposure to media violence has an impact on the neurological system. Watching media violence produces a heightening of arousal (Simons et al., 2003). The fast action that usually accompanies televised violence captures the viewer's attention. Watching this fast-paced programming has an effect on a young child's executive functioning. Experimental studies find that immediately after watching fast-paced programs, children have more trouble with self-regulation, delay of gratification, and focused attention (Lillard & Peterson, 2011). Watching a violent incident raises the child's level of emotionality, bringing to the fore other aggressive feelings, thoughts, memories, and action tendencies. The more frequently this network of elements is activated, the stronger their association will be. In some video games, the child selects a character and is encouraged to identify with that role. Violent acts are repeated over and over, with the possibility that the child increases the character's aggressive behaviors after each encounter, thereby escalating the level of emotional intensity and angry feelings as the play continues (Bushman & Anderson, 2002). Particularly for children who are temperamentally aggressive, watching violent television or playing violent video games increases their inclination toward aggressiveness in real-life situations (Wittman, Arce, & Santisteban, 2008).

Finally, exposure to media violence affects a young child's beliefs and values. Children who are exposed to frequent episodes of televised violence are more likely to believe that aggressive behavior is an acceptable way to resolve conflicts, and they become hardened to the use of aggression in peer interactions. They are also more accepting of the use of aggression as a response to frustration. Children (and adults) who are exposed to media violence are more likely to expect that others will be aggressive toward them, worry about being victims of aggression, and see the world as a dangerous place (Huesmann & Skoric, 2003).

Exposure to media violence has long-lasting effects. For example, in a longitudinal study, TV viewing habits in childhood (ages 6 to 10) were related to adult aggressive behavior 15 years later. The relationship between extensive exposure to televised violence in childhood and later aggressive behavior was observed for both men and women, even after controlling for mitigating factors such as intelligence, parenting characteristics, and family's socioeconomic status. The more children identified with aggressive TV characters, the stronger this relationship to adult aggressive behavior (Huesmann, Moise-Titus, Podolski, & Eron, 2003).

Prosocial Programming. If watching media violence can influence aggressive behavior, it makes sense to think that watching positive, prosocial behaviors can influence caring, helping, and other positive behaviors. One analysis found that in a week of television programming of over 2,000 shows, 73 percent included one act of altruism defined as helping, sharing, giving, or donating. Children's programming includes more frequent instances of prosocial behavior. A child who watches an average of three hours a day of children's television programming will see 4,380 acts of altruism a year (Wislon, 2008).

Children who are exposed to prosocial programming are influenced toward more positive social behavior. One study recontacted more than 500 adolescents whose television viewing had been studied when they were in early childhood. Watching educational programming in the early years was associated with many positive characteristics in adolescence, including higher grades, reading more books, greater creativity, and less aggression (Anderson, Huston, Schmitt, Linebarger, & Wright, 2001). In a meta-analysis of 34 studies on the prosocial effects of watching television, a clear relationship was observed between watching prosocial programming and children's positive behaviors including altruism, positive social interactions with others, and tolerance for differences (Mares & Woodard, 2005). The positive impact of these programs can be enhanced when adults and children talk about the moral message of the episode or about how the positive behaviors might be enacted in other situations. Other studies considered the relationship between playing prosocial video games, that is, games that include opportunities for characters to help one another or form friendships, and the players' real-life prosocial behaviors. There was a consistent relationship between time spent playing prosocial games and prosocial behaviors such as helping someone, cooperation and sharing, empathy, and emotional awareness (Gentile et. al., 2009).

Many programs—some developed for children and others intended for a broader viewing audience—convey positive ethical messages about the value of family life, the need to work hard and sacrifice in order to achieve important goals, the value of friendship, the importance of loyalty and commitment in relationships, and many other cultural values. A number of contemporary programs include characters of many races and ethnic backgrounds. Many feature women in positions of authority or performing acts of heroism. Increasingly, programs include characters with physical disabilities who play important roles. Through exposure to these programs, children learn to challenge social stereotypes and develop positive images of people from many ethnic groups (Rosenkoetter, 1999).

Review of Influences on Moral Development

In early school age, children are developing an initial moral code. The approaches to this issue are summarized in Table 7.3. Each contribution highlights an essential element of the larger, more complex phenomenon. *Learning theory* points out that an external reward structure inhibits or reinforces behavior. *Cognitive theory* suggests that in early childhood, children are most likely to take a pragmatic view about whether something is right or wrong, based largely on the consequences. *Psychoanalytic theory* is especially concerned with the relationship between parental identification and the development of conscience. *Object relations theory* stresses the importance of early, loving relationships with a sensitive caregiver as the path through which a child comes to value the self and to care about others. *Evolutionary theory* highlights benefits to groups that were able to create moral codes that emphasize protecting the kin from harm, behaving fairly and exercising reciprocity, being loyal to members of one's group, showing respect and obedience to authority, and maintaining bodily and spiritual purity.

Table 7.3   Contributions to the Study of Moral Development

Conceptual Source	Significant Contributions	Relevance for a Particular Aspect of Moral Development
Learning theory	Relevance of an external system of rewards and punishments. Imitation of models. Formation of expectations about the reward structure.	Moral behaviors. Internalization of a moral code.
Cognitive theory	Conceptual development of notions of intentionality, rules, justice, and authority. Stages of moral reasoning.	Moral judgments. Distinctions between moral transgressions and social convention transgressions.
Psychosexual theory	Parental identification. Formation of the superego and the ego ideal.	Internalization of parental values and moral standards. Experiences of guilt.
Object relations theory	The origins of morality in infancy with the development of object relations. The extension of self-love to love of the other and the desire to maintain connection with loved others.	Moral emotions. Formation of strong ties between self and others. Willing compliance with adult requests.
Evolutionary theory	Adaptive nature of moral intuition and moral reasoning. Morality as co-evolving with large cultural groups. Moral standards promoting the cohesiveness and stability of the group.	Moral emotions. Content of moral principles and their relationship to group survival.
Research on empathy, care, and perspective taking	Ability to experience another's feelings begins very early and changes with age. Care, the feelings of concern and desire to help, emerge early and continue to mature along with increases in cognitive development. Ability to recognize differences in point of view emerges slowly during early-school-age and middle childhood years.	Empathy heightens concern for others and helps inhibit actions that might cause distress. Perspective taking can foster helping and altruism. A caring orientation influences action—a willingness to reduce distress and provide help.
Research on parental discipline	Parents define moral content. Parents point out the implications of a child's behavior for others. Parents create a reward structure.	Standards for moral behavior. Moral reasoning. Internalization of moral values.
Research on media	Observing aggressive role models. Arousal of aggressive emotions, memories, and action tendencies. Formation of beliefs and values about the use of aggression to resolve conflict. Prosocial thoughts and behaviors can be stimulated.	New repertoire of aggressive behaviors. Lower threshold for aggressive actions. Expectations of aggression from others. Desensitization to acts of violence. Imitate models of prosocial behavior. Reduce aggressive behaviors and increase helpfulness.

© Cengage

The research on *empathy, care,* and *perspective taking* shows that moral behavior requires an emotional and cognitive understanding of the needs of others as well as a desire or even a sense of obligation to help. Research on *parental discipline* suggests that parents promote moral development when they establish clear standards, involve their children in dialogue, and try to increase children's understanding of the effects of their behavior on others. Research on *media*, including television and video games, shows that children who are exposed to many hours of violent programming or who engage in many hours of violent video game play are more likely to act aggressively, accept violence as a method for resolving conflicts, and interpret the behavior of others as having an aggressive intention. In contrast, watching prosocial programming can have a positive impact on young children's altruism and positive interactions with others.

FURTHER REFLECTION: What are your earliest recollections of your own moral development? What did you consider to be the essential "rights" and "wrongs" when you were very young? What difficulties did you face in trying to live up to the moral standards that were impressed upon you at that time?

What were the early influences on your moral code? Can you recall any stories, television programs, movies, books, or other cultural resources that shaped your sense of right and wrong?

Self-Theory

OBJECTIVE 3 Analyze changes in the self-theory, with special focus on the theory of mind and self-esteem during the early-school-age years.

The development of the self-concept is at the heart of psychosocial development. Psychosocial theory provides a framework for understanding how the ego is transformed through ongoing interactions with society over the life span. It describes the creative process through which basic experiences of the physical self in infancy are transformed through self-awareness, self-consciousness, self-control, a sense of self—other relationships, a personal identity, a style of life, and finally a sense of integrity about the life one has lived.

The self-concept can be viewed as a theory that links the child's understanding of the nature of the world, the nature of the self, and the meaning of interactions between the two (Epstein, 1973, 1991, 1998). Consider the two cases of Gloria and Lee. We see two very distinct approaches to the construction of a self-theory. Gloria is reserved; she takes refuge in her closet to read and pretend; she feels proud of her independence, but reluctant to face the adult world. Issues of race and discrimination enter into her sense of self at a very young age, creating a degree of cautiousness. Lee is rambunctious; she loves the outdoors; her fantasies are of adventure and daring; she is aware of the restrictions of the adult world, but they do not seem to worry her. Although she knows she is a girl, she aligns herself with the male world in scorning girls.

The function of the **self-theory** is to make transactions between the self and the world turn out as positively and beneficially as possible. One's theory about oneself draws on such inner phenomena as dreams, emotions, thoughts, fantasies, and feelings of pleasure or pain. One's self-theory is also based on logical thoughts and information such as assessments of one's abilities, comparisons with others, and analysis of experiences with the environment (Epstein, 2003, 2008). The complexity and logic of the self-theory depend on the maturation of cognitive functions, which is tied in part to the maturation of the brain. Furthermore, because the self-theory is based on personal experiences and observations, one would expect it to be modified over the life course as a result of changing physical, cognitive, and socioemotional competencies as well as by participation in new roles.

The Neuroscience of the Self

The self-concept is a complex construction based on many sources of information including one's physical appearance, an awareness of one's body, the sound of one's voice, memories of one's past experiences and the emotions tied to those experiences, current thoughts and feelings, one's tastes and preferences, hopes and dreams about one's future, and a wealth of information coming from others about how you are perceived and what is expected of you. Neuroscientists are striving to understand how the brain manages to integrate all these facets into a coherent sense of self (Morin, 2006).

The brain appears to have at least four functions that contribute to components of the self-concept:

1. Recognition and experiences of the physical self.
2. Self-representations. This includes use of personal pronouns, experiences of ownership ("mine"), awareness of one's personality traits and preferences, and self-appraisal (self-esteem).
3. Awareness of the expectations of others for oneself. Judging how you measure up to the expectations and social standards of others.
4. Awareness of the differences between the self and others. Distinguishing one's own thoughts and feelings from the thoughts and feelings of others; the "me" from the "not me."

Each of these four functions is associated with specific areas of the brain. Work by Uddin, Iacoboni, Lange, and Keenan (2007) suggests that there are two separate but interrelated areas that support the capacity for distinguishing the self and others, self-representation, and the ability to understand and learn from others. The right frontoparietal area is active when individuals view their own face as compared to faces of familiar others. This same area is also active in response to images of one's body and the sounds of one's voice. So it appears that the right frontoparietal area is involved in many of the physical aspects of the self-concept. This area overlaps with an area of the mirror neuron system described in chapter 6. The mirror neuron system supports the ability to understand and replicate the actions and goals of others (Neiworth, 2009).This helps explain how a child can observe and imitate the behaviors of others and then incorporate those behaviors into their own physical/motor patterns.

Other brain regions are associated with self-representations including self-recognition, use of personal pronouns, expression of ownership, self-appraisal, judging one's personality traits, and making judgments about the mental states of others (Lewis & Carmody, 2008). This brain structure (the cortical midline structure) is activated when the person is integrating information in order to make judgments about the self (Northoff & Bermpohl, 2004). As one might expect, these areas of the brain are interconnected, sending information back and forth so that experiences of viewing one's image and thinking about oneself form an integrated concept. The convergence and interaction of these brain areas with the mirror neuron system contribute to the ability for self-recognition, self–other distinctions, the ability to replicate another person's actions and understand the intentions of those actions, and the ability to reflect upon another person's experiences and perceptions in comparison to our own (Ruby & Decety, 2001, 2004).

This research, which considers the neural basis for self-concept, supports the underlying principle from psychosocial theory of an ongoing interaction between the person and the social environment. At the neural level, a variety of mechanisms operate to connect information about the self and others. As self-awareness and self-understanding mature, so does awareness of and understanding of the other.

In the sections that follow, the self-theory is discussed in relation to the distinction between the *me* and the *I*, a general description of how the self-theory changes from infancy through middle childhood, and the nature of self-esteem—the evaluative aspect of a child's sense of self.

The Me and the I

One of the earliest psychological analyses of self-theory was provided by William James (1892/1961). He described two elements of the self, the *me* and the *I*. The *me* is the self as object—the self one can describe—including physical characteristics, personality traits, social roles and relationships, thoughts, and feelings. The *I* is the self who is aware, the self that feels, knows, and plans one's actions. It can be characterized by four features: (1) a sense of agency or initiation of behaviors; a sense of voluntary action or free will; (2) a sense of uniqueness; (3) a sense of continuity from moment to moment and from day to day; and (4) an awareness of one's own awareness (i.e., metacognition).

Building on these ideas, Damon and Hart (1988) devised a model of self-understanding that includes both the *me* (*self as the object of awareness and as perceived by others*) and the *I* (*self as the subject, the one who experiences and knows*) changing over time. The Me, can be characterized along four dimensions: *physical self* (my physical appearance and observable characteristics), *active self* (my behaviors and actions), *social self* (my social bonds and social skills), and *psychological self* (my personality, emotions, and thoughts). The I, or self as subject, can be characterized along three dimensions: *continuity* (experiences that allow me to know that I am the same person from day to day), *distinctiveness* (experiences that illustrate how I differ from others and perceive myself to be a unique individual), and *agency* (experiences that allow me to believe that I have an impact, that I am a causal agent). At each stage of development from early school age through later adolescence, these seven dimensions of self-change.

One can recognize evidence of self-understanding in each domain even in early childhood. Development of the self is not viewed as a shift in awareness of the physical self in childhood to an awareness of the social self at a later age. Rather, there is a continuous awareness of the physical self, but the way it is evaluated and assessed changes as other aspects of the I and Me change. Self-understanding is transformed from a *categorical* and concrete assessment of the self in early school age to a *comparative* assessment of self and others in middle childhood. This is followed by a shift to an understanding of the *social implications of one's self-characteristics* in early adolescence. In later adolescence the organizing principle becomes the formulation of a *personal and social identity* that integrates the characteristics of the self into a set of beliefs and plans that guide future actions. By later adolescence, aspects of the self-theory, including personal values, experiences, and interpretations of life events, shape and are shaped by interpersonal relationships and moral choices.

Developmental Changes in the Self-Theory

The self-concept, including the I and the Me, is a product of a person's cognitive capacities and dominant motives as he or she comes into contact with the stage-related expectations of family, peers, teachers, and other members of the radius of significant others (Harter, 2012). As a result, one can expect the self-concept

to undergo developmental changes, brought about in part by changing cognitive capacities and in part by changing societal messages the child encounters at various periods of life.

In infancy, the self consists of a gradual awareness of one's independent existence. The infant discovers body boundaries, learns to identify recurring need states, and feels the comfort of loving contact with caregivers. Early efforts to reach and grab objects suggests an awareness of the distinction between the self and the other. Early gestures, like showing and pointing, offer additional evidence of the infant's awareness of this distinction (Rochat, 2012). Basic needs to maximize pleasure and avoid pain and to preserve closeness to the loving caregiver serve as organizing principles for the infant's behavior. Many theorists emphasize the close connection of the infant's internal working model of the self with the responsiveness of the other (Bretherton & Munholland, 2010). The infant relies on the other to be accessible, to permit exploration, and to comfort and reassure.

During the second year of life, self-recognition and the sense of the self as a causal agent add new dimensions to the self-theory. Gradually, these experiences are integrated into a sense of the self as a permanent being who has an impact on the environment, existing in the context of a group of other permanent beings who either do or do not respond adequately to the infant's internal states.

In toddlerhood, the self-theory grows through an active process of self-differentiation. Children explore the limits of their capacities and the nature of their impact on others. Because of toddlers' limited ability to entertain abstract concepts and their tendency to perceive themselves as the center of the world, their self-theories are based largely on the accumulation of daily experiences of competence, self-directed goal attainment, and praise

Claude is fascinated by his image reflected in the water. He notes his facial features and enjoys his appearance. His self-concept is emerging as he begins thinking about who he is, what he is like, and what the future holds for him.

or disapproval. There is little recognition of social comparisons (being better or worse than someone else), but an increasing sensitivity to the positive and negative reactions of others. Emotions including embarrassment and shame suggest an emerging awareness of the self as an object that is perceived by others.

During early school age, the self-theory becomes more complex. Children can distinguish between the real self (how one actually is) and the ideal self (how one would like to be). They recognize some discrepancies between how they describe themselves and how their parents or friends may describe them (Burton & Mitchell, 2003). They can differentiate among various areas of activities like math, reading, and music, indicating perceptions of strength in certain areas and weakness in others (Denissen, Zarrett, & Eccles, 2007).

According to Damon and Hart (1988), in early school age the self is understood as an accumulation of **categorical identifications**. No additional linkage or significance is taken from these categorical statements—simply a recognition that they exist.

> EXAMPLES: What kind of person are you? *I have blue eyes.*
>
> Why is that important? *It just is.*
>
> What kind of a person are you? *I'm Catholic.*
>
> What does that say about you? *I'm Catholic, and my mother is, and my father is, and my grandmother, and my grandfather, and I'm Catholic too.*
>
> (pp. 59–60)

In middle childhood, the organizing principle shifts to **comparative assessments**. Self-understanding relies on comparisons of oneself with social norms and standards or with specific other people.

> EXAMPLES: What are you like? *I'm bigger than most kids.*
>
> Why is that important? *I can run faster than everybody.*
>
> What are you like? *I'm not as smart as most kids.*
>
> Why is that important? *It takes me longer to do my homework.* (pp. 62–63)

The period of early school age brings with it heightened self-consciousness. Through conversations, stories, photographs, and rituals, early-school-age children begin to understand that their experiences have a uniqueness. With increasing capacities for perspective taking, children can appreciate that their view of themselves may differ from the view that others have of them. They realize that they exist in a specific time, not in the long ago of dinosaurs or pioneers, nor in near past of their grandmother's or their mother's childhood (Nelson, 2000). The ability to reflect on the self in the past and the self in the present contributes to a new aspect of the self-concept, bringing with it both the comfort of a sense of self-sameness, and the beginnings of an appreciation for the ability to change and grow. It is not uncommon for children in early school age to begin reflecting on what they hope to be when they grow up, a kind of speculation that links a self-appraisal of their strengths and interests with an understanding of the social positions that might be possible in their culture (D'Argembeau et al., 2008).

In order to collaborate on a project, children need to be able to take the point of view of the other person. As the self-concept matures, so does the ability to think about how situations may appear to someone else.

Culture and the Self-Theory

Certain aspects of culture influence the nature of self-concept. In many Western countries, values given to characteristics such as self-reliance, autonomy, and distinctiveness shape a relatively more *independent* view of the self. In many Asian cultures, values given to fitting in with the group and preserving harmonious relationships shape a relatively more *interdependent* view of the self. In both cultural views, individuals are able to differentiate a sense of self and other. They are aware of a continuous self who is the same today as yesterday and can make distinctions between a view of an inner or private self and a public self. However, in the independent orientation, greater emphasis is placed on an inherent distinctiveness in which the self is the figure and others are the ground. In the interdependent orientation, a greater emphasis is placed on the inherent interconnectedness of members of the group and an appreciation that one's thoughts, feelings, and behaviors fluctuate based on the desire to fit in to the larger social unit.

For example, one study reported on U.S. and Chinese college students' earliest childhood memories (Wang, 2001). The average age for these first memories was 3½ years for U.S. students, and 4 years for the Chinese students. The U.S. students' memories tended to be discreet events where they had the lead role in a drama or some emotional event or moment. The Chinese students' memories tended to be more routine events involving family and neighborhood. Students were asked to produce something that they actually remembered, not something someone had told them.

The following is a U.S. college student's response to a request to think of her earliest memory and to describe it as precisely as possible. This memory comes from a time when the student was about 3.

> I remember standing in my aunt's spacious blue bedroom and looking up at the ceiling. Then something caught my eye—it was the white wainscoting that bordered the top of the wall with the ceiling. I remember staring, fixated with its intricate design. And while I was doing this, all of sudden, I had an epiphany, a sort [of] realization. It was almost my first realization of a sense of "self." Because, as I was staring at the ceiling,

Kablonk/Golden Pixels LLC/Alamy Stock Photo

I realized that no one else was around. I remember being taken aback by the ability to amuse myself without any toys. (Wang, 2001, p. 220)

The next childhood memory was told by a Chinese female college student from the time when she was about age 5.

I was 5 years old. Dad taught me ancient poems. It was always when he was washing vegetables that he would explain a poem to me. It was very moving. I will never forget the poems such as "Pi-Ba-Xing" one of the poems I learned then. (Wang, 2001, appendix)

Cultural worldviews are preserved in each society's view of the self. In the United States, the self is valued as a unique, bounded, autonomous being that guides the life history through choices and action. In China and in other Asian cultures, the self is viewed as an interdependent, relational being. In these cultures, children are encouraged to show restraint in their interactions with certain others, particularly in public situations, in order to preserve social cohesion. Whereas self-expression may be encouraged in private, self-control is valued in public (Raeff, 2010). As we think about the emergence of a self-theory in early school age, it is important to keep in mind that cultures not only shape the value placed on certain attributes but also influence whether children are likely to think of the self as relatively stable and enduring across settings or relatively fluid and attuned to the demands and expectations of the social situation.

Self-Esteem

For every component of the self—the physical, emotional, social, and psychological self—a person makes an evaluation of worthiness. This self-evaluation, or **self-esteem**, is based on three sources: (1) messages of love, support, and approval from others; (2) specific attributes and competencies; and (3) the way one regards these specific aspects of the self in comparison with

Experiences of success build confidence and contribute to positive self-esteem.

michaeljung/Shutterstock.com

others and in relation to one's ideal self. The need to protect and enhance one's self-esteem is a basic psychological motive that drives behavior (Greenberg, 2008). Views of the self as being loved, valued, admired, and successful contribute to a sense of worth. Views of the self as being ignored, rejected, scorned, and inadequate contribute to a sense of worthlessness. These early affective experiences build a general sense of pride or shame, worthiness or worthlessness that is captured in the global statements children make about themselves even as early as age 3 or 4.

Information about specific aspects of the self is accumulated through experiences of success and failure in daily tasks or when particular aspects of one's competence are challenged. A young child may develop a positive sense of self in athletics, problem solving, or social skills through the encouraging reactions of others as well as through the pleasure associated with succeeding in each of these areas (Harter & Bukowski, 2012).

With experience in a variety of roles and settings, each specific ability takes on a certain level of importance. Not all abilities are equally valued at home, at school, and by friends. Children may believe they have abilities in some areas, but not in those they consider highly important. Others may believe they have only one or two areas of strength, but they may highly value those areas and believe them to be critically important to their overall success. Self-esteem is influenced by the value one assigns to specific competencies in relation to one's overall life goals and personal ideals. Thus, it is possible to be a success in the eyes of others and still feel a nagging sense of worthlessness. Similarly, it is possible to feel proud and confident even when others do not value the activities and traits in which one takes satisfaction.

Feelings of positive self-worth provide a protective buffer against insecurity or conditions that threaten to expose one's lack of value or meaning. If a person has a positive, optimistic self-evaluation, then messages that are negative and incongruent with it will be deflected. People with high self-esteem may explain a failure by examining the task, the amount of time needed for its completion, the other people involved, or the criteria for evaluating success and failure. They use strategies to minimize the importance of negative feedback. They do not permit a failure to increase doubt about their basic worth. Rather, their high self-esteem functions to protect their positive self-evaluation by coping effectively with negative feedback and reclaiming their view of the self as someone who has socially valued qualities (Brown, Dutton, & Cook, 2001).

By contrast, people with low self-esteem feel worse after a failure, tend to view failure as new evidence of their lack of worth, and are less likely to cope effectively with the negative feelings that accompany failure (Heimpel, Wood, Marshall, & Brown, 2002). People with low self-esteem appear to accept negative moods that follow a failure experience and are less likely to take action to try to improve their mood. Because negative feedback is so painful for those with low self-esteem, they avoid unfavorable comparisons with others, leading them to be more cautious in situations that might expose them to criticism (Bernichon, Cook, & Brown, 2003).

Despite the many positive correlates of high self-esteem, some question whether high self-esteem is always a positive quality. Some researchers have suggested that there is such a thing as

By the age of 5 or 6, children are trying hard to gain acceptance from adults and peers. Even mild criticism from a teacher is often enough to arouse feelings of guilt or remorse. What kind of teacher criticism do you imagine might be taking place in this photo?

unrealistic or fragile high self-esteem (Kernis, 2003). For example, people with high self-esteem seem to deflect failure messages in one area by emphasizing their abilities in another area. When employed consistently, this strategy can be perceived as a defensive reaction that allows the individual to preserve a sense of self-worth rather than to address underlying feelings of inferiority or shame (Jordan et al., 2003).

A different criticism concerning self-esteem is that the emphasis on high self-esteem is a value that reflects the individualist nature of Western culture. In contrast, Eastern cultures are less concerned with affirming the positive qualities of the individual, valuing instead self-discipline and self-improvement (Markus, Mullally, & Kitayama, 1997). A pan-cultural perspective suggests that it is a universal tendency for humans to strive for and protect their self-regard. However, the norms for what one considers evidence of self-worth and the strategies that human beings use to advance their self-regard are shaped by culture (Brown, 2003; Sedikides, Gaertner, & Toguchi, 2003; Sedikides, Gaertner, & Vevea, 2005).

A third concern is the confusion between self-esteem and narcissism. Both of these personality qualities arise as children internalize how other people perceive them. Whereas some scholars suggest that narcissism is an excessive expression of self-esteem, others suggest that these two traits are quite distinct. Narcissists feel superior to others; they believe they should be entitled to special treatment, respect, and privilege. Those with high self-esteem feel satisfied with themselves and confident in their abilities; they view themselves as worthy but not superior to others (Brummelman, Thomaes, & Sedikides, 2016). Socialization messages that express affection and appreciation nurture self-esteem, whereas messages that over value the child or convey that the child is superior to others can nurture narcissism (Brummelman et al., 2015).

Self-Esteem and the Early-School-Age Child. At each life stage, as individuals set new goals for themselves or as discrepancies in competence become apparent, temporary periods

of lowered self-esteem may be anticipated. Although we tend to think of self-esteem as a stable trait that characterizes individuals across settings, there are periods of life when self-esteem is more vulnerable to fluctuation, especially as individuals encounter dramatic changes in roles, environments, and normative expectations for behavior (Trzesniewski, Donnellan, & Robins, 2003). Early childhood appears to be one of those periods.

The family provides a critical context that can support or undermine a child's self- esteem. When parents speak in a positive way to their children, recall positive emotions and experiences, and offer explanations even when they are engaged in conflict with their children, the children have a more positive self-esteem (Reese, Bird, & Tripp, 2007). When parents make unfavorable comparisons of their child to other siblings or peers, or when they highlight shortcomings and make repeated reference to negative experiences and emotions, these interactions lower the child's self-esteem.

In early school age, children are increasingly able to make distinctions among areas of competence, such as math ability, reading, writing, athletic ability, or artistic or musical talents. They may also think that some aspects of competence are more important than others, and they are able to judge their own abilities in light of what they believe others expect of them. When children think an area is important and they believe they are competent in that area, it increases their self-esteem. When children think an area is important and they believe they are not very competent in that area, it decreases their self-esteem (Grier, 2013).

Children are also aware of the importance of acceptance by adults and peers outside the family, especially their teachers and classmates. When students have opportunities to present their work, or when their work is displayed in a personalized way in the classroom, it tends to increase their feelings of self-worth. In contrast, when teachers or children tease or belittle each other in the classroom, it has a negative impact on self-worth (Maxwell & Chmielewski, 2008).

In addition to the influences of families and school environments on self-esteem, young children are aware of the expectations and stereotypes conveyed by their peers and the media about body type and physical appearance. In a study of girls ages 5 through 8, the expression among peers about the desire to be thin and exposure to television programming that promoted the value of thinness was shown to promote body dissatisfaction. As the girls were followed over the course of a year, from age 5 to 6 or 6 to 7, body dissatisfaction in the first year was found to predict lower self-esteem 1 year later (Dohnt & Tiggemann, 2006). Even at this very young age, children are reacting to social messages about physical appearance that can negatively impact their feelings of self-worth.

Children's sense of self-esteem begins to crystallize in the early-school-age years. In research with kindergartners, children were faced with a challenging task. The way children approached the task, their hopefulness about succeeding, and their general expression of positive or negative attributes were combined to reflect a measure of helplessness. Five years later, the expressions of helplessness assessed in kindergarten proved to be a good predictor of depression and a low sense of self-worth. A scheme for low self-esteem and helplessness may begin to take shape in the early childhood period and, unless challenged through positive intervention, may color a child's sense of mastery and competence in the years ahead (Davis-Kean & Sandler, 2001; Kistner, Ziegert, Castro, & Robertson, 2001). Young children need frequent reassurance from adults that they are competent, safe, and loved. They need numerous opportunities to discover that their unique talents and abilities are useful and important and that they can have a positive impact on others. As competencies increase, as thought becomes more flexible, and as the child makes meaningful friendships, self-esteem is expected to increase.

FURTHER REFLECTION: Analyze the interaction of the developmental tasks of gender identification, moral development, and self-theory. How might gender identification and moral development influence a child's self-theory? How might a child's self-theory influence their gender identification and moral development?

Peer Play

OBJECTIVE 4 Describe the features of peer play, including group games, media play, and friendship in the early-school-age years.

Although experiences in the family provide the primary information that guides a young child's construction of the social world, interactions with peers contribute important opportunities for physical, cognitive, social, and emotional development. The quality of play expands during the early-school-age period, introducing more complex games with larger numbers of participants. Media in various forms have increasingly become play companions. Children form friendship groups that allow them to sustain more elaborate fantasy play, experience group cooperation and conflict, participate in group problem solving, and encounter varying ideas about the topics discussed previously: gender, morality, and the self.

Developmental scholars generally acknowledge the value of child-initiated, freely chosen play for the young child's cognitive and social development. Nonetheless, playtime at school and at home is dwindling. Estimates suggest that young children have 8 fewer hours a week of unstructured play time today than did children 20 years ago (Elkind, 2007; Miller & Almon, 2009). With the upward pressure on kindergarten and first grade to introduce new levels of competence in basic academic skills, there are fewer resources and less time available for child-initiated play. Outside of school, many families create a series of structured activities for their young children including music lessons, early sports experiences, and language enrichment, leaving little time for after-school or weekend unstructured play.

What is more, the toys and play resources that are marketed for young children are becoming increasingly oriented toward specific educational objectives such as vocabulary building and math facts. Through the insertion of computer chips, the play value of many modern toys is controlled in advance by the manufacturers rather than invented through the child's active exploration (Winerman, 2009). In the following sections we focus on group games, media play, and friendships as aspects of peer play in early school age.

Group Games

Early-school-age children continue to use vivid fantasies in play. However, during this period a new form of play emerges. Children show interest in **group games** that are more structured and somewhat more oriented to reality than social pretend play based primarily on imagination. Duck-Duck-Goose, London Bridges, and Farmer-in-the-Dell are examples of early group play. Simon Says, Hide-and-Seek, Hopscotch, and Statue-Maker are more complex games of early school age. They involve more cognitive complexity, physical skill, and ritual. These games combine fantasy with an emphasis on peer cooperation and competition. Group play is a transitional form between the fantasy play of the toddler and the team sports and other games with rules of middle childhood (Erikson, 1977).

Group games usually include a few rules that are simple enough so that a child can use them effectively to begin a game and determine a winner without the help of an adult. Usually, no team concept is involved. A game is played repeatedly so that many children have an opportunity to win. The particular pleasure that children derive from these games seems to result more from peer cooperation and interaction than from being a winner. Many of these games permit children to shift roles. A child is the hider and then the seeker, the catcher and then the thrower, the statue-maker and then the statue. Through group play, children experience the reciprocal nature of role relationships. Whereas many of their social roles are fixed—son or daughter, sibling, student—in play with peers, children have opportunities to experience a variety of perspectives.

Early-school-age children also play simple board games that involve two or more players. Games like Chutes and Ladders, Checkers, Candyland, Hi Ho Cherry-o, and card games like War and Go-Fish give young children opportunities to experience games with a few rules that set the stage for later, more complex play. These games introduce the idea of winning and losing. They typically combine elements of chance and a bit of skill, giving young children the idea of having good or bad luck. By the age of 5 most children understand that games involve both cooperation and competition. Cooperation is reflected in the willingness of the players to take turns and follow the rules. Competition is reflected in using one's best chances and strategies to win (Schmidt, Hardecker, & Tomasello, 2016). Once they understand about winning and losing, it is not unusual for early-school-age children to make up their own rules or ignore the rules in order to win.

Media Play

From a psychosocial perspective, development is a product of the ongoing interaction of the changing person in a changing environment. The media environment is an excellent example of this idea. Children are being exposed to electronic media at younger and younger ages, and new media platforms and resources are being developed for this young audience. A research literature is accumulating about the scope and extent of use of these electronic media by very young children and its impact on their social and cognitive development (Dill, 2009; Strasburger, Wilson, & Jordan, 2014).

A national survey sponsored by Common Sense Media was designed to address questions about young children's use of diverse media. How much time do children spend with electronic media including television, computers, video games, and mobile devices? How many children have access to new mobile media devices? What types of activities/content do children engage with using various media platforms (Rideout, 2013)? The study involved a nationally representative sample of families with children ages 0 to 8 years old. Survey responses were given by parents.

Children spent an average of 2 hours a day with some type of screen media. Television was the dominant media source; almost all the children (96 percent) had TVs in their homes and about half the daily screen time was spent watching television. Television is a major source of educational content, especially for 2- to 4-year-olds. Older children are more likely to watch children's entertainment programs. However, an increasing amount of this viewing (about one third) is spent watching programming that was recorded earlier, downloaded, or accessed on demand. In 38 percent of homes, the TV is on most or all of the time even if no one is watching. Over half the parents say that they sometimes or often have their children with them while they watch their own programs.

Children are not just passive consumers of electronic media—they are making choices and affecting their media environment. Table 7.4 shows the percentage of children ages 0 to 8 who use each type of resource on a daily basis. Of particular note is the increasing use of mobile media (smartphones and tablets). Almost three fourths of children have used a mobile device at some time, and 17 percent use one daily. For those who use one daily, the time spent was slightly over one hour. Surprisingly, even among the youngest children (0–2), parents report that 38 percent have used a mobile device. By the age 5 to 8, over 80 percent have used a mobile device, especially for playing games, and also for use with apps that involve creative art, music, photography, and as an e-reader.

Income Inequality and Media Access

The Common Sense Media survey divided the sample into three income groups: low-income ($30,000 and under), middle income ($30,000–$75,000), and higher income ($75,000 and above).

Table 7.4	Daily Media Activities
Among 0- to 8-year-olds, the percent who engage in each activity at least once or more per day	
Read/are read to	60%
Watch TV	58%
Watch DVDs	18%
Use a mobile device*	17%
Use a computer	14%
Use handheld video game	7%
Use console video game	6%
Read an ebook	4%

* Such as a smartphone or tablet
Source: Rideout, 2013, Table 4. p. 16.

Media use and access differ by income. Low-income families are less likely than high-income families to have high speed internet (46 percent versus 86 percent). As a result, in many homes children's access to media content is limited to broadcast, real-time programming. Low-income families are more likely to have the television going when no one is watching, and children in low-income families are more likely to have a television in their room. Parents say that a common reason is that the young child shares a room with an older sibling, an adult, or sleeps in a common bedroom. This means that children in lower-income families are more likely to be exposed to the programming and advertising that was intended for adult viewers. Although ownership of smartphones and tablets has been increasing, there is still a gap between low-income and higher income families (smartphone: 25 percent gap; tablet: 43 percent gap). As a result, fewer low-income families have downloaded an educational app or any type of child-orientated app to a smartphone or tablet. Even among low-income families that have a mobile device, fewer parents have downloaded educational apps for their children than among middle and higher-income families.

The media is an intimate part of family life. Various media are used by families in different ways, for play, learning, escape, to foster interactions, and to give parents a time when they are not interacting with their children.

> Being an adult is hard. There are times when my interacting with my children is best served by me having an opportunity to allow them to do something alone so I can regroup. When I got laid off a couple of weeks ago, I didn't know it was coming. I got blindsided. I couldn't have interacted with my children that night. I couldn't have done it. "Let's watch *Finding Nemo,* kids. Here are some chicken strips, here are sippy cups—I'll see you in about an hour and a half." (Rideout, Hamel, & Kaiser Family Foundation, 2006, p. 14)

Many videos, computer programs, and video games are marketed to parents as having an educational value. However, manufacturers argue that their first concern is that the materials have to be fun. They believe that if children don't experience the materials as fun, then the media won't be used and the educational value will never be realized. Parents seem to be divided in their views about the educational value of television and other media. Some are surprised about the positive things their children take away from watching TV. "My daughter started saying something to me in Spanish—I don't know a word of Spanish—TV is definitely educational" (Rideout, Hamel, & Kaiser Family Foundation, 2006, p. 14). At the same time, families appear to be setting more rules about how much television their children can watch and what types of video games, mobile apps, or hand held games they can play, implying some wariness about the impact of these resources on their children's emotional and cognitive development. A systematic review of the evidence found few if any published studies that document the advertised educational claims associated with these resources (Garrison & Christakis, 2005).

Children's media games seem to share certain features. The most popular games are action or combat scenarios, sports, and adventure games. At every age, boys spend more time playing media games than girls (Cherney & London, 2006; Rideout, 2013). That may be explained in part by the fact that most of the player-controlled characters in the most popular video games are male. Where female characters appear, they tend to be in supportive or helping roles (Mou & Peng, 2009). Boys may also be more interested in the themes that dominate many video games, especially sports, combat, and monster scenarios.

Studies that focus on the design features of interactive games find that experience with these games contributes to spatial visualization, visual attention, manual dexterity, and early readiness for computer literacy (Subrahmanyam, Kraut, Greenfield, & Gross, 2001). Most of the video games require some reading skills. Speed of response is a feature of many games. This rewards children who can think quickly, analyze the situation, and make a rapid-fire motor response. When you lose or the turn ends, it is easy to start over and try to do better the next time. Many of the games provide immediate reinforcement through increasing points, sounds, accumulation of virtual rewards, and access to new screens or levels. In some games, children can play with or against each other.

Studies of video game use among young children suggest that children link their experiences with television, videos, and video games into other areas of imagination and creativity. It is not unusual for children to form relationships with the on-screen characters, which seems to lead to increased motivation to pay attention to the information that these characters present and to learn from them (Richert, Robb, & Smith, 2011).

Eric is solving a puzzle on his tablet while his sister looks on. She gives him suggestions about what to do, and they plan their strategy together. The computer environment can be a zone of proximal development when siblings or friends work together to advance their reasoning and problem-solving skills.

The media themselves are often linked so that characters from a movie or television program are integrated in computer software or a video game. In role-playing videos, children may be able to choose a favorite character or switch characters as part of the play. Children use images from these media in their written narratives, their imaginative play, and their conversations with friends (Singer & Singer, 2008; Wohlwend, 2009).

Given the extensive exposure to electronic media at young ages, additional research is needed to help clarify their impact. Concerns about the relationship of extensive media use to childhood obesity, possible interference with social communication and language development, and exposure to non-educational content deserve empirical study. The media environment may also contribute positively to the emergence of self-directed goal attainment, new capacities for managing multiple stimuli at once (multitasking), and new appreciation for music, art, poetry, and the natural environment through early exposure.

Friendship Groups

What can we expect about the nature of friendship in early school age? Friends clearly matter to young children. They make play exciting; they provide experiences of emotional closeness; and they create opportunities for new and interesting activities. The friendships of young children may not have the degree of loyalty, emotional intensity, and disclosure that are seen among older children and adolescents, but they certainly provide important experiences of companionship and affection (Dunn, 2004).

Friendships, by definition, are voluntary and reciprocal. Even young children choose who they want to have as their friends. You cannot make children befriend another child. Of the many children in a play group, preschool class, or kindergarten, some children like each other and want to spend time playing together; other children have no friends. The precise reasons that children are drawn to one another are not entirely understood.

For young children, friendships are likely based on proximity (living in the same neighborhood, or going to the same preschool), and the mutual enjoyment of activities. Friendships are maintained through acts of affection, sharing, and collaboration in fantasy or play that involves building or making things like block construction, or water table or sandbox play. Children may build snow forts together, play dolls or cars, create space adventures, or sleep over at one another's homes. By the age of 4 or 5, children who have stable friendships become skilled at coordinating their interactions with their friends, creating elaborate pretend games, and being willing to modify their play preferences so that both members in the friendship have a chance to enjoy the kinds of play they like best. Because they care about their friend, young children have opportunities to expand their sense of empathy. They show concern for their friends' troubles and offer help when they perceive that their friends need assistance (Vaughn, Colvin, Azria, Caya, & Krzysik, 2001).

Young children are sensitive to the norms for fairness and cooperation among friends and are more likely to be generous with their friends than with children they know who are not friends (Moore, 2009). The opportunity to form friendships benefits young children by enhancing their interpersonal sensitivity, social reasoning skills, and conflict resolution skills

(Volling, Youngblade, & Belsky, 1997). Having a good friend who has effective social and cognitive skills leads to more meaningful conversations between friends, less frustration and aggression, and more mutually satisfying companionship (Engle, McElwain, & Lasky, 2011; Salvas et al., 2011).

Conflicts Among Friends.
Even though children appear to be drawn into the active world of peer friendships, it is an uneven, difficult, and often extremely frustrating terrain for many early-school-age children. Peer play is frequently disrupted by quarrels, tattling on others, and hard feelings about injustices. Friendships may be broken by taking away a toy, hitting, or name-calling.

Early-school-age children differ markedly in their social skills, language abilities, and the extent to which they understand or think about how another person is feeling or thinking. Moreover, some children have already achieved a fairly high level of self-control and are able to inhibit their angry impulses, while other children are still likely to take out their angry feelings on others by hitting, kicking, grabbing, and other aggressive acts.

Young children tend to evaluate situations on the basis of outcomes rather than intentions. Therefore, they are often harsh in assigning blame in the case of negative outcomes. For example, many 5- and 6-year-olds participate in play fighting. In a study of children's perceptions of play fighting, Italian and British children of ages 5, 8, and 11 were surveyed about the differences between real fighting and play fighting (Smith, Hunter, Carvalho, & Costabile, 1992). About half the children liked play fighting—a somewhat larger number of boys than girls. But about 80 percent thought there was a risk that play fighting could lead to a serious, real fight. This might happen if there was an accidental injury, if the play fighting got carried away into mean name-calling, or if, when one child accidentally hurt the other, the second child mistook the injury as purposeful and hurt the first child back. Five-year-olds said that if play fighting turned into real fighting, they would tell an adult. No matter whether the other child was a friend or not, they believed that such a transgression had to be handled with a serious intervention by a grown-up. The older children were more likely to forget about it, especially if the other person was a friend.

The quality of children's friendships and the extent to which their play is characterized by cooperative, positive interactions or conflicts and fighting depend on the social and cognitive maturity of the play companions. Some studies find that young children who have no or very few friends are also likely to be described by teachers as exhibiting more antisocial behaviors. They have difficulty controlling their anger and are likely to lash out at others (Engle, McElwain, & Lasky, 2011).

Some children seem especially preoccupied with violent fantasies, often fed by exposure to violent media, or as a result of exposure to power-assertive discipline and frequent angry interactions among adults at home. These children, who were described as "hard to manage," experience more conflicts in interactions with friends, are less willing to help other children, and are less effective at coordinating their play with others (Dunn & Hughes, 2001). Not surprising, when children find "best friends" who are similarly antisocial, it tends to accentuate their antisocial

behavior, especially among boys (Eivers, Brendgen, Vitaro, & Borge, 2012).

Sex Segregation Among Friends.
One of the most noticeable characteristics of young children's friendship groups is that they are likely to be segregated by sex. When boys and girls are free to choose play companions, they tend to choose others of their own sex. This pattern of same-sex social groupings among children is found not only in the United States, but also in most other cultures (Whiting & Edwards, 1992). In one longitudinal study, children at age 4½ were found playing with same-sex friends about three times more often than with opposite-sex friends. By age 6½, they were 11 times more likely to be playing with same-sex friends (Maccoby & Jacklin, 1987).

Sex segregation is promoted by cognitive, behavioral, and contextual/cultural factors (Martin, Fabes, Hanish, Leonard, & Dinella, 2011). Based on the earlier discussion of gender identification, it is clear that children expect others of the same sex to like similar activities, toys, and forms of play. Children form internal representations of what boys and girls are like as friends and playmates. These internal models guide the inferences they make as they engage in peer interaction (Markovits, Benenson, & Dolenszky, 2001). Thus, children are likely to seek others of the same sex because they believe these other children will have the same play preferences they have.

At the same time, boys and girls do appear to play differently, especially when in same-sex and mixed-sex groups. Thus, a preference for same-sex play groups may be fostered by feelings of comfort or discomfort as children accumulate play experiences. For instance, in the review of children's media play, researchers report a significant difference in boys' and girls' involvement in video game play. Seventeen percent of 5- to 8-year-old boys are daily video game players as compared to 5 percent of same age girls (Rideout, 2013). Some cultures discourage girls and boys from participating in the same types of play. For example, when children in a Brazilian tribal culture play family, the boys (husbands) go off to pretend to be hunting and fishing, returning with leaves that are then given to the girls (wives), who pretend to cook them and pass them out to the boys to eat (Gregor, 1977).

Environmental cues can enhance children's same-sex preferences. In an experimental study, some preschool teachers were asked to use gender-specific language when talking with the class while the control group teachers were asked to use gender-inclusive language. For example, in the experimental group a teacher might say: "Good morning girls and boys." In the control group a teacher might say: "Good morning children." After 2 weeks of this treatment, children's attitudes about gender stereotypes were measured and their preferences for play companions during free play were observed. Children in the experimental groups showed an increase in their agreement about gender stereotypes and a decrease in the amount of play with opposite sex children during free play (Hilliard & Liben, 2010).

The significance of the formation of same-sex social groups is that boys and girls grow up in distinct peer environments. The quality, tone, and content of social interactions differ depending on the sex of the child and the sex of their play companions (Fabes, Martin & Hanish, 2003; Sigelman & Holtz, 2013). The more children play with same-sex groups, the more they take on the gender-stereotypical attitudes and behaviors of their play companions (Maccoby, 1988, 1990; Martin, Fabes, & Hanish, 2011, 2014). Boys and girls use different strategies to achieve dominance or leadership in their groups. Boys are more likely to use physical assertiveness and direct demands; girls are more likely to use verbal persuasiveness and polite suggestions. The verbal exchanges in all-boy groups are apt to include frequent boasts, commands, interruptions, heckling, and generally playful teasing. Boys try to top one another's stories and to establish dominance through verbal threats. The interactions in all-girl groups, on the other hand, tend to include agreeing with and acknowledging the others' comments, listening carefully to one another's statements, and talking about things that bind the group together in a shared sentiment or experience. In mixed-sex groups, boys may be less controlling and dominating than they would be in all-boy groups, but this may still be more than girls find acceptable or comfortable. As a result, girls' negative views of boys are reinforced and their tendency to seek all-girl peer interactions increases.

In contemporary U.S. culture, children are not typically restricted from playing with opposite-sex friends. They actively construct their friendship groups and choose play companions with the help of parents and caregivers who may facilitate their play and coordinate with other families to arrange for playtime. Many young children form friendships with children of the opposite sex. In the case of Lee, she was best friends with her cousin, Bob. The two of them played endlessly, enjoying the same adventures and activities, getting into scrapes, and testing the limits of their initiative. These friendships may begin as early as infancy or toddlerhood between children who live in the same neighborhood or attend the same child care center. They are sustained by a compatibility of interests and play preferences and may survive the trend toward seeking same-sex friendships, even during early and middle childhood. There is evidence of a benefit to children who have more flexible preferences for play companions, including mixed-sex and same-sex play groups. Experiences with mixed-sex play groups are associated with exposure to a wider array of play activities and materials, and the emergence of positive emotional adjustment as children encounter the increasingly complex social environment of the mixed-sex classroom (DiDonato et al., 2012; Fabes, Hanish, & Martin, 2007).

However, the general preference for same-sex friendship groups is an important aspect of social development that is established during the early childhood years and continues into adolescence (Leaper & Bigler, 2011). Although a boy and a girl grow up in the same culture, the same neighborhood, and even the same family, the tendency to establish separate play and friendship groups fosters the development of distinctive gender-linked communication strategies and makes the achievement of mutual understanding between boys and girls difficult.

Groups and Dyads. In addition to the preference for same-sex friends, boys and girls tend to prefer to interact in groups of different sizes. Early-school-age girls seem to enjoy dyadic (two-person) interactions over larger groups, whereas boys seem to enjoy larger groups (Benenson, 1993; Markovits, Benenson, & Dolenszky, 2001). This is not to say that boys and girls cannot function effectively in both dyadic and larger peer group situations, but when given the choice, boys prefer the group and girls the dyad. These two configurations, the group and the dyad, provide different opportunities for intimacy, different needs to exercise dominance and control, and different problems in the coordination of action. They provide models for different forms of adult social relationships—the dyad being associated with intimacy between partners or in parent–child relationships, and the group being associated with sports teams, work groups, and families.

FURTHER REFLECTION: Try to recall your favorite pastimes from the early-school-age years. How much influence did the media have on the kinds of games and play you enjoyed? What were some differences in the kinds of play you engaged in by yourself, with just one friend, and with a group of friends? How "gendered" or sex-segregated was your play?

The Psychosocial Crisis: Initiative Versus Guilt

OBJECTIVE 5 Explain the psychosocial crisis of initiative versus guilt, the central process of identification, the prime adaptive ego quality of purpose, and the core pathology of inhibition.

As children positively resolve the psychosocial crisis of autonomy versus shame and doubt, they emerge from toddlerhood with a strong sense of themselves as unique individuals. During early school age, children shift their attention toward investigation of the external environment. They attempt to discover the same kind of stability, strength, and regularity in the external world that they have discovered in themselves.

Initiative

Initiative is an expression of agency and innovation—an outgrowth of early experiences of the self as a causal agent that continues to be demonstrated as children impose themselves and their ideas and questions onto their social world. You might think of imitation as a more conservative process in which a child copies behaviors that already exist in their family or community. In contrast, initiative suggests a creative expression of the child's imagination and curiosity (Nielsen, Tomaselli, Mushin, & Whiten, 2014). It is a manifestation of the *I*, the executive branch of the self that was discussed earlier in the section on self-concept. Initiative is the active, conceptual investigation of the world, in much the same sense that autonomy is the active, physical manipulation of it (Erikson, 1963). It can be recognized in a child's curiosity, inventiveness, exploratory behavior, and active coping strategies in the face of obstacles (Frese, 2001).

Children's curiosity about the order of the universe ranges from the physical to the metaphysical. They may ask questions about the color of the sky, the purpose of hair, the nature of God, the origin of babies, or the speed at which fingernails grow. They take things apart, explore the alleys and dark corners of their neighborhood, and invent toys and games out of odds and ends.

One expression of initiative is children's playful exploration of their own bodies and sometimes of their friends' bodies. It is not uncommon to find 5- and 6-year-olds intently involved in a game of doctor in which both doctor and patient have their pants off. Boys of this age may occasionally be observed in a game that is won by the child who can achieve the longest urine trajectory. Girls report occasions on which they have attempted to urinate from a standing position, attempting to imitate how a boy does. Both boys and girls engage in some form of masturbation. These behaviors are evidence of children's growing curiosity about and pleasure in their bodies and their physical functioning.

Children may express initiative while they are alone by attempting to discover how things work and by building or inventing novel devices.

> Donald kicked and knocked over an endless variety of things at hand. He put a block on top of a toy car, a leaf on top of that, then knocked the leaf off. Then he turned a truck over on its side, put a block on top of it, moved over to the car, stacked three blocks on top of it, and knocked the whole structure over. He took the car again, spanked it as if it were a doll, knocked it upside down, placed a leaf on top of it, then swept the leaf off. He played a little longer in this way, then ran out of the garage. (Murphy, 1962, p. 102)

In the home environment, many children express initiative by creating hiding places or private spaces. In these places, where children create a feeling of autonomy and control, they can impose their own form of creative play. These spaces, like under the table, in a closet, or behind the couch, can be used alone or with other play companions. Five-year-old Micah likes to use the space between the front door and the door to the house as a private play space. She fills the entry way with pillows and blankets, then she brings her little sister in with her and they pretend. It's definitely a "no grown ups" territory (Green, 2015).

Children may also express initiative in social play by asking questions, asserting their presence, taking leadership, and coordinating their ideas with their play companions. In play, children can express their agency by co-constructing fantasy situations, transforming materials to new uses, inventing roles, and establishing the rules of collaborative interactions. Pretend play is associated with enhanced creativity, divergent thinking, and emotional well-being, all features of a positive sense of initiative (Hoffmann & Russ, 2016; Stetsenko & Ho, 2015).

In one study of social competence, children described the strategies they used to enter a peer play group (Dodge, Pettit, McClaskey, & Brown, 1986). Two children were playing a game (they were referred to as the *hosts*), and a third child was asked to enter the room and try to initiate play with the others. The entry episode was videotaped and coded. The child who tried to initiate play and the two hosts were interviewed about the episode and asked to evaluate how successful the entry child had been. Three strategies for initiating interaction were judged to be effective and were associated with other evidence of social competence:

1. Children established common ground by giving meaningful information in response to questions.

2. Children engaged in a positive, friendly interchange with the others.
3. Children did not show evidence of negative, irritable behaviors.

The children who were least successful in initiating entry into the play "were disruptive, . . . made nagging, weak demands, . . . engaged in incoherent behaviors, or . . . disagreed with hosts without citing a rule or reason" (Dodge et al., 1986, p. 25).

The ability to engage with peers in a positive way is a key component of social competence. Children who are able to make their wishes and needs known, who can enter into peer activities easily and make appropriate contributions to group discussions and play are also more likely to become positively connected to their academic environment. The school is, after all, a social setting. In order for children to do well in school, they need to be able to establish and maintain positive peer relationships, a process that often requires initiative (Ladd, Herald-Brown, & Kochel, 2009; Oades-Sese, Esquivel, Kaliski, & Maniatis, 2011).

Children who experience a positive sense of initiative can apply this orientation to investigation of the physical as well as the social world. They innovate through the creation of magic potions mixed together with soap, perfume, pinecones, leaves, and other "powerful" ingredients. They create plays, stories, puppet shows, dances, and ceremonies. They dress up in costumes, entertain company by standing on their heads, engage in daring acts by hanging from tree limbs or walking on the tops of high ledges, and impose themselves in any and all curious and private discussions. They spend time trying to figure out ways to catch a glimpse of Santa Claus on Christmas Eve or the Tooth Fairy when she comes at night to collect her treasures. These are the years when a sense of initiative is associated with a naive, exuberant, entrepreneurial spirit and a desire to discover, direct, and dominate. All manner of investigation and inquiry is fair game.

The psychosocial crisis of initiative versus guilt is resolved positively when children develop the sense that an active, questioning investigation of the environment is informative and pleasurable. Inquiry is tempered by a respect for personal privacy and cultural values. However, the dominant state of mind is curiosity and experimentation. The child learns that, even though certain areas are off-limits, efforts to understand most aspects of the world are appropriate.

Guilt

Guilt is an emotion that accompanies the sense that one has been responsible for an unacceptable thought, fantasy, or action (Izard, 2004). It is a fundamental moral emotion usually accompanied by remorse and a desire to make reparation for real or imagined wrongdoing. It has the adaptive function of promoting social harmony because it disrupts or inhibits aggressive actions and leads people to ask for forgiveness or to compensate for wrongs they may have done. In comparison to *shame*, which often is accompanied by feelings of humiliation, anger, or resentment, guilt is typically tied to constructive efforts to repair the harm done to others (Bafunno & Camodeca, 2013; Tangney, 2001, 2012).

Sandy made her sister cry by calling her a bad name. Now she is in her room, thinking things over. For most children, occasional feelings of guilt lead to wanting to set things right and regain positive feelings with their family or friends.

Three theories offer different explanations for the dynamics that underlie feelings of guilt. The psychoanalytic perspective views guilt as an emotional reaction to one's unacceptable sexual and aggressive impulses. These impulses are especially threatening during the phallic stage, when hostility and feelings of sexuality toward one's parents become a focus of the child's wishes and must be repressed.

Research on empathy suggests that guilt may be awakened at a very early age through emotional arousal and sensitivity to another person's emotional distress. This view of guilt based on empathy is not defensive; it is closely linked to prosocial feelings and the basic emotional ties between infants and their caregivers.

The cognitive perspective suggests that guilt occurs when one fails to act in accord with one's own personal standards and beliefs. This view supposes a more advanced level of self-reflection and the ability to compare one's behaviors against personal standards.

Every culture imposes some limits on legitimate experimentation and investigation. Some questions may not be asked; some acts may not be performed. Adults' reactions determine whether the child learns to view specific behaviors, such as aggressiveness, sexual play, or masturbation, as wrong or acceptable. Children gradually internalize cultural prohibitions and learn to inhibit their curiosity in the taboo areas. One taboo shared by most cultures is the prohibition of incest. Most children learn that any behavior that suggests sexual intimacy between family members is absolutely forbidden. Even the thought of such a relationship comes to generate feelings of anxiety and guilt. The child's curiosity in other domains is limited to the extent that the family and the school impose restrictions on certain areas of inquiry or action. For example, children might be very curious to know what is happening in the teacher's lounge at school, but they are not allowed in there.

Guilt, like other negative poles of the psychosocial crises, can have an adaptive function. As children grow in their sense of empathy and ability to take responsibility for their actions, they are able to acknowledge when their actions or words may have caused harm to someone else. Normal levels of guilt have been associated with positive levels of prosocial behavior and high levels of empathy. Feelings of guilt generally lead to remorse and some attempt to set things right again, to restore the positive feelings in a relationship (Tangney, Malouf, Stuewig, & Mashek, 2012). In a longitudinal study, guilt-prone and shame-prone children were followed from elementary grades to later adolescence. At ages 18 to 21, the guilt-prone children were less likely to be involved in risky and illegal behaviors including less involvement with drugs and alcohol and less involvement with the criminal justice system (Stuewig et al., 2015).

Some children suffer from overwhelming guilt. They feel that each of their questions or doubts about the world is inappropriate. They may experience guilt about their own impulses and fantasies, even when they have taken no actions and no negative consequences have resulted. Moreover, these children begin to believe that their thoughts and actions are responsible for the misfortune or unhappiness of others. They do not seem to take any enjoyment in play, and their play is often characterized by negative or sad themes. Excessive guilt is one of the symptoms associated with early identification of depression in preschoolers (Luby, 2010).

Young children of depressed mothers express unusually high levels of distress, concern, rejection, and feelings of responsibility for others' unhappiness. Mothers who are consistently sad set an example of blaming themselves for most of the bad things that happen. Depressed mothers are likely to withdraw love when the child has misbehaved—a discipline technique associated with high levels of guilt and anxiety in children. In this environment, children learn to restrict new behaviors out of fear that they may cause harm or unhappiness to someone else (Rakow et al., 2011; Zahn-Waxler & Van Hulle, 2012). Children who resolve the crisis of initiative versus guilt in the direction of guilt are left to rely almost totally on their parents or other authorities for directions on how to operate in the world.

The psychosocial crisis of initiative versus guilt highlights the close tie between intellectual curiosity and emotional development. During this stage, parents and the school transmit the cultural attitudes toward experimentation, curiosity, and investigation. They also make demands that direct the child's curiosity away from familial, subgroup, and cultural areas of taboo. Children are expected to develop the ability to control their own questions and behavior. While violations may bring disapproval and punishment, successful self-control may attract no notice whatsoever. Children must develop a strong internal moral code that will help them avoid discipline. They must also develop the ability to reward themselves for correct behavior. The more areas of restriction that are imposed on children's thinking, the more difficult it is for children to distinguish between legitimate and inappropriate areas of investigation. One way that children have of coping with this problem is to develop a rigid moral code that restricts many aspects of thought and action.

FURTHER REFLECTION: Describe the behaviors that you would expect to observe in a child who had a strong sense of initiative or a strong sense of guilt. Speculate about how the sense of initiative is built on the earlier crises of trust versus mistrust and autonomy versus shame and doubt. Explain why guilt is more likely to be linked to reparation than shame.

The Central Process: Identification

Identification is the central process in the resolution of the conflict between initiative and guilt. We introduced the concept of identification in discussions of gender identity, moral development, and self-concept. In each of these tasks, the sense of self is clarified in the context of interactions with significant others. As a result of identification, children internalize salient cultural values. Children actively strive to enhance their self-concepts by incorporating into their own behavior some of the valued characteristics of their parents. Through a variety of processes, including watching the behavior of others, imitating others, engaging in activity where others are watching, and participating in play, conversation, and problem solving with others, children form an internal representation of the self that is coordinated with the representation of the other (Decety & Chaminade, 2003).

Four different theories suggest motives for identification (see Table 7.5). The *fear of loss of love* is founded on a child's initial realization of dependence on the parents. A child behaves like a parent in order to ensure a continued positive relationship. Eventually, the child incorporates aspects of the loved one's personality into the self-concept. The child can then feel close to the loved person even when they are not physically together (Jacobson, 1964).

Identification with the aggressor is aroused when children experience some fear of their parents. In order to protect themselves from harm, they perform behaviors that are similar to those they fear. Children identify even with parents who are extremely brutal. Because most of the behaviors that these children incorporate are aggressive, they often tend to be aggressive toward others. This kind of identification may give children a magical feeling of power and decrease the parents' tendency to mistreat them. Parents who see great similarity between themselves and their children are less likely to threaten or harm them (Freud, 1936).

A third motive for identification is the *need for status and power* (Bandura, 1977, 1986). Children are more likely to imitate the behavior of a model who controls resources than they are the behavior of a model who is rewarded. The imitative behavior is motivated by a vicarious feeling of power experienced when they behave in the same way as the powerful model. Within a family, children are likely to have personality characteristics similar to those of the more dominant parent.

A fourth motive for identification results from the *children's need to increase the perceived similarity with their parents* (Kagan, 1958). Children attribute a number of valued characteristics to their parents, including physical size, good looks, special competencies, power, success, and respect. Children more readily share these positive attributes when they perceive a similarity between themselves and their parents. They experience this sense of similarity in three principal ways: by (1) perceiving actual physical and psychological similarities, (2) adopting parental behaviors, and (3) being told about similarities by others. Increasing perceptions of similarity promote stronger identifications.

These four motives apply to the process of identification at all ages and regardless of the sex of the identifier or the model. For a particular child, one of these motives may dominate, but all four motives are involved in the process. Parental identification allows children to feel that their parents are with them even when they are not physically present. This feeling of connection with parents provides an underlying sense of security for children in a wide variety of situations.

Viewed from another perspective, identification allows children a growing sense of independence from their parents (Jacobson, 1964). Children who know how their parents would respond in a given situation no longer need the parents' physical presence to direct their behavior. Children who can praise or punish themselves for their actions are less dependent on their parents to perform these functions.

Parental identification affects children's development in two different ways. On the one hand, the closeness with parents provides the basis for the incorporation of parental sanctions and prohibitions. Once children have integrated these guidelines for behavior, they are bound to feel guilty whenever they anticipate abandoning them. On the other hand, the security that results from strong parental identification allows children increased freedom when they are away from their parents. The child whose parental identification is strong is more likely to engage the environment, take risks, and initiate actions.

An important outcome of early-school-age identification is the formation of an ideal self-image, sometimes referred to as the **ego ideal** (Freud, 1909/1955; Sandler, Holder, & Meers, 1963). The superego not only punishes misdeeds but also rewards actions that bring children closer to their ideal self-image. The ideal self is a complex view of the self as it may be in the future, including skills, profession, values, and personal relationships. It is a fantasy, a goal that is unlikely to be attained even in adulthood. Nonetheless, the discrepancy between the real self and the ideal self is a strong motivator. As children strive to achieve their ideal, they attempt new activities, set goals that strain the limits of their abilities, take risks, and resist temptations that might interfere with their desired goals.

The ego ideal is more unrealistic during early school age than at later stages. Young children fantasize anything they wish about themselves in the future. The ideal self may include the strength of Superman, the courage of Harriet Tubman, and the intellectual

Table 7.5	Four Motives for Parental Identification
Motive	**Definition**
Fear of loss of love	A child behaves like a parent in order to ensure a continued positive love relationship.
Identification with the aggressor	A child behaves like a parent in order to protect himself or herself from the parent's anger.
Identification to satisfy needs for power	A child behaves like a parent in order to achieve a vicarious sense of the power associated with the parent.
Identification to increase perceived similarity	A child behaves like a parent to increase a perceived similarity to the parent and thereby to share in the parent's positive attributes.

© Cengage

The Prime Adaptive Ego Quality and the Core Pathology

As a result of efforts to resolve the crisis of initiative versus guilt, children emerge from the period of early school age with the benefit of the prime adaptive ego quality of purpose or the core pathology of inhibition. These predispositions suggest an orientation that leaves a child with coping resources that will support directed, action-oriented problem solving or a more passive, self-protective approach to stress in which the child is more likely to allow others to guide the course of behavior.

Purpose

Purpose is thought or behavior with direction and meaning. "Purposefulness is the courage playfully to imagine and energetically to pursue valued goals," noted Erikson (1978, p. 29). Purpose is linked to personal aspirations. It is a cognitively more complex extension of the will gained in toddlerhood, in that it combines a sense of agency with a plan and a belief in one's ability to make something happen. In contrast to the toddler who exercises the will through the mere delight in action, the early-school-age child imposes intention and goals on action. This is the difference, for example, between running around the yard, laughing and shouting—typical behavior for toddlers—and saying to a friend, "Let's play tag," which is more likely for early-school-age children. Toddlers may enjoy stacking blocks and knocking them down, or splashing in water; in contrast early-school-age children want to turn materials and toys into a story or a project. Their actions are going in a direction; their play has a plan. Behind the process of planning is a complex sense of the situation, creating a goal, devising strategies to achieve it, implementing these strategies in action, and monitoring success in realizing the goal (Deci & Ryan, 2000). The sense of purpose, expressed in planning and enacting plans, reflects a significant expansion of the ego into the realm of the present and the future.

A sense of purpose suggests that the action has meaning and that the person initiating it has meaning. Purposeful behavior suggests that the child is aware of something meaningful in the world outside the self that needs attention, and a sense of confidence in the ability to contribute to that goal (Damon, 2014). Purpose can be nurtured by involving children in meaningful tasks that contribute to the well-being of the family; supporting children as they set some of their own goals and encouraging them to figure out how to achieve them; and by giving children opportunities to observe family members, friends, or relatives who are pursuing meaningful goals that they believe in. Ricky comes home from preschool and says, "Let's take all our plastic bags to the recycle bin at the grocery so we can save the planet." This suggestion reflects Ricky's ability to state a goal-directed plan that addresses a meaningful concern and a sense of confidence about introducing his idea into the ongoing activities of the family.

The sense of purpose is a key resource throughout life. The assumption introduced in chapter 1 that people contribute to their development relies on the emergence and elaboration of a sense of purpose. At later ages, especially in later adulthood and

Courtesy of Philip Newman

Identification is the central process through which children develop an ego ideal. A dad and his son talk about what it means to be a good person as they look out over the water.

brilliance of Einstein. The lack of realistic constraints on the ego ideal allows children to imagine the possibility of attaining human qualities that may always be beyond their reach. As people mature, they need to modify their ego ideal so that it remains inspiring, yet includes emerging insights about oneself, one's groups, and society. People who find it difficult to modify their ideal self-image from its childhood origins may become vulnerable to personal frustrations and psychological despair because they are unable to be what they wish. Many 6-year-old children may wish to become president of the United States. This fantasy is exciting and, for some, ennobling. However, few people actually achieve this position. By the time one reaches early adulthood, it is important to have developed an ego ideal that is closer to what is actually attainable.

The crisis of initiative versus guilt captures the child's need to question existing norms and the emerging feelings of moral concern when these norms are violated. This crisis does not focus specifically on intellectual development; however, one may assume that the level of questioning that takes place during this stage is possible only because of an increase in cognitive complexity. The process of positive parental identification promotes the incorporation of cultural norms and strengthens the child's sense of competence. Socialization during this stage may either foster a creative openness or an anxious dread of novelty.

The Prime Adaptive Ego Quality and the Core Pathology   **263**

self-control, pointing out the important adaptive value for young children of being able to resist temptations, regulate their emotions, and restrict behaviors when the situation requires it. As the executive functions mature, early-school-age children are expected to demonstrate an increasingly high level of behavioral inhibition especially in school and family settings where patience and delay of gratification are often required. Deficits in inhibitory control during early childhood are linked to later problems with externalizing behaviors as well as anxiety and depression (Kertz, Belden, Tillman, & Luby, 2015). However, as a core pathology, extreme inhibition can be observed in children who are intensely timid, overly cautious, and socially anxious.

Inhibited children are likely to emerge as shy, withdrawn, and often lonely during the subsequent period of middle childhood. Shyness is associated with self-consciousness and a fear of negative evaluation that can inhibit participation in desired activities and cause withdrawal from social situations. Without some form of social intervention, shy children may become increasingly withdrawn, not knowing how to impose their ideas into the ongoing activities of the group, and not experiencing the confidence-building effects of making suggestions and having them accepted. Consequently, their inhibition produces new deficits in social skill development (Henderson, Gilbert, & Zimbardo, 2014).

FURTHER REFLECTION: What does a sense of purpose look like in early-school-age children? How might a sense of purpose contribute to a child's ability to cope with difficult stressful situations? What advice might you offer to parents about how to foster the sense of purpose and minimize inhibition as children make the transition to kindergarten?

Coach Carl is guiding Billy to overcome his doubts and to keep trying to make a basket. Goal-directed play becomes increasingly important in early school age and requires a sense of purpose. A few successes will make a big difference in his confidence.

elderhood, many of the more structured and well-defined life roles are relinquished. In their place, adults need to invent and impose a new sense of purpose that provides satisfaction and meaning to daily life (Penick, 2004).

Inhibition

As a core pathology, **inhibition** refers to a self-conscious restraint or suppression of thoughts and behavior. As we discussed in chapter 5, inhibition has temperamental origins. As a core pathology, however, inhibition becomes problematic when parents or caregivers use high levels of love withdrawal and guilt-inducing interactions with their children. These kinds of interactions suggest that the parent's love, affection, and approval are based on the condition that the child must match certain specific parental standards. In order to adapt in this kind of environment and avoid risking loss of love, the child becomes unsure and restrained in action. In contrast to the sense of confidence and agency implied in the notion of purpose, a child who is inhibited does not want to take the risks associated with imposing a plan or suggesting a direction for fear that suggestions will result in parental or peer disapproval.

As with other core pathologies, some degree of inhibition is necessary and adaptive. In chapter 6, we addressed the topic of

Applied Topic School Readiness

OBJECTIVE 6 Define the concept of school readiness, and analyze its relation to the developmental tasks of early school age. Summarize the obstacles that may prevent children from being able to adapt and learn in the school environment.

The first years of schooling are critical in setting the long-term pathway for school achievement. A federal priority for improving the quality and access to educational opportunities in early childhood began with the establishment of the Head Start programs in the 1960s, continued with the emphasis on preparing young children to reach kindergarten "ready to learn" in the 1980s, and is an ongoing priority to ensure that children are prepared for success by their entry in kindergarten. In his State of the Union speech in 2013, President Obama proposed extending federal funds to expand high-quality public preschool to reach all low- and moderate-income 4-year olds (The Education Innovator, 2009; White House, 2013). This goal, which seems positive and appropriate on the face of it, has resulted in important dialogue about what is meant by **school readiness**, how to measure it, what obstacles stand in its way, and who should be responsible for achieving it (Wesley & Buysse, 2003).

What Do We Mean by Readiness?

The concept of readiness is a familiar idea in the study of development. Typically, the term is used to refer to a time when a child's physical, cognitive, social, and emotional maturation are at a level to undertake new learning or to engage in a more complex, demanding type of activity or relationship. It is sometimes referred to as a critical or sensitive period or a teachable moment. The idea of a *sensitive period* was identified in chapter 5 in relation to attachment relationships, in chapter 6 in relation to language use and toilet training, and in this chapter in relation to gender-role identification. Vygotsky's concept of a *zone of proximal development* is another way of conceptualizing readiness; it is the next higher level of performance one can achieve with the help of more competent mentors, teachers, and peers.

When thinking about the goal that all children should come to school ready to learn, the concept of readiness becomes somewhat more complicated. Does it refer to readiness to learn or readiness to be successful in school? One might argue that all children—except perhaps those with severe neurological damage—are both ready and eager to learn. However, not all children have the combined physical, cognitive, emotional, and social skills that allow them to adapt to the demands of the kindergarten environment or to succeed at the academic challenges of its curriculum without support (Bowman, Donovan, & Burns, 2000; Early, Pianta, Taylor, & Cox, 2001).

Measuring Kindergarten Readiness

In the past, kindergarten readiness was established largely by chronological age. School districts typically established a birthday cutoff. For example, if a child was 5 by December 1 of a given year, the child could start kindergarten in September of that year. Those who missed the December 1 date had to wait until the following year. In the 1980s, concern about the quality of education in the United States led to an upgrading of the elementary school curriculum. As part of this school reform, academic demands for school performance were raised, and children were exposed to a more challenging curriculum in earlier grades. Many skills that had been introduced in first grade are now part of the kindergarten curriculum, and more children are having trouble meeting the expectations for school performance. As they enter kindergarten, children are expected to have some experience with printed letters and sound recognition along with beginning writing skills. They are also expected to have a repertoire of behavioral and emotional skills that support attention, persistence, and cooperative social interactions with teachers and peers (Federal Interagency Forum on Child and Family Statistics, 2013; Hatcher, Nuner, & Paulsel, 2012).

In efforts to prevent early school failure, many states began to administer school readiness tests. However, there is no agreement or universal acceptance of a measure of kindergarten readiness. Some educators dispute whether any test given to 5-year-olds can accurately predict a child's ability to learn in the school environment (Pyle, 2002). The American Academy of Pediatrics suggests that these tests are more often used to keep some children out of kindergarten rather than to identify areas where children may need additional support in order to succeed (High, 2008).

According to the National Association for the Education of Young Children (NAEYC), there are four appropriate uses for assessment: to support instruction, to identify those with special needs, for program evaluation, and for high stakes accountability. "Use of kindergarten readiness assessments as a means of screening children into or out of kindergarten is **inconsistent** [emphasis added] with generally accepted best practices and NAEYC's formal position on the inappropriate use of kindergarten assessments to keep an age-eligible child from enrolling" (Snow, 2011). When it comes to school readiness, norm referenced assessment techniques typically fail to include the role of motivation, temperament, and social and cultural factors that may influence the various strategies and processes that young children use for learning (High, 2008).

Most 5-year-olds do not read or write, so mass testing is not feasible. Any approach to measuring kindergarten readiness must involve one-on-one evaluation. Many early childhood educators emphasize that cognitive skills in reading, mathematics, and general knowledge are not enough to understand the child's readiness for school. School readiness is a comprehensive construct which draws on many of the developmental tasks reviewed in the chapter. Physical development and motor coordination, attention and executive control, social skills, communication skills, and a child's enthusiasm for learning all play a part in how well a child will adapt to the school environment (Grimm, Steele, Mashburn, Burchinal, & Pianta, 2010).

Increasing attention is being given to social and emotional resources that support children's learning and ability to cope with the demands of the school environment (DeAngelis, 2010). The way a child approaches learning, such as task persistence, attentiveness, and organization; a child's capacity for self-control and behavioral regulation; and a child's interpersonal skills, such as getting along with others and being able to express one's feelings and ideas in a positive way are all aspects of social and emotional competence that contribute to school success (Galindo & Fuller, 2010; Ponitz, McClelland, Matthews, & Morrison, 2009).

These children are learning a fundamental skill for success in school: walking in line.

Given the lack of an objective, accepted measure, or screening test, what do parents and teachers think are essential markers of school readiness? How can a parent judge if a child is ready or should wait a year before beginning kindergarten? Advice about kindergarten readiness is diverse. States have issued their own readiness checklists. Online sources reflect at least three different perspectives: (1) recommendations for preschool educators, especially NAEYC, about how to assess the curriculum in order to prepare young children to be successful in the transition to kindergarten; (2) recommendations from teachers, especially the American Federation of Teachers, about how to evaluate kindergarten readiness; and (3) recommendations for parents, which come from many sources, both professional and informal. For example, the Urban Child Institute (2016) offers this advice to parents: "There are four key dimensions of readiness—language and literacy, thinking skills, self-control, and self-confidence." On their website they list the following skills that teachers and child development experts suggest for a child to be successful in the transition to kindergarten:

- Know her first and last name and her parents' first and last names.
- Recognize letters (both lowercase and uppercase) and numbers (up to 10).
- Communicate wants and needs (like hunger, pain, happiness) through words.
- Know basic colors and shapes.
- Use the bathroom and wash her hands all by herself.
- Solve problems without hitting, biting, or yelling.
- Follow instructions from teachers and parents.
- Be comfortable being apart from her parents during the school day.
- Sit quietly for short periods of time.
- Be curious and interested in activities like story and art time.

In an attempt to provide a systematic picture of what kindergartners are able to do at the start of school, the U.S. Department of Education initiated the Early Childhood Longitudinal Study, Kindergarten Class of 1998–1999 (Zill & West, 2000). A new cohort of kindergarteners was studied in the 2010–2011 school year. This national sample of more than 18,000 kindergartners from 970 schools will be followed through fifth grade (Federal Interagency Forum on Child and Family Statistics, 2013). In addition to one-on-one assessment of children, information was gathered from parents, teachers, special education teachers, school administrators, and child care providers. Reports from the first data collection focus on children's reading, math, and science knowledge; their body-mass index; and their approach to learning. This last category included a number of behaviors that reflect executive function, social competence, positive outlook, and emotional regulation: "the child's ability to keep belongings organized, pay attention well, persist in completing tasks, show eagerness to learn new things, work independently, adapt easily to changes in routine, and follow classroom rules." The expectation is that these assessments will provide norms for what most children can do when they come to kindergarten and allow consideration of how these early abilities predict subsequent school success (Federal Interagency Forum on Child and Family Statistics, 2013;

Mulligan, McCarroll, Flanagan, & Potter, 2015). A report of how kindergartners performed on each of the areas assessed can be found in *America's Children: Key National Indicators of Well-being, 2013, Special Feature, The Kindergarten Year* (Federal Interagency Forum on Child and Family Statistics, 2013).

Risk Factors for School Readiness

Most children are excited about going to kindergarten and want to do well. However, certain demographic characteristics are linked to school readiness skills and approaches to learning in kindergarten. In the fall of the year when children first started kindergarten, the following differences in approaches to learning were observed:

> Boys were rated lower than girls.
> Younger children were rated lower than the older children.
> Children whose parents had less than a high school education were rated lower than children whose parents had more formal education.
> Children whose families were below 100 percent of the poverty level were rated lower than children from families at 200 percent of the poverty level or higher.

FIGURE 7.2 ▶ shows the differences in approaches to learning for boys and girls, and for children from three different levels of family income measured in the fall and again in the spring of their kindergarten year. All children showed some gains in approaches to learning from fall to spring. However, after a year of kindergarten, differences between the groups were still evident.

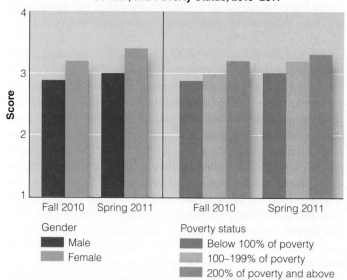

Mean Approaches to Learning Scores of
U.S. First-time Kindergartners by Time of Data Collection,
Gender, and Poverty Status, 2010–2011

Gender
■ Male
■ Female

Poverty status
■ Below 100% of poverty
■ 100–199% of poverty
■ 200% of poverty and above

FIGURE 7.2 ▶ KINDERGARTENERS' APPROACHES TO LEARNING BY GENDER AND POVERTY STATUS, FALL 2010 AND SPRING 2011

NOTE: Approaches to learning behaviors include children's ability to keep belongings organized, pay attention well, persist in completing tasks, show eagerness to learn new things, work independently, adapt easily to changes in routine, and follow classroom rules. Higher scores demonstrate more positive approaches to learning. Approaches to learning scores are derived from teacher ratings. Estimates pertain to a sample of children who were enrolled in kindergarten for the first time in the 2010–2011 school year. Potential approaches to learning scores range from 1 to 4.

SOURCE: U.S. Department of Education, National Center for Education Statistics, Early Childhood Longitudinal Study, Kindergarten Class of 2010–2011 (ECLS-K:2011) Restricted-Use Kindergarten Data File.

In the analysis of kindergartners from the earlier 1998–1999 cohort, four factors were identified as placing children at risk for poor early school experience: parents who had not graduated from high school, low income or welfare dependence, single-parent families, and families where a language other than English was the primary language spoken at home (Zill & West, 2000). Forty-six percent of kindergartners had one or more of these risk factors. Having one or more risk factors was associated with lower scores in reading and mathematics and poorer health. Children with multiple risk factors were more likely to be described by teachers as having difficulty paying attention or persisting in the completion of a task and were more likely to be described as sometimes or never eager to learn, in contrast to children with no risk factors.

Certain microsystem environments can undermine a child's cognitive, emotional, social, and physical readiness for school. Poverty, stress, and disorganization can all impact the quality of parenting and the nature of the early learning environment (Son & Peterson, 2016). Harsh, controlling parenting has been linked to poor executive functioning, withdrawal, and an increased risk of externalizing problems. Household disorganization and instability, especially frequent moving from one residence to another, changes in the presence or absence of adults in the home, particularly the mother and father figures, the total number of people in the home, and the continuous ambient noise in the home are all associated with less optimal parenting behaviors. Children in these family environments show evidence of poorer executive functioning and problems in behavioral regulation from ages 3 to 5 (Vernon-Feagans et al., 2016).

Despite the essential role of the family and home environment, quality early childhood programs can make a real contribution in reducing risk and supporting kindergarten readiness. For example, an enhanced, evidence-based curriculum that was incorporated into a number of Head Start centers was found to have long-lasting contributions to children's social-emotional functioning including improved social competence, less aggressive-oppositional behavior, more learning engagement, fewer attention problems, greater teacher–student closeness, and fewer experiences with peer rejection (Nix et al., 2016). Early childhood programs can also form effective partnerships with parents to alter the home environment for children. For example, within Head Start programs, those that have a targeted parent-involvement emphasis find evidence of more cognitive stimulation activities at home and less use of harsh, controlling parenting, both of which are tied to children's academic and behavioral skills (Ansari & Gershoff, 2016).

Who Is Responsible for Meeting the Goal for School Readiness?

School readiness and school success are products of the interaction of the individual child, the child's family environment and early learning experiences, the particular school that the child attends, and the larger community that does or does not invest in the support of teachers and school (U.S. Department of Health and Human Services, 2011). In establishing a national priority for children to start school ready to learn and prepared to succeed, we are faced with this question: "Whose responsibility is it to meet this goal?" Do we need to provide more support to families to provide the early experiences that will foster health, confidence, motivation, and cognitive and social development during the first 4 years of life? Do we need to place more responsibility on schools to work with children where they are by providing the environment, services, curriculum, and methods of instruction that will facilitate learning for an increasingly diverse group of students? Do we need to place more responsibility on local, state, and federal government to sustain and expand programs such as Head Start, so that more children can participate in early educational experiences that help offset the negative effects of poverty?

Since school attendance is not required by law before the age of 6, kindergarten is optional. A child's family has the primary role in deciding whether or not a child is ready to start kindergarten. Some parents worry or wonder if their child is ready. Their decision is based on their own day-to-day observations, information they have received from the child's preschool/Head Start program, guidelines provided by the elementary school where the child might begin kindergarten, advice from family and friends, and/or from books and websites about school readiness. What if parents decide the child is not ready? A few strategies are possible: (1) Delay entry. Evidence suggests that children who are older do better in kindergarten than those who have not yet turned five when school starts. (2) Meet with the school counselor and the kindergarten teachers at the elementary school, describe your observations and find out if these concerns would result in significant difficulties in school adjustment. Many schools have a pre-kindergarten program for children who are not old enough or not quite ready to approach the kindergarten environment. (3) Have the child evaluated by a pediatrician or assessed by a psychologist to determine whether the child has special needs that might require additional accommodations. See the **Human Development and Diversity** box for a discussion of how to support school readiness for children with disabilities.

The child's chances of success in school can be improved if *all* interacting systems support one another and keep the goal of academic success for the widest range of students in focus. Schools need to be attuned to the characteristics of their incoming kindergartners. Professionals need to identify the physical, cognitive, social, and motivational factors that support school success and find ways to support development in those domains during infancy and early childhood. Parents need to foster a home environment that supports their child's interest and motivation for learning as well as providing opportunities for the acquisition of specific school-related competences. Educators and parents must become partners for the optimal development of children, identifying those children who are at risk for school failure and making plans for integrated, multiyear, multiservice programs to support their success.

FURTHER REFLECTION: Analyze the biological, psychological, and societal factors that contribute to school readiness. Discuss ways that a caring community might support school success for a diverse group of learners in the transition to kindergarten.

Supporting School Readiness for Young Children with Disabilities

About 4 percent of young children ages 3 through 5 have been identified as having a disability described as (1) developmental delay; (2) difficulty walking, running, or playing; or (3) both of these (Brault, 2011). By definition, children with a developmental delay are performing at or below the 50th percentile of their age-mates in one or more domains, including motor skills, speech and language, social and emotional competence, and learning and memory (Siegel, 1996).

In the national longitudinal study of the kindergarten class of 1998 to 1999, about 10 percent of the children were identified by their parents as having a developmental difficulty. For that study, a child with a developmental difficulty was defined as one whose parents noted a problem by first grade and obtained "a diagnosis from a professional for problems related to attention, activity, communication, hearing, or sight that could not be corrected with eyeglasses" (Malone, West, Flanagan, & Park, 2006).

The term **disability** can refer to a wide variety of possible functional challenges. The two most common impairments are speech and language delays (55 percent of those receiving services) and developmental delays (25 percent of those receiving services). In the study of American kindergartners, parents reported that "substantial minorities of children are already experiencing risks for developmental difficulties, with one in five being described as overly active, one in six having problems concentrating for sustained periods, and one in nine

not articulating words clearly or fluently" (Zill & West, 2000).

Preschool and kindergarten programs that include children with disabilities face a significant task—to ensure that the inclusion benefits the child both socially and academically. Many children with disabilities are mainstreamed in a classroom without any provision for encouraging social interaction with the other children. One of the major concerns facing teachers is the ability to promote positive social skills, including appropriate levels of assertiveness, self-control, and cooperation among students of varying abilities (U.S. Department of Education, 2002). The school setting makes specific demands on children to function in more constrained, regulated ways than might be required at home. Some children benefit from the routine and predictability of the school setting, whereas others have difficulty regulating their behavior to comply with teacher and peer expectations.

Effective **inclusion** requires strategies for promoting contact between students with and without disabilities and creating an accepting social climate among students. Interventions must be tailored to address the unique areas of deficit. A child with autism, for example, may need to be taught how to imitate a model and may have difficulty cooperating with peers but might be able to play successfully with puzzles or listen to the teacher read a story. A child with moderate neurological deficits may have difficulty with tasks that require fast reaction time, such as competitive games among students, but

could perform well if speed of response is not a concern. Children with speech and language difficulties may find it difficult to express themselves or to engage in conversation with peers. As a result, they may withdraw from social interactions. Teachers need to find ways to build on each child's level of performance so the child is not stigmatized for a disability and continues to make progress toward an appropriate academic standard.

Critical Thinking Questions

1. Investigate the kinds of accommodations that schools make for children who have been identified as having serious, moderate, and mild disabilities. You may want to contact someone at a local elementary school or the school you attended to find out what they are required to provide. How might this have changed since you were in elementary school?
2. Evaluate the advantages and disadvantages of mainstreaming early-school-age children as compared to placing these children in special education classes.
3. Given what you know about the early-school-age period, summarize some of the challenges to effective inclusion. How might a course in human development help teachers meet these challenges?
4. Request permission to attend an IEP evaluation team meeting. How do the professionals from various disciplines approach the challenges for creating a supportive plan?

CHAPTER SUMMARY

Early school age marks the beginning of work on developmental tasks that will persist well into adulthood. The four tasks of early school age are closely interrelated.

OBJECTIVE 1 Describe the process of gender identification during early school age and explain its importance for the way a child interprets experiences.

The complex process of gender identification has cognitive, affective, physical, and interpersonal elements. Gender identification includes:

(1) understanding the concept of gender, (2) learning gender-role standards and stereotypes, (3) identifying with parents, and (4) forming a gender preference. As young children clarify the content of their gender identification, they create a set of beliefs about the self, including their self-worth, relationships with other children, and the kinds of activities and interests that are appropriate for them, not only in the present but also in the future. The gender identification of the early-school-age child will be revised and reintegrated as it becomes a core element of personal identity in adolescence.

OBJECTIVE 2 Summarize the process of early moral development, drawing from theories and research to explain how knowledge, emotion, and action combine to produce internalized morality.

Early moral development involves the integration of three components: knowledge of the moral standards, experiences of moral emotions, and the willingness and ability to take moral actions. The development of conscience, with its capacity to reward and punish, brings an internalization of moral standards. Five theories are discussed that offer different views on the process of internalization: learning theories, cognitive developmental theory, psychoanalytic and object relations theories, and evolutionary theory. Research on empathy, caring, and perspective taking add insights into the processes through which morality matures in early school age. Two significant environmental forces, parental discipline and exposure to models and messages in the media, shape a child's moral outlook. Moral development is accompanied by a heightened sensitivity to violating basic cultural standards, many of which relate to interpersonal behavior, especially toward adults and peers. The child's experiences with transgressions, guilt, or praise for prosocial behavior have implications for the elaboration of the self-theory and particularly for the establishment of self-esteem.

OBJECTIVE 3 Analyze changes in the self-theory, with special focus on the theory of mind and self-esteem during the early-school-age years.

The self-concept can be viewed as a theory that links the child's understanding of the nature of the world, the nature of the self, and the meaning of interactions between the two. Various neural structures are actively involved in processing and integrating information to support the self-concept. Two faces of the self—the I and the Me—contribute to self-understanding. One is the originator of thoughts and actions; the other is the self as object as perceived by oneself and others. The self-concept becomes increasingly complex as gains from infancy and toddlerhood undergo developmental changes, brought about in part by changing neural development, new cognitive capacities, and changing societal expectations. Although the self-theory is continuously revised with entry into new roles and the emergence of new cognitive capacities, the establishment of a positive sense of worth in early school age brings an important tone of optimism as the child faces new challenges. Competence and social acceptance are the essential antecedents of self-esteem.

OBJECTIVE 4 Describe the features of peer play, including group games, media play, and friendship in the early-school-age years.

Play takes on new complexities including games with rules and multiple roles, exposure to diverse forms of media, and participation in friendship relationships. Children spend an average of 2 hours a day with some type of screen media, making media an increasingly dominant feature of the family system and an important play companion even at this young age. The type and content of media exposure differs by family income. Increased involvement with peers brings about an appreciation of others' perspectives, social acceptance, and delight in the intimacy of friends as well as new experiences with conflict and conflict resolution. Children's sense of initiative and purpose are reflected in the ways they actively create their social environment through their choice of games, media entertainment, and friends. The social worlds of boys and girls become notably distinct as gender preferences are expressed in different patterns of play and play companions.

OBJECTIVE 5 Explain the psychosocial crisis of initiative versus guilt, the central process of identification, the prime adaptive ego quality of purpose, and the core pathology of inhibition.

The psychosocial crisis of initiative versus guilt has direct implications for such essential personality characteristics as self-esteem, creativity, curiosity, and risk taking. The child who resolves this crisis positively will be fortified with an active, exploratory approach to the environment. Guilt plays an important role in orienting children toward the implications of their actions for others. In moderation, guilt is an essential ingredient in preserving social bonds. In the extreme, however, guilt restricts creative thought and limits action. As a result of identification, children internalize salient cultural values. Four different theories suggest motives for identification: fear of loss of love, identification with the aggressor, need for status and power, and the need to increase perceived similarity with one's parent. The prime adaptive ego quality of purpose emerges as children become aware of something meaningful in the world outside the self that needs attention, and a sense of confidence in the ability to contribute to that goal. The core pathology of inhibition refers to a self-conscious restraint or suppression of thoughts and behavior.

OBJECTIVE 6 Define the concept of school readiness, and analyze its relation to the developmental tasks of early school age. Summarize the obstacles that may prevent children from being able to adapt and learn in the school environment.

The applied topic of school readiness illustrates the potential conflict between development and socialization. Society has determined that 5-year-old children will attend school. At the same time, 5-year-olds are at a wide array of developmental levels, bringing them to the door of the school with substantial differences in physical, cognitive, social, and emotional competence. There is lack of agreement as to the definition of school readiness and how to measure it. Risk factors such as disabilities, poverty, and a non-English-speaking home environment may all complicate the child's ability to adapt to the school environment.

CASEBOOK

For additional case material related to this chapter, see the case entitled "Delaney Goes to Kindergarten," in *Life Span Development: A Case Book*, by Barbara and Philip Newman, Laura Landry-Meyer, and Brenda J. Lohman, pp. 87–94. This case illustrates some of the challenges that children face in the transition to kindergarten and how home, preschool, and kindergarten systems can work together to foster a child's continuing school success.

University of Michigan Museum of Art

A major theme of middle childhood is the mastery of new, valued skills. Among those skills most highly valued in modern cultures is reading, which opens the door to endless sources of knowledge, stimulates imagination, and connects children with worlds past and future.

1. Examine the role of friendship in helping children learn to take the point of view of others, be sensitive to the norms and pressures of the peer group, and experience closeness in relationships. Summarize the negative consequences that result from social rejection and loneliness.

2. Describe the development of concrete operational thought, including conservation, classification skills, mathematical reasoning, and the child's ability to understand and monitor his or her own knowledge and understanding.

3. Analyze the nature of skill learning, and examine societal factors that provide the contexts in which skill learning occurs.

4. Outline the factors that contribute to self-evaluation, including feelings of pride, self-efficacy, and ways that social expectations of parents, teachers, and peers contribute to a child's self-evaluation.

5. Summarize new levels of complexity in play as children become involved in team sports, examine the benefits of participation in sports, and analyze the cognitive and emotional development that accompanies team play.

6. Explain the psychosocial crisis of industry versus inferiority, the central process through which the crisis is resolved, education, the prime adaptive ego quality of competence, and the core pathology of inertia.

7. Evaluate the impact of exposure to violence on development during middle childhood.

MIDDLE CHILDHOOD (6 TO 12 YEARS)

8

CASE STUDY Recollections of Childhood Friends

In my life-span class, every so often I ask students to answer a question on an index card so that I can have a better idea about their own experiences and opinions. The following cards were written by college students in response to a question asking them to tell about a best friend or close friends from middle childhood.

"When I was a young boy, I played soccer. At soccer we were placed with boys who were the same age. I made a friend named S. who had a lot of the same traits as me. S and I played soccer together all through elementary, middle, and high school and we are still friends today. I am so happy that I played this sport and was able to make new friends that were like me." J. U.

"Since I have no siblings, and live across the street from my cousins, we are all very close. I have 5 cousins ranging from ages 18 to 26 now. When we were in middle childhood we would all hang out all summer together and just have fun. We were able to walk to the store down the street to get ice cream, and we were allowed to swim to the raft in the ocean near our houses. They were, and still are, my best friends. We have each other's backs and we all care about each other. We also would do anything for each other so we are all very loyal. Now that we are older, we don't get to see each other much because of work, college, and conflicting schedules. Back then were some good times." J. M.

"My best friend in middle school was a girl named L. We were best friends since kindergarten, so we were pretty inseparable. We were both very imaginative and everywhere we went we were making up strange games. We came up with ridiculous plot lines and character names and would act them out everywhere. We used all kinds of props—anything around us was part of the story. We had so much fun letting our imaginations take us away. We did everything together and her family felt like part of my family, and my family felt like part of hers. We were really more like sisters." C. M.

"My friendships during middle childhood were brutal especially during middle school. I was a part of a clique where one day you were making fun of someone, but the next day everyone was making fun of you. It was often stressful because I felt like I had to fit in and besides a select few I knew I could count on, I didn't feel like I had many real friends." G. J.

CASE ANAYLSIS Using What You Know

1. Based on these accounts, describe the important characteristics of friendships that are formed in middle childhood.
2. Compare and contrast the four narratives. What are some similarities and differences in childhood experiences of friendship?
3. Thinking back to your middle childhood, how would you describe you own close childhood friendships? How similar or different are they to these narratives?
4. Consider how the themes of middle childhood, including cognitive maturation, social competence, self-evaluation, and team play, are implicated in these narratives about friendship.
5. Speculate about how experiences with friends can contribute to the resolution of the crisis of industry versus inferiority.

For many children, middle childhood is a joyful, vigorous time. The fears and vulnerabilities of their early school days are behind them. Energized by ego qualities of hope, will, and purpose, most children are able to enjoy the resources and opportunities of their communities. Even as their family members continue to be a comfort to them, they begin to explore more complex social relationships with peers and other significant adults.

In some parts of the world, however, life in middle childhood is marked by extreme disorganization and exploitation. Children are vulnerable to the violence of war as victims of terrorist attacks, civil wars, injury from explosions of abandoned land mines, and forced enlistment as soldiers among warring tribes (Beah, 2007; Pearn, 2003). Slavers travel through impoverished areas, kidnapping, buying, or luring children into forms of slave-like labor where they are often beaten or sexually abused. Children of impoverished families are being sold or given away as slaves or bonded laborers. In many cultures, child marriage has become a form of enforced servitude; a condition that primarily impacts young girls (antislavery.org, 2016).

> Over 100 million children around the world work in hazardous conditions in agriculture, mining, domestic labor, and other sectors. On tobacco farms, children work long hours in extreme heat, exposed to nicotine and toxic pesticides that can make them sick. In Africa, Asia, and Latin America, child laborers in artisanal and small-scale gold mines work underground in pits that easily collapse and use toxic mercury to process the gold, risking brain damage and other serious health conditions. (Human Rights Watch, 2016)

According to the International Labor Organization (2012), 5.5 million children are in slavery, trafficking, debt bondage, and other forms of forced labor, forced recruitment for armed conflict, prostitution, pornography, and other illicit activities. An estimated 250,000 to 300,000 children are being used as soldiers, couriers, and sex slaves in armed conflicts in at least 14 countries around the world (Peace Direct, 2016). They not only witness bloodshed but also may be used as spies, messengers, informants, and "soldiers' wives" (Annan, Brier & Aryemo, 2009). In cities and towns suffering from ongoing armed conflicts, hundreds of thousands of children are unable to attend school and millions more are fleeing with their families to refugee camps. Over the past 4 years of civil war, an estimated 2 million Syrian children are now refugees, many living in makeshift camps (UNICEF USA, 2016).

In such circumstances, the opportunity for children to work on the developmental tasks of friendship formation, concrete operational reasoning, skill learning, self-evaluation, and team play may be viewed as a great luxury. We do not know much about the developmental outcomes for these children. Having the time, resources, and security to promote areas of cognitive, social, and emotional development is possible only in the context of communities that are economically and politically stable and ideologically committed to the intellectual and interpersonal future of their children. ●

Developmental Tasks

New developmental tasks emerge as children become focused on friendship formation, concrete mental operations, skill learning, self-evaluation, and team play. This mix of tasks coupled with new capacities for complex social, emotional, and intellectual activity produce a remarkable energy. Whereas play dominates the behavior of early-school-age children, middle childhood is characterized by more purposeful, industrious behavior such as earning money for completing chores; planning and building toys, gardens, or play spaces; or participating in competitions, performances, and community events. This is not to say that play is lost. New thrills and excitement accompany the capacity to engage in new forms of play and games, and taking new risks—riding one's bike farther from home, jumping and then diving into a pool from the high board, or riding on the big, fast roller coasters.

Friendship

OBJECTIVE 1 Examine the role of friendship in helping children learn to take the point of view of others, be sensitive to the norms and pressures of the peer group, and experience closeness in relationships. Summarize the negative consequences that result from social rejection and loneliness.

Can you remember some things about a friend you had when you were 9 or 10 years old? As you can tell from the opening case quotations, the **friendships** of middle childhood are often quite memorable. At this age, children describe **close friends** as people who play together, like the same activities, share common interests, enjoy each other's company, and count on each other for help. Peer relationships include forming meaningful dyadic and group relationships, participating in larger peer networks, and experiencing peer acceptance or rejection (Gifford-Smith & Brownell, 2003).

Friendships clearly provide social and developmental advantages (Berndt & Murphy, 2002; Hruschka, 2010). Human beings are social animals whose development is intricately dependent on a network of close, supportive social relationships. In middle childhood, the radius of significant relationships expands to include classmates, teammates, and close friends. According to evolutionary theory, being a member of a group has protective advantages. Group cooperation gives a selective advantage to many social species, especially in tracking and hunting for food. Therefore, the skills of cooperation and sociability may advance the species as a whole as well as the individual (Seligman, 2011). On an individual level, children who are able to participate in positive peer friendships are embedded in an intellectually and socially stimulating environment. For children who have caring, responsive relationships with their family members, friendships provide additional reassurance about being integrated into the social community.

Time with friends, whether in school, after school, or on weekends and vacation days, makes up a large part of a child's daily life. Friendships are not only important for companionship but also to keep loneliness at bay. The peer group is a microsystem in which diverse socialization processes are at work. Peers influence one another's self-concepts, emotions, moral beliefs and behaviors, engagement in skill-building activities, and attitudes about school. Experiences of peer acceptance and rejection have powerful and enduring consequences for children's physical and mental health as well as for their cognitive and emotional well-being (Bukowski, Castellanos, Vitaro, & Brendgen, 2015).

Family Influences on Social Competence

Not all children enter middle childhood with the same capacity to make friends and enjoy the benefits of close peer relations. Early family experiences, including the quality of a child's attachment, the family's approach to discipline, and the nature of family conversations, all contribute to a child's **social competence**. By social competence, we mean all the skills involved in the child's ability to form and maintain positive relationships with others (Bloom, 2009). Social competence includes the ability to alter one's behavior to conform to the norms and expectations for interactions in various settings and with different social partners. For example, a socially competent child can be friendly but not overly friendly with an unfamiliar child, or respectful but not overly intimidated by an unfamiliar adult. Social competence includes strategies for initiating an interaction as well as for sustaining and building an ongoing relationship. Social competence also involves the ability to manage occasional social difficulties, such as being teased, excluded, or ignored. The features of social competence change as children mature because the expectations for social behavior change with a child's age and the social settings a child is likely to encounter become more diverse.

Early Attachment and Social Competence. Children who have secure attachments in infancy appear to be more socially competent in preschool as evidenced by their greater popularity and their ability to engage more freely in social interactions. They are perceived as more helpful and better able to consider the needs of others. By middle childhood, the children who were securely attached in infancy have more friends than those with insecure attachments, have more positive interactions with their friends, and are more highly regarded by their peers. When two children with histories of secure attachments are friends with one another, those friendships are likely to be more responsive, less critical, and offer more companionship than friendships between children whose attachment history is mismatched (e.g., secure-insecure) (Berlin, Cassidy, & Appleyard, 2008; Thompson, 2008).

Peer relationships may be more difficult for children with insecure attachments. Children with insecure attachments are less likely to be perceived as leaders among their peers. Children with an avoidant attachment tend to be more aggressive and rejecting of their peers; they are more likely to engage in unprovoked hostile actions that push peers away. Children with a resistant (sometimes referred to as an ambivalent) attachment tend to be tentative, inhibited, and more likely to appear needy, a quality that may also result in peer rejection (Berlin, Cassidy, & Appleyard, 2008).

Parent–Child Interactions and Social Competence.

Four ways that parents of securely attached children enhance their child's social competence include: (1) providing children with a greater number and a more diverse array of social experiences; (2) advising children on ways to develop and maintain positive relationships; (3) behaving in ways that provide children with role models for how to interact in sensitive ways with others; and (4) talking about emotions in an open, supportive style. Parents' discipline techniques, the way they speak to their child, and their parenting values are all linked to a child's development of social competence. Children whose parents interact with them in positive, agreeable ways by showing warmth, respect, empathy, interest, and affection, and who communicate frequently with their children are likely to have more positive friendship relations than children whose parents are harsh or neglectful (Biglan, Flay, Embry, & Sandler, 2012). These patterns are observable as early as preschool and continue to be found in the elementary grades.

Parents who use power-assertive, controlling discipline techniques and who believe that aggression is an acceptable way of resolving conflicts have children who expect to get their way by asserting power in peer conflicts (Deater-Deckard, Wang, Chen, & Bell, 2012; Malin, Cabrera, Karberg, Aldoney, & Rowe, 2014). A parent's discipline technique may influence what a child expects in a social interaction. Children who have been exposed to aggressive parenting or violence between their parents may believe that these same strategies will work to establish control and compliance with their peers. As a result, these children are more likely to have conflicts with their friends and to experience social rejection because of their aggressiveness.

Exposure to harsh and/or neglectful parenting in the early years is associated with a child's difficulties in emotional regulation, externalizing behaviors, and deceitful-callous behaviors, all of which make peer rejection more likely (Hallquist, Hipwell, & Stepp, 2015; Waller et al., 2012). Harsh parenting is typically associated with child aggression, and children's aggression is associated with a greater likelihood of peer rejection. However, there are some distinctions regarding both harsh parenting and child aggression that need to be considered when trying to understand their influence on children's peer friendships.

Variations in Harsh Parenting. First, harsh parenting can have a different impact on children when it is delivered by a parent who is emotionally controlled as compared to a parent who is out of control, administering the punishment in a context of rage (Deater-Deckard, Wang, Chen, & Bell, 2012). Second, harsh parenting can have a different impact on a child depending on the chaotic, disorganized, and stressful nature of the home environment (Vernon-Feagans, Willoughby, Garrett-Peters, & the Family Life Project Key Investigators, 2016). Third, harsh parenting appears to have a different impact on children depending on whether it is delivered by mothers or fathers (Chang, Schwartz, Dodge, & McBride-Chang, 2003).

Variations in Child Aggression. First, exposure to family stress and harsh parenting can result in different adaptive coping strategies. In the context of highly stressful environments, children may become highly vigilant, always on the lookout for the next possible threat. In some children, this vigilance is associated with increased risk taking, impulsivity, hostile social competition, and reactive aggression. In other children, vigilance is expressed in social anxiety, lower risk taking and impulsivity, and fearful or withdrawn behavior (Del Giudice, Hinnant, Ellis, & El-Sheikh, 2012). These distinctions have sometimes been described as the Hawk and Dove reactions to stress (Sturge-Apple, Davies, Martin, Cicchetti, & Hentges, 2012). Still other children appear to block information related to stress altogether, ignoring information about dangers and threats in the environment. These children may be described as callous or deceitful; they are low in empathy and cooperation, and more likely to be impulsive and antisocial, with frequent proactive/instrumental aggression (Del Giudice, Hinnant, Ellis, & El-Sheikh, 2012; Waller et al., 2012).

Second, different forms of aggression have been described, especially relational aggression and physical aggression. Relational aggression might include gossiping, mean teasing, or social exclusion; it is less directly confrontational.

> If a girl gets mad at someone, they often don't tell the person, or at least not in a straightforward way. They let them figure it out by ostracizing them. . . . A quick way to ostracize a girl is to start a rumor about her, which may or may not be based in a nugget of fact. There also may be pressure in the group to not defend the girl if one of the group members hears someone else repeat the rumor. (Maybury, 2015 p. 12)

Physical aggression might include hitting, kicking, or pushing and shoving. Aggression can take the form of victimization such as threatening harm, taking a child's belongings, or embarrassing a child in front of others (Schwartz, Lansford, Dodge,

Peopleimages/E+/Getty Images

Relational aggression is more common among girls. Sometimes bullies gang up on a target, using the power of their peer support to intimidate or humiliate another child.

Pettit, & Bates, 2013). These various types of aggression are used differently by different children and have different consequences for peer acceptance, friendship, and rejection.

Third, there may be some adaptive advantages to certain types of aggression. Frequent physical aggression is generally associated with peer rejection, but a modest amount of physical aggression is not necessarily disruptive to peer relations. Relational aggression may have functional advantages for preserving social status and popularity in the peer culture. Children who are well liked by their peers, especially girls, are likely to increase their use of relational aggression, which in turn results in increases in peer acceptance. Girls who use a fair amount of relational aggression and little physical aggression are viewed positively by their peers (Ettekal & Ladd, 2015).

Children may directly imitate their parents' interpersonal communication styles and positive or aggressive behaviors. If parents ask a lot of questions and invite their child's opinions, for example, the child is more likely to show interest in others' ideas and opinions. One study asked children and parents to describe characteristics of parental conflict and related this to the child's friendship quality (Kitzmann & Cohen, 2003). Children who perceived their parents' conflicts as poorly resolved (e.g., "Even after my parents stop arguing, they stay mad at each other") also had difficulty resolving conflicts in their own close friendships. Children's perceptions of poor parental conflict resolution were correlated with lower friendship quality, including seeing their friends as less of a source of companionship, help, or intimacy.

Parents who are highly restrictive and who try to control their children's behavior are less likely to permit their children to have frequent or diverse peer social interactions. Children in these families may arrive at the middle childhood years with less experience in peer play (Hart, Ladd, & Burleson, 1990; McCloskey & Stuewig, 2001).

Sibling Interactions and Social Competence.

Although parent–child relationships play an important role in the development of social competence, sibling relationships are also important. When asked about their close friends, many adolescents mention their siblings. Younger siblings are likely to be exposed to the toys, play companions, and play activities of their older siblings, bringing them into contact with more mature play partners at a young age. Depending on the age differences among siblings, many older siblings are expected to play a nurturing or protective role for their younger siblings, thereby advancing their own sense of responsibility and competence. Some families deliberately try to foster close sibling friendships by planning family activities and encouraging at-home playtime.

The study of sibling relationships is extremely difficult given the many possible configurations of sibling order, sibling spacing, sex composition of siblings, and family values regarding sibling relationships. There are few consistent results linking birth order to personality characteristics. What is more, relationships among siblings change over time as siblings develop new levels of social understanding.

It makes sense to consider that children learn patterns of peer interaction with their siblings that they bring to the larger arena of peer relationships at school or in the neighborhood. For example, firstborns are more likely to be self-assured in their position in the

These siblings are having a wonderful time together playing on a small stone beach. They are forging the basis for lifelong memories and friendship bonds. The younger sibs learn and benefit from advice from their older sibs; the older sibs enjoy their role as guides and mentors. The friendship among sibs may also be a source of support during their transition from childhood to adulthood.

family whereas later-borns, having less power or authority, need to devise unique strategies to get their needs met or opinions heard.

Not all sibling relationships are close and comfortable. The more a child feels trusting and positive about his or her sibling, the more likely the relationship is to be characterized by high levels of openness and disclosure (Howe, Aquan-Assee, Bukowski, Lehoux, & Rinaldi, 2001). The more positive the quality of a sibling relationship, the more likely the siblings are to use compromise or reconciliation to resolve conflicts; conflicts between siblings who do not like each other are more likely to result in aggression or submission, often with one child in tears (Recchia & Howe, 2009). In contrast to children with siblings, only children have less experience handling the day-to-day conflicts that arise among siblings, leaving them less prepared to manage peer conflicts outside the family (Kitzmann, Cohen, & Lockwood, 2002). Results from two large studies find that in adulthood, people are likely to form close friendships and romantic relationships with other people of the same birth order (Hartshorne & Salem-Hartshorne, 2009). This is an indication that people learn patterns of social interaction in their sibling relationships that contribute to their social competence and provide a foundation for the establishment of intimacy.

Three Contributions of Friendship to Social Development

Children learn at least three lessons from daily interactions with their peers. The first lesson is an increasing appreciation of the many points of view represented in the peer group. As children play together, they discover that there may be several versions of the same song, different rules for the same game, and different customs for the same holiday. In learning about others through the friendly exchange of ideas, children also learn about themselves. The second lesson teaches children to be sensitive to the social norms and pressures of their peer group. The third lesson is the value of emotional closeness to a peer (Bukowski, 2001).

Perspective Taking and Cognitive Flexibility.

The behavior of well-adjusted, competent children is maintained in part by a number of social cognitive abilities, including social perspective taking, interpersonal problem solving, information processing, and communicative competence. These cognitive abilities foster a child's entry into successful peer interactions. At the same time, active participation with peers promotes the development of these social cognitive abilities. In a longitudinal study of the influence of friendship on motivation and school adjustment, students who had a reciprocated friendship in sixth grade showed greater prosocial behavior, higher academic achievement, and less emotional distress than those who had no reciprocated friendship (Wentzel, Barry, & Caldwell, 2004).

You may recall the discussion of **perspective taking** from chapter 7 as one of the key factors that contributes to moral development, especially moral reasoning. As children interact with peers who see the world differently, they begin to understand the limits of their own points of view. Piaget (1932/1948) suggested that peers have an important influence in diminishing one another's self-centered outlook precisely because they interact as equals. Children are not forced to accept one another's ideas in quite the same way as they are with adults. They argue, bargain, and eventually compromise in order to maintain friendships. The opportunity to function in peer groups for problem solving and for play leads children away from the egocentrism of early childhood and closer to the eventual flexibility of adult thought. The benefit of these interactions is most likely to occur when peers have differences in perspective that result in conflicts that must be resolved. The benefits are especially positive for children who interact with slightly more competent peers who can introduce more advanced or flexible approaches to problem solving (Tudge, 1992).

Perspective-taking ability improves other social skills that contribute to the quality of a child's social relationships. Such skills include the ability to analyze social problems, recognize the emotional state of another person especially when that differs from their own emotional state, understand that others may view a situation differently because of their own information or beliefs, and accept individual differences in personality or abilities. Children who are sensitive to the variety of perspectives that coexist in a social situation are also likely to be more positively evaluated and trusted by their peers. Those who are perceived as more trustworthy and attuned to the concerns of others are likely to form more friendships (Rotenberg et al., 2004). An interactive process is thus set in motion. Children who have opportunities to participate in peer friendships make progress in achieving new levels of interpersonal understanding. As interpersonal understanding grows, children acquire the skills and sensitivity with which to be more effective with—and usually more valued by—their peers.

Social Norms and Peer Group Pressure.

The peer group evolves **norms** for acceptance and **rejection**. As children become aware of these norms, they begin to experience pressure to conform to the peer group. Adults, particularly teachers, then lose some of their power to influence children's behavior. In the

classroom, the early-school-age child focuses primarily on the teacher as a source of approval and acceptance. By age 9 or 10, children perceive the peer group as an equally significant audience. Children often *play* to the class instead of responding to the teacher. The roles of class joker, class snob, and class hero or heroine emerge during middle childhood and serve as ways of gaining approval from the peer group. Thinking back to the notion of relational aggression, you can see that some children use their knowledge of peer group norms to advance or preserve their social status. By spreading gossip, embarrassing children, or encouraging their friends to reject certain other children, they use social manipulation to sustain their power and prestige in the group.

The need for **peer approval** becomes a powerful force toward **conformity**. Children learn to dress, talk, and joke in ways that are acceptable to their peers. They learn to inhibit the expression of certain emotional reactions—especially sadness, vulnerability, and anger—in order to present a cool, competent public image to their peers (Salisch, 2001). Heterosexual antagonism, which is common at this stage, is perpetuated by pressures toward conformity. If all the fifth-grade boys hate girls, Johnny is not very likely to admit openly that he likes to play with Mary. Homophobic reactions are also evidenced at this age. Children who are gender atypical are often targeted for teasing, bullying, and social exclusion (Vaccaro, Kennedy, & August, 2012; Drury, Bukowksi, Vellásquez & Stella-Lopez, 2013). There are indications that perceived pressures to conform are stronger in the fifth and sixth grades than at later times, even though the importance of specific peer groups for group identity has not yet peaked (Gavin & Furman, 1989).

Close Friends.

Peer acceptance and popularity are not the same things as having a close or best friend. To gain peer acceptance, children may need to conform to group norms for dress, behaviors, and attitudes; they may need to adhere to gender stereotypes in order to appear gender-typical; and they may have to conceal certain strong feelings or hide facts about their family (Gifford-Smith & Brownell, 2003). Close friends experience a more intimate level of disclosure, trust, and supportiveness. Close friendships are often measured through a *mutual nomination strategy*. Children are given a roster of the names of their classmates and asked to circle the names of children who are their friends. When two children circle each other's names, they are identified as friends. Close friendships are then identified by the children as those characterized by high levels of shared activity, companionship, help or guidance, and ease of conflict resolution (Asher & Paquette, 2003). In the context of these friendships, children share private jokes, develop secret codes, tell family secrets, set out on adventures, and help each other in times of trouble. They enjoy spending time together. They also fight, threaten, break up, and reunite.

In his theory of interpersonal psychiatry, Harry Stack Sullivan (1949) pointed out the significance of these early friendships as building blocks for adult relationships. Best friend relationships provide a degree of understanding and openness that is often not possible with parents or family members. Within these friendships, private thoughts and fantasies are shared without the worry of being judged as silly, gross, or impractical. It is significant that the child experiences love for and closeness to a peer rather than

Carly and Michelle have been best friends since first grade. They love to spend time together whether they're washing the dog, going for bike rides, or listening to music. They depend on each other for fun, support, and problem solving.

an adult. The relationship is more likely to allow for mutuality of power, status, and access to resources (Youniss, 1980). Conflicts in these close relationships may be worked out in terms that the children control. One child cannot take away another child's allowance or send the other child out of the room when a conflict arises. The children must resolve their differences within the framework of their commitment to each other.

The stability of close friendships is quite variable. Some children remain friends over several years despite changes in classrooms and schools; other children seem to be in different friendship relationships every few months. The structure of a school or classroom influences friendship formation and stability. Close friends often see each other during the school day in classes and extracurricular activities. In schools that promote stable classroom groupings, where children remain in the same homeroom or class group from one grade to the next, friendship groups also remain more stable (Neckerman, 1996).

Close friendships are influenced by attractiveness, intelligence, classroom social status, and satisfaction with and commitment to the best friend. In a study of more than 800 children in grades 3 to 5, 78 percent had at least one reciprocating best friend (i.e., one child named another as one of three best friends, and that other child named the first child high on the list as well), and 55 percent had a *very* best friend. More girls than boys had best friends, and the quality of their best friendships was somewhat different. Girls and boys described their best friend relationships quite similarly with respect to having low levels of conflict or betrayal and high levels of companionship and shared recreational activities. However, girls described their best friend relationships as having higher levels of caring and personal validation ("makes me feel good about my ideas"), intimacy ("we always tell each other our problems"), help and guidance ("help each other

with schoolwork a lot"), and conflict resolution ("we make up easily when we have a fight") (Parker & Asher, 1993).

Girls and boys have somewhat different expectations about close friends. Girls tend to disclose more than boys about their worries and personal feelings. This seems to be related to how they feel about disclosure. Girls are more likely than boys to expect that by disclosing they will feel cared for and understood. Boys are more likely to feel weird about disclosing and see it as a "waste of time" (Rose et al., 2012). When asked to respond to a fictional scenario in which a close friend disappoints them by betraying a confidence, being unreliable, or failing to provide support or help, girls were more troubled by these transgressions than boys. Boys and girls were equally likely to say they would use some strategies to get revenge, but girls were more likely to say they would feel either sad or angry. These studies suggest that although having a close friend is highly valued for both boys and girls, the dynamics of these relationships are gendered (MacEvoy & Asher, 2012).

Having a close friend provides joyful experiences of companionship and feelings of being understood. As such, close friends can also play a protective role, reducing the impact of negative experiences. When a best friend is present during a negative experience, the experience itself seems to arouse less anxiety and is less damaging to a child's self-concept (Adams, Santo, & Bukowski, 2011). Children who have at least one best friend are less likely to experience depressive symptoms. Even among children who are characterized as withdrawn or inhibited, having at least one close friend seems to prevent the escalation of depression over time (Bukowski, Laursen, & Hoza 2010).

Loneliness

With the increased importance of friendship and peer acceptance come the risks of peer rejection and feelings of loneliness. In the period from preschool to middle childhood, issues of shyness, social anxiety, and peer victimization become increasingly salient. Experiences of social rejection or dissatisfaction in friendship quality become linked to a more general sense of anxiety in the school environment and a decline in self-worth (Asher & Gazelle, 1999; Asher, Parkhurst, Hymel, & Williams, 1999; Fordham & Stevenson-Hinde, 1999). By third grade, some children are characterized as anxious and solitary. They are shy, typically watching their peers without joining in, wanting to interact with their peers but afraid that they will be socially awkward or will not be accepted (Rubin, Coplan, & Bowker, 2009).

Three social characteristics combine to increase a child's experiences of **loneliness**. First, children who are anxious and solitary have trouble forming close friendships that provide emotional closeness and companionship; they are more likely to feel lonely. It is not necessary to have many friends. However, children who have at least one enduring, high-quality friendship are less likely to experience loneliness (Nangle, Erdley, Newan, Mason, & Carpenter, 2003).

Second, some children are systematically excluded. They don't get invited to children's parties or are the last to be chosen for teams. Peer rejection is especially powerful in producing feelings of loneliness. The relationship between peer rejection and loneliness has been found across countries and grades from kindergarten through middle school (Asher & Paquette, 2003; Crick & Ladd, 1993).

Lily is feeling sad and lonely. Her best friend said she doesn't want to play with her anymore; the other kids in the neighborhood laugh at her; and her mom told her to go outside and play because she needs to get some work done in the house.

Third, among the children who are anxious and solitary, those who experience exclusion or are rejected by peers become increasingly socially helpless, anticipating rejection and being unwilling to take new risks to reach out or initiate social exchanges (Gazelle & Druben, 2009). Children who tend to blame themselves for their lack of social acceptance feel more lonely and are less likely to believe that they can do anything to improve their situation. Those who are withdrawn, victimized, or bullied report higher levels of loneliness than other unpopular children (Kochenderfer-Ladd & Wardrop, 2001).

Although loneliness can be a transient experience, as when children move from one neighborhood or school to another, or when a best friend moves away, some children are chronically lonely. They may have unrealistic expectations about friendship and intense worries about the possibility of negative peer evaluations (MacEvoy, Papadakis, Fedigan, & Ash 2016). These children have strong negative emotional reactions to social messages of exclusion and tend to be suspicious of efforts to include them. They view social exclusion as evidence that there is something inadequate about them. Thus, their perceptions and attributions about social cues reinforce their reticence and increase feelings of loneliness (Vanhalst et al., 2015).

What can lonely or socially anxious children do to increase their sense of closeness to friends? **Cognitive restructuring** techniques may help children deal with social anxiety (Rapee, Wignall, Spence, Lynham, & Cobham, 2008). The central features of cognitive restructuring are (1) identify the thoughts that increase strong emotions such as anger, anxiety, or sadness; (2) challenge their accuracy; and (3) replace them with interpretations that are more realistic and less disruptive to adaptive behavior.

With regard to **social anxiety**, students learn to monitor changes in their anxiety level and to become aware of the thoughts that accompany this increase in anxiety. For example, a student may recognize that his anxiety rises in class when he thinks about answering a question out loud because he assumes that his classmates would think he is stupid if he were to give an incorrect answer. Once these assumptions have been identified, the student may be guided to look for evidence that these assumptions are correct and to consider alternative interpretations. The student may be encouraged to take a more accepting view, recognizing that everyone makes mistakes. When other students make mistakes, he does not usually think badly of them. To strengthen this perspective and remain calm, the student might practice self-talk, such as, "It's OK to make mistakes; that's how we learn." Through cognitive restructuring, socially anxious students learn to recognize the sources of their anxiety and practice strategies for redefining the situation so they can be more confident about taking the initiative in peer situations.

Some children have discovered that online communication provides an environment where they can experience greater levels of self-disclosure and depth of communication with friends. The Internet is increasingly used as a way to supplement face-to-face friendship interactions through a variety of social media including Facebook, Twitter, Instagram, texting, blogs, email, and instant messaging (Peter, Valkenburg, & Schouten, 2005; Walther, 2011). Although some children use the Internet to participate in chat with strangers, most use it to maintain their existing network of friends. Some form friendships with strangers through chat who then become face-to-face friends. In a study of Dutch children, 61 percent of the participants who were 10 and 11 years old used the Internet for online communication. Almost 90 percent of those children communicated with preexisting friends (Valkenburg & Peter, 2007). Children who described themselves as either lonely or socially anxious were more likely to perceive online communication as facilitating greater breadth and depth of communication. Those socially anxious children who perceived the Internet as offering a way to achieve greater intimacy in communication used the Internet more often and described their friendships as closer than socially anxious children who used online communication infrequently.

Socially anxious children may have more difficulty with face-to-face self-disclosure. For these children, the value of the Internet is not for increasing general social interaction or for forming new relationships but for allowing greater levels of intimacy with existing friends, unencumbered by the difficult visual and auditory cues that may disrupt disclosure in face-to-face interactions. Unfortunately, online technologies and text messaging can also be used in a hostile way to send messages of rejection, such as with cyberbullying. Youth can use electronic media to embarrass, harass, or threaten their peers.

Rejection

Rejection hurts. Studies of rejection find different patterns of reaction, including emotional numbness, changes in mood reflecting new levels of sadness or feeling bad, and decreases in self-esteem. Two basic needs appear to be thwarted when a child experiences social rejection—the need for control and the need for belonging. Under some conditions, children protect themselves from the negative feelings associated with rejection by withdrawing from social interactions; in other conditions they may act aggressively to try to reassert control (Baumeister, DeWall, & Vohs, 2009; Gerber & Wheeler, 2009).

Research has identified three types of children who experience peer rejection. Some children who are rejected are disruptive and aggressive with their peers; others are socially withdrawn but do not exhibit aggressive tendencies; a third group has been described as both aggressive and withdrawn (French, 1988, 1990; Hymel, Bowker, & Woody, 1993). Children who are physically aggressive are identified as early as toddlerhood. Aggressiveness has been noted as a feature of personality that is linked to difficulties in emotional regulation, exposure to power-assertive or harsh parenting, and reduced levels of empathy. Genetic and environmental factors combine to support a child's aggressive and oppositional behavior (Burt & Neiderhiser, 2009). **Aggressive-rejected** children, often referred to as *bullies*, are more likely than nonaggressive children to attribute hostile intentions to others. They see peer interactions as threatening and say they would be likely to use aggressive strategies in response to negative peer behaviors (Quiggle, Garber, Panak, & Dodge, 1992; Waldman, 1996). Aggressive-rejected children tend to have an exaggerated idea of their competence and social status. They are less accurate in reading their own social status among their classmates, although they are just as accurate as other children in reading the social status of others (Zakriski & Coie, 1996).

However, not all aggressive children are rejected. One study looked at the relationship of antisocial and prosocial characteristics of young children and their social standing in the classroom (Farmer & Rodkin, 1996). Children in four different types of classroom groups were compared: academic giftedness, emotional and behavioral disorders, general education, and learning disabilities. Across all four types of classrooms, aggressive, disruptive characteristics were strongly associated with peer rejection or isolation for girls. For boys in the general education classes, however, aggressive behavior was positively associated with popularity. In some classroom contexts, aggressiveness, particularly among boys, may be a viable path toward bonding with other boys and asserting one's leadership, especially for boys who cannot achieve notice through their academic performance (Ettekal & Ladd, 2015; Poulin & Boivin, 2000). In many cases, bullies deliberately choose targets who are already rejected by their peers, thus minimizing the risk of social rejection from other children. Moreover, boys who bully other boys are admired by some girls who are possibly being attracted to this gender-stereotyped dominant male behavior (Dijkstra, Lindenberg, & Veenstra, 2007; Veenstra, Lindenberg, Munniksma, & Dijkstra, 2010).

Children in the **withdrawn** group tend to be inhibited, anxious, and interpersonally reserved. They have a negative self-concept and tend to interpret negative peer reactions as resulting from their own personal failings (Hymel et al., 1993). They have difficulty dealing with stress. These children may exhibit inappropriate emotions and display various unusual behavioral mannerisms that are likely to draw ridicule from their peers (French, 1988). Withdrawn, non-aggressive rejected children were paired with popular children in a problem-solving and reasoning task. The withdrawn rejected children demonstrated difficulties in collaboration and communication that may help account in part for their social isolation (Crosby, Fireman, & Clopton, 2011). Studies of children with developmental disabilities and language disorders suggest that these children begin to have more relationship problems in the upper elementary school grades. As their social status among classmates declines, they may become targets of bullying, and they are less likely to be involved in reciprocal friendships. Over time, children who experience a combination of anxiety, lack of a close friend, and peer victimization are likely to continue to be targets of victimization (Asher & Gazelle, 1999; Gazelle, 2008; Goldbaum, Craig, Pepler, & Connolly, 2003).

Children in the **aggressive-withdrawn** group tend to be the least well liked of all three types of rejected children. They exhibit anxiety, poor self-control, and social withdrawal in addition to aggressive behavior. They are rated by other children as incompetent in school ability; unattractive; showing the poorest skills in leadership, cooperation, or sense of humor; and the most likely to behave inappropriately in school. Aggressive-withdrawn children are similar to the bully-victims described in the **Applying Theory and Research to Life** box Bullying (Marini, Dane, Bosacki, & YLC-CURA, 2006). Having been excluded or rejected by their peers, they respond by lashing out against children who are more vulnerable than they. Despite high levels of peer rejection, aggressive-withdrawn children do not have the same low self-concept and negative view of their abilities as the withdrawn children. They are likely to have future adjustment problems and often require psychiatric treatment in adolescence or adulthood (Coie & Krehbiel, 1984; Hymel et al., 1990).

Peer rejection has consequences for mental health and school adjustment. Children with problems in attention and self-regulation may become targets of peer victimization in the early school grades. The anxiety and distractions caused by this hostile peer environment can increase the demands on a child's self-regulation resources, making initial difficulties with hyperactivity, inattentiveness, and behavioral regulation worse. Beginning in the early school grades, peer rejection is associated with school problems, including school avoidance, negative attitudes about school, less engagement with school-related tasks, and a less cooperative orientation toward teacher requests and group activities. The longer this peer rejection lasts, the more impact it seems to have on a child's engagement with the learning environment and the academic challenges of school (Ladd, Herald-Brown, & Reiser, 2008; Schwartz, Lansford, Dodge, Pettit, & Bates, 2013; Stenseng, Belsky, Salicka, & Wichstrøm, 2016).

FURTHER REFLECTION: Analyze the relationship of social competence and friendship. Describe some ways that a child's social competence contributes to the quality of friendship in middle childhood. Describe some ways that a child's friendships might enhance social competence.

Given what you have read about loneliness and rejection, think about what might be done to help improve social competence among children who lack adequate social skills.

Bullying

Bullying is a common problem facing children in many cultures. Building on the work of Dan Olweus (1978, 1995), the Centers for Disease Control and Prevention (CDC) and the Department of Education offered a federal definition of bullying which includes three elements: "unwanted aggressive behavior; observed or perceived power imbalance; and repetition of behaviors or high likelihood of repetition" (stopbullying. gov, 2014). Bullying can take many forms such as physical harm, verbal threats, harming a child's reputation, ostracizing a child, or victimizing a child (for example by taking their belongings). Relational bullying is the most common form, such as name calling, teasing, and spreading rumors or lies. Physical bullying is next most common, and cyberbullying is least common (Bradshaw, Sawyer, & O'Brennan, 2007). Given the variety of forms that bullying can take, the age of the respondents, and the form of assessment, the prevalence of bullying is difficult to determine (Hymel & Swearer, 2015). The government website referred to above estimates that between 25 percent and 33 percent of children have been bullied at school, and as many as 30 percent of students admit to bullying others. In a national survey of parents' worries and concerns about their children, 60 percent were worried that their child might be bullied (Pew Research Center 2015c).

Bullying is most common in middle schools. Over 70 percent of school staff have observed bullying in their schools, with over 40 percent saying they have witnessed bullying once a week or more (Bradshaw et al., 2007). Although cyberbullying is less common than other forms, it can have a far-reaching impact. **Cyberbullying** involves "intimidation , hurt or harassment conducted using cell phones, the Internet or other electronic devices" (Svoboda, 2014). When an insult, threat, photo, or rumor is started online, it can spread through a network of contacts, allowing people to continue the bullying without any consequences. Meanwhile the victim may experience the insult over and over, unable to remove the message or stop the spread of the attack.

What are the characteristics of bullies and their victims? There appear to be two types of bullies, those who are socially integrated and enjoy a degree of peer popularity, and those who are marginalized and lack peer acceptance (Juvonen, Graham, & Schuster, 2003; Olweus, 1978; Rodkin, Espelage, & Hanish, 2015).

Socially Integrated Bullies. These children are identified by their peers as higher than average in aggression and low in victimization. Classmates often perceive them as "cool" but do not want to spend much time with them (Juvonen et al., 2003). Boys may be physically stronger than their peers; girls may be socially more popular. They have deep-seated needs for power and enjoy being in control. They are likely to have experienced a family environment characterized by harsh discipline or love withdrawal as well as indifference, low involvement, and lack of warmth. This context results in little sense of personal empathy and a high degree of hostility toward others. They have learned early in life that aggression is a tool for controlling others. These children are often aggressive toward teachers and other authority figures as well as toward peers.

It is not uncommon for aggressive boys to have best friends who are also aggressive. Within these relationships, the boys encourage each other toward rule breaking (Bagwell & Coie, 2004). Socially integrated bullies often find some reward or reinforcement for their behavior, especially when they coerce their victims into giving them money, taking things of value, and being treated with respect by other peers. For some, even the pain or humiliation they observe in their victims can be a rewarding source of satisfaction (American Society for the Positive Care of Children, 2016). The fact that bullies enjoy both high social status and report few psychological problems helps explain why bullying is so hard to modify. Bullies enjoy their social reputation and, although feared by others, do not seem to be bothered by the fact that many of the children avoid them.

Socially Marginalized Bullies. These children are described by their peers as both high in aggression and high in victimization (bully-victims). Socially marginalized bullies have themselves been targets of exclusion or victimization. As a result, their bullying may be an attempt to gain some control or to retaliate in a system that they perceive as rejecting or humiliating. In contrast to socially integrated bullies, bully-victims are more depressed and lonely, have lower social status, are less popular, and are more likely to be avoided by their classmates. Over time, they are likely to become increasingly friendless (Kechel, Ladd, Bagwell, & Yabko, 2015). These bullies are often described as "at risk" students who have negative attitudes about themselves and a tendency to perceive others as threatening or hostile toward them (Juvonen et al., 2003; Rodkin et al., 2015). Having been victimized by others, they may subsequently lash out to express a desire for revenge (American Society for the Positive Care of Children, 2016). In some cases, these marginalized children have been victimized at home as well as at school, resulting in a sense of being overwhelmed by unmanageable threats (Schwartz, Lansford, Dodge, Petit, & Bates, 2013).

Victims. If bullying involves a power differential between the bully and the victim, we can infer that in a specific school environment certain children are victimized because of a relative lack of essential resources. Victims may be singled out due to disabilities, gender atypicality, comparatively lower income, or due to personality qualities like shyness or low self-esteem. In comparison to the bullies, the victims, especially boys, are physically weaker. When attacked, they do not retaliate. As a result, the abuse continues and often escalates. Children who are perceived by their peers as victims also report the highest levels of depression, social anxiety, and loneliness; have the lowest social status as rated by peers; and are described by teachers as the least popular of the children (Juvonen et al., 2003). They are the most marginalized of the children, and, as a result, may be additionally vulnerable because they have no classmates who will defend them or intervene when they are being attacked.

Sexual orientation and race/ethnicity are two factors that are commonly intertwined with bullying. LGBTQ students are targets of frequent bullying. Surveys of LGBTQ youth find that 80 percent say that their teachers never or rarely intervened to stop homophobic joking or bullying (SPLC Report, 2010). Children who are members of a numeric ethnic minority in their school are more vulnerable to harassment than children who are in the ethnic majority. When a school is ethnically diverse and no group is in a clear numeric majority, children who are victims of bullying are more likely to attribute the problem to the bullies or to conditions of the school environment that allow this kind of harassment than to blame themselves (Graham, 2004; Graham & Juvonen, 2002).

Intervention. The complex social dynamics surrounding bullying call for a multidimensional approach to intervention. In order to be effective, interventions need to be sensitive to the microsystem in which the bullying is taking place. Who are the bullies? Who are the victims? Are there ethnic, gender, religious, social class, or sexual orientation issues involved? Is there evidence that bullies are being rewarded with social capital? If so, how does the intervention infiltrate the social reward system of the peer group? (Rodkin et al., 2015).

To date, evaluations of anti-bullying programs have reported modest success in preventing bullying and reducing victimization in schools (Ansary, Elias, Greene, & Green, 2015). In designing programs, one needs to be clear about the focus of the intervention. Violence prevention, harassment prevention, and bullying prevention are related, overlapping concepts, but programs focusing on one may not adequately address the others (Cornell & Limber, 2016). Some programs focus on prevention of bullying; others on addressing bullying once it has occurred. Some interventions are intended to support children who have been victimized to prevent long-term social, academic, health, and mental health consequences (Juvonen, Schacter, Sainio, & Salmivalli, 2016).

Four key areas need to be addressed in any effective bullying intervention (Ansary et al., 2015):

1. An overall holistic theoretical approach that addresses both in-school and out-of-school contexts and strives to create a positive school climate involving students, administrators, teachers, staff, and families.
2. Specific content areas, including social-emotional development, conflict resolution, character development, and efforts to increase "upstander" behavior that encourages others to speak out and intervene when they observe bullying.
3. Leadership and team management, including teacher/staff/administrator training, and clear policies for addressing bullying when it occurs.
4. Systematic use of assessments to understand the extent of bullying and victimization in the school, monitor program implementation, and improve effectiveness.

Critical Thinking Questions

1. Why do you think that some bullies are popular and have high status among their peers? Hypothesize about the implications of having popular bullies for the nature of the school climate.
2. What might be some consequences of being a victim of bullying? Summarize how being a victim affects subsequent school achievement, peer relationships, and mental health.
3. Predict the likely trajectories for bullies as they move into adolescence and adulthood. What factors might influence whether being a bully in middle childhood continues to be expressed in some fashion in later stages of life?
4. What strategies can you think of that would improve the school environment for LGBTQ students and reduce the chances that they are victims of bullying?
5. Imagine that you are asked to evaluate a school-based program to prevent bullying. What outcome measures would you select? In other words, what would you consider evidence that a program to prevent bullying was effective?

Concrete Operations

OBJECTIVE 2   Describe the development of concrete operational thought, including conservation, classification skills, mathematical reasoning, and the child's ability to understand and monitor his or her own knowledge and understanding.

Children's abilities to analyze and manage social relationships, including friendships, are linked to their ability to solve other kinds of problems. Advances in reasoning about the physical world may stimulate new ways of handling complex social situations; similarly, engaging in complex social situations may enhance the child's ability to bring flexibility and perspective to problems of the physical world. Observations across many different cultures confirm a shift in adults' expectations of children at around age 7, suggesting a convergence of advanced cognitive capacities and new cultural demands. By middle childhood, children are expected to be able to coordinate their thinking with others, cooperate with the group, and use ideas and information to solve applied problems (Gauvain & Reynolds, 2011).

Thinking back to the period of infancy, the discussion of intelligence focused on the establishment of sensory and motor patterns used to explore the environment, manipulate means–end relationships, clarify the nature of physical objects, and form simple categories. During toddlerhood, cognition moves beyond the experiential domain as children develop a variety of representational skills that free them from complete reliance on their immediate physical environment. Toddlers create novel situations and solve problems by using thought, fantasy, and language. Piaget (Piaget & Inhelder, 1969) suggested that at about age 6 or 7, a qualitatively new form of thinking develops, referred to as **concrete operational thought**. This type of reasoning guides thought by imposing logical rules on one's judgments, leading to the acceptance of certain inferences that adhere to the logic as more compelling or convincing than others (Moshman, 2004).

The word **operation** refers to an action that is performed on an object or a set of objects. A **mental operation** is an action that is carried out in thought rather than in behavior. Piaget argued that such mental operations are built on some physical relationship that the younger child can perform but cannot articulate. For example, a toddler can arrange a graduated set of circles on a stick so that the largest circle is at the bottom of the stick and the smallest circle is at the top. The child does not have a verbal label for the ordering operation but can perform it. With the emergence of concrete operations, children begin to consider a variety of actions that can be performed on objects and can do so mentally without having to do them physically. Thus, a mental operation is a representation or scheme for an alteration in the relationships among objects.

One of the most powerful mental operations is *reversibility*. One can imagine an action, such as filling a glass with water and then undoing the action by emptying the glass. One can even imagine adding salt to water and then removing the salt, even though this would be difficult in practice. In contrast to sensorimotor schemes, which unfold in a behavior sequence, operations can be done and undone in the mind (Newman & Newman, 2007).

Piaget (1972a) used the term concrete to contrast this quality of thinking to the more hypothetical reasoning of adolescents and adults. The child reasons about objects and the relations among them but has difficulty entertaining hypothetical statements or propositions. Thinking is typically focused on real objects that exist in the world, even if the child is not seeing or manipulating these objects at the moment. For example, children can reason about problems involving the grouping of trees into different categories and identifying the features of these categories. However, if you pose a problem involving trees that migrate from North to South with the seasons, a child in the concrete stage of thinking will have difficulty even entertaining the problem because trees do not migrate. During the stage of concrete operations, the three conceptual skills that have received the most attention are (1) conservation, (2) classification, and (3) computational skills; these are explained briefly in Table 8.1. Over the period of middle childhood, children apply these skills to achieve a clearer understanding of the logic, order, and predictability of the physical world. As children take a new approach to problem solving through the use of the logical principles associated with concrete operational thought, they generalize these principles to their thinking about friendships, team play and other games with rules, and their own self-evaluation. Children are able to consider two competing explanations, look at a problem from another person's point of view as well as their own, and, using this information, plan a strategy to reach a goal.

Conservation

The basic meaning of **conservation** is that physical matter does not magically appear or disappear despite changes in form, shape, or container. The concept of conservation can be applied to many dimensions, including mass, weight, number, length, and volume. A child who conserves is able to resist perceptual cues that alter

Tony has created a plan and is focusing seriously on how to implement his plan as he builds his brick structure. The combination of fine motor skills, computational skills, and logical reasoning come together in the design of his project. For many children, materials that offer opportunities to design and build new structures are a source of satisfaction throughout middle childhood.

the form of an object, insisting that the quantity remains the same despite the change in form. One of the most common problems of this type that Piaget investigated involves *conservation of mass*. The child is presented with two clay balls and is asked to tell whether or not they are equal. Once the child is satisfied that the balls are equal, one of them is flattened out into a pancake. The child is then asked, "Which has more—this one [the pancake] or this one [the ball]?" Sometimes, the child is also asked whether the clay pieces are still the same. The child who does not conserve might say that the pancake has more clay because it is a lot wider than the ball. This child is still in the preoperational stage of thought: She is using personal perceptions to make judgments rather than logic. In contrast, the child who conserves knows that the two pieces of clay are still identical in mass and can explain why.

Children eventually use the three concepts illustrated in FIGURE 8.1 ▶ to ascertain that equality in any physical dimension has not been altered. First, the child may explain that the pancake has the same amount of clay as the ball; no clay has been added or taken away. This is an example of the concept of **identity**: The pancake is still the *same* clay, and nothing has been

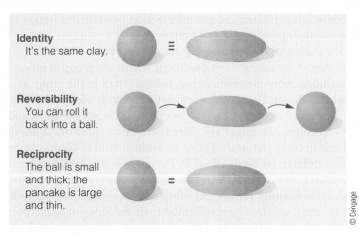

Identity
It's the same clay.

Reversibility
You can roll it back into a ball.

Reciprocity
The ball is small and thick; the pancake is large and thin.

FIGURE 8.1 ▶ Three Concepts That Contribute to Conservation

changed except its shape. Second, the child may point out that the experimenter can turn the pancake back into a ball. This is an example of the concept of **reversibility**. The child realizes that operations can be reversed so that their effects are nullified. Third, the child may notice that, although the pancake has a larger circumference, the ball is much thicker. When the child can simultaneously manipulate two dimensions, such as circumference and thickness, we observe the concept of **reciprocity**. In the clay ball example, change in one dimension is compensated for by change in another; the total mass remains the same. With consolidation of the concepts of identity, reversibility, and reciprocity, the child is able to conserve in any physical dimension. Children generally conserve mass and number earliest, weight later, and volume last.

Conservation may not generalize across all of the physical modes. For example, children who are unable to conserve quantity in an unfamiliar object, such as poker chips, can do so with a more familiar one, such as M&M's (Gulko, Doyle, Serbin, & White, 1988). In one study, girls were able to perform a conservation of liquid task when it was presented in the standard manner of comparing the experimenter's glass and their own. However, when the task was embedded in a story where juice had to be divided between two dolls, their performance declined. Evidence of a lack of generalizability of knowledge from in-school to out-of-school contexts is found in other areas of reasoning, especially mathematical codes and scientific principles (Perret-Clermont, Perret, & Bell, 1991).

Extensions of Piaget's Ideas About Conservation. Researchers have raised questions about the meaning of conservation tasks, the timing of the emergence of conservation, and the possibility of teaching children to conserve. The way the task is presented and the kinds of questions asked may influence a child's responses. For example, the task may emphasize identity or equivalence. In an *identity* task, the child is asked to judge whether a single clay ball has the same amount of clay after it has been rolled into a sausage. In an *equivalence* task, there are two balls of clay. The child is asked to judge whether the ball that is rolled into a sausage has the same amount of clay as the standard, comparison ball. Some studies have shown that children can perform the identity task earlier than the equivalence task; others have shown the opposite; and still others have argued that identity

and equivalence are achieved at the same time (Silverstein et al., 1982). In a study of 5- to 7-year-olds, children were asked to tell how the materials looked and then to tell how they really were. Giving the child this distinction between appearance and reality resulted in more correct answers than the standard procedure in which this distinction was not made (Bijstra, Van Geert, & Jackson, 1989). Approaches to instruction, including the use of gestures, the variety of materials, and the specific language used to present the problem all contribute to a child's ability to reason about conservation (Ping & Goldin-Meadow, 2008).

Piaget's view that children will enter the stage of concrete operational reasoning through active construction and experimentation at around the age of 6 or 7 is not universally true. In a study of the relationship of conservation of liquid and early mathematical skills, researchers found that only about half the 6 and 7 year olds could conserve volume (Wubbena, 2013). In a study of fifth graders, half the students were identified as being in the preoperational stage, even at age 10. The study examined strategies for enhancing concrete operational reasoning through guided intervention involving special activities intended to promote logical problem solving and abstract thinking. This intervention was found to be successful in promoting concrete operational thought (Bakken, Thompson, Clark, Johnson, & Dwyer, 2001).

Theoretically, Piaget's view of development suggests that there is a period of maturational readiness for the application of logical operations to physical objects. When left to their own exploration and experimentation, Piaget argued, children would discover the regularities and operations that underlie conservation. Showing a child a conservation problem and then explaining and reinforcing the correct answer should not be very effective if the child is not ready to assimilate this information. However, research has shown that it is possible to train young children of preschool age to conserve. Early training studies have both theoretical and practical implications. They demonstrate that it is possible to introduce such concepts as identity and reversibility so that children as young as 4 can achieve conservation. Children also transfer conservation from the tasks involved in training to other materials and dimensions (Field, 1981; May & Norton, 1981).

One way to advance a child's approach to conservation is to confront the child with alternative reasoning. For this contradiction to be effective, however, the child must be approaching a level of readiness to reorganize his thinking, and the gap between the child's current level of reasoning and the new ideas must not be too great. This reminds us of Vygotsky's concept of the zone of proximal development. The implication is that entry into a new stage of thought may emerge earlier and may be more readily influenced by the social environment than Piaget's cognitive developmental theory predicts. However, Piaget himself was not especially impressed by faster and sooner. He believed in the enduring benefits of personal discovery.

Practically speaking, research has demonstrated that preschool- and kindergarten-age children can integrate and apply more abstract concepts than educators once believed they could. For example, studies of children as young as 3 and 4 have shown that they understand the idea that materials are made of tiny particles that retain their properties even when they are invisible. They can use this notion of particles to explain how a substance, such as sugar, continues to exist in a solution and retain its sweetness even when it is invisible (Au, Sidle, & Rollins, 1993; Rosen & Rozin, 1993). In a study focused on estimating volume, many children in kindergarten and first grade were able to consider the integration of three dimensions—height, width, and depth—to guess how many small cubes would be needed to build a larger cube. Their estimates suggest that at even this young age, children can integrate information from three dimensions (Ebersbach, 2009). Early childhood educators have found that through a planned program of exploring, experimenting, and describing the transformation of materials, young children can be guided to conceptualize the physical world in a systematic, logical manner.

Classification Skills

Classification was first discussed in chapter 5, describing infants' basic categorization skills. **Classification** is the ability to identify the properties of categories, relate categories or classes to one another, and use categorical information to solve problems. Two components of classification provide the essential ability to apply knowledge from a known or familiar instance to a new instance: categorization and induction. **Categorization** simply means that if one apple belongs to the category of fruit, then *all* apples are fruit. You do not need to learn this categorization label for each type of apple. **Induction** refers to the realization that whatever holds true for one member of a category is likely to hold true for other members as well. For example, water and juice are both liquids. If you can pour water, you can pour juice. Other substances classified as liquids should also have this property—even substances one has never seen. The value of classification skills is not merely to organize objects or experiences into classes, but to take advantage of what is known about these categories to make inferences about the characteristics and dynamics of members of the same categories, members of hierarchically related categories, and objects that are not members of a specific category (Farrar, Raney, & Boyer, 1992; Kalish & Gelman, 1992; Lopez, Gelman, Gutheil, & Smith, 1992).

One component of classification skills is the ability to group objects according to some dimension that they share. Another component is the ability to order subgroups hierarchically so that each new grouping will include all previous subgroups. Vygotsky (1962) suggested a method for studying classification in young children. Children are presented with a variety of wooden blocks that differ in shape, size, and color. Under each block is a nonsense syllable that is hidden from view. The children are instructed to select, one at a time, all the blocks that have the same syllable. The youngest children, who would be characterized as preoperational in Piaget's stage theory, tend to select blocks by their color. Their technique for grouping is highly associative. They choose each new block to match some characteristic of the previous selection, but they do not hold in mind a single concept that guides their choices.

In the stage of concrete operations children tend to focus on one dimension at first, perhaps shape, and continue to select blocks until they discover that they have made an incorrect choice. They use this discovery to change their hypothesis about which characteristics of the blocks are associated with the nonsense syllable. This classification task demonstrates the child's ability to hold a concept in mind and to make a series of decisions based on it. It also demonstrates that during the stage of concrete

operations, children can use information from their mistakes to revise their problem-solving strategy.

Piaget studied reasoning about class hierarchies or class inclusion by asking questions about whether a group of objects included more members of one subtype than of the group as a whole (Piaget, 1941/1952; see also Chapman & McBride, 1992). Thus, when a set of pictures shows three ducks, six sparrows, and two robins, one might ask, "Are there more sparrows or more birds in these pictures?" This is an unusual kind of question, one that children are rarely asked. By the age of 8 or 9, however, many children can respond correctly because they recognize the distinction between classes and subclasses. In order to handle such problems, children have to inhibit their tendency to reinterpret the question in line with a more common comparison, such as, "Are there more sparrows than ducks?"

In one study of class inclusion reasoning, an intriguing pattern was found. Children of ages 3 and 4, who could not repeat the question and clearly had not learned any rules about classes, were more likely to answer correctly than children of ages 5 and 6. Children of ages 7 and 8 performed better than any of the younger children. The 5- and 6-year-olds, who answered quickly and confidently, were consistently incorrect. They seemed unable to inhibit the more obvious comparison in order to consider the actual question (McCabe, Siegel, Spence, & Wilkinson, 1982).

Laura loves to sit and sort her change into piles (categories) of coins and then to see how high she can stack each type of coin.

Two processes appear to contribute to classification judgments among young children. First, perceived similarities among target objects guide judgments about whether the objects belong to the same category. Second, verbal labels play an important role in cuing children into the similarities among objects. When no verbal labels are available, children judge whether two objects are members of the same category based on the number of similar features. In comparison to adults, who rely less on verbal labels than on similarity of features, young children expect the labels to provide important information about objects, but they do not rely solely on these labels to guide their judgment (Sloutsky & Fisher, 2004).

From ages 6 to 12, children's knowledge of categories and the information associated with them expands dramatically. Moreover, children have a broad range of categories available into which to incorporate a novel observation. The capacity for classifying and categorizing has been explored in relation to specific domains, such as health and illness or concepts of the family. For example, children were told about 21 different human groupings and asked to say whether these groupings were a family: "Here are Mr. Mead and his son, Tom. They live together, just the two of them. Are they a family?" The youngest participants (4- to 6-year-olds) had trouble accepting examples involving single parents or biologically related people who did not live in the same home as instances of a family. Principles of biological relatedness and shared physical residence were both important to these children's view of a family. By middle childhood, the children were able to accept a wider variety of groups as meeting certain essential criteria of a family, usually biological relatedness and emotional closeness. Emotional closeness was endorsed by 80 percent of the participants as a defining feature of a family and was used repeatedly as a basis for judging whether a specific instance of a grouping could be considered a family or not (Newman, Roberts, & Syre, 1993).

Categorization skills can be used in an active way to construct and constrain behavior. Butler and Weatherall (2006) observed the natural use of categorization in the play sequences of 6- and 7-year-olds. Children systematically mapped participants to categories of play roles and used these categories to establish appropriate behaviors within the play sequence. The use of membership categories, such as good and bad pirates, provides a guide toward the kinds of actions, props, and strengths or vulnerabilities children are allowed within the pretense. These categories are used to include new players to the situation and to guide the initiation of new play sequences that will fit with the established categories.

Computational Skills

A third characteristic of concrete operational thought is the development of **computational skills**. The number symbols (1, 2, etc.) can provide three types of information: nominal, cardinal, and ordinal. *Nominal numbers* are used like names, such as the number on a football player's jersey or a home address. They do not refer to an amount. *Cardinal numbers* refer to a quantity (e.g., two siblings or 5 minutes). *Ordinal numbers* refer to the position or progression of things in a set (e.g., first, second, third) rather than to a specific amount. In the transition from preoperational to concrete operational thought, children shift from using numbers in a nominal way (knowing and reciting the names of numbers, or reciting their street address) to the ordinal and cardinal nature of numbers (Canobe, 2008).

Conservation of number is achieved around age 6 or 7 (Halford & Boyle, 1985). Once they have acquired the operations underlying conservation of number, children understand that certain physical transformations will not alter the number of units in a set. If 10 poker chips are lined up in a row, the number remains constant whether they are spread out, squeezed tightly together, or stacked. Children can use counting to answer a "how many" question sometime between the ages of 3 and 4. For example, they can assign one number to each item in a set of four poker chips and tell you that there are four chips in all. However, young children have more difficulty selecting a set of six chips from a larger pile, or establishing that two sets of chips are equal in number. They also have trouble solving verbal story problems when no concrete objects are present (Jordan et al., 1992; Sophian, 1998).

Young children differ widely in their mathematical knowledge and problem-solving skills. Success in doing addition and subtraction requires counting knowledge, working memory, understanding of part–whole relationships, familiarity with the language and features of specific problems and experience with a variety of strategies for estimating answers, solving problems, and checking one's answers (Canobi, Reeve, & Pattison, 2003; Ginsburg & Pappas, 2004). The ability to solve addition problems begins with an understanding that cardinal numbers refer to quantities. There is clearly a link between conservation of matter, conservation of number, and the ability to add or subtract quantities (Sophian, 2007).

Early number competence includes an understanding that each number is one more than the number preceding it and one less than the number following it. This understanding allows children to make quick and accurate judgments about the value of small quantities and to understand the logic behind joining or separating of sets (e.g., 5 and 2 makes 7; 7 take away 2 leaves 5). During the first few elementary grades, most children acquire the complementary operations of addition, subtraction, multiplication, and division and learn to apply these operations no matter what specific objects or quantities are involved. Longitudinal studies show that children's number competence and rate of growth in understanding numbers in kindergarten and first grade are strong predictors of their mathematics achievement by third grade, a point at which many children are required to take mathematics assessment tests (Canobi, 2004; Jordan, Kaplan, Ramineni, & Locuniak, 2009; Zur & Gelman, 2004).

There is a difference between the cognitive understanding of single computational operations, such as addition and subtraction, and the coordination of computational abilities to solve mathematics problems (Montague, 2006). As the problems become more complex, involving larger numbers, more numbers, or numbers embedded in story problems, same-grade children demonstrate notable differences in the speed and accuracy of their solutions. The explanation for these differences may rest with the social and cultural context of learning, especially the quality of interactions between teachers and their students. Teachers differ in their confidence about their own mathematical abilities, as well as their ability to assess children's understanding of mathematics and to select appropriate approaches to mathematics instruction. In a detailed policy report on mathematics education for young children, the researchers concluded that early childhood mathematics instruction is poor, failing to build upon the basic capacities of mathematics understanding that most children bring to the preschool or kindergarten setting. "The typical situation is that (teachers) are poorly trained to teach the subject, are afraid of it, feel it is not important to teach, and typically teach it badly or not at all," noted Ginsburg, Lee, and Boyd (2008, p. 1). More research is needed to clarify factors that support the cognitive basis of computational skills and factors that support more advanced computational problem solving (Newcombe et al., 2009).

Central Conceptual Structures and Computational Reasoning.

A group of theorists, sometimes referred to as neo-Piagetians (Morra, Gobbo, Marini, & Sheese, 2008; Young, 2011) agree with Piaget's characterization of development as stage-like rather than continuous. They also consider biological maturation as providing the basic constraints on cognition at any given age. And they agree that children are developing internal mental structures that support logic and reasoning across problems. However, they argue that Piaget's broad characterization of stage-related mental structures is too general—it does not take into account the evidence from neuroscience about the maturation of the brain, and it does not consider the insights and skills derived from instruction and practice that can advance children's reasoning.

Robbie Case's theory of central conceptual structures is an example of this neo-Piagetian perspective (Case, 1998). Case drew on evidence about changes in processing speed, memory, and executive control to explain that as children get older they can keep more information in the mind at once, thereby allowing them to organize, coordinate, and compare data in order to solve problems. Case acknowledged the role of instruction through guided teaching, expanded opportunities for exploration, and encouragement for practice. Advances in reasoning emerge as operations become more and more efficient, a result of the integration of neurological maturation, independent exploration, practice, and instruction (Case, 1987). At the same time, he observed that children did not advance in their reasoning at the same rate across specific domains. The ability to coordinate dimensions related to number did not generalize to this same ability in problems involving spatial relations or interpersonal problems.

The product of this approach was the theory of central conceptual structures (Case & Okamoto, 1996). "Central conceptual structures were originally defined as networks of semantic modes and relations that have an extremely broad (but not system-wide) domain of application and that are central to children's functioning in that domain" (Case & Okamoto, 1996, p. 5). Through empirical study of children's understanding of number, Case provided an example of this idea of a conceptual structure. At the age of 4 many children can count to five, and they can judge quantity when groups of items are presented to them in order to say which group has more. However, they are often incorrect in answering a question like: which is bigger, 4 or 5? In other words, the central conceptual structure that links a number word, like two or four, to an idea of a set of items with a certain quantity, has not yet emerged. By the age of about 6, children understand that giving an item a new number tag or word is the same as changing its quantity. The conceptual structure of the relationship between numbers and quantity becomes a tool that can be used in many problems involving quantity such as assessing distance, or measuring length or weight.

Case suggested that structures, such as the one described here, depend upon the maturation of certain central processing capacities, especially processing speed and short term memory storage, and the development of executive functions that support the integration of information, especially the ability to attend to and organize multiple elements. Once a central conceptual structure is formed, it provides a way of understanding a variety of situations within and across content areas. These central conceptual structures are the basic building blocks upon which more complex structures are based.

The specific conceptual structure differs from one domain to another. For example the basic understanding of the relationship of number words and quantity is a central conceptual structure for arithmetic, and may apply to other domains where measuring and counting are important. It is not the central conceptual structure for social understanding, for example that behaviors of another person may be intentional and motivated by needs and desires. Each domain has its own conceptual structure. However, the process of moving from labeling states to recognizing the link between states and then attributing causal or relational characteristics to these states is roughly the same. Thus, Case offered a model of cognitive development that is at once content specific and developmentally general suggesting a common path of development while also accounting for individual differences based on biological maturation, experience with problems in a particular domain, and practice.

Metacognition

How do children know what they know? What reasons do they give to justify or support their answers? **Metacognition** refers to a range of processes and strategies used to assess and monitor knowledge. It includes the feeling of knowing that accompanies problem solving—the ability to distinguish those answers about which we are confident from those we doubt (Tarricone, 2011). One element of this feeling of knowing is understanding the source of one's beliefs. For example, we can be told about sand, we can see pictures of it for ourselves, or we can feel and touch it. All three of these sources of information may coincide to create a single belief, or we may discover that there are inconsistencies

Table 8.1	Components of Concrete Operational Thought	
Component	**New Abilities**
Conservation	Ability to apply the identity operation
	Ability to apply the reversibility operation
	Ability to apply the reciprocity operation
Classification	Ability to categorize objects according to some common dimensions
	Ability to induce that properties of one member of a class apply to others
	Ability to order subclasses in a hierarchy
Computational Skills	Ability to understand that numbers represent quantities
	Ability to manipulate quantities using the operations of addition, subtraction, multiplication, and division

© Cengage

between what someone says is true and what we perceive through sight or touch. By the ages of 4 and 5, children are able to understand how all three sources of information have contributed to their understanding of an experience (O'Neill & Gopnik, 1991).

Metacognition includes the ability to review various strategies for approaching a problem in order to choose the one that is most likely to result in a solution. It includes the ability to monitor one's comprehension of the material one has just read and to select strategies for increasing one's comprehension (Currie, 1999): "I need to reread this section." "I need to underline and take notes to focus my attention on new information." "I need to talk about this with someone in order to understand it better."

Psychological mindedness is an aspect of metacognition, the ability to think about what might be accounting for one's own or another person's behavior. It requires building a link between experiences, emotions, and behaviors. For example, a child who is feeling sad may think about what happened in the recent past that is producing this feeling. This would be a type of reflection on one's psychological state (Lagattuta & Wellman, 2001).

Metacognition develops in parallel with other cognitive capacities. As children develop their ability to attend to more variables in their approach to problems, they simultaneously increase their capacity to take an executive posture in relation to cognitive tasks. They can detect uncertainty and introduce strategies to reduce it. They are increasingly able to think about what is possible and from there to select what is the best answer or the most likely alternative (Gauffroy & Barrouillet, 2011). Children can learn study techniques that will enhance their ability to organize and recall information. These capacities continue to develop as the child becomes a more sophisticated learner (Veenman, Wilhelm, & Beishuizen, 2004).

Metacognition is a natural component of cognitive development. However, just like first-level cognitive capacities, it is constructed in a social context. Interactions between children and adults or peers may nurture and stimulate metacognition by helping children identify sources of information, talk about and recognize the differences between feelings of certainty and uncertainty in their knowledge, and devise effective strategies for increasing their feelings of knowing (Stright, Neitzel, Sears, & Hoke-Sinex, 2001; Teong, 2003).

FURTHER REFLECTION: Concrete operational thought is an approach to analyzing and solving problems. Think back to a task or activity that you were engaged in during middle childhood that required systematic problem solving. Describe the activity. Can you identify any aspects of concrete operational thought that were involved in this work? (For example, a project that involved coordinating two or three variables, using classification or categorization skills, and/ or using combinatorial skills.)

Skill Learning

OBJECTIVE 3 Analyze the nature of skill learning, and examine societal factors that provide the contexts in which skill learning occurs.

In addition to the cognitive achievement of concrete operational thought, middle childhood brings impressive growth in the acquisition of skills. **Skills** combine knowledge (knowing *about*) and practice (knowing *how*) directed toward identifying and solving significant, meaningful problems (Gardner, 1983, 2006; Kuhn, Garcia-Mila, Zohar, & Andersen, 1995). Typically, a person moves through a developmental progression within a skill area, starting off as a **novice**, becoming more proficient, and then, depending on a combination of aptitude, training, and practice, becoming an **expert.** The importance of skill development is highlighted by the United Nations declaration of July 15 as World Youth Skills Day. According to UN Secretary General Ban Ki-moon, "Skills development reduces poverty and better equips young people to find decent jobs. It triggers a process of empowerment and self-esteem that benefits everyone" (United Nations, 2016).

Cultures differ in the kinds of skills that are valued (Greenfield, Keller, Fuligni, & Maynard, 2003). In some societies, like ours, symbolic skills focusing on reading, mathematics, and abstract reasoning are highly valued. In other cultures, reading and mathematics are of less value than agricultural skills, hunting, or food preparation. In some cultures, parents consider social skills (knowing how to behave appropriately with peers and teachers), practical skills necessary for adjustment to school (completing one's homework), and motivation (working hard to understand a problem) as more important indications of intelligence than cognitive accomplishments (Neisser et al., 1996; Sternberg, 2007). In many African cultures, parents emphasize social intelligence, the ability to be attuned to the social intentions of others, and the ability to anticipate the social impact of one's actions and the actions of others. For example, in a study of the meaning of intelligence in rural Kenya, four different concepts were used: *rieko* (knowledge and skills), *luoro* (respect), *winjo* (comprehension of how to handle practical problems), and *paro* (initiative) (Sternberg, 2007, p. 149). Parents tend to view the acquisition of technical skills and academic knowledge as important primarily insofar as these skills can enhance social intelligence, social harmony, and social acceptance (Dasen, 1984; Nsamenang, 2004).

In the United States, one observes the emergence of a wide range of valued skills during middle childhood, including mathematics, science, writing, social skills, digital media skills, sports, mechanical skills, music, dance, theater, art, cooking, sewing, crafts, reading, and health-management skills. Many out-of-school programs designed for children ages 6 to 12 focus on skill development. Organizations such as 4-H, scouting, Olympics of the Mind, and Junior Guards, as well as team sports provide opportunities for children to acquire and advance their skills.

One area that is often overlooked in the focus on skill development is **health literacy**, knowing where to find trustworthy information about health concerns, understanding the information that is provided, and using the information to make informed decisions about one's health (Nemours, 2016). In a website on Kids' Health, the Nemours foundation provides information written specifically for children in middle childhood in order to foster health-related skills. Most children at this age are curious about their health and want to know how to stay healthy. They may be confused about the information they get about health, and, just as with other areas of skill development, they need opportunities to practice good health-related behaviors. Looking at the list in Table 8.2, you can appreciate the range of topics that are included and the need to foster knowledge, motivation, and behaviors that will build health-related skills and habits.

Table 8.2	Topics for Health Literacy
Being Good to My Body	

- A Kid's Guide to Shots
- Acne Myths
- Alcohol
- Are Your Bowels Moving?
- Bad Breath
- Be a Fit Kid
- Be a Fit Kid
- Chilling Out With Colds
- Glasses and Contact Lenses
- Going With the Flow of Nosebleeds
- How Does Fluoride Work?
- Learning About Proteins
- Quiz: Shots
- Should I Gain Weight?
- Sleepwalking
- Smoking Stinks!
- Taking Care of Your Ears
- Taking Care of Your Skin
- Taking Care of Your Teeth
- Time for Bed?
- What Being Overweight Means
- What Kids Say About: Their Health
- What Sleep Is and Why All Kids Need It
- What to Do if You Can't Sleep
- What's the Big Sweat About Dehydration?

Source: Nemours, 2016 Staying Healthy, for Kids. Being good to my body. Retrieved from the internet on May 8, 2016 at http://kidshealth.org/en/kids/stay-healthy/#catbody

The nature and diversity of skills and the fact that children can function at high levels in some but not in others raises the question of exactly what is meant by *intelligence*. The debate about intelligence is especially relevant in middle childhood because this is when intelligence tests are administered and school placement decisions are made. As children discover the results of these tests, they make personal attributions about their ability or potential. Thus, IQ tests have a direct impact on the kind of educational experiences that children encounter and on their sense of academic self-efficacy. Three theoretical approaches to the definition of intelligence are discussed in the **Applying Theory and Research** box What Is Intelligence?

Features of Skilled Learning

Skills are actions that take place in specific contexts (Fischer & Bidell, 2006). One uses the skill of manipulating a fork for eating,

not to type on a computer. Skills can be of varying levels of complexity, from whistling a tune to playing poker. In each case, they have a developmental trajectory—the skill begins in some rudimentary form of action, which may mature to increasingly high levels of performance. Skills are both context specific and culturally guided. The skill of managing a fork for eating is valued in most Western cultures; however, chopsticks are the preferred tool in many Eastern cultures.

Skills change as they become more advanced; they are also integrated with other skills that may permit new, more complex skills. Each skill is comprised of systems that must be coordinated in order for the skill to be effective. For example, the use of a fork for eating requires hand-eye-mouth coordination, judgments about the consistency and size of the food, and understanding cultural practices for eating. Once the basic skill of using a fork becomes well established, it can be integrated into more complex skills such as cutting food with a knife and a fork, or the use of a fork in food preparation. The systems that contribute to one skill, such as hand–eye coordination, may contribute to more than one skill. These contributing systems may develop at different rates, thus explaining why a skill may change slowly and then seem to advance to a new level rather suddenly.

Skills are self-organizing, goal-oriented actions designed to perform specific functions in a particular environment. As the goals or the contexts for skill performance change, the skills may be modified or integrated with other skills to produce new behavior. For example, think about playing the piano as a skill. Many components are required in order to play, including memory, auditory perception, manual dexterity, rhythm, and the ability to read music. As one area improves, the level of playing may improve so that the notes are smoother, more rhythmic, and more musical. At some point, simple tunes may be replaced by more complex compositions requiring new fingering, more complex rhythms, faster speed, and coordinated use of right and left hands. As the technical challenges of playing the piano are mastered, the person may introduce emotion, interpretation, liveliness, and a personal voice into the music. Now, the skill of playing the piano becomes a means of self-expression and possibly the entertainment of others.

Principles of Skill Development

Four principles have been identified for understanding how complex behavioral skills are achieved. First, the development of a skill depends on a combination of sensory, motor, perceptual, cognitive, linguistic, emotional, and social processes. In sports, for example, a child must learn to coordinate specific sensory information and motor activities, understand the rules of the game, be able to communicate with the coach and the other players, gain control over emotions such as fear or anger that might interfere with performance, and sustain motivation to keep trying despite errors or defeat.

Second, skills are attained through the simultaneous integration of many levels of the component behaviors. They are not acquired in strict sequence from simple to complex. Instead, children work on the simple and more complex components of the skill at the same time. For example, as children learn the game of baseball, they practice simple skills like throwing and catching, and at the same time, they have to learn more complex skills like

What Is Intelligence?

The term intelligence is used in many contexts, with a variety of meanings. Informally, it may refer to the ability to solve difficult problems, to draw on evidence in defending an argument, or to adapt to environmental conditions. When discussing measurement, it may refer to the score on a standardized test composed of one type of item (such as *Peabody's Picture Vocabulary Test*) or many kinds of items (such as the *Stanford-Binet Intelligence Test*). Some theorists emphasize a general underlying factor, *g*, that reflects what many different types of test items have in common (Spearman, 1927). Other models suggest multiple intelligences with distinct areas of specialization. The remarkable adaptive and inventive capacities that human beings exhibit suggest a diversity of intellectual abilities, which are captured in the three theories of intelligence described here (Sternberg & Kaufman, 2011).

Jean Piaget (1972b) analyzed intelligence from a developmental perspective. His theory focuses on the logical and analytic aspects of intelligence as they arise from infancy through adolescence. He described four types of intelligence, each emerging at a different period of life: (1) *sensorimotor intelligence* (the ability to know through direct observation and manipulation of objects), (2) *representational intelligence* (the ability to distinguish between the real and the pretend, and to think about and represent objects and events that are not present), (3) *concrete operational intelligence* (the ability to detect the logical relationships among objects, to place objects in sequences, and to comprehend and manipulate numbers), and (4) *formal operational intelligence* (the ability to use experimental techniques and hypothetical reasoning to solve problems, to generalize observations from one situation to another, and to relate cause and effect in complex, multidimensional problems). These approaches to problem solving are not lost as one moves from stage to stage. Rather, each is integrated into the next level, with lower levels of reasoning being viewed as inadequate as the person achieves new capacities.

Alan is solving mathematical problems involving unknowns. Piaget would consider this the beginning of formal operational thinking. Gardner would call it logical-mathematical intelligence, and Sternberg would call it analytic intelligence. What is its practical or adaptive value for Alan's future?

Howard Gardner's (1983, 2006; Davis, Christodoulou, Seider, & Gardner, 2011) theory of multiple intelligences identifies at least eight distinct intelligences, each with its own content and unique contribution to solving important, meaningful problems. These include *linguistic*, *musical*, *logical-mathematical*, *spatial*, *naturalist*, *bodily-kinesthetic*, and two forms of personal intelligence—one directed toward understanding one's own internal feelings (*intrapersonal*) and the other directed toward identifying and differentiating among the characteristics of others (*interpersonal*). This theory recognizes domains of human functioning that show evidence of high levels of achievement, not all of which are related to scientific, mathematical, or verbal reasoning. They cover a broader range of skills than are normally included in tests of intelligence, validating the variety of individual differences in competence typically observed among school-age children (Gardner, Kornhaber, & Wake, 1996).

A third view, devised by Robert Sternberg (1985; Sternberg, Castejon, Prieto, Hautamäki, & Grigorenko, 2001), described three universal processes of intelligence that are expressed in three different abilities—analytic, creative, and practical. The universal processes include: (1) executive processes including the ability to make a plan to achieve a goal, monitor progress toward the goal, and evaluate and/or modify the progress and plan; (2) performance components, which refer to the ability to carry out the steps indicated by the executive processes; and (3) knowledge components, which include the ability to the gather the information needed or the skills required to implement the plan (Education Encyclopedia, 2016). These processes can be exercised in each of the three domains: analytic, creative, or practical intelligence. Analytic intelligence usually involves evaluating information, comparing and contrasting alternatives, and applying principles of logic. This type of intelligence is systematically measured by tests of intelligence and is the primary focus of formal classroom teaching. Creative intelligence is a bit harder to define because it may be expressed differently in different fields such as writing, art, science, and music. Typically,

Alexey Fursov/Shutterstock.com

By the age of 6, Kim has already reached a very high level of bodily-kinesthetic intelligence in rhythmic gymnastics. As Gardner points out, intelligence can be evidenced in many different domains including music, drama, art, sports, mathematics, and invention.

creative intelligence involves producing a novel or unusual solution, often bringing together information or skills from diverse domains to address a situation in a new or unexpected way. Practical intelligence is knowledge about how to do something, how to assess a situation, and how to get a desired outcome. In his theory of successful intelligence, Sternberg strives to explain how the person integrates mental capacities and life experiences with the demands of the culture in order to achieve an effective adaptation with the environment (Sternberg, 2012).

Cultures differ in how they define intelligence, and the knowledge and skills required to be successfully intelligent (Sternberg, 2014). For example, some groups value social competence highly, recognizing that intelligence involves knowing how to maintain positive and cooperative group relations. In these cultures, intelligence is demonstrated by being able to interact effectively with people in various positions of authority and showing the proper respect in social contexts. Other cultural groups emphasize cognitive

skills, especially those skills that will result in good grades in school. A third cultural perspective might focus on a moral view of intelligence, that is, doing what is right and showing humility without judgment of others. The nature of intelligence and its key features are culturally constructed and passed along from teachers to students and from parents to their children (Castles, 2012; Sternberg, 2004).

Critical Thinking

1. Compare the three theories of Piaget, Gardner, and Sternberg. What, if anything, do they have in common? What are their distinguishing features?
2. Contrast the implications of the three theories of intelligence for educational practice. How might teachers approach the teaching/ learning process differently depending on which of these three views of intelligence they endorse?
3. Many scholars support the idea of a single underlying factor, often referred to as *g*, which refers to basic intelligence. Do you think there is such a thing as *g*? Summarize the evidence you have for your belief. How does the idea of *g* fit with the three theories presented here?
4. Explain the view that intelligence is culturally constructed. Do you believe there can be such a thing as a culture-free test of intelligence? Why or why not?

fielding a ground ball and throwing it accurately to the first baseman in order to make an out.

Third, the limits of the human system place constraints on an individual's capacity to perform skilled behavior. With practice, lower level processes begin to function automatically, so a person can attend to higher order processes. In writing, for example, young children struggle with the physical act of printing and writing, concentrating largely on the motor skills necessary to make each letter, word, and sentence. A skilled writer can write with little effort, focusing attention on the meaning of the writing, the plot, or the character development rather than on the physical aspects of the task.

Fourth, skilled behavior requires the use of strategies. Skillful people operate with purpose and continuously monitor their performance. They perceive breakdowns in performance, are selective in focusing attention on various aspects of what they are

working on, and refine higher order processes as they perform the skill. This model of skill development focuses on the elements that are necessary in order to move from what might be considered a novice level to a more advanced level in skill performance.

Early Deprivation and Skill Development

Studies of children who have experienced early and prolonged deprivation, for example children who have spent 12 months or more in institutional care before adoption, show evidence of neurological deficits in certain areas by the age of 8 or 9. For example, the children who experienced prolonged institutionalization perform less well on tests of visual memory, attention, and inhibitory control, but about the same as children who were adopted before 8 months and those who were never institutionalized on tests of auditory memory or executive function (Pollack et al., 2010).

The impact of early deprivation may be masked in the early years, when expectations for skill development are at a novice level. However, by age 8 or 9, these neurological deficits may have a more noticeable impact on a child's ability to reach advanced, sustained levels of competence or mastery. Children who are placed in foster care at an early age and who continue to reside with the same family appear to benefit the most from early intervention, and their cognitive abilities show the greatest degree of resilience (Fox, Almas, Degnan, Nelson, & Zeanah, 2011).

In each distinct area of skill development, a combination of maturational factors, aptitude or talent, opportunities for exposure and training, and the value placed on the skill by the family, school, or larger society all play a role in how rapidly and how well a skill will be developed. The **Human Development and Diversity** box presents a cross-national comparison of mathematics mastery, highlighting patterns of performance in the United States, Japan, and Taiwan. Given the societal emphasis on encouraging students to enter the STEM fields (science, technology, engineering, and mathematics), mathematics skills are essential to pursue this path.

In the sections that follow, we look at reading as a specific case of skill development and at the social and cultural contexts within which reading emerges. Whereas certain cognitive abilities are foundational in both math and reading, reading appears to be essential for initial competence in mathematics. At more advanced levels, however, each of these skill areas requires its own foundation of conceptual structures and opportunities for practice.

Reading

Reading may be the most significant skill that develops for children in the United States because it opens the door to all the others. **Literacy** transforms children, just as the advent of the written alphabet transformed civilization. Reading provides access to new information, new uses of language, and new forms of thinking. Children are limited in their ability to learn mathematics, social studies, and science if they cannot read. However, once they can read fluently, the possibilities for independent inquiry expand significantly.

Reading builds on language. Gradually children begin to appreciate the link between spoken words and their written or printed counterparts. Children begin to read in a variety of ways. Some children memorize the words they see in books or signs and repeat them. Some children begin to read by learning letters and the sounds linked to them and by experimenting with sounding out the letters when they are strung together. The bridge between spoken language and the written word requires experience with books as well as some types of instruction. Gradually, through a process of trial, feedback, and repetition, children learn to read simple words and sentences (Knight & Fischer, 1992; Rayner, Schotter, Masson, Potter, & Treiman, 2016). At some point, a child begins to articulate the concept "I can read" or "I am a reader." Once this idea is part of the self-concept, efforts to read increase and are energized by a confidence in one's potential for success.

Reading is a visual, cognitive, and social process that improves greatly with practice. In order to read, children have to perceive the printed marks that comprise letters and words with accuracy. They have to fixate on words and move their eyes along the lines and paragraphs to capture sentences. As this is happening, the reader has to recognize and recall the meaning of words before moving along. The recognition process is linked to the child's vocabulary and to the frequency with which the child has seen the word before. Thus, basic executive functions of attention, working memory, and flexibility are linked with visual processes and language competence to achieve reading skills (Cantin et al., 2016; Rayner et al., 2016).

Young children may have a large spoken or oral vocabulary. They understand the meaning of many words. However, in order to read, they have to realize that each spoken word is comprised of sounds that are represented in English by letters or letter combinations. **Phonemic awareness**, that is, knowing the sound of a letter and being able to hear it as one reads, is a key to reading. Children with **dyslexia** frequently have trouble with this process of connecting letters and their sounds. Another component of reading is the rapid naming of objects, referred to in the literature as RAN (rapid automatized naming). To measure RAN, children are asked to name 40 items including colors, objects, numbers, and letters as fast as possible. RAN, measured before children have begun formal reading instruction, is a predictor of reading fluency. Scholars who study reading argue that RAN is a general capacity for object recognition, not only letters but also numbers and other symbols, that contributes to the reading process; as a child learns to read the brain treats printed words as if they are objects to be recognized (Fuchs, Geary, Fuchs, Compton, & Hamlett, 2016; Lervåg & Hulme, 2009).

Reading involves more than recognizing one word at a time. **Reading fluency** refers to the accuracy and speed with which children can read words in a text. Children who struggle with figuring out each word may find it difficult to capture the meaning of a sentence or paragraph. Being a slow reader may be related to having a limited vocabulary, difficulties in attention, limited recognition or memory retrieval for words previously encountered, and limits in perceptual span (e.g. the amount of information captured in a single fixation on a line of text) (Sperlich, Meixner, & Laubrock, 2016). Over time, children who have difficulty reading are less willing to practice reading outside of class, and this lack of practice confounds their problems with fluency (Gabrieli, 2009). Certain interventions have been shown to be successful for children who are having difficulties with reading, especially when these interventions occur early in kindergarten or first grade and involve intensive, small group lessons with active, engaging interactions between students and their teachers (Cirino, Vaughn et al., 2009).

Parents Influence Their Child's Reading Abilities. Parents affect their children's reading in at least six ways (Tudge, Putnam, & Valsiner, 1996).

1. The value they place on literacy
2. The emphasis they place on academic achievement
3. The reading materials they make available at home
4. The time they spend reading with their children and listening to their children read
5. The way they read with their children
6. The opportunities they provide for verbal interaction in the home

Cross-national Comparisons of Mathematics Ability

In 1980, comparative studies showed that first and fifth grade children in Minneapolis, Minnesota, were substantially behind their age-mates in Sendai, Japan, and Taipei, Taiwan, in tests of mathematics achievement. In a 10-year follow-up, U.S. children still lagged behind, and by the 11th grade, the gap in achievement had widened (Stevenson, 1992; Stevenson, Chen, & Lee, 1993). Even the top 10 percent of the Minneapolis students scored at about the average level of the Taipei and Sendai students.

Beginning in 1995, and repeatedly to 2011, the U.S. National Center for Education Statistics sponsored the Trends in International Mathematics and Science Study (TIMSS), which examined mathematics and science teaching practices and student accomplishment for grades 4 and 8. The project involves 63 countries and other education systems (states and provinces). Analysis of the 2011 data indicated significant improvement in U.S. students' scores from 1995Nonetheless, the following non-U.S. educational systems had scores that were above the U.S. average in mathematics: Taiwan, Korea, Singapore, Hong Kong, Japan, the Russian Federation, and Quebec, Canada (Provasnik et al., 2012). Mathematics scores were grouped into four categories: low, intermediate, high, and advanced. In 2011, 7 percent of U.S. eighth grade students scored in the advanced level. Seven countries had significantly higher percentages of students scoring at this advanced level, led by 49 percent of students in Taipei, China.

Think about mathematics from an ecological systems perspective. At least five sociocultural factors interact to contribute to the advantages that Japanese and Chinese children show in comparison to U.S. children in mathematical skill development: (1) cultural beliefs and values placed on academic success; (2) the school resources available to children; (3) parents' beliefs and strategies that encourage or support mathematics achievement (4) teachers' preparation, training, and approach to teaching

mathematics; and (5) the peer culture that rewards school achievement.

1. *Culture.* There are cultural differences in beliefs about academic achievement that impact how parents and teachers approach the process of learning. U.S. parents and teachers highlight the importance of natural ability as a major factor in accounting for individual differences in mathematical ability. In contrast, Japanese and Chinese parents and teachers are more likely to see academic achievement as a result of studying hard. If you believe that math or science achievement depends on natural ability, you might conclude that not much can be done to improve performance. If you believe that math and science skill depends on effort, you may be more inclined to devote additional time and focused application to reach a new level of performance. Other comparisons suggest that Chinese parents emphasize their child's academic failures, encouraging children to strive to improve by paying special attention to their mistakes. U.S. parents emphasize their child's successes, hoping to bolster their self-esteem by pointing out how well they are doing (Ng, Pomerantz, & Lam, 2007).

2. *Resources.* School resources, which impact the number of teachers per student, the salaries for teachers, the availability of teaching materials, and the quality of the physical environment, are all associated with academic achievement. In the U.S., living in a poor community has a substantially negative impact on student achievement in comparison to other countries where health and educational resources are available to all children regardless of their family's income (Balfanz & Byrnes, 2006; Tucker-Drob & Bates, 2015).

3. *Parents'. expectations about schools.* Parents differ in their views about what they should expect of their children and their children's schools. U.S. parents appear to be satisfied with their children's level of mathematics performance and do not expect their children to do better. In contrast, Japanese and Chinese parents have high expectations for their children's performance. Parents differ in how they evaluate their children's schools. U.S. parents are generally satisfied with the school curriculum and think that the schools are doing a good job. Far fewer Japanese and Chinese parents view the schools as good or excellent. The public

christian kober/Alamy Stock Photo

Japanese mathematics classes involve two teachers, one who gives instruction to the whole class, and one who meets individually with students to help them in areas where they may be having difficulties. In this way, all the students are able to move ahead at the same pace and "no child is left behind."

pressure in these cultures is for greater improvement in the quality of education. Even though Japanese and Chinese children spend more time on homework than do U.S. children, their parents are more likely to encourage them to spend even more time on homework.

4. *Teachers*. Teachers' specialized preparation to teach mathematics and confidence in their ability to teach mathematics, as well as their satisfaction with their teaching assignments and work environment are all associated with students' mathematics achievement (Ker, 2016; Marcenaro-Gutierrez, Luque, & Lopez-Agudo, 2015). There are also notable differences in the approach to mathematics instruction across countries. In Japan, for example, the classroom teaching approach is quite distinct from that in the United States. Based on videotapes of U.S. and Japanese classrooms, one can observe Japanese teachers spending less time reviewing and more time presenting new content; more time focusing on complex problems that require four or more

steps to reach a solution; and more time on problems that require connections among mathematically related concepts rather than a repetition of the previous problem (National Center for Education Statistics 2015a). If you are interested in viewing examples of classroom teaching of math and science across countries, you can find sample lessons at the TIMSS video website.

5. *Peers*. Mathematics achievement is enhanced when students are embedded in a peer culture that rewards academic achievement and working hard at school. Having friends who do well in mathematics can help advance a child's mathematics ability. In contrast, being part of a peer group that is disengaged from school can undermine a child's academic goals and reduce their willingness to spend time on challenging mathematics homework. The academic and career aspirations of the friendship group can greatly impact a child's motivation and interest in math (DeLay, Laursen, Kiuru, Poikkeus,

Aunola, & Nurmi, 2015; Sebanc, Guimond, & Lutgen, 2016).

Critical Thinking Questions

1. Describe your experiences in mathematics and science instruction in elementary and secondary school. Did you leave high school feeling confident about your ability in these domains? What role did teachers, parents, and peers play in your interest and achievement in mathematics and science?

2. Analyze the distinctions among the U.S., Japanese, and Chinese cultures that you believe make the greatest difference with respect to science and mathematics achievement. Hypothesize about how the concepts of individualism and collectivism influence the teaching and learning process.

3. Assess whether differences in mathematics and science achievement are a result of differences in basic ability or differences in motivation and effort. Support your view.

There are different ways to approach the social occasion of reading. Some parents ask their children about the story as they read along to make sure the child understands. Some try to expand on the story, talking with their children about other things they notice in the pictures or experiences related to the story. Some parents point out words and specifically teach about the sounds of letters as they read (Justice & Ezell, 2000; Reese & Cox, 1999).

In a study of parents' contributions to their children's literacy development in the United States and Japan, family members in both countries were found to employ a range of strategies to encourage their children's ability to read. These included reading and telling stories, discussing stories, teaching vocabulary, writing about their experiences, playing board games, and watching certain types of television programs (Saracho & Shirakawa, 2004). Parents who value the ability to read do some direct teaching to promote reading, urge their children to do well in school, provide resources for reading, take turns reading and listening to their children read, and talk with them about what they are reading. All these strategies produce children who are more skilled readers (Bus, van IJzendoorn, & Pellegrini, 1995; Haney & Hill, 2004).

Parents also have an indirect effect on how well a child will learn to read by influencing the child's placement in a school reading group. Ability grouping for reading instruction is practically universal in elementary schools. Teachers depend on their perceptions of a child's ability, work habits, and behavior when they assign students to reading groups. The higher the level of the children's reading group, the better they learn how to read. Parents need to understand the school's approach to ability grouping and help their child understand it (National Association of School Psychologists, 2002). Parents who encourage good work habits and appropriate classroom behavior are likely to influence a teacher's perception of their child and, as a result, influence the child's assignment to a more advanced reading-level group.

The Social and Cultural Contexts of Reading. The analysis of reading provides many good examples of the importance of context. First, societies differ in their level of literacy. For example, in Afghanistan, a country of over 32.5 million people, 52 percent of men and 24 percent of women age 15 and older are literate. In Israel, a country of over 8 million, 99 percent of men and 98 percent of women are literate (Central Intelligence Agency, 2016). Expectations on how much children should be read to, when they should be able to read, and the level of skill development they are expected to reach at a certain age depend on cultural norms for literacy. The Progress in International Reading Literacy Study (PIRLS, 2011) assessed reading activities of fourth graders in 45 countries. In addition to assessing reading competence for literary and informational purposes, the study examined students' enjoyment of reading. There is a clear bi-directional relationship between reading

Children who enjoy reading books outside of school show the greatest gains in reading achievement between second and fifth grades.

ability and "reading for fun." Students who are better readers enjoy reading more, and students who enjoy reading become better readers. In the United States, 27 percent of the students reported that they liked reading; this includes enjoying reading, reading for fun daily or almost every day, and enjoying talking with others about what they read. In 23 countries, a larger percentage of fourth graders reported that they liked reading than was the case in the United States (Mullis, Martin, Foy, & Drucker, 2012).

Second, the purpose of literacy varies from one culture to the next. For example, missionaries introduced literacy to the Kaluli of New Guinea primarily as a way to teach the Bible. Among the Kaluli, reading is viewed as having limited purpose for daily life and as too difficult for children (Schieffelin & Cochran-Smith, 1984). In many societies, the ability to read the Bible, the Koran, or the Torah is the principal reason for literacy, and that one book is the primary written resource.

Third, the mark of a literate person varies by context. In the United States, we have age-graded expectations for reading achievement and tests to measure reading ability. By the time they are applying to college, students are expected to be able to analyze a complex text for meaning, know advanced principles

of grammar, write a well-organized essay under time constraints, use approved strategies for citing references, and understand principles of fair use and plagiarism. However, in the digital environment reading and writing follow other standards. Some environments, such as texting and Twitter, encourage the use of brief messages and replies. Online texting often integrates words, emoticons, symbols, abbreviations, and acronyms. At the same time, children can access a vast array of online sources. To take advantage of these resources requires skills in searching as well as reading and evaluating information. With the easy sharing of digital content, the written word can be read by a wide network of "friends" who can comment and respond, creating a social environment in which reading is a skill that can be used for peer group integration or exclusion.

In more traditional societies, a good reader might be someone who can read a letter for someone else, someone who can keep track of business accounts, or someone who can accurately make a copy of a text. The point is that the achievement of literacy is a product of cultural expectations, individual capacity, and opportunities to learn (Tudge, Putnam, & Valsiner, 1996).

The emphasis on skill building and the energy that children bring to the acquisition of new skills suggest a strong parallel to toddlerhood. At both stages, children's motives for competence and mastery are directed outward to the environment. At both stages, most children delight in the potential for learning that almost every new encounter offers. However, as a result of children's cognitive capacities and their awareness of social expectations, skill learning during middle childhood is embedded in a much more complex framework of continuous monitoring and self-assessment. Children's beliefs and attitudes about which skills are important, what they should expect of themselves, what others expect of them, and what kinds of competing demands should influence their dedication to skill development all contribute to the levels of performance they are likely to achieve.

FURTHER REFLECTION: Make a list of 15 to 20 skills that might be developed during middle childhood. Now create three lists: one for success in school, one for success in peer relationships, and one for life satisfaction and well-being after high school. Rank-order the skills from most to least important in each list. How much overlap is there in the three lists? To what extent do we need different skills to achieve different goals?

Self-Evaluation

OBJECTIVE 4   Outline the factors that contribute to self-evaluation, including feelings of pride, self-efficacy, and ways that social expectations of parents, teachers, and peers contribute to a child's self-evaluation.

During middle childhood, the emphasis on skill building is accompanied by a new focus on **self-evaluation**. Children strive to match their achievements to internalized goals and external standards. Simultaneously, they receive feedback from others about the quality of their performance. Some children may be asked to sit at one table to receive help; others may be told to go down the hall for tutoring. Some children are designated as peer tutors who assist their classmates. These and many other signs are sources of social evaluation that children incorporate into their own self-evaluations.

In middle childhood, the peer group joins the adult world as a source of social comparison, criticism, and approval. Toddlers and early-school-age children are likely to observe and imitate their peers in order to learn new strategies for approaching a task, or out of curiosity to see how their peers are doing a particular project. But in middle childhood, pressures toward conformity, competition, and the need for peer approval feed into the self-evaluation process. Children pay attention to the work of others in order to assess their own abilities. Their athletic skills, intellectual abilities, and artistic talents are no longer matters to which only teachers and parents respond. Peers also identify others' skills and begin to generate profiles of one another: "Oh, Rafael is good in math, but he's not much at sports"; "Jane is kind of fat, but she writes great stories"; "I like Rashidah best, because she's good at everything." Depending on their resolution of the psychosocial crises of toddlerhood and early school age, children approach the process of self-evaluation from a framework of either self-confidence or self-doubt. They may expect to find tasks easy to accomplish and approach them vigorously, or they may anticipate failure and approach tasks with hesitation.

Evaluation of competence is not the same as global self-esteem. In research involving children ages 8 to 13, Susan Harter (1982, 1993) devised a method for assessing children's perceptions of competence in five specific domains that are relevant for children in this age range: scholastic competence, athletic competence, likability by peers, physical appearance, and behavioral conduct. She also measured general or global self-esteem. Her research was guided by the idea that by the age of 8, children not only differentiate specific areas of competence but also view certain areas as more important than others. She found that self-esteem is highest in those children who view themselves as competent in domains that they judge to be important. Competence in relatively unimportant domains is not strongly related to overall self-esteem.

Feelings of Pride

Feelings of pride are typically associated with positive self-evaluations. In general, children as well as adults feel happy when they succeed at an achievement-related task. However, the experience of **pride** depends in part on the child's perceptions about the cause of their success. As children mature, their feelings of pride after a success become increasingly linked to whether they attribute the success to internal factors such as their own ability or effort as compared to external factors such as the poor preparation of the other children or a teacher who is an easy grader (Graham & Weiner, 1986). In experimental tests of these relationships, young children ages 5 and 6 felt about the same degree of pride whether the success was due to internal or external factors. However, by ages 8 to 10 children were making a clearer distinction. They felt greater pride when success was due to internal factors and less pride when success was due to external factors (Graham & Weiner, 1991). By middle childhood, children are engaged in a process of self-evaluation that includes several sources of information including their past performance, task difficulty, the reactions of others, and their assessment of their ability and effort.

Self-evaluation takes place in relation to internal frames of reference, as children compare how well they can perform in one domain versus another, or how well they performed in the current situation as compared to their past performances. The internal frame of reference includes an assessment of both ability and effort. Self-evaluation also takes place in relation to external frames of reference as children evaluate their performance in light of parent, teacher, or peer feedback and observations of the performance of others (Skaalvik & Skaalvik, 2004). In the sections that follow, we focus on two different paths toward self-evaluation: *self-efficacy*, which reflects a child's personal judgment of ability, and *social expectations*, which reflect the impact of the expectations of others on a child's performance.

Self-Efficacy

How do children assess their competence in a specific ability area? Albert Bandura (1982) theorized that judgments of self-efficacy are crucial to understanding this process. **Self-efficacy** is defined as the person's sense of confidence that he or she can perform the behaviors demanded in a specific situation. Expectations of efficacy vary with the specific ability. In other words, a child may view efficacy in one way in a situation requiring mathematical ability and in another way when the situation requires physical strength.

Bandura theorized that four sources of information contribute to judgments of self-efficacy (see FIGURE 8.2 ▶). The first source is **enactive attainments**, or prior experiences of mastery in the kinds of tasks that are being confronted. Children's general assessment of their ability in any area (e.g., mathematics, writing, or gymnastics) is based on their past accomplishments in that area. There is a bidirectional relationship between achievement in a domain and one's confidence about being able to perform well in that domain. High confidence will lead to better performance, and better performance will increase one's confidence. Over time, children establish a more stable view of areas where they expect to do well and areas where they anticipate greater difficulty (Denissen, Zarrett, & Eccles, 2007). Success experiences increase self-efficacy, whereas repeated failures diminish it. Failure experiences are especially detrimental when they occur early in the process of trying to master a task. Many boys and

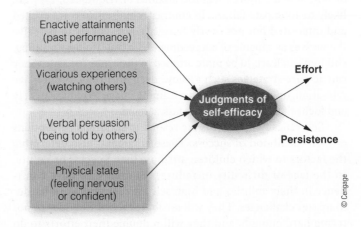

FIGURE 8.2 ▶ Four Components of Self-Efficacy

Three fifth-grade boys are celebrating their success at winning the Olympics of the Mind competition for their school.

give up in the face of difficulty because they attribute their failure to a basic lack of ability. The level of self-efficacy also affects how children prepare to handle new challenges. In their thoughts, emotions, and preparation for action, those who are preoccupied by self-doubts differ from those who believe in themselves (Bandura & Schunck, 1981; McAuley, Duncan, & McElroy, 1989; Pajares, 1996).

Children with high levels of self-efficacy related to academic achievement are likely to set challenging goals for themselves. They are also likely to regulate their learning behaviors by deliberately enlisting a number of strategies, including concentrating, organizing their work, finding a good place to study, taking notes in class, and completing their homework assignments so that they have the best chances of reaching their goals (Bandura, Barbaranelli, Caprara, & Pastorelli, 1996; Zimmerman, Bandura, & Martinez-Pons, 1992). The following case study of Becca illustrates the behaviors and thoughts of a middle school student whose sense of self-efficacy has been declining.

girls are diverted from mastering such sports as tennis and baseball because they have made mistakes early in their participation. They develop doubts about their abilities, which then prevent them from persisting in the task.

The second source of information is **vicarious experience.** Seeing a person similar to oneself perform a task successfully may raise one's sense of self-efficacy; seeing a person similar to oneself fail at a task may lower it.

Verbal persuasion is the third source. In a supportive environment, children are encouraged to believe in themselves and to try new tasks with confidence. This type of motivational talk is likely to be most effective with children who already have confidence in their abilities, and it helps boost their performance level.

The fourth source is **physical state.** People monitor their body states in making judgments about whether they can do well or not. When children feel too anxious or frightened, they are likely to anticipate failure. In contrast, children who are excited and interested but not overly tense are more likely to perceive themselves as capable of succeeding. With mindfulness training, children can learn to be more attuned to their internal state. They can acquire strategies such as slow, deep breathing, progressive relaxation, or concentrating on a calming image to reduce anxiety and focus their attention on the task at hand.

Self-efficacy judgments are related to children's perceptions of their likelihood of success. These judgments also determine the factors to which children attribute their success or failure. In the face of difficulty or failure, children who have confidence in their abilities and high self-efficacy will work harder to master challenges. They will attribute their difficulties to not trying hard enough, and they will redouble their efforts to do well. Children who have a low sense of self-efficacy tend to

— CASE STUDY   Becca —

Becca, an eighth grader, is disengaging from school.

Under the weight of her family burdens, Becca's academic confidence has begun to falter. . . . In sixth grade, Becca was an A student; at the end of seventh grade, she asked to be removed from the advanced math class; and by the middle of eighth grade, her grades in all of her classes were drifting to low Cs.

A quiet girl, Becca says she has never spoken much in class ("unless I'm really, really sure of an answer, and sometimes not even then"), but with her self-esteem flagging, she stops volunteering entirely. She even begins to see her silence as an advantage: As long as she's perceived as shy, her teachers won't notice that she has, in truth, disengaged from school. . . . In a sense, Becca is invisible. Her teachers don't see her as someone in need of counseling or special help because, although her grades have dropped, she is never combustible: She never, for instance, yells in class, pounds desks, fights with other children, or conspicuously challenges authority. Becca's is a passive resistance—a typically feminine resistance. By opting out rather than acting out, Becca still conforms to the image of the ideal female student—quiet, compliant, obedient; as such she is easily overlooked, or seen as making choices rather than expressing psychological distress. "Becca is so quiet," her math teacher admits, "she gets lost in the crowd. I don't like that to happen, but it has happened with her. She doesn't disrupt. She always looks like she's paying attention, but maybe she's not. I don't know."

"Maybe she thinks she'll be more cool as a C student," her history teacher says. "But she doesn't even get it together after she gets the bad grade. I'll say, 'Becca, you have a D, you may fail,' but then she doesn't turn in the next homework assignment, which is really easy. But I think of her as someone who's responsible for her own grade, and I let her be responsible for that."

Source: Orenstein, 1994, pp. 80–81.

CASE ANALYSIS Using What You Know

1. Describe Becca's sense of academic self-efficacy.
2. Apply Bandura's model, explaining how the four factors of enactive attainments, vicarious experiences, verbal persuasion, and physical states contribute to Becca's self-efficacy.
3. How does the case illustrate the relationship of gender and school engagement? In what ways is Becca's situation made possible because of gender stereotypes?
4. Propose ways that teachers might intervene to reverse Becca's decline in academic performance and school engagement.
5. Infer likely outcomes for Becca if this pattern of disengagement continues.

Social Expectations

In middle childhood, the appraisals and expectations of significant others become incorporated into one's own self-concept and become a source for self-evaluation (Chen, Boucher, & Tapias, 2006). Self-esteem is based on the general positive regard and approval of others and on the specific expectations they have for one's ability and achievement in certain areas of performance (Harter, 2012). In attempting to assess their own abilities, children rely on many external sources of evaluation, including school grades, teachers' comments, and parent and peer evaluations (Hergovich, Sirsch, & Felinger, 2002). If feedback from important adults suggests to children that they are cooperative, intelligent, and creative, these attributes are likely to be incorporated into their self-evaluations. Children who see themselves as cooperative and intelligent are likely to approach social and intellectual tasks with optimistic expectations about their performance. Conversely, feedback suggesting lack of cooperation, intelligence, or creativity can produce a pessimistic or antagonistic approach to the challenges of skill development. Thinking back to the concept of verbal persuasion, you can see that one's judgments of self-efficacy in a particular domain can be influenced by how a relevant person has evaluated one's performance in the past.

Repeated failure information or remarks that imply lack of ability tend to make children less confident of success in subsequent tasks. This pattern of expectations appears to crystallize during grades 2 and 3. Preschoolers do not make systematic use of success or failure feedback in predicting their next success. Even in the first grade, children's expectations about the grades they will receive on their first report cards are not clearly related to their IQs or to parents' or teachers' expectations, nor are they closely related to the children's later estimates of their grades. By the end of the first grade, however, children begin to be more accurate predictors of their performance. A combination of a parent's support for the child's schooling and the child's own motivation and temperament contribute to an orientation toward schooling in first grade that impacts school achievement.

School performance in first grade has been found to predict educational attainment into late adolescence and occupational attainment into early adulthood, suggesting the formation of an early and persistent view of the self as someone who can or cannot do well in school (Entwisle, Alexander, & Olson, 2005a; Alexander, Entwisle, & Olson, 2014). By middle childhood, children are clearly aware of their teachers' expectations for their performance and are likely to mirror those expectations in their own attitudes about school, academic achievement, and school behaviors (Alexander, Entwisle, & Kabbani, 2001; Weinstein et al., 1987).

Teachers' Expectations: The Self-Fulfilling Prophecy. The feedback that students receive from their teachers is not wholly objective. Teachers' expectations about their students' abilities may be based on objective assessments, but they may also be derived from stereotypes about certain types of children or from biases based on prior experiences, such as having a child's older siblings in class in prior years or hearing favorable or unfavorable comments from other teachers. Merton (1948) suggested that problems may arise through a process that he called the **self-fulfilling prophecy**. This concept refers to the idea that false or inaccurate beliefs can produce a personal reality that corresponds with them.

In the original study on the effect of teacher expectations on student performance, teachers were led to believe that certain students were late bloomers who would show major gains in IQ later on in the school year. These children, chosen at random from among first and second graders, actually did show increases in IQ of 10 to 15 points by the end of the school year in comparison to the control group (Rosenthal & Jacobson, 1968).

Subsequent studies of the self-fulfilling prophecy in classroom settings have shown that it has a consistent but comparatively small effect on student performance (Rosenthal, 1994, 1995). In one longitudinal study, students' math achievement and mathematics self-concept data were collected at the end of fifth grade, early in sixth grade, and at the beginning of seventh grade. Teachers' expectations about student performance were assessed early in sixth grade as well. Both student achievement at the end of fifth grade and teachers' expectations in sixth grade were predictive of students' achievement at the beginning of seventh grade. Researchers found that the self-fulfilling prophecy (the impact of teacher expectations separate from prior student achievement scores) was observable only for those students who were in the low achievement group. Both overestimates and underestimates of these students' abilities in sixth grade were predictive of the students' achievement in seventh grade. There was some tendency for overestimates to have a greater impact in boosting these students' performance than for underestimates to depress the students' performance (Madon, Jussim, & Eccles, 1997).

In a review of many studies that have attempted to examine the impact of self-fulfilling prophecies, the authors conclude that the impact of erroneous expectations is typically small. These incorrect expectations seem to have the most impact when children are starting a new school setting, like the start of elementary school or middle school. Evidence about whether the impact of erroneous expectations is positive or negative is mixed. Most studies find that erroneous expectations have the greatest influence when positive expectations are focused on children who are typically low-performing (Jussim, Robustelli, & Cain, 2009).

Teachers' Attributions of Ability and Effort. Teachers' expectations for a student's performance are influenced by their assessments of both the student's ability and effort. Teachers often reward what they perceive as greater effort with higher grades. It is important to appreciate that this judgement about effort may be subjective and open to bias or error (Jussim, Robustelli, & Cain, 2009). Studies of teachers' explanations for their students' math performance have noted an attributional gender bias. Teachers tend to believe that boys are somewhat more talented in math than girls. What is more, they are likely to attribute boys' successes in math to ability and girls' successes to effort. In contrast, they are likely to attribute boys' failures to lack of effort, and girls' failures to lack of ability. These attributions can be conveyed to students through subtle messages of encouragement or frustration, especially in response to students whom teachers perceive as not working up to their ability or not putting in the effort needed to do well (Espinoza, Arêas da Luz Fontes, & Arms-Chavez, 2014; Tiedemann, 2002).

Certain conditions make children more or less vulnerable to internalizing false expectations. Children who are unsure about their abilities and children who are learning something for the first time may be more likely to rely on the information they receive from others to assess their abilities. Being in a new situation, like moving to a new school or changing from elementary to middle school, may increase a child's dependence on social expectations for performance. In middle childhood, when many new domains of skill development are first being introduced, children may be more vulnerable to the effects of biased perceptions and erroneous expectations than are older children (Jussim, 1990).

Parents' Expectations. Parents' as well as teachers' expectations influence children's perceptions of their abilities, and these perceptions influence children's academic performance. This process is evident across cultures and within groups. In a comparison of Chinese and Anglo parents of primary school children, the parents' perceptions of their children's memory abilities and their expectations for their children's language and mathematics performance were consistent predictors of the children's achievement (Phillipson & Phillipson, 2007). In studies of African American families, parents reported lower academic expectations for their boys than for their girls. The relationship of gender to children's own expectations was strongly influenced by their parents' expectations (Wood, Kaplan, & McLoyd, 2007; Wood, Kurtz-Costes, Rowley, & Okeke-Adeyanju, 2010). In a longitudinal study of children in Baltimore, parents who had the fewest economic resources also had notably lower expectations for their boys' school performance, and these low expectations were mirrored in the boys' lower reading comprehension scores, even in first grade (Entwisle, Alexander, & Olson, 2007).

Expanding on the relationship between gender role bias and the socialization of children's competencies and interests, Eccles (1993) proposed the following model (see FIGURE 8.3 ▶): Parents' gender role stereotypes and beliefs influence their perceptions of their own children's competences and interests. These perceptions influence the kinds of experiences parents provide for their children and the types of encouragement or criticisms they communicate. Over time, this combination of parental beliefs and behaviors impact a child's assessment of his or her abilities and the amount of time and effort the child is willing to invest in various activities.

A number of studies support the underlying dynamics of this model. Parents' beliefs and behaviors, often influenced by gender stereotypes and social norms, influence their expectations for their children's academic futures (Davis-Kean, 2005). Independent of actual gender differences in specific domains, including math, sports, or English, parents' stereotypes about which gender is more talented in a particular area influence their perceptions of their own child's competence in that area. Parents' perceptions of competence are directly related to their children's perception of competence (Tiedemann, 2000).

Illusions of Incompetence and Competence

Some children who perform well on tests of academic achievement (at the 90th percentile or above) perceive themselves as below average in academic ability, a phenomenon described as the

Ms. Conrad is a caring teacher who encourages Diego even as she corrects his work. She knows he is trying hard, which makes her more patient as she explains his mistakes and how to fix them.

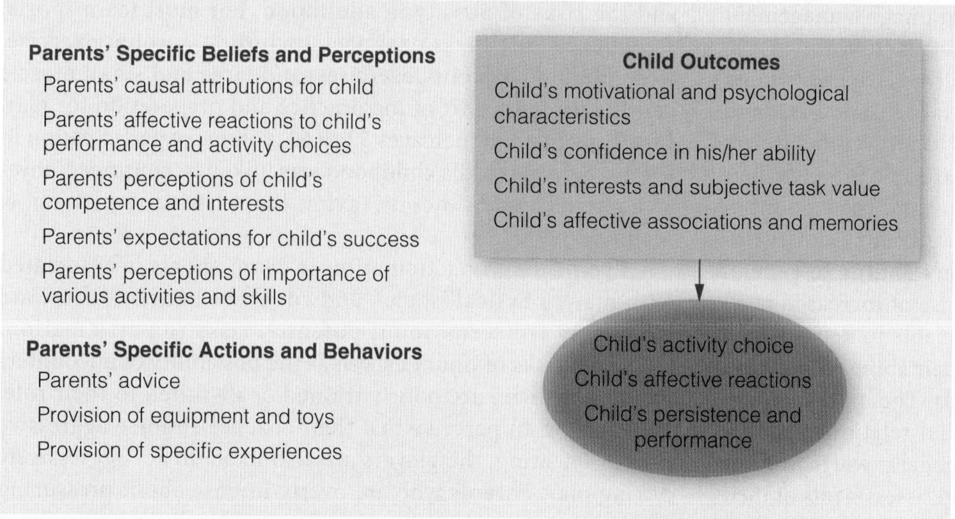

Parents' Specific Beliefs and Perceptions	Child Outcomes
Parents' causal attributions for child	Child's motivational and psychological characteristics
Parents' affective reactions to child's performance and activity choices	Child's confidence in his/her ability
Parents' perceptions of child's competence and interests	Child's interests and subjective task value
Parents' expectations for child's success	Child's affective associations and memories
Parents' perceptions of importance of various activities and skills	

Parents' Specific Actions and Behaviors

Parents' advice

Provision of equipment and toys

Provision of specific experiences

Child's activity choice

Child's affective reactions

Child's persistence and performance

© 2018 Cengage

FIGURE 8.3 ▶ The Relationship of Parents' Gender-Role Beliefs and Behaviors to Children's Beliefs and Behaviors

illusion of incompetence. In studies of gifted children, 20 percent to 30 percent underestimated their abilities (Phillips, 1984, 1987). The same phenomenon has been observed in regular classrooms of third and fourth graders. A subset of children systematically under value their abilities, despite objective test scores that indicate that they are performing as well as their peers (Bouffard, Boisvert, & Vezeau, 2003).

These children expect lower levels of success, are less confident, attempt less challenging tasks, and say that their schoolwork is more demanding than peers of similarly high ability who have more positive self-evaluations. They begin to identify with their lower-performing classmates. As the concept of self-efficacy would suggest, over time, children who have an illusion of incompetence are less likely to persist in the face of difficult work, and show a decline in school performance (Chayer & Bouffard, 2010; Larouche, Galand, & Bouffard, 2008).

Parents play a central role in establishing these children's low assessments of themselves. Children who have an illusion of incompetence see their parents as less available and more conditional in their support (Côté & Bouffard, 2011). They think that their parents have a low opinion of their abilities and expect little of them. They see their fathers, in particular, as having rigorous standards that they are not expected to meet. The parent–child dynamics that underlie this negative assessment were observed in a study involving children with high academic ability who had varying levels of perceived academic competence. Children worked with their mothers and fathers on solvable and unsolvable tasks. The fathers of children who had low perceptions of their own academic competence were found to interact with their children in more critical or unsupportive ways than did the fathers of children who had high perceptions of their academic competence. The children who had illusions of incompetence were more emotionally upset and dependent when they approached the unsolvable tasks (Wagner & Phillips, 1992).

Children may infer messages of incompetence from parental control. In a comparison of children in grades 2 through 5,

the older children interpreted parental helping, monitoring, and decision making as evidence that the parents thought they were incompetent. As children get older and their desire for autonomy, initiative, and industry increases, they may interpret parental monitoring as evidence of a lack of confidence in their ability to make good decisions or to function competently (Pomerantz & Eaton, 2000).

In contrast to illusions of incompetence, some people have **illusions of competence**. In four separate studies, researchers found that those participants who scored in the lowest 12 percent of test takers on measures of grammar, logic, and humor substantially overestimated their own abilities. The extreme lack of ability in an area is accompanied by the inability to distinguish accurate from inaccurate responses, thus leading to a misconception of competence. In contrast to illusions of incompetence, where children underestimate their abilities, illusions of competence occur when people have such deficiencies that they do not even realize the extent of their limitations (Kruger & Dunning, 1999).

The discussion of self-evaluation highlights children's sensitivity to their social environment. They become aware of existing roles and norms and of the sanctions for norm violation. Direct experiences with success and failure are important, but they are also embedded in the context of social expectations. In this age period, with the skills of metacognition and perspective taking, children come to understand that people may alter their behavior in order to project an image that will receive a favorable evaluation from others. Under certain circumstances they may wish to alter their own self-presentation in order to receive positive social evaluation from parents, teachers, or peers. This kind of motivated modification of self-presentation is sometimes referred to as *brownnosing* or *kissing up*. Even though this behavior can be a subject of critical taunts from peers, the motivated student may realize that this strategy is necessary in order to receive positive evaluations or high grades. For example, Perry notices that his English teacher is especially nice to a friend of his who reads poetry during their free time. Perry knows that his friend is not at all interested in poetry, but that the friend has received positive grades from the teacher who believes that the child is really interested in English literature. Taking a cue from this strategy, Perry brings a book of poetry to class and makes frequent eye contact with the teacher to convey interest. The teacher now smiles at him more often, shows new interest in his ideas, and gives his written work a more positive evaluation. Perry concludes that the image he is presenting of himself as one who likes English literature is influencing his teacher's evaluation of his work. Thus, the notion that self-evaluation is shaped by the reflected appraisal from others becomes more complicated as children become skilled in image management (Banerjee, 2002; Hergovich, Sirsch, & Felinger, 2002).

By the end of middle childhood, children have had enough school experience that they can detect favoritism, bias, and unfair treatment and can devise strategies to protect themselves from the impact of negative biases. They are able to judge their abilities by considering their mastery level and the amount of effort they have to exert in order to do well. They can evaluate their own learning based on an understanding of general standards for performance, their own sense of increased mastery, and the opinions of others. They are able to decide when someone else might be a better judge of their abilities than they are (Burton & Mitchell, 2003; Elder, 2010). The more children are embedded in strong, supportive social relationships, the more confidence they will have in their general worth and the more likely they will be to arrive at accurate assessments of their own abilities.

FURTHER REFLECTION: Examine the role of parents, peers, and teachers as they influence a child's self-evaluation in middle childhood. Explain how positive feedback and encouragement from one of these sources can make up for criticism or rejection from another.

Team Play

OBJECTIVE 5 Summarize new levels of complexity in play as children become involved in team sports, examine the benefits of participation in sports, and analyze the cognitive and emotional development that accompanies team play.

During middle childhood, many children participate in team sports, which are generally more complicated than the kinds of games described as group play in chapter 7. The rules are complex, and they may require a referee or an umpire if they are to be followed accurately. In these sports, children join together into teams that remain together for the duration of the game. Some children join teams that play together for an entire season, such as Little League. Many children play on more than one type of team, rotating across activities with the seasons.

According to the Pew Research Center national survey, 73 percent of parents say that their children participated in sports/athletic activities over the past year. For many families, a child's participation in team sports is a family affair. Among the parents whose children are under age 13, almost 4 in 10 have helped to coach one of their children's sports teams (Pew Research Center, 2015c). While team play may not be for every child, it appears to be a normative aspect of middle childhood and an aspect of life that is accompanied by a number of physical, cognitive, and social benefits.

Health and Fitness

A growing interest in physical activity and fitness in adulthood has shed new light on the importance of involvement in team sports in childhood and early adolescence. Regular participation in sports helps build bones and muscles, enhances endurance and balance, and lowers risks of high blood pressure and the risks of obesity in adulthood. For most team sports, a sequence of fitness exercises including aerobic exercise, strength and flexibility exercises, and large and small muscle coordination are part of the practice and preparation for play. In a study of adult men ages 32 to 60, voluntary participation in team sports in middle childhood was linked to continued physical activity in adulthood (Taylor, Blair, Cummings, Wun, & Malina, 1999).

Even though participation in team sports is associated with many physical, social, and cognitive benefits, there are increasing concerns about potential risks to participation, especially risks of injury as well as the possibility of encountering coaches who are poorly trained or ill-suited to their role. When children perceive that their coaches endorse aggressive play or cheating, the players are also likely to act aggressively during play. Parents who are overly intense about pressuring their child or coaches who use aggressive techniques can both become forces that encourage rough, unsportsmanlike conduct that may result in injury (Malete, Chow, & Feltz, 2013; Sánchez et al., 2014).

A growing national concern focuses on the risks of traumatic brain injuries associated with some team sports. This issue has received wide public attention in the professional sports world, especially football, hockey, and soccer. The study of the incidence of concussions and the long-term consequences for brain damage among professional athletes has led to greater efforts to monitor concussions in high school and college players. As a result, the focus has drifted down to concerns about head injuries among children at younger ages when brain development is undergoing rapid transformation. However, more systematic documentation of incidences of brain injury among these younger players is needed. For 80 to 90 percent of the players who experience a sports-related concussion, full recovery is experienced within about 2 weeks. However, for the other 10 to 20 percent, recovery is more prolonged and may be associated with an array of cognitive and affective difficulties.

Three policy issues are needed to address this problem: (1) Guidelines for returning to play after a possible head injury. Often players don't want to leave the game because they don't want to let down their team. Coaches and team members may encourage players to return to play or "play through the pain" despite a possible concussive injury. The risks of a repeated concussion appear to be especially serious for young players. (2) Guidelines for returning to school or regular activities in order to support full recovery. A plan for gradual return to school and to play is needed and considerations for this process need to be supported by family, friends, teachers, coaches, and team members. (3) Guidelines for injury prevention. This may involve changes in the rules of play for younger players, use of new equipment, and practice in techniques that protect the head. The CDC recommends that a player who sustains a concussion should be immediately removed from play and not permitted to return to play until he/she has been cleared by a knowledgeable health professional (Institute of Medicine & National Research Council, 2013; Wahowiak, 2015).

Parents are urged to be aware of the safety precautions needed for each type of sport and the kinds of warm-up exercises and equipment needed to help prevent injuries. Attending practices and games in a supportive role is an important aspect of preventing the team environment from becoming abusive (KidsHealth, 2014). Not all children are interested in team sports as a path toward activity and fitness. Other options for children in this age range include bicycling, horseback riding, tennis, swimming, karate, fencing, skateboarding, ice skating, hiking and climbing, and golf. Each of these activities offers opportunities to incorporate physical activity in a child's daily life. However, each also poses some risks of injury and requires appropriate preparation, training, monitoring, and safety considerations.

In addition to its contribution to fitness and physical activity, team participation provides opportunities to spend time with friends and to celebrate together (Mowling, Brock, & Hastie, 2006). In addition, participation in **team play** provides a context for learning the social and interpersonal skills and strategies that will apply to work and family life in the years ahead (Van der Vegt, Emans, & Van De Vliert, 2001). Participation on a team may create a climate for collectivist values such as cooperation, interdependence, and the subordination of the individual's goals to the team's success (Kernan & Greenfield, 2005). Team participation raises issues of moral judgment and moral behavior, especially regarding fair play, cheating, sportsmanship, and prosocial or antisocial behaviors (Lee, Whitehead, & Ntoumanis, 2007). The following five characteristics of the experience of team membership contribute to development during this stage: (1) interdependence, (2) the division of labor, (3) competition, (4) cooperation, and (5) in-group and out-group attitudes.

Interdependence

Team membership carries with it an awareness that one's acts may affect the success or failure of the entire group. Although team sports do provide opportunities for individual recognition, team success casts a halo over even the poorest players and team failure a shadow over even the best. Participation in team sports provides lessons in **interdependence**. Team members rely on one another, and ideally, it is to everyone's advantage to assist the weaker members in improving the quality of their play. As reflected in a favorite saying of coaches, players, and newspaper reporters, "There is no I in team." Over time, the team provides what is sometimes referred to as a **superordinate group identity**, such that the individual members are willing to suppress their distinct racial, religious, or cultural differences and work together for the success of the group (Jackson et al., 2002). The best coaches are noted for inspiring this sense of interdependence and mutual support among team members. They urge team members to work together to improve their skills. Often, when teams are closely matched, it is the unexpected success of the weaker players that contributes to a victory.

Division of Labor

Through participation with peers on teams, children discover that **division of labor** is an effective strategy for attaining a goal. Children learn that each position on a team has a unique

function and that the team has the best chance of winning if each player performs his or her specific function rather than trying to do the work of all the other players. The concept of the team suggests the notion of a system of interrelated roles and functions in which each of the team members actually engages.

A team becomes an experiential model for approaching problem solving in other complex organizations. Once children learn that certain goals can best be attained when tasks are divided among a group of people, they begin to conceptualize the principles behind the organization of social communities. They recognize that some children are better suited to handling one aspect of the task and others to handling another. Some children enjoy the skill development associated with team play; others enjoy learning the rules and devising strategies; others especially value peer companionship; and still others have a strong inner motive to compete and win (Ntoumanis, Vazou, & Duda, 2007). The distribution of roles to fit the children's individual skills and preferences is a subtle element of the learning that is acquired through team play.

Competition

Team play teaches children about **competition**. In team sports, both sides cannot win; success for one side must result in failure for the other. When children were asked to talk about their views of participating in team sports, they identified three major themes: sport as competition, sport as fun, and sport as fair play. From the children's point of view, coaches and parents are especially likely to be the ones to emphasize the competitive theme through the use of disciplinary techniques, language, and their relative power and authority (Walters, Payne, Schluter, & Thomson, 2015).

If the team experience is a laboratory for learning lessons about the larger social community, this characteristic promotes a view of social situations in competitive terms. Some adults think of business, politics, popularity, and even interpersonal conflicts as win-lose situations, in which the primary goal is to beat one's opponents. The idea of a win-win strategy to resolve conflict is very foreign in this context.

Many young adults have fond memories associated with winning an important game or a big match. They hope to re-experience the energy that occurs as a result of winning as they approach their adult activities. The metaphor of playing on a winning team is deeply interwoven into the world of work, helping to give focus and drive to day-to-day work-related obligations and tasks.

In contrast to those who are energized by the challenges of competition, some children are especially sensitive to the pain of failure. Children may be ostracized or ridiculed if they contribute to a team loss (Mowling, Brock, & Hastie, 2006). The public embarrassment and private shame that accompany failure are powerful emotions. Some children will go to remarkable extremes to avoid failing. In team sports, each game ends with a winning and a losing side. Some children who have a low sense of self-esteem may experience anxiety about losing in a competitive situation (Brustad, 1988). Involvement in

After a hard-fought game, the winners experience the positive emotions and feelings of pride and self-confidence that accompany winning.

team sports is guaranteed to bring with it some experience of losing—experiences that drive some children away from sports and into other domains of competence. On the other hand, some children just use the experience of losing to work harder. A trip for ice cream or milk shakes after a team loss can help erase any bad feelings and leave the team ready to face the next challenge.

Cooperation

Cooperation is a fundamental feature of evolution. Selection favors families and groups whose members are cooperative. In the evolutionary past, warfare between competing groups was common. Those groups that were able to foster greater cooperation among members had a better chance of survival (Pennisi, 2009). It appears that the human brain has evolved so that the individual acts to defend the group against threat, even if such efforts result in exposure to danger to the self. Under conditions of intergroup competition, the brain produces oxytocin, a hormone that enhances empathy, generosity, cooperation, and trust. The adaptive value of cooperation is supported by this hormonal activity, which strengthens the individual's positive sentiments toward the group and willingness to promote the group's welfare (De Dreu et al., 2010).

Team members learn that if the team as a whole is to do its best, the team members must help one another. Rather than playing all the roles, a team member tries to help every other member play his role as well as possible. In team play, **cooperation** takes many forms: Members share resources, take time to help other team members improve their skills, plan strategies together, work together on the field, encourage each other, bring out the equipment, or clean up after the game. Physical educators have found that they can use a cooperative teaching approach to enhance skills and strategy. When children are placed into groups to talk about the rules and skills needed for the sport, both motor skills and strategy use improved (Darnis & Lafont, 2015).

In many sports, there is a dynamic tension between competition and cooperation. Team members may compete with each other for a more desirable position or for the status of being the top player. At the same time, the team members know that they have to support each other, especially when they play against another team.

In-Group and Out-Group Attitudes

Team membership provides a microsystem for observing the formation of in-group and out-group attitudes and behaviors. All human societies observe distinctions between in-group and out-group attitudes and behaviors (Haidt, 2007). The **in-group** members share common norms, goals, and values. They also share a common fate—in sports, for example, the team wins or loses as a team. Feelings of cohesiveness with and similarity to members of an in-group prompt behaviors that are supportive of that group's survival. Members of a group typically behave in ways that are more accepting of other in-group members. This is referred to as **in-group bias**. Individuals distribute resources so that members of their in-group receive more and members of the out-group receive less. People are more forgiving of the limitations or weaknesses of members of their in-group and are more willing to give in-group members the benefit of the doubt. The more salient group membership is and the higher the status of the group in comparison to other groups, the more likely it is for group members to endorse positive attitudes toward other members of their group (Mullen, Brown, & Smith, 2006). When in-group norms emphasize fairness and reject discrimination, members are more likely to treat members of the out-group with fairness. Thus, in-group norms can influence the degree to which out-group hostilities are encouraged and expressed or suppressed (Jetten, Spears, & Manstead, 1996).

The **out-group** is any group whose goals are either in opposition to or inconsistent with the goals of the in-group. Any group may be perceived as an out-group, even though it does not actually pose any physical threat to members of the in-group. Students at one university may perceive students at another university as an out-group (e.g., the longstanding football rivalry between Ohio State University and the University of Michigan). Students enrolled in one program or major may view students in a similar but competing major as an out-group (e.g., chemical engineers versus electrical engineers). In experimental studies, in-groups and out-groups have been formed based simply on wearing a blue or yellow badge, or based on those with blue eyes and those with brown eyes (Verkuyten & De Wolf, 2007). Children as young as

Table 8.3	In-Group and Out-Group Attitudes That Develop Through Team Play Experiences	
In-Group Attitudes	**Out-Group Attitudes**	
The child learns	The child learns	
1. To value and contribute to team goals	1. To view the goals of the opponents as inconsistent with the goals of the in-group	
2. To subordinate personal goals to team goals	2. To view the outcome of competition as a zero-sum game, in which only one team can win	
3. To receive and use feedback and help from team members	3. To recognize that helping the other team to win is unethical	
4. To value one's role as an element in a larger system and the interdependence of the team members	4. To accept the necessity for antagonism between members of opposing teams	
5. To recognize that team members share a common fate	5. To devise strategies that will exploit the weaknesses of the opponent	

© Cengage

age 5 are aware of the status of their group. If they believe that their group has positive qualities and is valued, they are more likely to want to remain in the group and see themselves as similar to other group members (Bigler, Brown, & Markell, 2001; Nesdale & Flesser, 2001).

Children learn to see the outcome of competition as a win-lose situation. For sports teams, the out-group's goal of winning is in direct competition with the in-group's similar goal. The other team is seen as the enemy, and there is no alternative to trying one's hardest to defeat it. Antagonism toward the out-group is valued in team sports, and any attempt to assist the other team in winning is seen as unethical. Generalizing to the level of inter-ethnic or intertribal conflict, children may learn that moral principles that apply to members of the in-group do not necessarily apply to members of the out-group (Triandis, 1990). Here we see the primitive origins of inter-group prejudices. What can coaches do to help children understand the nature of these in-group and out-group processes and to minimize intergroup hostilities and prejudices?

Children may belong to more than one team. Depending on the situation, children can view one another as members of their in-group in one sport and as members of an out-group in another sport. For example, Ryan and his friend Tom were on the school soccer team together, but they belonged to different summer baseball leagues. During the summer, they had to compete against each other, so it usually turned out that they spent more time together and were closer friends during the school year than they were during the summers. Categorizing a peer as a member of an in-group or an out-group will lead to different attitudes and behaviors toward that person.

As children get older, their tendency to show unquestioning favoritism for their in-group is tempered by social reality and their experiences of participating in multiple groups (Verkuyten & De Wolf, 2007). They can evaluate information that suggests that one team or nationality or ethnic group is better than another and use that information to temper their in-group favoritism or their out-group prejudices. At the same time, functional messages that highlight the benefits of being in one group over another can strengthen in-group attitudes. For example, in one community, Japanese American families were

concerned that their third and fourth generation children were losing their ethnic identity. In an effort to address this concern, they formed a Japanese American basketball league. Through this sports league, a context was created that strengthened the cultural network of Japanese American children and their families while engaging in an activity that has a clearly American cultural connotation (Chin, 2016). Table 8.3 shows the in-group and out-group attitudes that may result from experiences in team play.

Team Play as a Context for Development

Participation in team sports provides socialization experiences that have both positive and negative consequences. For most children, belonging to a team, making friends, learning new skills, and enjoying the sense of success associated with a collaborative effort are positive experiences. For example, in a study of what young people value about their sports experiences, most children placed the greatest emphasis on enjoyment, positive time spent with peers, and personal achievement, and the least emphasis on winning (Lee, Whitehead, & Balchin, 2000; MacDonald, Côté, Eys, & Deakin, 2011). However, we all know of instances where rivalries escalate into peer hatreds, children from neighboring schools turn against each other, and coaches humiliate and degrade children in order to instill a commitment to the team and a determination to win. Perhaps the question is whether—particularly in team sports—the focal point of the activity is to enhance children's natural impulses for competence and skill elaboration, or whether the team activity becomes a way for adults to vent their own frustrated needs for domination and power. So much depends on the coaches and the kind of team environment they foster.

Team play has implications for both social and intellectual development. Children who play team sports see themselves as contributors to a larger effort and learn to anticipate the consequences of their behavior for the group. Team play creates a valuable context for the formation of interpersonal relationships. Inclusion in a positive team experience often results in a child's identification with the coach and other team members. These new emotional investments can expand the child's sense of well-being and social support (Blanchard, Perreault, &

Vallerand, 1998; Wylleman, 2000). In a comparison of seventh-grade children who were or were not involved in organized team sports, teachers rated the children who were involved in sports as more socially competent and less withdrawn. There were no differences between the groups in aggression. However, among the boys, those involved in sports also reported a broader range of delinquent behaviors (McHale et al., 2005). Participation in a team can help buffer experiences of peer victimization. Children who were victimized at age 7 were followed to the age of 10. Those victimized children who participated in team sports were less likely to be victimized at age 10, less likely to suffer experiences of depression, and less likely to exhibit externalizing problems. The team experiences apparently helped these children to form meaningful social bonds and to have a sense of belonging that contributed to their well-being (Perron et al., 2012).

Games that involve teams typically require children to learn many rules, make judgments about those rules, plan strategies, and assess the strengths and weaknesses of the other players. All of these characteristics of participation in team sports can stimulate cognitive growth. In one study, for example, children were divided into soccer experts and soccer novices (Schneider & Bjorklund, 1992). The experts had an impressive depth of knowledge about the game of soccer and, when given a memory task involving soccer-related items, were able to use their expertise to perform at a high level. Through participation in the teaching and learning environment of a collaborative sports experience, the more skilled players can help advance the knowledge of their less skilled teammates, and at the same time, consolidate their own understanding as they try to explain various rules, strategies, and techniques to others (Darnis & Lafont, 2015).

Interest in sports and competitive team play has been used as a motivational hook to promote other areas of school ability. For example, children diagnosed with attention deficit/hyperactivity disorder (ADHD) were recruited for a basketball camp. Many of these children had difficulties regulating their impulses and showed poor social skills. The camp focused on athletic competence and sportsmanship. The combined efforts resulted in improved communication skills, reduced aggressiveness, increased interest in basketball as an activity, and some improvement in sports ability (Hupp & Reitman, 1999). Well-designed sports programs can have a broad impact on intellectual and social development by combining increased competence in physical activity with related emphasis on the cognitive and social components of team play.

FURTHER REFLECTION: Consider the positive and negative aspects of participation in team sports during middle childhood. How can these experiences contribute to optimal development? How might they undermine development? Think about which kinds of experiences might benefit which kinds of children. How might a coach's attitudes about fair play, competition, cooperation, and the developmental needs of children influence the team atmosphere and children's experiences? What kinds of training and expertise should a person have about the process of team play and the sport he or she is coaching?

The Psychosocial Crisis: Industry Versus Inferiority

OBJECTIVE 6 Explain the psychosocial crisis of industry versus inferiority, the central process through which the crisis is resolved, education, the prime adaptive ego quality of competence, and the core pathology of inertia.

According to psychosocial theory, with the resolution of the psychosocial crisis of industry versus inferiority, a young person's fundamental attitude toward work is established (Erikson, 1963). As children develop skills and acquire standards of self-evaluation, they make an initial assessment of whether or not they will be able to make a contribution to the social community. They also make an inner commitment to strive for success. Some children are keenly motivated to compete against a standard of excellence and achieve success. Other children have low expectations about the possibility of success and are not motivated by achievement situations. The strength of a child's need to achieve success is well established by the end of this stage.

Supporting the psychosocial perspective, results of the American Psychological Association's *Stress in America* survey indicated that in middle childhood children experience a variety of worries linked to the themes of industry and inferiority (Munsey, 2010). Among children ages 8 to 12, 44 percent worried about doing well in school; 28 percent worried about whether their family would have enough money; and 22 percent worried about getting along with their friends. Their worries are associated with physical symptoms including headaches, sleep disturbances, and upset stomachs. The survey found that parents tended to underestimate the extent to which their children were worrying about family finances or doing well in school and were often unaware of the physical symptoms their children were experiencing. These findings illustrate the domains in which the conflict of industry versus inferiority is being played out for children in the United States. Most children are keenly attuned to themes of evaluation and competence, not only in their academic lives, but also in social relationships, their parents' work environments, and family financial well-being.

Industry

Industry is an eagerness to acquire skills and perform meaningful work. During middle childhood, many aspects of work are intrinsically motivating. The skills are new. They bring the child closer to the capacities of adults. Each new skill allows the child some degree of independence and may even bring new responsibilities that heighten their sense of worth. In addition, external sources of reward promote skill development. Parents and teachers may encourage children to get better grades by giving them material rewards, additional privileges, and praise. Peers also encourage the acquisition of some skills, although they may have some negative input with regard to others. Certain youth organizations, such as scouting and 4-H, make the acquisition of skills a specific route to success and higher status.

In many low and middle income countries, children work to support their families. Often this work takes place in the family context where children help with household tasks, watch younger siblings, or contribute to farm or family business tasks. Children may work alongside their same-sex parent, learning the skills associated with their gender roles and contributing to their family's effective functioning. Under the best conditions, this kind of work can contribute to a child's sense of industry as children see how their work contributes to supporting the family and to gaining competences that will be valuable to their own future families.

There are also some negative consequences of child labor. When families in low and middle income countries rely too heavily on their children's labor for economic survival, this may prevent the children from attending school or from doing well in school. Some children are exposed to hazardous labor conditions that undermine their health and expose them to risks of injury. They may feel that they must work in order for their family to survive. Under these conditions, early experiences of work may undermine the sense of industry, creating feelings of anxiety, depression, and dread (Putnick & Bornstein, 2016).

Kowaz and Marcia (1991) described the construct of industry as comprising three dimensions:

1. The *cognitive* component of industry was defined as the acquisition of the basic skills and knowledge that are valued by the culture.
2. The *behavioral* component of industry was defined as the ability to apply the skills and knowledge effectively through characteristics such as concentration, perseverance, work habits, and goal directedness.
3. The *affective* component of industry was defined as the positive emotional orientation toward the acquisition and application of skills and knowledge, such as a general curiosity and desire to know, a pride in one's efforts, and an ability to handle the distresses of failure as well as the joys of success.

Children who resolve the psychosocial crisis of industry versus inferiority in the direction of industry are likely to anticipate their vocational pathway with optimism and confidence. The contemporary world of occupational decision making is complex, and career paths are uncertain. In middle childhood, children may not yet have a clear idea of their specific career path, but with a sense of industry they experience satisfaction associated with work and an appreciation that through work they can contribute in meaningful ways to their community (Marcia, 2014). It is easy to appreciate the value of a sense of industry as a psychosocial resource for young children as they face the variety of decisions that will be required in order to carve out a satisfying vocational future.

Inferiority

What experiences of middle childhood might generate a sense of **inferiority**? Feelings of worthlessness and inadequacy come from two sources: the self and the social environment. Children who cannot master certain skills experience some feelings of inferiority. Individual differences in aptitude, physical development, and prior experience result in experiences of inadequacy in some domain. No one can do everything well. Children discover that they cannot master every skill they attempt. Even a child who feels quite positive toward work and finds new challenges invigorating will experience some degree of inferiority in a specific skill that he or she cannot master. For example, students who are born just after the age cutoff date for a particular sports competition may find that they have a hard time competing with the slightly older children in their age group. Especially at younger ages, children who are matched with others who are 10 to 12 months older may experience disappointment when they cannot compete successfully (Musch & Grondin, 2001). For many children who have developmental delays or motor impairments, the challenge of experiencing mastery in school-based skills can be very frustrating. Disabilities that influence school success are discussed in the **Human Development and Diversity** box.

If success in one area could compensate for failure in another, we would be safe in minimizing the effect of individual areas of inadequacy on the overall resolution of the psychosocial conflict of industry versus inferiority. However, the social environment does not reinforce success in all areas equally. In post-industrial societies, skills in reading and math are much more highly rewarded than fishing or tinkering with broken automobile engines. Likewise, athletic skills associated with team sports are

These young Honduran children experience a sense of industry as they help cultivate lettuce in their family field.

Disabilities of Childhood and School Success

What happens when children have significant difficulty accomplishing the tasks associated with basic areas of school achievement? The centrality of success in school-based learning for a positive resolution of the psychosocial crisis of industry versus inferiority brings the problem of childhood disabilities to our attention. In 2012–2013, 6.4 million children (about 13 percent of public school children) received special education services in the United States under the Individuals with Disabilities Education Act (IDEA) (National Center for Education Statistics, 2015a). The most prevalent groups of disabilities were specific learning disabilities (35 percent), speech and/or language impairments (21 percent), health impairments (this includes a diverse group of health problems; 12 percent). Four groups of disabilities are described here, each one posing significant challenges for academic and social success during middle childhood and beyond.

Learning Disabilities

Learning disabilities are diagnosed when a child's skills and measured abilities in reading, mathematics, or written communication are well below the child's grade level and the level expected from the child's measured IQ. "Learning disabilities arise from neurological differences in brain structure and function and affect a person's ability to receive, store, process, retrieve or communicate information" (Cortiella & Horowitz, 2014, p. 3).

Learning disorders have been identified in approximately 5 percent of public school children in the United States. These children are differentiated from others who show low performance because of mental retardation, poor teaching, or cultural factors that interfere with school performance. Typically, learning disabilities are linked with deficits in the primary processing system, including speed and accuracy of information processing, attention, and memory. These deficits may be a result of genetic disorders, neurological damage during the prenatal period, or lead poisoning during childhood, but

not all children with learning disorders have a history of these conditions. There have been many advances in early intervention, targeted instruction, and family support that contribute to school success for children with specific learning disabilities. Nonetheless, one third of students with a specific learning disability have been held back a grade at least once, and 19 percent drop out of school (Cortiella & Horowitz, 2014).

Communication Disorders

Some children experience difficulties in effective communication. Difficulties may include delays in acquiring new vocabulary; oversimplified grammatical expressions; limited variation in sentence types and structures; problems in sound production, such as lisping, omitting certain sounds in spoken speech, or stuttering; and problems in understanding certain types of words, expressions, and grammatical constructions. About 3 percent of children have some type of speech or language impairment that is distinct from mental retardation or a hearing impairment that influences speech (National Center for Education Statistics, 2015a). These difficulties interfere with academic performance especially because school learning involves the ongoing communication of information and ideas as well as the need to participate in social interactions with adults and peers. Children who have speech and language disabilities may have difficulty understanding social cues. They also likely to be the target of peer teasing and social ridicule, leading to a pattern of social withdrawal.

Health Problems

A range of health problems including a heart condition, asthma, sickle cell anemia, epilepsy, hemophilia, lead poisoning, and diabetes impact a child's vitality, strength, and/or alertness. Children with health problems may require the administration of medications during the school day. Depending on their health, some restrictions may be placed on their daily

activities due to increased sensitivity to injury, limited endurance, or increased vulnerability to infection. These children may also encounter frequent absences if their health problems become more severe. Some health conditions change with age, requiring new approaches to treatment and management in the school environment. Managing one's health problems may make it challenging to succeed in school because of disruptions in the school routine, absences, anxiety about one's health and stamina, and feelings of being treated differently by teachers and peers. On the other hand, many children with health problems become more self-reliant as they take responsibility for managing their health needs.

Motor Skill Disabilities

Motor skills disorders, often referred to as developmental coordination disorders, may manifest themselves in a variety of ways, from mild to severe, including difficulty with large or small muscle coordination, speed of movement, muscle tone and strength, motor planning, and sensory integration (Nelson & Jaskiewicz, 2015). Children with these disorders may appear clumsy and delayed in the typical acquisition of early motor skills such as walking, running, tying their shoes, or using scissors or a knife. In later school years, they have trouble writing with a pencil or pen, are slow to develop skills in putting together puzzles or models, and their athletic skills, such as throwing and catching a ball, are delayed. These children are distinguished from others who have some broader medical diagnosis such as cerebral palsy. Their lack of motor coordination interferes with academic achievement to the extent that these children struggle with any kind of written assignment and have difficulty completing projects that require manual dexterity. They lack the satisfaction of excelling in physical activities because even simple motor skills such as running or playing catch are sources of frustration.

Learning disabilities, speech and language disabilities, health problems,

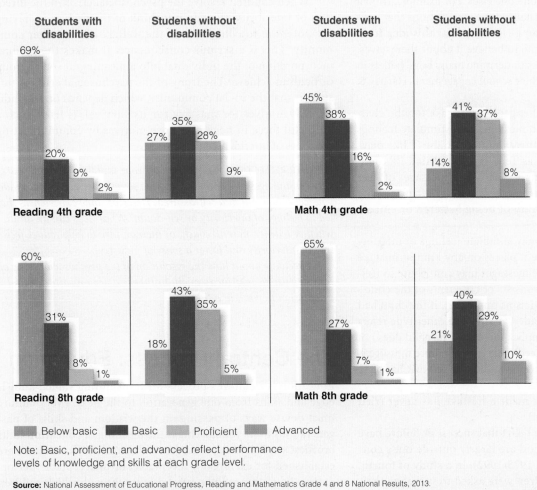

Reading 4th grade

Math 4th grade

Reading 8th grade

Math 8th grade

■ Below basic   ■ Basic   ■ Proficient   ■ Advanced

Note: Basic, proficient, and advanced reflect performance levels of knowledge and skills at each grade level.

Source: National Assessment of Educational Progress, Reading and Mathematics Grade 4 and 8 National Results, 2013. Students with disabilities includes students with both IEPs and 504 plans.

FIGURE 8.4 ▶ Children with and without Disabilities Performance on National Assessment of Educational Progress, 2013

and motor coordination disorders are among the variety of mental, emotional, and physical disabilities that children may face as they struggle to resolve the crisis of industry versus inferiority. Depending on their severity, each of these conditions requires an individualized plan in order to help succeed in the daily tasks of schooling. Children who experience these disorders may find it difficult to carry out projects or to complete assignments that others view as simple. They may also become targets of peer teasing, bullying, or rejection. As a result, they may define themselves as incompetent, inferior, or unable to learn. FIGURE 8.4 ▶ summarizes how students with and without disabilities performed on the National Assessment of Educational Progress in fourth and eighth grade assessments of reading and mathematics (Cortiella & Horowitz, 2015). The figure illustrates the substantial performance gaps between children with and without disabilities at both the fourth and eighth grade levels.

With appropriate diagnosis and effective intervention, children can learn strategies to manage or compensate for their disabilities. Success in coping with a disability may, in fact, strengthen a child's self-confidence and provide a basis for beliefs of self-efficacy. Many children use the experience of coping with a disability as evidence that they can face and overcome other difficult challenges in their lives.

Critical Thinking Questions

1. Compare and contrast the kinds of problems children with each type of disability described in this box might experience in school.
2. Describe some implications of each of these disabilities for peer relationships and friendship formation.
3. Propose the steps that a family might take to support a child with each of these disabilities. What role might family members play with regard to school? Peers? The child's own self-evaluation?
4. Investigate the laws that address the responsibility of schools for meeting the needs of children with various types of disabilities. What might be some better approaches for supporting children with various special needs?
5. Propose some coping strategies that children might use to sustain their positive self-regard and to pursue high levels of school achievement.

more highly valued than skills for building a camp fire or planting a garden. It is difficult for a child who does not excel in culturally valued skills to compensate through the mastery of others.

The social environment also generates feelings of inferiority through the process of *social comparison*. Particularly in the school setting, but even in the home, children are confronted by statements suggesting that they are not as good as some peer, sibling, or cultural subgroup. Performance suffers when children face negative expectations. Children may be grouped, tracked, graded, or publicly criticized on the basis of how their performance compares with someone else's. For example, from a young age, children have internalized the expectations that boys are less academically able than girls. They hear this idea from parents and teachers, and come to believe it about themselves. As a result, negative stereotypes undermine many boys' beliefs in their ability and detract from their school engagement (Hartley & Sutton, 2013).

The intrinsic pleasure of engaging in a task for the challenge it presents conflicts with messages that stimulate feelings of self-consciousness, competitiveness, and doubt: "I like playing ball, but I'm not as good as Ted, so I don't think I'll play." As children become increasingly sensitive to messages of peer acceptance and rejection, they may refuse to try a new activity because they fear the possibility of being bettered or embarrassed by their peers.

The social environment may stimulate feelings of inferiority through the negative value it places on any kind of mistake or failure. Two types of failure messages may contribute to feelings of inferiority. One type consists of criticisms of the child's motivation or effort. Such criticisms imply that, if the child had really tried, he could have avoided failure. The other type refers to a lack of ability. Here, the implication is that the child does not have the basic aptitude to succeed. This type of failure message is associated with a pattern of attitudes about the self that has been described as learned helplessness.

"A person who has never made a mistake has never tried anything new." (Albert Einstein)

Learned helplessness is a belief that success or failure have little to do with one's effort and are largely outside one's control (Nelson, 1987; Seligman, 1975/1992). In a study of fourth, fifth, and sixth graders, children were asked to verbalize their thoughts as they worked on various tasks. The children's verbalizations following failure showed a clear difference between the mastery-oriented children and the helpless ones. The mastery-oriented children were able to keep a positive attitude, increase their problem-solving efforts, and use their past mistakes to correct their approach. The helpless children began to blame themselves ("I never did have a good memory"). They emphasized the negative aspects of the task or criticized their own abilities and tried to find ways to escape from the situation (Diener & Dweck, 1980).

Helpless children tend to discount their successes and, in response to even a few remarks about their lack of ability, generate a self-definition that leads them to take a pessimistic view of their future success. When faced with a difficult or challenging situation, children described as helpless experience a negative mood while working on the task, give up quickly, blame their failures on a lack of ability, and expect to fail in the future (Cain & Dweck, 1995). Messages about failure usually suggest that there is an external standard of perfection—an ideal that the child did not meet. A few failures may generate such strong negative feelings that the child will avoid engaging in new tasks in order to avoid future failure. Longitudinal research suggests that children who are identified as helpless in their approach to tasks in kindergarten continue to show evidence of these same behaviors, expectations, and emotions as first graders and as fifth graders (Ziegert, Kistner, Castro, & Robertson, 2001).

When children resolve the psychosocial crisis in the direction of inferiority, they do not think of themselves as having the potential to contribute to the welfare of the larger community. This is a serious consequence. It makes the gradual incorporation of the individual into a meaningful social group difficult to achieve. The irony of the psychosocial crisis at this stage is that the social community, which depends on the individual's motives for mastery for its survival, is itself such a powerful force in negating those motives by communicating messages of inferiority.

FURTHER REFLECTION: Think back on your middle childhood years, between the ages of 6 and 12. Describe some experiences that made you feel competent and self-assured. Describe some experiences that led to feelings of inferiority or self-doubt. What steps can an adult, whether teacher, parent, coach, or mentor, take to help reduce feelings of inferiority and foster a sense of industry?

Speculate about how the resolution of the psychosocial crisis of industry versus inferiority might influence a person's attitude and orientation to work in adulthood.

The Central Process: Education

Education is a culture's process for transmitting valued knowledge and skills from one generation to the next. Every culture must devise ways of passing on the wisdom and skills of past generations to its young. This is the meaning of **education** in its broadest sense. It is also the process through which standards are established for exemplary, acceptable, or unacceptable performance. Education is the central process through which children experience the sense of mastery and accomplishment associated with industry and the critical feedback or negative evaluations that are associated with inferiority.

Education is different from schooling. The term *education* can have different meanings across cultural groups. For example, in Spanish the word *educación* refers to the internalization of proper, respectful social behavior. The goal of *educación* is character development. For children growing up in indigenous communities of South and Central America, the cultural tradition for education emphasizes learning by keenly observing the activities of the adults around them and then participating as they feel ready (López, Correa-Chávez, Rogoff, & Gutiérrez, 2010). In the United States, the term *education* focuses on an individual's acquisition of knowledge and skill development, typically gained within the context of school or a formal program of instruction (Greenfield, Keller, Fuligni, & Maynard, 2003). The literature on education places an emphasis on test scores and grades as well as grade retention and graduation rates as indicators of academic achievement. However, these outcome measures do not capture the dynamic process of education that takes place as children participate in the social, cognitive, and emotional work of learning.

The practice of separating formal educational experiences from the direct, intimate, hands-on activities of home and community is only about 200 years old. Before the industrial revolution, most children were educated by assisting their parents in the tasks of home life, farming, trading with neighbors, and participating in religious life (Coleman, 1987). In the case of the nobility, children often had tutors who supervised their education at home. Today, however, schools bear the primary responsibility for education.

Teaching, which began as an extension of the parental role, has become a distinct profession. In our culture, formal learning takes place in a special building during certain hours of the day. To be sure, the success of that experience in promoting a child's skills and a sense of the self as a learner depends heavily on the ongoing involvement and commitment of family members (Hill & Taylor, 2004). However, schools play a key role in providing opportunities for skill development and mastery, contexts for assessment, social comparison, and self-evaluation, and socialization for the behavioral characteristics—including focus, persistence, and organization—that contribute to the formation of a personal sense of industry.

During the elementary school years, the goal of education is to help children develop the basic tools of learning. Central to this process is an introduction to the language of concepts, theories, and relationships that allow children to organize their experiences. Schools strive to develop verbal and analytic problem solving. Instruction focuses on rules, descriptions, and abstract concepts. Children are exposed to a range of disciplines and methods of inquiry for dealing with complex problems. Throughout the educational process, children are presented with problems of increasing difficulty. They are given many opportunities to practice their newly developing skills, receiving continuous feedback about their level of competence.

In addition to the acquisition of skills and knowledge, schools emphasize an approach to behavior that can be described as a combination of *citizenship, social competence,* and *study habits* Schools impart a code of conduct that is intended to facilitate the teacher's ability to guide students' attention, help children organize and focus on the tasks at hand, and foster a respectful, cooperative attitude toward adults and peers. Within this framework, all of these qualities become part of the sense of industry for those children who adapt well to the culture of schooling.

Teachers' expectations about their students influence the kind of educational climate that they create (Jussim, Robustellli, & Cain, 2009). When teachers expect students to do well and to be highly motivated to learn, they tend to direct more encouraging emotional signals to those students. They smile more, offer them more encouragement, and interact in a warmer, more supportive tone. Their feedback to these students tends to focus more on their academic performance, and not as much on their behavior or their attitude. Teachers spend more time with the students whom they perceive as having academic potential, giving them more of their attention and challenging them with more interesting assignments. Finally, when teachers have high expectations for students, they give the students more opportunities to participate; they call on these students more often, give them more time to answer questions, and encourage them to be involved. All of these strategies convey to the students that the educational process is both welcoming and interesting.

Some children do not do well in this culture of schooling; they do not bring the expected social behaviors or study habits; they do not demonstrate the desired qualities of cooperation, self-regulation, or rule compliance. As a result, they receive negative evaluations, which contribute to feelings of inferiority, leading to a gradual disengagement from the educational experiences of school. Low school-engagement behaviors in the early elementary grades are as strong predictors of dropping out of school as are grades and test scores (Alexander, Entwisle, & Kabbani, 2001; Entwisle, Alexander, & Olson, 2007). In contrast, teachers who create classroom environments that are warm and supportive, well managed, and where students are encouraged to tackle challenging projects can help students overcome their reluctance and remain engaged in the learning process (Kim & Cappella, 2016).

In the United States, socioeconomic status (SES) and student achievement are strongly related. Differences in academic performance between children from low-resource and high-resource families are noted beginning as early as preschool. These differences have been attributed to variations in parents' investment in their children's schooling; disparities in the resources available to schools; differences in children's cognitive, social, and emotional maturity that support school engagement; and discrepancies in opportunities to learn, both in school, after school, and in the summer (Schmidt Burroughs, Zoido, & Houang, 2015).

Schools, as institutions of the larger communities they serve, may not have the same expectations for success for all the students who attend. And children and their families do not all bring the same degree of trust in the educational process to their schooling. In some cases, parents find that they have no access to or voice in decisions affecting their children. They and their children experience barriers to achieving success in the skills that schooling values. For example, in a study of Latino immigrant families, parents experienced language barriers, an inability of teachers to explain their children's school difficulties, and constraints in making contact with teachers. Even though parents expressed a desire to support their children's school success, they felt helpless and dismissed as they tried to make contact with the school (Ramirez, 2003). The sense of inferiority can be provoked for children when they perceive that the school devalues or disrespects their parents.

In some cases, inferiority is inflicted on children through abusive treatment by school adults. In the United States, in a single school year over 200,000 children were victims of corporal punishment in their schools, a practice that is legal in 20 states. African American children and children with disabilities were overrepresented in the percentages of groups who were punished by paddling and other physical means (Murphy, Vagins, & Parker, 2010).

Failure in school and the public ridicule that it brings play a central role in the establishment of a negative self-image, which can readily be linked to the sense of inferiority. Sometimes, children defend themselves against the threat of failure messages by blaming others for their failures or by bragging that they can succeed in other ways. Much as it may appear that these children do not care about school or the school's goals, the school remains a symbol of cultural authority. Children in these groups may conclude that the only way to retain a basic sense of self-confidence is to withdraw from school and try to establish their competence among their peers by accelerating their transition to adulthood through more risky paths (Alexander, Entwisle, & Kabbani, 2001; Clark, 1991; Gregory, 1995; Ogbu, 1987).

FURTHER REFLECTION: Describe how the environment of school changes from age 6 (grade 1) through age 12 (grade 6). How well do these changes in the school environment match the developmental changes that take place during these two stages of life?

Imagine that you were asked to provide guidance to a local school board about improving their elementary schools. What ideas from this chapter might inform your recommendations?

The Prime Adaptive Ego Quality and the Core Pathology

Competence

Erikson's (1982) notion of **competence** as the prime adaptive ego quality is a belief in the ability to make sense of and master the demands of a situation.

> Competence, in turn, is the free exercise of dexterity and intelligence in the completion of tasks, unimpaired by infantile inferiority. It is the basis for cooperative participation in technologies, and it relies, in turn, on the logic of tools and skills. (Erikson, 1978, p. 30)

Similar to the concept of self-efficacy, competence refers to confidence in one's ability to engage in new situations and do

well. This idea is illustrated by a study that monitored children's perceptions of competence during school transitions from grade 5 to 6 and from grade 6 to 7. The children who had the highest levels of perceived competence also had the strongest positive feelings about how they were doing in school and showed the highest scores on a measure of intrinsic motivation. They wanted to be challenged by their schoolwork and they liked working independently and figuring things out for themselves. They expressed curiosity about the tasks, saying they would work hard because of their own interest rather than to please the teacher or to get good grades (Harter, Whitesell, & Kowalski, 1992). Children who have positive assessments of their cognitive competence anticipate future school successes; children who have positive assessments of their social competence anticipate improvements in their future peer relationships (Wang & Koh, 2015).

Children who have internalized a sense of competence love to learn and work. They are excited about developing new skills and are optimistic about being able to achieve success. These children are the ones who sign up for new activities or start neighborhood clubs, want to be on two or three sports teams, look forward to field trips and school projects, and take pleasure in being asked to help with difficult tasks like planting trees along the highway, building a new playground, or raising money for earthquake victims.

Inertia

Inertia is the core pathology of middle childhood. In Erikson's words, "The antipathic counterpart of industry, the sense of competent mastery to be experienced in the school age, is that inertia that constantly threatens to paralyze an individual's productive life and is, of course, fatefully related to the inhibition of the preceding age, that of play" (1982, pp. 76–77).

Children who leave early school age with the core pathology of inhibition fail to participate and engage much during middle childhood. These are not the students who try and fail repeatedly, nor are they the ones whose sense of competence must be reconfirmed daily. Instead, they are students who tend to be passive and withdrawn, never engaging psychologically with the demands of their schools or their communities. Growing from this reticence to engage, the core pathology of inertia leaves a child listless and unable to summon the energy and will to participate in new activities or to prepare for a different, more positive future.

Children who leave middle childhood with a sense of inertia continue to be withdrawn and passive. They have trouble instigating actions or changing the course of events in their lives. As a result, they will not be likely to address challenges or problems by formulating plans of action, evaluating them, and then executing them. Children with a sense of inertia will not believe that they can master the challenges they face, and thus, they are likely to be swept along by the tide of events.

We all experience periods of inertia—times when we cannot muster the energy, enthusiasm, or confidence to take action. We may become besieged by

Erika is an excellent student who enjoys teaching others. Here she is demonstrating her reading and spelling competence as she guides the class in a word-recognition activity.

doubts about our competence and worth—doubts that can produce work blocks, writer's block, waves of fatigue, boredom, procrastination, or aimlessness. Typically, one can survive a few days or even weeks on automatic pilot, doing the bare minimum to survive. Children may be able to get by for quite a while without exercising much energy or direction, especially if they are being sustained by parents and teachers. Eventually, however, life brings demands for change and expectations to meet new challenges that have never been faced before. Children who believe in their competence and their ability to learn can direct their willpower to overcoming obstacles; they will respond to these challenges with resilience (Yeager & Dweck, 2012). Children who are burdened with a pervasive sense of inertia may be unable to cope.

Applied Topic: Violence in the Lives of Children

OBJECTIVE 7 Evaluate the impact of exposure to violence on development during middle childhood.

The problem of violence in families, schools, and neighborhoods threatens to undermine the quality of the psychosocial development and educational attainment for many American children. Exposure to violence has potential damaging effects on cognitive, emotional, social, and physical development. Based on a national survey conducted by the U.S. Department of Justice and the CDC, an estimated 58 percent of children under age 17 had experienced one or more incidences of violence in the past year including physical assault, sexual victimization,

maltreatment, property victimization, and witnessing violence. Almost half of the children had experienced more than one of these types of violence in the past year. Among children in the age group 14 to 17, almost 70 percent said that they have been a victim of some type of physical assault in their lifetime (Finkelhor, Turner, Shattuck Hamby, & Kracke, 2015). The topic of violence in the lives of children illustrates the interaction of the biological, psychological, and societal systems as they contribute to developmental trajectories.

Consequences of Exposure to Violence

Three consequences of exposure to violence are of especially grave concern: children are victims of violence; children become more violent; and exposure to violence disrupts cognitive functioning and mental health.

Children as Victims of Violence

As a result of the violence in their families and neighborhoods, large numbers of children and youth are victims of violent crimes. Among 14 to 17 year olds, almost a third said they had been injured as a result of an assault in their lifetime (Finkelhor et al., 2015). According to the CDC, 279 children ages 5 to 14 died due to homicide in 2014. Homicide was the third leading cause of death for adolescents and young adults ages 15 to 24 in the United States (CDC, 2016). Children who live in low-income neighborhoods are especially vulnerable to exposure to violence. According to a report issued by the National Center for Education Statistics and the Bureau of Justice Statistics, in 2009–2010, 1,183,700 violent crimes were committed in public schools (Robers, Zhang, & Truman, 2012). Findings from this report suggest that the younger students are more fearful than the older students about the chances of being harmed at school.

In a survey of fifth graders who live in a very poor urban district in the Northeast, 82 percent reported being victimized at school, including being hit by another student, kicked or pushed by a student, threatened with a knife or other weapon, verbally threatened, or robbed. Ninety-three percent of the children had observed one of these forms of violence being directed to other students at their school (Cedeno, Elias, Kelly, & Chu, 2010). Neighborhoods that are centers of illegal drug trade are also often the sites of violence, including stabbings, shootings, and gang raids. In these communities, the loss of a legitimate economic base, with few people in stable or high-status occupations, leads to takeovers by gangs and other organized criminal activities. Children may be lured into dangerous forms of drug-related transactions, which make them targets of violence on the streets as well as victims of abuse by drug-addicted family members and youth. Once involved in some aspect of drug trafficking, these children are more likely to be exposed to other forms of community violence (Li, Stanton, & Feigelman, 1999; Okundaye, 2004).

Anadolu Agency/Anadolu Agency/Getty Images

Syrian children have been exposed to years of violence. Two children leave the territory of their home as battle rages around them. Imagine the long-term impact of ongoing violence and family disruptions on this generation of children.

Exposure to Violence and Aggressive Behaviors

Many studies report a significant relationship between victimization or witnessing violence and carrying out violent actions on others. Initial reactions to community violence may lead younger children to feel wary, worrying that they or their friends or family members might become victims. However, over repeated exposure to community violence, children may come to accept violence as predictable and normative in their neighborhood. As a result, they may begin to see violence as an adaptive approach to conflict (Kennedy & Ceballo, 2016). The accumulation of exposure to violence across several settings, including community, school, and home, coupled with low parental monitoring and the likelihood of being a victim of violence, creates a context in which children engage in risky and more serious violent behaviors as an adaptive response to the chaos of their home and community (Boxer et al., 2013; Garbarino, 2001; Saltzinger, Rosario, Feldman, & Ng-Mak, 2008).

Exposure to Violence Disrupts Cognitive and Emotional Development

Intense, frequent, or prolonged exposure to one or more forms of violence can be considered toxic stressors. Exposure to these stressors has been associated with serious detrimental consequences for physical health, cognitive functioning, and mental health (Moffitt & the Klaus-Grawe 2012 Think Tank, 2013; Shern, Blanch, & Steverman, 2016). Children who have been severely abused or exposed to intense violence may be suffering from symptoms similar to post-traumatic stress disorder. **Post-traumatic stress disorder** can result from direct experience of a grave threat to personal safety or injury, witnessing the injury or death of another person, or learning about the violent death or injury of a family member or someone close. The response usually includes "intense fear, helplessness, or horror." The person typically has recurrent vivid recollections or dreams of the event with accompanying strong emotional reactions. Children may have recurring nightmares, repeat the same play sequences that re-enact some part of the traumatic event, withdraw interest from activities they used to enjoy, and show physical symptoms that they did not have before the event, such as stomach aches or headaches. School-age children may believe that there were warning signs that would have allowed them to avoid the trauma if they had been alert enough to recognize them. As a result, these children maintain a type of **hypervigilance** or increased arousal, directing their attention to threat-related stimuli (Dalgleish, Moradi, Taghavi, NeshatDoost, & Yule, 2001; Hamblen & Barnett, 2016; Osofsky, 1995). These symptoms often interfere with sleep, schoolwork, concentration, and normal social life.

Symptoms of post-traumatic stress disorder can be long lasting and, in some cases, can emerge long after the event has passed. For example, one study focused on 69 children who had lived within 100 miles of Oklahoma City in 1995 when the federal building was bombed. These children, studied in 1997, did not see the explosion, they did not live near the explosion, and no one they knew personally was injured or killed in the explosion. Yet 2 years after the event, many of these children showed evidence of post-traumatic stress disorder symptoms and related difficulties in functioning. Their symptoms were attributed to experiences of the event through the media and indirect loss through friends or family members who knew someone who was killed (Pfefferbaum et al., 2000). It is reasonable to expect that even when they are not the targets or victims of violence, the children who are present at school shootings, bombings, or beatings will have enduring symptoms associated with exposure to these violent events.

The Neurobiology of Exposure to Violence. Children preserve sensory and motor memories of the conditions associated with their trauma, which are then released under contemporary conditions of fear. In boys, these symptoms commonly reflect **hyperarousal**, including startle response, increases in heart rate, sleep disturbance, anxiety, and motor hyperactivity. In girls, the symptoms are more likely to be dissociation, gastrointestinal symptoms, and pain. Under threatening conditions, children who have been traumatized in the past automatically return to these disruptive states, making it difficult to access higher order problem-solving and reasoning skills.

Exposure to severe trauma may produce long-lasting changes in the way a child's brain regulates emotional reactions, the ability to concentrate, and the ability to inhibit impulses (Moffitt et al., 2013; Peckins, Dockray, Eckenrode, Heaton, & Susman, 2012). Simple regulatory and impulsive functions are governed by the more primitive, reactive areas of the brain, including the brain stem and the midbrain. More complex functions of language and abstract reasoning develop later and are located largely in the subcortical and cortical areas. The ability to modify and regulate impulses involves the coordination of two neurological pathways, one which provides intense signals about threats or dangers emerging from the brain stem, and the other which provides ideas about alternative coping strategies emerging from the cortex. An overreactive brain stem that produces intense and frequent impulses may result from any one or a combination of factors, including fetal exposure to alcohol and drugs, environmental exposure to lead, hormonal abnormalities, head injuries, or exposure to child abuse. Children reared in a socialization environment of chaos, violence, parental aggression, and harsh and abusive discipline lack the opportunity to develop empathy, self-control, and higher order problem-solving skills that might allow them to modulate their strong impulses.

Preventing Violence

Preventing violence in society and reducing exposure to violence among children have become significant public health issues (Shern, Blanch, & Steverman, 2016). Rather than focusing solely on the criminal justice definitions and strategies for deterrence, a public health perspective emphasizes the need to understand the contexts of violence from which strategies for prevention can be devised and evaluated. An ecological systems perspective leads us to consider the layers of influence that produce violence in the lives of children including the larger international conflicts that result in warfare and terrorism, the violent crimes that occur in neighborhoods, the aggressive acts that children experience in their homes and schools, and the representation and glorification of violence in music, movies, and video games. Some children are less able to regulate their impulsive reactions than others. Some children are more likely to perceive actions as threatening, and as a result, are more likely to strike out against others. We must try to determine what kinds of socialization environments can help children control their aggressiveness. Furthermore, we must discover strategies to reduce violence in families, neighborhoods, schools, and the media. Several directions for prevention have been identified and require coordination (Farrington, 2013; Low & Mulford, 2013; Matjasko et al., 2012):

1. Prevent prenatal and perinatal conditions that cause neurological damage and increase the biological vulnerability for violent behaviors.
2. Educate parents about ways to resolve their own conflicts so they do not continuously expose their young children to interpersonal violence in the home.
3. Develop techniques that parents and teachers can incorporate to help children acquire self-control, empathy, and perspective taking.
4. Strengthen the teaching and learning environment of schools in order to encourage greater school engagement and cooperative learning.
5. Develop effective techniques for teaching children how to reframe cognitions and beliefs that lead them to interpret the behaviors of others as threatening and develop alternative, nonaggressive strategies to handle and respond to insults, threats, and frustration.
6. Decrease children's access to guns and other weapons.
7. Increase the sense of social control and cohesion in neighborhoods so that mutual trust is higher, people help one another more, and people are more willing to take steps to intervene when children are acting destructively.

8. Improve coordination and cooperation among community agencies to strengthen the reach and effectiveness of interventions.
9. Implement social policies to reduce unemployment; improve safe, affordable housing; and encourage business development.

A variety of programs are being implemented to help reduce violence. Some focus on providing information about the problem and strategies for avoiding violence; some use role-playing, modeling, feedback, and reinforcement to alter students' behaviors; and some go beyond the classroom and the school environment by involving parents and community leaders to create a safe community where people are encouraged to practice positive behavioral interactions. In a review of 53 studies that evaluated universal school-based programs, researchers found that these programs were generally effective in decreasing violence (Hahn et al. & Task Force on Community Preventive Services, 2007). School-based programs that are delivered to all the children in the school rather than targeted to children who are at special risk for exposure to violence not only succeed in reducing violence but are also often associated with reduced truancy, improved school achievement, and improved social skills among students. One significant challenge facing these initiatives is discovering how to expand their reach from one school, community, or county to a wider population while preserving the specific features of the intervention (Hawkins et al., 2015). To learn more about strategies that are designed to prevent violence in schools, families, and communities, visit the website Blueprints for Healthy Youth Development (www.blueprintsprograms.com) to read about model programs that meet rigorous standards to evaluate effectiveness.

FURTHER REFLECTION: Investigate the neurobiological effects of exposure to violence for children. What might be the immediate and more long-term impacts of these experiences? Evaluate the concept of toxic stress. Given what you know about the developmental tasks and psychosocial crisis of middle childhood, how might exposure to toxic stress compromise development during the middle childhood years?

CHAPTER SUMMARY

During middle childhood, cognitive and social skills develop that are crucial to later life stages. Remarkable synergies occur across the cognitive domains, bringing new levels of skill development, expanded access to information, and complex strategies for approaching and solving problems. Children apply their cognitive abilities not only in academic, school-related domains, but also in an increased capacity for social competence, self-evaluation, and peer group participation. As a result of the combination of cognitive and social skill development, children are able to make significant contributions to the social groups to which they belong. They are also likely to seek approval and acceptance from these groups.

OBJECTIVE 1 Examine the role of friendship in helping children learn to take the point of view of others, be sensitive to the norms and pressures of the peer group, and experience closeness in relationships. Summarize the negative consequences that result from social rejection and loneliness.

The family environment provides the early context in which social competence emerges. The child's ability to establish and preserve friendships in middle childhood is built upon earlier capacities including temperament, attachment, sibling interactions, and the family's orientation toward peer relationships. Three important lessons are gained through participation in friendship: increasing appreciation for various points of view, awareness of peer norms and expectations, and a growing capacity for intimacy. As the role of friendship increases, problems tied to loneliness, rejection, and peer victimization become increasingly distressing.

OBJECTIVE 2   Describe the development of concrete operational thought, including conservation, classification skills, mathematical reasoning, and the child's ability to understand and monitor his or her own knowledge and understanding.

In early and middle childhood, new cognitive capacities focus on mental operations that provide a logical system of relationships among objects. Three achievements of this stage of reasoning include the scheme for conservation, classification, and combinatorial skills. A hallmark of this period is an increase in logical, focused problem solving. Children are able to consider competing explanations, look at a problem from another person's point of view as well as their own, and use information to plan a strategy to reach a goal.

OBJECTIVE 3   Analyze the nature of skill learning and examine societal factors that provide the contexts in which skill learning occurs.

An understanding of skill development combines an appreciation of the child's intellectual maturity with a sense of the significant motives that may influence willingness to learn. Skilled actions require adaptation to a cultural context. Skill development involves the integration of multiple domains that may mature at different rates. Skilled behavior involves the coordination of simple and complex elements as well as overarching strategies to achieve specific goals. Reading is discussed as an example of a skill that begins as a focus of its own (learning to read) and then becomes integrated into the achievement of many other skills (reading to learn). Health-related skills are discussed as an example of a domain that contributes to personal well-being.

OBJECTIVE 4   Outline the factors that contribute to self-evaluation, including feelings of pride, self-efficacy, and ways that social expectations of parents, teachers, and peers contribute to a child's self-evaluation.

The combination of advanced reasoning through concrete operational thought and engagement in a more complex peer environment contribute to new approaches to self-evaluation. The themes of pride, self-efficacy, and sensitivity to the social expectations of others are all relevant to understanding how children evaluate their competence or incompetence, and their willingness to strive toward new levels of achievement. The idea of domains of competence suggests that children are forming a more differentiated evaluation of their abilities. Children may form a self-evaluation as they reflect on their past performance, their comparison to peers, and messages from teachers and parents.

OBJECTIVE 5   Summarize new levels of complexity in play as children become involved in team sports, examine the benefits of participation in sports, and analyze the cognitive and emotional development that accompanies team play.

Participation in team sports can provide important health benefits that set the stage for continued activity in adulthood. They can also introduce risks of injury, with special attention to head injuries. Coaches and parents play a central role in creating a safe and cooperative environment for the unfolding of team experiences. Team sports offer a new and more complex form of play that combines the need for advanced levels of skill, cognitive capacities to understand rules and strategies for success, and interpersonal skills related to interdependence, cooperation, division of labor, and competition. Experiences regarding the formation of in-group and out-group attitudes are part of team sports. Team sports provide a microcosm of intergroup and intragroup relations that will be repeated in various contexts through adult life.

OBJECTIVE 6   Explain the psychosocial crisis of industry versus inferiority, the central process through which the crisis is resolved, education, the prime adaptive ego quality of competence, and the core pathology of inertia.

Industry focuses primarily on building competence. The family, peer group, and school all play their part in the support of feelings of mastery or failure, industry or inferiority. Education is the central process through which children discover the core understanding of the skills that are valued in a society and the paths toward their achievement. In our society, school is the environment in which continuous attention is given to the child's success or failure in basic skill areas. The child's emerging sense of industry is closely interwoven with the quality of the school environment and the extent to which the child encounters experiences that foster enthusiasm for new learning and provide objective feedback about levels of mastery. A positive resolution of the psychosocial crisis of industry versus inferiority is accompanied by a prime adaptive ego quality of competence. A negative resolution of the crisis is accompanied by the core pathology of inertia, leading to a passive disengagement from the opportunities and challenges of school and community life.

OBJECTIVE 7   Evaluate the impact of exposure to violence on development during middle childhood.

The Applied Topic illustrates the biological, psychological, and societal contexts of violence. Children can be exposed to prenatal and perinatal risks that disrupt their neurological development. They may be embedded in a family system in which abusive or disorganized parenting reduces their ability to cope with threats or stress. Violence in the neighborhood, media, and school strengthens impulsive, reactive responses and makes it increasingly difficult for children to draw on their higher order reasoning skills to reinterpret or interrupt their sense of anger and threat. Access to weapons, especially guns, leads to new heights of destructive expression for these children. Preventive interventions can be effective. However, they require a multilevel approach and coordination of family, school, and community agencies to support a positive, reassuring environment in which children can approach skill development and social relationships with confidence.

The achievements of middle childhood contribute in key ways to coping and adaptation in adulthood. Issues of industry, mastery, achievement, social expectations, social skills, cooperativeness, and interpersonal sensitivity are all salient themes during this stage. A person's orientation toward friendship and work—two essential aspects of adult life—begin to take shape.

CASEBOOK

For additional case material related to this chapter, see the case entitled "Ayesha and the Dinosaurs," in *Life Span Development: A Case Book*, by Barbara and Philip Newman, Laura Landry-Meyer, and Brenda J. Lohman, pp. 100–104. The case suggests how new cognitive skills, skill learning, and a sense of competence come together to promote new levels of leadership and problem solving in middle childhood. The case also illustrates some of the challenges that children face in the transition to kindergarten and how home, preschool, and kindergarten systems can work together to foster a child's continuing school success.

In early adolescence, physical changes of puberty are accompanied by alterations in the self-concept. The biological, psychological, and societal systems conspire to accelerate the transition along the path from childhood toward adulthood.

1. Describe the patterns of physical maturation during puberty for female and male adolescents, and analyze the impact of early and late maturing on self-concept and social relationships.

2. Summarize the development of romantic and sexual relationships, and evaluate the factors that influence the transition to first intercourse, the formation of a sexual orientation, and pregnancy and parenthood in early adolescence.

3. Identify the basic features of formal operational thought, and explain the factors that promote the development of advanced reasoning at this period of life.

4. Examine patterns of emotional development in early adolescence, characterize the neurological processes associated with emotional expression, and describe the nature of three problem areas: eating disorders, depression, and delinquency.

5. Analyze the nature of peer relations in early adolescence, especially the formation of cliques and crowds, and contrast the typical relationships with parents and peers during this stage.

6. Explain the psychosocial crisis of group identity versus alienation, the central process through which the crisis is resolved, peer pressure, the prime adaptive ego quality of fidelity to others, and the core pathology of isolation.

7. Apply your understanding of developmental issues of early adolescence to an analysis of factors that account for patterns of adolescent alcohol and drug use.

EARLY ADOLESCENCE (12 TO 18 YEARS)

9

— CASE STUDY Evelyn Cabrera: Balancing Autonomy and Closeness in Early Adolescence —

Evelyn Cabrera is a seventeen-year-old second generation Mexican-American living in a working class neighborhood of a large urban area in the southwest with her parents, three brothers, and one sister....She spends most of her time at school, her job, a local theme park, family events, and with her boyfriend.

Evelyn describes her relationship with her mother as very close:

> We're close, like really close; we communicate a lot. For example, when I have a problem, I tell her what's going on in my life, about my boyfriend, or about my friends, in school; yeah we're pretty close.

She doesn't communicate as often with her father because he works long hours, but she feels she can talk to him about anything as well—that is except for her relationship with her boyfriend. Evelyn and her boyfriend are serious, talking and thinking of marriage. He is older—in his twenties and has a steady job as an office manager for a health care company. Evelyn is Daddy's little girl, and he has a hard time thinking about letting her go....

Evelyn's father thinks she is too young for this level of seriousness in a relationship, and he tries to limit their contact by keeping her involved in family activities and responsibilities. Still, she spends a lot of time with her boyfriend....

(Evelyn) says her boyfriend wants her to go to college, as do her parents, but the seriousness of their relationship seems likely to complicate these plans, which is worrying her parents....Evelyn is adamant, however, that she is not having sex and will wait for marriage for that. She wants to go to college and become a detective, just like her uncle. After college, she plans to get married and have a child, but just one. Evelyn appears determined to achieve her goals. (Christerson, Edwards, & Flory, 2010, pp. 17–19)

CASE ANALYSIS Using What You Know

1. The case presents a number of tensions in Evelyn's life: between her family's goals and her relationship with her boyfriend; within Evelyn herself between her academic and career goals, and her relationship with her boyfriend; and between her father and her mother, who seem to be in agreement in their approach to Evelyn in some ways and in conflict in others. How typical would you say this array of tensions is for adolescents in the United States?

2. How might Evelyn's ethnic and social class identities be influencing her pathway through adolescence?

3. Evelyn has pretty specific goals about her next phases of life: college, marriage, a career, and parenthood. How common is it for early adolescents to have such specific future-oriented goals? How likely are Evelyn's goals to change in the next 5 years?

At this point in our discussion of life stages, we depart again from Erikson's conceptualization. In psychosocial theory, Erikson viewed adolescence as a single stage, unified by the resolution of the central conflict of identity versus identity confu-

sion. Erikson's approach attempted to address the tasks and needs of children and youth ranging in age from about 11 to 21 years within one developmental stage. Based on our own research on adolescence and our assessment of the research literature, we have identified two distinct periods of psychosocial development during these years—early adolescence (12 to 18 years) and later adolescence (18 to 24 years). This chapter discusses the stage of early adolescence; chapter 10 discusses later adolescence.

Early adolescence begins with the onset of puberty and ends roughly at age 18. This stage is characterized by rapid physical changes, significant cognitive and emotional maturation, newly energized sexual interests, and a heightened sensitivity to peer relations. We have called the psychosocial crisis of this stage **group identity** versus **alienation**. Later adolescence begins at approximately age 18 and continues for about 6 years. This stage is characterized by new advances in the establishment of autonomy from the family and the development of a personal identity. The psychosocial crisis of this period is **individual identity** versus **identity confusion**.

The elaboration of adolescence into two stages is closely tied to social and historical changes. At the beginning of the 20th century in the United States, few youths in the 12 to 18 age range were in school; at the turn of the 21st century, almost all of them were. The time between entry into puberty and entry into the self-sustaining roles of adulthood has expanded. In contrast to life 100 years ago, there is a longer period of required education and training, fewer opportunities to enter the full-time labor force without a high school education, laws restricting the employment of children under the age of 16, and a workplace that requires more advanced technical, representational, and interpersonal skills for success. At the same time, occupational choices are much more diverse, and the process of selecting a career path has become increasingly difficult. Young people reach the biological capacity to reproduce and the physical stature of an adult at an earlier age, but they do not yet have fully mature brain development or the education, skills, training, or sense of purpose to create a sustainable independent life. For adolescents, the challenge and the joy of the period is to construct a sense of self that is at once connected to meaningful individuals and groups and, at the same time, authentic and autonomous. Adolescence is a thrilling time of life, a time of lasting memories and first experiences. Young people emerge into a wider, more varied social environment. Their social relationships take on a new intensity and complexity. New and more intricate thoughts are possible, accompanied by new insights about the self as well as the physical, social, and political environments. Many adolescents experience new levels of emotional intensity, including positive feelings such as romantic sentiments, sexual desires, tenderness, loyalty, and spirituality, as well as the negative emotions of depression, anxiety, jealousy, hatred, and rage.

Early adolescence is a period of transition from the relatively weak and protected status of childhood to a more equal position in relation to adults and authority figures. In some cases, as adolescents strive to express their views and preferences, they are met with a strong resistance by adults who still treat teens as if they were young children who are not mature enough to make important decisions. In response to overbearing, harsh, or neglectful adult authorities, adolescents may display anger, rebellion, or depression. They may engage in risky behaviors, including self-harm and harming others. These are the problems that the media, television, and movies tend to highlight.

However, this is not an accurate portrayal of most teens. According to a special report by *U.S. News and World Report*, "adolescents now are less likely than their parents were to smoke, do hard drugs, get pregnant, commit violent crimes,... and drive drunk" (Baxter, 2009). Subsequent studies of adolescent risk behaviors support this trend. This group of teens, born beginning in the mid-1990s and sometimes referred to as "Generation Z," is described as conscientious and hardworking (Williams, 2015). In fact, some authors refer to the current generation of adolescents as conservative, even boring (Parker-Pope, 2012). Given a supportive environment in which their parents and other adults are able to balance autonomy-granting and warmth, most young people make important new strides toward maturity during this time. They reach new levels of mastery and a new appreciation of their interdependence with family, friends, community, and culture. ●

Developmental Tasks
Physical Maturation

OBJECTIVE 1 Describe the patterns of physical maturation during puberty for female and male adolescents, and analyze the impact of early and late maturing on self-concept and social relationships.

Coming on the heels of a period of gradual but steady physical development in middle childhood, early adolescence is marked by rapid physical changes, including a height spurt, maturation of the reproductive system, appearance of **secondary sex characteristics**, increased muscle strength, and the redistribution of body weight. At the same time, the brain continues to develop, with changes that increase emotionality, modify memory, and gradually improve connections among areas of the brain that regulate emotion, impulse control, and judgment (Mascarelli, 2012). Variability in the rate and sequence of development is well documented (Brooks-Gunn & Reiter, 1990; Tanner, 1990). The time from the appearance of breast buds to full maturity may range from 1 to 6 years for girls; the male genitalia may take from 2 to 5 years to reach adult size. These individual differences in maturation suggest that during early adolescence, the chronological peer group is biologically far more diverse than it was during early and middle childhood.

Puberty refers to the time in development when a person becomes able to reproduce. However, the changes associated with puberty are quite diverse. Puberty encompasses a group of interrelated neurological and endocrinological changes that influence brain development, changes in sexual maturation, cycles and levels of hormone production, and physical growth. Puberty starts when the hypothalamus begins releasing a hormone called gonadotropin-releasing hormone (GnRH). GnRH then signals the pituitary gland to release two more hormones—luteinizing hormone (LH) and follicle-stimulating hormone (FSH)—to start sexual development. This system—the hypothalamus, pituitary gland, and the gonads, often referred to as the HPG axis—is responsible for the production and regulation of the sex hormones that result in the growth and maturation of the reproductive organs (NICHD, 2013). The hypothalamus and pituitary glands are also linked to the adrenal gland (the HPA axis) which controls reactions to stress, regulates digestion, and influences the immune system, mood, energy use, and the sleep-wake cycle (see the **Applying Theory and Research to Life** box about changes in the sleep needs of adolescents). The HPA axis establishes a feedback system that integrates the brain, glands, and hormones to support adaptation. During adolescence, both the HPG axis and the HPA axis are emerging into new patterns of regulation and growth.

There is a great deal of individual variation in the timing, rate of change, and coordination of these changes. Some changes, such as the maturation of the adrenal glands, occur very early, at around ages 6 to 9, and some changes, such as growth in height, can continue well into the late teens and 20s. The term **pubertal status** refers to the extent to which physical changes associated with puberty have taken place, from the very earliest signs of physical development to full sexual and physical maturation. Thus, adolescents of the same chronological age may be at quite different points in their pubertal status. Thus, from a psychosocial perspective, one must think of pubertal development as a gradual transformation in which internal states and external appearance are coordinated with social expectations and a changing self-image (Dorn, Dahl, Woodward, & Biro, 2006).

Adaptation at puberty requires an integration of biological, psychological, and social changes. A young person may be responding to noticeable physical changes, such as a height spurt or the growth of pubic hair, or less readily observable biological changes in hormone production associated with new levels of arousal and emotionality. Psychological changes may be due to chronological age as well as physical changes, since some important societal changes are linked to age rather than to pubertal status. For example, many children make a school transition into sixth or seventh grade at ages 11 or 12, leading to new status, a new sense of responsibilities, and new expectations for school performance. Some responses to puberty are cued by the way other people, including parents, teachers, siblings, and peers, respond to a child whose physical appearance has changed.

In many cultures, **rites of passage**, ceremonies that mark important transitions, occur with entry into puberty, giving the young person new roles and new status within the community. In the United States, many students consider getting their driver's license as a kind of rite of passage—a societal recognition of a new level of autonomy and responsibility. Some responses to puberty have to do with the timing of these changes—whether pubertal changes are perceived to be early, on time, or late in relation to their peers. Thus, puberty is not one event, but a *biopsychosocial* transition that takes on meaning in the context of a child's culture and community.

Sleep Loss in Adolescence

Along with many changes in physical stature and appearance, puberty brings changes in sleep patterns. Research finds that when allowed to sleep as long as they wished, adolescents would sleep about 9 hours. However, as they get older, the quality of the sleep changes, with less time spent in deep sleep, leaving adolescents more tired during the day even when they get the same amount of sleep as younger children (Campbell, Grimm, de Bied, & Feinberg, 2012). In actuality, as adolescents make the transition to high school, they get less sleep than younger children, leaving them more tired and more likely to fall asleep during the day. The majority of 17-year-olds get less than 7 hours of sleep a night (Weintraub, 2016).

The study of sleep and its relation to psychosocial outcomes is a growing field. Questions of interest include how the biological changes of puberty contribute to changes in sleep quality, sociocultural factors that contribute to sleep deprivation, and the impact of sleep habits on cognition and memory, obesity, moodiness, self-esteem, depression, risky health behaviors, and school achievement (Johnson, 2004; Malone, 2011). A combination of societal and biological factors contributes to sleep deprivation in adolescence. Middle school tends to start earlier than elementary school, and high school starts earlier still. Many adolescents are in activities that involve before-school preparation. In many communities, bus schedules determine earlier wake times for older students. Adolescents are likely to stay up late on school nights doing homework, talking with friends, using the computer, or watching television. Some adolescents have jobs at restaurants and stores where they stay until closing time.

The family environment has also been studied as a factor that influences sleep time. For younger children ages 5 through 11, parental warmth is associated with more hours of sleep during the weekdays. However, for older children in the age range 12 to 19, those adolescents whose families had stricter rules actually got more sleep (Adam, Snell, & Pendry, 2007).

In addition to these contextual factors, the natural biorhythm for adolescents shifts toward a preference for a later sleep phase. In comparison with younger children, who sleep about the same amount during the weekdays as on weekends, adolescents tend to sleep much later on the weekends (Williams, Zimmerman, & Bell, 2013). When they have a choice, as on the weekends, older adolescents stay up later at night, when they feel alert and energized, and sleep later in the morning. This shift is tied to pubertal status; those teens who are in a more advanced pubertal status show a greater tendency toward this delay and a greater difference between weekend and weekday sleep (Laberge et al., 2001).

In a longitudinal study of more than 2,000 children, the amount of sleep that children said they got on a typical school night was tracked for 3 years, in sixth, seventh, and eighth grades (Fredriksen, Rhodes, Reddy, & Way, 2004). The amount of sleep for both boys and girls declined from sixth to eighth grade. In the sixth grade, children who got fewer hours of sleep also had lower self-esteem, lower grades, and more depressive symptoms. Those students who experienced the greatest decline in hours of sleep over the 3 years also showed greater increases in depressive symptoms and lower self-esteem by eighth grade. Other national studies

support the association between insufficient sleep and a range of risky health behaviors, lack of physical activity, and obesity (McKnight-Eily et al., 2011).

Increasing school start time to 8:30 a.m. or later has been shown to have a benefit. In a study of over 9,000 students in eight public high schools, researchers found the following benefits: better attendance and less tardiness, fewer students falling asleep during class, better academic performance in classes and on state and national achievement tests, and fewer teens involved in car crashes (Wahlstrom et al., 2014; Weintraub, 2016). What is more, students and teachers report that with a later start time comes a change in atmosphere in classrooms and in the school—less moodiness, fewer conflicts, more enthusiastic class participation, which mean happier teachers as well as students. Despite many sources of resistance to a later start time, a number of schools around the country have shifted their schedules and are reporting noticeable benefits. To learn more visit the advocacy website Start Schools Later at http://www.startschoollater.net/success-stories.html.

Critical Thinking Questions

1. Analyze how biological maturation and the social environment interact to alter the amount of sleep adolescents get.
2. Evaluate the implications of not getting enough sleep for adolescents' academic and social life.
3. Hypothesize about how learning and academic performance are influenced by sleep. What might be happening while a person sleeps that contributes to learning?

The degree to which one's body matches the socially valued body build of the culture influences social acceptance by peers and adults. This match between body shape and cultural values also influences the future course of psychosocial development. The European American culture gives self-esteem advantages to muscular, well-developed boys and petite, shapely girls. In contrast, it detracts from the self-esteem of thin, gangly boys, underdeveloped girls, and overweight boys and girls. Changes in body size and shape at puberty can bring advantages or disadvantages, depending on the context (see the case study on Simone Biles).

Simone Biles was born on March 14, 1997, in Columbus, Ohio. Her mother struggled with alcohol and drug abuse, so at the age of three, she and her little sister went to live with their grandparents, Nellie and Ron Biles, whom she considers her mom and dad. They live in Spring, Texas.

At the age of 6, Simone was on a field trip with her childcare program. They visited a gym where she watched students learning gymnastics. She began to imitate their moves, and the coach was so impressed that she wrote Simone's parents encouraging them to enroll her in their program. From that point on, she was devoted to gymnastics.

When she graduated from eighth grade, Simone made the decision to be homeschooled so that she could maintain her rigorous workout schedule. Now she devotes 30 hours a week to training and practice.

Simone is a tough, serious, determined athlete. Her mother says she has been a resilient survivor who took control of her life, even at a very young age. At 4'9" she is a powerful and vivacious competitor. She attributes much of her determination to her mother: "She always told me that although I am small, that doesn't limit my power or define me. For me, I don't think about size—I focus more on being powerful and confident" (Wallace, 2016).

In 2013, at the age of 16, Simone was the world all-around, floor exercise, and vault champion. She was named the 2014 Women's Sports Foundation's individual Sportswoman of the Year. She has won 10 world gold medals, the most in women's gymnastics history. In 2016, as a member of the U.S. Women's Olympic Gymnastics Team, she won four individual gold medals and one bronze medal (usagym.org, 2016).

But her mother, Nellie, says despite the championships, fans, requests for endorsements, and celebrity status, "at home, she's just a teenager who requested a belly ring after her first world title in 2013. [She's] the daughter whose chores include feeding the family's four dogs. The girl who better be at her seat for Sunday dinner regardless of whatever time zone she may have been in the day before" (Graves, 2015).

If you are interested in seeing Simone Biles in action, visit the YouTube videos of her floor exercises at the 2016 Pacific Rim championship competition and the Rio Olympic Games.

CASE ANALYSIS Using What You Know

1. Explain how the case illustrates the interactions among the biological, psychological, and societal systems in supporting unusual ability.

2. Apply what you know about physical development at puberty to the training of a gymnast from childhood into early adolescence. How might this training promote athletic ability and physical health? How might such training create health risks for adolescent girls?

3. You might think of Simone Biles as resilient. How do her personal characteristics and her support system contribute to her ability to thrive?

4. Think about Simone's decision to be home schooled for high school so she could devote herself more intensively to gymnastics training. What factors should a family take into account when determining whether to encourage a young person to follow an alternative educational path in order to pursue a special talent or ability?

Signposts of Puberty for Girls

The following changes are part of the normal pubertal transition for girls. The timing and sequence of these changes are variable, so any chart or table you may encounter about pubertal sequences should be viewed with caution. In general, if none of these signs of puberty are observed by age 13, girls are advised to see a pediatrician (HealthyChildren.org, 2015).

Breast Development. Breast development is typically the first of the secondary sex characteristics to be observed. Recent studies find that the average first sign of breast development (often referred to as "breast buds") is age 8.8 for African American girls, 9.3 for Hispanic girls, and 9.7 for Anglo, non-Hispanic girls (Herman-Geddes, 2013). Generally it takes from 3 to 5 years for breasts to reach their adult size and shape. The rate at which breasts mature and reach adult size and shape varies greatly from one girl to the next. The age at which breast development begins is not related to their adult size (Center for Young Women's Health, 2016).

Pubic Hair. Pubic hair begins to grow shortly after the beginning of breast development, around the age of 8 to 10. For some girls, pubic hair growth precedes breast development. Pubic hair

Olympic champion Simone Biles performing on the balance beam. At 4 foot 9 inches, she dominates her spo

first appears right around the genital area and then spreads to form an inverted triangle.

Growth Spurt. The growth spurt, including an increase in the rate of growth in height, weight gain, changes in muscle mass, and changes in the distribution of body fat, typically begins about 1 year after the start of puberty. Girls may grow an average of 3.5 inches a year, reaching their adult height at around age 14 or 15. As a result of these changes, a girl's body typically changes to the "hourglass" shape with curves at the breast, hips, and bottom.

Menarche. The first menstrual period usually occurs about 1 ½ to 2 years after the beginning of puberty. A national study reported that the average age at menarche was 11.5 for African American girls and 12.1 for non-Hispanic Anglo girls (Herman-Geddes, 2013). Menarche is often irregular at first, with cycles ranging from 24 to 45 days. After a few years, the cycles become shorter and more regular. Early cycles may occur without ovulation, but the earlier the onset of menarche, the more likely the cycles will include ovulation (American Academy of Pediatrics, 2006). Many young girls wonder how soon they might be able to get pregnant once they begin to menstruate. The answer to this question is not entirely known and differs from one girl to the next.

Underarm Hair, Increased Oil and Sweat Gland Production. Underarm hair appears about 2 years after the growth of pubic hair. At about the same time there is an increase in oil and sweat gland production resulting in a new probability of acne.

Reactions to Breast Development and Menarche

For girls, two of the most noticeable events of puberty are the development of breast buds and the onset of the menstrual cycle (menarche). The trend toward earlier breast development has parents and mental health experts concerned about the compression of childhood. Eight-year-old girls with breasts are still emotionally and cognitively like their undeveloped 8-year-old peers. Their physical development may result in new expectations for more mature behavior and new sexualized attention from older boys.

Menarche is a comparatively late event in a girl's pubertal development. Breast development and the growth of pubic hair are earlier evidence of pubertal growth and may provide the signal that a conversation about menarche is in order. Although most girls are prepared by their mothers for menstruation, the topic is often handled as a matter of hygiene rather than as a sexual transition. Many girls do not understand the relation of menstruation to reproduction. They simply accept their monthly periods as another sign of their femininity. The process of learning about menarche may be somewhat more anxiety producing for girls who are not living with their mothers or with a female caregiver. In a qualitative study of girls who were living without their mothers, the girls were often embarrassed to ask questions of their fathers and experienced more distress around this issue if they did not have access to a woman who could answer their questions (Kalman, 2003). This has special implications for the health of girls who may be separated from their mothers due to maternal death, war, or imprisonment.

Most girls seem to react to menstruation with a mix of positive and negative feelings. The positive feelings reflect their pride in maturing and the confirmation of their womanliness. The negative feelings reflect the inconvenience, unpleasant symptoms, and the possible embarrassment of menstruation (Brooks-Gunn & Reiter, 1990). Girls rarely tell their male peers or their fathers about the onset of menarche, but they do discuss it with their female friends and their mothers. Negative feelings are especially likely if a girl matures early, at age 9 or 10. In a retrospective study involving more than 1,500 Chinese American junior high school girls, students were asked about their knowledge and attitudes about menarche and their emotional responses to their first menstruation. Although 85 percent reported feeling annoyed and embarrassed by their first menstruation, about 66 percent also reported positive feelings, especially feeling more grown up. The more adequate their preparation for menarche and the more they saw menarche as a natural, healthy event, the more positive were their emotional responses (Tang, Yeung, & Lee, 2003).

Concerns About Obesity

The greatest concern that adolescent girls express about their bodies is the perception that they are too fat. This concern about **obesity** is that it results in peer rejection from both boys and girls.

Lisa is a seventh grader who attends a White, upper-middle-class middle school. She is clearly overweight. As a newcomer to her school, she found that her weight was the major factor in determining her social and academic experiences.

> At first I thought if I got good grades and tried to fit in it wouldn't matter how I looked. But I still got teased; it didn't make a difference. All the good things about me—like that I was smart—it was just, "You don't fit. You don't look good. You're fat." I felt like I was doing all the good things for no reason. So I just said, "Fine, if it's going to be that way, then I don't care." And I don't try at all anymore. I don't care about school. (Orenstein, 2000, pp. 100–101)

In a review of research on body dissatisfaction and eating disorders, Stice and Shaw (2002) found support for a relationship between body image disturbances and eating disorders (see FIGURE 9.1 ▶). Three factors appear to contribute to **body dissatisfaction** among adolescent girls: social pressures to be thin, an internalized thin ideal body type, and higher than average body mass. Those girls who have higher body dissatisfaction are likely to start dieting and also to experience negative emotional states, especially depression. In a longitudinal study of adolescents in grades 7 through 12, symptoms of depression predicted obesity 1 year later. The link between depression and obesity may be due to a decrease in physical activity, or for some, an increase in hunger eating and weight gain (Goodman & Whitaker, 2002; Needham Epel, Adler, & Kiefe, 2010). The combination of these factors can lead to future eating pathologies. In an attempt to attain a thin ideal and to reduce negative feelings about themselves, many early adolescent girls begin a process of strict and often faddish dieting. This strategy is ill-timed, because their bodies require well-balanced diets and increased caloric intake during the period of rapid growth (Stice & Shaw, 2004).

FIGURE 9.1 ▶ THE RELATIONSHIP OF BODY IMAGE TO EATING DISTURBANCES
Source: Based on Stice and Shaw, 2002.

Concern about being overweight is linked to the day-to-day experiences girls have with peers at school. Girls who face peer teasing about their body and physical appearance are likely to experience heightened body dissatisfaction and declines in their global feelings of self-worth (Jones & Newman, 2009). Girls who are overweight are more likely to try to lose weight if other girls at their school of similar body type are also trying to lose weight. Girls who are underweight are also more likely to try to lose weight if other underweight girls at their school are trying to lose weight. Even though girls are aware of a broad, cultural ideal about thinness, their own body satisfaction and behavior regarding weight control or weight loss are influenced by what other girls in their immediate social world say and do (Mueller, Pearson, Muller, Frank, & Turner, 2010).

For girls, one of the compounding factors in obesity is that they tend to reduce their activity level with age (Finne, Bucksch, & Lampert, 2011). One longitudinal study monitored common physical activities for children from grades 3 through 10. During grades 6 through 8, those girls who were more advanced in their pubertal status were less active than the girls who were less physically mature (Bradley, McMurray, Harrell, & Deng, 2000).

Signposts of Puberty for Boys

The following changes are part of the normal pubertal transition for boys. As with girls, the timing and sequence of these changes are variable, so any chart or table you may encounter about pubertal sequences should be viewed with caution. In general, if none of these signs of puberty are observed by age 14, boys are advised to see a pediatrician (HealthyChildren.org, 2015).

Testicles and Scrotal Sac. The first signpost of pubertal development for boys is usually an increase in the size of the testicles. The skin of the scrotum is likely to show some reddening and a rougher texture. Evidence from a sample of over 4,000 boys found that on average, the first signs of this pubertal development occurred at ages 9.1 for African American boys, 10.04 for Hispanic boys, and 10.14 for non-Hispanic Anglo boys (Herman-Giddens et al., 2012). The testes produce sperm and testosterone.

Pubic Hair. Pubic hair begins to grow about 1 ¼ years after the start of testicular growth (Herman-Giddens et al., 2012).

Growth Spurt. The growth spurt, which includes changes in height, weight, muscle mass, and body shape, begins about 2 years after the start of puberty and may continue for 2 to 5 years. Most boys stop growing between the ages of 17 and 19, although some continue to grow into their 20s. Growth does not take place at the same rate in all parts of the body. One particular discrepancy is the time lag between the height spurt and the increase in muscle strength. The peak increase in muscle strength usually occurs about 12 to 14 months after the peak height spurt (Brierley, 1993). Eventually, most boys' bodies change to acquire an inverted triangular shape—wider at the shoulders and narrower at the waist and hips.

Growth of the Penis. About 1 year after the testicles begin to enlarge, the penis starts to grow. As the penis grows, boys begin to experience erections. About a year after the penis starts to grow, most boys experience an ejaculation of semen. The semen may not carry sperm right away, but by the time the testes are fully grown, sperm are produced and the boy is fertile.

Change in Voice. At the same time as the penis is growing, a boy's voice is changing. This is caused by the increased size and thickening of the larynx. This is usually accompanied by some cracking or squeaking in the early phase, followed by a deepening in tone.

Facial and Underarm Hair. Body and facial hair begin to be noticeable about 2 years after the beginning growth of pubic hair.

Oil and Sweat Production. The production of oil and sweat glands increases at about the same time as the growth of underarm hair. This can result in acne if the oil clogs skin pores.

Boys' Reactions to the Physical Changes of Puberty

Boys generally welcome the changes involving increased height and muscle mass that bring them closer to adult maturity. Nonetheless, some ambivalence is likely as boys experience the transitions of puberty. On the one hand, a mature physique usually brings well-developed physical skills that are highly valued by peers and adults alike. On the other hand, the period of rapid growth may leave a boy feeling awkward and uncoordinated for a time. For boys, body image dissatisfaction is typically associated with frustration about not looking muscular, strong, or handsome—a concern that is magnified by the lag between the height spurt and the increase in muscle mass (Cohane & Pope, 2000). In a national survey of British teens, dissatisfaction with body image was the third most common worry for boys. Boys expressed concern about being too fat or not attractive enough; a third had been on a diet to improve their body image (Espinoza, 2016).

Spermarche, the production and release of sperm that can be detected in a boy's urine, occurs rather late in the pubertal process

(Dorn et al., 2006). Boys are generally not well prepared by their parents with information on the maturation of their reproductive organs. Specifically, they are not taught about the pattern of gradual genital changes that are likely to occur or about spontaneous ejaculation and may be surprised, scared, or embarrassed by it. The sexual connotation of the event may make it difficult for boys to seek an explanation from their parents. They are left to gain information from friends, or to go online for medical opinions and peer reactions (KidsHealth.org, 2013). For many boys, spontaneous ejaculation provides an important clue to the way in which physical adult sexuality and reproduction are accomplished. The pleasure of the ejaculation and the positive value of the new information that it provides are counterbalanced by a mild anxiety.

A third area of physical development that has psychological and social meaning for boys is the development of secondary sex characteristics, particularly the growth of facial and body hair. In many societies, the equipment and ritual behaviors associated with shaving are closely linked to the masculine gender role. Most boys are eager to express their identification with this role, and will use the slightest evidence of facial hair as an excuse to take razor in hand. The ritual of shaving not only provides some affirmation of the boy's masculinity, but it also allows him an acceptable outlet for his narcissism. As he shaves, it is legitimate for him to gaze at and admire his changing image. In some societies, the ability to grow a mustache or a beard is a sign of one's masculinity. In these cultures, boys cultivate and admire their mustaches or beards as evidence of their enhanced male status. See Table 9.1 for a summary of primary and secondary sex characteristics in boys and girls.

Cultural Contexts of Puberty

The way adolescents react to the physical changes of puberty depends in part on the cultural context (Buzney & DeCaro, 2012). For example, studies of Mexican youth find that girls become somewhat more depressed as they go through puberty, whereas boys experience an improved sense of body image and well-being (Benjet & Hernandez-Guzman, 2002). These gender differences may reflect the greater status and new responsibilities given to male children in Mexican culture, and the new restrictions that apply to female children as they enter puberty in order to protect their chastity.

A report on the reactions of female students in India who were following an undergraduate medical curriculum found that most of these young women said that they were ill prepared for their menarche. About half reported that their emotional reaction to their initial menstruation was panic. The cultural attitude toward menstruation among Indian women is typically one of secrecy and uncleanliness. The cultural transmission of these attitudes from mothers to daughters means that mothers generally try to keep their menstrual experiences hidden and are reluctant to talk to their daughters about it. As a result, menstruation remains a source of anxiety and embarrassment for many (Bharatwaj, 2014).

In another cultural comparison, several studies comparing African American and European American adolescent girls were summarized. In general, African American adolescent girls are more satisfied with their body image and less inclined toward eating disorders than European American girls. Furthermore, early pubertal onset and weight increases were not particularly strong predictors of negative body image and depression among African

Table 9.1	The Development of Primary and Secondary Sex Characteristics for Girls and Boys	
Girls	**Average Age of Occurrence**	**Boys**
Onset of height spurt	10–11	**Growth of testes**
Initial breast development	11	Development of pubic hair
Increased activity of oil and sweat glands (acne can result from clogged glands)	11–12	Increased activity of oil and sweat glands (acne can result from clogged glands)
Development of pubic hair	12	**Growth of penis**
Onset of menarche (age range is 9–17)	12–13	Onset of height spurt
Earliest normal pregnancy	14	Deepening of the voice
Completion of breast development (age range is 13–18)	15–16	**Production of mature spermatozoa**
		Nocturnal emissions
		Growth of underarm and facial hair
Maturation of skeletal system	17–18	Maturation of skeletal system
		Development of chest hair

Note: Primary sex characteristics are in boldface type.

The **primary sex characteristics** relate to the development of genitalia and reproductive organs. Secondary sex characteristics are other physical changes associated with puberty, such as body hair or breast development.

Source: Adapted from Turner and Rubinson, 1993.

This 15-year-old is getting ready for school. Shaving is now added to his regular morning preparations. Shaving is a symbol of a boy's transition into adolescence and continues to be an element of a young man's masculine identity throughout young adulthood.

American girls, as they are for European American girls (Franko & Streigel-Moore, 2002).

The Secular Growth Trend

A **secular growth trend** is a change over time in the average age at which physical maturation takes place (Godina, 2009). All over the world, changes in hygiene, nutrition, and health care have contributed to an earlier entry into puberty and earlier growth spurt over the past century (Richter, 2006). In the United States, children ages 10 to 14 increased in height by an average of 2 to 3 centimeters every decade from 1900 to 1960. Adult height is not necessarily greater due to this increase; it is simply attained at an earlier age.

Other evidence of a secular trend is the decrease in age for the onset of puberty, including an earlier age for the beginning of breast development in girls and for testicular development for boys (Herman-Geddes, 2013). In addition, average age at menarche has declined. Data reported by Tanner (1990) showed a decrease in the average age at menarche from the 1950s (13.5 to 14 years) to the 1970s (12.5 to 13 years). At present, the mean age at menarche in the United States is 12.1 for white, non-Hispanic girls and 11.2 for African American girls (Buttke, Sircar, & Martin, 2012).

Age at menarche varies among countries and even among socioeconomic groups within a country. Evidence from two rural counties in China illustrates the impact of improved living standards on age at menarche. In a survey of over 12,000 females, age at menarche decreased from an average of 16.5 to 13.7 over an approximate 40-year interval. Improvements were associated with a variety of environmental conditions including reduced pesticide exposure before age at menarche, the source of drinking water,

the amount of physical labor the girls were required to perform, and improved nutrition (Graham, Larsen, & Xu, 1999). Researchers in Italy report that Italian girls reach menarche about a quarter year earlier than their mothers' generation. A number of factors were associated with age at menarche in the Italian sample including the mother's menarcheal age, the region where the parents were born, family size, and the girl's body mass index (Rigon et al., 2010).

What is the relevance of the secular trend for understanding the development of contemporary adolescents in post-industrialized societies? Modern adolescents experience a mismatch between the biological and the societal systems as they make their transition from childhood to adulthood. Reproductive capacity and physical adult stature occur at a younger age than at the turn of the 20th century, but full engagement in the adult society requires more training, education, and complex preparation than in the past. Thus, adolescence is prolonged, with more time to experience the risks of unwanted pregnancy and the sense of being in a marginal social status. At the same time, many adolescents experience a longer "protected" status as students and legal minors, with delayed expectations for self-sufficiency and enactment of adult roles.

The concept of the secular trend alerts us to the importance of the psychosocial context of physical development. Because the period of reproductive capacity starts earlier than it did 50 years ago, young people must cope with special challenges in the expression and regulation of their sexual impulses. One consequence of the earlier onset of puberty is that adolescents may find themselves in potentially high-risk situations at a relatively young age, a reality that has become a major contemporary health and mental health concern (Weir, 2016).

Individual Differences in the Timing and Rate of Change

The age at onset of puberty and the rate of change in physical maturation vary. Children of the same chronological age can be at very different points in their pubertal maturation. Whereas individual differences in the onset of puberty are to be expected, **precocious puberty**, that is evidence of pubertal maturation before the age of 8 for girls or before the age of 9 for boys, may be an indication of a more serious medical problem (Boyse & Phelps, 2012).

The Impact of Pubertal Timing for Boys. Early and late maturing and the length of time it takes for a child's body to achieve adult physical and reproductive status have psychological and social consequences for both boys and girls. Research carried out in the 1950s and 1960s found that boys who matured early

Houts, Grimm, & Susman, 2011; Science Daily 2010). These early maturing boys have more hostile feelings, greater levels of anxiety and depression, more problems with drug and alcohol use, and more deviant activities and problems in school than boys who mature at a later age. The association of early maturation and heightened rates of violent and nonviolent delinquent behavior has been observed for African American, Mexican American, and European American youth (Cota-Robles, Neiss, & Rowe, 2002). In a longitudinal study of over 3,000 South African children born in the early 1990s, early maturing boys and girls were found to be more involved in high-risk behaviors such as smoking, experimenting with drugs, and sexual behavior than their less physically mature age-mates (Richter, 2006).

By grade 8, the physical diversity of the peer group is quite noticeable. Differences in height, weight, and body shape have implications for popularity, leadership, athletic success, and self-confidence.

experienced positive consequences, including greater opportunities for leadership and social status, and as a result, they had higher self-esteem (Clausen, 1975; Mussen & Jones, 1957). A similar advantage for early maturation for fifth- and sixth-grade boys was reported in the early 1990s. The boys who were more physically mature described more positive daily emotions, better attention, and feelings of being strong (Richards & Larson, 1993). In contrast to the early maturing boys, late maturing boys express greater body dissatisfaction, especially at the start of high school (de Guzman & Nishina, 2014). In a comparison of early maturing girls and boys, the early maturing boys reported less stress in opposite-sex relationships than the girls and less depression associated with these early other-sex relationships (Llewelyn, Rudolph, & Roisman, 2012).

Several explanations have been offered to account for the advantages of early maturing for boys. Early maturing boys are likely to be given increased responsibility by their parents and teachers. They are generally more satisfied with their bodies, feel more positive about being boys, and are likely to be more involved in school activities by the 10th grade than are late-maturing boys. Early maturing boys are likely to have more advantages in competitive sports, especially those that rely on height and muscle strength, and are likely to have advantages in peer popularity. In contrast, boys who mature later than their age-mates may experience psychological stress and develop a negative self-image. Late-maturing boys are treated as if they were younger than they really are. They may become isolated from their peers or behave in a silly, childish manner to gain attention.

In contrast to this picture of psychological and social advantages, other research tells a somewhat different story of the consequences of early maturing for boys, especially those who mature in grade 7 or before. Boys who experience early puberty are at greatest risk for externalizing problems (Marceau, Ram,

How can we account for these differences? Is early maturing a benefit or a risk for boys? Explanations for the impact of early maturation for boys vary. One explanation is that we are looking at a cohort effect. Maturing early in the 1950s may have been a more positive experience, whereas maturing early in the 1990s may expose adolescent boys to more stressors. Another explanation is that in today's society, physical maturation at age 12 and earlier converges with other stressful life events, especially school transitions, disruption of the peer network, more challenging expectations for school performance, and the related risk of failure. More stressful life events coupled with the pubertal transition increase uncertainty and may leave boys feeling out of control. The combination of heightened stress reactivity during early puberty and the possible exposure to environmental stressors such as peer violence, school demands, or harsh parenting alter the brain's response to stress-related hormones and increase the boy's anxiety and depression (Holder & Blaustein, 2014).

A third explanation is that boys who mature early have not had time to fully master the tasks of the middle childhood period. This explanation fits especially well for the studies that consider boys who experience puberty both early and quickly. With an early height spurt and a more mature physical appearance, they may be accelerated into situations where they are faced with expectations for a level of self-control, decision making, and leadership for which they are not prepared. They may be likely to spend time in the company of older boys who are also involved in more risky behaviors (Ge, Conger, & Elder, 2001; Ge & Natsuaki, 2009).

These different views of the impact of early maturing may all be correct. For example, it may be true that early maturing boys do experience greater opportunities for leadership and social status. The advantages of an earlier height spurt and related increases in muscle mass and endurance can make a significant difference as boys engage in athletic competitions with their age-mates (Gladwell, 2008). At the same time, because they look older, they may begin to engage in some of the high-risk behaviors of slightly older boys.

The Impact of Pubertal Timing for Girls. The literature on the effect of pubertal timing for girls is more consistent in finding that early pubertal onset is a source of stress (Joinson et al., 2012; Marceau et al., 2011; Weingarden & Renshaw, 2012). Because pubertal changes occur earlier for most girls than for boys, the early maturing girl stands out among all her male and female age-mates. Early onset of breast development is associated with a new surge of gonadal hormones, which may create heightened emotions of depression, self-consciousness, and anxiety (Peper & Dahl, 2013). Early maturing girls are less likely to have been prepared for the onset of menstruation, and they are less likely to have close friends with whom they can discuss it. Early pubertal maturation may result in feelings of social isolation and social anxiety for girls (Blumenthal et al., 2011). Early maturing girls experience higher levels of conflict with their parents and are more likely to report depression and anxiety (Wierson, Long, & Forehand, 1993; Winer, Parent, Forehand, & Breslend, 2016). Early maturing girls are less likely to be physically active than their age mates, are more dissatisfied with their physical appearance, and are especially vulnerable to low self-esteem (Cumming et al., 2012; Williams & Currie, 2000).

There is some evidence that early maturing girls earn lower grades and lower scores on academic achievement tests. They are also more likely to be identified as having behavior problems in school. Early maturing girls start dating earlier and perceive themselves as more popular with boys than do late maturing girls. Some studies report that early maturing girls are more likely to engage in high-risk, promiscuous sexual behavior. They are also more likely to be exposed to sexual harassment (Skoog & Ozdemir, 2016). Taken by itself, the timing of the transition to puberty is not a strong predictor of a girl's emotional well-being. Rather, this timing interacts with other contextual factors, including school transition, family conflict, peer acceptance, and unwanted sexual advances, to influence how girls construct the meaning of this physical transition (Booth, Johnson, Granger, Crouter, & McHale, 2003; Skoog, 2013).

Many books and websites emphasize the important role for parents in talking to their children about their physical, psychological, and social experiences as they go through puberty. Given the evidence about the hereditary influences on pubertal timing, it could be very helpful for parents to talk to their children about what it was like when they experienced these transitions. It is also important to be proactive, recognizing the early signs of puberty that may arise at ages 8 to 10, to help young people feel prepared for subsequent changes.

However, there are important limitations to this advice. First, not all children arrive at puberty in the context of a warm, sensitive parent–child relationship. Some children have been exposed to harsh or neglectful parenting in toddlerhood and early childhood, thus leaving them more vulnerable or reactive to the stressors of puberty. For these children, the opportunity to find support and encouragement in conversations with parents is unlikely; they need to have access to other supportive adults who can help them navigate this important transition. Second, as puberty progresses, parent support may not have the stress-buffering benefits that it had at earlier ages (Hostinar, 2015). There may be important benefits to forming supportive peer relationships and adult mentor relationships that can provide reassurance and positive regard while helping to strengthen adolescents' coping strategies during times of stress and uncertainty.

Romantic and Sexual Relationships

OBJECTIVE 2 Summarize the development of romantic and sexual relationships, and evaluate the factors that influence the transition to first intercourse, the formation of a sexual orientation, and pregnancy and parenthood in early adolescence.

During adolescence, romantic relationships, sexual fantasies, and sexual behaviors increase, partly as a result of biological changes and partly as a result of social, cultural, and historical contexts. Early in puberty, the HPG axis is reactivated leading to increases in the production of gonadal hormones, testosterone, and estradiol (a form of estrogen). The adrenal gland generates increases in DHEA and other hormones linked to the growth of pubic hair, body odor, acne, and pre-pubertal growth (Peper & Dahl, 2013; Shirtcliff, Dahl, & Pollack, 2009). The amount of these hormones that is absorbed in the blood reaches a peak between the ages of 10 and 12—a time when both boys and girls begin to be aware of sexual feelings toward others (Herdt & McClintock, 2000). Whereas the early onset of these feelings may be triggered by biological factors, the way they are expressed depends largely on socialization and cultural factors.

The Transition into Sexualized Relationships

Most young people are involved in a variety of romantic relationships during adolescence, including dating, feelings of tenderness and love, and deepening commitments (Temple-Smith, Moore, & Rosenthal, 2016). Components of both gender identity and sexual orientation, which have implications for the young person's motivation and opportunities for sexualized relationships, are formulated during this period of life. Some adolescents are reticent about sexual behavior. Others are sexually permissive and regularly active in sex play, from petting to intercourse. The manner in which early adolescents think about sexual relationships varies. Some are preoccupied by thoughts of very romantic, idealized relationships. They can become infatuated with rock stars, athletes, movie stars, or other sex symbols. Some have crushes on boys or girls in their school or neighborhood, and still others have obsessions with sexual material but do not have any tender or caring relationships with peers.

Sexual desire can be thought of as having at least two faces: sexual arousal and sexual motivation. Sexual arousal refers to the way a person's body and thoughts are stimulated by sexual fantasies, images, and reactions to others. Sexual motivation refers to a person's interest in initiating sexual behaviors (Diamond &

Developmental Tasks　　**327**

Savin-Williams, 2009). Adolescents do not arrive at puberty as complete novices in sexual desire. According to psychoanalytic theory, children are sexual beings from infancy, using and exploring their bodies in order to experience physical pleasures. Children experience erotic activity before puberty, including self-stimulation, viewing sexually explicit media, or experimenting with sexual role-playing with peers. Early adolescents' sexual interests reflect a system that has been running at a low level and is now energized by new hormonal levels, maturing sexual features, and changing cultural views about the acceptability of sexual behavior. As a result, adolescents begin to think of themselves as sexual, develop scripts and schemes for how to act sexually with others, and begin to formulate ideas about the qualities of people whom they find sexually attractive.

Dating. Pubertal changes may increase a young person's interest in sexual ideation and arousal, but the timing and rituals or *script* of dating depend on the norms of the peer group and the community. Most teens today do not use the term "dating." They use expressions like "seeing someone," "getting together," or "going with" someone. Regardless of the way they talk about it, young people learn the art of flirtation, practice how to approach and how to coyly refuse, and learn the rules of engagement between the sexes, which vary from culture to culture and from cohort to cohort. The hallways of a high school may not seem very romantic, but feelings of affection can blossom in the most unexpected places.

Contemporary youth describe a diversity of relationships that may involve sexual activity. Participation in mixed-sex friendship groups typically provides the context for the formation of romantic pairing that becomes more exclusive and less group oriented over time (Connolly, Craig, Goldberg, & Pepler, 2004; Dunphy, 1963). Most sexual activity occurs in the context of close relationships. However, teens also describe having sexual experiences in the context of noncommitted relationships with ex-boyfriends or

ex-girlfriends, people they have just met ("hooking up"), friends or acquaintances ("friends with benefits"), and people they just date every once in a while (Connolly & McIsaac, 2011). Both texting and "sexting" are ways that teens use electronic media to initiate and expand their sexualized or romantic feelings. Involvement in romantic relationships increases over the middle school and high school years, and the quality of these relationships becomes increasingly intimate.

One approach to understanding the nature of adolescent dating is to see this social behavior as meeting one or more central life goals, especially identity, intimacy, status, and sexuality (Kelly, Zimmer-Gembeck, & Boislard, 2012). Identity goals reflect a need for self-acceptance, self-assurance, and the ability to express and maintain personal interests. Teens use the concept of "respect" to emphasize the importance of identity in a relationship. Intimacy refers to the desired for committed, exclusive relationships that support emotional closeness, disclosure, and security. Status focuses on social validation, social striving, and support for a desirable group identity. Teens know that their peers are making judgments about their relationships; their choice of a partner can be a source of pride or embarrassment in the peer context. Sex may refer to opportunities to satisfy sexual urges, to enjoy sexual pleasure, or to experience various forms of sexual exploration and experimentation. Satisfaction in dating can be evaluated by how well the relationship allows a young person to achieve each of these goals.

First Intercourse. The sexual transition at first intercourse may take place in very different contexts. It may be a planned event or an unplanned impulse, often combined with alcohol use or a drug high. The sexual encounter may be viewed as a marker of independence or as an act of rebellion against and defiance of the family. It may take place in the context of an ongoing close relationship or as part of a casual encounter. Usually, the earlier the transition into sexual activity and intercourse, the more likely the act is to be part of a profile of high-risk behaviors, including alcohol use, drug use, and delinquent activity. For girls 14 years old and younger, 27 percent said that they did not want their first sexual experience. For many of these young teens, their first sexual experience was a result of being sexually assaulted. The later the transition, the more likely it is to be seen as a marker of the transition into adulthood or as a planned aspect of the deepening commitment to an ongoing relationship (Terry-Humen, Manlove, & Cottingham, 2006).

A national survey of students in grades 9 through 12 conducted in 2013 reported that 47 percent of students surveyed had had sexual intercourse. The prevalence of sexual intercourse increased with grade level, such that by 12th grade, 64 percent were sexually experienced, and 49 percent were currently sexually active. Eleventh grade seems to be the tipping point, by which time more than half the students (51 percent) are sexually experienced (Kann et al., 2014).

Boys report being sexually active at younger ages than girls. Boys are aware of sexual urges and

Romance begins to stir in the halls of the high school.

Hero Images/Superstock

interests at a younger age than girls; they report more frequent sexual arousal than girls; and boys report that their sexual feelings are more distracting than girls report (Diamond & Savin-Williams, 2009). Eight percent of boys and 3 percent of girls reported having sexual intercourse before age 13. Among ninth graders, 9 percent of boys and 4 percent of girls said they had already had sex with four or more partners; by 12th grade this had increased to 21 percent of girls and 26 percent of boys (Kann et al., 2014).

Roughly one third of U.S. adolescents have not had sexual intercourse by 12th grade. This does not mean that they are sexually inexperienced. In a study of 11- and 12-year-old girls, 46 percent of 12-year-old girls had hugged a boy. Other intimate behaviors that were reported at this age were spending time alone with a boy or girl, holding hands, and kissing (Hipwell, Keenan, Loeber, & Battista, 2010). It is not uncommon for teens to experience oral sex, even if they have not had sexual intercourse. Among 15 to 19 year olds, close to 50 percent of males and females have had oral sex (Copen, Changra, & Martinez, 2012).

There are at least five reasons why data regarding entry into sexual activity and age at first intercourse must be interpreted with caution (Diamond & Savin-Williams, 2009). First, teens who are uncomfortable or whose parents are uncomfortable participating in research on this topic will not be included. Second, studies rarely include questions about same-sex sexual activity that might be comparable to first intercourse. Third, the reporting is retrospective (i.e., asking adolescents to think back to when they first engaged in sexual activities) and thus is vulnerable to inconsistencies and memory errors. Fourth, cultural and social contexts may influence reporting. It may be socially desirable to exaggerate one's sexual experiences in some communities and socially responsible to conceal one's sexual experience in others. Finally, most studies focus on individual reports and do not gather data to confirm reported sexual experiences by participating partners.

Factors Affecting the Initiation of Sexual Intercourse

The unfolding of sexual behavior in adolescence includes many components such as feelings of arousal or sexual excitement, sexual fantasies, self-stimulation, awareness of a desired object, feelings about being a desirable partner, and intentions to abstain or engage in sexual activities. Although all of these aspects of sexual maturation are relevant to the eventual experiences of partnered sexual intercourse, many of them have not been documented in a systematic way (Fortenberry, 2013). In contrast, most of the research focuses on the experience of sexual intercourse, which typically occurs after many of these more private experiences arise. FIGURE 9.2 ▶ provides a useful model for thinking about factors that influence the transition to sexual intercourse in early adolescence (Udry, 1990; Udry & Billy 1987). In that model, three dimensions account for the adolescent's initiation of sexual activity: *motivation*, *social controls*, and *attractiveness*.

The first dimension, **sexual motivation**, includes the biologically organized drives associated with sexual arousal and sexual

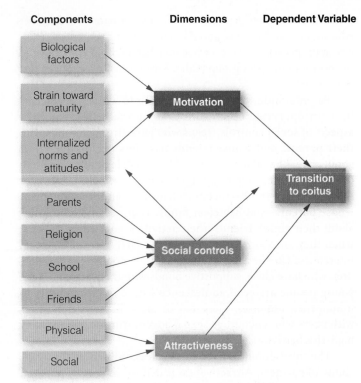

FIGURE 9.2 ▶ A MODEL OF THE TRANSITION TO FIRST COITUS IN EARLY ADOLESCENCE

Source: Adapted from Udry & Billy, 1987.

pleasure, as well as a range of social motives such as achieving new levels of intimacy in a relationship, pleasing one's partner, impressing one's peers, gaining sexual experience, or preventing conflict or dissolution by providing sexual satisfaction (Impett & Tolman, 2006). Some sexual motives can be considered approach motives in that sexual activity is viewed as a way of achieving a positive outcome, like increasing one's physical pleasure or enhancing intimacy. Some sexual motives can be considered avoidance motives if sexual activity is viewed as preventing a negative outcome, like reducing conflict in a relationship. In a study of positive sexual motives among ninth graders, females valued achieving intimacy more than males, and males valued sexual pleasure more than females. Adolescents expected that sexual experience would most likely satisfy motives for sexual pleasure, then for intimacy, and least for social status. Those ninth graders who were sexually active had greater expectations that sexual activity would result in greater intimacy in the relationship than those who were not sexually active (Ott, Millstein, Ofner, & Halpern-Felsher, 2006).

The second dimension, **social controls**, refers to the normative environment in which sexual activity is embedded. According to the model, these controls are a product of parental socialization and practices, school achievement and educational aspirations, and the attitudes and sexual experiences of friends. We have added the important influence of religious beliefs and values to the model's list of social controls.

For girls, various social controls—including parents, school achievement, friends' attitudes and behaviors, and religious values—all play an important part in predicting sexual intercourse. A girl's decision to become sexually active is influenced by her own self-esteem, her personal aspirations, her parents' values, her educational expectations, and the capacity of her parents to exercise appropriate control over her social and school activities and the norms of her peer group (Udry, Kovenock, Morris, & van den Berg, 1995).

Parental monitoring and the extent to which adolescents have unsupervised opportunities for sexual activity may be aspects of social controls. Teens who have stronger bonds with their parents and whose friends have less permissive views about sexual behavior are more likely to delay their transition into sexual intercourse (L'Engle, & Jackson, 2008). Even for those who live in low-income, chaotic neighborhoods, teens whose parents establish clear family routines and who know about their child's friends, their activities, and where they are when they are away from home have a later entry into sexual intercourse (Roche & Leventhal, 2009). In contrast to the children who have close, supportive bonds with their parents, some young people arrive at adolescence with a reduced ability to inhibit their impulses. They may be more likely to spend time with peers who encourage sexual adventuring as one of many high-risk behaviors.

The third dimension, **attractiveness**, influences the availability of partners. Attractiveness is defined in part by pubertal maturation, social acceptance or popularity, and also by the local peer environment in which one is judged to be pretty or handsome. Certain features of physical appearance, such as being overweight, or being a late maturing male may result in delayed entry into sexual experience.

Across cultures, boys typically experience a consistent message that being sexual is a valued aspect of the masculine gender identity. In contrast, girls are confronted by conflicting messages about the desirability and risks of being sexually active. These confusing messages operate to increase girls' sensitivity to the social context in which her decisions are made and are likely to delay coitus, even if they do not stifle her sexual desires. A separate reason that the link between hormonal levels and sexual debut is unclear for girls is that for many young girls their early sexual experiences were unwanted.

The Effects of Religious Beliefs on Sexual Behavior

One of the clearest cultural influences on adolescent sexual behavior is religious participation. Adolescents who frequently attend religious services and church-related activities and who value religion as an important aspect of their lives have less permissive attitudes toward premarital sex. They may believe that they should wait until after marriage to engage in sexual intercourse. However, within a religious framework the way adolescents define abstinence can vary from complete sexual denial to sexual activity that stops just short of vaginal intercourse (Uecker, Angotti, & Regenrus, 2008).

An adolescent's attitudes toward premarital sex are shaped by many factors in addition to religious beliefs. By the time young people are making independent decisions about religious participation, they also have opinions on premarital sex. Thus, those young people who have more permissive views on sex may be less likely to attend religious services and may find less satisfaction in religious participation.

As an example of how religious beliefs can affect sexual behavior, the Southern Baptist Church initiated a program that encouraged teens to make a public virginity pledge. Since 1993, more than 2.5 million youth have taken this pledge in which they vow to abstain from sex until marriage. In a study of those who participated in the program, the pledge was found to be most effective in delaying the age of first intercourse when taken by younger teens. It was also more effective for pledge takers who are a minority among their peers. Taking the pledge is then viewed as an act of independent decision making and identity commitment rather than as compliance to peer norms (Bearman & Brueckner, 2001; Martino et al., 2008).

Findings based on the National Longitudinal Study of Adolescent Health suggest that one of the hazards of taking the pledge is that when it is broken, youth are less well prepared to engage in protected sex and are therefore at risk for sexually transmitted diseases. Five years after making their pledge, 82 percent of teens denied having ever made this pledge. Those who had pledged were no different from matched non-pledgers in the percentage who had premarital sex, sexually transmitted diseases, or lifetime sexual partners (Rosenbaum, 2009).

Sexual Orientation

It is not always possible to distinguish sexual behaviors that reflect a form of experimentation and exploration from behaviors that reflect an eventual commitment to a same-sex or bisexual orientation. The language for describing a person's sexual orientation is expanding as the society becomes more aware of sexual diversity and information about sexual orientation becomes more widely available. Table 9.2 provides a brief glossary of terms that refer to alternative sexual orientations. One might assume that sexual orientation begins to take shape in early adolescence, yet research on this point suggests a more differentiated path. Many adolescents are unsure about their sexual orientation even by the end of high school, and others have known since early childhood that they do not fit the heterosexual model.

> Since childhood I felt attraction for both boys and girls, but gradually the feelings for girls went away. One day, a new guy to my school walked into class and I felt such an attraction that I simply knew. (Jordan, 17 years) (Hillier et al., 2010)

One's sexual orientation includes an awareness of sexual attraction to others, which may arise in fantasy, while watching videos or movies, observing one's peers, or as an aspect of any private thoughts. Thus, a young person may be aware of a non-traditional sexual orientation well before he or she is ready to engage in sexual activity with a partner. In the Adolescent Health survey, 13 percent of girls and 6 percent of boys reported that they had experienced same-sex attractions or same-sex relationships. However, only a subset of these youth identified as having a non-heterosexual sexual orientation. Teens who have same-sex sexual experiences may still identify as heterosexual; many teens who have self-identified as gay or lesbian have also had cross-sex

Table 9.2	A Brief Glossary of Terms and Definitions Related to Sexual Orientation
Term	**Definition**
Asexual	A person who is not interested in sex and may not experience sexual attraction, but who still has emotional bonds with others. Asexuality is not the same as celibacy or abstinence.
Bisexual	A person who is sexually and emotionally attracted to people of both sexes.
Gay	A person whose primary emotional and sexual attraction is toward people of the same sex. Commonly applied to men, although women sometimes use the term as well.
Heterosexual	A person whose primary emotional and sexual attraction is toward people of the opposite sex. Heterosexuals are sometimes called "straight."
Lesbian	A woman whose primary emotional and sexual attraction is toward other women.
Pansexual	A person whose emotional and sexual attractions are fluid and open to people of all types of sexual orientation and gender identities.
Queer	An umbrella term for anyone who identifies outside the norms of sexual or gender identity; an alternative term that resists the limitations of binary classifications.
Questioning	A term that describes a person who is in the process of exploring and discovering their sexual orientation, gender identity, and/or gender expression.

Source: Hillier, et al., 2010; PFLAG 2016b

experiences; and many who self-identify as gay or lesbian have not had sexual intercourse at all (Canadian Paediatric Society, 2008; Savin-Williams, 2005, 2006). These observations illustrate the complex process of forming a nontraditional sexual identity.

In the context of a strong heterosexual social norm in the family, community, and peer group, the idea of recognizing same-sex attractions and initiating same-sex sexual behaviors may not be enough to support a young person's decision to openly claim a minority sexual orientation. Even in the contemporary context of increasing awareness and acceptance of sexual diversity, many sexual minority youth perceive an atmosphere of rejection or hostility that inhibits their willingness to openly disclose an alternative sexual orientation (National Academies Press, 2011).

The development of a sexual identity for gay, lesbian, bisexual, and pan-sexual youth is an ongoing process which takes place in a social and historical context.

> Being pansexual is something I have always known to be true about myself. From a young age I was always aware that my attraction to people is not limited by their gender or sex, but I lacked the words to explain this. At 12 years old I was introduced to the term "bisexual" by a friend, who was attracted to both girls and boys. I finally felt as though I had a word for how I felt.
>
> As years passed, my knowledge expanded, and I discovered the many different gender identities on the spectrum. Pansexuality soon entered my vocabulary, and it has stayed with me ever since. (Kahn, 2015)

Four milestones of sexual identity development are relevant: awareness of sexual attractions; self-labeling as lesbian, gay, bisexual, pansexual, or queer; disclosure of one's sexual orientation; and sexual experiences (National Academies Press, 2011;

Savin-Williams, 1996). Self-labeling and disclosure are discussed in more detail below.

Self-Labeling. Self-labeling, applying a label such as gay, lesbian, or bisexual to oneself, may begin with experiences in early childhood when boys or girls recall feeling different from their peers. These feelings, typically captured in retrospective studies of gay or lesbian young adults, may include a general sense that they did not share the same interests as others of their same sex. Boys may recall being more sensitive than their peers or being drawn to more artistic and aesthetic interests. Girls may remember passionate, mysterious friendships in the pre-pubertal and early adolescent period (Diamond, 2000). In many instances, these feelings of being different are associated with confusion and a sense of isolation or lack of belonging. Ronan recalls his early awareness, before he was able to label his interests:

> I guess I have pretty much always been a bit queer. I liked wearing all the women's clothes in dress ups at preschool and kindergarten. In role playing games I was always female. I don't know why. I was different: I didn't like sport, I liked to read and was good academically. I've never had many male friends; the ones that mattered were always female. I think I've been a bit effeminate. Not that all gay people are like that, but I was and always felt different. (Hillier et al., 2010)

Often, at puberty, the implications of these earlier childhood experiences become more evident. A growing awareness of one's own sexual interests and fantasies, coupled with new information about the variety of sexual orientations that may exist in the peer group or community, leads to new insights about one's own sexual preferences. In some ways, this may be a shocking realization. In other ways, it may help focus and clarify feelings of uncertainty and dissociation that had been difficult for the child to understand at an earlier age. Ronan describes the clarifying experience of being sexually attracted to a male friend.

> I had a few platonic crushes on girls and would go home and masturbate over other guys. I didn't think there was anything wrong with that until grade 8 when I had my first crush on a boy. He was one of my few male friends. I had seen him with his shirt off during swimming and was attracted immediately. I realized other guys didn't feel this way, and I was different even more so than I thought. (Hillier et al., 2010)

Not all young people who eventually recognize their same-sex sexual orientation reach the point of self-labeling in adolescence. With the greater visibility, openness, and acceptance of differences in sexual orientation and the presence of gay, lesbian, and bisexual role models, it is increasingly likely that this will happen. However, some young people resist the labeling process altogether: "I don't like to pigeonhole myself as one thing or another, so *queer* works well for me" (Hillier et al., 2010).

Disclosure. Disclosure, sharing information about one's sexual orientation with others, may be a prolonged process in which young people carefully decide which individuals can be trusted with this information, or it can be a very open, obvious statement of personal identity. Reports of adolescents who are openly gay suggest that disclosure can be very stressful when it is accompanied by negative reactions from parents and friends and by acts of open hostility from school peers (Burton, Marshal, Chisolm, Sucato, & Friedman, 2013). Sexual minority youth continue to experience sexual minority specific victimization, which is associated with fears about attending school, stress-related behaviors such as smoking and binge drinking, and higher rates of depressive symptoms and suicidal thoughts (CDC 2015e; Human Rights Campaign, 2014). Anticipating the strong social censure attached to an unconventional sexual orientation, adolescents may deny or mask it by functioning as heterosexuals during early adolescence.

> I feared not being liked and being alienated. I was president of various school clubs, and once I beat up a guy for being a faggot. I was adamant that fags should be booted out of the Boy Scouts. Other kids asked me why I was so rough on them. I did not say. No one suspected me because I did sports and had several girlfriends. (Savin-Williams, 1996, p. 169)

Disclosure typically occurs first with close friends, and later, if at all, with family members. Studies of gay, lesbian, and bisexual youth suggest that parental acceptance and the ability to maintain closeness and autonomy with parents after disclosure are very important to a young person's continued identity development and well-being (Ryan, 2009). Even when disclosure is accompanied by negative reactions, it has many emotional and social advantages. By disclosing, the young person has a greater sense of authenticity and freedom. Once adolescents disclose to their friends and family, they can be more readily integrated into the gay community and find others

who will help support their emerging identity. They can direct more of their effort to the task of integrating their gender identity, sexual identity, and social relationships and figuring out how to cope with the challenges that their minority sexual orientation poses.

However, disclosure continues to be accompanied by risks in many communities. In a nationally representative sample of youth, those who self-identified as sexual minority youth were more isolated, had fewer social connections, and had lower social status in their peer network that youth who self-identified as heterosexual. For boys in particular, this degree of social isolation was a strong predictor of depression (Hatzenbuehler, McLaughlin, & Xuan, 2012). Despite growing societal awareness of the diversity of sexual orientations, sexual minority youth continue to face negative attitudes from teachers, peers, and community members; possible social rejection from family members; and difficulty finding age-appropriate, non-exploitive sexual partners. The formation of school-based support groups such as the Gay-Straight Alliance play an important role in creating a more inclusive, less threatening environment for adolescents who are questioning their sexual orientation (Heck, Flentje, & Cochran, 2011). PFLAG (Parents and Friends of Lesbians and Gays) is an advocacy group that provides education, information, and community services to support families and allies of LGBTQ youth. The Harvey Milk High School in New York was the first high school to purposefully focus on creating a safe, supportive environment for LGBTQ (lesbian, gay, bisexual, transgendered, and questioning) students. As the broader societal system becomes more open about diverse sexual orientations and practices, the process of identifying, labeling, and disclosing an alternative sexual orientation should

A group of several hundred people demonstrate in support of a new high school for lesbian and gay students in New York City. The Harvey Milk High School opened for the first day of school with 100 students. What might be some developmental outcomes of attending a LGBTQ high school?

become less stressful. For ideas and inspiration about how to bring about positive change for LGBTQ youth, check out the "It Gets Better" project, a collection of over 50,000 videos where people and groups tell their stories.

Transgender Youth

Transgender refers to gender identity, not to sexual orientation. It includes anyone whose gender identity differs from the sex assigned at birth. A transgender person may be straight, gay, lesbian, or bisexual. Although it is difficult to know for certain how many people are transgender, one estimate is that 0.3 percent of the U.S. population believes that their biological sex does not correspond to their gender identity. Transgender children are insistent that they have been labeled as the wrong sex. They are not just resisting the socialization norms for what is expected of boys and girls; they strongly feel that they are in the wrong body. By puberty, the reality of being transgender becomes clarified. In a study that followed gender dysphoric children under the age of 12, 37 percent persisted in their commitment to a transgender identity by age 15 (Russo, 2016).

Problems and Conflicts Associated with Sexuality

The sexual system is one of the most problematic components of psychosocial development for young people in the United States. Five issues are taken up: lack of a consistent approach to sexual health education, reactions to first intercourse, sexual victimization, inconsistent contraceptive use, and exposure to sexually transmitted diseases.

Sources of Sexual Health Information. Where do teens get their information about sexual health? Formal sex-education that takes place in schools is a primary source. Yet, the percentage of schools that provide education on a range of topics has declined from 2000 to 2014 (see FIGURE 9.3 ▶). The majority of teens say they have received formal instruction about HIV, other sexually transmitted infections, and how to say no to sex. But far fewer have received formal instruction about birth control, where to obtain birth control, or how to use a condom. What is more, the information about pregnancy prevention, contraception, and how to use a condom is more likely to be taught at the high school level than the middle school level. Many students are already sexually active before they have this formal sex education. And 88 percent of schools allow parents to exclude their children from sex education (Guttmacher Institute 2016b).

Parents are another important source of information about sexual health. The majority of teen girls and boys say they have talked with their parents about at least one of the topics typically covered in a course on sexual health. However, many parents acknowledge that their information about contraception and other topics is incomplete. Pediatricians and primary care physicians can provide confidential consultation about sexuality, but relatively few teens feel comfortable talking with their doctor about their sexual health. And likewise, most health care professionals don't feel comfortable talking with teens about sexual health (Guttmacher Institute 2016b).

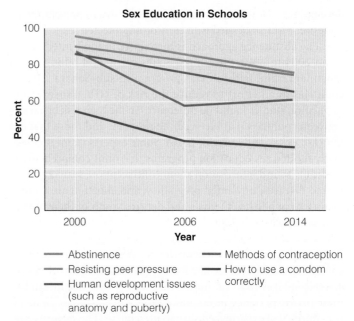

FIGURE 9.3 ▶ CONTENT OF SEXUAL HEALTH EDUCATION, 2000–2014

Source: Guttmacher Institute, (2016). American Teens' Sources of Sexual Health Education. Retrieved from the internet on May 29, 2016 at https://www.guttmacher.org/fact-sheet/facts-american-teens-sources -information-about-sex

Digital media provide another important source of information about sexual health. More than half of 7th through 12th graders say they have used the Internet to find information. Websites can offer medical information, information about sexual relationships, and interactive sites where teens can ask questions and get responses from experts as well as from other teens. The U.S. National Library of Medicine provides a website just for teens including links to information about sexuality and birth control. However, not all websites claiming to provide information about sexual health for teens are accurate or up-to-date (Guttmacher Institute 2016b).

Teens encounter information and approaches to sexual health that may be confusing or conflicting. For example, in the late 1990s, the U.S. Congress authorized funding to support programs that taught abstinence as the primary approach to sex education. These programs, referred to as Abstinence Only, were required to teach about the social, psychological, and health benefits of abstinence; the risks of sex outside of marriage; and the importance of monogamy. At the same time, national studies show that the vast majority of both men and women are not virgins when they marry. Adolescents realize that abstinence is not being practiced by most unmarried young adults, and was not practiced by their parents' generation when they were young. And imagine getting formal sex education that presents abstinence only when you are already sexually active.

Systematic evaluations of sex education programs find that comprehensive sex education based in a framework that emphasizes gender roles, empowerment, diversity, and human rights has a much greater impact on reducing unwanted pregnancy, improving contraceptive use, and reducing sexually transmitted diseases than abstinence only programs (United Nations Population Fund, 2015). Abstinence from sexual intercourse can be an effective strategy for reducing exposure to sexually transmitted diseases and is probably a good choice for teens in the early phases of pubertal development. However, it simply is not effective in preventing the undesired risks associated with early or unprotected sex.

The abstinence approach is ineffective in the United States. From 2004 to 2013, the United States spent $1.4 billion on an "abstinence and faithfulness" program in sub-Sahara African countries in an effort to reduce the risk of HIV transmission. Population studies found no differences in the high risk behaviors between countries that received the program and those that did not (Lo, Lowe, & Bendavid, 2016). Some experts claim that federally funded sex education programs that omit comprehensive, medically sound information about contraception, sexually transmitted diseases, unwanted pregnancy, and abortion are contradictory to public health goals and deprive youth of their human rights (Santelli et al., 2006).

Reactions to First Intercourse.
What is the first experience of sexual intercourse like for teens? A national survey of over 4,500 teens ages 15 to 19 showed that slightly over one fourth had their first experience intercourse experience; by ages 18 to 19, two-thirds had experienced sexual intercourse. The majority said their first experience was with someone they were "going steady" with (70 percent for females; 56 percent for males), but another significant group (16 percent of females and 28 percent of males) said they had intercourse the first time with someone they just met (Martinez, Copen, & Abma, 2011).

When college students were asked to reflect back on their first experience, about one fourth expressed regret, which was more likely among women than among men. Women who were young, age 15 or under, are more likely than older teens to feel bad or used, often because the first experience was with an older male who was not really committed to the girl. Those who had a first sexual experience while under the influence of alcohol or drugs were also more likely to express regret (Reissing, Andruff, & Wentland, 2011). Moreover, more than twice as many men than women described their first experience as physically satisfying (65 percent of men versus 25 percent of women). Fewer women than men described their first experience as emotionally or psychologically satisfying (38 percent of women versus 57 percent of men). When the first experience took place within a committed or steady relationship, it was more likely to be described as psychologically satisfying (Higgins, Trussell, Moore, & Davidson, 2010).

Sexual Victimization.
Adolescents' sexual experiences can occur in a variety of relationships from stable and serious to very intermittent and casual. Within these contexts, aggressive, abusive, and exploitive behaviors also take many shapes from the most serious forms of rape to unwanted touching to sexualized attention and teasing. A national survey of children's and teen's exposure to violence documented sexual victimization experiences in the following categories: sexual assault, statutory sex offense, peer flashing, dating violence, and Internet/cell phone harassment. Among 14 to 17 year olds, 27 percent reported experiencing sexual victimization in their lifetime. Among teens in this age group, 20.3 percent reported sexual Internet or cell phone harassment; 10.6 percent reported experiences of sexual assault; 8.3 percent experienced peer flashing; and 6.3 percent

experienced dating violence, which can include physical aggression, stalking, emotional or psychological threats, or sexual coercion (Finkelhor, Turner, Shattuck, Hamby, & Kracke, 2015). These figures are likely underestimates given that many teens are unwilling to report or reveal their experiences.

Beyond the more violent forms of sexual victimization, many adolescents are exposed to **unwanted sexual attention**, including teasing, verbal insults, and gestures, which can be perceived as threatening, embarrassing, or harmful. The impact of this sexualized attention is difficult to determine; it may be viewed as playful teasing or flirting by some, but it may be viewed as offensive or harassing by others. In a study of potentially offensive sexual behavior (POSB), three types of behavior were considered: (1) physical and verbal behavior like sexual jokes, sexual touching or pinching, pulling on someone's clothes in a sexual way, or making comments about someone's body parts that make them a boy or a girl; (2) electronic behavior like showing, sending, or leaving someone sexualized messages or pictures, or sending someone sexualized messages or photos on websites; and (3) homophobic behaviors like calling someone *gay, fag, dyke, queer,* or something similar. Among ninth graders who were surveyed, 72 percent reported at least one of these types of behaviors toward cross-sex peers and 77 percent reported at least one of these types of behaviors toward same-sex peers. For boys, the most common form of POSB was "made sexual comments, jokes, gestures or looks about someone." For girls, the most common form of POSB was "called someone *gay, fag, dyke,* or *queer* or something similar." It is not surprising to find common patterns of use between teens and their friends. Teens who were more likely to engage in POSBs also had friends who reported frequent POSBs (Jewell, Brown, & Perry, 2015).

Electronic media play an insidious role in the current environment of sexual victimization (Wildsmith, Barry, Manlove, & Vaughn, 2013). Teens are taking and sending pictures of their bodies, including nude images or images of their genitals, on their smartphones. In some cases, these pictures are sent as a way to "show off" or get someone's attention. In other instances, the pictures are taken without the person's awareness or consent and circulated to the peer community. Even when the original image was intended just for a boyfriend or girlfriend, the images posted on Facebook or Instagram or through a text message can be shared with the larger community, resulting in a barrage of harassing, insulting, and humiliating comments. Most states have laws that make the circulation of explicit sexual images of minors illegal; it is considered child pornography. However, the victim of the "sexting" has no way of stopping the spread of these images to a wider network. The results of this form of unwanted sexual exposure can be devastating (Burleigh, 2013; Rosen, 2014).

The boundaries for acceptable sexual contact are unclear; the sexual agenda for boys and girls is likely to be very different; the perceived potential rewards for sexual experimentation are great; and other risk-taking behaviors, including alcohol and drug use, may create an environment for these unwanted or violent sexual encounters (Vagi et al., 2013).

The lack of supervision and monitoring by adults, as well as the lack of opportunity to talk about sexuality with them, can place adolescents at risk for early sexual experiences that are abusive or associated with negative feelings. The sex-linked problems that many people encounter—unintended pregnancy, marital infidelity, rape and other forms of unwanted sexual contact, child sexual abuse, pornography addiction, and sexually transmitted diseases—are evidence that the socialization process—including efforts by parents, teachers, and religious leaders—is failing to promote mature sexuality in significant numbers of adolescents and adults in the United States.

Inconsistent Contraception. Despite the decline in the inclusion of information about methods of contraception and the use of condoms in formal sex education, the use of contraceptives by U.S. teens has increased. In a survey conducted between 2011 and 2013, 79 percent of females and 84 percent of males used some form of contraception during their first sexual intercourse. Among females who were sexually active, 97 percent had used a condom as a method of contraception at least once. However, the next most commonly used method reported by females was withdrawal (60 percent) (Martinez & Abma, 2015).

Although contraceptive use has increased among adolescents, its use continues to be inconsistent. In part, this is because sexual activity among many adolescents is sporadic. Other explanations for inconsistent use include misunderstanding about pregnancy risks and the need for **contraception**; lack of skills in the use of contraceptives and a desire to avoid embarrassment; barriers to acquiring contraceptives including cost, lack of anonymity, and religious or cultural barriers; poor communication among the partners about who is responsible for contraceptive use; experiencing side-effects associated with various forms of contraception; lack of knowledge about the effectiveness of various types of contraception; a view that using contraceptives, especially the use of a condom, intrudes on the spontaneity of sexual activity; and the involvement of drugs and alcohol with sexual activity, which

may increase impulsiveness and reduce reasoned decision making (Reed et al., 2014; U. S. Department of Health and Human Services, Centers for Disease Control and Prevention, 2006).

Many adolescents are confused about the difference between contraception for the prevention of pregnancy and contraception for the prevention of STIs. For example, girls might say that they were more likely to expect a boy to use a condom if this was a casual sexual relationship, but that it wasn't necessary if it was a steady relationship (Reed et al., 2014). As the quote below suggests, a young woman's intention to use contraceptives effectively may be at odds with her understanding about their various purposes.

> Jane answered unequivocally "yes" to the question whether young people she knew would use condoms every time they had sexual intercourse. But she added: "Depending on whether they didn't want to—and whether the girl's on the pill and they were in a steady relationship and they didn't want to use one. But otherwise most people would use them." (Kirkman et al., 1998)

One direction that is gaining increasing support in the public health community is offering teens the option of long-acting, reversible contraception (LARC), including an intrauterine device or an implant. These options avoid the need for frequent decision making, have proven to be highly effective in preventing pregnancy, and give young women greater protection against unwanted or unplanned pregnancies until they are ready to have a child (Northridge & Coupey, 2015). Evidence from a statewide initiative in Colorado that offered free long-active reversible contraceptives to teens resulted in a 40 percent decrease in teen pregnancies and an accompanying 42 percent reduction in abortions for this segment of the population over a 4 year period when the intervention was implemented (Tavernise, 2015). One concern with this direction is that the LARC does not prevent the spread of sexually transmitted infections.

Sexually Transmitted Infections. In 2014, the CDC reported increases in the number of the three sexually transmitted infections (STIs) that are tracked: chlamydia, gonorrhea, and syphilis. An estimated 20 million new cases of STIs are reported annually, roughly half to early and later adolescents aged 15 to 24. Adolescents aged 15 to 19 accounted for 20 percent of the new cases of gonorrhea and 26 percent of the new cases of chlamydia (CDC 2015e). Untreated, chlamydia and gonorrhea in young women can produce pelvic inflammatory disease, leading to infertility and abnormal pregnancies. In a study that tracked young women ages 14 to 17, within

Mary Kate Denny/PhotoEdit

In this classroom the teacher is showing students wrapped condoms as part of her instruction about safe sex. This is not always permitted as part of sex education, especially in programs that promote abstinence only.

1 year of their first sexual intercourse, 25 percent of the sample had their first sexually transmitted infection (Tu et al., 2009).

In 2014, 20 percent of the new HIV cases (9,731 cases) were among individuals in the age range 13 to 24. Most of these cases are a result of sexual transmission, the majority involving adolescent males who have sex with men or are bisexual (CDC 2015e). Although adolescents believe that they have a strong understanding of AIDS as a disease, including its transmission and prevention, often their knowledge is confused or incorrect (Meschke, Bartholomae, & Zentall, 2002). At the same time, adolescents express little interest in learning more about AIDS; 84 percent say that they have been taught about HIV/AIDS in school (Centers for Disease Control and Prevention, 2012d). However, HIV/AIDS instruction is not being covered soon enough, and the percentage of schools that include systematic HIV/AIDS prevention has declined from 64 percent in 2000 to just over 40 percent in 2014. Even when students have had classes on sexual health, many young people overestimate how well they understand this health problem. Others are cynical about getting the specific information they need from typical school-based sex education courses, especially when these courses teach abstinence as the most effective method to avoid pregnancy, HIV, and other STIs. These courses often fail to provide the practical information that is needed to resolve questions about contraception and other sexual health topics. For example, only 39 percent of health education courses taught the correct use of a condom in a required health education course, even in programs intended to focus on HIV/AIDS prevention (Centers for Disease Control and Prevention, 2012d).

Efforts at prevention are typically targeted to individuals. However, broader system factors need to be incorporated into efforts to reduce the risks of infection and disease among adolescents. A variety of factors specifically impacting teens includes ineffective sexual health education; peer norms; media influences; and the availability, privacy/confidentiality, and costs associated with health service resources (CDC 2015e).

Parenthood in Early Adolescence

One of the consequences of early entry into sexual activity and inconsistent use of contraception is **adolescent pregnancy**. In 2014, 249,078 infants were born to young women ages 15 to 19 in the United States. The birth rate was 10.9 births per 1,000 girls ages 15 to 17, and 43.8 per 1,000 girls ages 18 to 19. These rates are at an all-time low for the United States, with steady declines from 1991 to the present (Hamilton et al., 2015). Declines in teen pregnancy rates were observed for all race/ethnic groups.

In efforts to explain the decline in birthrates to young mothers, data were collected that focused on sexual activity and contraceptive use. Both delays in the initiation of sexual activity and more effective contraceptive use contributed to the decline in teen pregnancy. Despite the encouraging trends, health experts are concerned that 17 percent of births to teens 15 to 19 are repeat pregnancies (roughly 26 percent of the births to 19 year olds), a fact that places the young women at risk for negative health, educational, and social outcomes and also increases the chances that the infants will be born preterm and/or low birth weight (Martin et al., 2012; WebMD, 2014). What is more, even at this historic low level, the birth rate to teens in the United States is substantially higher than the rate in other developed nations.

Predictors of Teenage Pregnancy. Are there any characteristics of teenage girls or their family and community contexts that are systematically linked to the likelihood of becoming pregnant? Using two national samples, Mollborn and Morningstar (2009) compared teenage girls who were pregnant to similar age girls who did not become pregnant and to women who became pregnant at age 20 or older. The risk factors for becoming a teenage mother included low parental education, having low grades in school, being in a single-mother or stepparent family, and having had sexual intercourse. For those girls who lived in very low-resource households, being poor coupled with high levels of distress combined to predict the increased likelihood of teen pregnancy.

Consequences of Teenage Pregnancy. The phenomenon of teenage parenthood is complex, touching the lives of the adolescent mother and father, the child or children born to them, their parents, and the schools, counseling services, and family planning services that have been created to help young parents cope with parenthood. The consequences for the young mother and her infant depend on the psychosocial context of the pregnancy. Within the time period of early adolescence, there is a big difference between becoming a mother at 14 or at 18. For the younger teens (i.e., those younger than 14), the pregnancies are typically unplanned and often a result of involuntary or forced sexual encounters. Younger teens are more likely to end their pregnancy by abortion. For the older teens, the girl's partner is usually within 2 years of her age, and even if the pregnancy was unplanned, the majority of girls go ahead with the birth. Very few teen age girls decide to allow their babies to be placed for adoption.

The most significant measurable impact of early pregnancy is its association with subsequent poverty. Teens growing up in high-poverty neighborhoods are at greater risk for teenage pregnancy and dropping out of school, both of which contribute to continuing poverty in adulthood. By the time their children are 3 years old, 50 percent of women who had a child before the age of 20 were living in poverty (The National Campaign, 2012). This effect is mediated through other personal and family factors that unfold following the first birth, such as continuing in school, repeat pregnancies, the chances of getting married, the kind of work one does, one's personal earnings, and the earning capacity of other family members.

Complications during labor and delivery may be devastating to the newborn's health. Young mothers more likely than older ones to experience such complications. Mothers under 19 are less likely than older mothers to initiate prenatal care during the first trimester of pregnancy. Infants born to mothers under 17 are at greater risk than those born to women in their 20s and 30s. They have a higher risk of being born prematurely or with a low birth weight (WebMD, 2014). Thus, young parents are more likely to have to cope with the special needs of a child with developmental disabilities.

Complications of pregnancy and negative birth outcomes for adolescent mothers are linked to the contexts of pregnancy. One study found that in a sample of 170 African American teens, the pregnancy was unplanned or unwanted in about half the cases (Crosby, DiClemente, Wingood, Rose, & Lang, 2003). Other studies have linked sexual abuse in childhood with earlier sexual activity and teen pregnancy. Girls with a history of both poverty and reported child abuse are significantly more likely to be pregnant at least once by age 17 (Garwood et al., 2015). When pregnancy occurs in these abusive or exploitive contexts, it is often accompanied by alcohol or drug use, cigarette smoking, and heightened anxiety, all of which contribute to low birth weight and neurological impairments for the infants. Teens who become pregnant under these circumstances are more likely to be socially isolated and to become psychologically disengaged from their infants. In contrast, when pregnancy occurs in the context of family, peer, and partner support, teen mothers are likely to receive encouragement for their caregiving, greater financial support, and opportunities to engage in appropriate social and educational activities that contribute to their own psychosocial maturity (Bunting & McAuley, 2004; Salas-Wright, Vaughn, Ugalde, & Todic, 2015).

For some teens, the experience of motherhood has an enhancing or self-righting impact. In a comparison of adolescent mothers who ended their pregnancies through abortion and those who kept their babies, the latter group demonstrated some important changes in their behavior. Rates of delinquency declined in this group, and they reduced their cigarette smoking and marijuana use (Hope, Wilder, & Watt, 2003). Young mothers may be inspired by their infant to make a better future for themselves and their baby. This often means completing their education, creating a more stable home environment, and taking better care of their own health.

Adolescent Fathers.

There is growing interest in factors that predict early fatherhood, as well as concerns about the impact of early fatherhood on subsequent development. Data from the National Longitudinal Study of Youth provided information about approximately 1,500 boys ages 13 or 14 who were studied over a period of 8 years. Participants reported their age at the birth of their first child. Overall, 140 participants or slightly over 9 percent became fathers before the age of 20. The following combination of individual, family, peer, and environmental factors predicted early age of fatherhood: boys who were involved in more delinquent behaviors and more substance use, boys who started dating at a younger age, boys whose mothers had less education and who had their sons while they were adolescents, boys who were living in a single-parent home or not living with their biological father, and boys who were living in more dangerous neighborhoods. After taking all these factors into account, sons of adolescent fathers were at greater risk for becoming fathers themselves in adolescence than were boys whose fathers were 20 or older at their birth. These findings suggest an intergenerational pattern of early fathering in which young boys learn about early sexual activity as a pathway into adulthood as part of the family socialization process (Sipsma, Biello, Cole-Lewis, & Kershaw, 2010).

Adolescent fathers are a diverse group. One estimate is that about 25 percent of teen boys who impregnate a teenage girl are antisocial; they view girls as sex objects who exist for their own

EPF/Alamy Stock Photo

Not much is known about the impact of teen fathering on a boy's psychological development. What factors might influence whether the boy becomes committed to nurturing and supporting his child or leaves the parenting entirely to the mother and her family?

pleasure and power. They are likely to deny responsibility for the pregnancy by claiming that birth control is a woman's job and refer to their own "uncontrollable sexual desire" as well as their fertility as evidence of their masculinity. These boys are also likely to be involved in other high risk behaviors including having multiple sex partners. They are the boys who support the negative stereotype about teen fathers as selfish, exploitive, and uncaring (Kiselica & Kiselica, 2014; Weber, 2012).

In contrast to this negative evaluation of teen fathers, three fourths of adolescent boys want to be recognized as involved and responsible fathers (Kiselica & Kiselica, 2014). These boys are likely to have been in what they describe as a committed relationship, many for a year or more, before the pregnancy. They have provided emotional and instrumental support to their partner during the pregnancy, and in many cases well through the infant's first year of life. Some adolescent fathers marry the mothers; others live with them for a while. Often, the couple continues to date. In some instances, they marry the child's mother several years after the child is born. In many cases, the father contributes financial support to the mother and child, even when the couple does not marry (Bunting & McAuley, 2004; Paschal, 2006). Being embedded in a strong social support system with the partner and the extended family helps to sustain the co-parenting relationship, providing essential stability for the child. The ability to establish a positive connection with his child also reinforces the teen's confidence in being able to continue on a path to responsible adulthood (Lewin et al., 2015; Mollborn & Jacobs, 2015).

Despite the desire to be a good provider and nurturer, adolescent fathers face a variety of challenges that may lead to a decline in support and reduced contact with their children. Many adolescent fathers have little education and are minimally employed, so the material support they can provide is limited. Conflicts with the child's mother and/or her family can result in being pushed away. Troubles with the justice system or the legal system, and difficulty finding or using needed services can be roadblocks to continued involvement with their child (Kiselica & Kiselica, 2014).

Little systematic research has been done on the attitudes, knowledge, or behaviors of adolescent fathers or the impact of fatherhood on a teenage boy's subsequent development. One study followed a large sample of adolescent boys through their teen years. Those who became fathers were characterized as having lower self-esteem and a lower sense of internal control than their age-mates who did not become fathers. Shortly after fatherhood, these boys experienced a boost in self-esteem, but in the next several years, their self-esteem declined to its pre-fatherhood level (Pirog-Good, 1995).

Any effort to provide services to teen fathers must begin with a nonstigmatizing approach. Successful programs typically recognize the diversity of needs facing teen fathers including job skills training, legal advice, educational opportunities, family life skills, and parenting education. Efforts to include young fathers in family planning programs, parent education, and employment training initiatives help strengthen the social context for the young mother and her child and contribute to the young father's psychosocial development (Kisela & Kisela, 2014).

For both girls and boys, a key to the prevention of early pregnancy requires building greater confidence in and commitment to the consistent use of contraception as part of any sexual relationship and comfortable, user-friendly access to reproductive health care. For girls, fostering a sense of self-efficacy and investment in academic goals leading to postsecondary education or professional training is an especially important area for intervention. For boys, building greater social expectations and commitment to assuming the financial and social responsibilities associated with fatherhood—including sending clearer messages from family and community that boys have responsibilities in these areas and devising specific opportunities for them to enact these responsibilities—seem promising directions for future intervention. For more information on pregnancy prevention programs, visit the website of the Centers for Disease Control and Prevention (CDC) and go to the Communitywide Teen Pregnancy Prevention Initiatives home page; also see the website of the National Campaign to Prevent Teen and Unplanned Pregnancy.

FURTHER REFLECTION: Think about the impact of physical development, including the emergence of sexuality and sexual interests, on adaptation during early adolescence. Identify personal, family, cultural, and environmental factors that help adolescents cope

effectively with these changes. What factors lead to dissatisfaction with body image, risk taking, and harmful or unhealthy behaviors? What factors may be contributing to the steady decline in teen pregnancies in the United States? Why does teen pregnancy continue to be a focus of public health and public policy initiatives?

Formal Operations

OBJECTIVE 3 Identify the basic features of formal operational thought, and explain the factors that promote the development of advanced reasoning at this period of life.

Just as the body undergoes significant changes during puberty, so too does the brain and related mental activity. Early adolescents begin to think about themselves and their world in new ways that reflect a broadening of consciousness. This includes greater introspection or monitoring of thoughts, greater integration of information from various sources, and more focused planning and control of behaviors guided by goals and strategies. Young people are able to think about several dimensions at once rather than focusing on just one domain or issue at a time. They are able to generate hypotheses about events that they have never perceived and to use logical reasoning to evaluate evidence to support or disconfirm these hypotheses (Kuhn, 2009).

Brain Development in Adolescence

You will recall from chapter 4 that the brain is comprised of **gray matter**, the cell body of neurons and the non-myelinated sections of axons and dendrites, and **white matter**, the myelinated axons that connect gray matter and carry messages between nerve cells and brain regions. **Myelin** is a substance that forms around the axons, acting as an insulator that speeds signals from one neuron to the next. Gray matter volume and distribution are associated with competence in that region of the brain. White matter is associated with speed and efficiency of processing.

Brain development is ongoing throughout the prenatal period, infancy, childhood, adolescence, and adulthood. Like physical maturation, it is very individual, reflecting an ongoing interaction between genetics and environment. Brain development is characterized by periods of intense production of neurons and synapses followed by a process of sculpting and pruning when some connections are strengthened and others drop away. One of the most important discoveries related to adolescent brain development is that various areas of the cerebral cortex reach their peak in gray matter production during early adolescence, followed by a process of sculpting and pruning. The timing for these peak periods of gray matter production vary quite a bit from one person to the next, but the average is around ages 10 to 12 for the parietal lobe, ages 11 to 12 for the frontal lobe, and ages 16 to 17 for the temporal lobe (Lenroot & Giedd, 2006).

The process of sculpting and pruning that occurs during the course of the high school years strengthens certain neural networks while others fall into disuse. Whatever a young person does frequently will be woven into a strong, well-integrated network of neural signals. Through focused attention and repeated actions, a person can alter his or her brain architecture. Neural functions that are infrequently or rarely stimulated will weaken. Thus, the high school years provide a truly irreplaceable opportunity to shape a person's neural landscape, creating areas of unique competence and mastery that develop as a result of active engagement in certain thoughts and behaviors (Siegel, 2013).

In contrast to the production of gray matter, which shows an inverted U-shaped pattern, increasing from childhood through adolescence and declining in the late teens and early adulthood, there is a steady increase in the volume of white matter from ages 4 through the 20s. The prefrontal cortex, which is responsible for the full range of executive functions, is not fully developed until the late 20s.

Executive functions, sometimes called cognitive control functions, include:

Working memory. The memory system used for temporarily storing and managing the information required to carry out complex cognitive tasks such as learning, reasoning, and comprehension.

Planning and organizing. Devising an approach to a complex task, including following a sequence of steps to task completion and using feedback to revise one's plan.

Impulse control. Including resisting distractions, self-regulation, and behavioral inhibition.

The combination of changes in gray matter and white matter in the frontal, parietal, and temporal lobes and the resulting improvements in executive functions are associated with the following potential changes in mental competence during adolescence.

Ages 10.5 to 13: New growth in the visual and auditory regions of the brain; new ability to perform calculations; increasing ability to perceive new meanings and functions for familiar objects.

Ages 13 to 17: New growth in visuoauditory, visuospatial, and somatic systems; new ability to review mental operations (metacognition), especially the ability to find flaws in one's reasoning and to use information to revise problem-solving strategies.

Ages 17 to 30: New growth in prefrontal cortex: new abilities to question and evaluate information; new abilities to formulate hypotheses based on new information from a variety of sources.

The relationship of the brain and behaviors is bidirectional. Many studies have shown a relationship between maturation in the prefrontal cortex and improvements in executive functions including working memory and response inhibition (Giedd et al., 2012; Paus, 2005). At the same time, repeated activity, such as musical training, can alter brain structure. For example, a 3-month period of juggling practice was found to be related to an increase in gray-matter density in the motion-processing region of the brain (Draganski et al., 2004). In other words, the maturing brain makes new accomplishments possible for adolescents, and, at the same time, the effort and persistence an adolescent exerts toward advanced skill building stimulates new neural growth.

Piaget's Theory of Formal Operational Thought

Without the benefit of magnetic resonance imaging or other technologies, Jean Piaget proposed a qualitative shift in thinking during adolescence from concrete to **formal operational thought**. His theoretical formulation reflects what is now known as a dramatic advance in neural maturation that takes place during early and later adolescence (Inhelder & Piaget, 1958; Piaget, 1970, 1972a). In the period of concrete operational thought, children use mental operations to explain changes in tangible objects and events. Their approach to problem solving is concrete in that they rely heavily on observed features and direct experience to infer rules for solving problems. In the period of formal operational thought, young people use mental operations to manipulate and modify thoughts and other mental operations (Piaget, 1972b).

A central feature of formal operational reasoning is the ability to separate and distinguish between *reality* and *possibility*. Problem solving is altered as adolescents become better able to think about the bigger picture of choices and their likely consequences. As the brain matures, neural systems are linked together more quickly so that memories, concepts, language, sensory/perceptual capacities, and motor skills can be integrated for use in a faster, more efficient way. For example, in thinking about trying to get a part-time job, adolescents may consider the possibilities related to the kind of work they would like to do and the kind of work they think they are qualified to do. They may also consider realities such as the specific jobs that are available in their town, the number of hours they can work given other school and family commitments, the physical demands of the work, and their access to transportation. They are able to create different scenarios about working, based partly on what they want and partly on what they learn in the process of applying for jobs. Some of the possibilities they may have considered are no longer realistic, and some of the information suggests new possibilities that they may not have considered.

In the maturation of scientific reasoning, the ability to distinguish between reality and possibility results in the formal operational process of hypothesis testing. **Hypotheses** are tentative propositions or *possible* explanations about the causes of events or the systematic associations among factors that explain events. In the scientific process, one raises hypotheses to explain an event and then follows the chain of evidence to determine whether the evidence supports the hypothesis. One of the classic experiments that Piaget and Inhelder designed to demonstrate the development of hypothetical deductive reasoning involves the explanation of the swing of a pendulum. The task is to find out what variable or combination of variables controls the speed of the swing. Four factors can be varied: the mass of the object, the height from which the pendulum is pushed, the force with which it is pushed, and the length of the string. To investigate this problem, it is necessary to begin by isolating the separate factors and then varying only one factor at a time while keeping the others constant. As it happens, only the length of the string influences the speed of the pendulum. The challenge, then, is to demonstrate that the length of the string accounts for the speed of the pendulum and that the other factors do not. Children at the stage of concrete operational thought have difficulty coordinating the interaction among four separate variables and may lose track of what is being varied and what is held constant. After trying one or two strategies, they may simply give up. In contrast, being able to use formal operational thought, a child can create a matrix of variables and test each factor separately to evaluate its contribution (Flavell, 1963; Inhelder & Piaget, 1958).

Six Characteristics of Formal Operational Thought

Formal operational thought is not a specific skill or expertise; rather, it is a way of approaching and solving problems based on new capacities for abstract, probabilistic thinking. Six conceptual skills emerge during the stage of formal operations that have implications for how adolescents approach interpersonal relationships, the formulation of personal plans and goals, and for how they analyze scientific and mathematical information (see Table 9.3). First, adolescents are able to mentally manipulate more than two categories of variables at the same time; for example, they can consider the relationship of speed, distance, and time in planning a trip. Second, they are able to think about things changing in the future. They can realize, for instance, that their current friendships may not remain the same in the years ahead.

Third, adolescents are able to hypothesize about a logical sequence of possible events. For example, they are able to predict college and occupational options that may be open to them depending on how well they do in certain academic coursework in high school. Fourth, they are able to anticipate the consequences of their actions. For instance, they realize that if they drop out of school, certain career possibilities will be closed to them.

Fifth, they have the capacity to detect the logical consistency or inconsistency of a set of statements. They can test the truth of a statement by finding evidence that supports or disproves it. They are troubled, for example, by the apparent

The capacity for hypothesis testing makes it possible for students to evaluate the results of their experiments. How might you design chemistry experiments so that they are most likely to foster formal operational reasoning?

Jim Cummins/Lithium/AGE Fotostock

contradiction between statements such as "all people are equal before the law" and the reality that people who have more money can afford better legal representation and are likely to have different experiences with the legal system than those who live in poverty.

Sixth, adolescents are able to think in a relativistic way about themselves, other individuals, and their world. They know that they are expected to act in a particular way because of the norms of their community and their culture. Adolescents also know that in other families, communities, and cultures, different norms may govern the same behavior. They realize that people are the products of societies with different sets of rules and norms.

These qualities of thought reflect what is *possible* for adolescents rather than what is typical. Most adolescents and adults approach problem solving in a practical, concrete way in their common, daily functioning. However, under the most supportive conditions, more abstract, systematic, and self-reflective qualities of thought can be observed and bring a new perspective to the way adolescents approach the analysis of information and the acquisition of knowledge (Lee, Anzures, & Freire, 2011). Science education is just such a context, where students may be encouraged to think hypothetically about the systematic interactions among multiple variables.

Factors That Promote Formal Operational Thought

Neurological development alone is not enough to foster formal operational thought. We have already addressed the importance of a healthy diet, getting enough sleep, and adequate physical exercise for optimal cognitive functioning. Healthy brain development must be coupled with a social environment that encourages

Table 9.3	New Conceptual Skills That Emerge During the Stage of Formal Operational Thought
1.	Ability to mentally manipulate more than two categories of variables simultaneously.
2.	Ability to think about the changes that come with time.
3.	Ability to hypothesize logical sequences of events.
4.	Ability to foresee consequences of actions.
5.	Ability to detect logical consistency or inconsistency in a set of statements.
6.	Ability to think in relativistic ways about self, others, and the world.

hypothetical, abstract reasoning; opportunities to investigate and explore alternative solutions; and a symbolic capacity for carrying out mental representations and operations. The affective components of interest, motivation, and self-efficacy are also involved in sustaining engagement with complex problems and the emotional regulation that allows one to stay focused despite frustrations and failures.

Several environmental conditions facilitate the development of formal operational thought and reduce egocentrism. First, early adolescents function in a variety of role relationships that place both compatible and conflicting demands on them. Among these role relationships are son or daughter, worker, student, friend, dating partner, religious believer, and citizen. Early adolescents experience firsthand the pressures of multiple expectations for behavior. Conversations with parents provide a give and take where adolescents are expected to state their opinions, consider their parent's point of view, and reach a mutually acceptable decision. Participating in a variety of roles also facilitates relativistic thinking by demonstrating that what is acceptable and valued in one situation may not be in another.

Adolescents participate in a more heterogeneous peer group. When children move from their community elementary school to a more centralized junior high and high school, they are likely to meet other students whose family backgrounds and social class are different from their own. In studying and playing with these friends, they realize the extent to which their expectations for the future differ from those of their new acquaintances because their values are shaped by the families and neighborhood from which they come.

The use of formal operational skills can be observed in adolescent discussions of peer-related issues and in the formation of intimate or romantic relationships—domains that require a wide range of hypothesis raising and testing. An example of a conversation between a 15-year-old girl and her best friend follows.

CINDY: I'm so frustrated I can't stand it. Before Sean and I started to date, he was nice to me. I enjoyed being with him. He said hello to me in the halls; we'd walk along together. We talked about all kinds of things. Now that we're going out, he seems rude and uncaring. When we're with other people, he jumps in when I start to talk, and his eyes say "be quiet." He breezes by me in the halls sometimes, and when we talk about things (if we talk), he acts as if he is always right. I don't think he cares about me anymore. What's going on?

DONNA: I know he likes you because he tells me. Maybe you should talk to him and tell him what he does and how it makes you feel.

CINDY: No, if I do that he'll get mad and he won't like me anymore. Why don't you talk to him?

DONNA: No, that wouldn't do any good, because then he would know you talked to me about this and he would not like it, or he would just say what he thinks would make him look good.

As this conversation continues, many possible scenarios are proposed about why this behavior is occurring, and hypotheses are raised about what could be done. The girls propose likely outcomes of each set of possible actions and attempt to evaluate the results of each. Finally, a tentative conclusion is reached: Boys treat girls differently when they are involved in a boyfriend–girlfriend relationship than when they are not. In the just-friends situation, there is a tendency to treat the girl as an equal, but in the boyfriend–girlfriend situation, there is a tendency for the boy to expect that he should dominate the girl. A solution is derived: Cindy must shape up Sean. Because she still likes him and wants to go out with him, she must try to tell him how she feels and hope he will change his behavior so that it is supportive and comfortable for her.

The context of friendship between Cindy and Donna allows Cindy to trust discussing her problem with Donna so that they can examine it fully. It also allows Donna to disagree with Cindy without terminating the conversation. Thus, Cindy can get a somewhat different point of view on her situation and the two friends together can explore a personal problem on a more objective, rational basis than Cindy probably could have done on her own.

The third condition that fosters the development of the cognitive skills of early adolescence is the content

Conversations with parents often force adolescents to rethink their assumptions or come up with support for their decisions. Although this is not always pleasant, these kinds of interactions are an important stimulus for more advanced reasoning.

of the high school curriculum. Guided by Vygotsky's theory of a zone of proximal development, we assume that capacities for formal operational reasoning are ready to be nurtured and advanced through exposure to educational experiences that promote systematic logical reasoning and problem solving. Courses in science and mathematics formally introduce students to the logical relationships inherent in these disciplines and give them practice in a hypothetical deductive style of reasoning. Courses in the social sciences, such as child development, psychology, anthropology, or sociology, introduce students to the organization of societies, individual differences in perspective, and psychological mindedness. The fine arts and the humanities advance students' conceptions of ways the world has been or might be. They expand the repertoire of representational thought. According to Gardner's model of multiple intelligences (discussed in chapter 8), the visual arts provide a means of integrating and innovating spatial intelligence with interpersonal intelligence. Many high schools involve students in community service learning, an experience that helps promote a greater sense of connection to the community and appreciation for the diverse perspectives on community improvement. The more complex, differentiated academic environment of the high school can bring substantial gains in conceptual skills for those students who become actively engaged in its academic programs (Cohen & Sandy, 2007; Gehlbach, 2006; Yamauchi, Billig, Meyer, & Hofschire, 2006).

The following examples illustrate how high school course experiences contributed to students' formal operational reasoning.

> In my senior physics class we would learn new concepts then apply them by building something. For example we were learning about inertia so then we had to build a cart to hold a pumpkin and it had to go straight and travel a certain distance.
>
> An assignment that enhanced my logical reasoning and critical thinking was to design a school playground using specific software. I had to think about dimensions of my playground and logically think about safety issues in the design.
>
> In high school I took a money matters course that talked about saving money, stocks, loans, debt, and every other aspect of money. It made me think in a much more logical way because hearing it from someone other than my parents made it more real.
>
> In my AP art class my senior year my teacher gave us a topic and we had to do 20 pieces of artwork with that one topic/object. Mine was a seashell and water. It broadened my thinking to think of 20 different things to do with a seashell. (Newman, 2010)

Although schooling can be a vehicle that promotes formal operational reasoning, not all school experiences are equally effective in promoting abstract, hypothetical reasoning. In a review of over 1,500 literary assignments for students in six middle schools, only13 percent were characterized as encouraging higher level cognitive functioning, (The Education Trust, 2015).

Keating (1990) described the following characteristics that are important in creating a cognitively stimulating school experience.

> Students need to be engaged with meaningful material; training of thinking skills must be embedded in a knowledge of subject matter, for acquisition of isolated content knowledge is likely to be unproductive; serious engagement with real problems has to occur in depth and over time; students need experiences that lead to placing a high value on critical thinking, to acquiring it as a disposition, not just as a skill; and many of these factors occur most readily, and perhaps exclusively, when students have the opportunity for real, ongoing discourse with teachers who have reasonably expert command of the material to be taught. (p. 77)

One does not expect to see a mature scientist or a profound philosopher by the end of early adolescence. A young person's formal operational reasoning awaits further encounters with a specific discipline and its full range of significant problems. However, the opportunity for cognitive growth during this period is extensive. Adolescents are able to generate novel solutions and apply them to current life challenges. They also are able to be increasingly objective about the problem-solving process and to gain insight into their own mental activity (Lee, Anzures, & Friere, 2011).

Criticisms of the Concept of Formal Operational Thought

In Piaget's theory, formal operational reasoning is viewed as the final stage in the development of logical thought. A number of scholars have pointed to limitations in this construction. Six criticisms are discussed here.

1. Although qualitative changes in problem solving are observed, cognition is much more variable than the strict stage approach might suggest. Adolescents solve problems in different ways depending on the domain, and adolescents as a group differ more from one another in their approach to cognitive problem solving than Piaget's stage concept might imply. Studies of brain functioning and information processing capacities suggest considerable diversity in the timing of emerging capacities and the ability to apply effective strategies (Giedd et al., 2010).

2. Some question whether there really is a qualitative, stage-like consolidation in the use of formal reasoning. Although most researchers agree that formal operational thinking exists and does characterize the nature of mature, scientific reasoning, many studies show that adolescents and adults typically do not function at the formal operational level and that their use of formal reasoning is inconsistent across problem areas (Bradmetz, 1999; Kuhn, 2009). For example, Neimark (1975) followed changes in the problem-solving strategies of adolescents over a 3 ½-year period. Even the oldest participants in her study, who were 15,

did not apply formal operational strategies across all problems. Research has not been able to confirm Piaget's claims that thinking becomes consistently more propositional across problem areas or that formal operational reasoning is a universal characteristic of adolescent reasoning in a variety of cultures. At the same time, the evidence does suggest that adolescents become more aware of the need to coordinate logic and evidence as they evaluate propositions (Keating, 2004). Even Piaget speculated that people were most likely to use formal operational reasoning in the area of their greatest expertise.

3. Formal operational reasoning is not broad enough to encompass the many dimensions along which cognitive functioning matures in adolescence. Information processing, another aspect of cognitive science, focuses on specific mechanisms for perceiving, encoding, and retrieving bytes or units of information. Increases in speed, efficiency, and capacity of information storage and retrieval have been documented during the period from ages 11 to 16 (Kwon & Lawson, 2000). These capacities can be applied to hypothetical reasoning but are not the same as formal operational thought. Improvements in logical reasoning may result in part from the ability to handle greater quantities of information more quickly and efficiently.

4. In addition to development in basic processing, there are gains in knowledge, both as a result of schooling and experience. Knowledge in each specialized subject, such as mathematics, language, or science, expands, bringing not only increases in logic but also increases in understanding the procedures or strategies that are most likely to work for a given problem. Complementing changes in specialized knowledge, adolescents demonstrate increases in self-monitoring and conscious control of mental activity, such as the ability to hold conclusions in abeyance while they examine alternative solutions or gather new information. These capacities for cognitive flexibility contribute to the potential for more mature solutions (Donald, 2001).

5. Some scholars claim that formal operational thought does not represent the apex or endpoint of adult thought and reasoning. As adults mature, they face many problems in which abstract, logical-mathematical reasoning must be integrated with the specific demands of the circumstances. This type of thinking is sometimes referred to as **postformal reasoning** because it emerges after the establishment of formal operational thinking. In adult life, problems may need to be reframed to suit the situation. The solution may need to be evaluated for its impact on many interrelated parties. The cognitive processes associated with psychotherapy, diplomacy, and leadership are all examples of what might be considered postformal reasoning (Richards & Commons, 1990; Torbert, 1994). Adolescents are just at the beginning of an expanding capacity to think about big, multidimensional scientific and social problems.

6. The emphasis in formal operational reasoning is on well-structured, logical problems with one correct answer. This misses the enormous array of messy, poorly defined, ambiguous social and emotionally laden problems that adolescents face. Decision making in daily life requires a person to think about several possible solutions, each one with potential costs as well as benefits. Think about the reasoning that Evelyn Cabrera may have used to try to convince her parents that it was acceptable to continue to be serious about her boyfriend, even when she was planning to go to college. Adolescent reasoning is likely to look less logical and systematic because many of the problems they are trying to address are embedded in complex cultural and social circumstances, and the "right answer" depends on one's point of view (Berg & Strough, 2011).

FURTHER REFLECTION: Describe ways that schooling supports the development of formal operational reasoning. Judge how well the high school environment matches the cognitive developmental changes that take place during early adolescence. Identify two or three experiences from your own high school years that encouraged your abstract, multidimensional probabilistic or hypothetical thinking.

Think back to the case of Evelyn at the opening of the chapter. How might she be making use of her formal operational reasoning to develop her plans for the future? How do these qualities of thought help Evelyn confront her parents' objections to her relationship with her boyfriend?

Emotional Development

OBJECTIVE 4 Examine patterns of emotional development in early adolescence, characterize the neurological processes associated with emotional expression, and describe the nature of three problem areas: eating disorders, depression, and delinquency.

Descriptions of adolescence often refer to new levels of emotional variability, moodiness, and emotional outbursts. However, this is also a time of increased emotional complexity, with new capacities to identify, understand, and express a wider range of emotions (Kang & Shaver, 2004). These capacities illustrate the interdependence of cognition and emotion, including interpreting and evaluating emotional signals, and reasoning about the consequences of expressing emotions, which may result in the control or management of emotional expression (Hoeksma, Oosterlaan, & Schipper, 2004). A major task during this time is to gain insight into one's emotionality and to expand one's capacity for empathy with the emotional state of others. This means accepting one's feelings and not interpreting them as a sign of going crazy or being strange. Adolescents who are highly sensitive to social expectations or overly controlled about expressing or accepting their feelings may experience a sense of shame about their emotional states. Attempts to rigidly control or defend oneself against feelings are likely to result in social alienation or maladaptive behaviors. In contrast, those who experience a diverse and well-differentiated range of emotions are also more likely to be characterized by greater openness to experience, empathy, and interpersonal adaptability (Kang & Shaver, 2004).

In the following sections, we review the neuroscience of emotion and cognition, pointing to the overlapping network of neural systems that operate as emotions are aroused, recognized, interpreted, and expressed or controlled; the diversity and complexity of adolescents' emotional life; and specific examples of internalizing and externalizing problems that result from difficulties in the management and expression of emotions.

The Neuroscience of Emotion and Cognition

A key feature of the human's adaptive capacity is the ability to detect and respond quickly to situations that threaten our survival. Some areas of the brain, especially the limbic system, detect threats, react intuitively to information, and produce quick emotional reactions to situations. The **limbic system**, which includes the hypothalamus, the hippocampus, the amygdala, and several other nearby areas, produces signals that identify the immediate situation as threatening, or link the immediate situation to other previously experienced dangers. The sound of an explosion, being hit or threatened with violence, or the experience of being caught in a raging storm are all examples of situations that could trigger an immediate threat reaction in the limbic system. When the system is activated, signals are sent to the adrenal gland, which releases stress-related hormones, especially adrenaline and cortisol, which prepare the body to deal with the threat. Adrenaline boosts energy supplies and increases heart rate. Cortisol adds sugars to the blood, providing a burst of energy, improves memory, and lowers sensitivity to pain. These reactions are referred to as *bottom-up processing*. In other words, the reactions are quick and relatively automatic, taking place without much conscious control.

Other areas of the brain, especially the prefrontal cortex, are more analytic. Information is evaluated, decisions are made, and a logical plan is formulated. The prefrontal cortex receives information from the limbic system, evaluates this information in light of the context, and makes an assessment of possible consequences of action. Information is then transmitted back to the limbic system to modify emotional signals and to the sensory-motor cortex to guide subsequent behavior. The frontal cortex control is referred to as *top-down processing*, a cooler, slower cognitive process that helps to regulate and manage the initial emotional reactions. The coordination of the limbic system and the prefrontal cortex is referred to as vertical control (Greenberg, Riggs, & Blair, 2007).

The **vertical control system** undergoes a process of maturation that is usually not complete until the 20s. In comparison to adults, adolescents are more emotionally reactive to negative stimuli, most likely because of the immaturity of the prefrontal control system (Cohen et al., 2016; Yuan et al., 2015). As a result, they are more likely to react rather than to withdraw from negative social cues.

Adolescents are also especially sensitive to rewards (Galván, 2013; Paus, 2009). The reward circuitry of the brain is responsible for producing dopamine, a neurotransmitter that is released during pleasurable experiences and that encourages actions toward anticipated rewarding or pleasurable experiences. This circuitry is more active among adolescents than among children or adults when they are experiencing primary rewards like a sweet tasting liquid, secondary rewards like money or prizes, or social rewards like recognition or praise (Telzer, 2016).

While we tend to think of rewards in terms of food, money, tokens, and other material reinforcements, social cues can also serve as rewards. Research in the field of social cognitive neuroscience provides evidence that adolescents are increasingly attuned to interpersonal and social cues such as facial expressions, hand gestures, and body movement that convey approval or disapproval. The adolescent's emotional reactions are especially intense as the brain processes information relevant to social evaluation (Somerville, 2013). The adaptive value of reading social cues, especially for detecting threat and for assessing potential friendship and romantic relationships, makes the increased sensitivity to complex social expressions all the more relevant to the developmental progress of social competence in early adolescence (Garcia & Scherf, 2015).

The increased sensitivity of the reward circuitry in adolescence has been implicated in a variety of maladaptive behaviors. The assumption is that the intense responsiveness to risky activities including rule breaking, drug and alcohol abuse, fast driving, and peer-instigated antisocial behaviors are reinforced by the over-production of dopamine in these contexts, which "overpowers" the executive functions of the prefrontal cortex. However, one can also find evidence for the adaptive functions of this system. It makes sense to think that from an evolutionary perspective, the reward centers of the brain would direct behavior toward activities that have long-term fitness implications. Some possibilities include the positive associations of dopamine production with creative expression, curiosity and exploration, achieving valued goals, performing socially valued actions, participating in meaningful ways to family well-being, or excelling in valued domains like leadership, academics, athletics, or the performing arts. Whereas some teens may find risky behaviors or ruthless behaviors to be accompanied by the "dopamine rush" others find this same surge of reward-related glow from contributing in meaningful ways to the well-being of their families, friends, or communities (Telzer, 2016).

Given the state of their brain development, one challenge that adolescents face is how to use their maturing executive functions under conditions of intense emotional arousal in order to avoid unnecessary risk taking. The prefrontal cortex is the site of a variety of executive functions, some of which help to manage strong emotions through monitoring one's internal state, interpreting the emotions, and finding acceptable ways for expressing or, if needed, inhibiting the expression of emotions. Other executive functions are useful for planning a course of action, evaluating possible consequences, and adapting to changing circumstances as the situation requires. As illustrated in FIGURE 9.4 ▶, the combination of

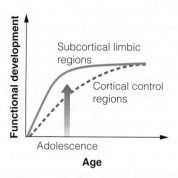

FIGURE 9.4 ▶ IMBALANCE MODEL OF NEUROBIOLOGICAL DEVELOPMENT
Source: Adpated from A. Galván (2013). The teenage brain: Sensitivity to rewards. *Current Directions in Psychological Science, 22,* 88–93.

these aspects of brain development may result in adolescents' need for greater stimulus seeking and the willingness for more risk taking. With a less fully developed prefrontal cortex, adolescents may have difficulty suppressing the immediate emotional responses of the limbic system. At the same time, they may engage in more intensely stimulating activities, some of which adults would judge to be highly risky, in order to achieve the desired experience of pleasure or arousal (Galván, 2012; Qu, Galvan, Fuligni, Lieberman, & Telzer, 2015).

Adolescents and adults are nearly equally able to understand information about the negative consequences of risky behavior. Early adolescents they may even overestimate the likelihood of their exposure to risk since they have relatively little life experience upon which to base their assessment of risks. However, if they engage in these behaviors frequently with no negative outcome, they are likely to conclude that the consequences are not as likely as they were led to believe. In gauging the risks and rewards of a decision, adolescents are likely to give greater weight to the rewards than to the possible negative consequences. Especially if the action is novel or one that provides social approval, its reward value can be quite high. What is more, the risks and rewards of certain behaviors are not the same for adolescents as they might be for adults. For example, the risk of being bullied, socially isolated, or embarrassed might be more serious for adolescents than for an adult. Imagine that Ken has to choose between calling his parents for a ride home from a party or getting a ride home from a friend who is intoxicated. While Ken's parents may view the risk of riding with an intoxicated friend as a great risk, Ken may view the risk of being seen by peers as overly dependent upon his parents as the greater risk.

In contrast to the vertical control system, through which the frontal cortex exerts control over the limbic system, there is also a horizontal control system that plays a role in risk taking and responses to threat. This **horizontal control system** refers to the flow of information between the right and left hemispheres of the brain. For right-handed children, the left hemisphere of the brain is the primary area involved in understanding spoken language, speech production, and the expression of positive emotions. The right hemisphere is involved in recognizing nonverbal expressions, processing positive and negative emotions, and

expressing uncomfortable or negative emotions. The effective flow of information between the two hemispheres provides teens with the ability to use verbal skills to identify and regulate their emotional states. With maturity, adolescents are increasingly able to use language to gain greater control over their behavior and to explain their internal states to themselves and to others. Although executive control and verbal behavior are two separate cognitive capacities, they can work together to manage strong emotional states as well as to guide effective action.

The Diversity of Emotions in Adolescence

Adolescents are more aware than younger children of distinctions in their emotional states and are able to attribute them to a wider range of causes. Given an increase in awareness of social cues and heightened motivation for peer approval, adolescents may experience new levels of intensity in moral or social emotions such as guilt, shame, embarrassment, and jealousy as well as strong feelings of sympathy and loyalty toward friends and family (Malti, 2013).

In a longitudinal study using internet responses, close to 400 adolescents were asked to rate their daily emotions for five consecutive days three times a year over 5 years from ages 13 to 18. Each teen provided ratings of four types of emotions: happiness, anger, sadness, and anxiety. As illustrated in FIGURES 9.5a and b ▶, over the period of early adolescence, happiness declined and anxiety increased for the total sample. At age 13, boys and girls were about equally happy, but by age 18 the girls' happiness had declined more steeply than the boys. As for worry, the girls started out more worried at age 13 and continued to be more worried than boys by age 18 (Maciejewski, van Lier, Branje, Meeus, & Koot, 2016).

Emotional development in adolescence goes beyond the experience of new gradations of emotion and fluctuations in emotional intensity. With increasing executive control, adolescents acquire new abilities to monitor and manage their emotions. They can observe the rise in their own emotional intensity and recognize when this intensity is adaptive or disruptive. For example, in a competitive sports context, in preparation for a class presentation, or when inviting someone to go to a party, an adolescent can learn to use intense emotions to increase motivation

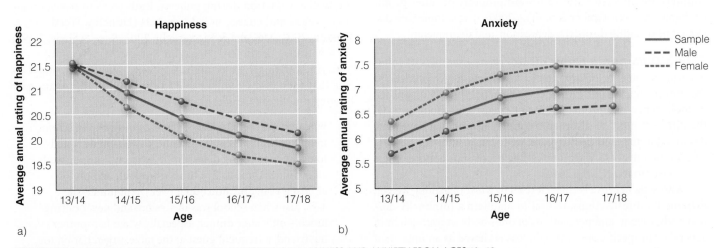

a)

b)

FIGURE 9.5 A AND B ▶ DEVELOPMENTAL TRAJECTORIES OF HAPPINESS AND ANXIETY FROM AGES 13–18.
Source: Maciejewski et al., (2016). p. 11

Sporting events provide settings where adolescents can express their exuberant and wild emotions, including joy, pride, and anger.

and focus. Certain contexts like sporting events and pep rallies give adolescents an opportunity to experience the intensity of these intense emotions.

An adolescent can also learn self-calming strategies to reduce emotional intensity if it is distracting or disruptive. Adolescents' lives are strewn with episodes of pleasurable and distressing emotions, and teens become increasingly able to see how these emotional reactions might alter or distort their perceptions and judgments (Larson & Brown, 2007).

Internalizing and Externalizing Problems

After puberty, boys and girls show noticeably different levels of aggression and depression, with girls showing more problems coping with depression and boys showing more problems managing and controlling their aggressive impulses (Farrington, 2009; Graber & Sontag, 2009). These differences are often expressed in terms of **internalizing problems**, in which feelings of hopelessness or worthlessness are directed inward on the self, and **externalizing problems**, sometimes referred to as conduct problems, such as aggression or delinquency, in which the adolescent's conflicts are directed outward toward property or other people (Achenbach, 1991; Graber & Sontag, 2009). Three topics are discussed next: eating disorders, depression, and delinquency.

Eating Disorders. **Eating disorders** are examples of internalizing problems—turning one's frustration, anger, anxiety, or fear inward on the self. Eating disorders are typically diagnosed in adolescence, and primarily but not exclusively among girls. Of the different types of disordered eating patterns that have been described in the medical literature, we focus on anorexia nervosa and bulimia nervosa. Each one can be expressed in more or less severe symptoms (NIMH, 2014).

Anorexia nervosa is characterized by a fear of gaining weight, extreme food restrictions, refusal to maintain a minimally normal body weight, and perceptions of one's body as overweight in general or in specific areas. Weight loss is viewed as an important accomplishment accompanied by increased self-esteem. Anorexia

is observed about 2 ½ times more frequently in girls than boys, with symptoms most commonly observed after the onset of puberty. Adolescents with this condition focus their behavior on weight loss. They take an obsessive, determined position in rejecting most foods, accompanied by dieting, fasting, or excessive exercise. They also tend to have a distorted perception of their body image, seeing themselves as much fatter than they really are. With treatment, some patients recover, some have periods of recovery with relapses, and others experience an ongoing battle with significant declines in health. Unfortunately, only about one third of those struggling with anorexia seek treatment (Eating Disorder Hope, 2016). Without effective treatment, anorexia nervosa can cause the deterioration of many physical functions including bone loss, damage to the heart, and organ failure. According to the National Institute of Mental Health, anorexia is associated with the highest mortality risk of any psychiatric disorder (NIMH, 2014).

Bulimia nervosa involves recurring spurts of binging and overeating, followed by the use of different strategies to prevent the absorption of food, such as induced vomiting, the use of laxatives, or strenuous exercise. People with bulimia are usually able to maintain their body weight, but tend to experience body shape and weight dissatisfaction. Bulimia is more common in female adolescents but is experienced somewhat more commonly by male adolescents than is anorexia. Individuals who suffer from bulimia are usually ashamed of their eating and often eat in secret. Their eating is often experienced as a frenzy or an intense loss of control, followed by self-criticism and depression. Health risks associated with bulimia are linked to induced vomiting and laxative abuse including acid reflux disorder, inflamed and sore throat, severe dehydration, and intestinal irritation (NIMH, 2014).

The origins of eating disorders are not fully understood. A preoccupation with body appearance may be provoked by the relatively rapid physical changes associated with puberty. Many authors implicate the cultural infatuation with thinness as a stimulus of this condition. Support for this view comes from evidence that anorexia nervosa and bulimia nervosa are almost nonexistent in nonindustrialized countries where there are often food shortages and where thinness is not a cultural ideal. A combination of parent, peer, and media idealization of thinness, coupled with a tendency for girls to experience body dissatisfaction during puberty, leads teens to restrict their food intake and engage in faddish diets (Dunkley, Wertheim, & Paxton, 2001; McCabe & Ricciardelli, 2001; Stice & Shaw, 2004). In a national Youth Risk Behavior Survey, 31 percent of teens described themselves as slightly to very overweight, suggesting that they may be vulnerable to engaging in risky eating or dieting practices (Kann et al., 2014).

> Evie tells me that she learned how to throw up in school, in fact in health class, from a one-day lesson designed to discourage eating disorders. . . . Evie says she vomited after dinner three to five times a week off and on for almost a year. She didn't do it over the summer, she says, just when school was in session; and never during lunch—only after dinner, especially when her mother's boyfriend, a frequent guest at the table, urged her on to extra helpings of Tater Tots or dessert. On those nights,

she'd wait until the dishes were done, then, a little while later, she'd mosey into the kitchen and pilfer a spoon. (Orenstein, 2000, p. 91)

The psychoanalytic view is that eating disorders link back to fear of sexual maturity and are an unconscious strategy to delay entry into adulthood. The family system perspective emphasizes the parents' control or over-control of their child's actions and preferences. Eating disorders, in this view, are a way for a child to exert control or power over one key area, eating, in a context where little power is permitted. In addition to these theories, some clinicians describe the adolescents who suffer from anorexia as having difficulty accepting and expressing their emotions. Compared with adolescents who have other types of emotional disorders, adolescents with anorexia show less emotional expressivity, greater timidity, and more submissiveness. Adolescents with anorexia have been described as "duty bound, rigidly disciplined, and moralistic with underlying doubts and anxious hesitancy" (Strober, 1981, pp. 289–290).

Certain genetic factors are associated with eating disorders. Twin studies provide evidence of a hereditary component to eating disorders. Three groups of genes are associated with eating disorders, especially through their role in emotional regulation, anxiety, and appetite suppression and weight gain or loss. The first group of genes influences the receptors and transporters of serotonin, which functions in the brain to control appetite, mood, sleep, memory, and learning. The second group of genes is related to brain-derived neurotrophic factor (BDNF), a protein that supports the growth of neurons in the brain. BDNF is also associated with appetite and weight gain or loss. Finally, genes associated with estrogen receptors have been tied to food intake as well as to depression and anxiety (Klump & Culbert, 2007). The exact role of each gene group in contributing to eating disorders or the severity of symptoms is not known. One hypothesis is that a few genes make the person vulnerable to eating disorders when they are exposed to certain environmental conditions. For example, girls who are engaged in specific types of activities such as ballet, gymnastics, or modeling, where weight is very important and where they are likely to be exposed to the stresses of competition and control, may be especially likely to develop eating disorders if they also have the genetic vulnerability that supports this condition.

Because of the seriousness and widespread nature of eating disorders, public health experts are working to create a more positive acceptance of people of various body types and shapes, with less focus on thinness. Advertisers are being urged to regulate ads promoting weight loss programs and products to children and adolescents and to disclose more accurately the amount of weight that can be lost. With the recent public health concerns about obesity, physicians may rely too heavily on height-weight tables as they discuss health with adolescents especially since those tables do not reflect individual variability in pubertal development at each chronological age. The current preoccupation with obesity may, in fact, contribute to a medically encouraged focus on thinness. The Academy for Eating Disorders has tried to encourage the fashion industry to support the health of models by setting minimal body mass index (BMI) guidelines for models. They oppose the trend of presenting design collections on extremely thin models. However, the United States does not regulate the fashion industry. In comparison to laws passed in France and Israel, there are no requirements for fashion models to have a medical exam to certify that they are of a healthy weight for their height and body type (Anvar, 2016).

Depression.   There is growing concern about the number of adolescents who experience **depression**. According to a national survey, 30 percent of teens in grades 9–12 felt sad or hopeless almost every day for two or more weeks in a row during the past 12 months, such that they had to stop doing some of their usual activities (Kann et al., 2014). Depression can be observed in different patterns. The most likely pattern observed in adolescence is depressed mood; however, major depressive disorder is estimated to be observed in 4 to 5 percent of adolescents worldwide (Petersen et al., 1993; Thapar, Collishaw, Pine, & Thepar, 2012).

Depressed mood refers to feeling sad or despondent, a loss of hope, a sense of being overwhelmed by the demands of the world, and general unhappiness. Almost everyone experiences this kind of depression at some time or another, describing it as the blues, feeling down in the dumps, or feeling low. Related symptoms include worrying, moodiness, crying, loss of appetite, difficulty sleeping, tiredness, loss of interest in or enjoyment of activities, and difficulty concentrating. These bouts of depression may range from mild, short-lived periods of being sad and discouraged to severe feelings of guilt and worthlessness. A depressed mood may be predictive of more serious emotional disorders, but it is not in itself a clinical diagnosis. Depression appears to increase for both boys and girls during adolescence, with a peak at about ages 17 or 18 (Petersen et al., 1993). For many girls, a few days each month of depressed mood are associated with their menstrual cycle.

For a diagnosis of *major depressive disorder*, the adolescent must have experienced at least 2 weeks of a depressed mood or loss of interest or irritability, and four or more of the following additional symptoms in that same 2-week period: weight loss or weight gain, insomnia or sleep problems, restlessness or having difficulty moving, fatigue or loss of energy, feelings of worthlessness or inappropriate guilt, difficulties concentrating, and recurring thoughts of death, suicide, or plans to commit suicide (Graber & Sontag, 2009; NIMH, 2016).

Factors Associated with Adolescent Depression. No single known cause is accepted as the explanation for depression. Neuroimaging of the brains of individuals with major depressive disorder has identified an area of the prefrontal cortex that is reduced in size and shows reduced functional links with the amygdala, a region of the brain that is associated with the regulation of emotions. This observation of a disruption in the link between a higher order system that evaluates information, and a lower order system that recognizes and reacts to threat coincides well with the symptoms of major depressive disorder that combine cognitive deficits and difficulties in emotion regulation (Insel, 2007).

Recalling the research on the interaction between depressed mothers and their infants discussed in chapter 5 (Infancy), it is hard to separate genetic and environmental factors in the etiology of clinical depression. Having a depressed mother increases the risk of depression during adolescence. Teens whose mothers are depressed are characterized by more anxious attachments, more suicidal thoughts, and more frequent episodes of depression than teens whose mothers are not depressed (Essau, 2004). The direction of influence between brain and behavior is difficult to establish. Are some children more vulnerable to the negative impact of disrupted parenting because of some genetic neurological abnormality, or does the disrupted parenting produce a change in emotional regulation that eventually results in structural and functional abnormalities in the brain? These questions have not been fully answered.

Parental loss or rejection increases an adolescent's vulnerability to depression. In one longitudinal study of the consequences of economic pressures on families, a connection was shown between the family's economic stresses and increased parental depression. Economic strain is associated with heightened marital conflict, increased hostility, and less nurturance toward the children, resulting in subsequent adjustment problems in adolescent daughters, especially problems with hostility and depression (Conger et al., 1993; Tomarken, Dichter, Garber, & Simien, 2004).

Psychosocial adversity is associated with increased risks for depression. Adolescents are often exposed to more negative events than are younger children. Adolescents are more aware of what other people are experiencing, and because more is expected of them, there is more to worry about. School is more demanding, and there are more instances of high-stakes testing; selection or rejection in teams, clubs, and activities; and new performance standards (Locker & Cropley, 2004). Teens have a wider circle of relationships than younger children through which they are exposed to more problems, expectations, and disappointments.

Adolescents report experiencing hassles in the following domains: social alienation (disagreements with teachers, disliking other students), excessive demands (not enough time to meet responsibilities, not enough time for sleep), romantic concerns (dissatisfaction in a romantic relationship), decisions about one's personal future (important decisions about a future career), loneliness and unpopularity (being ignored), assorted annoyances and concerns (money problems, disagreement with a boyfriend or girlfriend), social mistreatment (being taken advantage of, having one's trust betrayed), and academic challenge (struggling to meet other people's standards of performance at school) (Kohn & Milrose, 1993). In this list, peer relations, including romantic relations and the elements of interpersonal experience that are part of being a member of a friendship group, play a central role.

Depression is linked to experiencing negative peer comparisons in areas that are considered to be important to others, such as good looks, athletic ability, having money, or having good social skills (Thwaites & Dagnan, 2004). Problems with peer relations can be a source of stress that triggers depression. At the same time, depression can lead to disruptions in peer relationships. Adolescents who are depressed may make more negative meaning of social interactions, feel more dependent on others to confirm their sense of self-worth, and have less energy or emotional resources for coping with experiences of rejection. Whereas having close friends who are not depressed may be a protective factor against depression, having friends who are depressed may actually induce a depressed mood. Depressed teens may ruminate about their problems, focus largely on negative experiences, experience more conflicts with each other, and generally convey dissatisfaction in their relationships (Brendgen, Lamarche, Wanner, & Vitaro, 2010). There is some evidence that girls who are depressed at age

15 are more likely to enter long-term romantic relationships with partners who are coercive, nonsupportive, and physically violent (Hammen, 2009). The implication is that depression plays a role in continuing to be exposed to stressful interpersonal relationships, which, in turn, create new sources of depression.

Adolescents are relatively inexperienced in coping with these kinds of stressors. They may not have developed strategies for interrupting or reducing the feelings of grief or discouragement that accompany stressful life events. The combination of pressures on parents, especially marital conflicts and economic pressures that affect youth, plus exposure to their own failures, disappointments, and loss of relationships with peers and in school, are clearly linked to a negative mood in adolescents, especially sadness and depression. Feelings of depression may be intensified by accompanying hormonal changes (Hartlage, Brandenburg, & Kravitz, 2004). Young people may become convinced of their worthlessness, and this distortion of thought may lead them toward social withdrawal or self-destructive actions.

Gender Differences in Depression.

Most studies find no differences in depression between prepubescent boys and girls; however, during the period from about age 11 to 15, gender differences are systematically noted and continue to be evident into adulthood. Experiences of depression appear to be more common in adolescent girls than in boys (Graber & Sontag, 2009).

Several ideas have been offered to explain this gender difference. First, the estrogen cycle has been linked to changes in mood, with periods of low estrogen production linked to negative feelings and low self-esteem. One related hypothesis is that the estrogen cycle in girls is accompanied by a new sensitivity to stress, which results in new and more intense feelings of sadness, anxiety, and depression (Soares & Zitek, 2008). Second, at puberty, girls become critical of their bodies, especially concerns about being overweight and unattractive. This attitude may lead to prolonged feelings of dissatisfaction with the self and a consequent depression. When coupled with restricted dietary intake, girls may feel listless and drained of energy. Third, girls tend to look within for explanations of their failures and problems, blaming them on their own lack of ability; in contrast, boys tend to focus on factors outside the self, blaming other people or unfair conditions for their failures.

Fourth, even when girls receive strong social support from their parents and friends, they are also somewhat more sensitive to the problems that people in their support network are having. Girls who have higher levels of caring and are involved in the problems of their close friends are more vulnerable to depression (Gore, Aseltine, & Colten, 1993). Any negative experiences that a girl's best friend or members of her family are going through tend to add to her own negative mood. For example, one study found a significant link between mothers' emotional distress and their daughters' internalizing symptoms over the period from age 11 to 22. The same association was not found for adolescent boys and their mothers (Crawford et al., 2001).

Finally, adolescent girls may begin to experience numerous micro-aggressions in middle school and high school spawned by the sexist views of teachers, male peers, and even their parents. These negative messages create a picture of a world in which the adolescent girl is viewed as less important, less competent, and

Ironically, the fact that girls are likely to try to comfort and support their friends during periods of emotional turmoil makes them more vulnerable to negative moods and depression. How might adolescent girls protect themselves from this negative consequence of close friendships?

less entitled to her own independent views than her male peers. The result is increased feelings of insecurity, lack of confidence, and new feelings of worthlessness.

Depressed mood is of special concern during early adolescence for several reasons. First, it is associated with adolescent suicide. (For further discussion of adolescent suicide, see the **Applying Theory and Research to Life** box.) Second, depression is linked to alcohol and drug abuse. Adolescents who are struggling with strong feelings of depression may turn to alcohol or other drugs to try to alleviate or escape from these feelings. Third, adolescents who are depressed may be unable to participate effectively in the classroom, so their academic performance deteriorates. Finally, depression during adolescence may be a forerunner of severe depression later in adulthood.

Delinquency. **Delinquency** is an example of externalizing problems related to difficulties in controlling or regulating one's impulses. *Delinquent offenses* are actions for which an adult could be prosecuted. Then there are offenses such as truancy, running away, or underage drinking that are known as *status offenses*, which are illegal for adolescents. Many adolescents commit some type of delinquent act that goes undetected. For most young people, the fear and guilt that follow a delinquent act are usually enough punishment to prevent further violations.

In an examination of a 10-year period of delinquency cases handled by juvenile courts in the United States from 2004 to 2014, the number of cases declined by 37 percent (Furdella & Puzzanchera, 2015). Despite this promising decline, a substantial number of teens are involved in violent and property crimes. There were 38,414 teens under age 18 arrested for violent crimes and 173,500 teens arrested for property crimes in 2014 (Federal Bureau of Investigation, 2014). In a grey area, not listed as a crime, incidents of cyberbullying, harassment, and sexual intimidation among teens has become a focus in the field of violence prevention. According to the Youth Risk Behavior survey,

21 percent of girls and 8.5 percent of boys in grades 9 through 12 reported being electronically bullied in the past year (Kann et al., 2014).

Violent Teens. Not all teens who commit delinquent acts are involved in violent crimes or repeated offenses. In a longitudinal study of more than 4,500 high school seniors and high school dropouts in California and Oregon, more than half the sample reported being involved in violent behavior—65 percent of the boys and 41 percent of the girls. A subset of these youth, the repeat offenders, were persistently involved in violent acts and were also significantly more likely to be involved in other high-risk delinquent behaviors such as selling drugs, committing felonies, and using alcohol, marijuana, or other drugs. These extremely violent youths were also more likely to drop out of school and to have other mental health problems (Ellickson, Saner, & McGuigan, 1997). The teens who begin their delinquent behavior at a young age, do poorly in school and have low levels of school engagement, who are involved in drug use in middle school, and who hang out with peers who also use drugs are likely to engage in a pattern of increasing involvement in violence against others (Ellickson & McGuigan, 2000). Other studies implicate early negative childhood experiences, especially physical abuse, as a predictive factor of violent delinquent behavior among boys (Baglivio & Epps, 2016; van der Put & de Ruiter, 2016).

The idea that certain young offenders are more likely to follow a path toward continued violent crime makes decisions about sentencing especially troubling. Efforts to curb youth violence must pursue a differentiated approach—creating programs that are appropriate for the youth who engage in isolated acts of delinquency in their teen years and other interventions focusing on the serious offenders who have multiple problems and are likely to be involved in both aggressive behavior and antisocial delinquency well into their adulthood (Farrington, 2009).

Delinquency, especially acts against property or other people, is an expression of externalizing behavior. At his sentencing hearing, Trevor apologizes to the court and to the victim's family for his assault on a 5-year-old girl.

Adolescent Suicide

I thought how easily you could kill yourself when you were drunk. Take a bath, fall asleep, drown. No turtle would come floating by to rescue you, no spotter plane would find you. I took my mother's knife and played johnny johnny johnny on the playhouse floor. I was drunk, stabbed myself every few throws. I held my hand up and there was satisfaction at seeing my blood, the way there was when I saw the red gouges on my face that people stared at and turned away. (Fitch, 1999, pp. 184–185)

Suicide at any age is deeply troubling, but adolescent suicide is cause for special anguish and soul searching. Public concern over adolescent suicide has been increasing in response to the rise in the suicide rate among adolescents. The suicide rate across all age groups in the United States, including those 15 to 24, has been increasing since 1999. Suicide is the second leading cause of death among adolescents ages 15 to 19. In 2013, there were 3,652 suicides in this age group, a rate of 8.3 deaths per 100,000 (Heron, 2016). These suicide rates may be underestimated, as there is a social stigma to reporting a death as suicide, and there are financial consequences to identifying a death as a suicide rather than as an accident. It is suspected that a significant number of adolescent deaths involving automobile accidents were actually suicides.

Death by suicide is only part of the picture. Every year, large numbers of young people attempt suicide or engage in self-harming behaviors. According to the Youth Risk Behavior Surveillance System report, 17 percent of high school students had seriously considered suicide and 8 percent had attempted suicide in the preceding 12 months (Kann et al., 2014). Girls are twice as likely as boys to attempt suicide, but boys are four times as likely as girls to die in a suicide attempt.

The rate of adolescent suicide differs by racial and ethnic groups. The risk of suicide death is substantially higher among American Indian and Alaskan Natives, especially the boys, than among other racial/ethnic

groups. Suicide attempts are highest among American Indian and Alaskan Native girls. Differences in rates of suicide and suicide attempts across racial and ethnic groups suggest different risk and protective factors tied to culture, acculturation strains, exposure to stresses of poverty and community disorganization, the stigma of discussing mental health problems, and the strength of ties to a supportive community (Goldston et al., 2008).

Instances of suicides may be prompted by widely publicized suicides as well as by internal depression or as a reaction to humiliation or loss. In attempting to understand the causes of suicide, primary risk factors have been identified. These factors were reconstructed by studying the lives of adolescents who committed or attempted suicide. However, they may not be very useful in predicting whether a particular individual will commit or attempt suicide. Although depression and low self-esteem are often included in the profile of those who attempt suicide, they are usually coupled with other issues. Risk factors often come in combination with each other. The risk factors among adolescents include:

- Drug and alcohol abuse
- Mental health disorders, especially depression or schizophrenia
- A prior suicide attempt
- Family history of psychiatric illness or substance abuse disorders
- A victim of family violence, including physical, sexual, or verbal abuse
- Limited family or other close social support
- A family history of suicidal behavior
- A high number of stressful life events or recent losses, including discrimination, victims of bullying, or social rejection
- People who identify as a sexual minority
- Cultural values that discourage help-seeking
- The availability of a firearm
- Exposure to the suicidal behavior of others, including family, peers, in the news, or in fictional accounts

In addition to these factors, there is usually some precipitating event. Recent reports of teen suicides related to cyberbullying and sexting suggest a new context in which teens can experience humiliation. A shameful or humiliating experience, a notable failure, and rejection by a parent or a romantic partner are all examples. Use of drugs that alter cognitive functioning and decrease inhibitions, coupled with easy access to a gun, suggest one likely path from suicidal ideation to suicidal action.

Suicide and attempted suicide continue to be surrounded by social stigma for individuals and their families. Moreover, there is pervasive misunderstanding about the causes and possible approaches to prevention, thereby impeding efforts at intervention. The following myths about suicide illustrate these problems (Web MD, 2016):

1. *Discussing suicide might encourage it.* There is no evidence to support this statement.
2. *The only people who are suicidal are those who are mentally ill.* Suicidal thoughts may be an aspect of a mental illness. But many people who have mental illness are not suicidal; and not all people who attempt suicide have a mental illness.
3. *Individuals who talk about suicide won't really do it.* Talking about suicide may be a way to reach out for support or help. Any reference to thinking about suicide and any attempts at suicide should be taken seriously.
4. *There is no warning for suicides.* Suicide is usually accompanied by evidence of serious distress. There are warning signs that can be helpful in connecting a person who is thinking about suicide with appropriate help. However, it is very difficult to predict which people will attempt it.

The U.S. Department of Health and Human Services (2102) issued a monograph, *The 2012 National Strategy for Suicide Prevention: Goals and Objectives for Action*. A key premise of this monograph is that suicide is a public health problem that is preventable. Four action components of prevention include (1) creating supportive environments that promote healthy, empowered individuals and families; (2) strengthening clinical and community preventive services and reducing the stigma for seeking mental health services; (3) improving the availability of timely treatment and supportive services adapted to groups that are particularly at risk; and (4) improving data collection, research, and evaluation of suicide prevention initiatives.

A study of the impact of the Signs of Suicide (SOS) program in 92 schools demonstrated the potential impact of effective intervention. Students who participated in the program showed an increase in help seeking of 60 percent in the month following the introduction of the curriculum. School coordinators found no negative reactions among students who were exposed to information about suicide and suicide prevention, and some improvement in student and teacher communication following this intervention (Aseltine, 2003). A later replication, evaluating the program among ninth graders found a substantial decrease in reported suicide attempts, improved understanding of depression and suicide, more positive attitudes about intervening if a friend shows signs of suicidal intention, and more willingness to seek help for themselves (Schilling, Aseltine, & James, 2016). To learn more about suicide prevention, visit the website of the American Foundation for Suicide Prevention, or the Substance Abuse and Mental Health Services Administration of the U.S. Department of Health and Human Services.

Critical Thinking Questions

1. Propose an explanation to account for the fact that girls are more likely than boys to attempt suicide, but boys are much more likely than girls to die as a result of their attempts.

2. Evaluate the statement that suicide is a preventable public health problem. Why is suicide a public health problem? In your opinion, is suicide preventable? If so, what are the key steps to prevention? If not, why not?

3. Speculate about why school administrators, teachers, parents, and/or students might resist the implementation of an SOS program in their schools. What resources should schools and communities have available for teens and their families if they do implement such a program?

Risk Factors. A combination of biological, psychological, and societal risk factors are associated with delinquency. At the biological level, issues related to executive control, including impulsiveness, attention deficit disorder, and hyperactivity, are important considerations. The teen's neurological reward system is especially sensitive to social cues, especially the approval and encouragement of peers. Teens are more likely to engage in delinquent behavior when their peers are also involved in these kinds of activities. At the psychological level, issues of poor school performance, lack of empathy, a belief in the harmful intentions of others, and anxious-resistant attachment have been identified as predictors. At the societal level, childhood victimization, minimal parental supervision, modeling of criminal behavior of parents and other community adults, and an active criminal network in the community that recruits youth have all been identified as risk factors (Farrington, 2009). The neighborhood environment can play an important role in whether a teen engages in delinquent behavior. In a study that followed children in foster care, those who were relocated into neighborhoods characterized by greater poverty and instability had a greater likelihood of having a formal delinquency charge (Huang, Ryan, & Rhoden, 2016).

Delinquent Girls. Much of the literature on causes and characteristics of delinquent behavior has focused on boys. However, in 2004 the Office of Juvenile Justice and Delinquency Prevention created the Girls Study Group to understand more clearly girls' paths into delinquency, the way girls are treated in the juvenile justice system, and the risk and protective factors that can guide prevention programs. Results of this study group are published in *The Delinquent Girl* (M.A. Zahn, 2009). Although many of the same predictive factors are associated with delinquent behavior for boys and girls, a few factors seem to be particular to girls. Girls are exposed to a greater number of negative life events than boys and may be more biologically sensitive to the negative impact of stressors. Girls are more likely than boys to experience childhood sexual abuse and/or rape, which is predictive of subsequent depression, anxiety, and post-traumatic stress disorder. These mental health problems are implicated in subsequent delinquent behaviors. As a result of victimization, girls more than boys are likely to run away from home, which is a status offense. This often leads to other delinquent acts including prostitution, survival sex, and drug trafficking. Finally, early pubertal development is a risk factor, especially for girls in families that have ineffective parental monitoring or where affectionate bonds are disrupted through divorce, imprisonment, or desertion. Under these conditions, early maturing girls are more likely to engage in more risk taking, spend time with older peers who may encourage deviant behavior, and have older boyfriends whose influence may lead to engaging in delinquent behaviors.

Weapon Carrying. Within the larger context of delinquent and violent behavior, weapon carrying is a public health safety concern. As part of the National Youth Risk surveillance system, high school students are asked about their involvement in weapon carrying and experiences of being threatened by someone with a weapon. In 2015, 24 percent of male and 7.5 percent of female high school students said they carried a weapon at least one day in the past month. Six percent of students reported having been

In Austin, Texas, junior high school students go through a metal detector before entering their school. Teachers, students, and visitors are all subjected to this procedure.

while, at the same time, lowering one's sensitivity to the pain and suffering of others. Prior victimization and exposure to violence clearly influence teens, increasing their fears and their involvement in weapon carrying as a way to protect themselves (Yun & Hwang, 2011).

In a reanalysis of the Youth Risk Behavior surveillance survey data, researchers examined the relationship of having been bullied at school and carrying weapons on school grounds. They considered several aspects of school-based intimidation including not going to school because they felt unsafe there, having had property stolen or damaged at school, having been threatened or injured with a weapon, and having been in a physical fight. Among students who had experienced one of these risk factors, 28 percent reported having brought a weapon to school; among students who experienced three or more of these factors, 62 percent brought a weapon to school. These data suggest a picture of weapon carrying for protection and/or retaliation (Kemp, 2014).

FURTHER REFLECTION: Think back on your early adolescence, from the age of about 12 to the end of high school. Describe situations that made you feel happy, hopeful, competent, and self-assured. Describe situations that made you feel discouraged, angry, frustrated, or worthless. How would you characterize your emotional development during that time of your life? How did your emotions change over this period? How did your ability to express or control the expression of your emotions change? Four problem areas were discussed: eating disorders, depression, suicide, and delinquent behaviors. How aware were you of these problems when you were in high school? What, if any efforts were made to educate students about these topics?

threatened with a weapon on school property at least once in the past month (Kann et al., 2016).

Why do high school students carry weapons? In one analysis, teens who carried guns were found to differ from those who carried other weapons to school. Only three factors predicted carrying guns to school: having been involved in physical fights, knowing that one's peers have guns at school, and being male. The likelihood that boys would bring a gun to school increased as the incidence of gun ownership in the peer network increased, suggesting both fear of violence and a tendency toward violent behavior. In contrast, bringing other weapons to school was predicted by seven factors including having been in physical fights, knowing that peers carry guns, knowing about drug use among peers, knowing that that there were gang members at the school, skipping school, being male, and a perception that the school rules were unfair and not strictly enforced (Cao, Zhang, & He, 2008). In an effort to protect children from the violence associated with weapon-carrying, many schools have introduced metal detectors and security guards who screen all students as they enter the building.

Some authors suggest that many boys who commit violent crimes are suffering from a form of post-traumatic stress disorder that leaves them angry, disconnected from their feelings, and unable to anticipate or control overwhelming images of violence that surge up with minimal provocation (Slovak & Singer, 2001). Chronic exposure to violence has a disruptive impact on neurological development. Youth who are exposed to violence experience higher levels of symptoms associated with post-traumatic stress disorder, including difficulties regulating emotional reactions, difficulties concentrating, and difficulties inhibiting aggressive impulses. Exposure to violence also increases aggressive cognitions and the attribution of aggressive motives to others

Membership in the Peer Group

OBJECTIVE 5 Analyze the nature of peer relations in early adolescence, especially the formation of cliques and crowds, and contrast the typical relationships with parents and peers during this stage.

The importance of peer interaction for psychosocial development is a continuous theme across the life span. Friendships, many of which are formed in middle childhood or even earlier, remain important in early adolescence. However, during early adolescence, the peer group becomes more structured and organized than it was previously and **peer group membership** becomes much more salient (Newman, 1982). Before the adolescent period, it is important to have friends but not so important to be a member of a definable group. A child's friends are often found in the neighborhood, local clubs and sports teams, community centers, or classrooms. It is not unusual for children whose parents are friends to become friends. And in many families, children identify their siblings and their cousins as their good friends. In early adolescence, young people spend more time away from home. Teens are more likely to interact with each other across classroom boundaries, leading to the formation of larger, more loosely affiliated friendship groups. Dyadic (two-person) friendships become an increasingly important source of social support, and the quality of these friendships changes. In addition to dyadic friendships, adolescents form small groups of friends, sometimes referred to as *cliques*, and in most communities they also become identified with a larger constellation of teens who have a common social identity, usually referred to as a *crowd* (Brown and Larson, 2009).

Cliques and Crowds

Cliques are small friendship groups of 5 to 10 friends. Usually, these groups provide the framework for frequent interactions both within school and in the neighborhood. Adolescents usually do not refer to their group of friends as a clique, but the term is used to connote a certain closeness among the members. They hang out together, know about each other's families, plan activities together, and stay in touch with each other from day to day. Within cliques, intimate information is exchanged and, therefore, a high degree of loyalty is expected. In the transition from middle school or junior high school to the larger, more heterogeneous environment of high school, there is a reordering of students according to a variety of abilities and a corresponding reordering of friendship groups. It may take some time for adolescents to find their clique, the members of which may change from time to time over the first year or two of high school. There is quite a lot of variability in the stability of the cliques; some dissolve over the course of a school year, and others remain intact throughout high school.

Crowd refers to a large group that can be recognized by a few predominant characteristics, such as their orientation toward academics, involvement in athletics, use of drugs, or involvement in deviant behavior. Crowds are more reputational than cliques, reflecting students' values and attitudes, preferred activities, and school and nonschool engagement. Students can typically name the crowds at their school, but when asked, not all students clearly fit with a specific crowd, and some students are in more than one.

Membership in a crowd at the high school may be based on one or more of the following characteristics: good looks; athletic ability; social class; academic performance; future goals; affiliation with a religious, racial, or ethnic group; special talents; involvement with drugs or deviant behavior; or general alienation from school. Although the criteria for group membership may not be publicly articulated, the groups tend to include or exclude members according to consistent standards. In a racially diverse sample of more than

600 middle school and high school students, some of the most common crowds mentioned were floaters (belonging to more than one group), nice or regulars, populars, middles (related to income), jocks, nerds/unpopulars, preps, skateboarders, and misfits/alternatives. Roughly 20 percent of the students said they did not belong to any group (Lohman, 2000).

In racially and ethnically diverse schools, it is not uncommon for students to identify crowds based specifically on ethnic categories, such as the Asian American group, the Mexican Americans, and the African Americans. Given the language diversity of some communities, adolescents may be drawn to peers who have a common home language. Banding together with other students who speak one's native language can provide a buffer from the direct or inadvertent stigma of limited English proficiency in a predominantly English-speaking school (Hill & Torres, 2010).

Crowds can be identified in a school setting by their dress, their language, the activities in which they participate, and the school settings in which they are most likely to congregate. For example, in one school, the crowds took their names from the places in the school where they hang out: "the fashionable 'wall people' who favor a bench along the wall outside the cafeteria, and the punkish 'trophy-case' kids who sit on the floor under a display of memorabilia" (Adler, 1999, p. 57). The peer culture in any high school is determined largely by the nature of the crowds that exist and their characteristic patterns of interaction. These large, visible groups provide an array of prototypical identities. Although many adolescents resist being labeled as part of one crowd or another, they usually recognize that these categories of students exist in their school. Thus, the youth culture, as it is sometimes called, actually comprises a number of subcultures, each endorsing somewhat different attitudes toward adults and other authority figures, school and academic goals,

Hero Images/Hero Images/Getty Images

Selfies provide a new way for members of a clique to preserve their "groupness". What better way to document a cohesive group of friends.

drugs and deviant behavior, and expressing different orientations toward partying and social life.

The relationship of crowd affiliation to behavior, especially behavior problems, has been established in research in the United States and Australia (Prinstein & LaGreca, 2002). In an effort to expand this picture to adolescents in Europe, researchers carried out a study of crowd affiliation in the Netherlands (Delsing, ter Bogt, Engles, & Meeus, 2007). The sample included over 2,000 adolescents ages 12 to 19 from 12 schools who self-identified as Dutch, Antillean, Moroccan, and Turkish. Adolescents were asked to rate how much they identified as a member of one of 10 crowds: punks, metal heads, Gothics, rural youth, Christian youth, normals, hip-hoppers, Rastas, elites, and brains. They also completed measures of aggression, delinquency, anxiety, and depression. The crowds could be differentiated on the basis of four dimensions: their orientation toward conventional or adult values; achievement and financial independence; urban youth culture, rebelliousness, nonconformity; and enthusiasm for rock music. Crowds whose members had a stronger conventional or achievement orientation also had lower levels of aggression and delinquency. Crowds whose members had stronger urban or alternative orientations also had higher levels of depression, delinquency, and aggression.

Group Boundaries and Norms

Membership in cliques is relatively stable but always vulnerable to change. Three processes contribute to the similarity among members of a clique: selection, socialization, and deselection. **Selection** refers to the idea that teens find other teens who share certain common interests, values, or preferences (e.g., teens who smoke find friends who smoke). **Socialization** refers to the idea that friends influence one another to behave in similar ways and to endorse similar views (e.g., teens who hope to go to college encourage each other to study, do well, and keep their grades up). **Deselection** refers to the idea that if an adolescent begins to differ from his or her friends on important behaviors or values, the relationships typically drift apart (Brown & Larson, 2009).

Cliques often have some central members who serve as leaders, others who are regularly included in clique activities, and still others who are on the periphery. At the same time, there are the "wannabes" who would like to be part of the clique but for one reason or another are never fully included. Some students try to push their way into a certain group; others may fall out of a group. Dating someone who is a member of a clique or getting involved in a school activity (such as athletics or cheerleading) may be a way of moving into a new peer group. A more likely scenario is that through gossip, refusal to adhere to shared group expectations, or failure in heterosexual relationships, individuals may slip outside the boundaries of their clique. Even when the specific members of a clique change, new members tend to have some common characteristics. Cliques of druggies find new friends who do drugs; cliques of jocks find new friends who excel in sports.

With the use of social networking, members of a crowd can maintain boundaries and solidify identity across a large group of "friends." By sharing photos, comments, gossip, information and misinformation, and by posting images or comments about new technologies, fashion, or fads as "legit," "fine," or "dope," members of the crowd can influence one another's values and behaviors. The instantaneous nature of online communication can accelerate peer contagion, influencing risky health behaviors, offensive sexual behaviors, gun ownership, and other forms of deviance (Bowes et al., 2015; Dishion & Tipsord, 2011). But the use of social media can also influence positive behaviors like attendance at school functions, enthusiasm for movies and books, volunteering, or civic engagement. Peers can use social media to embarrass or exclude, but they can also recognize and "call out" accomplishments of their friends. Texting with friends is a valued way that teens stay in touch on a daily basis. Among those who use social media, a majority say that they feel more connected to their peers' lives and daily activities, they feel better connected to their friends' feelings, and they have felt support from peers when they have been going through difficult times (Pew Research Center 2015d).

Changing one's crowd identity may be more difficult than changing from one clique to another. Adolescents appear to be on a trajectory toward certain crowd identities beginning in middle childhood. This trajectory is influenced by their athletic interests and competence, their academic abilities, their physical attractiveness, and their orientation toward authority (Stone et al., 2008). When the school population is relatively stable, it is more difficult to lose one's identity as a member of a particular crowd. In some schools, specific crowds have strong animosity toward each other. Members of the opposing crowds may occupy different areas of the school, participate in different activities, mock or ridicule each other, or articulate their differences in symbolic ways through dress, art, and music. When these differences are widely known, it becomes even more difficult to shift crowd identities. More research is needed about the contexts that permit changes in crowd membership and the motives that students might have for wanting a new crowd affiliation.

Membership in an adolescent peer group is a forerunner of membership in adult social organizations. As teens develop a focused peer group affiliation, they become aware of that group's internal structure and norms, as well as its relationship to other groups in the school environment. The existence of a complex peer structure in the high school environment and the motivation to find one's place within it puts pressure on the maturing mind to understand this structure. At the same time, maturing cognitive capacities permit adolescents to consider multiple variables and to speculate about hypothetical relationships. These abilities, newly stimulated by social motives, are now applied to an analysis of the high school peer structure. The structure may include patterns of social status, dominance, popularity, privilege, and relationships with others outside the group. Associated with each of these dimensions of social structure are sets of norms or expectations for the behavior of peer group members. As adolescents discover their positions in the dominance hierarchy of the group, they learn how they may advance within it and what behaviors are expected at various levels. On the basis of all this information, they must decide whether their personal growth is compatible with the peer group affiliation they have made.

Parents and Peers

Under optimal conditions, the increasingly important role of peer relationships in early adolescence takes place within a background of continuing close, supportive relationships with family members. Adolescents describe a variety of overt signs of independence from their families: They may make decisions about clothes, dating, and so on; they may drive cars; they may stay out late; and they may earn their own money. However, they continue to maintain an emotional attachment to their families and to family values. Support from this close inner circle made up largely of family members is an important correlate of well-being and sociability.

Parent–Adolescent Interaction. Using the attachment paradigm as a frame of reference, one can think of adolescence as a time when young people strive to expand their range of exploration with reduced needs to return to the secure base. Adolescents try to decrease their dependence on their parents for setting goals, establishing patterns of tastes and preferences, and making decisions. This does not mean that the sense of closeness and connection with parents is less important. For example, adolescents may not want to seek help from parents when they are experiencing difficulty in their social relationships, but at the same time, if a serious problem arises, they want to know that their parent is available to be supportive and understanding. Adolescents who continue to experience parental warmth also report lower levels of emotional distress than those who report more distant relationships with parents and turn more to peers for support (Operario, Tschann, Flores, & Bridges, 2006). Adolescents can take the point of view of their parents. Although they may not always act as if they are aware, they realize when their behavior has been a source of distress to their parent, or if they have tested the limits of previously agreed-upon rules or boundaries. Within the context of a secure attachment, these times lead to a goal-corrected revision in the balance of autonomy and closeness. In many ways, the parent's desire to foster a child's self-reliance and a child's goal to reduce the parent's authority over day-to-day behaviors are compatible. In the process of achieving these goals, some loss of emotional closeness is likely (Allen, 2008; Collins & Laursen, 2006).

Parent–Adolescent Conflict. As adolescents go through puberty, conflicts with parents are likely. One way of understanding this conflict is to view it as a way for adolescents to achieve new levels of individuation and autonomy while still preserving bonds of closeness and connection (Collins & Laursen, 2006). A meta-analysis of patterns of conflict in White, middle-class families found that frequency of conflict and intensity of conflict were two distinct dimensions. Over time, the frequency of parent–adolescent conflict decreased from early adolescence (ages 10 to 12) to middle adolescence (12 to 16), but the intensity of those conflicts increased (Laursen, Coy, & Collins, 1998). Typically parent–adolescent conflicts are about daily issues, like household chores, cleaning up their room, how money will be spent, whether the child is spending enough time on schoolwork, or curfews, rather than about basic value issues like political ideology or religious beliefs. This same pattern has been observed in African American and White middle-class families (Smetana, Daddis, & Chuang, 2003).

With age, adolescents and their parents expand the range of issues that are considered personal issues that should be decided by teens and not subject to parental authority, such as how they spend their free time, how they dress, or the kind of television shows they watch. Nonetheless, certain areas of morality or safety, like using drugs or smoking cigarettes, still fall under parental authority. Some issues, such as hanging around with people your parents disapprove of, may be topics that require negotiation. They are not clearly in the parental authority or the personal preference domain.

Even though the trend is for the domain of personal preference to increase with age, families differ both within cultures and across cultures in how likely they are to view decisions as legitimately governed by parental authority, personal adolescent preferences, or shared control (Cumsille, Darling, Flaherty, & Martinez, 2009). These differences in perceptions about who has legitimate authority around issues of concern to adolescents are relevant for the extent to which parents and children experience conflict, the extent to which adolescents try to deceive their parents, and the opportunities that parents have to influence their children's decision making. Consider the following narrative written by a Chinese adolescent whose family had recently immigrated to Canada (Li, 2009).

Renee and her dad have a regular evening chess game. They have a relaxed conversation about other things while they play the game. The combination of competition, conversation, and companionship provides an important source of social support for both of them.

Tom & Dee Ann McCarthy/Corbis/Getty Images

My parents said we brought you to Canada because student life in China is too hard. But now I don't think my life has changed except for the place. I am still being pushed very hard.... They always press me like, "you should study, you should study, you should study.... like this." If I just watched TV for 10 minutes, by the 11th minute, they would say "go study, don't watch it" or they would say "if you are tired, you can rest for 5 minutes, then go back to your study." They say this to me almost every day. (Li, 2010, p. 488)

In European American families, as children get older, they are less likely to concede to their parents, and parents are increasingly likely to concede to their children. In African American families, most conflicts end with the child conceding to the parents, preserving the cultural value of obedience and respect for elders (Smetana, Daddis, & Chuang, 2003). In a study of Chinese American adolescents, expectations for personal autonomy seemed to be expressed at a somewhat later age. Urban Chinese American youth were more accepting of open disagreements with their parents than rural youth and described their relationships with parents as less cohesive and more conflictual than rural youth (Wenxin, Meiping, & Fuligni, 2006). Mild, periodic conflicts reflect a changing balance of power or control within the family, as adolescents give voice to their own opinions and defend their choices. The acceptability of these conflicts, their intensity and frequency, and the ways they are resolved appear to be shaped by the cultural context and values regarding individuation and interdependence.

One topic of special interest is parent–adolescent conflict about peer relationships. Parents use a variety of techniques to manage, monitor, and possibly control their adolescent children's peer interactions (Mounts, 2004). Whereas adolescents may seek parental advice from time to time about peer issues, they also view peer friendships, clique membership, and time spent with peers to fall into the category of personal choice. As they get older, adolescents are likely to defend their right to choose their friends and to spend time with friends as they see fit. In a study of an ethnically diverse sample of seventh and eighth graders, high levels of parent–adolescent conflict over peer relationships were associated with greater amounts of delinquent behavior, more drug use, and lower grades (Mounts, 2007). Because this was a correlational study, we do not know whether the parent–adolescent conflict is a result of the parents' assessment that the child's friends are antisocial and engaging in high-risk behaviors, or if the parent–child conflict about peers leads the child to seek out friends who are similarly distressed at home and resort to antisocial, high-risk behaviors.

Parenting and Peer Group Membership. The quality of the home environment, especially the nature of parenting practices, has implications for the adolescent's peer relationships. High levels of power assertion by parents are associated with a greater likelihood of peer rejection during middle childhood. Studies of the relationship of parenting practices to adolescent peer group membership extend this analysis. A model was proposed to examine the relationship of parenting practices to adolescent behaviors and ultimately to crowd affiliation (Brown, Mounts, Lamborn, & Steinberg, 1993; Durbin et al., 1993).

Parenting practices were operationally defined as the extent to which parents emphasized academic achievement, parental monitoring of adolescent behaviors, and the degree to which parents involved adolescents in decision making. Three adolescent behaviors were measured: the students' grade point averages, drug use, and self-reliance. Finally, the students were identified as members of one of six crowds: popular, jocks, brains, normals, druggies, or outcasts.

Parenting practices had both direct and indirect impacts on adolescents' crowd memberships. Parenting practices were linked to the children's behavior, which in turn was a strong predictor of their crowd affiliation. Parents who emphasized academic achievement were likely to have adolescents who had high grades and who were self-reliant, factors that also predicted being popular and not being members of the druggie or outcast groups. Low parental monitoring and little joint decision making were associated with drug use, low self-reliance, and membership in the druggie crowd. Adolescents may perceive their involvement with their peers as a matter of personal preference that is separate and distinct from their family life. However, this research suggests that parental socialization practices and features of the home environment establish a trajectory for the adolescent's likely path toward peer relations.

FURTHER REFLECTION: What are some lessons learned from high school peer relationships that continue to be meaningful to you today?

The Psychosocial Crisis: Group Identity Versus Alienation

OBJECTIVE 6 Explain the psychosocial crisis of group identity versus alienation, the central process through which the crisis is resolved, peer pressure, the prime adaptive ego quality of fidelity to others, and the core pathology of isolation.

Throughout life, tensions arise between the desires for individuality and for connection. Certain cultures emphasize connection over individuality, whereas others put individuality ahead of connection. However, all societies must deal with both aspects of the ego: the *I* as agent, originator, and executive of one's individual thoughts and actions, and the *We* as agent, originator, and executive of collective, cooperative enterprises that preserve and further the survival of the group (Triandis, 1990). During the early years of adolescence, one confronts a new psychosocial conflict, in which pressures to ally oneself with specific groups and to learn to be comfortable functioning as a member of a group are major preoccupations. This conflict is called *group identity versus alienation* (Newman & Newman, 2001).

Group Identity

In early adolescence, young people form a *scheme*—an integrated set of ideas about the norms, expectations, and status hierarchy of the salient groups in their social world. They build these representations from **reference groups**, the groups of which they are members or in which they aspire to hold membership (Gurin & Markus, 1988). Associated with these schemes are strong emotional investments, cognitions, and possibly behavioral patterns. Young people may be viewed by others as belonging to certain groups—for example their racial, religious, academic, school, immigrant status, disability status, or neighborhood identities. You might consider these groups part of the young person's "social address." But these groups are not necessarily salient to the young person's group identity. As a young person prepares to engage in the larger social world, a positive sense of group identity provides confidence that he or she is meaningfully connected to society, has a cognitive map of the characteristics of the social landscape, and the skills or tools to navigate the terrain. Perceiving oneself as a competent member of a group or groups is fundamental to one's self-concept as well as to one's willingness to participate in and contribute to society. The formation of social commitments in early adolescence provides a foundation for the capacity to establish meaningful ties to groups at the personal, community, national, and international levels in adult life (Lawler, Thye, & Yoon, 2009).

Early adolescents experience a search for membership—an internal questioning about the groups of which they are most naturally a part. They ask themselves, "Who am I, and with whom do I belong?" Although membership in a peer group may be the most pressing concern, questions about other group identifications also arise. Adolescents evaluate the nature of their ties to immediate and extended family members, and they begin to understand the unique characteristics of their racial, ethnic, cultural, and sexual identities. They may become identified with various organizations (e.g., religious, political, civic).

In the most positive pattern, peer group membership does not replace attachment to parents or closeness with family. Rather, the adolescent's network of supportive relations is anchored in the family and expands into the domain of meaningful peer relationships. Adolescents who show strong signs of mental health and adaptive coping strategies have positive communication and trusting relationships with parents or other close family members as well as strong feelings of trust and security among their friends.

In the process of seeking group affiliation, adolescents are confronted by the fit—or lack of fit—between their personal needs and the norms and values of relevant social groups in the environment. The process of self-evaluation takes place within the context of the meaningful groups whose members are available for comparison and identification. Needs for social approval, affiliation, leadership, power, and status are expressed in the kinds of group identifications that are made and rejected during the period from age 12 to 18. In a positive resolution of the conflict of group identity versus alienation, adolescents discover one or more groups that provide a sense of group belonging, meet their social needs, and allow them to express their social selves.

Cognitive Processes That Support the Formation of Group Identity

Adolescence is not the first time that children are aware of being a group member or of claiming an affiliation with a group. Young children may be on sports teams, play in an orchestra or band, or belong to a dance group. They tend to define groups on the basis of common activities. In comparison, adolescents have a mental representation of the social groups in their school or community and the relationships among these groups. They are able to analyze the norms and expectations associated with various groups. They can assess the status or prestige of being a member of a particular group, and the ways that group membership affects attitudes and values, shapes interests, and influences one's self-concept through acceptance and rejection (Bettencourt & Hume, 1999). For example, in a high school, teens can identify various crowds and describe distinctions among these groups with regard to their dress, where they hang out at the school, and behaviors or values that are associated with these crowds. Further, adolescents can characterize what it would take to be a member of one of these crowds, the possibility of being in more than one of these crowds, the possibility for interactions among members of these crowds, and the advantages or disadvantages linked to being associated with each of these crowds.

Three cognitive capacities are needed for an adolescent to establish a group identity: (1) group representations, the conceptualization and labeling or classification of groups; (2) group operations, the processes through which groups are formed, maintained, or dissolved; and (3) reflective thinking about groups, an ability to analyze the array of groups and their relationship to one another.

Group Representations. Group representations provide the earliest forms of group identity, reflecting the ability to use words and symbols to signify membership in a group. Children have a wide variety of group experiences and are able to represent their group membership using verbal labels and drawings. The capacity for representing groups and the relationships among groups expands in early adolescence so that youth are able to map more groups simultaneously, including those in their immediate family, school, and peer environments. The expansion of this representational ability may be stimulated by exposure to a greater variety of groups, by increases in representational skills, and by new social demands to establish one's place within the range of existing groups. It may also be a product of neurological changes that accompany puberty.

Group Operations. Group operations include such diverse processes as joining a group, forming in-group and out-group attitudes, stereotyping, quitting or rejecting a group, and exercising leadership in a group. Some of these operations can be observed among toddlers and early-school-age children. They recognize the common members of a group, use fantasy play to coordinate roles with other members of a group, and talk about themselves as part of a family, school, or friendship relationship. Group operations can be observed in neighborhoods, with some children experiencing exclusion and others experiencing acceptance and support. Children as young as 5 or 6 may join sports teams and learn lessons of team spirit, teamwork, and team pride. By the fourth and fifth grades, some children have already begun to experience social isolation and social rejection. In early adolescence, teens develop more advanced skills for connecting to their groups, experiencing bonding and acceptance, participating in leadership and team building, and detecting evidence about the possibility of rejection from their significant groups.

Table 9.4	Four Types of Experiences that Build a Sense of Group Identity
Type of Experience	**Explanation and Example**
Categorizing people and recognizing features of group membership	Awareness of group boundaries and shared markers of members like use of symbols, jargon, or common activities.
Experiencing a sense of history as a member of a group	Continuous interactions over time that create shared knowledge and shared experiences.
Emotional investment in the group	In-group bias, investment in the group members, and efforts to preserve the group's social reputation.
Social evaluation of one's group and its relation to other groups	A capacity to analyze the social hierarchy of the groups in your school or community; to differentiate between how others view one's group and how you value it.

Reflective Thinking About Groups. The formation of group identity involves reflective and comparative thinking. It requires decentering from one's own groups to consider how these groups may be perceived by others, evaluating the strengths and weaknesses of a group, and considering the implications of group membership for how one is treated in the community. Early adolescence is characterized by a new consciousness about one's membership in groups, the boundaries and barriers that separate groups or limit membership in groups, and the social implications of being in one group or another. The emergence of formal operational reasoning brings new capacities for reflection and speculation about social relationships and complex social systems.

Four Types of Experiences That Build a Group Identity

Given the three cognitive capacities that permit the conceptualization of a group identity, we hypothesize that the actual formation of a group identity requires four types of experiences: (1) categorizing people into groups and recognizing the distinguishing features that define members, (2) experiencing a sense of history as a member of a group, (3) having an emotional investment in the group, and (4) detecting the social evaluation of one's group and its relation to other groups (Table 9.4).

Categorizing People and Recognizing Distinguishing Features of Group Members. Groups typically have *boundaries* that limit membership and *shared markers* that bind the members together. In early adolescence, young people learn to read, categorize, and relate to informal peer networks where clique structures provide a comparatively egalitarian learning environment, determine social status, and help define a person's feelings of belonging and worth. Language use, nonverbal gestures, style of dress, use of certain spaces, behaviors such as cigarette smoking or drug use, and participation in specific activities may become markers that delineate group membership and provide a sense of group identification. Having a symbol, a logo, or a tattoo can increase a group's visibility, give it a greater sense of reality, and convey the cohesiveness of the group (Callahan & Ledgerwood, 2016). Friends may invent expressions or unique ways of speaking that help define a group and strengthen members' commitment. Over time, the similarities among members of a peer group are strengthened, thereby clarifying their com-mitment to certain values and behaviors. Although much of the literature that explores this process has focused on deviant or risky behaviors, such as cigarette smoking, alcohol use, or truancy, the process can support prosocial commitments as well.

Experiencing a Sense of History as a Group Member. In a gym class, one may be assigned to the red team one day and to the gray team another. These assignments do not foster a meaningful sense of group identity. However, if one joins the band and practices every day, performs at games, travels on the bus, and parties with the band members, the sense of being a "bandie" begins to take shape. Group identity emerges out of continuous interactions, through which one becomes visible and known to other group members while they become visible and known to you. What was done in fun last year may become next year's tradition as a group selects rituals to symbolize how important they all are to each other. Participation in group rituals, whether of a formalized nature, like an initiation ceremony, or an informal nature, like a group outing to the beach to celebrate the end of school, contribute to the cohesiveness of the group. They foster cooperation among the group members and mark group boundaries. Teens who participate in group rituals, especially rituals that involve resources, challenges, pain or danger, or time consuming planning to enact, are likely to experience heightened commitment to the group (Watson-Jones & Legare, 2016).

Of course, memberships in groups change. One may transfer to a new school, join a new team or club, or become part of a group that gets together only in the summers. In each case, the formation of a sense of group identity requires the accumulation of interactions and the sense of having a history of shared experiences. Here one sees the interconnection of the *I* and the *We*. One may think of the *I* as the agent that seeks out group membership, choosing to join one group or avoid another. At the same time, as one participates in a group and experiences a sense of shared history, one begins to internalize values, beliefs, and practices held in common by the group, thus leading to a revision of the *I* and strengthening of the *We*.

Emotional Investment in the Group. The intensification of emotions that occurs with puberty and early adolescence is often evidenced in a deepening dedication and commitment to one's groups, including family and kinship groups. One sees here the seeds of nationalism and patriotism—a redirection of feelings of self-worth to the group and a binding of energy to the group as an extension of oneself. Evidence of this emotional investment

These four friends are having a wonderful time joking, singing, and hanging out. They will look back on this special afternoon sitting in the big orange chair for a long time. It will provide a sense of shared history that will keep the group members emotionally invested in each other.

includes knowing that one is a member of a certain ethnic group, and recognizing that some aspects of one's thoughts, feelings, and actions are influenced by one's ethnic identity. One's ethnic group becomes a significant reference group, whose values, outlook, and goals are taken into account as one makes important life choices. Ethnic group identity varies across ethnic groups and among individuals within groups. For example, some young people have had more exposure to the cultural norms and values of their ethnic group than others. Some have had more guided parental socialization about the existence of prejudice and ways of coping with discrimination. Some children are born to mixed-race or multiracial parents, thus further complicating their definitions of ethnic group identity. Thus, ethnic group identity is more aptly viewed as a psychosocial rather than a demographic variable. It is based upon socially constructed meaning rather than biological or genetic differences (Ho, 2015; Phinney, 1996b; Quintana et al., 2006; Smedley & Smedley, 2005).

In the United States, a history of negative imagery, violence, discrimination, and invisibility has been linked to African Americans, Native Americans, Asian Americans, and Hispanic Americans. Young people in each of these groups encounter conflicting values as they consider the larger society and their own ethnic group identity. They may struggle with the negative or ambivalent feelings that are linked with their own ethnic group because of the cultural stereotypes that have been conveyed to them through the media and their schools, and because of the absence of role models from their own group who are in positions of leadership and authority.

Issues of ethnic group identity may not become salient until early adolescence. As children of color grow up, they are surrounded by members of their own ethnic group and socialized to internalize the values and beliefs of that group. At the same time, through participation in school, exposure to the media, and exploration of their community, they incorporate many of the ideals and values of European American culture. Several longitudinal studies describe a trajectory of development of racial/ethnic identity across adolescence (Altschul, Oyserman, & Bybee, 2006; Pahl & Way, 2006). With more advanced social and cognitive abilities, adolescents who are members of ethnic minorities are likely to think of themselves as bicultural or multicultural. This is most likely in school environments that are diverse and when teens experience peer acceptance in a multiracial/ethnic friendship group (Rutland et al., 2012).

In the transition to high school, adolescents may encounter more evidence of discrimination through overt rejection, academic hassles, being ignored, being harshly punished, or experiencing fewer opportunities to be recognized for school leadership roles (French, Seidman, Allen, & Aber, 2000; Seaton, Yip, & Sellers, 2009). In some communities sanctions against cross-race/cross-ethnic friendships and dating relationships may become more intense.

The nature and extent of racial or ethnic hostilities are related in part to the composition of the high school. In some schools, ethnic group hostilities are accentuated by their

is found in the expression of pride about one's group, a tendency to idealize the members of the group in comparison to others outside the group, and a willingness to make personal sacrifices in order to support or advance the group's goals. The emotional investment can be expressed as positive feelings of attraction to other members of the group and negative feelings of depression or jealousy associated with betrayal.

Social Evaluation of One's Group and Its relation to Other Groups. Adolescents become aware of the status hierarchy of the groups in their school and neighborhood. They recognize how their groups are viewed by others, and they form their own views of each group's value and importance to them (Dunbar, 1997). A strong, positive identification with one or more groups, coupled with a sense of belonging to valued groups, are associated with improved feelings of well-being (Wakefield et al., 2016). The group identity established during early adolescence occurs in the context of a social reality in which one's own group can be located in a status hierarchy leading to judgments about the merits of the group and about oneself as a member of the group. Studies of racial and ethnic identity clearly show that adolescents are able to differentiate between being viewed negatively by others or being a target of discrimination, and expressing personal pride in their racial group (Williams & Thornton, 1998).

Ethnic Group Identity

One of the most challenging aspects of establishing group identity facing many adolescents is the formation of an **ethnic group identity** (Spencer & Markstrom-Adams, 1990). Ethnic group identity convergence with other attitudes and values, like academic engagement, athletic participation, or economic resources (Laursen et al., 2010). Students who are in a racial or ethnic numeric minority within their school are more likely to experience intergroup hostilities than those who are in a more diverse, well-balanced school (Graham, 2004, 2011). Students may find that their family and ethnic group values conflict with the values of the majority culture. Acculturation strain may stimulate new levels of exploration and ethnic commitment, or new sentiments of alienation. During the high school years, most youth are in the process of exploring what their ethnic group membership means to them, not yet having made a clear commitment to embracing or crystallizing an ethnic identity (Yip, Seaton, & Sellers, 2006).

It is not uncommon to observe a gradual unfolding of ethnic identity as adolescents move from unexamined assumptions about their ethnic group to greater degrees of exploration, analysis, comparison, possible confusion, and eventual commitment to a version of ethnic group identity that fits with their other group identities. In a longitudinal study of Latinos' ethnic identity over a 4-year period, girls showed a steady growth in exploration of their ethnic identity, increased clarity about what their ethnic identity meant to them, and increasingly positive feelings about their Latina identity. For boys, there was little evidence of exploration or increased clarity, but there was growth in the positive feelings about being Latino. For both boys and girls, affirmation of their Latino ethnicity was positively associated with self-esteem (Umaña-Taylor, Gonzales-Backen, & Guimond, 2009).

In the transition from early to late adolescence, most minority youth experience some critical evaluation of the values and beliefs of the dominant culture and how they conflict with the values and beliefs of their own ethnic group. The more fully immersed young children are in the values and traditions of their ethnic heritage, the more likely it is that they will experience a *dual* or *multiple identity*—for example, seeing themselves as both American and African American or American and Chinese American (Phinney, 1997). Over time, and with the benefit of exposure to reading, conversations, and interactions with people from other subgroups, young people begin to synthesize a sense of how their ethnic identity fits into their overall personal identity and how it will influence the quality of their relationships with members of their own and other ethnic groups (Cross, 1991; Phinney, 1989, 1996; Yip, Seaton, & Sellers, 2006).

Most research on ethnic identity in the United States has focused on African American, Latino American, and Asian American youth. Relatively little attention has been given to the ethnic identity of the racially/ethnically privileged European American youth. There are substantial benefits to being a member of a racially/ethnically privileged group for social status, access to resources, and social expectations. Not much is known about how these benefits and their link to being a member of a privileged racial/ethnic group are conceptualized by European American youth (Spencer, 2006). One study examined how the ethnic label that White children gave themselves related to their attitudes toward other minority groups. Those White children who considered themselves biracial, or of some

For these Chinese American teens, their ethnic identity is integrated into their personal identity as they form friendships and make commitments to their families and community.

hyphenated ethnic identity (e.g., Greek-American or Polish-American) showed less in-group and out-group bias than those who viewed themselves as singularly White or American (Brown, Spatzier, & Tobin, 2010). This finding provides further evidence of the simultaneous emergence of the *I* and the *We* as part of group identity.

Alienation

Alienation refers to a sense of social estrangement, an absence of social support or meaningful social connection. Alienation at the individual level may result from societal norms and biases when individuals are denied resources or access to participation based on some aspect of their group identity. This type of exclusion can be experienced early in childhood when children are rejected from play groups or school activities. It can expand in middle childhood and early adolescence through barriers to educational or community resources. Family and community norms can create an environment in which some children emerge into early adolescence with a history of rejection and victimization due to their group identity (Killen, Elenbaas, & Rutland, 2016).

Alienation may arise from dilemmas associated with issues of **common identity**, **common bond**, or both. Alienation associated with issues of common identity may happen when young people are forced to take on roles or are expected to comply with group expectations to which they do not subscribe. This might occur as a result of stereotyping, racism, or elitism within a school or community. For example, in a study of Muslim adolescents ages 12 to 18, 84 percent said they experienced one or more acts of discrimination in the previous year, and 10 percent reported daily discrimination (Sirin & Fine, 2008). In the current political climate, with the president elect being very outspoken in his views against Muslims, teachers and students report heightened levels of hostility toward Muslims and fearfulness among Muslim students (Costello, 2016). In many schools, some subsets of students are marginalized due to some marker such as minority status, physical disabilities, or developmental delays, or as a result of poor social skills or low academic motivation. These students are often typed as nobodies, loners, disengaged, or outcasts.

Alienation associated with issues of common bond surfaces when adolescents are unable to form interpersonal ties that provide feelings of acceptance and emotional support. Under conditions of parental coldness, distancing, neglect, or rejection, children find that they cannot count on the family to serve as a source of emotional or instrumental support (Dishion, Poulin, & Medici-Skaggs, 2000). They lack a template for experiencing the foundational benefits of belonging that are associated with group identity. As a result of harsh parenting, some adolescents have poor social skills—they are either overly aggressive and domineering, or overly withdrawn and socially inept (Poulin, Dishion, & Haas, 1999). Over time, children with poor social skills are less likely to form satisfying social relationships with friends and are more likely to engage in delinquent behaviors that reflect their sense of alienation from family and peers.

In some families, children are exposed to a pattern of hostile, aggressive parenting in which the custodial parent insists in the most assertive and unkind way that their other parent is someone to be mistrusted, an enemy to be avoided and disrespected. This condition, referred to as **parental alienation** (PA), is defined as follows:

> a mental condition in which a child, usually one whose parents are engaged in a high-conflict separation or divorce, allies himself strongly with one parent (the preferred parent) and rejects a relationship with the other parent (the alienated parent) without legitimate justification. PA features abnormal, maladaptive behavior (refusal to have a relationship with a loving parent) that is driven by an abnormal mental state (the false belief that the rejected parent is evil, dangerous, or unworthy of love). (Bernet & Baker, 2013, p. 99)

These efforts to alienate a child from a parent are frightening, confusing, and a source of emotional distress. The child, exposed to this kind of emotional abuse, may experience a variety of symptoms such as anxiety, withdrawal, self-inflicted injuries, or uncontrolled aggression, any of which may make the establishment of effective peer relationships difficult. As the child gets older, he or she may question or challenge the hostile, aggressive parent, asserting his independent view about the absent parent and defying the custodial parent. The child may reach adolescence alienated from both the noncustodial parent and the custodial parent and lacking the social skills needed to form satisfying peer friendships (Baker, Burkhard, & Kelley, 2012).

Conditions that create parent–child alienation can spill over to impact children's mental health, school performance, and peer relationships. Evidence of parent–child alienation has been observed in some immigrant families where conflicts arise due to differences in the acculturation process for children and families. Having brought their children to a new country, some parents then proceed to withdraw support and become increasingly critical as their children embrace new, American values. The result is not only alienation within the parent–child relationship but also problems for the adolescents related to health, non-engagement with school, and feelings of depression and hopelessness (Cheng et al., 2013; Kim et al., 2013; Wang & Benner, 2016).

Alienation may result from personality characteristics, such as shyness, introversion, or lack of sociability. Some young people experience social anxiety, mistrust, or cautiousness that prevent them from forming interpersonal connections. Others are overly self-conscious, so preoccupied with their own feelings and thoughts that they withdraw from social interactions. Feelings of shame over an illness, disability, or perceived inadequacy may lead to perceptions of peer rejection or an unwillingness to form social bonds (Fife & Wright, 2000). Some teens who are alienated from peers in their face-to-face social environment may become invested in virtual relationships through various social media in order to satisfy their needs for peer group connections (Xu & Zhang, 2011). Social media can also serve as a vehicle to reinforce alienation, especially when teens block or "unfriend" a former friend, thus disconnecting them from their social network (Pew Research Center 2015d).

Finally, alienation may result from a combination of problems with common identity and common bond. For example, friendships across racial groups may be very difficult to preserve in a neighborhood but are supported in the school environment. If an African American and a European American adolescent become close friends at school, both may feel alienated from their same-race peers in their community. Youth who are recent immigrants may experience this conflict as they become acculturated. They may become increasingly distant from their families as they take on U.S. language and practices, but they may still be unable to form close, supportive relationships with U.S. adolescents who view them as outsiders. Nataša, an immigrant from Bosnia, described her experiences of alienation as a high school student:

> I was so different and so odd. I ended up in an all-girls Catholic school in the middle of Ohio where everyone is blond and everyone wants to get married and have babies.... And no one wanted to talk to me; *no one even wanted to talk to me.* I was the only person in the class that no one ever talked to because I'm so different, and they all made a point of seeing me as different. (Mosselson, 2009, p. 463)

In this case, Nataša's alienation is in part a result of her cultural displacement and the related lack of common identity and in part a result of the lack of common bond with other students in her school.

The Contribution of Alienation to Group Identity and Individual Identity

To some degree, experiences of alienation are important for the continued formulation of both group and individual identity. A period of feeling alone and lonely may help teens appreciate how good social acceptance feels and how important it is for their well-being. Moreover, experiences of alienation within a group may help a young person see the *I* against the backdrop of the

We. The discomfort of not fitting in helps one recognize the distinctiveness of one's point of view. In the extreme, however, the lack of social integration that may result from a negative resolution of this crisis can have significant implications for adjustment to school, self-esteem, and subsequent psychosocial development. Giving the important role of a sense of belonging for adaptation and well-being, chronic conflict about one's integration into a meaningful reference group can lead to lifelong difficulties in areas of personal health, work, controlling anger, and the formation of intimate family bonds.

The Central Process: Peer Pressure

Adolescents' family backgrounds, interests, and styles of dress quickly link them to subgroups of peers who lend continuity and meaning to life within the context of their neighborhoods or schools. The peer group social structure is usually well established in most high schools, and members of that structure exert pressure on newcomers to join one peer group or another. **Peer pressure** refers to demands for conformity to **group norms** and a demonstration of commitment and loyalty to group members. Young people outside the groups form expectations that reinforce adolescents' connections to specific peer groups and prohibit their movement to others. An individual who becomes a member of a group is more acceptable to the social system than one who tries to remain unaffiliated and aloof.

The term *peer pressure* is often used with a negative connotation, suggesting that young people behave in ways that go against their beliefs or values because of a fear of peer rejection. However, we suggest an alternative meaning that highlights the emerging role of the peer group in the radius of significant others. The pressure from those close by—those with whom a young person interacts each day—is not necessarily perceived as oppressive or coercive. It is, more often, the subtle co-adaptation of those who interact in the same social space, shaping and guiding one another toward intersubjectivity, much as an infant and a caregiver achieve mutual regulation. In a process of give and take, friends adapt to each other's preferences and interests, leading to a shared outlook on their world. We often read that the presence of peers can increase risk taking, especially when peer approval accompanies dangerous or hazardous actions. However peers can also encourage exploration and learning. When faced with new or challenging tasks, the presence of friends can improve learning, enhance exploration, and increase sensitivity to potential benefits of engaging in new behaviors. For example, Ellen is very shy, but it's Friday night and her good friend Pam wants to go to the basketball game and then to a party afterward. Ellen is reluctant. She knows there is often a lot of drinking at these parties, and she is not in with the popular crowd that usually goes to these parties. Pam promises her that she won't drink at the party and that if Ellen is really not having a good time Pam will leave with her. Ellen decides to go along with Pam and they end up having a very good time. Pam keeps her promise of no drinking, and at midnight they leave so they are home by their curfew. Pam and Ellen are now thinking about having a party at Ellen's house next week since this turned out to be a lot of fun.

Five modes of peer influence serve to encourage some behaviors and discourage others (Brown, Bakken, Ameringer, & Mahone, 2008). The most overt mode is the direct suggestion that a teen should perform a behavior (e.g., smoke marijuana) or risk group rejection. This is the usual connotation of peer pressure, and parents or educators are often focused on helping teens resist this type of influence. A second type of peer influence occurs through modeling. Teens who spend time with one another watch each other's style of dress, gestures, and use of language, and imitate those behaviors in an effort to consolidate their sense of group membership. A third type of influence is more subtle normative regulation, where peers use teasing, gossiping, or sarcasm to influence each other's attitudes and behavior. A fourth type of influence includes the many ways that peers reinforce one another's behaviors. Positive verbal statements, gestures like smiling, nodding, or giving "high fives," and Internet reinforcement such as "liking" on Facebook are all ways that teens convey encouragement for one another's behaviors. Among the teens who use social media, many report that they feel some pressure to post only content that will be viewed positively and make a good impression on their peers or to post content that will get lots of positive comments (Pew Research Center 2015d). Finally, peer influence occurs when friends create opportunities for unsupervised activities—having parties where beer is served, cruising in cars, or arranging to meet at a park or mall when adults are not likely to be present.

These teens influence each other's style of dress and facial expressions. They show solidarity by wearing their hoods up when they walk the streets. Even on a crowded street, people can sense that they are together.

Affiliating with a Peer Group

The process of affiliating with a peer group requires an adolescent to accept the pressure and social influence imposed by it. This process provides the context in which the crisis of group identity versus alienation is resolved. Adolescents are at the point in their intellectual development when they are able to conceptualize themselves as objects of expectations. They may perceive these expectations as forces urging them to be more than they think they are—braver, more outgoing, more confident, and so forth. These expectations help define the zone of proximal development for group skills and social competencies. Peer pressure may have a positive effect on the adolescent's self-image and self-esteem, serving as a motive for group identification. Those dimensions of the self that are valued by one's own peer group become especially salient in each young person's self-assessment.

As members of peer groups, adolescents have more influence than they would have as single individuals; they begin to understand the value of *collective enterprise*. In offering membership, peer groups expand adolescents' feelings of connection and protect them from loneliness. When family conflicts develop, adolescents can seek comfort and intimacy among peers. For adolescents to benefit in these ways from their affiliation with a peer group, they must be willing to suppress some of their individuality and find pleasure in focusing on the attributes they share with those peers.

Conflicts Between Belonging and Personal Autonomy

Peer groups do not command total conformity. In fact, most peer groups depend on the unique characteristics of their members to lend definition and vigor to the roles that emerge within them. However, the peer group places importance on some level of conformity in order to bolster its structure and strengthen its effectiveness in satisfying members' needs. Indeed, most adolescents find some security in peer group demands to conform. The few well-defined characteristics of the group lend stability and substance to adolescents' views of themselves. In complying with group pressure, adolescents have an opportunity to state unambiguously that they are someone and that they belong somewhere (see the **Applying Theory and Research to Life** box Gangs).

Adolescents may also find that some peer expectations conflict with their personal values or needs. For example, they may feel that intellectual skills are devalued by the peer group, that they are expected to participate in social functions they do not enjoy, or that they are encouraged to be more independent from their families than they prefer to be. In most cases, adolescents' personal values are altered and shaped by peer group pressure to increase their similarity with the other group members. If, however, the peer group's expectations are too distant from the adolescents' own values, establishing a satisfying group identification will become much more difficult. As a result, adolescents experience tension and conflict as they try to balance the allure of peer group membership with the cost of abandoning personal beliefs.

Susceptibility to coercive peer pressure seems to peak at age 13 or 14, when adolescents are most sensitive to peer approval and make the initial transition toward new levels of behavioral autonomy and emotional independence from parents (Lamborn & Steinberg, 1993; Urberg, Shyu, & Liang, 1990). During the years from 14 to 16, adolescents become more adept at resisting peer pressure. Through encounters with peer pressure and opportunities to see how it feels to conform or resist, they develop a growing appreciation for the content of their personal values against the backdrop of peer expectations. However, if the emotional costs of identifying with the peer group become too great, adolescents may not open themselves up to group pressures. An inability to reduce the tension and conflict between group pressure and personal values produces a state of alienation in which the individual is unable either to identify with social groups or to develop personal friendships.

The Prime Adaptive Ego Quality and the Core Pathology
Fidelity to Others

A positive resolution of the psychosocial crisis of group identity versus alienation results in the achievement of the prime adaptive ego quality referred to as **fidelity to others**—a capacity to freely pledge one's loyalty to a group and to sustain one's faithfulness to the promises and commitments one makes to others. Fidelity to others produces the sentiments that are necessary to preserve small groups and larger communities alike: dedication to family, civic pride, and patriotism. One of the by-products of fidelity to others is *mattering*, a "feeling that others depend upon us, are interested in us, are concerned with our fate" (Rosenberg & McCullough, 1981, p. 163). Mattering is a relational aspect of the self-concept that reflects an assessment of how aware others are of you, how important you are to others, and how much others rely on you (Elliott, Kao, & Grant, 2004). When we pledge ourselves to others, we also become salient for them. We make a difference in their lives, and that, in return, contributes to our sense of well-being (Taylor & Turner, 2001). Adolescents who perceive that they matter to their parents and friends report higher levels of well-being than those who matter only to their parents, or to neither group (Marshall, 2004). For adolescents, mattering is closely related to self-esteem. When adolescents believe that they matter to important others, especially their families and close friends, they are less likely to engage in antisocial behavior, experience less depression, and are less likely to have suicidal thoughts (Elliott, 2009; Elliott, Colangelo, & Gelles, 2005). The Applying Theory and Research to Life box on gangs illustrates how the desire for mattering may lead a young person to make an affiliation with a dangerous or deviant group where they feel valued and protected, when those needs that are not being met by family, school, or other community groups.

Looking ahead to subsequent life stages, one can appreciate the significant role that this ego quality plays in pledging long-term faithfulness to friends, marital partners, children, one's aging parents, and other groups. Research on factors that buffer the

Youth Gangs

In the late 1920s and 1930s, the study of delinquency included an analysis of the role of youth gangs. Early on, it was understood that delinquent behavior was typically group behavior, involving two or more boys in some type of criminal activity. Gangs were viewed as social groups, not unlike the kinds of groups that boys in more stable, prosperous neighborhoods create.

The motives for joining a gang—"desires for recognition, approbation, and esteem of his fellows, for stimulation, thrill, and excitement, for intimate companionship, and for security and protection" (Burgess & Bogue, 1967, p. 300)—do not differ much from the motives that adolescents have for joining any type of social group or club. However, the focus of these gangs developed a delinquent emphasis and tradition that was passed from one generation of gang members to the next in a neighborhood. The ethical standards and values of these groups were often contrary to conventional values. In fact, actions that might bring a nondelinquent boy dishonor or shame—such as being arrested, appearing in juvenile court, or being sent to a correctional institution—would be viewed as a source of pride and distinction to a gang member.

Street gangs and youth gangs are defined as groups with membership ranging from early adolescence through about age 24. They are differentiated from motorcycle gangs, prison gangs, and ideological or hate-based gangs, which have mostly adult members. Street gangs are groups that have a history over many years, even many generations, a relatively large membership, an organization that usually includes a leadership hierarchy, and involvement in various violent crimes typically committed in a neighbourhood or territory (Howell & Moore, 2010).

Gangs continue to thrive in communities all across the United States. According to a survey carried out by the National Youth Gang Center, 3,100 jurisdictions experienced gang problems in 2012. Based on this survey, there are 850,000 gang members in 30,700 gangs across the United States. There has been a spread of gang activity over the years into small cities and suburban and rural jurisdictions; however, the greatest amount of gang activity and serious gang crime occurs in large cities. Gang-related homicides (n=2,363) increased by more than 20 percent in 2012 compared to the previous 5 year average, accounting for 16 percent of all homicides nationally in the United States (Egley, Howell, & Harris, 2014).

Gangs flourish in the most disadvantaged neighborhoods where social institutions such as families and schools are inadequate and opportunities are limited. They are organized to dominate their neighborhood territories, and, as a result, they reflect the ethnic composition of their neighborhoods. Youth gangs are therefore typically segregated by racial and ethnic groups. Teens in these neighborhoods also have a lot of free time; many are in neither school nor work. For gangs to be established and persist over time, youth must have limited access to appealing conventional jobs and career paths. Finally, there must be a place for youth to congregate, often an unsupervised park, mall, or street (National Gang Center, 2013, 2016).

Gangs may actively recruit new members, engage in violent acts of initiation, and are becoming increasingly associated with drug trafficking and violent crime. Yet, few gangs are actually involved in the coordinated sale and distribution of drugs. Rather, individual gang members become involved in the sale of drugs, which then may lead them to related violent crimes. Most of the violence experienced by gang members is linked to rivalries and territorial disputes between gangs. Although we tend to think of gangs as predominantly male groups, many decades of research have documented that females have been involved in gangs, both female gangs and adolescent girls who are members of mixed-sex gangs (National Gang Center, 2016).

Jeff Greenberg/PhotoEdit

These young gang members give hand signals to convey their gang membership, send messages to each other, and taunt or "dis" other gangs.

Young people may join gangs for a variety of reasons. *Pulls* that attract youth to gangs include "the perception of increased reputation and social status, the desire to be with friends and/or family who are already gang-involved, the promise of money, drugs, and/or excitement, and cultural pride and identification with one's neighborhood." In contrast, some youth are *pushed* into gangs, possibly because of high levels of neighborhood crime, where they are coerced into joining or join because they hope to find protection within the gang (National Gang Center, 2016).

Adolescents who join gangs are often unsuccessful in school and may have been suspended or expelled. School failure leads to periods of unsupervised time in the community and an inability to find work. Modern gang activities are supported by a growing and spreading drug trade, easy access to guns, and the technology of cell phones with texting and voice mail, which allow gang members to coordinate their activities and preserve control over a wider area with increased mobility (Howell & Griffiths, 2016).

The concept of gangs is closely linked to the theme of group identity. Although gangs may have a violent, criminal, or antisocial value system, they provide a highly organized group for identification. Gangs have clothing, colors, symbols, and signs that provide recognition across settings. Being recruited into a gang may make a young person feel valued and protected by the older gang members. Despite the great risks associated with gang activities, the pervasive presence of gangs across all ethnic groups and diverse communities suggests that gangs address a number of needs that are not being met by communities, schools, and families.

To learn more about gangs and ideas about preventing adolescent involvement in gangs, visit the website of the National Gang Center sponsored by the U.S. Office of Juvenile Justice and Delinquency Prevention.

Critical Thinking Questions

1. Analyze the differences between being a gang member and being part of a clique or friendship group that is involved in delinquent activities. Describe the ways that gangs are similar to other kinds of tough or antisocial peer groups; describe the ways they are different.

2. Summarize the functions that are served by gang membership. Are the effects of gang membership only negative?

3. Evaluate how concepts presented in the chapter related to peer group membership and group identity versus alienation inform your understanding of gang membership.

4. Imagine that you are a school counselor, and a student has been brought to your attention who is suspected of being involved in criminal activity. Apply ideas from this chapter to develop an approach to working with this student to keep them engaged in school and to prevent future illegal behavior.

---

effects of stress often cite the contribution of social support to the long-term abilities of individuals to cope with change and to adapt positively to life challenges. Social support implies a capacity for fidelity. People who function as sources of support have the ability to remain compassionately connected to others during periods of hardship and loss as well as during periods of success and prosperity. When one thinks of a true friend, one pictures someone who stands by you even when it is not especially advantageous to do so. A true friend is someone who cares about you and supports you during moments of adversity as well as in times of joy.

Fidelity to others becomes a source of family solidarity as family members age and adults are called on to meet the needs of their own aging parents. The role one plays in caring for one's aging parents is largely voluntary. It is based on one's own definition of filial obligation, a sense of duty and responsibility for one's parents. Surely the way adults enact this role reflects their capacity for fidelity to others.

Dissociation

Dissociation refers to a sense of feeling removed and separate, withdrawal from others, and an inability to experience the bond of mutual commitment. It does not mean a preference for being by oneself, but rather a tendency toward social distancing and a reluctance to make the kinds of commitments to others that are required for the establishment and maintenance of enduring friendships and group memberships. Dissociation may involve a mental process that reflects lack of connection or continuity among thoughts, feelings, and actions. The following is an example of an adolescent who describes herself as floating along, disconnected from reality. Dissociation may be a symptom of more serious mental health problems such as schizophrenia, or an acute reaction to stress such as exposure to violence, rejection, or loss.

> What can I tell you about that time in my life? Hunger dominated every moment, hunger and its silent twin, the constant urge to sleep. School passed in a dream. I couldn't think. Logic fled, and memory drained away like motor oil. My stomach ached, my period stopped. I rose above the sidewalks, I was smoke. The rains came and I was sick and after school I had nowhere to go. (Fitch, 1999, p. 201)

Dissociation may occur as a result of rejection, abuse, or neglect. Adolescents who experience dissociation are likely to mistrust their peers and may even develop an attitude of hostile resentment toward the amiability and companionship they observe in others. Over time, dissociation results in the formulation of a mental world that is not well coordinated with social reality. A young person who experiences dissociation is likely to feel misunderstood and to lack confidence in her ability to communicate with or connect to others.

At a basic level, any sense of *we*-ness requires a shared understanding between at least two people and recognition that they experience some bond of investment in or identification with a common reality. This common reality could involve facing a common enemy, encountering a common crisis, or embracing a common goal. The core pathology of dissociation occurs when the young person is unable to experience the level of mutual understanding or symbolic connection that creates such bonds of *we*-ness.

FURTHER REFLECTION: How do the developmental tasks of early adolescence contribute to the capacity for forming group identity? The psychosocial crisis of group identity versus alienation is closely linked to the issue of intergroup relations. Analyze the forces in schools or communities that foster positive intergroup relations among adolescents. What factors promote intergroup hostilities? Propose a strategy to promote positive intergroup relations at the middle school and high school levels. Trace the path of social development from infancy to early adolescence. What experiences from earlier stages might result in the negative resolution of the psychosocial crisis of group identity versus alienation?

Applied Topic: Adolescent Alcohol and Drug Use

OBJECTIVE 7 Apply your understanding of developmental issues of early adolescence to an analysis of factors that account for patterns of adolescent alcohol and drug use.

American high-school-age youth show a higher level of illicit drug use than those of any other industrialized nation. By their senior year in high school (typically ages 17 and 18), almost half of American high school students have tried an illegal drug in their lifetime—whether marijuana/hashish, amphetamines, heroin or other opiates, cocaine/crack, methamphetamines, tranquilizers, or barbiturates (Johnston, O'Malley, Miech, Bachman, & Schulenberg, 2016).

FIGURES 9.6 a and b ▶ provide a historical overview of the lifetime prevalence of illicit drug use for 8th, 10th, and 12th graders from 1975 to 2015 based on the *Monitoring the Future* national survey sponsored by the National Institute on Drug Abuse (Johnston et al., 2016). Following a period of decline from 1981 through 1992, drug use among adolescents increased over the 1990s and then began a second decline. Recent versions of the survey have identified the use of certain prescription and over-the-counter drugs for nonmedical use such as Adderall, Vicodin, Percocet, OxyContin, and cough medicines containing dextromethorphan.

Underage drinking is a serious public health concern. Alcohol is widely used by teens and is associated with a range of health and safety risks. In 2015, 26 percent of eighth graders had tried alcohol, and 11 percent said that they had been drunk at least once in their lives; 19 percent had tried a flavored alcoholic beverage. By the 12th grade, 64 percent had tried alcohol, 47 percent had gotten drunk, and 56 percent had tried a flavored alcoholic beverage. About 17 percent of 12th graders had experienced binge drinking (five or more drinks in a row) in the past

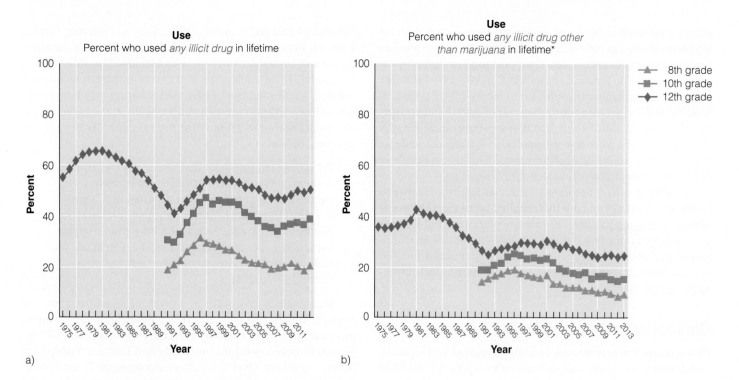

Source: The *Monitoring the Future* study, the University of Michigan.
*In 2001, a revised set of questions on other hallucinogen use and tranquilizer use were introduced. In 2013, a revised set of questions on amphetamine use was introduced. Data for any illicit drug other than marijuana were affected by these changes.

FIGURE 9.6 A AND B ▶ TRENDS IN LIFETIME USE FOR ANY ILLICIT DRUG; TRENDS IN LIFETIME USE FOR ANY ILLICIT DRUG OTHER THAN MARIJUANA
Source: Johnston, O'Malley, Bachman, & Schulenberg, 2013.

two weeks (Johnston et al., 2016). Alcohol use, binge drinking, and drunkenness among 12th graders have declined since their peak in the early 1980s.

Physical Effects of Alcohol

Alcohol depresses the central nervous system. People may think that alcohol makes one high; however, at its highest concentrations in the body it can cause death by suppressing breathing. Although this outcome is extremely rare, it may occur after chugging large quantities of alcohol, a practice that is sometimes included in certain adolescent initiation rites and drinking games. There are two other situations in which alcohol use has potentially lethal consequences. One is the use of alcohol in combination with other drugs, especially barbiturates. The other is its use in combination with driving.

The physical development accompanying puberty leads to a heightened awareness of body sensations. In small quantities, alcohol has a relaxing effect that may accentuate pleasurable bodily sensations. Adolescents may use alcohol in an attempt to increase their sense of physical arousal, reduce sexual inhibitions, and minimize the self-consciousness that is a barrier to social interactions. In larger quantities, alcohol may alter reality in such a way that adolescents are willing to take risks or ignore certain physical limitations. When adolescents are intoxicated, the barriers of physical appearance, height, weight, or sexual immaturity may be minimized. Thus, dissatisfaction with one's body image may contribute to an inclination to drink heavily in social situations.

The National Institute on Alcohol Abuse and Alcoholism provides information about the potential harm alcohol can have for health and brain functioning (NIAAA, 2016). The following information about health risks associated with underage drinking is taken from that source.

Underage drinking is associated with many deaths

Alcohol has been identified as a factor in the deaths of over 4,000 young people under age 21 each year in the U.S.

- 1,580 deaths from motor vehicle crashes
- 1,269 from homicides
- 245 from alcohol poisoning, falls, burns, and drowning
- 492 from suicides

Causes many injuries

In 2011 alone, about 188,000 people under age 21 visited an emergency room for alcohol-related injuries.

Impairs judgment

Drinking can lead to poor decisions about engaging in risky behavior, including drinking and driving, sexual activity (such as unprotected sex), and aggressive or violent behavior.

Increases the risk of physical and sexual assault

Underage drinkers are more likely to carry out or be the victim of a physical or sexual assault after drinking than others their age who do not drink.

Can lead to other problems

Drinking may cause youth to have trouble in school or with the law. Drinking alcohol also is associated with the use of other drugs.

Increases the risk of alcohol problems later in life

Research shows that people who start drinking before the age of 15 are four times more likely to meet the criteria for alcohol dependence at some point in their lives.

Interferes with brain development

Research shows that young people's brains keep developing well into their 20s. Alcohol can alter this development, potentially affecting both brain structure and function. This may cause cognitive or learning problems and/or make the brain more prone to alcohol dependence. This is especially a risk when people start drinking young and drink heavily.

Factors Associated with Alcohol Use

Consider some of the factors associated with the use of alcohol and the part it plays in the adolescent's life. We are especially concerned about understanding the relationship between alcohol use and the major themes of early adolescence—cognitive factors, motivation and emotion, parent and peer relations, and community contexts.

Cognitive Factors

Most adolescents do not view drinking alcohol as an especially risky activity. When it comes to binge drinking, however, nearly 50 percent of 12th graders consider binge drinking once or twice on weekends as very risky, and nearly 60 percent view binge drinking every day or two as very risky (Johnston et al., 2016). This perception is linked to increasing awareness of the dangers of drunk driving.

Adolescents typically see themselves as more vulnerable to negative consequences than do adults and overestimate their exposure to risks. However, with age these overestimations decline, most likely because teens have had more experiences, explored more, and may rarely encounter the negative consequences or have judged the consequences to be less serious than they expected. As a result, in the case of binge drinking, adolescents view the behavior as less risky as they get older (Reyna & Farley, 2006).

One component of the assessment of risk is concern about the anticipated future. Adolescents are increasingly able to speculate about possible futures and to consider the logical consequences of their actions. Teens are less likely to engage in binge drinking or heavy drinking if they anticipate that drinking could harm their future. This could involve physical harm, legal consequences, or harming or disappointing others (Schneider & Caffray, 2012).

Motivation and Emotion

At least four different patterns of motives and emotions have been linked to the willingness to engage in risky health behaviors, including drinking and drug use. Some adolescents can be characterized by high levels of **sensation seeking**, a tendency to pursue activities that are novel, thrilling, and exciting. Youth who have a great need for novel, complex sensory experiences may be willing to take physical risks in order to satisfy this need. Some teens are depressed; they may feel sad, lonely, worthless, or socially isolated. They engage in heavy drinking as a way to mask these feelings. Many teens experience periods of heightened tension. They are stressed as a result of school demands, parental expectations, conflicts with peers, and work. For these teens, drinking is a way to relieve stress and relax. Finally, some teens see drinking as a way to satisfy a desire for social interaction. They may be shy, they may want to impress their peers, or see drinking as part of their peer group's norms for social interaction. Social motives and a need to be part of a group can motivate drinking (Robbins & Bryan, 2004; Schneider & Caffray, 2012).

The Social Contexts of Alcohol Use

Adolescent alcohol use takes place in a complex social environment comprised of family, friends, school, and neighborhood. A study of over 6,000 adolescents ages 11 to 17 explored the importance of these four contexts in predicting alcohol misuse and how these contexts might interact to influence drinking among teens (Ennett et al., 2008). Each context made an independent contribution to the likelihood that adolescents would misuse alcohol. High levels of family conflict and alcohol use by parents were associated with a teen's drinking. Family closeness and parental supervision were associated with less drinking. In the peer context, peer modeling of drinking was associated with teens' drinking when the peer relationships were close and reciprocated. In the school and the neighborhood contexts, the most important factor was the frequency of alcohol use by students or neighbors. There was also evidence of some interaction among contexts. When family supervision was high, teens were less likely to misuse alcohol even if their friends and schoolmates were drinking. When family conflict and family alcohol use were high, teens were more likely to be influenced by their friends' and schoolmates' drinking.

Given the significance of social contexts and the socialization forces that may encourage or reward risky behavior, it is important to keep sight of the role of self-selection in alcohol and drug use as well. Some adolescents seek out friends who will support their involvement with alcohol or drugs as part of a more general pattern of deviance or thrill seeking, whereas other teens, who do not drink alcohol or use drugs, find friends who support this position. Both factors—socialization pressures toward alcohol and drug use and willingness to seek out peers who misuse drugs

and alcohol—increase over the high school years, with a consequent increase in the likelihood that adolescents will become involved in the misuse of alcohol and drugs themselves (Schulenberg & Maggs, 2001). When teens are in the presence of other teens, they tend to be especially responsive to peer approval and the possible rewards of social status. If their friends are impressed by binge drinking or drunkenness, the tendency for adolescents to engage in risky alcohol use is greatly enhanced (Albert, Chein, & Steinberg, 2013).

A final aspect of the social context is the perceived availability of access to alcohol. The legal drinking age in the United States is 21. However, teens differ in their perception of how easy or difficult it is to buy alcohol in their community. Among eighth graders, about 54 percent say it is fairly easy or very easy to get alcohol. Among 12th graders, 87 percent say it is fairly easy or very easy to get alcohol in their community. Even teens who may not be willing to purchase alcohol illegally themselves are likely to know someone who will buy it for them (Johnston et al., 2016).

Although the use of many legal and illegal substances is declining, a combination of biological, psychological, and societal factors converge to make alcohol and drug use a part of the life for many adolescents during the high school years. Experimentation with alcohol is relatively easy to understand in the context of the adolescent's psychosocial needs and the modeling of alcohol use in the family, peer group, and community. Although alcohol and drug use may be considered a normative rite of passage for most adolescents, it appears that children who begin to drink or use drugs early—that is, before ninth grade—are especially vulnerable to more serious involvement with alcohol and drug use later. They experience some combination of family, peer, and psychosocial pressures that increase their willingness to engage in deviant behavior and to ignore or minimize the risks. The risk factors associated with early alcohol and drug use are linked to social class and culture. Control over the sale of alcohol to minors, its cost, and the efforts of parents and other adults—including school officials and the police—to monitor its use among adolescents are all community factors that influence the use of alcohol in early adolescence.

FURTHER REFLECTION: *A number of health-related issues have been raised in this chapter. Suppose that you were asked to provide guidance to a parents' group about how to improve health among adolescents. What ideas from this chapter might inform your recommendations?*

CHAPTER SUMMARY

Early adolescence provides vivid evidence of the interaction of the biological, psychological, and societal systems during a period of rapid growth and development.

OBJECTIVE 1 Describe the patterns of physical maturation during puberty for female and male adolescents, and analyze the impact of early and late maturing on self-concept and social relationships.

Puberty encompasses a group of interrelated neurological and endocrinological changes that influence brain development, changes in sexual maturation, cycles and levels of hormone production, and physical growth. Coming on the heels of a period of gradual but steady physical development in middle childhood, early adolescence is marked by rapid physical changes, including a height spurt, maturation of the reproductive system, appearance of secondary sex characteristics, increased muscle strength, and the redistribution of body weight. At the same time, the brain continues to develop, with changes that increase emotionality, modify memory, and gradually improve connections among areas of the brain that regulate emotion, impulse control, and judgment. Variability in the rate and sequence of development is well documented. The time from the appearance of breast buds to full maturity may range from 1 to 6 years for girls; the male genitalia may take from 2 to 5 years to reach adult size. These individual differences in maturation suggest that during early adolescence, the chronological peer group is biologically far more diverse than it was during early and middle childhood.

OBJECTIVE 2 Summarize the development of romantic and sexual relationships, and evaluate the factors that influence the transition to first intercourse, the formation of a sexual orientation, and pregnancy and parenthood in early adolescence.

Physical maturation is accompanied by new romantic feelings and sexualized experiences, some desirable and some unwanted. Most adolescents find ways to express sexual impulses in the context of socially acceptable practices. Young people are involved in a variety of romantic relationships during adolescence, including dating, feelings of tenderness and love, and deepening commitments. Adolescent dating (although not necessarily using that term) can be understood as meeting one or more central life goals, especially identity, intimacy, status, and sexuality. A majority of adolescents engage in forms of sexual behavior, including intercourse, with its accompanying risks and rewards, by the end of high school. The transition into sexual activity involves individual motivations, family and peer influences, attractiveness, and religious values and beliefs. Teens face a variety of challenges associated with their emerging sexuality. A major theme is the clarification of one's sexual orientation including awareness of sexual attractions; self-labeling as straight, lesbian, gay, bisexual, pansexual, or queer; disclosure of one's sexual orientation; and sexual experiences. Transgender youth face special challenges in connecting their gender identity with desired romantic relationships. Problems associated with sexuality include difficulty obtaining accurate and applicable sexual health information, sexual victimization, inconsistent contraception, sexually transmitted infections, and unwanted/unplanned pregnancy.

OBJECTIVE 3 Identify the basic features of formal operational thought, and explain the factors that promote the development of advanced reasoning at this period of life.

The physical changes of adolescence are taking place in a context of new and more complex cognitive capacities. Various areas of the cerebral cortex reach their peak in gray matter production during early adolescence, followed by a process of sculpting and pruning. There is a steady increase in the volume of white matter from ages 4 through the 20s. The combination of changes in gray matter and white matter in the frontal, parietal, and temporal lobes result in improvements in executive functions including working memory, planning and organizing, and impulse control. Early adolescents begin to think about themselves and their world in new ways that reflect a broadening of

consciousness. This includes greater introspection or monitoring of thoughts, greater integration of information from various sources, and more focused planning and control of behaviors guided by goals and strategies. Young people are able to think about several dimensions at once rather than focusing on just one domain or issue at a time. They are able to generate hypotheses about events that they have never perceived and to use logical reasoning to evaluate evidence to support or disconfirm these hypotheses. The concept of formal operational reasoning is described, including factors that promote formal reasoning, and criticisms of this construct are reviewed. During this stage of life, the quality of experiences and the demands for higher order thinking can play a significant role in advancing a young person's cognitive abilities.

OBJECTIVE 4 Examine patterns of emotional development in early adolescence, characterize the neurological processes associated with emotional expression, and describe the nature of three problem areas: eating disorders, depression, and delinquency.

Adolescence is a time of increased emotional complexity, with new capacities to identify, understand, and express a wider range of emotions. These capacities illustrate the interdependence of cognition and emotion, including interpreting and evaluating emotional signals, and reasoning about the consequences of expressing emotions which may result in the control or management of emotional expression. The neuroscience of emotions is discussed, highlighting the emerging capacities for responding to emotionally arousing situations and new sensitivities to rewards, particularly social rewards that may motivate behavior. Emotional development is characterized by a more diverse range of emotions, greater awareness of one's emotions, and for most teens, a growing capacity to express and control the expression of emotions. After puberty, boys tend to have more externalizing problems reflecting the outward expression of anger and aggression whereas girls have more internalizing problems reflecting inward turning emotions of anxiety and depression. Three specific problem areas are described: eating disorders, depression, and delinquency.

OBJECTIVE 5 Analyze the nature of peer relations in early adolescence, especially the formation of cliques and crowds, and contrast the typical relationships with parents and peers during this stage.

The radius of significant relationships expands as adolescents enter new roles and new settings. During early adolescence, the peer group becomes more structured and organized than it was previously and peer group membership becomes much more salient. Dyadic (two-person) friendships become an increasingly important source of social support, and the quality of these friendships changes. In addition to dyadic friendships, adolescents form small groups of friends, sometimes referred to as *cliques*, and in most communities they also become identified with a larger constellation of teens who have a common social identity, usually referred to as a *crowd*. The processes of selection and socialization help explain how boundaries are formed around peer groups, and how membership in peer groups shapes individual attitudes and behaviors. Parents continue to be an important source of reassurance and support for many adolescents. However, the period is characterized by strong desires to find membership and acceptance among peers. Within this context, adolescents seek like-minded peers and are open to peer influence.

OBJECTIVE 6 Explain the psychosocial crisis of group identity versus alienation, the central process through which the crisis is resolved, peer pressure, the prime adaptive ego quality of fidelity to others, and the core pathology of isolation.

The crisis of group identity versus alienation involves a potential tension between the *I* and the *We*, the desire to feel meaningfully connected to a valued group and, at the same time, to have an authentic, autonomous sense of self. A positive sense of group identity provides confidence that one is meaningfully connected to society, has a cognitive map of the characteristics of the social landscape, and the skills or tools to navigate the terrain. Perceiving oneself as a competent member of a group or groups is fundamental to one's self-concept as well as to one's willingness to participate in and contribute to society. Three cognitive capacities are needed for an adolescent to establish a group identity: (1) group representations, the conceptualization and labeling or classification of groups; (2) group operations, the processes through which groups are formed, maintained, or dissolved; and (3) reflective thinking about groups, an ability to analyze the array of groups and their relationship to one another. The actual formation of a group identity requires four types of experiences: (1) categorizing people into groups and recognizing the distinguishing features that define members, (2) experiencing a sense of history as a member of a group, (3) having an emotional investment in the group, and (4) detecting the social evaluation of one's group and its relation to other groups. Issues associated with ethnic identity are reviewed—an aspect of group identity that may become more salient for some adolescents than for others.

In the process of resolving this conflict, most adolescents experience moments of alienation, a sense of separateness and disconnection, out of which can grow a new personal confidence or a deep well of resentment and rage. Alienation can be viewed as deriving from dilemmas associated with issues of common identity, common bond, or both. The central process of peer pressure refers to demands for conformity to group norms and a demonstration of commitment and loyalty to group members. Peer pressure can be experienced as oppressive or very subtle. The threat of peer rejection may push those adolescents who lack confidence in their own worth to violate essential values in the pursuit of acceptance. The prime adaptive ego quality, fidelity to others, is a capacity to freely pledge one's loyalty to a group and to sustain one's faithfulness to the promises and commitments one makes to others. Fidelity to others produces the sentiments that are necessary to preserve small groups and larger communities. The core pathology, dissociation refers to a sense of feeling removed and separate, withdrawal from others, and an inability to experience the bond of mutual commitment. It reflects a tendency toward social distancing and a reluctance to make the kinds of commitments to others that are required for the establishment and maintenance of enduring friendships and group memberships.

OBJECTIVE 7 Apply your understanding of developmental issues of early adolescence to an analysis of factors that account for patterns of adolescent alcohol and drug use.

Although alcohol and drug use among teens have declined from their recent high levels of the 1990s, they continue to be a major source of health and safety risks. Almost half of American high school students have tried an illegal drug in their lifetime. High concentrations of alcohol in the body it can cause death by suppressing breathing, an outcome that may occur after chugging large quantities of alcohol, a practice that is sometimes included in certain adolescent initiation rites and drinking games. Two other situations in which alcohol use has potentially lethal consequences are the use of alcohol in combination with other drugs, especially barbiturates, and its use in combination with driving. The risks associated with underage drinking are reviewed. Alcohol use is linked to other developmental tasks of early adolescence, including cognitive, emotional, and social factors. Alcohol misuse takes place in a context of family, peer, school, and community forces that may constrain or encourage drinking and drunkenness.

CASEBOOK

For additional case material related to this chapter, see the case entitled "The Early Bloomer," in *Life Span Development: A Case Book*, by Barbara and Philip Newman, Laura Landry Meyer, and Brenda J. Lohman, pp. 120–123. The case focuses on the challenges of early maturing for girls and how pubertal timing influences social relationships.

Portrait of the Artist's Wife, Jacqueline Kneeling, 1954 (oil on canvas), Picasso, Pablo (1881-1973)/Private Collection/Giraudon/The Bridgeman Art Library

Engaged in the active resolution of the identity crisis, young people make commitments that will shape the structure of their adult lives. In this portrait, Picasso suggests the balance, focus, and purposefulness of a young woman who is striving to achieve a sense of personal identity.

1. Explain the concept of autonomy from parents and examine the conditions under which autonomy is likely to be achieved.

2. Summarize the development of gender identity in later adolescence. Analyze how the components of gender-role identification that were relevant during the early-school-age period are revised and expanded.

3. Investigate the maturation of morality in later adolescence, with special focus on the role of new cognitive capacities that influence moral judgments and the various value orientations that underlie moral reasoning.

4. Trace the process of career choice, with attention to education and gender-role socialization as two major influential factors.

5. Define and describe the psychosocial crisis of later adolescence, individual identity versus identity confusion; the central process through which this crisis is resolved, role experimentation; the prime adaptive ego quality of fidelity to values and ideals; and the core pathology of repudiation.

6. Examine some of the predictors and consequences of dropping out of college and hypothesize how dropping out of college may influence development in later adolescence.

LATER ADOLESCENCE (18 to 24 YEARS)

10

*A 22-year old male wrote this account as part of an assignment in
a college course on interpersonal relationships. Students who self-
identified as coming from families of divorce were asked to write on
the pros and cons of divorce for all concerned, as well as how the
divorce affected them and their siblings.*

As the years went by after the divorce the emotional trauma still
lingered and I never felt like I was very close with my parents. The
responsibilities required of me living in the household of a single
parent were a tough initial adjustment, but I feel I am a much better
person because of it. I feel a sense of accomplishment and confidence
in working to keep our household functioning for so many years. I also
have been able to pinpoint one of my personality traits: the feeling that
I should always be pleasing people. For most of my teen years my mom
would get upset when I wouldn't meet her emotional needs; so I worked
to counter that by always trying to please her and make her happy in
order to prevent her from being upset, which always stressed me out.

Recently my dad has remarried, and it has been a very happy
time for all of us. The fact that he is in a stable, loving relationship is
just a huge ease to my mind. The weeks after the wedding I noticed
a difference in my psyche. I really felt a lot of closure on my parents'
divorce. I had never realized the weight my subconscious feelings
about the divorce had on my over-all mental health.

Coming to college was a very positive experience for me. It gave
me some perspective on the family I have come from, a family I love
very much; but for my own mental health, I needed some distance
from them. There is a lot of significance in my parents remarrying—
those events have brought closure on my lingering feelings of loss
from the divorce. (Harvey & Fine, 2004, p. 81)

CASE ANALYSIS Using What You Know

1. Describe how divorce propels this young man to deal with issues that require more responsibility and maturity than many
   of his age-mates. How typical do you think this is? What does
   it suggest about the diversity of adult-like roles that young
   people enact in later adolescence?

2. Evaluate the quality of the parent–child relationship that is
   described in this case. How well is this young man working on
   balancing his feelings of autonomy and closeness?

3. Generate ideas about how helping with household responsibilities as a teenager may be of value in adapting to the college environment or for establishing a sense of self-sufficiency.

4. List some ideas about how the college environment might enhance mental health and a sense of well-being in later
   adolescence.

There is general agreement among human development scholars
that the years from about 18 through 24 are a distinct stage of development, separate from early adolescence and from early adulthood.

Studies from a variety of industrialized countries confirm that
young people in these societies have characteristics that distinguish
them from younger teens, especially advanced cognitive reasoning
abilities, intensive personal identity exploration, a feeling of being
somewhere in between childhood and adulthood, and a preoccupation with future possibilities. These developmental capacities are
unfolding in the context of significant societal conditions including a prolonged period of education and training before entry into
and investment in an occupational role, delayed age at marriage and
childbearing, and difficulties becoming financially self-sufficient
(Arnett, 2006; Sirsch, Dreher, Mayr, & Willinger, 2009). Pathways
into adulthood are stretched out and diverse (Coté, 2014).

What should we call this stage of life? Despite a growing enthusiasm in the field of human development to refer to this as the
stage of emerging adulthood, we prefer the term later adolescence
for the following reasons:

1. Adulthood, a status that is socially and culturally constructed, is becoming an increasingly elusive state, difficult to define or achieve. The adult transition might be
   considered to be completed when three or more of the
   following five criteria have been achieved: leaving home,
   completing one's education, becoming financially independent, getting married, and, for most, having children
   (Furstenberg, 2010). FIGURE 10.1 ▶ provides a comparison of the percentage of men and women who completed
   all five of these markers of adult status by age 20, 25, and
   30 in 1960 and 2000. In 1960 this transition into adulthood was very unusual for men and women aged 20,
   but common for young men aged 25 and normative for
   young women aged 25. By 2000, it was no longer normative for all five markers of adult status to be achieved by
   men or women at age 25 or 30. These data illustrate that
   adulthood is not emerging in the ages of 18 to 24 years,
   but in fact, is further away than it was 55 years ago.

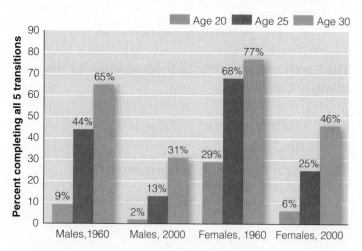

FIGURE 10.1 ▶ THE PERCENTAGE COMPLETING FIVE CRITERIA OF THE
ADULT TRANSITION, 1960 AND 2000, BY AGE AND GENDER

Source: Data are from the Integrated Public Use Microdata Series extracts (IPUMS) of the 1960 and 2000
U.S. Censuses. Men are defined as financially independent if they are in the labor force; women are defined
as financially independent if they have completed all transitions except employment in the labor force. Table
reprinted, with permission, from *Between Adolescence and Adulthood: Expectations about the Timing of Adulthood* (Working Paper No. 1), by F. F. Furstenberg, S. Kennedy, V. C. McLoyd, R. G. Rumbaut, and R. A. Settersten, (2003), Philadelphia: Network on Transitions to Adulthood. Used by permission of Frank Furstenberg, Jr.

2. In contemporary industrialized or post-industrialized countries, young people are enrolling in postsecondary education at greater rates than ever before. This includes associates degree, bachelor's degree, and professional degree programs. The student status, which by definition is transitional as one moves toward a level of new knowledge and expertise, has been extended. Typically the student status delays full-time entry into the labor market and fosters a prolonged period of temporary residential identification with a community.

3. The average age at first marriage is approaching 30. Although the majority of young people in the age range 18 to 24 are sexually active, their relationships are temporary. Relatively few young people in the age range 18 to 24 are involved in relationships that they expect will result in marriage.

4. The economic recession of 2008–2009 resulted in a growing number of young people who were out of work, underemployed, or working at jobs that were viewed as temporary. Among high school graduates ages 17 to 20, 19 percent are unemployed and 37 percent are underemployed (Davis & Kimball, 2015). The percentage of young people in this age group who can support themselves has declined even further than it was in 2000.

5. Close to 60 percent of people ages 20 to 24 years who are not married live with their parents. One recent change in the U.S. health policy was a provision to allow young people to remain on their parents' health insurance policies until age 26. These are just two indications of the continued financial dependence of young people on their parents.

The prospects of making a behavioral, psychological, or social transition into adulthood is not emerging in the age period of 18 to 24 years. We prefer the term later adolescence because it connotes a process of continued growth and maturation prior to adulthood. The executive decision-making capacities of the frontal cortex are still maturing, suggesting that later adolescents have new abilities for reflection, problem solving, and planning, but these capacities are not fully developed (Cohen et al., 2016). For many, this is a period of exploration, experimentation, and self-development. As one author described it, "between the late teens and late 20s...young Americans experience their 'odyssey years,' a time of wandering on the path to maturity" (Boonstra, 2009, p. 13).

An estimated 15 percent of youth ages 18 to 24 are disconnected; they are not in school, and they are not employed. Some are in jail, others are homeless or disabled, and others have been released from foster care but are having difficulty achieving independent lives (National Kids Count, 2016).

Later adolescence is a time of fewer constraints and greater self-determination than early adolescence. Young people ages 18 to 24 do not have to be in school even though many are. New legal rights and privileges become available. Life paths become increasingly divergent as young people make choices and pursue their goals. But, by and large, these paths are experimental and temporary, reflecting the flexibility of the stage and the lack of urgency to make long-term commitments.

Later adolescence is characterized by a heightened sensitivity to the process of identity development. Personal identity is developed as an individual struggles to answer the questions, "What is the meaning of my life? Who am I? Where am I headed?" Most young people are cognitively complex enough to conjure up alternative scenarios about their own future, including possible kinds of work and various meaningful relationships. They struggle with the uncertainty of having to choose their own life's directions. This period is often characterized by a high level of anxiety. Even though most young people are energetic and capable, they are also troubled by the lack of certainty about their future. Some worry whether they will be able to succeed in a chosen direction; others may be anxious because they do not even know what direction they wish to take.

FURTHER REFLECTION: Assess the distinguishing features of later adolescence as compared to early adolescence. Where do you place yourself on the ladder of development from early adolescence to adulthood? Why? ●

Developmental Tasks

Autonomy from Parents

OBJECTIVE 1 Explain the concept of autonomy from parents and examine the conditions under which autonomy is likely to be achieved.

Achieving a psychological sense of autonomy from one's parents is a multidimensional task that is faced gradually over the course of later adolescence and early adulthood. As illustrated in the opening case, young people enter the period of later adolescence carrying with them complex mental representations of their relationships with family members, including feelings of obligation, emotional closeness or distance, and some preoccupation about their parents' expectations for them. **Autonomy** from parents is the ability to regulate one's behavior and to select and guide one's decisions and actions in order to achieve meaningful personal goals without undue control from or dependence on one's parents. Autonomy suggests that decisions and behaviors are guided by personal will; they are voluntary rather than imposed or controlled by others (Ryan & Deci, 2000).

Autonomy is not the same as rejection, alienation, or physical separation from parents. Rather, it is an independent psychological status in which parents and children accept each other's individuality. Many areas of similarity between parents and children may provide bonds for a continued close, supportive relationship into adulthood. However, those bonds are re-created in later adolescence and early adulthood through a process of self-definition. Adolescents who achieve autonomy can recognize and accept both the similarities and the differences between themselves and their parents while still feeling love, understanding, and connection with them. It is not uncommon for later adolescents to experience a strengthening of their family identity and their sense of obligation to their family in later adolescence, recognizing the importance of family experiences to the way they think about themselves, a feeling that their parents value their ideas and opinions, and a sense of mutual responsibility and care (Tsai, Telzer, & Fuligni, 2013).

Autonomy may refer to independence of behavior, thoughts, and emotions (Steinberg, 2013). Much of the psychosocial development that has occurred in childhood and early adolescence can be understood as preparing for behavioral independence from one's parents. Such skills as dressing oneself, handling money, cooking, driving a car, reading, and writing have been mastered. Many of these skills are incorporated into the concept of activities of daily living (ADLs), a measure that is used to assess the self-sufficiency of older adults. Although it is easy to take these skills for granted, they are essential for someone who is living independently. The physical maturation that has taken place also contributes to the possibility of autonomy. Daily survival requires physical strength, coordination, and endurance—qualities that accompany the physical maturity of adolescence.

Beyond these physical requirements, autonomy involves a psychological sense of confidence about one's unique point of view and an ability to express opinions and beliefs that may differ from those of one's parents (Herman, Dornbusch, Herron, & Herting, 1997). In early school age, the process of identification and the accompanying internalization of parental values allow the young child to function with a sense of what is appropriate behavior. In early adolescence, the child's ability to emerge from the intimacy of the family may also be promoted by a growing involvement with the peer group. In early adolescence, a young person's autonomy is expressed in personal preferences and tastes that are considered legitimate domains for decision making. In later adolescence, a young person's cognitive maturity provides problem-solving abilities, the ability to consider multiple perspectives and to evaluate information from multiple sources, and a capacity to plan for the future, all of which support new levels of autonomous reasoning about important life choices. As later adolescents become more autonomous in thought, they are able to reflect upon their parents' opinions and advice and to set these views next to their own as well as the views of peers or other mentors or authorities in order to decide what makes sense for them.

The concept of **differentiation**, a term drawn from family systems theory, has been associated with emotional maturity and a healthy emergence of individuality. Differentiation is the extent to which a social system encourages intimacy while supporting the expression of differences (Bomar & Sabatelli, 1996). Within the family context, identity exploration is facilitated by an open exchange of ideas and a certain level of challenge. Adolescents must have opportunities to express their separateness within the boundaries of the family. They must feel that their parents accept and understand their need to have distinct opinions and views. This takes place as parents support their child's quest for autonomy and encourage their child to express new ideas and differing points of view without making them feel guilty when they disagree (Best, Hauser, & Allen, 1997). Adolescents who experience high levels of parental control and frequent exposure to parental conflict are likely to have difficulties achieving a comfortable sense of autonomy (Taylor & Oskay, 1995; Oudekerk, Allen, Hessel, & Molloy, 2015). In contrast, well-being is higher among college students who perceive their parents as supporting their autonomy

(Ratelle, Simard, & Guay, 2013; Van der Giessen, Branje, & Meeus, 2014). Ideally, individuality is achieved in a context of mutual caring and emotional support. A secure attachment to parents, based on a perception of them as committed to their child's well-being, is essential for growth toward independence (Buhl, 2007; Palladino-Schultheiss & Blustein, 1994; Perosa, Perosa, & Tam, 1996).

In response to a question about drinking and partying at college, one student explained how her parents' support influenced her decisions.

> I was very open with my parents before, my mom especially. We had a talk like the day before I moved in and both my parents told me that they don't mind if I just like try. They know I am curious. They told me that I know my limits and I do know. Like I know, they always told me like I'm pretty responsible so I know when too far is too far. So I feel like if I was to just try it once, I would know not to go crazy, because I know the consequences of it. So I just feel like they trust me a lot so that's kind of, it's been really good that I know that they trust me. (Adams, Kisler, Vaccaro, & Newman, 2013)

The meaning a young person gives to achieving autonomy from parents varies depending on personal, family, and cultural values, such as commitment to education, financial independence, and marriage. For example, some cultural groups are more accustomed to living in multigenerational families and place great value on the filial bond between children and their parents. Parents in these cultures may be more comfortable with the idea of having their later adolescent children living in their home without paying rent, and the children may perceive it as part of their obligation to stay near their parents and grandparents in order to provide social and instrumental support. In contrast, in some cultures, families expect their later adolescent children to achieve residential separateness. They may expect that children ages 18 to 24 who are living at home will contribute to the cost of housing.

Families have ways of remaining close while still giving their later adolescent children room to express their individuality.

As illustrated in the opening case, paths toward autonomy are influenced by the family context. The young man in the case tells us that as a teenager he had taken responsibility for many aspects of family life, preparing him for the instrumental aspects of autonomy. His experiences focus more on his emotional attachments and the opportunity to gain some distance from feelings of confusion, obligation, and loss. Children living with their two biological parents are likely to leave home later than are children living in a stepfamily. Children growing up in families with few financial resources are likely to have to assume responsibilities for their family's household tasks, sibling care, and economic needs at a younger age, thereby accelerating their sense of self-sufficiency (Benson & Elder, 2011). Three components of achieving autonomy from parents are discussed in the following sections: leaving home, attending college, and self-sufficiency.

Autonomy and Leaving Home

Living away from one's parents' household may be a symbol of independence; however, it is not as readily achievable in the age range from 18 to 24 as it was in the past. Before about 1960, marriage was the most traditional reason for moving to a new residence other than leaving temporarily for college or the military. Since that time, however, the median age at marriage has increased; in 2015, 87 percent of those in the age range from 20 to 24 have never been married (U.S. Census Bureau, 2015b). More than half of these later adolescents consider their parents' home as their permanent residence (U.S. Census Bureau, 2015c) (see FIGURE 10.2 ▶).

Parents and adolescent children have different views about the age at which children are expected to leave home. Parents tend to expect children to leave home at an older age—more closely tied to the expected age of marriage—than do adolescent children. Also, parents expect daughters to live at home longer than sons. However, these differences are not reflected in the expectations of the adolescents themselves. Thus, this issue is a potential source of family conflict. Family structure is also associated with the age of leaving home. Children in single-parent families and girls in stepfamilies leave at an earlier age (Cooney & Mortimer, 1999).

Economic factors and social norms play a significant role in the timing of leaving home. A child's ability to live away from home may depend on whether the family is willing and financially able to provide support during this period. This, in turn, depends in part on the family's values and the later adolescent's values. For example, many families are strongly committed to having their children complete college and are willing to provide financial support while the child is away at school. However, if the child gets married while still in college, some families may feel that their financial obligation to support the child is over.

Some parents are willing to support their children who are away from home if the child is in college but not willing to provide support if the child wants to live away from home but not attend school (Goldscheider, Thornton, & Yang, 2001). Imagine that, after 1 or 2 years of college, a child wants to move to a new city and seek opportunities in the entertainment industry. Some parents might encourage this path toward self-discovery; others might consider it risky or frivolous. When children and parents disagree about the appropriate path toward self-reliance and adulthood, parents may be unwilling to provide the financial resources that would make this level of autonomy possible.

What is the relationship of later adolescents' living arrangements to their well-being? Do young people who continue to live at home with their parents have the same sense of well-being and life satisfaction as young people who live in some type of group situation with other friends or who live independently? There are some conflicting views about this. Some studies show that later adolescents who live with peers or on their own have a more adult-like view of themselves and get along better with their parents than those who live with their parents (White, 2002). Other studies show that later adolescents who have a good relationship with their parents are more likely to live with them for a longer period (Lanz & Tagliabue, 2007).

When there is a stepparent involved or frequent conflict with parents, later adolescents may feel pushed out into independent living. A study of Belgian later adolescents examined the relationship of three types of living arrangements to well-being: living at home with parents, living with other students but returning home frequently, and living independently with a partner or alone. The most important factor was the young person's sense that the living arrangement was of their own choosing. In addition, later adolescents whose parents supported their autonomous decision were most confident about their decision and had the greatest sense of well-being, regardless of whether they lived at home with their parents, with friends, or on their own (Kins, Beyers, Soenens, & Vansteenkiste, 2009).

Autonomy and the College Experience

Going away to college is an intermediate step between living at home and establishing a separate permanent residence. The mere act of going to college does not in itself bring a sense of leaving home or of psychological autonomy from one's parents. In fact, most students do not go far from home when they enter college as freshmen; over half live 100 miles or less from home. Fifteen percent of freshmen continue to live at home while they attend college

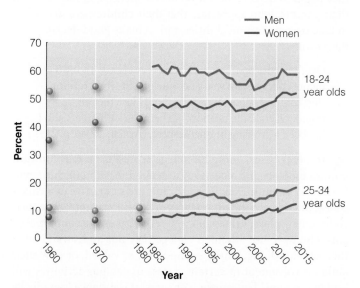

Note: Unmarried college students living in dormitories are counted as living in group quarters in decennial data but as living in their parental home in CPS data.

FIGURE 10.2 ▶ PERCENTAGE OF YOUNG ADULTS LIVING IN PARENTAL HOME

Source: U.S. Census Bureau, Decennial Censuses, 1960 to 1980, and Current Population Survey, Annual Social and Economic Supplements, 1983 to 2015.

Developmental Tasks   377

Students who go away to college use their group identity skills to form new relationships while creating a physical environment that preserves a connection to family, friends, and home.

and 18 percent say that enrolling in a college close to home was a very important factor in their choice of which college to attend (Eagan et al., 2015). The likelihood of attending college close to home depends in part on the number of colleges and universities in one's home state. In states like Utah, Arizona, and California, close to 90 percent of students attend college in state (Guo, 2015).

Most freshmen still request and receive both emotional and instrumental support from their parents. In an ongoing study of belonging among college freshmen, most students we have interviewed report frequent contact with their parents during the first few weeks including texting, emails, and phone conversations. Students often describe their sense of belonging by saying that the campus feels "like home." Many students hold on to their connection to family through the bits and pieces of home that they use to decorate their dorm rooms.

Some college-age students are more ready than others to embrace the demands for new levels of independence and responsibility. College freshmen express a variety of attitudes that suggest different views about their desire to be independent from their family. Of students entering college in the fall of 2015, 18 percent said that a very important reason for deciding to go to a specific college was that their parents wanted them to attend; 18 percent said that it was very important to live near home (Eagan et al., 2015). As they enter college, students differ markedly in how much work they have already done toward achieving autonomy from their parents, how much they desire autonomy, and what evidence they use to determine whether they have achieved autonomy.

Similarly, parents differ in how ready they are to support and encourage their child's autonomy. Many parents experience pangs of separation distress as their children leave for college. They know that their child will be entering a new period of self-discovery and maturation, and that their relationship will change. Despite feelings of sadness about separation, they are able to step back and let their child experience a new level of independence.

Whereas most parents are able to encourage and support their child's emerging autonomy, some have been given the dubious label of "helicopter parents," a term that suggests over-parenting. These parents may convey their own anxiety about their child's well-being through excessive levels of involvement, control, and problem solving. They engage in inappropriate levels of assistance and direct intervention on behalf of their children, either directly with their children or with advisors, faculty, and/or administrators. The impact of this "hovering" approach is to undermine the child's self-confidence and increase the young person's feelings of anxiety and stress (Segrin, Woszidlo, Givertz, & Montgomery, 2013).

Revision of Attachment to Parents

The experience of entering college focuses new attention on the changing quality of the attachment relationship between college students and their parents. Students who live at college are more likely to rely on the mental representations of their attachment figures, whereas students who live with their parents continue to be involved daily with concrete interactions. Issues of autonomy and control, establishing new guidelines and limits related to participation in family life, involvement in relationships with peers, and management of time and money are resolved in the absence of direct input from parents for most students who live at college, but these decisions continue to involve parental input for students who live at home.

For students who live on campus, preoccupation with thoughts and concerns about their parents tend to diminish over the course of the first semester while new relationships form and confidence in their independent decision making builds. The attachment scheme or representation, rather than the actual interactions with parents, is modified. Many students who attend college away from home begin to have more positive thoughts and feelings about their parents. At the same time, they begin to detect a new level of confidence and respect from their parents, who appreciate that their children are managing to take on new responsibilities and to make good decisions on their own.

> Over the past year I have become very close with my dad. Before college there was a definite parent–child relationship with my father. Now he is more like a mentor or friend. Overall, the relationship between my parents and I has been a growing mutual respect. (Arnett, 2004a, p. 215)

In other cases, going to college represents a move toward upward mobility and a decision to seek a life path quite different from one's parents. Even when parents are supportive of a child's college attendance, the experiences of college may introduce their child to new ideas, values, and interests that create conflict. Parents who have not attended college may not understand what their child is doing, why it is important or valued, or how their child's involvement in certain classes or campus activities will lead to economic betterment. For some, this distance is gradually bridged as parents become familiar with their children's lives, and children become more skilled at giving parents ways of understanding what they are doing. For others, as in the case of Mary, the distance widens over time:

I go home, we talk about the weather, talk about people in the family, people in the neighborhood.... The stuff I would like to talk about, [my mother] can't. She doesn't understand it. Stuff she'd like to talk about I think would be incredibly boring.... I learned very early on that they couldn't discuss [school]. To try to discuss it with them would be very frustrating to me and embarrassing for them.... I realized I had far educated myself past my parents. (Roberts & Rosenwald, 2001, p. 102)

The relationship between emotional closeness and living at home is culturally shaped. For example, in the United States, later adolescents who live at home and have frequent daily interactions with their parents tend to be *least* close to them. In comparison, studies of European later adolescents find that young people who live at home are quite happy with their living arrangements, find their parents to be an important source of emotional support, and experience considerable autonomy in the context of their parents' household (Arnett, 2000). The **Applying Theory and Research to Life** box Attachment and Identity Formation provides more detail on the relationship of parental attachment to identity formation in later adolescence.

The delay in age at marriage also has implications for the revision of the **parental attachment** relationship. When the majority of young people in the 20 to 24 age range were married, it was normal to expect that some of the emotional investment in one's family of origin would shift to the new intimate marital bond. Thus, emotional distancing from one's parents made sense in the context of forming a culturally approved marital commitment. Today, many young people have deeply valued love relationships, but they are not married and are not ready to make lifelong commitments to these relationships. This results in lengthening the period when both children and parents may feel that the child's primary emotional attachment is to the family of origin.

Autonomy and Self-Sufficiency

Despite the variety of life paths and demographic characteristics of those in the period of later adolescence, most young people can recognize when they have achieved a sense of autonomy from their parents. One important underlying theme is a sense of **self-sufficiency**, expressed by making independent decisions, taking responsibility for one's actions, and achieving a degree of financial independence.

The expression of self-sufficiency can be particularly challenging for college students with disabilities. In the transition to college, students with disabilities leave behind the structures in place in elementary and secondary school that are associated with the identification, assessment, and development of educational plans to support and accommodate their needs. The process of disclosing one's disability and receiving appropriate accommodations rests squarely on the student's shoulders in the post-secondary environment. In one national study, only 28 percent of students who had received accommodations in high school said that they informed their postsecondary institution of their disability (Newman et al., 2011). Yet, it is known that **self-advocacy**, "the ability to communicate one's needs and wants and to make decisions about the supports needed to

achieve them" is closely related to college persistence and success (Adams & Proctor, 2010). In one qualitative study, students with disabilities described a variety of ways that they learned self-advocacy skills from family members. Once at college, these students found that they had to adapt their approach in the new environment.

Before I had my parents to help me with meetings ... and this time I was all on my own ... I had to ... self-advocate, you know? But that's obviously a skill you need for life and that's a skill you learn in college. So I was happy I was doing that. But, that was just overwhelming because I [had] to go in to talk to my teachers and make that first move. (Daly-Cano, Vaccaro, & Newman, 2015)

Other aspects of self-sufficiency relate to financial needs. In one study, researchers asked students and their parents to select a question from a survey about autonomy and write why they might disagree about this issue. One of the items was, "My parents will give me money when I ask for it." The following responses illustrate the point of view of a student who would like to be as financially self-sufficient as possible, and the point of view of a parent who wants her daughter to know that there are some limits to the kind of support she can expect (Kenyon & Koerner, 2009, p. 307).

18-YEAR-OLD FEMALE: I think one of the things we would disagree about is money. My father is helping me with rent, and both of my parents are helping me financially, when I need it. They want me to come to them if I need money, but I want to be able to do things on my own, without having to run to mommy or daddy whenever I need money. They don't mind helping me out, but I would like to try and get by on my own as much as I can. It will be easier when I get a job.

44-YEAR-OLD MOTHER: She will think that I will give her money for 99% of the things that she thinks is important and that is not going to be the case. I will give her money when she needs it for the important things that you need to live on or with. No shopping sprees for the heck of it!

Although few college students who are enrolled full time expect to work full time, roughly 50 percent of college students who are enrolled full time are also employed. Data from six countries including the United States and Canada show that over the past 20 years there has been a decline in the percentage of later adolescents who are able to support themselves as defined by wages and salary above 50 percent of the national adjusted disposable personal income for their country (Bell, Burtless, Gornick, & Smeeding, 2007). The median annual income for 20- to 24-year-olds who were not in school was *lower* in 2012 than in 2000 for all levels of education (Federal Interagency Forum on Child and Family Statistics, 2014). In 2009, 21 percent of those in the 18- to 24-year-old age range had incomes below the poverty level. As shown in FIGURE 10.3 ▶, this rate varied by sex and level of educational attainment (Aud, KewalRomani, & Frohlich, 2011). These data help to explain the pattern of delays in self-sufficiency and the postponement of an independent lifestyle.

Attachment and Identity Formation

Identity formation is usually viewed as a process that requires young people to distance themselves from the socialization pressures and expectations imposed by parents and other family members. To achieve an individual identity, one must create a vision of the self that is authentic—a sense of having taken hold of one's destiny in an effort to reach goals that are personally meaningful. Yet research has demonstrated that the quality of family relationships contributes significantly to a young person's ability to achieve a personal identity (Allen, 2008).

The relationship between close parental bonds and identity achievement can be compared to the way that a secure attachment in infancy supports a willingness to explore the environment. Securely attached infants will move away physically from their caregiver, confident that the caregiver will be available when they are in need of help. For later adolescents, autonomy-seeking behaviors can be interpreted as a more advanced form of the exploratory activities observed in infancy. Later adolescents who have a secure relationship with their parents and who are comfortable in loosening these ties can begin to explore the ideological, occupational, and interpersonal alternatives that become the content for their own identities.

Attachment to parents in later adolescence and adulthood has been measured using the *Adult Attachment Interview* (AAI), which asks participants to describe their relationship with their parents when they were younger, including specific memories of that relationship; recall incidences of distress in the relationship; and discuss factors that have influenced their relationship (George, Kaplan, & Main, 1996; Hesse, 2008). The interview is then coded to characterize the attachment state of mind as (1) *autonomous*, reflective of an open, coherent narrative about the parent–child relationship; (2) *dismissive*, reflective of minimizing the importance of the parent–child relationship, inability to recall many details, and a tendency to idealize one's parents; or (3) *preoccupied*, reflective of continuing anger toward one's parents and a confused, vague,

or passive narrative (Bernier et al., 2004). Interviews with students at the beginning and end of the first year of college found that the preoccupied students had the most difficulty adapting to college and actually did worse with respect to adjustment and grades as the year went along. These students had the greatest difficulty transferring their emotional investment from parents to peers, even if that investment was negative (Bernier et al., 2004).

Students who have a positive attachment to their mothers are more likely to have an achieved identity and are less likely to be in a moratorium or identity-confused status than are students who have insecure, mistrustful relationships with their mothers. On the other hand, those whose attachments are insecure show a greater tendency to experience identity confusion and are more vulnerable to experiences of depression (Agerup, Lydersen, Wallander, & Sund, 2015; Benson, Harris, & Rogers, 1992).

By the time young people reach later adolescence, those who are securely attached to their parents are confident about parental affection and support. They can receive and implement parental advice insofar as it seems useful and practical. At the same time, they trust in their own worth and their ability to make decisions (Carlson, 2014). Later adolescents may make a point of *not* seeking parental support, but in a secure relationship, they know that help is available if needed. By imposing emotional distance and achieving greater self-reliance, later adolescents are able to reach a more objective evaluation of their parents as figures for identification and, thereby, to create the needed space for the emergence of their own identity (Kobak & Madsen, 2008).

A secure parental attachment supports identity formation in the following ways:

- It fosters confidence in the exploration of social relationships, ideologies, and settings.
- It establishes positive expectations in regard to interpersonal experiences outside the family.

- It fosters the formation of group identities apart from the family, thus providing a transitional context for work on individual identity.
- It provides a basic layer of self-acceptance, permitting the young person to approach the process of identity formation with optimism.

Critical Thinking Questions

1. Analyze how the typology of *preoccupied* attachment in adolescence or adulthood corresponds to the attachment styles described in the section on infant attachment in chapter 5. What do you think the mental representations of parents of the *preoccupied* later adolescent are like? Hypothesize about why these students have difficulty adjusting to college.

2. Explain the relationship between a secure attachment in infancy and an autonomous attachment in later adolescence. Describe the kinds of behaviors and attitudes you would expect to see among later adolescents who have an autonomous attachment style.

3. Infer from your readings how the formation of an avoidant, resistant, or disorganized attachment in infancy would relate to work on identity in later adolescence.

4. Create a matrix that compares the benefits and costs of living at home with parents and living on campus with respect to identity formation and self-acceptance.

5. Describe how cultural differences with regard to the values of independence and interdependence might influence the process of attachment and achieving autonomy from parents in later adolescence.

6. Imagine that you were asked to advise families about the optimal balance between autonomy from parents and connection to parents during the college years. What should parents and students do to try to achieve this balance? What should colleges and universities do to help families achieve this balance?

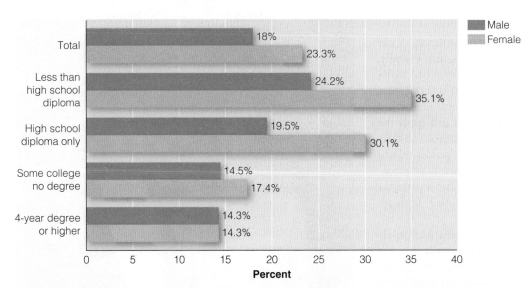

FIGURE 10.3 ▶ PERCENTAGE OF 18- TO 24-YEAR-OLDS IN POVERTY BY SEX AND EDUCATIONAL ATTAINMENT, 2009

Source: Aud, KewalRomani, & Frohlich, 2011.

In addition to poverty, one obstacle to financial self-sufficiency is the increasing burden of debt faced by many college students. Young people have mounting student loans as well as some credit card debt. Every year, about 12 million students borrow money to help cover the costs of higher education. For students who graduated from college in 2016, the average amount of student loan debt was $37,172 (Student Loan Hero.com, 2016). Repayment is a struggle for many, especially if they drop out of school before completing their degree, if they experience unemployment, or if they also accumulate credit card debt. A majority of students report that the amount of their student loan debt has impacted important life decisions like the choice of career, the ability to purchase a home, and saving for retirement. A substantial minority (over 20 percent) say that their student load debt has influenced a decision to delay marriage or to delay having children (ASA, 2015). Thus, although young people are encouraged to enroll in college, the rising costs and associated debt obligations slow their ability to achieve financial independence.

A sense of self-sufficiency goes beyond personal income. It is a subjective experience that is distinct from a person's living arrangement, student status, having a steady job, or being in a serious love relationship. A subjective sense of self-sufficiency is achieved gradually as young people face and meet important challenges of school, work, and family life and build confidence in their capacity to make good decisions. An appropriately structured, encouraging environment that scaffolds challenges so that students can experience increasing levels of competence fosters autonomy at the same time as it supports feelings of connection and belonging (Naude, Nel, van der Watt, & Tadi, 2016).

The process of achieving autonomy from parents opens the door to new considerations regarding gender identity, morality, and career aspirations. In each of these areas, a young person has the opportunity to *decenter*—to step back from the close socialization pressures of family and neighborhood—and construct his or her own point of view. After a period of role experimentation and **introspection**, some may choose to adopt the framework that was in place at the end of the high school years. Others may invent novel and nontraditional perspectives. The growth that takes place during the period of later adolescence in each of these areas reflects a willingness to evaluate multiple perspectives and to integrate personal commitments with societal expectations and resources.

FURTHER REFLECTION: Explain the idea of self-sufficiency. What does this term mean to you? What level of self-sufficiency would you expect someone in the age range 18–24 to have achieved? What are some of the obstacles to self-sufficiency?

Gender Identity

OBJECTIVE 2 Summarize the development of gender identity in later adolescence. Analyze how the components of gender-role identification that were relevant during the early-school-age period are revised and expanded.

In later adolescence, important revisions and elaborations of the child's earlier work on gender identification are taking place (see chapter 7). The formulation of **gender identity** refers to the acquisition of a set of beliefs, attitudes, and values about oneself as a man or a woman in many areas of social life, including intimate relations, family, work, community, and religion. The developmental task of forming one's gender identity reflects the need to integrate and synthesize three basic components of gender—its biological, psychological, and social meanings—into a view of oneself as a man or a woman entering the complex social world of adult life.

Four terms that are often used in discussing gender identity are masculinity, femininity, androgyny, and transgendered. **Masculinity** is typically associated with being instrumental, focusing on tasks and products, and *agentic* (i.e., having leadership abilities, being assertive, taking control); **femininity** is typically associated with being expressive, focusing on emotions and communication, and *communal* (i.e., valuing interpersonal and spiritual development, being tender, sympathetic, and concerned about the well-being of others). **Androgyny** refers to the capacity to express both masculine and feminine characteristics as the situation demands. **Transgendered** refers to people who do not identify with or present themselves as reflecting the **sex** they were born with and who move across or combine gender boundaries. The **Human Development and Diversity** box introduces the concept of the **third gender**, an idea that illustrates alternative pathways toward gender identity that exist in many cultures.

The Role of Culture

According to social role theory, *roles* are basic building blocks of social organizations. Every organization, including a family, workplace, community, and a culture, can be described by its roles. Individuals learn the roles of their social system throughout their lives. Through the socialization process, people internalize the expectations associated with many life roles and apply the socially shared norms and standards linked to these roles to their own behaviors. This process occurs with respect to gender-related roles as well as to kinship, age, occupation, and other socially constructed roles. For example, when a person becomes a parent, a man is called a *father* and a woman is called a *mother*. Both are parenting roles, but gender is identified.

All cultures construct gender-differentiated roles, and people expect one another to behave in certain ways because they are male or female. Perhaps more important, they form expectations of how men and women ought to act when they are together so that the distinctions between the genders are demarcated. These expectations are taught and learned, beginning early in life. Many important life events, such as the ritual of the wedding ceremony, highlight the distinctions between the male and female gender roles. For later adolescents, the gendered nature of the family is an especially important factor in shaping gender identity. Family experiences from the past provide the gender script with which they are most familiar. The family life they envision for themselves in the future creates many of the priorities that shape their current commitments and goals (Schlegel, 2009).

In the United States, many people argue that gender-based role distinctions are inappropriate, at least as a part of public life. They believe that men and women should be considered equal and treated identically in all public matters. But in many cultures, there are distinct, agreed-upon norms prescribing differences in how men and women are treated, which tasks they are expected to perform, and what status they hold in their family and community. Often, these norms establish specific power differences as part of the gender distinctions. Typically, men have more power than women, but this is not always the case.

Others argue that men and women should be considered equal, but that they should be treated in ways that take into account differences in their needs and capacities. For example current workplace guidelines recommend the creation of specific settings for nursing women.

> The Patient Protection and Affordable Care Act ("Affordable Care Act") amended section 7 of the Fair Labor Standards Act ("FLSA") to require employers to provide reasonable break time for an employee to express breast milk for her nursing child for one year after the child's birth each time such employee has need to express the milk. Employers are also required to provide a place, other than a bathroom, that is shielded from view and free from intrusion from coworkers and the public, which may be used by an employee to express breast milk. The break time requirement became effective when the Affordable Care Act was signed into law on March 23, 2010. (U.S. Department of Labor, 2016)

Courtesy of Philip Newman

Cultures construct gender-differentiated roles. In the United States, the traditional attire of the bride and groom symbolize ideal images of feminine beauty and masculine respectability to which many young people aspire.

The experiences of immigrant youth to the United States illustrate the role of culture in shaping gender identity. Young people who immigrate with their families, sometimes referred to as the 1.5 generation, find themselves in the position of having to navigate contrasting norms and values regarding gender. Having been born and raised in a culture in which men are elevated to a higher status position and strict rules are applied in defining women's roles, they find themselves in an environment where new opportunities for status and roles are available. For example, it is not uncommon for immigrant girls to do better in school and to adapt more quickly to the educational opportunities in their new community than the boys. At the same time, immigrant boys are likely to be allowed more freedom to explore outside the home. Girls are held to a traditional standard for chastity and are expected to preserve traditional practices that they will pass on to the next generation. As a result, boys may experience conflict between reduced status in the eyes of teachers and school authorities in comparison to girls; and girls may experience resentment of their male siblings' freedom given their better performance and recognition in the school environment. Both males and females in the 1.5 generation have to construct new meaning of their gender roles in this transitional process (Stritikus & Nguyen, 2007).

Third Genders

Biologically, humans may be sexually dimorphic, but in many cultures there is evidence of alternatives that expand the dualistic perspective of male and female gender. Three examples of cultural traditions that have *third gender* categories are provided here as a way of illustrating the potential diversity of gender concepts. Many more examples can be found in anthropological writings (Nanda, 2001). Many cultures include alternatives to the traditional male and female categories that broaden the possibilities for pathways that individuals may follow as they crystallize their gender identity.

In Oman, a country in the Persian Gulf, *Xanith* is a term used to refer to biological males who function mostly as women (Nanda, 1998). In some Middle Eastern countries, this term is used as insulting slang for effeminate men. When asked, *Xanith* say they are women, but they are not entirely like women according to Omani standards. *Xanith* falls in between that of men and women. Under Islamic law, *Xanith* have all the rights of men and are allowed to worship with the men at the mosque, yet they are allowed to visit with women, eat with women, and walk arm in arm with women. The facial expressions, voice, laugh, movements, and swaying walk of the *Xanith* imitate those of women, but they wear clothing that is a mixture of men's and women's styles. *Xanith* are prohibited by law from wearing some women's clothing, including the mask and veil that all adult women must wear. A *Xanith* wears the ankle-length tunic typical for men, but it is belted tightly at the waist as a woman might do. In Oman both men and women cover their heads, but *Xanith* go bareheaded. Unlike women, *Xanith* move around freely outside their houses, though only during the day. Most importantly, *Xanith* are openly prostitutes, an activity that is not acknowledged for Omani woman. Thus, the *Xanith* demonstrate a third gender role in many aspects of their public self-presentation.

In India and Pakistan, the *Hijra* provide another example of a third gender. The *Hijra* have an ancient tradition, inspired in part by the Hindu deity, Shiva. Shiva is sometimes portrayed as half male, half female. The Sanskrit name for this form of the deity, *Ardhanārīśvara*, is best translated as "the lord who is half woman." This image is used to symbolize the idea that the sacred powers of the universe are both feminine and masculine (Pettis, 2011). Hindu thought allows for overlapping and even contradictory categories that support flexibility in gender roles. In general, *Hijra* are men who dress in women's clothing but do not try to hide their masculine features. When asked, they say they are not trying to be women but view themselves as both male and female. In some writings, the *Hijra* are described as eunuchs, and some do undergo surgeries to have their male genitalia removed. They appear at weddings, usually uninvited, to sing and dance and bring wishes for fertility. They expect to be paid for these performances, and usually they are. *Hijras* refer to themselves using feminine pronouns and expect others to do so. They typically live together in a commune arrangement of five or more chelas (disciples), supervised by a guru.

Among American Indian tribes, the two-spirit person is a native tradition that anthropologists have associated with some of the earliest discoveries of native artifacts. Before colonization and contact with European cultures, Native people believed in the existence of three genders: the male, the female, and the male-female gender, or what is now called the two-spirit person, a term derived from interpretations of Native languages used to describe people who displayed both male and female characteristics (Roscoe, 2000).

In the religious views of many Native people, humans are seen as minor relatives of goddesses and gods. When a human person is born, only one or the other spirit usually comes into substance, into life on Earth—the other half remains in the spirit world as a higher self. A

The *Hijra* of India are men who think of themselves as both male and female.

woman may have her hidden male side, and a man may have his female side. Traditionally, the two-spirited person was one who had received a gift from the Creator, the privilege to house both male and female spirits in the body. Being given the gift of two spirits meant that this individual had the ability to see the world from two perspectives at the same time. This greater vision was a gift to be shared with all, and as such, two-spirited beings were revered as leaders, mediators, teachers, artists, seers, and spiritual guides. They were treated with the greatest respect and held important spiritual and ceremonial responsibilities (Williams, 1992).

These examples extend our thinking about gender. They illustrate cultural strategies for formalizing alternative understandings about gender. In some cultures and at certain times in history, people who embrace these alternatives have been persecuted or reviled, but in other cultures and at other times, people who claim a third gender identity have been recognized as having special powers or insights.

(Continued on next page)

Ladi Kirn/Alamy Stock Photo

Critical Thinking Questions

1. Express your reactions to the idea of a third gender. Explain how the concept of a third gender fits your own understanding of gender identity. How might it be possible to be neither male nor female? Or both male and female?

2. Explain why many indigenous people or cultures have conceived of a social identity for people who combine male and female qualities.

3. Whereas third gender individuals are respected and acknowledged as having their own social space in many non-Western cultures, individuals who exhibit these characteristics have been ostracized and stigmatized in many Western societies. Why is that?

Reevaluating Gender Constancy

Each of the components of gender identification discussed in chapter 7 undergoes some transformation as work on gender identity continues, including reevaluating gender constancy, reevaluating earlier gender role standards and learning new ones, and revising childhood gender identifications. What is more, a sexual dimension is added to gender identity.

Later adolescents can appreciate that the use of gender labels is a social convention and that, apart from the genital basis of this label, there are wide individual differences *within* gender groups in most traits and abilities. Moreover, information about genetic anomalies and medical technologies may lead later adolescents to realize that it is possible to have a conflict between one's genetic sex and one's gender identity.

Some young people, referred to as transgendered, develop a gender identity that is opposite to their biological sex. They feel certain of their gender, which is at odds with their genital features. In these cases, the possibility of sex-reassignment surgery combined with hormone treatments provides an alternative to the notion of gender constancy (Ettner, 2016). One study followed the adjustment of 20 adolescents who had experienced sex-reassignment surgery. In the 1 to 4 years following treatment, these young people were functioning well, and none of them expressed regrets about their decision (Smith, van Goozen, & Cohen-Kettenis, 2001). Later adolescents may realize that one's sex is not quite as fixed and constant as they may have believed. Furthermore, those who experience psychological conflict about their gender may learn that a new designation is not only possible but also desirable.

Reevaluating Earlier Gender-Role Standards and Learning New Ones

Gender-role expectations exist at the cultural, institutional, interpersonal, and individual levels. As later adolescents learn about these expectations, they must integrate and synthesize them with their assessments of their personal talents, temperament, needs, and goals. The content of gender-role standards—that is, the cultural and subcultural expectations concerning the appropriate behavior of male and female individuals—is different for later adolescents than for young children. For a 6- or 7-year-old boy, it may have been important to learn to be tough and not to cry or whimper, to stand up for himself, and not to hit girls. For a young man in later adolescence, the gender-role expectations may include holding

a steady job, demonstrating sexual prowess, or being competitive. For a 6- or 7-year-old girl, the emphasis may have been on taking turns, not being too bossy, and staying clean. For a young woman in later adolescence, gender-role expectations may focus on being a caring, supportive friend; expressing maternal, nurturant behavior; or having an attractive figure and knowing how to dress well.

In later adolescence, young men and women begin to develop an analysis of what it takes to get ahead in their social world, whether success is defined as finding a mate, getting a good job, being a good parent, or being popular. They may learn to be more flexible in their interpersonal behavior, modifying their strategy to suit their goals. They discover that such traits as assertiveness, goal-directed behavior, competitiveness, being a good communication partner, personal disclosure, and negotiation are all required in social situations, and they learn to develop and apply them as required. In previous generations, some of the aforementioned traits were considered masculine and some feminine. Today, however, they are perceived as helpful to both men and women to be able to succeed in work and family life.

Gender-role standards may change from one generation to the next, so that parents who are socializing their children may have grown up with one set of gender-role expectations, but their children may enter later adolescence with a very different set of norms and expectations. For example, in a national survey of college freshmen, students were asked to respond to a number of statements about attitudes and values. One of those statements was, "Activities of married women are best confined to home and family." In 1970, 48 percent of freshmen agreed with that statement; 34 years later, in 2004, only 21 percent of freshmen agreed (*Chronicle of Higher Education*, 2005; U.S. Bureau of the Census, 1996). One could speculate that many of the parents who were college freshmen in the 1970s had more traditional gender-role attitudes than their children currently have. Societal changes related to education, employment, and views about marriage and childbearing combine to modify the outlook of both men and women on their appropriate and normative roles.

The U.S. culture is moving toward more flexible standards. It is normative for women, including married women with young children, to be in the labor market. The prevalence of dual-earner couples, combined with the increased educational attainment of women, has led to increases in career achievement and leadership roles for women in many fields. As a result, young women in early and later adolescence have numerous role models of women who are assertive, competitive, and achievement oriented. Young men in early and later adolescence have numerous role models of men who are effectively combining career and family-life roles, and who take pride in their ability to nurture and mentor their own children as well as younger workers. Many gender-stereotyped expectations about behaviors that are appropriate for men or women have been relaxed and replaced by a greater diversity of behavior that is considered acceptable for both men and women in our society.

The greatest impact of this revision of tightly scripted gender roles is on the later adolescent population as they formulate their gender identities. There are more options, choices, and goals, and fewer obstacles to expressing personal preferences. Many social influences including family, friends, romantic partners, media, university culture, and religious and political figures contribute content to the young person's conception of gender norms. Later adolescents incorporate this diversity of views about gender-role standards and expectations into their self-concept, and these internalized standards guide their behavior. Yet, later adolescents are not simply passive recipients of these influences. They transform this information into conceptions of a future self; and as a generation they often bring about social change, endorsing new visions of how gender is expressed through song, fashion, media, creative arts, and in day to day interactions (Bussey, 2011). Research with college-age students demonstrates how gender-role standards serve a regulatory function. Students report increases in self-esteem and positive emotions when they behave in ways that conform to their own gender-role standards, and more distress when they behave in ways that conflict with these standards (Witt & Wood, 2010).

Even as gender-role standards are becoming more flexible in the United States, certain ethnic groups face new conflicts between adhering to traditional cultural expectations and embracing gender roles that are less scripted. For example, Mexican American women experience a strong cultural emphasis on the role of women as mothers who are nurturing, virtuous, and devoted to their husbands and children. This gender-role standard places pressure on them to restrict their occupational aspirations and to remain close to their family of origin, particularly when it comes to thinking about going to college or planning a career (Wright, Mindel, Tran, & Habenstein, 2012). In later adolescence, however, these young women must review these expectations, weighing the benefits they have had from this kind of close, attentive mothering with their own changing desire for higher levels of educational and occupational attainment. For some young women, this conflict results in psychological distress as they struggle to balance their commitments to home and family with their desires for challenging and rewarding careers. As economic demands and educational opportunities have expanded, Mexican American women have found ways to satisfy their community's traditional expectations while still claiming some space for their own personal goals (Denner & Dunbar, 2004).

Revising Childhood Identifications

The component of parental identification that contributes to gender identity is also reviewed and revised in later adolescence. During this time, young people begin to encounter a wide range of possible targets for identification. In the college environment, students meet teachers, residence hall counselors, and older students whose views and values may differ widely from those of their parents. Outside the college environment, workers meet supervisors, other workers, and social companions whose views and values may differ widely from those of their parents. Later adolescents may admire public figures, such as religious leaders, political leaders, artists, or scholars, whose work and ideas are especially inspiring. In the process, later adolescents revisit the content of their parental identifications. They analyze those beliefs, attitudes, and values that they may have swallowed whole as children, evaluating which of them are still relevant to their own personal vision of themselves functioning as a man or a woman in their current situation. They try to determine whether the lessons they learned as children about how husbands and wives, fathers and mothers, and men and women treat each other and think about each other remain applicable.

The opening case provides examples of how a young man may revise his childhood identifications. In his youth, the boy was always trying to meet his mother's emotional needs which also created a certain degree of stress. Now, in his later adolescence, he sees how this pattern of behavior tied to his identification with his mother led him to be preoccupied with worries about pleasing others. Coming to college and being away from his family allowed him to review and revise his childhood identifications. Hopefully, this insight will allow him to behave more flexibly in his own relationships in the future.

Adding a Sexual Dimension to Gender Identity

In addition to revising parental identifications, later adolescents add a sexual dimension to their gender identity. Biological changes of puberty, including changes in reproductive capacities, secondary sex characteristics, body shape, height, weight, and strength, must be incorporated into one's gender identity.

Satisfaction with one's physical appearance provides an important basis for approaching social relations with a positive, optimistic outlook. Furthermore, it may influence one's attractiveness or initial desirability as a sexual partner. In contrast, dissatisfaction with one's physical appearance as integrated into the self-concept may interfere with the formation of positive social relationships, causing the person to approach interpersonal contacts with self-consciousness and a pessimistic expectation that he will be rejected.

Maturation of the hormonal system, which influences emotional arousal as well as sexual urges, contributes to the development of one's gender identity. The hormonal changes of puberty bring new sexual impulses as well as the capacity for reproduction. Hormonal changes may also contribute to changes in the basis of relationships, increasing attention to new emotions, such as jealousy, love, depression over loss of love, sexual arousal, and passion. Individual differences in hormone levels are linked to gender-role characteristics.

The general term for male sex hormones is **androgens**, the most prevalent of which is *testosterone*. Androgens, especially testosterone, are associated with sexual arousal, interest, and behavior. This relationship is observed in both men and women. For men, higher levels of androgens are associated with both increased sexual motivation and increased involvement in sexual activity. For women, higher levels of androgens are associated with increased sexual motivation, but **estrogens** appear to be implicated in their willingness to engage in sexual activity. This may be a result of the fact that estrogens contribute to the maturation of primary and secondary sex characteristics that make women more sexually attractive. In general, hormone levels are not as good a predictor of sexual activity for women as are the social contexts of family and peer group and the woman's own internalized standards about sexual behavior (Crooks & Bauer, 2014).

There is growing concern about the sexual and reproductive health of young people in their early 20s (Boonstra, 2009). Later adolescents are more likely than those in their late 20s and 30s to be involved in multiple sexual relationships, with little intention of permanency or desire for having children. Norms within some college environments appear to be particularly supportive to casual relationships.

> Lydia just simply stated "I think it's hard to not be sexually active in college" because of an existing "culture of sex" on college campuses. She elaborated by stating:
>
> Like a lot of people always talk about freshman and sophomore year, they're very promiscuous … I don't know if I'd say that it's considered a good thing or a bad thing. But it's certainly not considered an unexpected thing, to sort of have casual sex … I think, there, that definitely is a culture thing like you should go out and you know it's cool if you can hook-up with someone on the weekend. (Fantasia, 2009, pp. 82–83)

College women describe a complex set of messages from friends about sex and romantic relationships. Despite the impression implied in the preceding quotation that campuses are characterized by a "hook-up" culture, friends actually provide a diverse and somewhat contradictory set of messages about how to navigate the landscape of sexuality. In one study, over 400 undergraduate women reported about the messages they received from their male and female friends about sex and romantic relationships. There was no consensus about advice. The messages were neither wholly permissive (do what you want) nor wholly conservative (wait until marriage). Few women received advice that focused on sexual desire (e.g. just do what you want and enjoy yourself). Many women described complex advice that combined encouragement within boundaries, especially from female friends (e.g. "My female friends have always said to enjoy yourself while in college but don't go overboard with sexual partners."). Most women reported a pretty traditional message—friends tell them to evaluate the context of the relationship before deciding to have sex. In addition, friends, both males and females warned of the double standard (e.g. "Men can sleep around and it's a good thing but when women sleep around it's *skanky*."). In addition, friends advised women to be *safe, smart, and careful* without giving specific advice about sexual health. In general, more messages from male friends were sex-positive messages; more messages from female friends emphasized reputational implications as well as emotional and health consequences of being too open or too casual about sexual behaviors (Trinh, 2016).

College students are well aware of the risks of unplanned pregnancy. Nonetheless, in 2014 there were 579,760 births to unmarried women ages 20 to 24, and approximately 200,000

abortions (Hamilton et al., 2015; Pazol, Creanga, & Jamieson, 2015). Later adolescent males and females are at especially high risk for sexually transmitted infections (STIs). In 2014, 20- to 24-year-old females and males had the highest rates of chlamydia, gonorrhea, and syphilis of any age groups, and there were 7,114 newly diagnosed cases of HIV in this age group (CDC, 2015f, 2015g).

As a group, later adolescents are more mobile, less connected to a specific community, and therefore less linked to health care services that might meet their needs. With the executive function still maturing, they are greater risk takers and more likely to have multiple, temporary sex partners than somewhat older adults. They are less likely to check with their intimate partners about their sexual health.

Sexual Orientation. During later adolescence, young people are engaged in an active process of integrating their sexual fantasies, experiences of sexual arousal, and understanding about sexual behavior into a sexual identity. Research on gay, lesbian, and bisexual (GLB) sexual orientation suggests the following sequence of milestones in the formation of sexual identity: initial attraction to a member of the same sex; identification of oneself as having a gay, lesbian, or bisexual orientation; first sexual experience; and first disclosure to others of one's sexual orientation (Calzo, Antonucci, Mays, & Cochran, 2011). Research with a large national sample found that there are different patterns to timing for the unfolding of this sequence, but that the sequence of milestones is relatively consistent no matter at what age a person begins this process. The most common pattern, for about 75 percent of the sample, begins in early adolescence; the next most common pattern begins in later adolescence; and the least common pattern begins in middle adulthood. Among those who begin self-identification early, about one third begin to have sexual attractions at around age 8 and final disclosure occurs by age 18. More commonly, initial attraction begins at around age 14, and disclosure takes place in the early 20s. Females report a somewhat older age at first attraction and first sexual experience, but an earlier age at disclosure to others than do males.

Later adolescents who may have struggled with acknowledging or accepting their sexual orientation during the high school period are likely to resolve these inner conflicts and disclose their sexual orientation to others. This process is fostered by support from at least one close person and by increasing involvement in the gay community. Although disclosure has its risks, failure to disclose or trying to continue to pass as heterosexual is typically associated with strong feelings of isolation and self-repudiation (Troiden, 1993).

Research on sexual identity development finds patterns of both consistency and change. One study followed a group of males and females recruited from a variety of GLB community and campus organizations over a 2-year period. About 40 percent self-identified as gay or lesbian, 40 percent self-identified as gay/lesbian and bisexual, and 20 percent self-identified as bisexual. Over the 2-year period, those who initially self-identified as gay or lesbian were most likely to remain in this group whereas those who self-identified as gay/lesbian and bisexual were most likely to identify as gay or lesbian. Among those who initially self-identified as bisexual, the majority continued to endorse this orientation, but about one third identified as gay or lesbian. In general, women were more consistent in their sexual identity over the period than were men. For both males and females, those who consistently self-identified as gay or lesbian rather than bisexual were also more certain and comfortable with their sexual identity, had more positive attitudes about homosexuality, and were more comfortable about allowing others to know about their sexual orientation. As later adolescents crystallize an alternative sexual identity, it appears that a less ambiguous status as either gay or lesbian is easier to navigate and is accompanied by less personal and social uncertainty than a bisexual orientation (Rosario, Schrimshaw, Hunter, & Braun, 2006).

Integrating One's Gender Identity

Young men and women formulate their gender identities as they encounter diverse and sometimes competing social messages, role relationships, sexual motives and activities, and dyadic interactions. These gender identities are situated in interpersonal, institutional, and cultural contexts. One of the salient factors contributing to the emergence of gender identity is gender-role preference. This preference is based on an assessment of two factors: how well one can meet the cultural and social expectations associated with one's gender, and how positively one views the status associated with it. The idea of gender typicality was introduced in chapter 7. As the norms for gender-related expectations shift, later adolescents may revise their view of whether their own physical appearance, traits, preferences, and talents are typical for their gender. Picasso illustrates the complexity of this process in his painting of the girl before the mirror. In this image, we observe the construction of an inner and an outer self, a reflected self, a physical self, and a desire to embrace all elements of the self.

Later adolescents' views about their gender typicality may become more differentiated. For example, Laura realizes that she has personal ambitions for career success and the accumulation of wealth that are not typical of other women in her friendship group or her family. Yet, she still sees herself as fitting in with her female friends and spending time in shared activities, including shopping for new clothes, volunteering at the senior center, and playing tennis. Her friends tease her about wanting to make her first million dollars by the age of 25, but they admire her for it as well. As her personal identity becomes clearer, she can accept that she is similar to other women in many respects and different from them in others.

Later adolescents can view themselves as personally and socially typical of their gender and still not be satisfied with their gender if the culture or context assigns a low status to their gender. If later adolescents become aware that their gender prevents them from having access to resources, influence, and decision-making authority, they are likely to experience a decline in their gender-role preference. This could happen to men as well as women, depending on the paths they choose to pursue and the gender biases they encounter. For example, in general, we tend to think of career aspirations as being stifled for women as a result of attitudes on the part of men who think that women are not suited to certain types of work. However, the reverse situation may apply to men who are interested in fields such as early childhood education or nursing.

SuperStock

The crystallization of gender identity requires the integration of one's sexuality, including physical appearance, primary and secondary sex characteristics, sexual drives, and fantasies. One's sexual identity is as much a mental representation as a physical reality.

If later adolescents perceive that, apart from real differences in ability, one gender group is treated with greater respect, given more opportunities, and responded to with more attention or greater rewards, then their gender-role preferences are likely to be recalibrated. During the high school years, adolescent girls are likely to encounter stereotyped expectations that restrict their behavior, judge their appearance, or label them as *sluts*. Sometimes, these stereotypes intersect with race and social class, especially as they encounter negative expectations from teachers or suspiciousness from shopkeepers (Abrams, 2003). Strict cultural norms regarding femininity, especially about body type and sexual behavior, can result in negative affect and alienation. Although some young women give in to these pressures, others resist, refusing to give up their voice or their autonomy in the face of adult judgments:

> Well, a lot of adults—they look at me kinda like, "ooh, she's like really crazy looking," or something like that. And my mom always says "oh, people are gonna think you're a bad girl." And I'm like "Whatever. I don't care." (Abrams, 2003, p. 71)

College students do not see much of this type of gender discrimination or preference. They tend to view the college environment as providing many opportunities and equal access to resources for both male and female students. In fact, women outnumber men as college students and exceed men in the percentage of students earning master's degrees in the United States. Women are the majority of students in all but a few majors including engineering, mathematics, chemistry, and physics (Diprete & Buchmann, 2013). Moreover, both male and female students feel equally oppressed by the stressors of college life and the uncertainties associated with the decisions they are trying to make. Typically, it is not until they enter the world of adult employment that they begin to experience the power differential that continues to operate to the benefit of White men in U.S. society (Heilman, 2001).

Later adolescents who enter the world of work at the end of high school are confronted by the power differential immediately and may experience intimidation that forces them to accept it. For example, a woman who makes $2 per hour less than a male counterpart may be afraid to say anything because she needs the job. She will have to integrate the reality of what she experiences into the formulation of her gender identity. One strategy is to accept that this is the way things should be according to gender-role norms—that women should defer to men and their contributions should be treated as less worthwhile. Another strategy may be to look for a different kind of work in a setting where women and men are paid equally.

The college population tends to set social trends by according more variety and less rigidity to sex-linked role expectations. Most studies find that during the college years, students become more flexible in their gender-role attitudes and more egalitarian in their views about how men and women ought to function in school, work, family, and community life. On the other hand, the non-college population tends to set employment trends by breaking down barriers in many male-dominated areas of work, such as construction, trucking, and public safety. Individuals can shape and strengthen the nature of their gender identity by spending time with other people who support their views and values about how men and women ought to behave toward one another and what life paths are most desirable for them.

FURTHER REFLECTION: Hypothesize about how experiences in college might influence gender identity. How might men and women differ in the ways they are affected by their experiences in college? How does one's gender identity influence a person's sexual behavior? Examine possible connections between academic performance, school engagement, the sense of belonging, and the sense of gender satisfaction.

Internalized Morality

OBJECTIVE 3 Investigate the maturation of morality in later adolescence, with special focus on the role of new cognitive capacities that influence moral judgments and the various value orientations that underlie moral reasoning.

In early school age, morality consists primarily of internalizing parental standards and values, recognizing the difference between right and wrong, and learning to control one's behavior in anticipation of its moral consequences. As young people

achieve new levels of autonomy from their parents and encounter new situations, they discover that some of the moral principles they learned as 6- or 7-year-olds neither apply to the new situation nor provide much of a rationale for why they should behave one way and not another. Later adolescents explore the distinction between *social conventions* and *moral issues*. Behaviors that may have been viewed as moral issues during childhood may be reevaluated as social conventions. The domain of personal preference or personal choice expands, resulting in a reorganization of one's moral thinking.

Within the overall process of formulating a personal identity, later adolescents devise a more mature **internalized morality**. They begin to see themselves as moral beings whose actions have implications for the well-being of others. They make moral commitments and judge their behavior and the behavior of others according to new moral standards (Damon, 1996, 2000). The three elements of morality—judgment, caring, and action—come together in an increasingly complex political, social, and interpersonal environment (Nucci & Turiel, 2009). Morality may be expressed in a variety of behaviors, including acts of consideration and kindness; resistance to temptation; opposition to unfair laws, rules, or practices; activism and civic engagement; and contributions of time, money, or other resources to enhance the well-being of others. The emerging moral synthesis suggests an active approach to moral situations in which young people evaluate the situation, consider salient values, and reflect on the consequences of possible actions as they decide on their response (Turiel, 2015a). The following sections examine Kohlberg's analysis regarding advances in moral reasoning, experiences that promote moral reasoning, and the expansion of research on moral development, which includes prosocial behavior and the ethics of care.

New Cognitive Capacities

Later adolescents bring new cognitive capacities to the arena of moral decision making. Research in cognitive neuroscience has emphasized the role of "hot" cognition, fueled by the limbic system, as contributing to risky behaviors and a focus on rewards. Nonetheless, the maturing executive functions cannot be overlooked. Later adolescents approach moral conflicts with new capacities for weighing alternatives and considering possible outcomes (Turiel, 2010). They are able to use abstract reasoning to consider the logical consequences of their actions, both for themselves and for others. They can project alternative paths in a probabilistic future and consider the multiple perspectives that are possible in a moral situation.

Most societies are structured around certain group inequalities in power, resources, and freedoms. Later adolescents can consider how resistance against certain laws, rules, or normative practices by a subordinated group, such as women, ethnic minorities, or religious or sexual minorities, can be viewed as morally justified by the less powerful group and morally wrong by the dominant group (Turiel, 2006). They are increasingly aware of the rights and needs of others, and to consider how an action may satisfy their own needs but harm others. They can reflect about how principles of social responsibility, human rights, and justice can be preserved in a moral decision.

Stages of Moral Reasoning

Building on Piaget's theory of cognitive development, Kohlberg (1964, 1969; Colby & Kohlberg, 1987) suggested that a qualitative change in a person's ability to reason about moral issues is expected from early school age to later adolescence. With age and exposure to moral conflicts, **moral reasoning** advances in much the same way that other domains of logical reasoning mature, from an early reliance on direct perceptions and immediate consequences to more complex, abstract, and relativistic judgments. Kohlberg's theory includes three levels of moral reasoning divided into six substages (see chapter 7, Table 7.1).

At Stage I, the **preconventional level**, from about age 4 to 10, children judge an action as morally justifiable based on the immediate consequences of the behavior and the approval of powerful authority figures. Stage II, the **conventional level**, from about age 10 to 18, reflects a concern about the maintenance of the existing rules and laws and a respect for legitimate authority. Stage III, the **postconventional level** of moral reasoning, from about age 18 into adulthood, brings an awareness of social, cultural, and political processes that result in the formulation of rules and laws. Morality is understood as a system of rules that are agreed upon in order to preserve human rights and social order. These rules have been created in cultural and historical contexts and can be altered as the norms of the community change. Beyond this appreciation for the **cultural relativism** of moral principles, a commitment emerges to overarching universal moral principles, including greater concern for the value of human life, human dignity, and justice for all members of society. The proportion of people who reach this final level of moral reasoning is small but increases during early and middle adulthood.

Longitudinal data provide evidence of the sequential nature of the stages during childhood and adolescence (Colby & Kohlberg, 1987; Colby, Kohlberg, Gibbs, & Lieberman, 1983; Nisan & Kohlberg, 1982; Snarey, Reimer, & Kohlberg, 1985). The sequence of stages proposed by Kohlberg is noted in a variety of countries outside the United States including Israel, Turkey, the Bahamas, Honduras, Mexico, India, Kenya, Nigeria, and Taiwan. Participants in these studies used forms of reasoning similar to those used by U.S. samples. The adults and adolescents in every culture used levels of reasoning that were higher than those used by the children (Colby & Kohlberg, 1987; Dawson, 2002; Nisan & Kohlberg, 1982; Rest, 1983; Snarey et al., 1985). The stages reflect qualitatively distinct ways of reasoning about moral dilemmas that are supported by increasingly complex cognitive capacities (Dawson, 2003).

Experiences That Promote Moral Reasoning

Later adolescents must formulate an integrated value system with which to guide their behavior, particularly in the face of strong pressures to violate their moral beliefs. Young people encounter situations that require moral evaluation, judgment, and decisions about action. Dilemmas about using illegal drugs, plagiarizing, or violating religious traditions and practices may confront a young person who is away from home for the first time. In these situations, the young person has the opportunity to envision the self as a moral actor and take a course of action most congruent with other facets of his personal identity.

Although the *sequence* of moral stages appears to be well established, the level of moral reasoning that an individual actually attains depends on the kinds of moral challenges and situations encountered. For college students, like the one in the following example, the academic curriculum itself often creates a degree of cognitive disequilibrium that promotes a revision in moral reasoning.

> I was taking a theology class as a freshman in college and was presented with "bold" alternatives to understand and interpret the creation story—primarily to understand it as a myth. My life up to that point was characterized by asking many questions but arriving at few answers. To those in my fundamentalist background, those questions were annoyances but not insurmountable problems. In my shift to some answers to those questions, I moved away from fundamentalism to a more broadly based and responsible manner of critical thinking. The professor was very bright and responsible, yet in a sophisticated way he was somewhat irreverent. I was troubled by the dilemmas that this posed for me in terms of my belief structures, but something about the information and the self-assurance of the professor encouraged me to embrace this new way of thinking. (Chickering & Reisser, 1993, p. 240)

Through participation in thought-provoking discussions or challenging life experiences, moral reasoning can advance to the next higher level. Social and educational experiences promote moral reasoning when they draw on existing constructs, but they also challenge those constructs by making their inadequacies clear. Many young people participate in community service, such as volunteering at a soup kitchen or tutoring younger children in reading or math (Seider, 2007). These experiences can stimulate discussions about differing points of view and a more complex analysis of the many interdependent factors that contribute to the social order. Many communities have established youth development programs that involve adolescents in community service. As a result, a growing number of young people gain new insights into moral situations (Nasir & Kirshner, 2003; Yates & Youniss, 1996). In a study of 12,000 college students, Sax and Astin (1997) found that participation in community service during college had long-term consequences for adult involvement in volunteering, community activism, and helping others. A student at UCLA described her experiences:

> As a volunteer for the UCLA Medical Center, my conversations with chronically ill patients made me realize the profound emotional drain caused by long-term hospitalization. With each visit, I wished there was something more than my compassion that I could use to bring vibrancy and warmth back into these patients' lives. In 2004, I used my background playing the piano and flute to create the volunteer organization, Music to Heal, through which I arrange for student musicians to bring music into the lives of hospital patients. (Mahanian, 2008, p. 27)

Exposure to a diversity of information, relationships, and worldviews stimulates moral reasoning. The change from conventional to postconventional morality that begins during adolescence involves a rethinking of traditional moral principles. During this period, there may be a loosening of ties to the family of origin and an increase in encounters with an expanding network of friends, students, and coworkers. Interactions with diverse reference groups stimulates an increasing recognition of the subcultural relativity of one's moral code. There may also be a degree of conflict over which moral values have personal meaning.

A Maturing Moral Identity

Kohlberg's view of moral development focuses on reasoning or moral knowledge, not on the emotional or behavioral aspects of morality. One criticism of the theory is that studies do not find a consistent relationship between a person's level of moral reasoning and that person's willingness to behave in a morally caring way. To address this concern, researchers have taken the approach of identifying **moral exemplars**—people who have dedicated themselves to improving the lives of others—and comparing them to others who are not especially exemplary (Hart & Fegley, 1995). The moral exemplars are not more complex or advanced in their *reasoning* than the comparison group. What the exemplars demonstrate is a **moral identity**—a sense in which they define themselves in moral terms and evaluate their behavior against moral standards. Moral identity reflects an integration of parental socialization about caring for others, an appreciation for the cultural and social contexts of moral actions, and experiences that have required moral action (Colby & Damon, 1999; Reimer, 2003). The formation of a moral identity implies a desire for a sense of congruence between one's values and one's actions. Once a moral identity is established, behaving in an immoral or indifferent manner to the plight of others produces strong negative emotions of shame and guilt (Blasi, 2013; Tangney, Stuewig, & Mashek, 2007).

A second criticism of Kohlberg's approach to understanding moral development is that his theory is based on a specific method that emphasizes **prohibitive moral judgments**, in which a person is asked to reach a decision about violating a law or breaking a promise in order to achieve some other goal. A typical example is the case of Heinz, a man who is faced with the dilemma of having to steal a drug from a pharmacist if he is to save his wife's life. These dilemmas place justice—usually framed in terms of the legitimate needs or rights of the individual—in conflict with rules, laws, authority figures, and the obligations associated with adhering to these rules or laws.

Not all moral dilemmas are of this type. Some moral judgments involve a conflict between doing something helpful for someone else and meeting one's own needs. An example would be stopping to help a person whose car has stalled on the highway at the risk of being late for a very important job interview. Some moral judgments involve doing something helpful or caring despite having to violate an existing law or social norm. These dilemmas are described as **prosocial moral judgments** (Turiel, 2015b). The prosocial aspect of morality includes a concern for the welfare and rights of others and a willingness to act in order to benefit or enhance the lives of others. Just as society depends on people adhering to rules and laws in order to preserve order, it also depends on a commitment to caring. People seem to be able to think more flexibly about a prosocial moral dilemma than about a prohibitive one. Moral decisions that draw on empathy and concern for the well-being of another person tend to evoke a higher level of moral reasoning than those that would require breaking a law (Eisenberg & Fabes, 1998; Eisenberg & Strayer, 1987).

Expanding on the theme of prosocial morality, Carol Gilligan (1977, 1982/1993, 1988) challenged Kohlberg's perspective. She argued that his description of the developmental course of reasoning about moral dilemmas is incomplete because it is based largely on the reasoning of male respondents about hypothetical rather than real-life situations. She claimed that men and women have distinct orientations toward moral dilemmas. According to Gilligan, women approach moral decisions with greater sensitivity to the context of the problem and a strong sense of **caring** focusing on one's responsibility for others and feelings of connection to them. Gilligan asserted that men, in contrast, emphasize abstract principles, rules, and laws, and the conflicts between the rights of the parties involved in the conflict. A woman, for example, might ask which outcome of a moral dilemma would result in the least harm for all concerned, whereas a man might ask whether one person has the right to infringe on the rights of others (Friedman, Robinson, & Friedman, 1987). These differences, according to Gilligan, are the product of different socialization patterns and result in different orientations to values, family life, and the basis of self-worth.

The research is inconclusive regarding whether men and women differ in their use of what have come to be called the **justice orientation** and the **caring orientation**. It appears that experiential and situational issues, as well as concerns about interpersonal obligations and caring, are more dominant in open-ended responses from both men and women than are issues of justice and individual rights. However, with age, both men and women add more autonomous, justice-oriented reasoning to their repertoire (Colby & Damon, 1994; Galotti, 1989; Galotti, Kozberg, & Farmer, 1991; Walker, de Vries, & Trevethan, 1987). The tendency of men and women to approach a moral dilemma using a justice-based or a care-based form of reasoning often depends on the social distance between the self and the other person involved. Regardless of gender, a caring orientation is more likely when the other person is viewed as a close friend or a member of one's relevant social group; a justice orientation is more likely when the other person is viewed as a member of an out-group, a stranger, or when the nature of the relationship to the other person is not specified (Ryan, David, & Reynolds, 2004).

In studies of prosocial behavior and empathic response to others, gender differences are commonly observed. Women report more caring behaviors, are rated as being more kind and considerate than men, emphasize the importance of helping others as a value, and exhibit more personal distress when faced with the distress of others (Eisenberg, Morris, McDaniel, & Spinrad, 2009). In many cultures, family socialization practices emphasize the importance of prosocial behavior and social responsibility for female children. As a result of this focus, perhaps women are more likely than men to integrate a prosocial orientation into their gender identity (Froming, Nasby, & McManus, 1998).

The process of achieving a moral identity is made more difficult in a pluralistic society, where one's moral perspective may be at odds with the perspective of others. Individuals emerge into later adolescence from different cultural and community groups whose moral frameworks derive from distinct configurations of basic principles. To some extent, these differences reflect divergent emphases on how moral agents and actions are understood. One approach to this idea of moral pluralism has been to identify three moral ethics: the Ethic of Autonomy, the Ethic of Community, and the Ethic of Divinity (Jensen, 2008, 2015). The Ethic of Autonomy refers to a focus on the moral agent as an individual and emphasizes principles such as the individual's well-being, welfare, and fairness to others. The Ethic of Community refers to a focus on the moral agent as a member of a social group and emphasizes principles of duty, the interests and well-being of the group, and the avoidance of social sanctions that would harm the group's reputation. The Ethic of Divinity refers to the person as an agent of a spiritual force and emphasizes religious or scriptural authority and spiritual duty. Whereas the Ethic of Autonomy is prevalent throughout childhood and into adolescence and adulthood, one sees new evidence of an emerging application of the Ethic of Community and the Ethic of Divinity in later adolescence and adulthood. What is more, the Ethic of Divinity may be applied more broadly by some religious subgroups whereas the Ethic of Community may be applied more broadly by others (Jensen & McKenzie, 2016). This can lead to different views about how a specific issue, such as capital punishment, or divorce or infidelity between marriage partners, is understood and judged.

Certain groups are consistently wronged by deeply ingrained inequalities in the social structure. Acts of resistance or subversion by groups in positions of less power may be labeled as immoral by those in higher positions and as heroic by those in the disenfranchised groups (Turiel, 2003). In later adolescence, young people begin to appreciate the moral ambiguities of their communities and may take action to express their commitments to justice and care through individual or group efforts. The concept of **civic purpose** captures this commitment to "contribute to the world beyond the self in the sociopolitical domain for example through community leadership, political activity, or participation in volunteer organizations" (Malin, Ballard, & Damon, 2015, p. 104).

Whereas some young people have been characterized in the media as self-indulgent and socially indifferent, others are intensely engaged in actions fueled by the passion of indignation about social injustice or commitments to service. The current cohort of college freshmen express a variety of attitudes and behaviors that suggest enthusiasm for civic engagement. About 75 percent say that helping others in difficulty is an important personal objective. Over 40 percent say that they want to influence social values, promote racial understanding, and believe that keeping up to date on political affairs is very important. Although a small minority (8.5 percent) say that there is a good chance they will participate in a student protest or demonstration while in college, this is the highest percentage reported since the survey first began asking the question in 1967 (Eagan et al., 2015). Evidence of this expression of moral identity through civic engagement can be seen in recent campus protests. These events were reported in *The Atlantic* (Wong, 2015):

- There was the confederate-flag fiasco at Bryn Mawr, which resulted in a mass demonstration by hundreds of students who, all dressed in black, called for an end to racism on the Pennsylvania campus.
- A week later, more than 350 students staged a similar protest further north, at New York's Colgate University. That one—dubbed #CanYouHearUsNow—likewise aimed to end bigotry among students and faculty; it was in part prompted by a series of racist Yik Yak posts.
- Students at the University of Chicago hosted a #LiabilityoftheMind social-media campaign last November to raise awareness about institutional intolerance.
- Roughly 600 Tufts students lay down in the middle of traffic in December for four and a half hours—the amount of time Michael Brown's body was left in the street after being shot. Students at numerous other colleges did the same.
- Early last fall, Emma Sulkowicz, then a student at Columbia, pledged to carry a mattress on campus daily to protest the school's refusal to expel her alleged rapist. Soon, hundreds of her classmates joined her, as did those at 130 other college campuses nationwide, according to reports. Anti-rape demonstrations became a frequent occurrence as colleges across the country came under scrutiny for their handling of campus sexual-assault cases. There were walkouts and sit-ins, canceled speeches and banner campaigns. Last May, the U.S. Department of Education reported that it was investigating 55 colleges and universities for possible violations of Title IX. As of this January, the number had gone up to 94.

Students who had a community service experience in high school were more likely to expect to continue this type of commitment during college. Volunteering has been found to be strongly associated with two aspects of moral commitment: social agency, or a personal goal of being politically and socially active in the community, and valuing and respecting other groups' points of view. This large and growing group of college students provides a very hopeful indication about the willingness of the new generation of young people for combining a caring and a justice orientation in order to make contributions to their communities.

College students, graduates and activists protest the ways banks finance college education which increases capitalist profits while creating student debt.

Describe an experience in later adolescence that has had an impact on your moral values or your approach to moral judgments. What should colleges and universities strive to achieve in the domain of fostering moral maturity among students? What messages does your college or university convey about moral and ethical behavior?

Career Choice

OBJECTIVE 4 Trace the process of career choice, with attention to education and gender-role socialization as two major influential factors.

The choice of occupation sets the tone for one's early adult lifestyle. The world of work determines daily routines, including the time one wakes up, daily activities, expenditures of physical and mental energy, and conditions for both immediate and long-term rewards. Because one's occupation has implications for income and earning potential, **career choice** will influence one's personal financial resources and opportunities. Occupation confers social status and provides varying opportunities for advancement. Finally, it represents a direct or indirect expression of one's value system. In subsequent chapters, we will discuss socialization in the work setting and the management of a career. Here, we focus on the process of career choice and its relationship to development during later adolescence.

Work Experiences in Early Adolescence

Later adolescence is not the first time young people encounter the world of work. Many early adolescents hold part-time jobs while they attend high school. In 2015, 34 percent of 16- to 19-year-olds were in the labor force. Of those in the labor force, 17 percent were unemployed—meaning that they were recently fired or had been unsuccessful in looking for work during the preceding 4 weeks (Bureau of Labor Statistics 2016a). These data suggest that it is currently more difficult for young people to enter or remain in the labor market than was the case 30 years ago when roughly 60 percent of teenage boys and slightly over 50 percent of teenage girls were employed.

There is some controversy about the benefits of working during high school and whether these work experiences make a positive contribution to the occupational component of identity development. A number of investigations have found that high school students who work long hours in stressful jobs are more likely to evidence increased cigarette smoking, marijuana and alcohol use, receive lower grades, earn fewer course credits, and are more likely to drop out of high school (Entwisle, Alexander, & Olson, 2005b; Marsh & Kleitman, 2005). Students who work long hours have less time for school activities, spending time with friends, or developing other areas of interest. The kinds of work opportunities that are available to adolescents are usually minimally skilled jobs with high turnover, low pay, little decision-making responsibility, and little stimulation of skill development. These kinds of jobs are likely to produce depression and low self-esteem and may contribute to feelings of alienation from the school environment. For some adolescents, the time spent in

these kinds of work settings is associated with the development of cynical attitudes toward work and greater acceptance of unethical practices by workers.

Other researchers have emphasized the diversity of work experiences and the potential benefits of certain kinds of work. Students who are able to find and keep a good job may feel more confident about themselves and their promise for future employment. When the work does not involve too many hours, and involves skill development that young people see as related to their future career direction, the experience is associated with higher levels of well-being and fewer problem behaviors. For girls, the perception of continuity between school and work and the feeling that work improves one's school performance had an especially positive relationship with mental health and well-being (Staff, Messersmith, & Schulenberg, 2009).

The transition at high school graduation is a clear societal cue that career decision making has to begin, placing the developmental task of career choice squarely in later adolescence. In order to achieve this task, four related processes must unfold: becoming aware of and concerned about career decision making, actively engaging in the process of self-understanding, actively examining career options, and analyzing the fit between the two (Savickas, 2011). Unfortunately, many young people leave high school with negative expectations about their career search because they have already experienced unemployment and perceive the job opportunities in their community to be very limited. What is more, many high school students focus narrowly on striving to be admitted to college, having done relatively little work on career exploration. They come to college with only a very vague idea about how their college education will be related to a career choice (Xiao, Newman, & Chu, 2016).

Factors Influencing Career Choice

Career choice is influenced by many factors (see FIGURE 10.4 ▶). Personal experiences and work on identity development contribute to career choice. Career choice is also influenced by a network of individual, socioeconomic, familial, school, peer, mentor, and neighborhood factors. These career decisions are embedded in a sociohistorical time period during which the labor market, economic conditions, and opportunities for various types of work will vary.

High school and college students say that individual factors, such as abilities, achievement needs, attitudes, and self-expectancies, most strongly affect their career decision making. They tend to think that familial, societal, and socioeconomic factors have little or no impact. This is contrary to social science research evidence. Family factors play a key role in shaping educational aspirations and occupational goals. Societal and socioeconomic conditions are major factors influencing the job market and the chances of both employment and advancement. Students who have a clearer understanding of the critical social and economic factors that influence the labor market are better able to consider career alternatives and to analyze the steps they need to take in order to achieve their career goals (Diemer & Blustein, 2006; Dietrich, Parker, & Salmela-Aro, 2012). In the following sections we highlight three of these influences: family environment, educational contexts, and gender.

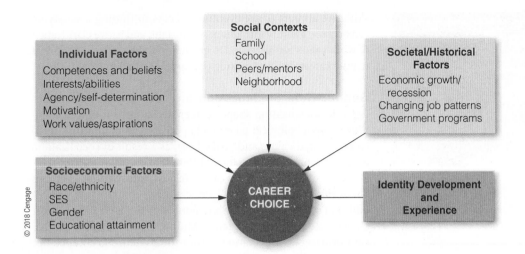

FIGURE 10.4 ▶ FACTORS AFFECTING
CAREER CHOICE IN LATER ADOLESCENCE

Social Contexts
Family
School
Peers/mentors
Neighborhood

Individual Factors
Competences and beliefs
Interests/abilities
Agency/self-determination
Motivation
Work values/aspirations

Societal/Historical Factors
Economic growth/
 recession
Changing job patterns
Government programs

Socioeconomic Factors
Race/ethnicity
SES
Gender
Educational attainment

CAREER CHOICE

Identity Development and Experience

© 2018 Cengage

Family Environment. A supportive, secure socioemotional family environment plays a key role in fostering effective career decision making. Parents influence their adolescent's career decision making through the values and expectations they convey about educational attainment, their own work activities and work ethic, and the way they encourage their children to develop and master their interests, talents, and abilities. Parents influence their children's school achievement from early childhood through the high school and college years. Parents are role models for their children, providing information about the specific kinds of work they perform. They provide opportunities for their children to hear the way they talk about their work and to observe their parents' success or frustration in the labor market (Staff, Messersmith, & Schulenberg, 2009). Most later adolescents continue to look to their parents for advice, resources, and emotional support throughout these years.

Differences in family resources result in diverging educational backgrounds, which have direct implications for the kinds of careers one is prepared to enter. We have addressed the educational achievement gap related to family income in earlier chapters, beginning with the topic of school readiness in chapter 6. In the period of early adolescence, children from low-income families and from families in which the parents did not graduate from high school are more likely to drop out of high school and less likely to be enrolled in postsecondary education. A national longitudinal study followed 15,000 students beginning at their sophomore year in high school. Ten years later, 14 percent of those in the lowest SES families had a bachelor's degree or higher; 60 percent of those in the highest SES families had a similar level of education. Even when students who scored in the top quartile in mathematics achievement in high school were compared, only 41 percent of those from the lowest SES families graduated from high school compared to 74 percent of those in the highest SES families (U.S. Department of Education, 2015). These data highlight a substantial impact of family income on educational attainment, which, of course, has implications for career choices and occupational opportunities. The gap in academic achievement between the children of families with the most and the least resources has been widening, at least as data for children born in the 1970s and in 2001 can tell us. Among those enrolled in college, about two thirds of students from families in the top income quartile graduate; fewer than one quarter of students

from families in the bottom quartile graduate (Bailey & Dynarski, 2011; Dynarski, 2015; Reardon, 2011). Differences in neighborhood poverty, family income, families' ability and willingness to support occupational exploration, and the parents' own educational and occupational attainment influence their children's educational access, persistence, and career decision-making process.

Education and Career Choice. Career advancement and the associated earnings are closely linked to levels of educational attainment. The metaphor of a pipeline is often used when thinking about educational attainment and career choice. As students move along the educational pipeline, their aspirations and intentions as well as their understanding of the requirements for educational advancement impact their decisions. One step along the pathway is students' intention to graduate from high school. For those who do not graduate from high school, career development is a bumpy path. In 2015, the unemployment rate for those who had dropped out of high school in the preceding year was 30 percent (Bureau of Labor Statistics 2016a).

While in high school, some students benefit from career counseling, assessment, and academic advising about postsecondary alternatives, but many do not have access to these resources. Preparation for the post-secondary transition is very uneven. For example, in a study of high school students in California, only about one third knew all of the curricular requirements for attendance at one of California's public colleges and universities, and fewer than 1 percent of students' parents knew these requirements. This is particularly disturbing in that California has one of the more fully articulated educational state systems with a well-developed set of application and transfer guidelines (Kirst & Bracco, 2004). Students who attend a well-resourced high school where most students attend college are likely to have access to a career resource center and individualized guidance about college applications and admissions. Students who attend less advantaged high schools have little access to guidance about postsecondary educational or employment avenues. In contrast to the myth that education is the great equalizer for opportunity, evidence is accumulating that social inequality is reproduced and extended through the organization and inequality of public schooling (Bailey & Dynarski, 2011; Dynarski, 2015).

Table 10.1	Median Annual Earnings of Men and Women 25–34 Years, 2014, by Level of School Completed and Sex		
	Average Annual Income ($)		
Education	**Men**	**Women**	
Less than high school completion	25,000	19,950	
High school graduate	32,970	25,000	
Some college, no degree	35,790	28,040	
Bachelor's degree or more	57,890	49,810	

Source: Table 502.30 National Center for Education Statistics, 2015d.

College is becoming an increasingly essential aspect of career development. In 2014, 68 percent of high school graduates in the United States were enrolled in some type of postsecondary institution, 64 percent of men and 73 percent of women. This compares to 49 percent of high school graduates in 1980 (National Center for Education Statistics, 2015b). Despite the large number of students who attend some type of college, many do not complete a degree. In 2015, 32.5 percent of the population ages 25 and older had a college degree or more. This percentage varied greatly by race/ethnicity: African Americans, 22.9 percent; Asian Americans and Pacific Islanders, 52.9 percent; European Americans, 36.2 percent; Hispanic/Latinos, 15.5 percent; American Indian/Alaskan Native, 19.8 percent; and two or more races/ethnicities 30.6 percent (National Center for Education Statistics, 2015c).

Table 10.1 shows the average annual income on the basis of educational attainment for men and women who were 25 to 34 years old in 2014. Educational attainment has a significant relationship to annual income. As the data indicate, however, educational achievement does not result in the same economic advantages for men and women. At all levels, women earn less than men, and women with 1 to 3 years of college but no degree earned less on average than men who were high school graduates (National Center for Education Statistics, 2015d). As more and more women earn college degrees and compete for higher paying jobs, the U.S. corporate environment appears to be getting quite a bargain by paying them less than their equally educated male colleagues. What is more, at every level of educational attainment, all groups are earning less in the most recent year than they were in 2009. The nature of the labor market leaves young people exposed to a range of what have been labeled as "bad jobs" (Kallenberg, 2011). Many are part-time, routine, with minimum wages and little job security.

The impact of educational experiences on subsequent career development goes beyond whether one plans to attend college or not. Vocational coursework of a specific nature, such as agricultural training, an emphasis on math and science courses, taking the sequence of courses that are required for college admission, and frequent conversations with teachers about one's work-related decisions are all associated with higher income and more stable work records after high school. Development of work-related habits such as attention to detail, the ability to plan and follow through on complex tasks, persistence in the face of difficulties, and communication skills are all part of the eventual success in finding a satisfying career path. Identity formation, self-insight, and active clarification of work values are all related to greater career confidence and more mature career decision making (Patton & McMahon, 2014).

Gender-Role Socialization and Career Choice. Gender-role socialization shapes career decisions through two significant psychological factors: (1) perceptions of ability and (2) career-related values and goals. First, as a result of socialization, men and women tend to form different expectations about their ability to succeed at various career-related skills. Self-expectancies about the ability to fulfill the educational requirements and job duties of specific careers are a major factor in determining career choices. Recall from chapter 8 (Middle Childhood) the discussion of parents' expectations about their children's competence in certain skill areas and its relation to the child's own perceptions of competence. In a longitudinal study, mothers' gender-stereotyped beliefs about their young child's math and science abilities predicted their child's self-perceptions of math and science self-efficacy 2 years after high school. Mothers' predictions of their child's ability to succeed in a math-oriented career was a significant predictor of their college-age child's career choice (Bleeker & Jacobs, 2004).

In the process of career decision making, strong gender-typed conceptualizations of the job demands of specific careers intervene to screen out some alternatives and highlight others. For example, there is a clear path from belief in one's competence in math to aspirations about careers in math, science, and engineering (Correll, 2001). Gendered beliefs about mathematics competence, influenced in part by parental expectations, teachers' evaluations, and career guidance advisors, may contribute to the persistent gender divide with respect to women enrolling in university and graduate programs in mathematics, physics, and engineering. In addition to gender socialization, persistent gender stereotypes attach to images of femininity. For example, in one study the same woman was dressed in a neutral outfit and in a "feminine" outfit. When being rated by both male and female students as a potential employee for a student IT job, when the woman was dressed in the feminine clothing she was considered as having less adequate computer skills, being less likely to succeed at a computer task, and as being less intelligent (Fleischman et al., 2016). Social feedback attached to one's gender image can impact one's own self-confidence and self-evaluation.

A national survey of students entering college in 2015 asked freshmen to rate their ability in a variety of areas. Even though women are now more likely than men to enter college and graduate, female students were less confident about their academic ability, less confident about their computer skills, and less confident about their mathematical abilities than male students (CIRP, 2015). Studies of career choice or career aspirations find that women with a strong sense of their own goals, an awareness of their personal needs, and an ability to cope realistically with stress are more likely to adopt a nontraditional career choice. A growing number of supportive groups, many funded in part by the National Science Foundation, have formed to encourage and mentor young women who have ability in mathematics to pursue college majors and occupations in the fields of science, mathematics, and technology.

Second, as a result of socialization, women and men are likely to establish different value hierarchies, reflecting different long-range life goals. Experiences in middle childhood set in motion images about one's preferred work and lifestyle in adulthood. In a study that followed children from about age 10 into their mid-twenties, researchers found that boys whose mothers had more traditional views about women's roles were more likely to choose traditional male occupational roles. Girls who spent more time with their fathers were more likely to enter nontraditional female occupations (Lawson, Crouter, & McHale, 2015). Among later adolescents, young men tend to prefer "jobs characterized by high salaries, power or influence over others, opportunities for advancement or achievement, risk taking, challenging tasks, a high level of responsibility, and a high level of prestige" (Weisgram, Bigler, & Liben, 2010, p. 779). Young women prefer "jobs that allow them to work with or help others, develop their knowledge or skills, and spend time with family" (Weisgram et al., p. 779). For example, one study compared what college students wanted from their careers, referred to as *work goals*, with what they thought certain careers might allow them to achieve, called *goal affordances*. Students who thought a career would help them achieve their work goals were also more interested in those careers (Morgan, Isaac, & Sansone, 2001). Women rated interpersonal goals as more important and high pay and high status goals as less important than did men. Both men and women viewed careers in physical and mathematical science as offering less in the way of interpersonal goals and more in the way of salary and status. As a result, women were less interested in careers in physical and mathematical science and less likely to identify those fields as career choices (Diekman, Brown, Johnston, & Clark, 2010). An additional factor is that women often encounter cultural stereotypes that imply that women are not as competent or well-suited for mathematics and science as men, which can undermine their motivation to persist in these fields (Zhang, Schmader, & Forbes, 2009). The internalization of gender-related goals is directly related to how motivated a young man or woman is in pursuing a career that promises to allow her to attain those goals (Evans & Diekman, 2009). Other contextual factors can also impact a decision to enter a gender atypical career. For example, in a study of U.S. teens, those boys who had a large number of female friends, whose parents were well-educated, and who expected growth in the field were more likely to aspire to a female-oriented career (Hardle, 2015).

The consequences of gender-role socialization for career choice can be seen in the distribution of men and women in the labor force (Bureau of Labor Statistics 2016a). Although there are many areas where men and women are equally involved, patterns of gender differentiation are quite notable. For example the large majority of those working in fields of preschool education, elementary or middle school teaching, special education, nursing, and office/administrative support are women. The large majority of those working as firefighters or police, or in engineering, computer programming, transportation, construction, and natural resources, are men.

Career Decision Making

The idea of **career decision making** must be evaluated in light of rapid changes in the nature of work. The pervasiveness of the two-earner family lifestyle, the increased likelihood of multiple job and career changes over the life course, and the constant reconfiguration of the job market—especially the trends toward downsizing, workforce reductions, retraining, and outsourcing are all factors that impact a young person's thinking about career choice. The idea of occupational choice should not be confused with choice about labor market participation. Although they may have a wide choice in the kind of work they will do, most people in the United States do not have a choice about whether to work or not. In fact, about 6 percent of young people in the 20 to 24 age range have more than one job (U.S. Bureau of Labor Statistics, 2015c, Table 36).

Career choice reflects a central component of a person's emerging identity. For some young people, occupational choice is a reflection of continued identification with their parents. They may select the same job or career as that of one of their parents, or they may select a career because it reflects their parents' aspirations for them. Little personal choice is involved. For some young people, primarily women, there continues to be a path of primary identification with the roles of wife and mother, with only secondary investment in the labor market. Many of these women, especially those who marry and have children after high school, return to school or to technical training in their 30s and 40s in order to pick up the thread of career development, either as a result of divorce or when their children get older. Increasing numbers of men and women realize that their occupational career will need to be coordinated and integrated with that of their spouse. In anticipation of a dual-earner lifestyle, young people begin to screen their career aspirations through the lens of the

Paul A. Souders/Corbis Documentary/Getty Images

After high school, Rick decided to work in a local fish market. He will probably quit when he has earned enough money to buy the truck he has been wanting. Then he'll travel for a while and get a job in another town.

compatibility of job demands with family commitments and personal aspirations.

Many people assume that the younger a person is when he makes a career choice, the better. Most career development professionals, however, advise that a decision about a career be delayed until later adolescence or early adulthood. The concept of **career maturity** suggests that with increased cognitive and affective development, a person develops decision-making strategies, gains access to information, and achieves a degree of self-insight that permit a realistic and consistent choice (Schmitt-Rodermund & Silbereisen, 1998). A person who delays the decision has a clearer sense of their adult interests and goals. By delaying the career decision, one also has more opportunities to explore alternative work scenarios and to understand more about the labor market.

Nonetheless, high schools, colleges, and various industries urge young people to make career choice decisions as early as possible. Thus, some of the tension that later adolescents experience in connection with a choice of career is a product of the lack of fit between socialization pressures and their own developmental timetable. With the increased likelihood of living to be 80 years old, there is no great rush to decide on a career by age 20. In the United States, the average person with a bachelor's degree is likely to have many jobs between the ages of 18 and 32, more in the period of later adolescence and fewer in their later 20s and 30s. These jobs may or may not be part of a coherent career. For example, many college students work in restaurants and local shops, but these jobs are not part of their intended career path. Other later adolescents work in a job they expect to be temporary, just to earn enough money to buy a car or pay their insurance until they are ready to move on to something new.

Phases of Career Decision Making. The literature on career decision making provides a variety of models that suggest phases or steps in a complex process including: an initial awareness of one's interests and abilities; identification of career values and goals; engagement in information gathering about the world of work and the requirements of specific occupations; exploration of work experiences; making an eventual commitment to a career path; and continuously evaluating the fit or lack of fit between these experiences and one's emerging identity (Dietrich, Parker, & Salmela-Aro, 2012; Gadassi, Gati, & Dayan, 2012). A career decision depends on the outcomes of several tasks during early and later adolescence and early adulthood. With effective problem solving, the person gains increased control over life events and is better prepared to meet the challenges of the next phase of decision making.

One such model, developed by Tiedeman and colleagues (Tiedeman & Miller-Tiedeman, 1985; Tiedeman & O'Hara, 1963), identifies seven **phases of career decision making**; the first four emphasize planning and clarification, whereas the last three emphasize implementation (FIGURE 10.5 ▶). The model illustrates how making career-related decisions helps to clarify one's occupational identity and, at the same time, uses the context of work to promote new learning about other aspects of the self. The model reflects an individual's capacity for ongoing adaptation and change. At each phase in the process, people can redefine

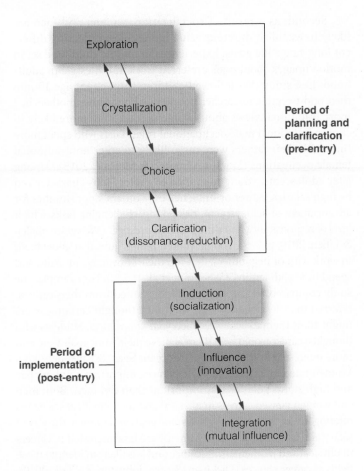

FIGURE 10.5 ▶ SEVEN PHASES OF CAREER DECISION MAKING
Source: Based on Tiedeman and O'Hara, 1963.

the self and transcend the conditions of the work environment to change their minds (Miller-Tiedeman, 1999).

In the **exploration phase**, the person realizes that a career decision must be made and therefore begins to learn more about those aspects of the self and the occupational world that are relevant to the impending decision. This is the point at which many young people use computer programs that help them identify their interests and abilities as well as the fit between these preferences and various occupations. The person begins to generate alternatives for action. Uncertainty about the future and the many possible alternatives are accompanied by feelings of anxiety. Concerns about future educational and career decisions constitute a major source of worry for college students. Many colleges and universities offer access to computer software programs including the Strong Interest Inventory, the Holland Self-Directed Search, and My Next Move sponsored by O'Net from the Bureau of Labor Statistics. These programs support exploration by incorporating a focus on a person's interests, talents, and values with descriptions of occupations and their features, requirements, and opportunities.

In the **crystallization phase**, the person becomes more aware of the alternatives for action and their consequences. Conflicts among alternatives are recognized, and some are discarded. The person develops a strategy for making the decision,

Paul is using the university's career exploration software to identify careers that are a good match for his interests and talents.

in part by weighing the costs and benefits of each alternative. This is a phase when a person might engage in volunteer work, short internships, or summer jobs that help to clarify the nature of the work and the fit or lack of fit with their own temperament, talents, and values.

In the **choice phase**, the person decides which action alternative to follow. The decision is solidified in the person's mind as he or she elaborates the reasons why the decision is beneficial. There is a sense of relief and optimism as the person develops a commitment to executing the decision. For college students, the choice phase might be the decision about a major. Of the students entering college as freshmen in 2012, 85 percent said that an important reason for going to college was to be able to get a better job (Eagan et al., 2015). For those who do not attend college, the decision might involve an apprenticeship or applying for a job that involves some extended training. The choice phase implies a willingness to invest time and effort in order to excel in this career.

In the **clarification phase**, the person more fully understands the consequences of the commitment to the decision that has been made. A person may tell others, including family and friends, about the decision, which may prompt the need to justify or explain the decision. There may be unexpected implications of the career choice. For example, the career decision may require additional education or training; the person may begin to be aware of some social advantages or disadvantages of the career; or the jobs that are open in the career may require moving to a new town. A person's self-concept is modified by the commitment to a career path and the desire to create congruity between one's decision and the demands that are likely to accompany that decision. For example, among students who made a commitment to an engineering major, the intention to persist was tested after two, three, and four semesters. The strongest predictor of commitment to persist was the student's self-efficacy. Having encountered the challenges and demands of the major, these students had confidence in their ability to succeed (Lent et al., 2015).

During the **induction phase** the person encounters the new career environment. The person wants to be accepted and looks to others for cues about how to behave. The person identifies with the new group and seeks recognition for his or her unique characteristics. If the choice is a good fit, the self-image is gradually modified as the person begins to believe in the values and goals of the new group. However, in some cases the person experiences incongruities between the demands of the career and personal values or goals. The work environment is not supportive; the work is more difficult, more tedious, or less rewarding than expected; or the person longs for opportunities that are not possible in this career. The model suggests that the person might start again with a new plan.

In the **influence phase**, the person is very much involved with the new group. The person becomes more assertive in encouraging the group to perform better. The person also tries to influence the group to accommodate some of his or her values. The self is strongly committed to group goals. During this phase, the group's values and goals may be modified to include the orientation of the new member. In some cases, these efforts to influence the group do not work out. Ideas that the worker brings from his or her education and training are rejected. The power hierarchy in the profession resists change. As the person matures, values and goals change, resulting in a new idea about one's occupational path.

Finally, in the **integration phase**, the group or the profession makes a more lasting investment in the person, whether by offering tenure, a long-term contract, licensure, or some other form of commitment. This process brings about a new degree of allegiance to the career and the specific work environment. The person now has a more complete understanding of the goals and operation of the group and has incorporated features of the career into his or her identity. A true collaboration between the new member and the group is achieved. The new member feels satisfied and is evaluated as successful by the self and others. Although this phase implies a degree of stability, conditions may arise that require reevaluation. Economic downturns may lead to layoffs; new government standards may require retraining; changes in the ownership or leadership of a company may result in a new work culture. In each of these conditions, the person may find that it is time to review and revise the career decision.

This model emphasizes continuous interaction between the individual and the work context. At first, interaction is necessary to clarify the person's talents and choice of career. Later, it is necessary to achieve a satisfactory level of adaptation to the work environment. At each juncture, whether the decision relates to college major, occupation, job change, or career redirection, effective decision making involves all seven phases. Each career is a unique story in its own right.

Career Decision-Making Self-Efficacy

The concept of career decision-making self-efficacy is widely used in the field of vocational education and development to highlight the role of a person's emerging confidence in the ability to make an effective career choice. Albert Bandura introduced the concept of self-efficacy to refer to the confidence that a person has that he or she can meet the standards for performance in a particular domain. We discussed self-efficacy in some detail in chapter 8, as a component of the developmental task of self-evaluation. Judgments of self-efficacy stem from four sources: prior experiences of success or failure in a specific domain, encouragement or discouragement from others (verbal persuasion), vicarious experiences of watching others succeed or fail, and the physical state of arousal that accompanies being engaged in the task.

Career **decision-making self-efficacy** includes assessments about whether one can make an accurate self-appraisal of one's abilities, gather relevant occupational information, formulate appropriate goals, make plans to achieve those goals, and solve the problems that pose barriers to the achievement of goals (Betz, 2001). For college students, the sense of career decision-making self-efficacy is closely tied to confidence in other domains, the most important of which is leadership. Students who believe that they have strong leadership abilities and who have had positive leadership experiences are also more confident about their ability to make effective career decisions. In addition, confidence in science, math, writing, using technology, and cultural sensitivity all contribute to career decision-making self-efficacy (Paulsen & Betz, 2004). Many courses and programs are introduced on college campuses to help support students' career decision making. The idea that self-efficacy about career decision making can be enhanced through deliberate interventions has guided many of these programs, resulting in measurable improvements in career confidence, especially for students who are unsure or highly anxious about their career direction (Betz, 2007).

The Impact of the Labor Market on Career Decision Making

Each cohort faces unique labor market conditions as they enter the career search process in later adolescence and early adulthood. Characteristics of the contemporary labor market may contribute to new difficulties as well as new opportunities that young people face as they attempt to move through the first four phases of Tiedeman's model.

- The increasing number of jobs and careers available make the exploration phase more difficult.
- As a result of changes in technology and organizational structure, some skills become obsolete and some job markets dry up. A career may become obsolete in the time it takes a young person to prepare for it.
- As established firms lose their identities in corporate mergers, identification with a particular company ceases to be appropriate.
- As most large companies go through restructuring and downsizing, the people who are left are asked to do more tasks of a greater variety. In addition to one's special area of training, it is important to develop support skills including data management, literature search skills, and verbal and written communication skills.
- New careers emerge at a rapid pace. From the time one enters the choice phase to the time one enters the influence phase, new kinds of work roles may become available.

- Career paths are less clear than they once were. Young people are being advised to expect three or four career changes in their lifetime. They may end up moving from the private to the nonprofit sector, from business to education, or from service provider to entrepreneur.
- The cost of living—especially the costs of housing, health care, and education—introduces concerns about the amount of money that will be needed to live comfortably. In addition, student loans must be repaid. Worries about making money may interfere with effective career decision making. There are many "bad jobs" even for college graduates. These jobs are defined as "those that pay less than $37,000 per year (in inflation-adjusted 2010 dollars); lack employer-provided health insurance; and have no employer-sponsored retirement plan." According to this definition, in 2010, 24 percent of all workers were in bad jobs. The percentage of workers in bad jobs was higher at all levels of educational attainment in 2010 than it was in 1979 (Schmitt & Jones, 2012).

Given the complexity of the world of work, **career indecision** is common in later adolescence. In contrast to those later adolescents who know what career they plan to enter, there are two different patterns of career indecision. One is a developmentally normal state that results from a lack of work experience, inadequate information about the world of work, and continuing emergence of personal identity. The other is considered to reflect chronic indecision, related to a pervasive lack of self-efficacy, dependency, and more serious identity confusion (Guay, Ratele, Senécal, Larose, & Deschênes, 2006).

Ideally, one's choice of occupation is the result of personal experimentation, introspection, self-evaluation, fact finding, and intuition. In order to make a career choice, people may first choose to pose difficult questions to themselves about their skills, temperament, values, and goals. When they make a decision based on this kind of personal evaluation, they are likely to see their careers as a well-integrated part of their personal identities rather than as activities from which they are alienated or by which they are dominated.

With advances in science, microbreweries have become a new option for careers. In this image, the French brewmaster demonstrates the latest techniques in beer making to students who are enrolled in a college course.

FURTHER REFLECTION: Describe some of the ways that career decision making influences identity development and the ways that identity development may influence career decisions.

How far along are most students in their career decisions by the time they enter college? By the time they graduate from college?

What are the most valuable experiences students have in later adolescence that support career decision-making?

The Psychosocial Crisis: Individual Identity Versus Identity Confusion

OBJECTIVE 5 Define and describe the psychosocial crisis of later adolescence, individual identity versus identity confusion; the central process through which this crisis is resolved, role experimentation; the prime adaptive ego quality of fidelity to values and ideals; and the core pathology of repudiation.

The psychosocial crisis of later adolescence is individual identity formation versus identity confusion. This crisis results from the enormous difficulty of pulling together the many components of the self—including changing perspectives on one's beliefs and values as well as new and changing social demands—into a unified image that can propel the person toward positive, meaningful action. As part of this process, a young person struggles to formulate a worldview, an outlook on those goals and values that are personally important and to which the person is willing to make a commitment. Over the period of later adolescence, whether in the context of college, the military, or in other work and community settings, young people begin to examine the beliefs and goals they may have internalized from childhood. Through self-reflection, role experimentation, and feedback from significant others, later adolescents make decisions about whether these beliefs and goals are still meaningful as they look ahead to the future.

Individual Identity

Erik Erikson provided a comprehensive treatment of the meaning and functions of **individual identity**, from his inclusion of this concept in the theory of psychosocial development in 1950 to his analysis of American identity in 1974 (Erikson, 1950, 1974). His notion of identity involves the integration of past, present, and future. From the past, young people undertake a process of reexamination of childhood identifications. From the present, young people identify and evaluate their talents, interests, and abilities. From the future, there is an articulation of valued life goals and aspirations. These three sources of identity content have to be woven into a meaningful sense of a purposeful self. The major works in which he discussed identity are the article "The Problem of Ego Identity" (Erikson, 1959) and the book *Identity: Youth and Crisis* (Erikson, 1968).

The construct of personal identity is not the same as the self-concept. The self-concept is a cognitive integration of one's physical qualities, personality traits, motives, and strivings, as well as an assessment of how one is viewed by others. The idea of personal identity is embedded in a lifespan perspective, reflecting the sense of meaning, purpose, and related commitments one embraces as one makes the transition from childhood into adulthood. Our discussion, which is grounded in Erikson's writings, is broadened to include the ideas of others whose work extends and operationalizes the concept of identity and links it to a sense of purpose (Crocetti, Rubini, & Meeus, 2008; Damon, 2008; Kroger, 2004; Lawler, Thye, & Yoon, 2009; Schwartz, 2001; Schwartz, Luyckx, & Vignoles, 2011).

Later adolescents are preoccupied with questions about their essential character in much the same way that early-school-age children are preoccupied with questions about their origins. In their efforts to establish an identity, later adolescents must take into account the bonds that have been built between them and others in the past as well as the direction they hope to take in the future. Identity serves as an anchor point, providing the person with an essential experience of continuity in social relationships:

> The young individual must learn to be most himself where he means the most to others—those others, to be sure, who have come to mean most to him. The term identity expresses such a mutual relation in that it connotes both a persistent sameness within oneself (self-sameness) and a persistent sharing of some kind of essential character with others. (Erikson, 1959, p. 102)

The Private and Public Faces of Identity

As the preceding quotation suggests, identity achievement is associated with an internal sense of individual uniqueness and direction accompanied by a social or community validation about the direction one has chosen. Thus identity includes both a private and a public self. The **private self**, often described as a *sense of self*, refers to one's uniqueness and unity, the subjective experience of being the originator of one's thoughts and actions and of being self-reflective. Through the private self, one recognizes the values and beliefs to which one is committed, and the extent to which certain thoughts and actions are consistent with those beliefs. The private, subjective sense of self, which develops over the course of the life span, includes four basic elements (Blasi, 1991; Glodis & Blasi, 1993):

- A sense of *agency*—Being the originator of thoughts and actions.
- A sense of *unity*—Sensing that one is the same basic self from one moment or one situation to the next.
- A sense of *otherness*—Recognizing the boundaries between the self and others.
- A sense of *decentering* or *distancing*—Reflecting on oneself so that one can recognize and own one's thoughts and actions.

The **public self** includes the many roles one plays and the expectations of others. As young people move through the stage of later adolescence, they find that social **reference groups**—including family members, neighbors, teachers, friends, religious

Woman with a Hat, Picasso, Pablo (1881–1973)/Private Collection/Photo © Bonhams, London, UK/The Bridgeman Art Library

This image captures a contemporary sense of the search for individual identity: a young woman with a broad-rimmed hat, hair flowing, one eye looking outward to the world, and one turned inward on the self.

groups, ethnic groups, and even national leaders—have expectations of their behavior. A young person may be expected to work, attend college, marry, serve the country in the military, attend religious services, vote, and provide economic support for family members. Persistent demands by meaningful others result in decisions that might have been made differently, or not made at all, if the individual were surrounded by a different configuration of social reference groups. In the process of achieving personal identity, one must synthesize the private sense of self with the public self derived from the many roles and relationships in which one is embedded.

The Content and Evaluation Components of Identity

The structure of identity has two components: content and evaluation. The *content* includes what one thinks about, cares about, and believes in, and the traits or characteristics by which one is recognized and known by others. Erikson suggested that identity was achieved by finding one's sense of direction with respect to salient roles and values, especially vocational decisions, political and religious ideologies, sexual expression and gender role, and interpersonal values. In many measures of identity formation,

these domains comprise the foundational content areas (Kroger, 2012). The second structural component of identity, *evaluation*, refers to the significance one places on various aspects of the identity content. Even though most people play many of the same roles, their identities differ in part because they place different values on some of these roles. Some people are single-minded, placing great value on success in one domain, such as their vocational goals, and little value on the others. Other people strive to maintain a balance in the roles they play; they consider themselves successful if they can find enjoyment in a variety of relationships and activities.

A person's assessment of the importance of certain content areas in relation to others influences the use of resources, the direction of certain decisions, and the kinds of experiences that may be perceived as most personally rewarding or threatening. College students, for example, may differ in whether academic success and professional preparation or interpersonal success is most central to their sense of identity. Students who are more concerned about academic success take a different approach to the college environment, become involved in different kinds of activities, and have a different reaction to academic feedback than do students who are more concerned about making friends and having new kinds of social and interpersonal success (Green & Hill, 2003).

Both the content and evaluation components of identity may change over the life course. In later adolescence, the focus is on integrating the various sources of content and determining which elements have the greatest salience. This is a major accomplishment that requires self-awareness, introspection, and the active exploration of a variety of roles and relationships. Insight into this process is provided in the case study of Houston A. Baker, Jr. However, the identity that is formed at the end of this period is often very abstract because later adolescents have not yet encountered many of the responsibilities, pressures, and conflicts of adult life. The ideological framework of identity has not yet been forged in the flames of reality.

— CASE STUDY   Houston A. Baker, Jr. —

A poet and literary scholar tells of the impact of one of his college professors on his personal identity.

He intrigued us. Slowly puffing on the obligatory pipe, he would chide us for the routineness of our analyses of revered works in the British and American literary canons. He wore—always—a tie and tweed of Ivy provenance, and at the end of the first session of his "World Literature" course at Howard University in the fall of 1963, I had but one response—I wanted to be exactly like him.

The task was to prove myself worthy. I labored furiously at the beginning assignment—an effort devoted to Marvellian coy mistresses and pounding parodies thereof. The result was a D and the comment: "This is a perfunctory effort. You have refused to be creative. There are worlds on worlds rolling ever. Try to make contact with them." I was more than annoyed; I was livid. Who did he think he was? I'd show him. My next essay would reveal (cleverly, of course) that I didn't give a tinker's dam for his grade or his comments. "Creative"—indeed!

My second essay might properly have been entitled: Love's labor loosed on William Blake. I strained to see every nuance of the "Songs of Innocence." I combed the poems for every mad hint that would help forward my own mad argument. I never turned my eyes from the text as I sought to construct the most infuriating (yet plausible) analysis imaginable. I felt my feet dancing to Muhammad Ali rhythms as I slaved away, darting logical jabs at Professor C. Watkins who would (I was certain) be utterly undone when I threw my irreverent straight right. The paper came back with the comment: "This is a maverick argument, but stubbornly logical—A–" Bingo! The grade in itself gave me almost enough courage to seek him out during office hours—but not quite. I corralled a friend to make the pilgrimage with me.

He was extraordinarily gracious on the mid-autumn afternoon when we had our first long talk. "Come in, Mr. Baker—Miss Pierce. How are you?" His tie was loose; he was reared back in his desk chair. There was a clutter of papers and blue books, and they provided a friendly setting for a two-hour conversation....We were thrilled that he considered us (potentially) enough like him to invite us to visit him and his wife two weeks hence—for dessert.

The evening surprisingly took on (in my youthful imagination) the cast of Greenwich Village "Beats" and verboten revelations. The greatest stimulation, however, came when he played the Library of Congress recording of T. S. Eliot reading "The Wasteland." In that moment, I became, willy-nilly, a party to "modernism" in its prototypical form. I was surprised and delighted. I had heard nothing like it before. The Eliotian reading initiated my habit of "listening" for poems rather than "looking" for them....I stepped into a late fall evening with an entirely new sense of myself and of "worlds on worlds rolling ever."

Source: From "An Apple for My Teacher: Twelve Writers Tell About Teachers Who Made All the Difference," by H. A. Baker, Jr., pp. 317–319 , in H. L. Gates, Jr. (Ed.), *Bearing Witness: Selections from African-American Autobiography in the Twentieth Century.* Copyright © 1991 Pantheon Books.

CASE ANALYSIS Using What You Know

1. Analyze the elements of the identity process that are evident in this case.
2. Describe some of the characteristics of Professor Watkins that made him a model for identification for Houston Baker.
3. Summarize aspects of the college environment that are likely to stimulate the identity process.
4. Have you ever had an intellectual experience that gave you a "new sense of yourself"? Explain the combination of factors that came together to permit this to happen.

Identity Status

Identity development takes place in historical and cultural contexts. During early and later adolescence, young people are aware of the age-graded expectations that exist in their families and communities, typically structured around specific tasks and roles, including educational attainment, occupation, intimacy, marriage, and childrearing. In most modern societies, each of these areas presents a variety of opportunities or possible paths as well as some constraints about which paths are possible given certain personal, financial, and cultural resources. In later adolescence, the **identity process** includes examining alternatives, selecting goals in these domains, making personal and interpersonal commitments to achieve these goals, and taking the active steps to achieve them (Nurmi, 2004). Throughout the chapter we have described contemporary circumstances that are prolonging the transition into adulthood, especially expectations for additional education, more diverse career alternatives, delayed entry into marriage, and less attachment to formal religious organizations. For all these reasons, one might expect the work on personal identity to take longer, require more time for exploration, and involve more revisions than may have been the case 40 years ago or in some other more traditional societies (Schwartz et al., 2013).

Identity formation is a dynamic process that unfolds as young people assess their competencies and aspirations within a changing social context of expectations, demands, and resources. A variety of potential resolutions of the psychosocial crisis of individual identity versus identity confusion have been described (Kroger, 2012; Kroger & Marcia, 2010). At the negative pole of the crisis, identity confusion or diffusion, the person is not able or possibly not willing to make any commitments to adult roles and values. At the positive pole, identity achievement, the person has made commitments to a defined set of values and goals.

Is it possible to compare later adolescents with regard to their progress in the formation of a personal identity? The concept of **identity status** is used to make these comparisons. It reflects different degrees of exploration and certainty about one's values and goals. One of the most widely used conceptual frameworks for assessing identity status was devised by James Marcia (1993, 2007). Drawing on Erikson's concepts, Marcia assessed identity status on the basis of two criteria: *crisis* and *commitment*. **Crisis,** sometimes referred to as exploration**,** refers to a period of trying out various roles, reviewing and sorting through one's options, and active decision making among alternative choices. **Commitment** consists of a demonstration of personal involvement and investment in the areas of occupational choice, religion, political ideology, and interpersonal relationships. On the basis of Marcia's interview, the status of respondents' identity development is assessed as identity achievement, foreclosure, moratorium, or confusion (see Table 10.2).

People who are classified as **identity achieved** have already experienced a crisis time and have made occupational and ideological commitments. They have struggled with experiences of uncertainty and have identified meaningful goals and values.

People who are classified as **foreclosed** have not experienced a crisis or a process of exploration, but demonstrate strong occupational and ideological commitments. Their occupational and ideological beliefs appear to be close to those of their parents. The foreclosed identity is deceptive. A young person of 18 or 19 who can say exactly what she wants in life and who has selected an occupational goal may appear to be mature. This kind of clarity of vision may impress peers and adults as evidence of a high level of self-insight. However, if this solution has been formulated through the wholesale adoption of a script that was devised by the young person's family, it may not actually reflect much depth

Table 10.2	Relationship of Crisis and Commitment to Identity Status		
Status		**Crisis**	**Commitment**
Identity achievement		+	+
Foreclosure		−	+
Moratorium		+	−
Identity confusion		+/−	−

© Cengage

of self-understanding. It is not surprising to find that of the four identity statuses, those in foreclosure also score highest in authoritarianism, a tendency to rely heavily on the values and expectations of authority figures to decide what is right and how to behave (Ryeng, Kroger, & Martinussen, 2010).

People who are classified as being in a state of **moratorium** are involved in ongoing exploration and experimentation. Their commitments are diffuse. The moratorium status is typically an active, open time for gathering information and discovering how one fits in certain roles. In an extension of Marcia's model, the idea of exploration has been expanded—exploration in *breadth*, which involves engaging in a diversity of roles and relationships, and exploration in *depth*, which involves taking a closer look at some earlier commitments in order to assess their fit with current goals and values. Within this framework, moratorium status can look rather different for those who are in a period of open-ended searching possibly accompanied with anxiety over uncertainty, and those engaged in focused examination of existing commitments with an eye toward replacing earlier commitments with new ones (Meeus et al., 2010).

Finally, people who are classified as **identity confused** may have had a limited or nonexistent exploratory phase and are unable to make commitments. Marcia described the identity-confused group as having a rather cavalier, party attitude that allows members to cope with the college environment. He suggested that the more seriously confused persons (such as those described by Erikson, 1959) may not appear in his sample because they are unable to cope with college. More recent analyses of the confused status support this idea of two subtypes: *troubled confusion* refers to those who have unrealistic expectations, are afraid of making the wrong kinds of decisions, and experience high levels of anxiety about their indecision; and *carefree confusion* refers to those who appear to be unconcerned with making any identity commitments (Luyckx, Goossens, Soenens, Beyers, & Vansteenkiste, 2005). Those in the identity confused status look to others to define their sense of self and purpose.

Sometimes, a young person develops a **negative identity**, because the society has labeled the person in a negative way (Erikson, 1959). *Failure, good-for-nothing, juvenile delinquent, hood, gangster,* and *loser* are some of the labels that the adult society applies to certain adolescents. Terms such as *illegal alien* or *terrorist* define individuals as without value to society, and as such, impose a negative identity (Lawler, 2014). These labels disconnect individuals from meaningful social bonds or valued

roles. The society creates a negative identity as "other" or "to be feared." The young person accepts such negative labels as a self-definition and proceeds to validate this identity by continuing to behave in ways that will strengthen it. Some young people grow up admiring people who have become very successful by following antisocial or criminal paths. Drug lords; gang leaders; leaders of groups that advocate hate, violence, and vengeance; and people who use elected political positions for personal gain are all examples of possible role models around which a negative identity may be formed.

A negative identity may also emerge as the result of a strong identification with someone who is devalued by the family or the community. A loving uncle who is an alcoholic or a clever, creative parent who commits suicide may stimulate the crystallization within the adolescent of a self-construal as one who may share these undesirable characteristics. Linda, for example, established the negative identity of a person going crazy:

> Her father was an alcoholic, physically abusive man, who terrified her when she was a child.... Linda, herself a bright child, became by turns the standard bearer for her father's proud aspirations and the target of his jealousy. Midway through grade school she began flunking all her courses and retreating to a private world of daydreams.... "I always expected hallucinations, being locked up, down the road coming toward me.... I always resisted seeing myself as an adult. I was afraid that at the point I stopped the tape [the years of wild experimentation] I'd become my parents.... My father was the closest person I knew to crazy." (Ochberg, 1986, pp. 296–297)

Identity Confusion

The maladaptive resolution of the crisis is identity confusion. Young people in this state are unable to make a commitment to any single view of themselves. They may be unable to integrate the various roles they play. They may be confronted by opposing value systems or by a lack of confidence in their ability to make meaningful decisions. Within the private, subjective self, some young people may reach later adolescence having difficulty accepting or establishing clear ego boundaries, or they may not experience feelings of agency. Individuals with identity confusion have been shown to have low self-esteem; they are more likely than individuals with other identity statuses to be influenced by peer pressures toward conformity; and they approach problem solving with tendencies toward procrastination and avoidance, which contribute to difficulties in adjusting to the college environment (Berzonsky & Kuk, 2000; Kroger, 2004). At an unconscious level, they may have incorporated two or more conflicting ideas about the self—for example, an abusive, harsh, rejecting powerful father and a wise, loving, nurturant, powerful grandmother—that stand in opposition to each other. Under any of these conditions, the demands for integration and synthesis of a personal identity arouse anxiety, apathy, and hostility toward the existing roles, none of which can be successfully adopted.

In comparison to the moratorium group, young people with a confused identity status are less conscientious, and are more likely to experience negative emotions and be more disagreeable. They have the lowest scores on multiple measures of well-being of all the identity status groups (Schwartz et al., 2011). They are generally not outgoing; rather, they describe themselves as self-conscious and likely to feel depressed. Their relationship with their parents is described as distant or rejecting. Difficulties in resolving earlier psychosocial crises—especially conflicts related to autonomy versus shame and doubt and initiative versus guilt—leave some young people with deficits in ego formation that interfere with the kind of energy and playful self-assertiveness that are necessary in the process of identity achievement (Marcia, 2006).

Dolores, an unemployed college dropout, describes the feeling of meaningless drifting that is associated with identity confusion:

> I have two sisters, and my father always told me I was the smartest of all, that I was smarter than he was, and that I could do anything I wanted to do…but somehow, I don't really know why, everything I turned to came to nothing.…I had every opportunity to find out what I really wanted to do. But…nothing I did satisfied me, and I would just stop.…Or turn away.…Or go on a trip. I worked for a big company for a while.…Then my parents went to Paris and I just went with them.…I came back…went to school…was a researcher at Time-Life…drifted…got married…divorced…drifted. [Her voice grew more halting.] I feel my life is such a waste. I'd like to write, I really would; but I don't know. I just can't get going. (Gornick, 1971)

A recent direction in the study of identity status has been to examine how identity processes relate to health-risk and health-promoting behaviors. Some studies have found a relationship between the *carefree* type of identity confusion and risky, reckless behaviors including rule breaking, use of dangerous drugs, risky sexual behaviors, and drunk driving (Schwartz et al., 2013). One interpretation of this link is that since these young people are not attached to any clear vision of purpose and meaning, they take risks with their health because they have nothing to lose. In contrast, those who have incorporated a well-integrated sense of self and commitments to a view of the self in the future are less likely to take these risks. In research focusing on specific health problems, such as diabetes or congenital heart disease, having a well-integrated identity and sense of purpose may operate to provide some protection against the anxieties associated with the disease and support commitment to the maintenance practices that help keep the disease under control (Schwartz et al., 2013).

Developmental Progression

The theoretical construct of identity status is built on the assumption that the process of exploring alternative roles and values, and making commitments requires a reconstruction of the self and associated strengthening of the ego. The identity statuses reflect different levels of both internal and external integration—an inner ability for self-reflection, review of alternatives, and hypothetical thinking about possible selves, and an external integration of the roles, expectations, and opportunities available in one's social and community contexts. Implied in this model is the assumption of a developmental progression where identity confusion is the least integrated status, movement from confusion to foreclosure and moratorium suggest greater ego strengths, and identity achievement reflects the most advanced status (Al-Owidha, Green, & Kroger, 2009; Kroger & Marcia, 2010). The following narrative illustrates the movement anticipated from moratorium to achieved identity:

> At the end of this summer, I left Canada for Scotland in order to pursue teaching education. This is something that I had planned on for a long time and was very sure about. I had been away from home before, but never as far away as another country. Although I only half completed the length of my time here, I have learned a great deal about myself that I didn't really see before. I have certainly proved that I am very independent. I had previously doubted this about myself. It felt rather fulfilling to feel such independence. I had the occasional doubt prior to coming here that it would be difficult, but little doubt exists in my mind now. (McLean & Pratt, 2006, p. 719)

Movement from achievement to one of the other statuses suggests regression. As a result of some destabilizing experiences, a person who has achieved identity at one period may conceivably return to a crisis period of moratorium or confusion. However, those who are in a moratorium or achieved status can never be accurately described as foreclosed, because by definition they have already experienced some degree of crisis (Meeus, 1996; Waterman, 1982). A number of cross-sectional and longitudinal studies have shown that over time, more young people have the mature identity statuses of moratorium and achievement, and fewer are in foreclosure or identity confusion (Kroger, Martinussen, & Marcia, 2010; Yip, Seaton, & Sellers, 2006).

In the process of evolving an individual identity, everyone experiences temporary periods of confusion and depression. The task of bringing together the many elements of one's experience into a coordinated, clear self-definition is difficult and time consuming. Most adolescents experience moments of self-preoccupation, isolation, and discouragement as the diverse pieces of their identity puzzle are shifted and reordered into the total picture. Thus, even the eventual attainment of positive identity formation will be the result of some degree of identity confusion. The negative outcome of identity confusion, however, suggests that the person is never able to formulate a satisfying identity that will provide for the convergence of multiple identifications, aspirations, and roles. Such individuals have persistent fears that they are losing their hold on themselves and on their future.

Identity Formation for Men and Women

Questions have been raised about whether the theory of identity formation, applies equally well to men and women. A summary of research comparing the course of identity development for males and females finds no evidence of gender differences in the timing or the process through which identity is formed (Coté, 2009). The kinds of ego strengths associated with identity achievement are equally important to the adaptive functioning of men and women. Men and women are equally likely to be distributed across the four identity statuses. Over the period of later adolescence, they show the same pattern of increasing frequencies in the moratorium and achievement categories and decreasing frequencies in the foreclosed and confused categories (Kroger, 2004).

Some have argued that the concept of identity as it has been formulated is a reflection of a male-oriented culture that focuses heavily on occupation and ideology rather than on interpersonal commitments as the foundation for identity content. These critics suggest that the construct of personal identity places greater value on self-sufficiency and autonomy, characteristics associated with the traditional male gender role, and less value on the building of close relationships and connections to the group, characteristics associated with the traditional female gender role (Archer, 1992; Sorrel & Montgomery, 2001).

Some evidence of gender differences has been found in the salience of various domains in the *content* of identity. Erikson's (1968, 1982) work suggested that ideological and vocational commitments are central to identity formation. Gilligan (1982/1993) criticized this orientation, arguing that interpersonal commitments may be more central for women and that its clarification opens the way for more advanced exploration of vocations and ideology. The early studies of identity status were conducted with male participants. As the approach gained traction, the interview method was modified to include domains that were thought to be especially relevant for young women, particularly ideas about relationships, sexuality, and family. These along with the focus on occupational and ideological commitments continue to be part of the assessment method for both men and women (Marcia et al., 1993). Research lends some support to this view. The quality of interpersonal relations and the establishment of satisfying social commitments are more central to the content of personal identity for women. Women are more likely to be in the identity achieved or moratorium status than men in relational domains such as family, friendship, or the values relating work and family (Kroger, 2002).

FURTHER REFLECTION: Evaluate factors that may make it difficult for someone to resolve the crisis of individual identity versus identity confusion during the period from 18 to 24 in contemporary U.S. society. Think about the idea of identity status. What experiences might foster movement from moratorium status to achieved status? What experiences might destabilize identity, resulting in regression from achievement to moratorium?

The Central Process: Role Experimentation

The concept of identity status, which has dominated the research on identity development, implies steps or levels of attainment in one's identity work. This approach may obscure the important question of how adolescents go about the task of figuring out their values and commitments. The central process of **role experimentation** suggests an answer to this question. Later adolescents

experiment with roles that represent the many possibilities for their future identities. They may imagine themselves in a variety of careers in an effort to anticipate what it would be like to be members of specific occupational groups. They may take a variety of summer jobs, change their college major, read extensively, and daydream about success in several occupations. They consider whether to marry, and they begin to define the ideal qualities they are looking for in a long-term intimate partner. Dating is one form of role experimentation; it allows for a different self-presentation with each new date. Friendship is another important context within which young people begin to clarify their interpersonal commitments. Later adolescents may also evaluate their commitment to their religion, consider religious conversion, or experiment with different rationales for moral behavior. They may examine a variety of political theories, join groups that work for political causes, or campaign for candidates.

Some researchers have conceptualized the process of role experimentation as a cycling of commitment formation and commitment reevaluation (Klimstra et al., 2010). Early in the identity formation process, this cycle may occur frequently, possibly daily, as young people vacillate between certainty about their values or commitments and uncertainty about whether these commitments make sense. For example, as a freshman in college Sam tells his parents that he wants to major in political science and become a lawyer. Then, after a few weeks he tells his folks that he wants to go into the field of foreign service and be a diplomat. By the time Sam comes home for Thanksgiving, he is talking about getting more involved in the student government and thinks that when he graduates from college he would like to go into politics. By his senior year, Sam has changed his mind about his future career five or six times, but each time he comes back to his interest in the law and ends up applying to law school. Over time, as commitments become more stable, the young person will experience greater confidence and fewer episodes of reevaluation.

Psychosocial Moratorium

The process of role experimentation takes many forms. Erikson (1959) used the term **psychosocial moratorium** to describe a period of free experimentation before a final identity is achieved. Ideally, the moratorium allows individuals freedom from the daily expectations for role performance. Their experimentation with new roles, values, and belief systems results in a personal conception of how they can fit into society so as to maximize their personal strengths and gain positive recognition from the community. The idea of being able to disconnect from daily demands and experiment with new roles may be more difficult for some later adolescents than for others. For example, young people who marry early and who go into the labor force right after high school may not have the luxury of a moratorium.

The concept of the psychosocial moratorium has been partially incorporated into some college programs that permit students to enroll in pass–fail courses before they select a major. The intention is to eliminate the problems of external evaluation during the decision-making process. The concept of a "Gap Year" is gaining traction. After graduation, some high school students take a year off for a combination of work, travel, or volunteer service

For some later adolescents, the psychosocial moratorium allows them to explore the wonders of nature and test the limits of their physical capabilities.

before deciding about college or career. Some colleges encourage students to take this year by offering a delayed admission (National Association for College Admission Counseling 2016; Ruiz, 2011). College students often express a need for a moratorium by leaving school for a while, disrupting the expected path of educational and career development. They assert their autonomy by imposing their own timetable and agenda on a socially prescribed sequence. Travel abroad is another strategy for experiencing moratorium. The time spent in another culture can give students an opportunity to demonstrate self-sufficiency, examine many of their assumptions about values and goals, express their individuality, and break out of whatever social environment they may feel is constraining or overshadowing their sense of self. The moratorium offers temporary relief from external demands and an opportunity to establish their identity.

As parents observe the process of role experimentation, they may become concerned because their adolescent son or daughter appears to lack direction or purpose. Parents are well advised to understand role experimentation as the expression of an appropriate developmental process in which a young person is trying on various roles, beliefs, and philosophies to see how they fit. If at all possible, parents need to trust in this process, giving their opinions and reactions when appropriate, but encouraging the young person to find the combination of roles, values, goals, and commitments that bring her the greatest feelings of enthusiasm and optimism about her own future.

Individual Differences in Role Experimentation

Not all young people approach the process of role experimentation with the same degree of openness to new experiences and new information. Michael Berzonsky (1989, 1993, 2011) hypothesized that in later adolescence, individuals differ in how they select, process, and apply self-relevant information. Three types of approaches to identity-related information processing were described. The *informational types* "actively seek out and evaluate self-diagnostic information when negotiating identity issues and making decisions" (Berzonsky, 1993, p. 289). The *normative types*

are "relatively more defensive and closed to feedback that may threaten hard core areas of the self" (Berzonsky, 1993, p. 290). The *diffuse-avoidant types* "procrastinate and delay dealing with self-relevant issues as long as possible. When push comes to shove, they tend to be influenced by immediate rewards and operate in a situation-sensitive fashion" (Berzonsky, 1993, p. 290). The three identity-processing styles are associated with distinct patterns of defense mechanisms that come into play when later adolescents encounter conflicts or threats to their identity. The informational types use cognitive strategies to minimize anxiety. The diffuse-avoidant types use defenses that turn aggression inward toward the self or outward, blaming others. The normative types use mechanisms of denial, distortion, and negation to defend against threatening information (Berzonsky & Kinney, 2008).

An implication of this theory that the path toward identity status depends in part on how willing a young person is to engage in role experimentation. The informational types are most likely to initiate role experimentation as a means of clarifying existing beliefs and values. The normative types have to process contradictions among the demands and expectations of the varying roles they play, but if possible, they will probably avoid novel experiences that would challenge their views. The diffuse-avoidant types may engage in role experimentation if it is viewed as cool or is positively regarded among others in their peer group, but they probably would not take the initiative to seek out new experiences as a conscious, proactive strategy. FIGURE 10.6 ▶ shows the relationship between the three information-seeking styles and the four identity statuses described earlier. In this model, exploration or seeking information is associated with both the moratorium and the achieved statuses (White, Wampler, & Winn, 1998).

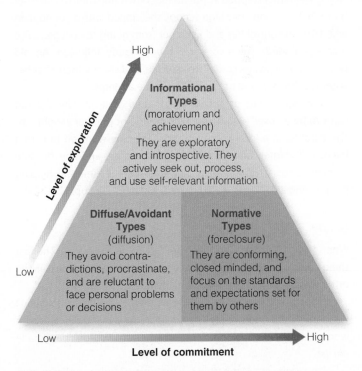

FIGURE 10.6 ▶ RELATIONS AMONG IDENTITY STATUS, LEVEL OF EXPLORATION, AND LEVEL OF COMMITMENT

Source: White, Wampler, and Winn, 1998, p. 226.

Role experimentation implies an active process by which later adolescents sort through various identifications, scripts, and social pressures in order to clarify their commitments. For some young people, however, a **turning point** or critical incident marks the point of commitment. Often, a dramatic loss, an unexpected victory, or an experience of victimization can help crystallize a young person's vision of how the self can fit in with the community or transcend the community. For later adolescents who experience stressful life events, the experience of suffering, struggle for meaning, and coping may result in new levels of personal insight that support the identity process (Marcia, 2010; McLean & Pratt, 2006). Two examples of turning points are illustrated in the following case study.

— CASE STUDY Turning Points in the Identity Process —

The following two examples illustrate how a critical life event can refocus personal identity toward a new consolidation of energy, purpose, and commitment. In the first example, Sullivan experiences personal losses that lead to a new occupational and value commitment. In the second example, Rachel experiences a national tragedy that reorients her political ideology.

Sullivan

Sullivan was living with her mother in a housing project. In high school, when life got very hard, she began drinking and using drugs. She often stayed out late "to all hours" without her mother knowing or caring. Her father stepped in, put his foot down, and tried to teach her better habits. Soon after high school, she eloped with a young man who tried to control her and keep her from going to college....The marriage ended after two years, then tragedy followed. An old boyfriend of Sullivan's committed suicide, and shortly thereafter her sister was hospitalized because of a suicide attempt.

The near-death of her sister changed Sullivan. She did not want to be a "loser"—someone who could not pull her weight—so she enrolled in a local community college. She went on to earn a bachelor's degree and then a master's degree, and she became a licensed social worker. Now Sullivan's work is aimed at helping people who are like she was. (Levine & Nidiffer, 1996, pp. 122–123)

Rachel

When I was 19, I moved to New York City to be a musician. The first thing I did was get a tattoo on each hand: One was a treble clef, the other was the insignia for Silvertone guitars....

If you asked me to describe myself then, I would have told you I was a musician, a poet, an artist and, on a somewhat political level, a woman, a lesbian, and a Jew. Being an American wouldn't have made my list.

I'm a junior at a Manhattan college. In my Gender and Economics class earlier this semester we discussed the benefits of socialism, which provides for all members of society, versus capitalism, which

values the self-interests of businesspeople. My girlfriend and I were so frustrated by inequality in America that we discussed moving to another country. On September 11, all that changed. I realized that I had been taking the freedoms I have here for granted. Now I have an American flag on my backpack, I cheer at the fighter jets as they pass overhead, and I am calling myself a patriot.

I had just stepped out of the shower when the first plane crashed into the North Tower of the World Trade Center. I stood looking out the window of my Brooklyn apartment, dumbfounded, as the second plane barreled into the South Tower. In that moment, the world as I had known it was redefined. (Newman, 2001, p. 9)

CASE ANALYSIS Using What You Know

1. Discuss the difference between turning points and role experimentation.
2. Examine the factors that might determine whether a turning point leads to identity achievement or identity confusion.
3. Contrast the events that Sullivan experienced and those that Rachel experienced. How might the differences in these two kinds of events relate to subsequent identity work?
4. Generate a list of factors that might be necessary to preserve the focus and sense of purpose that are evoked in these critical life events. For example, how might family support, the response of close friends, or opportunities for enacting new roles influence whether these changes are sustained?

Role Experimentation and Ethnic Identity

In chapter 9 (Early Adolescence), we introduced the idea that group identity precedes individual identity. One component of group identity is an orientation toward one's ethnic group. Efforts to understand one's **ethnic identity** and to clarify one's commitment to a particular ethnic subculture lead to self-definition that facilitates work on personal identity as well (Yip, Seaton, & Sellers, 2006). Part of forming a clear sense of personal identity may require an understanding of one's ancestry, especially one's cultural and ethnic heritage and the values, beliefs, and traditions that may have shaped one's childrearing environment as well as one's vision of the future. Ethnic group identity typically involves the incorporation of certain ideals, values, and beliefs that are specific to that ethnic group; a sense of how this ethnic group is regarded by outsiders; and the way in which one orients oneself with respect to this group—that is, whether one seeks out other members of the group, feels proud of one's membership in it, and has positive attitudes about it (Cross, 1991).

As you might imagine, young people make the transition from early to later adolescence having done different amounts of work in exploring their ethnic group identity. One theory of ethnic minority identity development offers a five-stage model (Atkinson, Morten, & Sue, 1983):

1. *Conformity.* Identification with the values, beliefs, and practices of the dominant culture.
2. *Dissonance.* Recognition and confusion about areas of conflict between the values, beliefs, and practices of the dominant culture and those of one's own ethnic group.

3. *Resistance and immersion.* Rejection of many elements of the dominant culture; education about and involvement in one's own ethnic group and its beliefs, values, and practices.
4. *Introspection.* Critical examination of the values, beliefs, and practices of both the dominant culture and one's own ethnic group's views.
5. *Articulation and awareness.* Identification of those values, beliefs, and practices from the dominant culture and from one's own ethnic group that are combined into a unique synthesis that forms a personal, cultural identity.

Exposure to the college curriculum offers an intellectual framework for understanding the historical, psychological, and sociological foundations of racism, prejudice, and cultural conflict (Phinney, 1996b). The complex interweaving of ethnic identity exploration, personal identity exploration, and the pursuit of academic goals results in a variety of individual trajectories (Syed, 2010). Over the period of later adolescence, young people gradually progress from an unexplored or unexamined ethnic identity to a more fully articulated understanding of how race and ethnicity contribute to their sense of self, and a stronger sense of ethnic group membership (Fuligni, Hughes, & Way, 2009). In one study of American Indian college students, the contribution of ethnic identity to well-being was examined. Those students who had a strong identification with their American Indian heritage and who socialized primarily with other American Indians were more likely to express feelings of historical loss. In contrast, the students who were more strongly assimilated into mainstream culture were less likely to struggle with these feelings (Tucker, Wingate, & O'Keefe, 2016). The implication of this research is that for some students, the formulation of a strong ethnic identity may increase one's sensitivity to the societal harms that have been inflicted on one's group.

This model highlights the interaction between ethnic identity and personal identity (Cross & Fhagen-Smith, 2001; Rotheram-Borus & Wyche, 1994). Not all young people experience all of these stages. Some children are raised in families where ethnic socialization begins at a young age, and they never experience a sense of tension between their ethnic background and that of other groups. If they are raised in an ethnically segregated community, they may not encounter members of other cultural or ethnic groups as significant figures during their early childhood years. For others, their family and community focus emphasizes religious affiliation or social standing over ethnic identity, placing relatively little emphasis on ethnicity as a defining aspect of the self.

But for many, later adolescence is the stage when exploration about ethnic identity is highlighted (see the **Human Development and Diversity** box Ethnic Identity and Adjustment). Ethnic identity exploration and commitment typically increase over the college years (Syed & Azmitia, 2009). Ethnic identity may become one lens through which students make decisions about their college major. As they participate in this major, they may experience new insights about the fit between their career aspirations and their social identity. The college environment also provides a social climate that may stimulate new ideas about ethnicity. Having attended an ethnically diverse high school, some students have already given thought to how their ethnicity fits in with their goals, career ambitions, and personal values. They may welcome opportunities to explore various cultural perspectives in coursework and student organizations. For others, arriving at college at the stage of conformity, the college environment brings a new awareness of conflicts that pervade contemporary culture. They may find that the student body is much more diverse than high school. Young people of many racial, ethnic, social-class, regional, and religious backgrounds come together in college and are expected to live together in the residence halls, learn together in the classrooms, and collaborate in college organizations, social activities, sports, and cultural events. Exposure to this diversity may be accompanied by experiences of racial and ethnic prejudice, cultural ethnocentrism, and intergroup conflict. The following example illustrates what some students encounter as aspects of a hostile or demeaning campus climate

Alejandra Padin-Dujon, a sophomore who is an Afro-Latina, said her experience has ranged from being called

The college environment provides an opportunity for students to learn about their cultural identities and the history of their ethnic groups.

Ethnic Identity and Adjustment

Ethnic identity has been studied as a component of the self-concept, usually focusing on how important people's ethnicity is to them, how often they think about themselves as members of their ethnic group, and how close they feel to other members of their ethnic group (Sears, Fu, Henry, & Bui, 2003). Ethnic identity has also been measured as a general concept, allowing one to compare the strength of ethnic identity across groups. The *Multigroup Ethnic Identity Measure* (MEIM) is one such measure, which consists of two subscales (Phinney, 1992; Roberts et al., 1999):

1. *Affirmation, belonging, and commitment*, which assesses one's feelings of connection and pride in membership.
2. *Ethnic identity search*, a developmental and cognitive component, which assesses a person's efforts to be involved in activities and practices associated with their ethnic group and to increase their understanding of the group and its history and traditions.

The MEIM allows one to characterize individuals along a continuum from an unexamined ethnic identity acquired with little exploration or commitment (*low ethnic identity*) to a well-developed, achieved ethnic identity (Yasui, Dorham, & Dishion, 2004). The parallels with personal identity status are striking, capturing the two processes of exploration (crisis) and commitment.

Ethnic identity, as measured by the MEIM, has been positively associated with self-esteem across middle childhood, early adolescence, and later adolescence. Individuals with positive ethnic identity deal more effectively with threatening social situations involving discrimination and stereotyping (Roberts et al., 1999). A sense of belonging to one's ethnic group may be important as part of one's social identity for all groups. However, the *salience* of ethnic identity is not the same for all groups. The establishment of a clear acceptance of their ethnic identity may be especially relevant for those who face discrimination or oppression on the basis of their ethnic membership.

A growing group of later adolescents identify themselves as multiracial or biracial. One estimate finds that close to 7 percent of Americans are multiracial and with the increase in multiracial marriages, this group is likely to grow (Pew Social Trends, 2015). However, many people with a multiracial heritage do not consider themselves multiracial. Others reject the traditional categories of race and ethnicity in favor of a more nuanced acceptance of diverse backgrounds and ancestries (Ojalvo, 2011). Having spent time figuring out how they fit into their families and communities, they come to later adolescence with a greater openness toward other groups and heightened appreciation for the value of cultural diversity.

I am Italian and African American and I am proud of all my heritages. My origins are diverse, but so is the world around me. I grew up in a national forest reserve which lent me a respect for rural America. Growing up I worked as a Thai sous chef for a Thai immigrant. He taught me to cook and I developed that skill in college where my primary supermarket in college became Patel's Cash and Carry. Two of my best friends are Muslim by way Bangladesh, but dress like 1930's French models. One is Polish and Irish who loves her Peruvian gay uncle. The love of my life is a first generation Cuban-American who works for a major East Asian Research Center. I am happy to consider myself uniquely American. I could have only happened here. (Ojalvo, 2011)

Critical Thinking Questions

1. Evaluate how well the two scales from the MEIM, ethnic identity search and affirmation, belonging, and commitment, capture the meaning of ethnic identity. What other dimensions would you add if you were going to modify this measure?
2. Describe the parallels between ethnic identity and personal identity. How might they relate to each other as the person matures? Can you imagine having an achieved personal identity without a clear ethnic identity? What about vice versa?
3. Summarize the personal, family, and community factors that might determine how important or salient ethnic identity is for an individual or for an ethnic group.
4. Predict how the increasing number of multiethnic youth may alter the way we think about and study ethnic identity in human development.

---

a "racial epithet" as a "joke" to what she sees as more subtle forms of racism: an advanced physics professor who suggested she might be better off in an easier class; students who suggested in various ways that she's at Yale because of affirmative action; and well-meaning friends who suggested that she would look prettier if she straightened her hair. (Megan, 2016)

At the same time, encounters with ethnic diversity may contribute to more divergent thinking, new perspectives about beliefs and values, and, as a result, more complex thinking about social issues (Antonio et al., 2004; Syed, 2010).

The Prime Adaptive Ego Quality and the Core Pathology

In the process of resolving the crisis of identity versus identity confusion, later adolescents have to examine their values and goals. This process relies upon more advanced executive functioning, including the capacity to take a step back from one's current commitments and reflect on their meaning as well as an ability to deliberately seek out new sources of information and ideas that can inform personal decisions (Klimstra et al., 2010). As a result of this reflective work, later adolescents who achieve a sense of personal identity are also likely to benefit from a clearer, more confident sense of their values and beliefs. In contrast, later adolescents who experience identity confusion are likely to leave this stage of life with the core pathology of repudiation—a rejection or standing *against* rather than standing *for* specific beliefs and values.

Fidelity to Values and Ideologies

Fidelity to values and ideologies is closely linked with the notion of *commitment*. In later adolescence, the ego strength of **fidelity** refers to "the ability to sustain loyalties freely pledged in spite of the inevitable contradictions and confusions of value systems" (Erikson, 1978, p. 28). Fidelity incorporates the trust and hope of infancy and directs it toward a belief in values and ideologies. Fidelity may be fostered by identification with inspirational role models or by participation in meaningful institutions. It is also achieved as a result of the new cognitive capacities of adolescence that permit self-reflection, relativistic thinking, and insight. Fidelity to values and ideals provides evidence of a reflective person who has taken time to struggle with opposing views and to select those that best reflect personal convictions (Waterman, 1992).

The emergence of fidelity to values provides a channel for guiding strong passions and drives toward the achievement of meaningful goals. At the close of later adolescence, young people who articulate specific values and goals, such as making a contribution to their community, gaining new levels of expertise in their chosen field, or establishing a loving, caring relationship, are more likely to experience a sense of subjective well-being in the years ahead as they take deliberate steps toward goal attainment (Bauer & McAdams, 2010). Fidelity to values strengthens one's ethical resolve, especially in the face of the many pressures and temptations of adult life. It also creates a bond of belonging with others who share the same loyalties. At the same time, fidelity in the individual strengthens the society by drawing on the commitments of those who share a common set of values to sustain and support basic institutions, such as religious organizations, political parties, educational institutions, and social service agencies.

Fidelity to values and ideologies is closely linked to the developmental tasks of autonomy, gender identity, moral development, and career choice. In each of these domains, the young person faces challenges that may undermine self-respect, or that may foster in-group favoritism over out-group derogation. When individuals perceive their own personal or group identity to be threatened, they are more likely to withdraw, lash out, or reject the values of others. When individuals perceive a context of acceptance, inclusion, and fair treatment, they are more likely to be open to dialogue and cooperation. We do not know which values a young person will embrace. However, the more individuals are treated in a humane, respectful, and inclusive manner, the greater the likelihood that these values will be reflected in their outlook toward others (Andersen, Downey, & Tyler, 2005).

Repudiation

Repudiation refers to a rejection of certain values, beliefs, and roles. In the diverse and pluralistic society of the United States, some degree of repudiation may be necessary in order to forge an integrated identity. One cannot embrace all ideologies and roles; each commitment brings some boundaries to one's values and limits one's investment to a certain vision of the self as continuing into the future. Repudiation can serve as a mechanism for intergenerational change. For example, a young person may decide that he will reject the characteristics of an unloving or abusive parent or a bigoted political figure. In this context, the young person will form an identity around suppressing certain negative qualities and learning to enact and endorse opposing positive qualities.

In the extreme case, repudiation results in a hostile rejection of all the ideas, values, and groups that do not adhere to one's own beliefs (Erikson, 1982). It fosters a rigid worldview that does not admit to the contributions of others' ideas. The roots of militancy, prejudice, and terrorism lie in the formation of the core pathology of repudiation. Imagine young people who, on the threshold of adulthood, see their future as grim or hopeless. They may perceive themselves as subjugated victims, rejected by the mainstream. They may believe that their culture, their ethnic identity, or their religion is mocked or berated. The energy of youth that can mobilize noble, courageous acts of fidelity can also crystallize around hate, turning against one or more groups in acts of violence.

Applied Topic: Dropping Out of College

OBJECTIVE 6 Examine some of the predictors and consequences of dropping out of college and hypothesize how dropping out of college may influence development in later adolescence.

A sizeable percentage of students who enroll in colleges leave without a degree. In general, the percentage of the U.S. population with advanced degrees has not grown much over the past 10 years. Among those ages 25 to 34, about 36 percent have a bachelor's or advanced graduate or professional degree (Ryan & Bauman, 2016). Although the majority of high school graduates (68 percent in 2014) attend some type of postsecondary institution in the year following high school, many do not graduate. The national graduation rate for students who enrolled full time at 4-year colleges and universities was 59 percent after 6 years. These rates differ by state, type of institution (public or private, research university or liberal arts college), and by students' race/ethnicity and family economic resources. Degree completion is notably lower for students entering college whose families have limited economic resources and for certain ethnic minorities, who tend to be overrepresented among low-income families (Kena et al., 2016). This picture is incomplete because the federal government does not track part-time students or those who enroll in one college and graduate from another.

Models of student retention and persistence suggest that degree completion is a result of the interaction of four classes of factors: financial factors, academic preparation, personal factors, and characteristics of the college environment (Newman & Newman, 1999).

Financial Factors

The cost of tuition, room, board, and fees increased 67 percent at public universities and 43 percent at private universities (in 2015 dollars) from the 2000–2001 academic year to the 2015–2016 academic year (College Board, 2016). These increases far outpaced the average increase in family income over the same period. Among college freshmen, about two thirds state that they are either somewhat or very concerned about their ability to finance their college education (Eagan et al., 2015).

It is no surprise that college students in the lowest quartile of family income are less likely to graduate than those in the higher quartiles. Students from poor families are more likely to be working several jobs to pay for school. Often they are troubled by the burden of growing debt and are uncomfortable about borrowing more. Many students have financial responsibilities for their family members. In some cases, they send some of their scholarship money or income from part-time work home to help support their family. Unexpected fees, and textbook and laboratory costs associated with college courses, are more difficult to cover for students from poor families because they have less access to supplemental financial resources. These students' parents have fewer resources and cannot help them meet unanticipated expenses. Students who dedicate their summer earnings to paying for tuition and fees do not have enough discretionary income to cover unanticipated costs.

In order to manage the financial requirements of attending college, many students make a combination of decisions that put them at risk for **dropping out of college**. They decide to save money by living at home, and they work more hours a week at jobs to help defray expenses. Both of these factors, living off campus and working long hours, are associated with an increased likelihood of dropping out of college (Bozick, 2007). Because they are not living on campus, they are less likely to feel a part of the college community and less likely to benefit from the friendship and social and academic support of other students. Working 20 hours or more per week makes it just about impossible to become involved with campus activities that might increase feelings of belonging or to take advantage of campus services and resources about how to cope with the academic and career preparation demands of college. When demands from classes conflict with demands from work, students from low-income families are less likely to be able to cut back on work hours.

In many cases, students from low-income families have had to establish independent financial status and do not receive any funds from parents. These students may also have attended high schools that did not provide adequate academic preparation, resulting in a requirement to take additional developmental coursework that does not count toward a college degree (Stinebrickner & Stinebrickner, 2008). Over time, students who are working at a job many hours a week just to keep up with tuition payments may find that life in college is more stressful and less enjoyable than it seems to be worth.

Academic Preparation

The following factors that precede college enrollment have all been found to relate to college retention and graduation:

- Attendance at a college-oriented high school
- Participation in a college-preparatory curriculum

- Parents' educational background
- Family's educational values and goals
- The student's intention to attend college
- Clarity of career goals
- High school coursework and grades

A rigorous high school curriculum is the strongest predictor of postsecondary persistence and success (Adelman, 2006). Students with inadequate academic preparation and lack of familiarity with the college environment are more likely to leave before graduating. High schools in low-resource neighborhoods are less likely to offer the rigorous curriculum that best prepares students for academic achievement in college.

There is growing concern among college faculty that students are not prepared to meet their expectations for writing, mathematics, independent work, critical thinking, detailed examination of information, and complex problem solving (Sanoff, 2006). Early failure experiences in college courses can result in a decision to drop out of college. Michael Van Adams' story illustrates this process:

> Van Adams...told himself that the University of Maine wasn't for him. He dropped out a couple of weeks before completing his first semester. "Frankly, I wasn't properly prepared for college," he says. "I didn't go into my freshman year with the right attitude. At age 18, I thought I had the world figured out; I thought I could ace my college classes like in high school. I couldn't have been more off. I was failing three classes, and I didn't see the point of sticking around." (Whitbourne, 2002)

Students may have an unrealistic idea about their academic preparation for college. A survey of college freshmen in 2015 found that over 70 percent rated their academic ability as in the top 10 percent or above average (Eagan et al., 2015). However, when they arrive in college, they discover that the combination of their academic preparation and their study skills are inadequate for the new demands of college-level courses. College mathematics and science courses are prerequisites for many majors. Students who fail an early mathematics or science course may realize that they will not be admitted to the major of their choice and decide to leave school. Students who have been accustomed to ranking in the top 10 percent of their high school class may be shocked to receive grades of C or D in college courses. They may assume that they do not have the ability to do college work. When students receive bad grades, especially when they expected to do well, they may begin to view college as less enjoyable and more stressful than they had hoped, leading to a decision to drop out (Stinebrickner & Stinebrickner, 2012). Many colleges have cut back on offering pre-collegiate or developmental courses in writing, mathematics, and science, thereby removing the support for students whose high school curriculum did not prepare them adequately for college-level work.

Personal Factors

The theme of personal identity and its salience in later adolescence is central to the decision to remain in college or leave. For many students, the decision to go to college is a commitment to a view of oneself in the future as a person who is more accomplished,

accomplish. Personal factors that can contribute to dropping out of college may include:

- Lack of a clear idea about one's interests; no sense of purpose
- An inability to cope with the new demands for autonomy, time management, and competition
- Disillusionment with the environment of college
- Discouragement or confusion about one's ability to achieve important goals
- The onset of mental health problems
- Alcohol or drug abuse/use
- Victimization

The college environment presents new challenges to mental health. Many students suffer from mental health problems that were managed satisfactorily in high school, but that become more challenging in the college environment. Away from family, friends, and familiar medical resources, students may stop taking their medication, become overwhelmed by anxiety or depression, or engage in new risky behaviors that impede their ability to concentrate. Being away from home may result in unexpected feelings of loneliness and isolation. The college environment typically introduces new opportunities to make decisions about daily life, and, as a result, brings new demands for time management. Students may feel unable to succeed at the academic or social demands of the environment. They may feel overwhelmed by the number of tasks or the social stimulation. Students who are participating in competitive athletics may have difficulty meeting expectations to perform at a new, high level. Feelings of being overwhelmed or overloaded may result in poor academic performance or low levels of life satisfaction that can lead to dropping out of school (Larson, 2006).

The college environment also poses new challenges for students with disabilities. As students with disabilities make the transition from a structured and guided educational support process in high school to the post-secondary environment, the importance of self-advocacy increases. However, many college students do not engage in even the most fundamental forms of self-advocacy such as registering with a disability services office and requesting accommodations. One national study found that although 87 percent of the sample had received accommodations in high school, only 19 percent reported receiving accommodations at their postsecondary institution (Newman et al., 2011). A combination of factors, including meeting the academic demands of the student role, learning and enacting self-advocacy skills, and forming meaningful relationships can all be particularly challenging for students with disabilities, leading to higher rates of dropping out. Eight years after high school, fewer students with disabilities who began college graduated within this time frame (41 percent) in comparison to the general population (52 percent). For students attending 4-year colleges and universities, the rate of completion for students with disabilities was even lower, with 34 percent graduating within the 8-year time frame (Murray, Lombardi, & Kosty, 2014; Newman et al., 2011).

African American and Hispanic American students leave college at a higher rate than European American students, even when controlling for family income. This pattern is often

Michelle is packing up her room. She is glad to be leaving; after two semesters she realized that college was just not for her.

Ute Grabowsky/photothek images UG/Alamy Stock Photo

prepared to function at a higher level, earning a better income, and being in a better position to direct the course of one's life. Students who have a clearly defined goal and strong motivation to persist are more likely to stay in college and graduate (Morrow & Ackerman, 2012). Within the college environment, identity work can be fostered as one is supported by others who validate the sense of a future self that is taking shape. It can be reassuring to be encouraged by family members and surrounded by peers who have similar academic aspirations. Interacting and identifying with faculty and graduate students who are pursuing interests as models for the future, the young person begins to see how personal goals may be attained (Kelly, LaVergne, Boone, & Boone, 2012). College coursework and interactions with peers can result in growth in worldview and exposure to new models of organizing, analyzing, and representing experience.

A variety of personal factors can interfere with this process. Once in college, the level of a student's social and academic integration, along with the wavering intention to complete college, can affect decisions to stay in school. Reflecting back on their first year in college, some students say they were not really sure why they enrolled. Going to college was the norm in their high school, or an expectation from their family (Hanford, 2013). They arrived at college without any clear idea about what they hoped to

attributed to a lack of a sense of connection or belonging in the college environment. Students who are doing well academically may decide to leave an environment where they are alienated, targets of discrimination, or disconnected from faculty and students (Walton & Cohen, 2011).

Characteristics of the College Environment

Characteristics of the college environment have also been associated with student retention. In a study of student retention at colleges and universities with large numbers of low-income students, the Pell Foundation compared schools with higher than average and lower than average graduation rates (Muraskin & Lee, 2004). School structure was associated with graduation rates. Universities characterized as Research I, where there were more graduate students and a greater emphasis on faculty research, had higher retention and graduation rates than the bachelor's degree/specialized colleges. Those institutions with higher graduation rates had more full-time students, a larger student enrollment, and more graduate students. These schools enrolled more students from the top half of their high school graduating classes. They had more full-time faculty, lower student/faculty ratios, and smaller classes. As a related factor, they spent more money per student full-time equivalent (FTE), and tuition and fees were higher, but these colleges were able to offset these costs with more grants to students.

Beyond these structural features, colleges and universities that were successful in graduating their low-income students focused on five aspects of the college environment (Muraskin & Lee, 2004):

- Building academic skills
- Providing financial support
- Working with students to help them clarify their academic direction
- Fostering a personalized environment for instruction and academic support
- Encouraging campus participation

Colleges that spend more money on student services have a lower dropout rate (Chen, 2012). At the colleges that are successful in graduating relatively large numbers of low-income students, one is likely to find pre-college or pre-enrollment courses to prepare students for the tone and tempo of college courses; supplemental services such as focused, proactive academic advising, study groups, and writing centers; and special housing groups, affinity groups, and interest groups to support students of common interest or background. Many of these campuses offer undergraduates research experiences with encouragement to consider graduate school. They create learning communities and organize students into social and academic groups in order to create a more personalized educational environment. These institutions express their commitment to retention and graduation through the ways faculty and staff interact with students, the care that is taken to create a supportive environment, and the encouragement that students experience to achieve their goals.

The Consequences of Dropping Out of College

In comparison to the research that has been done to predict student retention, relatively little is known about how students who drop out of college cope with this disrupted educational trajectory and its impact on their transition into adulthood. Dropping out of college does not necessarily solve the young person's problems and may introduce new ones. Abandoning the set of goals and activities that are linked to college attendance leaves the student in a directional vacuum. Formulating another set of goals and becoming involved in the activities required to achieve these goals may be difficult. There may be new pressures on the college dropout as people ask, "What are you going to do now?" While enrolled in college, students can cover some of their uncertainty by saying, "I'm in college." Dropping out means losing this protective, if somewhat ambiguous, role. This decision brings a need to recalculate and reorganize one's trajectory for the transition into adulthood. This task may be difficult and confusing because the identity work needed to flourish outside of college is different than the identity work required of the college student.

Dropping out has an impact on short-and long-term earnings. Leaving college has significant financial implications that will impact the young person's autonomy and capacity for financial self-sufficiency. As presented earlier in Table 10.1, the median income for a person who has some college but no degree is only slightly more than for a person who has graduated from high school. This difference in earning capacity increases as people move into their middle adulthood because opportunities for advancement are associated with higher levels of education. Moreover, those who attend college for a year or two and then leave are likely to have debts from tuition, fees, and other costs that they carry with them without hope of the increase in salary that might help them repay those debts.

Reduced educational attainment will have an impact on occupation. This in turn may have consequences for one's social status in the community. Dropping out of college may be accompanied by the loss of a peer group and the need to create a new social network and the possibility of disappointing family members. The lack of a college degree may make one a less desirable life partner and reduce one's marriage prospects.

Given the flexibility of the higher education system in the United States, there are many opportunities to reengage the college environment, including online enrollment, part-time status, evening and weekend courses, and continuing education. We do not know much about the process through which later adolescents who leave college without a degree decide to return or how they make meaning of their disrupted college years. Does the decision to leave college result in feelings of regret about unrealized promise? Or does the decision result in the formulation of a more authentic set of life goals that can be achieved without benefit of a college education? Perhaps this depends on whether the person views the decision to leave as an expression of agency or as evidence of failure.

There are many instances of people who do not graduate from high school or college, but who become engaged in creative, productive lives. A number of successful actors, singers, models, athletes, inventors, entrepreneurs, and authors have taken the non-collegiate route, choosing to use these years to become clearer about their life goals and to develop their talents (collegedropoutshalloffame.com, 2016).

FURTHER REFLECTION: Summarize the reasons that someone might drop out of college. Link each reason to possible consequences.

Examine the links between the developmental tasks of later adolescence and the decision to drop out of college.

Imagine that you are working as a residence hall advisor. What information from this chapter could you use to help counsel a student who is thinking of dropping out of school?

Analyze the possible positive and negative impact of this decision for career development, identity development, and psychosocial maturity.

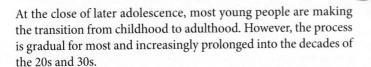

CHAPTER SUMMARY

At the close of later adolescence, most young people are making the transition from childhood to adulthood. However, the process is gradual for most and increasingly prolonged into the decades of the 20s and 30s.

OBJECTIVE 1 Explain the concept of autonomy from parents and examine the conditions under which autonomy is likely to be achieved.

Later adolescents are striving for self-sufficiency in a complex culture. Many have achieved a new degree of independence from their parents, so that ties of love, trust, and support are expressed within a framework of mutual respect and autonomous decision making. Three components of achieving autonomy from parents are discussed: leaving home, attending college, and self-sufficiency. Families and cultural groups differ in their expectations about the nature of ties to parents in young adulthood, the timing of home-leaving, and the contexts in which support for autonomy is or is not provided. In the college population, students differ in their desire and readiness to loosen ties with parents, and parents differ in the encouragement and support they provide for independent decision-making. The process of achieving autonomy from parents opens the door to new considerations of basic ego structures, including gender identity, morality, and career aspirations. In each of these areas, a young person has the cognitive ability to reflect on the earlier socialization pressures of family and neighborhood and to construct a personal point of view.

OBJECTIVE 2 Summarize the development of gender identity in later adolescence. Analyze how the components of gender-role identification that were relevant during the early-school-age period are revised and expanded.

The formulation of gender identity requires an integration of the biological, psychological, and societal meanings associated with being a man or a woman. During later adolescence, young men and women formulate their gender identities as they encounter diverse and sometimes competing social messages, role relationships, sexual motives and activities, and dyadic interactions. These gender identities are situated in interpersonal, institutional, and cultural contexts. The components of gender identification that were established in early childhood are revised and reevaluated.

New considerations are given to the ideas of gender constancy, gender role norms, and gender identifications. A sexual dimension is added to one's gender identity. These changes are taking place in the context of changing societal/historical conditions that have implications for how women and men are viewed and treated. Gender identity is a powerful lens through which many other aspects of personal identity are interpreted, including the content of values, commitment to family relationships, preferences and expectations for career choice, and beliefs about one's role in an intimate relationship.

OBJECTIVE 3 Investigate the maturation of morality in later adolescence, with special focus on the role of new cognitive capacities that influence moral judgments and the various value orientations that underlie moral reasoning.

Exposure to a diversity of information, relationships, and worldviews stimulates moral reasoning. The idea of an internalized morality is discussed as moral reasoning matures through progressive stages. Criticisms of Kohlberg's theory of moral reasoning are reviewed. Of particular interest is the focus on prosocial and caring aspects of morality. The concept of a maturing moral identity is discussed, including the expression of moral identity through a sense of purpose, civic engagement, and activism. The change from conventional to post-conventional morality that often occurs during later adolescence involves a rethinking of traditional moral principles. During this period, there may be a loosening of ties to the family of origin and an increase in encounters with an expanding network of friends, students, and coworkers. Through interactions with diverse reference groups, there is an increasing recognition of the cultural relativity of one's moral code. There may also be a degree of conflict over which moral values have personal meaning.

OBJECTIVE 4 Trace the process of career choice, with attention to education and gender-role socialization as two major influential factors.

The process of career choice, often accompanied by periods of uncertainty and confusion, is influenced by interacting factors, including personal abilities and attributes, emotional and motivational factors, family and societal factors, educational background, gender identity and gender-role socialization, and the situational realities of the current labor market. The work experiences of early adolescence are considered as a stepping stone in the career decision-making process. Three factors that influence career choice are reviewed: family context, education, and gender role socialization. A model of career decision making is presented that highlights the interaction of a maturing personal identity and a growing awareness of occupational opportunities and demands. Career decision-making self-efficacy is a concept used in the vocational development field to suggest that individuals differ in their confidence about making a sound decision. The role of the labor market and the changing nature of the world of work are discussed as they impact career decision-making. Ideally, one's choice of occupation is the result of personal experimentation, introspection, self-evaluation, fact finding, and intuition. As such, this choice becomes intimately interwoven with one's psychological development.

OBJECTIVE 5 Define and describe the psychosocial crisis of later adolescence, individual identity versus identity confusion; the central process through which this crisis is resolved, role experimentation; the prime adaptive ego quality of fidelity to values and ideals; and the core pathology of repudiation.

Those who have resolved the psychosocial crisis of individual identity versus identity confusion in the direction of identity achievement have an integrated identity that includes a definition of themselves as sexual, moral, political, and career participants. The sense of identity has both a public and a private face. It includes both content and evaluation suggesting that individuals may differ in the focus of their commitments to various aspects of work, family, ideology, and political life. The idea of identity status is explored, focusing on the two processes: crisis or exploration, and commitment. The four statuses that have received primary attention are: identity confusion, foreclosure, moratorium, and achievement.

The strain of this stage is felt in the tension between the person's need to question and experiment and the society's expectations for closure on significant themes, particularly occupation, gender identity, and political ideology. The expansion of roles and relationships exposes many young people to new views that require evaluation. The crisis of individual identity versus identity confusion suggests a new synthesis of earlier identifications, present values, and future goals into a consistent self-concept. This unity of self is achieved only after a period of uncertainty and open questioning. Role experimentation during this time is an essential strategy for coping with new information and new value orientations. Differences in how later adolescents approach the process of experimentation are reviewed. Once young people know what they stand for, they can commit themselves more deeply to others.

The prime adaptive ego quality of fidelity reflects the capacity to commit oneself to an ideology or belief system. The core pathology of repudiation suggests an intense rejection of certain values and beliefs. Although most later adolescents are forming a positive vision of the self that is connected to a shared community, some are defining themselves in opposition, as rebels, terrorists, or avengers.

OBJECTIVE 6 Examine some of the predictors and consequences of dropping out of college and hypothesize how dropping out of college may influence development in later adolescence.

The applied topic, dropping out of college, illustrates the fluidity of this period. Identity work, which requires an integration of one's biological, psychological, and social selves, takes place in concrete settings where daily demands and expectations must be met. Societal expectations set many young people on a path toward college that they cannot follow, whether for financial, academic, personal, or situational reasons. Colleges differ in their ability to foster a sense of belonging among diverse groups of students, as well as their readiness to provide academic, health, and mental health resources. The psychosocial consequences of dropping out of college are varied as reflected in individual accounts and narratives. The disruption of this academic trajectory poses significant challenges for establishing a life structure into adulthood. At the same time, it may invite more serious and considered reflection about what a person wants out of life and the activities and resources that will be required to achieve those goals.

CASEBOOK

For additional case material related to this chapter, see the case entitled "Life Turning Points and Career Choice," in *Life Span Development: A Case Book*, by Barbara and Philip Newman, Laura Landry-Meyer, and Brenda J. Lohman, pp. 153–156. The case illustrates how a young person's encounter with a difficult personal situation leads to a revised sense of self and a new focus on meaningful goals for the future.

The major themes of early adulthood—work, intimacy, marriage, and parenting—are all captured in this image of the young Harlequin family. We sense the vulnerability of a young family trying to create a life of love and tenderness in a difficult world.

1. Define and explain selected theoretical concepts that are especially relevant for understanding development during adulthood, including social roles, the life course, and fulfillment theories.

2. Analyze the process of forming intimate relationships, including initial attractions, mate selection, and commitment to a long-term relationship. Contrast the ways that different patterns of cohabitation contribute to the formation of close relationships. Summarize the challenges one faces in adjusting to the early years of marriage.

3. Describe the factors associated with the decision to have children, and evaluate the impact of childbearing on intimate relationships.

4. Define the concept of work in early adulthood and explore how work stimulates psychosocial development.

5. Examine the role of lifestyle development as an expression of an individual's personal identity, with consideration for the pace of life, balancing competing role demands, building a supportive social network, and adopting practices to promote health, fitness, and nutrition.

6. Define and describe the psychosocial crisis of intimacy versus isolation, the central process through which the crisis is resolved, mutuality among peers, the prime adaptive ego quality of love, and the core pathology of exclusivity.

7. Investigate divorce as a life stressor in early adulthood, including the factors contributing to it and the process of coping with it.

EARLY ADULTHOOD (24 TO 34 YEARS)

11

— CASE STUDY Changing Work to Recapture Love and Happiness —

A young man reflects on the delights of being in love, the disappointments of early career, and the decision to make a change.

In the course of our courting, there were frisbees-a-flying, beers-a-flowing, big bad barbeques, and more than a smattering of smooching and cuddles. Being together was easy and always.

We married in 1997, healthy, happy, and excited about our lives. All that we wanted was to be together and continue the fun and goofiness that attracted us to each other in the first place. Simple enough, seeing that we were getting married and all, right?

Change from 1998–2007 included such delights as increased pant sizes, long work hours, more doctor visits, decreased intimacy, a slump in the fun fund, fewer hours together, lack of peaceful sleep, lack of creative endeavors, and an increase in mindless spending, just to name a few.

What the hell happened during this nine year black hole of productivity, progress, and pleasure? Work happened. Two crappy jobs that we allowed to suck the life right out of us.

Fun, where ever did you go?

Mornings were filled with sullen grunts, brooding silences, sick heads and stomachs, and occasional weeping. Yes, even that. Evenings were a noxious mixture of prickliness and anxiety with the additional strain of trying to show love in the absence of the resources to make it so. The night was all tossing and turning with our minds running and repeating disturbing scenarios of the following day despite total exhaustion.

Finally, we admitted that we were very unhappy apart from each other, so we quit and opened our own guitar and tutoring studio.

Sullen morning grunts became laughter and five mile walks. The death defying and lonely commute became an animated discussion or business meeting on the way to the studio. Our commute now enjoyed together. Incompetent coworkers became employees of the month – every month. We really did hang an award on the wall of the studio too. Work hours got slashed by 50%. Evenings became filled with conversation, reading, and excitement over our tasty vittles. I can feel the excitement over the changes even now as I write and relive the lifting of the immense burdens of the past! Before we sleep, there is usually one more fit of giggles about some asinine thing we said or did. And night time now was filled with blissful, peaceful, complete, high-quality sleep – oblivion.

We wanted and got our time together back. And now that we have it, we clench it in our jaws like a rabid Tasmanian devil with a chip on its striped shoulder. And fun has returned screaming with vengeance.

Selected from "The more we get together," by C. J. Renzi, 2013. retrieved from http://www.thechangeblog.com/get-together/

CASE ANALYSIS Using What You Know

1. Discuss how concepts from social role theory are illustrated in this case. What are the key roles that a person is likely to enact in early adulthood? How might these roles enhance each other? Conflict with each other?

2. What are the sources of happiness and fulfillment that are central to this case? Describe some possible consequences of getting drawn into a work role that does not promote fulfillment.

3. Think about the period of early adulthood as a time for establishing a lifestyle that is in harmony with the goals, values, and commitments that were formed in later adolescence. Analyze how the case illustrates this idea. What are some reasons that young adults might experience uncertainty and a need to change? Evaluate the costs and benefits of making major lifestyle changes during this stage.

4. Speculate about the characteristics of the couple that will be central to their ability to weather their lifestyle change and support their marital satisfaction as well as their occupational well-being.

Welcome to the study of adulthood. All that has gone before can be seen as preparation; all that follows can be viewed as actualization. We have considered psychosocial development through seven preparatory stages of life, encompassing approximately 24 years. During these stages, an individual undergoes rapid physical, cognitive, social, and emotional development. In the United States, life expectancy at birth is currently about 79 years. Thus, 55 years or more remain after the seven preparatory stages. In our conceptual scheme, four stages of psychosocial development unfold during these 55 years. In this chapter, we discuss a few theoretical concepts that help account for the direction of development in adulthood. Then we address the developmental tasks and psychosocial crisis of the stage of early adulthood. ●

Expanding Theoretical Views of Adult Development

OBJECTIVE 1   Define and explain selected theoretical concepts that are especially relevant for understanding development during adulthood, including social roles, the life course, and fulfillment theories.

In chapter 2 (Major Theories for Understanding Human Development) and chapter 3 (Psychosocial Theory) we introduced a variety of theoretical concepts that explain the processes of continuity and change over the life span. In this chapter, we expand the discussion of theoretical constructs that help account for the directions of growth in adult life. The biological, psychological, and societal systems continue to interact, but the nature of lives becomes increasingly diverse and more difficult to characterize as stage-like over time. Life stories are guided by historical events, unexpected crises and opportunities, and personal choices. New levels of mastery, autonomy, and agency allow individuals to make decisions and choices about the kinds of environments in which they participate. In addition, the autonomy of adult life allows individuals to express their genetic predispositions to a greater degree than when their parents, teachers, and other authority figures were creating their environments and constraining their choices. The bidirectional nature of development is increasingly obvious in adulthood as interests, beliefs, and goals guide the direction and focus of actions, and these actions and their consequences in turn create the contexts for the revision of interests, beliefs, and goals. In the following sections, we review the concepts of social roles, the life course, and personal fulfillment, ideas that help explain the psychosocial dynamics of adulthood.

Social Roles

Social role is one of the concepts most frequently used for understanding adulthood. The major concepts of social role theory, which were introduced in chapter 2, are summarized in Table 11.1. We relied on concepts from social role theory frequently in the analysis of childhood and adolescent life stages, including chapter 7 when we discussed gender-role identification and again in chapter 10 when we examined individual identity versus identity confusion. The concept of role experimentation is the central process of that period. Clearly, many roles are learned and enacted during childhood. In adulthood, however, people assume multiple roles that expand their opportunities for self-expression and bring them into contact with new social demands. Adulthood can be seen as a series of increasingly differentiated and complex roles that the individual plays for substantial lengths of time. The salient roles of adulthood, such as worker, spouse, friend, parent, teacher, mentor, volunteer, or community leader, give structure to adult identity and meaning to life.

Social roles link individuals to their social environments. The roles that an individual plays exist as socially shared patterns of expectations for behavior. All roles can be characterized by costs and benefits that accumulate over time. For example, by assuming the role of worker, one has access to the benefits associated with the role, which might include social status, social support, health benefits, or financial resources. One also becomes responsible for meeting the expectations of the role, such as working for a certain number of hours each week or completing one's work to a certain

Bret's wife, Maureen, is already off to an early morning meeting. His daughter, Cheryl, is eating the breakfast that her mother left out on the counter for her. But she can't quite reach her milk. Bret is checking his emails and materials online for his first meeting while he talks to Cheryl's preschool to let them know that she will be picked up at noon by Suzie, her babysitter. Bret is getting pretty good at balancing the roles of husband, father, worker, and household manager. It's lucky they don't have a dog!

standard of quality. Over one's life, the costs and benefits of the roles accumulate, influencing the ease or difficulty with which new roles and role transitions can be managed (Jackson, 2004). For example, if a person's worker role involves many short-term jobs with no retirement benefits, the transition to retirement may be more difficult financially, but the person may have less identification with a specific worker role and find the transition into

Table 11.1	Major Concepts of Social Role Theory
Concept	**Explanation**
Social role	Parts or identities a person assumes that are also social positions: kinship roles, age roles, gender roles, occupational roles
Role enactment	Patterned characteristics of social behavior generated by a social role
Role expectations	Scripts or shared expectations for behavior that are linked to each role
Role gain	Addition of roles
Role strain	Stress caused by too many expectations within a role
Role conflict	Conflict caused by competing demands of different roles
Role loss	Ending of a role; may result in stress and disorientation
Dimensions of life roles that vary from person to person	Number of roles Intensity of involvement in roles Time demands of each role Structure or flexibility of the role

© Cengage

retirement psychologically easier. As illustrated in the opening case, young adults may conclude that the costs of the worker role outweigh the benefits, and new work roles have to be discovered.

Roles are *reciprocal*, requiring complementary role identities—such as teacher-student, parent-child—in order to be enacted and sustained. Thus, participation in multiple roles brings with it a form of **social integration** and social support (Thoits, 2012; Wethington, Moen, Glasgow, & Pillemer, 2000). Involvement in multiple roles allows adults to help socialize younger generations. Only in adulthood do individuals experience the behavioral requirements of many of their roles, which in turn provide a basis on which to socialize their children for the demands of adulthood (Kite, 1996).

The expectations associated with adult roles provide a frame of reference within which individuals make their own personal decisions. For example, a man may know what is expected of him in the worker role, but he may choose to ignore those expectations and strive for greater responsibilities, more power, or more autonomy. People can conform to role expectations, revise them, or reject them altogether. In addition to the tensions produced by role conflicts and role strain, some of the stresses of adulthood result from the need to redefine certain role expectations in order to preserve an authentic sense of self.

Role theory offers several ideas about factors that may impede optimal growth or increase the risks for disruptions in development (Newman & Newman, 2016). First, individuals may be unable to meet role expectations due to physical, cognitive, or emotional limitations. For example, chronic illness or injury may make it impossible for a person to continue in a particular job. Severe postpartum depression may impair a woman's ability to parent her infant. Being too short, too tall, or having poor eyesight may prevent someone from following a desired career path.

A second factor that may place individuals at risk is the possibility of role conflict, role overload, or role strain. Especially in adulthood, individuals experience many highly demanding roles. When these roles are particularly salient, as with parenting and work roles, a person may find that he or she simply cannot meet all the expectations of each role adequately. Role strain is a form of stress that can result in physical and mental health problems.

A third factor that may result in risk is uncontrolled or unwanted role loss, like unemployment, widowhood, or nonvoluntary retirement. To the extent that a social role provides a structure for personal identity and social integration, role loss can bring serious problems of alienation and social isolation.

Life Course

Life course refers to the integration and sequencing of phases of **work** and family life over time. Glen Elder (1985, 1996; Elder & Giele, 2009; Elder & Shanahan, 2006), a leader in the elaboration of the life course perspective, described the two central themes of **trajectories** and **transitions**. A trajectory is the path of one's life experiences in a specific domain, particularly work and family. The family trajectory might include marriage, parenthood, grandparenthood, and widowhood. A transition is the beginning or ending of an event or role relationship. In the work trajectory, for

example, transitions might be getting one's first job, being fired, and going back to school for an advanced degree. Transitions are the events that make up a lifelong trajectory. A person's work and family trajectories are embedded in a sociohistorical context. For example, for people born in the early 1920s, the events of World War II, occurring during their 20s, influenced their work and family formation. For many young men, the planned work trajectory was interrupted by military service, and many young women entered the labor market unexpectedly. At the close of the war, in the late 1940s and early 1950s, many couples who had delayed parenting started their families, which gave rise to the baby boom generation.

The life course concept can be applied to the content of individual life histories as they are expressed in a social and historical time period. Each person's life course can be thought of as a pattern of the adaptations to the configuration of cultural expectations, resources, and barriers experienced during a particular time period. One form of cultural expectations is what Bernice Neugarten and her colleagues (Neugarten, Moore, & Lowe, 1965) termed the **social clock**. This term refers to "age norms and age expectations [that] operate as prods and brakes upon behavior, in some instances hastening behavior and in some instances delaying it" (p. 710). Neugarten and her associates suggested that social class groups tend to agree on the appropriate age for significant life events, such as marriage, childrearing, and retirement. This consensus exerts social pressure on individuals in the group, pushing them to assume a particular role at an expected age. Age norms may also suppress behaviors that are considered inappropriate for one's age. Adults are aware of existing norms regarding the timing of certain behaviors and evaluate their own behaviors as being on time, too soon, or too late.

Implied in the notion of the social clock are expectations about **role sequencing**, the pattern or order of entry or exit from new roles and age-related role transitions. For example, European American adults in the United States tend to view an ideal sequence as work, marriage, and parenting, in that order. Research indicates that for women, following this sequence is associated with better mental health, including less depression and greater happiness in adulthood. Among African Americans, however, the sequence of work, parenting, and then marriage is associated with less depression and greater happiness. This suggests that different social norms for role sequencing may be operating in the respective ethnic communities (Jackson, 2004). The social clock is constantly being reset as people confront the challenges, demands, and new structures of modern society. For example, the age of first marriage in the United States is moving closer to 30; while it was very typical for young people in the 1960s to marry at age 21 or 22, very few college students today expect to be married at that age. In contemporary society, with the lengthening of the life expectancy and the increasing vitality of older adults, there are fewer and fewer domains in which a person is considered too old to participate (Neugarten, 1990).

FIGURE 11.1 ▶ provides a hypothetical view of the age-linked changes in occupational and family careers. The figure maps the convergence of transitions across the occupational and family trajectories, illustrating periods of potential harmony and conflict between the demands in the two trajectories. The bottom

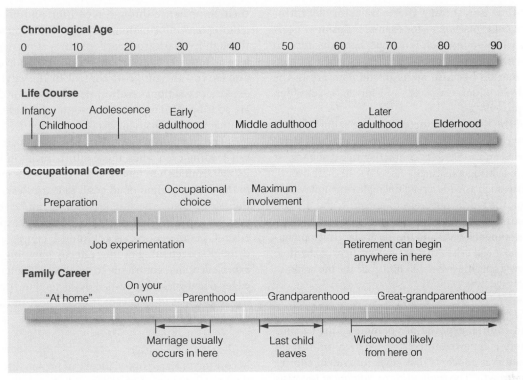

FIGURE 11.1 ▶ A HYPOTHETICAL LIFE COURSE
Source: Adapted from Atchley, 1975.

line shows transitions in a family career. The line above shows transitions in an occupational career. Sometimes these transitions occur around the same time in life. For example, in Figure 11.1, marriage occurs during a period of job experimentation when a person may be changing jobs. This could create tension in the marriage if it results in economic insecurity. Occupational experimentation might be cut short in order to establish financial stability for the marriage. The conflicts that arise in coordinating these family and occupational careers may contribute to the high divorce rate in the first years following marriage. Considering adult lives in contemporary society, one can appreciate that this is only one possible map of the interconnections between work and family in the course of a life. The timing and overlap of occupational and family careers look quite different for the following people: a woman who extends her educational preparation to include a professional degree, works before marriage, and delays childbearing into her middle to late 30s; a woman who remains single and voluntarily childless, and dedicates her energy to excellence in a career; and a woman who marries right after high school, begins having children at age 18, works during her childbearing years, and then retires at 55 to enjoy her grandchildren and her personal freedom.

The pattern of the life course is influenced by the *historical era* (Schaie & Elder, 2005). The life course of a person who was born in 1900 and died in 1975, including the ages of completion of educational attainment, entry into the labor market, marriage, and retirement, would look quite different from that of a person born in 1930 and reaching age 75 in 2005. The two people would have gone through the same chronological ages, but during different periods of history, with different opportunities, expectations,

and challenges. The first person would have been 30 at the time of the Great Depression. Her family could have been seriously influenced by loss of employment, difficulty in finding work, and loss of savings for retirement. The second person would have been 30 in 1960. Having served in the military during the Korean War, he would have been eligible for the GI Bill benefits to go to college, resulting in new occupational opportunities that contribute to occupational advancement during a booming economy (MacLean & Elder, 2007). There are many other possibilities of historical impact; these examples illustrate how historical factors might affect the life course.

All the people who are roughly the same age during a particular historical period are referred to as a **cohort**. The following list reflects the names given to particular generations in the United States and their estimated birth years. The cohorts are characterized by their shared exposure to historical events, prevailing economic conditions, and cultural/technological conditions (Robinson, 2016).

The Greatest Generation	1910–1925
The Silent Generation	1923–1944
Baby Boomer Generation	1945–1964
Generation X	1961–1981
Generation Y	1975–1995
The Millennials	
Generation Z	1995–2015

Differences in medical advances, occupational opportunities, educational resources, and the number of people in the cohort are four factors that may affect the pattern of life events for cohort members. Moreover, major crises, such as war, famine, and political unrest, may alter a trajectory by introducing unanticipated transitions—for example, closing off certain activities, as when young men interrupt their education to go to war, or opening up new opportunities, as when women enter the labor market because many of the men are in the military (Elder, 1986; Elder, Caspi, & van Nguyen, 1986; Elder, Shanahan, & Clipp, 1997).

The study of the life course focuses on the sequencing of events and the psychological growth that occurs as adults strive to adjust to changing and sometimes conflicting role demands. At different ages, people bring a distinct perspective to these events. For example, a crisis such as widespread unemployment may have a direct impact on the work trajectory of an adult, and also on the family environment or educational opportunities of a child. The person's developmental level and the particular developmental tasks and psychosocial crises that are most salient at the time will determine how a specific event will influence the life course.

Fulfillment Theories

As the norms and cultural expectations of modern life become more flexible, there is renewed interest in personal fulfillment and self-actualization as concepts that guide individual choices and directions for growth. The *humanistic* or *fulfillment* theorists emphasize the purposive, goal-oriented strivings that characterize adult life. The **fulfillment theories** have become integrated into the field of *positive psychology*, the scientific study of the strengths and virtues that enable individuals and communities to thrive (Seligman, 2011; Seligman, Parks, & Steen, 2006).

Charlotte Buhler was one of the earliest and most continuously productive of the humanistic or fulfillment theorists. Her work emphasized the centrality of life goals and intentionality through the life course (Buhler & Massarik, 1968). In her view, each person experiences life within a complex orientation to past, present, and future time. It is the hope for meeting future goals and for achieving a sense of fulfillment that prompts psychological growth. Buhler saw the years of early and middle adulthood as a time of setting definite goals and striving to achieve them. Toward the end of middle adulthood, there is focused preoccupation with the assessment of goals and the analysis of successes and failures. This process ends with a sense of fulfillment, partial fulfillment, or despair.

The last phase of life is seen as a reaction to this assessment. People may resign themselves to their successes and failures (as Erikson suggests in the concept of integrity). However, some people may be motivated to return to an earlier phase of striving to achieve unfulfilled goals or to undo past failures. Some people end their lives in a despondent state of unfulfillment, concluding that their existence has not been meaningful. Three concepts from fulfillment theory are especially relevant for understanding the directions of growth in adulthood: competence, self-acceptance, and self-actualization.

Competence

Robert White (1959; 1960, 1966) introduced the term **competence motivation** to explain behaviors that are motivated by a desire for new levels of mastery and control. People strive to increase their competence through repetition and practice of skills, by gaining new information, through education and training, and through feedback from earlier efforts at mastery. Exploration is a basic human behavior that results in opportunities to expand and extend the range of control in the environment. When exploratory actions result in new mastery or competence, they are accompanied by positive emotions of pride, satisfaction, and confidence (Heckhausen, 2011).

The competence motive can be seen in an infant's efforts at self-feeding even when those efforts result in less food making its way from dish to mouth. The competence motive can be seen in the determination of an adult to learn to ski despite the cold, the expense, and the sore muscles. It can be seen when retired persons enroll in adult education courses to expand their knowledge. Over the course of adulthood, competence is expanded through a deepening of interests, by pursuing information and experiences that contribute to what we often term expert knowledge. When goals are reached or deemed unattainable, the adaptive response is to disengage from the goal and set one's sights on new areas of mastery.

Self-Acceptance

According to Carl Rogers' theory of personality development, an essential component of continued growth is to experience and accept the authentic self (Rogers, 1959, 1961). This means achieving a sense of trust in one's ideas and impulses rather than denying or constantly disapproving of them. It means fostering acceptance and trust in relationships with others so that people bring their most authentic selves into interactions. **Self-acceptance** is a product of the positive feelings that come from being direct and from the acceptance one receives from others.

In Rogers' view, barriers to self-acceptance come largely from conditions that others place on their **love** or approval. If significant others give approval based only on meeting certain conditions, then the person learns to modify his behavior so that it conforms to those conditions. However, these modifications are made at the price of self-acceptance. They lead a person into a pattern of inhibiting or rejecting new thoughts and relying more and more on the opinions of others. The greater the discrepancy between the authentic self as one perceives it and daily experience, the more one is likely to experience life as threatening and stressful. The greater the harmony between the authentic self and experience, the more likely one is to experience a sense of trust, freedom, and creativity in daily functioning. An implication of this theory is that well-being is a product of person–environment coadaptation. In the search for self-acceptance, the person seeks social settings where his or her thoughts, beliefs, and actions are highly valued and where the social setting can be modified to value and endorse the talents of those who participate in it.

Self-Actualization

According to Abraham Maslow's theory, human beings are always in a state of striving (Maslow, 1968). **Self-actualization** is a powerful, growth-oriented motive that sits atop a pyramid of needs (see FIGURE 11.2 ▶). In Maslow's view, the primary human motives concern physiological needs, such as hunger, thirst, and

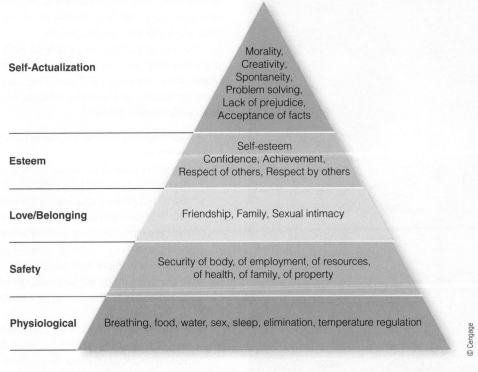

FIGURE 11.2 ▶ MASLOW'S HIERARCHY OF NEEDS

Self-Actualization
Morality,
Creativity,
Spontaneity,
Problem solving,
Lack of prejudice,
Acceptance of facts

Esteem
Self-esteem
Confidence, Achievement,
Respect of others, Respect by others

Love/Belonging
Friendship, Family, Sexual intimacy

Safety
Security of body, of employment, of resources,
of health, of family, of property

Physiological
Breathing, food, water, sex, sleep, elimination, temperature regulation

© Cengage

a need for sleep. The second level focuses on safety and security—the need to find protection from dangers and threats. At this level, one might include security of employment, safety for oneself and one's family, and concerns about one's health and the health of one's family. As those needs are satisfied and maintained at a relatively stable level, people direct their energy to satisfying needs for belongingness and love, including friendship, intimate relationships, family and kinship ties, and desired group belonging. At the next level, one is motivated to enhance and protect self-esteem by building confidence in oneself, achieving valued goals, and gaining the respect and admiration of others. Finally, if those needs can be met and sustained, the person directs energy to self-actualization, a motive to make optimal use of one's full potential, to become a fully effective, creative participant in daily life. The need for self-actualization, like White's idea of competence, becomes a driving force, urging the person to seek new levels of insight and fulfillment. People who are characterized as self-actualized are described as authentic, having a reality-based orientation about themselves and others. They are spontaneous, interested in solving problems, and accepting of others. They lack prejudice. These qualities result from a continuous force toward growth as the richness of a person's human capacities are allowed to flourish (Maslow, 1943).

The fulfillment theories suggest that growth and maturation in adulthood are characterized by successful encounters with life challenges that result in a sense of purpose, meaning, and mastery. Building on the concepts of fulfillment theories, Carol Ryff developed a measure of psychological well-being, a multidimensional construct based on six dimensions: self-acceptance, quality ties to others, a sense of autonomy in thought and action, environmental mastery, purpose in life, and continued growth (Ryff, 1989; Ryff & Keyes, 1995; Seifert, 2016). Well-being, measured according to these dimensions, is associated with the capacity to sustain a positive outlook in the face of discrimination and adversity. A sense of meaning and purpose can support resilience in the face of illness and serve as a protective factor to reduce the risks of disease (Ruini & Ryff, 2016; Ryff, 2014).

In summary, the concepts of life roles, the life course, and fulfillment theories extend our understanding of psychosocial development in adulthood. Childhood is over. One addresses life with great expectations and exhilaration as well as the realization that there is serious work to be done. Young adults engage in intense and meaningful relationships in marriage or with intimate partners, friends, and coworkers. They attempt to cope with the complex challenges of daily life by balancing multiple roles. At the same time, they put into action the practices that express the values and beliefs to which they became committed at the close of later adolescence. They establish and revise goals, setting new standards for competence and self-acceptance. Over the course of adulthood, people return periodically to reflect on the meaning of their life and the value of their accomplishments. The expanding periods of later adulthood and elderhood provide new opportunities to seek self-actualization and moments of joy through intense dedication to personal and interpersonal achievements.

FURTHER REFLECTION: Explain how the three theories—social role theory, life course theory, and fulfillment theory—extend psychosocial theory as a framework for understanding development in adulthood.

Oprah Winfrey personifies Maslow's theory of self-actualization. She has overcome the challenges of her early childhood to found a business empire that has made her one of the wealthiest women in the world. Along the way she won an Oscar for her performance in the movie *The Color Purple*, became a model of integrity, dignity, generosity, and compassion through her philanthropic initiatives, and inspired American television audiences with the highest rated television talk show for 25 years. In 2013 she received the Presidential Medal of Freedom. In making this award to Oprah and others, President Obama reflected the essence of fulfillment theory in these words: "These are the men and women who in their extraordinary lives remind us all of the beauty of the human spirit, the values that define us as Americans, the potential that lives inside of all of us."

How does culture shape the way adulthood is defined? Based on your experience and knowledge, how do cultures differ in the milestones that mark adult status or maturity?

Developmental Tasks

We have identified the period from ages 24 to 34 as early adulthood. For many, this is a time of continued uncertainty as people begin to make essential commitments to work, relationships, lifestyles, and ideologies that express the content of their personal identities. The nature of early adulthood has changed dramatically over the past 60 years, from a time when young people moved with some deliberate focus into roles that they expected would be stable and long-lasting to a time of many more transitions and temporary commitments.

The current cohort of people in early adulthood have been given the label of Generation Y, or millennials. These young adults, born between 1975 and 1995, are children of the baby boom generation and have shared some of the following life experiences (Robinson, 2016):

- Grew up in a time when the majority of homes had a computer.
- Explosive growth in online companies such as Google, Facebook, Amazon, LinkedIn, and Paypal. Widespread use of cell phones and Internet services.
- The 9/11 terrorist attacks on the World Trade Center and the Pentagon, resulting in the Patriot Act, which permitted new, pervasive changes in security practices, surveillance, and monitoring of individuals. The attack also resulted in the invasion of Afghanistan, the search for Osama Bin Laden and other leaders of Al-Qaeda, and the removal of the Taliban.
- President G. W. Bush, Vice President Cheney, and Secretary of Defense Rumsfeld deceived the nation about Iraq having weapons of mass destruction, resulting in the invasion of Iraq.
- In 2008, the largest economic decline since the Great Depression, with many families losing their homes to foreclosures, and widespread unemployment.
- Growing consensus about global warming, an accompanying emphasis on energy conservation and eco-friendly products and consumer practices.
- Widespread changes in the workplace including increases in part-time, flex-time, and work from home with accompanying decreases in health care benefits and retirement benefits.
- An increasing divide in fundamental beliefs and values between the Republican and Democratic parties, resulting in a growing public frustration with government's inability to address important domestic issues.

Recall Figure 10.1 from chapter 10 that compared the percentage of young people who completed the transition to adulthood in 1960 to those who completed this transition in 2000. The five criteria for the transition to adulthood as defined in that figure are leaving home, finishing school, becoming financially independent, getting married, and having a child. By 2000, only 31 percent of men and 46 percent of women had made this complete transition by the age of 30. It is certainly possible to feel like an adult even if one has not completed all of these behaviors. Yet, for most young people, the list captures the essence of a cultural definition of adult status, and, as such, provides a framework for the psychological sense of maturity. In the 10 years from age 24 to 34, most young adults are striving to enact the key life roles of worker, intimate partner, community member, and parent that will reflect their ability to take responsibility for themselves, make important decisions about their lives, and begin to care for others.

The developmental tasks of this period have a lot to do with the person's ability to form effective relationships. The establishment of a sense of intimacy with a marital or cohabiting partner requires movement toward a greater sharing of personal feelings, secrets, and ways of looking at the world. Sometimes the demand is to listen; sometimes to listen and offer advice; sometimes to be understanding and helpful. Another set of behaviors that develops during this period involves establishing effective relationships at work. Getting along with associates, responding to authority figures, and having respectful relationships with clients or customers are keys to success. Parenting is another type of relationship of considerable responsibility. Becoming a parent is a role that most people are not terribly well prepared for, and as a result, there is a great deal of learning by doing. Becoming a parent means creating a new relationship that is distinct from any role in one's past—blending the caregiver, planner, and disciplinarian in a balance that changes frequently as the child matures. These three key relationships—intimate partner, worker, and parent—form the basic structure of the lifestyle that is enacted in early adulthood.

The pathway into adulthood is taking longer and is more diverse today than it was in the 1960s. Some young adults who do not go to college directly after high school may later enroll in college. Some later adolescents enter the military and return to civilian life to begin their early adulthood as veterans. The period of job experimentation is lasting longer, with many young adults making multiple job and career changes before settling into a career. The nature of the labor market is changing, with new occupations emerging and others falling away. The average age of entry into marriage is now the late 20s for women and the early 30s for men. Many marriages end in divorce. For many, early adulthood is a time of multiple intimate relationships. A significant percentage of early adults are in cohabiting relationships that do not end in marriage. Later age at marriage is associated with an older age for first childbearing. All these factors reflect a lifestyle in early adulthood that is more fluid and transitional than it has been in the past. At the same time, one must keep in mind the diversity of life stories. Some young adults assume significant role responsibilities, autonomy from their family, and self-sufficiency at relatively young ages. Others delay the typical commitments of adulthood well into their 30s and beyond.

Exploring Intimate Relationships

OBJECTIVE 2 Analyze the process of forming intimate relationships, including initial attractions, mate selection, and commitment to a long-term relationship. Contrast the ways that different patterns of cohabitation contribute to the formation of close relationships. Summarize the challenges one faces in adjusting to the early years of marriage.

The period of early adulthood is a time when men and women explore the possibility of forming relationships that combine emotional closeness, shared interests, a shared vision of the future, and sexual intimacy. Most young people become involved in romantic relationships that involve both sexual and emotional intimacy. Many forms of intimate relationships in addition to

marriage are established including serious dating and **cohabitation** with or without the intention of marriage.

Marriage is one context in which work on intimate social relationships takes place. In 2015, 85 percent of the U.S. population had been married at least once by ages 40 to 49, and 96 percent had been married at least once by ages 75 to 84. The main change in the marriage pattern in the United States over the past 50 years is that more young adults postpone marriage until the end of their 20s. In 2015, 54 percent of women and 67 percent of men ages 25 to 29 had never been married. It is now normative for men and women to be single throughout their 20s (U.S. Census Bureau, 2015d, Table A1).

Delaying the age at marriage is related to other social trends, including having children at a later age, smaller projected family size, and, therefore, fewer years devoted to childrearing. Delaying age at marriage is also related to increased sexual exploration for single people. The 1980s brought the uncoupling of sexual activity, marriage, and childbearing. Younger age at entry into sexual activity and increases in rates of affairs and cohabitation suggest that even though many young adults do not marry, they become involved in intimate relationships during their twenties.

Readiness to Form Intimate Relationships

What factors are important in determining a person's readiness for a long-term commitment? From a psychosocial perspective, one can hypothesize that work on personal identity must be far enough along so that the possibility of a deep, emotional involvement with another person will be regarded as exciting rather than frightening. In studies of college students, a relationship has been found between identity status and the quality of intimacy. Students who had an achieved identity also reported the most genuine intimate relationships. In contrast, those who were characterized as identity confused were the least intimate and the most isolated (Montgomery, 2005; Seiffge-Krenke & Beyers, 2016). An overview of studies focusing on the relationship of identity and intimacy supports this relationship, although the link seems to be somewhat stronger for men than for women (Arseth, Kroger, Martinussen, & Marcia, 2009).

Early and later adolescents are likely to be thinking about intimacy issues long before their work on identity is completed. Thus, it makes sense to think that the capacity for intimacy emerges alongside identity work (Adams & Archer, 1994). However, when faced with dilemmas in which needs for identity and intimacy conflict, later adolescents tend to give identity issues higher priority. The following example and others like it were presented to adolescents to determine whether identity or intimacy would be the primary developmental issue guiding an important decision.

> Allison has been accepted to a very prestigious college with a reputation for a high-quality English department. She knows she wants to major in English. The main drawback to this college is that it is a 6-hour driving distance from her boyfriend. She also has been accepted to a college located within an hour away from her boyfriend, which has an average English department. She is unsure of which one to choose. How much

consideration should be given to each of the following issues in resolving this dilemma?

a. The quality of the program
b. The distance from her boyfriend

Why? (Lacombe & Gay, 1998, p. 801)

In this study, young people placed greater emphasis on the identity-oriented solutions, those that relate to the quality of the program and the importance of a high-quality education, rather than on the intimacy-oriented solutions. However, women were more likely than men to try to balance the two, seeking ways to meet identity and intimacy needs in the same solution (Lacombe & Gay, 1998).

In addition to identity achievement, school enrollment as well as educational and occupational aspirations are linked to relationship commitment. Young adults who are still in school are less likely to make a serious long-term commitment to an intimate partner, either through marriage or through cohabitation, than those who have completed school (Thornton, Axinn, & Teachman, 1995). Educational and occupational goals, and cultural views about the value of marriage create community expectations about the ideal age at marriage. The ideal age for marriage tends to be younger in a working-class community than in a middle-class community because expectations for continued education are not as great (Teachman, Tedrow, & Kim, 2012). In contrast, young people who attend college have a later timetable for marriage. Advanced education delays marriage more frequently for women than for men, perhaps because young women who have had more years of education have alternative means to secure economic resources. Nonetheless, college graduates are more likely to marry and less likely to intend to remain single than those who have never graduated from high school (Mahay & Lewin, 2007).

Readiness for a long-term intimate relationship may also be determined by other aspects of one's personal agenda, such as reaching a certain level of achievement in one's career, completing military service, or earning a certain income. Individuals with these ambitions are less likely to seek a long-term partner or to be receptive to expressions of love from someone than they may be once the goal is achieved.

Readiness to Marry

What determines whether an intimate relationship will end in matrimony? A basic factor is the person's underlying desire to marry. In the United States, most people hope to marry. In a national sample of individuals ages 18 to 89 in U.S. households, people who were single, heterosexual, and not in a steady romantic relationship were asked the following question: "If the right person came along, would you like to be married?" Over 3,000 respondents were categorized into five age groups: 18–24, 25–34, 35–44, 45–54, and 55–69. Answers were coded as yes or no. Overall, only 5 percent of respondents were single and had no desire to marry. This percentage was higher in the youngest age group (about 7 percent) and the oldest age group (about 10 percent), and lower in the three middle age groups (about 3 percent to 4 percent). In addition to age, having been divorced, having

children, and not being employed were all associated with a lack of intention to marry (Mahay & Lewin, 2007).

In the United States, although expectations that one will marry are strong, young adults have the freedom to follow their own timetables for marriage and choice of a partner. Cultural values of individualism and autonomy provide support and justification for addressing personal goals prior to making a commitment to an intimate relationship. With greater geographic mobility, young adults are more likely to make nontraditional partner choices, including interracial and same-sex unions (Rosenfeld & Kim, 2005). However, in some ethnic groups, such as Asian Indians and Arab Americans, there is still a strong expectation that parents will guide the selection of a marriage partner. In other groups, such as the Mormons, the high value placed on sexual abstinence prior to marriage results in an earlier age at marriage than for other groups (DeGenova, 1997).

Phases in the Selection of a Partner

In the United States and other individualist cultures, most people believe that **romantic love**, usually defined as a combination of physical attraction, exhilaration in the presence of the loved one, and a strong desire to care for, protect, and be physically close to the loved one, is the central reason for choosing a marriage partner. In societies with a more collectivist orientation, romantic love is not necessarily relevant to the selection of a partner. In these cultures, the choice may be made by family members, based on religious, financial, or family background factors believed to contribute to a good match, not only for the person, but also for the extended family system. In these cultural groups, the principle of **endogamy**, or marriage within one's well-defined group, is encouraged. An Asian Indian college student of Muslim faith describes her orientation toward marriage:

> A few years ago I fell in love with a Hindu guy, but after a while I realized I had to end the relationship. My mom, it would have broken her heart. I care too much about my family. People would look down on my parents if I married outside of our religion.... Muslims are good people. We are very focused. We have morals. I want to give my children that sense of identity. So I'm comfortable waiting until I meet an acceptable Muslim man. (Belsky, 1997, p. 279)

FIGURE 11.3 ▶ provides a theoretical model including four phases of increasing involvement in the mate selection process (Adams, 1986). The model suggests a dynamic process where movement toward new levels of intimacy and commitment can be advanced or deterred depending on how the partners interact, the nature of alternative attractions, and the social contexts that support or undermine the relationship. At each phase, the relationship may be terminated if the key issues produce undesirable information or negative assessment of the partner. Also, the relationship may end if an alternative attraction becomes so strong that it reduces investment in the first relationship. The alternative attraction may be another person, a job, school, or the desire to achieve a personal goal. In contrast, investment in the relationship may increase if no attractive or acceptable alternatives are available (Stanley, Rhoades, & Whitton, 2010).

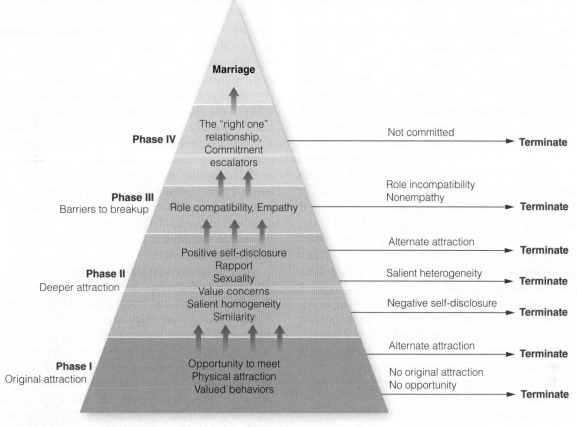

Marriage

Phase IV
The "right one" relationship, Commitment escalators
— Not committed → **Terminate**

Phase III
Barriers to breakup
Role compatibility, Empathy
— Role incompatibility / Nonempathy → **Terminate**

Phase II
Deeper attraction
Positive self-disclosure
Rapport
Sexuality
Value concerns
Salient homogeneity
Similarity
— Alternate attraction → **Terminate**
— Salient heterogeneity → **Terminate**
— Negative self-disclosure → **Terminate**

Phase I
Original attraction
Opportunity to meet
Physical attraction
Valued behaviors
— Alternate attraction → **Terminate**
— No original attraction / No opportunity → **Terminate**

FIGURE 11.3 ▶ THE MATE SELECTION PROCESS IN THE UNITED STATES
Source: Based on Adams, 1986.

Phase I: Original Attraction. Phase I, original attraction, captures the early process of partner identification. *Initial impressions* are formed in the first few seconds of an interaction. Many of these cues are captured through eye contact and a scan of a person's face (Jones et al., 2010; Perrett, 2012). Several brain circuits are involved in this rapid evaluation. One system is activated more when the face is a person of the desired sex; one system is activated when the face is attractive as compared to unattractive; and one system is activated when the person is judged as a "good match for me" (Cooper, Dunne, Furey, & O'Doherty, 2012; Hahn & Perrett, 2014). The positive "reward value" of these faces at the neural level has motivational implications. The observer is willing to expend more effort to see the face again, suggesting a path toward repeated contact.

In an experimental study, women were shown pictures of men's faces. These same men had been assessed as to whether they preferred pictures of adults or pictures of infants. Their testosterone levels were assessed using a saliva sample. Women were shown the photographs of these men and asked to rate them on four dimensions: likes children, masculine, physically attractive, and kind. They were also asked to rate each man's attractiveness as a short-term romantic partner and as a long-term partner in a committed relationship. Based on facial cues alone, women were able to differentiate the men who preferred the pictures of infants from those who preferred pictures of adults. From these photographs women also rated the men who had higher testosterone

levels as more masculine. In their assessment of short- and long-term relationships, the photos that women rated as more masculine and physically attractive were the ones they rated most highly for a short-term relationship. The photos women rated as kind, likes children, and physically attractive were most highly rated for a long-term relationship; masculinity was no longer a salient feature for these ratings. Research supports the view that for women, initial attraction can be based on facial cues and that the importance of various cues depends on the kind of relationship the woman is seeking (Roney, Hanson, Durante, & Maestripieri, 2006).

The principle of **homogamy** means that people are attracted to others who share important areas of similarity. Three salient aspects of similarity are race, religion, and educational level. In a study of three levels of relationship commitment—sexually intimate partners, cohabiting couples, and married couples—the couples showed high levels of similarity (Blackwell & Lichter, 2000, 2004). However, similarity extends beyond these basic demographic characteristics. For example, in a study of dating and mating preferences among college students, women preferred to date men who were similar to them in education and occupational level and preferred to marry someone who was also similar in religious values and desire for children (Knox, Zusman, & Nieves, 1997). Other studies show that couples are similar in their preferences for leisure, their political orientation, and whether their parents had been divorced or not (Wolfinger, 2003).

In a study of 12,000 Dutch couples, partners were found to be significantly similar with regard to health indicators. Individuals whose partners were in poor health were significantly more likely to report being in poor health themselves than individuals whose partners were in good health. Although there were patterns of accumulated health problems within households, the young couples who had been together only a short time were just as similar in their health as older couples who had been together for years. The researcher concluded that the similarity in health status was more a result of initial similarities than a product of the impact of shared circumstances over years of marriage (Monden, 2007).

Partners are selected from among those who are available for interaction. In the most general sense, the choice of a partner depends on the network of interactions in which one is involved. Many of the choices one makes during adolescence and young adulthood—such as where to go to college, where to work, which activities and social functions to attend, and where to take a vacation—determine who one meets. People who occupy similar settings such as neighborhoods, college environments, work settings, or religious institutions are likely to be similar in certain characteristics that contribute to the observed homogamy in couples (Kalmijn & Flap, 2001). People who do not perceive themselves as having desirable qualities or who view the pool of potential partners as undesirable are more pessimistic about finding a partner and may not be very active in seeking out romantic encounters (Bredow, Huston, & Glenn, 2011).

Some early adults are in situations in which it is difficult to find suitable mates. They might move to a new town for a job, return home after serving in the military, or be employed in a career that leaves little time for social life. The problem they face is how they are going to meet people and begin the dating process. Online dating is one strategy to expand access to potential partners. From 2013 to 2015, the use of online dating and mobile apps to find romantic partners has nearly tripled. A recent survey found that 22 percent of those in the age range 25 to 34 have used these services to identify potential partners, and about one third of respondents in this age range knew of someone who formed a long-term relationship through an online dating service (Pew Research Center, 2016).

Demographic realities influence the possibility of meeting suitable partners. In each community, for each age group of heterosexual women, the number of suitable, available male partners may differ, depending on such characteristics as the educational level, employment opportunities, and racial composition of the men in that community. For example, declines in the marriage rates for African Americans is linked to the decline in the availability of appropriate African American male partners. Single, never-married African American women increased from 17 percent of the total female African American population 18 years old and older in 1970 to 46 percent in 2014 (U.S. Census Bureau, 2015d, Table A1). This pattern is related in part to the high rates of mortality and imprisonment of African American men and in part to their economic marginality (Kaiser Family Foundation, 2006).

Once two people meet, what factors support their continued involvement? One's style of interaction—for example, whether one is shy and withdrawn or expressive and outgoing—influences the number and kinds of interactions one has with others. In contrast to the principle of homogamy, which emphasizes the role of similarity in the attraction process, **social evolutionary theory** suggests that men and women differ in the features they emphasize in evaluating someone as a desirable partner. The evolutionary perspective highlights the reproductive potential and the reproductive investment of one's partner. *Reproductive potential* refers to the physical, material, and social resources that a partner may be able to contribute to one's fertility and childrearing. *Reproductive investment* refers to the willingness of a potential partner to commit these resources to one's children. Men tend to emphasize the biological or physical resources of a potential partner, valuing youth and physical appearance in a partner more than do women. Women tend to emphasize the social status and economic resources of a potential partner, valuing earning potential and job stability in a partner more than do men (Geary, Vigil, & Byrd-Craven, 2004).

In a cross-national study of heterosexual mate preferences in samples collected in Africa, Asia, Australia, Europe, New Zealand, and North and South America, David Buss (2003) found that men placed more emphasis on a partner's youth and physical appearance, whereas women placed more emphasis on a partner's financial prospects, dependability, and industriousness. In addition to physical appearance and social status, people who behave in an admirable, effective manner may be viewed as attractive or desirable. People seek others who will support their goals, who can be encouraging and positive, and who appear to be able to collaborate effectively in shared experiences (Sanders, 1997).

Phase II: Deeper Attraction. Phase I, *original attraction*, moves on to Phase II, *deeper attraction*, as the partners begin to disclose information about themselves, interact in ways that deepen the relationship, and discover areas of important similarity. In Phase II, the discovery of basic similarities and a feeling of rapport are central to continuing the relationship (Bredow, Kate, & Huston, 2008).

— **CASE STUDY** Hannah and Matt: An Online Dating Couple's Story —

This case illustrates the process from first attraction to deepening commitment in the context of a relationship that started through an online dating service.

The way we met was actually a happy accident. I had not changed my location settings or my age settings from the default, so Matt kind of snuck in there, because there's a 13-year age difference and we lived 50 miles apart. So we got a match, but neither of us was really taking it seriously. Matt messaged me, and we talked a little bit, and just kind of got everything big, all of our baggage, out right away so we could see if it was even worth continuing to talk. I gave him my phone number and he texted me, "Hi, Hannah, it's Matt." And I said: "Which Matt?" as a joke. And that was it. We just talked nonstop from that point, and we went on our first date a week later. We went on a hike, and we put wine in water bottles and had a little picnic at the end of the hike.

Neither of us was looking for anything super-serious, but we kept hanging out regularly and it just kind of happened without either of us noticing. I have a son from a previous relationship—Jackson, he was 2 at the time—and they met and just really hit it off. I knew from the first date that I really, really liked Matt. It was great, because I couldn't get out a lot at the time—I could get out maybe once a week, if I had a babysitter. And you're not going to meet somebody at a bar if you're a single mom. So it saved me from meeting a lot of duds.

Five months into dating, he proposed, but we had already been talking about it for a few months. He had met my son, so we had to ask: Do we have a future? Is it worth dating and building a relationship with Jackson? We decided it was worth it, obviously. I'm grateful. I don't know what I did to deserve this, but I'm just going with it.

Source: Oswaks, M. (2015). Four couples share their online dating success stories: A casual online date really can turn into a marriage.

CASE ANALYSIS Using What You Know

1. Based on what you have read, what factors might have moved this relationship from initial interest to deeper attraction?

2. How does this case illustrate the idea of readiness to marry?

3. Have you ever tried online dating? What were your hopes or goals for this experience? How well were they met?

4. Hannah says that being a single mother made online dating a very valuable tool for meeting potential partners. What might be some other life conditions that could contribute to the appeal of using an online dating site?

Each person has key values and background characteristics that serve as a filter for assessing whether the other person is an eligible partner. Of course, eligibility is defined differently by different people. For some, any person who is conscious is eligible. Others have criteria that limit the choice of a marriage partner to someone of a certain age range, religion, race, educational background, and family history. Some adults would not consider marriage to someone who does not share their religious faith. Only members of their own religious group are perceived as eligible partners. Research conducted on religious homogamy finds a consistent relationship between the extent to which partners have similar religious beliefs and participate together in religious practices and their marital quality. However, over the past 20 years, this relationship has been weakening. Agreement about gender ideology, partner participation in the labor market, and agreement about the balance of work and family roles have emerged as salient values that rival religious values.

There are many dimensions along which two people may recognize similarities or differences. They may seem quite different on some dimensions, such as religion and social class, yet discover that they are quite similar on others, such as life goals and political ideology. For example, partners who have similar ideas about gender roles and how men and women ought to function in a marriage are likely to be drawn to one another. The more aware individuals are of the themes that are central to their own sense of personal identity, the better they can recognize the dimensions of similarity and difference in other people that will contribute to intimate relationships.

The process of finding partners who are similar in important values, goals, and lifestyle is incorporated into most online dating services. Rather than going through a gradual process of learning about someone through conversations, frequent or periodic interactions, and the gossip or wisdom of other people who know the person, the user can learn a lot of information about someone all at once and decide if that other person is worth pursuing in a face-to-face meeting. Through the use of a mathematical algorithm, online dating services identify potential partners who appear to be a good match for one's salient preferences (Finkel et al., 2012).

Many people may not even be aware of their own criteria for the eligibility of potential partners. For example, most heterosexual men expect to marry women who are a few years younger than they are. Although they do not deliberately state this as a criterion for marriage, they simply do not interact with or feel drawn to a partner who is perceived as too old. Similarly, if heterosexual women are looking for a long-term commitment, they tend to seek partners who are a few years older (Buunk et al., 2001).

Most people seek intimate partners who will understand them and provide a sense of security and emotional support. The attachment theory of romantic relationships expands on infant-caregiver attachment research. The seeds of one's expectations and mental representations about close relationships are formed in infancy through the quality of early care one received. Building on this early experience, the three features of attachment—secure, anxious, and avoidant—can be seen in the ways that adults approach romantic relationships. If you think back to the attachment system, its primary function is to provide reassurance about safety and security, especially under conditions of threat or stress. In a secure attachment, the mere physical presence of a loved one, as well as comforting words and touch, can reduce feelings of pain and distress. However, the anxiously attached person is constantly vigilant to potential loss, fearing rejection or abandonment. The avoidantly attached person downplays the importance of close relationships and tends to suppress emotional reactions in order to prevent being harmed by messages of rejection (Feeney, 2016; Zayas & Sellcuk, 2013; Zayas, Mischel, Shoda, & Aber, 2011). The **Applying Theory and Research to Life** box on attachment styles provides a way of understanding how implicit attachment representations influence the way people move toward or away from potential partners.

In addition to the preferences that individuals express about potential partners and the availability of those partners in a particular community, third parties can play a role in the progression or termination of a relationship during Phase II (Kalmijn, 1998). Family members can help enhance a partner's attractiveness if they are enthusiastic about the partner and encourage the relationship. As the earlier example of the Muslim college student illustrated, parent and family reactions can also interfere with a deepening attraction if the potential partner meets with family disapproval.

Research on interethnic dating has shown how social network diversity contributes to the likelihood of college students

Attachment Styles and Relationship Formation

Attachment theory is an influential framework for understanding the process of relationship formation in adulthood. One's attachment style, established in infancy, provides a template for orienting toward intimate relationships in adulthood. Anxiety over abandonment, comfort or discomfort with closeness and emotional disclosure, and the level of self-esteem associated with a secure or insecure attachment contribute to the type of partner one seeks and one's ability to sustain an intimate relationship. The threat of loss of access (both physical and emotional access) to an intimate partner is likely to produce anxiety, protest, and steps to regain proximity (Feeney, 2016; Shaver & Mikulincer, 2011).

Bartholomew (1990) developed an attachment typology based on one's attachment experiences in infancy and toddlerhood. One can have a positive or negative assessment of the self, and a positive or negative assessment of others (see Table 11.2).

Secure individuals have a positive model of themselves and of others: "It is easy for me to become emotionally close to others. I am comfortable depending on them and having them depend on me."

Preoccupied individuals have a positive model of others, but a negative model of the self: "I want to be completely emotionally intimate with others, but I often find that others are reluctant to get as close as I would like. I am uncomfortable being without close relationships, but I sometimes worry that others don't value me as much as I value them." Preoccupied individuals are both anxious about rejection and dependent on others for reassurance. When one

or both partners are characterized by a preoccupied attachment, the likelihood of abuse in the relationship increases (Henderson, Bartholomew, Trinke, & Kwong, 2005).

Dismissing avoidant individuals have a positive model of self, but a negative model of others: "I am comfortable without close emotional relationships. It is very important to me to feel independent and self-sufficient, and I prefer not to depend on others or have others depend on me." Dismissing avoidant individuals are low in anxiety, and also reluctant to get too close to others.

Fearful avoidant individuals have a negative model of both self and others: "I am uncomfortable getting close to others. I want emotionally close relationships, but I find it difficult to trust others completely, or to depend on them" (Crowell, Fraley, & Shaver, 1999, p. 451). These individuals are both socially avoidant and anxious about loss and rejection.

The secure and the dismissing individuals have high self-esteem; however, they differ markedly in the value they place on intimacy and in their interpersonal style. Secure individuals value relationships and are viewed as warm and nurturing. In contrast, dismissing individuals minimize relationships in favor of self-reliance and are viewed as cold or competitive. The fearful avoidant and the preoccupied individuals lack the self-esteem of the secure or dismissing groups. However, the fearful individuals avoid social contact, whereas the preoccupied individuals try hard to engage in relationships.

Although it may seem obvious that partners who both have secure attachment styles will enjoy a stable, trusting, and satisfying relationship, other combinations have been found to form stable relationships as well. Not everyone is looking for a partner with a secure attachment. The relationships of anxious women and avoidant men are quite stable. These relationships reflect gender-role stereotypes in which women work hard to be nurturing while men are more distant and pull away from conflict or intimate disclosure (Feeney, 2008).

The context of the relationship may also alter one's characteristic attachment responses. When a close romantic relationship is perceived to be deteriorating, insecure avoidant behaviors may increase, even among those who have a secure attachment style (Gillath & Shaver, 2007). In contrast, over time a person with an anxious attachment can be reassured when a partner is caring and trustworthy.

I had a real problem trusting anyone at the start of any relationship. A couple of things happened to me when I was young, which I had some emotional difficulties getting over. At the start of our relationship, if P. had been separated from me I would have been constantly thinking: "what was he doing?"; "was he with another girl?"; "was he cheating on me?"; all that would have been running through my head. Over a 3-year period of going out, you look at it in a different light; you learn to trust him. (Feeney, 2008, p. 465)

Critical Thinking Questions

1. Summarize the similarities and differences between the attachment styles described in infancy and those described here regarding adult romantic relationships.
2. Imagine that people have been set up on a blind date. How might the following couples get along?

   - Secure and Dismissing
   - Secure and Preoccupied

Table 11.2	The Attachment Typology		
		Working Model of Others	
		Positive	Negative
Working Model of the Self	Positive	Secure	Dismissing avoidant
	Negative	Preoccupied	Fearful avoidant

Source: Based on Bartholomew, 1990.

dating across ethnic boundaries (Clark-Ibanez & Felmlee, 2004). Students who had an ethnically diverse group of friends were significantly more likely to have had one or more experiences with interethnic dating relationships. Students of color and male students were more likely than White or female students to have had experiences of interethnic dating. Those students whose parents had a diverse group of friends were most likely to respond that they had experienced interethnic dating more than once or twice. In the open-ended responses, students were asked how easy or how difficult it might be to date someone of a different ethnic group. The majority mentioned social pressures and social networks in their responses. For most of the students, the social network exercised pressures against interethnic dating. As one Korean American student wrote, "My parents, just as most Korean parents that I have contact with, banish the idea of interracial dating." However, those who say it would be easy to date across ethnic lines often mention the role of friends and associates: "It is easy to date interethnically. I see people of different ethnicities every day. I'm used to them" (male Latino American).

Phase III: Role Compatibility and Barriers to Break Up.

The relationship is likely to proceed from Phase II to Phase III if the partners extend the domains in which self-disclosure occurs, including sexual needs, personal fears, and fantasies. With each new risk taken, the discovery of a positive, supportive reaction in the partner deepens the level of trust in the relationship. The discovery of **role compatibility** and empathy gives the relationship a life of its own. Role compatibility is a sense that the two partners approach a situation in ways that work well together. Whether it is a visit to a relative's home, an office party, a casual evening with friends, or running out of gas on the highway, the two people discover that they like the way each behaves and that their combined behavior is effective. Empathy builds through these observations, enabling each partner to know how the other responds and how to anticipate the other's needs. Here we see one of the significant limitations of online dating algorithms. They can be useful in finding matches, but once two people begin to interact, the algorithms are not able to predict how well they will face real life, new situations together (Finkel et al., 2012).

One aspect of this new level of intimacy is the special way in which romantic partners interact with one another. In affectionate and playful exchanges, partners often use baby talk, a type of gentle, high-pitched register, in which features of words are altered and new vocabulary may be created. Partners may give one another affectionate nicknames and create unique signals for communication. The establishment of this intimate communication system acts as another bond between the couple, creating a personal environment that is not shared with and often not even known to others (Bombar & Littig, 1996). At some point in Phase III, partners may begin to think that they are in love. They may even tell each other, "I love you."

In addition to the growing sense of compatibility, barriers to breaking up help consolidate the relationship. First, the partners have disclosed and taken risks with each other that they probably have not taken with others. Second, they have achieved

Courtesy of Philip Newman

As role compatibility and empathy grow, the relationship takes on a new degree of intimacy and the couple begins to conceptualize a future together.

Andy and Jennifer take a moment to celebrate their decision to move in together. What factors will influence the future of this cohabiting relationship?

& Acitelli, 2001). Both the positivity bias and the similarity bias are associated with the perceiver's satisfaction in the romantic relationship, thereby reducing the likelihood that an alternative attraction will deter the person from making a long-term commitment (Luo & Snider, 2009).

The right one relationship is characterized by both romantic love and friendship. The intensity of romantic love has been documented in studies that contrast romantic love and friendship. Lovers describe their relationships as characterized by *fascination*, *exclusiveness*, and *sexual desire*: "I would go to bed thinking about what we would do together, dream about it, and wake up ready to be with him again" (Davis, 1985, p. 24). They also express more intense caring for their loved ones than for friends. This caring includes giving their utmost, even to the point of self-sacrifice. The intensity of these characteristics accounts for some of the specialness and unsettling euphoria associated with being in love. It may also explain the relative instability of love relationships. Intense emotion is difficult to sustain. In contrast, friendship or companionate relationships reflect a high level of **disclosure** and a sense of having shared many life experiences. This leads to a sense of truly knowing the person, experiencing mutual understanding, and being concerned about each other's welfare (Driver, Tabares, Shapiro, & Gottman, 2012).

Even with the help of this model, the final step of commitment to marriage is not easy to understand. In today's society, many young couples agree to live together and make a commitment to their partnership without marriage.

comfortable feelings of predictability and empathy that make them more certain about each other than about possible alternative attractions. Third, once a person has become an object of romantic attachment, closeness to that person is accompanied with feelings of safety and trust. The attachment system operates to motivate the partners to maintain physical and emotional closeness. Strong feelings of loss and anxiety are likely to be associated with the possibility of disruption to this relationship. Fourth, the partners have been identified by others in their social network, including family and friends, as a couple. Support from one's social network provides a stabilizing force that may be especially important for couples in nontraditional relationships. Other barriers include procedures needed to end the relationship, such as moving to a new apartment or dividing up or selling off shared purchases, and the feelings of obligation that may have accompanied earlier expressions of love and sexual intimacy (Kurdek, 2006a). At this point, the costs of breaking up begin to be quite high, including loss of a confidant, a companion, and disruption or even disapproval in their social network.

Phase IV: The Right One Relationship.

Once the partners enjoy role compatibility and empathy, they move on to Phase IV, *the right one relationship*. Two processes unfold that contribute to the intensification of this romantic attachment: the positivity bias and the similarity bias. The **positivity bias** refers to the tendency to view one's romantic partner in an overly positive light. This bias contributes to the perceiver's belief that he or she has indeed found the absolutely perfect partner. It also makes the partner feel valued and cherished (Rusbult, VanLange, Wildschut, Yovetich, & Verette, 2000). The **similarity bias** refers to the tendency to exaggerate perceptions of similarity between partners, thereby increasing feelings of closeness and being understood (Kenny

Cohabitation

Cohabitation has become an increasingly common practice for people in early adulthood. In 2014 there were 6.7 million unmarried, opposite-sex couple households in the United States, and over 783,000 unmarried same-sex couple households (U.S. Census Bureau, 2014). What is the nature and meaning of cohabitation? Is it an informal alternative to marriage, or more like singlehood, except with ongoing bond of connection to a partner?

In a cross-national comparison of opposite-sex couples, six types of cohabiting relationships were described (Heuveline & Timberlake, 2004, pp. 1216–1218):

1. *Marginal.* Cohabiting is infrequent, its duration short, and few children are born within this relationship because the cultural norms strongly discourage this kind of union.
2. *Prelude to marriage.* In the face of high divorce rates, cohabiting may be viewed as a way for couples to test the relationship prior to marriage. The duration of cohabitation should be relatively brief, frequently transition into marriage, with few children born to cohabiting couples.
3. *Stage in the marriage process.* Couples in this type of relationship may see some disadvantages to marrying immediately, but they do intend to marry. Childbearing

in the context of this relationship is more common, because the partners expect to marry. The relationships are of longer duration than in type 2, more often involve childbearing, and end in transition to marriage.

4. *Alternative to being single.* Couples want to postpone marriage and family formation, perhaps because they think they are too young to marry. These couples are more like single, dating couples than like married couples. These relationships should be relatively short in duration, end in separation, and few children are born in these relationships.

5. *Alternative to marriage.* Couples view cohabiting as an alternative to marriage. These relationships are often established in the context of cultural support for children born outside the bonds of marriage. These relationships are of long duration, less likely to transition into marriage, and more likely to involve children.

6. *Indistinguishable from marriage.* Because of the cultural acceptability of unmarried couples and institutional support for all parents, couples consider cohabitation versus marriage on pragmatic grounds. These relationships are not a conscious alternative to marriage based on attitudes or values. The relationships are likely to involve children, but they may be of shorter duration than in the alternative to marriage, if only because many of them do transition into marriage.

The cross-national comparison was based on data from 14 European countries plus Canada, New Zealand, and the United States. Cohabitation among never-married women is comparatively rare in Spain, Italy, and Poland (less than 15 percent) and quite common in France, Finland, New Zealand, and Sweden (more than 60 percent). The median duration of cohabiting relationships is 3 years or longer in France, Sweden, and Canada, and comparatively short in the United States where the median duration is 1.2 years. Across 11 countries where there are substantial numbers of cohabiting relationships, 61 percent of these relationships end in marriage. In comparison, 64 percent of Canadian cohabitation relationships end in separation, as do 52 percent of cohabitation relationships in the United States.

Using the indicators of incidence of cohabitation, proportion ending in marriage, and incidence of children born to mothers in a cohabiting relationship, the researchers tried to match countries with the six types of cohabitation most characteristic of their population. In Italy, Poland, and Spain, cohabitation was considered marginal. In Belgium, the Czech Republic, Hungary, and Switzerland, cohabitation was most likely a prelude to marriage. In Austria, Finland, Germany, Latvia, and Slovenia, cohabitation was a stage in the marriage process. In New Zealand and the United States, cohabitation was an alternative to being single. In Canada and France, cohabitation was an alternative to being married. In Sweden, cohabitation was indistinguishable from being married. The authors warned, however, that these national patterns may not reflect all the differences that are present within a culturally diverse society such as the United States (Heuveline & Timberlake, 2004). As an example, among Latino couples in the United States, those who share the same religious faith and who frequently attend religious services together are likely to experience a stable, cohabiting relationship (Petts, 2016). These comparisons provide a frame of reference for interpreting the meaning of cohabitation in national contexts. They illustrate differences in cultural support for varying patterns of family formation by highlighting the frequency, duration, and path of cohabiting relationships.

Consensual union without a civil or religious marriage has been practiced in Latin America for centuries and is regarded as a form of marital union (Martin, 2002). For a variety of economic, political, and religious reasons, some couples were not able or willing to meet the formal or religious requirements of marriage. They entered into an informal but no less stable relationship. Women who had a child within such a relationship were more likely to describe it as informal marriage than as cohabitation. Women who had been married before were also more likely to describe their current relationship as informal marriage rather than cohabitation. It appears that consensual unions were perceived by women to be more like marriage than like singlehood. Long-term cohabiting couples are very similar to legally married couples with regard to the frequency of conflict, perceptions of equity, and relationship satisfaction (Willetts, 2006).

Even though cohabitation has become increasingly common in the United States, there is a consistent finding of a negative relationship between cohabitation and marital quality and stability. Individuals who have cohabited in the past have more conflict in their marriages, less marital happiness, and a greater probability of divorce. These findings have been repeated for cohorts of couples who married between 1964 and 1980 when cohabitation was less common, and those who married between 1981 and 1997 when cohabitation became more frequent (Dush, Cohan, & Amato, 2003). The relationship was observed in a meta-analysis involving numerous studies of premarital cohabitation and marital stability (Jose, O'Leary, & Moyer, 2010). However, the relationship of cohabitation and marital instability was not found for couples who married their cohabiting partner, suggesting that for these couples, the cohabiting experience was in fact a stage in the marriage process. More research is needed to understand why those who cohabit and then go on to marry someone else experience less marital satisfaction and greater marital instability.

Close Relationships Between Partners of the Same Sex

In many respects, the same dynamics that influence the formation of close relationships among opposite-sex couples apply to same-sex couples. Nonetheless, gay and lesbian couples face certain unique challenges that are not typically present for heterosexual couples: They often have to establish their relationship in a context of secrecy, they often experience disapproval from their family, and until very recently, many states refused access to legal recognition of their union should they desire it (Kurdek, 2005). Now, with the passage of the Supreme Court ruling of *Obergefell* v. *Hodges* in 2015, marriage between same-sex couples is viewed as a constitutional right that is to be respected across all states in the U.S. In the months following the Supreme Court ruling, the Gallup Poll reported increases in the percentage of same-sex couples who are married, both in states where it

As two professional women creating a life together, Jenny and Rachel have to invent many aspects of their relationship, but they do not have to invent the wonderful feelings of being in love.

Lesbian relationships often emerge out of close, same-sex friendships. Lesbians are somewhat more likely to be able to establish long-term relationships than gay men. Most lesbians describe their relationships as stable, sexually exclusive, and extremely close. They also describe their relationships as closer and more flexible than do gay men or heterosexual couples (Green, Bettinger, & Zacks, 1996). Greater levels of satisfaction in the relationship are associated with greater levels of equality and shared decision making. Equality in the relationship depends on equal resources and commitment to the relationship (Eldridge & Gilbert, 1990). In comparison with women in opposite-sex marriages, women in lesbian relationships are more likely to describe greater satisfaction in their sexual activity and greater dissatisfaction with inequalities in the relationship. These women place a strong value on companionship and on confiding in one another, but they also expect to experience high levels of autonomy within their relationships.

Gay men are also interested in long-term relationships. However, they are less likely than lesbians to be sexually exclusive, and there is less consensus among them about the importance of sexual exclusiveness to their sense of relationship satisfaction (Deenen, Gijs, & van Naerssen, 1994; Kitzinger & Coyle, 1995). In comparison to lesbian relationships, gay men often find partners in the context of a more active, competitive social scene that involves multiple short-term relationships. In comparison to men in heterosexual couples, gay men are more likely to be emotionally intimate. In the practical matters of household work, gay couples are more likely than heterosexual couples to divide tasks so that each partner does an equal number (Peplau & Beals, 2004). Gay couples report higher levels of closeness and flexibility than do heterosexual couples. Moreover, the combination of flexibility and closeness is strongly associated with couple satisfaction (Kurdek, 2006b).

had previously been legal and in states where it had been illegal (Jones & Gates, 2015).

Lesbian and gay relationships are similar in many respects and distinct in others. Lesbian and gay couples who are in a committed relationship tend to give great priority to maintaining and enhancing their relationship for several reasons. First, they share the conflicts around coming out and the complications that this poses in family and work settings. This provides a common bond and a need to protect the relationship from detractors. Second, because of the nontraditional nature of same-sex relationships, the partners have to invent many of the details of their relationship, thus making it more salient and less scripted than heterosexual relationships. Finally, they face ongoing challenges, such as the complexities associated with the decision about whether and how to have children and how to ritualize their commitment to one another (Mohr & Jackson, 2016).

In a comparison of gay and lesbian couples, the two types of couples were similar in many respects (Kurdek, 2003). They had similar approaches to conflict resolution, similar experiences with support from their social networks, and similar rates of dissolution or instability in their relationships. The same variables predicted relationship dissolution for gay and lesbian couples. Lesbian couples were more alike than gay couples at the start of their relationship and scored higher on measures of liking their partners, trusting their partners, and perceiving equality in their relationship. Overall, lesbian couples had higher rates of relationship satisfaction. This finding is puzzling given that lesbian and gay couples had the same degree of stability. However, it may be explained by observations that lesbian couples have somewhat lower levels of attachment anxiety, which can produce relationship distress (Mohr, Selterman, & Fassinger, 2013).

Many of the same factors are associated with relationship quality across all types of couples: valuing security, permanence, and closeness; expressiveness; perceived rewards for being in the relationship; trust in the partner; good problem-solving and conflict resolution skills; egalitarian decision making; openness to the expression of differences; and perceived social support (Kurdek, 2006b; Peplau & Fingerhut, 2007). Factors that are likely to lead to the dissolution of a gay or lesbian couple are a lack of investment in the relationship, a decline in expressions of positive affect and emotional support, an increase in conflicts, and an increased desire for personal autonomy. Interdependence sustains the relationships, and power inequalities disrupt them.

Given the heteronormative social context, one may ask about factors that support stability in same-sex relationships. From an attachment perspective, it is conceivable that exposure to stressors and threats associated with community prejudice and social rejection strengthen the couple's commitment to one another, and activate their efforts to seek security and safety in one another. From an identity perspective, we can expect that gay and lesbian couples have given extensive thought to the challenges they are

Abe and Craig are a perfect match. Having found each other by chance, they have formed a loving bond that will sustain them for a lifetime.

likely to face as a couple and that they form their relationship with extensive work already done on the expectations they have for one another as committed partners.

Adjustment During the Early Years of Marriage

What are the defining characteristics of a high-quality relationship and how are they sustained during the early years of marriage? Two different theories have been advanced by family scientists. One view, sometimes referred to as the **communal norm**, is that each person should pay close attention to the partner's needs and act in ways that will support the partner's welfare. In a communal relationship, each partner tries to meet the needs of the other within reason, without regard for or without keeping track of what has been received in return. Couples that are characterized as flexibly supportive are likely to view their relationship as positive and satisfying.

A second view, sometimes referred to as the **exchange norm**, is that each person expects to satisfy the needs of the partner and to have needs met in about the same amount. The exchange norm includes a sense of obligation so that what one receives from the partner should be returned in similar value. Partners keep track of the benefits given or received, so that there is a continuous sense of equity or balance in the relationship. Couples who perceive that what is given is equal to what is received will view their relationship as positive and satisfying (Clark & Lamay, 2010).

In a study of couples prior to their weddings and 2 years after they were married, most couples thought that the communal norm was ideal and preferable to the exchange norm. Over time, the couples that relied more on the exchange norm were also less satisfied in their relationship. Individuals who were characterized by an anxious or avoidant attachment became increasingly reliant on the exchange norm 2 years into their marriage as compared to individuals who were characterized by a secure attachment. Even though they viewed the communal norm as ideal, those who had an anxious or avoidant attachment had difficulty establishing a communal, mutually beneficial supportive relationship. The communal norm depends more on trust and reciprocity as compared to the exchange norm that reflects some doubt about the partner's ability to care for and respond to one's needs (Clark, Lemay,

Graham, Pataki, & Finkel, 2010). People who have an insecure attachment are likely to be mistrustful of the good intentions of their partner. As a result, they pay very close attention to the value of what they are receiving from their partner in relation to what they give to the partner. This preoccupation with a fair exchange seems to be associated with more marital conflict and lower levels of marital happiness.

Mutual Adaptation. Once the choice has been made and the thrill of courtship has passed, the first few years of a committed relationship involve a process of mutual adaptation. Couples who idealize one another and who see each other in a possibly unrealistically positive light are less likely to experience declines in marital satisfaction and feelings of love as they make their way through these early years (Miller, Niehuis, & Huston, 2006). The first few years of marriage can be extremely difficult, particularly because the couple does not anticipate the strains. The partners may be distressed to find their home becomes riddled with the tensions that are a normal part of carving out a life together. In one study of 1,000 newlywed husbands and wives, problems appear for many couples in the first few months of marriage. Results revealed that 8 percent of newlyweds scored in the distressed range on measures of marital satisfaction and 14 percent scored in the distressed range on measures of marital adjustment after the first few months of wedlock. For both husbands and wives, the most problematic areas in the early months of marriage were balancing employment and marriage and debt brought into marriage (Schramm, Marshall, Harris, & Lee, 2005).

There are many additional sources of tension in a new marriage. If the partners do not have similar religious, educational, or social class backgrounds, they will have to compromise on many value decisions. Assuming a shared value orientation, certain lifestyle decisions can generate tension. The couple must establish a mutually satisfying sexual relationship. They must work out an agreement about spending and saving money. They must also respond to each other's sleep patterns, food preferences, work patterns, and toilet habits. The couple may find the demands of their parents and in-laws to be an additional source of conflict. Often, it is the number of demands rather than any single one that makes the adjustment process so difficult.

As part of the adjustment to marriage, the partners must achieve a sense of psychological commitment to each other. The marriage ceremony is intended to make that commitment public and binding. It is safe to say that most people probably do not fully accept the reality of their marriage vows until they have tested the relationship. Each partner is likely to put strain on the relationship to see how strong it really is. The question of trust may be posed as, "Will you still love me even if I do…?" or, "Am I still free to do what I did before we were married?" Every marriage relationship is different. The partners must discover the limits of their particular relationship, but both partners must feel that they still have some freedom within these limits. They must also believe that the limits are balanced by the love, respect, and support they gain in return. As each test is successfully passed, the partners grow closer. They trust each other more and become increasingly sensitive to each other's feelings. Eventually, the tests diminish in number as the question of trust is resolved. In the study of newlyweds mentioned previously, the factors that worked to protect the marriages included respect, appreciation, commitment, mutual affection, and trust (Schramm et al., 2005).

Communication and Marital Adjustment. Intimacy and a high level of satisfaction require effective communication and the capacity to cope effectively with conflict. Happy couples enjoy being together. They start out their marriages being very much in love, and they view one another as responsive. They value the companionship aspects of their marriage, such as spending time together with friends or having dinner together. The causal nature of this relationship is not fully understood. One might assume that happy couples choose to spend more time together, but it may also be that couples who have opportunities to spend more time together come to feel more positive about their marriage as a result.

High levels of *disclosure* and *disclosure reciprocity* (i.e., you tell a person what you are thinking about, and that person tells you what she is thinking about) are associated with greater relationship satisfaction among marital partners (Finkenaure, Engles, Branje, & Meeus, 2004; Lippert & Prager, 2001). Self-disclosure and partner disclosure both contribute to high levels of intimacy as well as relationship satisfaction. Perceptions of responsiveness from one's spouse also contribute to daily feelings of intimacy. It is likely that the positive impact of self-disclosure and partner disclosure in strengthening intimacy and satisfaction is accompanied by simultaneous increases in perceived partner responsiveness (Laurenceau, Barrett, & Rovine, 2005). The sense of intimacy involves sharing an open, tender relationship with another person. Emotional expressiveness, especially by husbands, and a lack of ambivalence about expressing one's feelings are important elements in this communication process. In contrast, declines in affectionate and pleasurable interactions, lack of intimacy, and increases in ambivalence about the union predict a high probability of divorce (Huston et al., 2001).

Approaches to Marital Conflict. In contrast to factors such as self-disclosure, partner disclosure, and a sense of partner responsiveness, which predict marital satisfaction, negative interactions and conflict are associated with marital distress. Conflict can be a product of the interaction of two well-developed identities, each with a distinct temperament, values, and goals. Conflict can result from the simple day-to-day need to make decisions that the couple has never made before. It can be a reflection of one or both partners' personalities, a tendency toward irritability, mistrust, or an aggressive temperament. It can be a product of disillusionment, as one or both partners perceive that the relationship fails to meet critical expectations. Much of the research on marital distress points to differences in power between the partners, especially differences in the control of resources and ongoing disagreements about the allocation of resources as an underlying source of **marital conflict**. Whatever the source, marital stability and satisfaction are closely tied to how couples manage conflict (Caughlin & Huston, 2006).

Three dimensions of conflict seem especially important in differentiating happy and distressed marital relationships. First, instances of **negative communication**—especially nonverbal negative expressions and hostile put-downs—are more frequent in distressed than in happy couples, even in the first few years of married life.

Second, distressed couples show a pattern of **coercive escalation**—a style of interaction in which the probability that a negative remark will be followed by another negative remark increases as the chain of communication gets longer and longer. This pattern has been observed at the behavioral level by coding the verbal and nonverbal characteristics of an interaction and at the physiological level by monitoring heart rate, blood pressure, and release of stress hormones during communication. As the communication becomes increasingly negative, the partners become so physiologically disorganized that they lose access to their more rational ego functions. Over repeated instances, they become sensitive to this physiological state, reaching it sooner. In comparison, happy couples become more effective in soothing each other and in finding ways of preventing conflicts (Driver, Tabares, Shapiro, & Gottman, 2012).

Third, distressed couples have different perceptions of the approach that their partners are taking to resolve a conflict. For example, one partner may think that he is acting in a constructive way to find a solution, but the other partner may view the behavior as patronizing or minimizing the importance of the

To sustain a marriage, the partners must be able to interact even during periods of conflict. Withdrawal, rejection, and distancing are common reactions to conflict. These strategies may be effective during a brief cooling-off period, but they do not replace direct communication for exploring or resolving differences.

issue. **Congruence** between the partners in how they think they and their partners are approaching the resolution of conflict is significantly related to marital satisfaction, whereas **lack of congruence** is significantly related to marital dissatisfaction and distress (Acitelli, Douvan, & Veroff, 1997).

In an analysis of effective problem solving among newly married couples, partners were asked to identify the areas where they had their most significant disagreements (Tallman & Hsiao, 2004). The four most common issues were money, who does what around the house, communication, and time spent with the spouse (p. 177). The premise of the study was that couples who were able to resolve problems so that both partners were satisfied with the outcome would experience greater levels of marital satisfaction. Another assumption was that both trust in one another and cooperative approaches to problem solving were needed in order to come to mutually satisfying solutions. Over time, the couples who were able to use cooperative problem-solving strategies had greater marital satisfaction, which in turn contributed to improved cooperative behavior in subsequent problem-solving efforts. Moreover, those couples who exhibited cooperative, mutually respectful problem solving were able to maintain their relationship quality in the face of economic distress.

Communication Styles of Men and Women in Marriage.
One hypothesis to account for difficulties in adjustment during the early years of marriage is that men and women have different communication styles, resulting in problems in conflict resolution and emotional closeness. This idea has mixed empirical support. In many ways, men and women are alike. For example, both perceive the value of emotional skills in promoting and sustaining friendships and romantic relationships. They both expect close friends—and especially romantic partners—to have the ability to encourage, soothe, reassure, and validate one another (Burleson, Kunkel, Samter, & Werking, 1996). When faced with upsetting problems, both women and men are most likely to offer suggestions for how to solve the problem or to take some action, rather than simply empathize and identify with the person's problem (Goldsmith & Dun, 1997).

When asked about their preferred mode or style of interaction as a married couple, husbands and wives both prefer interactions that are **contactful**—that is, open to the other person's point of view—and that also clearly express the speaker's own position. They least prefer **controlling interactions**, in which one person expresses her point of view and does not take the other person's point of view into consideration (Hawkins, Weisberg, & Ray, 1980). These similarities suggest that men and women approach the process of establishing intimate relationships with many common skills and values. In constructive conflict resolution, partners are able to support their own position while engaging in interactions that show concern for the other person and for preserving a positive relationship. Both partners are able to disagree while preserving a good level of accuracy about the conflict; they don't exaggerate or overstate one another's position, or claim to know what the other person thinks without confirming their opinion by checking back with the other person (Feeney, 2008).

Couples' communication in conflicts is associated with, and predictive of, marital satisfaction and stability (Noller & Feeney,

2002; Weiss & Heyman, 1997). One pattern of communication that has been documented in the marital interaction literature is the **demand-withdraw pattern**, in which one member (the demander) nags, criticizes, and makes demands of the other to change, while the partner (the withdrawer) avoids confrontation, becomes silent, and withdraws. The demand-withdraw pattern has been found to be consistently associated with relationship dissatisfaction (Eldridge & Christensen, 2002). Further, research has demonstrated that the demand-withdraw pattern is associated with several central aspects of marriage, such as power differences and violence, differences in desire for closeness and independence, femininity and masculinity, gender roles, and division of labor (Eldridge & Christensen, 2002; Sagrestano, Heavey, & Christensen, 1999). The demand-withdraw pattern occurs most often in distressed marriages. The pattern is also extremely resistant to change in these relationships (Baucom et al., 2011; Eldridge et al., 2007).

Although both men and women can be in either role, women are more often in the demanding role and men more often in the withdrawing role. These gender distinctions have been observed in a variety of samples, including dating couples, cohabiting couples, married couples, clinic couples seeking therapy, violent couples, and divorcing couples (Eldridge & Christensen, 2002). The demand-withdraw pattern increases with the length of the marriage.

Some differences in the ways men and women approach communication have implications for the quality of an intimate relationship. The socialization of both sexes in U.S. culture is still sufficiently distinct to result in differences in expectations and competencies. For example, when faced with a problem, men are more likely to want to deny it or to spend time analyzing and defining it in comparison with women (Goldsmith & Dun, 1997). Men tend to value the skills of being a good conversationalist or storyteller and being able to laugh and joke as well as to argue and defend a position somewhat more than do women (Burleson et al., 1996). They tend to be more ambivalent than women about expressing emotions and withdraw to avoid escalating conflict. Women, on the other hand, tend to want to talk things out so that everyone feels comfortable with the situation. In conflicts, these styles can become incompatible, especially if the woman is trying to reach consensus and the man withdraws. In general, women expect and desire a degree of closeness that is often not reciprocated. Men, on the other hand, are more likely to be satisfied with the degree of intimacy that they find in marriage and have fewer expectations of or less desire for greater closeness (Dindia & Allen, 1992).

Adjustment in Dual-Earner Marriages. One of the greatest changes in U.S. families in the second half of the 20th century was the increase in the number of married women who were employed. It is normative for married women, including those with young children, to be in the labor market. The percentage of employed, married women whose husbands are present was 32 percent in 1960 and 56 percent in 2012. The number of women with young children who work outside the home has also grown substantially. In 2012, 60 percent of married women with children under 6 years of age were in the labor force, compared with 39 percent in 1960 (U.S. Bureau of Labor Statistics, 2013d). Rather than drop out of the labor force and return to work after their children are grown, the majority of women now remain in the labor force throughout the early years of parenthood.

There is no question that the involvement of both partners in the labor market requires the couple to arrive at a satisfactory approach to **work/life balance**. The partners' career ambitions and specific job demands need to be coordinated, and considered in the context of the couple's needs for time together, management of home and family life, and individual needs for fitness, leisure, and time with friends and family. Uncertainty about the expectations and behaviors of the spousal roles must be worked out between the partners. Sometimes, this uncertainty helps to produce greater intimacy by generating interactions that lead to greater self-disclosure by each partner. Personal preferences and habits must be examined if the partners are to arrive at a mutually satisfying division of labor. Sometimes, however, this process is threatening. The partners may not really be aware of their expectations of themselves or of the other person until they are married and faced with these work/family life challenges.

A potential area of conflict for dual-earner couples is the relative balance of power and demands for household labor for the two partners. In the traditional male-breadwinner, female-homemaker family model, the husband has more power as a result of his access to financial resources and participates little in the low-status household tasks. The wife, in contrast, has little power and carries the majority of responsibility for the household tasks. As women have entered the labor market, their access to financial resources has increased. To the extent that their husbands also help in sharing the household tasks, women's well-being and mental health improve.

For men, especially in families where there is a relatively high family income, as their wives' income matches or surpasses their own and they have to take on a greater role in domestic tasks, their well-being declines and their mental health suffers. This is true primarily for men who have traditional views about the importance of men as breadwinners (Brennan, Barnett, & Gareis, 2001). Men who feel demeaned or threatened by demands to participate in household labor are likely to experience depressive symptoms. These reactions are similar to the reactions that women have when they try to carry the full responsibility of household tasks while also participating in the labor market. Finding the balance of power and of household responsibilities that preserves mutual respect and support is a major challenge in the early years of the marriage and has to be fine-tuned and renegotiated throughout the marriage.

In contemporary U.S. society, there are a number of benefits for couples when husbands and wives have multiple roles that include marriage, career, and parenting (Barnett & Hyde, 2001). Four benefits are summarized here.

1. Involvement in multiple roles means that both partners are likely to be more fully integrated into meaningful social support systems.
2. Participation of both partners in the labor force increases financial resources and buffers the couple against fluctuations in each person's job situation.
3. Success in one role can buffer each person against negative experiences in other roles. For example, negative

work experiences can be offset by marital happiness and the centrality of parenting.
4. Involvement in similar roles provides husbands and wives with a shared frame of reference. Thus, partners are more likely to appreciate one another's point of view and to empathize with each other's struggles and accomplishments.

However, there are limits to the benefits of the dual-earner arrangement. The advantages of the dual-earner, multiple- role lifestyle can be offset when one or both partners experience role overload—for example, if the care of an ill parent is added to an already full basket of responsibilities. The quality of the roles can undermine the benefits, as when a person is in a terrible job with inadequate wages and oppressive work conditions. Chronic stressors at home that create feelings of overload or lack of control can make the daily hassles of home or work life seem even worse. These ongoing stressors, which result in frequent but unpredictable demands, can cause psychological distress in the individual and disrupt relationship satisfaction (Serido, Almeida, & Wetherington, 2004). Multiple roles can be disruptive if a partner holds traditional gender-role values that are in conflict with the enactment of multiple roles. Finally, couples may find that their actual work schedules do not fit well together, leaving too little time to be together or too little control over their non-work life (Barnett, Brennan, & Gareis, 1999).

Roughly 100 years of social science research has established that satisfaction in the relationship of marriage contributes significantly to psychological well-being, including a greater sense of social integration and protection from other life stressors. For most adults, happiness in life depends more on having a satisfying marriage than on any other domain of adult life, including work, friendships, hobbies, and community activities. Longitudinal studies of adults who either remained single or got married and remained married over a 7-year period found that those who were married had higher levels of well-being and fewer mental health problems (Horwitz, White, & Howell-White, 1996; Williams, 2003). The benefits of being married for mental health and life satisfaction accrue primarily in the context of happy marriages where the partners describe their relationship as one in which their spouse makes them feel valued and cared for (Williams, 2003).

FURTHER REFLECTION: Review the developmental tasks and psychosocial crises of earlier life stages, from infancy through later adolescence. What are some psychosocial resources from earlier stages that would contribute to a person's ability to form and sustain an intimate relationship in early adulthood? What are some areas of vulnerability that might prevent the formation of these relationships?

What characteristics are important to you in a long-term romantic partner? On what dimensions is homogamy important to you in the choice of a mate?

Childbearing

OBJECTIVE 3 Describe the factors associated with the decision to have children, and evaluate the impact of childbearing on intimate relationships.

During early adulthood, decisions about reproduction and child-bearing are confronted many times. Young adults make choices to delay parenting, have an abortion, have a child, wait before having another child, or stop having children altogether. Many couples undergo difficult and expensive procedures to conceive a child. Others who are unable to conceive decide to adopt children. Some adults become foster parents, whether or not they have children of their own. Even unplanned pregnancies are products of some kind of decision making—whether to have sexual relations knowing that pregnancy is possible, decisions about contraception, and decisions about whether to abort the pregnancy or to carry the child to term.

In all of these decisions, many powerful themes are reflected: one's sense of fulfilling a masculine or feminine life purpose by having children; one's childhood socialization and identification with parental figures; religious beliefs about sexuality, contraception, or abortion; and ideas about carrying on a family's ancestry and traditions. Reproduction is the means by which the species perpetuates itself. As people reflect on their lives, the birth of their children is commonly recalled as a life-story high point (McAdams & Bowman, 2001). Regardless of the decisions one reaches, this issue cannot help but heighten the sense that the decisions of adulthood make a difference (Lydon, Dunkel-Schetter, Cohan, & Pierce, 1996).

Fertility Rate

The average number of births required for the natural replacement of a population is calculated by assuming that for every adult woman in a population, a female child must be born who will reach reproductive maturity and have children. Because slightly more male than female children are born and because not all children reach childbearing age, the estimate for a population replacement reproductive rate is 2.1 births per adult woman (Bachu & O'Connell, 2001).

The **fertility rate** in the United States has fluctuated from the late 1950s, when the rate was 3.5 births per woman, to a low of 1.8 in the 1970s. In 2012, the rate was 1.989, slightly below the replacement estimate. Fertility rates in the United States vary by race, ethnicity, and socioeconomic status. Latinas have the highest fertility rate; Asian or Pacific Islanders have the lowest. Women who have graduated from high school or less have a higher fertility rate than women who graduated from college. Women who are not in the labor force have a higher fertility rate than those in the labor force. Women whose family income is below 200 percent of the poverty level have a higher fertility rate than those above 200 percent of the poverty level (Monte and Ellis, 2014).

Decisions About Childbearing

Decisions about **childbearing** are made in the context of other personal and family goals and commitments. Factors such as religious beliefs, career aspirations, ideals about family life, and social expectations in the family and culture all contribute to a couple's commitment to bearing children and the timing of first and subsequent pregnancies. Cultures differ in the norms and expectations they convey about the value of having children and the appropriate timing and frequency of pregnancies (see the **Human Development and Diversity** box The Reproductive Career of the Gusii).

Attitudes about the desire to have children and the importance of having children to personal happiness have changed over time. Thornton and Young-DeMarco (2001) compared responses from men and women as well as adolescents from five different national U.S. samples. Data were collected in the 1960s, 1970s, 1980s, and 1990s, with the most recent data coming from adolescents surveyed in 1997–1998. Over time, two themes emerged. First, in the more recent decades, people viewed childbearing within marriage as more of an option than an obligation. From the 1960s to the 1990s, respondents increasingly disagreed with the idea that all married couples who can have children ought to have children. This concept was positively endorsed by 84 percent of mothers in 1962, but by only 41 percent of mothers and 22 percent of their adult daughters in 1993. Similarly, in the 1980s and 1990s, the majority of people disagreed with the idea that having children is the main reason for getting married, or that people who did not have children led meaningless lives. Nonetheless, the study reported a steady endorsement of the value of parenting among young people. The majority of high school seniors who were surveyed from the mid-1970s through the late 1990s agreed that fatherhood and motherhood are among the most fulfilling experiences of adulthood; roughly 60% of these students (both male and female) said they were likely to want to have children.

Pursuing this line of inquiry, a recent national survey compared attitudes about the importance and the contexts for childbearing among men and women ages 15 to 44 in samples from 2006–2010 and 2011–2013. In 2011–2013, only a small percentage of women (6.4 percent) and men (9.4 percent) agreed with the statement that people can't be really happy unless they have children. However, a majority of men and women agreed that it is okay to have and raise children when the parents are living together and not married, and that it is okay for an unmarried woman to have and raise a child. Thus, current attitudes appear to be more accepting of a variety of contexts for childbearing and childrearing, while at the same time endorsing the view that childbearing is not an essential condition for life satisfaction (Daugherty & Copen, 2016).

Although the majority of married couples intend to have children, the timing of their entry into parenthood varies. From 1975 to 2010, the age of entry into parenthood has been getting older. Whereas the years from 20 to 29 are still the most typical age for having children, far fewer women have babies in their teens, and many more have babies in their 30s and beyond (see FIGURE 11.4 ▶). Both the social and biological clocks come into play in this decision. The social clock refers to expectations from family, friends, and coworkers about the optimal time to start a family. In recent years, many couples have decided to postpone childbearing. This decision is related to other developmental tasks of adult life and needs to be understood in the context of competing goals, including education, career aspirations, housing, and a desire to experience intimacy with a partner prior to having children. Dual earner couples have to consider the effect of children on their family income. They may try to anticipate the best timing for childbearing in relation to job security or career advancement. Some couples set certain material goals for themselves as a prerequisite to having children. For example, they may decide to wait until they can buy a home, establish a certain amount of

The Reproductive Career of the Gusii

Robert LeVine (1980) described the patterns of adulthood among the Gusii, a tribe living in the Kisii highlands of western Kenya, about 50 miles south of the equator. The Gusii lived in a well-protected, fertile area where they were able to expand their communities and grow their crops. LeVine characterized their adult life course as being composed of three interdependent spheres: reproductive, economic, and spiritual. His description of the reproductive career illustrates how personal and societal expectations influence the childbearing decisions of young adults.

The reproductive career seems to be the most salient for both sexes. Its goal is to become the ancestor of a maximally expanding genealogy. For women, this means to have children as frequently between marriage and menopause as is consistent with child health, which the Gusii believe to be every 2 years. A man who fails to impregnate his wife that often will be publicly accused by her of neglect. The woman must have at least one son to take care of her in her old age and whose wives work with her; to have nothing but daughters (who move away at marriage) is second only to barrenness as a disaster. If her husband dies, it is her right as well as her obligation to have a leviratic husband to impregnate her regularly so she will continue to bear children "for the dead man."

For men, the goal means not only maximizing his wife's offspring but also taking additional wives as he can afford them and so appending their reproductive careers to his. If a man has been a monogamist, he might take a younger second wife when his first wife reaches menopause, for that would extend his reproductive career by a decade or more. The reproductive career as I see it, however, is not limited to the individual's own procreation but

includes that of his or her offspring. Grandchildren are as fervently desired as one's own children and, not incidentally, play an essential role in the burial of the grandparents. (LeVine, 1980, p. 94)

The value placed on having children, the practice of child spacing, and the practice of extending the father's reproductive career by adding a second, younger wife all contribute to the high fertility rate of the Gussi (LeVine et al., 1996). In 2011, the fertility rate in Kenya was 4.7 births per woman. However, current conditions threaten the reproductive career of the Gusii. The mortality rate for children under 5 years old is 73/1,000 live births in Kenya (Countdown, 2013). The following issues impact the survival of children under the age of 5:

- Maternal mortality. Approximately 360 Kenyan women die in every 100,000 live births. Without their mothers, infants are at great risk for survival.
- Only 44 percent of women are attended by skilled health professionals at childbirth. There is a lack of comprehensive obstetrics, neonatal care services, and emergency obstetrics in many hospitals, particularity in rural areas, and there are delivery complications arising from many deliveries done outside health care facilities and not supervised by skilled health workers.
- HIV/AIDS and its related opportunistic infections—increasing HIV infection rates among pregnant mothers and mother to infant transmission. Roughly one third of pregnant women who are HIV positive lack access to Preventing Mother to Child Transmission (PMTCT) services.
- Hunger and the resultant protein-energy malnutrition (PEM) among children. Roughly 16 percent of children under age 5 are significantly underweight, and

35 percent are stunted, meaning that their overall growth in height is well below average.
- Widespread incidences of preventable diseases due in part to a lack of immunization, poor water quality, and lack of access to antibiotics. Only 50 percent of children diagnosed with pneumonia receive antibiotics. Malaria, diarrhea, and acute respiratory infections, which mainly impact children, currently contribute to about 50 percent of all reported morbidity and about 25 percent of all reported deaths.
- Literacy levels and low mothers' education levels in many parts of the country. Children of mothers with little or no education have the largest risk of mortality.
- Inadequate access to sustainable clean water sources and sanitation facilities.

These factors illustrate the potential disruptive forces of modernization on traditional cultural systems and practices.

Critical Thinking Questions

1. Analyze the differences in the orientation toward childbearing between the Gusii and young adults in the United States.
2. Evaluate the likely impact of greater contact with the more industrialized, commercial world on the Gusii and their reproductive values and behaviors.
3. How might the goal of becoming an ancestor of an expanded genealogy affect men and women's health and reproductive practices for the Gusii? For your own family?
4. Describe how taking a second, younger wife in order to continue a man's reproductive career may be perceived by his first wife. Speculate about a cultural equivalent to this practice in contemporary U.S. culture.

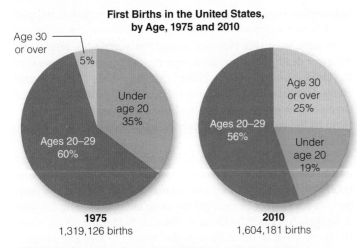

**First Births in the United States,
by Age, 1975 and 2010**

1975
1,319,126 births

Age 30 or over 5%
Under age 20 35%
Ages 20–29 60%

2010
1,604,181 births

Age 30 or over 25%
Ages 20–29 56%
Under age 20 19%

FIGURE 11.4 ▶ AGE AT FIRST CHILDBEARING, 1975 AND 2010

Source: CDC/NCHS, National Vital Statistics System

savings, or travel together before they have children. Given the high divorce rate, couples are likely to want to feel confident that their relationship is strong before deciding to have children.

Delayed entry into parenthood has typically been studied in relation to the characteristics of the woman. It has been found to be related to a woman's level of education, her career commitment, and the family's income.

> Zine Magubane (age 32) and her husband, Patrick McCabe, married in June. She's got a tenure-track university teaching job; he's a sports agent who travels constantly. They want to wait at least a year before beginning a family "to get a little more stability," says Magubane, whose mother delivered her at 36. Today she works hard to stay healthy, knowing she'll be an older mom. (Kalb, 2001, p. 43)

In a study of the timing of entry into fatherhood, men who were characterized as late-entry fathers (30 years old or older) were more involved with their children and had more positive feelings about them than did the on-time or early fathers (Cooney, Pedersen, Indelicato, & Palkovitz, 1993). Older fathers may feel that they have less conflict between their commitments to work and to family. They may feel that they have already demonstrated their ability to succeed in the breadwinner role and, therefore, can approach parenthood with more confidence and a greater sense of self-efficacy. Older fathers may have more emotional resources to bring to their marriage and their parenting relationship.

Decisions to postpone childbearing are also constrained by the *biological clock,* the closing of reproductive capacity for women and increasing risks of infertility and birth anomalies with age. After age 30, women's fertility rates decline, and by age 40, miscarriages increase. Reproductive technologies that involve fertilizing a woman's own eggs decrease from 40 percent effectiveness for women in their late 20s to less than 10 percent for women in their 40s. However, new ideas are being introduced that may push back these constraints, such as transferring the cell nucleus from an older woman's egg, transplanting it into the cytoplasm of a younger woman's egg, and implanting the new egg into the

older mother so that she can experience pregnancy and childbirth (Kalb, 2001).

The patterns discussed above may lead one to believe that couples are making very deliberate, strategic decisions about the timing for their childbearing. However, in 2011, 45 percent of the 6.1 million pregnancies in the United States were unintended, meaning that the pregnancy was mistimed (the woman did not intend to get pregnant at that time) or unwanted (the woman did not want to be pregnant at all). Later adolescents, ages 20 to 24 have the highest rate of unintended pregnancies of any age group (Guttmacher Institute, 2016c). Moreover, among women who have had one unintended child, about one third have another unintended birth (Wildsmith, Guzzo, & Hayford, 2010).

In addition to one's intentions about childbearing, certain other experiences feed into fertility decisions. For example, characteristics of the firstborn child influence a couple's decision about having another child. When the firstborn child has a sociable temperament, has relatively few behavioral problems, and shows a readiness and eagerness for learning, families are more

This couple's affection for and commitment to each other is expanding to include love for their unborn child. How might the quality of the parents' relationship influence the experience of pregnancy?

Developmental Tasks **441**

likely to be enthusiastic about having another child (Jokela, 2010). Sometimes the conditions leading up to pregnancy, such as sexual abuse or unusually difficult experiences of pregnancy, result in a reluctance to have additional children (Sperlich & Seng, 2008). Social policies, such as the one-child policy in China, or the welfare policy in the United States, which emphasizes labor force participation for mothers of young children, can have an impact on childbearing decisions.

Adjustment During Pregnancy and Childbearing

Although most women are healthy and happy about being pregnant, there is growing concern about how to treat mood disorders among women during pregnancy and after childbirth. Numerous studies document the disruptive impact of maternal depression on the infant's cognitive and emotional development and the associated mother–infant relationship (Pearson et al., 2010). Some women are chronically depressed prior to pregnancy and are being treated with psychotropic drugs. Other women become anxious or depressed during pregnancy. The challenge is whether to continue the use of these therapeutic drugs, weighing the risks of potential harm to the fetus and the risks of untreated or increased depressive symptoms for the pregnant woman (Cohen et al., 2010). Approximately 13 percent of women experience mild to moderate depression in the first 3 months following childbirth (Bick & Howard, 2010). Many cases of depression go undiagnosed and untreated, resulting in maternal distress, negative affect, reduced sensitivity to the infant's signals, and disengagement from the mothering role.

The Dual Roles of Intimate Partner and Parent

In contrast to the elation that usually accompanies the anticipation of and preparation for the newborn, the arrival of the first child often brings a period of stress to the relationship (Newman, 2000). Belsky and Rovine (1990) found clear evidence of individual differences in how couples adapted to the transition to parenthood. In their longitudinal study of 128 families, they observed four patterns of change in the assessment of marital quality: (1) Some couples showed a rapid decline in marital quality after the first baby was born. (2) Others showed a slow, steady decline. (3) A third group showed no significant change. (4) A fourth group showed slight increases in marital quality. These findings caution us not to overgeneralize group trends to individual cases.

The quality of marital adjustment during the transition to parenthood is closely related to marital quality before the child was born (Heinicke, 2002). Couples who are in close, confiding, satisfying marriages before their children are born tend to show higher levels of marital adjustment 3 months after childbirth than do couples in conflictual marriages. However, many couples experience increased conflict after the birth of their first child. If the relationship was negative and the partners had high levels of conflict prior to the baby's birth, these difficulties are likely to increase (Crohan, 1996).

In some couples, conflict escalates to physical violence. An estimated 4 percent to 8 percent of pregnant women experience violence from their intimate partner during the pregnancy. The risks of intimate partner violence are greater in low-income households, especially in communities where people feel trapped in a life of poverty and disorganization. Negative consequences associated with this violence include miscarriages, abortions, injury or death to the pregnant woman, and continued abuse after the child is born (Li et al., 2010; Silverman et al., 2010). Several characteristics of the partner relationship, especially shared involvement of the partners in household tasks and commitment to the relationship, reduce the likelihood of such violence (Bradley & Gottman, 2012).

In an attempt to understand how marital satisfaction changes during the transition to parenthood, researchers compared marital activities and evaluations of the marriage by parents and nonparents who had been married the same number of years (Huston & Vangelisti, 1995; MacDermid, Huston, & McHale, 1990). Over the first 3 years of marriage, couples' ratings of love and satisfaction declined somewhat. There were no differences in the magnitude of the decline for parents and nonparents. Having children did not account for a greater drop in love or satisfaction than occurred as a result of adjusting to marriage in general. This is an important observation that provides new insight into much of the earlier research on marital satisfaction and the transition to parenthood (Holmes, Huston, Vangelisti, & Guinn, 2013).

Having children did have an impact on **marital companionship**. The percentage of leisure activities shared by the husband and wife dropped sharply after the baby was born, but it declined only slightly for the couples without children. During the third year of marriage, parents had a greater number of shared activities per day than nonparents, but few when the child was not present. FIGURE 11.5 ▶ shows the number of minutes of joint leisure time per day without the child for two groups of parents in comparison with joint leisure time for nonparents in the first, second, and third years of marriage. After the birth of their child, couples have only about one third as many minutes together alone as they had when they were childless. The nature of companionship in marriage changes to incorporate a baby and therefore may become less intimate.

FIGURE 11.5 ▶ DURATION OF JOINT HUSBAND-WIFE LEISURE WITHOUT CHILD FOR PARENTS AND NONPARENTS

Source: Based on MacDermid, Huston, and McHale, 1990.

For most couples, coping with the early months of childrearing strengthens the bond between the partners. The partners begin to respect each other's competence in caring for their child. They also begin to conceptualize their roles as parents and to view the increasing complexity of their family structure as a challenge rather than a burden. The new baby adds a degree of energy to the family through expressions of satisfaction, pleasure, and affection.

As the roles of mother and father are added to the adults' repertoire of role relationships, adults face new challenges in balancing their work, intimate partner, and parent roles. A variety of factors influence adults' ability to achieve a positive sense of role balance. Access to financial resources helps couples enjoy leisure time and purchase services that can reduce some degree of role strain. When partners are equally highly invested in their parental roles, they are more readily able to make the trade-offs and compromises that parenting requires, including modifying their leisure time to incorporate each other's interests and the presence of their young child. In contrast, when partners have to work long hours, especially on the weekends, or try to pursue individual leisure interests that do not include their partner or child, they may have more difficulty achieving a comfortable sense of role balance (Claxton & Perry-Jenkins, 2008; Marks, Huston, Johnson, & MacDermid, 2001).

The daily demands of the child help the parents define their own roles more realistically. Instead of wondering what parents should do, they are occupied with the actual demands of parenting. Through this experiential learning, young adults formulate their own definitions of parental roles. Assuming that the early experiences are successful and the parents are able to meet their child's needs, they gradually achieve a new level of self-efficacy in the parenting role, gaining new confidence in their ability to provide a nurturing environment for their child.

The process of social attachment and its impact on the infant were discussed in chapter 5 (Infancy). The theme of mutuality as the central process for the establishment of trust was stressed. Mutuality also has an impact on parents. Infants actively engage their parents, evoke unique responses, and, through their differential behaviors, begin to shape parenting behaviors. Infants

respond to their parents with shrieks of delight, elaborate smiles, and the active pursuit of them. They are unrestrained in their loving. They mouth, bite, grab, laugh, smile, squeal, and coo in response to pleasure. Through their open demonstrations of affection, infants teach adults about the expression of love and increase their parents' ability to demonstrate it. As parents and children begin to engage in playful interactions, the capacity to establish and maintain reciprocal interactions expands. Children learn how to initiate a play sequence by bringing a toy or making a playful gesture. Parents then learn how to respond by complying to the request for play, sitting down on the floor, bringing out the box of favorite play materials, or tickling and tumbling. As children and parents experience mutual, congruent playful interactions, the bond of affection is strengthened and communication is enhanced (Lindsey, Mize, & Pettit, 1997).

Nonmarital Childbearing

In 2014, over 1.6 million babies were born in the United States to women who were not married. Of all births in 2014, 40.2 percent were to unmarried women (CDC, 2016). Within the age range 15 to 44, the birth rate (births per 1,000 unmarried women) was highest among unmarried women ages 25 to 29 (Hamilton et al., 2015). The decision to have children outside of a marriage relationship at this age may be a result of recent divorce or widowhood, a decision reached in the context of a lesbian or a cohabiting relationship, or a decision to start a family without a partner. A substantial number of nonmarital first births are taking place in the context of cohabiting unions. From 2002 to 2011–2013, there has been increasing social acceptance among men and women toward the idea of unmarried women having and raising children (Daughtery & Copen, 2016). The website of Single Mothers by Choice (http://singlemothersbychoice.org) provides some insights into the motivations and resources of women who deliberately choose to have a child without a partner.

Adoption

Adoption is an alternative to childbearing for individuals who want to start a family or expand their family. Data about the total number of adoptions taking place in the United States are difficult to obtain. No single agency is responsible for gathering these data, and adoptions can take place in a variety of contexts. Overall, adoption is relatively rare today. One government report found that in 2012, an estimated 119,514 children were adopted in the United States. This is a decline of 15 percent since 2001 (Child Welfare Information Gateway, 2016).

Adoption can occur between related family members or between unrelated individuals. Roughly half of adoptions involve family members who adopt, for example, when adults with children remarry and their children are adopted by their new partner, when adults adopt the children of siblings who have died, or when grandparents adopt their grandchildren because the adult children are not able to parent. Infertility is the most common reason that adults adopt unrelated children. Other reasons that adults give for adoption include religious or philosophical convictions, for example, a belief that it is more responsible to care for otherwise parentless children than to reproduce, to prevent passing an inheritable diseases (e.g., Tay-Sachs disease), to avoid

Couples with children find new ways to spend time together that includes their children. Rather than a romantic ski weekend for two, this family romps in the snow and builds a friendly snowman.

contributing to perceived overpopulation, and health concerns relating to pregnancy and childbirth.

Over the past 30 years, the context of adoption has changed, resulting in fewer children available for adoption. The fertility rate in the United States has declined, and teen births, which were a source of many adoptive babies, have also declined. Social welfare practices have become increasingly focused on family preservation, emphasizing the importance of keeping children with their birth parents. International adoptions have also decreased. Countries including Vietnam, Guatemala, China, and Russia have taken steps to try to arrange for local adoption rather than sending their children to the United States (Seabrook, 2010).

Within the Child Welfare System, the adoption process is intended to support the best interests of children; however, this is not always easy to assess. Parents may experience some continued feelings of sadness as a result of not having a biologically linked child. This sadness or disappointment might be conveyed to their adoptive child. Adopted children may also experience feelings of loss as they learn of the separation from the birth mother, or in the case of international adoption, as they begin to understand the separation from their cultural heritage (Grotevant, 2009). When children have been in foster care for 2 years or longer, the lack of continuity in the attachment process and harsh or unstimulating conditions of care can have significant negative consequences for children's emotional and cognitive development. Adults who adopt older children or children with special needs and disabilities require additional support in order to provide an appropriate environment. In a review of 36 studies of post-permanency adjustment, both risk and protective factors were identified that were associated with adoption outcomes. Risk factors included caring for a child with special needs, adopting a child that had been in multiple placements or who had experienced a history of abuse or neglect, adoption involving parents who had no prior parenting experience, families that were experiencing their own boundary ambiguity, and families that lacked adequate social support. Protective factors included having adoption preparation, adoptive parents who were married, high levels of openness about the adoption process, and a strong network of social and professional support (Liao, 2016). At present, the preparation and training for adoptive parents to help them address these concerns are not adequately developed (Palacios & Brodzinsky, 2010).

Open adoptions, which are becoming increasingly common, strive to preserve the sense of family origins and connections so that children have a clearer picture of their developmental history as they mature. The success of this openness depends on the willingness of the birth mother to share information, and on the skill of the adoptive parents to incorporate this information into the narrative for the child about how their family was formed (Neil, 2009).

The Decision Not to Have Children

Not all couples choose to have children. In 2014, 15.3 percent of women ages 40 to 44 were childless, twice as many as were childless 30 years ago. Fewer Hispanic women are childless than White non-Hispanic and Black women (U.S. Census, 2015e). Much like attitudes toward remaining single, attitudes toward a lifestyle in which a couple chooses not to have children are becoming more accepting. As discussed earlier, childbearing is increasingly viewed as a choice rather than an obligation. This shift is evidenced in part by a change in the sociological jargon from the term *childless* to the newer term *voluntarily childfree*. The decision not to have children is becoming increasingly common, not only in the United States, but also in other industrialized nations, especially as women's educational attainment, occupational commitments, and income reach new levels (Giles, Shaw, & Morgan, 2009).

Nonetheless, resisting social expectations that married couples ought to bear children requires a high level of personal autonomy and less need for social support from a wide range of reference groups. It may also require a competing positive identity, such as commitment to one's career goals, or a redefinition of gender roles to sustain and validate this decision.

Kelli Cooper (2016) shares her personal thoughts about not having children.

> I believe our purpose is to experience life from our unique perspective, and be happy—not simply reproduce. That is just one of the countless experiences available to us.
>
> But that conditioning runs deep, and I struggled at times. I worried I was "weird" or would regret it. There are some pretty unflattering assumptions about women like me, like we are selfish, cold or emotionally damaged. Harsh.
>
> I do know for certain there was never a time when I felt like I wanted children. I was never really "on the fence" and my journey was more of examining why I felt this way so strongly, and getting comfortable with it.
>
> The moment I truly realized how I felt was while doing some exercise from a book. I was to write down a list of things I wanted most, and then rank them in order of importance.
>
> I remember being really into it, and excitedly writing down all my desires without restraint. There was travel, devoting myself to personal growth, inspiring people to live a better life, being self-employed and living life on my own terms. I had a burning desire to be free. All of these things came to pass, and it's wonderful. And during this exercise, having children **literally** did not enter my mind, not even as a thought I rejected.

The U.S. culture continues to be *pronatalist,* placing a high value on the meaning of parenthood in adult life. Women's childbearing decisions are often influenced by their own mothers' religiosity and their childhood religious teachings (Pearce, 2002). In some ethnic and religious groups, having children is considered a sacred trust. For example, within the Mormon Church, children are highly valued. "Mormon doctrine states that children are the spirit sons and daughters of heavenly parents, and that God holds parents responsible for their stewardship in raising them in righteousness" (Lambert & Thomasson, 1997, p. 90).

Through a pronatalist lens, motherhood is viewed as the symbol of a woman's ultimate identity, regardless of her other talents or accomplishments. Mary Blair-Loy (2001) described a powerful *family devotion schema* among women—a view that the ideal mother should be committed full-time to her children and the well-being of her family. This view is contrasted to the *work devotion schema*, which suggests that an ideal employee should devote all time to the work setting. In comparison to people in many European countries, workers in the United States work longer days, take less vacation, have no paid maternity leave, and have limited access to quality infant care. The tensions between pronatalist cultural values, devotion to the work ideal, and the lack of workplace policies that support parenting result in many women leaving the labor market during their childbearing years or reducing their labor participation to part-time employment (Williams & Cooper, 2004).

FURTHER REFLECTION: Summarize your views about the importance of having children. How does childbearing fit into your concept of yourself as an adult and your plans for adult life?

Work

OBJECTIVE 4 Define the concept of work in early adulthood and explore how work stimulates psychosocial development.

Within the life course framework, the occupational career is a major trajectory in each person's life story. Efforts to balance and coordinate work and family life produce some of the greatest challenges of adult life. Work is the primary means of accumulating financial resources. It is the focus of attention for much of the waking day. One's work determines in large part the activities, social relationships, challenges, satisfactions, and hassles or frustrations of daily life. Work is the context in which many adults express their personal identity, experience a sense of personal value, and achieve their social status.

In chapter 10 (Later Adolescence), we discussed the developmental task of career choice, emphasizing the link between career decision making and other aspects of individual identity. Here we focus on adaptation to the world of work where the demands of work present new challenges and opportunities for development.

The concept of work is complex. The following discussion considers a few general characteristics of work and their potential impact on cognitive, social, and emotional development and on one's sense of self in adulthood. It is difficult to be more specific since occupational roles are so varied and each job role places the individual in a somewhat different psychosocial context, with a unique combination of expectations, resources, and strains.

The World of Work

To appreciate the variety of career paths and their impact on daily life, you may want to consult the Bureau of Labor Statistics' *Occupational Outlook Handbook,* which has projections

val lawless/Shutterstock.com

This typewriter was a staple technology of the publishing, secretarial, business and journalism fields. Now it is obsolete.

for jobs in hundreds of industries for the period 2014 to 2024 (www.bls.gov/ooh). For each career, the handbook provides information about the training and education needed, earnings, expected job prospects, what workers do on the job, and working conditions.

The nature of the workplace is changing rapidly. Many factors have introduced new levels of uncertainty into the process of choosing a career, finding work, and staying employed. These factors include: the transformation from agricultural to manufacturing to service, computer, and advanced technologies; the increasingly global nature of business; the higher educational standards required for entry into many careers; the expectation that workers will be able to perform across a variety of tasks; and the rapid evolution and extinction of specific types of work brought on by new technologies. Even as advanced technologies are creating new kinds of jobs and careers, automation and robotics are replacing others. Think of the way Amazon and other online services are replacing retail "brick and mortar" stores, or the way self-service kiosks are replacing cashiers. The most common occupations in the United States—retail salesperson, cashier, food and beverage server, and office clerk—may eventually be substantially reduced or replaced through automation (Thompson, 2015). Those who are writing about the future of the workforce suggest that growth areas include robotics, cybersecurity, the commercialization of genetically modified products, mining and application of big data sets, and the impact of digital technologies on money and markets (Ross, 2016). Preparation for these fields obviously begins with advanced courses at the high school level in science and math, continued education at the undergraduate and graduate levels, and ongoing workplace training.

Because economic, technical, and social conditions are changing so rapidly, young adults face two related challenges as they navigate the world of work. First, they cannot expect that strategies or patterns that led to success in the past will necessarily lead to success in the future. Second, they need to be more proactive in designing or inventing an occupational identity that conveys the way their unique education, talents, and experiences are a good fit for the demands of a particular kind of work (Handy, 2001, 2008; Patton & McMahon, 2006).

The early phases of career decision making, presented in Tiedeman's model in chapter 10, focus on self-understanding; career exploration; identifying a good match between personal interests, skills, and values, and particular careers; and learning as much as possible about the specific job opportunities in a career domain. However, because of the wide variety of occupational choices and associated work settings, one can make only limited progress in preparing to enact a specific occupational role during later adolescence. Even though many employers consider educational attainment a selection criterion, they often use it more as an element in determining one's eligibility for the job rather than as a detailed assessment of whether one has the background and skills to perform it. For that reason, many employers emphasize the importance of internships, apprenticeships, and/or course-related field experiences as valued qualifications. What is more, organizations are moving away from large numbers of permanent full-time employees toward more part-time, consulting, and project-based positions.

Most jobs require a period of training for the entry-level employee, which varies from a few weeks in the case of an assembly-line worker to 10 years in the case of a physician. This is the induction phase in Tiedeman's model. Most people do not stay at their first job. A national longitudinal study followed the work experiences of people who were 18 years old in 1978 through age 48. During this period, the average number of jobs they held was 11.7 (Bureau of Labor Statistics, 2015d). A job was defined as a period of uninterrupted employment with the same employer, even if the job responsibilities changed. Most of this job mobility occurred during later adolescence (18 to 24), when the average number of jobs held was 5.5. By the age of 30 to 34, the average number of jobs held was 2.4. Even at the age of 40 to 48, the average number of jobs held was 2.4, suggesting a degree of job mobility over the stages of early and middle adulthood. Job changes do not necessarily imply a complete career change. A person might work for different employers doing the same type of work. The formation of what has been called an attachment to one's career takes most adults a while to establish. Therefore, the training phase is not only about acquiring the specific knowledge and skills necessary to carry out the work, but also about developing the personal, interpersonal, and transferable skills that will be important as one moves around the labor market.

The training period involves a process of socialization of the new worker. During this time, the individual must evaluate the match between personal characteristics and goals and four central components of the work situation: (1) technical skills, (2) authority relations, (3) unique demands and hazards, and (4) interpersonal relations with coworkers. These are the major arenas for new learning in early adulthood. Each of these components might become a source of increasing satisfaction or personal dissatisfaction that might lead to the decision to look for a new position.

Technical Skills. Most jobs require a degree of technical expertise, which varies greatly from one occupation to another. The job training phase involves learning new skills. A report from the Organisation for Economic Cooperation and Development summarized the amount of informal training experienced by workers in 35 countries. More than 40 percent of adults reported being involved in some type of informal education or training each year, with a lifetime average of 715 hours of job-related informal education over their career. Workers with more formal education also sought and received more informal job-related education (OECD, 2011). Specific skill training and general technical competence are part of the job demands. The success of individuals in learning and applying new skills determines to some extent whether they will become attached to the occupation. At the same time, the opportunity to learn new skills is part of what permits new workers to advance and seek new employment.

As a result of the recession of 2007–2008, a large number of workers were forced to seek new skills through job retraining in the wake of massive firings and downsizing. Trade Adjustment Assistance is a government program for workers who were laid off as a result of shifting industry to foreign countries and who enroll in new training programs. Since its inception, over 2 million U.S. workers have taken advantage

Jeneen is just out of engineering school. She is working with a civil engineering firm to explore a career in the building and construction field. Here, she works with Ted, a master engineer with many years of experience on the job. He is teaching her how to read a blueprint and translate the plan into a reality in this partially constructed building. While she explores this field in order to determine if she enjoys this work, the firm observes how well she learns and performs in order to determine whether she should be encouraged to continue in this field.

iStockphoto.com

of this program to return to school and learn new skills in fields that have growth potential. Some colleges and universities have made a special effort to reach out to returning adult students to offer retraining to those whose jobs were lost as a result of the economic downturn. For example, Beverly Berndt was laid off from her job as a computer programmer for a cabinet hardware distributor. With help from the Trade Adjustment Assistance act, she went back to school to earn her nursing degree. "I hate to say it, but getting laid off from Belwith was probably the best thing that ever happened to me—getting help from the state for tuition and books, and drawing unemployment—I couldn't have done it without it" (Bauer, 2010).

Authority Relations. Each job role specifies status and decision-making relationships among workers. One aspect of job training is learning which people evaluate one's work, the criteria they use, and the limits of one's autonomy in the job. In today's organizational environment, career ladders are less obvious, and the authority hierarchy may be difficult to identify. Young workers may be assigned to a number of projects with different leaders, they may be asked to take on significant leadership roles early in their careers, and they may need to form interdependent, collaborative teams (Collin & Young, 2000). New workers must attend to both the authority structure and the people who occupy positions in it. They must also assess the channels for decision making and the ways in which they can influence decisions. With respect to the people who occupy positions of authority, new workers must be able to deal with a variety of personalities in positions of higher and lower status. Having a good relationship with one's supervisor is a key element in job satisfaction. The opportunity to form a cooperative relationship with an experienced mentor has been identified as a valued feature of career satisfaction and professional advancement. For early-career phase workers, the immediate supervisor can play a key role by recognizing the talents of a younger worker, encouraging a worker to apply for more training, or providing a positive recommendation for a promotion (Hudson et al., 2013).

Vic is a designer with a fashion magazine. He loves leading a relaxed, creative group of young designers as they prepare the next edition of the magazine. Part of his value to the firm is his ability to develop a creative team of designers to reach optimal productivity.

Roughly one third of American workers report that they experience some form of hostility from their supervisor at work in the form of being belittled, yelled at, or undermined. Typically, people in positions of authority are supposed to encourage and support those who work for them. However, when people in positions of power perceive threats to their competence or feel incompetent in a domain in which they are supposed to have authority, a likely reaction is to become aggressive. When bosses feel inadequate, they may lash out at those who are less powerful (Fast & Chen, 2009). It may not be possible for a new worker to achieve a good working relationship with a boss who is extremely defensive. Having an abusive supervisor is likely to produce negative emotions in the worker, resulting in work and job withdrawal. Especially among men, strong negative emotions produced by supervisory abuse are associated with an increased likelihood of quitting the job altogether (Atwater et al., 2016).

Demands and Hazards. Each job has unique occupational demands, including norms for self-preservation, productivity, and availability. In some work settings, the worker comes into contact with clients, patients, or customers who are very stressed, anxious, rude, or aggressive. The worker has to manage the hostile outbursts or attacks in a professional way in order to avoid escalation, but exposure to this type of negative affect can be very distressing for the worker who is trying to carry out a job as effectively as possible. For example, in some schools, teachers and other staff are exposed to student violence, creating a perception of a dangerous work environment. Experiences of victimization were linked to poor work engagement and high rates of staff burnout, especially in schools where staff perceived the school leadership as unable to limit or manage student violence (Bass et al., 2016).

A licensed vocational nurse described the tensions that come with being berated by a patient's family members.

> If you are working in an office and someone comes in and they're having words with you and maybe they're rude and you can say, "Listen, you've gone too far and you need to leave," whereas we have family members who come up to us and say, "How come you…? How dare you…?" And they can just be rude and say terrible things and we cannot, we really cannot, we really are not expected to, nor are we really allowed to answer back. (Bullock & Morales Waugh, 2004, p. 775)

Occupational hazards include a range of potential physical and psychological risks associated with the workplace, including exposure to toxins, work-related injuries, exposure to diseases or reproductive hazards, and working conditions that have negative psychological consequences, such as noise or shift work. The rate of work-related deaths and disabling injuries has decreased substantially since the 1960s. Nonetheless, in 2014, there were 4,821 deaths and 3 million disabling injuries and illnesses among U.S. workers in private industries, and over 700,000 injuries and illnesses among U.S. workers in public sector industries (e.g. police, firefighters, etc.) (U.S. Bureau of Labor Statistics, 2015b, c, 2016f).

Settings differ in the kinds of pressures or hazards they impose on workers. For example, mining is one of the most dangerous occupations. In 2014, 46 workers died in mining accidents, highlighting the fact that many workers continue to face hazardous conditions such as exposure to intense heat and humidity, exposure to toxic minerals and gases, poor air quality, and long hours underground (U.S. Department of Labor, 2016a). The most common source of fatal occupational injuries is transportation incidents, including crashes on public roadways (Byler et al., 2016).

Just as occupations vary in their risks, individuals differ in their vulnerability to occupational pressures and hazards, their willingness to risk certain potential dangers, and their evaluation of the payoff for enduring some degree of stress. People must ultimately decide whether the particular vulnerabilities are tolerable in light of the rewards.

In 2015, 17.5 percent of adults with disabilities were employed. Workers with disabilities were more likely than others to work part time, to be self-employed, and to work in service occupations. Since persons with disabilities were also likely to have fewer years of formal education, they were also less likely to be in management and professional occupations (Bureau of Labor Statistics, 2016g).

Interpersonal Relationships with Coworkers. The work setting can be a context for the formation of interpersonal relationships including friendship, collaborative teamwork, friendly competition, romantic feelings, and mentoring, as well as negative relationships like bullying, unwanted sexual attention or harassment, and hostile tactics that undermine the achievements of others. Although the potential for friendships in the work setting is usually not advertised as a central component of a job description, workplace friendships are often described as a key feature in the decision to be committed to a particular work setting. The need for friends with whom one can share the anxieties of learning the new job provides a strong motive for seeking comradeship on the job. The presence of congenial coworkers who can relax together and share feelings of accomplishment greatly enhances any work setting. In fact, the spirit of friendship on the job may compensate for many stressful situational demands. A workplace that creates space for collaboration and social interaction is likely to promote friendship formation and foster a more positive interpersonal environment.

Some work settings stress competition among coworkers; incentives are arranged to stimulate competition rather than cooperation. In such settings, new workers often must shoulder the strains of their new learning independently. Some settings create both competitive and cooperative norms by creating teams or production units that compete with one another for incentives. Under these arrangements intergroup relations tend to be more distrustful, whereas individual relations among team members tend to be more trusting and cooperative. The greater the commitment to the team's goal, especially under conditions of supportive leadership and encouragement for interdependence, the greater the team's effectiveness and the participants' sense of the team effort as a high-quality experience (Aubé & Rousseau, 2005). Knowledge sharing is one of the essential ingredients for successful team performance. However, in some settings, individuals who are rewarded for their individual achievement may be reluctant to share their knowledge or expertise with others, especially if this would result in reduced compensation for their individual performance. Support for shared leadership and shared knowledge within project teams may require the introduction of new limited-access web-based tools and new team-based incentives (Barnett & Weidenfeller, 2016; Jafari Navimipour & Charband, 2016). Many companies are introducing retreats that foster team-building and collaboration in order to bring a new spirit of interpersonal trust to the workplace.

Workplace bullying has become a growing concern. Managers recognize that bullying results in increased illness and absences as well as decreases in productivity (Meyers, 2006). Workers who have been bullied may be afraid or embarrassed to say anything about it. However, when interviewed about their experiences they describe the impact in powerful terms. "I feel that I have been maimed. . . . I've been beaten, abused, broken, scared. . . . I feel like I have 'kick me' tattooed on my forehead" (Tracy, Lutgen-Sandvik, & Alberts, 2006). The presence of egotistical, narcissistic, and aggressive coworkers can quickly disrupt the interpersonal climate of the workplace, making it harder to solve problems or collaborate on new initiatives. People who are exposed to insults or bullying at work are likely to suffer feelings of exclusion and depression, which may result in lashing out against other coworkers, thereby adding to the hostile climate.

Sexual harassment, defined as "unwelcome sexual advances, requests for sexual favors, and other verbal or physical harassment of a sexual nature... is illegal when it is so frequent or severe that it creates a hostile or offensive work environment or when it results in an adverse employment decision (such as the victim being fired or demoted)" (U.S. Equal Employment Opportunity Commission (EEOC), 2016). In 2015, the EEOC received over 6,800 allegations of workplace sexual harassment.

Many incidents of sexual harassment do not come to the level of federal investigation. A recent *Cosmopolitan* online survey found that in the more informal workplace, where coworkers interact on social media, through text messaging, and at informal gatherings, sexual harassment is pervasive.

Roughly 1 in 3 women ages 18 to 34 has been sexually harassed at work, reveals our study of 2,235 fulltime and part-time female employees, conducted by the polling firm SurveyMonkey. The problem is at its worst in the restaurant industry, where 42 percent of women say they've experienced it, but it has also affected 36 percent of women in retail, 31 percent in science/tech, 31 percent in arts/entertainment, and 30 percent in the legal field. . . .

Cosmopolitan's survey reveals a no-filter, say-anything workplace: Eight in 10 of those who were sexually harassed at work say it involves something said out loud. Forty-four percent of women who were sexually harassed say they've encountered unwanted touching and sexual advances. And about 1 in 4 have received lewd texts or e-mails. (Ruiz, 2015)

It is not uncommon for victims of sexual harassment to leave their workplace, thus suffering both humiliating abuse and job loss.

Poverty and Career Opportunities

Among the most obvious limiting factors the range of occupational opportunities open to a person during the work search phase are educational attainment, ability, and location. Discrimination on the basis of race and gender also continues to thwart the full participation of women and minorities in the workforce.

Since the 1970s there has been a growing gap between the quality of "good jobs" and "bad jobs" (Kalleberg, 2011). Factors including deregulation, global competition, increasing service sector work and declining manufacturing, weakening labor unions, and the reduced purchasing power of the minimum wage have all contributed to the expansion of precarious employment. Those with the most education are likely to be able to find jobs that have higher wages, some degree of job security, opportunities for control over their work schedule, and possibilities for advancement. However, a growing number of jobs pay low wages, offer few benefits, and offer no security. As a result, a large group of people are considered the "working poor;" they are working full time but are at less than 200 percent of the poverty level (Davis, 2010).

Recent economic conditions have added to a societal context in which relatively few resources are allocated to support low-income families. In a comparison of 21 rich nations, the overall poverty rate for all persons ranged from a low of 5.4 percent in Finland to a high of 20.2 percent in Mexico. The United States was second highest on the list, after Mexico. This dubious honor can be explained by a combination of two factors: (1) The United States has the highest proportion of workers in poorly paid jobs, and (2) the United States spends much less than most other countries on benefits that provide cash supplements, health, education, child care, or housing for low-wage workers (Smeeding, 2008). In 2014, about one third of the U.S. population earns 200 percent of the poverty level or less. The following example illustrates how close the working poor are to complete financial ruin.

> Karen Wall, 38, works as a teacher, cheerleading coach and weekend bartender. Yet money is tight, and all of it goes to keeping her family afloat and paying off her student loan debt. Both of her boys have special needs, so even with the multiple income sources, Wall knows she's only one disaster away from losing it all. "If I got in a car accident, I'd be homeless," she said. "If I get laid off from any of my jobs, my kids will end up going hungry." (Wing, 2014)

Successful programs that try to prepare individuals and families for self-sufficiency typically emphasize some combination of basic education, job skills training, and adaptive work orientation with supports such as child care subsidies and medical benefits. Some programs put more time and resources into improving the conditions of the jobs and fostering employee skills. Programs that combine work with career counseling, earnings supplements, health insurance, and child care subsidies have the combined benefits of decreasing poverty rates in a community, increasing long-term employment, and fostering children's well-being and school performance (Duncan, Huston, & Weisner, 2007). Nonetheless, the lack of jobs that consider the needs of single parents, families with children with special needs, or individuals with disabilities result in a constant struggle for significant subgroups of the population to find work that provides a healthy quality of life.

Career Phases and Individual Development

In an attempt to synthesize career and individual development, Kathy Kram (1985; Ragins & Kram, 2007) proposed a developmental model of career issues (see Table 11.3). Careers are delineated in three phases—early career, middle career, and late career—which correspond roughly to the phases of career exploration, career establishment and advancement, and career maintenance and disengagement. In each phase, career development reflects *concerns about self*, including questions of competence and identity; *concerns about career*, including questions of occupational commitment, advancement, and the quality of relationships in the work setting; and *concerns about family*, especially family-role definition and possible conflicts between work and family life. Typical issues facing the person at each phase are suggested in Table 11.3.

Issues of greatest concern during the early career phase reflect the need to demonstrate competence and to establish a satisfying lifestyle. Career development is never a completely rational process. As organizational loyalty gives way to a free-agent orientation to career development, individuals have to take a more assertive, risk-taking approach to their career development. In the early career phase, a person needs to reflect on his or her aspirations. This involves reviewing the central identity commitments that give meaning to one's life, including personal, career, and family values and goals. With respect to career goals, one must consider a mid-length time frame, looking ahead 3 to 5 years to think about the kinds of continuing education, experiences, and network of contacts that will contribute to the achievement of these goals. In this process, one confronts uncertainties about the meaning of work, worries about financial self-sufficiency, and potential conflicts between work and other spheres of life, especially intimate relations and family responsibilities.

In a survey conducted by the American Psychological Association, people were asked about various sources of stress in their lives (American Psychological Association, 2010). Even though about two thirds of the sample reported feeling satisfied with their jobs, 41 percent said they typically feel tense or stressed out during the workday. The younger workers, those in the age range 18 to 30, were most likely to report some lost productivity due to stress at work. Fears of the unknown—of taking on new responsibilities, of discovering the limits to one's abilities, and of disappointing important people in one's life—must all be faced and reframed if one is to achieve the adaptive flexibility necessary in today's world of work.

FURTHER REFLECTION: *Hypothesize about how meaningful work can stimulate adult development and how exploitation, discrimination, or thankless work can undermine development.*

What are your essential goals in the world of work? What steps are you taking to achieve those goals?

Lifestyle

OBJECTIVE 5 Examine the role of lifestyle development as an expression of an individual's personal identity, with consideration for the pace of life, balancing competing role demands, building a supportive social network, and adopting practices to promote health, fitness, and nutrition.

Table 11.3	Characteristic Developmental Tasks at Successive Career Stages		
	Early Career	**Middle Career**	**Late Career**
Concerns about self	Competence: Can I be effective in the managerial/professional role? Can I be effective in the role of spouse and/or parent?	Competence: How do I compare with my peers, with my subordinates, and with my own standards and expectations?	Competence: Can I be effective in a more consultative and less central role, still having influence as the time to leave the organization gets closer?
	Identity: Who am I as a manager/ professional? What are my skills and aspirations?	Identity: Who am I now that I am no longer a novice? What does it mean to be a "senior" adult?	Identity: What will I leave behind of value that will symbolize my contributions during my career? Who am I apart from a manager/professional, and how will it feel to be without the role?
Concerns about career	Commitment: How involved and committed to the organization do I want to become? Do I want to seriously explore other options?	Commitment: Do I still want to invest as heavily in my career as I did in previous years? What can I commit myself to if the goal of advancement no longer exists?	Commitment: What can I commit myself to outside of my career that will provide meaning and a sense of involvement? How can I let go of my involvement in my work role after so many years?
	Advancement: Do I want to advance? Can I advance without compromising important values?	Advancement: Will I have the opportunity to advance? How can I feel productive if I am not going to advance further?	Advancement: Given that my next move is likely to be out of the organization, how do I feel about my final level of advancement? Am I satisfied with what I have achieved?
	Relationships: How can I establish effective relationships with peers and supervisors? As I advance, how can I prove my competence and worth to others?	Relationships: How can I work effectively with peers with whom I am in direct competition? How can I work effectively with subordinates who may surpass me?	Relationships: How can I maintain positive relationships with my boss, peers, and subordinates as I get ready to disengage from this setting? Can I continue to mentor and sponsor as my career comes to an end? What will happen to significant work relationships when I leave?
Concerns about family	Family role definition: How can I establish a satisfying personal life? What kind of lifestyle do I want to establish?	Family role definition: What is my role in the family now that my children are grown?	Family role definition: What will my role in the family be when I am no longer involved in a career? How will my significant relationships with spouse and/or children change?
	Work/family conflict: How can I effectively balance work and family commitments? How can I spend time with my family without jeopardizing my career advancement?	Work/family conflict: How can I make up for the time away from my family when I was launching my career as a novice?	Work/family conflict: Will family and leisure activities suffice, or will I want to begin a new career?

Source: *From Mentoring at Work: Developmental Relationships in Organizational Life*, by K. E. Kram. © 1985 Scott Foresman.

Lifestyle is a social psychological construct that integrates personality characteristics, goals, convictions, and inner conflicts with social opportunities and resources into an organized pattern of actions and choices (Lombardi, Melchior, Murphy, & Brinkerhoff, 1996; Slavick, 1995). Simply put, a lifestyle is the self in action (Richman, 2001). Central components of the lifestyle include the tempo or pace of activities, the balance between work and leisure, the focus of time and energy in specific arenas, and the establishment of social relationships at varying degrees of intimacy. One's lifestyle guides decisions about how to organize time and prioritize the use of resources. One can think of lifestyle as the first translation of the values and commitments of individual identity into action through the devotion of time and energy to

certain tasks and relationships and the development of domains of competence.

In the United States, a strong cultural assumption is that individuals are active agents who make choices (Savani et al., 2010). These choices reflect one's preferences and values. In early adulthood, the desire to create a life that is satisfying and meaningful is expressed through choices and decisions one makes about work, leisure, living arrangements, relationships, health, and **fitness**. In general, the more one perceives that there is freedom of choice about these decisions, the greater one's sense of happiness and satisfaction with life (Inglehart, Foa, Peterson, & Welzel, 2008).

Even though a person may experience considerable social pressure to build an identity around an occupational focus, the concept of lifestyle reinforces the idea that a person's work or career is not the same as a meaningful life (Allan, Douglass, Duffy, & McCarty, 2016). Because career choices can have such an impact on other aspects of life, it is important to select a career that supports a life, not the other way around. The following discussion illustrates some ways in which the overlapping systems of early adulthood—intimate relationships, parenting, and career—interact to organize characteristics of the lifestyle.

Pace of Life

Some counselors use the metaphor of a three-dimensional space to describe the lifestyle (Amundson, 2001). *Length* is the length of life, or where one is along a developmental continuum. For example, in early adulthood one is likely to view life as stretching out for many years into the future, as compared to middle adulthood when one is likely to think that one's life is about half over. *Width* is the busyness of life, including multiple role demands and how much activity one tries to jam into each day. *Depth* is the sense of purpose and meaning in life and the experiences of satisfaction or fulfillment that come with it. This three-dimensional configuration changes over the course of life, both as a result of personal changes in goals or developmental needs and as a result of situational changes in demands or resources.

The **pace of life**, or the busyness of life, is shaped by work, family, personality, and environmental context. For most young adults, the work setting largely determines the structure of time, including when one goes to work and returns, what one feels energetic enough to do after work, how much time is free for leisure or vacations, and the amount of preparation required during nonworking hours to prepare for the next day. People who are trying to combine parenting with a long workday experience the greatest time bind. Schedule control, rather than reducing the number of hours of work, seems to be especially important for helping people maintain a sense of lifestyle balance (Tausig & Fenwick, 2001).

Activity level, or the pace of life, is influenced in part by one's temperament, health, and fitness. This is a circular issue. Adults whose lives are very sedentary are likely to have lower levels of endurance and to feel the strain of daily exertion. Those who are more active and who include physical activity in their lifestyle are likely to have more energy and to be able to handle the demands of an active life.

The pace of life is also influenced by the climate and community. In a comparison of pace of life in 31 countries, the pace was faster in colder climates, more economically productive countries, and more individualistic countries (Levine & Norenzayan, 1999). In that study, Japan had the fastest pace of life. Pace of life may also be seasonal. In northern climates, for example, there may be fewer social events away from home during the winter, and life may therefore revolve primarily around the home. In spring and summer, neighborhood activities become a more important stimulus for social life as people emerge and renew their friendships. Rural communities often provide a calmer pace of life than urban communities. People often choose to live in rural or rural-like communities, even when they work in the city, to escape from the hectic pace of urban life. Pace of life is both a feature of personal lifestyle and a feature of a community or culture.

Social Network

Most people expand their social network during early adulthood. They form friendships in their neighborhood and at work. In some work settings, coworkers help each other balance their work and family life by taking shifts for one another, covering special family holidays, or carpooling to save expenses. Young adults may become involved in the social life of their religious community or civic associations. They may engage in community volunteer projects with friends and become more invested in the social needs of their neighborhood. If they have young children, the parents of other young children at the child care center or preschool may become important sources of social support. When options are possible, individuals often look for housing in neighborhoods where there are others in their same life stage and lifestyle orientation. For example, when couples with young children live in a community with other young families, they tend to rate the community more favorably than couples living in the community who do not have children (Swisher, Sweet, & Moen, 2004). The contribution of friendships to personal satisfaction and lifestyle differs widely during this time, with single adults and couples without children typically having more time for adult friendships than do parents.

The rapid and continuously expanding growth in the use of online social networking sites including Facebook, Twitter, and LinkedIn reflects the important role of social networks in the lives of contemporary young adults. There are over 2 billion users worldwide of online social networking sites, with the estimate projected to reach 3 billion by the year 2020 (Statista, 2016). About 90 percent of those ages 18 to 29 use these sites (Perrin, 2015). Social networking sites have a variety of functions, including staying connected with the activities of friends and relatives, sharing information and opinions about products or experiences, gaining recognition for accomplishments, and encouraging participation in upcoming events (Back et al., 2010; Boyd and Ellison, 2007). The online social networking sites function as

The social network for new mothers often includes other new mothers who are facing similar demands and challenges. They discuss their strategies, share information and resources, and give each other emotional support.

mass communication vehicles powered by individual users who share their experiences and ideas with friends and associates. As these sites have grown, the possibility of making personalized contact with a wide and diverse audience has changed the nature and meaning of social networks so that they are now potentially quite vast, fluid, and include individuals who have never met face-to-face.

Online social network sites have become an indispensable resource for enacting and enhancing one's lifestyle. No matter what one's interests, hobbies, or needs, it is possible to find others who are willing to share their opinions or who have information about the availability, cost, and quality of community resources.

Striving for Work/Life Balance

A challenge faced in early adulthood is the management of competing role demands. Adults struggle with the tensions between the demands of the work setting and the demands of building an intimate relationship; with the tension between the desire to have children and the desire to achieve in the workplace; and with legitimate expectations for commitment to the worker role and the desire to experience fulfillment in other domains such as sports, arts, or community service. As more and more women with young children entered the labor market, the concept of work/life balance originally focused on issues related to conflicts between worker and parent roles. Research addressed the strains created by competing demands of work and family roles, including health-related impact, absenteeism, and reduced productivity (van Emmerik, Bakker, Westman, & Peeters, 2016).

Recent literature has expanded the idea of balance to consider the broader scope of work and *personal life,* reflecting the diversity of roles, commitments, and personal goals that dominate a person's lifestyle. The emphasis of this work is on approaches that support a healthy, satisfying quality of life for workers and a productive work/life organizational culture. Studies differ in how the term "balance" is defined and the factors that are considered important determinants for achieving balance. An ecological framework suggests that factors that contribute to the achievement of balance can be found at the individual, couple, family, job, corporate, and larger societal levels (Grawitch & Ballard, 2016).

For both men and women, the world of work is likely to provide the most rigorous test of commitment and the greatest pressures for productivity during the early adult years. For example, researchers have documented the impact of daily workplace events and the way men and women behave when they come home at the end of the day. At the end of a negatively arousing and stressful day of work, women are more likely to be angry at home whereas men are more likely to be withdrawn (Schulz, Cowan, Pape, Cowan, & Brennan, 2004).

Pressures in the work setting may come from a number of sources such as unpleasant interpersonal interactions, being bullied, increased pace and demands of work, feelings of incompetence, or frustration at being undervalued. Women who work full time in an inflexible work setting and who experience a high degree of work-related pressure have to deal with spillover into home and family life. This spillover competes directly with needs for intimacy and also with the time and energy needed

for parenting. As a result, these women also exhibit a variety of depressive symptoms that make it difficult to cope with work demands. The greater these workplace stressors, the more likely they are to disrupt the quality of partner interactions at home, thereby reducing the availability of social support that might help buffer women from unrealistic work expectations (Goodman & Crouter, 2009).

As the opening case suggests, poor work/life balance can erode the quality of one's most valued relationships. It is also associated with a number of negative health consequences: fatigue, poor health, increased leg and back pain, stress-related impact on the immune system, loss of joy in living, and related depression and burnout (Mayo Clinic, 2015c).

In an analysis of the role demands of dual-earner families, researchers identified three distinct dual-earner lifestyles—high status, low stress, and main-secondary—each with its own pattern of role relationships, costs, and benefits (Crouter & Manke, 1997; Crouter, 2006). In the *high-status* couples, both partners had high-prestige careers, earned comparatively high salaries, and were involved in their work. In these couples, the division of household work was more equal than in the other two types. They experienced the greatest amount of role overload, had lower levels of love and marital satisfaction, and had more marital conflict than the other two groups.

The *low-stress* couples worked about the same amount of hours as the high-status couples, but their jobs were less prestigious. Examples were a mechanic and a secretary, and a salesman and a substitute teacher. Although the couples had levels of involvement similar to the high-status group, they had the lowest amount of role overload. This group had the highest scores in marital satisfaction and love for their spouse, and the lowest scores in marital conflict. These couples monitored their children more closely and seemed to be more accurate in describing their children's daily activities.

The *main-secondary* couples reflected a lifestyle in which husbands were the primary workers, with higher occupational prestige, more hours worked, and more work involvement than their wives, who typically worked part time. Women in these relationships had less education and tended to have more household responsibilities. A gender-typed division of labor was reflected in the pattern for female children, who performed more household tasks than girls in the other family types, whereas male children in these families performed fewer household tasks than boys in the other family types. This research illustrates the role of individuals and couples in managing work/life balance in part by decisions they make about the kinds of careers they pursue and the ways they support their partners' career choices.

Successful work/life balance depends upon a combination of personal coping strategies and workplace policies that support flexibility (Daverth, Hyde, & Cassell, 2016; Russo, Shteigman, & Carmeli, 2016). Given the vast differences in job demands and schedules, no one set of policies can apply across all workplace settings. The U.S. Department of Labor has created a Workplace Flexibility Toolkit to help workers, employers, and policy makers in identifying strategies that can address this importance aspect of modern life (U.S. Department of Labor, 2016b).

Health, Fitness, and Nutrition

The contemporary emphasis on health, fitness, and nutrition highlights the importance of lifestyle decisions for illness prevention, wellness, and longevity. Research on health and health-related risks has begun to identify characteristics of a healthy lifestyle, including factors that operate at an individual level and those that reflect community commitment (see Healthy People, 2000, 2010, 2020). Leading health indicators include such practices as the use of preventive health services, regular exercise, eating a well-balanced diet high in fruits and vegetables and low in fat, avoiding smoking, limiting the number of sexual partners, and using contraceptives.

Many nutritionists recommend having a healthy breakfast, increasing the amount of fruits and vegetables, focusing on lean proteins, drinking 6 to 8 glasses of water a day, and eating 4 to 6 small meals rather than three big meals a day. Consider how often one of the following situations might interfere with a young adult's intention to eat a healthy, nutritious diet (Taylor, 2016):

- You have an unexpected early conference call, so you miss breakfast.
- You're at work and have an unexpected meeting to attend right before your usual break. No time to grab a snack.
- You're traveling; no chance to prepare healthy meals to take along.
- You're in a meeting and it's gone into overtime; you only have time to grab whatever is nearby (donuts or bagels).
- You're running errands and lose track of time, and there's nowhere to get a good healthy meal.
- You get home late; you're too stressed, too tired, or too overworked to eat a good nutritious meal and end up eating junk food.

An aspect of lifestyle that is often overlooked is the daily pattern of sleep and waking hours. A growing concern focuses on the large number of people who do not get the nightly sleep they require. This can lead to serious health problems, deficits in performance and alertness, increased risk of motor vehicle accidents, and impaired memory and cognitive functioning. In addition to problems with disrupted sleep or inadequate sleep, shifting one's bedtime by more than 2 hours can cause difficulties in falling asleep, staying asleep, or waking up on time and feeling restored by sleep (Vital Signs, 2010). Conditions of one's lifestyle, including living arrangements, the time one has to be at work or return from work; the noise level of the neighborhood; one's involvement in leisure activities including television viewing, online social networking, or gaming; and the use of drugs or alcohol, can all influence the amount and quality of one's sleep.

The concept of encouraging young adults to adopt a lifestyle that promotes health is becoming a focus for preventive health care. Lifestyle patterns established in early and middle adulthood, including one's diet, activity level, exercise, encounters with challenging and intellectually stimulating tasks, and reduced involvement with cigarette smoking and alcohol, all influence health and vitality in later life.

Although the establishment of a healthy lifestyle can be viewed as an individual's responsibility, healthy communities

Shawn Hempel/Alamy Stock Photo

Here in Amsterdam, thousands of health conscious adults ride their bicycles to work, school, and recreational activities. You can see from the parking arrangements the vast number of people who use their bicycles daily.

are shaped by adults who share a common vision about the lifestyle they want for themselves and their families. Many aspects of fitness can be achieved at the individual or family level; however, some, such as air and water quality, access to health care, reduction of violence, or access to safe settings that promote physical activity, require a community commitment. Adults may join together to create resources and programs that increase the involvement of children and adults in regular physical activity. They may form a coalition of parents, health care professionals, educators, business leaders, and law enforcement agencies to devise a plan to decrease incidents of violence in their community.

Commitment to a healthy lifestyle may be enacted through efforts to improve air and water quality, reduce exposure to secondhand smoke, improve availability and access to health care services and health education, or increase support for environmental resources that sustain physical activity. For example, a report on walking and biking provides information about patterns of biking and walking in the 50 states, infrastructure that supports safe biking and walking, the relationship of biking and walking to health and well-being, and funding for projects that improve opportunities and resources for walking and biking (Steele, 2010). FIGURES 11.6 and 11.7 ▶ provide international comparisons for

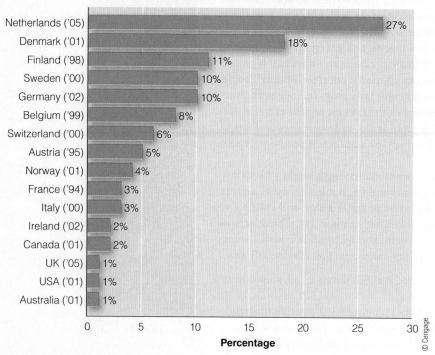

FIGURE 11.6 ▶ COMPARISON OF THE PERCENTAGE OF TRIPS MADE BY BICYCLE IN 16 COUNTRIES

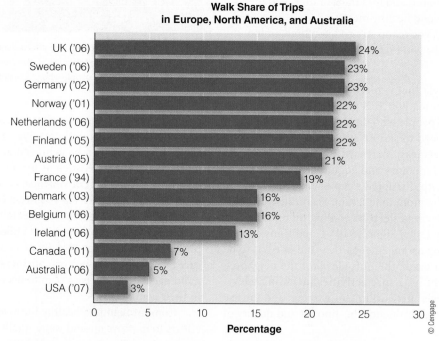

FIGURE 11.7 ▶ COMPARISON OF THE PERCENTAGE OF TRIPS MADE BY WALKING IN 14 COUNTRIES

the percentage of individual trips that are carried out by biking and walking in Europe, North America, and Australia. As the data show, people in the United States are at the bottom with respect to the frequency with which they bike or walk to their destinations. The relationship of limited physical activity to significant health problems, especially obesity, diabetes, and high blood pressure, is well documented. Efforts by communities to improve the infrastructure to support walking and bicycling can have important benefits for public health, as well as improvements in pedestrian safety and reduced traffic and air pollution.

FURTHER REFLECTION: Describe your current lifestyle. How do you use your time? What do you consider to be the essential structure of your lifestyle?

Are you comfortable and satisfied with the pace of your life and the meaningfulness of your lifestyle? If not, what could you do to modify your lifestyle?

The Psychosocial Crisis: Intimacy Versus Isolation

OBJECTIVE 6 Define and describe the psychosocial crisis of intimacy versus isolation, the central process through which the crisis is resolved, mutuality among peers, the prime adaptive ego quality of love, and the core pathology of exclusivity.

We have seen the importance of a sense of belonging in every stage of the life span. Accompanying these feelings of belonging, a sense of mattering emerges that helps a person experience the psychological and physiological benefits of social support. In contrast to the relationships that create a sense of belonging and mattering, some people are unable to engage in the trusting, open, mutually responsive relationships. They may experience rejection, exclusion, or an inability to accept the affection of others, resulting in a sense of isolation.

Intimacy

Intimacy is defined as the ability to experience an open, supportive, tender relationship with another person without fear of losing one's own identity in the process. An **intimate relationship** has both cognitive and affective components. The partners are able to understand each other's point of view. They usually experience a sense of confidence and mutual regard that reflects their respect as well as their affection for each other. Intimacy in a relationship supports independent judgments by each partner. It also permits the disclosure of personal feelings, as well as the sharing and developing of ideas and plans.

There is a sense of mutual enrichment in intimate interactions. Each person perceives enhancement of well-being through affectionate or intellectually stimulating interactions with the other (Erikson, 1963, 1980). Coming as it does after the establishment of personal identity, the possibility of establishing intimacy depends on individuals' perceptions of themselves as valuable, competent, and meaningful people. In an intimate relationship, the partners are aware of one another's aspirations. Under the best of circumstances, the partners interact in such a way as to promote one another's self-fulfillment, reassuring their partner about the possibility of achieving their most important goals and encouraging their self-actualization (Rusbult, Finkel, & Kumashiro, 2009). As exemplified in the following case study, intimacy also supports health and well-being. Intimate partners look after one another, respond to signs of stress or illness with concern, and monitor and contribute to one another's recovery during times of illness or injury.

— CASE STUDY In Sickness and in Health —

"Is that your husband?" The ER nurse is pointing to you, the fever-spiked lump who is snoring softly and muttering beside me. We've been here for hours, and for hours I've returned my lips over and over to your scalding forehead, as if to cool it, or, perhaps, to comfort myself. In just a little while longer, we'll find out that what you have is a severe case of strep, and you will swallow the prescribed pills, and I will finally put my lips to your quietly sleeping forehead and feel a welcome coolness. But for now the nurse's face is creased with compassion and weariness—she is waiting—and it's not really the right time to tell her about your gentle strength: the way you rocked our baby in the sling for hours on end while you graded papers, rocked another baby three years later while you did your anatomy homework, babies peacefully asleep across your broad chest for what feels like my entire adult life. It's not the right time to explain what a funny contradiction you are, a hockey-playing massage therapist, or how just last week you lay your hands on a friend's father while he lay dying in hospice. She wouldn't understand how funny it is that you gave me bedtime coupons—promising to turn in early on the nights I redeem them—because you're a night owl and I miss you in bed, or how it feels when I come down in the morning to a toasty kitchen because you've already lit a fire in our wood stove. She doesn't know that I'm strangely euphoric, sitting here thinking about how lucky I am to have so much to lose — my rock, my mystery, the love of my life—that I'm sitting here thinking *in sickness and in health. I will*, I think. *I do.* But all I can say is yes. "Yes. That's my husband."

Source: C. Newman (2009) *Redbook,* Is this what romance looks like?

CASE ANALYSIS Using What You Know

1. What evidence does this case provide about the feelings of intimacy?
2. How might experiences of a partner's serious illness or injury foster a sense of intimacy?
3. Although the narrative is told by one partner, what can you detect that suggests mutual regard and the partners' interdependence?

It is not difficult to understand that a person would be on intimate terms with parents and siblings. The family is a central context for sharing confidences, expressing love, and revealing weaknesses and areas of dependence. In fact, there is growing evidence that the nature of one's parental attachment orientation influences the ability to form new intimate relationships (Khalifian & Barry, 2016). The unique task of young adulthood is to establish an intimate relationship with someone outside of one's family. Two people who eventually establish intimacy may begin as complete strangers who have very few, if any, common cultural bonds.

The obstacles to attainment of intimacy in a romantic relationship are many. Some arise from childhood experiences of shame, guilt, inferiority, or alienation, which undermine the achievement of personal identity. Others result from incompatibility between partners. The number of adjustments that intimacy requires may overwhelm some young adults. Obstacles to intimacy derive from environmental circumstances that may erode the person's feelings of self-worth or interfere with the establishment of mutuality. These obstacles may be embedded in the socialization process as children learn distinct gender roles that introduce antagonism between men and women and foster interpersonal styles that stand in the way of forming open, caring interpersonal relationships.

Intimacy in the Work Setting

Although we tend to think of intimacy as a quality of romantic bonds, it is increasingly common for young adults to form close, intimate relationships with coworkers. Building on the experiences of group identity in early adolescence, young adults who achieved a positive sense of belonging in a peer group strive to reproduce this sense of loyalty, connection, and collegiality in the workplace. Affiliation and close friendships are likely to develop among coworkers. Workers may express devotion to an older leader or teacher, or with peers who share long hours every day in offices, schools, hospitals, and field settings. Through conversations around projects, solving team problems, attending conferences, or informal interactions on the golf course, the bowling alley, or at the tavern after work, coworkers can achieve an affectionate, playful, and enriching relationship. This kind of intimacy is demonstrated in the following reflection about a coworker.

> Alan was very influential. I respected him as being pretty sharp and pretty astute. He had a lot of guts to tackle the problems that existed in the area and that was the union-management business. I was really identifying with him in terms of what and how you run something, how you manage something. You would sit down and talk about or debate how you do certain things, what should we do in this kind of situation. We would be right in line. I think it was the way I came at a problem; it might be similar to the way he would come at a problem. (Kram, 1985, p. 33)

It may not be surprising to learn that having a "best friend" at work is associated with job satisfaction, engagement in one's work, and productivity. According to research gathered through a Gallup poll, about 30 percent of employees say that they have a best friend at work, and those that do are more productive, produce higher quality work, have a greater feeling of well-being, and are less likely to be injured on the job (Rath & Harter, 2010). Here are some speculations about the reasons for this link between having a best friend at work and positive work-related outcomes.

> [best] friends are more likely to invite and share candid information, suggestions, and opinions and to accept them without feeling threatened. Friends tolerate disagreements better than do those who are not friends. The good feelings friends share make them more likely to cheer each other on. Friends are more committed to the goals of the group and work harder, regardless of the type of task. (Wagner & Harter, 2008)

Despite the positive associations between having a best friend at work and both personal and work-related outcomes, some authors advise navigating these relationships with care. Information shared between close friends outside of work may slip out at work, undermining a friend's reputation or credibility. Best friends may find themselves in competition for a raise or promotion, resulting in hard feelings. In some situations, one person may be asked to provide evaluation to a supervisor about a coworker who is also a best friend, thereby creating an ethical conflict. When it comes to job security, pay, or advancement, close friendships may end up taking a second place to economic considerations or career success.

Isolation

The negative pole of the psychosocial crisis of early adulthood is **isolation**, a fear or unwillingness to have close, confiding, meaningful relationships. As social beings, people have a deep need for a sense of connection and belonging. Social isolation and the accompanying feeling of being unable to experience intersubjectivity or shared meaning are major sources of psychological distress (Jordan, 1997).

As with the negative poles of other psychosocial crises, most people experience some periods of the negative dimension of isolation. The more fully developed the ego becomes, the more it is characterized by clear boundaries. One by-product of individuality and independence is a heightened sense of separateness from others. During a period of intense personal growth and discovery, a person may experience interpersonal isolation, feeling preoccupied by thoughts and emotions that cannot be easily shared with others (Rokach & Neto, 2001).

Seven themes discussed in the following sections illustrate experiences of isolation: social anxiety, loneliness, depression, fragile identity, sexual disorders, situational factors, and drifting apart.

Social Anxiety

Isolation may come about because a person is anxious about all types of social activities (Cacioppo et al., 2000). They believe that success in social relationships is important but expect social encounters to be difficult and to end poorly. People who have high levels of **social anxiety** have a fear of being watched, judged, and criticized. They are very self-conscious in social situations, fearing that they will be embarrassed or humiliated. In anticipation of these possible outcomes, they avoid social situations, thereby minimizing exposure to potential negative experiences (Richards, 2016). The following narrative offers a glimpse into the challenges of daily life that are associated with social anxiety:

> Many times I'd be too fearful to speak up and be assertive at jobs. So, I'd get afraid and look like a "deer in the headlights." I didn't make good decisions at jobs. I had a hard time staying employed. I quit jobs I couldn't tolerate and got fired from others.
> I was fortunate to have great friends growing up, so I didn't struggle as much with social isolation as other social anxiety sufferers do. But then they went away to

college, and I went to a different college than they did. I'd spend the whole weekend playing videogames (literally 20 hours+) because I was too afraid to go out and meet people. I wouldn't go to the gym because I believed people there were just waiting for me to "screw up" so they could "attack" me verbally. I didn't go outside for a jog as frequently for the same reasons. And asking people in class for their phone numbers? Forget it—too scary. It rarely happened.

Even simple things like ordering food at a restaurant were hard. I'd get nervous and stutter when the waiter looked at me and forget what I wanted to order. Then on top of that, I'd get ashamed of myself afterwards for being such a "fool." (Stelter, 2014)

Not surprising, those with high levels of social anxiety are also uncomfortable about communicating with an intimate partner about sexuality, which in turn results in lower levels of sexual satisfaction (Montesi et al., 2013). Social anxiety disorder is the third most common mental disorder after depression and alcohol dependence, affecting over 19 million adults (WebMD, 2013).

Loneliness

Feelings of **loneliness**, a sadness when one's connection with others is disrupted or inadequate, can be separated into three categories: transient, situational, and chronic (Meer, 1985). *Transient loneliness* lasts a short time and passes, as when you hear a song or an expression that reminds you of someone you love who is far away. *Situational loneliness* accompanies a sudden loss or a move to a new city. *Chronic loneliness* lasts a long time and cannot be linked to a specific stressor. Chronically lonely people may have an average number of social contacts, but they do not achieve the desired level of intimacy in these interactions. Alana Massey reflects on the peculiar meaning of experiencing and expressing loneliness for this generation of young adults:

Expressing loneliness has the rare distinction of making a person appear both pitiful and callous. As members of a generation raised on the virtues of self-esteem and self-reliance, confessing that we are lonely is to admit we've failed to sufficiently absorb the personal motto we were assigned from birth: "I am enough." Adding insult to injury, admitting loneliness to an audience of one or more puts the listener on the defense. "You've got me! Aren't I enough?" they reply, having so thoroughly internalized the self-affirmation that they have expanded "I am enough" to mean "I am enough for everyone." The assumption is a category error. I would be terribly lonely if I had a romantic relationship but no friends, but that's never happened. I have, however, experienced prolonged bouts of singleness, and the crushing loneliness those long stretches pressed onto me. (Massey, 2016)

Experiences of loneliness are associated with a variety of social skills and personality characteristics. People who have higher levels of social skills, including friendliness, communication skills, appropriate nonverbal behavior, and appropriate

responses to others, have more adequate social support systems and lower levels of loneliness (Rokach, Bacanli, & Ramberan, 2000). In contrast, those who are lonely are more angry and anxious, have greater fear of negative evaluation, and a more pessimistic outlook about the future of a relationship (Cacioppo et al., 2006). Chronically lonely people are more likely to have a depressed immune system making them more vulnerable to illness. Their inability to form satisfying interpersonal relationships makes them vulnerable to exploitation, which creates a cycle of mistrust and social withdrawal (Cacioppo, 2008). Although it may seem logical to suggest that the lonely person should try harder to meet new people or develop new social skills, it is possible that the sense of isolation interferes with more active coping strategies (Goossens, 2012).

Depression

Depression is a worldwide health problem (Moussavi et al., 2007). When combined with one or more other chronic diseases such as arthritis, asthma, or diabetes, it substantially worsens a person's health. As a result, people who have a chronic health problem and depression are less able to engage in the kinds of social activities and pleasurable interactions that are likely to result in the formation of intimate relationships. Isolation may be a cause as well as a consequence of depression.

For some women, clinical depression appears to be linked to an orientation toward intimacy in which the self is systematically inhibited and devalued (Jack & Dill, 1992). They have a rigid view of how they should act in an intimate relationship, which is characterized by four major themes:

1. They judge themselves by external standards, feeling that they never quite measure up to what other people expect of them.
2. They believe they should build a close relationship with a man by putting his needs ahead of their own, and that to do otherwise is selfish.
3. They try to maintain a relationship by avoiding conflict and repressing their own views if they think those views may lead to disagreement.
4. They perceive themselves as presenting a false front in which they appear happy and satisfied on the outside although they are angry or resentful inside.

Over time, women who endorse this outlook lose contact with their authentic self, and even if the relationship remains stable, they become increasingly depressed. Longitudinal studies find that depression in one of the partners and relationship distress occur together. Depression has a negative impact on relationship quality, and poor relationship quality increases depression (Papp, 2010).

For some, the roots of depression begin in adolescence. Young people who tend to internalize their feelings under conditions of stress are likely to experience feelings of loneliness, lack of self-worth, anxiety, and depression. People who develop internalizing disorders in adolescence are at greater risk of continuing to experience depression as adults (Pine, Cohen, Gurley, Brook, & Ma, 1998). One of the most common stressors that may set off a bout of depression in adolescence is the breakup of a romantic relationship (Monroe, Rohde, Seeley, & Lewinsohn, 1999). As adolescents move into early adulthood, they may be more inclined to isolation as a way of protecting themselves from the depression that they have learned to associate with risks of rejection in romantic relationships.

Fragile Identity

According to the psychosocial perspective, work on personal identity precedes the capacity for adult intimacy. Longitudinal research that followed a group of adolescents from ages 15 to 24 supported this developmental sequence, demonstrating a clear relationship between the ego strengths associated with personal identity in middle and later adolescence with the capacity for mature intimate relationships in early adulthood (Beyers & Seiffge-Krenke, 2010). For some people, the possibility of closeness with another person seriously threatens the sense of self. They imagine intimate relationships to be a blurring of the boundaries of their own identities and cannot let themselves engage in them. People who fear a loss of identity continually erect barriers between themselves and others in order to keep their sense of self intact. Their fragile sense of self results from accumulated experiences of childhood that have fostered the development of personal identities that are either rigid and brittle or totally confused. Such a tenuous sense of identity requires that individuals constantly remind themselves who they are. They may not allow their identities to stand on their own strength while they lose themselves, even momentarily, in others. They are so busy maintaining their identities or struggling to make sense out of confusion that they feel isolated and cannot attain intimacy.

Sexual Disorders

Isolation may be linked to sexual disorders. Two widely cited desire disorders are *hypoactive sexual desire*, a decrease or absence of interest in sexual activity, and *compulsive sexual behavior*, a compulsive need to relieve anxiety through sex (Coleman, 2003). A loss of sexual desire is usually accompanied by physical withdrawal from the partner and by feelings of guilt and dread about losing intimacy. At the same time, the unafflicted partner often feels angry and guilty about imposing sexual needs on an unresponsive and uninterested partner, as in the following example.

> At first it was fun: feverish kisses in his red Chevy, giggly nights of passion in the apartment. But then came marriage, two kids, and suddenly her husband's hands on her flesh felt like tentacles, and the sight of him approaching made her body stiffen with revulsion. Then the disagreements began, hurtful scenes ending with each of them lying wedged against opposite sides of the bed, praying for sleep. (From L. Rosellini, 1992, "Sexual Desire," *U.S. News & World Report, 113*(1), p. 62. Reprinted by permission.)

In the case of compulsive sexual behavior, as in the following anecdote, sex is disconnected from pleasure or intimacy. Satisfaction of sexual drives is often accompanied by shame and disgust.

> Gary's pattern was always the same: First, the unbearable anxiety, never feeling good enough to handle the latest stress at his architect's job. Then, the familiar response—a furtive scanning of newspaper ads, a drive to a strip show, two straight Scotches to catch a buzz, and finally a massage parlor.... Afterward, he'd sit naked on the edge of the bed, his thought roiling in disgust: "I must be sick ... I can't change." But a few days later, the anxiety would begin again and he'd pore over the ads. (From L. Rosellini, 1992, "Sexual Desire," *U.S. News & World Report, 113*(1), p. 64. Reprinted by permission.)

Some psychologists view compulsive sexual behavior as an anxiety-based disorder, like other compulsions. Others argue that it is an addiction, like alcoholism. All agree that those who suffer from this disorder are not able to integrate sexual behavior as a meaningful component of an intimate relationship and therefore experience feelings of isolation.

Situational Factors

Isolation can also result from situational factors. A young man goes off to war in Afghanistan and returns after being seriously wounded, resulting in the amputation of his left leg. As a result of

Job loss is a common correlate of social isolation. Sarah stops to sit down and cry after having been laid off in a corporate restructuring. Her job was everything to her. She can't think of facing her family or her friends with this news. The idea of starting all over again to look for work is simply overwhelming.

his injuries, he doubts whether he could be an attractive or effective partner, and he is reluctant to engage in social activities to pursue romantic interests. A young woman rejects marriage in order to attend medical school and finds little time for the formation of intimate relationships. By the time she completes her internship and residency, she has many fewer options for finding an intimate partner. Due to the economic recession, a young adult loses her job, thus losing contact with many coworkers, and has to move to a new town to find employment. She faces the loss of multiple relationships in her social network as well as the undermining experience of unemployment. Under these and other similar circumstances, isolation is the result.

Drifting Apart

Isolation can arise even within an ongoing relationship. Some couples drift apart due to diverging spheres of interest and activity. For example, the partners may participate in distinct roles and activities. Marriages characterized by such a division of life spheres are sometimes referred to as *his-and-her* marriages (Bernard, 1972). The wife stays home most of the day, interacting with the children and the other wives in the neighborhood. The husband is away from home all day, interacting with his coworkers. When the partners have leisure time, they pursue different interests; for instance, the woman likes to play cards and the man likes to hunt. Over the years, the partners have less and less in common. Isolation is reflected in their lack of mutual understanding and lack of support for each other's life goals and needs.

In other cases, the partners create a widening body of unexpressed or undisclosed thoughts and feelings. They may have started out as a couple who could tell one another everything and share all their thoughts; but over time more and more topics become "hot" or uncomfortable. Talk about work is too upsetting; they disagree about politics; they can't talk about family members; and money is a source of tension as well. Eventually, the partners retreat into their own private worlds. They may go out to dinner, but have nothing to talk about; sit at home reading separate books they never discuss with each other; and spend time with separate friends. The feelings of closeness that accompany shared disclosure are lost, and replaced with a sense of isolation.

FURTHER REFLECTION: Imagine a culture in which commitment to family and intimate relationships was valued above commitment to work. What policies and practices would provide evidence of this priority? How might the salience of these values influence the experience of development in early adulthood?

The Central Process: Mutuality Among Peers

The central process through which intimacy is acquired is **mutuality among peers**. Mutuality refers to empathic awareness of one another, understanding of self and other, and the ability and willingness to regulate one's needs in order to respond to the needs of one's partner (Skerrett, 1996). John Gottman (2011) describes an essential feature of mutuality as **emotional attunement**, a couple's capacity to fully listen and understand one another, respect one

Santiago and Alysse look into each other's eyes. They have just decided to get married, and that decision fills them with joy and hope.

another's opinions, and show affection. Through attunement, the couple can manage conflicts and reduce the strong negative emotions that may threaten to burst through from time to time.

The two young adults must bring equal strengths and resources to the relationship. Their intimacy is built on their ability to meet each other's needs and accept each other's weaknesses. When one partner needs to be dependent, the other is strong and supportive; at other times, the roles may be reversed. Each partner understands that the other is capable of many kinds of relationships. Mutuality facilitates the couple's ability to meet each other's needs in different ways over time rather than producing a static, unitary relationship. In fact, mutuality should enhance both individual and couple development. In the process of supporting each other, both partners perform in ways that they might not have adopted had they been alone (Van Lange & Rusbult, 2012).

The concept of mutuality has been used in previous chapters to describe the development of a sense of basic trust during infancy. In that context, the distribution of resources, experience, and strength is quite uneven. Mutuality is possible only because the caregiver is committed to the infant's well-being. Through caregivers' consistent efforts, children eventually learn to regulate their needs to fit the family pattern. However, children at this stage are not expected to be sophisticated enough to assess and meet their caregivers' needs. In young adulthood, the partners are responsible for fulfilling each other's needs. In most cases, there is no benevolent, superordinate caregiver. Just as the infant learns to trust the caregiver's ability to meet personal needs, each adult partner learns to trust the other's ability to anticipate and satisfy the partner's needs. By expressing trust and commitment to one another, each partner strengthens the other's ability to believe in and invest in the relationship (Avery, 1989). The partners may also realize that they depend on each other to solve the problems they face as a couple.

Mutuality in relationships has been studied by asking participants to read brief descriptions of relationship styles and to say which style characterizes their relationship with their mother, father, best friend, and romantic partner (Neff & Harter, 2003). Three relationship styles were described: one that emphasized autonomy and one's personal needs; one that emphasized connection and the needs and feelings of the other person; and one that described an effort to balance autonomy and connection by reflecting on what would be an effective response to the other person as well as meeting one's own needs. This last style was considered evidence of mutuality. Mutuality in a romantic relationship was associated with the most ideal outcomes, including relationship satisfaction, relational self-worth, and lack of relational depression. Think back to the process of individuation in later adolescence discussed in chapter 10. One can imagine that young people whose families had difficulty balancing autonomy and closeness while they were adolescents might have difficulty themselves in achieving this balance in order to create optimal mutuality in their intimate relationships (Kerig, Swanson, & Ward, 2012).

Mutuality is strengthened as the two partners learn to rely on each other and as they discover that their combined efforts are more effective than their individual efforts would be. Mutuality, like attachment, is a characteristic of the dyadic relationship rather than of the individual members in it. It is formed as two individuals, each of whom has a well-defined identity, discover that they can have open, direct communication, hold each other in high regard, and respond effectively to each other.

The Prime Adaptive Ego Quality and the Core Pathology

Love

Take 5 minutes and write down all the song titles you can think of that focus on the theme of love. For thousands of years, the nature of love and the qualities of a loving relationship have been described in songs and stories. In the resolution of the crisis of intimacy versus isolation in early adulthood, the ego quality of love emerges as the capacity for devotion and deep affection. Robert Sternberg (1988) described interpersonal **love** as a set of feelings, thoughts, and motives that contribute to communication, sharing, and support. According to his theory, almost all types of love may be viewed as a combination of three dimensions: *intimacy*, the emotional investment in a relationship that promotes closeness and connection; *passion*, the expression of physical and psychological needs and desires in the relationship; and *commitment*, the cognitive decision to remain in the relationship. These dimensions form a triangle that helps characterize the different types of love (see FIGURE 11.8 ▶). Each of these dimensions changes over time. Passion is the most fleeting and, without commitment, is likely to result in a short-lived love. Intimacy and commitment can grow stronger over time. However, if passion and intimacy both decline, commitment may dwindle as well (Belsky, 1997). An important aspect of this theory is that it helps account for many types of loving relationships including those that do not follow the romantic ideal of U.S. culture. Commitment, which may originate from valued kinship obligations or economic practicalities, can sustain a relationship and foster an enduring love with or without intimacy or passion.

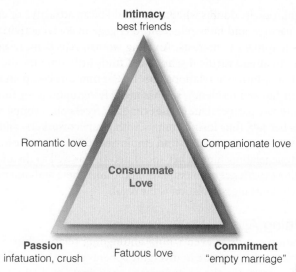

FIGURE 11.8 ▶ STERNBERG'S TRIANGLE OF TYPES OF LOVE

Conceptions of love usually include four aspects: ideas about the beloved, feelings that are associated with love, thoughts associated with love, and actions that are likely to occur between the lover and the beloved (Beall & Sternberg, 1995). The exact content of these feelings, beliefs, and actions differs from culture to culture, based on the culture's ideals about human nature, relationships, and cultural roles, especially courtship, marriage, child-rearing, and religion.

In Western cultures, 10 components of a loving relationship have been identified:

1. Promoting the welfare of the loved one
2. Experiencing happiness with the loved one
3. Highly regarding the loved one
4. Being able to count on the loved one in time of need
5. Mutually understanding the loved one
6. Sharing oneself and one's possessions with the loved one
7. Receiving emotional support from the loved one
8. Giving emotional support to the loved one
9. Communicating intimately with the loved one
10. Valuing the loved one in one's own life

These 10 dimensions are present in relationships with parents, siblings, friends, and lovers. The weighting of the 10 components, however, may vary. Also, some love relationships include a dimension of sexual attraction, and others do not.

Romantic love has a motivational quality that is similar to other basic drives such as thirst and hunger. In brain imaging studies, people who have recently fallen deeply in love are shown photographs of their loved one (Aron et al., 2005). Although participants experience a variety of emotions, both positive and negative as they gaze at the photo, they all typically show activation of the area of the brain associated with motivation and reward, areas that are rich in dopamine production. In addition to other cognitive and affective characteristics of love, there is a neurological response associated with focused attention, new levels of energy, and feeling that a deep need is being satisfied. The association with dopamine-rich areas of the brain helps explain feelings similar to other types of craving, including mental preoccupation with the loved one, anxiety when separated from the loved one, and a desire to maintain contact with the loved one.

From an evolutionary perspective, it makes sense to think that features of love have adaptive value. The passionate and romantic features of love open a person up to including another person in one's life. In order to form a long-term relationship, a person has to reorganize activities, alter existing relationships, and modify living arrangements. All these changes require a lot of energy and time. The passionate and romantic feelings of love probably contribute to a person's willingness to make all these changes. In contrast, the dimensions of intimacy and commitment contribute to the ability to sustain a relationship over long periods of time. Love between partners must be sustained in order to have and rear children, accumulate resources, fend off competitors, and preserve the social bonds of the family and community. The feelings of companionate love help motivate a person to remain devoted to one's partner in order to maintain the family system (Reis & Aron, 2008).

Exclusivity

The core pathology of this period is **exclusivity**—a shutting out of others. To some extent, exclusivity is a natural element in intimate relations. For example, sexual exclusivity tends to be valued in monogamous sexual relationships. From an evolutionary perspective, women value their male partner's sexual exclusivity in order to ensure that his resources will be directed toward her and her offspring. Men value their female partner's sexual exclusivity in order to insure their paternity.

At some level, however, exclusivity can become destructive to one's ability to have relationships. Exclusivity of this type is characterized by intense jealousy, a rivalrous orientation toward anyone who shows an interest in one's loved one, and preoccupation with intense feelings of anger and resentment, both toward the loved one and toward others (Firestone, Firestone, & Catlett, 2006). The person has to expend tremendous energy monitoring the activities of the loved one. As a result, the person is cut off from relationships and ends up isolated. Ideally, the experiences of intimacy and love should broaden one's sense of connection and **social integration**. Through exclusivity, however, one's social support network is limited.

Exclusivity may be extended to the overestimation of one's family, religious group, and national group. Exclusivity may be expressed in various forms of prejudice including sexism, racism, and ethnocentrism. As the result of a belief about one's superiority, individuals become unwilling to seek out new people or new experiences. Exclusivity may limit one's willingness to entertain new ideas. In order to preserve the belief in the value of one's exclusive world, one has to distort reality, limit access to new information, and restrict movement in the social environment. Thus, exclusivity becomes a substantial impediment to coping.

Applied Topic: Divorce

OBJECTIVE 7 Investigate divorce as a life stressor in early adulthood, including the factors contributing to it and the process of coping with it.

Americans have one of the highest rates of marriage among modern industrial societies. Almost everyone in the United States wants to get married and does. However, the divorce rate is also high. In 2010, almost half of those in their late 50s who had ever been married had also been divorced or separated (Kennedy & Ruggles, 2014). In international comparisons, the divorce rate in the United States is higher than that of 34 other countries including the United Kingdom, Canada, New Zealand, and Australia (Cherlin, 2009). An analysis of the marriage history of a national sample of 3 million house units and 200,000 people living in group quarters provided an estimate of the duration of first marriages in the United States in 2009 (Elliot & Simmons, 2011). Thirteen percent of all first marriages had dissolved through separation or **divorce** at the end of 5 years; another 13 percent dissolved between 5 and 9 years; and an additional 22 percent dissolved between 10 and 19 years. Fifty-three percent of first marriages lasted 20 years or more. This study did not include information about the rate of dissolution of cohabiting couples, which would add another dimension to our understanding of relationship instability.

The focus of the following section is on the experiences of adults who are going through divorce rather than on the impact of divorce on children. Thus, our focus is on the nature of the divorce experience and its relationship to development during early adulthood.

Factors Contributing to Divorce

Following are some of the many hypotheses offered to account for the high divorce rate in the United States.

- We have an overly romantic idea about marriage; the reality of married life cannot live up to our expectations.
- We are overly individualistic and unprepared to make the commitment to achieve a collective goal.
- Men and women are socialized to fear and mistrust or devalue one another.
- We are an overly secular culture with too little commitment to religious values.
- The need for both partners to be involved in the world of work interferes with the establishment and nurturing of intimate relationships.
- Marriage is an outmoded institution, perpetuated by a patriarchal power structure.
- Women who work do not need to remain in unsupportive marriages.
- Men whose wives work do not feel obligated to remain in a marriage to support their wives.
- Smaller family size means less time devoted to childrearing, and more opportunity for nonparental, adult exploration.
- The longer life span makes it unrealistic that marriages can endure throughout adulthood.

- Children who experience insecure attachments and marital instability grow up to be young adults who are unable to sustain intimate relationships.
- Marriage is a status that requires access to financial resources; lack of equitable employment opportunities and high risks of unemployment threaten the stability of marriage among low-income populations.
- As the age at first marriage increases, people who get married are more "set in their ways" and find it difficult to adapt to the interdependence required of marriage.

A large number of variables have been examined as correlates or predictors of divorce. These analyses encompass cross-national studies, historical cohort analyses, multicounty comparisons, and cross-sectional comparisons of couples (Amato, 2010). At the societal level, countries where there are fewer women than men and where women marry at a later age have lower divorce rates. In traditional patrilineal societies, the social order is organized around families linked through ties of blood and marriage. Relationships are organized in a hierarchy of obligations and privileges that are maintained through an interdependence of family ties. Divorce rates are low in cultures where the stigma of disrupting a marriage is not only felt at the individual level but also results in harming important kinship bonds that are critical to the larger social structure (Savaya & Cohen, 2003). In countries or regions where traditional gender attitudes are combined with traditional division of labor, that is where men are in the labor market and women are responsible for the home, the divorce rate is lower. In countries or regions where women endorse more emancipatory gender values, divorce rates are higher regardless of women's participation in the labor market (Gelissen, 2003; Kalmijn, De Graaf, & Poortman, 2004).

In a comparison of divorce rates across more than 3,000 counties in the United States, another important construct was identified—social integration, or the degree to which "people are tied or connected to one another, shared values being an important element in such integration" (Breault & Kposowa, 1987, p. 556). The characteristics of a community influence this sense of connectedness. Among the most significant of these characteristics are *population change*, the number of people who move in or out of a community each year; *religious integration*, the percentage of the population that belongs to a religious organization; and *urbanity*, the percentage of people in each county who live in an urban area. Divorce rates are significantly linked to each of these characteristics: They are higher in counties with high population change, low religious integration, and high urbanity. These findings suggest that the difficulties that individual couples experience in their marriages may be aggravated by the community context. In contrast, marriages may be buffered and supported by a sense of community identity and shared destiny (Rosenfeld, 2007).

In couple-to-couple comparisons, four variables have been associated with the likelihood of divorce: age at marriage, socioeconomic level, differences in socioemotional development of the partners, and the family's history of divorce.

Age at Marriage

The relationship of divorce to age at marriage appears to be changing (see FIGURE 11.9 ▶). From 1970 to 2010, marriages among

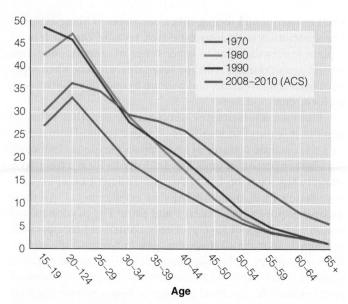

FIGURE 11.9 ▶ AGE-SPECIFIC DIVORCE RATES PER 1,000 MARRIED WOMEN, DIVORCE REGISTRATION AREA, 1970–2010
Source: Kennedy & Ruggles, 2014.

young people in the age groups 15 to 19 and 20 to 24 have been high. In earlier decades, the divorce rate showed a significant decline for those who married at the ages 25 to 29 and older. We can see the link here between the range of developmental differences between later adolescence and early adulthood including differences in the clarity of personal goals and commitments, maturation of executive functions, integration of one's moral identity and opportunities to establish meaningful ties to community supports. However, in the recent period, 2008–2010, the decline in the divorce rate with age is much more gradual, with those marrying in their mid to late 30s showing a much higher rate of divorce than in any of the previous periods (Kennedy & Ruggles, 2014; Wolfinger, 2015).

Both for couples who marry young and for those who marry later, dissatisfaction with role performance is a significant factor in marital instability. For young couples, dissatisfaction centers on sexual infidelity and jealousy. For older couples, it focuses on interpersonal conflict, a domineering style, and lack of companionship. Age at marriage is associated with different developmental needs and varying threats to marital stability. Of course, age at marriage is not a single explanatory dimension. For those who marry young, there is also a greater incidence of premarital pregnancy, dropping out of school, and lower-paying employment—all of which contribute to the likelihood of divorce.

Socioeconomic Level

The concept of **socioeconomic level** is a complex combination of education, occupation, and income. Each of these components is uniquely related to the divorce rate (White & Rogers, 2000). Men with more education have lower divorce rates. Women with more education also have lower divorce rates, except that those with 5 or more years of college are somewhat more likely to divorce than those who have had only 4 years (that is, have graduated from college). Within this overall pattern, there is also evidence of the **Glick effect**: Men and women who have dropped out of high school or college have higher divorce rates than those who have completed high school or college. Furthermore, those who have graduated from high school have a lower divorce rate than those who have had 1 to 3 years of college. Glick (1957) explained this pattern as evidence of lack of persistence. Those who are not able to complete a unit of schooling may also lack the resources to work at resolving the problems they encounter in marriage.

Many people believe that divorce is a privilege of the rich, but the evidence suggests that the opposite is true. The divorce and separation rates are generally higher among couples with minimal education and low incomes. Total family income is related to marital stability in some distinct ways. First, an erratic income and a high level of debt are more strongly associated with marital disruption than a low, steady income. Second, the relationship between income and marital instability is different for men and women. For men, higher income is associated with low divorce rates. For women, when wives contribute 50 percent to 60 percent of the total family income and when they express low to moderate marital happiness, divorce is more likely. When both partners bring about equal economic resources to the marriage, there is less of a sense of obligation to remain in an unhappy relationship (Rogers, 2004).

Socioemotional Development of the Partners

Socioemotional development is reflected in such dimensions as the partners' self-acceptance, autonomy, and expressiveness. Personality factors associated with emotionality and constraint have been linked with the risk of divorce. Both positive and negative emotionality increase the risk of divorce, whereas constraint decreases it. The genetic basis of these personality factors and the study of the link between personality factors and marital history among twins have led to the recognition that genetic factors play a role in the risk of divorce (Jersky et al., 2010).

Problems in communication are frequently cited by men and women as a major cause of divorce. Couples who are characterized as conflicted in their relationship during the premarital period, who have frequent disagreements, and who have different perceptions of how to resolve arguments are more likely to be separated or divorced 3 years after marriage (Fowers, Montel, & Olson, 1996). Generally, women experience more stress and report more problems in adjusting to marriage than men (Cotten, 1999). They tend to be more dissatisfied with the level of intimacy in their marriage than are men. These factors were examined earlier in the discussion of adjustment to marriage. Mutual satisfaction in marriage depends heavily on the husband's qualities. The stability of the husband's masculine identity, the happiness of his parents' marriage, his educational level, his social status, and his ability to be comfortable with the expression of emotions all affect marital happiness. Many husbands, however, enter marriage with a deep need to be nurtured and to continue the pattern of care that they received in childhood. The stability of a marriage depends on both partners' achieving a sense of their own identity. This achievement helps to establish the balance of power and mutual respect that is so central to emotional and intellectual intimacy.

Family History of Divorce

The partners' family history of divorce is yet another factor that contributes to marital instability. Children of divorced parents are more likely to get divorced than are children of intact marriages. A number of large national studies find that parental divorce markedly increases the chances that an adult child's marriage will end in divorce. For example, Amato (1996) reported that "the odds of divorce increased by 69% if the wife's parents had been divorced and by 189% if both the wife's and the husband's parents had been divorced" (Amato & DeBoer, 2001, p. 1038).

There are many interpretations of this *intergenerational transmission of divorce* (Amato & DeBoer, 2001). One interpretation is that, having seen their parents voluntarily end their marriage, children of divorce do not view marriage as a lifelong commitment and hold more favorable attitudes toward divorce as a reasonable strategy for resolving marital conflict (Greenberg & Nay, 1982). Another explanation is that children from single-parent and remarried families are likely to marry at an earlier age than children in intact marriages, thus increasing the probability of divorce. A third explanation is that parental hostility resulting in divorce harms children's psychosocial development. Children who have been exposed to high levels of negative affect and parental conflict may suffer from social anxiety, poor self-concept, and difficulties in concentrating, all of which may harm their ability to form supportive, intimate relationships in adulthood (Amato & Kane, 2011).

In a 17-year longitudinal study of marital stability, Amato and DeBoer (2001) were able to link the quality of the parents' marriage to the probability that their children's marriage would end in divorce. Of 335 married children, 20 percent had experienced a divorce or separation. Discord in the parents' marriage was not a strong predictor of divorce among the children. Rather, the study

For couples who are dissolving a distressed marriage, hostility and resentment that have been characteristic of their relationship are likely to escalate during the divorce process. Despite the fact that attorneys are present, negotiations are likely to be riddled with angry interactions and communication failures.

found that children who divorced were in families in which there was relatively little conflict, but which nonetheless ended in divorce. This lends support to the explanation that these children are not as committed to a lifelong view of marriage. When marital unhappiness occurs, these children have less inhibition about ending the relationship, especially if a more attractive alternative is likely.

Coping with Divorce

Divorce is not a single event, but a relatively long process starting with thoughts about the possibility of divorce, through possible steps of marital counseling, reconciliation, mediation, trial separation, and legal action. It is an understatement to say that divorce is stressful. Divorce is associated with numerous losses, including the loss of financial resources, emotional support, one's marital and parental role, social support, and social integration (Fine, Ganong, & Demo, 2010). Loss of income may result in other kinds of material loss. For example, a divorced woman and her children may have to move to less expensive housing, sell many of their possessions, and leave the community where they have established a network of friends and social support.

Divorce can also bring role loss and social isolation. Even when a divorce is viewed as a desirable solution, the period from the suggestion of divorce to its conclusion involves a variety of decisions and conflicts that may be painful. In an analysis of a large national sample, researchers found that people experience increases in depression after divorce, regardless of whether they are leaving a negative marriage with high levels of conflict or a marriage that was not as unpleasant (Kalmijn & Monden, 2006). Divorced partners may lose contact with family and friends as each person's social support system takes sides in the split (Kunz & Kunz, 1995). In communities where there is high disapproval of divorce, men and women who decide to continue to live in their neighborhood following divorce are likely to suffer social rejection and loss of contact with neighbors and former friends (Kalmijn & Uunk, 2007).

Many people who experience divorce go through a time of intense self-analysis. They try to integrate the failure of their marriage with their personal definition of masculinity or femininity, competence as loving people, and long-held aspirations to enact the role of husband or wife, father or mother. The stress-related correlates of divorce include increased health problems, a higher incidence of suicide, and the overrepresentation of divorced adults in all forms of psychiatric settings (Stack, 1990).

The process of leaving a marriage is different for the partner who initiates the divorce than for the partner who is being left. The initiators view the process as more voluntary and tend to be more aware of support services and feel more in control, even if they experience some sentiments of self-doubt and redefinition. Those who do not initiate the divorce are more likely to experience a period of shock and disbelief. They, too, must go through a process of identity redefinition, which often takes longer and may be associated with stronger feelings of emotional turmoil (Duran-Aydintug, 1995; Vannoy, 1995).

Attachment to a Former Spouse

One challenge in coping with divorce is that many divorced people retain a strong attachment to their former spouse. Grief in divorce has been compared to bereavement in widowhood. In both cases, there is a loss and a need to adjust to it. Although the loss due to death may be more intense, especially if it is sudden, the loss due to divorce may be more bitter. If an intimate bond was once formed, there is certain to be ambivalence about losing it even when the divorce is desired.

In a study of more than 200 divorced people, 42 percent expressed moderate or strong attachment to their former spouse. Some people wondered what their former spouse was doing, spent a lot of time thinking about them, expressed disbelief that the divorce had really taken place, and felt that they would never get over it. The attachment was stronger for those who had not initiated the divorce. The lingering feelings of attachment were associated with greater difficulties in adjustment to divorce, especially problems of loneliness and doubt about being able to cope with single life (Kitson, 1982). The stronger the positive or negative post-divorce attachment, the more difficult the adjustment in the years following the divorce (Tschann, Johnston, & Wallerstein, 1989).

In contrast to mental preoccupation or rumination about a former spouse, many former spouses continue to have contact with each other. Divorced couples with children may be encouraged to maintain cooperative parenting arrangements that require ongoing conversations about the best interests of their child. These interactions are likely to preserve certain aspects of the relationship between partners that were formed during the marriage. In a Dutch study of about 1,800 former spouses, almost half continued to have contact 10 years after the divorce (Fischer, DeGraaf, & Kalmihn, 2005). Over time, contact with a former spouse decreases, especially antagonistic contact. Yet, even 10 years after divorce about 5 percent of the sample reported antagonistic contact, women reporting threats of physical harm from their former husbands and men reporting verbal aggression from their former wives. Contact was most frequent for couples who had children together before the divorce. For couples who did not have children, about 60 percent no longer had any contact with a former spouse 10 years after divorce. For couples with children, about 70 percent have contact with each other 10 years after divorce. For these couples, antagonistic contact declined and friendly contact increased over this time.

The fact that divorce is stressful and that people have lingering attachments to their former spouse does not mean that they consider the divorce undesirable. Studies that ask divorcing people what went wrong in the relationship suggest that for many, the conditions of the marriage were demeaning, exploitive, or oppressive.

> Common complaints by wives include their husband's authoritarianism, mental cruelty, verbal and physical abuse, excessive drinking, lack of love, neglect of children, emotional and personality problems, and extramarital sex…. More men than women describe themselves as having problems with alcohol, drugs, or physical abuse that contributed to the divorce. (Demo, Fine, & Ganong, 2000, pp. 283–284)

Many divorced parents report that, despite the difficulties of single parenting, life is more manageable than it was in the midst of the arguments and hostility that preceded the divorce.

Coping Strategies

Most people who experience divorce are determined to cope with the stresses it brings. Unfortunately, many adults do not anticipate the specific kinds of stressors that they will encounter. Of course, they have different coping strategies, some of which may not be effective for the special demands of divorce. In a longitudinal study that focused on how people adjusted to divorce, the researchers emphasized (1) the *kinds of stressors* that the individuals encountered, (2) the *resources* they had to help them cope, and (3) the *meaning* they gave to the divorce situation (Wang & Amato, 2000). The major stressors were large losses in income, losing friends, and having to move. Those whose post-divorce adjustment was most positive had higher income levels, were dating someone steadily or remarried, were most favorable about the marital dissolution before the divorce, or actually initiated the divorce. The magnitude of the stressors was not as important in predicting adjustment as were the coping strategies (resources and meaning).

In another study comparing widowed and divorced women, the contribution of social support to coping was examined in more detail. Those women who were most stressed by their loss received increased social support from friends and relatives in the following year. For the two groups, the most beneficial type of support differed. For widows, practical support, such as transportation or help with household chores, was positive; for those who had been divorced, having someone who would listen to their personal problems was especially helpful. For both groups, receiving monetary support was associated with an increase in distress. Thus, some types of social support appear to foster recovery, whereas others may serve to highlight the extent of one's loss (Miller, Smerglia, Gaudet, & Kitson, 1998).

It is not uncommon to read narratives that describe the personal and interpersonal growth that accompanies effective coping with divorce. Erin Smith (2015) described important ways she matured after 4 years in a troubled marriage.

1. After spending time in therapy, she learned that by understanding more fully who she was she could also be better at forming relationships.

2. She realized that after 4 years of being told that she was a terrible person, she had been beaten down. After the divorce, she learned to be more accepting of herself.

3. She realized that she had given up many of the things that had made her happy. After the divorce she rediscovered those activities.

4. She learned that in a "normal relationship" she should expect someone to treat her with kindness and respect.

Divorce is typically accompanied by a diversity of emotions including grief, anger, guilt, depression, fear, and self-doubt. It may also involve feelings of identity confusion, numbness, and loss. Coping typically requires some time to allow the grieving process to unfold, facing these emotions and finding ways to manage them. In addition to psychotherapy and support groups, coping strategies might include the following: striving to regain a healthy lifestyle including diet, exercise, sleep, and other positive routines; using a journal to provide an outlet for feelings and thoughts; making a list of enjoyable distractions that can be used when feelings of numbness or depression seem overwhelming; exploring some new interests or returning to earlier hobbies that bring feelings of competence and self-worth (Dombeck, 2016).

Coping with divorce requires strategies devised to deal with the aspects of it that are perceived as most troublesome. Further, many coping strategies, including becoming involved in new activities, spending more time with family and friends, gaining new skills, or taking a new job, may promote new levels of functioning. Human service professionals can be effective in helping adults develop coping skills for resolving some of the stressors of divorce and transforming a difficult life event into an opportunity for personal growth.

FURTHER REFLECTION: Account for the high divorce rate in the United States. Distinguish five or more levels of explanation: historical, economic, cultural, familial, and personal. How are the developmental tasks of early adulthood related to the challenges of divorce? How might the circumstances of the divorce determine the most effective coping strategies?

CHAPTER SUMMARY

OBJECTIVE 1 Define and explain selected theoretical concepts that are especially relevant for understanding development during adulthood, including social roles, the life course, and fulfillment theories.

Three theoretical concepts were introduced to help consider the challenges and directions of growth in adulthood: social roles, the life course, and fulfillment theories. Adulthood comprises a series of increasingly complex and demanding roles, experiences of role gain and role loss, and new challenges of balancing multiple roles. The life course perspective is a framework for examining adulthood as the interface of family and occupational careers against the backdrop of chronological age, historical period, and societal norms and expectations. Through the life course lens,

one gains appreciation for the developing person and the changing historical context. Fulfillment theories emphasize the ability of adults to go beyond meeting daily needs and achieving equilibrium to make plans, strive toward goals, and seek personal meaning in life.

The developmental tasks of early adulthood require that individuals apply the many competencies they have acquired in childhood and adolescence to solving new and complex challenges. They may marry or make a commitment to an intimate partner, have children or decide to delay or forgo childbearing, and choose work roles. Gradually, they evolve a style of life. In this process, their commitment to social institutions and to significant others expands. Their worldview becomes more diverse, and their appreciation of the interdependence of systems increases. One of the major sources of stress at this life stage is the need to balance and integrate multiple roles.

OBJECTIVE 2 Analyze the process of forming intimate relationships, including initial attractions, mate selection, and commitment to a long-term relationship. Contrast the ways that different patterns of cohabitation contribute to the formation of close relationships. Summarize the challenges one faces in adjusting to the early years of marriage.

The exploration of intimate relationships requires a readiness to engage in the complex set of dyadic interactions that move a relationship from initial attraction to deeper levels of disclosure, role compatibility, mutual support, and commitment. These close relationships can take a variety of forms, some of which set the stage for long-term commitment and others that seem to be more marginal or temporary. A major theme in the establishment and maintenance of satisfying intimate relationships is the quality of communication and the ability of couples to coordinate their interactions, particularly under conditions of conflict or role strain.

OBJECTIVE 3 Describe the factors associated with the decision to have children, and evaluate the impact of childbearing on intimate relationships.

The decision to have children is becoming increasingly one of choice rather than obligation. Age at childbearing is delayed in line with later age at marriage. At the same time, there is an increase in nonmarital childbearing and in voluntarily child-free couples. Having children alters the adults' intimate relationship, especially the amount of time parents spend with one another when the children are not present. Couples differ in the ways they balance their roles as parents and intimate partners; some couples grow closer and more companionate, whereas others experience new levels of conflict and declines in marital satisfaction.

OBJECTIVE 4 Define the concept of work in early adulthood and explore how work stimulates psychosocial development.

In the period of occupational training, many new areas of intellectual awareness are stimulated. Self-understanding is integrated with social expectations and historical opportunities as men and women embark on their career paths. The nature of the world of work and the possible kinds of jobs and careers are rapidly changing. A growing concern is the divide between "good jobs" and "bad jobs," leaving many young adults in jobs that have little security, few benefits, and low pay. Four components of the work environment must be mastered: technical skills, authority relations, interpersonal relations with coworkers, and ways of coping with the demands, hazards, and risks of the workplace. Career development implies

changing phases of emphasis and preoccupation with self, family, and occupational goals. One of the most challenging aspects of career development in this early phase is the coordination of work with the establishment of meaningful intimate relationships.

OBJECTIVE 5 Examine the role of lifestyle development as an expression of an individual's personal identity, with consideration for the pace of life, balancing competing role demands, building a supportive social network, and adopting practices to promote health, fitness, and nutrition.

Lifestyle is the translation into action of the values, goals, and personal preferences that were crystallized into a personal identity in later adolescence. Components of lifestyle that impact the sense of well-being and personal life satisfaction include the pace of life, the quality of one's social network, the ability to balance competing role demands, and behaviors that contribute to one's fitness and overall health.

OBJECTIVE 6 Define and describe the psychosocial crisis of intimacy versus isolation, the central process through which the crisis is resolved, mutuality among peers, the prime adaptive ego quality of love, and the core pathology of exclusivity.

The psychosocial crisis of intimacy versus isolation emphasizes the evolution of adult sexuality into an interpersonal commitment. This crisis requires that needs for personal gratification be subordinated to needs for mutual satisfaction. Success is comparatively difficult to achieve in our culture because of the basic tension between the norm of independence and the desire for closeness. The varieties of circumstances and personal characteristics that can result in a sense of isolation are discussed. The research on marriage suggests that willingness to make a personal commitment to another adult is one of the key aspects of success. The elaboration of communication skills, the ability to engage in and resolve conflict, and the ability to find time for companionate, leisurely interaction are emphasized as central to marital stability.

OBJECTIVE 7 Investigate divorce as a life stressor in early adulthood, including the factors contributing to it and the process of coping with it.

The high rate of divorce suggests that many societal, community, and interpersonal factors work against the support of stable intimate relationships. Linked to the increase in the age at first marriage, there appears to be an increasing risk of divorce among those in their 30s. In the process of coping with divorce, there is a clear need for daily problem solving and emotional expression to manage the grief, loss, and role transitions that accompany the disruption of an intimate relationship.

CASEBOOK

For additional cases related to this chapter, see the case entitled "To Marry or Not," in *Life Span Development: A Case Book*, by Barbara and Philip Newman, Laura Landry-Meyer, and Brenda J. Lohman, pp. 163–170. The case focuses on the development of

Jonah's and Abby's dating relationship, their decision to marry, and the early years of their married life as they are influenced by work and extended family relationships.

Album/sfgp/Newscom

Gertrude Stein was Picasso's friend and mentor. She provided an environment where creative people could get together and share ideas. This portrait was the only one that Stein felt represented her true sense of self. Middle adulthood is the period when one's energy and talent are directed toward building and maintaining the structures upon which future generations depend. It is the stage when self-fulfillment is integrated with caring for others.

1. Analyze features of the world of work as a context for development, focusing on interpersonal demands, authority relations, and demands for the acquisition of new skills.

2. Define the concept of a vital, intimate relationship and examine factors that support this goal in middle adulthood, especially a commitment to growth, effective communication, creative use of conflict, and preserving passion.

3. Evaluate the expansion of caring in middle adulthood as it applies to two specific roles—that of a parent and that of an adult child caring for one's aging parents. Clarify your assumptions about the costs and benefits of enacting these roles.

4. Summarize the tasks required for effective management of the household and explain why they are necessary.

Describe the diversity of households, including blended families, single-parent families, and adults who live alone, and hypothesize about the implications of these various household structures for individual development.

5. Define and explain the psychosocial crisis of generativity versus stagnation and the central processes through which the crisis is resolved: person–environment interaction and creativity, the primary adaptive ego strength of care, and the core pathology of rejectivity.

6. Apply a psychosocial analysis to the issue of discrimination in the workplace, and evaluate the cost to society and to the individual when discrimination operates to restrict career access and advancement.

MIDDLE ADULTHOOD (34 TO 60 YEARS)

12

— CASE STUDY Reinventing Family in Middle Adulthood —

This dad started his blog when he was in his late 30s in anticipation of the birth of his first child. Now he is divorced, in a new relationship, and marveling at the possibility of life in a blended family.

The Girlfriend and I have been living together for almost a year now. Since we both have joint custody of our children, this means that for 50% of our time, we have three children from two separate marriages living under one roof.

It's pure heaven and we don't take any of our happiness for granted. Luck and fate somehow conspired to bring us together. For that, we're eternally grateful.

When the Boss Lady and I split up, I was forty years old with a four-year-old daughter. I had no idea what was in store for my future and my mind raced with a million questions.

Will I ever find someone who shares my perspective on life?

Does that woman even exist?

Will she mind that I have a kid?

Will she even like kids?

What if she wants one of her own?

What if she already has kids?

What if her kids hate me?

What if my kid hates her?

What if the kids hate each other?

The Girlfriend and I have been extremely lucky to find one another. I'll get into the trial and tribulations of forming a modern-day blended family in another post but, right now, I'll just say that things are going great.

The two of us have a very loving relationship, and it's important for us to show our kids what a healthy relationship looks like. We're firm believers that children live what they learn. But in a way, that's all besides the point. What makes all of it so much easier is the fact that our kids truly do love one another. They love like sisters. They fight like sisters. And they make up like sisters.

While the Peanut may have had a bit of a tougher time acclimating from being an only child to a middle one, it's been a major adjustment for all of us. Yet despite the fact that so many things could have gone wrong, we couldn't be happier about how well things have worked out. Three girls under one roof can be intimidating but, at the end of the day, they care for each other. They love one another. And they're lucky to have one another. What more could two divorced parents ask for?

Blog from "Microphone Check, One, Two...," by MetroDad, May 2013. Retrieved June 10, 2013.

CASE ANALYSIS Using What You Know

1. Evaluate the assumption that children live what they learn. What evidence supports the idea that the quality of parenting is a major influence on the development of children as they mature into adolescence and adulthood?

2. Describe the features of a healthy relationship in middle adulthood. What features of the partners and the couple contribute to a healthy relationship?

3. Given what you learned about divorce in chapter 11, what challenges do you expect this man to face in adjusting to divorce and to the new intimate relationship?

4. Reflecting on this case, describe the new outlook on parenting, intimacy, and meaning in life that may emerge in middle adulthood.

Middle adulthood lasts from about age 34 to 60. According to psychosocial theory, a new reorganization of personality occurs that focuses on the achievement of a sense of generativity—a concern about the well-being of future generations. This new stage integrates the skills and perspectives of the preceding life stages with a commitment of energy to the future. During this period, individual and societal development are intimately interwoven. In order for societies to thrive and grow, adults must dedicate their energy and resources to preserving the quality of life for future generations. In order for individuals to continue to thrive and grow, societies must provide opportunities for adults to express and fulfill their generative strivings.

The current cohort of middle adults is sometimes referred to as Generation X, born between the 1960s and 1980. They are a noticeably smaller generation than the older baby boomers or the younger millennials, coming of age in the 1980s and 90s, and associated with the popular culture of MTV, video rental stores, and cable television. Generation X experienced the end of the Cold War, with the fall of the Berlin Wall, and the splitting apart of the Soviet Union. Ronald Reagan, George H. W. Bush, and William Clinton were the presidents during their "coming of age" years. Among other events, these years brought heightened awareness of the AIDS virus and its impact on the gay community, the emerging use of the World Wide Web, the bombing of the Oklahoma City federal building, and the founding of Google (Robinson, 2016; Taylor & Gao, 2014). Generation Xers have been described as accepting of diversity, pragmatic, and self-reliant/individualistic. Many saw their parents getting laid off, and have redefined corporate loyalty; they take employment seriously but dislike rigid, authority relations; they prefer having autonomy to learn new skills and devise new approaches in order to get the job done. They are somewhat pessimistic about the future of their retirement (Thielfoldt & Scheef, 2004).

Because middle adulthood covers a relatively long period, there are opportunities to review and revise one's commitments and goals along the way. People experience many transitions in their work and family roles during this time, encountering a widening circle of relationships and new responsibilities for the care and guidance of others. Many situations call for decisions that have no single correct answer. Several alternatives are possible, and adults must rely on their ability to gather and evaluate information to determine which choice is best for them and their loved ones. Flexibility coupled with a good sense of humor and creative problem solving emerge in this stage as key coping strategies. ●

Developmental Tasks

Every adult typically engages in all of the following developmental tasks during middle adulthood: managing a career, nurturing intimate relationships, expanding caring relationships, and managing the household. Through their roles in the family, at work, and in the community, middle adults have broad responsibilities for the nurturance, education, and care of children, adolescents, young adults, and older adults. The strains of middle adulthood result largely from difficulties in balancing many roles and striving to navigate through predictable as well as sudden role transitions. The emotional well-being of the society as a whole rests largely on the capacity of middle adults to succeed in the developmental tasks of this life stage.

Managing a Career

OBJECTIVE 1 Analyze features of the world of work as a context for development, focusing on interpersonal demands, authority relations, and demands for the acquisition of new skills.

Work is a major context for adult development. Every person who enters the labor market has an occupational **career**. However, this career may not appear to be orderly or progressive. It may involve changes in the kind of work performed over time, short- or long-term exit from the labor market due to unemployment or family responsibilities, and periodic return to school for new training. One can argue that as long as a person is involved in an effort to make use of **skills** and talents, there will be significant interactions between the world of work and the person's individual development.

Using the framework of systems theory, one can appreciate that the microsystem of work is embedded in a larger societal macrosystem. Each society has an economic orientation that influences policies and practices related to work. The climate for the U.S. worker is one that encourages a relatively long work week and few benefits. For example, there is no law requiring companies to provide paid vacation. In comparison to European countries, the labor union structure is less powerful in the United States and often cannot protect workers from new demands for productivity. According to data gathered by the Organization for Economic Cooperation and Development, the average U.S. worker works over 1,790 hours a year. This is over 250 hours a year more than in Denmark, France, Germany, Netherlands, or Norway, but less than in Chile, Korea, Greece, Mexico, or Poland (OECD, 2016). Over the period from 2004 to 2013, an average of 5.2 million employed workers ages 25 to 54 were working more than one job (Lalé, 2015). The demands on U.S. workers are substantial, resulting in significant role strain as middle adults strive to balance work with other important life roles, especially those of parent, caregiver for aging parents, intimate partner, and community member.

The buying power of wages has declined, so that most families find it necessary for both partners to work in order to have a reasonable standard of living. The costs of housing, education, and health care have increased dramatically, and the projection of a longer life expectancy has placed new pressures on workers to save for a more diverse set of needs in retirement. The costs of medical care adds to the financial worries of many middle adults, both out of concern for their ability to pay for their own immediate family's medical expenses and for their ability to support their aging parents whose health care costs are often not fully covered by insurance. All these features of the macrosystem in the United States have implications for the way individuals orient to the world of work and for the potential conflicts between work and family life (Warren, 2003/2016, 2007).

There is reciprocity between work experiences and individual growth. People with certain kinds of experiences, abilities, and values will enter certain kinds of work roles (Holland, 1997). Once those roles have been entered, the work environment and the kinds of activities that the person performs also influence intellectual, social, and value orientation. One's lifelong occupational career is a fluid structure of changing activities, ambitions, and sources of satisfaction. As people move through middle adulthood, the management of their occupational career becomes central to their sense of personal effectiveness, identity, and social integration. Four themes in the management of a career are discussed for their contribution to adaptation and individual development: achieving new levels of competence, midlife career changes, balancing work and family life, and the impact of joblessness.

Achieving New Levels of Competence in the World of Work

Middle adulthood brings new challenges, a reformulation of ambitions and goals, and new levels of competence in the workplace. Three areas are emphasized here as they relate to the interpersonal and cognitive components of career development: understanding and managing leadership and authority

Dr. Riva is explaining the results of Chuck's examination by showing him his chest x-ray. She thinks of her role as a physician as a combination of teacher, caregiver, and scientist.

relationships, expanding interpersonal skills and relationships, and achieving new levels of mastery in critical skill areas.

Understanding and Managing Leadership and Authority.

Authority relations encompass all the hierarchical relationships that give people decision-making power and supervisory responsibility for others. Returning to Tiedeman's model that was introduced in chapter 10 (Later Adolescence), in the *induction* phase of career development one must identify the authority structure operating in the work setting and begin to establish one's position in it. In the *integration* phase, which typically occurs in middle adulthood, advancement in a career inevitably involves taking on positions of increased responsibility and power to make decisions. Career advancement means assuming authority in some areas, while recognizing the authority of others. However, not everyone in a position of authority provides effective leadership. A common complaint among workers is that their organization lacks leadership, or that their boss or supervisor does not provide adequate leadership.

What is **leadership**? Organizational theory suggests that leadership is not a quality of personality as much as it is a relationship among people. Woyach (1991) defined leadership as "the process of helping a group shape a vision of its purpose and goals and of getting people, both inside and outside the group, to commit and recommit themselves to accomplishing that vision" (p. 7).

This definition embodies three basic assumptions: (1) Leadership is a relationship among people, (2) leaders provide a sense of vision or direction, and (3) leaders motivate the group to work toward achieving its vision. Building on this view of leadership, Woyach (1993) argued that effective leaders try to balance the good of the group with their own self-interest. They try to take into account the best interests of individuals, groups, and communities while they also participate and lead.

The requirements of leadership may change as the group develops and as the team or organization faces new, emerging challenges. Groups may go through phases when everyone is overloaded and distracted. During those times, leaders help the group return to its mission and recommit to working together by communicating a clear, coherent sense of direction that others can understand and follow (Dewan & Myatt, 2008). At other times, the group members may understand their roles and tasks so clearly that the primary acts of leadership involve delegating responsibilities and removing obstacles to the group's success. Effective leadership involves the ability to assess the changing needs and challenges faced by the team or organization and to adapt to those changes through the use of flexible problem-solving strategies. **Adaptive leadership** is required when the organization faces new conditions or complex problems that cannot be solved with the current use of technologies or techniques. Under these conditions, leaders need to help frame new ways of defining problems and engaging workers, consumers, or clients in a search for solutions (Heifetz, Grashow, & Linsky, 2009).

Some requirements of leadership are perceived differently across cultures. For example, in a study comparing full-time, white-collar workers in China and Australia, participants were asked to rate traits that were important for effective leadership. The Australians, who expect their leaders to be able to work collaboratively with employees, rated friendly and respectful traits higher than did the Chinese workers. For the Chinese workers, a hierarchical authority structure is valued. A person in a leadership position might be perceived as weakening authority through friendly interactions with subordinates (Casimir & Waldman, 2007).

Other aspects of leadership appear to be universally effective. Leaders who are described as charismatic or visionary are more likely to be rated as highly effective by their subordinates. Charismatic leaders are able to convey a vision by distilling complex ideas into a simple message and linking their message through symbols, analogies, or stories to experiences that are personally relevant to their followers. Charismatic leaders are confident and optimistic. They might be idiosyncratic or theatrical in their approach and inspirational in their delivery. They are willing to take risks and often suggest a direction that is a noticeable departure from the way the organization has been heading. Charismatic leaders are sensitive to the needs of their members and actively monitor and listen to people at all levels of an organization in order to retain rapport with their group members and to stay attuned to changes in the organizational climate (Conger & Kanungo, 1998).

Across many types of groups and different degrees of organizational complexity, charismatic leaders encourage followers to become deeply committed to the organizational mission, make

Alan has been with the company for a long time and has been very successful as a manager. His team is creating a mission statement for their department. Team members are pleased that he respects their ideas and provides this mechanism for them to express their ideas as they build the vision for the future.

personal sacrifices for this mission, and perform above expectations (Maxwell, 2011). They do this in part through their positive and encouraging emotional messages and their ability to form constructive relationships with workers. Under the guidance of this positive leadership, workers are happier, less likely to miss work, and more willing to engage in training and development activities (Campbell, Ward, Sonnenfeld, & Agle, 2008; Den Hartog, De Hoogh, & Keegan, 2007; Erez, Misangyi, Johnson, LePine, & Halverson, 2008; Rowold & Laukamp, 2009).

The reorganization of many large companies has resulted in fewer employees, who are then asked to be more productive. In this context, leaders need to develop adaptive leadership to accompany their technical expertise. This involves communicating a clear view of the challenges, mobilizing and guiding the direction of innovation, coordinating people and projects, and increasing workers' willingness and readiness for change. Adaptive leadership may involve increasing employees' sense of confidence in their ability to initiate changes as well as increasing their commitment to the organization during a period of uncertainty or transition (Heifetz, Grashow, & Linsky, 2009; Strauss, Griffin, & Rafferty, 2009).

The idea that leaders are able to motivate others is explored in detail by Rosabeth Moss Kanter in her analysis of how organizations are able to turn a losing streak around. Based on hundreds of interviews and a national survey of more than 1,000 companies, Kanter (2004) identified strategies that successful leaders use to encourage members of their organization to reach new, higher levels of performance. When leaders believe in the goals of the organization and in the ability of people to achieve those goals, people will rise to meet those expectations. In inspiring confidence, leaders set high standards and are role models for these standards. They establish systems for individual and system accountability. They foster collaboration through mutual respect and effective communication. They recognize and encourage initiative, imagination, and innovation. They are able to convince others outside the organization to invest in the goals of the organization, which makes their success more attainable. Thus, it falls to the leader of a group to embrace a vision of success and to build commitment to that vision rather than to be caught up in the many obstacles that prevent success.

The focus on leadership highlights the importance of ego strengths for middle adults in positions of authority, not only for their own personal occupational achievements but also for the future of organizations and the well-being of workers. Especially during periods of uncertainty and transition, middle adults who are optimistic, flexible, open to new ideas, and confident can create environments where people are able to address their work in a productive, proactive manner. Through effective leadership, middle adults convey a vision about the possibilities for their organization and guide others toward the achievement of this vision. Success in this enterprise contributes to the sense of meaning and mattering, essential elements of subjective well-being in adulthood.

Expanding Interpersonal Skills and Relationships.
Many occupations place a great deal of emphasis on the development and use of **interpersonal skills**—especially the ability to interact well with customers and coworkers and the ability to communicate effectively—as criteria in the selection and promotion process. Interpersonal skills include at least three components: self-presentation, or how a person introduces oneself to others and conveys openness to further interactions; social scanning, or the ability to read the social cues in the situation; and social flexibility, or the ability to respond adaptively to the social demands of the situation, for example by being assertive or cooperative as the circumstances require (Wu, 2010). Even if these skills are not mentioned explicitly in the job description, success in career management requires the ability to influence others, appear credible, develop a fluent conversational style, and learn to work effectively in groups or teams. Problems in interpersonal relationships can have a negative impact on employees, on the image of the organization, and on overall productivity.

Another essential feature of many work environments is the ability to work in teams or groups. Teams that work well together are able to maintain positive social relationships among the members as they work to complete their group's tasks, all the while supporting the personal and professional development of team members. Eight features of effective teams, many of which reflect the importance of interpersonal skills and relationships, have been identified in the literature (Marquardt, Seng, & Goodson, 2010):

1. Clear and meaningful goals
2. Clearly stated expectations for positive interpersonal behavior
3. Strong interpersonal and communication skills
4. Competence and commitment to solving problems and performing tasks
5. Trust, openness, and group cohesiveness
6. The ability to manage conflict to preserve positive relationships among members
7. Shared leadership
8. Continuous individual and team commitment to learning and improvement

When individuals work in teams, especially when there is frequent interaction, there is a tendency toward **social comparison**. One may learn that a colleague has made a lot of sales, received recognition for an accomplishment, or solved an important work-related problem. This might be viewed as an *upward* comparison—a person believes that the colleague performed better than others. In contrast, one may learn that a colleague made a lot of errors, worked too slowly, or failed to make a sales quota. This might be viewed as a *downward* comparison—a person believes that the colleague performed worse than others. Social comparison is an ongoing aspect of the interpersonal environment at work, with some people being more likely to base their self-evaluation on comparisons with others (Buunk et al., 2005).

In a cooperative work environment, people view the fate of their colleagues as directly affecting each member of the team. In such a setting, one can imagine an interpersonal dynamic such that people feel proud of those who are doing better than they are and are encouraged to seek out these high performers to learn from. People who feel bad when others are not doing as well as they are may be willing to help them raise their skills or improve their performance.

Those in leadership positions have an opportunity to foster a cooperative or competitive work climate and to manage the process of social comparison in the interest of productivity or effectiveness. More senior workers are often in a position to influence the interpersonal atmosphere, serving as models for others, demonstrating pride in their achievements, providing encouragement for appropriate work-related behavior, and fostering respect and trust among coworkers.

Whether a person is in a supervisory role or not, experienced and highly qualified workers can be extremely valuable to newer workers as **mentors**. Among the major Fortune 500 companies, over 70 percent have a mentoring program to help workers manage the demands of their job, make wise career decisions, and progress through the milestones of career advancement (Wharton School, 2007). The mentor–mentee relationship may be informal or assigned. In either case, the mentee is hoping to find someone who will provide safe, confidential advice; honest feedback; and insights into how to succeed. Mentors need to be sensitive to the needs of the mentee and their career ambitions, be able to convey the values and organization of the corporate culture, and help link the mentee to an expanded and varied network of colleagues. Effective mentors are "trustworthy, accessible, sincere, and active listeners. [They] have mentoring experiences, professional experience, a good reputation, and a large professional network" (Giancola, Heaney, Metzger, & Whitman, 2016, p. 212). Successful mentor–mentee relationships involve a good matching process including shared interests, commitment to the relationship, and a willingness on the part of the mentee to accept feedback and follow through on recommendations. Whereas having an effective mentor is clearly beneficial for the career and psychosocial well-being of the mentee, this kind of interaction has also been found to have benefits for the mentor. By interacting with their mentee, the mentors can learn new aspects of their organization, get insights into new technologies, and expand their network through the mentee's contacts. The success of the mentee becomes a source of pride for the mentor, and in some cases, the mentee's success can be of direct benefit to the career advancement of the mentor (Giancola et al., 2016; Wharton School, 2007).

Meeting New Skill Demands. The characteristics of the occupation and the work setting determine what kinds of work-related skills will dominate the adult's energies. It makes sense to expect that the actual tasks a person performs from day to day will influence their intellectual development. The *Dictionary of Occupational Titles* (U.S. Department of Labor, Employment and Training Administration, 1993) was updated and converted to a Web-based resource called *O*NET* by the U.S. Department of Labor, Employment and Training Administration. O*NET describes and updates over 900 occupational titles with regard to skills, abilities, knowledge, tasks, work activities, work context, experience levels required, job interests, and work values and needs. Each of these dimensions has implications for workers' adaptation to their work setting. In the process of adapting to these dimensions, adults often carry over aspects of work-related competence to family and community roles.

The idea that social structure influences personality through occupational demands was developed in some detail by Melvin Kohn (1980, 1999). One of the strongest relationships he identified was between the *substantive complexity* of the job and *intellectual flexibility*. **Substantive complexity** is the degree to which the work requires thought, independent judgment, and frequent decision making. Those whose work is characterized by substantive complexity also tend to have relatively low levels of supervision, and their work is not overly routinized. As a result of these work conditions, they tend to value self-direction, encourage self-direction in others—including their children—and show evidence of **intellectual flexibility**, the ability to handle conflicting information, grasp several perspectives on a problem, and reflect on one's own values and solutions.

This relationship between substantive complexity at work and personal intellectual flexibility was found among workers in the United States, Poland, and Japan (Kohn, 2006). In the cross-national comparison, U.S. workers whose jobs were characterized as substantively complex also had greater personal satisfaction and a sense of well-being, whereas those whose work was highly routinized and supervised had a lower sense of well-being. In contrast, in Poland, when these data were collected in 1978, the workers who had the more substantively complex work were also more distressed. The workers at the more routinized jobs were more confident of job security and less threatened by instability. Although the Polish workers at the routinized jobs had the least self-direction of all three countries, they felt a high sense of satisfaction about their current and future employment. However, the managers, whose jobs were more substantively complex, were also at greater risk. They were held accountable for productivity with little opportunity to influence rewards or working conditions.

One of the most frequently cited areas of skill development in the contemporary labor market is *creative problem solving*. The combination of increasingly complex technology, instant international communication, and continuing reorganization of the network of interrelated businesses results in the emergence of a new and changing array of problems. These problems may relate to the need to recruit and train the workforce, bring together changing teams of workers depending on the task, find new strategies for the manufacture and delivery of products, or integrate technologies. The concept of **managerial resourcefulness** captures the nature of this problem solving. Managerial resourcefulness combines three critical features: a cognitive capacity to gather and analyze information, sensitivity to the emotional and motivational aspects of change, and a readiness to take appropriate actions (Kanungo & Menon, 2005; Kanungo & Misra, 1992).

By middle adulthood, individuals have accumulated a deep knowledge of the specific tasks and routines associated with their work. At the same time, they have either tried or observed a variety of problem-solving strategies. Thus, the challenge for the middle adult worker is to synthesize these two bodies of knowledge to create a flexible approach to emerging problems. Successful development in this area requires recognizing when conditions have changed such that past solutions will not be adequate. At the same time, it requires confidence in one's ability to find new solutions and remain creative under stressful conditions.

Midlife Career Changes

Management of a career does not necessarily mean remaining within the same occupational structure throughout adult life.

Recall from the discussion of work in chapter 11 (Early Adulthood) that between the ages of 18 and 48, the average number of jobs held was 11.7. Although the rate of job turnover slows down after age 30, people still need to remain flexible about their attachment to a specific job. The segment of workers employed fulltime by corporations is a shrinking percentage of working-age adults. A growing number of middle adults are experiencing work-role transitions, including new assignments within the same company, the same type of work in a different company, combining self-employment with part-time work, and making a transition into an entirely new field of work (Mahler, 2011).

As today's working-age labor force moves through middle adulthood, from age 34 to 60, the nature of the labor market is also changing to a more decentralized, fee-for-services model. This requires individuals to create a "portfolio approach" to their career—developing a document that is more detailed and three-dimensional than a resume that highlights one's products, skills, talents, and experiences (Handy, 1996). The portfolio approach assumes that people need to market themselves, whether in hopes of advancement within a company, or as they seek new employment opportunities. People who change jobs relatively often or who work as consultants and project managers can take this approach in order to convey the range of skills they have developed and the diverse products or activities in which they have played a major role.

Work activities or work-related goals may change for at least six reasons during middle adulthood. First, some careers end during middle adulthood. One example is the career of the professional athlete, whose strength, speed of reaction time, and endurance decline to the point where the athlete can no longer compete.

Second, some adults cannot resolve conflicts between job demands and personal goals. Some workers recognize that the kinds of contributions they thought they could make in the workplace are simply not possible within their chosen work structure. Others feel like outsiders within their corporations.

> Trish Millines Dziko didn't discover her affinity for computers until she attended college on a basketball scholarship. Later, while she was rising through the mostly White, male ranks at Microsoft, she felt uncomfortable being one of the few African Americans in Redmond. At age 39, she retired as one of many Microsoft millionaires and used $100,000 of her kitty to establish the Technology Access Foundation, designed to bring more kids of color into the game. . . . "I want to change the dynamics of the [corporation] club," says Dziko, "by changing the demographics." (Schultz, 2001, pp. 68–69)

A third explanation for midlife career change is the realization that one has succeeded as much as possible in a given career. Adults may realize that they will not be promoted further or that changing technology has made their expertise obsolete. Consequently, they may decide to retrain for new kinds of work or return to school to move in new career directions.

Fourth, family transitions may prompt career changes. In some instances, adults leave the labor market or move to part-time work in order to care for their children or their aging parents. In other cases, adults enter the labor market following divorce or widowhood. According to a New York Times/CBS News/ Kaiser Family Foundation poll of people who were not in the labor force, 61 percent of women and 37 percent of men ages 25 to 54 said that family responsibilities were the reason they were not working (Miller & Alderman, 2014).

Fifth, with the restructuring of the workforce, some workers are laid off and cannot be rehired in the same field. They have to retrain for a new line of work or for similar work in a new industry. Other workers may remain with the same company but find that they are being asked to perform new tasks that require a new set of skills and responsibilities. When people are laid off, they may have to find work that is below their level of training and previous salary.

Sixth, some jobs are too stressful or physically demanding to continue over many years. In order to preserve their physical and/ or mental health, people may have to find a kind of work that is a better fit with their energy, physical strength, and coping capacity.

One must be cautious not to idealize midlife career change. It is not uncommon to experience a variety of fears or worries about leaving one occupation and starting something new: fear of making an unfavorable discovery about one's abilities as a result of the change, fear of failing to satisfy the expectations of important others, fear of taking on new responsibilities, and fear of giving up a known present for an unknown future. For many middle adults, the process of career change requires a reassessment of assumptions that were made in adolescence and early adulthood about gender expectations, family roles, and their attached career ambitions. The process of career change involves gaining insights into one's hopes and ambitions as well as the changing nature of the labor market in order to conceptualize a path forward (Markel, 2016).

The ease or difficulty of work transitions depends in part on the extent to which workers perceive that they have control over the conditions of the change. Voluntary transitions usually occur with some control over the timing of the change and the opportunity to prepare financially and to acquire new credentials or skills. What is more, in the case of voluntary work transitions, the person has the sense of agency about making decisions that advance desired goals. Involuntary transitions often occur with little chance to select the optimal time or to save up for the possibility of a period of unemployment or reduced income. There is less opportunity to consider the impact of the transition on family members. The person who is making an involuntary transition may feel compelled to take a position in order to support the family or to meet existing financial obligations even if the position is not a very good fit with personal values or goals (Fouad & Bynner, 2008).

The Impact of Joblessness

Even though the workplace can be a major source of stress, **joblessness** can be even more disruptive to personal mental health and family functioning. As a result of the restructuring of the labor market, plant closings, downturns in the economy, and workforce reorganizations, many workers who had a history of steady employment, including increased responsibility and advancement, have faced job loss in their middle adulthood. Unemployment in middle adulthood has a major psychological impact on an individual's sense of self-worth and hope for the future. Among middle-aged workers, job loss is associated with material deprivation, disruption in family life, and increases in marital conflict.

Al Franken made a dramatic midlife career change. He left his role as a comedian and ran for the United States Senate. He won a hard-fought contest and has become a respected senator.

Children and spouses are acutely involved in the effects of job loss on a middle-aged parent, and often the entire family experiences new feelings of alienation from social institutions as a result of the experience (Stevens, 2014).

Job loss has been associated with both physical health and mental health consequences, such as self-doubt, passivity, and social withdrawal. Depression is a common consequence, and the associated family strains may lead to new levels of conflict and family violence. In some instances, adjustments that families make to a husband's unemployment result in a further reduction of his sense of importance and accentuate the decline in his self-respect. Social support—especially family strengths and marital satisfaction—are important buffers for the negative effects of unemployment (Bambra, 2010; Blustein, 2008).

In 2004, the U.S. unemployment rate was 4.4 percent, slightly higher for men than for women. The modal period of unemployment was less than 5 weeks, but about 22 percent were unemployed for 27 weeks or more. By the end of 2009, the rate was 10 percent, and 40 percent of those who were unemployed, or 6.1 million people, were long-term unemployed (e.g. had been jobless 27 weeks or more). At the end of July 2016, the unemployment rate had dropped to

4.9 percent among whom 2 million were considered long-term unemployed (U.S. Bureau of Labor Statistics, 2013a, 2016b). An additional 2 million adults were marginally attached to the labor market (they were willing to work but had not looked for work in the last 4 weeks), and another 600,000 were discouraged workers (they were not looking for work because they did not believe there were any jobs available for them).

Table 12.1 summarizes the unemployment rates in 2015 by race/ethnicity and educational attainment for individuals ages 25 years old and older. African Americans and those with less education were at especially high risk for unemployment (U.S. Bureau of Labor Statistics, 2016c).

There is a difference in how people cope with seasonal or short-term (less than 5 weeks) unemployment and long-term or chronic unemployment (Morin, 2010). From 2011 to 2015, 3.2 million workers who had been at their jobs for 3 years or more were displaced from their job because their plant or company closed or moved, there was insufficient work for them to do, or their position or shift was abolished. Although two-thirds of these workers were eventually re-employed, the experience of job loss, job search, and prolonged unemployment was deeply distressing (U.S. Bureau of Labor Statistics, 2016d).

Because of the cultural emphasis on productive work, people are especially likely to experience guilt about being unemployed. Moreover, for men, unemployment disrupts the self-concept of the traditional definition of the adult male role as breadwinner for the family. As a result of guilt, shame, and anger, men may

These blue collar workers have lost their jobs, and they are angry about it. Their jobs have been outsourced to other countries. They do not foresee new jobs that would be right for them emerging in the recovery. They have banded together in an organization through which they are asserting their right to work.

Table 12.1	Unemployment Rates by Ethnicity and Educational Attainment, 2015			
	Educational Level			
Race	**Less Than High School**	**High School Graduate**	**Some College, No Degree**	**Bachelors Degree or Higher**
European American	6.8	4.6	4.4	2.4
African American	15.9	9.7	8.0	4.0
Asian American	5.4	4.1	3.4	2.8
Hispanic/Latino	6.6	5.9	5.3	3.4

Source: U.S. Bureau of Labor Statistics, 2016, Table 7.

find it hard to direct their energy toward creative solutions to life problems. The inability to work can be expected to become a serious hurdle to the resolution of the psychosocial conflict of generativity versus stagnation for men. In a comparison of men and women who had a combination of breadwinner and childrearing responsibilities, the men were more likely to view unemployment as a defeat, whereas the women were more likely to view unemployment as an opportunity (Forret, Sullivan, & Mainiero, 2010).

In a qualitative study of 13 men and women who were unemployed or underemployed, different stories of job loss and coping emerged (Blustein, Kozan, & Connors-Kellgren, 2013). First, some were shocked by the sudden news that they were being laid off whereas others anticipated the possible job loss. Those for whom job loss came "out of the blue" had a harder time reacting to the news and experienced more immediate emotional distress. Second, some saw the reason for their job loss as personal, e.g. they had a long-term illness or they had fewer qualifications than others, while others saw the reason as due to a larger corporate or societal factor, e.g. good jobs are being sent overseas or companies are downsizing to give more money to corporate executives. Third, participants differed in the kinds and levels of support during their unemployment. Some felt a particular loss of social support whereas others had a strong friendship and family support network; some were more severely impacted by financial loss than others; and some found that their physical health prevented them from being considered for new jobs. Those with serious financial limitations also had more limited access to education or training for new kinds of work. Not unexpectedly, participants differed in their ability to cope with the job loss and to redirect toward new work. Some participants were more proactive, networking, volunteering, retraining, and focusing on their own improved physical and mental health. Others suffered with the combined stressors of increased economic insecurity, loss of self-esteem, and anxiety about the uncertainties of future employment.

Aaron has been unemployed for slightly less than 1 year. He is being interviewed at a one-stop career counseling center.

Being unemployed does humble you. It makes you think, it makes you see things in a different perspective, it makes you test your humanity and how others treat you when you are not working. Cause when I was working I was the hero, you know why? Cause I was paying the bills. I had a home you know, I was able to go

to certain places, buy certain things . . . And they said that you had counselors here but a counselor cannot do anything for me. You have a job—what can you possibly do for me that you've got a job . . . And when I leave you, you still have a job. I'm out here hustling the best I can to make sure that I still have a roof over my head and still able to eat and I can still apply myself and get some a little bit of satisfaction in the process. (Blustein, Kozan, & Connors-Kellgren, 2013, p. 262)

The threats of job loss and job insecurity can also create stress for those who remain employed as well as for those who become unemployed. For example, in a study of employment conditions on job-related distress, workers in industries that were experiencing high levels of unemployment had a higher incidence of depression than did workers in industries where unemployment was low. Similarly, studies have shown that workers who are spared during downsizing and mergers show signs of anxiety and depression.

These observations highlight the salience that work has in middle adulthood and the role that meaningful work plays in supporting well-being. At its best, work provides resources for survival, creates a context for social relatedness, and offers opportunities for self-determination. As such, involuntary long-term or chronic unemployment or underemployment can undermine a middle adult's sense of mattering and establish conditions for alienation or self-loathing (Blustein, 2008; Garrett-Peters, 2009).

Balancing Work and Family Life

Almost everyone manages a career while juggling commitments to spouse, children, parents, other household members, and friends. A decision to assume more authority, work longer hours, accept an offer with another company, quit a job, accept a transfer to a new location, or start up one's own business will touch the lives of other household and family members.

In thinking about balancing work and family life, it is useful to consider three interrelated concepts: role overload, role conflict, and role spillover. **Role overload** occurs as a result of too many demands and expectations to handle in the time allowed. For example, a parent with three children ages 8, 11, and 15 may find that the demands of getting the children ready for school, attending functions at three different schools, picking children up and dropping them off at various places, and trying to be emotionally available for the problem of the day are exhausting. Role overload can be experienced within a particular role as well as across roles.

Role conflict occurs when demands and expectations of various roles conflict with each other. For example, role conflict occurs when a worker is expected to stay late at the job to finish a project, but that same night is a spouse's birthday or a child's performance.

Role spillover occurs when the demands or preoccupations about one role interfere with the ability to carry out another role. For example, a person may be disrupted at work by worries about an ill parent or distracted at home by a work assignment that is due the next day.

Role overload in the workplace is consistently perceived as a source of stress and is typically associated with negative attitudes toward the organization, reducing a worker's organizational commitment and job satisfaction (Eatough, Chang, Miloslavic, & Johnson, 2011). Some occupations are more likely to create work overload, especially when companies are downsizing and increasing the demands on a reduced workforce. Studies of role overload are also beginning to address the health-related implications. For example, adults who suffer from arthritis are likely to report that work-related strains can exacerbate their symptoms (Gignac et al., 2014; Mustafa et al., 2012).

Two features of the workplace that are thought to relieve this strain are empowerment in the job and a cooperative workplace climate. **Empowerment** can include strategies to increase a sense of job control, such as opportunities to be creative and innovative in one's work, to have a role in decisions that impact how one performs one's work, and to be encouraged by one's supervisor to have adequate authority about how to get one's job done. A cooperative climate reflects a spirit of teamwork and collaboration among coworkers who are willing to help one another to get the job done (Fisher, 2014). In a large, cross-national study involving workers in 18 countries, the negative relationship between role overload and organizational commitment was observed across all contexts. A cooperative climate was found to modify this relationship. However, a sense of empowerment was only effective in cultures that had a more egalitarian work climate. In cultures where the power distance between supervisors and workers was great, the institution of workplace empowerment practices did not ease the tensions around overload (Fisher, 2014).

The combination of role overload, role conflict, and role spillover can lead to reduced satisfaction at work and in family roles and a decline in the person's sense of well-being (Kinnunen, Feldt, Mauno, & Rantanen, 2010). However, some studies find that multiple role involvement may contribute to health and well-being. Spousal support for the partner's involvement in work can increase work satisfaction, and feelings of success and pride in one's accomplishments at work can contribute to marital satisfaction (Dreman, 1997). In a large, longitudinal study of British women born in 1946, those women who had participated in multiple work and family roles over the course of their adulthood were healthier at age 54 than women from the same birth cohort who were long-time homemakers (McMunn, Bartley, Hardy, & Kuh, 2006).

The domains of work and family, both central to adult lives across cultures, are likely to conflict under certain circumstances and complement each other in other circumstances. In order to understand the nature of this relationship, researchers have identified the elements of work and the elements of family life that appear to be most central to this conflict. A model of how job characteristics and family characteristics might contribute to work–family conflict and family–work conflict is presented in FIGURE 12.1 ▶.

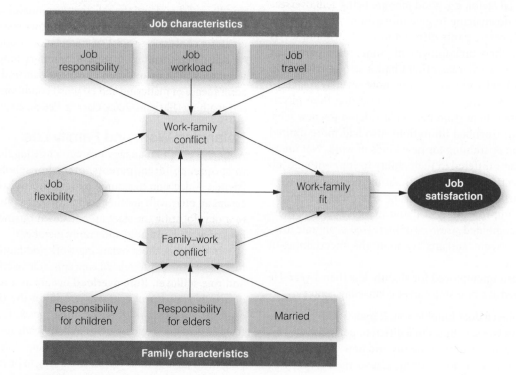

FIGURE 12.1▶ A MODEL OF THE WORK–FAMILY INTERFACE

Source: Hill, Yang, Hawkins, and Ferris, 2004, Fig. 1, p. 1302.

The basic assumption is that there are role pressures from work and family that are mutually incompatible, so that meeting the expectations in one domain makes it very difficult to meet expectations in the other. Moreover, there may be interactions such that conflicts from work make it difficult to meet role expectations in the family, but then the disruptions in the family make it difficult to meet role expectations at work (Greenhaus & Allen, 2011). Despite these tensions between work and family obligations, people strive to find ways for the two roles to work together (work–family fit), which leads to greater job satisfaction. Job flexibility, for example, a workplace policy that supports taking hours off to carry out family-related responsibilities, is one factor that can contribute to this successful adaptation.

The model presented in Figure 12.1 was tested in 48 countries (Hill, Yang, Hawkins, & Ferris, 2004). The characteristics of a job that were hypothesized to produce work–family conflict were job responsibility, job workload, and job travel. The characteristics of the family that were hypothesized to produce family–work conflict were responsibility for children, responsibility for elders, and being married. The model was tested by analyzing survey responses of more than 25,000 IBM workers whose average age was 39. The countries were divided into 11 Eastern countries with a collectivist orientation, and three groups of countries with a more individualist orientation: Western developing countries, Western affluent countries, and the United States.

The model was a good fit for all four groups of countries. The three job characteristics were significantly related to work–family conflict across all 48 countries, although the strength of the relationship was greater in the three individualist groups of countries. Responsibility for children and elders was related to family–work conflict across all the countries, but this relationship was stronger for women than for men. Contrary to expectations, marriage was related to less family–work conflict across all the countries. Job flexibility was associated with less work–family conflict in the Eastern countries and the Western developing countries, but not in the Western affluent countries or the United States. Across all the countries, work was much more likely to create conflict in family life than family life was to be disruptive for work. The general model was a good predictor of job satisfaction across these very different work environments. One might ask whether the global corporate environment of IBM might have smoothed out some of the cultural variations that would have been observed had workers been drawn from a greater diversity of businesses. However, this research is a very exciting approach in trying to understand the dynamics of work–family interactions at a global level.

This cross-national study also adds to a growing literature documenting that women are more distressed by family–work conflict than are men, possibly because responsibilities for household and child care continue to rest more on the shoulders of employed women than on those of employed men (Voydanoff, 2004). Nonetheless, trends in the United States are moving toward a more egalitarian model. Men and women increasingly agree on the value of having women in the labor market and the importance of family-friendly workplace policies. Employed men are spending an increasing amount of time on household and child care tasks, both on workdays and nonworkdays.

Balancing work and family life is challenging; it involves the interface of multiple, interacting systems—each partner's work environment, each partner's role demands within the family, and the partners' relationships with one another and with their children. Over time, the partners adapt to the changing demands of the workplace by modifying their involvement in household tasks. As adults become increasingly invested in their work, they may do less household work. If one partner becomes more involved at work, the other partner may take on more of the household responsibilities (Lam, McHale, & Crouter, 2012). One study found that for professional couples with children, when husbands were required to work long hours at their job, the probability of the wife quitting her job increased (Cha, 2010).

Work conditions involving high demands and little support have an impact on parents and their children. Mothers who worked long hours and felt overloaded were less warm and accepting toward their adolescent children. Fathers who worked long hours and felt overloaded experienced more conflict with their adolescent children. Husbands' negative work-related stressors also increased their wives' sense of overload beyond what the wives were experiencing because of their own work situation (Crouter & Bumpus, 2001). When either partner experiences a lot of work pressure, multiple role demands and little support from the boss or supervisor, the impact on the couple and the family is negative. Under these conditions, adults have more marital conflict, less quality time for each other, and more conflict with their adolescent children (Ransford, Crouter, & McHale, 2008).

When couples have a shared view of one another as co-providers who contribute equally to their economic and personal well-being, they tend to experience less stress associated with role overload and higher levels of marital satisfaction (Helms, Walls, Crouter, & McHale, 2010). Ellen Galinsky (2007) has coined the term *dual-centric* to describe people who put the same emphasis and priority on their work and their personal lives. These people are equally likely to be men and women. They are more likely to have children at home, and they spend an average of about 5 hours a week more at home than those who place a higher priority on work than on their personal lives. These dual-centric individuals feel more successful at work and at home, and by objective measures, such as their level in the organization or their salary, feel equally successful as those who place a greater priority on their work. In comparison to those who place a higher priority on either their work or their personal lives, dual-centric people experience lower levels of stress, and fewer say that they find it difficult to manage their multiple roles. These dual-centric adults were very clear and intentional about having both domains as priorities in their lives, they set some clear boundaries between the domains, they practiced being emotionally as well as physically present in the sphere where they were functioning at the time, and they took time to rest or redirect their energy away from work from time to time.

After the birth of her twins, Karen decided to try working from home. She balances work and family life by having a babysitter 3 half days and trying to work on small projects for a half hour here and there while the twins are awake. The twins love their mom's computer and are eager to help.

Although much of the responsibility for managing multiple roles falls to individuals and couples, **work–family facilitation** can be supported by resources in the workplace that make it easier for employees to address pressing family demands within the scope of their daily work (Voydanoff, 2004). When the workplace is organized to recognize and sustain the multiple-role responsibilities of employees, people are likely to experience an increase in their sense of self-worth, competence, and fulfillment, resulting in a more positive outlook on their interpersonal relationships at home and greater productivity at work. These policies are often referred to as supporting "work-life fit." Some examples include policies that allow workers to take family-related leaves without risking their job security, to take time off during the day to take a child to the doctor or meet with a teacher, or to focus on work accomplished regardless of where it is done as opposed to hours at the office. A supportive work climate in which supervisors help workers feel comfortable about using these flexible policies and accommodating significant personal obligations contribute to work–family facilitation. Given that most people in middle adulthood are expected to be functioning in multiple roles, it makes sense that the responsibility for success in achieving an effective balance between work and family demands should rest not only on the coping strategies of individuals and couples, but also on the policies and climate of the work setting, and the practices of managers and supervisors (Kelly et al., 2014).

FURTHER REFLECTION: Summarize how the demands of managing a career change from early to middle adulthood.

Describe some of the conditions that have occurred over the past 25 years that have changed the work environment for American workers. What are your conclusions about the implications of these changes for development in middle adulthood?

What characteristics of the work environment are most likely to foster intellectual growth, job satisfaction, and the ability to effectively balance work and family life? How common are these characteristics for jobs at the top, middle, and bottom of the economic ladder?

How does home life facilitate or interfere with job performance for men? For women?

Nurturing an Intimate Relationship

OBJECTIVE 2 Define the concept of a vital, intimate relationship and examine factors that support this goal in middle adulthood, especially a commitment to growth, effective communication, creative use of conflict, and preserving passion.

Although people derive a significant sense of personal identity from their jobs and may worry a lot about them, happiness in an intimate relationship is a stronger predictor of overall well-being in adulthood than is satisfaction with work. According to a survey conducted by the AARP (American Association of Retired Persons, 2010), over 90 percent of men and 86 percent of women in middle adulthood reported that having a good relationship with a spouse or partner was very important to their quality of life. Marriage and other long-term intimate bonds are salient, dynamic relationships. They change as the partners mature, as the family constellation changes, and in response to changing events, including divorce and remarriage, family crises, and historical events. Focus and effort are required to keep these relationships healthy and vital throughout middle adulthood.

What is a **vital marriage**? Four themes have been identified as contributing to long-lasting, happy marriages: the characteristics of the individual partners, the nature of the partners' **interpersonal interactions**, the partners' commitment to nurturing the future of the relationship, and the preservation of passion in the relationship (Crooks & Bauer, 2010).

Characteristics of the Partners

Happy marriages are built on love and affection between two people who are basically even tempered and warm hearted (Huston & Melz, 2004). Continuing ego development and adaptive restructuring of personal identity in the context of meaningful social roles provide a core of personal strengths that help sustain interdependence and care in the face of the many challenges of middle adulthood (Marcia, 2002, 2010). The partners in a vital marriage are not overly anxious, depressed, or impulsive. They are nurturing, expressive, gentle, understanding, and conscientious. They care about each other, rather than being self-absorbed or indifferent to one another's fate.

These individuals also contribute other types of social capital that help sustain the relationship. For example, they may have a supportive network of family members and friends, they may contribute financial resources to the family, they are cooperative rather than domineering in the way they participate in decision making, and they bring unique competencies to the tasks of household maintenance (Edin, 2000).

Early childhood trauma, especially childhood sexual, emotional, and physical abuse, have been found to derail the capacity for sustaining close, trusting adult relationships (McCarthy & Sypeck, 2003). Adults who were abused as children report fear of intimacy, dysfunctional sexual behaviors, strong feelings of jealousy, and patterns of re-enacting earlier abusive relationships with contemporary partners. Symptoms of post-traumatic stress disorder continue to arise, which result in dissociation and self-criticism (Davis, Petretic-Jackson, & Ting, 2001; Liang Williams & Siegel, 2006). Many first person accounts suggest that adults who have had repeated abusive relationships eventually give up on intimacy and prefer to live a more peaceful life without a partner. As the following narrative suggests, it is possible to find a secure, loving relationship, but it may take a special partner (Buczynski, 2016).

> I experienced trauma as a child through being adopted into a family where my parents were themselves dealing with trauma (dad from the war). I was a very insecure child. I can remember my mother telling me I had an "inferiority complex". She was authoritative and we clashed later in life. I married at 18 to a violent man and spent the next 18 years dealing with that—by this stage I argued back and on the surface I seemed confident, but I was very self-critical inside. After the marriage ended, I had a series of same-sex relationships in which I was described as emotionally volatile—I worked hard at being wanted—it was exhausting. I am now in a relationship of 12 years and until recently I pushed my partner away, always planning to escape especially when we argued. It seemed like a trigger—if I went to my "cubby" everything would be alright. My partner is steadfast and would not give up on me. Something recently changed in me (I had exhausted all my escape plans perhaps) and I am able to truly commit to the relationship. I feel safe. I feel as if I belong here. The peripherals are not important anymore. (first person narrative comment from Helen, in Buczynski, 2016)

Partners' Interpersonal Interactions

Long-term stable relationships are typically based on a strong bond of friendship. The partners support each other and like each other. They have shared interests, enjoy similar activities, and are supportive and appreciative of one another's accomplishments. The couple must develop an effective communication system. This requires adequate opportunities for interaction. If competing life roles, including work and parenting, dramatically reduce opportunities for interaction, the couple will risk drifting apart. They will have increasingly fewer shared experiences

and be less readily influenced by each other's observations and reactions. There is a reciprocal relationship between interaction and happiness. In a longitudinal study, couples who were happier early in their marriage showed higher levels of interaction in later years (Zuo, 1992). After a number of years of marriage, the two variables were strong predictors of each other: Those who were happy were involved in more frequent interactions, and, similarly, those who were involved in frequent interactions were happier.

John Gottman and his colleagues have examined the nature of interactions among heterosexual married couples. Based on their research, they have been able to predict with a high degree of accuracy whether couples will separate in the first few years of their marriage or stay together (Driver, Tabares, Shapiro, & Gottman, 2012; Gottman, Coan, Carrere, & Swanson, 1998; Gottman & Silver, 2000). Enduring relationships are characterized by a high ratio of positive to negative interactions. Couples

Monkey Business Images/Shutterstock.com

Omar and Vidya have been married for 10 years, and they have two young children. He works as a field agent for the gas company. She works from home as a copywriter for a catalog company. This allows her to devote time and attention to caring for the children and managing the household. They are still deeply in love and delight in sharing a few moments to cuddle and laugh together.

in satisfied marriages did argue, but the balance of five positive statements to one negative statement was an important constant in predicting relationship stability. In stable, satisfied heterosexual couples, the woman tends to use a gentle, diplomatic beginning when she introduces a problem or concern, and the man accepts his wife's influence. When the woman expresses contempt, is overly negative, or aggressive and the man is overly domineering or defensive in the face of conflict, the relationship is less likely to endure.

Do men and women have different ways of expressing their love? In many ways, men and women are alike in the ways they express affection and in the importance they place in trust as a component of a loving relationship. Couples have many personal and private ways of conveying their love—a joke, a caress, a look, a word or expression that captures a shared experience, the preparation of a special dish. When observed in day-to-day interactions, some differences have also been found. Women show their love through their positive interactions, expressing less whining, complaining, or criticizing of their husbands. Men show their love by initiating lovemaking, participating in shared leisure time activities, and joining their wives in carrying out daily household work (Schneider, Konijn, Righetti, & Rusbult, 2011; Schoenfield, Bredow, & Huston, 2012).

For couples that do not have an effective communication system, resentments accumulate with no opportunity to resolve them. A common pattern is that the wife wants to talk things over, but the husband does not see what good this will do. Harmonious, satisfied couples listen to and consider each other's problems. They validate each other's concerns by expressing understanding, even if they cannot offer solutions. In contrast, dissatisfied couples avoid problems or engage in counterattack. Instead of validating the spouse's concern, the partner raises complaints and criticisms or withdraws. Over the years, expressions of affection, enjoyment, laughter, and support decline. Even if negative or critical interactions do not increase, they are embedded in a less positive overall context. The ideal 5 to 1 ratio may drop to 3 or 2 to 1, making the negative interactions more salient. This takes the couple along the path to marital disruption.

Partners' Commitment to Nurturing the Future of the Relationship

In order for a marriage to last over the long period of middle and later adulthood, the partners have to see a long-term commitment as one of their values. Research on cohabitation and research on marriage stability among children whose parents divorced both illustrate contexts in which adults may view marriage as a more temporary alliance than as a lifelong relationship. Assuming that couples share a view of their relationship as long term, the partners must learn to work toward change in areas where it is possible and to accept one another and the characteristics of the relationship in areas where change cannot be accomplished. By expanding their tolerance for differences and admiration for their strengths, couples can achieve new levels of intimacy. Research on long-lasting, satisfying marriages identified a set of psychosocial tasks that couples have to master (Wallerstein & Blakeslee, 1995). Salient in this list are the following challenges:

- Preserving a balance between intimacy in the couple and autonomy for the individuals
- Expanding the bonds of affection to include children while preserving and nurturing the couple relationship
- Shifting the focus of energy from the family of origin to the newly formed family while preserving relationships with the extended kinship network
- Managing the adversities in life, such as serious illness, death, or disaster, in ways that strengthen the relationship
- Sharing laughter and delight in daily life

The partners must be committed to growth both as individuals and as a couple. This means that they accept the idea that they will change in important ways and that the relationship, too, will change. Within any enduring relationship, each person experiences a dynamic tension between pressures and desires for personal growth on the one hand and the pressures and desires to preserve the relationship on the other hand. Both of these forces have the potential to overwhelm or dominate the sense of mutuality, as is illustrated in the case study on the struggle for commitment to growth in a vital marriage. A vital marriage requires both partners to be open to the need to be themselves (as they continue to discover new dimensions of self) and an energizing, interpersonal chemistry that is resilient even in the face of the harshest challenges. Partners in an enduring relationship repeatedly act in ways that take into account their own self-interest and the well-being of their partner (Rusbult & Agnew, 2010).

— CASE STUDY The Struggle for Commitment to Growth in a Vital Marriage —

One common example of the need to permit individual growth within a marriage occurs when a woman who has been primarily responsible for child care and household management expresses an interest in entering or returning to the paid labor force.

Annette, who had worked as a nurse before she married, decided that it was time to go back to work. Her three children were in elementary and middle school, and her husband had a full-time job, so she was by herself for long hours during the day. She began to feel depressed and jealous of everyone else's active lives, so she took a position at a local hospital, working three afternoons and on Saturday each week.

At first, her husband, Gary, fussed and resisted. "Why did she need to go to work?" he asked. They didn't really need the money, and Gary liked to know that she would be at home when he came back from work. He wasn't used to having to take the kids to their activities after school. Plus, Saturday used to be his day to hang out with his friends from work. The kids fussed at being asked to get dinner ready. But Annette insisted that she had to get back to work—her mental health and happiness depended on it.

The first months were terrible. Annette wondered if she was doing the right thing, and Gary used every trick in the book to lure her back to the house. But there was no denying the value of this new job for Annette's self-confidence, her renewed feeling of personal identity, and her ability to return to the home with new energy and enthusiasm for her husband, children, and family life. Gary began to get more involved in the children's lives and actually looked forward to the Saturdays they spent together. Soon the children began to see their mother in a new light, as a professional who took care of other people as well as them. They also felt a new surge of independence in being able to handle the dinner meal on their own. Gary and Annette felt closer to each other as a result of Annette's self-confidence and Gary's new level of involvement in the lives of the children.

CASE ANALYSIS Using What You Know

1. Summarize the features of a vital marriage that are evident in this case. What features of a vital marriage are missing?

2. Describe the changes in the family system that take place from Annette's initial decision to return to work to the eventual pattern of family adaptation.

3. Explain how Annette's decision leads to new opportunities for growth for Gary, her children, and herself.

4. Imagine that Gary had been the one looking for a new structure—perhaps going into business for himself or going back to school for a new profession. What types of changes might this have caused in the family system? On the marital relationship?

Preserving Passion in a Long-Term Relationship

According to Sternberg's three-dimensional model of love presented in chapter 11, passion is the first thing to go. However, preserving an erotic and sexual aspect to intimacy continues to play a role in fostering long-term **intimate relationships** throughout adulthood. Relationship satisfaction is associated with openness about sexual needs, satisfaction with sexual frequency, and experiencing a playful enjoyment of sexual pleasure (Crooks & Bauer, 2016). This means coping with the physiological changes in sexual responsiveness that accompany aging and finding new ways to enjoy sexual contact in the context of parenting demands, chronic illness or disability, or other stressful life events that interfere with one's sexual interest. Results of an AARP survey found that having a satisfying sexual relationship was somewhat more important to men than to women in middle adulthood. However, for both men and women, those who had a satisfying sexual relationship had higher life satisfaction than those who did not (AARP, 2010).

Changes in sexual responsiveness over the middle adult years have been well documented (Crooks & Bauer, 2016; Masters & Johnson, 1966). For men, erections take longer to develop, orgasm is less intense, and the erection fades more quickly. With age, it may take a longer period, from several hours to days, to experience a new erection. Even though the sexual response changes, orgasm continues to be a source of pleasure. Although there is a reduction in sperm production, most men remain fertile well into elderhood. Most men are able to enjoy sexual activity throughout their life provided they continue to have a partner.

For some men, periods of illness, certain medications, heart disease, or high blood pressure can interfere with the ability to have an erection. Anxiety about being able to have an erection or a preoccupation with the quality of sexual performance may interfere with the ability to become aroused. The availability of drugs to treat erectile disorders has increased openness and awareness of this problem and provided new avenues for couples to discuss changes in their sexual vitality. An estimated 18 million men age 20 and older in the United States have erectile dysfunction (Selvin, Burnett, & Platz, 2007). Although the incidence increases with age, usually it is not age itself, but illnesses that are associated with aging and the accompanying medications that account for this relationship.

One of the common changes experienced by men in midlife is inflammation or increased size of the prostate gland. This gland produces fluids that are released during ejaculation. When the prostate becomes enlarged, it may put pressure on the urethra and restrict the flow of urine. A significant number of men experience prostate cancer. Although treatments for prostate cancer vary, they can interfere with sexual functioning (Ofman, 2004).

Physical changes that affect the sexual response also occur for women. At some time during their late 40s or in their 50s, women experience the **climacteric**, or the involution and atrophy of the reproductive organs. Many physiological changes accompany the close of fertility, including the cessation of menstruation (**menopause**), gradual reduction in the production of estrogen, atrophy of the breasts and genital tissues, and shrinkage of the uterus (Carroll, 2012). The most commonly reported symptom is a frequent hot flash, a sudden onset of warmth in the face and neck that lasts several minutes. Sometimes it is accompanied by dizziness, nausea, sweating, or headaches. About 75 percent to 85 percent of women going through natural menopause report this symptom. Other physiological symptoms are the reduction of vaginal fluid and loss of elasticity, sleeplessness, and increased anxiety (Nelson, 2008). The symptoms appear to be closely related to a drastic drop in the production of estrogen. Postmenopausal women produce only one sixth as much estrogen as do women who regularly menstruate.

The use of estrogen treatment alleviates or even prevents menopausal symptoms. Results of research from the Women's Health Initiative found a relationship of hormone replacement therapy to decreased risk of osteoporosis, cardiovascular disease, and colorectal and lung cancers, but an increased risk of breast cancer. As a result, many physicians have stopped prescribing hormone replacement therapy and have begun to seek alternative therapies to help reduce severe symptoms of menopause for those women who experience them (Beck, 2008).

The reduction in estrogen is associated with changes in the sexual response cycle. The most noticeable change is decreased lubrication and less expansion of the vagina during the excitement phase. This can cause pain during intercourse and reduced sensitivity, which interfere with sexual pleasure. Although the number of orgasmic contractions may be fewer, orgasm remains a pleasurable experience for postmenopausal women. Without the risk of pregnancy, many women are more enthusiastic about sexual relations after menopause than they were before. As discussed in the **Human Development and Diversity** box Menopause, the

Menopause

The experiences associated with menopause differ widely from one person to the next. The severity of symptoms is associated with both the biological changes related to decreases in estrogen production and the attitude of the culture toward the infertile, older woman. In cultures that reward women for reaching the end of the fertile period, menopause is associated with fewer physiological symptoms. In a study describing the reaction of women in India, menopause was associated with increased social status: "The absence of menstrual flow signaled an incredible elevation of stature for these women. Women were released from a veiled, secluded life in a compound to talk and socialize (even drink) with menfolk. They then became revered as models of wisdom and experience by the younger generation" (Gillespie, 1989, p. 46). Women from different cultural groups have diverse attitudes about menopause that may create a more or less positive context for the end of the reproductive stage of life (Lerner-Geva, Boyko, Blumstein, & Benyamini, 2010).

Within a society, a woman's attitudes toward aging and her involvement in adult roles influence the ease or difficulty with which she experiences menopause. In U.S. society, for example, a woman who is going through menopause at age 50 may also be experiencing the severe illness or death of her parents and the marriage of her youngest child. The severity of menopausal symptoms and the extent to which women experience changes in their sexual motivation may depend largely on their involvement in a satisfying intimate relationship (Hinchiff, Gott, & Ingleton, 2010).

In the U.S. medical culture, the tendency is to view menopause as a normal developmental transition associated with symptoms that can be alleviated with various hormonal and dietary supplements. Many publications dealing with menopause focus on issues such as the treatment of symptoms and the pros and cons of hormone replacement therapy (Womenshealth. gov, 2010). Comparatively few studies have focused on the social and psychological correlates of menopause.

Women differ in how they interpret the meaning of menopause. Some are embarrassed by the hot flashes when they occur in a public setting. Others see the symptoms of menopause as a reminder that they are aging in a culture that values youth and physical attractiveness in women above other characteristics. An emerging group has recast hot flashes as *power surges*, suggesting the beginning of a new, competent period of life.

In an online survey, women from four ethnic groups were asked to describe their menopausal symptoms (Im, Lee, Chee, Dormire, & Brown, 2010). Asian American women reported the fewest symptoms; European American women reported the most. Among African American women, there was a cultural theme of being strong, accepting menopause as a natural process, and keeping silent or downplaying their symptoms. Individual variability was noted, with sensitivity to symptoms linked to the woman's health and concurrent life stressors, as well as her cultural beliefs about the meaning of this transition in her life.

The North American Menopause Society (NAMS) provides resources to address women's concerns about menopause. Health-related issues, including concerns about weight gain, osteoporosis, sleep disturbances, and sexual dysfunction are associated with the hormonal changes of menopause. Many women are frustrated by the lack of clear information they receive from their health care providers. At the same time NAMS advises women to see this transition as a stimulus for new beginnings, a time to take a closer look at one's health, one's relationships, and one's investment in satisfying activities (North American Menopause Society, 2013, 2015). They note the similarities between menopause and puberty as significant biopsychosocial transitions, except that with menopause most middle adults have the advantage of life experience to shape the direction of their development.

For more information about menopause, see the North American Menopause Society website and the National Institute on Aging.

Critical Thinking Questions

1. How does menopause relate to the developmental tasks of middle adulthood?
2. Talk to three or four women who have not yet experienced menopause and three or four who have experienced menopause. Summarize the factors that account for differences in the ways that women interpret the meaning of menopause. What factors are most likely to be associated with a positive transition?
3. Design a study that focuses on either the psychological or social correlates of menopause. What are your research questions? What might be some difficulties in doing research on this topic?
4. Examine the medical culture in the United States. What challenges do women face in striving to gain information about menopause and their health in a culture that is hierarchical, male-dominated, and heavily influenced by the profit motive of pharmaceutical and insurance companies?

impact of menopause for women is determined in part by its cultural meaning. As with other aspects of an intimate relationship, preserving the sexual dimension requires good communication and a sense of humor.

Nurturing vitality in an intimate relationship is relevant for the ongoing social support it provides as the couple enters later life. What is more, the quality of the parents' marital relationship during middle adulthood has significant consequences for the well-being of children in the family and provides the context for the children's emerging understanding of intimacy and marital roles. As children mature into middle childhood and early adolescence, they pay attention to and try to make sense of the quality of their parents' interactions with each other. As children observe their parents, they acquire a sense of how they function as intimate partners as well as parents. Of course, children will not perfectly replicate their parents' marriages. However, the degree of egalitarianism, the approach to conflict resolution, and the expression of affection that children observe can influence their ideas about the kind of partner they seek, their ability to manage conflict in an intimate relationship, and their expectations about marital interaction (Schulz, Pruett, Kerig, & Parke, 2010).

FURTHER REFLECTION: Clarify your assumptions about the quality of intimate relationships in middle adulthood. How does the evidence you have read confirm or disconfirm these assumptions?

Describe how a couple might work to preserve a vital intimate relationship in the face of other competing demands and stressors of adult life.

Speculate about alternative outlets for experiencing intimacy for adults who do not have a life partner.

Expanding Caring Relationships

OBJECTIVE 3 Evaluate the expansion of caring in middle adulthood as it applies to two specific roles—that of a parent and that of an adult child caring for one's aging parents. Clarify your assumptions about the costs and benefits of enacting these roles.

Middle adults have opportunities to express caring in many roles. This section focuses on two of those: parenting and the care of one's aging parents. Both domains offer numerous challenges to the intellectual, emotional, and physical **resources** of the adult caregiver. Beyond family roles, middle adults may also express their caring through charitable giving, a wide variety of careers in caregiving, volunteerism, community action, care of ill or disabled friends and family, foster care, and support of religious and charitable organizations.

Parenting

In parenting, we see the critical intersection of adult development and child development. As parents, adults bring a psychosocial history of ego strengths and core pathologies, coping skills and defenses, and adequate or inadequate resolutions of previous psychosocial crises to the task of nurturing their children. They have scripts from their own childhood, modified by information from friends, relatives, and experts about how to approach the task. With all this, they have to adapt to the unique temperament, developmental level, and strengths or vulnerabilities of each of their children and to the work, family, cultural, and community contexts in which childrearing is taking place.

Parenting takes place over a long period of time. In a two-parent family, the partners have many opportunities to observe and appreciate each other's approaches to the care, nurturing, and guidance of their children. The concept of a **parenting alliance** captures the importance of the working relationship between the partners as they engage in parenting behaviors. The parenting alliance is defined as "the capacity of a spouse to acknowledge, respect, and value the parenting roles and tasks

of the partner" (Cohen & Weissman, 1984, p. 35). The parents' personalities, their attachment orientations, the quality of their shared parenting activities, and the infant's temperament all contribute to the quality of this alliance (Goldiolo & Roskam, 2016). It is not surprising that there is a close association between marital satisfaction and the formation of an effective parenting alliance (Hughes, 2006). As adults establish their parenting alliance, they benefit from knowing that their partner values, trusts, and respects the way they enact their parenting role. The confidence and sense of appreciation that come with this knowledge help adults engage more joyfully in their parenting and weather periods of stress. It also provides a context of reassurance for children who observe the way their parents encourage and sustain each other (Hughes, Gordon, & Gaertner, 2004; McHale, Kuersten-Hogan, & Rao, 2004).

Being a parent is a difficult, demanding task that requires a great deal of learning. Because children are constantly changing and are often unpredictable, adults must be sensitive and flexible in new situations in order to cope successfully with their demands. Each period of the child's development calls for new and innovative parenting strategies. Childrearing experiences are different with each child, and the changing family constellation brings new demands for flexibility and learning. With each successive child, however, there seems to be less anxiety about parenting skills. Children help adults learn about parenting through their responses to their parents' efforts and their own persistence in following the path of development.

Fathering

In the history of the field of family science, the research on parenting has focused almost exclusively on mothers. Most research involved interviews or surveys of mothers, and even when the study used the term *parent*, the informant was typically a mother. In an effort to balance this one-sided view of parenting, a growing literature is clarifying the multidimensional nature of the father role and fathering in middle adulthood (Pleck, 2010). Paternal involvement has been characterized along a variety of dimensions, including how men perceive their connection with their children; the frequency and nature of their one-to-one interactions with their children; their responsibility for specific child care needs, such as taking children to school, caring for them when they are ill, or helping with homework; and their accessibility when the child wants to initiate interactions. Research has also focused on men's views and values regarding fatherhood, the impact of fathers on children, and the relationship of marital quality to men's competence as fathers.

Most men find personal meaning and emotional support in their roles as husband and father (Palkovitz, Trask, & Adamsons, 2014). When men were interviewed about their experiences of divorce, many expressed deep grief over the loss of contact with their children. For example:

> For Tim Scott, 49, the hardest part of his decision to end his marriage to his wife, Jane, a doctor, was what would happen to his relationship with his son Robert, then three. "I know I'd miss him. I didn't realize how much. . . . I don't think I realized quite how strongly

I identified with myself as being a husband and father until it wasn't there anymore. I was absolutely poleaxed by losing Robert, by not having the day-to-day relationship with him." (Cavendish, 2013)

For many men, the positive quality of their marital and parental roles helps them cope more effectively with the stresses of work (Palkowitz, 2002). In many instances, specific lessons from home—including the patience and communication necessary to be an effective parent, willingness to plan and work out alternative strategies for managing daily tasks with his wife, and the admiration he has for his wife in her paid labor force activities—actually help a man function more effectively at work.

In some families, fathers face a particularly difficult challenge in finding time to interact effectively with their children. For example, one naturalistic observational study focused on the quality of family interactions in dual-earner families when parents returned home from work and in the evening when everyone was at home. Fathers typically returned home from work later than mothers. When mothers came home from work, they were usually greeted positively by their children who filled them in on the day's activities. When fathers returned from work, they were greeted positively, but often the children then resumed their activities and little conversation took place about the events of the day. Over the course of the evening, mothers were more likely to spend time with their children; fathers were more likely to spend time alone (Campos, Graesch, Repetti, Bradbury, & Ochs, 2009). One can infer from this pattern that fathers who want to have a more detailed picture of their children's daily lives may have to develop deliberate strategies for engaging their children in conversations when they are together.

In many families, fathers perceive that they are in a "secondary" role during the period of pregnancy and early infancy, especially while mothers are breastfeeding (Datta, Graham, & Welling, 2012). However, as children get older, fathers and mothers modify their caregiving roles. Fathers tend to become more involved in their children's care, and mothers' involvement decreases somewhat. This is especially true when there are more boys than girls in the family. The more hours mothers work, the more responsibility fathers have for their children. Within the context of a loving marital relationship, the traits associated with a competent, caring parental role are learned and practiced so that fathers become increasingly involved and attuned to their child's needs (Bradford & Hawkins, 2006; Jacobs & Kelley, 2006; Wood & Repetti, 2004).

Many children grow up in families where there is no father living in the household. This may be a result of divorce, cohabiting couples who have children and then break up, or unmarried women who have children. A growing literature in child development provides evidence of the important role that fathers can play in the lives of children. As a result, there is a new appreciation for the establishment of **coparenting**, a respectful relationship in which parents who are not living together encourage active involvement with their children. This is in direct contrast to the pattern of parental alienation observed in some couples where one parent, typically the mother, deliberately tries to undermine the attachment relationship of the child to the other parent. Support and encouragement for coparenting is especially important for the continuing engagement of nonresidential fathers who face many barriers to positive involvement with their children (Fagan & Palkovitz, 2011; Palkovitz, Fagan, & Hull, 2013).

Developmental Stages of Families

At each stage of a child's life, the demands on parents change. Infants require constant care and attention. Preschoolers require educational toys and interaction with peers. They can spend a great deal of time in independent or peer play, but they require close, mindful supervision. Early and middle school-age children require parental reassurance about their skills, talents, and fears. Early adolescents require less in the way of physical care but need continuing emotional support and guidance. They pose new financial demands, and they need help clarifying academic and personal goals, and support to foster participation in athletics, after-school activities, peer relations, and social life.

In the following discussion of parenting, we consider the potential influences of the phases of family development on adult development. This approach illustrates the links in psychosocial development across generations. Parents monitor and assess how their children are doing; they continually evaluate their children's struggles, their successes and failures. The more engaged parents are in the parenting process, the more their own well-being is likely to be linked to their perceptions of how their children are faring. When the children are adults, the parents' assessment of their children's health, happiness, and success in life have a direct impact on their own sense of personal fulfilment (Fingerman, Cheng, Birditt, & Zarit, 2012). Parenting highlights the processes through which the development of children may prompt new growth among parents. Although middle adults might be parenting children of any age, we focus on the following four periods that correspond to the most likely transitions that take place as parents age from 34 to 60:

1. The years when children are in early and middle childhood.
2. The years when children are adolescents.
3. The years when children are adults.
4. Grandparenthood.

The Years When Children Are in Early and Middle Childhood. School-age children tap parents' resources for ideas about things to do, places to go, and friends to meet. They seek new experiences in order to expand their competence and investigate the larger world outside the home. The role that parents play in exposing their children to cultural resources, such as music, art, travel, theater, and science, contributes positively to the children's school achievement, even beyond the impact of the parents' own educational background, beliefs, and expectations (Roscigno & Ainsworth-Darnell, 1999). Parents become active as chauffeurs, secretaries, and sometimes as buffers between their children and the rest of the community.

During this time, parents have many opportunities to function as educators for their children. They actively contribute to their children's academic success through such activities as reading with them, helping them with homework, praising them for school success, and school involvement, including talking with teachers, visiting the school, participating in school projects, or joining school committees. Research on academic success makes it clear that parents' aspirations for their children, their overall parenting skills, and their involvement in their children's education make a substantial contribution to their children's progress (Gutman & Midgley, 2000). Parents who combine appropriate challenges with warmth and support typically have children who are highly motivated, think of themselves as academically capable, and want to do well in school (Bronstein et al., 1998). Parents of early and middle school age children typically believe that they are responsible for their children's school performance, and they want their friends, family, and community members to think well of them in their parenting role (Pew Research Center, 2015).

Parenting during this period has the potential for boosting an adult's sense of pride in the skills and knowledge already accumulated. Parents are gatekeepers to the resources of the community. They come to see themselves through their children's eyes, as people who know about the world—its rewards, treasures, secrets, and dangers. Adults often function as advocates for their children in order to make sure that school, community, and health care professionals provide needed resources.

The Years When Children Are Adolescents. Parents tend to view the years of their children's adolescence as extremely trying. In a national survey, over half of parents of adolescents say they worry that their children will struggle with anxiety or depression. Many worry that their children will have problems with drugs or alcohol, or with unwanted pregnancy. Especially among those with family incomes under $30,000, parents of adolescents worry that their children might get beat up, shot, or be in trouble with the law. These worries are linked to their view that their neighborhood is not a very good place to raise kids (Pew Research Center, 2015).

Adolescents are likely to seek new levels of behavioral independence. They spend most of the day away from home and apart from adult supervision. As adolescents gain in physical stature and cognitive skills, they are likely to challenge parental authority. During this time, the principles that parents have emphasized as important for responsible, moral behavior are frequently tested. Children are exposed to many voices—including the media, popular heroes and heroines, peers, and school adults—that suggest there may be more than one ideal way to behave and more than one definition of success. Successful parents of adolescents attempt to balance autonomy granting (opportunities for their children to make their own decisions), responsiveness, warmth and support, communication about high standards, and limit setting in the needed proportions so that their children can grow increasingly independent while still being able to rely on an atmosphere of family guidance and reassurance (Steinberg, 2001).

Adolescent children are the front line of each new generation. The questions they raise and the choices they make reflect not only what they have learned, but also what they are experiencing in the present and what they anticipate in the future. Parents of adolescents are likely to feel persistent pressure to reevaluate their own socialization and their effectiveness as parents. Questions are raised about their preparation for their own future as well as their children's. The ego boost parents experienced from being viewed as wise and resourceful when their children were young is likely to be replaced by doubt as they and their children face an uncertain future. Parents who can respond to their adolescents in an open, supportive way can benefit by finding opportunities to clarify their own values. They can begin building new parent–child relationships that will carry them and their emerging adult children into later adulthood.

The Years When Children Are Adults. When children make their own transitions into adulthood results in new patterns of interaction between parents and children and new opportunities

The demands of parenting change as children move through different stages of development. In early and middle childhood parents lead the way in guiding their children on new experiences and adventures. In adolescence, parents often try to support their children's emerging interests and goals.

for the middle adult parents. Alternative patterns are clearly evident as children take a variety of paths toward self-sufficiency and entry into adult roles. In general, adult children and their middle adult parents are more involved in each other's lives and in closer contact today than they were 30 years ago. There is some speculation that middle adult parents, having grown up in an era when parents and children were more distant, have made a more deliberate effort to create a family environment of interdependence and open communication. Adult children and their parents interact often on the phone, texts, through email, or face-to-face interactions. Middle adult parents provide frequent financial, emotional, and practical support, and children typically view their parents' support as contributing in important ways to their quality of life (Fingerman, Cheng, Tighe, Birditt, & Zarit, 2012).

Family roles change during this time. Most women enter menopause bringing a close to the couple's natural childbearing years. The relationship between the parents also changes as parenting activities diminish. Some couples become closer—closer than they have been since they first fell in love. However, divorces also occur after the children leave home. Parents begin a review and evaluation of their performance as parents as they see the kinds of lives their children have established for themselves. Erikson (Erikson et al., 1986) found that during this period, many parents continue to build their identities on the accomplishments of their children.

The period when children leave home does not seem to be a negative time for adults. A woman who was anticipating her children leaving home described her feelings this way:

> From the day the kids are born, if it's not one thing, it's another. After all these years of being responsible for them, you finally get to the point where you want to scream, "Fall out of the nest already, you guys, will you? It's time." It's as if I want to take myself back after all these years—to give me back to me, if you know what I mean. Of course, that's providing there's any "me" left. (Rubin, 1980, p. 313)

Parents are usually pleased as they follow their children's accomplishments. According to a national survey of parents whose children were ages 18 to 29, 73 percent responded that they had mostly positive relationships with their children, and 86 percent named their children as a source of enjoyment (*U.S.A. Today*, 2013). Of course, adults maintain certain parental functions during this stage. Many children remain fully or partly financially dependent on their parents during their 20s and 30s. If the children are in college or in postgraduate study, their parents may experience greater financial demands than at any earlier period in their parenting history. In many families, parents take on additional jobs and loans to meet the financial requirements of their children's education. Adult children may turn to their parents to provide financial resources in order to take advantage of new opportunities, like training or advanced degrees, or to provide a safety net when their own financial situation deteriorates.

Children who have left home may not have resolved decisions about occupation and marriage. Their parents may remain a source of advice and support as they go through periods of identity and intimacy formation and consolidation. Parents begin to feel the pressure of challenges to their value orientation as their children experiment with new roles and lifestyles. During this stage, parents may serve as sounding boards or as jousting partners in young people's attempts to conceptualize their own lifestyle.

As less time is taken up with direct parenting responsibilities, parents may alter their roles and redirect their energies. However, some parents experience resistance from their children, who expect their parents to remain the same as they themselves change and grow. Young adult children may return home for intervals when they look for a new job, find a new roommate, recover from a love relationship that has ended, return from military service, or drop out of college. Throughout these transitions, young adults look to their parents as a source of stability and to their home as a safe harbor while they try to establish their own life structure.

One of the major family events that may occur during this period is the child's decision to cohabit or marry. Along with this new relationship comes a connection to an entirely new network of relationships, the partner's family. In the United States, most parents have little influence on their child's decisions in this matter. They may find themselves associated through marriage or intimate partnership with a family kinship group that differs significantly from their own or with one that shares many of their own family's beliefs and values.

The first few years of marriage can be somewhat precarious. Parents may have to reintegrate an adult child into the family at this stage if the marriage is not successful. An adult child who leaves a marriage may need some temporary parental reassurance and support in order to regain confidence in the ability to form an intimate relationship. Thus, at times of crisis, middle adults may need to practice parenting skills they have not used for a while and develop new skills in helping their children deal with new challenges.

Grandparenthood. Grandparenthood—the time when an adult witnesses the birth of a new generation—might be considered the beginning of an additional stage in family development. This transition to grandparenthood is outside one's own control. Whenever one's children have children of their own, the adult parent is propelled into a new ancestral role, and membership in an expanding kinship network. With grandparenthood, adults begin to observe their children as parents. Reflecting on their own roles 20 to 30 years earlier, they may attribute some of their children's successes to their own parenting techniques and may take responsibility for some of the failures (Erikson et al., 1986). In chapter 13 (Later Adulthood), we consider in greater detail the role of grandparenthood and its significance for adult development. Suffice it to say that as grandparents, adults have the opportunity to relate to small children as an expression of the continuity of their lives into the future. Of course, not all grandparents relate to their grandchildren from this philosophical point of view. However, the attainment of the grandparent role has the potential for bringing with it a new perspective on time, purpose, and the meaning of life that may serve as a source of reassurance during later adulthood.

Adults differ in how they define the role of grandparent. Most grandparents do not live with their grandchildren. The nature of their relationship and the quality of their influence depend largely on how often they interact. Grandparents may have the greatest

require facing challenges that are difficult or intriguingly complex in hopes of growing while struggling to meet them.

Caring for One's Aging Parents

In addition to meeting the challenges of parenting, another test of one's capacity for generativity comes in the form of commitment to one's aging parents. One of the significant challenges of middle adulthood is the struggle to respond effectively to one's parents as well as to one's children and grandchildren. That is why middle adults are sometimes referred to as the *sandwich generation*, tucked in the middle between caring for one's children and caring for one's aging parents. This dual obligation may create new sources of role overload. As one ages from 30 to 50, one's parents may age from 60 to 80. With the advancing life expectancy, it is becoming increasingly likely that middle adults will be involved in meeting the needs of their own aging parents and grandparents. It is also increasingly probable that their aging parents will survive through a period of vigorous and independent later adulthood into a period of frail later life.

Grandparents and their grandchildren are having fun in a friendly board game. Everyone is a winner when they get to spend time together.

impact on their grandchildren indirectly in the way they support the child's adult parents, especially in times of crisis or distress, by providing emotional or instrumental support to the parents.

The better the relationship of grandparents to their adult children, the more likely it is that the grandparents and grandchildren will interact frequently and form a bond of affection and care (Dunifon, 2013). Grandparents may see themselves as carriers of the family traditions and dispensers of wisdom, as needed experts in child care, as convenient and trusted babysitters, or as admirers from afar. As grandparents, adults are asked to reinvest energy in small children. The quality of the relationship that develops between grandparents and their grandchildren depends not so much on the fact that they are relatives as on the kinds of experiences that the two generations share. Grandparents may also find that the quality of their relationship with their grandchildren is mediated by the child's parents. Especially when the grandchildren are little, the amount of time they spend with their grandparents and the way the grandparents view them are filtered through the quality of the adult relationship that their parents have with their own parents, the grandparents (Brubaker, 1990; Erber, 2013).

The process of expanding caring relationships through parenting can be stressful. It is full of conflicts and challenges, demanding time that the partners might otherwise spend with each other or in pursuit of their own interests and ambitions. However, parenting generates the kind of conflict that promises an enormous potential for personal growth. By providing a meaningful, responsive context for their children's lives, parents have the opportunity to articulate their own value systems and to observe the consequences of their efforts in the continuous development of their children. Psychosocial growth requires a willingness to engage in tasks that may temporarily increase stress, uncertainty, and complexity. Rather than turning away from or minimizing tension, development may

What Is Filial Obligation? **Filial obligation** is a feeling of responsibility to care for one's parents. One way of thinking about filial obligation is that it is a sense of responsibility that adult children have to help their parents as they get old, especially when their physical or mental health declines. Another view is that filial obligation is a moral sense of duty that arises as one realizes and acknowledges the sacrifices one's parents have made and the sense of indebtedness for those sacrifices. This view is more compatible with the observation that a sense of filial obligation can be very salient in adolescence or early adulthood, not only in middle adulthood when one's parents are aging (Stein, 2009).

How do adult children define their responsibilities for their parents? One measure of filial obligation included five components: providing needed assistance, maintaining frequent contact, avoiding conflict, sharing appropriate personal information, and maintaining appropriate levels of self-sufficiency (Stein, 2009). Using this measure with a sample of middle adults whose parents were all living in assisted living communities, researchers found that the kind of help adults provided depended in part on their assessment of their parents' physical and mental health. The healthier the parents, the less sense of obligation the middle adults felt. When middle adults evaluated their parents' mental health as better than average but their physical health as worse, they were more inclined to provide more sharing of personal information. When they evaluated their parents' physical health as better than average but their mental health as worse, they were more inclined to provide assistance. Thus, the adults' sense of obligation was tailored to support their parents' strengths.

The expression of filial obligation is affected by one's culture as well as by the aging parent's well-being. A cross-national study of filial obligation compared responses from 1,200 adults in each of five countries: Norway, England, Germany, Spain, and Israel (Lowenstein & Daatland, 2006). Across all countries, most respondents acknowledged some level of filial obligation, although the extent of support was greater in Spain and Israel than in the northern European countries. The nature of the obligation was varied, more prescriptive in Spain and Israel, and more open to negotiation in the northern countries. Across countries, more help was given to older parents when they were unmarried and suffering from some kind of physical disability. Across countries, help was bidirectional, with aging adults providing emotional and financial support to their adult children as well as receiving support from them.

In fact, studies of intergenerational economic transfers find that, on average, adults 65 and older give more in cash and gifts than they receive from younger generations and that it is more likely that an adult child will live in the household of an older parent than the reverse (Fingerman, Miller, Birditt, & Zarit, 2009; Litwin, Vogel, Kunemund, & Kohli, 2008).

Who Provides Help? Family members play a key role in providing help to their aging parents. In a longitudinal study, mothers were asked about which of their children they expected to provide help if they became ill. Seven years later, they were interviewed again. It turned out that the child they expected to provide help was indeed more likely to be the one who did provide help as needed. Caregivers were more likely to share their mothers' values, to live close by, and to be daughters rather than sons (Pillemer & Suitor, 2014).

Daughters typically assume more responsibility for their aging parents than do sons—including care for their spouse's parents as well as their own (Allen, Blieszner, & Roberto, 2001). This involvement is one element of the basic kin-keeping tasks that have traditionally been incorporated into women's socialization. Daughters are more likely than sons to provide care for their aging parents even when the daughters are employed. However, several structural aspects of an adult child's employment may influence this gender difference (Sarkisian & Gerstel, 2004). Women typically earn less than men, and more men than women are self-employed. Both of these factors predict how much time an adult child will spend helping their aging parents. Adult children who earn lower wages are more likely to take time off to help their aging parent, and adults who are self-employed are less likely to take time off to help their aging parent. Thus, some of the gender difference in caregiving is interdependent with the nature of workplace commitments and demands.

In addition to the amount of time that adult children spend helping their parents, daughters also provide somewhat different kinds of help. Daughters provide more direct care, such as bathing or dressing a parent, as well as emotional support, such as listening to a parent's concerns or helping the parent feel important and loved. However, both sons and daughters are about equally likely to assist in some of the tasks involving relations with health and human service organizations, scheduling medical checkups, and reviewing insurance and other financial matters. Research shows that aging adults who have three or more children—whether they are sons or daughters—are more likely to end up living with one of them than are adults with fewer than three children. However, for other forms of support, such as receiving telephone calls, visiting, and help in daily tasks, older adults who have one daughter receive more support than those who have only sons (Spitze & Logan, 1990).

Although adult children provide much of the family support to aging parents, young adult grandchildren also report

Rolf Bruderer/Jupiter Images

Robyn derives a great deal of satisfaction from taking a walk with her mother. Because of physical frailty, her mother lives with her now. Robyn thinks about all the things her mother has done for her and all the sacrifices she made so that Robyn could go to college and have the life she now has. Robyn is very happy to take care of her mother and to still have her mother's company and wisdom.

a sense of filial obligation and participate in the caregiving role (Fruhauf, Jarrott, & Allen, 2006). In a qualitative study of 17 grandchildren ages 21 to 29 who were actively involved in their grandparents' care, some began to take a more active role when another family member was no longer able to help. Eleven said that they respected and valued the time their grandparents spent with them as children, and this was a way for them to reciprocate.

Josh, who has been caring for his paternal grandparents since he started driving, voiced the sentiment of several grandchildren when he stated, "It just felt like it was what I was supposed to do. They helped me out . . . helped raise me and so now they need us. . . . Now it is time to give back" (Fruhauf et al., 2006, p. 899).

What Factors Promote an Optimal Relationship Between Adults and Their Aging Parents? The nature of the continuing relationship between adult children and their aging parents is not focused solely on caregiving. The norms of independence and self-sufficiency are strong among the current aging population, many of whom state that they do not need assistance from their adult children. However, when asked whom they view as their preferred source of assistance should they need it, aging parents mention their children first, before their friends, siblings, or other relatives. Likewise, adult children view themselves as being primarily responsible for meeting their parents' needs; however, most do not expect to have to meet a variety of such needs (Zarit & Eggebeen, 2002).

In adulthood, preserving and building a positive parent–child relationship is a dyadic process in which both middle adults and aging parents may need to gather new information and change old behaviors (AgriLife Extension, 2010; Lyons, Zarit, Sayer, & Whitlach, 2002). Thinking back to later adolescence and early adulthood, children may feel a sense of obligation to their parents, but they may not be in a position to reciprocate for the many ways their parents have helped them. During those stages of life, they continue to be dependent on their parents for emotional and instrumental support. However, sometime during early and middle adulthood, a socioemotional transition occurs. Middle adult children are likely to have achieved a greater sense of independence from their parents and to have the experience and resources needed to assist them in some valued ways.

However, the relationship of adults and their aging parents has a history. For some, this history is one of a positive attachment, mutual positive regard, and experiences in which parents skillfully balanced autonomy granting and closeness to create a family environment in which the children could emerge with the resources needed to form a strong personal identity. In other families in which children feel they were rejected or undermined by their parents, they emerge into adulthood with strong feelings of resentment or rebellion toward their parents. Their relationships with their parents are never close, and as they go off on their own, interactions become increasingly infrequent. These antecedents influence the nature and quality of filial obligation. Adult children and aging parents may find that they have predictable areas of conflict. They may not always share the same goals regarding care. In one qualitative study, researchers focused on how the parents and their adult daughters navigated situations when their goals about care differed. Daughters typically tried to reason with their mothers, expressing their concerns for their mothers' safety and health. Aging parents often ignored their daughters' requests. When goals differed, aging parents were described as "insisting, resisting, and persisting" suggesting that the path toward negotiated agreement was much more difficult. When goals were similar, the dyads seemed to find that their suggestions were respected and things went along well (Heid, Zerit, & Van Haitsma, 2016). Adult children who are providing care are likely to see this kind of resistance as a form of "stubbornness." Of course, some older adults just have a more disagreeable personality; they are stubborn by nature. What is more, the more severe their disability, the more their resistance is viewed by their children as stubbornness (Heid, Zarit, & Fingerman, 2015).

In a desire to reduce conflict, adults and aging parents may need to improve their approach to communication, or redefine problems so they do not continue to disrupt a caring relationship. Similarly, adult children and aging parents need to identify the activities they enjoy together and talk openly about how much time they want to spend together. For some parent–child bonds, a few hours a week or a weekend visit every so often may be all that is desired; for others, daily contact may be pleasant and satisfying. Adult children need to learn more about the changes associated with aging and begin to identify specific aspects of their parents' mental or physical health that may be impacted by aging. Aging parents need to learn more about the demands and stressors their children are facing in order to appreciate the constraints these demands place on their child's helping behaviors.

Adult children are sometimes in a position of trying to supplement the care and support they provide their parents by coordinating social services and interacting with various public agencies. Many feel unprepared for this aspect of the caring relationship (Zarit & Eggebeen, 2002). They are not comfortable dealing with hospitals, insurance agencies, social service agencies, or residential treatment facilities. However, when older adults require the services of these organizations, their adult children typically know their parents' unique needs and are among the best people to interpret them for service providers. Through such contacts, middle adults have the opportunity to modify and improve the services offered by these agencies, making them more effective for future generations of aging adults.

Research on caregiving within the family has begun to examine the rewards as well as the costs in this relationship (Robertson, Zarit, Duncan, Rovine, & Femia, 2007). Although quite a bit of attention has been given to caregiver strain, caregivers experience both positive and negative aspects of this role. The costs may include feelings of exhaustion, never having time for oneself, feeling overwhelmed by the demands of multiple roles, or experiencing the physical strain of caregiving. Rewards of the caregiving role may include feelings of being appreciated, putting life's demands into a new perspective, or feeling closer to the care recipient. In some cases, the care recipient is able to exchange resources with the caregiver, for example, by providing babysitting time for help with the grocery shopping.

In a study of the costs and rewards experienced by children and spouses who were caring for an aging parent or partner, adult children experienced more rewards in their caregiving role than did spouses, and women experienced more caregiving costs than did men. An unexpected finding was that for women, companionship from their spouse was an especially rewarding response from the care recipients (i.e., their husbands). Thus, the research underscores the reciprocal nature of caregiving, with rewards and costs flowing in both directions (Raschick & Ingersoll-Dayton, 2004). These ideas are reflected in the case study of a daughter caring for her ailing mother.

— **CASE STUDY** A Daughter Cares for Her Ailing Mother —

Lois Lyles reflects on what she learns from her mother as she provides care during her mother's last days of life.

Mama is down, I am up. Up, and up, and up. She wants Vaseline for her char-dry lips, her St. Francis church bulletin, her rosary. The vase on the dresser must be moved out of the way of the black-faced digital clock. Two twenty-five, New Year's afternoon. She stares at the red numerals each like an imp or an infernal flame, as the five becomes a six; the six, a seven. "Water the plants, Lois."

Nervously, I dribble water into the flower pots. I work fast. She has approximately one request every three minutes.

"Thank you, darling. I feel so worthless and useless. Why can't I do anything?"

"Mama, you are not worthless. You are a beautiful person. You still look beautiful to me," I say, and mean it. She was my childhood idol. Her soulful-eyed, smooth-haired beauty was my first acquaintance with romance.

"No, I'm not," she whimpers; then says, "Thank you, darling."

"Mama, whatever happens, I'm with you, and I'm for you." She cries. Her misery makes me recall how my fear of death had once made me, to my mortal shame, abandon a sick woman I loved. I am the namesake of Mama's sister Florence, who died of cancer four summers ago. Florence is my middle name. Mama must be thinking of Aunt Flo, too, for she says, "I took care of Sister when she went up to her bedroom three days before she died and never came downstairs again. I remember she was amazed that I would wash her down there, you know, her private parts. She didn't want me to have to do that." After pausing, my mother adds, "I thought, Lois, it would help you after this is over, to be with me now when I need you, and do things for me."

I am astonished at her, the good mother. She has called me to her sickbed, not so much as to help her as to help *me*. I, in childhood, was never hungry, never homeless, never seriously ill; and was never exposed to the sight of physical suffering. My parents had made sure of all that. But an easy ride of a life is only a half-truth. Now, Mama's gift is to let me know her pain. She is letting me see if I am strong enough to grapple, by proxy, with Death. (Lyles, 1991, p. 242)

CASE ANALYSIS Using What You Know

1. Explain the concept of filial obligation and how it is illustrated in this case.
2. List the costs of and rewards of caregiving in this case.
3. Based on the evidence, infer the quality of the mother–daughter relationship in this case.
4. Hypothesize how caring for her dying mother may influence Lois's development as an adult.

FURTHER REFLECTION: Summarize the changing nature of the relationship of adults and their children as the children mature from middle childhood into early adulthood. Hypothesize how these changes may stimulate new psychosocial development for parents during their middle adulthood.

Explain the concept of filial obligation. What have you observed about your parents and their relationship to their aging parents? What are your assumptions about how you will meet the needs of your parents as they age?

Consider the role of culture in shaping expectations about the relationship of adults and their aging parents. How do various ethnic practices and religious beliefs influence the way adults view their obligations to their parents?

Managing the Household

OBJECTIVE 4 Summarize the tasks required for effective management of the household and explain why they are necessary. Describe the diversity of households, including blended families, single-parent families, and adults who live alone, and hypothesize about the implications of these various household structures for individual development.

Household is a term that describes an entity that is created by people for a particular style of living. The household is a physical setting and a shared psychological context for a group of people. Households are bounded units of people who pool their resources, earn and spend money, interact with the labor market, and engage in social interaction with their neighbors (Wallerstein & Smith, 1991). The demands and tasks of household management stimulate cognitive, social, and personal development during adulthood.

The household provides a basic life structure for people in all cultures. The Hindu joint family illustrates the way that household management is culturally constructed, based on norms for gender, age, and kinship ties. In the traditional form of the joint family, parents, their children, and eventually their sons and the sons' wives and children live together. When daughters marry, they go to live with their husbands' families. Respect for age creates a dominance hierarchy. The eldest male is considered the head of the whole family, with the eldest son holding a position of dominance over other men in the family. The eldest is the head of the household. When a woman becomes a mother-in-law, her status increases. She supervises her daughters-in-law who are expected to make and serve the meals, wash the dishes, and keep the house clean. When daughters-in-law give birth to sons, their status increases. The dominance hierarchy, related roles, and approach to family decision-making are internalized as children grow up in this family and observe the relationships among parents and their children, husbands and their wives (Valsiner, 2000; Gardiner & Kosmitzki, 2011).

Management of the household refers to all the planning, problem solving, and activities adults undertake in order to take care of themselves and others who are entrusted to their care. At present, society's ability to recognize and value the accomplishments linked to the management of the household is poorly developed. At the same time, more emphasis is being placed on the centrality of the home environment in fostering intellectual development, social competence, health, and emotional well-being.

The household is a system. The stability and predictability of life for members of the household is supported by the shared understanding of roles and rules. The roles refer to expectations about how each person in the household is expected to behave; rules refer to explicit or implicit norms about such matters as the quality of interactions, decision-making, and use of resources (Palkovitz, Trask, & Adamsons, 2014). The household system has the potential for providing an environment that facilitates human growth and mental health. Learning to create such an environment is a developmental task of the middle adult years. Households have the potential for much greater variety and flexibility than most work settings. However, many of the tasks required for household maintenance are tedious, physically demanding, repetitive, and time consuming. As women have become more intensively involved in the labor market, research has focused on how much time people spend at the tasks of household maintenance and who is performing those tasks.

Managing Resources and Meeting Needs

Data gathered through daily time diaries provide a picture of the amount of time devoted to various household tasks and the involvement of men and women in those tasks in the United States (Bureau of Labor Statistics, 2015). These data help clarify the diversity of household tasks, the amount of time devoted to those tasks, and the way the division of labor between men and women is played out in the management of the household. FIGURE 12.2 ▶ shows the average number of hours spent in each activity per day by men and women. With the exception of lawn and garden care, and indoor and outdoor maintenance, women spend more time than men in each of these household activities. In comparison to patterns of time use from the 1960s, fewer hours are devoted to household tasks overall, and more time is devoted to child care by both men and women. Dual-career couples are more likely to purchase services for household tasks and are especially likely to order in meals or to eat out as a way of saving time (Casper & Bianchi, 2002).

The challenge of household management is to create an environment that supports both individual and group functioning. The significance of the household can be appreciated by thinking about the consequences of its absence, especially in the case of homeless individuals and families (see the **Applying Theory and Research** box Homelessness), or in crises such as hurricanes, fires, or floods when people are displaced from their homes. Management of the household, much like the workplace, requires leadership in order to set priorities and goals, manage resources,

and operationalize plans. The scarcer the resources, the greater the pressure on the adult to make careful decisions and to find creative solutions to the daily challenges of meeting the household's physical and psychological needs. Leadership begins as adults model the process of shared decision making and children (if there are any) learn to participate in problem solving. Household members discover ways to work together to achieve a shared vision of the future. The home environment is the first place where many children discover that they can have a voice. Parents can create a family atmosphere in which the spirit of democracy comes alive through a careful balance of freedom and responsibility, respect for individuality, and commitment to the welfare of others.

Building Networks and Coalitions

One of the most difficult and subtle kinds of new learning that occurs during middle adulthood is the development of an understanding of how the structures of other organizations affect one's life and the lives of family members. These other organizations may include (1) members of the **extended family** (e.g., one's in-laws), (2) other families, (3) business or work-related associations, (4) religious groups, (5) educational groups, and (6) community groups. The family is interconnected with other social systems that can expand its resources. Its contact with social groups must include the maintenance of goodwill and some evidence of group identification and commitment. Social groups also generate norms that may make demands on the family. Hence, adults must be able to protect the family from excessive external demands, while retaining valuable and satisfying external relationships.

Families differ in their investment in relationships outside the family unit. In some households, the nuclear family is more

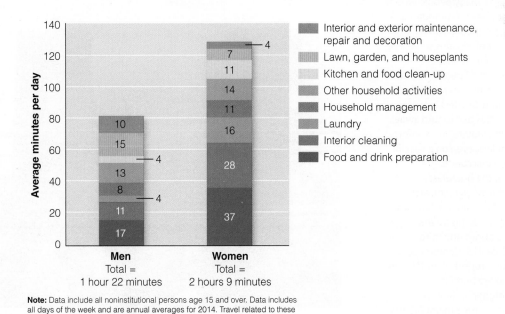

Note: Data include all noninstitutional persons age 15 and over. Data includes all days of the week and are annual averages for 2014. Travel related to these activities is not included in these estimates.

Source: Bureau of Labor Statistics, American Time Use Survey.

FIGURE 12.2 ▶ AVERAGE MINUTES PER DAY MEN AND WOMEN SPEND IN HOUSEHOLD ACTIVITIES

Homelessness

The term homeless refers to people who have no permanent resting place and no private space (Nunez, 2004). Although many estimates focus on individuals who are living on the streets, in emergency shelters, or in transitional housing, there are also individuals who are living with friends or relatives, moving from one location to the next every few weeks. It is difficult to assess the exact number of people who experience homelessness; the numbers often reflect a specific point in time rather than a lifetime estimate. The National Alliance to End Homelessness reported a point-in-time estimate of 564,708 people experiencing homelessness in January 2015, a decrease of 2 percent since 2014. Whereas 33 states and DC reported decreases in homelessness from 2014 to 2015, 16 states reported increases (National Alliance to End Homelessness, 2016). This count did not include people who were in shelters for abused women, people who were living in outdoor areas typically inhabited by the homeless, people who may have avoided the shelter on that day in order to prevent being counted, and people who were housed in some other form of temporary housing with family and friends.

In some locations, many people who seek shelter cannot be accommodated. A survey by the U.S. Conference of Mayors (2014) reported that of 25 cities surveyed, "because no beds were available, emergency shelters in 73 percent of the survey cities had to turn away homeless families with children. Shelters in 61 percent of the cities had to turn away unaccompanied individuals." Thus, efforts to count the homeless, even on a specific day, are likely to be inaccurate.

The majority of the homeless population, roughly 63 percent, are individuals, and 37 percent are families. A survey of 25 U.S. cities found that children comprise about one third of all homeless people (U.S. Conference of Mayors, 2014). The proportion of families with children who are homeless is estimated to be higher in rural areas.

A combination of three major factors contributes to the continued risk of homelessness for families with children

in the United States: (1) the decline in the value of the minimum wage, coupled with the prevalence of insecure jobs with few or no benefits; (2) the decline in the availability and value of social welfare benefits; and (3) shortages in low-income housing and public-assistance housing (National Coalition for the Homeless, 2014). Many adults are described as "rent poor," meaning that they are using 50 percent or more of their income for housing.

Paths toward homelessness for families are diverse. Some of the most common precursors are job loss, domestic violence, substance abuse, mental illness, and divorce. Although some homeless individuals are in a sudden crisis, many have stumbled from one temporary living situation to the next, and others have never been able to establish a permanent home. Some of these people are singularly alone and unable to develop minimal social relationships. This is an unusual phenomenon because most people have some ability to have meaningful social ties. Among homeless mothers, for example, many have friends or family but cannot count on them for housing support. For some, the nature of their

housing crisis may disrupt their social network, making it impossible to ask for help from family or friends. Following an episode of homelessness, some families are relocated far from their social network, making it likely that they will become vulnerable to homelessness in the future (Toohey, Shinn, & Weitzman, 2004). As a result of victimization earlier in their lives, some women suffer from a degree of emotional dysfunction, exacerbated by the use of alcohol and drugs. An estimated 10 percent to 15 percent of homeless parents have a problem with drug addiction, making it difficult for them to hold a job, sustain a relationship, or be approved for low-cost housing (Nunez, 2004).

In homelessness, society exhibits a painful example of psychosocial stagnation—the inability of mature adults to meet their (and their children's) basic needs for shelter, food, and clothing—combined with its own failure to prevent this degree of vulnerability. In the face of the cultural value placed on independence, self-sufficiency, and hard work, U.S. society has difficulty making effective public responses. In fact, national policies have operated to increase

Louise earns a bit of money by redeeming aluminum cans and bottles. She lives in a temporary shelter in Battery Park, and walks daily in full view of the Statue of Liberty.

homelessness and the stressors of living on the streets. Since 1975, there has been a steady decrease in federal funding for low-income rural and urban housing accompanied by the loss of low-cost units that qualify for public assistance. There was a temporary increase in funding from 2009 to 2012 with the Homeless Prevention and Rapid Rehousing program, which was part of the American Recovery and Reinvestment Act of 2009, but the program ended in 2012. Recent across-the-board budget cuts have further compromised funds for public housing.

Over this time, a growing number of cities have enacted laws that criminalize homelessness, making it illegal to sleep, camp, eat, beg, or store personal belongings in public places. The police make periodic sweeps of areas known as gathering places for the homeless, forcing them to leave their personal belongings and to move to outlying areas.

Critical Thinking Questions

1. What are you assumptions about the causes of homelessness? How does the evidence support your assumptions?
2. Describe how the experiences of homelessness may interfere with psychosocial development in adulthood.
3. Summarize the physical, psychological, and social needs of people who are homeless. As a student of human development, what two suggestions would you give to policy makers regarding reducing homelessness in the United States?
4. Look up the approach to homelessness in one of the following major cities: Los Angeles, New York, Boston, Atlanta, and Miami. What are the primary strategies being implemented in this city? Who is responsible for the success of these programs? How are they funded? How do these programs address basic themes of human development in middle adulthood?
5. Roughly 10 percent of the homeless are veterans. Investigate the conditions that are associated with homelessness for veterans.

important than any other group. Such households expend little energy outside the family boundaries. At the other extreme are families who are involved in a number of community groups and who incorporate their extended families into frequent group activities. In some families, each person is encouraged to establish a group of close friends. In others, each person's friends are screened or evaluated by the other family members. The adult's task is to define the family's preferred stance toward other individuals and social groups and to create opportunities to build desired relationships.

Friendships are known to contribute to well-being in adulthood. However, among people in middle adulthood one observes different patterns in the approach to friendship. Some people are very selective, preserving a small number of close friends who have been in their network over a long time and with whom they experience frequent interactions and emotional closeness. Others prefer to keep their distance, having relatively few contacts with friends. Still others acquire new friends throughout their adulthood. Circumstances can solidify or disrupt these friendship networks. For example, some people continue to live in the same community where they went to high school; they maintain ties with these friends well into midlife. Adults whose children attended school together may continue to be friends as their children grow up. For others, experiences of job loss, divorce, illness, or moving to a new community may disrupt friendship networks (Miche, Huxhold, & Stevens, 2013).

Preserving relationships within the extended family is a delicate matter. This is the realm of family politics. In close family relations, it is likely that positive feelings of warmth and affection are coupled with negative feelings of irritation and aggravation (Fingerman, Hay, & Birditt, 2004). Failed expectations about courtesies and obligations or thoughtless insults and slights from family members are typical stressors that occur within the family network. Family members may have opposing political, religious, or childrearing views; they may have competing motivations; or they may try to form alliances among family subgroups. When children decide to marry, they bring two family networks together that may or may not get along. Parents may or may not convey support to their child's partner or spouse; sisters and brothers have partners who may or may not support each other. Likewise, parents may divorce and remarry, bringing one family system into contact with another. All these transitions introduce challenges to sustaining valued coalitions within the extended family and protecting the family from disruptive forces.

Much of this chapter has focused on two-adult families, especially those with children, often in the dual-earner arrangement. In the following sections, three alternative forms of households are described: remarriage and **blended families**, one-parent families, and single-person households, each of which poses unique opportunities and challenges for household management.

Remarriage and Blended families

According to a national survey of marriages and divorce in the United States in 2013, by the age of 50 to 59, roughly 20 percent of men and women had been married twice and 6 percent had been married three or more times (Kreider & Ellis, 2011; Livingston, 2014). The psychosocial reality of **remarriage** is unique for each family. Partners come to the remarriage with different marital histories. One or both have a former spouse and in-laws from a previous marriage.

In some cases, the relationships with the former spouse or the in-laws may involve unresolved conflicts. In other cases, relationships with the former spouse or in-laws from a previous marriage may continue to be close. If either partner has children, the remarriage involves a family formation between the adult partners, and the establishment of new parental roles and the negotiation of ties with noncustodial parents and grandparents. Custody arrangements may require that the parents remain in the same state or community in order to facilitate visitation. As a result, the remarried couple's life choices are constrained. The complexities of considering these extended family bonds can become difficult as the new, blended family approaches traditional holidays, celebrations, and transitions (Portrie & Hill, 2005).

One of the significant sources of ambiguity in a blended family is the relationship of stepparents to their nonbiological stepchildren. Although the most typical character in fairytales and myths about blended families is the stepmother, in fact the most common blended family is one in which a man marries a woman who has custody of her children, thereby entering into the role of stepfather. What determines whether a man will embrace this role, investing in another man's children as his own? William Marsiglio (2004) has provided a glimpse into the complexity of this process as men approach the social, personal, and interpersonal nature of becoming invested in their stepfather role. For some men, like Monty, the role is continuously ambiguous:

> I never really understood what I was to her; I still don't. I felt, I've always felt, like I should have been her father, but I never was, and I never will be. . . . I was always there for her, in positive ways, and he never was; I mean, never. (Marsiglio, 2004, p. 28)

For others, like Terry, there is an openness to the possibility of sharing the role with the biological father:

> Look, it's OK to have two dads. You have a couple sets of grandparents and whatever. It's OK to have two different fathers. I'm the one that's here with you all the time and he's the one up there. If he gets more involved in your life, then great! If he doesn't, nothing changes. I'm still here. I'm the one that's going to be here every day. (Marsiglio, 2004, p. 30)

For still others, like Doug, there is no room for ambiguity:

> I told her, I'll marry you, but that's my son legally. No step involved, nothing like that. That's my son. She said, "Fine; I don't see anything wrong with that." So that's when she went back to him [biological father] and said she don't want any alimony, child support, nothing. Just want you out of the picture. He signed the papers; he said, "No problem. I won't cause any trouble." So when the papers came back, they just simply read my name, didn't say stepfather or nothing else. (Marsiglio, 2004, p. 33)

The American Psychological Association (2016) identified three key issues that couples want to address as they consider remarriage and the formation of a blended family:

1. Living arrangements and financial issues. These two concerns involve making plans for where the new family is going to live, particularly the desirability of

In this blended family, Tony is Berta's stepfather and Andrew's biological father. The children mean everything to Tony, and they both adore him.

creating a new home for the new family, and how to coordinate and share financial resources so that the partners have a sense of shared financial decision-making.

2. Addressing and resolving dynamics associated with the former partner/parent. This is especially important when former spouses continue to have relationships with children in the newly formed family.

3. Anticipating and communicating about new parenting roles, especially how the new spouse will interact with and form a meaningful role in the care, supervision, guidance, and discipline of their partner's children.

In remarriage, partners must find ways to create boundaries around the blended family so that children can benefit from the love and support of their parents, grandparents, and other relatives, while protecting the new family from unwanted intrusions and pressures for competing loyalties. Blended families have to find new traditions and rituals to mark their distinctiveness while preserving links to valued relationships from the past.

One-Parent Families
In 2012, about 27 percent of all families with children under the age of 18 were one-parent families: 77 percent were headed by women, 23 percent by men (Vesp, Lewis & Kreider, 2013). This compares to 22 percent of all U.S. families in 1980.

The greatest stressor for single mothers is the lack of financial resources. Roughly 38 percent of families with single-mother households and children under the age of 18 had family incomes less than 100 percent of the poverty level in 2012 (Vespa, Lewis, & Kreider, 2013). To put this figure in context, 9 percent of children in families with two married parents had family incomes at 100 percent of the poverty level or less. Thus, children in single-mother families are over four times more likely to live in poverty than children in two-parent families. Poverty in these families is the result of a number of factors: Single mothers tend to have a lower earning capacity, they work fewer hours, and even when they receive some support from the child's father, they bear a substantial portion of their children's expenses.

In addition to stresses associated with poverty, single parents may suffer from social isolation, continuous pressure to meet the needs of their children, and overload in trying to combine work, parenting, and household decision making without a partner. How well can single mothers manage their parenting role in the face of their many role demands? Some studies emphasize a deficit perspective—for example, identifying factors that place children or adolescents from single-parent families at risk for antisocial behavior and delinquency. Other studies focus on adaptation and coping within the single-parent structure. They consider factors that help sustain a positive parent–child relationship, such as sharing a strong emotional connection with other family members, being able to help one another in concrete ways, talking with one another and listening, and spending time together as parent–child and with other family members (McCreary & Dancy, 2004; Simons, Beaman, Conger, & Chao, 1993).

Retrospective studies show that many children who are identified as having psychological problems, especially temper tantrums, being a bully, cheating, stealing, and fighting, are from divorced, single-mother families. However, prospective studies—those that look at childrearing practices and subsequent child outcomes—show that poor parenting practices, especially emotional unavailability, ineffective discipline, minimal supervision, and a dominating, hostile style of interaction, produce these negative child outcomes in both single-parent and two-parent families. Family instability, especially the loss of parental figures and frequent changes in adults in the household, are more predictive of negative cognitive and health outcomes for children than the single-parent structure itself (Waldfogel, Craigie, & Brooks-Gunn, 2010). Although single-parent families face many additional problems, it is clearly inaccurate to label all of them as problem families.

Among single-mother families, one of the fastest growing subgroups is low-income women who have never been married (Casper & Bianchi, 2002). These women may be in cohabiting or serious romantic relationships, but for a variety of reasons they have rejected the idea of getting married. It is not that marriage is devalued; in fact, some argue that it is the high standards that these women have for marriage that makes them decide to stay single (Edin, Kefalas, & Reed, 2004). Women want to be able to find a partner whom they can trust to be faithful—someone who is not addicted to drugs or alcohol, who will treat them and their children with kindness, and who will be able to contribute financially to their family. In many communities, this type of partner is difficult to find. Rushing into a marriage with someone who does not have these qualities just because one has a child seems foolhardy. These women know of too many instances of couples who start out with great expectations and then run into job loss, infidelity, abuse, drunkenness, or criminal behavior. Thus, for many women, being an unmarried, single parent is a deliberate strategy for avoiding a difficult relationship and a potentially costly divorce (Edin & Kefalas, 2011).

People Who Live Alone

In 2012, about 32 million people in the United States lived alone. These one-person households were more likely to consist of men in the younger age groups (under 44) and women in the older age groups (45 and older) (Vespa, Lewis, & Kreider, 2013). Single-person households include people who have never married, are divorced or separated, and are widowed. The reasons for living alone and the backgrounds for this life pattern vary considerably.

Little is known about the differences in psychosocial development between adults who live alone and those who live with others. Some of the aspects of household management, including organizing time, planning for the future, making decisions,

Reggie Casagrande/Jupiterimages

Jolene is very pleased to be able to spend time with her daughter Karen and granddaughter Margaret. As a single mom, she knows how important it is for Karen to have someone to help her and to spend time with her. When Ray walked out, Karen was devastated financially and depressed emotionally. Jolene helped Karen get a lawyer who was able to get Ray to fulfill his obligation to provide child support. She also babysat with Margaret while Karen pursued her MFA. With the new degree, Karen was able to get a good job and to regain her joie de vivre.

and establishing relationships with other social groups, pose challenges to the person living alone. On the other hand, assigning responsibility and establishing a pattern for group decision making are clearly not required. People who live alone may not feel the need to engage in elaborate planning and evaluation when they are the only ones who will be immediately affected by their choices. They may be freer to decide spontaneously as each opportunity presents itself. Living alone allows some freedom from adapting to the demands and needs of others, thus leaving time to focus on one's own preferences, projects, and interests. Some studies find that people who live alone are more likely to get out of the home, spend time with friends and neighbors, go to restaurants, and attend art classes and lectures than those in married or cohabiting relationships. These trends are not only observed in early adulthood, but also in middle and later adulthood. The freedom to initiate interactions and activities and the desire to remain socially connected may stimulate a more proactive approach to selecting and engaging in social life (Klinenberg, 2012).

FURTHER REFLECTION: *Describe the primary functions required for managing a household. Explain how the ability to perform these functions might contribute to the physical and mental health of the members of the household. How might failure to perform these functions undermine the physical and mental well-being of members of the household?*

Reflect on the way your parent(s) managed the household as you were growing up. How aware were you of their decision making and how much did you participate in the decisions that were made regarding household management?

How will your approach to household management differ from that of your parents? Explain the reasons behind these similarities and differences.

The Psychosocial Crisis: Generativity Versus Stagnation

OBJECTIVE 5 Define and explain the psychosocial crisis of generativity versus stagnation and the central processes through which the crisis is resolved: person–environment interaction and creativity, the primary adaptive ego strength of care, and the core pathology of rejectivity.

The psychosocial crisis of *generativity versus stagnation* can be understood as pressure to be committed to improving the life conditions of future generations (Erikson, 1963). Generativity is essential for both personal well-being and for the survival of any society. The maturing person experiences an increasing urgency to clarify the meaning and purpose of life beyond the satisfaction of immediate safety and security needs. To some degree, this motive is aroused as one recognizes the inevitability of mortality—that one will not be around forever to direct the course of events. Therefore, one must make contributions to the society, on both personal and public levels, that will stand some chance of continuing after one's death. At the same time, adult members of the

society, who are typically in positions of authority and in control of resources, must begin to feel an obligation to contribute their resources, skills, and creativity to improving the quality of life for future generations in the hopes that the younger members of society will survive and thrive (de St. Aubin, McAdams, & Kim, 2004; Hofer et al., 2008).

There is an old story about three men who were observed laying bricks for the wall of a church. When asked what they were doing, the first man said he was laying bricks, the second said he was building a wall, and the third said he was building a church. As the story implies, during middle adulthood one must arrive at a philosophy of life that will impart significance to daily activities. One part of generativity lies in the actual attainment of creative goals. The other part lies in the perspective one brings to one's lifework, an outlook that appreciates the relationship of one's life and one's efforts to promoting well-being for the next generation. In contrast, stagnation reflects an outlook dedicated to preserving or embellishing one's power and resources without regard for the impact of this self-centeredness on the long-term well-being of the larger community.

Generativity

Generativity "encompasses procreativity, productivity, and creativity, and thus the generation of new beings, as well as of new products and new ideas, including a kind of self-generation concerned with further identity development" (Erikson, 1982, p. 67). Generativity is formed as a result of experiences of maintaining the world, nurturing and being concerned, and caring (Erikson et al., 1986).

It is worth pausing to consider what it means to *generate*. A basic dictionary definition is "to bring into existence." Through generativity, adults may change the world by introducing new things, ideas, beings, or bonds of relationship—all of which had not existed before. Although Erikson directed us to the heightened importance of generativity for development in middle adulthood, it makes sense to view this critical capacity as emerging over the life course. Stewart and Vandewater (1998) suggested that generativity arises through three phases: (1) generative desire or motivation, (2) a belief in one's capacity for generative action, and (3) a subjective sense of generative accomplishment.

The most obvious expression of generativity in middle adulthood is through parenting. Although not all parents are generative, those who are create a family environment that nurtures agreeable, conscientious children (Peterson, 2006). Adolescents whose parents have strong generative motives and who exhibit generative actions are likely to identify with these values and express generative concern in their own goals (Pratt, Norris, Hebblethwaite, & Arnold, 2008). This motive might be expressed in the formation of caring relationships with friends or siblings, as well as in the articulation of broader generative goals. For example, young people who want to promote better interracial understanding or to improve the educational experiences of young children might be said to have generative motives (Pratt, Arnold, & Lawford, 2009).

Studies have linked generativity to environmental practices. Parents who have strong generative motives are also likely to embrace environmental values and to socialize their children to enact environmentally conscious behaviors. As a result, the adolescent children also share their parents' environmental values and behaviors. Thus, generativity not only makes its impact on future generations through the care and concern of adults for their physical environment, but also through the passing on of these values to the next generation (Matsuba et al., 2012; Pratt, Norris, Alisat, & Bisson, 2013).

Parenting is by no means the only path to a sense of generativity. In a comparison of parents and childless adults, the link between generativity and psychological well-being was equally strong for both groups (Rothrauff & Cooney, 2008). Generativity may be expressed through a variety of actions, including procreation, parenting, invention, teaching, mentoring in the workplace, expanding the knowledge base, improving the physical or social environment, and artistic creation (Clark & Arnold, 2008; Kotre, 1995a). Generativity may be expressed by volunteering for a program like Big Brothers, Big Sisters; teaching skills or passing on knowledge to others; through innovations in the workplace; in the scientist's lab; in poetry, art, music, or literature; or in creating some splendid form of recreation, like a theme park or a refreshing new food like frozen yogurt.

Generative concern may involve recognition that there are problems or challenges facing the community that need to be addressed in order to ensure the well-being of the next generation. This awareness suggests a commitment to social involvement and community engagement. In a study designed to examine this relationship, generativity was assessed in a sample of African American and European American adults ages 34 to 65. Individual differences in generativity were associated with social support from family and friends, involvement in religious activities, and political participation. Those individuals who scored higher in measures of generativity were also more likely to emphasize pro-social values in raising their children and were especially conscious of the way they served as role models for their children. African Americans scored significantly higher on measures of generative concern and generative action than European Americans, suggesting a cultural context for the support and value of generativity within various ethnic communities (Hart, McAdams, Hirsch, & Bauer, 2001; Newton & Jones, 2016).

In looking back on one's life, one can assess one's actions and make a judgment about whether one's generative aspirations or motives have been realized. Erikson suggested that the outcome of the crisis of generativity versus stagnation has implications for adults at the next life stage in the form of *grand-generativity*:

> The reconciling of generativity and stagnation involves the elder in expressing a "grand-generativity" that is somehow beyond middle age's direct responsibility for maintaining the world. The roles of aging parent, grandparent, old friend, consultant, adviser, and mentor all provide the aging adult with essential social opportunities to experience grand-generativity in current relationships with people of all ages. In these relationships, the individual seeks to integrate outward-looking care for others with inward-looking concern for self. As a complement to caring for others, the elder is also challenged to accept from others that caring which is required, and to do so in a way that is itself caring. In the context of the generational cycle, it is incumbent upon the aged to enhance feelings of generativity in their caregivers from the younger generations. (Erikson et al., 1986, pp. 74–75)

Measuring Generativity

The meaning of generativity is being clarified through attempts to measure it (Hawkins & Dollahite, 1997; McAdams & de St. Aubin, 1998; Peterson & Stewart, 1993). In a cross-sectional comparison of dimensions of generativity among participants in early (22–27), middle (37–42), and later (67–72) adulthood, four aspects of generativity were measured (McAdams, de St. Aubin, & Logan, 1993):

- Generative concern—A sense that one is making a difference in the lives of others
- Generative commitment—Personal strivings or goals that have a generative nature
- Generative action—A checklist of actions that the person has performed in the past 2 months that involved creating, maintaining, or offering
- Generative narrative—Autobiographical recollections coded for generative meaning

A proud mentor and her outstanding graduate student celebrate commencement. The relationship of mentor and student expresses a form of generativity—a dedication to learning and discovery that is passed along from one generation to the next.

Courtesy of Philip Newman

Results suggest the following trends:

1. Across all age groups, generative concern was significantly correlated with happiness and life satisfaction.
2. When all four measures of generativity were combined, the middle adults scored higher than the young or older age groups.
3. The measures of generative commitment and generative narration were higher for the middle adult group.
4. The pattern of responses showed significant differences between the middle adult and the younger adult groups, but the middle adults and the older adults were not significantly different.

Once the generative orientation emerges, it appears to endure in the life goals and activities of a person into later adulthood (Villar, 2012).

Another approach to the measurement of generativity takes its inspiration from the construct of identity status that was introduced in chapter 10. In this view, generativity is defined as a commitment to "establish and guide the next generation through one's acts of care" (Bradley, 1997; Bradley & Marcia, 1998). Using a semi-structured interview, individuals are characterized along two dimensions: a person's level of involvement and active concern for the growth of the self and others, and a person's level of tolerance for differences in values, ideas, and traditions that reflects the inclusivity of their generative concern. Using these two dimensions, five types of generative status were described as fitting into one of five types:

- Generative: Vital involvement in growth for self and others and tolerance for a wide range of ideas
- Pseudogenerative-agentic: Active involvement in one's own growth and openness to a wide range of ideas for oneself, but not for others
- Pseudogenerative-communal: Active involvement to promote growth and tolerance for ideas in others, but not for oneself
- Conventional: Active involvement in growth for oneself and others, but low tolerance for different ideas and values
- Stagnant: Low involvement in growth for oneself and others and low tolerance for different ideas and values

This model expands the definition of generativity by making a distinction between people who are committed to growth for their own immediate circle and those who are committed to growth for humanity or a wider and more diverse population. It recognizes a group of middle adults who are generative toward those who are part of their in-group but not toward people whose ideas and values differ from their own.

— CASE STUDY   My Leadership Journey:
Health and Generative Action —

Lourie Campos describes how a leadership training experience transformed her generative strivings into action.

In the fall of 1999, I was encouraged to apply to the Women's Health Leadership program by my former boss. At that time, my job was a hodgepodge of responsibilities, although I was beginning to focus more and more on policy work. I felt that I lacked direction and the tools to make changes in my job. I didn't consider myself a "leader" even though my colleagues saw me as one. I wanted to be proactive in making positive changes in my job so I decided to apply to WHL. What I didn't expect was to learn as much about myself as I did about women's health issues.

In 1997, I was diagnosed with metastatic cancer. Years earlier, I saw my father lose his battle with colon cancer, which he courageously fought for 12 years, and in 1999 my brother was diagnosed with the same cancer. It has changed the way I think about my future. While work was important to me, I needed to set limits. While it may seem that participating in the WHL program would have added more stress to my life, it was just the opposite. Through WHL, I worked on an individual leadership development program that not only allowed me to be effective at my job by sharpening my skills and learning new ones but [also included] activities that I wanted to concentrate on outside of work. I spent more time having fun, learning new things, and spending quality time with my family and friends. WHL encourages personal and professional growth as well as teaching women to be advocates for themselves and other women in their community.

My major accomplishment was the creation of the *Women's Health Advocacy Guidebook*. The guidebook is specific to Santa Clara County and is full of information on the gaps and barriers low-income, medically underserved women face in Santa Clara County. It is a tool to help women's health advocates understand the legislative process and how they can participate in the process. I distributed 40 guidebooks to women in my community and I have had such a positive response from them. The guidebook is something I wish I had when I began doing policy work.

Prior to WHL, I had never spoken about my experience with cancer. I did not fully understand or recognize the positive impact my story could have. I was always afraid that if I spoke about my cancer and my family's experience with cancer people would just feel sorry for me, and that is the last thing I wanted. But WHL has taught me to take risks and to find my voice. This past year, I have been a featured speaker in a "Living with Cancer" series in Santa Cruz; I submitted my cancer story to the *San Jose Mercury News* and it was printed with a picture of me and my dog on the front page; I was a panelist on assembly member Elaine Alquist's "Women's Health Forum"; and I was selected as one of 8 people to represent California and to provide testimony to the President's Cancer Panel. Many people, especially women, have shared their experiences with me and I have felt so honored to listen to their stories.

Source: Littlefield, Robison, Engelbrecht, Gonzalez, & Hutcheson, 2002, p. 579.

CASE ANALYSIS Using What You Know

1. Describe the generative changes Lourie Campos experienced as a result of the Women's Health Leadership training experience.
2. Summarize how the case illustrates the following concepts: generative concern, generative commitment, generative action, generative narrative.

3. Explain the links between the developmental tasks of middle adulthood and the process of resolving the psychosocial crisis of generativity versus stagnation as they are evidenced in this case.

4. What role does the environment play in promoting generativity? Identify some examples of community programs or workplace initiatives that may foster psychosocial development in adulthood.

5. Speculate about possible causal links between a generative commitment in middle adulthood and health and longevity in later life. What evidence would you need to support this connection?

Stagnation

Stagnation suggests a lack of psychological movement or growth. Those unable to cope with managing a household, raising children, or managing their career are likely to feel psychological stagnation at the end of middle adulthood. Stagnation has been operationalized as an absence of investment in the growth of self or others and a rejection of ideas and values that differ from one's own. Stagnation is a distinct construct, not simply the absence of generativity. It is associated with the personality characteristic of neuroticism, indicating high levels of worry, and negatively associated with the personality characteristics of extraversion and openness to experience, indicating difficulties in social relationships, problems achieving a sense of social acceptance, and being highly controlled. Taken together, these characteristics suggest a person who is not only closed off to experiences with others but is also lacking in the kinds of experiences that would promote self-development (Van Hiel, Mervielde, & DeFruyt, 2006).

Narcissism

The experience of stagnation may differ for the narcissistic adult and the depressed adult. Thinking well of oneself, having a high opinion of one's abilities, and having more confidence in one's abilities than in the abilities and opinions of others, can be adaptive. However, in the extreme, narcissism is associated with "arrogance, feelings of superiority, a sense of entitlement, and lack of empathy for others" (Miller & Campbell, 2010). **Narcissistic people**—adults who devote their energy and skills to self-aggrandizement and personal satisfaction—are likely to have difficulty looking beyond their own needs or experiencing satisfaction in taking care of others. They are self-serving and defensive, expending energy to accumulate wealth and material possessions. They relate to others in terms of how people can serve them. Narcissistic people can exist quite happily until the physical and psychological consequences of aging begin to make an impact. At that point, and continuing toward elderhood, self-satisfaction is easily undermined by anxieties related to death. It is not uncommon for such people to undergo some form of religious or humanitarian "conversion" after a serious illness or an emotional crisis forces them to acknowledge the limitations of a totally self-involved lifestyle.

Depression

Chronically depressed people do not feel a sense of accomplishment during middle adulthood—they think of themselves as worthless. They are unable to perceive themselves as having sufficient resources to make any contribution to their society. They may have low self-esteem, doubt their opportunities for future improvement, and therefore become unwilling to invest energy in conceptualizing future progress. Adults who lack a belief in their own inner resources are vulnerable to chronic feelings of envy of others, which may be transformed into devaluation of others, and feelings of resentment or vengeance (Navaro & Schwartzberg, 2007). People who are chronically depressed and facing stagnation may lose their will to live. Their stagnation is tied to a loss of hope about the future and may increase the likelihood of suicidal thoughts and plans. The U.S. Centers for Disease Control and Prevention found that suicide among middle adults has risen steadily from 1999 to 2014, increasing by 43 percent for males and 63 percent for females in the age range 45 to 64 (Curtin, Warner, & Hedegaard, 2016). A combination of loss of financial resources, lack of control over one's life, feelings of being overwhelmed by stress, and loss of a sense of meaning and mattering may increase the level of stagnation to a point of giving up on life (Parker-Pope, 2013).

One source of stagnation in middle adulthood is **career stagnation**. Career stagnation can be a product of subjective factors at the personal or interpersonal levels or a product of objective conditions of the workplace. At the subjective level, people may be dissatisfied with their work; they may feel threatened by younger workers; they may be unable to attain valued work-related goals; or they may be stifled because of efforts to coordinate their career with that of their partner. Some people have been described as taking a "career maintenance" posture. They do everything possible to hold on to their position, even at the expense of undermining others or taking advantage of younger workers (Arnold & Clark, 2016).

At the objective level, people may be passed over for promotion, they may be a target of bullying, a victim of discrimination, or they may be fired or reassigned to a less desirable position (Abele, Volmer, & Spurk, 2012). Rather than taking up the challenge to mentor new employees, to invent new approaches to their work, or to seek another type of work, they become resentful, avoidant, and withdrawn. Career stagnation is likely to be associated with physical or emotional symptoms associated with the stress of work-related frustration (Clark & Arnold, 2008). The case of Lourie Campos illustrates how important the encouragement of professional development can be in forestalling stagnation and promoting continued generative growth in the workplace.

Middle adulthood extends over many years. During this stage, people encounter complex challenges for which they may not be fully prepared. Stressful life events are a certainty. Promotion to an administrative position, the need to care for an aging parent, and the negotiation of a divorce are examples. Both success and failure force people to redefine and reexamine their goals (Brim, 1992). At many points, adults doubt their ability to move ahead, achieve their goals, or make meaningful contributions. Feelings of stagnation surge temporarily.

The conditions that create uncertainty, struggle, and doubt are also times when new ego development is possible (Marcia, 2010). People may recognize that unless they redefine their situation or take some new risks, the quality of their lives will deteriorate. They face the possibility of feeling outdated by new technology, outmoded by new lifestyles, overburdened by role demands, or alienated from meaningful social contacts. At these moments of crisis, adults may become entangled in a process of self-protection and withdrawal that results in permanent stagnation. However, they may also be able to muster new resources and see things from a new perspective that will permit continuing growth and the expansion of generativity.

The Central Process: Person–Environment Interaction and Creativity

Two aspects of the central process that lead to the development of generativity in middle adulthood are **person–environment interaction** and **creativity**. The first refers to ongoing experiences between the individual and the social environment including family, work setting, neighborhood, and the larger political community. Day-to-day interactions, the expectations for behavior, the available resources, and the social supports that are necessary for the growth of self-confidence are elements of the social environment. The second part of the central process in the establishment of generativity is personal creativity. Although creativity has been defined in many ways, for our purposes we define it as the willingness to abandon old forms or patterns of doing things in favor of new ways. This requires the production, evaluation, and implementation of new ideas.

Person–Environment Interaction

Successful personality growth depends on the interaction between the demands of a person's immediate environment and one's own needs, skills, and interpersonal style. The concept of interaction suggests a potential for reciprocal influence between individuals and settings. People have an impact on the settings in which they participate. The structure and demands of settings may alter a person's behavior, values, goals, and sense of self-worth.

People have multiple identities and, as a result, participate in a variety of settings within their community. Person–environment interactions take place as employers modify work settings to enhance productivity, or as workers bargain through their unions to improve work benefits and conditions. Person–environment interactions take place as parents establish rules for family life, and as adolescent children react, resist, or redefine those rules. Person–environment interactions occur as community members protest police brutality and law enforcement officials respond with new training. Adults do more than maintain or respond to their environments; they shape them.

Adults with higher status—that is, more resources and power—are more able to influence the quality of interactions they have with others in their environment. In turn, they are more likely to create conditions in which they receive validation for their identities because they are treated with greater respect and recognition from others for the roles they play (Stets & Harrod, 2004).

In creating their environments, adults may decide whom they will marry, whether to have children, which occupation they will follow, and where they will live. To the degree that they have a choice in these matters, they are able to influence the kinds of transactions that occur between their personality and their social milieu. They build families with lifestyles that suit the members. Making good decisions about social settings requires that they understand themselves, the nature of other people, and the social institutions that are part of their social environment. The degree of fit between family needs and community characteristics helps support the essential functions of middle adulthood, including caring for children or aging parents, coordinating work and family life, and sustaining a vital marriage. When the community consists of other families facing similar tasks, the resources,

Some Chinese Americans choose to live and work in a Chinese ethnic community. They experience a sense of acceptance and support while contributing to the continuity of their cultural heritage.

mutual support, and validation for one's life choices are likely to be greater (Swisher, Sweet, & Moen, 2004).

Although participation in some settings is a matter of choice, many others are the result of chance. Some settings can be abandoned or altered if they do not meet the individual's needs; other settings are permanent and difficult to alter. If one is in an unsuitable setting, one must be willing to leave it if possible or discover a way to influence it so that it meets one's needs more adequately.

When one is forced to remain in social settings that are contrary to one's needs, the possibility of developing generativity is seriously diminished. If one is unable to experience a personal sense of effectiveness at home, at work, or in the community, then one is unlikely to feel capable of contributing to future growth in these spheres. Fortunately, the social environment is so multifaceted that individuals are likely to experience satisfaction in their participation in at least one setting, even if they are dissatisfied in others. For example, people are likely to experience a sense of validation in their relationships with friends and close family members even when they have difficulty experiencing recognition at work. This may require that individuals reorder their priorities. If there is little opportunity to find satisfaction in work, for example, one might begin to reinvest in contributions to one's family, religion, or community. Creativity is required in order to find a new balance among competing role demands while retaining a sense of joy and optimism.

Creativity

The importance of a creative response, no matter how small, is that it redefines the world and opens the door to new possibilities. Although the idea of creativity tends to be associated with the arts, we are using the term in a broader sense to suggest a novel transformation in any of a variety of domains from the practical to the theoretical—from creating a new recipe to creating a painting, a dance, or a theory of human behavior. Through creative effort, adults impose a new perspective on the organization, expression, or formulation of ideas.

Human evolution provides a rich history of the capacity for innovation. Archeological evidence stretching as far back as 3.4 million years shows remains of animal bones that were cut and marked for tool use. At some point, roughly 90,000 to 100,000 years ago, human creativity burst into a frenzy of innovation resulting in art, carvings, tools, hunting instruments, musical instruments, bowls, and bedding. Human capacities for symbolic representation, communication, and social interaction have combined to foster a rich production of new ideas. As humans come into contact with each other, they share information, pass on techniques, and build on one another's achievements to form a continuing thread of creative expression (Pringle, 2013).

Creativity is supported by aspects of brain function, personality, and experiences (Kaufman & Gregoire, 2016). At the neurological level, creativity is a product of the interplay among various large neural networks: executive attention, imagination, and the salience network. "Converging research findings do suggest that creative cognition recruits brain regions that are critical

for daydreaming, imagining the future, remembering deeply personal memories, constructive internal reflection, meaning making, and social cognition" (Kaufman, 2013).

The neurotransmitter dopamine is responsible for the pleasurable experiences associated with exploration. The motivation to seek new experiences and to enjoy the stimulation associated with novelty is sustained in part by the release of dopamine. In addition to the motivating nature of dopamine release, creative individuals are thought to have a tendency to tune in to more details in their environment. They are less likely to screen out what others might consider redundant or irrelevant information. As a result, their minds are processing more information with the possible benefit of finding new connections among ideas or experiences that others have tuned out.

At the personality level, creativity is closely tied to the dimension of openness to experience. This can be expressed at the cognitive level in enjoyment of engaging with complex problems or ideas; at the emotional level in exploration of deep human emotions; and at the aesthetic level in the exploration of art, music, or natural beauty. People with this kind of open personality have a tendency to ask big questions, to look deeply into the meaning of their experiences, and to feel strong emotional reactions to sensory experiences. Finally, the combination of neurological factors that motivate exploration and personality factors that support openness to novelty contribute to an exploratory approach to life—engaging with new and novel experiences that open one's thinking and result in new ways to approach life's challenges (Kaufman & Gregoire, 2016).

Creative adults are not dominated by social forces but are able to direct the course of events themselves. They are at a point in their development at which their own creative responses can become a source of influence on others. Think about the menopausal woman who referred to her first hot flash as a *power surge*. Imagine the person who invented wheelchair basketball or the person who invented Post-Its. Consider the influence of parents who, by creating a flexible, open, and loosely structured home environment, nurture the self-expression of their children. In Columbus, Ohio, Dr. Alexander Bandar transformed an empty 65,000 square foot old shoe factory into the Columbus Idea Foundry, a makerspace where people learn to use old and new technologies and create their ideas. The Foundry is "stocked with woodworking machinery, metalworking equipment, welding rigs, CNC routers, laser cutters, 3D printers, glassworking facilities, photography studios and even an area for metal casting and blacksmithing. There's an area to learn coding, an Arduino room, a youth incubator, a leather stitchery, and equipment for making soap" (Noe, 2014). Through the process of creative problem solving, adults help reshape the social and physical environments in order to meet both personal and social needs.

Throughout middle adulthood, adults are faced with situations in family, childrearing, and work settings that provide stimuli for creative problem solving. In their efforts to take into account the requirements of the social setting and to be productive in it, people must develop creative plans. They must also attempt to carry out those plans—a task that may require further creativity. The essence of creative problem solving is to think outside the box—to resist defining the situation as it has been defined for you by others, then to formulate a new plan, and translate the plan into action.

The roots of creativity can be found in childhood, in the semiotic, representational, playful thinking of toddlerhood. As-if thinking—the ability to imagine a situation in some different configuration, to use objects to stand for something else, to give new names to familiar objects, to devise private symbols for common experiences, to take on imagined roles—all these capacities of symbolic play are the foundational building blocks of creativity. In our view, all humans are creative in the sense that they can pretend. All humans are creative when they cope effectively in a changing, unpredictable environment. All humans are creative in that they can invent games, songs, tools, artifacts, or messages that are new to them. It is not so important that the creative act is new to the world, but that it is new to the person who is inventing it (Sternberg, Grigorenko, & Singer, 2004).

From the outset, the creative process involves frustrations and risk. Typically, a creative solution is required because the standard way—the scripted way—is not working. In order to try new things, people must give up some old, reliable ways of thinking or behaving. In this process, people must anticipate the possibility that their efforts will fail. They may flounder for a seemingly long period, unable to identify the solution that will allow forward movement. They may worry about public embarrassment or humiliation. Given one's embeddedness in many demanding social roles, it is often difficult to step aside and view one's situation from a fresh perspective. For some, the anxiety and self-consciousness associated with prolonged uncertainty and possible failure may be so great that creative solutions are never realized. Their creativity is blocked by a fear of the unknown, or by an inability to violate conventional norms of behavior.

People who are hopeful about the future are more likely to overcome their reservations and doubts in order to press ahead with a creative plan. For those who are not inhibited by the fear of failure, the achievement of a creative solution is invigorating. For the great creative geniuses—such as Sigmund Freud, Albert Einstein, Isadora Duncan, or Pablo Picasso—a breakthrough or a profound creative insight fueled their commitment to pursue the creative path with increased energy (Gardner, 2011). Personal talent combined with an appreciation of the inadequacies of the current situation can lead to a significant creative act, which then promotes future efforts. Creativity provides an outlet for caring for something that has not yet been defined or experienced. Repeated efforts to generate creative solutions eventually result in the formulation of a transforming philosophy of life. Through risk taking, occasional failure, and a predominance of successful creative efforts, adults achieve a sense of what they believe in and what gives meaning to life. With this remarkable integration of experience and information, people enter later adulthood.

The Prime Adaptive Ego Quality and the Core Pathology

Implied in the concept of generativity is a moral directive to *take care of* and to *care for and about* the development of others. As generativity is fully achieved and expressed in action, it will be linked to the prime adaptive ego quality of care (Leffel, Fritz, & Stephens, 2008). In contrast, experiences of stagnation are likely to be accompanied by the core pathology of rejectivity—a defensive, self-protective outlook. The person who develops rejectivity blames the target of envy and possibly justifies expressions of vengefulness or rage.

Care

The ego strength associated with the achievement of generativity is **care**.

> Care "is a widening commitment to take care of the persons, the products, and the ideas one has learned to care for. All the strengths arising from earlier developments in the ascending order from infancy to young adulthood (hope and will, purpose and skill, fidelity and love) now prove, on closer study, to be essential to the generative task of cultivating strength in the next generation, for this is indeed the 'store' of human life." (Erikson, 1982, p. 67)

Parenting contributes to the expansion of caring. Seven aspects of emotional development can be identified as potential consequences of parenting. First, parenting brings a depth of commitment that is tied to the responsibility for the survival of a child. This depth of commitment is strengthened through the reinforcing nature of the child's responses to attempts to meet his or her needs. Second, parenting brings adults into contact with new channels for expressing affection. Third, it requires that adults achieve a balance between meeting their own needs and those of

Creativity is expressed in many forms. The puppet maker surrounds himself with the creations of his imagination, inventing new characters and new ways of moving to entertain future generations.

others. Fourth, parenting enhances adults' feelings of value and well-being through the significant role they play in the child's life. Fifth, parents achieve a degree of empathy for their child that widens the array of their emotional experiences. Sixth, parents may experience new levels of emotional intensity in reaction to their child's behavior. Finally, many parents learn to help their children express and understand emotions. By playing a therapeutic role for their children, parents may become more effective in accepting and expressing their own emotions.

Parenting is not the only role through which adults experience the expansion of caring. A growing field of care-work jobs and careers contribute to the health, well-being, and development of others (Dwyer, 2013). A diversity of philanthropic organizations reflects this value in efforts to improve the quality of life and expand opportunities for others. The psychosocial achievement of middle adulthood is to identify the domains in which one has opportunities to influence the quality of the social environment so that it becomes more hospitable, humane, nurturing, or supportive of one's own visions for the future. Caring expands in different domains for different people, but it always leads to having the welfare of people and enduring things (including ideas) at heart. There is an action component to caring, in that people work to care for what they can. As the crisis of generativity versus stagnation is resolved in a positive direction, adults find new energy and innovative ways to express their capacity for care.

Rejectivity

Caring strongly for certain people, products, and ideas can cause people to reject any person or group that appears to threaten one's objects of care. **Rejectivity** refers to an unwillingness to embrace or include certain individuals, groups, or ideas in one's circle of care and, at an extreme level, to view these threats as appropriate targets for hostility, even annihilation. Ironically, one may exhibit great courage and dedication to protect the objects of one's care by directing intense aggression toward the objects that one rejects.

Erikson (1982) referred to this process as **pseudospeciation**, in which one defines another group as different, dangerous, and potentially less human than one's own. Seen through the lens of pseudospeciation, family members can become scapegoats, neighboring communities can establish intense rivalries, racial or religious groups can terrorize each other, and regions or countries can go to war. Albert Bandura (1999, 2015) has developed an analysis of how the core pathology of rejectivity and accompanying pseudospeciation can result in moral disengagement. By dehumanizing their victims or perceiving them as deserving of punishment, people can justify their cruel, harmful, and vicious behavior.

Thus, rejectivity goes beyond an intellectual selectivity of certain ideas and groups as more central to one's identity than others. It is transformed into harmful action, taking on an aggressive energy, drawn from the power and authority of one's status in middle adulthood. The risk of rejectivity for the society is that certain groups will become so powerful that they can cause the extermination or domination of other groups. Through control of the media, the legislature, the military, or the police, people in power can establish justifications for inhumane behaviors toward members of certain groups. As each subgroup falls out of the circle of caring, the society as a whole reaches a new level of stagnation.

FURTHER REFLECTION: *Describe the basic features of generativity and a generative outlook. Summarize the nature of a society in which the majority of adults are characterized as generative and contrast that to the nature of a society in which the majority of adults are characterized as stagnant.*

Explain why adults might resolve the psychosocial crisis of middle adulthood with a tendency toward stagnation. What are the implications for family, workplace, and community when adults with a tendency toward stagnation are in positions of authority?

Illustrate how creativity operates as a central process to resolve the psychosocial crisis of generativity versus stagnation.

Applied Topic: Discrimination in the Workplace

OBJECTIVE 6 Apply a psychosocial analysis to the issue of discrimination in the workplace, and evaluate the cost to society and to the individual when discrimination operates to restrict career access and advancement.

The United States has been characterized as an achieving society. As a cultural group, we value individual achievement, usually expressed through accomplishments in the world of work. In the United States, the mark of successful adulthood is frequently equated with success at work, which is typically attributed to personal characteristics of ability, intelligence, and motivation. Conversely, a lack of success in the labor market is attributed to deficiencies in personal characteristics—lack of ability, low intelligence, and poor motivation. Yet many Americans face serious and persistent disadvantages in the workplace that are linked to race, ethnicity, age, cultural practices, national origin, gender, sexual orientation, disability, or religion (MacLean, 2006).

Types of Discrimination

The following examples illustrate four areas of discrimination: sex discrimination, race discrimination, age discrimination, and discrimination based on disability.

Sex Discrimination

Promotion

Marilyn has worked as a sales clerk at a retail store for 10 years but has been repeatedly denied the opportunity to advance. Men with less experience, including men that she trained and/or supervised, received the promotions instead.

Pay

Carla worked her way up from the position of cook's helper to chef. Now another chef has been hired. He has similar training and work experience, but she finds out that he is being paid more than she is.

Sexual Harassment

Rita's boss is the vice president of the company. He repeatedly makes unwelcome comments about her body and routinely puts his arm around her waist when discussing work-related matters. Rita tells him his behavior makes her uncomfortable and asks him to stop. He says, "Maybe you are too uptight for this job. I probably should never have hired you." Now Rita is afraid of losing her job if she doesn't "loosen up." (equalrights.org, 2010)

Race Discrimination

Hoping to become lieutenants, 77 New Haven firefighters took a promotion test—but when none of the 19 Black firefighters qualified, the city jettisoned the results. Their hopes dashed, 17 White firefighters sued the city for racial discrimination, and the case went to the Supreme Court (newser.com, 2009). The Supreme Court found in favor of the White firefighters, stating that they were subject to race discrimination. The new standards announced by the Court will make it much more difficult for employers to discard the results of hiring or promotion tests once they are administered, even if the results have a disproportionately negative impact on members of a given racial group (Liptak, 2009).

Age Discrimination

Two years ago I worked at a nonprofit organization and was the oldest person employed in that facility as a teacher. It was an experience that will stay with me for the rest of my life. Working with people that thought of you as being too old to work with 3- to 5-year-old children was a nightmare. I endured being called an old lady that had no business being there and why would they hire someone that old? (about.com, 2010)

Disability Discrimination

An employer requires all job applicants to use an online recruitment portal. The portal is not accessible for people with visual impairments and you cannot use screen reading software with it. Unless the employer offered alternative ways for job applicants to apply, this would be indirect disability discrimination. (Equality and Human Rights Commission, 2016)

Overview of Discrimination

In the past, women and minority workers in the United States were restricted to low-paying jobs in the agricultural, service, or factory sectors. In 1964, the Civil Rights Act made it illegal to refuse to hire a person or discriminate in compensation, firing practices, or any other employment benefits based on race, color, religion, sex, or national origin. This act made the practice of restricting access to employment opportunities illegal and opened up many arenas for professional development that had previously been denied to minorities (Hodson & Sullivan, 2011).

With additional legislation, other groups were included in the umbrella of legal protections. Currently, the U.S. Equal Employment Opportunity Commission (EEOC) lists types of discrimination to include age, disability, genetic information, national origin, pregnancy, race, religion, and sex-based factors including sex, gender identity, and sexual orientation. This office also addresses cases of retaliation against individuals who file charges of discrimination and cases of harassment including sexual harassment. The Civil Rights Act prohibits both intentional discrimination and otherwise neutral workplace policies that disproportionately disadvantage persons of a certain protected group (EEOC, 2016a).

Nonetheless, barriers to full and equitable involvement in the labor market for women, minorities, and persons with disabilities as well as persons in other protected groups continue to exist (Robert & Harlan, 2006). For example, some women find that their workplace sets limits on their achievement through gender-stereotyped assumptions about the woman's commitment to her family role (Ridgeway & Correll, 2004). In these settings, women do not tend to be promoted to high-level administrative or managerial positions in which work demands would begin to invade family commitments. Some companies are reluctant to put married women in positions in which they may have to be transferred for fear that their husbands will refuse to make the move.

In 2015, 89,385 charges of discrimination were filed with the EEOC (EEOC, 2016b). Retaliation was the leading cause of charges, almost 40,000 cases. Charges of discrimination on the basis of disability increased by 6 percent from the prior year, and were the third most frequent basis of discrimination after retaliation and discrimination on the basis of race. In addition to blatant discrimination in hiring practices, working conditions, salary, and dismissals, individuals have to cope with subtle acts of discrimination such as marginalization, harassment, and rumors or fictionalized stories that are embarrassing or imply that they are incompetent. Incivility and bullying are widespread problems that create a hostile environment for workers. National surveys indicate that 25 percent to 45 percent of workers report incidents of workplace bullying or harassment, often by supervisors, but sometimes by coworkers. Workers who are especially capable might be targeted for intimidation in hopes that they will quit (Barnes, 2012).

Workplace discrimination is an exceedingly costly problem for the society as a whole. Discriminatory practices that lead to the disaffection of individuals from the world of work is costly in economic terms—in lower levels of productivity, high turnover, high levels of irritability and conflict among workers, lawsuits, and less identification with the company and its goals. It is costly in personal terms as well. Workplace discrimination has both health and mental health consequences (Lim, Cortina, & Magley, 2008). Feelings of frustration about not being recognized for one's competence or being passed over for promotion by less competent workers interfere with the development of a generative orientation. These experiences may lead to a more self-serving orientation, focusing exclusively on self-protection or to a pervasive sense of futility about the future.

Disparities in Income and the Occupational Structure

The Equal Pay Act of 1963 "requires that men and women be given equal pay for equal work in the same establishment. The jobs need not be identical, but they must be substantially equal. It is job content, not job titles, that determines whether jobs are substantially equal . . . All forms of compensation are covered, including salary, overtime pay, bonuses, stock options, profit sharing and bonus plans, life insurance, vacation and holiday pay, cleaning or gasoline allowances, hotel accommodations, reimbursement for travel expenses, and benefits" (EEOC, 2016c). Nonetheless, disparities in salary, benefits, and other forms of compensation between women and men, and across racial/ethnic groups continue to exist, resulting in substantial differences in annual salary, rates of unemployment, and rates of poverty for people of comparable educational attainment by race and gender.

One explanation for the racial, ethnic, and gender differences in salary, rates of poverty, and rates of unemployment is that workers from different groups are distributed unevenly in the occupational structure. Jobs continue to be gender stereotyped, with women being socialized and encouraged to work in vocations that involve helping and serving others. In the food service industry, 70 percent of the waiter/waitress workers are women, but only 20 percent of the chefs and head cooks are women. In the health care industry, 73 percent of the physicians' assistants are women, but only 38 percent of the physicians and surgeons. Women are underrepresented as chief executive officers in corporations, architects and engineers, and the skilled trades where strong unions can protect salary scale and benefits (U.S. Bureau of Labor Statistics, 2016e). The wage gap can also be explained in part by the priority that different industries give to fixed versus flexible hours. In this context, women suffer, especially during their "childbearing and parenting" years. When industries reward time in the office or on the job, the wage gap between men and women is larger; when industries reward "getting the job done" and allow flexibility, the wage gap between men and women is smaller (Kliff, 2016).

Group differences in occupational position that result in different salary structures and risks of layoffs are not necessarily

In Miami Beach, Florida, these women are saying in no uncertain terms that for equal work they should receive equal pay.

evidence of discrimination. Discrimination exists when two people doing the same job are paid substantially different wages. It occurs when factors other than merit prevent a person from being hired, promoted, or rewarded through various forms of compensation or increase a person's risk of being fired. Specifically, discrimination occurs when a person is evaluated on the basis of group membership rather than individual performance. In the workplace, this process operates as an in-group versus out-group dynamic, in which members of the in-group view members of the out-group as deficient and, at some level, possibly threatening to their own continued success and well-being.

How Discrimination Perpetuates Itself

Employers, supervisors, and others in positions of power typically establish a normative profile for their employees and judge each new employee against it. In some work settings, the judgment about competence is equated with a willingness to dedicate long hours to the job, be available at a moment's notice, and keep one's cell phone on at all times, including evenings and weekends. Gender stereotypes (beliefs about what men and women are like or should be like) can influence workplace decisions about hiring and promotions, as well as creating penalties or disadvantages when these stereotypes are violated (Heilman, 2012). In some instances, women who are mothers are expected to direct their time and energy toward their parenting role and, thus, are often judged to be less committed and less competent workers than women who are not mothers or than men who are fathers (Ridgeway & Correll, 2004). For example, in one study, participants rated women who were mothers as less competent—and thus less worthy of investing in hiring, training, or promoting them—than women who did not have children. Participants also rated women as less competent after they had children than before they became mothers (Cuddy, Fiske, & Glick, 2004).

These internalized norms about the ideal worker may include beliefs and values about the superiority of men in comparison to women. Men may wonder whether women can perform the same kinds of jobs as men and can effectively assume responsibility to supervise men, whether clients will place their trust in female executives, or whether women will be dedicated to their work when conflicts between work and family arise.

In the same vein, these norms may include beliefs and values on the part of Whites about people of color—especially beliefs that they are superior to people of color in ability, that the cultural characteristics of people of color will be disruptive or damaging to productivity in the workplace, or that people of color are better suited to some types of jobs than others (Feagin & McKinney, 2003). White men are twice as likely as men of color to be promoted to positions of authority and leadership (Cook & Glass, 2013). In many organizations, one can observe what has been called racial segmentation—the creation of specific kinds of administrative positions that were created to carry out affirmative action agendas, community relations with specific racial or ethnic communities, or to promote the recruitment of minority employees (Forman, 2003). Because of the historical and continuing separation of neighborhoods, schools, and churches on the basis of race, few White adults have firsthand, personal relationships with people of color. In many companies, promotions come about as a result of networks of contacts, which results in new opportunities and informal assessments of ability. Exclusion from personal and professional networks contributes to the continuing disadvantage of minorities. Decisions about promotions or assignments to positions of increased responsibility are often made in situations where senior employees, mostly White, make decisions that do not take into account the values, beliefs, and practices of non-White groups.

Consider the following situation: "FedEx's prohibition against individuals involved in customer contact from wearing dreadlocks, beards, ponytails or braids had been company policy for years but it was not enforced until 1999 when the Memphis, Tennessee-based company gave at least seven couriers who wore dreadlocks and worked in New York an ultimatum to cut them off or lose their jobs" (Cukan, 2001).

The employees were Rastafarians, who wear dreadlocks for religious reasons. They all offered to cover their hair with a hat or some other businesslike attire. However, FedEx refused this arrangement. The men were placed on a 90-day unpaid leave and then fired because no noncustomer contact positions could be found. These men had worked for FedEx for 5 years and had excellent service records with the company. The state of New York sued FedEx for violation of antidiscrimination laws, arguing that they fired the employees based on their religious observances. In response, FedEx changed its policy, allowing individuals to request an exception to the company's policy regarding hairstyles in order to respect their religious beliefs. This example illustrates the continuing need for examination of workplace practices that create hostile or disrespectful environments for workers.

Psychosocial Analysis: Discrimination and Coping

In general, in discussing psychosocial development, one examines the outcome for the individual in achieving a positive resolution of the psychosocial crisis. But when considering discrimination in the workplace, one must also look at the consequences for a society. Discrimination in the workplace is one expression of *societal stagnation*. It is a defensive posture, in which those in power try to protect their own status and profits by preventing members of less powerful groups from gaining a foothold. Rather than treating diversity as a factor that can improve productivity in the work setting, discrimination operates to reduce it.

Over time, the fate of individuals who have been discriminated against becomes a great cost to the society at large. Perceived discrimination in the workplace has been associated with lower job satisfaction, reduced life satisfaction, health problems, depression, and general anxiety (Feagin & McKinney, 2003; Jang, Chiriboga, & Small, 2008). Some targets of discrimination give up and become chronically unemployed or underemployed, resulting in a loss of human capital. Others remain in a discriminatory workplace, trying to get by, not making trouble, and yet operating behind a veil of caution.

Two approaches to reducing the impact of discrimination have been described as identity switching and identity redefinition. Identity switching involves concealing or deemphasizing the stigmatized identity and emphasizing a more valued identity. A gay worker might try to conceal his sexual orientation at work, and engage coworkers in conversations about his attachment to his college or his hometown. Identity redefinition involves highlighting the positive or valued aspects of one's social identity rather than those that are devalued. A woman who is aware of the negative assumptions that women are not good at math and science might try to emphasize her communication and negotiation skills in the workplace. Rather than concealing their identity, people may try to convey the strengths or benefits of their group membership. These two strategies can be effective in deflecting hostile or discriminatory practices, but they can also be costly in terms of the psychological energy needed to preserve the altered identity and in social isolation from others in one's stigmatized group (Shih, Young, & Bucher, 2013). One outcome of the various forms of discrimination is the development within a person of an unspoken resentment of work that may be communicated in some form to one's children, thus transmitting a cross-generational, cynical outlook on work.

However, the history of the United States is also filled with many cases of individuals who succeed against the odds. Adults recognize the risks of staying in a setting that does not fit well with their desire to create, produce, and care. They may strike out on their own by setting up their own companies, they may challenge unfair practices through the courts, and they may mentor younger workers to help them cope with the conflicts they face in the workplace.

The responsibility for coping with discrimination cannot rest entirely on its victims. There are examples of work settings that have taken active steps to challenge their own practices. Company policies that value diversity and multiculturalism can be conveyed in their mission statement, their training of managers and supervisors, and in the images they use in their promotional materials, corporate events, and hiring and promotion practices. Companies have been recognized for their policies to support the hiring and promotion of women into senior positions, and for their innovations in weaving new levels of understanding about diversity into all aspects of employee development. A growing focus on corporate social responsibility suggests that many companies strive to go beyond compliance with the law to engage in practices that reflect high ethical standards and address specific aspects of community welfare. These practices can benefit the reputation of the company, but they also create a positive workforce identification and sense of attachment to the workplace (Bauman & Skitka, 2012). Companies are recognizing that by being more visibly attuned to the interests and needs of culturally diverse communities, they can increase their brand reputation and increase their client base (Purdie-Vaughn, Steele, Davies, Dilmann, & Crosby, 2008; Rodriquez, 2006).

The American workforce of the 21st century is becoming increasingly diverse. Women and ethnic minorities are the fastest growing groups of new employees. Slightly more than 25 percent of children who were under the age of 5 in 2009 were children of color (U.S. Census Bureau, 2012a, Table 10). Their preparation for and participation in the labor market will be determining factors in the quality and productivity of the U.S. economy in the years ahead. The psychosocial approach, which highlights the interdependence of the individual and the society, is dramatically illustrated in the connection between contemporary workplace policies and practices and their implications for the maturation of a sense of initiative and industry during childhood. Children who believe that their parents and other adult members of the community are thriving in work environments that respect and value them are more likely to make the commitment to schooling that is needed to participate fully when it is their turn to enter the labor market.

FURTHER REFLECTION: Define the concept of workplace discrimination. List the various forms of discrimination that can arise. Describe the evidence you have seen of discrimination in the settings where you work, where you attend school, or where you function as a consumer.

Investigate factors that are associated with workplace discrimination. What personal, cultural, or societal factors might account for workplace discrimination? What might motivate individuals to harass, undermine, or reject their coworkers?

Based on your understanding of psychosocial development, predict what kinds of experiences in earlier stages of life might protect a person from the negative impact of discrimination and foster effective coping.

CHAPTER SUMMARY

During the middle adult years, people have an opportunity to make significant contributions to their culture. Through work, home, childrearing, and other caring relationships, people express their own value orientations, moral codes, personalities, and talents. They grow more sensitive to the multiple needs of those around them and more skillful in influencing the social environment.

OBJECTIVE 1 Analyze features of the world of work as a context for development, focusing on interpersonal demands, authority relations, and demands for the acquisition of new skills.

The developmental tasks of middle adulthood are complex and require long-term persistence. People gauge their self-worth largely in relation to their contributions to complex social units, especially work, family, and community. Each task calls for a new level of conceptualization of the interaction of the self with immediate and more remote social systems and an increased ability to balance one's individual needs with system goals.

In the process of managing a career, one observes the bidirectional influence of individuals and their work settings. Occupational environments have an impact on the cognitive, interpersonal, and emotional development of middle adults, and middle adults influence work settings through their positions of authority, leadership, and the achievement of new levels of expertise. Effective leaders try to balance the good of the group with their own self-interest. They try to take into account the best interests of individuals, groups, and communities while they also participate and lead. The requirements of leadership may change as the group develops and as the team or organization faces new, emerging challenges.

The concept of interpersonal skills is complex and includes at least three components: self-presentation, or how a person introduces oneself to others and conveys openness to further interactions; social scanning, or the ability to read the social cues in the situation; and social flexibility, or the ability to respond adaptively to the social demands of the situation, for example by being assertive or cooperative as the circumstances require.

A key area of skill development in the contemporary labor market is *creative problem solving*. The combination of increasingly complex technology, instant international communication, and continuing reorganization of the network of interrelated businesses results in the emergence of a new and changing array of problems. The concept of managerial resourcefulness captures the nature of this problem solving. Managerial resourcefulness combines three critical features: a cognitive capacity to gather and analyze information, sensitivity to the emotional and motivational aspects of change, and a readiness to take appropriate actions.

One of the significant challenges of middle adulthood is the effective coordination of work and family life. Three concepts are reviewed: role overload, role conflict, and spillover. Role overload in the workplace is consistently perceived as a source of stress and is typically associated with negative attitudes toward the organization, reducing a worker's organizational commitment and job satisfaction. Although much of the responsibility for managing multiple roles falls to individuals and couples, work–family facilitation can be supported by resources and policies in the workplace that make it easier for employees to address pressing family demands within the scope of their daily work.

OBJECTIVE 2 Define the concept of a vital, intimate relationship and examine factors that support this goal in middle adulthood, especially a commitment to growth, effective communication, creative use of conflict, and preserving passion.

Happiness in an intimate relationship is a cornerstone of well-being in middle adulthood. The establishment and preservation of close, nurturing relationships require ego strengths of the partners, effective communication strategies, a commitment to the future of the relationship, and creative strategies for preserving passion and excitement within a framework of close companionship. Long-term stable relationships are typically based on a strong bond of friendship. The partners support each other and like each other. They have shared interests, enjoy similar activities, and are supportive and appreciative of one another's accomplishments. A vital marriage requires both partners to be open to the need to be themselves (as they continue to discover new dimensions of self) and an energizing, interpersonal chemistry that is resilient even in the face of the harshest challenges. Partners in an enduring relationship repeatedly act in ways that take into account their own self-interest and the well-being of their partner.

OBJECTIVE 3 Evaluate the expansion of caring in middle adulthood as it applies to two specific roles—that of a parent and that of an adult child caring for one's aging parents. Clarify your assumptions about the costs and benefits of enacting these roles.

The maturity and commitment to care of those in middle adulthood are closely linked to the psychosocial well-being of children as well as the elderly. Through parenting, adults create the supportive environment for children's safety, health, and development. The parents' personalities, their attachment orientations, the quality of their shared parenting activities, and the infant's temperament all contribute to the quality of this alliance. The quality of the parental alliance provides the model that children observe and internalize as they conceptualize the nature of adult relationships. The demands on adults as parents change as children mature. With each stage of family life, adults experience new opportunities for growth that are stimulated in part by their children's new capacities and relationships, as well as by the settings that link parents, children, and their activities.

Through their relationship with their aging parents, adult children can support their parents' optimal functioning and, at the same time, grow in their understanding of the challenges of aging. **Filial** obligation is a feeling of responsibility to care for one's parents; a sense of responsibility that adult children have to help their parents as they get old, especially when their physical or mental health declines; or a moral sense of duty that arises as one realizes and acknowledges the sacrifices one's parents have made and the sense of indebtedness for those sacrifices. Aging parents and adult children may have different ideas about how to enact filial obligation. Effective communication is a key to preserving positive relationships when goals and views about providing care conflict.

OBJECTIVE 4 Summarize the tasks required for effective management of the household and explain why they are necessary. Describe the diversity of households, including blended families, single-parent families, and adults who live alone, and hypothesize about the implications of these various household structures for individual development.

Management of the household involves the creation of a safe, stimulating, and comforting environment for those who live there. The capacity to maintain a household and nurture those who live there is linked to the middle adult's ability to identify needed resources and to create the network of relationships that will support the members of the household. The skills that are needed to achieve these goals will differ depending on the structure of the household and the ages, abilities, and relationships of the household members. In addition to the two-adult family with children, alternatives that are described include blended families, single parent families, and people who live alone. The topic of homelessness is highlighted as a particular challenge in the context of the importance of home in middle adulthood.

OBJECTIVE 5 Define and explain the psychosocial crisis of generativity versus stagnation and the central processes through which the crisis is resolved: person–environment interaction and creativity, the primary adaptive ego strength of care, and the core pathology of rejectivity.

The psychosocial crisis of the middle adult years—generativity versus stagnation—is really a moral crisis of commitment to a better way of life. The well-being of the community as a whole rests largely on the effectiveness of people in middle adulthood in reaching new levels of psychosocial maturity. The society must encourage adults to care for others besides themselves. The egocentrism of toddlerhood, early school age, and adolescence must eventually come to an end if the social group is to survive. In the same way that intimacy (giving oneself to another) requires identity, generativity (giving oneself to the next generation) requires love of specific others. Interpersonal sources of satisfaction are the primary forces propelling people toward a generative approach to society as a whole.

As generativity is fully achieved and expressed in action, it will be linked to the prime adaptive ego quality of care, a capacity to look after and promote the optimal development of others. In contrast, experiences of stagnation are likely to be accompanied by the core pathology of rejectivity—a defensive, self-protective outlook in which self-interest and self-aggrandizement are heightened by devaluing or degrading others.

OBJECTIVE 6 Apply a psychosocial analysis to the issue of discrimination in the workplace, and evaluate the cost to society and to the individual when discrimination operates to restrict career access and advancement.

The applied topic of discrimination in the workplace provides evidence of societal stagnation. Laws have been enacted to protect members of specific groups from discriminatory practices, and regulatory agencies are charged with the monitoring and prosecution of unlawful practices. Nonetheless, discrimination in the workplace continues, along with retaliation against those who file complaints and harassment of workers by supervisors and coworkers. Often, it is middle adults in leadership positions who, by deliberate practice or informal example, set a tone that promotes the exclusion of certain workers on the basis of age, gender, racial or ethnic group, ability status, or other group characteristics. At the same time, others in middle adulthood suffer from discriminatory policies and are unable to reach the levels of achievement and contribution that their talents merit. Social policies and practices that interfere with individuals' abilities to perform meaningful work or to achieve recognition and respect for their work pose a hazard to individual psychosocial development and to the future of the social group. These practices, born from the core pathology of rejectivity, act in opposition to the fundamental needs of a society to care about its members and foster the most optimistic ambitions and goals possible in younger generations.

CASEBOOK

For additional case material related to this chapter, see the case of "Annie and Career Contemplation," in *Life Span Development: A Case Book*, by Barbara and Philip Newman, Laura Landry-Meyer, and Brenda J. Lohman, pp. 176–179. In this case, Annie evaluates her current work situation in light of health concerns and a desire for greater personal satisfaction.

akg-images/akg-images/Superstock

The integrating theme of later adulthood is a search for personal meaning. When older adults achieve a sense of integrity, it leads to inner peace and serves as a source of reassurance to the next generation.

1. Examine the construct of life satisfaction in later adult-hood and analyze factors associated with subjective well-being.

2. Define intellectual vigor, and describe factors that promote it in later life. Evaluate evidence about the interaction of heredity and environment on intelligence in later life.

3. Explain the process of redirecting energy to new roles and activities, with special focus on role gain, such as grandparenthood; role loss, such as widowhood; and new opportunities for leisure.

4. Summarize the development of a point of view about death.

5. Define and explain the psychosocial crisis of integrity versus despair, the central process of introspection, the prime adaptive ego quality of wisdom, and the core pathology of disdain.

6. Apply theory and research to understanding the process of adjustment to retirement.

LATER ADULTHOOD (60 TO 75 YEARS)

13

Mary Gergen is Professor Emerita of Psychology and Women's Studies at Penn State University, Brandywine and co-founder of the Taos Institute, focusing on the integration of social constructionist ideas and professional practice. Here she reflects on the experience of retiring.

Younger people believe that health is something one takes for granted. Middle aged people worry as they start to see chinks in their armor, but older people learn to adjust. By and large, people manage to live well, even with major decrements in their youthful capacities. It is a good idea to eat well, sleep long, and laugh heartily in one's career days as extra insurance against falling apart too soon. Keeping up good habits helps in retirement as well.

Overall, life is not that different for me today from what it was ten years ago: I don't envy people who have a full time job at all. I often wonder why some people are still carrying the burdens of fulltime employment when they don't really need to. It's snowing out right now, and the highway is packed with cars going about 10 miles an hour. In those cars are people going home from work, tense and tired, and eagerly awaiting the chance to kick off their shoes and relax with their loved ones. (At least that is my fantasy.) And here I am, writing up the joys of not being out there, struggling to get home. I'm already home. (Gergen, 2012, pp. 307–308)

CASE ANALYSIS Using What You Know

1. Based on what you have read about the nature of work and career development, explain how the concept of retirement might be viewed differently and have different meaning depending on one's stage of life, including early adulthood, middle adulthood, and later adulthood.

2. Speculate about how retirement contributes to Mary's sense of control over her life and general well-being.

3. List some reasons why people might continue to work well into their later adulthood. Explain how work might contribute to life satisfaction, personal identity, health, and financial and psychosocial well-being in later life. How might continuing to work undermine these domains?

In this chapter and the next, we consider the challenges, changes, and new avenues for development in later life. This chapter focuses on the period from 60 to 75; the next chapter focuses on the years from 75 to the end of life. The French refer to the years from 60 onward as the troisième age, the third stage of life (Rubenstein, 2002). One can think of the first 30 years of life as a period of construction and learning, when many avenues are open and the person is building the skills and knowledge to engage in the roles of adulthood. The second 30 years, from 30 to 60, are a period of enactment, when commitments established during identity formation are translated into roles and relationships. In this period, life is shaped by the interaction of work, family, and community demands and expectations. The individual strives to achieve personal ambitions and goals and to meet cultural expectations for maturity while coping with planned and unexpected changes in adjoining systems. The final 30 years are a period of reinvention. The integrating theme of later adulthood is a search for personal meaning. For many, this stage of life brings a gradual release from the daily demands of work and family and, depending on one's health and resources, provides the opportunity to invent a new life structure. This is a time when one faces both significant adversity and great joy.

Psychosocial theory assumes that new opportunities for growth emerge at each life stage. Like each of the preceding stages, later adulthood is marked by stressors, risks, and forces that can disrupt growth. However, in strong contrast to the stereotype of aging as an undesirable process associated with accumulated deficits and decline, these chapters highlight continuous growth through coping and adaptation.

One cannot understand the full unfolding of human life without appreciating the beliefs, practices, and social relationships of those in later adulthood and old age. The interdependence of the stages in a human life story suggests that the ways in which older adults function and are treated will have immediate impact on the psychosocial development of individuals in all the earlier periods of life. The courage and vitality of older adults are sources of inspiration that motivate children and younger adults to continue facing the challenges of their lives with optimism.

Physical, social, emotional, and intellectual developments are intricately interrelated during later life. Patterns of aging are neither universal nor irreversible. For example, although many older adults become more sedentary and lose aerobic capacity, others continue to perform strenuous labor and remain free from heart disease and respiratory difficulties. Many life conditions, especially poverty, malnutrition, poor sanitation, and limited health care, can accelerate the aging process. Other life conditions, such as access to a stimulating social environment, participation in a program of physical activity, and a well-balanced diet, can increase physical and intellectual functioning (Jeste, Depp, & Vahia, 2010; Rowe & Kahn, 1998). It is essential to keep in mind the individual differences in physical and mental health when thinking about patterns of growth in later adulthood.

Most of the people in today's cohort of later adults are part of the baby boom generation (born between 1945 and 1964). At the close of World War II, there was a spike in the birthrate over a period of 14 years resulting in a substantial increase in the population. Because of its size, the baby boom generation put pressure on many social institutions, pushing for more resources at every stage of its development including building new elementary schools, new high schools, community colleges, and increasing competition for college enrollment.

This cohort grew up in a time of national optimism following the close of the war and economic prosperity in the 1950s. It was a time of remarkable contradictions. Competition with the Soviet Union brought about the space race resulting in landing humans on the moon and the expansion of space exploration. This same political tension resulted in the Cold War, fear of communism, and threats of a nuclear attack. Coming of age in the 1960s and early 70s, this cohort faced the challenging social and political issues associated with the war in Vietnam with accompanying protests and devastating loss of life, the civil rights movement, the hippie counterculture, and the assassinations of John F. Kennedy, Robert Kennedy, and Martin Luther King, Jr. (Robinson, 2016).

In the context of the sexual revolution and the women's movement, baby boomers resumed the trend to delayed age of marriage which was noted at the start of the 20th century. They experienced an increase and destigmatization of divorce, and had smaller families. These changes have led some to wonder who will meet the social support and care needs of the baby boomers as they age. As they enter later adulthood, they are putting new pressures on the health care system, the Social Security system, and the demand for new leisure, education, and community services. Having challenged social institutions over the course of earlier life stages and innovated in family, work, and community contexts, the baby boomers are redefining the nature of later adulthood including new ideas about continuing education, work, retirement, and family life.

For people in the United States who were 65 years old in 2014, the average life expectancy was an additional 18 years for men, and an additional 20.5 years for women (National Center for Health Statistics, 2016a, Table 15). Major improvements in hygiene, nutrition, preventive medicine, and medical treatments and technologies have allowed more people to experience a vigorous later adulthood today than was true 70 years ago. As a result, more and more people are living to face the developmental tasks of later adulthood and elderhood. ●

Developmental Tasks

The developmental tasks confronted in later adulthood include: accepting one's life and achieving a sense of life satisfaction, promoting intellectual vigor, redirecting energy to new roles and activities, and developing a point of view about death. These themes suggest new barriers to adaptation as well as new opportunities. Changes in memory and reduced speed of neural processing may make the accomplishment of daily tasks more difficult. Role loss and the death of loved ones stimulate needs for new kinds of support and changes in daily lifestyle. Success in these tasks requires considerable psychological effort. As the more structured roles of parent and worker become less demanding, a person has to find new sources of personal meaning and a new pattern to daily life. In some cultures, aging takes place in a context of reverence and high regard, which makes the loss of certain instrumental activities less significant. In other cultures, emphasis on autonomy, instrumentality, and achievement form a challenging context for the preservation of dignity in late life.

Accepting One's Life

OBJECTIVE 1 Examine the construct of life satisfaction in later adulthood and analyze factors associated with subjective well-being.

One of the significant challenges of aging is learning to accept the reality of one's life and formulate a vision of this new phase of later adulthood.

"Weren't you ever afraid to grow old?" I asked.

"Mitch, I *embrace* aging."

"Embrace it?"

"It's very simple. As you grow, you learn more. If you stayed at twenty-two, you'd always be as ignorant as you were at twenty-two. Aging is not just decay, you know. It's growth. It's more than the negative that you're going to die, it's also the positive that you *understand* you're going to die, and that you live a better life because of it." (Albom, 1997, p. 118)

By later adulthood, evidence about one's successes and failures in the major tasks of middle adulthood—marriage, childrearing, and work—has begun to accumulate. Data by which to judge one's adequacy in these areas are abundant. The process of accepting one's past life as it has been may be a difficult personal challenge. One must incorporate certain areas of failure, crisis, or disappointment into one's self-image without being overburdened by a sense of inadequacy. Individuals also must be able to take pride in areas of achievement, even when those accomplishments fall short of personal expectations. At the same time, older adults face the challenge of defining new goals for the future.

We have used the language of "accepting one's life" as a developmental task for later adulthood. This language reflects the reality that many people experience some disappointment, regret or frustration in their middle adulthood at being unable to achieve the hopes and dreams that they may have set for themselves at earlier ages (Rauch, 2014).

K. is a 54-year old woman [who] had an exciting launch in her 20s ("working my dream job"), a sense of continuing achievement but slowing momentum in her 30s ("sort of a slog"), and an ambush in her 40s, when her father died, her mother had a stroke, her husband left her after their daughter was born, and she was laid off. Despite coping with all of that and doing well professionally, even with her layoff ("I did better in my career; I made more money") she developed what she describes as a dark sense of humor about her life, ruefully telling herself that at least she had so many troubles that she couldn't dwell on all of them at once. (Rauch, 2014, p. 9)

The challenge facing later adults is to accept their disappointments, to view the life they have led with satisfaction, and to find meaning and purpose in the life they have yet to live. Much of the literature on successful or positive aging includes terms such as well-being, life satisfaction, and happiness to examine how well older adults are able to attain this state of acceptance and positive outlook. Studies differ in the way these concepts are defined and measured (Martin et al., 2015). Table 13.1 provides definitions of successful aging from six sources, giving a sense of the variety of dimensions that might be included under this conceptual umbrella. From these definitions, you can appreciate that successful aging is a biopsychosocial process. The discussion that follows describes several models for understanding how older adults establish a satisfying approach to the developmental task of accepting one's life in light of changing resources, goals, and accomplishments.

Table 13.1	Definitions of Successful Aging
Author	Definitions
Baltes & Baltes, 1990	Selective optimization with compensation
Depp & Jeste, 2006	Disability/physical function, cognitive functioning, life satisfaction/well-being, social/productive engagement, presence of illness, longevity, self-rated health, personality, environment/finances, self-rated successful aging
Kahana & Kahana, 1996, 2003	Social and psychological resources, preventive and corrective adaptations, psychological, existential, and social well-being
Phelan & Larson, 2002	Freedom from disability, independent functioning, life satisfaction, active engagement with life, longevity, positive adaptation, mastery/growth
Rowe & Kahn, 1997, 1998	Low probability of disease and disease related disability, high cognitive and physical functional capacity, active engagement with life
Ryff & Keyes, 1995	Self-acceptance, quality ties to others, autonomy of thought and action, ability to manage complex environments to suit personal needs and values, pursuit of meaningful goals and a sense of purpose in life, continued growth and development as a person

© 2018 Cengage

The SOC Model

Over the life span, people confront the challenges of balancing and matching a variety of opportunities with fluctuations in resources (Baltes & Baltes, 1990; Freund & Baltes, 1998). At every period of life, there are limited resources—whether time, energy, or money—to address all the opportunities that present themselves. For example, in later adulthood, a person may want to continue to work (an opportunity) but find that a chronic heart condition makes it difficult to bring the required energy and resilience to the task (loss of a resource). According to the **SOC model**, adaptation requires the integration of three processes:

Selection: Identifying the opportunities or domains of activity that are of the greatest value or importance.

Optimization: Allocating and refining resources in order to achieve higher levels of functioning in the selected domains.

Compensation: Under conditions of reduced resources, identifying strategies to counteract the loss and minimize the negative impact on functioning in the selected domains.

In later life, adults are inevitably faced with changes in resources. They may have more time, but less physical stamina and fewer financial resources. Life satisfaction and a sense of well-being are linked to selecting specific goals as important areas of functioning and then effectively directing both internal (e.g., energy, thought, planning) and external (e.g., hiring help, taking classes, technical assistance) resources in order to maximize their level of functioning. Demographic factors alone—such as

gender, race, age, and income—are not adequate predictors of life satisfaction. Instead, well-being rests on two related coping strategies: (1) An ability to anticipate potential losses and prevent them through proactive coping in order to prolong the availability of resources and maintain engagement with desired activities (Ouwehand, de Riller, & Bensing, 2006) and (2) an ability to manage or reduce the impact of stressful life events by redirecting resources in order to continue engaging in valued roles and activities (Hamarat et al., 2001; Salvatore & Sastre, 2001). For example, preventive adaptation can include purchasing a stationary bicycle to support daily aerobic exercise, especially if you live in a climate that makes outdoor exercise difficult in extreme heat or freezing weather. Knowing that older adults can be the target of financial scams, people can reduce the impact of these stressors by having a reliable contact like an adult child, grandchild, or financial professional to contact when in doubt about a phone or email request for personal or financial information. Building in time to relax each day can help reduce the toll of daily stress on physical and mental health.

Life Goals and Life Satisfaction

Life satisfaction is an overall assessment of feelings and attitudes about one's life, rather than a momentary feeling of happiness or unhappiness. It can be assessed as a global overview (e.g. "How satisfied are you with your life at present?") or as a composite of satisfaction with various domains such as work, leisure activities, social/family life, health, and finances/income (Kapteyn, Smith, & van Soest, 2009). Many older adults have high levels of life satisfaction even though they face serious stressors and physical limitations (Brandtsadter, 2002). In part, this is due to their ability to achieve or realize important personal goals, and in part it is due to the ability to modify or adjust their goals in light of changing resources. Goals are linked to daily actions, related to desired states in the present or the future, and controllable, at least in so far as the person can choose to invest resources in certain goals or not (Mayser, Scheibe, & Riediger, 2008).

In later adulthood, individuals continue to aspire to new goals and strive to achieve new levels of optimal functioning. A person's life goals and needs may change over the course of later adulthood, depending on life circumstances. Rather than viewing satisfaction in later adulthood in terms of wrapping things up and facing a roleless, undifferentiated future, older adults continue to formulate personal goals and assess their current life satisfaction in light of how well they are able to achieve those goals. In order to appreciate the link between life goals and life satisfaction, it is important to consider three aspects of life goals: goal domains, **goal orientation**, and goal-related activities that are aligned with achieving valued goals (see FIGURE 13.1 ▶).

Goal Domains. What are the achievements that stand out as important areas of accomplishment in later adulthood? Studies of life goals and life satisfaction present different typologies of life goals. One international study of life goals compared older adults in the United States and Holland. Four domains were relevant to both groups: job or daily activity goals, social contact and family goals, health goals, and income goals. Across the two cultures, attainment of social contact and family goals were the strongest

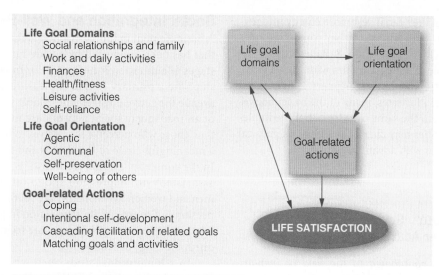

Life Goal Domains
  Social relationships and family
  Work and daily activities
  Finances
  Health/fitness
  Leisure activities
  Self-reliance
Life Goal Orientation
  Agentic
  Communal
  Self-preservation
  Well-being of others
Goal-related Actions
  Coping
  Intentional self-development
  Cascading facilitation of related goals
  Matching goals and activities

FIGURE 13.1 ▶ LIFE GOALS AND LIFE SATISFACTION
Source: © Cengage

predictor of overall life satisfaction (Kapteyn, Smith, & van Soest, 2010). Other studies include self-reliance or autonomy goals and leisure time and physical activity goals in their analyses of the link between life goals and life satisfaction (Straechen, Brawley, Spink, & Glazebrook, 2010; Wong & Lou, 2010).

Individuals show different patterns of investment in these **goal domains**, and in the specific activities or achievements within domains. To some extent, a person's profile of meaningful goals takes shape in the stages of later adolescence and early adulthood. At that time, individuals are crystallizing their identity and creating a lifestyle. The combination of one's culture and life experiences shapes an imagined self, moving into the future. As a person begins the process of accepting one's life in later adulthood, there is a tendency to return to the personal goals that were envisioned at that earlier time of life in order to assess the extent to which they were realized and perhaps to reevaluate their importance given the 40 years or more of life that have transpired since these goals were formed (Cappeliez, 2008).

Goal Orientation. In addition to the specific goals one aspires to, people differ in their goal orientation. Some people are more agentic in their goal strivings. Their important goals focus on achievement, power, and the expression of personal abilities. Other people are more communal in their goal strivings. Their goals focus on intimacy, affiliation, and contributions to the moral community (Pohlmann, 2001). Other studies have contrasted goals that seem to emphasize self-preservation with those that focus on the interest in and well-being of others. One might look back at the psychosocial crisis of middle adulthood, generativity versus stagnation, and consider that the profile of goals emerging from that period of life might differ for those who resolved the crisis in the direction of generativity compared to those who resolved it in the direction of stagnation (Lapierre, Bouffard, & Bastin, 1997).

Goal-Related Actions. As people make progress on the developmental task of accepting their life, they are able to integrate their goals and their **goal-related activities** in order to experience

a sense of personal fulfillment. For those in later adulthood who have a strong sense of self-directed goal attainment, sentiments of life satisfaction feed back into life goals, strengthening their sense of purpose and providing renewed energy. Activities that are not satisfying or that bring negative social exchanges will be abandoned in favor of activities that are enjoyable and that contribute to feelings of confidence or well-being. With age, it appears that a person's goals become more supportive of each other, so that one activity, for example, joining a book club, can provide support for both intellectual goals and social goals; spending time with grandchildren can be an opportunity to experience family support and physical activity. Couples who enjoy cooking may find that this shared interest also allows them to spend time together, planning, shopping, and preparing meals. Older adults find that their goals

Chuck Savage/Corbis/Getty Images

Ray and Carla have more time for each other now that they are getting closer to retirement. Their happiness as a couple is an important source of life satisfaction. A shared interest in cooking combines physical activity, cognitive planning, cooperative efforts, and enjoyment of the results.

support each other and that they can invest more energy into personal goal pursuits as their obligations to other competing roles and role demands decline (Riediger, Freund, & Baltes, 2005). The more closely a person is able to match activities with valued goals, the greater the life satisfaction (Halisch & Geppert, 2001). As the case of Orville Brim's father illustrates, many of the basic motives for goal pursuits may remain the same over time, but the implementation of specific activities may change as a person's physical health or endurance declines with advanced age.

— CASE STUDY Goal Adjustment in Later Adulthood —

Orville Gilbert Brim, who contributed to the field of human development through his work on social role theory (see chapter 3), became increasingly interested in ambition and self-directed goal attainment in adulthood. He described his father's successful adaptations in later life as an example of this process (Brim, 1992).

Brim's father, also named Orville, lived to be 103. He was born in a small farming community in a rural area of Ohio in 1883. After receiving his bachelor's degree in education at Valparaiso University, he taught school in a one-room schoolhouse for 2 years and then became principal of a high school in Indiana. Eventually he left the rural Midwest to attend Harvard and then Columbia to get his PhD. He was a professor at Ohio State University until he retired at age 60. Then Orville and his wife, Helen, bought an abandoned farm of several hundred acres in Connecticut, remodeled the farmhouse, and settled into farming. In the early years of retirement, he cleared and thinned the trees on the hills and mountains of his farm. After a while, he stopped working the hillsides and planted a large vegetable and flower garden. Orville tilled the garden with a power tiller. When he was 90, he bought a riding tractor. When he could no longer manage the large garden, he focused on a small border garden and four large window boxes that he planted with flowers. As his eyesight became more impaired, he shifted from reading to listening to "talking books," and when he had to give up actually planting the window boxes, he enjoyed watering them and looking at the flowers. Orville approached each new challenge of physical decline by correctly assessing his abilities, investing in a new project, and taking pride in his achievements within that domain.

CASE ANALYSIS Using What You Know

1. In this case, Brim's father drew on early life experiences growing up on a farm to guide his goals in later adulthood. Describe how a person might integrate other prior life roles into a satisfying lifestyle in later adulthood.

2. Explain how goal readjustment is related to life satisfaction in this case. Analyze some of challenges people might face in later life as they realize the need to revise their life goals.

3. Describe the resources Brim's father had that allowed him to achieve new goals for mastery.

Social Integration and Well-Being

A basic element in life satisfaction is the sense of belonging, a fact that has been supported by a wide range of research across life stages (Baumeister & Leary, 1995). In later life, social relationships are a primary source of pleasure and meaning and are an avenue for active engagement. People who experience loneliness or an inadequate social network are much less satisfied with life than those who perceive themselves to be positively connected to a meaningful circle of loved ones and friends (Gow et al., 2007). In the context of marital relationships, high levels of conflict are associated with depression and lower life satisfaction for both men and women (Whisman et al., 2006). Even though social connection is a source of life satisfaction in later adulthood, negative relationships and ongoing exposure to interpersonal conflict can disrupt feelings of satisfaction.

In a longitudinal study, men who had participated in the Terman Study of Gifted Children when they were in early childhood were interviewed about their life satisfaction at ages 58 to 72. Four styles of adaptation emerged: (1) poorly adjusted, (2) career focused but socially disengaged, (3) family focused, and (4) well rounded. Three family experiences from early childhood and adolescence, including parent–child attachment, family socioeconomic status, and early parental divorce, were associated either directly or indirectly with life satisfaction in later life (Crosnoe & Elder, 2004). In addition, contemporary factors including health and socioeconomic resources were generally predictive of life satisfaction for the group as a whole. Goals related to family life and religious life provided a greater sense of meaning, social benefits, and emotional support than occupational goals, especially for the family-focused and well-rounded groups (Crosnoe & Elder, 2002b). The family-focused and well-rounded groups had many areas of similarity, as did the career-focused and poorly adjusted groups. There is some suggestion that people who place too great a priority on occupational attainment during middle adulthood may find it difficult to reorient toward satisfying life goals in later adulthood.

Personality and Well-Being

We all know people who have lived difficult lives yet appear to be full of zest and enthusiasm. We also know people who appear to have had the benefits of many of life's resources yet are continually complaining about problems. Whether specific events will contribute to feelings of satisfaction or dismay depends in part on how they are interpreted. Some people are more likely to be grumblers; others are more likely to be celebrants of life. In efforts to understand these differences, some researchers have looked to personality factors to predict subjective life satisfaction in later adulthood.

The term **personality** refers to patterns of thoughts, feelings, and actions that are characteristic of a person across situations. Personality provides ways of understanding individual differences in coping, goal orientation, and self-evaluative processes. Confusing as it may seem, personality is both stable and changing over one's life. Personality is stable in the sense that people who are high in one aspect of personality in comparison to their peers remain relatively high in that quality over time. For example, a person who is outgoing and sociable in comparison to others will continue to rank high in sociability over time. Personality is also changing in the sense that certain personality qualities seem to increase with age, while others decline. For example, studies find that agreeableness increases with age, whereas openness to new experiences declines (Lodi-Smith, Turiano, & Mroczek, 2011).

A number of personality characteristics have been linked with life satisfaction in later life, including extroversion, openness to experiences, lack of neuroticism, usefulness/competence, optimism, a sense of humor, and a sense of control. **Extroversion** includes such qualities as sociability, vigor, sensation seeking, and positive emotions. People who are outgoing and enjoy social interaction tend also to report high levels of life satisfaction (Costa, Metter, & McCrae, 1994). In a comparison of two cohorts of older adults, those assessed in 1976–1977 and those assessed in 2005–2006, the more recent group of older adults were more extraverted and less constrained by social desirability, suggesting a generational shift toward a more outgoing, trusting interpersonal style (Billstedt et al., 2013).

Openness to experience includes characteristics such as curiosity, imaginativeness, and enthusiasm about exploring different music, art, foods, travel, or points of view. Older adults who are open to new ideas and are aware of their feelings are more likely to have a high level of life satisfaction because they seek and take advantage of the novelty and unpredictability of their lives (Stephen, 2009).

A personality dimension described as **neuroticism** is characterized by anxiety, hostility, and impulsiveness. People who are neurotic experience discouragement, unhappiness, and hopelessness. For them, real-life events are screened and interpreted through a negative filter, resulting in low levels of satisfaction. In the study of Terman's gifted sample, high levels of neuroticism predicted worse physical health and lower life satisfaction (Friedman, Kern, & Reynolds, 2010).

The personality factor of **usefulness/competence** is related to **well-being** and high self-esteem in older adults. This quality is associated with informal volunteer work, higher levels of involvement with others, and a greater sense of purpose and structure in the use of time (Ranzijn, Keeves, Luszcz, & Feather, 1998). Continuing to work in later adulthood may also contribute to this sense of usefulness/competence, or perhaps those who have a high sense of usefulness/competence choose to work longer. Those older adults who take on the role of mentor for new or younger workers can enhance their sense of life satisfaction through this role to the extent that it creates opportunities to feel useful, to be involved as a valued resource, and to achieve their own career goals in this relationship (Stevens-Roseman, 2009).

Optimism is another predictor of life satisfaction. **Optimism** is a belief that one's decisions will lead to positive consequences and that uncertain situations will turn out well. Under conditions of uncertainty and stress, adults who are optimistic have less depression, greater hopefulness, and, as a result, a greater sense of well-being (Chang & Sanna, 2001). In contrast, those who are pessimistic experience more social strain, have lower social support, and as a result, are likely to have lower life satisfaction (Luger, Cotter, & Sherman, 2009).

Along with optimism, a sense of humor has been found to predict life satisfaction. Given the many changes associated with aging, it helps to see events as amusing rather than embarrassing or demeaning. Older adults who have a good sense of humor are likely to experience life in a more playful, engaged way, even if they view life as somewhat more absurd (Ruch, Proyer, & Weber, 2010).

A **sense of control** is systematically associated with life satisfaction (McConatha, McConatha, Jackson, & Bergen, 1998). Life experiences such as engaging in physical activity, the opportunity to select one's leisure activities, or the ability to decide when to retire are all examples of factors that can improve an older adult's sense of control. A study that monitored daily activity of older adults over 2 years found that people who were able to alternate social, physical, and cognitive activities with periods of rest and relaxation had the greatest sense of happiness (Oerlemans, Bakker, & Veenhoven, 2011). Taken together these studies suggest that people who are extroverted, open to new experiences, optimistic, experience a sense of usefulness, have a good sense of humor, and feel that they are in control of events in their life will also express high levels of satisfaction.

Illness, Disability and Health

Illness and disability pose increasing challenges in later adulthood. In addition to an increase in vulnerability to acute illnesses, such as influenza, more than 80 percent of people over the age

RMN-Grand Palais/Art Resource, NY

In his later life, Renoir suffered from severe arthritis. To compensate, he tied paint brushes to his hands so he could continue to function in this highly valued domain.

of 65 have at least one chronic condition such as arthritis, hypertension, coronary heart disease, diabetes, or cancer. **Chronic illnesses** are long lasting and can be characterized by periods of intense illness followed by periods of remission or progressive decline. The most common chronic conditions in the 65 to 74 age range are arthritis, hearing impairments, heart conditions, and high blood pressure (Warshaw, 2006).

Heart disease is the leading cause of death for men and women in the United States. However, it begins about 10 years earlier for men than for women. After menopause, the risk of heart disease for women increases. Moreover, women are less likely than men to be accurately diagnosed as suffering from a heart attack, less likely to recover from it, and more likely to suffer the complications of stroke. The lifestyle factors associated with heart disease are about the same for men and women. However, men are more likely to be at risk because they do not get the physical activity they need, eat more meat and fat and less fruit and fiber than women, are less likely to go to the doctor for regular checkups, and are generally more likely to deny being sick (National Center for Health Statistics, 2013). Longitudinal studies of men consistently find that current health status and functional autonomy are significant predictors of life satisfaction (Barger, Donoho, & Wayment, 2009).

Experiencing a sense of well-being and acceptance of one's life is associated with physical health. Physical functioning and freedom from disability are included as components in the vast majority of definitions of successful aging (Depp & Jest, 2006). However, the relationship of health to life satisfaction is mediated by personality, resources, and personal goals. A chronic illness, such as arthritis, may result in a significant loss of control and reduced opportunities for physical activity or social interaction. A person who is characterized by a neurotic personality may be more discouraged and embittered by these losses than one who is optimistic or agreeable. A person whose leisure activities have focused on physical activities, such as skiing or running, may find the restrictions of arthritis more frustrating than someone whose hobbies and lifestyle are more sedentary. Subjective well-being and life satisfaction appear to be more closely tied to psychological traits, like optimism or agreeableness, and to the quality of social relationships, like having caring family and friends or being involved in community activities, than to the severity or specific nature of one's illness or disability (Jeste, Depp, & Vahia, 2010).

In a study of more than 3,000 U.S. adults, the personality traits of **conscientiousness** and neuroticism were found to be associated with mental and physical health. Adults who were more conscientious had reduced risks of health problems, whereas those who were more neurotic had increased risk. Among adults with diagnosed physical illnesses, those who were conscientious were less likely to be limited by these conditions. One explanation for this association is that the more conscientious a person is, the more likely the person will follow a recommended plan of treatment and incorporate recognized healthy behaviors into daily life (Goodwin & Friedman, 2006). Another interpretation is that those who are more neurotic are also more likely to alienate their social support system, thereby losing the important functions of social support that

are associated with health and life satisfaction (Barger, Donoho, & Wayment, 2009).

It will come as no surprise that the onset of a significant disability, especially one that limits mobility or restricts the ability to work, would result in a decrease in life satisfaction. However, there is also evidence of resilience in the face of disability, more so for some than for others. In a longitudinal study of German adults, over 300 encountered a disability that led to the reduced ability to work. There was a loss in life satisfaction accompanying the disability, but over 4 years following the disability, life satisfaction began to rise. What is more, for some adults, especially those characterized by the personality quality of agreeableness, the adaptation resulted in levels of life satisfaction that returned to the same level as before the disability occurred (Boyce & Wood, 2011).

In the face of disability, the nature and quality of social relationships are especially important for promoting life satisfaction. Without support for involvement in community activities and close family and friends, older adults with disabilities are likely to become inactive and lonely, characteristics that are associated with depression (Pagan, 2015; Stancliffe, Bigby, Balandin, Wilson, & Craig, 2015). Especially for people with physical disabilities who live alone, having valued close friends can serve as a key factor in sustaining life satisfaction (Kim, Hong, & Kim, 2015).

Erikson on Accepting One's Life

Erikson's psychosocial theory places accepting one's life at the center of the psychosocial crisis of this life stage: ego integrity versus despair. The tension of this stage is created as people strive to make peace with the disappointments of the past as well as the new frailties and limitations associated with aging. Erikson et al. (1986) highlighted the importance of trust in the acceptance of one's life and the challenge of accepting support as it becomes needed.

> Maples and aspens every October bear flamboyant witness to this possibility of a final spurt of growth. Nature unfortunately has not ordained that mortals put on such a fine show. As aging continues, in fact, human bodies begin to deteriorate and physical and psychosocial capacities diminish in a seeming reversal of the course their development takes. When physical frailty demands assistance, one must accept again an appropriate dependence without the loss of trust and hope. The old, of course, are not endowed with the endearing survival skills of the infant. Old bodies are more difficult to care for, and the task itself is less satisfying to the caretaker than that of caring for infants. Such skills as elders possess have been hard won and are maintained only with determined grace. Only a lifetime of slowly developing trust is adequate to meet this situation, which so naturally elicits despair and disgust at one's own helplessness. Of how many elders could one say, "He surrendered every vestige of his old life with a sort of courteous, half humorous gentleness"? (p. 327)

The U-Shaped Curve of Well-Being

The general sense of subjective well-being can be defined as a combination of beliefs and feelings about whether one is leading a desirable, rewarding life (Diener, 2012). Studies across cultures find that certain factors including social support, trust, and a sense of mastery or control predict well-being. What is more surprising is that many studies find a U-shaped relationship of age and well-being (see FIGURE 13.2 ▶). The sense of well-being decreases to a low point in the late 40s and early 50s and then increases steadily with advanced age (Blanchflower & Oswald, 2007; Stone, Schwartz, Broderick, & Deaton, 2010). Controlling for income, employment status, and having children, the U-shaped pattern is still observed.

In an analysis of well-being across 46 countries, the U-shaped curve held up in 44. In this study, well-being was measured using the Cantril ladder question: "Please imagine a ladder, with steps numbered from 0 at the bottom to 10 at the top. On which step of the ladder would you say you personally feel you stand at this time?" The data came from the Gallup World Poll for the years 2005–2014, with an average of 9,000 observations per country. The bottom of the well-being curve occurred in the age range 40 to 60, depending on the country. Two additional observations emerged from this cross-national study: (1) The curve begins to ascend at a younger age in countries where the national level of well-being is higher, and (2) within countries, the curve ascends at a younger age for individuals who are more satisfied with life as compared to those who are less satisfied overall. The implication is that even though they will experience a decline in life satisfaction during a period of middle adulthood, people who are satisfied with their lives and who live in places where most people are satisfied have more years of middle and later adulthood when they experience satisfaction with life (Graham & Pozuelo, 2016).

Four explanations may account for this U-shaped trend in life satisfaction:

- Happiness is associated with health. Since health and happiness are both associated with longevity, it is possible that those who are unhappy with their lives also die younger.

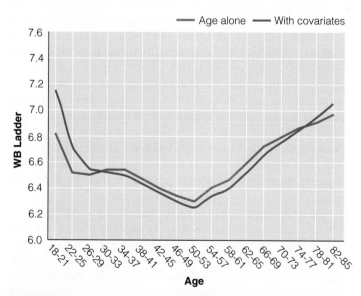

FIGURE 13.2 ▶ THE U-SHAPED CURVE OF WELL-BEING

Source: Stone, A. A., Schwartz, J. E., Broderick, J. E., & Deaton, A. (2010). A snapshot of the age distribution of psychological well-being in the United States. *Proceedings of the National Academic of Sciences.* Retrieved from http://www.pnas.org/cgi/doi/10.1073/pnas.1003744107

Thus, the older sample includes more people who have been happier with their lives all along whereas more of the unhappy people have died.

- Older people are less angry, less likely to engage in conflicts, and better able to find solutions to conflicts, resulting in lower experiences of stress.
- Older people are more likely to focus on what matters in the present and not worry as much about what the future holds.
- Older people may give up certain kinds of strivings and accept the life they have.

FURTHER REFLECTION: Explain how people might modify their goals in later adulthood in order to optimize life satisfaction. Give an example from your own experience or from the life of someone you know that illustrates this idea.

Promoting Intellectual Vigor

OBJECTIVE 2 Define intellectual vigor, and describe factors that promote it in later life. Evaluate evidence about the interaction of heredity and environment on intelligence in later life.

Over the life span, adaptation and survival depend on a person's ability to meet the demands of their environment. Problem solving, which begins in infancy at the sensory and motor levels, becomes increasingly flexible, abstract, and adapted to the context and situation, over the life course. **Memory**, reasoning, information processing, problem-solving abilities, and mental rigidity or fluidity all influence an adult's **intellectual vigor**, the capacity to introspect, select meaningful goals, manage changing resources, and plan for the future. These intellectual capacities also influence the adult's ability to remain involved in productive work, advise and guide others, and invent new solutions to the problems of daily life. The person's capacity to cope with the challenges of later adulthood, and thereby preserve a high level of life satisfaction, depends on the ability to promote and sustain intellectual vigor. It is not surprising to know that there is a link between well-being and cognitive functioning. Among older adults, well-being is associated with better performance on tests of cognitive functioning. What is more, people who perform better on certain tests of cognitive functioning are likely to be better able to handle tasks of daily life, engage in challenging problem-solving, and as a result, experience more positive mood and higher quality of life (Allerhand, Gale, & Deary, 2014).

In the following section, we review problems associated with the study of intelligence and aging that make it difficult to make broad generalizations. Specific topics are then discussed including neuroplasticity in later life, memory, problem solving in loosely defined situations, and an overview of age-related changes in various mental abilities. The focus then shifts to an analysis of the impact of heredity and environment on intelligence and factors that help to sustain high levels of intellectual functioning in later life.

Problems in Defining and Studying Intelligence in Later Adulthood

The primary goals in the study of development are to describe and explain patterns of change and continuity over time. Four problems arise in evaluating the research on intelligence in later life (Stuart-Hamilton, 1996). First, one must differentiate between **age differences** and **age changes**. Suppose that in a cross-sectional study conducted in 2000, 70-year-olds performed less well on tests of flexible problem solving than 40-year-olds. The difference may be clear, but it may not be a result of age alone. The 70-year-olds would have been born in 1930, and the 40-year-olds in 1960. Differences in performance may be a product of different educational opportunities, varying experiences with standardized tests, or other cohort-related factors. Educational opportunities increased markedly during the 20th century so that younger cohorts are much more likely to have benefited from formal schooling at both the high school and college levels (U.S. Bureau of the Census, 2000). For example, only 10 percent of people ages 65 to 74 in 2000 had completed a bachelor's degree, whereas 18 percent of adults ages 35 to 44 had attained this level of education. In the older cohort, 26 percent had not graduated from high school, compared to 11 percent in the younger cohort. Advanced education is associated with greater reflectiveness, flexibility, and relativistic thinking (King & Kitchener, 1994; Labouvie-Vief & Diehl, 2000).

In cross-sectional studies of cognitive functioning, historical factors may be confounded with developmental or aging factors that contribute to observed differences in performance. In longitudinal studies that follow change over time, if only one cohort is sampled, it is impossible to tell whether changes from one period to the next are products of age and development or a result of fluctuations in resources and challenges faced by that particular generation.

A second problem is the *definition of abilities*. Cognitive functioning is a broad term that encompasses such varied abilities as vocabulary, problem solving, and short-term memory. It is possible that the pattern of change in abilities with age depends on which abilities are tested. Some abilities are frequently used and have been developed to a high level of efficiency. For example, an architect is more likely to retain abilities in spatial relations and reasoning than is someone whose work is not intimately connected with the construction and organization of spatial dimensions.

A third related problem is the *relevance of the tasks* used to measure adult cognitive functioning. The definition of intelligence that is used in the design and application of most intelligence tests refers to capacities that are predictive of school-related success. The criteria for assessing adult intelligence are necessarily more varied than the ability to succeed in a school curriculum. Furthermore, motivational factors come into play in the measurement of intelligence. This raises the distinction between *ability* and *performance*. If a test is perceived as irrelevant or unimportant, an adult may not give much effort to performing well.

Finally, *factors associated with health* are intertwined with the functioning of older adults, although they are often not directly measured. A number of age-related diseases impact an individual's ability to learn and retain new information. However, the boundaries between what might be considered normal cognitive changes associated with age and disease-related changes are not easy to detect, especially in the early stages of an illness (Albert, 2002). In a longitudinal study of intelligence, Riegel and Riegel (1972) found clear declines in performance among participants who died before the next testing period. Vocabulary skills, which normally remain high or continue to show increases with age, are especially likely to decline in older individuals who will die within the coming few years. Adults who are in the early stages of dementia but have not yet been diagnosed as suffering from the disease are often included in samples described as normal or normative. This inclusion lowers the mean of the total group and overestimates the negative association of age and intelligence (Sliwinski, Hofer, Hall, Buschke, & Lipton, 2003). At each older age, the inclusion of adults who are in an early phase of a progressive illness lowers the average performance of the group as a whole.

Neuroplasticity and Aging

Aging is normally accompanied by some decline in cognitive abilities, especially abilities that rely heavily on processing speed, working memory, and long-term memory. Cognitive capacities are impacted by a variety of changes in the brain including shrinking volume of brain structures, deterioration of white matter, and amyloid plaque deposits in the arteries and between nerve cells as well as tau tangles in the brain cells (Park & Bischof, 2013). The decline in cognitive ability can be minimal or serious enough to interfere with a person's ability to live independently. In chapter 14 we discuss Alzheimer's disease, a form of dementia that results in the extreme deterioration of cognitive capacities.

Despite these patterns of possible loss in cognitive functioning, the aging brain has continuing capacity for plasticity. A variety of mentally stimulating and challenging experiences that are carried out over time can result in increases in the number of synapses, the actual thickness or volume of brain structures, the development of new connections among neural networks, and the activation of brain areas related to new skills and abilities. The most striking evidence of this plasticity comes from experiences with patients who have had a stroke, resulting in permanent damage to a specific region of the brain. With many hours of training to develop specific skills, brain areas that are not normally involved can be recruited to take over for the damaged areas. For healthy adults, the nature of plasticity may not be as dramatic. However, there is evidence that when older adults face new tasks that place repeated demands on basic capacities like speed of response, memory, and reasoning, new neural networks may be formed, and new regions of the brain are activated.

Reserve capacity has been theorized to protect cognitive functioning in healthy adults. **Reserve capacity** refers to the idea that with age, older adults are able to maintain a high level of cognitive ability by drawing on bilateral frontal regions to accomplish tasks of working memory and episodic encoding. They use additional neural resources to achieve the same level of competence that was previously accomplished with less neural activation. Certain life experiences, especially education (including early childhood education), high levels of literacy, engagement in cognitively and socially stimulating activities, a healthy diet, and physical activity are all thought to contribute to "brain health" and the maintenance of neural reserve that supports plasticity (Baltes & Baltes, 1990; Erikson, Gildengers, & Butters, 2013; Max Planck Institute for Human Development and Stanford Center on Longevity, 2014; McDonough, Haber, Bischof, & Park, 2015).

Memory

The exact nature of changes in memory with age is a topic of active and ongoing research (Hertzog & Shing, 2011; Johnson, 2003; Lustig & Lin, 2016). A common model breaks memory into three forms: the sensory register, working member (including short-term memory), and long-term memory; and three functions: encoding, storage, and retrieval. In this model, the **sensory register** is the neurological processing activity that is required to take in visual, auditory, tactile, and olfactory information. **Encoding**, which involves attending to information, perceiving it, and catching the gist or drift of the information, begins with the sensory register. **Speed of processing** which is most closely linked to the sensory register, can be slowed as a result of illness. Illness does not seem to affect higher order aspects of memory, particularly the recall of past life events (Rosnick et al., 2004).

Once information is encoded, it has to be stored. **Working memory** has been described as comprising several different capacities (Cowan, 2008). It includes, **short-term memory**, which is the capacity to encode and store five to nine bits of information in the span of a few seconds to a minute or two. This is the scratch pad of memory that is used when someone tells you a telephone number or gives you an address. Short term memory has a limited capacity and fades rapidly.

Working memory uses attention and other executive functions to manipulate and manage information in short term memory, especially when cognitive tasks are involved. For example, you use working memory when you are looking for airline flights online. You may scan quickly through the schedule of flights to see which ones have the best departure times, number of stops, and cost. You are very briefly comparing bits of information, not intending to recall all of them, but hoping to spot one or two that will work for you.

Long-term memory is a complex network of information, concepts, and schemes related by associations, knowledge, and use. It is the storehouse of a lifetime of information. Remembering something for more than a few minutes involves moving the information from short-term to long-term memory, storing it in relation to other associated knowledge, and being able to recognize, retrieve, or reconstruct it at a later time (Hoyer & Verhaeghen, 2006).

The memory functions most relevant to understanding cognitive ability in aging have to do with the ability to transfer and store information from short-term to long-term memory and then retrieve it. Studies that compare the short-term memory abilities of older and younger adults find that age is not associated directly with the capacity of short-term memory, but with the ability to transfer newly learned information to long-term memory and then retrieve it on demand. Older adults are just as effective as younger adults in recognizing information that was learned in the past, but they have difficulty summoning up a specific name or number when they want to find it (Hertzog, Fulton, Mandviwala, & Dunlosky, 2013; Rowe & Kahn, 1998).

Furthermore, older adults find that their memory functions are especially likely to be disrupted under conditions in which information is presented rapidly and contextual cues are absent. Older adults rely on meaning to store and retrieve new information. With each passing year of life, there is more to remember. We do not really know the limits of the storage capacity of long-term memory.

Studies of memory focus on different kinds of tasks, each with its own trajectory of growth and decline. **Semantic memory** focuses on basic knowledge, such as recalling the meaning of words like *vegetable*, *democracy*, or *insect*. Once learned, semantic memory seems very resistant to loss. People continue to grow in the accumulation of new ideas and information over adulthood.

Episodic memory focuses on specific situations and data. Measures of episodic memory may ask people to recall words from a list or remember what they had for breakfast 3 days ago. In general, episodic memory declines modestly with age. With age, so many daily events and bits of information are encountered that unless the events have some particular importance, they may not be encoded, or may become difficult to retrieve in the accumulated network of memories. There are exceptions to this decline, however, depending on the type of task involved (Zelinski, 2009).

A third type of memory task is called **prospective memory**. This is memory about events or actions taking place in the future. An example would be remembering to take pills at 4 p.m. or to call a spouse when arriving at a hotel after traveling on a business trip. This type of memory task requires recalling that something needs to happen at a future time or under some future condition and also remembering specifically what needs to be done. Older adults do not do as well as young adults on prospective memory tasks in laboratory conditions. However, in naturalistic studies, the older adults do better than the young adults (Henry, MacLeod, Phillips, & Crawford, 2004). Prospective memory is a critical component of adaptive coping, and older adults use a variety of strategies to help stay attuned to their functional future.

Research using the narrative method suggests that people construct memories that make sense of their past. They tell a story about the past that puts events in a chronological sequence, highlighting events that, in retrospect, are important achievements or turning points. For example, in one study, participants were asked to provide a narrative about a time when they said, thought, or did something wise. Adolescents as well as younger and older adults were all able to retell experiences where wisdom helped them to turn a negative experience into something positive. Adults were also able to describe how the wisdom experience helped shape their outlook or life philosophy (Bluck & Gluck, 2004). Memory may be used in a new way in later adulthood in order to resolve the conflict of integrity versus despair. Memory is used to recall and evaluate certain salient life events until the role of these events can be integrated into a meaningful sense of one's purpose. This process may interfere with an adult's ability to attend to current minutiae or to rehearse and recall new information.

There is wide variability in people's memory skills (Zelinski & Lewis, 2003). Some people pay great attention to details and are more able to recall them. Others ignore many details and are not able to retrieve them. A salesman or politician may have a knack for remembering the names of friends, acquaintances, and family members. A historian may have a memory for historical events and personalities. A police detective may pay great attention to the details of the physical environment from specific cases. As the demands of work and family life accumulate, people adapt by focusing attention on the details and events that are most salient for their success. Over time, the differences in people's approaches to what they have learned, recalled, and found useful in coping with life shape the context for whether and how new information is encoded and retrieved.

In addition to actual declines in some kinds of memory performance, older adults complain of memory problems. Anxiety and frustration over memory loss nag many, even those older adults whose memory performance has not dramatically declined. However, memory complaints may reflect the person's accurate subjective assessment of a slowing in the retrieval process, or a decline in their episodic memory (Price, Hertzog, & Dunlosky, 2010). A loss of memory self-efficacy can become a hindrance to effective performance on memory tasks. Low self-efficacy regarding one's memory may lead to an avoidance of tasks that require episodic memory, such as playing certain types of games or attending social events where one is expected to recall the names of new associates.

In hopes of understanding the degree of resilience or plasticity available in the memory capacity of older adults, various training studies have been performed. Training strategies have been shown to improve the memory of older adults. However, when younger and older adults are given the same training, the younger adults benefit significantly more and show greater improvement in their memory skills than the older adults. In one study, training was found to improve performance in memory, attention, processing speed, and word recall, but after 3 months of no training, the group receiving training was no different from the control group. Thus, training was viewed as having a short term impact rather than a long term benefit (Singer, Lindenberger, & Baltes, 2003; Zelinski et al., 2011).

Solving Loosely Defined Problems

Research based on the standard Piagetian tasks has been criticized for its lack of relevance and familiarity to older participants. These tasks are dominated by the role of pure logic, disconnected from the situation. They emphasize problems that have a scientific rather than a pragmatic focus. Although the solution to most formal operational problems requires the manipulation of multiple variables, there is typically only one correct solution. In adult life, most problems involve multiple dimensions with changing or poorly defined variables and more than one solution. For example, given my limited resources, should I buy more life insurance, put cash in a certificate of deposit, or invest in the stock and bond market to best protect my family's financial future?

As a result of these limitations or criticisms of formal operational reasoning, scholars have formulated a view of **postformal thought**, which has been characterized in the following ways

(Commons & Richards, 2003; Labouvie-Vief, 1992; Sinnott & Cavanaugh, 1991).

- A greater reliance on reflection on self, emotions, values, and the specific situation in addressing a problem
- A willingness to shift gears or take a different approach depending on the specific problem
- An ability to draw on personal knowledge to find pragmatic solutions
- An awareness of the contradictions in life and a willingness to try to include conflicting or contradictory thoughts, emotions, and experiences in finding a solution
- A flexible integration of cognition and emotion so that solutions are adaptive, reality oriented, and emotionally satisfying
- An enthusiasm for seeking new questions, finding new problems, and new frameworks for understanding experience

Different types of problems require different strategies. When a problem has clear parameters and needs a single solution, concrete or formal operations may work. However, when a problem is loosely defined, value laden, ambiguous, or involves many interpersonal implications, a more flexible approach may be required. Given the complexity of adult life, adaptive problem solving requires flexibility, differentiation of positive and negative aspects of a single alternative, and the ability to consider the implications of a course of action. When older adults face a loosely defined problem, they tend to consider multiple aspects of the situation. Their solution is altered depending on the larger overall goal they are striving to achieve (Berg & Strough, 2011).

Increasingly, problem solving becomes a social task, whereby several people or groups of people work together to arrive at solutions. Older adults tend to be sensitive to the emotional impact of their solution, especially when the problem is embedded in a social situation. Older adults are likely to strive for a solution that maintains harmony and avoids conflict. They benefit from collaboration with a close or trusted colleague or partner in solving complex problems, drawing on the collective experience of their partner in identifying alternative strategies. Collaborative problem solving includes the ability to balance the interpersonal and analytical aspects of the work. Because members of groups are vulnerable to pressures toward conformity or groupthink, it is important for individuals to retain their capacity to differentiate or distance themselves from the group in order to examine the group's product in a more objective light. At the same time, when trusted and valued colleagues work together, the product may become a more creative, innovative solution than any single individual may have been able to produce alone (Martin & Wight, 2008).

Patterns of Change in Different Mental Abilities

How readily can older adults improve their skills or learn new skills? This question seems to produce two different kinds of answers (Kühn & Lindenberger, 2016). One line of research finds evidence of DNA damage in the human brain with reduced capacity for repair beginning after about age 40. Damage of this kind has negative consequences for plasticity leading to declines

Diplomacy is an example of advanced problem solving that requires interpersonal skills, collaboration, and an awareness of the rules and conditions impacting the political constraints on the partners.

in learning and memory. Certain brain areas are more vulnerable to the accumulated stressors of aging than others, and certain individuals are more vulnerable to the neurological diseases of aging than others (Erraji-Benchekroun et al., 2005; Lu et al., 2004; Mattson & Magnus, 2006).

In contrast, other researchers find that among people in their 60s and 70s, continuing improvement in performance is possible through training and practice. According to this view, much of the decline in cognitive performance is a result of limited educational opportunities and disuse. Following training, improvement has been observed in tasks involving memory, reasoning, perceptual-motor speed, and visual attention, as well as specific areas of expertise (Krampe & Charness, 2006; Yang, Krampe, & Baltes, 2006). In one longitudinal study, cognitive interventions resulted in a long-term benefit lasting from 7 to 14 years after the training (Schaie & Willis, 2010). One possible way to reconcile these opposing observations is to consider how different types of mental abilities might change with age.

John Horn (1979) proposed that the course of mental abilities across the life span is not uniform. Some areas are strengthened, and others decline. Horn suggested differentiating **crystallized intelligence** (*Gc*) and **fluid intelligence** (*Gf*). *Gc* is the ability to bring knowledge accumulated through past learning into play in appropriate situations. *Gf* is the ability to impose organization on information and generate new hypotheses. Both kinds of intelligence are required for optimal human functioning.

Gc and *Gf* can be identified as integrated structures in both early and later adulthood (McArdle, Ferrer-Caja, Hamagami, &

Woodcock, 2002). However, Horn argued that these two kinds of thinking draw on different neurological and experiential sources. *Gc* reflects the consequences of life experiences within a society. Socialization in the family; exposure to the media; and participation in school, work, and community settings all emphasize the use and improvement of *Gc*. *Gc* increases with age, experience, and physical maturation, and remains at a high level of functioning throughout adulthood.

Gf is characteristic of what is meant by someone having common sense. Finding a general relationship and applying it without having been schooled in that problem-solving area is an example of *Gf*, as is being able to approach new problems logically, systematically, and quickly. Horn hypothesized that *Gf* depends more on the specific number of neurons available for its functioning than does *Gc*. Thus, neurological loss would be more damaging to *Gf* than to *Gc*. Neural efficiency, often recognized through changes in sensory functioning and speed of response, is closely related to fluid intelligence and shows an age-related decline, independent of disease (Baltes & Lindenberger, 1997). However, the extent of this decline may be related to the domain in which it is studied. For example, one study focused on men who had different levels of expertise in playing the game of Go. Measures of reasoning, memory, and cognitive speed were developed to apply specifically to that game. Older players generally showed the expected decline in deductive reasoning and cognitive speed. However, for those older men who were very expert players, no decline was observed (Masunaga & Horn, 2000). The implication is that in areas where there is highly developed expertise, aging is not necessarily accompanied by declines in either *Gf* or *Gc*.

In an analysis of the pattern of cognitive abilities across the life span, Tucker-Drob (2009) gathered data from a nationally representative sample of over 6,000 individuals from ages 4 to 101. He compared high and low scoring individuals at different ages to address two basic questions: (1) How do various abilities change with age? (2) Do abilities cluster together (e.g., people who are good at visual-spatial thinking are also good at short-term memory), or is there differentiation among abilities with age (people can be very good in one area, and average or not so strong in another)? Seven areas of cognitive ability were measured: comprehension knowledge (similar to *Gc*), fluid reasoning (*Gf*), visual-spatial thinking (e.g., identifying the pieces needed to complete a pattern), processing speed (e.g., quickly identifying two identical numbers in a row of numbers), short-term memory (e.g., repeating a list of unrelated words), long-term retrieval (e.g., naming as many examples as possible from a specific category of places or objects), and auditory processing (e.g., identifying a word when it is presented against a competing background of distracting sounds).

As illustrated in FIGURE 13.3 ▶, all the abilities with the exception of *Gc* increased in childhood and adolescence, peaked in later adolescence and early adulthood, and then declined through adulthood and aging. In contrast, crystallized intelligence continued to increase throughout adulthood, until about age 60, and then declined slightly into later life. Among those of higher general intelligence, there was less commonality in the scores across the various cognitive abilities suggesting that with greater intelligence comes a greater capacity to express certain abilities to a

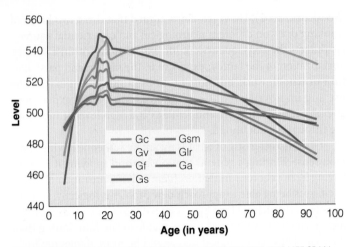

FIGURE 13.3 ▶ CHANGES IN COGNITIVE ABILITIES OVER THE LIFE SPAN

Source: Tucker-Drob, 2009, Figure 5, Page 1107.

Legend: *Gc* = comprehension knowledge; *Gv* = visual spatial thinking; *Gf* = fluid reasoning; *Gs* = processing speed; *Gsm* = short term memory; *Glr* = long-term retrieval; *Ga* = auditory processing.

uniquely high level. Over the life span, the abilities were more differentiated; that is, people in middle adulthood and later life showed more variability in their cognitive capacities than did younger children and adolescents.

The Interaction of Heredity and Environment on Mental Functioning

For years, it was assumed that the environment played an increasingly major role in intellectual functioning over time. The accumulation of life experiences, education, and socialization were expected to introduce new bases of knowledge and problem-solving structures. Recent work suggests that the construct of the norm of reaction, introduced in chapter 4 (The Period of Pregnancy and Prenatal Development), provides a more appropriate framework for understanding intelligence in adulthood. Genetic factors, early childhood family environment, and contemporary work and family environments all contribute to adult cognitive functioning (Reynolds & Finkel, 2016).

Research on identical and fraternal twins who were 80 years old or older found that the heritability of general cognitive ability was about 60 percent (McClearn et al., 1997). In other words, genetic factors substantially contribute to the stability of cognitive capacities over the life span. Hereditary factors related to health also impact cognitive functioning. For example, genetic factors that contribute to longevity are associated with resistance to disease and greater vitality in late life. Likewise, hereditary factors associated with diseases that have a late-life onset such as Parkinson's or Alzheimer's disease contribute to changes in cognitive functioning with age (Wilcox, Wilcox, Hsueh, & Suzuki, 2006).

Evidence also supports the increasing role of the environment on cognitive functioning in late life. Long-term exposure to environmental toxins, poor nutrition, or social isolation can impair optimal cognitive abilities. The stimulating or stifling nature of the environment—including access to social support, the quality of health care, exposure to disease, and opportunities for continuing involvement in challenging work—transforms the

genotype into an observed phenotype (Baird & Bergeman, 2011; Gottesman, 1997; Shanahan & Hofer, 2005).

The noted learning theorist B. F. Skinner (1983) described some possible environmental qualities that fail to reinforce systematic thinking or new ideas in aging people. Many people who live alone, for example, lack the diversity of social interaction that produces cognitive discrepancy and new concepts. Older people may be reinforced for talking about the past. Their recollections of early memories are interesting to students and younger colleagues. However, preoccupation with these reminiscences does not encourage thinking in new directions.

Skinner claimed that one is more likely to repeat oneself as one ages. It may be important for older adults to move into new areas of work in order to prevent the repetition of old ideas. Skinner believed that it is possible to analyze how the quality of one's thinking is influenced by the circumstances of aging and to identify interventions that will prevent the deterioration of cognitive abilities. These interventions include attempts to be sensitive to the signs of fatigue, planning for regular opportunities for stimulating verbal interactions with others, making careful outlines of written work to avoid distraction, and acting on ideas as they come to one's mind rather than counting on remembering them later.

In summary, cognitive functioning in later adulthood is multidimensional, with substantial differences among individuals as well as differences among cognitive domains within the same person (McArdle et al., 2002). Within these domains, many complex networks of information, strategies, and frameworks of meaning are elaborated that may result in high-level, flexible functioning. The overall level of functioning is subject to environmental influences that promote particular specialization and cognitive organization based on the demands of the situation, the stresses and challenges of daily life, and the opportunities for mastery in particular areas of competence. At the same time, certain aspects of the processing base that are dependent on neural functioning may decline with age. This decline, however, is not always great, and capacities described as elements of fluid intelligence, such as speed of response, inductive reasoning, and spatial orientation, can benefit from targeted interventions (Saczynski, Willis, & Schaie, 2002; Yu, Ryan, Schaie, Willis, & Kolanowski, 2009). As the baby boomers have entered the stage of later adulthood, their desire to maintain intellectual vigor and to hold at bay the risks of cognitive decline have made them a ready market for a burgeoning computer-based brain game industry. The **Applying Theory and Research** box reviews the opinions of scientists regarding the effectiveness of these games for enhancing intelligence among older adults.

On the basis of extensive longitudinal research, the following factors have been identified as effective for retaining a high level of cognitive functioning in later adulthood:

1. Absence of cardiovascular and other chronic diseases
2. Favorable environment linked to high socioeconomic status
3. Involvement in a complex and intellectually stimulating environment

Can Computer "Brain Games" Prevent or Reverse Cognitive Decline Associated with Aging?

Two seemingly opposing processes are at work in relation to cognition and aging. First, there is evidence of decline in certain capacities, especially those related to fluid intelligence, including speed of processing, working memory, auditory processing, and short-term memory. Second, there is evidence of plasticity with aging, especially when adults engage in activities that place a repeated and significant demand on their cognitive abilities. In the face of these facts, a growing industry has emerged to produce and market computer-based cognitive training software, sometimes called "brain games." Advertisers often claim that playing the games will increase alertness, allow one to learn faster, increase intelligence, and improve memory. What does the scientific community of cognitive psychologists and neuroscientists make of these claims? Does the research evidence support these claims?

The Stanford Center on Longevity and the Max Planck Institute on Human Development invited a large group of scientists to evaluate the existing research and offer a consensus report to the public. Some studies show that practicing certain skills results in improvement, including improvement in other cognitive tasks. Some studies find long lasting improvements, whereas others find that improvements fade in a few months. When there are improvements in performance, it is difficult to determine whether the gains are due to changes in strategies the player uses to manage the challenges of the game or to changes in brain plasticity at the neural level, such as increases in the number of synapses, activation of neural regions, or changes in the connections among neural networks (Park & Bischof, 2013).

Overall, the consensus is that the existing scientific evidence does not support claims that playing brain games improves "underlying broad cognitive abilities or that it enables one to better navigate a complex realm of everyday life" (Stanford Center on Longevity and the Max Planck Institute on Human Development, 2014). Claims that brain games can reduce or reverse the effects of cognitive decline associated with aging are not supported by scientific evidence. Their report provides the following recommendations/conclusions:

1. No studies have demonstrated that playing computer-based games cures or prevents Alzheimer's disease or other forms of dementia.
2. Before the benefits of these games can be accepted, research findings need to be replicated in different laboratories with different investigators. Studies need to demonstrate advantages of playing the computer games in comparison to appropriate control groups that do not play the games but are treated in a similar way.

3. The limited evidence does not support the transfer of gains in a particular skill, even if the gains endure, to other more global cognitive abilities or capacities for functioning in daily life.
4. Researchers need to consider the relative benefits of playing computer brain games against the benefits of other activities a person might be doing. Currently the known benefits of engaging in socially complex, physically and intellectually challenging activities on brain health and plasticity have not been systematically compared to the benefits of spending a similar amount of time playing brain games.
5. The known benefits of physical exercise for general health and brain health include increased blood flow to the brain and associated improvements in attention, reasoning, some aspects of memory, and well-being. The cognitive benefits of sitting in front of the computer playing brain games versus engaging in physical activity that increases blood flow have not been assessed.

Critical Thinking Questions

1. How would you design a study to test the hypothesis that playing "brain games" has a benefit for neural plasticity above and beyond improvements in strategy?
2. Which cognitive abilities do you think might benefit most from playing computer brain games? Why?
3. Talk to some people in later adulthood about their concerns regarding cognitive decline. Analyze how brain games are marketed to appeal to people with these concerns.
4. Do you play brain games? What do you like about them? What makes them fun? If you have never played them, try one or two just for the experience. What is your assessment? Would you pay money to keep playing? Why or why not?

Source: Boston Globe, Michael Fitzgerald, Do brain games work? October 9, 2014. Retrieved from the internet on September 18, 2016 at https://www.bostonglobe.com/magazine/2014/10/09/brain-games-work/rXjTWOKUYK5UOiNQ6St0fN/story.html

4. A strong sense of control over one's work
5. Flexible personality style at midlife
6. High cognitive functioning of spouse
7. Maintenance of a high level of perceptual processing speed
8. Rating oneself as being satisfied with life accomplishments in midlife

This list illustrates the interplay of the biological, psychological, and social systems that contribute to cognitive functioning in the later years (Schaie, 1994; Schaie & Willis, 2010). Retaining one's intellectual vigor and problem-solving abilities is closely linked to the ability to cope with the inevitable role transitions that occur in later life.

FURTHER REFLECTION: *Summarize the aspects of intellectual functioning that are most vulnerable to the effects of aging. What are some strategies that individuals can use to preserve and/or promote intellectual vigor?*

Explain some ways that the social environment, including immediate family, friends, and community resources, may influence cognitive functioning in later life.

Redirecting Energy to New Roles and Activities

OBJECTIVE 3 Explain the process of redirecting energy to new roles and activities, with special focus on role gain, such as grandparenthood; role loss, such as widowhood; and new opportunities for leisure.

Role transition, role gain, and role loss occur in each life stage. In later adulthood, however, a convergence of role transitions is likely to lead to a revision of major life functions and a reformulation of one's lifestyle. Roles are lost through widowhood, retirement, and the death of friends. At the same time, new roles, such as grandparent, senior adviser, or community leader, require the formation of new patterns of behavior and relationships. In the following sections, we focus on three specific role transitions: grandparenthood, widowhood, and leisure roles.

Grandparenthood

Grandparenthood provides opportunities for psychosocial growth, both for individuals and for grandparent couples (Taubman-Ben-Ari, Findler, Ben Shlomo, 2013). Becoming a grandmother or grandfather brings a psychological transformation as well as a change in the family system. With the birth of a first grandchild, an adult may begin to reflect on one's own life phases of childhood, parenthood, and **grandparenthood**, revisiting earlier personal and interpersonal themes, and possibly revising earlier understandings of the parent–child relationship. Depending on one's level of engagement in the grandparent role, grandparenthood may require a renewal of parenting skills that have been stored away along with the bottles, bibs, and potty chairs. Grandparents begin to rekindle

their acquaintance with the delights of childhood, including diapering the baby, telling fairy tales, taking trips to the zoo, or having the pleasure of small helping hands with baking, gardening, or carpentry. A person's parenting skills, patience, and knowledge come into play in a new configuration and may be more in demand in the grandparent role than they were in the parent role.

Grandparenting Styles. Grandparenthood involves a three-generational family system. The average age for becoming a grandparent is in the decade of the 50s, resulting in the potential of a 20- to 30-year relationship with one's grandchildren. The enactment of the grandparent role depends on the timing of entry into this role and on the outlook or interest of each generation in having interactions and access to one another. The quality of the grandparent–grandchild relationship is negotiated through the adult child and is likely to change as the grandchildren mature (Giarrusso, Silverstein, & Bengston, 1996; Smith & Drew, 2002).

Certain common factors appear to predict feelings of closeness between grandchildren and their grandparents. These include frequent contact, grandparents' educational level, younger age of the grandparent, and general health. Maternal grandmothers tend to be more involved in their grandchildren's lives than other grandparents (Danielsbacka & Tanskanen, 2012; Hakoyama & MaloneBeach, 2013).

People differ in the way they enact the grandparent role. In one of the first empirical studies of grandparenthood, Neugarten and Weinstein (1964) interviewed grandparents in 70 middle-class families. Five grandparenting styles were identified, each expressing a distinct interpretation of the role:

1. *Formal.* Grandparents were interested in the grandchildren but careful not to become involved in parenting them other than by occasional babysitting.
2. *Fun seeker.* Grandparents had informal, playful interactions with the grandchildren, enjoying mutually self-indulgent fun with them.
3. *Surrogate parent.* This style was especially likely for grandmothers who assumed major child care responsibilities when the mother worked outside the home.
4. *Reservoir of family wisdom.* This style was an authoritarian relationship in which a grandparent, usually the grandfather, dispensed skills and resources. Parents as well as grandchildren were subordinate to this older authority figure.
5. *Distant figure.* Grandparents appeared on birthdays and holidays but generally had little contact with the grandchildren.

More than 35 years later, Bengston (2001) offered a revised picture of the nature of multigenerational family bonds based on the Longitudinal Study of Generations (LSOG), begun in 1971, and continuing with data collection every 3 years. This study of more than 2,000 members of three-generational families, provided the assessment of relationship characteristics between parents and their adult children, adult children and their children, and grandparents and grandchildren. The study found that the way a person enacts the grandparent role is not only a product of a personal definition of the role, but also a result of how the interconnected family members permit and support intergenerational interactions.

The LSOG identified five aspects of **intergenerational solidarity**—a construct that reflects closeness and commitment within the parent–child and grandparent–grandchild relationships.

1. *Affectional solidarity*: Feelings of affection and emotional closeness
2. *Associational solidarity*: Type and frequency of contact
3. *Consensual solidarity*: Agreement in opinions and expectations
4. *Functional solidarity*: Giving and receiving emotional and instrumental support
5. *Structural solidarity*: Geographic proximity that would allow for interaction

Based on these dimensions, five intergenerational family types were identified, which closely resemble the grandparenting roles characterized by Neugarten and Weinstein. The *tight-knit* families were emotionally close, lived near one another, interacted often, and both gave and received help. The *sociable* families were emotionally close and had frequent contact but did not offer much functional help. The *intimate but distant* families had high levels of agreement and felt emotionally close but did not interact often, lived far apart, and offered little functional help. The *obligatory* families lived near one another and had frequent contact but were not emotionally close and did not share much in the way of common opinions or expectations. Finally, the *detached* families had low levels of all measures of solidarity.

Looking at the adult children's views of their parents, the sample was divided rather evenly across the five groups. Tight-knit and sociable families were each about 25 percent of the sample, obligatory and intimate but distant families were each about 16 percent, and detached families were about 17 percent. When ethnic groups were compared, European Americans were more likely than African Americans or Hispanic Americans to describe their relationship with their mother as obligatory or detached. Cultural dimensions including the emphasis on filial obligation, immigration or acculturation status, and the symbolic meaning of linkages to one's ancestry all influence the emphasis that various cultures place on the grandparent role (Ikels, 1998). Some cultural differences observed in the enactment of the grandparent role are described in the **Human Development and Diversity** box Intergenerational Relationships in Various Ethnic Groups.

Two important ideas emerge from these descriptions. First, contemporary U.S. families are characterized by a variety of intergenerational relationships. No single type is normative. Second, about two thirds of these relationships can be characterized as showing high levels of affectional and consensual solidarity. This has been observed in repeated measurements between 1971 and 1997. Thus, despite many changes in family characteristics, including decreased family size, increased

involvement of mothers in the labor force, parental divorce, and increasing educational attainment of the parent generation, sentiments of intergenerational closeness are strong. This implies an important stabilizing role for the grandparent generation—a role that may become increasingly important for the large number of children growing up in single-parent and dual-earner parent families.

The Meaning of the Grandparent Role.

Grandparenthood has a variety of personal meanings that contribute to the grandparent's overall sense of purpose and worth (Gattai & Musatti, 1999; Kivnick, 1988; Scraton & Holland, 2006). Grandchildren symbolize an extension of personal influence that will most assuredly persist well beyond the grandparent's death. To this extent, grandchildren may help older adults feel more comfortable about their own death. Grandchildren offer concrete evidence that some thread of their lives will persist into the future, giving a dimension of immortality to themselves and the family ancestry that they represent.

Active grandparenting may promote a process of life review, stimulating a revisitation of one's own parenting role and possibly supporting the achievement of a psychosocial sense of integrity. In an interview study, grandsons shared the ways that their grandfathers helped them make meaning of fatherhood. In these conversations, themes included consciousness of the family's lineage, a sense of who they are and what they do as fathers, ideas about multigenerational family bonds, and intergenerational and intragenerational improvement (Bates & Goodsell, 2013). In all of these ways, grandparents transmit their generative concern.

In an analysis of the sources of vitality in later life, Erikson, Erikson, and Kivnick (1986) found that relationships with grandchildren played the following critical role:

> The major involvement that uniformly makes life worth living is the thought of and participation in their relationships with children and grandchildren. Their pride in their own achievement in having brought up their young, through thick and thin, and their satisfaction in the way these young have developed gives them, for the most part, deep gratification. With the arrival of grandchildren, they may identify themselves as ancestors, graduated to venerability. Listen to their voices as they trace their own ancestry and that of their children's traits: "She has her mother's fire, that first girl of ours. She has more energy and more projects than anyone. Come to think of it, my mother had that fire, too. And my wife's two grandmothers." "My son is a perfectionist, like me." "The kids are innately smart, like their father." (p. 326)

Grandchildren also stimulate older adults' thoughts about time, the changing of cultural norms across generations, and the patterning of history. In relating to their grandchildren as they grow up, grandparents discover elements of the culture that remain stable. Some familiar stories and songs retain their appeal

Intergenerational Relationships in Various Ethnic Groups

Grandparents play a variety of roles in U.S. families from remote and minimally involved to actively engaged. A cross-cultural perspective highlights the qualitatively different ways that grandparents are viewed in ethnic groups that emerge from a more collectivist orientation, and the central role that grandparents play in the socialization process and family support systems. Although the majority of U.S. families do not have three generations living together in one household, the presence of grandparents living with their grandchildren is more than twice as likely in African American, Asian American, and Hispanic American families than in European American families. This may, in part, be a result of the financial pressures on ethnic families, but it is also a result of a more collectivist outlook in which family and kinship relationships are central to the value system and priorities of many ethnic groups.

In an interview study of African Americans, Latin Americans, Filipino Americans, and Cambodian Americans, older adults (ages 50 and up) described the importance of mutual assistance and its critical role in fostering a sense of continuity across the generations. This can be especially important for immigrant families. Older adults provide care, guidance, and instrumental assistance for families, especially when there are young children in the home and the parents have to work (Becker et al., 2003). Immigrant families from collectivist cultures express a strong sense of family obligation, which has an intergenerational pull. Children and adolescents strive to respect and please their adult family members, and aging adults offer instrumental support, guidance, and affection to their children and grandchildren (Merz, Ozeke-Kocabaas, Oort, & Schuengel, 2009).

In many ethnic groups, the grandparent generation is highly revered. In others, the intimacy of the family's daily concerns extends to grandparents, aunts and uncles, and

other kin (Burnett, 1999; Lockery, 1991). The following brief descriptions suggest the outlook of four U.S. ethnic groups on intergenerational relations. Each has a slightly different flavor.

African Americans value strong kinship bonds and a supportive extended family system. Caregiving responsibilities are shared among kin and non-kin as needed. Grandparents tend to support working parents by providing care to young children and are cared for in return. Their active role in the family often contributes a strong moral and religious strength and provides emotional support to the parent generation that reduces stress in the household (Pellebon, 2012).

Chinese Americans place a strong value on bringing honor to the family. Filial piety is one of the highest values, evidenced in a great sense of obligation, respect, and responsibility for parents. Contemporary Chinese American adolescents place a great deal of importance on treating their elders with respect, and spend more time assisting and being with their parents and grandparents than their Anglo age-mates (Wong, 2012).

Japanese American families value and promote a high degree of interdependence. The Japanese children feel a strong motivation to seek their parents' approval for their own self-esteem, and Japanese parents' sense of well-being depends heavily on their children's achievements. The intergenerational transmission of this mutual interdependence results in a deep sense of obligation for the care of aging parents. Retired parents may live with their adult child who takes on the leadership role for the family (Sakamoto, Kim, & Takei, 2012).

Puerto Rican and many other Latino cultures embrace the value of familialism, a sense of closeness and interdependence among members of the nuclear and extended family, which includes a deep respect for elders. Family members serve many functions, including socialization, protection, companionship, social and business contacts, and economic support. Puerto Rican families create a formal intergenerational link through the role of the *compadrazgo*, or godparent, who has

Chinese American families continue to feel closeness across generations. These family members obviously have a strong sense of affection for one another as they enjoy a relaxing day in the park.

a responsibility for the child's well-being through life (Negroni, 2012).

Critical Thinking Questions

1. If you have a living grandparent, describe your relationship. Summarize the impact that your grandparents had on your development at different stages. How has your ethnic or religious group shaped the way you view your aging family members and the quality of your relationship with them?

2. Summarize the idea of different styles of grandparenting. How do you think your grandparents conceptualize their role? Talk to them about the kind of grandparent they are and how they would like to be. How does their sense of themselves compare with how you think of them in their grandparent role? What are the implications of the similarities and differences in these conceptualizations?

3. For each American ethnic group discussed above, consider some likely tensions between the grandparent and the grandchild generation. Speculate about problems that might arise if the adult children and the grandchildren identify with American individualistic values and grandparents identify with more collectivist values.

4. Imagine yourself as a grandparent. Based on the information presented in the chapter, what kind of grandparent would you like to be? Why? How do you think having a grandchild would influence your psychosocial development?

from generation to generation. Certain toys, games, and preoccupations of children of the current generation are remembered by grandparents from their own childhood. Grandparents may become aware of changes in the culture that are reflected in new childrearing practices; new equipment, toys, games, and forms of entertainment; and new expectations for children's behavior at each life stage.

For example, when grandmothers were interviewed about their experiences of breastfeeding, it became clear that though many women wanted to be helpful to their adult daughters, they came from a generation where breastfeeding was not typically practiced. Some women had very negative memories of how their own mothers and grandmothers viewed breastfeeding as vulgar, unsanitary, or lower class. Others recalled resisting the negative pressure and going ahead with breastfeeding. These personal experiences were very salient as they tried to support and encourage their own daughters in an era when breastfeeding was much more highly valued (Grassley & Eschiti, 2011).

By maintaining communication with their grandchildren, older adults keep abreast of the continuities and changes in their culture that are reflected in the experiences of childhood. Through their grandchildren, adults avoid a sense of alienation from the contemporary world. The more involved grandparents are in the daily care and routines of their grandchildren, the more central they become to a child's sense of security and well-being. This kind of importance is a benefit not only to the child, but also to the older adult's assessment of personal worth. Over time, the grandparent–grandchild relationship has the potential for becoming increasingly meaningful as grandchildren mature into adulthood. This relationship, typically sustained through mutual personal choice, combines love, respect, mutual support, and a unique form of shared as well as diverging history (Crosnoe & Elder, 2002a; Kemp, 2005).

Some adults interpret the role of grandparent as an opportunity to pass on to their grandchildren the wisdom and cultural heritage of their ancestry. Through interactions with their grandchildren, grandparents can transmit cultural values, providing insights that they hope will guide and protect future generations and preserve something of the cultural heritage that they treasure from their own past (Quéniart & Charpentier, 2013; Thompson, Cameron, & Fuller-Thompson, 2013). In the process of fulfilling this role, older adults communicate the meaning of their life experiences to their grandchildren. Grandparents select many avenues to educate their grandchildren, influencing their thoughts and fantasies. Storytelling, special trips, long walks, attending religious services, and working on special projects are all activities that allow grandparents moments of intimacy with their grandchildren. Educating one's grandchildren involves a deep sense of investment in experiences and ideals that one believes to be central to a fruitful life.

In a variety of ways, the transition into grandparenthood can serve as an opportunity for personal growth. Through interactions with grandchildren, older adults have the opportunity to reflect upon and understand their place in the chain of generations, to gain new insights into their own character, and to expand their capacity for love and affection.

> The transition to grandparenthood enabled me to come to terms with my parenting and maybe to give myself another chance to give, influence and be an important figure in my grandchildren's lives. (first time grandmother) (Taubman Ben-Ari, 2012)

Grandparent Caregivers. Roughly 10 percent of U.S. children under the age of 18 live in households with at least one grandparent present. In comparison to other ethnic groups, African American and Asian American children are more likely than Anglo or Latino children to be living in households with one or both grandparents. For about one third of these children, their parents are the primary householders and one or more grandparents live

Jakob invited his grandmother to come to school with him. First she read a story to the class; then Jakob read one. Reading aloud is one of the things they have enjoyed doing together ever since Jakob was small.

Courtesy of Barbara Newman

at home with them (Ellis & Simmons, 2014). These grandparents are likely benefiting from some type of support or care from their adult children. They may also provide direct and indirect support for their grandchildren, including being home when the children return from school, taking care of the children when they are ill and the parents have to work, and taking over household tasks so that parents and children can have time together.

In the other two thirds of this group, the grandparents are the householders, suggesting that many grandparents are using their resources to help support their adult children and grandchildren. About 1.5 million children live with their grandparents with no parents in the household. These children are more likely to be living in poverty, without health insurance, and receiving some type of public assistance than are children who live in their grandparents' household with their own parents present (Ellis & Simmons, 2014). Among grandparents who have custody of their grandchildren, an estimated 40 percent cared for their grandchildren for 5 years or more (Abel, 2010). This is a long-term commitment when the adult children are unable to parent.

Many grandparents play an important role in supporting the development of their grandchildren during times of family stress (Goodman, 2003; Mills, Gomez-Smith, & DeLeon, 2005; Villar, Celdrán, & Triadó, 2012). In contemporary American society, grandparents are a potential resource that can becalled into active duty when certain difficulties arise for parents. In cases of parental divorce, grandparents often assume a central role in the lives of young children. Some custodial mothers move back home with their parents. Grandparents often assume more child care responsibilities during this time.

Grandparents also play a key role when their young, unmarried daughters become pregnant. The pattern of unmarried teen mothers living with parents is especially common in African American families (Minkler & Fuller-Thomson, 2005). Among young adult African American parents, the grandmother is most often viewed as the person to count on for child care assistance, advice, and emotional support (Hunter, 1997). These grandmothers may be young themselves, just entering middle adulthood, when they assume the grandparent role. The presence of grandmothers appears to affect the family atmosphere as well as the childrearing environment. Having a grandmother in the home allows the mother to be more flexible in managing daily demands, thereby reducing much of the stress that characterizes single-parent families.

Maternal employment is another condition in which grandparents are likely to give direct support. Increasingly, parents of young children call on grandparents to provide all or part of daily child care (Brandon, 2000; Goodfellow & Laverty, 2003). These grandparents are intimately involved in the lives of their grandchildren, directing significant energy, talent, and time to this role. For more information on resources for grandparents who are raising their grandchildren, visit the government website USA.gov, and search for the topic "grandparents raising their grandchildren." Resources differ by state.

Grandparents who take on primary responsibility for their grandchildren face challenges as well as experiencing satisfactions in this off-time role. Grandparents who are raising their grandchildren are likely to have fewer financial resources than other families. Many grandparents are working as well as caring for their children. They may have to support their grandchildren with little access to social and financial services that would be available to other low-income families or foster families because they do not have legal guardianship of their grandchildren.

Increasingly, more grandparents fall into the involved category, taking on parenting responsibilities for their grandchildren on a daily basis.

Michael Newman/PhotoEdit

Depending on their age and their own health, grandparent caregivers may feel they have less energy and that they are less effective when it comes to discipline strategies. In some instances, they face conflicts and ambiguities in the relationship with their adult children that create a negative interpersonal environment (Barnett, Mills-Koonce, Gustafsson, & Cox, 2012). Caregiver stress is associated with poverty, absence of social services or financial support for child care, loss of freedom, and lack of involvement with friends and interests outside their family circle. When the grandchildren have been exposed to chaotic or neglectful parenting, they may have physical and mental health problems that place additional strain on grandparent caregivers (Dunifon, 2013; Longoria, 2010).

In contrast to these stressors, grandparent caregivers may perceive that they are expressing their generative motives in caring for their grandchildren. They are in a unique position to form a close emotional bond with their grandchildren, helping their grandchildren to cope during periods of family disruption and preserving kinship and community ties (Bullock, 2005; Dolbin-MacNab & Keiley, 2006; Landry-Meyer, Gerard, & Guzell, 2005; Minkler & Fuller-Thomson, 2005).

Bill and Sharon Hicks were interviewed about raising their granddaughter, Brittany:

> "It has not been easy. Sometimes we feel a little bitter because our anticipated freedom has been taken away." But when asked if he and his wife would open their home to Brittany again, he answered: "Positively, yes! Brittany has been a shining light in our lives. She has forced us to stay young at heart. And that's not such a bad thing to happen." (Abel, 2010)

Loss of Grandparent–Grandchild Contact. In contrast to the picture of an increasing role for grandparents in caring for their grandchildren, a growing number of grandparents are losing contact with their grandchildren as a result of parental divorce, conflict between the parents, death of an adult child, or adoption of a grandchild after remarriage. Disruption in the grandparent–grandchild relationship is especially likely when the grandparent's adult child is not named as the custodial parent after a divorce. In the 1980s, most states created statutes allowing grandparents to file for a legal right to enforced visitation with their grandchildren, even over parental objections. The laws differ from state to state, establishing different conditions under which grandparents may be granted visitation. In 1998, a law was passed to ensure that grandparents who have visitation rights in one state may visit their grandchildren in any state. However, in some states, earlier visitation laws have been overturned, finding that they interfere with parental rights regarding the rearing of their children. States vary in the possibility for legal recourse if grandparents are denied visitation with their grandchildren.

> In states that do allow grandparents to petition for visitation, the standard for determining whether or not visitation is awarded varies. Some states ask grandparents to prove that it is in the "best interest of the child" to have a relationship with them. Other states require grandparents to prove it will "harm" the child if they do not have a relationship. Proving harm is much harder

than proving that it is in the best interest of the child to see grandparents. Unfortunately, there are also states that don't allow grandparents to petition the court for visitation with grandchildren under any circumstances. While some grandparents do obtain court-ordered visitation arrangements with their grandchildren, most do not. (Goyer 2009)

For more information about grandparent visitation rights, visit the website of the Foundation for Grandparenting (www.grandparenting.org/) or AARP (aarp.org) on grandparents' visitation rights.

Widowhood

Among those ages 65 to 74, 6.8 percent of men and 20 percent of women describe their marital status as widowed; by the ages 75 to 84 these rates increase to 15.6 percent for men and 43 percent for women (U.S. Census Bureau, 2015f, Table A1). For many adults, the psychosocial consequences of **widowhood** include intense emotional grief, loss of social and emotional support, and loss of material and instrumental support. Emotions of depression, anger, shock, and overall grief as well as yearning for the deceased partner are observed 6 and 18 months after the loss (Carr, House, Wortman, Neese, & Kessler, 2001). The nature and intensity of emotional reactions to this loss will vary depending on how much the partners relied on one another for instrumental and emotional support, and on the quality of their marital relationship prior to the death of one partner. Most older widowers remarry, whereas the majority of widows remain unmarried and live alone.

Widows. Widows must learn to function socially and in their own households without the presence of a marriage partner. Adaptation to this role requires resilience, creative problem solving, and a strong belief in one's personal worth. A woman who is widowed at age 60 can expect more than 20 years of life in which to create a new, single head-of-household lifestyle.

In addition to bereavement, a number of stressors challenge the coping resources of widows. Studies of economic changes among widows show that many experience increased expenses just prior to widowhood, as well as decreases in their financial resources for years following widowhood (Fan & Zick, 2006; Gillen & Kim, 2009). Women who have never participated in the labor market during their married years may have no marketable skills and feel insecure about entering the labor force. They may be uninformed or uneasy about using social service agencies to meet their needs. For most women, the loss of their husband is most keenly felt as a loss of emotional support, as expressed in the following quote. "He is most apt to be mentioned as the person the widow most enjoyed being with, who made her feel important and secure" (Lopata, 1978, p. 221). The transition to widowhood may be especially difficult for those who have been caring for an ill partner, hoping for recovery yet observing constant decline (Bass & Bowman, 1990).

Despite the pain and grief that accompany widowhood, most women cope with it successfully. In a study of women ages 60 through 98 who had recently become widows, there was a high degree of self-sufficiency (O'Bryant & Morgan, 1990). The majority said they performed a variety of daily tasks, including transportation, housekeeping, shopping, preparing meals, personal care and hygiene, financial and other decisions, and providing financial support, without help from others. More than 30 percent said they managed their own home repairs, yard work, and legal questions without help. From this study, a picture emerges of older, widowed women functioning at a high level of independence and autonomy yet benefiting from assistance from others, especially their children, in specific domains, depending on where help is needed.

Research from other national samples in the United States, Australia, and Hong Kong confirm this picture. Resilience, which may be expressed in a variety of ways, including recovery of positive mood, engaging in new activities, or experiencing new levels of efficacy, are commonly observed in the months and years following widowhood. Women report that widowhood is a very difficult negative life event, but that after a period of bereavement they find themselves making a shift to a new, positive phase of adult life in which they both receive and provide social support to others (Cheng & Chan, 2006; Dolbin-MacNab & Keiley, 2006; Dutton Zisook, 2005; Feldman, Byles, & Beaumont, 2000; Ha, Carr, Utz, & Nesse, 2006).

Widows are likely to find support from their siblings, children, and friends. Over time, a widow's siblings, especially her sisters, may become a key source of emotional support and direct, instrumental assistance with home repairs and shopping. In an exploratory analysis of the responses of widows in a support-group discussion, comments about the positive and negative contributions of their social support network were analyzed (Morgan, 1989). The widows described their non-family, reciprocal friendship relationships as somewhat more positive than their family relationships. In many cases, widows found that as a result of their own sense of family obligation, they were drawn into negative events occurring in their families, especially divorce, illness, and the death of other family members. These negative events added to their distress and prevented them from receiving the support they felt they needed at the time of their own loss.

The analysis also concluded that the most positive form of immediate support from family, especially children, was a willingness to accept the widow's feelings of grief and to talk openly about their father. Social support from friends included a similar willingness to allow the widow to take her time in finding a new identity. These women did not want to be forced to mourn too quickly or be told how strong they were and how well they were handling their grief: "The fact that you're using the strength that you have, just to cope, and to stay alive (another voice: "to survive") is a big job and they don't recognize that, you know it makes you angry" (Morgan, 1989, p. 105). The widows wanted to have their anger, grief, and the disruption in their lives acknowledged and accepted by their friends. Then they felt they could begin to come to terms with their loss and build a new life.

Widowers. Widowers suffer greater increases in depression following the loss of their spouses than do widows (Lee, DeMaris,

Two long-time friends provide social support for each other. After they became widows, they moved into an apartment together to help manage costs. They're reviewing a box of bills and receipts as they get ready to do their income taxes. This also helps them reminisce about what they did during the past year.

Bavin, & Sullivan, 2001; Umberson, Wortman, & Kessler, 1992). Perhaps because men in traditional heterosexual marriages rely heavily on their wives for the instrumental support of managing daily household tasks and the emotional and social support of companionship and social activity, their lives are more intensely disrupted when their wives die. However, many men are resilient, especially if the death of their partner occurs at an older age. Despite an initial painful period of grief and loss, these men are able to bring a sense of optimism and a positive outlook to their lives. They may cope by reorganizing their lives, by changing their environment, or by finding a new partner (Bennett & Soulsby, 2012).

In a 2-year follow-up study of dating and remarriage after the death of their spouses, 61 percent of men and 19 percent of women had remarried or were in a new romantic relationship by 25 months. For men, a higher monthly income and level of education were the best predictors of being remarried. For both men and women, involvement in a new relationship was positively associated with psychological well-being and interpreted as a positive coping strategy (Schneider, Sledge, Shuchter, & Zisook, 1996).

Widowhood is associated with increased death rates among surviving spouses. In a longitudinal study of married couples in the United States, the death of one spouse from any of a variety of causes, such as cancers, infections, and cardiovascular diseases, was associated with an increased risk of death for the surviving spouse (Elwert & Christakis, 2008). The process of bereavement seems to accelerate the course of preexisting diseases and leads to increased rates of suicides, accidents, and alcohol-related deaths. To some degree, the relationship of widowhood to mortality is tied to the well-known health effects of marriage. Depending upon the way that spouses support each other's health, the loss of a spouse may result in less effective adherence to medical care, less adequate diet, and less social interaction and social stimulation, all of which support physical and mental health in later life (Elwert & Christakis, 2006). In a meta-analysis of 15 studies, the relationship of widowhood to risk of mortality was found to be especially significant in the first 6 months following bereavement, and the risk was greater for men than for women (Moon, Kondo, Glymour, & Subramanian, 2011). Most adults cope successfully with widowhood, either by forming a new intimate relationship or establishing a new, independent lifestyle; however, others find it difficult to recover from the impact of their loss. The **Applying Theory and Research to Life** box on Patterns of Adaptation During Widowhood illustrates the variety of patterns of adaptation to widowhood.

Leisure Activities

As the role responsibilities of parenthood and employment decrease, older adults have more time and resources to devote to leisure activities. Involvement in leisure activities is associated with higher levels of well-being and lower stress.

Different types of leisure activities are available that meet a variety of psychosocial needs. Table 13.2 shows the percentage of older adults, ages 55 to 64, 65 to 74, and 75 and older, who participated in five types of leisure activities at least once in the prior year: exercise programs, playing sports, charity work, going to the movies, and gardening (U.S. Census Bureau, 2012b, Table 1202). Gardening tops the list in each of these age groups, with relatively little difference between those 55 to 64 and those 65 to 74.

A range of needs may be met through leisure pursuits, including companionship and social integration, experiencing something new and unusual, opportunities to enhance one's

APPLYING THEORY AND RESEARCH TO LIFE

Patterns of Adaptation During Widowhood

In a prospective, longitudinal study of widowhood, researchers surveyed married couples where the husband was 65 years old or older. Following the death of one partner, the surviving spouse was surveyed again at 6 and 18 months (Bonanno, Wortman, & Nesse, 2004). Five patterns of adjustment following the death of a spouse were described:

1. Common grief
2. Chronic grief
3. Chronic depression
4. Depression followed by improvement
5. Resilience

The most common patterns, for 56 percent of the sample, were common grief and resilience. These two groups had no signs of depression before the loss. The common grief group had evidence of depression at 6 months but returned to pre-loss levels at 18 months. The resilient group had low levels of depression even at 6 months following loss. Although these groups experienced fond memories and moments of yearning for their partners, they did not experience long-term grief at 18 months. A second, unexpected pattern, characteristic of about 10 percent of the sample, was a group that showed a change for the better following widowhood. The

participants in this group had high levels of depression before the loss and lower levels at 6 and 18 months following the loss. Participants in this group were in unhappy marriages, and many of them had been caring for chronically ill partners. They reported being more confident and having found a new sense of personal strength in coping with the events of widowhood.

Two other groups were described as chronically grieving and chronically depressed. The chronically grieving group was not depressed before the death of their spouse but continued to show high levels of depression at 6 and 18 months following the death. These widows and widowers were often coping with the sudden loss of a healthy spouse and had trouble finding meaning in the death of their partners. The chronically depressed were already depressed prior to the death of their spouse. The death added a new stressor that increased their levels of depression at 6 and 18 months after the loss.

Subsequent studies of the transition from caregiver to widow support the idea that the conditions that surround the caregiving role and the quality of the marital bond, as well as the physical and mental health of the surviving spouse, will influence the coping process (Pruchno, Cartwright, &

Wilson-Genderson, 2009). The majority of adults are able to cope effectively with the loss of a spouse. However, an understanding of the context of the loss and the emotional well-being of the surviving spouse before the loss are important factors that influence the bereavement process. Those striving to support widows and widowers need to be mindful of these differences in order to offer appropriate interventions.

Critical Thinking Questions

1. Summarize the contexts of widowhood that might determine how a person adjusts to loss.
2. Imagine that a person has spent several years caring for a dying spouse. Describe the aspects of role loss that might result upon the death of the spouse.
3. Consider the case of couples who have been happily married for 40 years or more. List the challenges of widowhood when one spouse dies. Identify the resources that might be useful to support adjustment under these conditions.
4. Explain how widowhood might influence the resolution of the psychosocial crisis of integrity versus despair for the surviving spouse, either positively or negatively.

Table 13.2 Participation in Various Leisure Activities by Age, 2008

Age Program	ACTIVITY* (% PARTICIPATION)				
	Exercise	Play Sports	Charity Work	Go to Movies	Gardening
55 to 64	52	17	33	46	52
65 to 74	48	13	30	32	55
75 and older	30	6	23	19	41

*Respondent has participated in the activity at least once in the last 12 months.

Source: U.S. Census Bureau, Statistical Abstract of the United States, 2012b. Table No. 1202.

competence and mastery, finding solitude and relaxation, opportunities for creativity and self-expression, opportunities for intellectual stimulation, and opportunities for community service.

Gardening. There is growing awareness of the health and therapeutic value of gardening. Gardening provides regular physical activity, including stretching, coordination, and weight resistance. Depending on the size and demands of the garden, gardening can help an older adult meet the recommendations for half an hour of physical activity each day. Gardening requires planning, research, and problem solving. Preparing a garden, evaluating plants and their care, and monitoring their health and growth are natural forms of cognitive stimulation that can be enhanced with classes, books and magazines, and online resources.

Gardening is a stress-reducing activity, especially when approached in an appropriate pace and with tools that are well adapted to one's physical capacities. The sensory components of the garden, including smells, colors, and textures, can have a soothing, reassuring impact. Gardening can be an expression of generative motives, providing a lasting contribution to the community through the planting of public gardens or the enhancement of public spaces. Gardens are increasingly incorporated into senior centers and nursing homes to encourage cognitive, sensory, and motor activity and to provide a positive opportunity for exercising mastery. Master Gardener programs are sponsored by many universities where adult volunteers learn about up-to-date research-based information on horticulture to share with home gardeners and implement in the beautification of their communities (Morgan, 2005).

Volunteerism. In the United States, among those 65 and older, about 25 percent volunteer, giving a median of 90 hours annually of unpaid time (U.S. Bureau of Labor Statistics, 2013d). Especially in the year or two following retirement, individuals who are not already involved in volunteer service are especially open to considering it (Caro & Bass, 1997). **Volunteerism** provides a meaningful structure to daily life, especially when other significant work and family roles are becoming less demanding. Volunteering is associated with increases in life satisfaction and improved perceptions of physical health (Van Willigen, 2000). The opportunities to assume new responsibilities and learn new skills are two of the rewards of volunteering in later adulthood. At the same time, certain types of volunteer work have been shown to have a positive impact on cognitive complexity and memory functions.

Johns Hopkins University researchers compared the health of volunteer tutors in Baltimore's public schools with that of nonvolunteers, ages 59 to 86 (Fried et al., 2004). The following benefits were observed:

- Sixty-three percent of volunteers had increased their activity level, compared with 43 percent of nonvolunteers.
- Volunteers boosted their weekly calorie burn by 25 percent.
- Volunteers reduced TV-watching time 4 percent whereas nonvolunteers increased theirs by 18 percent.
- Their networks of friends expanded, whereas nonvolunteers' social circles shrank.
- Volunteers perceived that they were making a difference: The students they tutored became better readers, and had fewer behavior problems at school.

Expanded research built upon this study through collaboration with Experience Corps Project, a high-intensity volunteer program. Older adults were trained as volunteers to tutor elementary school children. The program combined goals to support health among older adults and reading competence among children. Studies of the health impact of this program on older adults across 17 national sites found evidence of significant health benefits and reduced symptoms of depression among volunteers as well as some evidence of increased neural activation in the prefrontal cortex and associated improvement in executive function (Carlson et al., 2009; Hong & Morrow- Howell, 2010; Park & Bischof, 2013).

Exercise. Physical exercise is becoming a focus of leisure activity for increasing numbers of older adults because the benefits are linked to better health and cognitive functioning, positive self-esteem, and a new zest for life. Almost 50 percent of adults ages 65 to 74 reported being involved in physical exercise during the prior 12 months. In a time use study reported by the Bureau of Labor Statistics (2016d), adults ages 65 to 74 reported engaging in sports, exercise, and related physical activities about 19 minutes a day during the week and 15 minutes on the weekends.

Research supports a clear relationship between physical activity—especially a regular pattern of aerobic exercise—and reduced atrophy of brain cells as well as better brain functioning and related cognitive abilities. "Physical activity takes advantage of the brain's capacity for plasticity," improving brain health (Erickson, Gildengers, & Butters, 2013). Improvements in cognitive function are associated with improved executive control processes mood and well-being (Kramer & Willis, 2002).

In the past, professionals were reluctant to encourage vigorous activity for older adults. They believed that a person who was unaccustomed to active physical exercise might be harmed by it. However, research on exercise in adulthood suggests that adults profit from a program of exercise, and that through systematic exercise, some of the negative consequences of a sedentary lifestyle can be reversed (Riebe, Burbank, & Garber, 2002).

Physical exercise is a component of optimal aging. Regular participation in moderate activity, such as walking, biking, or gardening, for 30 minutes a day may provide protection from certain chronic diseases and ease the discomfort of arthritis (DiPietro, 2001). Exercise is associated with increased muscle tone, strength, and endurance, which build confidence about one's body movement, coordination, and stamina. Exercise also increases perceptions of self-control and self-efficacy in meeting one's own needs. As a result, people who exercise tend to have a generally more positive self-evaluation and higher levels of self-confidence than their inactive peers (Clark, Long, & Schiffman, 1999; Fontane, 1996). Many community organizations and agencies are exploring group fitness programs to engage older adults in regular exercise. Group programs have the benefit of providing valued social interaction as well as a regular schedule of meetings and a clear routine of aerobic, strengthening, balance, and flexibility exercises. Research on participant perspectives in one such program highlights the value of the social nature of these classes as well as the practical benefits for improving participants' ability to manage daily activities at home (Kohn, Belza, Petrescu-Prahova, & Miyawaki, 2016).

Redirection of energy to new roles in later adulthood requires a degree of flexibility and resilience that often goes unnoticed in observations of older adults. Try to imagine what life might be like for you 30 or 40 years from now. We are impressed by how readily most older adults adapt to new roles, especially those of retiree and widow, for which there is little early preparation or social reward.

FURTHER REFLECTION: Describe some of the challenges of redirecting energy to new roles in later adulthood. What might prevent a person from giving up earlier identities or engaging in new activities?

Speculate about the relationship between life satisfaction and redirecting energy to new roles. If you are satisfied with your life, why would you want to redirect energy to new roles? If you experience significant role loss, will it undermine life satisfaction?

Think about the nature of leisure activities. What are you doing now that you expect to continue into later adulthood? What activities might you "pick up" or engage in when you reach later adulthood that create new cognitive demands and thereby support well-being?

Developing a Point of View About Death

OBJECTIVE 4 Summarize the development of a point of view about death.

During later adulthood, it is inevitable that serious, possibly frightening, preoccupations about death fill the individual's thoughts. In middle adulthood, most people experience the death of their parents. During later adulthood, one's peers, including siblings and spouses, may die. These deaths typically evoke grief and mourning as well as the cognitive strain of trying to accept or understand them. At the same time, these deaths stimulate a more immediate recognition of one's own mortality. Although death can occur at any stage of life, in this section we focus on the psychosocial work that is likely in later adulthood as one confronts the possibility of one's own death. In chapter 15, we review the research on death, dying, and bereavement within the broader biological, psychological, and cultural perspectives, considering the experiences not only of the dying person but also of those left to mourn.

Changing Perspectives About Death

The development of a perspective on death is a continuous process that begins in childhood and is not fully resolved until later adulthood. The earliest concern with death, which occurs during toddlerhood, reflects an inability to conceive of an irreversible state of lifelessness. Toddlers are likely to think that a person may be dead at one moment and "undeaded" the next. By middle school age, children have a more realistic concept of death, but they are unlikely to relate that concept to themselves or to others close to them (Kastenbaum, 2000). A conceptualization of death becomes increasingly accurate from early through later adolescence (Noppe & Noppe, 1997). In the process of forming a personal identity, young people ask new questions about mortality, the meaning of life, and the possibility of life after death.

During middle adulthood, people recognize that they have already lived more than half of their lives. Death becomes increasingly concrete as parents and older relatives die. At the same time, middle adults have a larger impact on their families and communities. Increased feelings of effectiveness and vitality lessen the threat of death. The degree to which individuals gain satisfaction from their own contributions to future generations influences the extent of their anxiety about death during this stage. The achievement of a sense of generativity usually allows adults to accept that their impact will continue to be felt even after death.

In the 1960s, Elisabeth Kübler-Ross engaged in groundbreaking work to understand the thoughts, feelings, and needs of patients who were dying. Through her interviews with more than 400 patients, she clarified a process of coping with one's death. She identified five stages that are likely to occur between the awareness of a terminal illness and ultimate acceptance of one's death: denial, anger and resentment, bargaining for a reprieve, depression and mourning one's death, and acceptance or a willingness to face the reality of one's death. She also discovered how eager most people were to have someone who would listen to their thoughts and how grateful they were to interact with someone about their death rather than have it treated as a taboo or unmentionable topic (Kübler-Ross, 1969/1997 reprint edition, 1981/1997 reprint edition).

Subsequent research suggests that there is no single, typical path in the dying process. Some people alternate between accepting and denying their death. They understand their situation, yet fall into periods of disbelief. Some people are able to bring what they view as an acceptable close to their life, saying good-bye to family and friends, and finding comfort in the support of others.

Others die while still in a state of fear or denial (Kastenbaum, 1985, 2012). Kübler-Ross's stages are neither a universal nor fixed sequence, but they provide a useful model for considering the dynamic ego processes that are engaged as one faces death. The capacity to confront the reality of death can be a profound occasion for new insight.

Ideally, during later adulthood, ego concerns about death decrease. Individuals come to accept their own lives as they have lived them and begin to see death as a natural part of the life span. Death no longer poses a threat to personal value, the potential for accomplishment, or the desire to influence the lives of others. As a result of having accepted one's life, one can accept its end without discouragement. As the case of Morrie Schwartz suggests, coming to terms with death does not imply a desire for, but an acceptance of the fact of death. Along with this acceptance may come a greater appreciation for life itself. It takes great courage to face the fact of one's own death and, at the same time, to live out the days of one's life with optimism and enthusiasm (Kübler-Ross, 1969, 1972).

— CASE STUDY   Morrie Schwartz Reflects on His Views About Death —

Mitch Albom, in his 40s, rediscovered his former college professor Morrie Schwartz, who was dying from amyotrophic lateral sclerosis (ALS), a progressive neurological disease that attacks body muscles and leaves one increasingly paralyzed. Mitch and Morrie met every Tuesday for the last 4 months of Morrie's life.

"Everyone knows they're going to die," he said again, "but nobody believes it. If we did, we would do things differently."

"So we kid ourselves about death," I said.

"Yes. But there's a better approach. To know you're going to die, and to be *prepared* for it at any time. That's better. That way you can actually be *more* involved in your life while you're living."

"How can you ever be prepared to die?"

"Do what the Buddhists do. Every day, have a little bird on your shoulder that asks, 'Is today the day? Am I ready? Am I doing all I need to do? Am I being the person I want to be?'" He turned his head to his shoulder as if the bird were there now.

"Is today the day I die?" he said. . . .

"The truth is, Mitch," he said, "once you learn how to die, you learn how to live." I nodded.

"I'm going to say it again," he said. "Once you learn how to die, you learn how to live." He smiled, and I realized what he was doing. He was making sure I absorbed this point, without embarrassing me by asking. It was part of what made him a good teacher.

"Did you think much about death before you got sick?" I asked.

"No." Morrie smiled. "I was like everyone else. I once told a friend of mine, in a moment of exuberance, 'I'm gonna be the healthiest old man you ever met!'"

"How old were you?"

"In my sixties."

"So you were optimistic."

"Why not? Like I said, no one really believes they're going to die."

"But everyone knows someone who has died," I said. "Why is it so hard to think about dying?"

"Because," Morrie continued, "most of us all walk around as if we're sleepwalking. We really don't experience the world fully, because we're half-asleep, doing things we automatically think we have to do." . . .

"Mitch. Can I tell you something?"

"Of course," I said.

"You might not like it."

"Why not?"

"Well, the truth is, if you really listen to that bird on your shoulder, *if you accept that you can die at any time*—then you might not be as ambitious as you are." I forced a small grin. "The things you spend so much time on—all the work you do—might not seem as important. You might have to make room for some more spiritual things."

"Spiritual things?"

"You hate that word, don't you? 'Spiritual.' You think it's touchy-feely stuff."

"Well," I said.

He tried to wink, a bad try, and I broke down and laughed. "Mitch," he said, laughing along, "even I don't know what 'spiritual development' really means. But I do know we're deficient in some way. We are too involved in materialistic things, and they don't satisfy us. The loving relationships we have, the universe around us, we take these things for granted."

He nodded toward the window with the sunshine streaming in. "You see that? You can go out there, outside, anytime. You can run up and down the block and go crazy. I can't do that. I can't go out. I can't run. I can't be out there without fear of getting sick. But you know what? I *appreciate* that window more than you do."

Source: From *Tuesdays with Morrie: An Old Man, a Young Man, and Life's Greatest Lessons*, by Mitch Albom, pp. 81–84. Copyright © 1997 Doubleday.

Case Analysis Using What You Know

1. Summarize the point of view about life and death that Morrie is developing.

2. Analyze what this conversation suggests about Morrie's psychosocial development, including how issues of intimacy, generativity, and integrity are reflected in this dialogue.

3. Hypothesize how the conditions of Morrie's illness might influence his outlook on death.

4. Describe the issues you would want to discuss if you had a mentor like Morrie who was willing to help you learn about living and dying.

The formulation of a **point of view about death** requires the capacity to absorb the loss of one's close relatives and friends and to accept one's own death. The former task may be even more difficult than the latter, in that the death of peers begins to destroy one's social group. Losing one's friends and relatives means losing daily companionship, a shared world of memories and plans and a source of support for values and social norms. The circumstances surrounding the deaths of others may also be very frightening. Older adults observe their peers suffering through long illnesses, dying abruptly in the midst of a thriving and vigorous life, or dying in absurd, meaningless accidents. After each death, the surviving adults must ask themselves about the value of these lives and subsequently about the value of their own life.

Death Anxiety

Fear of personal death, or **death anxiety**, is natural and normal. Death may be feared for a variety of reasons, some of which relate to the actual process of dying and others to the consequences of it. Concerns about dying include fears of being alone, being in pain, having others see one suffering, or losing control of one's mind and body. Concerns about the consequences of dying include fears of the unknown, loss of identity ("People will forget about me"), the grief that others will feel, the decomposition of the body, and punishment or pain in the hereafter (Tomer & Eliason, 2000).

Several researchers have considered the sources of personal anxiety about death and the changes in preoccupation with death at various ages. Although older adults seem to think about death more frequently than do young adults, they do not appear to feel more threatened by it. In comparison to middle-aged adults, older adults experience lower death anxiety (Sinoff, Iosipovici, Almog, & Barnett-Greens, 2008). Among the elderly, it appears that those who have higher levels of self-worth and sense of mastery also have lower levels of death anxiety (Ron, 2010). In comparison to those in early or middle adulthood, those in later adulthood know more people who have died and are more likely to have visited a cemetery or attended a funeral. Those in later adulthood are more likely to have made some specific arrangements related to their death, including purchasing cemetery space, writing a will, or making plans for their funeral. Their concrete experiences with the events of death, coupled with their own sense of mastery in preparing for their death, may allow them to cope more effectively with their fears (Cicirelli, 2001).

What factors help older people cope with fears about death? Psychosocial theory predicts that through acts of generativity, people experience satisfaction in guiding and nurturing future generations. Achieving a positive resolution to the psychosocial crisis of generativity versus stagnation should help reduce death anxiety. One study designed to test this hypothesis found that the relationship of generativity to the fear of death was mediated by ego integrity, the positive pole of the crisis of later adulthood. Among those who were described as generative, the older adults who had high levels of ego integrity had the least fear of death, supporting the theoretical notion of a progressive integration of ego strengths from one stage of life to the next (Bringle, 2007).

In addition to the achievement of a generative orientation, people who describe themselves as religious may be less troubled by the fear of death. Most religions offer a point of view about death, as well as death-related rituals and practices that help structure this great unknown. Those who have a strong social support system, and those who have a strong sense of self-worth are less likely to be preoccupied with the fear of death (Tomer & Eliason, 2000). Frey (2003) extended this perspective by focusing on the relationship of self-beliefs to death anxiety. Older adults who have a positive sense of spiritual self-efficacy, perceived

The ritual of a graveside service helps mourners separate from their loved one before the burial. Many elements of a traditional funeral are depicted here: the flowers, the tombstone, and the mourners gathered and supporting each other in a tree-lined cemetery.

ability to generate spiritually based faith and inner strength, have less fear of the unknown following death and less fear of the pain and suffering associated with dying.

FURTHER REFLECTION: Developing a point of view about death may be one of the most universal tasks across cultures. What are the societal resources that help people address their mortality? What are the most helpful ideas you have encountered in your life so far that will aid you in dealing with the challenges of this task?

The Psychosocial Crisis: Integrity Versus Despair

OBJECTIVE 5   Define and explain the psychosocial crisis of integrity versus despair, the central process of introspection, the prime adaptive ego quality of wisdom, and the core pathology of disdain.

On entering later adulthood, adults draw on the competence and creativity attained during middle adulthood to invent solutions to their changing conditions. You may appreciate the common theme of a search for meaning, especially a desire to understand one's purpose in life, between the psychosocial crisis of later adolescence and the psychosocial crisis of later adulthood. In later adolescence, young people strive to create a coherent vision of the self in society that will guide future choices. In later adulthood, adults strive to reconcile and accept the events of their life. At this stage, adults apply the wealth of their life experiences, their perspective on time, and their adaptation to life crises to construct personally satisfying answers to the questions of life's meaning.

The conflict of integrity versus despair is resolved through a dynamic process of life review, introspection, and self-evaluation. Contemporary factors, such as health, family relationships, and role loss or role transitions, are integrated with an assessment of one's past aspirations and accomplishments. Thoughts of the past may be fleeting or a constant obsession. Memories may be altered to fit contemporary events, or contemporary events may be reinterpreted to fit memories. The achievement of integrity is the culmination of a life of psychosocial growth. It is the peak of the pyramid in that it addresses the ultimate question, "How do I find meaning in life given the ultimate reality of death?"

Integrity

The term **integrity**, as it is used in psychosocial theory, refers to the ability to accept the facts of one's life and face death without great fear. As people get older, they need to find a way to integrate or reconcile the events of their life with the hopes and dreams they may have had in their early or middle adulthood. This process of meaning making involves an assessment of one's life and the extent to which worthwhile goals were sought and achieved. In a search for life's meaning, a person looks for a way to assemble a coherent story of order, purpose, and value out of the complex puzzle pieces of a life (Krause, 2004; Reker, 1997). The sense of meaning in life provides a higher order belief that can unify many disparate experiences, give direction to life decisions, and contribute to an overall feeling of well-being. People differ in what they find meaningful and where they realize the greatest personal inspiration including such dimensions as achievement, relationships, religion, self-transcendence, self-acceptance, intimacy, and fair treatment. These sources of meaning can motivate action, increase commitment and persistence, and add a sense of enjoyment to life (Macdonald, Wong, & Gingras, 2011).

The attainment of integrity is ultimately a result of the balance of all the psychosocial crises that have come earlier, accompanied by all the ego strengths and core pathologies that have accumulated along the way. Integrity comes only after some considerable thought about the meaning of one's life. Older adults who have achieved a sense of integrity view their past in an existential light. They appreciate that their lives and individuality are due to an accumulation of personal satisfactions and crises. Integrity is not so much a quality of honesty and trustworthiness—as the term is used in daily speech—as it is an ability to integrate one's past history with one's present circumstances and to feel content with the outcome.

Most people have some regrets. One may look back and wish that one had taken advantage of certain opportunities, been smarter about saving or investing money, or spent more time with one's children while they were young. The challenge in achieving integrity is to face the decisions and experiences of the past with acceptance. In this process, a person seeks to find an integrative thread that makes sense of the life one has led without belaboring past mistakes. The concept of **sense of coherence** has been linked to integrity and well-being in later life (Antonovsky, 1987; Wiesmann & Hannich, 2011). People who view their lives as understandable, manageable, and meaningful are thought to benefit from this sense of coherence. It is a construct that combines a cognitive ability to make sense of life experiences, an emotional optimism that things will, by and large, work out favorably, and a behavioral component that involves taking steps to achieve desired goals (Eriksson & Lindstrom, 2005).

Given the abstract and subjective construct of integrity, how can it be measured? A variety of approaches have been developed (Hearn, Saulnier, Strayer, Glenham, Koopman, & Marica, 2011). One approach, devised by Neil Krause (2007), provides a four-dimensional measure of meaning in life. These dimensions include (1) having a system of values, (2) having a sense of purpose, (3) having goals to strive for, and (4) reflecting on the past to reconcile one's accomplishments with one's goals. Taken together, these four dimensions comprise a meaning in life scale. In a longitudinal study of older adults, Krause examined how various forms of social support as well as anticipated social support related to meaning in life over a 4-year period. Those older adults who received high levels of emotional support had higher meaning in life, but those who received tangible support had lower meaning in life. Anticipated support, that is, believing that you could call upon close family and friends for help if it were needed, was the strongest predictor of meaning in life. Over time, anticipated support was also a significant predictor of changes in a person's sense of meaning.

When older adults are confident that they will be able to count on others for help in the future, their sense of meaning in life is bolstered. This finding speaks to the role of the radius of significant relationships in predicting and sustaining a sense of integrity in later adulthood. It also suggests a continuing role for trust and hope, the very earliest psychosocial concepts of infancy, in fostering integrity in late life.

In addition, research suggests a link between generativity and integrity. Older adults who have made meaningful contributions to the quality of life for future generations can draw on these experiences to find meaning in their own lives. As suggested by the data on volunteerism, for many adults generative action continues into later adulthood and extends beyond care for one's immediate family to concern about the larger community (Ehlman & Ligon, 2012; Schoklitsch & Baumann, 2012).

Despair

The opposite pole of integrity is **despair**, a feeling of regret about one's past and a continuous, haunting desire to be able to do things differently, or of bitterness over how one's life has turned out. People who resolve the crisis of later adulthood in the direction of despair cannot resist speculating about how things might have been or what actions might have been taken if conditions had only been different. They are preoccupied with the *if-onlys* of their past, without any hope of altering or repairing these regrets in the future. Despairing individuals either seek death as a way of ending a miserable existence or desperately fear death because it makes impossible any hope of compensating for past failures.

In response to the interview question, "Overall, how do you feel your life has gone so far?" a despairing woman gave the following answer:

> Well, (sighs), it could have been worse. I'm satisfied.
> I've had a lot of problems, and ah, yes, there are regrets.
> That's life. I don't think you're supposed to be happy
> on earth. If you're happy you're lucky. Or if you get
> everything you want you're lucky. I haven't had a happy

marriage and I always felt that I could have, you know that there must be. . .my husband is not a man that I can lean on, and in my younger days I wanted somebody to lean on because I lost my father and there was no father figure in my life. (Hearn et al., 2011, p. 5)

Most older adults do not resolve the psychosocial crisis of later adulthood in the direction of despair. Over a long life, most people have opportunities to review and redefine earlier life challenges in a way that makes them seem acceptable. Recall the U-shaped curve of life satisfaction. At older ages, people generally experience less anger and sadness, and a more positive sense of well-being. At the same time, there are experiences and societal contexts that may contribute to periodic feelings of disappointment and regret.

Older adults may face some degree of **ageism**—devaluation and even hostility from the social community. The negative attitudes expressed by family members, colleagues, and younger people toward the perceived lack of competence, dependence, slowness, or old-fashioned ways of older people may lead some later adults to feel discouraged about their self-worth. The gradual deterioration or loss of certain physical capacities—particularly hearing, vision, and motor agility—may add to an older person's frustration and discouragement. Older adults recognize that they cannot perform certain tasks as well as they did in the past or that their domains of independent functioning and mastery have diminished.

Furthermore, there is a general cultural sentiment that the death of an older person—in contrast, for example, with the death of a child or youth—though sad, is not a great loss to society, because that person had already contributed to society and lived a full life. Thus, older adults may perceive that society is already letting go of them, even before they are ready to let go of life (Jecker & Schneiderman, 1994).

Depression

People who are in a state of despair are also more likely to experience **depression** as well as problems with perceived ill health (Hearn et al., 2011). However, depression is not a normal aspect of aging. Nearly 8 percent of all people in the United States aged 12 and older (6 percent of males and 10 percent of females) reported moderate or severe depressive symptoms in the past 2 weeks. Females had higher rates of depression than males in every age group. Middle adulthood appears to be the peak for the incidence of depression. Males aged 40 to 59 had higher rates of depression (7 percent) than males aged 60 years and older (3.4 percent). Females aged 40 to 59 had higher rates of depression (12 percent) than females aged 60 years and older (7 percent) (Pratt & Brody, 2014).

Many of the same factors that are associated with depression in younger age groups are associated with depression in older age groups: poverty, poor physical health, lack of social involvement, and being single, divorced, or widowed. The risk of depression in later life cannot be attributed to the aging process itself. The physiological changes associated with aging—such as high blood pressure, reduced breathing capacity, reduced muscle strength, slower reaction time, memory loss, and loss of visual or auditory

acuity—are not associated with depression in and of themselves (Hinrichsen & Clougherty, 2006). However, some of these conditions or the medications that are given to address these problems may trigger feelings of depression. The symptoms of depression may look somewhat different among older adults; less evidence of sadness or feelings of worthlessness, and more complaints of being tired, having trouble sleeping, being irritable, or having trouble concentrating (National Institute of Health, 2016; Mayo Clinic, 2016).

Older adults who have a clear sense of coherence about life, those who view their situation as comprehensible, manageable, and meaningful, are more likely to be resilient in the face of chronic physical illness than those who view their lives as chaotic and out of their control. Depression as a complex affective and cognitive syndrome does not automatically come with the territory of aging. However, it is especially likely among those who have experienced decreased activity level associated with pain or illness; death of a loved one and associated loss of significant, close, confiding relationships; and accumulated physical health problems that limit their independence and dampen their sense of enthusiasm for pleasant activities (Wiesmann & Hannich, 2013).

The Central Process: Introspection

In order to achieve a sense of integrity, a person must engage in **introspection**, a deliberate process of private, personal reflection and self-evaluation. The achievement of a sense of integrity requires the ability to introspect about the gradual evolution of life events and to appreciate their significance in the formation of adult personality. This state can be reached only through individual effort. It may require temporary isolation, shutting out the influences of potentially competitive or resentful associates, or deliberately stepping away from daily tasks in order to have time to relax and think. A national survey of time use finds that the time spent relaxing and thinking increases with age, from just under 7 minutes a day for those in their early 20s to 22 minutes a day in the period of later adulthood (Bureau of Labor Statistics, 2016d).

One mode for engaging in self-evaluation is **reminiscence**, the recollection of past experiences and the recalling or retelling of memories from long ago. This process of nostalgic remembering allows adults to recapture some of the memorable events in their life histories. Reminiscence may be a playful recalling of a life adventure or a painful review of some personal or family crisis. The process of reminiscence is comprised of four elements: the *selection* of an event or story to retell or review; *immersion* in the details of the story, including the strong emotions linked to the event; *withdrawal* from the past by distancing oneself from the event or comparing past and present; and bringing *closure* to the memory by summing up, finding some lesson, or making a general observation. Through this process, a person builds a mental and emotional bridge between the past and the present (Meacham, 1995).

The process of nostalgic remembering allows adults to recapture some of the memorable people and events in their life histories.

Reminiscence is linked to positive adjustment in later life, especially better health, a more positive outlook, and a better ability to cope with the challenges of daily life (Kunz & Soltys, 2007). However, not all forms of reminiscence are of equal benefit. In particular, reminiscences of the integrative or instrumental type tend to be associated with high levels of well-being, whereas obsessive reminiscences are not. Integrative reminiscence involves reviewing one's past in order to find meaning or to reconcile one's current and prior feelings about certain life events. Instrumental reminiscence focuses on the past, on accomplishments, efforts to overcome difficulties, and experiences to help cope with current difficulties. *Obsessive reminiscence* suggests an inability to resolve or accept certain past events and a persistent guilt or despair about them (Korte, Cappeliez, Bohlmeijer, & Westerhof, 2012; Wong & Watt, 1991). Contrast the following two narratives:

> When I was a teenager, my parents broke up and both remarried. I was very resentful because they did not seem to care about my feelings or needs. But as I grow older and look back, I understand that they were really not compatible with each other. They had suffered for many years before their divorce. [Integrative reminiscence]

> My husband died when I was away for two days visiting my friends in the West. He fell in the bathtub and eventually died because there was no one there to help him. It has been years now, but I still cannot forgive myself for leaving him home alone for two days. [Obsessive reminiscence] (Wong & Watt, 1991, p. 276)

Reminiscence lends continuity to older adults' self-concepts. They can trace the path of their own development through time and identify moments that were of central importance in the crystallization of their personal philosophies. Through reminiscence, older adults can revise the meaning of past events by using current wisdom to understand or accept what took place in the past. For example, reminiscence was encouraged in a group of veterans who had been involved in the Normandy invasion at the end of World War II. The veterans retold their experiences of loss, grief, and shock and how those experiences influenced their lives over the subsequent 50-year period. Formulating their experiences in a story-like format and retelling their stories to others provided a means of coping with the stressors of this past experience (Harvey, Stein, & Scott, 1995).

Reminiscence serves as an integrating process that has positive value in an eventual attainment of integrity. In a review of 20 studies with older adults who suffered from depression, guided reminiscence was found to be as effective as drug treatment or psychotherapy for alleviating depressive symptoms (Bohlmeijer, Smit, & Cuijpers, 2003). In excess, however, reminiscence can dominate reality, taking over the time and energy that might be directed toward more appropriate active social involvement. Some adults dwell on sad events and allow earlier disappointments to preoccupy their current thoughts. Their past lives take precedence over their current circumstances. No new events can compete successfully with past memories for their attention.

The benefit of introspection for well-being and the sense of integrity depends on the person's ability to cope with the material that was called up from the past. Two effective coping strategies that have been linked to mental health in older adults are assimilative and accommodative coping. In assimilative coping, the person recognizes the significance of past events and their links to important life goals. This provides a positive sense of continuity, affirming the focus and meaning of life events, even if the past events were troubling. In accommodative coping, the person recognizes the need to revise his or her appraisal of the situation. The person realizes how the difficult events of the past led to the modification of goals which, in turn, created a new and valued sense of meaning (Cappeliez & O'Rourke, 2002; Cappeliez & Robitaille, 2010).

The Prime Adaptive Ego Quality and the Core Pathology

Wisdom

Erikson identified wisdom as the prime adaptive ego quality of later adulthood. It reflects a concern for life and a desire to learn and communicate essential lessons from experience in the face of impending death (Erikson et al., 1986).

Wisdom has been characterized by six features (Ardelt, 2004; Baltes, Smith, & Staudinger, 1992, p. 272; Bangen, Meeks, & Jeste, 2013; Kramer, 2003; Staudinger, Dorner, & Mickler, 2005):

1. *Factual knowledge* about fundamental life matters, such as general knowledge about the human condition and specific knowledge about life events, their age-related occurrence, and their expected and unexpected course.

2. *Procedural knowledge*, composed of strategies for approaching the management and interpretation of life matters, including linking past, present, and future.

3. *Life-span contextualism*, approaching problems with the realization that events are embedded in a multidimensional context—including age-related, culturally defined, role-related, and sociohistorical frameworks—and that events take their meaning from certain distinct domains, especially family, work, and leisure.

4. *Relativism of values and life goals*, allowing the person to appreciate differences among individuals and societies with respect to the priorities they place on certain values, as well as the ability to preserve a certain core of universal values.

5. *Recognition and management of uncertainty*, incorporating the realization that the future cannot be totally predicted and that many aspects of the past and present are not fully known, plus an ability to manage and cope with this uncertainty.

6. *Self-insight*, including self-understanding, a sense of humor, and emotional balance (e.g. self-control and emotional regulation).

One concept that helps link the idea of intelligence in later adulthood with the ego strength of wisdom is **expertise**. With age, individuals who focus their intelligence in intensive study, training, and repeated opportunities for problem solving within a domain become *experts*. A variety of intellectual processes support expertise, including deductive reasoning, a rich and complex working memory, and the ability to organize large amounts of information for storage and subsequent recall. We rely on experts to help inform important and difficult decisions. We see experts as having wisdom in their particular specialization. Although we may be inclined to look to experts in one field to help us solve a wide range of problems, the assumption behind expertise is that it is discipline specific. In that sense, expertise and wisdom are not identical (Horn & Masunaga, 2000; Masunaga & Horn, 2001).

Not all people who live to old age function at a high level of wisdom. However, studies that compare younger and older adults find that there are contexts in which older adults demonstrate a greater degree of insight and problem-solving skill. When asked to analyze situations involving intergroup and interpersonal conflicts, older adults made greater use of advanced reasoning, multiple perspectives, and the need for compromise than younger adults. They also more readily acknowledged the limits of their knowledge and the need to take the specific context into account when predicting the outcome of the situation (Grossmann et al., 2010). There is a path toward increasing wisdom among certain individuals who are especially able to find insights about life from their daily experiences (Ardelt, 2010; Choi & Landeros, 2011).

Jose Galvez/PhotoEdit

Joseph looks forward to these quiet talks with his father. He knows he will always come away with new insight about planning, managing, or understanding the challenges he is facing in his own life.

Three dimensions that have been hypothesized to promote wisdom are (1) opportunities to experience a wide variety of life situations and circumstances; (2) encouragement by a mentor or guide to expand one's capacity for thinking about problems from a multidimensional, psychohistorical perspective; and (3) a strong generative orientation or desire to continue to gain insight into how people meet the challenges of life (Baltes & Smith, 1990).

Disdain

Wisdom reflects flexibility of thought, openness to new interpretations, and a willingness to accept the complexity of life. In contrast, **disdain** refers to feelings of contempt for ideas or people who are viewed as inferior or unworthy. Disdain conveys rejection and scorn for ideas and persons and an arrogance that implies one's own opinions and views are superior. It can be understood as a defensive response to the repulsion for one's physical self and failed past. Disdain for others may be a mechanism to enhance one's own status and prestige. Rather than becoming more patient, more compassionate, more forgiving, and less critical in their later life, older adults who develop disdain are more likely to disparage others and detach from the world around them (Erikson et al., 1986).

FURTHER REFLECTION: Explain how reminiscence and introspection contribute to the resolution of the psychosocial crisis of integrity versus despair. What experiences from earlier stages might contribute to a person's ability to reflect upon and evaluate the meaning of her or his life?

What is your own definition of wisdom? Where do you seek wisdom? What wisdoms would you want to pass along to others that might help them cope with life's uncertainties and achieve a sense of well-being?

The psychosocial perspective assumes that new growth takes place at every stage of life. Summarize the new directions for growth in later adulthood.

Applied Topic: Retirement

OBJECTIVE 6 Apply theory and research to understanding the process of adjustment to retirement.

Retirement is a societal and psychological construct that has a variety of definitions. One definition is that the person works less than full-time year round and receives income from a retirement pension earned during earlier periods of employment. Some people define retirement as the time at which people begin to receive Social Security or other pension benefits, regardless of their employment status. However, retirement also refers to a psychosocial transition involving role loss and role gain—a time for redirecting energy to new roles, new opportunities to promote intellectual vigor, and new sources of life satisfaction. As one withdraws from the formal structure of work and alters one's occupational identity, the transition brings increased time for reflection about the meaning and purpose of one's life. To the extent that work has provided a basic structure for one's lifestyle, withdrawal from the structure and significance of paid employment can be replaced by other activities, new relationships, and a new sense of purpose.

Of course, some people never retire, some die before they reach retirement age, and others continue to work on a part-time schedule. Some people of retirement age leave their primary job and take another full-time or part-time job in a related field or in a totally different one. Many adults who are self-employed or whose work involves creative skills, such as acting, music, painting, or writing, continue to work into their late adulthood. Projections from the U.S. Bureau of Labor Statistics indicate that in the coming years there will be an increasing involvement of older adults in the labor force. Table 13.3 shows the percentage of men and women at two ages, 65 to 74 and 75 and older, who were in the labor force in 1994, 2004, and 2014, as well as projections for 2024. Over the 20 years from 1994 to 2014, the rate of labor force participation increased for both men and women at both ages and is projected to continue to rise in the coming 10 years. By 2024, about one third of men and one fourth of women in later adulthood will be working, and a substantial subset of elders (10 percent of those 75 and older) will continue their labor force participation. Thus, although retirement will still be normative in later life, a growing segment of the older population will be working (U.S. Bureau of Labor Statistics, 2015).

Income Loss

Much of the information about retirement planning and the decision to retire focuses on financial considerations (USA.gov, 2016).

Based on data regarding life expectancy, for those who reach the age of 65, there may be another 20 to 25 years of life ahead. Think about what is required to support 25 years of retirement during 40 years of paid employment. Most financial planners suggest that there is about a 25 percent to 30 percent reduction in income after retirement, which is somewhat greater for those who retire before age 65. Although work-related expenses, taxes, and child care expenses may decrease, health and recreational expenses may increase. In addition to reduced income, not all the sources of income are adjusted to keep pace with inflation. Thus, the value of retirees' fixed income declines over time (USA.gov, 2016).

Older householders' annual income is derived from five primary sources: Social Security, property and other assets, pensions, earnings, and supplemental security income (Social Security Administration, 2016) (see FIGURE 13.4 ▶). Access to these various resources varies by race and ethnicity, with older Whites having greater access to personal assets and pensions, and Asian Americans and Hispanics drawing more on supplemental security income due to their poverty status. In 2014–2015, the median income for households headed by someone 66 years old and older was $38,515. This can be compared to a median household income of $73,857 for a household headed by someone ages 45 to 54. About 9 percent of individuals 66 years and older had incomes below the poverty level. Poverty is greater for older minorities and older adults who live alone (Proctor, Semega, & Kollar, 2016).

Economic factors account, in part, for why people are staying in the labor market for a longer time. The age at which one can receive full Social Security benefits has increased to an older age for more recent cohorts, and there is no penalty for continuing to work after the normal retirement age. Many employer-provided retirement benefits have shifted from guaranteed pension plans to defined contribution plans, so that workers can continue to contribute to their retirement fund for every year they work. Employer-sponsored health care benefits after retirement have decreased, so there is an incentive to continue working until one reaches the age at which Medicare benefits are available (Mermin, Johnson, & Murphy, 2007). Factors including grandparents who are the primary caregivers for their grandchildren, unemployment or underemployment of children in middle adulthood, and the poor quality of benefits associated with many jobs contribute to financial decisions to continue in the labor market in later adulthood.

Adjustment to Retirement

Adjustment during the retirement transition is an individual process. Although we think of retirement as an event, it is really a long period during which people have to clarify their sense of

Table 13.3	Civilian Labor Force Participation Rates by Age and Sex for 1994, 2004, 2014, and Projections for 2024							
	1994		2004		2014		2024	
	Men	Women	Men	Women	Men	Women	Men	Women
65–74	21.7%	13.6%	26.7%	18.0%	30.6%	22.4%	34%	26.2%
75+	8.6%	3.5%	9.0%	4.3%	11%	5.9%	13.5%	8.4%

Source: U.S. Bureau of Labor Statistics. (2015). Table 3.3. Civilian labor force participation rates by age, sex, race and ethnicity, 1994, 2004, 2014 and projected 2024. Retrieved from http://www.bls.gov/emp/ep_table_303.htm.

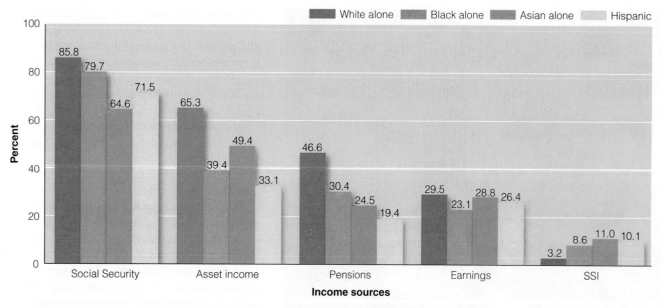

FIGURE 13.4▶ PERCENTAGE RECEIVING INCOME FROM MAJOR SOURCES, BY RACE AND HISPANIC ORIGIN, 2014
Source: Social Security Administration, 2010.

purpose and meaning, and redefine the nature of their daily activities. Adjustment to retirement is expected to change with time. Atchley (1999) proposed phases of anticipation, transition, and eventual adaptation to retirement. Four markers in this process include (1) a *honeymoon* period, which is busy and positive; (2) a *disenchantment* or letdown phase, in which the meaning and structure of work are missed; (3) a *reorientation* phase, in which a more realistic lifestyle is created; and (4) a *stable* period, which may last 10 or 15 years until changes in health, financial resources, or one's social support system require a significant revision.

Most older adults cope effectively with the changes associated with retirement, viewing it as a desired transition (Atchley, 2003). In retrospect, however, they often realize that preparation for retirement should have included more emphasis on the psychosocial aspects of this change rather than focusing so exclusively on its financial impact. Nancy Schlossberg (2009) refers to this as assembling a "Psychological Portfolio" in which a person articulates and clarifies aspects of identity, relationships, and sense of purpose that will serve as resources during the post-retirement years. In her research, she characterized seven paths through retirement and beyond that capture differences in how people shape their future lives:

1. Continuers: They maintain their former identity, but in a modified way. They stay connected to their former work and work-related identities while expanding in new directions.
2. Adventurers: They pursue an unrealized dream or try something new.
3. Easy-gliders: They take each day as it comes; no agenda and no pressures.
4. Involved spectators: They are still psychologically involved in their former life but are no longer active in it.

5. Searchers: They are looking for their special niche, exploring, and then moving on.
6. Retreaters: They are stepping back, taking a break to decide what to do next.
7. Disengaged: They are depressed, uninvolved, and unable to find a path forward.

Benefits of Retirement

What do people look forward to in retirement? Weiss (1997) described a longitudinal study of men and women who were over age 63 and intended to retire in the coming year or had recently retired. Most anticipated that retirement would bring a reduction in stress, especially in coping with the challenges and crises of the workplace. Workplace conditions such as lack of challenge, reorganization, and downsizing (with its accompanying increased demands on the remaining employees) are stressors that workers are glad to leave behind when they retire (Henkens & Tazelaar, 1997). According to the American Time Use Survey, retirees have a newfound 7–8 hours of leisure time each day. They use this time in many ways including getting more sleep; watching more TV; doing household maintenance including lawn and garden care, cooking, and housework; working for pay; eating more slowly and lingering over meals with family and friends; shopping, including comparison shopping; volunteering and participating in spiritual, civic, or community activities; reading; using the Internet for entertainment, information, and contacting others; socializing with friends, family, and neighbors; relaxing and thinking; and exercising (Brandon, 2016).

People who come to retirement from a context of lifelong well-being are likely to adapt well to this transition. They have had experiences of goal attainment, management of their time, effective social support, and invigorating intellectual stimulation, which

Using his knowledge of camping and exploration of the out-of-doors, Grandpa Victor teaches his grandchildren how to build a fire from gathered twigs, bark, and small branches. Victor loves being with his grandchildren and now that he is retired, he spends as much time as possible with them.

provide continuing resources after retirement. We can imagine that they will fit into one of the positive pathways described above and find a satisfying direction (Halleröd, Örestig, & Stattin, 2013).

Difficulties with Retirement

In contrast to those who are adjusting easily, a subset of retirees report declines in life satisfaction, especially those who experience significant income loss, poor health, or death of a spouse, events that are age-related and may not be attributed specifically to retirement. Approximately one third of adults report significant difficulties during this process (Pinquart & Schindler, 2007).

Perceptions of retirement involve a person's enthusiasm, positive anticipation, or resentment about it. These perceptions are linked to the ways in which work structures one's lifestyle throughout early and middle adulthood. In addition to the obvious functions of paid employment—especially income and social status—a number of latent functions provide important psychological benefits (Jahoda, 1982; Lo & Brown, 1999). Work provides a structure for the use of time; a context for social contact; a content for self-identity; regular, predictable activities into which one can channel intellectual, physical, and emotional energy; and a sense of participation in a collective effort. If retirement is perceived as resulting in deprivation in these areas, it presents a threat to psychological well-being.

The concept of **retirement anxiety** refers to apprehensions that adults have as they anticipate retirement (Fletcher and Hansson, 1991; Osborne, 2012). Sharpley (1997) found that when retirees reflected on factors that caused them stress in everyday living, three areas emerged: missing work, problems with personal health, and relationship issues. Psychological aspects of retirement that can create anxiety include identity disruption, a loss

of a sense of meaning or purpose, uncertainty about ways to continue to engage meaningfully in society, and the loss of meaningful social relationships. For those who suffer from retirement anxiety, two factors were especially troubling. First, people worried about the loss of structured social involvement and connection. This concern was linked to worry about losing friendships, being lonely, and having little in common with former coworkers after retirement. Second, people worried about having to be assertive or proactive in finding new relationships and activities that would meet their needs. This concern was linked to a general difficulty in handling life transitions, a high level of uncertainty about the future, and a general feeling of loss of identity. Although one might think that people who have high levels of retirement anxiety would use services that help people plan for retirement, this was not the case. They may try to deny this transition by avoiding planning and counseling sessions.

In addition to worries about being unable to meet social needs following retirement, some adults experience anxiety because they feel a lack of control. People have expectations about how long they plan to work and at what age they will retire. When people perceive that they are working or not working by their own choice and that they can determine how much work to do, they have higher levels of health and well-being. However, when they perceive that their level of involvement in work is being decided by someone else and have little say in it, they are likely to have more difficulty adjusting to retirement, more health problems, and a greater incidence of depression (Gall, Evans, & Howard, 1997; Schultz, Morton, & Weckerle, 1998). Especially for men who expect to work on into their late 60s and are forced into retirement, this lack of control over exiting from the workplace is predictive of lower well-being and reduced life satisfaction (Clarke, Marshall, & Weir, 2013).

— **CASE STUDY**   Anna Quindlen Writes About Retiring as "Stepping Aside" for the Next Generation of Writers —

Anna Quindlen, who wrote "the last word" for Newsweek for 9 years, explains why it's time for her to move on.

The baby-boom generation has created an interesting conundrum for this country. Born between 1946 and 1964, boomers take up more room than any other generation in American History. They now account for about a quarter of the population. And so, inevitably, they have created a kind of bottleneck, in the work world, in politics, in power. The frustration this poses for the young and talented should be obvious. In my personal life it was reflected powerfully on the day when, talking of the unwillingness of my friends to retire, my eldest child noted, "You guys just won't go." . . .

Today we have an entire generation of Americans who seem dedicated to the proposition that they will fight aging to the death. Quite literally. And that means staying front and center professionally.

The unspoken synonym for "emeritus" is "old." And old is a word we don't even use anymore in polite conversation, a modern obscenity....

I believe that many of our old ways of doing things are out of date, including some of our old ways of looking at, and reporting on, the world around us. Since the day he delivered his Inaugural Address, when I was 8 years old, people have been quoting the youthful John F. Kennedy saying that the torch had been passed to a new generation. But torches don't really get passed very much because people love to hold on to them....

If I had any lingering doubts about giving it up after almost nine years, they were quelled by those binders on my desk, full of exemplary work by reporters young enough to be my children. Flipping through their pages, reading such essential and beautifully rendered accounts of life in America and around the world, I felt certain of the future of the news business in some form or another. But between the lines I read another message, delivered without rancor or contempt, the same one I once heard from my own son: It's our turn. Step aside. And now I will.

Source: Quindlen, 2009.

Case Analysis Using What You Know

1. Explain how the developmental tasks of later adulthood are reflected in this narrative.
2. Evaluate the accuracy of Ms. Quindlen's analysis about the reluctance of the baby boom generation to retire. Discuss the factors that might account for the baby boom cohort's approach to retirement.
3. Summarize the ways the psychosocial crises of generativity versus stagnation and integrity versus despair are related to Ms. Quindlen's decision to retire.

Retirement for Couples

From a systems perspective, it makes sense to think about adaptation to retirement in the context of the other life roles one is playing. One of the most relevant is the marital relationship. With the large number of dual earner couples, it is important to consider the impact of retirement for a couple as well as for the individual. Retirement transitions can involve one partner remaining in the labor market when the other retires, both partners retiring at about the same time, and one or both partners retiring from their primary work and becoming involved in secondary work after retirement. These configurations can have consequences for the couple's marital satisfaction because the change in work status affects their relationship.

The Cornell Retirement and Well-Being Study focused on workers and retirees ages 50 to 72. Participants were interviewed once in 1994–1995 and again in 1996–1997. Among the people in this sample, 25 percent were not yet retired and their spouses were also not yet retired. For another 36 percent, both the respondent and the respondent's spouse were retired. In the remainder, one spouse was working and the other spouse was retired. Several observations were made about marital quality during this transition. First, both men and women reported decreases in marital quality when they moved from work to retirement. The role transition from work to retirement appears to have a short-term negative impact on the marriage. Second, if one spouse remains in

the labor market and the other retires, the retired partner reports more marital conflict. In this case, the stress of the role transition from work to retirement seems to be compounded by the lack of synchrony between the partners in the structure of their daily lives (Moen, Kim, & Hofmeister, 2001). The greatest satisfaction with retirement was reported by couples where both partners were retired, and the wives said that their husbands did not influence their decision to retire (Smith & Moen, 2004).

In an AARP national survey of individuals who were married (or living as married) and were retired or had a partner who was retired, couples where both spouses were retired were happier than couples where one partner was still in the labor force. Although the retirement decision is often treated as an individual one, in about one third of cases where one partner retired first, that person encouraged the other partner to retire. For some couples, dissatisfaction with retirement tended to spill into the marital relationship. Individuals who were dissatisfied with retirement also said their relationship with their partner was weaker. This lack of satisfaction could be a product of another underlying issue such lack of control or purpose. For most couples, retirement was positively associated with more travel, more exercise, volunteering, and involvement in hobbies (Kopper, 2008).

The Future of Retirement

A combination of demographic, economic, and organizational changes are contributing to more varied, flexible alternatives to full retirement (Lytle, Clancy, Foley, & Cotter, 2015). Certain social forces are influencing continuing involvement in the labor market after age 65. An increasing number of businesses are eliminating a mandatory retirement age. In 2000, the earnings limit for receiving full Social Security benefits after age 65 was lifted. Finally, the age for full eligibility for Social Security retirement benefits will rise to 67 for those born in 1960 or later. At the same time, movements toward reducing labor force participation for older workers include the development of early retirement plans, phased retirement, part-time work, and reduced or redefined job expectations. Innovation in retirement options seems to be taking two directions at the same time: how to retain older workers in meaningful work roles and how to permit more flexible earlier retirement programs (AARP, 2000).

Several long-range concerns suggest a need to reexamine the right to retirement concept. Prospects for a longer, healthier adulthood mean that a large proportion of the population will be out of the labor force for nearly one third of their adult lives if people continue to retire fully at age 65. Between 2010 and 2030 the large baby boom generation will reach retirement age, placing new demands on the Social Security system and new expectations for services to support quality of life. With a reduced fertility rate in Generation X, there may not be enough younger workers available to support this large nonworking population. If adults work to an older age, they will continue to contribute to the Social Security system, which will keep it financially sound for a longer time.

Among older adults who are well educated and have enjoyed working, many want to continue some of their positive experiences through constructive work. They do not want to retire, and with the lifting of the mandatory retirement age, they do not have to. It is not uncommon for men and women to take new jobs, perhaps with fewer or more flexible hours after they retire from their primary work. A great majority of these older workers remain in the labor market by choice. In a national survey of people ages 50 to 70 sponsored by AARP, nearly 70 percent thought that age 65 or older was an ideal age to retire, 37 percent said they would continue some type of paid work when they retired from their current job, and 6 percent said they thought they would never retire (Anderson, 2015). Reflecting on the next phase of their "post-retirement" career, the following features of an ideal job were mentioned: working part-time, working from home, opportunities for travel, helping others, and earning a good income from their work. Couples often want to coordinate their retirement. Since men typically marry younger women, they may continue working to an older age until their wives reach age 65.

People who reenter the labor force during midlife or make major career changes then want to persist in these new activities in order to fulfill achievement goals. Many women who delayed their entry into the labor market or achieved a professional degree after their spouse had completed his degree want to extend their work life into their late 60s and 70s (Austria, 2012).

The current cohort of workers who are now in their 50s and 60s have become used to a more fluctuating work history, moving from one company or employer to another. They are more accustomed to taking charge of their occupational career rather than relying on the built-in career ladder of a single occupation or employer. The idea of switching companies or occupations is a more familiar process for current workers, giving them confidence to retire from one position, withdraw from work for a while, and start over somewhere else. Technologies that allow people to work from home increase the chances that older workers, especially those who are well-educated, can continue to participate in the paid labor force. At the same time, fluctuating labor-market conditions create the risk that older workers who want to reenter the job market will not be able to find suitable employment (Rosegrant, 2013). Thus, just as the earlier generations grew accustomed to expecting to retire, new generations of older adults are finding ways to prolong their productive work lives, negotiating new and innovative ways of making transitions in and out of the paid labor force.

FURTHER REFLECTION: *Given the information and evidence you have read about later adulthood, what are your thoughts about retirement? Is age a relevant factor in deciding when to retire? If not, what other factors should a person consider?*

What is your own plan regarding retirement? Do you expect to retire? How does work fit into your sense of life satisfaction? How important is work to your personal identity? Describe an approach to retirement that inspires you.

CHAPTER SUMMARY

Variability in the patterns of adjustment during later adulthood results from the interaction among biological, psychological, and societal factors including personality characteristics, health, coping strategies, ego strengths, social support, and the range of life circumstances. Certain regularities can be anticipated in the termination of old roles and the establishment of new ones. The tasks of later adulthood—accepting one's life, promoting intellectual vigor, redirecting energy to new roles and activities, and developing a point of view about death—require a balance among investments in past, present, and future.

OBJECTIVE 1 Examine the construct of life satisfaction in later adulthood and analyze factors associated with subjective well-being.

There is an expectation that energy will be spent in the evaluative process of reviewing and accepting one's past achievements. However, this focus on the past must be complemented by the enactment of new roles, the resolution of new problems, and efforts to find new, engaging challenges in the present. People who are extroverted, optimistic, experiencing a sense of usefulness, and who feel they are in control of events in their life are also likely to experience high levels of satisfaction. Development in this period of life requires an ability to selectively direct resources to optimize functioning in the areas of life that are of primary value and satisfaction. Studies of life satisfaction and well-being find evidence of a U-shaped curve in which well-being reaches a low point in middle adulthood and rises in later adulthood and elderhood.

OBJECTIVE 2 Define intellectual vigor, and describe factors that promote it in later life. Evaluate evidence about the interaction of heredity and environment on intelligence in later life.

Genetic factors contribute to the stability of cognitive capacities over the life course, whereas the impact of the environment, including access to social support, engagement in challenging work and social relationships, health, and education all contribute to variability in cognitive functioning. Certain abilities, especially general knowledge and verbal abilities, remain relatively unchanged with age, whereas speed of processing and numeric abilities tend to decline. These patterns differ depending on overall intelligence of the person, the career focus, and expertise of the individual. Research in cognitive neuroscience provides evidence of both decline in brain functions with age, and continued plasticity, depending on health, and repeated engagement with demanding tasks.

OBJECTIVE 3 Explain the process of redirecting energy to new roles and activities, with special focus on role gain, such as grandparenthood; role loss, such as widowhood; and new opportunities for leisure.

The nature of the grandparent role differs across cultures, and within cultures across families. No single type of grandparent–adult child–grandchild relationship is normative in the United States, but most are characterized by feelings of affection and agreement about basic opinions and values. Adaptation to widowhood also varies across individuals and between men and women. Men are more likely to remarry, women to live alone after the death of their spouse. The pattern of adjustment depends heavily on the quality of the relationship before the partner died and the conditions surrounding the partner's death. Leisure time represents another domain in which there can be both role gain and role loss. Leisure activities can serve a wide range of physical, cognitive, and interpersonal goals. Volunteerism, through which later adults make substantial contributions to their communities, also has the potential for sustaining cognitive functioning and subjective well-being.

OBJECTIVE 4 Summarize the development of a point of view about death.

In later adulthood, people's thoughts about death tend to become more practical, focusing on the preparation of a will and planning for one's burial. However, anxiety about death seems to diminish with age. A strong sense of generativity and integrity contribute to the ability to face death with less fear while continuing to find joy in the satisfactions of daily life.

OBJECTIVE 5 Define and explain the psychosocial crisis of integrity versus despair, the central process of introspection, the prime adaptive ego quality of wisdom, and the core pathology of disdain.

The psychosocial crisis of integrity versus despair captures the courage and creative synthesis required in later adulthood. In the face of an increasingly evident mortality, experiences in physical changes, role loss, and the death of peers, most older adults are able to define and articulate the thread of meaning in their lives. They are able to look back with satisfaction at past achievements and with acceptance of past failures. The central process of introspection acknowledges the need for self-awareness as well as time for reflection in order to carry out the psychological work required to reach a sense of integrity. In this process, many older adults find a certain practical wisdom that is shared with others and becomes their legacy for the future.

OBJECTIVE 6 Apply theory and research to understanding the process of adjustment to retirement.

The role transitions that accompany retirement illustrate the challenge of later adulthood. Retirement usually results in leaving a major life structure—one that provided social status, focus, purpose, and economic resources. The potential loss of daily stimulation poses threats to both cognitive and social functioning. Because so much of one's social status is linked to occupational attainment, leaving a work role is almost like giving up a social identity. Older adults face numerous adjustments after retirement, including role loss. They must restructure their lives so that they continue to feel pride in past achievements without dwelling on the past, and so that they seek new and realistic opportunities for making use of their talents in the present. With the prospect of a long, healthy later adulthood, many in the current cohort of older adults expect to continue participation in the paid labor force even if they intend to change jobs or shift their occupational focus.

It is critical to be sensitive to the image that children, adolescents, young and middle-aged adults, and older adults themselves have of later adulthood. One should not underestimate the impact that one's perceptions of later life have on well-being and optimism at every earlier life stage. If the later years hold no promise, all earlier stages will be tainted with a sense of desperation. On the other hand, if the later years can be anticipated with optimism, people will be free at each earlier stage to experience life in a more confident, accepting manner.

CASEBOOK

For additional case material related to this chapter, see the case of "Lola," in *Life Span Development: A Case Book*, by Barbara and Philip Newman, Laura Landry-Meyer, and Brenda J. Lohman, pp. 209–212.

This case focuses on the role of reminiscence in resolving the psychosocial crisis of integrity versus despair and the opportunity for earlier expertise to be used in redirecting energy to new roles.

At the age of 91, shortly before his death, Picasso painted this remarkable self-portrait. He faces his death with eyes wide open—no pretenses, some fear, some wonder.

1. Explain the rationale for identifying elderhood as a unique developmental stage for those of unusual longevity with its own developmental tasks and psychosocial crisis.

2. List the physical changes associated with aging, and evaluate the challenges that these changes pose for continued psychosocial well-being.

3. Describe the concept of a psychohistorical perspective, an altered perspective on time and history that emerges among the long-lived.

4. Summarize elements of the lifestyle structure in elderhood, especially living arrangements and gender roles, and analyze the impact of these life structures for continued well-being.

5. Define and explain the psychosocial crisis of immortality versus extinction, the central process of social support, the prime adaptive ego quality of confidence, and the core pathology of diffidence.

6. Apply research and theory to concerns about meeting the needs of the frail elderly.

ELDERHOOD (75 UNTIL DEATH)

14

Fred Hale was born December 1, 1890, in New Sharon, Maine. His biography and photo portrait are included in a book on "supercentenarians," people who have lived to be 110 or more.

Earth's Elders: The Wisdom of the World's Oldest People, by Jerry Friedman.

Perhaps the most amusing story from Fred came about when he was 107 and still living on his own. At that age, he was the world's oldest licensed driver.

There had been a heavy snowfall in Maine and Fred was up on his porch roof shoveling off the snow. When he finished, he hopped off into a snow bank and then went into his house to change his wet clothes. Suddenly he noticed there were flashing lights outside. When he opened the door, there were the firemen and police who'd come to his rescue. When he was told that a passerby had seen someone fall of the roof, Fred quipped, "I didn't fall, I jumped" and slammed the door.

Fred has been confined to a wheelchair and the assisted care facility after he tripped and broke his hip. That hasn't dulled his mind however. He still jokes and plays cards with his son of eighty. He read a little and loved to watch the Red Sox. Clearly, he was the oldest Red Sox fan in the world. When asked why he had lived so long he jibed, "Oh, I don't know, punishment I guess. I've enjoyed all my years, each one. I even like the recent one."

The last time we spoke I asked, "If there was one piece of wisdom you'd like to pass on to your grandchildren what would it be?"

"You have one life to live, live it well, and don't disgrace your family."

Source: Jerry Friedman, 2005, p. 80.

CASE ANALYSIS Using What You Know

1. Summarize your assumptions about the lifestyle and behaviors of elders. How does this case confirm or disconfirm those assumptions?
2. List five of Fred's personality characteristics. Explain how these qualities may contribute to longevity.
3. Analyze Fred's final wisdom. What are the implications of this advice for you and your family? For others in your generation?

P ablo Picasso, whose works illustrate this book, lived to be 91 years old. When he was 79, he married Jacqueline Roque with whom he enjoyed 12 years of married life. During the last 20 years of his life, he remained productive and energetic, persistently experimenting with new art forms and ideas.

Here are some other examples of people who achieved major accomplishments after the age of 80 (Wallechinsky & Wallace, 1993; Wallechinsky, Wallace, & Wallace, 1977):

At 100, Grandma Moses was still painting.
At 99, twin sisters Kin Narita and Gin Kanie recorded a hit CD single in Japan and starred in a television commercial.

At 94, George Burns, who won an Oscar at age 80 for his role in *The Sunshine Boys*, performed at Proctor's Theater in Schenectady, New York, 63 years after he had first played there.
At 93, George Bernard Shaw wrote the play *Farfetched Fables*.
At 91, Eamon de Valera served as president of Ireland.
At 91, Hulda Crooks climbed Mount Whitney, the highest mountain in the continental United States.
At 89, Arthur Rubenstein gave one of his greatest piano recitals in New York's Carnegie Hall.
At 88, Konrad Adenauer was chancellor of Germany.
At 87, Mary Baker Eddy founded the *Christian Science Monitor*.
At 81, Benjamin Franklin provided leadership for the political compromises that led to the adoption of the U.S. Constitution. ●

The Longevity Revolution

We have entered a period in which increasing numbers of people are living into old age. As the previous examples illustrate, it's not that we have no models of the long-lived in earlier periods of history, but that so many more adults are living into their 80s and 90s than ever before. In 2016, 6 percent of the U.S. population was 75 and older, and as the baby boomers (those born between 1946 and 1964) mature, this age group is expected to reach 11 percent of the population. In 1980, more than 2 million people were 85 and older; by 2015, this group had grown to 6.2 million (U.S. Census Bureau, 2016). At the 2010 census, 53,364 people were 100 years and older. The 85-and-older population is the fastest-growing age group in the United States (Werner, 2011).

The 20th century was unique in human history in the large percentage of people who lived well beyond their reproductive and childrearing years into later adulthood and elderhood. This new facet of life raises questions about the pattern of mortality after achieving reproductive success and about what, if any, limit there might be to the human life span. Current projections suggest that in the United States the average life expectancy at birth will be 80 by the year 2020 (U.S. Census Bureau, 2010e). Genetically based diseases that emerge only in the second half of life, such as breast and colon cancer or adult-onset diabetes, become more common as larger numbers of people reach advanced age. At the same time, the mapping of the human genome along with medical and technical innovations hold the promise of preventing some of the diseases now associated with later life. Life expectancy is most influenced by interventions that prevent infants and children from dying, ensuring that more people reach advanced ages of 70 or older. Interventions that influence the life expectancy at ages 70 and older increase overall life expectancy by only a few years. Nonetheless, significant discoveries that might prevent death from cancers or cardiovascular diseases could affect large populations and continue to extend human longevity.

The human species is a highly complex organism designed to survive over a relatively long period in order to find a mate, reproduce, and rear and nurture the young until they are old enough to reproduce. From an evolutionary perspective, the adaptive value of life after this sequence is not well understood. One hypothesis is that the extended family—composed of grandparents as well as parents—provides more resources for the support of the young and forms an added protective layer against crises that might leave the younger generation vulnerable (Baudisch & Vaupel, 2012).

It is clear that there is a genetic basis to longevity. Studies of centenarians (people 100 years old and over) find a relatively large number of genetic markers involving over 130 genes that predict extreme longevity. These markers become increasingly accurate in predicting which individuals will live to advanced ages of 100 and older. Studies of these centenarians find three different patterns of resilience that are associated with longevity. One group has many of the same diseases of aging before age 80 as those who are not so long lived, but they recover and continue on to advanced age. One group has delayed age-related illness after the age of 80. And one group had no age-related illnesses even at age 100. Genetic factors contribute to the compression of illness toward the very end of life and enhanced capacities for recovery (Andersen, S. L., 2012; Sebastiani et al., 2012).

The current cohort of elders (those 75 and older) includes the older group from the greatest generation (sometimes called the GI Joe generation) born between 1910 and 1925, and the younger group from the silent generation, born between 1925 and 1945. The greatest generation grew up during the Great Depression; many men served during World War II, and many women worked in factories in order to sustain war-related production. Over 400,000 U.S. deaths were attributed to war-related military actions, civilian deaths related to military actions, and disease associated with the war. The harsh and stressful conditions of the war are known to have shortened the life expectancy of those who served in battle. Following a period of economic and war-related hardships, the survivors, both veterans and civilians, went on to rebuild the country in a spirit of optimism and patriotism.

The silent generation, most of whom were too young to serve in World War II, experienced the war during their childhood. In the 1950s, during the McCarthy anti-communist era, the atmosphere was one of suspicion and suppression of criticism of government. This generation was socialized to accept society, to adopt a conservative outlook, and to work hard at a time of economic recovery. They entered the labor market in a time of economic growth, formed families at an early age, and adopted traditional gender roles (Howe, 2014; Robinson, 2016).

Each new cohort of the very old will benefit from the information and technologies that are being developed. The more knowledge is gained about the biological processes of aging and the genetic basis of diseases and health that emerge in later life, the more likely it is that human longevity can be extended. Those adults in the current baby boom generation (born between 1946 and 1964) are quite likely to be high school graduates, to have benefited from many of the health-related innovations of the late 20th and early 21st centuries, and to be even more vigorous than our current older population. The projections of increased numbers of people reaching advanced age are due to improvements in health care and fitness and to the size of the baby boom cohort.

Secrets to Longevity

The very long lived, like Jeanne Calment, inspire others to ask about the factors that contribute to a long life. Jim Heynen (1990)

Jeanne Calment, who died in 1997 at the age of 122, was the world's longest living person whose birth date could be verified. Mme. Calment liked chocolates, smoked cigarettes, and had a wonderful sense of humor. Here she displays her Guinness certificate acknowledging her record-winning longevity.

interviewed 100 people who were 100 years or older. He found wide variations in their lifestyles and philosophical perspectives. Some of the advice they offered on how to live a long life follows:

"Mind your own business, have a good cigar, and take a shot of brandy." *Brother Adelard Beaudet, Harrisville, Rhode Island*

"I've lived long because I was so mean." *Pearl Rombach, Melbourne, Florida*

"I always walked several miles a day. I'd talk to the flowers." *Mary Frances Annand, Pasadena, California*

"Don't smoke before noon. Don't drink or smoke after midnight. The body needs 12 hours of the day to clear itself." *Harry Wander, Boise, Idaho*

"I've been a tofu eater all my life; a mild, gentle man, never a worrier." *Frank Morimitsu, Chicago, Illinois*

"I picked my ancestors carefully." *Stella H. Harris, Manhattan, Kansas*

"Regular hours, taking it easy, smiling, whistling at the women when they walk by." *John Hilton, Fort Lauderdale, Florida*

A team of nutritionists, psychologists, physicians, and gerontologists interviewed 12 Cuban men and women who were reported to be more than 100 years old about their daily diets and lifestyles. The one theme they all agreed upon was the importance of an optimistic outlook on life. The coordinator of the meeting, Dr. Eugenio Selman, said that the six basic elements to longevity are (1) motivation to live, (2) appropriate diet, (3) medical attention, (4) intense physical activity, (5) cultural activities, and (6) a healthy environment. In this analysis, one sees the interaction of the biological, psychological, and societal systems (CNN.com,

2005). Surprisingly absent from this list is the role of social integration and social support. A growing literature highlights the contribution of a sense of belonging to overall health and resilience in the face of crisis (Gow et al., 2007).

The Blue Zone

The Blue Zone refers to specific geographic areas of the world where people are known to live a long, healthy life. Early work by Poulain et al. (2004), identified an area of Sardinia in Italy where a large number of men were found to live to 100 years and more. Following this research, Dan Buettner (2008; 2012) identified other regions where similar patterns of longevity and low incidence of certain diseases, especially heart disease, cancer, and dementia, were observed. By overlaying the qualities associated with three of these special geographic areas: Okinawa, Japan; Sardinia; and the Seventh Day Adventist community of Loma Linda, California, Buettner identified features of the lifestyle that were common to all three:

Moderate daily activity as a regular aspect of life
A strong sense of life purpose
A low-stress, slower pace of life
Moderate calorie intake including a largely plant-based diet
Moderate alcohol consumption, especially red wine
Engagement in spirituality or religion
Engagement in family life
Engagement in social life with good friends

Building on the Blue Zone analysis, the Blue Zone Project is striving to adapt these features of a healthy, happy lifestyle to U.S. communities. They hope to introduce changes at the family, school, neighborhood, and health care levels in order to "make it easier to get up and move, eat healthy, make new friends, find a reason for being—and live longer, better" (Blue Zone Project, 2016). Currently eight cities/regions have embraced the Blue Zone guidelines to improve the health, community involvement, and well-being of their citizens.

Although the concept seems positive, there is also pushback and some scientific reservation about this idea. First, the population of isolated communities may spring from long-lived ancestors, thus ignoring the genetic basis to longevity among the residents. Second, adapting lifestyle characteristics from small isolated communities to modern towns may not be appropriate. Third, the Blue Zone characteristics identify features that are present, but not necessarily features that are absent from these lifestyles that may contribute to longevity, for example, lack of air pollution, traffic, noise, and other environmental features that create stress. Fourth, some critics view the Blue Zone guidelines as an imposition on their family privacy and a restriction of their personal freedoms. Finally, interviews with centenarians find quite a diversity of lifestyle features, suggesting that for the very long lived, there may not be one secret, or even one pattern of secrets (Murray, 2015).

The Gender Gap Among the Very Old

A discussion of aging in the United States must acknowledge the shifting sex composition of the population at older ages. In 2010, 60 percent of those 75 to 84 were women, 70 percent of those 85 to 94 were women, and 80 percent of those 95 and older were women (Werner, 2011). This **gender gap** in longevity is observed in virtually all countries of the world, but the differences are accentuated in the developed countries. The imbalance in the sex composition is much more noticeable today than it was 50 years ago when there were about as many men as women in the older-than-65 category. Because those currently at the stage of elderhood are predominantly women, many of the social issues of aging—especially poverty, health care, the future of Social Security, and housing—are also viewed as women's issues.

FURTHER REFLECTION: The majority of the elderly are women. Generate some implications of this for social policy and community development.

A New Psychosocial Stage: Elderhood

OBJECTIVE 1 Explain the rationale for identifying elderhood as a unique developmental stage for those of unusual longevity with its own developmental tasks and psychosocial crisis.

An increasing number of people are reaching advanced years and share certain personal and behavioral characteristics. This leads us to hypothesize a new stage of psychosocial development that emerges at the upper end of the life span after one has exceeded the life expectancy for one's birth cohort. This stage of life is experienced by the long-lived in a community who have outlived most of their age-mates. Drawing on the concept of village elders who share their wisdom and help resolve community disputes, we call this stage **elderhood**. Although it was not specifically identified in Erikson's original formulation of life stages, Erikson began to characterize the dynamics of psychosocial adaptation in this period of life in the book *Vital Involvement in Old Age* (Erikson et al., 1986). Throughout this chapter, we have drawn on Erikson's insights to enrich our appreciation of the courage, vitality, and transformations that accompany elderhood.

We have formulated a psychosocial analysis of development in elderhood based on research literature, firsthand reports, and personal observations to describe the developmental tasks, psychosocial crisis, central process, prime adaptive ego quality, and core pathology of this stage. We acknowledge that in many domains—especially physical functioning, reaction time, memories, and cognitive abilities—variability increases significantly with age. With advanced age, a person is less constrained by pressures of institutionalized roles and social demands. As a result, personal preferences and genetically based sources of individuality are freer to be expressed. In addition, individual differences reflect the diversity of educational experiences, health or illness, exposure to harsh conditions, and patterns of work and family life.

The concept of *norm of reaction* introduced in chapter 4 (The Period of Pregnancy and Prenatal Development) offers a framework for understanding the enormous variability in vitality and functioning during elderhood. The quality of functioning in elderhood is a product of the interaction among genetic factors, lifestyle choices, and environmental conditions. *Genetic factors* influence longevity, vulnerability to illnesses, intelligence, and personality factors that contribute to coping (Underwood, 2015).

Former U.S. President Jimmy Carter continues to function in an informal role as a diplomat and advocate of peaceful solutions to world problems. Here he is at age 88. In 1982 he established the Carter Center, focusing on efforts to resolve conflict, promote democracy, protect human rights, and prevent disease. In 2002 he was awarded the Nobel Peace Prize.

Support for a genetic basis to longevity is provided from observations from the New England Centenarian Study that found that half the centenarians had grandparents, siblings, and other close relatives who also reached very advanced ages (Perls, Kunkel, & Puca, 2002; Sebastiani & Persl, 2012). An analysis of data from five studies of centenarians found that genetic profiles were increasingly accurate in predicting those who live to especially advanced ages—102 and beyond (Sebastiani et al., 2013).

Lifestyle factors include physical activity, diet, control over one's life, not smoking, moderate alcohol use, and the quality of one's social network. *Environmental conditions* that reduce longevity include poverty, discrimination, social alienation, and lack of social support. Data comparing the life expectancy across countries suggest that environmental conditions, including air and water quality, health care services, housing, and educational resources, all impact longevity beyond what the individual person can control (Katch, 2013).

Variations in life experiences and outlook among the very old are great. As a result, chronological age becomes less useful as an indicator of aging. Neugarten (1981) offered a distinction that helps clarify the functional differences among elders. She described two groups: the **old-old** and the **young-old**. The old-old have "suffered major physical or mental decrements," which increase their dependence on health and social services. This group will grow as the number of adults over 75 increases.

The majority of people over 75 can be described as young-old. They are competent, vigorous, and relatively healthy. They live in their own households and participate in activities in their communities. For example, among the New England centenarians studied, 90 percent were functionally independent and relatively healthy up until age 92 (Perls & Terry, 2007).

FURTHER REFLECTION: Evaluate the argument that it is necessary to introduce a new stage of elderhood in the life-span perspective. What evidence supports the need to differentiate elderhood from the stage of later adulthood?

Developmental Tasks

Despite the wide variability in capacities, lifestyles, and worldviews in later life, three themes characterize the challenges that face individuals in elderhood. First, they must adapt to *physical changes*, monitoring their health and modifying their lifestyles to accommodate these changes. Second, they must conceptualize their lives within a new *time frame*, realigning their thoughts about past, present, and future in order to stay connected to the present in a meaningful way. Third, they must develop new **life structures**—especially living arrangements and social relationships—that provide comfort, interest, and appropriate levels of care.

Coping with the Physical Changes of Aging

OBJECTIVE 2 List the physical changes associated with aging, and evaluate the challenges that these changes pose for continued psychosocial well-being.

There is no way to avoid the realization that with advanced age one's body is not what it used to be. Erikson described it as follows:

> With aging, as the overall tonus of the body begins to sag and innumerable inner parts call attention to themselves through their malfunction, the aging body is forced into a new sense of invalidness. Some problems may be fairly petty, like the almost inevitable appearance of wrinkles. Others are painful, debilitating, and shaming. Whatever the severity of these ailments, the elder is obliged to turn attention from more interesting aspects of life to the demanding requirements of the body. This can be frustrating and depressing. (Erikson et al., 1986, p. 309)

Aging, which is a continuous process over the life span, includes both development and decline. Some physical changes are considered to be normal or expected, and not especially related to disease. People who are well educated, have access to health care and other resources, and have observed healthy lifestyle practices in earlier stages of life are still going to experience some of the normative changes of aging when they reach advanced age, such as some loss of muscle strength or difficulty returning to normal respiration after periods of exertion. However, certain lifestyle practices including smoking cigarettes, alcohol and drug abuse, poor diet, and a sedentary life are likely to accelerate these patterns of normal decline. Other changes are disease related and not a result of normal aging. Genetic factors appear to increase vulnerability to these diseases, but so do lifestyle factors, exposure to toxins, and stress. Thus, we want to emphasize that the **physical changes of aging** are multidimensional and variable across individuals. Some people who have observed a healthy lifestyle in early and middle adulthood still experience diseases whereas others who have led a more risky lifestyle do not experience these diseases. We do not fully understand the extent to which genetic, environmental, social, and lifestyle factors help support continued health or vulnerability to disease in elderhood.

The theme of the physical changes of aging can be approached much like its counterpart in early adolescence. Although the rate of change may be slower, older adults notice changes in a range of areas, including appearance, body shape, strength and stamina, and the accumulation of chronic illnesses. Just as in adolescence, the rate and sequence of changes vary from person to person. The following sections identify major areas of physical change. Not all adults experience all of these changes, nor to the same degree. The level of fitness that was established and maintained during early and middle adulthood influence the progression of physical changes associated with aging. Important issues include the meaning that adults attribute to their physical condition and the coping strategies they invent to adapt to these changes. The topics of fitness, sleep and rest, behavioral slowing, sensory changes, health, illness, and functional independence combine to provide a picture of the physical changes of aging.

Fitness

There is a great deal of variation in **fitness** among people after age 75 as patterns of activity or inactivity, endurance or frailty, and illness or health take their toll. What is described here might be thought of as the usual patterns of aging. However, these changes are not inevitable and, in many instances, are reversible or modifiable with appropriate intervention (Dobek, White, & Gunter, 2007).

Seven components are often included in measures intended to assess fitness among the elderly: coordination, reaction time, balance, muscle strength, muscle endurance, flexibility, and cardiorespiratory endurance (Hilgenkamp, van Wijck, & Evenhuis, 2010). Among those 75 and older, elders who exhibit high levels of fitness are also likely to report a better overall quality of life, higher cognitive functioning, lower levels of depression, and a lower likelihood of encountering physical disabilities as they age (Tainaka, Takizawa, Katamoto, & Aoki, 2009; Takata et al., 2010; Voelker-Rehage, Godde, & Staudinger, 2010).

Most people begin to notice declines in their physical health and fitness in their late 20s and early 30s. As those who love baseball are likely to claim, "The legs are the first to go." On a more positive note, most people's strength and capacity for moderate effort are about the same at age 70 as they were at age 40 (Stevens-Long & Commons, 1992). However, older people are less resilient after a period of prolonged exertion. The respiratory and circulatory systems usually degenerate to some extent and are less capable of providing the heart and muscle tissue with oxygenated blood as quickly as they once could. One result is that sudden changes in posture can cause an older person to feel lightheaded. In order to adapt successfully to this kind of bodily change, an older person may find it necessary to move more slowly and to change positions more deliberately. This observable change in the tempo of movement may be incorrectly interpreted as fatigue or weakness when, in fact, it is often a purposeful strategy for preventing dizziness.

Nutrition and Fitness. Slowed metabolism reduces the need for calories, but there are new risks. Blood sugar levels are likely to rise after eating and body fat increases. These conditions increase the risk of type 2 diabetes. Reduction in food intake—particularly the elimination of foods such as milk—may result in the lack of essential vitamins and minerals in an older person's diet. The resulting malnutrition may then contribute to osteoporosis and iron deficiencies, which produce feelings of weakness, fatigue, and a lack of resilience (Klesges et al., 2001). In order to cope successfully with a diminished appetite, elders must become more conscientious in selecting foods that will provide the nutritional elements necessary for healthy functioning.

Many health concerns of later adulthood that may have been attributed to the aging process itself are in fact a direct or indirect result of malnutrition. In the years from 2007 to 2009, a period of severe economic downturn in the United States, researchers reported substantial increases in food insecurity among adults including those in middle and later adulthood as well as elderhood (Ziliak & Gunderson, 2011). Food insecurity is associated with lower nutritional intake, fewer calories, less protein, fewer essential vitamins, greater likelihood of reporting poor or fair health, and significant increases in functional limitations, requiring assistance in activities of daily living (Lee & Frongillo, 2001). There is speculation that adults who suffered from food insecurity in their middle and later adult years may reach elderhood in a state of greater frailty and in need of more health services.

Lifestyle and Fitness. A number of factors make it difficult to maintain a high level of physical fitness in later life. Some aspects of aging that impact fitness are a result of the body's natural process as cells replicate again and again and, through metabolism, produce by-products that can be harmful to the body itself. Some aspects of aging that reduce fitness are a result of choices and circumstances such as a sedentary lifestyle, smoking, a diet heavy in fats, too much time in the sun, exposure to environmental toxins, and lack of health care.

Commitment to physical fitness is important for adults in order to face their later years in the best possible physical condition. In its report *Healthy People 2020*, the U.S. government identified physical activity as a key factor in promoting health and

Those who survive into their 90s demonstrate surprising good health. Solly has been bowling since he was 10; at age 96, he still enjoys the sport and carries a 123 average in the 80 and older league.

preventing illness (U.S. Department of Health and Human Services, 2013). A primary goal is to improve health, function, and quality of life for older adults. Among the recommendations to achieve this goal is to encourage regular, daily physical activity. The recommended level of physical activities includes 2 hours and 30 minutes a week of moderate aerobic activity, strengthening activities 2 days a week, and balancing activities 3 days or more a week.

Regular physical activity is associated with decreased rates of death from heart disease, lower risk of diabetes and colon cancer, and prevention of high blood pressure. Physical activity also improves muscle and bone strength, contributes to weight control, and improves strength, flexibility, and balance. These latter factors all reduce chances of serious injury, thereby preserving functional independence. Despite these advantages, only 27.6 percent of people ages 75 and older meet the guidelines for aerobic activity, and 9 percent meet the combined guidelines for aerobic and strengthening (National Center for Health Statistics, 2016b).

With advancing age, some people tend to become more sedentary and lose interest in physical activity. In order to maintain optimal functioning and to retard the degenerative effects of aging, very old adults must continue to have frequent and regular opportunities for physical exercise. A regular program of walking or other aerobic exercise can enhance cardiovascular functioning and reverse some of the effects of a sedentary adult lifestyle,

resulting in both improved mood, increased reaction time, and improved performance on tests of working memory (Hogan, Mata, & Carstensen, 2013). Research on weight, or resistance, training shows that even among the very old, a steady program of exercise builds muscle strength, which contributes to agility and an overall sense of well-being (Ades, Ballor, Ashikaga, Utton, & Nair, 1996; Seguin, Epping, Buchner, Bloch, & Nelson, 2002). Weight-bearing exercises help offset the normal processes of loss of muscle tone and bone density, improving balance and reducing the likelihood of falls. Experimental studies of the effects of exercise on cognitive functioning show that it also leads to improvements in various central nervous system functions. These benefits of exercise are attributed in part to higher levels of oxygen that improve the metabolism of glucose and neurotransmitters in the brain, as well as to increased levels of arousal that increase response speed (Newell, Vaillancourt, & Sosnoff, 2006).

Sleep and Rest

Older adults seem to need about 7 to 9 hours of sleep a night. However, older adults tend to go to sleep earlier and wake up earlier than when they were younger and spend less time in deep sleep, which may be why older adults often report being light sleepers (National Institute on Aging, 2016). Sleep problems, including difficulty falling asleep, periods of wakefulness after falling asleep, and shorter length of sleep are often observed among the elderly, even among older adults who say their quality of sleep is fine (Cavuoto et al., 2016). These sleep problems are associated with poorer performance on memory tasks and poor consolidation of newly learned information, especially tasks requiring visual and motor coordination (Mantua, Bran, & Spencer, 2016). More significant sleep problems occur for older adults who have various medical conditions that involve pain, sleep apnea, movement disorders, and urinary problems. In a large sample of elderly women, those who suffered from arthritis and heart disease also reported the greatest sleep difficulties (Leigh, Hudson, & Byles, 2016; Ohayon, Carskadon, Guilleminault, & Vitiello, 2004).

The most common sleep problem in elderhood is *insomnia*, which involves difficulties falling asleep or staying asleep. Insomnia may be a temporary problem associated with particular worries, excitement over an upcoming event, or preoccupation with an unresolved challenge. On the other hand, insomnia may be a symptom of other medical conditions, such as unmanaged pain or difficulty breathing. People who have had a bout of insomnia may exacerbate their problem by worrying about whether they will be able to fall asleep (National Institute on Aging, 2016).

> Ever since he retired, Edward dreads going to bed at night. He's afraid that when he turns off his light, he will just lie there with his eyes open and his mind racing. "How can I break this cycle?" he asks. "I'm so tired—I need to get some sleep." (National Institute on Aging, 2016)

Problems with sleep may also lead to subsequent difficulties in cognition and a sense of well-being. Given the role of sleep for supporting memory, consolidation of new learning, and positive mood, older adults who have sleep difficulties may also be at greater risk for depression, declines in cognitive functioning, and disease. One analysis of five longitudinal studies found that insomnia was a significant predictor of subsequent risk of dementia (de Almondes, Costa, Malloy-Diniz, & Diniz, 2016; Leigh, Hudson, & Byles, 2016).

Many older adults take daytime naps; an estimated 15 percent of those ages 55 to 64 and 25 percent of those ages 75 to 84 nap. There may be benefits from the practice of napping. In a study that tracked over 23,000 Greek adults for 6 years, those who napped three times a week or more for about half an hour had a substantially lower risk of heart attacks than those who did not nap (Naska et al., 2007). Napping has also been associated with improved memory consolidation among the elderly, especially for visual memories (Ladenbauer et al., 2016). Napping may help reduce stress and allow a person to engage the remainder of the day with more energy. In a study of napping among older adults, those who had a regular habit of sleeping at about the same time each day and waking themselves up after about half an hour had a greater sense of self-efficacy and less experience of sluggishness in the afternoon and evening (Kaida et al., 2006).

Several hypotheses link napping to well-being. People who are able to nap during the day may also be in greater control of their lives and less exposed to stress. Taking a nap may be a deliberate way to reduce stress, relax, and prepare to engage more fully in the remaining hours of the day. Cognitive benefits of a nap may contribute to feelings of well-being. Despite the benefits of a brief nap, when a person is napping several times a day this may be linked to unusual feelings of sleepiness, depression, and pain, which may indicate a more serious health problem (Foley et al., 2007).

Behavioral Slowing

One of the most commonly noted markers of aging is a gradual slowing in response to stimuli. **Behavioral slowing** is observed in motor responses, reaction time, problem-solving abilities, memory skills, and information processing (Salthouse, 1996). Reaction time is a composite outcome of the time it takes to perceive a stimulus, retrieve related information from memory, integrate it with other relevant stored information, reason as necessary about the required action, and then take action—whether that means the time it takes to press a button after detecting a signal, or the time it takes to complete a crossword puzzle or solve a math problem. Age-related slowing is more readily observable in complex tasks requiring mental processing than in routine tasks (Lemaire, Arnaud, & Lecacheur, 2004). The more complex the task, the greater the **processing load**—that is, the more domains of information called into play, the more time it takes to select response strategies.

The number of tasks presented in a sequence and the complexity of choice required to make a response are all factors that influence response time. Under conditions where a choice of response is required, older adults do not show evidence of slowing in the early phase of processing the stimuli, but in the executive functions associated with enacting the appropriate response (Yordanova, Kolev, Hohnsbein, & Falkenstein, 2004). In many studies, older adults show improvements in response time when given opportunity for practice. However, when older and younger adults are both given opportunities for practice, the older adults do not improve as much as the younger adults, and the performance gap may actually increase (Hein & Schubert, 2004).

Biological, learned, and motivational factors may account for behavioral slowing. At the biological level, there is evidence of the slowing of neural firing in certain brain areas, which may result in a slower speed of information processing. This is due in part to age-related damage to the myelin sheath that insulates neurons and facilitates speed of firing (Salat, 2011). The extent of this slowing depends on the kinds of tasks and specific cognitive processes involved. Speed of processing may be only one of many factors responsible for age-related changes in cognitive processing (Hartley, 2006). Older adults appear to be effective in recruiting various brain regions to compensate for declines in processing speed, which stimulates new patterns of connections across the hemispheres of the brain. Research on brain functioning in later life finds evidence for plasticity and adaptive reorganization (Davis, Kragel, Madden, & Cabeza, 2012).

The slowing of responses may also be a product of learned cautiousness. With experience, people learn to respond slowly in order to avoid making mistakes. When confronted with new, experimental problem-solving tasks, older adults may take longer because they are not confident in using a new strategy. They may revert to a more familiar, if more time-consuming, approach in order to solve the problem correctly. Thus, a conservative orientation to the selection of problem-solving strategies may result in slower responses but not be strictly due to neurological causes (Touron & Hertzog, 2004). Depending upon the task, cautiousness may be related to prior experiences of instability or falling. As older adults step down from the sidewalk to the street, or step off an elevator or onto an escalator, they move more slowly to ensure that they have good footing and will not slip or fall. Finally, response slowing may be a product of a low level of motivation to perform a task. In experiments in which reaction time is being tested, adult participants may be uninterested in the task and thus unwilling to try to respond quickly.

The implications of the consequences of behavioral slowing are currently being examined. Some researchers argue that even the slightest reduction in the speed of neural firing may result in reduced sensory and information-processing capacities. Furthermore, response slowing may reduce a person's chances of survival if a situation arises in which a sudden evasive action or immediate response is required. Others have suggested that if a moment of thought is required before an action is taken, slowness may increase a person's chances of survival.

The impact of slowing on cognitive functioning continues to be debated. If the nervous system functions at a slower rate, it takes more time to scan and perceive information, search long-term memory, integrate information from various knowledge domains, and make a response (Madden, 2001). However, mental abilities that rely on speed, which are often assessed under laboratory conditions, do not predict cognitive functioning for elders in their real-world environments. Although it is well established that speed of performance declines with age, there are few real-world situations that require the rapid speed that is typically measured in laboratory conditions. As they age, people typically create living conditions that are adapted to their abilities, allowing them to preserve effective problem-solving strategies as well as possible (Salthouse, 2012). Recall from chapter 13 (Later Adulthood) that crystallized intelligence tends to increase with age, whereas fluid intelligence declines. When the factor of speed of responding was removed from the tests of fluid intelligence, the decline with age was significantly less. Contemporary circumstances—especially physical fitness and health, as well as the kinds of medications one is taking and the presence of immediate stressors in one's life—influence the speed of responding. In each situation, motor performance results from the adaptive self-organization of responses that are a product of how the person assesses the situation; the person's physical strength, flexibility, and endurance; and the person's ability to control posture, movement, and dexterity. Speed of responding will vary depending on what type of response is required and which systems constrain behavior (Newell, Vaillancourt, & Sosnoff, 2006). One 80-year-old woman may be able to walk through an airport quickly to get to her gate but may be slow in reading and evaluating the information that tells whether her flight is on time or delayed. Another 80-year-old woman may be able to read the information about the flight and quickly assess whether her flight is on time but may take much longer to get to the departure gate.

Because slowing occurs gradually, most adults compensate for it by making their environments more convenient or by changing their lifestyles. However, slowing becomes more hazardous in situations that require the older adult to keep pace with a tempo that cannot be modified, such as highway driving or crossing the street with the light. For instance, some older people encounter problems because the amount of time the light stays green at a pedestrian crosswalk is insufficient to permit them to get to the other side of the street safely. Elders may become more selective in their choice of activities so that they can allocate enough time for the tasks most important to them and perform them satisfactorily. This means exercising greater control over their time and being less concerned about whether they are in harmony with the tempo of others.

Sensory Changes

The story of sensory development began in our discussion of fetal development (chapter 4). The term "sensorimotor intelligence" reflects the key role that the sensory system plays in supporting cognition, from infancy and beyond. From an evolutionary perspective, the sensory capacities are vital for survival, providing information about threats, decay, and dangers. The sensory

As a result of behavioral slowing, it takes longer for elders to perform daily tasks. Her trips to the market take May more time than they did 10 years ago, but she still enjoys her shopping and the satisfaction of preparing her meals with the best ingredients.

system also supports experiences of comfort, beauty, joy, and transcendence.

Every sense modality—vision, hearing, taste, touch, and smell—is vulnerable to age-related changes. With age, greater intensity of stimulation is required to make the same impact on the sensory system that was once achieved with lower levels of stimulation. Some of the changes in vision, hearing, and taste and smell are listed in Table 14.1. These changes begin in early adulthood, and their effects increase throughout the remainder of life

Table 14.1	Changes in Sensory Systems After Age 20		
Age Group	**Vision**	**Hearing**	**Taste and Smell**
20–35	Constant decline in accommodation as lenses begin to harden at about age 20	Pitch discrimination for high-frequency tones begins to decline	No documented changes
35–65	Sharp decline in acuity after 40; delayed adjustment to shifts in light and dark	Continued gradual loss in pitch discrimination to age 50	Loss of taste buds begins
65+	Sensitivity to glare; increased problems with daily visual tasks; increases in diseases of the eye that produce partial or total blindness	Sharp loss in pitch discrimination after 70; sound must be more intense to be heard	Higher thresholds for detecting sour, salt, and bitter tastes; higher threshold for detecting smells, and errors in identifying odors

Source: Based on Newman & Newman, 1983.

(Erber, 2005). Results from a large, national sample of adults aged 57 to 85 found that roughly two thirds of the respondents experienced a significant deficit in at least one sense, and that the incidence of multiple sensory deficits increased with age. Among the oldest participants, difficulties in hearing, vision, and smell were more prominent (Correia et al., 2016). About 20 percent of those ages 75 and older have multiple sensory impairments. Those who have both visual and hearing impairments are more likely to report reduced social interactions, difficulty getting together with friends, and are at greater risk for falls, possibly due to the lack of sensory cues that help support navigation in unfamiliar settings (He et al., 2005).

Vision.   **Visual adaptation** involves the ability to adjust to changes in the level of illumination. Pupil size decreases with age, so that less light reaches the retina. Thus, older adults need higher levels of illumination to see clearly, and it takes them longer to adjust from dark to light and from light to dark. Many older adults are increasingly sensitive to glare and may draw the shades in their rooms to prevent bright light from striking their eyes. Slower adaptation time and sensitivity to glare interfere with night driving. Some of the visual problems of people older than 75 are difficulties with tasks that require speed of visual performance, such as reading signs in a moving vehicle; a decline in near vision, which interferes with reading and daily tasks; and difficulties in searching for or tracking visual information (National Institute on Aging, 2009a). About 16.5 percent of those 75 and older report that they have trouble seeing (National Center for Health Statistics, 2010).

Several physiological conditions seriously impair vision and can result in partial or total blindness. These conditions include cataracts, which are a clouding of the lenses, making them less penetrable by light; deterioration or detachment of the retina including age-related macular degeneration, which can result in blurring details needed for sewing, reading, and driving or complete vision loss; corneal disease, which can result in redness, watery eyes, pain, and difficulties seeing; and glaucoma, which is an increase in pressure from the fluid in the eyeball. The incidence of visual impairments, especially cataracts, increases dramatically from later adulthood (65 to 74) to elderhood (beyond 75) (He, Sengupta, Velkoff, & Barros, 2005; National Institute of Health, 2016).

By age 75, half of Anglo Americans have cataracts or have had them removed. By age 80, 70 percent of Anglo Americans have cataracts compared with 53 percent of African Americans and 61 percent of Hispanic Americans (National Eye Institute, 2016). According to vision experts, recent medical innovations have made cataract surgery much less complicated than it was in the past. Nine out of 10 people who have cataract surgery regain very good vision, somewhere between 20/40 and 20/20 (Lee, 2002).

Loss of vision poses serious challenges to adaptation—it has the effect of separating people from contact with the world. Such impairment is especially linked with feelings of helplessness. Most older adults are not ready to cope with the challenge of learning to function in their daily world without being able to see. For them, the loss of vision reduces their activity level, autonomy,

and willingness to leave a familiar setting. For many older adults, impaired vision results in the decision to give up driving altogether, or at least night driving, causing a significant loss of independence. However, this loss can be minimized by the availability of inexpensive, flexible public transportation.

Hearing.   Hearing loss increases with age. About 47 percent of those ages 75 and older have some trouble with their hearing (National Institute of Health, 2016). The most common effects of hearing loss are a reduced sensitivity to both high-frequency (high-pitched) and low-intensity (quiet) sounds and a somewhat decreased ability to understand spoken messages. Tinnitus, a ringing or buzzing sound that can come and go, and appear to be loud or soft, often accompanies other forms of hearing loss or as a side effect of certain medications. Certain environmental factors—including exposure to loud, unpredictable noise, and injuries, such as damage to the bones in the middle ear—influence the extent of hearing loss.

Loss of hearing interferes with a basic mode of human connectedness—the ability to participate in conversation. Hearing impairment may be linked to feelings of isolation or suspiciousness. A person may hear things imperfectly, miss parts of conversations, or perceive conversations as occurring in whispers rather than in ordinary tones. There are a variety of devices that can help support individuals who have hearing loss. These include hearing aids, amplifying devices that can make it easier to hear on the phone, alert systems coordinated with doorbells or smoke detectors, and cochlear implants that are surgically implanted to help overcome certain specific types of hearing loss (National Institute on Aging, 2009b).

Being aware of one's hearing loss and its impact on social interactions is the first step in learning to compensate for diminished auditory sensitivity. Knowing the people one is with and believing that one is valued by them can help reassure a person about the nature of conversations and allay suspicions. Elders with hearing loss may ask for a quiet spot in a restaurant or ask friends to speak one at a time in a group setting. Self-esteem plays an important part in this process. An older person with high self-esteem is more likely to make the intellectual adjustment needed to interpret interactions and to request clarification when necessary. Such requests may even serve to stimulate greater interaction and produce greater clarity in communication. Older people with a hearing loss and high self-esteem tend to insist that people who want to communicate with them should face them when they speak.

In contrast, older people who have low self-esteem are likely to be more vulnerable to suspicions about the behavior of others. They are more likely to perceive inaudible comments as attempts to ridicule or exclude them. These experiences contribute to feelings of rejection and can produce irritability and social withdrawal.

Taste and Smell.   There are taste receptors throughout the mouth, including on your tongue, the roof of your mouth, and your throat. These receptors detect flavors of food based on five tastes: sweet, salty, bitter, sour, and tangy. In addition, the smell of food contributes to its flavor, and many would argue that the

Irina Afonskaya/Shutterstock.com

The sense of smell invigorates daily experiences and continues to be a source of pleasant memories. Greta smells the lilacs, a delightful sign that spring has come. She remembers gathering lilacs as a gift for her mother on Mother's Day.

appearance of food contributes to its appeal. With age, the number of taste buds decreases. Older adults have a higher threshold than young adults for detecting sweet, sour, bitter, and salty tastes. Some of this reduced sensitivity may be related to the impact of certain medications, gum disease, dentures, some infections, cancer treatments, or alcohol consumption (National Institute on Aging, 2009c). In order to improve the taste of food, older adults may add salt or sugar, which may aggravate existing conditions such as high blood pressure or diabetes. An impaired sense of taste can interfere with the ability to detect spoiled foods or ingredients that are likely to cause indigestion.

Smell and taste are closely linked. Much of the flavor that we experience from foods comes from its aroma. Deficits in the sensory capacity for smell occur in about 22 percent of adults, with problems increasing with age (Correia et al., 2016). Older adults may require greater intensity to detect odors and are more likely to misidentify them. Loss or change in the sense of smell can be a symptom of other diseases. The sense of smell can keep a person safe. Smells related to smoke, gas leaks, spoiled food, or household chemicals are important indications of a possible environmental problem. Loss of smell in older adults can increase their vulnerability to illness or accidents. Changes in the senses of smell and taste may result in a loss of appetite or a disruption of normal eating habits. Loss of appetite (which may accompany illness and new medications), pain due to dental problems, and changes in the digestive system all contribute to malnutrition among the elderly.

Coping with Sensory Changes

As a result of the various patterns of aging among the very old, it is impossible to prescribe an ideal pattern of coping with sensory

changes. The first step is awareness. Elders need to be aware that changes in sensory systems are likely and pay attention to these changes, especially reductions in sensitivity that might impact their safety and health. The second step is evaluation. Most annual check-ups do not focus on the full sensory systems. If a person has diabetes, or a history of diabetes, annual eye exams are customary. However, problems in other sensory systems may not be included in an annual exam unless a person indicates a problem. Elders need to check with their physician about possible side effects of their medications that might impact the sense of smell, taste, touch, vision, or hearing. The third step is intervention. In some cases, a sensory deficit can be improved through medications or devices (e.g., eyeglasses or hearing aids). If deficits are not reversible, new coping strategies can be implemented that compensate for the loss of certain sensory stimuli. Guided by the SOC model, older adults must select the areas where they are most invested in sustaining optimal functioning and direct their resources to enhancing those areas while compensating for the areas in which functioning is more limited. What one hopes to achieve is a balance between self-sufficiency and willingness to accept help, preserving one's dignity as much as possible and optimizing the enjoyment of daily experiences.

Health, Illness, Disability, and Functional Independence

How can we characterize the level of health, illness, disability, and **functional independence** in later life? A mild but persistent decline in the immune system is observed as a correlate of aging. As a result, older adults are more susceptible to infections and take a longer time to heal. Substantial numbers of older adults are afflicted with one or more chronic conditions, such as arthritis, osteoporosis, diabetes, or high blood pressure, which may require medication and interfere with daily functioning. Older adults are at increased risk for developing chronic conditions, the most common of which are diabetes, arthritis, congestive heart failure, and dementia (U.S. Department of Health and Human Service, 2013). Nonetheless, 39 percent of those aged 75 and older describe their health as very good or excellent, and 35 percent report their health as good (Schiller, Lucas, Ward, & Peregoy, 2012).

Disability. What is disability? Some diseases result in impairments in organs; others result in limitations in physical or mental functioning. Functional limitations are typically measured by asking about specific tasks like walking up a flight of stairs or driving a car. Some functional limitations are significant for carrying out tasks of daily life, like preparing food, showering/bathing, or getting dressed. Other limitations may only be relevant for certain people, depending on the work they do, where they live, or their family responsibilities. The term **dependence** refers to health-related limitations that impact a person's ability for independent life including self-care and more complex tasks like shopping or using the phone. Two indicators of disability in later life are whether a person needs assistance with basic activities of daily life (ADLs), including eating, bathing, dressing, and moving from the bed to a chair or to the bathroom, and **instrumental activities of daily life (IADLs)** including light housework, grocery shopping, or preparing meals. Depending on how it is measured, the term

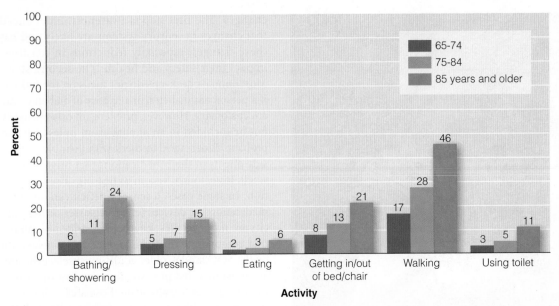

FIGURE 14.1 ▶ PERCENT OF PERSONS WITH LIMITATIONS IN ACTIVITIES OF DAILY LIVING BY AGE GROUP: 2010

Source: Administration on Aging (2012).

disability can include functional limitations and/or dependence (Cutler, 2001).

In contrast to negative stereotypes about later life, the level of independent functioning among adults 80 years and older is high. FIGURE 14.1 ▶ shows the percentages of noninstitutionalized people in three age groups who needed help in six **activities of daily living (ADLs)**: bathing/showering, dressing, eating, getting in and out of bed or a chair, walking, and using the toilet. The area of greatest limitation is walking. The percentage of adults needing assistance is small for those ages 65 to 74, increases slightly for those 75 to 84, and increases further for those 85 and older. However, even among this oldest group, fewer than half require help with walking, and fewer than 25 percent need help with other basic tasks of self-care (Administration on Aging, 2012).

From 1992 to 2013, the percentage of people aged 65 and older who report having ADLs or IADLs has *decreased* from 48.9 percent to 44 percent (Federal Interagency Forum on Aging-Related Statistics, 2016). Many factors account for this improvement in daily functioning for recent cohorts including improved education of recent elders, fewer people smoking, improved design of interior spaces in senior housing, new devices that make it easier for older adults to compensate for physical limitations, and medications that help alleviate the symptoms of chronic illness. Improved treatment of cataracts and heart disease are especially important contributors to this reduction in disability (Chernew, Cutler, Ghosh, & Landrum, 2016).

Osteoarthritis is the most common type of arthritis for older adults. This type of arthritis results when the cartilage that pads bones in a joint wears away. The joints may feel stiff when a person has not moved for a while. Other symptoms include temporary or chronic pain and gradual loss of mobility in the affected joints. Fifty-four percent of those 75 and older have osteoarthritis. *Osteoporosis* is a disease that weakens bones so that they break easily. Bone tissue is continuously broken down and replaced.

With age, more bone is lost than is replaced. Although women are at greater risk of osteoporosis than men, after age 70 men and women lose bone at about the same rate (National Institute on Aging, 2009d, 2009e).

Data from the National Health Interview Survey (Schiller, Lucas, Ward, & Peregoy, 2012) provide a look at the relationship of age to difficulties in physical functioning. Participants were asked about whether they had certain upper-body and lower-body limitations. Upper-body limitations included such things as reaching up over one's head or using one's fingers to grasp a handle. Lower-body limitations included walking for a quarter mile or stooping, crouching, or kneeling. The percentage of respondents who reported difficulty in one or more areas increased from 30 percent of those ages 65 to 74, to 46 percent among those 75 and older. The area of most difficulty was standing for 2 hours, with 30 percent of those over age 75 reporting difficulties. This suggests that many elders would not go to an outdoor concert without bringing a chair.

One of the most difficult health challenges of elderhood is a group of disorders referred to as **organic brain syndromes**. These conditions, which result in confusion, disorientation, and loss of control over basic daily functions, present obstacles for adaptation to the person with the disease as well as the caregivers who are responsible for the older person's well-being (see the **Applying Theory and Research** box Dementia).

Do people generally experience a rapid, general decline in health after age 65 or 70? Not according to self-ratings. In a national survey of older adults, people were asked to rate their health from poor to excellent. In the 75 to 84 age range, 76 percent of non-Hispanic Whites, 57 percent of non-Hispanic Blacks, and 60 percent of Hispanics rated their health as good, very good, or excellent. Among those 85 and older, the percentage who rated their health as good, very good, or excellent declined somewhat for the three groups, to 69 percent, 55 percent, and 52 percent,

Dementia

Dementia is the loss of thinking, memory, and reasoning skills that significantly impairs a person's ability to carry out daily tasks. Symptoms include the inability to remember information, asking the same questions over and over again, becoming lost or confused in familiar places, being unable to follow directions, or neglecting personal safety, hygiene, or nutrition (National Institute on Aging, 2009f). Two of the most common causes of dementia in older people are vascular dementia or repeated small strokes and Alzheimer's disease. With **vascular dementia**, the supply of blood to the brain is disrupted, resulting in the death of brain cells. The loss of function may be gradual or relatively sudden. The symptoms vary depending upon which area of the brain has been damaged. Memory, language, reasoning, or motor coordination can be disrupted. Supportive counseling, attention to diet, and skilled physical therapy to reestablish control of daily functions may restore much of the person's previous level of adaptive behavior provided that additional strokes do not occur.

Alzheimer's disease produces a more gradual loss of memory, reduced intellectual functioning, and an increase of mood disturbances—especially hostility and depression. An estimated 5.4 million Americans had Alzheimer's disease in 2012. The incidence of this disease increases with age, with few people below the age of 60 affected by it, whereas an estimated 45 percent of those ages 85 and older have the diagnosis. The severity of the disease also increases with age (Alzheimer's Association, 2013).

A person with Alzheimer's disease experiences gradual brain failure over a period of 7 to 10 years. Symptoms include severe problems in cognitive functioning, especially increased memory impairment and a rapid decline in the complexity of written and spoken language; problems with self-care; and behavioral problems, such as wandering, asking the same questions repeatedly, and becoming suddenly angry or stubborn (Kemper, Thompson,

& Marquis, 2001; O'Leary, Haley, & Paul, 1993). Currently, there is no cure for Alzheimer's disease. Treatments address specific symptoms—especially mood and memory problems—and attempt to slow its progress.

As the number of older adults with Alzheimer's disease and related disorders has grown, the plight of their caregivers has aroused concern (Roth et al., 2001; Zarit, Femia, Kim, & Whitlatch, 2010). Most Alzheimer's patients are cared for at home, often by their adult children and their spouse. The caregiving process is ongoing, with an accumulation of stressors and periodic transitions as the patient's condition changes. As the symptoms of the disease progress, caregivers have to restructure their personal, work, and family life. Caregivers often experience stress and depression as they attempt to cope with their responsibilities and assess the effectiveness or ineffectiveness of their efforts. Over time, they are likely to experience physical symptoms of their own, associated with the physical and emotional strains of this role.

When people with dementia are cared for at home by their spouse, children, or other relatives, three spheres of functioning intersect: home life, intimate or close relationships, and custodial care. Custodial care often involves routinization, surveillance, and indignities as a result of lost capacities, such as needing help with toileting, bathing, or dressing. Observations and interviews with caregivers and care recipients who live together suggest that these features of custodial care disrupt intimate relationships and home life, making daily experiences more monotonous, restrictive, and constraining. As their symptoms worsen, care recipients gradually lose many of the functions that support their identities as homemakers, parents, or intimate partners (Askham, Briggs, Norman, & Redfern, 2007).

The care of an older person with some form of dementia is fraught with problems and frustrations, but it also provides some opportunities for satisfaction and feelings of

encouragement (Pinquart & Sörensen, 2003). The uplifts and hassles frequently reported by caregivers give some insight into the typical day-to-day experience of caring for a person who is suffering from Alzheimer's disease (Donovan & Corcoran, 2010; Kinney & Stephens, 1989).

The uplifts include the following:

- Seeing care recipient calm
- Sharing a joke, laughing together with the care recipient
- Seeing care recipient responsive
- Care recipient showing affection
- Friends and family showing understanding about caregiving
- Care recipient recognizing familiar people, smiling, or winking
- Care recipient being cooperative
- Leaving care recipients with others at home

Some of the hassles include:

- Care recipient being confused or not making sense
- Care recipient's forgetfulness, asking repetitive questions
- Care recipient's agitation, anger, or refusing help
- Care recipient's bowel or bladder accidents
- Seeing care recipient withdrawn or unresponsive
- Dressing and bathing care recipient, assisting with toileting
- Care recipient declining physically
- Care recipient not sleeping through the night

Two symptoms that are most difficult to manage are sleep disturbances and wandering. As cognitive functioning declines, the pattern of sleep deteriorates. A person with Alzheimer's disease sleeps for only short periods, napping on and off during the day and night. Often, the napping is accompanied by wakeful periods at night, during which the person is confused, upset, and likely to wander. Caregivers must therefore be continuously alert, night and day. Their own sleep is disturbed as they try to remain alert to the person's whereabouts. When the disease reaches this level, family caregivers are likely to institutionalize the family member. Alzheimer's disease is a major cause of hospitalization and nursing home placement among the elderly; an estimated 50 percent of nursing home residents have Alzheimer's disease or a related form of dementia (He, Sengupta, Velkoff, & DeBarros, 2005).

A woman who remembers her mother as independent, with strong views and a deep commitment to social justice, describes some of the ups and downs as she witnesses her mother's condition:

> My mother also had strong views on quality of life issues for the elderly. We had often spoken about the importance of being able to die in a dignified way. She has a living will and opposes heroic measures to prolong life. I am convinced that Mom wouldn't want the quality of life she now has. She can't express herself, is

unable to hold a knife or fork, has no control over her bodily functions and can't walk.

However, on a recent visit to her mother, who is living in a group home, she describes the following scene:

> I worried. . . . that Mom wouldn't recognize me this time. But when I got there, she looked up at me and broke into a huge smile. She was truly excited to see me. She laughed and as I hugged her, we both cried. Then she began to speak nonstop gibberish. Although she can't tell us otherwise, my mother appears to be happy. . . . I honestly don't know if she has any thoughts about quality of life. (Simon, 2002, p. B7)

Critical Thinking Questions

1. Imagine that you are responsible for the care of a loved one who has Alzheimer's disease. What steps could you take to help support their optimal functioning?
2. Hypothesize about psychosocial development for adult caregivers. How might the responsibilities of care contribute to or impede their psychosocial development?
3. Explain why sleep disturbances and wandering are the symptoms that are most likely to lead to institutionalization for those with Alzheimer's disease.
4. Hypothesize about why an adult child may want to care for a parent who has Alzheimer's disease rather than place him or her in a nursing home or extended care facility.
5. Imagine being responsible for someone with dementia. Describe how you would prepare for this role. How would you plan for the long-term nature of this responsibility and cope with the continuing deterioration of your loved one?

---

respectively (Federal Interagency Forum on Aging Related Statistics, 2012). However, the majority continue to view their health in a positive light.

Among those in their 80s and early 90s, one health-related crisis may result in a marked decline in other areas. For example, the loss of a spouse may result in social withdrawal, loss of appetite, sleep disturbance, loss of energy, unwillingness to take medication, and decline in physical activity. All these changes can produce a rapid deterioration of the respiratory, circulatory, and metabolic systems.

People in their late 90s and older demonstrate unexpectedly good health. They appear to be more disease free than those who are 10 or 15 years younger. Perls (2004) suggested that a combination of genetic factors protect some people from the diseases of aging through two complementary processes. First, they are less vulnerable to some of the damaging effects of *oxygen radicals* that destroy DNA and cells. Thus, during their 70s and 80s, they do not suffer from the major diseases such as heart disease, cancer, stroke, or Alzheimer's disease. Second, they have a greater *functional reserve*, meaning that they require less of their organs to perform basic adaptive functions so they can tolerate a degree of damage without losing basic capacities. Studies of centenarians confirm this view of aging; they typically have a short period of poor health before death rather than suffering from prolonged disease-torn illness and disability.

FURTHER REFLECTION: Describe someone you know well who is in the life stage of elderhood. What physical challenges is this person facing? How is he or she coping with these challenges? What environmental and/or social supports are required to help sustain this person's optimal functioning?

Developing a Psychohistorical Perspective

OBJECTIVE 3 Describe the concept of a psychohistorical perspective, an altered outlook on time and history that emerges among the long-lived.

A psychohistorical perspective, achieved in elderhood, is the product of an integration of past, present, and future. Through a process of creative coping, elders in each generation blend the ideas, experiences, and salient events of their past histories with the contexts of current reality. Elders reach new levels of conscious thought. They are more aware of alternatives; they can look deeply into both the past and the future and can recognize that opposing forces can exist side by side (Kunzmann & Baltes, 2005; Riegel, 1973). In a rapidly changing society, elders may be perplexed by the emergence of new technologies, new social norms, and new products. At the same time, they have seen a history of change and recognize the enduring values and qualities of a good life in the midst of change. Having lived a long time, and envisioning less time in the future, elders are more likely to be more forgiving, less interested in material accumulation, and more focused on the emotional satisfactions of life (Allemand, 2008; Brandtstädter, Rothermund, Kranz, & Kühn, 2010). The idea of a *psycho*historical perspective suggests that people will differ in the meanings and interpretations they give to the events of their lives. Nonetheless all elders have to face the inevitability of change and strive to create a meaningful narrative around the decisions and directions of their life in the context of change.

Wendell tells his young listeners what it was like to be a soldier in World War II. Through his stories, he makes this period of American history come alive for a new generation.

Think about what it means to have lived for 75 or more years. Those adults who were 85 years old in 2016 were born in the Great Depression. They are members of the silent generation. They lived through World War II but were too young to serve; the Korean war; the Vietnam war; the Gulf war; the Afghan and Iraqi wars; the assassinations of President Kennedy, Robert Kennedy, and Martin Luther King, Jr.; Watergate; the Clinton impeachment trials; the AIDS epidemic; the terrorist attacks of September 11, 2001; Hurricane Katrina; and the election of the first African American president. They have experienced the political leadership of 15 presidents. During their lives, they have adapted to dramatic technological innovations in communication, transportation, manufacturing, economics, food production, leisure activities, and health care. They have also experienced striking changes in cultural and political values.

One consequence of a long life is the realization that change is a basic element of all life at the individual and societal levels. Sometimes, these changes appear cyclical; at other times, they appear to bring real transformations. For example, people who are now age 80 lived during World War II when women were involved in the labor market while men served in the military; the 1950s, when many women withdrew from the labor market and committed themselves to working at home; and the 1970s up to the present when it has become normative for women to be employed outside the home, even when they have very young children. The patterns of behavior that younger adults might view as normative and necessary, elders may recognize as part of fluctuating social or historical conditions.

Within the framework of an extended life, elders have opportunities to gain a special perspective on conditions of continuity and change within their culture. As society becomes more accustomed to having a significant group of elders functioning in the community, some scholars anticipate that a *culture of aging* will emerge in technological societies. This culture is likely to provide more opportunities for the expression of the pragmatic wisdom accumulated over a long lifetime through theater, music, the arts, and critical commentary. At the same time, new roles will evolve for successful agers as mentors and advisors to the young (Kunzmann & Baltes, 2005). Some professional societies, like the American Sociological Society, have created a network for retirees to share their views and exchange ideas. In the United Kingdom, pensioners have created the Retirement Lounge, an online setting where retirees can interact and share their experiences:

> Social interaction is extremely important when we leave work for good. We are no longer in the working environment to share a joke or gossip with our colleagues. Sadly, many retirees get trapped in their home environment with no one to talk to apart from their family members, if they are fortunate to have them around. With that in mind, this portal is set up to serve the needs of senior citizens. This is a Pensioners Corner. With our pool of experience and knowledge base we should be able to help each other. (retirement-lounge .com, 2013)

Another online resource is sponsored by TIAA, myretirement. org. It has thousands of members who share ideas about weekly topics, access information about current trends, respond to surveys about topics of relevance to older adults and read about the results, share aspirations, thoughts, and photos with others. Other sites where older adults are sharing their expertise include cool-grandma.com, senior.com, seniornet.org, and senioryears.com.

An international group of leaders, *The Elders*, is a different example of how people can bring their life experiences to bear to address critical issues (www.theelders.org). *The Elders*, founded by Nelson Mandela, was formed to help address some of the serious and seemingly intractable problems that plague our world. A premise of this group is that in traditional societies, the oldest members of the group were looked to for their wisdom and guidance in efforts to resolve difficult conflicts. In today's world, where the conflicts are often of an international and intercultural nature, the global community is in need of a group of respected and trusted leaders who can offer guidance without a vested interest in a particular national, industrial, or religious advantage. The founding members of *The Elders* are characterized as "trusted, respected worldly-wise individuals with a proven commitment and record of contributing to solving global problems." *The Elders* hope to share their wisdom, forged over their long lifetimes and opportunities for international leadership.

As the example of *The Elders* suggests, a psychohistorical perspective contributes to the wisdom that the very old bring to their understanding of the meaning of life. As a result of living a long time, a person becomes aware of life's lessons as well as its uncertainties. The integration of a long-term past, present, and future combined with an appreciation for the relativistic nature of human experience allows these adults to bring an acceptance of alternative solutions and a commitment to essential positive values.

We are all part of the process of psychosocial evolution. Each generation adds to the existing knowledge base and reinterprets the norms of society for succeeding generations. Elders are likely to be parents, grandparents, and great-grandparents. Many are seeing their lines of descent continue into the fourth generation, which will dominate the 21st century. The opportunity to see generations of offspring brings a new degree of continuity to life, linking memories of one's own grandparents to observations of one's great-grandchildren. We can expect the value of the oral tradition of history and storytelling to take on new meaning as the elders help their great-grandchildren feel connected to the distant past. We can also expect a greater investment in the future, as elders see in their great-grandchildren the concrete extension of their ancestry three generations into the future.

Erikson (Erikson et al., 1986) identified the emergence of these tendencies in the very old in the following excerpt:

> The elder has a reservoir of strength in the wellsprings of history and storytelling. As collectors of time and preservers of memory, those healthy elders who have survived into a reasonably fit old age have time on their side—time that is to be dispensed wisely and creatively, usually in the form of stories, to those younger ones who will one day follow in their footsteps. Telling these stories, and telling them well, marks a certain capacity for one generation to entrust itself to the next, by passing on a certain shared and collective identity to the survivors of the next generation: the future. (p. 331)

FURTHER REFLECTION: Explain the concept of a psychohistorical perspective and evaluate how it contributes to psychosocial development in elderhood. Reflect on any conversations you have had with someone who offered a unique perspective on time, history, and self-awareness.

Traveling Uncharted Territory: Life Structures in Elderhood

OBJECTIVE 4 Summarize elements of the lifestyle structure in elderhood, especially living arrangements and gender roles, and analyze the impact of these life structures for continued well-being.

How should elders behave? What norms exist to guide their social relationships or the structure of their daily lives? When we talk about traveling uncharted territory, we are assuming that elderhood is a time of life for which there are few age-specific social norms. Elders are creating their own definitions of this life stage.

Changes in role relationships—especially role loss in later adulthood—present significant challenges to the preservation of a coherent self-concept. In early adulthood, there is an opportunity to engage in many new roles and to establish a lifestyle that expresses the priorities of one's personal identity. In middle adulthood, the pressure of life roles and their competing demands may be at their peak. During later adulthood, the challenge is to establish an integrated sense of self that helps to compensate for the loss of salient life roles and to protect the person from a sense of despair.

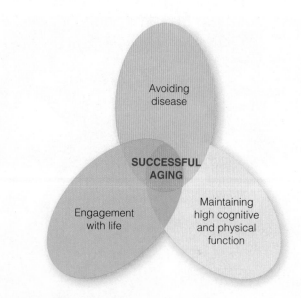

FIGURE 14.2 ▶ COMPONENTS OF SUCCESSFUL AGING

Source: Adapted from *Successful Aging*, by J. W. Rowe & R. L. Kahn, 1998, New York: Pantheon.

In elderhood, those who cope most effectively create a new, modified lifestyle. They are able to focus on certain valued characteristics of the self and to optimize them despite changes in their social and physical resources (Diehl, Hastings, & Stanton, 2001). One of the key features of this emerging lifestyle is a sense of purpose in life. Those who have a strong sense of meaning, who view their lives as meaningful to the self and significant for the lives of others, live longer, healthier lives than those without this sense of meaning (Krause, 2009; Macdonald, Wong, & Gingras, 2011).

Successful aging is a biopsychosocial process. The MacArthur Foundation Research Network on Successful Aging (Rowe & Kahn, 1998) introduced an interdisciplinary perspective on the distinction between usual and successful aging. Those characterized by **usual aging** may be functioning well but are at high risk for disease, disability, and reduced capacity for functional independence. In contrast, the **successful agers** are characterized by three interdependent features (see FIGURE 14.2 ▶). They have a "low risk of disease and disease-related disabilities; high mental and physical function; and active engagement with life" (p. 38). This last feature, **active engagement,** is a frequently repeated theme in the field of gerontology.

In an effort to describe the norms that older adults use to guide their conduct, researchers asked older adults from New York City and Savannah, Georgia, to respond to six pictures similar to the two drawings in FIGURE 14.3 ▶ (Offenbacher & Poster, 1985). The responses to the following two questions were used to construct a code of conduct: "How do you think that people who know this person, such as family or friends, feel about him or her?" and "How do you feel about this person?" Four normative principles were found in the responses:

1. Don't be sorry for yourself.
2. Try to be independent.
3. Don't just sit there; do something.
4. Above all, be sociable.

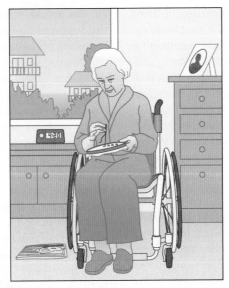

FIGURE 14.3 ▶ TYPICAL DRAWINGS THAT RESEARCHERS MIGHT USE TO ESTABLISH THE SOCIAL NORMS OF VERY OLD PEOPLE

Source: Drawings based on Offenbacher and Poster, 1985.

women, freedom from the burdens of care for their aging family members or children was a valued opportunity for empowerment in later life. A number of women engaged in forms of group religious services and the related opportunities for social interaction, volunteer work, and prayer, which created feelings of social inclusion and agency.

> I am baptized Sikh and value religion to guide me and have focus in life. My religion has influenced my life very positively; this has helped me to care for my husband and cope with stressful events. I have planned days when I visit friends and attend religious activities. These are also my means of socializing. We offer each other support and get involved in charity work. (Wray, 2003, p. 519)

This code of conduct suggests that older people believe that being sociable, active, and independent constitute successful living in later life. Of course, older adults are not alone in valuing these qualities. However, these norms are important as sources of self-esteem for this age group. They promote a sense of vigor and a shield against depression or discouragement.

The themes "Don't be sorry for yourself" and "Don't just sit there" suggest that elders continue to see their lives as precious resources that are not to be wasted in self-pity and passivity. The emphasis on activity as opposed to meditation reflects the Western cultural value of a *sense of agency*—thinking is not as highly valued as action. In contrast, doing things, having an impact, and receiving the feedback that action stimulates provide the keys to successful living. Subsequent studies have supported the idea that finding meaning in one's existence, continuing to experience a sense of social competence, and perceptions of self-efficacy help older adults maintain a sense of well-being (Onedera & Stickle, 2008). In today's technologically rich environment, there are many opportunities for engaging in intellectually stimulating and socially engaging activities, even if one's physical mobility is limited. By continuing to participate in intellectually complex and challenging leisure activities—such as reading stimulating books and magazines; participating in online discussion groups; going to museums, concerts, and plays; traveling; or participating in hobbies that require decision making and problem solving—older adults contribute to preserving their intellectual flexibility (McDonough, Haber, Bischof, & Park, 2015; Schooler & Mulatu, 2001).

The desire to preserve a sense of control and agency is expressed across ethnic groups despite differences in health problems, loss of loved ones, and poverty. However, the ways that women define empowerment and experience successful aging is related, in part, to their cultural values and worldview. In a study of women between the ages of 60 and 80, nine different ethnic groups were self-defined by the participants: English, British Muslim, African Caribbean, Dominican, British Irish, Pakistani, British Polish, Indian, and Bangladeshi (Wray, 2003). For some of these

For some women, paid employment or volunteer work keeps them connected to society and provides feelings of being in control of their daily lives. Some women spoke of their time with their grandchildren and the responsibilities they had for their grandchildren's care as contributing to a sense of purpose and well-being. In some cultural groups, the opportunity to strengthen their connection with their religious and ethnic communities created a form of collective agency. In other cultural groups, the opportunity to continue to express self-reliance and control over daily life was especially significant. Among most of the women, some form of interdependence and participation in meaningful social relationships played a key role in sustaining feelings of agency and continued self-worth.

The fact that elders must carve out new patterns of adapting to later life is illustrated in three specific areas of functioning: living arrangements, gender-role definitions, and romance and sexuality.

Living Arrangements

Approximately 78 percent of U.S. adults ages 75 and older own their own homes. However, the pattern of **living arrangements** changes after age 75, especially for women. Before that age, the majority of older adults live in family households, mostly as married couples. Among adults ages 75 to 84, however, only 53 percent live with a spouse; the others either live alone or with family or nonrelatives. The pattern differs by gender. Among women ages 75 to 84, 37 percent are married and live with their spouse; among men ages 75 to 84, 71 percent are married and live with their spouse (U.S. Census Bureau, 2013d). Older women are less likely than men to remarry after the death of their spouse, and older women are less likely to live with other family members than they were in the past. For unmarried elders, functional status and cognitive functioning are key factors that lead to living with one's children or other relatives (Liang et al., 2005).

Living arrangements among older adults are linked to cultural values associated with individualism and independence or collectivism and interdependence. In a comparison of living arrangements in 43 countries, older adults were the most likely age group to live alone. However, in Africa it was more common for older adults to head up a large household that included young children than in other countries. In Asia, co-residence with adult children was more common than in Africa. When older adults lived with their children, co-residence with adult sons and their families was more common in Asia and Africa, but co-residence with adult daughters and their families was more common in Latin America. In countries with higher levels of education for the general population, families were more likely to have nuclear households with older adults living alone (Bongaarts & Zimmer, 2002).

Living Alone. Increasing numbers of women are establishing a new single lifestyle in which they function as heads of households at ages 75 and older. In 2014, 46 percent of women aged 75 and older lived alone. Anglo American and African American women are more likely than Asian American women and Latinas to live alone (Administration on Aging, 2014). Older unmarried Asian American women, for example, are much more likely to live with other family members than to live alone in comparison to Anglo American women of similar economic and educational backgrounds. Though still in need of social interaction and support services, they are often relieved of the responsibilities of caring for spouses who were ill. Depending on their own health, these women may be freer to direct their time and interests toward their friends, grandchildren, hobbies, and activities than they have been at any other time in their lives. In a qualitative study of older widows' experiences, four themes emerged: (1) making aloneness acceptable, (2) going my own way, (3) reducing my risks, and (4) sustaining myself (Porter, 1994). One aspect of this process of adaptation, often linked to "going my own way" and "reducing my risks," is a decision to move from one's residence. In a longitudinal study of residential mobility, individuals were interviewed over a

Most older women who live alone adapt well to this independent life style. Charlotte enjoys her needlepoint, has frequent visits from family and friends, and does not have to take care of anyone but herself.

20-year period. Widowhood was found to be a significant event that triggered a decision to move, often within the first year after becoming widowed (Chevan, 1995).

The pattern of elderly women living alone is similar in Canada, the United Kingdom, and many other northern European countries, but it is not as common in southern Europe and developing countries where both older men and women, whether married or widowed, live in multigenerational families. For example, data gathered in four Asian countries—Thailand, Singapore, Philippines, and Vietnam—in the mid-1990s found that from 60 percent to 90 percent of older adults lived with their children and grandchildren.

The case of Japan illustrates the possible impact of modernization on the living arrangements of the elderly. In 1960, about 90 percent of older adults lived with their children (or one might say that the children lived with them in their households). By 1990, this type of living arrangement had declined to 50 percent. Both the increasing longevity and improved financial resources of older adults contribute to this trend toward independent housing, which is coupled with a continued desire for close kinship ties (Kinsella & Velkoff, 2001).

In contrast to those older women who live alone and those who live with a male partner, an emerging strategy is for several older women to live together. This alternative addresses the increasing costs of housing in many communities as well as the problem of the health and mental health risks of social isolation and loneliness in later life. Women of the baby boom generation are more likely to have experienced divorce and have smaller families than the previous generation of older adults. Many of these women have developed and nurtured friendships with other women from their high school and college years, in the workplace, and through community participation. As they begin planning for later adulthood, the idea of sharing the costs and responsibilities with good friends can be quite appealing. "We lived together in dorms and sororities. We shared apartments after graduation. We traveled together. We helped each other through divorce and the death of our parents. Why not take it to the next level?" (Gross, 2004, p. 1). A number of online services and agencies, like Golden Girls Housing in Minneapolis, are emerging to help women find others who want to live in shared housing (Abrahams, 2013).

Interstate Migration. The great majority of older adults (more than 95 percent) remain in their home communities as they age, many preferring to stay in their own home even after their children move out and their spouse dies. Yet the trend toward interstate migration has increased since the mid-1960s. In 2012–2013, 48,000 people aged 75 and older moved from one region of the country to another (U.S. Census Bureau, 2013d). Many of these older interstate migrants will live out their lives in communities in which they did not grow up, work, or raise their children. They are pioneers, establishing new friendships, community involvements, and lifestyles. Another group of older adults return to their birth state, especially after one's spouse dies or, in the case of serious disability, in order to be close to family caregivers (Stoller & Longino, 2001). In the face of new physical limitations, older adults may want to remain independent but require more help. By moving back to their home community, they are more confident about being able to draw on needed support from family and friends (Rowles & Ravdal, 2002). In addition to these permanent moves, many older adults participate in seasonal migration—residents from southern states go north for the summer, and residents of northern states go south for the winter. Over time, some of these seasonal migrants decide to establish a permanent residence in the state they visit. This is especially likely for northern residents who establish permanent residence in the South (Smith & House, 2006).

Housing Options. Differences in lifestyle, health, interest, ability to perform daily activities, marital status, and income enter into the very old person's preference for housing arrangements. Housing for the elderly has expanded dramatically, and developers have experimented with a great variety of housing configurations that are intended to meet the special needs of particular aging populations (Shapiro, 2001). These options range from inner-city hotels for those with minimal incomes to sprawling luxury villages with apartments, medical clinics, and sponsored activities. Retirement communities are typically age-restricted residences. They may be apartments in a high-rise, townhouses, or homes with shared recreational resources. Often, they provide the option for prepared meals or a communal dining center.

The baby boomers are "pushing the envelope" in many social institutions, not the least of which is housing. Their ideals about aging influence the kinds of living arrangements they seek: "Stay active, keep learning, develop and preserve relationships; and have fun for as long as possible" (Abrahms, 2011). The following housing alternatives suggest innovative approaches to benefit today's elders (Abrahms, 2011).

Niche Communities. For people with similar backgrounds and interests. These communities are for people who are still active and relatively healthy, but who may want some assisted care resources. The most common of these are the 50 or more university-based communities where alumnae, retired faculty, and others can enjoy classes, lectures, cultural and sporting events, as well as the health care resources of the university.

Intergenerational Co-housing. For families with children as well as elders. The group of residents buy a property, design the housing units and common features, and share the responsibilities of the management of the property. Residents live in separate homes but share communal space for large group meals, recreational facilities, some guest quarters, and resources like, arts, media, exercise, or meditation rooms depending on the interests of the residents.

The Village Model. For people who want to remain in their own homes, the village model provides a collaborative approach to resources. People join the village with a membership fee for the individual or household. With this fee, they have access to services including transportation, health professionals, home maintenance services, and other resources. The village may offer group prices for tickets, sponsor outings and group activities, and hold suppers for members.

Life satisfaction in a retirement community may depend on the fit between one's marital status and the demographics of the community. One study assessed the life satisfaction of widows who were living alone in retirement communities. When widows outnumbered married couples in the community, the widows had a high frequency of seeing friends and participating in activities. However, when married couples outnumbered widows, the widows experienced less satisfaction and were more socially isolated (Hong & Duff, 1994).

The majority of elders live in urban areas. As a result, any economic factors that affect the **housing options** in urban communities have a significant impact on the living arrangements of older adults (see the **Applying Theory and Research** box The Impact of Gentrification on the Elderly). Roughly 23 percent of women and 14 percent of men over the age of 80 live below the supplemental poverty threshold (Cubansi, Casillas, & Damico, 2015). Many have a fixed income and depend on the quality of community resources and social support for their well-being; moving can be an especially difficult life event, adversely affecting overall well-being (Pynoos, Caraviello, & Cicero, 2010).

Institutional Care. About 1.3 million adults older than 65 live in **skill care facilities** (sometimes referred to as nursing homes). This includes any arrangement with three or more beds that provides nursing and personal care services (U.S. Census Bureau, 2012). **Nursing homes** provide nursing care and rehabilitation for people who have severe functional limitations as a result of acute illness, surgery, or advanced dementia. The likelihood of institutionalization increases with age and limitations in family support. In 2011, about 1 percent of those ages 65 to 74 were living in a nursing home, but 11 percent of those 85 and older were in this kind of facility. About 75 percent of people in nursing homes do not have spouses. The likelihood of a person living in a nursing home increases when there is no family member who can help to manage daily living needs (Harris-Kojetin et al., 2016).

The Green House is a new style of nursing home on a smaller scale. Typically 10 residents live in private bedrooms and bathrooms but share a living and dining room area that looks like a single-family home. These rooms open onto a porch or backyard. The group of 10 is supported by a nursing staff that provides daily medical care as well as meals. The residents take care of themselves to the extent of their ability, and the staff gets to know the residents quite well (Gustke, 2015).

People tend to think that once older adults are admitted to a nursing home, they stay there until they die. In fact, there is a high annual turnover among nursing home residents. The average length of stay is 6 months. The U.S Department of Health and Human Services estimates that about 37 percent of people will use some type of nursing or assisted living care facility in their lifetime, and that people use this type of care for an average of 12 months in their lifetime (longtermcare.gov, 2013). Often, a person enters a nursing home for a period of convalescence after hospitalization and then returns home or to a setting that provides less intensive care.

Many nursing homes are part of a **continuing care retirement community**—a residential setting offering housing and medical, preventive health, and social services to residents who are well at the time they enter the community. In 2014 there were over 800,000 residents living in residential care communities. Once admitted, they are guaranteed nursing care if they become ill or disabled (Harris-Kojetin et al., 2016).

The Impact of Gentrification on the Elderly

Gentrification is a process of urban renewal or renovation in which new home owners and developers invest in the rehabilitation of neighborhoods that have been deteriorating due to lack of maintenance and upkeep of the properties. Middle and upper income residents move into areas that have been deteriorating, often displacing poorer residents who have lived in that area for some time. To make investment in new construction and rehabilitation of older housing stock profitable, developers must be able to attract residents who can pay higher rents such as professionals and managers (the urban gentry). Once this process gets under way, landlords have an incentive to evict low-income residents who may have lived in the neighborhood for a long time in favor of more affluent tenants who can afford higher rent (Renn, 2013).

Several consequences of gentrification can have a negative impact on the housing options of older adults. First, rental apartments are converted to condominiums that older adults cannot afford. Second, in areas where there is no rent control, the rent rises above the rate that the older person is able to pay. In a report on the gentrifying process in New York City, rents in gentrifying neighborhoods increased 34 percent from 1990 to 2014. In citywide plans for 51,000 new rental units, only 3,000 were identified as low-income housing (NYU Furman Center, 2016). Some developers promise to build low-income housing and may receive state and federal funds to support these units, but the low-income housing and related community improvements never materialize (Patel, 2013).

Where there is rent regulation, some landlords use harassment to force out the original residents. Third, properties that have been used as single-room-occupancy hotels are demolished and new structures are built. Single-room-occupancy hotels provide low-cost housing and social support to many older adults who live alone. From 1970 to 1982, more than half the single-room-

occupancy units in the United States were lost to various urban gentrification projects (Hopper & Hamberg, 1986). A similar study of gentrification in London found a significant displacement of the elderly, with the hidden costs of overcrowding in family, friends', or relatives' homes; homelessness; and expanded unmet housing needs (Atkinson, 2000).

In addition to reducing access to affordable housing, the disruption in older adults' living arrangements can have health implications due to dispersion of the person's social support network, reduced access to public transportation, and less readily accessible sources of basic goods and services (Centers for Disease Control and Prevention, 2012a).

Although gentrification poses threats to housing for the elderly, the alternative of ongoing neglect and decay in urban neighborhoods brings its own risks—especially increased crime, health and safety hazards, and lack of services. Over time, people with more resources leave these neighborhoods, making them vulnerable to continued deterioration.

Writing about the process of gentrification in Los Angeles, David Zahniser described it as follows:

That, in a nutshell, is the most maddening thing about gentrification—its very duality, the way in which it simultaneously delivers pleasure and pain, miraculous benefits and terrible consequences. As middle-income residents move in, neighborhoods that once heard low-flying helicopters and automatic-weapons fire have found a greater measure of peace. Working-class families who scraped together the money to buy homes in the mid-1990s have happily cashed out, making hundreds of thousands of dollars en route to a five-bedroom home in Fontana, Las Vegas or Phoenix. Those who stay behind, however, frequently find themselves in a neighborhood they don't recognize. And those

who rent in a rapidly gentrifying neighborhood discover that they gained physical security while losing economic security, with rents rising steadily and the inventory of reasonably priced homes shrinking. (Zahniser, 2006, p. 2)

More positive approaches suggest a gradual rehabilitation or redevelopment of urban communities that preserves the identity of the neighborhood but encourages new building and new businesses at a slower rate of growth (Centers for Disease Control and Prevention, 2012a). One idea is to offer developers incentives to include rental or sale units for low- and moderate-income residents as part of their design. Some cities have placed a freeze on the conversions of rental units to condominiums. Others have created community land trusts where residents own the units or homes they live in, but the community owns the land, thus helping to control its use. This strategy is intended to help protect the neighborhood atmosphere and tone that have been created by its long-term residents.

Critical Thinking Questions

1. Explain why older adults are especially likely to be impacted by gentrification. Why might the increased housing costs be especially difficult for them?
2. Describe the particular stressors that an older adult might face if gentrification results in a loss of their long-term residence.
3. Speculate about impact on psychosocial development of moving to a new neighborhood for people who are in their 80s or 90s.
4. Hypothesize about why the elderly might want to remain in their apartment or home, even if the neighborhood is deteriorating.
5. State your opinion about the obligations that local governments and developers should assume for the housing needs of the elderly when older housing stock is renovated or replaced.

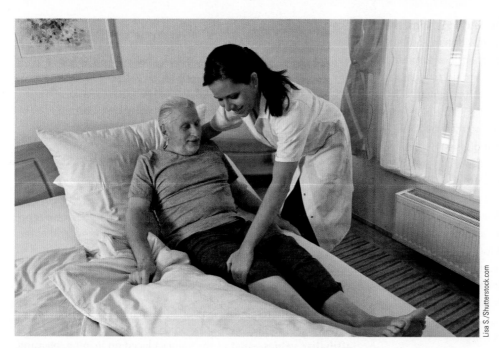

At age 82, Randall is receiving physical therapy and rehabilitation in a nursing care facility. He expects to return to independent living in a few weeks.

The advantages of a continuing care community are described by Glenn Smith:

"We'd seen a lot of people our age struggle when one went into a skilled nursing facility 6 miles away," says 76-year-old Glenn Smith. "Then someone has to drive Momma over to see Daddy every day." So Smith and his wife, Kathleen, moved to a CCRC (continuing care retirement community) atop a hill overlooking Oregon's Rogue River Valley. A nursing home is just a short walk from their spacious three bedroom cottage. Smith, who is a retired college administrator, has one bit of advice: Move in while you are younger and healthy in order to take full advantage of the activities—and pay a lower entry fee. (Shapiro, 2001, p. 60)

Aging in Place. The fastest growing component of the Medicare program is **community-based long-term health care**, which provides medical and social services to those who are chronically ill and eligible for institutionalization but who live in the community. In 2013 close to 5 million clients received services from home health agencies; 57 percent were age 75 and older (Harris-Kojetin et al., 2016). At their best, these programs are designed to complement and support informal caregiving, supplementing and providing relief for family members and friends who are trying to care for the very old. They bring comfort to the very old clients who prefer to remain in their homes.

These programs also offer flexibility by providing needed services and modifying them as a person's condition changes. A home health service may provide a case manager who can identify the required services and coordinate a program of home care providers, services, and adult day care to meet the needs of the client and the client's support system. Funding is person-centered rather than institution-centered, which allows services to be altered in order to support movement from institution to home-based care. Long-term home health care programs evolve in response to the pattern of need that emerges in a community and the quality of the services available. As the programs develop, their emphasis tends to shift from providing services to those who would otherwise be institutionalized to preventing institutionalization among a high-risk population (Kasper, 1997; Kaye, 1995; Medicaid.gov, 2013; U.S. Department of Health and Human Services, 2005).

The benefits of remaining in one's home, despite serious limitations in functional independence, are (1) preserving one's sense of autonomy and dignity, (2) reducing expenses, and (3) sustaining relationships with family and friends. By remaining in one's home, a person has greater control over the way the environment is adapted to one's changing abilities and needs. The personal and private meaning of the home environment supports one's identity and helps preserve a sense of "keeping up with dignity and pride" (Rowles & Bernard, 2013; Witse, Vik & Ytterhus, 2012). In contrast, the move to a nursing home tends to be associated with higher levels of dependence and greater emphasis on "going along with the program" rather than initiating one's own plans and projects.

In a comparison of older women living in their homes and those living in a nursing care facility, researchers were interested in how the living arrangements might influence cognitive problem solving. The home-based group became more engaged in the hypothetical problems, their solutions suggested a greater sense of perceived control over the solutions, and they approached the problems in a more abstract, relativistic manner (Collins, Luszcz, Lawson, & Keeves, 1997). These results suggest that nursing home environments may undermine cognitive functioning by reducing the need for independent problem-solving activity. However, as the case study about Mr. Z suggests, there are nursing home residents who retain their positive spirit and are able to help others while receiving the support they require given serious physical disabilities.

— Case Study Mr. Z —

The following case illustrates the importance of psychological attitudes in allowing a person with serious physical problems to play a meaningful role in a social setting for the frail elderly. Mr. Z's outlook helps him maintain his vitality and express his love of life.

Mr. M. L. Z is an 89-year-old White male of Eastern European origin. He lives in a midsized nursing home in the Midwest. Many of his daily activities revolve around circulating among the facility's residents, chatting, playing cards, reading to them, and "fetching things." Most important, Mr. Z carries his old battered violin with him and at the drop of a hat will play a tune or break into song in a surprisingly strong, clear, melodic voice. He claims to be able to sing songs in any one of seven languages, and with the least encouragement will try out several for anyone who will listen.

Mr. Z is small (5′ 3″), frail looking, and completely bald. He has facial scars and wears extremely thick-lensed glasses. He seems to be known and well liked by practically all residents and staff of the facility in which he resides, and by many visitors there as well.

He recalls a colorful history. He "escaped" his homeland at the tender age of 16 to avoid compulsory military service and fled to Russia. There he was inducted into the army, and was subsequently sent off to duty in Siberia, where he lived for about 6 years. After another tour of duty in a border patrol he deserted, he made his way across Europe, and eventually came to the United States. Here he took odd jobs, educated himself, and in time "got into show business"; he became a vaudeville prompter. In time his contacts in entertainment took him around the world. Yet time took its toll.

He tells of marrying a woman with whom he lived for almost 40 years. They had no children and she died some 15 years ago. Following her death, he began to experience a series of physical difficulties. An operation for cataracts left him with the need for very thick glasses. At one time he had a toupee made, which he has not worn for some time. One leg was amputated because of a diabetic condition, and he now wears a prosthetic leg. In addition, he wears a hearing aid, false teeth, and, for the last year, a heart pacer. Several years ago he experienced what he calls a small stroke, which left him "mixed up" for a few days. But he "worked this out," he reports, by "walking a lot," an activity in which he engages frequently.

Mr. Z says he has never smoked and drinks only on occasions or holidays, and then only to a limited degree. He scorns food fads, and eats mostly fresh fruits and lots of vegetables; he loves fish and drinks lots of tea.

Despite all his troubles, Mr. Z maintains what is apparently a cheerful, optimistic view of life and circumstances, while he pursues his hobby of energetically helping his fellow residents keep their spirits up and their interests high. He is very highly regarded and seen as filling a very important role in his nursing home as a storyteller and entertainer.

Source: Excerpt from Aging and Life: An Introduction to Gerontology (2nd ed.). A.N. Schwartz, C.L. Snyder, & J.A. Peterson, pp. 33–34. Copyright © 1984. Austin, TX: Holt, Rinehart & Winston, Inc.

CASE ANALYSIS Using What You Know

1. Imagine that you were having lunch with Mr. Z. What questions would you want to ask him?
2. Summarize the physical challenges of aging with which Mr. Z must cope.
3. Explain why Mr. Z might be living in a nursing home. What supports does he need?
4. Describe Mr. Z's psychohistorical perspective. What insights does he have about history, time, and self-awareness?

Gender-Role Definitions

The way in which elders view masculinity and femininity is yet another aspect of traveling uncharted territory. The idea of **gender-role convergence** suggests a transformation of gender-role orientation during midlife. According to this theoretical perspective, men become more nurturant and more concerned with social relationships. Women become more assertive and concerned with independence and achievement. As a result, men and women become more androgynous and, in that sense, more similar in gender orientation during later life (Gutmann, 1987).

Evaluating the Concept of Gender-Role Convergence. The extent to which men and women become more similar in outlook and behavior in later adulthood and elderhood is a subject of controversy. Few data from longitudinal or cohort sequential studies are available to address this topic. Cross-sectional data collected from earlier cohorts of men and women across a wide age span from early adulthood to elderhood have focused on men's and women's endorsement of affiliative and instrumental values. Men and women appear to be similar in their **affiliative values**—that is, the values placed on helping, pleasing, or enjoying the companionship of others. At each age, men are more invested than women in **instrumental values**—that is, the values placed on having an impact, engaging in challenging activities, and making things happen. However, the youngest age groups value instrumentality more highly and devote more time to it than the oldest age group. Thus, gender differences in instrumentality persist, but instrumentality becomes somewhat less important for older men and women. Affiliative behavior is equally important for men and women at both ages (Fultz & Herzog, 1991).

The stereotypes that are applied to aging men and women reflect similar patterns. College students and older adults (with a mean age of 70) were asked to generate characteristics in response to one of four target stimuli: a 35-year-old man, a 35-year-old woman, a 65-year-old man, and a 65-year-old woman (Kite, Deaux, & Miele, 1991). Age stereotypes were more prevalent than gender stereotypes. The attributes that were used to characterize older men and women were similar and distinct from the attributes used to characterize younger men and women.

The older target people were evaluated more negatively by the younger participants, but not as negatively by the older participants. These negative judgments included unattractive physical qualities as well as irritable and depressed personality qualities. Moreover, younger participants were more likely to characterize both male and female older target people as lacking in instrumental traits, such as achievement orientation and self-confidence. However, they did not view older target people as lacking in affiliative traits, such as caring about others or being kind or generous. Thus, the gender-role convergence that has been hypothesized as taking place with advanced age is reflected in the stereotypes that younger people apply to older adults.

Gender-role convergence, where it is observed, may be due to changing circumstances rather than to a normative pattern of development in later life. For example, many older women experience a transition from living with their husbands to living alone after age 75. This change is linked to new demands for independence, self-reliance, and agency. Women who are able to meet these challenges by developing independent living skills, making effective use of social supports and community resources, and initiating new relationships are likely to experience a heightened sense of well-being.

For many older married couples, the physical effects of aging bring new needs for assistance in some of the tasks of daily living. Because men usually marry younger women, they are more likely to require the assistance of their wives in the later years of marriage, thus shifting the balance of power by increasing the sense of **dependency** among older men and the sense of instrumentality among older women. This may be especially true when husbands retire while their wives continue to work, when husbands can no longer drive and depend on their wives for transportation, or when, due to health constraints, husbands are restricted from performing the household tasks that once were their domain, such as mowing the grass, shoveling snow, repairing the home, or other tasks requiring muscle strength and endurance.

In contrast, among adults 75 years and older more women than men have difficulties with mobility and require assistance in the tasks of independent living. For these couples, men may assume new caregiving roles, combining nurturance with feelings of agency. Thus, health and fitness more than gender may guide the nature of dyadic interactions among older couples. As men and women become more equal with respect to power and resources in their marital relationship, there may be fewer clear-cut gender expectations. Still, to the extent that gender-role distinctions help stabilize a relationship, older adults may be reluctant to make dramatic changes to the way their relationships have been structured (Silver, 2003). We do not know whether new cohorts of the elderly, especially the baby boomers, who are accustomed to balancing work and family life, will arrive at later life with different views about instrumentality and its association with gender (Muhlbauer, Chrisler, & Denmark, 2015; Robbins, Wester, & McKean, 2016).

Romance and Sexuality

Romance, intimacy, and sexuality remain important among older couples. The majority of couples who have enjoyed a close, sexually active relationship report little change in satisfaction from age 60 to 85. Some couples explore different ways of experiencing sexual pleasure in later life, and others report a more relaxed, sexually satisfying quality in their lovemaking. Thinking back to Sternberg's (1988) model of the three dimensions of love, long-lasting marriages tend to be more companionate in nature, emphasizing intimacy and commitment over passion.

Research on sexuality in later life confirms that many older adults have sexual needs, benefit from sexual expression, and are able to be sexually active. A national survey of adults ages 60 and older found that more than half were sexually active, meaning that they had intercourse, oral sex, anal intercourse, or masturbated at least once a month (Dunn & Cutler, 2000). Sexual activity declined with age, but 20 percent to 25 percent of those in their 80s were still sexually active. Older couples may find greater

After 60 years of marriage, Ann and Ted still get quite a kick out of being together. Their lives are sprinkled with many moments like this, when a glance or an expression brings out a loving smile.

satisfaction in intimate physical contact, such as kissing and caressing, and experimentation with new ways of experiencing sexual stimulation as genital intercourse becomes less frequent. Following along with the idea of gender-role convergence, men and women become more similar in their sexual behavior and more harmonious in their lovemaking (Crooks & Bauer, 2013).

One of the greatest challenges to continued romantic and sexual intimacy in later life is widowhood. Despite the fact that older men are much more likely to remarry than older women, remarriage is relatively uncommon in later adulthood and elderhood. In a study of older couples that followed men and women 6 and 18 months after widowhood participants were asked two questions about their romantic interests: "At this point do you have any interest in dating?" which was answered *yes* or *no*, and "Someday I would like to remarry," answered on a scale from *not true at all* to *very true*. They were also asked if they were dating. At 6 months after widowhood, men were more likely to want to be dating than women (17 percent versus 6 percent), more likely to want to remarry (30 percent versus 16 percent), and more likely to be dating (15 percent versus less than 1 percent). At 18 months after widowhood, men were still more likely to want to be dating (37 percent versus 15 percent) and more likely to be dating (23 percent versus 9 percent), but about equally likely to want to remarry (26 percent versus 19 percent). The most important predictor of whether men or women wanted to date or remarry was the quality of their social support system. In general, women had more supportive relationships with friends than did men prior to widowhood. The more social support men had, the less likely they were to express interest in remarriage. Men and women who had comparable levels of social support from friends were equally disinterested in remarriage (Carr, 2004).

This research suggests that the picture we have about gender differences in motivations to find a new partner after widowhood may need to be revised. First, although more men than women are interested in new romantic relationships, the majority of men do not express this interest. Second, when social support systems are comparable, men and women are about equally likely to reject the idea of a new romantic relationship.

One criticism of this research was the way in which interest in a new partner was defined, limiting the alternatives for romantic relationships to dating and marriage. Potential financial consequences may make remarriage undesirable. For instance, a widow may lose her husband's pension or Social Security benefits if she remarries. Given the potential costs of remarriage in later life, older adults may be looking for a different kind of intimacy that does not require the responsibilities of co-residence or the legal and financial considerations of marriage (Davidson, 2002; Ghazanfareeon, Karlsson, & Borrell, 2002; Moorman, Booth, & Fingerman, 2006). Some older couples cope with this problem by living together instead of marrying. From 2000 to 2010, in the United States the number of unmarried, heterosexual couples over the age of 65 who were living together increased from 193,000 to 575,000 (Creamer, 2011).

Ageism and Sexuality. Older adults continue to face negative attitudes about sexual activity that may inhibit their sexual behavior. These attitudes include assumptions that very old adults do not have sexual desires, they cannot have intercourse because of sexual dysfunction, sex may be dangerous to their health, they are physically and sexually unattractive, and it is morally wrong or perverted for older adults to be sexually active (Crooks & Bauer, 2013). Current cohorts of elders may have limited knowledge about sexuality and aging. Increasing knowledge through various sex education programs can increase permissive attitudes about sexuality among older adults (Hillman & Stricker, 1994). These interventions have involved elderly people, nursing students, college students, nursing home staff, and adult children of aging parents. However, increased knowledge does not always result in more permissive attitudes. Especially among health care staff in institutional settings, the institutional regulations, personal moral values, and practical problems of permitting sexual activity among residents may combine to promote a negative attitude even with advanced information about sexuality and aging.

As the value of intimacy for health and well-being is more fully recognized, we expect future groups of elders to be more comfortable about forming intimate relationships. Cohort factors may change the current societal attitudes toward sexuality among the very old. Because so many more adult women are in the workplace, they have more experience with male colleagues. Acceptance of forming new sexual relationships in later life is more likely because many adults have experienced nonmarital sexual relationships in their earlier years of adulthood. The high divorce rate since the mid-1970s means that in the future more women will have had the experience of developing a single lifestyle that includes a network of both male and female friends. With an estimated 1.5 million LGBT adults age 65 and over and a growing openness about same-sex intimate relationships, we see the emergence of niche communities that support the lifestyles of same-sex couples.

FURTHER REFLECTION: Imagine that you are now 85 years old. Describe the kind of life you hope to be living. What kind of living arrangement, social relationships, and activities would you like to have? What concerns for physical health, safety, intellectual stimulation, and social interaction will you have then? How will you design your life structure to support your needs in these domains?

The Psychosocial Crisis: Immortality Versus Extinction

OBJECTIVE 5 Define and explain the psychosocial crisis of immortality versus extinction, the central process of social support, the prime adaptive ego quality of confidence, and the core pathology of diffidence.

By the end of later adulthood, most people have developed a point of view about death. Although they may continue to experience anxiety about their impending death, they have found the courage to confront their fears and overcome them. If older adults have achieved integrity, they believe that their life has made sense. This amplifies their confidence about the choices they have made and the goals they have achieved without despair over the failures, missed opportunities, or misfortunes that may have occurred. Thus, elders can accept the end of life and view it as a natural part of the life span. They are capable of distilling wisdom from the events of their lives, including their successes and mistakes.

However, elders are faced with a new challenge—a conflict between the acceptance of death and the intensifying hope for immortality. Having lived longer than their cohort of friends, family members, and even, in some cases, their children, elders struggle to find meaning in their survival. All of us face a certain disbelief about our own mortality. Although we know that death is a certainty, an element of human thought prevents us from facing the full realization of death; we continue to hope for immortality. This quality may be adaptive in that people who have a sense of hope cope with the reality of death better than those who do not (Kesebir, 2011).

Immortality

Elders have a unique appreciation of time. They recognize that there is a finite amount of future time until their death, as well as an unlimited transcendental future time that begins with their death and extends onward into infinity (Boyd & Zimbardo, 1996; Zimbardo & Boyd, 2008). They begin to see themselves as links in a long, fluid chain of historical and biological growth and change. The positive pole of this crisis is a confidence in the continuity of life, a transcendence of death through the development of a symbolic sense of immortality. The achievement of this perspective, which may include the incorporation of transcendental goals such as reuniting with loved ones after death or being released from the limitations of an aging body, may be accompanied with sentiments of joy, which contribute to feelings of well-being, flexibility, and acceptance of the challenges of aging.

A psychosocial sense of **immortality** may be achieved and expressed in many ways (Lifton, 1973). Here, we explore

The Responsibility of Native Hawaiians for Their Ancestors' Remains

The following narrative describes the psychosocial crisis of immortality versus extinction in the context of the desecration of a native Hawaiian burial site. In fighting to stop the destruction, those involved were reminded of the commitment that the living have for the care and protection of the burial grounds of their ancestors:

Hawai'i Nei was born December 1988 from the *kaumah a* (heaviness) and *aokanaka* (enlightenment) caused by the archaeological disinterment of over 1,100 ancestral Native Hawaiians from Honokahua, Maui. The ancestral remains were removed over the protests of the Native Hawaiian community in order to build the Ritz Carlton Hotel. The desecration was stopped following a 24-hour vigil at the State Capital. Governor John Waihe'e, a Native Hawaiian, approved of a settlement that returned the ancestral remains to their *one hanau* (birth sands), set aside the reburial site in perpetuity, and moved the hotel inland and away from the ancestral resting place.

In one sense Honokahua represents balance for from this tragedy came enlightenment: the realization by living Native Hawaiians that we were responsible for the care and protection of our ancestors and that cultural protocols needed to be relearned and laws effectively changed to create the empowerment necessary to carry out this important and time-honored responsibility to *malama* (take care) and *kupale* (protect) our ancestors.

Hui Malama I Na Kupuna O Hawai'i Nei members have trained under the direction of Edward and Pualani Kanahele of Hilo in traditional protocols relating to the care of *na iwi kupuna* (ancestral remains). These commitments were undertaken as a form of *aloha* and respect for our own families, ancestors, parents, and children.

Hui Malama I Na Kupuna O Hawai'i Nei has been taught by the Kanahele family about the importance of *pule* (prayer) necessary to *ho'olohe* (listen) to the calling of our ancestors. Through *pule* we request the assistance of *ke akua* and our ancestors to provide us with the tools necessary to conduct our work:

E homai ka ike, e homai ka ikaika, e homai ka akamai, e homai ka maopop o pono, e homai ka 'ike papalua, e homai ka man a.

(Grant us knowledge, grant us strength, grant us intelligence, grant us righteous understanding, grant us visions and avenues of communication, grant us mana.)

Moreover, we have been taught that the relationship between our ancestors and ourselves is one of interdependence—as the living, we have a *kuleana* (responsibility) to care for our *kupuna* (ancestors). In turn, our ancestors respond by protecting us on the spiritual side. Hence, one side cannot completely exist without the other.

Source: Pell (2002), http://huimalama.tripod.com/

Critical Thinking Questions

1. Describe the belief system that connects native Hawaiians and their ancestors. How does this belief system contribute to the resolution of the psychosocial crisis of immortality versus extinction?
2. Predict how the sense of interdependence between the living and the dead might influence the day-to-day behavior of native Hawaiians.
3. Select a culture of interest to you. Investigate and describe the relationship of the living to their ancestors in this culture. Summarize the beliefs, rituals, and actions that reflect this relationship.
4. Analyze the trends of modernization that may explain why Hawaiians have lost touch with the traditional practices associated with the care of ancestral remains. Propose what may be gained by reviving these traditions.

---

five possible paths toward immortality. First, one may live on through one's children and grandchildren, sensing a connection and attachment to the future through one's life and the lives of one's offspring. This type of immortality can be extended to include devotion to one's country, social organizations or groups, or humankind.

Second, one may believe in an afterlife, an immortal soul, or a spiritual plane of existence that extends beyond one's biological life (Pereira, Falsca, & de Sá-Saraiva, 2012). Most religions espouse the concept of a state of harmony with natural forces, so that after death, one endures beyond this earthly life.

Among many indigenous peoples, there is a sacred link between the living and the dead—a responsibility on the part of the living to protect and respect the sacred burial grounds and a responsibility on the part of the dead ancestors to look after the spiritual well-being of the living. This belief is illustrated in the **Human Development and Diversity** box, The Responsibility of Native Hawaiians for Their Ancestors' Remains.

Third, one may achieve a sense of immortality through creative achievements and their impact on others. Many people find comfort in believing that they are part of a chain of positive influences on the lives of others. This sense of immortality is linked to the achievement of generativity in middle adulthood. Adults who have made a commitment to improving the quality of life for others during middle adulthood are likely to see evidence of this effort by the time they reach elderhood.

Perhaps it was only in the later years of my practice— I saw the results of my labors in the unfolding lives of my

Through prayer and inspiration, this minister shares her faith and sense of immortality with her congregation.

about feelings of cosmic communion with the spirit of the universe, and a redefinition of time, space, life, and death (Tornstam, 2005). This expression of immortality is independent of religion, offspring, or creative achievement. It is an insight derived from moments of rapture or ecstasy in which all that one senses is the power of the moment. In these experiences, the duality of life and death dissolve, and what remains is continuous being.

Extinction

The negative pole of the psychosocial crisis of elderhood is a sense of being bound by the limits of one's life history. In place of a belief in continuous existence and transformation, one views the end of life as an end to motion, attachment, and change. Instead of faith in the ideas of connection and continuity, one experiences a fear of **extinction**—a fear that one's life and its end amount to nothing. Erikson's advice on coping with aging concerns responding to loss and dealing with diminished capacities (see the **Applying Theory and Research to Life** box Erikson on Coping with Aging). It is not difficult to imagine that as a person reflects on the many losses encountered over a long life, there will be periods when it seems that all the effort, striving, hoping, and struggle did not amount to much. In the process of resolving this psychosocial crisis, it is to be expected that people will have at least momentary thoughts that there is nothing more; that the end is truly an end.

The following quotations from a study of very old men suggest the range in sentiment about immortality and extinction (Rosenfeld, 1978, p. 10). About 28 percent of the adults in the study were described as having low morale and made statements such as "I feel I'm a forgotten man. I don't exist anymore.... I don't feel old.... I'm just living out my life." About 25 percent were stoic but not very positive about their condition: "You know you're getting old. You have to put your mind to it and take it as it comes. You can't get out of it. Take it gracefully." Almost half found their lives full and rewarding: "I go home with my cup overflowing. There are so many opportunities to do things for people. These are the happiest days of my life."

Conditions in long-term care facilities may contribute to the sense of extinction for some elders. Imagine living in a facility where the staff consistently mistreats older adults. In one study, incidents of physical abuse, intimidation, and neglect were reported by 44 percent of nursing care residents. Being a victim of violence or being exposed to violent treatment of others in a setting where a person has no way to retaliate or punish the abuser can certainly produce feelings of despair and withdrawal (National Center on Elder Abuse, 2012).

The possibility of ending one's life with a sense of extinction is reflected in the public health concern about suicide among the elderly. In the United States, the highest suicide rate in 2014 was among those 85 years old and older (American Foundation for Suicide Prevention, 2016). Data from the *World Health Organization* provide a basis for describing the incidence of suicide for men and women by age. Men commit suicide at higher rates than women at all ages, and those aged 70 and older have the highest suicide rates. National differences are substantial, with suicide rates higher in the high income as compared to the middle and low income countries (World Health Organization, 2014).

patients—that once again I appreciated the value of my link in the chain of life. (Young, 2011)

The bond between an individual and community makes death less final. An African proverb advises that you live as long as someone knows your name. The more embedded you are in your community and the more lives you have touched, the greater the sense of continuity or transcendence.

Fourth, one may develop the notion of participation in the chain of nature. In death, one's body returns to the earth and one's energy is brought forth in a new form.

Fifth, one may achieve a sense of immortality through what Lifton (1973) described as **experiential transcendence**:

This state is characterized by extraordinary psychic unity and perceptual intensity. But there also occurs … a process of symbolic reordering…. Experiential transcendence includes a feeling of … "continuous present" that can be equated with eternity or with "mythical time." This continuous present is perceived as not only "here and now" but as inseparable from past and future. (p. 10)

The notion of **cosmic transcendence** has been developed further by Lars Tornstam, a Swedish gerontologist, who writes

Erikson on Coping with Aging

The Eriksons' advice (Erikson et al., 1986, pp. 332–333) suggests the achievement of experiential transcendence:

> With aging, there are inevitably constant losses—losses of those very close, and friends near and far. Those who have been rich in intimacy also have the most to lose. Recollection is one form of adaptation, but the effort skillfully to form new relationships is adaptive and more rewarding. Old age is necessarily a time of relinquishing— of giving up old friends, old roles, earlier work that was once meaningful, and even possessions that belong to a previous stage of life and are now an impediment to the resiliency and freedom that seem to be requisite for adapting to the unknown challenges that determine the final stage of life.
>
> Trust in interdependence. Give and accept help when it is needed. Old Oedipus well knew that the aged sometimes need three legs; pride can be an asset but not a cane. When frailty takes over, dependence is appropriate, and one has no choice but to trust in the compassion of others and be consistently surprised at how faithful some caretakers can be.
>
> Much living, however, can teach us only how little is known. Accept that essential "not-knowingness" of childhood and with it also that playful curiosity. Growing old can be an interesting adventure and is certainly full of surprises.
>
> One is reminded here of the image Hindu philosophy uses to describe the final letting go—that of merely being. The mother cat picks up in her mouth the kitten, which completely collapses every tension and hangs limp and infinitely trusting in the maternal benevolence. The kitten responds instinctively. We human beings require at least a whole lifetime of practice to do this.

Source: From *Vital Involvement in Old Age,* E.H. Erikson, J.M. Erikson, & H.Q. Kivnick (1986), pp. 332–333.

Critical Thinking Questions

1. Critically evaluate the advice provided by Erikson. Would this be good advice to help elders cope with the challenges of aging? If not, what advice would you offer in its place?
2. Given the full course of psychosocial development, speculate about why it may be especially difficult for the elderly to accept help and depend upon others when they need it. What lessons from earlier stages of life might prepare a person to do this?
3. Erikson suggests adopting an outlook of playful "not-knowingness" and adventure. Summarize the cultural, religious, and personal factors that might help a person attain this view of elderhood.
4. Read more about Erik Erikson. What can you find out about how well he was able to accept this advice in the last years of his life?

Relatively few of the elderly in the United States experience a level of discouragement that is implied by the sense of extinction. Among those ages 75 and older, roughly 5 percent reported pervasive feelings of worthlessness or hopelessness (Blackwell, Lucas, & Clarke, 2014). A caution about these data is that elders may be reluctant to report feelings of discouragement or hopelessness.

The Central Process: Social Support

Social support has been defined as the social experiences that lead people to believe that they are cared for and loved, esteemed and valued, and belong to a network of communication and mutual obligation (Cobb, 1979). Social support includes the quantity and interconnectedness or web of social relationships in which a person is embedded, the strength of those ties, the frequency of contact, and the extent to which the support system is perceived as helpful and caring (Bergeman, Plomin, Pedersen, McClearn, & Nesselroade, 1990). It is commonly divided into two different but complementary categories: **socioemotional support**, which refers to expressions of affection, respect, and esteem, and **instrumental support**, which refers to direct assistance, including help with chores, medical care, or transportation. Both types of social support—but especially socioemotional support—contribute to maintaining well-being and fostering the possibility of transcending the physical limitations that accompany aging (Rowe & Kahn, 1998).

The Benefits of Social Support

Social support plays a direct role in promoting health, well-being, and life satisfaction even when a person is not facing a specific stressful situation (Gow et al., 2007; White, Philoogene, Fine, & Sinha, 2009). Because social support involves meaningful social relationships, it reduces isolation. People who have intimate companions in later life have higher levels of life satisfaction. They feel valued and valuable. This kind of social support is likely to be most appreciated when it comes from friends and neighbors— members of the community who are not bound by familial obligation to care about the person, but who do so anyway.

The presence of caring, familiar people provides a flow of affection, information, advice, transportation, and assistance with meals and daily activities, finances, and health care—all critical resources. The support system tends to reduce the impact of stressors and protect people from some of their negative consequences, especially serious illnesses and depression (Krause, 2006).

Social support can contribute to improved health. Jean and Carol exercise together three times a week, talking and laughing as they ride.

Social integration and membership in a meaningful social support network are associated with increased longevity. A high level of social integration is associated with lower mortality rates (Cherry et al., 2013; Rowe & Kahn, 1997). The support system often serves to encourage an older person to maintain health care practices and to seek medical attention when it is needed. Members of the immediate family, close relatives, and friends provide direct care during times of grave illness or loss, encouraging the older person to cope with difficulties and to remain hopeful. Elders are likely to experience declines in physical stamina. They may also have limited financial resources. In order to transcend the limitations of their daily living situations, elders must be convinced that they are embedded in a network of social relationships in which they are valued. But their value cannot be based solely on a physical exchange of goods and services. Rather, it must be founded on an appreciation of the person's dignity and a history of reciprocal caring.

The Dynamics of Social Support

The benefits of receiving social support can be diminished if the recipients adhere to a strong cultural norm for reciprocity. The **norm of reciprocity** implies that you are obligated to return in full value what you receive: "One good turn deserves another." People want and expect to be able to give about the same as or more than they receive. What is given does not have to be identical to what is received, but it has to be perceived as having equal worth. Being in someone's debt may be considered stressful and shameful. In a study of Japanese American elderly people, receiving material support from their family was associated with higher levels of depression and less satisfaction in life, especially for those who had very traditional values about reciprocity. In efforts

to mobilize social support to enhance the functioning of the very old, one needs to be sensitive to the context and meaning of that support (Nemoto, 1998).

Most elders continue to see themselves as involved in a reciprocal, supportive relationship with their friends. Feelings of usefulness and competence continue to be important correlates of well-being in later life. Older adults are especially likely to experience positive feelings of life satisfaction when they are able to provide assistance to others at times of significant life transition or need, such as widowhood or the divorce of a child (Davey & Eggebeen, 1998). Even though they are comforted by knowing that support would be available when needed, older adults are likely to experience negative feelings when the support received is more than was needed or when there is no opportunity for them to reciprocate (Liang, Krause, & Bennett, 2001).

Elders may expect to receive more care from their children when they are ill than they can provide in exchange. By shifting to a life-span perspective, however, they can retain a sense of balance by seeing the help they receive now as comparable to the help they gave their children at earlier life stages (Ingersoll-Dayton & Antonucci, 1988). When elders are highly valued, it is not as important that they reciprocate in the exchange of tangible resources. Wisdom, affection, joie de vivre, and a positive model of surviving into old age are intangible resources that are highly valued by members of the very old person's social support network. Being valued may also mean that the person's advice and conversation are adequate exchange for some of the services and assistance provided by family and friends.

Social relationships can include both positive and negative interactions. Within one's social network, positive interactions might include enjoying shared activities, confiding about one's worries, or asking for help when one is ill. Negative interactions might include being taken advantage of, having one's privacy invaded, or being insulted. Sometimes, the same people can be sources of both positive and negative interactions. Not surprisingly, the overall frequency of positive exchanges is related to lower levels of depression. When older adults experience the effects of negative social interactions in one relationship—for example, when they have an argument with their adult child—they can buffer these emotions by having positive interactions with another member of their social network—for example, a friend or spouse (Okun & Keith, 1998).

Many older adults are selective about the people in their social network, striving to interact primarily with people who engage in harmonious interactions. They also take steps to prevent conflict in the relationships they value. For example, they impose certain constraints on their interactions—not criticizing someone in public, respecting others' privacy, and keeping a confidence. These strategies help avoid negative interactions and maximize the satisfaction and stability of their relationships (Sorkin & Rook, 2004).

The Social Support Network

Of course, being an integral part of a social system does not begin in later life. It has its origins in infancy, with the formation of a mutual relationship with a caregiver. Social support systems are extended in childhood and early adolescence through identification with a peer group, and in early and middle adulthood through marriage, childrearing, and relationships with coworkers and adult friends. In later life, family members are usually the primary sources of social support, especially one's spouse, children, and siblings. The quality of the relationship between an adult child and an aging parent has a long history. Clearly, the nature of the support that an aging parent is able to receive or that an adult child is willing to provide is influenced by the feelings of closeness and connection that were fashioned during the childrearing process and also by the child's relationship to the parents during early adulthood years.

In the United States, age is a predictor of the size of the social support network. Younger people have larger social support networks than do older people. This may be true for a variety of reasons. For elder women, the likelihood of living alone is high. After the death of a spouse, men and women must realign their social support systems from among relationships that include their adult children, friends, relatives, neighbors, and new acquaintances in order to satisfy their needs for interaction and companionship. In a study of social relationships following widowhood, women clearly benefited from the social network that existed prior to their husband's death. However, contrary to expectations, efforts to modify this network by renewing old acquaintances or forming new friendships did not help to reduce feelings of depression or loneliness, even 2 years after the loss (Zettel & Rook, 2004).

Elders differ in the composition of their social networks. Whereas some elders rely heavily on close family members, others are closely linked to friends and neighbors, and others find their closest ties in church or community organizations. What is more, each social network component may contribute a unique resource. A sibling might provide emotional support whereas a friend might provide companionship, shared activities, or health-related advice. Elders who are childless or have no surviving children or siblings are especially vulnerable to ending their lives in isolation. In contrast, those who are able to preserve a diverse social network are more likely to be the healthiest, make the most use of appropriate community services, and experience the highest levels of well-being (Antonucci et al., 2001; Bosworth & Schaie, 1997; Litwin, 1997; Litwin & Shiovitz-Ezra, 2011).

Social media are becoming an increasingly valued resource among the elderly for preserving and even expanding their social support network. In a recent national survey conducted by the Pew Research Center, 56 percent of those ages 65 and older said they were regular users of Facebook (Duggan, 2015). Older adults use this resource for a variety of reasons including preserving bonds of friendship with their long-time friends, joining new interest groups, and staying connected with family and loved ones (Rogers, 2016). An especially valued feature of Skype and FaceTime are the real-time interactions that are possible, allowing elders who are not able to visit their family and friends or who have limited mobility to engage in face-to-face conversations.

For many elders, religious participation provides an additional source of social support. Older adults are more likely than younger adults to describe themselves as religious in their beliefs and behavior. Mary, who at age 80 has experienced the deaths of three brothers, her husband, and her daughter-in-law, gives and receives emotional support through her faith:

> I always have a lot of faith. The good Lord has always given me the strength to go on. I was raised to believe and pray when I have problems. I go to Mass every Sunday, and we have other special days when we go to Mass. I'm a Eucharistic minister. God makes me do things to feel better—I serve people and God. I go to buildings to give communion to people who can't get out. (Rowe & Kahn, 1998, p. 164)

Members of religious congregations may provide one another with both emotional and instrumental social support. The place of religion in the lives of the very old is especially significant for African Americans, who are more likely than European Americans to attend religious services regularly, even at advanced ages. They are also more likely to describe themselves as very religious—a characterization that reflects the frequency of their private prayer, their strong emotional commitment, and their reading of religious material. Religious involvement among elderly African Americans is not predicted by income or education. Over time, elders who are active in their religious communities give and receive increasing amounts of emotional support to one another and express increased satisfaction from these church-based relationships (Hayward & Krause, 2013).

Ethnic identity may also become an important vehicle for social support in later life. It can provide sources of nonfamilial support, from a loose network of associations to membership in formal clubs and organizations. Members of an ethnic group may feel a strong sense of community as a result of their shared exposure to past discrimination, a realization of common concerns, and a sense of responsibility to preserve the authenticity of their ethnic identity for future generations. Participation in such a support network may be a way to contribute wisdom gained through life experiences to those who will follow. Insofar as members of ethnic groups have felt marginal in the larger society in the past, their mutual support in later life may protect them from some of the negative stereotypes that the society imposes on the very old.

Involvement in a social support system can be an essential ingredient in the achievement of a sense of immortality. The social support system confirms the value of elders, providing direct evidence of their positive impact on others and embeddedness in their social communities. The social support system of elders usually includes adult children. Positive interactions with them contribute to the sense of living on through one's offspring and their descendants. Interactions with members of the social support system—especially those marked by feelings of warmth, caring, and celebration—may be moments of experiential transcendence for elders. They feel the fullness and joy of existence that transcend physical and material barriers (Sadler et al., 2006).

The Prime Adaptive Ego Quality and the Core Pathology

Confidence

Confidence, as a prime adaptive ego quality, refers to a conscious trust in oneself, an appreciation of one's abilities, and an assurance about the meaningfulness of life. In this definition, one finds the earliest psychosocial crisis of trust versus mistrust integrated with the crisis of integrity versus despair. In elderhood, after a lifetime of facing challenges and experiencing losses and gains, one has a new belief in the validity of one's intuition, a trust in one's worldview, and a continued belief in one's capacity to participate in the world on one's own terms. Confidence is sustained by a stable, supportive social network (Krause, 2007; Lang, Featherman, & Nesselroade, 1997). Older adults who feel they are able to engage in the activities they enjoy and interact with people they value are also more likely to believe that they can adapt to the challenges they face. As a result of their confidence, they are less disrupted by stressful events and more hopeful about being able to find successful solutions in the face of negative events (Pushkar, Arbuckle, Conway, Chaikelson, & Maag, 1997).

Physical health and age, per se, are not the best predictors of confidence. One's perceptions of physical health problems and how one sees oneself in comparison to others may be more important predictors of confidence than any objective measure of health status. Some people view themselves as more impaired and dependent than they actually are; others, who may be suffering from serious illnesses, continue to view their situation with optimism (Ryff, 1995). Similarly, one's perception of the adequacy of social support and its appropriateness in response to one's needs is more important to a sense of confidence than the material value of the resources exchanged (Davey & Eggebeen, 1998).

Over the course of life, psychosocial theory predicts that each individual will confront issues related to the negative poles of the psychosocial crisis of each stage. Finding ways to integrate the negative pole of each stage into an overall positive worldview strengthens and humanizes one's character. Encounters with each negative pole provide a deeper sense of empathy for the suffering of others and a more profound appreciation for the courage that it takes to live out one's life with an open, generous, hopeful outlook. Confidence emerges not because of a life of one success after the next, but out of a sequence of struggles in which creative energy is required to find a positive balance between positive and negative forces (J. M. Erikson, 1988).

Diffidence

Diffidence, the core pathology of elderhood, refers to an inability to act because of overwhelming self-doubt. It is considered one of the basic factors underlying personality disorders (Livesley, Jackson, & Schroeder, 1992). Diffidence is evidenced by an unusual amount of difficulty in making daily decisions without advice and reassurance from others, great reluctance in undertaking projects or becoming involved in activities because of lack of confidence, and fears of being unable to care for oneself, which result in the fear of being alone (American Psychiatric Association, 1994).

Experiences with ageism, being ignored, devalued, or dismissed as irrelevant can promote diffidence. In an era of rapid technological advances and transformations of communities through renovation and renewal, an older person can feel dislocated in space and in relationships, losing the sense of competence about how to navigate in the community. Diffidence can be a product of an earlier form of socialization about "politeness" that no longer guides contemporary social interactions. People call on the phone and, out of politeness, you answer only to find that they want your money, they threaten you with a lawsuit, or they want you to buy some product you don't need. You receive letters in the mail from people you don't know, asking for donations, telling you that you owe money, or that you have been specially selected for some prize. It all turns out to be a sham, leaving you reluctant to answer the next call or open the next piece of mail. Exploitation of the elderly contributes to diffidence—an inability to trust long-learned patterns of courteous behavior.

Diffidence is likely to be associated with hopelessness. Among the elderly, hopelessness is experienced as a negative expectancy about the future and a sense of futility about having an impact on impending events. The combination of hopelessness and depression are strongly associated with suicidal ideation among the elderly (Uncapher, Gallagher-Thompson, Osgood, & Bongar, 1998). Feelings of diffidence can result from increased dependency and loss of control due to physical illness, loss of social support, or marked reduction in the quality of life, or they can be a product of a continuous process of ego pathology, building on the negative resolutions of earlier psychosocial crises. It is clear that in later life, the courage and energy required to remain flexible and adaptive to change must be derived from a depth of ego resources established over the life course. For some of the very old, this precious resource has been eroded and they face the end of life in a state of passivity and doubt.

FURTHER REFLECTION: Explain what is meant by the psychosocial concept of immortality. Analyze ways that a person's social support system contributes to the resolution of the crisis of immortality versus extinction.

Evaluate the notion that spirituality becomes a stronger feature of well-being in later life. Why might this be true? What evidence is there to support this idea?

Speculate about how positive resolutions of the crises of generativity versus stagnation and integrity versus despair contribute to the resolution of the crisis of immortality versus extinction.

Applied Topic: Meeting the Needs of the Frail Elderly

OBJECTIVE 6 Apply research and theory to concerns about meeting the needs of the frail elderly.

The goal of providing services or community resources to the frail elderly should be to enhance a realistic level of performance. On the one hand, one should not try to encourage 80-year-olds to live the lives of teenagers or people in their 50s. On the other hand, one should not hold such minimal expectations for the elderly that they are robbed of their autonomy and ability to meet challenges or to strive toward achievable goals. A current focus of research and policy is the extent to which physical frailty in elderhood is treatable or preventable and how to reduce dependency, especially in long-term nursing care.

In 2004, the U.S. Administration on Aging announced an initiative focused on supporting "Seniors Aging in Place" (ageinplace.org) in response to the strong preference among the very old to remain independent. Projects were funded that provided new resources or access to services in the community so that older adults with a wide range of needs and abilities could retain an optimal level of independent functioning. The National Aging in Place Council is a forum whose mission is to encourage professionals and corporations in specific communities to work together to provide the system of community resources that will permit older adults to remain in their homes as long as possible. The council provides suggestions to individuals about how to modify their homes to make them accessible and how to take advantage of community resources and services. It also sponsors innovative collaboration between health care, transportation, and corporate interests to create products and services that will facilitate optimal residential communities for the very old (National Aging in Place Council, 2016).

Because of his problems walking, Caleb was practically homebound. But once his children bought him this motorized chair he was able to enjoy going outdoors, interacting with neighbors, and taking Pebbles for a walk. What other technological inventions help support optimal functioning in elderhood?

Defining Frailty

Frailty has typically been defined in terms of dependency. One common approach is to list any difficulties in the ADLs, including bathing, dressing, transferring from the bed to a chair, using the toilet, and eating. Sometimes, these assessments include walking a short distance because this degree of motor ability is usually required to function independently. Beyond these basic types of self-care, an expanded notion of dependency refers to difficulties in managing IADLs, such as shopping, preparing meals, doing light housework, using transportation, or using the telephone. These tasks, though more complex than the basic ADLs, are essential to maintaining one's daily life without dependence on informal or formal community support services.

Measures of functional limitations often fail to differentiate between what people say they might be able to do (as when completing a survey) and what they actually do in their day-to-day lives. For example, some people may respond to a questionnaire saying that they are able to walk half a mile without help, but they do not ever walk that much. Others may respond that they cannot walk half a mile without help, but in fact they walk several blocks on most days to go to the store near their home. When observed in their natural setting, many older adults use compensatory strategies to overcome some physical impairment or integrate the support of others so they can enact certain functions even though they have serious disabilities. For example, in a sample of women who needed assistance in more than three areas of daily living, more than one fourth still managed to get to church services once

a week or more. They did not allow their physical limitations to restrict their role involvement (Glass, 1998; Hayward & Krause, 2013).

Dependency or difficulty in managing ADLs increases markedly after age 85. Many factors combine to produce this dependency. In most postindustrial societies, later adulthood is characterized by a sedentary lifestyle. Estimates suggest that only about 10 percent of older adults are active enough to sustain appropriate levels of muscle strength and cardiovascular capacity. Weakness resulting from disuse combines with certain biological changes, diseases, medications, and malnutrition to produce muscle atrophy, risk of falling, reduced arousal and cognitive capacity, and a gradual decline in confidence in being able to cope with even moderate types of physical exertion.

For many older adults, problems with remaining independent change from time to time. For example, a 20 minute walk each day is known to help support endurance, balance and overall health. However, in the winter, when streets are icy and the weather is cold, a person living in a cold climate may need more help because it is difficult to walk outside. In the event of an acute illness requiring a period of hospitalization, a person may temporarily need support during the post-hospital recovery but does not require long-term institutionalization. Full recovery from a week or two of being bedridden may require additional physical therapy, rebuilding muscle tone and endurance and rebuilding confidence in managing daily tasks. The outcome for the older person depends on the patient, caregiver, and health care system—all sharing expectations for recovery and rehabilitation rather than viewing the person as permanently weakened and destined for prolonged dependency (U.S. Department of Health and Human Services, 2013).

Supporting Optimal Functioning

Optimal functioning is what a person is capable of doing when motivated and well prepared. To support optimal functioning of elderly people, one must accurately assess their limitations. One does not want to take away the supports that help elders sustain their independence or overreact to their physical or intellectual limitations. This tendency, however, is observed in the responses of some adult children to their aging parents. Once children realize that their parents are not functioning at the same high level of competence that they enjoyed previously, the children may move toward a **role reversal**. The children may infantilize or dominate their parents, insisting on taking over all financial matters or attempting to relocate their parents to a more protective housing arrangement. Gradually, some children take away all their parents' decision-making responsibilities.

Although children may view such actions as being in their parents' best interests, they may fail to take their parents' preferences into account. Adult children tend to overemphasize the importance of health and financial considerations for their parents and overlook the significance of familiar housing in preserving the companionship and daily support that are critical to their parents' sense of well-being. Adult children may fail to realize how important decision-making tasks and responsibility for personal care are to the maintenance of their parents' personality structure. In mutually satisfying relationships between adult daughters and their aging mothers, the daughters made sure that their mothers were consistently involved in decisions that affected their lives, even when the mothers were heavily dependent on their daughters for daily care (APA, 2016; Kahana, 1982; Pratt, Jones, Shin, & Walker, 1989).

In many nursing homes, there is a similar tendency to reduce or eliminate expectations of autonomy by failing to give residents responsibilities for planning or performing the activities of daily life. Routine chores such as cooking, cleaning, shopping for groceries, doing laundry, planning meals, answering the phone, paying bills, and writing letters give older adults the sense that life is going along as usual. Replacing these responsibilities with unstructured time may subject very old people to more stress than continuing to expect some forms of regular contribution to daily life. Thus, paid work assignments and structured daily responsibilities are activities that an institutional setting can provide to help maintain a high level of social and intellectual functioning among the residents.

The Eden Alternative (2016), an emerging philosophy in elder care, proposed that loneliness, helplessness, and boredom are the primary sources of suffering in late life. Principles of intervention, training, and care are applied to home and nursing home interventions to address these three concerns. "An Elder-centered community commits to creating a Human Habitat where life revolves around close and continuing contact with people of all ages and abilities, as well as plants and animals. It is these relationships that provide the young and old alike with a pathway to a life worth living." With this principle in mind, the Eden Care approach in nursing home care is to foster meaningful, close relationships; to incorporate unexpected and spontaneous events to prevent boredom; and to give residents responsibilities

for decision making and activities depending on their level of functioning. These responsibilities, which might include watering plants, volunteering in a nearby child care center, or reading to other residents, help overcome the negative impact of dependency and institutionalization.

Supporting the optimal functioning of frail elderly people requires an individualized approach. Each person has a unique profile of competencies and limitations. For some, the physical environment presents the greatest barriers to optimal functioning. For example, older adults who are in a wheelchair are likely to experience a fall every so often. However, those who have installed modifications in their home—including widened doorways and halls, railings, and easy-open doors—are less likely to fall than those whose homes have not been modified (Berg, Hines, & Allen, 2002). A person who cannot walk without fear of falling, see well, or grasp objects because of arthritis may need to have modifications in the home that will compensate for these limitations.

The Role of the Community

Most older adults want to remain in their community as long as possible. However, they may not be able to afford to pay for supplemental services. Economic security is more fragile for those 80 and older than for those 65 to 74. Two explanations for this economic vulnerability are the increases in medical and long-term health costs and the fact that Social Security income has not kept up with these increased costs. Fifty-eight percent of older adults are considered economically vulnerable, that is their income is less than two times the supplemental poverty level (Cooper & Gould, 2013; LaPonsie, 2016). Future generations of elders are projected to be at even greater risk since almost one third of those aged 55 and older have no work-related defined retirement plan or retirement savings (National Council on Aging, 2015). Interventions at the community level may be necessary to meet the safety, health, and social needs of elders. Housing, transportation, and health care resources and services are essential elements of a community response. States that invest in these resources are able to reduce the growth in the costs of long-term care expenses for elders (U.S. Department of Health and Human Services, 2013).

In promoting optimal functioning in urban settings, it is important to provide health care settings that are easily accessible for elderly people with limited mobility. As the number of elderly people in the urban centers of the United States increases, health care organizations and providers supported by local, state, and federal governments must be prepared to reach out to the growing population of elderly people (Andrulis, 2000). Many of these people are poor, have physical limitations, and experience psychological barriers such as perceived threat of violence, confusion, fear, and embarrassment over lack of financial resources. As a result, they may be unable or unwilling to leave their immediate environment. Community outreach would have to provide a wide variety of services to a culturally diverse population with special attention to poverty-related concerns.

Community resources that have been found to be useful to elders as they strive to remain in their communities include: transportation resources, educational opportunities, volunteer opportunities, food and nutrition support, housing and home modification services, in-home health care and services, and the creation of social settings where elders can interact including senior centers and adult day service centers. Information and referral services for elders and their caregivers provide access to a diverse array of resources as needs arise and change. Many people are unaware of programs and services for which they are eligible. Community services must include outreach efforts to let elders know about the available resources. The more knowledgeable people are about community resources and services, the longer they are likely to remain living independently in their home (Aging Services Council of Central Texas, 2013; National Institute of Health 2016; Tang & Lee, 2011).

A unique set of coordinated services for elders is described as Project Care, in San Diego, California (County of San Diego, 2016). The project supports frail older adults in living independently and feeling secure. This program has several components:

Are You OK?: A daily telephone call is made to individuals who have signed up for this service. A computer automatically makes the calls at a regularly scheduled time selected by the participant. If the call goes unanswered, volunteers will check to see if the individual is OK.

Gatekeeper: Utility and refuse collection companies provide training for their meter readers and refuse collectors to recognize the warning signs that their customers may be in trouble. These signs include newspapers piling up by the door or garbage not being set out for collection. If a problem is noted, it will be reported to the appropriate authority for follow up.

Minor Home Modification: Volunteers and local business groups are recruited to assist in making minor home repairs for seniors and the disabled. Many of these repairs are related to basic health and safety, such as obtaining grab bars, ramps, handrails, and security lighting.

Safe Return: A nationwide identification system of the Alzheimer's Association that helps authorities locate, identify, and safely return persons with dementia (and other cognitive impairments) who wander and become lost.

Vial of Life: Seniors and adult with disabilities who sign up for this no-cost program will be given a plastic box or a magnetic plastic container that holds specific information on the individual's medical history. Should the paramedics be called in an emergency situation, they use the information in the box to save precious time in providing medical assistance.

You Are Not Alone (YANA): A personalized phone call or home visit by the Senior Volunteer Patrol run by an associated law enforcement in various communities. (County of San Diego, 2016)

In recent years, more elders are choosing to live in urban centers (Abrahms, 2011). Living in areas that are densely populated

J&L Images/Getty Images

Many communities are sensitive to the need for informal recreational resources for elderly residents. Bocce ball is a favorite pastime where friends gather to socialize, get a bit of exercise, and engage in friendly competition.

means access to more markets, specialty shops, and interesting things to do in walking distance. People in New York City are more likely to walk a mile to get to something than people who live in suburban or rural areas. In a shift from earlier views of cities as crime-ridden, disease-promoting, alienating environments, some social scientists are starting to write about urban health advantages. Friendship groups are likely to form in neighborhoods; cities may have bigger, more fully equipped hospitals; and population density can attract more parks, gyms, and recreational facilities. The causal relationship between urban life and health is probably bidirectional. As cities become safer, people with more resources (who generally have greater longevity) want to live there, attracting more of the lifestyle resources that support health.

Urban areas are likely to be comprised of "naturally occurring retirement communities" (NORCs), places where over 50 percent of the residents are over age 60. Communities where people of shared interests and needs live near one another allow community members to voice their collective needs and concerns in order to influence the distribution or creation of appropriate resources. At the same time, a community with a certain density of elders provides an efficient approach for locating services that will meet the needs of the residents.

For some elderly adults, the absence of meaningful interpersonal relationships is the greatest barrier to optimal functioning. The role of the informal social support system in meeting the needs of the frail elderly cannot be underestimated. Children, spouses, other relatives, and neighbors are all important sources of help. Within communities, the elderly are themselves likely to provide significant help to age-mates who may be ill, bereaved, or impaired in some way. Most older adults prefer not to have to ask for help. However, they are much better off if they have someone to whom they can turn than if they have no one.

Beyond personal networks of social support, communities have been characterized by different levels of **collective efficacy**, which combines a strong sense of social cohesion with a high level of informal social control (Sampson, Raudenbush, & Earls, 1997). People who live in communities characterized by high collective efficacy are willing to take on important community concerns and to intervene on each other's behalf even if they do not know one another on a personal level. Examples of the impact of collective efficacy include reducing violent victimization, child or elder abuse, and illicit drug trafficking in a neighborhood. Communities that are high in collective efficacy will act to draw on the required resources to attract health care services, create new recreational settings, and improve transportation resources.

At age 85, George and his grandchild enjoy some pretense, building a high rise while making sure to be safe with their hard hats. George finds that the time he spends in pretend play fosters his own capacity for creative action.

Communities characterized by collective efficacy can enhance the health and optimal functioning of the frail elderly (Browning & Cagney, 2003).

The Role of Creative Action

People can do a lot for themselves to promote a fulfilling later life. By identifying meaningful goals and coordinating action to achieve these goals, elders can create lives that are both meaningful and manageable (Riediger, Freund, & Baltes, 2005). Elders can alter the structure of their environment to preserve optimal functioning and enhance their sense of well-being. They may move to a warmer climate, to a homogeneous-age community, or to a more modest home or apartment that entails fewer maintenance responsibilities. They may participate in exercise classes or other guided physical activity to improve their strength, endurance, and flexibility. Elders may select some family and friendship relationships that they sustain through frequent interaction, mutual help giving, and shared activities. They may participate in activities in community settings, including churches, senior centers, libraries,

and volunteer organizations through which they retain a sense of purpose and social connection. They may decide to focus their interest on a single role that is most important to them. Maintaining a sense of control over important life roles and activities contributes to longevity and well-being. As at earlier ages, elders make choices that direct the course of their lives, provide a sense of meaning, and influence their overall level of adjustment.

In summary, the quality of life for the frail elderly depends on four factors: (1) the specific nature and timing of the health-related limitations that accompany aging; (2) the availability of appropriate resources within the home, family, and community to help compensate for or minimize these limitations; (3) the selective emphasis that the person gives to some life experiences over others as being central to well-being; and (4) the person's motivational orientation to continue to find creative strategies to adapt to change.

FURTHER REFLECTION: *Explain the concept of optimal functioning. Based on what you have read about the developmental tasks and psychosocial crisis of elderhood, what suggestions would you make for enhancing the care of the frail elderly?*

CHAPTER SUMMARY

OBJECTIVE 1 Explain the rationale for identifying elderhood as a unique developmental stage for those of unusual longevity with its own developmental tasks and psychosocial crisis.

Elderhood is a period of new challenges and opportunities that will be faced by an increasing number of people in the years ahead. Those who are 80 years old and older are the fastest growing

segment of the U.S. population. Having reached a sense of acceptance of one's death, the task is to find meaning and enjoyment in the "bonus" years of life. This requires ongoing adaptation to changing physical and cognitive capacities, a deepening sense of time and the place of one's life in the history of one's people, and a willingness to find new and flexible solutions to the demands of daily life. This period of life requires ongoing adaptive self-organization.

In attempting to describe the psychosocial development of the very old, we are drawn to concepts that have a strong non-Western philosophical flavor. We have introduced such concepts as psychohistorical perspective, experiential transcendence, immortality, and social support—themes that reflect the need to assume a long-range perspective on life and its meaning.

OBJECTIVE 2 List the physical changes associated with aging, and evaluate the challenges that these changes pose for continued psychosocial well-being.

The quality of daily life for the very old is influenced to a great extent by their physical health. For some, daily activities are restricted by one or more chronic diseases. Nevertheless, the majority of elders continue to live in their own households and perform tasks of daily living independently. The topics addressed in this section include physical fitness, sleep and rest, behavioral slowing, sensory changes, illness, disability, and functional independence. The box on dementia outlines features of the disease and the experiences of caregivers, including both hassles and "uplifts."

OBJECTIVE 3 Describe the concept of a psychohistorical perspective, an altered perspective on time and history that emerges among the long-lived.

The concept of time changes with advanced age so that the continuity of past, present, and future becomes clearer. At age 50, someone who is 20 seems young, but at age 80, someone who is age 50 seems young. People who have lived a long time have had the chance to observe social and historical changes, to adapt to new technologies, and to observe the similarities and differences in the realities they faced growing up as compared to the lives of subsequent generations. This long time perspective brings insights into enduring values of life as well as an appreciation for the process of change.

OBJECTIVE 4 Summarize elements of the lifestyle structure in elderhood, especially living arrangements and gender roles, and analyze the impact of these life structures for continued well-being.

An increasingly wide range of lifestyle alternatives are being invented in elderhood, including opportunities for travel, housing that provides varying levels of care, and patterns of close relationships in which traditional gender roles are modified to take into consideration new capacities and interests. Living arrangements including living alone, aging in place, and living in any one of a variety of styles of "retirement" communities. Each alternative introduces new social and cognitive challenges, and new possibilities for purposeful engagement with community life.

OBJECTIVE 5 Define and explain the psychosocial crisis of immortality versus extinction, the central process of social support, the prime adaptive ego quality of confidence, and the core pathology of diffidence.

Having lived well beyond their life expectancy, elders face the psychosocial crisis of immortality versus extinction. A key to their quality of life lies in whether they are integrated into effective social support networks. Social support provides help, resources, meaningful social interaction, and a psychological sense of being valued. Elders who survive within a support system can transcend the limitations of their mortality, finding comfort and continuity in their participation in a chain of loving relationships. Those who are isolated, however, are more likely to face the end of their lives bound to the tedium of struggling with their physical limitations and resenting their survival. The themes of purpose and meaning are central to the resolution of this crisis. A positive resolution results in a prime adaptive ego quality of competence; a negative resolution results in diffidence, a pervasive sense of self-doubt.

OBJECTIVE 6 Apply research and theory to concerns about meeting the needs of the frail elderly.

The topic of the care of the frail elderly illustrates the relevance of a biopsychosocial framework. The quality of life for the frail elderly depends on four factors: (1) the specific nature and timing of the health-related limitations that accompany aging; (2) the availability of appropriate resources within the home, family, and community to help compensate for or minimize these limitations; (3) the selective emphasis that the person gives to some life experiences over others as being central to well-being; and (4) the person's motivational orientation to continue to find creative strategies to adapt to change. Elders can guide the direction of their care by the decisions they make, both in earlier periods of life and as they detect new signs of frailty.

CASEBOOK

For additional cases related to this chapter, see "Still Going Strong," in *Life Span Development: A Case Book*, by Barbara and Philip Newman, Laura Landry-Meyer, and Brenda J. Lohman, pp. 215–218. This case highlights the importance of living arrangements for the health and well-being of an active 93-year-old woman.

When the dove returned to the ark with an olive branch in its beak, Noah and his family perceived the sign that the period of turmoil was at an end and that life could begin anew. The dove has become a symbol of peace and hope—an image of comfort in a time of grief—providing the sense that rebirth accompanies death.

1. Explain how mortality influences psychosocial development.

2. Define the biological state of death, including the distinctions between cardiopulmonary and whole-brain death.

3. Describe factors associated with the process of dying and the modern ideal of a good death.

4. Summarize the role of cultural death-related rituals and their functions.

5. Analyze factors that affect grief and bereavement.

UNDERSTANDING DEATH, DYING, AND BEREAVEMENT

15

5. Describe some of Harriet's coping strengths and weaknesses.

6. Imagine that you were Harriet's parents. What would you do to try to prepare Harriet for her life? For her death?

CASE STUDY   Too Late to Die Young

Harriet McBryde Johnson was diagnosed with muscular dystrophy as a little girl. She has faced a life of surviving the expectation that she would die young.

I'm 3 or 4 years old. I'm sitting on the living room floor, playing with dolls. I look up at the TV and see a little boy. He's sitting on the floor, playing with toy soldiers. Then he's in Little League; he stumbles on his way to first base. He visits a doctor. His parents are sad. He's in a wheelchair. Then a bed. Then I see the toy soldiers. No boy. An unseen narrator says, "Little Billy's toy soldiers have lost their general." It's a commercial for the Muscular Dystrophy Association. As the narrator makes the pitch, a realization comes to me: I will die.

Is it really one of my earliest memories? Or was it manufactured by my imagination? I don't suppose it matters. Either way, it was my truth. I'm a little girl who knows she will die, but I don't say anything. Somehow my mother guesses. "That boy," she says, "has a different kind of muscular dystrophy. Girls don't get it." Maybe, I think, but he looks a lot like me. And pretty soon I see little girls on the telethon and hear that girls too have "killer diseases." I don't know the word, but I figure my mother is in denial.

By the time I am 5, I think of myself as a dying child. I've been sick a lot. There is some discussion before my parents decide to send me to kindergarten. I am glad they do. When I die, I think, I might as well die a kindergartner.

I've just turned 30. I've been lolling in bed for nearly 3 weeks; I say I've strained my neck, but really it's major depression. Just before my birthday my mother had brain surgery. She's come through it beautifully, but I'm terrified to think I could actually outlive my parents. I am further set adrift by the sudden death of the crazy German doctor who nursed me with pea soup and sausages when I refused to go to the hospital with pneumonia. My thoughts race by, but I manage to grab them and take a look. I find that I'm bonkers but rational. I know what's bothering me; my plan to die young hasn't worked out. What do I do now? My thoughts take on the structure of a song with a repeated chorus; it's too late to die young.

I decide to embrace the death sentence. No need to fear it; no need to hasten it. Mortality is something all people share, a unifying force. Every life, whether long or short, is a treasure of infinite value. These things are true, I figure, and it's my job to say so. When I die, I might as well die honest.

Source: Johnson, 2005, pp. 44–46.

CASE ANALYSIS Using What You Know

1. Death is a biological, psychological, and societal reality. Explain how the case illustrates these three interrelated systems.

2. Discuss the challenges of facing an ambiguous dying trajectory for the dying person and for close relatives.

3. Hypothesize about some of the possible reasons for Harriet's depression at age 30.

4. Apply psychosocial theory to account for the life themes that Harriet is facing at age 4; and at age 30.

Like bookends, birth and death bracket the story of development. Birth is preceded by a long chain of biological transformations, in which the biochemical thread of DNA is passed from generation to generation. Pregnancy and birth occur in a psychosocial context of relationships, resources, and cultural beliefs and practices. So, too, it is with death. The biological process of dying takes place in a psychosocial context of relationships, resources, and cultural beliefs and practices. Death is accompanied by transformations at the biological, psychological, and societal levels. It is the role of culture and religion to provide narratives or explanations for the transformations of energy that occur in death. Because we cannot empirically test many of these explanations, it is the role of the ego to cope with the unknown aspects of death, to give it personal meaning.

Death is at once a certainty in that all living things die, and a random event, in that the timing of death is unknown. Moreover, whereas through observation, systematic study, and the transmission of knowledge from generation to generation, we have a good idea about the trajectory of development beginning with the prenatal period until death, we have only speculations and belief systems to guide our understanding of what occurs at death and beyond. Thus, death is both inevitable and unknowable.

Thanatology is the field of science that addresses dying, death, and the psychological mechanisms of coping with them. This field includes an analysis of the attitudes toward dying, the meaning of death for individuals and societies, the rituals and practices associated with death, the bereavement process, and the expressions of bereavement across situations and cultures. ●

Mortality and Psychosocial Development

OBJECTIVE 1   Explain how mortality influences psychosocial development.

Psychosocial development focuses on the ongoing interactions between the person and the environment. A person's ability to understand the self and others matures and changes with each psychosocial crisis. At each stage of life, the ego is shaped by the perplexing nature of mortality. In infancy, as one achieves a balance between trust and mistrust, an outlook of hopefulness emerges. This outlook shapes one's orientation toward risk, transitions, and ultimately death. If one has lived a life of hopefulness about the future, this same orientation is likely to extend toward one's beliefs about death—a sense that whatever follows the death of the physical body is going to be good.

In the resolution of the crisis of identity versus role confusion, one confronts the need to impose a sense of meaning on one's life: Where am I going? What do I want out of life? What is my path? Even though one may believe that death is in the distant future, the creation of a personal identity reflects an understanding that since one's life is finite, one's choices should count for something.

The crisis of generativity versus stagnation brings the issue of mortality even more to center stage. Here, one begins to consider the impact of one's life on future generations: What can I do to contribute to the quality of life for others, even after my death? How can I use my resources, talents, and creative abilities to ensure a good future for those who come after me? While still in the throes of caring for children, aging parents, colleagues, and communities, the generative action of middle adults suggests a concern for a time when the ego is not present to nurture and maintain.

Developing a point of view about death is a major developmental task during later adulthood. The resolution of the crisis of integrity versus despair requires recognition that death is increasingly imminent. Integrity is achieved on the shoulders of earlier ego strengths that allow the person to celebrate personal achievements, cherish meaningful relationships, and look with satisfaction at the life thus far lived. The integrity expressed by those in later adulthood—an ability to celebrate life in the face of impending death—is a model for younger generations.

Finally, the crisis of immortality versus extinction brings the confidence of continuity. One is ready—though not necessarily eager—to close one door, confident that another will open. In this period, the possibility of death cannot dampen the joy of being and the certainty that one's life is intimately connected with all life.

Over time, direct personal experiences with dying and death have changed. One hundred years ago, most people died in their homes. Many women and infants died in childbirth. As a result, death was experienced by family members who cared for the dying and were present at the death. As you travel through New England, it is common to find small cemeteries near churches and homes where you sense the intimate gathering of families who buried their dead nearby.

With the growth of modern medicine, people who were very ill were taken to hospitals. Those who were dying were removed from the home, and death occurred more in hospitals or nursing homes. Death was sanitized through embalming practices. A culture of death as medical failure emerged, leaving people increasingly alienated from the realities of dying. The discussion of topics related to death and dying became taboo. Children were shielded from experiences with death. Doctors often tried to protect people from the knowledge that they were dying. Once people became terminally ill, they were deprived of the right to have a voice in decisions related to their treatment and the conditions surrounding the end of life (Kastenbaum, 2012).

Beginning with the works of Elisabeth Kübler-Ross (1969/1997, 1983/1997), the needs of the dying person were given a voice again. Concern about allowing people to talk about their fears, to plan for their funeral, and to bring closure to their

Courtesy of Philip Newman

In older communities it is common to find small family cemeteries where people are buried near their home or farmland. These cemeteries suggest a time when there was a greater intimacy between the living and their ancestors.

personal affairs led people to face death more openly and directly. This approach also led to new ways of thinking about the care of the dying. Currently, we have new technologies that allow for the prolongation of life but we continue to face conflicts about how long and under what conditions life should be sustained.

FURTHER REFLECTION: Explain how the inevitability of death affects your own approach to life. Do you think about death when making important life decisions? Can you give an example?

Definitions of Death

OBJECTIVE 2 Define the biological state of death, including the distinctions between cardiopulmonary and whole-brain death.

The definition of death has changed. Historically, the criteria for death were lack of a heartbeat and lack of respiration, called **cardiopulmonary death**. This definition was used for hundreds of years. In 1981, the President's Commission for the Ethical Study of Problems in Medicine and Biomedical and Behavioral Research identified eight criteria for the determination of **whole-brain death**:

1. No spontaneous movement in response to any stimuli
2. No spontaneous respirations for at least 1 hour
3. Total lack of responsiveness to even the most painful stimuli

4. No eye movements, blinking, or pupil responses
5. No postural activity, swallowing, yawning, or vocalizing
6. No motor reflexes
7. A flat electroencephalogram (EEG) for at least 10 minutes
8. No change in any of these criteria when they are tested again 24 hours later

In addition to these eight criteria, certain other conditions, such as deep coma, have to be ruled out. Two areas in the brain control different types of life functions: the *brainstem* controls heartbeat and respiration, and the *cortex* controls sensory integration and cognitive function. It is possible for a person's brainstem functions to continue even when there is no cortical functioning. This condition is called **persistent vegetative state**. If you refer back to the list of eight criteria, you can see that the person in this state is not technically dead. When this state occurs, family members, doctors, and sometimes the courts are faced with the difficult decision about whether to let the person die.

In response to the report of the President's Commission, Congress passed the Uniform Determination of Death Act (UDDA). All 50 states and the District of Columbia recognize whole-brain death as the one legal standard. However, the UDDA allows physicians or hospitals to apply the cardiopulmonary definition or the whole-brain death definition, whichever applies first. Despite what we see on television, where a person leans over a body and proclaims, "He's dead," there is ambiguity about whether or not a person is dead.

> First, the diagnosis of brain death may be unreliable. Many patients who meet all the criteria for brain death do not in fact have "irreversible cessation of all functions of the entire brain," because some of the brain stem's homeostatic functions remain, such as temperature control and water and electrolyte balance. To counter this observation, some argue that not all the functions of the brain need to be lost for a patient to be dead, only those that are critical to maintaining integration of the body functions; loss of these critical functions will inevitably lead over hours or days to cardiac arrest, even with continuing intensive life-support. Yet, even though this is often true, the bodies of some patients who meet all the criteria for brain death can survive for many years with all their bodily functions intact except for consciousness and brain stem reflexes. (Sade, 2011, p. 2)

On the one hand, because of the great need for transplantable organs, there is urgency in deciding whether or not a person has died. On the other hand, it is not legal to remove an organ when that removal would cause a person's death. Therefore, the decision whether to harvest organs from people who are experiencing whole-brain death poses a difficult ethical question (DeGrazia, 1998; Sade, 2011).

Advance Directives

Because there are a variety of technologies that can extend life when a person is no longer able to communicate, adults are urged to prepare some form of **advance directive**, such as a living will

or durable power of attorney (Doukas & Reichel, 2007). These documents inform a physician or hospital of a person's wishes about life-sustaining procedures in the face of terminal illness or imminent death, and designate someone to act on one's behalf. Through a **living will**, a person can direct physicians or a hospital to withhold life-sustaining procedures and prevent the use of unwanted medical measures when that person is unable to convey those wishes. Some people wear bracelets that say, "living will—do not resuscitate (DNR)" or a medallion stamped NO CODE, which means they do not want to be resuscitated. The **durable power of attorney** authorizes someone to act on behalf of the person regarding financial and property matters and health care decisions. This directive can go into effect when either the agreement is signed or the disability occurs (Hooyman & Kiyak, 2011). One benefit of the living will is that it helps resolve potential conflicts between a dying person's wishes and family members' feelings of obligation to do everything possible to keep the person alive.

Without a "Do Not Resuscitate" directive, when a patient in a hospital stops breathing and has no pulse, a *code blue* team, with 5 to 10 physicians, nurses, and intensive care specialists, is likely to be called in. They initiate mechanical and medical procedures involving shock, IVs, and tubes down the throat aimed at resuscitation for a person who is probably dead (Ofri, 2012). It is possible to register a living will online at www.uslivingwillregistry.com.

The following quotation describes the benefit that accompanied a woman's decision to register her advanced directive with the U.S. Living Will Registry:

> I am very glad I registered my advanced directive. As caregiver to my mother, my father, and my stepmother I cannot express the peace of mind that registering gives. My husband and daughter will never go through the stress of wondering if they are acting according to my wishes. It will be very clear for them. In a way, making my advanced directive is protecting my husband and daughter, even when I am seriously ill. When a loved one is seriously ill is the worst possible time to deal with the subtleties and ramifications of hospital and legal bureaucracies. This will free them from a lot of those worries. (U.S. Living Will Registry, 2010)

One of the more troubling health conditions is Alzheimer's disease, in which there is a gradual loss of mental competence. A decision must be made about when the person is no longer competent and the living will or durable power of attorney will go into effect. Preparation of advance directives requires that people think about the kind of care they want to receive and the conditions under which they want treatment to be withheld. Currently, most Americans do not complete advance directives, and many interventions that are designed to increase completion of advance directives are not effective (Jezewski, Meeker, Sessana, & Finnell, 2007; Kersting, 2004). Even though it is recommended that people consider these issues while they are flourishing, the fact remains that it is difficult for people to face these issues and make decisions about their death.

FURTHER REFLECTION: Explain the functions of advance directives. How are they related to the various medical conditions that can occur at the end of life?

The Process of Dying

OBJECTIVE 3 Describe factors associated with the process of dying and the modern ideal of a good death.

People can experience death in many different ways. Their psychological coping strategies differ depending on the context of dying. Kübler-Ross's concept of stages in coming to terms with one's death included: denial, anger and resentment, bargaining, depression and mourning one's death, and acceptance. Although these emotional reactions are all important aspects of understanding how people may cope with the reality of their death, differences in the conditions of death mean that this stage process is not experienced universally. The 10 leading causes of death for 2014 are listed in Table 15.1 (National Center for Health Statistics, 2016c). As you can imagine, the conditions surrounding each of these causes will create different experiences of dying.

Confronting One's Death

In contrast to the notion of stages, some people write about the **dying trajectory** (Lawton, 2001)—that is, the time during which the person's health goes from good to death. Certain illnesses such as some cancers or AIDS result in a gradual decline. Under these conditions, people have more time to acknowledge their death and to plan for it. They may be asked to make a number of decisions about their treatment, in each case weighing the risks or side effects of treatment against the chances of prolonging life. Some people experience unpredictable, sudden death in the midst of a healthy life, as in an automobile accident, by homicide, or a heart attack. This trajectory does not allow the person to confront the reality of death. For some, death involves an ambiguous decline, in which periods of illness may alternate with periods of remission, as in the case of leukemia or muscular dystrophy. These people face a process of learning to live with a disease in which there may be periods of health as well as periods of decline. The person may wrestle with the question of whether they are dying from the illness or living with the illness. The opening case of Harriet McBryde Johnson illustrates the difficulties of making meaning in the face of an ambiguous trajectory.

The dying process may bring a high **degree of suffering**, including shortness of breath, inability to eat, limited mobility, and pain. In some instances, this suffering can be alleviated with medications, but in some cases it grows worse. Health care providers and family members often express great dissatisfaction with these end-of-life conditions for the dying person and the surviving loved ones.

The dying process may be conceptualized in different ways depending on the *age* of the dying person. The primary cause of death differs for people of various age groups, creating different contexts for dying. Children and adolescents are most likely to die from accidents including injuries due to fire and auto accidents, or abuse. In middle adulthood, cancer, heart disease, and liver disease are common causes of death, along with unintentional accidents and suicide. Older adults are most likely to die of the complications from chronic diseases, such as heart disease, diabetes, pneumonia, or cancer (National Center for Health Statistics, 2016c).

People of different ages have differing cognitive abilities, psychological coping mechanisms, and views of the future that they bring to the tasks of preparing for death. Kübler-Ross reported the following poem that was written by Mike, a teenage boy, to his parents on the day of his death:

> The time has come,
> My job is done.
> Now it's time for another one
> The gates will open, open soon
> I now will go.
> See you soon.
> Time, time will never stop
> Everlasting time
> Love is eternal
> Forevermore love
> I will always love you. (Kübler-Ross, 1983, p. 189)

Because of the nature of his illness, Mike had time to prepare for his death. His mother reports that he taped messages to his family and friends, helped plan his funeral, and gave a few things away before he died. At this age, Mike appears to have a hopeful view about an everlasting life. He is able to conceptualize dying as a transition that allows some continuity between the life he had and the life he is going to have. He also sees a future in which he will be reunited with the other loved ones in his life before too long. Another teenager, John, who was terminally ill, stated that before he died he wanted two things: to own a van and to make love to a woman (Kübler-Ross, 1983, p. 184). Here we see a

Table 15.1	Ten Leading Causes of Death and Numbers of Deaths, 2014
Causes of Death	**Number of Deaths**
All Causes	**2,626,418**
Diseases of the heart	614,348
Malignant neoplasms	591,699
Chronic lower respiratory diseases	147,101
Unintentional injuries	136,053
Cerebrovascular diseases	133,103
Alzheimer's disease	93,541
Diabetes mellitus	76,488
Influenza and pneumonia	55,227
Nephritis, nephrotic syndrome, and nephrosis	48,146
Suicide	42,773

Source: CDC. (2015). Health United States, 2015. Table 19. Leading causes of death and numbers of deaths: United States, 1980 and 2014.

youthful approach to the dying process. John's goals are more fun loving and pragmatic, whereas Mike's approach is more spiritual and interpersonal.

Ray Bradbury provided a portrait of a great-grandmother's approach to her own death. At 90, Great-Grandma told her children and grandchildren:

> I don't want any Halloween parties here tomorrow. Don't want anyone saying anything sweet about me; I said it all in my time and my pride. I've tasted every victual and danced every dance; now there's one last tart I haven't bit on, one tune I haven't whistled. But I'm not afraid. I'm truly curious. Death won't get a crumb by my mouth I won't keep and savor. So don't you worry over me. Now, all of you go, and let me find my sleep. (Bradbury, 1957/1964, pp. 140–141)

In this case, Great-Grandma reassures her children that she is ready—that she has experienced a full life and sees death as the next dance. In addition to the way death is perceived by the dying, the death will be perceived and conceptualized differently by caregivers. The death of a child or adolescent may be seen as quite tragic in the minds and hearts of parents and friends; the death of an older person may be seen as the natural close to a full life. In some cultures, the death of an elder is especially painful, as it results in the loss of wisdom and guidance for younger generations. In other cultures, the death of a child is especially tragic, because it results in the loss of promise and potential for the future.

The Good Death

Professionals who are responsible for the care of the dying have begun to define the characteristics of a good death or dying well. Certain themes stand out across various groups (Emanuel & Emanuel, 1998; Kehl, 2006; Meier et al., 2016; Webb, 1997). One British group offered the following 12 principles of a good death (Smith, 2000):

- To know when death is coming, and to understand what can be expected
- To be able to retain control of what happens
- To be afforded dignity and privacy
- To have control over pain relief and other symptom control
- To have choice and control over where death occurs (at home or elsewhere)
- To have access to information and expertise of whatever kind is necessary
- To have access to any spiritual or emotional support required
- To have access to hospice care in any location, not only in the hospital
- To have control over who is present and who shares the end
- To be able to issue advanced directives which ensure wishes are respected
- To have time to say good-bye and control over other aspects of timing

- To be able to leave when it is time to go and not to have life prolonged pointlessly

Research on perspectives about dying find that the definition of a **good death** is highly individual, shaped by the context of dying and changing over the course of the illness. The ideals of a good death were studied by asking recent widows and widowers to rate their spouses' end-of-life experiences along the following dimensions (Carr, 2003):

- Spouse was at peace with the idea of dying
- Spouse was aware of the impending death
- Respondent and spouse discussed the death
- Respondent was with spouse at the moment of death
- Spouse led a full life
- Spouse was not in pain
- Spouse did not receive negligent care

These dimensions represent concrete evidence of what people perceive to be a good death. Of all these features, the greatest psychological distress for the survivor was associated with seeing the spouse in great pain at the end of life. Although roughly 70 percent of Americans say they would prefer to die at home, about 75 percent actually die in a hospital, many undergoing painful medical interventions in attempts to prolong life (Cloud, 2000).

In a study of what patients, family members, and their health care professionals were concerned about in preparing for the end of life, the following issues were highlighted: naming someone to make decisions, knowing what to expect about one's physical condition, having one's financial affairs in order, having one's treatment preferences in writing, and knowing that one's physician is comfortable talking about death. Dying patients were also concerned about planning their funeral (Steinhauser et al., 2001).

How well are people's needs being met at the end of their lives? Researchers addressed this question through a telephone interview with family members or close associates of more than 1,500 people who had died in the previous 9 to 15 months (Teno et al., 2004). The focus was on the location where people die and the quality of care received by the person in the last 48 hours of life. Two thirds of the deceased had been in a hospital or nursing home in the last 48 hours of life. Of the one third who died at home, 38 percent had no nursing services, 12 percent had some home nursing services, and 50 percent had home hospice services. Over 70 percent of those whose loved ones received hospice care rated that care as excellent. Fewer than 50 percent of those whose loved ones died in a hospital, nursing home, or at home with home nursing services rated their care as excellent. With the exception of those receiving hospice care, many of the bereaved felt that their loved ones did not receive the pain relief, respect, or emotional support they needed in the 2 days before their death.

Two different paths to achieving a good death among people who are in a slow, painful death trajectory include hospice care and euthanasia.

Hospice Care

Hospice care is an integrated system of medicine, nursing, counseling, and spiritual care for the dying person and their family. Its goal is to achieve the highest possible quality of life for the dying

The quality of a good death is fostered when caregivers are able to minimize discomfort and support the patient's positive emotional state.

person and the family, alleviating physical and emotional pain to the highest degree possible while supporting family strengths to cope with the process of dying, loss of the loved one, and long-term bereavement (Bruera & Yennurajalingam, 2011; Knee, 2010). Hospice care can take place in a hospice setting or at home.

The Hospice Education Institute (2001) offers the following goals for high-quality end-of-life care:

- Promote relief from pain
- Integrate the psychological and spiritual aspects of patient care
- Offer a support system to help patients live as actively as possible until death
- Help the family cope during the patient's illness and their own bereavement

Hospice care differs from traditional hospital care in that the focus is on enhancing the quality of life for the dying person and the loved ones rather than on treating the disease or intervening to delay the end of life. The first role of hospice care is to relieve the person's pain and suffering through medical, physical, psychological, and spiritual means. Dying patients are encouraged to take an active role in as many aspects of their end-of-life care as their cognitive functioning and health permit. They are supported in talking about their death and interacting with their family. Hospice care has many advantages for those with a terminal illness. It prevents the experience of dying alone for those who do not have family and friends nearby. It allows the person to die in a more natural, familiar setting rather than in a hospital or nursing home. It offers emotional, spiritual, and physical comfort, helping more people experience a good death.

Mary Wasacz is a spiritual care coordinator who works for the Hospice and Palliative Care of Westchester in New York.

Her job is to care for the spiritual lives of the dying and those who love them. She visits their homes.... She helps (patients) face their relationship with God, address their doubts, come to terms with their religious shortcomings, hold tighter to their faith (whether it's rich or flickering) and prepare for death.... "This is sacred ground," says Wasacz. "It is such a sad time, but a privilege to be there, on this journey with them. It can be uplifting. What I do is facilitate peace." (Stern, 2007)

People come to the role of hospice work through many paths. Mary Wasacz is a devout Roman Catholic and Eucharistic minister (she has been specially trained by the clergy to administer the sacrament of the Eucharist or communion). She does not advocate her religion, or any particular religious orientation as a spiritual care coordinator, but her own faith helps her reassure people as they deal with their many fears and doubts. In contrast, Loretta Downs came to her role as a Hospice Partners volunteer patient companion after having experienced the death of many close friends who died of AIDS. She approaches her role in hospice through the lens of yoga training.

Hospice is ... a blanket of hope. It is a safe haven in which a team of specialists form a cocoon around the dying one and guide him or her through physical transformation while encouraging spiritual healing along the way. I am to be present in silence as well as in laughter and tears. I am to encourage all the appropriate activity and behavior my patients are able to perform while I create a space for them to engage in spiritual healing.... I am to be open to learn how to die myself. Now my patients and their families are my teachers. (Downs, 2004)

Angela Morrow described a third path, from intensive care nursing to hospice:

I began my nursing career in an intensive care unit. The majority of deaths I witnessed there involved patients, most of whom were elderly, undergoing painful tests and treatments.... I'll never forget the 90-year-old male patient who had terminal cancer and was admitted to the intensive care unit with severe breathing problems. We had to place a tube down his throat to help him breathe and inserted several IV lines to give him medicine. His hands were tied to the bed and he was given medication to put him into a coma-like state. Then his heart stopped. We spent a long time trying to revive him and with every chest compression I gave him, I thought, "What are we doing? Why are we doing this?"

Now that I'm working in hospice, I have the pleasure of helping my patients achieve a "good death," one that is in accordance with their goals and priorities. (Morrow, 2008)

The story of the hospice movement illustrates how many factors converge to create a new set of policies and practices. The concept of the hospice as a setting for the care of terminally ill patients is attributed to Dr. Cicely Saunders, who founded St. Christopher's Hospice in London in 1967. In 1963, she gave a talk at Yale University about her work with terminally ill cancer patients and their families, illustrating the many ways in which patients benefited from an integrated approach to care. Following her talk, Florence Wald, the Dean of the Yale School of Nursing, invited Dr. Saunders to be a visiting faculty member for a semester. Subsequently, in 1968, Dr. Wald took a sabbatical and spent time with Dr. Saunders at St. Christopher's. These two health care leaders were supported in their efforts to create hospice settings in the United States by the publication of Dr. Kübler-Ross' book, *On Death and Dying*, in 1969. In 1972, the U.S. Senate Special Committee on Aging heard testimony from Dr. Kübler-Ross about the negative impact of institutionalizing and isolating the dying. Between 1978 and 1982, several demonstration programs to explore the benefits of hospice care were funded by federal agencies and private foundations. As a result, the U.S. Congress included hospice care as a reimbursable Medicare benefit in 1982—a provision that became permanent in 1986.

Since that time, Congress has increased the level of reimbursement for hospice care, included hospice care as part of veterans' benefits, and included hospice care in the review of efforts to reduce waste and abuse in the Medicare and Medicaid systems. Clear guidelines have been established for the range and quality of services that hospices must offer in order to receive Medicare reimbursements, and an increasing range of educational and training programs have emerged to provide interdisciplinary training for professionals working in hospice and end-of-life care settings. In 1999, the U.S. Postal Service issued the Hospice Care Commemorative Stamp, marking the recognition of this successful model as part of the continuum of health care (National Hospice and Palliative Care Organization, 2005).

To take advantage of hospice through Medicare, one must make a decision to forgo any further life-saving or life-prolonging treatments. A physician must also submit certification that the person is terminally ill, with 6 months or less to live. This provision is one of the current limitations in the use of hospice care within the Medicare system. In 2014, an estimated 1.3 million people received hospice services, 77 percent of whom were age 75 or older (Harris-Kojetin et al. 2016). In advanced stages of Alzheimer's disease and other forms of dementia, the demands on caregivers can be intense, but survival can be prolonged beyond 6 months. As a result, only a small percentage of those with Medicare hospice coverage are patients with Alzheimer's disease (Kersting, 2004). To learn more about hospice care, you can visit the website of the National Hospice and Palliative Care Organization.

Euthanasia

Euthanasia is the practice of ending someone's life for reasons of mercy. In comparison to hospice care, euthanasia is considered when pain medication is ineffective in reducing suffering, when a person is in a persistent vegetative state being kept alive by mechanical equipment, or when a person is in the final stages of a terminal illness. Euthanasia generally involves hastening the end of life by allowing people to have control over their death (Kastenbaum 2012).

Passive Euthanasia. Imagine that a person in the late stages of Alzheimer's disease is diagnosed as having cancer. Should treatments including surgery, chemotherapy, and radiation be administered to prolong the life of someone who is already near death? Passive euthanasia refers to withholding treatment or removing life-sustaining nourishment and breathing aids. The result is that death occurs more quickly than if these procedures were continued. Through a living will, a person can make wishes known to others, including the hospital or care center, physicians, and family members or legal representatives. Through the durable power of attorney, a person assigns life-prolonging or life-ending decision making to a representative. Thus, by refusing treatment or by granting discretion to others to end extraordinary treatment, individuals may hasten their own death. In the preceding example of a person suffering from dementia, if the person had a living will or durable power of attorney, a decision could be made by someone else to withhold treatment for the cancer, if the person is no longer capable of decision making.

Active Euthanasia. Activities designed to end a person's life are referred to as active euthanasia. There are several ways in which this may happen. **Mercy killing** involves actively taking a person's life. This is sometimes done in order to end a person's suffering. In our society, this is considered to be murder. States vary widely on whether the killer will be prosecuted for this act and whether juries will be willing to convict. In a Michigan case of a nurse who ended the lives of more than 20 patients at the Ann Arbor VA hospital, the jury found the nurse to be guilty of murder and sentenced her to life imprisonment. In a California case of a spouse who strangled her husband to end his suffering because she could not help him any longer, the state decided not to prosecute.

Physician-assisted suicide (PAS) involves either the administration of a lethal dose of some medication by a physician or arranging for a terminally ill patient to administer his or her own lethal dose of medication using a suicide machine. This is a controversial procedure. In 1994, Oregon passed a Death with Dignity Act (ODDA) allowing individuals who are terminally ill to request a prescription from their physician for a lethal dose of medication. According to that act, doctors would be allowed to help patients commit suicide by prescribing a lethal dose of medication under the following conditions (Oregon Health Services, 2010a):

1. Patients must be 18 years old or over and be residents of the state of Oregon.
2. Patients have been informed that they have a terminal disease and that they have less than 6 months to live; this must be confirmed by a second opinion.
3. The patient must make a written request for the lethal medication twice, at least 15 days apart, in the presence of two witnesses.
4. There must be an evaluation to determine that the person is capable of making an informed decision, that there is no psychological disorder that would impair the ability to make the decision, and that the person is not suffering from depression.

5. The patient must be informed of the risks and possible results of taking the medication and counseled as to feasible alternatives such as hospice or palliative care.

6. The patient must be advised to have someone present at the time of taking the medication and urged not to take the medication in public.

7. The patient is advised of the right to rescind the request at any time.

In 1997, the U.S. Supreme Court ruled that there is no constitutional right to physician-assisted suicide, leaving the issue up to the states. They did not overturn the Oregon law. In 1997, Oregon voters affirmed the decision to allow physician-assisted suicide by passing the measure again. In 2009, 95 people received prescriptions, and 53 took the medication. The most frequently mentioned end-of-life concerns were loss of autonomy (96.6 percent), loss of dignity (91.5 percent), and decreasing ability to participate in activities that made life enjoyable (86.4 percent) (Oregon Human Services, 2010b).

How common are these measures? In the United States, legislation regarding Death with Dignity has been passed in four states—California, Washington, Oregon, and Vermont—and has been approved through court ruling in Montana (Death with Dignity, 2016). In all other states, assisted suicide and active euthanasia are illegal, which makes it difficult to know how often these strategies are used. A study of the use of PAS in the state of Washington found that over a 3-year period, 255 people received lethal prescriptions from a physician. This is in the context of 50,000 deaths per year in that state (Gordon, 2013). Although the provision is used infrequently, the people who requested it typically had a terminal form of cancer and were grateful that this alternative was open to them.

PAS is legal in several European countries including Belgium, Germany, Luxembourg, The Netherlands, and Switzerland, and it has also been recently approved in Canada (Lewis, 2015). In a study in The Netherlands, which has accurate records about requests for PAS, Wolf (1996) found that 38 percent of all deaths involved some kind of medical decision. Of these, 18 percent were the result of passive euthanasia where treatment was not provided, and 18 percent involved hastening death by providing pain medication or other care that led to death occurring more quickly than it might have by not using these treatments. Only about 2 percent of all cases involved the administration of a lethal drug or physician-assisted suicide. Thus, even in a country where assisted suicide is permitted, it is approached cautiously and used sparingly.

Ethical Issues at the End of Life

Ethical principles focus on standards of right and wrong, especially as they govern areas of moral and professional

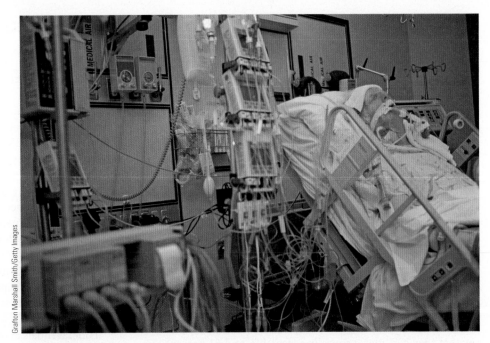

Technological innovations allow physicians to keep a person alive with the hope of saving them. These advances raise many ethical questions about conditions under which life should be sustained and treatment continued. Under what conditions do you think treatment should be terminated?

responsibility. Ethical issues surrounding end-of-life decisions bring to mind the applied topic of abortion that was discussed in chapter 4. One might view abortion as a special case of decisions about ending life. End-of-life decisions are relevant not only for elderly people; they may also be addressed when parents decide to limit treatment for a terminally ill child, when family members decide to remove life support for an adult who is in a vegetative state, or when a person seeks assisted suicide in order to avoid a decline into an immobile or helpless state. The matter is made even more complex because decisions about ending life conflict with the commitment of the medical profession to prolong life. As a result of many new technologies, medications, and genetic interventions, there are ongoing innovations that may be effective in slowing the progression of a disease or sustaining life even if the condition cannot be cured.

Public opinion about the acceptability of physicians helping patients end their lives depends on how the question is framed. The following question has been asked in polls from 1947 to 2016: "When a person has a disease that cannot be cured, do you think doctors should be allowed by law to end the patient's life by some painless means if the patient and his family request it?" In 1947, 37 percent of respondents said yes; in 2016, 69 percent said yes. Clearly, the public has a more accepting view of involving doctors in euthanasia today than in the past (Swift, 2016). The range of techniques that are available to prolong life has expanded profoundly since 1947. One consequence is the need for a new level of decision making among those who are dying and their families about the point at which medical treatment should be discontinued.

In contrast to PAS, some dying patients exercise a right to voluntarily refuse food and fluids as a way to hasten death. In interviews with 20 hospice workers, both nurses and social workers, 33 different cases were described where people wanted to hasten their death (Harvath et al., 2006). Two thirds sought PAS; one third chose refusal of food and fluids. The hospice workers who were interviewed perceived these two paths as substantially different with different ethical considerations. Voluntary refusal of food and fluids was seen as "letting go of life" and most hospice workers viewed it as an expression of a dying person's autonomy.

> I don't have any dilemmas or ethical issues with a person not eating or drinking. It's a part of hospice that people have a right to determine what they will and will not do, how they want to die. There's a big difference between that and somebody taking (a lethal dose of) medicine. Nobody makes a decision to tell a person not to eat or drink. (Harvath et al., 2006, p. 209)

Despite public opinion supporting PAS, issues around voluntarily ending one's life continue to be a matter of ethical controversy (Fraser & Walters, 2001; Walker, 2001). In the recent Gallup poll where a large majority favor PAS, only 53 percent say that they consider it morally acceptable, and 51 percent say they would consider ending their own lives if they were facing an incurable disease or living in great pain (Swift, 2016). Those who support PAS argue that it respects the individual liberties and personal autonomy of those who are terminally ill but competent to make an informed decision about the end of life. It is also a compassionate response to help end suffering. Finally legalizing PAS would open the possibility for more reasoned, full discussion of alternatives between patients and their physicians. At present, these conversations are taking place covertly, without full access to information about alternatives.

Opponents of PAS argue that legalizing assisted suicide might put undue pressure on elderly people to end their lives rather than be a burden to their families or to use scarce financial resources for end-of-life care. For those who have struggled to have access to quality health care during their adult lives, there is great mistrust about giving someone the right to withhold care or accelerate their death. Other opponents suggest that permitting those who are terminally ill to choose death would be one step toward a process of killing people who have mental disabilities or are born with serious defects that affect their quality of life. Some contend that the dying person who is in a great deal of pain may be depressed and lose sight of the possibilities for medical treatments that could improve their medical condition. With effective counseling, the person might be less desperate about the suffering and find ways to achieve a new sense of closeness with loved ones. Finally, there are those who feel that allowing someone to decide to end his or her own life is a violation of their religious values and is unacceptable regardless of the conditions faced by the ill person.

FURTHER REFLECTION: Explain the concept of the "good death." How does culture influence the way people think about ideal or optimal end-of-life experiences?

Critically evaluate the proposition that people should have as much control as possible over the conditions surrounding their death and dying.

Death-Related Rituals

OBJECTIVE 4 Summarize the role of cultural death-related rituals and their functions.

Death is a powerful change of state that has mysterious qualities. Typically, it is accompanied by a range of symbolic rituals. These rituals address at least three critical aspects of death: (1) how to treat the physical body—the corpse—in an appropriate way (2) how to address the fate of the spiritual aspect of the person—the soul, and (3) how to meet the emotional needs of the survivors and the needs of the society as a whole. Across cultures, people feel a strong need to carry out funeral rituals for the burial or cremation of the dead. Rituals have the advantage of offering a prescribed set of practices at a time when people may be too distressed to make complex decisions. Over one's life span, prior attendance and participation in funeral rituals provide some comfort and familiarity that may help reduce the distress when a loved one dies.

Funeral rituals allow survivors to say good-bye to their loved one, honor the dead person, and begin to detach themselves from the dead person. The concrete evidence of the body proves beyond a doubt to survivors that the person is dead. This helps break down natural tendencies to want to deny the loss. When there is no body, as sometimes happens in natural disasters, mass killings, and war, survivors may be overcome by distress and anxiety caused by uncertainty. Under these conditions, communities sometimes create memorial services or monuments to symbolically bury their dead (Boss, 2002a). The following section provides examples of traditional customs, and community practices in the context of the death.

Care of the Body

Most funeral preparations include specific practices for caring for the corpse. Often, the corpse is washed and wrapped in a funeral shroud or cloth. Muslims wash the body in warm water and soap and, finally, with a scented water. Among Native Americans, a powdery substance made of corn is used to cover the dead person's face. Among Protestants and Catholics in Europe and the United States, the body is usually washed, embalmed, and dressed in clothes selected by the family. Often, cosmetics are applied to make the person look as if he or she is sleeping. The corpse is placed in a casket and laid out for viewing. According to Jewish tradition, the deceased person is to be attended by a guardian, usually a family member or close friend, for the period from death to burial. The body is to be cleansed according to specific rituals by a specially trained person or a Jewish funeral director.

Cultures have different practices concerning how quickly the body is to be disposed of after death. In most Protestant and Catholic families, there is a 1- to 3-day viewing period after death, when family and friends come to the funeral home to see the body and pay respects to family members. This precedes the actual funeral service and burial. In contrast, among Islamic families, the body is prepared by family members when possible, men

In India, the body of a dead woman is prepared for cremation as family members, friends, and members of the community look on.

Yadid Levy/Alamy Stock Photo

caring for the body of men and women for the body of women. The burial is expected to take place as soon as possible after the death, preferably within 24 hours (Aisha, 2013). In Japan, Buddhists allow 3 days to pass before the body is burned. On the first day, a priest comes to the home and recites a prayer called a *sutra*. On the second day, the family members burn incense sticks before the family altar. On the third day, the body is burned at a funeral hall, and the ashes are brought back to the house and then taken to the cemetery.

Care of the Spirit

Most cultures believe that there is a spiritual component of a person's being that is not destroyed as the body decomposes or burns. Certain ritual practices are designed to help the spirit make a transition to whatever existence the culture believes takes place after death. According to a Gallup Poll taken in 2016, 71 percent of Americans believe in heaven and 14 percent say they are not sure (Newport, 2016). The concept of heaven, whether it is viewed as a beautiful garden or a perfect, golden city, is typically conceptualized as a paradise of safety and abundance where some form of pleasant existence continues after death (Miller, 2010).

The pathway to heaven depends on one's religious and cultural beliefs. For example, in the Roman Catholic religion, the Last Rites, or Viaticum (which in Latin refers to provision for the journey), is a ritual that is carried out at the end of life or in instances of serious illness. The ritual is a celebration of faith; a prayer for God to deliver the person from the illness of body, mind, and spirit; and a process of absolving the person of sins in preparation for life after death in a state of grace. As part of the ritual, the person confesses sins, takes communion, and prays with the priest or Eucharistic minister, reciting a set of familiar prayers and blessing (beliefnet, 2007).

Preparation of the spirit or soul may be achieved by reciting specific prayers or burying the person with possessions that may be useful in the afterlife. Singing, dancing, and playing musical instruments are sometimes used to speed the departed spirit on its way to the next life. Hindus believe that at death, the spirit leaves the body and enters a small flame that is lit next to the body. The spirit remains in the home because of attachments to family and possessions. The body is cremated, and there is a period of prayers in the person's home that lasts for 12 days. On the 10th day, the flame with the spirit is taken to the sea. Placing the flame in the sea is a signal to the spirit to leave the attachments of the earthly life and begin the transition to the afterlife.

The Navajo believe that the dead person will need certain resources in the afterlife. The dead are often buried with an extra set of clothes, food, water, and other items that may be of value in the afterworld. The Navajo believe that everything a person creates has some part of the person's spirit in it. As a result, at death, many of the artifacts a person made, such as pottery or blankets, are cracked or torn in order to release the person's spirit (Santillanes, 1997).

Many societies also observe rituals in the years following the death to nurture and respect the spirit of the ancestor and establish a link between the living and the departed. In Estonia, it is thought that there is a day each year when the dead return to their home for a visit. Rooms are cleaned, and food is laid out for a banquet. This is to preserve and strengthen relationships between the living and the souls of the dead. In Mexican tradition, The Day of the Dead, or All Souls Day, November 2, is a similar ritual. Many families believe that the souls of deceased loved ones return on this day to comfort and advise their family members. Many Japanese families visit the cemetery four times each year. They also have small altars in their homes, where they pray to their ancestors. They believe that the ancestors are always with them, guiding their lives and providing protection. In America, many people of different cultures visit the cemetery for periods of reflection, solitude, and discussion with dead relatives. Practices of leaving flowers and wreaths at the gravesite are expressions of respect.

Care of the Surviving Family, Friends, and Community

In addition to addressing the treatment of the body and soul, death rituals are important for helping the people who remain to cope with their grief and reorient their lives in a world without the person who died. These rituals also allow the society to elaborate the meaning of death and decrease the ambiguity surrounding death. Most cultures have funerals for the dead. These funerals involve a gathering of family, friends, and spiritual leaders to carry out the rites for the dead person, provide a social context for expressions of grief, celebrate the life of the person who died, and begin the process of social support for those who remain. Depending on cultural custom, these gatherings may occur before or after the burial or cremation. Funerals or memorial services provide a transition period surrounding death when people often have difficulty believing that the loved one has really died.

Among Africans who have migrated to the United States in recent years, a complex set of funeral rituals are observed that help mark the status of the deceased and to reaffirm traditional customs of the African community. The wake may last many days as mourners gather from distant locations. The entire community contributes money to cover the costs of food, burial expenses, and the family's support during the period of mourning. The funeral begins with drumming, singing, and dancing, which continue when the funeral procession moves to the burial site or the airport if the person is returned to Africa to be buried with his or her ancestors. The more important the social position of the deceased, the more elaborate the funeral (Hazell, 1997).

In the Jewish tradition, the period of mourning is prescribed in some detail, taking the bereaved from the days immediately following the funeral through the first year and annually thereafter. Special focus is given to the practices expected of children on the death of their parents. This may be related to the importance placed on the fifth commandment to honor one's father and mother. Upon returning to the home after the burial, the family members light a *shiva* (shiva means 7) candle, which represents the everlasting soul of the deceased. They then begin 7 days of mourning. This is a time when family members stay at home and focus their attention on their grief and recollections of the deceased. Friends usually come by to visit, but no business is transacted. It is a solemn time, when luxuries and recreation are set aside. The Kaddish, a prayer that affirms life and faith in God, is recited daily. On the seventh day, the *shiva* candle is extinguished and the family members take a walk outside, symbolically escorting the loved one's soul out of the house and indicating that the family is strong enough to carry on their lives. The period of mourning typically lasts 12 months for those who have lost a parent and is marked by the unveiling of the tombstone or grave marker. After that time, children note the anniversary of their parents' death by lighting a *yahrzeit* (year's time) candle and attending services where the Kaddish is said (Louchheim, 1997).

Other rituals help to address the impact of the death on the larger social system. In the United States, people typically have a will, which is read to the heirs. This ritual provides for the distribution of resources and assets according to the deceased person's wishes. The reading of the will and distribution of the assets help to realign the social system following a death. Obituaries, which are published in local newspapers, are another custom that notifies the larger community of a death. These statements often acknowledge the person's accomplishments and recognize their family members. This public statement can provide an opportunity for community members to offer support and condolences to the bereaved family members.

A recent innovation is the practice of posting a **tribute** to a loved one on a memorial website (Miller, 2014). A memorial website can be set up so that family and friends can share photos, videos, fond memories, and anecdotes of the deceased. Often the website includes a biography of the person and key life events. People can send condolences to family members, and may be directed to special charities where contributions can be given in memory of the deceased. The following is a tribute posted on a memorial website.

> My grandma was the strongest and most beautiful person that I've ever known. She would light up a room when she walked in and had a wonderful warmth to her that made everyone love her. Although she has been gone from us for nearly 7 years—her spirit remains in each one of us. Life has not been the same without her here but we know that she is in a better place and that she looks over all of us. I've heard from many the famous quote of "it will get easier with time" but when you love someone that much it doesn't ever get easier. I think you just come to accept the outcome. Grandma—We miss you and Love you so much!! Not just today but Everyday!!! Love–your family. (Hospice of Michigan, 2007)

The concept of **legacy** refers to what a person leaves behind after death. People may leave a legacy to their loved ones, such as passing on material possessions, a business, or a family history. They may have a larger societal impact in mind, even an impact on future generations, as when people endow a professorship at a university or a wing of a hospital. Legacies are a way to transmit one's resources, values, and wisdom in order to support and comfort those who survive one's death (Newton & Jones, 2016).

There are also many ways that the living can memorialize the deceased, including making contributions to charities in the name of the dead person, creating monuments, naming buildings or programs, listing names on a wall or plaque, and establishing scholarships, grants, or other types of endowments. It is not uncommon to see a small memorial set up at a place on the road where someone was killed in an auto accident. At the park where we often go to enjoy the ocean, people have dedicated benches to family members who used to come there. Every year, the family and friends of a loved one participate in the "Boston Brain Tumor Ride" to raise money for research about brain cancer in her memory. In these and many other ways, people cherish the memory of their departed family and friends.

Memorializing can be at a personal level, but it can also occur on a larger scale. In the face of widespread catastrophes or deaths during wartime, a monument can be erected that honors the victims and also reminds the public of the meaning and impact of the events surrounding the loss (Pollack, 2003). In the wake of the terrorist attacks of September 11, 2001, public memorial services were televised to permit national and international mourning. A National September 11 Memorial and Museum has been created to keep the individuality of the victims alive, to teach about the historical and social contexts of the attack, and to examine its continuing influence as we strive toward a more peaceful, hopeful future.

The **Human Development and Diversity** box The Amish Way of Death illustrates how one culture openly incorporates

The Amish Way of Death

The importance that the Amish place on their funeral ceremonies is reflected not only in familiarity with death, but also in an intensified awareness of community. As an Amish man reported in a family interview, "The funeral is not for the one who dies, you know; it is for the family."

The Amish community takes care of all aspects of the funeral occasion, with the exception of the embalming procedure, coffin, and horse-drawn wagon. These matters are taken care of by a non-Amish funeral director who provides the type of service that the Amish desire.

The embalmed body is returned to the home within a day of the death. Family members dress the body in white garments in accordance with the biblical injunction found in Revelation 3:5. For a man, this consists of white trousers, a white shirt, and a white vest. For a woman, the usual clothing is a white cape and apron that she wore at both her baptism and marriage. At baptism, a black dress is worn with the white cape and apron; at marriage, a purple or blue dress is worn with the white cape and apron. It is only at her death that an Amish woman wears a white dress with the cape and apron that she put away for the occasion of her death. This is an example of the lifelong preparation for death as sanctioned by Amish society. The wearing of white clothes signifies the high ceremonial emphasis on the death event as the final rite of passage into a new and better life.

Several Amish women stated that making their parents', husbands', or children's funeral garments was a labor of love that represented the last thing they could do for their loved ones. One Amish woman related that each month, her aged grandmother carefully washed, starched, and ironed her own funeral clothing so it would be in readiness for her death. This act appears to have reinforced for herself and her family her lifelong acceptance of

At the time of death, the whole Amish community comes together to support the mourners and say farewell to their friend.

death and to have contributed to laying the foundation for effective grief work for herself and her family. This can be seen as an example of the technique of preventive intervention called *anticipatory guidance* (Caplan, 1964) which focuses on helping individuals to cope with impending loss through open discussion and problem solving before the actual death.

After the body is dressed, it is placed in a plain wooden coffin that is made to specifications handed down through the centuries. The coffin is placed in a room that has been emptied of all furnishings, in order to accommodate the several hundred relatives, friends, and neighbors who will begin arriving as soon as the body is prepared for viewing. The coffin is placed in a central position in the house, both for practical considerations of seating and to underscore the importance of the death ceremony.

The funeral service is held in the barn in the warmer months and in the house during the colder seasons. The service is conducted in German and lasts 1½ hours, with the same order of service for every funeral. The guests view the body when they

arrive and again when they leave to take their places in the single-file procession of the carriages to the burial place.

Source: From The Amish Way of Death: A Study of Family Support Systems, by K.B. Bryer, *American Psychologist, 34,* 255–261. Copyright 1979 American Psychological Association.

Critical Thinking Questions

1. Summarize how the Amish way of death addresses the care of the body, spirit, and surviving loved ones.
2. Analyze the cultural worldview, values, and beliefs about life after death that are reflected in this narrative about death-related rituals among the Amish.
3. What can you find out about the Amish beliefs regarding the afterlife?
4. Interpret the meaning of the various symbols in this narrative, including the white clothing, plain coffin, funeral taking place in the barn, and procession of horse-drawn carriages.
5. Compare the funeral rituals of the Amish with the rituals described for the Hindus and Navajo Indians. What might be some similarities and differences in beliefs that are reflected in these practices?

death into every aspect of life. The service and ritual are expressions of the belief in a spiritual immortality and a simultaneous recognition of separation. Families customarily care for their aging parents in their own homes. Dying persons are surrounded by their families, who provide reassurance of generational continuity (Greksa & Korbin, 2004). In one study, Amish families found six conditions especially helpful for coping with death (Bryer, 1979, p. 260):

1. The continued presence of the family, both during the course of the illness and at the moment of death
2. Open communication about the process of dying and its impact on the family
3. Maintenance of a normal lifestyle by the family during the course of the illness
4. Commitment to as much independence of the dying person as possible
5. The opportunity to plan and organize one's own death
6. Continued support for the bereaved for at least a year following the funeral, with long-term support given to those who do not remarry

FURTHER REFLECTION: Describe the elements of a funeral you have attended or observed. What are the features of a funeral that address the care of the body, the spirit, and the surviving family and community?

What are some strategies for memorializing the deceased? Which ones have you found to be especially effective?

Bereavement and Grief

OBJECTIVE 5 Analyze factors that affect grief and bereavement.

Three terms—bereavement, grief, and mourning—are associated with the death or loss of a close relationship. Bereavement refers to the loss of a meaningful relationship; grief is the complex set of emotions and thoughts that accompany this loss; and mourning is the social and behavioral expressions of loss, often guided by cultural practices (Fontana & Keene, 2009).

Bereavement

Bereavement is a long-term process of adjustment to the death of a loved one and is more all-encompassing than grief. It commonly includes physical symptoms; role loss; cognitive manifestations, such as seeking meaning in the loss or trying to solve problems that arise as a result of loss of the loved one; and a variety of intense emotions, including anger, sorrow, anxiety, and depression. Bereavement may be expressed in very individual ways and may also be guided by cultural practices that shape the behaviors and activities of those in mourning. The bereavement process can include both confronting the loss and seeking ways to move away from or beyond the loss. It can include the expression of pain, sorrow, and loneliness as well as the possibility of self-insight, redefinition, and psychosocial growth. The bereavement process

can be viewed as a form of coping as the person confronts the loss and its secondary stressors (Hansson & Stroebe, 2007).

Bereavement and Coping with Stress

Some authors conceptualize bereavement within a more general framework of coping with stress. In Reuben Hill's (1958) ABCX model of coping with stress, adaptation (X) is determined by the interaction among three factors: the initial stressor (A), the resources and social support a person has to deal with the stressor (B), and the perception or meaning the person makes of the situation (C). The model was expanded into the double ABCX model (McCubbin & Patterson, 1983) to reflect the changes in the family system over time as the initial stressor is met and subsequent events bring new stressors, alter the existing resources, and change perceptions of the event (FIGURE 15.1 ▶). As this model suggests, efforts to cope with the initial stressor result in changes in the situation that alter the family's adjustment. Initial coping strategies may reduce or improve the family's resources, perceptions of the original stressor may change with time, and new secondary stressors may arise that impact the family system.

The value of this model for understanding bereavement is its emphasis on individual contexts of the death, the dynamic and changing nature of the stressor and its impact over time, and the key role that meaning making plays in how a person will adapt to the loss of a loved one. For example, a death might be perceived as unfair, sudden, cruel, or too soon by some but perceived as a blessing, or timely, by others. Positive or negative appraisal of the loss may influence the emotional state that emerges. If the person gains new insights into the loss and is able to construct positive meaning in the situation, some of the distressing negative emotions may subside and be replaced by positive emotions that could foster subsequent adjustment (Hansson & Stroebe, 2007).

With respect to resources, the loss of a life partner might be followed by the loss of social status, income, and companionship, but this same loss might result in new financial resources such as life insurance, fewer medical bills, and freedom from caregiving responsibilities. Over time, bereavement might have an impact on a survivor's health. The depression and confusion that accompany

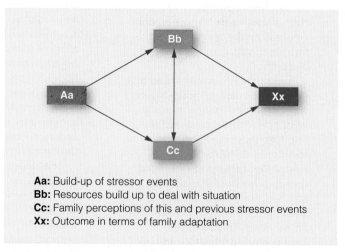

Aa: Build-up of stressor events
Bb: Resources build up to deal with situation
Cc: Family perceptions of this and previous stressor events
Xx: Outcome in terms of family adaptation

FIGURE 15.1 ▶ THE DOUBLE ABCX MODEL OF COPING WITH STRESS
Source: © Cengage Learning.

grieving may decrease the survivors' sensitivity to their own physical health and pose risks to their mental health as well. People in deep mourning may have feelings of uselessness or emptiness that prevent them from seeking help for their own physical or emotional health problems. Some people try to cope with their grief by increasing their use of medication, alcohol, or tranquilizers, which may threaten their physical health. Loss of appetite and lack of sleep are other symptoms of grief that contribute to the pattern of increased vulnerability during this time. In contrast, others may find a new sense of purpose and commitment to life as a consequence of bereavement. They may take new steps to improve their own health and to treasure their days, realizing that life is precious. In order to understand the adaptive nature of the bereavement process, one must appreciate that the meaning a surviving loved one gives to the death and the resources that are available to cope with the loss are changing over time.

Grief

Grief refers to the cognitive and emotional reactions that follow the death of a loved one. Grief reactions can vary in duration and intensity and can fade and reappear at unexpected moments. In a study of family members who were responsible for caring for a person suffering from later-life dementia, five aspects of grief were identified: (1) preoccupation with thoughts of the deceased person, (2) longing for the person, (3) painful emotions, (4) feelings of dissociation—feeling disconnected from reality, and (5) sensory illusions that led to the impression that the deceased person was still present. Of these five aspects of grief, preoccupation was the most common and lasted the longest after the person's death (Aneshensel et al., 1995).

Sometimes intense grief reactions are very similar to symptoms of mental illness (Hospice of Michigan, 2007). The following symptoms are not unusual:

> *Time distortion:* Time seems to be frozen, the person is unsure what day it is, time moves unusually slowly or speeds by.
> *Obsessive rumination:* Telling a story or incident over and over; thinking about a situation involving the dead person over and over.
> *Suicidal thoughts:* Thoughts that the person cannot go on living without the deceased person in their lives.
> *Mystical experiences:* Experiences of seeing or hearing the person who died, sensing them with you.
> *Identification symptoms:* Experiences of symptoms that are similar to those of the person who died.
> *Increased use of drugs and alcohol:* Used to buffer experiences of pain from the loss.
> *Confusion:* Difficulty concentrating or making decisions.

There is no timetable for grief. One study followed the grief reactions of family members whose loved one died from cancer (Ringdal, Jordhov, Ringdal, & Kaasa, 2001). The intensity of grief response showed significant declines by the end of the first year after the death. In monitoring the grief response, however, one often finds conflicting evidence of devastation and impressive coping. A widow may be handling daily tasks at a high level of competence and still find herself in tears at seeing her husband's hat in the closet. Over time, one expects to see gradual improvement in the intense, disruptive feelings of grief, but it is hard to say if there is a time when mourning is completed. Perhaps the most important sign is that the person is able to reinvest in new activities and relationships, even while preserving affection for the deceased loved one.

Grief Work

In the face of the death of a loved one, there is a need to work through the reality of the loss as well as the feelings that accompany it. The experience of the bereaved person is not that different from the experience of the person who is coping with his or her own death. Psychiatrist Erich Lindemann (1944) worked with people whose relatives died in the Coconut Grove fire in Boston. His writings continue to provide a basis for understanding the bereavement process.

Lindemann described three phases to the normal grief reaction. First, the person must achieve "emancipation from bondage to the deceased." This bondage may include feelings of guilt about ways in which he or she had criticized or even harmed the person who had died, or feelings of regret for things left unsaid or undone. Second, the person must make an adjustment to all the aspects of the environment from which the deceased is missing. The more closely linked the lives of the living and the dead, the more difficult this may be. Third, the person must begin to form new relationships—what we have called redirecting energy to new roles. One major obstacle to working through this loss is a desire to avoid the accompanying emotions and intense physical distress. According to Lindemann's analysis, the strategy of avoiding grief only prolongs the survivor's physical, mental, and emotional preoccupation with the dead person.

Questions have been raised about how universally applicable Lindemann's idea of **grief work** really is. In some cultures, intense emotional expressions of grief are considered inappropriate. Under conditions of grave trauma, some counselors suggest that an early period of denial helps the person cope with immediate demands. For some, the death of a loved one comes after a long period of painful illness. Death may be viewed as a relief from suffering and, as such, brings a form of comfort to those who are still living. Thus, the context of death and its meaning for those who mourn suggests a more individualized view of the adaptive process of bereavement (Hansson & Stroebe, 2007).

Bereavement and Grief Among Older Widows and Widowers

Among people who have lost a spouse, intense depression is more likely to be experienced by those who described their marriage as positive and vital. This loss strikes at the core of an older adult's sense of attachment, social integration, and personal worth (Futterman, Gallagher, Thompson, Lovett, & Gilewski, 1990). In a comparison of older widows and widowers with adults who were not experiencing bereavement, the widowed adults showed greater signs of depression, psychopathology, and grief at 2 months after the loss (Thompson, Gallagher-Thompson, Futterman, Gilewski, &

Peterson, 1991). At 12 and 30 months after the loss, the two groups were comparable in levels of depression and psychopathology, but the bereaved group continued to experience higher levels of grief than the nonbereaved. Among older adults, one may not expect a full resolution of the grief work associated with the death of a spouse. Rather, older adults come to accept a certain empty place in their hearts for their deceased partner and learn to find appropriate times to experience their profound sense of loss.

Five Patterns of Bereavement Among Widows and Widowers

The complexity of bereavement as a coping process is illustrated in a study that followed older couples from before the death of a spouse until 18 months after the death. Five **patterns of bereavement**-related adjustment were identified (Bonanno, Wortman, & Nesse, 2004). These patterns, shown in FIGURE 15.2 ▶, were:

1. *Common grief pattern.* These people had low levels of depression before the spouse died. They experienced an increase in depression 6 months after the loss. After 18 months, they returned to the same low level of depression that characterized them before the loss.
2. *Resilient pattern.* People in this group had low levels of depression before the death of their spouse and continued to have low levels after the death of the spouse.
3. *Chronic grief pattern.* These people had low levels of depression before the loss but showed increased grief responses at both 6 months and 18 months after the loss.
4. *Chronic depression pattern.* These people had high levels of depression before the loss, and depression continued at high levels at both 6 and 18 months.

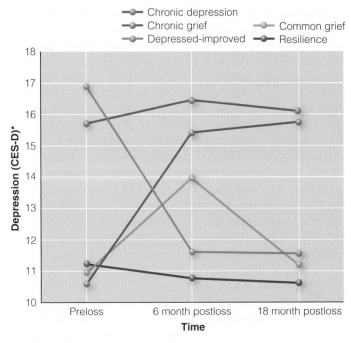

FIGURE 15.2 ▶ FIVE PATTERNS OF BEREAVEMENT

*Note: Depression measured by the Center for Epidemiologic Studies of Depression (CES-D). Bonanno, Wortman, & Nesse, 2004, Fig. 1, p. 263. Copyright © 2004 by the American Psychological Association. Reprinted with permission.

5. *Depressed-improved pattern.* These people had elevated levels of depression before the loss, but lower depression scores at 6 and 18 months after the loss.

This research helps clarify the importance of the context of loss as it affects the bereavement process. The context of the loss can include the nature of the relationship between the deceased person and the survivor, the sudden or gradual trajectory of death, the causes of death, the psychological health of the surviving spouse before the death of the partner, and the extent to which a spouse believes that the deceased had led a full life. The depressed-improved group, for example, was composed of people who were in unhappy or unsatisfying marriages; many had a substantial caregiving burden for an ailing spouse. Although people in this group did show evidence of grief responses at 6 months, they also reported benefits of widowhood and pride in the ability to cope with their new status.

In contrast, the chronic grievers comprised people whose lives were suddenly disrupted by the death of a healthy spouse. This group was especially preoccupied with a search for meaning as they tried to make sense of their spouse's death. They had sustained experiences of yearning for their spouse, thinking about their spouse, and talking with others about their spouse at 6 months, with some evidence of improvement in these aspects of grief by 18 months. The results of the study suggest that for some groups, especially the resilient and depressed-improved groups, the

Bernice comes each month to visit with her husband at the cemetery. She never remarried and still thinks of herself as Bill's wife. She finds comfort knowing that her husband died bravely in the service of his country.

relative lack of expression of grief-related symptoms may not be due to denial of their loss, but to evidence of appropriate coping.

Complicated Grief

The pattern of chronic grievers described above can be considered an example of **complicated grief**. Where the typical symptoms of grief gradually fade with time, in complicated grief the person remains in a continuing state of deep mourning for 6 months or more. In some instances, the grief reactions become more intense over time. Some signs of complicated grief include the following: intense sorrow and pain when thinking about the loved one, intense longing for the loved one, problems accepting the death, an inability to focus on anything other than the loss, a feeling of numbness or detachment, and a loss of ability to think about periods of enjoyment in the past or to experience enjoyment in the present. The combination of these symptoms may create anxiety, depression, an inability to sleep, increased risk of illness, and difficulty engaging in basic tasks of work or family life. Dr. M. K. Shear reported on the following case:

> A 68-year-old widow who continued to be seriously impaired by grief four years after her husband died. The woman slept on the couch because she could not bear to sleep in the bed she had shared with him. She found it too painful to engage in activities they used to do together. She no longer ate regular meals because preparing them was a too-distressing reminder of her loss. And she remained alternately angry with the medical staff who cared for him and with herself for not recognizing his illness earlier. (Brody, 2015; Shear, 2015)

The causes of complicated grief are not entirely understood. They may be related to the context of the loss, a lack of an adequate support system, a vulnerability to depression, or some co-occurring stressors that overwhelm the person's typical coping capacities (Mayo Clinic, 2014d).

Factors That Affect the Distress of Survivors

As illustrated in the study of patterns of bereavement among widows, the bereavement path depends in part on the context of the loss. Grief may be more intense for those who lose a loved one in a sudden death. Under these conditions, there is no opportunity to discuss end-of-life decisions, for final expressions of caring and love, and for the bereaved to begin to anticipate life without the loved one (Howarth, 2007). In cases of natural disaster, the death of loved ones may be accompanied by loss of home, neighbors, and a sense of place.

Bereavement may be difficult if the dying person is unable to receive effective pain control in their last days of life. Survivors who feel that the death of their loved one was brought about by physicians' negligence feel greater distress and anger than survivors who feel that the loved one received high-quality medical care. An aspect of the dying process that is seen as negative for the dying person but is protective for the survivor is nursing

HECTOR RETAMAL/AFP/Getty Images

In October, 2016, Hurricane Matthew brought devastating destruction and loss of life to families in Haiti. The combination of sudden loss and disruption of family life can result in complicated grief.

home usage. It leads to reduced anxiety for the survivor and may prepare them for the separation that death finalizes while sparing them from the burden and strain of direct caregiving.

Ambiguous loss is another especially difficult challenge for loved ones. Two types of ambiguous loss have been described (Boss, 1999). In the first instance, the person is missing and may be dead, as in soldiers who are missing in action or people who may have died in a disaster, but there are no physical remains. In the second instance, the person is physically present but unable to participate in any meaningful way in family interactions, as when a person is in a coma or in the late stages of Alzheimer's disease. As a result of the destruction of the World Trade Center in New York, some children experienced both types of losses: One parent died in the destruction of the towers, but no remains were recovered, and the other parent was so distraught by the spouse's death that he or she became unable to enact the parent role (Boss, 2004). The **Applying Theory and Research to Life** box Ambiguous Loss describes some of the issues surrounding this unique context of bereavement.

Finally, bereavement may be especially difficult if the survivor has experienced many positive benefits of caregiving, including feelings of being needed, important, and effective, as they addressed the needs of an ailing spouse (Boerner, Schulz, & Horowitz, 2004). Although family caregiving is often viewed as a source of stress, some people find that they gain comfort and even a personal sense of worth through caregiving. In this context, the death of the ailing spouse or parent brings a double loss—loss of the loved one and loss of the meaningful caregiving role.

Unacknowledged and Stigmatized Loss

The bereavement process is influenced by a society's interpretation of who the legitimate mourners are and who has experienced a legitimate death. Some people who grieve may not be recognized as legitimate mourners. These might include former spouses, foster children, partners in a gay relationship, professional caregivers, extramarital lovers, families of addicts and criminals, or women who have had abortions. When communities do not

Ambiguous Loss

Of the 2,749 people who were reported missing after the attack on the World Trade Center in New York on Sept. 11, 2001, 1,640 have now been positively identified (Dunlop, 2015). Despite the use of a variety of approaches to identification, more than 9,000 body fragments were not identified. These fragments were stored for future analysis, in case new technologies are developed that allow for their identification. At some point after the tragedy, the mayor of New York offered presumed-death certificates to families when there was no body that could be identified. Some families accepted those certificates, whereas others continued to wait for DNA testing results. In ensuing years, through the process of cleaning up debris from roads and nearby buildings, and the excavation of the Ground Zero site, some additional human remains were discovered (9-11 Research, 2013). Thousands of families suffered ambiguous loss—some for days not knowing if their loved one was in the buildings, many for months as they waited for the remains to be excavated from Ground Zero, and some are still suffering because there is no physical evidence of their loved one's body.

Pauline Boss (2002b, 2004, 2007) developed an understanding of ambiguous loss through clinical observation, theory, and research. She worked with many families who have experienced this type of loss, including merchant marine families, soldiers' families, families whose loved ones died in the terrorist attacks of September 11, 2001, and families in Kosovo. Much of this discussion is based on her observation and methods.

Ambiguous loss poses significant challenges to the structural and functional characteristics of a family. Families may try to hold a place for the person in daily life. Confusion about whether a loved one is dead or alive may lead some families to ignore parental roles, put off decisions, neglect daily tasks, and isolate living family members. Many families stop carrying out rituals and celebrations, which leads to further disconnection among family members.

Psychologically, the chronic uncertainty and lack of new information produce feelings of hopelessness, passivity, and immobilization. Because they do not have proof of death, family members may become confused—they do not know what to think or how to act. They may become stagnant by denying the loss and continuing to hope. The result is that family members are not grieving, and they are not coping with their loss.

Questions arise such as, "Should you have a funeral if you do not have a body?" Families would get into protracted arguments about this. Some parents did not want to tell their children that their father or mother was dead. Many children got the impression that they were not supposed to talk about the missing parent. People in these families are trying to hold two opposing ideas in their minds: (1) the loved one is still alive, and (2) the loved one is dead. As a result, their grief process is blocked. It takes a very long time to create a family life that includes acceptance and integration of this ambiguity.

Boss used several techniques that helped people cope with their loss. First, she created family storytelling meetings, where adults and children were encouraged to tell something they remembered about the missing person. Second, she arranged for groups of families who lived in the same community to meet together and tell stories about their missing family members. These meetings helped foster community connections. People were able to identify others who had the same needs, and they began to find ways to meet those needs. Third, she explained the idea of ambiguous loss and helped people see why it was causing them so much distress. This helped reduce self-blame and family discord. Fourth, she encouraged families to revise family rituals and celebrations but to continue having them because they are so important to preserving the unity of a family. Fifth, she told them not to become agitated and distressed by pushing for closure. She believes that closure is a myth and that death always produces ambiguity and uncertainty. Being done with grief, putting an end to mourning, and moving on are unrealistic expectations. Some families were less distressed than others. The characteristics of these families included a belief that the loss of the loved one was predestined and perhaps a product of the will of God; some had a deep faith that God would care for their loved one and guide them; some had prior experience in coping with ambiguous loss; and some were cognitively or temperamentally better able to hold the two opposing ideas in their minds and still retain the ability to function. Boss (2004) reported some comments that were made to her by people who were less distressed: "My son has been missing so long now—he's probably dead, but I feel he's here with me, and always will be" (p. 559). "I must move on and organize life without my son, but at the same time I can hope and remember" (p. 559).

Critical Thinking Questions

1. Summarize the challenges of ambiguous loss that interfere with the bereavement process.
2. Critically evaluate the five techniques Boss has developed to help people cope with their loss. What might be helpful about these strategies? Why might these techniques be helpful? Are there aspects of these strategies that might not be helpful? Why not?
3. Classify people into those who might be more or less troubled by ambiguous loss. Why? Which types of people would be most likely to benefit from Boss's approach? Why?
4. Propose other kinds of interventions, aside from those mentioned here, that might be helpful in supporting survivors of ambiguous loss.
5. Compare differences in the challenges of coping with ambiguous loss and stigmatized loss.

sanction or support their grief, it may be difficult for these people to acknowledge that they have suffered a loss or to experience closure after the death. These **unacknowledged mourners** may be confused about their status and feel guilty or embarrassed by their attachment to the dead person (Murray, Toth, Larsen, & Moulton, 2010).

There are also situations in which a person survives a loved one who had a stigmatized death. **Stigmatized deaths** are those in which people attribute the death to an immoral, illegal, or evil cause. Some survivors feel conflict in their grief and anger toward the dead person because they believe that person was involved in immoral or unclean behavior. These feelings may lead the griever to secrecy and misrepresentations about the death. Social networks may shun people who are grieving for someone who died a stigmatized death. Negative stereotypes surround these deaths and are often extended to include survivors (Murray, Toth, Larsen, & Moulton, 2010).

Death by suicide is an example of a stigmatized death, in which survivors may feel guilty about not having been able to prevent the death and angry at that person for the suicide. They may experience great conflict because of their love for the person who died and their belief that death by suicide is immoral. Communities look down on death by suicide and may not provide the customary rituals that help support the grieving persons. Many religions consider suicide to be a sin and will not provide religious services or burial rights for the deceased. In a qualitative study of adults who were mourning people who had committed suicide, two persistent themes were trying to make sense of the death and struggling to manage the social uneasiness in interactions with others. Meaning making was a key factor in the coping process for these survivors, including the meaning of the suicide, the meaning of the relationship between the survivor and the person who committed suicide, and the meaning of the survivor's own life (Begley & Quayle, 2007).

Death as a result of AIDS is another example of a stigmatized loss. In the 1980s, as the AIDS epidemic was taking hold, many survivors found that there was little support for their grief. The devastating effects of AIDS and the associated end-of-life conditions, compounded by fear of contamination, left many survivors isolated and traumatized by their stigmatized loss. In 1985, gay rights activist Cleve Jones discovered that more than 1,000 people had died of AIDS in San Francisco alone. He and other activists conceived of the NAMES Project AIDS Memorial Quilt as a way of honoring and memorializing this loss. The first national display of the AIDS Quilt took place on the National Mall in Washington, DC, at a lesbian and gay rights march in 1987. At the time, the quilt had 1,920 panels and was seen by more than half a million people. By 1988, the quilt was taken on a 20-city tour and had grown to 6,000 panels. In 2005, the quilt was named an American Treasure, resulting in a grant to support the conservation of the quilt. Today, there are 10 NAMES chapters in the United States and 29 affiliates around the world. The quilt has 46,000 panels commemorating the memory of over 96,000 people who have died from AIDS (The NAMES Project Foundation, 2016). As a result of this and other initiatives, the focus shifted from shunning the ill to investing in new medical research for causes and

CORBIS/AGE Fotostock

The AIDS Memorial Quilt displayed on the Mall in Washington DC.

cures. Resources were invested in research about AIDS, AIDS education, and the discovery of treatments to slow the course of the illness and prolong life.

In the United States and throughout the world, the death of adult children as a result of AIDS is resulting in the increased involvement of grandparents who are parenting their orphaned grandchildren (Linsk & Mason, 2004; Winston, 2006). In a qualitative study of South Africans who had lost a loved one to AIDS, bereaved adults described their situation as so overwhelming that there was little time for the typical experiences of grief (Demmer, 2007). The struggle for daily survival was intensified as a result of the economic losses associated with the death of an adult member of the household. Older women were burdened with the tasks of caring for the sick and looking after the surviving children. In this context, customary practices associated with mourning and loss were set aside in order to continue to meet the pressing demands of daily life.

Comforting the Bereaved

You can appreciate that there is no single way of experiencing loss, no right or best way to mourn, no specific timetable for recovering from the strong feelings of loss, and therefore, no one best way to comfort a bereaved person. The person in mourning is probably experiencing a range of emotions that fluctuate from moment to moment, and in the intensity of their grief they may also feel isolated and exhausted. The more you understand about grief and bereavement, the better able you are to provide comfort and support. And the way of approaching the role of providing comfort depends on the context of the loss, the meaning the loss has for the person, and the nature of the relationship between a bereaved person and one trying to offer comfort. Nonetheless, the literature on bereavement consistently mentions the importance of having a supportive social network as one factor that helps people cope with their loss. The role of the supportive network may be clearly defined by religion or culture, or it may have to be "improvised" by those close to the person who is mourning. The following suggestions are offered by therapists and grief counselors (Smith & Segal, 2016):

Listen with compassion. Acknowledge the situation, and let the person know you care and are there to listen or to help. Without forcing a person to talk about their loss, be ready to listen openly without judgement. You may ask, "Do you feel like talking?" Be patient if the person needs to tell their story over and over. Share your experience if you feel it's appropriate, but don't tell the person you know how they feel since each person experiences their loss in a very personal way.

Check in often and continuously. Friends who continue to call, stop in, or send emails or text messages in the initial few weeks after the death are especially valued. Often, the person can't even respond, but this doesn't mean they are unaware or unappreciative of this continuing support. "From pure exhaustion I often chose not to respond, but I felt incredibly supported by these messages and much less alone" (Tempesta, 2015).

Take the initiative in offering simple acts of help or service. The general statement, "What can I do to help?" is often impossible for the bereaved person to answer. They may feel so overwhelmed or confused that they can't even figure out what they need. But specific suggestions like bringing over a meal, offering to go grocery shopping, coming over to help fold the laundry, suggesting to go for a walk together, or picking the kids up after school might be really appreciated. Since the process of bereavement may continue for months, continuing to make these efforts is highly valued. Special efforts may be particularly important at certain times, like holidays, birthdays or anniversaries, and the anniversary of the death.

Watch for signs of complicated grief or the emergence of serious depression. After 4 to 6 months, you ought to notice some easing of the signs of grief. If you begin to realize that the person is unable to function in daily tasks, neglecting personal hygiene, unable to sleep, withdrawing from others, or expressing continued feelings of helplessness or hopelessness, you might share your concern with them, "I am troubled that you aren't sleeping and you seem to have given up on many of the things you used to enjoy." Any mention of suicide or increasing use of alcohol or drugs are to be taken seriously as signs that professional intervention is needed (Smith & Segal, 2016).

FURTHER REFLECTION: Summarize the various contexts that can impact the nature and severity of the bereavement process. How might the reason for a person's death, the age of the person, or the role of the person in one's life impact bereavement? How might stigmatized loss impact the bereavement process?

Psychosocial Growth Through Bereavement

Bereavement brings new possibilities for psychosocial growth. Just as happiness and joy are innate human emotions, so is sadness. Having these feelings is part of the human experience. Even though they are unpleasant, the emotions associated with grief connect people to their essential human nature. Expressions of grief have a social consequence. An infant's cries have the effect of bringing the caregiver into contact with the infant; the tears of grief communicate to others a person's needs for comfort and reassurance. Without experiences of grief, the moments of treasured happiness would mean less. These experiences help people understand the essence and limits of their existence. They provide a bridge for understanding the grief and unhappiness of others. Grief leads to greater levels of understanding of oneself and others.

The adaptive process of bereavement involves an oscillation between **loss-oriented coping** and **restoration-oriented coping**. The former refers to confronting one's pain, sadness, and the loss of a loved one and finding a place for the deceased loved one in one's thoughts and memories in order to achieve emotional health and cognitive functioning. The latter refers to finding ways to master the practical challenges of the loss in order to make meaning of the death and move along in one's life (Caserta & Lund, 2007; Hansson & Stroebe, 2007). When a person who is close dies, it stimulates reflection about that relationship. There may be a new appreciation of the qualities of the relationship and its importance. One may consider what the other person did to make the relationship especially valued. The bereaved person may begin to examine his or her own behavior, thinking of ways to bring some of the valued qualities of the relationship with the dead person to ongoing friendships and family ties. People may make resolutions to do a better job of supporting valued relationships by staying in touch, writing more often, or calling home. In the process of experiencing the death of a loved one, a person may become more appreciative of the value of these special, close relationships, realizing that they will not last forever. It is important to give valued relationships appropriate care and nurturance. This may lead to a growth in commitment to one's radius of significant relationships and to maintaining excellent quality in them.

The death of a loved one may stimulate a process of life review, leading one to reflect on the meaning of one's life. This process of taking stock may involve posing some of the big questions of life: What is the purpose of your life? Are you spending time in ways that are meaningful? Is your work an expression of your real values? Are your relationships satisfying and meaningful? Are you making any contribution to your community and to the well-being of others? This kind of reflection may lead to a reformulation of one's lifestyle or a re-evaluation of certain life experiences.

The death of someone whose presence serves to help define your identity requires a redefinition of your identity. Social roles are typically reciprocal—children have parents, husbands have wives. The death of someone in a reciprocal role leads to the reorganization of that role and its enactment. When a parent dies, children may have to assume some elements of the parental role. These elements are often concerned with greater levels of responsibility and caregiving. When a spouse dies, the remaining spouse has a new identity as a widow or widower. This brings with it new social meaning and, sometimes, a change in social status.

When a person dies, the links to social identity and social network may no longer exist for the person who remains. As a result, the survivors have to redefine themselves and establish new personal identities. For example, when Carl died, his wife Lois was no longer invited to social events that were hosted by Carl's coworkers. Lois no longer maintained her membership at Carl's golf club. She found that it was awkward to introduce herself to new people without being able to say that she was Carl's wife. She recognized that her social status was based on Carl's work and leisure activities. Being Carl's widow did not carry the high level of social status and value that she was used to. Lois had to begin to create a new identity in her community. This work is not easy, but it is very important and necessary.

The death of a loved one may stimulate a revisitation of psychosocial crises. For example, upon the death of a parent, one may reflect on earlier issues of autonomy versus shame and doubt, realizing a new sense of responsibility for one's actions. When parents are alive, even as they get older, an adult child is somehow buffered from the full weight of autonomous self-determination. When parents die, one may reflect on the many ways in which their values and beliefs have guided one's attitudes and behavior.

When a spouse dies, in addition to the need to reconfigure one's identity, issues of intimacy versus isolation may be revisited. A person may reflect on the quality of his or her intimate relationship, thinking about the nature of trust, levels of disclosure, sense of mutual respect, and openness to change. One may reexamine the ways in which intimacy was expressed and the ways in which isolation was experienced in the relationship. If the opportunity arises for the formation of a new intimate relationship, this revisitation could lead the person to approach that new relationship with different strategies, assumptions, or expectations for self and other.

When a person you admire dies, it often promotes new levels of identification with the deceased. This process sometimes begins with the eulogy where the community is reminded of the strengths and accomplishments of the person who died. In reflecting on the person's life, a survivor may take on a valued characteristic, such as integrity, fairness, sense of humor, or patience. Survivors may find themselves using expressions or participating in activities that were associated with the person who died. In this way, they expand their repertoire of behaviors, activities, and ego strengths. In addition to identification, the survivor may *introject* the lost person (i.e., take the person's essence inside themselves in thought and feelings). **Introjection** is different from identification in that the person feels that the lost person is in them. They may carry on meaningful conversations with this person and sense their guiding presence. This is similar to having an imaginary companion. Introjection allows the bereaved person to keep the dead person alive and to preserve their relationship. While still carrying on a mature and sensible existence, the bereaved add a psychological dimension to their abilities by preserving the characteristics of the revered and adored loved one.

In bereavement, thoughts are likely to turn to one's own mortality. The manner of the loved one's death and the way he or she faced death may help survivors prepare for their own death. The dead person's courage may lead the living person to work to develop courage. The creation of a living will by the deceased may be seen as beneficial by the surviving people, who proceed to establish their own living wills. The depth of emotion created by the death of someone close helps individuals recognize the value of their own lives and the emotions that significant others will experience when they die. In bereavement, a person can find comfort in the faith, confidence, and hopefulness of the person who died and be inspired to achieve that sense of integrity with regard to his or her own death.

FURTHER REFLECTION: Create a memorial ritual that would help support continued psychosocial growth for bereaved loved ones.

CHAPTER SUMMARY

The field of human development has come to a new openness about the topics of death and dying. There is an increasing sense that people can make decisions about the quality of their death and that these decisions can and should be discussed with family members as well as with health care professionals. In addition to experiences with death and the anticipation of one's own mortality, dialogues about death are taking place in families to a greater degree than they did in the past.

OBJECTIVE 1 Explain how mortality influences psychosocial development

The psychosocial perspective helps direct attention to how people determine the meaning of the events of their lives as they interact with the environment over time. Death presents one of the greatest challenges to meaning making. At each stage of life, our understanding of death changes because of the different cognitive and emotional resources we have available and as a result of the salience and proximity to death. The way people conceptualize their own death and the death of others is influenced by the cultural context.

OBJECTIVE 2 Define the biological state of death, including the distinctions between cardiopulmonary and whole-brain death.

The definition of the biological state of death has changed as a result of the development of new technologies. In addition to the lack of a heartbeat and the lack of respiration, death is determined by a combination of eight criteria that confirm the end of brain functioning. New legal procedures or advance directives allow people to convey their preferences about end-of-life treatment and to appoint people to make decisions for them if they are incapacitated.

OBJECTIVE 3 Describe factors associated with the process of dying and the modern ideal of a good death.

The process of dying can follow different trajectories, involve different degrees of suffering, and occur at different ages. Professionals have begun to define characteristics of a good death, and dying patients are having a greater voice in determining the nature of their death. Hospice care and euthanasia are two paths that people may choose when they are experiencing a slow, painful death trajectory. End-of-life decisions are a focus of ongoing ethical controversies and debate.

OBJECTIVE 4 Summarize the role of cultural death-related rituals and their functions.

Death-related rituals are found in all cultures. They tend to focus on three aspects of the meaning of death: (1) care of the body, (2) care of the spirit, and (3) care of the surviving family, friends, and community. These rituals provide a context for acknowledging the death, preparing the spirit for its transition, and legitimizing the grief of the bereaved survivors and providing support for their recovery from the loss over time.

OBJECTIVE 5 Analyze factors that affect grief and bereavement.

Bereavement is the long-term process of adjustment to the death of a loved one. Grief is the cognitive and emotional reaction to loss. The concept of grief work refers to the emotional expression, cognitive reorganization, and social adjustments that take place as a result of the death of a loved one. There are many patterns of bereavement depending on the context of the death, relationship of the survivor to the dead person, religious orientation of the survivor, and finality or ambiguity surrounding the death. Communities play a role in supporting the bereavement process by the way they respect or stigmatize the death and the way they memorialize and honor the dead.

CASEBOOK

For additional case material related to this chapter, see the case "Till Death Do Us Part," in *Life Span Development: A Case Book*, by Barbara and Philip Newman, Laura Landry-Meyer, and Brenda J. Lohman, pp. 195–199. This case focuses on the role of a sudden illness in opening up communication about end-of-life issues for an older couple.

This appendix highlights basic principles of the scientific process, including the positivist and qualitative approaches to inquiry. This process guides inquiry, and imposes constraints of logic, methodology, and ethics in hopes of building a sound, unbiased understanding of patterns and processes of development. The Appendix reviews basic topics in research design including sampling, research methods, and designs for studying development. A section on evaluating research highlights the need to approach the results of research as a critical and informed consumer, recognizing some of the limitations and biases that may be imbedded in the research process. Finally we review ethical guidelines for conducting research with human participants.

In approaching the challenges of conducting and interpreting research about development, it is useful to think of the following wisdom: Each individual is, in some ways, like every other human being; in some ways like certain groups of human beings more than others; and in some ways like no one else (Kluckhohn, 1961). This wisdom helps explain why the study of development requires a variety of methods including cross-national and cross-cultural comparisons, large sample surveys that rely on statistical analysis for their interpretation, and qualitative studies that give voice to individuals who share their unique life experiences. Studies that summarize the responses or behaviors of groups of people will not necessarily account for the experiences of specific individuals. Similarly, the experiences of individuals will not necessarily be generalizable to larger groups. The study of life-span development is a quest for patterns of continuity and change over time and across historical eras. Some patterns that might characterize the experiences of one cohort may not apply across historical periods.

Appendix
THE RESEARCH PROCESS

The Scientific Process

The **scientific process** consists of techniques for acquiring new knowledge, investigating questions of interest, and modifying or correcting previous knowledge. By adhering to a scientific process, researchers are better able to overcome the tendency to want to confirm what they already believe and to discard or ignore evidence that disconfirms their views. As human beings who are studying human behavior, the likelihood of making this kind error is especially great (Lilienfeld, 2012). Two major positions have been taken on how to approach the discovery of knowledge: *positivism* and *qualitative inquiry*, sometimes referred to as *post-positivism* or phenomenology (Bordens & Abbott, 2013).

Positivism seeks causal relationships with the goal of trying to predict outcomes. This approach typically applies statistical analyses to data gathered from many participants in order to test specific hypotheses. In the positivist approach, research hypotheses guide decisions about the nature and size of the sample needed, the site(s) where data are collected, the methods of data collection, and the statistical procedures used to analyze the data.

Qualitative inquiry strives to understand the meanings, motives, and beliefs that underlie a person's experiences. This approach emphasizes the individual's point of view and the subjective understandings that help account for a person's actions. Often this approach begins with examination of a *personal experience*, such as a parent's experience of caring for a child who has a developmental disability; a *process*, such as staff–parent communication in a neonatal unit; or a *unique phenomenon*, such as a near-death experience. Approaches to data collection may change as the study evolves, depending on the nature of the participants, the ideas that emerge, and the researcher's reactions and **interpretations**. Both positivism and qualitative inquiry contribute to a new level of understanding of human behavior.

The Positivist Approach to Research

The positivist research approach is described in FIGURE A.1.▶ The research process usually begins with a puzzling idea or observation. Something needs to be explained or clarified that is currently not explained, or current explanations are inadequate or incorrect. In this process of searching for explanations, one develops a set of interrelated ideas to account for the observation. These ideas—referred to as assumptions, hypotheses, or predictions—constitute a **theory**. The theory is not an end in itself, but a way to begin.

Scientific Observation

The next step of the scientific process is to test the theory through **systematic observation**. A good theory contains specific predictions about cause and effect. After the predictions are stated, one must figure out how to test whether they are accurate. One must **operationalize** the concepts of a theory in order to test them by translating these concepts into variables that can be observed and measured.

Scientific observation is characterized by three essential qualities: It must be *objective, repeatable, and systematic* (Creswell, 2013a). **Objective observations** accurately reflect the events that are taking

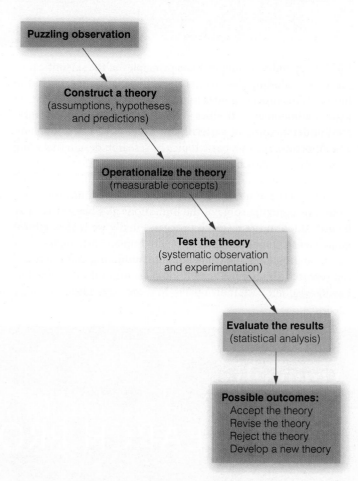

FIGURE A.1 ▶ THE SCIENTIFIC PROCESS

place. They are not unduly influenced by what the observer expects or hopes to see. Suppose, for example, that you want an objective assessment of your child's talent for playing the guitar. You are unlikely to get objective feedback from friends or relatives. Because they know you and presumably would not like to insult you, they may be inclined to slant their answers to please you.

A more objective approach might be to include an audiotape of your child's guitar playing with tapes of 10 other children. You would then ask another person to play the tapes for 10 people who do not know you or your child and ask each of them to rate the quality of musical ability demonstrated on each tape. You may or may not like the outcome, but at least your method would be more objective. It would reveal what other people think of your child's musical ability without being biased by any feelings. Scientific research is always vulnerable to the theoretical biases and value orientations of the researchers. Certain practices of research design, sampling, and methodology are used to help overcome biases and enhance objectivity. However, many will argue that it is impossible to be entirely objective. One's orientation toward framing research questions and interpreting the results are always influenced by cultural and historical contexts that shape the values, beliefs, and assumptions that guide the research process. That is why it is important that the research be replicated by other investigators and that the procedures are explained in enough detail to be repeatable.

In order for research to be **repeatable**, the original investigator must carefully explain all the procedures used in the study, describe all the essential characteristics of the participants (e.g., age, sex, social class), and describe the setting or situation where the observations were made. When you read a research report in a scholarly journal, these are the details that are included in the Methods section. Because there are many ways that one group of participants might differ from another and many different ways that observations can be made, replication is an important part of building a body of social science knowledge.

A **systematic approach** ensures that research is done in a careful, orderly way. Researchers have a framework of essential questions that they strive to answer based on what is already known and what certain theories predict. They approach research by having clear objectives, carefully defining the purpose of the research, and the specific methods they will use to reach those objectives. Although some discoveries are made by accident, scientific research typically does not poke here and there at unrelated events.

Often the theory is not tested by the same person who develops it because this person may have some personal investment in demonstrating that the theory is correct. The scientific process usually involves the ideas of more than one person. Sometimes, people with different points of view engage in debate, trying to refute positions they find flawed. At other times, two or more people work on different phases of theory building, experimentation, and **evaluation**.

If a theory is fruitful, many researchers working in independent groups devise ways of testing and clarifying it. Working in this way, as a community of scholars, helps to ensure that a theory will not be confirmed simply because of the theorist's personal biases. For example, Erik Erikson was not the person who tested his own psychosocial theory. Many other researchers have devised strategies for operationalizing Erikson's concepts, thereby expanding our understanding of concepts such as hope, identity, intimacy, generativity, and wisdom—to name a few—and clarifying the relationship of development in childhood and adolescence to adulthood and later life.

Statistical techniques help determine the likelihood that observations could have happened by chance. Observations that appear to be a result of chance do not confirm the theory. If the observations have a low probability of having occurred by chance, one says that they are statistically significant. If statistically significant results support the theory's predictions, one is likely to accept them as providing evidence for the theory. However, given the variability of samples, methods, and statistical techniques, no single study can be considered as sufficient evidence to establish a scientific fact (Tryon, 2016).

If the results do not fit the theory's predictions one must reexamine the methods and design of the study. Perhaps the key concepts were not measured appropriately or the sample was limited in some way. When results of research are inconclusive or contrary to the predictions, scholars may try another research approach before revising the theory. But when several different studies fail to support the hypotheses, we tend to lose confidence in the theory. We may revise or discard the theory and begin to develop an alternative explanation for the observations.

In summary, in the positivist approach, the scientific process consists of creating a theory, testing it through research, and modifying, rejecting, or accepting it.

The Qualitative Inquiry Approach to Research

Whereas the positivist perspective assumes that there is a truth that can be captured through the research process, qualitative inquiry assumes that there are many versions of truth, depending on the informant and the context. Knowledge is not out there to be discovered; rather, it is invented, constructed, and continuously revised as one accumulates new information (Creswell, 2013b). The qualitative approach focuses on processes of meaning making. It strives to uncover the ways that individuals understand and cope with the complicated experiences of their lives. In particular, it focuses on the value of "interpretation," recognizing that the same set of events can have different meaning depending on a person's social identity, personal history, and life stage (Karp & Birk, 2013).

The qualitative approach begins with an open mind. One looks at the world as if it were ripe for discovery. Theory typically emerges from the data, rather than starting with a theory that guides the methodology and data collection. When evidence is gathered that contradicts the theory, the theory is rejected or modified. Multiple methods are employed in order to learn as much as possible about the setting, the participants, and the contexts of behavior. In some instances, the observer's own experiences and beliefs are included as a guide to the meaningfulness of the observation. In other instances, the observer attempts to challenge a personal point of view by gathering as many different perspectives about the process as possible. Because qualitative inquiry assumes that there is not one truth, all perspectives and insights are considered equally valid. A major emphasis is on interpretation, made possible by the close acquaintance of the researcher with the details and voices of the participants.

In the study of human development, both positivist and qualitative inquiry are applied, often as complementary approaches to the same issue. Generalizations and categories used in the positivist approach can be reframed or refined using data from qualitative inquiry. Assumptions from the positivist perspective may be challenged by observations made through qualitative inquiry. For example, many children who live in female-headed, single-parent families actually have fathers, uncles, and grandfathers who participate actively in their daily lives. Conversely, many children who live in two-parent families actually have little daily contact with their fathers. Categories and definitions that are assumed to be meaningful from a positivist perspective are often shown to be more ambiguous or diversely defined when considered through the qualitative lens.

Research Design

Regardless of whether the positivist or qualitative approach is used, each empirical study needs to be designed. Research investigations are designed just as cars, bridges, and buildings are designed. Scientists know that the information they gain from conducting research will be influenced by the characteristics of the participants who are involved in their study, the kinds of data that are gathered, and the conditions under which the data are gathered. The principles of **research design** focus on the approach to selecting a sample, the methods used to gather information, the design for studying change, and the techniques used to analyze the data (Gliner, Morgan, & Leech, 2009).

Sampling

Sampling is the method for choosing participants who will be included in the study. The nature of the research questions has implications for the best way to identify the sample. If the study is about some universal principle of development, it should apply to individuals from a wide variety of family and social backgrounds. For example, studies of normal language development should include children from various ethnic, racial, social class, and cultural backgrounds. One cannot argue for universal principles if the research has shown the processes or patterns to be true only for a homogeneous group of children.

Every *sample* is taken from a population. The **population** is the large group to which the findings of the research are intended to apply. There is no single, predetermined population; the relevant population depends on the purpose and scope of the research. The sample is a smaller subgroup of the larger population that will participate in the study. For example, the population of interest might be adolescents in the United States who graduate from high school but do not go on to college. Roughly 906,000 adolescents who graduated from high school in the spring of 2014 were not enrolled in any postsecondary school in the fall of 2014 (National Center for Educational Statistics, 2015e). No study is likely to include all of those adolescents, so a sample is drawn that is expected to be representative of the population. Under ideal conditions, the participants in any study of this population ought to have the same general characteristics (e.g., family income; race; gender; urban, suburban, or rural environment; disability status; and high school academic background) as the population from which the sample was selected.

The sample and the population from which the sample is taken determine the **generalizability** of the research findings—the extent to which we can say with confidence that the observations made for this sample would apply to other groups. We must be careful not to assume that research findings based on one sample are generalizable for all ages, both sexes, all racial and ethnic groups, all social classes, or individuals from other cultures.

Five approaches to sampling, described in more detail in the following sections, are common in the research literature: *random samples, stratified samples, matched groups, volunteer samples,* and *qualitative sampling.* Each one has different implications for the generalizability of the findings (Henry, 2009).

Random Samples

In a **random sample**, each person in a given population has an equal chance of being included. The researcher may ensure equal opportunity by putting each person's name on a slip of paper and then choosing some of the slips blindly, or by selecting names from a list at random, using numbers produced by a random number generator. The Kaiser Family Foundation study of media use by infants, toddlers, and preschoolers discussed in chapter 7 is an example of a study that used a random sampling of households (Rideout, Hamel, & Kaiser Family Foundation, 2006). The study was a random, national telephone survey of families with children ages 6 months to 6 years old. The parent who spent the most time with the child was asked to complete the survey.

Stratified Samples

In a **stratified sample**, participants are deliberately selected from a variety of levels (strata) or subgroups within the population. For example, one study used a stratified, random sample to examine the care received from family members by African American and European American adults ages 65 and older who live in their own homes. The sample groups were selected in proportion to their numbers in the community. Within the African American and European American groups, participants were selected at random (Peek, Coward, & Peek, 2000).

Matched Groups

Researchers can also select two or more groups of participants who are similar on many dimensions. In most studies using **matched groups**, participants in one group receive some type of treatment or participate in some type of experimental intervention that the participants in the other group do not receive or participate in. In other studies, the impact of a naturally occurring difference is examined. For example, a matched group design was used to study the impact of low birth weight on subsequent academic performance. At age 11, children who had weighed less than 750 grams (1.65 pounds) at birth were compared to children who had weighed 750 to 1,400 grams (1.65 to 3.08 pounds) and to children of normal birth weight. The groups were matched on age, sex, and other background variables. The design allowed researchers to evaluate the long-term risks for very small babies (Taylor, Klein, Minich, & Hack, 2000).

Volunteer Samples

Participants can be solicited by asking people directly, placing advertisements in newspapers or on bulletin boards, sending letters to teachers or parents asking for participants, or writing to professionals or groups of potential participants. Those who are included in the study are selected from among those who **volunteer**. Most studies that are conducted with students enrolled in introductory psychology courses involve volunteer samples. Although the students may be required to participate in research, they usually have a choice about the study for which they will volunteer. People can register online to participate in computer-based research. Companies have emerged that provide samples of participants who have volunteered to carry out online studies. Some provide convenience samples of workers who choose which projects they will respond to; other services will identify samples that meet a researcher's specifications (DeSoto, 2016). In some sense, all research with human participants uses a volunteer sample. One cannot compel a person to participate in research.

The Qualitative Approach to Sampling

The primary objective of the qualitative approach to sampling is to learn as much as possible from each informant. Researchers begin with some general idea of questions they seek to understand. The strategy is to remain open to the information that is provided. Researchers may learn that they cannot get information about the question they started out with. For example, in a study of institutional wards for people with severe and profound retardation, Taylor (1987) wanted to know about residents' perspectives. However, many residents were nonverbal, and others were reticent to share their opinions so Taylor shifted his attention to staff perspectives on the environment. Qualitative researchers emphasize that the **informants** should have the knowledge and experience that the researcher requires, be able to reflect and verbalize about the experiences, and be willing to participate in the study. The number of informants or settings in which research occurs is not decided in advance. Typically, the greater the depth and detail in each case, the fewer the cases will be included. Additional cases are added as needed until the researcher believes that the variety of perspectives within a setting has been captured and the theoretical insights are well confirmed (Maxwell, 2009).

Strengths and Weaknesses of Approaches to Sampling

There are both strengths and limitations to the different approaches to sampling. Random sampling and stratified sampling are the most likely to ensure that a sample is representative of the population from which it is drawn. If each person in the population has an equal chance of being included in a study, then the results of the study ought to be equally likely to apply to those in the population who did not participate as to those who did. These sampling approaches provide statistical information about a population. They do not provide information about any specific person within the population. For example, the mean or arithmetic average income of a group of 100 people may not be the exact income of any single person in the group.

The use of matched samples allows one to examine the impact of naturally occurring events—such as unemployment, parental divorce, or low birth weight—that cannot be randomly assigned. By matching participants on a variety of background factors, such as IQ, family income, or birth order, one might be able to detect the impact of these events on emotional, social, or cognitive development. However, critics argue that one cannot match groups perfectly, and one might omit an important variable for which there is no match. For example, in the study described earlier about the impact of low birth weight on school achievement, sibling order was not included in the match. Because we know that firstborns typically do better on tests of academic achievement than siblings born later, this factor might explain more about the outcome than birth weight.

The method that places the greatest limits on generalization is volunteer sampling. One never knows what type of person will volunteer to participate in social science research. Reliance on volunteers may produce special problems. For example, imagine a study that promises to pay $25 to those who participate. People who volunteer to participate in this research may be especially in need of money. Sometimes, volunteers have more free time, are hoping to find some kind of help as a result of participating in the research, or have greater faith in science than those who choose not to volunteer.

Regardless of these limitations, volunteer samples are widely used. Most of the studies cited in this textbook are based on volunteer samples. All studies involving observation, interview, or experimentation with children require formal consent from parents and could be classified as volunteer samples. Frequently, the only way to study a certain question is to ask for volunteers.

Some of the research findings discussed in this text are based on **clinical samples**. The participants have been involved in some type of treatment program or are on a waiting list to receive clinical treatment. These studies are especially important for understanding the causes of clinical conditions, the developmental paths or patterns that these conditions exhibit, or the impact of certain interventions on these conditions. Without voluntary participation, there would be no way to begin to document the effectiveness of treatment. At the same time, one must be cautious not to generalize findings from clinical studies to the population as a whole.

It will come as no surprise that the vast majority of studies reported in U.S. journals are based on U.S. samples. The U.S. population comprises only 5 percent of the world population. Thus, studies that presume to characterize normal development are limited to the extent that the results have not been repeated or confirmed across countries and cultures (Arnett, 2008). As international communication improves and the use of the Internet supports international collaboration, we expect that cross-national research will increase.

Similarly, many studies of development during the period that we refer to as later adolescence are carried out with college students. Since roughly one third of later adolescents do not attend college, the results of these studies cannot be accurately generalized to the noncollege population.

From a qualitative perspective, the best informants are those who willingly volunteer to share their experiences and reflect on them. If the informant is providing an authentic, open narrative, then insights can be drawn. Each informant's perspective is treated as one way of making meaning of the situation. The researcher's job is to try to build a complex picture of the topic by synthesizing and comparing the views of multiple informants.

Research Methods

A variety of methods have been used to study development. Each one has strengths and weaknesses, allowing the investigator to focus on one set of behaviors at the expense of others. The choice of method must fit the problem under study. Six categories of research methods are described here: *observation, case study, interviews, surveys, tests,* and *experimentation.* These methods have all contributed to the discovery of knowledge. Some techniques—especially observation, case study, and interviews—are more commonly used in qualitative inquiry as investigators try to uncover basic themes or dimensions of a problem. Other methods—especially observation using a predetermined coding scheme, experimentation, structured interviews, surveys, and tests—tend to be used in the positivist approach to the research process.

Observation

At the heart of all science is observation—taking note of events and trying to make sense of them. Direct **observation** of children in their home and school environments is one of the oldest methods for studying development (Kessen, 1965). Researchers have used mothers' diaries and observation logs to gather information about behavior in intimate settings that could not be known in any other way. Jean Piaget was guided by the observations of his own children in the formulation of his theory of cognition. Today, researchers conduct observations in homes, schools, playgrounds, and child care centers where children typically spend their time. Others bring children and their families or friends into homelike laboratory settings, where they can watch children's behaviors under more constant and controlled physical conditions (Kochanska, Murray, & Harlan, 2000).

Naturalistic Observation.
Naturalistic observation refers to research in which behavior in a setting is carefully observed without any other kinds of manipulation. This type of observation, sometimes referred to as **ethnography**, provides insight about how things occur in the real world (Fetterman, 2010). In some instances, researchers go into a setting to observe the full range of interactions and behavior patterns. Based on their field notes, they begin to develop hypotheses about the meaning of the behaviors. Then, they may test these hypotheses through more focused observation or controlled experimentation. In other instances, researchers use observation to examine a specific behavior or relationship. They may be looking for different forms of peer aggression, patterns of social cooperation, or conditions that promote cross-gender interactions. In these studies, the observers limit their observations to behaviors that are relevant to their focus.

Participant Observation.
In **participant observation** the researcher actively engages in interactions with other people in a setting in order to understand how they experience the world. To engage in this type of work, one must obtain access to the setting and then gain the trust of the people in the setting. Some participant observation takes place in public settings, such as parks, street corners, pool halls, or train stations, where the researcher can be accepted as a nonthreatening participant. Even in these situations, it may take time for people to interact with the observers or be willing to confide in them. In Elliot Liebow's (1967, 2003) famous study of Black street-corner men, *Tally's Corner*, Liebow met his primary informant, Tally, while playing with a puppy outside a carryout restaurant. The friendship he formed with Tally led to introductions to other men on the street.

The participant observer usually gathers data through field notes, which are made after an observational session. Over time, the skilled observer learns to retain information about the details of a session and to record it in a systematic way. This is a very demanding process; it may take several hours to summarize what was observed in a single hour in the field. In addition to the observations, researchers try to capture their own reactions to the situation, using personal feelings and responses as a way of empathizing with the participants. In a study of a mental institution, Taylor made the following field notes:

> O.C. [observer's comments]: Although I don't show it, I tense up when the residents approach me when they're covered with food or excrement. Maybe this is what the attendants feel and why they often treat the residents as lepers. (Taylor & Bogdan, 1998, p. 73)

One of the challenges in participant observation is to check out and confirm one's insights from observation by comparing them with information drawn from other sources. This is especially important the more involved one becomes in the setting and the more attached one becomes to the participants. This confirmatory approach, called *triangulation*, can be achieved by looking at written documents about the setting, interviewing other informants, and sharing observations with other members of a research team (Taylor & Bogdan, 1998).

Correlation.
Observational studies lend themselves to an examination of correlation rather than causation. **Correlation** refers to a statistical analysis of the strength and direction of the relationships among variables. It reflects the degree to which knowing the value of one variable, such as popularity, allows one to predict the level of another variable, such as aggressiveness.

The correlation coefficient is a numeric index of the strength of relationship between variables that can range from a value of $+1.0$ to -1.0. As an example, consider the correlation between popularity with peers and aggressiveness. If, as popularity increases so does aggressiveness, the correlation is *positive* (between 0 and $+1.0$). If, as popularity increases, aggressiveness decreases, the correlation is *negative* (between 0 and -1.0). If there is no systematic relationship between aggressiveness and popularity, the correlation is close to 0 (see FIGURE A.2 ▸). A correlation of 0.40 suggests that

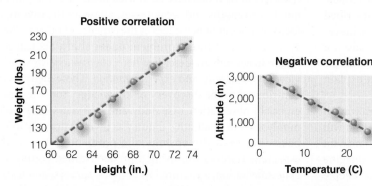

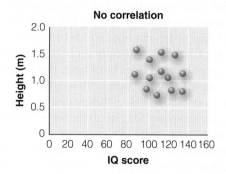

FIGURE A.2 ▸ PATTERNS REFLECTING POSITIVE, NEGATIVE, AND ZERO CORRELATIONS

there is a positive relationship between aggressiveness and popularity, but that aggressiveness cannot be predicted entirely or even predominantly by knowing about a person's popularity.

A strong correlation between two variables shows only that there is an association between them. It does not provide information about causation. Knowing that aggression is negatively correlated with popularity does not necessarily mean that being aggressive causes children to be rejected by peers. It could be that some other factor, such as mistrust of others, accounts for both aggression and peer rejection.

Strengths and Limitations of the Observational Method

Many scholars agree that direct observation is an ideal way to study behavior. It avoids the interpretive issues that are raised when one asks people to report on their behavior, and it allows for the documentation of patterns of behavior that may not have been anticipated by the investigator. For example, in studying patterns of dominance among children, one might assume that hitting is a form of dominance. However, in observing play behavior, one may find that certain kinds of hitting are a type of affectionate interaction rather than a mechanism for achieving dominance. The observational method allows participants' behaviors to guide the researcher's conceptualization. Rather than setting up a specific task or group of questions and having people respond, the observer examines the full range of relevant behaviors and builds an interpretation of the meaning of the events from the patterns that have been observed.

Observational research also has weaknesses. It is often difficult to establish agreement among observers about exactly what occurred. Think about the times that you and a friend have been in the same situation but have entirely different reactions to what is happening or describe it very differently to a third party. Typically, two or more observers' codings of the same situation are compared to determine whether different observers interpreted the same event in the same way. This is called **interobserver reliability**. When interobserver reliability is high, one has confidence that all the observers are describing or coding the events in the same way. When interobserver reliability is low, the researchers must determine why and then correct the differences in observation techniques. This may result in changing the category scheme so that it is easier to link each behavior with a category, or it may result in more training, so that the observers know more precisely how to code each behavior.

Another difficulty with the observational method occurs when so much activity is taking place that it is difficult to select specific behaviors or to code fast enough to keep up with the pace of activity in the setting. The technology of video recording has helped address this problem. A video record can be reviewed over and over again. Several observers can watch a video, stop it, and discuss what they saw. The same events can be observed from several points of view. Video records allow one to track the sequences of interaction, turn taking, and the formation of cycles of interaction among family members, which often occur too subtly or quickly to be captured by direct observation (Heath, Hindmarsh, & Luff, 2010; Johnson, Cowan, & Cowan, 1999). Because of the rich potential for sharing and reusing video files

for different research purposes, the National Science Foundation and the National Institutes of Health have created a web-based video library, Databrary. This resource will preserve recordings relevant for developmental research and encourage their reuse (Adolph, 2016).

Some research focuses on a particular kind of behavior or behavioral sequence, such as helping behavior, peer rejection, or conflict. In naturalistic observation, one cannot be sure that the behavior of interest will take place during the observational period. Finally, some researchers fear that the presence of the observer or the introduction of audio recording, videotaping, or even note taking, may change the nature of the behaviors that take place in the setting. Although there are techniques to limit the impact of the observer on the setting, this is always a concern in direct observation.

Case Study

A **case study** is an in-depth description of a single person, family, social group, or social setting. The purpose of a case study may be to illuminate something very particular and interesting about the person or organization being studied, illustrate a general principle by providing specific details, examine a phenomenon that does not conform to theoretical predictions, or stimulate theory development in an area that has not been investigated (Yin, 2014).

Some case studies document the lives of great individuals. In *Gandhi's Truth*, Erikson (1969) provided a psychosocial analysis of the life of Mahatma Gandhi. Erikson considered Gandhi's childhood, adolescence, and young adulthood as they contributed to his personality, his moral philosophy, and the contradictions between his personal relationships and his role as a powerful social leader.

Case studies can also focus on social groups, families, and organizations. One of Anna Freud's most famous cases described the attachments that developed among a group of orphans who had lived together in a concentration camp during World War II (Freud & Dann, 1951). The study focused on the strong feelings the children had for one another and their strategies for maintaining their sense of connectedness once they were placed in a more normal social environment. The case illustrated a unique phenomenon—the intense emotional attachment of young children to each other—that had not been documented before.

Case studies can be based on a variety of sources of information, including interviews, therapy sessions, prolonged observation, narrative stories, diaries or journals, letters, historical documents, and talks with people who know the subject of the study. The researcher usually spends a great deal of time with the subject of the case, in conversation, observation, and gathering information from documents and informants. In addition to gathering information, the researcher engages in ongoing reflection in order to reach a new depth of insight about the case.

Strengths and Limitations of the Case Study Method

Case studies have the advantage of illustrating the complexity and uniqueness of the subject. Studies carried out with large samples often identify general principles, whereas case studies provide concrete examples of how these principles play out in the lives of specific individuals or groups. Some cases give the details of an experience that is rare and might not be captured in a large-scale study. Sometimes, the case study brings a problem to the attention of researchers, who then pursue it through other methods. Although case studies cannot provide the basis for broad generalizations, they can provide specific examples of instances where a broad generalization does not hold true. Throughout this book, you will find case material that is intended to help you apply concepts from the text to specific examples and to stimulate reflection about links among theory, research, and your own life experiences.

Case studies have been criticized as unscientific. They are obviously not representative of large groups of individuals. Moreover, if the information that provides the basis of the case study is gathered in a biased or subjective way, then the results or conclusions of the study will be of little worth. Of course, this criticism applies to any type of research. Critics argue that there is no reliability in case studies. If different people were writing a case study on the same individual, they might come up with very different views of the events and their significance.

One must have a very clear idea of the study's purpose and a systematic approach to gathering information in order to conduct case studies that meet the standards of scientific observation. At the same time, vividly written, compelling case material has had a consistent impact in stimulating theory and research in the field of development. In some instances, the lucid recounting of case material is more convincing to policymakers than the results of studies based on large, national samples.

Interviews

Many case studies are based on face-to-face interviews. The **interview** method can also be used to gather data from large numbers of individuals or from individuals in clinical settings. Interviews can be highly structured, almost like a verbal survey, or very open ended, allowing the participant to respond freely to general questions. There are at least three common uses of in-depth interviewing (Roulston, 2010). First, the life history or personal narrative allows the researcher to learn about a person's key life experiences and the meaning of those experiences. The researcher's role is to encourage the person being interviewed to cover all the important issues and to foster elaboration and reflection.

Second, through interviews, informants are asked to describe in detail events that occurred when the researcher was not present. This might be a historical event, a natural disaster, or the behaviors of a group to which the researcher does not have access. For example, a researcher may want to interview informants who have been members of a gang about the gang's initiation rites or practices. Third, interviews can be useful in gathering information from a number of people about a similar topic. For example, Harrington and Boardman (2000) interviewed 100 people whom they called pathmakers—people who achieved career success despite growing up in impoverished families and communities.

The success of the interview method depends heavily on the skill of the interviewer. Interviewers are trained to be nonjudgmental as they listen to a participant's responses. They try to create **rapport** with the participant by conveying a feeling of trustworthiness and acceptance. The goal, especially in qualitative

interviewing, is to create a conversational atmosphere where the person feels at ease to talk. In unstructured interviews, the interviewer makes use of this rapport to encourage the participant to say more about a topic and to share thoughts that may be private or personal. Matching the race and gender of the interviewer and the participant being interviewed has been found to help foster rapport and improve the quality of the data that are produced.

The interview method has traditionally been associated with clinical research; however, it is becoming a common method in the study of cognition and language as well. Piaget's structured interview technique (Piaget, 1929) provided a model for the investigation of cognitive development. The researcher who uses this technique asks a child a question (e.g., "Are clouds living or dead?") and then follows up on the child's answer with questions about how the child arrived at his or her conclusion. In other studies, Piaget asked children to solve a problem and then asked them to explain how they arrived at the solution. The child becomes an informant about his or her own conceptual capacities. This approach has been adapted in the study of moral development, interpersonal development, and positive, helping behavior.

Strengths and Limitations of the Interview Method

The interview method has the advantage of allowing individuals to contribute their own views on the topic being studied. They can tell the interviewer what is important to them, why they might choose one alternative over another, or what they think is wrong with the investigator's view of the situation. Interviews have the advantage of expediency when it might be difficult to gain access to a setting for observation or when one wants to gather information from a larger number of participants, rather than observing just a few.

There are also limitations to the interview method. Participants may present themselves in the way they want the interviewer to see them. This is referred to as **self-presentation bias**. Young children's responses are especially vulnerable to influence by the interviewer. By smiling, nodding, frowning, or looking away, the interviewer can deliberately or inadvertently communicate approval or disapproval. There is a fine line between establishing rapport and influencing responses.

Another limitation of interviews is that people may not be aware of all the factors that influence their behaviors or decisions. Thus, in asking people about their lives and why they behave as they do, one is limited by the participants' level of insight into their own situation. As compared to participant observation, relying solely on interviews limits the researcher's access to contextual factors that may influence a person's behavior (Taylor & Bogdan, 1998).

Surveys and Tests

Survey research is a means of collecting specific information from a large number of participants (Fowler, 2013). If people are to respond directly to surveys, they must be able to read and write unless the survey questions are read to them. The survey method is, therefore, most commonly used with participants in middle childhood, adolescence, and adulthood. However, survey information about infants and toddlers is often collected from parents, child care workers, physicians, nurses, and others who are responsible for meeting the needs of young children. Surveys have contributed a great deal to our knowledge about the way adults perceive the behaviors and needs of young children.

Survey methods can be used to collect information about attitudes ("Do you believe teachers should be permitted to use corporal punishment with their students?"), current behaviors and practices ("How many hours per day do you watch television?"), aspirations ("What do you hope to do when you graduate from high school?"), and perceptions ("How well does your mother/father or son/daughter understand your views?").

Survey questions are prepared in a standard form, and the responses are usually coded according to a prearranged set of categories. In well-designed surveys, the questions are stated clearly and offer response choices that are not ambiguous or overlapping. Surveys may be conducted by telephone, through the mail, on the Internet, in classrooms, at work, or in the participants' homes (Fowler, 2013).

Tests are often similar in form to surveys. They consist of groups of questions or problems that the person is expected to answer. Usually, tests are designed to measure a specific ability or characteristic. You are no doubt familiar with the kinds of tests typically given in school. You are presented with a group of items and asked to produce the correct answer or select the correct answer from among several choices. Intelligence and achievement tests are of this nature. A researcher might give these tests along with some other measures in order to learn how intelligence relates to social life, emotions, or self-understanding.

Other tests are designed to measure specific psychological constructs such as creativity, conformity, depression, or extroversion. Some tests are administered to assess whether a person has some form of mental illness, learning disorder, or developmental or physical disability.

Psychological tests must be reliable and valid to be useful. Tests are **reliable** when the results are consistent. A person who takes a reliable test on two consecutive days should get approximately the same score on both days, unless some deliberate training or intervention has been introduced between test sessions. There ought to be a positive correlation (between 0 and +1.0) between the two scores.

Tests are **valid** when they measure what they claim to measure. The people who design the tests have to define what it is they are trying to measure. They also have to provide evidence that their test really measures this construct (Ray, 2011). For example, when designing a test to measure self-esteem, one should first consider, "What is meant by self-esteem?" and "What type of questions or tasks would provide evidence of self-esteem?"

Consider the various tests that have been designed to measure intelligence in infants and very young children. The results of these tests are not very closely related to the results of tests of intelligence given in adolescence and adulthood (Slater, Carrick, Bell, & Roberts, 1999). In other words, infant intelligence tests are not valid measures of intelligence for older children or adults. The infant tests are not really tests of broad, adaptive intelligence, but measures of sensory processing and central nervous system coordination.

Strengths and Limitations of Surveys and Tests

Surveys and tests have advantages that make them widely used in developmental research. They allow the summary and comparison of responses by large groups of respondents. Surveys and tests have been designed to address a wide variety of topics. With a prearranged coding or scoring system, many tests can be administered and evaluated without the extensive training that is usually necessary with observation or interview methods.

This method also has limitations. Some surveys create attitudes where none existed before. This is referred to as the **reactive** nature of surveys. For example, you might ask sixth-grade children questions about their satisfaction with their school curriculum. The students may answer a lot of questions on this topic, even though they had not given much thought to the issue before. Thus, reading the questions and response options on a survey may influence participants to formulate their opinions (Wilson, LaFleur, & Anderson, 1996).

Another problem is the gap between answers to survey questions or scores on tests and actual behavior. Parents may respond to a survey by indicating that they allow their children to participate in family decisions, but when it comes to real family decisions, they may not give their children much voice. Some survey questions are more difficult for some respondents to answer accurately than others. For example, consider the following question: "How often did you go for medical treatment over the past 6 months?" It would be easier for a person who went only once to respond accurately and with confidence than for a person who went six or eight times (Mathiowetz, 1999).

Experimentation

Experimentation is best suited for examining causal relationships. In an **experiment**, some variable or group of variables is systematically manipulated to examine the effect on an outcome. For example, in research on memory among older adults, the complexity of the material and the speed of presentation are varied in order to learn more about how these factors influence the ability of adults to recall information. The factor (or factors) manipulated by the experimenter is called the **independent variable**. The dimension of the participant's responses or reactions that is measured is the **dependent variable**. The research is carried out to determine whether the independent variable or some combination of independent variables can produce a change in the dependent variable.

In some experiments, one group of participants has a certain set of experiences or receives information (usually referred to as a **treatment**) that is not provided to another group. The group that experiences the experimenter's manipulation is called the **experimental group**. The group that does not experience the treatment or manipulation is called the **control group**. Participants are randomly assigned to the treatment and control groups so that differences in their behavior can be attributed to the treatment. For example, in a study of academic performance in human development courses, some students enrolled in a course are randomly assigned to the experimental group, in which they are linked as a study group through email, so they can contact one another, discuss questions from the course, and share their ideas. Other students, who are in the control group, do not receive this

Internet support. Differences in course grades between the experimental and the control groups would be attributed to the Internet intervention.

In other experiments, the behavior of a single group of participants is compared before and after a treatment or across several treatments. Once again, systematic differences in behavior before and after the treatment are attributed to the experimental manipulation. In this case, each participant serves as his or her own control.

Control is the key to successful experimentation. The experimenter exercises control in selecting the participants who must be able to bring equivalent competencies to the situation. The task presentation must be the same for the experimental and the control group. If these conditions are not met, one cannot assume that differences between groups are due to the treatment.

Many studies in human development are **quasi-experimental**. This means that the treatment was not controlled by the experimenter but was the result of some life events (Fife-Shaw, 2012). Suppose we are interested in the impact of unemployment on conflict between married couples. We cannot (nor do we want to) cause some adults to lose their jobs while others remain employed. We can, however, compare couples of about the same age and social class who have experienced unemployment with couples who have not. In these studies, assignment to a treatment occurs as a result of real-world events. One would select participants for the study who are as much alike as possible (e.g. a matched sample), except for their encounters with unemployment. It is the task of the researcher to compare some of the consequences of this treatment—the experience of unemployment—and to address the limitations that are imposed on the results because of how individuals come to be in one group or the other.

Strengths and Limitations of the Experimental Method

The experimental method has the advantage of providing conclusions about causal relationships. If the results suggest that the participants' behavior changes only when something about the experimental situation changes, we can conclude that the manipulation caused the changes. This is a very powerful statement, particularly as we search for explanations for how conditions that occur early in development might influence later outcomes.

Experiments also have limitations. Despite careful control, one cannot entirely rule out factors that can interfere with the impact of the treatment or that influence the respondents in ways that were not anticipated (Ray, 1993). In studies on the impact of Head Start, researchers wanted to compare the cognitive performance of children who were and were not enrolled in Head Start. However, it was impossible to control for the diverse educational experiences of children who were not in Head Start. Some enrolled in other early childhood programs; some enrolled in a different Head Start when an opening came up later in the school year; and some attended family child care with an adult who emphasized educational activities (Cooper & Lanza, 2014). Any factor occurring outside the specific design of the study that influences the participants' responses is a threat to the **internal validity** or meaningfulness of the experiment.

Experiments may also be challenged on the basis of their **external validity**. We cannot be certain how applicable a controlled laboratory situation is to the real world. For example, through studies of infant attachment we have learned that infants and young children do not behave the same way in the presence of their mothers as they do when their mothers are absent. Thus, experimental research conducted with children that does not allow their mothers to be present may produce behaviors that differ in quantity, quality, and sequence from the behavior that would be observed under conditions when the mothers are present.

Experimental studies suggest that event A causes response B. In many domains of development, however, a multifaceted, reciprocal process promotes change. Think about the development of *friendship*. A friendship depends on so many domains and on the fit or lack of fit along each domain for the two people. Friendships may be influenced by physical appearance, abilities, temperaments, intelligence, family background, whether others support the friendship or ridicule it, and so on. Friendships are sustained and promoted by continuous feedback and interaction among the friends rather than by one or two factors that could be said to promote or inhibit friendship. Experiments tend to suggest a unidirectional, causal explanation for behaviors that may more accurately be described using an interactional model.

Advantages and disadvantages of the five research methods are summarized in Table A.1.

Designs for Studying Development

The primary concern of developmental research is to describe and account for patterns of continuity and change over time, including explanations for why individuals who have been exposed to similar life situations differ from one another as they age. This challenging task requires strategies for considering changing individuals in changing environments. Four major research approaches have been created for examining development: *retrospective studies, cross-sectional studies, longitudinal studies,* and *cohort sequential studies.*

Retrospective Studies

Retrospective studies ask participants to report on experiences from an earlier time in their lives. Many early studies of childrearing used parents' recollections of their parenting techniques to evaluate their patterns of child care. Researchers who studied the effects of stress during pregnancy often asked women to recall their emotional state before, during, and after their child was born. Investigators of personality development use retrospective data by asking adolescent or adult subjects to recall important events of their childhood.

This approach produces a record of what a person has retained of past events. We cannot be certain that these events really occurred as they are remembered or, for that matter,

Table A.1   Advantages and Disadvantages of the Methods of Developmental Research

Method	Definition	Advantages	Disadvantages
Observation	Systematic recording of behavior	Documents the variety of ongoing behavior; captures what happens naturally, without intervention	Time consuming: difficult to achieve inter-rater agreement; requires careful training; observer may interfere with what would normally occur; difficult to capture and code full range of ongoing activity
Case Study	In-depth description of a single person, family, or group	Focuses on complexity and unique experiences of individual; permits analysis of unusual cases	Lacks generalizability; conclusions may reflect bias of investigator; hard to replicate
Interviews	Face-to-face interaction in which each person can give a full account of his or her views	Provides complex, first-person account; flexible method; allows access to the other person's own meaning	Vulnerable to investigator bias; self-presentation bias; relies on participant's self-insight
Surveys and Tests	Standard questions adminis- tered to many participants	Permits data collection from large samples; permits group compari- sons of responses in standard form; requires little training; flexible	Wording and way of presenting questions may influence responses; responses may not be closely related to behavior; tests may not be valid for certain groups
Experimentation	Analysis of cause–effects relations; manipulation of some conditions while others are held constant	Permits testing of causal hypotheses; permits isolation and control of specific variables; allows evaluation of treatment effects	Laboratory findings may lack ecological validity; unable to control for all threats to internal valid- ity; focuses on a unidirectional model of causality

whether they occurred at all. Piaget (1951) described a vivid memory from his second year of life:

> I was sitting in my pram, which my nurse was pushing in the Champs Elysées, when a man tried to kidnap me. I was held in by the strap fastened around me while my nurse bravely tried to stand between me and the thief. She received various scratches, and I can still see vaguely those on her face. (Piaget, 1951, p. 188)

Thirteen years later, when Piaget was 15, the nurse joined a religious order. She wrote to his parents and returned a watch they had given her for protecting Jean from the kidnapper. She confessed that she had made up the story, even to the point of scratching her own face. Piaget believed he created the visual memory from the story his parents had told him.

The passage of time may change the significance of past events in a person's memory. As we gain new levels of cognitive complexity or change our attitudes, we reorganize our memo- ries of the past so as to bring them into line with our current level of understanding (Kotre, 1995b). Sometimes, people claim to have recovered memories of past events that have been long forgotten or repressed. It is difficult to determine the accuracy of these memories (Loftus, 1993). They may be entangled with current experiences or with ideas taken from books, movies, or conversations with others. They may be altered by the sugges- tion that something happened that actually did not, or by the suggestion that something did not happen that actually did. Because memory is easily modified by suggestion, its usefulness in uncovering systematic data about the past is limited. How- ever, retrospective data provide insight into how people make sense of their past and the role they give to past experiences in

determining their present way of thinking. Studies that use the technique of life review provide insight into the way adults orga- nize and structure key periods and events from their life history (McAdams et al., 1997).

Cross-Sectional Studies

Studies that compare people of different ages, social backgrounds, or from different school or community settings are called **cross-sectional studies**. Such studies are quite common. Investigators may compare children at different levels of biological maturity or different chronological ages to learn how a particular devel- opmental domain changes with age. The main limitation of the cross-sectional method is that it measures group differences, not patterns of individual change over time. However, these group differences are interpreted to suggest a pattern of development. With respect to studies on cognitive problem solving, the cross- sectional approach tells us that most 12-year-olds are more flex- ible in their reasoning than most 7-year-olds. It does not tell us how the same children actually change from the time they are 7 until they are 12 or how the children who were most flexible at age 7 would perform at age 12 in comparison with those who were the least flexible.

Longitudinal Studies

A **longitudinal study** involves repeated observations of the same participants at different times. The time between observations may be brief, as from immediately after birth to 2 or 3 days after birth. Observations may be repeated over the entire life course, as in Leo Terman's longitudinal study of gifted children (Crosnoe &

Elder, 2004; Holahan, Sears, & Cronbach, 1995; Sears & Barbee, 1978; Terman & Oden, 1947, 1959).

An emerging approach to longitudinal research is called the *intensive longitudinal method*. Using a smartphone, for example, participants can be prompted to respond many times a day, wherever they are. Physiological, psychological, and environmental information can be gathered repeatedly to produce a personalized network of data that can create a portrait of a person's fluctuating activities, moods, or stress levels. The results of this type of intensive longitudinal data can be useful in identifying subtle patterns of individual stability or change such as emotional state fluctuations or the relationship of activity and mood (Drew, 2016).

Longitudinal studies have the advantage of tracking the course of development. We can discover how certain characteristics of children in infancy or toddlerhood relate to those same characteristics when the individuals reach adolescence or adulthood. We can learn whether certain qualities of childhood, such as intelligence or sociability , are related to overall social adjustment or life satisfaction in later years. Longitudinal studies permit us to trace intra-individual patterns over time—that is, how individuals change, for example, from the use of one-word expressions to two-word phrases. They also allow us to monitor changes in groups, for example, by comparing adults who have children in their early 20s to those who remain childfree and looking at their economic or occupational attainment by midlife (Schaie, 1994).

Longitudinal studies may be difficult to complete, especially if they are intended to cover a significant time period, such as the years from childhood to adulthood. Over this span of time, participants may drop out of the study, the investigators may lose funding or interest in the project, or the methods may become outdated. Questions that once seemed important may no longer be seen as vital. Another limitation is that repeated interactions with the participants may influence their behaviors. Participation in the study could itself become a factor in their development. One of the greatest limitations of longitudinal studies is that they focus on only one generation or cohort of participants. Imagine studying the academic achievement and occupational attainment of a group of children born in 1980. Historical and social factors that may influence the course of this group's development will be inextricably intertwined in the observations. One cannot tell if people growing up at other times in history would exhibit the pattern of changes that characterize this particular group.

Cohort Sequential Studies

A **cohort sequential design** combines the cross-sectional and longitudinal approaches into one method of study (Prinzie & Onghena, 2005; Schaie, 1965, 1992). Groups of participants, called *cohorts*, are selected because they are a certain number of years apart in age. For example, imagine a study that begins with three groups of adolescents who are 11, 14, and 17, respectively. Every 3 years, these groups would be interviewed until the 11-year-olds have turned 17. Every 3 years, a new group of 11-year-olds would be added to the study. This combination of a longitudinal and cross-sectional design is a powerful developmental research

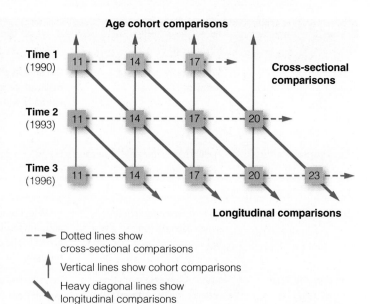

--→ Dotted lines show cross-sectional comparisons

↑ Vertical lines show cohort comparisons

↘ Heavy diagonal lines show longitudinal comparisons

FIGURE A.3 ▶ THE COHORT SEQUENTIAL DESIGN

method. It produces immediate cross-sectional data, longitudinal data after 3 and 6 years, and a comparison of children who were the same age (11, 14, or 17) at three different times. This third comparison allows one to identify social and historical factors that may influence age-related differences. This comparison also provides control for the possible impact of repeated measurement on the participants.

Comparisons of cohorts over time offers a way of controlling for the many historical factors—such as access to schooling, health, medical treatment, and nutrition—that might influence performance by separating these factors from age-related changes. The elements of a cohort sequential design are shown in FIGURE A.3.▶ One drawback to the cohort sequential design is that data analysis requires more complex techniques in which time of response and frequency of response can both be included.

Evaluating Existing Research

In addition to collecting new data, considerable scholarly effort is directed to reviewing and evaluating existing research. As a student, you may be asked to review research findings on a topic of interest to you. You will probably rely on online databases to find books, book chapters, and journal articles relevant to your topic. These sources provide information from published sources, many of which have undergone a **peer review** process. This means that other professionals have read and critically evaluated the materials before they were published. You may also find information using Internet search engines. Internet resources are of a much more varied nature, including Web pages from professionals, reports of research institutes and centers, government documents, and blogs from teachers, students, and others who have opinions on the topic. The challenge in reviewing all this information is to apply a standard for judging its quality and validity as you formulate your own analysis of the topic.

Most researchers use this method of reading and reviewing the research of others to keep well informed about the research in their subject area. They analyze the work of others to generate new questions and to formulate well-founded conclusions about issues in their field of specialization. The study, analysis, and evaluation of current research literature constitute special skills in their own right (Fink, 2013).

The evaluation of published research poses its own challenges. Recent reports of research fraud alert us to the hazards of relying too heavily on the results of any one specific study. For example, the Dutch researcher, Diederik Stapel was found to have made up the data for 55 published studies (Cossins, 2012). The scientific process argues for relying on replications to ensure that a research finding is credible. However, relatively few published articles are replications (Pashler & Wagenmakers, 2012). Research journals tend to have a bias toward publishing novel, unexpected, and possibly media-noteworthy results. This may increase the tendency of scholars to focus their research on the unexpected or surprising results rather than the replication of prior studies. Many journals will not publish "null findings." In other words, studies, including replications, that do not find statistically significant results are unlikely to be published (Ferguson & Heene, 2012; Shea, 2011). Recent efforts by scientific associations have encouraged the publication of replications in order to build a more trustworthy knowledge base.

The approaches to statistical analyses of data have become so complicated that only a small group of experts can really evaluate whether the techniques have been used properly. Critics have suggested that researchers should be required to state the analytic technique they plan to use before conducting the research in order to prevent post-hoc manipulations that disguise the basic results of the research (Wagenmakers, Wetzels, Bosboom, Van der Maas, & Kievit, 2012).

Increasingly, websites provide information for researchers and report results of research. Because of the open access nature of the Web, there is no guarantee about the quality or validity of information. Using information from the Web requires a degree of care and caution over and above that used in the review of peer-reviewed journals. In reading about research from a website, one should ask the same questions about the research process that one would ask of a peer-reviewed journal article. In addition, the following issues need to be considered when evaluating Web-based information: the authority and **credibility** of the authors of the Web-based information; the scope, relevance, and timeliness of the information; and the potential **bias** of the author's point of view.

Authority and Credibility

- Who publishes the website?
- Who is the author(s) of the website?
- What makes the author an authority on this subject?
- Does the author cite his/her experience/credentials?
- Does the website contain footnotes or references?
- If so, does material taken from other sources appear to be fully credited?

Scope, Relevance, and Timeliness

- Who is the intended audience? (general, specialized, scholars)
- What is the level of the material? (basic, advanced)
- Is new research being reported or is the author reviewing/summarizing previously conducted research?
- What time period is covered?
- How recently has the website been updated?

Bias and Accuracy

- How is the information presented? (fact, opinion, propaganda, etc.)
- If presented as fact, is it accurate?
- Is there a bias? (cultural, political, religious, etc.)
- If so, is the bias clearly stated or acknowledged by the authors?

One strategy in making use of Web-based information is to look for several sources on the same topic.

There are some wonderful resources of online information. You have come across many of them cited as references throughout this book. All branches of the federal government have websites with information about policies, programs, and research reports. The U.S. Census Bureau publishes extensive reports on a range of topics of interest in human development including population trends, household characteristics, labor market trends, and health. Medical information is available from the National Institutes of Health as well as from ongoing medical research projects that provide results of their research online. The Bureau of Labor Statistics provides information on employment, occupational opportunities, and career trends. The Administration on Aging is a rich resource for programs, services, and surveys of older adults. Advocacy groups, such as the National Center for Children in Poverty, provide up-to-date information about the impact of policies or programs.

Beyond the United States, there are websites from other countries and sources about international trends such as the World Health Organization. The United Nations monitors international trends such as child poverty, women's rights, and access to education. With all this information available, the research process is at once more open, more accessible, and more vulnerable to viral mischief, just like an election. The effectiveness of your searches will depend on the way you define the topic of interest, your patience in visiting a variety of sources, and your critical evaluation of the quality of information you uncover.

Ethics

Ethics refers to principles of conduct that are founded on a society's moral code. In conducting research with living beings, and especially with children, social scientists continually confront ethical questions. Researchers are obligated to maintain humane, morally acceptable treatment of all living study participants.

Three reports have influenced the conceptualization of ethical guidelines for research with human participants: The Declaration of Helsinki (1964), the Belmont Report (1979), and the International Ethical Guidelines for Biomedical Research Involving Human Subjects (1993). Five key dimensions emerged from these three documents that provide a framework for ethical medical and behavioral research (Presidential Commission for the Study of Bioethical Issues, 2015; Yan & Munir, 2004):

1. Human rights: The fundamental right for human well-being where each can achieve his/her full potential.
2. Validity: Accuracy and closeness to the stated scientific goals.
3. Distributive justice: The fair distribution of research benefits and risks.
4. Beneficence/nonmaleficence: The obligation to maximize benefits and minimize risks.
5. Autonomy: The permission granted by subjects to allow research.

The American Psychological Association has published a guide for researchers entitled *Ethics in Research with Human Participants* (American Psychological Association, 2002; Sales & Folkman, 2000). This guide provides advice to researchers about how to manage all aspects of the research process in order to maintain the trust and safety of participants. Participants have a right to know how their **privacy** will be preserved and what steps will be taken to ensure that responses or behaviors observed in the research will remain **confidential**. The guidelines require that participants be told about all aspects of the research that may influence their decision to participate. This is referred to as **informed consent**. Individuals must not be coerced into participating in a research project, and their refusal to participate should have no negative consequences. If children in a classroom decide that they do not want to participate in a research project, or if their parents do not give permission for them to participate, they should not be shamed, given an undesirable alternate assignment, or given a lower grade.

Researchers must protect participants from unnecessary painful physical and emotional experiences, including shame, failure, and social rejection. Researchers must weigh the benefits of the new information they may discover in a particular study against the potential risks or harm to the participants. Two questions must guide the researcher's decisions:

1. How would you feel if you or one of your family members were a participant in this study?
2. Can the problem be studied in ways that do not involve pain, deception, or emotional or physical stress?

These questions are especially relevant for studies involving young children where it may not be easy to know how stressful or anxiety-provoking an experimental procedure is. For some children, just going into the laboratory setting may be stressful. For some adolescents, being observed in a decision-making situation with peers may be stressful. For some couples, being asked to resolve a conflict in the presence of observers may be anxiety-provoking. Participants must be aware of the fact that they are free to withdraw from the study at any time. They are entitled to a full explanation of the study once it has been completed. When the participants are children, their parents must be given this information and must approve their children's participation.

In thinking about research in the field of human development, certain of the basic principles may conflict. For example, on the one hand, children and those with significant developmental disabilities may not be able to fully understand the nature of the research in order to provide informed consent to participate. As a result, decisions may be made to eliminate these groups from research or to impose strict limitations on their participation in order to protect them from harm. On the other hand, these vulnerable populations may be the ones most likely to benefit from research. By preventing research that focuses on these populations, they may be less likely to benefit from new practices, interventions, or basic knowledge (Yan & Munir, 2012).

When children under the age of 18 are involved as research participants, it is typically the practice to require a parent or guardian to provide consent. However, researchers need to be sensitive to cultural patterns and practices regarding parental authority and community responsibility for children. In some Native American tribes, the tribal leader has authority to make decisions about whether children can be included in research. In some African American families, grandparents, aunts, uncles, or older siblings may be the primary decision makers even if they are not legal guardians. They need to be consulted concerning a child's participation in research. In these examples, a person who is responsible for the child's protection may not be the child's legal guardian (Fisher et al., 2002).

Researchers are obligated to stipulate **conflicts of interest** and to avoid them wherever possible. Conflict of interest can arise when a researcher has a financial or personal investment that might influence his or her judgment. Since publication of research is an expectation for faculty promotion and tenure in most universities, faculty members are typically highly motivated to conduct research that can be published. They may fail to give people an accurate description of the time, effort, or risks of participation involved in their study when recruiting participants. They may be tempted to design studies in which recruitment of participants is most easily and quickly accomplished.

In addition to violations of ethical practices regarding the treatment of human participants, some researchers engage in questionable practices that undermine the credibility of their work and violate the principles that ensure accuracy of scientific knowledge. These practices include **plagiarism**, which involves the use of written material by others without providing credit or citation of their work in the application for funding or in a written report; failure to cite studies that do not confirm the author's hypotheses; falsification by modifying or deleting data that alter the statistical significance of the findings; or failing to give credit to students or colleagues who contributed in important ways to the design, implementation, or written report of the research (John, Loewenstein, & Prelec, 2010; Rapp, 2016).

Each university has an **institutional review** process that applies guidelines for the ethical conduct of research to proposals being prepared by faculty and students. Before a study can begin, the institutional review board considers the design of the study and its potential impact on participants and the potential conflicts of interest identified by the investigators. The investigators have to commit to a procedure of informed consent, so that participants are aware of the nature of the research, potential risks, conditions of confidentiality, and their freedom to withdraw from the study at any time if they choose. Approval for the research is typically given for 1 year. The institutional review process includes a mechanism for ongoing evaluation of research that takes place over longer periods of time. Most schools, child care centers, hospitals, nursing homes, and other treatment centers have their own review procedures for determining whether they will permit research to be carried out with the people in their programs. Ethical guidelines are important in order to prevent exploitation of participants and to prevent unintended negative consequences of participation in research. In cases when the results of published research reports have been challenged and misconduct has been proven, the researcher may be required to withdraw prior research from publication sites.

Glossary

abortion Termination of a pregnancy before the fetus is capable of surviving outside the uterus.

accommodation (1) In Piaget's theory of cognitive development, the process of changing existing schemes in order to account for novel elements in the object or the event. (2) In vision, changes in the curvature of the lens in response to the distance of the stimulus.

active engagement Continuing to be sociable and involved in doing things as you get older.

active euthanasia Activities—such as mercy killing or physician-assisted suicide—that are designed to end a person's life, often to end a person's suffering.

activities of daily living (ADLs) Basic types of self-care that are required to function independently.

adaptation (1) In evolutionary theory, the total process of change in response to environmental conditions. (2) In Piaget's theory of cognitive development, a process of gradually modifying existing schemes and operations in order to take into account changes or discrepancies between what is known and what is being experienced.

adaptive leadership A leadership style that is required when an organization faces new conditions or complex problems that cannot be solved with the current use of technologies or techniques. Leaders help frame new ways of defining problems and engaging workers, consumers, or clients in a search for solutions.

adaptive self-organization The process by which an open system retains its essential identity when confronted with new and constant environmental conditions. It creates new substructures, revises the relationships among components, and establishes new, higher levels of organization that coordinate existing substructures.

adaptive self-regulation Adjustments made by an operating system in which feedback mechanisms identify and respond to environmental changes in order to maintain and enhance the functioning of the system.

adequacy versus vulnerability A two-dimensional spectrum of cultural attitudes toward pregnant women. Adequacy is the idea that pregnancy is a sign of sexual prowess and a means of access to social status. Vulnerability is the idea that

child-making is exhausting, pregnant women are vulnerable, and women grow more frail with each pregnancy. Combined with solicitude versus shame, these attitudes create a matrix within which the birth culture of any society or subculture can be located.

adolescent pregnancy When a woman becomes pregnant under age 19.

adoption An alternative to biological reproduction for those who believe that there are already enough children who need families and for those who have tried alternative reproductive technologies to no avail.

advance directive A document that allows people to say what type of care they want to receive in case they cannot speak for themselves.

advocate (plural: advocates) A person who pleads another's cause.

affect (plural: affects) Emotion, feeling, or mood.

affiliative value The values placed on helping or pleasing others, reflected in the amount of time spent in and the degree of satisfaction achieved from such actions.

age changes Changes that are due to the natural aging process.

age differences In the comparison of age groups, differences between populations that may be due to development, aging, or a variety of cohort-related opportunities and experiences.

age-graded expectations Views held within societies about what would be appropriate behavior at a given time in life.

ageism A devaluation of older adults by the social community.

agency Viewing the self as the originator of action.

aggressive-rejected A path to peer rejection in which children are aggressive and attribute hostile intentions to others.

aggressive-withdrawn A path to peer rejection in which children are both aggressive and self-conscious.

alcohol and drug use The illegal use of alcohol and/or drugs.

alienation Withdrawal or separation of people or their affections from an object or position of former attachment.

allele (plural: alleles) The alternate state of a gene at a given locus.

Alzheimer's disease The most common form of chronic organic brain syndrome,

involving gradual brain failure over a period of 7 to 10 years.

ambiguous loss A condition in which death is uncertain because there is no verification of death, as when a soldier is missing in action and there is no body, or when a person is physically present but unable to participate in any meaningful way in interactions with others.

amniocentesis The surgical insertion of a hollow needle through the abdominal wall and into the uterus of a pregnant woman to obtain fluid for the determination of sex or chromosomal abnormality of the fetus.

amniotic sac A thin membrane forming a closed sac around the embryo that contains a fluid in which the embryo is immersed.

anal stage In psychosexual theory, a period of life in which the anus is the most sexualized body part, typically during the second year of life.

androgens General term for male sex hormones, the most prevalent of which is testosterone.

androgyny The capacity to express both masculine and feminine characteristics as the situation demands.

anomaly Irregularity, something that is inconsistent with the normal condition; abnormality.

anorexia nervosa An emotional disorder in which the person loses the ability to regulate eating behavior; the person is obsessed with a fear of being overweight and avoids food or becomes nauseated after eating.

Apgar scoring method Assessment method of the newborn based on heart rate, respiration, muscle tone, response to stimulation, and skin color.

aphasia A language impairment involving the loss of ability to understand or use speech.

applied behavioral analysis An intervention that uses systematic operant-conditioning strategies to assist people who have severe behavior problems, including aggressive disorders and autism.

appraisal In coping, an estimate of the nature, quality, and importance of the stressors in a situation.

artificial insemination Injection of donor sperm into a woman's vagina to promote conception.

assimilation In Piaget's theory of cognitive development, the process of incorporating objects or events into existing schemes.

assisted living Housing or living arrangements for the elderly, infirm, or disabled, in which housekeeping, meals, medical care, and other assistance is available to residents as needed.

assisted reproductive technology (ART) (plural: assisted reproductive technologies) Includes all fertility treatments in which both eggs and sperm are handled. In general, ART procedures involve surgically removing eggs from a woman's ovaries, combining them with sperm in the laboratory, and returning them to the woman's body or donating them to another woman.

assumption (plural: assumptions) A fact, statement, or premise that is considered true and that guides the underlying logic of a theory.

attachment The tendency to remain close to a familiar individual who is ready and willing to give care, comfort, and aid in time of need.

attachment behavior system A complex set of reflexes and signaling behaviors that inspire caregiving and protective responses in adults; these responses shape a baby's expectations and help create an image of the parent in the child's mind.

attachment scheme A set of internal mental representations that an infant has of the anticipated responses of a caregiver.

attention An infant's ability to focus on an object or task as well as to shift or redirect focus from one object to another.

attractiveness Having a pleasing or handsome appearance that may play a role in the arousal of romantic or sexual feelings.

auditory acuity The ability to recognize sounds of varying pitch and loudness.

autonomous morality A relatively mature moral perspective in which rules are viewed as a product of cooperative agreements.

autonomy The ability to behave independently, to do things on one's own.

autosomal Being or pertaining to a chromosome other than a sex chromosome.

avoidance conditioning A kind of learning in which specific stimuli are identified as painful or unpleasant and are therefore avoided.

avoidant attachment A form of insecure attachment in which infants avoid contact with their mothers during the reunion segment of the strange situations or ignore their mothers' efforts to interact. At home, these babies cry a lot, they are not readily soothed by contact with the caregiver, and yet they are quite distressed by separations.

babbling The vocal sounds of infants after about the sixth week that are initially characterized by sounds used in many languages and then begin to reflect the sounds and intonation infants are most likely to hear in their caregivers' speech.

behavioral inhibition A combination of fearfulness, a low threshold for arousal in the presence of novel or unusual stimuli, and general cautiousness.

behavioral slowing Age-related delay in the speed of response to stimuli.

bereavement The long-term process of adjustment to the death of a loved one that is more all-encompassing than grief and is commonly accompanied by physical symptoms, role loss, and a variety of intense emotions, including anger, sorrow, anxiety, and depression.

bias In research, a systematic error or distortion introduced by selecting or encouraging one outcome over others; a tendency to create conditions or interpret results in such a way as to confirm a previously held belief.

bidirectional In developmental systems theory, the back-and-forth regulation of the person and the environment over time.

bilingualism The ability to speak two languages fluently.

binge drinking Quickly consuming five or more drinks in a row.

biological system Includes all those processes necessary for the physical functioning of the organism. Sensory capacities, motor responses, and the workings of the respiratory, endocrine, and circulatory systems are all biological processes.

biopsychosocial Of or pertaining to the interaction among biological, social, and psychological factors.

birth culture A culture's beliefs, values, and guidelines for behavior regarding pregnancy and childbirth.

blended families A family that includes children from the previous marriage of one or both of the marital partners.

body dissatisfaction Body image disturbances; the state of feeling sad or angry at the way one's body looks.

boundaries In family systems theory, what determines who is considered to be a family member and who is an outsider. They influence the way information, support, and validation of the family unit are sought and the way new members are admitted into the family.

bulimia nervosa A habitual disturbance in eating behavior, mostly affecting young women of normal weight which is characterized by frequent episodes of grossly excessive food intake followed by self-induced vomiting to prevent weight gain.

cardiopulmonary death A set of criteria for death that includes lack of a heartbeat and lack of respiration.

care The commitment to be concerned.

career A period of time spent in a particular occupation or profession, often involving transitions, and a trajectory from one phase to another.

career choice A choice of occupation that will influence one's personal financial resources and opportunities.

career decision making A process which takes place at various points in one's occupational life that involves reviewing alternatives and assimilating factors such as social and historical contexts, socioeconomic factors, individual talents, identity development and experience into work-related decisions.

career decision-making self-efficacy The state of confidence about being able to accurately assess one's abilities, gather relevant information, formulate appropriate goals, make plans to achieve those goals, and solve the problems that pose barriers to the achievement of goals.

career indecision The inability to choose an occupation; common in later adolescence due to the complexity of the work world.

career maturity The stage at which a person has developed decision-making strategies and the self-insight that permit a realistic career choice.

career stagnation A lack of advancement or growth in one's occupational path; a sense of disillusion about the meaning or value of one's work.

caregiving The nurturing responses of the caregiver that form a corresponding behavioral system we often refer to as parenting.

caring Displaying kindness and concern for others.

caring orientation Moral decision making based on one's responsibility for others and feelings of connection to them.

case study An in-depth description of a single person, family, social group, or social setting.

categorical identification Self-understanding that relies on the categories one fits into, such as physical characteristics and religion.

categorization The process of arranging, classifying, or describing by labeling or naming.

causality The relation between a cause and an effect.

causal schemes The capacity to anticipate that certain actions will have specific consequences.

cell differentiation A process whereby cells take on specialized structures related to their function.

cell nucleus The part of the cell that contains the genetic material essential to reproduction and protein synthesis.

central process The dominant context or mechanism through which the psychosocial crisis is resolved.

cervix The narrow lower end of the uterus which forms the beginning of the birth canal.

cesarean section A procedure that removes a baby from its mother surgically through an incision in the uterine wall when a spontaneous vaginal delivery would be dangerous to the mother or the newborn.

childbearing Related to the process of having babies.

child care The wide diversity of arrangements that provide for the physical, emotional, social, nutritional and financial needs of children.

choice phase In Tiedeman's career decision model, the phase when the person decides which action alternative to follow. The decision is solidified in the person's mind as he or she elaborates the reasons why the decision is beneficial. There is a sense of relief and optimism as the person develops a commitment to executing the decision.

chromosomal disorders A disorder or birth defect that is linked to a specific chromosomal abnormality.

chromosome (plural: chromosomes) One of the rod-like bodies in a cell nucleus that contains genetic material and that divides when the cell divides. In humans, there are 23 pairs of chromosomes.

chronic illnesses Long-lasting, ongoing illnesses.

chronically depressed Experiencing depression over a long period of time.

clarification phase In Tiedeman's career decision model, the phase when the person more fully understands the consequences of his or her commitment to the decision that has been made. He or she plans definite steps to take and may actually take them or may delay them until a more appropriate time. The self-image is prepared to be modified by the decision.

classification The action of grouping objects according to some specific characteristics they have in common, including all objects that show the characteristic and none that do not.

climacteric The period of menopause for women and a parallel period of reduced reproductive competence for men.

clinical samples Populations who are or have been treated for a problem, or who are waiting to be treated.

clique (plural: cliques) A small friendship group of 5 to 10 people.

close friends People who play together, like the same activities, share common interests, enjoy each other's company, and count on each other for help.

code switching Switching from one language to another as the conversational situation demands.

codominance A condition in which both alleles of a specific gene contribute to the characteristic that is expressed, as in AB blood type.

coercive escalation A style of interaction in which the probability that a negative remark will be followed by another negative remark increases as the chain of communication gets longer and longer.

cognition The capacity for knowing, organizing perceptions, and problem solving.

cognitive competencies A person's knowledge, skills, and abilities.

cognitive functioning A very broad term that encompasses the range of cognitive abilities.

cognitive map An internal mental representation of the environment.

cognitive restructuring A process that helps people cope with social anxiety by identifying thoughts that increase their strong emotions such as anger, anxiety, or sadness, challenge the accuracy of those thoughts, and replace them with interpretations that are more realistic and less disruptive to adaptive behavior.

cognitive unconscious The range of mental structures and processes that operate outside awareness but play a significant role in conscious thought and action.

cohabitation Two or more people living together, with or without the intention of marriage.

cohort In research design, a group of individuals who are studied during the same time period. In life course analysis, a cohort is a group of people who are roughly the same age during a particular historical period.

cohort sequential design See cohort sequential study.

cohort sequential study A research design that combines cross-sectional and longitudinal methods. Cohorts consist of participants in a certain age group. Different cohorts are studied at different times. New cohorts of younger groups are added in successive data collections to replace those who have grown older. This design allows the analysis of age differences, changes over time, and the effects of social and historical factors.

collective efficacy A strong sense of social cohesion with a high level of informal social control in a community.

collectivism Worldview in which social behavior is guided largely by the shared goals of a family, tribe, work group, or other collective.

combinatorial skills The ability to perform mathematical operations, including addition, subtraction, and multiplication. These skills are acquired during the stage of concrete operational thought.

commitment Consists of a demonstration of personal involvement in the areas of occupational choice, religion, and political ideology.

common bond Interpersonal ties that provide feelings of acceptance and emotional support.

common identity Shared roles involving pressure to comply with group expectations.

communal norm A family science theory that suggests each person pays close attention to their partner's needs and acts in ways that will support the partner's welfare. In a communal relationship, each partner tries to meet the needs of the other within reason.

communication The act or process of using words, sounds, signs, or behaviors to express or exchange information or to express your ideas, thoughts, feelings, to someone else.

communication repairs Periods of recovery in normal mother–infant interactions that follow periods of mismatch so that infants and mothers cycle again through points of coordination in their interactions.

communicative competence The ability to use all the aspects of language in one's culture, such as systems of meaning, rules of sentence formation, and adjustments for the social setting.

communion The commitment to and consideration for the well-being of others.

community-based long-term health care A component of the Medicare program which provides medical and social services to those who are chronically ill and eligible for institutionalization but who, nevertheless, live in the community.

comparative assessments Self-understanding that relies on comparisons of oneself with social norms and standards or of oneself with specific other people.

competence The exercise of skill and intelligence in the completion of tasks; the sense that one is capable of exercising mastery over one's environment.

competence motivation The desire to exercise mastery by effectively manipulating objects or social interactions.

competition A contest between rivals.

complicated grief Persistent signs of bereavement that impair functioning including intense sorrow or inability to think about anything other than the loss after more than six months following the loss or death of a loved one.

compulsions Repetitive ritualized actions that serve as mechanisms for controlling anxiety.

compulsive sexual behavior A compulsive need to relieve anxiety through sex.

computational skills Comprehending and using numbers in the arithmetic processes of addition, subtraction, multiplication, and division.

concrete operational thought In Piaget's theory, a stage of cognitive development in which rules of logic can be applied to observable or manipulable physical relations.

confidence A conscious trust in oneself and in the meaningfulness of life.

confidential Private.

conflict of interest Something that may influence a researcher's judgment, such as when a researcher has a financial or personal investment in a study.

conformity Behavior, such as dress, talk, or jokes, that is the same as the behavior of most other people in a particular group.

congruence In a romantic or marital relationship, the state in which the partners are similar or agree in how they approach conflict.

conscientiousness A personality dimension associated with doing what is right and doing one's work or duty well.

conscious processes The mental capacities that contribute to awareness of one's immediate surroundings as well as one's thoughts, feelings, and actions. Conscious processes are under the control of the person.

conservation The concept that physical changes do not alter the mass, weight, number, or volume of matter. This concept is acquired during the concrete operational stage of cognitive development.

conservation of number Understanding that certain physical transformations will not alter the number of units in a set.

constructivist perspective The view that gender differences are a product of particular interactions that have a socially agreed-upon, gender-related meaning. In this view, the specific behaviors that are described as masculine or feminine depend largely on the situation, including expectations that people will behave in gender appropriate ways.

contactful A mode or style of interaction that is open to the other person's point of view and that also clearly expresses the speaker's own position.

contactful interactions Interactions that are open to the other's point of view and clearly express the speaker's point of view.

contexts of development The interrelated conditions in which development occurs.

Family, culture, and ethnic group are three of the major contexts that have an effect on development. Work organizations, community settings, child care programs, schools, religious groups, community clubs, athletic teams, cities, counties, states, and nations may also have influence. Economic and historical factors such as war, political revolution, famine, or economic collapse are additional factors that have been shown to affect development.

contextual dissonance The difference between the characteristics of the primary childrearing and home environment and other environments in which the child participates.

contextualization of learning Offering instruction in ways that first draw of a child's existing experiences, knowledge, and concepts and then expand them in new directions.

continuing care retirement community A residential setting offering housing and medical, preventive health, and social services to residents who are well at the time they enter the community.

continuity A condition that characterizes a culture when a child is given information and responsibilities that apply directly to his or her adult behavior.

contraception Deliberate prevention of conception, impregnation, or the spread of disease through sexual behaviors.

control group The participants in an experiment who do not experience the manipulation or treatment and whose responses or reactions are compared with those of participants who are treated actively to determine the effects of the manipulation.

controlling interactions Interactions in which one person expresses his or her point of view and does not take the other person's point of view into consideration.

conventional level Stage II of Kohlberg's moral reasoning theory which reflects a concern about the maintenance of the existing rules and laws and a respect for legitimate authority.

conventional morality A stage of moral reasoning described by Kohlberg in which right and wrong are closely associated with the rules created by legitimate authorities, including parents, teachers, or political leaders.

cooperation Working or acting together for a common purpose or benefit.

coordination Refers to two related characteristics of interaction—matching and synchrony.

coparenting A respectful relationship in which parents who are not living together encourage active involvement with their children.

coping Active efforts to respond to stress. Coping includes gathering new information, maintaining control over one's emotions, and preserving freedom of movement.

core pathologies Destructive forces that result from severe, negative resolutions of the psychosocial crises.

correlation A measure of the strength and direction of the relationship among variables.

cosmic transcendence Feelings of cosmic communion with the spirit of the universe and a redefinition of time, space, life, and death.

couvade A ritual in which an expectant father takes to his bed and observes specific taboos during the period shortly before birth.

creativity The ability to abandon old forms or patterns of doing things and to think in new ways.

credibility The quality of being accepted as true, real, or honest; having acknowledged expertise in a field.

crisis A dramatic emotional or circumstantial upheaval in a person's life. In psychosocial theory, this often refers to a normal set of stresses and strains rather than to an extraordinary set of events, and it consists of a period of role experimentation and active decision making among alternative choices.

critical period A time of maximum sensitivity to or readiness for the development of a particular skill or behavior pattern.

cross-sectional study (plural: cross-sectional studies) A research design in which the behavior of individuals of different ages, social backgrounds, or environmental settings is measured once to acquire information about the effects of these differences.

crowd (plural: crowds) A large group that is usually recognized by a few predominant characteristics, such as the "preppies," the "jocks," or the "druggies."

crystallization phase In Tiedeman's career decision model, the phase when the person becomes more aware of the alternatives for action and their consequences. Conflicts among alternatives are recognized, and some alternatives are discarded. The person develops a strategy for making the decision, in part by weighing the costs and benefits of each alternative.

crystallized intelligence (Gc) Skills and information that are acquired through education and socialization.

cultural determinism The theoretical concept that culture shapes individual experience.

cultural pathways   Adults in each culture have values and goals for themselves and for their children that shape and organize the socialization process and activities of daily life.

cultural relativism   Morality is viewed as a system of rules that are agreed upon in order to preserve human rights and social order. These rules are understood as having been created in cultural and historical contexts, and can be altered as the norms of the community change.

cultural tools   Symbol systems such as language of one's society that permit individuals to alter their environments and guide, regulate, and redefine themselves.

culture   Refers to the socially standardized ways of thinking, feeling, and acting that are shared by members of a society.

culture carriers   People, such as parents, teachers, religious leaders, and elders, who use strategies to transmit critical practices and values.

cumulative relation   In heredity, when the allelic states of a gene in a single pair of chromosomes combine to influence a trait.

cyberbullying   The use of electronic media to send threatening, intimidating, or humiliating messages.

death anxiety   Personal fear and worry about death.

decentering   Gaining some objectivity over one's own point of view; reducing the dominance of one's subjective perspective in the interpretation of events.

defense mechanism   A technique, usually unconscious, that attempts to alleviate the anxiety caused by the conflicting desires of the id and the superego in relation to impulses (e.g., repression, denial, projection).

degree of suffering   Amount or intensity of pain and other symptoms, including shortness of breath, inability to eat, and limited mobility, that a person experiences at the end of life.

delay of gratification   The exertion of willpower in order to resist the strong immediate pull or temptation of something desirable.

delinquency   Crimes for which an adult could be prosecuted when committed by an adolescent, and status offenses which are illegal for adolescents, such as underage drinking.

demand-withdrawal pattern   A pattern of communication in which one member of a marital relationship (the demander) nags, criticizes, and makes demands of the other to change, while the partner (the withdrawer) avoids confrontation, becomes silent, and withdraws.

dementia   Deterioration of intellectual faculties, such as memory, concentration, and judgment, sometimes accompanied by emotional disturbance and personality changes. Dementia is caused by organic damage to the brain (as in Alzheimer's disease), head trauma, metabolic disorders, or the presence of a tumor.

dependency   In the study of aging, an assessment of difficulties in the activities of daily living usually required to function independently. Beyond very basic types of self-care, an expanded notion of dependency refers to difficulties in managing instrumental activities of daily living.

dependent variable   A factor that is defined by a participants responses or reactions and that may or may not be affected by the experimenter's manipulation of the independent variable.

depressed mood   Refers to feelings of sadness, a loss of hope, a sense of being overwhelmed by the demands of the world, and general unhappiness.

depression   A state of feeling sad, often accompanied by feelings of low personal worth and withdrawal from relations with others.

depressive syndrome   This term refers to a constellation of behaviors and emotions that occur together. The syndrome usually includes complaints about feeling depressed, anxious, fearful, worried, guilty, and worthless.

deselection   The process in which an adolescent begins to differ from his or her friends on important behaviors or values, which usually causes the relationship to drift apart.

despair   Feeling a loss of all hope and confidence.

developmental change   Patterns of growth and reorganization.

developmental stage   A period of life dominated by a particular quality of thinking or a particular mode of social relationships. The notion of stages suggests qualitative changes in competence at each phase of development.

developmental systems theory   This perspective emphasizes the ongoing interaction and integration across many levels of the human organism from the genetic to the behavioral level, within the nested contexts of the person, family, community, and culture, to consider both continuity and change over individual and historical time.

developmental task   A set of skills or competencies acquired at a specific stage of development.

developmental viability   A point at which a fetus may survive outside the uterus.

differentiation   The extent to which a social system encourages closeness while supporting the expression of differences.

diffidence   The inability to act due to overwhelming self-doubt.

dilation   In childbirth, the gradual enlargement of the woman's cervix.

disability   An umbrella term that includes a wide variety of possible functional challenges.

disclosure   Sharing personal information with others.

discontinuity   A condition that characterizes a culture when a child is either barred from activities that are open only to adults or forced to unlearn information or behaviors that are accepted in children but considered inappropriate for adults.

disdain   A feeling of scorn for the weakness and frailty of oneself or others.

disengaged relationships   Infrequent contact and a sense that the members of the family do not really seem to care about one another.

disequilibrium   In Piaget's theory, a condition when changes in the organism or changes in the environment require a revision of schemes or mental structures.

dismissing avoidant attachment   An attachment outcome in which people have a positive model of the self and a negative model of others.

disorganized attachment   Babies' responses are particularly notable in the reunion sequence. In the other three attachment patterns, infants appear to use a coherent strategy for managing the stress of the situation. The disorganized babies have no consistent strategy: They behave in contradictory, unpredictable ways that seem to convey feelings of extreme fear or utter confusion.

dissociation   A sense of separateness or withdrawal from others; an inability to experience the bond of mutual commitment.

divorce   The legal dissolution of a marriage.

division of labor   Splitting the activities needed to accomplish a task between participants.

dizygotic twins   Twins developed from two separate fertilized ova; also called fraternal twins.

dominance   If one allele is present, its characteristic is always observed, whether the other allele of the allelic pair is the same or not.

doubt   A sense of uncertainty about one's abilities and one's worth.

Down syndrome   A chromosomal irregularity in which the child has an extra chromosome 21. The condition results in mental retardation.

drives In psychosexual theory, sexual and aggressive forces that have a biological or somatic origin. They are a result of some metabolic functions but are also intimately linked to psychological processes.

dropping out of college Leaving a college or university in which one is enrolled before completing a degree.

dual-earner marriages A marriage in which both partners earn income for the household.

durable power of attorney A document that authorizes someone to act on behalf of a person in financial and property matters and health care decisions that can go into effect either when the agreement is signed or when a disability occurs.

dying trajectory The time during which a person goes from good health to death.

dyslexia A learning disability involving difficulties in reading, spelling, and writing.

eating disorders Any of several psychological disorders such as anorexia nervosa and bulimia characterized by disturbances in the daily consumption of food, preoccupation with thinness, or binge and purge behaviors.

ecological niche The place where an organism lives and the role it plays in the ecosystem.

ecological validity The applicability of a controlled laboratory situation in the real world.

education In the broadest sense, a culture's process for transmitting valued knowledge and skills from one generation to the next.

effacement The shortening of the cervical canal preceding childbirth.

efficacy The capacity for producing a desired result, including planning intentional actions, guiding and directing one's own behaviors toward a goal, and reflecting on ones actions to assess their quality, impact, and purpose.

effortful control A child's ability to suppress a dominant response and perform a subdominant response instead.

ego In psychosexual theory, the mental structure that experiences and interprets reality. The ego includes most cognitive capacities, including perception, memory, reasoning, and problem solving.

egocentric empathy When one recognizes distress in another person and responds to it in the same way one would respond if the distress were one's own.

egocentric speech In Piaget's observation, toddlers use this to control and direct their behavior. The speech is considered egocentric because it is not intended to communicate with anyone else and often doesn't make sense to anyone else. Vygotsky suggested that egocentric speech is a component of the problem-solving function.

egocentrism The perception of oneself at the center of the world; the view that others and events base their behavior on or occur as a result of one's own perceptions.

ego ideal A set of positive standards, ideals, and ambitions that represent the way a person would like to be.

ego psychology The study of the development and differentiation of the ego as integrative, adaptive, and goal directed.

Electra complex In psychosexual theory, a conflict that results from ambivalence surrounding heightened sexuality during the phallic stage. The daughter has a strong, sexualized attraction to her father, and her mother becomes a fantasized rival. See Oedipal complex for boys.

electronic fetal heart rate monitoring The continuous monitoring of fetal heart rate using an electronic amplification device.

embryo The developing human individual from the time of implantation to the end of the eighth week after conception.

embryonic period A stage of pregnancy in the first trimester that occur after the germinal period, and is devoted primarily to elaboration of the supportive elements that will house the embryo. The embryonic period lasts about 10 weeks after the last menstrual period.

emotional regulation Strategies for coping with intense emotions, both positive and negative. Caregiver behavior and observation are important factors in the development of emotional regulation.

empathy The capacity to recognize and experience the emotional state of another person.

empathy for another's feelings When one shows empathy for a wide range of feelings and anticipates the kinds of reactions that might really comfort someone else.

empathy for another's life conditions When one experiences empathy in understanding the life conditions or personal circumstances of a person or group.

empowerment Sharing information and authority so that people can take initiative and make decisions to solve problems; a concept applied in any context where power is typically unequal, such as parent–child , doctor–patient, or supervisor–subordinate.

enactive attainment (plural: enactive attainments) Personal experience of mastery.

encoding (plural: encodings) In cognitive behaviorism, the construct that a person has about the self, the situation, and others in the situation.

enculturation The process by which culture carriers teach, model, reward, punish, and use other symbolic strategies to transmit critical practices and values.

endogamy Marriage within one's well-defined group, such as one's ethnic or religious group.

enmeshed relationships Characterized by over involvement in one another to the extent that any change in one family member is met by strong resistance by the others; individuality is viewed as a threat to the relationship.

environmental toxins Poisonous substances in a pregnant woman's environment that may cause malformations to the fetus she carries, such as lead, mold, and chemicals in plastics and pesticides.

enzymes Complex proteins produced by living cells that act as catalysts for biochemical reactions.

epigenetic marks Chemicals that sit on top of the genes and instruct them to switch on or off.

epigenetic principle A biological plan for growth such that each function emerges in a systematic sequence until the fully functioning organism has developed.

epigenetics Activities at the biochemical level that alter gene expression but do not alter the genome itself.

episodic memory Recall of situations and data.

equilibration Efforts to reconcile new perspectives and ideas about basic moral concepts, such as justice, intentionality, and social responsibility with one's existing views about what is right and wrong when a stage change occurs.

equilibrium In Piaget's theory, the balance that every organism strives to attain in which organized structures (sensory, motor, or cognitive) provide effective ways of interacting with the environment.

estrogen (plural: estrogens) The major female sex hormone.

ethical principles Standards of right and wrong, especially as they govern areas of moral and professional responsibility.

ethics Principles of conduct founded on a society's moral code.

ethnic group (plural: ethnic groups) A group of people who share a common cultural ancestry, language, or religion within a larger cultural context.

ethnic group identity Knowing that one is a member of a certain ethnic group; recognizing that aspects of one's thoughts, feelings, and actions are influenced by ones ethnic membership; and taking the ethnic group's values, outlook, and goals into account when making life choices.

ethnic identity   An aspect of self-concept related to one's sense of belonging and connection to one or more ethnic groups.

ethnography   A type of observation in which behavior in a setting is carefully observed and recorded without any other kind of manipulation; often used to describe complex cultural activities.

ethology   The comparative investigation of the biological basis of behavior from an evolutionary perspective to determine the proximal causes of behavioral acts, the relative contribution of inheritance and learning to these acts, and the adaptive significance and evolutionary history of different patterns of behavior within and across species.

euthanasia   The practice of ending someone's life for reasons of mercy.

evaluation   A judgment of the accuracy and/or usefulness of research findings, and their implications for the confirmation or revision of theory.

evolutionary psychology   The study of the long-term, historical origins of behavior.

exchange norm   A family science theory that suggests each person expects to satisfy the needs of the partner and to have needs met in about the same amount. It includes a sense of obligation so that what one receives from the partner should be returned in similar value.

exclusivity   A shutting out of others for elitist reasons.

executive functioning (noun: executive functions)   Includes several cognitive capacities, including the ability to reject irrelevant information, formulate complex hypothetical arguments, organize an approach to a complex task, and follow a sequence of steps to task completion. Often associated with advances in the development of the prefrontal cortex.

exosystem   One or more settings that do not involve the developing person as an active participant but in which events occur that affect or are affected by what happens in the setting containing the developing person.

expansion   Elaborating on a child's expression by adding more words.

expectancies   Expectations about one's ability to perform, the consequences of one's behavior, and the meaning of events in one's environment.

expectations   Views held by oneself or by others about what would be appropriate behavior in a given situation or at a given stage of development.

experiential transcendence   A way of experiencing immortality through achieving a sense of continuous presence.

experiment   A research method best suited for examining causal relationships in which some variable or group of variables is systematically manipulated to examine its effect on an outcome.

experimental group   The participants who experience the manipulation or treatment in an experiment.

expert   A person who has become proficient at a skill due to a combination of aptitude, training, and practice. The final stage of a developmental progression to acquire a skill.

expertise   A quality of individuals who focus their intelligence on intensive study, training, and repeated opportunities for problem solving within a domain in which they become specialists.

exploration phase   In Tiedeman's career decision model, the phase when a person realizes that a career decision must be made and therefore begins to learn more about those aspects of the self and the occupational world that are relevant to the impending decision. The person begins to generate alternatives for action. Uncertainty about the future and the many alternatives is accompanied by feelings of anxiety.

external frames of reference   When a child evaluates his or her own performance in light of parent, teacher, or peer feedback and observations of the performance of other children in the class.

externalizing problems   Having the inability to suppress impulses. Intense anger in conditions of frustration, an inability to delay gratification, and lack of empathy are experienced. Anger and frustration are directed outward to other people or objects.

external validity   The degree to which the results of an experiment are applicable to situations beyond the experiment itself.

extinction   (1) In psychosocial theory, the negative pole of the psychosocial crisis of elderhood, in which it is feared that the end of one's life is the end of all continuity. (2) In evolutionary theory, the failure of a species to adapt to changing environmental conditions results in a gradual process in which the species no longer exists.

extroversion   Personality dimension that includes such qualities as sociability, vigor, sensation seeking, and positive emotions.

faceness   The properties of appearing like a human face. Infants seem to have a special visual category for the properties of a human face, showing surprise when facial features are disorganized or upside down.

fallopian tube   The tube, extending from the uterus to the ovary, in which fertilization takes place.

family   Two or more individuals living together who are related by birth, marriage, partnership agreement, or adoption.

family constellation   The many variables that describe a family group, including the presence or absence of mother and father; the number, spacing, and sex of siblings; and the presence or absence of extended family members in the household.

family of origin   The family into which one is born.

family of procreation   The family one begins as an adult.

fast–mapping (verb: fast-map)   Forming a rapid, initial, partial understanding of the meaning of a word by relating it to the known vocabulary and restructuring the known-word storage space and its related conceptual categories.

fearful avoidant attachment   An attachment outcome in which people have a negative model of both self and others.

feedback   The process by which a system, often biological or ecological, is modulated, controlled, or changed by the product, output, or response it produces.

feedback loop (plural: feedback loops)   The section of a control system that allows for feedback and self-correction and that adjusts its operation according to differences between the actual output and the desired output.

feedback mechanisms   In systems theory, the operations in an open system that produce adaptive self-regulation by identifying and responding to changes in the environment.

femininity   Gender traits associated with being expressive and communal (e.g., valuing interpersonal and spiritual development, and being tender, sympathetic, and concerned about the well-being of others).

fertility rate   The average number of births per woman of childbearing age.

fertilization   The penetration of an egg by a sperm.

fetal alcohol spectrum disorders   An umbrella term for the range of effects that can occur in an individual whose mother drank alcohol during pregnancy. These effects include physical, mental, behavioral, and learning disabilities with possible life-long implications.

fetal alcohol syndrome   A condition of the fetus involving central nervous system disorders, growth deficiency, low birth weight, and malformations of the skull and face; the condition is associated with use of alcohol by mothers during pregnancy.

fetal period   A stage of pregnancy beginning in the first trimester after the embryonic period. During this period the fetus continues to grow and the sex organs form. The fetus's heartbeat can be heard with an amplified stethoscope, called a Doppler. This period lasts until birth.

fetal viability The maturational age at which the fetus can survive outside the uterus.

fetoscopy Examination of the fetus through the use of a fiber-optic lens.

fetus The unborn infant. Usually, the term fetus refers to infants between 8 weeks of gestational age and birth. See embryo.

fidelity (to others) The ability to freely pledge and sustain loyalties to others; the ability to freely pledge and sustain loyalties to values and ideologies.

filial obligation The responsibilities of adult children for their aging parents.

first word The first words a baby uses, typically between the ages of 12 and 18 months. Most first words have a shared meaning between the baby and the caregiver.

fitness (1) The genetic contribution of an individual to the next generation's gene pool relative to the average for the population, usually measured by the number of that individual's offspring or close kin that survive to reproductive age. (2) Patterns of activity or inactivity, endurance or frailty, and illness or health that influence the ability to manage tasks of independent daily living.

fixation In psychosexual theory, the continued use of pleasure-seeking or anxiety-reducing behaviors appropriate to an earlier stage of development.

fluid intelligence (Gf) The ability to impose organization on information and to generate new hypotheses.

foreclosure See identity foreclosure.

formal operational thought In Piaget's theory, the final stage of cognitive development, characterized by reasoning, hypothesis generation, and hypothesis testing.

formal operations Complex cognitive capacities, such as reasoning, hypothesis generation, and hypothesis testing.

foundational category In cognitive development, a fundamental mental classification, such as the distinction between human beings and inanimate objects.

frailty Physical weakness or disease, often stemming from old age, that prevents individuals from performing activities of daily living.

fraternal twins Children born at the same time who developed from two different ova.

friendship (plural: friendships) The relationship between people who are attached to one another by affection, esteem, shared interests, etc.

functional independence Requiring little or no help with the activities of daily living.

fulfillment theories Theories that emphasizes the purposive, goal-oriented strivings that characterize adult life, particularly those strivings for personal fulfilment and self-actualization.

gamete (plural: gametes) A mature germ cell involved in reproduction; a sperm or an ovum.

gender Refers to the integrated cognitive, social, and emotional schemes associated with being male or female.

gender constancy When children learn the biological basis of gender and that one's gender does not change.

gender contentedness A feeling of satisfaction with one's biological sex and related gender expectations.

gender dysphoria A condition in which one has a strong aversion to some or all of the physical characteristics or social roles associated with one's biological sex.

gender gap Systematic differences between men and women in some measurable variable such as income, length of life, or elected representation in government.

gender identification Incorporation into one's self-concept of the valued characteristics of male or female that become integrated into an early scheme for thinking of oneself as either male or female.

gender identity A set of beliefs, attitudes, and values about oneself as a man or woman in many areas of social life, including intimate relations, family, work, community, and religion.

gender label (plural: gender labels) The word boy or girl. First component of gender identity, in which children learn to refer to themselves as a boy or girl and to identify other children by applying the word correctly.

gender permanence An appreciation that a boy grows up to be a man and a girl grows up to be a woman. One's sex is permanent over time, even though many things about one might change.

gender-role convergence A transformation in which men and women become more androgynous and more similar in gender orientation during later life.

gender-role expectations The cultural and subcultural expectations concerning the appropriate behavior of male and female individuals.

gender-role standards Attributes held by the culture for males and females. These attributes can include both precepts and sanctions.

gender scheme (plural: gender schemes) A personal theory about cultural expectations and stereotypes related to gender.

gene (plural: genes) The fundamental physical unit of heredity. A gene is a linear sequence of nucleotides along a segment of DNA that carries the coded instructions for the synthesis of RNA, which, when translated into protein, leads to hereditary characteristics.

gene pool The genetic information contained in the genes of the population or culture that provides the ancestry for an individual.

generalizability The extent to which we can say with confidence that the observations made for a sample would apply to other groups.

generativity The capacity to contribute to the quality of life for future generations. A sense of generativity is attained toward the end of middle adulthood.

genetic anomalies Neurological or physical abnormalities that have a genetic cause.

genetic counseling Recent discoveries make it possible to identify the genes responsible for certain forms of disease and genetic anomalies. Couples who have reason to believe that they may carry genes for one of these disorders can be tested and advised about the probability of having children who may be afflicted.

genital basis of gender labels An understanding that a person's genitals provide the physical basis for distinguishing male and female gender roles.

genital stage In psychosexual theory, a period in which a person finds ways of satisfying sexual impulses in mature, dyadic relationships, typically beginning with the onset of puberty.

genome The full set of chromosomes that carries all the inheritable traits of an organism.

genotype The hereditary information contained in the cells of an individual. Genotype may or may not be observable in the phenotype. See phenotype.

gentrification A pattern of real estate change in which a higher income group buys property and develops residential and commercial projects in an area that has previously been serving a lower income group.

germinal period A stage of pregnancy in the first trimester that occur immediately after fertilization and lasts until implantation, typically six days after fertilization. During this stage, the egg begins to divide and is referred to as a zygote. After implantation, the zygote is called an embryo and the pregnancy enters the embryonic period.

gestation The period from conception to birth.

gestational age The age of the fetus from the time of conception until birth.

Glick effect   Statistical evidence of a lack of persistence that relates dropping out of high school or college with a high probability of divorce.

global empathy   Distress experienced and expressed as a result of witnessing someone else in distress.

globalization   A process that includes the rapid spread of materials and products, ideas, images, capital flows, and people across spaces and borders (national or otherwise) that formerly were far more difficult if not impossible to connect.

goal (plural: goals)   The result or achievement toward which effort is directed.

goal-corrected partnership   In Bowlby's attachment theory, the capacity that emerges in toddlerhood and early school age in which children begin to find more flexible and adaptive ways to maintain proximity with the object of attachment and to seek reassurance under stressful situations. As a result, children are able to manage negotiated separations more easily.

goal domains   Areas of life that are viewed as important and that contribute to life satisfaction such as job or daily activities, social contact and family, health, income, self-reliance, leisure time, and physical activity.

goal orientation   Guiding direction of one's life goals, especially the distinction between agentic (such as focusing on achievement, power, and the expression of personal abilities) and communal (focusing on intimacy, affiliation, and contributions to the welfare of others).

goal-related activities   The actions one takes to achieve one's life goals.

good death   The ideal conditions a person envisions surrounding death and dying.

grammar   Rules for the arrangement of words and phrases in a sentence and for the inflections that convey gender, tense, and number.

grandparenthood   The stage of life one enters when one's first grandchild is born.

gray matter   The cell body of neurons and the nonmyelinated sections of axons and dendrites.

grief   The cognitive and emotional reactions that follow the death of a loved one.

grief work   A person's psychological efforts to work through the reality of loss of a loved one and the feelings in which the person must (1) achieve freedom from feelings of guilt about ways he or she had criticized or even harmed the person who died and feelings of regret for things left unsaid or undone; (2) make an adjustment to all the aspects of the environment from which the deceased is missing; and (3) begin to form new relationships.

group games   Games that are more structured and somewhat more oriented to reality than play that is based primarily on imagination. These games combine fantasy with an emphasis on peer cooperation and competition.

group identity   The positive pole of the psychosocial crisis of early adolescence, in which the person finds membership in and value convergence with a peer group.

group norms   Collective expectations or rules for behavior held by members of a particular group.

guilt   An emotion associated with doing something wrong or the anticipation of doing something wrong.

habituation   A form of adaptation in which the child no longer responds to a stimulus that has been repeatedly presented.

harsh discipline   A form of discipline that includes physical punishment, yelling, angry and prolonged timeouts, and threatening violence.

health literacy   Knowing where to find trustworthy information about health concerns, understanding the information that is provided, and using the information to make informed decisions about one's health.

heteronomous morality   A child's moral perspective, in which rules are viewed as fixed and unchangeable.

heterozygous   Characterized by the presence of different alleles of a particular gene at the same locus.

higher mental processes   In Vygotsky's theory, processes, particularly language and meaning, that emerge from a child's ongoing interactions within social, historical, and cultural contexts, as well as from the child's biological maturation.

holophrase (plural: holophrases)   A single word functioning as a phrase or sentence.

homeostasis   A relatively stable state of equilibrium.

homogamy   When people are attracted to others who share important areas of similarity.

homozygous   Characterized by the presence of two matched alleles of a particular gene at the same locus.

hope   An enduring belief that one can attain one's essential wishes.

horizontal control system   The flow of information between the right and left hemispheres of the brain.

hormones   A group of chemicals, each of which is released into the bloodstream by a particular gland or tissue and has a specific effect on tissues elsewhere in the body.

hospice care   An integrated system of medicine, nursing, counseling, and spiritual care for the terminally ill and their family that emphasizes pain control and emotional support and typically refrains from extraordinary measures to prolong life.

household   All persons who occupy a housing unit, including both related family members and all unrelated persons.

housing options   Alternative living arrangements including single-family homes, apartments, continuing care facilities, and nursing homes.

hyperarousal   A response to exposure to violence and trauma, including low threshold for startle response, increases in heart rate, sleep disturbance, anxiety, and motor hyperactivity.

hypervigilance   An increased arousal for threat-related stimuli, often as a result of experiencing trauma.

hypoactive sexual desire   A decrease or absence of interest in sexual activity.

hypothesis   A tentative proposition that can provide a basis for further inquiry.

hypothetico deductive reasoning   A method of reasoning in which a hypothetical model based on observations is first proposed and then tested by deducing consequences from the model.

id   In psychoanalytic theory, the mental structure that expresses impulses and wishes. Much of the content of the id is unconscious.

identical twins   Children born at the same time who developed from the same ovum.

identification   The process through which one person incorporates the values and beliefs of a valued other such as a parent.

identity achievement   Individual identity status in which, after a crisis, a sense of commitment to family, work, political, and religious values is established.

identity confusion   The negative pole of the psychosocial crisis of later adolescence in which a person is unable to integrate various roles or make commitments.

identity foreclosure   Individual identity status in which a commitment to family, work, politics, and religious values is established prematurely without crisis.

identity process   A process in which the older adolescent examines alternatives, selects goals in various domains (personal, occupational, financial cultural), makes personal and interpersonal commitments to achieve these goals, and takes the active steps to achieve them.

identity status   One of four levels in the identity process characterized by different degrees of crisis and commitment.

illusion of competence   An overestimation of one's abilities despite poor academic achievement or test performance.

illusion of incompetence Expressed by children who perform well in academic achievement tests yet perceive themselves as below average in academic ability and behave in accordance with this perception.

imaginary audience The preoccupation with what you believe other people are thinking about you.

imaginary companion (plural: imaginary companions) A make-believe friend, which may be an animal, a child, or some other creature, that springs complete in concept from the mind of a child. It is thought to occupy space. It has its own personality, which is consistent from day to day. It has its own likes and dislikes, which are not necessarily the same as those of its creator.

imitation Repetition of another person's words, gestures, or behaviors.

immortality The positive pole of the psychosocial crisis of very old age, in which the person transcends death through a sense of symbolic continuity.

impulse control The ability to delay gratification and to suppress a dominant response in order to perform a subdominant response.

inclusion In a school environment, the process of promoting contact between students with and without disabilities and creating an accepting social climate among students.

inclusive fitness The fitness of an individual organism as measured by the survival and reproductive success of its kin, each relative being valued according to the probability of shared genetic information, with an offspring or sibling having a value of 50 percent and a first cousin having a value of 25 percent.

independent variable The factor that is manipulated in an experiment, and the measured effects of the manipulation.

individual differences perspective The view that gender differences exist within the individual as persistent, internal attributes and that differences between boys and girls are stable characteristics that individuals bring to various situations.

individual identity The commitment to a personal integration of values, goals, and abilities that occurs as personal choices are made in response to anticipated or actual environmental demands at the end of adolescence.

individualism Worldview in which social behavior is guided largely by personal goals, ambitions, and pleasures.

induction (1) A form of discipline that points out the consequences of a child's actions for others. (2) In cognitive development, the

realization that whatever holds true for one member of a category is likely to hold true for other members as well.

induction phase In Tiedeman's career decision model, the phase when a person encounters the new work environment for the first time. He or she wants to be accepted and looks to others for cues about how to behave. The person identifies with the new group and seeks recognition for his or her unique characteristics. Gradually, the self-image is modified as the person begins to believe in the values and goals of the work group.

industry A sense of pride and pleasure in acquiring culturally valued competences. The sense of industry is usually acquired by the end of the middle childhood years.

inertia A paralysis of thought and action that prevents productive work.

infant mortality rate The number of infants who die during the first year of life per 1,000 live births during that year.

infertility Inability to conceive or carry a fetus through the gestational period.

influence phase In Tiedeman's career decision model, the phase when the person is very much involved with the new group. He or she becomes more assertive in asking that the group perform better. The person also tries to influence the group to accommodate some of his or her values. The self is strongly committed to group goals. During this phase, the group's values and goals may be modified to include the orientation of the new member.

informants Participants in a researcher's study who will provide their insight, experience, and knowledge.

informed consent Telling all participants in a research study all aspects of the research that may influence their decision to participate.

in-group A group of which one is a member; contrasted with out-group.

in-group bias The tendency for members of a group to behave in ways that are more acceptable to other in-group members and to view members of the in-group more positively than people who are not members of the in-group.

inhibition A psychological restraint that prevents freedom of thought, expression, and activity.

initiative The ability to offer new solutions, to begin new projects, or to seek new social encounters; active investigation of the environment.

inner speech Language spoken softly or even silently to the self which guides behavior. In Vygotsky's theory, the internalization of social language is a transition between spoken language and thought.

institutional review A process in which representatives of an organization read and react to research proposals, applying guidelines for the ethical conduct of research and approving, modifying, or rejecting proposals based on these guidelines.

instrumental activities of daily living (IADLs) Basic tasks that are essential to maintaining one's daily life without dependence on informal or formal community support services.

instrumental reminiscence Reminiscence that emphasizes past accomplishments, past efforts to overcome difficulties, and the use of past experiences to approach current difficulties.

instrumental support Direct assistance, including help with chores, medical care, or transportation.

instrumental values The values placed on doing things that are challenging, reflected in the amount of time spent on and the degree of satisfaction achieved in such actions.

integration phase In Tiedeman's career decision model, the phase when group members react against the new member's attempts to influence them. The new member then compromises. In the process, he or she attains a more objective understanding of the self and the group. A true collaboration between the new member and the group is achieved. The new member feels satisfied and is evaluated as successful by the self and others.

integrative reminiscence Reminiscence that involves reviewing one's past in order to find meaning or to reconcile one's current and prior feelings about certain life events.

integrity The ability to accept the facts of one's life and to face death without great fear. The sense of integrity is usually acquired toward the end of later adulthood.

intellectual flexibility A person's ability to handle conflicting information, to take several perspectives on a problem, and to reflect on personal values in solving ethical problems.

intellectual vigor A person's ability to maintain and successfully utilize cognitive abilities.

interdependence A condition in which systems depend on each other, or in which all the elements in a system rely on one another for their continued growth.

intergenerational solidarity The closeness and commitment within parent–child and grandparent–grandchild relationships.

intermental In Vygotsky's theory, understanding or shared meaning between two or more people.

internal frames of reference When a child compares how well he or she can perform in one domain versus another.

internalization A process in which the values, beliefs, and norms of the culture become the values, beliefs, and norms of the individual.

internalized morality The ability to see oneself as a moral being whose actions have implications for the well-being of others; using closely held standards to judge their own behavior and the behavior of others.

internalizing problems Having overcontrol, intense worries and fears, and suppression of emotions. Anxiety is focused inward on the self.

internal validity The sample and methods are appropriate in an experiment.

interobserver reliability Two or more observers' codings of the same situation are compared to determine whether different observers rated the same event in the same way.

interpersonal interactions The frequency and quality of communication and time shared in a relationship.

interpersonal skills Skills that promote relationships and include at least three components: self-presentation, social scanning, and social flexibility.

interpretation The result of explaining or understanding something.

intersubjectivity A shared repertoire of emotions that enables infants and their caregivers to understand each other and create shared meanings. They can engage in reciprocal, rhythmic interactions, appreciate state changes in one another, and modify their actions in response to emotional information about one another.

interview A conversation used to discover people's opinions or experiences; information can be gathered in face-to-face encounters, via telephone, or other media.

intimacy The ability to experience an open, supportive, tender relationship with another person without fear of losing one's own identity in the process of growing close. The sense of intimacy is usually acquired toward the end of early adulthood.

intimate relationship (plural: intimate relationships) An open, supportive, tender relationship with another person without fear of losing one's own identity in the process.

intramental In Vygotsky's theory, an understanding of the special relationship between the desired goal and the communication required to achieve that goal.

introjection An unconscious psychic process by which a person incorporates the characteristics of another person into his or her own personality.

introspection Deliberate self-evaluation and examination of private thoughts and feelings.

in vitro fertilization A process where eggs are removed from the ovary and placed in a petri dish inside an incubator. A few drops of sperm are then added to the dish. If the eggs are fertilized and the cells begin to divide, they are implanted in the uterus for subsequent development.

iron deficiency anemia A nutrient disorder where there is not enough iron available for proper brain development. Babies who have severe iron deficiencies test lower in motor and cognitive development and show evidence of fearfulness, fatigue, and wariness.

isolation A crisis resolution in which situational factors or a fragile sense of self lead a person to remain psychologically distant from others; the state of being alone.

joblessness The state of not having work.

justice orientation Moral decision making based on human rights, respect for others, and fairness.

labor In pregnancy, involuntary contractions of the uterine muscles that occur prior to giving birth.

lack of congruence In a romantic or marital relationship, the state in which the partners are dissimilar or disagree in how they approach conflict.

language environment The sounds, system of meanings, rules for word and sentence formation, and guidelines for communication in social settings of a particular language. This includes the nature of language partners and language stimulation such as television, books, and other media.

language perception The ability to recognize sounds and differentiate among sound combinations before the meanings of these sounds are understood.

language production The generation of language material by an individual. One of the first significant events is the naming of objects.

latency In psychosexual theory, a period of development that occurs after the Oedipal or Electra conflict is resolved and lasts from about 7 years until puberty. No new significant conflicts or impulses arise. The primary personality development during this period is the maturation of the ego.

launching period The time in family life during which children leave home.

leadership A relationship between people; the process of helping a group shape a vision of its purpose and goals and of getting people, both inside and outside the group, to commit and recommit themselves to accomplishing that vision.

learned helplessness A belief that one's efforts have little to do with success or failure and that the outcome of task situations is largely outside one's control.

learning Any relatively permanent change in thought or behavior that is the consequence of experience.

legacy A bequest; something handed down from one generation to the next.

life course Reference to the integration and sequencing of phases of work and family life.

life expectancy The average number of years from birth to death, as based on statistical analyses of the length of life for people born in a particular period.

life satisfaction A sense of well-being based on an evaluation of one's progress toward achieving important life goals.

life span Refers to the typical length of time that any particular organism can be expected to live.

life structure One's living arrangement and social relationships that support one's physical and mental health.

lifestyle A relatively permanent structure of activity and experience, including the tempo of activity, the balance between work and leisure, and patterns of family and social relationships.

literacy The ability to read and write.

living arrangements The type of household or facility in which someone lives and the people an individual choose to live with.

living will A document instructing physicians, relatives, or others to refrain from the use of extraordinary measures, such as life support equipment, to prolong one's life in the event of a terminal illness.

locomotion The ability to move from one place to another.

loneliness The state of feeling sad because one is apart from other people, rejected by others, or because one has fewer social interactions than are desired.

longevity The length or duration of life.

longitudinal study A research design in which repeated observations of the same participants are made at different times in order to examine change over time.

long-term memory A complex network of information, concepts, and schemes related by associations, knowledge, and use. It is the storehouse of a lifetime of information.

loss-oriented coping Confronting one's pain, sadness, and the loss of a loved one and finding a place for the deceased in one's thoughts and memories in order to achieve emotional health and cognitive functioning.

love A profoundly tender affection for another person. Characterized by intimacy, passion and commitment.

love withdrawal A form of discipline in which parents express disappointment or disapproval and become emotionally cold or distant.

low-birth-weight babies Infants who weigh less than 2,500 grams (about 5 pounds, 8 ounces) at birth. This may be a result of being born before the full period of gestation, or it may result from the mother's inadequate diet, smoking, or use of drugs.

lower mental processes In Vygotsky's theory, natural processes that can be observed in animal behavior and in the problem-solving behaviors of infants and very young children.

macrosystem Refers to consistencies in the form and content of lower order systems (micro-, meso-, and exosystems) that exist or could exist at the level of the subculture or the culture as whole along with any belief systems of ideology underlying such consistencies.

major depressive disorder A disorder in which a person will have experienced five or more of the following symptoms for at least 2 weeks: depressed mood or irritable mood most of the day; decreased interest in pleasurable activities; changes in weight, or perhaps failure to make necessary weight gains in adolescence; sleep problems; psychomotor agitation or retardation; fatigue or loss of energy; feelings of worthlessness or abnormal amounts of guilt; reduced concentration and decision-making ability; and repeated suicidal ideation, attempts, or plans of suicide.

management of the household All the planning, problem solving, and activities adults undertake in order to take care of themselves and others who are entrusted to their care.

managerial resourcefulness Flexible, creative problem solving in the workplace, particularly when facing new problems and changing conditions.

marital companionship Leisure activities shared by a married couple.

marital conflict Disagreement between partners in a marital relationship, often over opposing goals, needs, values, and the control of resources.

marriage The relationship that exists between two people who are in a consensual and contractual relationship recognized by law.

masculinity Gender traits associated with being instrumental and agentic (e.g., having leadership abilities, being assertive, taking control).

matched groups Two or more groups who are similar on many dimensions; in experimental research often one group of participants receives some type of treatment or experimental intervention but the other group does not.

matched groups sampling Two or more groups of participants who are similar on many dimensions are selected as the sample for an experiment. The effects of different treatments or manipulations are determined by comparing the behavior of these groups.

matching The infant and the caregiver are involved in similar behaviors or states at the same time.

meaning making The psychological system that seeks out information, integrates information from many sources, and evaluates experiences as positive or negative, encouraging or threatening.

memory Complex capacity that includes recognizing something similar to something one has seen or experienced in the past, holding information in mind for a brief period before using it, and recalling information as needed.

menopause The natural cessation of menstruation, usually occurring in the fifth decade of life; one aspect of the close of a woman's fertility.

mental image A form of representational thought that involves the ability to hold the picture of a person, object, or event in one's mind even in the absence of the stimulus itself.

mental operation (plural: mental operations) A transformation—carried out in thought rather than action—that modifies an object, event, or idea.

mercy killing Taking a person's life in order to end their suffering. In our society, this is considered to be murder.

mesosystem The interrelations among two or more settings in which the developing person actively participates (e.g., for a child, the relations between home, school, and neighborhood peer groups; for an adult, between family, work, and social life).

metabolism A collective term for all the chemical processes that take place in the body: in some (catabolic), a complex substance is broken down into simpler ones, usually with the release of energy; in others (anabolic), a complex substance is built up from simpler ones, usually with the consumption of energy.

metacognition Thinking about one's own thinking, including what individuals understand about their reasoning capacities and about how information is organized, how knowledge develops, how reality is distinguished from belief or opinion, how to achieve a sense of certainty about what is known, and how to improve understanding.

microsystem A pattern of activities, roles, and interpersonal relations experienced by the developing person in a given setting with specific physical and material characteristics.

mirror neuron system A coordinated network of neural areas that underlies a person's ability to observe and then recreate the actions of others as well as to understand the emotions and intentions of others.

miscarriage Spontaneous termination of a pregnancy.

mismatch The infant and caregiver are not involved in the same behaviors or states at the same time.

mistrust A sense of unpredictability in the environment and suspicion about one's own worth. Experiences with mistrust are most critical during infancy.

model In social learning theory, the person being observed.

modeling In social learning theory, the process of observing a person.

monozygotic twins Twins who develop from a single fertilized egg. These twins have identical genetic characteristics.

moral development The acquisition of the principles or rules of right conduct and the distinction between right and wrong.

moral exemplars People who have dedicated themselves to improving the lives of others.

moral identity The sense in which a person defines himself or herself in moral terms and evaluates his or her behavior against moral standards that represent an integration of parental socialization about caring for others, an appreciation for the cultural and social contexts of moral actions, and experiences that have required moral action.

moral intuition An emotional or affective aspect to morality; a more primitive, immediate, almost automatic system that evaluates experiences as positive or negative, without going through steps of searching for more information or weighing evidence.

morality Conforming to rules of right or virtuous conduct that involves conceptions of the rights, dignity, and welfare of others.

moral reasoning (1) A cognitive aspect to morality that is based on assessments of intention, fairness, justice, and social obligation. (2) The ability to use logic in order to evaluate what is right and wrong; this capacity matures along with other cognitive abilities from childhood to adulthood.

moratorium An identity status in which people are involved in ongoing exploration and experimentation; typically an active, open time for gathering information and discovering how one fits in certain roles.

motor development All the changes in a child's ability to control, coordinate, and direct movement, including movement of the eyes and head, as well as movement of fingers, arms, legs, and torso.

multiply determined In psychosexual theory, behaviors that may appear to be somewhat unusual or extremely intense—a single behavior expresses many motives, some of which the person can recognize and control and others that are guided by unconscious thought.

mutation The change in the structure of a gene that can be passed along to the next generation.

mutuality The ability of two people to meet each other's needs and to share each other's concerns and feelings.

mutuality among peers Empathic awareness of one another, understanding of self and other, and the ability and willingness to regulate one's needs in order to respond to the needs of one's partner.

mutuality with the caregiver The ability of the caregiver to understand and meet the infant's needs; and the infant's understanding that his or her needs will be met.

myelin A substance that forms around the axons of some neurons, acting as an insulator that speeds signals from one neuron to the next.

myelination The formation of a soft, white, fatty material called myelin around certain nerve axons to serve as an electrical insulator that speeds nerve impulses to muscles and other effectors.

narcissistic Extremely self-absorbed and self-loving.

narcissistic people Adults who devote their energy and skills to the sole end of self-aggrandizement and personal satisfaction.

naturalistic observation See ethnography.

natural selection A process whereby those individuals best suited to the characteristics of the immediate environment are most likely to survive and reproduce.

negative communication Verbal and nonverbal negative expressions and hostile put-downs.

negative identity A clearly defined self-image that is contrary to the cultural values of the community.

network Individuals in significant relationships who interact with each other as well as with the target person.

neural plasticity All the changes in the brain's neural pathways that occur as a result of learning and experience. Also, the ways the brain compensates for injury by making use of alternate resources.

neural tube The tube formed during the early embryonic period that later develops into the brain, spinal cord, nerves, and ganglia.

neuron (plural: neurons) A nerve cell with specialized processes; the fundamental functional unit of nervous tissue.

neuroticism A personality dimension consistently associated with discouragement, unhappiness, and hopelessness. Neuroticism includes such qualities as anxiety, hostility, and impulsiveness.

neurotransmitters Chemicals that influence how the nerves grow, how they respond to stimulation, and whether they result in the firing or the inhibition of firing of the neurons.

nonparental care Child care arrangements in which infants and toddlers are taken care of by persons who are not their parents. Center-based care includes day care centers, Head Start programs, preschool, prekindergarten, and other early childhood programs.

norm of reaction A pattern of possible phenotypes that are likely to be observed under different environmental conditions.

norm of reciprocity The cultural norm that you are obligated to return in full value what you receive.

norms Collective expectations or rules for behavior held by members of a group or society.

novice A person who has just started learning something. The first stage of a developmental progression to acquiring a new skill.

nuclear family A household grouping that includes one or two parents and their children.

nursing home A facility that provides housing, food, nursing care, and rehabilitation for people who have severe functional limitations as a result of illness, surgery, aging, or advanced dementia.

obesity A condition of extreme overweight.

objective observations No prior bias; based solely on facts or what is taking place.

object permanence A scheme acquired during the sensorimotor stage of development, in which children become aware that an object continues to exist even when it is hidden or moved from place to place.

object relations The component of ego development that is concerned with the self, self-understanding, and self–other relationships.

object relations theory A modern adaptation of psychoanalytic theory that places less emphasis on the drives of aggression and sexuality as motivational forces and more emphasis on human relationships as the primary motivational force in life.

objective Based on facts and not influenced by personal feelings, interpretations, or prejudices.

observation A research method in which behavior is watched and recorded.

observation of models A mechanism for learning; the process in which a person watches and imitates others.

obsessions Persistent repetitive thoughts that serve as mechanisms for controlling anxiety.

obsessive-compulsive disorder An anxiety disorder that is characterized by recurrent, unwanted thoughts (obsessions) and/or repetitive behaviors (compulsions).

obsessive reminiscence Reminiscence that suggests an inability to resolve or accept certain past events and a persistent guilt or despair over these events.

occupational hazards Potential physical and psychological risks associated with the workplace, including exposure to toxins, work-related injuries, and exposure to diseases, reproductive hazards, and working conditions that have negative psychological consequences.

Oedipal complex In psychosexual theory, a conflict that results from ambivalence surrounding heightened sexuality during the phallic stage. The son has a strong, sexualized attraction to his mother, and his father becomes a fantasized rival. See Electra complex for girls.

old-old Among the very old, those who have suffered major physical or mental decrements.

openness to experience A personality characteristic that includes curiosity, imaginativeness, and enthusiasm for novelty.

operation (plural: operations) In Piaget's theory, an action that is performed on an object or a set of objects.

operational definition In research, the way an abstract concept is defined in terms of how it will be measured.

operationalize To translate an abstract concept into something that can be observed and measured.

optimal functioning What a person is capable of doing when motivated and well prepared.

optimism   A belief that one's decisions will lead to positive consequences and that situations will turn out well.

oral stage   In psychosexual theory, a period of life in which the mouth is the site of sexual and aggressive gratification, typically during the first year of life.

organic brain syndromes   Disorders involving memory loss, confusion, loss of ability to manage daily functions, and loss of ability to focus attention.

out-group   A group that competes with one's own group; contrasted with in-group.

overregularization (verb: overregularize)   In language acquisition, the tendency to use a grammar rule for the formation of regular verbs or nouns when one cannot remember the irregular form. As a child's vocabulary grows, the need to apply the rule to unfamiliar words declines.

ovum   An egg; the female germ cell.

oxytocin   A hormone that plays a key role in social attachment, produces a general sense of calm relaxation, reducing wariness and increasing approach behavior.

pace of life   The busyness of life, including activity, leisure, and rest, which is shaped by work, family, personality, and environmental contexts.

parental alienation   A psychological condition in which a child becomes strongly allied with one parent and rejects a relationship with the other parent, without legitimate justification; often a result of one parent's manipulation of the image of the other parent.

parental attachment   The relationship of a child to his or her parents characterized by different possible levels of stability and security.

parental identification   A developmental process through which a child incorporates the values, beliefs, and behaviors of the parent.

parenting   The rearing of children.

parenting alliance   The capacity of a spouse to acknowledge, respect, and value the parenting roles and tasks of the partner.

participant observation   Observation in which the researcher actively engages in interactions with other members of the setting.

passive euthanasia   Withholding treatment or removing life-sustaining nourishment and breathing aids for the dying person with the result that death occurs more quickly than if these procedures were continued.

patterns of bereavement   Five categories of adjustments an individual may make to the loss of a loved one that include common grief, resilient, chronic grief, chronic depression, and depressed-improved.

peer approval   Receiving positive reactions from peers and inhibiting behaviors that evoke peer ridicule in order to fit in with one's social group.

peer group membership   Inclusion in a group of people of similar age, grade, or status.

peer play   Play interactions with one's peers that provide opportunities for physical, cognitive, social, and emotional development.

peer pressure   Expectations to conform and commit to the norms of one's peer group.

peer review   The process in which other professionals read and critically evaluate a researcher's materials before they are published.

persistent vegetative state   State in which a person's brainstem functions to continue to maintain heartbeat and respiration even when there is no cortical functioning.

personal choice   When children recognize a domain of personal freedom in decision making that is not guided by adult authority and regulations but by the child's own preferences.

personal fable   An intense investment in one's own thoughts and feelings and a belief that these thoughts are unique.

personality   A pattern of thoughts, feelings, and actions that are characteristic of a person across situations.

person–environment interaction   Ongoing experiences between the individual and the physical and social environment that includes the family, work setting, neighborhood, and larger political community.

person in the setting   In developmental systems theory, the focus of analysis.

perspective taking   The ability to consider a situation from a point of view other than one's own.

phallic stage   In psychosexual theory, a period of heightened genital sensitivity in the absence of the hormonal changes that accompany puberty, typically starting during the third year of life and lasting until the child is 6.

phases of career decision making   A model for choosing an occupation and making occupation-related decisions; includes seven stages: exploration phase, crystallization phase, choice phase, clarification phase, induction phase, influence phase, and integration phase.

phenotype   The observable characteristics that result from the interaction of a particular genotype and a particular environment.

phonemic awareness   Knowing the sound of letters and being able to hear these sounds as one reads.

physical changes of aging   Multidimensional and variable changes that affect all individuals as they age, caused by an interaction of genetic, environmental, social, and lifestyle factors.

physical culture   Encompasses the objects, technologies, structures, tools, and other artifacts of a culture.

physical state   In self-efficacy theory, the state of arousal or excitement that provides information as one makes a judgment whether one is likely to succeed or fail in a certain task.

physician-assisted suicide   The administration of a lethal dose of some medication by a physician or arranging for a terminally ill patient to administer his or her own lethal dose of medication using a suicide machine.

placenta   The vascular organ that connects the fetus to the maternal uterus and mediates metabolic exchanges.

plagiarism   Using someone's words or ideas without giving them credit or taking credit as if they were one's own.

plasticity   (1) The capability of being shaped and molded. (2) The capacity for continuous alteration of the neural circuits and synapses of the living brain and nervous system in response to experience or injury that involves the formation of new circuits and synapses and the elimination or modification of existing ones.

play companions   The people who play with a child, including parents, siblings, peers, and child care professionals.

pleasure principle   From psychosexual theory, the instinctive drive to seek pleasure and avoid pain that originates and is expressed in the id.

point of view about death   A considered and/or evaluated perspective about death, including the death of others and oneself.

population   All units for potential observation.

positivism   An approach to the study of human behavior that seeks causal relationships among factors, with the goal of trying to predict outcomes.

positivity bias   The tendency to view one's romantic partner in an overly positive light, thereby making one feel he or she has found the absolutely perfect partner, and making the partner feel valued and cherished.

postconventional level   Stage III of Kohlberg's moral reasoning theory, bringing an awareness that rules and laws are a product of social, cultural, and political processes; individuals can evaluate the fairness and appropriateness of these rules and laws based on their own values and the social conditions.

postformal reasoning The integration of abstract, logical-mathematical reasoning with the special emotional and social demands of the circumstances.

postformal thought A qualitatively new form of thinking that emerges after formal operational thought which involves a higher use of reflection and the integration of contextual, relativistic, and subjective knowledge.

postpartum depression A period of sadness that may be experienced by the mother after giving birth, which appears to be related to hormonal activity.

post-traumatic stress disorder A mental disorder that occurs after a traumatic event outside the range of usual human experience, characterized by symptoms such as reliving the event, reduced involvement with others, and manifestations of autonomic arousal such as hyperalertness and exaggerated startle response.

poverty Commonly understood as the condition of having little money and few material possessions. Since poverty is defined at the family level and not the household level, the poverty status of the household is determined by the poverty status of the householder. Households are classified as poor when the total income of the householder's family is below the appropriate poverty threshold. (For nonfamily householders, their own income is compared with the appropriate threshold.) The income of people living in the household who are unrelated to the householder is not considered when determining the poverty status of a household, nor does their presence affect the family size in determining the appropriate threshold. The poverty thresholds vary depending on three criteria: size of family, number of related children, and, for one- and two-person families, age of householder.

poverty threshold The minimum cash income needed to support a person or a family in meeting basic needs of daily living.

power assertion A discipline technique involving physical force, harsh language, or control of resources.

pragmatics The relationship of the social setting to the production and interpretation of language. Vocabulary, grammar, and pragmatics combine to form communication.

precocious puberty Changes in pubertal maturation that occur before the age of 8 for girls and before the age of 9 for boys.

preconscious From psychosexual theory, a part of the mind just below conscious awareness from which memories and emotions can be recalled or retrieved.

preconventional level Stage I of Kohlberg's moral reasoning theory in which children judge an action as morally justifiable based on the immediate consequences of the behavior and the approval of powerful authority figures.

preconventional morality In Kohlberg's stages of moral reasoning, the most immature form of moral judgment.   Moral decisions are based on whether the act has positive or negative consequences, or whether it is rewarded or punished.

prediction Declaration in advance, usually with precision of calculation.

prefrontal cortex The area of the brain that appears to be responsible for supporting the capacities of executive functions including deriving abstract concepts, rules, and generalizations from sensory and motor experiences and applying them in new situations.

pre-literacy Describing the skills and knowledge necessary before a child can learn to read independently.

preoccupied attachment An outcome of attachment in which a person has a positive model of others and a negative model of the self.

preoperational thought In Piaget's theory of cognitive development, the stage in which representational skills are acquired.

pretense Imagination or make-believe.

pride A feeling of satisfaction derived from success in one's own achievements or the achievements of others with whom one is closely associated.

primary narcissism In psychosexual theory, a process in which the sense of ego emerges as psychic energy and is directed toward the self: the sense of self is born out of self-love, an enthusiasm and excitement for one's body, one's experiences, and one's emerging sense of agency.

primary process thought From psychosexual theory, the quality of unconscious thought derived from the pleasure principle that is characteristic of the id and is observed in dreams. This kind of thinking lacks many of the constraints of time, social convention, and shared meaning.

primary sex characteristics Physical structures in males and females directly related to the reproductive capacity.

prime adaptive ego qualities Mental states that form a basic orientation toward the interpretation of life experiences; new ego qualities emerge in the positive resolution of each psychosocial crisis.

principal of care A sense of duty or obligation to help someone who is in need.

privacy Keeping an individual's confidential information secret, especially in a research study.

private self Refers to a person's inner uniqueness and unity and the subjective experience of being the originator of one's thoughts and actions and of being self-reflective.

process An ongoing operation or activity, not directly observable, that takes place in small increments over time and leads to a natural transformation.

processing load In problem solving, the number of domains of information called into play and the amount of work necessary to select response strategies.

processing speed The time it takes to identify a stimulus and figure out its meaning.

prohibitive moral judgment (plural: prohibitive moral judgements) A judgment involving a conflict between violating a law and breaking a promise in order to achieve some other goal.

prompting Urging a child to say more about an incomplete expression.

prosocial moral judgment (plural: prosocial moral judgements) A judgment involving a conflict between doing something helpful for someone else and meeting one's own needs.

prospective memory Memory about events or actions taking place in the future.

proteome Constellation of all proteins in a cell. Unlike the relatively unchanging genome, the dynamic proteome changes from minute to minute in response to tens of thousands of intra- and extracellular environmental signals. A protein's chemistry and behavior are specified by the gene sequence and by the number and identities of other proteins made in the same cell at the same time and with which it associates and reacts. Thus, at the cellular level, genetic and environmental information are continuously interacting to influence the functions of the cells.

pruning A process of sculpting synapses, in which infrequently used connections drop away.

psychological system Includes those mental processes central to the person's ability to make meaning of experiences and take action. Emotion, memory and perception, problem solving, language, symbolic abilities, and orientation to the future all require the use of psychological processes. The psychological system provides the resources for processing information and navigating reality.

psychosocial Of or pertaining to the interaction between social and psychological factors.

psychosocial approach A process that seeks to understand development as a product of interactions among biological, psychological, and societal processes.

psychosocial crisis A predictable life tension that arises as people experience some conflict between their own competencies and the expectations of their society.

psychosocial evolution The contribution of each generation to the knowledge and norms of society.

psychosocial moratorium A period of free experimentation before a final identity is achieved.

psychosocial theory A theory of psychological development that proposes that cognitive, emotional, and social growth are the result of the interaction between social expectations at each life stage and the competencies that people bring to each life challenge.

pubertal status The extent to which physical markers have emerged in the transition to adult reproductive and sexual maturity.

puberty The period of physical development at the onset of adolescence when the reproductive system matures.

public self The many roles that one plays and the expectations that social reference groups, including family members, neighbors, teachers, friends, religious groups, ethnic groups, and even national leaders, have for one's behavior.

punishment A penalty or negative experience imposed on a person for improper behavior.

purpose The ability to imagine and pursue valued goals.

qualitative inquiry An approach to the study of human behavior that tries to understand the meanings, motives, and beliefs underlying a person's actions.

quasi-experimental Treatment in a human development study that is not controlled by the experimenter but was the result of some pattern of life events.

quasi-experimental study A study in which the assignment of participants to treatment was not controlled by the experimenter but was a result of some pattern of life events.

question-asking Using inquiry to gather information, accomplish goals, or clarify a situation.

quickening Sensations of fetal movement, usually beginning during the second trimester of fetal growth.

radius of significant relationship The groups of important people in one's life. The breadth and complexity of these groups change over the life span.

random sample A sample in which each person in a given population has an equal chance of being included.

random sampling A method for choosing the sample for a study in which each member of the population under investigation has an equal chance of being included.

range of applicability The nature of the concepts and principles that a theory is trying to explain.

rapport Conveying a feeling of trustworthiness and acceptance in an interview or in a counseling setting.

reaction range The range of possible responses to environmental conditions that is established through genetic influences.

reaction time The interval between the onset of a stimulus and a behavior in response.

reactive With regard to surveys, the quality of creating attitudes where none existed before.

reactive nature of surveys The ability of some surveys to create attitudes where none existed before.

reactivity A child's threshold for arousal, which indicates the likelihood of becoming distressed.

readiness A time when a child's physical, cognitive, social, and emotional maturation is at a level to undertake new learning or to engage in a more complex, demanding type of activity or relationship.

reading fluency The accuracy and speed with which one can read words in a text.

reality principle In psychosexual theory, a principle in which the ego protects the person by waiting to gratify id impulses until a socially acceptable form of expression or gratification can be found.

receptive language The ability to understand words.

reciprocal role Social roles that are partly defined by the other roles that support them such as the student and the teacher, the parent and the child, and the salesperson and the customer.

reciprocity A scheme describing the interdependence of related dimensions, such as height and width or time and speed.

reference group (plural: reference groups) A group with which an individual identifies and whose values the individual accepts as guiding principles.

reflex (plural: reflexes) An involuntary motor response to a simple stimulus.

regression In psychosexual theory, a defense mechanism where a person reverts to an earlier form of drive satisfaction, immature forms of relationships with others, lower moral standards, or more simplistic ways of thinking and solving problems.

rejection Refusal to accept someone in a social group.

rejectivity The unwillingness to include certain others or groups of others in one's generative concerns.

relational paradigm In contemporary psychoanalytic theory, the view that humans have basic needs for connection, contact, and meaningful interpersonal relationships and that the self is formed in an interpersonal context and emerges through interactions with others. Maturity requires the achievement of a sense of vitality, stability, and inner cohesiveness formulated through interpersonal transactions. Psychopathology or dysfunction arises when a person internalizes rigid, rejecting, or neglectful relational experiences and then uses these internalizations to anticipate or respond to real-life social encounters.

reliable With regard to tests, the quality of being repeated consistently. For example, a person who takes the same test on two consecutive days and earns approximately the same score both times has taken a reliable test.

reliability The consistency of a test in measuring something.

remarriage Marrying two or more times.

reminiscence The process of thinking or telling about past experiences.

repair (plural: repairs) See communication repairs.

repeatable In research, it is important that others carry out a similar investigation and observe the same results as the original investigator. For this to occur, the original investigator must carefully define all the procedures and equipment used, describe all the essential characteristics of the participants (e.g., age, sex, and social class background), and describe the setting or situation where the observations were made.

representational skills Skills learned in the preoperational stage—including mental imagery, symbolic play, symbolic drawing, imitation, and language—that permit the child to represent experiences or feelings in a symbolic form.

repression In psychosexual theory, a defense mechanism where unacceptable impulses are pushed into the unconscious.

repudiation Rejection of roles and values that are viewed as alien to oneself.

reputational identity Identity characteristics assigned to someone by those in their environment (such as a school) that is derived from their being associated with a crowd in the setting.

research design A process that outlines an empirical study, focusing on the approach to selecting a sample, the methods used to gather information, the design for studying change, and the techniques to analyze the data.

reserve capacity A person's resources to protect themselves from illness or recover from illness or stress, especially as they age.

resilience   The capacity to recover from stress, or the ability to withstand the effects of stressors that are typically associated with negative outcomes.

resilient   Able to withstand or recover quickly from difficult conditions.

resistant attachment   A form of insecure attachment in which the child is anxious about exploring the environment, even when the mother is present, shows distress and anxiety in the Strange Situation when the mother is absent, and may be ambivalent about being comforted even after the mother returns.

resources   Skills, talents, wealth, or other goods that can be used as needed.

restoration-oriented coping   Refers to finding ways to master the practical challenges of the loss of a loved one in order to make meaning of the death and move along in one's life.

retirement   A societal and psychological construct in which an individual ceases to work year-round full time, often withdrawing from the formal structure of work.

retirement anxiety   Apprehensions that adults have as they anticipate retirement.

retrospective study   Research that asks the participants to report on experiences from an earlier time in their lives.

reversibility   A scheme describing the ability to undo an action and return to the original state.

rites of passage   A ceremony or ritual associated with an important transition in a person's life.

ritual   A formal and customarily repeated act or series of acts.

role   A set of behaviors with some socially agreed-upon functions and for which there exists an accepted code of norms, such as the role of teacher, child, or minister.

role compatibility   When partners in a relationship approach situations in a manner that works well, their behaviors and responses complement one another.

role conflict   The state of tension that occurs when the demands and expectations of various roles conflict with each other.

role enactment   Patterned characteristics of social behavior that one performs as a result of being in a specific role.

role expectations   Shared expectations for behavior that are linked to a social role.

role experimentation   The central process for the resolution of the psychosocial crisis of later adolescence which involves participation in a variety of roles before any final commitments are made.

role overload   The state of tension that occurs when there are too many role demands and expectations to handle in the time allowed.

role reversal   Assuming the behaviors of a person in a reciprocal role, as when a child acts toward his or her parent as a parent.

role sequencing   The order of entry into new roles and age-related role transitions often based on normative expectations of members of one's ethnic group.

role spillover   The state of tension that occurs when the demands or preoccupations about one role interfere with the ability to carry out another role.

role strain   The conflict and competing demands made by several roles that the person holds simultaneously.

romantic love   A form of love that combines passion and commitment; an exhilarating, emotional, and preoccupying experience of affection and attachment to the loved object.

rule (plural: rules)   Principle or regulation governing conduct, action, procedure, or ritual.

sampling   A method of choosing participants in a study.

scaffolding   A process through which a child and an adult attempt to arrive at a shared understanding about a communication, at which point the adult interacts so as to expand or enrich the child's communicative competence.

scheme (plural: schemes)   In Piaget's theory, the organization of actions into a unified whole, a mental construct.

school readiness   When a child's physical, cognitive, social, and emotional maturity are at a level to undertake the rigors of formalized schooling.

scientific process   A set of techniques for acquiring new knowledge, investigating questions of interest, and modifying or correcting previous knowledge.

secondary process thought   In psychosexual theory, a reality-oriented thinking; a logical, sequential thinking.

secondary sex characteristics   The physical characteristics other than genitals that indicate sexual maturity, such as body hair, breasts, and deepened voice.

secular growth trend   A tendency, observed since approximately 1900, for more rapid physical maturation from one generation to the next, probably as a result of favorable nutrition, increased mobility, and greater protection from childhood diseases.

secure attachment   Infants actively explore their environment and interact with strangers while their mothers are present. After separation, the babies actively greet their mothers or seek interaction. If the babies were distressed during separation, the mothers' return reduces their distress,

and the babies return to exploration of the environment. In adulthood, this is an attachment outcome in which a person has a positive model of the self and of others.

selection   The process in which adolescents form relationships with other adolescents who share certain common interests, values, or preferences.

selection forces   Adolescents seek out friends who will support their involvement or their resistance to the use of alcohol and drugs as part of a more general pattern of behavior.

self-acceptance   The product of the positive feelings that come from expressing and trusting one's ideas and feelings; and from the acceptance one receives from others.

self-actualization   A motive that urges the person to make optimal use of his or her full potential to become a more effective, creative participant in daily life.

self-control   For toddlers, the ability to comply with a request, modify behavior according to the situation, initiate or postpone action, and behave in a socially acceptable way without having to be guided or directed by someone else.

self-efficacy   A sense of confidence that one can perform the behaviors that are demanded in a specific situation.

self-esteem   The evaluative dimension of the self that includes feelings of worthiness, pride, and discouragement.

self-evaluation   The ability to assess one's own abilities and skills.

self-fulfilling prophecy   False or inaccurate beliefs can produce a reality that corresponds with these beliefs.

self-insight   An understanding and awareness of one's true nature.

self-monitoring children   Some children appear to monitor their social environment more self-consciously than others. High self-monitoring children are more aware of the emotional and nonverbal behavior of others and make more use of social information to evaluate and regulate their own behavior than low self-monitoring children.

self-presentation bias   Research participants may present themselves in the way they want the interviewer to see them.

self-regulation   Behavior inhibition in response to stimuli.

self-regulatory plan (plural: self-regulatory plans)   A strategy for achieving one's goals, including techniques for managing internal emotional states, creating a plan, and putting the plan into action.

self-sufficiency   The state of making independent decisions, taking responsibility for one's actions, and achieving a degree of financial independence.

self-theory An organized set of ideas about the self, the world, and the meaning of interactions between the self and the environment.

semantic memory Recall of basic knowledge, such as the meaning of words like "vegetable," "democracy," or "insect."

semiotic thinking The understanding that one thing can stand for another.

sensation seeking A tendency to pursue activities that are novel, thrilling, and exciting.

sense of coherence A process in which one seeks to find an integrative thread that makes sense of the life one has led without belaboring past mistakes.

sense of control A feeling that one has the authority or power to direct one's behavior in various aspects of one's life, such as selecting one's leisure activities or choosing when to retire. In older adults, a sense of control is associated with life satisfaction.

sensitive period (plural: sensitive periods) A span of time during which a particular skill or behavior is most likely to develop.

sensitivity (of caregiver) Attentiveness to an infant's state, accurate interpretation of the infant's signals, and well-timed responses that promote mutually rewarding interactions.

sensorimotor adaptation Infants use their reflexes to explore their world, and they gradually alter their reflexive responses to take into account the unique properties of objects around them. This provides the basis for sensorimotor intelligence.

sensorimotor intelligence In Piaget's theory of development, the first stage of cognitive growth, during which schemes are built on sensory and motor experiences.

sensorimotor play Sensory exploration and motor manipulation that produce pleasure.

sensory register The neurological processing activity that is required to take in visual, auditory, tactile, and olfactory information.

separation anxiety Feelings of fear or sadness associated with the departure of the object of attachment.

sex Refers to biological features or distinctions of men and women that are determined by chromosomal information.

sex linked Genetic material that is located on the 23rd chromosome.

sex-linked characteristics Characteristics for which the allele is found on the sex chromosomes.

sex segregation A characteristic of young children's friendships where boys and girls tend to choose play companions of their own sex.

sexual motivation A person's interest in initiating sexual behaviors.

shame An intense emotional reaction to being ridiculed or to a negative self-assessment.

short-term memory The working capacity to encode and retrieve five to nine bits of information in the span of a minute or two. This is the scratch pad of memory that is used when someone tells you a telephone number or gives you his or her address.

sign (plural: signs) Something that represents something else, usually in an abstract, arbitrary way, for example, a word for an object.

significant relationship Important relationships that provide opportunities for great depth and intimacy and which allow age-related demands on individuals to be communicated.

similarity bias The tendency to exaggerate perceptions of similarity between partners, thereby increasing feelings of closeness and being understood.

skill (plural: skills) An ability to do something competently in a particular area that combines knowledge, practice, and training.

skill care facility See nursing homes.

small for gestational age (SGA) Fetus who does not weigh as much as a normal fetus of the same age. These fetuses are at greater risk for health problems than those who are born prematurely but are of average weight for their gestational age.

SOC model A model of adaption that requires the integration of three processes: selection, optimization, and compensation.

social anxiety A fear of being watched, judged, and criticized in social situations.

social clock Expectations for orderly and sequential changes that occur with the passage of time as individuals move through life.

social cognition Concepts related to understanding interpersonal behavior and the point of view of others.

social cognitive neuroscience The field of study that explores the neurological processes associated with the ways we perceive social information and reason about others. It is premised on the idea that articulating the biological, cognitive, and social levels of analysis contribute to more comprehensive explanations of human mind and behavior. While higher order metacognitive processes affect how we consciously operate in social interactions, automatic and unconscious mechanisms also account for much social interaction.

social comparison Comparing oneself to others in a particular social environment.

social competence The skills involved in one's ability to form and maintain positive relationships with others.

social construction In the study of gender, the view that gender differences are a product of cultural scripts and contextualized social expectations.

social controls Guiding models and influences that encourage or restrict one's behavior; common sources of influence include parents, friends, authority figures, and religious values and beliefs.

social conventions Socially accepted norms and regulations that guide behavior.

social culture Encompasses the norms, roles, beliefs, values, rites, and customs of a culture.

social evolutionary theory A theory that emphasizes reproductive potential and reproductive investment in the selection of a desirable partner.

social expectations The appraisals and beliefs of significant others about what is valued or desirable that impact a person's performance.

social identity The aspect of the self-concept that is based on membership in a group or groups and the importance and emotional salience of that membership.

social integration Being comfortably involved in meaningful interpersonal associations and friendship relations.

socialization The process of teaching and enforcing group norms and values to the new group members.

social learning theory A theory of learning that emphasizes the ability to learn new responses through observation and imitation of others.

social play Children joining with other children in some activity.

social pretend play Children who coordinate their pretense. They establish a fantasy structure, take roles, agree on the make-believe meaning of props, and solve pretend problems.

social referencing The process by which infants use facial features and verbal expressions as clues to the emotional responses of another person, often the mother, and as information about how to approach an unfamiliar, ambiguous situation.

social role A set of behaviors with some socially agreed-upon functions and for which there exists an accepted code of norms, such as the role of teacher, child, or minister.

social role theory The theory that emphasizes participation in varied and more complex roles as a major factor in human development.

social support   The social experiences leading people to believe that they are cared for and loved, that they are esteemed and valued, and that they belong to a network of communication and mutual obligation.

societal system   Includes those processes through which a person becomes integrated into society. Societal influences include social roles, rituals, cultural myths, social expectations, leadership styles, communication patterns, family organization, ethnic and subcultural influences, political and religious ideologies, patterns of economic prosperity or poverty and war or peace, and exposure to racism, sexism, and other forms of discrimination, intolerance, or intergroup hostility. The impact of the societal system on psychosocial development results largely from interpersonal relationships, often relationships with close or significant others.

sociobiology   The scientific study of the biological basis of social behavior that focuses on practices within populations that increase the likelihood of certain genes surviving in subsequent generations of offspring.

socioeconomic level   One's ranking based on a number of social and financial indicators, including years of education, occupation, and income.

socioeconomic status (SES)   Refers to a combination of resources including income, education, and occupation.

socioemotional support   Expressions of affection, care, respect, and esteem.

solicitude   State of caring, attentiveness, and helpfulness.

solicitude versus shame   A two-dimensional spectrum of cultural attitudes toward pregnant women. Solicitude is shown in the care, interest, and help of the pregnant woman and fetus. Shame is instilled through humiliation or separation of the pregnant woman. Combined with adequacy versus vulnerability, these attitudes create a matrix within which the birth culture of any society or subculture can be located.

solitary pretense   Children are involved in their own fantasy activities, such as pretending that they are driving a car or giving a baby a bath.

speciation   A process that contributes to biological diversity wherein a new species is established by breaking away from an earlier evolutionary lineage.

speed of processing   The amount of time it takes to detect and interpret sensory stimuli.

sperm   The male germ cell.

spermarche   The production and release of sperm that can be detected in a boy's urine; typically happens late in the pubertal process.

stagnation   A lack of psychological movement or growth during middle adulthood that may result from self-aggrandizement or from the inability to cope with developmental tasks.

statistically significant   Pertaining to observations that are unlikely to occur by chance and that therefore indicate a systematic cause.

status offense   Behavior that is criminalized for minors, such as running away or truancy, which would not be against the law for adults.

stigmatized death (plural: stigmatized deaths)   People attributing someone's death to an immoral, illegal, or evil cause.

strange situation   A standard laboratory procedure designed to study patterns of attachment behavior. A child is exposed during a 20-minute period to a series of events that are likely to stimulate the attachment system. Child and caregiver enter an unfamiliar laboratory setting; a stranger enters; the caregiver leaves briefly; and the caregiver and infant have opportunities for reunion while researchers observe child, caregiver, and their interactions.

stranger anxiety   Feelings of fear or apprehension in the presence of unfamiliar people, especially during infancy.

stratified sampling   A method for choosing the sample for a research study in which participants are selected from a variety of levels or types of people in the population.

statistical techniques   During the final, evaluation phase of the scientific process, techniques that help determine the likelihood that observations could have happened by chance.

subculture (plural: subcultures)   A cultural group within a larger group that may or may not have beliefs at variance with a larger cultural group.

sublimation   In psychosexual theory, a process that channels the energy from impulses into activities that either symbolize the impulses or express them in a socially acceptable form.

substantive complexity   The degree to which one's work requires thought, independent judgment, and frequent decision making.

successful agers   Elderly individuals who are characterized by three interdependent features: they have a low risk of disease and disease-related disabilities; high mental and physical function; and active engagement with life.

sudden infant death syndrome   A cause of infant death in which apparently healthy babies are put to bed and are later found dead with no clear explanation, even after autopsy.

superego   In psychoanalytic theory, the mental function that embodies moral precepts and moral sanctions. The superego includes the ego ideal, or the goals toward which one strives as well as the punishing conscience.

superordinate group identity   The members of a team or other group who bring their own individual racial/ethnic, cultural, or socioeconomic group identities to a situation and are willing to suppress their differences and work together for the success of the group.

surrogacy   An alternative to biological reproduction in which a woman is implanted through one of a variety of methods and carries the fetus through the full gestational period at which time she releases the infant to the individual or couple who enlisted her participation.

survey research   A means of collecting specific information from a large number of participants.

swaddling   The practice of wrapping a baby snugly in a soft blanket, which is a common technique for soothing a newborn in many cultures.

symbol (plural: symbols)   An object or image that represents something. A symbol can be an image that represents an object, such as "chair," or an object that represents a concept, such as a dove.

symbolic play   Imaginative or pretend activities that express emotions, problems, or roles.

synchrony   Infant and caregiver move from one state to the next in a fluid manner. Interactions of the infant and caregiver are rhythmic, well timed, and mutually rewarding.

system   An entity—a cell, an organ, an individual, a family, or a corporation—that is composed of interdependent elements that share some common goals, interrelated functions, boundaries, and an identity.

systematic   In a careful, orderly way. Scientists have a framework of questions that they strive to answer based on what is already known and what theories predict. They approach research by having clear objectives, carefully defining the purpose of their work, and describing the specific methods they will use.

systematic approach   An approach that ensures research is done in a careful, orderly way by having clear objectives, carefully defining the purpose of the research, and the specific methods researchers will use to reach those objectives.

systematic observation   A step of the scientific process that tests a theory by translating an abstract concept into something that can be measured and observed. Observations must be objective, repeatable, and systematic.

Taegyo   A Korean set of practices that defines the behavior of pregnant women based on the belief that the fetus is able to feel what the mother feels.

tantrums   In young children, sudden, uncontrollable outbursts of anger and frustration.

teachable moment   A time when a person is most ready to acquire a new ability.

team play   Sports or games played with a group that generally have complex rules and that provide a context for early learning about the skills and orientations that will apply to the world of work and to functioning in the family group.

telegraphic speech   Two-word sentences used by children that omit many parts of speech but convey meaning.

temperament   Innate characteristics that determine the person's sensitivity to various sense experiences and his or her responsiveness to patterns of social interaction.

teratogens   Agents that produce malformations during the formation of organs and tissues.

testosterone   A hormone that fosters the development of male sex characteristics and growth.

thanatology   The field of science that addresses dying and death as well as the psychological mechanisms of coping with them.

theory   A logically interrelated system of concepts and statements that provides a framework for organizing, interpreting, and understanding observations, with the goal of explaining and predicting behavior.

third gender   A concept that expands our way of thinking about gender by including more options than just man and woman.

time   In ecological systems theory, the period in which change among the systems occurs.

trajectory (plural: trajectories)   In the life course, the path of one's life experiences in a specific domain, particularly work and family life.

transgendered   Refers to people who do not identify with or present themselves as reflecting the sex they were born with and who move across or combine gender boundaries.

transient exuberance   A rapid increase in the number of neurons, dendrites, and synapses that form in the brain during the first 2 years of life.

transition (plural: transitions)   In the life course, the beginning or close of an event or role relationship. For example, work transitions might be getting one's first job, being laid off, and going back to school for an advanced degree.

treatment   In an experiment, the set of experiences or information a group of participants receives.

triangulation   Confirming a researcher's insights by looking at written documents about the setting, interviewing other informants, and sharing observations with other members of the research team.

tribute   A gift, testimonial, compliment, establishment of a public monument, or good works in the name of a deceased person given in acknowledgment of gratitude or esteem.

trimester (plural: trimesters)   A conceptualized period of pregnancy that lasts three months. There are three trimesters in a typical pregnancy.

trust   An emotional sense that both the environment and oneself are reliable and capable of satisfying basic needs.

turning point   A critical incident that brings about a significant change in commitment.

ultrasound   A technique for producing visual images of the fetus in utero through a pattern of deflected sound waves.

unacknowledged mourners   People whose grief over a death is not sanctioned or supported by the community.

unconscious   Psychological processes that occur outside of awareness, including problem solving.

unwanted sexual attention   Sexual attention that is perceived as threatening, embarrassing, or harmful.

usefulness/competence   Personality dimension associated with well-being and high self-esteem through volunteer work, involvement with others, and a sense of purpose and structure in the use of time.

usual aging   A state of typical aging in which individuals may be functioning well but are at high risk for disease, disability, and reduced capacity for functional independence.

uterus   In the female reproductive system, the hollow muscular organ in which the fertilized ovum normally becomes embedded and in which the developing embryo and fetus is nourished and grows.

vagal tone   A process through which changes in heart rate vary during changes in environmental conditions. Typically, when you breathe in, heart rate increases, and when you breathe out, heart rate decreases. Under conditions when a task requires attention and concentration, heart rate increases, which allows for adaptive mobilization of resources. When the situation becomes more intense or threatening, heart rate slows, leading to conservation of resources and the ability to achieve a more calm state. The vagal system contributes to regulation of arousal and reactivity and is considered to be a basic neural component of self-regulation, information processing, and emotion.

valid   With regard to tests, the quality of actually measuring what the test intends to measure.

validity   The extent to which a test measures what it is supposed to measure.

value (plural: values)   A principle or quality that is intrinsically desirable.

vascular dementia   A form of dementia that occurs when the blood vessels to the brain are blocked or narrow; the brain does not get the blood flow, oxygen, and nutrients needed for adequate functioning.

verbal persuasion   Encouragement from others.

viability   Reaching the stage of development in which a fetus is capable of living outside the uterus.

vicarious experience   An experience achieved through the imagined participation in events that happen to another person.

vicarious reinforcement   Through observing others, a person can learn a behavior and also acquire the motivation to perform the behavior or resist performing that behavior depending on what is observed about the consequences of that behavior.

visual acuity   The ability to detect visual stimuli under various levels of illumination.

visual adaptation   The ability to adapt to changes in the level of illumination.

visual tracking   Following an object's movement with one's eyes.

vital marriage   The partners enjoy spending time together; they resolve conflicts quickly, often using compromise; they are willing to make sacrifices for each other; and they have a satisfying, pleasurable sex life.

vocabulary   All the words a person uses and understands.

volunteer   With regard to research, an individual who agrees to participate in a study. One cannot compel a person to participate in research.

volunteerism   Involvement in some form of volunteer service.

volunteer sampling   Sampling in which participants for a study are selected from volunteers.

well-being   The state of being happy, healthy, or prosperous.

white matter   Myelinated axons that connect gray matter and carry messages between nerve cells and brain regions.

whole-brain death   A technical definition of death with eight criteria that was developed in 1981 by the President's Commission for the Ethical Study of Problems in Medicine and Biomedical and Behavioral Research.

widowhood   The stage of life one enters when one's spouse dies.

will   The determination to exercise free choice and self-control.

wisdom   A type of expert knowledge that reflects sound judgment and good advice in the face of high levels of uncertainty.

withdrawal   General orientation of wariness toward people and objects.

withdrawn   A path to peer rejection in which children are shy and self-conscious.

word (plural: words)   A unit of language, consisting of one or more spoken sounds or their written representation, that functions as a principal carrier of meaning.

work   A job or activity that a person does regularly, especially to earn money.

work-family facilitation   Individual coping strategies and family-friendly attitudes and resources of the workplace that make it easier for employees to address pressing family demands within the scope of their daily work.

work/life balance   A concept that reflects the ability to prioritize career ambitions and goals with lifestyle goals to achieve a sense of well-being and life satisfaction.

working memory   A type of memory that uses attention to hold and manipulate information in the short term.

working model of attachment   An infant's expectations of the behavior of their caregiver that is based on the quality of attachment.

workplace discrimination   Practices that occur in the workplace that involve the unjust or prejudicial treatment of one person or group of people.

worldview   A way of making meaning of the relationships, situations, and objects encountered in daily life in a culture.

young-old   Among the very old, those who remain healthy, vigorous, and competent.

zone of proximal development   The emergent developmental capacity that is just ahead of the level at which the person is currently functioning.

zygote   The first phase of fetal development, when a single cell is formed from two gametes.

References

AARP. (2000). *Update on the older worker: 2000*. Retrieved from http://research.aarp.org/econ/dd62_worker.html

AARP. (2002). *AARP national survey on consumer preparedness and e-commerce: A survey of computer users age 45 and older.* Retrieved from http://research.aarp.org/consume/ecommerce_1.html

Abbey, A. (1995). Provision and receipt of social support and disregard: What is their impact on the marital life quality of infertile and fertile couples? *Journal of Personality and Social Psychology, 68*, 455–469.

Abel, E. L. (1984). *Fetal alcohol syndrome and fetal alcohol effects.* New York, NY: Plenum.

Abel, K. (2010). *Grandfamilies: Grandparents raising grandchildren.* Retrieved from http://life.familyeducation.com/grandparents/family/29678.html

Abele, A. E., Volmer, J., & Spurk, D. (2012). Career stagnation: Underlying dilemmas and solutions in contemporary work environments. In N. P. Reilly, M. J. Sirgy, & C. A. Gorman (Eds.), *Work and quality of life: Ethical practices in organizations* (pp. 107–132). International handbooks of quality-of-life. New York, NY: Springer Science + Business Media.

Abele, A. E., & Wojciszke, B. (2007). Agency and communion from the perspective of self and others. *Journal of Personality and Social Psychology, 93*, 751–763.

Aber, J. L. (1994). Poverty, violence, and child development: Untangling family and community level effects. In C. A. Nelson (Ed.), *Threats to optimal development: Integrating biological, psychological, and social risk factors* (pp. 229–272). Hillsdale, NJ: Erlbaum.

Abma, J. C., & Martinez, G. M. (2006). Childlessness among older women in the United States: Trends and profiles. *Journal of Marriage and Family, 68*, 1045–1056.

About.com. (2010). *Discrimination stories.* Retrieved from http://jobsearch.about.com/u/sty/tipsforolderjobseekers/agediscrimination/I-Was-Called-an-Old-Lady.htm

Abrams, L. (2003). Contextual variations in young women's gender identity negotiations. *Psychology of Women Quarterly, 27*, 64–74.

Abrahms, S. (2011). Boomers redefine retirement living. *AARP.* Retrieved from http://www.aarp.org/home-garden/housing/info-04-2011/elder-housing.html

Abrahms, S. (2013). House sharing for boomer women who would rather not live alone. *AARP,* Retrieved from http://www.aarp.org/home-family/your-home/info-05-2013/older-women-roommates-house-sharing.html

Academy of Medical Royal Colleges (AMRC). (2011). *Induced abortion and mental health—A systematic review of the mental health outcomes of induced abortion, including their prevalence and associated factors.* London: Academy of Medical Royal Colleges/National Collaborating Center for Mental Health.

Achenbach, T. M. (1991). *Manual for the youth self-report and 1991 profile.* Burlington: University of Vermont, Department of Psychiatry.

Acitelli, L. K., Douvan, E., & Veroff, J. (1997). The changing influence of interpersonal perceptions on marital well-being among Black and White couples. *Journal of Social and Personal Relationships, 14*, 291–304.

Ackerman, G. L. (1993). A congressional view of youth suicide. *American Psychologist, 48*, 183–184.

Acredolo, L., Goodwyn, S., & Abrams, D. (2009). *Baby signs: How to talk with your baby before your baby can talk* (3rd ed.). New York, NY: McGraw-Hill.

Adam, E. K., Snell, E. K., & Pendry, P. (2007). Sleep timing and quantity in ecological and family context: A nationally representative time-diary study. *Journal of Family Psychology, 21*, 4–19.

Adams, B. N. (1986). *The family: A sociological interpretation* (4th ed.). San Diego, CA: Harcourt Brace Jovanovich.

Adams, G. R., & Archer, S. L. (1994). Identity: A precursor to intimacy. In S. L. Archer (Ed.), *Interventions for adolescent identity development* (pp. 193–213). Thousand Oaks, CA: Sage.

Adams, K. S., & Proctor, B. E. (2010). Adaptation to college for students with and without disabilities: Group differences and predictors. *Journal of Postsecondary Education and Disability, 22*, 166–184.

Adams, R. B., Franklin, R. G., Nelson, A. J., & Stevenson, M. T. (2010). Compound social cues in human face processing. A brain's eye view. In R. B. Adams, N. Ambady, K. Nakayama, & S. Shimojo (Eds.), *The science of social vision* (pp. 90–106). New York, NY: Oxford University Press.

Adams, R. E., Santo, J. B., & Bukowski, W. M. (2011). The presence of a best friend buffers the effects of negative experiences. *Developmental Psychology, 47*, 1786–1791.

Adams, S., Kisler, T., Vaccaro, A., & Newman, B. M. (2013). Unpublished research interviews.

Addy, S., & Wight, V. R. (2012). *Basic facts about low-income children, 2010.* National Center for Children in Poverty. Retrieved from http://www.nccp.org/publications/pub_1049.html

Adelman, C. (2006). *The toolbox revisited: Paths to degree completion from high school through college.* Washington, DC: U.S. Department of Education.

Adelson, J., & Doehrman, M. J. (1980). The psychodynamic approach to adolescence. In J. Adelson (Ed.), *Handbook of adolescent psychology* (pp. 99–116). New York, NY: Wiley.

Ades, P. A., Ballor, D. L., Ashikaga, T., Utton, J. L., & Nair, K. S. (1996). Weight training improves walking endurance in healthy elderly persons. *Annals of Internal Medicine, 124*, 568–572.

Adler, J. (1999, May 10). The truth about high school. *Newsweek*, pp. 56–58.

Adler, N. E., David, H. P., Major, B. N., Roth, S. H., Russo, N. F., & Wyatt, G. (1990). Psychological responses after abortion. *Science, 248*, 41–44.

Administration on Aging. (2012). *A profile of older Americans: 2012.* Retrieved from http://www.aoa.gov/Aging_Statistics/Profile/2012/16.asp

Administration on Aging. (2014). *Highlights.* Retrieved from http://www.aoa.acl.gov/Aging_Statistics/Profile/2014/2.aspx

Adolph, K. (2016). Video as data. *Observer, 29*, 23–25.

Adolph, K. D. (2008). Learning to move. *Current Directions in Psychological Science, 17*, 213–218.

Adolph, K. E., & Berger, S. E. (2006). Motor development. In D. Kuhn, R. S. Siegler, W. Damon, & R. M. Lerner (Eds.), *Handbook of child psychology: Vol. 2. Cognition, perception, and language* (6th ed., pp. 161–213). Hoboken, NJ: John Wiley & Sons.

Adolph, K. E., & Berger, S. E. (2011). Physical and motor development. In M. H. Bornstein & M. E. Lamb (Eds.), *Cognitive development: An advanced textbook* (pp. 257–318). New York, NY: Psychology Press.

Adolph, K. E., Berger, S. E., & Leo, A. J. (2011). Developmental continuity? Crawling, cruising and walking. *Developmental Science, 14*, 306–318.

Adolph, K. E., Cole, W. G., Komati, M., Garciaguirre, J. S., Badaly, D., Lingeman, J. M., Chan, G. L. Y., Sotsky, R. B. (2012). How do you learn to walk? Thousands of steps and dozens of falls per day. *Psychological Science, 23*, 1387–1394.

Adolph, K. E., & Eppler, M. A. (2002). Flexibility and specificity in infant motor skill acquisition. In J. W. Fagen & H. Hayne (Eds.), *Progress in infancy research* (Vol. 2, pp. 121–167). Mahwah, NJ: Erlbaum.

Adolph, K. E., & Robinson, S. R. (2015). Motor development. In R. M. Lerner (Series Eds.) & L. Liben & U. Muller (Vol. Eds),

Handbook of child psychology and developmental science: Vol. 2: Cognitive processes (7th ed., pp. 114–157). New York: Wiley.

Adolph, K. E., & Tamis-LeMonda, C. S. (2014). The costs and benefits of development: The transition from crawling to walking. *Child Development Perspectives, 8*, 187–192.

Adolph, K. E., Vereijken, B., & Denny, M. A. (1998). Learning to crawl. *Child Development, 69*, 1299–1312.

Adolphs, R. (2009). The social brain: Neural basis of social knowledge. *Annual Review of Psychology, 60*, 693–716.

Agerup, T., Lydersen, S., Wallander, J., & Sund, A. M. (2015). Associations between parental attachment and course of depression between adolescence and young adulthood. *Child Psychiatry and Human Development, 46*, 632–642.

Ageworks.com. (2012). *World and U.S. Population Pyramids, The U.S.* Retrieved from http://www .ageworks.com/course _demo/200/module2/module2b.htm#us

Aging Services Council of Central Texas. (2013). *Best practices.* Retrieved from http://www.agingservicescouncil.org /documents/Report/00AGINGSERVICESS CANhowcancommunitysupport.htm

AgriLife Extension. (2010). *Building positive relationships: Adult children and their aging parents.* Retrieved from http://fcs.tamu .edu/families/aging/elder_care/building _positive_relation-ships.php

Ahlqvist, S., Halim, M. L., Greulich, F. K., Lurye, L. E., & Ruble, D. (2013). Potential benefits and risks of identifying as a tomboy: A social identity perspective. *Self and Identity, 12*, 563–581.

Ainsworth, C. (2015). Sex redefined. *Nature, 518*, 288–291.

Ainsworth, M. D. S. (1973). The development of infant–mother attachment. In B. M. Caldwell & H. N. Ricciuti (Eds.), *Review of child development research* (Vol. 3). Chicago, IL: University of Chicago Press.

Ainsworth, M. D. S. (1979). Infant-mother attachment. *American Psychologist, 34*, 932–937.

Ainsworth, M. D. S. (1985). Patterns of infant–mother attachments: Antecedents and effects on development. *Bulletin of the New York Academy of Medicine, 61*, 771–791.

Ainsworth, M. D. S. (1989). Attachments beyond infancy. *American Psychologist, 44*, 709–716.

Ainsworth, M. D. S., Bell, S. M. V., & Stayton, D. J. (1971). Individual differences in strange situational behavior of one-year-olds. In H. A. Schaffer (Ed.), *The origins of human social relations.* London: Academic Press.

Ainsworth, M. D. S., Blehar, M. C., Waters, E., & Wall, S. (1978). *Patterns of attachment: A psychological study of the strange situation.* Hillsdale, NJ: Erlbaum.

Ainsworth, M. D. S., & Eichberg, C. (1991). Effects on infant-mother attachment of mother's unresolved loss of an attachment figure or other traumatic experience. In

C. M. Parkes, J. Stevenson-Hinde, & P. Marris (Eds.), *Attachment across the life cycle* (pp. 160–186). Alameda, CA: Tavistock Books.

Aisha, B.A. (2013). *Funeral rites and regulations in Islam.* Retrieved from http://www .missionislam.com/knowledge/funeral.htm

Akhtar, N., & Gernsbacher, M. A. (2008). On privileging the role of gaze in infant social cognition. *Child Development Perspectives, 2*, 59–65.

Aksan, N., & Kochanska, G. (2005). Conscience in childhood: Old questions, new answers. *Developmental Psychology, 41*, 506–516.

Alan Guttmacher Institute. (2002). *Sexuality education. Facts in brief.* Retrieved from http://www .agi-usa.org/pubs/fb_sex_ed02 .pdf

Alan Guttmacher Institute. (2002). *Teenagers' sexual and reproductive health. Facts in brief.* Retrieved from http://www.agi-usa .org/pubs/fb_sex _ed02 .pdf

Albert, D., Chein, J., & Steinberg, L. (2013). The teenage brain: Peer influence on adolescent decision making. *Current Directions in Psychological Science, 22*, 114–120.

Albert, M. S. (2002). Memory decline: The boundary between aging and age-related disease. *Annals of Neurology, 51*, 282–284.

Albom, M. (1997). *Tuesdays with Morrie: An old man, a young man, and life's greatest lesson.* New York, NY: Doubleday.

Aldwin, C. (2011). Stress and coping across the lifespan. In S. Folkman (Ed.), *The Oxford handbook of stress, health, and coping* (pp. 15–34). Oxford Library of Psychology. New York, NY: Oxford University Press.

Aldwin, C. M., & Gilmer, D. F. (2013). *Health, illness and optimal aging* (2nd ed.). New York: Springer.

Aldwin, C. M., Spiro, III., A., & Park, C. L. (2006). Health behavior and optimal aging: A developmental perspective. In J. E. Birren & K. W. Schaie (Eds.) *Handbook of psychology of aging* (6th ed., pp. 77–104). San Diego CA: Elsevier.

Alexander, C. S., Somerfield, M. R., Ensminge, M. E., Johnson, K. E., & Kim, Y. J. (1993). Consistency of adolescents' self-report of sexual behavior in a longitudinal study. *Journal of Youth and Adolescence, 22*, 455–473.

Alexander, K. L., Entwisle, D. R., & Kabbani, N. S. (2001). The dropout process in life course perspective: Early risk factors at home and school. *Teachers College Record, 103*, 760–822.

Alexander, K. L., Entwisle, D. R., & Olson, L. S. (2007). Lasting consequences of the summer learning gap. *American Sociological Review, 72*, 167–180.

Alexander, K., Entwisle, D., & Olson, L. (2014). *The long shadow: Family background disadvantaged urban youth, and the transition to adulthood.* New York: Russell Sage Foundation.

Alexander, K. L., Entwisle, D. R., & Thompson, M. S. (1987). School performance, status relations, and the structure

of sentiment: Bringing the teacher back in. *American Sociological Review, 52*, 655–682.

Allan, B. A., Douglass, R. P., Duffy, R. D., & McCarty, R. J. (2016). Meaningful work as a moderator of the relation between work stress and meaning in life. *Journal of Career Assessment, 24*, 429–440.

Allemand, M. (2008). Age differences in forgiveness: The role of future time perspective. *Journal of Research in Personality, 42*, 1137–1147.

Allen, J. P. (2008). The attachment system in adolescence. In J. Cassidy & P. R. Shaver (Eds.), *Handbook of attachment: Theory, research and clinical applications* (2nd ed., pp. 419–435). New York, NY: Guilford.

Allen, K. R., Blieszner, R., & Roberto, K. (2001). Families in the middle and later years: A review and critique of the research in the 1990s. *Journal of Marriage and the Family, 62*, 911–926.

Allen, T. D. (2001). Family-supportive work environment. *Journal of Vocational Behavior, 38*, 414–435.

Allen, T.D., French, K.A., Dumani, S. & Shockley, K.M. (2015). Meta-analysis of work-family conflict mean differences: Does national context matter? *Journal of Vocational Behavior, 90*, 90–100.

Allerhand, M., Gale, C. R., & Deary, I. J. (2014). The dynamic relationship between cognitive function and positive well-being in older people: A prospective study using the English Longitudinal Study of Aging. *Psychology and Aging, 29*, 306–318.

Allhusen, V., Belsky, J., Booth-La Force, C., et al. (2005). Duration and developmental timing of poverty and children's cognitive and social development from birth through third grade. *Child Development, 76*, 795–810.

Al-Owidha, A., Green, K. E., & Kroger, J. (2009). On the question of an identity status category order: Rasch model step and scale statistics used to identify category order. *International Journal of Behavioral Development, 33*, 88–96.

Altschul, I., Oyserman, D., & Bybee, D. (2006). Racial-ethnic identity in mid-adolescence: Content and change as predictors of academic achievement. *Child Development, 77*, 1155–1169.

Altvater-Mackensen, N., Mani, N., & Grossman, T. (2016). Audiovisual speech perception in infancy: The influence of vowel identity and infants' productive abilities on sensitivity to (mis)matches between auditory and visual speech cues. *Developmental Psychology, 52*, 191–204.

Alzheimer's Association. (2013). *2012 Alzheimer's disease facts and figures.* Retrieved from http:// www.alz.org /downloads/facts_figures_2012.pdf

Amato, P. R. (1988). Parental divorce and attitudes toward marriage and family. *Journal of Marriage and the Family, 50*, 453–462.

Amato, P. R. (1996). Explaining the intergenerational transmission of divorce. *Journal of Marriage and the Family, 58*, 628–640.

Amato, P. R. (2010). Research on divorce: Continuing trends and new developments. *Journal of Marriage and the Family, 72,* 650–666.

Amato, P. R., & De Boer, D. D. (2001). The transmission of marital instability across generations: Relationship skills or commitment to marriage? *Journal of Marriage and the Family, 63,* 1038–1051.

Amato, P. R., & Kane, J. B. (2011). Parents' marital distress, divorce and remarriage: Links with daughters' early family formation transitions. *Journal of Family Issues, 32,* 1073–1103.

Ambady, N. & Bharucha, J. (2009). Culture and the brain. *Current Directions in Psychological Science, 18,* 342–345.

American Academy of Pediatrics. (1995). The inappropriate use of school "readiness" tests. *Pediatrics, 95,* 437–438.

American Academy of Pediatrics. (1999). *Caring for your baby and young child.* New York, NY: Bantam.

American Academy of Pediatrics. (2006). Menstruation in girls and adolescents: Using the menstrual cycle as a vital sign. *Pediatrics, 118,* 2245–2250.

American Academic of Pediatrics. (2012). Breastfeeding and the use of human milk. Policy Statement. *Pediatrics, 129,* e827–e841.

American Academy of Pediatrics. (2013). *Children, adolescents and the media.* Retrieved from http://pediatrics.aappublications.org/content/132/5/958

American Academy of Pediatrics. (2014). *Caring for your baby and young child, 6th edition: Birth to age 5.* New York: Bantam.

American Academy of Pediatrics. (2016a). *Breastfeeding initiatives: Frequently asked questions (FAQs).* Retrieved from https://www2.aap.org/breastfeeding/faqsBreastfeeding.html

American Academy of Pediatrics. (2016b). *Cognitive and verbal skills needed for toilet training.* Retrieved from www.healthychildren.org/English/ages-stages/toddler/toilet-training/Pages/Cognitive-and-Verbal-Skills

American Administration on Aging. (2010). *Profile of older Americans, 2009.* U.S. Government Printing Office: U.S. Department of Health and Human Services.

American Association of Retired Persons. (2010). *Sex, romance and relationships. AARP survey of midlife and older adults.* Retrieved from http://assets.aarp.org/rgcenter/general/srr_09.pdf

American Civil Liberties Union. (1996). *Violence chip.* Retrieved from http://www.aclu.org/library/aavchip .html

American College of Obstetricians and Gynecologists. (2014). *Committee opinion, #613.* Retrieved from http://www.acog.org/Resources-And-Publications/Committee-Opinions/Committee-on-Health-Care-for-Underserved-Women/Increasing-Access-to-Abortion

American Foundation for Suicide Prevention. (2016). Retrieved from https://afsp.org/about-suicide/suicide-statistics/

American Medical Association. (2004). *American Medical Association Family Medical Guide* (4th ed.). Hoboken, NJ: John Wiley & Sons.

American Pregnancy Association. (2013). *Abusing prescription drugs during pregnancy.* Retrieved from http://www.americanpregancy.org/pregnancyhealth/abusingprescriptiondrugs

American Pregnancy Association. (2015a). *Miscarriage signs, symptoms, treatment and prevention.* Retrieved from http://americanpregnancy.org/pregnancy-complications//miscarriage

American Pregnancy Association. (2015b). *Abusing prescription drugs during pregnancy.* Retrieved from http://americanpregnancy.org/pregnancy-health/abusing-prescription-drugs-during-pregnancy/

American Pregnancy Association. (2015c). *Abortion procedures.* Retrieved from http://americanpregnancy.org/unplanned-pregnancy/abortion-procedures/

American Psychiatric Association. (2016). *What is gender dysphoria?* Retrieved from https://www.psychiatry.org/patients-families/gender-dysphoria/what-is-gender-dysphoria

American Psychological Association. (1992). Ethical principles of psychologists and code of conduct. *American Psychologist, 47,* 1597–1611.

American Psychological Association. (2002). Ethical principles of psychologists and code of conduct. *American Psychologist, 57,* 1060–1073.

American Psychological Association. (2008). *Answers to your questions: For a better understanding of sexual orientation and homosexuality.* Washington, DC: author. Retrieved from www.apa.org/topics/sorientation.pdf

American Psychological Association. (2010). *Stress in America, 2009.* Washington, DC: Author.

American Psychological Association. (2016). *Making stepfamilies work.* Retrieved from http://www.apa.org/helpcenter/stepfamilies.aspx

American Psychological Association Task Force in Gender Identity and Gender Variance. (2009). *Report of the task force on gender identity and gender variance.* Washington, DC: Author.

American Society for the Positive Care of Children. (2016). *Causes of bullying.* Retrieved from http://www.americanspcc.org/wp-content/uploads/2013/04/Bullying-Causes-of-Courtesy-of-nobullying.pdf

American Speech-Language-Hearing Association. (2013). *Two to three years; Three to four years.* Retrieved from www.asha.org/public/speech/development/

American Speech-Language-Hearing Association (ASHA). (2016). *Social language use (Pragmatics).* Retrieved from http://www.asha.org/public/speech/development/Pragmatics/

Amundson, N. E. (2001). Three-dimensional living. *Journal of Employment Counseling, 38,* 114–127.

Andersen, S. L., Sebastiani, P., Dworkis, D. A., Feldman, L., & Perls T. (2012). Health span approximates life span among many supercentenarians: Compression of morbidity at the approximate limit of life span. *Journal of Gerontology, A: Biological Science and Medical Science, 67,* 395–405.

Anderson, D. R., Huston, A. C., Schmitt, K., Linebarger, D. L., & Wright, J. C. (2001). Early childhood television viewing and adolescent behavior: The recontact study. *Monographs of the Society for Research in Child Development, 66* (Serial No. 264).

Anderson, G. O. (2015). *AARP post-retirement career study.* Retrieved from http://www.aarp.org/content/dam/aarp/research/surveys_statistics/econ/2015/aarp-work-jobs-report-res-econ.pdf

Anderson, K. H., Foster, J. E., & Frisvold, D. E. (2010). Investing in health: The long-term impact of Head Start on smoking. *Economic Inquiry, 48,* 587–602.

Anderson, K. J., & Leaper, C. (1998). Meta-analyses of gender effects on conversational interruption: Who, what, when where, and how. *Sex roles, 39,* 225–252.

Anderson, S. M., Downey, G., & Tyler, T. R. (2005). Becoming engaged in the community: A relational perspective on social identity and community engagement. In G. Downey, J. S. Eccles, & C. M. Chatman (Eds.), *Navigating the future: Social identity, coping and life tasks* (pp. 210–251). New York, NY: Russell Sage Foundation.

Anderssen, N., Amlie, C., & Ytteroy, E. A. (2002). Outcomes for children with lesbian or gay parents: A review of studies from 1978 to 2000. *Scandinavian Journal of Psychology, 43,* 335–351.

Andrulis, D. P. (2000). Community, service, and policy strategies to improve health care access in the changing urban environment. *American Journal of Public Health, 90,* 858–862.

Aneshensel, C. S., Pearlin, L. I., Mullan, J. T., Zarit, S. H., & Whitlatch, C. J. (1995). *Profiles in caegiving: The unexpected career.* San Diego, CA: Academic Press.

Anglin, J. M. (1993). Vocabulary development: A morphological analysis. *Monographs of the Society for Research in Child Development,* Serial No. 238, 58.

Annan, J., Brier, M., & Aryemo, F. (2009). From "rebel" to "returnee": Daily life and reintegration for young soldiers in Northern Uganda. *Journal of Adolescent Research, 24,* 639–667.

Annie, E. Casey Foundation. (1999). *Kids count data book.* Baltimore MD: Author.

Ansari, A., & Gershoff, E. (2016). Parent involvement in Head Start and children's development: Indirect effects through parenting. *Journal of Marriage and the Family, 78,* 562–579.

Ansary, N. S., Elias, M. J., Greene, M. B., & Green, S. (2015). Guidance for schools selecting antibullying approaches: Translating evidence-based strategies to contemporary implementation realities. *Educational Researcher, 44,* 27–36.

Anthony, S. (1972). *The discovery of death in childhood and after.* New York, NY: Basic Books.

Antislavery.org. (2016). *Child slavery.* Retrieved from http://www.antislavery .org/english/slavery_today/child_slavery /default.aspx

Antonio, A. L., Chang, M. J., Hakuta, K., Kenny, D. A., Levin, S., & Milem, J. F. (2004). Effects of racial diversity on complex thinking in college students. *Psychological Science, 15,* 507–510.

Antonovsky, A. (1987). *Unraveling the mystery of health. How people manage stress and stay well.* San Francisco, CA: Jossey-Bass.

Antonucci, T. C., Lansford, J. E., Schaberg, L., Smith, J., Baltes, M., Akiyama, H., et al. (2001). Widowhood and illness: A comparison of social network characteristics in France, Germany, Japan, and the United States. *Psychology and Aging, 16,* 655–665.

Antzoulatos, E. G., & Miller, E. K. (2014). Increases in functional connectivity between the prefrontal cortex and striatum during category learning. *Neuron, 83,* 216–225.

Anvar, M. (2016). An anorexic fashion industry. *The Daily Californian.* Retrieved from http://www.dailycal.org/2016/02/26 /france-modeling-laws/

Aoki, C., & Siekevitz, P. (1988). Plasticity in brain development. *Scientific American, 259,* 56–64.

APA. (2016). *Elder care: More than "parenting a parent."* Retrieved from http://www.apa .org/helpcenter/elder-care.aspx

Apgar, V. (1953). Proposal for a new method of evaluating the newborn infant. *Anesthesia and Analgesia, 32,* 260–267.

Aptekar, S. (2015). *The road to citizenship: What naturalization means for immigrants and the United States.* New Brunswick, NJ: Rutgers University Press.

Arbuckle, T. Y., Gold, D. P., Andres, D., Schwartzman, A., & Chaikelson, J. (1992). The role of psychosocial context, age, and intelligence in memory performance of older men. *Psychology and Aging, 7,* 25–36.

Arcus, D., & Chambers, P. (2008). Childhood risks associated with adoption: Family influences on childhood behavior and development. In T. P. Gulotta & G. M. Blau (Eds.), *Family influences on childhood behavior and development: Evidence-based prevention and treatment approaches* (pp. 117–142). New York, NY: Routledge /Taylor & Francis.

Archer, J. (1991). Human sociobiology: Basic concepts and limitations. *Journal of Social Issues, 47,* 11–26.

Archer, S. L. (1992). A feminist's approach to identity research. In G. R. Adams, T. P. Gullotta, & R. Montemayor (Eds.), *Adolescent identity formation: Advances in adolescent development* (pp. 25–49). Newbury Park, CA: Sage.

Ardelt, M. (2004). Wisdom as expert knowledge system: A critical review of a contemporary operationalization of an ancient concept. *Human Development, 47,* 257–285.

Ardelt, M. (2010). Are older adults wiser than college students? A comparison of two age cohorts. *Journal of Adult Development, 17,* 193–207.

Arias, E. (2007). United States life tables, 2004. *National Vital Statistics Reports, 56*(9).

Arias, E. (2014). United States life tables, 2010. *National Vital Statistics Reports, 63, No.7,* Hyattsville, MD: National Center for Health Statistics.

Aries, E. (1998). Gender differences in interaction: A reexamination. In D. J. Canary & K. Dindia (Eds.), *Sex differences and similarities in communication: Critical essays and empirical investigations of sex and gender in interaction* (pp. 65–81). Mahwah, NJ: Erlbaum.

Armour, N. (2012, August 4). Golden again, U.S. wins first Olympic title since '96. NBCOlympics.com. London: NBCUniversal Media, Associated Press.

Arnett, J. J. (2004a). *Adolescence and emerging adulthood: A cultural approach* (2nd ed.). Upper Saddle River, NJ: Prentice Hall.

Arnett, J. J. (2006). Emerging adulthood: Understanding the new way of coming of age. In J. J. Arnett & J. L. Tanner (Eds.), *Emerging adults in America: Coming of age in the 21st century* (pp. 3–19). Washington, DC: American Psychological Association.

Arnold, J., & Clark, M. (2016). Running the penultimate lap of the race: A multimethod analysis of growth generativity, career-orientation, and personality amongst men in mid/late career. *Journal of Occupational and Organizational Psychology, 89,* 308–329.

Arnold, M. L. (2000). Stage, sequence, and sequels: Changing conceptions of morality, post-Kohlberg. *Educational Psychology Review, 12,* 365–383.

Aron, A., Fisher, H., Mashek, D., Strong, G., Li, H., & Brown, L. (2005). Reward, motivation and emotion systems associated with early-stage intense romantic love. *Journal of Neurophysiology, 93,* 327–337.

Aronson, D. (2009). Nutrition for health and longevity. *Today's Dietician, 11,* 40.

Arsenio, W. F., & Gold, J. (2006). The effects of social injustice and inequality on children's moral judgments and behavior: Towards a theoretical model. *Cognitive Development, 21,* 388–400.

Arseth, A. K., Kroger, J., Martinussen, M., & Marcia, J. E. (2009). Meta-analytic studies of identity status and the relational issues of attachment and intimacy. *Identity:*

An International Journal of Theory and Research, 9, 1–32.

ASA. (2015). *Life delayed: The impact of student debt on the daily lives of young Americans. 2015 edition.* Retrieved from http://www.asa.org/site/assets/files/4743 /life_delayed_whitepaper_2015.pdf

Aseltine, R. H., Jr. (2003). Evaluation of a school based suicide prevention program. *Adolescent & Family Health, 3,* 81–88.

Asher, S. R., & Gazelle, H. (1999). Loneliness, peer relations, and language disorder in childhood. *Topics in Language Disorders, 19,* 16–33.

Asher, S. R., & Paquette, J. A. (2003). Loneliness and peer relations in childhood. *Current Directions in Psychological Science, 12,* 75–78.

Asher, S. R., Parkhurst, J. T., Hymel, S., & Williams, G. A. (1999). Peer rejection and loneliness in childhood. In S. R. Asher & J. D. Coie (Eds.), *Peer rejection in childhood* (pp. 253–273). New York, NY: Cambridge University Press.

Ashley, J. M., Harper, B. D., Arms-Chaves, C. J., & LoBello, S. G. (2015). Estimated prevalence of antenatal depression in the U.S. population. *Archives of Women's Mental Health, December 21, 2015.*

Askham, J., Briggs, K., Norman, I., & Redfern, S. (2007). Care at home for people with dementia: As in a total institution? *Aging and Society, 27,* 3–24.

Aslin, R. N. (1987). Visual and auditory development in infancy. In J. D. Osofsky (Ed.), *Handbook of infant development* (2nd ed., pp. 5–97). New York, NY: Wiley.

Astone, N. M. (1993). Are adolescent mothers just single mothers? *Journal of Research on Adolescence, 3,* 353–372.

Atchley, R. C. (1975). The life course, age grading, and age-linked demands for decision making. In N. Datan & L. H. Ginsberg (Eds.), *Life-span developmental psychology: Normative life crises.* New York, NY: Academic Press.

Atchley, R. C. (2001). *Continuity and adaptation in aging.* Baltimore, MD: Johns Hopkins University Press.

Atchley, R. C. (2003). Why most people cope well with retirement. In J. L. Ronch and J. A. Goldfield (Ed.), *Mental wellness in aging: Strengths-based approaches* (pp. 123–138). Baltimore, MD: Health Professions Press.

Atkinson, A. P., Heberlein, A. S., & Adolphs, R. (2010). Are people special? A brain's eye view. In R. B. Adams, N. Ambady, K. Nakayama, & S. Shimojo (Eds.), *The science of social vision* (pp. 363–392). New York, NY: Oxford University Press.

Atkinson, D. R., Morten, G., & Sue, D. W. (1983). *Counseling American minorities: A cross-cultural perspective* (2nd ed.). Dubuque, IA: William C. Brown.

Atkinson, R. H. (2000). Measuring gentrification and displacement in Greater London. *Urban Studies, 37,* 149–166.

Atkinson, R. H. (2001). *Standardized tests and access to American universities.* Retrieved from http://www .ucop.edu/news/sat /speech.html

Attachment and Trauma Network. (2014). *What are attachment disorders?* Retrieved from http://www.attachmenttraumanetwork .org/understanding-attachment/ attachment-disorders/

Atwater, L., Kim, K. Y., Witt, A., Latheef, Z., Callison, K., Elkins, T. J., & Zheng, D. (2016). Reactions to abusive supervision: Examining the roles of emotions and gender in the USA. *The International Journal of Human Resource Management, 27*, 1874–1899.

Au, T. K., Sidle, A. L., & Rollins, K. B. (1993). Developing an intuitive understanding of conservation: Invisible particles as a plausible mechanism. *Developmental Psychology, 29*, 286–299.

Aubé, C., & Rousseau, V. (2005). Team goal commitment and team effectiveness: The role of task interdependence and supportive behaviors. *Group Dynamics: Theory, Research, and Practice, 9*, 189–204.

Aud, S., KewalRamani, A., & Frohlich, L. (2011). *America's youth: Transitions to adulthood.* (NCES2012-026). U.S. Department of Education, National Center for Education Statistics. Washington, DC: U.S. Government Printing Office.

Auger, A., Farkas, G., Burchinal, M. R., Duncan, G. J., &Vandell, D. L. (2014). Preschool center care quality effects on academic achievement: An instrumental variables analysis. *Developmental Psychology, 50*, 2559–2571.

Augustine, J. M., Nelson, T., & Edin, K. (2009). Why do poor men have children? Intentions among low-income unmarried U.S. fathers. *The Annals of the American Academy of Political and Social Science, 624*, 99–117.

Austria, A. M. (2012). The retiree as a professor, a woman, and an ethnic minority. In E. Cole & M. Gergen (Eds.), *Retiring but not shy: Feminist psychologists create their post-careers* (pp. 24–43). Chagrin Falls, OH: Taos Institute Publications.

Avert.org. (2010). *Global HIV/AIDS estimates, end of 2008.* Retrieved from www.avert .org/worldstats.htm

Avery, C. S. (1989). How do you build intimacy in an age of divorce? *Psychology Today, 23*(5), 21–31.

Azar, S.T. (2012). Parenting and child mal-treatment. In M. H. Bornstein (Ed.), *Handbook of parenting: Vol. 4. Social conditions and applied parenting* (2nd ed.). New York, NY: Psychology Press.

BabyCenter.com. (2007). *17 surprising facts about birth in the U.S.* Retrieved from http://www.babycenter.com/refcap /pregnancy/childbirth/

Bachu, A., & O'Connell, M. (2001). Fertility of American women: June 2000. *Current Population Reports*, P20-543RV. Washington, DC: U.S. Bureau of the Census.

Back, M. D., Stopfer, J. M., Vazire, S., Gaddis, S., Schmukle, S. C., Egloff, B., et al. (2010). Facebook profiles reflect actual personality, not self-idealization. *Psychological Science, 21*, 372–374.

Bafunno, D., & Camodeca, M. (2013). Shame and guilt development: The role of context, audience and individual characteristics. *European Journal of Developmental Psychology, 10*, 128–143.

Baglivio, M. T., & Epps, N. (2016). The interrelatedness of adverse childhood experiences among high-risk juvenile offenders. *Youth Violence and Juvenile Justice, 14*, 179–196.

Bagnini, C. (2014). Men in the nursery: A discussion-play group with fathers and their infants and toddlers. In J. Magagna & P. Pasquini (Eds.), *Being present for your nursery age child: Observing, understanding, and helping children* (pp. 249–253). London, England: Karnac Books.

Bagwell, C. L., & Coie, J. D. (2004). The best friendships of aggressive boys: Relationship quality, conflict management, and rule-breaking behavior. *Journal of Experimental Child Psychology, 88*, 5–24.

Bahrick, L. E., Lickliter, R., & Flom, R. (2006). Up versus down: The role of intersensory redundancy in the development of infants' sensitivity to the orientation of moving objects. *Infancy, 9*, 73–96.

Bailey, B. A. (2010). Partner violence during pregnancy: Prevalence, effects, screening and management. *International Journal of Women's Health, 2*, 183–197.

Bailey, B. A. & Daugherty, R. A. (2007). Intimate partner violence during pregnancy: Incidence and associated health behaviors in a rural population. *Maternal and Child Health, 11*, 495–503.

Bailey, J. M., & Pillard, R. (1991). A genetic study of male sexual orientation. *Archives of General Psychiatry, 48*, 1089–1096.

Bailey, J. M., & Pillard, R. (1994). The innateness of homosexuality. *The Harvard Mental Health Letter, 10*, 4–6.

Bailey, M. J., & Dynarski, S. M. (2011). Inequality in postsecondary education. In R. Murnane & G. Duncan (Eds.), *Whither opportunity? Rising inequality and the uncertain life chances of low-income children* (pp. 117–132). New York: The Russell Sage Foundation Press.

Balfanz, R., & Byrnes, V. (2006). Closing the mathematics achievement gap in high-poverty middle schools: Enablers and constraints. *Journal of Education for Students Placed at Risk, 11*, 143–159.

Baillargeon, R. (1987). Object permanence in 3½- and 4½- month-old infants. *Developmental Psychology, 23*, 655–664.

Baillargeon, R. (2004). Infants' physical world. *Current Directions in Psychological Science, 13*, 89–94.

Baillargeon, R. (2008). Innate ideas revisited: For a principles of persistence in infants' physical reasoning. *Perspectives on Psychological Science, 3*, 2–13.

Baillargeon, R., & DeVos, J. (1991). Object permanence in young infants: Further evidence. *Child Development, 62*, 1227–1246.

Baillargeon, R., & Graber, M. (1988). Evidence of location memory in 8-month-old infants in a nonsearch AB task. *Developmental Psychology, 24*, 502–511.

Baillargeon, R. H., Zoccolillo, M., Kenan, K., Côte, S., Perusse, D., Wu, H.-X., et al. (2007). Gender differences in physical aggression: A prospective population-based survey of children before and after 2 years of age. *Developmental Psychology, 43*, 13–36.

Baird, B. M., & Bergeman, C. S. (2011). Life-span developmental behavior genetics. In K. L. Fingerman, C. A. Berg, J. Smith, & T. C. Antonucci (Eds.), *Handbook of life-span development* (pp. 701–726). New York, NY: Springer.

Bakalar, N. (2012). Partners in flavor. *Nature, 486*, S4–S5.

Baker, A. J. L., Burkhard, B., & Kelley, J. (2012). Differentiating alienated from not alienated children: A pilot study. *Journal of Divorce and Remarriage, 53*, 178–193.

Baker, H. A., Jr. (1991). An apple for my teacher: Twelve writers tell about teachers who made all the difference. In H. L. Gates, Jr. (Ed.), *Bearing witness: Selections from African-American autobiography in the twentieth century* (pp. 317–319). New York, NY: Pantheon Books.

Baker, T. B., McFall, R. M., & Shoham, V. (2009). Current status and future prospects of clinical psychology. *Psychological Science in the Public Interest, 9*, 67–103.

Bakken, L., Thompson, J., Clark, F. L., Johnson, N., & Dwyer, K. (2001). Making conservationists and classifiers of preoperational fifth-grade children. *Journal of Educational Research, 95*, 56–61.

Baltes, P. B. (1997). On the incomplete architecture of human ontogeny: Selection, optimization, and compensation as foundation of developmental theory. *American Psychologist, 52*, 366–380.

Baltes, P. B., & Baltes, M. M. (1990). Psychological perspectives on successful aging: The model of selective optimization with compensation. In P. B. Baltes & M. M. Baltes (Eds.), *Successful aging: Perspectives from the behavioral sciences* (pp. 1–34). United Kingdom: Cambridge University Press.

Baltes, P. B., & Lindenberger, U. (1997). Emergence of a powerful connection between sensory and cognitive functions across the adult life span. A new window to the study of cognitive aging? *Psychology and Aging, 12*, 12–21.

Baltes, P. B., & Smith, J. (1990). The psychology of wisdom and its ontogenesis. In R. J. Sternberg (Ed.), *Wisdom: Its nature, origins and development* (pp. 87–120). New York, NY: Cambridge University Press.

Baltes, P. B., Smith, J., & Staudinger, U. M. (1992). Wisdom and successful aging. In T. B. Sonderegger (Ed.), *Psychology and aging* (pp. 123–168). Lincoln, NE: University of Nebraska Press.

Bambra, C. (2010). Yesterday once more? Unemployment and health in the 21st century. *Journal of Epidemiology and Community Health, 64*, 213–215.

Ban, M., & Uchiyama, I. (2015). Mothers' adjustment of behavior to pretend play. *North American Journal of Psychology, 17*, 17–26.

Bandura, A. (1971/2006). *Psychological modeling: Conflicting theories.* Chicago: Aldine-Atherton. Reprinted New Brunswick, NJ: Aldine Transaction.

Bandura, A. (1973). *Aggression: A social learning analysis.* Englewood Cliffs, NJ: Prentice Hall.

Bandura, A. (1977). *Social learning theory.* Englewood Cliffs, NJ: Prentice Hall.

Bandura, A. (1982). Self-efficacy mechanism in human agency. *American Psychologist, 37*, 122–147.

Bandura, A. (1986). *Social foundations of thought and action: A social cognitive theory.* Englewood Cliffs, NJ: Prentice Hall.

Bandura, A. (1989a). Regulation of cognitive processes through perceived self-efficacy. *Developmental Psychology, 25*, 729–735.

Bandura, A. (1989b). Social cognitive theory. *Annals of Child Development, 6*, 1–60.

Bandura, A. (1991). Social cognitive theory of moral thought and action. In W. M. Kurtines & J. L. Gewirtz (Eds.), *Handbook of moral behavior and development: Vol. 1. Theory* (pp. 45–103). Hillsdale, NJ: Erlbaum.

Bandura, A. (1999). Moral disengagement in the perpetration of inhumanities. *Personality and Social Psychology Review, 3*, 193–209.

Bandura, A. (2000). Self efficacy: The foundation of agency. In W. J. Perrig & A. Grob (Eds.), *Control of human behavior, mental processes, and consciousness: Essays in honor of the 60th birthday of August Flammer* (pp. 17–33). Mahwah, NJ: Erlbaum.

Bandura, A. (2001). Social cognitive theory: An agentic perspective. *Annual Review of Psychology, 52*, 1–26.

Bandura, A. (2008). An agentic perspective on positive psychology. In S. J. Lopez (Ed.), *Positive psychology: Exploring the best in people. Vol. 1. Discovering human strengths* (pp. 167–196). Westport, CT: Greenwood.

Bandura, A. (2015). *Moral disengagement: How people do harm and live with themselves.* New York: Worth Publishers.

Bandura, A., Barbaranelli, C., Caprara, G. V., & Pastorelli, C. (1996). Multifaceted impact of self-efficacy beliefs on academic functioning. *Child Development, 67*, 1206–1222.

Bandura, A., & Schunk, D. H. (1981). Cultivating competence, self-efficacy, and intrinsic interest through proximal self-motivation. *Journal of Personality and Social Psychology, 41*, 586–598.

Bandura, A., & Walters, R. H. (1963). *Social learning and personality development.* New York, NY: Holt, Rinehart & Winston.

Banerjee, R. (2002). Individual differences in children's understanding of social evaluation concerns. *Infant and Child Development, 11*, 237–252.

Bangen, K. J., Meeks, T. W., & Jeste, D. V. (2013). Defining and assessing wisdom: A review of the literature. *American Journal of Geriatric Psychiatry, 21*, 1254–1266.

Barajas-Gonzalez, R. G., & Brooks-Gunn, J. (2014). Income, neighborhood stressors, and harsh parenting: Test of moderation by ethnicity, age, and gender. *Journal of Family Psychology, 28*, 855–866.

Barbu-Roth, M., Anderson, D. I., Després, A., Provasi, J., Cabrol, D., & Campos, J. J. (2009). Neonatal stepping in relation to terrestrial optic flow. *Child Development, 80*, 8–14.

Bard, K. A., Coles, C. D., Platzman, K. A., & Lynch, M. E. (2000). The effects of prenatal drug exposure, term status and caregiving on arousal and arousal modulation in 8-week-old infants. *Psychobiology, 36*, 194–212.

Barger, S. D., Donoho, C. J., & Wayment, H. A. (2009). The relative contributions of race/ethnicity, socioeconomic status, health, and social relationships to life satisfaction in the United States. *Quality of Life Research: An International Journal of Quality of Life Aspects of Treatment, Care and Rehabilitation, 18*, 179–189.

Barnard, K. E., & Morisset, C. E. (1995). Preventive health and developmental care for children: Relationships as a primary factor in service delivery with at risk populations. In H. E. Fitzgerald, B. M. Lester, (Eds.), *Children of poverty: Research, health, and policy issues* (pp. 167–195). New York, NY: Garland.

Barnes, P. G. (2012). *Surviving bullies, queen bees & psychopaths in the workplace.* P. G. Barnes.

Barnett, M. A., Deng, M., Mills-Koonce, W. R., Willoughby, M., & Cox, M. (2008). Inter-dependence of parenting of mothers and fathers of infants. *Journal of Family Psychology, 22*, 561–573.

Barnett, M. A., Mills-Koonce, W. R., Gustafsson, H., & Cox, M. (2012). Mother-grandmother conflict, negative paenting, and young children's social development in multigenerational families. *Family Relations: An Inter-disciplinary Journal of Applied Family Studies, 61*, 864–877.

Barnett, R. C. (2004). Preface: Women and work: Where are we, where did we come from, and where are we going? *Journal of Social Issues, 60*, 667–674.

Barnett, R. C., Brennan, R. T., & Gareis, K. C. (1999). A closer look at the measurement of burnout. *Journal of Applied Biobehavioral Research, 4*, 65–78.

Barnett, R. C., & Hyde, J. S. (2001). Women, men, work, and family. *American Psychologist, 56*, 781–796.

Barnett, R. C., & Weidenfeller, N. K. (2016). Shared leadership and team performance. *Advances in Developing Human Resources, 18*, 334–351.

Barnett, W. S. (1996). *Lives in the balance: Age-27 benefit-cost analysis of the High/Scope Perry Preschool Program* (Monographs of the High/Scope Educational Research Foundation, 11). Ypsilanti, MI: High/Scope Press.

Barnett, W. S., Carolan, M. E., Squires, J. H., Clarke Brown, K., & Horowitz, M. (2015). *The state of preschool 2014: State preschool yearbook.* New Brunswick, NJ: National Institute for Early Education Research.

Barondes, S. (2011). *Making sense of people: Decoding the mysteries of personality.* Upper Saddle River, NJ: F. T. Press.

Barth, F. D. (2015). Social media and adolescent development: Hazards, pitfalls, and opportunities for growth. *Clinical Social Work Journal, 43*, 201–208.

Bartholomew, K. (1990). Avoidance of intimacy: An attachment perspective. *Journal of Social and Personal Relationships, 7*, 147–178.

Bartz, K. W., & Levine, E. S. (1978, November). Child rearing by black parents: A description and comparison to Anglo and Chicano parents. *Journal of Marriage and the Family, 40*, 709–719.

Bashore, T. R., Osman, A., & Heffle, E. F., III. (1989). Mental slowing in elderly persons: A cognitive psychophysiological analysis. *Psychology and Aging, 4*, 235–244.

Bass, B. I., Cigularov, K. P., Chen, P. Y., Henry, K. L., Tomazic, R. G., & Li, Y. (2016). The effects of student violence against school employees on employee burnout and work engagement: The roles of perceived school unsafety and transformation leadership. *International Journal of Stress Management, 23*, 318–336.

Bass, D. M., & Bowman, K. (1990). The transition from caregiving to bereavement: The relationship of care-related strain and adjustment to death. *The Gerontologist, 30*, 35–42.

Bassett, M. T. (2001). Keeping the M in MTCT: Women, mothers, and HIV prevention. *American Journal of Public Health, 91*, 701–702.

Bates, E., & Goodman, J. C. (2001). On the inseparability of grammar and the lexicon: Evidence from acquisition. In M. Tomasello & E. Bates (Eds.), *Language development: The essential readings* (pp. 134–162). Malden, MA: Blackwell.

Bates, E., Reilly, J., Wulgeck, B., Dronkers, N., Opei, M., Fenson, J., et al. (2001). Differential effects of unilateral lesions on language production in children and adults. *Brain & Language, 79*, 223–265.

Bates, E., & Roe, K. (2001). Language development in children with unilateral brain injury. In C. A. Nelson & M. Luciana (Eds.), *Handbook of developmental cognitive neuroscience* (pp. 281–308). Cambridge, MA: MIT Press.

Bates, J. E. (1987). Temperament in infancy. In J. D. Osofsky (Ed.), *Handbook of infant development* (2nd ed., pp. 1101–1149). New York, NY: Wiley.

Bates, J. S., & Goodsell, T. L. (2013). Male kin relationships: Grandfathers, grandsons, and generativity. *Marriage and Family Review, 49*, 26–50.

Baucom, B. R., Atkins, D. C., Eldridge, K., McFarland, P., Sevier, M., & Christensen, A. (2011). The language of demand/withdraw: Verbal and vocal expression in dyadic interactions. *Journal of Family Psychology, 25*, 50–580.

Baudisch, A., & Vaupel, J. W. (2012). Getting to the root of aging. *Science, 338*, 618–619.

Bauer, J. (2010). *Workers tell stories on how job retraining changed their lives.* Grand Rapids Press. Retrieved from http://www.mlive.com/news/index.ssf/2010/02/job_retraining_trade_readjustm.html

Bauer, J. J., & McAdams, D. P. (2010). Eudaimonic growth: Narrative growth goals predict increases in ego development and subjective well-being 3 years later. *Developmental Psychology, 46*, 761–772.

Bauer, M. (2014). *Men fall pregnant too. Look at couvade syndrome.* Retrieved from http://www.pregnancy.org/article/men-fall-pregnant-too-look-couvade-syndrome

Bauman, C. W., & Skitka, L. J. (2012). Corporate responsibility as a source of employee satisfaction. *Research and Organizational Behavior, 32*, 63–86.

Baumeister, R. F., DeWall, C. N., & Vohs, K. D. (2009). Social rejection, control, numbness, and emotion: How not to be fooled by Gerber and Wheeler, 2009. *Perspectives on Psychological Science, 4*, 489–493.

Baumeister, R. F., & Leary, M. R. (1995). The need to belong: Desire for interpersonal attachments as a fundamental human motivation. *Psychological Bulletin, 117*, 497–529.

Baumgardner, A. H. (1990). To know oneself is to like oneself: Self-certainty and self-affect. *Journal of Personality and Social Psychology, 58*, 1062–1072.

Baumgartner, T., Heinrichs, M., VonLanthen, A., Fischbacher, U., & Fehr, E. (2008). Oxytocin shapes the neural circuitry of trust and trust adaptation in humans. *Neuron, 58*, 639–650.

Baumrind, D. (1995). Commentary on sexual orientation: Research and social policy implications. *Developmental Psychology, 31*, 130–136.

Baxter, K. (2009). (Re)inventing adolescence. *The Hedgehog Review, 11*, 18–30.

Beah, I. (2007). *A long way gone: Memoirs of a boy soldier.* New York, NY: Farrar, Straus, & Giroux.

Beall, A. E., & Sternberg, R. J. (1995). The social construction of love. *Journal of Social and Personal Relationships, 12*, 417–438.

Beardsley, T. (1996). Vital data. *Scientific American, 274*, 100–105.

Bearman, P. S., & Brueckner, H. (2001). Promising the future: Virginity pledges and first intecourse. *American Journal of Sociology, 106*, 859–912.

Beauchamp, G. K., & Mennella, J. A. (2009). Early flavoring and its impact on later feeding behavior. *Journal of Pediatric Gastroenterological Nutrition, 48*, Supplement 1, S25–30.

Beauchamp, G. K., & Mennella, J. A. (2011). Flavor perception in human infants: Development and functional significance. *Digestion, 83*, Supplement 1, 1–6.

Beaver, K. M., DeLisi, M., Vaughn, M. S., Wright, J. P., & Boutwell, B. B. (2008). The relationship between self-control and language: Evidence of a shared etiological pathway. *Criminology: An Interdisciplinary Journal, 46*, 939–970.

Beck, A. T. (1976/1979). Cognitive therapy and the emotional disorders. New York, NY: Penguin Books.

Beck, J. C., & Schouten, R. (2000). Workplace violence and psychiatric practice. *Bulletin of the Menninger Clinic, 64*, 36–48.

Beck, M. (2008, March 11). Sorting through the choices for menopause hormones. *Wall Street Journal*, p. D1.

Becker, G., Beyene, Y., Newsom, E., & Mayen, N. (2003). Creating continuity through mutual assistance: Intergenerational reciprocity in four ethnic groups. *Journals of Gerontology: Series B: Psychological Sciences and Social Sciences, 58B*, S151–S159.

Beckman, L. J., & Harvey, S. M. (2005). Current reproductive technologies: Increased access and choice? *Journal of Social Issues, 61*, 1–20.

Beere, C. A. (1990). *Gender roles: A handbook of tests and measures.* New York, NY: Greenwood.

Begley, M., & Quayle, E. (2007). The lived experience of adults bereaved by suicide: A phenomenological study. *Crisis: The Journal of Crisis Intervention and Suicide Prevention, 28*, 26–34.

Begley, S. (1995, September 2). The baby myth. *Newsweek*, pp. 38–41.

Behrman, R. E., & Butler, A. S. (2007). *Preterm birth: Causes, consequences and prevention.* Washington, DC: National Academies Press.

Beins, B. C. (2012). Jean Piaget: Theorist of the child's mind. In W. E. Pickren, D. A. Dewsbury, & M. Wertheimer (Eds.). *Portraits of pioneers in developmental psychology* (pp. 89–107). New York, NY: Psychology Press.

Belanger, N. D., & Desrochers, S. (2001). Can 6-month-old infants process causality in different types of causal events? *British Journal of Developmental Psychology, 19*, 11–21.

Beliefnet. (2007). *What are the last rites?* Retrieved from http://www.beliefnet.com/story/163/story_16366.html

Bell, L., Burtless, G., Gornich, J., & Smeeding, T. M. (2007). Failure to launch: Cross-national trends in the transition to economic independence. In S. Danzinger & C. E. Rouse (Eds.), *The price of independence* (pp. 27–55). New York, NY: Russell Sage Foundation.

Bell, S. M., & Ainsworth, M. D. S. (1972). Infant crying and maternal responsiveness. *Child Development, 43*, 1171–1190.

Belsky, J. (1997). *The adult experience.* St. Paul, MN: West.

Belsky, J. (2006). Determinants and consequences of infant-parent attachment. In L. Balter & C. S. Tamis-LeMonda (Eds.), *Child psychology: A handbook of contemporary issues* (2nd ed., pp. 53–77). New York, NY: Psychology Press.

Belsky, J. (2011). The determinants of parenting in GXE perspective: A case of differential susceptibility? In A. Booth, S. M. McHale, & N. S. Landale (Eds.), *Biosocial foundations of family processes. National Symposium on Family Issues* (pp. 61–68). New York, NY: Springer Science + Business Media.

Belsky, J., Campbell, S. B., Cohn, J. F., & Moore, G. (1996). Instability of infant–parent attachment security. *Developmental Psychology, 32*, 921–924.

Belsky, J., & Pluess, M. (2009). The nature (and nurture?) of plasticity in early human development. *Perspectives on Psychological Science, 4*, 345–351.

Belsky, J., & Rovine, M. (1990). Patterns of marital change across the transition to parenthood. *Journal of Marriage and the Family, 52*, 5–20.

Belsky, J., Vandell, D. L., Burchinal, M., Clarke-Stewart, K. A., McCartney, K., & Owen, M. T. (2007). Are there long-term effects of early child care? *Child Development, 78*, 681–701.

Bem, S. L. (1981). Gender schema theory: A cognitive account of sex-typing. *Psychological Review, 88*, 354–364.

Bem, S. L. (1989). Genital knowledge and gender constancy in preschool children. *Child Development, 60*, 649–662.

Benasich, A. A., & Leevers, H. J. (2003). Processing of rapidly presented auditory cues in infancy: Implications for later language development. In H. Hayne & J. W. Fagen (Eds.), *Progress in infancy research* (Vol. 3, pp. 245–288). Mahwah, NJ: Lawrence Erlbaum.

Ben-Dat Fisher, D., Serbin, L. A., Stack, D. M., Ruttle, P. L., Ledingham, J. E., & Schwartzman, A. E. (2007). Intergenerational predictors of diurnal cortisol secretions in early adulthood. *Infant and Child Development, 16*, 151–170.

Benedict, R. (1934/1950). *Patterns of culture.* New York, NY: New American Library.

Benenson, J. F. (1993). Greater preference among females than males for dyadic interaction in early childhood. *Child Development, 64*, 544–555.

Bengston, V. L. (2001). Beyond the nuclear family: The increasing importance of multigenerational bonds. *Journal of Marriage and the Family, 63*, 1–16.

Benjet, C., & Hernandez-Guzman, L. (2002). A short-term longitudinal study of pubertal change, gender, and psychological well-being of Mexican early adolescents. *Journal of Youth and Adolescence, 31,* 429–442.

Bennett, K. M., & Soulsby, L. K. (2012). Well-being in bereavement and widowhood. *Illness, Crisis, and Loss, 20,* 321–337.

Benson, J. B., & Uzgiris, I. C. (1985). Effect of self-initiated locomotion on infant search activity. *Developmental Psychology, 21,* 923–931.

Benson, J. E., & Elder, G. H., Jr. (2011). Young adult identities and their pathways: A developmental and life course model. *Developmental Psychology, 47,* 1646–1657.

Benson, M. J., Harris, P. B., & Rogers, C. S. (1992). Identity consequences of attachment to mothers and fathers among late adolescents. *Journal of Research on Adolescence, 2,* 187–204.

Benson, P. L. (1992). *The troubled journey: A profile of American youth.* Minneapolis, MN: Lutheran Brotherhood.

Berg, C. A., & Strough, J. (2011). Problem solving across the lifespan. In K. L. Fingerman, C. A. Berg, J. Smith, & T. C. Antonucci (Eds.), *Handbook of life-span development* (pp. 239–268). New York, NY: Springer.

Berg, K., Hines, M., & Allen, S. (2002). Wheelchair users at home: Few home modifications and many injurious falls. *American Journal of Public Health, 92,* 48.

Bergen, D. (2002, Spring). The role of pretend play in children's cognitive development. *Early Childhood Research and Practice, 4*(1).

Bergeman, C. S., Plomin, R., Pedersen, N. L., McClearn, G. E., & Nesselroade, J. R. (1990). Genetic and environmental influences on social support: The Swedish adoption/twin study of aging. *Journal of Gerontology, 45,* P101–P106.

Berger, A. (2011). *Self-regulation: Brain, cognition and development.* Washington, DC: American Psychological Association.

Berk, L. E. (2004). *Infants, children, and adolescents* (5th ed.). Needham Heights, MA: Allyn & Bacon.

Berkman, L. F., Glass, T., Brisette, I., & Seeman, T. E. (2000). From social integration to health: Durkheim in the new millennium. *Social Science and Medicine, 51,* 843–857.

Berlin, L. J., Appleyard, K., & Dodge, K. A. (2011). Intergenerational continuity in child maltreatment: Mediating mechanisms and implications for prevention. *Child Development, 82,* 162–176.

Berlin, L. J., Cassidy, J., & Appleyard, K. (2010). The influence of early attachments on other relationships. In J. Cassidy & P. R. Shaver (Eds.), *Handbook of attachment: Theory research and clinical applications* (2nd ed., pp. 317–333). New York, NY: Guilford Press.

Berlin, L. J., Ispa, J. M., Fine, M. A., Malone, P. S., Brooks-Gunn, J., Brady-Smith, C., et al. (2009). Correlates and consequences of spanking and verbal punishment for low-income white, African American, and Mexican American toddlers. *Child Development, 80,* 1403–1420.

Bernard, J. (1972). *The future of marriage.* New York, NY: World.

Berndt, T. J., & Murphy, L. M. (2002). Influences of friends and friendships: Myths, truths, and research recommendations. In R. V. Kail (Ed.), *Advances in child development and behavior* (Vol. 30, pp. 275–310). San Diego, CA: Academic Press.

Bernet, W., & Baker, A. J. L. (2013). Parental alienation, DSM-5, and ICD-II. *Journal of the American Academy of Psychiatry and the Law, 41,* 98–104.

Bernichon, T., Cook, K. E., & Brown, J. D. (2003). Seeking self-evaluative feedback: The interactive role of global self-esteem and specific self-views. *Journal of Personality and Social Psychology, 84,* 194–204.

Bernier, A., Larose, S., Boivin, M., & Soucy, N. (2004). Attachment state of mind: Implications for adjustment to college. *Journal of Adolescent Research, 19,* 783–806.

Berrueta-Clement, J. R., Schweinhart, L. J., Barnett, W. S., Epstein, A. S., & Weikart, D. P. (1984). *Changed lives: The effects of the Perry Preschool Program on youths through age 19.* Ypsilanti, MI: High/Scope Press.

Bertalanffy, L. von (1950). The theory of open systems in physics and biology. *Science, 111,* 23–28.

Bertalanffy, L. von (1968). *General systems theory* (Rev. ed.). New York, NY: Braziller.

Berzonsky, M. D. (1989). Identity style: Conceptualization and measurement. *Journal of Adolescent Research, 4,* 267–281.

Berzonsky, M. D. (1993). Identity style, gender, and social-cognitive reasoning. *Journal of Adolescent Research, 8,* 289–296.

Berzonsky, M. D. (2011). A social-cognitive perspective on identity construction. In S. J. Schwartz, K. Luyckx, & V. L. Vignoles, (Eds.), *Handbook of identity theory and research* (Vol. 1, pp. 55–76). New York, NY: Springer Science + Business Media.

Berzonsky, M. D., & Kinney, A. (2008). Identity processing style and defense mechanisms. *Polish Psychological Bulletin, 39,* 111–117.

Berzonsky, M. D., & Kuk, L. S. (2000). Identity status, identity processing style, and the transition to university. *Journal of Adolescent Research, 15,* 81–98.

Best, K. M., Hauser, S. T., & Allen, J. P. (1997). Predicting young adult competencies: Adolescent era parent and individual influences. *Journal of Adolescent Research, 12,* 90–112.

Betancourt, H., & Lopez, S. R. (1993). The study of culture, ethnicity, and race in American psychology. *American Psychologist, 48,* 629–637.

Bettencourt, B. A., & Hume, D. (1999). The cognitive contents of social-group identity: Values, emotions, and relationships. *European Journal of Social Psychology, 29,* 113–121.

Betz, N. E. (2001). Career self-efficacy. In F. Leong & A. Barak (Eds.), *Contemporary models in vocational psychology* (pp. 55–78). New York, NY: Routledge.

Betz, N. E. (2007). Career self efficacy: Exemplary recent research and emerging directions. *Journal of Career Assessment, 15,* 403–422.

Beyers, W., & Seiffge-Krenke, I. (2010). Does identity precede intimacy? Testing Erikson's theory on romantic development in emerging adults of the 21st century. *Journal of Adolescent Research, 25,* 387–415.

Bharatwaj, R. S. (2014). Preparation for menarche is still a concern even among urban girls irrespective of their education. *International Journal of Clinical and Surgical Advances, 2,* 68–69.

Bialystok, E., & Craik, F. I. M. (2010). Cognitive and linguistic processing in the bilingual mind. *Current Directions in Psychological Science, 19,* 19–23.

Bick, D., & Howard, L. (2010). When should women be screened for postnatal depression? *The Expert Review of Neurotherapeutics, 10,* 151–154.

Biddle, B. J. (1979). *Role theory: Expectations, identities, and behaviors.* New York, NY: Academic Press.

Biddle, B. J. (1986). Recent developments in role theory. In R. H. Turner & S. F. Short, Jr. (Eds.). *Annual Review of Sociology, 12,* 67–92.

Biddle, B. J., & Thomas, E. J. (1966). *Role theory: Concepts and research.* New York, NY: Wiley.

Biglan, A., Flay, B. R., Embry, D. D., & Sandler, I. N. (2012). The critical role of nurturing environments for promoting human well-being. *American Psychologist, 67,* 257–271.

Bigler, R. S., Spears Brown, C., & Markell, M. (2001). When groups are not created equal: Effects of group status on the formation of intergroup attitudes in children. *Child Development, 72,* 1151–1162.

Bijstra, J., Van Geert, P., & Jackson, S. (1989). Conservation and the appearance–reality distinction: What do children really know and what do they answer? *British Journal of Developmental Psychology, 7,* 43–53.

Billstedt, E., Waern, M., Duberstein, P., Marlow, T., Hellstrom, T., Östling, S., et al. (2013). Secular changes in personality: Study on 75-year-olds examined in 1976–1977 and 2005–2006. *International Journal of Geriatric Psychiatry, 28,* 298–304.

Bilsker, D., Schiedel, D., & Marcia, J. (1988). Sex differences in identity status. *Sex Roles, 18,* 231–236.

Bindman, S. W., Pomerantz, E. M., & Roisman, G. I. (2015). Do children's executive functions account for associations between early autonomy-supportive parenting and achievement through high school? *Journal of Educational Psychology, 107,* 756–770.

Birsch, K. H., Munz, D., Bemmerer-Mayer, K., Terinde, R., Kreienberg, R., & Kachele, H. (2003). Coping styles of pregnant women after prenatal ultrasound screening for fetal malformation. *Journal of Psychosomatic Research, 55,* 91–97.

Bishaw, A. (2012). *Poverty: 2010 and 2011.* American Community Survey Briefs. U.S. Department of Commerce, ACSBR/11-01.

Blackwell, D. L, & Lichter, D. T. (2000). Mate selection among married and cohabiting couples. *Journal of Family Issues, 21,* 275–302.

Blackwell, D. L., & Lichter, D. T. (2004). Homogamy among dating, cohabiting and married couples. *Sociological Quarterly, 45,* 719–737.

Blackwell, D. L., Lucas, J. W., Clarke T. C. (2014). Summary health statistics for U.S. adults: National Health Interview Study, 2012. National Center for Health Statistics. *Vital Health Statistics, 10.* Retrieved from https://www.ncbi.nlm.nih.gov/pubmed/

Blair-Loy, M. (2001). Cultural constructions of family schemas: The case of women finance executives. *Gender & Society, 15,* 687–709.

Blanchard, C., Perreault, S., & Vallerand, R. J. (1998). Participation in team sport: A self-expansion perspective. *International Journal of Sport Psychology, 29,* 289–302.

Blanchflowe, D. G., & Oswald, A. (2007). *Is well-being U-shaped over the life cycle?* National Bureau of Economic Research Working Paper: No. 12935. Retrieved from http://www.nber.org/papers/w12935

Blanck, R., & Blanck, G. (1986). *Beyond ego psychology.* New York, NY: Columbia University Press.

Blasi, A. (1991). The self as subject in the study of personality. In D. Ozer, J. Healy, & A. Stewart (Eds.), *Perspectives in personality* (Vol. 3, Part A, pp. 19–37). London: Kingsley.

Blasi, A. (2013). Moral functioning: Moral understanding and personality. In D. K. Lapsley & D. Narvaez (Eds.), *Moral development, self and identity* (pp. 335–348). New York, NY: Psychology Press.

Bleakley, A., Jordan, A. B., & Hennessy, M. (2013). The relationship between parents' and children's television viewing. *Pediatrics, 132,* e364–e371.

Bleeker, M. M., & Jacobs, J. E. (2004). Achievement in math and science: Do mothers' beliefs matter 12 years later? *Journal of Educational Psychology, 96,* 97–109.

Bloom, L. (2004). The integration of expression in the stream of everyday activity. In I. Stockman (Ed.), *Movement and action in learning and development: Clinical implications for pervasive developmental disorders* (pp. 139–168). San Diego, CA: Academic Press.

Bloom, M. (2009). Social competency: A blueprint for promoting academic and social competence in after-school programs. In T. P. Gullotta, M. Bloom, C. P. Gullotta, & J. C. Messina (Eds.), *A blueprint for promoting academic and social competence in after-school programs: Issues in children's and families' lives* (pp. 1–19). New York, NY: Springer.

Blos, P. (1962). *On adolescence: A psychoanalytic interpretation.* New York, NY: The Free Press.

Blos, P. (1967). The second individuation process of adolescence. *Psychoanalytic Study of the Child, 23,* 162–186.

Blos, P. (1979). *The adolescent passage.* New York, NY: International Universities Press.

Bluck, S., & Gluck, J. (2004). Making things better and learning a lesson: Experiencing wisdom across the lifespan. *Journal of Personality, 72,* 543–572.

Blue Zone Project. (2016). Retrieved from https://communities.bluezonesproject.com/

Blumenthal, H., Leen-Feldner, E. W., Babson, K. A., Gahr, J. L., Trainor, C. D., & Fralah, J. L. (2011). Elevated social anxiety among early maturing girls. *Developmental Psychology, 47,* 1133–1140.

Blustein, D. L. (2008). The role of work in psychological health and well-being: A conceptual, historical and public policy perspective. *American Psychologist, 63,* 228–240.

Blustein, D. L., Kozan, S., & Connors-Kelllgren, A. (2013). Unemployment and underemployment: A narrative analysis. *Journal of Vocational Behavior, 82,* 256–265.

Boerner, K., Schulz, R., & Horowitz, A. (2004). Positive aspects of caregiving and adaptation to bereavement. *Psychology and Aging, 19,* 668–675.

Bohan, J. S. (1993). Regarding gender. *Psychology of Women Quarterly, 17,* 5–21.

Bohlin, G., Bengtsgard, K., & Andersson, K. (2000). Social inhibition and over-friendliness as related to socioemotional functioning in 7- and 8-year-old children. *Journal of Clinical Child Psychology, 29,* 414–423.

Bohlmeijer, E., Smit, F., & Cuijpers, P. (2003). Effects of reminiscence and life review on late-life depression: A metaanalysis. *International Journal of Geriatric Psychiatry, 18,* 1088–1094.

Bolton, F. G., Jr., & MacEachron, A. E. (1988). Adolescent male sexuality: A developmental perspective. *Journal of Adolescent Research, 3,* 259–273.

Bomar, J. A., & Sabatelli, R. M. (1996). Family system dynamics, gender, and psychosocial maturity in late adolescence. *Journal of Adolescent Research, 11,* 421–439.

Bombar, M. L., & Littig, L. W. (1996). Babytalk as a communication of intimate attachment: An initial study in adult romances and friendships. *Personal Relationships, 3,* 137–158. .

Bonanno, G. A., Wortman, C. B., & Nesse, R. M. (2004). Prospective patterns of resilience and maladjustment during widowhood. *Psychology and Aging, 19,* 260–271.

Bongaarts, J., & Zimmer, Z. (2002). Living arrangements of older adults in the developing world. *The Journals of Gerontology Series B: Psychological Sciences and Social Sciences, 57,* S145–S157.

Boom, J., Brugman, D., & van der Heijden, P. G. M. (2001). Hierarchical structure of moral stages assessed by a sorting task. *Child Development, 72,* 535–548.

Boonstra, H. (2013). Medication abortion restrictions burden women and providers—and threaten U.S. trend toward very early abortion. *Guttmacher Policy Review, 16*(1).

Booth, A. E. (2009). Causal supports for early word learning. *Child Development, 80,* 1243–1250.

Booth, A., Johnson, D. R., Granger, D. A., Crouter, A. C., & McHale, S. (2003). Testosterone and child and adolescent adjustment: The moderating role of parent–child relationships. *Developmental Psychology, 39,* 85–98.

Boonstra, H. D. (2009). The challenge in helping young adults better manage their reproductive lives. *Guttmacher Policy Review, 12,* 13–18.

Borca, G., Bina, M., Keller, P. S., Gilbert, L. R., & Begotti, T. (2015). Internet use and developmental tasks: Adolescents' point of view. *Computers in Human Behavior, 52,* 49–58.

Borden, W. (2000). The relational paradigm in contemporary psychoanalysis: Toward a psychodynamically informed social work perspective. *Social Service Review, 74,* 352–380.

Bordens, K., & Abbott, B. B. (2013). *Research design and methods: A process approach* (9th ed.). New York, NY: McGraw-Hill.

Borkenau, P., Riemann, R., Angleitner, A., & Spinath, F. M. (2001). Genetic and environmental influences on observed personality: Evidence from the German Observational Study of Adult Twins. *Journal of Personality and Social Psychology, 80,* 655–668.

Borman, K. M., & Hopkins, M. (1987). Leaving school for work. *Research in the Sociology of Education and Socialization, 7,* 131–159.

Bornstein, M. H. (1985). How infant and mother jointly contribute to developing cognitive competence in the child. *Proceedings of the National Academy of Science, USA, 82,* 7470–7473.

Bornstein, M. H. (Ed.). (1987). *Sensitive periods in development: Interdisciplinary perspectives* (pp. 211–221). Hillsdale, NJ: Erlbaum.

Bornstein, M. H. (2001). Mother–infant interaction. In G. Bremner & A. Fogel (Eds.), *Blackwell handbook of infant development* (pp. 269–295). Malden, MA: Blackwell.

Bornstein, M. H. (2002). Parenting infants. In M. H. Bornstein (Ed.), *Handbook of parenting Vol. 1. Children and parenting* (2nd ed., pp. 3–43). Mahwah, NJ: Erlbaum.

Bornstein, M. H. (2012). Parenting infants. In M. H Bornstein (Ed.), *Handbook of parenting* (Vol. 1, 2nd ed., pp 3–44). New York, NY: Psychology Press.

Bornstein, M. H., Arterberry, M. E., Mash, C., & Manian, N. (2011). Discrimination of facial expression by 5-month old infants of non-depressed and clinically depressed mothers. *Infant Behavior and Development, 34,* 100–106.

Bornstein, M. H., Cote, L. R., Haynes, O. M., Suwalsky, J. T. D., & Bakeman, R. (2012).

Modalities of infant-mother interaction in Japanese, Japanese American immigrant, and European American dyads. *Child Development, 83*, 2073–2088.

Bornstein, M. H., Kessen, W., & Weiskopf, S. (1976). The categories of hue in infancy. *Science, 191*, 201–202.

Bornstein, M. H., & Lansford, J. E. (2010). Parenting. In M. H. Bornstein (Ed.), *Handbook of cultural developmental science* (pp. 259–277). New York, NY: Taylor & Francis.

Bornstein, M. H., Putnick, D. L., Lansford, J. E., Deater-Deckard, K., & Bradley, R. H. (2015). A developmental analysis of caregiving modalities across infancy in 38 low-and middle-income countries. *Child Development, 86*, 1571–1587.

Bornstein, M. H., Putnick, D. L., Lansford, J. E., Deater-Deckard, K., & Bradley, R.H. (2016). Gender in low-and-middle income countries. *Monographs of the Society for Research in Child Development, Serial No. 320, Vol. 81, whole*.

Bornstein, M. H., & Suess, P. E. (2000). Child and mother cardiac vagal tone: Continuity, stability and concordance across the first years. *Developmental Psychology, 36*, 54–65.

Bornstein, M. H., & Tamis-LeMonda, C. S. (2010). Parent–infant interaction. In J. G. Bremner & T. D. Wachs (Eds.), *Wiley-Blackwell handbook of infant development: Vol. 1. Basic research* (pp. 458–482). Wiley-Blackwell handbooks of developmental psychology. Malden, MA: Blackwell Publishing.

Boss, P. (1999). *Ambiguous loss*. Cambridge, MA: Harvard University Press.

Boss, P. (2002a). Ambiguous loss: Working with the families of the missing. *Family Process, 41*, 14–17.

Boss, P. (2002b). *Family stress management: A contextual approach* (2nd ed.). Thousand Oaks, CA: Sage.

Boss, P. (2004). Ambiguous loss research, theory, and practice: Reflections after 9/11. *Journal of Marriage and the Family, 66*, 551–566.

Boss, P. (2007). Ambiguous loss theory: Challenges for scholars and practitioners. *Family Relations, 56*, 105–111.

Bosworth, H. B., & Schaie, K. W. (1997). The relationship of social environment, social networks, and health outcomes in the Seattle longitudinal study: Two analytical approaches. *Journal of Gerontology, 52*, P197–P205.

Bouchard, T. J. & McGue, M. (1981). Familial studies of intelligence: A review. *Science, 212*, 1055–1059.

Bouchard, T. J., Jr., & Pederson, N. (1999). Twins reared apart: Nature's double experiment. In M. C. LaBuda & E. L. Grigorenko (Eds.), *On the way to individuality: Current methodological issues in behavioral genetics* (pp. 71–93). Huntington, NY: Nova Science.

Bouffard, T, Boisvert, M., & Vezeau, C. (2003). Illusion of incompetence and school functioning among elementary school children. *Learning and Individual Difference, 14*, 31–46.

Bouldin, P. (2006). An investigation of the fantasy predisposition and fantasy style of children with imaginary companions. *Journal of Genetic Psychology, 167*, 17–29.

Bouldin, P., & Pratt, C. (1999). Characteristics of preschool and school-age children with imaginary companions. *Journal of Genetic Psychology, 160*, 397–410.

Bowen, M. (1978). *Family therapy and clinical practice*. New York, NY: Aronson.

Bowes, L., Carnegie, R., Pearson, R. et al. (2015). Risk of depression and self-harm in teenagers identifying with Goth subculture: A longitudinal cohort study. *Lancet Psychiatry, 2*, 793–800.

Bowlby, J. (1960). Separation anxiety. *International Journal of Psychoanalysis, 41*, 69–113.

Bowlby, J. (1969/1982). *Attachment and loss: Vol. 1. Attachment*. New York, NY: Basic Books.

Bowlby, J. (1980). *Attachment and loss: Vol. 3. Loss, sadness, and depression*. New York, NY: Basic Books.

Bowlby, J. (1988). *A secure base: Parent–child attachment and healthy human development*. New York, NY: Basic Books.

Bowman, B. T., Donovan, M. S., & Burns, M. S. (2000). *Eager to learn: Educating our preschoolers*. Washington, DC: National Academy Press.

Boxer, P., Huesmann, L. R., Dubow, E. F., Landau, S. F., Gvirsman, S. D., Shikaki, K., & Ginges, J. (2013). Exposure to violence across the social ecosystem and the development of aggression: A test of ecological theory in the Israeli-Palestinian conflict. *Child Development, 84*, 163–177.

Boyce. C. J., & Wood, A. M. (2011). Personality prior to disability determines adaptation: Agreeable individuals recover lost life satisfaction faster and more completely. *Psychological Science, 22*, 1397–1402.

Boyd, D. M., & Ellison, N. B. (2007). Social network sites: Definition, history and scholarship. *The Journal of Computer-Mediated Communication, 13*, 210–230.

Boyd, J., & Zimbardo, P. G. (1996). Constructing time after death: The transcendental-future time perspective. *Time and Society, 6*, 35–54.

Boykin, A. W. (1994). Harvesting talent and culture. In R. J. Rossi (Ed.), *Schools and students at risk: Context and framework for positive change* (pp. 116–138). New York, NY: Teachers College Press.

Boyse, K., & Phelps, R. (2012). *Precocious puberty*. University of Michigan Health System. Retrieved from http://www.med.umich.edu/yourchild/topics/puberty.htm

Bozick, R. (2007). Making it through the first year of college: The role of students' economic resources, employment and living arrangements. *Sociology of Education, 80*, 261–285.

Bradbury, R. (1957/1964). *Dandelion wine*. New York, NY: Bantam Books.

Bradford, K., & Hawkins, A. J. (2006). Learning competent fathering: A longitudinal analysis of marital intimacy and fathering. *Fathering, 4*, 215–234.

Bradley, C. B., McMurray, R. G., Harrell, J. S., & Deng, S. (2000). Changes in common activities of 3rd through 10th graders: The CHIC study. *Medicine and Science in Sports and Exercise, 32*, 2071–2078.

Bradley, C. L. (1997). Generativity-stagnation: Development of a status model. *Developmental Review, 17*, 262–290.

Bradley, C. L., & Marcia, J. E. (1998). Generativity-stagnation: A five-category model. *Journal of Personality, 66*, 39–64.

Bradley, R. H., Caldwell, B. M., & Rock, S. L. (1988). Home environment and school performance. A ten-year follow up and examination of three models of environmental action. *Child Development, 59*, 852–867.

Bradley, R. H., McKelvey, L. M., & Whiteside-Mansell, L. (2011). Does the quality of stimulation and support in the home environment moderate the effect of early education programs? *Child Development, 82*, 2110–2122.

Bradley, R. P. C, & Gottman, J. M. (2012). Reducing situational violence in low-income couples by fostering health relationships. *Journal of Marital and Family Therapy, 38*, Supplement 1, 187–198.

Bradmetz, J. (1999). Precursors of formal thought: A longitudinal study. *British Journal of Developmental Psychology, 17*, 61–81.

Bradshaw, C. P., Sawyer, A. L., & O'Brennan, L. M. (2007). Bullying and peer victimization at school: Perceptual differences between students and school staff. *School Psychology Review, 36*, 361–382.

Bradshaw, Z., & Slade, P. (2003). The effects of induced abortion on emotional experiences and relationships: A critical review of the literature. *Clinical Psychology Review, 23*, 929–948.

Braine, M. D. S. (1976). Children's first word combinations. *Monographs of the Society for Research in Child Development, Serial No. 164, 41*(1).

Braithwaite, V. (2004). The hope process and social inclusion. In V. Braithwaite (Ed.), Hope, power, and governance. *The Annals of the American Academy of Political and Social Science* (pp. 128–151). Thousand Oaks, CA: Sage.

Brandon, E. (2016). 12 ways retirees spend their new found free time. *U.S. News and World Report*. Retrieved from http://money.usnews.com/money/retirement/slideshows/12-ways-retirees-spend-their-newfound-free-time

Brandon, P. E. (2000). An analysis of kin provided child care in the context of intrafamily exchanges: Linking components of family support for parents raising young children. *The American Journal of Economics and Sociology, 59*, 191.

Brandtstadter, J. (2002). Searching for paths to successful development and aging: Integrating developmental and action theoretical perspectives. In L. Pulkkinen & A. Caspi (Eds.), *Paths to successful development: Personality in the life course* (pp. 380–408). New York, NY: Cambridge University Press.

Brandtstädter, J., Rothermund, K., Kranz, D., & Kühn, W. (2010). Final decentrations, personal goals, rationality perspectives, and the awareness of life's finitude. *European Psychologist, 15*, 152–163.

Brault, M. W. (2011). School-age children with disabilities in U.S. metropolitan statistical areas: 2010. *American Community Survey Briefs, November 2011*. Retrieved from https://www.census.gov/prod/2011pubs /acsbr10-12.pdf

Braungart, J. M., Plomin, R., Defries, J. C., & Fulker, D. W. (1992). Genetic influence on tester-rated infant temperament as assessed by Bayley's Infant Behavior Record: Non-adoptive and adoptive siblings and twins. *Developmental Psychology, 28*(1), 40–47.

Braungart-Rieker, J. M., Garwood, M. M., Powers, B. P., & Wang, X. (2001). Parental sensitivity, infant affect, and affect regulation: Predictors of later attachment. *Child Development, 72*, 252–270.

Brazelton, T. B. (1974). *Toddlers and parents: A declaration of independence*. New York, NY: Delacorte Press.

Brazelton, T. B., Koslowski, B., & Main, M. (1974). The origins of reciprocity: The early mother–infant interaction. In M. Lewis & L. A. Rosenblum (Eds.), *The effect of the infant on its caregiver* (pp. 49–76). New York, NY: Wiley-Interscience.

Brazelton, T. B., Nugent, J. K., & Lester, B. M. (1987). Neonatal behavioral assessment scale. In J. D. Osofsky (Ed.), *Handbook of infant development* (2nd ed., pp. 780–817). New York, NY: Wiley.

Breault, K. D., & Kposowa, A. J. (1987). Explaining divorce in the United States, 1980. *Journal of Marriage and the Family, 49*, 549–558.

Bredow, C. A., Cate, R. M., & Huston, T. L. (2008). Have we met before?: A conceptual model of first romantic encounters. In S. Sprecher, A. Wenzel, & J. Harvey (Eds.), *Handbook of relationship initiation* (pp. 3–28). New York, NY: Psychology Press.

Bredow, C. A., Huston, T. L., & Glenn, N. D. (2011). Market value, quality of the pool of potential mates, and single's confidence about marrying. *Personal Relationships, 18*, 39–57.

Brendgen, M., Lamarche, V., Wanner, B., & Vitaro, F. (2010). Links between friendship relations and early adolescents' trajec-tories of depressed mood. *Developmental Psychology, 46*, 491–501.

Brennan, A. (2010). *Couvade syndrome in Australian men: A national survey, 2010*. Retrieved from http://www.abc.net.au /catalyst/fatherhood /CatalystCouvadeSurveyAustralia.pdf

Brennan, A., Ayers, S., Marshall-Lucette, S., & Ahmed, H. (2007a). A critical review of the couvade syndrome: The pregnant male. *Journal of Reproductive and Infant Psychology, 25*(3), 173–189.

Brennan, R. T., Barnett, R. C., & Gareis, K. C. (2001). When she earns more than he

does: A longitudinal study of dual-earner couples. *Journal of Marriage and the Family, 63*, 168–182.

Bretherton, I. (1985). Attachment theory: Retrospect and prospect. In I. Bretherton & E. Everett (Eds.), *Growing points of attachment theory and research* (pp. 3–35). Monographs of the Society for Research in Child Development, 50(1–2, Serial No. 209).

Bretherton, I. (1988). Open communication and internal working models: Their roles in the development of attachment relationships. In R. Dienstbier & R. A. Thompson (Eds.), *Nebraska symposium on motivation, 1988: Socioemotional development* (Vol. 36, pp. 60–61). Lincoln, NE: University of Nebraska Press.

Bretherton, I. (1990). Open communication and internal working models: Their role in the development of attachment relationships. In R. Dienstbier & R. A. Thompson (Eds.), *Nebraska symposium on motivation 1988: Vol. 36. Socioemotional development* (pp. 57–113). Lincoln, NE: University of Nebraska Press.

Bretherton, I., & Munholland, K. A. (2010). Internal working models in attachment relationships: Elaborating a central construct in attachment theory. In J. Cassidy & P. R. Shaver (Eds.), *Handbook of attachment: Theory, research and clinical applications* (2nd ed., pp. 102–131). New York, NY: Guilford Press.

Bretschneider, J. G., & McCoy, N. L. (1988). Sexual interest and behavior in healthy 80- to 102-year-olds. *Archives of Sexual Behavior, 17*, 109–129.

Brezina, P. R. & Zhao, Y. (2012). The ethical, legal and social issues impacted by modern assisted reproductive technologies. *Obstetrics and Gynecology International, 2012*, 7 pages. Open access article.

Bridges, L. J., Connell, J. P., & Belsky, J. (1988). Similarities and differences in infant–mother and infant–father interaction in the strange situation: A component process analysis. *Developmental Psychology, 24*, 92–100.

Brierley, J. (1993). *Growth in children*. London: Cassell.

Brim, G. (1992). *Ambition: How we manage success and failure throughout our lives*. New York, NY: Basic Books.

Brim, O. G. (1966). Socialization through the life cycle. In O. G. Brim and S. Wheeler (Eds.) *Socialization after childhood: Two essays*. New York, NY: Wiley.

Brind'Amour, Katherine. (2010). Induced pluripotent stem cells. *Embryo Project Encyclopedia*. Retrieved from http:// embryo.asu.edu/handle/10776/1974

Bringle, J. R. (2007). Psychosocial processes at the end of life: The relationship between generativity and fear of death. *Dissertation Abstracts International: Section B: The Sciences and Engineering, 68*, 1296.

Brinkmeyer, M. Y., & Eyberg, S. M. (2003). Parent–child interaction therapy for oppositional children. In A. E. Kazdin & J. R. Weisz (Eds.), *Evidence-based psy-chotherapies for

children and adolescents* (pp. 204–223). New York, NY: Guilford Press.

Brisch, K. H., Bechinger, D., Betzler, S., Heinemann, H., Kächele, H., Pohlandt, F., et al. (2005). Attachment quality in very low-birthweight premature infants in relation to maternal attachment representations and neurological development. *Parenting: Science and Practice, 5*, 311–331.

Brisch, K. H., Munz, D., Bemmerer-Mayer, K., Terinde, R., Kreienberg, R., & Kächele, H., (2003). Coping styles of pregnant women after prenatal ultrasound screening for fetal malformation. *Journal of Psychosomatic Research, 55*, 91–97.

Brockner, J. (1984). Low self-esteem and behavioral plasticity. In L. Wheeler (Ed.), *Review of personality and social psychology* (Vol. 4, pp. 237–271). Beverly Hills, CA: Sage.

Broderick, C. B. (1993). *Understanding family process: Basics of family systems theory*. Newbury Park, CA: Sage.

Brody, J. E. (2015). When grief won't relent. *New York Times*. Retrieved from http:// well.blogs.nytimes.com/2015/02/16 /when-grief-wont-relent/

Brodzinsky, D. M., & Pertman, A. (2012). *Adoption by lesbians and gay men: A new dimension in family diversity*. New York, NY: Oxford University Press.

Broen, A. N., Moum, T., Bodtker, A. S., & Ekeberg, O. (2005). Reasons for induced abortion and their relation to women's emotional distress: A prospective, two-year follow-up study. *General Hospital Psychiatry, 27*, 36–43.

Bronfenbrenner, U. (1979). *The ecology of human development*. Cambridge, MA: Harvard University Press.

Bronfenbrenner, U. (1995). Developmental ecology through space and time: A future perspective. In P. Moen, G. H. Elder, and K. Luscher (Eds.), *Examining lives in context: Perspectives on the ecology of human development* (pp. 619–647). Washington, DC: American Psychological Association.

Bronfenbrenner, U. (1999). Environments in developmental perspective: Theoretical and operational models. In S. L. Friedman, T. D., & Wachs (Eds), *Measuring environment across the life span: Emerging methods and concepts* (pp. 3–28). Washington, DC: American Psychological Association.

Bronfenbrenner, U. (2004). *Making human beings human: Bioecological perspectives on human development*. Thousand Oaks, CA: Sage.

Bronfenbrenner, U., & Morris, P. A. (2006). The bioecological model of human development. In W. Damon & R. M. Lerner (Eds.), *Handbook of child psychology: Vol. 1. Theoretical models of human development* (6th ed., pp. 793–828). New York, NY: Wiley.

Bronson, G. W. (1973). Infants' reactions to an unfamiliar person. In L. J. Stone, H. T. Smith, & L. B. Murphy (Eds.), *The competent infant*. New York, NY: Basic Books.

Bronstein, P., Duncan, P., Clauson, J., Abrams, C., Yannett, N., Ginsburg, G., et al. (1998).

Preventing middle school adjustment problems for children from lower income families: A program for aware parenting. *Journal of Applied Developmental Psychology, 19,* 129–152.

Brookes, H., Slater, A., Quinn, P. C., Lewkowizc, D. J., Hayes, R., & Brown, E. (2001). Three-month-old infants learn arbitrary auditory-visual pairings between voices and faces. *Infant and Child Development, 10,* 75–82.

Brooks, S. (2015). Does personal social media usage affect efficiency and well-being? *Computers in Human Behavior, 46,* 26–37.

Brooks-Gunn, J., & Reiter, E. O. (1990). The role of pubertal processes. In S. S. Feldman & G. R. Elliott (Eds.), *At the threshold: The developing adolescent* (pp. 16–53). Cambridge, MA: Harvard University Press.

Brooks-Gunn, J., & Warren, M. P. (1988). The psychological significance of secondary sexual characteristics in 9- to 11-year-old girls. *Child Development, 59,* 161–169.

Brown, B. B. (1990). Peer groups and peer cultures. In S. S. Feldman & G. R. Elliott (Eds.), *At the threshold: The developing adolescent* (pp. 171–196). Cambridge, MA: Harvard University Press.

Brown, B. B., Bakken, J. P., Ameringer, S.W., & Mahon, S. D. (2008). A comprehensive conceptualization of the peer influence process in adolescence. In M. J. Prinstein & K. Dodge, (Eds.), *Understanding peer influence in children and adolescents* (pp. 17–44). New York, NY: Guilford Press.

Brown, B. B., & Larson, J. (2009). Peer relationships in adolescence. In R. M. Lerner & L. Steinberg (Eds.), *Handbook of adolescent psychology: Vol. 2. Contextual influences on adolescent development* (3rd ed., pp. 74–102). Hoboken, NJ: John Wiley.

Brown, B. B., Mounts, N., Lamborn, S. D., & Steinberg, L. (1993). Parenting practices and peer group affiliation in adolescence. *Child Development, 64,* 467–482.

Brown, C. S., Spatzier, A., & Tobin, M. (2010). Variability in the inter-group attitudes of white children: What we can learn from their ethnic identity labels. *Social Development, 19,* 758–778.

Brown, I., Jr., & Inouye, D. K. (1978). Learned helplessness through modeling: The role of perceived similarity in competence. *Journal of Personality and Social Psychology, 36,* 900–908.

Brown, J. D., Dutton, K. A., & Cook, K. E. (2001). From the top down: Self-esteem and self-evaluation. *Cognition and Emotion, 15,* 615–631.

Brown, J. D., & Gallagher, F. M. (1992). Coming to terms with failure: Private self-enhancement and public self-effacement. *Journal of Experimental Social Psychology, 28,* 3–22.

Brown, J. D., & Mankowski, T. A. (1993). Self-esteem, mood, and self-evaluation: Changes in mood and the way you see you. *Journal of Personality and Social Psychology, 64,* 421–430.

Brown, J. L., & Pollitt, E. (1996). Malnutrition, poverty, and intellectual development. *Scientific American, 27,* 38–43.

Brown, J. R., & Dunn, J. (1992). Talk with your mother or your sibling? Developmental changes in early family conversations about feelings. *Child Development, 63,* 336–349.

Brown, J. V., Bakeman, R., Coles, C. D., Platzman, K. A., & Lynch, M. E. (2004). Prenatal cocaine exposure: A comparison of 2-year-old children in parental and nonparental care. *Child Development, 75,* 1282–1295.

Brown, R. (1965). *Social psychology.* New York, NY: Free Press.

Brown, S. K. (2003). *Staying ahead of the curve 2003: The AARP working in retirement study.* Washington, DC: AARP. Retrieved from http://www.aarp .org/research/reference/publicopinions/aresearch-import-417.html

Brown, S. L., & Booth, A. (1996). Cohabitation versus marriage: A comparison of relationship quality. *Journal of Marriage and the Family, 58,* 668–678.

Brown, W. H., Pfeiffer, K. A., McIver, K. L., Dowda, M., Addy, C. L., & Pate, R. R. (2009). Social and environmental factors associated with preschoolers' non-sedentary physical activity. *Child Development, 80,* 45–58.

Browning, C. R., & Cagney, K. A. (2003). Moving beyond poverty: Neighborhood structure, social processes, and health. *Journal of Health and Social Behavior, 44,* 552–571.

Brown University. (2004). *The female athlete triad.* Health Education. Retrieved from http://www.brown .edu/Student_Services /Health_Services/Health_Education /nutrition/ec_fatriad .htm

Brownell, C. A., & Kopp, C. B. (2007a). *Socioemotional development in the toddler years: Transitions and transformations.* New York, NY: Guilford Press.

Brownell, C. A., & Kopp, C. B. (2007b). Transitions in toddler socioemotional development: Behavior, understanding, and relationships. In C. A. Brownell & C. B. Kopp (Eds.), *Socioemotional development in the toddler years: Transitions and transformations* (pp. 1–30). New York, NY: Guilford Press.

Brubaker, T. H. (1990). Families in later life: A burgeoning research area. *Journal of Marriage and the Family, 52,* 959–981.

Bruera, E., & Yennurajalingam, S. (2011). *Oxford American handbook of hospice and palliative medicine.* New York, NY: Oxford University Press.

Brummelman, E., Thomaes, S., Nelemans, S. A., Orobio de Castro, B., Overbeek, G., & Bushman, B. J. (2015). Origins of narcissism in children. *Proceedings of the National Academy of Sciences, U.S.A., 112,* 3659–3662.

Brummelman, E., Thomaes, S., & Sedikides, C. (2016). Separating narcissism from self-esteem. *Current Directions in Psychological Science, 25,* 8–13.

Bruner, J. (2001). Human infancy and the beginnings of human competence. In J. A. Bargh & D. K Apsley (Eds.), *Unraveling the complexities of social life: A festschrift in honor of Robert B. Zajonc* (pp. 133–139). Washington, DC: American Psychological Association.

Brustad, R. J. (1988). Affective outcomes in competitive youth sport: The influence of intrapersonal and socialization factors. *Journal of Sport and Exercise Psychology, 10,* 307–321.

Bryant, J., Carveth, R. A., & Brown, D. (1981). Television viewing and anxiety: An experimental examination. *Journal of Communication, 31,* 106–119.

Bryer, K. B. (1979). The Amish way of death: A study of family support systems. *American Psychologist, 34,* 255–261.

Buczynski, R. (2016). How does childhood trauma impact adult relationships? *National Institute for the Application of Behavioral Medicine.* Retrieved from http://www.nicabm.com/could-childhood-trauma-affect-adult-relationships/

Buettner, D. (2008). *The Blue Zones: Lessons for living longer from the people who lived the longest.* Washington, DC: National Geographic.

Buettner, D. (2012). *The Blue Zones, 2nd ed.: 9 lessons for living longer from the people who lived the longest.* Washington, DC: National Geographic.

Buhl, H. M. (2007). Well-being and the child-parent relationship at the transition from university to work life. *Journal of Adolescent Research, 22,* 550–571.

Buhler, C., & Massarik, F. (1968). *The course of human life: A study of goals in the humanistic perspective.* New York, NY: Springer-Verlag.

Bukowski, W. M. (2001). Friendship and the worlds of childhood. In D. W. Nangle & C. A. Erdley (Eds.), *The role of friendship in psychological adjustment* (pp. 93–105). San Francisco, CA: Jossey-Bass.

Bukowski, W. M., Castellanos, M., Vitaro, F., & Brendgen, M. (2015). Socialization and experience with peers. In J. E. Grusec & P. D. Hastings (Eds.), *Handbook of socialization: Theory and Research* (2nd ed.) (pp. 228–250). New York: Guilford Press, pp. 228-250.

Bukowski, W. M., Gauze, C., Hoza, B., & Newcomb, A. F. (1993). Differences and consistency between same-sex and other-sex peer relationships during early adolescence. *Developmental Psychology, 29,* 255–263.

Bukowski, W. M., Laursen, B., & Hoza, B. (2010). The snowball effect: Friendship moderates escalations in depressed affect among avoidant and excluded children. *Development and Psychopathology, 22,* 749–757.

Bulotsky-Shearer, R .J., Manz, P. H., Mendez, J. L., McWayne, C. M., Sekino, Y., & Fantuzzo, J. W. (2012). Peer play interactions and readiness to learn: A protective influence for African American preschool children from low-income households. *Child Development Perspectives, 6,* 225–231.

Bullock, H. E., & Morales Waugh, I. (2004). Caregiving around the clock: How women in nursing manage career and family demands. *Journal of Social Issues, 60,* 767–786.

Bullock, K. (2005). Grandfathers and the impact of raising grandchildren. *Journal of Sociology and Social Welfare, 32,* 43–59.

Bullock, M., & Lutkenhaus, P. (1988). The development of volitional behavior in the toddler years. *Child Development, 59,* 664–674.

Bunting, L., & McAuley, C. (2004). Teenage pregnancy and motherhood: The contribution of support. *Child & Family Social Work, 9,* 201–215.

Burchinal, M. R., Magnuson, K., Powell, D., & Hong, S. S. (2015). Early child care and education. In M.H. Bornstein, T. Leventhal, & R.M. Lerner (Eds.), *Handbook of child psychology and developmental science, Vol. 4: Ecological settings and processes* (7th ed., pp. 223–267). Hoboken NJ: John Wiley & Sons.

Burchinal, M. R., Roberts, J. E., Riggins, R., Jr., Zeisel, S. A., Neebe, E., & Bryant, D. (2000). Relating quality of center-based child care to early cognitive and language development longitudinally. *Child Development, 71,* 338–357.

Burchinal, M. R, Vandell, D. L., & Belsky, J. (2014). Is the prediction of adolescent outcomes from early child care moderated by later maternal sensitivity? Results from the NICHD study of early child care and youth development. *Developmental Psychology, 50,* 542–553.

Bureau of Labor Statistics. (2014). *Women in the labor force: A databook.* Retrieved from http://www.bls.gov/cps/wlf-databook-2013.pdf

Bureau of Labor Statistics. (2015a). *Employment and unemployment of recent high school graduates and dropouts. 2013–2014.* Retrieved from http://www.bls.gov/careeroutlook/2015/data-on-display/dod_q4.htm

Bureau of Labor Statistics, (2015b). *Employer-reported workplace illnesses and injuries, 2014.* Retrieved from the internet on August 14, 2016 at http://www.bls.gov/news.release/pdf/osh.pdf

Bureau of Labor Statistics. (2015b). *Table 11. Employed persons by detailed occupation, sex, race, & Hispanic/Latino ethnicity.* Retrieved from http://www.bls.gov/cps/cpsaat11.pdf

Bureau of Labor Statistics, (2015c). *National census of fatal occupational injuries, 2014.* Retrieved from the internet on August 14, 2016 at http://www.bls.gov/news.release/pdf/cfoi.pdf

Bureau of Labor Statistics. (2015c). *Table 36. Multiple jobholders by selected characteristics, 2014, 2015.* Retrieved from http://www.bls.gov/cps/cpsaat36.pdf

Bureau of Labor Statistics. (2015d). *Number of jobs held, labor market activity and earnings growth among the youngest baby boomers:* Results from a longitudinal study. Retrieved from http://www.bls.gov/news.release/pdf/nlsoy.pdf

Bureau of Labor Statistics. (2015e). *Employer-reported workplace illnesses and injuries, 2014.* Retrieved from http://www.bls.gov/news.release/pdf/osh.pdf

Bureau of Labor Statistics. (2015f). *National census of fatal occupational injuries, 2014.* Retrieved from http://www.bls.gov/news.release/pdf/cfoi.pdf

Bureau of Labor Statistics, (2016f). *Number of fatal work injuries, 1992-2014.* Retrieved from the internet on August 13, 2016 at http://www.bls.gov/iif/oshwc/cfoi/cfch0013.pdf

Bureau of Labor Statistics, (2016g) *Persons with a disability- Labor force characteristics, 2015.* Retrieved from the internet on August 14, 2016 at http://www.bls.gov/news.release/pdf/disabl.pdf

Bureau of Labor Statistics. (2016a). Table 3. *Employment status of the civilian noninstitutionalized populations by age, sex and race. 2015.* Retrieved from http://www.bls.gov/cps/cpsaat03.htm

Bureau of Labor Statistics. (2016b). *Number of fatal work injuries, 1992–2014.* Retrieved from http://www.bls.gov/iif/oshwc/cfoi/cfch0013.pdf

Bureau of Labor Statistics. (2016c) *Persons with a disability- Labor force characteristics, 2015.* Retrieved from http://www.bls.gov/news.release/pdf/disabl.pdf

Bureau of Labor Statistics. (2016d) *Time spent in leisure and sports activities for the civilian population by selected characteristics, 2015 annual averages.* Table 11. Retrieved from http://www.bls.gov/news.release/atus.t11.htm

Burgard, S. A. & King, M. M. (2015). Health. *Pathways: A Magazine on Poverty, Inequality and Social Policy, Special Issue, State of the States, 2015.*

Burgess, E. W., & Bogue, D. J. (1967). The delinquency research of Clifford R. Shaw and Henry D. McKay and associates. In E. W. Burgess & D. J. Bogue (Eds.), *Urban sociology* (pp. 293–317). Chicago, IL: University of Chicago Press.

Burleigh, N. (2013). Sexting, shame and suicide: A shocking tale of sexual assault in the digital age. *Rolling Stone Magazine, The Archives Issue 1192, September 26, 2013.* Retrieved from http://www.rollingstone.com/culture/news/sexting-shame-and-suicide-20130917

Burleson, B. R., Kunkel, A. W., Samter, W., & Werking, K. J. (1996). Men's and women's evaluations of communication skills in personal relationships: When sex differences make a difference—and when they don't. *Journal of Social and Personal Relationships, 13,* 201–224.

Burnett, D. (1999). Social relationships of Latino grandparent caregivers: A role theory perspective. *The Gerontologist, 39,* 49–58.

Burr, D., & Gori, M. (2012). Multisensory integration develops late in humans. In M. M. Murray & M. T. Wallace (Eds.), *The neural basis of multisensory processes* (pp. 345–362). Boca Raton, FL: CRC Press/Taylor and Francis.

Burr, W. R., & Christensen, C. (1992). Undesirable side effects of enhancing self-esteem. *Family Relations, 41,* 480–484.

Burt, R. D., Vaughan, T. L., & Daling, J. R. (1988). Evaluating the risks of cesarean section: Low Apgar score in repeat C- section and vaginal deliveries. *American Journal of Public Health, 78,* 1312–1314.

Burt, S. A., & Neiderhiser, J.M. (2009). Aggressive versus non-aggressive antisocial behavior: Distinctive etiological moderation by age. *Developmental Psychology, 45,* 1164–1176.

Burton, C. M., Marshall, M. P., Chisolm, D. J., Sucato, G. S., & Friedman, M. S. (2013). Sexual minority-related victimization as a mediator of mental health disparities in sexual minority youth: A longitudinal analysis. *Journal of Youth and Adolescence, 42,* 394–402.

Burton, S., & Mitchell, P. (2003). Judging who knows best about yourself: Developmental change in citing the self across middle childhood. *Child Development, 74,* 426–443.

Bus, A. G., van IJzendoorn, M. H., & Pellegrini, A. D. (1995). Joint book reading makes for success in learning to read: A meta-analysis on intergenerational transmission of literacy. *Review of Educational Research, 65,* 1–21.

Busby. P., Huesmann, L. R., Dubow, E. F., Landau, S. F., Gvirsman, S. D., Shikaki, K., et al. (2013). Exposure to violence across the social ecosystem and the development of aggression: A test of ecological theory in the Israeli-Palestinian conflict. *Child Development, 84,* 163–177.

Buschman, T. J., & Miller, E. K. (2007). Top-down versus bottom-up control of attention in the prefrontal and posterior parietal cortices. *Science, 315,* 1860–1862.

Bushman, B., & Anderson, C. (2002). Violent video games and hostile expectations: A test of the general aggression model. *Personality and Social Psychology Bulletin, 28,* 1679–1686.

Bushman, B. J., Huesmann, L. R., & Whitaker, J. L. (2009). Violent media effects. In R. L. Nabi & M. B. Oliver (Eds.), *Media processes and effects* (pp. 361–376). Thousand Oaks, CA: Sage.

Businessballs.com. (1984). Free online learning for career development and training. In A. H., & Plomin, R. (Eds.), *Temperament: Early developing personality traits.* Hillsdale, NJ: Erlbaum.

Buss, A. H., & Plomin, R. (1984/2015). *Emotion: Temperament: Early developing personality traits, Vol. 3.* Mahwah, NJ: Erlbaum, Reissued edition by New York: Psychology Press.

Buss, A. H., & Plomin, R. (1986). The EAS approach to temperament. In R. Plomin &

J. Dunn (Eds.), *The study of temperament: Changes, continuities, and challenges.* Hillsdale, NJ: Erlbaum.

Buss, D. M. (2003). *The evolution of desire* (Rev. 4th ed.). New York, NY: Basic Books.

Buss, D. M. (2006). Strategies of human mating. *Psychological Topics, 15,* 239–260.

Buss, D. M., Haselton, M. G., Shackelford, T. K., Bleske, A. L., & Wakefield, J. C.(1998). Adaptations, exaptations, and spandrels. *American Psychologist, 53,* 533–548.

Buss, F. L. (1985). *Dignity: Lower income women tell of their lives and struggles* (pp. 153–154). Ann Arbor, MI: University of Michigan Press.

Buss, K. A. (2011).Which fearful toddlers should we worry about? Context, fear regulation and anxiety risk. *Developmental Psychology, 47,* 804–819.

Bussey, K. (2011). Gender identity development. In S.J. Schwartz, K. Luyckx, & V.L. Vignoles (Eds.), *Handbook of identity theory and research. Vols. 1 and 2* (pp. 603–628). New York: Springer Science + Business Media.

Butler, C., & Weatherall, A. (2006). "No, we're not playing families": Membership categorization in children's play. *Research on Language and Social Interaction, 39,* 441–470.

Butler, R. (1990). The effects of mastery and competitive conditions on self-assessment at different ages. *Child Development, 61,* 201–210.

Buttke, D. E., Sircar, K., & Martin, C. (2012). Exposures to endocrine-disrupting chemicals and age of menarche in adolescent girls in NHANES (2003–2008). *Environmental Health Perspectives, 120,* 1613–1618.

Buunk, B. P., Kijkstra, P., Kenrick, D. T., & Warntjes, A. (2001). Age preferences for mates as related to gender, own age, and involvement level. *Evolution and Human Behavior, 22,* 241–250.

Buunk, B. P., Zurriaga, R., Peiro, J. M., Nauta, A., & Gosalvez, I. (2005). Social comparisons at work as related to cooperative social climate and to individual differences in social comparison orientation. *Applied Psychology: An International Review, 54,* 61–80.

Buysse, A. (1996). Adolescents, young adults, and AIDS: A study of actual knowledge vs. perceived need for additional information. *Journal of Youth and Adolescence, 25,* 259–271.

Buzney, C. D., & DeCaro, J. A. (2012). Explanatory models of female pubertal timing: Discordances between cultural models of maturation and the recollection and interpretation of personal developmental experiences. *Culture, Medicine, and Psychiatry, 36,* 601–620.

Byers-Heinlein, K., Burns, T. C., & Werker, J. F. (2010). The roots of bilingualism in newborns. *Psychological Science, 21,* 343–348.

Byler, C., Kesy, L., Richardson, S., Pratt, S. G., & Rodriguez-Acosta, R. L. (2016). Work-related fatal motor vehicle traffic crashes: Matching of 2010 data from the census of fatal occupational injuries and the fatality analysis reporting system. *Accidents: Analysis and Prevention, 92,* 97–106.

Cacioppo, J. T., & Cacioppo, S. (2012). The phenotype of loneliness. *European Journal of Developmental Psychology, 9,* 446–452.

Cacioppo, J. T., Ernst, J. M, Burleson, M. H., McClintock, M. K., Malarkey, W. B., Hawkley, L. C., et al. (2000). Lonely traits and concomitant physiological processes: The MacArthur social neuroscience studies. *International Journal of Psychophysiology, 35,* 143–154.

Cacioppo, J. T., Hawkley, L. C., Ernst, J. M, Burleson, M., Bernstson, G. G., Bita, N., et al. (2006). Loneliness within a nomological net: An evolutionary perspective. *Journal of Research in Personality, 40,* 1054–1085.

Cacioppo, J. T., & Patrick, W. (2008). *Loneliness: Human nature and the need for social connection.* New York, NY: Norton.

Cacioppo, S., & Cacioppo, J. T. (2012). Decoding the invisible forces of social connections. *Frontiers in Integrative Neuro Science, 6,* Article 51.

Cain, K. M., & Dweck, C. S. (1995). The relation between motivational patterns and achievement cognitions through the elementary school years. *Merrill-Palmer Quarterly, 41,* 25–52.

Cain, P. S., & Treiman, D. J. (1981). The DOT as a source of occupational data. *American Sociological Review, 46,* 253–278.

Caldas, S. J. (1993). Current theoretical perspectives on adolescent pregnancy and childbearing in the United States. *Journal of Adolescent Research, 8,* 4–20.

Caldera, Y. M., Huston, A. C., & O'Brien, M. (1989). Social interactions and play patterns of parents and toddlers with feminine, masculine, and neutral toys. *Child Development, 60,* 70–76.

Caldwell, C. A., & Millen, A. E. (2009). Social learning mechanisms and cumulative cultural evolution. Is imitation necessary? *Psychological Science, 20,* 1478–1483.

California Department of Public Health. (2016). *Comprehensive perinatal health services program.* Retrieved from http://www.cdph.ca.gov/programs/CPSP/Pages/default.aspx

Calkins, S. D., & Dedmon, S. E. (2000). Physiological and behavioral regulation in two-year-old children with aggressive/destructive behavior problems. *Journal of Abnormal Child Psychology, 28,* 103–118.

Calkins, S. D., & Fox, N. A. (1992). The relations among infant temperament, security of attachment, and behavioral inhibition at twenty-four months. *Child Development, 63,* 1456–1472.

Calkins, S. D., & Fox, N. A. (2002). Self-regulatory processes in early personality development: A multilevel approach to the study of childhood, social withdrawal, and aggression. *Development and Psychopathology, 14,* 477–498.

Calkins, S. D., & Howse, R. B. (2004). Individual differences in self-regulation: Implications for childhood adjustment. In P. Philippot & R. S. Feldman (Eds.), *The regulation of emotion* (pp. 307–332). Mahwah, NJ: Erlbaum.

Calkins, S. D., & Leerkes, E. M. (2011). The early attachment processes and the development of emotional self-regulation. In K.D. Vohs & R.F. Baumeister (Eds.), *Handbook of self-regulation: Research, theory, and application* (2nd ed., pp. 355–373). New York: Guilford.

Callahan, C. L., Stevens, M. L., & Eyberg, S. (2010). Parent–child interaction therapy. In C. E. Schaefer (Ed.), *Play therapy for preschool children* (pp. 199–221). Washington, DC: American Psychological Association.

Callahan, S. P., & Ledgerwood, A. (2016). On the psychological function of flags and logos: Group identity symbols increase perceived entitativity. *Journal of Personality and Social Psychology, 110,* 528–550.

Calvert, G., Spence, C., & Stein, B. E. (2004). *The handbook of multisensory processes.* Cambridge, MA: MIT Press.

Calzo, J. P., Antonucci, T. C., Mays, V. M., & Cochran, S. D. (2011). Retrospective recall of sexual orientation identity development among gay, lesbian, and bisexual adults. *Developmental Psychology, 47,* 1658–1673.

Campbell, I. G., Grimm, K. J., de Bie, E., & Feinberg, I. (2012). Sex, puberty and the timing of sleep EEG measured adolescent brain maturation. *PNAS Proceedings of the National Academic of Sciences of the United States of America, 109,* 5740–5743.

Campbell, J. (1990). Self-esteem and clarity of the self-concept. *Journal of Personality and Social Psychology, 59,* 538–549.

Campbell, R., MacSweeney, M., & Waters, D. (2007). Sign language and the brain: A review. *Journal of Deaf Studies and Deaf Education, 13,* 3–20.

Campbell, S. M., Ward, A. J., Sonnenfeld, J. A., & Agle, B. R. (2008). Relational ties that bind: Leader-follower relation-ship dimensions and charismatic attribution. *The Leadership Quarterly, 19,* 556–568.

Campos, B., Dunkel-Schetter, C., Aboud C. M., Hobel, C. J., Glynn, L. M. & Sandman, C. A. (2008). Familialism, social support, and stress: Positive implications for pregnant Latinas. *Cultural Diversity and Ethnic Minority Psychology, 14,* 155–162.

Campos, B., Graesch, A. P., Repetti, R., Bradbury, T., & Ochs, E. (2009). Opportunity for interaction? A naturalistic observation study of dual-earner families after work and school. *Journal of Family Psychology, 23,* 798–807.

Canadian Paediatric Society. (2008). Adolescent sexual orientation. *Paediatrics and Child Health, 13,* 619–623.

Cannella, C., Savina, C., & Donini, L. M. (2009). Nutrition, longevity and behavior. *Archives of Gerontology and Geriatrics, 49,* 19–27.

Canobi, K. (2008). Number words in young children's conceptual and procedural knowledge of addition, subtraction, and inversion. *Cognition, 108*, 675–686.

Canobi, K. H. (2004). Individual differences in children's addition and subtraction knowledge. *Cognitive Development, 19*, 81–93.

Canobi, K. H., Reeve, R. A., & Pattison, P. E. (2003). Patterns of knowledge in children's addition. *Developmental Psychology, 39*, 521–534.

Cantin, R. H., Gnaedinger, E. K., Gallaway, K. C., Hesson-McInnis, M. S., & Hund, A. M. (2016). Executive functioning predicts reading, mathematics, and theory of mind during the elementary years. *Journal of Experimental Child Psychology, 146*, 66–78.

Cao, L., Zhang, Y., & He, N. (2008). Carrying weapons to school for protection: An analysis of the 2001 school crime supplement data. *Journal of Criminal Justice, 36*, 154–164.

Capaldi, D. M. (1996). The reliability of retrospective report for timing first intercourse for adolescent males. *Journal of Adolescent Research, 11*, 375–387.

Caplan, G. (1964). *Principles of preventive psychiatry*. New York, NY: Basic Books.

Caplan, L. J., & Schooler, C. (2007). Socioeconomic status and financial coping strategies: The mediating role of perceived control. *Social Psychology Quarterly, 70*, 43–58.

Cappeliez, P. (2008). An explanation of the reminiscence bump in the dreams of older adults in terms of life goals and identity. *Self and Identity, 7*, 25–33.

Cappeliez, P., & O'Rourke, N. (2002). Profiles of reminiscence among older adults: Perceived stress, life attitudes, and personality variables. *International Journal of Aging and Human Development, 54*, 255–266.

Cappeliez, P., & Robitaille, A. (2010). Coping mediates the relationships between reminiscence and psychological well-being among older adults. *Aging and Mental Health, 14*, 807–818.

Carlo, G., Knight, G. P., Eisenberg, N., & Rotenberg, K. J. (1991). Cognitive processes and prosocial behaviors among children: The role of affective attributions and reconciliations. *Developmental Psychology, 27*, 456–461.

Carlson, C. L. (2014). Seeking self-sufficiency: Why emerging adult college students receive and implement parental advice. *Emerging Adulthood, 2*, 257–269.

Carlson, M., & Earls, F. (1997). Psychological and neuroendocrinological sequelae of early social deprivation in institutionalized children in Romania. *Annals of the New York Academy of Sciences, 807*, 419–426.

Carlson, M. C., Erickson, K. I., Kramer, A. F. et al., (2009). Evidence for neurocognitive plasticity in at-risk older adults: The Experience Corps Program. *Journals of Gerontology, Series A: Biological Sciences and Medical Science, 64*, 1275–1282.

Carnagey, N. L., & Anderson, C. A. (2004). Violent video game exposure and aggression: A literature review. *Minerva Psichiatrica, 45*, 1–18.

Caro, F. G., & Bass, S. A. (1997). Receptivity to volunteering in the immediate postretirement period. *Journal of Applied Gerontology, 16*, 427–441.

Carpendale, J. I. M., & Krebs, D. L. (1992). Situational variation in moral judgment: In a stage or on a stage? *Journal of Youth and Adolescence, 21*, 203–224.

Carr, D. (2003). A "good death" for whom? Quality of spouse's death and psychological distress among older widowed per-sons. *Journal of Health and Social Behavior, 44*, 215–232.

Carr, D. (2004). The desire to date and remarry among older widows and widowers. *Journal of Marriage and the Family, 66*, 1051–1068.

Carr, D., House, J. S., Wortman, C., Neese, R., & Kessler, R. C. (2001). Psychological adjustment to sudden and anticipated spousal loss among older widowed persons. *Journal of Gerontology, 56B*, S237–S248.

Carroll, J. L. (2012). *Sexuality now: Embracing diversity* (4th ed.). Belmont, CA: Cengage.

Carter, C. S. (2014). Oxytocin pathways and the evolution of human behavior. *Annual Review of Psychology, 65*, 17–39.

Carver, C. S., & Scheier, M. F. (2016). Self-regulation of action and affect. In K. D. Vohs & R. F. Baumeister (Eds.), *Handbook of self-regulation: Research, theory and applications* (3rd ed., pp. 3–21). New York, NY: Guilford.

Carver, L. J., & Vaccaro, B. G. (2007). 12 month old infants allocate increased neural resources to stimuli associated with negative adult emotion. *Developmental Psychology, 43*, 54–69.

Casalin, S., Luyten, P., Vliegen, N., & Meurs, P. (2012). The structure and stability of temperament from infancy to toddlerhood: A one-year prospective study. *Infant Behavior and Development, 35*, 94–108.

Case, R. (1987). The structure and process of intellectual development. *International Journal of Psychology, 22*, 571–607.

Case, R. (1998). The development of conceptual structures. In W. Damon (Ed.), *Handbook of child psychology, Vol. 2: Cognition, perception and language* (pp. 745–800). Hoboken, NJ: John Wiley and Sons.

Case, R., & Okamoto, Y. (1996). The role of central conceptual structures in the development of children's thought. *Monographs of the Society for Research in Child Development, 61*.

Caserta, M. S., & Lund, D. A. (2007). Toward the development of an inventory of daily widowed life (IDWL): Guided by the dual process model of coping with bereavement. *Death Studies, 31*, 505–534.

Cashon, C. H. (2011). Development of specialized face perception in infants: An information processing perspective. In L. M. Oakes, C. H. Cashon, M. Casasola, & D. H. Rakison (Eds.), *Infant perception and cognition: Recent advances, emerging theories, and future directions* (pp. 69–83). New York, NY: Oxford University Press.

Casimir, G., & Waldman, D. A. (2007). A cross cultural comparison of the importance of leadership traits for effective low-level and high-level leaders: Australia and China. *International Journal of Cross Cultural Management, 7*, 47–60.

Casper, L. M., & Bianchi, S. M. (2002). *Continuity and change in the American family*. Thousand Oaks, CA: Sage.

Caspi, A., Hariri, A. R., Holmes, A., Uher, R., & Moffitt, E. (2010). Genetic sensitivity to the environment: The case of the serotonin gene and its implications for studying complex diseases and traits. *American Journal of Psychiatry, 167*, 509–527.

Caspi, A., & Shiner, R. L. (2006). Personality development. In W. Damon & R. Lerner (Series Eds.) & N. Eisenberg (Vol. Ed.), *Handbook of child psychology: Vol. 3. Social, emotional, and personality development* (6th ed) (pp. 300–365). New York: Wiley.

Cassia, V. M., Turati, C., & Simion, F. (2004). Can a nonspecific bias toward top-heavy patterns explain newborns' face preference? *Psychological Science, 15*, 379–383.

Cassidy, J. (2016). The nature of the child's ties. In J. Cassidy & P. R. Shaver (Eds.), *Handbook of attachment: Theory, research and clinical applications* (3rd ed., pp. 3–22). New York, NY: Guilford.

Castles, E. E. (2012). *Inventing intelligence: How America came to worship IQ*. Westport, CT: Praeger Publishing.

Caughlin, J. P., & Huston, T. L. (2006). The affective structure of marriage. In A. L. Vangelisti & D. Perlman (Eds.), *The Cambridge handbook of personal relationships* (pp. 131–155). New York, NY: Cambridge University Press.

Caughy, M. O., Nettles, S. M., O'Campo, P. J., & Lohrfink, K. (2006). Neighborhood matters: Racial socialization of African American children. *Child Development, 77*, 1220–1236.

Cavuoto, M. G., Ong, B., Pike, K. E. et al. (2016). Objective but not subjective sleep predicts memory in community-dwelling older adults. *Journal of Sleep Research, 25*, 475–485.

Ceballo, R., & McLoyd, V. C. (2002). Social support and parenting in poor, dangerous neighborhoods. *Child Development, 73*, 1320–1321.

Cedeno, L. A., Elias, M. J., Kelly, S., & Chu, B. C. (2010). School violence, adjustment, and the influence of hope on low-income, African American youth. *American Journal of Orthopsychiatry, 80*, 213–226.

Center on the Developing Child. (2007). *The impact of early adversity on child development* (In Brief). Retrieved from www.developingchild.harvard.edu

Center on the Developing Child. (2016). *Key concepts*. Retrieved from http://developingchild.harvard.edu/

Center for the Study and Prevention of Violence. (2001). *Bullying prevention: Recommendations for schools*. Safe Communities-Safe Schools Fact Sheet. Retrieved from http://www.colorado.edu/cspv/publications/factsheets/safeschools/pdf/FS-SC08.pdf

Center for Young Women's Health. (2016). *Breast health: General information*. Retrieved from http://youngwomenshealth.org/2014/02/27/breast-health

Centers for Disease Control and Prevention (CDC). (2003). *2001 Assisted reproductive technology success rates: National summary and fertility clinic reports*. Washington, DC: U.S. Department of Health and Human Services.

Centers for Disease Control and Prevention (CDC). (2007). *Fetal alcohol spectrum disorders*. Retrieved from http://www.cdc.gov/ncbddd/fas/

Centers for Disease Control and Prevention (CDC). (2012a). *Health effects of gentrification*. Retrieved from http://www.cdc.gov/healthyplaces/healthtopics/gentrificationhtm

Centers for Disease Control and Prevention (CDC). (2012b). *PRAMS and smoking*. Retrieved from http://www.CDC.gov/PRAMS/Tobacco andPrams.htm

Centers for Disease Control and Prevention. (2015a). American Society for Reproductive Medicine, Society for Assisted Reproductive Technology. 2013 *Assisted Reproductive Technology Fertility Clinic Success Rates Report*. Atlanta, GA: U.S. Dept. of Health and Human Services. Retrieved from http://www.cdc.gov/art/reports/

Centers for Disease Control and Prevention. (2015b). *Preterm birth*. Retrieved from www.cdc.gov/reproductivehealth/maternalinfanthealth/pretermbirth.htm

Centers for Disease Control and Prevention. (2015c). *Birthweight and gestation*. Retrieved from www.cdc.gov/nchs/fastats/birthweight.htm

Centers for Disease Control and Prevention. (2015d). *Facts about FASDs*. Retrieved from http://www.cdc.gov/ncbddd/fasd/facts.html

Centers for Disease Control and Prevention. (2015e). *Health risks among sexual minority youth*. Retrieved from http://www.cdc.gov/healthyyouth/disparities/smy.htm

Centers for Disease Control and Prevention. (2015f). *STDs in adolescents and young adults, 2014*. Retrieved from http://www.cdc.gov/std/stats14/adol.htm

Centers for Disease Control and Prevention. (2015g). *HIV surveillance report, 2014; vol. 26*. Retrieved from http://www.cdc.gov/hiv/library/reports/surveillance/

Centers for Disease Control and Prevention. (2016). *Ten leading causes of death and injury by age group, 2014*. Retrieved from http://www.cdc.gov/injury/wisqars/leadingcauses.html

Central Intelligence Agency. (2007). *Afghanistan*. The World Fact Book. Retrieved from http://www.cia.gov/library/publications/the-world -factbook/geos/af.html# People

Central Intelligence Agency. (2013). *World fact book*. Retrieved from https://www.cia.gov/library/publications/the-world-factbook/rankorder/2091rank.html

Central Intelligence Agency. (2015). *Change reference from 2013 to 2015*. Retrieved from https://www.cia.gov/library/publications/resources/the-world-factbook/rankorder/2091rank.html

Central Intelligence Agency. (2016). *World fact book*. Afghanistan. Retrieved from https://www.cia.gov/library/publications/resources/the-world-factbook/geos/af.html

CEO Forum on Education and Technology. (2001). *The CEO forum: School technology and readiness report. Key building blocks for student achievement in the 21st century*. Retrieved from http://www.ceoforum.org/downloads/report4.pdf

Cerella, J. (1990). Aging and information processing rate. In J. E. Birren & K. W. Schaie (Eds.), *Handbook of cognitive aging* (3rd ed., pp. 201–221). New York, NY: Academic Press.

Cernoch, J. M., & Porter, R. H. (1985). Recognition of maternal axillary odors by infants. *Child Development, 56*, 1593–1598.

Cesarone, B. (1994). *Video games and children*. ERIC Digest EDO-PS-94-3. Retrieved from http://www .kidsource.com/kidsource/content2/video.games.html

Cha, Y. (2010). Reinforcing separate spheres: The effect of spousal overwork on men's and women's employment in dual earner households. *American Sociological Review, 75*, 303–329.

Chalmers, B. (2012). Childbirth across cultures: Research and practice. *Birth: Issues in Perinatal Care, 39*, 276–280.

Chandler, L. S., & Lane, S. J. (Eds.). (1996). *Children with prenatal drug exposure* (pp. 111–128). New York, NY: Haworth Press.

Chang, E. C., & Sanna, L. J. (2001). Optimism, pessimism, and positive and negative affectivity in middle-aged adults: A test of a cognitive-affective model of psychological adjustment. *Psychology and Aging, 16*, 524–531.

Chang, J. (1991). *Wild swans: Three daughters of China*. New York, NY: Random House.

Chang, L., Schwartz, D., Dodge, K.A., & McBride-Chang, C. (2003). Harsh parenting and relation to child emotion regulation and aggression. *Journal of Family Psychology, 17*, 598–606.

Chang, P., Wray, L., & Lin, Y. (2014). Social relationships, leisure activity and health in older adults. *Health Psychology, 33*, 516–523.

Chapman, M. (1988). *Constructive evolution: Origin and development of Piaget's thought*. New York, NY: Cambridge University Press.

Chapman, M., & McBride, M. L. (1992). Beyond competence and performance. Children's class inclusion strategies, superordinate class cues, and verbal justifications. *Developmental Psychology, 28*, 319–327.

Charlesworth, W. R. (1992). Darwin and developmental psychology: Past and present. *Developmental Psychology, 28*, 5–16.

Chayer, M., & Bouffard, T. (2010). Relations between impostor feelings and upward and downward identification and contrast among 10- to12-year old students. *European Journal of Psychology of Education, 25*, 125–140.

Chazan, S. E. (1981). Development of object permanence as a correlate of dimensions of maternal care. *Developmental Psychology, 17*, 79–81.

Chen, R. (2012). Institutional characteristics and college student drop out risks: Multilevel event history analysis. *Research in Higher Education, 53*, 487–505.

Chen, S., Boucher, H. C., & Tapias, M. P. (2006). The relational self revealed: Integrative conceptualization and implications for interpersonal life. *Psychological Bulletin, 132*, 151–179.

Cheng, S.-T., & Chan, A. C. M. (2006). Relationship with others and life satisfaction in later life: Do gender and widowhood make a difference? *Journals of Gerontology: Series B: Psycho-logical Sciences and Social Sciences, 61B*, P46–P53.

Cheng, T. K., Ho, D. Y. F, Xie, W., Wong, H. Y. K., & Cheng-Lai, A. (2013). Alienation, despair and hope as predictors of health, coping, and non-engagement among non-engaged youth: Manifestations of spiritual emptiness. *Asia Pacific Journal of Counseling and Psychotherapy, 4*, 18–30.

Cherlin, A. J. (2009). *The marriage-go-round: The state of marriage and the family in America today*. New York, NY: Random House.

Cherney, I. D., & London, K. (2006). Gender-linked differences in the toys, television shows, computer games and outdoor activities of 5- to 13-year-old children. *Sex Roles, 54*, 717–726.

Chernew, M., Cutler, D. M., Ghosh, K., & Landrum, M. B. (2016). Understanding the improvement in disability free life expectancy in the U.S. elderly population. *Working paper 22306*. Cambridge MA: National Bureau of Economic Research. Retrieved from http://www.nber.org/papers/w22306

Cherry, K. E., Walker, E. J., Brown, J. S., Volaufova, J., et al. (2013). Social engagement and health, in younger, older and oldest-old adults in the Louisiana Healthy Aging study. *Journal of Applied Gerontology, 32*, 51–75.

Chevan, A. (1995). Holding on and letting go: Residential mobility during widowhood. *Research on Aging, 17*, 278–302.

Chickering, A. W., & Reisser, L. (1993). *Education and identity* (2nd ed.). San Francisco, CA: Jossey-Bass.

Childbirthconnection.org. (2007). *Quotes from mothers. Labor induction*. Retrieved from http://www.childbirthconnection.org

Children's Defense Fund. (2003). *Key facts about America's children*. Retrieved from http://www .childrensdefense.org/data/default.aspx

Chin, C.B. (2016). "We've got team spirit"!: Ethnic community building and Japanese American youth basketball leagues. *Ethnic and Racial Studies, 39,* 1070–1088.

Choe, D. W., Olson, S. L., & Sameroff, A. (2013). The interplay of externalizing problems and physical and inductive discipline during childhood. *Developmental Psychology, 49,* 2029–2039.

Choi, N. G., & Landeros, C. (2011). Wisdom from life's challenges: Qualitative interviews with low- and moderate-income older adults who were nominated as being wise. *Journal of Gerontological Social Work, 54,* 592–614.

Chouinard, M. M. (2007). Children's questions: A mechanism for cognitive development. *Monographs of the Society for Research in Child Development, 72*(1, Serial No. 286), 1–112.

Christakis, N. A., & Fowler, J. H. (2009). *Connected: The surprising power of our social networks and how they shape our lives.* New York, NY: Little, Brown.

Christerson, B., Edwards, K. L., & Flory, R. (2010). *Growing up in America: The power of race in the lives of teens.* Stanford, CA: Stanford University Press.

Christiansen, S. L., & Palkovitz, R. (1998). Exploring Erikson's psychosocial theory of development: Generativity and its relationship to paternal identity, intimacy, and involvement in childcare. *Journal of Men's Studies, 7,* 133–156.

Chronicle of Higher Education. (2005, August 26). Life objectives considered essential or very important by college freshmen, 2004. *Almanac Issue,* 14–18.

Church, J. (1966). *Three babies: Biographies of cognitive development.* New York, NY: Random House.

Cicirelli, V. G. (1999). Personality and demographic factors in older adults' fear of death. *The Gerontologist, 39,* 569–579.

Cicirelli, V. G. (2001). Personal meanings of death in older adults and young adults in relation to their fears of death. *Death Studies, 25,* 663–683.

Cincinnati Children's Hospital Medical Center. (1998). *Wellness: Infant safety tips.* Retrieved from http://www .cincinnatichildrens.org/health/info / newborn/well/infant-tips.htm

Cincinnati Children's Hospital Medical Center. (2004). *Installing and using child safety seats and booster seats.* Retrieved from http:// www .cincinnati childrens.org/health/info /safety/vehicle/harness.htm

Cirino, P. T., Vaughn, S., Linan-Thompson, S., Cardena-Hagan, E., Fletcher, J. M., & Francis, D. J. (2009). One-year follow-up outcomes of Spanish and English interventions for English language learners at risk for reading problems. *American Educational Research Journal, 46,* 744–781.

CIRP. (2006). *American freshman national norms for fall 2006.* Retrieved from www .gseis.ucla.edu/heri/PDFs/06CIRPFS _Norms_Narrative.pdf

Clark, A. L., & Howland, R. I. (1978). The American Samoan. In A. L. Clark (Ed.), *Culture, childbearing, and the health professionals* (pp. 154–172). Philadelphia, PA: Davis.

Clark, D. A., Holifield, M., Leah, R., & Beck, J. S. (2009). In G. O. Gabbard (Ed.), *Textbook of psychotherapeutic treatments* (pp. 165–200). Arlington, VA: American Psychiatric Publishing Company.

Clark, J. E., Phillips, S. J., & Petersen, R. (1989). Developmental stability in jumping. *Developmental Psychology, 25,* 929–935.

Clark, M., & Arnold, J. (2008). The nature, prevalence, and correlates of generativity among men in middle career. *Journal of Vocational Behavior, 73,* 473–484.

Clark, M. L. (1991). Social identity, peer relations, and academic competence of African-American adolescents. *Education and Urban Society, 24,* 41–52.

Clark, M. S., & Lemay, E. P., Jr. (2010). Close relationships. In S. T. Fiske & D. Gilbert (Eds.), *Handbook of social psychology* (pp. 898–940). New York, NY: Oxford University Press.

Clark, M. S., Lemay, E. P., Jr., Graham, S. M., Pataki, S. P., & Finkel, E. J. (2010). Ways of giving benefits in marriage: Norm use, relationship satisfaction, and attachment-related variability. *Psychological Science, 21,* 944–951.

Clark, S. D., Long, M. M., & Schiffman, L. G. (1999). The mind–body connection: The relationship among physical activity level, life satisfaction, and cognitive age among mature females. *Journal of Social Behavior and Personality, 14,* 221–240.

Clarke, P., Marshall, V. W., & Weir, D. (2013). Unexpected retirement from full time work after age 62: Consequences for life satisfaction in older Americans. *European Journal of Ageing, 9,* 207–219.

Clarke-Stewart, K. A. (1989). Infant day care: Maligned or malignant? *American Psychologist, 44,* 266–273.

Clarke-Stewart, K. A., & Fein, G. G. (1983). Early childhood programs. In P. H. Mussen (Ed.), *Handbook of child psychology: Vol. 2. Infancy and developmental psychobiology* (pp. 917–1000). New York, NY: Wiley.

Clark-Ibanez, M., & Felmlee, D. (2004). Inter-ethnic relationship: The role of social network diversity. *Journal of Marriage and the Family, 66,* 293–305.

Clasen, D. R., & Brown, B. B. (1985). The multidimensionality of peer pressure in adolescence. *Journal of Youth and Adolescence, 14,* 451–468.

Clausen, J. A. (1975). The social meaning of differential physical and sexual maturation. In S. E. Dragastin & G. H. Elder (Eds.), *Adolescence in the life cycle: Psychological change and social context.* Washington, DC: Hemisphere.

Claxton, A., & Perry-Jenkins, M. (2008). No fun anymore: Leisure and marital quality across the transition to parenthood. *Journal of Marriage and the Family, 70,* 28–43.

Cloud, J. (2000, September 18). A kinder, gentler death. *Time, 156,* 60–67.

Cloud, J. (2001). Should SATs matter? *Time, 157,* 62–76.

Cloud, J. (2010). Why genes aren't destiny. *Time, 175,* 48–53.

CNN.com. (2005, February 10). *Centenarians reveal longevity secrets.* World. Retrieved from http://www .cnn.com/2005/WORLD /americas/02/09/cuban.centenarians.ap/

Coan, J. A. (2008). Toward a neuroscience of attachment. In J. Cassidy & P. R. Shaver (Eds.), *Handbook of attachment: Theory, research and clinical applications* (pp. 241–268). New York, NY: Guilford.

Coan, J. (2016). Toward a neuroscience of attachment. In J. Cassidy & P..R. Shaver (Eds.) *Handbook of attachment: Theory, research and clinical applications* (pp. 242–269). New York: Guilford.

Cobb, S. (1979). Social support and health through the life course. In M. W. Riley (Ed.), *Aging from birth to death.* Boulder, CO: Westview.

Cohane, G. H., & Pope, H. G., Jr. (2000). Body image in boys: A review of the literature. *International Journal of Eating Disorders, 29,* 373–379.

Cohen, A. O., Breiner, K., Steinberg, L., Bonnie, R. J., Scott, E. S., Taylor-Thompson, K. A., Rudolph, M. D., Schein, J., Richeson, J. A., Heller, A. S., Silverman, M. R., Dellarco, D. V., Fair, D. A., Galván, A., & Casey, B. J. (2016). When is an adolescent an adult? Assessing cognitive control in emotional and nonemotional contexts. *Psychological Science, 27,* 549–562.

Cohen, B. (2004). Introduction. In N.B. Ander-son, R. A. Bulatao, & B. Cohen (Eds.), *Critical perspectives on racial and ethnic differences in health in late life* (p. 6). National Research Council, Panel on Race, Ethnicity, and Health in Later Life, Committee on Population, Division of Behavioral and Social Sciences and Education. Washington, DC: The National Academies Press.

Cohen, D. L. (2013). Surrogate pregnancies on rise despite cost hurdles. *Reuters U.S. Edition.* Retrieved from http://www.reuters .com/article/us-parent-surrogate -idUSBRE92H11Q20130318

Cohen, J., & Sandy, S. V. (2007). The social, emotional and academic education of children: Theories, goals, methods and assessments. In R. Bar-On, J. G. Maree, & M. J. Elias (Eds.), *Educating people to be emotionally intelligent* (pp. 63–77). Westport, CT: Praeger.

Cohen, L. S., Wang, B., Nonacs, R., Viguera, A. C., Lemon, E. L., & Freeman, M. P. (2010). Treatment of mood disorders during pregnancy and postpartum. *Psychiatric Clinics of North America, 33,* 273–293.

Cohen, R. S., & Weissman, S. H. (1984). The parenting alliance. In R. S. Cohen, B. J. Cohler, & S. H. Weissman (Eds.),

Parenthood: A psychodynamic perspective (pp. 33–49). New York, NY: Guilford Press.

Cohn, B. (1998, March/April). What a wife's worth. *Stanford,* 14–15.

Cohn, J. (2013). The complexities of Obama's universal pre-kindergarten plan. *New Republic.* Retrieved from http://www.newrepublic.com/article/112403/state-union-2013-obamas-universal-pre-kindergarten-plan#

Coie, J. D., & Krehbiel, G. (1984). Effects of academic tutoring on the social status of low achieving, socially rejected children. *Child Development, 55,* 1465–1478.

Colasante, T., Zuffianò, A., Bae, N. Y., & Malti, T. (2014). Inhibitory control and moral emotions: Relations to reparation in early and middle childhood. *Journal of Genetic Psychology: Research and Theory on Human Development, 175,* 511–527.

Colby, A., & Damon, W. (1994). Listening to a different voice: A review of Gilligan's "In a Different Voice." In B. Puka (Ed.), *Caring voices and women's moral frames: Gilligan's view. Moral development: A compendium* (Vol. 6, pp. 275–283). New York, NY: Garland.

Colby, A., & Damon, W. (1999). The development of extraordinary moral commitment. In M. Killen & D. Hart (Eds.), *Morality in everyday life: Developmental perspectives* (pp. 342–370). New York, NY: Cambridge University Press.

Colby, A., & Kohlberg, L. (1987). *The measurement of moral judgment: Vol. 1. Theoretical foundations and research validation.* Cambridge, England: Cambridge University Press.

Colby, A., Kohlberg, L., Gibbs, J., & Lieberman, M. (1983). A longitudinal study of moral judgment. *Monographs of the Society for Research in Child Development, 48* (1, Serial No. 200).

Cole, C. L., & Cole, A. L. (1985). Husbands and wives should have an equal share in making the marriage work. In H. Feldman & M. Feldman (Eds.), *Current controversies in marriage and family* (pp. 131–141). Newbury Park, CA: Sage.

Cole, D., & La Voie, J. C. (1985). Fantasy play and related cognitive development in 2 to 6 year olds. *Developmental Psychology, 21,* 233–240.

Coleman, E. (2003). Compulsive sexual behavior: What to call it, how to treat it? *SIECUS Report, 31,* 12–16.

Coleman, J. S. (1987). Families and schools. *Educational Researcher, 16,* 32–38.

Coll, C. G. (2004). The interpenetration of culture and biology in human development. *Research in Human Development, 1,* 145–160.

Coll, C. G., & Marks, A. K. (2009). *Immigrant stories: Ethnicity and academics in middle childhood.* New York, NY: Oxford University Press.

Coll, C. G., & Marks, A. K. (2012). *Is becoming an American a developmental risk?* Washington, DC: American Psychological Association.

Coll, C. T. G. (1990). Developmental outcome of minority infants: A process-oriented look into our beginnings. *Child Development, 61,* 270–289.

College Board. (2016). *Tuition and fees and room and board over time, 1975–76 to 2015–16, selected years.* Retrieved from https://trends.collegeboard.org/college-pricing/figures-tables/tuition-and-fees-and-room-and-board-over-time-1975-76-2015-16-selected-years

Collin, A., & Young, R. A. (2000). *The future of career.* New York, NY: Cambridge University Press.

Collins, K., Luszcz, M., Lawson, M., & Keeves, J. (1997). Everyday problem solving in elderly women: Contributions of residence, perceived control and age. *The Gerontologist, 37,* 293–302.

Collins, W. (1995). Relationship and development: Family adaptation to individual change. In S. Shulman (Ed.), *Close relationships and socioemotional development* (pp. 128–154). Norwood, NJ: Ablex.

Collins, W. A., & Laursen, B. (2006). Parent-adolescent relationships. In P. Noller & J. A. Feeney (Eds.), *Close relationships: Functions, forms and processes* (pp. 111–125). Hove, England: Taylor & Francis.

Common Dreams. (2012). *UNICEF: US among highest child poverty rates in developed countries.* Retrieved from https://www.commondreams.org/headline/2012/05/30-6

Commons, M. L., & Richards, F. A. (2003). Four postformal stages. In J. Demick & C. Andreoletti (Eds.), *Handbook of adult development* (pp. 199–219). New York, NY: Plenum Publishers.

Conger, J. A., & Kanungo, R. N. (1998). *Charismatic leadership in organizations.* Thousand Oaks, CA: Sage.

Conger, R. D., Conger, K. J., Elder, G. H., Lorenz, F. O., Simons, R. L., & Whitbeck, L. B. (1993). Family economic stress and adjustment of early adolescent girls. *Developmental Psychology, 29,* 206–219.

Conger, R. D., Wallace, L. E., Sun, Y., Simons, R. L., McLoyd, V. C., & Brody, G. H. (2002). Economic pressure in African American families: A replication and extension of the family stress model. *Developmental Psychology, 38,* 179–193.

Congress and RU-486. (2001, April 26). *Washington Post,* p. A26.

Connolly, J., Craig, W., Goldberg, A., & Pepler, D. (2004). Mixed-gender groups, dating, and romantic relationships in early adolescence. *Journal of Research on Adolescence, 14,* 185–207.

Connolly, J., & McIsaac, C. (2011). Romantic relationships in adolescence. In M. K. Underwood & L. H. Rosen (Eds.), *Social development: Relationships in infancy, childhood, and adolescence* (pp. 180–203). New York, NY: Guilford Press.

Connolly, K., & Dalgleish, M. (1989). The emergence of a tool-using skill in infancy. *Developmental Psychology, 25,* 894–912.

Constantinople, A. (1969). An Eriksonian measure of personality development in college students. *Developmental Psychology, 1,* 357–372.

Conte, H. R., Weiner, M. B., & Plutchik, R. (1982). Measuring death anxiety: Conceptual, psychometric, and factor-analytic aspects. *Journal of Personality and Social Psychology, 43,* 775–785.

Conway, M. A., & Holmes, A. (2004). Psychosocial stages and the accessibility of autobiographical memories across the life cycle. *Journal of Personality, 73,* 461–480.

Cook, A., & Glass, C. (2013). Glass cliffs and organizational saviors: Barriers to minority leadership in work organizations. *Social Problems, 60,* 168–187.

Cook, K. S., Levi, M., & Hardin, R. (Eds.). (2009). *Whom can we trust? How groups, networks and institutions make trust possible.* New York, NY: Russell Sage Foundation.

Coolhart, D. (2014, March 5–8). Being transparent about having a trans-parent: Experiences of children of transgender parents. *Conference Abstract from the International Therapy Association's 22nd World Family Therapy Congress, Panama City, Panama.*

Cooney, T. M., & Mortimer, J. T. (1999). Family structure differences in the timing of leaving home: Exploring mediating factors. *Journal of Research in Adolescence, 9,* 367–393.

Cooney, T. M., Pedersen, F. A., Indelicato, S., & Palkovitz, R. (1993). Timing of fatherhood: Is "on-time" optimal? *Journal of Marriage and the Family, 55,* 205–215.

Cooper, B. R., & Lanza, S. T. (2014). Who benefits from Head Start? Using latent class moderation to examine differential treatment effects. *Child Development, 85,* 2317–2338.

Cooper, D., & Gould, E. (2013). Financial security of elderly Americans at risk. *Economic Policy Institute.* Retrieved from http://www.epi.org/publication/economic-security-elderly-americans-risk/

Cooper, J. C., Dunne, S., Furey, R., & O'Doherty, J. P. (2012). Dorsomedial prefrontal cortex mediates rapid evaluations predicting the outcome of romantic interactions. *The Journal of Neuroscience, 32,* 15647–15656.

Cooper, K. (2016). Why I chose not to have children and how I'm making peace with my decision. *Huffington Post July 13, 2015.* Retrieved from http://www.huffingtonpost.com/kelli-cooper/why-i-chose-not-to-have-children-and-how-im-making-peace-with-my-decision_b_7741408.html

Cooper, L. (2013). *Protecting the rights of transgender parents and their children.* New York: ACLU/Washington, DC: National Center for Transgender Equality.

Copen, C. E., Chandra, A., & Martinez, G. (2012, August 16). Prevalence and timing of oral sex with opposite-sex partners among females and males age 15–24 years: United States, 2007–2010. *National Health Statistics Reports, 56.*

Corcoran, M. E., & Chaudry, A. (1997). The dynamics of childhood poverty. *Future of Children, 7,* 40–54.

Coreter, C. M., & Fleming, A. S. (2002). Psychobiology of maternal behavior in human beings. In M. H. Bornstein (Ed.), *Handbook of parenting: Vol. 2. Biology and ecology of parenting* (pp. 141–181). Mahwah, NJ: Erlbaum.

Corijn, M., Liefbroer, A. C., & Gierveld, J. De J. (1996). It takes two to tango, doesn't it? The influence of couple characteristics on the timing of the birth of the first child. *Journal of Marriage and the Family, 58,* 117–126.

Cornell, D. G., & Limber, S. P. (2016). Do U.S. laws go far enough to prevent bullying at school? *Monitor on Psychology, 47,* 64–73.

Correia, C., Lopez, K. J., Wroblewski, K. E., et al. (2016). Global sensory impairment in older adults in the United States. *Journal of the American Geriatric Society, 64,* 306–313.

Correll, S. J. (2001). Gender and the career choice process: The role of biased self-assessments. *American Journal of Sociology, 106,* 1691–1730.

Corter, C. M., & Fleming, A. S. (2002). Psychobiology of maternal behavior in human beings. In M. H. Bornstein (Ed.), *Handbook of parenting: Vol. 2. Biology and ecology of parenting* (pp. 141–181). Mahwah, NJ: Erlbaum.

Cortiella, C., & Horowitz, S. H. (2014). *The state of learning disabilities: Facts, trends and emerging issues.* New York: National Center for Learning Disabilities.

Cosmides, L., & Tooby, J. (1997). *Evolutionary psychology: A primer.* Retrieved from http://www.psych.ucsb.edu/research/cep/primer.html

Cossins, D. (2012). Social psychology damned again. *The Scientist Magazine.* Retrieved from http ://www.The-Scientist.com/?articles.view/articleNo/33509/title/Social-Psychology-Damned-Again/

Costa, P. T., Metter, E. J., & McCrae, R. R. (1994). Personality stability and its contribution to successful aging. *Journal of Geriatric Psychiatry, 27,* 41–59.

Costello, M. B. (2016). *Teaching the 2016 election: The Trump effect; the impact of the presidential campaign on our nation's schools.* Montgomery, AL: Southern Poverty Law Center.

Cota-Robles, S., Neiss, M., & Rowe, D. C. (2002). The role of puberty in violent and nonviolent delinquency among Anglo American, Mexican American, and African American boys. *Journal of Adolescent Research, 17,* 364–376.

Côté, J. E. (2009). Identity formation and self-development in adolescence. In R. M. Lerner & L. Steinberg (Eds.), *Handbook of adolescent psychology, Vol. 1. Individual bases of adolescent development* (3rd ed., pp. 266–304). New York, NY: Wiley.

Coté, J. E. (2014). The dangerous myth of emerging adulthood: An evidence-based critique of a flawed developmental theory. *Applied Developmental Science, 18,* 177–188.

Côté, S., & Bouffard, T. (2011). Role of parental emotional support in illusion of scholastic incompetence. *European Review of Applied Psychology, 61,* 137–145.

Cotten, S. R. (1999). Marital status and mental health revisited: Examining the importance of risk factors and resources. *Family Relations, 48,* 225–233.

Cougle, J. R., Reardon, D. C., & Coleman, P. K. (2005). Generalized anxiety following unintended pregnancies resolved through childbirth and abortion: A cohort study of the 1995 National Survey of Family Growth. *Journal of Anxiety Disorders, 19,* 137–142.

Council for International Organizations of Medical Sciences. (1993). *International ethical guidelines for biomedical research involving human subjects.* Geneva, Switzerland: Author.

Countdown. (2013). *Maternal, newborn and child survival, Kenya.* Retrieved from http://www .countdown2015mnch.org /documents/2013Report/Kenya _Accountability_profile_2013.pdf

County of San Diego. (2013). *Project Care.* Retrieved from at http://www .sandiegocounty.gov/content/sdc/hhsa /programs/ais/project_care.html

Couzin, J. (2003, October). Is long life in the blood? *Science, 2–4(302),* 373–375.

Covington, S. N. (Ed.). (2015). *Fertility counseling: Clinical guide and case studies.* Cambridge, U.K.: Cambridge University Press.

Cowan, N. (2008). What are the differences in long-term, short-term and working memory? *Progress in Brain Research, 169,* 323–338.

Cowan, P. A., & Cowan, C.P. (2012). Normative family transitions, couple relationship quality, and healthy child development. In F. Walsh, (Ed) *Normal family processes: Growing diversity and complexity* (4th ed.) (pp. 428–451). New York, NY: Guilford Press.

Cowley, G. (1997, June 30). How to live to 100. *Newsweek,* 56–67.

Cox, M. J., Owen, M. T., Henderson, V. K., & Margand, N. A. (1992). Prediction of infant–father and infant–mother attachment. *Developmental Psychology, 28,* 474–483.

Cox, M. J., Owen, M. T., Lewis, J. M., & Henderson, V. K. (1989). Marriage, adult adjustment, and early parenting. *Child Development, 60,* 1015–1024.

Coyle, C. T. (2007). Men and abortion: A review of empirical reports concerning the impact of abortion on men. *Internet Journal of Mental Health, 32.*

Crain, W. (2011). *Theories of development: Concepts and applications* (6th ed.). Upper Saddle River, NJ: Prentice Hall.

Crawford, T. N., Cohen, P., Midlarsky, E., & Brook, J. (2001). Internalizing symptoms in adolescents: Gender differences in vulnerability to parental distress and discord. *Journal of Research on Adolescence, 11,* 95–118.

Creamer, A. (2011). More elderly unmarried couples are living together. *The Sacramento Bee.* Retrieved from at http://www.mcclatchydc.com/2011/09/01/v-print/122807/more-elderly-unmarried-couples.html

Creswell, J. W. (2013a). *Research design: Qualitative, quantitative and mixed methods approaches* (4th ed.). Thousand Oaks, CA: Sage.

Creswell, J. W. (2013b). *Qualitative inquiry & research design: Choosing among five approaches* (3rd ed.). Thousand Oaks, CA: Sage.

Crick, N. R., & Ladd, G. W. (1993). Children's perceptions of their peer experiences: Attributions, loneliness, social anxiety, and social avoidance. *Developmental Psychology, 29,* 244–254.

Crinion, J., Turner, R., Grogan, A., Hanakawa, T., Noppeney, U., Devlin, J. T., et al. (2006). Language control in the bilingual brain. *Science, 312,* 1537–1540.

Crocetti, E., Rubini, M., & Meeus, W. (2008). Capturing the dynamics of identity formation in various ethnic groups: Development and validation of a three-dimensional model. *Journal of Adolescence, 31,* 207–222.

Crockenberg, S. C., Leerkes, E. M., & Lekka, S. K. (2007). Pathways from marital aggression to infant emotion regulation: The development of withdrawal in infancy. *Infant Behavior and Development, 30,* 97–113.

Crohan, S. E. (1996). Marital quality and conflict across the transition to parenthood in African American and White couples. *Journal of Marriage and the Family, 58,* 933–944.

Crooks, R. L., & Baur, K. (2016). *Our sexuality* (13th ed.). Belmont CA: Cengage.

Crooks, T. J. (1988). The impact of classroom evaluation practices on students. *Review of Educational Research, 58,* 438–481.

Crosby, K. A., Fireman, G. D., & Klopton, J. R. (2011). Differences between non-aggressive rejected children and popular children during peer collaboration. *Child and Family Behavior Therapy, 33,* 1–19.

Crosby, R. A., DiClemente, R. J., Wingood, G. M., Rose, E., & Lang, D. (2003). Correlates of unplanned and unwanted pregnancy among African-American female teens. *American Journal of Preventive Medicine, 25,* 255–258.

Crosnoe, R. (2009). Low-income students and the socioeconomic composition of public high schools. *American Sociological Review, 74,* 709–730.

Crosnoe, R., & Elder, G. H., Jr. (2002a). Life course transitions, the generational stake, and grandparent–grandchild relationships. *Journal of Marriage and Family, 64,* 1089–1096.

Crosnoe, R., & Elder, G. H., Jr. (2002b). Successful adaptation in the later years: A life course approach to aging. *Social Psychology Quarterly, 65,* 309–328.

Crosnoe, R., & Elder, G. H., Jr. (2004). From childhood to the later years: Pathways of human development. *Research on Aging, 26,* 623–654.

Crosnoe, R., & Huston, A. (2007). Socio-economic status, schooling, and the developmental trajectories of adolescents. *Developmental Psychology, 43*, 1097–1110.

Crosnoe, R., Purtell, K. M., Davis-Kean, P., Ansari, A., & Benner, A. D. (2016). The selection of children from low-income families into preschool. *Developmental Psychology, 52*, 599–612.

Cross, W. E., Jr. (1991). *Shades of black: Diversity in African-American identity*. Philadelphia: Temple University Press.

Cross, W. E., Jr., & Fhagen-Smith, P. (2001). Patterns of African American identity development: A life span perspective. In B. Jackson & C. Wijeyesinghe (Eds.), *New perspectives on racial identity development: A theoretical and practical anthology* (pp. 199–219). New York, NY: New York University Press.

Crouter, A. C. (2006). Mothers and fathers at work: Implications for families and children. In A. Clarke-Stewart & J. Dunn (Eds.), *Families count: Effects on child and adolescent development*. The Jacobs Foundation series on adolescence (pp. 135–154). New York, NY: Cambridge University Press.

Crouter, A. C., & Bumpus, M. F. (2001). Linking parents' work stress to children's and adolescents' psychological adjustment. *Current Directions in Psychological Science, 10*, 156–159.

Crouter, A. C., & Manke, B. (1997). Development of a typology of dual-earner families: A window into differences between and within families in relationships, roles, and activities. *Journal of Family Psychology, 11*, 62–75.

Crowe, J. (2001). *Elementary school social worker*. Retrieved from www.wetfeet.com

Crowell, J. A., Fraley, R. C., & Shaver, P. R. (1999). Measurement of individual differences in adolescent and adult attachment. In J. Cassidy & P. R. Shaver (Eds.), *Handbook of attachment: Theory, research, and clinical applications* (pp. 434–465). New York, NY: Guilford Press.

C. S. Mott Children's Hospital-University of Michigan Health Systems. (2015). *Caring for your baby*. Retrieved from www.mottchildren.org/conditions-treatments/caring-your-baby

Cubansi, J., Casllas, G., & Damico, A. (2015). Poverty among seniors: An updated analysis of national and state level poverty rates under the official and supplemental poverty measures. Retrieved from http://kff.org/medicare/issue-brief/poverty-among-seniors-an-updated-analysis-of-national-and-state-level-poverty-rates-under-the-official-and-supplemental-poverty-measures/

Cuddy, A. J. C., Fiske, S. T., & Glick, P. (2004). When professionals become mothers, warmth doesn't cut the ice. *Journal of Social Issues, 60*, 701–718.

Cukan, A. (2001). FedEx sued for dreadlocks discrimination. *United Press International*.

Retrieved from http://www.hirediversity.com/news/newsbyid.asp?id_4736

Cumming, S. P., Sherar, L. B., Hunter Smart, J. E., Rodrigues, A. M. M., Standage, M., Gillison, F. P., & Malina, R. M. (2012). Physical activity, physical self-concept, and health-related quality of life of extreme early and late maturing adolescent girls. *The Journal of Early Adolescence, 32*, 269–292.

Cumsille, P., Darling, N., Flaherty, B., & Martinez, M. L. (2009). Heterogeneity and change in the patterning of adolescents' perceptions of the legitimacy of parental authority: A latent transition model. Child Development, 80, 418–432.

Cunningham, F. G., Leveno, K. J., Bloom, S. L., Spong, C. Y., Dashi, J. S., Hoffman, B. L., Casey, B. M., & Sheffield, J. S. (2014). *Williams obstetrics* (24th ed.). New York: McGraw Hill Education.

Currie, L. A. (1999). "Mr. Homunculus the Reading Detective": A cognitive approach to improving reading comprehension. *Educational and Child Psychology, 16*, 37–42.

Curtin, S. C., Warner, M., & Hedegaard, H. (2016). Increase in suicide in the United States: 1999–2014. *National Center for Health Statistics*. Retrieved from http://www.cdc.gov/nchs/products/databriefs/db241.htm

Cutler, A. (2012). *Native listening: Language experience and the recognition of spoken words*. Cambridge, MA: MIT Press.

Cutler, D. M. (2001). Declining disability among the elderly. *Health Affairs, 20*, 11–27.

Dake, C. L. (2002). *Infertility: A survival guide for couples and those who love them* (p. 49). Birmingham, AL: New Hope Publishers.

Dalai Lama & Ekman, P. (2008). *Emotional awareness: Overcoming the obstacles to psychological balance and compassion*. New York: Times Books.

Dalgleish, T., Moradi, A. R., Taghavi, M. R., Neshat-Doost, H. T., & Yule, W. (2001). An experimental investigation of hyper-vigilance for threat in children and adolescents with post-traumatic stress disorder. *Psychological Medicine, 31*, 541–547.

Dalirazar, N. (2007). *Reasons people do not work: 2004*. Current Population Reports, Washington, DC: U.S. Census Bureau.

Daly-Cano, M., Vaccaro, A., & Newman, B. (2015). College student narratives about learning and using self-advocacy skills. *Journal of Postsecondary Education and Disability, 28*, 213–227.

Damasio, A. (2005). Brain trust. *Nature, 435*, 571–572.

Damianova, M. K., Lucas, M., & Sullivan, G. B. (2012). Verbal mediation of problem solving in pre-primary and junior primary school children. *South African Journal of Psychology, 42*, 445–455.

Damon, W. (1996). The lifelong transformation of moral goals through social influence. In P. B. Baltes & V. M. Staudinger (Eds.), *Interactive minds: Life-span perspectives on the social foundation of cognition* (pp. 198–220). New York, NY: Cambridge University Press.

Damon, W. (2000). Setting the stage for the development of wisdom: Self-understanding and moral identity during adolescence. In W. S. Brown (Ed.), *Understanding wisdom: Sources, science, and society. Laws of science symposia series* (Vol. 3, pp. 339–360). West Conshohocken, PA: Templeton Foundation Press.

Damon, W. (2014). *How can we encourage a sense of purpose and meaning early in life?* Published in Big Questions online. Retrieved from https:.www.bigquestionsonline.com/content/how-can-we-encourage-sense-purpose-and-meaning-early-life

Damon, W. (2008). *The path to purpose: How young people find their calling in life*. New York: Free Press.

Damon, W., & Hart, D. (1988). *Self-understanding in childhood and adolescence*. New York, NY: Cambridge University Press.

Danielsbacka, M., & Tanskanen, A. O. (2012). Adolescent grandchildren's perceptions of grandparents' involvement in UK: An interpretation from life course and evolutionary theory perspectives. *European Journal of Ageing, 9*, 329–341.

Daniluk, J. C. (1999). When biology isn't destiny: Implications for the sexuality of women without children. *Canadian Journal of Counseling, 33*, 79–94.

D'Argembeau, A., Feyers, D., Majerus, S., Collette, F., Van der Linden, M., Maquet, P., et al. (2008). Self-reflection across time: Cortical midline structures differentiate between present and past selves. *Social Cognitive Affective Neuroscience, 3*, 244–252.

Darling-Fisher, C. S., & Leidy, N. K. (1988). Measuring Eriksonian development in the adult: The Modified Erikson Psychosocial Stage Inventory. *Psychological Reports, 62*, 747–754.

Darnis, F., & LaFont, L. (2015). Cooperative learning and dyadic interactions: Two modes of knowledge construction in socio-constructivist settings for team-sport teaching. *Physical Education and Sport Pedagogy, 20*, 459–473.

Darwin, C. (1859/1979). *The illustrated "Origin of species."* (Abridged and introduced by Richard E. Leakey). New York, NY: Hill & Wang.

Darwin, C. (1872/1965). *The expression of emotions in man and animals*. Chicago, IL: University of Chicago Press.

Dasen, P. R. (1984). The cross cultural study of intelligence: Piaget and the Baoulé. *The International Journal of Psychology, 19*, 407–434.

Datta, J., Graham, B., & Wellings, K. (2012). The role of fathers in breastfeeding decision-making and support. *British Journal of Midwifery, 20*, 159–167.

Daugherty, J., & Copen, C. (2016). Trends in attitudes about marriage, childbearing and sexual behavior: United States, 2002, 2006–2010, and 2011–2013. *National Health Statistics Reports, 92*.

Daverth, G., Hyde, P., & Cassell, C. (2016). Uptake of organizational work-life balance opportunities: The context of support. *The International Journal of Human Resource Management, 27,* 1710–1729.

Davey, A., & Eggebeen, D. J. (1998). Patterns of intergenerational exchange and mental health. *Journal of Gerontology, 53,* P86–P95.

Davidson, K. (2002). Gender differences in new partnership choices and constraints for older widows and widowers. *Ageing International, 27,* 43–60.

Davies, P. L., & Rose, J. D. (1999). Assessment of cognitive development in adolescents by means of neuropsychological tasks. *Developmental Neuropsychology, 15,* 227–248.

Davies, P. T., & Woitach, M. J. (2008). Children's emotional security in the interparental relationship. *Current Directions in Psychological Science, 17,* 269–274.

Davis, A. (1995). The experimental method in psychology. In G. Breakwell, S. Hammond, & C. Fyfe-Schaw (Eds.), *Research methods in psychology* (pp. 42–58). Thousand Oaks, CA: Sage.

Davis, A., & Kimball, W. (2015). *Job prospects have improved for graduates, but the class of 2015 still faces a challenging labor market.* Economic Policy Institute. Retrieved from http://www.epi.org/blog /job-prospects-have-improved-for-graduates-but-the-class-of-2015-still-faces-a-challenging-labor-market/

Davis, J. E. (2010). Painful numbers. *The Hedgehog Review, 12*(3), 42–45.

Davis, J. L., Petretic-Jackson, P. A., & Ting, L. (2001). Intimacy dysfunction and trauma symptomatology: Long-term correlates of different types of child abuse. *Journal of Traumatic Stress, 14,* 63–79.

Davis, K., Christodoulou, J., Seider, S., & Gardner, H. (2011). The theory of multiple intelligences. In R. J. Sternberg & S. B. Kaufman (Eds.), *The Cambridge Handbook of Intelligence. Cambridge Handbooks in Psychology* (pp. 485–503). New York: Cambridge University Press.

Davis, K. E. (1985, February). Near and dear: Friendship and love compared. *Psychology Today, 19,* 22–30.

Davis, P. E., Meins, E., & Fernyhough, C. (2011). Self-knowledge in childhood: Relations with children's imaginary companions and understanding of mind. *British Journal of Developmental Psychology, 29,* 680–686.

Davis, P. E., Meins, E., & Fernyhough, C. (2013). Individual differences in children's private speech: The role of imaginary companions. *Journal of Experimental Child Psychology, 116,* 561–571.

Davis-Floyd, R. E. (1990). The role of obstetrical rituals in the resolution of cultural anomaly. *Social Science and Medicine, 31,* 175–189.

Davis-Kean, P. E. (2005). The influence of parent education and family income on child achievement: The indirect role of parental

expectations and the home environment. *Journal of Family Psychology, 19,* 294–304.

Davis-Kean, P. E., & Sandler, H. M. (2001). A meta-analysis of measures of self-esteem for young children: A framework for future measures. *Child Development, 72,* 887–906.

Davis, S. W., Kragel, J. E., Madden, D. J., & Cabeza, R. (2012). The architecture of cross-hemispheric communication in the aging brain: Linking behavior to functional and structural connectivity. *Cerebral Cortex, 22,* 232–242.

Davydov, V. V. (1995). The influence of L. S.Vygotsky on education theory, research, and practice (S. T. Kerr, Trans.). *Educational Researcher, 24,* 12–21.

Daw, J. (2001). Road rage, air rage and now "desk rage." *Monitor on Psychology, 32,* 52–54.

Dawson, T. L. (2002). New tools, new insights: Kohlberg's moral judgement stages revisited. *International Journal of Behavioral Development, 26,* 154–166.

Dawson, T. L. (2003). A stage is a stage is a stage: A direct comparison of two scoring systems. *Journal of Genetic Psychology, 164,* 335–364.

Dawson-Tunik, T. L., Commons, M., Wilson, M., & Fischer, K. W. (2005). The shape of development. *European Journal of Developmental Psychology, 2,* 163–195.

Dayton, C. J., Walsh, T. B., Oh, W., & Volling, B. (2015). Hush now baby: Mothers' and fathers' strategies for soothing their infants and associated parenting outcomes. *Journal of Pediatric Health Care, 29,* 145–155.

de Guzman, N. S., & Nichina, A. (2014). A longitudinal study of body dissatisfaction and pubertal timing in an ethnically diverse adolescent sample. *Body Image, 11,* 68–71.

deAlmondes, K. M., Costa, M. V., Malloy-Diniz, L .F. & Diniz, B. S. (2016). Insomnia and risk of dementia in older adults: Systematic review and meta-analysis. *Journal of Psychiatric Research, 77,* 109–115.

DeAngelis, T. (2010). Social awareness and emotional skills equal successful kids. *Monitor on Psychology, 41,* 46–49.

Dearing, E., McCartney, K., & Taylor, B. A. (2009). Does higher quality early child care promote low-income children's math and reading achievement in middle childhood? *Child Development, 80,* 1329–1349.

Deater-Deckard, K., & O'Connor, T. G. (2000). Parent–child mutuality in early childhood: Two behavioral genetic studies. *Developmental Psychology, 36,* 561–570.

Deater-Deckard, K., Pickering, K., Dunn, J. F., & Golding, J. (1998). Family structure and depressive symptoms in men preceding and following the birth of a child. *American Journal of Psychiatry, 155,* 818–823.

Deater-Deckard, K., Wang, Z., Chen, N., & Bell, M. A. (2012). Maternal executive function, harsh parenting, and child conduct problems. *Journal of Child Psychology and Psychiatry, 53,* 1084–1091.

Death with Dignity. (2016). *How to access and use Death with Dignity laws.* Retrieved from https://www.deathwithdignity.org /learn/access

DeCasper, A., Granier-Deferre, C., Fifer, W. P., & Moon, C. M. (2011). Measuring fetal cognitive development. When methods and conclusions don't match. *Developmental Science, 14,* 224–225.

DeCasper, A. J., & Fifer, W. (1980). Of human bonding: Newborns prefer their mothers' voices. *Science, 208,* 1174–1176.

DeCasper, A. J., Lecanuet, J. P., Busnel, M. C., Granier-Deferre, C., & Maugeais, R. (1994). Fetal reactions to recurrent maternal speech. *Infant Behavior and Development, 17,* 159–164.

DeCasper, A. J., & Spence, M. J. (1986). Prenatal maternal speech influences newborns' perception of speech sounds. *Infant Behavior and Development, 9,* 133–150.

Decety, J., & Chaminade, T. (2003). When the self represents the other: A new cognitive neuroscience view on psychological identification. *Consciousness and Cognition, 12,* 577–596.

Deci, E. L., & Ryan, R. M. (2000) The "what" and "why" of goal pursuits: Human needs and the self-determination of behavior. *Psychological Inquiry, 11,* 227–268.

Declerq, E. R., Sakala, C., Corry, M. P., & Applebaum, S. (2006). Executive summary. In *Listening to Mothers II: Report of the second national U.S. survey of women's childbearing experiences* (pp. 1–9). New York, NY: Childbirth Connection.

De Dreu, C. K. W., Greer, L. L., Handgraaf, M. J. J., et al. (2010). The neuropeptide oxytocin regulates parochial altruism in intergroup conflict among humans. *Science, 328,* 1408–1411.

Deenen, A. A., Gijs, L., & van Naerssen, A. X. (1994). Intimacy and sexuality in gay male couples. *Archives of Sexual Behavior, 23,* 421–431.

DeGrazia, D. (1998). Biology, consciousness, and the definition of death. *Report from the Institute for Philosophy and Public Policy, 18,* 18–22.

DeHaan, M., & Carver, L. J. (2013). Development of brain networks for visual social-emotional information processing in infancy. In M. Legerstee, D. W. Haley, & M. H. Bornstein (Eds.), *The infant mind: Origins of the social brain* (pp. 123–145). New York, NY: Guilford.

Dekeyser, M., Verfaillie, K., & Vanrie, J. (2002). Creating stimuli for the study of biological motion perception. *Behavior Research Methods, Instruments, & Computers, 34,* 375–382.

DeLay, D., Laursen, B., Kiuru, N., Poikkeus, A., Aunola, K., & Nurmi, J. (2015). Stable same-sex friendships with higher achieving partners promote mathematical reasoning in lower-achieving primary school children. *British Journal of Developmental Psychology, 33,* 519–532.

Del Giudice, M., Hinnant, J. B., Ellis, B. J., & El-Sheikh, M. (2012). Adaptive patterns of stress responsivity: A preliminary investigation. *Developmental Psychology, 48,* 775–790.

Delsing, M. J.M. H., ter Bogt, T. F. M., Engles, R. C. M. E., & Meeus, W. H. J. (2007). Adolescents' peer crowd identification in the Netherlands: Structure and associations with problem behaviors. *Journal of Research on Adolescence, 17,* 467–480.

De Magalhaes, J. P. (2003). Winning the war against aging. *Futurist, 37,* 48–51.

DeMaris, A., & Rao, K. V. (1992). Premarital cohabitation and subsequent marital stability in the United States: A reassessment. *Journal of Marriage and the Family, 54,* 178–190.

Deming, D. (2009). Early childhood intervention and life-cycle skill development: Evidence from Head Start. *American Economic Journal: Applied Economics, 1*(3), 111–134.

Demmer, C. (2007). Grief is a luxury: AIDS-related loss among the poor in South Africa. *Illness, Crisis & Loss, 15,* 39–51.

Demo, D. H., Fine, M. A., & Ganong, L. H. (2000). Divorce as a family stressor. In P. C. McKenry & S. J. Price (Eds.), *Families and change: Coping with stressful events and transitions* (pp. 279–302). Thousand Oaks, CA: Sage.

DeNavas-Walt, C., & Proctor, B. D. (2015). *U.S. Census Bureau, current population reports, P60-252, income and poverty in the United States: 2014.* Washington, DC: U.S. Government Printing Office.

DenHartog, D. N., DeHoogh, A. H. B., & Keegan, A. E. (2007). The interactive effects of belongingness and charisma on helping and compliance. *Journal of Applied Psychology, 92,* 1131–1139.

Denissen, J. J. A., Zarrett, N. R., & Eccles, J. S. (2007). I like to do it, I'm able, and I know I am: Longitudinal couplings between domain-specific achievement, self-concept, and interest. *Child Development, 78,* 430–447.

Denmark, F. L., Griffin, A., & Blumenthal, S. J. (Eds.). (1996). Women and mental health. *Annals of the New York Academy of Sciences, 789,* 101–117.

Denner, J., & Dunbar, N. (2004). Negotiating femininity: Power and strategies of Mexican American girls. *Sex Roles, 50,* 301–314.

Denton, W. H., Burleson, B. R., & Sprenkle, D. H. (1994). Motivation in marital communication: Comparison of distressed and non-distressed husbands and wives. *American Journal of Family Therapy, 22,* 17–26.

Denzin, N. K., & Lincoln, Y. S. (1998). *Strategies of qualitative inquiry.* Thousand Oaks, CA: Sage.

Depp, C. A., & Jeste, D. V. (2006). Definitions and predictors of successful aging: A comprehensive review of larger quantitative studies. *American Journal of Geriatric Psychiatry, 14,* 6–20.

de Rosnay, M., Cooper, P. J., Tsigara, N., & Murray, L. (2006). Transmission of social anxiety from mother to infant: An experimental study using a social referencing paradigm. *Behaviour Research and Therapy, 44,* 1165–1175.

DeSoto, K. A. (2016). Under the hood of the MechanicalTurk. *Observer, 29,* 17–19.

de St. Aubin, E., McAdams, D. P., & Kim, T.-C. (2003). *The generative society: Caring for future generations.* Washington, DC: American Psychological Association.

de St. Aubin, E., McAdams, D. P., & Kim, T. (2004). *The generative society: Caring for future generations.* Washington, DC: American Psychological Association.

DeVries, M. W., & DeVries, M. R. (1977). Cultural relativity of toilet training readiness: A perspective from East Africa. *Pediatrics, 60,* 170–177.

DeVries, R., Hildebrandt, C., & Zan, B. (2000). Constructivist early education for moral development. *Early Education and Development, 11,* 9–35.

Dewan, T., & Myatt, D. P. (2008). The qualities of leadership: Direction, communication and obfuscation. *American Political Science Review, 102,* 351–368.

Dewey, J. (1896). The reflex arc concept in psychology. *Psychological Review, 3,* 357–370.

De Wolff, M. S., & van IJzendoorn, M. H. (1997). Sensitivity and attachment: A meta-analysis on parental antecedents of infant attachment. *Child Development, 68,* 571–591.

Diamond, A. (2002). Normal development of the prefrontal cortex from birth to young adulthood: Cognitive functions, anatomy, and biochemistry. In D. T. Stuss & R. T. Knight (Eds.), *Principles of frontal lobe function* (pp. 466–503). London: Oxford University Press.

Diamond, A. (2007). Interrelated and interdependent. *Developmental Science, 10,* 152–158.

Diamond, L. M. (2000). Passionate friendships among adolescent sexual-minority women. *Journal of Research on Adolescence, 10,* 191–209.

Diamond, L. M., & Savin-Williams, R. C. (2009). Adolescent sexuality. In R. M. Lerner & L. Steinberg (Eds.), *Handbook of adolescent psychology. Vol. 1. Individual bases of adolescent development* (3rd ed., pp. 479–523). Hoboken, NJ: John Wiley.

Diaz, R. M. (1983). Thought and two languages: The impact of bilingualism on cognitive development. *Review of Research in Education, 10,* 23–54.

Dickstein, S., & Parke, R. D. (1988). Social referencing in infancy: A glance at fathers and marriage. *Child Development, 59,* 506–511.

DiDonato, M. D., Martin, C. L., Hessler, E. E., Amazeen, P. G., Hanish, L. D., & Fabes, R. A. (2012). Gender consistency and flexibility: Using dynamics to understand the relation between gender and adjustment. *Nonlinear Dynamics, Psychology, and Life Sciences, 16,* 159–184.

Diehl, M., Hastings, C. T., & Stanton, J. M. (2001). Self-concept differentiation across the adult life span. *Psychology and Aging, 16,* 643–654.

Diekman, A. B., Brown, E. R., Johnston, A. M., & Clark, E. K. (2010). Seeking congruity between goals and roles: A new look at why women opt out of science, technology, and engineering and mathematics careers. *Psychological Science, 21,* 1051–1057.

Diemer, M. A., & Blustein, D. L. (2006). Critical consciousness and career development among urban youth. *Journal of Vocational Behavior, 68,* 220–232.

Diener, C. I., & Dweck, C. S. (1980). An analysis of learned helplessness: 2. The processing of success. *Journal of Personality and Social Psychology, 39,* 940–952.

Diener, E. F. (2012). New findings and future directions for subjective well-being research. *American Psychologist, 67,* 590–597.

Dietrich, J., Parker, P., & Salmela-Aro, K. (2012). Phase-adequate engagement at the post-school transition. *Developmental Psychology, 48,* 1575–1593.

Dijkstra, J. K., Lindenberg, S., & Veenstra, R. (2007). Same-gender and cross-gender peer acceptance and peer rejection and their relation with bullying and helping among preadolescents: A goal-framing approach. *Developmental Psychology, 43,* 1377–1389.

Dill, K. E. (2009). *How fantasy becomes reality: Seeing through media influence.* New York, NY: Oxford University Press.

DiMatteo, M. R., Morton, S. C., Lepper, H. S., Damush, T. M., et al. (1996). Cesarean childbirth and psychosocial out-comes: A meta-analysis. *Health Psychology, 15,* 303–314.

Dimidjian, S., Goodman, S. H., Felder, J. N., Gallop, R., Brown, A. P., & Beck, A. (2016). Staying well during pregnancy and the postpartum: A pilot randomized-trial of mindfulness-based cognitive therapy for the prevention of depressive relapse/recurrence. *Journal of Consulting and Clinical Psychology, 84,* 134–145.

Dindia, K., & Allen, M. (1992). Sex differences in self-disclosure: A meta-analysis. *Psychological Bulletin, 112,* 106–124.

Dionne-Dostie, E., Paquette, N., Lassonde, M., & Gallagher, A. (2015). Multisensory integration and child neurodevelopment. *Brain Sciences, 5,* 32–57.

DiPietro, J. A. (2004). The role of prenatal maternal stress in child development. *Current Directions in Psychological Science, 13,* 71–74.

DiPietro, J. A. (2012). Maternal stress in pregnancy: Considerations for fetal development. *Journal of Adolescent Health, 51*(2), Supplement, S3–S8.

DiPietro, J. A., Caulfield, L. E., Costigan K. A., Merialdi, M., Nguyen, R. H. N., Zavaleta, N., et al. (2004). Fetal neurobehavioral development: A tale of two cities. *Developmental Psychology, 40,* 445–456.

DiPietro, J. A., Caulfield, L. E., Irizary, R. A., Chen, P., Merialdi, M., & Zavaleta, N. (2006). Prenatal development of intrafetal and maternal-fetal synchrony. *Behavioral Neuroscience, 120,* 687–701.

DiPietro, J. A., Kivlighan, K. T., Costigan, K. A., Rubin, S. E., Shiffle, D. E., Henderson, J. L., et al. (2010). Prenatal antecedents of newborn neurological maturation. *Child Development, 81,* 115–130.

DiPietro, L. (2001). Physical activity in aging: Changes in patterns and their relationship to health and function. *Journals of Gerontology: Series A: Biological Sciences and Medical Sciences, 56A,* 13–22.

Diprete, T. A., & Buchmann, C. (2013). *The rise of women: The growing gender gap and what it means for American schools.* New York, NY: Russell Sage Foundation.

Dirix, C. E. H., Nijhuis, J. G., Jongsma, H. W., & Hornstra, G. (2009). Aspects of fetal learning and memory. *Child Development, 80,* 1251–1258.

Dishion, T. J., Poulin, F., & Medici-Skaggs, N. (2000). The ecology of premature autonomy in adolescence: Biological and social influences. In K. A. Kens, A. M. Neal-Barnett, & J. M. Contreras (Eds.), *Family and peers: Linking two social worlds* (pp. 27–46). Westport, CT: Praeger.

Dishion, T. J., & Tipsord, J. M. (2011). Peer contagion in child and adolescent social and emotional development. *Annual Review of Psychology, 62,* 189–214.

Dobek, J. C., White, K.N., & Gunter, K.B. (2007). The effect of a Nevel ADL-based training program on performance of activities of daily living and physical fitness. *Journal of Aging and Physical Activity, 15,* 13–25.

Dodge, K. A. (1989). Coordinating responses to aversive stimuli: Introduction to a special section on the development of emotion regulation. *Developmental Psychology, 25,* 339–342.

Dodge, K. A., Pettit, G. S., McClaskey, C. L., & Brown, M. M. (1986). Social competence in children. *Monographs of the Society for Research in Child Development, 51* (2, Serial No. 213).

Dohnt, H., & Tiggemann, M. (2006). The contribution of peer and media influences to the development of body satisfaction and self-esteem in young girls: A prospective study. *Developmental Psychology, 42,* 929–936.

Doi, H., & Shinohara, K. (2012). Event-related potentials elicited in mothers by their own and unfamiliar infants' faces with crying and smiling expression. *Neuropsychologia, 50,* 1297–1307.

Dolbin-MacNab, M. L., & Keiley, M. K. (2006). A systemic examination of grandparents' emotional closeness with their custodial grandchildren. *Research in Human Development, 3,* 59–71.

Dole, N., Savitz, D. A., Siega-Riz, A. M., Hertz-Picciotto, I., McMahon, M. J., & Buekens, P. (2004). Psychosocial factors and preterm birth among African American and White women in central North Carolina. *American Journal of Public Health, 94,* 1358–1365.

Dombeck, M. (2016). *Emotional coping and divorce.* Retrieved from https://www.mentalhelp.net/articles/emotional-coping-and-divorce/

Dominguez, T. P., Dunkel-Schetter, C., Glynn, L. M., et al. (2008). Racial differences in birth outcomes: The role of general, pregnancy, and racism stress. *Health Psychology, 27,* 194–203.

Domino, G., & Affonso, D. D. (1990). Erikson's life stages: The inventory of psychosocial balance. *Journal of Personality Assessment, 54,* 576–588.

Donald, M. (2001). A mind so rare: The evolution of human consciousness. New York, NY: Norton.

Donovan, M. L. & Corcoran, M. A. (2010). Description of dementia caregiver uplifts and implications for occupational therapists. *American Journal of Occupational Therapy, 64,* 590–595.

Dorn, L. D., Dahl, R. E., Woodward, H. R., & Biro, F. (2006). Defining the boundaries of early adolescence: A user's guide to assessing pubertal status and pubertal timing in research with adolescents. *Applied Developmental Science, 10,* 30–56.

Doucet, A. (2009). Dad and baby in the first year: Gendered responsibilities and embodiment. *Annals of the Academy of Political and Social Science, 624,* 78–98.

Doukas, D. J., & Reichel, W. (2007). *Planning for uncertainty: Living wills and other advance directives for you and your family* (2nd ed.) Baltimore, MD: Johns Hopkins University Press.

Doula of North America (DONA). (2016). *Birth doula FAQs.* Retrieved from www.dona.org/mothers/faqs_birth.php

Downey, G., & Walker, E. (1989). Social cognition and adjustment in children at risk for psychopathology. *Developmental Psychology, 25,* 835–845.

Downs, L. S. (2004). Facing dying: A hospice worker tells how. *Yoga Chicago.* Retrieved from http://www.yogachicago.com/may04/dying.shtml

Dowrick, P. W. (1991). *Practical guide to using video in the behavioral sciences.* New York, NY: Wiley.

Draganski, B.,Winkler, J., Flügel, D., May, A. (2004). Selective activation of ectopic grey matter during motor task. *Neuroreport: For Rapid Communication of Neuroscience Research, 15*(2), 251–253.

Drake, N. (2015). Human evolution 101. *National Geographic.* Retrieved from http://news.nationalgeographic.com/2015/09//human-evolution-101.html

Dreman, S. (1997). *The family on the threshold of the 21st century: Trends and implications.* Mahwah, NJ: Erlbaum.

Drew, A. (2016). Across your universe: Intensive longitudinal data and dynamical systems. *Observer, 29,* 27–29.

Driver, J., Tabares, A., Shapiro, A. & Gottman, J. (2012). Couple interaction in happy and unhappy marriages: Gottman laboratory studies. In F. Walsh (Ed.), *Normal family*

processes: Growing diversity and complexity (4th ed., pp. 57–77). New York, NY: Guilford.

Drury, K., Bukowski, W. M., Velásquez, A. M., & Stella-Lopez, L. (2013). Victimization and gender identity in single-sex and mixed-sex schools: Examining contextual variations in pressure to conform to gender norms. *Sex Roles, 69,* 442–454.

Dubler, N. N., & Sabatino, C. P. (1991). Age-based rationing and the law: An exploration. In R. H. Binstock & S. G. Post (Eds.), *Too old for health care? Controversies in medicine, law, economics, and ethics* (pp. 92–119). Baltimore, MD: Johns Hopkins University.

Duckworth, A. L., Peterson, C., Matthews, M. D., & Kelly, D. R. (2007). Grit: Perseverance and passion for long-term goals. *Journal of Personality and Social Psychology, 92,* 1087–1101.

Duckworth, A. L., & Seligman, M. E. P. (2005). Self-discipline outdoes IQ in predicting academic performance of adolescents. *Psychological Science, 16,* 939–944.

Dudgeon, M. R., & Inhorn, M. C. (2004). Men's influence on women's reproductive health: Medical anthropological perspectives. *Social Science and Medicine, 59,* 1379–1395.

Duggan, M. (2015). The demographics of social media users. *Pew Research Center.* Retrieved from http://www.pewinternet.org/2015/08/19/the-demographics-of-social-media-users/

Dunbar, E. (1997). The personal dimensions of difference scale: Measuring multigroup identity with four ethnic groups. *International Journal of Intercultural Relations, 21,* 1–28.

Dunbar, K. (2000). How scientists think in the real world: Implications for science education. *Journal of Applied Developmental Psychology, 21,* 49–58.

Duncan, G. J., Huston, A. C., & Weisner, T. S. (2007). *Higher ground: New Hope for the working poor and their children.* New York, NY: Russell Sage Foundation.

Duncan, G. J., Ziol-Guest, K. M., & Kalil, A. (2010). Early-childhood poverty and adult attainment, behavior, and health. *Child Development, 81,* 306–325.

Dundes, L. (2003). *The manner born: Birth rites in cross-cultural perspective.* Lanham, MD: Alta Mira Press.

Dunham, Y., Baron, A. S., & Banaji, M. R. (2008). The development of implicit group cognition. *Trends in Cognitive Sciences, 12,* 248–253.

Dunham, Y., Baron, A. S., & Carey, S. (2011). Consequences of "minimal" group affiliations in children. *Child Development, 82,* 793–811.

Dunifon, R. (2013). The influence of grandparents on the lives of children and adolescents. *Child Development Perspectives, 7,* 55–60.

Dunkel Schetter, C. (2009). Stress processes in pregnancy and preterm birth. *Current*

Directions in Psychological Science, 18(4), 205–209.

Dunkel-Schetter, C., Sagrestano, L. F., Feldman, P., & Killingsworth, C. (1996). Social support and pregnancy: A comprehensive review focusing on ethnicity and culture. In G. R. Pierce & B. R. Sarason (Eds.), *Handbook of social support and the family* (pp. 375–412). New York, NY: Plenum.

Dunkley, T. L., Wertheim, E. H., & Paxton, S. J. (2001). Examination of a model of multiple sociocultural influences on adolescent girls' body dissatisfaction and dietary restraint. *Adolescence, 36,* 265–279.

Dunlop, D. W. (2015). Remains of 9/11 victim at World Trade Center are identified. *New York Times.* Retrieved from http://www .nytimes.com/2015/03/20/nyregion/victim -of-9-11-trade-center-attack-is-positively -identified.html?_r=0

Dunn, J. (2004). *Children's friendships: The beginnings of intimacy.* Malden, MA: Wiley-Blackwell.

Dunn, J. (2006). Moral development in early childhood and social interaction in the family. In M. Killen & J. G. Smetana (Eds.), *Handbook of moral development* (pp. 331–350). New York, NY: Psychology Press.

Dunn, J., Brown, J., & Beardsall, L. (1991). Family talk about feeling states and children's later understanding of others' emotions. *Developmental Psychology, 27,* 448–455.

Dunn, J., & Hughes, C. (2001). "I got some swords and you're dead!": Violent fantasy, antisocial behavior, friendship, and moral sensibility in young children. *Child Development, 72,* 491–505.

Dunn, M., & Cutler, N. (2000). Sexual issues in older adults. *AIDS Patient Care and STDs, 14,* 67–69.

Dunphy, D. C. (1963). The social structure of urban adolescent peer groups. *Sociometry, 26,* 230–246.

Duran-Aydintug, C. (1995). Former spouses exiting role-identities. *Journal of Divorce and Remarriage, 24,* 23–40.

Durbin, D. L., Darling, N., Steinberg, L., & Brown, B. B. (1993). Parenting style and peer group membership among European-American adolescents. *Journal of Research on Adolescence, 3,* 87–100.

Durik, A. M., Hyde, J. S., & Clark, R. (2000). Sequelae of cesarean and vaginal deliveries: Psychosocial outcomes for mothers and infants. *Developmental Psychology, 36,* 251–260.

Dush, C. M. K., Cohan, C L., & Amato, P. R. (2003). The relationship between cohabitation and marital quality and stability: Change across cohorts? *Journal of Marriage and Family, 65,* 539–549.

Duster, T. (2010, May 28). Welcome, freshmen. DNA swabs please. *The Chronicle of Higher Education.*

Dutton, Y. C., & Zisook, S. (2005). Adaptation to bereavement. *Death Studies, 29,* 877–903.

Dwyer, R. E. (2013). The care economy? Gender, economic restructuring, and job polarization in the U.S. labor market. *American Sociological Review, 78,* 390–416.

Dynarski, S. M. (2015). For poor, the graduation gap is even wider than the enrollment gap. *The New York Times.* Retrieved from www.nytimes.com/2015/06/02 /upshot/for-the-poor-the-graduation-gap -is-even-wider-than-the-enrollment-gap .html?_r=0

Eagan, K., Stolzenberg, E. B., Bates, A. K., Aragon, M. C., Suchard, M. R., & Rios-Aguilar, C. (2015). *The American freshman: National Norms Fall 2015.* Los Angeles: Higher Education Research Institute, UCLA.

Eagly, A. H. (2009). The his and hers of prosocial behavior: An examination of the social psychology of gender. *American Psychologist, 64,* 644–658.

Early, D. M., Pianta, R. C., Taylor, L. C., & Cox, M. J. (2001). Transition practices: Findings from a national survey of kindergarten teachers. *Early Childhood Education Journal, 28,* 199–206.

East, P. L., & Rook, K. S. (1992). Compensatory patterns of support among children's peer relationships: A test using school friends, nonschool friends, and siblings. *Developmental Psychology, 28,* 163–172.

Eating Disorder Hope. (2016). *Eating disorder statistics and research.* Retrieved from www.eatingdisorderhope.com/information /statistics-studies

Eatough, E. M., Chang, C.-H., Miloslavic, S. A., & Johnson, R. E. (2011). Relationships of role stressors and organizational citizenship behavior: A meta-analysis. *Journal of Applied Psychology, 96,* 619–632.

Ebersbach, M. (2009). Achieving a new dimension: Children integrate three stimulus dimensions in volume estimations. *Developmental Psychology, 45,* 877–883.

Eccles, J. S. (1993). School and family effects on the ontogeny of children's interests, self-perceptions, and activity choices. In J. E. Jacobs (Ed.), *Developmental perspectives on motivation: Nebraska Symposium on Motivation, 1992* (pp. 145–208). Lincoln, NE: University of Nebraska Press.

Eckerman, C. O., & Didow, S. M. (1996). Nonverbal imitation and toddlers' mastery of verbal means of achieving coordinated action. *Developmental Psychology, 32,* 141–152.

Eckstein, S., & Shemesh, M. (1992). The rate of acquisition of formal operational schemata in adolescence: A secondary analysis. *Journal of Research in Science Teaching, 29,* 441–451.

Edelstein, R. S., Alexander, K. W., Shaver, P. R., Schaaf, J. M., Quas, J. A., Lovas, G. S., et al. (2004). Adult attachment style and parental responsiveness during a stressful event. *Attachment and Human Development, 6,* 31–52.

Eden Alternative. (2016). *Mission, vision, values, principles.* Retrieved from http://www .edenalt.org/about-the-eden-alternative /mission-vision-values/

Edin, K. (2000). What do low-income single mothers say about marriage? *Social Problems, 47,* 112–133.

Edin, K., & Kefalas, M. (2011). *Promises I can keep: Why poor women put motherhood before marriage* (Rev. 3rd ed.). Berkeley, CA: University of California Press.

Edin, K., Kefalas, M. J., & Reed, J. M. (2004). A peek inside the black box: What marriage means for poor unmarried parents. *Journal of Marriage and the Family, 66,* 1007–1014.

Education Encyclopedia. (2016). *Intelligence—Triarchic theory of intelligence.* Retrieved from http://education.stateuniversity.com /pages/2104/Intelligence-TRIARCHIC -THEORY-INTELLIGENCE.html

Education Innovator. (2009). Getting it right, right from the start: Birth to five kindergarten readiness. *Education Innovator, 7*(5), 1. Retrieved from http://www2.ed.gov/news /newsletters/innovator/2009/0529.html

Education Week. (2001). Harris interactive poll of students and technology. *Technology Counts, 2001,* 7–8.

Edwards, C. P., & Liu, W. -L. (2012). Parenting toddlers. In M. H. Bornstein (Ed.), *Handbook of parenting, Vol. 1. Children and parenting* (2nd ed., pp. 45–72). New York, NY: Psychology Press.

Egan, S. K., & Perry, D. G. (2001). Gender identity: A multidimensional analysis with implications for psychosocial adjustment. *Developmental Psychology, 37,* 451–463.

Egeland, B., Jacobvitz, D., & Sroufe, L. A. (1988). Breaking the cycle of abuse. *Child Development, 59,* 1080–1088.

Egeland, B., & Sroufe, L. A. (1981). Attachment and early maltreatment. *Child Development, 52,* 44–52.

Egley, A. Jr., Howell, J. C., & Harris, M. (2014). *Highlights of the 2012 National Youth Gang Survey.* Washington, DC: U.S. Department of Justice, Office of Justice Programs, Office of Juvenile Justice and Delinquency Prevention. Retrieved from http://www .ojjdp.gov/pubs/248025.pdf

Egley, A., Howell, J. C., & Moore, J. P. (2010). *Highlights of the 2008 National Youth Gang Survey.* Washington, DC: Office of Juvenile Justice and Delinquency Prevention.

Egley, A., Jr., & Major, A. K. (2004). Highlights of the 2002 National Youth Gang Survey. *Office of Juvenile Justice and Delinquency Prevention Fact Sheet.* Retrieved from http://www .ncjrs.org/pdffiles1/ojjdp /fs200401.pdf

Ehlman, K., & Ligon, M. (2012). Application of a generativity model for older adults. *The International Journal of Aging and Human Development, 74,* 331–344.

Eibl-Eibesfeldt, I. (2007). *Human ethology.* Piscataway, NJ: Aldine Transaction.

Eiden, R. D., Veira, Y., & Granger, D. A. (2009). Prenatal cocaine exposure and infant cortisol reactivity. *Child Development, 80,* 528–543.

Einav, M., Levi, U., & Margalit, M. (2012). Mothers' coping and hope in early intervention. *European Journal of Special Needs Education, 27,* 265–279.

Ein-Dor, T., Mikulincer, M., Doron, G., & Shaver, P. R. (2010). The attachment paradox: How can so many of us (the insecure ones) have no adaptive advantages? *Perspectives on Psychological Science, 5,* 123–141.

Eisenberg, N., Fabes, R. A., Guthrie, I. K., & Reiser, M. (2002). The role of emotionality and regulation in children's social competence and adjustment. In L. Pulkkinen & A. Caspi (Eds.), *Paths to successful development: Personality in the life course* (pp. 46–70). New York, NY: Cambridge University Press.

Eisenberg, N., Fabes, R. A., & Spinrad, T. L. (2006). Prosocial development. In W. Damon, R. L. Lerner, & N. Eisenberg (Eds.), *The handbook of child psychology: Vol. 3. Social, emotional and personality development* (6th ed., pp. 646–718). New York, NY: John Wiley & Sons.

Eisenberg, N., Guthrie, I. K., Murphy, B. C., Shepard, S. A., Cumberland, A., & Carlo, G. (1999). Consistency and development of prosocial dispositions: A longitudinal study. *Child Development, 70,* 1360–1372.

Eisenberg, N., Morris, A. S., McDaniel, B., & Spinrad, T. L. (2009). Moral cognitions and prosocial responding in adolescence. In R. M. Lerner & L. Steinberg (Eds.), *Handbook of adolescent psychology: Vol. Individual bases of adolescent development* (3rd ed., pp. 229–265). New York, NY: Wiley.

Eisenberg, N., & Strayer, J. (1987). Critical issues in the study of empathy. In N. Eisenberg & J. Strayer (Eds.), *Empathy and its development* (pp. 3–13). Cambridge, UK: Cambridge University Press.

Eivers, A. R., Brendgen, M., Vitaro, F., & Borge, A. I. H. (2012). Concurrent and longitudinal links between children's and their friends' antisocial and prosocial behavior in preschool. *Early Childhood Research Quarterly, 27,* 137–146.

Ekas, N. V., Lickenbrock, D. M., Braungart-Rieker, J. M. (2013). Developmental trajectories of emotion regulation across infancy: Do age and the social partner influence temporal patterns? *Infancy, 18,* 729–754.

Ela, E. J. (2011). *Adoption motivations among U.S. parents. (FP-11-06).* National Center for Family and Marriage Research. Retrieved from http://ncfmr.bgsu.edu/pdf/family_profiles/file99486.pdf

Elder, A. D. (2010). Children's self-assessment of their school work in elementary school. *Education 3-13, 38,* 5–11.

Elder, G. H. (1985). *Life course dynamics: Trajectories and transitions, 1968-1980.* Ithaca, NY: Cornell University Press.

Elder, G. H. (1986). Military times and turning points in men's lives. *Developmental Psychology, 22,* 233–245.

Elder, G. H., Jr., Caspi, A., & van Nguyen, T. (1986). Resourceful and vulnerable children: Family influences in had times. In R. K. Silbereisen, K. Eyferth, & G. Rudinger (Eds.), *Development as*

action in context* (pp. 167–186). Berlin: Springer-Verlag.

Elder, G. H., Jr., George, L. K., & Shanahan, M. J. (1996). Psychosocial stress over the life course. In H. B. Kaplan (Ed.), *Psychosocial stress: Perspectives on structure, theory, life course, and methods* (pp. 247–291). Orlando, FL: Academic Press.

Elder, G. H., Jr., & Giele, J. Z. (2009). *The craft of life course research.* New York, NY: Guilford Press.

Elder, G. H., Jr., & Shanahan, M. J. (2006). The life course and human development. In R. M. Lerner, & W. Damon (Eds.), *Handbook of child psychology: Vol. 1. Theoretical models of human development* (6th ed., pp. 665–715). Hoboken, NJ: John Wiley & Sons.

Elder, G. H., Jr., Shanahan, M. J., & Clipp, E. C. (1997). Linking combat and physical health: The legacy of World War II in men's lives. *American Journal of Psychiatry, 154,* 330–336.

Eldridge, K. A., & Christensen, A. (2002). Demand-withdraw communication during couple conflict: A review and analysis. In P. Noller & J. A. Feeney (Eds.), *Understanding marriage: Developments in the study of couple interaction* (pp. 289–322). Cambridge, England: Cambridge University Press.

Eldridge, K. A., Sevier, M., Jones, J., Atkins, D. C., & Christensen, A. (2007). Demand-withdraw communication in severely distressed, moderately distressed, and non-distressed couples: Rigidity and polarity during relationship and personal problem discussions. *Journal of Family Psychology, 21,* 218–226.

Eldridge, N. S., & Gilbert, L. S. (1990). Correlates of relationship satisfaction in lesbian couples. *Psychology of Women Quarterly, 14,* 43–62.

Elias, M. J., Beier, J. J., & Gara, M. A. (1989). Children's responses to interpersonal obstacles as a predictor of social competence. *Journal of Youth and Adolescence, 18,* 451–465.

Elkind, D. (2007). *The power of play: Learning what comes naturally.* Philadelphia, PA: Da Capo Press.

Ellickson, P., Saner, H., & McGuigan, K. A. (1997). Profiles of violent youth: Substance use and other concurrent problems. *American Journal of Public Health, 87,* 985–991.

Ellickson, P. L., & McGuigan, K. A. (2000). Early predictors of adolescent violence. *American Journal of Public Health, 90,* 566–572.

Elliott, D. B., & Simmons, T. (2011). Marital events of Americans: 2009. *American Community Survey Reports.* Retrieved from https://www.census.gov/prod/2011pubs/acs-13.pdf

Elliott, G. C. (2009). *Family matters: The importance of mattering to family and adolescence.* Hoboken, NJ: Wiley-Blackwell.

Elliott, G. C., Colangelo, M. F., & Gelles, R. J. (2005). Mattering and suicide ideation: Establishing and elaborating a relationship. *Social Psychology Quarterly, 68,* 223–238.

Elliott, G. C., Kao, S., & Grant, A. (2004). Mattering: Empirical validation of a social psychological concept. *Self and Identity, 3,* 339–354.

Ellis, R. R., & Simmons, T. (2014). Co-resident grandparents and their grandchildren: 2012. *Current population reports, P20-576.* Washington, DC: U.S. Census Bureau.

Elwert, F., & Christakis, N. A. (2006). Widowhood and race. *American Sociological Review, 71,* 16–41.

Elwert, F., & Christakis, N. A. (2008). The effect of widowhood on mortality by the causes of death of both spouses. *American Journal of Public Health, 98,* 2092–2098.

Emanuel, E. J., & Emanuel, L. (1998). The promise of a good death. *The Lancet, 251,* 21–29.

Emde, R. N., & Buchsbaum, H. K. (1990). "Didn't you hear my mommy?" Autonomy with connectedness in moral self-emergence. In D. Cicchetti & M. Beeghly (Eds.), *The self in transition: Infancy to child-hood* (pp. 35–60). Chicago, IL: University of Chicago Press.

eMedicineHealth. (2015). *Motor skills disorder.* Retrieved from http://www.emedicinehealth.com/motor_skills_disorder/article_em.htm

Enard, W., Przeworski, M., Fisher, S. E., Lai, C. S., Wiebe, V., Eitano, T., et al. (2002). Molecular evolution of FOXP2, a gene involved in speech and language. *Nature, 418,* 869–872.

Encarta. (2004). *Finland.* Retrieved from http://encarta.msn.com/encyclopedia_761578960_5/ Finland.html

Engle, J. M., McElwain, N. L., & Lasky, N. (2011). Presence and quality of kindergarten children's friendships: Concurrent and longitudinal associations with child adjustment in the early school years. *Infant and Child Development, 20,* 365–386.

Enkelis, L. (2000). *On being 100: 31 centenarians share their extraordinary lives and wisdom.* Roseville, CA: Prima Publishing.

Ennett, S. T., Foshee, V. A., Bauman, K. E., et al. (2008). The social ecology of adolescent alcohol misuse. *Child Development, 79,* 1777–1791.

Entwisle, D. R., & Alexander, K. L. (1987). Long-term effects of cesarean delivery on parents' beliefs and children's schooling. *Developmental Psychology, 23,* 676–682.

Entwisle, D. R., Alexander, K. L., & Olson, L .S. (2005a). First grade and educational attainment by age 22: A new story. *American Journal of Sociology, 110,* 1458–1502.

Entwisle, D. R., Alexander, K. L., & Olson, L. S. (2005b). Urban teenagers: Work and dropout. *Youth and Society, 37,* 3–32.

Entwisle, D. R., Alexander, K. L., & Olson, L. S. (2007). Early schooling: The handicap of being poor and male. *Sociology of Education, 80,* 114–138.

Epstein, S. (1973). The self-concept revisited; or, a theory of a theory. *American Psychologist, 28,* 404–416.

Epstein, S. (1991). Cognitive-experiential self theory: An integrative theory of personality. In R. Cutis (Ed.), *The self with others: Convergences in psychoanalytic, social, and personality psychology* (pp. 111–137). New York, NY: Guilford Press.

Epstein, S. (1998). Cognitive-experiential self-theory. In D. F. Barone & M. Hersen (Eds.), *Advanced personality* (pp. 211–238). New York, NY: Plenum Press.

Epstein, S. (2003). Cognitive-experiential self theory of personality. In T. Millon & M. J. Lerner (Eds.), *Handbook of psychology: Personality and social psychology* (Vol. 5, pp. 159–184). Hoboken, NJ: John Wiley & Sons.

Epstein, S. (2008). Intuition from the perspective of cognitive-experiential self theory. In H. Plessner, C. Betsch, & T. Betsch (Eds.), *Intuition in judgment and decision making* (pp. 23–37). Mahwah, NJ: Lawrence Erlbaum.

Epstein, S., Lipson, A., Holstein, C., & Huh, E. (1993). Irrational reactions to negative outcomes: Evidence for two conceptual systems. *Journal of Personality and Social Psychology, 62,* 328–339.

Equal Employment Opportunity Commission. (2016a). *Discrimination by type.* Retrieved from https://www.eeoc.gov/laws/types/index.cfm

Equal Employment Opportunity Commission. (2016b). *EEOC releases fiscal year 2015 enforcement and litigation data.* Retrieved from https://www.eeoc.gov/eeoc/newsroom/release/2-11-16.cfm

Equal Employment Opportunity Commission. (2016c). *Facts about equal pay and compensation discrimination.* Retrieved from https://www.eeoc.gov/eeoc/publications/fs-epa.cfm

Equality and Human Rights Commission. (2016). *Disability discrimination.* Retrieved from https://www.equalityhumanrights.com/en/advice-and-guidance/disability-discrimination

Equalrights.org. (2010). *Sex discrimination.* Retrieved from www.equalrights.org/publications/kyr/sexdiscrim.asp

Erber, J. T. (2013). *Aging and older adulthood* (3rd ed.). Hoboken, NJ: Wiley.

Erez, A., Misangyi, V.F., Johnson, D.E., LePine, M.A., & Halverson, K.C. (2008). Stirring the hearts of followers: Charismatic leadership as the transferal of affect. *Journal of Applied Psychology, 93,* 601–616.

Erickson, K. I., Gildengers, A. G., & Butters, M. A. (2013). Physical activity and brain plasticity in late adulthood. *Dialogues in Clinical Neuroscience, 15,* 99–108.

Erikson, E. H. (1950). *Childhood and society.* New York: Norton.

Erikson, E. H. (1959). The problem of ego identity. *Psychological Issues, 1,* 101–164.

Erikson, E. H. (1963). *Childhood and society* (2nd ed.). New York, NY: Norton.

Erikson, E. H. (1968). *Identity: Youth and crisis.* New York, NY: Norton.

Erikson, E. H. (1969). *Gandhi's truth: On the origins of militant nonviolence.* New York, NY: Norton.

Erikson, E. H. (1972). Play and actuality. In M. W. Piers (Ed.), *Play and development* (pp. 127–167). New York, NY: Norton.

Erikson, E. H. (1974). *Dimensions of a new identity: The 1973 Jefferson Lectures in the Humanities.* New York: Norton.

Erikson, E. H. (1975). "Identity crisis" in autobiographic perspective. In E. H. Erikson (Ed.), *Life history and the historical moment* (pp. 17–47). New York, NY: Norton.

Erikson, E. H. (1977). *Toys and reasons.* New York, NY: Norton.

Erikson, E. H. (1978). Reflections on D. Borg's life cycle. In E. H. Erikson (Ed.), *Adulthood* (pp. 1–31). New York, NY: Norton.

Erikson, E. H. (1980). Themes of adulthood in the Freud-Jung correspondence. In N. J. Smelser & E. H. Erikson (Eds.), *Themes of work and love in adulthood* (pp. 43–74). Cambridge, MA: Harvard University Press.

Erikson, E. H. (1982). *The life cycle completed: A review.* New York, NY: Norton.

Erikson, E. H., Erikson, J. M., & Kivnick, H. Q. (1986). *Vital involvement in old age.* New York, NY: Norton.

Erikson, J. M. (1988). *Wisdom and the senses: The way of creativity.* New York, NY: Norton.

Erikson, M., & Lindström, B. (2005). Validity of Antonovsky's Sense of Coherence scale: A systematic review. *Journal of Epidemiological Community Health, 59,* 460–466.

Erraji-Benchekroun, L., Underwood, M. D., Arango, V., Galfalvy, H., Pavlidis, P., Smyrniotopoulos, P., et al. (2005). Molecular aging in human prefrontal cortex is selective and continuous throughout adult life. *Biological Psychiatry, 57,* 549–558.

Escalona, S. K. (1968). *The roots of individuality.* Chicago, IL: Aldine.

Espinoza, J. (2016). Teenage boys are increasingly worried about their body image, research finds. *Telegraph.* Retrieved from http://www.telegraph.co.uk/education/12158200/Teenage-boys-are-increasingly-worried-about-their-body-image-research-finds.html

Espinoza, P., Arêas da Luz Fontes, A. B., & Arms-Chavez, C. J. (2014). Attributional gender bias: Teachers' ability and effort explanations for students' math performance. *Social Psychology of Education, 17,* 105–126.

Essau, C. A. (2004). Association between family factors and depressive disorders in adolescents. *Journal of Youth and Adolescence, 33,* 365–372.

Ettekal, I., & Ladd, G. W. (2015). Costs and benefits of children's physical and relational aggression trajectories on peer rejection, acceptance and friendships: Variations by aggression subtypes, gender, and age. *Developmental Psychology, 51,* 1756–1770.

Evans, C. D., & Diekman, A. B. (2009). On motivated role selection: Gender beliefs, distant goals, and career interest. *Psychology of Women Quarterly, 33,* 235–249.

Evans, D. W., Gray, F. L., & Leckman, J. F. (1999). The rituals, fears, and phobias of young children: Insights from development, psychopathology, and neurobiology. *Child Psychiatry and Human Development, 29,* 261–276.

Evans, G. W., Gonnella, C., Marcynyszyn, L. A., Gentile, L., & Salpekar, N. (2005). The role of chaos in poverty and children's socioemotional adjustment. *Psychological Science, 16,* 560–565.

Evans, N., Gilpin, E., Farkas, A. J., Shenassa, E., & Pierce, J. P. (1995). Adolescents' perceptions of their peers' health norms. *American Journal of Public Health, 85,* 1064–1069.

Fabes, R. A., Hanish, L. D., & Martin, C. L. (2007). Peer interactions and the gendered social ecology of preparing young children for school. *Early Childhood Services: An Interdisciplinary Journal of Effectiveness, 1,* 205–218.

Fabes, R. A., Martin, C. L. & Hanish, L. D. (2003). Young children's play qualities in same-other- and mixed-sex peer groups. *Child Development, 74,* 921–932.

Fagan, J., & Palkovitz, R. (2011). Coparenting and relationship quality effects on father engagement: Variations by residence, romance. *Journal of Marriage and Family, 73,* 637–653.

Fan, J. X., & Zick, C. D. (2006). Expenditure flows near widowhood. *Journal of Family and Economic Issues, 27,* 335–353.

Fantasia, H. C. (2009). Late adolescents' perceptions of factors that influence their sexual decision-making: A narrative inquiry. A dissertation submitted in partial fulfillment of the doctoral program in the School of Nursing. Boston College. This work is posted on eScholarship@BC, Boston College University Libraries. Retrieved from https://dlib.bc.edu/islandora/object/bc-ir:101170/datastream/PDF/view

Farid, W. O., Dunlop, S. A., Tait, R. J., & Hulse, G. K. (2008). The effects of maternally administered methadone, buprenorphine and naltrexone on offspring: Review of human and animal data. *Current Neuropharmacology, 6,* 125–150.

Farkas, G., Grobe, R. P., Sheehan, D., & Shuan, Y. (1990). Cultural resources and school success: Gender, ethnicity, and poverty groups. *American Sociological Review, 55,* 127–142.

Farmer, T. W., & Rodkin, P. C. (1996). Antisocial and prosocial correlates of classroom social positions: The social network centrality perspective. *Social Development, 5,* 174–188.

Farrar, M. J., Raney, G. E., & Boyer, M. E. (1992). Knowledge, concepts, and inferences in childhood. *Child Development, 63,* 673–691.

Farrell, A. D., Danish, S. J., & Howard, C. W. (1992). Risk factors for drug use in urban adolescents: Identification and cross-validation. *American Journal of Community Psychology, 20*, 263–286.

Farrell, M. P., & Rosenberg, S. D. (1981). *Men at midlife*. Boston, MA: Auburn House.

Farrington, D. P. (2009). Conduct disorder, aggression, and delinquency. In R. M. Lerner & L. Steinberg (Eds.), *Handbook of adolescent psychology. Vol. 1. Individual bases of adolescent development* (3rd ed., pp. 683–722). Hoboken, NJ: John Wiley.

Farrington, D. P. (2013). Longitudinal and experimental research in criminology. *Crime and Justice, 42*(1), 453–527.

Fast, N.J., & Chen, S. (2009). When the boss feels inadequate: Power, incompetence and aggression. *Psychological Science, 20*, 1406–1413.

Fava, E., Hull, R., & Bortfeld, H. (2014). Dissociating cortical activity during processing of native and non-native audiovisual speech from early to late infancy. *Brain Sciences, 4*, 471–487.

Fay-Stammbach, T., Hawes, D. J., & Meredith, P. (2014). Parenting influences on executive function in early childhood: A review. *Child Development Perspectives, 8*, 258–264.

Feagin, J. R., & McKinney, K. D. (2003). *The many costs of racism*. Lanham, MD: Rowman & Littlefield.

Fearon, R. P., Bakermans-Kranenburg, M. J., van IJzendoorn, M. H., Lapsley, A., & Roisman, G. I. (2010). The significance of insecure attachment and disorganization in the development of children's externalizing behavior: A meta-analytic study. *Child Development, 81*, 435–456.

Federal Bureau of Investigation. (2005). *Uniform Crime Reports, 1996 and 2005*. Retrieved from http://www.fbi.gov/ucr/ucr.htm

Federal Bureau of Investigation. (2013). *Uniform Crime Reports. Tables 32 and 33*. Retrieved from http:// www.fbi.gov/about-us/cjis/ucr /crime -in-the-u.s/2011/crime-in-the -u.s.-2011/fbi-releases-2011-crime-statistics

Federal Bureau of Investigation. (2014). *Uniform crime reports, 2014. Table 37*. Retrieved from https://www.fbi.gov/about -us/cjis/ucr/crime-in-the-u.s/2014/crime -in-the-u.s.-2014/tables/table-37

Federal Interagency Forum on Aging Related Statistics. (2004). *Older Americans 2004: Key indicators of well-being*. Retrieved from http://www .agingstats .gov /chartbook2004/default.htm

Federal Interagency Forum on Aging-Related Statistics. (2012). *2012 Older Americans: Key indicators of well-being; health status*. Retrieved www.agingstats.gov/Main_Site /Data/2012_Documents/docs /HealthStatus.pdf

Federal Interagency Forum on Aging-Related Statistics. (2016). *Older Americans 2016: Key indicators of well-being*. Retrieved from http://www.agingstats.gov/

Federal Interagency Forum on Child and Family Statistics. (2013). *America's children: Key national indicators of well-being, 2013. Special feature, the kindergarten year.*

Washington, DC: U.S. Government Printing Office.

Federman, J. (1998). *National television violence study* (Vol. 3). Thousand Oaks, CA: Sage.

Feeney, J. A. (1999). Adult romantic attachment and couple relationships. In J. Cassidy & P. R. Shaver (Eds.), *Handbook of attachment: Theory, research, and clinical applications* (pp. 355–377). New York, NY: Guilford Press.

Feeney, J. A. (2008). Adult romantic attachment: Developments in the study of couple relationships. In J. Cassidy & P. R. Shaver (Eds.), *Handbook of attachment: Theory, research and clinical applications* (2nd ed., pp. 456–481). New York, NY: Guilford Press.

Feeney, J. A. (2016). Adult romantic attachment: Developments in the study of couple relationships. In J. Cassidy & P. R. Shaver (Eds.), *Handbook of attachment: Theory, research, and clinical applications* (pp. 435–463) (3rd ed.). New York: Guilford Press.

Feinman, S., & Lewis, M. (1983). Social referencing at ten months: A second-order effect on infants' responses to strangers. *Child Development, 54*, 878–887.

Feinman, S., Roberts, D., Hsieh, K.-F., Sawyer, D., & Swanson, D. (1992). A critical review of social referencing in infancy. In S. Feinman (Ed.), *Social referencing and the social construction of reality in infancy* (pp. 15–54). New York, NY: Plenum Press.

Feldman, R. (2004). Mother infant skin-to-skin contact and the development of emotion regulation. In S. P. Shohov (Ed.) *Advances in psychology research* (Vol. 27, pp. 113–131). Hauppauge, NY: Nova Science.

Feldman, R. (2007). Maternal–infant contact and child development: Insights from the Kangaroo intervention. In L. L'Abate (Ed.), *Low cost approaches to promote physical and mental health: Theory and practice* (pp. 323–351). New York, NY: Springer Science + Business Media.

Feldman, R. (2011). Maternal touch and the developing infant. In M. Hertenstein & S. Weiss (Eds.), *The handbook of touch: Neuroscience, behavioral, and health perspectives* (pp. 373–407). New York, NY: Springer Publishing.

Feldman, R., & Eidelman, A. I. (2004). Mother–infant skin-to-skin contact (Kangaroo Care) accelerates autonomic and neurobehavioral maturation in premature infants. *Developmental Medicine and Child Neurology, 45*, 274–280.

Feldman, S., Byles, J. E., & Beaumont, R. (2000). "Is anybody listening?" The experiences of widowhood for older Australian women. *Journal of Women and Aging, 12*, 155–176.

Fenson, L., Dale, P. S., Reznick, J. S., Bates, E., Thal, D. J., & Pethick, S. J. (1994). Variability in early communicative development. *Monographs of the Society for Research in Child Development, 59* (Serial No. 5).

Ferguson, C. J. (2012). A vast graveyard of undead theories: Publication bias and psychological science's aversion to the null. *Perspectives on Psychological Science, 7*, 555–561.

Ferguson, C. J. (2013). Violent video games and the Supreme Court: Lessons for the scientific community in the wake of Brown v. Entertainment Merchants Association. *American Psychologist, 68*, 57–74.

Fergusson, D. M., Horwood, L. J., & Boden, J. M (2009). Reactions to abortion and subsequent mental health. *The British Journal of Psychiatry, 195*, 420–426.

Fetterman, D. M. (2010). *Ethnography: Step by step* (3rd ed.). Thousand Oaks, CA: Sage.

Fiedler, K. (2008). Language: A toolbox for sharing and influencing social reality. *Perspectives on Psychological Science, 3*, 38–47.

Fiel, C. M., Harris, D., & House, R. (1999). Charismatic leadership: Strategies for effecting social change. *Leadership Quarterly, 10*, 449–482.

Field, D. (1981). Can preschool children really learn to conserve? *Child Development, 52*, 326–334.

Field, T., Diego, M., & Hernandez-Reif, M. (2009). Depressed mothers' infants are less responsive to faces and voices. *Infant Behavior and Development, 32*, 239–244.

Field, T., Hernandez-Reif, M., & Diego, M. (2006). Intrusive and withdrawn depressed mothers and their infants. *Developmental Review, 26*, 15–30.

Field, T. M., Diego, M., Hernandez-Reif, M., Schanberg, S., Kuhn, C., Yando, R., et al. (2003). Pregnancy anxiety and comorbid depression and anger: Effects on the fetus and neonate. *Depression & Anxiety, 17*, 140–151.

Fife, B. L., & Wright, E. R. (2000). The dimensionality of stigma: A comparison of its impact on the self of persons with HIV/ AIDS and Cancer. *Journal of Health and Social Behavior, 41*, 50–67.

Fife-Shaw, C. (2012). Quasi-experimental designs. In G. M. Breakwell, J. A. Smith, & D. B. Wright (Eds.), *Research methods in psychology* (4th ed.). Thousand Oaks, CA: Sage.

Filion, K. (2009). Fact sheet for 2009 minimum wage increase. *Economic Policy Institute*. Retrieved from www.epi.org/publications /entry/mwig_fact_sheet/

FindLaw. (2016). *Fathers' rights and abortion*. Retrieved from http://www.family.findlaw. com/paternity/fathers-rights-and-abortion .html

Fine, M. A., Ganong, L. H., & Demo, D. H. (2010). Divorce, a risk and resilience perspective. In S. J. Price, C. A. Price, & P. C. McKenry (Eds.), *Families and change: Coping with stressful events and transitions* (4th ed., pp. 211–233). Thousand Oaks, CA: Sage.

Finer, L. B., & Henshaw, S. K. (2003). Abortion incidence and services in the United States in 2000. *Perspectives on Sexual and Reproductive Health, 35*(1), 1–15.

Finer, L. B., & Henshaw, S. K. (2006). *Estimates of U.S. abortion incidence, 2001–2003*. New York, NY: Guttmacher Institute.

Fingerman, K., Miller, L., Birditt, K., & Zarit, S. (2009). Giving to the good and the needy: Parental support of grown children. *Journal of Marriage and the Family, 71*, 1220–1233.

Fingerman, K. L., Cheng, Y., Birditt, K. S., & Zarit, S. (2012). Only as happy as the least happy child: Multiple grown children's problems and successes and middle-aged parents' well-being. *The Journals of Gerontology: Series B. Psychological Sciences and Social Sciences, 67B*, 184–193.

Fingerman, K. L., Cheng, Y., Tighe, L., Burditt, K. S., & Zarit, S. (2011). Relationships between young adults and their parents. In A. Booth, S. A. Brown, N. S. Landale, W. S. Manning, & S. M. McHale (Eds.), *Early adulthood in a family context* (Vol. 2, pp. 59–85). New York, NY: Springer, pp. 59–85.

Fingerman, K. L., Hay, E. L., & Birditt, K. S. (2004). The best of ties, the worst of ties: Close, problematic, and ambivalent social relationships. *Journal of Marriage and the Family, 66*, 792–808.

Fink, A. (2013) *Conducting research literature reviews: From the Internet to paper* (4th ed.). Thousand Oaks, CA: Sage.

Finkel, E. J., Eastwick, P. W., Karney, B. R., Reis, H. T., & Sprecher, S. (2012). Online dating: A critical analysis from the perspective of psychological science. *Psychological Science in the Public Interest, 13*, 3–66.

Finkelhor, D., Turner, H., Shattuck, A., Hamby, S., & Kracke, K. (2015). Children's exposure to violence, crime and abuse: An update. U.S. Department of Justice, Office of Juvenile Justice and Delinquency Prevention. Retrieved from http://www.ojjdp.gov/pubs/248547.pdf

Finkenauer, C., Engels, R. C. M. E., Branje, S. J. T., & Meeus, W. (2004). Disclosure and relationship satisfaction in families. *Journal of Marriage and the Family, 66*, 195–209.

Finley, N. J. (1989). Gender differences in caregiving for elderly parents. *Journal of Marriage and the Family, 51*, 79–86.

Finne, E., Bucksch, J., Lampert, T., & Kolip, P. (2011). Age, puberty, body satisfaction and physical activity decline in adolescence. Results of the German Health Interview and Examination Survey (KiGGS). *International Journal of Behavioral Nutrition and Physical Activity, 8*, Article 119.

Firestone, R. W., Firestone, L. A., & Catlett, J. (2006). Couple relationships: Jealousy and sexual rivals. In F. W. Firestone, L. A. Firestone, & J. Catlett (Eds.), *Sex and love in intimate relationships* (pp. 197–225). Washington, DC: American Psychological Association.

Fischer, K. W. (1980). A theory of cognitive development: The control and construction of hierarchies of skills. *Psychological Review, 87*, 477–531.

Fischer, K. W., & Bidell, T. R. (1992, Winter). Ever younger ages: Constructive use of nativist findings about early development. *Newsletter of the Society for Research in Child Development, 1*, 10, 11, 14.

Fischer, K. W., & Bidell, T. R. (2006). Dynamic development of action and thought. In W. Damon & R. M. Lerner (Eds.), *Theoretical models of human development: Handbook of child psychology* (Vol. 1, 6th ed., pp. 313–399). New York, NY: Wiley.

Fischer, K. W., Bullock, D., Rotenberg, E. J., & Raya, P. (1993). The dynamics of competence: How context contributes directly to skill. In R. Wozniak & K. Fischer (Eds.), *Development in context: Acting and thinking in specific environments*, JPS Series on Knowledge and Development (Vol. 1, pp. 93–117). Hillsdale, NJ: Erlbaum.

Fischer, K. W., & Wozniak, R. (Eds.). (2002). *Development in context: Acting and thinking in specific environments*. JPS Series on Knowledge and Development (Vol. 1, pp. 93–117). Hillsdale, NJ: Erlbaum.

Fischer, T. F. C., De Graaf, P. M., & Kalmijn, M. (2005). Friendly and antagonistic contact between former spouses after divorce: Patterns and determinants. *Journal of Family Issues, 26*, 1131–1163.

Fisher, C. B., Hoagwood, K., Boyce, C., et al. (2002). Research ethics for mental health science involving ethnic minority children and youths. *American Psychologist, 57*, 1024–1040.

Fisher, D. M. (2014). A multilevel cross-cultural examination of role overload and organizational commitment: Investigating the interactive effects of context. *Journal of Applied Psychology, 99*, 723–736.

Fisher, L. & Trenkamp, B. (2010). *Income of the aged chartbook, 2008*. Social Security Administration. Retrieved from http://www.socialsecurity.gov/policy/docs/chartbooks/income_aged/2008/iac08.pdf

Fitch, J. (1999). *White oleander*. Boston, MA: Little, Brown.

Fitzgerald, B. (1999). Children of lesbian and gay parents: A review of the literature. *Marriage and Family Review, 29*, 57–75.

Fitzsimons, G. M., & Finkel, E. J. (2010). Interpersonal influences on self-regulation. *Current Directions in Psychological Science, 19*, 101–105.

Flavell, J. H. (1963). *The developmental psychology of Jean Piaget*. Princeton, NJ: Van Nostrand.

Flavell, J. H. (1974). The development of inferences about others. In W. Mischel (Ed.), *Understanding other persons*. Oxford, England: Blackwell, Basil & Mott.

Flavell, J. H. (1982). Structures, stages, and sequences in cognitive development. In W. A. Collins (Ed.), *The concept of development* (pp. 1–28). Hillsdale, NJ: Erlbaum.

Flavell, J. H., Flavell, E. R., & Green, F. L. (1987). Young children's knowledge about the apparent-real and pretend-real distinctions. *Developmental Psychology, 23*, 816–822.

Fleischmann, A., Sieverding, M., Hespenheide, U., Weiss, M., & Koch, S. B. (2016). See feminine-think incompetent? The effects of a feminine outfit on the evaluation of women's computer competence. *Computers and Education, 95*, 63–74.

Fleming, A. S., Ruble, D. N., Flett, G. L., & Shaul, D. L. (1988). Postpartum adjustment in first-time mothers: Relations between mood, maternal attitudes, and mother–infant interactions. *Developmental Psychology, 24*, 71–81.

Fletcher, W. L., & Hansson, R. O. (1991). Assessing the social components of retirement anxiety. *Psychology and Aging, 6*, 76–85.

Floet, A. M. W., & Maldonado-Duran, J. M. (2006). Motor skills disorders. *eMedicine*. Retrieved from http://www.emedicine.com/ped/topic2640.htm

Flom, R. & Bahrick, L. E. (2010). The effects of intersensory redundancy on attention and memory: Infants' long-term memory for orientation in audiovisual events. *Developmental Psychology, 46*, 428–436.

Florian, V., & Kravetz, S. (1983). Fear of personal death: Attribution structure and relation to religious belief. *Journal of Personality and Social Psychology, 44*, 600–607.

Floyd, F. J., Haynes, S. N., Doll, E. R., Winemiller, D., Lemsky, C., Burgy, T. M., et al. (1992). Assessing retirement satisfaction and perceptions of retirement experiences. *Psychology and Aging, 7*, 609–621.

Fogel, A., Hsu, H-C., Shaprio, A. F., Nelson-Goens, G. C., & Secrist, C. (2006). Effects of normal and perturbed social play on the duration and amplitude of different types of infant smiles. *Developmental Psychology, 42*, 459–473.

Foley, D. J., Vitiello, M. V., Bilwise, D. L., Ancoli-Israel, S., Monjan, A. A., & Walsh, J. K. (2007). Frequent napping is associated with excessive daytime sleepiness, depression, pain, and nocturia in older adults. *American Journal of Geriatric Psychiatry, 15*, 344–350.

Folkman, S., & Moskowitz, J. T. (2000). Positive affect and the other side of coping. *American Psychologist, 55*, 647–654.

Fonagy, P. (2003). The development of psychopathology from infancy to adulthood: The mysterious unfolding of disturbance in time. *Infant Mental Health Journal, 24*, 212–239.

Fonagy, P., Gergely, G., & Target, M. (2010). Psychoanalytic constructs and attachment theory and research. In J. K. Cassidy & P. R. Shaver (Eds.), *Handbook of attachment: Theory, research and applications* (2nd ed., pp. 783–810). New York, NY: Guilford Press.

Fonagy, P., Luyten, P., Allison, E., & Campbell, C. (2016). Reconciling psychoanalytic ideas with attachment theory. In J.Cassidy & P.R. Shaver (Eds.), *Handbook of attachment:*

Theory, research and applications (3rd ed., pp. 780–804). New York: Guilford Press.

Fontana, A., & Keene, J. R. (2009). *Death and dying in America*. Malden, MA: Polity Press.

Fontane, P. E. (1996). Exercise, fitness, feeling well. *American Behavioral Scientist, 39*, 288–305.

Foodsafety.gov. (2016). *Baby food and infant formula*. Retrieved from http://www .foodsafety.gov/keep/types/babyfood/

Food Safety.gov. (2016). *Food safety for pregnant women*. Retrieved from http://www .foodsafety.gov/risk/pregnant/

Ford, C. S. (1945). *A comparative study of human reproduction*. Yale University Publications in Anthropology (No. 32).

Fordham, K., & Stevenson-Hinde, J. (1999). Shyness, friendship quality, and adjustment during middle childhood. *Journal of Child Psychology and Psychiatry and Allied Disciplines, 40*, 757–768.

Forman, T. A. (2003). The social psychological costs of racial segmentation in the workplace: A study of African Americans' well-being. *Journal of Health and Social Behavior, 44*, 332–352.

Forret, M. L., Sullivan, S. E., & Miniero, L. A. (2010). Gender role differences in reactions to unemployment: Exploring psychological mobility and boundaryless careers. *Journal of Organizational Behavior, 31*, 647–666.

Fortenberry, J .D. (2013). Puberty and adolescent sexuality. *Hormones and Behavior, 64*, 280–287.

Fosburgh, L. (1977, August 7). The make-believe world of teenage maturity. *New York Times Magazine*, pp. 29–34.

Fouad, N. A., & Bynner, J. (2008). Work transitions. *American Psychologist, 63*, 241–251.

Fowers, B. J., Montel, K. H., & Olson, D. H. (1996). Predicting marital success for pre-marital couple types based on PREPARE. *Journal of Marital and Family Therapy, 22*, 103–119.

Fowler, F. J. (2013). *Survey research methods* (5th ed.). Thousand Oaks, CA: Sage.

Fox, N. A., Almas, A. N., Degnan, K. A., Nelson, C. A., & Zeanah, C. H. (2011). The effects of severe psychosocial deprivation and foster care intervention on cognitive development at 8 years of age: Findings from the Bucharest early intervention project. *Journal of Child Psychology and Psychiatry, 52*, 919–928.

Fox, N. A., Hane, A. A., & Pine, D. S. (2007). Plasticity for affective neurocircuitry. *Current Directions in Psychological Science, 16*, 1–5.

Fragile Families and Child Wellbeing Study. (2012). *Fact sheet*. Retrieved from www .fragilefamilies.princeton .edu/documents /Fragile Families

Fragile Families and Child Wellbeing Study. (2016). *Fragile families and child wellbeing study fact sheet*. Retrieved from http:// www.fragilefamilies.princeton.edu /documents/FragileFamiliesandChild WellbeingStudyFactsSheet.pdf

Fraley, R. C., & Spieker, S. J. (2003). Are infant attachment patterns continuously or categorically distributed? A taxometric analysis of strange situation behavior. *Developmental Psychology, 39*, 387–404.

Frankenberg, W. K., & Dodds, J. B. (1967). The Developmental Screening Test. *Journal of Pediatrics, 71*, 181–191.

Franklin, D. L. (1988). Race, class, and adolescent pregnancy: An ecological analysis. American Journal of Orthopsychiatry, 58, 339–355.

Franko, D. L., & Striegel-Moore, R. H. (2002). The role of body dissatisfaction as a risk factor for depression in adolescent girls: Are the differences Black and White? *Journal of Psychosomatic Research, 53*, 975–983.

Fraser, S. I., & Walters, J. W. (2000). Death—whose decision? Euthanasia and the terminally ill. *Journal of Medical Ethics, 26*, 121–125.

Fredriksen, K., Rhodes, J., Reddy, R., & Way, N. (2004). Sleepless in Chicago: Tracking the effects of adolescent sleep loss during the middle school years. *Child Development, 75*, 84–95.

Freeman, R. B., & Wise, D. A. (1982). *The youth labor market: Problems in the United States*. Chicago, IL: University of Chicago Press.

Freiberg, K., Tually, K., & Crassini, B. (2001). Use of an auditory looming task to test infants' sensitivity to sound pressure level as an auditory distance cue. *British Journal of Developmental Psychology, 19*, 1–10.

French, D. C. (1984). Children's knowledge of the social functions of younger, older and same-age peers. *Child Development, 55*, 1429–1433.

French, D. C. (1988). Heterogeneity of peer-rejected boys: Aggressive and nonaggressive subtypes. *Child Development, 59*, 976–985.

French, D. C. (1990). Heterogeneity of peer-rejected girls. *Child Development, 61*, 2028–2031.

French, S. B., Seidman, E., Allen, L., & Aber, J. L. (2000). Racial/ethnic identity, congruence with the social context, and the transition to high school. *Journal of Adolescent Research, 15*, 587–603.

Frese, M. (2001). Personal initiative: The theoretical concept and empirical findings. In M. Erez & U. Kleinbeck (Eds.), *Work motivation in the context of a globalizing economy* (pp. 99–110). Mahwah, NJ: Erlbaum.

Freud, A. (1936/1946). *The ego and the mechanisms of defense*. New York, NY: International Universities Press.

Freud, A. (1965). Normality and pathology in childhood. In *Writings of Anna Freud* (Vol.6, pp. 3–235). New York, NY: International Universities Press.

Freud, A., & Dann, S. (1951). An experiment in group upbringing. In R. Eissler, A. Freud, H. Hartmann, & E. Kris (Eds.), *The psychoanalytic study of the child* (Vol. 6,

pp. 127–168). New York, NY: International Universities Press.

Freud, S. (1905/1953). Three essays on the theory of sexuality. In J. Strachey (Ed.), *The standard edition of the complete psychological works of Sigmund Freud* (Vol. 7, pp. 125–245). London: Hogarth Press.

Freud, S. (1909/1955). An analysis of a phobia in a 5-year-old boy. In J. Strachey (Ed.), *The standard edition of the complete psychological works of Sigmund Freud* (Vol. 10, pp. 5–149). London: Hogarth Press.

Freud, S. (1925/1961). Some psychical consequences of the anatomical distinction between the sexes. In J. Strachey (Ed.), *The standard edition of the complete psychological works of Sigmund Freud* (Vol. 19, pp. 248–258). London: Hogarth Press.

Freud, S. (1933/1964). New introductory lectures on psychoanalysis. In J. Strachey (Ed.), *The standard edition of the complete psychological works of Sigmund Freud* (Vol. 22, pp. 3–182). London: Hogarth Press.

Freund, A. M., & Baltes, P. B. (1998). Selection, optimization, and compensation as strategies of life management: Correlations with subjective indicators of successful aging. *Psychology and Aging, 13*, 531–543.

Frey, K. S., & Ruble, D. N. (1987). What children say about classroom performance: Sex and grade differences in perceived competence. *Child Development, 58*, 1066–1078.

Frey, P. S. (2003). Perceived self-efficacy domains as predictors of fear of the unknown and fear of dying among older adults. *Psychology and Aging, 18*, 474–486.

Fried, L. P., Carlson, M. C., Freedman, M., Frick, K. D., Glass, T. A., Hill, J., et al. (2004). A social model for health promotion for an aging population: Initial evidence on the Experience Corps. *Journal of Urban Health, 81*, 64–74.

Fried, M. G. (2013). Reproductive rights activism in the post-Roe era. *American Journal of Public Health, 103*, 10–14.

Friederici, A. D. (2008). Brain correlates of language processing during the first years of life. In C. A. Nelson an M. Luciana (Eds.), *The handbook of developmental cognitive neuroscience* (2nd ed., pp. 117–126). Cambridge, MA: MIT Press.

Friedman, C. K., Leaper, C., & Bigler, R. S. (2007). Do mothers' gender-related attitudes or comments predict young children's gender beliefs? *Parenting: Science and Practice, 7*, 357–366.

Friedman, H. S., Kern, M. L., & Reynolds, C. A. (2010). Personality and health: Subjective well-being and longevity. *Journal of Personality, 78*, 179–216.

Friedman, J. (2005). *Earth's elders: The wisdom of the world's oldest people*. South Kent, CT: The Earth's Elders Foundation.

Friedman, W. J., Robinson, A. B., & Friedman, B. L. (1987). Sex differences in moral judgments? A test of Gilligan's theory. *Psychology of Women Quarterly, 11*, 37–46.

Froming, W. J., Nasby, W., & McManus, J. (1998). Prosocial self-schemas, self-awareness, and children's prosocial behavior. *Journal of Personality and Social Psychology, 75,* 766–777.

Fruhauf, C. A., Jarrott, S. E., & Allen, K. R. (2006). Grandchildren's perceptions of caring for grandparents. *Journal of Family Issues, 27,* 887–911.

Fuchs, L. S., Geary, D. C., Fuchs, D., Compton, D. L., & Hamlett, C. L. (2016). Pathways to third-grade calculation versus word-reading competence: Are they more alike or different? *Child Development, 87,* 558–567.

Fulcher, M., Sutfin, E. L., & Patterson, C. J. (2008). Individual differences in gender development: Associations with parental sexual orientation, attitudes, and division of labor. *Sex Roles, 58,* 330–341.

Fuligni, A. J., Hughes, D. L., & Way, N. (2009). Ethnicity and immigration. In R. M. Lerner & L. Steinberg (Eds.), *Handbook of adolescent psychology, Vol. 2. Contextual influence of adolescent development* (3rd ed., pp. 527–569). New York, NY: John Wiley.

Fuller-Rowell, T. E., Evans, G. W., & Ong, A. D. (2012). Poverty and health: The mediating role of perceived discrimination. *Psychological Science, 23,* 734–739.

Fultz, N. H., & Herzog, A. R. (1991). Gender differences in affiliation and instrumentality across adulthood. *Psychology and Aging, 6,* 579–586.

Funk, J. B., Baldacci, H. B., Pasold, T., & Baumgardner, J. (2004). Violence exposure in real-life, video games, television, movies, and the Internet: Is there desensitization? *Journal of Adolescence, 27,* 23–39.

Furdella, J., & Puzzanchera, C. (2015, October). Delinquency cases in juvenile court, 2013. Office of Juvenile Justice and Delinquency Prevention, National Report Series.

Furstenberg, F. F. (2010). Passage to adulthood. *The Prevention Researcher, 17,* 3–7.

Fuster, J. (2008). *The prefrontal cortex.* San Diego, CA: Elsevier.

Futterman, A., Gallagher, D., Thompson, L. W., Lovett, S., & Gilewski, M. (1990). Retrospective assessment of marital adjustment and depression during the first two years of spousal bereavement. *Psychology and Aging, 5,* 277–283.

Gabrieli, J. D. E. (2009). Dyslexia: A new synergy between education and cognitive neuroscience. *Science, 325,* 280–283.

Gadalla, T. M. (2009). Impact of marital dissolution on men's and women's incomes: A longitudinal study. *Journal of Divorce and Remarriage, 50,* 55–65.

Gadassi, R., Gati, I., & Dayan, A. (2012). The adaptability of career decision-making profiles. *Journal of Counseling Psychology, 59,* 612–622.

Gadassi, R., Gati, I., & Dayan, A. (2012). The adaptability of career decision-making profiles. *Journal of Counseling Psychology, 59,* 612–622.

Gagne, J. R., & Saudino, K. J. (2010). Wait for it! A twin study of inhibitory control in early childhood. *Behavior Genetics, 40,* 327–337.

Gagne, J. R. & Saudino, K. J. (2016). The development of inhibitory control in early childhood: A twin study from 2–3 years. *Developmental Psychology, 52,* 391–399.

Galindo, C., & Fuller, B. (2010). The social competence of Latino kindergarteners and growth in mathematical understanding. *Developmental Psychology, 46,* 579–592.

Galinsky, E. (2007). *Dual-centric: A new concept of work-life.* Retrieved from http://familiesandwork.org/site/research/reports/main.html

Gall, T. L., Evans, D. R., & Howard, J. (1997). The retirement adjustment process: Changes in the well-being of male retirees across time. *Journal of Gerontology, 52,* P110–P117.

Gallagher, S. (2013). When the problem of intersubjectivity becomes the solution. In M. Legerstee, D. W. Haley, & M. H. Bornstein (Eds.), *The infant mind: Origins of the social brain* (pp. 48–76). New York, NY: Guilford Press.

Galler, J. R., & Tonkiss, J. (1998). The effects of prenatal protein malnutrition and cocaine on the development of the rat. In J. A. Harvey & B. E. Kosofsky (Eds.), *Cocaine: Effects on the developing brain* (pp. 29–39). New York, NY: New York Academy of Sciences.

Gallese, V. (2006). Intentional attunement: A neurophysiological perspective on social cognition and its disruption in autism. *Brain Research, 1079,* 15–24.

Gallitto, E. (2015). Temperament as a moderator of the effects of parenting on children's behavior. *Development and Psychopathology, 27,* 757–773.

Galotti, K. M. (1989). Gender differences in self-reported moral reasoning: A review of new evidence. *Journal of Youth and Adolescence, 18,* 475–488.

Galotti, K. M., Kozberg, S. F., & Farmer, M. C. (1991). Gender and developmental differences in adolescents' conceptions of moral reasoning. *Journal of Youth and Adolescence, 20,* 13–30.

Galt, A. H. (1991). Magical misfortune in Locorotondo. *American Ethnologist, 18,* 735–750.

Galván, A. (2012). Risky behavior in adolescence: The role of the developing brain. In V. F. Reyna, S. B. Chapman, M. R. Dougherty, & J. Confrey (Eds.), *The adolescent brain: Learning, reasoning, and decision-making* (pp. 267–289). Washington, DC: American Psychological Association.

Galván, A. (2013a). The teenage brain: Sensitivity to rewards. *Current Directions in Psychological Science, 22,* 88–93.

Galván, A. (2013b). Sensitivity to reward in adolescence. *Current Directions in Psychological Science, 22,* 100–105.

Galyer, K. T., & Evans, I. M. (2001). Pretend play and the development of emotion regulation in preschool children. *Early Child Development and Care, 166,* 93–108.

Ganea, P. A., Lillard, A. S., & Turkheimer, E. (2004). Preschoolers' understanding of the role of mental states and action in pretense. *Journal of Cognition and Development, 5,* 213–238.

Garbarino, J. (2001). An ecological perspective on the effects of violence on children. *Journal of Community Psychology, 29,* 361–378.

Garcia, N. V., & Scherf, K. S. (2015). Emerging sensitivity to socially complex expressions: A unique role for adolescence? *Child Development Perspectives, 9,* 84–90.

Gardner, H. (1983). *Frames of mind: The theory of multiple intelligences.* New York, NY: Basic Books.

Gardner, H., Kornhaber, M. L., & Wake, W. K. (1996). *Intelligence: Multiple perspectives.* Fort Worth, TX: Harcourt Brace.

Gardner, H. E. (2006). *Multiple intelligences: New horizons in theory and practice.* New York, NY: Basic Books.

Gardner, H. E. (2011). *Creating minds.* New York, NY: Basic Books.

Gardner, H. W., & Kosmitzki, C. (2011). *Lives across cultures: Cross-cultural human development* (5th ed.). Boston, MA: Pearson.

Garmezy, N. (1991). Resilience in children's adaptation to negative life events and stressed environments. *Pediatric Annals, 20,* 459–466.

Garrett-Peters, R. (2009). "If I don't have to work anymore, who am I?": Job loss and collaborative self-concept repair. *Journal of Contemporary Ethnography, 38,* 547–583.

Garrison, C. Z., Schluchter, M. D., Schoenbach, V. J., & Kaplan, B. K. (1989). Epidemiology of depressive symptoms in young adolescents. *Journal of the American Academy of Child and Adolescent Psychiatry, 28,* 343–351.

Garrison, M. M., & Christakis, D. A. (2005). A teacher in the living room. *The Kaiser Family Foundation.* Retrieved from www.kff.org/entmedia/upload/7427.pdf

Garton, A. F. (1992). *Social interaction and the development of language and cognition.* Hillsdale, NJ: Erlbaum.

Gartrell, D. (2011). Aggression, the prequel preventing the need. *Young Children, 66,* 62–64.

Gartstein, M. A., Bridgett, D. J., Rothbart, M. K., Robertson, C., Iddins, E., Ramsay, K., et al. (2010). A latent growth examination of fear development in infancy: Contributions of maternal depression and the risk for toddler anxiety. *Developmental Psychology, 46,* 651–668.

Garwood, S. K., Gerassi, L., Jonson-Reid, M., Plax, K., & Drake, B. (2015). More than poverty: The effect of child abuse and neglect on teen pregnancy risk. *Journal of Adolescent Health, 57,* 164–168.

Gattai, F. B., & Musatti, T. (1999). Grandmothers' involvement in grandchildren's care: Attitudes, feelings, and emotions. *Family Relations: Interdisciplinary Journal of Applied Family Studies, 48,* 35–42.

Gauffroy, C., & Barrouillet, P. (2011). The primacy of thinking about possibilities in the development of reasoning. *Developmental Psychology, 47*, 1000–1011.

Gauvain, M., & Reynolds, C. A. (2011). The sociocultural context of cognition across the lifespan. In K. L. Fingerman, C. A. Berg, J. Smith, & T. C. Antonucci (Eds.), *Handbook of lifespan development* (pp. 269–298). New York, NY: Springer.

Gavin, L. A., & Furman, W. (1989). Age differences in adolescents' perceptions of their peer groups. *Developmental Psychology, 25*, 827–834.

Gazelle, H. (2008). Behavioral profiles of anxious solitary children and heterogeneity in peer relations. *Developmental Psychology, 44*, 1604–1624.

Gazelle, H., & Druhen, M. J. (2009). Anxious solitude and peer exclusion predict social helplessness, upset affect, and vagal regulation in response to behavioral rejection from a friend. *Developmental Psychology, 45*, 1077–1096.

Ge, X., Conger, R. D., & Elder, G. H., Jr. (2001). The relation between puberty and psychological distress in adolescent boys. *Journal of Research on Adolescence, 11*, 49–70.

Ge, X., & Natsuaki, M. N. (2009). In search of explanations for early pubertal timing effects on developmental psychopathology. *Current Directions in Psychological Science, 18*, 327–331.

Geary, D. C., Brown, S. C., & Samaranayake, V. A. (1991). Cognitive addition: A short longitudinal study of strategy choice and speed-of-processing differences in normal and mathematically disabled children. *Developmental Psychology, 27*, 787–797.

Geary, D. C., Vigil, J., & Byrd-Craven, J. (2004). Evolution of human mate choice. *Journal of Sex Research, 41*, 27–42.

Geffken, G., Sajid, M., & MacNaughton, K. (2005). The course of childhood OCD, its antecedents, onset, comorbidities, remission, and reemergence: A 12-year case report. *Clinical Case Studies, 4*, 380–394.

Gelbach, H. (2006). How changes in students' goal orientations relate to outcomes in social studies. *Journal of Educational Research, 99*, 358–370.

Gelissen, J. P. T. M. (2003). Cross-national differences in public consent to divorce: Effects of cultural, structural and com-positional factors. In W. Arts, L. C. J. M. Halman, & J. A. P. Hagenaars (Eds.), *The cultural diversity of European unity: Findings, explanations and reflections from the European values study* (pp. 339–370). Leiden, Netherlands: Brill Academic Publishers.

Gelles, R. J. (1989). Child abuse and violence in single-parent families: Parent absence and economic deprivation. *American Journal of Orthopsychiatry, 59*, 492–501.

Gelman, S. A., Taylor, M. G., & Nguyen, S. P. (2004). Mother–child conversations about gender: Understanding the acquisition of essentialist beliefs. *The Monographs of the Society for Research in Child Development, 69*.

Genetic Science Learning Center. (2014). Genomic imprinting. *Learn.Genetics.* Retrieved from http://learn.genetics.utah.edu/content/epigenetics/imprinting

Genetic Science Learning Center. (2015a). Epigenetics and inheritance. *Learn.Genetics.* Retrieved from http://learn.genetics.utah.edu/content/epigenetics/inheritance/

Genetic Science Learning Center. (2015b). What is a mutation? *Learn.Genetics.* Retrieved from http://learn.genetics.utah.edu/content/variation/mutation/

Genetics Home Reference. (2015a). *What is a mutation and how do mutations occur?* Retrieved from http://ghr.nlm.nih.gov/handbook/mutationsanddisorders/genemutation

Genetics Home Reference. (2015b). *Genetic disorders A-Z.* Retrieved from http://ghr.nlm.nih.gov/

Gentile, D. A., Anderson, C. A., Yukawa, S., Ihori, N., Saleem, M., Ming, L. K., et al. (2009). The effects of prosocial video games on prosocial behaviors: International evidence from correlational, longitudinal, and experimental studies. *Personality and Social Psychology Bulletin, 35*, 752–763.

Gentile, D. A., & Walsh, D. A. (2002). A normative study of family media habits. *Applied Developmental Psychology, 23*, 157–178.

George, C., Kaplan, N., & Main, M. (1996). *Adult attachment interview protocol* (3rd ed.) Unpublished manuscript, Department of Psychology, University of California at Berkeley.

George, C., & Solomon, J. (2008). The caregiving system: A behavioral systems approach to parenting. In J. Cassidy & P. R. Shaver (Eds.), *Handbook of attachment: Theory, research and clinical applications* (pp. 833–856). New York, NY: Guilford.

Georgieff, M. K. (2008). The role of iron in neurodevelopment: Fetal iron deficiency and the developing hippocampus. *Biochemical Society Transactions, 36*, 1267–1271.

Gerber, J., & Wheeler, L. (2009). On being rejected: A meta-analysis of experimental research on rejection. *Perspectives on Psychological Science, 4*, 468–488.

Gerbner, G., Gross, L., Morgan, M., & Signorelli, N. (1980). The "mainstreaming" of America: Violence profile no. 11. *Journal of Communication, 30*, 10–29.

Gergen, M. (2012). Revisions and visions of retirement: My story. In E. Cole & M. Gergen (2012), *Retiring but not shy: Feminist psychologists create their post-careers* (pp. 290–308). Chagrin Falls, OH: Taos Institute Publications.

Gerhold, M., Laucht, M., Texdorf, C., Schmidt, M. H., & Esser, G. (2002). Early mother–infant interaction as a precursor to childhood social withdrawal. *Child Psychiatry & Human Development, 32*, 277–293.

Gernsbacher, M. A., & Kaschak, M. P. (2003). Neuroimaging studies of language production and comprehension. *Annual Review of Psychology, 54*, 91–114.

Getchell, N., & Robertson, M. A. (1989). Whole body stiffness as a function of developmental level in children's hopping. *Developmental Psychology, 25*, 920–928.

Ghazanfareeon Karlsson, S., & Borrell, K. (2002). Intimacy and autonomy, gender and ageing: Living apart together. *Ageing International, 27*, 11–26.

Gialamas, A., Mittinty M. N., Sawyer, M. G., Zubrick, S. R., & Lynch, J. (2015). Social inequalities and child care quality and their effects on children's development at school entry: Findings from the longitudinal study of Australian children. *Journal of Epidemiology and Community Health, 69*, 841–848.

Gialamas, A., Sawyer, A. C. P., Mittinty, M. N., Zubrick, S. R., Sawyer, M. G., & Lynch, J. (2014). Quality of childcare influences children's attentiveness and emotional regulation at school entry. *The Journal of Pediatrics, 165*, 813–819.

Giambra, L. M., Arenberg, D., Zonderman, A. B., & Kawas, C. (1995). Adult life span changes in immediate visual memory and verbal intelligence. *Psychology and Aging, 10*, 123–139.

Giancola, J. K., Heaney, M. S., Metzger, A. J., & Whitman, B. (2016). An organizational-development approach to implementing mentoring partnerships: Best practices from physician programs. *Consulting Psychology Journal: Practice and Research, 68*, 208–221.

Giarrusso, R., Silverstein, M., & Bengston, V. L. (1996). Family complexity and the grandparenting role. *Generations: Quarterly Journal of the American Society on Aging, 20*, 17–23.

Gibbons, A. (2008). The birth of childhood. *Science, 322*, 1040–1043.

Gibson, E. J., & Pick, A. D. (2000). *An ecological approach to perceptual learning and development.* London: Oxford University Press.

Gibson, F. L., Ungerer, J. A., McMahon, C. A., Leslie, G. I., & Saunders, D. M. (2000). The mother–child relationship following in vitro fertilisation (IVF): Infant attachment, responsivity, and maternal sensitivity. *Journal of Child Psychology and Psychiatry and Allied Disciplines, 41*, 1015–1023.

Gied, J. N., Stockman, M., Weddle, C., et al. (2012). Anatomic magnetic resonance imaging of the developing child and adolescent brain. In V. F. Reyna, S. B. Chapman, M. R. Dougherty, & J. Confrey (Eds.), *The adolescent brain: Learning, reasoning, and decision making* (pp. 15–35). Washington, DC: American Psychological Association.

Gielen, U. P., & Markoulis, D. C. (2001). Preference for principled moral reasoning: A developmental and cross-cultural perspective. In L. L Adler & U. P. Gielen (Eds.), *Cross-cultural topics in psychology* (2nd ed., pp. 81–101). Westport, CT: Greenwood.

Gielen, U. P., & Miao, E. S. C. Y. (2000). Perceived parental behavior and the development of moral reasoning in students from Taiwan. In A. L. Comunian & U. P. Gielen (Eds.), *International perspectives on human development* (pp. 479–503). Lengerich, Germany: Pabst.

Gifford-Smith, M. E., & Brownell, C. A. (2003). Childhood peer relationships: Social acceptance, friendships, and peer networks. *Journal of School Psychology, 41,* 235–284.

Gignac, M. A. M., Lacaille, D., Beaton, D. E., Backman, C. L. Cao, X., & Badley, E. M. (2014). Striking a balance: Work-health -personal life conflict in women and men with arthritis and its association with work outcomes. *Journal of Occupational Rehabilitation, 24,* 573–584.

Gilbert, R. M. (2006). *The eight concepts of Bowen theory.* Falls Church, VA: Leading Systems Press.

Giles, D., Shaw, R. L., & Morgan, W. (2009). Representations of voluntary childlessness in the U.K. press, 1990–2008. *Journal of Health Psychology, 14,* 1218–1228.

Gilissen, R., Koolstra, C. M., van IJzendoorn, M. H., Bakermans-Kranenburg, M. J., & van der Veer, R. (2007). Physiological reactions of preschoolers to fear-inducing film clips: Effects of temperamental fearfulness and quality of the parent–child relationship. *Developmental Psychobiology, 49,* 187–195.

Gillath, O., & Shaver, P. R. (2007). Effects of attachment style and relationship context on selection among relational strategies. *Journal of Research in Personality, 41,* 968–976.

Gillen, M. & Kim, H. (2009). Older women and poverty transition: Consequences of income source changes from widowhood. *Journal of Applied Gerontology, 28,* 320–341.

Gillespie, C. (1989). *Hormones, hot flashes, and mood swings.* New York, NY: Harper & Row.

Gilligan, C. (1977). In a different voice: Women's conceptions of self and morality. *Harvard Educational Review, 47,* 481–517.

Gilligan, C. (1982/1993). *In a different voice: Psychological theory and women's development.* Cambridge, MA: Harvard University Press.

Gilligan, C. (1988). *Mapping the moral domain: A contribution of women's thinking to psycho-logical theory and education.* Cambridge, MA: Harvard University Press.

Ginsburg, H. P., Lee, J. S., & Boyd, J. S. (2008). Mathematics education for young children: What it is and how to promote it. *Social Policy Report, 22.*

Ginsburg, H. P., & Pappas, S. (2004). SES, ethnic, and gender differences in young children's informal addition and subtraction: A clinical interview investigation. *Journal of Applied Developmental Psychology, 25,* 171–192.

Gladwell, M. (2008). *Outliers: The story of success.* Boston, MA: Little, Brown.

Glass, T. A. (1998). Conjugating the "tenses" of function: Discordance among hypothetical, experimental, and enacted function in older adults. *The Gerontologist, 38,* 101–112.

Gleason, T. R. (2002). Social provisions of real and imaginary relationships in early childhood. *Developmental Psychology, 38,* 979–992.

Gleason, T. R., Sebanc, A. M., & Hartup, W. W. (2003). Imaginary companions of preschool children. In M. E. Hertzig & E. A. Farber (Eds.), *Annual progress in child psychiatry and child development: 2000–2001* (pp. 101–121). New York, NY: Brunner-Routledge.

Glenn, N. D., & Kramer, K. B. (1987). Marriages and divorces of children of divorce. *Journal of Marriage and the Family, 49,* 811–826.

Glick, P. C. (1957). *American families.* New York, NY: Wiley.

Gliner, J. A., Morgan, G. A., & Leech, N. L. (2009). *Research methods in applied settings: An integrated approach to design and analysis* (2nd ed.). New York, NY: Routledge.

Glodis, K. A., & Blasi, A. (1993). The sense of self and identity among adolescents and adults. *Journal of Adolescent Research, 8,* 356–380.

Glover, V. (1997). Maternal stress or anxiety in pregnancy and emotional development of the child. *British Journal of Psychiatry, 171,* 105–106.

Godina, E. Z. (2009). The secular trend: History and prospects. *Human Physiology, 35,* 770–776.

Goldbaum, S., Craig, W. M., Pepler, D., & Connolly, J. (2003). Developmental trajectories of victimization: Identifying risk and protective factors. *Journal of Applied School Psychology, 19,* 139–156.

Goldberg, E. (2001). Starboys. In A. Walker, M. Manoogan-O'Dell, L. McGraw, & D. L. White (Eds.), *Families in later life: Connections and transitions* (pp. 250–251). Thousand Oaks, CA: Sage Publications.

Goldberg, S. (1977). Infant development and mother–infant interaction in urban Zambia. In P. H. Leiderman, S. R. Tulkin, & A. Rosenfeld (Eds.), *Culture and infancy: Variations in the human experience* (pp. 211–244). New York: Academic Press.

Goldberg, S., & DiVitto, B. (1995). Parenting children born preterm. In M. H. Bornstein (Ed.), *Handbook of parenting, Vol. 1. Children and parenting* (pp. 209–232). Mahwah, NJ: Erlbaum.

Goldberg, W. A., Clarke-Stewart, K. A., Rice, J. A., & Dellis, E. (2002). Emotional energy as an explanatory construct for fathers' engagement with their infants. *Parenting: Science & Practice, 2,* 379–408.

Golden, J., Conroy, R. M., Lawlor, B. A. (2009). Social support network structure in older people: Underlying dimensions and association with psychological and physical health. *Psychology, Health and Medicine, 14,* 280–290.

Goldenberg, C. N. (1989). Parents' effects on academic grouping for reading: Three case studies. *American Educational Research Journal, 26,* 329–352.

Goldfield, E. C. (1989). Transition from rocking to crawling: Postural constraints on infant movement. *Developmental Psychology, 25,* 913–919.

Goldman, H. I. (2001). Parental reports of "MAMA" sounds in infants: An exploratory study. *Journal of Child Language, 28,* 497–506.

Goldscheider, F. K., Thornton, A., & Yang, L. (2001). Helping out the kids: Expectations about parental support in young adulthood. *Journal of Marriage and the Family, 63,* 727–740.

Goldsmith, D. J., & Dun, S. A. (1997). Sex differences and similarities in the communication of social support. *Journal of Social and Personal Relationships, 14,* 317–337.

Goldsmith, H. H., Buss, A. H., Plomin, R., Rothbart, M. K., Thomas, A., Chess, S., et al. (1987). Roundtable: What is temperament? Four approaches. *Child Development, 58,* 505–529.

Goldsmith, H. H., & Campos, J. J. (1986). Fundamental issues in the study of early development: The Denver twin temperament study. In M. E. Lamb, A. Brown, & B. Rogoff (Eds.), *Advances in developmental psychology* (Vol. 4, pp. 231–283). New York: Psychology Press.

Goldston, D. B., Molock, S. D., Whitbeck, L. B., Murakami, J. L., Zayas, L. H., & Hall, G. C. N. (2008). Cultural considerations in adolescent suicide prevention and psychosocial treatment. *American Psychologist, 63,* 14–31.

Goleman, D. (2006). *Social intelligence: The new science of human relationships.* New York, NY: Bantam Books.

Golinkoff, R. M., Can, D. D., Soderstrom, M., & Hirsh-Pasek, K. (2015). (Baby) talk to me: The social context of infant-directed speech and its effects on early language acquisition. *Current Directions in Psychological Science, 24,* 339–344.

Golinkoff, R. M., Hirsh-Pasek, K., Bailey, L. M., & Wenger, N. R. (1992). Young children and adults use lexical principles to learn new nouns. *Developmental Psychology, 28,* 99–108.

Golombok, S. (2013). Families created by reproductive donation: Issues and research. *Child Development Perspectives, 7,* 61–65.

Golombok, S. (2015). *Modern families: Parents and children in new family forms.* Cambridge, U.K.: Cambridge University Press.

Golombok, S., Murray, C., Jadva, V., MacCallum, F., & Lycett, E. (2004). Families created through surrogacy arrangements: Parent–child relationships in the first year of life. *Developmental Psychology, 40,* 400–411.

Golombok, S., Readings, J., Blake, L., Casey, P., Marks, A., & Jadva, V. (2011). Families created through surrogacy: Mother-child relationships and children's psychological adjustment at age 7. *Developmental Psychology, 47*, 1579–1588.

Goodfellow, J., & Laverty, J. (2003). Grandparents supporting working families: Satisfaction and choice in the provision of child care. *Family Matters, 66*, 14–19.

Goodman, C. C. (2003). Intergenerational triads in grandparent-headed families. *Journal of Gerontology: Series B: Psychological Sciences and Social Sciences, 58B*, S281–S289.

Goodman, E., & Whitaker, R. C. (2002). A prospective study of the role of depression in the development and persistence of adolescent obesity. *Pediatrics, 110*, 497–504.

Goodman, W. B., & Crouter, A. C. (2009). Longitudinal associations between maternal work stress, negative work-family spillover, and depressive symptoms. *Family Relations: An Interdisciplinary Journal of Applied Family Studies, 58*, 245–258.

Goodway, Ozman, & Gallahue. (2012). Motor development in young children. In O. N. Saracho and B. Spodek (Eds.), *Handbook of research on the education of young children*. New York, NY: Routledge.

Goodwin, R. D., & Friedman, H. S. (2006). Health status and the five-factor personality traits in a nationally representative sample. *Journal of Health Psychology, 11*, 643–654.

Goodwyn, S., Acredolo, L., & Brown, C. (2000). Impact of symbolic gesturing on early language development. *Journal of Nonverbal Behavior, 24*, 81–103.

Goossens, L. (2012). Genes, environments, and interactions as new challenges for European developmental psychology: The sample case of adolescent loneliness. *European Journal of Developmental Psychology, 9*, 432–445.

Gopnik, A., & Meltzoff, A. N. (1987). The development of categorization in the second year and its relation to other cognitive and linguistic developments. *Child Development, 58*, 1523–1531.

Gopnik, A., & Meltzoff, A. N. (1992). Categorization and naming: Basic-level sorting in eighteen-month-olds and its relation to language. *Child Development, 63*, 1091–1103.

Gordon, S. (2013). Physician-assisted suicide program rarely used study finds. *U.S. News and World Report, Health.* Retrieved from http://health.usnews.com/health-news/news/articles/2013/04/10/physician-assisted-suicide-program-rarely-used-study-find

Gore, S., Aseltine, R. H., & Colten, M. E. (1993). Gender, social-relational involvement, and depression. *Journal of Research on Adolescence, 3*, 101–126.

Gorer, G. (1938). *Himalayan village: An account of the Lepchas of Sikkim*. London: Michael Joseph.

Gornick, J. C., & Jäntti, M. (2016). Poverty. *Pathways, The Poverty and Inequality Report, 2016*. The Stanford Center on Poverty and Inequality, pp. 15–24.

Gornick, V. (1971, January 10). Consciousness. *New York Times Magazine.*

Gottesman, I. I. (1997). Twins: En route to QTLs for cognition. *Science, 276*, 1522–1523.

Gottfried, M. A. (2015). Can center-based childcare reduce the odds of early chronic absenteeism? *Early Childhood Research Quarterly, 32*, 160–173.

Gottman, J. M. (2011). *The science of trust: Emotional attunement for couples.* New York, NY: Norton.

Gottman, J. M., Coan, J., Carrere, S., & Swanson, C. (1998). Predicting marital happiness and stability from newlywed interactions. *Journal of Marriage and the Family, 60*, 5–22.

Gottman, J. M., & Silver, N. (2000). *The seven principles for making marriage work.* New York, NY: Crown.

Gow, A. J., Pattie, A., Whiteman, M. C., Whalley, L. J., & Deary, I. J. (2007). Social support and successful aging: Investigating the relationships between lifetime cognitive change and life satisfaction. *Journal of Individual Differences, 28*, 103–115.

Goyer, A. (2009). *Grandparents' visitation rights.* AARP. Retrieved from http://www.aarp.org/relationships/grandparenting/info-05-2009/goyer_grandparent_visitation.html

Graber, J. A., & Sontag, L. M. (2009). Internalizing problems during adolescence. In R. M. Lerner & L. Steinberg (Eds.), *Handbook of adolescent psychology. Vol. 1. Individual bases of adolescent development* (3rd ed., pp. 642–682). Hoboken, NJ: John Wiley.

Graham, A. M., Pfeifer, J. H., Fisher, P. A. Carpenter, S., & Fair, D. A. (2015). Early life stress is associated with default system integrity and emotionality during infancy. *Journal of Child Psychology and Psychiatry, 56*, 1212–1222.

Graham, C., & Pozuelo, J. R. (2016). *Happiness, stress, and age: How the U-curve varies people and places.* Retrieved from https://www.brookings.edu/research/happiness-stress-and-age-how-the-u-curve-varies-across-people-and-places/

Graham, J., Nosek, B. A., Haidt, J., Iyer, R., Koleva, S., & Ditto, P. H. (2011). Mapping the moral domain. *Journal of Personality and Social Psychology, 101*, 366–385.

Graham, M. J., Larsen, U., & Xu, X. (1999). Secular trend in age at menarche in China: A case study of two rural counties in Anhui province. *Journal of Biosocial Science, 31*, 257–267.

Graham, S. (2004). Ethnicity and peer harassment during early adolescence. In T. Urdan & F. Pajares (Eds.), *Educating adolescents: Challenges and strategies.* Greenwich, CT: Information Age Publishing.

Graham, S. (2011). School racial/ethnic diversity and disparities in mental health and academic outcomes. In G. Carlo, L. J. Crockett, & M. A. Carranza (Eds.), *Health disparities in youth and families, Nebraska Symposium on Motivation* (pp. 73–96). New York: Springer.

Graham, S., & Juvonen, J. (2002). Ethnicity, peer harassment, and adjustment in middle school: An exploratory study. *Journal of Early Adolescence, 22*, 173–199.

Graham, S., & Weiner, B. (1986). From an attributional theory of emotion to developmental psychology: A round-trip ticket? *Social Cognition, 4*, 152–179.

Graham, S., & Weiner, B. (1991). Testing judgments about attribution-emotion-action linkages: A lifespan approach. *Social Cognition, 9*, 254–276.

Grandquist, H. (1950). *Child problems among the Arabs.* Helsinki, Finland: Soderstrom.

Grant, B. (2003). What is gentrification? *PBS.org.* Retrieved from http://www.pbs.org/pov/flagwars/special_gentrification.ph

Grantham-McGregor, S., Cheung, Y. B., Cueto, S., Glewwe, P., Richter, L., & Strupp, B. (2007). Developmental potential in the first 5 years for children in developing countries. *The Lancet, 369*, 60–70.

Grassley, J. S., & Eschiti, V. (2011). The value of listening to grandmothers' infant-feeding stories. *Journal of Perinatal Education, 20*, 134–141.

Graves, W. (2016). *World champion Biles begins run-up to Rio at Pac-Rims.* Retrieved from http://bigstory.ap.org/article/89f5cb6318bd46bb91f97ac697a8ad82/world-champion-biles-begins-run-rio-pac-rims

Grawitch, M. J., & Ballard, D. W. (Eds.). (2016). *The psychologically healthy workplace: Building a win-win environment for organizations and employees.* Washington, DC: American Psychological Association.

Green, C. (2015). "Because we like to": Young children hiding in their home environment. *Early Childhood Education Journal, 43*, 327–336.

Green, C. D. (2009). Darwinian theory, functionalism, and the first American psychological revolution. *American Psychologist, 64*, 75–83.

Green, R. J., Bettinger, M., & Zacks, E. (1996). Are lesbian couples fused and gay male couples disengaged? Questioning gender straightjackets. In J. Laird & R. J. Green (Eds.), *Lesbians and gays in couples and families: A handbook for therapists* (pp. 185–230). San Francisco, CA: Jossey-Bass.

Green, R. J., & Hill, J. H. (2003). Sex and higher education: Do men and women attend college for different reasons? *College Student Journal, 37*, 557–563.

Greenberg, E. F., & Nay, W. R. (1982). The intergenerational transmission of marital instability reconsidered. *Journal of Marriage and the Family, 44*, 335–347.

Greenberg, J. (2008). Understanding the vital human quest for self-esteem. *Perspectives on Psychological Science, 3*, 48–55.

Greenberg, M. T., Riggs, N. R., & Blair, C. (2007). The role of preventive interventions in enhancing neurocognitive functioning and promoting competence in adolescence. In D. Romer & E. F. Walker (Eds.), *Adolescent psychopathology and the developing* brain: Integrating brain and prevention science (pp. 441–462). New York, NY: Oxford University Press.

Greene, R. R. (2008). Psychosocial theory. In B. A. Thyer, K. M. Sowers, & C. N. Dulmus (Eds.), *Comprehensive handbook of social work and social welfare, Vol. 2. Human behavior in the social environment* (pp. 229–255). Hoboken, NJ: John Wiley & Sons.

Greenfield, P. M. (2009). Linking social change and developmental change: Shifting pathways of human development. *Developmental Psychology, 45*, 401–418.

Greenfield, P. M., & Childs, C. P. (1991). Developmental continuity in biocultural context. In R. Cohen & A. W. Siegel (Eds.), *Context and development* (pp. 135–159). Hillsdale, NJ: Erlbaum.

Greenfield, P. M., Keller, H., Fuglini, A., & Maynard, A. (2003). Cultural pathways through universal development. *Annual Review of Psychology, 54*, 461–490.

Greenfield, P. M., Suzuki, L. K., & Rothstein-Fisch, C. (2006). Cultural pathways through human development. In W. Damon (Series Ed.), I. E. Sigel & K. A. Renninger (Vol. Eds.), *Handbook of cultural psychology Vol. 4. Child psychology and practice* (6th ed., pp. 655–699). New York, NY: Wiley.

Greenfield, P. M., Trumbull, E., & Rothstein-Fisch, C. (2003). Bridging cultures. *Cross-Cultural Psychology Bulletin, 37*, 6–17.

Greenhaus, J. H., & Allen, T. D. (2011). Work–family balance: A review and extension of the literature. In J. C. Quick & L. E. Tetrick (Eds.), *Handbook of occupational health psychology* (2nd ed., pp. 165–183). Washington, DC: American Psychological Association.

Gregor, T. (1977). *Mehinaku: The drama of daily life in a Brazilian Indian village.* Chicago, IL: University of Chicago Press.

Gregory, K. M., Kim, A. S., & Whiren, A. (2003). The effect of verbal scaffolding on the complexity of preschool children's block constructions. In D. E. Lytle (Ed.), *Play and educational theory and practice* (pp. 117–133). Westport, CT: Greenwood.

Gregory, L. W. (1995). The "turnaround" process: Factors influencing the school success of urban youth. *Journal of Adolescent Research, 10*, 136–154.

Greksa, L. P., & Korbin, J. E. (2004). Amish. In C. R. Ember & M. Ember (Eds.), *Encyclopedia of medical anthropology* (pp. 557–563). New York, NY: Springer.

Grier, L. K. (2013). Relations between perceived competence, importance ratings, and self-worth among African American school-age children. *Journal of Black Psychology, 39*, 3–27.

Grigsby, C., Baumann, D., Gregorich, S. E., & Roberts-Gray, C. (1990). Disaffiliation to entrenchment: A model for understanding homelessness. *Journal of Social Issues, 46*, 141–156.

Grimm, K. J., Steele, J. S., Mashburn, A. J., Burchinal, M., & Pianta, R. C. (2010). Early behavioral associations of achievement trajectories. *Developmental Psychology, 46*, 976–983.

Groh, A. M., & Roisman, G. I. (2009). Adults' autonomic and subjective emotional responses to infant vocalizations: The role of secure base script knowledge. *Developmental Psychology, 45*, 889–893.

Grolnick, W. S., & Farkas, M. (2012). Parenting and self-regulation. In M. H. Bornstein (Ed.), *Handbook of parenting, Vol. 5. Practical issues in parenting* (2nd ed., pp. 89–110). New York, NY: Psychology Press.

Groome, L. J., Mooney, D. M., Holland, S. B., Smith, Y. D., Atterbury, J. L., & Dykman, R. A. (2000). Temporal pattern and spectral complexity as stimulus parameters for eliciting a cardiac orienting reflex inhuman fetuses. *Perception and Psychophysics, 62*, 313–320.

Groome, L. J., Swiber, M. J., Bentz, L. S., Lynn, S., Holland, S. B., et al. (1995). Maternal anxiety during pregnancy: Effect on fetal behavior at 38 to 40 weeks of gestation. *Journal of Developmental and Behavioral Pediatrics, 16*, 391–396.

Gross, H., & Pattison, H. (2007). *Sanctioning pregnancy.* London: Routledge.

Gross, J. (2004). Older women team up to face future together. *New York Times.* Retrieved from http://query.nytimes.com/gst/fullpage.html?res=9F01E3DF113CF934A15751C0A9629C8B63&sec=&spon=&pagewanted=1

Grossman, F. K., Eichler, L. S., Winickoff, S. A., with Anzalone, M. K., Gofseyeff, M. H., & Sargent, S. P. (1980). *Pregnancy, birth, and parenthood.* San Francisco, CA: Jossey-Bass.

Grossmann, I., Na, J., Varnuma, M. E. W., Park, D. C., Kitayama, S., & Nisbett, R. E. (2010). Reasoning about social conflicts improves into old age. *PNAS Proceedings of the National Academy of Sciences of the United States of America, 107*, 7246–7250.

Grossman, T. (2013). The role of the medial prefrontal cortex in early social cognition. *Frontiers in Human Neuroscience, 7*, article 340, 1–6.

Grossman, T. (2013). The early development of processing emotions in voice and face. In P. Belin, Pasca, S. Campanella, & T. Ethofer, (Eds.), *Integrating face and voice in person perception* (pp. 95–116). New York, NY: Springer Science + Business Media.

Grotevant, H. D. (2009). Emotional distance regulation over the life course in adoptive kinship networks. In G. M. Wrobel & E. Neil (Eds.), *International advances in adoption research for practice* (pp. 295–316). New York, NY: Wiley-Blackwell.

Growing Bolder. (2008). *Ruth1898. Ruth's first blog.* Retrieved from http://growingbolder.com/media/health/aging/ruths-first-blog-start-hee-140968.html

Gruber, K. J., Cupito, S. H., & Dobson, C. F. (2013). Impact of doulas on health birth outcomes. *The Journal of Perinatal Education, 22*, 49–58.

Grunewaldt, K. H., Fjørtoft, T., Bjuland, K. H. et al. (2014). Follow-up at age 10 years in ELBW children: Functional outcome, brain morphology and results from motor assessments in infancy. *Early Human Development, 90*, 571–578.

Grusec, J. E. (1992). Social learning theory and developmental psychology: The legacies of Robert Sears and Albert Bandura. *Developmental Psychology, 28*, 776–786.

Grusec, J. E., & Abramovitch, R. (1982). Imitation of peers and adults in a natural setting: A functional analysis. *Child Development, 53*, 636–642.

Grusky, D. B., Mattingly, M. J., & Varner, C. (2015). Executive summary. *Pathways: The Poverty and Inequality Report, 2015.* Stanford, CA: The Stanford Center on Poverty and Inequality.

Guay, R., Ratelle, C. F., Senécal, C., Larose, S., & Deschênes, A. (2006). Distinguishing developmental from chronic career indecision: Self-efficacy, autonomy, and social support. *Journal of Career Assessment, 14*, 235–251.

Gulko, J., Doyle, A., Serbin, L. A., & White, D. R. (1988). Conservation skills: A replicated study of order of acquisition across tasks. *Journal of Genetic Psychology, 149*, 425–439.

Gunnar, M. R. (2000). Early adversity and the development of stress reactivity and regulation. In C. Nelson (Ed.), *Minnesota Symposium on Child Psychology: Vol. 31. The effects of adversity on neurobehavioral development* (pp. 163–200). Mahwah, NJ: Erlbaum.

Günther, K-B., & Hennies, J. (2012). From pre-symbolic gestures to language: Multisensory early intervention in deaf children. In A. Foolen, U. M. Lüdtke, T. P. Racine, P. Timothy, & J. Zlatev (Eds.), *Moving ourselves, moving others: Motion and emotion in intersubjectivity, consciousness and language. Consciousness & emotion book series. Vol 6.* (pp. 369–382). Amsterdam, Netherlands: John Benjamins Publishing Company.

Guo, J. (2015). These states are terrible at hanging on to their college-bound students. *Washington Post.* Retrieved from https://www.washingtonpost.com/blogs/govbeat/wp/2015/04/08/these-states-are-terrible-at-hanging-on-to-their-college-bound-students/

Gur, R. C., Turetsky, B. I., Matsui, M., Yan, M., Bilker, W., Hughett, P., et al. (1999). Sex differences in brain gray and white matter in healthy young adults: Correlations with cognitive performance. *The Journal of Neuroscience, 19*, 4065–4072.

Guralnik, J. M., & Kaplan, G. A. (1989). Predictors of healthy aging: Prospective evidence from the Alameda County study. *American Journal of Public Health, 79*, 703–708.

Guralnik, J. M., & Simonsick, E. M. (1993). Physical disability in older Americans. *Journal of Gerontology, 48*, 3–10.

Gurin, P., & Markus, H. (1988). Group identity: The psychological mechanisms of durable salience. *Revue Internationale de Psychologie Sociale, 1,* 257–274.

Gurung, R.A.R., Dunkel-Schetter, C., Collins, C., et al. (2004). Psychosocial predictors of prenatal anxiety. *Journal of Social and Clinical Psychology, 24,* 497–519.

Gustke, C. (2015). Small residences for the elderly provide more personal homelike care. *The New York Times.* Retrieved from the internet at https://www.nytimes .com/2015/11/21/your-money/small -residences-for-the-elderly-provide-more -personal-homelike-care.html?_r=0

Gutman, L., & Midgley, C. (2000). The role of protective factors in supporting the academic achievement of poor African American students during the middle school transition. *Journal of Youth and Adolescence, 29,* 223–248.

Gutmann, D. (1987). *Reclaimed powers: Toward a new psychology of men and women in later life.* New York, NY: Basic Books.

Guttmacher Institute. (2007). *Get in the know: Medical abortions.* Retrieved from http:// www.guttmacher .org/in-the-know /medical.html

Guttmacher Institute. (2008). *Facts on induced abortion in the United States.* Retrieved from www.guttmacher.org/pubs /fb_induced _abortion.html

Guttmacher Institute. (2013). Substance abuse during pregnancy. *State Policies in Brief.* Retrieved from www .guttmacher.org/;ubs /spib_SADP.pdf

Guttmacher Institute. (2016a). Substance abuse during pregnancy: *State Policies in Brief.* Retrieved from http://www.guttmacher.org /statecenter/spibs/spib_SADP.pdf

Guttmacher Institute. (2016b). American teens' sources of sexual health education. Retrieved from https://www.guttmacher .org/fact-sheet/facts-american-teens -sources-information-about-sex

Guttmacher Institute. (2016c). *Unintended pregnancy.* Retrieved from https://www .guttmacher.org/sites/default/files/factsheet /fb-unintended-pregnancy-us_0.pdf

Guttmann, B. (1932). *Die Stammeslehvender des Chagga* (Vol. 1). Munich, Germany: Beck.

Ha, J.-H., Carr, D., Utz, R. L., & Nesse, R. (2006). Older adults' perceptions of inter-generational support after widowhood: How do men and women differ? *Journal of Family Issues, 27,* 3–30.

Hack, M., & Fanaroff, A. A. (1999). Outcomes of children of extremely low birth weight and gestational age in the 1990s. *Early Human Development, 53,* 192–218.

Hack, M., Taylor, H. G., Drotar, D., Schluchter, M., Cartar, L., Andreias, L., et al. (2005). Chronic conditions, functional limitations, and special health care needs of school aged children born with extremely low-birth-weight in the 1990s. *Journal of the Medical Association, 294,* 318–325.

Haffner, D. W. (1998). Facing facts: Sexual health for American adolescents. *Journal of Adolescent Health, 22,* 453–459.

Hahn, A. C., & Perrett, D. I. (2014). Neural and behavioral responses to attractiveness in adult and infant faces. *Neuroscience and Biobehavioral Reviews, 46*(Part 4), 591–603.

Hahn, R., Fuqua-Whitley, D., Wethington, H., Lowy, J., Crosby, A., Fullilove, M., Johnson, R., Liberman, A., Moscicki, E., Price, L., Snyder, S., Tuma, F., Cory, S., Stone, G., Mukhopadhaya, K., Chattopadhyay, S., Dahlberg, L., & Task Force on Community Preventive Services. (2007). Effectiveness of universal school-based programs to prevent violent and aggressive behavior: A systematic review. *American Journal of Preventive Medicine, 33*(Suppl 2), S114–S129.

Hahn, R. A., & Muecke, M. A. (1987). The anthropology of birth in five U.S. ethnic populations: Implications for obstetrical practice. *Current Problems in Obstetrics, Gynecology, and Fertility, 10,* 133–171.

Haidt, J. (2007). The new synthesis in moral psychology. *Science, 316,* 998–1002.

Haidt, J. (2008). Morality. *Perspective on Psychological Science, 3,* 65–72.

Hakoyama, M., & MaloneBeach, E. E. (2013). Predictors of grandparent-grandchild close-ness: An ecological perspective. *Journal of Intergenerational Relationships, 11,* 32–49.

Hakuta, K., & Garcia, E. E. (1989). Bilingual-ism and education. *American Psychologist, 44,* 374–379.

Halberstadt, A. G., & Lozada, F. T. (2011). Emotion development in infancy through the lens of culture. *Emotion Review, 3,* 158–168.

Halfon, N., Inkelas, M., & Hochstein, M. (2000). The health development orga-nization: An organizational approach to achieving child health development. *Milbank Quarterly, 78,* 447–497.

Halford, G. S., & Boyle, F. M. (1985). Do young children understand conservation of number? *Child Development, 56,* 165–176.

Halford, W. K., Hahlweg, K., & Dunne, M. (1990). Cross-cultural study of marital communication and marital distress. *Journal of Marriage and the Family, 52,* 487–500.

Halim, M. L., Ruble, D. N., Tamis-LeMonda, C. S., Zosuls, K. M., Lurye, L. E., & Greulich, F. K. (2014). Pink frilly dresses and the avoidance of all things "girly": Children's appearance rigidity and cogni-tive theories of gender development. *Developmental Psychology, 50,* 1091–1101.

Halisch, F., & Geppert, U. (2001). Motives, personal goals and life satisfaction in old age: First results from the Munich twin study (GOLD). In A. Efklides, J. Kuhl, & R. M. Sorrentino (Eds.), *Trends and pros-pects in motivation research* (pp. 389–409). Dordrecht, Netherlands: Kluwer Academic Publishers.

Halleröd, B., Örestig, J., & Stattin, M. (2013). Leaving the labor market: The impact of exit routes from employment to retirement on health and well-being in old age. *European Journal of Aging, 10,* 25–35.

Hallquist, M. N., Hipwell, A. E., & Stepp, S. D. (2015). Poor self-control and harsh punishment in childhood prospectively predict borderline personality symptoms in adolescent girls. *Journal of Abnormal Psychology, 124,* 549–564.

Hamachek, D. (1985). The self's development and ego growth: Conceptual analysis and implications for counselors. *Journal of Counseling and Development, 64,* 136–142.

Hamachek, D. (1994). Changes in the self from a developmental/psychosocial perspective. In T. M. Brinthaupt & R. P. Lipka (Eds.), *Changing the self: Philosophies, techniques, and experiences* (pp. 21–68). Albany, NY: State University of New York Press.

Hamarat, E., Thompson, D., Zabrucky, K. M., Steele, D., Matheny, K. B., & Aysan, F. (2001). Perceived stress and coping resource availability as predictors of life satisfaction in young, middle-aged, and older adults. *Experimental Aging Research, 27,* 181–196.

Hamblen, J., & Barnett, E. (2016). PTSD in children and adolescents. *PTSD: National Center for PTSD.* Retrieved from http://www .ptsd.va.gov/professional/treatment/children /ptsd_in_children_and_adolescents _overview_for_professionals.asp

Hamilton, B. E. (2004). Reproduction rates for 1990–2002 and intrinsic rates for 2000–2001: United States. *National Vital Statistics Reports, 52* (Whole No. 17).

Hamilton, B. E., Martin, J. A., Osterman, M. J. K., et al. (2015). Births: Final data for 2014. *National Vital Statistics Reports, 64* no 12. Hyattsville, MD: National Center for Health Statistics.

Hamilton, W. D. (1964). The genetical evolu-tion of social behavior. *Journal of Theoreti-cal Biology, 7,* 1–52.

Hammen, C. (2009). Adolescent depression: Stressful interpersonal contexts and risk for recurrence. *Current Direction in Psycho-logical Science, 18,* 200–204.

Hammer, C. S. (2001). Come and sit down and let Mama read: Book reading interac-tions between African American mothers and their infants. In J. L. Harris & A. G. Kamhi (Eds.), *Literacy in African American communities* (pp. 21–43). Mahwah, NJ: Erlbaum.

Hammill, D. D. (2004). What we know about correlates of reading. *Exceptional Children, 70,* 453–468.

Hamon, R. R., & Blieszner, R. (1990). Filial responsibility expectations among adult child–older parent pairs. *Journal of Geron-tology, 45,* P110–P112.

Han, W. -J. & Huang, C.-C. (2010). The for-gotten treasure: Bilingualism and Asian children's emotional and behavioral health. *American Journal of Public Health, 100,* 831–838.

Handy, C. (1996). *Beyond certainty: The chang-ing worlds of organizations.* Cambridge, MA: Harvard Business School Press.

Handy, C. (2001). A world of fleas and elephants. In W. Bennis & G. M. Spreitzer (Eds.), *The future of leadership: Today's top leadership thinkers speak to tomorrow's* leaders (pp. 29–40). San Francisco, CA: Jossey-Bass.

Handy, C. (2008). *Myself and other more important matters.* New York, NY: AMACOM.

Haney, M., & Hill, J. (2004). Relationships between parent-teaching activities and emergent literacy in preschool children. *Early Child Development and Care, 174,* 215–228.

Hanford, E. (2013). Quitting college. *American Radio Works.* Retrieved http://americanradioworks.publicradio.org/features/tomorrows-college/dropouts/quitting-college.html

Hanna-Attisha, M., LaChance, J., Sadler, R. C., & Schnepp, A. C. (2016). Elevated blood lead levels in children associated with the Flint drinking water crisis: A spatial analysis of risk and public health response. *American Journal of Public Health, 106,* 283–290.

Hans, S. L. (1987). Maternal drug addiction and young children. *Division of Child, Youth, and Family Services Newsletter, 10,* 5, 15.

Hansson, R. D., & Stroebe, M. S. (2007). *Bereavement in late life: Coping, adaptation and developmental influences.* Washington, DC: American Psychological Association.

Harder, S., Lange, T., Hansen, G. F., Væver, M., & Køppe, S. (2015). A longitudinal study of coordination in mother-infant vocal interaction from age 4 to 10 months. *Developmental Psychology, 51,* 1778–1790.

Hardie, J. H. (2015). Women's work? Predictors of young men's aspirations for entering traditionally female-dominated occupations. *Sex Roles, 72,* 349–362.

Hardy, J. B., & Duggan, A. K. (1988). Teenage fathers and the fathers of infants of urban teenage mothers. *American Journal of Public Health, 78,* 919–922.

Harel, J., & Scher, A. (2003). Insufficient responsiveness in ambivalent mother–infant relationships: Contextual and affective aspects. *Infant Behavior and Development, 26,* 371–383.

Harkness, S., & Super, C. M. (2012). Culture and parenting. In M. H. Bornstein (Ed.), *Handbook of parenting, Vol. 1. Children and parenting* (2nd ed., pp. 253–280). New York, NY: Psychology Press.

Harrington, C. C., & Boardman, S. K. (2000). *Paths to success: Beating the odds in American society.* Cambridge, MA: Harvard University Press.

Harris, P. L., & Kavanaugh, R. D. (1993). Young children's understanding of pretense. *Monographs of the Society for Research in Child Development, Serial No. 231, 58*(1).

Harris, P. L. (2007). Commentary: Time for questions. *Monographs of the Society for Research in Child Development, Serial No. 286, 72*(1), 113–120.

Harris, T., Kovar, M. G., Suzman, R., Kleinman, J. C., & Feldman, J. J. (1989). Longitudinal study of physical ability in the oldest old. *American Journal of Public Health, 79,* 698–702.

Harris-Kojetin, L., Sengupta, M., Park-Lee, E., et al. (2016). *Long-term care providers and services users in the United States: Data from the National Study of Long-Term Care Providers, 2013–2014.* National Center for Health Statistics. *VitalHealth Statistics, 3*(38). Retrieved from http://www.cdc.gov/nchs/data/series/sr_03/sr03_038.pdf

Harrison, D., Bueno, M., Yamada, J., Adams-Webber, T., & Stevens, B. (2010). Analgesic effects of sweet tasting solutions for infants: Current state of equipoise. *Pediatrics, 126,* 894–902.

Hart, B., & Risley, T. R. (1992). American parenting of language-learning children: Persisting differences in family-child interactions observed in natural home environments. *Developmental Psychology, 28,* 1096–1105.

Hart, C. H., Ladd, G. W., & Burleson, B. R. (1990). Children's expectations of the outcomes of social strategies: Relations with sociometric status and maternal disciplinary styles. *Child Development, 61,* 127–137.

Hart, C. H., Newell, L. D., & Olsen, S. F. (2003). Parenting skills and social- communicative competence in childhood. In J. O. Greene & B. R. Burleson (Eds.), *Handbook of communication and social interaction skills* (pp. 753–797). Mahwah, NJ: Erlbaum.

Hart, D., & Fegley, S. (1995). Prosocial behavior and caring in adolescence: Relations to self-understanding and social judgment. *Child Development, 66,* 1346–1359.

Hart, H. M., McAdams, D. P., Hirsch, B. J., & Bauer, J. J. (2001). Generativity and social involvement among African Americans and White adults. *Journal of Research in Personality, 35,* 209–230.

Harter, S. (1982). The perceived competence scale for children. *Child Development, 53,* 87–97.

Harter, S. (1993). Visions of self: Beyond the me in the mirror. In J. E. Jacobs (Ed.), *Nebraska Symposium on Motivation: 1992* (Vol. 40, pp. 99–144). Lincoln, NE: University of Nebraska Press.

Harter, S. (2012). Emerging self processes during childhood and adolescence. In M. R. Leary & J. P. Tangney (Eds.), *Handbook of self and identity* (2nd ed., pp. 680–715). New York, NY: Guilford Press.

Harter, S., & Bukowski, W. M. (2012). *The construction of the self: Developmental and sociocultural foundations* (2nd ed.). New York, NY: Guilford Press.

Harter, S., Whitesell, N. R., & Kowalski, P. (1992). Individual differences in the effects of educational transitions on young adolescents' perceptions of competence and motivational orientation. *American Educational Research Journal, 29,* 777–807.

Hartlage, S. A., Brandenburg, D. L., & Kravitz, H. M. (2004). Premenstrual exacerbation of depressive disorders in a community-based sample in the United States. *Psychosomatic Medicine, 66,* 698–706.

Hartley, A. (2006). Changing role of the speed of processing construct in the cognitive psychology of human aging. In J. E. Birren & K. W. Schaie (Eds.), *Handbook of the psychology of aging* (6th ed., pp. 183–207). Amsterdam, Netherlands: Elsevier.

Hartley, B. L., & Sutton, R. M. (2013). A stereotype threat account of boys' academic underachievement. *Child Development, 84,* 1716–1733.

Hartmann, H. (1939/1964). *Ego psychology and the problem of adaptation.* New York, NY: International Universities Press.

Hartshorne, J. K., & Salem-Hartshorne, N. (2009). Birth order effects in the formation of long-term relationships. *Journal of Individual Psychology, 65,* 156–176.

Hartup, W. W. (1989). Social relationships and their developmental significance. *American Psychologist, 44,* 120–126.

Harvath, T. S., Miller, L. L., Smith, K. A., Clark, L. D., Jackson, A., & Ganzini, L. (2006). Dilemmas encountered by hospice workers when patients wish to hasten death. *Journal of Hospice and Palliative Nursing, 8,* 200–209.

Harvey, B., Mette-Gagné, C., Stack, D. M., Serbin, L. A., Ledingham, J. E., & Schwartzman, A. E. (2016). Risk and protective factors for autonomy-supportive and controlling parenting in high-risk families. *Journal of Applied Developmental Psychology, 43,* 18–28.

Harvey, J. H., & Fine, M. A. (2004). *Children of divorce: Stories of loss and growth.* Mahwah, NJ: Lawrence Erlbaum.

Harvey, J. H., Stein, S. K., & Scott, P. K. (1995). Fifty years of grief: Accounts and reported psychological reactions of Normandy invasion veterans. *Journal of Narrative and Life History, 5,* 315–332.

Hawkins, J. D., Jenson, J. M., Catalano, R., Fraser, M. W., Botvin, G. J., Shapiro, V., Brown, C. H., Beardslee, W., Brent, D., Leslie, L. K., Rotheram-Borus, M. J., Shea, P., Shih, A., Anthony, E., Haggerty, K. P., Bender, K., Gorman-Smith, D., Casey, E., & Stone, S. (2015). *Unleashing the power of prevention.* Discussion Paper, Institute of Medicine and National Research Council, Washington, DC.

Harwood, R. L. (1992). The influence of culturally derived values on Anglo and Puerto Rican mothers' perceptions of attachment behavior. *Child Development, 63,* 822–839.

Hatcher, B., Nuner, J., & Paulsel, J. (2012). Kindergarten readiness and preschools: Teachers' and parents' beliefs within and across programs. *Early Childhood Research and Practice, 14,* 1–17.

Hatfield, E., & Specher, S. (1995). Men's and women's preferences in marital partners in the United States, Russia, and Japan. *Journal of Cross-Cultural Psychology, 26,* 728–750.

Hatzenbuehler, M. L., McLaughlin, K. A., & Xuan, Z. (2012). Social networks and risk for depressive symptoms in a national sample of sexual minority youth. *Social Science and Medicine, 75*, 1184–1191.

Hauser, M. (2006). *Moral minds: How nature designed our universal sense of right and wrong.* New York, NY: HarperCollins.

Havighurst, R. J. (1972). *Developmental tasks and education* (3rd ed.). New York, NY: David McKay.

Hawkins, A. J., & Dollahite, D. C. (1997). *Generative fathering: Beyond the deficit perspectives.* Thousand Oaks, CA: Sage.

Hawkins, J. L., Weisberg, C., & Ray, D. W. (1980). Spouse differences in communication style preference, perception, behavior. *Journal of Marriage and the Family, 42*, 585–593.

Hawley, G. A. (1988). *Measures of psychosocial development.* Odessa, FL: Psychological Assessment Resources.

Hay, D. F., & Cook, K. V. (2007). The transformation of prosocial behavior from infancy to childhood. In C. A. Brownell, & C. B. Kopp (Eds.), *Socioemotional development in the toddler years: Transitions and transformations* (pp. 100–131). New York, NY: Guilford Press.

Hayflick, L. (2000). The future of aging. *Nature, 408*, 267–269.

Haynes, J., & Miller, J. (2003). *Inconceivable conceptions: Psychological aspects of infertility and reproductive technology.* New York, NY: Brunner-Routledge.

Hayward, M. D., Crimmins, E. M., Miles, T. P., & Yang, Y. (2000). The significance of socioeconomic status in explaining the racial gap in chronic health conditions. *American Sociological Review, 65*, 910–930.

Hayward, R. D., & Krause, N. (2013). Change in church-based social support relationships during older adulthood. *The Journals of Gerontology: Series B. Psychological Sciences and Social Sciences. 68B*, 85–96.

Hazan, C., Campa, M., & Gur-Yaish, N. (2006). Attachment across the lifespan. In P. Noller & J. Feeney (Eds.), *Close relationships: Functions, forms and processes* (pp. 189–209). Hove, England: Psychology Press.

Hazan, C., & Shaver, P. R. (1987). Attachment as an organizational framework for research on close relationships. *Journal of Personality and Social Psychology, 52*, 511–524.

Hazell, L. V. (1997). Cross-cultural funeral rites. *The Director, 69*, 53–55.

Hazlett, H. C., Hammer, J., Hooper, S. R., & Kamphaus, R. W. (2011). Down syndrome. In S. Goldstein & C.R. Reynolds (Eds.), *Handbook of neurological development and genetic disorders in children* (pp. 362–381). NY: Guilford.

He, W., Sengupta, M., Velkoff, V., & DeBarros, K.A. (2005). *65+ in the United States: 2005. Current Population Reports, P23-209.* Washington, DC: U.S. Government Printing Office.

Healthy Children.org. (2015). *Physical changes during puberty.* Retrieved from http://www .healthychildren.org/English/ages-stages /gradeschool/puberty/Pages/Stages-of -Puberty.aspx

Healthy People 2000: National Health Promotion and Disease Prevention Objectives. (1990). Washington, DC: U.S. Department of Health and Human Services, Public Health Service, DHHS publication PHS 91-50212.

Healthy People 2010. (2001). Retrieved from http://www.health .gov/healthypeople/LHI /lhiwhat.htm

Healthy People 2020. (2010). Proposed Healthy People 2020 objectives. Retrieved from www.healthypeople.gov/hp2020/objectives /TopicAreas.aspx

Healthy People 2020. (2016). *Framework.* Retrieved from https://www.healthypeople .gov/2020/About-Healthy-People

Hearn, S., Saulnier, G., Strayer, J., Glenham, M., Koopman R., & Marcia, J. E. (2012). Between integrity and despair: Construct validation of Erikson's eighth stage. *Journal of Adult Development, 19*, 1–20.

Hearold, S. (1986). A synthesis of 1043 effects of television on social behavior. In G. Comstock (Ed.), *Public communications and behavior* (Vol. 1, pp. 65–133). New York, NY: Academic Press.

Heath, C., Hindmarsh, J., & Luff, P. (2010). *Video in qualitative research.* Thousand Oaks, CA: Sage.

Heath, S. B. (1989). Oral and literate traditions among black Americans living in poverty. *American Psychologist, 44*, 367–372.

Hebert-Myers, H., Guttentag, C. L., Swank, P. R., Smith, K. E., & Landry, S. H. (2006). The importance of language, social, and behavioral skills across early and later childhood as predictors of social competence with peers. *Applied Developmental Science, 10*, 174–187.

Hebl, M. R., King, E. B., Glick, P., Singletary, S. L., & Kazama, S. (2007). Hostile and benevolent reactions toward pregnant women: Complementary interpersonal punishments and rewards that maintain traditional roles. *Journal of Applied Psychology, 92*, 1499–1511.

Heck, N. C., Flentje, A., & Cochran, B. N. (2011). Offsetting risks: High school gay-straight alliances and lesbian, gay, bisexual, and transgender (LGBT) youth. *School Psychology Quarterly, 26*, 161–174.

Heckhausen, J. (1987). Balancing for weaknesses and challenging developmental potential: A longitudinal study of mother-infant dyads in apprenticeship interactions. *Developmental Psychology, 23*, 762–770.

Heckhausen, J. (2011). Agency and control striving across the lifespan. In K. L. Fingerman, C. A. Berg, J. Smith, & T. C. Antonucci (Eds.), *Handbook of lifespan development* (pp. 183–212). New York, NY: Springer.

Heckhausen, J., Dixon, R. A., & Baltes, P. B. (1989). Gains and losses in development throughout adulthood as perceived by different adult age groups. *Developmental Psychology, 25*, 109–121.

Hegarty, P. (2009). Toward an LGBT-informed paradigm for children who break gender norms: Comment on Drummond et al. (2008) and Rieger et al. (2008). *Developmental Psychology, 45*, 895–900.

Heid, A., Zarit, S. H., & Fingerman, K. L. (2016). My parent is so stubborn: Perceptions of aging parents' insistence, persistence, and resistance. *The Journals of Gerontology: Psychological Sciences, 71*, 602–612.

Heifetz, R., Grashow, A., & Linsky, M. (2009). *The practice of adaptive leadership: Tools and tactics for changing your organization and the world.* Cambridge, MA: Harvard Business Press.

Heilman, M. E. (2001). Description and prescription: How gender stereotypes prevent women's ascent up the organizational ladder. *Journal of Social Issues, 57*, 657–674.

Heilman, M. E. (2012). Gender stereotypes and workplace bias. *Research in Organizational Behavior, 32*, 113–135.

Heimpel, S. A., Wood, J. V., Marshall, M. A., & Brown, J. D. (2002). Do people with low self-esteem really want to feel better? Self-esteem differences in motivation to repair negative moods. *Journal of Personality and Social Psychology, 82*, 128–147.

Hein, G., & Schubert, T. (2004). Aging and input processing in dual-task situations. *Psychology and Aging, 19*, 416–432.

Heinicke, C. M. (2002). The transition to parenting. In M. H. Bornstein (Ed.), *Handbook of parenting: Vol. 3. Being and becoming a parent* (2nd ed., pp. 363–389). New York, NY: Routledge.

Helman, C. G. (1990). *Culture, health, and illness* (2nd ed.). London: Wright.

Helman, C. G. (2007). *Culture, health and illness* (5th ed.). London: Hodder Arnold.

Helms, H. M., Walls, J. K., Crouter, A. C., & McHale, S. M. (2010). Provider role attitudes, marital satisfaction, role overload, and housework: A dyadic approach. *Journal of Family Psychology, 24*, 568–577.

Helwig, C. C., Zelazo, P. D., & Wilson, M. (2001). Children's judgments of psychological harm in normal and noncanonical situations. *Child Development, 72*, 66–81.

Henderson, A. J. Z., Bartholomew, K., Trinke, S. J., & Kwong, M. J. (2005). When loving means hurting: An exploration of attachment and intimate abuse in a community sample. *Journal of Family Violence, 20*, 219–230.

Henderson, H. A., Fox, N. A., & Rubin, K. H. (2001). Temperamental contributions to social behavior: The moderating roles of frontal EEG asymmetry and gender. *Journal of the American Academy of Child and Adolescent Psychiatry, 40*, 68–74.

Henderson, K. E., Grode, G. M., O'Connell, M. L., & Schwartz, M. B. (2015, March 29). Environmental factors associated with physical activity in childcare centers. *The International Journal of Behavioral Nutrition and Physical Activity, 12*, article 43.

Henderson, L., Gilbert, P., & Zimbardo, P. (2014). Shyness, social anxiety and social phobia. In S. G. Hofmann & P. M. DiBartolo (Eds.), *Social anxiety* (3rd ed.) (pp. 95–115). San Diego, CA: Academic Press.

Henkens, K., & Tazelaar, F. (1997). Explaining retirement decisions of civil servants in the Netherlands: Intentions, behavior, and the discrepancy between the two. *Research on Aging, 19,* 139–173.

Henrich, C. C., Brown, J. L., & Aber, J. L. (1999). Evaluating the effectiveness of school-based violence prevention: Developmental approaches. *Social Policy Report, 13,* 1–17.

Henry, G. T. (2009). Practical sampling. In L. Bickman & D. Rog (Eds.), *The Sage handbook of applied social research methods* (2nd ed., pp. 77–106). Thousand Oaks, CA: Sage.

Henry, J. D., MacLeod, M. S., Phillips, L. H., & Crawford, J. R. (2004). A meta-analytic review of prospective memory and aging. *Psychology and Aging, 19,* 27–39.

Hepach, R., Vaish, A., & Tomasello, M. (2012). Young children are intrinsically motivated to see others helped. *Psychological Science, 23,* 967–972.

Hepper, P. G., Doman, J. C., & Lynch, C. (2012). Fetal brain function and response to maternal alcohol consumption: Early evidence of damage. *Alcoholism: Clinical and Experimental Research, 36,* 2168–2175.

Herbert, W. (1996). The moral child. *U.S. News and World Report, 120,* 52–59.

Herdt, G., & McClintock, M. (2000). The magical age of 10. *Archives of Sexual Behavior, 29,* 587–606.

Herek, G. M. (2006). Legal recognition of same-sex relationships in the United States: A social science perspective. *American Psychologist, 61,* 607–621.

Hergovich, A., Sirsch, U., & Felinger, M. (2002). Self-appraisals, actual appraisals, and reflected appraisals of preadolescent children. *Social Behavior and Personality, 30,* 603–612.

Herkovits, M. (1948). *Man and his works.* New York, NY: Knopf.

Herman, M. R., Dornbusch, S. M., Herron, M. C., & Herting, J. R. (1997). The influence of family regulation, connection, and psychological autonomy on six measures of adolescent functioning. *Journal of Adolescent Research, 12,* 34–67.

Herman-Giddens, M. E. (2013). The enigmatic pursuit of puberty in girls. *Pediatrics, 132,* 1125–1127.

Herman-Giddens, M. E., Slora, E. J., Wasserman, R. C., Bourdony, C. J., Bhapkar, M. V., Koch, G. G., et al. (1997). Secondary sex characteristics and menses in young girls seen in office practice: A study from the pediatric research in office settings network. *Pediatrics, 99,* 505–512.

Herman-Giddens, M. E., Steffes, J., Harris, D., Slora, E., Hussey, M., Dowshen, S. A., Wasserman, R., Serwint, J. R., Smitherman, L., & Reiter, E. O. (2012). Secondary sexual characteristics in boys: Data from the Pediatric Research in Office Settings (PROS) network. *Pediatrics, 130,* e1058–e1068.

Herman-Giddens, M. E., Wang, L., & Koch, G. (2001). Secondary sexual characteristics in boys. *Archives of Pediatric and Adolescent Medicine, 155,* 1022–1028.

Hernandez, C. L., Elliott, T. R., Berry, J. W., Underhill, A. T., Fine, P. R., & Lai, M. H. C. (2014). Trajectories of life satisfaction five years after medical discharge for traumatically acquired disability. *Rehabilitation Psychology, 59,* 183–192.

Heron, M. (2016, February 16). Deaths: Leading causes for 2013. *National Vital Statistics Reports, 65*(2).

Herring, C., & Wilson-Sadberry, K. R. (1993). Preference or necessity? Changing work roles of Black and White women, 1973–1990. *Journal of Marriage and the Family, 55,* 315–325.

Hertzog, C., Fulton, E. K., Mandviwala, L., Dunlosky, J. (2013). Older adults show deficits in retrieving and decoding associative mediators generated at study. *Developmental Psychology, 49,* 1127–1131.

Hertzog, C., & Shing, Y. L. (2011). Memory development across the lifespan. In K. L. Fingerman, C. A. Berg, J. Smith, & T. C. Antonucci (Eds.), *Handbook of life-span development* (pp. 299–330). New York, NY: Springer.

Hertzog, D., & Schaie, K. W. (1988). Stability and change in adult intelligence: 2. Simultaneous analysis of longitudinal means and covariance structures. *Psychology and Aging, 3,* 122–130.

Hesketh, K. R., Griffin, S. J., & van Sluijs, E. M. F. (2015, September 26). UK preschool-aged children's physical activity levels in childcare and at home: A cross-sectional exploration. *The International Journal of Behavioral Nutrition and Physical Activity, 12,* article 123.

Hespos, S. J., & Baillargeon, R. (2001). Reasoning about containment events in very young infants. *Cognition, 78,* 207–245.

Hesse, E. (2008). The adult attachment interview: Protocol, method of analysis, and empirical studies. In J. Cassidy & P. R. Shaver (Eds.), *Handbook of attachment: Theory, research, and clinical applications* (2nd ed., pp. 552–598). New York, NY: Guilford Press.

Heuveline, P., & Timberlake, J. M. (2004). The role of cohabitation in family formation: The United States in comparative perspective. *Journal of Marriage and the Family, 66,* 1214–1230.

Heynen, J. (1990). *One hundred over 100: Moments with one hundred North American centenarians.* Golden, CO: Fulcrum.

Hicks, S. (2013). Lesbian, gay, bisexual and transgender parents and the question of gender. In A. E.Goldberg & K. R. Allen (Eds.), *LGBT-parent families: Innovations in research and implications for practice* (pp. 149–162). New York: Springer Science + Business Media.

Hickson, F. C., Davies, P. M., Hunt, A. J., & Weatherburn, P. (1992). Maintenance of open gay relationships: Some strategies for protection against HIV. *AIDS Care, 4,* 409–419.

Higgins, J. A., Trussell, J., Moore, N. B., & Davidson, J. K. (2010). Virginity lost, satisfaction gained? Physiological and psychological sexual satisfaction at heterosexual debut. *Journal of Sex Research, 47,* 384–394.

High, P. C. (2008). School readiness. *Pediatrics, 121,* 1008–1015.

High/Scope. (2003). *Perry Preschool Project: Significant benefit.* Retrieved from http://www.highscope.org/Research/PerryProject/perrymain.htm

Hilgenkamp, T. I. M., van Wijck, R., & Evenhuis, H.M. (2010). Physical fitness in older people with ID—Concept and measuring instruments: A review. *Research in Developmental Disabilities, 31,* 1027–1038.

Hill, E. J., Yang, C., Hawkins, A. J., & Ferris, M. (2004). A cross-cultural test of the work–family interface in 48 countries. *Journal of Marriage and the Family, 66,* 1300–1316.

Hill, H. M., & Kuczaj, S. A. (2011). The development of language. In A. Slater & B. Bremner (Eds.), *An introduction to developmental psychology* (2nd ed.). West Sussex, England: Wiley.

Hill, N. E., & Taylor, L. C. (2004). Parental school involvement and children's academic achievement: Pragmatics and issues. *Current Directions in Psychological Science, 13,* 161–164.

Hill, N. E., & Torres, K. (2010). Negotiating the American dream: The paradox of aspirations and achievement among Latino students and engagement between their families and schools. *Journal of Social Issues, 66,* 95–112.

Hill, R. (1958). Generic features of families under stress. *Social Casework, 39,* 139–150.

Hill, S. E., Prokosch, M. L., DelPriore, D. J., Griskevicius, V., & Kramer, A. (2016). Low childhood socioeconomic status promotes eating in the absence of energy need. *Psychological Science, 27,* 354–364.

Hilliard, L. J., & Liben, L. S. (2010). Differing levels of gender salience in preschool classrooms: Effects on children's gender attitudes and intergroup bias. *Child Development, 81,* 1787–1798.

Hillier, L., Jones, T., Monagle, M., Overton, N., Gahan, L., Blackman, J., & Mitchell, A. (2010). *Writing themselves in 3 (WTi3): The Third National Study on the Sexual Health and Well-being of Same-sex Attracted and Gender Questioning Young People.* Monograph Series No. 78. La Trobe University.

Hillman, J. L., & Stricker, G. (1994). A linkage of knowledge and attitudes toward elderly sexuality: Not necessarily a uniform relationship. *The Gerontologist, 34,* 256–260.

Hinchliff, S., Gott, M., & Ingleton, C. (2010). Sex, menopause and social context: A qualitative study with heterosexual women. *Journal of Health Psychology, 15,* 724–733.

Hing, E., & Bloom, B. (1990). Long-term care for the functionally dependent elderly. *Vital Health Statistics, 13,* No. 104.

Hinrichsen, G. A., & Clougherty, K. F. (2006). Depression and older adults. In G. A. Hinrichsen & K. F. Clougherty (Eds.), *Interpersonal psychotherapy for depressed older adults* (pp. 21–41). Washington, DC: American Psychological Association.

Hippensteele, K. A. (2011). "Best interest" analysis and the power of legal language. In K. A. Davis (Ed.), *Agency and advocacy. Contemporary language education* (pp. 39–59). Charlotte: Information Age Publishing.

Hipwell, A. E., Keenan, K., Loeber, R., & Battista, D. (2010). Early predictors of sexually intimate behaviors in an urban sample of young girls. *Developmental Psychology, 46,* 366–378.

Hirsh-Pasek, K., Adamson, L. B., Bakeman, R., Owen, M. T., Golinkoff, R. M., Pace, A., Yust, P. K. S., & Suma, K. (2015). The contribution of early communication quality to low-income children's language success. *Psychological Science, 26,* 1071–1083.

Hirsh-Pasek, K., Golinkoff, R. M., Berk, L. E., & Singer, D. G. (2009). *A mandate for playful learning in preschool: Presenting the evidence.* New York: Oxford University Press.

Ho, J. A. (2015). *Racial ambiguity in Asian American culture.* New Brunswick. NJ: Rutgers University Press.

Hobfoll, S. E. (2011). Conservation of resources theory: Its implications for stress, health and resilience. In S. Folkman (Ed.) *Handbook of stress, health, and coping* (pp. 127–147). New York: Oxford Univ. Press.

Hodges, J., & Tizard, B. (1989). Social and family relationships of ex-institutional adolescents. *Journal of Child Psychology and Psychiatry, 30,* 77–97.

Hodnett, E. D. (2003). Caregiver support for women during childbirth. *The Cochrane Library, 2,* 1–72. Retrieved from http://www.maternitywise .org/pdfs/continuous_support.pdf

Hodson, D. S., & Skeen, P. (1994). Sexuality and aging: The hammerlock of myths. *Journal of Applied Gerontology, 13,* 219–235.

Hodson, R., & Sullivan, T. A. (2011). *The social organization of work* (5th ed.). Belmont, CA: Cengage.

Hoehl, S., Reid, V. M., Parise, E., Handle, A., Palumbo, L., & Striano, T. (2009). Looking at eye gaze processing and its neural correlates in infancy—Implications for social development and autism spectrum disorder. *Child Development, 80,* 968–985.

Hoeksma, J. B., Oosterlaan, J., & Schipper, E. M. (2004). Emotion regulation and the dynamics of feelings: A conceptual and methodological framework. *Child Development, 75,* 354–360.

Hof, L., & Miller, W. R. (1981). *Marriage enrichment: Philosophy, process, and program.* Bowie, MD: Brady.

Hofer, J., Busch, H., Chasiotis, A., Kärtner, J., & Campos, D. (2008). Concern for generativity and its relation to implicit prosocial power motivation, generative goals, and satisfaction with life: A cross-cultural investigation. *Journal of Personality, 76,* 1–30.

Hoff, E. (2004). *Language development* (3rd ed.). Pacific Gove, CA: Wadsworth.

Hoff, E. (2013). *Language development* (5th ed.). Belmont, CA: Wadsworth.

Hoffman, M. L. (1970). Moral development. In P. H. Mussen (Ed.), *Carmichael's manual of child psychology* (Vol. 2, 3rd ed.). New York, NY: Wiley.

Hoffman, M. L. (1977). Moral internalization: Current theory and research. In L. Berkowitz (Ed.), *Advances in experimental social psychology* (Vol. 10). New York, NY: Academic Press.

Hoffman, M. L. (2000). *Empathy and moral development: Implications for caring and justice.* Cambridge, UK: Cambridge University Press.

Hoffman, M. L. (2007). The origins of empathic morality in toddlerhood. In C. A. Brownell & C. B. Kopp (Eds.), *Socioemotional development in the toddler years: Transitions and transformations* (pp. 132–148). New York, NY: Guilford Press.

Hoffman, M. L., & Powlishta, K. K. (2001). Gender segregation in childhood: A test of the interaction style theory. *Journal of Genetic Psychology, 162,* 298–313.

Hoffman, S. J. (1985). Play and the acquisition of literacy. *Quarterly Newsletter of the Laboratory of Comparative Human Cognition, 7,* 89–95.

Hoffmann, J. D., & Russ, S. W. (2016). Fostering pretend play skills and creativity in elementary school girls: A group play intervention. *Psychology of Aesthetics, Creativity, and the Arts, 10,* 114–125.

Hofmann, S. G. (2012). The future of cognitive therapy and research is bright and clear. *Cognitive Therapy and Research, 36,* 259–260.

Hofmann, S. G., Asnaani, A., Vonk, I. J. J., Sawyer, A. T. & Fang, A. (2012). The efficacy of cognitive behavioral therapy: A review of meta-analyses. *Cognitive Therapy Research, 36,* 427–440.

Hogan, C. L., Mata, J., & Carstensen, L. L. (2013). Exercise holds immediate benefits for affect and cognition in younger and older adults. *Psychology of Aging, 28,* 587–594.

Hogan, D. P., Eggebeen, D. J., & Clogg, C. C. (1993). The structure of intergenerational exchanges in American families. *American Journal of Sociology, 98,* 1428–1458.

Holahan, C. K., Sears, R. R., & Cronbach, L. J. (1995). *The gifted group in later maturity.* Stanford, CA: Stanford University Press.

Holder, M. K., & Blaustein, J. D. (2014). Puberty and adolescence as a time of vulnerability to stressors that alter neurobehavioral processes. *Frontiers in Neuroendocrinology, 35,* 89–110.

Holland, J. L. (1997). *Making vocational choices: A theory of vocational personalities and work environments* (3rd ed.). Odessa, FL: Psychological Assessment Resources.

Hollingsworth, L. D. (2005). Ethical considerations in prenatal sex selection. *Health and Social Work, 30,* 126–134.

Holmboe, K., Nemoda, Z., Fearon, R. M. P., Csibra, G., Sasvari-Szekely, M., & Johnson, M. H. (2010). Polymorphisms in dopamine system genes are associated with individual differences in attention in infancy. *Developmental Psychology, 46,* 404–416.

Holmes, C., Levy, M., Smith, A., Pinne, S., and Neese, P. (2015). A model for creating a supportive trauma-informed culture for children in preschool settings. *Journal of Child and Family Studies, 24,* 1650–1659.

Holmes, E. K., Huston, T. L., Vangelisti, A. L., & Guinn, T. D. (2013). On becoming parents. In A. L. Vangelisti (Ed.), *The Routledge handbook of family communication* (2nd ed., pp. 80–96). New York, NY: Routledge.

Holmes, T. H., & Rahe, R. H. (1967). The social readjustment rating scale. *Journal of Psychosomatic Research, 11,* 213–218.

Holokawa, S., Brosseau-Laprè, F., & Pettito, L. A. (2002). Semantic and conceptual knowledge underlying bilingual babies' first signs and words. *Language Learning, 52,* 205–262.

Holstein, J. A., & Gubrium, J. F. (1995). *The active interview.* Thousand Oaks, CA: Sage.

Holzman, C., Eyster, J., Kleyn, M., Messer, L. C., Kaufman, J. S., Laraia, B. A., et al. (2009). Maternal weathering and risk of preterm delivery. *American Journal of Public Health, 99,* 1864–1869.

Hong, L. K., & Duff, R. W. (1994). Widows in retirement communities: The social context of subjective well-being. *The Gerontologist, 34,* 347–352.

Hong, S. I., & Morrow-Howell, N. (2010). Health outcomes of Experience Corps: A high commitment volunteer program. *Social Science and Medicine, 71,* 414–420.

Honig, A. S. (1995). Choosing child care for young children. In M. H. Bornstein (Ed.), *Handbook of parenting: Applied and practical parenting* (Vol. 4, pp. 411–435). Mahwah, NJ: Erlbaum.

Honig, A. S. (2012). Choosing childcare for young children. In M. H. Bornstein (Ed.), *Handbook of parenting: Practical issues in parenting* (Vol. 5, 2nd ed., pp. 375–405). New York, NY: Psychology Press.

Hooyman, N., & Kiyak, H. A. (2011). *Social gerontology: A multidisciplinary perspective* (9th ed.). Boston, MA: Pearson.

Hope, T. L., Wilder, E. I., & Watt, T. T. (2003). The relationship among adolescent pregnancy, pregnancy resolution, and juvenile delinquency. *Sociological Inquiry, 44,* 555–576.

Hopkins, E. J., Dore, R. A., & Lillard, A. S. (2015). Do children learn from pretense? *Journal of Experimental Child Psychology, 130,* 1–18.

Hopkins, J. R. (1995). Erik Homburger Erikson (1902–1994). *American Psychologist, 50,* 796–797.

Hopper, K., & Hamberg, L. (1986). The making of America's homeless: From skid row to new poor, 1945–1984. In R. Bratt, C. Harman, & A. Meyerson (Eds.), *Critical perspectives on housing*. Philadelphia, PE: Temple University Press.

Horn, J. L. (1979). The rise and fall of human abilities. *Journal of Research and Development in Education, 12*, 59–78.

Horn, J. L., & Masunaga, H. (2000). New directions for research into aging and intelligence: The development of expertise. In T. J. Perfect & E. A. Maylor (Eds.), *Models of cognitive aging* (pp. 125–159). London: Oxford University Press.

Hornik, R., & Gunnar, M. R. (1988). A descriptive analysis of infant social referencing. *Child Development, 59*, 626–634.

Hornik, R., Risenhoover, N., & Gunnar, M. (1987). The effects of maternal positive, neutral, and negative affective communications on infant responses to new toys. *Child Development, 58*, 937–944.

Horobin, K., & Acredolo, C. (1989). The impact of probability judgments on reasoning about multiple possibilities. *Child Development, 60*(1), 183–200.

Horwitz, A. V., White, H. R., & Howell-White, S. (1996). Becoming married and mental health: A longitudinal study of a cohort of young adults. *Journal of Marriage and the Family, 58*, 895–907.

Hospice Education Institute. (2001). *A short history of hospice and palliative care*. Essex, CT: The Hospice Education Institute.

Hospice of Michigan. (2007). *Grief support services*. Retrieved from http://www.hom.org/griefami.asp

Hostinar, C. E. (2015). Recent developments in the study of social relationships, stress responses and physical health. *Current Opinion in Psychology, 5*, 90–95.

Howarth, G. (2007). *Death and dying: A sociological introduction*. Malden, MA: Polity Press.

Howe, N. (2014). The silent generation, "The Lucky Few." *Forbes*. Retrieved from http://www.forbes.com/sites/neilhowe/2014/08/13/the-silent-generation-the-lucky-few-part-3-of-7/#605556521e54

Howe, N., Aquan-Assee, J., Bukowski, W. M., Lehoux, P. M., & Rinaldi, C. M. (2001). Siblings as confidants: Emotional understanding, relationship warmth, and sibling self-disclosure. *Social Development, 10*, 439–454.

Howell, C. (1994, February 2). Coroner delivers primer to directors. *Arkansas-Democrat Gazette*.

Howell, J. C. (2012). *Gangs in America's communities*. Thousand Oaks, CA: Sage.

Howell, J. C., & Moore, J. P. (2010). History of street gangs in the U.S. *National Gang Center Bulletin, 4*.

Howell, J. C., & Griffiths, E. (2016). *Gangs in America's communities* (2nd ed.). Thousand Oaks, CA: Sage.

Howell, K. K. (2005) *Ten most frequently asked questions about consuming caffeine during pregnancy*. Emory Department of Psychiatry and Behavioral Sciences. Retrieved from http://www.psychiatry.emory.edu/PROGRAMS/GADrug/caffeine.htm

Howes, C. (1987). Peer interaction of young children. *Monographs of the Society for Research in Child Development, 53* (1, Serial No. 217).

Howes, C., & Spieker, S. (2016). Attachment relationships in the context of multiple caregivers. In J. Cassidy & P. R. Shaver (Eds.), *Handbook of attachment: Theory, research and clinical applications* (3rd ed., pp. 317–332). New York, NY: Guilford.

Howes, C., & Stewart, P. (1987). Child's play with adults, toys, and peers: An examination of family and child-care influences. *Developmental Psychology, 23*, 423–430.

Howes, C., Unger, O., & Seidner, L. B. (1989). Social pretend play in toddlers: Parallels with social play and with solitary pretend. *Child Development, 60*, 77–84.

How RU-486 works. (1997, March 3). *U.S. News and World Report*, 66–69.

Hoyer, W. J., & Rybash, J. M. (1994). Characterizing adult cognitive development. *Journal of Adult Development, 1*, 7–12.

Hoyer, W. J., & Verhaeghen, P. (2006). Memory aging. In J. E. Birren and K. W. Schaie (Eds.), *Handbook of the psychology of aging* (pp. 209–232). Amsterdam, Netherlands: Elsevier.

Hruschka, D. J. (2010). *Friendship: Development, ecology and evolution of a relationship*. Berkeley, CA: University of California Press.

Huang, H., Ryan, J. P., & Rhoden, M. (2016). Foster care, geographic neighborhood change, and the risk of delinquency. *Children and Youth Services Review, 65*, 32–41.

Huber, J. (1990). Macro-micro links in gender stratification. *American Sociological Review, 55*, 1–10.

Hubert, N. C., Wachs, T. D., Peters-Martin, P., & Gandour, M. J. (1982). The study of early temperament: Measurement and conceptual issues. *Child Development, 53*, 571–600.

Hudson, M., Netto, G., et al., (2013). In-work poverty, ethnicity and workplace cultures. *A report of the Joseph Rowntree Foundation*. Retrieved from https://www.jrf.org.uk/report/work-poverty-ethnicity-and-workplace-cultures

Huesmann, L. R., Moise-Titus, J., Podolski, C. L., & Eron, L. D. (2003). Longitudinal relations between children's exposure to TV violence and their aggressive behavior in young adulthood: 1977–1992. *Developmental Psychology, 39*, 210–221.

Huesmann, L. R., & Skoric, M. M. (2003). Regulating media violence: Why, how, and by whom? In E. L. Palmer & B. M. Young (Eds.), *The faces of televisual media: Teaching, violence, selling to children* (2nd ed., pp. 219–240). Mahwah, NJ: Erlbaum.

Hughes, F. M. (2006). Longitudinal prediction of parenting alliance strength: The roles of marital satisfaction and depression. *Dissertation Abstracts International: Section B: The Sciences and Engineering, 66*, 5684.

Hughes, F. M., Gordon, K. C., & Gaertner, L. (2004). Predicting spouses' perceptions of their parenting alliance. *Journal of Marriage and the Family, 66*, 506–514.

Human Rights Campaign. (2014). *While resilient, LGB students in AL face challenges as school year begins*. Retrieved from http://www.hrc.org/press/while-resilient-lgbt-students-in-ms-face-challenges-as-school-year-begins

Human Rights Watch. (2016) *Child labor*. Retrieved from https://www.hrw.org/topic/childrens-rights/child-labor

Huhtala, M., Korja, R., Rautava, L. et al. (2016). Health-related quality of life in very low birth weight children at nearly 8 years of age. *Acta Paediatrica, 105*, 53–59.

Hunter, A. G. (1997). Counting on grandmothers: Black mothers' and fathers' reliance on grandmothers for parenting support. *Journal of Family Issues, 18*, 251–269.

Hupp, S. D. A., & Reitman, D. (1999). Improving sports skills and sportsmanship in children diagnosed with attention-deficit/hyperactivity disorder. *Child and Family Behavior Therapy, 21*, 35–51.

Hurley, D. (2015). Grandma's experiences leave a mark on your genes. *Discover*. Retrieved from http://discovermagazine.com/2013/may/13-grandmas-experiences-leave-epigenetic-mark-on-your-genes

Huston, T. L., Caughlin, J. P., Houts, R. M., Smith, S. E., & George, L. J. (2001). The connubial crucible: Newlywed years as predictors of marital delight, distress, and divorce. *Journal of Personality and Social Psychology, 80*, 237–252.

Huston, T. L., & Melz, H. (2004). The case for (promoting) marriage: The devil is in the details. *Journal of Marriage and the Family, 66*, 943–958.

Huston, T. L. & Vangelisti, A. L. (1995). How parenthood affects marriage: Explaining family interactions. In M. A. Fitzpatrick & A. L. Vagelisti (Eds.), *Exploring family interactions* (pp. 147–176). Thousand Oaks, CA: Sage.

Hutt, S. J., Tyler, S., Hutt, C., & Foy, H. (1988). *Play exploration and learning: A natural history of the preschool*. New York, NY: Routledge.

Huttenlocher, J., Vasilyeva, M., Waterfall, H. R., Vevea, J. L., & Hedges, L.V. (2007). The varieties of speech to young children. *Developmental Psychology, 43*, 1062–1083.

Huxley, J. (1941). *The uniqueness of man*. London: Chatto & Windus.

Huxley, J. (1942). *Evolution: The magic synthesis*. New York, NY: Harper.

Hwa-Froelich, D. A. (2015). Social communication development. In D.A. Hwa-Froelich (Ed.), *Social communication development and disorders* (pp. 108–137). New York: Psychology Press.

Hyde, J. S. (2005). The gender similarities hypothesis. *American Psychologist, 60*, 581–592.

Hymel, S., Bowker, A., & Woody, E. (1993). Aggressive versus withdrawn unpopular children: Variations in peer and self-perceptions of multiple domains. *Child Development, 64*, 879–896.

Hymel, S., & Swearer, S. M. (2015). Four decades of research on school bullying: An introduction. *American Psychologist, 70*, 293–299.

Hymel, S., Wagner, E., & Butler, L. J. (1990). Reputational bias: View from the peer group. In S. Asher & J. D. Coie (Eds.). *Peer rejection in childhood* (pp. 156–186). New York, NY: Cambridge University Press.

Iacoboni, M. (2009). Imitation, empathy and mirror neurons. *Annual Review of Psychology, 60*, 653–670.

Iacoboni, M., & Dapretto, M. (2006). The mirror neuron system and the consequences of its dysfunction. *Nature Reviews/Neuroscience, 7*, 942–951. Retrieved from http://www.nature.com/reviews/neuro

Iannotti, R. J. (1985). Naturalistic and structured assessments of prosocial behavior in preschool children: The influence of empathy and perspective taking. *Developmental Psychology, 21*, 46–55.

Iannotti, R. J., & Bush, P. J. (1992). Perceived versus actual friends' use of alcohol, cigarettes, marijuana, and cocaine: Which has the most influence? *Journal of Youth and Adolescence, 21*, 375–389.

Iliescu, B. F., & Dannemiller, J. L. (2008). Brain behavior relationships in early visual development. In C. A. Nelson & M. Luciana (Eds), *Handbook of developmental cognitive neuroscience* (2nd ed., pp. 127–146). Cambridge, MA: MIT Press.

Ikels, C. (1998). Grandparenthood in cross-cultural perspective. In M. Szinovacz (Ed.), *Handbook on grandparenthood* (pp. 40–52). Westport, CT: Greenwood Press.

Im, E. –O., Lee, B. I., Chee, W., Dormire, S., & Brown, A. (2010). A national multi-ethnic online forum study on menopausal symptom experience. *Nursing Research, 59*, 26–33.

Impett, E. A., & Tolman, D. L. (2006). Late adolescent girls' sexual experiences and sexual satisfaction. *Journal of Adolescent Research, 21*, 628–646.

Inglehart, R., Foa, R., Peterson, C., & Welzel, C. (2008). Development, freedom and rising happiness: A global perspective 1981–2007. *Perspectives in Psychological Science, 3*, 264–285.

Ingersoll-Dayton, B., & Antonucci, T. C. (1988). Reciprocal and nonreciprocal social support: Contrasting sides of intimate relationships. *Journal of Gerontology, 43*, S65–S73.

Inhelder, B., & Piaget, J. (1958). *The growth of logical thinking from childhood to adolescence.* New York, NY: Basic Books.

Insel, T. R. (2007). Shining light on depression. *Science, 317*, 757–758.

Institute on Aging. (2013). *Aging in America.* Retrieved from http://www.ioaging.org/aging-in-america

Institute of Medicine. (2007). Chapter 10: Mortality and acute complications in pre-term infants. In Behrman R. E., & Butler A. S. (Eds.), *Preterm birth: Causes, consequences, and prevention.* Washington, DC: National Academies Press. Retrieved from http://www.ncbi.nlm.nih.gov/books/NBK11385/

Institute of Medicine & National Research Council. (2013). *Sports-related concussions in youth: Improving the science, changing the culture.* Washington, DC: The National Academies Press.

InteliHealth.com. (2002). *Words, not bullets, make the workplace hostile.* Retrieved from http://www.intelihealth.com/IH/ihtIH/WSIHW000/20813/23598/263562.html?d_dmt-Content

International Labour Organzation. (2012). *ILO global estimate of forced labour.* Retrieved from http://www.ilo.org/wcmsp5/groups/public/@ed_norm/@declaration/documents/publication/wcms_182004.pdf

Iowa Women's Archives. (2012). *Ruth Hamilton.* Retrieved from http://sdrc.lib.uiowa.edu/iwa/findingaids/html/HamiltonRuth.ht

Isaacowitz, D. M., Vaillant, G. E., & Seligman, M. E. P. (2003). Strengths and satisfaction across the lifespan. *International Journal of Aging & Human Development, 57*, 181–201.

Ishii-Kuntz, M. (1997). Japanese American families. In M. K. DeGenova (Ed.), *Families in cultural context: Strengths and challenges in diversity* (pp. 131–153). Mountain View, CA: Mayfield.

Ivarsson, T., & Valderhaug, R. (2006). Symptom patterns in children and adolescents with obsessive-compulsive disorder (OCD). *Behaviour Research and Therapy, 44*, 1105–1116.

IVF-infertility.com. (2013). *Artificial insemination.* Retrieved from http://www.ivf-infertility.com/insemination/insemination13.php

Izard, C.E. (2004) *The psychology of emotions* (paperback ed.). New York, NY: Springer.

Izard, C. E., Haynes, O. M., Chisholm, G., & Baak, K. (1991). Emotional determinants of infant-mother attachment. *Child Development, 62*, 906–917.

Jabr, F. (2010, July 6). Exposing the student body: Stanford joins U.S. Berkeley in controversial genetic testing of students. *Scientific American.*

Jack, D. C., & Dill, D. (1992). The silencing the self scale: The schemas of intimacy associated with depression in women. *Psychology of Women Quarterly, 16*, 97–106.

Jacklin, C. N., & Maccoby, E. E. (1978). Social behavior at 33 months in same-sex and mixed-sex dyads. *Child Development, 49*, 557–569.

Jackson, J. S., Keioper, S. K., Brown, K. T., Brown, T. N., & Manuel, W. (2002). Athletic identity, racial attitudes and aggression in first-year Black and White intercollegiate athletes. In M. Gatz, M. A. Messner, & S. J. Ball-Rokeach (Eds.), *Paradoxes of youth and sport* (pp. 159–172). Albany, NY: SUNY Press.

Jackson, P. B. (2004). Role sequencing: Does order matter for mental health? *Journal of Health and Social Behavior, 45*, 132–154.

Jacobs, J. N., & Kelley, M. L. (2006). Predictors of paternal involvement in childcare in dual-earner families with young children. *Fathering, 4*, 23–47.

Jacobson, E. (1964). *The self and the object world.* New York, NY: International Universities Press.

Jafari Navimipour, N., & Charband, Y. (2016). Knowledge sharing mechanisms and techniques in project teams: Literature review, classification, and current trends. *Computers in Human Behavior, 62*, 730–742.

Jahoda, M. (1982). *Employment and unemployment.* Cambridge, England: Cambridge University Press.

Jahromi, L. B., Putnam, S. P., & Stifter, C. A. (2004). Maternal regulation of infant reactivity from 2 to 6 months. *Developmental Psychology, 40*, 477–487.

James, W. (1890). *Principles of psychology* (2 vols.). New York, NY: Henry Holt.

James, W. (1892/1961). *Psychology: The briefer course.* New York, NY: Harper & Row.

Jamieson, A., Curry, A., & Martinez, G. (2001). School enrollment in the United States—Social and economic characteristics of students: 1999. *Current Population Reports, P20-533.*

Jang, Y., Chiriboga, D. A., & Small, B. J. (2008). Perceived discrimination and psychological well-being: The mediating and moderating role of sense of control. *International Journal of Aging and Human Development, 66*, 213–227.

Jarboe, P. J. (1986). A comparison study of distress and marital adjustment in infertile and expectant couples. Unpublished doctoral dissertation, Ohio State University.

Jayakody, R., Chatters, L. M., & Taylor, R. J. (1993). Family support to single and married African-American mothers: The provision of financial, emotional, and childcare assistance. *Journal of Marriage and the Family, 55*, 261–276.

Jean, A. D. L., Stack, D. M., & Fogel, A. (2009). A longitudinal investigation of maternal touching across the first 6months of life: Age and context effects. *Infant Behavioral Development, 32*, 344–349.

Jecker, N. S., & Schneiderman, L. J. (1994). Is dying young worse than dying old? *The Gerontologist, 34*, 66–72.

Jeffries, V. (1993). Virtue and attraction: Validation of measure of love. *Journal of Social and Personal Relationships, 10*, 99–118.

Jenkins, J. M., Turrell, S. L., Kogushi, Y., Lollis, S., & Ross, H. S. (2003). A longitudinal investigation of the dynamics of mental state talk in families. *Child Development, 74*, 905–920.

Jenkins, L. E. (1989). The Black family and academic achievement. In G. L. Berry & J. K. Asamen (Eds.), *Black students* (pp. 138–152). Newbury Park, CA: Sage.

Jensen, L. A. (2008). Through two lenses: A cultural-developmental approach to moral reasoning. *Developmental Review, 28,* 289–315.

Jensen, L. A. (2015). *Moral development in a global world: Research from a cultural-development perspective.* New York: Cambridge University Press.

Jensen, L. A., & McKenzie, J. (2016). The moral reasoning of U.S. evangelical and mainline Protestant children, adolescents, and adults: A cultural-developmental study. *Child Development, 87,* 446–464.

Jerskey, B. A., Panizzon, M. S., Jacobson, K. C., et al. (2010). Marriage and divorce: A genetic perspective. *Personality and Individual Differences, 49,* 473–478.

Jeste, D. V., Depp, C. A., & Vahia, I. V. (2010). Successful cognitive and emotional aging. *World Psychiatry, 9,* 78–84.

Jetten, J., Spears, R., & Manstead, A. S. R. (1996). Intergroup norms and intergroup discrimination: Distinctive self-categorization and social identity effects. *Journal of Personality and Social Psychology, 71,* 1222–1233.

Jewell, J., Brown, C. S., & Perry, B. (2015). All my friends are doing it: Potentially offensive sexual behavior perpetration within adolescent social networks. *Journal of Research on Adolescence 25,* 592–604.

Jezewski, M. A., Meeker, M. S., Sessanna, L., & Finnell, D. S. (2007). The effectiveness of interventions to increase advance directive completion rates. *Journal of Aging and Health, 19,* 519–536.

Jiang, Y., Ekono, M., & Skinner, C. (2015). *Basic facts about low-income children: Children 12 through 17 years, 2013.* New York: National Center for Children in Poverty, Mailman School of Public Health, Columbia University.

Jiang, Y., Ekono, M., & Skinner, C. (2016). *Basic facts about low-income children: Children under 6 years, 2014.* Retrieved from http://www.nccp.org/publications/pdf/text_1149.pdf

Jirtle, R. L., & Weidman, J. R. (2007). Imprinted and more equal. *American Scientist, 95,* 143–149.

John, L. K., Loewenstein, G., & Prelec, D. (2010). Measuring the prevalence of questionable research practices with incentives for truth telling. *Psychological Science, 23,* 524–532.

Johnson, C., Heron, J., Araya, R., Paus, T., Croudace, T., Rubin, C., et al., (2012). Association between pubertal development and depressive symptoms in girls from a U. K. cohort. *Psychological Medicine, 42,* 2579–2589.

Johnson, H. B. (2005, March–April). My word. Too late to die young. *AARP: The Magazine, 48,* 44–46.

Johnson, K. P. (2004). Adolescent sleep patterns: Biological, social, and psychological influences. *Journal of the American Academy of Child and Adolescent Psychiatry, 43,* 374–375.

Johnson, L. (2014). Regulation of assisted reproductive treatments (ART) in Australia and current ethical issues. *Indian Journal of Medical Research, 140,* S9–S12.

Johnson, L. D., O'Malley, P. M., Bachman, J. G., & Schulenberg, J. E. (2013). *Monitoring the Future national results on drug use: 2012 overview key findings on adolescent drug use.* Ann Arbor, MI: Institute for Social Research, University of Michigan.

Johnson, M. H. (2001). Functional brain development in humans. *Nature Reviews Neuroscience, 2,* 475–483.

Johnson, M. P. (2002). An exploration of men's experience and role at childbirth. *Journal of Men's Studies, 10,* 165–182.

Johnson, R. C. (2010). The health returns of education policies from preschool to high school and beyond. *American Economic Review: Papers & Proceedings,* 188–194.

Johnson, R. E. (2003). Age and the remembering of text. *Developmental Review, 23,* 261–346.

Johnson, S. P. (2000). The development of visual surface perception: Insights into the ontogeny of knowledge. In C. Rovee-Collier, L. P. Lipsitt, & H. Hayne (Eds.), *Progress in infancy research* (Vol. 1, pp. 113–154). Mahwah, NJ: Erlbaum.

Johnson, V. K., Cowan, P. A., & Cowan, C. P. (1999). Children's classroom behavior: The unique contribution of family organization. *Journal of Family Psychology, 13,* 355–371.

Johnson-Powell, G. (1996). Alice's little sister: The self-concealed behind the self. In B. Thompson & S. Tyagi (Eds.), *Names we call home: Autobiography on racial identity* (pp. 53–62). New York, NY: Routledge.

Johnston, L. D., O'Malley, P. M., Bachman, J. G., & Schulenberg, J. E. (2004). *Monitoring the Future: National results on adolescent drug use: Overview of key finding, 2003* (NIH Publication No. 04-5506). Bethesda, MD: National Institute on Drug Abuse.

Johnston, L. D., O'Malley, P. M., Bachman, J. G., & Schulenberg, J. E. (2010). *Monitoring the future: National results on adolescent drug use. Overview of key findings: 200.* (NIH Publication yet to be assigned). Bethesda, MD: National Institute on Drug Abuse.

Johnston, L. D., O'Malley, P. M., Bachman, J. G., & Schulenberg, J. E. (2013). *Monitoring the future: National results on drug use: 2012 overview key findings on adolescent drug use.* Ann Arbor, MI: Institute for Social Research, University of Michigan.

Johnston, L. D., O'Malley, P. M., Miech, R. A., Bachman, J. G., & Schulenberg, J. E. (2016). *Monitoring the Future national survey results on drug use, 1975–2015: Overview, key findings on adolescent drug use.* Ann Arbor: Institute for Social Research, University of Michigan.

Johnston, T. (2005). In one's own image: Ethics and the reproduction of deafness. *Journal of Deaf Studies and Deaf Education, 10,* 426–441.

Joinson, C., Heron, J., Araya, R., et al. (2012). Association between pubertal development and depressive symptoms in girls from a UK cohort. *Psychological Medicine, 42,* 2579–2589.

Jokela, M. (2010). Characteristics of the first child predict the parents' probability of having another child. *Developmental Psychology, 46,* 915–926.

Jones, B. C., Main, J. C., DeBruine, L. M., Little, A. C., & Welling, L. L. M. (2010). Reading the look of love: Sexually dimorphic cues in opposite sex faces influence gaze categorization. *Psychological Science, 21,* 796–798.

Jones, D. C. (2004). Body image among adolescent girls and boys: A longitudinal study. *Developmental Psychology, 40,* 823–835.

Jones, D. C., & Newman, J. B. (2009). Early adolescent adjustment and critical evaluations by self and other: The prospective impact of body image dissatisfaction and peer appearance teasing on global self-esteem. *European Journal of Developmental Science, 3,* 17–26.

Jones, J. M., & Gates, G. J. (2015). Same-sex marriages up after Supreme Court ruling. *Gallup,* Retrieved from http://www.gallup.com/poll/186518/sex-marriages-supreme-court-ruling.aspx

Jones, N. A. & Bullock, J. (2012). The two or more races population: 2010. *2010 Census Briefs,* Washington DC: U.S. Census Bureau.

Jones, S. S., & Fox, S. (2009). Generations online in 2009. *PEW Internet and American Life Project.* Retrieved from http://pewinternet.org/Reports/2009/Generations-Online-in-2009/Generational-Differences-in-Online-Activities.aspx

Jones, S. S., Smith, L. B., & Landau, B. (1991). Object properties and knowledge in early lexical learning. *Child Development, 62,* 499–516.

Jordan, B. (1983). *Birth in four cultures: A cross-cultural investigation of childbirth in Yucatan, Holland, Sweden and the United States* (3rd ed.). Montreal, Canada: Eden Press.

Jordan, C. H., Spencer, S. J., Zanna, M. P., Hoshino-Browne, E., & Correll, J. (2003). Secure and defensive high self-esteem. *Journal of Personality and Social Psychology, 85,* 969–978.

Jordan, J. V. (1997). Relational development through mutual empathy. In A. C. Bohart & L. S. Greenberg (Eds.), *Empathy reconsidered: New directions in psychotherapy* (pp. 343–351). Washington, DC: American Psychological Association.

Jordan, K. F., Lyons, T. S., & McDonough, J. T. (1992). *Funding and financing for programs to serve K–3 at-risk children: A research review.* Washington, DC: National Education Association.

Jordan, N. C., Kaplan, D., Ramineni, C., & Locuniak, M. N. (2009). Early math matters: Kindergarten number competence and later mathematics outcomes. *Developmental Psychology, 45,* 850–867.

Jose, A., O'Leary, D.K., & Moyer, A. (2010). Does premarital cohabitation predict subsequent marital stability and marital quality? A meta-analysis. *Journal of Marriage and the Family, 72,* 105–116.

Josselson, R., Lieblich, A., & McAdams, D. P. (Eds.). (2007). *The meaning of others; Narrative studies of relationships.* Washington, DC: American Psychological Association.

Joussemet, M., Landry, R., & Koestner, R. (2008). A self-determination theory of parenting. *Canadian Psychology, 49,* 194–200.

Jussim, L. (1990). Social realities and social problems: The role of expectancies. *Journal of Social Issues, 46,* 9–34.

Jussim, L., Robustelli, S. L., & Cain, T. R. (2009). Teacher expectations and self-fulfilling pophecies. In K. Wentzel & A. Wigfield (Eds.), *Handbook of motivation at school.* (Educational Psychology Handbook). New York, NY: Routledge, pp. 349–380.

Justice, L. M., & Ezell, H. K. (2000). Enhancing children's print and word awareness through home-based parent intervention. *American Journal of Speech-Language Pathology, 9,* 257–269.

Juvonen, J., Graham, S., & Schuster, M. A. (2003). Bullying among young adolescents: The strong, the weak, and the troubled. *Pediatrics, 112,* 1231–1237.

Juvonen, J., Schacter, H. L., Sanio, M., & Salmivalli, C. (2016). Can a school-wide bullying prevention program improve the plight of victims? Evidence for riskXintervention effects. *Journal of Consulting and Clinical Psychology, 84,* 334–344.

Kagan, J. (1958). The concept of identification. *Psychological Review, 65,* 296–305.

Kagan, J., & Snidman, N. (2004). *The long shadow of temperament.* Cambridge, MA: Harvard University Press.

Kagan, S. L. (1990). Readiness 2000: Rethinking rhetoric and responsibility. *Phi Delta Kappan, 1,* 21–23.

Kagitcibasi, C. (1990). Family and socialization in cross-cultural perspective: A model of change. In J. J. Berman (Ed.), *Nebraska Symposium on Motivation, 1989: Crosscultural perspectives* (pp. 135–200). Lincoln, NE: University of Nebraska Press.

Kagitcibasi, C. (2007/2009). *Family, self, and human development across cultures: Theory and applications* (2nd ed.). Mahwah, NJ: Lawrence Erlbaum, Reprinted by Psychology Press.

Kahana, B. (1982). Social behavior and aging. In B. B. Wolman (Ed.), *Handbook of developmental psychology* (pp. 871–889). Englewood Cliffs, NJ: Prentice Hall.

Kahana, E., & Kahana, B. (1996). Conceptual and empirical advances in understanding aging well through proactive adaptation. In V. Bengston (Ed.), *Adulthood and aging: Research on continuities and discontinuities* (pp. 18–40). New York: Springer.

Kahana, E., & Kahana, B. (2003). Contextualizing successful aging: New direction in age-old search. In R. Settersten, Jr. (Ed.), *Invitation to the life course: A new look at old age* (pp. 225–255). Amityville, NY: Baywood Publishing Company.

Kahn, F. (2015). *Being pansexual.* Retrieved from http://www.independent.co.uk /voices/comment/im-pansexual-here-are -the-five-biggest-misconceptions-about -my-sexuality-10480878.html

Kaida, K., Ogawa, K., Matsuura, N., Takkahashi, M., & Hori, T. (2006). Relationship between the habit of napping with self-awakening and generalized self-efficacy. *Japanese Journal of Health Psychology, 19,* 1–9.

Kalb, C. (2001, August 13). Should you have your baby now? *Newsweek,* pp. 40–48.

Kalish, C. W., & Gelman, S. A. (1992). On wooden pillows: Multiple classification and children's category-based inductions. *Child Development, 63,* 1536–1557.

Kalleberg, A. L. (2011). *Good jobs, bad jobs.* New York, NY: Russell Sage Foundation.

Kalleberg, A. L., & Rosenfeld, R. A. (1990). Work in the family and in the labor market. *Journal of Marriage and the Family, 52,* 331–346.

Kalman, M. B. (2003). Taking a different path: Menstrual preparation for adolescent girls living apart from their mothers. *Health Care for Women International, 24,* 868–879.

Kalmijn, M. (1998). Intermarriage and homogamy: Causes, patterns, trends. *Annual Review of Sociology, 24,* 395–421.

Kalmijn, M., De Graaf, P. M., & Poortman, A. R. (2004). Interactions between cultural and economic determinants of divorce in the Netherlands. *Journal of Marriage and Family. 66,* 75–89.

Kalmijn, M., & Flap, H. (2001). Assortative meeting and mating: Unintended consequences of organized settings for partner choices. *Social Forces, 79,* 1289–1312.

Kalmijn, M., & Monden, C. W. S. (2006). Are the negative effects of divorce on well-being dependent on marital quality? *Journal of Marriage and Family, 68,* 1197–1213.

Kalmijn, M., & Uunk, W. (2007). Regional value difference in Europe and the social consequences of divorce: A test of the stigmatization hypothesis. *Social Science Research, 36,* 447–468.

Kamii, C., Lewis, B.A., & Kirkland, L. (2001). Manipulatives: When are they useful? *Journal of Mathematical Behavior, 20,* 21–31.

Kamii, C., Rummelsburg, J., & Kari, A. (2005). Teaching arithmetic to low-performing, low-SES first graders. *Journal of Mathematical Behavior, 24,* 39–50.

Kamii, C. K. (1985). *Young children reinvent arithmetic.* New York, NY: Teachers College Press.

Kamii, C. K. (1994). *Young children continue to reinvent arithmetic: 3rd grade.* New York, NY: Teachers College Press.

Kanazawa, S. (2015). Breast feeding is positively associated with child intelligence even net of parental IQ. *Developmental Psychology 51,* 1683–1689.

Kaneshige, T., & Haryu, E. (2015). Categorization and understanding of facial expressions in 4-month-old infants. *Japanese Psychological Research, 57,* 135–142.

Kang, S. M., & Shaver, P. R. (2004). Individual differences in emotional complexity: Their psychological implications. *Journal of Personality, 72,* 687–726.

Kann, L., Kinchen, S., Shanklin, S, et al. (2014). High school youth risk behavior surveillance—United States, 2013. *Morbidity and Mortality Weekly Report, 63*(4).

Kann, L., McManus, T., Harris, W. A. et al. (2016). Youth risk behavior surveillance—United States, 2015. MMWR.Surveill summ 2016, 65(6).

Kanter, R. M. (2004). *Confidence: How winning and losing streaks begin and end.* New York, NY: Crown.

Kanungo, R. N., & Menon, S. T. (2005). Managerial resourcefulness: Measuring a critical component of leadership effectiveness. *Journal of Entrepreneurship, 14,* 39–55.

Kanungo, R. N., & Misra, S. (1992). Managerial resourcefulness: A reconceptualization of management skills. *Human Relations, 45,* 1311–1332.

Kaplowitz, P. B. (2008). Link between body fat and the timing of puberty. *Pediatrics, 121,* S208-S217.

Kapteyn, A., Smith, J. P., & van Soest, A. (2009). *Life satisfaction.* Discussion Paper No, 4015. Retrieved from http://ftp.iza.org /dp4015.pdf

Kapteyn, A., Smith, J. P., & van Soest, A. (2010). Life satisfaction. International differences in well-being. In E. Diener, J. F. Helliwell, & D. Kahneman (Eds.), *International differences in well-being* (pp. 70–104). New York, NY: Oxford University Press.

Karevold, E., Røysamb, E., Ystrom, E., & Mathiesen, K. S. (2009). Predictors and pathways from infancy to symptoms of anxiety and depression in early adolescence. *Developmental Psychology, 45,* 1051–1060.

Karmel, M. (1983). *Thank you, Dr. Lamaze.* Philadelphia, PA: Lippincott.

Kasper, J. D. (1997). Long-term care moves into the mainstream. *The Gerontologist, 37,* 274–276.

Kastenbaum, R. (1985). Dying and death: A life-span approach. In J. Birren and K. W. Schaie (Eds.), *Handbook of the psychology of aging* (pp. 619–643). New York, NY: Van Nostrand Reinhold.

Kastenbaum, R. (2000). *Psychology of death* (3rd ed.). New York, NY: Springer.

Kastenbaum, R. (2012). *Death, society and human experience* (11th ed.). Boston, MA: Pearson.

Katch, V. (2013). Dare to be 100. *Michigan Today.* Retrieved from http://michigantoday. umich.edu/2013/06/story .php?id=8643#.UtBSirRl3bo

Katchadourian, H. (1990). Sexuality. In S. S. Feldman & G. R. Elliott (Eds.), *At the threshold: The developing adolescent* (pp. 330–351). Cambridge, MA: Harvard University Press.

Kaufman, S. B. (2013). The real neuroscience of creativity. *Scientific American*. Retrieved from http://blogs.scientificamerican.com /beautiful-minds/the-real-neuroscience -of-creativity/

Kaufman, S. B., & Gregoire, C. (2016). How to cultivate creativity. *Scientific American Mind, 27*, 62–67.

Kavanaugh, R. D., & Engel, S. (1998). The development of pretense and narrative in early childhood. In O. N. Saracho & B. Spodek (Eds.), *Multiple perspectives on play in early childhood education* (pp. 80–99). Albany, NY: University of New York Press.

Kaye, L. W. (1995). *New developments in home care services for the elderly: Innovations in policy, program, and practice.* Binghamton, NY: Haworth Press.

Keating, D. P. (1990). Adolescent thinking. In S. S. Feldman & G. R. Elliott (Eds.), *At the threshold: The developing adolescent* (pp. 54–90). Cambridge, MA: Harvard University Press.

Keating, D. P. (2004). Cognitive and brain development. In R. M. Lerner & L. Steinberg (Eds.), *Handbook of adolescent psychology* (2nd ed., pp. 45–84). New York, NY: Wiley.

Kechel, K. P., Ladd, G. W., Bagwell, C. L., & Yabko, B. A. (2015). Bully-victim profiles differential risk for worsening peer acceptance: The role of friendship. *Journal of Applied Developmental Psychology, 41*, 38–45.

Kegan, R. (1982). *The evolving self: Problems and process in human development.* Cambridge, MA: Harvard University Press.

Kehl, K. (2006). Moving toward peace: An analysis of the concept of a good death. *American Journal of Hospice and Palliative Medicine, 23*, 277–286.

Keith, V. M., & Finlay, B. (1988). Parental divorce and children's education, marriage, and divorce. *Journal of Marriage and the Family, 50*, 797–810.

Keller, H., Lohaus, A., Kuensemueller, M. A., Yovsi, R., Voelker, S., Jensen, H., et al. (2004). The bioculture of parenting: Evidence from five cultural communities. *Parenting: Science and Practice, 4*, 25–50.

Kelly, E. L., Moen, P., Oakes, J. M., et al. (2014). Changing work and work-family conflict: Evidence from the work, family, and health network. *American Sociological Review, 79*, 485–516.

Kelly, J. L., LaVergne, D. D., Boone, H. N., Jr., & Boone, D. A. (2012). Perceptions of college students on social factors that influence student matriculation. *College Student Journal, 46*, 653–664.

Kelly, M., Zimmer-Gembeck, M. J., & Boislard, M. (2012). Identity, intimacy, status and sex dating goals as correlates of goal-consistent behavior and satisfaction in Australian youth. *Journal of Adolescence, 35*, 441–454.

Kelly, M. L., Power, T. G., & Wimbush, D. D. (1992). Determinants of disciplinary practices in low-income Black mothers. *Child Development, 63*, 573–582.

Kelly, S. J., Ostrowski, N. L., & Wilson, M. A. (1999). Gender differences in brain and behavior: Hormonal and neural bases. *Pharmacology, Biochemistry and Behavior, 64*, 655–664.

Kelly, Y., Sacker, A., Schoon, I., & Nazroo, J. (2006). Ethnic differences in achievement of developmental milestones by 9 months of age: The Millenium Cohort Study. *Developmental Medicine & Child Neurology, 48*, 825–830.

Kelsey G, Bartolomei, M. S. (2012) Imprinted Genes . . . and the Number Is? *PLoS Genetics* 8(3): e1002601. doi:10.1371/journal .pgen.1002601

Kemp, C. (2014). *Scores of bullying victims bringing weapons to school.* Retrieved from http://www.aappublications.org/content /early/2014/05/04/aapnews.20140504-3

Kemp, C. L. (2005). Dimensions of grandparent-adult grandchild relationships: From family ties to intergenerational friendships. *Canadian Journal on Aging, 24*, 161–178.

Kemper, S., Thompson, M., & Marquis, J. (2001). Longitudinal change in language production: Effects of aging and dementia on grammatical complexity and propositional content. *Psychology and Aging, 16*, 600–614.

Kena, G., Hussar, W., McFarland, J., de Brey, C., Musu-Gillette, L., Wang, X., Zhang, J., Rathbun, A., Wilkinson- Flicker, S., Diliberti, M., Barmer, A., Bullock Mann, F., and Dunlop Velez, E. (2016). *The condition of education 2016* (NCES 2016-144). U.S. Department of Education, National Center for Education Statistics. Washington, DC. Retrieved from http://nces.ed.gov/pubsearch.

Kennedy, A. C. (2006). Urban adolescent mothers exposed to community, family, and partner violence: Prevalence, outcomes and welfare policy implications. *American Journal of Orthopsychiatry, 76*, 44–54.

Kennedy, S., & Ruggles, S. (2014). Breaking up is hard to count: The rise of divorce in the United States, 1980-2010. *Demography, 51*, 587–598.

Kennedy, T. M., & Ceballo, R. (2016). Emotionally numb: Desensitization to community violence exposure among urban youth. *Developmental Psychology, 52*, 778–789.

Kenny, D. A. & Acitelli, L. K. (2001). Accuracy and bias in the perception of the partner in a close relationship. *Journal of Personality and Social Psychology, 80*, 439–448.

Kenyan, D. B., & Koerner, S. S. (2009). Examining emerging adults' and parents' expectations about autonomy during the transition to college. *Journal of Adolescent Research, 24*, 293–320.

Ker, H. W. (2016). The impacts of student-, teacher-, and school-level factors on mathematics achievement: An exploratory comparative investigation of Singaporean students and the U.S.A. students. *Educational Psychology, 36*, 254–276.

Kerig, P. K., Swanson, J. A., & Ward, R. M. (2012). Autonomy with connection: Influences of parental psychological control on mutuality in emerging adults' close relationships. In P. K. Kerig, M. S. Schultz, & S. T. Hauser (Eds.), *Adolescence and beyond: Family processes and development* (pp. 134–153). New York, NY: Oxford University Press.

Kermoian, R., & Campos, J. J. (1988). Locomotor experience: A facilitator of spatial cognitive development. *Child Development, 59*, 908–917.

Kernan, C. L., & Greenfield, . M. (2005). Becoming a team: Individualism, collectivism, ethnicity and group socialization in Los Angeles girls' basketball. *Ethos, 33*, 542–566.

Kernberg, O. F. (2005). Object relations theories and technique. In E. S. Person, A. M. Cooper, & G. O. Gabbard (Eds.), *The American psychiatric publishing textbook of psychoanalysis* (pp. 57–75). Washington, DC: American Psychiatric Publishing, Inc.

Kernis, M. H. (2003). Toward a conceptualization of optimal self-esteem. *Psychological Inquiry, 14*, 1–26.

Kersting, K. (2004). Improving the end of life for older adults. *Monitor on Psychology, 35*, 53–54.

Kertz, S. J., Belden, A. C., Tillman, R., & Luby, J. (2015). Cognitive control deficits in shifting and inhibition in preschool aged children are associated with increased depression and anxiety over 7.5 years of development. *Journal of Abnormal Child Psychology, 44*, 1185–1196.

Kesebir, P. (2011). Existential functions of culture: The monumental immortality project. In A. K. Leung, C. Chiu, & Hong, Y. (Eds.), *Cultural processes: A social psychological perspective.* Culture and Psychology New York, NY: Cambridge University Press, pp. 96–110.

Kessen, W. (1965). *The child.* New York, NY: Wiley.

Ketch, V. (2013, June 18). Dare to be 100? *Michigan Today.* Retrieved from http:// michigantoday.umich.edu/story .php?id=8643

Khalifian, C. E., & Barry, R. A. (2016). Trust, attachment and mindfulness influence intimacy and disengagement during newlyweds' discussions of relationship transgression. *Journal of Family Psychology, 30*, 592–601.

Kids Count. (2016). *Persons age 18 to 24 not attending school, not working, and no degree beyond high school.* Retrieved from http:// datacenter.kidscount.org/data/tables/5063 -persons-age-18-to-24-not-attending -school-not-working-and-no-degree -beyond-high-school?loc=1&loct =1#detailed/1/any/false/869,36,868,867,133 /any/11484,11485

KidsHealth.org. (2013). *Everything you wanted to know about puberty.* Retrieved from http://kidshealth.org/teen/sexual_health /changing_body/puberty.html#

KidsHealth. (2014a). *Fitness and your 2-to-3-year old.* Retrieved from http://kidshealth.org/en/parents/fitness-2-3.html

KidsHealth. (2014b). *Fitness and your 6- to 12-year olds.* Retrieved from http://kidshealth.org/en/parents/fitness-6-12.html#

Killen, M., Elenbaas, L., & Rutland, A. (2016). Balancing the fair treatment of others while preserving group identity and autonomy. *Human Development, 58*, 253–272.

Kim, H., Hong, S., & Kim, M. (2015). Living arrangement and social connectedness and life satisfaction among Korean older adults with physical disabilities: The results from the National Survey on Persons with Disabilities. *Journal of Developmental and Physical Disabilities, 27*, 307–321.

Kim, H. -J. K. (2002). *Taegyo (fetal education).* Retrieved from http://fieldworking.com/historical/kim.html

Kim, H. Y., & Cappella, E. (2016). Mapping the social world of classrooms: A multi-level, mult-reporter approach to social processes and behavioral engagement. *American Journal of Community Psychology, 57*, 20–35.

Kim, P., Rigo, P., Mayes, L. C., Feldman, R., Leckman, J. F., & Swain, J. (2014). Neural plasticity in fathers of human infants. *Social Neuroscience, 9*, 522–535.

Kim, S., & Kochanska, G. (2012). Child temperament moderates effects of parent-child mutuality on self-regulation: A relationship-based path for emotionally negative infants. *Child Development, 83*, 1275–1289.

Kim, S. Y., Chen, Q., Wang, Y., Shen, Y., & Orozco-Lapray, D. (2013). Longitudinal linkages among parent-child acculturation discrepancy, parenting, parent-child sense of alienation, and adolescent adjustment in Chinese immigrant families. *Developmental Psychology, 49*, 900–912.

Kimura, D. (2002). Sex differences in the brain. *Scientific American.com.* Retrieved from http://www.sciam.com

Kimura, D. (2004). Human sex differences in cognition, fact, not predicament. *Sexualities, Evolution & Gender, 6*, 45–53.

King, L. A. (1993). Emotional expression, ambivalence over expression, and marital satisfaction. *Journal of Social and Personal Relationships, 10*, 601–607.

King, P. M., & Kitchener, K. S. (1994). *Developing reflective judgment: Understanding and promoting intellectual growth and critical thinking in adolescents and adults.* San Francisco, CA: Jossey-Bass.

Kinney, J. M., & Stephens, M. A. P. (1989). Hassles and uplifts of giving care to a family member with dementia. *Psychology and Aging, 4*, 402–408.

Kinnunen, U., Feldt, T., Mauno, S., & Rantanen, J. (2010). Interface between work and family: A longitudinal individual and crossover perspective. *Journal of Occupational and Organizational Psychology, 83*, 119–137.

Kins, E., Beyers, W., Soenens, B., & Vansteenkiste, M. (2009). Patterns of home leaving and subjective well-being in emerging adulthood: The role of motivational processes and parental autonomy support. *Developmental Psychology, 45*, 1416–1429.

Kinsella, K., & Velkoff, V. A. (2001). *An aging world: 2001.* U.S. Census Bureau, Series P95/01-1. Washington, DC: U.S. Government Printing Office.

Kirkman, M., Rosenthal, D., & Smtih, A. M. A. (1998). Adolescent sex and the romantic narrative: Why some young heterosexuals use condoms to prevent pregnancy but not disease. *Psychology, Health & Medicine, 3*, 355–370.

Kirkorian, H. L., Pempek, T. A., Murphy, L. A., Schmidt, M. E., & Anderson, D. R. (2009). The impact of background television on parent–child interactions. *Child Development, 80*, 1350–1359.

Kirkwood, T. B. L. (2001). Where will it all end? *The Lancet, 357*, 576–577.

Kirsch, P., Esslinger, C., Chen, Q., Mier, D., Lis, S., Siddhanti, S., et al. (2005). Oxytocin modulates neural circuitry for social cognition and fear in humans. *Neuroscience, 25*, 11489–11493.

Kirst, M. W., & Bracco, K. R. (2004). Bridging the great divide: How the K–12 and post-secondary split hurts students, and what can be done about it. In M. W. Kirst & A. Venezia (Eds.). *From high school to college: Improving opportunities for success in post-secondary education* (pp. 1–30). San Francisco, CA: Jossey Bass.

Kiselica, M. S., & Kiselica, A. M. (2014). The complicated worlds of adolescent fathers: Implications for clinical practice, public policy and research. *Psychology of Men and Masculinity, 15*, 260–274.

Kisilevsky, B.S., Hains, S. M. J., Brown, C. A., et al. (2009). Fetal sensitivity to properties of maternal speech and language. *Infant Behavior and Development, 32*, 59–71.

Kisilevsky, B. S., Hains, S. M., Brown, C. A. et al. (2009). Fetal sensitivity to properties of maternal speech and language. *Infant Behavior and Development, 32*, 59–71.

Kissil, K. & Davey, M. (2012). Health disparities in procreation: Unequal access to assisted reproductive technologies. *Journal of Feminist Family Therapy: An International Forum, 24*, 197–212.

Kistner, J. A., Ziegert, D. I., Castro, R., & Robertson, B. (2001). Helplessness in early childhood: Prediction of symptoms associated with depression and negative self-worth. *Merrill-Palmer Quarterly, 47*, 336–354.

Kiston, J. M. (1994). Contemporary Eriksonian theory: A psychobiographical illustration. *Gerontology and Geriatrics Education, 14*, 81–91.

Kitayama, S., Karasawa, M., & Mesquita, B. (2004). Collective and personal processes in regulating emotions: Emotion and self in Japan and the United States. In P. Philippot & R. S. Feldman (Eds.), *The regulation of emotion* (pp. 251–276). Mahwah, NJ: Erlbaum.

Kite, M. E. (1996). Age, gender, and occupational label: A test of social role theory. *Psychology of Women Quarterly, 20*, 361–374.

Kite, M. E., Deaux, K., & Miele, M. (1991). Stereotypes of young and old: Does age outweigh gender? *Psychology and Aging, 6*, 19–27.

Kitson, G. C. (1982). Attachment to the spouse in divorce: A scale and its application. *Journal of Marriage and the Family, 44*, 379–393.

Kitzinger, C., & Coyle, A. (1995). Lesbian and gay couples: Speaking of difference. *Psychologist, 8*, 64–69.

Kitzmann, K. M., & Cohen, R. (2003). Parents' versus children's perceptions of interparental conflict as pedictors of children's friendship quality. *Journal of Social and Personal Relationships, 20*, 689–700.

Kitzmann, K. M., Cohen, R., & Lockwood, R. L. (2002). Are only children missing out? Comparison of the peer-related social competence of only children and siblings. *Journal of Social and Personal Relationships, 19*, 295–316.

Kivnick, H. Q. (1988). Grandparenthood, life review, and psychosocial development. *Journal of Gerontological Social Work, 12*, 63–81.

Klein, H. (1991). Couvade syndrome: Male counterpart to pregnancy. *International Journal of Psychiatry in Medicine, 21*, 57–69.

Klein, L. & Knitzer, J. (2007). *Promoting effective early learning: What every policy maker and educator should know.* New York, NY: National Center for Children in Poverty, Columbia University Mailman School of Public Health.

Klein, M. (1932/1975). *The psychoanalysis of children* (The International Psychoanalytic Library, No. 22). Oxford, England: Hogarth Press.

Klein, M. (1948). *Contributions to psychoanalysis, 1921–1945.* London: Hogarth Press.

Klesges, L. M., Pahor, M., Shorr, R. I., Wan, J. Y., Williamson, J. D., & Guralnik, J. M. (2001). Financial difficulty in acquiring food among elderly disabled women: Results from the Women's Health and Aging Study. *American Journal of Public Health, 91*, 68–75.

Kliff, S. (2016). *The truth about the gender wage gap.* Retrieved from www.vox.com/2016/8/1/12108126/gender-wage-gap-explained-real

Klimstra, T. A., Luyckx, K., Hale, K. K., et al. (2010). Short-term fluctuations in identity: Introducing a micro-level approach to identity formation. *Journal of Personality and Social Psychology, 99*, 191–202.

Kline, D. W., & Scialfa, C. T. (1997). Sensory and perceptual functioning: Basic research and human factors implications. In A. D. Fisk & W. A. Rogers (Eds.), *Handbook of human factors and the older adult* (pp. 27–54). San Diego, CA: Academic Press.

Klinenberg, E. (2012). *Going solo: The extraordinary rise and surprising appeal of living alone.* New York, NY: Penguin Press.

Kluger, J. (1997, March 10). Will we follow the sheep? *Time, 149*, 67–72.

Kluckhohn, C. (1961). *Culture and behavior: The collected essays of Clyde Kluckholn.* Glencoe, IL: The Free Press.

Klump, K. L., & Culbert, K. M. (2007). Molecular genetic studies of eating disorders: Current status and future directions. *Current Directions in Psychological Science, 16,* 37–41.

Knee, D. O. (2010). Hospice care for the aging population in the United States. In J. C. Cavanaugh & C. K. Cavanaugh (Eds.), *Aging in America* (Vol. 3, pp. 203–221). Santa Barbara, CA: Praeger.

Knight, C. C., & Fischer, K. W. (1992). Learning to read words: Individual differences in developmental sequences. *Journal of Applied Developmental Psychology, 13,* 377–404.

Knitzer, J. (2007). Testimony of Jane Knitzer, Ed.D. to the House Ways and Means Committee, U.S. Congress Hearing on Economic and Societal Costs of Poverty. New York, NY: National Center for Children in Poverty, Columbia University Mailman School of Public Health. Retrieved from http://nccp.org/media/wmt07_text.pdf

Knitzer, J. & Cooper, J. (2006). Beyond integration: Challenges for children's mental health. *Health Affairs, 25,* 670.

Knox, D., Zusman, M., & Nieves, W. (1997). College students' homogamous preferences for a date and mate. *College Student Journal, 31,* 445–448.

Ko, E.-S., Seidl, A., Cristia, A., Reimchen, M., & Soderstrom, M. (2015). Entrainment of prosody in the interaction of mothers with young children. *Journal of Child Language,* advance online publication. Doi: 10.1017/S0305000915000203

Kobak, R., & Madsen, S. (2008). Disruptions in attachment bonds: Implications for theory, research, and clinical interventions. In J. Cassidy & P. R. Shaver (Eds.), *Handbook of attachment: Theory, research, and clinical applications* (2nd ed., pp. 23–47). New York, NY: Guilford Press.

Koblinsky, S. A., & Anderson, E. A. (1993, Spring–Summer). Studying homeless children and their families: Issues and challenges. *Division 7 Newsletter,* 1–3.

Kochanska, G., Aksan, N., & Joy, M. E. (2007). Children's fearfulness as a moderator of parenting in early socialization: Two longitudinal studies. *Developmental Psychology, 43,* 222–237.

Kochanska, G., Aksan, N., & Koenig, A. L. (1995). A longitudinal study of the roots of preschoolers' conscience: Committed compliance and emerging internalization. *Child Development, 66,* 1752–1769.

Kochanska, G., Forman, D. R., Aksan, N., & Dunbar, S. B. (2005). Pathways to conscience: Early mother-child mutually responsive orientation and children's moral emotion, conduct, and cognition. *Journal of Child Psychology and Psychiatry, 46,* 19–34.

Kochanska, G., & Knaack, A. (2003). Effortful control as a personality characteristic of young children: Antecedents, correlates, and consequences. *Journal of Personality, 71,* 1087–1112.

Kochanska, G., & Radke-Yarrow, M. (1992). Inhibition in toddlerhood and the dynamics of the child's interactions with an unfamiliar peer at age 5. *Child Development, 63,* 325–335.

Kochanska, G., Woodard, J., Kim, S., Koenig, J. L., Yoon, J. E., & Barry, R. A. (2010). Positive socialization mechanisms in secure and insecure parent child dyads: Two longitudinal studies. *Journal of Child Psychology and Psychiatry, 51,* 998–1009.

Kochenderfer-Ladd, B. J., & Wardrop, J. L. (2001). Chronicity and instability of children's peer victimization experiences as predictors of loneliness and social satisfaction trajectories. *Child Development, 72,* 134–151.

Kohlberg, L. (1964). Development of moral character and moral ideology. In M. L. Hoffman & L. W. Hoffman (Eds.), *Review of child development research* (Vol. 1). New York, NY: Sage.

Kohlberg, L. (1966). A cognitive-developmental analysis of children's sex-role concepts and attitudes. In E. E. Maccoby (Ed.), *The development of sex differences.* Stanford, CA: Stanford University Press.

Kohlberg, L. (1969). Stage and sequence: The cognitive-developmental approach to socialization. In D. A. Goslin (Ed.), *Handbook of socialization theory and research.* Chicago, IL: Rand McNally.

Kohlberg, L. (1976). Moral stages and moralization: The cognitive-developmental approach. In T. Lickona (Ed.), *Moral development and behavior.* New York, NY: Holt, Rinehart & Winston.

Kohn, M. L. (1980). Job complexity and adult personality. In N. J. Smelser & E. H. Erikson (Eds.), *Themes of work and love in adulthood* (pp. 193–210). Cambridge, MA: Harvard University Press.

Kohn, M. L. (1999). Social structure and personality under conditions of apparent social stability and radical social change. In A. Jasinska-Kania, M. L. Kohn, & K. Slomczynski (Eds.), *Power and social structure: Essays in honor of W. L. Odzimierz Wesolowski.* Warsaw, Poland: University of Warsaw Press.

Kohn, M. L. (2006). *Change and stability: A cross national analysis of social structure and personality.* Greenbrae, CA: Paradigm Press.

Kohn, M., Belza, B., Petrescu-Prahova, M., & Miyawaki, C. E. (2016). Beyond strength: Participant perspectives on the benefits of an older adult exercise program. *Health Education and Behavior, 43,* 305–312.

Kohn, P. M., & Milrose, J. A. (1993). The inventory of high-school students' recent life experiences: A decontaminated measure of adolescents' life hassles. *Journal of Youth and Adolescence, 22,* 43–55.

Kohut, H. (1971). *The analysis of the self.* New York, NY: International Universities Press.

Kolata, G. (2007, January 3). A surprising secret to long life, according to studies: Stay in school. *New York Times,* pp. A1, A16.

Kolb, B., Mychasivk, R., Muhammad, A. et al., (2012). Experience and the developing prefrontal cortex. *Proceedings of the National Academy of Science, 109,* 17186–17193.

Konopka, G. (1976). *Young girls: A portrait of adolescence.* Englewood Cliffs, NJ: Prentice Hall.

Konrad, P. (1990, August 6). Welcome to the woman-friendly company. *Business Week,* 48–55.

Kopp, C. B. (1989). Regulation of distress and negative emotions: A developmental view. *Developmental Psychology, 25,* 343–354.

Koppen, J. (2008). Retired spouses: A national survey of adults 55–75. *AARP, The Magazine.* Retrieved from www.aarp.org/relationships/love-sex/info-11-2008/retired_spouses.html

Korte, J., Cappeliez, P., Bohlmeijer, E. T., & Westerhof, G. B. (2012). Meaning in life and mastery mediate the relationship of negative reminiscence with psychological distress among older adults with mild to moderate depressive symptoms. *European Journal of Ageing, 9,* 343–351.

Kosfield, M., Heinrichs, M., Zak, . J., Fischbacher, U., & Fehr, E. (2005). Oxytocin increases trust in humans. *Nature, 435,* 673–676.

Kotre, J. N. (1995a). Generative outcome. *Journal of Aging Studies, 9,* 33–41.

Kotre, J. N. (1995b). *White gloves: How we create ourselves through memory.* New York, NY: Free Press.

Kotre, J. N., & Kotre, K. B. (1998). Intergenerational buffers: The damage stops here. In D. P. McAdams & E. de St. Aubin (Eds.), *Generativity and adult development: Psychosocial perspectives on caring for and contributing to the next generation* (pp. 367–389). Washington, DC: American Psychological Association.

Kovacs, A. M., & Mehler, J. (2009). Flexible learning of multiple speech structures in bilingual infants. *Science, 325,* 611–612.

Kowaz, A. M., & Marcia, J. E. (1991). Development and validation of a measure of Eriksonian industry. *Journal of Personality and Social Psychology, 60,* 390–397.

Kozhimannil, K. B., Almanza, J., Vogelsang, C. A.,& Hardeman, R. R. (2015). *Medicaid coverage of doula services in Minnesota: Findings from the first year.* University of Minnesota. Executive Summary. December 2015. Retrieved from http://sph.umn.edu/faculty1/hpm/name/katy-kozhimannil/

Kram, K. E. (1985). *Mentoring at work: Developmental relationships in organizational life.* Glenview, IL: Scott, Foresman.

Kramer, A. F., & Willis, S. L. (2002). Enhancing the cognitive vitality of older adults. *Current Directions in Psychological Science, 11,* 173–177.

Kramer, D. A. (2003). The ontogeny of wisdom in its variations. In J. Demick & C.

Andreoletti (Eds.), *Handbook of adult development* (pp. 131–151). New York, NY: Plenum Press.

Kramer, M. R., Waller, L. A., Dunlop, A. L., & Hogue, C. R. (2012). Housing transitions and low-birth weight among low-income women: Longitudinal study of the perinatal consequences of changing public housing policy. *The American Journal of Public Health, 102*, 2255–2261.

Krampe, R. T., & Charness N. (2006). Aging and expertise. In K. A. Ericsson, N. Charness, P. Feltovich, & R. Hoffman (Eds.), *Cambridge handbook of expertise and expert performance* (pp. 725–744). New York, NY: Cambridge University Press.

Krause, N. (2004). Stressors in highly valued roles, meaning in life, and the physical health status of older adults. *Journals of Gerontology, Series B: Psychological Sciences and Social Sciences, 59*, S287–S297.

Krause, N. (2006). Social relationships in late life. In R. H. Binstock & L. K. George (Eds.), *Handbook of aging and the social sciences* (pp. 181–200). San Diego, CA: Academic Press.

Krause, N. (2007). Longitudinal study of social support and meaning in life. *Psychology and Aging, 22*, 456–469.

Krause, N. (2009). Meaning in life and mortality. *Journal of Gerontology: Social Sciences, 64b*, 517–527.

Kreider, R. M., & Ellis, R. (2011). Number, timing and duration of marriages and divorces: 2009. *Current Population Reports,* P70–125. Washington, DC: U.S. Census Bureau.

Kremar, M., & Cooke, M. C. (2001). Children's moral reasoning and their perceptions of television violence. *Journal of Communication, 51*, 300–316.

Kremer, M., Smith, A. B., & Lawrence, J. A. (2010). Family discipline incidents: An analysis of parental diaries. *Journal of Family Studies, 16*, 251–263.

Krier, J. (2009). *Social networking and peer relationships: The benefits and drawbacks of children (9–12) using online social networking sites.* Retrieved September from http://smhp.pysch.ucla.edu/pdfdocs /socialnet.pdf

Kroger, J. (1997). Gender and identity: The intersection of structure, content, and context. *Sex Roles, 36*, 747–770.

Kroger, J. (2002). Commentary on "Feminist perspectives on Erikson's theory: Their relevance for contemporary identity development research." *Identity: An International Journal of Theory and Research, 2*(3), 257–266.

Kroger, J. (2004). *Identity in adolescence: The balance between self and other.* New York, NY: Routledge.

Kroger, J. (2007). *Identity development: Adolescence through adulthood* (2nd ed.). Thousand Oaks, CA: Sage.

Kroger, J. (2012). The status of identity: Developments in identity status research. In P. K.

Kerig, M. S. Schultz, & S. T. Hauser (Eds.), *Adolescence and beyond: Family processes and development* (pp. 64–83). New York, NY: Oxford University Press.

Kroger, J., & Marcia, J. E. (2011). The identity statuses: Origins, meanings, and interpretations. In S. J. Schwartz, K. Luyckx, & V. L. Vignoles (Eds.) *Handbook of identity theory and research* (pp. 31–53). New York: Springer.

Kroger, J., Martinussen, M., & Marcia, J. E. (2010). Identity status change during adolescence and young adulthood: A meta-analysis. *Journal of Adolescence, 33,* 683–698.

Krones, T., Schlüter, E., Neuwohner, E., Ansari, S. E., Wissner, T., & Richter, G. (2006). What is the preimplantation embryo? *Social Science and Medicine, 63,* 1–20.

Kropp, J. P., & Haynes, O. M. (1987). Abusive and nonabusive mothers' ability to identify general and specific emotion signals ofinfants. *Child Development, 58,* 187–190.

Kross, E., Mischel, W., & Shoda, Y. (2010). Enabling self-control: A cognitive-affective processing system approach to problematic behaviour. In J. E. Maddux & J. P Tangney (Eds.), *Social psychological foundations of clinical psychology* (pp. 375–394). New York, NY: Guilford Press.

Kruger, J., & Dunning, D. (1999). Unskilled and unaware of it: How difficulties in recognizing one's own incompetence lead to inflated self-assessments. *Journal of Personality and Social Psychology, 77,* 1121–1134.

Kruk, E. (1995). Grandparent–grandchild contact loss: Findings from a study of "grandparents' rights" members. *Canadian Journal on Aging, 14,* 737–754.

Kübler-Ross, E. (1969). *On death and dying.* New York, NY: Macmillan.

Kübler-Ross, E. (1969/1997). *On death and dying* (Reprint). New York, NY: Scribner Classics.

Kübler-Ross, E. (1972, February). On death and dying. *Journal of the American Medical Association, 219,* 10–15.

Kübler-Ross, E. (1981/1997). *Living with death and dying* (Reprint). New York, NY: Scribner.

Kübler-Ross, E. (1981). *Living with dying.* New York, NY: Macmillan.

Kübler-Ross, E. (1983). *On children and death.* New York, NY: Macmillan.

Kübler-Ross, E. (1983/1997). *On children and death: How children and their parents can and do cope with death* (Reprint). New York, NY: Touchstone.

Kuhl, P. K. (1987). Perception of speech and sound in early infancy. In P. Salapatek & L. Cohen (Eds.), *Handbook of infant perception* (Vol. 1). Orlando, FL: Academic Press.

Kuhn, D. (2009). Adolescent thinking. In R. M. Lerner & L. Steinberg (Eds.), *Handbook of adolescent psychology. Vol. 1. Individual bases of adolescent development* (3rd ed., pp. 152–186). Hoboken, NJ: John Wiley.

Kuhn, D., Garcia-Mila, M., Zohar, A., & Andersen, C. (1995). Strategies of

knowledge acquisition. *Monographs of the Society for Research in Child Development, 60* (4, Serial No. 245).

Kühn, S., & Lindenberger, U. (2016). Research on human plasticity in adulthood: A lifespan approach. In K.Warner-Schaie & S. Willis (Eds.), *Handbook of the psychology of aging* (8th ed.) (pp. 106–124). San Diego, CA: Academic Press/Elsevier.

Kunjufu. (2004). *Fathers and childbirth.* Retrieved from http://www.blackchat .co.uk/theblackforum/forum2/2969.html

Kunz, J., & Kunz, P. R. (1995). Social support during the process of divorce: It does make a difference. *Journal of Divorce and Remarriage, 24,* 111–119.

Kunz, J. A., & Soltys, F. G. (2007). *Transformational reminiscence: Life story work.* New York, NY: Springer.

Kunzmann, U., & Baltes, P. B. (2005). The psychology of wisdom: Theoretical and empirical challenges. In R. J. Sternberg & J. Jordan (Eds.). *A handbook of wisdom: Psychological perspectives* (pp. 110–135). New York, NY: Cambridge University Press.

Kuo, P. X., Carp, J., Light, K. C., & Grewen, K. M. (2012). Neural responses to infants linked with behavioral interactions and testosterone in fathers. *Biological Psychology, 91,* 302–306.

Kurdek, L. A. (1995). Lesbian and gay couples. In A. R. D'Augelli & C. J. Patterson (Eds.), *Lesbian, gay, and bisexual identities over the lifespan: Psychological perspectives* (pp. 243–261). New York, NY: Oxford University Press.

Kurdek, L. A. (2003). Differences between gay and lesbian cohabiting couples. *Journal of Social and Personal Relationships, 20,* 411–436.

Kurdek, L. A. (2004). Are gay and lesbian cohabiting couples really different from heterosexual married couples? *Journal of Marriage and the Family, 66,* 880–900.

Kurdek, L. A. (2005). What do we know about gay and lesbian couples? *Current Directions in Psychological Science, 14,* 251–254.

Kurdek, L. A. (2006a). The nature and correlates of deterrents to leaving a relationship. *Personal Relationships, 13,* 521–535.

Kurdek, L. A. (2006b). Differences between partners from heterosexual, gay and lesbian cohabiting couples. *Journal of Marriage and Family, 68,* 509–528.

Kwon, Y. -J., & Lawson, A. E. (2000). Linking brain growth with the development of scientific reasoning ability and conceptual change during adolescence. *Journal of Research in Science Teaching, 37,* 44–62.

Laberge, L., Petit, D., Simard, C., Vitaro, F., Tremblay, R. E., & Montplaisir, J. (2001). Development of sleep patterns in early adolescence. *Journal of Sleep Research, 10,* 59–67.

Labouvie-Vief, G. (1992). A neo-Piagetian perspective on adult cognitive development. In R. J. Sternberg & C. A. Berg (Eds.),

Intellectual development (pp. 197–228). New York, NY: Cambridge University Press.

Labouvie-Vief, G., & Diehl, M. (2000). Cognitive complexity and cognitive-affective integration: Related or separate domains of adult development? *Psychology and Aging, 15,* 490–504.

Lack, E. (2016). *Strange but true: Couvade syndrome (sympathetic pregnancy).* Retrieved from http://www.babycenter.com /0_strange-but-true-couvade-syndrome -sympathetic-pregnancy_10364940.bc

Lacombe, A. C., & Gay, J. (1998). The role of gender in adolescent identity and intimacy decisions. *Journal of Youth and Adolescence, 27,* 795–802.

Lacroix, V., Pomerleau, A., Malcuit, G., Seguin, R., & Lamarre, G. (2001). Language and cognitive development of the child during the first thee years in relation to the duration of maternal vocalizations and the toys present in the environment: Longitudinal study of populations at risk. *Canadian Journal of Behavioural Science, 33,* 65–76.

Ladd, G. W., Herald-Brown, S. L., & Kochel, K. P. (2009). Peers and motivation. In K. R. Wenzel & A. Wigfield (Eds.), *Handbook of motivation at school* (pp. 323–348). Educational Psychology Handbook series New York, NY: Taylor and Francis Group.

Ladd, G. W., Herald-Brown, S. L., & Reiser, M. (2008). Does chronic peer rejection predict the development of children's classroom participation during the grade school years? *Child Development, 79,* 1001–1015.

Ladenbauer, J., Kützow, N., Passmann, S. et al. (2016, July 2). Brain stimulation during an afternoon nap boosts slow oscillatory activity and memory consolidation in older adults. *NeuroImage.* http://dx.doi .org/10.1016/j.neuroimage.2016.06.057

Laflamme, D., Pomerleau, A., & Malcuit, G. (2002). A comparison of fathers' and mothers' involvement in childcare and stimulation behaviors during free-play with their infants at 9 and 15 months. *Sex Roles, 47,* 507–518.

Lagattuta, K. H., & Wellman, H. M. (2001). Thinking about the past: Early knowledge about links between prior experience, thinking, and emotion. *Child Development, 72,* 82–102.

Lagercrantz, H., Hanson, M. A., Ment, L. R. & Peebles, D. M (Eds.). (2010). *The newborn brain: Neuroscience and clinical applications.* New York, NY: Cambridge University Press.

Laible, D. J., & Thompson, R. A. (2000). Mother–child discourse, attachment security, shared positive affect, and early conscience development. *Child Development, 71,* 1424–1440.

Lakin, J. L., Chartrand, T. L., & Arkin, R. M. (2008). I am too just like you. *Psychological Science, 19,* 816–822.

Lalé, E. (2015). Multiple job holding over the past two decades. *Monthly Labor Review.* Retrieved from http://www.bls.gov/opub /mlr/2015/article/multiple-jobholding -over-the-past-two-decades.htm

Lam, C. B., McHale, S. M., & Crouter, A. C. (2012). The division of household labor: Longitudinal changes and within-couple variation. *Journal of Marriage and Family, 74,* 944–952.

LaMastro, V. (2001). Childless by choice? Attributions and attitudes concerning family size. *Social Behavior and Personality, 29,* 231–243.

Lamb, M. E. (2012). Mothers, fathers, families, and circumstances: Factors affecting children's adjustment. *Applied Developmental Science, 16,* 98–111.

Lambert, J. D., & Thomasson, G. C. (1997). Mormon American families. In M. K. DeGenova (Ed.), *Families in cultural context: Strengths and challenges in diversity* (pp. 85–108). Mountain View, CA: Mayfield.

Lambert, S. (2005). Gay and lesbian families: What we know and where to go from here. *The Family Journal, 13,* 43–51.

Lamborn, S. D., & Steinberg, L. D. (1993). Emotional autonomy redux: Revisiting Ryan and Lynch. *Child Development, 64,* 483–499.

Lamm, B., & Keller, H. (2007). Understanding cultural models of parenting. *Journal of Cross-Cultural Psychology, 38,* 50–57.

Landale, N. S., & Fennelly, K. S. (1992). Informal unions among mainland Puerto Ricans: Cohabitation or an alternative to legal marriage. *Journal of Marriage and the Family, 54,* 269–280.

Landry, S. H., Miller-Loncar, C. L., Smith, K. E., & Swank, P. R. (2002). The role of early parenting in children's development of executive processes. *Developmental Neuropsychology, 21,* 15–41.

Landry, S. H., Smith, K. E., Swank, P. R., Assel, M. A., & Vellet, S. (2001). Does early responsive parenting have a special importance for children's development or is consistency across early childhood necessary? *Developmental Psychology, 37,* 387–403.

Landry-Meyer, L., Gerard, J. M., & Guzell, J. R. (2005). Caregiver stress among grandparents raising grandchildren: The functional role of social support. *Marriage and Family Review, 37,* 171–190.

Lang, F. R., Featherman, D. L., & Nesselroade, J. R. (1997). Social self-efficacy and short-term variability in social relationships: The MacArthur successful aging study. *Psychology and Aging, 12,* 657–666.

Langley-Evans, S. C. (2006). Developmental programming of health and disease. *Proceedings of the Nutrition Society, 65,* 97–105.

Lanz, M., & Tagliabue, S. (2007). Do I really need someone in order to become an adult? Romantic relationships during emerging adulthood in Italy. *Journal of Adolescent Research, 22,* 531–549.

Lapierre, S., Bouffard, L., & Bastin, E. (1997). Personal goals and subjective well-being in later life. *The International Journal of Aging and Human Development, 45,* 287–303.

LaPonsie, M. (2016). Why seniors have the greatest financial security. *U.S. News and World Report.* Retrieved from http:// money.usnews.com/money/personal -finance/articles/2016-02-26/why-seniors -have-the-greatest-financial-security

Larouche, M., Galand, B., & Bouffard, T. (2008). The illusion of scholastic incompetence and peer acceptance in primary school. *European Journal of Psychology of Education, 23,* 25–39.

Larson, E. A. (2006). Stress in the lives of college women: "Lots to do and not much time." *Journal of Adolescent Research, 21,* 579–606.

Larson, R. W., & Brown, J. R. (2007). Emotional development in adolesdence: What can be learned from a high school theater program? *Child Development, 78,* 1083–1099.

Laszlo, E. (1972). *Introduction to systems philosophy: Toward a new paradigm of contemporary thought.* New York, NY: Harper & Row.

Laughlin, L. (2013). Who's minding the kids? Child care arrangements: Spring, 2011. *Household Economic Studies, P70-135.* Retrieved from https://www.census.gov /prod/2013pubs/p70-135.pdf

Laumann, E. Q., Ganon, J. H., Michael, R. T., & Michaels, S. (1994). *The social organization of sexuality.* Chicago, IL: University of Chicago Press.

Laurenceau, J., Barrett, L. F., & Rovine, M. J. (2005). The interpersonal process model of intimacy in marriage: A daily-diary and multilevel modeling approach. *Journal of Family Psychology, 19,* 314–323.

Laursen, B., Bukowski, W. M., Nurmi, J. et al. (2010). Opposites detract: Middle school peer group antipathies. *Journal of Experimental Child Psychology, 106,* 240–256.

Laursen, B., Coy, K., & Collins, W.A. (1998). Reconsidering changes in parent-child conflict across adolescence: A meta-analysis. *Child Development, 69,* 817–832.

Lawler, E. J., Thye, S. R., & Yoon, J. (2009). *Social commitments in a depersonalized world.* New York, NY: Russell Sage Foundation.

Lawler, S. (2014). *Identityt: Sociologicial perspectives* (2nd ed.). Hoboken, NJ: Wiley.

Lawson, K. M., Crouter, A. C., & McHale, S. M. (2015). Links between family gender socialization experiences in childhood and gendered occupational attainment in young adulthood. *Journal of Vocational Behavior, 90,* 26–35.

Lawton, M. P. (2001). Quality of life and the end of life. In J. E. Birren & K. W. Schaie (Eds.), *Handbook of the psychology of aging* (5th ed., pp. 592–616) San Diego, CA: Academic Press.

Lazarus, R. S. (2000). Toward better research on stress and coping. *American Psychologist, 55,* 655–673.

Lazarus, R. S., & Folkman, S. (1984). *Stress, appraisal, and coping.* New York, NY: Springer-Verlag.

Le, H.-N., Munoz, R. F., Ippen, C. G., & Stoddard, J. L. (2003). Treatment is not enough: We must prevent major depression in women. *Prevention & Treatment, 6.*

Leaper, C. (2000). Gender, affiliation, assertion, and the interactive context of parent-child play. *Developmental Psychology, 36,* 381–393.

Leaper, C., Anderson, K. J., & Sanders, P. (1998). Moderators of gender effects on parents' talk to their children: A meta-analysis. *Developmental Psychology, 34,* 3–27.

Leaper, C., & Bigler, R. S. (2011). Gender. In M. K. Underwood & L. H. Rosen (Eds.), *Social development: Relationships in infancy, childhood, and adolescence* (pp. 289–315). New York, NY: Guilford Press.

Lebel, C., & Beaulieu, C. (2011). Longitudinal development of human brain wiring continues from childhood to adulthood. *Journal of Neuroscience, 31,* 10937–10947.

Lecanuet, J. P., Graniere-Deferre, C., Jacquet, A. Y., & DeCasper, A. J. (2000). Fetal discrimination of low-pitched musical notes. *Developmental Psychobiology, 36,* 29–39.

Lee, C. (2002). *Cataracts.* Retrieved from http://www.allaboutvision.com/conditions/cataracts.htm

Lee, G. R., DeMaris, A., Bavin, S., & Sullivan, R. (2001). Gender differences in the depressive effect of widowhood in later life. *Journal of Gerontology, 56,* S56–S61.

Lee, J. S., & Frongillo, E. A. (2001). Nutritional and health consequences are associated with food insecurity among U.S. elderly persons. *Journal of Nutrition, 131,* 1503–1509.

Lee, H. C., Green, C., Hintz, S. R., et al. (2010). Prediction of death for extremely premature infants in a population-based cohort. *Pediatrics, 126,* e644–e650.

Lee, K., & Allen, N. J. (2002). Organizational citizenship behavior and workplace deviance: The role of affect and cognitions. *Journal of Applied Psychology, 87,* 131–142.

Lee, K., Anzures, G., & Freire, A. (2011). Cognitive development in adolescence. In A. Slater & G. Bremner (Eds.), *An introduction to developmental psychology* (pp. 519–546). West Sussex, England: BPS Blackwell.

Lee, K., Ashton, M. C., & Shin, K.-H. (2005). Correlates of workplace anti-social behavior. *Applied Psychology, 54,* 81–98.

Lee, M. J., Whitehead, J., & Balchin, N. (2000). The measurement of values in youth sport: Development of the Youth Sport Values Questionnaire. *Journal of Sport and Exercise Psychology, 22,* 307–326.

Lee, M. J., Whitehead, J., & Ntoumanis, N. (2007). Development of the attitudes to moral decision-making in youth sport questionnaire. *Psychology of Sport and Exercise, 8,* 369–392.

Lee, R., Zhai, F., Han, W.-J., Brooks-Gunn, J., & Waldfogel, J. (2013). Head Start and children's nutrition, weight, and health care receipt. *Early Childhood Research Quarterly, 28,* 10.1016, 723–733.

Leech, K. A., & Rowe, M. L. (2014). A comparison of preschool children's discussions with parents during picture book and chapter book reading. *First Language, 34,* 205–226.

Leech, K. A., Salo, V. C., Rowe, M. L., & Cabrera, N. J. (2013). Father input and child vocabulary development: The importance of *wh* questions and clarification requests. *Seminars in Speech and Language, 34,* 249–259.

Leerkes, E. M., Blankson, A. N., & O'Brien, M. (2009). Differential effects of maternal sensitivity to infant distress and non-distress on social-emotional functioning. *Child Development, 80,* 762–775.

Leffel, G. M., Fritz, M. E., & Stevens, M. R. (2008). Who cares? Generativity and the moral emotions, Part III. A social intuitionist "ecology of virtue." *Journal of Psychology and Theology, 36,* 202–221.

Lehr, U., Seiler, E., & Thomae, H. (2000). Aging in a cross-cultural perspective. In A. L. Comunian & U. P. Gielen (Eds.), *International perspectives on human development* (pp. 571–589). Lengerich, Germany: Pabst.

Leiderman, S., Tulkin, R., & Rosenfeld, A. (Eds.), (1977). *Culture and infancy: Variations in the human experience* (pp. 15–28). New York, NY: Academic Press.

Leigh, L., Hudson, I. L., & Biles, J. E. (2016). Sleep difficulty and disease in a cohort of very old women. *Journal of Aging and Health 28,* 1090–1104.

Leiras-Muney, A. (2005). The relationship between education and adult mortality in the United States. *The Review of Economic Studies, 72,* 189–221.

Lemaire, P., Arnaud, L., & Lecacheur, M. (2004). Adults' age-related differences in adaptivity of strategy choices: Evidence from computational estimation. *Psychology and Aging, 19,* 467–481.

Lempinen, E.W. (2012). AAAS Briefing: Links between poverty, brain development raise key policy issues. *AAAS News Release.* Retrieved from http://www.aaas.org//news/releases/2012/0731early_brain.shtml

L'Engle, K. L., & Jackson, C. (2008). Socialization influences on early adolescents' cognitive susceptibility and transition to sexual intercourse. *Journal of Research on Adolescence, 18,* 353–378.

Lengua, L. J. (2009). Effortful control in the context of socioeconomic and psychosocial risk. *Psychological Science Agenda, 23*(1).

Lengua, L. J., Honorado, E., & Bush, N. (2007). Cumulative risk and parenting as predictors of effortful control and social competence in preschool children. *Journal of Applied Developmental Psychology, 28,* 40–55.

Lenneberg, E. H. (1967). *Biological foundations of language.* Oxford, England: Wiley.

Lenroot, R. K., & Giedd, J. N. (2006). Brain development in children and adolescents: Insights from anatomical magnetic resonance imaging. *Neuroscience and Biobehavioral Reviews, 30,* 718–729.

Lent, R. W., Miller, M. J., Smith, P. E., Watford, B. A., Hui, K., & Lim, R. H. (2015). Social cognitive model of adjustment to engineering majors: Longitudinal test across gender and race/ethnicity. *Journal of Vocational Behavior, 86,* 77–85.

Lenton, A. P., & Francesconi, M. (2010). How humans cognitive manage of abundance of mate options. *Psychological Sciences, 21,* 528–533.

Lerner, J. V., & Lerner, R. M. (1983). Temperament and adaptation across life: Theoretical and empirical issues. In P. B. Baltes & O. G. Brim (Eds.), *Life span development and behavior, 5* (pp. 197–231). New York, NY: Academic Press.

Lerner-Geva, L., Boyko, V., Blumstein, T., & Benyamini, Y. (2010). The impact of education, cultural background, and lifestyle on symptoms of the menopausal transition: The Woman's Health at Midlife study. *The Journal of Women's Health, 19,* 975–985.

Lervåg, A., & Hulme, C. (2009). Rapid automatized naming (RAN) taps a mechanism that places constraints on the development of early reading fluency. *Psychological Science, 20,* 1040–1048.

Lev, A. I., & Alie, L. (2012). Transgender and gender nonconforming children and youth: Developing culturally competent systems of care. In S. K. Fisher, J. M. Poirier, & G. M. Blau (Eds.), *Improving emotional and behavioral outcomes for LGBT youth: A guide for professionals* (pp. 43–66). Systems of Care for Children's Mental Health. Baltimore, MD: Paul H. Brookes Publishing.

LeVay, S. (1991). A difference in hypothalamic structure between heterosexual and homosexual men. *Science, 253,* 1034–1037.

LeVay, S. (2011). *Gay, straight, and the reason why: The science of sexual orientation.* New York, NY: Oxford University Press.

Levenson, H. (2010). *Brief dynamic therapy.* Washington, DC: American Psychological Association.

Levine, A., & Nidiffer, J. (1996). *Beating the odds: How the poor get to college.* San Francisco, CA: Jossey-Bass.

Levine, R. A. (1977). Child rearing as cultural adaptation. In P. H. Leiderman, S. R. Tulkin, & A. Rosenfeld (Eds.), *Culture and infancy: Variations in the human experience* (pp. 15–28). New York, NY: Academic Press.

Levine, R. A. (1980). Adulthood among the Gusii of Kenya. In N. J. Smelser & E. H. Erikson (Eds.), *Themes of work and love in adulthood* (pp. 77–119). Cambridge, MA: Harvard University Press.

Levine, R. A., Levine, S., Dixon, S., Richman, A., Liederman, P. H., Keefer, C. H., et al. (1996). *Child care and culture: Lessons from Africa.* New York, NY: Cambridge University Press.

Levine, R. V., & Norenzayan, A. (1999).The pace of life in 31 countries. *Journal of Cross-Cultural Psychology, 30,* 178–205.

Levinger, G. (1983). Development and change. In H. H. Kelley, E. Berscheid, A. Christensen, J. H. Harvey, T. L. Huston, G. Levinger, E. McClintock, L. A. Peplau, & D. R., Peterson (Eds.), *Close relationships* (pp. 315–359). New York, NY: Freeman.

Levitt, M. J., Weber, R. A., & Clark, M. C. (1986). Social network relationships as sources of maternal support and wellbeing. *Developmental Psychology, 22,* 310–316.

Levitt, M. J., Weber, R. A., & Guacci, N. (1993). Convoys of social support: An intergenerational analysis. *Psychology and Aging, 8,* 323–326.

Levy, G. D. (1998). Effects of gender constancy and figure's height and sex on young children's gender-typed attributions. *Journal of General Psychology, 125,* 65–68.

Levy, R. I. (1996). Essential contrasts: Differences in parental ideas about learners and teaching in Tahiti and Nepal. In S. Harkness & C. M. Super (Eds.), *Parents' cultural belief systems* (pp. 123–142). New York, NY: Guilford Press.

Lewin, A., Hodgkinson, S., Waters, D. M., Prempeh, H. A., Beers, L. S., & Feinberg, M. E. (2015). Strengthening positive coparenting in teen parents: A cultural adaptation of an evidence-based intervention. *The Journal of Primary Prevention, 36,* 139–154.

Lewis, M. (2005). The child and its family: The social network model. *Human Development, 48,* 8–27.

Lewis, M., & Carmody, D. P. (2008). Self representation and brain development. *Developmental Psychology, 44,* 1329–1334.

Lewis, P. (2015). Assisted dying: What does the law in different countries say? *BBC News.* Retrieved from http://www.bbc.com/news/world-34445715

Lewis, T. T., Cogburn, C. D., & Williams, D. R. (2015). Self-reported experiences of discrimination and health: Scientific advances, ongoing controversies, and emerging issues. *Annual Review of Clinical Psychology, 11,* 407–440.

Li, J. (2009). Forging the future between two different worlds: Recent Chinese immigrant adolescents tell their cross-cultural experiences. *Journal of Adolescent Research, 24,* 477–504.

Li, J., Hestenes, L. L., & Wang, Y. C. (2016). Links between preschool children's social skills and observed pretend play in outdoor childcare environments. *Early Childhood Education Journal, 44,* 61–68.

Li, Q., Kirby, R. S., Sigler, R. T., Hwang, S-S., LaGory, M. E., & Goldenberg, R. L. (2010). A multilevel analysis of individual, household, and neighborhood correlates of intimate partner violence among low-income pregnant women in Jefferson County, Alabama. *American Journal of Public Health, 100,* 531–539.

Li, X., Stanton, B., & Feigelman, S. (1999). Exposure to drug trafficking among urban, low-income African American children and adolescents. *Archives of Pediatric Medicine, 155,* 161–168.

Liang, B., Williams, L. M., & Siegel, J. A. (2006). Relational outcomes of childhood sexual trauma in female survivors: A longitudinal study. *Journal of Interpersonal Violence, 21,* 42–57.

Liang, J., Brown, J. W., Krause, N. M., Ofstedal, M. B., & Bennett, J. (2005). Health and living arrangements among older Americans. *Journal of Aging and Health, 17,* 305–335.

Liang, J., Krause, N. M., & Bennett, J. M. (2001). Social exchange and well-being: Is giving better than receiving? *Psychology and Aging, 16,* 511–523.

Liao, M. (2016). Factors affecting post-permanency adjustment for children in adoption or guardianship placements: An ecological systems analysis. *Children and Youth Services Revies, 66,* 131–143.

Lieberman, A. F., Weston, D. R., & Pawl, J. H. (1991). Preventive intervention and outcome with anxiously attached dyads. *Child Development, 62,* 199–209.

Liebow, E. (1967). *Tally's corner: A study of Negro streetcorner men.* Boston, MA: Little Brown.

Liebow, E. (2003). *Tally's corner: A study of Negro streetcorner men* (2nd ed.). Lanham, MD: Roman and Littlefield Publishers.

ton, R. J. (1973). The sense of immortality: On death and the continuity of life. *American Journal of Psychoanalysis, 33,* 3–15.

Li-Grining, C. P. (2007). Effortful control among low-income preschoolers in three cities: Stability, change and individual differences. *Developmental Psychology, 43,* 208–221.

Lilienfeld, S. O. (2012). Public skepticism of psychology. *American Psychologist, 67,* 111–129.

Lillard, A. S., Lerner, M. D., Hopkins, E. J., et al. (2013). The impact of pretend play on children's development: A review of the evidence. *Psychological Bulletin, 139,* 1–34.

Lillard, A. S., & Peterson, J. (2011). The immediate impact of different types of television on young children's executive function. *Pediatrics, 128,* 644–649.

Lim, S., Cortina, L. M., & Magley, V. J. (2008). Personal and work group incivility: Impact on work and health outcomes. *Journal of Applied Psychology, 93,* 85–107.

Lin, R. -G., II. (2001, February 23). Nation's colleges anticipate end of SATs at UC schools. *Daily Californian, University of California, Berkeley.* Retrieved from http://www.studentadvantage.com_article_0,1075,c0-i0-t0-a1333686,00.html

Lindemann, E. (1944). Symptomology and management of acute grief. *American Journal of Psychiatry, 101,* 141–148.

Lindsey, E. W. (1994). Homelessness. In P. C. McKenry & S. J. Price (Eds.), *Families and change: Coping with stressful events* (pp. 281–302). Thousand Oaks, CA: Sage.

Lindsey, E. W., & Colwell, M. J. (2003). Preschoolers' emotional competence: Links to pretend and physical play. *Child Study Journal, 33,* 39–52.

Lindsey, E. W., Mize, J., & Pettit, G. S. (1997). Mutuality in parent–child play: Consequences for children's peer competence. *Journal of Social and Personal Relationships, 14,* 523–538.

Link, B., Phelan, J., Bresnahan, M., & Stueve, A. (1995). Lifetime and five-year pevalence of homelessness in the United States: New evidence on an old debate. *American Journal of Orthopsychiatry, 65,* 347–354.

Linsk, N. L., & Mason, S. (2004). Stresses on grandparents and other relatives caring for children affected by HIV/AIDS. *Health & Social Work, 29,* 127–136.

Lipina, S. J., & Colombo, J. A. (2009). *Poverty and brain development during childhood: An approach from cognitive psychology and neuroscience.* Washington, DC: American Psychological Association.

Lippert, T., & Prager, K. J. (2001). Daily experiences of intimacy: A study of couples. *Personal Relationships, 8,* 283–298.

Liptak, A. (2009, June 29). Supreme Court finds bias against white firefighters. *New York Times,* Page A1.

Littlefield, D., Robison, C. C., Engelbecht, L., Gonzalez, B., & Hutcheson, H. (2002). Mobilizing women for minority health and social justice in California. *American Journal of Public Health, 92,* 576–579.

Litwin, H. (1997). Support network type and health service utilization. *Research on Aging, 19,* 274–299.

Litwin, H., & Shiovitz-Ezra, S. (2011). Social network type and subjective well-being in a national sample of older Americans. *The Gerontologist, 51,* 379–388.

Litwin, H., Vogel, C., Künemund, H., & Kohli, M. (2008). The balance of intergenerational exchange: Correlates of net transfers in Germany and Israel. *European Journal of Ageing, 5,* 91–102.

Live Science Staff. (2011). Why are "Mama" and "Dada" a baby's first words? Retrieved from http://www.livescience.com/32191-why-are-mama-and-dada-a-babys-first-words.html\

Livesley, W. J., Jackson, D. N., & Schroeder, M. L. (1992). Factorial structure of traits delineating personality disorders in clinical and general population samples. *Journal of Abnormal Psychology, 101,* 432–440.

Llewellyn, N., Rudolph, K. D., & Roisman, G. I. (2012). Other-sex relationship stress and sex differences in the contribution of puberty to depression. *The Journal of Early Adolescence, 32,* 824–850.

Lo, N. C., Lowe, A., & Bendavid, E. (2016). Abstinence funding was not associated with reduction in HIV risk behavior in Sub Saharan Africa. *Health Affairs, 35,* 856–863.

Lo, R., & Brown, R. (1999). Stress and adaptation: Preparation for successful retirement. *Australian and New Zealand Journal of Mental Health Nursing, 8,* 30–38.

Lobel, T. E., & Menashri, J. (1993). Relations of conceptions of gender-role transgressions and gender constancy to gender-typed toy preferences. *Developmental Psychology, 29,* 150–155.

Locker, J., & Cropley, M. (2004). Anxiety, depression, and self-esteem in secondary school children: An investigation into the impact of standard assessment tests (SATs) and other important school examinations. *School Psychology International, 25,* 333–345.

Lockery, S. (1991). Caregiving among racial and ethnic minority elders. *Generations, 15,* 58–62.

Lodi-Smith, J., Turiano, N., & Mroczek, D. (2011). Personality trait development across the lifespan. In K. L. Fingerman, C. A. Berg, J. Smith, & T. C. Antonucci (Eds.), *Handbook of lifespan development* (pp. 513–530). New York, NY: Springer.

Loevinger, J. (1976). *Ego development.* San Francisco, CA: Jossey-Bass.

Loftus, E. F. (1993). The reality of repressed memories. *American Psychologist, 48,* 518–537.

Lohman, B. J. (2000). School and family contexts: Relationship to coping with conflictduring the individuation process. Unpublished doctoral dissertation, Ohio State University.

Loizou, E. (2005). Infant humor: The theory of the absurd and the empowerment theory. *International Journal of Early Years Education, 13,* 43–53.

Lombardi, D. N., Melchior, E. J., Murphy, J. G., & Brinkerhoff, A. L. (1996). The ubiquity of life-style. *Individual Psychology: Journal of Adlerian Theory, Research and Practice, 52,* 31–41.

Longoria, R. A. (2010). Grandparents raising grandchildren: The association of grandparents' self-reported use of alcohol and drugs and their emotional well-being. *American Journal of Orthopsychiatry, 80,* 401–411.

Longtermcare.gov. (2013). *How much care will you need?* Retrieved from http://longtermcare.gov/the-basics/how-much-care-will-you-need/

Lopata, H. Z. (1978). Widowhood: Social norms and social integration. In H. Z. Lopata (Ed.), *Family factbook.* Chicago, IL: Marquis Academic Media.

López, A., Correa-Chávez, M., Rogoff, B., & Gutiérrez, K. (2010). Attention to instruction directed to another by U.S. Mexican-heritage children of varying cultural backgrounds. *Developmental Psychology, 46,* 593–601.

Lopez, A., Gelman, S. A., Gutheil, G., & Smith, E. (1992). The development of category-based inductions. *Child Development, 63,* 1070–1090.

Lopez, S. J., & Snyder, C. R. (2003). *Positive psychological assessment: A handbook of models and measures.* Washington, DC: American Psychological Association.

Lorenz, K. F. (1935). Der Kumpan in der Urwelt des Vogels. *Journal Ornithologie, 83,* 137.

Lorenz, K. F. (1937/1961). Imprinting. In R. C. Birney & R. C. Teevan (Eds.), *Instinct.* Princeton, NJ: Van Nostrand.

Lott, B. (2012). The social psychology of class and classism. *American Psychologist, 67,* 650–658.

Lott, B., & Bullock, H. E. (2001). Who are the poor? *Journal of Social Issues, 57,* 189–206.

Louchheim, T. (1997). *Jewish customs of mourning.* Retrieved from http://scheinerman.net/judaism/ life-cycle/mourning.html

Lourenço, O. (2012). Piaget and Vygotsky: Many resemblances and a crucial difference. *New Ideas in Psychology, 30,* 281–295.

Love, J. M., Chazan-Cohen, R., Raikes, H., & Brooks-Gunn, J. (2013). What makes a difference: Early Head Start evaluation findings in a developmental context. *Monographs of the Society for Research in Child Development, 78* (Serial No. 306).

Low, S., & Mulford, C. (2013). Use of a social-ecological framework to understand how and under what conditions family violence exposure affects children's adjustment. *Journal of Family Violence, 28,* 1–3.

Lowenstein, A., & Daatland, S. O. (2006). Filial norms and family support in a comparative cross-national context: Evidence from the OASIS study. *Ageing and Society, 26,* 203–223.

Lu, T., Pan, Y., Kao, S-Y., Li, C., Kohane, I., Chan, J., et al. (2004). Gene regulation and DNA damage in the ageing human brain. *Nature, 429,* 883–891.

Luby, J. L. (2010). Preschool depression: The importance of identification of depression early in development. *Current Directions in Psychological Science, 19,* 91–95.

Luby, J., Belden, A., Sullivan, J., Hayen, R., McCadney, A., & Spitznagel, E. (2009). Shame and guilt in preschool depression: Evidence for elevations in self-conscious emotions in depression as early as age 3. *Journal of Child Psychology and Psychiatry, 50,* 1156–1166.

Lucariello, J. (1987). Spinning fantasy: Themes, structure, and the knowledge base. *Child Development, 58,* 434–442.

Lucassen, N., Kok, R., Bakermans-Kranenburg, M. J., Van Ijzendoorn, M. H., et al. (2015). Executive functions in early childhood: The role of maternal and paternal parenting practices. *British Journal of Developmental Psychology, 33,* 489–505.

Ludemann, P. M., & Nelson, C. A. (1988). Categorical-representation of facial expressions by 7-month-old infants. *Developmental Psychology, 24,* 492–501.

Ludwig, J., & Miller, D. (2007). Does Head Start improve children's life chances? Evidence from a regression discontinuity design. *The Quarterly Journal of Economics, 122,* 159–208.

Ludwig, J., & Phillips, D. (2007). The ben-efits and costs of Head Start. *SRCD Social Policy Report, 21,* 3–18.

Luedi, P. P., Dietrich, F. S., Weidman, J. R., Bosko, J. N., Jirtle, R. L., & Hartemink, A. J. (2007). Computational and experimental identification of novel human imprinted genes. *Genome Research, 17,* 1723–1730.

Luger, T., Cotter, K. A., & Sherman, A. M. (2009). It's all in how you view it: Pessimism, social relations, and life satisfaction in older adults with osteoarthritis. *Aging and Mental Health, 13,* 635–647.

Lugo-Gil, J. & Tamis-LeMonda, C. S. (2008). Family resources and parenting quality: Links to children's cognitive development across the first thee years. *Child Development, 79,* 1065–1085.

Lukas, W. D., & Campbell, B. C. (2000). Evolutionary and ecological aspects of early brain malnutrition in humans. *Human Nature, 11,* 1–26.

Lumeng, J., Kaciroti, N., Sutrza, J., Krusky, A. M., Miller, A. L., Peterson, K. E., Lipton, R., & Reischl, T. M. (2015). Changes in body mass index associated with Head Start participation. *Pediatrics, 135,* 1–8.

Luna, B., Paulsen, D. J., Padmanabhan, A., & Geier, C. (2013). The teenage brain: Cognitive control and motivation. *Current Directions in Psychological Science, 22,* 94–100.

Luo, S., & Snider, A. G. (2009). Accuracy and biases in newlyweds' perceptions of each other. *Psychological Science, 11,* 1332–1339.

Lustig, C., & Lin, Z. (2016). Memory: Behavior and neural basis. In K.Warner-Schaie & S. Willis (Eds.), *Handbook of the psychology of aging* (8th ed.) (pp. 147–165). San Diego, CA: Academic Press/Elsevier.

Luyckx, K., Goossens, L., Soenens, B., Beyers, W., & Vansteenkiste, M. (2005). Identity statuses based on four rather than two identity dimensions: Extending and refining Marcia's paradigm. *Journal of Youth and Adolescence, 34,* 605–618.

Lydon, J., Dunkel-Schetter, C., Cohan, C. L., & Pierce, T. (1996). Pregnancy decision making as a significant life event: A commitment approach. *Journal of Personality and Social Psychology, 71,* 141–151.

Lyerly, A. D., Little, M. O., & Faden, R. R. (2009). The National Children's Study: A golden opportunity to advance the health of pregnant women. *American Journal of Public Health, 99,* 1742–1745.

Lyles, L. (1991). What I learned from my mother. In H. L. Gates Jr. (Ed.), *Bearing witness: Selections from African-American autobiography in the twentieth century* (p. 242). New York, NY: Pantheon Books.

Lynam, D. R., & Henry, G. (2001). The role of neuropsychological deficits in conduct disorders. In J. Hill & B. Maughan (Eds.), *Conduct disorders in childhood and adolescence* (pp. 235–263). New York, NY: Cambridge University Press.

Lyons, K. S., Zarit, S. H., Sayer, A. G., & Whitlatch, C. J. (2002). Caregiving as a dyadic process: Perspectives from caregiver and receiver. *Journal of Gerontology: Psychological Science 57B,* P195–P204.

Lyons-Ruth, K., Connell, D. B., Zoll, D., & Stahl, J. (1987). Infants at social risk: Relations among infant maltreatment, maternal behavior, and infant attachment behavior. *Developmental Psychology, 23*, 223–232.

Lyons-Ruth, K., & Jacobvitz, D. (2016). Attachment disorganization from infancy to adulthood: Neurobiological correlates, parenting contexts, and pathways to disorder. In J. Cassidy & P.R. Shaver (Eds.), *Handbook of attachment* (3rd ed.). New York: Guilford Press.

Lyons-Ruth, K., Lyubchik, A., Wolfe, R., & Bronfman, E. (2002). Parental depression and child attachment: Hostile and helpless profiles of paent and child behavior among families at risk. In S. H. Goodman & I. H. Gotlib (Eds.), *Children of depressed parents: Mechanisms of risk and implications for treatment* (pp. 89–120). Washington, DC: American Psychological Association.

Lytle, M. C., Clancy, M. E., Foley, P. F., & Cotter, E. W. (2015). Current trends in retirement: Implications for career counseling and vocational psychology. *Journal of Career Development, 42*, 170–184.

Ma, L., & Woolley, J. D. (2013). Young children's sensitivity to speaker gender when learning from others. *Journal of Cognition and Development, 14*, 100–119.

Maccoby, E. E. (1988). Gender as a social category. *Developmental Psychology, 24*, 755–765.

Maccoby, E. E. (1990). Gender and relationships: A developmental account. *American Psychologist, 45*, 513–520.

Maccoby, E. E. (1992). The role of parents in the socialization of children: An historical overview. *Developmental Psychology, 28*, 1006–1017.

Maccoby, E. E. (2002). Perspectives on gender development. In W. W. Hartup & R. K. Silbereisen (Eds.), *Growing points in developmental science* (pp. 202–222). New York, NY: Psychology Press.

Maccoby, E. E., & Jacklin, C. N. (1987). Gender segregation in childhood. In E. H. Reese (Ed.), *Advances in child development and behavior* (Vol. 20, pp. 239–287). New York, NY: Academic Press.

MacCormack, C. P. (1994). *Ethnography of fertility and birth* (2nd ed.). Long Grove, IL: Waveland Press.

MacDermid, S. M., Huston, T. L., & McHale, S. M. (1990). Changes in marriage associated with transition to parenthood. *Journal of Marriage and the Family, 52*, 475–486.

MacDonald, D. J., Côté, J., Eys, M., & Deakin, J. (2011). The role of enjoyment and motivational climate in relation to the personal development of team sport athletes. *The Sport Psychologist, 25*, 32–46.

MacDonald, M. G. & Seshia, M. M. K. (2016). *Avery's neonatology: Pathophysiology and management of the newborn* (7th ed.). Philadelphia: Wolters Kluwer.

Macdonald, M. J., Wong, P. T. P., & Gingras, D. T. (2011). Meaning-in-life measures and development of fa brief version of the personal meaning profile. In P. T. P. Wong (Ed.), *The human question for meaning* (2nd ed.) (pp. 357–382). New York: Routledge.

Mace, D. R. (1982). *Close companions*. New York, NY: Continuum.

MacEvoy, J. P., & Asher, S. R. (2012). When friends disappoint: Boys' and girls' responses to transgressions of friendship expectations. *Child Development, 83*, 104–119.

MacEvoy, J. P., Papadakis, A. A., Fedigan, S. K., & Ash, S. E. (2016). Friendship expectations and children's friendship-related behavior and adjustment. *Merrill-Palmer Quarterly, 62*, 74–104.

Maciejewski, D. F., van Lier, P. A. C., Branje, S. J. T., Meeus, W. H. J., & Koot, H. M. (2016, April 21). A daily diary study on adolescent emotional experiences: Measurement invariance and developmental trajectories. *Psychological Assessment.*

MacKain, S. J. (1997). "I know he's a boy because my tummy tells me": Social and cognitive contributions to children's understanding of gender. Unpublished doctoral dissertation, University of North Carolina, Chapel Hill.

MacLean, A., & Elder, G. H., Jr. (2007). Military service in the life course. *Annual Review of Sociology 36*, 175–196.

MacLean, D. J., & Schuler, M. (1989). Conceptual development in infancy: The understanding of containment. *Child Development, 60*, 1126–1137.

MacLean, N. (2006). *Freedom is not enough: The opening of the American workplace.* Cambridge, MA: Harvard University Press.

MacMurray, B., & Aslin, R. N. (2004). Anticipatory eye movements reveal infants' auditory and visual categories. *Infancy, 6*, 203–229.

MacTurk, R. H., McCarthy, M. E., Vietze, P. M., & Yarrow, L. J. (1987). Sequential analysis of mastery behavior in 6- and 12-month-old infants. *Developmental Psychology, 23*, 199–203.

MacWhinney, B. (2015). Language development. In R.M. Lerner, L. S. Liben & U. Mueller (Eds.), *Handbook of child psychology and developmental science: Cognitive processes, Vol. 2.* (7th ed., pp. 296–338). Hoboken NJ: Wiley.

Madden, D. J. (2001). Speed and timing of behavioral processes. In J. E. Birren & K. W. Schaie (Eds.), *Handbook of the psychology of aging* (5th ed., pp. 288–312). San Diego, CA: Academic Press.

Madden, N. A., Slavin, R. E., Karweit, N. L., Doaln, L. J., & Wasik, B. A. (1993). Success for all: Longitudinal effects of a restructuring program for inner-city elementary schools. *American Educational Research Journal, 30*, 123–148.

Madon, S., Jussim, L., & Eccles, J. (1997). In search of the powerful self-fulfillingprophecy. *Journal of Personality and Social Psychology, 72*, 791–809.

Mahanian, M. (2008). In their own words. *UCLA College Report, 10*, 27.

Mahay, J., & Lewin, A. C. (2007). Age and the desire to marry. *Journal of Family Issues, 28*, 706–723.

Mahler, E. B. (2011). Midlife work role transitions: Generativity and learning in 21st century careers. In C. Hoare (Ed.), *The Oxford handbook of reciprocal adult development and learning* (2nd ed., pp. 186–214). New York, NY: Oxford University Press.

Mahler, M. S. (1963). Thoughts about development and individuation. *Psychoanalytic Study of the Child, 18*, 307–324.

Mahler, M. S., & Furer, M. (1968). *On human symbiosis and the vicissitudes of individuation.* New York, NY: International Universities Press.

Mahler, M., Pine, F., & Bergman, A. (1975). *The psychological birth of the human infant.* New York, NY: Basic Books.

Main, M., & Solomon, J. (1990). Procedures for identifying infants as disorganized /disoriented during the Ainsworth Strange Situation. In M. T. Greenberg, D. Cicchetti, & E. M. Cummings (Eds.), *Attachment during the preschool years: Theory, research and intervention* (pp. 121–160). Chicago, IL: University of Chicago Press.

Main, N., Kaplan, N., & Cassidy, J. (1985). Security in infancy, childhood, and adulthood: A move to the level of representation. In I. Bretherton & E. Everett (Eds.), Growing points of attachment theory and research (pp. 60–104). *Monographs of the Society for Research in Child Development, 50*(1–2, Serial No. 209).

Major, B., Appelbaum, M., Beckman, L., Dutton, M. A., Russo, N. F., & West, C. (2009). Abortion and mental health. *American Psychologist, 64*, 863–890.

Majors, K. (2013). Children's perceptions of their imaginary companions and the purposes they serve: An exploratory in the United Kingdom. *Childhood: A Global Journal of Child Research, 20*, 550–565.

Makin, S. (2015). What really causes autism? *Scientific American Mind, 26*, 56–63.

Malanowski, J. (1997, November 3). Generation. *www.Time* (digital), 42–49.

Malatesta, C. A., & Izard, C. E. (1984). The ontogenesis of human social signals: From biological imperative to symbol utilization. In N. A. Fox & R. J. Davidson (Eds.), *The psychobiology of affective development* (pp. 161–206). Hillsdale, NJ: Erlbaum.

Malete, L., Chow, G. M., & Feltz, D. L. (2013). Influence of coaching efficacy and coaching competency on athlete-level moral variables in Botswana youth soccer. *Journal of Applied Social Psychology, 43*, 2107–2119.

Malin, H., Ballard, P. J., & Damon, W. (2015). Civic purpose: An integrated construct or understanding civic development in adolescence. *Human Development, 58*, 103–130.

Malin, J. L., Cabrera, N. J., Karberg, E., Aldoney, D., & Rowe, M. L. (2014). Low-income, minority fathers' control strategies and their children's regulatory skills. *Infant Mental Health Journal, 35*, 462–472.

Malle, B. F., & Horowitz, L. M. (1995). The puzzle of negative self-views: An explanation using the schema concept. *Journal of Personality and Social Psychology, 68,* 470–484.

Malone, L., West, J., Flanagan, K. D., & Park, J. (2006). The early reading and mathematics achievement of children who repeated kindergarten or who began school a year late. *Statistics in Brief.* Retrieved from http://nces.ed.gov/pubs2006/2006064.pdf

Malone, S. K. (2011). Early to bed, early to rise?: An exploration of adolescent sleep hygiene practices. *The Journal of School Nursing, 27,* 348–354.

Malti, T. (2013). *Adolescent emotions: Development, morality, and adaptation: New Directions for Youth Development, #136.* San Francisco, CA: Jossey-Bass.

Mandel, D. R., Jusczyk, P. W., & Pisoni, D. B. (1995). Infants' recognition of the sound patterns of their own names. *Psychological Science, 6,* 314–317.

Mandel, J. L., Monaco, A. P., Nelson, D. L., Schlessinger, D., & Willard, H. (1992). Genome analysis and the human X chromosome. *Science, 258,* 103–109.

Mangelsdorf, S. C., Plunkett, J. W., Dedrick, C. F., Berlin, M., Meisels, S. J., McHale, J. L., et al. (1996). Attachment security in very low birth weight infants. *Developmental Psychology, 32,* 914–920.

Mannella, J. A., & Trabulsi, J. C. (2012). Complementary foods and flavor experiences: Setting the foundation. *Annual Nutrition and Metabolism, 60,* Supplement 2, 40–50.

Mantua, J., Baran, B., & Spencer, R. M. C. (2016). Sleep benefits consolidation of visuo-motor adaptation learning in older adults. *Experimental Brain Research, 234,* 587–595.

Marceau, K., Ram, N., Houts, R. M., Grimm, K. G., & Susman, E. J. (2011). Individual differences in boys' and girls' timing and tempo of puberty: Modeling development with nonlinear growth models. *Developmental Psychology, 47,* 1389–1409.

Marcenaro-Gutierrez, O. D., Lugue, M., & Lopez-Agudo, L. A. (2015, October 28). Balancing teachers' math satisfaction and other indicators of the education system's performance. *Social Indicators Research.*

March of Dimes. (2013). *Emotional and life changes.* Retrieved from www.marchofdimes.com/pregnancy/lifechanges_indepth.html

March of Dimes. (2016). *Caffeine in pregnancy.* Retrieved from http://www.marchofdimes.org/pregnancy/caffeine-in-pregnancy.aspx

Marchman, V. A., & Fernald, A. (2008). Speed of word recognition and vocabulary knowledge in infancy predict cognitive and language outcomes in later childhood. *Developmental Science, 11,* 9–16.

Marcia, J. E. (1980). Identity in adolescence. In J. Adelson (Ed.), *Handbook of adolescent psychology* (pp. 159–187). New York, NY: Wiley.

Marcia, J. E. (1993). The relational roots of identity. In J. Kroger (Ed.), *Discussions on ego identity* (pp. 101–120). Hillsdale, NJ: Erlbaum.

Marcia, J. E. (2002). Identity and psychosocial development in adulthood. *Identity, 2,* 7–28.

Marcia, J. E. (2006). Ego identity and personality disorders. *Journal of Personality Disorders, 20,* 577–596.

Marcia, J. E. (2007). Theory and measure: The identity status interview. In M. Watz-lawik & A Born (Eds.), *Capturing identity: Quantitative and qualitative methods* (pp. 186–214). Lanham, MD: University Press of America.

Marcia, J. E. (2010). Life transitions and stress in the context of psychosocial development. In T. W. Miller (Ed.), *Handbook of stressful transitions across the lifespan* (pp. 19–34). New York, NY: Springer Science + Business Media.

Marcia, J. E. (2014). From industry to integrity. *Identity: An International Journal of Theory and Research, 14,* 165–176.

Marcia, J. E., Waterman, A. S., Matteson, D. R., Archer, S. L., & Orlofsky, J. L. (1993). *Ego identity: A handbook for psychosocial research.* New York: Springer.

Marcus, G. F. (1996). Why do children say "breaked"? *Current Directions in Psychological Science, 5,* 81–85.

Marcus, G. F. (2000). Pabiku and Ga Ti Ga: Two mechanisms infants use to learn about the world. *Current Directions in Psychological Science, 9,* 145–147.

Mares, M-L., & Woodard, E. (2005). Positive effects of television on children's social interactions: A meta-analysis, *Media Psychology 7,* 301–322.

Margolin, G., Ramos, M. C., Timmons, A. C., Miller, K. F., & Han, S. C. (2016). Intergenerational transmission of aggression: Physiological regulatory processes. *Child Development Perspectives, 10,* 15–21.

Marini, Z. A., Dane, A. V., Bosacki, S. L., & YLC-CURA. (2006). Direct and indirect bully-victims: Different psychosocial risk factors associated with adolescents involved in bullying and victimization. *Aggressive Behavior, 32,* 551–569.

Markel, A. (2016). *Pivot: The art and science of reinventing your career and life.* New York: Atria Books.

Markovits, H., Benenson, J., & Dolenszky, E. (2001). Evidence that children and adolescents have internal models of peer interactions that are gender differentiated. *Child Development, 72,* 879–886.

Marks, S. R. (1989). Toward a systems theory of marital quality. *Journal of Marriage and the Family, 51,* 15–26.

Marks, S. R., Huston, T. L., Johnston, E. M., & MacDermid, S. M. (2001). Role balance among white married couples. *Journal of Marriage and the Family, 63,* 1083–1098.

Markstrom, C. A., & Marshall, S. K. (2007). The psychosocial inventory of ego strengths: Examination of theory and psychometric properties. *Journal of Adolescence, 30,* 63–79.

Markstrom, C. A., Sabino, V. M., Turner, B. J., & Berman, R. C. (1997). The psychosocial inventory of ego strengths: Development and validation of a new Eriksonian measure. *Journal of Youth and Adolescence, 26,* 705–732.

Markus, H. R., Mullally, P., & Kitayama, S. (1997). Selfways: Diversity in modes of cultural participation. In U. Neisser & D. A. Jopling (Eds.), *The conceptual self in context: Culture, experience, self-understanding* (pp. 13–61). Cambridge, England: Cambridge University Press.

Marquardt, M., Seng, N.C., & Goodson, H. (2010). Team development via action learning. *Advances in Developing Human Resources, 12,* 241–259.

Marsh, H. W., & Kleitman, S. (2005). Consequences of employment during high school: Character building, subversion of academic goals, or a threshold? *American Educational Research Journal, 42,* 331–370.

Marshall, S. K. (2004). Relative contributions of perceived mattering to parents and friends in predicting adolescents' psychological well-being. *Perceptual and Motor Skills, 99,* 591–601.

Marsiglio, W. (1989). Adolescent males' pregnancy resolution preferences and family formation intentions: Does family background make a difference for Blacks and Whites? *Journal of Adolescent Research, 4,* 214–237.

Marsiglio, W. (1993). Adolescent males' orientation toward paternity and contraception. *Family Planning Perspectives, 25,* 22–31.

Marsiglio, W. (2004). When stepfathers claim stepchildren: A conceptual analysis. *Journal of Marriage and the Family, 66,* 22–39.

Marsiglio, W., & Pleck, J. H. (2005). Fatherhood and masculinities. In R. W. Connell, J. Hearn, & M. Kimmel (Eds.), *The handbook of studies on men and masculinities* (pp. 249–269). Thousand Oaks CA: Sage.

Martin, C. L. (1989). Children's use of gender-related information in making social judgments. *Developmental Psychology, 25,* 80–88.

Martin, C. L., Eisenbud, L., & Rose, H. (1995). Children's gender-based reasoning about toys. *Child Development, 66,* 1453–1471.

Martin, C. L., Fabes, R. A., & Hanish, L. D. (2011). Gender and temperament in young children's social interactions. In A. D. Pellegrini (Ed.), *The Oxford handbook of the development of play* (pp. 214–230). New York, NY: Oxford University Press.

Martin, C. L., Fabes, R. A., & Hanish, L. (2014). Gendered-peer relationships in educational contexts. In L.S. Liben & R.S. Bigler (Vol. Eds) and J. Benson (Series Ed.), *The role of gender in educational contexts and outcomes. Advances in child development and behavior* (pp. 151–187). San Diego, CA: Elsevier.

Martin, C. L., Fabes, R. A. Hanish, L. D., Leonard, S., & Dinella, L.M. (2011). Experienced and expected similarity to same gendered peers: Moving toward a comprehensive model of gender segregation. *Sex Roles, 65,* 421–434.

Martin, C. L., & Halverson, C. F. (1987). The roles of cognition in sex roles acquisition. In D. B. Carter (Ed.), *Current conceptions of sex roles and sex typing: Theory and research* (pp. 123–137). New York, NY: Praeger.

Martin, C. L., & Ruble, D. N. (2004). Children's search for gender cues: Cognitive perspectives on gender development. *Current Directions in Psychological Science, 13,* 67–70.

Martin, C. L., & Ruble, D. N. (2010). Patterns of gender development. *Annual Review of Psychology, 61,* 353–381.

Martin, C. L., Ruble, D. N., & Szkrybalo, J. (2002). Cognitive theories of early gender development. *Psychological Bulletin, 128,* 903–933.

Martin, J. A., Hamilton, B. E., Osterman, M. J. K., Curtin, S. C. & Mathews, T. J. (2015). Births: Final data for 2013. *National Vital Statistics Reports, 64*(1). Hyattsville, MD: National Center for Health Statistics.

Martin, J. A., Hamilton, B. E., Ventura, S. J., Osterman, M. J. K., Wilson, E. C., & Matthews, T. J., (2012). Births: Final data for 2010. *National Vital Statistics Report, 61.*

Martin, M., & Wright, M. (2008). Dyadic cog-nition in old age: Paradigms, findings, anddirections. In S. M. Hoffer & D. F. Alwin (Eds.), *Handbook of cognitive aging: Interdisciplinary perspectives* (pp. 629–646). Thousand Oaks, CA: Sage.

Martin, P., Kelly, N., Kahana, B., Kahana, E., Willcox, B. J., Willcox, D. C., & Poon, L. W. (2015). Defining successful aging: A tangible or elusive concept? *The Gerontologist, 55,* 14–25.

Martin, T. C. (2002). Consensual unions in Latin America: Persistence of a dual nuptiality system. *Journal of Comparative Family Studies, 33,* 35–55.

Martinez, G. M., & Abma, J. C. (2015, July). Sexual activity, contraceptive use, and childbearing of teenagers aged 15–19 in the United States. *NCHS Data Brief, No. 209.* Hyattsville, MD: National Center for Health Statistics.

Martinez, G., Copen, C. E., & Abma, J. C. (2011). Teenagers in the United States: Sexual activity, contraceptive use, and childbearing, 2006–2010. National Survey of Family Growth. *Vital and Health Statistics, Series 23*(31).

Martino, S. C., Elliott, M. N., Collins, R. L., Kanouse, D. E., & Berry, S. H. (2008). Virginity pledges among the willing: Delays in first intercourse and consistency of condom use. *Journal of Adolescent Health, 43,* 341–348.

Marvin, R. S., & Britner, P. A. (2008). Normative development: The ontogeny of attachment. In J. Cassidy & P. R. Shaver (Eds.), *Handbook of attachment: Theory, research and clinical applications* (pp. 269–294). New York, NY: Guilford.

Mascarelli, A. L. (2012). The teenage brain. *Science News for Students.* Retrieved from https://student.society-forscience.org /article/teenage-brain

Maslow, A. H. (1943). A theory of human motivation. *Psychological Review, 50,* 370–396.

Maslow, A. H. (1968). *Toward a psychology of being* (2nd ed.). Princeton, NJ: Van Nostrand.

Massey, A. (2016). Feeling lonely when you're single doesn't mean you're weak. *New York Magazine.* Retrieved from http://nymag .com/thecut/2016/03/feeling-lonely-when -single-not-weakness.html

Massey, Z., Rising, S. S., & Ickovics, J. (2005). Centering Pregnancy group prenatal care: Promoting relationship-centered care. *Journal of Obstetric Gynecologic and Neonatal Nursing, 35,* 286–294.

Masten, A. S. (2001). Ordinary magic: Resilience processes in development. *American Psychologist, 56,* 227–238.

Masten, A. S., Obradovi´c. J., & Burt, K. B. (2006). Resilience in emerging adulthood: Developmental perspectives on continuity and transformation. In J. J. Arnett & J. S. Tanner (Eds.), *Emerging adults in America: Coming of age in the 21st century* (pp. 173–190). Washington, DC: American Psychological Association.

Masters, W., & Johnson, V. (1966). *Human sexual response.* Boston, MA: Little, Brown.

Masuda, M. (1994). Exclusivity in heterosexual romantic relationships. *Japanese Journal of Experimental Social Psychology, 34,* 164–182.

Masunaga, H., & Horn, J. (2000). Characterizing mature human intelligence: Expertise development. *Learning and Individual Differences, 12,* 5–33.

Masunaga, H., & Horn, J. (2001). Expertise and age-related changes in components of intelligence. *Psychology and Aging, 16,* 293–311.

Mathews, T. J., MacDorman, M. F. & Thoma, M. E. (2015). Infant mortality statistics from the 2013 period linked birth/infant death data set. *National Vital Statistics Reports. 64*(9). Hyattsville, MD: National Center for Health Statistics.

Mathiowetz, N. A. (1999). Respondent uncertainty as indicator of response quality. *International Journal of Public Opinion Research, 11,* 289–296.

Matjasko, J. L., Vivolo-Kantor, A. M., Massetti, G. M., Holland, K. M., Holt, M. K., & Cruz, J. D. (2012). A systematic meta-review of evaluations of youth violence prevention programs: Common and divergent findings fom 25 years of meta-analyses and systematic reviews. *Aggression and Violent Behavior, 17,* 540–552.

Matsuba, M. K., Pratt, M. W., Norris, J. E., Mohle, E., Alisat, S., & McAdams, D. P. (2012). Environmentalism as a context for expressing identity and generativity: Patterns among activists and uninvolved youth and midlife adults. *Journal of Personality, 80,* 1091–1115.

Matte-Gagné, C., Harvey, B., Stack, D. M., & Serbin, L. A. (2015). Contextual specificity in the relationship between maternal autonomy support and children's socioemotional development: A longitudinal study from preschool to preadolescence. *Journal of Youth and Adolescence, 44,* 1528–1541.

Mattessich, P., & Hill, R. (1987). Life cycle and family development. In M. B. Suss-man & S. K. Steinmetz (Eds.), *Handbook of marriage and the family* (pp. 437–469). New York, NY: Plenum Press.

Mattson, M. P., & Magnus, T. (2006). Ageing and neuronal vulnerability. *Nature Reviews Neuroscience, 7,* 278–294.

Maupin, H. (2011). *Designing the adaptive enterprise—Part II strategy and structure.* Retrieved from http://righttojoy.com /uncategorized/transformation /organizational-transformation/designing- the-adaptive-enterprise%E2%80%94part -ii-strategy-and-structure

Max Planck Institute for Human Development and Stanford Center on Longevity. (2014). *A consensus on the brain training industry from the scientific community.* Retrieved from http://longevity3.stanford.edu/blog /2014/10/15/the-consensus-on-the-brain -training-industry-from-the-scientific -community/

Maxwell, J. A. (2009). Designing a qualitative study. In L. Bickman & D. Rog (Eds.), *The Sage handbook of applied social research methods* (2nd ed., pp. 214–253). Thousand Oaks, CA: Sage.

Maxwell, J. C. (2011). *The five levels of leadership: Proven steps to maximize your potential.* New York: Hachette Book Group.

Maxwell, L. E., & Chmielewski, E. J. (2008). Environmental personalization and elementary school children's self-esteem. *Journal of Environmental Psychology, 28,* 143–153.

May, R. B., & Norton, J. M. (1981). Training task orders and transfer in conservation. *Child Development, 52,* 904–913.

Maybury, K. (2015). Peer rejection: An interview with a teen and some tips for coping. *The Feminist Psychologist, 42,* 11–14.

Mayer, R. (1992). *Thinking, problem solving, and cognition* (2nd ed.). New York, NY: Freeman.

Mayo Clinic. (2012). *Antidepressants: Safe during pregnancy?* Retrieved from http://www .mayoclinic.com/health/antidepressants /DN00007

Mayo Clinic. (2013). *Child development chart: Preschool milestones.* Retrieved from www .mayoclinic.com/health/child -development/MY00136

Mayo Clinic. (2014a). *Pregnancy nutrition: Foods to avoid during pregnancy.* Retrieved from http://www.mayoclinic.org/healthy -lifestyle/pregnancy-week-by-week /in-depth/pregnancy-nutrition /art-20043844

Mayo Clinic. (2014b). *Oxytocin: The social hormone.* Retrieved from www.HealthLetter.MayoClinic.com

Mayo Clinic. (2014c). *Infant and toddler health. Potty training as a major milestone.* Retrieved from http://www.mayoclinic.org/healthy-lifestyle/infant-and-toddler-health/in-depth/potty-training/art-20045230

Mayo Clinic. (2014d). *Complicated grief.* Retrieved from http://www.mayoclinic.org/diseases-conditions/complicated-grief/basics/definition/con-20032765

Mayo Clinic. (2015a). *Antidepressants: Safe during pregnancy?* Retrieved from http://www.mayoclinic.org/healthy-lifestyle/pregnancy-week-by-week/in-depth/antidepressants/art-20046420?pg=1

Mayo Clinic. (2015b). *Infant and toddler health.* Retrieved from http://www.mayoclinic.org/healthy-lifestyle/infant-and-toddlerhealth

Mayo Clinic. (2015c). *Healthy Lifestyle: Adult Health, When your work life and personal life are out of balance, your stress level is likely to soar.* Retrieved from http://www.mayoclinic.org/healthy-lifestyle/adult-health/in-depth/work-life-balance/art-20048134?p=1

Mayo Clinic. (2016). Depression (major depressive disorder). Retrieved from http://www.mayoclinic.org/diseases-conditions/depression/basics/definition/con-20032977

Mayr, E. W. (1991). *One long argument: Charles Darwin and the genesis of modern evolutionary thought.* Cambridge, MA: Harvard University Press.

Mayser, S., Scheib, S., & Riediger, M. (2008). Unreachable? An empirical differentiation of goals and life longings. *European Psychologist, 13*, 126–140.

McAdams, D. P., & Bowman, P. J. (2001). Narrating life's turning points: Redemption and contamination. In D. P. McAdams, R. Josselson, & A. Lieblich (Eds.), *Turns in the road: Narrative studies of lives in transition.* Washington, DC: American Psychological Association.

McAdams, D. P., & de St. Aubin, E. (1992). A theory of generativity and its assessment through self-report, behavioral acts, and narrative themes in autobiography. *Journal of Personality and Social Psychology, 62*, 1003–1015.

McAdams, D. P., de St. Aubin, E., & Logan, R. L. (1993). Generativity among young, midlife, and older adults. *Psychology and Aging, 8*, 221–230.

McAdams, D. P., Diamond, A., de St. Aubin, E., & Mansfield, E. D. (1997). Stories of commitment: The psychosocial construction of generative lives. *Journal of Personality and Social Psychology, 72*, 678–694.

McAdoo, H. P. (1985). Racial attitude and self-concept of young Black children over time. In H. P. McAdoo & J. L. McAdoo (Eds.), *Black children: Social, educational, and parental environments* (pp. 213–242). Newbury Park, CA: Sage.

McAllister, L. E., & Boyle, J. S. (1998). Without money, means, or men: African American women receiving prenatal care in a housing project. *Family and Community Health, 21*, 67–79.

McArdle, J. J., Ferrer-Caja, E., Hamagami, F., & Woodcock, R. W. (2002). Comparative longitudinal structural analyses of the growth and decline of multiple intellectual abilities over the lifespan. *Developmental Psychology, 38*, 115–142.

McAuley, E., Duncan, T. E., & McElroy, M. (1989). Self-efficacy cognitions and causal attributions for children's motor performance: An exploratory investigation. *Journal of Genetic Psychology, 150*, 65–73.

McCabe, A. E., Siegel, L. S., Spence, I., & Wilkinson, A. (1982). Class-inclusion reasoning: Patterns of performance from three to eight years. *Child Development, 53*, 780–785.

McCabe, M. P., & Ricciardelli, L. A. (2001). Parent, peer, and media influence on body image and strategies to both increase and decrease body size among adolescent boys and girls. *Adolescence, 36*, 225–240.

McCarthy, B. W., & Sypeck, M. (2003). Childhood sexual trauma. In D. K. Snyder & M. A. Whisman (Eds.), *Treating difficult couples: Helping clients with co-existing mental and relationship disorders* (pp. 330–349). New York: Guilford Press.

McCarthy, E. (2013, June 6). For men, infertility often becomes a private heartache. *Washington Post Magazine.*

McCarthy, M. M. (2015). Sex differences in the brain. *The Scientist.* Retrieved from http://www.the-scientist.com/?articles.view/articleNo/44096/title/Sex-Differences-in-the-Brain/

McCarthy, M. P. (2008). Women's lived experience of infertility after unsuccessful medical intervention. *Journal of Midwifery and Women's Health, 53*, 319–324.

McClearn, G. E., Johansson, B., Berg, S., Pedersen, N. L., Ahern, F., Petrill, S. A., et al. (1997). Substantial genetic influenceon cognitive abilities in twins 80 or more years old. *Science, 276*, 1560–1563.

McClelland, J. L., & Rumelhart, D. E. (1986). *Parallel distributed processing* (Vol. 2). Cambridge, MA: MIT Press.

McCloskey, L. A., & Stuewig, J. (2001). The quality of peer relationship among children exposed to family violence. *Development and Psychopathology, 13*, 83–96.

McClure, E. B. (2000). A meta-analytic review of sex differences in facial expression processing and their development in infants, children and adolescents. *Psychological Bulletin, 126*, 424–453.

McComish, J. F., & Visger, J. M. (2009). Domains of postpartum doula care and maternal responsiveness and competence. *Journal of Obstetric Gynecologic and Neonatal Nursing: Clinical Scholarship for the Care of Women, Childbearing Families, and Newborns, 38*, 148–156.

McConatha, J. T., McConatha, D., Jackson, J. A., & Bergen, A. (1998). The control factor: Life satisfaction in later adulthood. *Journal of Clinical Geropsychology, 4*, 159–168.

McCool, W. R., Dorn, L. D., & Susman, E. J. (1994). The relation to cortisol reactivity and anxiety to perinatal outcome in primiparous adolescents. *Research in Nursing and Health, 17*, 411–420.

McCord, J. (1990). Problem behaviors. In S. S. Feldman & G. R. Elliott (Eds.), *At the threshold: The developing adolescent* (pp. 414–430). Cambridge, MA: Harvard University Press.

McCormick, C. M., Kuo, S. I., & Masten, A. S., (2011). Developmental tasks across the lifespan. In K. L. Fingerman, C. A. Berg, J. Smith, & T. C. Antonucci (Eds.), *Handbook of lifespan development* (pp. 117–139). New York, NY: Springer.

McCreary, L. L., & Dancy, B. L. (2004). Dimensions of family functioning: Perspectives of low-income African American single-parent families. *Journal of Marriage and the Family, 66*, 690–701.

McCubbin, H. I., & Patterson, J. M. (1982). Family adaptation to crisis. In H. I. McCubbin, A. E. Cauble, & J. M. Patterson (Eds.), *Family stress, coping, and social support* (pp. 26–47). Springfield, IL: Thomas.

McCubbin, H. I., & Patterson, J. M. (1983). The family stress process: The double ABCX model of adjustment and adaptation. *Marriage and Family Review, 6*, 7–37.

McDonough, L. (2002). Basic-level nouns: First learned but misunderstood. *Journal of Child Language, 29*, 357–377.

McDonough, C., Song, L., Hirsha-Pasek, K., Golinkoff, R. M., & Lannon, R. (2011). An image is worth a thousand words: Why nouns tend to dominate verbs in early word learning. *Developmental Science, 14*, 181–189.

McDonough, I. M., Haber, S., Bischof, G. N., & Park, D. C. (2015). The Synapse Project: Engagement in mentally challenging activities enhances neural efficiency. *Restorative Neurology and Neuroscience, 33*, 865–882.

McGonagle, K. A., Kessler, R. C., & Gotlib, I. H. (1993). The effects of marital disagreement style, frequency, and outcome on marital disruption. *Journal of Social and Personal Relationships, 10*, 385–404.

McGowen, K. R., & Hart, L. E. (1990). Still different after all these years: Gender differences in professional identity formation. *Professional Psychology: Research and Practice, 21*, 118–123.

McGuffin, Riley, B., & Plomin, R. (2001). Toward behavioral genomics. *Science, 291*, 1232–1249.

McHale, J. P., Kuersten-Hogan, R., & Rao, M. (2004). Growing points for coparenting theory and research. *Journal of Adult Development, II*(3), 221–234.

McHale, J. P., Vinden, P. G., Bush, L., Richer, D., Shaw, D., & Smith, B. (2005). Patterns of personal and social adjustment among sport-involved and non-involved urban middle-school children. *Sociology of Sport Journal, 22,* 119–136.

McIntosh, J. L. (1999). *U.S.A. Suicide: 1999 official final data.* Retrieved from http://www.suicidology.org/index.html

McKnight-Eily, L. R., Eaton, D. K., Lowry, R., Croft, J. B., Presley-Cantrell, L., & Perry, G. S. (2011). Relationships between hours of sleep and health-risk behaviors in U.S. adolescent students. *Preventive Medicine: An International Journal Devoted to Practice and Theory, 53,* 271–273.

McLean, K. C., & Pratt, M. W. (2006). Life's little (and big) lessons: Identity statuses and meaning-making in the turning point narratives of emerging adults. *Developmental Psychology, 42,* 714–722.

McLeod, J. D., & Shanahan, M. J. (1993). Poverty, parenting, and children's mental health. *American Sociological Review, 58,* 351–366.

McLoyd, V. C. (1990). The impact of economic hardship on Black families and children: Psychological distress, parenting, and socioemotional development. *Child Development, 61,* 311–346.

McLoyd, V. C. (1998). Socioeconomic disadvantage and child development. *American Psychologist, 53,* 185–204.

McLoyd, V. C., & Smith, J. (2002). Physical discipline and behavior problems in African American, European American, and Hispanic children: Emotional support as a moderator. *Journal of Marriage and the Family, 64,* 40–63.

McMunn, A., Bartley, M., Hardy, R., & Kuh, D. (2006). Life course social roles and women's health in mid-life: Causation or selection. *Journal of Epidemiology & Community Health, 60,* 484–489.

McRae, S. (1997). Cohabitation: A trial run for marriage? *Sexual and Marital Therapy, 12,* 259–273.

Meacham, J. A. (1995). Reminiscing as a process of social construction. In B. K. Haight & J. D. Webster (Eds.), *The art and science of reminiscing: Theory, research, methods, and applications* (pp. 37–48). Philadelphia, PA: Taylor & Francis.

Mead, G. H. (1934). *Mind, self, and society.* Chicago: University of Chicago Press.

Mead, M. (1928/1950). *Coming of age in Samoa.* New York, NY: New American Library.

Mead, M. (1935). *Sex and temperament in three primitive societies.* New York, NY: Morrow.

Mead, M. (1949/1955). *Male and female: A study of the sexes in a changing world.* New York, NY: Mentor.

Mead, M., & Newton, N. (1967). Cultural patterning of perinatal behavior. In S. A. Richardson & A. F. Guttmacher (Eds.), *Childbearing: Its social and psychological aspects.* Baltimore, MD: Williams & Wilkins.

Means-Christensen, A., Snyder, D., & Negy, C. (2003). Assessing nontraditional couples: Validity of the marital satisfaction inventory–Revised with gay, lesbian, and cohabiting heterosexual couples. *Journal of Marital and Family Therapy, 29,* 69–83.

Medicaid.gov. (2013). *Community-based long-term services and supports.* Retrieved from http://www.medicaid.gov/AffordableCareAct/Provisions/Community-Based-Long-Term-Services-and-Supports.html

Medline Plus. (2014). Hemophilia A. *A.D.A.M. Medical Encyclopedia.* Retrieved from https://www.nlm.nih.gov/medlineplus/ency/article/000538.htm

Medline Plus. (2015). *Genetic counseling.* Retrieved from https://www.nlm.nih.gov/medlineplus/geneticcounseling.htmlMeer, J. (1985, July). Loneliness. *Psychology Today, 19,* 28–33.

Meer, J. (1985). Loneliness. *Psychology Today, 19,* 28–33.

Meeus, W. (1996). Studies on identity development in adolescence: An overview of research and some new data. *Journal of Youth and Adolescence, 25,* 569–598.

Meeus, W., Iedema, J., Helsen, M., & Vollenbergh, W. (1999). Patterns of adolescent identity development: Review of literature and longitudinal analysis. *Developmental Review, 19,* 419–461.

Meeus, W., van de Schoot, R., Keijsers, L., Schwartz, S. J., & Branje, S. (2010). On the progression and stability of adolescent identity formation: A five-wave longitudinal study in early-to-middle and middle-to-late adolescence. *Child Development, 81,* 1565–1581.

Megan, K. (2016). Yale students speak out on campus racism; make demands. *Hartford Courant,* Retrieved from http://www.courant.com/education/hc-yale-racism-students-speak--20151115-story.html

Meier, E. A., Gallegos, J. V., Thomas, L. P., Depp, C. A., Irwin, S. A., & Jeste, D. V. (2016). Defining a good death (successful dying): Literature review and a call for research and public dialogue. *American Journal of Geriatric Psychiatry, 24,* 261–271.

Meins, E. (2011). Emotional development and attachment relationships. In A. Slater & J. D. Bremner (Eds.), *An introduction to developmental psychology* (2nd ed.) (pp. 183–216). Leicester, UK: The British Psychological Society and Blackwell Publishing, Ltd.

Melender, H. (2002). Experiences of fears associated with pregnancy and childbirth: A study of 329 pregnant women. *Birth: Issues in Perinatal Care, 29,* 101–111.

Mellor, S. (1989). Gender differences in identity formation as a function of self–other relationships. *Journal of Youth and Adolescence, 18,* 361–375.

Meltzoff, A. N. (2010). Social cognition and the origins of imitation, empathy and theory of mind. In U. Goswami (Ed.), *Wiley-Blackwell handbook of childhood cognitive development* (pp. 49–75). Malden, MA: John Wiley & Sons.

Mendel, G. (1866). Experiments with plant hybrids. *Proceedings of the Brunn Natural History Society.*

Mennella, J. A., & Trabulsi, J. C. (2012). Complementary foods and flavor experiences: Setting the foundation. *Annals of Nutrition and Metabolism, 60,* 40–50.

Mermin, G. B. T., Johnson, R. W., & Murphy, D. (2007). How long do Boomers plan to work? *The Retirement Project, Urban Institute.* www.urban.org

Merton, R. K. (1948). The self-fulfillingprophecy. *Antioch Review, 8,* 193–210.

Merz, E., Özeke-Kocabas, E., Oort, F. J., & Schuengel, C. (2009). Intergenerational family solidarity: Value differences between immigrant groups and generations. *Journal of Family Psychology, 23,* 291–300.

Meschke, L. L., Bartholomae, S., & Zentall, S. R. (2002). Adolescent sexuality and parent–adolescent processes: Promoting healthy teen choices. *Journal of Adolescent Health, 31,* 264–279.

Mesman, J., Oster, H., & Camras, L. (2012). Parental sensitivity to infant distress: What do discreet negative emotions have to do with it? *Attachment and Human Development, 14,* 337–348.

Mesman, J., van IJzendoorn, M. H., & Sagi-Schwartz, A. (2016). Cross-cultural patterns of attachment: Universal and contextual dimensions. In J. Cassidy & P. R. Shaver (Eds.) *Handbook of attachment* (3rd ed., pp. 852–877). New York: Guilford Press.

Mesquita, B., De Leersnyder, J., & Albert, D. (2014). The cultural regulation of emotions. In J. J. Gross (Ed.), *Handbook of emotion regulation* (2nd ed., pp. 284–304). New York: Guilford Press.

Messer, S., & Warren, S. (1995). *Models of brief psychodynamic therapy.* New York, NY: Guilford Press.

MetroDad. (2013, May). *Blog from MetroDad.* Retrieved from http://metrodad.typepad.com/index/2013/05/

Metz, T., & Gaie, J. B. R. (2010). The African ethic of Ubuntu/Botho: Implications for research on morality. *Journal of Moral Education, 39,* 273–290.

Meyer, V. (1991). A critique of adolescent pregnancy prevention research: The invisible White male. *Adolescence, 26,* 217–222.

Meyers, L. (2006). Office bullies: Still wearingthe "kick me" sign. *Monitor on Psychology, 37,* 68–70.

Miche, M., Huxhold, O., & Stevens, N. L. (2013). A latent class analysis of friendship types and their predictors in the second half of life. *The Journals of Gerontology: Series B: Psychological Sciences and Social Science, 68B,* 644–652.

Mikulincer, M., & Shaver, P. R. (2007). *Attachment in adulthood: Structure, dynamics and change.* New York, NY: Guilford Press.

Miles, L. K., Nind, L. K., & Macrae, C. N. (2010). Moving through time. *Psychological Science, 21,* 222–223.

Milkman, K. L., Rogers, T., & Bazerman, M. H. (2008). Harnessing our inner angels and demons: What we have learned about want/should conflicts and how that knowledge can help us reduce short-sighted decision making. *Perspectives on Psychological Science, 3*, 324–338.

Miller, C. C., & Alderman, L. (2014). Why U.S. women are leaving jobs behind. *The Upshot*. Retrieved from http://www.nytimes.com/2014/12/14/upshot/us-employment-women-not-working.html?_r=0

Miller, E., & Almon, J. (2009). *Crisis in the kindergarten: Why children need to play in school*. College Park, MD: Alliance for Childhood.

Miller, E. K., Freedman, D. J., & Wallis, J. D. (2003). The prefrontal cortex: Categories, concepts, and cognition. In A. Parker, A. Derrington, & C. Blakemore (Eds.), *The physiology of cognitive processes* (pp. 252–273). New York, NY: Oxford University Press.

Miller, G. A., & Gildea, P. M. (1987). How children learn words. *Scientific American, 257*, 94–99.

Miller, J., Slomczynski, K. M., & Kohn, M. L. (1988). Continuity of learning-generalization: The effect of job on men's intellective process in the United States and Poland. In J. T. Mortimer & K. M. Borman (Eds.), *Work experience and psychological development through the lifespan* (pp. 79–107). Boulder, CO: Westview Press.

Miller, J. D., & Campbell, W. K. (2010). The case for using research on trait narcissism as a building block for understanding narcissistic personality disorder. *Personality Disorders: Theory, research and treatment, 1*, 180–191.

Miller, J. T. (2014). How to make an online memorial for a departed loved one. *Huffington Post*. Retrieved from http://www.huffingtonpost.com/jim-t-miller/how-to-make-and-online-me_b_5459622.html

Miller, L. (2010). *Heaven: Our enduring fascination with the afterlife*. New York, NY: Harper Collins.

Miller, N. B., Smerglia, V. L., Gaudet, D. S., & Kitson, G. C. (1998). Stressful life events, social support, and the distress of widowed and divorced women: A counteractive model. *Journal of Family Issues, 19*, 181–203.

Miller, P. H. (2016). *Theories of developmental psychology* (6th ed.). New York: Worth.

Miller, P. J., & Sperry, L. L. (1987). The socialization of anger and aggression. *Merrill-Palmer Quarterly, 34*, 217–222.

Miller, P. J. E., Niehuis, S., & Huston, T. L. (2006). Positive illusions in marital relationships: A 13-year longitudinal study. *Personality and Social Psychology Bulletin, 32*, 1579–1594.

Miller, R. (2011). *Vygotsky in perspective*. New York, NY: Cambridge University Press.

Miller, W. B. (1992). An empirical study of the psychological antecedents and consequences of induced abortion. *Journal of Social Issues, 48*, 67–93.

Miller-Tiedeman, A. (1999). Development, decision making, and the new (quantum) careering. In A. Miller-Tiedeman (Ed.), *Learning, practicing, and living the new*

careering (pp. 96–120). Philadelphia, PA: Accelerated Development.

Mills, T. L., Gomez-Smith, Z., & DeLeon, J. M. (2005). Skipped generation families: Sources of psychological distress among grandmothers of grandchildren who live in homes where neither parent is present. *Marriage and Family Review, 37*, 191–212.

Minkler, M., & Fuller-Thomson, E. (2005). African American grandparents raising grandchildren: A national study using the census 2000 American Community Survey. *Journals of Gerontology: Series B: Psychological Sciences and Social Sciences, 60B*, S82–S92.

Mischel, W. (2012). Self-control theory. In P. A. M. Van Lange, A. W. Kruglanski, & E. T. Higgins (Eds.), *Handbook of theories of social psychology* (Vol. 2, pp. 1–22). Thousand Oaks, CA: Sage Publications.

Mischel, W., & Ayduk, O. (2002). Self-regulation in a cognitive-affective personality system: Attentional control in the service of the self. *Self & Identity, 1*, 113–120.

Mischel, W., & Ayduk, O. (2011), Willpower in a cognitive-affective processing system: The dynamics of delay of gratification. In K. D. Vohs & R. F. Baumeister (Eds.), *Handbook of self-regulation: Research, theory, and applications* (2nd ed., pp. 83–105). New York, NY: Guilford.

Mischel, W., Shoda, Y., & Rodriguez, M. L. (1989). Delay of gratification in childen. *Science, 244*, 933–938.

Misjak, L. (2012). Jordyn Wieber has gold medal regimen. *Lansing State Journal*. Retrieved from www.lansingstatejournal.com/article/20120717/Sports/307170026/Jordyn-Weiber-has-gold-medal-regimen

Mistretta, C. M., & Bradley, R. M. (1977). Taste in utero: Theoretical considerations. In J. M. Weiffenbach (Ed.), *Taste and development* (pp. 279–291). DHEW Publication No. NIH 77-1068. Bethesda, MD: U.S. Department of Health, Education, and Welfare.

Mitchell, R. W. (2001). Americans' talk to dogs: Similarities and differences with talk to infants. *Research on Language and Social Interaction, 34*, 183–210.

Moen, P., Kim, J., & Hofmeister, H. (2001). Couples' work/retirement transitions, gender, and marital quality. *Social Psychology Quarterly, 64*, 55–71.

Moffitt, . E., Caspi, A., Harrington, H., Milne, B. J., Melchior, M., Goldberg, D., et al. (2007). Generalized anxiety disorder and depression: Childhood risk factors in a birth cohort followed to age 32. *Psychological Medicine, 37*, 441–452.

Moffitt, T. E., & The Klaus-Grawe 2012 Think Tank. (2013). Childhood exposure to violence and lifelong health: Clinical intervention science and stress biology research join forces. *Development and Psychopathology, 25*, 1619–1634.

Mohr, J. J., & Jackson, S. D. (2016). Same-sex romantic attachment. In J. Cassidy & P. R. Shaver (Eds.), *Handbook of attachment: Theory, research, and clinical application*

(pp. 484–506) (3rd ed) New York: Guilford Press.

Mohr, J. J., Selterman, D., & Fassinger, R. E. (2013). Romantic attachment and relationship functioning in same-sex couples. *Journal of Counseling Psychology, 60*, 72–82.

Molenaar, P. C. M., Lerner, R. M., & Newell, K. M. (Eds.). (2014). *Handbook of developmental systems theory and methodology*. New York: Guilford.

Mollborn, S., & Jacobs, J. (2015). "I'll be there for you": Teen parents' coparenting relationships. *Journal of Marriage and Family, 77*, 373–387.

Mollborn, S., & Morningstar, E. (2009). Investigating the relationship between teenage childbearing and psychological distress using longitudinal evidence. *Journal of Health and Social Behavior, 50*, 310–326.

Monden, C. (2007). Partners in health? Exploring resemblance in health between partners in married and cohabiting couples. *Sociology of Health & Illness, 29*, 391–411.

Monroe, S., Rohde, P., Seeley, J., & Lewisohn, P. (1999). Life events and depression in adolescence: Relationship loss as a prospective risk factor for first onse of major depressive disorder. *Journal of Abnormal Psychology, 108*, 606–614.

Montague, M. (2006). Self-regulation strategies for better math performance in middle school. In M. Montague & A.K. Jitendra (Eds.), *Teaching mathematics to middle school students with learning difficulties* (pp. 89–107). New York, NY: Guilford.

Monte, L. M., & Ellis, R. R. (2014). Fertility of women in the United States: June 2012, *Current Population Reports*, P20–575, Washington, DC: U.S. Census Bureau.

Montemayor, R. (1983). Parents and adolescents in conflict: All families some of the time and some families most of the time. *Journal of Early Adolescence, 3*, 83–103.

Montesi, J. L., Conner, B. T., Gordon, E. A., Fauber, R. L., Kim, K. H., & Heimberg, R. G. (2013). On the relationship among social anxiety, intimacy, sexual communication, and sexual satisfaction in young couples. *Archives of Sexual Behavior, 42*, 81–91.

Montgomery, M. (2005). Psychosocial intimacy and identity: From early adolescence to emerging adulthood. *Journal of Adolescent Research, 20*, 346–374.

Moon, J. R., Kondo, N., Glymour, M. M., & Subramanian, S. V. (2011). Widowhood and mortality: A meta-analysis. *PLoS One, 6*, e23465.

Moore, C. (2008). The development of gaze following. *Child Development Perspectives, 2*, 66–70.

Moore, C. (2009). Fairness in children's resource allocation depends on the recipient. *Psychological Science, 20*, 944–948.

Moore, D. S. (2015). *The developing genome: An introduction to behavioral genetics*. New York: Oxford University Press.

Moore, K. L., & Persaud, T. V. N. (2003). *Before we were born: Essentials of embryology and birth defects*. Philadelphia, PA: Saunders.

Moore, K. L., Persaud, T. V. N., & Torchia, M. G. (2015). *Before we are born: Essentials of embryology and birth defects* (9th ed.). Philadelphia, PA: Saunders.

Moore, S. C., Patel, A.V., Matthews, C. E., Berrington de Gonzalez, A., Park, Y., et al. (2012). Leisure time physical activity of moderate to vigorous intensity and mortality: A large pooled cohort analysis. *PLoS Med, 9*(11): e1001335. doi:10.1371/journal .pmed.1001335.

Moore, S. R., & Depue, R. A. (2016). Neurobehavioral foundation of environmental reactivity. *Psychological Bulletin, 142*, 107–164.

Moorman, S. M., Booth, A., & Fingerman, K. L. (2006). Women's romantic relationships after widowhood. *Journal of Family Issues, 27*, 1281–1304.

Morawska, A., & Sanders, M. (2011). Parental use of time out revisited: A useful or a harmful parenting strategy? *Journal of Child and Family Studies, 20*, 1–8.

Morf, C. C., & Mischel, W. (2002). Epilogue: Self-regulation, vulnerability, and implications for mental health. *Self & Identity, 1*, 191–199.

Morgan, C., Isaac, J. D., & Sansone, C. (2001). The role of interest in understanding the career choices of female and male college students. *Sex Roles, 44*, 295–320.

Morgan, D. M. (1989). Adjusting to widowhood: Do social networks really make it easier? *The Gerontologist, 29*, 101–107.

Morgan, S. (2005). Health benefits of gardening. *University of Illinois Cooperative Extension.* Retrieved from http://web.extension.uiuc .edu/chapaign/homeowners/050103.html

Morin, A. (2006). Levels of consciousness and self-awareness: A comparison and integration of various neurocognitive views. *Conscious Cognition, 15*, 358–371.

Morin, R., & Kochhar, R. (2010). Lost income, lost friends—and loss of self-respect. *Pew Research Center.* Retrieved from http:// www.pewsocialtrends.org/2010/07/22/hard -times-have-hit-nearly-everyone-and -hammered-the-long-term-unemployed/

Morra, S., Gobbo, C., Marini, Z., & Sheese, R. (Eds.). (2008). *Cognitive development: Neo-Piagetian perspectives.* New York: Taylor and Francis Group/Erlbaum.

Morrison, A. P. (1989). *Shame: The underside of narcissism.* Hillsdale, NJ: Analytic Press.

Morrissey, T. W. (2009). Multiple child care arrangements and young children's behavioral outcomes. *Child Development, 80*, 59–76.

Morrow, A. (2008). "A good death"? *Palliative care blog.* Retrieved from http://dying.about .com/b/2008/02/25/a-good-death.htm

Morrow, J. A., & Ackermann, M. E. (2012). Intention to persist and retention of first-year students: The importance of motivation and sense of belonging. *College Student Journal, 46*, 483–491.

Moseman, A. (2010). UC Berkeley halts its freshman DNA testing project. *Discover:*

The Magazine of Science, Technology and the Future. Retrieved from http://blogs .discovermagazine.com/80beats /2010/08/13/uc-berkeley

Moshman, D. (2004). From inference to reasoning: The construction of rationality. *Thinking and Reasoning, 10*, 221–239.

Mosselson, J. R. (2009). Where am I? Refugee youth living in the United States. *Journal of the History of Childhood and Youth, 2.3*, 453–469.

Mottweiler, C. M., & Taylor, M. (2014). Elaborated role play and creativity in preschool age children. *Psychology of Aesthetics, Creativity, and the Arts, 8*, 277–286.

Mou, Y., & Peng, W. (2009). Gender and racial stereotypes in popular video games. In R. F. Ferdig (Ed.), *Handbook of research on effective electronic gaming in education* (Vol. 2, pp. 922–935). Hershey, PA: IGI Global.

Mounts, N. S. (2004). Adolescents' perceptions of parental management of adolescent peer relationships in an ethnically diverse sample. *Journal of Adolescent Research, 19*, 446–467.

Mounts, N. S. (2007). Adolescents' and their mothers' perceptions of parental management of peer relationships. *Journal of Research on Adolescence, 17*, 169–178.

Moussavi, S., Chatterji, S., Verdes, E., Tandon, A., Patel, V., & Ustan, B. (2007). Depression, chronic diseases, and decrements in health: Results for the World Health Surveys. *Lancet, 370*, 851–858.

Moutsiana, C., Johstone, T., Murray, L., Fearon, P. et al., (2015). Insecure attachment during infancy predicts greater amygdala volumes in early adulthood. *Journal of Child Psychology and Psychiatry, 56*, 540–548.

Mowling, C. M., Brock, S. J., & Hastie, P. A. (2006). Fourth grade students' drawing interpretations of a sport education soccer unit. *Journal of Teaching in Physical Education, 25*, 9–35.

Mueller, A. S., Pearson, J., Muller, C., Frank, K., & Turner, A. (2010). Sizing up peers: Adolescent girls' weight control and social comparison in the school context. *Journal of Health and Social Behavior, 51*, 64–78.

Muhlbauer, V., Chrisler, J. C., & Denmark, F. L. (Eds.). (2015). *Women and aging: An international, intersectional power perspective.* Cham, Switzerland: Springer International Publishing.

Muir, D., & Lee, K. (2003). The still face effect: Methodological issues and new applications. *Infancy, 4*, 483–491.

Mulder, E. J. H., deMedina, P. G. R., Huizink, A. C., Van den Bergh, B. R. H., Buitelaar, J. K., & Visser, G. H. A. (2002). Prenatal maternal stress: Effects on pregnancy and the (unborn) child. *Early Human Development, 70*, 3–14.

Mullen, B., Brown, R., & Smith, C. (2006). In-group bias as a function of salience, relevance and status: An integration. *European Journal of Social Psychology, 22*, 103–122.

Mulligan, G.M., Hastedt, S., & McCarroll, J. C. (2012). *First-time kindergartners in 2010–11: First findings from the kindergarten rounds of the early childhood longitudinal study, kindergarten class of 2010–11* (ECLS-K:2011) (NCES 2012-049). U.S. Department of Education. Washington, DC: National Center for Education Statistics. Retrieved from http://nces.ed.gov/pubsearch.

Mulligan, G. M., McCarroll, J. C., Flanagan, K. D., & Potter, D. (2015). *Findings from the 2nd grade rounds of the early childhood longitudinal study, kindergarten class of 2010–11.(ECLS-K:2011). (NCES 2015-077).* U.S. Department of Education, Washington DC: National Center for Education Statistics. Retrieved from http://nces.ed.gov /pubsearch

Mullis, I. V. S., Martin, M. O., Foy, P., & Drucker, K. T. (2012). *PIRLS 2011: International results in reading.* Chestnut Hill, MA: TIMSS & PIRLS International Study Center, Boston College.

Mulrane, A. (2001). Are boys the weaker sex? *U.S. News and World Report, 131*, 40–47.

Munsey, C. (2010). The kids aren't all right. *Monitor on Psychology, 41*, 22–25.

Muraskin, L., & Lee, J. (2004). *Raising the graduation rates of low-income college students.* Washington, DC: The Pell Institute for the Study of Opportunity in Higher Education.

Murphy, L. B. (1956). *Personality in young children: Vol. 2. Colin, a normal child.* New York, NY: Basic Books.

Murphy, L. B. (1962). *The widening world of childhood: Paths toward mastery.* New York, NY: Basic Books.

Murphy, L. B. (1972). *Infant's play and cognitive development* (pp. 99–126). New York, NY: Norton.

Murphy, L. W., Vagins, D. J., & Parker, A. (2010). Statement before the House Education and Labor Subcommittee on healthy families and communities hearing on corporal punishment in schools and its effect on academic success. *American Civil Liberties Union and Human Rights Watch.* Retrieved from www.hrw.org

Murray, C., Lombardi, A., & Kosty, D. (2014). Profiling adjustment among post secondary students with disabilities: A person-centered approach. *Journal of Diversity in Higher Education 7*(1) 31–44.

Murray, C. I., Toth, K., Larsen, B. L., & Moulton, S. (2010). Death, dying and grief in families. In S. J. Price, C. A. Price (Eds.) with P. C. McKenry, *Families and change: Coping with stressful events and transitions* (4th ed., pp. 73–96). Thousand Oaks, CA: Sage.

Murray, L. (2015). *People who have lived to 100 share their longevity secrets.* Retrieved from http://www.cnn.com/2015/09/01/health /longevity-secrets-live-to-100/

Murray, L., De Rosnay, M., Pearson, J., Bergeron, C., Schofield, E., Royal-Lawson M., & Cooper, P. J. (2008). Intergenerational transmission of social anxiety: The role of social referencing processes in infancy. *Child Development, 79,* 1049–1064.

Murray, M. M., & Wallace, M. T. (Eds.). (2012). *The neural basis of multisensory processes.* Boca Raton, FL: CRC Press/Taylor and Francis.

Murray-Close, D., & Ostrov, J. M. (2009). A longitudinal study of forms and functions of aggressive behavior in early childhood. *Child Development, 80,* 828–842.

Murthy, D., Gross, A., & Pensavalle, A. (2015). Urban social media demographics: An exploration of Twitter© use in major American cities. *Journal of Computer-Mediated Communication,* November 19, 2015.

Musch, J., & Grondin, S. (2001). Unequal competition as an impediment to personal development: A review of the relative age effect in sport. *Developmental Review, 21,* 147–167.

Mussen, P. H., & Jones, M. C. (1957). Self-conceptions, motivations, and interpersonal attitudes of late and early maturing boys. *Child Development, 28,* 243–256.

Mustafa, S. S., Looper, K. J., Zelkowitz, P., Purden, M., & Baron, M. (2012). Role overload pain and physical dysfunction in early rheumatoid or undifferentiated inflammatory arthritis in Canada. *BioPsychoSocial Medicine, 6,* article 13.

Myers, S. M. (2006). Religious homogamy and marital quality: Historical and generational patterns, 1980-1997. *Journal of Marriage and Family, 68,* 292–304.

Myrseth, K. O. R., & Fishbach, A. (2009). Self control: A function of knowing when and how to exercise restraint. *Current Directions in Psychological Science, 18,* 247–252.

NACBT.org. (2007). *Cognitive behavior therapy.* Retrieved from http://nacbt.org/whatiscbt.htm

Nakato, E., Otsuka, Y., Kanazawa, S., et al. (2011). I know this face: Neural activity during mother's face perception in 7- to 8-month old infants as investigated by near-infrared spectroscopy. *Early Human Development, 87,* 1–7.

Namy, L. L., & Waxman, S. R. (2002). Patterns of spontaneous production of novel words and gestures within an experimental setting in children ages 1.6 and 2.2. *Journal of Child Language, 29,* 911–921.

Nanda, S. (1998). *Neither man nor woman: The Hijras of India.* Belmont, CA: Wadsworth Publishing.

Nanda, S. (1999). *Gender diversity: Cross-cultural variations.* Prospect Heights, IL: Waveland Press.

Nanda, S. (2004). *The Xanith: An intermediate gender in Oman.* Retrieved from www.galva108.org/xanith.html

Nangle, D. W., Erdley, C. A., Newman, J. E., Mason, C. A., & Carpenter, E. M. (2003). Popularity, friendship quantity, and friendship quality: Interactive influences on children's loneliness and depression. *Journal of Clinical Child and Adolescent Psychology, 32,* 546–555.

Nash, E., Gold, R. B., Rathbun, G. & Vierboom, Y. (2015). *Laws affecting reproductive health and rights: State trends at midyear, 2015.* Retrieved from http://www.guttmacher.org/statecenter/updates/2015/statetrends22015.html

Nasir, N. S., & Kirshner, B. (2003). The cultural construction of moral and civic identities. *Applied Developmental Science, 7,* 138–147.

Naska, A., Oikonomou, E., Trichopoulou, A., Psaltopoulou, T., & Trichopouolos, D. (2007). Siesta in healthy adults and coronary mortality in the general population. *Archives of Internal Medicine, 167,* 296–301.

Nathanielsz, P. W. (1996). The timing of birth. *American Scientist, 84,* 562–569.

National Academies Press. (2011). *The health of lesbian, gay, bisexual and transgender people: Building a foundation for better understanding.* Washington DC: National Academies Press.

National Aging in Place Council. (2013). www.ageinplace.

National Association of Cognitive Behavioral Therapists. (2014). *What is cognitive behavioral therapy?* Retrieved from http://nacbt.org/whatiscbt.aspx

National Association for College Admission Counseling. (2016). *The gap year.* Retrieved from http://www.nacacnet.org/studentinfo/articles/pages/gap-year-.aspx

National Association of School Psychologists. (2002). *Position paper on ability grouping.* Retrieved from http://www.nasponline.org/information/pospaper_ag.html

National Center for Education Statistics. (2003). *The condition of education.* Washington, DC: U.S. Government Printing Office.

National Center for Education Statistics. (2004). *Highlights from the TIMSS 1999 video study of eighth-grade mathematics teaching study.* Retrieved from http://nces.ed.gov/pubs2003/timssvideo/3E.asp?nav_3

National Center for Education Statistics. (2006). *Digest for Education Statistics.* Tables 187, 317. Retrieved from http://nces.ed.gov/programs/digest/d06/tables/dt06_187.asp

National Center for Education Statistics. (2015a). *Children and youth with disabilities.* Retrieved from http://nces.ed.gov/programs/coe/indicator_cgg.asp

National Center for Education Statistics. (2015b). *Recent high school completers and their enrollments in 2-year and 4-year colleges by sex: 1960 through 2014.* Retrieved from http://nces.ed.gov/programs/digest/d15/tables/dt15_302.10.asp

National Center for Education Statistics. (2015c). *Rates of high school completion and bachelor's degree attainment among persons 25 and over, by race/ethnicity and sex: Selected years, 1910 through 2015.* Retrieved from http://nces.ed.gov/programs/digest/d15/tables/dt15_104.10.asp

National Center for Education Statistics. (2015d). *Median annual earnings of full-time year-round workers 25 to 34 years old and full-time year round workers as a percentage of the labor force, by sex, race/ethnicity, and educational attainment: Selected years, 1995 through 2014.* Retrieved from http://nces.ed.gov/programs/digest/d15/tables/dt15_502.30.asp

National Center for Education Statistics. (2015e). *Digest for education statistics, 2015.* Table 302.10. Recent high school completers and their enrollment in 2-year and 4-year college by sex: 1960–2014. Retrieved from https://nces.ed.gov/programs/digest/d15/tables/dt15_302.10.asp

National Center for Education Statistics. (2016). *TIMSS video studies.* Retrieved from https://nces.ed.gov/timss/video.asp

National Center for Health Statistics. (2007). *Healthy People 2010.* Retrieved from http://www.cdc.gov/nchs/hphome.htm

National Center for Health Statistics. (2010). *Summary health statistics for U.S. adults: National Health Interview study, 2009.* U.S. Department of Health and Human Services.

National Center for Health Statistics. (2012). *Health, United States, 2011. With special features on socioeconomic status and health.* Hyattsville, MD: Author.

National Center for Health Statistics. (2013). *Health, United States, 2012: With Special Feature on Emergency Care.* Hyattsville, MD: U.S. Department of Health and Human Services.

National Center for Health Statistics. (2016a). *Health, United States, 2015: With special feature on racial and ethnic health disparities.* Hyattsville, MD. Table 15. Retrieved from http://www.cdc.gov/nchs/data/hus/hus15.pdf#015

National Center for Health Statistics. (2016b). *Early release of selected estimates based on data from the National Health Interview Survey,* January–March 2016. Retrieved from http://www.cdc.gov/nchs/data/nhis/earlyrelease/earlyrelease201609_07.pdf

National Center for Health Statistics. (2016c). *Health, United States, 2015: With special feature on racial and ethnic health disparities.* Hyattsville, MD: U.S. Government Printing Office.

National Center for Higher Education Management. (2004). *Graduation rates. Six-year graduation rates of Bachelor's students—2004.* Retrieved from http://www.higheredinfo.org/dbrowser/index.php?year=2004&level=nation&mode=map&state=0&submeasure=27

National Center for Higher Education Management. (2007). *Difference in median earnings between a high school diploma and a bachelor's degree by age group.* Retrieved from thttp://www.higheredinfo.org/dbrowser/index.php ?measure=83

National Center on Elder Abuse. (2012). *Fact Sheet: Abuse of residents of long-term care facilities.* Retrieved from www.centeronelderabuse.org/docs/Abuse_of_Residents_of_Long _Term_Care_Facilities.pdf

National Coalition on Television Violence. (1990). Nintendo tainted by extreme violence. *NCTV News, 11*(1–2), 1, 3–4.

National Commission on Children. (1993). *Just the facts: A summary of recent information on America's children and their families.* Washington, DC: Author.

National Council on Aging. (2015). *Economic security fact sheet.* Retrieved from https://www.ncoa.org/news/resources-for-reporters/get-the-facts/economic-security-facts/

National Dissemination Center for Children with Disabilities. (2004). *Speech and language impairments.* Retrieved from http://www.nichcy.org/pubs/factshe/fs11txt.htm

National Dissemination Center for Children with Disabilities. (2013). *Overview of early intervention.* Retrieved from http://nichcy.org/babies/overview#what

National Down Syndrome Society. (2013). *What Is Down syndrome?* Retrieved from at http://www.ndss.org/Down-Syndrome/What-Is-Down-Syndrome

National Eye Institute. (2016). *Cataracts.* Retrieved from https://nei.nih.gov/eyedata/cataract

National Gang Center. (2013). *Frequently asked questions about gangs.* Retrieved from http://www.nationalgangcenter.gov

National Gang Center. (2016). *Frequently asked questions.* Retrieved from https://www.nationalgangcenter.gov/About/FAQ

National Hospice and Palliative Care Organization. (2005). *History of hospice care.* Retrieved from http://www.nhpco.org/i4a/pages/index .cfm?pageid_3285

National Institute on Aging. (2009a). *Hearing loss.* Retrieved from http://www.nia.nih.gov/HealthInformation/Publications/hearing.htm

National Institute on Aging. (2009b). *A good night's sleep.* Retrieved from http://www.nia.nih.gov/HealthInformation/Publications/sleep.htm

National Institute on Aging. (2009c). *Smell and taste: Spice of life.* Retrieved from http://www.nia.nih.gov/HealthInformation/Publications/smell.htm

National Institute on Aging. (2009d). *Arthritis advice.* Retrieved from http://www.nia.nih.gov/HealthInformation/Publications/arthritis.htm

National Institute on Aging. (2009e). *Osteoporosis: The bone thief.* Retrieved from http://www.nia.nih.gov/HealthInformation/Publications/osteoporosis.htm

National Institute on Aging. (2009f). *Forgetfulness: Knowing when to ask for help.* Retrieved from http://www.nia.nih.gov/HealthInformation/Publications/forgetfulness.htm

National Institute on Aging. (2016). *A good night's sleep.* Retrieved from https://www.nia.nih.gov/health/publication/good-nights-sleep

National Institute on Alcohol Abuse and Alcoholism (NIAAA). (2011). Fetal alcohol spectrum disorders: Understanding the effects of prenatal alcohol exposure. *Alcohol Research and Health, 34.* Retrieved from http://pubs.niaaa.nih.gov/publications/AA82/AA82.htm

National Institute for Drug Abuse (NIDA). (2010). *Cocaine: What are the effects of maternal cocaine use?* Retrieved from http://www.drugabuse.gov/publications/research-reports/cocaine/what-are-effects-maternal-cocaine-use

National Institutes of Health. (2000). The relation of child care to cognitive and language development. *Child Development, 71,* 960–980.

National Institutes of Health. (2009). *Stem cell information.* Retrieved from http://stemcells.nih.gov/info/basics/basics1.asp

National Institutes of Health. (2011). *Specific genetic disoders.* Retrieved from http://www.genome.gov/10001204

National Institutes of Health. (2014). *Down syndrome.* Retrieved from https://www.nichd.nih.gov/health/topics/down/conditioninfo/Pages/faqs.aspx

National Institutes of Health. (2015a). *Specific genetic disorders.* Retrieved from http://www.genome.gov/10001204

National Institutes of Health. (2015b). *Stem cell information.* Retrieved from http://stemcells.nil,gov/info/basics/pages/basics1.aspx

National Institutes of Health. (2016a). Depression. *NIHSeniorHealth.* Retrieved from https://nihseniorhealth.gov/depression/aboutdepression/01.html

National Institutes of Health. (2016b). *Senior health. Long-term care: Community-based services.* Retrieved from https://nihseniorhealth.gov/longtermcare/communitybasedservices/01.html

National Research Council and Institute of Medicine. (2000). *From neurons to neighborhoods: The science of early childhood development.* Washington, DC: National Academy Press.

Natural Resources Defense Council. (2013). *Mercury contamination in fish.* Retrieved from www.nrdc.org/health/effects/mercury/effects.asp

National Safety Council. (2013). *Safety and health.* Retrieved from www.nsc.org/safetyhealth/Pages/8 11HarmfulExposure.aspx

National Telecommunications and Information Administration. (2002). *Trendline study on electronic access by households: 1984–1998.* Retrieved from http://www.ntia.doc.gov/ntiahome/fttn99/appendix.html

National Urban League. (1987). *Adolescent male responsibility, pregnancy prevention, and parenting program: A program development guide.* New York, NY: Author.

Naude, L., Nei, L, van der Waat, R., & Tadi, F. (2016). If it's going to be, it's up to me: First-year psychology students' experiences regarding academic success. *Teaching in Higher Education, 21,* 37–46.

Naughton, K., & Thomas, E. (2000, March 13). Did Kayla have to die? *Newsweek,* 24–29.

Navaro, L., & Schwartzberg, S.L. (2007). *Envy, competition, and gender: Theory, clinical applications and group work.* New York, NY: Taylor & Francis Group.

Nazzi, T., & Gopnik, A. (2001). Linguistic cognitive abilities in infancy: When does language become a tool for categorization? *Cognition, 80,* B11–B20.

NCES (2010). *Contexts of postsecondary education.* Retrieved from http://nces.ed.gov/programs/coe/2010/section5/table-cst-1.asp

NCES. (2012). *Condition of education, 2011* (NCES 2012-045) Indicator 45. Retrieved from http://neces.ed.gov/fastfacts/display.asp?id=40

NCHEMS (2010). *Information center.* Retrieved from www.higheredinfo.org/

Neckerman, H. J. (1996). The stability of social groups in childhood and adolescence: The role of the classroom social environment. *Social Development, 5,* 131–145.

Needham, A. (2001). Object recognition and object segregation in 4.5-month-old infants. *Journal of Experimental Child Psychology, 78,* 3–24.

Needham, B. L., Epel, E. S., Adler, N. E., & Kiefe, C. (2010). Trajectories of change in obesity and symptoms of depression: The CARDIA study. *American Journal of Public Health, 100,* 1040–1046.

Neese, R. M. (2001). Motivation and melancholy: A Darwinian perspective. In R. A. Dienstbier, J. A. French, A. C. Kamil, & D. W. Leder (Eds.), Evolutionary psychology and motivation: Vol. 47. *Nebraska Symposium on Motivation* (pp. 179–204). Lincoln, NE: University of Nebraska Press.

Neff, K. D., & Harter, S. (2003). Relationship styles of self-focused autonomy, other-focused connectedness, and mutuality across multiple relationship contexts. *Journal of Social and Personal Relationships, 20,* 81–99.

Negroni, L. K. (2012). The Puerto Rican American family. In R. Wright, C. H. Mindel, T.V. Tran, & R. W. Habenstein (Eds.), *Ethnic families in America: Patterns and variations* (pp. 129–147). Boston, MA: Pearson.

Neil, E. (2009). The corresponding experiences of adoptive parents and birth relatives in open adoptions. In G. M. Wrobel & E. Neil (Eds.), *International advances in adoption research for practice* (pp. 269–293). New York, NY: Wiley-Blackwell.

Neimark, E. D. (1975). Longitudinal development of formal operations thought. *Genetic Psychology Monographs, 91,* 171–225.

Neisser, U., Boodoo, G., Bouchard, T. J., Jr., Bodkin, A. W., Brody, N., Ceci, S. J., et al. (1996). Intelligence: Knowns and unknowns. *American Psychologist, 51,* 77–101.

Neiworth, J. J. (2009). Thinking about me: How social awareness evolved. *Current Directions in Psychological Science, 18,* 143–147.

Nelson, C. A. (2001). The development and neural bases of face recognition. *Infant and Child Development, 10*, 3–18.

Nelson, E. (1987). Learned helplessness and children's achievement. In S. Moore & K. Kolb (Eds.), *Reviews of research for practitioners and parents* (Vol. no. 3, pp. 11–22). Minneapolis, MN: Center for Early Education and Development.

Nelson, H. D. (2008). Menopause. *The Lancet, 372*, 760–770.

Nelson, K. (1981). Individual differences in language development: Implications for development and language. *Developmental Psychology, 17*, 170–187.

Nelson, K. (2000). Narrative, time and the emergence of the encultured self. *Culture and Psychology, 6*, 183–196.

Nelson, K. (2007). *Young minds in social worlds: Experience, meaning and memory.* Cambridge, MA: Harvard University Press.

Nelson, K. (2010). Developmental narratives of the experiencing child. *Child Development Perspectives, 4*, 43–47.

Nelson, K. (2012). Cognitive functions of lan-guage in early childhood. In B. D. Homer & C. S. Thomas-LeMonda (Eds.), *The development of social cognition and communication* (pp. 7–28). New York, NY: Psychology Press.

Nelson, S. L., & Jaskiewicz, J. L. (2015). *Developmental coordination disorder.* Retrieved from http://emedicine.medscape.com/article/915251-overview

Nemours. (2014). Individualized Education Programs (IEPs). *Kids Health. org.* Retrieved from www.kidshealth.org/en/parents/iep.html

Nemoto, T. (1998). Subjective norms toward social support among Japanese American elderly in New York City: Why help does not always help. *Journal of Community Psychology, 26*, 293–316.

Nepomnyaschy, L. (2009). Socioeconomic gradients in infant health across race and ethnicity. *Maternal and child Health Journal, 13*, 720–731.

Nesdale, D., & Flesser, D. (2001). Social identity and the development of children's group attitudes. *Child Development, 72*, 506–517.

Nesi, J. & Prinstein, M. J. (2015). Using social media for social comparison and feedback seeking: Gender and popularity moderate associations with depressive symptoms. *Journal of Abnormal Child Psychology, 43*, 1427–1438.

Neugarten, B. L. (1981). Growing old in 2020: How will it be different? *National Forum, 61*(3), 28–30.

Neugarten, B. L. (1990). The changing meanings of age. In M. Bergener & S. I. Finkel (Eds.), *Clinical and scientific psychogeriatrics: Vol. 1. The holistic approaches* (pp. 1–6). New York, NY: Springer-Verlag.

Neugarten, B. L., Moore, J. W., & Lowe, J. C. (1965). Age norms, age constraints, and adult socialization. *American Journal of Sociology, 70*, 710–717.

Neugarten, B. L., & Weinstein, R. (1964). The changing American grandparent. *Journal of Marriage and the Family, 26*, 199–204.

Neugebauer, R., Hoek, H. W., & Susser, E. (1999). Prenatal exposure to wartime famine and development of antisocial personality disorder in early adulthood. *Journal of the American Medical Association, 282*, 455–462.

Neumann, I. D. & Landgraf, R. (2012). Balance of brain oxytocin and vasopressin: Implications for anxiety, depression, and social behaviors. *Trends in Neurosciences, 35*, 649–659.

Neville, H. J., Bavelier, D., Corina, D., Rauschecker, J., Karni, A., Lalwani, A., et al. (1998). Cerebral organization for language in deaf and hearing subjects: Biological constraints and effects of experience. *Proceedings of the National Academy of Sciences, 95*, 922–929.

Neville, H. J., & Mills, D. I. (1997). Epigenesis of language. *Mental Retardation and Developmental Disabilities Research Reviews, 3*, 1–11.

Newcombe, N. S., Ambady, N., Eccles, J., et al. (2009). Psychology's role in mathematics and science education. *American Psychologist, 64*, 538–550.

Newell, K. M., Vaillancourt, D. E., & Sosnoff, J. J. (2006). Aging, complexity and motor performance. In J. E. Birren & K. W. Schaie (Eds.), *Handbook of the psychology of aging* (6th ed., pp. 163–182). Amsterdam, Netherlands: Elsevier.

Newman, A. J., Bavelier, D., Corina, D., Jezzard, P., & Neville, H. J. (2002). A critical period for right hemisphere recruitment in American Sign language processing. *Nature Neuroscience, 5*, 76–80.

Newman, B. M. (1989). The changing nature of the parent–adolescent relationship from early to late adolescence. *Adolescence, 24*, 916–924.

Newman, B. M. (2000). The challenges of parenting infants and children. In P. C. McKenry & S. J. Price (Eds.), *Families and change: Coping with stressful events and transitions* (pp. 45–70). Thousand Oaks, CA: Sage.

Newman, B. M. (2010). Teacher's corner. *Developments, 53*(1), 6–7.

Newman, B. M., & Newman, P. R. (2001). Group identity and alienation: Giving the We its due. *Journal of Youth and Adolescence, 30*, 515–538.

Newman, B. M., & Newman, P. R. (2007). *Theories of Human Development.* Mahwah, NJ: Lawrence Erlbaum Associates (now published by Psychology Press).

Newman, B. M., & Newman, P. R. (2016). *Theories of human development* (2nd ed.). New York: Psychology Press.

Newman, C. (2009). Sickness and health. *Redbook.* Retrieved from http://www.redbookmag.com/love-sex/relationships/advice/a4659/real-life-love-stories/

Newman, J. L., Roberts, L. R., & Syre, C. R. (1993). Concepts of family among children and adolescents: Effect of cognitive level, gender, and family structure. *Developmental Psychology, 29*, 951–962.

Newman, L., Wagner, M., Knokey, A. M., Marder, C., Nagle, K., Shaver, D., Wei, X., et al. (2011). *The post-high school outcomes of young adults with disabilities up to 8 years after high school. A report from the National Longitudinal Transition Study-2 (NLTS-2) (NCSER 2011–3005).* Menlo Park, CA: SRI International.

Newman, P. R. (1982). The peer group. In B. B. Wolman (Ed.), *Handbook of developmental psychology* (pp. 526–535). Englewood Cliffs, NJ: Prentice Hall.

Newman, P. R. & Newman, B. M. (1983). *Principles of psychology.* Homewood, IL: Dorsey Press.

Newman, P. R., & Newman, B. M. (1999). What does it take to have a positive impact on minority students' college retention? *Adolescence, 34*, 483–492.

Newman, R. (2001, October 1). The day the world changed, I did too. *Newsweek,* 9.

Newport, F. (2016). Most Americans still believe in God. *Gallup.* Retrieved from http://www.gallup.com/poll/193271/americans-believe-god.aspx?version=print

Newser.com.(2010). *Race discrimination.* Retrieved from www .newser.com/story/55858/white-fiefighters-bias-claims-head-to-high-court.html#ixzz0x4OZM8dZ

Newton, N. J., & Jones, B. K. (2016). Passing on: Personal attributes associated with midlife expressions of intended legacies. *Developmental Psychology, 52*, 341–353.

Ng, F. F., Pomerantz, E. M., & Lam, S. (2007). European American and Chinese parents' responses to children's success and failure: Implications for children's responses. *Developmental Psychology, 43*, 1239–1255.

Ngun, T. C. & Vilain, E. (2014). The biological basis of sexual orientation: Is there a role for epigenetics? *Advances in Genetics, 86*, 167–184.

NHSA.org. (2016) Website of the National Head Start Association.

NIAAA. (2016). *Underage drinking.* Retrieved from http://pubs.niaaa.nih.gov/publications/UnderageDrinking/Underage_Fact.pdf

NICHD Early Child Care Research Network. (2002). Early child care and children's development prior to school entry: Results from the NICHD Study of Early Child Care. *American Educational Research Journal, 39*, 51–62.

NICHD (2012a). *Infertility and fertility overview.* Retrieved from http://www.nichd.nih.gov/health/topics/infertility/Pages/default.aspx

NICHD. (2012b). *What causes normal puberty, precocious puberty and delayed puberty?* Retrieved from http://www.nichd.nih.gov/health/topics/puberty/conditioninfo/Pages/causes.aspx

NICHD. (2006). *The NICHD study of early child care and youth development.* NIH Publication No. 05-4318. Retrieved from https://www.nichd.nih.gov/publications/pubs/documents/seccyd_06.pdf

Nichols, M. R. (1993). Paternal perspectives of the childbirth experience. *Maternal-Child Nursing Journal, 21,* 99–108.

Nicoladis, E. (1998). First clues to the existence of two input languages: Pragmatic and lexical differentiation in a bilingual child. *Bilingualism: Language and Cognition, 1,* 105–116.

Nicoladis, E., & Secco, G. (2000). The role of a child's productive vocabulary in the language choice of a bilingual family. *First Language, 20,* 3–28.

Nielsen. (2009). TV viewing among kids at an 8 year high. Retrieved from http://www .nielsen.com/us/en/insights/news/2009 /tv-viewing-among-kids-at-an-eight -year-high.html

Nielsen, M., Tomaselli, K., Mushin, I., & Whiten, A. (2014). Exploring tool innovation: A comparison of Western and Bushman children. *Journal of Experimental Child Psychology, 126,* 384–394.

NIH/CEPH Collaborative Mapping Group. (1992). A comprehensive genetic linkage map of the human genome. *Science, 258,* 7–86.

Nijhuis, J. G. (2003). Fetal behavior. *Neurobiology of Aging, 24,* Supplement 1, S41–S46.

NIMH. (2010). *Obsessive-Compulsive Disorder: When unwanted thoughts take over.* Retrieved from http://www.nimh.nih.gov /health/publications/obsessive-compulsive -disorder-when-unwanted-thoughts-take -over/index.shtml

NIMH. (2014). *Eating disorders: About more than food.* Retrieved from https://www .nimh.nih.gov/health/publications/eating -disorders-new-trifold-index.shtml

NIMH. (2015). *Autism spectrum disorder.* Retrieved from http://www.nimh.nih.gov /health/publications/autism-spectrum -disorder-qf-15-5511/index.shtml

NIMH. (2016). *Depression.* Retrieved from http://www.nimh.nih.gov/health/topics /depression/index.shtml

9-11 Research. (2013). *Missing bodies.* Retrieved from http://911research.wtc7 .net/wtc/evidence/bodies.html

Ninio, A., & Rinott, N. (1988). Fathers' involvement in the care of their infants and their attributions of cognitive competence to infants. *Child Development, 59,* 652–663.

Nippoldt, T. B. (2016). *What can you tell me about couvade syndrome? Do men really experience pregnancy related symptoms?* Retrieved from http://www.mayoclinic.org /healthy-lifestyle/pregnancy-week-by-week /expert-answers/couvade-syndrome /faq-20058047

Nisan, M., & Kohlberg, L. (1982). Universality and variation in moral judgment: A longitudinal and cross-sectional study in Turkey. *Child Development, 53,* 865–876.

Nix, R. L., Bierman, K. L., Heinrichs, B. S., Gest, S. D., Welsh, J. A., & Domitrovich, C. E. (2016). The randomized controlled trial of Head Start REDI: Sustained effects on developmental trajectories of social-emotional functioning. *Journal of*

Consulting and Clinical Psychology, 84, 310–322.

Noe, R. (2014). *Massive makerspace: The Columbus Idea Foundry.* Retrieved from http://www.core77.com/posts/27908 /Massive-Makerspace-The-Columbus -Idea-Foundry

Nolen-Hoeksema, S., & Girgus, J. S. (1994). The emergence of gender differences in depression during adolescence. *Psychology Bulletin, 115,* 424–443.

Noller, P., & Feeney, J. A. (2002). Communication, relationship concerns, and satisfaction in early marriage. In A. L.Vangelisti, H. T. Reis, & M. A. Fitzpatrick, (Eds.) *Stability and change in relationships: Advances in personal relationships* (pp. 129–155). New York, NY: Cambridge University Press.

Nommsen-Rivers, L. A., Mastergeorge, A. M., Hansen, R. L., Cullum, A. S., & Dewey, K. G. (2009). Doula care and early breastfeeding outcomes and breastfeeding status at 6 weeks postpartum among low-income primapara. *Journal of Obstetric Gynecologic and Neonatal Nursing: Clinical Scholarship for the Care of Women, Childbearing Families, and Newborns, 38,* 157–173.

Noppe, I. C., & Noppe, L. D. (1997). Evolving meanings of death during early, middle, and later adolescence. *Death Studies, 21,* 253–275.

Norlin, D., Axberg, U., & Broberg, M. (2014). Predictors of harsh parenting practices in parents of children with disabilities. *Early Child Development and Care, 184,* 1472–1484.

North American Menopause Society. (2013). *Make your menopause a positive experience.* Retrieved from http://www.menopause. org/for-women/menopauseflashes/make-you-menopause-a-positive-experience

North American Menopause Society. (2015). *The menopause guidebook* (8th ed.). Pepper Pike, OH: North American Menopause Society.

Northoff, G., & Bermpohl, F. (2004). Cortical midline structures and the self. *Trends in Cognitive Science, 8,* 102–127.

Northridge, J. L., & Coupey, S. (2015). Realizing reproductive health equity for adolescents and young adults. *American Journal of Public Health, 105,* 1284.

Nsamenang, A. B. (2004). *Cultures of human development and education: The challenge of growing up African.* Hauppauge, NY: Nova Science Publishers.

Ntoumanis, N., Vazou, S., & Duda, J. L. (2007). Peer-created motivational climate. In S. Jowette & D. Lavallee (Eds.), *Social psychology in sport* (pp. 145–156). Champaign, IL: Human Kinetics.

Nucci, L. P., & Turiel, E. (2002). The moral and the personal: Sources of social conflict. In L. Nucci & Saxe G. B. (Eds.), *Culture, thought, and development* (pp. 115–137). Mahwah, NJ: Erlbaum.

Nucci, L., & Turiel, E. (2009). Capturing the complexity of moral development and

education. *Mind, Brain, and Education, 3,* 151–159.

Nunez, R. (2004). *Beyond the shelter wall: Homeless families speak out.* New York, NY: White Tiger Press.

Nurmi, J.-E. (2004). Socialization and self-development: Channeling, selection, adjustment, and reflection. In R. M. Lerner & L. Steinberg (Eds.), *Handbook of adolescent psychology* (2nd ed., pp. 85–124). New York, NY: Wiley.

NYU Furman Center. (2016). *Focus on gentrification.* Retrieved from http:// furmancenter.org/files/sotc/Part_1 _Gentrification_SOCin2015_9JUNE2016.pdf

O'Brien, S. F., & Bierman, K. L. (1988). Conceptions and perceived influence of peer groups: Interviews with preadolescents and adolescents. *Child Development, 59,* 1360–1365.

O'Bryant, S. L., & Morgan, L. A. (1990). Recent widows' kin support and orientations to self-sufficienc. *The Gerontologist, 30,* 391–398.

O'Leary, P. A., Haley, W. E., & Paul, P. B. (1993). Behavioral assessment in Alzheimer's dis-ease: Use of a 24-hr log. *Psychology and Aging, 8,* 139–143.

O'Leary, S. (1995). Parental discipline mistakes. *Current Directions in Psychological Science, 4,* 11–13.

O'Neill, D. K., & Gopnik, A. (1991). Young children's ability to identify the sources of their beliefs. *Developmental Psychology, 27,* 390–397. O'Neil, J. M., Ohlde, C., Barke, C., Prosser-Gelwick, B., & Garfield, N. (1980).Research on a workshop to reduce the effects of sexism and sex-role socialization on women's career planning. Journal of Counseling Psychology, 27, 355–363.

O'Rahilly, R., & Muller, F. (2001). *Human embryology and teratology* (3rd ed.). New York, NY: Wiley.

Oades-Sese, G. V., Esquivel, G. B., Kaliski, P. K., Maniatis, L. (2011). A longitudinal study of the social and academic competence of economically disadvantaged bilingual preschool children. *Devepmental Psychology, 47,* 747–764.

Oakes, L. M. (2009). The Humpty Dumpty problem in the study of early cognitive development: Putting the infant back together again. *Current Perspectives in Psychological Science. 4,* 352–358.

Oates, J., Karmiloff-Smith, A., & Johnson, M. (Eds.) (2012). Developing brains. *Early-Childhood in Focus, 7.* Milton Keynes: The Open University

Obeidallah, D. A., Brennan, R. T., Brooks-Gunn, J., Kindlon, D., & Earls, F. (2000). Socioeconomic status, race, and girls' pubertal maturation: Results from the project on human development in Chicago neighborhoods. *Journal of Research on Adolescence, 10,* 443–464.

Ochberg, R. L. (1986). College dropouts: The developmental logic of psychosocial moratoria. *Journal of Youth and Adolescence, 15,* 287–302.

ODPHP. (2016). *Physical activities guidelines.* Retrieved from http://health.gov/paguidelines/

OECD. (2010). *Average annual hours actually worked per worker, 2009.* Retrieved from http://stats.oecd.org/Index.aspx?DatasetCode=ANHRS

OECD. (2011). How many adults participate in education and learning? *Indicator C5.* Retrieved from http://www.oecd.org/education/skills-beyond-school/48631098.pdf

OECD. (2016). Hours worked: Average annual hours actually worked, *OECD Employment and Labour Market Statistics* (database). DOI: http://dx.doi.org/10.1787/data-00303-en

Oerlemans, W. G. M., Bakker, A. B., & Veenhoven, R. (2011). Finding the key to happy aging: A day reconstruction study of happiness. *The Journals of Gerontology: Series B: Psychological Sciences and Social Sciences, 66B,* 665–674.

Offenbacher, D. I., & Poster, C. H. (1985). Aging and the baseline code: An alternative to the "normless elderly." *The Gerontologist, 25,* 526–531.

Ofman, U. (2004). ". . . And how are things sexually?": Helping patients adjust to sexual changes before, during and after cancer treatment. *Supportive Cancer Therapy, 1,* 243–247.

Ofri, D. (2012, Summer). Against nature. *Proto: Massachusetts General Hospital Dispatches from the Frontiers of Medicine,* 35–36.

Ogbu, J. U. (1987). Variability in minority school performance: A problem in search of an explanation. *Anthropology and Education Quarterly, 18,* 312–334.

Ohannessian, C. M., & Crockett, L. J. (1993). A longitudinal investigation of the relationship between educational investment and adolescent sexual activity. *Journal of Adolescent Research, 8,* 167–182.

Ohayon, M. M., Carskadon, M. A., Guilleminault, C., & Vitiello, M. V. (2004). Meta-analysis of quantitative sleep parameters from childhood to old age in healthy individuals: Development normative sleep values across the human lifespan. *Journal of Sleep and Sleep Disorder Research, 27,* 1255–1273.

Ojalvo, H. E. (2011). What is your racial and ethnic identity? *Student Opinion.* Retrieved from http:// learning.blogs.nytimes.com/2011/02/01/what-is-your-racial-and-ethnic-identity/

Okimoto, J. T. (2001). The appeal cycle in three cultures: An exploratory comparison of child development. *Journal of the American Psychoanalytic Association, 49,* 187–215.

Okun, M. A., & Keith, V. M. (1998). Effects of positive and negative social exchanges with various sources on depressive symptoms in younger and older adults. *Journal*

of Gerontology: Psychological Sciences, 53B,* 4–20.

Okundaye, J. N. (2004). Drug trafficking andurban African American youth: Risk factors for PTSD. *Child & Adolescent Social Work Journal, 21,* 285–302.

Olds, D. L., Henderson, C. R., Jr., Tatelbaum, R., & Chamberlin, R. (1988). Improving the life-course development of socially disadvantaged mothers: A randomized trial of nurse home visitation. *American Journal of Public Health, 78,* 1436–1445.

Olweus, D. (1978). *Aggression in school: Bullies and whipping boys.* Washington, DC: Hemisphere.

Olshansky, S. J., Antonucci, T., Berkman, L., Binstock, R. H., Boersch-Supan, A., Cacioppo, J. T., et al. (2012). Differences in life expectancy due to race and educational differences are widening, and many may not catch up. *Health Affairs, 31,* 1803–1813.

Olshansky, S. J., Carnes, B. A., & Desesquelles, A. (2001). Prospects for human longevity. *Science, 291,* 1492–1492.

Olson, K. R., Key, A. C., & Eaton, N. R. (2015). Gender cognition in transgender children. *Psychological Science, 26,* 467–474.

Olson, S. L., Tardif, T. Z., Miller, A., Felt, B., Grabell, S., et al. (2011). Inhibitory control and harsh discipline as predictors of externalizing problems in young children: A comparative study of U.S., Chinese, and Japanese preschoolers. *Journal of Abnormal Child Psychology, 39,* 1163–1175.

Olweus, D. (1993). *Bullying at school: What we know and what we can do.* Cambridge, MA: Blackwell Press.

Olweus, D. (1995). Bullying or peer abuse at school: Facts and intervention. *Current Directions in Psychological Science, 4,* 196–200.

Olweus, D. (2007). *Olweus bullying prevention program: Schoolwide guide.* Center City, MN: Hazelden.

Onedera, J. D., & Stickle, F. (2008). Healthy aging in later life. *The Family Journal, 16,* 73–77.

Operario, D., Tschann, J., Flores, E., Bridges, M. (2006). Brief report: Associations of parental warmth, peer support, and gender with adolescent emotional distress. *Journal of Adolescence, 29*(2), 299–305.

OPSIC. (2015). *OPSIC at a glance.* Retrieved from http://opsic.eu/wp-content/uploads/2013/07/OPSIC-Factsheet-new.pdf

Oregon Health Services. (2010a). *Death with dignity act.* Retrieved from http://www.oregon.gov/DHS/ph/pas/pasforms.shtml

Oregon Health Services. (2010b). *2009 Summary of Oregon's death with dignity act.* Retrieved from http://www.oregon.gov/DHS/ph/pas/docs/year12.pdf

Orenstein, P. (1994). *Schoolgirls: Young women, self-esteem, and the confidence game.* New York, NY: Anchor Books.

Orenstein, P. (2000). *Schoolgirls: Young women, self-esteem, and the confidence*

game* (2nd paperback ed.). New York, NY: Anchor Books.

Osborne, J. W. (2012). Psychological effects of the transition to retirement. *Canadian Journal of Counseling and Psychotherapy, 46,* 45–58.

Osofsky, J. D. (1995). The effect of exposure to violence on young children. *American Psychologist, 50,* 782–788.

Oster, H., Hegley, D., & Nagel, L. (1992). Adult judgments and fine-grained analysis of infant facial expressions: Testing the validity of a priori coding formulas. *Developmental Psychology, 28,* 1115–1131.

Ostrov, E., Offer, D., & Howard, K. I. (1989). Gender differences in adolescent symptomatology: A normative study. *Journal of the American Academy of Child and Adolescent Psychiatry, 28,* 394–398.

Oswaks, M. (2015). Four couples share their online dating success stories: A casual online date really can turn into a marriage. *Cosmopolitan.* Retrieved from http://www.cosmopolitan.com/sex-love/a36793/couples-share-their-online-dating-success-stories/

Ott, M. A., Millstein, S. G., Ofner, S., & Halpern-Felsher, B. L. (2006). Greater expectations: Adolescents' positive motivations for sex. *Perspectives on Sexual and Reproductive Health, 38,* 84–89.

Oudekerk, B. A., Allen, J. P., Hessel, E. T., & Molloy, L. E. (2015). The cascading development of autonomy and relatedness from adolescence to adulthood. *Child Development, 86,* 472–485.

Ouwehand, C., de Ridder, D. T. D., & Bensing, J. M. (2007). A review of successful aging models: Proposing proactive coping as an important additional strategy. *Clinical Psychology Review, 27,* 873–884.

Over, H., & Carpenter, M. (2013). The social side of imitation. *Child Development Perspectives. 7,* 6–11.

Overby, M. S., Trainin, G., Smit, A. B., Bernthal, J. E., & Nelson, R. (2012). Preliteracy speech sound production skill and later literacy outcomes: A study using the Templin archive. *Language, Speech and Hearing Services in Schools, 43,* 97–115.

Owens, R., Jr. (2015). *Language development: An introduction* (9th ed.). Upper Saddle River, NJ: Pearson.

Ozturk, O., & Papafragou, A. (2015). The acquisition of epistemic modality: From semantic meaning to pragmatic interpretation. *Language Learning and Development, 11,* 191–214.

Pagan, R. (2015, August 11). Are relational goods important for people with disabilities? *Applied Research in Quality of Life.*

Pahl, K., & Way, N. (2006). Longitudinal trajectories of ethnic identity among urban, low-income Black and Latino adolescents. *Child Development, 77,* 1403–1415.

Pajares, F. (1996). Self-efficacy beliefs inacademic settings. *Review of Educational Research, 66,* 543–578.

Palacios, J., & Brodzinsky, D. (2010). Adoption research: Trends, topics and outcomes. *International Journal of Behavioral Development, 34*, 270–284.

Palermo, G. B. (1995). Should physician-assisted suicide be legalized? A challenge for the 21st century. *International Journal of Offender Therapy and Comparative Criminology, 39*, 367–376.

Palkovitz, R. (1985). Fathers' attendance, early contact, and extended care with their newborns: A critical review. *Child Development, 56*, 392–406.

Palkovitz, R. (2002). *Involved fathering and men's adult development: Provisional balances.* Mahwah, NJ: Erlbaum.

Palkovitz, R., Fagan, J., & Hull, J. (2013). Coparenting and children's well-being. In N. J. Cabrera & C. S. Tamis-LeMonda (Eds.), *Handbook of father involvement: Multidisciplinary perspectives* (2nd ed., pp. 202–219). New York, NY: Routledge.

Palkovitz, R., Trask, B. S., & Adamson, K. (2014). Essential differences in the meaning and processes of mothering and fathering: Family systems, feminist and qualitative perspectives. *Journal of Family Theory and Review, 6*, 406–420.

Palladino-Schultheiss, D., & Blustein, D. (1994). Contributions of family relationship factors to the identity formation process. *Journal of Counseling Development, 73*, 159–166.

Palm, G. F., & Palkovitz, R. (1988). The challenge of working with new fathers: Implications for support providers. In R. Palkovitz & M. B. Sussman (Eds.), *Transitions to parenthood* (pp. 357–376). New York, NY: Haworth.

Palmer, C. F. (1989). The discriminating nature of infants' exploratory actions. *Developmental Psychology, 25*, 885–893.

Palmer, S. B., Fais, L., Golinkoff, R. M., & Werker, J. F. (2012). Perceptual narrowing of linguistic sign occurs in the 1st year of life. *Child Development, 83*, 543–553.

Palmore, E. B., Nowlin, J. B., & Wang, H. S. (1985). Predictors of function among the old-old: A 10-year follow-up. *Journal of Gerontology, 40*, 244–250.

Papp, L.M. (2010). Course and quality of intimate relationships among psychologically distressed mothers. *American Journal of Orthopsychiatry, 80*, 71–79.

Parents should talk to college students about alcohol. (1997, October 12). *Columbus Dispatch*, p. 7H.

Park, D. C., & Bischof, G. N. (2013). The aging mind: Neuroplasticity in response to cognitive training. *Dialogues in Clinical Neuroscience, 15*, 109–119.

Park, K. (2002). Stigma management among the voluntarily childless. *Sociological Perspectives, 45*, 21–45.

Parker, A. E., Halberstadt, A. G., Dunsmore, J. C., Townley, G., Bryant, A., Jr., Thompson, J. A., et al. (2012). "Emotions are a window into one's heart": A qualitative analysis of parental beliefs about children's emotions across three ethnic groups. *Monographs of the Society for Research in Child Development, 77*(3, Serial No. 304).

Parker, J. G., & Asher, S. R. (1993). Friendship and friendship quality in middle childhood: Links with peer group acceptance and feelings of loneliness and social dissatisfaction. *Developmental Psychology, 29*, 611–621.

Parker, S. E., Mai, C. T., Canfield, M. A., et al.(2010). Updated national birth prevalence estimates for selected birth defects in the United States, 2004–2006. *Birth defects research, Part A, 88*, 1008–1016.

Parker-Pope, T. (2012, February 5). The kids are more than all right. *The New York Times Magazine.* Retrieved from http://well.blogs.nytimes.com/2012/02/02/the-kids-are-more-than-all-right/?_r=0

Parker-Pope, T. (2013). Suicide rise sharply in U.S. *The New York Times.* Retrieved from http://www.nytimes.com/2013/05/03/health/suicide-rate-rises-sharply-in-US.html?nl=todaysheadlinesandemc=edit_th_20130503

Parkhurst, J. T., & Asher, S. R. (1992). Peer rejection in middle school: Subgroup differences in behavior, loneliness, and interpersonal concerns. *Developmental Psychology, 28*, 231–241.

Parrish-Morris, J., Golinkoff, R. M., & Hirsh-Pasek K. (2013). From coo to code: A brief story of language development. In P. D. Zelazo (Ed.), *The Oxford handbook of developmental psychology (Vol 1): Body and mind* (pp. 867–908). New York, NY: Oxford University Press.

Parsons, T., & Bales, R. F. (Eds.). (1955). *Family socialization and interaction process.* Glencoe, IL: Free Press.

Partanen, E., Kujala, T., Tervaniemi, M., & Huotilainen, M. (2013). Prenatal music exposure induces long-term neural effects. *PLoS ONE, 8*, e78946.

Paschal, A. M. (2006). *Voices of African American teen fathers: I'm doing what I got to do.* New York, NY: Haworth Press.

Pashler, H., & Wagenmakers, E. (2012). Editors' introduction to the special section on replicability in psychological science: A crisis of confidence? *Perspectives on Psychological Science, 7*, 528–530.

Patel, J. (2013). *Empty promises: Developers often don't deliver.* Retrieved from http://wamu.org/news/13/05/22/empty_promises_developers_often_dont_deliver

Paterson, G., & Sanson, A. (1999). The association of behavioural adjustment to temperament, parenting and family characteristics among 5-year-old children. *Social Development, 8*, 293–309.

Patterson, C. J. (1995). Families of the lesbian baby boom: Parents' division of labor and children's adjustment. *Developmental Psychology, 31*, 115–123.

Patterson, C. J. (2006). Children of lesbian and gay parents. *Current Directions in Psychological Science, 15*, 241–244.

Patterson, C. J. (2009). Children of lesbian and gay parents: Psychology, law, and policy. *American Psychologist, 64*, 727–736.

Patterson, G. R. (1982). *Coercive family processes.* Eugene, OR: Castalia.

Patton, W., & McMahon, M. (2006). *Career development and systems theory* (2nd ed.). Rotterdam, Netherlands: Sense Publishers.

Patton, W., & McMahon, M. (2014). *Career development and systems theory: Connecting theory and practice* (3rd ed.). Rotterdam, The Netherlands: Sense Publishers.

Pauli-Pott, U., Mertesacker, B., & Beckman, D. (2004). Predicting the development of infant emotionality from maternal characteristics. *Development and Psychopathology, 16*, 19–42.

Paulsen, A. M., & Betz, N. E. (2004, June). Basic confidence pedictors of career decision-making self efficacy. *Career Development Quarterly.* Retrieved from http://findarticles.com/p/articles/mi_m0JAX/is_4_52/ai_n6148413/

Paulussen-Hoogeboom, M. C., Stams, G. J. J. M., Hermanns, J. M. A., & Peetsma, T. T. D. (2007). Child negative emotionality and parenting from infancy to preschool: A meta-analytic review. *Developmental Psychology, 43*, 438–453.

Paus, T. (2005). Mapping brain maturation and cognitive development during adolescence. *Trends in Cognitive Science, 9*, 60–68.

Paus, T. (2009). Brain development. In R. M. Lerner & L. Steinberg (Eds.), *Handbook of adolescent psychology. Vol. 1. Individual bases of adolescent development* (3rd ed., pp. 95–115). Hoboken, NJ: John Wiley.

Pazol, K., Creanga, A. A., & Jamieson, D. J. (2015). Abortion surveillance - United States, 2012. *Morbidity and Mortality Weekly Report, 64*, 1–40.

Peace Direct. (2016). *Child soldiers.* Retrieved from at http://www.peacedirect.org/us/child-soldiers/?gclid=CM2ElOKVtMwCFQeRfgodhOsCdw

Pearce, L. D. (2002). The influence of earlylife course religious exposure on young adults' dispositions toward childbearing. *Journal for the Scientific Study of Religion, 41*, 325–340.

Pearn, J. (2003). Children and war. *Journal of Paediatrics & Child Health, 39*, 166–172.

Pearson, D., Rouse, H., Doswell, S., Ainsworth, C., Dawson, O., Simms, K., et al. (2001). Prevalence of imaginary companions in a normal child population. *Child Care, Health, & Development, 27*, 13–22.

Pearson, R. M., Cooper, R. M., Penton-Voak, I. S., Lightman, S. L., & Evans, J. (2010). Depressive symptoms in early pregnancy disrupt attentional processing of infant emotion. *Psychological Medicine: A Journal of Research in Psychiatry and the Allied Sciences, 40*, 621–631.

Peckins, M. K., Dockray, S., Eckenrode, J. L., Heaton, J., & Susman, E. J. (2012). The longitudinal impact of exposure to violence on cortisol reactivity in adolescents. *Journal of Adolescent Health, 51*, 366–372.

Peek, C. W., Koropeckyj-Cox, T., Zsembik, B. A., & Coward, R. T. (2004). Race comparisons of household dynamics of older adults. *Research on Aging, 26,* 179–201.

Peek, M. K., Coward, R. T., & Peek, C. W. (2000). Race aging and care: Can differences in family and household account for race variations in informal care? *Research on Aging, 22,* 117–142.

Pelham, B. W. (1991). On the benefits of misery: Self-serving biases in the depressive self concept. *Journal of Personality and Social Psychology, 61,* 670–681.

Pell, R. W. (2002). *Hui Malama I Na Kupuna 'O Hawai'i Nei.* Retrieved from http://www.pixi.com/huimalam/#beliefs

Pellebon, D. A. (2012). The African American family. In R. Wright, C. H. Mindel, T.V. Tran, & R.W. Habenstein (Eds.), *Ethnic families in America: Patterns and variations* (pp. 326–36). Boston, MA: Pearson.

Pellegrini, A. D. (2009). Research and policy on children's play. *Child Development Perspectives, 3,* 131–136.

Pellegrini, A. D. (2011). The development and function of locomotor play. In A. D. Pellegrini (Ed.), *The Oxford handbook of the development of play* (pp. 172–184). New York: Oxford University Press.

Pellegrini, A. D., & Bjorklund, D. F. (2004). The ontogeny and phylogeny of children's object and fantasy play. *Human Nature, 15,* 23–43.

Pellegrini, D. S. (1985). Social cognition and competence in middle childhood. *Child Development, 56,* 253–264.

Peltonen, L., & McKusick, V. A. (2001). Dissecting human disease in the postgenomic era. *Science, 291,* 1224–1229.

Pembrey, M. E. (2008). Human inheritance, differences and diseases: Putting genes in their place. Part I & II. *Paediatric and Perinatal Epidemiology, 22,* 497–513.

Pembrey, M. E., Bygren, L. O., Kaati, G., Edvinsson, S., Northstone, K., Sjöström, M., et al. (2006). Sex-specific, male line-transgenerational responses in humans. *European Journal of Human Genetics, 14,* 159–166.

Penick, J. M. (2004). Purposeful aging: Teleological perspectives on the development of social interest in late adulthood. *The Journal of Individual Psychology, 60,* 219–233.

Pennisi, E. (2009). On the origin of cooperation. *Science, 325,* 1196–1199.

Peper, J. S., & Dahl, R. E. (2013). The teenage brain: Surging hormones—brain-behavior interactions during puberty. *Current Directions in Psychological Science, 22,* 134–139.

Peplau, L., & Fingerhut, A. W. (2007). The close relationships of lesbians and gay men. *Annual Review of Psychology, 58,* 405–424.

Peplau, L. A., & Beals, K. P. (2004). The family lives of lesbians and gay men. In A. L. Vangelisti (Ed.), *Handbook of family communication* (pp. 233–248). Mahwah, NJ: Erlbaum.

Pereira, M., Negrao, M., Soares, I., & Messman, J. (2015). Predicting harsh discipline in at-risk mothers: The moderating effect of socioeconomic deprivation severity. *Journal of Child and Family Studies, 24,* 725–733.

Pereira, V., Falsca, L., & de Sá-Saraiva, R. (2012). Immortality of the soul as an intuitive idea: Towards a psychological explanation of the origins of afterlife beliefs. *Journal of Cognition and Culture, 12,* 101–127.

Perfect, T. J. (1994). What can Brinley Plots tell us about cognitive aging? *Journal of Gerontology, 49,* P60–P64.

Peris, A. (2000). *Therapies: Artificial insemination.* Retrieved from http://www.fertilitext.org/p2_doctor/ai.html

Perls, T. T. (2004). The oldest old. *Scientific American, 14,* 6–11.

Perls T. T., Kunkel L., & Puca, A. (2002). The genetics of exceptional human longevity. *Journal of the American Geriatric Society, 50,* 359–368.

Perls, T. T., & Terry, D. (2007). *The New England centenarian study. Overview.* Retrieved from http://www.bumc.bu.edu/Dept/Content .aspx?DepartmentID=361&PageID=5924

Perosa, L. M., Perosa, S. L., & Tam, H. P. (1996). The contribution of family structure and differentiation to identity development in females. *Journal of Youth and Adolescence, 25,* 817–837.

Perret-Clermont, A., Perret, J., & Bell, N. (1991). The social construction of meaning and cognitive activity in elementary school children. In L. B. Resnick, J. M. Levine, & S. D. Teasley (Eds.), *Perspectives on socially shared cognition* (pp. 41–62). Washington, DC: American Psychological Association.

Perrett, D. (2012). *In your face: The new science of human attraction.* New York: Palgrave Macmillan.

Perrin, A. (2015). Social media usage: 2005–2015. *Pew Research Center.* Retrieved from http://www.pewinternet.org/2015/10/08/social-networking-usage-2005-2015/

Perron, A., Brengen, M., Vitaro, F., Côté, S. M., Tremblay, R. E., & Boivin, M. (2012). Moderating effects of team sports participation on the link between peer victimization and mental health problems. *Mental Health and Physical Activity, 5,* 107–115.

Perry, B. D., Pollard, R., Blakley, T., Baker, W., & Vigilante, D. (1995). Childhood trauma, the neurobiology of adaptation and "use-dependent" development of the brain: How states become traits. *Infant Mental Health Journal, 16,* 271–291.

Perry, M. A., & Fantuzzo, J. W. (2010). A multivariate investigation of maternal risks and their relationship to low-income, preschool children's competences. *Applied Developmental Science, 14,* 1–17.

Pertman, A. (2011). *How the adoption revolution is transforming families and America* (Revised). Boston, MA: The Harvard Common Press.

Perusse, D. (1994). Mate choice in modern societies: Testing evolutionary hypotheses with behavioral data. *Human Nature, 5,* 255–278.

Pete, J. M., & DeSantis, L. (1990). Sexual decision making in young Black adolescent females. *Adolescence, 25,* 145–154.

Peter, J., Valkenburg, P. M., & Schouten, A. P. (2005). Developing a model of adolescent friendship formation on the Internet. *CyberPsychology & Behavior, 8,* 423–430.

Petersen, A. C., Compas, B. E., Brooks-Gunn, J., Stemmler, M., Ey, S., & Grant, K. E. (1993). Depression in adolescence. *American Psychologist, 48,* 155–168.

Petersen, A. C., Sarigiani, P. A., & Kennedy, R. E. (1991). Adolescent depression: Why more girls? *Journal of Youth and Adolescence, 20,* 247–272.

Peterson, B. D., Newton, C. R., & Rosen, K. H. (2003). Examining congruence between partners' perceived infertility-related stress and its relationship to marital adjustment and depression in infertile couples. *Family Process, 42,* 59–70.

Peterson, B. E. (2006). Generativity and successful parenting: An analysis of young adult outcomes. *Journal of Personality, 74,* 874–869.

Peterson, B. E., & Stewart, A. J. (1993). Generativity and social motives in young adults. *Journal of Personality and Social Psychology, 65,* 186–198.

Peterson, G. (2001). *Infertility is taking its toll.* Retrieved from http://www.parentsplace.com/fertility/conception/qas/0,,238711_270929,00.html

Peterson, M. M. (2005). Assisted reproductive technologies and equity of access issues. *Journal of Medical Ethics, 31,* 280–285.

Pettis, R. M. (2011). *Hijras. Glbtq: An encyclopedia of gay, lesbian, bisexual, transgender, and queer culture.* Retrieved from at http://www.glbtq.com/social-sciences/hijras.html

Petts, R. J. (2016). Religious homogamy, race/ethnicity, and parents' relationship stability. *Sociological Focus, 49,* 163–179.

Pew Research Center. (2015a). *Parenting in America. Section 3. Parenting approaches and concerns.* Retrieved from http://www.pewsocialtrends.org/2015/12/17/3-parenting-approaches-and-concerns

Pew Research Center. (2015b). *Parenting in America. Section 4. Childcare and education: Quality, availability, and parental involvement.* Retrieved from http://www.pewsocialtrends.org/2015/12/17/4-child-care-and-education-quality-availability-and-parental-involvement/

Pew Research Center. (2015c). *Parenting in America: Outlook, worries, aspirations are strongly linked to financial situations. Survey of Parents with Children Under 18: September 15-October 13, 2015.* Retrieved from https://www.pewsocialtrends.org/2015/12/17/parenting-in-america/st_2015-12-17_parenting-01/

Pew Research Center. (2015d). *Teens, technology and friendships.* Retrieved from http://www.pewinternet.org/2015/08/06/teens-technology-and-friendships

Pew Research Center. (2016). *15% of American adults have used online dating sites or mobile dating apps.* Retrieved from http://

www.pewinternet.org/2016/02/11/15
-percent-of-american-adults-have-used
-online-dating-sites-or-mobile-dating-apps/

Pew Social Trends. (2015). *Multiracial in America*. Retrieved from http://www.pewsocialtrends.org/2015/06/11/multiracial-in-america/

Pfefferbaum, B., Seale, T. W., McDonald, N. B., Brandt, E. N., Jr., Rainwater, S. C., Maynard, B. T., et al. (2000). Posttraumatic stress two years after the Oklahoma City bombing in youth geographically distant from the explosion. *Psychiatry: Interpersonal and Biological Processes, 63*, 358–370.

PFLAG. (2016a). *A definition of "Queer."* Retrieved from https://community.pflag.org/abouttheq

PFLAG. (2016b). *The PFLAG national glossary of terms*. Retrieved from http://community.pflag.org/glossary

Phelan, E. A., & Larson, E. B. (2002). "Successful aging"- where next? *Journal of the American Geriatric Society, 50*, 1306–1308.

Phillips, D. A. (1984). The illusion of incompetence among academically competent children. *Child Development, 55*, 2000–2016.

Phillips, D. A. (1987). Socialization of perceived academic competence among highly competent children. *Child Development, 58*, 1308–1320.

Phillipson, S., & Phillipson, S. N. (2007). Academic expectations, belief of ability, and involvement by parents as predictors of child achievement: A cross-cultural comparison. *Educational Psychology, 27*, 329–348.

Phinney, J. S. (1989). Stages of ethnic identity development in minority group adolescents. *Journal of Early Adolescence, 9*, 34–49.

Phinney, J. S. (1992). The multigroup ethnic identity measure: A new scale for use with adolescents and young adults from diverse groups. *Journal of Adolescent Research, 7*, 156–176.

Phinney, J. S. (1996a). Understanding ethnic diversity: The role of ethnic identity. *American Behavioral Scientist, 40*, 143–152.

Phinney, J. S. (1996b). When we talk about American ethnic groups, what do we mean? *American Psychologist, 51*, 918–927.

Phinney, J. S. (1997). Variations in bicultural identification among African American and Mexican American adolescents. *Journal of Research on Adolescence, 7*, 3–32.

Piaget, J. (1926). *The language and thought of the child*. New York, NY: Harcourt Brace.

Piaget, J. (1929). *The child's conception of physical causality*. New York, NY: Harcourt Brace.

Piaget, J. (1932/1948). *The moral judgment of the child*. Glencoe, IL: Free Press.

Piaget, J. (1936/1952). *The origins of intelligence in children*. New York, NY: International Universities Press.

Piaget, J. (1941/1952). *The child's conception of number*. London: Kegan Paul, Trench & Trubner.

Piaget, J. (1951). *Play, dreams, and imitation in childhood*. New York, NY: Norton.

Piaget, J. (1952). *The language and thought of the child*. London: Routledge & Kegan Paul.

Piaget, J. (1954). *The construction of reality in the child*. New York, NY: Basic Books.

Piaget, J. (1962). *Play, dreams, and imitation in childhood*. New York, NY: Norton.

Piaget, J. (1963). The attainment of invariant and reversible operations in the development of thinking. *Social Research, 30*, 283–299.

Piaget, J. (1970). Piaget's theory. In P. H. Mussen (Ed.), *Carmichael's manual of child psychology* (Vol. 1, 3rd ed.). New York, NY: Wiley.

Piaget, J. (1972a). Intellectual evolution from adolescence to adulthood. *Human Development, 15*, 1–12.

Piaget, J. (1972b). *The psychology of intelligence*. Totowa, NJ: Littlefield Adams.

Piaget, J. (1978/1985). *The equilibration of cognitive structures*. Chicago, IL: University of Chicago Press.

Piaget, J., & Inhelder, B. (1966/1969). *The psychology of the child*. New York, NY: Basic Books.

Pick, H. L., Jr. (1989). Motor development: The control of action. *Developmental Psychology, 25*, 867–870.

Pick, H. L., Jr., & Rosengren, K. S. (1991). Perception and representation in the development of mobility. In R. R. Hoffman & D. S. Palermo (Eds.), *Cognition and the symbolic processes: Applied and ecological perspectives* (pp. 433–454). Hillsdale, NJ: Erlbaum.

Piers, M. W., & Landau, G. M. (1980). *The gift of play*. New York, NY: Walker.

Pillemer, K., & Suitor, J. J. (2014). Who provides care? A prospective study of caregiving among adult siblings. *The Gerontologist, 54*, 589–598.

Pine, D., Cohen, P., Gurley, D., Brook, J., & Ma, Y. (1998). The risk for early adulthood anxiety and depressive disorders in adolescents with anxiety and depressive disorders. *Archives of General Psychiatry, 55*, 56–64.

Ping, R. M., & Goldin-Meadow, S. (2008). Hands in the air: Using ungrounded iconic gestures to teach children conservation of quantity. *Developmental Psychology, 44*, 1277–1287.

Pinquart, M., & Schindler, I. (2007). Changes in life satisfaction in the transition to retirement: A latent-class approach. *Psychology and Aging, 22*, 442–455.

Pinquart, M., & Sörensen, S. (2003). Associations of stressors and uplifts of caregiving with caregiver burden and depressive moods: A meta-analysis. *Journals of Gerontology B: Psychological Science and Social Science, 58*, P112–P128.

Pirog-Good, M. A. (1995). The family background and attitudes of teen fathers. *Youth and Society, 26*, 351–376.

Planned Parenthood. (2000). *Mifepristone: A brief history*. Retrieved from http://www.plannedparenthood.org/library/ABORTION/Mifepristone.html

Planned Parenthood. (2013). *The emotional effects of induced abortion*. Retrieved from https://www.plannedparenthood.org/files/8413/9611/5708/Abortion_Emotional_Effects.pdf

Pleck, J. H. (2010). Paternal involvement: Revised conceptualization and theoretical linkages with child outcomes. In M. E. Lamb (Ed.), *The role of the father in child development* (5th ed., pp. 58–94). Hoboken, NJ: Wiley.

Plomin, R. (2004). Genetics and developmental psychology. *Merrill-Palmer Quarterly, 50*(3) 341–352.

Plomin, R. & Deary, I. J. (2015). Genetics and intelligence differences: Five special findings. *Molecular Psychiatry, 20*, 98–108.

Plomin, R., DeFries, J. C., Knopik, V. S., & Neiderhiser, J. M. (2012). *Behavioral genetics* (6th ed.). New York, NY: Worth Publishers.

Plomin, R., & Spinath, F. M. (2004). Intelligence, genetics, genes, and genomics. *Journal of Personality and Social Psychology, 86*(1) 112–129.

Plotnick, R. D. (1992). The effects of attitudes on teenage premarital pregnancy and its resolution. *American Sociological Review, 57*, 800–811.

Pluess, M., & Belsky, J. (2010). Differential susceptibility to parenting and quality child care. *Developmental Psychology, 46*, 379–390.

Plutchik, R. (2001). The nature of emotions. *American Scientist, 89*, 344–350.

Pöhlmann, K. (2001). Agency- and communion-orientation in life goals: Impacts on goal pursuit strategies and psychological well-being. In P. Schmuck & K. M. Sheldon (Eds.), *Life goals and well-being: Towards a positive psychology of human striving* (pp. 68–84). Ashland, OH: Hogrefe and Huber.

Polednak, A. P. (1991). Black-White differences in infant mortality in 38 standard metropolitan statistical areas. *American Journal of Public Health, 81*, 1480–1482.

Polka, L., Rvatchew, S., & Mattock, K. (2009). Experiential influences on speech perception and speech production in infancy. In E. Hoff & M. Schatz (Eds.), *The Blackwell handbook of language development* (pp. 153–172). Malden, MA: Wiley-Blackwell.

Pollack, C. E. (2003). Intentions of burial: Mourning, politics and memorials following the massacre at Srebrenica. *Death Studies, 27*, 125–142.

Pollak, S. D. (2008). Mechanisms linking early experience and the emergence of emotions: Illustrations from the study of maltreated children. *Current Directions in Psychological Science, 17*, 370–375.

Pollak, S. D., Nelson, C. A., Schlak, M. F., Roeber, B. J., Wewerka, S. S., Wiik, K. L., et al. (2010). Neurodevelopmental effects of early deprivation in post-institutionalized children. *Child Development, 81*, 224–236.

Pollard, I. (2000). Substance abuse and parenthood: Biological mechanisms— bioethical challenges. *Women and Health, 30*, 1–24.

Pollitt, E. (1994). Poverty and child development: Relevance of research in developing countries to the United States. *Child Development, 65*, 283–295.

Pomerantz, E. M., & Easton, M. M. (2000). Developmental differences in children's conceptions of parental control: "They love me, but they make me feel incompetent." *Merrill-Palmer Quarterly, 46*, 140–167.

Ponitz, C. C., McClelland, M. M., Matthews, J. S., & Morrison, F. J. (2009). A structured observation of behavioral self-regulation and its contribution to kindergarten outcomes. *Developmental Psychology, 45*, 605–619.

Poon, L. W., & Harrington, C. A. (2006). Commonalities in aging- and fitness-related impact on cognition. In L. W. Poon, W. Chodzko-Zajko, & P. D. Tomporowski (Eds.), *Activity, cognitive functioning and aging* (Vol. 1, pp. 33–50). Champaign, IL: Human Kinetics.

Popova, S., Lange, S., Burd, L., & Rehm, J. (2012). Health care burden and cost associated with Fetal Alcohol Syndrome: Based on official Canadian data. *PLoS. ONE, 7*, e43024. doi: 10.1371/journal. pone.0043024.

Porcaro, C., Zappasodi, F., Barbati, G., Salustri, C., Pizzella, V., Rossini, P. M., et al.(2006). Fetal auditory responses to external sounds and mother's heart beat: Detection improved by Independent Component Analysis. *Brain Research, 1101*, 51–58.

Porter, E. J. (1994). Older widows' experiences of living alone at home. *Image: Journal of Nursing Scholarship, 26*, 19–24.

Portes, A. & Rumbaut, R. G. (2014). *Immigrant America: A portrait, updated, and expanded* (4th ed.). Berkeley, CA: University of California Press.

Portrie, T., & Hill, N. R. (2005). Blended families: A critical review of the current research. *The Family Journal, 13*, 445–451.

Posada, G., Gao, Y., Wu, F., Posada, R., Tascon, M., & Schoelmerich, A. (1995). The secure-base phenomenon across cultures: Children's behavior, mothers' preferences, and experts' concepts. *Monographs of the Society for Research in Child Development, 60*, 27–48.

Posada, G., Jacobs, A., Richmond, M. K., Carbonell, O. A., Alzate, G., Bustamante, M. R., et al. (2002). Maternal caregiving and infant security in two cultures. *Developmental Psychology, 38*, 67–78.

Posttraumatic stress two years after the Oklahoma City bombing in youth geographically distant from the explosion. *Psychiatry: Interpersonal and Biological Processes, 63*, 358–370.

Poulain, M., Pes, G. M., Grasland, C. et al. (2004). Identification of a geographic area characterized by extreme longevity in the Sardinia Island: The AKEA study. *Experimental Gerontology, 39*, 1423–1429.

Poulin, F. W., & Boivin, M. (2000). The role of proactive and reactive aggression in the formation and development of boys' friendships. *Developmental Psychology, 36*, 233–240.

Poulin, R., Dishion, T. J., & Haas, E. (1999). The peer influence paradox: Friendship quality and deviancy training within male adolescent friendships. *Merrill-Palmer Quarterly, 45*, 42–61.

Power, T. G. (1985). Mother- and father-infant play: A developmental analysis. *Child Development, 56*, 1514–1524.

Powers, S. M. (2002). Merge as a basic mechanism of language: Evidence from language acquisition. In E. Witruk & A. D. Friederici (Eds.), *Basic functions of language, reading and reading disability* (pp. 105–117). Dordrecht, Netherlands: Kluwer.

Powledge, T. M. (2014). How much of the human DNA is doing something? *Genetic Literacy Project,* Retrieved from https://www.geneticliteracyproject. org/2014/08/05/how-much-of-human -dna-is-doing-something/

Pratt, C. C., Jones, L. L., Shin, H., & Walker, A. J. (1989). Autonomy and decision making between single older women and their caregiving daughters. *The Gerontologist, 29*, 792–797.

Pratt, L. A., & Brody, D. J. (2014). Depression in the U.S. household population 2009–2012. *NCHS data brief No. 172, December, 2014.* Retrieved from http://www.cdc.gov /nchs/data/databriefs/db172.htm

Pratt, M. W., Arnold, M. L., & Lawford, H. (2009). Growing toward care: A psychosocial approach to moral identity and generativity of personality in emerging adulthood. In D. Narvaez & D.K. Lapsley (Eds.), *Personality, identity, and character: Explorations in moral psychology* (pp. 295–315). New York, NY: Cambridge University Press.

Pratt, M. W., Norris, J. E., Alisat, S., & Bisson, E. (2013). Earth mothers (and fathers): Examining generativity and environmental concerns in adolescents and their parents. *Journal of Moral Education, 42*, 12–27.

Pratt, M. W., Norris, J. E., Hebblethwaite, S., & Arnold, M. L. (2008). Intergenerational transmission of values: Family generativity and adolescents' narratives of parent and grandparent value teaching. *Journal of Personality, 76*, 171–198.

Prawat, R. S., Byers, J. L., & Anderson, A. H. (1983). An attributional analysis of teachers' affective reactions to student success and failure. *American Educational Research Journal, 20*, 137–152.

Premack, D. (2010). Why humans are unique: Three theories. *Perspectives on Psychological Science, 5*, 22–32.

Price, J., Hertzog, C., & Dunlosky, J. (2010). Self-regulated learning in younger and older adults: Does aging affect cognitive control? *Aging, Neuropsychology,and Cognition, 17*, 329–359.

Price, S., Price, C., & McKenry, P. (2010). *Families and change.* Thousand Oaks, CA: Sage.

Pringle, H. (2013). The origins of creativity. *Scientific American, 308,*36–43.

Prinstein, M. J., & LaGreca, A. M. (2002). Peer crowd identification and intenalizing distress in childhood and adolescence: A longitudinal follow-back study. *Journal of Research on Adolescence, 12*, 325–351.

Prinzie, P., & Onghena, P. (2005). Cohort sequential design. *Encyclopedia of Statistics in Behavioral Science.* Retrieved from ahttp://onlinelibrary.wiley.com /doi/10.1002/0470013192.bsa110/abstract

Proctor, B. D., Semega J. L., & Kollar, M. A. (2016). *Income and poverty in the United States: 2015.* Retrieved from https://www .census.gov/library/publications/2016 /demo/p60-256.html

Provasnik, S., Kastberg, D., Ferraro, D., Lemanski, N., Roey, S., & Jenkins, F. (2012). Highlights from TIMSS 2011: Mathematics and science achievement of U.S. fourth- and eighth-grade students in an international context (NCES 2013-009). *National Center for Education Statistics, Institute of Education Sciences, U.S. Department of Education.* Washington, DC: U.S. Department of Education.

Pruchno, R. A., Cartwright, F. P., & Wilson-Genderson, M. (2009). Effects of marital closeness on the transition to caregiving to widowhood. *Aging and Mental Health, 13*, 808–817.

Puma, M., Bell, S., Cook, R., Heid, C., Broene, P., Jenkins, F., et al. (2012). *Third grade follow-up to the Head Start impact study, final eport, executive summary, OPRE Report, 2012-45b.* Washington, DC: Office of Planning, Reseach and Evaluation, Administration for Children and Families, U.S. Department of Health and Human Services.

Puma, M., Bell, S., Cook, R., Heid, C., & Lopez, M. (2005). *Head Start impact study: First year findings.* Washington, DC: U.S. Department of Health and Human Services.

Purdie-Vaughns, V., Steele, C. M., Davies, P. G., Ditlmann, R., & Crosby, J. R. (2008). Social identity contingencies: How diversity cures signal threat or safety for African Americans in mainstream institutions. *Journal of Personality and Social Psychology, 94*, 615–630.

Purhonen, M., Kilpelainen-Lees, R., Valkonen-Korhonen, M., Karhu, J., & Lehtonen, J. (2005). Four-month-old infants process own mother's voice faster than unfamiliar voices. *Cognitive Brain Research, 24*, 627–633.

Purhonen, M., Kilpeläinen-Lees, R., Valkonen-Korhonen, M., Karhu, J., Lehtonen, J. R. H. T. (2006). Implications of attachment theory for research on intimacy. In M. Mikulincer & G. S. Goodman (Eds.), *Dynamics of romantic love: Attachment, caregiving, and sex* (pp. 383–403). New York, NY: Guilford Press.

Pushkar, D., Arbuckle, T., Conway, M., Chaikelson, J., & Maag, U. (1997). Everyday activity parameters and competence in older adults. *Psychology and Aging, 12*, 600–609.

Putnam, S. P., Sanson, A.V., & Rothbart, M. K. (2012). Child temperament and parenting. In M. H Bornstein (Ed.), *Handbook of parenting* (Vol. 1, 2nd ed., pp. 255–277). New York, NY: Psychology Press.

Putnick, D. L., & Bornstein, M. H. (2016). Girls' and boys' labor and household chores in low-. and middle-income countries. In M. H. Bornstein, D. L. Putnick, J. E. Lansford, K. Deater-Deckard, & R. H. Bradley (Eds.), *Gender in low- and middle-income countries. Monographs of the Society for Research in Child Development, Serial 320, 81*(1) (pp. 104–122).

Putze, D. (2014). Custodial parents living in poverty. *Child Support Fact Sheet Series, No. 3.* Retrieved from www.acf.hhs.gov /sites/default/files/programs/css/sbtn _custodial_parents_living_in_poverty.pdf

Pye, C. (1986). Quiché Mayan speech to children. *Journal of Child Language, 13,* 85–100.

Pyle, R. P. (2002). Best practices in assessing kindergarten readiness. *California School Psychologist, 7,* 63–73.

Pyne, J. (2016). "Parenting is not a job...it's a relationship": Recognition and relational knowledge among parents of gender non-conforming children. *Journal of Progressive Human Services, 27,* 21–48.

Pynoos, J., Caraviello, R., & Cicero, C. (2010). Housing in an aging America. In J. C. Cavanaugh & C. K. Cavanaugh (Eds.), *Aging in America, Vol. 3. Societal Issues* (pp. 128–159). Santa Barbara, CA: Praeger.

Qu, Y., Galván, A., Fuligni, A. J., Lieberman, M. D., & Telzer, E. H. (2015). Longitudinal changes in prefrontal cortex activation underly declines in adolescence risk taking. *Journal of Neuroscience, 35,* 11308–11314.

Quadrel, M. J., Fischhoff, B., & Davis, W. (1993). Adolescent (in)vulnerability. *American Psychologist, 48,* 102–116.

Quakenbush, S. W., & Barnett, M. A. (1995). Correlates of reminiscence activity among elderly individuals. *International Journal of Aging and Human Development, 41,* 169–181.

Queensland Government. (2012). *Multicultural health.* Retrieved from www .health.qld.gov.au/multicultural /support_tools/14MCRS-Pregnancy.pdf

Quéniart, A., & Charpentier, M. (2013). Initiate, bequeath, and remember: Older women's transmission role within the family. *Journal of Women and Aging, 25,* 45–65.

Quiggle, N. L., Garber, J., Panak, W. F., & Dodge, K. A. (1992). Social information processing in aggressive and depressed children. *Child Development, 63,* 1305–1320.

Quindlen, A. (2009, May 11–18). Stepping aside. *Newsweek,* 69–70.

Quinn, P. C., Doran, M. M., Reiss, J. E., & Hoffman, J. E. (2009). Time course of visual attention in infant categorization of cats versus dogs: Evidence for a head bias as revealed through eye tracking. *Child Development, 80,* 151–161.

Quinn, P. C., Eimas, P. D., & Tarr, M. J. (2001). Perceptual categorization of cat and dog silhouettes by 3- to 4-month-old infants. *Journal of Experimental Child Psychology, 79,* 78–94.

Quintana, S. M., Aboud, F. E., Chao, R. K., Contreras-Grau, J., Cross, W. E., Jr., Hudley, C., et al. (2006). Race, ethnicity and culture in child development: Contemporary research and future directions. *Child Development, 77,* 1129–1141.

Rabagliati, H., Senghas, A., Johnson, S., & Marcus, G. F. (2012). Infant rule learning: Advantage language or advantage speech? *PLoS ONE, 7,* e40517, doe:10.1371/journal .pone.0040517.

Raeff, C. (2010). Independence and interdependence in children's developmental experiences. *Child Development Perspectives, 4,* 31–36.

Ragins, B. R. & Kram, K. E. (2007). *The handbook of mentoring at work: Theory, research and practice.* Thousand Oaks, CA: Sage.

Raimbault, C., Saliba, E., & Porter, R. H. (2007). The effect of the odour of the mother's milk on breastfeeding behavior of premature neonates. *Acta Paediatrica, 96,* 368–371.

Rakison, D. H., & Poulin-Dubois, D. (2001). Developmental origin of the animate–inanimate distinction. *Psychological Bulletin, 127,* 209–228.

Rakoczy, J., Tomasello, M., & Striano, T. (2004). Young children know that trying is not pretending: A test of the "behaving as if" construal of children's early concept of pretense. *Developmental Psychology, 40,* 388–399.

Rakow, A., Forehand, R., Haker, K., McKee, L. G., Champion, J. E., Potts, J., Hardcastle, E., Roberts, L., & Compas, B. E. (2011). Use of parental guilt induction among depressed parents. *Journal of Family Psychology, 25,* 147–151.

Ramirez, A. Y. F. (2003). Dismay and disappointment: Parental involvement of Latino immigrant parents. *Urban Review, 35*(2) 93–110.

Randall, G. K., Martin, P., Bishop, A. J., Johnson, M. A., & Poon, L.W. (2012). Social resources and change in functional health: Comparing three age groups. *The International Journal of Aging and Development, 75,* 1–29.

Rands, C. M., Meader, S., Ponting, C. P., & Lunter, G. (2014). 8.2% of the human genome is constrained: Variation in rates of turnover across functional element classes in the human lineage. *PLoS Genet, 10,* e1004525.

Ransford, C. R., Crouter, A. C., & McHale, S. M. (2008). Implications of work pressure and supervisor support for fathers', mothers', and adolescents' relationships and well-being in dual-earner families. *Community,Work and Family, 11,* 37–60.

Ranzijn, R., Keeves, J., Luszcz, M., & Feather, N. T. (1998). The role of self-perceived usefulness and competence in the self-esteem of elderly adults: Confirmatory factor analyses of the Bachman revision of Rosenberg's self-esteem scale. *Journal of Gerontology, 53,* P96–P104.

Rapee, R., Wignall, A., Spence, S., Lyne-ham, H., & Cobham, V. (2008). *Helping your anxious child: A step-by-step guide for parents.* Oakland, CA: New Harbinger Publications.

Rapp, A. (2016). Research ethics at the graduate level. *Observer, 29,* 38–39.

Raschick, M., & Ingersoll-Dayton, B. (2004). The costs and rewards of caregiving among aging spouses and adult children. *Family Relations, 53,* 317–325.

Ratelle, C. F., Simard, K., & Guay, F. (2013). University students' subjective well-being: The role of autonomy support from parents, friends, and the romantic partner. *Journal of Happiness Studies, 14,* 893–910.

Rath, T., & Harter, J. (2010). Your friends and your social wellbeing. *Gallup Business Journal.* Retrieved from http://www.gallup.com /businessjournal/127043/Friends-Social -wellbeing.aspx?g_source=ELEMENT_10 _BEST_FRIEND&g_medium=topic&g _campaign=tiles

Rauch, J. (2014). The real roots of midlife crisis. *The Atlantic.* Retrieved from http:// www.theatlantic.com/magazine /archive/2014/12/the-real -roots-of-midlife-crisis/382235/

Ray, W. J. (2011). *Methods toward a science of behavior and experience* (10th ed.). Belmont, CA: Cengage Learning.

Raymond, E. G. & Grimes, D. A. (2012). The comparative safety of legal induced abortion and childbirth in the United States. *Obstetrics and Gynecology, 119,* 215–219.

Rayner, K., Schotter, E. R., Masson, M. E. J., Potter, M. C., & Treiman, R. (2016). So much to read, so little time: How do we read and can speed reading help? *Psychological Science in the Public Interest, 17,* 4–34.

Reardon, S. F. (2011). The widening academic achievement gap between the rich and the poor: New evidence and possible explanations. In R. Murnane & G. Duncan (Eds.) *Whither opportunity? Rising inequality and the uncertain life chances of low-income children* (pp. 91–116). New York: The Russell Sage Foundation Press.

Recchia, H. E., & Howe, N. (2009). Associations between social understanding, sibling relationship quality, and siblings' conflict strategies and outcomes. *Child Development, 80,* 1564–1578.

Receputo, G., Mazzoleni, G., DiFazio, I., & Alessandria, I. (1996). Study on the sense of taste in a group of Sicilian centenarians. *Archives of Gerontology and Geriatrics, 22*(5), 411–414.

Reck, C., Noe, D., Stefenelli, U., et.al. (2011). Interactive coordination of currently depressed in-patient mothers and their infants during the postpartum period. *Infant Mental Health Journal, 32,* 542–562.

Reddy, V. (2000). Coyness in infancy. *Developmental Science, 3,* 186–192.

Reed, J., England, P., Littlejohn, K., Bass, B. C., & Caudillo, M. L. (2014). Consistent and inconsistent contraception among young women: Insights from qualitative interviews. *Family Relations: An Interdisciplinary Journal of Applied Family Studies, 63,* 244–258.

Reed, R. K. (2005). *Birthing fathers: The transformation of men in American rites of birth.* New Brunswick, NJ: Rutgers University Press.

Reese, E., Bird, A., & Tripp, G. (2007). Children's self-esteem and moral self: Links to parent-child conversations. *Social Development, 16,* 460–478.

Reese, E., & Cox, A. (1999). Quality of adult book reading affects children's emergent literacy. *Developmental Psychology, 35,* 20–28.

Reich, J. A., & Brindis, C. D. (2006). Conceiving risk and responsibility: A qualitative examination of men's experiences of unintended pregnancy and abortion. *Journal of Men's Health, 5,* 133–152.

Reid, V. M., Hoehl, S., Grigutsch, M., Groen-dahl, A., Parise, E., & Striano, T. (2009). The neural correlates of infant and adult goal prediction: Evidence for semantic processing systems. *Developmental Psychology, 45,* 620–629.

Reidiger, M., Freund, A. M., & Baltes, P. B. (2005). Managing life through personal goals: Intergoal facilitations and intensity of goal pursuit in younger and older adulthood. *Journals of Gerontology: Series B: Psychological Sciences and Social Sciences, 60B,* P84–P91.

Reimer, K. (2003). Committed to caring: Transformation in adolescent moral identity. *Applied Developmental Science, 7,* 129–137.

Reis, H. T. (2006). Implications of attachment theory for research on intimacy. In M. Mikulincer and G. S. Goodman (Eds.), *Dynamics of Romantic Love: Attachment, Caregiving, and Sex* (pp. 383–403). New York, NY: Guilford Press.

Reis, H. T. & Aron, A. (2008). Love: What is it, why does it matter, and how does it operate? *Perspectives on Psychological Science, 3,* 80–86.

Reischl, T. M., & Hirsch, B. J. (1989). Identity commitments and coping with a difficult developmental transition. *Journal of Youth and Adolescence, 18,* 55–70.

Riessing, E. D., Andruff, H. L., & Wentland, J. J. (2011). Looking back: The experience of first sexual intercourse and current sexual adjustment in young heterosexual adults. *Journal of Sex Research, 49,* 27–35.

Reker, G. T. (1997). Personal meaning, optimism and choice: Existential predictors of depression in community and institutional elderly. *The Gerontologist, 37,* 709–716.

Remennick, L. (2000). Childless in the land of imperative motherhood: Stigma and coping among infertile Israeli women. *Sex Roles, 43,* 821–841.

Renn, A. M. (2013). Why gentrification? *Newgeography.com.* Retrieved from http://www.newgeography .com/content /003701-y-gentrification

Repacholi, B. M., & Meltzoff, A. N. (2007). Emotional eavesdropping: Infants selectively respond to indirect emotional signals. *Child Development, 78,* 503–521.

Repetti, R. L., Robles, T. F., & Reynolds, B. (2011). Allostatic processes in the family. *Development and Psychopathology, 23,* 921–938.

Repetti, R. L., Taylor, S. E., & Seeman, T. E. (2002). Risky families: Family social environments and the mental and physical health of offspring. *Psychological Bulletin, 128,* 330–366.

Repokari, L., Punamaki, R, Poikkeus, P., Tiitinen, A., Vilska, S., Unkila-Kallio, L., et al. (2006). Ante- and perinatal factors and child characteristics predicting parenting experience among formerly infertile couples during the child's first year: A controlled study. *Journal of Family Psychology, 20,* 670–679.

Republic of Kenya Ministry of Health. (2004). *Status and trends of Millennium Development Goals (MDG) in Kenya.* Retrieved from http://www.health.go.ke/

Rest, J. R. (1983). Morality. In P. H. Mussen (Gen. Ed.), J. H. Flavell, & E. M. Markman (Vol. Eds.), *Handbook of child psychology: Vol. 3. Cognitive development.* New York, NY: Wiley.

Retirement-lounge.com. (2013). Retrieved from www.retirement-lounge.com

Rettew, D. C., Stanger, C., McKee, L., Doyle, A., & Hudziak, J. J. (2006). Interactions between child and parent temperament and child behavior problems. *Comprehensive Psychiatry, 47,* 412–420.

Reyna, V. F., & Farley, F. (2006). Risk and rationality in adolescent decision making: Implications for theory, practice, and public policy. *Psychological Science in the Public Interest, 7,* 2–44.

Reynolds, C. A., & Finkel, D. G. (2016). Cognitive and physical aging: Genetic influences and gene-environment interplay. In K. Warner-Schaie & S. Willis (Eds.), *Handbook of the psychology of aging* (8th ed., pp. 125–146). San Diego, CA: Academic Press/Elsevier.

Rhee, S. H., Boeldt, D. L., Friedman, N. P., Corley, R. P., Hewitt, J. K., Young, S. E., Knafo, A., Robinson, J., Waldman, I. D., Van Hulle, C. A., Zahn-Waxler, C. (2013). The role of language in concern and disregard for others in the first years of life. *Developmental Psychology, 49,* 197–214.

Rhee, S. H., Friedman, N. P., Boeldt, D. L., Corley, R. P., Hewitt, J. K., Knafo, A., Lahey, B. B., Robinson, J., Van Hulle, C. A., Waldman, I. D., Young, S. E., & Zahn-Waxler, C. (2013). Early concern and disregard for others as predictors of anti-social behavior. *Journal of Child Psychology and Psychiatry, 54,* 157–166.

Rice, P. L. (2000). Baby, souls, name, and health: Traditional customs for a newborn infant among the Hmong in Melbourne. *Early Human Development, 57,* 189–203.

Richards, F., & Commons, M. L. (1990). Post-formal cognitive-developmental theory and research: A review of its current status. In C. N. Alexander & E. J. Langer (Eds.), *Higher stages of human development: Perspectives on adult growth* (pp. 229–257). New York, NY: Oxford University Press.

Richards, M., Pennings, G., & Appleby, J. (2012). *Reproductive donation: Practice, policy, and bioethics.* Cambridge, England: Cambridge University Press.

Richards, M. H., & Larson, R. (1993). Pubertal development and the daily subjective states of young adolescents. *Journal of Research on Adolescence, 3,* 145–169.

Richards, T. A. (2016). What is social anxiety? *Social Anxiety Institute.* Retrieved from https://socialanxietyinstitute.org /what-is-social-anxiety

Richert, R. A., Robb, M. B., & Smith, E. I. (2011). Media as social partners: The social nature of young children's learning from screen media. *Child Development, 82,* 82–95.

Richman, J. (2001). Humor and creative life styles. *American Journal of Psychotherapy, 55,* 420–428.

Richter, L. M. (2006). Studying adolescence, *Science, 312,* 1902–1905.

Ricks, M. H. (1985). The social transmission of parental behavior: Attachment across generations. In I. Bretherton & E. Waters (Eds.), Growing points of attachment: Theory and research (pp. 211–227). *Monographs of the Society for Research in Child Development, 50*(1–2, Serial No. 209).

Rideout, V. (2013). *Zero to eight: Children's media use in America, 2013.* A Common Sense Media Research Study. Retrieved from https://www.commonsensemedia .org/research/zero-to-eight-childrens -media-use-in-america-2013

Rideout, V., Hamel, E., & Kaiser Family Foundation, (2006). *The media family: Electronic media in the lives of infants, toddlers, preschoolers and their parents.* Menlo Park, CA: Henry J. Kaiser Family Foundation.

Ridgeway, C. L., & Correll, S. J. (2004). Motherhood as a status characteristic. *Journal of Social Issues, 60,* 683–700.

Riebe, D., Burbank, P., & Garber, C. E. (2002). Setting the stage for active older adults. In P. M. Burbank & D. Riebe (Eds.), *Promoting exercise and behavior change in older adults: Interventions with the transtheoretical model* (pp. 1–28). New York, NY: Springer-Verlag.

Riediger, M., Freund, A. M., & Baltes, B. (2005). Managing life through personal goals: Intergoal facilitation and intensity of goal pursuit in younger and older adulthood. *The Journals of Gerontology: Series B: Psychological Sciences and Social Sciences, 60B,* 84–91.

Riegel, K. F. (1973). Dialectic operations: The final period of cognitive development. *Human Development, 16,* 346–370.

Riegel, K. F., & Riegel, R. M. (1972). Development, drop, and death. *Developmental Psychology, 6*, 306–319.

Rieser-Danner, L. A. (2003). Individual differences in infant fearfulness and cognitive performance: A testing, performance, or competence effect? *Genetic, Social, and General Psychology Monographs, 129*, 41–71.

Rigon, F., Bianchin, L., Bernasconi, S., Bona, G., Bozzola, M., Buzi, F., Cicognani, A., et al. (2010). Update on age at menarche in Italy: Toward the leveling off of the secular trend. *Journal of Adolescent Health, 46*, 238–244.

Rindfuss, R. R., & VandenHeuvel, A. (1990). Cohabitation: Precursor to marriage or alternative to being single? *Population and Development Review, 16*, 703–726.

Ringdal, G. I., Jordhoy, M. S., Ringdal, K., & Kaasa, S. (2001). The first year of grief and bereavement in close family members to individuals who have died of cancer. *Palliative Medicine, 15*, 91–105.

Rispoli, M. (2003). Changes in the nature of sentence production during the period of grammatical development. *Journal of Speech, Language, & Hearing Research, 46*, 818–830.

Ritchie, S., & Howes, C. (2003). Program practices, caregiver stability, and child-caregiver relationships. *Journal of Applied Developmental Psychology, 24*, 497–516.

Ritter, C., Hobfoll, S. E., Lavin, J., Cameron, R. P., & Hulsizer, M. R. (2000). Stress, psychosocial resources, and depressive symptomatology during pregnancy in low-income, inner-city women. *Health Psychology, 19*, 576–585.

Robbins, M. J., Wester, S. R., & McKean, N. B. (2016). Masculinity across the lifespan: Implications for older men. In Y.J. Wong & S.R. Wester (Eds.), *APA handbook of men and masculinities* (pp. 389–409). Washington, DC: American Psychological Association.

Robbins, R., Stagman, S., & Smith, S. (2012). Young children at risk. *National Center for Children in Poverty.* Retrieved from http://www.nccp.org/publications/pub_1073html

Robbins, R. N., & Bryan, A. (2004). Relationships between future orientation, impulsive sensation seeking, and risk behavior among adjudicated adolescents. *Journal of Adolescent Research, 19*, 428–445.

Robers, S., Zhang, J., & Truman, J. (2012). *Indicators of School crime and safety: 2011.* (NCES 2012-002/NCJ 236021). National Center for Education Statistics, U.S. Department of Education, and Bureau of Justice Statistics, Office of Justice Programs, U.S. Department of Justice, Washington, DC.

Robert, P. M., & Harlan, S. L. (2006). Mechanisms of disability discrimination in large bureaucratic organizations: Ascriptive inequalities in the workplace. *Sociological Quarterly, 47*, 599–630.

Roberts, J. S., & Rosenwald, G. C. (2001). Ever upward and not turning back: Social mobility and identity formation among first-generation college students. In D.P. McAdams, R. Josselson, & A. Lieblich (Eds.), *Turns in the road: Narrative studies of lives in transition* (pp. 91–119). Washington, DC: American Psychological Association.

Roberts, L. J., & Krokoff, L. J. (1990). Withdrawal, hostility, and displeasure in marriage. *Journal of Marriage and the Family, 52*, 95–105.

Roberts, R. E., Phinney, J. S., Masse, L. C., Chen, Y. R., Roberts, C. R., & Romero. A. (1999). The structure of ethnic identity of young adolescents from diverse ethnocultural groups. *Journal of Early Adolescence, 19*, 301–322.

Robertson, J., & Robertson, J. (1989). *Separation and the very young.* New York, NY: Free Association Books.

Robertson, S. M., Zarit, S. H., Duncan, L. G., Rovine, M. J., & Femia, E. E. (2007). Family caregivers' patterns of positive and negative affect. *Family Relations, 56*, 12–23.

Robin, D. J., Berthier, N. E., & Clifton, R. K. (1996). Infants' predictive reaching for moving objects in the dark. *Developmental Psychology, 32*, 824–835.

Robinson, B. E. (1988). Teenage pregnancy from the father's perspective. *American Journal of Orthopsychiatry, 58*, 46–51.

Robinson, J. L., & Emde, R. N. (2004). Mental health moderators of Early Head Start on parenting and child development: Maternal depression and relationship attitudes. *Parenting: Science and Practice, 4*, 73–97.

Robinson, M. T. (2016). *The generations.* Retrieved from http://www.careerpanner.com/Career-Articles/Gerneations.cfm

Rochat, P. (1989). Object manipulation and exploration in 2- to 5-month-old infants. *Developmental Psychology, 25*, 871–884.

Rochat, P. (2012). Primordial sense of embodied self-unity. In V. Slaughter & C. A. Brownell (Eds.), *Early development of body representations. Cambridge studies in cognitive and perceptual development* (pp. 3–18). New York: Cambridge University Press.

Rochat, P., & Passos-Ferreira, C. (2009). From imitation to reciprocation and mutual recognition. In J. A. Pineda (Ed.), *Mirror neuron systems: The role of mirroring processes in social cognition* (pp. 191–212). Totowa, NJ: Humana Press.

Roche, K. M., & Leventhal, T. (2009). Beyond neighborhood poverty: Family management, neighborhood disorder, and adolescents' early sexual onset. *Journal of Family Psychology, 23*, 819–827.

Rodgers, A., & Rodgers, E. M. (2004.) *Scaffolding literacy instruction: Strategies for K-4 classrooms.* Portsmouth, NH: Heinemann.

Rodier, P. (2004). Environmental causes of central nervous system maldevelopment. *Pediatrics, 113*, 1076–1083.

Rodkin, P. C., Espelage, D. L., & Hanish, L. D. (2015). A relational framework for understanding bullying: Developmental antecedents and outcomes. *American Psychologist, 70*, 311–321.

Rodriguez, R. (2006). Diversity finds its place. *HRMagazine, 51*(8). Retrieved from http://www.shrm.org/hrmaga-zine/articles/0806/0806rodriguez.asp

Rodriguez-Fornells, A., Rotte, M., Heinze, H.-J., Nosselt, T., & Munte, T. F. (2002). Brain potential and functional MRI evidence for how to handle two languages with one brain. *Nature, 415*, 1026–1029.

Rogers, C. R. (1972). *Becoming partners: Marriage and its alternatives.* New York, NY: Delacorte Press.

Rogers, C. R. A. (1959). A theory of therapy, personality, and interpersonal relationships as developed in the client-centered framework. In S. Koch (Ed.), *Psychology: A study of a science* (Vol. 3, pp. 184–156). New York, NY: McGraw-Hill.

Rogers, C. R. A. (1961). *On becoming a person.* Boston, MA: Houghton Mifflin.

Rogers, K. (2016, April 15). Why do older people love Facebook©? Let's ask my dad. *The New York Times.* Retrieved from http://www.nytimes.com/2016/04/15/technology/why-do-older-people-love-facebook-lets-ask-my-dad.html

Rogers, S. J. (2004). Dollars, dependency, and divorce: Four perspectives on the role of wives' income. *Journal of Marriage and the Family, 66*, 59–74.

Rogers, S. J., & Williams, J. H. G. (2006). *Imitation and the social mind: Autism and typical development.* New York, NY: Guilford.

Rogoff, B., & Angelillo, C. (2002). Investigating the coordinated functioning of multifaceted cultural practices in human development. *Human Development, 45*, 211–216.

Rogoff, B., Mistry, J., Goncu, A., & Mosier, C. (1993). Guided participation in cultural activity by toddlers and caregivers. *Monograph of the Society for Research in Child Development, 58* (8, Serial No. 236).

Rogoff, B., & Morelli, G. (1989). Perspectives on children's development from cultural psychology. *American Psychologist, 44*, 343–348.

Rogoff, B., Morelli, G. A., & Chavajay, P. (2010). Children's integration in communities and segregation from people of different ages. *Perspectives on Psychological Science, 5*, 431–440.

Rogoff, B., Paradise, R., Arauz, R. M., Correa-Chavez, M., & Angelillo, C. (2003). Firsthand learning through intent participation. *Annual Review of Psychology, 54*, 175–203.

Rohner, R. P. (1984). Toward a conception of culture for cross-cultural psychology. *Journal of Cross-Cultural Psychology, 15*, 111–138.

Rokach, A., Bacanli, H., & Ramberan, G., (2000). Coping with loneliness: A cross-cultural comparison. *European Psychologist, 5*, 302–311.

Rokach, A., & Neto, F. (2001). The experience of loneliness in adolescence: A cross-cultural comparison. *International Journal of Adolescence and Youth, 9*, 159–173.

Ron, P. (2010). Elderly people's death and dying anxiety. A comparison between elderly living within the community and in nursing homes in Israel. *Illness, Crisis & Loss, 18*, 3–17.

Roney, J. R., Hanson, K. N., Durante, K. M., & Maestripieri, D. (2006). Reading men's faces: Women's mate attractiveness judgments track men's testosterone and interest in infants. *Proceedings of the Royal Society: B, 273*, 2169–2175.

Rosario, M., Schrimshaw, E. W., Hunter, J., & Braun, L. (2006). Sexual identity development among gay, lesbian, and bisexual youths: Consistency and change over time. *Journal of Sex Research, 43*, 46–58.

Roscigno, V., & Ainsworth-Darnell, J. (1999). Race, cultural capital and educational resources: Persistent inequalities and achievement returns. *Sociology of Education, 72*, 158–178.

Roscoe, W. (2000). *Changing ones: Third and fourth genders in Native North America*. New York, NY: Palgrave Macmillan.

Rose, A. J., Schwartz-Mette, R. A., Smith, R. L., Asher, S. R., Swenson, L. P., Carlson, W., & Waller, E. M. (2012). How girls and boys expect disclosure about problems will make them feel: Implications for friendship. *Child Development, 83*, 844–863.

Rose, S. A., Feldman, J. A., & Jankowski, J. J. (2009). Information processing in toddlers: Continuity from infancy and persistence of preterm deficits. *Intelligence, 37*, 311–320.

Rosegrant, S. (2013). To retire or not to retire? *Michigan Today*. Retrieved from http://michigantoday.umich.edu/story.php?id=8646

Rosellini, L. (1992, July 6). Sexual desire. *U.S. News and World Report, 113*(1), 60–66.

Rosen, A. B., & Rozin, P. (1993). Now you see it, now you don't: The preschool child's conception of invisible particles in the context of dissolving. *Developmental Psychology, 29*, 300–311.

Rosen, C. S., Schwebel, D. C., & Singer, J. L. (1997). Preschoolers' attributions of mental states in pretense. *Child Development, 68*, 1133–1142.

Rosen, W. D., Adamson, L. B., & Bakeman, R. (1992). An experimental investigation of infant social referencing: Mothers' messages and gender differences. *Developmental Psychology, 28*, 1172–1178.

Rosenbaum, J. E. (2009). Patient teenagers: A comparison of the sexual behavior of virgin pledgers and matched nonpledgers. *Pediatrics, 123*, 110–120.

Rosenberg, M. (1979). *Conceiving the self*. New York, NY: Basic Books.

Rosenberg, M., & McCullough, B. C. (1981). Mattering: Inferred significance and mental health among adolescents. *Research in Community and Mental Health, 2*, 163–182.

Rosenblatt, R. A., Mattis, R., & Hart, L. G. (1995). Abortions in rural Idaho: Physicians' attitudes and practices. *American Journal of Public Health, 85*, 1423–1425.

Rosenblum, L. D. (2013). A confederacy of senses. *Scientific American, 30*, 72–75.

Rosenfeld, A. H. (1978). *New views on older lives*. Rockville, MD: National Institute of Mental Health.

Rosenfeld, M. J. (2007). *The age of independence: Interracial unions, same-sex unions, and the changing American family*. Cambridge, MA: Harvard University Press.

Rosenfeld, M. J., & Kim, B-S. (2005). The independence of young adults and the rise of interracial and same-sex unions. *American Sociological Review, 70*, 541–562.

Rosenfield, A., & Figdo, E. (2001). Where is the M in MTCT? The broader issues in mother-to-child transmission of HIV. *American Journal of Public Health, 91*, 703–704.

Rosenkoetter, L. I. (1999). The television situation comedy and children's prosocial behavior. *Journal of Applied Social Psychology, 29*, 979–993.

Rosenthal, R. (1994). Interpersonal expectancy effects: A 30-year perspective. *Current Directions in Psychological Science, 3*, 176–179.

Rosenthal, R. (1995). Critiquing Pygmalion: A 25-year perspective. *Current Directions in Psychological Science, 4*, 171–172.

Rosenthal, R., & Jacobson, L. (1968). *Pygmalion in the classroom: Teacher expectations and student intellectual development*. New York, NY: Holt, Rinehart & Winston.

Rosin, H. (2014, November). Why kids sext. *The Atlantic*. Retrieved from http://www.theatlantic.com/magazine/archive/2014/11/why-kids-sext/380798

Rosnick, C. B., Small, B. J., Graves, A. B., & Mortimer, J. A. (2004). The association between health and cognitive performance in a population-based study of older adults: The Charlotte county healthy aging study (CCHAS). *Aging, Neuropsychology, & Cognition, 11*, 89–99.

Ross, A. (2016). *Industries of the future*. New York: Simon and Schuster.

Rotenberg, K. J., McDougall, P., Boulton, M. J., Vaillancourt, T., Fox, C., & Hymel, S. (2004). Cross-sectional and longitudinal relations among peer-reported trustworthiness, social relationships, and psychological adjustment in children and early adolescents from the United Kingdom and Canada. *Journal of Experimental Child Psychology, 88*, 46–67.

Roth, D. L., Haley, W. E., Owen, J. E., Clay, O. J., & Goode, K. T. (2001). Latent growth models of the longitudinal effects of dementia caregiving: A comparison of African American and White family caregivers. *Psychology and Aging, 16*, 427–436.

Rothbart, M. K. (1981). Measurement of temperament in infancy. *Child Development, 52*, 569–578.

Rothbart, M. K. (1991). Temperament: A developmental framework. In J. Strelau

& A. Angleitner (Eds.), *Explorations in temperament: International perspectives on theory and measurement* (pp. 235–260). London: Plenum Press.

Rothbart, M. K., Ahadi, S. A., & Evans, D. E. (2000). Temperament and personality: Origins and outcomes. *Journal of Personality and Social Psychology, 78*, 122–135.

Rothbart, M. K., & Bates, J. E. (2006). Temperament. In W. Damon & R. M. Lerner (Series Eds.) & N. Eisenberg (Vol. Ed.), *Handbook of child psychology: Vol. 3. Social, emotional, and personality development* (6th ed., pp. 99–166). New York, NY: Wiley.

Rothbart, M. K., & Derryberry, D. (1981). Development of individual differences in temperament. In M. E. Lamb & A. L. Brown (Eds.), *Advances in developmental psychology* (Vol. 1, pp. 37–86). Hillsdale, NJ: Erlbaum.

Rothbaum, F., Morelli, G., & Rusk, N. (2011). Attachment, learning and coping: The interplay of cultural similarities and differences. In M. J. Gelfand, C. Chiu, & Y. Hong (Eds.), *Advances in culture and psychology* (Vol. 1, pp.153–215). New York, NY: Oxford University Press.

Rotheram-Borus, M. J., & Wyche, K. F. (1994). Ethnic differences in identity development in the United States. In S. L. Archer (Ed.), *Interventions for adolescent identity development* (pp. 62–83). Thousand Oaks, CA: Sage.

Rothrauff, T., & Cooney, T. M. (2008). The role of generativity in psychological well-being: Does it differ for childless adults and parents? *Journal of Adult Development, 15*, 148–159.

Roulston, K. (2010). *Reflective inteviewing: A guide to theory and practice*. Thousand Oaks, CA: Sage.

Rovee-Collier, C. (1987). Learning and memory in infancy. In J. D. Osofsky (Ed.), *Handbook of infant development* (2nd ed., pp. 98–148). New York, NY: Wiley.

Rowe, J. W., & Kahn, R. L. (1997). Successful aging. *The Gerontologist, 37*, 433–440.

Rowe, J. W., & Kahn, R. L. (1998). *Successful aging*. New York, NY: Pantheon Books.

Rowe, M. L. (2012). A longitudinal investigation of the role of quantity and quality of child-directed speech in vocabulary development. *Child Development, 83*, 1762–1774.

Rowe, M. L. (2013). Decontextualized language input and preschoolers' vocabulary development. *Seminars in Speech and Language, 34*, 260–266.

Rowe, M. L., & Goldin-Meadow, S. (2009). Differences in early gesture explain SES disparities in child vocabulary size at school entry. *Science, 323*, 951–953.

Rowland, C. F., Pine, J. M., Lieven, E. V. M., & Theakston, A. L. (2003). Determinants of acquisition order in wh- questions: Reevaluating the role of caregiver speech. *Journal of Child Language, 30*, 609–635.

Rowles, G. D., & Bernard, M. (2013). The meaning and significance of place in oldage. In G. D. Rowles & M. Bernard (eds.), *Environmental gerontology: Making meaningful places in old age* (pp. 3–24). New York, NY: Springer.

Rowles, G. D., & Ravdal, H. (2002). Aging, place, and meaning in the face of changing circumstances. In R. S. Weiss & S. P. Bass (Eds.), *Challenges of the third age: Meaning and purpose in later life* (pp. 81–114). New York, NY: Oxford University Press.

Rowold, J., & Laukamp, L. (2009). Charismatic leadership and objective performance indicators. *Applied Psychology: An International Review, 58*, 602–621.

Rubenstein, R. L. (2002). The third age. In R. S. Weiss & S. A. Bass (Eds.), *Challenges of the third age: Meaning and purpose in later life* (pp. 29–40). London: Oxford University Press.

Rubia, K., Smith, A. B., Woolley, J., Nosarti, C., Heyman, I., Taylor, E., et al. (2006). Progressive increase of frontostriatal brain activation from childhood to adulthood during event-related tasks of cognitive control. *Human Brain Mapping, 27*, 973–993.

Rubin, K. H. (1980). Fantasy play: Its role in the development of social skills and social cognition. *New Directions in Child Development, 9*, 69–84.

Rubin, K. H., Bukowski, W. M., & Parker, J. G. (2006). Peer interactions, relationships and groups. In N. Eisenberg, W. Damon, & R. M. Lerner (Eds.), *Handbook of child psychology, Vol. 3. Social emotional and personality development* (6th ed., pp. 571–645). Hoboken, NJ: John Wiley & Sons, Inc.

Rubin, K. H., Coplan, R. J., & Bowker, J. C. (2009). Social withdrawal in childhood. *Annual Review of Psychology, 60*, 141–171.

Rubin, K. H., Hastings, P., Stewart, S. L., Henderson, H. A., & Chen, X. (1997). The consistency and concomitants of inhibition: Some of the children all of the time. *Child Development, 68*, 467–483.

Ruble, D. N., Alvarez, J., Bachman, M., Cameron, J., Fuligni, A., Coll, C. G., et al. (2004). The development of a sense of "WE": The emergence and implications of children's collective identity. In M. Bennett & F. Sani (Eds.), *The development of the social self* (pp. 29–76). New York, NY: Psychology Press.

Ruby, P., & Decety, J. (2001). Effect of subjective perspective taking during simulation of action: A PET investigation of agency. *Nature Neuroscience, 4*, 546–550.

Ruby, P., & Decety, J. (2004). How would you feel versus how do you think she would feel? A neuroimaging study of perspective-taking with social emotions. *Journal of Cognitive Neuroscience, 16*, 988–999.

Ruch, W., Proyer, R. T., & Weber, M. (2010). Humor as a character strength among the elderly: Empirical findings on age-related changes and its contribution to satisfaction with life. *Zeitschrift für Gerontologie und Geriatriei, 43*, 13–18.

Ruini, C., & Ryff, C. D. (2016). Using eudaimonic well-being to improve lives. In A. M. Wood & J. Johnson (Eds.), *The Wiley Handbook of Positive Clinical Psychology: An integrative approach to studying and improving well-being* (pp. 153–166). Hoboken, NJ: Wiley-Blackwell.

Ruiz, M. (2015). What Sexual Harassment at Work Really Looks Like. *Cosmopolitan.* Retrieved from http://www.cosmopolitan.com/career/a36462/sexual-harassment-at-work/

Ruiz, R. R. (2011). *The Gap Year: Breaking up the "Cradle to College to Cubicle to Cemetery" Cycle.* Retrieved from http://thechoice.blogs.nytimes.com/2011/09/24/the-gap-year-breaking-up-the-cradle-to-college-to-cubicle-to -cemetery-cycle

Rumelhart, D. E., & McClelland, J. L. (1986). *Parallel distributed processing* (Vol. 1). Cambridge, MA: MIT Press.

Runyan, D. K., Shankar, V., Hassan, F., Hunter, W. M., et al. (2010). International variations in harsh discipline. *Pediatrics, 126*, e701–e711.

Rusbult, C. E., & Agnew, C. R. (2010). Prosocial motivation and behavior in close relationships. In M. Mikulincer & P. R. Shaver (Eds.), *Prosocial motives, emotions and behavior: The better angels of our nature* (pp. 327–345). Washington, DC: American Psychological Association.

Rusbult, C. E., Agnew, C. R., & Arriaga, X. B. (2012). The investment model of commitment processes. In P. A. M. Van Lange, A.W. Kruglanski, & E. T. Higgins (Eds.), *Handbook of theories of social psychology* (Vol. 2, pp. 218–231).Thousand Oaks, CA: Sage.

Rusbult, C. E., Finkel, E. J., & Kumashiro, M. (2009). The Michael Angelo phenomenon. *Current Directions in Psychological Science, 18*, 305–309.

Rusbult, C. E., Van Lange, P. A. M., Wildschut, T., Yovetich, N. A., & Verette, J. (2000). Perceived superiority in close relationships: Why it exists and persists. *Journal of Personality and Social Psychology, 79*, 521–545.

Russo, F. (2016). Debate is growing about how to meet the urgent needs of transgender kids. *Scientific American Mind, 27*, 27–35.

Russo, M., Shteigman, A., & Carmeli, A. (2016). Workplace and family support and work-life balance: Implications for individual psychological availability and energy at work. *The Journal of Positive Psychology, 11*, 173–188.

Rutland, A., Cameron, L., Jugert, P., Nigbur, D., Brown, R., Watters, C., et al. (2012). Group identity and peer relations: A longitudinal study of group identity, perceived peer acceptance, and friendships amongst ethnic minority English children. *British Journal of Developmental Psychology, 30*, 283–302.

Rutter, M. (2012). Maternal deprivation. In M. H. Bornstein (Ed.), *Handbook of parenting: Vol. 4. Applied and practical parenting* (pp. 181-203). New York, NY: Psychology Press.

Rutter, M., Sonuga-Barke, E. J., & Castle, J. (2010). Investigating the impact of early institutional deprivation on development: Background and research strategy of the English and Romanian adoptees (ERA) study. *Monographs of the Society for Research in Child Development, 75*, 1–20.

Ryan, C. (2009). *Supportive families, healthy children: Helping families with lesbian, gay, bisexual and transgender children.* San Francisco, CA: Marian Wright Edelman Institute, Family Acceptance Project. San Francisco State University.

Ryan, C. L., & Bauman, K. (2016). Educational attainment in the United States: 2015. *Current Population Reports.* Retrieved from http://www.census.gov/content/dam/Census/library/publications/2016/demo/p20-578.pdf

Ryan, C. L., Patraw, J. M., & Bednar, M. (2013). Discussing princess boys and pregnant men: Teaching about gender diversity and transgender experiences within an elementary school curriculum. *Journal of LGBT Youth, 10*, 83–105.

Ryan, M. K., David, B., & Reynolds, K. J. (2004). Who cares? The effect of gender and context on the self and moral reasoning. *Psychology of Women Quarterly, 28*, 246–255.

Ryan, R. M., & Deci, E. L. (2000). Self-determination theory and the facilitation of intrinsic motivation, social development, and well-being. *American Psychologist, 55*, 68–78.

Ryan, R. M., & Lynch, J. H. (1989). Emotional autonomy versus detachment: Revisiting the vicissitudes of adolescence and young adulthood. *Child Development, 60*, 340–356.

Ryeng, M. S., Kroger, J., & Martinussen, M. (2010). Identity status and authoritarianism: A meta-analysis. *Identity: An International Journal of Theory and Research, 13, Special issue No.3.*

Ryff, C. D. (1989). Happiness is everything, or is it? Explorations on the meaning of psychological well-being. *Journal of Personality and Social Psychology, 57*, 1069–1081.

Ryff, C. D. (1995). Psychological well-being in adult life. *Current Directions in Psychological Science, 4*, 99–104.

Ryff, C. D. (2014). Psychological well-being revisited: Advances in the science and practice of eudaimonia. *Psychotherapy and Psychosomatics, 83*, 10–28.

Ryff, C., & Keyes, C. (1995). The structure of psychological well-being revisited. *Journal of Personality and Social Psychology, 69*, 719–727.

Sabatelli, R. M., Meth, R. L., & Gavazzi, S. M. (1988). Factors mediating the adjustment to involuntary childlessness. *Family Relations, 37*, 338–343.

Sabbagh, M. A., & Baldwin, D. A. (2001). Learning words from knowledgeable versus ignorant speakers: Links between preschoolers' theory of mind and semantic development. *Child Development, 72*, 1054–1070.

Sachs, S. (2001, October 7). The two worlds of Muslim American teenagers. *New York Times*, p. B1.

Saczynski, J. S., Willis, S. L., & Schaie, K. W. (2002). Strategy use in reasoning training with older adults. *Aging, Neuropsychology, & Cognition, 9*, 48–60.

Sade, R. M. (2011). Brain death, cardiac death and the dead donor rule. *Journal of South Carolina Medical Association, 107*, 146–149.

Sadler, E. A., Braam, A. W., Broese van Groenou, M. I., Deeg, D. J. H., & van der Geest, S. (2006). Cosmic transcendence, loneliness, and exchange of emotional support with adult children: A study among older parents in The Netherlands. *European Journal of Ageing, 3*, 146–154.

Safran, J. D. (2012). *Psychoanalysis and psychoanalytic therapies.* Washington, DC: American Psychological Association.

Sagrestano, L. M., Felman, P., Killingsworth Rini, C., Woo, G., & Dunkel-Schetter, C. (1999). Ethnicity and social support during pregnancy. *American Journal of Community Psychology, 27*, 869–898.

Sagrestano, L. M., Heavey, C. L., & Christensen, A. (1999). Perceived power and physical violence in marital conflict. *Journal of Social Issues, 55*, 65–79.

Sakamoto, A., Kim, C. -H., & Takei, I. (2012). The Japanese American family. In R. Wright, C. H. Mindel, T. V. Tran, & R. W. Habenstein (Eds.), *Ethnic families in America: Patterns and variations* (pp. 252–276). Boston, MA: Pearson.

Salas-Wright, C. P., Vaughn, M. G., Ugalde, J., & Todik, J. (2015). Substance use and teen pregnancy in the United States: Evidence from the NSDUH 2002–2012. *Addictive Behaviors, 45*, 218–225.

Salat, D. H. (2011). The declining infrastructure of the aging brain. *Brain Connectivity, 4*, 279–293.

Sales, B. C., & Folkman, S. (Eds.). (2000). *Ethics in research with human participants.* Washington, DC: American Psychological Association.

Salisch, M. von (2001). Children's emotional development: Challenges in their relationships to parents, peers, and friends. *International Journal of Behavioral Development, 25*, 310–319.

Salter, J. (2014). Premature babies: How 24-week-old babies are now able to survive. *Telegraph.* Retrieved from http://www.telegraph.co.uk/women/womens-health/11121592/Premature-babies-How-24-week-old-babies-are-now-able-to-survive.html

Salthouse, T. (2012). Consequences of age-related cognitive declines. *Annual Review of Psychology, 63*, 201–226.

Salthouse, T. A. (1985). Speed of behavior and its implications for cognition. In J. W. Birren & K. W. Shaie (Eds.), *Handbook of the psychology of aging* (pp. 400–426). New York, NY: Van Nostrand Reinhold.

Salthouse, T. A. (1996). The processing-speed theory of adult age differences in cognition. *Psychological Review, 103*, 403–428.

Saltz, R., & Saltz, E. (1986). Pretend play training and its outcomes. In G. Fein & M. Rivkin (Eds.), *The young child at play: Reviews of research* (Vol. 4, pp. 155–173). Washington, DC: National Association for the Education of Young Children.

Salvas, M., Vitaro, F., Brendgen, M., Lacourse, E., Boivin, M., & Tremblay, R.E., (2011). Interplay between friends' aggression and friendship quality in the development of child aggression during the early school years. *Social Development, 20*, 645–663.

Salvatore, N., & Sastre, M. T. M. (2001). Appraisal of life: "Area" versus "dimension" conceptualizations. *Social Indicators Research, 53*, 229–240.

Salzinger, S., Rosario, M., Feldman, R. S., & Ng-Mak, D. S. (2008). Aggressive behavior in response to violence exposure: Is it adaptive for middle school children? *Journal of Community Psychology, 36*, 1008–1025.

Sameroff, A. J. (1982). Development and the dialectic: The need for a systems approach. In W. A. Collins (Ed.), *The concept of development: The Minnesota Symposia on Child Psychology* (Vol. 15). Hillsdale, NJ: Erlbaum.

SAMHSA. (2001). *National Strategy for Suicide Prevention Goals and Objectives for Action.* Washington, DC: U.S. Department of Health and Human Services, Inventory Number SMA01-3517. Retrieved from http://mentalhealth.samhsa.gov/suicideprevention/strategy.asp

Sampson, R. J., Raudenbush, S. W., & Earls, F. (1997). Neighborhoods and violent crime: A multilevel study of collective efficacy. *Science, 227*, 918–923.

Sánchez Miguel, P. A., Pulido González, J. J., Alonso, D. A., Oliva, D. S., & Leo Marcos, F. M. (2014). Perception of parents' conducts on antisocial behaviors shown by team sports youth athletes. *Universitas Psychologica, 13*, 299–309.

Sanders, L. D., Weber-Fox, C. M., & Neville, H. J. (2008). Varying degrees of plasticity in different subsystems within language. In J. R. Pomerantz (Ed.), *Topics in integrative neuroscience: From cells to cognition* (pp. 125–153). New York, NY: Cambridge University Press.

Sanders, R. E. (1997). Find your partner and do-si-do: The formation of personal relationships between social beings. *Journal of Social and Personal Relationships, 14*, 387–415.

Sandler, J., Holder, A., & Meers, P. M. (1963). The ego ideal and the ideal self. *Psychoanalytic Study of the Child, 18*, 139–158.

San Martin Martinez, C., Boada i Calbet, H., & Feigenbaum, P. (2011). Private and inner speech and the regulation of social speech communication. *Cognitive Development, 26*, 214–229.

Sanoff, A. P. (2006, March 10). A perception gap over students' preparation. *The Chronicle of Higher Education, School & College Special Report*, B9–B14.

Santelli, J. S., Abma, J., Ventura, S., Lindberg, L., Morrow, B., Anderson, J., et al. (2004). Can changes in sexual behaviors among high school students explain the decline in teen pregnancy rates in the 1990s? *Journal of Adolescent Health, 34*, 80–90.

Santelli, J., Ott, M. A., Lyon, M., Rogers, J., Summers, D., & Schleifer, R. (2006). Abstinence and abstinence-only education: A review of U.S. policies and programs. *Journal of Adolescent Health, 38*, 72–81.

Santillanes, G. F. (1997). Releasing the spirit: A lesson in Native American funeral rituals. *The Director, 69*, 32–34.

Saracho, O. N., & Shirakawa, Y. (2004). A comparison of the literacy development context of United States and Japanese families. *Early Childhood Education Journal, 31*, 261–266.

Sargrestano, L. M., Heavey, C. L., & Chistensen, A. (1999). Perceived power and physical violence in marital conflict. *Journal of Social Issues, 55*, 65–79.

Sarkisian, N., & Gerstel, N. (2004). Explaining the gender gap in help to parents: The importance of employment. *Journal of Marriage and the Family, 66*, 431–451.

Saudino, K. J. & Zapfe, J. A. (2008). Genetic influences on activity level in early childhood: Do situations matter? *Child Development, 79*, 930–943.

Savani, K., Markus, H. R., Naidu, N. V. R., Kumar, S., & Berlia, N. (2010). What counts as a choice? U.S. Americans are more likely than Indians to construe actions as choices. *Psychological Science, 21*, 391–398.

Savaya, R., & Cohen, O. (2003). Perceptions of the societal image of Muslim Arab divorced men and women in Israel. *Journal of Social and Personal Relationships, 20*, 193–202.

Savickas, M. L. (2011). *Career counseling.* Washington, DC: American Psychological Association.

Savin-Williams, R. C. (1996). Self-labeling and disclosure among gay, lesbian, and bisexual youths. In J. Laird & R. -J. Green (Eds.), *Lesbians and gays in couples and families: A Handbook for therapists* (pp. 153–182). San Francisco: Jossey-Bass.

Sax, L., & Astin, A. (1997). The benefits of service: Evidence from undergraduates. *Educational Record, 78*, 25–32.

Scarbrough, J. W. (2001). Welfare mothers' reflections on personal responsibility. *Journal of Social Issues, 57*, 261–276.

Scarrier, M., Schmader, T., & Lickel, B. (2009). Parental shame and guilt: Distinguishing emotional responses to a child's wrongdoings. *Personal Relationships, 16*, 205–220.

Schaffer, H. R., & Emerson, P. E. (1964). The development of social attachments in infancy. *Monographs of the Society for Research in Child Development, 29*(94).

Schaie, K. W. (1965). A general model for the study of developmental problems. *Psychological Bulletin, 64*, 92–107.

Schaie, K. W. (1992). The impact of methodological changes in gerontology. *International Journal of Aging and Human Development, 35*, 19–29.

Schaie, K. W. (1994). The course of adult intellectual development. *American Psychologist, 49*, 304–313.

Schaie, K. W., & Elder, G. H. (Ed.). (2005). *Historical influences on lives and agin. Societal impact on aging series*. New York, NY: Springer Publishing Company.

Schaie, K. W., & Hertzog, C. (1983). Fourteen-year cohort-sequential analyses of adult intellectual development. *Developmental Psychology, 19*, 531–543.

Schaie, K. W., & Willis, S. L. (2010). The Seattle Longitudinal Study of Adult Cognitive Development. *ISSBD Bulletin, 57*, 2429.

Schatz, M. (1983). Communication. In J. H. Flavell & E. M. Markman (Eds.), *Handbook of child psychology* (Vol. 3, pp. 841–889). New York, NY: Wiley.

Scheff, T. J. (2003). Shame in self and society. *Symbolic Interaction, 26*, 239–262.

Schlein, S. (2007, Summer). Dimensions of relatedness, activation, and engagement: Erikson's interpersonal-relational method of psychoanalysis. *Psychologist-Psychoanalyst Newsletter, 59*.

Schickedanz, J. A. (1986). *More than the ABCs: The early stages of reading and writing*. Washington, DC: National Association for the Education of Young People.

Schiedel, D. G., & Marcia, J. E. (1985). Ego identity, intimacy, sex-role orientation, and gender. *Developmental Psychology, 21*, 149–160.

Schieffelin, B. B., & Cochran-Smith, M. (1984). Learning to read culturally: Literacy before schooling. In H. Goelman, A. A. Oberg, & F. Smith (Eds.), *Awakening to literacy* (pp. 3–23). Exeter, NH: Heinemann.

Schiller, J. S., Lucas, J. W., Ward, B. W., & Peregoy, J. A. (2012). Summary health statistics for U.S. adults: National health interview survey, 2010. *National Center for Health Statistics, Vital Health Statistics, 10*, No. 252.

Schilling, E. A., Aseltine, R. H. Jr., & James, A. (2016). The SOS suicide prevention program: Further evidence of efficacy and effectiveness. *Prevention Science, 17*, 157–166.

Schlegel, A. (2009). Cross-cultural issues in the study of adolescent development. In R. M. Lerner & L. Steinberg (Eds.), *Handbook of adolescent psychology, Vol. 2. Contextual influences of adolescent development* (3rd ed., pp. 570–589). New York, NY: John Wiley.

Schlein, S. (1987). *A way of looking at things: Selected papers from 1930 to 1980*. Erik H. Erikson. New York, NY: Norton.

Schlein, S. (2007, Summer). Dimensions of relatedness, activation, and engagement: Erikson's interpersonal-relational method of psychoanalysis. *Psychologist-Psychoanalyst Newsletter, 59*.

Schlossberg, N. K. (2012). Creating a lifetime of possibilities: A look at retirement. In E. Cole & M. Gergen, *Retiring but not shy: Feminist psychologists create their post-careers* (pp. 204–221). Chagrin Falls, OH: Taos Institute Publications.

Schmidt, L. A., Fox, N. A., Perez-Edar, K., & Hamer, D. H. (2009). Linking gene, brain, and behavior. *Psychological Science, 20*, 831–837.

Schmidt, M. F. H., Hardecker, S., & Tomasello, M. (2016). Preschoolers understand the normativity of cooperatively structured competition. *Journal of Experimental Child Psychology, 143*, 34–47.

Schmidt, W. H., Burroughs, N. A., Zoido, P., & Houang, R. T. (2015). The role of schooling in perpetuating educational inequality: An international perspective. *Educational Researcher, 44*, 371–386.

Schmiege, S., & Russo, N. F. (2005). Depression and unwanted first pegnancy: Longitudinal cohort study. *British Medical Journal, 331*.

Schmitt, J. & Jones, J. (2012). *Bad jobs on the rise*. Center for Economic and Policy Research. Retrieved from http://cepr.net/documents/publications/bad-jobs-2012-09.pdf

Schmitt-Rodermund, E., & Silbereisen, R. K. (1998). Career maturity determinants: Individual development, social context, and historical time. *Career Development Quarterly, 47*, 16–31.

Schnall, S., Roper, J., & Fessler, D. M. T. (2010). Elevation leads to altruistic behavior. *Psychological Science, 21*, 315–320.

Schnarch, D. (2000). Desire problems: A systematic perspective. In S. Leiblum & R. Rosen (Eds.), *Principles and practice of sex therapy* (pp. 17–56). New York, NY: Guilford Press.

Schneider, B. H., Atkinson, L., & Tardif, C. (2001). Child-parent attachment and children's peer relations: A quantitative review. *Developmental Psychology, 37*, 86–100.

Schneider, D. S., Sledge, P. A., Shuchter, S. R., & Zisook, S. (1996). Dating and remarriage over the first two years of widowhood. *Annals of Clinical Psychiatry, 8*, 51–57.

Schneider, I. K., Konijn, E. A., Righetti, F., & Rusbult, C. E. (2011). A healthy dose of trust: The relationship between interpersonal trust and health. *Personal Relationships, 18*, 668–676.

Schneider, S. L., & Caffray, C. M. (2012). Affective motivators and experience in adolescents' development of health-related behavior patterns. In V. F. Reyna, S. B. Chapman, M. R. Dougherty, & J. Confrey (Eds.), *The adolescent brain: Learning, reasoning, and decision-making* (pp. 291–335). Washington, DC: American Psychological Association.

Schneider, W., & Bjorklund, D. F. (1992). Expertise, aptitude, and strategic remembering. *Child Development, 63*, 461–473.

Schoen, R. (1992). First unions and the stability of first marriages. *Journal of Marriage and the Family, 54*, 281–284.

Schoenfeld, E. A., Bredow, C. A. & Huston, T. L. (2012). Do men and women show love differently in marriage? *Personality and Social Psychology Bulletin, 38*, 1396–1409.

Schoklitsch, A., & Baumann, U. (2012). Generativity and aging: A promising future research topic? *Journal of Aging Studies, 26*, 262–272.

Schooler, C., & Mulatu, M. S. (2001). The reciprocal effects of leisure time activities and intellectual functioning in older people: A longitudinal analysis. *Psychology and Aging, 16*, 466–482.

Schootman, M., Fuortes, L. J., Zwerling, C., Albanese, M. A., & Watson, C. A. (1993). Safety behavior among Iowa junior high and high school students. *American Journal of Public Health, 83*, 1628–1629.

Schore, A. N. (2013). Bowlby's "environment of evolutionary adaptedness": Recent studies on the interpersonal neurobiology of attachment and emotional development. In D. Narvaez, J. Panksepp, A. N. Schore, & T. R. Gleason (Eds.), *Evolution, early experience and human development: From research to practice and policy* (pp. 31–67). New York, NY: Oxford University Press.

Schramm, D. G., Marshall, J. P., Harris, V. W., & Lee, T. R. (2005). After "I do": The newlywed transition. *Marriage & Family Review, 38*, 45–67.

Schulenberg, J., & Maggs, J. L. (2001). Moving targets: Modeling developmental trajectories of adolescent alcohol misuse, individual and peer risk factors, and intervention effects. *Applied Developmental Science, 5*, 237–253.

Schulenberg, J., Vondracek, F. W., & Kim, J. (1993). Career certainty and short-term changes in work values during adolescence. *Career Development Quarterly, 41*, 268–284.

Schultz, A. (2001, March). 25 women making it big. *Fortune Small Business*, 17–24.

Schultz, K. S., Morton, K. R., & Weckerle, J. R. (1998). The influence of push andpull factors on voluntary and involuntary early retirees' retirement decision and adjustment. *Journal of Vocational Behavior, 53*, 45–57.

Schultz, M. S., Cowan, P. A., Pape Cowan, C., & Brennan, R. T. (2004). Coming home upset: Gender, marital satisfaction and the daily spillover of workday experience into couple interactions. *Journal of Family Psychology, 18*, 250–253.

Schulz, M. S., Pruett, M. K., Kerig, P. K., & Parke, R. D. (2010). *Strengthening couple relationship for optimal child development: Lessons from research and intervention*. Washington, DC: American Psychological Association.

Schultz, R. I., Grelotti, D. J., & Pober, B. (2001). Genetics of childhood disorders: Vol. 26. Williams syndrome and brain–behavior relationships. *Journal of the American Academy of Child and Adolescent Psychiatry, 40*, 606–609.

Schuster, C. S. (1986). Intrauterine development. In C. S. Schuster & S. S. Ashburn (Eds.), *The process of human development* (pp. 67–94). Boston, MA: Little, Brown.

Schwartz, A. N., Snyder, C. L., & Peterson, J. A. (1984). *Aging and life: An introduction to gerontology* (2nd ed.). New York, NY: Holt, Rinehart & Winston.

Schwartz, D., Lansford, J. E., Dodge, K. A., Pettit, G. S., & Bates, J. E. (2013). The link between harsh home environments and negative trajectories is exacerbated by victimization in the elementary peer group. *Developmental Psychology, 49,* 305–316.

Schwartz, S. J. (2001). The evolution of Eriksonian and neo-Eriksonian identity theory and research: A review and integration. *Identity, 1*, 7–58.

Schwartz, S. J., Beyers, W., Luyckx, K., Soenens, B., Zamboanga, B. L., & Forthun, L.F., et al. (2011). Examining the light and dark sides of emerging adults' identity: A study of identity status differences in positive and negative psychosocial functioning. *Journal of Youth and Adolescence, 40,* 839–859.

Schwartz, S. J., Luyckx, K., & Vignoles, V. L. (2011). *Handbook of identity theory and research* (Vols. 1 and 2). New York, NY: Springer Science + Business Media.

Schwartz, S. J., Zamboanga, B. L., Luyckx, K., Meca, A., & Ritchie, R. A. (2013). Identity and emerging adulthood: Reviewing the field and looking forward. *Emerging Adulthood, 1,* 96–113.

Schweinhart, L. J., Montie, J., Xiang, Z., Barnett, W.S., Belfield, C. R., & Norse,M. (2005). *Lifetime effects: The High/Scope Perry Preschool study through age 40.* Ypsilanti, MI: High/Scope Press.

Schweinhart, L. J., & Weikart, D. P. (1988). The High/Scope Perry Preschool Program. In R. H. Price, E. L. Cowen, R. P. Lorion, & J. Ramos-McKay (Eds.), *Fourteen ounces of prevention* (pp. 53–66). Washington, DC: American Psychological Association.

Science Daily. (2005). *Fetal exposure to toxins could be behind rise in asthma.* Retrieved from http://www .sciencedaily.com /releases/2005/10/051011063818.htm

ScienceDaily. (2010). *Earlier, later puberty may trigger aggression in boys researchers find.* Penn State. Retrieved from https://www .sciencedaily.com/releases/2010/05 /100503111750.htm

Scogin, F., Storandt, M., & Lott, L. (1985). Memory-skills training, memory complaints, and depression in older adults. *Journal of Gerontology, 40*, 562–568.

Scopesi, A., Zanobini, M., & Carossino, P. (1997). Childbirth in different cultures: Psychophysical reactions of women delivering in U.S., German, French, and Italian hospitals. *Journal of Reproductive and Infant Psychology, 15*, 9–30.

Scott, J. P. (1987). Critical periods in processes of social organization. In M. H. Bornstein (Ed.), *Sensitive periods in development: Interdisciplinary perspectives* (pp. 247–268). Hillsdale, NJ: Erlbaum.

Scraton, S., & Holland, S. (2006). Grandfatherhood and leisure. *Leisure Studies, 25*, 233–250.

Scrimgeour, M. B., Davis, E. L., & Buss, K. A. (2016). You get what you get and you don't throw a fit!: Emotion socialization and child physiology jointly predict early prosocial development. *Developmental Psychology, 52*, 102–116.

Seabrook, J. (2010, May 10). The last babylift: Adopting a child in Haiti. *The New Yorker, 86*(12), 44–53.

Sears, D. O., Fu, M., Henry, P. J., & Bui, K. (2003). The origins and persistence of ethnic identity among the "new immigrant" groups. *Social Psychology Quarterly, 66*, 419–437.

Sears, P. S., & Barbee, A. H. (1978). Career and life satisfaction among Terman's gifted women. In J. Stanley, W. George, & C. Solano (Eds.), *The gifted and the creative: Fifty year perspective*. Baltimore, MD: Johns Hopkins University Press.

Seaton, E. K., Yip, T., & Sellers, R. M. (2009). A longitudinal examination of racial identity and racial discrimination among African American adolescents. *Child Development, 80*, 406–417.

Sebanc, A. M., Guimond, A. B., & Lutgen, J. (2016). Transactional relationships between Latinos' friendship quality and academic achievement during the transition to middle school. *The Journal of Early Adolescence, 36*, 108–134.

Sebastiani, P., Bael, H., Sun, F. X. et al. (2013). Meta-analysis of genetic variants associated with human exceptional longevity. *Aging, 5*, 653–661.

Sebastiani, P., & Perls, T. T. (2012). The genetics of extreme longevity: Lessons from the New England Centenarian Study. *Frontiers in Genetics, 3*, 277.

Sebastiani, P., Solovieff, N., DeWan, A. T., Walsh, K. M., Puca, A,, Hartley, S.W., et al. (2012). Genetic signatures of exceptional longevity in humans. *PloS ONE, 7*: e29848.

Seccombe, K. (1991). Assessing the costs and benefits of childen: Gender comparisons among child-free husbands and wives. *Journal of Marriage and the Family, 53*, 191–202.

Seccombe, K. (2000). Families in poverty in the 1990s: Trends, causes, consequences, and lessons learned. *Journal of Marriage and the Family, 62*, 1094–1113.

Sedikides, C., Gaertner, L., & Toguchi, Y. (2003). Pancultural self-enhancement. *Journal of Personality and Social Psychology, 84*, 60–79.

Sedikides, C., Gaertner, L., & Vevea, J. L. (2005). Pancultural self-enhancement reloaded: A meta-analytic reply to Heine (2005). *Journal of Personality and Social Psychology, 89*, 539–551.

Segal, L. B., Oster, H., Cohen, M., Caspi, B., Myers, M., & Brown, D. (1995). Smiling and fussing in seven-month-old preterm and full-term Black infants in the still-face situation. *Child Development, 66*, 1829–1843.

Segal, N. L. (2010). Twins: The finest naturalexperiment. *Personality and Individual Differences, 49*, 317–323.

Segal, N. L., & Johnson, W. (2009). Twin studies of general mental ability. In Y.-K. Kim (Ed.) *Handbook of behavior genetics* (pp. 81–99). New York, NY: U.S. Springer Science and Business Media.

Seger, C. A. & Miller, E. K. (2010). Category learning in the brain. *Annual Review of Neuroscience, 33*, 203–219.

Segrin, C., Woszidlo, A., Givertz, M., & Montgomery, N. (2013). Parent and child traits associated with overparenting. *Journal of Social and Clinical Psychology, 32*, 569–595.

Seguin, R. A., Epping, J. N., Buchner, D. M., Bloch, R., & Nelson, M. E. (2002). *Growing stronger: Strength training for older adults.* Retrieved from the internet on September 28, 2016 at https://www.cdc.gov /physicalactivity/downloads/growing _stronger.pdf

Seiffge-Krenke, I. & Beyers, W. (2016). Was Erikson right after all? Identity, attachment and intimacy of couples in young adulthood. *Psychotherapeut, 61*, 16–21.

Seider, S. (2007). Catalyzing a commitment to community service in emerging adults. *Journal of Adolescent Research, 22*, 612–639.

Seligman, M. E. P. (1975/1992). *Helplessness.* San Francisco, CA: Freeman.

Seligman, M. E. P. (2011). *Flourish: A visionary new understanding of happiness and well-being.* New York, NY: Free Press/Simon & Schuster.

Seligman, M. E. P., Parks, A. C., & Steen, T. (2006). A balanced psychology and a full life. In F. Huppert, B. Keverne, & N. Baylis (Eds.), *The science of well-being* (pp. 275–283), Oxford, England: Oxford University Press.

Sells, C. W., & Blum, R. W. (1996). Morbidity and mortality among U.S. adolescents: An overview of data and trends. *American Journal of Public Health*, 86, 513–519.

Selvin, E., Burnett, A. L., & Platz, E. A. (2007). Prevalence and risk factors for erectile dysfunction in the US. *American Journal of Medicine, 120*, 151–157.

Semeniuk, I. (2013). How poverty influencesa child's brain development. *The Globe and Mail.* Retrieved from www.theglobeandmail .com/technology/science/brain/how -poverty -influences-a-childs-brain -development/article7882957/?page=all

SeniorJournal.com. (2004, September 13). *AoA awards $5.1 million to support seniors aging in place.* Retrieved from http://www .seniorjournal .com/NEWS/Eldercare /4-09-13AOA.htm

Sera, M. D., Troyer, D., & Smith, L. B. (1988). What do two-year-olds know about the sizes of things? *Child Development, 59,* 1489–1496.

Serbin, L. A., Powlishta, K. K., & Gulko, J. (1993). The development of sex typing in middle childhood. *Monographs of the Society for Research in Child Development, 58*(232).

Seriido, J., Almeida, D. M., & Wetherington, E. (2004). Chronic stressors and daily hassles: Unique and interactive relationship with psychological distress. *Journal of Health and Social Behavior, 45,* 17–33.

Setterlund, M. B., & Niedenthal, P. M. (1993). "Who am I? Why am I here?": Self-esteem, self-clarity, and prototype matching. *Journal of Personality and Social Psychology, 65,* 769–780.

Seymour, S. C. (2004). Multiple Caretaking of Infants and Young Children: An Area in Critical Need of a Feminist Psychological Anthropology. *Ethos, 32*(4).

Shaffer, K., & Kipp, D. R. *Developmental psychology, childhood & adolescence* (7th ed., p. 202). Belmont, MA: Thomson Wadsworth.

Shah, P. E., Fonagy, P., & Strathearn, L. (2010). Is attachment transmitted across generations? The plot thickens. *Clinical Child Psychology and Psychiatry, 15,* 329–345.

Shanahan, M. J., & Hofer, S. M. (2005). Social context in gene-environment interactions: Retrospect and prospect. *Journals of Gerontology: Series B: Psychological Sciences and Social Sciences, 60B,* 65–76.

Shapiro, J. P. (2001). Growing old in a good home. *U.S. News and World Report, 130,* 56–61.

Sharp, C., Fonagy, P., & Goodyer, I. (Eds). (2008). *Social cognition and developmental psychopathology.* Oxford, England: Oxford University Press.

Sharpley, C. F. (1997). Psychometric properties of the Self-Perceived Stress in Retirement Scale. *Psychological Reports, 81,* 319–322.

Shaver, P. R., Collins, N., & Clark, C. L. (1996). Attachment styles and internal working models of self and relationship partners. In G. J. O. Fletcher & J. Fitness (Eds.), *Knowledge structures in close relationships: A social psychological approach* (pp. 25–61). Hillsdale, NJ: Erlbaum.

Shaver, P. R., & Mikulincer, M. (2011). A general attachment-theoretical framework for conceptualizing interpersonal behavior: Cognitive-motivational predispositions and patterns of social information processing. In L. M. Horowitz & S. Strack (Eds), *Handbook of interpersonal psychology: Theory, research, assessment and therapeutic interventions* (pp. 17–35). New York, NY: Wiley.

Shea, C. (2011). Fraud scandal fuels debate over practices of social psychology. *The Chronicle of Higher Education, Research.* Retrieved from http://chronicle.com/article/As-Dutch-Research-Scandal/129746

Sher, T. G., & Weiss, R. L. (1991). Negativity in marital communication? Where's the beef? Special Issue: Negative communication in marital interaction: A misnomer? *Behavioral Assessment, 13,* 1–5.

Shern, D. L., Blanch, A. K., & Steverman, S. M. (2016). Toxic stress, behavioral health, and the next major era in public health. *American Journal of Orthopsychiatry, 86,* 109–123.

Sherraden, M. S., & Barrera, R. E. (1996). Maternal support and cultural influences among Mexican immigrant mothers. *Families in Society, 77,* 298–313.

Shibley, P. K. (2000). The concept of revisitation and the transition to parenthood. Unpublished doctoral dissertation, Ohio State University.

Shih, M., Young, M. J., & Bucher, A. (2013). Working to reduce the effects of discrimination: Identity management strategies in organizations. *American Psychologist, 68,* 145–157.

Shiner, R. L., Buss, K. A., McClowry, S. G. et al. (2012). What is temperament *NOW?* Assessing progress in temperament research on the twenty-fifth anniversary of Goldsmith et al. (1987). *Child Development Perspectives,* 1–9.

Shirtcliff, E. A., Dahl, R. E., & Pollack, S. D. (2009). Pubertal development: Correspondence between hormonal and physical development. *Child Development, 80,* 327–337.

Shrestha, L. B. (2006). Life expectancy in the United States. *CRS Report for Congress. Congressional Research Service of the Library of Congress.*

Shrestha, L. B., & Heisler, E. J. (2011). The changing demographic profile of the United States. *CRS Report for Congress.* Washington, DC: The Congressional Research Service of the Library of Congress.

Shutts, K., Roben, C. K., Pemberton, C. K., & Spelke, E. S. (2013). Children's use of social categories in thinking about people and social relationships. *Journal of Cognition and Development, 14,* 35–62.

Siefert, T. A. (2005). The Ryff scales of psychological well-being. *Technical Report. The Center of Inquiry in the Liberal Arts.* Retrieved from http://www.liberalarts.wabash.edu/ryff-scales/

Siegel, B. (1996). Is the emperor wearing clothes? Social policy and the empirical support for full inclusion of children with disabilities in the preschool and early elementary grades. *Social Policy Report, 10,* 2–17.

Siegel, D. J. (2013). *Brainstorm: The power and purpose of the teenage brain.* New York: Jeremy P. Tarcher/Penguin and imprint of Penguin Random House.

Siegler, I. C., Poon, L. W., Madden, D. J., & Welsh, K. A. (1996). Psychological aspects of normal aging. In E. W. Busse & D. G. Blazer (Eds.), *The American Psychiatric Press textbook of geriatric psychiatry* (pp. 105–127). Washington, DC: American Psychiatric Press.

Siegler, R. S. (2000). Unconscious insights. *Current Directions in Psychological Science, 9,* 79–83.

Siegler, R. S., & Stern, E. (1998). A micro-genetic analysis of conscious and unconscious

strategy discoveries. *Journal of Experimental Psychology: General, 127,* 377–397.

Siegmund, F. (2015). Inflation and the buying power of the minimum wage. *Automatic Finances.* Retrieved from http://www.automaticfinances.com/inflation-buying-power-minimum-wage/

Sigelman, C. K., & Holtz, K. D. (2013). Gender differences in preschool children's commentary on self and other. *The Journal of Genetic Psychology: Research and Theory on Human Development, 17,* 192–206.

Silven, M., & Rubinov, E. (2010). Language and preliteracy skills in bilinguals and monolinguals at preschool age: Effects of exposure to richly inflected speech fom birth. *Reading and Writing, 23,* 385–414.

Silver, C. B. (2003). Gendered identities in old age: Toward (de)gendering? *Journal of Aging Studies, 17,* 379–397.

Silverman, J. G., Decker, M. R., McCauley, H. L., Gupta, J., Miller, E., Raj, A., & Goldberg, A. B. (2010). Male perpetration of intimate partner violence and involvement in abortions and abortion-related conflict. *American Journal of Public Health, 100,* 1415–1417.

Silverstein, A. B., Pearson, L. B., Aguinaldo, N. E., Friedman, S. L., Tokayama, D. L., & Weiss, Z. T. (1982). Identity conservation and equivalence conservation: A question of developmental priority. *Child Development, 53,* 819–821.

Simon, B., & Klandermans, B. (2001). Politicized collective identity. *American Psychologist, 56,* 319–331.

Simon, T. (2002, January 19). Dreaming of the mother who was. *Providence Journal,* p. B7.

Simons, F., Detenber, B. H., Cuthbert, B. N., Schwartz, D. D., & Reiss, J. E. (2003). Attention to Television: Alpha Power and Its Relationship to Image Motion and Emotional Content. *Media Psychology, 5*(3), 283–301.

Simons, R. L., Beaman, J., Conger, R. D., & Chao, W. (1993). Stress, support and antisocial behavior traits as determinants of emotional well-being and parenting practices among single mothers. *Journal of Marriage and the Family, 55,* 385–398.

Simonton, D. K. (1990). Creativity in the later years: Optimistic prospects for achievement. *The Gerontologist, 30,* 626–631.

Simonton, D. K. (1991). Creative productivity through the adult years. *Generations, 15,* 13–16.

Simonton, D. K. (1997). Creative productivity: A predictive and explanatory model of career trajectories and landmarks. *Psychological Review, 104,* 66–89.

Singer, D. G., Golinkoff, R. M., & Hirsh-Pasek, K. (Eds.). (2006). *Play=Learning: How play motivates and enhances children's cognitive and social-emotional growth.* New York: Oxford University Press.

Singer, D. G., & Singer, J. L. (1990). *The house of make-believe: Children's play and developing imagination.* Cambridge, MA: Harvard University Press.

Singer, D. G., & Singer, J. L. (2008). Make-believe play, imagination, and creativity: Links to children's media exposure. In S. L. Calvert & B. J. Wilson (Eds.), *The handbook of children, media and development. Handbooks in communication and media* (pp. 290–308). Malden, MA: Blackwell.

Singer, L. T. Minnes, S. Min, M. O., Lewis, B. A., & Short, E. J. (2015). Prenatal cocaine exposure and child outcomes: A conference report based on a prospective study from Cleveland. *Human Psychopharmacology: Clinical and Experimental, 30*, 285–289.

Singer, T., Lindenberger, U., & Baltes, P. B. (2003). Plasticity of memory for new learning in very old age: A story of major loss? *Psychology and Aging, 18*, 306–317.

Singer, W. (1995). Development and plasticity of cortical processing architectures. *Science, 270*, 758–764.

Singh, L., Morgan, J. L., & Best, C. T. (2002). Infants' listening preferences: Baby talk or happy talk? *Infancy, 3*, 365–394.

Sinnott, J. D., & Cavanaugh, J. C. (1991). *Bridging paradigms: Positive development in adulthood and cognitive aging.* New York, NY: Praeger.

Sinoff, G., Iosipovici, A., Almog, R., & Barnett-Greens, O. (2008). Children of the elderly are inept in assessing death anxiety in their own parents. *International Journal of Geriatric Psychiatry, 23*, 1207–1208.

Sipsma, H., Biello, K. B., Cole-Lewis, H., & Kershaw, T. (2010). Like father like son: The intergenerational cycle of adolescent fatherhood. *American Journal of Public Health, 100*, 517–524.

Sirin, S. R., & Fine, M. (2008). *Muslim American youth: Understanding hyphenated identities through multiple methods.* New York, NY: New York University Press.

Sirsch, U., Dreher, E., Mayr, E., & Willinger, U. (2009). What does it take to be an adult in Austria? Views of adulthood in Austrian adolescents, emerging adults and adults. *Journal of Adolescent Research, 24*, 275–292.

Skaalvik, S., & Skaalvik, E. M. (2004). Frames of reference for self-evaluation of ability in mathematics. *Psychological Reports, 94*, 619–632.

Skerrett, K. (1996). From isolation to mutuality: A feminist collaborative model of couples therapy. *Women and Therapy, 19*, 93–106.

Skinner, B. F. (1983). Intellectual self-management in old age. *American Psychologist, 38*, 239–244.

Skoog, T. (2013). Adolescent and adult implications of girls' pubertal timing. In A. Andershed (Ed.), *Girls as risk: Swedish longitudinal research on adjustment. Advancing responsible adolescent development* (pp. 9–34). New York, NY: Spring Science + Business Media.

Skoog, T., & Özdemir, S. B. (2016). Explaining why early-maturing girls are more exposed to sexual harassment in early adolescence. *The Journal of Early Adolescence, 36*, 490–509.

Slade, A. (1987). A longitudinal study of maternal involvement and symbolic play during the toddler period. *Child Development, 58*, 367–375.

Slater, A., Carrick, R., Bell, C., & Roberts, E. (1999). Can measures of infant information processing predict later intellectual ability? In A. Slater & D. Muir (Eds.), *The Blackwell reader in developmental psychology* (pp. 55–64). Malden, MA: Blackwell.

Slavik, S. (1995). Presenting social interest to different life-styles. Special Issue: Counseling homosexuals and bisexuals. *Individual Psychology: Journal of Adlerian Theory, Research and Practice, 51*, 166–177.

Sliwinski, M., Lipton, R. B., Buschke, H., & Stewart, W. (1996). The effects of pre-clinical dementia on estimates of normal cognitive functioning in aging. *Journal of Gerontology, 51*, P217–P225.

Sliwinski, M. J., Hofer, S.M., Hall, C., Buschke, H., & Lipton, R. B. (2003). Modeling memory decline in older adults: The importance of preclinical dementia, attrition, and chronological age. *Psychology and Aging, 18*, 658–671.

Slobin, D. I. (1985). *The cross-linguistic study of language acquisition* (Vols. 1and 2). Hillsdale, NJ: Erlbaum.

Sloutsky, V. M., & Fisher, A. V. (2004). Induction and categorization in young children: A similarity-based model. *Journal of Experimental Psychology: General, 133*, 166–188.

Slovak, K., & Singer, M. (2001). Gun violence exposure and trauma among rural youth. *Violence and Victims, 16*, 389–400.

Small, R., Rice, P. L., Yelland, J., & Lumley, J. (1999). Mothers in a new country: The role of culture and communication in Vietnamese, Turkish, and Filipino women's experiences of giving birth in Australia. *Women and Health, 28*, 77–101.

Small, S. A., Silverberg, S. B., & Kerns, D. (1993). Adolescents' perceptions of the costs and benefits of engaging in health-compromising behaviors. *Journal of Youth and Adolescence, 22*, 73–88.

Smedley, A., & Smedley, B. (2005). Race as biology is fiction, racism as a social problem is real: Anthropological and historical perspectives on the social construction of race. *American Psychologist, 60*, 16–26.

Smeeding, T. M. (2008, Winter). Poorer by comparison: Poverty, work and public policy in comparative perspective. *Pathways*, 3–5.

Smetana, J. G. (1986). Preschool children's conceptions of sex-role transgressions. *Child Development, 57*, 862–871.

Smetana, J. G. (2013). Social domain theory: Consistencies and variations in children's moral and social judgments. In M. Killen & J. G. Smetana (Eds.), *Handbook of moral development* (2nd ed., pp. 23–46). New York, NY: Psychology Press.

Smetana, J. G., Daddis, C., & Chuang, S. S. (2003). "Clean your room!" A longitudinal investigation of adolescent-parent conflict and conflict resolution in middle class African American families. *Journal of Adolescent Research, 18*, 631–650.

Smetana, J. G., Schlagman, N., & Adams, P. W. (1993). Preschool children's judgments about hypothetical and actual transgressions. *Child Development, 64*, 202–214.

Smetana, J. G., Yau, J., & Hanson, S. (1991). Conflict resolution in families with adolescents. *Journal of Research on Adolescence, 1*, 189–206.

Smith, A. C., & Smith, D. I. (2001). Emergency and transitional shelter population: 2000. *Census Special Reports, Series CENSR/01-2.* Washington, DC: U.S. Government Printing Office.

Smith, D. B., & Moen, P. (2004). Retirement satisfaction for retirees and their spouses: Do gender and the retirement decision-making process matter? *Journal of Family Issues, 25*, 262–285.

Smith, E. (2016). Five reasons my divorce was the best thing that happened to me. *Huffington Post.* Retrieved from http://www.huffingtonpost.com/erin-smith2/five-reasons-my-divorce-w_b_7693184.html

Smith, L. B., Jones, S. S., & Landau, B. (1992). Count nouns, adjectives, and perceptual properties in children's novel word interpretations. *Developmental Psychology, 28*, 273–286.

Smith, M., & Segal, J. (2016). *What you need to know about bereavement and grief.* Retrieved from http://www.helpguide.org/articles/grief-loss/supporting-a-grieving-person.htm

Smith, P. B., Ambalavanan, N., Li, L., et al. (2012). Approach to infants born at 22-24 weeks' gestation: Relationship to outcomes of more-mature infants. *Pediatrics, 129*, e1508–e1516.

Smith, P. K. (Ed.). (1991). *The psychology of grandparenthood: An international perspective.* London: Routledge.

Smith, P. K., & Drew, L. M. (2002). Grandparenthood. In M. H. Bornstein (Ed.), *Handbook of parenting: Vol. 3. Being and becoming a parent* (pp. 141–147). Mahwah, NJ: Erlbaum.

Smith, P. K., Hunter, T., Carvalho, A. M. A., & Costabile, A. (1992). Children's perceptions of play fighting, play chasing and real fighting: A cross-national interview study. *Social Development, 1*, 211–221.

Smith, R. (2000). A good death. *British Medical Journal, 320*, 129–130.

Smith, S. K., & House, M. (2006). Snowbirds, sunbirds and stayers: Seasonal migration of elderly adults in Florida. *Journal of Gerontology: Social Sciences, 61B*, S232–S239.

Smith, Y. L. S., van Goozen, S. H. M., & Cohen-Kettenis, P. T. (2001). Adolescents with gender identity disorder who were accepted or rejected for sex reassignment surgery: A prospective follow-up study. *Journal of the American Academy of Child and Adolescent Psychiatry, 40*, 472–481.

Smolowe, J. (1997). A battle against biology; a victory in adoption. *Time, 150*, 46.

Snarey, J. R., Reimer, J., & Kohlberg, L. (1985). Development of social-moral reasoning among kibbutz adolescents: A longitudinal cross-sectional study. *Developmental Psychology, 21*, 3–17.

Snedeker, J., Geren, J., & Shafto, C. I. (2007). Starting over: International adoption as a natural experiment in language development. *Psychological Science, 18*, 79–87.

Snow, C. E. (1984). Parent-child interaction and the development of communicative ability. In R. L. Schiefelbusch & J. Pickar (Eds.), *Communicative competence: Acquisition and intervention* (pp. 69–108). Baltimore, MD: University Park Press.

Snow, K. (2011). *Developing kindergarten readiness and other large-scale assessment systems: Necessary considerations in the assessment of young children.* Washington, DC: National Association for the Education of Young Children.

Snow, K. (2016). Research news you can use: Pretend play is important but its role in learning is complex. *NAEYC.* Retrieved from www.naeyc.org/content/research-news-pretend-play-is-important

Snyder, C. R. (1994). *The psychology of hope: You can get there from here.* New York, NY: Free Press.

Snyder, C. R. (2002). Hope theory: Rainbows in the mind. *Psychological Inquiry, 13*, 249–275.

Snyder, C. R., Cheavens, J., & Sympson, S. C. (1997). Hope: An individual motive for social commerce. *Group Dynamics: Theory, Research, and Practice, 1*, 107–118.

Snyder, C. R., Harris, C., Anderson, J. R., Holleran, S. A., Irving, L. M., Sigmon, S. T., et al. (1991). The will and the ways: Development and validation of an individual-differences measure of hope. *Journal of Personality and Social Psychology, 60*, 570–585.

Snyder, H. N., & Sickmund, M. (2006). Juvenile Offenders and Victims: 2006 National Report. *National Center for Juvenile Justice.* Retrieved from http://ojjdp.ncjrs.gov/ojstatbb/nr2006/downloads/NR2006.pdf

Soares, C. N., & Zitek, B. (2008). Reproductive hormone sensitivity and risk for depression across the female life cycle: A continuum of vulnerability? *Journal of Psychiatry and Neuroscience, 33*, 331–343.

Sobel, D. M. (2004). Children's developing knowledge of the relationship between mental awareness and pretense. *Child Development, 75*, 704–729.

Social Security Administration. (2016). *Income of the aged chartbook, 2014.* Retrieved from https://www.ssa.gov/policy/docs/chartbooks/income_aged/2014/iac14.html#chart8

Soderstrom, M. (2007). Beyond baby talk: Re-evaluating the nature and content of speech input to preverbal infants. *Developmental Review, 27*, 501–532.

Soet, J. E., Brack, G. A., & DiIorio, C. (2003). Prevalence and predictors of women's experience of psychological trauma during childbirth. *Birth: Issues in Perinatal Care, 30*, 36–46.

Sokol, R. J., Delaney-Black, V., & Nordstrom, B. (2003). Fetal alcohol spectrum disorder. *Journal of the American Medical Association, 290*, 2996–2999.

Sommerville, L. H. (2013). Teenage brain: Sensitivity to social evaluation. *Current Directions in Psychological Science, 22*, 122–127.

Sommerfield, M. J., & McCrae, R. R. (2000). Stress and coping research: Methodological challenges, theoretical advances, and clinical applications. *American Psychologist, 55*, 620–625.

Son, S. C., & Peterson, M. F. (2016, March 30). Marital status, home environments, and family strain: Complex effects on preschool children's school readiness skills. *Infant and Child Development.*

Sonfield, A. (2002). Looking at men's sexual and reproductive health needs. *Guttmacher Report on Public Policy, 5.*

Sophian, C. (1998). A developmental perspective in children's counting. In C. Donlan (Ed.), *The development of mathematical skills* (pp. 27–46). Hove, England: Psychology Press/Taylor & Francis.

Sophian, C. (2007). *The origins of mathematical knowledge in childhood.* New York, NY: Routledge.

Sorkin, D. H., & Rook, K. S. (2004). Interpersonal control strivings and vulnerability to negative social exchanges in later life. *Psychology and Aging, 19*, 555–564.

Sorrell, G. T., & Montgomery, M. J. (2001). Feminist perspectives on Erikson's theory: Their relevance for contemporary identity development research. *Identity: An International Journal of Theory and Research, 1*, 97–128.

Soska, K. C., Robinson, S. R., & Adolph, K. E. (2015). A new twist on old ideas: How sitting reorients crawlers. *Developmental Science, 18*, 206–218.

Spearman, C. (1927). *The abilities of man.* New York, NY: Macmillan.

Spelke, E. S., von Hofsten, C., & Kestenbaum, R. (1989). Object perception in infancy: Interaction of spatial and kinetic information for object boundaries. *Developmental Psychology, 25*, 185–186.

Spencer, M. B. (2006). Revisiting the 1990 Special Issue on Minority Children: An editorial perspective 15 years later. *Child Development, 77*, 1149–1154.

Spencer, M. B., & Markstrom-Adams, C. (1990). Identity processes among racial and ethnic minority children in America. *Child Development, 61*, 290–310.

Sperlich, A., Meixner, J., & Laubrock, J. (2016). Development of the perceptual span in reading: A longitudinal study. *Journal of Experimental Child Psychology, 146*, 181–201.

Sperlich, M., & Seng, J. (2008). *Survivor moms: Women's stories of birthing, mothering and healing after sexual abuse.* Eugene, OR: Motherbaby Press.

Sperling, D. (1989, March 10). Success rate for in vitro is only 9%. *USA Today*, p. D1.

Spitz, R. A. (1945). Hospitalism: An inquiry into the genesis of psychiatric conditions in early childhood. *Psychoanalytic Study of the Child, 1*, 113–117.

Spitz, R. A. (1946). Anaclitic depression. *Psychoanalytic Study of the Child, 2*, 313–342.

Spitze, G., & Logan, J. (1990). Sons, daughters, and intergenerational social support. *Journal of Marriage and the Family, 52*, 420–430.

SPLC Report. (2010, Spring). *New SPLC film to addess anti-gay bullying in schools*, p. 5.

Sprecher, S., Sullivan, Q., & Hatfield, E. (1994). Mate selection preferences: Gender differences examined in a national sample. *Journal of Personality and Social Psychology, 66*, 1074–1080.

Stack, D. M., & Muir, D. W. (1992). Adult tactile stimulation during face-to-face interactions modulates five-month-olds' affect and attention. *Child Development, 63*, 1509–1525.

Stack, S. (1990). The impact of divorce on suicide, 1959–1980. *Journal of Marriage and the Family, 52*, 119–128.

Stadtler, A. C., Gorski, P. A., & Brazelton, T. B. (1999). Toilet training methods, clinical interventions, and recommendations. *Pediatrics, 103*, 1359–1361.

Staff, J., Messersmith, E. E., & Schulenberg, J. E. (2009). Adolescents and the world of work. In R. M. Lerner & L. Steinberg (Eds.), *Handbook of adolescent psychology, Vol. 2. Contextual influences of adolescent development* (3rd ed., pp. 270–313). New York, NY: John Wiley.

Stake, R. E. (1998). Case studies. In N. K. Denzin & Y. S. Lincoln (Eds.), *Strategies of qualitative inquiry* (pp. 86–109). Thousand Oaks, CA: Sage.

Stallings, J. A. (1995). Ensuring teaching and learning in the 21st century. *Educational Researcher, 24*, 4–8.

Stancliffe, R. J., Bigby, C., Balandin, S., Wilson, N. J., & Craig, D. (2015). Transition to retirement and participation in mainstream community groups using active mentoring: A feasibility and outcomes evaluation with a matched comparison group. *Journal of Intellectual Disability Research, 59*, 703–718.

Standley, K., Soule, B., & Copans, S. A. (1979). Dimensions of prenatal anxiety and their influence on pegnancy outcome. *American Journal of Obstetrics and Gynecology, 135*, 22–26.

Stanley, S. M., Rhoades, G. K., & Whitton, S. W. (2010). Commitment: Functions, formation, and the securing of romantic attachment. *Journal of Family Theory and Review, 2*(4), 243–257.

Stapley, J. C., & Haviland, J. M. (1989). Beyond depression: Gender differences in normal adolescents' emotional experiences. *Sex Roles, 20,* 295–308.

Statista. (2016). *Number of social network users worldwide from 2010 to 2020 (in billions).* Retrieved from http://www.statista.com /statistics/278414/number-of-worldwide -social-network-users/

Staudinger, U. M., Dorner, J., & Mickler, C. (2005). Wisdom and personality. In R. J. Sternberg & J. Jordan (Eds.), *A handbook of wisdom: Psychological perspectives* (pp. 191–219). New York, NY: Cambridge University Press.

Steele, K. (2010). *Biking and walking in the U.S. 2010: Benchmark report.* Washington, DC: Alliance for Biking and Walking.

Stein, B. E. (Ed.). (2012). *The new handbook of multisensory processing.* Cambridge, MA: MIT Press.

Stein, C. H. (2009). "I owe it to them": Understanding felt obligation toward parents in adulthood. In K. Shifren (Ed.), *How caregiving affects development: Psychological implications for child, adolescent, and adult caregivers* (pp. 119–145). Washington, DC: American Psychological Association.

Steinberg, L. (2001). We know some things: Parent-adolescent relationships in retrospect and prospect. *Journal of Research on Adolescence, 11,* 1–19.

Steinberg, L. (2013). *Adolescence* (10th ed.). New York, NY: McGraw-Hill.

Steinhauser, K. E., Christakis, N. A., Clipp, E. C., McNeilly, M., Grambow, S., Parker, J., & Tulsky, J. A. (2001). Preparing for the end of life: Preferences of patients, families, physicians, and other care providers. *Journal of Pain and Symptom Management, 22,* 727–737.

Stelter, D. (2014). Living with social anxiety. *Anxiety Resource Center.* Retrieved from http://anxietyresourcecenter.org/2014/04 /living-social-anxiety/

Stenberg, G. (2013). Do 12-month-old infants trust a competent adult? *Infancy, 18,* 873–904.

Stenseng, F., Belsky, J., Skalicka, V., & Wichstrøm, L. (2016). Peer rejection and attention deficit hyperactivity disorder symptoms: Reciprocal relations through ages 4 6, and 8. *Child Development, 87,* 365–373.

Stephan, Y. (2009). Openness to experience and active older adults' life satisfaction: A trait and facet-level analysis. *Personality and Individual Differences, 47,* 637–641.

Stern, G. (2007, Ocober 28). Hospice worker attends to spiritual needs of the dying. *The Journal News.* Retrieved from http://www .thejournalnews.com/apps/pbcs.dll /article?AID=2007710280354

Sternberg, R. J. (1985). *Beyond IQ: A triarchic theory of human intelligence.* Cambridge, England: Cambridge University Press.

Sternberg, R. J. (1988). *The triangle of love.* New York, NY: Basic Books.

Sternberg, R. J. (1990). *Wisdom: Its nature, origins and development.* New York, NY: Cambridge University Press.

Sternberg, R. J. (2004). Culture and intelligence. *American Psychologist, 59,* 325–338.

Sternberg. R. J. (2007). Who are the bright children? The cultural context of being and acting intelligent. *Educational Researcher, 36,* 148–155.

Sternberg, R. J. (2012). The triarchic theory of intelligence. In D. P. Flanagan & P. L. Harrison (Eds.), *Contemporary intellectual assessment: Theories, tests, and issues* (3rd ed.) (pp. 156–177). New York: Guilford Press.

Sternberg, R. J. (2014). The development of adaptive competence: Why cultural psychology is necessary and not just nice. *Developmental Review, 34,* 208–224.

Sternberg, R. J., Castejon, J. L., Prieto, M. D., Hautamaki, J., & Grigorenko, E. L. (2001). Confirmatoy factor analysis of the Sternberg Triarchic Abilities Test in three international samples: An empirical test of the triarchic theory of intelligence. *European Journal of Psychological Assessment, 17,* 1–16.

Sternberg, R. J., Grigorenko, E. L., & Singer, J. (2004). *Creativity: From potential to realization.* Washington, DC: American Psychological Association.

Sternberg, R. J., & Kaufman, S. B. (Eds.). (2011). *The Cambridge Handbook of Intelligence. Cambridge Handbooks in Psychology.* New York: Cambridge University Press.

Stets, J. E., & Harrod, M. M. (2004). Verification across multiple identities: The role of status. *Social Psychology Quarterly, 67,* 155–171.

Stetsenko, A., & Ho, P. G. (2015). The serious joy and the joyful work of play: Children becoming agentive actors in co-authoring themselves and their world through play. *International Journal of Early Childhood, 47,* 221–234.

Stevens, A. H. (2014, Summer). Labor market shocks: Are there lessons for anti-poverty policy? *Pathways,* 19–22.

Stevens, J. H., Jr. (1988). Social support, locus of control, and parenting in three low-income groups of mothers: Black teenagers, Black adults, and White adults. *Child Development, 59,* 635–642.

Stevens, J. H., Jr., & Bakeman, R. (1985). A factor analytic study of the HOME scale for infants. *Developmental Psychology, 21,* 1196–1203.

Stevens-Long, J., & Commons, M. L. (1992). *Adult life: Developmental processes* (4th ed.). Mountain View, CA: Mayfield.

Stevens-Roseman, E. S. (2009). Older mentors for newer workers: Impact of a worker-driven intervention on later life satisfaction. *Journal of Workplace Behavioral Health, 24,* 419–426.

Stevenson, D. L., & Baker, D. P. (1987). The family-school relation and the child's school performance. *Child Development, 58,* 1348–1357.

Stevenson, H. W. (1992, December). Learning from Asian schools. *Scientific American, 267*(6), 70–77.

Stevenson, H. W., Chen, C., & Lee, S. (1993). Mathematics achievement of Chinese, Japanese, and American children: Ten years later. *Science, 259,* 53–58.

Stewart, A. J., & Vandewater, E. A. (1998). The course of generativity. In D. P. McAdams & E. de St. Aubin (Eds.), *Generativity and adult development* (pp. 75–100). Washington, DC: American Psychological Association.

Stice, E., & Shaw, H. (2002). Role of body dissatisfaction in the onset and maintenance of eating pathology: A synthesis of research findings. *Journal of Psychosomatic Research, 53,* 985–993. Stice, E., & Shaw, H. (2004). Eating disorder prevention programs: A meta-analytic review. *Psychological Bulletin, 130,* 206–227.

Sticker, E. J. (1991). The importance of grandparenthood during the life cycle in Germany. In P. K. Smith (Ed.), *The psychology of grandparenthood: An international perspective* (pp. 32–49). London: Routledge.

Stinebrickner, R. S., & Stinebrickner, T. R. (2008). The effect of credit constraints on the college drop-out decision: A direct approach using a new panel study. *American Economic Review, 98,* 2163–2184.

Stinebrickner, T. R., & Stinebrickner, R. S. (2012). Learning about academic ability and the college dropout decision. *Journal of Labor Economics, 30,* 707–748.

Stoller, E. P., & Longino, C. F., Jr. (2001). "Going home" or "leaving home"? The impact of person and place ties on anticipated counterstream migration. *The Gerontologist, 41,* 96–102.

Stone, A. A., Schwartz, J. E., Broderick, J. E., & Deaton, A. (2010). A snapshot of the age distribution of psychological well-being in the United States. *Proceedings of the National Academic of Sciences.* Retrieved from www.pnas.org/cgi/doi/10.1073 /pnas.1003744107

Stone, M. R., Barber, B. L., & Eccles, J. S. (2008). We knew them when: Sixth grade characteristics that predict adolescent high school social identities. *Journal of Early Adolescence, 28,* 304–328.

Stone, P. K., & Selin, E. (2009). *Childbirth across cultures: Ideas and practices.* New York, NY: Springer Science + Business Media.

Stopbullying.gov. (2014). *Facts about bullying.* Retrieved from https://www.stopbullying .gov/kids/facts/

Stovall-McClough, K. C., & Dozier, M. (2016). Attachment states of mind and psychopathology in adulthood. In J. Cassidy & P.R. Shaver (Ed.), *Handbook of attachment: Theory, research and clinical applications* (3rd ed., pp. 715–738). New York: Guilford Press.

Strachan, S. M., Brawley, L. R., Spink, K., & Glazebrook, K. (2010). Older adults' physically-active identity: Relationships between social cognitions, physical activity, and satisfaction with life. *Psychology of Sport and Exercise, 11,* 114–121.

Strasburger, V. C., Wilson, B. J., & Jordan, A. B. (2014). *Children, adolescents, and the media* (3rd ed.). Thousand Oaks, CA: Sage.

Strauss, K., Griffin, M. A., & Raferty, A. E. (2009). Proactivity directed toward the team and organization: The role of leadership, commitment and role-breadth self-efficacy. *British Journal of Management, 20,* 279–291.

Streri, A. (2005). Touching for knowing in infancy: The development of manual abilities in very young infants. *European Journal of Developmental Psychology, 2,* 325–343.

Stright, A. D., Neitzel, C., Sears, K. G., & Hoke-Sinex, L. (2001). Instruction begins in the home: Relations between parental instruction and children's self-regulation in the classroom. *Journal of Educational Psychology, 93,* 456–466.

Stringer, C. (2012). *Lone survivors: How we came to be the only humans on earth.* New York: Macmillan.

Stringfellow, L. (1978). The Vietnamese. In A. L. Clark (Ed.), *Culture, childbearing, and the health professionals* (pp. 174–182). Philadelphia, PA: Davis.

Stritikus, T., & Nguyen, D. (2007). Strategic transformation: Cultural and gender identity negotiation in first generation Vietnamese youth. *American Educational Research Journal, 44,* 853–895.

Strober, M. (1981). A comparative analysis of personality organization in juvenile anorexia nervosa. *Journal of Youth and Adolescence, 10,* 285–295.

Stroebe, M. S. (2011). Coping with bereavement. In S. Folkman (Ed.) *Handbook of stress, health, and coping* (pp. 148-172). New York: Oxford Univ. Press.

Stuart-Hamilton, I. (1996). Intellectual changes in late life. In R. T. Woods (Ed.), *Handbook of the clinical psychology of ageing* (pp. 23–41). Oxford, England: John Wiley & Sons.

Stuewig, J., Tangney, J. P., Kendall, S., Folk, J., Meyer, C. R., & Dearing, R. (2015). Children's proneness to shame and guilt predict risky and illegal behaviors in young adulthood. *Child Psychiatry and Human Development, 46,* 217–227.

Sturge-Apple, M. L., Davies P. T., Martin, M. J., Cicchetti, D., & Hentges, R. F. (2012). An examination of the impact of harsh parenting contexts on children's adaptation within an evolutionary framework. *Developmental Psychology, 48,* 791–805.

Subrahmanyam, K., Kraut, R., Greenfield,P., & Gross, E. (2001). New forms of electronic media. In D. Singer & J. Singer (Eds.), *Handbook of children and the family* (pp. 73–99). Thousand Oaks, CA: Sage.

Sui, J., Liu, C. H., & Han, S. (2009). Cultural difference in neural mechanisms of self-recognition. *Social Neuroscience, 4,* 402–411.

Sullivan, H. S. (1949). *The collected works of Harry Stack Sullivan* (Vols. 1 and 2). New York, NY: Norton.

Sullivan, H. S. (1953). *The interpersonal theory of psychiatry.* New York, NY: Norton.

Sullivan, M. D. (2003). Hope and hopelessness at the end of life. *American Journal of Geriatric Psychiatry, 11,* 393–405.

Sullivan, M & Lewis, M. (2003). Contextual determinants of anger and other negative expressions in young infants. *Developmental Psychology, 39,* 693–705.

Sullivan, M. W., Lewis, M., & Allesandri, S. M. (1992). Cross-age stability in emotional expressions during learning and extinction. *Developmental Psychology, 28,* 58–63.

Super, C. M., Kagan, J., Morrison, F. J., Haith, M. M., & Weiffenbach, J. (1972). Discrepancy and attention in the five-month infant. *Genetic Psychology Monographs, 85,* 305–331.

Susman, E. J., Dorn, L. D., & Chrousos, G. P. (1991). Negative hormones and affect levels in young adolescents: Concurrent and predictive perspectives. *Journal of Youth and Adolescence, 20,* 167–190.

Svetina, M. (2014). Resilience in the context of Erikson's theory of human development. *Current Psychology: A Journal for Diverse Perspectives on Diverse Psychological Issues, 33,* 393–404.

Svoboda, E. (2014). Virtual assault. *Scientific American Mind, 25,* 46–55.

Swann, W. B., Jr. (1990). To be known or be adored? The interplay of self-enhancement and self-verification. In E. . Higgins & R. M. Sorrentino (Eds.), *Handbook of motivation and cognition: Foundations of social behavior* (pp. 404–448). New York, NY: Guilford Press.

Swift, A. (2016). Euthanasia still acceptable to solid majority in U.S. *Gallup,* Retrieved from http://www.gallup.com/poll/193082 /euthanasia-acceptable-majority.aspx

Swing, E. L., & Anderson, C. A. (2007). The unintended negative consequences of exposure to violent video games. *International Journal of Cognitive Technology, 12,* 3–13.

Swingler, M. M., Sweet, M. A., & Carver, L. J. (2010). Brain behavior correlations: Relationships between mother-stranger face processing and infant's behavior responses to a separation from mother. *Developmental Psychology, 46,* 669–680.

Swingley, D. (2007). Lexical exposure and word-form encoding in 1.5-year olds. *Developmental Psychology, 43,* 454–464.

Swisher, R., Sweet, S., & Moen, P. L. (2004). The family-friendly community and its life course fit for dual eaner couples. *Journal of Marriage and the Family, 66,* 281–292.

Swyer, P. R. (1987). The organization of perinatal care with particular reference to the newborn. In G. B. Avery (Ed.), *Neonatology: Pathophysiology and management of the newborn* (pp. 13–44). Philadelphia, PA: Lippincott.

Sydney Morning Herald. (2011). *Oldest new mother gives birth at 63.* Retrieved from http://www.smh.com.au/lifestyle /life/oldest-new-mother-gives-birth-at -63-20110322-1c437.html

Syed, M. (2010). Developing an integrated self: Academic and ethnic identities among ethnically diverse college students. *Developmental Psychology, 46,* 1590–1604.

Syed, M., & Azmitia, M. (2009). Longitudinal trajectories of ethnic identity during the college years. *Journal of Research on Adolescence, 19,* 587–600.

Tainaka, K., Takizawa, T., Katamoto, S., & Aoki, J. (2009). Six-year prospective study of physical fitness and incidents of disability among community-dwelling Japanese elderly women. *Geriatrics and Gerontology International, 9,* 21–28.

Tajfel, H. (1981). *Human groups and social categories.* Cambridge, England: Cambridge University Press.

Takahashi, L. K., Baker, E. W., & Kalin, N. H. (1990). Ontogeny of behavioral and hormonal responses to stress in prenatally stressed male rat pups. *Physiology and Behavior, 47,* 357–364.

Takahashi, L. K., & Kalin, N. H. (1991). Early developmental and temporal characteristics of stress-induced secretion of pituitary-adrenal hormones in prenatally stressed rat pups. *Brain Research, 558,* 75–78.

Takata, Y., Ansai, T., Soh, I., et al. (2010). Quality of life and physical fitness in an 85-year-old population. *Archives of Gerontology and Geriatrics, 50,* 272–276.

Tallman, I., & Hsiao, Y.-L. (2004). Resources, cooperation, and problem solving in early marriages. *Social Psychology Quarterly, 67,* 172–188.

Tamis-LeMonda, C. S., Uzgiris, I. C., & Bornstein, M. H. (2012). Play in parent-child interactions. In M. H. Bornstein (Ed.), *Handbook of parenting, Vol. 5. Practical issues in parenting* (pp. 221–242). New York, NY: Psychology Press.

Tanfer, K. (1987). Premarital cohabitation among never-married women. *Journal of Marriage and the Family, 49,* 483–497.

Tang, C. S. K., Yeung, D. Y., & Lee, A. M. (2003). Psychosocial correlates of emotional responses to menarche among Chinese adolescent girls. *Journal of Adolescent Health, 33,* 193–201.

Tang, F., & Lee, Y. (2011). Social support networks and expectations for aging in place and moving. *Research on Aging, 33,* 444–464.

Tangney, J. P. (2001). Constructive and destructive aspects of shame and guilt. In A. C. Bohart & D. J. Stipek (Eds.), *Constructive and destructive behavior: Implications for family, school and society* (pp. 127–145). Washington, DC: American Psychological Association.

Tangney, J. P., Baumeister, R. F., & Boone, A. L. (2004). High self-control predicts good adjustment, less pathology, better grades, and interpersonal success. *Journal of Personality, 72,* 271–322.

Tangney, J. P., & Dearing, R. L. (2002). *Shame and guilt.* New York, NY: Guilford Press.

Tangney, J. P., Malouf, E., Stuewig, J., & Mashek, D. (2012). Emotions and morality:

You don't have to feel really bad to be good. In M. W. Eysenck, M. Fajkowska, & T. Maruszewski (Eds.), *Personality, cognition and emotion. Warsaw lectures in personality and social psychology* (Vol. 2, pp. 141–154). Clinton Corners, NY: Eliot Werner Publications.

Tangney, J. P., & Mashek, D. J. (2004). In search of the moral person: Do you have to feel really bad to be good? In J. Greenberg, S. L. Koole, & T. Pyszczynski (Eds.), *Handbook of experimental existential psychology* (pp. 156–166). New York, NY: Guilford Press.

Tangney, J. P., Stuewig, J., & Moshek, D. J.(2007). Moral emotions and moral behavior. *Annual Review of Psychology, 58*, 345–372.

Tangney, J. P., Wagner, P., Fletcher, C., & Gramzow, R. (1992). Shamed into anger? The relation of shame and guilt to anger and self-reported aggression. *Journal of Personality and Social Psychology, 62*, 669–675.

Tanner, E. M., & Finn-Stevenson, M. (2002). Nutrition and brain development: Social policy implications. *American Journal of Orthopsychiatry, 72*, 182–193.

Tantibanchachai, C. & Zhang, M. (2015). Cocaine as a teratogen. *Embryo Project Encyclopedia*, Retrieved from https://embryo.asu.edu/pages/cocaine-teratogen

Tanner, J. M. (1990). *Foetus into man: Physical growth from conception to maturity* (rev. ed.). Cambridge, MA: Harvard University Press.

Tarricone, P. (2011). *The taxonomy of metacognition.* New York, NY: Psychology Press.

Task Force on Community Preventive Services. (2007). *The effectiveness of universal school-based programs for the prevention of violent and aggressive behavior.* A report on recommendations of the Task Force on Community Preventive Services. Retrieved from http://www.cdc.gov/mmwr/preview/mmwrhtml/rr5607a1.htm

Tasker, F. (2005). Lesbian mothers, gay fathers, and their children: A review. *Developmental and Behavioral Pediatrics, 26*, 224–240.

Taubman-Ben-Ari, O., Findler, L., & Ben Shlomo, S. (2013). When couples become grandparents: Factors associated with the growth of each spouse. *Social Work Research*, published online February 13, 2013, doi: 10.1093/swr/svt005.

Tausig, M., & Fenwick, R. (2001). Unbinding time: Alternate work schedules and work-life balance. *Journal of Family and Economic Issues, 22*, 101–119.

Tavernise, S. (2015). *Colorado's effort against teenage pregnancies is a startling success.* Retrieved from http://www.nytimes.com/2015/07/06/science/colorados-push-against-teenage-pregnancies-is-a-startling-success.html?_r=0

Taylor, H. G., Klein, N., Minich, N. M., & Hack, M. (2000). Middle-school-age outcomes in children with very low birth weight. *Child Development, 71*, 1495–1511.

Taylor, J., & Turner, R. J. (2001). A longitudinal study of the role and significance of mattering to others for depressive symptoms. *Journal of Health and Social Behavior, 42*, 310–325.

Taylor, L. L. (2016). *Healthy eating tips for busy people.* Retrieved from http://www.shapefit.com/diet/healthy-eating-tips-busy-people.html

Taylor, M., & Mannering, A. M. (2006). Of Hobbes and Harvey: The imaginary companions created by children and adults. In A. Göncü & S. Gaskins (Eds.), *Play and development: Evolutionary, sociocultural, and functional perspectives* (pp. 227–245). The Jean Piaget symposium series. Mahwah, NJ: Lawrence Erlbaum.

Taylor, P., & Gao, G. (2014). Generation X: America's neglected "middle child." *Pew Research Center.* Retrieved from http://www.pewresearch.org/fact-tank/2014/06/05/generation-x-americas-neglected-middle-child/

Taylor, R. D., & Oskay, G. (1995). Identity formation in Turkish and American late adolescents. *Journal of Cross-Cultural Psychology, 26*, 8–22.

Taylor, S. E., Way, B. M., Welch, W. T., Hilmert, C. J., Lehman, B. J., & Eisenberger, N. I. (2006). Early family environment, cultural adversity, the serotonin transporter promoter polymorphism and depressive symptomatology. *Biological Psychiatry, 60*, 671–676.

Taylor, S. J. (1987) "They're not like you and me": Institutional attendants' perspectives on residents. *Children and Youth Services, 8*, 109–125.

Taylor, S. J., & Bogdan, R. (1998). *Introduction to qualitative research methods* (3rd ed.). New York, NY: Wiley.

Taylor, W. C., Blair, S. N., Cummings, S. S., Wun, C. C., & Malina, R. M. (1999). Childhood and adolescent physical activity patterns and adult physical activity. *Medicine and Science in Sports and Exercise, 31*, 118–123.

Teachman, J., Tedrow, L., & Kim, G. (2012). Demography of the family. In G. Peterson & K. Bush (Eds.), *Handbook of Marriage and the Family* (pp. 39–64). New York, NY: Springer.

Telingator, C. J., & Patterson, C. (2008). Children and adolescents of lesbian and gay parents. *The Journal of the American Academy of Child and Adolescent Psychiatry, 47*, 1364–1368.

Teller, D. Y., & Bornstein, J. H. (1987). Infant color vision and color perception. In P. Salapatek & L. Cohen (Eds.), *Handbook of infant perception* (Vol. 1). Orlando, FL: Academic Press.

Telzer, E. H. (2016). Dopaminergic reward sensitivity can promote adolescent health: A new perspective on the mechanism of ventral striatum activation. *Developmental Cognitive Neuroscience, 17*, 57–67.

Tempesta, D. (2015). *How to help someone who is grieving.* Retrieved from http://www.huffingtonpost.com/daniela-tempesta-lcsw/how-to-help-someone-who-i_b_6331568.html

Temple-Smith, M., Moore, S., & Rosenthal, D. (2016). *Sexuality in adolescence: The digital generation.* New York: Routledge.

Tenenbaum, H. R., & Leaper, C. (2002). Are parents' gender schemas related to their children's gender-related cognitions? A meta-analysis. *Developmental Psychology, 38*, 615–630.

Teno, J. M., Clarridge, B. R., Casey, V., Welch, L. C., Wetle, T., Shield, R., et al. (2004). Family perspectives on end-of-life care at the last place of care. *Journal of the American Medical Association, 291*, 88–93.

Teong, S. K. (2003). The effect of metacognitive training on mathematical word- problem solving. *Journal of Computer Assisted Learning, 19*, 46–55.

Terman, L. M., & Oden, M. H. (1947). *The gifted child grows up: Twenty-five years' follow-up of a superior group.* Stanford, CA: Stanford University Press.

Terman, L. M., & Oden, M. H. (1959). *The gifted group at mid-life: Thirty-five years' follow-up of a superior group.* Stanford, CA: Stanford University Press.

Terry-Humen, E., Manlove, J., & Cottingham, S. (2006). Trends and recent estimates: Sexual activity among U.S. teens. *Child Trends Research Brief, Publication #2006-08.*

Teti, D. M., & Lamb, M. E. (1989). Outcomes of adolescent marriage and adolescent childbirth. *Journal of Marriage and the Family, 51*, 203–212.

TFMHA-Task Force on Mental Health and Abortion. (2008). *Report of the APA Task Force on Mental Health and Abortion.* Washington, DC: American Psychological Association on Mental Health and Abortion.

Thapar, A., Collishaw, S., Pine, D. S., & Thapar, A. K. (2012). Depression in adolescence. *Lancet, 379*, 1056–1067.

Tharp, R. G., & Gallimore, R. (1988). *Rousing minds to life: Teaching, learning, and schooling in social context.* Cambridge, England: Cambridge University Press.

The Chronicle of Higher Education. (2005, August 26). *Almanac.*

The Education Trust. (2015). *Checking In: Do classroom assignments reflect today's higher standards?* Retrieved from http://edtrust.org/wp-content/uploads/2014/09/CheckingIn_TheEducationTrust_Sept20152.pdf

The Names Project Foundation. (2005). *History of the quilt.* Retrieved from http://www.aidsquilt.org/history.htm

The NAMES Project Foundation. (2016). *Mission, goals, values and history.* Retrieved from http://www.aidsquilt.org/about/the-names-project-foundation

The National Campaign. (2012). Teen childbearing, education, and economic well-being. Retrieved from www.thenationalcampaign.org

The National Commission for the Protection of Human Subjects of Biomedical and Behavioral Research. (1979). *The Belmont Report: Ethical principles and guidelines for the protection of human subjects*. Federal Registered Document 79-12065. Washington, DC: Government Printing Office.

Thelen, E. (1995). Motor development: A new synthesis. *American Psychologist, 50,* 79–95.

Thelen, E., & Fisher, D. M. (1982). Newborn stepping: An explanation for a "disappearing" reflex. *Developmental Psychology, 18,* 760–775.

Thelen, E., Fisher, D. M., & Ridley-Johnson, R. (1984). The relationship between physical growth and a newborn reflex. *Infant Behavior and Development, 7,* 479–493.

Thelen, E., & Smith, L. B. (1994). *A dynamic systems approach to the development of cognition and action*. Cambridge, MA: MIT Press.

The Retirement-Lounge.com. (2010). *Retirement—It's great to be out of the rat race*. Retrieved from http://www.retirement-lounge.com/index.html

Thielfoldt, D., & Scheef, D. (2004). Generation X and the millennials: What you need to know about mentoring the new generations. *Law Practice Today,* Retrieved from http://Americanbar.org/lpm/lpt/articles/mg08044.html

Thoits, P. A. (2012). Self, identity, stress, and mental health. In C. S. Aneshensel, J. C. Phelan, & A. Bierman (Eds.) *Handbook of the sociologoy of mental health* (pp. 141–154). New York, NY: Springer.

Thomas, A., & Chess, S. (1977). *Temperament and development*. New York , NY: Brunner/Mazel.

Thomas, A., & Chess, S. (1980). *The dynamics of psychological development*. New York, NY: Brunner/Mazel.

Thomas, A., & Chess, S. (1986). The New York longitudinal study: From infancy to early adult life. In R. Plomin & J. Dunn (Eds.), *The study of temperament: Changes, continuities, and challenges*. Hillsdale, NJ: Erlbaum.

Thomas, A., Chess, S., & Birch, H. (1970). The origin of personality. *Scientific American, 223,* 102–109.

Thomas, A. J., & Schwarzbaum, S. (2011). Culture and identity: Life stories for counselors and therapists (2nd ed.). Thousand Oaks, CA: Sage.

Thomas, M. H., & Drabman, R. S. (1977). Effects of television violence on expectations of others' aggression. Paper presented at the annual convention of the American Psychological Association, San Francisco, CA.

Thomas, R. M. (2009). *Human development theories: Windows on culture*. Thousand Oaks, CA: Sage.

Thompson, D. (2015). A world without work. *The Atlantic*. Retrieved from http://www.theatlantic.com/magazine/archive/2015/07/world-without-work/395294/

Thompson, G. E., Cameron, R. E., & Fuller-Thomson, E. (2013). Walking the red road: The role of First Nations grandparents in promoting cultural well-being. *The International Journal of Aging and Human Development, 76,* 55–78.

Thompson, L. (1993). Conceptualizing gender in marriage: The case of marital care. *Journal of Marriage and the Family, 55,* 557–569.

Thompson, L. W., Gallagher-Thompson, D., Futterman, A., Gilewski, M. J., & Peterson, J. (1991). The effects of late-life spousal bereavement over a 30-month interval. *Psychology and Aging, 6,* 434–441.

Thompson, R. A. (1990). Emotion and self-regulation. In R. A. Thompson (Ed.), *Nebraska Symposium on Motivation, 1988* (Vol. 36, pp. 367–467). Lincoln, NE: University of Nebraska Press.

Thompson, R. A. (2010). Early attachment and later development: Familiar questions, new answers. In J. Cassidy & P. R. Shaver (Eds.), *Handbook of attachment: Theory research and clinical applications* (2nd ed., pp. 348–365). New York, NY: Guilford Press.

Thompson, R. A. (2014). Socialization of emotion and emotion regulation in the family. In J. J. Gross (Ed.), *Handbook of emotional regulation* (2nd ed.) (pp. 173–186). New York: Guilford Press.

Thompson, R. A., Connell, J. P., & Bridges, L. J. (1988). Temperament, emotion, and social interactive behavior in the strange situation: A component process analysis of attachment system functioning. *Child Development, 59,* 1102–1110.

Thomson, E., & Colella, U. (1992). Cohabitation and marital stability: Quality or commitment? *Journal of Marriage and the Family, 54,* 259–267.

Thornton, A., Axinn, W. G., & Teachman, J. D. (1995). The influence of schoolenrollment and accumulation on cohabitation and marriage in early adulthood. *American Sociological Review, 60,* 762–774.

Thornton, A., & Young-DeMarco, L. (2001). Four decades of trends in attitudes toward family issues in the United States: The 1960s through the 1990s. *Journal of Marriage and the Family, 63,* 1009–1037.

Thornton, A., Young-DeMarco, L., & Goldscheider, F. (1993). Leaving the parental nest: The experience of a young wife cohort in the 1980s. *Journal of Marriage and the Family, 55,* 216–229.

Thorpe, I. (2001). *Ian Thorpe's home page*. Retrieved from http://www.ianthorpe.telstra.com.au/

Thwaites, R., & Dagnan, D. (2004). Moderating variables in the relationship between social comparison and depression: An evolutionary perspective. *Psychology & Psychotherapy: Theory, Research & Practice, 77,* 309–323.

Tichauer, R. (1963). The Aymara children of Bolivia. *Journal of Pediatrics, 62,* 399–412.

Tiedeman, D. V., & Miller-Tiedeman, A. (1985). The trend of life in the human career. *Journal of Career Development, 11,* 221–250.

Tiedeman, D. V., & O'Hara, R. P. (1963). *Career development: Choice and adjustment*. New York, NY: College Entrance Examination Board.

Tiedemann, J. (2000). Parents' gender stereotypes and teachers' beliefs as predictors of children's concept of their mathematical ability in elementary school. *Journal of Educational Psychology, 92,* 144–151.

Tiedemann, J. (2002). Teachers' gender stereotypes as determinants of teacher perceptions in elementary school mathematics. *Educational Studies in Mathematics, 50,* 49–62.

Tiedje, L. G. (2004). Processes of change in work/home incompatibilities: Employed mothers 1986–1999. *Journal of Social Issues, 60,* 787–800.

Timberlake, J. M., & Heuveline, P. (2005). Changes in nonmarital cohabitation and the family structure experiences of children across 17 countries. In L.E. Bass (Ed.), *Sociological studies of children and youth: Special international volume* (Vol. 10, pp. 257–278). Oxford, England: Elsevier Science/JAI Press.

Tither, J. M., & Ellis, B. J. (2008). Impact of fathers on daughters' age at menarche: A genetically and environmentally controlled sibling study. *Developmental Psychology, 44,* 1409–1420.

Tolman, E. C. (1932/1967). *Purposive behavior in rats and men*. New York, NY: Appleton-Century-Crofts.

Tolman, E. C. (1948). Cognitive maps in rats and men. *Psychological Review, 55,* 189–208.

Tomarken, A. J., Dichter, G. S., Garber, J., & Simien, C. (2004). Resting frontal brain activity: Linkages to maternal depression and socioeconomic status among adolescents. *Biological Psychology, 67,* 77–102.

Tomasik, M. J., & Silbereisen, R. K. (2012). Social change and adolescent developmental tasks: The case of post-communist Europe. *Child Development Perspectives, 6,* 326–334.

Tomer, A., & Eliason, G. (2000). Attitudes about life and death: Toward a comprehensive model of death anxiety. In A. Tomer (Ed.), *Death attitudes and the older adult: Theories, concepts, and applications* (pp. 3–22). New York, NY: Brunner-Routledge.

Toohey, S. B., Shinn, M., & Weitzman, B. C. (2004). Social networks and homelessness among women heads of household. *American Journal of Community Psychology, 33,* 7–20.

Torbert, W. R. (1994). Cultivating postformal adult development: Higher stages and contrasting interventions. In M. E. Miller & S. R. Cook-Greuter (Eds.), *Transcendence and mature thought in adulthood: The further reaches of adult development* (pp. 181–203). Lanham, MD: Rowman & Littlefield.

Tornstam, L. (2005). *Gerotranscendence: A developmental theory of positive aging*. New York, NY: Springer.

Toth, S. L., Rogosch, F. A., Sturge-Apple, M., & Cicchetti, D. (2009). Maternal depression, children's attachment security, and representational development: An organizational perspective. *Child Development, 80*, 192–208.

Touron, D. R., & Hertzog, C. (2004). Distinguishing age differences in knowledge, strategy use, and confidence during strategic skill acquisition. *Psychology and Aging, 19*, 452–466.

Tracy, J. L., Shaver, P. R., Albino, A. W., & Cooper, M. L. (2003). Attachment styles and adolescent sexuality. In P. Florsheim (Ed.), *Adolescent romantic relationships and sexual behavior: Theory, research, and practical implications* (pp. 137–159). Mahwah, NJ: Erlbaum.

Tracy, R. L., & Ainsworth, M. D. S. (1981). Maternal affectionate behavior and infant-mother attachment patterns. *Child Development, 52*, 1341–1343.

Tracy, S. J., Lutgen-Sandvik, P., & Alberts, J. K. (2006). Nightmares, demons, and slaves: Exploring the painful metaphor of workplace bullying. *Management Communication Quarterly, 20*, 148–185.

Trawick-Smith, J. (1988). "Let's say you're the baby, OK?": Play leadership and following behavior of young children. *Young Children, 43*, 51–59.

Tremblay, R. E., Nagin, D. S., Séguin, J. R., Zoccolillo, M., Zelazo, P. D., Boivin, M., et al., (2004). Physical aggression during early childhood: Trajectories and predictors. *Pediatrics, 114*, 43–50.

Trethowan, W. (1972). The couvade syndrome. In J. Howells (Ed.), *Modern perspectives in psycho-obstetrics*. New York, NY: Brunner/Mazel.

Trevarthen, C., & Aitken, K. J. (2001). Infant intersubjectivity: Research, theory, and clinical applications. *Journal of Child Psychology and Psychiatry and Allied Disciplines, 42*, 3–48.

Triandis, H. C. (1990). Cross-cultural studies of individualism and collectivism. In J. J. Berman (Ed.), *Nebraska Symposium on Motivation, 1989: Cross-cultural perspectives* (pp. 41–133). Lincoln, NE: University of Nebraska Press.

Triandis, H. C. (1994). *Culture and social behavior*. New York, NY: McGraw-Hill.

Triandis, H. C. (Ser. Ed.). (1995). *New directions in social psychology: Individualism and collectivism*. Boulder, CO: Westview Press.

Triandis, H. C. (1998). Vertical and horizontal individualism and collectivism: Theory and research implications for international comparative management. In J. L. C. Cheng & R. B. Peterson (Eds.), *Advances in international comparative management* (Vol. 12, pp. 7–35). Stamford, CT: JAI Press.

Triandis, H. C., Lambert, W., Berry, J., Lonner, W., Heron, A., Brislin, R., & Draguns, J. (Eds.). (1980). *Handbook of cross-cultural psychology: Vols. 1–6*. Boston, MA: Allyn & Bacon.

Trinh, S. L. (2016). "Enjoy your sexuality, but do it in secret": Exploring undergraduate women's reports of friends' sexual communications. *Psychology of Women Quarterly, 40*, 96–107.

Trionfi, G., & Reese, E. (2009). A good stoy: Children with imaginary companions create richer narratives. *Child Development, 80*, 1301–1313.

Troiden, R. R. (1993). The formation of homosexual identities. In L. D. Garnets & D. C. Kimmel (Eds.), *Psychological perspectives on lesbian and gay male experiences. Between men—between women* (pp. 191–217). New York, NY: Columbia University Press.

Tronick, E. (2008). Multilevel meaning-making and dyadic expansion of consciousness theory: The emotional and the polymorphic polysemic flow of meaning. In D.Fosha, D. J. Siegel, & M. Solomon, (Eds.), *The healing power of emotion: Affective neuroscience, development, and clinical practice* (pp. 86–110). New York, NY: Norton.

Tronick, E., & Beeghly, M. (2011). Infants' meaning-making and the development of mental health problems. *American Psychologist, 66*, 107–119.

Tronick, E. Z. (1989). Emotions and emotional communications in infants. *American Psychologist, 44*, 112–119.

Tronick, E. Z. (2003). Emotions and emotional communication with others. In J. Raphael-Leff (Ed.), *Parent-infant psychodynamics: Wild things, mirrors, and ghosts* (pp. 35–53). London: Whurr.

Tronick, E. Z., Als, H., & Brazelton, R. B. (1979). Early development of neonatal and infant behavior. In F. Falkner & J. M. Tanner (Eds.), *Human growth, Vol. 3. Neurobiology and nutrition* (pp. 305–328). New York, NY: Plenum Press.

Tryon, W. W. (2016). Replication is about effect size: Comment on Maxwell, Lau, and Howard (2015). *American Psychologist, 71*, 236–237.

Trzesniewski, K. H., Donnellan, M. B., & Robins, R. W. (2003). Stability of self-esteem across the life span. *Journal of Personality and Social Psychology, 84*, 205–220.

Tsai, K. M., Telzer, E. H., & Fuligni, A. J. (2013). Continuity and discontinuity in perceptions of family relationships from adolescence to young adulthood. *Child Development, 84*, 471–484.

Tsao, D. (2006). A dedicated system for processing faces. *Science, 314*, 72–73.

Tsao, F. -M., Liu, H. -M., & Kuhl, P. K. (2004). Speech perception in infancy predicts language development in the second year of life: A longitudinal study. *Child Development, 75*, 1067–1084.

Tschann, J. M., Johnston, J. R, & Wallerstein, J. S. (1989). Factors in adults' adjustment after divorce. *Journal of Marriage and the Family, 51*, 1033–1046.

Tu, W., Batteiger, B. E., Weihe, S., Offner, S., VanDerPol, B., Katz, B. P., et al. (2009). Time from first intecourse to firs sexually transmitted infection diagnosis among adolescent women. *Archives of Pediatric and Adolescent Medicine, 163*, 1106–1111.

Tucker, M. B., Taylor, R. J., & Mitchell-Kernan, C. (1993). Marriage and romantic involvement among aged African Americans. *Journal of Gerontology, 48*, S123– S132.

Tucker, R. P., Wingate, L. R., & O'Keefe, V. M. (2016). Historical loss thinking and symptoms of depression are influenced by ethnic experience in American Indian college students. *Cultural Diversity and Ethnic Minority Psychology, 22*, 350–358.

Tucker-Drob, E. M. (2009). Differentiation of cognitive abilities across the life span. *Developmental Psychology, 45*, 1097–1118.

Tucker-Drob, E. M., & Bates, T. C. (2016). Large cross-national differences in gene × socioeconomic status interaction on intelligence. *Psychological Science, 27*, 138–149.

Tudge, J., Putnam, S., & Valsiner, J. (1996). Culture and cognition in developmental perspective. In R. B. Cairns, G. H. Elder, Jr., & E. J. Costello (Eds.), *Developmental science* (pp. 190–222). Cambridge, England: Cambridge University Press.

Tudge, J. R. H. (1992). Processes and consequences of peer collaboration: A Vygotskian analysis. *Child Development, 63*, 1364–1379.

Tudge, J. R. H., & Winterhoff, P. A. (1993). Vygotsky, Piaget, and Bandura: Perspectives on the relations between the social world and cognitive development. *Human Development, 36*, 61–81.

Turiel, E. (2002). *The culture of morality: Social development, context, and conflict*. Cambridge, England: Cambridge University Press.

Turiel, E. (2003). Resistance and subversion in everyday life. *Journal of Moral Education, 32*, 397–409.

Turiel, E. (2006). Social hierarchy, social conflicts and moral development. In C. Daiute, Z. Beykont, C. Higson-Smith, & L. Nucci (Eds.), *International perspectives on youth conflict and development* (pp. 86–99). New York, NY: Oxford University Press.

Turiel, E. (2010). Snap judgement? Not so fast: Thought, reasoning and choice as psychological realities. *Human Development, 53*, 105–109.

Turiel, E. (2015a). Moral development. In W. F. Overton, P. C. M. Molenaar, & R. M. Lerner (Eds.), *Handbook of child psychology and developmental science, Vol.1: Theory and Method* (7th ed.) (pp. 484–522). Hoboken, NJ: John Wiley & Sons.

Turiel, E. (2015b). Morality and prosocial judgments and behavior. In D. A. Schroeder & W. G. Graziano (Eds.), *The Oxford handbook of prosocial behavior. Oxford library of psychology* (pp. 137–152). New York: Oxford University Press.

Turner, J. S., & Rubinson, L. (1993). *Contemporary human sexuality*. Englewood Cliffs, NJ: Prentice Hall.

Twain, M. (1962). *The Adventures of Huckleberry Finn*. New York, NY: Scholastic Book Services.

Twomey, J., LaGasse, L., Derauf, C., Newman, E., Shah, R., et al., (2013). Prenatal methamphetamine exposure, home environment, and primary caregiver risk factors predict child behavioral problems at 5 years. *American Journal of Orthopsychiatry, 83*, 64–72.

Tyson, P. (1996). Object relations, affect management, and psychic structure formation: The concept of object constancy. *Psychoanalytic Study of the Child, 51*, 172–189.

Uchino, B. N., Cacciopo, J. T., & Kiecolt-Glaser, J. K. (1996). The relationship between social support and physiological processes: A review with emphasis on underlying mechanisms and implications for health. *Psychological Bulletin, 119*, 488–531.

UCLA Health System. (2010). Lack of sleep can lead to serious health problems. *Vital Signs, 47*, 6–7.

UCSF Medical Center. (2015). *Infertility in men: Treatment*. Retrieved from http://www.ucsfhealth.org/conditions/infertility_in_men/treatment.html

Uddin, L. Q., Iacoboni, M., Lange, C., & Keenan, J. P. (2007). The self and social cognition: The role of cortical midline structures and mirror neurons. *Trends in Cognitive Science, 11*, 153–157.

Udry, J. R. (1990). Hormonal and social determinants of adolescent sexual initiation. In J. Bancroft & J. M. Reinisch (Eds.), *Adolescence and puberty* (pp. 70–87). New York, NY: Oxford University Press.

Udry, J. R., & Billy, J. O. (1987). Initiation of coitus in early adolescence. *American Sociological Review, 52*, 841–855.

Udry, J. R., Billy, J. O., Morris, N. M., Groff, T. R, & Raj, M. S. (1985). Serum androgenic hormones motivate sexual behavior in adolescent boys. *Fertility and Sterility, 43*, 90–94.

Udry, J. R., Kovenock, J., Morris, N. M., & van den Berg, B. J. (1995). Childhood precursors of age at first intercourse for females. *Archives of Sexual Behavior, 24*, 329–337.

Uecker, J. E., Angotti, N., & Regnerus, M. D. (2008). Going most of the way: "Technical virginity" among American adolescents. *Social Science Research, 37*, 1200–1215.

Umaña-Taylor, A. J., Gonzales-Backen, M. A., & Guimond, A. B. (2009). Latino adolescents' ethnic identity: Is there a developmental progression and does growth in ethnic identity predict growth in self-esteem? *Child Development, 80*, 392–405.

Umbel, V. M., Pearson, B. Z., Fernandez, M. C., & Oller, D. K. (1992). Measuring bilingual children's receptive vocabularies. *Child Development, 63*, 1012–1020.

Umberson, D., Wortman, C. B., & Kessler, R. C. (1992). Widowhood and depression: Explaining long-term gender differences in vulnerability. *Journal of Health and Social Behavior, 33*, 10–24.

UNAIDS. (2006). *Report on the global AIDS epidemic: Executive summary*. Geneva, Switzerland: Author.

Uncapher, H., Gallagher-Thompson, D., Osgood, N. J., & Bongar, B. (1998). Hopelessness and suicidal ideation in older adults. *The Gerontologist, 38*, 62–70.

Underhill, P. A., Shen, P. Lin, Li Jin, A. A., Passarino, G., Yang, W. H., Kauffman, E., et al. (2000). Y chromosome sequence variation and the history of human populations. *Nature Genetics 26*, 358–361.

Underwood, E. (2015). The final countdown: In the race to find a biological clock there are plenty contenders. *Science, 350*, 1188–1190.

Unicef USA. (2016). *Syrian children under siege*. Retrieved from https://www.unicefusa.org/mission/emergencies/child-refugees/syria-crisis

United Nations. (2000). *Child labor, conflict-induced trauma in childen, among key topics in Third Committee Survey of children's rights*. Press Release GA/SHC/3590. Retrieved from http://srch1.un.org/plwebcgi/fastweb?state_id_999965071&view_unsearch&docrank_3&numhitsfound_12&query_child%20slavery&&docid_1804&docdb_pr2000&dbname_web&sorting_BYRELEVANCE&operato_adj&TemplateName_predoc.tmpl&set-Cookie_1

United Nations. (2012). *The Millenium Development Goals Report: Gender Chart, 2012*. Retrieved from http://mdgs.un.org/unsd/mdg/Resources/Static/Products/Progress2012/MDG -Gender-2012.pdf

United Nations. (2015). Millennial development goals and beyond 2015. Goal 5. Improve maternal health. Retrieved from http://www.un.org/millenniumgoals/maternal.shtml

United Nations. (2016). *World Youth Skills Day*. Retrieved from http://www.un.org/en/events/youthskillsday/

United Nations Population Fund. (2015). *The evaluation of comprehensive sexuality education programmes: A focus on the gender and empowerment outcomes*. Retrieved from http://www.unfpa.org/sites/default/files/pub-pdf/UNFPAEvaluationWEB4.pdf

Urban Child Institute. (2016). What is school readiness? Retrieved from http://www.urbanchildinstitute.org/articles/research-to-policy/research/what-do-we-mean-by-school-readiness

U.S. Bureau of Labor Statistics. (2009). *Volunteers by selected characteristics, September 2009*. Retrieved from http://www.bls.gov/news.release/volun.t01.htm

U.S. Bureau of Labor Statistics (2010). *Table 2. Labor force status of persons 16 to 24 years old by school enrollment, educational attainment, sex, race, and Hispanic or Latino ethnicity, October 2009*. Retrieved from www.bls.gov/news.release/hsgec.t02.htm

U.S. Bureau of Labor Statistics. (2010). *Table 7. Employment status of the civilian non-institutional population 25 years and over by educational attainment, sex, race, and Hispanic or Latino ethnicity*. Retrieved from www.bls.gov/cps/cpsaat7.pdfU.S.

U.S. Bureau of Labor Statistics. (2013a). *Employment projections*. Retrieved from http://www.bls.gov/news.release/hsgec.t01.htm

U.S. Bureau of Labor Statistics. (2013b). *Volunteering in the United States, 2012*. Retrieved from http://www.bls.gov/news.release/pdf/volun.pdf

U.S. Bureau of Labor Statistics (2013c). Labor force projections to 2022: The labor force participation rate continues to fall. December, 2013, *Monthly Labor Review*.

U.S. Bureau of Labor Statistics, 2013d. *Employment characteristics of families- 2012*. Retrieved from the internet at HYPERLINK "http://www.bls.gov/news.release/archives/famee_04262013.pdf" http://www.bls.gov/news.release/archives/famee_04262013.pdf

U.S. Bureau of Labor Statistics. (2016a). *American time use survey. Married parents*. Retrieved from http://www.bls.gov/tus/tables/a6_0913.pdf

U.S. Bureau of Labor Statistics. (2016b). *Employment situation summary—July 2016*. Retrieved from http://www.bls.gov/news.release/empsit.nr0.htm

U.S. Bureau of Labor Statistics. (2016c). *Employment status of the civilian noninstitutionalized population 25 years old and over by educational attainment, sex, race, and Hispanic or Latino ethnicity*. Retrieved from http://www.bls.gov/cps/cpsaat07.htm

U.S. Bureau of Labor Statistics. (2016d). *Worker displacement: 2013–2015*. Retrieved from http://www.bls.gov/news.release/pdf/disp.pdf

U.S. Bureau of Labor Statistics. (2016e). *Employed persons by detailed occupation, sex, race and Hispanic or Latino ethnicity*. Retrieved from http://www.bls.gov/cps/cpsaat11.htm

U.S. Census Bureau. (1976). *Population profile of the United State, 1975*. Current Population Reports (Ser. P-20, No. 292). Washington, DC: U.S. Government Printing Office.

U.S. Census Bureau. (1984). *Demographic and socioeconomic aspects of aging in the United States*. Current Population Reports (Ser. P-23, No. 138), 59. Washington, DC: U.S. Government Printing Office.

U.S. Census Bureau. (1986). *Statistical abstract of the United States: 1986*. Washington, DC: U.S. Government Printing Office.

U.S. Census Bureau. (1987). *An aging world*. International Population Reports (Ser. P-95, No. 78). Washington, DC: U.S. Government Printing Office.

U.S. Census Bureau. (1989a). *Population profile of the United States, 1989*. Current Population Reports (Ser. P-23, No. 159). Washington, DC: U.S. Government Printing Office.

U.S. Census Bureau. (1989b). *The Black population in the United States, March, 1988*. Current Population Reports (Ser. P-20, No. 442). Washington, DC: U.S. Government Printing Office.

U.S. Census Bureau. (1991). *Statistical abstract of the United States: 1991*. Washington, DC: U.S. Government Printing Office.

U.S. Census Bureau. (1992). *Statistical abstract of the United States: 1992*. Washington, DC: U.S. Government Printing Office.

U.S. Census Bureau. (1995). *Statistical abstract of the United States: 1995*. Washington, DC: U.S. Government Printing Office.

U.S. Census Bureau. (1996). *Statistical abstract of the United States: 1996*. Washington, DC: U.S. Government Printing Office.

U.S. Census Bureau. (1997). *Statistical abstract of the United States: 1997*. Washington, DC: U.S. Government Printing Office.

U.S. Census Bureau. (1999). *Statistical abstract of the United States: 1999*. Washington, DC: U.S. Government Printing Office.

U.S. Census Bureau. (2000). *Statistical abstract of the United States: 2000*. Washington, DC: U.S. Government Printing Office.

U.S. Census Bureau. (2003). *Current Population Survey, Table 429*. Retrieved from http://nces.ed.gov/programs/digest/d03/tables/dt429.

U.S. Census Bureau. (2006a). *Statistical abstract of the United States: 2006*. Table 85. Washington, DC: U.S. Government Printing Office.

U.S. Census Bureau. (2006b). *Statistical abstract of the United States: 2006*. Table 183. Retrieved from http://www.census.gov/compendia/statab/2006/2006edition.html

U.S. Census Bureau. (2006c). *Statistical abstract of the United States: 2006*. Tables 50, 51, 624, 626. Retrieved from http://www.census.gov/compendia/statab/2006/population/pop.pdf

U.S. Census Bureau. (2006d). *Statistical abstract of the United States: 2006*. Tables 51, 577, 685, 696. Retrieved from http://www.census.gov/compendia/statab/2006/2006edition.html

U.S. Census Bureau. (2006e). *Statistical abstract of the United States: 2006*. Tables 52, 58, 604, 610, 615, 698. Retrieved from http://www.census.gov/compendia/statab/2006/2006edition.html

U.S. Census Bureau. (2006f). *Statistical abstract of the United States: 2006*. Tables 577, 610. Retrieved from http://www.census.gov/compendia/statab/2006/labor_force_employment_earnings/labor.pdf

U.S. Census Bureau. (2007a). *Statistical abstract of the United States: 2007*. Table 111. Deaths and death rates by leading causes of death and age: 2003. Retrieved from http://www.census.gov/prod/2006pubs/07statab/vitstat.pdf

U.S. Census Bureau. (2007b). *Marital history by sex for selected birth cohorts, 1935–39 to 1980 –84: 2004*. Retrieved from http://www.census.gov/population/socdemo/marital-hist/2004/Table1.2004.xls

U.S. Census Bureau. (2007c). *Statistical abstract of the United States: 2006*. Washington, DC: U.S. Government Printing Office.

U.S. Census Bureau. (2007d). *Statistical abstract of the United States: 2007*. Tables 55, 1222. Retrieved from http://www.census.gov/compendia/statab/population/

U.S. Census Bureau. (2007e). *Statistical abstract of the United States: 2007*. Tables 78, 81, 584. Retrieved from http://www.census.gov/compendia/statab/tables/07s0584.xls

U.S. Census Bureau. (2008). *Statistical abstract of the United States, 2008*. Tables 56, 57, 72. Retrieved from http://www.census.gov/prod/2007pubs/08abstract/pop.pdf

U.S. Census Bureau. (2009a). *America's families and living arrangements: 2009*. Table A2. Retrieved from www.census.gov/population/www/socdemo/hh-fam/cps2009.html

U.S. Census Bureau. (2009b). *Statistical abstract of the United States: 2009*. Tables 100, 102. Retrieved from at http://www.census.gov/compendia/statab/cats/births_deaths_marriages_divorces.html

U.S. Census Bureau. (2009c). *Statistical abstract of the United States: 2009*. Tables 676, 697, 1199. Retrieved from http://www.census.gov/prod/2008pubs/09statab/arts.pdf

U.S. Census Bureau. (2010a). *America's families and living arrangements: Current Population Survey, 2009 Annual Social and Economic Supplement*. Table C8. Retrieved from www.census.gov/population/www/socdemo/hh-fam/cps2009.html

U.S. Census Bureau. (2010b). *Statistical abstract of the United States: 2010*. Table 80. Retrieved from www.census.gov/compendia/statab/2010/tables/10s0080.pdf

U.S. Census Bureau. (2010c). *Statistical abstract of the United States: 2010*. Table 232. Preprimary school enrollment—Summary: 1970 to 2007. Retrieved from www.census.gov/compendia/statab/2010/tables/10s0232.pdf

U.S. Census Bureau. (2010d). *Statistical abstract of the United States: 2010*. Table 117. Retrieved from http://www.census.gov/compendia/statab/2010/tables/10s0117.pdf

U.S. Census Bureau. (2010e). *Statistical abstract of the United States: 2010*. Tables 7, 102, 207. Retrieved from http://www.census.gov/compendia/statab/

U.S. Census Bureau. (2010f). *Statistical abstract of the United States: 2010*. Table 57. Retrieved from http://www.census.gov/compendia/statab/2010/tables/10s0057.pdf

U.S. Census Bureau. (2010g). *Statistical abstract of the United States: 2010*. Tables 7, 65. Retrieved from www.census.gov/compendia/statab/cats/population.html

U.S. Census Bureau. (2010h). *Statistical abstract of the United States: 2010*. Tables 100, 113. Retrieved from http://www.census.gov/compendia/statab/

U.S. Census Bureau. (2011a). *More young adults living in their parents' home, Census Bureau Reports*. Retrieved from http://www.census.gov/newsroom/releases/archives/families_households/cb11-183.html

U.S. Census Bureau. (2011b). *Statistical abstract of the United States: 2011*. Table 103. Retrieved from http://www.census.gov/prod/2011pubs/11statab/vitstat.pdf

U.S. Census Bureau. (2012a). *The 2012 Statistical Abstract of the United States*. Table 56. Marital status. Retrieved from http://www.census.gov/compendia/statab/2012/tables/12s0056.pdf

U.S. Census Bureau. (2012b). *2012 Statistical Abstract of the United States*. Table 1202. Retrieved from at http://www.census.gov/compendia/statab/2012/tables/12s1202.pdf

U.S. Census Bureau. (2013a). *America's families and living arrangements: 2011*. Table A1, Marital status of people 15 years old and older by age, sex, personal earnings, race, and Hispanic origin. Retrieved from http://www.census.gov/population/www/socdemo/hh-fam/cps2011.html

U.S. Census Bureau. (2013b). *The older population in the United States: 2011*. Retrieved from http://www.census.gov/population/age/data/2011.html

U.S. Census Bureau. (2013c). *The older population in the United States: 2011*. Retrieved from http://www.census.gov/population/age/data/2011 .html

U.S. Census Bureau. (2013d). *Table 13. Migration flows between regions by sex, age, race and Hispanic origin, 2012 to 2013*. Retrieved from http://www.census.gov/library/publications/2014/demo/p20-574.html

U.S. Census Bureau. (2014). *American Community Survey. Table 1. Household characteristics of opposite-sex and same-sex couple households*. Retrieved from https://www.census.gov/hhes/samesex/data/acs.html

U.S. Census Bureau. (2015a). *Poverty*. Retrieved from https://www.census.gov/hhes/www/poverty/about/overview/

U.S. Census Bureau. (2015b). *Median age at first marriage*. Retrieved from https://www.census.gov/hhes/families/files/graphics/MS-2.pdf

U.S. Census Bureau. (2015c). Young adults living in the parental home. 1960 to present. *Current population survey. Annual social and economic supplements. 1983 to 2015*. Retrieved from http://www.census.gov/hhes/families/files/graphics/AD-1.pdf

U.S. Census Bureau. (2015d). *Current Population Survey. Table A1. Marital status of people 15 years old and over by age, sex, race, and personal earnings, 2015*. Retrieved from https://www.census.gov/hhes/families/files/cps2015/tabA1-all.xls

U.S. Census Bureau. (2015e). *Current Population Survey, 2014. Table 3. Children ever born per 1000 women and percent childless by age and marital status, June 2014*. Retrieved from http://www.census.gov/hhes/fertility/data/cps/2014.html

U.S. Census Bureau. (2015f). *America's families and living arrangements: 2015: Adults*. Retrieved from https://www.census.gov/hhes/families/data/cps2015A.html

U.S. Census Bureau. (2016). *Annual estimates of the resident population for selected age groups by sex for the United States, states, counties, and Puerto Rico commonwealth and municipios: April 1, 2010 to July 1, 2015; 2015 population estimates*. Retrieved from http://factfinder.census.gov/faces/tableservices/jsf/pages/productview.xhtml?src=bkmk

U.S. Department of Labor. (2016a). Mine Safety and Health Administration, MSHA fatality statistics. Retrieved from http://arlweb.msha.gov/stats/charts/chartshome.htm

U.S. Department of Labor. (2016b). Workplace flexibility toolkit. Retrieved from https://www.dol.gov/odep/workplaceflexibility/

U.S. Code of Federal Regulations. (2015). *U.S. Code of Federal Regulations 45*, Head Start Program Performance Standards, CH. XIII (10-1-14 edition) ἐ1304.20 Child health and developmental services.

U.S. Code of Federal Regulations 45, CH. XIII (10-01-02 edition), §1304.21. Program Performance Standards for Operation of Head Start-Education and Early Childhood Development.

U.S. Department of Education. (1995). *Digest of education statistics, 1995*. Washington, DC: U.S. Government Printing Office.

U.S. Department of Education. (2003). *Digest of education statistics, Student use of computers by level of enrollment and selected characteristics: 1993, 1997, and 2001, Table 429*. Washington, DC: U. S. Government Printing Office.

U.S. Department of Education. (2015). *Postsecondary attainment: Differences by socioeconomic status*. National Center for Educational Statistics, Education Longitudinal Study of 2002. Retrieved from http://nces.ed.gov/programs/coe/indicator_tva.asp

U.S. Department of Education. (2016). *IDEA 2005: Building the legacy*. Retrieved from http://idea.ed.gov/part-c/search/new

U.S. Department of Energy. (2003). Human Genome Project: Genomics and Its Impact on Science and Society. The Human Genome Project and Beyond. *Genomics 101: A Primer*. Retrieved from http://www.ornl.gov/sci/techresources/Human_Genome/publicat/primer2001/1.shtml

U.S. Department of Health and Human Services. (2001). *Healthy people 2010*. Washington, DC: U.S. Government Printing Office.

U.S. Department of Health and Human Services. (2005). *Home Health Care Fact Sheet*. Retrieved from http://www.eldercare.gov/eldercare/Public/resources/fact_sheets/home_care.asp

U.S. Department of Health and Human Services (2009a). *Assisted Reproductive Technologies (ART) report*. Retrieved from http://apps.nccd.cdc.gov/ART/Marquee.aspx

U.S. Department of Health and Human Services (2009b). *Healthy People 2020: Public Meetings*. Retrieved from www.healthypeople.gov/HP2020/

U.S. Department of Health and Human Services. (2010). Office of Disease Prevention and Health Promotion. Maternal, infant, and child health. *Healthy People 2020*. Washington, DC. Available at http://healthypeople.gov/2020/topicsobjectives2020/overview.aspx?topicid=26#

U.S. Department of Health and Human Services. (2011). *Head Start approach to school readiness—Overview*. Retrieved from http://eclkc.ohs.acf.hhs.gov/hslc/hs/sr/approach

U.S. Department of Health and Human Services, Office of the Sugeon General, and National Action Allliance for Suicide Prevention. (2012, September). *2012 national strategy for suicide prevention: Goals and objectives for action*. Washington, DC: Department of Health and Human Services.

U.S. Department of Health and Human Services. (2013). Healthy People 2020. *Older Adults-2020*. Retrieved from http://www.healthypeople.gov/2020/topicsobjectives2020/overview.aspx?topicid=31

U.S. Department of Health and Human Services. (2015). Children's Bureau. *The adoption and foster care analysis and reporting system (AFCARS) Report, FY 2014, No. 22*.

U.S. Department of Health and Human Services, Centers for Disease Control and Prevention. (2006). *2004 Assisted Reproductive Technology (ART) report*. Washington, DC: U.S. Government Printing Office.

U.S. Department of Health and Human Services, Office of the Sugeon General, and National Action Alliance for Suicide Prevention. (2012). *2012 National strategy for suicide prevention: Goals and objectives for action*. Washington, DC: Department of Health and Human Services.

U.S. Department of Labor. (1993). *Work and family: Turning thirty–job mobility and labor market attachment*. Report 862. Bureau of Labor Statistics.

U.S. Department of Labor. (2003). *O*NET*. Retrieved from http://www.doleta.gov/programs/onet/

U.S. Department of Labor. (2010). *Occupational outlook handbook: 2008–2018*. Retrieved from www.bls.gov/oco/

U.S. Department of Labor, Employment and Training Administration. (1993). *Selected characteristics of occupations defined inthe revised dictionary of occupational titles*. Washington, DC: U.S. Government Printing Office.

USDA. (2016). *Women, infants and children (WIC)*. Retrieved from http://www.fns.usda.gov/wic/women-infants-and-children-wic

U.S. EEOC. (2013). *Enforcement and litigation statistics*. Retrieved from http://www.eeoc.gov/eeoc/statistics/enforcement/index.cfm

U.S. Living Will Registry. (2010). *Testimonials from registrants*. Retrieved from http://www.uslivingwillregistry.com/testimonials_registrants.shtm

U.S. National Library of Medicine. (2014). *Apgar score*. Retrieved from https://www.nlm.nih.gov/medlineplus/ency/article/003402.htm

U.S. News & World Report. (2005). *Mysteries of the teen years: An essential guide for parents* (Special Edition).

University of California. (2004). *UC and the SAT*. Retrieved from http://www.ucop.edu/news/sat/welcome.html

Urberg, K. A. (1992). Locus of peer influence: Social crowd and best friend. *Journal of Youth and Adolescence, 21*, 439–450.

Urberg, K. A., Shyu, S. J., & Liang, J. (1990). Peer influence in adolescent cigarette smoking. *Addictive Behavior, 115*, 247–255.

USA TODAY. (2013). *Parents say they feel positive about young adult kids*. Retrieved from http:// www.usatoday.com/story/news/nation/2013/05/06/parents-young-adults-survey/2138727/

Usagym.org. (2016). *Simone Biles*. Retrieved from https://usagym.org/pages/athletes/athleteListDetail.html?id=164887

USA.gov. (2016). *Retirement*. Retrieved from https://www.usa.gov/retirement

Vaccaro, A., Kennedy, M. S., & August, G. (2012). *Safe spaces: Making schools and communities welcoming to LGBT youth*. Santa Barbara, CA: Praeger.

Vagi, K. J., Rothman, E. R., Latzman, N. E., et al. (2013). Beyond correlates: A review of risk and protective factors for adolescent dating violence perpetration. *Journal of Youth and Adolescence, 42*, 633–649.

Valas, H. (2001). Learned helplessness and psychological adjustment II: Effects of learning disabilities and low achievement. *Scandinavian Journal of Educational Research, 45*, 101–114.

Valkenburg, P. M., & Peter, J. (2007). Preadolescents' and adolescents' online communication and their closeness to friends. *Developmental Psychology, 43*, 267–277.

Vallotton, C., & Ayoub, C. (2011). Use your words: The role of language in the development of toddlers' self-regulation. *Early Childhood Research Quarterly, 26*, 169–181.

Valsiner, J. (2000). *Culture and human development*. Thousand Oaks, CA: Sage.

Valvano, J., & Rapport, M. J. (2006). Activity-focused motor interventions for infants and young children with neurological conditions. *Infants and Youth Children, 19*, 292–307.

Van der Giessen, D., Branje, S., & Meeus, W. (2014). Perceived autonomy support from parents and best friends: Longitudinal associations with adolescents' depressive symptoms. *Social Development, 23*, 537–555.

van der Kolk B. (2005). Developmental Trauma Disorder: Toward a rational diagnosis for children with complex trauma histories. *Psychiatric Annals, 35*, 401–408.

Van der Mark, I. L., van IJzendoorn, M. H., & Bakermans-Kranenburg, M. J. (2002). Development of empathy in girls during the second year of life: Associations with parenting, attachment, and temperament. *Social Development, 11*, 451–468.

van der Put, C. E., & de Ruiter, C. (2016, December 16). Child maltreatment victimization by type in relation to criminal recidivism in juvenile offenders. *BMC Psychiatry, 16*, article 24.

Van der Vegt, G., Emans, B. J. M., & Van De Vliert, E. (2001). Patterns of interdependence in work teams: A two-level investigation of the relations with job and team satisfaction. *Personnel Psychology, 54*, 51–69.

van Emmerik, H., Bakker, A. B., Westman, M., & Peeters, M. C. W. (2016). Spillover and crossover processes: Consequences for work/life balance. In S. G. Baugh & S. E. Sullivan (Eds.), *Striving for balance* (pp.97–111). Charlotte, NC: U.S.IAP Information Age Publishing.

Van Geert, P. (1998). A dynamic systems model of basic developmental mechanisms: Piaget, Vygotsky and beyond. *Psychological Review, 105*, 634–677.

Van Hiel, A., Mervielde, I., & DeFruyt, F. (2006). Stagnation and generativity: Structure, validity and differential relationship with adaptive and maladaptive personality. *Journal of Personality, 74*, 543–574.

van IJzendoorn, M. H., Goldberg, S., Kroonenberg, P. M., & Frenkel, O. J. (1992). The relative effects of maternal and child problems on the quality of attachment: A meta-analysis of attachment in clinical samples. *Child Development, 63*, 840–858.

van IJzendoorn, M. H., & Kroonenberg, P. M. (1988). Cross-cultural patterns of attachment: A meta-analysis of the strange situation. *Child Development, 59*, 147–156.

Van Lange, P. A. M., & Rusbult, C. E. (2012). Interdependence theory. In P. A. M. Van Lange. A. W. Kruglanski, & E. T. Higgins (Eds.), *Handbook of theories of social psychology* (Vol. 2, pp. 251–272).Thousand Oaks, CA: Sage.

Van Willigen, M. (2000). Differential benefitsof volunteering across the life course. *Journal of Gerontology, 55*, S308–S318.

Vandell, D., Belsky, J., Burchinal, M., Steinberg, L., Vandergrift, N., & the NICHD Early Child Care Research Network. (2010). Do effects of early child care extend to age 15 years? Results from the NICHD Study of Early Child Care and Youth Development. *Child Development, 81*(3).

Vanhalst, J., Soenens, B., Luyckx, K., Van Petegem, S., Weeks, M. S., & Asher, S. R. (2015). Why do the lonely stay lonely? Chronically lonely adolescents' attributions and emotions in situations of social inclusion and exclusion. *Journal of Personality and Social Psychology, 109*, 232–248.

Vannoy, D. (1995). A paradigm of roles in the divorce process: Implications for divorce adjustment, future commitments, and personal growth. *Journal of Divorce and Remarriage, 24*, 71–87.

Vassoler, F. M., Byrnes, E. M., & Pierce, R. C. (2014). The impact of exposure to addictive drugs on future generations: Physiological and behavioral effects. *Neuropharmacology, 76.*

Vatička, P., & Vuilleumier, P. (2012). Neuroscience of human social interactions and adult attachment style. *Frontiers in Human Neuroscience, 6*, Article 212.

Vaughn, B., Egeland, B., Sroufe, L. A., & Waters, E. (1979). Individual differences in infant-mother attachment at 12 and 18 months: Stability and change in families under stress. *Child Development, 50*, 971–975.

Vaughn, B. E., Bost, K. K., & van Ijzendoorn, M. H. (2008). Attachment and temperament: Additive and interactive influenceson behavior, affect and cognition during infancy and childhood. In J. Cassidy & P. R. Shaver (Eds.), *Handbook of attachment: Theory, research and clinical applications* (pp. 192–216). New York, NY: Guilford.

Vaughn, B. E. & Bost, K. K. (2016). Attachment and temperament as intersecting developmental products and interacting developmental contexts throughout infancy and childhood. In J. Cassidy & P.R. Shaver (Eds.), *Handbook of attachment* (3rd ed.). New York: Guilford Press.

Vaughn, B. E., Colvin, T. N., Azria, M. R., Caya, L., & Krzysik, L. (2001). Dyadic analyses of friendship in a sample of preschool-age children attending Head Start: Correspondence between measures and implications for social competence. *Child Development, 72*, 862–878.

Vaughn, B. E., Lefever, G. B., Seifer, R., & Barglow, P. (1989). Attachment behavior, attachment security, and temperament during infancy. *Child Development, 60*, 728–737.

Veenhoven, R. (2000). Freedom and happiness: A comparative study in forty-four nations in the early 1990s. In E. Diener & E. M. Suh (Eds.), *Culture and subjective well-being* (pp. 257–288). Cambridge, MA: MIT Press.

Veenman, M. V. J., Wilhelm, P., & Beishuizen, J. J. (2004). The relation between intellectual and metacognitive skills from a developmental perspective. *Learning and Instruction, 14*, 89–109.

Veenstra, R., Lindenberg, S., Munniksma, A., & Dijkstra, J. K. (2010). The complex relation between bullying, victimization, acceptance, and rejection: Giving special attention to status, affection and sex differences. *Child Development, 81*, 480–486.

Vega, W. A., Zimmerman, R. S., Warheit, G. J., Apospori, E., & Gil, A. G. (1993). Risk factors for adolescent drug use in four ethnic and racial groups. *American Journal of Public Health, 83*, 185–189.

Venables, P. H. & Raine, A. (2016). The impact of malnutrition on intelligence at 3 and 11 years of age: The mediating role of temperament. *Developmental Psychology, 52*, 205–220.

Venter, J. C., Adams, M. D., Myers, E. W., et al. (2001). The sequence of the human genome. *Science, 291*, 1304–1351.

Ventura, S. J., & Hamilton, B. E. (2011). U.S. teenage birth rate resumes decline. *NCHS Data Brief, 58.*

Verhaeghen, P., Geraerts, N., & Marcoen, A. (2000). Memory complaints, coping, and well-being in old age: A systemic approach. *The Gerontologist, 40*, 540–548.

Verhoef, H., & Michel, C. (1997). Studying morality within the African context: Model of moral analysis and construction. *Journal of Moral Education, 26*, 389–407.

Verhoeven, L. (2001). Prevention of reading difficulties. In L. Verhoeven & C. Snow (Eds.), *Literacy and motivation: Reading engagement in individuals and groups* (pp. 123–134). Mahwah, NJ: Erlbaum.

Verkuyten, M., & DeWolf, A. (2007). The development of in-group favoritism: Between social reality and group identity. *Developmental Psychology, 43*, 901–911.

Vernon-Feagans, L., Willougby, M., Garrett-Peters, P., & the Family Life Project Key Investigators. (2016). Predictors of behavioral regulation in kindergarten: Household chaos, parenting, and early executive functions. *Developmental Psychology, 52*, 430–441.

Vespa, J., Lewis, J. M., & Kreider, R. M. (2013). *America's families and living arrangements: 2012.* Retrieved from https://www.census .gov/prod/2013pubs/p20-570.pdf

Villar, F. (2012). Successful ageing and development: The contribution of generativity in older age. *Ageing and Society, 32*, 1078–1105.

Villar, F., Celdrán, M., Triadó, C. (2012). Grandmothers offering regular auxiliary care for their grandchildren: An expression of generativity in later life? *Journal of Women and Aging, 24*, 292–312.

Vinokur, A., Caplan, R. D., & Williams, C. C. (1987). Effects of recent and past stress on mental health: Coping with unemployment among Vietnam veterans and non-veterans. *Journal of Applied Social Psychology, 17*, 708–728.

Violato, C., & Holden, W. B. (1988). A confirmatoy factor analysis of a four-factor model of adolescent concerns. *Journal of Youth and Adolescence, 17*, 101–113.

Vizziello, G. F., Antonioloi, M. E., Cocci, V., & Invernizzi, R. (1993). From pregnancy to motherhood: The structure of representative and narrative change. *Infant Mental Health Journal, 14*, 4–16.

Voelker-Rehage, C., Godde, B., & Staudinger, U.M. (2010). Physical and motor fitness are both related to cognition in old age. *European Journal of Neuroscience, 31*, 167–176.

Vogel, G. (2001). Human cloning plans spark talk of U.S. ban. *Science, 292*, 31.

Vogel, E. A., Rose, J. P., Okdie, B. M., Eckles, K. & Franz, B. (2015). Who compares and despairs? The effect of social comparison orientation on social media use and its outcomes. *Personality and Individual Differences, 86,* 249–256.

Vogl-Bauer, S. (2003). Maintaining family relationships. In D. J. Canary & M. Dainton (Eds.), *Maintaining relationships through communication: Relational, contextual, and cultural variations* (pp. 31–49). Mahwah, NJ: Erlbaum.

Volling, B. L., Youngblade, L. M., & Belsky, J. (1997). Young children's social relationships with siblings and friends. *American Journal of Orthopsychiatry, 67,* 102–111.

Vondracek, F. W., Schulenberg, J., Skorikov, V., & Gillespie, L. (1995). The relationship of identity status to career indecision during adolescence. *Journal of Adolescence, 18,* 17–29.

Vouloumanos, A., Hauser, M. D., Werker, J. F., & Martin, A. (2010). The tuning of human neonates' preference for speech. *Child Development, 81,* 517–527.

Voydanoff, P. (2004). The effects of work demands and resources on work-to-family conflict and facilitation. *Journal of Marriage and the Family, 66,* 398–412.

Voydanoff, P. (2005). Consequences of boundary-spanning demands and resources for work-to-family conflict and perceived stress. *Journal of Occupational Health Psychology, 10,* 491–503.

Vreeswijk, C. M. J. M., Maas, A., Janneke, B. M., et al. (2014). Stability of fathers' representations of their infants during the transition to parenthood. *Attachment and Human Development, 16,* 292–306.

Vrijkotte, T. G. M., van der Wal, M. F., van Eijsden, M. & Bonsel, G. J. (2009). First-trimester working conditions and birth weight: A prospective cohort study. *American Journal of Public Health, 99,* 1409–1416.

Vuchinich, S. (1987). Starting and stopping spontaneous family conflicts. *Journal of Marriage and the Family, 49,* 591–601.

Vygotsky, L. S. (1962). *Thought and language.* Cambridge, MA: MIT Press.

Vygotsky, L. S. (1978a). Tool and symbol in child development. In M. L. S. Cole, V. John-Steiner, S. Scribner, & E. Souberman, (Eds.), *Mind in society: The development of higher psychological processes* (pp. 19–30). Cambridge, MA: Harvard University Press.

Vygotsky, L. S. (1978b). Interaction between learning and development. In M. L. S. Cole, V. John-Steiner, S. Scribner, & E. Souberman (Eds.), *Mind in society: The development of higher psychological processes* (pp. 79–92). Cambridge, MA: Harvard University Press.

Vygotsky, L. S. (1978c). *Mind in society.* Cambridge, MA: Harvard University Press.

Vygotsky, L. S. (1987). Genetic roots of thinking and speech. In R. W. Rieber & A. S. Carton (Eds.), *The collected works of L. S. Vygotsky: Vol. 1. Problems of general psychology* (pp. 101–120). New York, NY: Plenum.

Waas, G. A. (1988). Social attributional biases of peer-rejected and aggressive children. *Child Development, 59,* 969–975.

Wagenmakers, E., Wetzels, R., Borsboom, D., Van der Maas, H. L. J., & Kievit, R. A. (2012). An agenda for purely confirmatory research. *Perspectives on Psychological Science, 7,* 632–638.

Wagner, B. M., & Phillips, D. A. (1992). Beyond beliefs: Parent and child behaviors and children's perceived academic competence. *Child Development, 63,* 1380–1391.

Wagner, R., & Harter, J. (2008). The tenth element of great managing. *Gallup Business Journal.* Retrieved from http://www.gallup.com/businessjournal /104197/Tenth-Element-Great-Managing .aspx?g_source=ELEMENT_10_BEST _FRIEND&g_medium=topic&g_ campaign=tiles

Wahlstrom, K., Dretzke, B., Gordon, M., Peterson, K., Edwards, K., & Gdula, J. (2014). *Examining the impact of later school start times on the health and academic performance of high school students: A multi-site study.* Center for Applied Research and Educational Improvement. St. Paul, MN: University of Minnesota.

Wahowiak, L. (2015). Health advocates working to prevent athlete concussions. *The Nation's Health, October, 2015,* 1, 16.

Wakefield, J. R. H., Sani, F., Madhok, V. et al. (2016, May 6). The relationship between group identification and satisfaction with life in a cross-cultural community sample. *Journal of Happiness Studies.*

Walcott, C. M., Scheemaker, A., Bielski, K. (2010). A longitudinal investigation of inattention and preliteracy development. *Journal of Attention Disorders, 14,* 79–85.

Waldfogel, J., Craigie, T., & Brooks-Gunn, J. (2010). Fragile families and child wellbeing. *The Future of Children, 20,* 87–112.

Waldman, I. R. (1996). Aggressive boys' hostile perceptual and response biases: The role of attention and impulsivity. *Child Development, 67,* 1015–1033.

Walker, A. (1991). Beauty: When the other dancer is the self. In H. L. Gates, Jr. (Ed.), *Bearing witness: Selections from African-American autobiography in the twentieth century* (pp. 257–258). New York, NY: Pantheon Books.

Walker, L J., de Vries, B., & Trevethan, S. D. (1987). Moral stages and moral orientations in real-life and hypothetical dilemmas. *Child Development, 58,* 842–858.

Walker, L. J., Gustafson, P., & Hennig, K. H. (2001). The consolidation/transition model in moral reasoning development. *Developmental Psychology, 37,* 187–197.

Walker, R. (2002). Case study, case records, and multimedia. *Cambridge Journal of Education, 32,* 109–127.

Walker, R. M. (2001). Physician-assisted suicide: The legal slippery slope. *Cancer Control, 8,* 25–31.

Walker-Andrews, A. S. (1986). Intermodal perception of expressive behaviors: Relation of eye and voice? *Developmental Psychology, 22,* 373–377.

Walker-Andrews, A. S., & Harris, P. L. (1993). Young children's comprehension of pretend causal sequences. *Developmental Psychology, 29,* 915–921.

Wallace, E., Hayes, D., & Jerger, J. (1994). Neurotology of aging: The auditory system. In M. L. Albert & J. E. Knoefel (Eds.), *Clinical neurology of aging* (2nd ed., pp. 448–464). New York, NY: Oxford University Press.

Wallace, K. (2016). Olympic gymnast Simone Biles' lessons from mom. *CNN.* Retrieved from http://www.cnn.com/2016/04/27 /health/simone-biles-olympics-mom-100 -days-until-rio/index.html?eref=rss_health

Wallechinsky, D., & Wallace, A. (1993). *The book of lists.* New York, NY: Little, Brown.

Wallechinsky, D., Wallace, I., & Wallace, A. (1977). *The book of lists.* New York, NY: Morrow.

Waller, R., Gardner, F., Hyde, L. W., Shaw, D. S., Dishion, T. J., & Wilson, M. N. (2012). Do harsh and positive parenting predict parent reports of deceitful-callous behavior in early childhood? *Journal of Child Psychology and Psychiatry, 53,* 946–953.

Wallerstein, I., & Smith, J. (1991). Households as an institution of the world economy. In R. L. Blumberg (Ed.), *Gender, family, and economy: The triple overlap* (pp. 225–242). Newbury Park, CA: Sage.

Wallerstein, J. S., & Blakeslee, S. (1995). *The good marriage.* New York, NY: Houghton Mifflin.

Wallerstein, J. S., & Corbin, S. B. (1989). Daughters of divorce: Report from a 10-year follow-up. *American Journal of Orthopsychiatry, 59,* 593–604.

Wallien, M. S. C., van Goozen, S. H. M., & Cohen-Kettenis, P. T. (2007). Physiological correlates of anxiety in children with gender identity disorder. *European Child and Adolescent Psychiatry, 16,* 309–315.

Walters, S. R., Payne, D., Schluter, P. J., & Thomson, R. W. (2015). "It just makes you feel invincible.": A Foucauldian analysis of children's experiences of organized team sports. *Sport, Education and Society, 20,* 241–257.

Walther, J. B. (2011). Theories of computer-mediated communication and interpersonal relations. In M. L. Knapp & J. A. Daly (Eds.) *The Sage handbook of interpersonal communication* (4th ed., pp. 443–480). Thousand Oaks, CA: Sage.

Walton, G. M., & Cohen, G. L. (2011). A brief social-belonging intervention improves academic and health outcomes of minority students. *Science, 331,* 1447–1451.

Wang, G. -Z., & Buffalo, M. D. (2004). Social and cultural determinants of attitudes toward abortion. *Social Science Journal, 41,* 93–105.

Wang, H., & Amato, P. R. (2000). Predictors of divorce adjustment: Stressors, resources, and definition. *Journal of Marriage and the Family, 62,* 655–668.

Wang, Q. (2001). Culture effects on adults' earliest childhood recollection and self-description: Implications for the relation between memory and the self. *Journal of Personality and Social Psychology, 81,* 220–233.

Wang, Q. I., & Koh, J. B. K. (2015). How will things be the next time? Self in the construction of future events among school-aged children. *Consciousness and Cognition: An International Journal, 36,* 131–138.

Wang, Q., Leichtman, M. D., & Davies, K. (2000). Sharing memories and telling stories: American and Chinese mothers and their 3-year-olds. *Memory, 8,* 159–177.

Wang, Y., & Benner, A. D. (2016). Cultural socialization across contexts: Family-peer congruence and adolescent well-being. *Journal of Youth and Adolescence, 45,* 594–611.

Wargo, E. (2008). Talk to the hand: New insights into the evolution of language and gesture. *Observer, 21,* 16–21.

Warneken, F. (2015). Precocious prosociality: Why do children help? *Child Development Perspectives, 9,* 1–6.

Warren, E. (2003). *The two-income family trap: Why middle class mothers and fathers are going broke.* New York, NY: Basic Books.

Warren, E. (2007). The vanishing middle class. In J. Edwards, M. Crain, & A. L. Kalleberg (Eds.), *Ending poverty in America: How to restore the American dream.* Chapel Hill, NC: The New Press.

Warren, E., & Tyagi, E. W. (2003/2016). *The two income trap. Why middle-class parents are (still) going broke.* New York: Basic Books. Updated and revised paperback, 2016.

Warshaw, G. (2006). Advances and challenges in care of older people with chronic illness. *Generations, 30,* 5–10.

Waterman, A. S. (1982). Identity development from adolescence to adulthood: An extension of theory and review of research. *Developmental Psychology, 18,* 341–358.

Waterman, A. S. (1992). Identity as an aspect of optimal psychological functioning. In G. Adams, T. P. Gullotta, & R. Mon-temayor (Eds.), *Adolescent identity formation: Advances in adolescent development* (Vol. 4., pp. 50–72). Newbury Park, CA: Sage.

Waterman, A. S., & Whitbourne, S. K. (1981). The inventory of psychosocial development. *Journal Supplement Abstract Service: Catalog of Selected Documents in Psychology, 11* (Ms. No. 2179).

Waters, E., & Beauchaine, T. P. (2003). Are there really patterns of attachment? Comment on Fraley and Spieker. *Developmental Psychology, 39,* 417–422.

Waters, E., Merick, S., Treboux, D., Crowell, J., & Albersheim, L. (2000). Attachment security in infancy and early adulthood: A twenty-year longitudinal study. *Child Development, 71,* 684–689.

Waters, S. F., West, T. V., & Mendes, W. B. (2014). Stress contagion: Physiological co-variation between mothers and infants. *Psychological Science, 25,* 934–942.

Watson, W., Koehn, J., & Desrochers, L. (2012). Expanding quality for infants and toddlers: Colorado implements Touchpoints. *Young Children, 67,* 58–64.

Watson-Jones, R. E., & Legare, C. H. (2016). The social functions of group rituals. *Current Directions in Psychological Science, 25,* 42–46.

Watson-Jones, R. E., Whitestone, H., & Legare, C. H. (2016). In-group ostracism increases high-fidelity imitation in early childhood. *Psychological Science, 27,* 34–42.

Waxman, S. R., & Lidz, J. (2006). Early word learning. In W. Damon, R. M. Lerner, D. Kuhn, & R. Siegler (Eds.), *Handbook of child psychology: Cognition, perception, and language* (6th ed., pp. 299–335). New York, NY: Wiley.

Weatherston, D. J. (2001). Infant mental health: A review of relevant literature. *Psychoanalytic Social Work, 8,* 39–69.

Weaver, I. C. G, Cervoni, N., Champagne, F. A., D'Alessio A. C., Sharma, S., Seckl, J. R., Dymov, S., Szyf, M., & Meaney, M. J. (2004). Epigenetic programming by maternal behavior. *Nature Neuroscience, 7,* 847–854.

Webb, M. (1997). *The good death: The new American search to reshape the end of life.* New York, NY: Bantam Books.

Weber, C., Hahne, A., Friedrich, M., & Friederici, A. D. (2004). Discrimination of word stress in early infant perception: Electrophysiological evidence. *Cognitive Brain Research, 18,* 149–161.

Weber, J. B. (2012). Becoming teen fathers: Stories of teen pregnancy, responsibility, and masculinity. *Gender and Society, 26,* 900–921.

WebMD. (2013). *Social Anxiety Disorder, Topic overview.* Retrieved from http://www.webmd.com/anxiety-panic/tc/social-anxiety-disorder-topic

WebMD. (2014). *Teen pregnancy: Medical risks and realities.* Retrieved from http://www.webmd.com/baby/guide/teen-pregnancy-medical-risks-and-realities?page=2

WebMD. (2015). Suicidal thoughts. *eMedicine Health,* Retrieved from http://www.emedicinehealth.com/suicidal_thoughts/article_em.htm

Weinfield, N. S., Soufe, L. A., Egeland, B., & Carlson, E. A. (2008). The nature of individual differences in infant-caregiver attachment. In J. Cassidy & P. R. Shaver (Eds.), *Handbook of attachment: Theory, research and clinical applications* (pp. 78–101). New York, NY: Guilford.

Weingarden, H., & Renshaw, K. D. (2012). Early and late perceived pubertal timing as risk factors for anxiety disorders in adult women. *Journal of Psychiatric Research, 46,* 1524–1529.

Weinreb, L., & Buckner, J. C. (1993). Homeless families: Program responses and public policies. *American Journal of Orthopsychiatry, 63,* 400–409.

Weinstein, R. S., Marshall, H. H., Sharp, L., & Botkin, M. (1987). Pygmalion and the student: Age and classroom differences in children's awareness of teacher expectations. *Child Development, 58,* 1079–1093.

Weintraub, K. (2016). Young and sleep deprived. *Monitor on Psychology, 47,* 46–50.

Weir, K. (2016). The risks of earlier puberty. *Monitor on Psychology, 47,* 41–44.

Weisgram, E. S., Bigler, R. S., & Liben, L. S. (2010). Gender, values, and occupational interests among children, adolescents and adults. *Child Development, 81,* 778–796.

Weismantle, M. (2001). Reasons people do not work, 1996. *Current Population Reports* (pp. 70–76). Washington, DC: U.S. Department of Commerce.

Weisner, T. S. (2005). Attachment as a cultural and ecological problem with pluralistic solutions. *Human Development, 48,* 89–94.

Weisner, T. S., & Lowe, E. (2004). Globalization and the psychological anthropology of childhood and adolescence. In C. Casey & R. Edgerton (Eds.), *A companion to psychological anthropology: Modernity and psychocultural change* (pp. 1–48). Oxford, England: Blackwell.

Weiss, B., Dodge, K. A., Bates, J. E., & Petit, G. S. (1992). Some consequences of early harsh discipline: Child aggression and a maladaptive social information processing style. *Child Development, 63,* 1321–1335.

Weiss, R. L., & Heyman, R. E. (1997). A clinical-research overview of couples interactions. In W. K. Halford & H. J. Markman (Eds.), *Clinical handbook of marriage and couples intervention* (pp. 13–41). Chichester, England: Wiley.

Weiss, R. S. (1997). Adaptation to retirement. In I. H. Gotlib & B. Wheaton (Eds.), *Stress and adversity over the life course: Trajectories and turning points* (pp. 232–245). New York, NY: Cambridge University Press.

Wellman, H. M. (2014). *Making minds: How theory of mind develops.* New York: Oxford University Press.

Wellman, H. M., Cross, D., & Bartsch, K. (1986). Infant search and object permanence: A meta-analysis of the A-not-B error. *Monographs of the Society for Research in Child Development, 51*(3, No. 214).

Wellman, H. M., Cross, D., & Watson, J. (2001). Meta-analysis of theory-of-mind development: The truth about false belief. *Child Development, 71,* 655–684.

Wentowski, G. J. (1985). Older women's perceptions of great-grandmotherhood: A research note. *The Gerontologist, 25,* 593–596.

Wentzel, K. R., Barry, C. M., & Caldwell, K. A. (2004). Friendships in middle school: Influences on motivation and schooladjustment. *Journal of Educational Psychology, 96,* 195–203.

Wenxin, Z., Meiping, W., & Fuligni, A. (2006). Expectations for autonomy, beliefs about parental authority, and parent-adolescent conflict. *Acta Psychologica Sinica, 38,* 868–876.

Werker, J. F., Yeung, H. H., & Yoshida, K. A. (2012). How do infants become experts at native speech perception? *Current Directions in Psychological Science, 21,* 221–226.

Werner, C. A. (2011). The older population: 2010. *2010 Census Briefs.* Retrieved from http://www.census.gov/prod/cen2010/briefs/c2010br-09.pdf

Wesley, P. W., & Buysse, V. (2003). Making meaning of school readiness in schools and communities. *Early Childhood Research Quarterly, 18,* 351–375.

West, J. R. (1986). *Alcohol and brain development.* London: Oxford University Press.

West, M., & Newton, P. (1983). *The transition from school to work.* London: Croom Helm.

West, R. L., Crook, T. H., & Barron, K. L. (1992). Everyday memory performance across the life span: Effects of age and non-cognitive individual differences. *Psychology and Aging, 7,* 72–82.

Wethington, E., Moen, P., Glasgow, N., & Pillemer, K. (2000). Multiple roles, social integration, and health. In K. Pillemer & P. Moen (Eds.), *Social integration in the second half of life* (pp. 48–71). Baltimore, MD: Johns Hopkins University Press.

Wharton School. (2007). *Workplace loyalties change, but the value of mentoring doesn't.* Retrieved from http://knowledge.wharton.upenn.edu/article/workplace-loyalties-change-but-the-value-of-mentoring-doesn't/

Whipple, N., Bernier, A., & Mageau, G. A. (2011). Broadening the study of infant security of attachment: Maternal autonomy-support in the context of infant exploration. *Social Development, 20,* 17–32.

Whisman, M. A., Uebelacker, L. A., Tolejko, N., Chatav, Y., & McKelvie, M. (2006). Marital discord and well-being in older adults: Is the association confounded by personality? *Psychology and Aging, 21,* 626–631.

Whitall, J., & Getchell, N. (1995). From walking to running: Applying a dynamical systems approach to the development of locomotor skills. *Child Development, 66,* 1541–1553.

Whitbourne, J. (2002). The dropout dilemma: One in four college freshmen drop out. What is going on here? What does it take to stay in? *Findarticles.com.* Retrieved from http://findarticles.com/p/articles/mi_m0BTR/is_4-22/ai_84599442/

Whitbourne, S. K., Sneed, J. R., & Sayer, A. (2009). Psychosocial development from college through midlife: A 34-year sequential study. *Developmental Psychology, 45,* 1328–1340.

Whitbourne, S. K., Zuschlag, M. K., Elliot, L. B., & Waterman, A. S. (1992). Psychosocial development in adulthood: A 22-year sequential study. *Journal of Personality and Social Psychology, 63,* 260–271.

White, A. M., Philogene, G. S., Fine, L., & Sarbajit, S. (2009). Social support and self-reported health status of older adults in the United States. *American Journal of Public Health, 99,* 1872–1878.

White, B. L., Kaban, B. T., & Attanucci, J. S. (1979). *The origins of human competence.* Lexington, MA: Heath.

White, J. M., Wampler, R. S., & Winn, K. I. (1998). The identity style inventory: A revision with a sixth grade reading level (ISI-6G). *Journal of Adolescent Research, 13,* 223–245.

White, L., & Rogers, S. J. (2000). Economic circumstances and family outcomes: A review of the 1990s. *Journal of Marriage and the Family, 62,* 1035–1051.

White, N. R. (2002). "Not under my roof!" Young people's experience of home. *Youth and Society, 34,* 214–231.

White, R. W. (1959). Motivation reconsidered. The concept of competence. *Psychological Review, 66,* 297–333.

White, R. W. (1960). Competence and the psychosexual stages of development. In M. R. Jones (Ed.), *Nebraska Symposium on Motivation* (Vol. 8). Lincoln, NE: University of Nebraska Press.

White, R. W. (1966). *Lives in progress* (2nd ed.). New York, NY: Holt, Rinehart & Winston.

White, R. W. (1974). Strategies of adaptation: An attempt at systematic description. In G. V. Coelho, D. A. Hamburg, & J. E. Adams (Eds.), *Coping and adaptation* (pp. 47–68). New York, NY: Basic Books.

White, T., & Ettner, R. (2007). Adaptation and adjustment in children of transsexual parents. *European Child and Adolescent Psychiatry, 16,* 215–221.

White House. (2013). *Fact Sheet President Obama's Plan for Early Education for All Americans.* Retrieved from https://www.whitehouse.gov/the-press-office/2013/02/13/fact-sheet-president-obama-s-plan-early-education-all-americans

Whiting, B. B., & Edwards, C. P. (1992). *Children of different worlds: The formation of social behavior.* Cambridge, MA: Harvard University Press.

Wholwend, K. E. (2009). Early adopters: Playing new literacies and pretending new technologies in print-centric classrooms. *Journal of Early Childhood Literacy, 9,* 117–140.

Wieber, J. (2013). *Jordyn Wieber.* Retrieved from www.jordynweiber.com

Wierson, M., Long, P. J., & Forehand, R. L. (1993). Toward a new understanding of early menarche: The role of environmental stress in pubertal timing. *Adolescence, 28,* 912–924.

Wiesmann, U., & Hannich, H. -J. (2011). A salutogenic analysis of developmental tasks and ego integrity versus despair. *The International Journal of Aging and Human Development, 73,* 351–369.

Wiesmann, U., & Hannich, H. -J. (2013, March 7). A salutogenic analysis of the well-being paradox in older age. *Journal of Happiness Studies.* First posting.

Wilcox, A. J., & Skjoerven, R. (1992). Birth weight and perinatal mortality. The effect of gestational age. *American Journal of Public Health, 82,* 378–382.

Wilcox, D. C., Wilcox, B. J., Hsueh, W. C., & Suzuki, M. (2006). Genetic determinants of exceptional human longevity: Insights from the Okinawa Centenarian Study. *Age, 28,* 313–332.

Wilcox, T., Schweinle, A., & Chapa, C. (2003). Object individuation in infancy. In H. Hayne & J. Fagen (Eds.), *Progress in infancy research* (Vol. 3, pp. 193–243). Mahwah, NJ: Erlbaum.

Wilcox, T., Woods, R., Tuggy, L., & Napoli, R. (2006). Shake, rattle, and . . . one or two objects? Young infants' use of auditory information to individuate objects. *Infancy, 9,* 97–123.

Wildsmith, E., Barry, M., Manlove, J., & Vaughn, B. (2013). Dating and sexual relationships. *Child Trends, Adolescent Health Highlight, No.1,* 1–10.

Wildsmith, E., Guzzo, K. B., & Hayford, S. R. (2010). Repeat unintended, unwanted and seriously mistimed childbearing in the United States. *Perspectives on Sexual and Reproductive Health, 42,* 14–22.

Wilhelm, M. O., & Bekkers, R. (2010). Helping behavior, dispositional empathic concern, and the principle of care. *Social Psychology Quarterly, 73,* 11–32.

Willetts, M. C. (2006). Union quality comparisons between long-term heterosexual cohabitation and legal marriage. *Journal of Family Issues, 27,* 110–127.

Williams, A. (2015, September 20). Move over millennials here comes Generation Z. *The New York Times.* Retrieved from http://www.nytimes.com/2015/09/20/fashion/move-over-millennials-here-comes-generation-z.html

Williams, D. (2000). Ian Thorpe. *Time, 156,* 76–77.

Williams, D. R. (2012). Miles to go before we sleep: Racial inequities in health. *Journal of Health and Social Behavior, 53,* 279–295.

Williams, H., & Monsma, E. V. (2006). Assessment of gross motor development. In B. A. Bracken & R. J. Nagle (Eds.), *Psychoeducational Assessment of Preschool Children* (4th ed., pp. 397–433). New York, NY: Routledge.

Williams, J. A., Zimmerman, F. J., & Bell, J. F. (2013). Norms and trends of sleep time among U.S. children and adolescents. *JAMA Pediatrics, 167,* 55–60.

Williams, J. C., & Cooper, H. C. (2004). The public policy of motherhood. *Journal of Social Issues, 60,* 849–865.

Williams, J. M., & Currie, C. (2000). Self-esteem and physical development in early adolescence: Pubertal timing and body image. *Journal of Early Adolescence, 20,* 129–149.

Williams, K. (2003). Has the future of marriage arrived? A contemporary examination of gender, marriage, and psychological well-being. *Journal of Health and Social Behavior, 44,* 470–487.

Williams, T. K., & Thornton, M. C. (1998). Social construction of ethnicity versus personal experience: The case of

Afro-Amerasians. *Journal of Comparative Family Studies, 29,* 255–267.

Williams, W. L. (1992). *Spirit and the flesh: Sexual diversity in American Indian culture.* Boston, MA: Beacon Press.

Wilson, B. (2008). Media and children's aggression, fear and altruism. *Children and Electronic Media, 18,* 87–118.

Wilson, B. J., Smith, S. L., Potter, W. J., Kunkel, D., Linz, D., Colvin, C. M., et al. (2002). Violence in children's television programming: Assessing the risks. *Journal of Communication, 52,* 5–35.

Wilson, R. S., & Matheny, A. P., Jr. (1986). Behavior genetics research in infant temperament: The Louisville twin study. In R. Plomin & J. Dunn (Eds.), *The study of temperament: Changes, continuities, and challenges.* Hillsdale, NJ: Erlbaum.

Wilson, S. M., Peterson, G. W., & Wilson, P. (1993). The process of educational and occupational attainment of adolescent females from low-income, rural families. *Journal of Marriage and the Family, 55,* 158–175.

Wilson, T. A. (2006). Congenital adrenal hyperplasia. *eMedicine.* Retrieved from http://www.emedicine.com/ped/topic48.htm

Wilson, T. D. (2009). Know thyself. *Perspectives on Psychological Science, 4,* 384–389.

Wilson, T. D., LaFleur, S. J., & Anderson, D. E. (1996). The validity and consequences of verbal reports about attitudes. In N. Schwarz & S. Sudum (Eds.), *Answering questions: Methodology for determining cognitive processes in survey research* (pp. 91–114). San Francisco, CA: Jossey Bass.

Winer, J. P., Parent, J., Forehand, R., & Breslend, N. L. (2016). Interactive effects of psychosocial stress and early pubertal timing on youth depression and anxiety: Contextual amplification in family and peer environments. *Journal of Child and Family Studies, 25,* 1375–1384.

Winerman, L. (2009). Playtime in peril. *Monitor on Psychology, 40,* 50–52.

Wing, N. (2014). Here's the painful truth about what it means to be "working poor" in America. *Huffington Post.* Retrieved from http://www.huffingtonpost.com/2014/05/19/working-poor-stories_n_5297694.html

Wingert, S., Harvey, C. D. H., Duncan, K. A., & Berry, R. E. (2005). Assessing the needs of assisted reproductive technology users on an online bulletin board. *International Journal of Consumer Studies, 29,* 468–478.

Winkleby, M. A., & Cubbin, C. (2004). Racial/ethnic disparities in health behaviors: A challenge to current assumptions. In N. B. Anderson, R. A. Bulatao, & B. Cohen (Eds.), *Critical perspectives on racial and ethnic differences in health in late life* (pp. 310–352). National Research Council, Panel on Race, Ethnicity, and Health in Later Life, Committee on Population, Division of Behavioral and Social Sciences and Education. Washington, DC: The National Academies Press.

Winnicut, D. W. (1948/1958). Paediatrics and psychiatry. In *Collected papers: Through paediatrics to psychoanalysis* (pp. 157–173). London: Tavistock.

Winston, C. A. (2006). African American grandmothers parenting AIDS orphans: Grieving and coping. *Qualitative Social Work: Research and Practice, 5,* 33–43.

Witherspoon, D., Schotland, M., Way, N., & Hughes, D. (2009). Connecting the dots: How connectedness to multiple contexts influences the psychological and academic adjustment of urban youth. *Applied Developmental Science, 13,* 199–216.

Witsø, A. E., Vik, K., & Ytterhus, B. (2012). Participation in older home care recipients: A value-based process. *Activities, Adaptation and Aging, 36,* 297–316.

Witt, M. G., & Wood, W. (2010). Self-regulation of gendered behavior in everyday life. *Sex Roles, 62,* 635–646.

Wittmann, M., Arce, E., & Santisteban, C. (2008). How impulsiveness, trait anger, and extracurricular activities might affect aggression in school children. *Personality and Individual Differences, 45,* 618–623.

Wohlwend, K. (2009). Early adopters: Playing new literacies and pretending new technologies in print-centric classrooms. *Journal of Early Childhood Literacy, 9,* 117–140.

Wolf, S. M. (1996). Gender, feminism, and death: Physician-assisted suicide and euthanasia. In S. M. Wolf (Ed.), *Feminism and bioethics: Beyond reproduction.* New York, NY: Oxford University Press.

Wolff, P. H. (1966). Causes, controls, and organization of behavior in the neonate. *Psychological Issues, 5*(1, No. 17).

Wolfinger, N. H. (2003). Family structure homogamy: The effects of parental divorce on partner selection and marital stability. *Social Science Research, 32,* 80–97.

Wolfinger, N. H. (2015). *Want to avoid divorce? Wait to get married but not too long.* Retrieved from http://family-studies.org/want-to-avoid-divorce-wait-to-get-married-but-not-too-long/

Womenshealth.gov. (2010). *Menopause.* Retrieved from http://womenshelath.gove/menopause/symptoms-relief-treatment

Wong, A. (2015, May 21). The renaissance of student activism. *The Atlantic.* Retrieved from http://www.theatlantic.com/education/archive/2015/05/the-renaissance-of-student-activism/393749/

Wong, C. -K. & Lou, V.W.Q. (2010). "I wish to be self-reliant": Aspiration for self-reliance, need and life satisfaction, and exit dilemma of welfare recipients in Hong Kong. *Social Indicators Research, 95,* 519–534.

Wong, M. G. (2012). The Chinese-American family. In R. Wright, C. H. Mindel, T. V. Tran, & R. W. Habenstein (Eds.), *Ethnic families in America: Patterns and variations* (pp. 227–251). Boston, MA: Pearson.

Wong, P. T. P., & Watt, L. M. (1991). What types of reminiscence are associated with

successful aging? *Psychology and Aging, 6,* 272–279.

Wood, C. (2002). Parent-child preschool activities can affect the development of literacy skills. *Journal of Research in Reading, 25,* 241–258.

Wood, D., Kaplan, R., & McLoyd, V. C. (2007). Gender differences in the educational expectations of urban, low-income African American youth: The role of parents and the school. *Journal of Youth and Adolescence, 36,* 417–427.

Wood, D., Kurtz-Costes, B., Rowley, S. J., & Okeke-Adeyanju, N. (2010). Mothers' academic gender stereotypes and education-related beliefs about sons and daughters in African American families. *Journal of Educational Psychology, 102,* 521–530.

Wood, J. J., & Repetti, R. L. (2004). What gets dad involved? A longitudinal study of change in parental child caregiving involvement. *Journal of Family Psychology, 18,* 237–249.

Wood, W., & Eagly, A. H. (2002). A cross-cultural analysis of the behavior of women and men: Implications for the origins of sex differences. *Psychological Bulletin, 128,* 699–727.

Wood, W., Rhodes, N., & Biek, M. (1995). Working knowledge and attitude strength: An information-processing analysis. In K. E. Petty & J. A. Krosnick (Eds.), *Attitude strength: Antecedents and consequences* (pp. 283–313). Mahwah, NJ: Erlbaum.

Woods, R. J. & Wilcox, T. (2010). Covariation of color and luminance facilitate object individuation in infancy. *Developmental Psychology, 46,* 681–690.

Woodward, K. L. (1997, March 10). Today the sheep. *Newsweek,* 60.

Woolley, J. D., & Wellman, H. M. (1993). Origin and truth: Young children's understanding of imaginary mental representations. *Child Development, 64,* 1–17.

Worchel, F. F., & Allen, M. (1997). Mothers' ability to discriminate cry types in low birth-weight premature and full-term infants. *Children's Health Care, 26,* 183–195.

World Health Organization. (2012). *Statistical annual. Suicides rates by age.* Retrieved from www.who.int/entity/mental_health/media/germ.pdf

World Health Organization. (2014). *Preventing suicide: A global imperative.* Retrieved from http://apps.who.int/iris/bitstream/10665/131056/1/9789241564779_eng.pdf?ua=1&ua=1

World Medical Association. (1979). Declaration of Helsinki. *Journal of the American Medical Association, 277,* 925–926.

Wortman, C. B., & Boerner, K. (2007). Beyond the myths of coping with loss: Prevailing assumptions versus scientific evidence. In H. S. Friedman & R. C. Silver (Eds.), *Foundations of Health Psychology* (pp. 285–324). New York, NY: Oxford University Press.

Woyach, R. B. (1991). *Preparing for leadership: A young adult's guide to leadership skills in a global age*. Columbus, OH: Mershon Center, Ohio State University.

Woyach, R. B. (1993). *Preparing for leadership: A young adult's guide to leadership skills in a global age*. Westport, CT: Greenwood Press.

Wray, S. (2003). Women growing older: Agency, ethnicity and culture. *Sociology, 37*, 511–527.

Wright, J. D., & Devine, J. A. (1993). Family backgrounds and the substance-abusive homeless: The New Orleans experience. *The Community Psychologist, 26*, 35–37.

Wright, R. H., Jr., Mindel, C. H., Tran, T. V., & Habenstein, R. W. (2012). *Ethnic families in American: Patterns and variations* (5th ed.). Upper Saddle River, NJ: Pearson.

Wrosch, C., Amir, E., & Miller, G. E. (2011). Goal adjustment capacities, coping, and subjective well-being: The sample case of caregiving for a family member with mental illness. *Journal of Personality and Social Psychology, 100*, 934–946.

Wu, S., & Keysar, B. (2007). The effect of culture on perspective taking. *Psychological Science, 18*, 600–606.

Wu, Y. (2010). Social skill in the workplace: What is social skill and how does it matter? *Dissertation Abstracts International Section A: Humanities and Social Sciences*, p. 3544.

Wubbena, Z. C. (2013). Mathematical fluency as a function of conservation ability in young children. *Learning and Individual Differences*. http://dx.dooi.org/10/1016/j.lindif.2013.01.013

Wulf, S. (1997). How to teach our children well. (It can be done.) *Time, 150*, 62–69.

Wylleman, P. (2000). Interpersonal relationships in sport: Uncharted territory in sport psychology research. *International Journal of Sport Psychology, 31*, 555–572.

www.IVF-infertility.com. *Artificial insemination*. Retrieved from http://www.IVF-infertility.com

Xiao, J. J., Newman, B. M., & Chu, B. (2016). Career preparation of high school students: A multi-country study. *Youth and Society*, First published online on March 18, 2016.

Xu, F. (2003). The development of object individuation in infancy. In H. Hayne & J. Fagen (Eds.), *Progress in infancy research* (Vol. 3, pp. 159–192). Mahwah, NJ: Erlbaum.

Xu, F. & Kushnir, T. (2013). Infants are rational constructivist learners. *Current Directions in Psychological Science, 22*, 28–32.

Xu, F., & Zhang, W. (2011). Relationship between adolescents' alienation and pathological internet use: Testing the moderating effect of family functioning and peer acceptance. *Acta Psychologica Sinica, 43*, 410–419.

Yamauchi, L. A., Billig, S. H., Meyer, S., & Hofschire, L. (2006). Student outcomes associated with service-learning in a culturally relevant high school program. *Journal of Prevention & Intervention in the Community, 32*, 149–164.

Yan, E. G., & Munir, K. M. (2004). Regulatory and ethical principles in research involving children and individuals with developmental disabilities. *Ethics and Behavior, 14*, 31–49.

Yang, L., Krampe, R. T., & Baltes, P. B. (2006). Basic forms of cognitive plasticitiy extended into the oldest-old: Retest learning, age and cognitive functioning. *Psychology and Aging, 21*, 372–378.

Yang, R. K., Zweig, A. R., Douthitt, T. C., & Federman, E. J. (1976). Successive relationships between maternal attitudes during pregnancy, analgesic medication during labor and delivery, and newborn behavior. *Developmental Psychology, 12*, 6–14.

Yanow, S. (2013). It is time to integrate abortion into primary care. *American Journal of Public Health, 103*, 14–16.

Yarrow, L. J. (1963). Research in dimensions of early maternal care. *Merrill-Palmer Quarterly, 9*, 101–114.

Yarrow, L. J. (1964). Separation from parents in early childhood. In M. L. Hoffman & L. W. Hoffman (Eds.), *Review of child development research* (Vol. 1). New York, NY: Sage.

Yarrow, L. J. (1970). The development of focused relationships during infancy. In J. Hellmuth (Ed.), *Exceptional infant* (Vol. 1). New York, NY: Brunner/Mazel.

Yarrow, L. J., McQuiston, S., MacTurk, R. H., McCarthy, M. E., Klein, R. P., & Vietze, P. M. (1983). The assessment of mastery motivation during the first year of life. *Developmental Psychology, 19*, 159–171.

Yasui, M., Dorham, C. L., & Dishion, T. Y. (2004). Ethnic identity and psychological adjustment: A validity analysis for European American and African American adolescents. *Journal of Adolescent Research, 19*, 807–825.

Yates, A. (1989). Current perspectives on the eating disorders: 1. History, psychological, and biological aspects. *Journal of the American Academy of Child and Adolescent Psychiatry, 28*, 813–828.

Yates, M., & Youniss, J. (1996). Community service and political-moral identity in adolescents. *Journal of Research on Adolescence, 6*, 271–284.

Yeager, D. S., & Dweck, C. S. (2012). Mindsets that promote resilience: When students believe that personal characteristics can be developed. *Educational Psychologist, 47*, 302–314.

Yin, R. K. (1994). *Case study research: Design and methods*. Thousand Oaks, CA: Sage.

Yin, R. K. (2014). *Case study research: Design and methods* (5th ed.). Thousand Oaks, CA: Sage.

Yip, T., Seaton, E. K., & Sellers, R. M. (2006). African American racial identity across the lifespan: Identity status, identity content, and depressive symptoms. *Child Development, 77*, 1504–1517.

Yoder, S. (2013). Why millions of seniors are moving back to cities. *The Fiscal Times*. Retrieved from http://www.thefiscaltimes.com/Articles/2013/06/05/Why-Millions-of-Seniors-Are-Moving-Back-to-Cities

Yoo, J. P., Slack, K. S., & Holl, J. I. (2009). Material hardship and the physical health of school-aged children in low-income households. *American Journal of Public Health, 99*, 829–836.

Yordanova, J., Kolev, V., Hohnsbein, J., & Falkenstein, M. (2004). Sensory slowing with ageing is mediated by a functional dys-regulation of motor-generation processes: Evidence from high-resolution event-related potentials. *Brain, 127*, 351–362.

Yoshikawa, H. (2005). *Placing the first-year findings of the National Head Start Impact Study in context*. Brief prepared for the Society for Research in Child Development. Retrieved from http://srcd.org/documents/policy/Impact-study.pdf

Yoshikawa, H., Aber, J. L., & Beardslee, W. R. (2012). The effects of poverty, emotional and behavioral health of children and youth: Implications for prevention. *American Psychologist, 67*, 272–284.

Young, B. (2011). T he psychological life, religion and immortality: Musings of a venerable psychoanalyst. *International Journal of Applied Psychoanalytic Studies, 8*, 288–300.

Young, G. (2011). *Development and causality: Neo-Piagetian perspectives*. New York: Springer.

Youngblade, L. M., & Belsky, J. (1992). Parent-child antecedents of 5-year-olds' close friendships: A longitudinal analysis. *Developmental Psychology, 28*, 700–713.

Youniss, J. (1980). *Parents and peers in social development: A Sullivan-Piaget perspective*. Chicago, IL: University of Chicago Press.

YourGenome. (2015). *What is gene therapy?* Retrieved from http://www.yourgenome.org/facts/what-is-gene-therapy

Youth Risk Behavior Surveillance System. (2010a). *Trends in the prevalence of sexual behaviors: 1991–2009*. Retrieved from www.cdc.gov/healthyyouth/yrbs/pdf/us_sexual_trend_yrbs.pdf

Youth Risk Behavior Surveillance System. (2010b). *Trends in the prevalence of suicide related behaviors: 1991–2009*. Retrieved from www.cdc.gov/healthyyouth/yrbs/pdf/us_suicide_trend_yrbs.pdf

Yow, W. Q., & Markman, E. M. (2015). A bilingual advantage in how children integrate multiple cues to understand a speaker's referential intent. *Bilingualism: Language and Cognition, 18*, 391–399.

Yu, F., Ryan, L. H., Schaie, K. W., Willis, S. L., & Kolanowski, A. (2009). Factors associated with cognition in adults: The Seattle Longitudinal Study. *Research in Nursing and Health, 32*, 540–550.

Yuan, J., Ju, E., Meng, X., Chen, X., Zhu, S., Yang, J., & Li, H. (2015). Enhanced brain susceptibility to negative stimuli in adolescents: ERP evidences. *Frontiers in Behavioral Neuroscience, 9*, Article 98.

Yun, I., & Hwang, E. (2011). A study of occasional and intensive weapon carrying among adolescents using a nationally representative sample. *Youth Violence and Juvenile Justice, 9,* 366–382.

Yurdakok, K., Yavuz, T., & Taylor, C. E. (1990). Swaddling and acute respiratory infections. *American Journal of Public Health, 80,* 873–875.

Yuri, J., Chiriboga, D. A., & Small, B. J. (2008). Perceived discrimination and psychological well-being: The mediating and moderating role of sense of control. *International Journal of Aging and Human Development, 66,* 213–227.

Zahn, M. A. (Ed.). (2009). *The delinquent girl.* Philadelphia, PA: Temple University Press.

Zahn-Waxler, C., & Kochanska, G. (1990). The origins of guilt. In R. A. Thompson (Ed.), *Nebraska Symposium on Motivation, 1988* (Vol. 36, pp. 183–258). Lincoln, NE: University of Nebraska Press.

Zahn-Waxler, C., Radke-Yarrow, M., & King, R. A. (1977). *The impact of the affective environment on young children.* Paper presented at the biennial meeting of the Society for Research in Child Development, New Orleans, LA.

Zahn-Waxler, C., Radke-Yarrow, M., Wagner, E., & Chapman, M. (1992). Development of concern for others. *Developmental Psychology, 28,* 126–136.

Zahn-Waxler, C., Robinson, J. L., & Emde, R. N. (1992). The development of empathy in twins. *Developmental Psychology, 28,* 1038–1047.

Zahn-Waxler, C., & Van Hulle, C. (2012). Empathy, guilt, and depression: When caring for others becomes costly to children. In B. Oakley, A. Knafo, G. Madhavan, & D.S. Wilson (Eds.), *Pathological altruism* (pp. 321–344). New York: Oxford University Press.

Zahniser, D. (2006). Welcome to gentrification city. *LA Weekly News.* Retrieved from http://www.laweekly.com/news/features/welcome-to-gentrification-city/14285

Zakriski, A. L., & Coie, J. D. (1996). A comparison of aggressive-rejected and nonaggressive-rejected children's interpretations of self-directed and other-directed rejection. *Child Development, 67,* 1048–1070.

Zarit, S. H., & Eggebeen, D. A. (2002). Parent-child relationships in adulthood and old age. In M. H. Bornstein (Ed.), *Handbook of parenting* (2nd ed., pp. 135–164). Mahwah, NJ: Erlbaum.

Zarit, S. H., Femia, E. E., Kim, K., & Whitlatch, C. J. (2010). The structure of risk factors and outcomes for family caregivers: Implications for assessment and treatment. *Aging and Mental Health, 14,* 220–231.

Zayas, L. H., & Solari, F. (1994). Early childhood socialization in Hispanic families: Context, culture, and practice implications. *Professional Psychology: Research and Practice, 25,* 200–206.

Zayas, V., Mischel, W., Shoda, Y., & Aber, J. L. (2011). Roots of adult attachment: Maternal caregiving at 18 months predicts adult attachment to peers and partners. *Social

Psychological and Personality Science, 2, 289–297.

Zayas, V., & Selcuk, E. (2013, February 1). What implicit processes tell us about romantic attachment: Understanding adult attachment from different levels of analysis. *Association for Psychological Science Observer.*

Zebrowitz, L. A., Bronstad, P. M., & Montepare, J. M. (2010). An ecological theory of face perception. In R. B. Adams, N. Ambady, K. Nakayama, & S. Shimojo (Eds.), *The science of social vision* (pp. 3–30). New York, NY: Oxford University Press.

Zelinski, E. (2009). The IMPACT study: Maintenance of gains after a brain plasticity-based intervention for aged-related cognitive decline. *Journal of the American Geriatric Society, 57,* 168–169.

Zelinski, E. M., & Lewis, K. L. (2003). Adult age differences in multiple cognitive functions: Differentiation, dedifferentiation, or process-specific change. *Psychology and Aging, 18,* 727–745.

Zelinski, E. M., Spina, L. M., Yaffe, K., Ruff, R., Kennison, R. F., Mahncke, H. W., & Smith, G. E. (2011). Improvement in memory with plasticity-based adaptive cognitive training: Results of the 3-month follow-up. *Journal of the American Geriatric Society, 59,* 258–265.

Zeskind, P. S. (1983). Cross-cultural differences in maternal perceptions of cries of low- and high-risk infants. *Child Development, 54,* 1119–1128.

Zeskind, P. S., Klein, L., & Marshall, T. R. (1992). Adult's perceptions of experimental modifications of durations of pauses and expiratory sounds in infant crying. *Developmental Psychology, 28,* 1153–1162.

Zettel, L. A., & Rook, K. S. (2004). Substitution and compensation in the social networks of older widowed women. *Psychology and Aging, 19,* 433–443.

Zhang, S., Schmader, T., & Forbes, C. (2009). The effects of gender stereotypes on women's career choice: Opening the glass door. In M. Barreto, M. K. Ryan, & M. T Schmitt (Eds.), *The glass ceiling in the 21st century: Understanding barriers to gender equality. Psychology of Women Book Series* (pp. 125–150). Washington, DC: American Psychological Association.

Zhang, Y., Haraksingh, R., Grubert, F., Abyzov, A., Gerstein, M., Weissman, S., et al. (2013). Child development and structural variation in the human genome. *Child Development,* 1–15.

Zhao, H., Brooks-Gunn, J., McLanahan, S., & Singer, B. (2000). Studying the real child rather than the ideal child: Bringing the person into developmental studies. In L. R. Bergman, R. B. Cairns, L. Nilsson, & L. Nystedt (Eds.), *Developmental science and the holistic approach* (pp. 393–419). Mahwah, NJ: Erlbaum.

Zhu, Y., Zhang, L., Fan, J., & Han, S. (2007). Neural basis of cultural influence on

self-representation. *NeuroImage, 34,* 1320–1316.

Ziegert, D. I., Kistner, J. A., Castro, R., & Robertson, B. (2001). Longitudinal study of young children's responses to challenging achievement situations. *Child Development, 72,* 609–624.

Zigler, E. F., & Styfco, S. (2004). Moving Head Start to the states: One experiment too many. *Applied Developmental Science, 8,* 51–55.

Ziliak, J. P., & Gundersen, C. (2011). *Food insecurity among older adults. A report submitted to AARP Foundation.* Retrieved from www.aarp.org/content/dam/aarp/aarp_foundation/pdf_2011/AARPFoundation_HungerReport_2011.pdf

Zill, N., & West, J. (2000). *Entering kindergarten: A portrait of American children when they begin school.* Washington, DC: National Center for Educational Statistics. Retrieved from http://nces.ed.gov/pubs2000/coe2000/entering_kindergarten.html

Zimbardo, P. G. & Boyd, J. (2008). *The time paradox: The new psychology of time that will change your life.* New York, NY: Free Press.

Zimmerman, B. J., Bandura, A., & Martinez-Pons, M. (1992). Self-motivation for academic attainment: The role of self-efficacy beliefs and personal goal setting. *American Educational Research Journal, 29,* 663–676.

Zimmerman, M. (2009, Spring). Why evolution is the organizing principle for biology. *Phi Kappa Phi Forum,* 4–7.

Zimmerman, M. A., Salem, D. A., & Maton, K. I. (1995). Family structure and psychosocial correlates among urban African-American adolescent males. *Child Development, 66,* 1598–1613.

Zosuls, K. M., Ruble, D. N., Tamis-LeMonda, C. S., Shrout, P. E., Bornstein, M. H., & Greulich, F. K. (2009). The acquisition of gender labels in infancy: Implications for gender-typed play. *Developmental Psychology, 45,* 688–701.

Zuckerman, B., Frank, D. A., & Hingson, R. (1989). Effects of maternal marijuana and cocaine use on fetal growth. *The New England Journal of Medicine, 320,* 762–768.

Zuckerman, C. (1997). Issues concerning end-of-life care. *Journal of Long Term Home Health Care, 16,* 26–34.

Zuo, J. (1992). The reciprocal relationship between marital interaction and marital happiness: A three-wave study. *Journal of Marriage and the Family, 54,* 870–878.

Zur, O., & Gelman, R. (2004). Young children can add and subtract by predicting and checking. *Early Childhood Research Quarterly, 19,* 121–137.

Zuravin, S. J. (1988). Child maltreatment and teenage first births: A relationship mediated by chronic sociodemographic stress? *American Journal of Orthopsychiatry, 58,* 91–103.

Name Index

Boss, P., 596, 603
Bost, K. K., 163–164
Bosworth, H. B., 579
Bouchard, T. J., 87, 90
Boucher, H. C., 297
Bouffard, L., 517
Bouffard, T., 299
Bouldin, P., 203
Boutwell, B. B., 193
Bowen, M., 50
Bowes, L., 354
Bowker, A., 279
Bowker, J. C., 277
Bowlby, J., 151–152, 156
Bowman, B. T., 265
Bowman, K., 533
Bowman, P. J., 439
Boxer, P., 312
Boyce, C. J., 520
Boyd, D. M., 451
Boyd, J., 574
Boyd, J. S., 286
Boyer, M. E., 284
Boykin, A. W., 76
Boyko, V., 484
Boyle, F. M., 285
Boyle, J. S., 198
Boyse, K., 325
Bozick, R., 410
Bracco, K. R., 393
Brack, G. A., 104
Bradbury, R., 592
Bradbury, T., 486
Bradford, K., 486
Bradley, C. B., 323
Bradley, C. L., 500
Bradley, R., 235
Bradley, R. H., 176, 196
Bradley, R. P. C., 442
Bradmetz, J., 342
Bradshaw, C. P., 280
Bradshaw, Z., 124
Braine, M., 191
Braithwaite, V., 172
Brandenburg, D. L., 348
Brandon, E., 545
Brandon, P. E., 532
Brandstädter, J., 516, 564
Branje, S., 376, 436
Branje, S. J. T., 345
Brault, M. W., 268
Braungart, J. M., 164
Braungart-Rieker, J. M., 156, 163
Braun, L., 387
Brawley, L. R., 517
Brazelton, T. B., 214, 215, 462
Bredow, C. A., 428, 482
Brendgen, M., 258, 348
Brennan, A., 116
Brennan, R. T., 438, 452
Bresland, N. L., 327
Bretherton, I., 154, 251

Brezina, P. R., 94
Bridges, M., 355
Briggs, K., 563
Brim, G., 501
Brim, O. G., 44
Brind-Amour, K., 90
Brindis, C. D., 125
Bringle, J. R., 539
Brinkmeyer, M. Y., 206
Brisch, K. H., 104
Brisette, I., 15
Britner, P. A., 152
Broberg, M., 208
Brock, S. J., 301
Broderick, C. B., 49
Broderick, J. E., 521, 521f
Brody, D. J., 541
Brody, J. E., 603
Brodzinsky, D., 444
Brodzinsky, D. M., 236
Broen, A. N., 124
Bronfenbrenner, U., 47–49
Bronfman, E., 155
Bronstad, P. M., 147
Bronstein, P., 487
Brookes, H., 138
Brook, J., 457
Brooks-Gunn, J., 208, 221, 222, 319, 322, 497
Brooks, S., 70
Brosseau-Lapré, F., 195
Brown, A., 484
Brown, B. B., 353, 354, 356, 362
Brown, C., 150
Brown, C. S., 334, 360
Brown, E. R., 395
Brown, J., 199
Brown, J. D., 253
Brown, J. L., 219
Brown, J. R., 198, 346
Brown, J. V., 111
Brown, M. M., 260
Brown, R., 44, 302, 546
Brown, S. K., 254
Brownell, C. A., 204, 206, 273, 276
Browning, C. R., 584
Brubaker, T. H., 489
Brueckner, H., 330
Bruera, E., 593
Brugman, D., 241
Brummelman, E., 254
Bruner, J., 146
Brustad, R. J., 301
Bryan, A., 368
Bryer, K. B., 599, 600
Bucher, A., 508
Buchmann, C., 388
Buchner, D. M., 557
Bucksch, J., 323
Buczynski, R., 481

Bueno, M., 139
Buettner, D., 554
Buffalo, M. D., 124
Buhler, C., 422
Buhl, H. M., 376
Bukowski, W., 277
Bukowski, W. M., 200, 253, 273, 275–276, 277
Bullock, H. E., 447
Bullock, J., 70
Bullock, K., 533
Bulotsky-Shearer, R. J., 202
Bumpus, M. F., 479
Bunting, L., 337
Burbank, P., 537
Burchinal, M. R., 221, 222, 223
Burd, L., 110
Bureau of Labor Statistics, 392, 393, 395, 446, 448, 493, 536, 541
Burgard, S. A., 108
Burgess, E. W., 364
Burkhard, B., 361
Burleigh, N., 334
Burleson, B. R., 275, 437
Burnett A. L., 483
Burnett, D., 530
Burns, M., 265
Burns, T. C., 101
Burr, D., 140
Burroughs, N. A., 309
Burt, K. B., 63, 72
Burt, S. A., 279
Burtless, G., 379
Burton, C. M., 332
Burton, S., 252, 300
Bus, A. G., 293
Buschke, H., 522
Buschman, T. J., 136
Bushman, B., 247, 248
Bush, N., 209
Buss, A. H., 164
Buss, D., 24, 428
Buss, F. L., 232
Buss, K. A., 166, 246
Bussey, K., 385
Buunk, B. P., 429, 473
Buysse, V., 264
Buzney, C. D., 324
Bybee, D., 359
Byers-Heinlein, C. D., 101
Bygren, L. O., 85
Byler, C., 448
Byles, J. E., 534
Bynner, J., 475
Byrd-Craven, J., 428
Byrnes, E. M., 110
Byrnes, V., 292

Cabeza, R., 558
Cabrera, N., 196
Cacioppo, J., 24
Cacioppo, J. T., 15, 456, 457
Cacioppo, S., 24
Cavuoto et al 2016, 557
Caffray, C. M., 367, 368
Cagney, K. A., 584
Cain, K. M., 308
Cain, T. R., 298, 309
Caldwell, C. A., 213
Caldwell, K. A., 276
California Department of Public Health, 108
Calkins, S. D., 163, 166, 172, 205
Callahan, S. P., 358
Callahan, C. L., 207
Calment, J., 553
Calvert, G., 139
Calzo, J. P., 386
Cameron, R. E., 531
Cameron, R. P., 104
Camodeca, M., 213, 260
Campa, M., 158
Campbell, B. C., 113
Campbell, C., 242
Campbell, I. G., 320
Campbell, R., 187, 188
Campbell, S. B., 155
Campbell, S. M., 473
Campbell, W. K., 500
Campos, B., 104, 486
Campos, J. J., 164
Canadian Paediatric Society 2008, 331
Canfield, M. A., 92
Cannella, C., 16
Canobe, K., 285
Canobe, K. H., 285
Cantin, R. H., 291
Cao, L., 352
Caplan, G., 599
Caplan, L. J., 71
Cappeliez, P., 517, 542
Cappella, E., 309
Caprara, G. V., 296
Caraviello, R., 569
Carbera, N. J., 274
Carlson, C. L., 380
Carlson, E. A., 154, 158
Carlson, M. C., 157, 536
Carmeli, A., 452
Carmody, D. P., 250
Carnagey, N. L., 247
Caro, F. G., 536
Carossino, P., 119
Carp, J., 177
Carpenter, E. M., 277
Carpenter, M., 215
Carr, D., 533, 534, 573, 592
Carrere, S., 481
Carroll, J. L., 483

Crawford, J. R., 523
Crawford, T. N., 348
Creamer, A., 574
Creanga, A. A., 122
Crick, N. R., 277
Crimmins, E. M., 9
Crinion, J., 195
Cristia, A., 194
Crocetti, E., 399
Crockenberg, S. C., 172, 178
Crohan, S. E., 442
Crooks, R. L., 99, 386, 480, 483, 573, 574
Cropley, M., 348
Crosby, J. R., 508
Crosby, K. A., 279
Crosby, R. A., 337
Crosnoe, R., 9, 10, 219, 518, 531, 619–620
Cross, W. E., Jr., 360, 406, 407
Crouter, A. C., 327, 395, 452, 472, 479
Crowell, J. A., 430
C. S. Mott Children's Hospital-University of Michigan Health System, 131
Cubansi, J., 569
Cubbin, C., 16
Cuddy, A. J. C., 507
Cuijpers, P., 542
Cukan, A., 508
Culbert, K. M., 347
Cullum, A. S., 105
Cumming, S. P., 327
Cummings, S. S., 300
Cumsille, P., 355
Cunningham, F. G., 88, 101, 102, 120
Cupito, S. H., 105
Currie, C., 327
Currie, L. A., 287
Curtin, S. C., 501
Cutler, A., 187
Cutler, D. M., 562
Cutler, N., 573

Daatland, S. O., 489
Daddis, C., 355, 356
Dagnan, D., 348
Dahl, R. E., 319, 327
Dake, C. L., 94
Dalai Lama, 244
Dalgleish, M., 145
Dalgleish, T., 312
Daly-Cano-Vaccaro, A., 379
Damasio, A., 168
Damianov, M. K., 211
Damico, A., 569
Damon, W., 251, 252, 263, 388, 389, 390, 391, 399
Dancy, B. L., 397
Dane, A. V., 279

Dannemiller, J. L., 137
Dapretto, M., 215
D'Argembeau, A., 252
Darling-Fisher, C. S., 74
Darling, N., 355
Darnis, F., 302, 304
Darwin, C., 21, 23
Dasen, P. R., 287
Datta, J., 486
Daugherty, J., 439, 443
Daverth, G., 452
Davey, A., 578, 580
Davey, M., 94
David, B., 390
Davidson, J. K., 334
Davidson, K., 574
Davies, P. G., 508
Davies, P. T., 169, 274
Davis, A., 375, 432
Davis, E. L., 246
Davis, J. E., 449
Davis, J. L., 481
Davis, K., 289
Davis-Kean, P. E., 219, 255, 298
Davis, P. E., 203
Davis, S. W., 558
Davydov, V. V., 36
Dawson, T. L., 389
Dawson-Tunick, T. L., 60
Dayan, A., 396
Dayton, C. J., 177
Deakin, J., 303
de Almondes, K. M., 558
DeAngelis, T., 265
Dearing, E., 222
Dearing, R., 390
Dearing, R. L., 213
Deary, I. J., 90, 521
Deater-Deckard, K., 106, 170, 176, 208, 235, 272, 274
Deaton, A., 521, 521f
Deaton, J. E., 521f
DeBarros, K. A., 560, 564
de Bie, E., 320
De Boer, D. D., 463
DeCaro, J. A., 324
DeCasper, A. J., 101, 136
Decety, J., 250, 262
Deci, E. L., 211, 263, 375
Declercq, E. R., 118
Dedmon, S. E., 205
de Dreu, C. K. W., 302
Deenen, A. A., 434
Defries, J. C., 164
DeFruyt, F., 501
DeGenova 1997, 426
Degnan, K. A., 291
De Graaf, P. M., 462, 464
DeGrazia, D., 590
de Guzman, N. S., 326
DeHaan, M., 138
DeHoogh, A. H.B., 473

Delaney-Black, V., 110
DeLay, D., 293
De Leersnyder, J., 166
DeLeon, J., 532
Del Giudice, M., 274
Delsing, M. J. M., 354
DeMaris, A., 534
Deming, D., 224
Demmer, C., 605
Demo, D. H., 464
Deng, M., 177
DenHartog, D. N., 473
Denissen, J. J. A., 252, 295
Denmark, F. L., 573
Denner, J., 385
Denny, M. A., 142
Depp, C. A., 514, 520
Depue, R. A., 165
de Ridder, D. T. D., 516
de Rosnay, M., 153, 167
de Ruiter, C., 349
de Sá-Saraiva, R., 575
Deschenes, A., 398
Desrochers, L., 220
Desrochers, S., 147
de St. Aubin, E., 8, 62, 74, 398, 499
de Vries, B., 390
DeVries, M. R., 214
De Vries, M. W., 214
DeVries, R., 242
DeWall, C. N., 279
Dewan, T., 472
Dewey, J., 25
Dewey, K. G., 105
DeWolf, A., 303
De Wolff, M. S., 174
Diamond, A., 140, 146
Diamond, L. M., 327–328, 329, 331
Dichter, G. S., 348
DiClemente, R. J., 337
DiDonato, M. D., 259
Didow, S. M., 203
Diego, M., 170, 171
Diehl, M., 522, 566
Diekman, A. B., 395
Diemer, M. A., 392
Diener, C. I., 308
Diener, E. F., 521
Dietrich, J., 392, 396
Dijkstra, J. K., 279
Dill, D., 457
Dill, K. E., 255
Dilorio, C., 104
Dimidjian, S., 112
Dindia, K., 437
Diniz, B. S., 558
Dionne-Dostie, E., 140
DiPietro, J. A., 101, 103, 113, 537
Diprete, T. A., 388
Dirix, C. E. H., 101

Dishion, T. J., 354, 361
Ditlmann, R., 508
Dobek, J. C., 556
Dobson, C. F., 105
Dockray, S., 312
Dodge, K. A., 205, 207, 260, 274, 279
Dohnt, H., 254
Doi, H., 166
Dolbin-MacNab, M. L., 533, 534
Dolesnszky, E., 258, 259
Doman, J. C., 110
Dombeck, M., 465
Dominguez, T. P., 113
Domino, G., 74
Donald, M., 343
Donini, L. M., 16
Donnellan, M. B., 254
Donoho, C. J., 520
Donovan, M. L., 563
Donovan, M. S., 265
Doran, M. M., 147
Dore, R. A., 202
Dormire, S., 484
Dornbusch, S. M., 376
Dorner, J., 543
Dorn, L. D., 319, 323–324
Doucet, A., 177
Douglass, R. P., 451
Doulas of North America, 105
Douvan, E., 437
Downey, G., 409
Downs, L., 2004
Doyle, A., 283
Dozier, M., 158
Draganski, B., 339
Drake, N., 23
Dreher, E., 374
Dreman, S., 477
Drew, P. K., 528
Driver, J., 432, 436, 481
Druhen, M. J., 278
Drury, K., 276
Duckworth, A. L., 209
Duda, J. L., 301
Dudgeon, M. R., 125
Duff, R. W., 569
Duffy, R. D., 451
Duggan, M., 579
Dumani, S., 45
Dunbar, E., 359
Dunbar, K., 56
Dunbar, N., 385
Dunbar, S. B., 243
Duncan, G. J., 219, 449
Duncan, K. A., 96
Duncan, L. G., 391
Duncan, T. E., 296
Dundes, L., 117
Dunham, Y., 233
Dunifon, R., 489, 533
Dunkel-Schetter, C., 118, 439

Park, D. C., 522, 527, 536
Park, J., 268
Parker, A., 309
Parke, R. D., 485
Parker, J. G., 200, 277
Parker, P., 392, 396
Parker-Pope, T., 319, 501
Parker, S. E., 63, 92, 210
Parkhurst, J. T., 277
Parks, A. C., 422
Parrish-Morris, J., 148
Parsons, T., 44
Partanen, E., 101
Paschal, A. M., 337
Pasold, T., 247
Passos-Ferreira, C., 167
Pastorelli, C., 296
Pataki, S. P., 435
Patel, J., 570
Patterson, C., 237
Patterson, C. J., 236
Patterson, G., 165
Patterson, J. M., 71, 600
Pattison, H., 115
Pattison, P. E., 285
Patton, W., 394, 446
Paul, P. B., 563
Pauli-Pott, U., 163, 166
Paulsen, A. M., 398
Paulsen, J., 265
Paulussen-Hoogeboom, M. C., 164, 205
Paus, T., 339, 344
Paxton, S. J., 346
Payne, D., 301
Pazol, K., 122
Peace Direct, 272
Pearn, J., 272
Pearson, B. Z., 195
Pearson, D., 203
Pearson, J., 323
Pearson, R. M., 442
Peckins, M. K., 312
Pedersen, F., 442
Pedersen, N., 577
Pederson, N., 87
Peeters, M. C. W., 452
Peetsma, T. T. D., 164, 205
Pell, R. W., 575
Pellebon, D. A., 530
Pellegrini, A. D., 186, 187, 201, 293
Peltonen, L., 89
Pemberton, C. K., 234
Pembrey, M. E., 85
Pempek, T. A., 196
Pendry, P., 320
Peng, W., 257
Penick, J. M., 264
Pennings, G., 236
Pennisi, E., 302
Pensavalle, A., 70

Peper, J. S., 327
Peplau, L. A., 434
Pepler, D., 279, 328
Peregoy, J. A., 561, 562
Pereira, M., 208
Pereira, V., 575
Perez-Edar, K., 164
Perls, T. T., 555, 564
Perosa, L. M., 376
Perosa, S. L., 376
Perreault, S., 303–304
Perret-Clermont, A., 283
Perret, J., 283
Perrett, D. I., 427
Perrin, A., 451
Perron, A., 304
Perry, B., 334
Perry, D. G., 235
Perry-Jenkins, M., 443
Perry, M. A., 219
Persaud, T. V. N., 88, 97
Pertman, A., 97, 236
Peter, J., 278
Petersen, A. C., 347
Petersen, R., 185
Peterson, B. D., 94
Peterson, B. E., 74, 498
Peterson, C., 450
Peterson, G., 93
Peterson, J., 248, 501–502
Peterson, J. A., 571–572
Peterson, M. F., 267
Peterson, M. M., 94
Petit, G. S., 207
Petrescu-Prahova, M., 537
Petretic-Jackson, P. A., 481
Pettis, R. M., 383
Pettit, G. S., 260, 443
Pettito, L. A., 195
Pew Research Center, 208, 219, 220, 280, 300, 354, 361, 362, 428, 487
Pew Social Trends, 408
Pfefferbaum, B., 312
Phelps, R., 325
Phillips, D., 221, 222
Phillips, D. A., 299
Phillips, L. H., 523
Phillips, S. J., 185
Phillipson, S., 298
Phillipson, S. N., 298
Philogene, G. S., 577
Phinney, J. S., 359, 360, 407, 408
Piaget, J., 32–33, 35, 36, 144, 145, 146, 201, 240, 241, 245, 276, 281, 282, 284, 289, 339, 340
Pianta, R. C., 265
Pick, A. D., 185
Pickering, K., 106
Pierce, R. C., 110
Pierce, T., 439
Pillard, R., 87
Pillemer, K., 420, 490

Pine, D., 457
Pine, D. S., 89, 91, 347
Pine, F., 29, 185
Pine, J. M., 196
Ping, R. M., 283
Pinquart, M., 546, 563
Pirog-Good, M. A., 338
Pisoni, D. B., 149
Platz, E. A., 483
Pleck, J. H., 485
Plomin, R., 83, 87, 90, 91, 164, 577
Pluess, M., 91
Pober, B., 148
Podolski, C. L., 248
Pöhlmann, K., 517
Poikkeus, A., 293
Polka, L., 151
Pollack, C. E., 598
Pollack, S. D., 290, 327
Pollak, S. D., 169
Pollard, I., 110
Pollitt, E., 219
Pomerantz, E. M., 212, 292, 299
Pomerleau, A., 198
Ponitz, C. C., 265
Ponting, C. P., 83
Poon, L. W., 75
Poortman, A., 462
Pope, H. G., Jr., 323
Popova, S., 110
Porcaro, C., 136
Porter, E. J., 568
Porter, R. H., 139
Portes, A., 70
Portrie, T., 496
Posada, G., 169, 174
Poster, C. H., 566
Potter, D., 266
Potter, M. C., 291
Poulain, M., 554
Poulin-Dubois, D., 147
Poulin, F., 361
Poulin, R., 279, 361
Powell, D., 223
Powers, B. P., 156
Powers, S. M., 191
Powledge, T. M., 83
Powlishta, K. K., 233, 235
Pozuelo, J. R., 521
Prager, K. J., 436
Pratt, C., 203
Pratt, C. C., 582
Pratt, L. A., 541
Pratt, M. W., 403, 406, 498, 499
Pratt, S. G., 448
Prelec, D., 622
Premack 2010, 37
Price, C., 69
Price, J., 524
Price, S., 69
Prieto, M. D., 289

Pringle, H., 503
Prinstein, M. J., 70, 354
Proctor, B. D., 544
Proctor, B. E., 379
Progress in International Reading Literacy Study (PIRLS), 293
Provasnik, S., 292
Proyer, R. T., 519
Pruchno, R. A., 535
Pruett, M. K., 485
Puca, A., 555
Puma, M., 222, 224
Purdie-Vaughn, V., 508
Purhonen, M., 136
Purtell, K. M., 219
Pushkar, D., 580
Putnam, S., 294
Putnam, S. P., 158, 163, 166
Putnick, D. L., 176, 235, 305
Putze, D., 10
Puzzanchera, C., 349
Pyle, R. P., 265
Pyne, J., 238
Pynoos, J., 569

Quayle, E., 605
Queensland Government, 115, 116, 120
Quéniart, A., 531
Quiggle, N. L., 279
Quindlen, A., 546–547
Quinn, P. C., 147
Quintana, S. M., 359
Qu, Y., 345

Rabagliati, H., 150
Raeff, C., 253
Raferty, A. E., 473
Ragins, B. R., 449
Raikes, H., 221, 222
Raimbault, C., 139
Raine, A., 175
Rakison, D. H., 147
Rakoczy, J., 199
Rakow, A., 261
Ram, N., 326
Ramberan, G., 457
Ramineni, C., 285
Ramirez, A. Y. F., 309
Ramos, M. C., 205
Randall, G. K., 75
Rands, C. M., 83
Raney, G. E., 284
Ransford, C. R., 479
Rantanen, J., 477
Ranzijn, R., 519
Rao, M., 485
Rapee, R., 278
Rapport, M. J., 187
Raschick, M., 491
Ratelle, C. F., 376, 398
Rath, T., 456

Subject Index

Note: Figures are denoted by *f*; tables by *t*.

child labor, 305
childlessness, 444
children with disabilities
    communication disorders, 306
    learning disabilities, 306
    motor skill disabilities, 306–307
    peer rejection and, 279
    school readiness for, 268
    school success and, 306–307,
        307f
chlamydia, 335
choice phase, of career decision
    making, 397
chromosomal disorders, 88–89, 88f
chromosomes, 83
chromosomes, as sources of
    genetic information, 82–83
chronic illnesses, 520
chronic loneliness, 457
chronological age, distinctions
    made based on, 75
circular reactions, 145t, 146
citizenship, 309
civic purpose, 391
clarification phase, of career
    decision making, 397
class hierarchies/class inclusion,
    284
classification skills, 284–285
climacteric, 483
Clinton, Hillary, 525f
cliques, 353, 354
cloning, 90
close friends, in middle
    childhood, 273, 276–277
cocaine, fetal development and, 111
code switching, 195
codominance, 84
coercive escalation, 436
cognition
    defined, 32
    impact of child care on, 221–222
    intellectual vigor in later adult-
        hood, 521–528
    locomotion and, 185
    metacognition, 286–287
    moral decision making in later
        adolescence, 388
    neuroscience of, 344–345
cognitive ability
    behavioral slowing in
        elderhood and, 558–559
    "brain games" and, 527
    changes in, across the life span,
        525–526, 526f
    genetics and, 90–91
    interaction of heredity and
        environment on, 526, 528
    neuroplasticity and aging and,
        522–523
cognitive behavioral therapy, 39
cognitive behaviorism, 38–40, 38f

cognitive competencies, 38, 38f
cognitive control functions, 339
cognitive development
    exposure to violence and, 312
    during infancy, 175–176
    metacognition and, 286–287
cognitive developmental theory,
    20, 51t
    basic concepts of, 36t
    on moral development,
        240–242
    Piaget's theory, 32–34, 36t
    psychosocial approach and, 36
    Vygotsky's theory, 34–36, 36t
cognitive factors, alcohol use and,
    367
cognitive map, 38
cognitive processes, supporting
    formation of group identity,
    357–358
cognitive restructuring, 278
cognitive smile, 163
cognitive theory, on moral
    development, 248, 249t
cohabitation, 432–433
coherence, sense of, 540
cohort, 421
cohort effect, 326
colic, 158
collective efficacy, 584
collective enterprise, 363
collectivism, 9, 41–42
    individualism compared with,
        42t
    intergenerational relationships
        and, 530
    living arrangements in elder-
        hood and, 567–568
    migration and, 43
    parenting practices and, 42f
college
    autonomy and, 377–378
    dropping out of, 409–413
    "gap year" before, 404–405
    gender identity and, 385,
        387–388
    number of students
        completing, 394
    romantic and sex relationships
        in, 386
    student loan debt, 381
    students employed while in, 379
    women in, 387–388
college debt/loans, 381
color blindness, 88t
Columbus Idea Foundry, 503
commitment
    generative, 499
    to nurturing future of a rela-
        tionship, 482
commitment (identity status),
    401

common bond, 360–361
common identity, 360–361
communal (femininity), 381
communal norm, 435
communication
    demand-withdraw pattern,
        437
    divorce and problems with,
        463
    emotions as channel for adult-
        infant, 166–167, 166–168
    with gestures, 149–150
    in infancy, 148–151
    marital adjustment and, 436
    milestones of early, 151t
    negative, 436
    styles of men and women in
        marriage, 437
communication disorders, 306
communication repairs, 170
communicative competence,
    189
communion, 75
community-based long-term
    health care, 571
community resources for elders,
    582–583
community service, moral
    reasoning and, 389, 391
comparative assessments, 252
competence, 310. See also social
    competence
    achieving new levels of, in
        work, 471–474
    children's perceptions of, 295
    illusions of, 298–300
    in middle childhood, 310
competence motivation, 422
competition
    team play and, 301–302
    in the workplace, 448
complicated grief, 603
compulsion, in toddlerhood,
    216–217
compulsive sexual behavior, 458
computational skills, 285–286
computer "brain games," 527
concrete operational intelligence,
    289
concrete operational thought, 33
    classification skills, 284–285
    components of, 286t
    computational skills, 285–286
    conservation, 282–284
    in middle childhood, 281–287
concussions, 300
confidence, in elderhood, 580
conflict
    among friends, 258
    associated with sexuality in
        early adolescence, 333–336
    marital, 436–437

parent-adolescent, about peer
    relations, 356
conformity, 276
    ethnic minority identity devel-
        opment and, 406
congruence, 437
conscience, 27
conscientiousness, 520
consciousness, 25
    domains of, 26–27
conscious processes, 26, 27f
consensual union, 433
conservation, 282–284
conservation of number, 285
contactful communication, 437
context. See also social context
    of development, 69–70
    individual development
        within, 22–23
continuing care retirement
    community, 569, 571
continuity, 5
    cultural, 41
continuity of self, 251
continuous self, 252
contraception, 335
controlling interactions, 437
conventional level of moral
    reasoning, 389
conventional morality, 241
cooperation, team play and, 302
coordination, 170
coordination of means and ends,
    145t, 146
coparenting, 486
coping
    in adolescence, 30
    with aging, 577
    assimilative, 542
    discrimination and, 508–509
    divorce and, 464–465
    emotion-focused, 71
    in later adulthood, 542
    problem-focused, 71
    psychosocial theory, 57,
        70–72
core pathologies, 59t, 72, 73t
Cornell Retirement and Well-
    Being Study, 547
coronary artery disease, 89
cortex, sensory and motor areas
    of the human, 136f
cortisal, 111
cosmic transcendence, 576
couvade, 116
coy smile, 163
crawling, 142
creative achievements,
    immortality through, 575
creative action, in elderhood,
    584
creative intelligence, 289–290

creativity
    generativity and, 502
    in middle adulthood, 503–504
creeping reflex, 141t
crisis (identity crisis), 401
cross-national comparisons
    of mathematics ability,
    292–293
crowds
    in early adolescence, 353–354
crying, in infants, 161–162
crystallization phase, of career
    decision making, 396–397
crystallized intelligence, 525
cultural continuity, 41
cultural determination, 40
cultural discontinuity, 41
cultural pathways, 40, 43
cultural relativism, 389
cultural theory, 40–43, 42t, 43t,
    51t
cultural tools, as mediator of
    cognitive structuring, 34–35
culture
    attachment and, 158, 161
    attitude toward intelligence
        and, 290
    autonomy from parents and,
        376
    beliefs about academic
        achievement, 292
    biological system and, 7
    birth, 115
    childbirth and, 117–120, 119t
    as context for reading, 293–294
    as context of development in
        psychosocial theory, 69–70
    cross-national comparisons
        of mathematics ability,
        292–293
    death-related rituals and,
        596–597
    decision to become a parent
        and, 444
    defined, 40, 69–70
    developmental tasks and, 63
    eating disorders and, 346
    emotional distancing from
        parents and, 379
    emotional regulation in in-
        fancy and, 166
    ethnic identity and, 406–408
    filial obligation and, 489–490
    funeral and mourning rituals,
        598
    gender identity and, 382–384,
        387
    gender preferences and,
        237–238
    gender-role standards and,
        384–385
    guilt and, 261

    language development and,
        189, 191
    living arrangements in elder-
        hood and, 567–568
    mathematics ability and, 292
    as mediator of cognitive struc-
        turing, 34–35
    menopause and, 484
    moral development and, 239
    motor development and, 142
    norm of reaction and, 92
    parent-adolescent conflict and,
        355–356
    parental expectations and,
        292–293, 298
    perspective taking and, 245
    physical, 40
    physical maturation and,
        319–320
    pregnancy and, 104, 115–117
    pretend play and, 203
    in psychosocial approach, 43
    puberty and, 324–325
    role in societal system, 9
    selection of a partner and,
        426
    self-esteem and, 254
    self-theory and, 252–253
    shame and, 213
    skill learning and, 287
    social, 40
    societal system and, 8, 9
    in Vygotsky's theory of human
        development, 35–36
    worldview and, 40–41
culture carriers, 40–41
culture of aging, 565
cumulative relation, 84
cyberbullying, 278, 280
cystic fibrosis, 88t

Darwin's theory of evolution,
    23, 25
dating
    in early adolescence, 328
    interethnic, 429, 431
    online, 428–429
    role experimentation and, 404
dating violence, 334
death
    advance directives and, 590
    ambiguous loss, 603, 604
    bereavement and grief,
        600–606
    case study on, 538, 588
    changing perspectives of,
        537–538
    confronting one's, 591–592
    definitions of, 589–590
    developing a point of view on,
        537–539, 589
    dying process, 591–596

    ethical issues at end of life,
        595–596
    euthanasia, 594–595
    good death, 592–595
    hospice care and, 592–594
    immortality and, 574–576
    psychosocial development
        and, 588–589
    rituals related to, 596–600
    stages in coming to terms
        with, 591
    stigmatized, 605
    ten leading causes of, 591t
death anxiety, 539
death rates, after widowhood, 534
Death with Dignity Act (ODDA),
    594
decentering, private self and, 399
decisions and decision-making
    career, 397–398
    on childbearing, 439, 441
    on parenthood, 439–440
deeper attraction phase of mate
    selection, 428–429, 431
defense mechanisms, in
    psychoanalytic theory,
    28–29
degree of suffering, dying process
    and, 591
delay of gratification, 209, 211
delinquency
    adolescent parents and, 337
    in early adolescence, 349, 351
    early maturation and, 326
delinquent offenses, 349
demand-withdraw pattern, 437
dementia, 563–564
dendrites, 134f
dependence, 561
depressed mood, 347
depression
    anaclitic, 172
    close friends and, 277
    cognitive behavioral therapy
        and, 39
    in early adolescence, 346,
        347–349
    in early adulthood, 457–458
    in father, 106
    gender differences in, 348–349
    genetic makeup and, 22
    joblessness and, 476
    in later adulthood, 541
    maternal (See maternal
        depression)
    obesity and, 322
    poverty and, 11
    in pregnant women, 112
deselection, 354
despair, in later adulthood,
    540–541
detached families, 529

development. See also
    developmental stages
    basic assumptions about, 5–6
    contexts of, 69–70
    fetal (See fetal development)
    genetic determinants of the
        rate and sequence of, 87
    individual contributions to, 5
    requirements for theories of,
        22–23
    team play as context for,
        303–304
    theoretical views on contri-
        butions of fantasy play to,
        201–202
developmental changes, 5
    in self-theory, 251–252
developmental delays, school
    readiness and, 268
developmental disabilities,
    rejection and, 279
developmental progression, in
    later adolescence, 403
developmental stages
    of families, 486–489
    Piaget's theory of cognitive
        development, 32–33
    psychoanalytic theory, 28
    psychoanalytic theory on, 28
    psychosocial theory, 57, 60–62,
        60f
developmental systems theory, 49
developmental tasks, 57, 62–64,
    64t
    in early adolescence, 319–356
    in early adulthood, 424–454,
        450t
    in early school age childhood,
        230–259
    in elderhood, 555–574
    in infancy, 130, 133–167
    in later adolescence, 375–398
    in later adulthood, 515–539
    in life stages, 58t
    in middle adulthood, 471–498
    in middle childhood, 273–304
    in toddlerhood, 184–211
developmental trauma disorder,
    160
developmental viability, 121
The Dictionary of Occupational
    Titles, 474
diet. See also nutrition
    intelligence and, 91
    longevity and, 16
    during pregnancy, fetal devel-
        opment and, 112–113
differentiation, 376
difficult temperament, 164t
diffidence, in elderhood, 580
diffuse-avoidant types, for role
    experimentation, 405, 405f

dilation, 102

disability(ies). *See also* children with disabilities
autonomy at college, 379
defined, 268
in elderhood, 561–562, 564
in later adulthood, 519–520

disability discrimination, 506

discipline
harsh, 208
impulse control and, 206–207
moral development and, 245–246
social competence and, 274
three general categories of, 207
time-outs and, 207

disclosure, 432
marital adjustment and, 436
on sexual orientation, 332–333

disclosure reciprocity, 436

discontinuity, cultural, 41

discrimination
coping with, 508–509
overview of workplace, 506
perpetuating itself, 507–508
types of, 505–506
well-being and, 423

disdain, in later adulthood, 543

disequilibrium, 32, 36

disinhibited social engagement disorder, 159–160

dismissing avoidant individuals, in relationship formation, 430

dismissive attachment, 380

disorganized attachment, 155, 158

dissociation, 365–366

dissonance
ethnic minority identity development and, 406

distancing, private self and, 399

distinctiveness, of self, 251

diversity, 5–6

division of labor, 301

divorce
cohabitation and, 433
coping with, 464–465
in early adulthood, 461–465
factors contributing to, 461–464
poverty and, 10

dizygotic (DZ) twins, 93

DNA methylation, 85*f*

DNA molecule, 83*f*

DNA, mutations and, 86

domains of consciousness, 26–27

dominance, 84

dominant allele, 84

"Do Not Resuscitate" directives, 590

doubt, in toddlerhood, 213

doulas, 105

Downs, Loreta, 593

Down syndrome, 88*t*, 92, 109

downward comparison, 473

drives, 26

dropping out of college, 409–413

drug use
in early adolescence, 335, 349, 366–368
maternal, and fetal development, 109–112
trends in lifetime use of, 366*f*

drug use/abuse
depression and, 349

dual-centric individuals, 479

dual-earner families, 437–438, 439–440, 452

dual identity, 360

Duchenne smile, 162

durable power of attorney, 590

dyadic attachment, 161

dyadic friendships, 353

dyadic interactions, 259

dying process and trajectory, 591–596

dynamic systems theory, on motor development, 185

dyslexia, 291

early adolescence
alcohol and drug use during, 366–368, 366*f*
alienation in, 360–362
brain development in, 338–339
case study, 318
central process in, 59*t*, 68*t*, 362–363
characteristics of, 318–319
core pathology in, 59*t*
delinquency in, 349, 351
developmental tasks in, 58*t*, 64*t*, 319–356
dissociation in, 365–366
eating disorders in, 346–347
emotional development in, 343–352
ethnic group identity in, 359–360
fidelity to others in, 363–365
first intercourse in, 328–329, 329*f*
formal operational thought in, 339–343, 340*t*
formal operations in, 338–343
group identity in, 356–360
individual differences in timing and rate of physical change in, 325–327
parenthood in, 336–338
parenting children in, 487
peer group membership in, 352–356
peer pressure in, 362–363
physical maturation in, 319–338

prime adaptive ego quality, 59*t*, 73*t*, 363–366
problems/conflicts associated with sexuality in, 333–336
psychosocial crisis, 58*t*, 65*t*, 318, 356–362
puberty, 321–323
relationship with parents, 355–356
romantic and sexual relationships in, 327–330
secular growth trend, 325
sexual orientation in, 330–333, 331*t*
suicide, 350–351
youth gangs and, 364–365

early adulthood
case study, 418
central process in, 59*t*, 68*t*, 459–460
childbearing in, 438–445
cohabitation in, 432–433
core pathology in, 59*t*
developmental tasks in, 58*t*, 64*t*, 424–454, 450*t*
divorce in, 461–465
intimacy in, 455–456
intimate relationships in, 425–438
isolation in, 456–459
life course and, 420–422
lifestyle, 449–455
marriage i, 425, 426, 435–438
pace of life in, 451
parenting children in, 487–488
prime adaptive ego quality, 59*t*, 73*t*, 460–461
psychosocial crisis, 58*t*, 65*t*, 455–459
same-sex relationships in, 433–435
selection of a partner in, 426–429, 427*f*, 431–432
social roles, 419–420
theoretical views of adult development and, 418–424
work in, 445–449
work/life balance in, 452

Early Childhood Longitudinal Study, 266

Early Head Start, 221–222, 224

early school age childhood
case study, 230
central process in, 59*t*, 68*t*, 262
core pathology in, 59*t*
developmental tasks, 58*t*, 64*t*, 230–259
friendship groups in, 257–259
gender identification, 231–235, 237–238
group games in, 255
guilt in, 260–261

inhibition in, 264
initiative in, 259–260
media play in, 255–257
moral development, 238–249
parenting children in, 486–487
peer play in, 255–259
prime adaptive ego quality, 59*t*, 73*t*, 263–264
psychosocial crisis, 58*t*, 65*t*, 259–261
purpose in, 263–264
school readiness, 264–268
self-esteem and, 253–254
self-theory and, 250–254

earning, dual-earner marriages, 437–438

easy temperament, 164*t*

eating disorders, 346

ecological niche, 23

ecological systems theory, 47–49

Eden Care, 582

education, 308–310. *See also* college
age at marriage and, 426
career choices and, 393–394
childhood disorders interfering with success in, 306–307, 307*f*
contributing to formal operational reasoning, 340, 341–342
earnings and, 394, 394*t*
HIV/AIDS, 336
longevity influenced by, 15
maternal, parenthood and, 441, 444
in middle childhood, 308–310
parent, 338
poverty and, 10, 11
relationship commitment and, 426
sexual health information, 333–334
unemployment and, 477*t*

educational apps, 256

effacement, 102

efficacy, 38

effortful control, 209

Ego and the Mechanisms of Defense, The (Freud, A.), 30

egocentric speech, 35, 211

ego ideal, 27–28, 262–263

ego psychology, 30

ego, the, 27, 28–29. *See also* prime adaptive ego qualities

elderhood
behavioral slowing in, 558–559
case studies, 552, 571–572
central process in, 59*t*, 68*t*, 577–579
core pathology in, 59*t*
dementia in, 563–564

fertilization, 92–93
  in vitro, 94, 95
  in vivo, 95
fetal alcohol spectrum disorders (FASDs), 110
fetal alcohol syndrome (FAS), 110, 110*f*
fetal development, 92–93
  critical periods, 98*f*
  environmental toxins and, 112
  fertilization, 92–93
  first trimester, 97, 97*t*, 99
  impact of pregnant woman on, 108–113
  maternal age and, 108–109
  maternal diet and, 112–113
  maternal drug use and, 109–112
  maternal impact on, 103–104, 108–114
  poverty's impact on, 108
  second trimester, 97*t*
  stress and, 113–114
  taegyo (fetal education) and, 115
  third trimester, 97*t*
fetal memory, 101
fetal period, 97, 99
fetal position, 99, 100, 100*f*
fetal viability, 121
fetus, 99, 100*f*
fidelity to others, 363–365
fidelity to values and ideologies, 409
filial obligation, 489–490
financial factors, dropping out of college, 410
fine motor skills, 140–141
first habits, 145*t*, 146
first intercourse, 328, 329*f*, 334
first words, 151
fitness, 23
  in early adulthood, 453–454
  in elderhood, 556–557
  inclusive, 23
fixation, 28
flexion reflex, 141*t*
fluid intelligence, 525
follicle-stimulating hormone (FSH), 319
food insecurity, 556
food safety, 114*f*
foreclosed (identity status), 401
formal operational intelligence, 289
formal operational thought, 34
  criticisms of the concept of, 342–343
  in early adolescence, 338–343
  explained, 339
  factors promoting, 340–342
  six characteristics of, 340
foster care
  attachment and, 156
  skill development and, 291

foundational category, 147
fragile identity, 458
frail elderly, 580–584
fraternal twins, 93
Friedman, Jerry, 552
friends/friendships
  care of surviving, after death, 597–598, 600
  case study on, 272
  close, 276–277
  conflicts among, 258
  dyadic, 353
  early school age childhood, 257–259
  loneliness and, 277–278
  in middle adulthood, 495
  in middle childhood, 272–279
  recollections of middle childhood, 272
  rejection and, 279
  role experimentation and, 404
  sex segregation among, 258–259
  social competence and, 273–275
  social development and, 275–277
frontal cortex, 345
frontal lobe, 136*f*
fulfillment theories, 422–424
functional independence, 561
functional reserve, 564
funerals and funeral rituals, 596, 598, 599

games
  board, 255
  "brain," 527
  group, in early school age childhood, 255
  language, 198
  team, 304
  video, 247, 248, 249, 256–257, 258
gamete intrafallopian transfer (GIFT), 95
gametes, 93
gangs, 364–365
Gap Year, before college, 404–405
gardening, in later adulthood, 536
Gardner's theory of multiple intelligences, 289, 342
gay (sexual orientation), 330–331, 331*t*. See also LGBTQ youth
gay men, relationship satisfaction of, 433–435
gay parents, 236–237
Gay-Straight Alliance, 332
gender. See also men; women
  adolescent depression and, 346, 348–349
  aggression and, 346

college attendance and, 394
communication patterns in marriage, 437
components for understanding, 233, 233*f*
defined, 231
depression and, 348–349
discrimination, 505–506
early maturation and, 325–327
expression of love and, 482
finding a new partner after widowhood and, 573–574
identity formation in later adolescence and, 403–404
income disparities and, 507
life expectancy and, 14–15, 14*f*
living arrangements in elderhood and, 567
media use and, 256–257
moral reasoning and, 390
prosocial behavior and, 390
third, 381, 383–384
widowhood and, 534
gender constancy, 233, 384
gender contentedness, 235, 237
gender dysphoria, 238
gender gap, in longevity, 554
gender identity
  case study, 231–232
  in early school age childhood, 231–235, 237–238
  integrating one's, 387–388
  in later adolescence, 381–388
  learning new gender-role standards, 384–385
  reevaluating gender constancy, 384
  third gender and, 383–384
gender labels, 233
gender permanence, 233
gender preferences, 232, 235, 237–238
gender-role convergence, 572–573
gender-role expectations, 384
gender-role socialization
  career choices and, 394–395
  gender-role socialization and, 394–395
  LGBT parents and, 236
gender-role standards, 234
gender schemes, 234
gender typicality, 235, 237, 387
Generation X, 421, 470
Generation Y, 421, 424
Generation Z, 421
generativity
  case study on, 500
  death anxiety and, 539
  five types of generative status, 500
  immortality and, 575–576

measuring, 499–500
  in middle adulthood, 498–500
  paths to, 499
generativity *versus* stagnation, 58*t*, 65*t*, 498–502, 589
genes, 82–83
gene therapy, 89
genetic counseling, 89
genetic disorders, 88–89, 88*t*
Genetic Information Nondiscrimination Act (2008), 89
genetic mutations, 86–87
genetics
  abnormal development and, 88–89
  development and, 82–86
  eating disorders and, 347
  environment and, 90–92
  ethical considerations, 89–90
  evolutionary theory and, 23, 25
  fetal development and, 99
  intelligence and, 90–91, 90*f*, 90*t*
  longevity and, 15, 553, 554–555
  motor development and, 142
  principles of heredity, 83–86
  psychological changes and, 7
  sources of individual differences, 86–89
genetic technology, psychosocial evolution and, 89–90
genital basis of gender labels, 233
genital stage, 28
genome, human, 82
genome mapping, 83
Genome-wide Complex Trait Analysis (GCTA), 90
genotype, 84, 87, 87*f*
genotypes, 91–92
gentrification, impact on elderly, 570
Gergen, Mary, 514
germinal period, 97
gestational age, 103
gestures
  communication with, 149–150
  in toddlerhood, 189, 191
GI Joe generation, 553
girls
  body image and dissatisfaction in, 322–323
  delinquent, 351
  first menstrual period, 322
  impact of pubertal timing for, 327
  nonconforming gender preference and, 237
  physical maturation in, 319
  preferring dyadic interactions, 259
  signposts of puberty for, 321–322

immortality *versus* extinction, 58t, 65t, 574–575, 589

imprinting, 85, 156

impulse control, 204–210
  in early adolescence, 339
  role of language and fantasy in, 209–210
  in toddlerhood, 204–210

incest taboo, 261

inclusion, for children with disabilities, 268

inclusive fitness, 23

income
  autonomy in late adolescence and, 379
  discrimination and, 505
  disparities in, 507
  dropping out of college and, 410–411
  educational attainment and, 393, 394, 394t
  quality of preschool and, 219
  in retirement, 582

incompetence, illusions of, 298–299

individual differences
  in ability to control impulses, 208–209
  genetic sources of, 86–89
  in physical maturation in early adolescence, 325–327
  in role experimentation, 405–406, 405f

individual identity
  alienation and, 361–362
  in later adolescence, 399–402

individual identity *versus* identity confusion, 58t, 65t, 318, 399–404

individualism, 9, 41–42, 42t
  collectivism compared with, 42t
  living arrangements in elderhood and, 567–568
  migration and, 43
  parenting practices and, 42

Individuals with Disabilities Education Act (IDEA), 178

individual traits, genetic determinants of, 87

induction phase of career development, 472

inductions, 284

industry, in middle childhood, 304–305

industry *versus* inferiority, 58t, 65t, 304–305, 307–308

inertia, in middle childhood, 310–311

infancy, 130–179
  Apgar scoring method, 131, 131t
  attachment during, 151–161
  brain development in, 133–136
  case study, 130
  categorization during, 147–148
  causal schemes in, 145–146, 145t
  central process in, 59t, 68t, 169–171
  communication during, 148–151, 151t
  core pathology in, 59t
  developmental tasks, 58t, 64t, 130, 133–167
  emotional development in, 161–168
  evolutionary theory and, 25
  faceness in, 137–138, 138f
  hearing, 136–137
  information-processing abilities, 144–145
  low-birth weight babies, 131, 132
  motor development during, 140–144, 142t
  nature of objects in, 146–148
  nutrition in, 175
  optimizing development in, 179t
  parental roles during, 172–179, 179t
  prefrontal cortex and intelligence in, 148
  prime adaptive ego quality, 59t, 73t, 171–172
  psychosocial crisis, 58t, 65t, 168–172
  reaching and grasping in, 140–141
  reflexes, 140, 141t
  safety during, 173, 175
  self-theory in, 251
  sensorimotor intelligence, 144–145
  sensory/perceptual and motor function development, 133–144
  sensory/perceptual development, 136–139, 136f
  taste and smell development in, 138–139
  taste in, 138–139
  temperament, 163–165, 164t
  touch development in, 139
  very-low-birth-weight babies (VLBW), 132–133
  vision, 137–138
  withdrawal in, 172

infant mortality rate, 102–103

inferiority, in middle childhood, 305, 307–308

infertility, 93–94

influence phase, in career decision making, 397

informational types, for role experimentation, 405, 405f

information-processing abilities, in infancy, 144–145

in-group attitudes, 302, 303t

"inherited characteristics," 82–83

inhibition, 87, 92
  in early school-age childhood, 264

initial impressions, 427

initiative, in early school age childhood, 259–260

initiative *versus* guilt, 58t, 65t, 259–261

inner speech, 35, 211

insecure attachment, 169

insight, 145t, 146

insomnia, 557–558

Instagram, 278

institutional care, in elderhood, 569, 571

instrumental activities of daily life (IADLs), 561–562

instrumental support, 577

instrumental values, 572

integration phase of career development, 397, 472

integrity, in later adulthood, 540

integrity *versus* despair, 58t, 65t, 539–541

intellectual flexibility, 474

intellectual vigor, in later adulthood, 521–528

intelligence
  creative, 280–290
  crystallized, 525
  fluid, 525
  genetics and, 90–91, 90f, 91f
  impact of child care on, 221–222
  in later adulthood, 521–528
  plasticity of, 91f
  problems in defining and studying in later adulthood, 522
  sensorimotor, 33, 144–145, 289
  theories approaching definition of, 289–290

intelligence tests, 288, 289

interdependence, 49, 213, 301

interethnic dating, 429, 431

intergenerational co-housing, 569

intergenerational relationships, 530

intergenerational solidarity, 529

intergenerational transmission of divorce, 463

intermental coordination, 35, 36

internalization, moral development and, 239

internalized morality, 388–392

internalizing problems, 209, 346

Internet
  communication with friends on, 278
  sexual health information on, 333

interpersonal interactions, 480, 481–482

interpersonal relationships. *See* intimacy/intimate relationships; relationships

interpersonal skills, 473

intersex, 231

interstate migration, in elderhood, 568–569

intersubjectivity, 149, 166

intimacy/intimate relationships. *See also* marriage; relationships
  childbearing and, 438–439, 441–444
  depression and, 457–458
  drifting apart and, 459
  in early adulthood, 425–438
  in middle adulthood, 480–485
  between partners of the same sex, 433–435
  preserving passion in, 483–485
  readiness to form, 425–426

intimacy *versus* isolation, 58t, 65t, 455–459

intimate but distance families, 529

intimate partner violence (IPV), 107

intracytoplasmic sperm injection, 95

intramental process, 35

intrauterine insemination, 95

introjection, 607

introspection
  ethnic group identity development and, 407
  in late adolescence, 381
  in later adulthood, 541–542

in vitro fertilization, 94, 95

in vivo fertilization, 95

IQ tests/score, 221, 288

iron deficiency anemia, 113

isolation
  divorce and, 464
  drifting apart and, 459
  in early adulthood, 456–459
  single-parent families and, 497
  social anxiety and, 456

joblessness, 475–477, 477t

Johnson, Harriet McBryde, 588, 591

Johnson-Powell, Gloria, 230

joint family, 492

jumping, in toddlerhood, 185–186, 186t

justice orientation, 390

marital conflict, 436–437
marriage
    adjustment during early years of, 435–438
    age at first, 377, 379, 420, 425, 462
    case study on, 482–483
    childbearing outside of, 443
    cohabitation and, 432–433
    in collectivist *vs.* individualistic cultures, 42
    communication in, 437
    delaying age at, 425
    divorce and age at, 462
    dual-earner, 437–438
    ideal age, 426
    in middle adulthood, 480–483
    readiness for, 426
    remarriage, 495–496
    same-sex, 433
    statistics on, 425
    themes contributing to long-lasting and happy, 480–485
    transition to parenthood in, 442–444
    vital, 480
masculinity, 381
Maslow's hierarchy of needs, 422–423, 423f
mastery smile, 163
matching of interactions, in infancy, 170
maternal depression
    anxiety in infancy and, 163
    child guilt and, 261
    fetal development and, 113
    infant psychosocial development and, 162–163
    treatment of, 112
maternal morality rate, 108
mate selection, 426–429, 427f, 431–432
mathematics
    ability, cross-national comparisons of, 292–293
    middle childhood, 285–286
mating strategies, 24
mattering, 363
maturation, individual differences in adolescent physical, 325–327
maturity, 60f
    stage of development in psychosocial theory, 60f
Max Planck Institute on Human Development, 527
meaning-making, 6, 7–8
Me, concept of, 251
media. *See also* television
    amount of time spent with, 247, 256
    daily activities, 256, 256t

features of games, 256–257
income inequality and access to, 256–257
mobile devices, 256
moral development and, 249
national survey on, 255–256
self-esteem and, 254
media play, 255–256
media violence, 247–248, 247t
meditation, 7
memorializing the deceased, 598
memories, used to explore psychosocial stages of life, 66
memory
    fetal, 101
    in infancy, 144
    in later adulthood, 521, 523
    working, 339, 523
men. *See also* fathers; gender
    communication style in marriage, 437
    drug use among, and fetal development, 109–110
    fathers' involvement during pregnancy, 105–107
    first intercourse experience, 334
    infertility and, 94
    middle adulthood sexuality in, 483
    reactions to abortion, 124–125
    reactions to pregnancy (couvade), 116
    relationship satisfaction of gay, 434
    widowed, 534
menarche, 322, 324t
    age at, 325
menopause, 483–484
menstruation, 43
mental health
    college environment and, 411
    poverty's impact on, 11
mental operation, 282
mental processes, lower and higher, 34
mental representation, attachment and, 152, 157–158
mental states, 72
mentors, 474
mercury, fetal development and exposure to, 112
mesosystem, 48
metacognition, 34, 286–287
methadone, fetal development and, 111
methamphetamine use, during pregnancy, 111
micro-aggressions, 348
Microsystems, 48
middle adulthood
    building networks and coalitions in, 493, 495

caring for aging parents in, 489–492
case study, 470
central process in, 59t, 68t, 502–504
characteristics of, 470
core pathology in, 59t
developmental tasks, 58t, 64t, 471–498
generativity in, 498–500
grandparenthood in, 488–489
intimate relationships in, 480–485
living alone in, 497–498
management of the household in, 492–493, 493f, 495–498
menopause in, 484
parenting in, 485–488, 496–497
person-environment interaction in, 502–503
prime adaptive ego quality, 59t, 73t, 504–505
psychosocial crisis, 58t, 65t, 498–502
remarriage and blended families in, 495–496
stagnation in, 501–502
workplace discrimination in, 505–509
middle childhood
    case study, 272
    central process in, 59t, 68t, 308–310
    children experiencing war and violence, 272–273, 311–312
    concrete operations in, 281–287
    core pathology in, 59t
    developmental tasks, 58t, 64t, 273–304
    friends/friendships in, 272, 273–281
    industry in, 304–305
    inferiority in, 305, 307–308
    parenting children in, 486–487
    prime adaptive ego quality, 59t, 73t, 310–311
    psychosocial crisis, 58t, 65t, 304–305, 307–308
    self-evaluation in, 294–300
    self theory and, 251
    skill learning in, 287–294
    team play in, 300–304
midlife career changes, 474–475
mifepristone, 120
Mifeprix, 120
milestones
    early communication, 151t
    in language development, during toddlerhood, 189–193, 192t
    motor development, 141, 142t

Millenials, 421, 424
Millennium Development Goals, 108
mindfulness, 7
mirror neuron system, 166–167, 215
miscarriage, 88
mismatch of interactions, in infancy, 170
mistrust, in infancy, 168–169
mobile devices, 256
modeling, 37
    peer influence and, 362, 368
monozygotic (MZ) twins, 93
moral development
    caring, 244–245
    case study, 243–244
    contributions to the study of, 249t
    in early school age childhood, 238–249, 249t
    empathy, 244
    evolutionary theory and, 243
    internalization and, 239
    in later adolescence, 388–392
    media's impact on, 246–248
    object relations theory and, 242–243
    parental discipline and, 245–246
    perspective taking, 245
    psychoanalytic theory and, 242
    theoretical perspectives on, 239–243
moral exemplars, 390
moral identity, 390
moral intuition, 243
moral judgments, 390
moral reasoning, 240
    experiences promoting, 389–390
    stages of, 389
moral transgressions, 241
moratorium
    in later adolescence, 402
    psychosocial, 404–405
moratorium (identity status), 402
Mormon church, pronatalist view in, 444–445
Morrow, Angela, 593
mortality
    psychosocial development and, 588–589
mothers
    adolescent, 336–337
    age of expectant, 108–109, 109f
    case study on mother-infant interaction, 130
    depressed, 171
    diet of pregnant, fetal development and, 112–113

prime adaptive ego qualities
(*continued*)
in infancy, 171–172
in later adolescence, 408–409
in later adulthood, 541–542
in life stages, 59*t*
in middle adulthood, 504–505
in middle childhood, 310–311
in toddlerhood, 215–217
principle of care, 244–245
private self, 252, 399
problem-focused coping, 71
procedural knowledge, wisdom
and, 543
process, 67. *See also* central
processes
in systems theory, 49
processing load, 558
processing speed, in infancy, 144
Progress in International Reading
Literacy Study (PIRLS),
293–294
prohibitive moral judgments, 390
Project Care, San Diego,
California, 583
prompting, 197
pronatalist view, 444–445
proprioception, 133
prosocial moral judgments, 390
prosocial programming, 248, 249
prospective memory, 523
proteome, 83
pruning of synapses, 134
pseudospeciation, 505
psychoanalytic theory, 20, 51*t*
basic concepts of, 31*t*
ego psychology, 30
five components of, 26–29
links to psychosocial ap-
proach, 31
on moral development, 242,
248, 249*t*
object relations theory, 29–30
psychosocial theory and, 31
psychohistorical perspective,
564–566
psychological change, 7
psychological change, self-
directed, 7
psychological mindedness, 287
psychological self, 251
psychological system, 11–12
components of, 7, 7*f*
meaning-making and, 6, 7–8
as meaning-making system, 6
psychological tools, 34
psychosocial approach
case study, 12
cognitive developmental
theory and, 36
cultural theory and, 43
evolutionary theory and, 25

learning theories and, 40
psychoanalytic theory and, 31
role theory and, 46
systems theory and, 50
psychosocial crises, 36, 57, 64–67
central process for resolving
(*See* central processes)
in early adolescence, 318,
356–362
in early adulthood, 455–459
in elderhood: immortality *versus* extinction, 574–577
in later adolescence, 399–404
in later adulthood, 539–541
in later adulthood: integrity
versus despair, 539–541
in life stages, 58*t*
in middle adulthood, 498–502
in middle adulthood: gen-
erativity *versus* stagnation,
498–502
trust *versus* mistrust, 168–169
unforeseen crises, 65–67
psychosocial development
11 stages of, 62, 62*f*
impact of poverty on, in toddlerhood, 217, 219–220
mortality and, 588–589
psychosocial environment
pregnancy and, 103–104
psychosocial evolution, 57
genetic technology and, 89–90
psychosocial growth, through
bereavement, 606–607
psychosocial impact
of abortion, 122–123
of poverty, 9–11
*The Psychosocial Inventory of Ego
Strength*, 72
*The Psychosocial Inventory of Ego
Strengths*, 72
psychosocial moratorium,
404–405
psychosocial theory, 56–77
assumptions of, 77
basic concepts of, 57, 59, 76*f*
biological system and, 6–7
case study, 12–13
explained, 6
life stages, 58*t*–59*t*
overview, 11–12, 76–77
psychological system and, 6,
7–8
rationale for emphasis on,
56–57
societal system, 8–11
strengths of, 73–74, 74*t*
theme of connection in, 76
weaknesses of, 74–76, 74*t*
puberty
in boys, 323–324
cultural contexts of, 324–325

in Erikson's model of psychosocial stages of develop-
ment, 60*f*
explained, 319
impact of timing for, 325–327
stage of development in psychosocial theory, 60*f*
puberty status, 319
pubic hair, 321–322, 323
public self, 252, 399–400
punishment
harsh, 165
in psychoanalytic theory, 28
pupillary reflex, 141*t*
purpose, in early school age
childhood, 263–264

queer, defined, 331*t*. *See also*
LGBTQ youth
question-asking, language
development and, 196
questioning (sexual orientation),
defined, 331*t*
quickening, 100
Quinceañera, 41*f*

race. *See also* African Americans
adolescent suicide and, 350
body image during adoles-
cence and, 324–325
bullying and, 281
cliques/crowds and, 353
college attendance and, 394
group identity and, 359
income disparities and,
507–508
life expectancy and, 15, 15*t*
pride in, 359
stress and fetal development
and, 113
unemployment and, 476, 477*t*
youth gangs and, 364
race discrimination, 506
racial discrimination, 15, 506
radius of significant relationships,
68–70, 68*f*, 70, 76
RAN (rapid automized naming),
291
range of applicability, of a theory,
21
reaching, during infancy, 140–
141
reactive attachment disorder,
159
reading, 193, 291, 293–294
reading aloud, 197–198
reading fluency, 291
reality principle, 27
receptive language, 151
receptor sites, 134*f*
recessive allele, 84
reciprocal roles, 44

reciprocity, 283, 283*f*
disclosure, 436
norm of, 578
reference groups, 356–357
reflective thinking about groups,
357, 358
reflexes, infant, 140, 141*t* 145*t*
145
refugee children, 272
regression, 29
regulation, emotional, 163–166
rejection (peer), 274, 275, 276,
279
aggression and, 274, 275
loneliness and, 277–278
in middle childhood, 279
social norms and, 276
rejectivity, 505
relational aggression, 205, 274.
See also intimacy/intimate
relationships
relationships. *See also* intimacy/
intimate relationships;
marriage
between adults and their aging
parents, 489–492
attachment styles and formation of, 430
caring, in middle adulthood,
485–492
with coworkers, 448
intergenerational, 530–531
intimate, in early adulthood,
425–438
isolation and, 456–459
in later adulthood, 518
in object relations theory, 29
psychosocial development
and, 12
radius of significant, 68–70, 68*f*
religion/religious beliefs
discrimination and, 508
in elderhood, 579
influence on adolescent sexual
behavior, 330
point of view on death and,
539
pronatalist view, 444–445
role experimentation and,
404
social support in elderhood
and, 567, 579
remarriage, 495–496, 573–574
reminiscence, in later adulthood,
541–542
repair of interactions, in infancy,
170
representational intelligence, 289
representational skills, 144, 189
representational (semiotic)
thinking, 187, 189
repression, 29

sexual orientation
  biological basis of, 87
  defined, 231
  in early adolescence, 330–333
  four types of, 231
  in later adolescence, 386–387
sexual victimization, 334–335
shame
  cultural practices in pregnancy
    and, 115, 117
  guilt and, 213, 260
  in toddlerhood, 213
shared markers, of group
  members, 358
short-term memory, 523
showing objects, 149
sibling relationships, 275, 275f
sickle-cell anemia, 88t
significant relationships, radius
  of, 68–70, 68f, 76
sign language, 188
signs, 189
Signs of Suicide (SOS) program,
  351
Silent Generation, 421, 553
similarity bias, 432
situational factors, in isolation,
  458–459
situational loneliness, 457
skill care facilities, 569
skill learning, in middle
  childhood, 287–294
sleep loss, in adolescence, 320
sleep patterns
  in early adulthood, 453
  in elderhood, 557–558
  puberty and, 320
sleep-wake cycle, in very small
  babies, 132
slow to warm up temperament,
  164t
small for their gestational age
  (SGA), 131
smell
  after age 20, 559t
  in elderhood, 560–561
  during infancy, 139
smiles, infant, 162, 163
smiling, 23–24
smoking, life expectancy
  and, 15
sociability, 87
  temperament and, 164
sociable families, 529
social anxiety, 278, 456–457
  cognitive restructuring and,
    278
  in early adulthood, 456–457
  loneliness and, 277
social clock, 420, 439
social cognitive theory, 37
social comparison, 307–308, 473

social competence
  early attachment and, 273
  education and, 309
  family influences on, 273–275
  impact of child care on,
    222–223
  influence of child care on,
    222–223
social connections, evolutionary
  psychology on, 24–25
social context
  of alcohol use, 268, 368
  of metacognition, 287
  of reading, 293–294
social controls, initiation of
  sexual intercourse and,
    329–330
social conventions, 388
social culture, 40
social development
  contribution of friendships to,
    275–277
  team play and, 303–304
social evolutionary theory, 428
social expectations, in middle
  childhood, 295, 297–300
social identity, 6, 46, 251
social integration, 461
  in early adulthood, 420
  longevity influenced by, 15–16
socialization, 354
social learning
  on moral learning, 239–240
social learning theory, 22, 37–38,
  40t
socially integrated bullies, 280
socially marginalized bullies, 280
social media
  influence on development, 70
  language development and,
    193
  in middle childhood, 278
social networking, in early
  adulthood, 451–452
social norms, 234, 252, 276
social pretend play, 200
social referencing, 167
social roles, 44
  in early adulthood, 419–420
social role theory, 44–46, 46t, 51t,
  419, 419t, 420
Social Security income, 582
social self, 251
social skills, loneliness and, 457
social smiles, 163
social status, pregnancy and
  changes in, 103–104
social support
  for caregivers, in infancy,
    178–179
  in elderhood, 577–579
  during infancy, 178–179

social transgressions, 241
societal expectations, of
  developmental tasks, 63
societal system, 8–9, 8f, 11
socioeconomic status (SES). See
  also poverty
  career choice and, 393
  coping and, 71
  influencing parent-child inter-
    actions and language devel-
    opment, 196
socioemotional development,
  during infancy, 175–176
socioemotional support, 577
SOC (selection, optimization,
  compensation) model, 516
solicitude versus shame, 115
spanking, 208
speciation, 23
species extinction, 23
speech
  egocentric, 35, 211
  inner, 35, 211
  telegraphic, 191
  in Vygotsky's theory of cogni-
    tive development, 35
speed of processing, 523
spermarche, 323–324
spinal cord, 136f
sports, in middle childhood,
  300–304
springing reflex, 141t
stages of development. See
  developmental stages
stagnation
  career, 501
  in middle adulthood, 501–502
standardized tests, 289
Stanford-Binet Intelligence Test,
  289
Stanford Center on Longevity, 527
startle reflex, 141t
status offenses, 349
steering, 186f
stem cell research, 90
stem cells, 97
stepparents, 377, 495–496
stepping, 143
stepping reflex, 141t
Sternberg's theory of intelligence,
  289–290
stigmatized deaths, 605
stranger anxiety, 153, 162
strange situation, 154–155, 154t,
  160–161
stress
  ABCX model of coping with,
    600, 600f
  bereavement and coping with,
    600–601, 600f
  fetal development and,
    113–114

  impact on brain development
    during infancy, 135
  infertility and, 93
  parent-child interactions and,
    274
  violence in middle childhood
    and, 312
Stress in America survey, 304
student loan debt, 381
study habits, 309
subcultures, 43
sublimation, 28
substantive flexibility, 474
successful aging, 566–567, 566f
success, self-efficacy and, 295,
  296
sucking, 139, 140
sucking reflex, 141t
sudden infant death syndrome
  (SIDS), 103, 110
suffering, dying and, 591
suicide
  adolescent, 349, 350–351
  among the elderly, 576
  physician-assisted, 594–596
  as stigmatized death, 605
superego, 27–28, 242
superordinate group identity, 301
surrogacy, 94, 95–96
survivors
  factors affecting distress of,
    603–606
  funeral rituals and, 596
  identity of, 607
swaddling, 139, 173
sweat production, in early
  adolescence, 322, 323
swimming reflex, 141t
symbolic play, 201, 202, 210
symbols, 187, 189
synapses, 134, 135
synaptic cleft, 134f
synchrony, 170
syphilis, 335
system(s)
  changes in, 48–49
  open, 47
  topography of relationship
    among, 48f
systems theory, 47–50, 50t, 51t

Taegyo (fetal education), 115
tantrums, 185
taste
  after age 20, 559t
  in elderhood, 560–561
  infancy, 138–139
Tay-Sachs disease, 88t, 89
teachable moments, 62
teachers
  expectations by, influence of,
    309